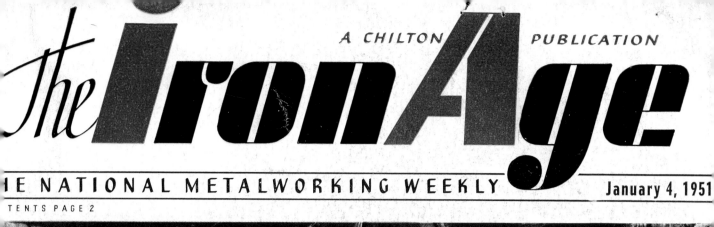

The Iron Age

A CHILTON PUBLICATION

THE NATIONAL METALWORKING WEEKLY

January 4, 1951

CONTENTS PAGE 2

Designed for Durability!

Hoskins Chromel*-equipped Electric Heat Treating Furnaces

Take a good look inside any Hoskins Electric Furnace and you'll quickly understand why they're known for dependability. For beneath their sturdy rugged external construction . . . inside their heavy heat-containing insulation . . . you'll find that every one is equipped with long-lasting heating elements made of CHROMEL resistance alloy.

CHROMEL, you know, is the original nickel-chromium alloy that first made electrical heating practical. It's highly resistant to oxidation . . . possesses close-to-constant "hot" resistance between 700° and 2000° F., delivers full rated power throughout its long and useful life. And, as the most vital part of every Hoskins Furnace, it represents your best assurance of long-life satisfactory service.

So next time you're in the market for good, dependable heat treating equipment . . . equipment designed for durability, efficient low-cost operation, and the production of uniformly high quality work . . . you'll do well to get the facts on the Hoskins line of CHROMEL-equipped Electric Furnaces.

Our Catalog 59-R contains complete information . . . want a copy?

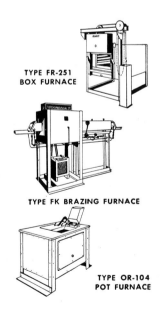

**TYPE FR-251
BOX FURNACE**

TYPE FK BRAZING FURNACE

**TYPE OR-104
POT FURNACE**

HOSKINS MANUFACTURING COMPANY

4445 LAWTON AVE. • DETROIT 8, MICHIGAN

NEW YORK • CLEVELAND • CHICAGO

West Coast Representatives in Seattle, San Francisco, Los Angeles
In Canada: Walker Metal Products, Ltd., Walkerville, Ontario

the original nickel-chromium resistance alloy that first made electrical heating practical

MILLION TONS MORE STEEL

Latest Increase in Bethlehem's Annual Capacity Climaxes 5 Years of Postwar 3,100,000-Ton Expansion

On January 1 of this year Bethlehem's steel making capacity stood at 16 million ingot-tons annually—*an increase of 1 million tons* over a year ago.

Since the war ended we have increased our annual steelmaking capacity *3,100,000 tons, or 24 per cent.*

Moreover, as the chart at the right shows, Bethlehem's steel capacity has nearly doubled in 25 years. Additional capacity can and will be created as it is needed.

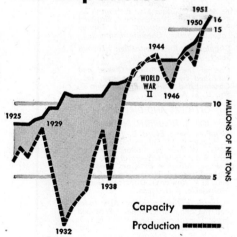

BETHLEHEM STEEL ★ ★

IRON AGE

CONTENTS

THE IRON AGE
Editorial, Advertising and Circulation Offices, 100 E. 42nd St., New York 17, N. Y.
GEORGE T. HOOK, Publisher
TOM C. CAMPBELL, Editor

EDITORIAL STAFF
Managing Editor   George F. Sullivan
Feature Editor   Darwyn I. Brown
News-Markets Editor   Wm. V. Packard
Machinery Editor   George Elwers
Associate Editors: William Czygan, H. W. Van Camp, F. J. Winters; Assistant Editors: R. L. Hatschek, J. Kolb, Ted Metaxas, W. B. Olson; Regional Editors: E. C. Beaudet, Chicago; W. A. Lloyd, Cleveland; W. G. Patton, Detroit; John B. Delaney, Pittsburgh; Osgood Murdock, R. T. Reinhardt, San Francisco; Eugene J. Hardy, Karl Rannells, George H. Baker, Washington; Correspondents: Fred L. Allen, Birmingham; N. Levenson, Boston; Fred Edmunds, Los Angeles; James Douglas, Seattle; Roy Edmonds, St. Louis; F. Sanderson, Toronto; F. H. Harley, London, England; Chilton Editorial Board: Paul Wooton, Washington Representative.

BUSINESS STAFF
Production Manager   B. H. Hayes
Director of Research   Oliver Johnson
Mgr. Circul'n & Promotion   C. T. Post
Asst. Promotion Mgr.   James A. Crites
Asst. Dir. of Research   Wm. Laimbeer

REGIONAL BUSINESS MANAGERS
B. L. Herman, Philadelphia; Stanley J. Smith, Chicago; Peirce Lewis, Detroit; Paul Bachman, New England; Robert F. Blair, Cleveland; R. Raymond Kay, Los Angeles; C. H. Ober, New York; J. M. Spackman, Pittsburgh; Harry Becker, European Representative.

REGIONAL OFFICES
Chicago 3, 1134 Otis Bldg.; Cleveland 14, 1016 National City Bank Bldg.; Detroit 2, 103 Pallister Ave.; Los Angeles 28, 2420 Cheremoya Ave.; New England, 62 La Salle Rd., W. Hartford 7; New York 17, 100 E. 42nd St.; Philadelphia 39, 56th & Chestnut Sts.; Pittsburgh 22, 814 Park Bldg.; Washington 4, National Press Bldg.; European, 111 Thorley Lane, Timperley, Cheshire England.

Circulation Representatives: Thomas Scott, James Richardson.

One of the Publications Owned and Published by Chilton Company, Inc., Chestnut and 56th Sts., Philadelphia 39, Pa., U. S. A.

OFFICERS AND DIRECTORS
JOS. S. HILDRETH, President
Vice-Presidents: Everit B. Terhune, G. C. Buzby, P. M. Fahrendorf, Harry V. Duffy. William H. Vallar, Treasurer; John Blair Moffett, Secretary; D. Allyn Garber, Maurice E. Cox, Frank P. Tighe, George T. Hook, Tom C. Campbell, L. V. Rowlands, Directors. George Maiswinkle, Asst. Treas.

Indexed in the Industrial Arts Index and the Engineering Index. Published every Thursday by the CHILTON CO. (INC.), Chestnut and 56th Sts., Philadelphia 39, Pa. Entered as second class matter Nov. 8, 1932, at the Post Office at Philadelphia under the act of March 3, 1879. $8 yearly in United States, its territories and Canada· other Western Hemisphere Countries $15; other Foreign Countries $25 per year. Single Copies 35c. Annual Review and Metal Industry Facts Issue, $2.00. Cable address "Ironage" N. Y.

Member Audit Bureau of Circulations. Member Society of Business Magazine Editors.

Copyright, 1951, by Chilton Co. (Inc.)

DIGEST

JANUARY FOURTH · NINETEEN FIFTY-ONE · VOLUME 167 · NUMBER 1

ALL SHEARING BY CINCINNATI...

All the steel parts requiring shearing operations on these engine jacket water coolers are handled by Cincinnati Shears.

The rapid stroking and gauging of Cincinnati Shears save time, and the square corners and straight edges of blanks produced on Cincinnati Shears cut assembly costs and speed production.

For best results, consult our Engineering Department. We will gladly cooperate with you on your shearing needs.

Write for Catalog S-5 for a description of the complete line of powerful, speedy, all-steel Cincinnati Shears.

The Young-Happy Full Flow Engine Jacket Water Cooler with 93" variable pitch fan.

THE CINCINNATI SHAPER CO.

CINCINNATI 25, OHIO U.S.A.

SHAPERS · SHEARS · BRAKES

What's Ahead?

LET'S say goodbye to pretty words and phrases about the New Year and what to expect. It will be some time before we again reach that blissful period when we work for the love of it and for "gracious" living.

The going will not only be rough—it will be something we have not seen before. We will have a war without a declaration. We will have controls and directions that are foreign to us. But we will have them in the name of democracy. If we do things right it will be worth the price.

We will have to clean up our own house. Before 1951 is out we will know the hollowness of politics as usual. It will come the hard way. We will know soon that business as usual is an empty phrase—when we are an outpost for freedom.

We have a lot of things to overcome this year before we can be the knights in shining armor fighting the crusade for freedom—whether it be a declared war or a hot-cold undeclared war of defense.

A $50 billion defense program is more than six times the total gross sales of the whole steel industry in one year. It is not necessary to dwell here on the details of what will happen to steel and other metals.

At least 50 pct of total steel output will be going for direct defense and essential civilian needs by the middle of the year. That means close to 60 or 70 pct of flat-rolled steel will be slated for those uses.

When Washington makes up its mind on what the armed force needs it might be 5 or 6 million men instead of $3\frac{1}{2}$ million. That means we will be using in industry older people, women, pensioners and anyone who can work.

We haven't seen anything in taxes yet. They will be much heavier. There will be little or no profit before this debacle either straightens out or topples over everything.

A tight hold will come on prices and wages. Attempts will be made to do it the easy way. They won't work in the period we talk about—late 1951 and 1952.

Business and labor will have to get along. Business and government will have to cooperate. This year we put up or shut up.

Tom Campbell

Editor

Giant fork truck

Morse cable chain like that in truck's lift mechanism is available in four pitch sizes, with average ultimate breaking strength ranging from 3,900 to 49,400 pounds.

Tough-built Morse roller chain drives give you on-the-job stamina and long life. They use teeth, not tension. Morse roller chain drives are positive, can't slip. They are 99% efficient.

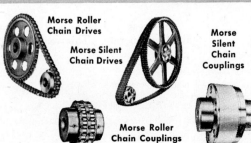

IRON AGE *newsfront*

news

methods

and product

forecast

▶ A greatly expanded merchant shipbuilding program is expected this year, despite some initial setbacks. Many of the ships now in reserve are too slow for use in an emergency. This will mean a further increase in steel plate production at the expense of sheets and strip.

If the Navy expands its building schedules, production of brass and bronze ingots may surpass that of the peak war years of 1943 and 1944.

▶ Fabricated copper will be in tight supply during 1951. Production will probably consume all available materials. Finding substitutes for copper is one of the toughest jobs there is. Copper fabricators can expect a year of steady production, after some initial dislocations due to government controls.

▶ The machine tool industry's 1951 order volume will probably total $1 billion. Most machine tool companies rated orders are less than 10 pct of their total but 75 pct or more could be rated as industry converts to defense production.

▶ Estimates are that stainless steel production in 1950 was almost 25 pct higher than the previous 617,378 ingot ton record set in 1948. This despite the handicap of alloy shortages during the last half of the year.

▶ The aluminum pinch will take a big bite out of automatic transmission production this year. Extensive plans have already been made to substitute gray iron for many of the aluminum castings now in production.

▶ Before the year is out new plants will be built for cold extrusion of steel products. Most of the work is expected to be in ordnance items. Details will be kept under wraps because the steel savings in the process would be relatively more valuable to the enemy than to the United States.

▶ Titanium will become firmly established as an engineering material during the coming year. Production will be greatly increased; prices may be reduced; new melting and extraction methods will be perfected. Reliable phase diagrams of ternary alloys and faster methods of analyzing for oxygen and nitrogen will emerge.

▶ Power steering for passenger cars--being introduced on the new Chrysler--is regarded in Detroit as one of the most important engineering developments since the automatic transmission. The wheel can be turned with one finger even when the car is standing still.

Chances of completing new high compression auto engines for 1952 models grow dimmer with each forward step in the arms programs. Currently, eight new high compression engines are tooling but only Chrysler is ready for production.

▶ Mandatory price controls are almost a certainty just as soon as an enforcement staff can be built up. The Economic Stabilization Agency now has a staff of less than 400, contrasted with OPA's administrative and police force of more than 20,000.

▶ New continuous casting units will be publicized this year, firmly establishing the soundness of making steel by this technique. Savings as high as $100 a ton on some grades are indicated.

Why the sea is salty

IN Norse mythology, a poor man got a magic mill from the elves. With it he could grind whatever he wanted--food, clothing, furniture, and best of all, gold. Of course, the poor peasant's lot changed from poverty to riches.

An envious brother borrowed the mill. He commanded it to "grind herrings and broth and grind them good and fast." But having taken the mill in such haste, he didn't know the magic words to shut it off. He was almost drowned in broth when the brother came to the rescue.

Finally, the magic mill was stolen by a salt dealer, who put it on his ship. Safely at sea, the skipper demanded, "Grind salt and grind it good and fast." Alas, he hadn't learned the control words either. The mill ground salt endlessly, filling all his kegs

and his hold, covering the decks and at last sinking the ship. There at the bottom of the sea, so people say, the magic mill still grinds--and that's why the sea is salty.

From time immemorial, men have dreamed about magic mills and schemes to bring abundance and riches. Here in America, today, there are plans that are flooding us with superabundance of certain commodities. But what about the magic words to shut off the mill?

Isn't it time we see the truth in this ancient Norse myth, that "too much" is just as foolish as "too little?" We may well remember this first law of economics: In a *free* market, supply can adjust itself to demand-- whether it be potatoes or steel--without sinking the ship. Here is a must job for all thinking Americans.

The Youngstown Sheet and Tube Company
General Offices--Youngstown 1, Ohio
Export Offices--500 Fifth Avenue, New York
MANUFACTURERS OF CARBON ALLOY AND YOLOY STEELS

RAILROAD TRACK SPIKES · CONDUIT · HOT AND COLD FINISHED CARBON AND ALLOY BARS · PIPE AND TUBULAR PRODUCTS · WIRE · ELECTROLYTIC TIN PLATE · COKE TIN PLATE · RODS · SHEETS · PLATES.

IRON AGE *summary*

ANNUAL REVIEW

STEEL production in the United States during 1950 was about equal to the combined output of all the other countries of the world. American steel companies produced 96,954,000 net tons of steel ingots and castings last year, compared with total world output of 194,154,000 net tons.

Steel production in the United States was more than three times the total output of the Soviet Union. U. S. output, 96,954,000; Russia, 26,500,000. When satellite countries and U. S. allies are included, the weight of steel production is even more heavily in favor of the U. S.

100 Million Ton Year Due

Barring unforseen trouble, the American steel industry can produce more than 100,000,000 net tons during 1951. It is already obvious that steel expansion during the next 2 years will be far greater than was reported to the Secretary of Commerce several months ago.

The 5-year write-off of taxes on defense plants is a strategic factor in increased expansion plans. This inducement to expansion has already greatly stimulated steel company plans.

U. S. Steel Corp.'s announcement of detailed plans for the huge Fairless Works to be built near Trenton, N. J., had been anticipated. The announced capacity of almost 2 million ingot tons is larger than was expected in some quarters.

An integrated steel corporation in New England moved closer to reality last week, marked by formal application for 5-year amortization of facilities. This plant, to be constructed near New London, Conn., would be rated above 1 million tons capacity. Its production would be concentrated in vital flat-rolled products. While the New England Steel Mill Development Corp. indicated that the way was being left open for participation by an existing steel company, it seemed that the way had already been cleared for financial assistance from the government if such help were not forthcoming.

This week it is clear that steel priority machinery is being strained to the utmost. Many steel consumers with DO orders are having difficulty locating a steel source. NPA personnel were being hard-pressed to answer inquiries and help frustrated holders of priority orders.

CMP Only Question of Time

Even sources close to NPA this week are convinced that a controlled materials plan is only a question of time. However, it will take from 3 to 5 months to collect sufficient personnel to adminster the plan.

Mandatory price-wage controls will probably come sooner. The first enforced controls will be on a selective basis. Nonferrous metals, scrap, and steel will probably be covered in that order. Controls will be broadened to include more commodities and industries as the administrating and policing staff of ESA is increased.

This week steel consumers are fighting what may be their last catch-as-catch-can procurement battle for many months. In anticipation of a controlled materials plan they are all vying for available tonnages of "free" steel. Defense and essential civilian steel orders are growing rapidly. Within a few months they will be taking at least one third of total steel output. Of special concern to steel consumers, they will be taking more than half the total production of flat-rolled steel products.

Steel Was Never Healthier

The steel industry enters the new year in the healthiest condition of its history. Earnings for the past 2 years have been highly satisfactory, due chiefly to the high rate of operations. Expansion plans are being encouraged by fast tax write-offs. New raw materials sources are being exploited to meet the demands of stepped-up capacity. All this adds up to more steel.

Steelmaking operations this week are estimated at 101 pct of rated capacity, up 2 points from last week's revised rate.

(nonferrous summary, p. 464)

Investigate →

THE ADVANTAGES OF DOING YOUR OWN SLITTING

Send for this book—a practical discussion of important questions as to operation, production and cost.

It contains time studies of output per cycle and per day, in slitting different widths, gauges and coil weights.

It shows how cycle time is affected by these and other factors; advantages of big coils and high speeds for big tonnages; economies of smaller, less expensive, standardized sizes of slitters for the more moderate requirements of most metal working plants.

Cost analyses show how Yoder slitters, operating only three or four days per month, often pay for themselves in a year or two. In addition, they greatly reduce inventory requirements of slit strands and facilitate production planning.

Phone or write today for free copy. Estimates and recommendations for the asking.

THE YODER COMPANY • 5510 Walworth Avenue, Cleveland 2, Ohio

Complete Production Lines

- ★ COLD-ROLL-FORMING and auxiliary machinery
- ★ GANG SLITTING LINES for Coils and Sheets
- ★ PIPE and TUBE MILLS — cold forming and welding

DESIGNERS AND BUILDERS OF THE WORLD'S LARGEST CRANES . . .

Alliance

LADLE CRANES · GANTRY CRANES · STRIPPER CRANES · SOAKING PIT CRANES · FORGING MANIPULATORS · OPEN HEARTH CHARGING MACHINES SLAB AND BILLET CHARGING MACHINES · SPECIAL MILL MACHINERY STRUCTURAL FABRICATION

THE ALLIANCE MACHINE COMPANY

Main Office
ALLIANCE, OHIO

Pittsburgh Office
1622 OLIVER BLDG., PITTSBURGH, PA.

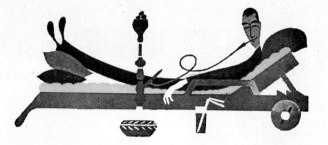

fatigue cracks

by charles t. post

The Look Back

Not so long ago that we can't remember, this first issue of each year was devoted to ponderous reports of what had taken place in the past 52 weeks and studded with brave visions of the year ahead.

Unfailingly, the description of the year past had the same relation to reality as a poor color photograph. If it was a good year, the annual reviews were as faultless as an obituary write-up. A bum one never was painted quite so black as it really was. Speak no evil of the dead. Never must future generations suspect what fools we really were.

Vistas of the future always are fenced with caution by those who make a profession of writing for publication. Amateur seers, business leaders particularly, tend to rosy predictions. Dusting off the Jan. 7, 1932, issue, you gain the unmistakable impression that prosperity was just around the corner, notwithstanding the paucity of paid advertising that is a barometer of business expectations.

This year the brains department has been hobbled in its appraisal of the past in the assumption that 1950 can be interpreted in as many different ways as there are readers of your favorite family journal. The logical course, then, is to give the readers as many facts as they can stuff down their gullets, and let them draw their own conclusions. Sitting here on Jan. 4, 1951, the odds against a successful forecast of the year ahead are slightly greater than those against naming the winner of the Kentucky Derby in 1954. As for controlling the future, well—do you have Stalin's ear?

Destiny's Child

Our own conviction as to the futility of planning ahead came many years ago, when a brilliant future at the bar (of justice) was thrust aside.

We were still in knee pants when a judge, a family friend, watched us win a fluke victory against par-
ental authority, stating our case with what seemed to us to be complete logic. Of course, if the judge had not been present, and had not dad wished to spare him embarrassment, the decision on our case would most certainly have gone the other way and sentence would have been executed immediately with a razor strop.

But the judge saw us win and clapped us on the shoulder. "There's a boy with a great future as an attorney," he predicted. Thereafter, for years and years we didn't have to worry about what the future held for us. We were going to be an attorney.

When we hit college, we discovered that reporters on the college paper got free tickets to all the local events. That caused a slight detour in our plans, but once we had our bachelor's degree we headed towards law school without the slightest hesitation.

Not until we were immersed in legal tomes and mock trials did we discover that the law for centuries had consisted of eternal bickering over trivial points of limited interest. Right then and there we wiped clean the crystal ball of our future, excused ourselves from this contentious atmosphere, fell into the arms of your f.f.j. and stopped worrying about the future altogether.

Now, our oldest girl is going to be a doctor, the boy an engineer, but the littlest angel gives evidence of deeper thought.

"I'm going to catch me a nice man," she confides, "and settle down and take life easy." Her mother says that even this is not an accurate appraisal of the future.

Here You See Them

Every once in a while some loyal reader of your f.f.j. writes us that he sits down and "reads it from cover to cover." If we get any letters like that about this issue, we'll have a strong suspicion that the writer either is straying from the truth or has a darn sore seat. But we do feel, and hope, that

Brass and Bronze Free Turning Rods

Produced in all sizes from 1/16" for small diameter rods up to 10" diameter for cast and turned.

Extruded Brass Shapes

Squares, hexagons, half rounds, half ovals and special shapes. Hexagons up to 4½" and rectangles up to 5½" (maximum diagonal).

Brass and Bronze Forgings

From ¼ oz. to 100 lbs. in weight. Produced to meet specified physical properties, corrosion resistance and finish.

Brass Pressure Die Castings

Parts having thin sections and intricate cored parts readily produced. Titan die castings have better finish, stronger structure, and greater accuracy than sand castings.

Bronze Welding Rods

Titan's exclusive double deoxidation process assures ductile, high-strength, non-porous welds.

Titan

Brass and Bronze Products

Write for descriptive catalogs on any of these products.

Titan
Metal Manufacturing Co.
GENERAL OFFICES AND PLANTS: BELLEFONTE, PA.
Offices and Agencies in Principal Cities

FATIGUE CRACKS
Continued

nearly all the readers will have this issue close at hand the rest of the year and will be looking at it many times.

We explained it to the advertisers in terms of the Sears Roebuck catalog. "If you've ever sat down with a Sears' catalog," we told them, "you can appreciate the hypnotic pull created by a vast display of varied products. In the IRON AGE Annual Review, the reader sees advertising at its best, with each advertiser making a special effort to please readers holding high expectations.

"Like Easter Sunday at church, nearly everybody 'attends,' whether or not he's advertised during the past year. Here are all the celebrities supplying metal-working, with comparisons among them to be expected. In no other issue of any magazine, or any specialized metalworking catalog service, is there such a dazzling array . . . This is the issue to catch the attention of the reader looking at advertising as a feature attraction rather than just an adjunct to editorial material."

All told, you will find 368 pages of advertising, most of it excellent educational reading. Whenever you get discouraged about America's military sinews, take a quick tour through the issue.

Signs of the Times

Clem Caditz, Northern Metal Products Company's irrepressible president, has posted this notice in the shop:

NOTICE

To All Doctors and First Aid Men

Any steel slivers removed from the fingers of our employees are to be carefully handled, stored and inventoried as to gauge.

In the event any slivers turn out to be 16 or 18 gauge H.R. or C.R., please notify our material control department immediately.

Your cooperation in this regard might keep a production line going.

Puzzlers

Instead of the usual puzzler for this issue, we'll merely give you a scripture taken from a letter submitted by a reader associated with one of the country's leading armaments manufacturers: "Enclosed is a solution to the problem. I have checked the calculations by working the problem by a different method, and the result is the same. To date this problem has only cost the ———— Co. about $1,500." Now get back to work before the rearmament effort folds up.

Dear EDITOR

letters from readers

Stone Tome

Sir:

It is part of the writers duties to purchase industrial diamonds in 2 to 3 and 5 karat size, mounted. It will be very much appreciated if you can furnish any literature or refer us to some good authorities, that will give technical advice on how to select diamonds for dressing wheels of all grades.

K. C. PHELPS
Alameda, Calif.

We haven't heard of any book that fills the bill exactly on selection of diamonds for dressing wheels, but the closest thing to it is the book "Diamond and Gem Stone Industrial Production" by Paul Grodzinski, published in London in 1942. In this country it is available through Henry Paulson & Co., 131 S. Wabash Ave., Chicago, at $4.95 per copy. It is quite a complete work on all phases of selection and use of industrial diamonds, and contains some charts which may be helpful.—Ed.

Currently Appropriate

Sir:

Our association publishes a monthly paper called *The Integrator*, and from time to time like to reprint editorials from some of the professional magazines.

You published in your Oct. 26, 1950, issue an editorial by Tom C. Campbell entitled "Take Care of Your Key Men." Since the article strikes us as especially appropriate at this time, we are asking your permission to reprint the editorial.

C. R. BROTHERTON
Editor, The Integrator
General Electric Engineers Assn.
Schenectady

A Reason For It

Sir:

In the Nov. 23, 1950, issue under the heading Briefs and Bulletins, the following item is included: "Urgent Business?—Some steel people who regarded speedy fulfillment of DO orders as an urgent matter have been given cause to wonder. Recently an alloy producer completed an order for stainless steel plate for the atomic energy program. When he asked for shipping instructions, the producer was advised to ship the steel to a warehouse."

You may be interested to know that the General Electric Co., which is the prime contractor for operations of the Atomic Energy Commission at Hanford, is purchasing alloy steel for the atomic energy program and, in many cases, having it shipped to a warehouse. This is because the steel is often being ordered in bulk in sizes and shapes which can be easily produced by the mill, yet is required in special sizes by the fabricators of equipment and vessels.

We have made arrangements that our orders are shipped to a central warehouse in the east where they are cut to size and rerouted to these fabricators in accordance with their requirements. This frees the mills from the necessity of breaking bulk orders down into large numbers of small shipments and tying up their vitally needed equipment with the work of making up small quantities of special sizes.

While we have no direct knowledge that the article refers to our activity, we are sure that the effect of the above quotation will be to do us a disservice. If the article does, in fact, refer to our operations, I think you will agree that the inclusion of this article has done a disservice to the atomic energy program and has placed the AEC in a poor light. Again assuming that the article referred to our activity, both of these regrettable conditions could have been avoided by a check of the facts.

F. K. McCUNE
Assistant General Mgr.,
Nucleonics Dept.
General Electric Co., Hanford Works
Richland, Wash.

The item was not checked because, from past experience, we have found that AEC apparently prefers to neither confirm nor deny most reports on atomic energy. In this case, such a check might have produced a clear answer and we would not have run the item.—Ed.

Ground Iron Powder

Sir:

I was very much interested in an article appearing in the Nov. 3, 1949, issue on the subject of domestic iron powder. I have been making a study of finely ground iron produced by abrasive wheels. This, of course, is mixed with the abrasive of which the wheel is made.

This study was being made in the interests of construction. We are anxious to learn all we can about "iron dust," as mentioned in the account. Where can we procure a sample of say 2 or 3 oz.? Kindly refer us to some paper, books or what not that discuss this subject.

G. R. HOUSTON
Birmingham

There are several books on powder metallurgy, including descriptions of the methods of producing and classifying iron powders. Two of the best known are: "Powder Metallurgy," by Dr. Paul Schwarykopf, MacMillan Co., New York, 1947; $8.00. "Powder Metallurgy," edited by John Wulff, published by American Society for Metals, Cleveland, 1942; $7.50.

Iron powder produced by machining is relatively coarse in comparison with the chemical and electrolytic powders; unless further reduction is made, it is generally

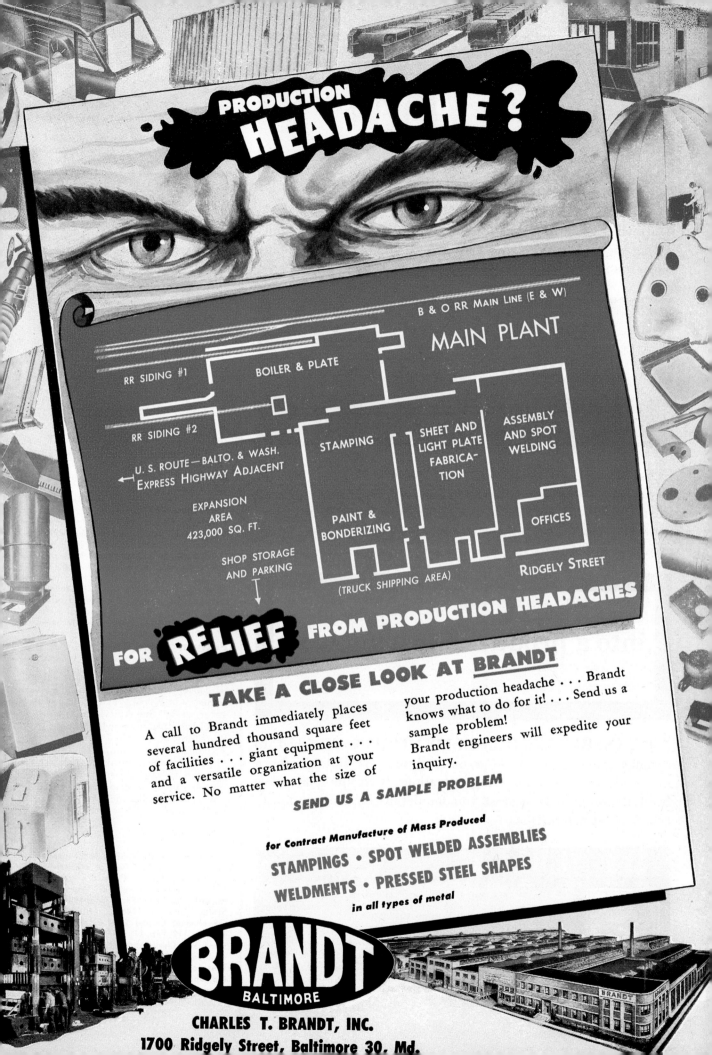

DEAR EDITOR

Continued

suitable only for use as a chemical reducing agent or precipitating agent, or as a hardener in concrete.

Quite possibly laboratory quantities of commercial iron powders can be obtained through either Ekstrand & Tholand Inc., 441 Lexington Ave., New York 17, one of the leading importers of Swedish powders or Metals Refining Co., Div. of the Blidden Co., P. O. Box 309, Hammond, Ind., a domestic producer. For coarser powders, try Pittsburgh Crushed Steel Co., 49th & Harrison Sts., Pittsburgh.—Ed.

Shooting For Work

Sir:

Can you advise me where I can get information on defense work that might be done in my shop. I make commercial rifle barrels, in calibers from .22 to .45. As my steel supply will no doubt be shut off, I must look around for something to do. It appears that we are all a little late in getting about the current unpleasant business.

I have, now, a capacity of 30 unfinished rifle barrels per day, of one caliber, and of simple shape. It is possible that this capacity can be put to good use in defense work. Where can I find out if my small shop could be of any use.

G. R. DOUGLAS
Charleston, W. Va.

As was the case last time, the country seems to be having considerable difficulty getting organized, and the small shops, which normally are sub-contractors, are the last to be fitted in. According to the Army Procurement Chart, however, rifles in such calibers are procured through the following: Commanding Officer, Rock Island Arsenal, Rock Island, Ill.; Commanding Officer, Springfield Armory, Springfield, Mass.—Ed.

Postwar Plant Disposal

Sir:

I am writing a report on the extent of concentration in the iron and steel industry in World War II. I have been referred by the American Iron and Steel Institute to your booklet entitled "A Study of Wartime Steel Industry Expansion." I would appreciate greatly your forwarding this booklet to me, along with any information you can give me pertaining to the disposal of government built and/or owned steel facilities after the year 1947.

R. D. LEVIDOW
Cornell University
Ithaca, N. Y.

Although IRON AGE did not publish a booklet entitled "A Study of Wartime Steel Industry Expansion," there are several articles which may be helpful: "Wartime Steel Records Revised; Show Mid-1945, Trade Status," Jan. 10, 1946, p. 110; "Tables of Government Owned Steel Plants," Feb. 13, 1947, p. 112, Feb. 27, 1947, p. 102; "Government Still Owns About 150 Million Dollars of Steel Facilities," Feb. 10, 1949, p. 116. These articles give both a brief summary of the wartime expansion and the later disposal to private industry.—Ed.

"you can get an extra half ton in that one . . .
it's a MAGNESIUM body"

One thousand, fifteen hundred, and even two thousand pounds of extra payload! That's what magnesium has meant to progressive haulers across the country. What used to be costly dead weight becomes profitable payload when magnesium, a full third lighter than any other light metal, is used in truck body and trailer construction.

Motor transportation is just one field where magnesium has proved its value. Others are business machines, optical instruments, portable tools, and materials handling equipment. All have been improved—made more efficient, easier to handle, more profitable to sell by the proper use of magnesium. If you make or plan to make anything in which lightness is important, it will pay you to investigate magnesium.

MAGNESIUM

LIGHTENS THE LOADS OF AMERICA

When lightness is important, consider MAGNESIUM first!

In magnesium you'll find a full third greater lightness combined with surprising strength and many other excellent properties. For full information call your nearest Dow sales office or write direct.

Magnesium Division, Dept. MG-21

THE DOW CHEMICAL COMPANY • MIDLAND, MICHIGAN

New York • Boston • Philadelphia • Washington • Atlanta • Cleveland • Detroit
Chicago • St. Louis • Houston • Los Angeles • San Francisco • Seattle
Dow Chemical of Canada, Limited, Toronto, Canada

DATES
to remember

Jan. 6—American Home Laundry Manufacturers Assn., winter meeting, Hotel Morrison, Chicago. Association headquarters are at 38 S. Dearborn St., Chicago.

Jan. 8-12—Society of Automotive Engineers, annual meeting, Hotel Book-Cadillac, Detroit. Society headquarters are at 29 W. 39th St., New York.

Jan. 9—Mining & Metallurgical Society of America, annual meeting, Mining Club, New York. Society headquarters are at 11 Broadway, New York.

Jan. 10-12—Heat Exchange Institute, annual meeting, Seaview Country Club, Absecon, N. J. Institute headquarters are at 122 E. 42nd St., New York.

Jan. 14-16—Institute of Scrap Iron & Steel, annual convention, Commodore Hotel, New York. Institute headquarters are at 1346 Connecticut Ave., N.W., Washington.

Jan. 15-16—Industrial Furnace Manufacturers Assn., mid-winter meeting, Edgewater Beach Hotel, Chicago. Association headquarters are at 420 Lexington Ave., New York.

Jan. 15-18—Plant Maintenance Show, Public Auditorium, Cleveland. Exposition management Clapp & Poliak, Inc., 341 Madison Ave., New York.

Jan. 16—American Boiler Manufacturers Assn. & Affiliated Industries, mid-winter meeting, Cleveland. Association headquarters are at 264 Rockefeller Bldg., Cleveland.

Jan. 18-20—Society of Plastics Engineers, annual national technical conference, Statler Hotel, New York. Society president is J. H. Dubois, 160 Coit St., Irvington, N. J.

Jan. 19—Malleable Founders Society, semiannual meeting, Hotel Cleveland, Cleveland. Society headquarters are at 1800 Union Commerce Bldg., Cleveland.

Jan. 21-23—Truck Trailer Manufacturers Assn., annual convention, Edgewater Gulf Hotel, Edgewater Park, Miss. Association headquarters are in the National Press Bldg., Washington.

Jan. 22-23—Compressed Gas Assn., annual convention, Waldorf Astoria Hotel, New York. Association headquarters are at 11 W. 42nd St., New York.

Jan. 24-25—Caster & Floor Truck Manufacturers Assn., winter meeting, Hotel New Yorker, New York. Association headquarters are at 7 W. Madison St., Chicago.

Jan. 28-Feb. 1 — Associated Equipment Distributors, annual meeting, Stevens Hotel, Chicago. Association headquarters are at 360 N. Michigan Ave., Chicago.

Feb. 19-22—American Institute of Mining & Metallurgical Engineers, annual meeting, Jefferson Hotel, St. Louis. Institute headquarters are at 29 W. 39th St., New York.

Mar. 5-7—Hydraulic Institute, quarterly meeting, Santa Barbara Biltmore Hotel, Santa Barbara, Calif. Institute headquarters are at 122 E. 42nd St., New York.

Mar. 5-7—Manufacturers Standardization Society of the Valve and Fittings Industry, annual meeting, Commodore Hotel, New York. Society headquarters are at 420 Lexington Ave., New York.

machine tool high spots

sales inquiries and production

by w. a. lloyd

Big War, Big Role—If it's true that a great country can have no such thing as a little war, the fortunes of the United States in the present emergency will depend to a great extent on the performance of the machine tool industry. A big war means big quantities of material, which is another way of saying that national defense begins in the factories.

Machine tool order volume in 1951 will be very large. During the last quarter of 1950, new orders averaged $80 million a month, most of which were unrated. As the defense program gains impetus and foreign business is placed, the machine tool industry's 1950 order volume will probably surpass $1 billion and possibly reach $1.5 billion, according to reliable trade sources.

Unknowns Limit Forecast—However, any appraisal of 1951 order volume is limited by a number of unknowns in the military planning equation and by the fact that some machine tool companies are already refusing unrated orders.

It is reliably reported that the industry will get $150 million in ECA orders and possibly $250 million under the Mutual Defense Assistance Program, both of which may be subject to revision.

Some of the foreign business the industry will get will be diverted from the European machine tool industry, which is swamped. British builders are quoting 1953 delivery on some machines.

Tooling for War Work—The growing volume of domestic defense production will require additional tooling for aircraft engines, shells, guns, guided missiles and many other projects, secret and urgent.

It has been predicted that the government may anticipate some of these tooling requirements by activating the Emergency Production Schedules or "phantom orders." This would provide the industry with some working capital which some companies could probably use, but would seriously overload it. Objective of EPS is production of 100,000 machine tools in the first 6 months following the outbreak of hostilities.

Those who oppose EPS activation say the plan was set up for an emergency of the Pearl Harbor type, and that many or most of the tools presently on commercial order could be diverted to defense contractors. In other words, the cushion is already on the order books.

Spotlight on Capacity—A potential order volume of $1 billion

ANNUAL REVIEW

brings the plant capacity of the industry into sharp focus. Capacity is larger than it was in 1939, but smaller than it was in 1942, peak of World War II machine tool production. In 1945, the capacity had dropped to an estimated $500 million on a one-shift operation. In 1942 the industry's shipments were $1,320,000,000. In today's dollars and prices, the industry would have to make shipment of $2,100,000,000 to reach the World War II peak, which was accomplished with subcontracting.

Shipments in 1950 were about $280 million. The industry will do well to raise its shipments to $600 million this year.

Consider Capacity Rise—In the interval from 1943, when 80 pct of its war production task was finished, to 1950, about 40 companies went out of the machine tool business, through merger, consolidation, or outright sale. Some capacity was lost as a result.

Increases in the industry's capacity are under consideration, however, as it is known that at least seven companies have filed applications for certificates of necessity for expansion.

Blanket Priority Needed—To double 1950 shipments, the industry will need a blanket priority for materials, which is not immediately

M. & M. DUPLEX MILLING AND CENTERING MACHINE

Part — automotive pinion
Operation — mill both ends and center drill
Production — 220 pieces per hour at 100%

FOR HIGHER PRODUCTION

Combine Operations

ON **MOTCH & MERRYWEATHER**
SPECIAL MACHINES

The Motch & Merryweather milling head features rigidity at the tool point.

You can be sure of getting higher production with lower cost per piece by using Motch & Merryweather machines designed for multiple operations. The machine pictured here mills and center drills a vast range of parts, some of which are shown in white above. Our representative will help you obtain thorough-going accuracy, together with *production, PRODUCTION,* and *MORE PRODUCTION.* Contact us *now.*

Manufactured by

THE MOTCH & MERRYWEATHER MACHINERY COMPANY
715 PENTON BUILDING • CLEVELAND 13, OHIO
Builders of Circular Sawing Equipment, Production Milling, Automatic and Special Machines

PRODUCTION-WITH-ACCURACY MACHINES AND EQUIPMENT

in sight. In World War II, the industry was able to increase production quickly, because it had a high priority for materials early and manpower was available.

Most serious problem facing the industry at the start of a critical year is a shortage of materials. These shortages vary with plant locations and are widespread. Most common items in short supply are steel, sheets and plate, ground shafting, bearings, anti-friction, fractional horsepower motors, oil pumps and copper wire. In some plants, machines are backing up on the assembly floors as a result.

Production Down the Drain—At present, the machine tool builder has priorities for materials for rated orders only. According to Tell Berna, general manager, National Machine Tool Builders' Assn., most companies' backlogs contain only 10 pct rated orders, a few have 30 pct of their business rated and one or two have more.

As a priority system develops the industry will get more materials, but in the meantime, production is being lost.

Warning for New Year—In a year-end statement, Richard E. LeBlond, president of NMTBA, and president of the R. K. LeBlond Machine Tool Co., warned, "From the volume of its unfilled orders one might assume that the industry is headed for unprecedented activity in 1951. As matters stand now, there is grave danger, however, that such may not be the case. There is every probability that while orders continue to rise, output will actually decline, this trend is already in evidence.

Can't Get Materials—"The industry has been unable to get priorities, therefore it can't get steel and other vital materials. Such rated defense orders as the industry does receive constitute a minor portion of its business. Furthermore, while in theory a rating on an order for a particular machine "enables" the builder to get the steel required, in practice steel cannot be bought in such small quantities.

"Unfilled orders are approximately 12 times the volume of current monthly output. During World War II, in spite of the tremendous load suddenly placed upon the industry, the backlog was never more than seven times its then current monthly output. But in World War II the industry was given a blanket priority which enabled it to buy everything it needed for production," Mr. LeBlond pointed out.

Don't Know Industry—Big stumbling block in the granting of a blanket priority at the present time seems to be a lack of recognition on the part of some government officials of the basic nature of the machine tool industry.

On the other hand, MSRB head, S. Stuart Symington has some understanding of the machine tool industry in war production. In January, 1946, Mr. Symington, then Surplus Property Administrator, declared, "Machine tools are the essential backbone of all industrial production."

Labor Supply Important—Manpower is another important problem. In September 1950, latest month for which figures are available, makers of metal cutting machine tools employed 44,500. Total employment in the industry, including metal forming machinery builders, was 80,000.

To produce $1,320,000,000 in 1942, metal cutting machine tool builders employed 112,000 men plus subcontracting. Outlines of the manpower problem in an emergency were apparent to some observers as far back as 1948. A. G. Bryant, president of Bryant Machinery & Engineering Co., and a vice-president of Cleereman Machine Tool Co., and president of NMTBA in 1948, warned that machine tool builders have had to let their working forces dwindle and there are no available reserves of skilled workmen that could be immediately tapped for a rebuilding of working shifts to normal operations.

Transition Takes Months—Supplies of steel, castings, scrap, pig iron and other essentials are on such a scanty basis that months would be required to get machine tool production in the average plant to an emergency basis.

Toll on Manpower—Nucleus of the industry's shop personnel is probably older than it was at the start of World War II, and the poor business of the past 5 years has not been conducive to apprentice training programs. Some of the industry's personnel is subject to the draft, or in the reserves. Finally, the industry has been losing men to other industries which are expanding and paying higher wages.

A diversion of skilled manpower from non-essential production will probably be required to pull the machine tool industry out of the manpower doldrums.

But It Can Be Done—In World War II, production practically doubled every year until the peak was reached and the industry had had 3 years to prepare for the big push. Doubling present production in view of present materials and manpower will be a tremendous accomplishment, but the machine tool industry is noted for such accomplishments.

Fortunately, in the National Security Reserve there are some tools in the grease. The exact number is known only to the government, since many have been released since K-Day, but at one time there were 110,000. According to one estimate, the AAF alone has taken out about 10,000 during the past 4 years. Some are being released to defense contractors at the present time. These tools are somewhat obsolescent and some are being rebuilt by their original manufacturers, but they are a temporary cushion.

Also, some aircraft engines, tank and shell lines have been kept in stand-by condition.

Cash Surplus Gone—Excess profits taxes and renegotiation will again prevent the industry from accumulating the cash surplus that is a recognized necessity in a cyclical business.

But apart from manpower, and materials, the industry is well prepared for the present emergency. It has good plants and equipment, determination, and good leaders.

8 SURFACES MACHINED ...1046 PIECES PER HOUR...

...ON EX-CELL-O PRECISION BORING MACHINE

Operator placing pistons on loading pins. Movement of the loading lever controls the automatic machine cycle.

Two Style 112-C Ex-Cell-O Precision Boring Machines finish eighteen surfaces of the parts shown in the drawings at right below. One machine finishes 8 surfaces at the net rate of 1046 pieces per hour; the companion machine finishes 10 surfaces at the net rate of 640 pieces per hour. The parts are automotive shock absorber pistons, approximately one inch in diameter.

The spindles, four on each machine, operate continuously. Work loading equipment and automatic ejection of finished parts contribute to the extremely fast machine cycles.

Whether your work involves precision machining in large volume or in small lots you'll find that it's economical to use *standard machines* whenever possible. Ask your Ex-Cell-O representative for complete information on standard Ex-Cell-O Precision Boring Machines.

Here the loading bracket has been turned down toward the spindles. Further movement of the loading lever seats parts in the chucks.

These enlarged drawings show in heavy lines the surfaces finished on the two Ex-Cell-O Precision Boring Machines. One machine finishes the surfaces numbered 1-10; the other 11-18.

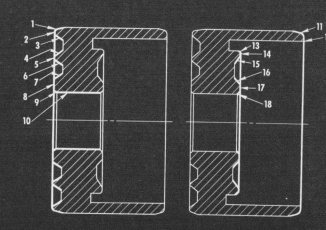

50-20

EX-CELL-O CORPORATION
DETROIT 32 MICHIGAN

FREE *publications*

Portable Hardness Tester

Four models of Ames portable hardness testers, for quick and accurate on-the-spot tests, reading directly in Rockwell hardness scales, are described in a new 6-p. folder. The different models shown vary in maximum capacities for testing flats and rounds up to 1 in., 2 in., and 4 in., all of which can be used to test long bars and large sheets right where they are, without cutting off samples. The simple steps for operation of the tester are illustrated in the folder. *Ames Precision Machine Works.*

For free copy insert No. 1 on postcard.

Vertical Boring Mills

Construction and operating features of 10 different sizes of King vertical boring mills are shown in a series of 4 new 16-p. catalogs. Photos and diagrams illustrate operation of the unit; and the booklet describes various head combinations and attachments. Complete specifications and capacities are listed in the catalogs. *King Machine Tool Div., American Steel Foundries.*

For free copy insert No. 2 on postcard.

Stocks Listed

A new 1951 general stock list, thumb-indexed for easy reference, contains all pertinent information on such items as beams, channels, angles, tees and zees, plates, hot-rolled bars and strip, cold-finished bars and shafting, alloy bars, steel sheets, strip, flat wire, spring steel, brass and copper alloys, aluminum, stainless steel, steel tubing, nails, bolts, rivets and washers, silver brazing materials and welding wire, tool steel and drill rod. Other sections list specifications, physical properties and weights on various materials, and give useful engineering data and conversion tables. *Central Steel & Wire Co.*

For free copy insert No. 3 on postcard.

For Track or Road

The Whiting Trackmobile, providing flexibility in spotting, switching and hauling railway cars, is described in a new bulletin telling how combination track and road operation saves time and cuts costs. By use of hydraulic jacks, the unit can be switched from road to track operation in less than ½ minute, as shown in the folder. A few examples of the hundreds of varied applications for the truck are shown, and construction features are listed. *Whiting Corp.*

For free copy insert No. 4 on postcard.

Heavy Duty Contactor

The A-C Type 256 high voltage air contactor, designed for general alternating current motor starting applications, is described in a new 8-p. booklet. The simplified construction and operating features of the unit are shown, illustrating its compact design. Special arc chutes are also detailed, and the A-C line of high voltage starters are described. *Allis-Chalmers Mfg. Co.*

For free copy insert No. 5 on postcard.

Investment Casting

A new 4-p. folder describes the investment casting process and applications, and the manner in which this process is used to make substantial savings in machining, tooling, and elimination of waste metal. Metals which can be cast are described, and a diagram illustrates a case history to demonstrate potentialities of investment casting. *Investment Casting Co.*

For free copy insert No. 6 on postcard.

Welding Electrodes

The full line of P & H shielded arc welding electrodes in all practical sizes for various types of welding and hard surfacing are listed in a new 56-p. thumb-indexed, pocket-size booklet. Specifications and operating procedures, along with other up-to-the-minute information on the new low hydrogen electrodes are presented. Section headings in the booklet deal with welding mild steels, cast iron, alloy steels, stainless steels, and electrodes for hard surfacing. *Harnischfeger Corp.*

For free copy insert No. 7 on postcard.

Protective Coatings

A new 4-p. bulletin presents data on five groups of chemical resisting Ucilon protective coatings. Described are coatings based on vinyl resins, phenolic resins, fish oils, chlorinated rubber, and also water emulsion coatings. The coatings are resistant to acids, alkalies, petroleum and its derivatives, water, oxidants, salt solutions, alcohols, and many solvents. *United Chromium, Inc.*

For free copy insert No. 8 on postcard.

Economics Chart

The high spots and the low points of the American economy since 1796 are graphically shown in the 1951 edition of the "Business Booms and Depressions" chart available from the warehousing subsidiary of U. S. Steel. Several new and timely features have been added to this year's edition; including census significance, employment and unemployment, wage rates, retail sales, and per capita income. Of particular interest are indices which show the effect of war production on the nation's economy.

Turn to Page 414D

NEW *production ideas*

Acetylene-Air Torch

Features built-in pilot light and diaphragm type valve.

The valve of a new Sod-R-Braze acetylene-air torch is designed and positioned so that the operator can turn the torch on and off, adjust the flame and regulate the pilot light all with the thumb of the hand holding the torch. A fire-resistant, plastic handle is grooved to provide cool operation and a firm grip. Six tips, with individual mixers, ranging from 3/32 to ¼ in. diam, permit a wide range of work, from soldering fine parts to sweat fitting and heavy heating. A carrying stand of aluminum tubing makes the Sod-R-Braze outfit completely portable. It holds a 40 cu ft acetylene cylinder, torch, hose, wrench and torch lighter. *National Cylinder Gas Co.*

For more data insert No. 24 on postcard.

Finish for Aluminum

Can be used as a base for paint or to protect bare metal from corrosion.

The new material called Protecto-Cote is already mixed and needs only to be dissolved in water, 6 oz per gal. Work is immersed in the solution at 185°F, remaining in the bath about 5 min. No electric current is required. The solution is self-cleaning, making the process a one-operation job. *Chemclean Products Corp.*

For more data insert No. 25 on postcard.

Storage System

One-man pushbutton control provides selectivity in handling any item.

A new method of storing materials is said to provide 100 pct selectivity in handling items such as rough stock, pallets, rolled goods, drums, bundles, dies, patterns and tote boxes. With only one attendant the Stak-Rak storage system delivers in-coming materials to the exact position specified, or quickly and accurately selects required units or materials from storage and makes prompt, speedy delivery at the required point. The system consists of self-standing rack-columns designed to receive the required material. A crane bridge spans the entire width of the storage area and travels lengthwise on tracks to any depth. It is equipped with an overhead trolley from which is suspended an electric fork lift. *Chicago Tramrail Corp.*

For more data insert No. 26 on postcard.

Water-Displacer

Insures a chemically moisture-free surface on all metals.

Used as a cold dip, Hydrolift instantly forms a molecular film, even in deep crevices, it is stated, lifting the moisture to the surface where it runs off. The film, when dry, is transparent and can neither be seen nor felt. Coverage is 8200 sq ft per gal. It is suited as a dip, spray, or brush-on after water rinsing of metal surfaces, assuring protection of the surfaces during inter-operational and short term finished product storage. After

use postcard below

pickling and rinsing, parts immediately dipped in Hydrolift will not rust and there are no after reactions. The film dries in 15 min, leaving a clean, desirable surface for further plating or finishing. *London Chemical Co.*

For more data insert No. 27 on postcard.

Power Hoist Unit

Portable drill one minute; power hoist the next.

A Skil 1-in. drill model 163 combined with an American handiwinch makes a complete power hoist unit in a matter of minutes. A simple adapter kit locks the drill and handiwinch in perfect alignment, assuring safe, big-capacity hoisting on all jobs. The drill can be taken out of the hoist bracket and is ready for drilling jobs. With a hoisting capacity of 1000 lb at 10 fpm, the drill-handiwinch combination is designed for use by contractors, machine shops, foundries, garages and warehouses. *Skilsaw, Inc.*

For more data insert No. 28 on postcard.

Welders Coat

Sleeve fronts are double thickness of leather to assure long wear.

A new model welders coat is a 26-in. length coat made of soft, pliable chrome tanned split cowhide in small, medium, large, and extra large sizes. It is generously cut for greatest comfort. Other features include double stitching, snap fasteners, adjustable wrist snaps, seam end reinforcement with copper rivets. *Metal & Thermit Corp.*

For more data insert No. 29 on postcard.

Fire Protection System

Dry chemical piped system for total flooding or for local application.

A new fire protection system using dry chemical as extinguishing agent is operated by an H.A.D. (heat-actuated device) mechanism. When fire starts and temperature increases, air expands within the H.A.D. This trips a nitrogen cylinder release, pressurizing the dry chemical container. Dry chemical is then discharged through strategically located distribution heads onto the fire area. Automatic controls can be added to close doors, windows, ventilation ducts and to operate valves on pipes carrying flammable liquids. Electric controls can be included to shut off motors and fans, sound alarms and transmit signals to central stations or fire alarm headquarters. Manual operation as well as automatic is provided. *Ansul Chemical Co.*

For more data insert No. 30 on postcard.

Improved Coolant

Hydrodyne said to improve coolants regardless of oils or additives used.

Increased coolant efficiency is said to result from the addition of minute quantities of Hydrodyne, a new multiphase wetting agent. It reduces the interfacial tension of the coolant assuring its intimate contact with working surfaces and it speeds dissipation of harmful heat. The coolant lasts longer, spreads faster and splashes less. *Aquadyne Corp.*

For more data insert No. 31 on postcard.

Vane Filing Fixture

Speeds up fitting a set of vanes to a cold spot compressor.

A simple tool is said to enable an unskilled helper to fit a set of vanes in 5 min within the extreme tolerances of 0.0001 in. The tool is micro-adjustable to the 5 sizes of vanes, including those of sealed units. It is precision made of case hardened tool steel, heavily plated to insure lifetime service. *Wagner Tool & Supply Corp.*

For more data insert No. 32 on postcard.

Hydraulic Grinder

Wheelhead swivels 180°; mounts internal and external spindles.

The wheelhead on the new universal hydraulic grinder is designed to eliminate dual work setups for internal and external grinding. The operator can quickly present either spindle to the same work. A feature providing added accuracy and speed is the mounting of draw-in collets and step chucks directly in the lathe type workhead and the operation of a lever closer to reduce chucking time. Internal spindle speeds range from 6000

use postcard below

production ideas
Continued

spindle speeds range from 6000 to 35,000 rpm. All spindles are flanged mounted, sealed from grit and life lubricated. The external spindle with double-row roller bearings for radial load and ball

bearings for end thrust permits maximum rigidity with no adjustment required. Other features include micrometer table stop and fine feed for shoulder and blind-hole grinding; sine bar for setting workhead on table swivel for perfect tapers; double swivels on cross slide for two angle internal and external grinding. *Rivett Lathe & Grinder, Inc.*
For more data insert No. 33 on postcard, p. 37.

Electronic Equipment
Speeds machining of jet engine blade

Accurate machining of the holding surfaces with respect to the airfoil surfaces of blades for jet engines is speeded up by a new machine developed for positioning the blade and drilling center holes used

for location purposes in a subsequent machining operation on the holding surfaces. The blade is supported in a cradle that adjustably pivots about two axes and is adjustable vertically. Each of the three movements can be clamped independently of the others. Proper positioning is effected by observation of six strain gage indicator points in contact with the airfoil surface and adjusting the three movements to zero position. After positioning the blade three combination center drill and facing cutters advance to make three operations on bosses on the blade. The setup is accomplished from a master blade. The machine accommodates 17 blade sizes. It is estimated that one man can operate the machine at a rate of 100 blades per hr. *Brown & Sharpe Mfg. Co.*
For more data insert No. 34 on postcard, p. 37.

Lapping Equipment
Adaptable for the finishing of small flat parts continuously.

A new arrangement of the No. 26 Hyprolap vertical lapping machine for finishing small flat parts continuously is suitable for products having an unusually high production requirement. It is reportedly well adapted to the production lap-

ping of small flat washers and similar parts that offer no unusual problems in the way of rapid loading. The new design features automatic loading and unloading during lapping cycle. Lapping is continuous with no down time except for dressing laps. Handling time is reduced to a minimum and the machine operator can be unskilled. Lapping operations require special work holder design with the machine operator loading and unloading each part individually and controlling the lapping cycle. Where the continuous feed arrangement is feasible, these duties have become almost completely eliminated. The photograph shows equipment furnished for continuous or through feed lapping of small brass washers. *Norton Co.*
For more data insert No. 35 on postcard, p. 37.

Injection Molding Machine
300-oz capacity, 1500-ton clamping pressure, and 4x6-ft mold size

Fully hydraulic, a plastics injection molding machine having a 300-oz capacity is equipped with manual as well as automatic single cycle control and adjustable speed control of the injection ram. Indi-

vidual adjustable control of injection and clamping pressures is also provided. The machine's immense capacity, clamping pressure and mold size accommodation, and its 4 ft maximum stroke and 6 ft daylight opening will enable molders to produce parts with deeper draw and opens up new production possibilities. *Watson-Stillman Co.*
For more data insert No. 36 on postcard, p. 37.

Tumbling Machine
Has increased capacity for grinding, de-burring and finishing metal parts.

A new tumbling machine employing the Grav-i-Flo tumbling process uses Grav-i-Flo chips and compounds to produce smooth and high luster surfaces. The machine is 5 ft 8 in. wide x 5 ft 4 in. deep x 5 ft 8 in. high. With its two 24 x 40 in. ID compartments, it is claimed to

handle a 30 pct larger work load than comparable machines occupying the same square feet of floor space. Compartments are furnished with ½ in. plate unlined or ¼ in. plate rubber-lined. Doors have cam locks with manually released safety
Turn to Page 410

METALWORKING MEETINGS SCHEDULED FOR 1951

Technical Meetings, Conventions and Expositions on Various Phases of Metalworking and Metal Production.

JANUARY

Jan. 6—American Home Laundry Manufacturers Assn., winter meeting, Hotel Morrison, Chicago. Association headquarters are at 38 S. Dearborn St., Chicago.

Jan. 8-12—Society of Automotive Engineers, annual meeting, Hotel Book-Cadillac, Detroit. Society headquarters are at 29 W. 39th St., New York.

Jan. 9—Mining & Metallurgical Society of America, annual meeting, Mining Club, New York. Society headquarters are at 11 Broadway, New York.

Jan. 10-12—Heat Exchange Institute, annual meeting, Seaview Country Club, Absecon, N. J. Institute headquarters are at 122 E. 42nd St., New York.

Jan. 14-16—Institute of Scrap Iron & Steel, annual convention, Commodore Hotel, New York. Institute headquarters are at 1346 Connecticut Ave., N.W., Washington.

Jan. 15-16—Industrial Furnace Manufacturers Assn., mid-winter meeting, Edgewater Beach Hotel, Chicago. Association headquarters are at 420 Lexington Ave., New York.

Jan. 15-18—Plant Maintenance Show, Public Auditorium, Cleveland. Exposition management Clapp & Poliak, Inc., 341 Madison Ave., New York.

Jan. 16—American Boiler Manufacturers Assn. & Affiliated Industries, mid-winter meeting, Cleveland. Association headquarters are at 264 Rockefeller Bldg., Cleveland.

Jan. 18-20—Society of Plastics Engineers, annual national technical conference, Statler Hotel, New York. Society president is J. H. DuBois, 160 Coit St., Irvington, N. J.

Jan. 19—Malleable Founders Society, semiannual meeting, Hotel Cleveland, Cleveland. Society headquarters are at 1800 Union Commerce Bldg., Cleveland.

Jan. 21-23—Truck Trailer Manufacturers Assn., annual convention, Edgewater Gulf Hotel, Edgewater Park, Miss. Association headquarters are in the National Press Bldg., Washington.

Jan. 22-23—Compressed Gas Assn., annual convention, Waldorf-Astoria Hotel, New York. Association headquarters are at 11 W. 42nd St., New York.

Jan. 24-25—Caster & Floor Truck Manufacturers Assn., winter meeting, Hotel New Yorker, New York. Association headquarters are at 7 W. Madison St., Chicago.

Jan. 28-Feb. 1—Associated Equipment Distributors, annual meeting, Stevens Hotel, Chicago. Association headquarters are at 360 N. Michigan Ave., Chicago.

FEBRUARY

Feb. 19-22—American Institute of Mining & Metallurgical Engineers, annual meeting, Jefferson Hotel, St. Louis. Institute headquarters are at 29 W. 39th St., New York.

MARCH

Mar. 5-7—Hydraulic Institute, quarterly meeting, Santa Barbara Biltmore Hotel, Santa Barbara, Calif. Institute headquarters are at 122 E. 42nd St., New York.

Mar. 5-7—Manufacturers Standardization Society of the Valve and Fittings Industry, annual meeting, Commodore Hotel, New York. Society headquarters are at 420 Lexington Ave., New York.

Mar. 5-7—Pittsburgh Conference on Analytical Chemistry and Applied Spectroscopy, William Penn Hotel, Pittsburgh. American Chemical Society national headquarters are at 1155 16th St., Washington.

Mar. 5-9—American Society for Testing Materials, spring meeting, Cincinnati. Society headquarters are at 1916 Race St., Philadelphia.

Mar. 6-8—Society of Automotive Engineers, passenger car, body and materials meeting, Hotel Book-Cadillac, Detroit. Society headquarters are at 29 W. 39th St., New York.

Mar. 12-15—National Electrical Manufacturers Assn., spring meeting, Edgewater Beach Hotel, Chicago. Association headquarters are at 155 E. 44th St., New York.

Mar. 13-15—Assn. of American Railroads, Engineering Div. and Construction & Maintenance Section, annual meeting, Palmer House, Chicago. Association headquarters are in the Transportation Bldg., Washington.

Mar. 13-16—National Assn. of Corrosion Engineers, conference and exhibition, Statler Hotel, New York. Association

Turn to Page 117

Meetings for 1951

headquarters are in the Southern Standard Bldg., Houston.

Mar. 14-17—American Society of Tool Engineers, annual meeting, Hotel New Yorker, New York. Society headquarters are at 10700 Puritan Ave., Detroit.

Mar. 19-21—National Assn. of Waste Material Dealers, annual convention, Stevens Hotel, Chicago. Association headquarters are at 1109 Times Bldg., New York.

Mar. 19-21—Steel Founders Society of America, annual meeting, Edgewater Beach Hotel, Chicago. Society headquarters are at 920 Midland Bldg., Cleveland.

Mar. 22-23—Pressed Metal Institute, annual technical meeting, Hotel Carter, Cleveland. Institute headquarters are at 13210 Shaker Square, Cleveland.

APRIL

Apr. 2-3—Diamond Core Drill Manufacturers Assn., annual meeting, The Homestead, Hot Springs, Va. Association headquarters are at 122 E. 42nd St., New York.

Apr. 2-4—American Institute of Mining & Metallurgical Engineers, openhearth and blast furnace, coke oven and raw materials conference, Statler Hotel, Cleveland. Institute headquarters are at 29 W. 39th St., New York.

Apr. 2-5—American Society of Mechanical Engineers, spring meeting, Atlanta Biltmore Hotel, Atlanta. Society headquarters are at 29 W. 39th St., New York.

Apr. 2-7—Steel Shipping Container Institute, annual meeting, Palm Beach-Biltmore Hotel, Palm Beach, Fla. Institute headquarters are at 570 Lexington Ave., New York.

Apr. 5-6—Compressed Air & Gas Institute, quarterly meeting. The Homestead, Hot Springs, Va. Institute headquarters are at 122 E. 42nd St., New York.

Apr. 8-11—Electrochemical Society, spring meeting, Wardman Park Hotel, Washington. Society headquarters are at 235 W. 102nd St., New York.

Apr. 8-12—American Hardware Manufacturers Assn., annual convention, Palm Beach, Fla. Association headquarters are at 342 Madison Ave., New York.

Apr. 9-10—American Institute of Steel Construction, spring engineering conference, Hotel William Penn, Pittsburgh. Institute headquarters are at 101 Park Ave., New York.

Apr. 15-18—Scientific Apparatus Makers Assn., annual meeting, Greenbrier White Sulphur Springs, W. Va. Association headquarters are at 20 N. Wacker Drive, Chicago.

Apr. 16-18—American Gas Assn., distribution, motor vehicle and corrosion conference, Hotel Peabody, Memphis, Tenn. Association headquarters are at 420 Lexington Ave., New York.

Apr. 16-18—American Society of Lubrication Engineers, annual convention and lubrication show, Bellevue-Stratford Hotel, Philadelphia. Society headquarters are at 343 S. Dearborn St., Chicago.

Apr. 16-18—Gas Appliance Manufacturers Assn., annual meeting, Drake Hotel, Chicago. Association headquarters are at 60 E. 42nd St., New York.

Apr. 16-18—Society of Automotive Engineers, aeronautic meeting and aircraft engineering display, Hotel Statler, New York. Society headquarters are at 29 W. 39th St., New York.

Apr. 16-21—Concrete Reinforcing Steel Institute, annual meeting, The Homestead, Hot Springs, Va. Institute headquarters are at 38 S. Dearborn St., Chicago.

Apr. 16-21—Wire Reinforcement Institute, annual meeting, The Homestead, Hot

Turn to Page 118

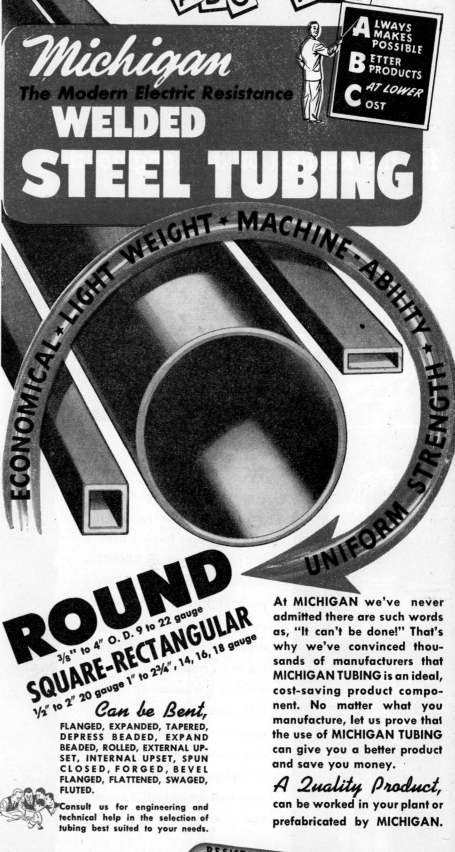

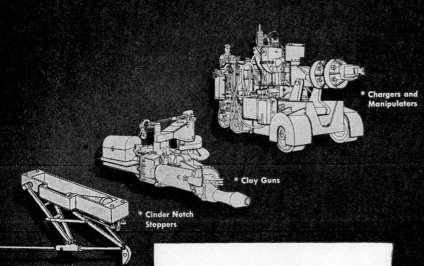

THE IRON AGE

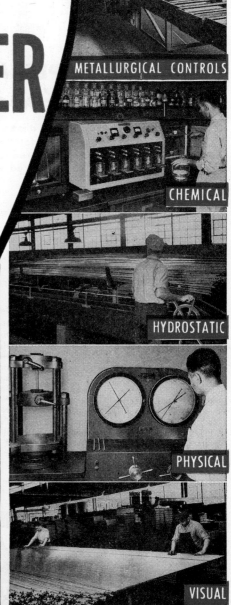

Meetings for 1951

ing, Netherland Plaza Hotel, Cincinnati. Association headquarters are at 209 Cedar Ave., Washington.

May 28-30—Grinding Wheel Institute, meeting, The Homestead, Hot Springs, Va. Institute headquarters are in Greendale, Mass.

May 30-June 2—Metal Treating Institute, spring meeting, Hotel Colorado, Glenwood Springs, Colo. Institute headquarters are at 271 North Ave., New Rochelle, N. Y.

May 31-June 2—Machinery Dealers National Assn., annual convention, Drake Hotel, Chicago. Association headquarters are at 20 N. Wacker Drive, Chicago.

JUNE

June 3-8—Society of Automotive Engineers, summer meeting, French Lick Springs Hotel, French Lick, Ind. Society headquarters are at 29 W. 39th St., New York.

June 4-6—American Gear Manufacturers Assn., annual meeting, The Homestead, Hot Springs, Va. Association headquarters are in the Empire Bldg., Pittsburgh.

June 4-6—Assn. of American Railroads, Purchases & Stores Div., annual meeting, Palmer House, Chicago. Association headquarters are in the Transportation Bldg., Washington.

June 4-6—Institute of Cooking & Heating Appliance Manufacturers, annual meeting and exhibit, Netherland Plaza Hotel, Cincinnati. Institute headquarters are in the Shoreham Hotel, Washington.

June 4-7—Edison Electric Institute, annual convention, Denver. Institute headquarters are at 420 Lexington Ave., New York.

June 7-8—Compressed Air & Gas Institute, quarterly meeting, Seaview Country Club, Absecon, N. J. Institute headquarters are at 122 E. 42nd St., New York.

June 11-13—Hydraulic Institute, quarterly meeting, Seaview Country Club, Absecon, N. J. Institute headquarters are at 122 E. 42nd St., New York.

June 11-13—Triple Industrial Supply Convention, St. Francis Hotel, San Francisco. National Supply & Machinery Distributors Assn. headquarters are at 505 Arch St., Philadelphia.

June 11-14—American Boiler Manufacturers Assn. & Affiliated Industries, annual meeting, Skytop Lodge, Skytop, Pa. Association headquarters are at 264 Rockefeller Bldg., Cleveland.

June 11-15—American Society of Mechanical Engineers, semiannual meeting, Royal York Hotel, Toronto. Society headquarters are at 29 W. 39th St., New York.

June 16—American Home Laundry Manufacturers Assn., summer meeting, Ho-

Turn to Page 122

Battery of individually controlled Annealing Furnaces for heat treating Unitcastings.

UNITCAST Heat Treating Facilities MEET ALL PHYSICAL REQUIREMENTS

To meet Unitcast's standards, there is more than enough heat treating capacity to handle production. Because of Unitcast's and customer's requirements, these facilities are a necessity.

In heat treating, Unitcastings are grouped according to the grade of metal and thickness of cross section to assure meeting all physical requirements. And all Unitcastings are heat treated in this manner to insure better performance. Here's just one illustration of the many ways Unitcast's adequate plant facilities benefit you.

tel Morrison, Chicago. Association headquarters are at 38 S. Dearborn St., Chicago.

June 18-22—American Society for Testing Materials, annual meeting, Atlantic City, N. J. Society headquarters are at 1916 Race St., Philadelphia.

June 20-22—Compressed Gas Assn., summer meeting, Seaview Country Club, Absecon, N. J. Association headquarters are at 11 W. 42nd St., New York.

June 21-22—Malleable Founders Society, annual meeting, The Homestead, Hot Springs, Va. Society headquarters are at 1800 Union Commerce Bldg., Cleveland.

June 24-26—Alloy Casting Institute, annual meeting, The Homestead, Hot Springs, Va. Institute headquarters are at 32 Third Ave., Mineola, N. Y.

June 25-28—American Electroplaters' Society, annual meeting, Hotel Biltmore, Los Angeles. Society address is P.O. Box 168, Jenkintown, Pa.

June 26-28—Assn. of American Railroads, Mechanical Div., annual meeting, Congress Hotel, Chicago. Association headquarters are in the Transportation Bldg., Washington.

SEPTEMBER

Sept. 6-7—Rail Steel Bar Assn., semiannual meeting, Broadmoor Hotel, Colorado Springs. Association headquarters are at 38 S. Dearborn St., Chicago.

Sept. 10-14 — Instrument Society of America, national instrument conference and exhibit, Sam Houston Coliseum, Houston. Society headquarters are at 921 Ridge Ave., Pittsburgh.

Sept. 11-13—Society of Automotive Engineers, tractor meeting, Hotel Schroeder, Milwaukee. Society headquarters are at 29 W. 39th St., New York.

Sept. 25-26—Steel Founders Society of America, fall meeting, The Homestead, Hot Springs, Va. Society headquarters are at 920 Midland Bldg., Cleveland.

Sept. 25-28—American Society of Mechanical Engineers, fall meeting, Hotel Radisson, Minneapolis. Society headquarters are at 29 W. 39th St., New York.

Sept. 26-28—National Metal Trades Assn., annual convention, Palmer House, Chicago. Association headquarters are at 122 S. Michigan Ave., Chicago.

Sept. 26-29—Marking Device Assn., national convention, Edgewater Beach Hotel, Chicago. Association headquarters are at 134 N. LaSalle St., Chicago.

OCTOBER

Oct. 1-4—Assn. of Iron & Steel Engineers, annual convention, Chicago. Association headquarters are at 1010 Empire Bldg., Pittsburgh.

Oct. 3-6—Pressed Metal Institute, annual meeting, Hotel Drake, Chicago. Institute headquarters are at 13210 Shaker Square, Cleveland.

Oct. 8-13—Concrete Reinforcing Steel Institute, semiannual meeting, Grove Park Inn, Asheville, N. C. Institute headquarters are at 38 S. Dearborn St., Chicago.

Oct. 10-12—Porcelain Enamel Institute, annual forum, Ohio State University, Columbus. Institute headquarters are at 1010 Vermont Ave., Washington.

Oct. 14-19—National Metal Congress & Exposition, Detroit. American Society for Metals headquarters are at 7301 Euclid Ave., Cleveland.

Oct. 15-17—American Institute of Mining & Metallurgical Engineers, Institute of Metals Div., fall meeting, Detroit. Institute headquarters are at 29 W. 39th St., New York.

Oct. 15-18—American Gas Assn., annual convention, St. Louis. Association headquarters are at 420 Lexington Ave., New York.

Oct. 18-20—**Anti-Friction Bearing Manufacturers Assn.**, fall meeting, The Homestead, Hot Springs, Va. Association headquarters are at 60 E. 42nd St., New York.

Oct. 20-23—**Steel Boiler Institute**, fall meeting, The Greenbrier, White Sulphur Springs, W. Va. Institute headquarters are at 1207 Land Title Bldg., Philadelphia.

Oct. 21-25—**American Institute of Steel Construction**, annual convention, Greenbrier Hotel, White Sulphur Springs, W. Va. Institute headquarters are at 101 Park Ave., New York.

Oct. 22-24—**American Mining Congress**, metal mining convention, Biltmore Hotel, Los Angeles. Association headquarters are in the Ring Bldg., Washington.

Oct. 25-26—**Gray Iron Founders' Society**, annual meeting, Edgewater Beach Hotel, Chicago. Society headquarters are at 210 National City—E. 6th Bldg., Cleveland.

Oct. 28-30—**Conveyor Equipment Manufacturers Assn.**, annual meeting, The Homestead, Hot Springs, Va. Association headquarters are at 1129 Vermont Ave., N. W., Washington.

Oct. 29-Nov. 3 — **American Institute of Mining & Metallurgical Engineers**, fall meeting, Mexico City. Institute headquarters are at 29 W. 39th St., New York.

Oct. 31 - Nov. 2 — **Foundry Equipment Manufacturers Assn.**, annual meeting, The Homestead, Hot Springs, Va. Association headquarters are in the Engineers Bldg., Cleveland.

NOVEMBER

Nov. 12-15—**National Electrical Manufacturers Assn.**, annual meeting, Haddon Hall, Atlantic City, N. J. Association headquarters are at 155 E. 44th St., New York.

Nov. 25-30 — **American Society of Mechanical Engineers**, annual meeting, Chalfonte-Haddon Hall Hotel, Atlantic City, N. J. Society headquarters are at 29 W. 39th St., New York.

DECEMBER

Dec. 3-5—**Institute of Cooking & Heating Appliance Manufacturers**, winter convention and management conference, Netherland Plaza Hotel, Cincinnati. Institute headquarters are in the Shoreham Hotel, Washington.

Dec. 6-8—**American Institute of Mining & Metallurgical Engineers**, electric furnace steel conference, Hotel William Penn, Pittsburgh. Institute headquarters are at 29 W. 39th St., New York.

Dec. 10—**Can Manufacturers Institute**, annual meeting, New York. Institute headquarters are at 1126 Shoreham Bldg., Washington.

Helping America's

ASK BAIRD ABOUT IT!

HIGH PRODUCTION TOOLING

5 LONGITUDINAL, 5 CROSS SLIDES
with a BAIRD *automatic* CHUCKER

MACHINING A CAST IRON OIL PUMP BODY

1ST OPERATION: Face flange, finish counter-bore I D and depth, cut groove in flange, drill and tap 5 ²⁹⁄₆₄" holes. Work held stationary for drilling and tapping . . . OTHERWISE WORK ROTATES. Production: 308 pieces per hour.

Completely Automatic Operations . . . Hands Free

THE OPERATOR of a Baird 7", 6 spindle horizontal chucking machine likes his job. The open construction gives him easy access to all tooling . . . fast set-up. The automatic mechanism that operates the chucks does away with chucking levers, valves and gages . . . leaves both hands free. Reliable mechanical and electrical safety devices protect him, his machine, and the work. He clearly sees the advantages of independently operated tool slides, many combinations of spindle speeds and the means to mill and cross mill. He's proud of his accomplishments for every shift.

THE PRODUCTION MANAGER likes the way the time sheets read (note this typical job). You can't go far wrong with such production.

MANAGEMENT, that makes the investment in Baird high production machinery, sees the favorable financial returns . . . the many profitable operating years of the Baird 7.6H Chucker . . . the machine that keeps young in performance, even when it becomes old in years.

2ND OPERATION: Face and turn shank end, undercut spot drill and drill center hole thru to cored section, turn OD of shank, ream center hole, drill 2 ¹⁵⁄₃₂" holes. Production: 222 pieces per hour.

FULL DETAILS AND BULLETIN ON REQUEST

the BAIRD MACHINE COMPANY
STRATFORD • CONNECTICUT

AUTOMATIC MACHINE TOOLS • AUTOMATIC WIRE & RIBBON METAL FORMING MACHINES • AUTOMATIC PRESSES • TUMBLING BARRELS

2BA51

January 4, 1951

149

NATIONAL TRADE ASSOCIATIONS AND TECHNICAL SOCIETIES

A list of some 200 Professional and Technical Societies and Trade Associations in Metalworking and Metal Production.

Air Conditioning and Refrigerating Machinery Assn.
Southern Bldg., Washington 5, D. C.
Exec. Vice-Pres.: Wm. B. Henderson

Aircraft Industries Assn. of America
Shoreham Bldg., Washington 5, D. C.
Pres.: DeWitt C. Ramsey

Alloy Casting Institute
32 Third Ave., Mineola, N. Y.
Exec. Secy.: E. A. Schoefer

Alloy Tank Manufacturers Council
Keith Bldg., Cleveland 15, Ohio
Commissioner: Harry A. Sieck

Aluminum Assn.
420 Lexington Ave., New York 17, N. Y.
Secy.: Donald M. White

Aluminum Research Institute
20 N. Wacker Drive, Chicago 6, Ill.
Secy.: Carl H. Burton

Aluminum Roofing Institute
209 Cedar Ave., Washington 12, D. C.
Secy.: O. J. Condon

Aluminum Wares Assn.
First National Bank Bldg., Pittsburgh 22, Pa.
Secy.: Stuart J. Swensson

Aluminum Window Manufacturers Assn.
74 Trinity Place, New York 6, N. Y.
Secy. & Counsel: Herbert S. Blake, Jr.

American Boiler and Affiliated Industries
15 Park Row, New York 7, N. Y.
Mgr.: Henry E. Aldrich

American Boiler Manufacturers Assn. and Affiliated Industries
264 Rockefeller Bldg., Cleveland 13, Ohio
Secy.: A. C. Baker

American Bureau of Metal Statistics
50 Broadway, New York, N. Y.
Director: R. R. Eckert

American Die Casting Institute
366 Madison Ave., New York 17, N. Y.
Secy.: W. J. Parker

American Electroplaters' Society
P. O. Box 168, Jenkintown, Pa.
Exec. Secy.: A. Kenneth Graham

American Foundrymen's Society
616 S. Michigan Ave., Chicago 5, Ill.
Secy.-Treas.: W. W. Maloney

American Gas Assn.
420 Lexington Ave., New York 17, N. Y.
Managing Dir.: H. Carl Wolf

American Gear Manufacturers Assn.
Empire Bldg., Pittsburgh 22, Pa.
Exec. Secy.: Newbold C. Goin

American Hardware Manufacturers Assoc.
342 Madison Ave., New York 17, N. Y.
Secy.: Arthur Faubel

American Home Laundry Manufacturers Assn.
38 S. Dearborn St., Chicago 3, Ill.
Exec. Secy.: A. H. Noelke

American Hot Dip Galvanizers Assn.
First National Bank Bldg., Pittsburgh 22, Pa.
Secy.: Stuart J. Swensson

American Institute of Mining & Metallurgical Engineers
29 W. 39th St., New York 18, N. Y.
Secy.: Edward H. Robie

American Institute of Steel Construction
101 Park Ave., New York 17, N. Y.
Exec. Vice-Pres.: L. Abbett Post

American Institute of Tack Manufacturers
80 Federal St., Boston 10, Mass.
Director: Ray A. Stevens

American Iron and Steel Institute
350 Fifth Ave., New York 1, N. Y.
Pres.: Walter S. Tower

American Machine Tool Distributors Assn.
1900 Arch St., Philadelphia 3, Pa.
Exec. Secy.: Thos. A. Fernley, Jr.

American Manganese Producers Assn.
National Press Bldg., Washington 4, D. C.
Pres.: J. C. Adkerson

American Mining Congress
1200—18th St., Washington 6, D. C.
Secy.: Julian D. Conover

American Ordnance Assn.
Mills Bldg., Washington 6, D. C.
Exec. Vice-Pres.: L. A. Codd

American Railway Car Institute
19 Rector St., New York 6, N. Y.
Secy.: W. C. Tabbert

Turn to Page 152

MORE *Power* for Manpower

IN EVERY CLARK MACHINE

STEADILY RISING COSTS—growing user demands—imminent labor shortages! These very real conditions need not pose frightening problems to alert and able management. Given proper machines, manpower can deliver a great deal *more* power—and enjoy doing it; more power that translates into greater production at lower cost. Now that CLARK has added Powered Hand Trucks to its *Leadership Line* of Fork Lift Trucks and Industrial Towing Tractors, it is better fitted than ever before to help Management meet the challenges of a most critical era. For it is in the field of Materials Handling that the greatest opportunities for savings, for increased production, for improved efficiency and for the betterment of employee relations are to be found. In every piece of CLARK materials-handling equipment, there is MORE POWER FOR MANPOWER. And it is yours to employ— yours to enjoy.

CLARK will exhibit at the Plant Maintenance Show, Cleveland, Ohio, January 15-18, 1951.

Let us send you a concise, easy-to-read catalog on CLARK'S Leadership Line. Just fill out and mail the coupon.

CLARK FORK TRUCKS ELECTRIC AND GAS POWERED

AND POWERED HAND TRUCKS • INDUSTRIAL TOWING TRACTORS

INDUSTRIAL TRUCK DIVISION • CLARK EQUIPMENT COMPANY • BATTLE CREEK 51, MICHIGAN
Please send: ☐ Condensed Catalog ☐ Movie Digest
Name_____
Firm Name_____
Street_____
City_____ Zone_____ State_____

AUTHORIZED CLARK INDUSTRIAL TRUCK PARTS AND SERVICE STATIONS IN STRATEGIC LOCATIONS

Associations

American Society of Lubrication Engineers
343 S. Dearborn St., Chicago 4, Ill.
Secy. & Asst. Treas.: W. F. Leonard

American Society of Mechanical Engineers
29 W. 39th St., New York 18, N. Y.
Secy.: C. E. Davies

American Society for Metals
7301 Euclid Ave., Cleveland 3, Ohio
Secy.: W. H. Eisenman

American Society for Testing Materials
1916 Race St., Philadelphia 3, Pa.
Exec. Secy.: C. L. Warwick

American Society of Tool Engineers
10700 Puritan Ave., Detroit 21, Mich.
Exec. Secy.: Harry E. Conrad

American Standards Assn.
70 E. 45th St., New York 17, N. Y.
Managing Dir. & Secy.: George F. Hussey, Jr.

American Steel Warehouse Assn., Inc.
442 Terminal Tower, Cleveland 13, Ohio
Pres.: Walter S. Doxsey

American Supply and Machinery Manufacturers Assn.
Clark Bldg., Pittsburgh 22, Pa.
Secy.: R. Kennedy Hanson

American Tin Trade Assn.
75 West St., New York 6, N. Y.
Secy.: Ethel M. Foley

American Welding Society
33 W. 39th St., New York 18, N. Y.
Secy.: J. G. Magrath

American Weldment Manufacturers Assn.
332 S. Michigan Ave., Chicago 4, Ill.
Pres.: Byrne Marcellus

American Zinc Institute, Inc.
60 E. 42nd St., New York 17, N. Y.
Exec. Vice-Pres. & Secy.: E. V. Gent

Amtea Corp.
30 Church St., New York 7, N. Y.
Secy.: Ralph W. Burk

Anti-Friction Bearing Manufacturers Assn., Inc.
60 E. 42nd St., New York 17, N. Y.
Secy.: H. O. Smith

Assn. of American Battery Manufacturers
First National Tower Bldg., Akron 8, Ohio
Commissioner: V. L. Smithers

Assn. of American Railroads
Transportation Bldg., Washington 6, D. C.
Pres.: Wm. T. Faricy

Assn. of Iron and Steel Engineers
1010 Empire Bldg., Pittsburgh 22, Pa.
Managing Dir.: T. J. Ess

Assn. of Lift Truck and Portable Elevator Manufacturers
P. O. Box 66, Medfield, Mass.
Exec. Secy.: J. A. Goldthwait

Assn. of Roller and Silent Chain Manufacturers
c/o Morse Chain Co., 7601 Central Ave., Detroit 8, Mich.
Secy.: Robert J. Howison

Assn. of Sprocket Chain Manufacturers
11 S. La Salle St., Chicago 3, Ill.
Exec. Secy.: Mark L. Patterson

Assn. of Steel Distributors
150 Broadway, New York 7, N. Y.
General Counsel: Morris Rosoff

Automobile Manufacturers Assn.
New Center Bldg., Detroit, Mich.
Managing Dir.: W. J. Cronin

Automotive and Aviation Parts Manufacturers
800 Michigan Bldg., Detroit 26, Mich.
Gen. Mgr.: Frank Rising

Automotive Tool & Die Mfrs. Assn.
103 Pallister Ave., Detroit 2, Mich.
Exec. Secy.: C. A. Cahn

Brass and Bronze Ingot Institute
308 W. Washington St., Chicago 6, Ill.
Secy.-Mgr.: Isadore Glueck

Bright Wire Goods Manufacturers Service Bureau
53 Park Pl., New York 7, N. Y.
Secy.: George P. Byrne

Broaching Tool Institute
74 Trinity Place, New York 6, N. Y.
Secy.: Montgomery S. Blake

Can Manufacturers Institute
Shoreham Bldg., Washington 5, D. C.
Exec. Vice-Pres.: H. Ferris White

Carbon Wrench Statistical Service
53 Park Pl., New York 7, N. Y.
Secy.: George P. Byrne

Turn to Page 154

The smoothest way to transmit power
from engine to load!

EASIER ON OPERATOR — EASIER ON LOAD!

The new Plymouth Torque Converter Locomotive combines rugged, economical Plymouth power with the smoothest way to transmit that power to the load—hydraulic torque conversion. Tests in both factory and field have proved that this new, efficient conversion, with its unlimited number of speed ratios, protects the load with "cushioned starts"—eliminating shock, and breakage because of shock. Acceleration is fast and smooth . . . adjustment to the speed and power required by varying loads is automatic. In addition, absence of clutching and shifting plus sensitive response provide ease of control which cuts down on fatigue and increases operator efficiency.

Easily accessible for inspection and service, the Plymouth Torque Converter can be installed in any Plymouth Locomotive. Write now for all the facts about this great new feature of "Industries' Favorite Switchers." Plymouth Locomotive Works, Division of The Fate-Root-Heath Company, Dept. A-2, Plymouth, Ohio.

GASOLINE, DIESEL AND DIESEL ELECTRIC

PLYMOUTH
TORQUE CONVERTER
LOCOMOTIVES

PLYMOUTH LOCOMOTIVE WORKS, Division of the Fate-Root-Heath Co., Plymouth, Ohio

When the World Needs a Lift

UNIT 357 on "earth moving" job, lifting globe into position at Midwest Fair exhibit.

It Picks a UNIT to do the Job!

Yes ... it's really amazing what you can do with a UNIT Crane or Excavator. Take a UNIT 357 Mobile Crane, for example. It travels anywhere! Any time! Powered by ONE engine ... controlled and operated by ONE man. Compact, it has light-truck mobility — the smoothest operating and easiest handling crane made. Works efficiently even in small yards where space is limited. FULL VISION CAB gives operator complete visibility in all directions.

UNIT 357 is self-propelled ... mounted on six pneumatic tires ... duals on the rear ... singles on the front. Balanced weight distribution keeps entire undercarriage on ground while working. Dimensions meet all highway requirements. Get the complete UNIT 357 story. Write for bulletin.

CONVERTIBLE TO ALL ATTACHMENTS

Rapid conversion, from one attachment or boom to another, is one of the many important UNIT 357 features. If the material handling operations in your plant call for magnet, crane, or clamshell, the UNIT 357 is the logical, and economical, answer to your problem. There is no limit to UNIT 357 versatility!

UNIT CRANE AND SHOVEL CORP.

6517 WEST BURNHAM STREET • MILWAUKEE 14, WISCONSIN, U. S. A.

SHOVELS • DRAGLINES • CLAMSHELLS
CRANES • TRENCHOES • MAGNETS

Turn to Page 156

"Ni-Carb"

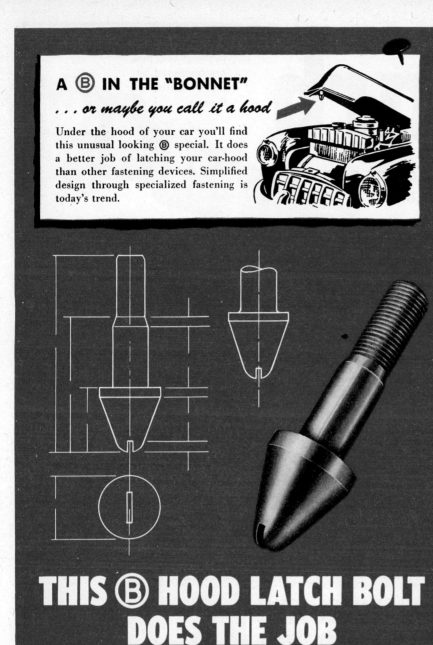
Associations

Fine and Specialty Wire Manufacturers Assn.
839 17th St., Washington 6, D. C.
Exec. Secy.: Wm. A. Penrose

Forged Tool Society
Law & Finance Bldg., Pittsburgh 19, Pa.
Exec. Secy.: G. D. Shrum

Forging Manufacturers Assn.
366 Madison Ave., New York 17, N. Y.
Secy.: W. J. Parker

Formed Steel Tube Institute
Keith Bldg., Cleveland 15, Ohio
Exec. Secy.: N. Myles Brown

Foundry Equipment Manufacturers Assn.
Engineers Bldg., Cleveland 14, Ohio
Exec. Dir.: Arthur J. Tuscany

Foundry Supply Manufacturers Assn.
1508 Law & Finance Bldg., Pittsburgh 19, Pa.
Exec. Secy.: G. D. Shrum

Galvanized Ware Manufacturers Council
Keith Bldg., Cleveland 15, Ohio
Commissioners: Hunter-Thomas Associates

Gas Appliance Manufacturers Assn., Inc.
60 E. 42nd St., New York 17, N. Y.
Managing Dir.: H. Leigh Whitelaw

Gasoline Pump Manufacturers Assn.
420 Lexington Ave., New York 17, N. Y.
Managing Dir.: G. Denny Moore

Gold Mining Assn. of America
251 Kearney St., San Francisco 8, Calif.
Mgr.: Claude M. Chaplin

Gray Iron Founders' Society, Inc.
210 National City—E 6th Bldg., Cleveland 14, Ohio
Exec. Vice-Pres.: R. L. Collier

Grinding Wheel Institute
Greendale, Mass.
Secy.-Treas.: Harry B. Lindsay

Hack Saw Manufacturers Assn. of America
50 Broadway, New York 4, N. Y.
Secy.: Wm. P. Jeffery

Hardware Cloth and Poultry Netting Institute
74 Trinity Place, New York 6, N. Y.
Secy.: Ralph W. Bacon

Heat Exchange Institute
90 West St., New York 6, N. Y.
Secy.: C. C. Rohrbach

Hollow Metal Door and Buck Assn.
7 E. 42 St., New York 17, N. Y.
Exec. Secy.: Sidney O. Raphael

Hydraulic Institute
122 E. 42 St., New York 17, N. Y.
Secy.: C. C. Rohrbach

Industrial Fasteners Institute
3648 Euclid Ave., Cleveland 15, Ohio
Secy.-Treas.: J. D. Eggers

Industrial Furnace Manufacturers Assn., Inc.
420 Lexington Ave., New York 17, N. Y.
Exec. Vice-Pres.: Stewart N. Clarkson

Industrial Safety Equipment Assn.
366 Madison Ave., New York 17, N. Y.
Secy.: W. J. Parker

Industrial Wire Cloth Institute
74 Trinity Pl., New York 6, N. Y.
Secy.: Ralph W. Bacon

Insect Wire Screening Bureau
74 Trinity Pl., New York 6, N. Y.
Secy.: Ralph W. Bacon

Institute of Boiler and Radiator Manufacturers
60 E. 42 St., New York 17, N. Y.
Gen. Mgr.: R. E. Ferry

Institute of Cooking and Heating Appliance Manufacturers
Shoreham Hotel, Washington 8, D. C.

Institute of Metals Div., AIME
29 W. 39th St., New York 18, N. Y.
Secy.: E. O. Kirkendall

Institute of Scrap Iron and Steel
1346 Connecticut Ave., Washington 6, D. C.
Exec. Vice-Pres.: Edwin C. Barringer

Instrument Society of America
921 Ridge Ave., Pittsburgh 12, Pa.
Secy.: Richard Rimbach

Internal Combustion Engine Institute
201 N. Wells St., Chicago 6, Ill.
Exec. Secy.: Charles G. Spice

International Acetylene Assn.
30 E. 42nd St., New York 17, N. Y.
Secy.: H. F. Reinhard

International Tin Study Group
7 Carel van Bylandtlaan, The Hague, Netherlands
Secy.: W. Fox

Turn to Page 158

Associations

Iron & Steel Div., AIME
29 W. 39th St., New York 18, N. Y.
Secy.: E. O. Kirkendall

The Lake Superior Iron Ore Assn.
1170 Hanna Bldg., Cleveland 15, Ohio
Vice-Pres. & Secy.: M. D. Harbaugh

Lead Industries Assn.
420 Lexington Ave., New York 17, N. Y.
Secy.: Robert L. Ziegfeld

Machine Knife Assn.
Wabash, Ind.
Secy.: Fred A. Collinge

Machinery and Allied Products Institute
120 S. La Salle St., Chicago 3, Ill.
Pres.: W. J. Kelly

Machinery Dealers National Assn.
20 N. Wacker Drive, Chicago 6, Ill.
Exec. Dir.: J. M. P. Fox

Machinery-Metals Export Club
330 W. 42 St., New York 18, N. Y.
Secy. & Treas.: F. J. Muller

Machinists Vise Assn.
c/o Desmond Stephan Manufacturers Co., Urbana, Ohio
Secy.: R. S. McConnell

The Magnesium Assn.
122 E. 42 St., New York 17, N. Y.
Asst. Secy.: (Miss) M. I. Hansen

Malleable Chain Manufacturers Institute
11 S. La Salle St., Chicago 3, Ill.
Exec. Secy.: Mark L. Patterson

Malleable Founders Society
1800 Union Commerce Bldg., Cleveland 14, Ohio
Managing Dir.: Lowell D. Ryan

Manufacturers of Hard Edge, Flexible Back, Metal Cutting Band Saws
50 Broadway, New York 4, N. Y.
Secy.: W. P. Jeffery

Manufacturers Standardization Society of the Valve and Fittings Industry
420 Lexington Ave., New York 17, N. Y.
Exec. Secy.: Lester W. Benoit

Marking Device Assn.
134 N. La Salle St., Chicago 2, Ill.
Secy. & Gen. Man.: Elmer F. Way

Material Handling Institute
Clark Bldg., Pittsburgh 22, Pa.
Secy.: R. Kennedy Hanson

Metal Abrasive Council
Engineers Bldg., Cleveland 14, Ohio
Exec. Secy.: Arthur J. Tuscany

Metal Cutting Tool Institute
405 Lexington Ave., New York 17, N. Y.
Pres.: Mason Britton

Metal Lath Manufacturers Assn.
Engineers Bldg., Cleveland 14, Ohio
Commissioner: Donald R. Wadle

Metal Powder Assn.
420 Lexington Ave., New York 17, N. Y.
Acting Secy.: Robert L. Ziegfeld

Metal Treating Institute
271 North Ave., New Rochelle, N. Y.
Exec. Secy.: C. E. Herington

Metal Window Institute
806 Rowland Rd., Cheltenham, Pa.
Exec. Secy.: George Hingston

Mining Assn. of Montana
505 Montana Standard Bldg., Butte, Mont.
Secy.-Treas.: Carl J. Trauerman

Mining and Metallurgical Society of America
11 Broadway, New York 4, N. Y.
Secy.: Donald M. Liddell

Multiple V-Belt Drive and Mechanical Power Transmission Assn.
7 W. Madison St., Chicago 2, Ill.
Exec. Secy.: Harry P. Dolan

National Assn. of Corrosion Engineers
Room 919, Milam Bldg., 803 Texas Ave., Houston 2, Texas
Exec. Secy.: A. B. Campbell

National Assn. of Engineering Co.'s
1601-13 Dime Bldg., Detroit 26
Exec. Secy.: A. Stewart Kerr

National Assn. of Fan Manufacturers, Inc.
2159 Guardian Bldg., Detroit 26, Mich.
Secy.: Lewis O. Monroe

National Assn. of Manufacturers
14 W. 49th St., New York, N. Y.
Managing Dir.: E. Bunting

National Assn. of Metal Finishers
Dime Bldg., Detroit 26, Mich.
Exec. Secy.: Raymond M. Shock

Turn to Page 160

Saved:
$39 per 1000 pieces

BY switching from bar stock to Timken®seamless tubing for this automatic transmission part, the manufacturer cut his cost 23.7%. The saving amounted to $39 per 1000 pieces. Actual cost figures below give the whole story.

Biggest saving with Timken seamless tubing is in production costs, as the figures show. With tubing the center hole is already there; there's less stock to machine away; speeds and feeds can be increased.

Timken tubing often saves you money on material costs, as well. Although tubing costs more per ton than bar stock, it usually comes to *less per foot*, because of its lighter weight. This also results in lower freight and handling costs.

Switching to Timken tubing can improve the *quality* of your product, too. With tubing, internal working tools may be flooded better with coolant. As a result you get closer dimensional control and better finish. And your product has greater strength because of the fine forged quality of Timken tubing.

For maximum savings with Timken tubing, use our Tube Engineering Service. We recommend the most economical tube size for your job—guaranteed to clean up to your finish dimensions. Let our Tube Engineering Service analyze your requirements. Write The Timken Roller Bearing Company, Steel and Tube Division, Canton 6, Ohio. Cable address: "TIMROSCO".

HOW 24% WAS SAVED:

	BAR STOCK	TUBING
Material costs per 1000 pieces	$79.56	$76.77 a saving of $2.79
Freight costs per 1000 pieces	$ 3.57	$ 2.18 a saving of $1.39
Number of pieces produced per hour on 6-spindle 2⅝" capacity automatic screw machine	80	140
Machining cost per 1000 pieces (estimated machine operating cost—$6.50 per hour)	$81.25	$46.43 a saving of $34.82

TOTAL COST SAVING WITH TUBING
$39.00 per 1000 pieces, or 23.7%

YEARS AHEAD—THROUGH EXPERIENCE AND RESEARCH

TIMKEN
TRADE-MARK REG. U.S. PAT. OFF.
Fine Alloy
STEEL
and Seamless Tubes

Specialists in alloy steel—including hot rolled and cold finished alloy steel bars—a complete range of stainless, graphitic and standard tool analyses—and alloy and stainless seamless steel tubing.

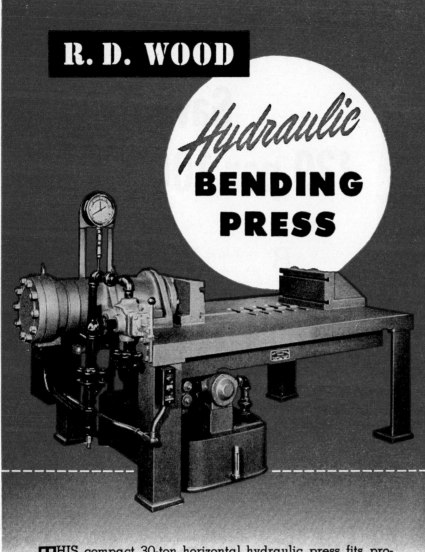

R. D. WOOD

Hydraulic BENDING PRESS

THIS compact 30-ton horizontal hydraulic press fits productively into general shop use—in the bending and straightening of rods, bars, light structural sections, and for similar work. Self-contained, it is well designed and constructed, with a smooth tool finished 3' x 4' steel work table, and 9" x 18" ram and resistance heads, machine tee slotted for dies or bending forms. Distance between rams is adjustable in 4" increments from 1' to 3'. The press stands 2½' above the floor at the work table, and occupies an approximate floor space of 7'3" x 4'6". Higher capacities and various size tables can be furnished. Write, without obligation, to R. D. Wood Company for additional information.

HYDRAULIC PRESSES AND VALVES FOR EVERY PURPOSE • ACCUMULATORS • ALLEVIATORS • INTENSIFIERS

R. D. Wood Company

EST. 1803 PUBLIC LEDGER BUILDING, PHILADELPHIA 5, PA.

Turn to Page 162

Electro HIGH-SPEED CUT-OFF WHEELS

K-385

Electro's NEW CUTRITE CUT-OFF WHEELS

Cut 2″ x 1¾″ Risers On Nickel Iron Castings in 16 Seconds!

With all this new defense work coming up, you've got to save *time;* minimize waste; and get jobs done right the first time.

On preparatory jobs, Electro's New Cutrite Cut-Off Wheels already have proved their worth by setting such records as . . .

9500 cuts on ¼″ alloy valve stock; cutting 2″ x 1¾″ risers on nickel-iron castings in 16 seconds; showed no binding or breakage on 5½″ x 2½″ heavy, stainless, alloy steel castings which are normally burned; outlived and outperformed competitive wheels on 15/32″ carbon steel, drill bit rod; and gave 46.6% longer service than the average of competitive wheels on stainless, low carbon, beryllium copper, silicon bronze and manganese bronze 1″ stock.

Let us show you on the job *what these new wheels can do for you;* and what other Electro High Speed Grinding Wheels can do for you on both rough and precision grinding. Write, wire or phone. No obligation for Field Engineer cooperation.

Electro manufacturers: HIGH-SPEED resin-bonded GRINDING WHEELS • CRUCIBLES • REFRACTORIES, Standard and Special Shapes • Electro-Carb BRIQUETS SiC Deoxidizer • STOPPER HEADS • POROUS MEDIA ELECTRO-CARB (SiC) ABRASIVE GRAIN and GRITS.

Electro Refractories & Alloys Corporation
344 DELAWARE AVENUE • BUFFALO 2, NEW YORK
West Coast Warehouse . . . Los Angeles • Canadian Electric Furnace Plant, P. Q.

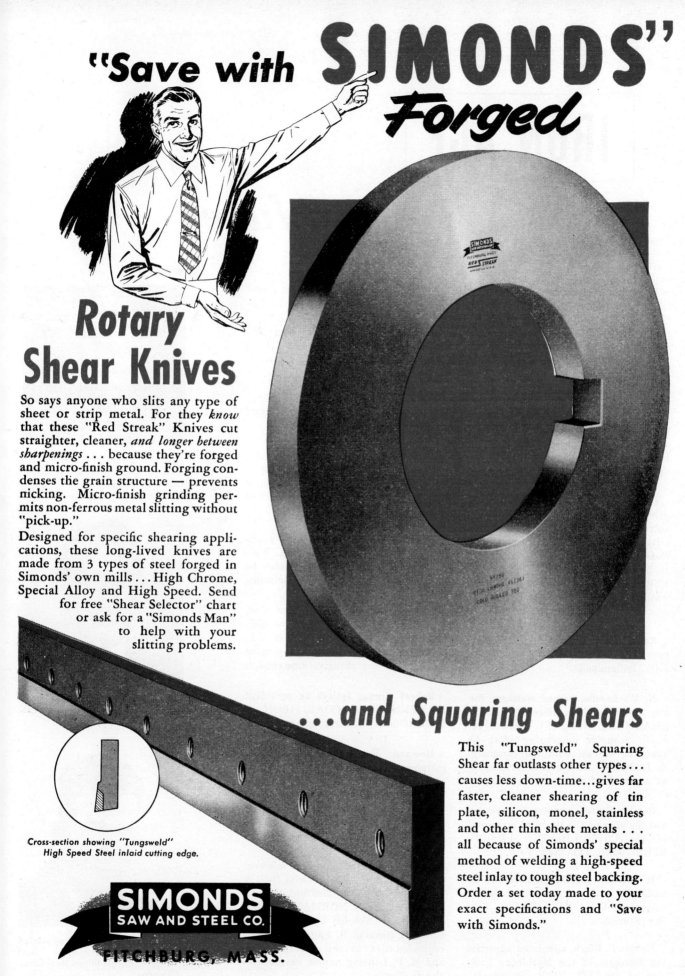

"Save with SIMONDS" Forged

Rotary Shear Knives

So says anyone who slits any type of sheet or strip metal. For they *know* that these "Red Streak" Knives cut straighter, cleaner, *and longer between sharpenings* . . . because they're forged and micro-finish ground. Forging condenses the grain structure — prevents nicking. Micro-finish grinding permits non-ferrous metal slitting without "pick-up."

Designed for specific shearing applications, these long-lived knives are made from 3 types of steel forged in Simonds' own mills . . . High Chrome, Special Alloy and High Speed. Send for free "Shear Selector" chart or ask for a "Simonds Man" to help with your slitting problems.

Cross-section showing "Tungsweld" High Speed Steel inlaid cutting edge.

. . . and Squaring Shears

This "Tungsweld" Squaring Shear far outlasts other types . . . causes less down-time . . . gives far faster, cleaner shearing of tin plate, silicon, monel, stainless and other thin sheet metals . . . all because of Simonds' special method of welding a high-speed steel inlay to tough steel backing. Order a set today made to your exact specifications and "Save with Simonds."

SIMONDS
SAW AND STEEL CO.
FITCHBURG, MASS.

BRANCH OFFICES IN: *Boston, Chicago, San Francisco and Portland, Ore.* Canadian Factory in Montreal, Que.

IRON AGE

introduces

William G. Rogers, elected executive vice-president of the EAST OHIO GAS CO., Cleveland. George W. Horsley, Robert W. Ramsdell and John H. Carson were named vice-presidents.

E. S. Quarngesser, elected vice-president in charge of the eastern sales division of the FRUEHAUF TRAILER CO., Detroit. W. W. Siegrist named vice-president in charge of truck body division and Harry R. Badger, vice-president in charge of scheduling.

Lorenzo Semple, elected vice-president and treasurer, John W. Brennan, secretary of the U. S. PIPE & FOUNDRY CO., Burlington, N. J. Donald Ross resigned as secretary-treasurer, to become first vice-president of the United Concrete Pipe Corp., at Baldwin Park, Calif., a partially owned subsidiary.

Ray F. Sparrow, named senior vice-president of P. R. MALLORY & CO., INC., Indianapolis.

N. W. Landis, named manager for the Detroit district office of ALLIS-CHALMERS MFG. CO., Milwaukee. F. S. Schuyler is retiring after 43 years of service with the company. A. J. Mestier, Jr., succeeds Mr. Landis as manager of the Syracuse office.

Roy J. Foster, appointed secretary and member of the board of directors, of the CONSOLIDATED IRON-STEEL MFG. CO., New York.

H. Stanley Worthington, retires as assistant to the vice-president—operations, of COLUMBIA STEEL CO., San Francisco.

Robert C. Black, appointed advertising manager of the Machinery Division of DRAVO CORP., Pittsburgh.

E. Preston Calvert, appointed director of public relations for PULLMAN-STANDARD CAR MFG. CO., Chicago. Other appointees: Hugh W. Foster, advertising manager, Paul Ackerman, editor of employee publications.

Evan Price, appointed turbine sales manager, of the WHITON MACHINE Co., New London, Conn.

Carl Brooks, named general sales manager of GENERAL DRY BATTERIES, INC., Cleveland. Mr. Brooks has held various positions with the company since 1933.

David R. Hull, elected vice-president of RAYTHEON MFG. CO., Waltham, Mass. Mr. Hull will also be manager of the equipment divisions.

Norman C. Minehart, elected vice-president in charge of abrasive division, CHARLES H. BESLY & CO., Chicago. Jack T. LeBeau, appointed manager of the abrasive department.

Robert Gregg, retires as president of TENNESSEE COAL, IRON & RAILROAD CO., Birmingham.

Howard E. Maloney, appointed manager of sales, Electric Wire Div. of JOHN A. ROEBLING'S SONS CO., Trenton, N. J. Frank T. Craven, appointed assistant manager of sales; Roy H. Hainsworth became eastern regional manager.

F. C. Helms, Jr., appointed midwest branch manager, Morse Twist Drill & Machine Co., New Bedford, Mass.; division of VAN NORMAN CO. Mr. Helms will make his headquarters in Chicago. Norman S. Fagerson named representative in the Chicago area, and M. P. Lansing named representative in Texas.

EDWARD J. HANLEY, elected president of Allegheny Ludlum Steel Corp., Pittsburgh.

ARTHUR V. WIEBEL, named president, Tennessee Coal, Iron & Railroad Co., Birmingham.

HAROLD B. WISHART, appointed chief metallurgist, Gary Steel Works, Carnegie-Illinois Steel Corp., Chicago.

IRON AGE

salutes

Clark W. King

To be informed these days is to be alive. To get things done with the minimum amount of confusion and frustration is to be almost a genius. To work at full steam and yet have everyone keep from blowing his top is worth talking about.

These things may sound like fairy tales. They aren't as far as some people are concerned. One who fills this bill is Clark W. King, executive vice-president and treasurer of Allegheny Ludlum Steel Corp. This fellow has the background and experience to shine under today's handicaps.

He is a type which we will call vice-president in charge of the president. His knowledge of his industry is broad—yet it is detailed. His background started years ago when he went with the American Steel & Wire Co.

His baptism of fire came during the National Recovery Administration when he helped to administer the NRA Steel Code. Later he joined Bethlehem Steel.

His ulcer days were soon to come. In 1941 he went to Washington on loan to the War Production Board. There he had headaches and gained experience—he served under seven different directors. Clark went with Allegheny Ludlum in 1945 as executive assistant; he was boosted to vice-president a year later. He was made treasurer and a member of the board of directors in 1949 and elected executive vice-president in December 1950.

He gives himself to more worthy causes than you can shake a stick at. He rates a salute because he represents the type of people coming along who will keep the steel industry where it belongs—and also keep it moving.

CLARK CONTROL for HIGH SPEED TIN MILL SHEARING LINE

5 Aetna-Standard
Shearing Lines

Clark DC
Control for One
Shearing Line

●**In a Midwest Tin Plate Mill,** the Aetna Standard Engineering Company installed five Flying Shear Lines with Side Trimmer, Sheet Classifiers and Conveyors, **ALL CLARK CONTROLLED.**

These lines handle coils up to a maximum of 30,000 pounds, and are capable of operating up to a maximum speed of 1000 feet per minute.

To maintain this high speed, the **CLARK** mill type apparatus ably co-operates to control the many motors that drive the heavy duty lines.

The build-down of the Payoff and the Speed-match, between the Side Trimmer and Shear, are automatically controlled by **CLARK** Photo-Electric Modulated Loop Control.

This is a typical **CLARK ENGINEERED** installation, accurately and efficiently co-ordinating both A.C. and D.C. operation to maintain high speed, and quantity production.

For all steel mill auxiliary control applications, consult your nearest **CLARK** *office for approved time-proved and accepted* **CLARK CONTROL.**

THE **CLARK CONTROLLER** CO.

ENGINEERED ELECTRICAL CONTROL • 1146 EAST 152ND STREET, CLEVELAND 10, OHIO

Patterns in Pensions

Streamlining a Pension Pattern
TO FIT YOUR BUSINESS

THE success of your pension plan will depend upon a streamlining job which gears your pension system with *your* particular financial, personnel and industrial problems. And, if your pension plan is not streamlined to fit your company's circumstances, you may suffer serious loss in dollars and greatly reduce the effectiveness of your plan.

Our Pension Trust Division has helped develop hundreds of pension plans. This broad experience with all types of pension systems is yours for the asking. We shall be glad to estimate the cost of a pension plan for your company or discuss with you any pension problem you may have. No obligation, of course.

Write or call the
PENSION TRUST DIVISION
City Bank Farmers Trust Company
or
The National City Bank of New York
Ask for Booklet I. A. 2

We Act As Trustee Under Pension Plans and as Agent for Individual Trustees

CITY BANK FARMERS TRUST COMPANY
CHARTERED 1822
HEAD OFFICE: 22 WILLIAM STREET, NEW YORK
Affiliate of
THE NATIONAL CITY BANK OF NEW YORK
ESTABLISHED 1812

on the assembly line

automotive
news and
opinions

by walter g. patton

Output records fall like leaves in 1950 ... Detroit now worries about war cutbacks and girds for war production.

From Records to Cutbacks—Practically all of the automobile industry's production, sales and profit records were shattered in 1950.

Trouble was signaled by war clouds rising in the Far East. Europe was uneasy. By the year's end, serious cutbacks in auto production for 1951 were certain. A reduction in schedules of 30 to 35 pct by the end of March was a definite possibility.

Rollback in Car Prices—By mid-December Washington had already made cuts in raw materials and ordered a rollback of car prices. The industry was waiting for more and more restrictions to come out of Washington as the year ended.

Output Fools Prophets—During 1950 passenger car output established an all-time record. An estimated 6,550,000 passenger cars and 1,300,000 trucks were built. Total U. S. vehicle assemblies plus an estimated 400,000 Canadian output reached 8,200,000 units. As the year began, the industry's most optimistic prophets would have settled for 7 million units.

Wholesale Values Soar — Coupled with price increases, the record production sent wholesale values to an all-time peak of $10,250 million. This is a gain of 25 pct for the industry. The increase over the previous year is 28 pct for passenger cars and 14 pct for trucks and buses.

Replacement part sales were off from the 1948 peak. Compared with a record $2,553 million in 1948, the auto service parts business in 1950 aggregated about $2 billion.

Exports Drag Feet — Exports were still dragging their feet. Only 145,000 passenger cars and 135,000 trucks were sold abroad during the year. Passenger car export business was off again by 7 pct although trucks sold abroad were up 3 pct compared with 1949.

Output Fills Highways—If the nation's highways seemed crowded there was a good reason. At the year's end 39,710,000 passenger cars were registered. Adding 8,774,000 trucks brought the 1950 total to an unprecedented 48,484,000 vehicles on the public roads. This is a net gain of 9 pct.

Employment at Peak — Despite the use of much greater machine capacity and electric power, direct employment in the industry hit a new peak of 715,000 production workers and 125,000 salaried employees. Total payrolls, swelled by

wage hikes during the year, hit $2,700 million. This is a gain of 22 pct.

Cars Get Older — Statisticians could point to the fact that despite its record production in the postwar period, the industry actually produced fewer passenger cars in the 1941-1950 decade than it assembled during the two previous 10-year periods ending in 1939 and 1929. The average age of vehicles on the highway in 1950 was 8 years compared with a 5.5 year average for the prewar years.

Faith in Future—During the year the industry showed its faith in its future by (1) advancing millions of dollars to build new steel capacity, (2) greatly extending its facilities for production and research, (3) buying 25 pct or more of its steel via the costly conversion route.

Industry Milestones—Early in the year Chevrolet introduced its new automatic transmission made entirely of metal stampings. In late January, Chrysler was hit by a strike that lasted 100 days, second only to the 113-day GM strike. Ford announced plans to build a foundry and engine plant in Cleveland.

The cost-of-living index was fading as late as March, and GM simultaneously reduced wages and

assembly line

Continued

prices. This is in sharp contrast to the runaway prices that hit the industry before the end of the year. By December the industry reported the price jump for raw materials ranged from 7 pct on steel to 300 pct on rubber.

Engine Hopes Sink—During the year it became clear that a large segment of the industry was committed to new high compression engines of the type introduced earlier by Oldsmobile and Cadillac. Chrysler Div. and Studebaker were in actual production.

Four new Ford engines, a new Ford tractor powerplant and engine programs for Dodge, DeSoto and Buick were under way. The prospect of these engines being in production on schedule in 1951 sank with every new report of reverses in Korea.

New Assembly Plants—During the year, Oldsmobile opened a new assembly plant. Ford also brought in a new assembly plant at Buffalo and a new transmission plant at Cincinnati. Another milestone was the decision by Fisher Body to halt production of wooden bodies for station wagons in favor of all-metal bodies.

GM Sets Pattern—During March, Nash granted a pension plan to its workers. This was followed by the Chrysler pension in May. In June, GM announced its unprecedented 5-year peace plan with the UAW-CIO. This set the wage pattern.

By the end of the year, it was estimated that more than 80 U. S. manufacturers employing 2 million workers had hitched their wages to the cost-of-living index. Each major auto producer now has a 5-year peace plan with labor. The industry had no way of knowing how its agreements would stand up in a wage freeze.

Light Cars Debut—The light car made history during 1950. Introduction of the Nash Rambler in April was followed later in the year by the Henry J produced by Kaiser-Frazer. The Big Three

were still holding off on a light car but Nash and K-F saw promising markets for small passenger and utility vehicles.

Ups and Downs—On June 25 shooting started in Korea and an auto market that was just so-so spurted for a few weeks. Then sales began to taper off. Late in the year serious reverses to the American forces abroad again revived the threat of limited auto production.

Once again, a fading new car market got a shot-in-the-arm although credit restrictions imposed by the government undoubtedly limited the public response. Independent producers reported serious sales obstacles had been placed in their path.

Arms from Detroit—National defense entered the automobile picture in a substantial way in June when the new Cadillac tank plant at Cleveland was announced. By the end of the year, Continental had a contract to build tank engines. GM Diesel was turning out war materials. Ford announced it would build aircraft engines in the old Tucker plant in Chicago.

Buick will build tank transmissions. A few Detroit firms had defense sub-contracts. Chrysler, Reo, Willys and GM had truck contracts. However, the total volume of defense business in the Detroit area was hardly more than 5 pct of total production as the year ended.

Stalin vs. Crystal Balls—Joe Stalin may not have planned it, but during 1950 he ruined one of Detroit's favorite indoor sports—making rosy predictions about the future. Unqualified predictions about the coming year were out the window. The industry may be fortunate to reach 50 to 60 pct of its 1950 output.

Even before the government declared a state of national emergency, these Detroit developments could be seen for 1951: Automatic transmission output will be severely curtailed. Buick, Ford and Studebaker will be hard hit by the aluminum shortage. Chevrolet, which uses metal stampings instead of aluminum castings for its major transmission components, may also feel the aluminum cutback. Cast iron pistons will be widely used in the industry.

THE BULL OF THE WOODS   BY J. R. WILLIAMS

PROGRESS

west coast progress report

digest of far west industrial activity

by r.t. reinhardt

It's Been a Good Year—Clearly discernible above the grousing and griping over material and manpower shortages in the metal producing and metalworking trade of the West can be heard a note of satisfaction with last year's business.

Steel producers showed an average 1950 operating rate of approximately 98 pct, which includes several dismal weeks during the coal strike. As the year closed it appeared production of rolled steel in the seven Western states would exceed the forecast here last year by some 400,000 tons.

Preliminary estimates indicate nine western steel producers made approximately 3,200,000 tons of rolled products in 1950.

A Few Highlights—Steel production in the West followed the national pattern closely with operations running from 90 to 95 pct of capacity until the Korean war, when producers began hitting from 100 to 106 pct.

Expansions and modernization of furnaces made some contributions to production capacity. Bethlehem Pacific Coast Steel Corp. last year began furnace enlargement which will ultimately increase the capacity of its South San Francisco plant approximately 25 pct and the company

got its 75-ton electric furnace operating in Los Angeles.

Two Openhearth Furnaces—Pacific States Steel Corp. at Niles, Calif., put two 125-ton openhearth furnaces in operation. Kaiser Steel Corp. started its 86-in. hot strip mill rolling in May.

Kaiser's Yoder pipe mill, with a capacity of approximately 100,000 tons per year of 5-in. to 14-in. diameter pipe, was put in production. Geneva Steel Co. put its expanded plate mill into production of hot-rolled coil early in 1950.

Fabricators Happy—With few exceptions steel fabricators wound up 1950 with a total volume almost as good as in 1949. Only complaints were shortages and restrictions of some specialty items such as wide flange beams. As 1950 ended, the material pinch became more acute, perhaps more so in the West because of the mills' tendency to ship larger lots of specialty items to nearby users.

Warehousemen's Worry — Steel warehouse operators were not too happy at year end because government steel allotments were based on a period of considerable depression for most western jobbers.

ANNUAL REVIEW

During the first 6 months of 1950 many jobbers showed only 60 pct as much business as in 1949.

Under government allocation, 1950 dollar volume was probably considerably less than in 1949. No immediate relief is in sight and the only consolation operators have is that they are reasonably sure to dispose of all their steel.

Historically, a larger percentage of steel used in the West, 30 to 35 pct, is sold through jobbers than is the practice nationally. Hence a drop in inventories is having greater impact on small users of steel here than elsewhere.

Aluminum Hot Spot—Aluminum was poured at record rates in the Pacific Northwest during 1950. Kaiser Aluminum & Chemical Corp.'s installation of the eighth pot line of 140 electrolytic cells at Mead, Wash., is expected to begin producing early this month. Production of the Mead plant will be 145,000 tons per year and the Tacoma plant, 25,000 tons per year. The company is planning installation of a plant or plants to produce approximately 100,000 tons in the southwest.

Operate at Capacity—Plants of Reynolds Metals Co. at Troutdale, Ore., and Longview, Wash., and

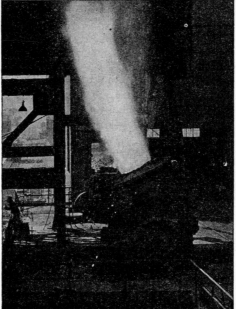

west coast report

Continued

that of the Aluminum Co. of America at Vancouver have also been operating at capacity. Longview is rated at 31,000 tons; Troutdale, 70,500 tons; and Vancouver, Wash., at 85,000 tons. Last year the Aluminum Co. of America officially opened its aluminum rod and wire mill at Vancouver.

California is out of the aluminum production picture. The plants built by Alcoa for the DPC at Los Angeles and Riverbank, Calif., have been gutted and the equipment dispersed.

Harvey Machine Co. of Los Angeles entered the aluminum production field last year with start of construction on the first unit of a reduction plant at Kalispell, Mont. This company purchased one of the 140 cell pot lines from the government which had been installed at Riverbank.

Crystal Gazing—It is too early to accurately predict production of rolled steel in the seven western states for 1951 but preliminary surveys indicate it will be in the neighborhood of 3,500,000 tons.

By the second quarter of this year Kaiser Steel Corp. will have its eighth openhearth in operation at Fontana, Calif., to bring Kaiser's total ingot capacity to 1,380,000 tons per year. Geneva Steel Co. intends to increase ingot capacity by 160,000 tons.

Kaiser will have under construction this year an electrolytic and hot-dip tin plant with a production of approximately 200,000 tons of tinplate per year which will be fed from a new 5-stand, 44-in. cold mill.

More Tinplate Production—Kaiser in 1951 will be getting a greater portion of its ore from Eagle Mountain when a screening station is completed which will permit reclamation of fines.

Columbia Steel Co. at Pittsburg, Calif., has under construction additional cold-reduction facilities which will have a capacity of approximately 250,000 net tons of cold-rolled sheet and tinplate.

This unit is expected to be completed by mid-year.

Geneva Expands—Geneva Steel Co. at Geneva, Utah, is installing facilities for production of 100,000 net tons of hot-rolled sheets annually, most of which will go to Columbia Steel for cold-reduction. This gives Columbia and Geneva a combined capacity of 640,000 tons of sheet and tinplate plus large capacity for production of other steel products.

There is still no definite announcement as to plans of the U. S. Steel Corp. subsidiary, Columbia Steel Co., on what will be done with the old Alcoa aluminum plant in Los Angeles, purchased by Columbia in October, 1948.

Was to Be Sheet Mill—At that time it was stated that it was to be made into a sheet mill with an annual capacity of approximately 300,000 tons.

Corporation officials since then have been evasive as to what will be done while at the same time they have given public assurance that a steel facility of some type would be installed there.

General Outlook—Additional ingot capacity and finishing facilities will be installed in the West. Even with production of 3½ million tons of rolled products per year there is still a deficiency of at least a million tons which is being supplied from eastern and, to a limited extent, foreign sources.

There is no indication of an appreciable let-up in population growth with 16 million people already making their homes in the seven western states. Experts anticipate that by 1965 this territory will have a population of more than 23 million.

Increased Steel Market — This continuing growth indicates a sizable increased market for steel. Taking average consumption of steel in California at 600 lb per person, which is below the national average, a potential market of 7½ million tons is developed.

Balanced Economy—It should be pointed out that even though

the rate of growth of manufacturing and industry in the West has exceeded the national pattern, the balance between manufacturing, service industries and agriculture in relation to the West's economy remains almost constant.

There is no indication that unbalance in favor of manufacturing is imminent.

Expansion Trend—A Federal Reserve Bank survey shows that although all industries expanded between 1939 and 1947, the second and third most important expansions in terms of both value added and number of production workers occurred in the machinery and metals industry.

The number of metal plants (primary and fabricated) has increased from 1421 in 1939 to 2715 in 1947 with an increase in production workers from 40,500 to 110,000. Since the 1947 census was taken, the rate of increase has been phenomenal, but reliable figures reflecting this increase in the metalworking industry in the West are lacking. The best estimate would be that the number has increased to at least 125,000.

Steel Users Increase—The 1939 census showed 700 of the plants included in the metals category as processing plants of steel users and a conservative estimate of the number of such steel users today is approximately 2000 in the seven western states.

Bright New Year—Under the existing garrison economy, there is no question every metal producer and metalworking plant will enjoy a profitable 1951 with the only limiting factors being availability of materials and men.

Even industries already affected by government allocations of materials will, after a period of adjustment, work out a modified operating rate which should return profits.

As severe as material shortages may be in curtailing production, skilled and semi-skilled manpower shortages will be far more important in limiting production.

January 4, 1951

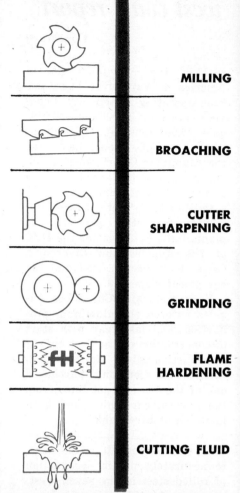
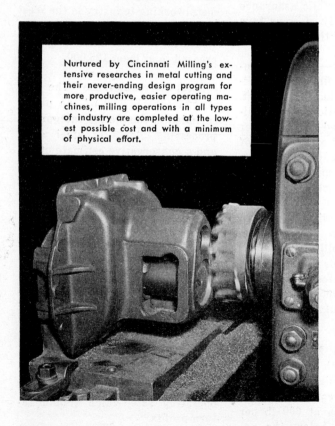

the federal view

by eugene j. hardy

1951????—Official Washington is confronted with a situation different from anything recorded in history. In partial mobilization to meet a war which may be a long time coming or could burst overnight, the control agencies are following the World War II pattern. The big unanswered question in 1951 is whether such a pattern will suffice in a lengthy period of mobilization, provided all-out war is staved off. This is one of the major problems facing C. E. Wilson in his new post as director of Office of Defense Mobilization.

More and More Controls—The 1951 outlook for business on two major fronts is a rapidly expanding controlled materials system and an almost equally rapid excursion into direct price, wage control.

Complete allocation of nonferrous metals and the ferroalloys is expected before a CMP for steel. The National Production Authority had indicated a possible easing in steel during the first half of 1951.

Cut in Steel Use—Three major factors are: (1) a coming cut in the allocation for freight cars; (2) a substantial drop in auto production due to inability to obtain metals other than steel; and, (3) relatively stable military demand for steel in the first half amounting to about 10 pct of product tonnage.

If this easing does develop, it will be only the lull before the storm and will not necessarily mean more steel for civilian products, but will provide more leeway in planning essential programs. It is the basic reason for the belief other metals will come under complete allocation before steel.

Agency Lacks Personnel—Lack of manpower to administer CMP is one of the major problems facing NPA and at the root of this problem is almost complete lack of available office space.

Private office space is being taken up and government offices are moving into new and unfinished residential apartments, in an effort to ease the shortage caused by ever-expanding civil agencies. At year end, NPA was operating with some 750 people. A complete allocation system would require between 10,000 and 12,000 employees.

Price and Wage Controls—Price and wage controls will blanket the economy. Again, the World War II pattern will be followed, with wages being allowed to rise within an area similar to that established by the "Little Steel" formula.

Direct price controls will de-

ANNUAL REVIEW

velop from a selective system applying to key commodities.

Office Space Needed—ESA is also troubled by problems of office space. Having only several hundred employees at the beginning of 1951, ESA will need a minimum of about 30,000 to effectively administer price, wage and ration controls. OPA's World War II employment ran to about 67,000.

Centralization—A strong effort to centralize all controls, production, price, wage transportation, and manpower, within one powerful agency, will be seen in 1951. The drive for such action will probably be sparked by Capitol Hill.

Bureaucratic prerogatives are expected to stall this movement, except for possible centralization of production controls powers.

On the hand, actual administration of various controls is slated for decentralization with regional and field offices being given wider latitude than in World War II.

Demand for Workers — Manpower problems will be accentuated. It is expected general manpower needs for defense industries will be met, since workers will gravitate from civilian plants as materials become scarce.

Skilled labor shortages present a tougher problem and one of the an-

258

the federal view

Continued

swers will be a step-up in the apprentice program. Controls will not be mandatory but will follow the World War II "voluntary" outline.

Hiring at State Offices — Primary control will force all hiring through state employment service offices with essential industries getting first crack at available workers.

Nothing will prevent employers from trying to hire workers on their own, but in a tight market the state offices will be the only **real** source and will, for all practical purposes, control the flow of labor. There will be a recruiting drive to attract women and older workers who have retired.

Military Spending—The movement toward tighter controls will depend on how fast the military translates money into orders. Chances for getting a slice of military business during the first half of 1951 are more than doubled.

Military buying will increase by at least 50 pct, and prime contractors must step up letting of subcontracts if delivery dates are to be met. Procurement funds available to military services total $18 billion, which must be spent or obligated before June 30.

Stockpiling — The materials headache will increase as the government tries to make up for stalling tactics in stockpile building. Whether from reluctance of the Munitions Board to press for funds or refusal of Congress to recognize needs, or both, stockpiling is far behind schedule.

First-half buying will be stepped up sharply as the remaining $440 million of the original $800 million (for current fiscal year) appropriations are committed.

Seek Additional Funds — The White House has asked Congress for $1.8 billion in supplemental funds so that advantage could be taken of any and all opportunities for stockpile purchases.

The Munitions Board is in a vicious cross-fire in this situation. Congress is screaming about the low state of the stockpile. If stockpile buying is increased rapidly, adding to materials shortages and causing unemployment, Congress will scream again.

A compromise between normal peacetime buying for the stockpile and NSRB Chairman Stuart Symington's desire to complete the stockpile by the original 1952 target date will provide the solution.

Industrial Expansion—Increasing defense needs and growing shortages of non-defense goods will shove plant and new equipment expansion above the $19 billion record of 1948.

Allowing for higher costs, 1951 investment in new industrial facilities will far exceed that of any war year. On the basis of preliminary reports to government agencies, the Securities & Exchange Commission looks for first quarter expansion to top $5 billion.

Expansion in Industry—A major portion of expected expansion will center in the industrial and manufacturing fields. Electric power and gas facilities will continue to increase.

Expansion of commercial facilities such as mercantile and other trade fields will slow down, partly because of diversion of goods and materials to more direct defense uses.

Congress to Oversee Program— As far as Congress is concerned, the metalworking industries are faced with long-range economic problems not concerned with day-to-day administration of controls by executive departments and agencies in the year ahead.

Congress takes the view that the pattern of business controls necessary for U. S. industry to wage its part in the battle against Communism has been pretty well defined.

Enforcement Up to President— Controls over materials, prices, wages and manpower all have been authorized in the Defense Production Act of 1950. How well—or how badly—these controls are enforced is now entirely up to President Truman and his staff of control experts.

This does not mean Capitol Hill has washed its hands of the overall Federal defense program. Plans are in the works in both Senate and House for creation of new "watchdog" committees to keep an eye on the way Mr. Truman and his staff administer the control powers.

"Watchdog" Groups—Based on performance during the last Congress, one of the most important of these "watchdog" groups will be a Senate Armed Services subcommittee headed by Senator Lyndon Johnson, Texas Democrat.

With his subcommittee counsel, Securities and Exchange Commissioner Donald C. Cook, he has raised honest criticism of some aspects of the defense program (steel, rubber, and surplus property, for example) that have won plaudits from businessmen and politicians.

Keep a close watch on this committee. Unless it unexpectedly puts its foot in its mouth politically—as Congressman Celler's "antimonopoly" group did last year—it will travel far in 1951.

Higher Taxes—Tax-wise, it appears certain corporations and individuals will be hit with new and sharper increases this year.

These increases will be apart from an excess profits tax. Few businessmen—and just as few congressmen—are fully aware today of the tremendous sums of revenue the government will need in the months ahead. A rude awakening is in store for both groups when the Treasury Dept. unfolds its new requests for additional revenue.

"Monopoly" Fights Off—In the antitrust field, comparatively little legislative activity is expected. As long as the nation is at war, or at least preparing to defend itself, Congress will be inclined to postpone moving against what some members call "trends toward monopoly."

Following the World War II pattern in this regard, the government will offer the highest praise of U. S. industrial might during time of crisis, and follow it up a few years later with criticism in peace.

Anti-Trust Let-Up — Another wartime moratorium on anti-trust suits will highlight activities of the Justice Dept. and FTC in '51.

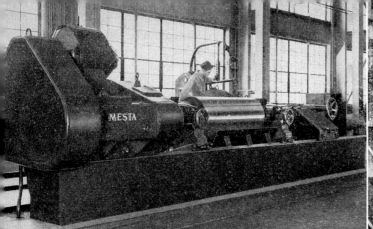

MESTA HEAVY DUTY TRAVELING WHEEL TYPE ROLL GRINDER

MESTA 68" FOUR-HIGH CONTINUOUS HOT STRIP MILL, UNIVERSAL STANDS

MACHINING A FORGED STEEL ROTOR SHAFT FOR A TURBINE DRIVEN GENERATOR

MESTA 80" FOUR-HIGH CONTINUOUS HOT STRIP MILL

MESTA 32" BAR MILL SHOWING INTERMEDIATE, LEADER, AND FINISHING STANDS

FORGING LARGE INGOT ON A MESTA 6,000 TON HYDRAULIC PRESS

GROUP OF THREE 32" MESTA PATENTED

MESTA-THOMSON FLASH WELDER INSTALLED IN A

STRAITJACKET

Industry's Future:

FREEDOM

OR *HOBBLE?*

By Tom C. Campbell

EDITOR

TOP management people today face a bleak future—if you look at the hurdles set for them. Industrialists know they are over the barrel too often—many times unfairly so. Those being trained to take key jobs may not know all the facts of industrial life but they will learn soon.

Now is the time to gird for battles to come; to work for changes that are needed. The goals, hard work and rewards will be worth it.

Why all this fuss about management? Management is good today—it has to be. But being good is not enough. This year will see the steel industry and other metalworking groups almost under complete control. What they can do and what they can't do will be largely dictated by government. This hobble may extend for as long as 4 years or more. If management is not alert, informed and on the ball we may wake up some day and find that we have controls forever.

Just as America must be strong to contain Russian communistic expansion so must American industry fight for its freedom on the home front.

This calls for housecleaning in management's talking, thinking and acting. The alternative is creeping control over business by socialistic, security-crazy and mediocre elements in our government.

Creeping paralysis of personal initiative means a strait jacket for industry, not for a short time but forever. Industry needs freedom to act and to expand if it is to carry out its responsibility.

It is silly to say that all people in government are mediocre. Thousands of workers in Washington and elsewhere are talented and loyal. They can match any setup in industry—in quality or number.

Some Hobbles Needed

But just as there are misfits in industry so are there in government. They are more dangerous in government because they can exercise power. Power compensates them for their own shortcomings. They can cost the people much in money, prestige and freedom.

There must be many hobbles in business if defense requirements are to be met promptly and if our system is to retain its stamina to oppose Communism. Productive power of the American people must be kept high or increased so that the greatest number benefit.

There is only one way to raise production — more output per man. This means better methods, better tools and a greater housecleaning on the use of inferior machinery.

The job goes further than this. There must be a real reawakening—an intellectual and spiritual approach to the human problems in industry

Whether industry winds up in a strait jacket or has the freedom it needs to expand and nourish this country is largely up to industry itself. Creeping paralysis will put it in a strait jacket if the current trend in socialistic thinking continues. One trouble is that top management is not as informed as it ought to be. Yet, to be informed today is to be alive. There are a lot of pitfalls along industry's rocky road. Here some direction signs have been posted. If you can't hire a vice-president in charge of the president you may be able to appoint a man to do his job.

and government. The mechanical phase is bound to forge ahead—it may have left behind the human phase.

We are a mass-producing nation. Many of our skilled jobs are monotonous to the workers. They do the same thing day in and day out, year in and year out. The work week and the work day are much shorter than they were 15 or 20 years ago. That is also true of routine jobs—of which there are millions.

All workers do not know how to use their spare time in a positive way. Some do, but we don't have to worry about them. Those who meander after working hours feel the oppressive effects of mass production or routine job jitters.

These effects are often expressed in bigger wage demands, sunshine security for old age, readiness to gripe and a sense of frustration. If these are multiplied by millions, management faces a negative force which must be met with patience, explanation and education.

Government has not helped people too much. Much of the social progress would have come one way or the other. A lot of it is good. A lot of it came about through expediency, to corral the greatest number of votes. Some of it is downright dishonesty.

We Need "Know Why" Too

Industry has furnished the tools and the "know how" but has it furnished the "know why?" Many industrialists individually know the answer but as a group can't get it across. If the real case for personal initiative is not sold by industrial leaders to the public and to workers, then private enterprise—as we know it—may not survive the next decade or two.

What has business to do with all this? It has plenty. Leaders must come from industry. They must think in broader terms than just chasing the dollar, cutting costs or making better products. They must do the impossible. They must

sell the basic usefulness of the capitalistic system to the greatest number of people—quickly.

Years ago industry's problem was restricted to our own country. Now it must sell its bill of goods not only at home but throughout the world. If it doesn't it will be duck soup for communistic salesmen who have been making hay in other parts of the world.

Obstacles to a better understanding by Americans for the way business succeeds are great. They involve hostile elements of the government and unnecessary mistakes by management.

For many years industry has faced an ingrained Administration that is inherently against business—no matter what political hacks may say in conciliatory speeches.

Some Administration politicians have developed doubletalk to perfection. They have garnered support from some segments of industry and at the same time pulled the props from under that very segment.

Poor pay, political favors and the pressure for workless prosperity have brought an unsurpassed mediocrity in government. Sincere and honest men cannot act. They are chained. Any attempt to loyally serve the people is often hindered by red tape, a sense of frustration and a general attitude of "what's the use." This attitude—understandable at times—plays into the hands of the vote getters who attempt to keep a perverted caricature of Santa Claus in office forever.

"Rabble Rousing" Is Tool

Most of the crack-brain, log rolling, below-the-belt projects coming from the Administration are obtained fairly easy. Putting these ideas over is easy because they appeal to a people who are becoming more conditioned to them; it is easy because the methods used are the toughest to fight.

The major technique has been, and will be,

"Government doubletalk"

"The receptionist who gives the firm a bad name"

"rabble rousing." In every day language this means "he has more than you; you ought to have as much as he; we will show you how to get it." This works well with flocks of people.

No politician bothers to tell the people that you can't get something for nothing. Or that you have to work hard for what you do get. Or that every man doesn't have the same capabilities or capacities.

Another tried and true tool for putting across a campaign against business is known as the "smear" technique. No facts are necessary. Just make up a good story; palm if off on a friendly columnist or news man. Then sit back and wait. The person being smeared can't answer except to deny the charges. Even then it takes so long that the retort never gets the attention the smear gets.

People would rather hear things than read them. A smear campaign usually turns into a first class whispering campaign. By that time it is almost too late to do anything.

These same tactics apply to congressmen who follow in the footsteps of that segment of the Administration and government which wants the fruits of the capitalistic system but at the same time wants to tie it in knots.

But all obstacles to a better understanding of individual freedom do not come from government. There are drawbacks in business which encourage strait jackets or too tight a hobble. Many of these road blocks are simple—which make it all the harder to do something about them.

Management Not Informed

Statistics, conversation and interviews show that top management is not as informed as it ought to be. There are good reasons for this but they do not excuse the condition. To be informed today is to be alive. If they don't know what goes on industry leaders can't fight back quickly, answer trick questions and keep their own business up to snuff.

Every top management man knows his own business. If he didn't he wouldn't be where he is. He spends hours of his time away from his home or his family pouring over reports, studies and recommendations.

There are only so many waking hours. Because of this our executive hasn't time to be properly informed about trends in: other lines of business, government, international affairs, medical advances, competitive situations (in other fields which will affect him), religion, "human" research, politics, and man-on-the-street viewpoints.

Too Many "Yes" Men?

Many men are informed—they are the leaders. They get recreation and they take vacations. They know they are not indispensable. But they are selfish with their time. They don't waste it doing things that somebody else can do as well as they can, if not better. There are not enough of these men. Industry needs thousands of them.

Because of the science (?) of "getting ahead" these days it is hard to tell whether those on the way up are sincere or whether they just read somebody's book on how to influence people and make friends. This may explain why we have too many "yes" men; or it might be that top executives are beaten over the head so much by politicians and have so little to say at home that they fall for the "yes" man patter.

Too many "yes" men will not equip industry to fight for its life. Too many top people feeling indispensable will not put industry ahead or help the country to any great extent. Delegation of authority has been proven on paper but in practice there is plenty of room for improvement.

What industry needs is a vice-president in charge of the president. Top management jobs today are too much for one man who must operate in a vacuum much of the time. No wonder a recent curbstone question "Would you like your boss' job?" got eight "No's" out of each ten answers. Management's job is not going to get any easier—it's going to get harder. Sacrifices may extend to a man's family and even his health unless the job is streamlined.

No Apple Polishing Necessary

A vice-president in charge of the president is not an attempt at being funny. This man won't have to polish apples because his contract says he can never become president. His salary will be close to the president's so he won't want the top job. He will be the man in the company who must say "No!" as often as other people say yes.

He will read and digest everything in the domestic and international news picture. He will know what gives in his own business and in every other one even remotely connected with his. He must see the fancy, well tabulated, well dressed and sparkling reports made up for the president's attention—before the president sees them.

He will not only censor the president's proposed speeches but he will disappear for a few days to try them out on the kind of people who will be listening to them. He will be the man who goes through the organization and gets the "feel" of the way things are. Top officials often

"Management often talks down"

Don't Miss It!

want a report on the way employees feel but they get what other people would like to have them believe.

This vice-president in charge of the president will insist that his boss participate in community events; get publicity in his own local community and quickly attack enemies with facts, fast words and a human touch. He will argue against too much emphasis on polls and statistics. To him people are not numbers; they insist on being people.

This reasonable facsimile of superman knows that management often talks down to people instead of to them. Our man would probably also hire a hall once a year where the top people can meet their employees if the company is not too large. He would also knock out the fanfare, the salaaming and the furious fussing which accompany plant visits by top management.

The Job Is Frightening

Our much needed friend would also toss overboard the receptionist, the phone operator and the people who by their manners give the firm a bad name to visitors before they have a chance to see the president or his staff.

He would also recommend that newspaper people only be called in when the people in the company have something to say. He would go to bat for the key men in the organization and see that they are not kept on the hook too long. He might even help weed out the ones who look like they have it but don't and give those who have it a fling at new jobs.

Those who can best fight for freedom are industrial leaders. Their job is frightening. If they lose, our way of living will go. If that goes so will most of the things which make this country what it is today—the watchdog of individual freedom and dignity.

Mid-Century Reference of
HEAT TREATING

By F. R. MORRAL, *Dept. of Materials Engineering*
Syracuse University, East Syracuse, N. Y.

THE curiosity of the scientist and of the engineer, together with the tools they have devised and developed, have made possible some systematization in the art of heat treating. The modern generation is taught with fair ease why steel hardens, and why an interrupted quench is successful. One explanation is enough for all steels, while some years ago each steel was considered to be a special class. The scientific approach, now aided by thermodynamics (C-154) has been used to explain the transformations of austenite. The diffusionless hardening by martensite transformation has been found in some nonferrous alloys, and others will no doubt be studied. No references are given in the table to the other method of hardening, which is accomplished by precipitation reactions.

No historical review will be attempted, but suffice it to mention that Biringuccio about 1540 A.D. (B-90) may have referred to a version of the interrupted quench. Early this century some metallurgists wondered why a treatment similar to the patenting given to steel wire could not be given to other steels. Fabian in 1934 (F-1) advocated a technique similar to martempering to obtain stress and crack-free martensite. Austin (A-216) has summarized the history of the hardening of steel in the last 50 years.

To the iron-carbon constitution diagram has been added the Time-Temperature-Transforma-

This is the most complete and modern index of references on time-temperature-transformation reactions ever assembled. Ferrous and nonferrous metals are included. Austenite transformations are affected by chemistry, grain size, segregation, cleanliness, etc., as well as by time and temperature. Many different references on these and isothermal heat treating practices are covered with a complete, modern reference index of each. Important foreign work is also used.

Continued

accurate design of heat treatment (H-161).

tion diagrams, and more recently the Temperature-Time-Hardness tempering diagrams which permit an

The table is divided into a number of subjects which are and have been of interest and which are related to the science of heat treating and for which work has been published. This table is the index to the complete list of references which follow the table.

SUBJECT	REFERENCE NO.
I. Historical	A-216, B-90, D-5
II. Surveys and General Reviews (American and foreign)	1, 2, B-26, B-200, C-10, C-180, D-1, D-9, D-50, D-54, D-55, D-56, D-140, D-210, E-125, G-200, H-3, H-151, H-161, I-10, J-60, M-18, M-150, M-151, M-152, O-10, P-6, R-55, R-90, R-220, U-1, W-54, W-100, W-101, W-250, and others
III. TTT Diagrams	
1. Nonferrous alloys	
a. Aluminum bronze	A-130, G-187, M-1, S-130
b. Silicon bronze	H-90
c. Other	I-50
2. Ferrous alloys	
a. Effect of analysis	
A. Carbon	B-200, D-5, M-150, M-152, P-6, U-1
B. Manganese	A-211, D-5, H210, J-50, K-180, L-10, M-152, P-6, R-221, W-52
C. Nickel	D-5, I-10, M-152, P-6, S-40, S-81, U-1
D. Chromium	D-5, D52, G210, J-51, L-155, L-250, L-251, M-152, P-6, U-1
E. Molybdenum	A-180, B-120, B-121, C-120, D-5, H-153, M-60, M-150, M-152, N-1, O-1, P6, R-210
F. Tungsten	D-5, H-210, M-152, P-6
G. Cobalt	D-5, H-15, M-152, P-6, S-250
H. Boron	D-5, G-240, M-152, P-6, T-150
I. Vanadium	C-180, R-210, W-53
J. Aluminum	G-181, P-4, T-60
K. Copper	G-190, K-120, P-4, T-210
L. Silicon	1, L-110, O-1
M. Others (O₂, H₂, N₂, Zr, U)	B-151, M-152, P-6, S-160, T-81, T-210, U-1, Z-90
b. Effect of	
A. Grain size	D-7, M-152, T-80
B. Austenitizing temperature	G-182, H-210, M-150, M-152
C. Homogenization	D-5, M-10, R-151
D. Segregation and banding	D-5, M-14
E. Carburizing	C-185, E-2, I-10, R-185, T-182
F. Overheating and burning	P-180, T-81, W-81, W-110
G. Powdered alloys	K-1
H. Rolling of ingot steel	M-152
I. Induction heating	L-100, M-14
J. Stress	A-220, A-221, J-55
c. Cast irons	N-1, O-1
3. Methods of determining TTT diagrams	

SUBJECT	REFERENCE NO.
a. Metallographic	D-5
b. Dilatometric	A-140, C-80
c. Welding	P-210
d. Hot hardness	E-140
e. Magnetometric	E-200, R-220
f. Electrical resistance	F-150, M-30
g. X-ray diffraction	H-11, W-180
h. Electron diffraction	
IV. Austenite Transformation	
1. Theory and mechanism	A-145, A-214, A-215, A-221, A-223, B-27, C-153, D-4, D-5, D-160, F-90, F-92, F-131, F-150, G-150, G-180, G-191, H-170, J-1, J-150, J-151, L-15, L-150, M-60, M-200, N-50, N-51, N-100, P-140, P-141, P-221, S-110, S-150, S-151, W-50, W-51, W-200, Z-1, Z-50, Z-250
2. To spheroidized cementite	P-1
3. To pearlite	G-183, H-200, P-2
4. To bainite	G-190, W-90
5. To martensite	B-40, C-190, F-1, F-90, H-8, J-10, M-16, M-17, M-90, P-6, S-250
a. Ms—determined	G-186, M-152, P-4, and others
b. Calculated	C-5, G-182, H-161, N-60, P-4, P-6, G-186, T-181
c. Mf	
d. Mechanism of martensite formation	C-154, F-91, G-185, G-186, G-188, J-20, K-210, K-211, M-15, M-16
e. Stability of martensite	L-70
f. Tempering	A-222, C-75, C-155, F-121, G-151, H-161, P-55
6. Retained austenite	A-223, A-224, C-150, C-151, E-123, H-11, T-184
a. Stabilization	C-150, C-151
b. Decomposition	A-222, F-120, F-121, H-10, H-160, T-82
V. Isothermal Heat Treating Practice	
1. General practice	9, B-155, D-8, H-1, P-100, S-60, S-70, S-90, V-2, V-3, W-95
a. Austempering	3, 5, D-6, L-50, O-80, W-251
b. Martempering	A-21, F-1, H-85, O-120, O-121, R-170, S-55, S-86, S-87, S-87a, W-85
c. Cyclic annealing	A-120, A-125, C-160, L-120, M-55, N-150, P-10, S-71, T-60
d. Spheroidizing	P-1, P-2, P-50
e. Bainitic hardening	B-20, B-21, H-161, P-3
f. Modified isothermal	B-154, B-180, F-190, L-60, L-61, S-50

SUBJECT	REFERENCE NO.
2. Comparison of properties	O-250
a. Static	C-170, D-53, D-57, G-190, P-180, R-50, S-1, S-2
b. Dynamic	B-96, C-100, D-150, F-155, F-180, F-181, J-10, P-180, S-131, T-85
c. Others (machinability, etc.)	8, F-155, P-5, S-87, S-87a
3. Applications	C-153, W-120
a. Tool and high-speed steels	B-30, B-31, C-153, K-150, P-3
b. Forgings	4, 6, A-125, L-121, R-160
c. Welding	A-20, B-152, B-181, H-50, H-52, H-180, L-20, P-210
d. Irons	I-16, L-1, M-220
A. Gray	11, O-80
B. Malleable	B-182, L-110
C. Nodular	A-210
e. Cast steel	E-40, G-50, M-50, R-171, R-180
f. Accuracy	S-88
g. Miscellaneous	A-200, B-1, B-153, C-210, D-60, D-90, D-200, E-120, G-155, H-95, H-150, H-169, M-20, M-80, P-130, S-151, T-180, Z-2
4. Martempering v. conventional hardening	
5. Cost comparison	B-30, D-60, S-35
6. Quenching media and cooling rates	B-156, B-157, D-O, F-51, F-179, L-200, M-153, P-60, P-61, P-142, P-150, P-230, R-155, S-80, S-87, S-87a, T-70, W-80
VI. Continuous Cooling	G-180, G-184, H-50, H-51, H-161, J-1, L-90, L-91, L-92, L-93, L-94, L-95, L-96, L-97, M-5
VII. Hardenability	B-150, C-75, G-184, P-220, R-91, S-30, T-183, V-1, W-94

TTT BIBLIOGRAPHY

Authors are listed alphabetically using name of author which appears first in the various publications.

1. "Atlas of Isothermal Transformation," Iron and Steel Institute, March 1949, special report No. 40.

2. T-T-T data sheets, Metal Progress, miscellaneous issues.

3. "Austempering in Successful Commercial Operation," Heat Treating and Forging, October 1939, p. 499.

4. "Salt Baths for Forgings," The Iron Age, Newsfront, May 6, 1947.

5. "Austempering and Isothermal Trans-

Turn to Page 448

How to Sell to UNCLE SAM

You need not call your Congressman or rush to Washington in person to sell to the Army, Navy or Air Force. Field offices of various government agencies handle a great deal of buying. Bid lists are easy to get on. More contracts will be negotiated directly as the defense program gets rolling. There are several other major sources for detailed information on government procurement.

Uncle Sam, the nation's biggest buyer, is annually spending billions of dollars for literally millions of items ranging from lead pencils to tanks and planes, from toothpicks to aircraft carriers. Other millions are spent for services from laundry work to research on hydrogen bombs.

Whether they want to help for defense or whether they have been forced to curtail production on account of materials shortages, how to get some of this business is uppermost in many minds—especially among the so-called small businessmen.

There are two ways of selling to the government—by competitive bidding and by negotiated contract. About 85 pct of all peacetime federal procurement was through the bid method.

First, the procurement agency or its office announces that it is in the market for specific quantities of certain goods. Next, suppliers who have these goods or services for sale must obtain bid forms. Finally, the bid forms are filled out in their many parts and mailed to the designated place to be opened on the scheduled date.

It's as simple as that. But the supplier putting in the lowest bid doesn't necessarily get the contract. There was a time when government procurement offices were required to accept the lowest bid. The law has been amended to allow the contract to be given the lowest "responsible" bidder whose bid is judged to be the "most advantageous to the government, price and other factors considered."

This means that the procurement officials are required to make sure that the bidder is a recognized manufacturer or regular dealer, that the product meets government specs, and—if there are restrictions—that the supplier is on the qualified list and that the plant has been approved for restricted or classified work.

Most buying offices keep on file a list of sup-

See p. 371 for a list of major metal products bought by the armed forces. P. 372 carries addresses of the most important offices where these products are bought.

"One must first catch the cat" *(In order to find out who is buying what)*

pliers to whom invitations to bid are sent automatically each time procurements are to be made. (See p. 372 for list of military buying offices.) If it is a long list and purchases are made fairly regularly, the invitations may be sent only to a portion of the list in rotation, that is, in turn.

It is easy to get on these lists. Merely request it in writing; a form will be sent to be filled out and returned. This form indicates the responsibility, the qualifications, and ability to deliver on the part of the supplier.

Inactive Names Are Dropped

But—a supplier should never fail to reply to an invitation to bid. If he isn't interested in that specific contract, the buying office should be notified to that effect. Names are automatically dropped from the mailing list after they are not heard from once or twice.

If the supplier does not have the specifications for the particular item he wants to sell, he should request them. Most procurement offices do not mail specs with invitations to bid unless so requested; they assume that the bidder is familiar with whether his goods meet government requirements.

Although the government normally bought about 15 pct of its supplies through negotiated contracts, there is now an increasing amount of items so obtained and some 15 or so conditions are specified under which contracts may be so made.

Some of the more important conditions are: national emergency, public exigency, procurements totalling less than $1000, supplies or services for which there is no competition, purchases in the interest of national defense or

industrial mobilization, and in cases where no bids result after advertising of invitation to bid.

Goods normally bought through negotiated contract include the following: purchases outside the United States, purchases for post exchanges or other authorized resale, perishable subsistence, medicines and medical supplies, classified items, various classifications of technical equipment, personal and professional services, and experimental, development and research work.

Now that the nation is in a declared state of emergency it means that all contracts can be negotiated. To speed up procurement a great many will be negotiated, and the former 15 pct figure will start climbing fast.

Tell What You Can Make

The procedure for obtaining negotiated contracts is somewhat similar to obtaining invitations to bid. In other words, (a) the supplier enrolls or informs the buying office that he would like to sell the government certain items or groups of items; (b) the buying offfice asks the supplier for all the necessary information, including price quotations and statements of actual or estimated costs or other evidence to show it is a reasonable price; and (c) when such goods are needed, the procurement agent begins negotiations by mail or phone for drawing up of a contract.

An important point concerns obtaining of contracts with the aid of an agent (a full-time employee is not considered an agent) or what is cometimes known as a "five percenter" because he works on a commission basis. There is no law against employing an agent to look after a supplier's interests or even to obtain government contracts. But, and this is a big if, if such is done it must be reported on the contract together with the amount of the fee paid. Failure to do so is cause for cancellation. And payment on a contingency or commission basis is definitely forbidden—only specific salaries or fees are permitted.

Still another point is that many contracts (those for more than $10,000) must be performed under provisions of the Fair Labor Standards Act. These conditions can be discussed with the procurement office and copies of the Walsh-Healy Act can be obtained from the Labor Dept.

Now, it is a well known maxim that in order to put a bell on the cat, one must first catch the cat. In this case, it is a problem of first finding who is buying what or more particularly, what department wants the widgets that a supplier has to sell.

Don't Rush to Washington

The first impulse of the uninitiated is usually to either write to his Congressman or to rush to Washington in person. In both cases, this is time consuming and the supplier usually ends up by being referred back to the field installation which does the actual buying. The same result can be obtained faster and easier by other means.

There are six major sources of information concerning what the government and, more particularly, what the armed services are buying. The first and best port of call is the nearest field office of the Commerce Dept. It can be contacted by letter, telephone call, or personal visit. (See p. 374 for list of Commerce Dept. field offices.)

These offices are supplied with copies of Department's daily Synopses of Procurement Information. These list the current proposed purchases of both military and civilian type items as well as the procurement office or officer that does the buying.

Because of the cost, the Commerce Dept. does not mail these out individually; arrangements must be made to pick them up. Many local Chambers of Commerce or other business groups have arranged to obtain these for local distribution.

Major Information Sources

There are five other major sources of obtaining procurement information. These are: (a) The Munitions Board; (b) the Army Procurement Information Center; (c) the Office of Navy Materiel; (d) the Air Force Procurement Division; and (e) the Federal Supply Service. The latter, with the exception of stockpile buying, confines its purchases largely to non-military items.

It should be noted in passing that with few exceptions the government buys only finished goods. One exception is procurement of parts for repair or replacement. But the government does not even *recommend* parts suppliers to holders of prime contracts. In other words, a supplier who wants to get a subcontract to supply parts or materials must deal directly with the prime contractor. He won't get any help from Uncle Sam.

However, it is not too difficult to find out the names of potential customers. Here again the Dept. of Commerce and its field offices are useful. In addition to the Synopses already mentioned, it publishes a weekly synopses of Award Information; this lists contract awards of $25,-000 or more with the names of the successful bidders.

FOR MORE DETAILS—

Information in this article is necessarily general in nature and limited in scope. More detailed data may be obtained by writing to the following major sources and asking for the publications named in parentheses:

Central Military Procurement Information Office, The Pentagon, Washington 25, D. C. ("*Index of Military Purchasing Offices and Guide to Indusrty in Selling to the Military Departments*");

Army Procurement Information Center, The Pentagon, Washington, (*How to Sell to the U. S. Army*);

Office of Navy Material, Main Navy Building, 17th St., & Constitution Ave., N. W., Washington 25, (*Purchased Items, Navy Purchasing Locations, and Selling to the Navy*);

Air Force Procurement Division, Air Material Command, Wright-Patterson Air Base, Dayton, Ohio, (*Guide for Selling to the U. S. Air Force*);

Federal Supply Inquiry Office, General Services Administration, 7th & D Sts., S. W., Washington 25, (*Basic Facts About Selling to the Government*); and

Senate Select Committee on Small Business, Senate Office Building Washington 25, (*Selling to Your Government*).

TECHNICAL PROGRESS

The Horizon Broadens

Growth of titanium production, heavy nickel plating, dielectric core drying and radioactive cobalt 60 are just a few of the fields in which startling progress occurred. Continuous casting of steel was put into production for the first time and cold extrusion of steel for ordnance items was tooled up and is ready for mass production.

TECHNICAL articles carried in the feature section of THE IRON AGE during 1950 highlight the industry's technological progress and problems during the past year. Late developments not yet fully documented in print are included in this summary. They are woven in to permit a better evaluation of the eventual effect of industry's newest developments.

Titanium still has everyone gasping. The year started off with the country producing laboratory quantities and ended at an annual rate of about 275 net tons productive capacity. For the entire 12 months, only about 60 net tons were made, so that the real expansion occurred in the last half of the year.

The accompanying box lists technical articles on developments as they occurred. The last story in the box of the government's pressure for more of the metal is still up to date as far as commercial aspects are concerned. No single person, company or government agency can predict where titanium is going as techically no one person is entirely up to date, developments are moving too fast. It is acknowledged that the Kroll process will have to be drastically refined or replaced before the present $40,000 per net ton price for titanium sheets can be shaved. The sponge makers are on a hotter seat as the supply of sponge is the present limiting factor to higher titanium metal production. It takes a $1500 capital investment per annual ton of titanium produced. Hence. money is a big road block.

New alloys of high strength, 200,000 psi ultimate strength and over are under development. New processes and additional facilities will continue to pop up. The aircraft industry will take a lion's share of the sheets and bars. AEC is taking practically all the tubing made so far and Navy is vitally interested for marine applications where titanium's superior corrosion resistance is needed. Ordnance so far is just talking, but more fire power per man means lighter weapons and titanium could well be applied in some of these cases not to mention the light weight airborne equipment, tanks, vehicles, etc.

Free machining steels MX and E, which made their appearance early last year, THE IRON AGE, Feb. 2, p. 86 and p. 79, lived up to expectations. Some day they may push the regular Bessemer screw stock out of first place. This might happen very soon. These steels have been under development for 2 or 3 years and, fortunately, arguments about patent rights were forgotten in the final rush to get the product on the mar-

TITANIUM BOOM—

Articles published in The Iron Age during 1950

"Forging and Welding Titanium," Jan. 19, p. 63
"And Now—Titanium Tubing," Apr. 6, p. 85
"Alloys Widen Use of Titanium," July 27, p. 60
"Two New Titanium Alloys Now In Production," Sept. 14, p. 85
"Wanted Huge Titanium Expansion," Nov. 30, p. 87

ket. Another article, THE IRON AGE, May 18, p. 95, from the consumers' viewpoint confirmed all the early claims made by the steelmakers.

Marforming a new press drawing tool, THE IRON AGE, Feb. 23, p. 78, which combines the best features of rubber forming and steel die drawing for deeper draws at lower tool cost was announced. A nice feature of this process is that the sheets can be pre-painted before forming so that in cases finishing costs can be reduced. There are other methods yet to be announced in the deep drawing field which promise to keep the press forming industry particularly active.

Electroplating, of heavy nickel coating 0.50 in. and over has long been a dream. Last year it came true, THE IRON AGE, Apr. 6, p. 98. Perhaps salvaging of parts was a back door entré, but it was a good way to prove the process. Nickel plating has advantages over chromium plating; nickel plates faster, requires less current, is machinable and has a coefficient of expansion close to that of iron which, when coupled with high ductility, makes nickel suitable in applications involving severe temperature changes.

Sonic Testing of heavy pieces of steel has reached a high state of perfection, THE IRON AGE, Apr. 13, p. 77. Sonic testing is now a standard inspection practice in one plant and is being adopted elsewhere. No longer does the supplier or customer have to wonder about the soundness of large forgings or castings. Sonic testing even charts the size of an interior defect. Going further, a new method of obtaining acoustical images of interiors of large metal objects is under development. Borrowed from the Germans, but being perfected here, this testing method will be the next big development.

The metal powder industry got back on its feet last year, THE IRON AGE, pp. 79-97. New applications and methods have brought these engineering materials into their rightful place

INDUCTION HARDENING is being done on the sixth station of an 8-spindle automatic screw machine. The arbor carrying the induction coil and quench chamber is in the center of the photograph. The coil and piece to be hardened appear within the white circle.

of design and application. Copper infiltration of iron powder has raised strength levels. Machining of powder parts is now common and satisfactory plating of powder parts, which are more porous than wrought or cast parts, was perfected. Overseas, iron powder is being successfully prefabricated as semifinished sections for regular wrought steel products. This practice may spread fast, especially in heavy sections of some of the new metals that are such good "getters" in the molten condition.

Hot dip galvanizing received a shot in the arm when a new galvanizing furnace which cuts dross formation to the bone was announced. THE IRON AGE, Apr. 13, p. 93. At long last the iron kettles can be discarded and, except for the dross formed by the work itself, the bath will not make dross but instead will coat more product and stretch a given supply of zinc at least 20 pct further. Low frequency induction units and modern refractories made this development possible.

Synthetic core binders and dielectric drying ovens have overcome one of the biggest bottlenecks in foundry operations. THE IRON AGE, May 4, p. 90. The method is cleaner, faster and safer than older methods. Overbaking is impossible and materials handling is drastically cut. Better and more uniform core surfaces are obtained with fewer manhours. Some new installations are pushbutton controlled from start to finish and skilled help is not needed. This isolated improvement should not be confused with the much rumored, but little written

ONE OF THE LARGEST ductile iron castings produced to date weighs 60,000 lb. This forging hammer anvil was cast of ductile Cecolloy.

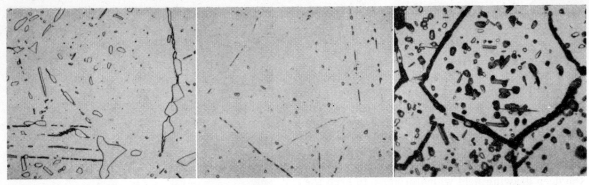

Hydrochloric and picric acids in alcohol.

Alkaline ferricyanide at room temperature for 1 min staining carbide only

Chromic acid electrolytically—3 v. lamp, 15 sec, carbide and sigma attacked.

SIGMA PHASE identification metallographically requires good technique. Actions of different etchants upon 18 Cr-8 Ni-Mo, type 316 stainless containing austenite, carbide and sigma appear above. 850X

about, "C" or Croning process. When all the "t's" are crossed, the lawyers retire and the Croning a-la-American story is fully told, the foundry industry will have reached an ultramodern, mechanized and highly efficient operation equal to that in any industry.

Glass as an engineering material in the metals field is cracking the ice in ingenious ways. As a heating element the English and Italians swear by it, THE IRON AGE, June 15, p. 95. Reduced carbon electrode consumption, simplification of atmosphere control and fast rates to high temperatures are the chief attraction so far. Yet to come are even more surprising applications of the material we choose to call glass, but which foreigners really exploit for what it is—an undercooled liquid. The secret to the success of the French hot extrusion practice of making steel tubes is glass. Here the glass, molten again, turns up as a lubricant par excellence. With metal shortages ahead of undreamed proportions, glass, even the old wine bottle, will be regurgitated no end by scientists, engineers, purchasing agents, et al in the months to come.

Nodular graphitic irons zoomed into production records in both light and heavy sections, THE IRON AGE, Aug. 3, p. 75 and Aug. 10, p. 79. Serving as a bridge between the properties of cast iron and steel or semisteel, wide use of these new irons were made. Cross-section thicknesses up to 12 in. or down to 3/32 in. are being cast every day and both dimensions are in the state of revision as the industry applies the metal to more parts. Castings as heavy as 30 tons or as light as 1/3 oz are being produced. Melting practices are improving and last year's production is estimated at 20,000 net tons.

Behind the iron curtain the Russians are very serious about the Korean peninsula, THE IRON AGE, Aug. 3, p. 67 and Aug. 10, p. 65. The 4 billion tons of iron ore, 700 million tons of coking coal, plenty of manganese, tungsten, molybe-

num and magnesite are enough economic reasons for Russia to sacrifice every able-bodied Chinaman alive if need be to secure the only promising base for large steel production in East Asia. Europe's captured iron and steel facilities are a drain on Russia's natural resources. With only 20 million ingot tons annual steel production within her old boundaries, Russia needs the riches of the Satellite countries. Manchuria and North Korea have the most of what Russia wants.

Induction coils on one station arbor of an 8-spindle automatic screw machine is the latest example of the versatility of tool designers, THE IRON AGE, Aug. 24, p. 65. A completely machined and heat treated piece for every indexing of these high production machines is about as fast as even Detroit's mass production men ever dreamed of. Copper plating, carburizing, drawing, internal grinding and cleaning of a part have been eliminated in the one application completely engineered to date.

Radioactive cobalt 60 once considered a waste or byproduct, is now a lusty infant in one phase of nondestructive testing, THE IRON AGE, Aug. 24, p. 68. Co[60] is fast replacing radium in the radiographic inspection departments of forging and casting plants. The cobalt isotope can be purchased for less than 2 months' rental cost of radium. Many small shops can now have radiographic inspection at a fraction of former prohibitive high costs.

It costs less to rent than to buy machine tools. A machine tool distributor who decided to think instead of cry about business came up last year with a rental plan for machines that was so solid a Philadelphia bank put up the money, THE IRON AGE, Aug. 31, p. 51. This plan permits deduction of the cost of new machinery as an expense before taxes which came as a surprise to a lot of industrialists as well as the Treasury Dept.

OH and BF designs are changing. Last year

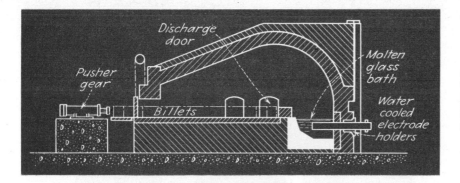

A MOLTEN GLASS bath at the discharge end is used in this pusher-type billet reheating furnace. Other types of reheating furnaces are in operation overseas.

the Japanese built an openhearth without a front wall, the English ran carbon brick linings all the way up to the throat of some blast furnaces and a wellknown American designed an all-welded shower-cooled carbon-lined O_2 fed blast furnace that promises more iron for less money, The Iron Age, Sept. 21, p. 85, 88 and 93. Faster scrap charging is the main feature of the new openhearth. Charging machines are burning out their bearings trying to keep up with O_2 melting practices. An American openhearth plant was built last year with one thing in mind, faster scrap charging via elevators; they still have a front wall.

Higher top pressures, O_2 in the blast and other improvements in squeezing more iron from blast furnaces may really pay off soon. A furnace designed primarily to use the new improvements may be built this year. Before the dust settles on this development, the coke charge may be cut as much as 1/3 per ton of iron produced. Some of the sulfur troubles now plaguing the steelmaker will be reduced when this program is put into practice.

Cold extrusion saves steel, critical alloys and produces parts with a better surface than can be had by machining, The Iron Age, Oct. 19, p. 69. Given impetus by the Ordnance Dept., this 5 in 1 process promises wide application. The fourth advantage is that strengths up to about 110,000 psi U. S. ultimate strength can be achieved without heat treatment. The fifth attraction is that precise tolerances are a natural function of the process and much machining is obviated. From here on, the process will be kept slightly under wraps. Exact pressures required, punch speeds, punch and die design, and lubrication details are now considered classified information. Press makers who neglected to pay serious attention to this development have done an abrupt about face. More plants will be built. Natural products for the process are those of cylindrical or tubular shape. Adherents to older methods of forming who have been somewhat resentful of the new method have an uphill battle ahead as long as steel and alloys are in short supply.

Sigma phase, nightmare of the stainless metallurgist, continued to haunt the industry, The Iron Age, Nov. 30, p. 63 and Dec. 7, p. 127. It even scared the testing engineers at the Atlantic City annual meeting. Methods of identification, effects on properties and causes of formation, however, were more clearly defined late in the year and some of the mysteries are beginning to be understood. Some of the stabilizers used to inhibit intergranular corrosion cause more sigma to form. That is bad enough, but last year tantalum started to appear in ever-increasing amounts which, for a while, caused some consternation to users and makers of type 347. Latest research shows that most of these fears were ill founded. The two alternates, the titanium grade 321 or low-carbon 18 8, also can be used judiciously when necessary and the industry is expected to be more calm this year provided they can get nickel and chromium to make it stainless in the first place.

Continuous casting of steel reached a new high last year, The Iron Age, Dec. 28, p. 66. Two new plants were authorized and another will be completed by late 1951. Savings as high as $100 a ton on special grades are predicted by continuous casting methods over former steelmaking practice. The mold is "the thing." The two major exponents of the process as a process agree only on the fact that continuous casting is the coming steelmaking method. From there on, there are two very distinct schools of thought. The black horse in the race may be the moving mold idea but to date, this process has yet to prove itself on aluminum. Aluminum shapes up to 10x48 in. are being continuous cast abroad. Steel sections of 3x15 in. are in production in this country. Molds to produce 100 sq in. sections in rectangular and oval form are being designed. A new company of former steel company officials is in the process of incorporating and building a plant to make slabs by a process as yet unannounced. Machines to continuous cast aluminum billets in 1-in. equilateral triangles, has been sold to the British. One such American unit is operating and another machine will arrive here in the spring. Someone is going to prove who is right in the approach to continuous casting steel before the year is out and the stakes are pretty high.

Out-of-round

means

out-of-stock

This studied revolution of a Federal XLS Ball Bearing is the forerunner of many thousands at high-speed every minute of its long operating life. The O.D. high and low spots, which mean taper and out-of-round, are intercepted at this point of Federal's inspection control. I.D. grinding, too, is held to such critical account to assure that bores are cylindrical, not bellmouthed, tapered or out-of-round.

Proper operating fit is the end result...correct running clearances maintained between the housing and shaft.

Taking the "measure" of a bearing to Federal's rigid standards involves over 100 individual production, inspection and cleaning operations—with *every fourth operator an inspector*. Out of this system of check and re-check,

fifty years in the developing, Federal Ball Bearings are equipped to deliver friction-free performance on any assignment.

Your application may benefit from a Federal Ball Bearing installation. Write for catalog "K." Its 260 pages describe the complete line of Federal Ball Bearings.

Also write for a copy of our latest Ball Bearing Conversion Tables which contain complete up-to-date interchange information.

THE FEDERAL BEARINGS CO., INC. · POUGHKEEPSIE, NEW YORK

Makers of Fine Ball Bearings

Quality since 1908

FEDERAL BALL BEARINGS

ONE OF AMERICA'S LEADING BALL BEARING MANUFACTURERS

1951

THE IRON AGE

METAL INDUSTRY FACTS

E

F

G

H

I

J

L

M

SPOTLIGHTING 1950

IMPORTANT EVENTS OF THE YEAR

Markets and Prices

Jan. 12—Machine tool shipment index reaches postwar low of 52.8, reflecting order low reached in July 1949, and begins uninterrupted upturn.

Mar. 13—RFC withdraws fixed price quotations on tin; adopts basis of selling on weekly average price.

May 31—Nickel price advances 8¢ to 48¢ per lb.

June 16—President Truman vetoes freight absorption bill.

June 25—Invasion of South Korea starts metals in rising price spiral.

Aug. 31—Iron Age reports new lease plan for new machine tools and other production equipment.

Sept. 7—National Machine Tool Builders Assn. backs up Winston Churchill's blast against sale of machine tools to Iron Curtain countries.

Sept. 12—Formula prices set on steelmaking scrap as mills try to hold price line. Formula tops on No. 1 heavy melting: Pittsburgh, $44; Chicago, $40; Detroit, $37.50; Philadelphia, $39; and Cleveland, $43.50.

Sept. 21—Steel gray market stronger; cold-rolled sheets bringing up to $360 per ton.

Sept. 30—Dow Chemical Co. announces new magnesium ingot price of 24.5¢ per lb.

Oct. 2—Last two copper producers raise prices to 24.5¢ per lb. Import duty of 2¢ per lb, which went back into effect July 1, brings imported metal to 26.5¢.

Oct. 3—Kaiser Aluminum & Chemical Co. and Reynolds Metals Co. follow Aluminum Co. of America in increasing aluminum ingot price to 19¢ per lb. This followed a 1/2¢ increase May 19.

Oct. 20—Titanium Metals Corp. of America establishes mill prices and sets up standards and extras for titanium metal products.

Nov. 21—Ferromanganese prices advance again to $181.20. Previous advance, Nov. 14, was to $178.60 per gross ton.

Nov. 8—Tin hits peak of $1.55 per lb.

Dec. 1—Steel prices advanced. Iron Age base price composite rises $5.88 a ton.

Dec. 2—Tool steel prices advance by 10 pct.

Dec. 5—General Motors says 1951 car prices will go up about 5 pct, setting off rhubarb with Washington, which replied with Ceiling Price Regulation No. 1.

Dec. 6—Scrap buying prices raised by mills, sending The Iron Age scrap composite to $45.08 on Dec. 12 and to $45.13 a week later.

Dec. 7—Steel gray market prices continue to soar; averages reported around $400 per ton.

Dec. 7—The Iron Age pig iron composite jumps from November's $49.69 to $51.94 per gross ton.

Dec. 13—Nickel price advances 2 1/2¢ to 50 1/2¢ per lb.

Dec. 14—The Iron Age pig iron composite advances to $52.69 a gross ton as all producers complete price increases.

Dec. 14—Lake Superior iron ore prices rise 60¢ a ton. Old range non-bessemer becomes $8.55 a ton and old range bessemer, $8.70 per gross ton.

Production

Feb. 2—U. S. Steel Corp. to build eastern mill near Trenton, N. J. Bethlehem Steel Co. to boost Sparrows Point flat-rolled capacity by 40 pct.

Apr. 20—A Venezuelan iron ore mountain, San Isidro, near U. S. Steel's fabulous Cerro Bolivar, contains more than 300 million tons of ore, Iron Age discloses. In no other recent year has the steel industry been so energetic or so successful in its search for new ore bodies to replace dwindling Lake Superior reserves.

Apr. 27—First gas turbine power plant for an automotive vehicle revealed as Boeing Aircraft announces completion of tests on 200-hp gas turbine for trucks.

Oct. 2—Steel industry plans to expand capacity to 109,-963,000 net tons by end of 1952, an increase of 9.4 million net tons over July 1 1950 capacity.

Oct. 19—Preliminary construction of the Quebec-Labrador iron ore project starts by the Hanna-Hollinger group of five companies. Contracts for railroad and docks let and financing arranged.

Nov. 23—Steel industry started this year to build up its coke capacity. Contracts for about 400 new byproduct ovens—with capacity of 2,240,000 net tons of coke—were let in 1950. This does not include oven replacement and rebuilding.

Dec. 2—First pig from reactivated Badin, N. C., Alcoa plant is presented to Jess Larson, General Service Administrator. Capacity expansion of 320,000 tons planned by members of aluminum industry along with reactivation of 79,000 tons of idle capacity.

Dec. 31—Auto production in 1950 exceeded 1949 figures by over a million units, despite hampering strikes and material shortages.

Labor

Mar. 9—Coal strike during February cost 1 million tons of steel production.

May 4—Chrysler Corp. lost production worth $1,022 billion during a 100-day strike (started Jan. 25). Chrysler and supplier plant employees lost an estimated $115.4 million in wages.

Aug. 1—A pronounced influx of labor into the aircraft industry became obvious, with expanding aircraft production programs.

Aug. 31—General Motors escalator clause gains more adherents.

Aug. 31—Weirton Steel labor harmony stalls USWA organizing.

Sept. 7—Fifth round labor pattern: 5 to 10¢ an hr plus cost of living adjustments and $125 pension.

Sept. 28—Aluminum Co. of America offers 10 pct wage increase effective first week in October.

Oct. 12—Most steelworkers decline retirement at 65. With 40 pct of those eligible still on the job, the actuaries have a new problem.

Nov. 9—Skilled labor in tool and die industry not available for big programs ahead. Youngsters can't be trained as Selective Service will get them.

Dec. 1—Steel wages raised average of 16¢ an hr.

IN THIS SECTION:

THE IRON AGE

SECTION 1

METAL INDUSTRY FACTS

Steel Production, Prices and Markets

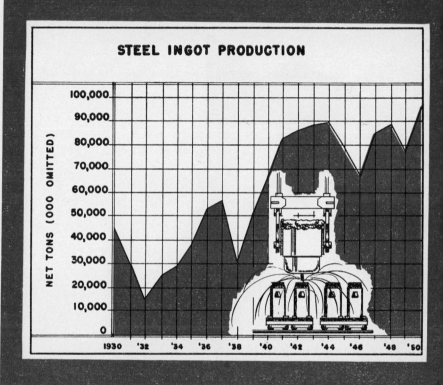

STEEL INGOT PRODUCTION

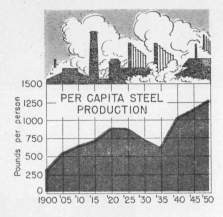

PER CAPITA STEEL PRODUCTION

PER CAPITA STEEL OUTPUT
Of the United States

Year	Pounds Per Person	Year	Pounds Per Person
1900	300	1925	878
1901	389	1926	921
1902	423	1927	846
1903	404	1928	958
1904	367	1929	1038
1905	535	1930	741
1906	613	1931	489
1907	602	1932	245
1908	354	1933	414
1909	593	1934	462
1910	633	1935	600
1911	565	1936	836
1912	734	1937	879
1913	712	1938	489
1914	531	1939	807
1915	716	1940	1015
1916	940	1941	1244
1917	976	1942	1278
1918	953	1943	1302
1919	739	1944	1298
1920	886	1945	1142
1921	408	1946	949
1922	725	1947	1184
1923	899	1948	1213
1924	745	1949	1036
		1950	1263*

* Estimated.

STEEL CAPACITY, PRODUCTION AND RATES

Ingots and Steel for Castings, Net Tons

	Total Capacity	Openhearth Production	Openhearth Percent of Total Output	Bessemer Production	Bessemer Percent of Total Output	Electric* Production	Electric* Percent of Total Output	Total Production	Total Percent of Capacity
1950†	**	86,483,134	89.2	4,556,847	4.7	5,941,205	6.1	96,954,186	97.0
1949	96,120,930	70,248,803	90.1	3,946,656	5.1	3,782,717	4.8	77,978,176	81.1
1948	94,243,460	79,340,157	89.5	4,243,172	4.8	5,057,141	5.7	88,640,470	94.1
1947	91,241,250	76,873,793	90.5	4,232,543	5.0	3,787,785	4.5	84,894,071	93.0
1946	91,890,560	60,711,963	91.2	3,327,737	5.0	2,563,024	3.8	66,602,724	72.5
1945	95,505,280	71,939,602	90.3	4,305,318	5.4	3,456,728	4.3	79,701,648	83.5
1944	93,854,420	80,363,953	89.7	5,039,923	5.6	4,237,724	4.7	89,641,600	95.5
1943	90,589,190	78,621,804	88.5	5,625,492	6.3	4,589,216	5.2	88,836,512	98.1
1942	88,886,550	76,501,957	88.9	5,553,424	6.5	3,976,550	4.6	86,031,931	96.8
1941	85,158,150	74,389,619	89.8	5,578,071	6.7	2,871,569	3.5	82,839,259	97.3
1940	81,619,496	61,573,083	91.9	3,708,573	5.6	1,701,030	2.5	66,982,686	82.1
1939	81,828,958	48,409,800	91.7	3,358,916	6.4	1,029,998	1.9	52,798,714	64.5
1938	80,158,638	29,080,016	91.6	2,106,340	6.6	565,634	1.8	31,751,990	39.6
1937	78,148,374	51,824,979	91.5	3,863,918	6.8	948,048	1.7	56,636,945	72.5
1936	78,164,300	48,760,463	91.2	3,873,472	7.2	866,064	1.6	53,499,999	68.4
1935	78,451,930	34,401,280	90.1	3,175,235	8.3	607,190	1.6	38,183,705	48.7
1934	78,128,416	26,354,838	90.3	2,421,840	8.3	405,246	1.4	29,181,924	37.4
1933	78,614,403	22,827,473	87.7	2,720,246	10.5	472,510	1.8	26,020,229	33.1
1932	78,780,913	13,336,210	87.0	1,715,925	11.2	270,766	1.8	15,322,901	19.5
1931	77,257,803	25,210,714	86.8	3,386,259	11.6	461,988	1.6	29,058,961	37.6
1930	72,985,406	39,255,073	86.1	5,639,714	12.4	688,634	1.5	45,583,421	62.5
1929	71,438,516	54,155,235	85.7	7,977,210	12.6	1,073,045	1.7	63,205,490	88.5
1928	68,840,912	49,407,631	85.6	7,414,618	12.8	907,232	1.6	57,729,481	83.9
1927	67,236,117	42,636,535	84.7	6,934,734	13.8	756,138	1.5	50,327,407	74.9
1926	67,750,035	45,575,016	84.2	7,766,716	14.4	747,282	1.4	54,089,014	83.5
1925	68,473,222	42,598,627	83.8	7,530,837	14.8	711,283	1.4	50,840,747	74.2

* Includes very small tonnages of crucible steel.

** Jan. 1, 1950 to June 30, 1950 capacity was 99,392,800 net tons. Beginning July 1, 1950 capacity was revised to 100,563,500 net tons.

† Preliminary

Source: American Iron & Steel Institute

STEEL INGOT PRODUCTION

Openhearth, Bessemer and Electric Furnace Ingots and Steel for Castings, Net Tons; U. S. Only

	1925	1926	1927	1928	1929	1930	1931	1932	1933	1934	1935	1936	1937
Jan.	4,719,919	4,656,029	4,302,172	4,531,172	5,115,195	4,288,212	2,852,540	1,685,665	1,157,745	2,276,596	3,279,473	3,474,353	5,398,326
Feb.	4,223,613	4,264,863	4,327,341	4,590,842	4,920,348	4,579,761	2,892,154	1,681,421	1,221,664	2,521,472	3,169,909	3,379,587	5,050,824
March	4,721,111	5,035,081	5,148,330	5,117,384	5,760,878	4,828,571	3,468,208	1,627,030	1,022,675	3,190,040	3,273,910	3,810,436	5,970,247
April	4,033,752	4,626,271	4,685,249	4,888,226	5,626,610	4,664,182	3,141,887	1,429,848	1,531,813	3,346,922	3,017,177	4,494,782	5,801,540
May	3,888,883	4,425,910	4,594,340	4,776,766	6,008,754	4,520,520	2,897,385	1,277,302	2,250,236	3,875,202	3,009,245	4,614,529	5,894,260
June	3,606,900	4,207,512	3,969,129	4,250,736	5,573,076	3,879,960	2,416,078	1,036,102	2,919,687	3,487,612	2,580,771	4,543,888	4,787,710
July	3,471,854	4,095,783	3,637,255	4,320,783	5,513,546	3,316,654	2,143,351	915,738	3,607,288	1,697,879	2,591,240	4,473,940	5,212,832
Aug.	3,850,644	4,492,374	3,971,467	4,744,291	5,614,144	3,473,898	1,949,462	961,153	3,260,279	1,574,649	3,331,770	4,782,442	5,580,683
Sept.	3,927,822	4,409,463	3,710,754	4,709,416	5,146,744	3,223,766	1,754,817	1,125,892	2,599,370	1,446,551	3,227,876	4,744,841	4,907,592
Oct.	4,377,214	4,591,053	3,764,573	5,279,460	5,154,063	3,055,972	1,805,653	1,233,957	2,373,729	1,689,272	3,590,945	5,182,430	3,881,819
Nov.	4,393,068	4,175,502	3,549,711	4,844,460	4,002,365	2,510,820	1,807,315	1,171,710	1,731,930	1,836,068	3,599,687	4,941,014	2,464,793
Dec.	4,469,629	3,906,230	3,604,731	4,562,175	3,299,786	2,246,742	1,477,529	977,389	2,047,780	2,239,126	3,511,702	5,056,843	1,685,273
Total	49,684,409	52,886,071	49,264,052	56,615,711	61,735,509	44,589,058	28,608,379	15,123,207	25,724,196	29,181,329	38,183,705	53,449,085	58,635,899

	1938	1939	1940	1941	1942	1943	1944	1945	1946	1947	1948	1949	1950
Jan.	1,984,815	3,663,004	5,764,723	6,928,085	7,112,106	7,424,522	7,592,603	7,204,312	3,872,887	7,222,612	7,480,878	8,197,390	7,930,372
Feb.	1,942,795	3,448,120	4,525,797	6,237,900	6,512,535	6,824,604	7,194,009	6,652,765	1,392,682	6,430,401	6,948,017	7,493,942	6,793,245
March	2,293,884	3,929,387	4,389,183	7,131,641	7,392,111	7,674,578	7,826,257	7,705,929	6,508,764	7,316,974	7,618,770	8,401,796	7,487,036
April	2,198,413	3,431,600	4,100,474	6,755,949	7,121,291	7,373,703	7,593,683	7,289,887	5,801,195	7,051,842	6,224,487	7,796,165	8,212,672
May	2,061,169	3,372,636	4,967,782	7,053,238	7,382,578	7,549,691	7,702,576	7,449,667	4,072,620	7,339,014	7,580,642	7,598,990	8,551,982
June	1,868,848	3,606,729	5,657,443	6,800,730	7,015,302	7,039,353	7,234,257	6,840,522	5,625,773	6,977,714	7,265,249	6,504,656	8,131,515
July	2,259,677	3,648,639	5,724,625	6,821,682	7,144,958	7,407,876	7,948,387	6,985,571	6,618,683	6,578,685	7,075,517	5,784,831	8,071,294
Aug.	2,903,805	4,341,726	6,186,383	7,000,957	7,227,655	7,586,464	7,498,913	5,735,317	6,924,522	6,991,152	7,446,834	6,722,771	8,230,317
Sept.	3,029,736	4,881,601	6,056,246	6,819,706	7,057,519	7,514,339	7,235,111	5,982,475	6,555,566	6,797,457	7,424,844	6,597,935	8,200,020
Oct.	3,554,912	6,223,126	6,644,542	7,242,683	7,579,514	7,814,117	7,620,885	5,596,776	6,951,742	7,570,152	7,996,895	928,347	8,718,978
Nov.	4,072,676	6,292,322	6,469,107	6,969,987	7,179,812	7,371,975	7,278,719	6,200,466	6,457,771	7,242,427	7,797,558	4,223,129	6,108,730*
Dec.	3,583,253	5,958,893	6,495,357	7,163,999	7,304,540	7,255,144	7,336,170	6,057,937	5,760,501	7,375,641	7,780,779	7,728,224	8,524,947*
Total	31,751,983	52,797,783	66,981,662	82,927,557	86,029,921	88,836,386	89,641,575	79,701,624	66,602,706	84,894,071	88,640,470	77,978,176	96,954,186*

* Estimate.

Source: American Iron & Steel Institute

Steel Operating Rates, Production of Stainless and Alloy Ingots, World Production.

METAL FACTS SECTION 1

STEEL INDUSTRY OPERATING RATES

Openhearth, Bessemer and Electric Furnace Ingots and Steel for Castings—Percent of Capacity; U. S. Only.

Percent of Capacity

	1929	1932	1933	1936	1937	1938
Jan.	86.56	25.88	17.76	52,46	81.32	29.14
Feb.	92.21	26.62	20.75	54.61	84.26	31.59
Mar.	97.48	24.98	15.68	57.54	89.93	33.67
Apr.	98.32	22.67	24.26	70.09	90.24	33.70
May	101.68	19.61	34.51	69.68	88.79	30.26
June	97.38	16.42	46.24	70.85	74.47	23.33
July	93.51	14.09	55.45	67.71	78.37	33.25
Aug.	95.00	14.76	50.00	72.22	83.71	42.63
Sept.	90.14	17.89	41.29	74.16	76.19	46.03
Oct.	87.22	18.94	36.40	78.26	53.23	52.19
Nov.	69.94	18.57	27.43	77.05	38.18	61.74
Dec.	55.96	15.04	31.48	76.53	25.34	52.72
Average	88.76	19.67	33.52	68.45	72.33	39.60

	1939	1940	1941	1942	1943	1944
Jan.	52.69	83.40	96.90	94.50	96.80	95.70
Feb.	54.93	70.00	96.60	95.90	98.50	97.00
Mar.	56.52	63.50	99.70	98.20	100.00	98.60
Apr.	50.97	61.20	97.60	97.70	99.30	98.80
May	48.51	71.80	98.70	98.10	98.40	97.10
June	53.57	84.50	98.20	96.30	94.80	94.10
July	52.60	83.00	93.40	94.50	96.20	94.30
Aug.	62.45	89.50	95.70	95.40	98.30	94.10
Sept.	72.68	90.60	96.40	96.40	100.70	94.00
Oct.	89.52	96.10	99.00	100.00	101.20	95.60
Nov.	93.46	96.60	98.30	97 80	98.60	94.30
Dec.	85.91	94.10	98.10	96.60	94.20	92.60
Average	64.53	82.10	97.40	96.80	98.10	95.50

	1945	1946	1947	1948	1949	1950†
Jan.	88.80	49.60	93.20	93.60	100.4	93.9
Feb.	90.80	19.80	91.90	93.00	101.6	89.1
Mar.	95.00	83.30	94.40	95.30	102.9	88.7
Apr.	92.80	77.50	93.90	80.40	98.6	100.4
May	91.80	52.20	94.70	94.80	93.0	101.3
June	87.10	74.40	92.90	93.80	82.2	99.4
July	86.30	84.90	85.10	88.70	71.0	94.7
Aug.	70.70	86.90	92.20	93.10	82.3	98.3
Sept.	76.30	86.90	90.80	96.10	83.6	99.3
Oct.	69.00	89.00	97.70	99.90	11.4	102.0
Nov.	78.90	85.40	96.50	100.50	53.4	97.8
Dec.	74.80	73.90	95.40	97.7	94.8	100.0
Average	83.50	72.50	93.00	94.1	81.1	97.0

* Estimated. † Preliminary.

Source: American Iron & Steel Institute

ALLOY STEEL INGOT PRODUCTION

Other Than Stainless, by Grade, Net Tons

	1950 10 Months	1949	1948	1947	1946	1945	1944
Nickel	129,293	108,062	408,401	322,058	200,317	205,285	318,396
Molybdenum	503,962	475,691	653,823	592,462	426,521	400,027	403,202
Manganese	261,352	264,898	244,678	213,955	168,405	510,010	689,684
Manganese-Molybdenum	173,458	204,653	*	*	*	*	*
Chromium	942,704	768.917	1,001,738	880,101	655,885	616,900	880,196
Chromium-Vanadium	32,748	28,314	*	*	*	*	*
Nickel-Chromium	161,930	156,080	686,918	630,705	456,456	503,604	861,967
Chromium-Molybdenum	441,220	313,195	489,931	347,867	384,571	343,147	1,117,780
Nickel-Molybdenum	412,638	309,971	*	*	461,689	426,594	433,262
Nickel-Chromium-Molybdenum—NE Steels	979,791	797,941	1,164,200	878,353	680,804	2,031,302	2,301,671
Nickel-Chromium-Molybdenum—All Other	*	*	*	*	*	1,031,159	1,326,671
Silico-Manganese	113,404	177,831	233,167	221,386	204,661	1,940,185	1,717,184
All Other	1,692,950	1,738,718	2,877,964	2,711,891	1,793,347	*	*
Total	5,845,450	5,342,271	7,760,820	6,798,778	5,432,656	8,008,213	10,050,013
Percentage of alloy ingots to total ingot output	7.3	6.4	8.8	8.0	8.2	10.1	11.3

* Included in "All Other."

Source: American Iron & Steel Institute

STAINLESS STEEL

Ingot Production, Net Tons

Type	First 6 mos. 1950	1949	1948	1947
301	33,535	34,144	61,565	24,485
302	96,813	93,666	145,426	124,542
302B	878	515	1,623	629
303	10,362	9,189	14,633	9,171
304	69,036	68,996	100,966	115,367
308	1,273	1,972	2,947	2.564
309	1,679	2,647	4,902	4,137
310	3,453	4,528	5,663	3,849
316	15,840	19,119	28,622	29,630
321	3,616	5,306	7,528	6,949
347	17,470	24,052	33,346	22,966
All Other	6,044	10,548	9,266	8,748
Total	259,999	274,682	416,387	353,037
403	2,890	5,526	6,423	5,921
405	1,670	2,156	4,126	2,259
406	1,091	1,621	2,580	1,842
410	10,567	15,961	25,614	19,568
414	1,553	2,165	5,562	2,090
416	11,350	9,285	16,284	9,905
420	2,628	3,315	4,852	4,818
430	99,764	122,286	122,437	105,783
430F	788	921	1,526	1,098
431	727	1,157	1,120	1,476
440A	918	1,334	1,433	800
440B	202	592	218	125
440C	766	873	1,220	1,223
442	229	298	318	439
443	5	4	33	13
446	1,481	2,321	2,573	1,753
All Other	3,047	2,528	4,692	7,783
Total	139,676	172,343	200,991	166,896
Total all types	399,675	447,025	617,378	519,933
Ratio stainless to total ingot output	1:118	1:174	1:144	1:163

Source: American Iron and Steel Institute

WORLD STEEL PRODUCTION

Ingots and Steel for Castings, Thousands of Net Tons

Compiled by THE IRON AGE from the United Nations Bulletin of Statistics, Chambre Syndicate de la Siderurgie Francaise, British Iron and Steel Federation and the American Iron and Steel Institute.

	1950*	1949[1]	1948[1]	1947	1946	1945	1944	1943	1942	1941	1940	1939
Australia	1,519	1,309	1,425	1,373	1,164	1,505	1,703	1,822	1,901	1,835	1,439	1,307
Austria	1,017	920	713	394	207	189	....	....	....	....	....	....
Belgium	3,863	4,242	4,318	3,181	2,508	805	670	1,834	1,518	1,782	2,086	3,429
Brazil	798	671	545	426	379	227	243	205	176	170	156	125
Canada	3,270	3,186	3,159	2,902	2,293	2,803	2,930	2,872	2,986	2,623	2,174	1,509
Czechoslovakia	2,850	2,756	2,910*	2,520	1,843	1,045	2,778	2,831	2,619	2,659	2,606	2,526
France	9,108	10,086	7,984	6,338	4,859	1,822	3,408	5,651	4,947	4,751	4,864	8,763
Germany	13,101[2]	10,090[2]	6,127[2]	4,739[2]	3,604[2]	5,500	28,481	33,706	31,684	25,804	23,732	26,152
Hungary	875	882	794*	658	389	142	766	856	865	861	827	808
India	1,525	1,517	1,237	1,346	1,373	1,426	1,465	1,518	1,452	1,531	1,399	1,135
Italy	2,503	2,265	2,342	1,874	1,269	436	1,138	1,905	2,130	2,275	2,487	2,513
Japan	4,970	3,352	1,916	1,041	608	1,177	7,032	9,676	8,760	8,349	8,288	8,124
Luxembourg	2,560	2,507	2,705	1,888	1,426	291	1,389	2,368	1,720	1,376	1,138	1,931
Mexico	390	380	268	353	277	201	199	194	104	104	104	085
Poland	2,525	2,539	2,116*	1,731	1,344	546	755	870	....	....	1,600	1,790
Saar	1,925	1,936	1,922	780	317	....	....	....	....	....	....	2,235
South Africa	849	699	750	660	568	594	541	462	370	370	396	343
Spain	904	793	604	581	656	617	546	721	663	633	766	644
Sweden	1,071	1,511	1,270	1,311	1,335	1,327	1,320	1,338	1,354	1,275	1,280	1,270
United Kingdom	18,078	17,256	16,662	14,246	14,220	13,243	13,599	14,595	14,495	13,790	14,527	14,808
U.S.S.R.	26,500	23,500	18,700	14,700*	13,400*	12,300*	13,300	12,200	10,900	16,600	20,130	20,719
United States	96,954	77,978	88,640	84,894	66,603	79,702	89,642	88,837	86,032	82,839	66,983	52,799
Totals	194,154	173,386	167,107	147,156*	120,345*	125,898*	171,905	184,461	174,676	169,627	156,982	150,780

* Estimated. [1]Revised. [2] British, French and United States Zones.

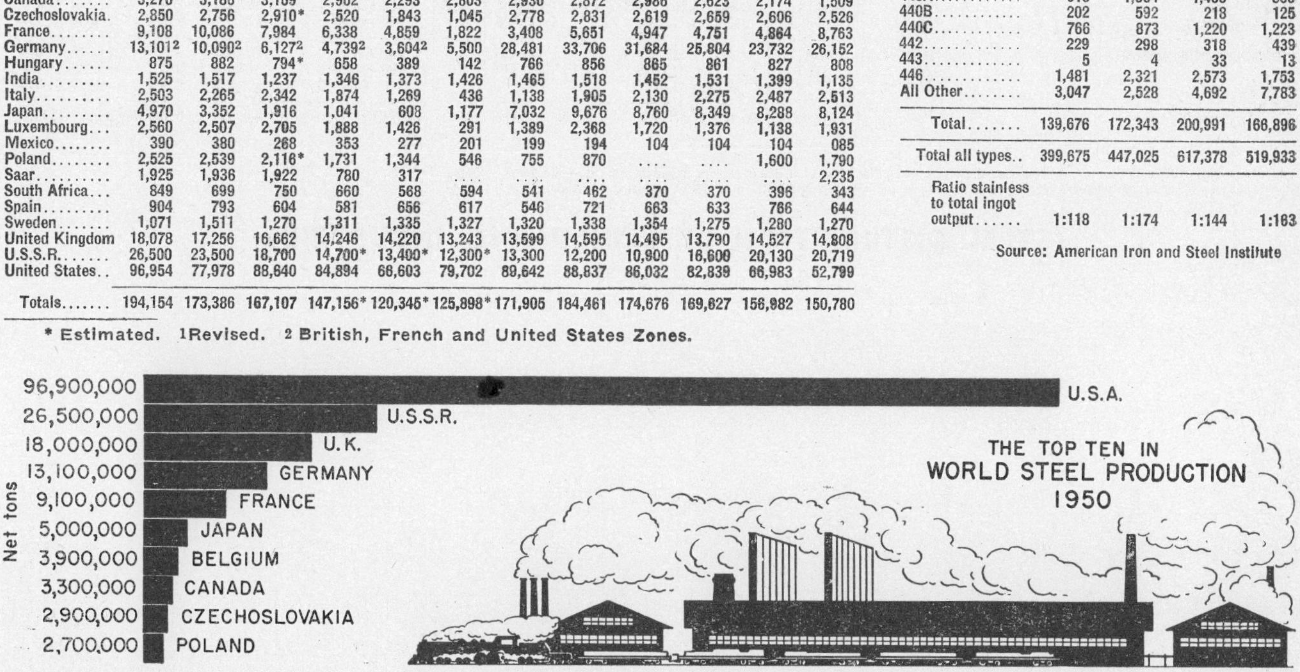

THE TOP TEN IN
WORLD STEEL PRODUCTION
1950
Net tons
96,900,000
U.S.A.
26,500,000
U.S.S.R.
18,000,000
U.K.
13,100,000
GERMANY
9,100,000
FRANCE
5,000,000
JAPAN
3,900,000
BELGIUM
3,300,000
CANADA
2,900,000
CZECHOSLOVAKIA
2,700,000
POLAND

SHIPMENTS AND PRODUCTION FOR SALE OF STEEL PRODUCTS
By Companies Who Made More Than 95 Pct of Total Rolled Steel Produced in the U. S.

Steel Products	1950—9 Months Shipments (N.T.)	Pct of Total	1949 Shipments (N.T.)	Pct of Total	1948 Shipments (N.T.)	Pct of Total	1947 Shipments (N.T.)	Pct of Total	1946 Shipments (N.T.)	Pct of Total	1945 Shipments (N.T.)	Pct of Total	1940 Production for Sale (N.T.)	Pct of Total
Ingots, blooms, billets, tube rounds, sheet and tin bars, etc.	2,174,838	4.1	2,261,285	3.9	3,150,754	4.8	2,966,748	4.7	1,949,624	4.0	4,724,688	8.3	4,532,745	9.9
Structural shapes (heavy)	3,068,992	5.8	3,669,503	6.3	4,255,355	6.5	4,436,129	7.0	3,474,284	7.1	3,545,673	6.3	3,149,036	6.9
Steel piling	243,778	0.5	301,824	0.5	299,537	0.5	324,224	0.5	205,313	0.4	217,336	0.4	215,234	0.5
Plates (sheared and universal)	3,924,394	7.4	5,759,065	9.9	7,000,199	10.6	6,345,216	10.1	4,152,181	8.5	6,508,130	11.5	4,171,158	9.1
Skelp	88,834	0.2	118,533	0.2	75,252	0.1	160,989	0.3	227,033	0.5	378,985	0.7	527,574	1.1
Rails, Standard (over 60 lbs.)	1,316,933	2.5	1,772,734	3.0	1,976,520	3.0	2,207,146	3.5	1,790,311	3.7	2,224,148	3.9	1,487,113	3.2
All other	86,831	0.2	117,154	0.2	214,880	0.3	211,900	0.3	144,999	0.3	170,055	0.3	162,622	0.4
Joint bars and tie plates	410,785	0.8	491,896	0.8	626,573	1.0	678,702	1.1	624,299	1.3	779,057	1.4	481,271	1.0
Track spikes	105,157	0.2	95,345	0.2	145,830	0.2	163,746	0.3	146,194	0.3	165,038	0.3	107,197	0.2
Hot Rolled Bars, Carbon	5,866,241	11.1	6,416.102	11.0	6,196,444	9.4	6,242,416	9.9	5,006,859	10.3	5,590,154	9.9	4,465,549	9.7
Reinf., New billet	1,210,461	2.3	1,572,588	2.7	1,329,945	2.0	1,277,075	2.0	1,048,483	2.1	750,442	1.3	1,299,455	2.8
Rerolled					212,021	0.3	175,833	0.3	141,346	0.3	85,006	0.1	142,480	0.3
Alloy	†	....	†	....	1,927,309	2.9	1,741,432	2.8	1,390,278	2.8	1,741,075	3.1	962,450	2.1
Total	7,076,702	13.4	7,988,690	13.7	9,665,719	14.6	9,436,756	15.0	7,586,966	15.5	8,166,677	14.4	6,869,934	14.9
Cold Finished Bars, Carbon				2.1	1,349,719	2.0	1,426,701	2.3	1,316,579	2.7	1,614,136	2.8	724,504	1.6
Alloy					244,248	0.4	218,802	0.4	196,237	0.4	326,173	0.6	99,589	0.2
Total	1,186,658	2.3	1,213,052	2.1	1,593,967	2.4	1,645,503	2.6	1,512,816	3.1	1,940,309	3.4	824,093	1.8
Tool steel bars	60,407	0.1	57,395	0.1	88,376	0.1	87,279	0.1	96,020	0.2	122,149	0.2	74,176	0.2
Pipes and Tubes, Buttweld	6,593,055	12.5	6,317,557	10.9	2,045,361	3.1	1,706,415	2.7	1,276,289	2.6	1,517,927	2.7	1,157,144	2.5
Lapweld					339,633	0.5	389,762	0.6	305,516	0.6	503,951	0.9	360,188	0.8
Electricweld					1,572,139	2.4	1,122,350	1.8	674,459	1.4	857,478	1.5	288,424	0.6
Seamless					2,924,416	4.4	2,082,686	3.3	1,871,540	3.8	2,235,294	4.0	1,759,567	3.8
Conduit							155,335	0.2	98,521	0.2	88,112	0.1	82,042	0.2
Mech., Press. Tubes			617,663	1.1			661,336	1.1	429,180	0.9	669,130	1.2	313,877	0.7
Wire rods	603,984	1.2	570,397	1.0	610,348	0.9	667,282	1.1	679,998	1.4	862,393	1.5	1,041,557	2.3
Wire, Drawn	2,077,512	3.9	2,138,878	3.7	2,673,276	4.1	2,590,963	4.1	1,933,124	4.0	1,942,168	3.4	1,540,357	3.4
Nails and staples	652,734	1.2	731,356	1.3	859,540	1.3	799,436	1.3	636,632	1.3	602,558	1.1	641,453	1.4
Barbed and twisted	175,049	0.3	215,047	0.4	254,629	0.4	256,991	0.4	207,610	0.4	234,209	0.4	213,825	0.5
Woven wire fence	363,993	0.7	358,162	0.6	399,457	0.6	407,295	0.6	383,230	0.8	373,920	0.7	230,278	0.5
Bale ties	59,464	0.1	42,828	0.1	113,892	0.2	119,917	0.2	99,993	0.2	82,809	0.1	67,610	0.1
All other wire products													5,302	0.0
Fence posts													54,434	0.1
Black Plate, Ordinary	391,284	0.7	452,014	0.8	821,398	1.3	801,745	1.3	781,167	1.6	628,634	1.1	282,551	0.6
Chemically treated					17,268	....	19,252	....	125,170	0.3	114,949	0.2		
Tin and Terne Plate, Hot dipped	1,438,246	2.7	1,699,355	2.9	2,167,912	3.3	2,093,149	3.3	1,924,657	3.9	2,046,153	3.6	2,689,856	5.9
Electrolytic	2,149,674	4.1	1,993,468	3.4	1,784,288	2.7	1,617,659	2.6	909,173	1.9	861,634	1.5		
Sheets, Hot rolled	5,750,499	10.9	6,192,610	10.7	7,786,056	11.8	7,891,798	12.5	5,956,633	12.2	6,327,995	11.2	6,197,810	13.5
Cold rolled	6,796,653	12.9	6,886,946	11.8	6,867,775	10.4	5,504,578	8.7	4,075,554	8.4	2,891,180	5.1	2,436,539	5.3
Galvanized	1,732,640	3.3	1,755,067	3.0	1,643,337	2.5	1,609,881	2.5	1,462,053	3.0	1,693,796	3.0	1,551,374	3.4
Strip, Hot rolled	1,693,627	3.2	1,674,818	2.9	1,662,787	2.5	1,740,085	2.7	1,363,812	2.8	1,369,094	2.4	1,349,188	2.9
Cold rolled	1,333,783	2.5	1,465,297	2.5	1,783,383	2.7	1,613,005	2.6	1,282,146	2.6	1,275,670	2.3	790,346	1.7
Wheels (car, rolled steel)	182,709	0.4	285,733	0.5	337,376	0.5	356,873	0.6	252,308	0.5	292,637	0.5	191,870	0.4
Axles	80,972	0.2	159,628	0.3	215,905	0.3	185,019	0.3	130,461	0.3	146,867	0.3	108,088	0.2
All other	883,470**	1.7	693,113*	1.2					6,266	0.0	41,719	0.1	10,138	0.0
Total Steel Products		....	58,104,010	100.0	65,973,138	100.0	63,057,150	100.0	48,775,532	100.0	56,602,322	100.0	45,965,971	100.0

† Included with carbon.   * Includes long ternes, 151,118 tons; enameling sheets, 162,815 tons; and electrical sheets, 519,821 tons.
** Includes other coated sheets, 172,610 tons; enameling sheets, 191,039 tons; and electrical sheets and strip, 519,821 tons.

STEEL DISTRIBUTION BY CONSUMING INDUSTRIES
In Thousands of Net Tons

	1939 Tons	Pct	Yearly Average 1941–44 Inc. Tons	Pct	1945 Tons	Pct	1946 Tons	Pct	1947 Tons	Pct	1948 Tons	Pct	1949* Tons	Pct	1950† Tons	Pct
Agriculture	1,421	3.6	1,565	2.4	2,426	4.3	2,100	4.3	2,422	3.84	2,743	4.16	2,644	4.55	3,047	4.25
Aircraft			5,557	8.8	5,521	9.7	32	.06	44	.07	39	.06	44	.08	54	.08
Automotive	5,906	15.1					7,379	15.1	10,292	16.32	11,330	17.17	11,880	20.45	15,518	21.63
Construction and Maintenance	6,100	15.6	8,379	13.3	8,353	14.7	8,130	16.7	10,039	15.92	10,157	15.40	10,200	17.25	12,288	17.13
Containers	2,978	7.6	4,216	6.7	4,333	7.6	4,749	9.7	5,598	8.87	5,844	8.85	5,026	8.65	6,472	9.02
Machinery, Tools	1,460	3.7	3,191	5.1	4,739	8.3	4,438	9.1	5,648	8.96	5,337	8.09	4,274	7.36	5,695	7.94
Oil, Gas, Water, Mining	1,842	4.7	2,221	3.5	2,670	4.7	2,480	5.1	3,833	6.08	5,080	7.70	5,455	9.39	6,689	9.32
Pressing, Forming, Stamping	1,842	4.7	2,809	4.5	3,800	6.7	3,127	6.4	3,770	5.98	4,256	6.45	3,124	5.38	4,490	6.26
Railroads	3,250	8.3	5,422	8.6	5,268	9.3	4,764	9.8	5,999	9.51	5,866	8.89	4,038	6.95	5,120	7.14
Shipbuilding	518	1.3	9,657	15.3	3,374	5.9	320	.64	373	.59	716	1.09	722	1.24	381	.53
Exports	2,817	7.2	7,701	12.2	3,793	6.7	3,378	6.9	4,639	7.36	3,798	5.42	3,798	6.54	2,417	3.37
All Others	10,933	28.2	12,212	19.4	12,669	22.2	7,879	16.2	10,402	16.50	11,029	16.72	7,077	12.18	9,575	13.36
Total	39,067	100.0	63,490	99.8	56,946	100.0	48,776	100.00	63,057	100.00	65,973	100.00	58,104	100.0	71,746	100.00

* Revised.   † Preliminary.

Data by American Iron & Steel Institute; Compilation, THE IRON AGE

STEEL USED BY THE METALWORKING INDUSTRY
1948 Consumption of All Grades by the Metalworking Industry, Net Tons

STATE	Hot-Rolled Sheets and Strip Including Galvanized	Cold-Rolled Sheets and Strip	Tin and Terne Plate Blackplate	Plates	Structural Shapes	Hot-Rolled Bars	Cold-Finished Bars	Pipe and Tubes	Wire and Wire Rods	Unclassified	Total	Pct. of Total
Alabama	54,380	26,304	1,182	76,583	81,427	43,531	5,333	17,012	15,506	21,475	342,733	0.75
Arizona	3,814	1,863	51	4,798	13,347	4,155	276	1,240	549	2,115	32,208	0.07
Arkansas	3,369	2,716	2,129	2,373	5,215	2,147	356	764	849	1,273	21,191	0.05
California	364,900	223,477	454,758	288,341	255,841	176,358	42,505	88,203	94,214	106,951	2,095,548	4.58
Colorado	14,905	6,737	2,649	19,693	22,106	16,745	2,739	5,179	2,530	8,102	101,385	0.22
Connecticut	251,832	266,159	16,781	79,467	25,067	190,101	81,203	65,817	165,607	52,660	1,194,694	2.60
Delaware	12,291	4,644	263	44,745	14,840	5,674	1,227	3,322	3,786	8,267	99,059	0.22
District of Columbia	2,488	1,532	117	2,822	6,230	5,839	1,496	834	318	1,498	23,174	0.05
Florida	18,000	8,207	53,422	13,681	14,129	6,705	1,018	2,010	878	3,811	121,861	0.26
Georgia	47,854	21,403	9,406	24,620	19,677	16,913	4,228	7,901	10,625	7,476	170,103	0.37
Idaho	802	584	21	756	1,045	1,885	379	318	553	419	6,762	0.02
Illinois	1,090,245	770,380	908,313	578,384	379,790	1,036,269	271,257	177,755	376,463	317,029	5,905,895	12.85
Indiana	708,255	477,368	70,606	216,193	133,013	468,969	127,593	82,378	112,441	119,694	2,516,510	5.48
Iowa	129,149	50,894	3,889	61,812	55,675	119,554	27,456	22,094	23,623	31,046	525,192	1.14
Kansas	25,028	13,537	619	32,061	30,271	24,188	4,425	9,494	3,377	8,501	151,501	0.33
Kentucky	77,224	56,836	46,078	32,214	26,394	44,733	9,474	15,588	10,083	29,398	348,022	0.76
Louisiana	32,790	8,550	50,083	24,939	19,039	8,657	1,382	7,474	1,847	4,082	158,843	0.35
Maine	4,557	3,497	32,886	7,694	6,398	7,312	3,235	2,495	4,472	1,412	73,958	0.16
Maryland	150,304	92,957	264,050	64,232	25,347	26,020	9,386	10,941	23,458	21,380	688,075	1.50
Massachusetts	287,051	201,151	54,618	144,513	82,272	205,643	70,403	53,247	134,943	81,390	1,315,231	2.86
Michigan	1,967,594	2,397,759	58,930	410,075	154,624	1,149,191	311,643	148,880	276,777	197,848	7,073,321	15.39
Minnesota	82,289	55,060	46,884	60,600	56,456	71,478	20,402	20,089	17,970	22,177	453,403	0.99
Mississippi	2,521	882	82	11,154	4,388	2,910	676	1,173	2,039	1,957	27,782	0.06
Missouri	198,432	135,880	76,154	110,180	61,719	89,947	25,144	39,497	51,286	35,135	823,374	1.79
Montana	1,153	135	8	2,826	1,673	1,081	110	1,440	188	156	8,770	0.02
Nebraska	29,828	11,367	858	16,043	25,840	18,722	3,707	4,515	2,667	6,384	119,931	0.26
Nevada	104	7	1	501	159	110	17	164	10	41	1,114	......
New Hampshire	8,749	5,068	290	9,644	4,571	7,606	2,876	1,801	11,683	1,850	54,138	0.12
New Jersey	325,447	237,507	312,480	176,543	110,974	188,917	56,213	82,529	120,480	73,609	1,684,699	3.66
New Mexico	312	91	5	160	157	96	16	31	21	43	932	......
New York	681,742	501,092	352,484	440,221	236,621	441,253	143,345	115,378	142,992	177,228	3,232,356	7.04
North Carolina	11,918	7,301	314	8,747	15,185	11,237	2,686	2,875	4,331	3,853	68,447	0.15
North Dakota	802	290	10	1,486	4,495	1,374	45	187	143	771	9,603	0.02
Ohio	1,383,791	1,108,124	213,011	571,659	331,836	838,364	281,767	225,538	374,599	305,601	5,634,335	12.26
Oklahoma	19,775	5,941	360	51,975	49,116	23,717	2,802	15,448	2,751	9,791	181,676	0.39
Oregon	14,172	9,990	31,029	11,756	12,277	10,510	2,462	3,780	4,337	4,902	105,215	0.23
Pennsylvania	997,057	672,793	352,875	1,065,941	584,863	850,001	119,763	218,713	269,582	367,066	5,498,654	11.96
Rhode Island	23,839	28,100	21,266	9,868	6,084	43,610	16,395	6,151	37,178	4,112	196,603	0.43
South Carolina	2,235	1,387	59	7,577	3,850	1,378	559	769	1,010	1,203	20,027	0.04
South Dakota	2,266	870	31	929	998	1,421	350	239	155	400	7,659	0.02
Tennessee	63,538	55,286	10,347	55,590	37,739	26,879	6,244	20,317	10,567	17,002	303,509	0.66
Texas	99,257	34,005	133,994	108,383	111,537	97,149	10,831	33,927	14,835	31,556	675,474	1.47
Utah	3,969	1,247	8,711	9,222	9,559	4,586	508	3,366	1,024	1,674	43,866	0.09
Vermont	8,447	6,317	219	3,052	2,667	6,403	4,361	1,137	1,668	1,383	35,654	0.08
Virginia	29,859	15,184	11,895	88,511	61,022	25,100	2,022	8,579	5,680	12,822	260,674	0.57
Washington	29,245	17,638	52,633	36,674	21,633	26,834	4,439	7,633	4,393	8,590	209,712	0.46
West Virginia	46,859	42,293	71,146	33,745	23,049	19,641	3,584	9,797	5,201	10,027	265,342	0.58
Wisconsin	803,297	370,022	51,508	863,866	155,846	386,286	100,772	83,697	92,330	153,933	3,061,557	6.66
Wyoming	339	364	14	138	94	430	110	87	86	122	1,784	......
National Total	10,118,074	7,960,796	3,779,519	5,886,987	3,306,155	6,757,627	1,789,220	1,631,848	2,442,105	2,279,215	45,951,546	100.00

Source: The IRON AGE Market Research Dept.

STAINLESS STEEL SHIPMENTS
Finished and Semifinished Products, Net Tons

PRODUCTS	1950—First 9 Months Shipments	Pct of Total	1949 Shipments	Pct of Total	1948 Shipments	Pct of Total	1947 Shipments	Pct of Total
Ingots, Blooms, Billets, Slabs, Sheet Bars, Tube Rounds, etc.	19,460	6.1	16,292	6.1	19,916	6.1	15,720	5.3
Plates	8,068	2.5	8,670	3.2	12,071	3.7	11,273	3.8
Sheets—Hot Rolled	21,415	6.7	15,515	5.8	19,510	6.0	32,358	11.0
Sheets—Cold Rolled	78,322	24.4	54,780	20.5	77,841	24.0	67,480	22.8
Strip—Hot Rolled	5,767	1.8	5,741	2.2	3,883	1.2	1,034	0.4
Strip—Cold Rolled	125,112	39.0	105,072	39.3	113,414	34.9	101,288	34.3
Bars—Hot Rolled	18,904	5.9	19,652	7.3	26,419	8.1	25,176	8.5
Bars—Cold Finished	20,585	6.4	17,928	6.7	26,784	8.2	22,762	7.7
Pipe and Tubes	7,965	2.5	7,336	2.7	9,689	3.0	8,296	2.8
Wire Rods	810	0.3	361	0.1	136	0.1	708	0.2
Wire Drawn	14,383	4.5	15,696	5.9	14,031	4.3	8,891	3.0
All Other (Incl. Structural Shapes)	219	0.1	634	0.2	1,272	0.4	560	0.2
Total Stainless Steel Products	321,010	100.0	267,677	100.0	324,966	100.0	295,516	100.0
All Products—4 Pct to 6 Pct Chromium (Types 501 and 502)	......	.....	8,528	.....	11,865	.....	12,044	.....

Source: American Iron & Steel Institute

1 METAL FACTS SECTION

Steel Shipments: Alloy and Alloy and High Speed Bars. Canadian Steel: Capacity, Production of Ingots and Finished Steel.

HIGH SPEED AND TOOL STEEL BARS

Shipments, Net Tons, Excluding Drill Steel

Class A High Speed Steel

Grade	C (Min.)	Cr (Max.)	W (Max.)	Mo (Max.)	V	Co	1950 10 Mo.	1949	1948	1947	1946
I	0.60	4.5	6.0	5.5	1.9 Max.	0.0	4,723	2,540	5,622	4,008	4,798
I-b	0.90	4.5	6.5	6.5	2.25 Min.	0.0	133	104	51	85	37
I-c	0.60	4.5	6.0	5.5	2.2 Max.	3.5 Min.	438	208	316	135	242
II	0.60	4.5	1.8	8.75	1.3 Max.	0.0	923	560	1,499	1,009	1,721
II-c	0.60	4.5	1.8	8.75	2.2 Max.	3.5 Min.	25	26	35	26	30
III	0.60	4.5	...	8.75	2.2 Max.	0.0	606	151	665	289	400
III-c	0.60	4.5	...	8.75	2.2 Max.	3.5 Min.	51	29	83	45	26
Total							6,899	3,618	8,305	5,563	7,254

Class B High Speed Steel

Grade	C (Min.)	Cr (Max.)	W (Max.)	Mo	V	Co	1950 10 Mo.	1949	1948	1947	1946
IV	0.55	4.5	19.0	0.0	1.2 Max.	0.0	5,180	4,041	7,949	9,804	8,574
IV-b	0.55	4.5	19.0	1.1 Max.	2.0 Min.	0.0	447	391	436	500	307
IV-c	0.55	4.5	22.0	1.1 Max.	2.2 Min.	3.5 Min.	819	884	1,071	1,054	778
Total							6,446	5,316	9,456	11,358	9,659

Other Tool Steels

		1950 10 Mo.	1949	1948	1947	1946
V	All hot-work steel	6,728	5,140	7,127	6,088	5,942
VI	High chromium (4% Cr. minimum) die steels	5,683	4,707	6,707	5,897	5,444
VII	All other alloy tool steels	32,683	26,251	37,988	36,605	40,043
VIII	Carbon tool steels excluding hollow drill steel	14,497	12,968	20,251	23,438	28,049
Total		59,591	49,066	72,073	72,028	79,478
Grand Total		72,936	58,000	89,834	88,949	96,391

Source: American Iron and Steel Institute

ALLOY STEEL SHIPMENTS

Except Stainless Steel and Types 501 and 502, Net Tons*

Products	1950—First 9 Months Full Alloy Shipments	1950—First 9 Months Hi-Str. Low Alloy Shipments	1950—First 9 Months Pct of Total	1949 Shipments	1949 Pct of Total	1948 Shipments	1948 Pct of Total	1947 Shipments	1947 Pct of Total
Ingots, blooms, billets, slabs, tube rounds, etc.	399,178	62	11.9	374,150	10.9	489,536	10.5	379,551	9.1
Structural shapes (heavy)	2,280	24,887	0.8	40,606	1.2	64,621	1.4	67,578	1.6
Galvanized Sheets	18,118	2,228	0.6						
Plates (sheared and universal)	35,164	90,549	3.7	153,220	4.5	225,450	4.8	186,106	4.0
Rails—standard (over 60 lbs)	284		0.0	120	0.0	76	0.0	157	0.0
Rails—all other	53		0.0	55	0.0	33	0.0	75	0.0
Bars—hot rolled	1,422,501	8,849	42.6	1,459,744	42.6	1,900,414	40.6	1,716,187	41.3
Bars—cold finished	181,491		5.4	173,420	5.1	217,833	4.7	196,200	4.7
Bars—tool steel	48,393		1.4	44,508	1.3	68,210	1.4	62,780	1.5
Pipe and tubes—oil country	165,165		4.9						
Pipe and tubes—mechanical	150,750		4.5	353,248	10.3	415,758	8.9	362,420	8.7
Pipes and tubes—pressure	17,960		0.5						
Electrical sheets and strip	444,640		13.2						
Wire rods	10,795		0.3	8,081	0.2	282	0.0	1,311	0.0
Wire drawn	28,424		0.9	26,286	0.8	34,485	0.7	28,436	0.7
Sheets—hot rolled	20,155	166,551	5.6	446,263	13.0	712,393	15.2	745,370	17.9
Sheets—cold rolled	5,169	73,251	2.3	223,210	6.5	349,756	7.5	251,474	6.1
Strip—hot rolled	13,777	17,685	0.9	54,354	1.6	90,364	1.9	67,972	1.7
Strip—cold rolled	7,882	2,803	0.3	66,840	1.9	103,405	2.2	103,719	2.5
Wheels (car, rolled steel)	65		0.0	93	0.0	23	0.0	53	0.0
Axles	463		0.0	550	0.0	942	0.0	558	0.0
All other	260	286	0.0	3,180	0.1	7,685	0.2	6,061	0.2
Total	2,972,975	387,151	100.0	3,427,928	100.0	4,681,066	100.0	4,156,008	100.0

*1947-1949 data includes high-strength low-alloy steels.

Source: American Iron & Steel Institute

> For steel used in automobile, appliances, etc., see Section 4. Steelmaking raw materials are in Section 3.

CANADIAN STEEL OUTPUT

Ingots and Steel for Castings, Net Tons

	Ingots	Castings	Total Steel Ingots and Castings
1923	940,475	33,213	973,688
1924	700,196	28,576	728,772
1925	836,016	21,100	868,116
1926	877,917	37,338	915,255
1927	972,079	44,475	1,016,554
1928	1,332,801	50,058	1,382,859
1929	1,466,688	78,562	1,545,250
1930	1,072,321	60,830	1,133,151
1931	744,605	41,501	786,106
1932	349,843	25,664	375,507
1933	441,346	17,830	459,176
1934	827,041	23,116	850,157
1935	1,016,814	35,123	1,051,937
1936	1,211,334	38,337	1,249,671
1937	1,496,575	74,652	1,571,137
1938	1,238,078	56,636	1,294,714
1939	1,266,056	60,997	1,327,053
1940	2,177,973	77,899	2,255,872
1941	2,578,063	123,250	2,701,313
1942	2,942,921	178,440	3,121,361
1943	2,848,235	148,743	2,996,978
1944	2,878,407	146,003	3,024,410
1945	2,747,206	134,117	2,881,323
1946	2,253,437	81,194	2,334,631
1947	2,854,532	90,634	2,945,166
1948	3,089,027	112,629	3,201,656
1949	3,089,368	97,562	3,186,930
1950: Jan.	283,894	6,055	289,949
Feb.	251,890	6,233	258,123
Mar.	287,719	6,584	294,303
Apr.	272,936	6,384	279,320
May	283,810	7,096	290,906
June	269,816	6,607	276,423
July	259,025	5,165	264,190
Aug.	275,009	6,213	281,312
Sept.	266,997	7,950	274,947
Year 1950*	3,200,000	70,230	3,270,230

* Estimated.

CANADIAN STEEL CAPACITY

Ingot Capacity and Operating Rates

	Steel Ingot Capacity	Steel Ingot Output	Percent of Capacity
1936	2,346,000	1,211,334	51.6
1937	2,346,000	1,496,575	63.7
1938	2,346,000	1,238,078	52.7
1939	2,346,000	1,266,056	53.9
1940	2,667,000	2,177,973	81.6
1941	2,964,000	2,578,063	86.9
1942	3,172,000	2,942,921	92.7
1943	3,257,500	2,848,235	87.4
1944	3,338,200	2,878,407	86.2
1945	3,358,600	2,787,206	81.7
1946	3,358,600	2,253,437	67.0
1947	3,245,000	2,854,532	87.9
1948	3,490,000	3,089,027	88.5
1949	3,598,000	3,089,368	84.1
1950	3,672,500	3,200,000*	87.1

* December estimated.

CANADIAN FINISHED STEEL

Production and Shipments, Net Tons

	Production Carbon Steel Shapes	Shipments* Carbon Steel Shapes	Production Alloy Steel Shapes	Shipments* Alloy Steel Shapes
1946	2,300,088	2,298,986	75,442	73,180
1947	3,042,727	2,343,688	117,684	111,776
1948	3,421,669	2,475,577	153,595	147,323
1949	3,556,507	2,604,884	109,735	103,307
1950:				
Jan.	310,925	203,045	9,204	8,386
Feb.	311,565	191,302	8,648	7,045
Mar.	347,760	345,292	14,001	13,664
Apr.	314,884	207,095	10,564	9,628
May	365,248	237,064	15,810	11,725
June	360,389	237,134	9,394	9,117
July	335,797	212,675	10,243	9,117
Aug.	354,031	211,669	10,094	10,326
Total 8 Mo.	2,700,599	1,733,553	87,958	81,004

* Excluding shipments to members of the industry for further conversion Source of above three tables: Dominion Bureau of Statistics.

FABRICATED STRUCTURAL STEEL

Estimated Bookings, Net Tons

Month	1923	1924	1925	1926	1927	1928	1929	1930	1931	1932	1933	1934	1935	1936
Jan.	227,760	224,940	187,380	208,800	195,000	207,900	256,025	238,800	158,000	48,400	98,239	91,594	64,306	120,364
Feb.	243,360	228,200	194,320	208,800	240,000	265,650	250,635	267,600	158,800	62,000	67,953	75,294	75,841	140,943
March	290,160	218,420	225,550	237,600	232,500	257,950	334,565	236,800	178,800	64,400	92,409	105,537	102,325	108,826
April	246,480	208,640	253,310	252,000	262,500	234,850	313,775	222,800	284,800	64,800	59,096	121,552	95,330	112,195
May	180,960	192,340	229,020	266,400	232,500	308,000	321,475	279,200	152,400	90,800	54,726	78,608	60,448	147,261
June	165,360	202,120	284,540	262,800	225,000	296,450	324,170	253,600	172,400	86,800	106,476	122,603	120,690	132,387
July	162,240	215,160	270,660	248,400	341,250	296,450	329,175	270,000	159,600	69,200	72,531	75,257	65,957	199,057
Aug.	184,080	189,080	263,720	284,400	270,000	354,200	340,725	252,000	124,000	78,800	101,832	95,489	102,859	110,687
Sept.	168,480	208,640	270,660	212,400	262,500	319,550	297,990	155,600	194,400	111,200	76,250	66,586	90,161	118,158
Oct.	159,120	208,640	298,420	230,400	288,750	257,950	319,550	209,200	109,200	74,400	67,119	64,723	102,708	130,989
Nov.	171,600	260,800	239,430	219,600	236,250	242,550	212,135	151,200	90,800	51,600	75,180	89,340	91,693	121,607
Dec.	249,600	247,760	249,840	255,600	262,500	246,400	297,605	152,800	97,600	145,600	103,931	66,196	96,235	166,542
Total	2,449,200	2,604,740	2,966,850	2,887,200	3,048,750	3,287,900	3,597,825	2,689,600	1,880,800	948,000	975,742	1,052,979	1,068,603	1,609,018
Mo. av.	204,100	217,062	247,238	240,600	254,063	273,992	299,819	224,133	156,733	79,000	81,312	87,732	89,050	134,085

Month	1937	1938	1939	1940	1941	1942	1943†	1944†	1945†	1946	1947	1948	1949	1950
Jan.	153,806	80,320	101,712	81,689	281,235	183,387	50,172	45,109	51,678	235,817	104,973	160,634	130,418	119,317
Feb.	101,710	57,144	82,719	98,882	173,559	228,688	34,657	37,477	62,856	132,707	125,681	130,119	108,764	117,664
Mar.	206,321	84,257	95,065	128,321	206,072	248,319	32,000	27,836	79,730	173,871	149,634	213,123	149,079	189,420
Apr.	158,471	91,158	118,309	73,780	218,018	313,953	50,726	61,498	97,188	128,671	161,338	154,082	98,802	155,011
May.	122,939	77,322	156,848	126,815	179,884	161,039	32,020	34,840	52,982	165,290	112,954	141,784	116,975	192,319
June.	175,552	99,899	111,594	109,744	246,910	184,516	79,409	56,239	104,283	131,010	103,273	162,367	96,952	266,612
July.	158,341	96,013	114,056	194,940	214,756	125,243	56,712	90,043	77,760	137,241	153,540	177,687	126,255	272,583
Aug.	124,897	106,772	100,849	122,468	158,658	80,605	37,563	44,740	97,682	165,590	146,382	172,485	98,953	259,015
Sept.	132,432	92,469	121,357	225,494	158,782	68,520	61,659	51,133	139,420	114,295	134,630	180,422	120,373	249,315
Oct.	62,267	154,756	118,841	240,942	128,658	50,946	59,282	80,521	124,707	142,565	159,132	162,739	158,593	250,000*
Nov.	132,835	153,084	99,316	141,945	184,043	49,637	34,093	62,437	117,755	102,399	132,916	140,794	103,557	225,000*
Dec.	99,070	163,445	84,383	203,124	146,379	67,600	35,282	37,004	108,048	96,601	144,103	169,553	124,251	225,000*
Total	1,628,641	1,256,639	1,305,049	1,748,144	2,296,954	1,762,453	563,584	628,877	1,114,087	1,726,057	1,628,756	1,965,769	1,432,972	2,551,256*
Mo. av.	135,720	104,720	108,754	145,679	191,413	146,871	46,965	52,406	92,841	143,838	135,729	163,814	119,414	210,105*

Approximate yearly total for industry: 707,480 — 786,096 — 1,392,608

Years 1910–1932 incl. Dept. of Commerce records; years 1933–1949 incl. A.I.S.C. records.
† The tonnages shown for 1936 to 1942 inclusive, 1946, 1947, 1948 and 1949 are estimated for the entire industry; for the years 1943, 1944 and 1945, they are on basis of tonnage actually reported to the institute. It is estimated that these reporting companies in 1943, 1944 and 1945 represented 80 pct of the total industry for the base years of 1923–1925.
* Estimated.

Source: American Institute of Steel Construction

EMPLOYMENT, AVERAGE HOURS AND EARNINGS

Reported by Companies Having More Than 93 Pct of the Total Employment of the Steel Industry

Year	Employees Receiving Wages					Employees Receiving Salaries			All Employees Receiving Wages and Salaries				
	Number of Employees	Total Hours Worked	Average hrs. per Week per Employee	Total Wages	Average Earnings per hr. (Cents)	Number of Employees	Total Hours Worked	Total Salaries	Number of Employees	Total Hours Worked	Average hrs. per Week per Employee	Total Wages and Salaries	Average Earnings per hr. (Cents)
1950:													
Jan.	480,875	82,040,999	38.5	141,097,315	172.0	87,103	15,529,724	36,130,373	567,978	97,570,723	38.8	177,227,688	181.6
Feb.	484,145	75,100,414	38.8	127,937,662	170.4	87,520	15,396,168	35,603,212	571,665	90,496,582	39.6	163,540,874	180.7
Mar.	486,193	83,583,434	38.8	141,850,887	169.7	87,573	15,781,652	39,955,261	573,766	99,365,086	39.1	177,806,148	178.9
April	491,035	81,058,051	38.5	138,372,937	170.7	87,790	15,521,309	35,896,627	578,825	96,579,360	38.9	174,269,564	180.4
May	497,447	87,461,830	39.7	150,586,449	172.2	88,076	15,885,591	36,524,166	585,523	103,347,421	39.8	187,110,615	181.1
June	503,943	85,052,917	39.3	145,781,365	171.4	88,670	15,872,423	37,049,671	592,613	100,925,340	39.7	182,831,036	181.2
July	509,700	79,903,708	35.5	139,357,645	174.4	89,611	15,841,572	37,275,582	599,311	95,745,280	36.1	176,633,227	184.5
Aug.	514,888	90,662,340	39.7	155,323,393	172.0	89,928	16,388,833	37,776,860	604,816	107,051,173	40.0	193,399,253	180.7
Sept.	515,261	86,936,542	39.4	152,759,103	175.7	90,099	16,044,003	37,981,882	605,360	102,980,545	39.7	190,740,985	185.2
1949	491,615	884,655,294	34.5	1,506,465,668	170.3	82,209	188,549,627	432,827,472	580,824	1,073,204,921	35.4	1,939,293,140	180.7
1948	509,351	1,028,519,481	39.1	1,675,913,066	162.9	88,196	191,044,219	412,845,319	591,547	1,219,563,700	39.4	2,088,758,385	171.3
1947	489,138	984,410,347	38.6	1,489,531,509	151.3	84,531	183,172,600	368,726,376	573,669	1,167,582,947	39.0	1,858,257,885	159.2
1946	458,259	836,870,389	35.0	1,133,503,371	135.4	79,889	173,301,314	317,760,089	538,148	1,010,171,703	36.0	1,451,263,460	143.7
1945	438,825	1,009,033,709	44.1	1,268,048,553	125.7	76,178	175,093,573	278,038,234	515,003	1,184,127,282	44.1	1,546,086,787	130.6
1944	456,682	1,112,029,921	46.6	1,365,342,466	122.8	76,969	178,320,937	275,170,922	533,651	1,290,350,858	46.3	1,640,513,388	127.1
1943	487,187	1,089,760,555	42.9	1,242,032,184	114.0	77,121	168,264,429	251,002,372	564,308	1,258,024,984	42.8	1,493,034,556	118.7
1942	511,414	1,036,968,871	38.9	1,101,787,008	106.3	71,511	151,390,870	226,941,787	582,925	1,188,359,741	39.1	1,328,728,795	111.8
1941	507,306	1,019,103,012	38.5	980,845,190	96.2	63,430	133,933,316	196,892,173	570,736	1,153,036,328	38.7	1,177,737,363	102.1
1940	453,990	857,770,926	36.1	733,364,058	85.5	57,338	122,522,777	169,864,608	511,328	980,293,703	36.7	903,228,666	92.1
1939	396,220	719,125,101	34.8	608,310,659	84.6	53,421	113,744,629	153,456,397	449,641	832,869,730	35.5	761,767,056	91.5
1938	360,365	518,406,035	27.6	433,372,123	83.6	52,742	107,763,785	143,236,899	413,107	626,169,820	29.1	576,609,022	92.1
1937	479,022	918,354,646	36.8	756,950,364	82.4	55,132	121,459,120	161,161,935	534,154	1,039,813,766	37.3	918,112,299	88.3
1936	429,111	893,745,272	39.8	599,629,059	67.1	45,162	98,673,490	123,280,276	474,273	992,418,762	40.0	722,909,335	72.8
1935	383,855	685,238,237	34.2	448,941,105	65.5	40,437	86,226,092	106,870,413	424,292	771,464,329	34.9	555,811,518	72.0

Source: American Iron & Steel Institute

THE IRON AGE FINISHED STEEL COMPOSITE PRICE
Current Series, 1929 to 1950, Cents Per Pound

	1929	1930	1931	1932	1933	1934	1935	1936	1937	1938	1939	1940		1945	1946	1947	1948	1949	1950
Jan.	2.278	2.229	1.991	1.852	1.830	1.958	2.065	2.076	2.323	2.584	2.354	2.305		2.412	2.464	2.877	3.193	3.720	3.837
Feb.	2.278	2.212	1.996	1.843	1.812	1.958	2.065	2.065	2.323	2.581	2.354	2.305		2.427	2.555	2.884	3.125	3.719	3.837
March	2.276	2.208	1.992	1.852	1.808	1.958	2.065	2.055	2.532	2.578	2.354	2.305		2.432	2.719	2.881	3.241	3.715	3.837
April	2.304	2.400	1.974	1.892	1.780	2.007	2.065	2.062	2.584	2.578	2.354	2.267		2.433	2.719	2.884	3.241	3.709	3.837
May	2.307	2.118	1.968	1.891	1.770	2.154	2.065	2.062	2.584	2.569	2.308	2.305	1941	2.436	2.719	2.884	3.214	3.706	3.837
June	2.318	2.093	1.961	1.888	1.786	2.154	2.065	2.067	2.584	2.513	2.283	2.305	1942	2.464	2.719	2.884	3.211	3.705	3.837
													1943						
July	2.312	2.056	1.940	1.892	1.841	2.107	2.065	2.139	2.584	2.359	2.283	2.305	1944	2.464	2.719	2.914	3.293	3.705	3.837
Aug.	2.294	2.031	1.943	1.889	1.851	2.065	2.065	2.139	2.584	2.359	2.283	2.305		2.464	2.719	3.193	3.720	3.705	3.837
Sept.	2.282	2.011	1.943	1.883	1.879	2.065	2.065	2.146	2.584	2.357	2.283	2.305		2.464	2.719	3.193	3.720	3.705	3.837
Oct.	2.270	2.001	1.942	1.873	1.955	2.065	2.076	2.172	2.584	2.320	2.283	2.305		2.464	2.719	3.193	3.720	3.705	3.837
Nov.	2.265	1.993	1.937	1.866	1.947	2.065	2.076	2.172	2.584	2.354	2.288	2.305		2.464	2.719	3.193	3.720	3.705	3.837
Dec.	2.278	1.975	1.902	1.861	1.958	2.085	2.076	2.263	2.584	2.354	2.305	2.305		2.464	2.747	3.193	3.720	3.758	4,131
Average	2.288	2.111	1.957	1.873	1.851	2.051	2.068	2.118	2.536	2.459	2.311	2.273	2.396	2.449	2.686	3.014	3.434	3.713	3,862

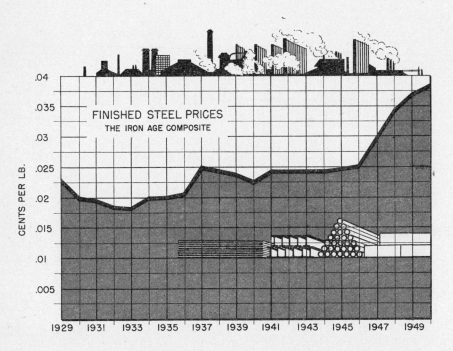

FINISHED STEEL PRICES — THE IRON AGE COMPOSITE

THE IRON AGE finished steel composite price is a weighted average of the base prices of 10 major steel products which account for the majority of finished steel shipments. It is weighted by the percentage that each of these products is to total finished steel shipments during the base period. With the base constant, the only changes in the composite from 1929 through 1940 or from 1941 through 1949 occur when one or more steel products prices were changed.

In the composite shown here there are two base periods. For the years 1929 through 1940 the base is finished steel shipments for 1929-1939 inclusive. For 1941 through 1950 the base is finished steel shipments for the 7 years 1937 to 1940 inclusive and 1946 to 1948 inclusive. Two base periods are used because of basic changes in the shipment pattern in the 20 years covered. In each case the products remain the same. They are hot-rolled bars, structural shapes, plates, rails, pipe, wire and hot- and cold-rolled sheets and strip. To eliminate variations due to nonferrous metals price fluctuations, no coated products are included.

The composite price was first published on a weighted basis on August 28, 1941, at which time it was revised for the years 1929 to 1940 inclusive. These figures are shown here. In 1941, 1942 and 1943 the composite was based on shipments for those years and on November 16, 1944, it was changed to reflect quarterly shipments. After consultation with industrial and government statisticians all figures from 1941 forward were discarded as too sensitive. The revision, shown here, has been substituted from 1941 to the present because it is a more accurate method of reflecting price changes, eliminating changes due to short term and seasonal variations in the shipment pattern. Details of this revision appeared in THE IRON AGE, May 12, 1949, p. 139.

COLD-ROLLED SHEETS
At Pittsburgh, Cents Per Pound

	1929	1933	1936	1937	1938	1939
Jan.	4.10	2.35	2.95	3.25	3.55	3.20
Feb.	4.10	2.25	2.95	3.25	3.50	3.20
Mar.	4.10	2.30	2.95	3.49	3.45	3.20
Apr.	4.10	2.30	2.95	3.55	3.45	3.20
May	4.10	2.34	2.95	3.55	3.43	3.11
June	4.10	2.29	2.95	3.55	3.32	3.05
July	4.10	2.40	3.05	3.55	3.20	3.05
Aug.	4.08	2.47	3.05	3.55	3.20	3.05
Sept.	4.00	2.75	3.05	3.55	3.20	3.05
Oct.	4.00	2.75	3.05	3.55	3.08	3.05
Nov.	4.00	2.75	3.05	3.55	3.20	3.05
Dec.	3.98	2.75	3.25	3.55	3.20	3.05
Average	4.06	2.48	3.02	3.49	3.31	3.10

	1940*	1946*	1947	1948	1949	1950
Jan.	3.05	3.05	3.20	3.55	4.00	4.10
Feb.	3.05	3.16	3.20	3.55	4.00	4.10
Mar.	3.05	3.275	3.20	3.55	4.00	4.10
Apr.	2.93	3.275	3.20	3.55	4.00	4.10
May	3.05	3.275	3.20	3.49	4.00	4.10
June	3.05	3.275	3.20	3.49	4.00	4.10
July	3.05	3.275	3.27	3.62	4.00	4.10
Aug.	3.05	3.275	3.55	4.00	4.00	4.10
Sept.	3.05	3.275	3.55	4.00	4.00	4.10
Oct.	3.05	3.275	3.55	4.00	4.00	4.10
Nov.	3.05	3.275	3.55	4.00	4.00	4.10
Dec.	3.05	3.215	3.55	4.00	4.04	4.35
Average	3.04	3.242	3.35	3.73	4.00	4.12

*1941-1945 = 3.05¢.

HOT-ROLLED SHEETS
At Pittsburgh, Cents Per Pound

	1929	1934	1937	1938	1939	1940*
Jan.	2.10	1.75	2.15	2.40	2.15	2.10
Feb.	2.10	1.75	2.15	2.40	2.15	2.10
Mar.	2.10	1.75	2.35	2.40	2.15	2.10
Apr.	2.10	1.81	2.40	2.40	2.15	2.10
May	2.13	2.00	2.40	2.38	2.06	1.98
June	2.20	2.00	2.40	2.27	2.00	2.10
July	2.14	1.88	2.40	2.15	2.00	2.10
Aug.	2.10	1.85	2.40	2.15	2.00	2.10
Sept.	2.10	1.85	2.40	2.15	2.00	2.10
Oct.	2.10	1.85	2.40	2.03	2.00	2.10
Nov.	2.10	1.85	2.40	2.15	2.02	2.10
Dec.	2.18	1.85	2.40	2.15	2.10	2.10
Average	2.12	1.85	2.35	2.25	2.06	2.09

	1945*	1946	1947	1948	1949	1950
Jan.	2.10	2.20	2.50	2.80	3.28	3.35
Feb.	2.10	2.31	2.50	2.80	3.28	3.35
Mar.	2.18	2.43	2.50	2.80	3.28	3.35
Apr.	2.20	2.43	2.50	2.80	3.26	3.35
May	2.20	2.43	2.50	2.77	3.25	3.35
June	2.20	2.43	2.50	2.77	3.25	3.35
July	2.20	2.43	2.56	2.89	3.25	3.35
Aug.	2.20	2.43	2.80	3.28	3.25	3.35
Sept.	2.20	2.43	2.80	3.28	3.25	3.35
Oct.	2.20	2.43	2.80	3.28	3.25	3.35
Nov.	2.20	2.43	2.80	3.28	3.25	3.35
Dec.	2.20	2.49	2.80	3.28	3.29	3.60
Average	2.18	2.40	2.63	3.00	3.26	3.37

*1941-1944 = 2.10¢.

GALVANIZED SHEETS
At Pittsburgh, Cents Per Pound

	1929	1933	1934	1936	1937	1938
Jan.	3.60	2.68	2.85	3.10	3.40	3.80
Feb.	3.60	2.50	2.85	3.10	3.40	3.80
Mar.	3.60	2.60	2.85	3.10	3.72	3.80
Apr.	3.60	2.63	2.95	3.10	3.80	3.80
May	3.60	2.70	3.25	3.10	3.80	3.80
June	3.60	2.70	3.25	3.10	3.80	3.68
July	3.60	2.85	3.13	3.20	3.80	3.50
Aug.	3.50	2.85	3.10	3.20	3.80	3.50
Sept.	3.50	2.85	3.10	3.20	3.80	3.50
Oct.	3.50	2.85	3.10	3.20	3.80	3.45
Nov.	3.48	2.85	3.10	3.20	3.80	3.50
Dec.	3.40	2.85	3.10	3.40	3.80	3.50
Average	3.55	2.74	3.05	3.17	3.73	3.64

	1945†	1946	1947	1948	1959	1950
Jan.	3.50	3.70	3.55	3.95	4.40	4.40
Feb.	3.50	3.88	3.55	3.95	4.40	4.40
Mar.	3.62	4.05	3.55	3.95	4.40	4.40
Apr.	3.65	4.05	3.55	3.95	4.40	4.40
May	3.66	4.05	3.55	3.91	4.40	4.40
June	3.70	4.05	3.55	3.91	4.40	4.40
July	3.70	4.05	3.63	4.03	4.40	4.40
Aug.	3.70	4.05	3.95	4.40	4.40	4.40
Sept.	3.70	4.05	3.95	4.40	4.40	4.40
Oct.	3.70	4.05	3.95	4.40	4.40	4.40
Nov.	3.70	4.05	3.95	4.40	4.40	4.80
Dec.	3.70	*3.65	3.95	4.40	4.40	4.80
Average	3.65	3.99	3.72	4.13	4.40	4.43

* Based on 10 gage since December 1946; 24 gage base up to that time.
† 1939-1944 = 3.50¢.

STEEL RAILS AT PITTSBURGH, No. 1 OH

Including Prices by Months and Yearly Averages in Dollars Per 100 lb*

	1929	1932	1934	1936	1937	1938†		1945†	1946	1947	1948	1949	1950
Jan.	$43.00	$43.00	$36.37	$36.37	$39.00	$42.50	Jan.	$40.00	$43.00	$2.50	$2.75	$3.20	$3.40
Feb.	43.00	43.00	36.37	36.37	39.00	42.50	Feb.	40.00	*43.19	2.50	2.75	3.20	3.40
Mar.	43.00	43.00	36.37	36.37	41.80	42.50	Mar.	42.25	43.39	2.50	2.75	3.20	3.40
Apr.	43.00	43.00	36.37	36.37	42.50	42.50	Apr.	43.00	43.39	2.50	2.75	3.20	3.40
May	43.00	43.00	36.37	36.37	42.50	42.50	May	43.00	43.39	2.50	2.70	3.20	3.40
June	43.00	43.00	36.37	36.37	42.50	42.50	June	43.00	43.39	2.50	2.70	3.20	3.40
July	43.00	43.00	36.37	36.37	42.50	42.50	July	43.00	43.39	2.50	2.80	3.20	3.40
Aug.	43.00	43.00	36.37	36.37	42.50	42.50	Aug.	43.00	43.39	2.75	3.20	3.20	3.40
Sept.	43.00	43.00	36.37	36.37	42.50	41.25	Sept.	43.00	43.39	2.75	3.20	3.20	3.40
Oct.	43.00	42.25	36.37	36.37	42.50	40.00	Oct.	43.00	43.39	2.75	3.20	3.20	3.40
Nov.	43.00	40.00	36.37	36.37	42.50	40.00	Nov.	43.00	43.39	2.75	3.20	3.20	3.40
Dec.	43.00	40.00	36.37	39.00	42.50	40.00	Dec.	43.00	47.36	2.75	3.20	3.28	3.60
Average	43.00	42.44	36.37	36.59	41.86	41.77	Average	42.44	43.67	2.60	2.93	3.21	3.42

* Prices quoted dollars per gross ton prior to Feb. 15, 1946. Net tons, Feb. 15 to Dec. 13, 1946.
† 1939-1944 = $40.00 per gross ton.

TINPLATE AT PITTSBURGH

Dollars Per Base Box, 1.50-lb Coating

	1929	1930	1931	1933	1934	1936
Jan.	$5.35	$5.25	$5.00	$4.25	$5.25	$5.25
Feb.	5.35	5.25	5.00	4.25	5.25	5.25
March	5.35	5.25	5.00	4.25	5.25	5.25
April	5.35	5.25	5.00	4.25	5.25	5.25
May	5.35	5.25	5.00	4.25	5.25	5.25
June	5.35	5.25	5.00	4.25	5.25	5.25
July	5.35	5.25	5.00	4.25	5.25	5.25
Aug.	5.35	5.25	5.00	4.25	5.25	5.25
Sept.	5.35	5.25	5.00	4.65	5.25	5.25
Oct.	5.35	5.00	4.75	4.65	5.25	5.25
Nov.	5.35	5.00	4.75	4.65	5.25	5.25
Dec.	5.35	5.00	4.75	5.25	5.25	5.25
Average	5.35	5.19	4.94	4.43	5.25	5.25

	1937	1938*	1947*	1948	1949	1950
Jan.	$4.85	$5.35	$5.75	$6.80	$7.75	$7.50
Feb.	4.85	5.35	5.75	6.80	7.75	7.50
March	4.85	5.35	5.75	6.80	7.75	7.50
April	5.35	5.35	5.75	6.80	7.75	7.50
May	5.35	5.35	5.75	6.70	7.75	7.50
June	5.35	5.35	5.75	6.70	7.75	7.50
July	5.35	5.35	5.75	6.72	7.75	7.50
Aug.	5.35	5.35	5.75	6.80	7.75	7.50
Sept.	5.35	5.35	5.75	6.80	7.75	7.50
Oct.	5.35	5.35	5.75	6.80	7.75	7.50
Nov.	5.35	5.18	5.75	6.80	7.75	7.50
Dec.	5.35	5.00	5.75	6.80	7.75	7.50
Average	5.22	5.31	5.75	6.77	7.75	7.50

* 1939-1946 = $5.00.

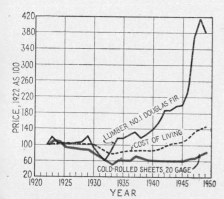

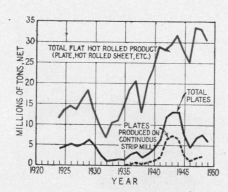

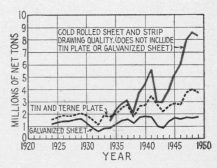

STEEL PRICES AND PRODUCTION show some interesting aspects in these charts. The chart at the left above shows steel prices lagging behind and lumber prices exceeding the cost of living index. The tremendous increase in plate production on continuous strip mills, above right, during World War II is likely to be repeated this year. And cold-rolled sheet and strip output, right, will suffer.

COLD-ROLLED STRIP

At Pittsburgh, Cents Per Pound

	1929	1933	1936	1937	1938	1939
Jan.	2.85	1.88	2.60	2.85	3.20	2.95
Feb.	2.85	1.80	2.60	2.85	3.20	2.95
March	2.80	1.80	2.60	3.13	3.20	2.95
April	2.75	1.80	2.60	3.20	3.20	2.95
May	2.75	1.88	2.60	3.20	3.18	2.86
June	2.75	2.00	2.60	3.20	3.07	2.80
July	2.75	2.19	2.60	3.20	2.95	2.80
Aug.	2.75	2.25	2.60	3.20	2.95	2.80
Sept.	2.75	2.29	2.60	3.20	2.95	2.80
Oct.	2.75	2.40	2.60	3.20	2.83	2.80
Nov.	2.75	2.40	2.60	3.20	2.95	2.80
Dec.	2.75	2.40	2.80	3.20	2.95	2.80
Average	2.77	2.09	2.62	3.14	3.05	2.86

	1940*	1946*	1947	1948	1949	1950
Jan.	2.80	2.80	3.20	3.55	4.00	4.20
Feb.	2.80	2.93	3.20	3.55	4.00	4.21
March	2.80	3.05	3.20	3.55	4.00	4.21
April	2.68	3.05	3.20	3.55	4.00	4.21
May	2.80	3.05	3.20	3.53	4.00	4.21
June	2.80	3.05	3.20	3.53	4.00	4.21
July	2.80	3.05	3.27	3.85	4.00	4.21
Aug.	2.80	3.05	3.55	4.00	4.00	4.21
Sept.	2.80	3.05	3.55	4.00	4.00	4.21
Oct.	2.80	3.05	3.55	4.00	4.00	4.21
Nov.	2.80	3.05	3.55	4.00	4.00	4.21
Dec.	2.80	3.17	3.55	4.00	4.06	4.75
Average	2.79	3.03	3.35	3.76	4.01	4.25

* 1941-1945 = 2.80¢.

HOT-ROLLED STRIP

At Pittsburgh, Cents Per Pound

	1929	1933	1936	1937	1938	1939
Jan.	1.80	1.45	1.85	2.15	2.40	2.15
Feb.	1.80	1.45	1.85	2.15	2.40	2.15
Mar.	1.80	1.45	1.85	2.35	2.40	2.15
Apr.	1.90	1.45	1.85	2.40	2.40	2.15
May	1.90	1.49	1.85	2.40	2.38	2.06
June	1.90	1.55	1.85	2.40	2.27	2.00
July	1.90	1.60	1.95	2.40	2.15	2.00
Aug.	1.90	1.64	1.95	2.40	2.15	2.00
Sept.	1.97	1.68	1.95	2.40	2.15	2.00
Oct.	1.90	1.75	1.95	2.40	2.03	2.00
Nov.	1.90	1.75	1.95	2.40	2.15	2.02
Dec.	1.90	1.75	2.11	2.40	2.15	2.10
Average	1.88	1.58	1.91	2.35	2.25	2.06

	1940†	1946*	1947	1948	1949	1950
Jan.	2.10	2.10	2.50	2.80	3.28	3.25
Feb.	2.10	2.23	2.50	2.80	3.28	3.25
Mar.	2.10	2.35	2.50	2.80	3.28	3.25
Apr.	1.98	2.35	2.50	2.80	3.26	3.25
May	2.10	2.35	2.50	2.80	3.25	3.25
June	2.10	2.35	2.50	2.80	3.25	3.25
July	2.10	2.35	2.58	2.90	3.25	3.25
Aug.	2.10	2.35	2.80	3.28	3.25	3.25
Sept.	2.10	2.35	2.80	3.28	3.25	3.25
Oct.	2.10	2.35	2.80	3.28	3.25	3.25
Nov.	2.10	2.35	2.80	3.28	3.25	3.25
Dec.	2.10	2.47	2.80	3.28	3.25	3.50
Average	2.09	2.33	2.63	3.03	3.26	3.27

* Over 6 in.: add 0.10¢ for 6 in. and under from February through November 1946.
† 1941-1945 = 2.10¢.

PLATES AT PITTSBURGH

Cents Per Pound, 1929 to 1950

	1929	1932	1933	1936	1937	1938*
Jan.	1.90	1.50	1.60	1.80	2.05	2.25
Feb.	1.90	1.50	1.60	1.80	2.05	2.25
Mar.	1.90	1.52	1.60	1.80	2.21	2.25
Apr.	1.95	1.60	1.55	1.80	2.25	2.25
May	1.95	1.60	1.50	1.80	2.25	2.25
June	1.95	1.60	1.53	1.80	2.25	2.22
July	1.95	1.60	1.60	1.90	2.25	2.10
Aug.	1.95	1.60	1.60	1.90	2.25	2.10
Sept.	1.95	1.60	1.60	1.90	2.25	2.10
Oct.	1.94	1.60	1.70	1.90	2.25	2.10
Nov.	1.90	1.60	1.70	1.90	2.25	2.10
Dec.	1.90	1.60	1.70	1.90	2.25	2.10
Average	1.93	1.57	1.61	1.85	2.21	2.17

	1945*	1946	1947	1948	1949	1950
Jan.	2.10	2.25	2.65	2.95	3.50	3.50
Feb.	2.10	2.38	2.65	2.95	3.50	3.50
Mar.	2.20	2.50	2.65	2.95	3.50	3.50
Apr.	2.20	2.50	2.65	2.95	3.50	3.50
May	2.21	2.50	2.65	2.93	3.40	3.50
June	2.25	2.50	2.71	2.93	3.40	3.50
July	2.25	2.50	2.95	3.07	3.40	3.50
Aug.	2.25	2.50	2.95	3.50	3.40	3.50
Sept.	2.25	2.50	2.95	3.50	3.40	3.50
Oct.	2.25	2.50	2.95	3.50	3.40	3.50
Nov.	2.25	2.50	2.95	3.50	3.40	3.50
Dec.	2.25	2.50	2.95	3.50	3.44	3.70
Average	2.21	2.47	2.80	3.19	3.43	3.52

* 1939-1944 = 2.10¢.

1 METAL FACTS SECTION

Steel Prices: Bars, Wire, Shapes, Stainless Steel Sheets, Iron and Steel Pipe and Tool Steel.

COLD-FINISHED STEEL BARS

At Pittsburgh, Cents Per Pound

	1929	1933	1936	1937	1938	1939*
Jan.	1.90	1.70	2.10	2.55	2.90	2.70
Feb.	1.90	1.70	2.10	2.55	2.90	2.70
Mar.	1.90	1.70	2.10	2.83	2.90	2.70
Apr.	1.95	1.70	2.10	2.90	2.90	2.70
May	1.95	1.70	2.10	2.90	2.90	2.68
June	1.95	1.70	2.10	2.90	2.70	2.65
July	1.95	1.70	2.25	2.90	2.70	2.65
Aug.	1.95	1.70	2.25	2.90	2.70	2.65
Sept.	1.94	1.95	2.25	2.90	2.70	2.65
Oct.	1.90	1.95	2.35	2.90	2.70	2.65
Nov.	1.90	1.95	2.35	2.90	2.70	2.65
Dec.	1.90	2.10	2.35	2.90	2.70	2.65
Average	1.92	1.80	2.20	2.84	2.78	2.67
	1945*	1946	1947	1948	1949	1950
Jan.	2.65	2.75	3.20	3.55	3.98	4.145
Feb.	2.65	2.93	3.20	3.55	3.98	4.145
Mar.	2.65	3.10	3.20	3.55	3.98	4.145
Apr.	2.65	3.10	3.20	3.55	3.98	4.145
May	2.65	3.10	3.20	3.50	3.98	4.145
June	2.65	3.10	3.20	3.50	3.98	4.145
July	2.65	3.10	3.27	3.82	3.98	4.145
Aug.	2.73	3.10	3.55	3.98	3.98	4.145
Sept.	2.75	3.10	3.55	3.98	3.98	4.145
Oct.	2.75	3.10	3.55	3.98	3.98	4.148
Nov.	2.75	3.10	3.55	3.98	3.98	4.15
Dec.	2.75	3.10	3.55	3.98	4.01	4.55
Average	2.69	3.06	3.35	3.74	3.98	4.179

* 1940-1944 = 2.65¢.

MERCHANT BARS

At Pittsburgh, Cents Per Pound

	1929	1933	1936	1937	1938	1939*
Jan.	$1.90	$1.60	$1.85	$2.20	$2.45	$2.25
Feb.	1.90	1.60	1.85	2.20	2.45	2.25
Mar.	1.90	1.60	1.85	2.40	2.45	2.25
Apr.	1.95	1.60	1.85	2.45	2.45	2.25
May	1.95	1.60	1.85	2.45	2.45	2.19
June	1.95	1.60	1.85	2.45	2.41	2.15
July	1.95	1.60	1.95	2.45	2.25	2.15
Aug.	1.95	1.60	1.95	2.45	2.25	2.15
Sept.	1.94	1.60	1.95	2.45	2.25	2.15
Oct.	1.90	1.75	2.07	2.45	2.25	2.15
Nov.	1.90	1.75	2.05	2.45	2.25	2.15
Dec.	1.90	1.75	2.03	2.45	2.25	2.15
Average	1.92	1.64	1.95	2.40	2.35	2.19
	1945*	1946	1947	1948	1949	1950
Jan.	$2.15	$2.25	$2.60	$2.90	$3.45	$3.45
Feb.	2.15	2.38	2.60	2.90	3.45	3.45
Mar.	2.15	2.50	2.60	2.90	3.43	3.45
Apr.	2.15	2.50	2.60	2.90	3.35	3.45
May	2.17	2.50	2.60	2.87	3.35	3.45
June	2.25	2.50	2.60	2.87	3.35	3.45
July	2.25	2.50	2.66	3.00	3.35	3.45
Aug.	2.25	2.50	2.90	3.45	3.35	3.45
Sept.	2.25	2.50	2.90	3.45	3.35	3.45
Oct.	2.25	2.50	2.90	3.45	3.35	3.45
Nov.	2.25	2.50	2.90	3.45	3.39	3.45
Dec.	2.25	2.56	2.90	3.45	3.38	3.70
Average	2.21	2.47	2.73	3.13	3.37	3.47

* 1940-1944 = 2.15¢.

MANUFACTURER'S BRIGHT WIRE

At Pittsburgh, Cents Per Pound

	1929	1931	1933	1934	1937	1938*
Jan.	2.50	2.20	2.16	2.20	2.60	2.90
Feb.	2.50	2.20	2.10	2.20	2.60	2.90
Mar.	2.50	2.20	2.10	2.20	2.84	2.90
Apr.	2.50	2.20	2.10	2.23	2.90	2.90
May	2.50	2.20	2.10	2.30	2.90	2.90
June	2.50	2.20	2.10	2.30	2.90	2.84
July	2.50	2.20	2.10	2.30	2.90	2.60
Aug.	2.43	2.20	2.10	2.30	2.90	2.60
Sept.	2.40	2.20	2.10	2.30	2.90	2.60
Oct.	2.40	2.20	2.10	2.30	2.90	2.60
Nov.	2.40	2.20	2.10	2.30	2.90	2.60
Dec.	2.40	2.20	2.20	2.30	2.90	2.60
Average	2.46	2.20	2.11	2.27	2.84	2.74
	1945*	1946	1947	1948	1949	1950
Jan.	2.60	2.75	3.30	3.55	4.33	4.50
Feb.	2.60	2.90	3.30	3.55	4.33	4.50
Mar.	2.60	3.05	3.30	3.55	4.22	4.50
Apr.	2.60	3.05	3.30	3.55	4.15	4.50
May	2.63	3.05	3.30	3.60	4.15	4.50
June	2.75	3.05	3.30	3.60	4.15	4.50
July	2.75	3.05	3.35	3.77	4.15	4.50
Aug.	2.75	3.05	3.55	4.33	4.15	4.50
Sept.	2,75	3,05	3.55	4.33	4.15	4.50
Oct.	2.75	3.05	3.55	4.33	4.15	4.50
Nov.	2.75	3.05	3.55	4.33	4.15	4.50
Dec.	2.75	3.10	3.55	4.33	4.29	4.85
Average	2.69	3.02	3.41	3.90	4.20	4.53

* 1939-1944 = 2.60¢.

STAINLESS STEEL SHEETS

No. 304, Cents Per Pound

	1937*	1946*	1948	1949	1950
Jan.	35.00	36.00	39.00	41.25	39.50
Feb.	35.00	36.00	39.00	41.25	39.50
March	36.00	36.00	39.00	41.25	39.50
April	36.00	38.21	39.00	40.81	39.50
May	36.00	38.95	39.00	39.50	39.50
June	36.00	38.95	39.00	39.50	39.50
July	36.00	38.95	39.00	39.50	40.62
Aug.	36.00	38.95	40.80	39.50	41.00
Sept.	36.00	38.95	40.37	39.50	41.00
Oct.	36.00	38.95	40.81	39.50	41.00
Nov.	36.00	38.95	41.25	39.50	41.00
Dec.	36.00	38.95	41.25	39.50	43.00
Average	35.90	38.15	39.79	40.05	40.38

* 1938-1945 = 36.00¢

HIGH SPEED TOOL STEEL

18-4-1, Cents Per Pound

	1938*	1946*	1947	1948	1949	1950
Jan.	80.0	67.00	72.494	82.0	90.5	100.0
Feb.	76.8	69.792	72.494	82.0	90.5	100.0
Mar.	67.0	72.494	72.494	82.0	90.5	100.0
Apr.	67.0	72.494	74.00	82.0	90.5	100.0
May	67.0	72.494	74.00	82.0	90.5	100.0
June	67.0	72.494	74.00	82.0	90.5	100.0
July	67.0	72.494	74.00	82.0	90.5	100.0
Aug.	67.0	72.494	82.00	90.5	90.5	100.0
Sept.	67.0	72.494	82.00	90.5	90.5	100.0
Oct.	67.0	72.494	82.00	90.5	90.5	100.0
Nov.	67.0	72.494	82.00	90.5	90.5	100.0
Dec.	67.0	72.494	82.00	90.5	90.5	110.0
Average	68.9	71.81	75.58	85.5	90.5	100.8

* 1939-1945 = 67.0¢.

CAST IRON WATER PIPE

At New York, Net Ton, 6-in. and Larger

	1929	1932	1933	1936	1937	1938
Jan.	$39.60	$30.20	$35.20	$45.20	$48.00	$53.00
Feb.	39.35	29.70	35.30	45.20	48.00	53.00
Mar.	38.60	28.40	35.30	45.20	51.00	53.00
Apr.	37.40	28.20	35.30	45.20	53.00	53.00
May	35.85	28.20	35.30	45.20	53.00	53.00
June	35.10	28.20	38.30	45.20	53.00	52.20
July	33.20	28.73	38.30	45.90	53.00	49.00
Aug.	33.60	31.10	38.30	45.90	53.00	49.00
Sept.	33.60	31.30	38.30	45.90	53.00	49.00
Oct.	34.60	33.30	38.00	45.90	53.00	49.00
Nov.	34.60	33.30	43.00	45.90	53.00	49.00
Dec.	34.60	34.30	43.00	47.90	53.00	49.00
Average	35.84	30.41	37.81	45.71	52.00	50.93
	1939*	1946*	1947	1948	1949	1950
Jan.	$49.00	$57.20	$73.60	$89.18	$105.95	$94.95
Feb.	49.00	57.20	73.75	89.18	105.95	92.36
Mar.	49.00	60.20	76.80	89.18	105.95	91.50
Apr.	49.00	62.20	79.80	89.18	103.98	91.50
May	49.00	62.20	79.80	92.34	94.95	91.50
June	49.00	62.20	79.80	95.50	94.95	91.50
July	49.00	69.60	80.50	95.50	94.95	91.50
Aug.	49.00	69.60	83.30	103.86	94.95	91.50
Sept.	49.00	69.60	83.30	105.95	94.95	91.50
Oct.	52.20	69.60	83.96	105.95	94.95	95.00
Nov.	52.20	69.60	84.18	105.95	94.95	95.00
Dec.	52.20	73.60	84.18	105.95	94.95	98.00
Average	49.80	65.23	80.25	97.31	98.45	92.98

* 1940-1945 = $52.20.

BUTWELD STEEL PIPE

At Pittsburgh, Per Net Ton, Carload Lots

	1929	1931	1933	1934	1936	1937
Jan.	$70.30	$66.50	$65.00	$61.75	$68.40	$61.00
Feb.	70.30	66.50	65.00	61.75	64.98	61.00
Mar.	70.30	66.50	65.00	61.75	61.80	69.00
Apr.	70.30	66.50	58.00	63.41	61.00	71.00
May	70.30	63.59	58.00	68.40	61.00	71.00
June	70.30	64.84	58.00	68.40	61.00	71.00
July	70.30	64.84	61.75	68.40	61.00	71.00
Aug.	70.30	64.84	61.75	68.40	61.00	71.00
Sept.	70.30	64.84	61.75	68.40	61.00	71.00
Oct.	70.30	64.84	61.75	68.40	61.00	71.00
Nov.	70.30	64.84	61.75	68.40	61.00	71.00
Dec.	70.30	64.84	61.75	68.40	61.00	71.00
Average	70.30	65.29	61.63	66.32	62.01	69.17
	1938*	1946*	1947	1948	1949	1950
Jan.	$71.00	$63.00	$79.00	$88.00	$103.00	$108.00
Feb.	71.00	66.00	79.00	91.50	103.00	108.00
Mar.	71.00	69.00	79.00	95.00	103.00	108.00
Apr.	71.00	69.00	79.00	95.00	103.00	108.00
May	71.00	69.00	79.00	94.00	103.00	108.00
June	71.00	69.00	79.00	93.00	103.00	108.00
July	63.00	69.00	79.00	95.00	103.00	108.00
Aug.	63.00	69.00	88.00	103.00	103.00	108.00
Sept.	63.00	69.00	88.00	103.00	103.00	108.00
Oct.	63.00	69.00	88.00	103.00	103.00	108.00
Nov.	63.00	69.00	88.00	103.00	103.00	108.00
Dec.	63.00	71.00	88.00	103.00	105.00	117.00
Average	67.00	68.42	82.75	97.21	103.17	108.75

* 1939-1945 = $63.00.

Computed from list discounts, for carload lots; price for base size pipe, 1 to 3 in.; 1 in. only since August, 1947; ¾ to 3 in. prior to Apr. 13, 1931

STRUCTURAL STEEL SHAPES

At Pittsburgh, Cents Per Pound

	1929	1931	1932	1934	1936	1937
Jan.	1.90	1.64	1.50	1.70	1.80	2.05
Feb.	1.90	1.65	1.50	1.70	1.80	2.05
Mar.	1.90	1.65	1.52	1.70	1.80	2.21
Apr.	1.95	1.65	1.60	1.74	1.80	2.25
May	1.95	1.65	1.60	1.85	1.80	2.25
June	1.95	1.65	1.60	1.85	1.80	2.25
July	1.95	1.63	1.60	1.81	1.90	2.25
Aug.	1.95	1.60	1.60	1.80	1.90	2.25
Sept.	1.95	1.60	1.60	1.80	1.90	2.25
Oct.	1.90	1.60	1.60	1.80	1.90	2.25
Nov.	1.90	1.60	1.60	1.80	1.90	2.25
Dec.	1.90	1.50	1.60	1.80	1.90	2.25
Average	1.92	1.62	1.57	1.78	1.85	2.21
	1938*	1946*	1947	1948	1949	1950
Jan.	2.25	2.10	2.50	2.80	3.25	3.40
Feb.	2.25	2.23	2.50	2.80	3.25	3.40
Mar.	2.25	2.35	2.50	2.80	3.25	3.40
Apr.	2.25	2.35	2.50	2.80	3.25	3.40
May	2.25	2.35	2.50	2.75	3.25	3.40
June	2.22	2.35	2.50	2.75	3.25	3.40
July	2.10	2.35	2.56	2.85	3.25	3.40
Aug.	2.10	2.35	2.80	3.25	3.25	3.40
Sept.	2.10	2.35	2.80	3.25	3.25	3.40
Oct.	2.10	2.35	2.80	3.25	3.25	3.40
Nov.	2.10	2.35	2.80	3.25	3.25	3.40
Dec.	2.10	2.35	2.80	3.25	3.31	3.65
Average	2.17	2.32	2.63	3.00	3.26	3.42

* 1939-1945 = 2.10¢.

Steel Shipments to Warehouses: Sheets and Strips,
Plates, Shapes, Bars, Wire, Pipe and Tubing and
Total Shipments.

METAL FACTS
SECTION 1

STEEL SHIPMENTS TO WAREHOUSES

Net tons

HOT ROLLED STRIP

	Shipments to Warehouses	Total Mill Shipments	Percent of Total
1950 (9 Mo.)..	99,052	1,693,627	5.85
1949........	125,079	1,628,917	7.68
1948........	142,873	1,568,540	9.11
1947........	129,352	1,740,085	7.43
1946........	107,905	1,363,812	7.91

COLD-ROLLED STRIP

	Shipments to Warehouses	Total Mill Shipments	Percent of Total
1950 (9 Mo.)..	73,862	1,333,830	5.52
1949........	83,534	1,380,477	6.05
1948........	91,343	1,519,753	6.01
1947........	47,349	1,499,121	3.16
1946........	45,088	1,282,146	3.52

GALVANIZED SHEETS*

	Shipments to Warehouses	Total Mill Shipments	Percent of Total
1950 (9 Mo.)..	691,557	1,732,640	39.9
1949........	623,897	1,755,067	35.5
1948........	481,266	1,643,337	29.3
1947........	440,021	1,609,881	27.3
1946........	440,457	1,462,053	30.1
1945........	647,748	1,695,796	38.2
1944........	537,020	1,370,175	39.2
1943........	318,674	869,109	36.7
1942........	283,196	998,584	28.4
1941........	676,835	1,708,050	39.6
1940........	733,848	1,586,723	46.2
1939........	857,519	1,635,336	52.4

* 1946–47 includes coated sheets except tinplate and terneplate.

HOT-ROLLED SHEETS

	Shipments to Warehouses	Total Mill Shipments	Percent of Total
1950 (9 Mo.)..	706,697	5,750,499	12.29
1949........	673,680	6,211,458	10.85
1948........	824,023	6,704,654	12.29
1947........	871,393	7,300,881	11.94
1946........	810,196	5,521,463	14.67

COLD-ROLLED SHEETS

	Shipments to Warehouses	Total Mill Shipments	Percent of Total
1950 (9 Mo.)..	692,075	6,795,653	10.18
1949........	590,779	6,942,201	8.51
1948........	516,273	6,361,378	8.12
1947........	459,335	5,504,578	8.34
1946........	453,491	4,075,554	11.13

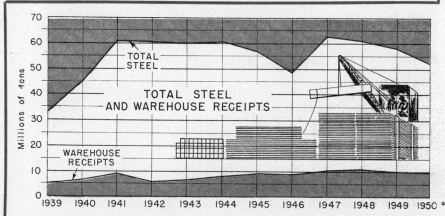

TOTAL STEEL PRODUCTS

	Shipments to Warehouses	Total Mill Shipments	Percent of Total
1950 (9*......	9,713,028	52,703,661	18.4
1949........	10,219,983	58,104,010	17.59
1948........	10,949,920	60,966,999	17.96
1947........	10,484,144	63,057,150	16.63
1946........	9,304,817	48,775,532	19.08
1945........	9,571,436	57,242,240	16.72
1944........	8,008,076	60,352,690	13.27
1943........	6,823,780	59,905,646	11.39
1942........	5,962,068	60,464,774	9.86
1941........	9,155,159	61,229,873	14.95
1940........	6,686,534	45,850,825	14.58
1939........	5,179,660	33,122,628	15.63

* 9 Months.

PLATES

	Shipments to Warehouses	Total Mill Shipments	Percent of Total
1950 (9 Mo.)..	581,535	3,926,105	14.8
1949........	661,348	5,759,065	11.5
1948........	822,149	6,762,678	12.2
1947........	922,459	6,345,216	14.5
1946........	709,728	4,152,181	17.1
1945........	745,663	6,841,304	10.9
1944........	778,498	11,955,559	6.5
1943........	565,290	12,937,230	4.4
1942........	456,582	11,612,987	3.9
1941........	438,540	5,842,809	7.5
1940........	313,663	4,065,383	7.7
1939........	215,241	2,584,057	8.4

HOT-ROLLED BARS

	Shipments to Warehouses	Total Mill Shipments	Percent of Total
1950 (9 Mo.)..	792,402	5,886,241	13.5
1949........	988,695	6,416,102	15.4
1948........	1,100,931	6,196,444	17.8
1947........	1,219,939	7,983,848	15.3
1946........	1,026,873	6,397,137	16.1
1945........	1,114,462	5,727,367	19.5
1944........	915,527	6,020,464	15.2
1943........	923,598	5,982,873	15.4
1942........	684,881	5,519,035	12.4
1941........	750,821	5,788,821	13.0
1940........	604,285	4,854,731	12.4

PIPE AND TUBING

	Shipments to Warehouses	Total Mill Shipments	Percent of Total
1950 (9 Mo.)..	3,026,710	6,592,782	45.9
1949........	3,266,231	6,935,220	47.1
1948........	3,302,127	6,456,102	51.1
1947........	2,825,666	6,117,884	46.2
1946........	2,601,500	4,655,505	55.9
1945........	2,243,123	5,752,752	39.0
1944........	2,054,560	5,259,503	39.1
1943........	1,647,543	5,116,671	32.2
1942........	1,633,738	4,716,061	34.6
1941........	2,692,424	5,888,939	45.7
1940........	2,142,147	3,920,200	54.6
1939........	983,957	3,318,746	29.6

WIRE AND WIRE PRODUCTS

	Shipments to Warehouses	Total Mill Shipments	Percent of Total
1950 (9 Mo.)..	1,255,767	3,328,683	37.7
1949........	1,297,742	3,486,271	37.2
1948........	1,559,676	4,300,794	36.3
1947........	1,366,090	4,174,602	32.7
1946........	1,151,316	3,260,589	35.3
1945........	1,248,596	3,228,716	38.7
1944........	1,262,525	3,200,852	39.4
1943........	1,306,300	3,276,874	39.9
1942........	935,104	3,314,361	28.2
1941........	1,536,347	3,794,538	40.5
1940........	1,054,843	2,569,337	41.1
1939........	1,045,367	2,614,962	39.9

STRUCTURAL SHAPES*

	Shipments to Warehouses	Total Mill Shipments	Percent of Total
1950 (9 Mo.)..	591,576	3,069,569	16.0
1949........	679,719	3,669,503	18.5
1948........	772,815	4,190,934	18.4
1947........	857,082	4,436,129	19.3
1946........	786,651	3,474,284	22.6
1945........	917,142	3,763,952	24.4
1944........	571,884	3,912,951	14.6
1943........	412,727	3,918,126	10.5
1942........	410,708	5,290,162	7.8
1941........	547,511	4,941,818	11.1
1940........	331,523	3,333,450	9.9
1939........	283,235	2,583,101	11.0

* 1940–45 includes piling.

Source for all tables on this page is American Iron & Steel Institute, compilation by American Steel Warehouse Assn. and THE IRON AGE

FINANCIAL ANALYSIS OF THE STEEL INDUSTRY

For Years 1947, 1948, 1949. Data Cover 26 Companies Representing 92 Pct of Ingot Capacity

COMPANY	Year	Ingot Capacity Net Tons	Ingot Production Net Tons	Percent of Capacity Operated	Steel Shipments Net Tons	Net Sales and Operating Revenue	Provision for Federal Income Taxes	Net Income	Net Income Percent of Sales	Earnings Per Common Share	Invested Capital
U. S. Steel Corp.	1949	32,000,000	25,807,000	82.5	18,212,000	$2,301,685,689	$126,000,000	$165,908,829	7.2	$5.39	$1,983,557,284
	1948	31,300,000	29,300,000	93.8	20,700,000	2,481,508,535	109,000,000	129,627,845	5.2	12.00	1,904,614,189
	1947	31,200,000	28,600,000	96.7	20,200,000	2,122,786,243	91,000,000	127,098,148	6.0	11.71	1,588,100,650
Bethlehem Steel Corp.	1949	14,200,000	12,596,949	88.7	9,217,188	1,271,040,076	66,500,000	93,283,539	7.8	9.68	903,760,929
	1948	13,800,000	13,411,492	97.2	9,993,481	1,315,188,536	57,225,000	90,347,560	6.9	9.36	766,985,287
	1947	12,900,000	12,806,940	99.3	9,403,067	1,034,856,444	31,000,000	51,088,375	4.9	4.98	689,236,892
Republic Steel Corp.	1949	8,700,000	6,804,020	79.1	5,123,608	651,952,835	35,000,000	46,142,323	7.1	7.54	400,744,821
	1948	8,600,000	8,324,172	96.8	6,405,581	772,000,047	34,000,000	46,438,382	6.0	7.61	372,895,488
	1947	8,600,000	7,987,170	92.9	6,073,125	649,824,006	23,250,000	31,018,410	4.8	5.17	324,527,137
Jones & Laughlin Steel Corp.	1949	4,816,500	4,170,432	87.0	3,042,296	386,046,149	13,150,000	20,961,245	5.4	7.50	311,167,816
	1948	4,815,000	4,633,558	97.0	3,695,414	446,057,301	18,950,000	31,222,451	7.0	12.01	288,320,131
	1947	4,740,000	4,520,387	95.0	3,486,305	350,132,366	11,482,000	19,225,184	5.5	7.17	294,829,694
National Steel Corp.	1949	4,200,000	....	....	....	424,892,845	37,400,000	39,311,269	9.3	16.02	268,804,722
	1948	4,050,000	....	....	....	436,522,051	33,300,000	40,121,506	9.2	16.35	239,837,256
	1947	3,900,000	....	....	....	328,957,189	19,270,000	26,838,788	8.2	12.03	239,837,256
Youngstown Sheet & Tube Co.	1949	4,082,000	3,478,259	85.2	2,550,380	338,344,004	19,894,000	31,777,010	9.5	18.97	272,689,691
	1948	4,002,000	3,966,099	99.1	2,982,057	381,742,264	25,400,000	35,711,732	9.4	21.32	250,962,729
	1947	4,002,000	3,959,343	98.9	2,853,801	308,571,405	16,635,000	26,299,923	8.5	15.70	213,226,037
Armco Steel Corp.	1949	3,793,000	3,131,020	82.5	2,389,103	341,350,147	19,315,315	30,918,202	9.1	7.68	261,897,665
	1948	3,563,000	3,332,261	93.5	2,572,608	382,563,811	20,072,015	32,030,712	8.4	8.00	255,678,366
	1947	3,367,000	3,078,487	91.4	2,413,406	311,685,322	16,464,876	25,002,211	8.0	7.44	196,500,603
Inland Steel Co.	1949	3,400,000	3,019,655	88.8	2,715,398	347,640,710	15,935,000	25,013,707	7.2	5.11	256,763,206
	1948	3,400,000	3,533,374	103.9	3,252,681	394,716,908	23,221,000	38,606,898	9.8	7.88	231,311,697
	1947	3,400,000	3,299,528	97.0	2,941,990	315,031,042	18,485,000	29,888,558	9.5	6.10	192,002,744
Sharon Steel Corp.	1949	1,672,000	1,001,625	59.9	738,584	90,068,564	1,650,000	3,325,964	3.7	5.39	49,917,062
	1948	1,672,000	1,298,383	77.7	964,987	118,849,560	5,811,000	9,234,983	7.8	14.96	48,525,580
	1947	1,672,000	1,222,887	76.6	912,962	94,130,807	4,225,000	6,722,019	7.1	10.89	33,994,671
Wheeling Steel Corp.	1949	1,536,000	1,227,600	79.9	....	143,419,446	5,819,000	7,896,265	5.5	10.68	158,195,963
	1948	1,409,000	1,303,424	92.5	....	154,953,406	10,000,000	15,050,045	9.7	23.24	155,546,764
	1947	1,409,000	1,285,832	91.3	....	131,721,128	7,760,000	11,651,579	8.8	17.27	144,625,836
Colorado Fuel & Iron Corp.	1949	1,472,000	1,446,693	98.3	1,348,138	138,344,200	6,059,200	10,182,919	7.4	8.46	77,408,438
	1948	1,472,000	1,395,717	94.8	1,225,027	118,858,896	3,659,100	6,181,777	5.2	5.04	66,942,398
	1947	1,448,640	1,369,460	94.5	1,046,008	94,740,442	2,676,815	5,088,676	5.4	4.07	60,314,493
Crucible Steel Co. of America	1949	1,112,984	....	....	....	99,393,228	351,827	1,352,764	1.4	None	92,304,721
	1948	1,277,133	....	....	....	131,360,030	2,748,021	3,596,177	2.7	4.15	93,418,780
	1947	1,253,650	....	....	....	110,503,836	1,084,466	2,064,887	1.9	1.12	89,762,980
Pittsburgh Steel Co.	1949	1,072,000	717,253	66.9	595,486	80,559,351	624,000	844,810	1.1	.04	54,186,177
	1948	1,072,557	976,218	91.0	774,108	102,858,785	4,350,000	5,484,090	5.3	9.07	54,841,029
	1947	1,072,557	1,006,888	93.9	737,978	85,873,537	3,175,000	4,019,637	4.7	6.20	51,810,390
Allegheny Ludlum Steel Corp.	1949	832,360	362,813	57.8	297,635	105,863,359	1,200,000	1,967,324	1.9	1.15	52,659,400
	1948	496,360	462,306	93.1	428,000	126,780,255	4,601,358	6,833,384	5.4	5.05	54,069,677
	1947	496,360	411,107	82.8	357,000	106,783,183	4,068,068	6,002,657	5.6	4.66	39,738,371
Lukens Steel Co.	1949	675,000	545,253	80.8	306,450	55,825,306	1,640,330	1,930,045	3.5	6.07	23,107,877
	1948	624,000	647,876	103.8	....	61,460,919	1,675,000	2,411,604	3.9	7.35	17,866,645
	1947	624,000	637,347	102.1	442,550	48,591,687	1,746,200	2,697,117	5.6	8.92	15,912,819
Portsmouth Steel Co.	1949	660,000	511,647	77.5	326,386	49,744,601	3,012,000	4,885,424	9.8	3.87	21,750,173
	1948	660,000	647,816	98.2	523,096	58,904,664	2,600,000	4,511,550	7.7	3.54	19,300,975
	1947	660,000	667,011	101.1	528,968	49,459,952	2,358,000	3,944,969	8.0	3.03	16,412,741
Granite City Steel Co.	1949	620,000	531,824	85.8	464,131	46,496,523	1,890,000	2,958,109[4]	6.4	7.44	21,050,032
	1948	620,000	493,720	79.6	408,449	41,370,688	2,370,000	3,267,707	7.9	8.54	20,396,133
	1947	500,000	440,398	88.1	347,047	25,869,719	880,000	1,941,899	7.5	5.08	18,491,504
Copperweld Steel Co.	1949	554,400	....	....	....	42,708,329	900,000	1,737,506	4.1	3.24	15,620,337
	1948	554,400	....	....	....	75,570,115	3,414,500	4,989,019	6.6	9.54	13,814,294
	1947	480,000	....	....	....	53,303,245	1,179,500	1,546,711	2.9	2.85	14,784,035
Alan Wood Steel Co.	1949	550,000	381,710	69.4	270,803	35,895,460	1,480,000	2,255,840	6.3	3.76	27,548,014
	1948	550,000	530,691	96.5	425,114	47,480,574	2,842,000	4,116,444	8.7	7.78	25,738,866
	1947	550,000	449,945	81.8	323,853	35,971,661	1,238,000	1,955,446	5.4	7.26	17,209,001
The Midvale Co.	1949	449,950	67,647	15.0	....	13,739,443	None	*1,094,387*	8.0	1.82	15,784,139
	1948	517,322	64,962	12.6	....	10,509,015	None	*1,665,718*	15.9	2.78	17,734,454
	1947	517,322	84,020	16.2	....	14,829,373	None	*1,186,727*	8.0	1.98	20,449,121
Barium Steel Corp.	1949	406,000	186,485	45.9	131,414	33,885,546	809,463	711,452	2.1	.33	13,295,963
	1948	441,000	390,000	88.4	310,000	51,257,670	2,048,176	2,615,270	5.3	1.32	12,552,420
	1947	387,000	318,000	82.2	280,000	41,365,948	1,104,564	1,689,213	4.1	.84	10,252,135
Continental Steel Corp.	1949	364,000	239,736	65.9	....	22,505,562	785,000	636,716	2.8	1.27	14,978,249
	1948	364,000	317,927	87.3	....	29,743,309	1,200,000	1,625,150	5.5	3.24	15,093,600
	1947	364,000	316,644	87.0	....	27,086,139	890,000	1,296,874	4.8	2.58	13,909,323
Rotary Electric Steel Co.	1949	420,000	247,350	58.9	213,976	16,865,512	955,000	1,287,063	7.6	6.7	10,093,290
	1948	340,000	247,658	94.5	227,280	18,940,250	1,500,000	2,496,859	13.2	12.94	6,081,237
	1947	255,000	201,556	79.0	176,246	16,500,149	544,000	903,360	5.5	5.41	4,469,191
Laclede Steel Co.	1949	326,025	283,488	87.0	263,862	31,209,110	1,815,000	2,718,352	8.7	13.18	12,733,916
	1948	326,025	278,170	85.3	284,538	34,072,411	1,165,000	1,767,863	5.2	8.57	11,178,504
	1947	326,025	288,038	88.3	272,852	26,283,120	956,913	1,429,035	5.4	6.93	9,772,843
Northwestern Steel & Wire Co.	1949	321,000	288,814	90.0	231,193	28,564,916	1,195,000	2,243,938	7.9	2.74	6,761,176
	1948	321,000	287,670	89.6	235,385	26,641,518	1,180,000	1,680,477	7.0	2.27	5,539,518
	1947	321,000	261,045	81.3	....	21,185,519	1,319,000	1,932,747	9.1	2.36	4,676,866
Keystone Steel & Wire Co.	1949	302,400	308,131	101.9	276,683	36,735,489	2,600,053	5,084,181	13.8	2.71	16,582,398
	1948	302,400	298,882	98.8	265,264	34,504,429	2,060,598	4,167,550	12.1	2.22	15,373,217
	1947	302,400	288,561	95.4	273,151	31,573,658	2,458,436	4,672,934	14.8	7.48	13,580,666
GRAND TOTAL	1948	86,549,197	80,565,700	94.0[2]	60,035,000[3]	$7,859,579,001	$374,392,768	$522,734,361	6.7	....	$5,026,661,545
	1947	84,747,954	77,153,400	92.9[2]	57,382,000[3]	6,437,617,120	265,250,838	394,832,630	6.1	....	4,360,286,787
Percent change, 1948 over 1947		+2.1	+4.4			+22.1	+41.1	+32.4			+15.3
GRAND TOTAL	1949	88,537,619	71,700,000[1]	81.0[2]	53,705,000[3]	$7,134,776,400	$365,240,409	$510,240,409	7.2	....	$5,395,896,275
	1948	86,549,197	80,565,700[1]	94.0[2]	60,035,000[3]	7,861,587,539	374,392,768	522,471,317	6.7	....	5,044,411,545
Percent change, 1949 over 1948		+2.3	—11	—13.8	—11	—9.2	—2.2	—2.3	+7.5		+7.0

[1] Estimated, based on national operating rate so as to include companies listed above that do not publish production figures.
[2] National rate for entire industry by American Iron & Steel Institute.
[3] Estimated.
[4] After $100,000 appropriation for inventory price declines.
Italics indicate loss.

ROLLING MILLS DISMANTLED—1950

Companies, Location of Works and Products

Company	Location of Works	Products
Colorado Fuel & Iron Corp.	Pueblo, Colo.	Rods.
Jones & Laughlin Steel Corp.	Pittsburgh	Large hot-rolled rounds and squares.
Jones & Laughlin Steel Corp.	Pittsburgh	Small hot-rolled bars and shapes.
Jones & Laughlin Steel Corp.	Pittsburgh	Small hot-rolled bars and shapes.
Youngstown Sheet & Tube Co.	East Chicago	2" to 8" dia. lap weld pipe
Rotary Electric Steel Co.	Detroit	Bars (temporary facilities)
Republic Steel Corp.	Pittsburgh	Tie plate bars

REROLLED RAIL STEEL SHIPMENTS
NET TONS

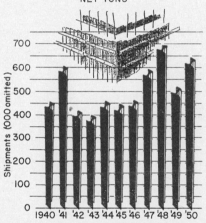

REROLLED RAIL STEEL
(Shipments—Net Tons)

Year	Concrete Bars	Carbon Bars	Other Products	Total
1940	155,188	213,551	85,331	454,070
1941	224,761	290,732	92,050	607,543
1942	223,015	136,161	65,243	424,419
1943	100,376	199,567	102,927	402,870
1944	96,265	246,274	118,242	460,781
1945	115,159	236,009	99,527	450,695
1946	181,141	225,632	61,877	468,650
1947	236,322	263,066	90,085	589,473
1948	248,768	308,661	145,649	703,079
1949	223,325	234,877	71,013	529,215
1950*	223,600	321,000	105,000	649,600

* Includes estimate on last 2 months.
Source: Rail Steel Bar Assn.

Is American industry, including steel, heading into a strait-jacket? Read "Industry's Future" on p. 263 for the duties of the vice-president in charge of the president. . . . Everyone will be selling to the Government this year; "How to Sell to Uncle Sam" (p. 269) is a briefing on the fundamentals of selling to the armed forces.

STEEL ROLLING MILL INSTALLATIONS

Built or Modernized During 1950—As Reported To The Iron Age

Company	Location of Works	Builder	Date Delivered	New or Modernized	Type
Allegheny Ludlum Steel Corp.	W. Leechburg, Pa.	Lewis Foundry & Machine Co.	1950	New	28-in. x 42-in. 2-H skin pass
Armco Steel Corp.	Middletown, O.	United	Dec. 1950	Modernized	80-in. hot strip
Bethlehem	Lackawanna	Birdsboro Foundry & Machine Co.	1950	New	18-in.—16-in.—12-in. cross-country bar mill
Bethlehem Steel Co.	Lackawanna	Mesta	1950	New	25-in. & 49-in. x 79-in. hot strip
Bethlehem Steel Co.	Lackawanna	Mesta	1950	New	54-in. slabbing-blooming stand
Bethlehem Steel Co.	Lackawanna	Mesta	1950	Modernized	79-in. hot strip
Bethlehem Steel Co.	Lackawanna	Mesta	1950	Modernized	20-in. & 49-in. x 54-in. 4-H cold
Columbia Steel Co.	Torrance	Mesta	1950	New	21-in. & 50-in. x 60-in. 4-stand 4-H tandem cold
Granite City Steel Co.	Granite City	United	Nov. 1950	Modernized	Tandem temper
Jones & Laughlin Steel Corp.	Cleveland	United	May 1950	Modernized	77-in. hot strip
Jones & Laughlin Steel Corp.	Pittsburgh	Mesta	1950	Modernized	96-in. hot strip
Kaiser Engineering	Fontana	United	Jan. 1950	New	80-in. hot strip finishing
Midvale Steel Co.	Philadelphia	Birdsboro Foundry & Machine Co.	1950	New	24-in. ring mill
Northwestern Steel & Wire	Sterling, Ill.	Birdsboro Foundry & Machine Co.	1950	New	16-in.—14-in.—12-in. merch. & narrow strip mill
Republic Steel Corp.	Cleveland	United	Nov. 1950	Modernized	98-in. hot strip
Republic Steel Corp.	Cleveland	United	Dec. 1950	New	54-in. skin pass
Sheffield Steel Corp.	Houston	Lewis Foundry & Machine Co.	1950	Modernized	100-in. plate
Sheffield Steel Corp.	Kansas City	Morgan Const. Co.	1950	Modernized	10-in. rod mill
Sheffield Steel Corp.	Houston	Morgan Const. Co.	1950	Modernized	19-in. sheet bar & billet
Sheffield Steel Corp.	Houston	United	June 1950	Modernized	110-in. plate
Sheffield Steel Corp.	Houston	United	Aug. 1950	New	130-in. 4-H Rev. Plate
Thompson Wire Co.	Franklin Park, Ill.	United	Sept. 1950	New	10½-in. & 33-in. x 24-in. Rev. cold mill
Thomas Steel	Warren, O.	United	May 1950	New	10½-in. & 26-in. x 24-in. tandem cold mill
Washburn Wire	Phillipsdale, R. I.	Morgan Const. Co.	1950	Modernized	No. 2 rod mill
Wallace Barnes	Bristol, Conn.	United	Feb. 1950	New	7¼-in. & 26-in. x 17-in. rev. cold mill
Weirton Steel Co.	Weirton	United	Dec. 1950	Modernized	66-in. hot strip
Youngstown Sheet & Tube Co.	Indiana Harbor	Morgan Const. Co.	1950	Modernized	10-in. skelp mill
Youngstown Sheet & Tube Co.	Indiana Harbor	Morgan Const. Co.	1950	Modernized	21-in. sheet bar mill
Youngstown Sheet & Tube Co.	Youngstown	United	Sept. 1950	Modernized	44-in. bloomer

STEELMAKING CAPACITY INSTALLED IN 1950

Reported by Companies and Location With Description of Facilities and Capacity

Openhearth Furnaces Company	Number of Furnaces	Rated Capacity per Heat (N.T.)	Annual Capacity Increase (N.T.)	Location	Furnace Builder	Operation Started	Remarks
U. S. Steel Corp.	57	182	610,000	Pittsbgh. Dist.		1950	Furnaces enlarged, improved facilities added, existing facilities altered and re-rearranged.
U. S. Steel Corp.	31	186	190,000	Chicago Dist.		1950	Addition of improved facilities, alteration and enlargement of existing facilities.
Armco Steel Co.	3	250	400,000	Middletown, O.	Loftus	Oct.	New furnaces
Colorado Fuel & Iron Corp.	16	—	48,000	Pueblo, Colo.		1950	Change in design of furnaces
Colorado Fuel & Iron Corp.	4	—	40,000	Buffalo, N. Y.	—	1950	Change in design of furnaces
Keystone Steel & Wire Co.	—	—	22,000	Peoria, Ill.		1950	Change in method of operation
Wheeling Steel Corp.	—	—	144,000	Wheeling, W. Va.		1950	Technological improvements, increased use of hot metal
Inland Steel Co.	36	—	350,000	Indiana Harbor		1950	Changes to accommodate larger cranes and ladles; technological improvements
Armco Steel Corp.	1	—	47,000	Ashland, Ky.	—	1950	Furnace modernized
Armco Steel Corp.	1	—	72,000	Houston, Tex.	—	1950	Furnace modernized.
Total openhearth furnaces			1,923,000				
Electric Furnaces							
Bethlehem Steel Co.	1	75	132,000	Los Angeles	Lectromelt	April	New furnace
Armco Steel Corp.	1	—	6,000	Butler, Pa.	—	1950	Furnace modernized
Armco Steel Corp.	1	—	12,000	Middletown, O.	—	1950	Furnace modernized
Allegheny Ludlum Steel Corp.	1	60	72,000	Brackenridge, Pa.	Swindell	May	New furnace.
Total Electric Furnaces			222,000				
Grand Total			2,145,000				

IRON AND STEEL EXPORTS—1937 TO 1950
Including Semi-Finished and Finished Products, In Net Tons

	1950*	1949	1948	1947	1946	1940	1939	1938	1937
Ingots, blooms, billets, slabs, sheet bars	33,982	257,156	219,340	491,214	452,533	2,822,428	241,671	187,758	379,369
Wire rods	5,453	53,312	38,142	71,237	62,857	320,981	35,224	24,957	67,209
Skelp	73,455	117,368	57,920	67,403	56,569	167,309	91,461	66,849	85,655
Iron bars	567	1,469	3,658	34,752	25,575	16,190	970	1,467	3,486
Concrete reinforcement bars	11,753	107,902	130,298	248,373	194,652	155,172	52,926	29,237 }	20,048
Steel bars, cold finished	10,326	37,923	46,496	106,270	88,152	74,602	12,747	7,225 }	
Other steel bars (excluding alloy)	43,343	273,923	309,475	535,370	339,905	524,211	150,247	121,823	148,419
Alloy steel bars	4,155	20,540	53,006	208,113	50,978	49,370	16,707	9,178	7,415
Welding rods, electric	7,739	15,945	15,834	14,842	9,470	4,800	1,795	1,324	
Boiler plate	74,572	417,092	28,877	32,558	61,706	12,510	10,391	7,564	11,704
Other plates, not fab. }			318,820	530,309	470,263	631,239	274,176	240,077	421,533
Plates, fab., punched or shaped	5,378	30,326	23,550	37,230	34,857	30,818	7,505	2,629	28,247
Iron sheets, black	11,269	22,651	17,773	30,215	31,179	29,622	11,702	8,474	12,082
Steel sheets, black	317,319	551,243	416,481	568,964	482,785	533,882	301,308	229,912	320,891
Galvanized sheets	69,821	85,594	62,782	74,552	77,747	184,370	124,284	85,161	90,741
Strip steel, cold rolled	28,687	57,378	59,483	89,617	64,626	72,804	29,392	28,575	40,682
Strip steel, hot rolled	32,036	82,367	69,094	107,147	84,376	150,558	70,235	41,486	83,900
Tin plate and tagger's tin	356,336	594,635	604,739	609,423	377,946	422,484	342,188	176,044	398,192
Terne plate (incl. long ternes)	5,402	10,427	9,046	12,851	20,503	6,846	6,149	4,921	5,771
Structural shapes, plain	128,848	408,702	292,176	463,651	319,102	456,015	129,321	93,734	151,991
Structural shapes, fab.	80,323	157,999	161,174	246,130	99,477	80,960	41,612	42,624	43,824
Frames and sashes	978	2,751	3,164	3,546	1,714	2,265	1,329	1,584	1,922
Sheet piling	7,428	19,751	34,523	34,163	25,641	13,506	8,615	3,913	8,374
Rails, 60 lbs. per yard and over	73,050	195,552	265,820	353,444	286,760	227,645	39,878	51,429	123,916
Rails, less than 60 lbs. per yard	10,469	7,875	9,718	59,286	38,455	41,487	7,364	4,917	11,341
Rails, relaying	23,819	33,563	32,837	87,855	60,368	19,888	18,941	36,301	30,707
Splice bars and tie plates	15,915	19,796	49,356	119,411	53,072	11,595	9,872	8,224	16,332
Frogs and switches	1,612	6,043	5,467	7,190	6,763	3,268	2,250	1,843	2,862
Railroad spikes	6,578	3,635	9,268	23,459	12,045	5,618	3,935	2,918	3,442
Railroad bolts, nuts, and washers	1,138	1,994	7,666	7,759	8,470	3,724	2,184	1,384	1,246
Car wheels, tires and axles	20,449	62,062	38,714	88,801	68,371	21,483	31,225	23,450	31,110
Seamless black pipe	12,578	25,962	21,692	18,717	14,870	34,027	11,445	8,354	13,980
Seamless casing and oil line pipe	112,581	268,276	227,524	243,038	123,757	165,584	87,501	56,092	84,031
Seamless boiler tubes	8,083	42,186	36,700	62,636	41,767	27,800	15,940	8,764	18,788
Welded black pipe	42,346	101,759	61,560	90,995	85,278	57,968	26,832	15,433	28,978
Welded galvanized pipe	50,018	98,531	41,760	70,219	61,062	71,827	37,405	19,492	23,025
Welded casing and oil line pipe	237,999	224,650	144,390	90,462	56,024	36,589	10,952	15,255	9,467
Welded boiler tubes	1,710	4,882	1,755	7,315	2,798	3,317	1,050	335	765
Other pipe and fittings	47,556	132,872	68,938	101,850	72,984	19,263	8,483	1,058	1,098
Plain wire	16,287	73,827	76,828	83,346	52,575	98,112	36,103	26,970	37,118
Galvanized wire	7,575	56,902	50,314	101,026	65,221	74,011	31,651	28,887	25,713
Barbed wire	6,534	75,735	39,789	78,862	46,803	49,510	59,721	38,015	37,894
Woven wire fencing	3,721	16,324	11,620	12,371	9,739	5,302	3,774	2,480	3,540
Woven wire screen cloth	1,436	4,296	5,737	5,985	3,523	3,751	2,154	1,486	1,779
Wire rope and strand	7,752	12,915	13,643	30,829	33,710	14,963	6,785	4,897	8,763
Wire nails	2,012	25,909	19,682	25,755	19,102	54,478	28,892	23,207	19,497
Other wire and manufactures	8,061	20,237	41,517	52,600	26,098	18,699	11,532	7,013	9,803
Horseshoe nails			428	1,025	2,080	1,650	1,043	995	1,092
Tacks	793	1,681	3,537	1,960	1,787	962	434	294	456
Other nails, incl. staples	1,764	9,889	10,949	13,010	7,782	6,150	5,756	4,576	3,473
Bolts, nuts, rivets and washers, except railroad	10,281	26,128	54,311	48,234	31,622	37,387	9,919	9,024	12,506
Forgings	10,569	23,747	27,063	35,818	19,358	35,952	18,595	10,183	11,332
Horseshoes	255	418	582	897	1,859	400	251	115	201
Castings other than car wheels, tires and axles	30,176	50,112							
Grand Total	2,083,838	4,957,097	4,354,996	6,543,085	4,747,397	7,914,352	2,493,822	1,829,907	4,593,735

* 8 months.

Source: Office of International Trade

IRON AND STEEL IMPORTS—1937 TO 1950
Including Semi-Finished and Finished Products, In Net Tons

	1950*	1949	1948	1947	1946	1940	1939	1938	1937
Steel ingots, blooms, etc.	77,775	52,312	23,284	1,516	1,193	493	845	857	2,499
Wire rods	65,270	5,733	6,613	6,016	6,053	4,464	11,981	5,918	17,735
Iron bars and slabs	305	353	190	249	404	222	1,042	564	2,192
Concrete reinforcement bars	29,142	10,269	790	2	1	9	2,648	1,714	4,361
Hollow bar and drill steel	446	92	63	111	146	976	1,571	969	2,841
Other steel bars	55,610	35,267	5,018	696	873	2,075	19,137	21,182	49,590
Boiler and other plate	20,700	30,519	30,316	664	2,048	17	31	398	239
Sheets, skelp, sawplate, n. e. s.	11,709	12,836	3,918	1,179	206	137	1,576	6,772	9,857
Tin plate, tagger's tin and terne plate	1,074	13,683	206	655	334	154	111	122	276
Other hoops and bands	15,215	5,671	2,803	35	53	795	26,48i	29,267	30,496
Structural shapes and sheet piling	79,368	119,501	65,811	1,730	757	860	44,276	44,379	87,666
Rails and fastenings	1,985	1,103	6,784	10,257	7,997	1,780	8,719	4,059	9,294
Wheels and axles	44	88	38	76	243				
Pipe and tubes	828	5,712	2,545	6,778	206	3,446	34,297	32,629	47,701
Round wire	8,052	2,307	23	97	208	995	2,814	1,886	5,452
Barbed wire	4,174	99				96	17,079	14,031	18,666
Flat wire and strip	2,028	1,574	2,122	2,171	3,03	2,481	3,534	3,020	4,518
Telegraph and telephone wire	14	455	2	242	6	1	9	30	38
Wire rope and strand	1,222	890	280	312	295	586	1,864	2,263	3,974
Miscellaneous wire	12,644	2,964		3	9	1	1,659	1,634	3,641
Nails, tacks and staples	33,266	2,383	2,019	116	183	125	8,187	8,510	16,836
Bolts, nuts and rivets	249	96	312	134	74	147	132	241	660
Castings and forgings	231	106	613	1,152	805	685	1,287	4,286	5,151
Die blocks and blanks	118	660	48	239	285	13	100	106	114
Total	421,469	304,673	153,798	34,430	25,410	20,473	189,805	185,321	324,27

* 8 Months.

Source: Office of International Trade

THE IRON AGE

SECTION 2

METAL INDUSTRY FACTS

Nonferrous Metals Production, Prices Markets

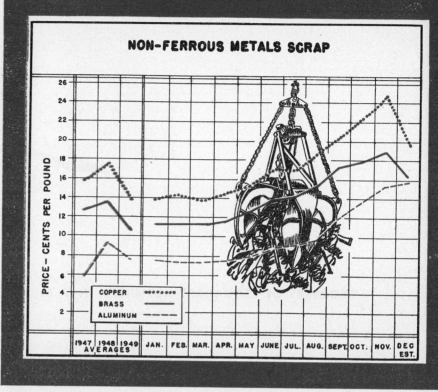

NON-FERROUS METALS SCRAP

COPPER
BRASS
ALUMINUM

1947 1948 1949 AVERAGES | JAN. | FEB. | MAR. | APR. | MAY | JUNE | JUL. | AUG. | SEPT. | OCT. | NOV. | DEC. EST.

PRICE — CENTS PER POUND

IN THIS SECTION:

January 4, 1951

2 METAL FACTS SECTION

U. S. Aluminum Production, Primary and Secondary; Aluminum Imports and Exports; Shipments of Wrought Aluminum and Aluminum Castings; Scrap and Secondary Aluminum Prices.

U. S. ALUMINUM PRODUCTION

Short Tons, Primary Metal Only

	1943	1944	1945	1946
Jan.	60,650	84,750	48,650	24,750
Feb.	55,600	74,400	45,650	22,250
March	64,600	80,200	53,100	26,000
April	66,800	77,800	51,600	25,900
May	72,850	76,450	52,000	24,850
June	74,150	66,400	47,500	27,800
July	78,450	67,550	47,900	35,750
Aug.	81,350	61,650	45,800	39,850
Sept.	86,400	47,450	31,600	41,100
Oct.	94,050	48,400	25,000	45,000
Nov.	91,350	44,450	20,800	46,300
Dec.	93,600	46,850	24,000	50,700
Total	920,179	776,446	495,060	409,630

	1947	1948	1949	1950
Jan.	50,045	48,767	53,356	52,023
Feb.	47,002	45,699	49,749	50,668
March	53,032	51,874	54,852	58,747
April	51,007	53,277	54,076	58,024
May	51,116	55,450	56,909	61,929
June	46,259	48,557	54,184	60,400
July	47,998	52,937	55,777	63,518
Aug.	47,054	54,953	52,005	63,006
Sept.	43,228	53,255	49,742	59,540
Oct.	43,959	54,526	45,790	62,916
Nov.	43,461	50,714	35,865	63,000*
Dec.	47,580	53,474	41,161	64,000*
Total	571,750	623,483	603,462	718,000*

* Estimate

Source: U. S. Bureau of Mines and Aluminum Association

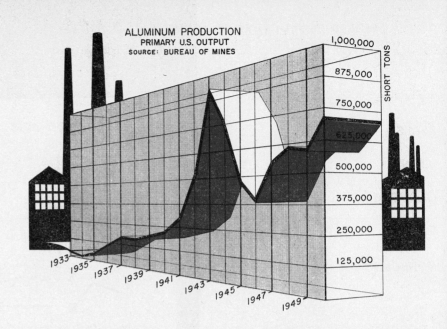

ALUMINUM PRODUCTION
PRIMARY U.S. OUTPUT
SOURCE: BUREAU OF MINES

RECOVERY OF SECONDARY ALUMINUM IN U. S.

Short Tons, Broken Down by Form of Recovery, Since 1943.

Form of Recovery	1943	1944	1945	1946	1947	1948	1949
As Metal	5,926	2,336	2,145	2,075	5,105	2,384	343
Aluminum Alloys	305,357	320,040	293,967	274,068	338,200	282,302	178,502
In Brass and Bronze	1,279	1,466	1,182	597	307	455	450
In Zinc-Base Alloys	219	187	267	504	624	776	600
In Magnesium Alloys				266	222	354	426
In Chemical Compounds	1,180	1,616	846	563	379	506	441
	313,961	325,645	298,387	278,073	344,837	286,777	180,762

Source: U. S. Bureau of Mines

ALUMINUM CASTINGS

Short Tons of Shipments, Since 1942

	Total	Sand	Permanent Mold	Die	Others
1942	162,050				
1943	230,250				
1944	257,450				
1945	186,950				
1946	194,356	80,423	78,569	38,851	513
1947	220,998	77,556	87,258	55,269	916
1948	212,245	69,891	80,667	59,369	2,319
1949	304,616	106,825	102,908	88,019	6,864
1950	270,524*	91,876*	86,751*	85,690*	6,207*

* First 8 Months

Source: U. S. Bureau of the Census

ALUMINUM WROUGHT PRODUCTS

Short Tons of Shipments Since 1942

	Total	Plate, Sheet and Strip	Rolled Structurals, Rod, Bar, Wire	Extruded Shapes, Tubing and Blooms	Powder, Flake, Paste
1942	270,200				
1943	420,500				
1944	448,900				
1945	369,300				
1946	570,425	433,491	65,319	63,039	8,576
1947	704,076	555,580	78,690	61,524	8,283
1948	820,103	634,149	91,496	85,982	8,477
1949	579,073	395,013	101,825	74,998	7,238
1950†	693,149	470,462	109,392	104,325	8,971

† 10 month total.

Source: U. S. Bureau the of Census

U. S. ALUMINUM IMPORTS

Short Tons, Imports for Consumption

	Semi-Finished Products†	Metal, Alloys Crude	Scrap
1934	110	9,186	
1935	108	10,538	
1936	202	12,579	
1937	238	22,351	
1938	114	8,756	
1939	306	8,984	5,046
1940	562	17,435	648
1941	528	12,830	55
1942	5,855	106,257	24
1943	76	135,505	241
1944	654	100,315	1,784
1945	1,688	332,437	5,168
1946	1,120	41,487	14,493
1947	31	15,579	15,719
1948	5,912	83,277	71,768
1949	7,863	77,342	40,120
1950:			
Jan.	476	10,809	6,321
Feb.	358	12,529	3,938
March	288	17,652	4,853
April	99	17,117	2,769
May	443	14,921	6,456
June	231	11,741	8,122
July	621	20,352	4,492
1950:			
First 7 Months	2,516	105,121	36,951

† Plates, sheets, bars, etc.

Source: U. S. Bureau of Mines

ALUMINUM SCRAP, CAST

Cents Per Pound, f.o.b. New York*

	1947	1948	1949	1950
Jan.	7.35	6.15	12.00	7.38
Feb.	6.70	6.75	10.25	7.25
March	6.50	6.75	8.10	7.25
April	6.47	7.05	6.72	7.38
May	6.30	8.25	6.25	7.88
June	5.63	9.00	5.65	8.65
July	5.25	10.65	5.38	8.75
Aug.	5.25	11.00	6.25	9.88
Sept.	5.25	9.85	7.30	12.00
Oct.	5.25	9.88	7.50	13.88
Nov.	5.38	11.88	8.00	15.15
Dec.	5.75	12.55	7.75	15.75†
Average	5.92	9.15	7.60	10.10†

* Dealers' Buying Price † Estimate

REMELT ALUMINUM INGOT

No. 12, Cents Per Pound, Cars*

	1947	1948	1949	1950
Jan.	16.47	15.60	25.50	16.50
Feb.	16.31	16.31	23.53	16.50
March	15.62	16.50	20.25	16.30
April	14.88	16.92	17.59	16.06
May	14.40	19.00	16.50	16.75
June	13.81	19.81	15.04	17.73
July	13.25	23.67	14.63	18.13
Aug.	13.50	23.75	15.38	21.85
Sept.	13.63	23.60	15.75	26.25
Oct.	13.75	23.63	15.75	27.06
Nov.	14.28	25.84	16.13	30.175
Dec.	15.34	26.50	16.50	31.00†
Average	14.60	20.93	17.71	21.19†

* Delivered † Estimate

U. S. ALUMINUM EXPORTS

Short Tons, by Form, Since 1934

	Semi-Finished Products†	Manu-factured Products*	Ingots, Slabs Crude	Scrap
1934	102	257	4,026	
1935	310	475	1,681	
1936	326	728	477	
1937	332	1,047	2,360	
1938	1,474	738	4,835	
1939	8,488	1,610	28,121	476
1940	14,659	3,497	12,227	955
1941	6,655	1,178	750	57
1942	20,913	4,979	17,834	32
1943	60,851	7,533	56,741	14
1944	55,019	19,326	133,089	413
1945	3,532	6,512	2,209	802
1946	15,587	5,427	1,107	640
1947	50,235	10,204	12,098	788
1948	47,869	7,199	1,239	438
1949	28,764	4,932	8,018	397

† Plates, sheet, bars, etc.
* Includes only Tubes, moldings, foil and leaf, table, kitchen and hospital utensils, powders and pastes up to 1948. In 1949, wire and manufactures, and materials for construction were also included.

Source: U. S. Bureau of Mines

World Production of Aluminum and Copper; Shipments of Aluminum Extrusions; Bauxite Imports; Primary Aluminum Prices.

METAL FACTS SECTION 2

WORLD PRODUCTION OF ALUMINUM SINCE 1941

Short Tons, Not Including Russian Production and the Small Output in Brazil.

Country	1941	1942	1943	1944	1945	1946	1947	1948	1949
United States	309,067	521,106	920,179	776,446	495,060	409,630	571,750	‡623,456	603,462
Canada	213,873	340,596	495,750	462,065	215,713	193,400	297,838	‡367,079	366,850
Total America	522,940	861,702	1,415,929	1,238,511	710,773	603,030	869,588	‡990,535	970,312
Austria	23,606	40,561	50,700	57,430	5,787	1,138	4,786	14,723	16,309
France	70,437	49,824	51,257	28,825	41,033	52,729	58,670	71,418	59,679
Germany	233,981	250,367	223,842	210,539	*22,000	....	(c)8,053	31,797
Great Britain	25,385	52,387	62,341	39,724	35,722	35,329	32,407	33,629	33,986
Italy	53,125	50,044	50,926	18,514	4,792	12,169	27,628	36,466	28,271
Hungary	5,489	6,570	10,428	10,880	*5,000	2,172	*3,000	5,679	
Norway	19,321	22,595	25,919	22,085	5,079	18,400	23,947	‡34,216	39,392
Spain	1,234	818	879	227	653	1,110	1,065	‡577	728
Sweden	1,206	1,426	3,937	4,104	3,567	3,931	3,188	‡3,707	*4,400
Switzerland	26,676	26,455	*22,000	*8,000	*5,500	15,400	19,800	‡20,994	23,148
Total Europe (a)	460,460	501,047	502,229	400,328	129,133	142,378	174,491	‡229,462	237,710
Others (c):									
Taiwan Province, China	13,452	13,315	11,777	8,807	653				
India			1,402	1,899	2,485	3,576	3,553	3,771	3,911
Japan	55,556	83,069	119,062	120,728	18,135	3,519	2,976	7,672	23,389
Korea	3,439	4,813	13,811	14,267					
Manchuria (b)	8,853	8,198	9,432	8,800					

(a) Excluding Yugoslavia. (b) Fiscal year beginning April 1. (c) Practically all by the Toeging works in American Zone.
* Estimated.
‡ Revised.

Source: American Bureau of Metal Statistics

ALUMINUM 99 PCT PLUS

Cents Per Pound, Freight Allowed

	1929	1934	1936	1937	1938	1939
Jan.	23.90	23.30	20.50	20.50	20.00	20.00
Feb.	23.90	21.65	20.50	20.50	20.00	20.00
March	23.90	21.65	20.50	20.00	20.00	20.00
April	23.90	21.65	20.50	20.00	20.00	20.00
May	23.90	21.65	20.50	20.00	20.00	20.00
June	23.90	21.65	20.50	20.00	20.00	20.00
July	23.90	21.65	20.50	20.00	20.00	20.00
Aug.	23.90	21.65	20.50	20.00	20.00	20.00
Sept.	23.90	21.65	20.50	20.00	20.00	20.00
Oct.	23.90	21.49	20.50	20.00	20.00	20.00
Nov.	23.90	20.50	20.00	20.00	20.00	20.00
Dec.	23.90	20.50	20.50	20.00	20.00	20.00
Average	23.90	21.58	20.50	20.08	20.00	20.00

	1940	1941			1948	1949	1950
Jan.	20.00	17.00			15.00	17.00	17.00
Feb.	20.00	17.00	1947		15.00	17.00	17.00
March	20.00	17.00	1946		15.00	17.00	17.00
April	19.00	17.00	1945		15.00	17.00	17.00
May	19.00	17.00	1944		15.00	17.00	17.20
June	19.00	17.00	1943		15.00	17.00	17.50
			1942				
July	19.00	17.00	price		16.00	17.00	17.50
Aug.	18.00	17.00	fixed		16.00	17.00	17.50
Sept.	18.00	17.00	at		16.00	17.00	17.69
Oct.	18.00	15.00	15.00		16.70	17.00	19.00
Nov.	17.50	15.00			17.00	17.00	19.00
Dec.	17.50	15.00			17.00	17.00	19.00
Average	18.71	16.50			15.66	17.00	17.70

U. S. BAUXITE IMPORTS

Long Tons, By Country of Origin

	Total	Surinam	British Guiana	Indonesia
1943	1,547,854	....	42,253	....
1944	560,461	518,208	42,253	....
1945	739,581	713,854	25,727	....
1946	852,005	802,288	40,595	....
1947	1,821,580	1,660,823	108,562	52,195
1948	2,448,915	2,051,265	114,764	302,079
1949	2,688,164	2,013,187	99,821	575,137
1950:				
Jan.	232,813	190,291	7,220	35,302
Feb.	142,324	110,475	8,805	23,044
Mar.	253,181	185,207	2,750	55,895
Apr.	248,354	145,194	13,139	85,674
May	225,388	137,064	7,470	80,854
June	167,154	138,061	10,893	18,200
July	182,954	148,891	11,801	22,262

Source: U. S. Department of Commerce

ALUMINUM EXTRUSIONS

Pounds Shipped, With Tubes, Blooms

	1948	1949	1950
Jan.	12,565,000	14,237,000	15,686,000
Feb.	14,323,000	13,828,000	15,513,000
March	16,032,000	15,745,000	19,523,000
April	16,110,000	13,692,000	18,494,000
May	15,566,000	12,055,000	20,255,000
June	16,850,000	11,246,000	22,081,000
July	14,833,000	9,525,000	20,176,000
Aug.	14,552,000	9,805,000	25,244,000
Sept.	11,224,000	10,516,000	25,600,000
Oct.	12,159,000	11,846,000	26,077,000
Nov.	13,682,000	13,056,000	....
Dec.	14,068,000	14,444,000	....
Total	171,964,000	149,995,000	*208,649,000

* Ten months.   Source: Bureau of Census

WORLD PRODUCTION OF COPPER FROM ORES

Short Tons, Not Including Copper Derived From Scrap. Russia Not Included.

Country	1941	1942	1943	1944	1945	1946	1947	1948	1949
United States	983,103	1,097,175	1,114,149	1,006,653	805,174	603,868	874,105	855,198	761,904
Mexico	56,911	56,907	50,642	47,589	67,784	64,693	72,675	63,928	70,662
Canada	321,658	301,831	287,595	273,535	237,457	183,968	225,861	240,732*	259,512
Cuba	8,212	11,023	8,075	6,256	9,053	12,340	14,600	16,800	15,990
Newfoundland	5,500	6,500	6,200	5,500	5,200	4,900	4,250	4,550	3,479
Bolivia	8,018	7,028	6,626	6,800	6,721	6,754	6,879	7,293	5,593
Chile	516,633	533,902	548,013	549,517	518,304	397,972	470,318	490,467	409,055
Peru	40,589	38,935	36,825	35,703	35,181	27,108	24,793	19,917	30,819
Ecuador	3,250	3,000	3,000	4,065	4,216	2,886	158	450	713
Total America	1,943,874	2,056,301	2,061,125	1,935,618	1,689,090	1,304,489	1,693,639	1,699,335*	1,557,727
Austria	816	1,082	1,505	1,653	353	138	285	1,082	1,429
Finland	18,213	17,221	17,073	17,462	16,510	19,400	19,200	25,713	26,811
Germany	25,059	25,240	25,766	23,148	....	(e)516	(e)263	(e)401	962
Italy	4,000	4,500	(b)2,800	400	2,400	....		99	33
Norway	19,828	17,054	17,900	15,900	5,735	13,500	16,212	16,658*	17,637
Spain	10,200	11,800	12,200	12,100	9,100	13,400	11,900	6,066	7,388
Sweden	14,760	19,903	19,656	17,770	16,453	16,934	14,489	16,353*	17,938
Yugoslavia	25,400	35,300	29,800	25,000					
Total Europe	118,276	132,100	126,700	113,433	50,551(a)	83,488(a)	82,349(a)	86,372(a)*	92,198(a)
Formosa	6,196	5,585	6,636	4,393					
Japan	84,921	91,561	104,419	95,728	30,847	18,889	24,127	28,353	36,090
India (c)	6,741	6,579	6,832	6,418	6,720	7,068	6,643	6,567	7,157
Turkey	11,585	9,103	10,725	12,076	10,80^	10,979	11,111	12,102	12,010
Philippines	7,800	(d)	(d)	(d)	(d)			2,300	7,712
Cyprus			5,706	1,695	1,100	2,950	17,400	21,500	30,912
Total Asia	117,243	112,828	134,318	120,310	49,467(a)	39,896(a)	59,281(a)	70,822(a)	93,881(a)
Belgian Congo	178,757	182,916	172,896	182,413	176,600	158,604	166,271	171,424*	155,864
Rhodesia	258,417	279,859	276,955	246,498	215,572	204,922	218,222	234,647	289,946
Southwest Africa							4,575	6,616	9,514
Union of South Africa	22,200	28,200	25,100	25,935	27,211	30,000	32,400	32,300	33,060
Total Africa	459,374	490,975	474,951	454,846	419,383	393,526	421,468	444,987*	488,384
Australia	23,000	22,500	27,300	31,500	27,500	19,886	14,698	13,852	12,052
Total World, as Reported	2,661,767	2,814,704	2,824,394	2,655,707	2,227,991a	1,841,275a	2,271,435a	2315368a*	2,244,242a

(a) Total based on incomplete returns. (b) January-June. (c) Including Burma through 1940. (d) Production of ores and concentrates (copper content) in Philippines during 1942-45 has been reported as about 14,500 short tons. (e) The production of Germany beginning 1946 is that of the British zone. Production in the Russian zone, in which are situated the Mansfeld mines, has been given as 19,600 short tons in 1946, and 9,500 tons in January-June, 1947.

In this table, which surveys mine production, the credits to the several countries are for copper smelted domestically plus copper in ores smelted from them smelted in other countries; or copper content of ores and concentrates produced in countries which do no smelting.

Source: American Bureau of Metal Statistics

2 METAL FACTS SECTION

Copper Production, Recovery, Consumption, Imports and Exports; Copper Scrap and Electrolytic Copper Prices.

DOMESTIC COPPER MINE PRODUCTION, MONTHLY

Short Tons, Based On Smelter Receipts of 1944; Actual Mine Output Since 1944

Month	1943	1944	1945	1946	1947	1948	1949	1950
Jan.	91,729	88,820	70,088	55,381	70,056	73,150	50,002	71,464
Feb.	85,367	87,622	63,962	41,934	68,416	68,943	56,410	67,296
Mar.	93,479	94,446	70,004	42,018	74,651	74,092	77,912	78,083
Apr.	91,420	88,106	67,493	32,295	72,418	74,344	72,843	73,351
May	94,919	88,055	72,018	33,526	75,164	74,779	67,412	74,522
June	89,826	83,480	67,910	33,171	70,150	75,596	61,254	74,860
July	88,352	76,172	62,100	53,948	73,310	71,340	56,615	72,525
Aug.	87,510	77,390	61,817	57,163	72,005	73,546	55,898	80,199
Sept.	90,398	74,846	59,854	62,667	70,770	69,630	58,111	76,645
Oct.	94,821	73,045	61,555	65,625	66,145	68,256	60,515	......
Nov.	99,942	68,909	58,664	62,336	63,278	51,318	66,044	......
Dec.	92,055	71,658	57,429	68,673	71,200	50,668	69,734	......
Total	1,090,818	972,549	772,894	608,737	847,563	825,666	752,750	666,945*

* First 9 Months.

Source: U. S. Bureau of Mines

CRUDE COPPER PRODUCTION

Short Tons, From Domestic Ores**

Year	Tons	Year	Tons
1845 to 1880	10,111*	1939	712,675
1881 to 1900	149,738*	1940	909,084
1901 to 1910	428,172*	1941	966,072
1911 to 1920	716,056*	1942	1,087,991
1921 to 1930	742,340*	1943	1,092,939
1931	521,356	1944	1,003,379
1932	272,005	1945	782,726
1933	225,000	1946	599,656
1934	244,227	1947	862,872
1935	381,294	1948	842,447
1936	611,410	1949	772,986
1937	834,661	1950†	689,137
1938	562,328		

* Yearly averages. † Nine Months.
** Smelter Output.

Source: Bureau of Mines

SECONDARY COPPER RECOVERY

Net Tons, Showing Form of Recovery

Form of Recovery	1944	1945	1946
As unalloyed copper:			
At primary plants	86,398	96,662	105,572
At other plants	15,737	16,194	31,337
	102,135	112,856	136,909
In brass and bronze	814,898	860,287	630,588
In alloy iron and steel	2,454	2,133	1,932
In aluminum alloys	17,054	12,055	14,434
In other alloys	1,044	519	491
In chemical compounds	13,357	18,666	19,192
	848,807	893,660	666,637
	950,942	1,006,516	803,546

Form of Recovery	1947	1948	1949
As unalloyed copper:			
At primary plants	269,085	245,376	212,392
At other plants	34,007	38,650	37,697
	303,092	284,026	250,089
In brass and bronze	619,576	653,281	436,457
In alloy iron and steel	2,830	2,911	1,552
In aluminum alloys	16,962	14,678	9,951
In other alloys	443	280	254
In chemical compounds	18,838	17,612	14,840
	658,649	688,762	463,054
	961,741	972,788	713,143

Source: Bureau of Mines

For data on government controls, defense plant loans and accelerated amortization, see "You and Government Controls," beginning on p. 365.

REFINED COPPER CONSUMPTION

Primary and Secondary, Short Tons

	1948	1949
Cathodes	85,725	66,119
Wire bars	806,073	668,591
Ingots and ingot bars	140,875	89,777
Cakes and slabs	210,170	163,359
Billets	170,413	109,786
Other	7,328	165
	1,420,584	1,097,797

Source: U. S. Bureau of Mines

No. 1 HEAVY COPPER SCRAP

Cents Per Pound, f.o.b. New York*

	1947	1948	1949	1950
Jan.	15.50	16.85	18.75	13.97
Feb.	15.88	16.44	18.13	14.06
March	16.50	16.25	16.66	13.88
April	17.00	16.60	14.13	14.19
May	16.30	16.75	11.97	15.13
June	14.50	16.75	10.60	16.98
July	14.65	17.00	11.88	16.94
Aug.	15.88	17.88	12.31	18.66
Sept.	15.75	17.65	12.93	20.38
Oct.	15.75	17.72	12.25	22.25
Nov.	15.88	18.47	12.44	24.75
Dec.	16.50	19.25	13.26	19.75†
Average	15.84	17.30	13.78	17.58†

* Dealers Buying Price.
† Estimate.

U. S. COPPER IMPORTS

Net Tons, Except Manufactures

Year	Tons	Year	Tons
1929	267,156	1940	491,342
1930	408,577	1941	735,545
1931	292,946	1942	757,974
1932	195,996	1943	716,596
1933	148,717	1944	785,211
1934	213,286	1945	853,196
1935	257,182	1946	393,275
1936	190,339	1947	413,890
1937	279,875	1948	507,251
1938	252,164	1949	552,704
1939	336,297	1950	512,515*

Imports for consumption plus entries under bond.
* First 9 Months.

Source: Bureau of Mines, Dept. of Commerce, and American Bureau of Metal Statistics

U. S. REFINED COPPER EXPORTS

Net Tons, With Primary Manufactures

Year	Tons	Year	Tons
1929	496,448	1940	427,650
1930	376,557	1941	158,893
1931	278,787	1942	212,309
1932	147,678	1943	294,459
1933	151,913	1944	237,515
1934	296,359	1945	132,555
1935	295,198	1946	97,475
1936	259,032	1947	196,999
1937	345,584	1948	206,567
1938	421,012	1949	195,990
1939	427,517	1950	144,551*

* First 9 Months.

Source: Bureau of Mines, Dept. of Commerce, and American Bureau of Metal Statistics

ELECTROLYTIC COPPER

Cents Per Pound, Conn. Valley

	1929	1934	1936	1938	1939	1940
Jan.	16.84	8.18	9.25	10.42	11.25	12.22
Feb.	18.05	8.00	9.25	10.00	11.25	11.40
March	21.38	8.00	9.25	10.00	11.25	11.38
April	19.93	8.39	9.40	10.00	10.47	11.33
May	18.00	8.50	9.50	9.60	10.06	11.32
June	18.00	8.82	9.50	9.00	10.00	11.37
July	18.00	9.00	9.60	9.81	10.22	10.81
Aug.	18.00	9.00	9.75	10.12	10.49	10.95
Sept.	18.03	9.00	9.75	10.25	11.93	11.54
Oct.	18.00	9.00	9.85	10.98	12.44	12.00
Nov.	18.00	9.00	10.43	11.25	12.50	12.00
Dec.	18.00	9.00	11.00	11.25	12.50	12.00
Average	18.35	8.66	9.71	10.22	11.20	11.53

		1946	1947	1948	1949	1950
Jan.		12.00	19.56	21.50	23.50	18.50
Feb.		12.00	19.75	21.50	23.50	18.50
March	1945	12.00	21.50	21.50	23.49	18.50
April	1944	12.00	21.50	21.50	21.72	18.94
May	1943	12.00	22.63	21.50	18.05	19.92
June	1942	14.28	21.63	21.50	16.66	22.27
	1941					
July	price	14.375	21.50	21.50	17.33	22.50
Aug.	fixed	14.375	21.50	23.43	17.63	22.54
Sept.	at	14.375	21.50	23.50	17.63	23.25
Oct.	12.00	14.375	21.50	23.50	17.63	24.50
Nov.		17.19	21.50	23.50	18.42	24.50
Dec.		19.50	21.50	23.50	18.50	24.50*
Average		14.04	21.30	22.33	19.51	21.54*

* Estimate.

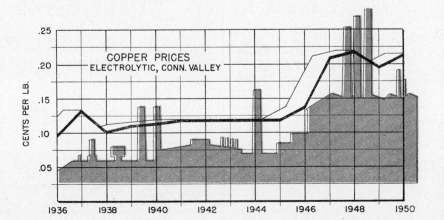

COPPER PRICES
ELECTROLYTIC, CONN. VALLEY

BRASS SCRAP, No. 1 COMP.

Cents Per Pound, f.o.b. New York*

	1947	1948	1949	1950
Jan.	14.45	12.45	14.19	11.13
Feb.	14.22	12.44	13.06	11.13
March	14.37	13.33	11.83	11.13
April	14.43	12.85	9.19	11.50
May	13.20	12.88	8.56	12.44
June	11.50	12.75	8.13	13.95
July	10.75	13.75	8.69	14.13
Aug.	10.75	14.28	8.88	15.50
Sept.	10.75	13.57	9.23	17.25
Oct.	10.85	14.41	9.13	17.75
Nov.	11.38	15.19	11.06	18.88
Dec.	12.00	14.95	10.73	16.38†
Average	12.39	13.57	10.22	14.26†

* Dealers' Buying Price.
† Estimate.

BRONZE INGOTS, 88-10-2

No. 245, Cents Per Pound, Cars*

	1947	1948	1949	1950
Jan.	21.75	23.25	24.13	19.63
Feb.	21.75	22.13	23.26	19.63
March	23.06	21.42	21.61	19.63
April	23.69	21.95	20.26	20.00
May	22.55	22.25	17.82	20.72
June	21.38	23.00	16.71	23.70
July	20.55	23.25	16.51	24.38
Aug.	21.25	24.38	16.76	27.55
Sept.	20.50	24.80	17.41	29.88
Oct.	19.75	24.38	17.63	32.50
Nov.	19.75	25.57	18.81	36.20
Dec.	21.88	25.16	18.35	37.00†
Average	21.49	23.46	19.11	25.90†

* Delivered.
† Estimate.

BRASS INGOTS, 85-5-5-5

No. 115, Cents Per Pound, Cars*

	1947	1948	1949	1950
Jan.	20.50	19.60	20.38	17.50
Feb.	20.50	19.31	19.01	17.50
March	21.25	18.95	17.96	17.50
April	21.50	19.22	16.94	17.81
May	20.30	19.19	15.07	18.41
June	19.13	19.12	13.96	21.33
July	18.20	19.75	13.76	22.11
Aug.	19.00	21.06	14.13	23.80
Sept.	18.38	21.30	14.41	25.50
Oct.	17.75	20.94	15.13	26.63
Nov.	17.75	21.65	16.81	28.60
Dec.	18.31	21.21	16.85	29.00†
Average	19.38	20.11	16.24	21.14†

* Delivered.
† Estimate.

INGOT BRASS AND BRONZE

Short Tons of Shipments, Monthly*

	1947	1948	1949	1950
Jan.	27,841	26,998	19,456	18,874
Feb.	24,686	22,487	15,026	18,487
Mar.	27,477	24,282	14,550	22,494
Apr.	24,577	25,177	10,695	22,118
May	19,525	23,718	11,114	23,643
June	16,929	24,401	9,696	25,093
July	16,728	20,456	10,220	21,609
Aug.	18,589	24,098	14,194	29,689
Sept.	19,025	23,641	16,208	28,811
Oct.	22,806	21,559	18,036	......
Nov.	21,666	21,731	18,488	......
Dec.	23,862	20,954	17,960	......
	263,711	279,500	175,643	......

* Delivered.
Source: Ingot Brass & Bronze Institute.

WORLD PRODUCTION OF ANTIMONY, SINCE 1942

Metric Tons, Estimated Production of Other Nations is Included in Total

Country	1942	1943	1944	1945	1946	1947	1948	49
Canada	1,269	465	809	696	286	480	124	64
Mexico[2]	10,759	12,585	10,056	8,053	6,046	6,371	6,790	5,293
United States	2,487	4,638	3,952	1,611	2,091	4,437	5,416	1,365
Bolivia (exports)	16,231	16,536	6,852	5,093	6,407	9,989	11,280	9,453
Peru	1,457	2,472	932	2,041	969	1,140	1,770	750
Austria	391	571	658	132	15	82	247	349 [10]
Czechoslovakia	[3] 3,130	(4)	(4)	1,115	2,156	1,434	1,593	(4)
France	128	153	116	153	202	200	(4)	(4)
Hungary[3]	2,200	1,500	[5] 61,160	(6)	......	......	(4)	(4)
Italy	667	522	403	348	330	450	430	330
Spain	210	176	128	108	96	84	[7] 270	150
Burma[3]	843	843	843	(4)	(4)	66	(4)	(4)
China	[8] 3,510	[8] 505	[8] 203	......	426	1,909	3,251	(4)
Japan	350	600	450	210	49	100	124	158
Turkey (Asia Minor)	40	8	58	33	36	103	520	420
Algeria	304	902	170	423	......	110	817	1,288
Morocco:								
French	322	409	166	353	260	390	411	600
Spanish	144	153	72	52	103	128	(9)	150
Southern Rhodesia	169	164	116	29	15	38	10	34
Union of South Africa	990	1,560	2,570	2,250	2,330	3,020	3,700	4,100
Australia	1,042	532	454	172	460	162	39	40 [11]
Total (except U. S. S. R.)	51,400	53,200	36,400	26,900	25,400	34,800	41,300	......

[1] Approximate recoverable metal content of ore produced, exclusive of antimonial lead ores; 92 pct of reported gross content is used as basis for calculations in nearly every instance. U. S. S. R. and Yugoslavia produce antimony but data on production are not available; an estimate for Yugoslavia is included in the total. Minor producing nations include Honduras, Argentina, Portugal, Indochina, Iran, Pakistan, Siam and New Zealand.
[2] Includes antimony content of antimonial lead.
[3] Estimate.
[4] Data not available; estimate included in total.
[5] January to June inclusive.
[6] Data represent Trianon Hungary after October 1944.
[7] Includes Spanish Morocco.
[8] Data represent area designated as Free China during the period of Japanese occupation.
[9] Included under Spain.
[10] Excludes Soviet Zone, data not available.
[11] Excluding New South Wales, data not available.

Source: U. S. Bureau of Mines

IMPORTS OF ANTIMONY INTO UNITED STATES

Short Tons, Imports of Antimony for Consumption Plus Entries in Bond

	1949 Ore Content	1949 Metal	1948 Ore Content	1948 Metal	1947 Ore Content	1947 Metal	1946 Ore Content	1946 Metal	1945 Ore Content	1945 Metal
Belgium and Luxembourg			210		56					
Bolivia†	3,153	......	3,310		2,435		758		11,348	
Canada	49	11	31	1	145					
Chile†	544		260		348		39		1,564	
China		313		2,986		5,815		1,720		571
French Morocco			95							
Honduras	8		6				8		17	
Italy		44		30						
Japan								873		
Mexico	2,985	767	8,674	54	6,138		5,031		8,303	
Netherlands		11								
Peru†	727		1,062		156		48		1,443	56
Portugal	7		17							
Siam			55	3	12		21			
South Africa									61	
Trieste		5								
Turkey					53					
United Kingdom		78				28				
Yugoslavia		472	22	132						
Total imports	7,473	2,081	13,532	3,416	9,287	5,899	5,905	2,593	22,736	627

† Imports shown from Chile were probably mined in Bolivia or Peru.

Source: U. S. Dept. of Commerce

ANTIMONY PRICES, MONTHLY, 1929 TO 1950

Cents per pound for American metal f.o.b. Laredo, Tex., since Apr. 1, 1942

	1929	1934	1936	1937	1938	1939*	1942*†	1946†	1947	1948	1949	1950
Jan.	9.62	7.23¾	13.22	14.06¼	15.47	14.00	16.50	14.50	28.25	33.00	38.50	30.05
Feb.	9.61	7.15	12.97	14.68¾	15.72	14.00	16.50	14.50	28.25	33.00	38.50	27.75
Mar.	9.52	7.45	13.37½	16.81¼	15.75	14.00	16.50	14.50	30.62½	33.00	38.50	24.50
Apr.	9.59	7.86¼	13.50	17.00	15.62½	14.00	14.50	14.50	33.00	33.00	38.50	24.50
May	9.12½	8.35½	13.50	15.81¼	14.75	14.00	14.50	14.50	33.00	33.00	38.50	24.50
June	8.90	7.98¾	13.25	14.81¼	13.90	14.00	14.50	14.50	33.00	35.00	38.50	24.50
July	8.56	7.93¾	13.00	14.72½	14.00	14.00	14.50	14.50	33.00	35.00	38.50	24.50
Aug.	8.83¾	8.40	12.62½	15.34	14.00	14.00	14.50	14.50	33.00	35.00	38.50	24.50
Sept.	8.81	8.31⅞	12.50	17.85	14.00	14.00	14.50	14.50	33.00	35.00	38.50	31.13
Oct.	8.58	9.21⅞	12.50	18.31¼	14.00	14.00	14.50	14.50	33.00	36.75	33.62	32.00
Nov.	8.62½	11.12½	12.50	16.43¾	14.00	16.50	15.50	21.25	33.00	38.50	32.00	32.00
Dec.	8.53	13.75	12.72½	14.60	14.00	16.50	14.50	24.68¾	33.00	38.50	32.00	32.00
Average	9.03	8.73¼	12.97¼	15.87	14.60	14.42	15.00	15.91	32.01	34.90	37.01	27.66

Asiatic antimony, New York, quoted until the end of March, 1942.
* Price unchanged at 16.50¢ during 1940 and 1941
† Price unchanged at 14.50¢ from 1943 through 1945.

U. S. ANTIMONY PRODUCTION
Short Tons, Ore and Concentrates

	Antimony Content	Average % Sb
1932	419	46.6
1933	587	51.8
1934	404	45.0
1935	559	15.5
1936	755	19.5
1937	1,266	29.8
1938	650	23.8
1939	393	12.4
1940	494	44.0
1941	1,214	35.1
1942	2,944	42.2
1943	5,556	33.1
1944	4,735	35.1
1945	1,930	12.9
1946	2,505	17.9
1947	5,316	26.8
1948	6,489	40.0
1949	1,636	31.1

Source: U. S. Bureau of Mines

WORLD PRODUCTION OF NICKEL, SINCE 1941

Metric Tons, Nickel Content of Ore, Minor Producing Nations in Total

Country	1941	1942	1943	1944	1945	1946	1947	1948	1949
Burma	[2] 471							(1)	(1)
Canada	128,029	129,369	130,642	124,555	111,189	87,146	107,616	118,909	116,417
Cuba		(1)	2,430	4,679	10,900	11,241	2,014		
Finland	97	1,630	8,970	313	900	622	(1)	(1)	(1)
Germany	674	577	951	(1)	(1)				
Greece	185	706	495						
Indonesia	[3] 1,200	[3] 1,200	[3] 1,200	(1)	(1)				
Japan	2,311	1,252	1,613	1,720	650				
New Caledonia	10,395	9,415	7,374	8,115	4,328	2,779	3,345	4,882	3,371
Norway	907	911	577	529	516	55		(1)	(1)
Sweden	101	377	702	698	390			(1)	(1)
South Africa	581	449	343	481	499	497	529	458	618
U. S. S. R.[3]	13,600	(1)	11,160	(1)	13,400	20,000	25,000	25,000	25,000
United States[4]	599	555	582	896	1,048	319	586	801	717
Total (estimate)	162,000	158,000	167,000	157,000	145,000	123,000	139,000	150,000	148,000

[1] Data not available; estimate included in total.
[2] Data cover 9 months ended Mar. 31, 1942.
[3] Estimate.
[4] Byproduct in electrolytic refining of copper. In 1941 includes also production from ore and as byproduct of talc; in 1944 and 1945 includes also production from ore.
Source: U. S. Bureau of Mines

U. S. NICKEL PRODUCTION
Short Tons, Primary and Secondary

	Primary	Secondary Recovery
1930	308	2,900
1931	373	2,070
1932	195	1,450
1933	126	1,650
1934	157	1,850
1935	160	1,950
1936	107	1,965
1937	219	2,400
1938	416	2,300
1939	394	2,920
1940	554	4,152
1941	660	5,315
1942	612	4,142
1943	642	6,917
1944	988	4,321
1945	1,155	6,483
1946	352	8,248
1947	646	9,541
1948	883	8,850
1949	790	5,680

Source: U. S. Bureau of Mines

U. S. NICKEL CONSUMPTION
Short Tons, Excludes Scrap Recovery

	1949	1948	1947	1946
Stainless steel	11,909	16,244	15,350	17,993
Alloy steel	13,474	21,782	17,379	15,597
Cast iron	3,396	4,216	3,953	2,987
Nonferrous alloys*	18,971	28,03	27,378	25,910
High temperature and resistance alloys	4,054	6,168	5,130	6,798
Anodes	13,810	14,213	8,988	8,530
Plating salts	724	609	664	771
Catalysts	497	595	439	272
Ceramics	149	185	193	194
Other	1,340	1,457	1,347	1,053
Total	68,326	93,558	80,757	80,105

* Includes copper-nickel alloys, nickel silver, brass, bronze, beryllium, magnesium and aluminum alloys; and Monel, Inconel and malleable nickel.
Source: U. S. Bureau of Mines

NICKEL IMPORTED INTO THE UNITED STATES

Short Tons, Nickel Imported for Consumption, Since 1926

	Ore and Matte	Pigs, Ingots, Shot, Bars, Rods, Tubes, etc.	Oxide	Nickel Silver	Gross Weight	Nickel Content*
1926		7,318	14,704	743	3	22,768	19,300
1927		5,372	14,610	507	8	20,497	17,900
1928		9,295	24,559	872	13	34,738	30,300
1929		14,491	32,355	1,638	7	48,486	41,500
1930		10,297	19,162	677	8	30,143	25,300
1931		5,815	11,817	152	5	17,789	15,100
1932		2,959	7,512	344	1	10,816	9,400
1933		9,610	15,811	1,010		26,430	21,900
1934		5,923	22,900	475		29,298	21,000
1935		7,962	29,429	456		37,848	34,200
1936		11,597	40,269	1,275		53,141	47,600
1937		12,543	40,615	1,022		54,180	47,884
1938		7,290	21,978	278		29,546	26,200
1939		14,217	49,763	816		64,795	58,200
1940		17,445	70,530	4,493		92,468	83,760
1941		39,946	74,993	9,189	1	124,130	106,182
1942		40,189	80,788	11,977		132,954	114,275
1943		43,486	92,579	5,184		141,249	122,492
1944		36,414	93,053	5,465		134,932	118,293
1945		25,039	78,402	19,087		122,528	107,433
1946		19,048	71,163	14,521	5	104,734	92,800
1947		14,636	58,687	15,074	11	88,408	80,718
1948		13,854	71,567	21,514	4	106,939	96,880
1949		11,128	73,769	12,242		97,139	879,107

* Estimate by Bureau of Mines.
Source: U. S. Bureau of Mines

ELECTROLYTIC NICKEL
Cents Per Pound, New York, Duty Paid

1929 to Nov. 24, 1946	35.00
Nov. 25, 1946 to Dec. 31, 1947	37.67
Jan. 1, 1948 to July 21, 1948	36.56
July 22, 1948 to Dec. 31, 1948	36.56
Jan. 1, 1949 to Aug. 31, 1949	42.93
Sept. 1, 1949 to May 31, 1950	42.97
June 1, 1950 to Dec. 31, 1950	51.22
Dec. 13, 1950 to Dec. 31, 1950	53.55

Prices of Tin, Lead and Cobalt; Production and Consumption of Cobalt.

METAL FACTS
SECTION 2

STRAITS TIN, PROMPT PRICE

Cents Per Pound, at New York

	1929	1936	1938	1939	1940	1941
Jan.	49.21	47.23	41.54	46.39	46.73	50.16
Feb.	49.39	47.94	41.23	45.64	45.85	51.41
March	48.85	48.00	41.16	46.17	47.07	52.07
April	45.93	46.97	38.41	47.16	46.96	52.03
May	43.88	46.31	36.83	49.00	51.51	52.18
June	44.20	42.24	40.36	48.81	54.64	52.68
July	46.29	42.96	43.38	48.53	51.61	53.41
Aug.	46.60	42.57	43.26	48.80	51.21	52.45
Sept.	45.32	44.77	43.40	Nom.	50.30	52.00
Oct.	42.25	44.95	45.25	55.68	51.50	52.00
Nov.	40.18	51.30	46.29	52.65	50.57	52.00
Dec.	39.87	51.85	46.21	51.40	50.11	52.00
Average	45.16	46.42	42.28	49.11	49.84	52.03

		1946	1947	1948	1949	1950
Jan.		52.00	70.00	94.00	$1.03	75.75
Feb.		52.00	70.00	94.00	$1.03	74.50
March		52.00	70.00	94.00	$1.03	75.62
April	1945	52.00	80.00	94.00	$1.03	76.38
May	1944	52.00	80.00	94.00	$1.03	77.50
June	1943	52.00	80.00	$1.03	$1.03	77.70
	1942					
July	price	52.00	80.00	$1.03	$1.03	89.88
Aug.	fixed	52.00	80.00	$1.03	$1.03	$1.02
Sept.	at	52.00	80.00	$1.03	$1.02	$1.01
Oct.	52.00	52.00	80.00	$1.03	95.49	$1.13
Nov.		61.00	80.00	$1.03	90.11	$1.38
Dec.		70.00	85.38	$1.03	79.06	$1.45*
Average		54.00	77.95	99.25	99.22	95.53*

* Estimate.

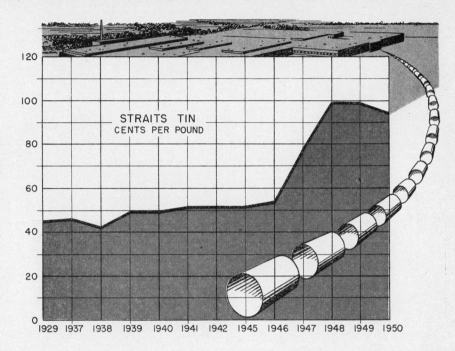

STRAITS TIN
CENTS PER POUND

1929 1937 1938 1939 1940 1941 1942 1945 1946 1947 1948 1949 1950

WORLD PRODUCTION OF COBALT, SINCE 1940

Metric Tons of Cobalt Contained in Mine Production of Ores

Country[1]	1940	1941	1942	1943	1944	1945	1946	1947	1948	1949
Australia	12	13	14	15	9	10	11	12	15	(2)
Belgian Congo	2,301	2,256	1,656	2,061	1,877	2,800	2,150	3,563	4,322	4,350
Bolivia (Exports)	2	2	(2)	(3)	....	....	....	....	....	(2)
Burma	218	73	(2)	(2)	(2)	(2)	(2)	(2)	(2)	....
Canada[1]	360	119	38	80	16	49	34	280	701	278
Chile	(2)	2	(2)	3	5	1	(2)	(2)	(2)	(2)
Finland	(2)	(2)	98	79	86	84	101	50	(2)	(2)
Italy	89	81	(2)	(2)	(2)	(2)	(2)	(2)	(2)	(2)
Japan	....	(2)	1	3	15	11	7	6	(2)	(2)
Morocco, French	330	65	(2)	216	243	100	200	370	278	209
Northern Rhodesia[4]	1,223	650	914	943	978	874	552	420	367	402
Sweden	....	....	....	....	....	9	....	....	....	(2)
United States (Shipments)	58	237	300	346	253	581	230	307	263	306
Total (Estimate)	5,000	4,000	3,500	4,200	3,900	4,700	3,500	5,200	6,200	5,900

In addition to countries listed, Brazil, China, Germany, and Spain produce cobalt, but production data are not available. Estimate included in total.
[1] Excludes cobalt recovered by Mond Nickel Co. at Clydach, Wales, from nickel copper ores of Sudbury, Ont. district.
[2] Data not available; estimate included in total.
[3] Less than 1 ton.
[4] Year ended June 30 of year stated.

Source: Bureau of Mines

COBALT, 97 TO 99 PCT.

Per Pound, 550 lb Lots Since 1947

1940 to June 30, 1947[1]	$1.50
July 1, 1947 to Mar. 31, 1949	1.65
Apr. 1, 1949 to Dec. 31, 1950	1.80

[1] 100 lb lots.

A list of trade associations and technical societies in nonferrous and other fields begins on p. 150.

CONSUMPTION OF COBALT IN UNITED STATES

Pounds of Cobalt Contained, Broken Down According to Use

	1946	1947	1948	1949
Metallic:				
High-Speed Steel	224,049	223,148	289,391	283,496
Magnet Steel	} 1,463,539	121,223	165,698	42,965
Permanent Magnet Alloys		894,924	1,186,673	1,194,920
Other Steel	201,949	386,354	503,082	472,193
Cast Cobalt-Chromium-Tungsten-Type Alloys	526,504	642,452	826,329	928,528
Alloy Hard-Facing Rods and Materials	53,874	71,545	116,313	82,965
Cemented Carbides	[1]45,100	82,734	115,687	118,522
Other	81,988	99,476	115,255	116,344
Total Metallic	2,597,003	2,501,856	3,318,428	3,239,933
Nonmetallic (Exclusive of Salts and Driers):				
Ground-Coat Frit	412,766	607,316	613,745	424,051
Pigments	170,662	207,928	232,725	188,606
Other	39,596	51,439	66,699	84,336
Total Nonmetallic	623,024	866,683	913,169	696,993
Salts and Driers: Lacquers, Varnishes, Paints, Inks, Pigments, Enamels, Glazes, Feed, Electroplating, etc. (Estimate)	885,000	797,000	818,000	765,000
Grand Total	4,105,027	4,165,539	5,049,597	4,701,926

[1] Revised figure

Source: Bureau of Mines

LEAD PRICE, COMMON GRADE

Cents Per Pound, at New York

	1929	1936	1938	1939	1940	1941
Jan.	6.65	4.50	4.87	4.83	5.47	5.50
Feb.	6.85	4.51	4.63	4.80	5.08	5.60
Mar.	7.41	4.60	4.50	4.82	5.19	5.77
Apr.	7.19	4.60	4.50	4.78	5.07	5.85
May	7.00	4.60	4.40	4.75	5.02	5.85
June	7.00	4.60	4.15	4.80	5.00	5.85
July	6.80	4.60	4.88	4.85	5.00	5.85
Aug.	6.75	4.60	4.90	5.04	4.85	5.85
Sept.	6.88	4.60	5.00	5.45	4.93	5.85
Oct.	6.87	4.63	5.10	5.50	5.31	5.85
Nov.	6.29	5.11	5.09	5.50	5.73	5.85
Dec.	6.25	5.55	4.84	5.50	5.50	5.85
Average	6.83	4.71	4.74	5.05	5.18	5.79

		1946	1947	1948	1949	1950
Jan.		6.50	13.00	15.00	21.50	12.00
Feb.		6.50	13.25	15.00	21.50	12.00
Mar.		6.50	15.00	15.00	18.98	10.96
Apr.	1945	6.50	15.00	17.21	15.15	10.63
May	1944	6.50	15.00	17.50	13.72	11.72
June	1943	8.18	15.00	17.50	12.00	11.81
	1942					
July	price	9.18	15.00	17.80	13.56	11.66
Aug.	fixed	8.25	15.00	19.50	14.99	12.93
Sept.	at	8.25	15.00	19.50	15.05	15.80
Oct.	6.50	8.25	15.00	19.50	13.42	16.00
Nov.		10.41	15.00	21.50	12.52	17.00
Dec.		12.20	15.00	21.50	12.00	*17.00
Average		8.10	14.69	18.04	15.37	*13.29

*Estimate

WORLD PRODUCTION OF MAGNESIUM SINCE 1941

Metric Tons, Production or Estimates for Minor Producing Nations in Total

Country	1941	1942	1943	1944	1945	1946	1947	1948	1949
Canada	5	367	3,245	4,799	3,338	145	136	......	[1]
France	1,989	1,334	1,542	703	279	707	800	1,507	[3]700
Germany	24,000	30,000	32,400	33,600	[2]4,225			17	
Italy	1,857	2,379	[3]2,000	[3]3,000	[3]400	[3]1,000	[3]600	1	......
Japan	2,575	2,020	2,777	2,904	1,020				
Korea	263	240	532	1,628	1,014	......	......	1	
Norway[3]	100	2,000	2,000	2,000			[3]500		
Switzerland[3]	700	1,500	1,500	1,000	500	300			
U. S. S. R.[3]	4,000	5,000	5,000	5,000	2,170	3,000	4,000	5,000	5,000
United Kingdom	9,380	14,865	19,096	13,094	[1]6,900	[1]1,700	[1]2,500	3,500	45,100
United States	14,782	44,418	166,544	142,518	29,748	4,823	11,198	9,075	10,521
Total	59,825	104,876	237,760	211,182	49,815	11,675	19,734	19,300	21,500

[1] Includes secondary.
[2] January–February only. Planned production for March, 2,830 tons.
[3] Estimated by Bureau of Mines.

Source: U. S. Bureau of Mines

MAGNESIUM OUTPUT AND USE

With Secondary, Short Tons

	1950
Primary ingot produced	15,750
Primary ingot sold and used by producer:	
For magnesium alloys	12,500
For aluminum alloys and other non-magnesium use	8,000
Total sold and used	20,500
Magnesium cast and wrought products shipped	14,000
Metals required for cast and wrought products	15,500
Secondary magnesium:	
Used in magnesium alloys	3,000
Used in aluminum and non-magnesium industries	3,000
Total secondary used	6,000
Total consumption of primary and secondary	26,500

Source: Estimated by Magnesium Assn.

U. S. MAGNESIUM PRODUCTION SHORT TONS

183,584 / 157,100 / 48,963 / 32,792 / 5,317 / 12,344 / 10,003 / 11,598 / 16,300

1942 1943 1944 1945 1946 1947 1948 1949 1950

SLAB ZINC CONSUMPTION

Short Tons, by Industry and Product

Industry and Product[1]	1948	1949
Galvanizing:[2]		
Sheet and strip	120,360	146,923
Wire and wire rope	49,906	39,231
Tube and pipe	81,874	78,030
Fittings	14,037	11,487
Other	104,792	75,209
Total	370,969	350,880
Brass products:		
Sheet, strip, and plate	51,813	43,157
Rod and wire	32,076	23,651
Tube	15,890	12,816
Castings and billets	4,228	2,620
Copper-base ingots	3,546	2,701
Other copper-base products	1,587	589
Total	109,140	85,534
Zinc-base alloy:		
Die castings	230,995	199,665
Alloy dies and rod	3,171	2,024
Slush and sand castings	462	492
Total	234,628	202,181
Rolled zinc	76,672	55,200
Zinc oxide	15,657	10,292
Other uses:		
Wet batteries	1,368	1,359
Desilverizing lead	2,654	2,448
Light-metal alloys	1,125	1,060
Other[3]	5,522	2,887
Total	10,669	7,754
Total: All uses	[4]817,735	[4]711,841

[1] Based on a canvass of 610 plants.
[2] Includes zinc used in electrogalvanizing, but excludes sherardizing.
[3] Includes zinc used in making zinc dust, bronze powder, alloys, chemicals, castings and miscellaneous uses not elsewhere mentioned.
[4] Includes 3,141 tons of remelt zinc in 1948 and 2,394 tons in 1949.
Source: Bureau of Mines

ZINC IMPORTS INTO U. S.

Short Tons, Imports for Consumption

	Ores (Zn content)	Blocks, Pigs, Slabs	Old Dross, Skimmings
1929	......	226	......
1930	......	281	35
1931	......	274	......
1932	......	310	......
1933	2,133*	1,890	......
1934	14,277*	1,725	......
1935	10,520*	4,444	29
1936	172*	11,660	16
1937	8,812*	37,208	678
1938	4,860	7,230	96
1939	33,503	30,960	203
1940	44,637	10,146	520
1941	154,520	40,288	456
1942	283,167	36,352	3,357
1943	518,646	56,155	5,146
1944	415,004	63,626	5,603
1945	330,397	96,710	7,331
1946	166,885	104,015	4,137
1947	194,822	72,063	5,105
1948	133,814	92,495	10,273
1949	240,881	126,925	3,746
1950†	171,628	107,621	1,036

* Includes entries under bond.
† Eight Months.
Source: Bureau of Mines, Department of Commerce, and American Bureau of Metal Statistics

Is industry headed for a strait-jacket, freedom or a hobble? Read Tom Campbell's proposal for a vice-president in charge of the president, on p. 263.

MAGNESIUM CONSUMPTION

Short Tons, Primary Metal Only

Product	1948	1949
Structural products:		
Castings:		
Sand	1,930	3,088
Die	213	127
Permanent mold	12	44
Sheet	1,122	2,155
Extrusions	2,529	3,364
Forgings	103	200
Total structural	5,909	8,978
Other products:		
Powder	......	......
Aluminum alloys	2,324	1,759
Other alloys	43	39
Scavenger and deoxidizer	418	404
Chemical	407	224
Cathodic protection	367	235
Other[1]	193	308
Total other products	3,752	2,969
Grand Total	9,661	11,947

[1] Included primary metal consumed in making secondary alloy.
Source: Bureau of Mines

U. S. PRODUCTION OF PRIMARY MAGNESIUM

Short Tons, Excludes Crystal Equivalent of Mg Content of Fire Bombs in 1943, 1944

Month	1942	1943	1944	1945	1946	1947	1948	1949	1950
January	2,512	10,300	20,056	3,816	98	1,398	883	988	1,000
February	2,337	10,666	19,537	2,958	48	1,232	830	884	900
March	2,591	13,008	19,571	3,297	10	1,472	887	988	950
April	2,506	13,558	17,986	3,174	......	1,153	801	958	950
May	2,635	15,093	16,217	3,171	......	926	797	987	950
June	2,631	15,077	13,750	3,404	241	848	766	950	1,150
July	3,299	16,584	14,134	4,586	692	905	792	985	1,350
August	3,426	17,160	11,561	4,500	889	886	809	970	1,400
September	4,120	16,199	8,296	2,063	986	912	873	941	1,700
October	5,838	18,011	7,370	1,017	1,000	870	814	969	1,850
November	7,953	18,374	5,301	715	558	870	814	969	1,850
December	9,115	19,554	3,321	101	795	893	932	1,004	1,900
Total	48,963	183,584	157,100	32,792	5,317	12,344	10,003	11,598	15,750

Producers' reports to WPB, Jan. 1942 to Aug. 1945, thereafter to Bureau of Mines and Magnesium Assn.

Magnesium Prices, Use and Recovery; Zinc Exports and Prices; Cadmium Prices and Production. Cadmium Imports and Exports.

METAL FACTS SECTION 2

MAGNESIUM, 99.8 PCT PLUS

Cents Per Pound, at Freeport, Tex.

1929	56.00	1935	30.00	1941	27.00
1930	48.00	1936	30.00	1942	22.50
1931	34.00	1937	30.00		1943
1932	29.00	1938	30.00		through
1933	28.00	1939	27.00		1949
1934	26.00	1940	27.00		20.50

1950

Jan.	20.50	May	20.50	Sept.	22.50
Feb.	20.50	June	21.50	Oct.	24.50
Mar.	20.50	July	21.75	Nov.	24.50
Apr.	20.50	Aug.	22.50	Dec.	24.50

1950 Average 22.02

RECOVERY OF SECONDARY MAGNESIUM IN U. S.

Short Tons, Broken Down by Form of Recovery, Since 1943

Form of Recovery	1943	1944	1945	1946	1947	1948	1949
Magnesium-Alloy Ingot[1] (Gross Weight)	11,009	13,379	7,359	2,506	5,138	4,713	4,249
Magnesium-Alloy Castings (Gross Weight)	327	235	496	1,145	1,377	1,301	681
Magnesium-Alloy Shapes	.....	.....	864	136	85	1	96
In Aluminum Alloys	34	23	274	1,218	1,883	998	294
In Zinc Alloys	1	5	3	4	3	6	4
In Other Alloys	.....	2	10	2	.....	.....	.....
Chemical and Incendiary Uses	33	541	241	106	199	84	83
Cathodic Protection	.....	.....	.....	.....	818	450	555
	11,404	14,185	9,247	5,117	9,503	7,553[2]	5,962

[1] Figures include secondary magnesium incorporated in primary magnesium ingot. Source: U. S. Bureau of Mines

ZINC EXPORTS FROM U. S.

Short Tons, Ore and Manufactures

	Ore, Concentrates, Dross	Slabs, Plates, Blocks	Sheet, Strip etc.	Dust
1929	3,561	14,411	5,265	1,256
1930	1,162	4,633	3,868	1,177
1931	395	643	2,759	1,400
1932	178	6,471	3,010	1,378
1933	809	1,145	3,189	1,569
1934	3,452	5,105	3,462	1,658
1935	461	1,617	4,813	1,613
1936	245	37	4,483	1,793
1937	314	249	5,813	2,145
1938	135	(1)	5,736	2,253
1939	303	4,515	6,708	2,384
1940	448	79,091	7,490	3,044
1941	.....	89,309	5,246	2,901
1942	.....	133,981	4,767	1,772
1943	.....	97,439	3,167	5,859
1944	.....	21,576	4,020	295
1945	.....	7,782	6,235	330
1946	89	37,431	13,846	366
1947	1,404	106,669	10,898	1,646
1948	3,547	65,537	7,344	891
1949*	2,925	58,709	7,456	690
1950*		2,677	.....	.....

* Eight months. (1) Pigs and slabs not shown separately; included with sheets, strip, etc.

Source: Bureau of Mines, Department of Commerce, and American Bureau of Metal Statistics

PRIME WESTERN ZINC PRICE

Cents Per Pound, at New York

	1929	1936	1938	1939	1940	1941
Jan.	6.70	5.22	5.35	4.89	6.03	7.65
Feb.	6.70	5.23	5.17	4.89	5.93	7.65
Mar.	6.80	5.27	4.77	4.89	6.14	7.65
Apr.	7.04	5.27	4.53	4.89	6.14	7.65
May	6.98	5.27	4.43	4.89	6.20	7.65
June	7.00	5.26	4.53	4.89	6.63	7.65
July	7.10	5.16	5.14	4.91	6.64	7.65
Aug.	7.15	5.17	5.14	5.11	6.79	7.65
Sept.	7.15	5.22	5.24	6.51	7.33	7.65
Oct.	7.09	5.22	5.40	6.89	7.64	8.36
Nov.	6.63	5.35	5.12	6.89	7.64	8.65
Dec.	6.09	5.64	4.89	6.46	7.65	8.65
Average	**6.87**	**5.27**	**4.98**	**5.51**	**6.73**	**7.88**

		1946	1947	1948	1949	1950
Jan.		8.65	11.005	11.69	18.18	9.48
Feb.		8.65	11.005	12.61	18.20	10.47
Mar.		8.65	11.005	12.61	17.76	10.66
Apr.	1945	8.65	11.005	12.61	14.76	11.41
May	1944	8.65	11.005	12.64	12.58	12.71
June	1943	8.65	11.005	12.65	10.27	15.49
July	1942 price	8.69	11.005	13.09	10.06	15.72
Aug.	fixed	8.69	11.005	15.65	10.70	15.72
Sept.	at	8.69	11.005	15.65	10.77	17.82
Oct.	8.85	9.28	11.03	15.74	10.04	18.22
Nov.		10.88	11.06	17.27	10.46	18.22
Dec.		10.94	11.06	18.15	10.47	18.22
Average		**9.09**	**11.02**	**14.20**	**12.85**	**14.51**

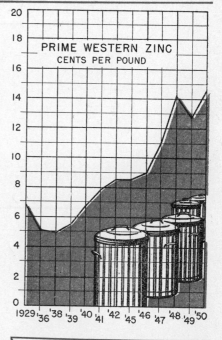

PRIME WESTERN ZINC
CENTS PER POUND

CADMIUM PRICES, STICKS, BARS

Dollars Per Pound, 1 to 5-Ton Lots

June 3, 1943 to July 17, 1946	$0.90
July 18, 1946 to Nov. 20, 1946	1.25
Nov. 21, 1946 to Dec. 4, 1946	1.37½
Dec. 5, 1946 to Feb. 19, 1947	1.50
Feb. 20, 1947 to Aug. 11, 1948	1.75
Aug. 12, 1948 to Nov. 17, 1948	1.90
Nov. 18, 1948 to June 14, 1950	2.00
June 15, 1950 to Sept. 10, 1950	2.15
Sept. 11, 1950 to Nov. 30, 1950	2.40
Dec. 1, 1950 to Dec. 31, 1950	2.55

U. S. CADMIUM EXPORTS

Gross Weight in Pounds, 1947-1949

Kind	1947	1948	1949
Dross, flue dust, residues, scrap	18,251	92,847	500
Metal	303,401	955,701	566,135
Alloys		1,506	3,000
Total	321,652	1,050,054	569,635

See Section 5 for data on various nonferrous castings and prices and production of nonferrous powders. . . . It also contains an analysis of jet engine alloys.

U. S. CADMIUM PRODUCTION

Short Tons of Contained Cadmium

	Metallic Cadmium	Compounds	Secondary Recovery
1932	400	130	...
1933	1,138	201	...
1934	1,389	283	...
1935	1,739	254	...
1936	1,817	313	...
1937	2,133	414	...
1938	2,039	216	...
1939	2,206	340	...
1940	2,961	423	114
1941	3,469	148	190
1942	3,662	24	158
1943	4,198	35	31
1944	4,227	163	53
1945	3,966	226	36
1946	3,100	135	178
1947	4,004	250	52
1948	3,791	96	61
1949	4,012	175	87

Source: U. S. Bureau of Mines

CADMIUM IMPORTED INTO THE UNITED STATES

Metal in Pounds, Flue Dust and Total 000 Omitted, Imports for Consumption

Metallic Cadmium	1949	1948	1947	1946	1945	1944	1943	1942
Australia	7,210	.....						
Belgian Congo				6,700	25,798	53,082	40,355	53,298
Belgium and Luxembourg	48,503		2,000	2,240		.....	.....	.....
Canada	68,140	6,300	14,612	3,568	672	.....		
Italy						8,656		
Japan	31,640							
Peru	1,711	3,509	3,658	4,907	2,254	4,889	8,536	
Switzerland	.....	.....	2	.....				
United Kingdom	.....	.....	20					
Total			20,292	17,415	28,724	66,627	48,891	53,298
Flue Dust								
Australia		621	.....					
Brazil	2,906							
Mexico	1,786,761	1,827,518	2,356	1,609	2,193	1,689	1,643	(1)
Netherlands			44	.....	.....	.....		(1)
Total Metallic Cadmium and Flue Dust			2,376	1,670	2,221	1,756	1,692	(1)

[1] Data not published. Source: U. S. Dept. of Commerce

2 METAL FACTS SECTION

Production of Molybdenum, Vanadium, and Mercury; Recovery of Secondary Lead; Employment, Hours and Earnings in Nonferrous Metal Industry.

WORLD PRODUCTION OF MOLYBDENUM, FROM 1941

Metric Tons of Ores and Concentrates, Molybdenum From Other Nations in Total[1]

Country[1]	1941	1942	1943	1944	1945	1946	1947	1948	1949
Canada	47	43	178	509	228	184	207	79	....
Chile	229	580	680	1,051	841	560	402	532	558
China: Manchuria[2]	75	384	516	516	30	......	......	......	......
Finland	148	126	108	110	92	99	......	......	......
Japan	41	56	87	189	108	52	18	1	......
Korea, South	122	217	291	394	54	......	5	2	11
Mexico	522	855	1,138	717	468	818	136	......	......
Norway	229	368	227	248	76	10	103	79	70
Peru	146	154	85	62	29	4	3	3	2
United States	18,309	25,829	27,972	17,545	13,972	8,264	12,268	12,114	10,219
Total	20,300	29,000	31,400	21,400	15,900	10,800	14,000	13,600	11,500

[1] Molybdenum is also produced in Greece, Rumania, Turkey, U. S. S. R., and Yugoslavia, but production data are not available. [2] Exports to Japan proper.

Source: U. S. Bureau of Mines

U. S. MOLYBDENUM OUTPUT

Short Tons of Contained Molybdenum

1926	697	1938	16,648
1927	1,150	1939	15,162
1928	1,714	1940	17,157
1929	2,011	1941	20,182
1930	1,862	1942	28,471
1931	1,567	1943	30,834
1932	1,216	1944	19,340
1933	2,841	1945	15,401
1934	4,681	1946	9,109
1935	5,756	1947	13,524
1936	8,593	1948	13,353
1937	14,710	1949	11,265

Source: U. S. Bureau of Mines

U. S. VANADIUM ORE OUTPUT

Short Tons, Contained Vanadium

1936	70	1942	2,220
1937	543	1943	2,793
1938	807	1944	1,764
1939	992	1945	1,482
1940	1,081	1946	636
1941	1,257	1947	1,059

Vanadium content of carnotite ore, vanadium and complex ores. Data for 1940 and 1947 are receipts at mills and government purchasing depots. Data following 1947 not released for publication.

Source: U. S. Bureau of Mines

WORLD PRODUCTION OF VANADIUM, SINCE 1940

Metric Tons, Total Excludes Russia, French Morocco and Spain, also Byproduct

	1940	1941	1942	1943	1944	1945	1946	1947	1948	1949
Argentina	1	6		4	3	6	7	(1)	(1)	
Mexico	32	(2)								
Northern Rhodesia	368	342	388	426	254	219	68	56	173	153
Peru	1,214	1,017	1,010	847	514	698	322	435	511	456
South-West Africa	428	269	453	577	385	420	430	282	187	165
United States (shipments)[3]	981	1,140	2,014	2,534	1,600	1,344	577	961	(4)	(4)
Total[5]	3,024	2,774	3,865	4,384	2,757	2,674	1,403	1,741	(4)	(4)

[1] Figure not available. [2] Less than 1 ton. [3] Includes also vanadium recovered as a byproduct of phosphate-rock mining.
[4] Bureau of Mines not at liberty to publish figure. [5] Total represents data only for countries shown in table.

Source: U. S. Bureau of Mines

RECOVERY OF SECONDARY LEAD IN THE U. S.

Short Tons of Metal, Showing Form of Recovery

Form of Recovery	1943	1944	1945	1946	1947	1948	1949
As Metal:							
At Primary Plants	21,634	11,368	18,525	8,013	15,662	4,952	23,230
At Other Plants	36,688	43,678	42,598	65,691	95,843	126,951	129,396
	58,322	55,046	61,123	73,704	111,505	131,903	152,626
In Antimonial Lead[1]	176,076	180,818	194,079	193,684	265,935	243,552	172,742
In Other Lead Alloys	76,474	68,271	77,051	94,653	103,799	102,603	78,894
In Copper-Base Alloys	28,625	26,667	30,346	30,101	30,137	21,449	7,440
In Tin-Base Alloys	1,746	614	440	645	594	514	481
	341,243	331,416	363,039	392,787	511,970	500,071	412,183

[1] Includes lead recovered in secondary antimonial lead at primary plants.

Source: U. S. Bureau of Mines

EMPLOYMENT, HOURS, EARNINGS

Nonferrous Metal Finishing*

	Production and Related Workers				All Employees
	Average Weekly Earnings	Average Weekly Hours	Average Hourly Earnings	Number (thousands)	Number (thousands)
1947	$51.89	39.7	$1.307	93.3	111.5
1948	57.81	40.2	1.438	86.0	103.8
1949	58.05	38.7	1.500	70.6	87.0
1950					
Jan.	61.97	40.5	1.530	73.7	89.0
Feb.	63.29	41.1	1.540	75.0	90.6
Mar.	64.29	41.4	1.553	76.5	92.4
Apr.	64.29	41.4	1.553	77.1	93.2
May	64.29	42.2	1.579	78.9	95.1
June	67.75	42.8	1.583	80.3	96.6
July	67.76	42.4	1.598	79.5	96.0

* Rolling, Drawing, and Alloying

Source: Bureau of Labor Statistics

EMPLOYMENT, HOURS, EARNINGS

Nonferrous Metal Manufacturing*

	Production and Related Workers				All Employees
	Average Weekly Earnings	Average Weekly Hours	Average Hourly Earnings	Number (thousands)	Number (thousands)
1947	$52.73	41.0	$1.286	46.9	55.1
1948	58.22	41.0	1.420	46.8	55.6
1949	60.36	40.4	1.494	43.3	52.3
1950					
Jan.	62.07	41.3	1.503	42.5	51.1
Feb.	60.24	40.4	1.491	45.3	54.1
Mar.	61.13	40.7	1.502	45.4	54.4
Apr.	61.61	40.8	1.510	45.2	54.2
May	61.98	40.8	1.519	45.5	54.6
June	62.58	40.9	1.530	46.0	55.2
July	62.83	40.3	1.559	45.1	54.3

* Primary Metal Industries Group, Primary Smelting and Refining.

Source: Bureau of Labor Statistics

WORLD PRODUCTION OF MERCURY, SINCE 1942

Number of 76 Pound Flasks, Estimated Production of Other Nations Is in Total

Country[1]	1942	1943	1944	1945	1946	1947	1948	1949
Algeria	121	146	165	326	340	348	381	102
Canada	13,630	22,240	9,682	......	......	......	......	......
Chile	2,256	2,563	1,181	862	827	445	467	(2)
China	4,293	3,133	3,510	1,828	1,189	290	290	(2)
Czechoslovakia	(2)	(2)	(2)	(2)	(2)	768	800	(2)
Germany	493	3,480	3,480	(2)	(2)	(2)	(2)	(2)
Italy	75,921	58,004	28,704	25,410	50,822	53,984	38,233	44,000
Japan	5,197	6,706	7,096	3,139	1,361	1,619	1,689	2,461
Mexico	32,443	28,321	26,063	16,443	11,661	9,700	4,788	5,250
Peru	145	326	152	209	5	......	......	......
Spain	72,288	47,756	34,349	40,694	41,801	55,608	22,684	32,289
Turkey	271	186	97	158	......	98	(2)	......
Union of South Africa	579	1,189	1,192	852	764	......	......	......
United States	50,846	51,929	37,688	30,763	25,348	23,244	14,388	9,930
Total	265,000	236,000	163,000	131,000	144,000	164,000	102,000	112,000

[1] Mercury is also produced in Korea (Chosen) and U. S. S. R., but production data are not available; estimates included in the total. Totals include output or estimates for minor producing nations, including Australia, Austria, Bolivia, New Zealand, Rumania, Southern Rhodesia, Sweden, Tunisia and Yugoslavia. [2] Data not yet available; estimates included in the total.

Source: U. S. Bureau of Mines

IN THIS SECTION:

THE IRON AGE 3
SECTION
METAL INDUSTRY FACTS
Raw Materials, Ore, Scrap, Coal and Coke

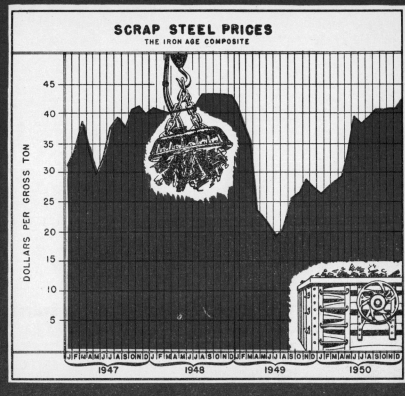

SCRAP STEEL PRICES
THE IRON AGE COMPOSITE

3 METAL FACTS SECTION

Production of Pig Iron in 22 Countries
U. S. Imports and Exports of Pig Iron
Number, Capacity, Materials Used—U. S. Blast Furnaces

WORLD PRODUCTION OF PIG IRON

(Net Tons in Thousands)

	1950*	1949	1948	1947	1946	1945	1944	1943	1942	1941	1940	1939
United States	65,000	54,206	61,912	60,117	48,515	54,919	62,866	62,770	60,903	56,687	47,399	38,677
Canada	2,465	2,367	2,335	2,152	1,525	1,976	2,012	1,930	2,156	1,708	1,448	930
United Kingdom	10,600	10,637	10,389	8,457	8,692	7,960	7,545	8,049	8,653	8,280	9,189	8,937
Belgium	4,200	4,130	4,346	3,109	2,393	802	780	1,801	1,398	1,572	1,976	3,382
Luxemburg	2,684	2,615	2,896	2,004	1,505	344	1,481	2,526	1,865	1,481	1,164	2,024
France	9,000	9,188	7,248	5,383	3,796	1,304	3,189	5,424	4,231	3,694	4,060	8,131
Netherlands	521	478	487		180	128					305	304
Hungary†			336	330	176	1	326	460	460	487	471	451
Germany†	10,411	7,870	6,394	2,491	2,425	1,550	14,737	17,606	17,021	17,012	15,383	19,266
Saar	1,801	1,743	1,252	721	271		1,634	2,411	2,224	2,258	2,008	2,091
Austria	867	924	679	306	64							
Czechoslovakia			1,822	1,569	1,058	635	1,746	1,878	1,759	1,733	1,786	1,773
Poland			1,199	944	800	252	271	290				1,100
Yugoslavia	225	211								83	92	67
Rumania											150	149
Russia	19,500	18,960	15,750*	12,450*	11,250*	10,140*	16,800	11,100	7,700	14,300	16,500	16,810
Italy	691	490	580	425	226	83	341	802	1,077	1,229	1,239	1,212
Spain	733	693	582	551	540	519	607	941	874	592	591	639
Sweden	965	948	861	779	771	839						
Japan‡	2,205	1,767	922	391	202	556	3,434	5,089	5,475	5,268	4,422	4,016
Australia**	1,354	1,171	1,384	1,329	1,204	1,252	1,462	1,466	1,745	1,653	1,357	1,279
Total	139,432	118,398	121,354	103,687	83,541	83,132	120,171	125,121	118,095	118,847	110,455	108,830

Includes ferroalloys made in the blast furnace.
* Estimate by THE IRON AGE.
† 1948 and 1949 figures do not include production in the Russian Zone. Saar and Austria are not included.
‡ Home islands, Korea and Manchuria in 1944 and previous years.
** Year ending June 30.

Source: American Iron and Steel Institute, Chambre Syndicale de la Siderurgie Francaise and Statistical Office of the United Nations

PIG IRON EXPORTS FROM THE UNITED STATES

Ranging from 1940 Through First 8 Months of 1950; in Short Tons

	1950*	1949	1948	1947	1946	1945	1944	1943	1942	1941	1940
Argentina				125	4,772	5,659	431		336		3,537
Belgium & Luxembourg				29,262		7,790					
Canada	4,223	19,164	6,520	9,524	11,789	6,106	8,984	7,673	1,691	5,117	30,496
Chile	40	863					2,331	1,229	578	2,119	
China					12,155						8,290
Colombia	396	242					2,887	148		441	
Costa Rica		28									
Cuba	135	111									
Dominican Republic	140	182									
Ecuador		129									
France					14,000	14,000					
Greece	33	1,690									
Italy					16,856	10,643					
Korea		8,346									
Mexico	338	2,280	175								
New Zealand	56	175									
Nicaragua		56									
Paraguay		5									
Peru		580									
Philippines	134	223									
Sweden					24,082	22,066					11,883
Trinidad & Tobago		11									
United Kingdom	10	46,990				1,524	132,001	121,534	105,495	555,339	515,061
Uruguay		235			3,366	3,078	1,202	2,557		195	
U.S.S.R.							4,036	3,729	430		
Other Countries			512	1,290	12,044	23,180	9,664	7,685	3,125	15,322	51,069
Total	5,505	81,310	7,032	40,201	99,064	94,046	161,536	144,555	111,655	578,533	620,336

* Eight months.

Source: Dept. of Commerce and AISI

U. S. IMPORTS OF PIG IRON

Ranging from 1940 Through First 8 Months of 1950; in Short Tons

	1950*	1949	1948	1947	1946	1945	1944	1943†	1941	1940
Netherlands	142,429	20,527	45,020	2,710						
Belgium	6,160	15,688	32,809							
Australia		19,599	26,901					336	3,367	
Germany	68,858	2,382	24,558							
Norway	1,984	145	23,920	9,482						
Austria	18,135	5,145	18,594	281						
France	14,944	340	17,876							
India		23,078	16,100					500		7,645
Canada	138,454	12,270	5,729	1,747	1,287	21,433	5,778	49	308	3,828
Italy			5,001							
United Kingdom	293	193			1,528			560		
French Morocco								165		
Mexico					11,248					
Other Countries	2,704	435	2,192	18,404	28					
Total	393,961	99,802	218,700	32,624	14,091	21,433	5,778	1,610	3,675	11,471

* Nine months.
† No imports for 1942.

Source: U. S. Dept. of Commerce

BLAST FURNACES IN THE U. S.

Producing pig iron, ferroalloys*

Massachusetts	1	Texas	2
New York	16	Ohio	50
Pennsylvania	75	Indiana	22
Maryland	8	Illinois	22
Virginia	1	Michigan	6
West Virginia	4	Minnesota	3
Kentucky	3	Colorado	4
Tennessee	2	Utah	5
Alabama	20	California	2
		Total	**247**

Capacity on tonnage basis, as of Jan. 1, 1949=71,497,540 net tons.
*As of Jan. 1, 1950

Source: American Iron & Steel Institute

BLAST FURNACE CAPACITY*

Net Ton Totals for Active Units

	Pig Iron	Ferro-alloys	Charcoal Iron	Total
1938	55,618,752	1,060,416	103,040	56,782,208
1939	55,162,374	1,060,416	103,040	56,325,830
1940	54,635,740	992,320	95,580	55,723,640
1941	56,522,370	980,660	106,560	57,609,590
1942	59,211,850	1,075,570	106,560	60,393,980
1943	62,859,330	987,000	107,200	63,933,530
1944	66,344,780	990,300	56,190	67,391,270
1945	66,256,810	992,600	64,480	67,313,890
1946	66,311,410	996,700	32,480	67,340,590
1947	64,674,020	1,002,700	32,480	65,709,200
1948	66,301,610	1,097,000	40,320	67,438,930
1949	69,435,130	1,066,400	40,320	70,541,860
1950	70,348,920	1,108,300	40,320	71,497,540

* Capacities are for year beginning Jan. 1. Capacities of furnaces long idle not included.

Source: American Iron & Steel Institute

BLAST FURNACE MATERIALS

Net Tons Used in 1949 for pig iron

Iron Ore	93,609,003
Scrap*	2,276,701
Mill Cinder, Scale, etc.	6,572,062
Total	**102,457,766**

* Scrap used less scrap produced.

Source: American Iron & Steel Institute

CANADIAN STATISTICS

PIG IRON PRODUCTION
Includes Ferroalloys, in Net Tons

	Pig Iron		
	1950	1949	1948
Jan.	190,432	183,074	160,042
Feb.	157,200	172,724	151,123
Mar.	174,944	202,130	172,675
Apr.	185,259	180,740	170,785
May	195,893	202,148	193,305
June	198,462	194,255	183,763
July	194,016	175,381	187,940
Aug.	201,830	180,115	191,383
Sept.	199,415	168,436	182,465
Oct.	200,000*	166,020	186,424
Nov.	200,000*	157,327	166,771
Dec.	200,000*	172,002	174,233
Total	2,297,451*	2,154,352	2,120,909

	Ferroalloys		
	1950	1949	1948
Jan.	9,961	21,931	17,125
Feb.	9,652	21,713	11,823
Mar.	17,157	22,457	14,293
Apr.	14,627	24,427	14,474
May	12,707	20,652	18,436
June	15,350	19,264	13,502
July	16,118	14,280	12,939
Aug.	19,018	12,562	12,700
Sept.	17,765	12,250	12,318
Oct.	18,000*	15,456	19,489
Nov.	18,000*	14,758	17,594
Dec.	18,000*	11,853	23,708
Total	167,337*	211,603	250,659†

* Estimate.
† Total figures includes additional tonnage for which monthly data are not reported.
Source: Dominion Bureau of Statistics

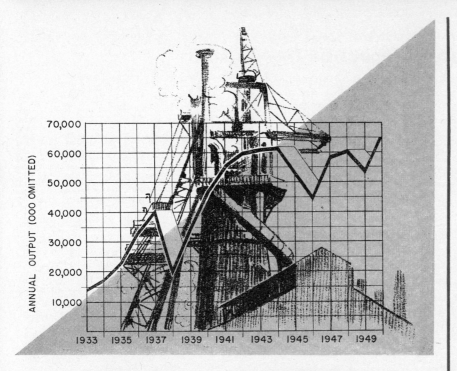

ANNUAL OUTPUT (000 OMITTED)								
70,000								
60,000								
50,000								
40,000								
30,000								
20,000								
10,000								
	1933	1935	1937	1939	1941	1943	1945	1947	1949

UNITED STATES PIG IRON PRODUCTION

Blast Furnace, Thousands of Net Tons, Includes Ferroalloys, Not Charcoal Iron

	Jan.	Feb.	Mar.	April	May	June	First Half	July	Aug.	Sept.	Oct.	Nov.	Dec.	Second Half	Year
1901	1301	1270	1433	1408	1500	1476	8,388	1523	1496	1456	1548	1526	1418	8,967	17,355
1910	2922	2685	2932	2782	2677	2537	16,535	2407	2360	2303	2344	2139	1991	13,544	30,079
1920	3377	3337	3781	3068	3344	3409	20,316	3435	3525	3504	3688	3287	3029	20,468	40,784
1921	2705	2169	1788	1336	1368	1193	10,559	969	1069	1104	1396	1585	1847	7,970	18,529
1922	1842	1826	2280	2321	2583	2644	13,496	2694	2034	2278	2956	3191	3457	16,610	30,106
1923	3617	3353	3947	3976	4332	4117	23,342	4119	3864	3501	3527	3241	3272	21,524	44,866
1924	3382	3441	3883	3822	2929	2269	19,526	1999	2114	2299	2774	2811	3318	15,315	34,841
1925	3774	3600	3992	3650	3283	2995	21,294	2964	3030	3052	3386	3386	3640	19,478	40,772
1926	3714	3274	3855	3864	3900	3623	22,230	3610	3586	3512	3734	3626	3461	21,529	43,759
1927	3477	3294	3901	3832	3798	3461	21,763	3305	3300	3108	3118	2966	3020	18,817	40,580
1928	3214	3248	3585	3567	3678	3452	20,744	3441	3514	3429	3779	3698	3774	21,635	42,379
1929	3855	3591	4160	4102	4366	4163	24,237	4239	4218	3918	4019	3563	3177	23,133	47,360
1930	3166	3180	3636	3564	3820	3286	20,452	2956	2827	2580	2425	2092	1866	14,716	35,168
1931	1920	1912	2276	2261	2233	1836	12,438	1639	1435	1309	1314	1235	1098	8,030	20,468
1932	1089	1080	1084	954	877	704	5,788	640	582	663	721	707	612	3,925	9,713
1933	637	621	607	699	993	1417	4,974	2007	2053	1705	1519	1215	1323	9,822	14,796
1934	1361	1416	1813	1934	2288	2162	10,974	1372	1181	1006	1065	1072	1151	6,847	17,821
1935	1654	1802	1983	1863	1934	1739	10,975	1702	1701	1990	2215	2315	2360	12,554	23,529
1936	2269	2042	2285	2693	2966	2896	15,151	2905	3037	3058	3351	3301	3489	19,141	34,292
1937	3597	3359	3875	3799	3961	3481	22,072	3919	4039	3819	3239	2248	1669	18,933	41,005
1938	1601	1454	1627	1541	1406	1189	8,818	1346	1673	1882	2298	2543	2476	12,218	21,036
1939	2436	2307	2882	2303	1924	2373	14,025	2639	2979	3224	4063	4167	4220	21,292	35,317
1940	4032	3311	3270	3137	3514	3819	21,083	4054	4238	4177	4446	4403	4548	25,866	46,949
1941	4664	4198	4704	4334	4600	4553	27,053	4771	4791	4717	4856	4703	5012	28,850	55,903
1942	4971	4500	5055	4896	5073	4935	29,430	5051	5020	4937	5237	4966	5201	30,552	59,982
1943	5137	4786	5314	5035	5178	4836	30,343	5023	5316	5226	5324	5096	5213	31,434	61,777
1944	5283	5091	5442	5251	5351	5064	31,482	5157	6210	4988	5200	4904	4998	30,457	61,939
1945	4945	4563	5228	4786	5016	4605	29,142	4861	4249	4227	3388	4026	4323	25,925	54,167
1946	2645	1148	4424	3614	2275	3682	17,807	4705	4898	4687	4815	4435	3992	27,672	45,379
1947	5071	4550	5123	4830	5081	4810	29,480	4585	4917	4801	5228	5015	5177	29,723	59,209
1948	5195	4838	5019	3840	5077	4990	28,961	4899	5254	5207	5520	5399	5955	31,888	60,849
1949	5725	5223	5820	5531	5517	4819	32,642	4173	4477	4350	612	2721	5231	21,564	54,206
1950	5294	4173	4601	5577	5855	5633	31,133	5879	5770	5697	5924	*5950	*5900	*35,020	*66,153

*Preliminary figure, subject to revision.   Source: 1901 to 1942, THE IRON AGE; October 1942 to 1949, AISI

PIG IRON PRODUCTION BY STATES

In U. S., Short Tons in Thousands, Includes 17 Major Producing States

	1949	1948	1947	1946	1945
Pennsylvania	15,037	17,742	17,563	13,251	16,171
Ohio	10,640	12,471	12,317	9,534	11,259
Indiana	5,991	6,493	6,401	4,829	5,982
Illinois	4,913	5,513	5,600	4,357	5,045
Md., W. Virginia	4,383	4,240	3,682	2,949	3,519
Alabama	3,663	4,013	3,929	3,149	3,582
Mass., New York	3,541	3,875	3,869	2,780	3,295
Colo., Utah, Calif.	2,154	2,379	2,245	1,381	1,642
Mich., Minn.	2,002	2,101	1,924	1,893	1,921
Ky., Tenn., Tex.	1,089	1,228	818	656	808

Source: American Iron & Steel Institute

BLAST FURNACE PRODUCTION
Net Tons

Year	Pig Iron	Ferro-alloys	Total Pig Iron and Ferro-alloys
1923	985,620	33,545	1,019,165
1924	664,186	29,624	693,810
1925	638,844	28,794	667,638
1926	826,003	64,305	890,308
1927	792,624	62,977	855,601
1928	1,162,254	50,267	1,212,521
1929	1,220,961	89,611	1,310,572
1930	836,839	73,049	909,888
1931	470,442	52,375	522,817
1932	161,425	18,100	179,525
1933	254,592	33,737	288,329
1934	455,789	37,055	492,844
1935	678,302	61,182	740,484
1936	759,618	87,679	847,297
1937	1,006,717	91,931	1,098,648
1938	789,710	59,720	849,430
1939	846,418	85,531	931,949
1940	1,309,161	151,661	1,460,822
1941	1,528,054	213,218	1,741,272
1942	1,975,015	213,636	2,188,651
1943	1,758,265	218,687	1,852,626
1944	1,852,626	182,428	4,012,006
1945	1,777,958	186,978	1,964,936
1946	1,403,758	116,995	1,520,753
1947	1,969,847	149,832	2,119,679
1948	2,120,909	250,659	2,371,568
1949	2,154,352	211,603	2,365,955
1950*	2,257,450	183,355	2,440,705

* December output estimated.
Source: Dominion Bureau of Statistics

PIG IRON CAPACITY, OUTPUT
Excluding Ferroalloys, Net Tons

	Capacity	Production	Percent of Capacity
1936	1,450,875	759,618	52.3
1937	1,450,875	1,006,717	69.3
1938	1,450,875	789,710	54.4
1939	1,450,875	846,418	58.3
1940	1,450,875	1,309,161	90.2
1941	1,815,875	1,528,054	84.1
1942	2,123,320	1,975,015	93.0
1943	2,756,160	1,758,265	63.7
1944	2,770,760	1,852,628	66.8
1945	2,770,760	1,777,958	64.1
1946	2,770,760	1,403,758	50.6
1947	2,745,760	1,969,847	71.7
1948	2,745,760	2,120,909	77.2
1949	2,754,760	2,154,352	78.4
1950	2,754,760	2,257,450*	82.2

* December output estimated.
Source: Dominion Bureau of Statistics

3 METAL FACTS SECTION

Composite Pig Iron Prices
Basic, Foundry, and Charcoal Iron Prices

GRANITE CITY, ILL., PIG IRON

No. 2 Foundry, Gross Ton, at Furnace

	1929	1934	1937	1938	1939	1940*
Jan.	$20.75	$17.50	$21.00	$24.00	$21.00	$23.00
Feb.	20.75	17.50	21.25	24.00	21.00	23.00
Mar.	20.75	17.50	23.60	24.00	21.00	23.00
Apr.	20.75	17.75	24.00	24.00	21.00	23.00
May	20.75	18.50	24.00	24.00	21.00	23.00
June	20.75	18.50	24.00	23.00	21.00	23.00
July	20.75	18.50	24.00	20.00	21.00	23.00
Aug.	20.69	18.50	24.00	20.00	21.00	23.00
Sept.	20.50	18.50	24.00	20.25	22.00	23.00
Oct.	20.50	18.50	24.00	21.00	23.00	23.00
Nov.	20.50	18.50	24.00	21.00	23.00	23.00
Dec.	20.50	18.50	24.00	21.00	23.00	23.50
Average	20.66	18.19	23.49	22.20	21.59	23.04

	1945*	1946	1947	1948	1949	1950
Jan.	$24.00	$25.75	$30.50	$39.25	$48.40	$48.40
Feb.	24.50	25.75	30.50	40.00	48.40	48.40
Mar.	25.00	26.13	32.00	40.00	48.40	48.40
Apr.	25.00	26.50	33.50	40.00	48.40	48.40
May	25.00	26.50	33.50	41.43	48.40	48.40
June	25.00	28.50	33.50	45.75	48.40	48.40
July	25.00	28.50	34.60	45.75	48.40	48.40
Aug.	25.00	28.50	36.63	47.34	48.40	48.40
Sept.	25.00	28.50	37.00	48.40	48.40	48.40
Oct.	25.30	28.50	37.00	48.40	48.40	51.40
Nov.	25.75	28.50	37.00	48.40	48.40	51.40
Dec.	25.75	29.70	37.00	48.40	48.40	53.65
Average	25.02	27.44	34.39	44.42	48.40	49.34

† Prior to September 1933. St. Louis prices are given.
* Price unchanged at $24.00 from 1941 through 1944.

BIRMINGHAM PIG IRON PRICES

No. 2 Foundry Grade, Per Gross Ton

	1929	1936	1937	1938	1939*	1941**
Jan.	$16.50	$15.50	$17.38	$20.38	$17.38	$19.38
Feb.	16.50	15.50	17.68	20.38	17.38	19.38
Mar.	16.00	15.50	19.93	20.38	17.38	19.89
Apr.	15.40	15.50	20.38	20.38	17.38	20.38
May	15.00	15.50	20.38	20.38	17.38	20.38
June	15.00	15.50	20.38	19.58	17.38	20.38
July	14.63	15.50	20.38	16.38	17.38	20.38
Aug.	14.50	15.88	20.38	16.38	17.38	20.38
Sept.	14.50	15.88	20.38	16.63	18.38	20.38
Oct.	14.50	15.88	20.38	17.38	19.38	20.38
Nov.	14.50	16.13	20.38	17.38	19.38	20.38
Dec.	14.50	16.88	20.38	17.38	19.38	20.38
Average	15.13	15.76	19.87	18.58	17.96	20.17

	1945**	1946	1947	1948	1949	1950
Jan.	$20.38	$22.13	$26.88	$37.38	$43.38	$39.38
Feb.	20.86	22.13	26.88	37.38	43.38	42.38
Mar.	21.38	22.51	29.13	37.38	43.38	42.38
Apr.	21.38	22.88	29.88	37.38	43.38	42.38
May	21.38	22.88	29.88	38.38	39.71	42.38
June	21.38	24.38	29.88	39.38	39.38	42.38
July	21.38	24.88	31.28	31.04	39.38	42.38
Aug.	21.38	24.88	34.13	43.38	39.38	42.38
Sept.	21.38	24.88	34.88	43.38	39.38	42.67
Oct.	21.68	24.88	34.88	43.38	39.38	45.88
Nov.	22.13	24.88	34.88	43.38	39.38	45.88
Dec.	22.13	26.88	34.60	43.38	39.38	48.88
Average	21.40	24.06	31.43	40.43	40.74	43.53

† Subject to 38c a ton deduction for 0.70 phosphorus and over.
* Price unchanged at $19.38 through 1940.
** Price unchanged at $20.38 from 1942 through 1944.

NO. 2 FOUNDRY PIG IRON PRICES

Mahoning, Shenango Valley, Per Gross Ton

	1929	1934	1936	1937	1938	1939
Jan.	$17.50	$17.50	$19.50	$21.00	$24.00	$21.00
Feb.	17.50	17.50	19.50	21.25	24.00	21.00
Mar.	17.75	17.50	19.50	23.60	24.00	21.00
Apr.	18.00	17.75	19.50	24.00	24.00	21.00
May	18.50	18.50	19.50	24.00	24.00	21.00
June	18.50	18.50	19.50	24.00	23.20	21.00
July	18.50	18.50	19.50	24.00	20.00	21.00
Aug.	18.50	18.50	19.50	24.00	20.00	21.00
Sept.	18.50	18.50	19.50	24.00	20.25	22.00
Oct.	18.50	18.50	19.50	24.00	21.00	23.00
Nov.	18.50	18.50	19.75	24.00	21.00	23.00
Dec.	18.50	18.50	20.25	24.00	21.00	23.00
Average	18.23	18.19	19.60	23.49	22.20	21.59

	1940*	1945*	1946	1947	1948**	1950
Jan.	$23.00	$24.00	$25.75	$30.50	$39.37	$46.50
Feb.	23.00	24.50	25.75	30.50	39.50	46.50
Mar.	23.00	25.00	26.13	33.50	39.50	46.50
Apr.	23.00	25.00	26.50	33.50	39.50	46.50
May	23.00	25.00	26.50	33.50	39.50	46.50
June	23.00	25.00	28.50	33.50	39.50	46.50
July	23.00	25.00	28.50	34.70	42.50	46.50
Aug.	23.00	25.00	28.50	36.50	43.50	46.50
Sept.	23.00	25.00	28.50	36.50	43.50	47.50
Oct.	23.00	25.30	28.50	36.50	46.12	49.50
Nov.	23.00	25.75	28.50	36.50	46.50	49.50
Dec.	23.40	25.75	30.10	36.70	46.50	52.50
Average	23.03	25.02	27.64	34.36	42.12	47.58

* Price unchanged at $24.00 from 1941 through 1944.
** Price unchanged at $46.50 through 1949.

COMPOSITE PIG IRON PRICE

Average of THE IRON AGE quotations on basic pig iron at Valley furnaces and foundry iron at Chicago. Birmingham. Buffalo. Valley and Philadelphia. in gross tons,

	1929	1930	1931	1932	1933	1934
Jan.	$18.43	$18.19	$15.90	$14.68	$13.56	$16.90
Feb.	18.38	18.02	15.80	14.51	13.56	16.90
Mar.	18.36	17.75	15.71	14.45	13.56	16.90
Apr.	18.52	17.73	15.79	14.35	13.76	17.07
May	18.70	17.60	15.76	14.12	14.48	17.90
June	18.65	17.48	15.62	14.01	15.01	17.90
July	18.48	17.16	15.56	13.76	15.50	17.90
Aug.	18.39	16.90	15.51	13.69	16.09	17.90
Sept.	18.27	16.70	15.44	13.64	16.71	17.90
Oct.	18.33	16.31	15.21	13.63	16.61	17.90
Nov.	18.36	16.21	14.97	13.59	16.61	17.90
Dec.	18.24	15.95	14.86	13.56	16.90	17.90
Average	18.43	17.17	15.51	14.00	15.20	17.58

	1936	1937	1938	1939	1940	1941*
Jan.	$18.84	$20.25	$23.25	$20.61	$22.61	$23.45
Feb.	18.84	20.50	23.25	20.61	22.61	23.45
Mar.	18.84	22.85	23.25	20.61	22.61	23.53
Apr.	18.84	23.25	23.25	20.61	22.61	23.61
May	18.84	23.25	23.25	20.61	22.61	23.61
June	18.84	23.25	22.98	20.61	22.61	23.61
July	18.84	23.25	19.61	20.61	22.61	23.61
Aug.	18.73	23.25	19.61	20.61	22.61	23.61
Sept.	18.73	23.25	19.82	21.61	22.61	23.61
Oct.	18.73	23.25	20.57	22.61	22.61	23.61
Nov.	18.98	23.25	20.61	22.61	22.61	23.61
Dec.	19.73	23.25	20.61	22.61	22.95	23.61
Average	18.90	22.74	21.67	21.19	22.64	23.58

	1945*	1946	1947	1948	1949	1950
Jan.	$23.61	$25.37	$30.14	$39.83	$46.79	$45.98
Feb.	24.11	25.37	30.15	40.27	46.74	46.38
Mar.	24.61	25.75	32.92	40.32	46.74	46.38
Apr.	24.61	26.12	33.15	40.11	46.64	46.38
May	24.61	26.45	33.15	40.33	45.97	46.38
June	24.61	28.13	33.15	40.51	45.91	46.38
July	24.61	28.13	34.52	42.25	45.91	46.38
Aug.	24.61	28.13	36.84	44.34	45.91	46.56
Sept.	24.61	28.13	36.95	44.96	45.90	47.16
Oct.	24.91	28.13	36.95	46.63	45.88	49.29
Nov.	25.37	28.13	37.04	48.84	45.88	49.69
Dec.	25.37	29.64	37.24	46.91	45.88	52.50
Average	24.61	27.29	34.35	42.94	46.18	47.85

* Price unchanged at $23.61 from 1942 through 1944.

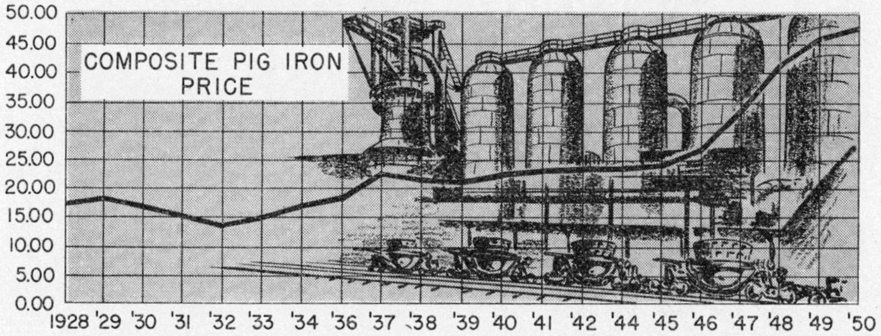

CHICAGO CHARCOAL PIG IRON

Prices Per Gross Ton

	1929	1938	1939	1940	1941*	1943**
Jan.	$27.04	$30.24	$28.34	$30.34	$30.34	$31.34
Feb.	27.04	30.24	28.34	30.34	30.34	31.34
Mar.	27.04	30.24	28.34	30.34	30.34	31.34
Apr.	27.04	30.32	28.34	30.34	30.34	31.34
May	27.04	30.34	28.34	30.34	31.09	31.34
June	27.04	30.34	28.34	30.34	31.34	31.34
July	27.04	28.34	28.34	30.34	31.34	31.34
Aug.	27.04	28.34	28.34	30.34	31.34	31.34
Sept.	27.04	28.34	29.34	30.34	31.34	37.34
Oct.	27.04	28.34	30.34	30.34	31.34	37.34
Nov.	27.04	28.34	30.34	30.34	31.34	37.34
Dec.	27.04	28.34	30.34	30.34	31.34	37.34
Average	27.04	29.31	28.92	30.34	30.99	33.34

	1945**	1946	1947	1948	1949	1950
Jan.	$37.34	$42.34	$42.99	$61.21	$73.78	$68.56
Feb.	37.34	42.34	42.99	62.46	73.78	68.56
Mar.	41.09	42.34	45.24	62.46	73.78	68.56
Apr.	42.34	42.34	45.99	62.46	73.78	68.56
May	42.34	42.34	45.99	63.27	73.78	68.56
June	42.34	42.34	45.99	65.55	69.35	68.56
July	42.34	42.34	47.01	67.55	68.24	68.56
Aug.	42.34	42.34	49.49	69.55	68.24	68.56
Sept.	42.34	42.34	49.49	69.55	68.50	69.06
Oct.	42.34	42.34	52.77	73.78	68.56	70.56
Nov.	42.34	42.34	56.04	73.78	68.56	70.56
Dec.	42.34	42.60	56.04	73.78	68.56	70.56
Average	41.40	42.36	48.34	67.11	70.74	69.10

* Price unchanged at $31.44 through 1942.
** Price unchanged at $37.34 through 1944.

BASIC PIG IRON PRICES

Mahoning, Shenango Valley, Gross Ton

	1929	1934	1936	1937	1938	1939
Jan.	$17.50	$17.00	$19.00	$20.50	$23.50	$20.50
Feb.	17.50	17.00	19.00	20.75	23.50	20.50
Mar.	17.50	17.00	19.00	23.10	23.50	20.50
Apr.	17.90	17.25	19.00	23.50	23.50	20.50
May	18.38	18.00	19.00	23.50	23.50	20.50
June	18.50	18.00	19.00	23.50	22.70	20.50
July	18.50	18.00	19.00	23.50	19.50	20.50
Aug.	18.50	18.00	19.00	23.50	19.50	20.50
Sept.	18.50	18.00	19.00	23.50	19.75	21.50
Oct.	18.50	18.00	19.00	23.50	20.50	22.50
Nov.	18.50	18.00	19.25	23.50	20.50	22.50
Dec.	18.50	18.00	20.00	23.50	20.50	22.50
Average	18.19	17.69	19.10	22.99	21.70	21.09

	1940*	1945*	1946	1947	1948**	1950
Jan.	$22.50	$23.50	$25.25	$30.00	$38.87	$46.00
Feb.	22.50	24.00	25.25	30.00	39.00	46.00
Mar.	22.50	24.50	25.63	33.00	39.00	46.00
Apr.	22.50	24.50	26.00	33.00	39.00	46.00
May	22.50	24.50	26.00	33.00	39.00	46.00
June	22.50	24.50	28.00	33.00	39.00	46.00
July	22.50	24.50	28.00	34.20	42.00	46.00
Aug.	22.50	24.50	28.00	36.00	43.00	46.00
Sept.	22.50	24.50	28.00	36.00	43.00	46.75
Oct.	22.50	24.80	28.00	36.00	45.62	49.00
Nov.	22.50	25.25	28.00	36.00	46.00	49.00
Dec.	22.90	25.25	29.60	36.20	46.00	52.00
Average	22.53	24.52	27.14	34.78	41.62	47.06

* Price unchanged at $23.50 from 1941 through 1944.
** Price unchanged at $46.00 through 1949.

CHICAGO FOUNDRY PIG IRON

No. 2, Per Gross Ton, at Furnace

	1929	1934	1936	1937	1938	1940*
Jan.	$20.00	$17.50	$19.50	$21.00	$24.00	$23.00
Feb.	20.00	17.50	19.50	21.25	24.00	23.00
Mar.	20.00	17.50	19.50	23.60	24.00	23.00
Apr.	20.00	17.75	19.50	24.00	24.00	23.00
May	20.00	18.50	19.50	24.00	24.00	23.00
June	20.00	18.50	19.50	24.00	23.20	23.00
July	20.00	18.50	19.50	24.00	20.00	23.00
Aug.	20.00	18.50	19.50	24.00	20.00	23.00
Sept.	20.00	18.50	19.50	24.00	20.25	23.00
Oct.	20.00	18.50	19.50	24.00	21.00	23.00
Nov.	20.00	18.50	19.75	24.00	21.00	23.00
Dec.	20.00	18.50	20.50	24.00	21.00	23.40
Average	20.00	18.19	19.60	23.49	22.20	23.03

	1945*	1946	1947	1948	1949	1950
Jan.	$24.00	$25.75	$30.50	$38.75	$46.50	$46.50
Feb.	24.50	25.75	30.50	39.00	46.50	46.50
Mar.	25.00	26.13	33.00	39.00	46.50	46.50
Apr.	25.00	26.50	33.00	39.00	46.50	46.50
May	25.00	26.50	33.00	39.00	46.50	46.50
June	25.00	28.50	33.00	39.00	46.50	46.50
July	25.00	28.50	34.20	42.00	46.50	46.50
Aug.	25.00	28.50	36.00	43.00	46.50	46.50
Sept.	25.00	28.50	36.00	43.00	46.50	47.50
Oct.	25.30	28.50	36.00	46.50	46.50	49.50
Nov.	25.75	28.50	36.00	46.50	46.50	49.50
Dec.	25.75	30.10	36.40	46.50	46.50	52.50
Average	25.02	27.64	34.80	41.77	46.50	47.58

* Price unchanged at $24.00 from 1941 through 1944.

BUFFALO FOUNDRY PIG IRON

No. 2 Grade, Per Gross Ton, at Furnace

	1929	1934	1937	1938	1939	1940*
Jan.	$18.00	$17.50	$21.00	$24.00	$21.00	$23.00
Feb.	18.39	17.50	21.25	24.00	21.00	23.00
March	18.50	17.50	23.60	24.00	21.00	23.00
April	18.50	17.50	24.00	24.00	21.00	23.00
May	18.50	18.50	24.00	24.00	21.00	23.00
June	18.75	18.50	24.00	23.20	21.00	23.00
July	19.50	18.50	24.00	20.00	21.00	23.00
Aug.	19.50	18.50	24.00	20.00	21.00	23.00
Sept.	19.50	18.50	24.00	20.13	22.00	23.00
Oct.	19.50	18.50	24.00	20.88	23.00	23.00
Nov.	19.50	18.50	24.00	21.00	23.00	23.00
Dec.	19.50	18.50	24.00	21.00	23.00	23.00
Average	18.97	18.17	23.40	22.18	21.59	23.03

	1945*	1946	1947	1948	1949	1950
Jan.	$24.00	$25.75	$30.50	$40.37	$47.28	$46.50
Feb.	24.50	25.75	30.50	42.12	47.00	46.50
March	25.00	26.13	32.38	42.45	47.00	46.50
April	25.00	26.50	33.00	41.19	46.75	46.50
May	25.00	26.50	33.00	41.37	46.50	46.50
June	25.00	28.50	33.00	41.44	46.50	46.50
July	25.00	28.50	34.20	42.08	46.50	46.50
Aug.	25.00	28.50	37.37	44.90	46.50	46.50
Sept.	25.00	28.50	37.18	45.87	46.50	47.25
Oct.	25.30	28.50	37.00	47.12	46.50	49.50
Nov.	25.75	28.50	37.75	47.50	46.50	49.50
Dec.	25.75	30.10	38.00	47.50	46.50	52.50
Average	25.02	27.64	34.49	43.65	46.67	47.56

* Price unchanged at $24.00 from 1941 through 1944.

MALLEABLE PIG IRON PRICES

Per Gross Ton, Mahoning, Shenango Valley

	1929	1934	1936	1937	1938	1939
Jan.	$18.00	$17.50	$19.50	$21.00	$24.00	$21.00
Feb.	18.00	17.50	19.50	21.25	24.00	21.00
Mar.	18.25	17.50	19.50	23.60	24.00	21.00
Apr.	18.50	17.75	19.50	24.00	24.00	21.00
May	19.00	18.50	19.50	24.00	24.00	21.00
June	19.00	18.50	19.50	24.00	23.00	21.00
July	19.00	18.50	19.50	24.00	20.00	21.00
Aug.	19.00	18.50	19.50	24.00	20.00	21.00
Sept.	19.00	18.50	19.50	24.00	20.25	22.00
Oct.	19.00	18.50	19.50	24.00	21.00	23.00
Nov.	19.00	18.50	19.75	24.00	21.00	23.00
Dec.	19.00	18.50	20.00	24.00	21.00	23.00
Average	18.73	18.19	19.60	23.49	22.20	21.59

	1940*	1945*	1946	1947	1948**	1950
Jan.	$23.00	$24.00	$25.75	$30.50	$39.50	$46.50
Feb.	23.00	24.50	25.75	30.50	39.50	46.50
Mar.	23.00	25.00	26.13	33.50	39.50	46.50
Apr.	23.00	25.00	26.50	33.50	39.50	46.50
May	23.00	25.00	26.50	33.50	39.50	46.50
June	23.00	25.00	28.50	33.50	39.50	46.50
July	23.00	25.00	28.50	34.70	42.50	46.50
Aug.	23.00	25.00	28.50	36.50	43.50	46.50
Sept.	23.00	25.00	28.50	36.50	43.50	47.50
Oct.	23.00	25.30	28.50	36.50	46.12	49.50
Nov.	23.00	25.75	28.50	36.50	46.50	49.50
Dec.	23.50	25.75	30.10	36.70	46.50	52.50
Average	23.04	25.02	27.48	34.36	42.13	47.58

* Price unchanged at $24.00 from 1941 through 1944.
** Price unchanged at $46.50 through 1949.

LAKE SUPERIOR IRON ORES

Avge. Analyses, Combined Ranges, Grades

		Analyses, Pct			
Year	Iron, Natural	Phos.	Silica	Mang.	Moisture
1949	50.39	0.096	9.72	0.78	11.12
1948	50.49	0.093	9.30	0.76	11.35
1947	50.91	0.093	9.09	0.75	11.28
1946	51.32	0.087	8.83	0.74	11.22
1945	51.69	0.089	8.52	0.72	10.96
1944	51.72	0.088	8.42	0.74	11.02
1943	51.58	0.091	8.32	0.82	11.06
1942	51.65	0.089	8.21	0.79	10.98
1941	51.83	0.085	8.18	0.78	11.01
1940	52.09	0.085	8.00	0.77	10.93
1939	51.75	0.085	8.27	0.76	10.73
1938	51.90	0.089	8.25	0.81	10.13
1937	51.53	0.091	8.27	0.82	11.31
1936	51.45	0.091	8.62	0.81	10.92
1935	51.44	0.093	8.93	0.79	10.75
1934	51.49	0.087	8.93	0.76	10.66
1933	51.85	0.090	8.96	0.71	10.47
1932	52.16	0.099	9.05	0.68	9.92
1931	51.53	0.087	8.60	0.80	10.84
1930	51.33	0.095	8.70	0.82	10.92

Source: Lake Superior Iron Ore Assn.

PRICE OF MESABI NON-BESSEMER ORE PER GROSS TON

LAKE SUPERIOR IRON ORES

Per Gross Ton at Lower Lake Ports

BESSEMER ORES

	Guarantee		Price	
	Iron Natural	Phosphorus Dry	Old Range	Mesabi
1915	55.00	0.045	$3.75	$3.45
1916	55.00	0.045	4.45	4.20
1917	55.00	0.045	5.95	5.70
1918 to July 1	55.00	0.045	5.95	5.70
1918-July 1 to Sept. 30	55.00	0.045	6.40	6.15
1918-Oct. 1 on	55.00	0.045	6.65	6.40
1919	55.00	0.045	6.45	6.20
1920	55.00	0.045	7.45	7.20
1921	55.00	0.045	6.45	6.20
1922	55.00	0.045	5.95	5.70
1923	55.00	0.045	6.45	6.20
1924	55.00	0.045	4.65	5.40
1925 through 1928	51.50	0.045	4.55	4.40
1929 through 1936	51.50	0.045	4.80	4.65
1937 to Apr. 15, 1940.	51.50	0.045	5.25	5.10
1940-Apr. 16 on	51.50	0.045	4.75	4.80
1941 through 1944	51.50	0.045	4.75	4.60
1945 to June 24, 1946.	51.50	0.045	4.95	4.70
1946-June 24 to Dec. 31	51.50	0.045	5.45	5.20
1947 to Apr. 1, 1948.	51.50	0.045	5.95	5.70
1948-Apr. 1 on	51.50	0.045	6.60	6.35
1949	51.50	0.045	7.60	7.35
1950 Feb. 1 to Dec. 1.	51.50	0.045	8.10	7.85
1950 Dec. 1 on	51.50	0.045	8.70	8.45

NON-BESSEMER ORES

	Guarantee	Price		
	Iron Natural	Old Range	Mesabi	High Phosphorus
1915	51.50	$3.00	$2.80	....
1916	51.50	3.70	3.55	....
1917	51.50	5.20	5.05	....
1918 to July 1	51.50	5.20	5.05	....
1918-July 1 to Sept. 30	51.50	5.65	5.50	....
1918-Oct. 1 on	51.50	5.90	5.75	....
1919	51.50	5.70	5.55	$5.35
1920	51.50	6.70	6.55	6.35
1921	51.50	5.70	5.55	5.35
1922	51.50	5.20	5.05	4.85
1923	51.50	5.70	5.55	5.35
1924	51.50	4.90	4.75	4.55
1925 through 1928	51.50	4.40	4.25	4.15
1929 through 1936	51.50	4.65	4.50	4.40
1937 to Apr. 15, 1940.	51.50	5.10	4.95	4.85
1940-Apr. 16 on	51.50	4.60	4.45	4.35
1941 through 1944	51.50	4.60	4.45	4.35
1945 to June 24, 1946.	51.50	4.80	4.55	4.55
1946-June 24 to Dec. 31	51.50	5.30	5.05	5.05
1947 to Apr. 1, 1948.	51.50	5.80	5.55	5.55
1948-Apr. 1 on	51.50	6.45	6.20	6.20
1949	51.50	7.45	7.20	7.20
1950 Feb. 1 to Dec. 1.	51.50	7.95	7.70	7.70
1950 Dec. 1 on	51.50	8.55	8.30	8.30

SHIPMENTS OF IRON ORE

Lake Superior Shipments, Gross Tons

1950	*78,300,000
1949	69,556,269
1948	82,655,757
1947	77,210,278
1946	58,975,000
1945	75,207,000
1944	81,039,000
1943	85,116,000
1942	92,070,000
1941	79,941,000
1940	63,308,000
1939	44,984,000
1938	19,353,000
1937	61,973,000
1936	44,746,000
1935	28,214,000
1934	21,841,000
1933	21,455,000
1932	3,553,000
1931	23,281,000

Source: Lake Superior Iron Ore Assn.
* Estimate by Lake Superior Iron Ore Assn.

U. S. IRON ORE CONSUMPTION

In Long Tons

Year	Tons
1944	99,942,454
1945	85,158,495
1946	72,174,844
1947	96,115,549
1948	100,498,557
1949	91,123,220
1950*	120,535,700

* Estimate by The Iron Age

WORLD RESERVES OF IRON ORE AND COKING COAL *

	IRON ORE — Probable (Millions of Metric Tons)	Approximate Iron Content (Percent)	Approximate Iron Content (Millions of Metric Tons)	IRON ORE — Potential (Millions of Metric Tons)	Approximate Iron Content (Percent)	Approximate Iron Content (Millions of Metric Tons)	Per Capita Metallic Content — Probable (Metric Tons)	Per Capita Metallic Content — Potential (Metric Tons)	COAL — Probable (Millions of Metric Tons)	Proportion of Coking Coal	Estimated Population Mid-1948 (Millions)
AFRICA:											
1 Algeria	88	50	44	88	50	44	5.1	5.1	100	....	8.68
2 Belgian Congo	100	50	50	100	50	50	4.6	4.6	95	....	10.86
3 Egypt	14	47	7	14	47	7	0.4	0.4	....	....	19.53
4 French West Africa	2,000	50	1,000	2,030	50	1,015	63.0	63.0	....	....	16.00
5 Liberia	....	....	....	14	67	9	....	5.6	....	....	1.60
6 Morocco (French)	6	47	3	45	49	22	0.4	2.6	21	....	8.30
7 Morocco (Spanish)	30	55	16	30	55	16	14.0	14.0	....	....	1.14
8 Sierra Leone	100	58	58	100	58	58	29.0	29.0	....	....	2.00
9 South-West Africa	....	....	....	569	38	216	....	583.7	....	....	0.37
10 Southern Rhodesia	2,240	51	1,142	105,564	48	50,671	576.8	25,591.0	7,224	Low	1.98
11 Togoland (French)	....	....	....	20	50	10	....	10.5	....	....	0.95
12 Tunisia	25	54	14	25	54	14	4.4	4.4	....	....	3.40
13 Union of South Africa	2,712	47	1,275	10,828	47	5,089	107.2	428.0	67,325	Moderate	11.89
14 **TOTAL**	7,315		3,609	119,427	48	57,221	18.6	295.2	74,765	Moderate	193.83
NORTH AMERICA:											
15 Canada	1,937	48	930	4,355	51	2,221	70.4	168.1	65,053	Low	13.21
16 United States	3,800	45	1,710	70,800	36	25,488	11.7	173.9	2,028,000	High	146.57
17 **TOTAL**	5,737	46	2,640	75,155	37	27,709	16.5	173.3	2,093,053	High	159.86
LATIN AMERICA:											
18 Argentina	....	....	....	80	40	32	....	2.0	50	....	16.30
19 Brazil	6,300	65	4,095	19,650	55	10,807	84.5	223.0	5,000	Low	48.45
20 Chile	72	60	43	262	58	152	7.7	27.0	110	Moderate	5.62
21 Colombia	20	45	9	20	45	9	0.8	0.8	27,000	....	10.78
22 Cuba	3,000	40	1,200	15,000	36	5,400	232.6	1,046.5	....	....	5.16
23 Honduras	10	47	5	10	47	5	4.0	4.0	1	....	1.26
24 Mexico	315	61	189	315	61	189	7.9	7.9	3,000	High	23.88
25 Peru	11	50	6	22	50	11	0.7	1.4	2,000	....	8.06
26 Venezuela	360	60	216	960	51	490	48.1	109.1	5	....	4.49
27 **TOTAL**	10,088	57	5,763	36,319	47	17,090	37.0	109.7	37,166	Low	155.72
ASIA:											
28 China	1,800	45	810	2,700	45	1,215	1.7	2.6	244,000	Moderate	463.49
29 India	9,347	60	5,608	20,320	51	10,272	16.1	30.0	62,143	Low	342.10
30 Indochina	10	60	6	56	50	28	0.2	1.0	3,500	Low	27.03
31 Indonesia	100	49	49	1,500	43	720	0.6	9.4	400	Low	76.36
32 Japan	....	....	....	62	61	38	....	0.5	18,218	Moderate-Low	80.17
33 Korea	70	35	24	370	31	115	0.9	4.1	5,585	Moderate-Low	28.20
34 Malaya	....	....	....	66	65	43	....	7.2	12	....	5.96
35 Philippines	1,016	47	478	1,016	47	478	24.0	24.0	50	Low	19.96
36 Thailand	2	66	1	5	54	3	0.1	0.2	....	....	17.67
37 Turkey	22	55	12	22	55	12	0.6	0.6	400	Moderate-Low	19.50
38 **TOTAL**	12,367	56	6,988	26,117	49	12,924	5.6	10.3	332,308	Low	1,248.92
EUROPE:											
39 Albania	20	50	10	20	50	10	8.5	8.5	....	....	1.18
40 Austria	....	....	....	242	35	85	....	12.1	19	....	6.97
41 Belgium	....	....	....	1	63	1	....	0.1	3,000	High	8.56
42 Bulgaria	....	....	....	1	63	1	....	0.1	1	....	7.10
43 Czechoslovakia	50	35	18	200	32	64	1.5	5.2	6,000	High	12.34
44 Finland	....	....	....	213	32	68	....	17.2	....	....	3.96
45 France	6,700	38	2,546	10,500	37	3,876	61.3	93.4	11,772	High	41.50
46 Germany	800	32	256	2,800	30	840	3.8	12.3	260,000	High	68.25
47 Greece	50	46	23	130	44	57	3.0	7.3	....	....	7.78
48 Hungary	80	40	32	80	40	32	3.5	3.5	210	High	9.16
49 Italy	60	50	30	60	50	30	0.7	0.7	155	....	45.71
50 Luxembourg	200	28	56	300	26	78	193.1	269.0	....	High	0.29
51 Norway	170	48	82	2,170	34	738	25.8	232.1	8,000	....	3.18
52 Poland	59	35	21	175	35	61	0.9	2.6	60,000	Moderate	23.90
53 Portugal	50	45	22	50	45	22	2.6	2.6	20	....	8.40
54 Romania	....	....	....	20	45	9	....	0.6	48	Moderate	16.00
55 Spain	800	45	360	1,800	35	630	13.0	22.7	8,000	Moderate	27.76
56 Sweden	2,200	64	1,408	2,500	64	1,600	204.6	232.8	100	....	6.88
57 Switzerland	....	....	....	55	30	16	....	3.5	....	....	4.61
58 United Kingdom	2,400	28	672	3,400	27	918	13.4	18.3	175,776	High	50.06
59 Yugoslavia	55	47	26	430	46	198	1.6	12.5	39	....	15.80
60 **TOTAL**	13,694	41	5,562	25,146	37	9,333	14.4	24.1	533,140	High	387.37
OCEANIA:											
61 Australia	203	62	126	330	60	198	16.3	25.7	15,241	High	7.71
62 New Caledonia	....	....	....	20	52	10	....	200.0	....	....	0.05
63 New Zealand	10	40	4	15	53	8	2.2	4.3	57	....	1.84
64 **TOTAL**	213	61	130	365	59	216	10.7	17.7	15,298	High	12.19
USSR:											
65 In Europe	3,133	45	1,410	7,124	40	2,850	7.3	14.8	....	....	....
66 In Asia	1,371	45	617	3,738	40	1,495	3.2	7.7	....	....	....
67 **TOTAL**	4,504	45	2,027	10,862	40	4,345	10.5	22.5	1,443,000	High	193.00
68 **GRAND TOTAL**	53,918	50	26,719	293,391	44	128,838	11.4	54.8	4,528,730	....	2,350.89

* For source and detailed information on table see United Nations booklet, "World Iron Ore Resources and Their Utilization," p. 66.

WORLD PRODUCTION OF IRON ORE
In Metric Tons, 1943 to 1949

COUNTRY [1]	1943	1944	1945	1946	1947	1948	1949
North America:							
Canada	581,769	501,899	1,030,052	1,405,696	1,741,210	1,213,121	3,424,174
Newfoundland	551,515	471,824	1,000,449	1,264,141	1,466,577	1,491,618	
Cuba	47,113	28,370		275,445	63,276	36,595	11,961
Mexico	252,437	301,550	282,524	275,445	332,446	333,100	362,600
United States	102,872,863	95,628,294	89,794,834	71,980,145	94,585,639	102,624,598	86,300,693
South America:							
Argentina	150	1,921	43,353	55,400	60,500	(2)	(2)
Brazil	792,217	782,000	716,000	517,785	926,625	1,441,119	
Chile[3]	299,411	674,529	944,863	1,352,886	1,607,929	2,545,401	2,597,330
Europe:							
Austria	3,188,459	3,014,909	323,189	462,016	884,856	1,269,100	10,487,616
Belgium	127,890	430,590	29,800	39,910	58,209	98,720	41,760
Czechoslovakia	1,944,000	1,584,000	276,000	1,116,074	1,363,491	1,428,000	1,400,000[4]
France[5]	31,934,000	19,012,800	7,712,760	16,232,220	18,718,510	23,031,000	31,424,000
Germany[6]	10,763,000	10,269,000[5]	(2)	4,140,100	4,463,000[8]	7,276,000[8]	9,112,000
Hungary	837,640	427,660[9,10]	47,800[9]	132,970	243,940	255,240	293,000
Italy	835,773	390,438	133,951	131,617	226,254	543,241	520,842
Luxembourg	5,253,025	2,912,500	1,405,877	2,246,908	1,992,167	3,399,274	4,137,327
Norway	219,000	264,426	78,538	59,972	127,798	287,992	375,878
Poland	717,331	680,754	105,669	395,470	504,454	602,000	506,801[11]
Rumania	252,058	243,418	140,797	111,502	120,870	140,000[4]	200,000[4]
Spain	1,587,817	1,508,610	1,171,377	1,598,212	1,513,911	1,630,728	1,811,112
Sweden	10,819,997	7,253,359	3,929,662	6,867,208	8,894,544	13,287,118	14,000,000[4]
Switzerland	276,959	214,499	17,436	18,000	45,000	75,000[4]	40,000
U. S. S. R.[12]	14,000,000[4]	16,000,000[4]	18,000,000[4]	21,000,000[4]	24,000,000[4]	(2)	(2)
United Kingdom:							
Great Britain[13]	18,790,524	15,720,021	14,425,878	12,368,377	11,268,909	13,299,282	13,620,000
Northern Ireland	6,660	579	(2)				(2)
Asia:							
China	10,560,500	8,445,700	4,178,000	15,114[14]	18,694[14]	248,600[4,14]	(2)
French Indochina	80,576	21,975	7,925				
India	2,697,813	2,401,576	2,300,524	2,446,325	2,538,559	2,321,255	(2)
Japan[15]	3,057,177[16]	4,367,879[16]	1,356,260[16]	566,470	500,212	561,063	779,674
Korea:							
North }	2,359,000	3,387,000	832,953	75,000[4]	93,000[4]	(2)	(2)
South }							
Malaya	49,137	10,621	13,590	205	902	651	8,525
Philippines	(2)	(2)	(2)			18,289	370,172
Portuguese India	(2)	(2)	(2)	(2)	(2)	(2)	151,000
Turkey	91,751	90,430	125,708	112,210	145,620	185,434	216,043
U. S. S. R.	(2)	(2)	(12)	(12)	(2)	(2)	(2)
Africa:							
Algeria	183,492	783,928	1,202,448	1,671,244	1,558,055	1,871,522	2,538,518
Belgian Congo	23,964						(2)
French Morocco	10,670	6,600	104	124,870	156,310	301,300	356,800
Northern Rhodesia	624	212	76	162	1,528	149	1,749
Sierra Leone	517,727	641,165	840,611	741,105	854,128	967,888	(2)
Southern Rhodesia	182				286	30,478	51,485
Spanish Morocco	547,625	690,880	764,816	787,340	869,016	904,330	943,539
Tunisia	29,703	88,863	132,450	182,705	403,691	690,200	711,894
Union of South Africa	738,128	768,392	775,470	946,828	1,162,127	1,163,723	1,248,000
Oceania:							
Australia:							
New South Wales	205,691	154,326	43,358				
Queensland	3,095	2,375	1,743	1,681	1,364	2,156	(2)
South Australia	2,217,865	2,061,810	1,543,983	1,847,398	2,179,965	2,067,485	762,917[11]
Western Australia	86					7,338	9,277[11]
New Caledonia	36,280	60,406			(2)	(2)	(2)
New Zealand	5,068	6,133	6,164	7,525	6,326	4,853	(2)
Total (estimate)	231,000,000	203,000,000	162,000,000	153,500,000	186,000,000	216,000,000	218,000,000

[1] In addition to countries listed Bulgaria, Burma, Egypt, Eritrea, French West Africa, Greece, Madagascar, Portugal, South-West Africa, and Yugoslavia report production of iron ore in past years, but quantity produced is believed insufficient to affect estimate of world total, except for Yugoslavia for which estimate has been included in the total. [2] Data not available; estimate by author of the chapter included in total. [3] Production of Tofo mines. [4] Estimate. [5] Including Moselle (Lorraine). [6] Exclusive of manganiferous iron ore carrying 12 to 30 pct manganese. [7] Includes Eastern Upper Silesia. [8] Excluding Russian zone. [9] Data represent Trianon Hungary subsequent to October 1944. [10] January to June, inclusive. [11] January to September, inclusive. [12] U.S.S.R. in Asia included with U.S.S.R. in Europe. [13] Exclusive of bog ore, which is used mainly for purification of gas. [14] Production of National Resources Commission only. [15] Includes iron sand production as follows: 1943-44, 427,000 tons; 1944-45, 858,782 tons; 1945-46, 235,094 tons; 1946, 10,472 tons; 1947, 3772 tons; 1948, 2588 tons; 1949, 23,724 tons. [16] Fiscal year ended March 31 of year following that stated.
Source: Bureau of Mines

U. S. PRODUCTION OF IRON ORE
In Gross Tons, Includes Lake Superior, Northeastern, Southeastern, Western

Year	Lake Superior	Northeastern	Southeastern	Western	Total
1930	49,383,383	2,248,682	5,838,105	938,492	58,408,664
1931	25,877,416	936,960	3,644,606	672,520	31,131,502
1932	8,139,427	165,009	1,375,459	167,021	9,846,916
1933	14,611,032	396,228	2,159,958	385,970	17,553,188
1934	21,031,019	908,944	2,347,625	300,028	24,587,616
1935	25,368,637	1,349,247	3,295,684	526,684	30,540,252
1936	41,781,215	2,069,764	4,214,587	723,179	48,788,745
1937	61,657,635	3,145,177	6,351,053	939,683	72,093,548
1938	21,308,410	2,306,910	4,325,729	506,233	28,447,282
1939	41,679,608	3,112,893	[1]6,021,781	917,448	51,731,730
1940	61,471,323	3,559,924	[1]7,446,103	1,218,549	73,695,899
1941	78,858,332	3,962,072	8,145,900	1,443,275	92,409,579
1942	91,005,021	3,119,506	9,159,228	1,599,429	[2]105,526,195
1943	85,789,017	3,487,575	8,478,736	2,859,994	[2]101,247,835
1944	79,111,320	3,849,396	7,121,676	3,442,405	[2]94,117,705
1945	74,821,045	3,620,147	6,329,987	3,087,774	[2]88,376,393
1946	59,042,154	2,596,349	6,247,096	2,450,611	[2]70,843,113
1947	76,531,789	3,987,195	7,527,321	4,502,512	[2]93,091,520
1948	82,630,430	4,422,971	8,365,390	5,104,703	[2]101,003,492
1949	68,494,123	3,893,833	7,601,822	4,441,671	[2]84,937,447
1950	[3]79,000,000	[3]4,800,000	[3]8,000,000	[3]5,200,000	[3]97,000,000

[1] Includes Texas.
[2] Includes by-product ore not assigned to districts.
[3] Estimate by Bureau of Mines.

Source: U. S. Bureau of Mines

IRON MINING EMPLOYMENT, WAGES

	Production and Related Workers				All Employees Number (thousands)
	Average Weekly Earnings	Average Weekly Hours	Average Hourly Earnings	Number (thousands)	
1947	$52.34	40.2	$1.302	31.6	34.3
1948	58.32	41.3	1.412	33.6	36.6
1949	59.06	39.8	1.484	30.4	33.7
1950:					
Jan.	58.68	39.7	1.478	30.4	34.0
Feb.	59.62	40.5	1.472	30.2	33.6
Mar.	57.57	38.9	1.480	30.5	33.9
Apr.	59.62	40.2	1.483	30.3	33.8
May	63.11	41.6	1.517	31.8	35.4
June	63.40	41.6	1.524	32.4	36.1
July	64.11	41.6	1.541	33.0	36.6

Source: Bureau of Labor Statistics

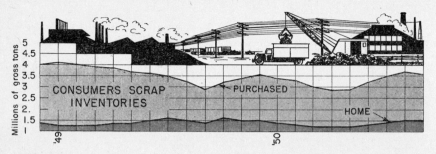

CONSUMERS' SCRAP INVENTORIES
In Gross Tons, Purchased and Home

Date	Purchased	Home
December 31, 1948	4,031,000	1,384,000
January 31, 1949	4,058,000	1,326,000
February 28, 1949	3,999,000	1,253,000
March 31, 1949	3,907,000	1,309,000
April 30, 1949	3,764,000	1,388,000
May 31, 1949	3,678,000	1,452,000
June 30, 1949	3,637,000	1,563,000
July 31, 1949	3,507,000	1,597,000
September 30, 1949	2,940,000	1,367,000
October 31, 1949	3,217,000	1,551,000
November 30, 1949	3,396,000	1,512,000
December 31, 1949	3,639,000	1,466,000
January 31, 1950	3,439,000	1,382,000
February 28, 1950	3,291,000	1,311,000
March 31, 1950	3,033,000	1,199,000
April 30, 1950	2,854,000	1,174,000
May 31, 1950	2,924,000	1,224,000
June 30, 1950	3,261,000	1,338,000
July 31, 1950	3,528,000	1,430,000
August 31, 1950	3,676,000	1,517,000
September 30, 1950	3,621,000	1,528,000

Source: U. S. Bureau of Mines

MACHINERY CAST AT CHICAGO
Prices of No. 1 Scrap, Per Gross Ton‡

	1929	1934	1936	1937	1939	1940
Jan.	$15.81	$9.50	$12.00	$15.87	$12.56	$14.00
Feb.	16.25	9.50	12.75	16.25	12.75	13.75
March	16.00	9.50	13.10	17.40	12.75	13.56
April	16.00	9.50	12.50	17.12	12.12	14.81
May	15.39	8.90	12.00	15.25	11.75	16.31
June	14.75	7.50	12.00	15.00	12.15	17.31
July	14.50	8.05	12.12	15.75	12.25	16.75
Aug.	14.50	8.00	13.37	16.55	12.25	16.88
Sept.	14.50	8.00	13.60	14.38	14.50	17.13
Oct.	14.50	8.00	14.00	13.18	16.87	17.75
Nov.	13.63	8.25	14.00	11.65	15.65	18.00
Dec.	13.50	9.65	14.75	12.12	14.50	19.13
Average	15.11	8.69	13.02	15.04	13.34	16.28

	1941*	1946*	1947	1948	1949	1950
Jan.	$18.88	$20.00	$43.38	$68.00	$57.25	$38.50
Feb.	19.25	20.00	44.56	65.25	46.00	39.00
March	20.75	20.00	46.00	68.50	41.20	39.75
April	‡22.33	20.00	42.70	73.12	29.63	41.50
May	21.40	20.00	38.00	72.50	27.90	45.70
June	20.00	20.00	41.81	69.90	28.69	47.25
July	20.00	20.00	46.00	71.50	30.75	45.50
Aug.	20.00	20.00	49.38	74.30	39.30	49.10
Sept.	20.00	22.50	49.50	71.25	42.25	50.25
Oct.	20.00	25.00	51.00	69.87	41.25	52.80
Nov.	20.00	32.28	52.75	72.20	43.88	60.38
Dec.	20.00	41.05	60.30	69.50	39.85	65.00†
Average	20.21	23.40	47.12	70.48	39.00	47.89

† Estimate.
‡ Changed from net ton basis April 30, 1941.
* Price unchanged at $20.00 from 1942 through 1945. Ceiling price does not include delivery costs.

PHILADELPHIA HEAVY MELTING
Prices of No. 1 Scrap, Per Gross Ton

	1929	1937	1939	1940	1941*	1944*
Jan.	$16.39	$17.37	$15.25	$18.00	$20.50	$18.75
Feb.	16.39	18.50	15.25	17.38	20.00	18.75
March	16.13	19.60	15.38	17.12	20.00	18.75
April	17.00	20.00	15.62	16.75	19.00	18.75
May	16.39	18.62	15.25	17.56	18.75	18.75
June	16.00	17.20	15.41	19.69	18.75	18.75
July	16.50	19.00	15.62	18.95	18.75	18.75
Aug.	16.50	19.75	18.25	19.56	18.75	18.60
Sept.	16.39	19.00	18.87	20.50	18.75	16.66
Oct.	15.70	16.38	22.35	20.70	18.75	14.60
Nov.	15.00	13.75	20.75	20.75	18.75	15.50
Dec.	14.50	14.25	18.92	20.85	18.75	18.50
Average	16.07	17.78	17.08	18.98	19.13	17.01

	1945	1946	1947	1948	1949	1950
Jan.	$18.75	$18.75	$31.00	$42.50	$42.75	$23.10
Feb.	18.75	18.75	33.38	41.50	39.75	23.00
March	18.75	18.75	39.38	40.80	35.10	23.85
April	18.75	18.75	33.10	41.50	23.00	25.39
May	18.40	18.75	29.69	42.31	22.00	28.70
June	18.25	18.75	33.63	42.50	19.50	34.63
July	18.75	18.75	38.45	43.12	17.50	32.81
Aug.	18.75	18.75	38.50	45.00	18.31	36.50
Sept.	18.75	18.75	36.80	45.00	23.35	38.50
Oct.	18.75	18.75	40.25	45.00	24.25	38.50
Nov.	18.75	22.94	42.63	44.75	24.50	39.44
Dec.	18.75	28.00	41.10	44.50	24.25	44.50†
Average	18.68	19.87	36.50	43.20	26.19	32.41

* Price unchanged at $18.75 throughout 1942 and 1943.
† Estimate.

PITTSBURGH HEAVY MELTING
Prices of No. 1 Scrap, Per Gross Ton

	1929	1937	1939	1940	1941*	1944*
Jan.	$19.31	$19.50	$15.72	$18.25	$22.13	$20.00
Feb.	18.63	19.81	15.72	17.50	21.00	20.00
Mar.	18.44	23.15	15.97	16.88	21.00	20.00
Apr.	18.60	22.25	15.61	16.55	20.20	20.00
May	17.88	19.38	14.48	18.37	20.00	20.00
June	18.25	18.45	15.12	20.06	20.00	20.00
July	18.55	19.75	15.56	19.10	20.00	20.00
Aug.	19.00	21.85	16.15	18.56	20.00	19.95
Sept.	18.31	19.62	19.88	20.00	20.00	18.25
Oct.	17.30	16.62	23.05	21.45	20.00	16.10
Nov.	16.39	13.75	20.58	21.69	20.00	17.13
Dec.	15.45	13.75	18.58	22.28	20.00	19.94
Average	18.01	18.86	17.17	19.23	20.36	19.28

	1945	1946	1947	1948	1949	1950
Jan.	$20.00	$20.00	$32.25	$40.37	$41.25	$29.95
Feb.	20.00	20.00	34.94	40.43	39.25	31.25
Mar.	20.00	20.00	39.85	40.25	36.30	32.13
Apr.	20.00	20.00	35.40	40.25	24.94	33.00
May	20.00	20.00	30.38	40.25	23.00	37.75
June	20.00	20.00	33.88	40.25	22.00	44.50
July	20.00	20.00	38.45	40.87	20.75	41.50
Aug.	20.00	20.00	40.00	42.75	21.94	43.90
Sept.	20.00	20.00	37.75	42.75	27.35	43.75
Oct.	20.00	20.00	40.75	42.75	29.44	43.75
Nov.	20.00	23.94	41.88	42.75	31.95	43.75
Dec.	20.00	29.00	40.00	42.75	30.75	46.25†
Average	20.00	21.08	37.13	41.36	29.08	39.29

* Price unchanged at $20.00 throughout 1942 and 1943.
† Estimate.

MACHINERY CAST AT CINCINNATI
Prices of No. 1 Scrap, Per Gross Ton

	1929	1934	1936	1937	1939	1940
Jan.	$17.14	$ 9.50	$11.37	$15.75	$13.75	$17.65
Feb.	17.24	9.50	11.75	16.12	13.75	16.69
March	17.19	10.00	12.40	17.30	14.38	16.25
April	17.19	10.00	12.19	17.37	13.56	16.05
May	17.19	9.45	11.50	14.44	12.00	16.88
June	17.19	9.00	11.20	14.00	12.13	19.38
July	17.19	9.00	11.19	14.87	12.25	18.65
Aug.	17.05	8.88	12.43	16.25	11.80	18.75
Sept.	16.98	8.75	13.60	14.25	15.38	20.12
Oct.	16.92	8.75	14.00	13.38	19.55	20.55
Nov.	16.57	8.88	14.00	11.85	18.88	21.00
Dec.	16.52	9.85	15.12	10.75	17.75	22.50
Average	17.03	9.30	12.56	14.69	14.68	18.71

	1941*	1946*	1947	1948†	1949†	1950†
Jan.	$22.75	$20.00	$34.00	$60.00	$60.00	$36.90
Feb.	22.50	20.00	35.38	66.75	49.00	35.75
March	‡22.50	20.00	47.00	63.70	42.00	38.50
April		20.00	45.60	63.50	32.00	40.50
May		20.00	43.25	63.50	27.50	44.90
June		20.00	44.88	63.50	26.30	46.75
July		20.00	46.50	64.75	25.50	46.50
Aug.		20.00	45.50	67.00	29.88	49.10
Sept.	‡22.50	22.50	44.50	67.00	36.50	53.50
Oct.		22.50	45.50	65.50	40.50	59.20
Nov.	22.50	26.25	50.38	65.50	41.00	63.75
Dec.	22.50	30.80	53.60	65.50	40.25	66.00**
Average	22.05	22.04	44.67	64.68	37.54	48.45

† Average of No. 1 cupola cast prices.
‡ In transition from open market quotations to OPA price maximums, this grade not quoted. However, in September, the maximum schedules were revised to include this grade.
* Price unchanged at $20.00 from 1942 through 1945.
** Estimate.

CHICAGO HEAVY MELTING SCRAP
Prices of No. 1 Scrap, Per Gross Ton‡

	1929	1937	1939	1940	1941*	1944*
Jan.	$15.39	$17.81	$13.87	$16.38	$20.00	$18.75
Feb.	15.88	19.25	13.94	15.75	19.25	18.75
March	15.66	20.60	14.25	15.69	19.88	18.75
April	15.95	20.56	13.37	15.33	18.95	18.75
May	15.39	17.12	12.75	17.00	18.75	18.75
June	14.94	15.70	13.45	18.19	18.75	18.75
July	14.75	17.62	13.50	17.35	18.75	18.75
Aug.	15.03	19.70	13.87	18.03	18.75	18.75
Sept.	15.13	17.56	16.22	19.22	18.75	18.69
Oct.	14.30	14.69	19.16	19.75	18.75	16.90
Nov.	13.15	12.50	17.85	20.06	18.75	17.00
Dec.	12.50	12.38	16.67	20.60	18.75	18.69
Average	14.84	17.12	14.91	17.73	19.01	18.27

	1945	1946	1947	1948	1949	1950
Jan.	$18.75	$18.75	$29.75	$39.56	$40.06	$26.70
Feb.	18.75	18.75	31.63	39.12	35.63	27.50
March	18.75	18.75	36.69	38.95	33.70	28.25
April	18.75	18.75	33.05	39.18	23.63	28.75
May	18.75	18.75	29.38	39.25	23.00	33.75
June	18.75	18.75	30.88	39.25	20.85	38.75
July	18.75	18.75	36.97	40.81	19.75	37.25
Aug.	18.75	18.75	39.88	41.75	22.00	39.15
Sept.	18.75	18.75	38.75	41.75	26.30	39.81
Oct.	18.75	18.75	40.50	41.75	25.50	39.75
Nov.	18.75	23.13	39.13	41.75	30.30	39.75
Dec.	18.75	27.25	38.90	41.75	26.75	44.50†
Average	18.75	19.87	35.45	40.40	27.29	35.33

* Price unchanged at $18.75 throughout 1942 and 1943.
† Estimate.
‡ Changed from net ton basis April 30, 1941.

COAL EMPLOYMENT AND WAGES
Bituminous Production, Related Workers

	Production and Related Workers				All Employees
	Average Weekly Earnings	Average Weekly Hours	Average Hourly Earnings	Number (thousands)	Number (thousands)
1947	$66.59	40.7	$1.636	402.1	425.6
1948	72.12	38.0	1.898	413.1	438.2
1949	63.28	32.6	1.941	373.4	399.0
1950:					
Jan.	47.36	24.5	1.933	322.5	347.7
Feb.	49.83	25.4	1.962	60.0	82.6
Mar.	78.75	39.2	2.009	398.4	422.9
Apr.	72.79	36.0	2.022	393.8	419.0
May	68.37	34.1	2.005	387.9	413.1
June	70.09	34.8	2.014	385.4	410.9
July	68.88	34.2	2.014	357.0	381.8

Source: Bureau of Labor Statistics

U. S. CONSUMPTION OF SCRAP
Gross Tons, Domestic, Exports, Imports

	Domestic Consumption (Purchased and Home)	Exports (Purchased)	Imports (Purchased)
1910	13,100,000	25,825	72,764
1911	12,100,000	77,918	17,272
1912	16,100,000	105,965	23,612
1913	15,300,000	94,429	44,154
1914	12,200,000	33,134	34,839
1915	18,600,000	79,361	79,982
1916	23,400,000	212,765	116,039
1917	26,800,000	145,574	180,034
1918	25,400,000	2,160	63,730
1919	20,700,000	27,275	177,293
1920	26,000,000	219,250	140,645
1921	12,400,000	37,592	41,469
1922	23,700,000	67,784	142,969
1923	27,000,000	65,980	162,066
1924	26,200,000	97,748	66,841
1925	30,700,000	82,573	99,815
1926	32,200,000	104,838	86,725
1927	30,700,000	239,209	60,207
1928	34,000,000	516,148	63,314
1929	37,600,000	557,044	90,479
1930	26,600,000	358,649	27,482
1931	18,300,000	136,125	16,279
1932	10,000,000	227,522	9,775
1933	17,400,000	773,406	56,133
1934	18,800,000	1,835,170	44,421
1935	26,415,330	2,103,959	64,768
1936	36,358,133	1,936,132	142,245
1937	38,006,272	4,092,590	81,640
1938	21,344,934	2,998,591	24,451
1939	32,434,407	3,577,427	29,492
1940	39,758,635	2,820,789	1,927
1941	52,871,657	792,760	64,085
1942	53,808,171	126,473	82,257
1943	55,045,495	48,957	128,018
1944	54,776,072	85,430	97,162
1945	50,170,612	76,318	41,313
1946	44,182,240	121,679	26,984
1947	54,343,000	173,413	32,312
1948	58,285,000	216,093	370,600
1949	49,281,000	307,468	977,154
1950	60,910,000*	340,000*	553,000*

* Estimate by Institute of Scrap Iron & Steel.

Source: U. S. Bureau of Mines, and Institute of Scrap Iron and Steel

INGOT RATE AND SCRAP PRICE -1949-50

COMPOSITE PRICE OF NO. 1 HEAVY MELTING SCRAP
Average of Iron Age scrap prices, Pittsburgh, Chicago, Phila., Per Gross Ton

	1929	1937	1939	1940	1941*	1944*		1945	1946	1947	1948	1949	1950
Jan.	$17.02	$18.33	$14.94	$17.58	$20.88	$19.17	Jan.	$19.17	$19.17	$31.00	$40.81	$41.36	$26.58
Feb.	16.96	19.27	15.01	16.88	20.08	19.17	Feb.	19.17	19.17	33.31	40.35	38.21	27.25
Mar.	16.71	21.25	15.20	16.56	20.29	19.17	Mar.	19.17	19.17	38.65	40.00	35.43	28.05
Apr.	17.18	21.02	14.77	16.14	19.22	19.17	Apr.	19.17	19.17	33.85	40.31	23.86	29.04
May	16.54	18.54	14.17	17.60	19.17	19.17	May	19.05	19.17	29.81	40.60	22.67	33.40
June	16.39	17.28	14.71	19.31	19.17	19.17	June	19.00	19.17	32.79	40.66	20.78	39.29
July	16.60	18.79	14.92	18.47	19.17	19.17	July	19.17	19.17	37.95	41.60	19.33	37.25
Aug.	16.86	20.43	15.43	18.72	19.17	19.10	Aug.	19.17	19.17	39.46	43.16	20.85	39.85
Sept.	16.60	18.73	18.32	19.91	19.17	17.87	Sept.	19.17	19.17	37.77	43.16	25.67	40.69
Oct.	15.78	15.89	21.48	20.63	19.17	15.87	Oct.	19.17	19.17	40.50	43.16	26.40	40.67
Nov.	14.83	13.34	19.66	20.83	19.17	16.54	Nov.	19.17	23.34	41.21	43.04	29.98	40.98
Dec.	14.15	13.46	18.05	21.42	19.17	19.04	Dec.	19.17	28.23	40.00	43.00	27.18	44.00
Average	16.30	18.03	16.39	18.67	19.49	18.55	Average	19.15	20.27	36.36	41.65	27.58	34.75

* Price unchanged at $19.17 throughout 1942 and 1943.   † Estimate,

U. S. COAL PRODUCTION
In Short Tons, Bituminous, Anthracite

	Bituminous	Anthracite
1930	467,526,299	69,384,837
1931	382,089,396	59,645,652
1932	309,709,872	49,855,221
1933	333,630,533	49,541,344
1934	359,368,022	57,168,291
1935	372,373,122	52,158,783
1936	439,087,903	54,579,535
1937	445,531,449	51,586,433
1938	348,544,764	46,099,027
1939	394,855,325	51,487,377
1940	460,771,500	51,484,640
1941	514,149,245	56,368,267
1942	582,692,937	60,327,729
1943	590,177,069	60,643,620
1944	619,576,240	63,701,363
1945	577,617,327	54,933,909
1946	533,922,068	60,506,873
1947	630,623,722	57,190,009
1948	599,518,229	57,139,948
1949	437,868,036	42,701,724
1950*	413,541,000	37,653,000

* Ten months.   Source: U. S. Bureau of Mines

U. S. COAL CONSUMPTION
In Short Tons, Bituminous, Anthracite

	Bituminous	Anthracite
1930	454,990,000	1
1931	371,869,000	58,400,000
1932	306,917,000	50,500,000
1933	321,748,000	49,600,000
1934	347,043,000	55,500,000
1935	360,292,000	51,100,000
1936	422,795,000	53,200,000
1937	432,603,000	50,400,000
1938	338,086,000	45,200,000
1939	377,773,000	49,700,000
1940	432,757,000	49,000,000
1941	494,088,000	52,700,000
1942	542,214,000	56,500,000
1943	596,164,000	57,100,000
1944	591,830,000	59,400,000
1945	559,567,000	51,600,000
1946	500,386,000	53,900,000
1947	557,243,000	48,200,000
1948	536,672,000	50,200,000
1949	445,538,000	37,700,700

¹ Not Available.   Source: U. S. Bureau of Mines

U. S. COAL EXPORTS
In Short Tons, Bituminous, Anthracite

	Bituminous	Anthracite
1930	15,877,407	2,551,659
1931	12,126,299	1,778,308
1932	8,814,047	1,303,355
1933	9,036,947	1,034,562
1934	10,868,552	1,297,610
1935	9,742,430	1,608,549
1936	10,654,959	1,678,024
1937	13,144,678	1,914,173
1938	10,490,269	1,908,911
1939	11,590,478	2,590,000
1940	16,465,928	2,687,632
1941	20,740,471	3,380,189
1942	22,943,305	4,438,588
1943	25,836,208	4,138,680
1944	26,032,348	4,185,933
1945	27,941,857	3,691,247
1946	41,208,578	6,506,829
1947	68,666,963	8,509,995
1948	45,930,133	6,675,914
1949	27,842,056	4,942,670
1950*	15,038,415	2,277,288

* Eight months.   Source: U. S. Bureau of Mines

PRODUCTION OF COKE IN THE U. S.

In Net Tons, Beehive and Byproduct Cokes

	Beehive	By-Product Merchant Plants	By-Product Furnace Plants	By-Product Total	Total
1928	4,492,803	10,068,771	38,244,254	48,313,025	52,805,828
1929	6,472,019	12,187,439	41,224,387	53,411,826	59,883,845
1930	2,776,316	11,989,651	33,206,054	45,195,705	47,972,021
1931	1,128,337	11,538,309	20,817,240	32,355,549	33,483,886
1932	651,888	9,762,471	11,374,371	21,136,842	21,788,730
1933	911,058	10,533,968	16,144,168	26,678,136	27,589,194
1934	1,028,765	11,550,961	19,241,850	30,792,811	31,821,576
1935	917,208	11,189,792	23,034,261	34,224,053	35,141,261
1936	1,706,063	12,493,032	32,076,089	44,569,121	46,275,184
1937	3,164,721	13,076,539	36,134,209	49,210,748	52,375,469
1938	837,412	10,989,525	20,668,878	31,658,403	32,495,815
1939	1,444,328	11,070,506	31,811,807	42,882,313	44,326,641
1940	3,057,825	12,549,132	41,465,177	54,014,309	57,072,134
1941	6,704,156	13,494,509	44,987,913	58,482,422	65,186,578
1942	8,274,035	15,134,866	47,160,043	62,294,909	70,568,944
1943	7,933,387	14,750,033	48,992,643	63,742,676	71,676,063
1944	6,973,022	14,144,951	52,919,844	67,064,795	74,037,817
1945	5,213,893	13,399,116	48,695,172	62,094,288	67,308,181
1946	4,568,401	12,388,485	41,540,962	53,929,447	58,497,848
1947	6,687,301	13,387,699	52,880,850	66,758,549	73,445,850
1948	6,577,571	13,332,499	54,951,858	68,284,357	74,861,928
1949	3,414,948	12,112,922	48,109,559	60,222,481	63,637,429
1950¹	3,756,737	9,004,356	39,749,608	48,753,964	52,510,701

¹Nine months only.

Source: U. S. Bureau of Mines

BLAST FURNACE COKE RECEIPTS

In Short Tons

	By-Product	Total, By-Product and Beehive
1928	37,731,610	40,952,638
1929	40,577,068	45,468,149
1930	31,413,599	33,037,680
1931	18,448,986	18,916,535
1932	8,766,118	8,867,686
1933	13,110,485	13,262,408
1934	15,857,087	16,027,682
1935	20,815,385	20,934,821
1936	30,228,314	30,772,156
1937	34,730,491	36,751,969
1938	18,755,989	19,070,186
1939	30,640,220	31,498,557
1940	40,057,325	42,483,624
1941	44,646,004	50,454,325
1942	48,360,913	55,491,570
1943	50,885,639	57,690,160
1944	51,670,789	57,481,353
1945	46,910,622	51,002,921
1946	40,406,056	43,700,492
1947	52,268,441	57,836,505
1948	53,953,343	59,285,506
1949	48,229,358	51,104,570
1950*	54,000,000	58,000,000

* Estimated by THE IRON AGE.

Source: Bureau of Mines

CONNELLSVILLE FOUNDRY COKE

Net Ton at Oven, Monthly Review

	1929	1939	1940	1941*	1943*	1944
Jan.	$3.75	$4.75	$5.50	$5.75	$6.88	$8.06
Feb.	3.75	4.75	5.31	5.75	7.13	8.25
Mar.	3.75	4.75	5.25	5.85	7.38	8.25
Apr.	3.75	4.75	5.25	5.62	7.38	8.25
May.	3.75	4.75	5.25	6.72	7.44	8.25
June	3.75	4.75	5.25	6.88	7.50	8.25
July.	3.75	4.75	5.25	6.88	7.50	8.25
Aug.	3.75	4.75	5.25	6.88	7.50	8.25
Sept.	3.75	5.12	5.25	6.88	7.50	8.25
Oct.	3.75	5.65	5.25	6.88	7.50	8.25
Nov.	3.75	5.75	5.68	6.88	7.50	8.25
Dec.	3.50	5.75	5.75	6.88	7.50	8.25
Average	3.73	5.02	5.35	6.49	7.39	8.24

	1945	1946	1947	1948	1949	1950
Jan.	$8.25	$9.00	$8.50	$14.00	$16.94	$15.75
Feb.	8.25	9.00	9.38	14.00	16.75	15.75
Mar.	8.25	9.00	10.25	14.00	16.50	16.25
Apr.	8.25	9.00	10.65	14.00	16.50	16.25
May.	8.47	9.00	11.25	14.00	16.38	16.25
June	9.00	9.00	11.25	16.00	16.25	16.25
July.	9.00	9.68	12.75	16.50	16.13	16.25
Aug.	9.00	8.50	13.75	17.00	15.75	16.25
Sept.	9.00	8.50	13.75	17.00	15.75	16.25
Oct.	9.00	8.50	13.94	17.00	15.75	16.75
Nov.	9.00	8.50	14.00	17.00	15.75	16.75
Dec.	9.00	8.50	14.00	17.00	15.75	†16.75
Average	8.71	8.85	11.98	15.62	16.18	16.18

* Price unchanged at $6.88 throughout 1942.
† Tentative.

CONNELLSVILLE FURNACE COKE

Net Ton at Oven, Monthly Review

	1929	1939	1940	1941	1942	1943*
Jan.	$2.75	$3.75	$4.20	$5.50	$6.13	$6.00
Feb.	2.90	3.75	4.00	5.50	6.00	6.25
Mar.	2.98	3.75	4.00	5.52	6.00	6.50
Apr.	2.78	3.75	4.00	5.63	6.00	6.50
May.	2.75	3.75	4.00	6.00	6.00	6.50
June	2.75	3.75	4.00	6.13	6.00	6.50
July.	2.75	3.75	4.20	6.13	6.00	6.50
Aug.	2.73	3.75	4.63	6.13	6.00	6.50
Sept.	2.65	4.25	4.75	6.13	6.00	6.50
Oct.	2.65	4.90	4.75	6.13	6.00	6.50
Nov.	2.65	5.00	5.10	6.13	6.00	6.50
Dec.	2.63	5.00	5.38	6.13	6.00	6.60
Average	2.75	4.09	4.42	5.92	6.01	6.45

	1945*	1946	1947	1948	1949	1950
Jan.	$7.00	$7.50	$8.75	$12.50	$16.56	$14.00
Feb.	7.00	7.50	8.88	12.50	15.25	14.00
Mar.	7.00	7.50	9.00	12.50	14.50	14.13
Apr.	7.00	7.50	9.60	12.50	14.50	14.25
May.	7.15	7.50	10.50	12.50	14.38	14.25
June	7.50	7.50	10.50	12.70	14.25	14.25
July.	7.50	8.50	11.40	13.68	14.25	14.25
Aug.	7.50	8.75	12.00	14.75	14.25	14.25
Sept.	7.50	8.75	12.00	15.00	14.25	14.25
Oct.	7.50	8.75	12.38	15.00	14.25	14.25
Nov.	7.50	8.75	12.50	15.00	14.20	14.25
Dec.	7.50	8.75	12.50	15.00	14.00	†14.25
Average	7.30	8.10	10.83	13.63	14.58	†14.20

* Price unchanged at $7.00 throughout 1944.
† Tentative.

U. S. FOREIGN COKE TRADE

In Short Tons

	Exports	Imports for Consumption
1928	1,097,666	147,701
1929	1,238,035	119,724
1930	1,003,866	132,674
1931	754,302	103,563
1932	630,151	117,275
1933	637,819	160,873
1934	942,765	160,934
1935	613,975	317,379
1936	670,312	329,987
1937	526,683	286,364
1938	486,571	135,240
1939	589,925	141,911
1940	804,095	112,550
1941	708,971	267,886
1942	839,582	108,782
1943	994,607	98,127
1944	868,835	63,004
1945	1,478,746	51,964
1946	1,231,327	52,188
1947	835,069	104,093
1948	706,190	161,400
1949	548,256	277,507
1950 (7 months)	197,041	255,016

Source: U. S. Dept. of Commerce

BLAST FURNACE COKE

Consumption in Short Tons

1938	19,035,270
1939	31,422,272
1940	41,839,039
1941	49,469,972
1942	54,694,746
1943	56,701,419
1944	57,071,689
1945	50,653,221
1946	43,178,789
1947	57,147,644
1948	59,128,129
1949	51,356,617
1950	58,000,000

Source: American Iron & Steel Institute

U. S. COKE PRODUCTION — STEEL PLANTS, MERCHANT PLANTS, BEEHIVE (Millions of tons, 1928–1950)

Manganese Ore: World Production, U. S. Imports, U. S. Production.

METAL FACTS SECTION 3

MANGANESE ORE, U. S. IMPORTS FOR CONSUMPTION

In Short Tons, Manganese Content, Totals Include Small Producers, Not Listed

	1941	1942	1943	1944	1945	1946	1947	1948	1949	1950*
Angola									2,466	3,892
Belgian Congo		1,545	9,075	7,544			1,608	1,371	3,191	732
Brazil	156,711	147,908	168,234	88,899	115,916	38,985	70,234	71,561	88,164	28,561
Chile	8,669	2,113	7,893	2,885	42,699	65,222	19,930	4,927	6,836	1,008
Cuba	129,896	73,098	101,789	223,392	140,325	77,469	26,893	15,931	27,337	32,526
Egypt										21,305
France									101	
French Morocco									186	7,619
Gold Coast	113,737	95,698	112,700	82,408	108,747	144,275	112,102	112,503	138,566	127,448
Greece										178
India	219,756	301,777	231,596	172,385	103,586	160,958	140,007	152,852	172,503	211,662
Iran										1
Mexico	515	16,270	26,662	35,610	22,240	18,570	22,805	23,894	23,769	11,524
Mozambique									283	
Philippines	30,797						1,141	5,099	6,944	1,748
So. Africa									3	
Turkey										473
Union of South Africa	142,838	110,093	58,812	19,028	29,544	113,037	87,154	130,114	131,319	142,859
United Kingdom									31	
U.S.S.R.	16,929	9,200	2,341		70,082	121,753	141,975	182,455	71,357	17,590
W. Portuguese Africa. N.E.S.										1,554
Total Imports†	824,956	766,399	729,305	633,197	633,859	740,277	624,431	702,211	673,668	610,680

* Eight months,   † Total import figures include small imports from minor producing countries not otherwise listed.   Source: Dept. of Commerce.

U. S. MANGANESE ORES
Shipped by U. S. mines, Metallurgical*

State	1939	1940	1942	1943	1944
Ala.	115	64	26		49
Ariz.		348	2,946	5,779	8,519
Ark.	6,009	6,808	4,132	5,319	7,109
Calif.		177	10,112	20,604	21,540
Colo.		251	513	707	
Ga.	2,964	4,001	4,890	2,467	1,135
Idaho				36	
Mo.			239	180	
Mont.	2,512	9,218	120,409	130,789	153,665
Nev.		235	6,112	10,451	21,799
N. Mex.	380	50	1,267	469	273
N. C.	48			140	
Okla.			31	265	
Oreg.			45	143	
S. C.				312	1,400
So. Dak.			81	12	
Tenn.	8,183	7,821	2,247	2,501	418
Utah	56	30	970	91	30
Va.	532	1,168	11,024	7,040	20,034
Wash.	11		10,660	7,731	5,199
W. Va.		245	2,240		
Wyo.				60	
Total	20,810	30,416	177,966	195,096	241,170

State	1945	1946	1947	1948	1949
Ala.	32				
Ariz.	1,093		133	240	223
Ark.	6,663	1,101	841	212	2,851
Calif.	1,668				280
Colo.					
Ga.	1,056				
Idaho					
Mo.					
Mont.	143,888	129,227	123,490	119,339	107,399
Nev.	960	1,064	67		
N. Mex.	3,334	1,166	858		
N. C.					
Okla.					
Oreg.					
S. C.	41	78			
S. Dak.					
Tenn.			39	37	175
Utah.					
Va.	8,566	321			
Wash.	6,994	1,424			
W. Va.					
Wyo.					
Total	174,295	134,381	125,428	119,828	110,928

* In short tons.

Source: U. S. Bureau of Mines

WORLD PRODUCTION OF MANGANESE ORE

In Metric Tons, Includes Pct Manganese, World Total, Through 1949

	Percent Mn	1942	1943	1944	1945	1946	1947	1948	1949
U.S.S.R. (estimate)	41–48	1,823,000³	1,000,000	461,000	2,251,000	1,700,000	1,800,000	1,900,000	(6)
Gold Coast	50†	691,016	534,362⁴	479,499⁴	713,013⁴⁵	777,583⁴⁵	598,655⁴⁵	640,088⁵	285,501⁵,⁷
India	47–52	769,423	604,922	376,251	213,602	258,975	350,000	318,220⁵	551,828⁵
Union of South Africa	30–51	394,445	219,122	106,883	114,546	237,897	288,213	276,393	655,181
Brazil (exports)	38–50	306,241	275,552	146,983	244,649	149,149	142,092	141,253	(6)
United States (shipments)	35†	173,043	186,129	224,632	165,412	130,303	119,409	118,931	114,427
Morocco, French	32–50	44,273	49,010	27,550	45,292	57,080	109,452	214,412	233,830
Cuba	36–50†	249,255	311,214⁴	257,864⁴	198,243	130,764	50,397	29,073	62,503
Japan²	32–40	254,254	342,884	400,679	85,700	29,394	33,194	47,500	92,947
Mexico	41–45	40,000	70,503	80,671	51,959	25,000	31,400	53,800	54,671⁸
Chile	40–50	71,292	114,074	43,989	7,445	20,538	19,352	20,498	(6)
World total¹		5,167,000	4,040,000	2,900,000	4,260,000	3,700,000	3,800,000	3,900,000	4,530,000

† Total world production figures include production of smaller producing countries not otherwise listed and estimates by the Bureau of Mines for countries not reporting.
² Preliminary figures.
³ Estimate excludes Ukraine.
⁴ Dry weight.
⁵ Exports.
⁶ Data not available, estimate included in total.
⁷ January to May inclusive.
⁸ U. S. Imports from Mexico.

Source: U. S. Bureau of Mines

SHIPMENTS OF MANGANIFEROUS ORES

By U. S. Producers in Short Tons, Metallurgical and Battery Ores

Year	Manganese Ore (35 Pct or more Mn)	Ferruginous Manganese Ore (10 to 35 Pct Mn)	Manganiferous Iron Ore (5 to 10 Pct Mn)	Manganiferous Zinc Residuum	Battery Ore (35 Pct or more Mn)
1939	20,810	268,289	526,067	144,747	8,699
1940	30,416	358,406	914,526	172,990	10,383
1941	73,852	512,162	918,725	282,049	11,399
1942	177,966	265,663	1,500,613	292,051	15,410
1943	195,096	468,862	1,251,275	270,328	*12,704
1944	241,170	296,981	1,190,476	247,402	6,224
1945	174,295	114,327	1,408,527	224,331	8,042
1946	134,381	100,402	1,070,694	205,786	8,295
1947	125,428	128,562	1,044,961	227,547	6,188
1948	119,828	139,580	1,198,523	291,383	10,845
1949	110,928	24,885	1,052,231	158,902	14,983

* Includes 2,731 tons containing 27 pct Mn.

Source: U. S. Bureau of Mines

3 METAL FACTS SECTION

Prices: Ferromanganese, Ferrosilicon, Spiegel.
Chromite: Production, Prices, Shipments

FERROMANGANESE, 80 PCT

Eastern Producers, Carloads, Gross Ton

	1929	1934	1936	1937	1938	1939
Jan.	$105.00	$85.00	$75.00	$80.00	$102.50	$85.00
Feb.	105.00	85.00	75.00	80.00	102.50	80.00
Mar.	105.00	85.00	75.00	89.00	102.50	80.00
Apr.	105.00	85.00	75.00	95.00	102.50	80.00
May	105.00	85.00	75.00	100.62	102.50	80.00
June	105.00	85.00	75.00	102.50	102.50	80.00
July	105.00	85.00	75.00	102.50	92.50	80.00
Aug.	105.00	85.00	75.00	102.50	92.50	80.00
Sept.	105.00	85.00	75.00	102.50	92.50	95.00
Oct.	105.00	85.00	75.00	102.50	92.50	100.00
Nov.	105.00	85.00	80.00	102.50	92.50	100.00
Dec.	105.00	85.00	80.00	102.50	92.50	100.00
Average	105.00	85.00	75.83	96.84	97.50	86.67

	1940	1942**	1947**	1948	1949	1950
Jan.	$100.00	$120.00	$135.00	$145.00	$161.40	$173.40
Feb.	100.00	120.00	135.00	145.00	161.40	173.40
Mar.	100.00	120.00	135.00	145.00	169.35	173.40
Apr.	100.00	120.00	135.00	145.00	173.40	173.40
May	100.00	135.00	135.00	145.00	173.40	173.40
June	110.00	135.00	135.00	145.00	173.40	173.40
July	120.00	135.00	135.00	145.00	173.40	173.40
Aug.	120.00	135.00	135.00	145.00	173.40	173.40
Sept.	120.00	135.00	135.00	145.00	173.40	173.40
Oct.	120.00	135.00	145.00	162.00	173.40	173.40
Nov.	120.00	135.00	145.00	162.00	173.40	178.60
Dec.	120.00	135.00	145.00	162.00	173.40	181.20
Average	110.84	130.00	137.50	149.25	171.08	174.48

†Seaboard price prior to October 7. 1948.
*Price unchanged at $120.00 through 1941.
**Price unchanged at $135.00 from 1943 through 1946.

50 PCT FERROSILICON

Carloads per Gross Ton, Delivered*

	1929	1937*	1939	1940**	1943*	1944
Jan.	$83.50	$69.50	$69.50	$69.50	$74.50	$6.65
Feb.	83.50	69.50	69.50	69.50	74.50	6.65
March	83.50	69.50	69.50	69.50	74.50	6.65
April	83.50	69.50	69.50	69.50	74.50	6.65
May	83.50	69.50	69.50	69.50	74.50	6.65
June	83.50	69.50	69.50	72.00	74.50	6.65
July	83.50	69.50	69.50	74.50	6.65	6.65
Aug.	83.50	69.50	69.50	74.50	6.65	6.65
Sept.	83.50	69.50	69.50	74.50	6.65	6.65
Oct.	83.50	69.50	69.50	74.50	6.65	6.65
Nov.	83.50	69.50	69.50	74.50	6.65	6.65
Dec.	83.50	69.50	69.50	74.50	6.65	6.65
Average	83.50	69.50	69.50	72.11	6.65	6.65

	1945	1946	1947	1948	1949	1950
Jan.	$6.65	$6.65	$7.45	$9.80	$11.30	$11.30
Feb.	6.65	6.65	7.45	9.80	11.30	11.30
March	6.65	6.65	7.45	9.80	11.30	11.30
April	6.65	6.65	7.80	9.80	11.30	11.30
May	6.65	6.65	7.80	9.80	11.30	11.30
June	6.65	6.65	7.80	9.80	11.30	11.30
July	6.65	7.05	7.80	9.80	11.30	11.30
Aug.	6.65	7.05	7.80	9.80	11.30	11.30
Sept.	6.65	7.05	7.80	9.80	11.30	11.30
Oct.	6.65	7.05	8.80	10.50	11.30	11.30
Nov.	6.65	7.05	8.80	10.50	11.30	12.00
Dec.	6.65	7.05	9.18	10.50	11.30	12.00
Average	6.65	6.85	7.99	9.98	11.30	11.42

† Cents per lb of contained Si, since July 1943. Delivered east of Mississippi only, prior to October 7, 1948.
* Price unchanged at $69.50 throughout 1938.
** Price unchanged at $74.50 throughout 1941 and 1942.

SPIEGELEISEN, 19 TO 21 PCT.

Palmerton, Pa., Carloads, Gross Ton

	1929	1933	1936	1937	1938	1939
Jan.	$31.00	$24.00	$26.00	$26.00	$33.00	$28.00
Feb.	31.00	24.00	26.00	26.00	33.00	28.00
March	31.00	24.00	26.00	28.40	33.00	28.00
April	31.00	24.00	26.00	30.00	33.00	28.00
May	31.00	24.00	26.00	32.25	33.00	28.00
June	31.00	24.00	26.00	33.00	33.00	28.00
July	31.00	27.00	26.00	33.00	28.00	28.00
Aug.	31.00	27.00	26.00	33.00	28.00	28.00
Sept.	31.00	27.00	26.00	33.00	28.00	31.00
Oct.	31.00	27.00	26.00	33.00	28.00	32.00
Nov.	31.00	27.00	26.00	33.00	28.00	32.00
Dec.	31.00	27.00	26.00	33.00	28.00	32.00
Average	31.00	25.50	26.00	31.14	30.50	29.25

	1940*	1946*	1947	1948	1949	1950
Jan.	$32.00	$36.00	$40.00	$47.00	$62.00	$65.00
Feb.	32.00	36.00	40.00	47.00	62.00	65.00
March	32.00	36.00	42.00	48.00	63.20	65.00
April	32.00	36.00	44.00	52.00	65.00	65.00
May	32.00	36.00	44.00	52.00	65.00	65.00
June	34.40	36.00	44.00	52.00	65.00	65.00
July	36.00	36.00	44.00	52.00	65.00	65.00
Aug.	36.00	36.00	46.25	53.00	65.00	65.00
Sept.	36.00	36.00	47.00	60.75	65.00	67.50
Oct.	36.00	36.00	47.00	62.00	65.00	70.00
Nov.	36.00	38.00	47.00	62.00	65.00	70.00
Dec.	36.00	40.00	47.00	62.00	65.00	70.00
Average	34.20	36.50	44.35	54.15	64.35	63.13

* Price unchanged at $36.00 from 1941 through 1945.

WORLD PRODUCTION OF CHROMITE

In Metric Tons

	1942	1943	1944	1945	1946	1947	1948	1949
Union of South Africa	337,620	163,232	88,909	99,090	212,253	373,094	412,783	326,976
U.S.S.R.	400,000[4]	325,000[1]	(2)	(2)	(2)	(2)	(2)	350,000[1]
Philippines, Republic of	50,000[1]	60,000[1]	70,000[1]	(2)	58,000	195,185	256,854	246,744
Cuba	286,470	354,152	192,131	172,626	174,350	159,209	116,624	97,368
Southern Rhodesia	348,314	287,453	277,051	186,318	151,433	154,242	230,703	243,506
Turkey	130,053	165,633	139,397	146,716	103,167	102,875	285,353	434,117
New Caledonia	67,610	46,952	55,229	40,826	24,946	50,530	75,021	75,000[1]
India	50,380	33,789	40,190	31,105	45,510	32,000[1]	(2)	(2)
Sierra Leone	10,726	16,306	9,851	578	33,641[5]	18,000[1]	7,886	(2)
Greece	24,300	15,500	18,295	2,413	8.500	8,000[1]	1,500	3,381
Cyprus (exports)	2,936	7,986	469	1,070	1,158	5,283	6,899	14,875
Yugoslavia	100,000[1]	65,000[1]	(2)	(2)	(2)	(2)	(2)	(2)
Bulgaria	6,500[1]	7,000[1]	(2)	(2)	(2)	(2)	(2)	(2)
Canada	10,393	26,848	24,543	5,221	2,821	1,814	1,497	242
Japan[3]	67,540	58,520	71,135	28,539	7,079	2,347	9,340	(2)
United States	102,400	145,259	41,394	12,676	3,726	860	3,283	393
Albania	5,000[1]	....	....	....	....	....	16,500[4]	(2)
Brazil (exports)	5,776	7,813	4,721	1,490	....	(2)	1,626	(2)
Total World production[1]	2,012,000	1,798,000	1,350,000	1,100,000	1,140,000	1,650,000	2,113,000	1,859,000

1 Estimate.
2 Data not available; estimates by Bureau of Mines included in total.
3 Preliminary.
4 Planned production.
5 Exports.

Source: U. S. Bureau of Mines

CHROMITE ORE SHIPMENTS

In Short Tons, Shipments by U. S. Mines

1917	48,972	1934	413
1918	92,322	1935	577
1919	5,688	1936	301
1920	2,802	1937	2,600
1921	316	1938	909
1922	398	1939	4,048
1923	254	1940	2,982
1924	323	1941	14,259
1925	121	1942	112,876
1926	158	1943	160,120
1927	225	1944	45,629
1928	739	1945	13,973
1929	301	1946	4,107
1930	90	1947	948
1931	300	1948	3,619
1932	174	1949	433
1933	944	1950	425*

* Nine months.

Source: Bureau of Mines

CHROMITE IMPORTS FOR CONSUMPTION

In Short Tons, Cr_2O_3 Content, By U. S.

	1943	1944	1945	1946	1947	1948	1949	1950*
Brazil	4,233	2,008	1,272	....	....	860	....	....
British West Africa	....	....	....	14,164	8,968	3,481	4,122	....
Canada	8,016	9,533	1,804	4,090	34	82	....	....
Cuba	112,554	123,504	103,482	73,129	59,399	57,813	32,221	23,080
Cyprus	3,729	....	....	....	....	2,509	....	....
French Pacific Isles	....	....	....	....	....	....	....	22,280
Guatemala	....	....	....	....	....	....	....	423
India	1,372	....	....	8,500	5,065	....	3,837	....
Mozambique	....	....	....	....	....	....	....	6,910
New Caledonia	15,821	16,486	17,806	11,326	10,185	24,884	36,969	....
Pakistan	....	....	....	....	....	....	....	4,471
Philippines	....	....	....	10,469	71,793	81,669	102,008	51,498
Southern Rhodesia	116,718	90,251	104,048	47,228	36,402	59,620	44,531	55,688
Turkey	42,363	47,810	34,829	4,328	28,854	119,646	131,634	69,898
Union of South Africa	50,340	17,754	48,265	105,831	118,446	133,498	122,001	95,851
U,S,S,R,	48,227	57,816	86,378	53,391	136,021	190,118	51,424	13,295
Yugoslavia	....	....	....	....	10,824	5,863	4,844	....
Total Imports	404,361	365,694	400,742	332,456	485,991	680,723	533,591	343,394

* Eight Months.

Source: Dept, of Commerce

PRODUCTION OF SPIEGELEISEN

In Short Tons, U. S. Output

1930	97,506	1941	177,915
1931	75,936	1942	186,026
1932	41,795	1943	149,036
1933	29,885	1944	165,530
1934	51,261*	1945	139,039
1936	106,553	1946	111,696
1937	151,181*	1947	134,329
1938	12,668	1948	112,610
1939	102,470	1949	78,167
1940	114,119	1950	26,797**

* Shipments from mines.
† Estimated by The Iron Age.
** Nine Months. Source: U. S. Bureau of Mines

FERROMANGANESE SHIPMENTS

By U. S. Furnaces, in Short Tons

1931	178,268	1941	619,395
1932	78,867	1942	659,219
1933	142,747	1943	722,658
1934	165,701	1944	715,059
1935	217,982	1945	610,376
1936	361,035	1946	493,808
1937	403,023	1947	614,647
1938	250,566	1948	659,193
1939	322,227	1949	560,180
1940	503,291	1950	501,203*

* Nine months. Source: U. S. Bureau of Mines

FERROSILICON IMPORTS FOR CONSUMPTION

In Short Tons, Silicon Content

1933	1,290	1942	4,337
1934	1,102	1943	901
1935	875	1944	4,189
1936	590	1945	7,191
1937	2,269	1946	1,331
1938	701	1947	2,141
1939	1,160	1948	734
1940	1,235	1949	931
1941	6,190	1950	1,915*

Nine months. Source: U. S. Bureau of Mines

FERROSILICON PRODUCTION

By U. S. Furnaces, in Short Tons

1934	233,555	1943	818,351
1935	294,856*	1944	700,358
1936	329,774	1945	660,403
1937	405,989	1946	614,422
1938	279,808	1947	769,653
1939	313,560	1948	814,297
1940	409,699	1949	647,981
1941	618,227	1950	542,226†
1942	712,710		

* Shipments.
† Nine months. Source: U. S. Bureau of Mines

CHEMICALLY BONDED MAGNESITE BRICK

Per Short Ton, Baltimore, F.o.b. Plant

	1939	1941*	1947*	1948	1949	1950
Jan	$57.00	$61.00	$65.00	$75.00	$80.00	$80.00
Feb	57.00	61.00	65.00	75.00	80.00	80.00
Mar	57.00	61.00	69.00	75.00	80.00	80.00
Apr	57.00	61.00	70.00	75.00	80.00	80.00
May	57.00	61.00	70.00	75.00	80.00	80.00
June	57.00	62.00	70.00	75.00	80.00	80.00
July	57.00	65.00	70.00	76.00	80.00	80.00
Aug	57.00	65.00	70.00	80.00	80.00	83.00
Sept	57.00	65.00	70.00	80.00	80.00	83.00
Oct	57.00	65.00	70.00	80.00	80.00	86.00
Nov	57.00	65.00	70.00	80.00	80.00	88.00
Dec	57.00	65.00	74.00	80.00	80.00	88.00
Average	57.00	63.00	69.00	77.00	80.00	82.08

* Price unchanged at $65.00 from 1942 through 1948.

SILICA BRICK STANDARD GRADE PRICES

Mt. Union, Pa., Ensley, Ala., Carloads per 1000 Brick, F.o.b. plant

	1939*	1941*†	1945†	1946	1947	1948	1949	1950
January	$43.75	$47.50	$51.30	$54.40	$65.00	$73.00	$80.00	$86.00
February	40.00	47.50	51.69	54.40	65.00	73.00	80.00	86.00
March	40.00	47.50	52.85	54.40	65.00	73.00	80.00	86.00
April	47.50	47.50	52.85	58.90	66.00	73.00	80.00	86.00
May	47.50	47.50	52.85	60.40	70.00	73.00	80.00	86.00
June	47.50	48.45	52.85	60.40	70.00	73.00	80.00	86.00
July	47.50	51.30	52.85	60.40	70.00	74.00	80.00	86.00
August	47.50	51.30	52.85	60.40	70.00	80.00	80.00	86.00
September	47.50	51.30	54.45	60.40	70.00	80.00	80.00	86.00
October	47.50	51.30	54.44	64.08	70.00	80.00	80.00	91.16
November	47.50	51.30	54.40	65.00	70.00	80.00	80.00	94.60
December	47.50	51.30	54.40	65.00	72.00	80.00	80.00	94.60‡
Average	45.94	49.48	53.15	59.85	69.00	76.00	80.00	88.03

* Price unchanged at $47.50 through 1940.
† Price unchanged at $51.30 from 1942 through 1944.
‡ Tentative.

FIRST QUALITY FIRE CLAY BRICK

Pa.,* Ky., Mo., Ill., Md., Ohio, F.o.b. Plant**

	1941†‡	1945‡	1946	1947	1948§	1950
Jan	$47.50	$51.30	$54.40	$65.00	$73.00	$86.00
Feb	47.50	51.69	54.40	65.00	73.00	86.00
Mar	47.50	52.85	54.40	65.00	73.00	86.00
Apr	47.50	52.85	58.90	66.00	73.00	86.00
May	47.50	52.85	60.40	70.00	73.00	86.00
June	48.45	52.85	60.40	70.00	73.00	86.00
July	51.30	52.85	60.40	70.00	74.00	86.00
Aug	51.30	52.85	60.40	70.00	80.00	86.00
Sept	51.30	54.45	60.40	70.00	80.00	86.00
Oct	51.30	54.44	64.08	70.00	80.00	91.16
Nov	51.30	54.40	65.00	70.00	80.00	94.60
Dec	51.30	54.40	65.00	72.00	80.00	94.60
Average	49.48	53.13	59.85	69.00	76.00	88.03

† Price unchanged at $47.50 throughout 1939 and 1940.
‡ Price unchanged at $51.30 from 1942 through 1944.
§ Price unchanged at $80.00 through 1949.
* Add $5.00 for Salina. Pa.. after May. 1949.
** Carloads, per i00 brick

BURNED MAGNESITE BRICK

Baltimore, F.o.b. Plant, short ton

	1939	1941*	1947*	1948	1949	1950
Jan	$67.00	$72.00	$76.00	$86.00	$91.00	$91.00
Feb	67.00	72.00	76.00	86.00	91.00	91.00
Mar	67.00	72.00	80.00	86.00	91.00	91.00
Apr	67.00	72.00	81.00	86.00	91.00	91.00
May	67.00	72.00	81.00	f86.00	91.00	91.00
June	67.00	73.00	81.00	86.00	91.00	91.00
July	67.00	76.00	81.00	87.00	91.00	91.00
Aug	67.00	76.00	81.00	91.00	91.00	93.40
Sept	67.00	76.00	81.00	91.00	91.00	94.00
Oct	67.00	76.00	81.00	91.00	91.00	97.00
Nov	67.00	76.00	81.00	91.00	91.00	99.00
Dec	67.00	76.00	81.00	91.00	91.00	99.00
Average	67.00	74.00	80.00	88.00	91.00	93.28

* Price unchanged at $76.00 from 1942 through 1946.

CHEM. BONDED CHROME BRICK

Baltimore, F.o.b. Plant, Per Short Ton

	1939	1941*	1947*	1948	1949	1950
Jan	$47.00	$50.00	$54.00	$64.00	$69.00	$69.00
Feb	47.00	50.00	54.00	64.00	69.00	69.00
Mar	47.00	50.00	58.00	64.00	69.00	69.00
Apr	47.00	50.00	59.00	64.00	69.00	69.00
May	47.00	50.00	59.00	64.00	69.00	69.00
June	47.00	51.00	59.00	64.00	69.00	69.00
July	47.00	54.00	59.00	65.00	69.00	69.00
Aug	47.00	54.00	59.00	69.00	69.00	71.40
Sept	47.00	54.00	59.00	69.00	69.00	72.00
Oct	47.00	54.00	59.00	69.00	69.00	75.00
Nov	47.00	54.00	59.00	69.00	69.00	77.00
Dec	47.00	54.00	63.00	69.00	69.00	77.00
Average	47.00	52.00	59.00	66.00	69.00	71.28

* Price unchanged at $54.00 from 1942 through 1946.

IRON ORE RESERVES OF MINNESOTA

In Gross Tons, Mesabi Range, Vermilion Range, and Cayuna Range

	Mesabi Range	Vermilion Range	Cuyuna Range	Total
May 1, 1920	1,305,926,735	10,927,844	24,819,959	1,341,674,538
May 1, 1930	1,154,434,031	14,250,540	66,542,939	1,235,227,510
May 1, 1940	1,139,314,272	13,841,272	65,431,104	1,218,586,648
May 1, 1945	973,129,581	12,715,183	59,787,900	1,045,632,664
May 1, 1946	935,323,167	11,850,889	59,228,985	1,006,403,041
May 1 1947	937,071,161	11,135,293	56,089,288	1,004,482,442*
May 1, 1948	930,828,130	10,760,141	38,430,351	980,412,870*
May 1, 1949	909,484,014	12,515,362	37,718,580	960,265,700
**May 1, 1950	....	....	....	....

Note: Figures represent the estimated reserve tonnages as reported by the Minnesota Department of Taxation, and comprise the tonnage of ore in the ground plus the ore in reserve and current stockpiles. The figures do not include ore on state lands that were not under ease as of May 1 of each year: the estimated total tonnage for May 1, 1948 was 3,584,084 tons.
* Includes Fillmore County District: 186,700 tons in 1947; 394,248 tons in 1948 and 548,000 tons in 1949.
** 1950 figures not available.

Source: Minnesota Department of Taxation

Iron Ore Imports
(long tons)

1932	582,498
1933	861,153
1934	1,427,521
1935	1,492,435
1936	2,232,229
1937	2,442,069
1938	2,122,455
1939	2,412,515
1940	2,479,326
1941	1,707,811
1942	731,352
1943	399,117
1944	463,532
1945	1,197,925
1946	2,754,216
1947	4,903,484
1948	6,108,754
1949	*7,402,157
1950	*7,800,000

* Estimate by U. S. Bureau of Mines.
Source: U. S. Bureau of Mines

COAL USED IN STEELMAKING

In Net Tons for Coke, Steam, Other Production, And Use in Gas Producers

Purpose		1949	1948	1947	1946
Production of coke	Anthracite	139,501	*199,826	290,122	125,428
	Bituminous	73,100,113	*85,261,623	81,893,509	63,603,409
	Total	73,239,614	86,461,449	82,183,631	63,728,837
In gas producers	Anthracite	47,657	77,573	93,858	75,590
	Bituminous	748,219	1,121,619	1,410,092	1,275,536
	Total	795,876	1,199,192	1,503,950	1,351,126
Production of steam	Anthracite	233,771	294,981	323,821	413,493
	Bituminous	7,681,152	9,355,835	8,994,066	7,787,894
	Total	7,914,923	9,650,816	9,317,887	8,181,397
All other purposes	Anthracite	133,323	*259,687	142,140	94,673
	Bituminous	786,557	*1,087,562	1,124,384	1,057,149
	Total	919,880	1,347,249	1,266,524	1,152,022
Total consumption	Anthracite	554,252	*832,067	849,941	709,384
	Bituminous	82,316,041	*96,826,639	93,422,051	73,703,988
	Total	82,870,293	97,658,706	94,271,992	74,413,372

* Revised.

Source: American Iron & Steel Institute

CONSUMPTION OF NATURAL GAS

In Millions of Cu Ft in Melting, Annealing Furnaces for Steelmaking

Purpose	1949	1948	1947	1946
Melting furnaces	36,589	39,278	34,708	30,313
Heating and annealing furnaces	268,444	202,072	195,978	166,787
All other	93,852	33,130	24,776	27,319
Total	398,885	274,480	255,462	224,419

Source: American Iron & Steel Institute

USE OF ALLOYING MATERIALS

In Pounds; 7 Materials Used in Steelmaking

	Pounds of Total Metal Contained		
	1949	1948	1947
Chromium	148,442,803	212,708,570	179,023,934
Cobalt	991,645	916,953	692,813
Columbium	632,051	796,495	572,406
Molybdenum	11,243,780	16,348,818	13,447,003
Nickel	51,882,941	76,763,848	66,481,899
Titanium	4,222,221	3,784,965	3,335,646
Tungsten	2,170,483	4,313,518	4,027,315
Vanadium	1,079,024	1,550,147	1,329,490
Zirconium	1,440,141	2,069,335	1,835,506

Source: American Iron & Steel Institute

CONSUMPTION OF FUEL OIL

Use by Gallons in Melting and Annealing Furnaces in Steel Industry

Purpose	1949	1948	1947	1946
Melting furnaces	1,272,367,038	1,533,128,862	1,511,944,791	1,225,903,798
Heating and annealing furnaces	425,900,664	524,517,885	507,211,651	390,801,444
All other	137,028,931	137,892,300	148,671,659	166,474,828
Total	1,835,296,633	2,195,539,047	2,167,828,101	1,783,180,070

Source: American Iron & Steel Institute

NONFERROUS METALS CONSUMPTION

In Net Tons by the Steel Industry in 1949

Purpose	Copper	Lead	Tin	Zinc
For coating	25,811	2,785	35,377	265,317
All other	37,219	16,457	573	1,702
Total for 1949	63,030	19,242	35,950	267,019
Total for 1948	66,588	22,518	38,363	252,588
Total for 1947	58,239	21,233	37,470	251,132

Source: American Iron & Steel Institute

STEELMAKING USE OF FLUXES

In Net Tons Used in Furnaces; Fluorspar, Limestone, Lime, Other Fluxes.

Years	Fluorspar	Limestone	Lime	Other Fluxes	Total
1949	197,018	4,662,526	735,579	179,469	5,775,592
1948	226,594	5,355,905	933,438	230,427	6,746,364
1947	204,392	5,132,400	813,020	219,502	6,369,314
1946	158,056	4,060,870	612,097	184,942	5,015,965

Source: American Iron & Steel Institute

CONSUMPTION OF TAR AND PITCH

Use by Gallons in Melting Furnaces and Annealing Furnaces in Steel Industry

Purpose	1949	1948	1947	1946
Melting furnaces	270,139,839	287,035,244	259,136,561	159,565,596
Heating and annealing furnaces	4,610,706	4,180,405	3,082,304	8,489,945
All other	8,487,774	5,109,764	3,895,368	5,257,583
Total	280,238,319	296,325,413	266,114,233	173,313,124

Source: American Iron & Steel Institute

CONSUMPTION OF ELECTRIC POWER

Millions of Kw Hours for Iron, Steelmaking

Years	Generated	Purchased	Total
1949	8,124	11,577	19,701
1948	9,766	13,404	23,170
1947	9,204	11,811	21,015
1946	8,030	9,477	17,507

Source: American Iron & Steel Institute

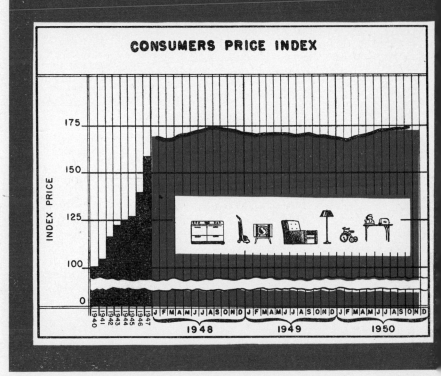

THE IRON AGE 4

SECTION

METAL INDUSTRY FACTS

Metal Products, Automotive, Railroad

STEEL PRODUCTS USED IN ELECTRICAL APPLIANCES

Shipments to Electric Appliance Industry Shown in Net Tons From 1946

Item	1946	1947	1948	1949	1950 9 Months
Ingots, blooms, billets, slabs, sheet bars, and seamless tube rounds	....	2,092	99	7	139
Wire rods	....	465	178	142	127
Structural shapes	1,174	1,376	3,321	1,890	1,167
Plates (sheared and universal)	9,400	10,417	8,915	6,205	5,670
Bars:					
Hot-rolled	11,149	14,716	12,567	9,648	12,464
Cold-finished	23,648	44,412	53,609	33,941	36,567
Tool steel	33	35	19	4	1
Pipe and tubes:					
Mechanical tubing }	4,940 }	10,359	5,493	3,818	5,221
Pressure tubing }			6,039	2,996	8,880
Standard pipe }			13,567	8,756	256
Line pipe }	14,775 }	16,371	382	114	....
Misc. tubular products }			2,910	1,156	....
Wire:					
Drawn	17,617	21,744	30,741	24,512	40,877
Nails and staples	168	47	559	269	439
Barbed and twisted	....	....	4	....	....
Black plate:					
Ordinary	8,073	8,738	10,699	6,914 }	53,587
Chemically treated	20	12	8	.... }	
Tin and ternplate:					
Hot dipped	836	1,237	1,696	1.470	9,543
Electrolytic	1,098	1,938	548	290	12,036
Hot-rolled sheets	183,306	307,067	363,015	197,288	238,664
Cold-rolled sheets	457,623	534,642	758,649	575,563	715,417
Galvanized sheets:					
Hot-dipped }			39,696	29,149 }	77,135
Electrolytic }	48,670 }	70,939	26,048	16,123 }	
Coated sheets—all other }			2,423	2,008	15,240
Electrical sheets and strip	5,165	3,316	26,240	14,663	25,639
Enameling sheets	106,266	147,767	187,482	112,733	129,692
Strip:					
Hot rolled	27,392	32,045	28,790	17,643	20,881
Cold rolled	56,343	63,288	98,888	100,937	106,260
All other	....	....	3	....	....
Total steel products	977,696	1,293,023	1,682,618	1,168,239	1,544,381

* IRON AGE estimate.
† Includes cooking stoves and ranges, refrigerators, washing machines and ironers, and other household appliances.
Source: American Iron & Steel Institute

A lot of the steel used in the products listed here will go into arms production for some time to come. Hints on selling to the armed forces will be found in "How to Sell to Uncle Sam," on p. 269. A list of items bought by the Army, Navy and Air Force and locations of their buying offices begins on p. 371. Government controls are digested on p. 365.

USE OF STEEL IN HOMES

Some Steel Items In Six-Room House

	Lb.
Metal lath	1800
Gas, water and heating pipe	1200
Steel window frames (16 at 50 lb each)	800
Kitchen equipment	800
Stove, refrigerator, sink, table top, kitchen cabinets, ventilators, washing machine, steel tile	
Structural shapes and columns	680
Heating equipment	640
Steel furnace, hot water tank, fuel oil tank	
Nails and miscellaneous wire	600
Door frames and sills	480
Gutters and downspouts	475
Bathroom	300
Bathtub, lavatory, medicine cabinet, shower cabinet, toilet (porcelain)	
Flashing and miscellaneous sheets	200
Steel doors (fire protection)	160
Electrical steel conduit	140
Hardware	90
Locks, knobs, hinges	
Radiator grilles	75
Screens	32
Laundry tubs	10
Total* Lb.	8482

* Some of the items may be lacking in some homes, or may be fashioned of other materials so that the total weight may be less than that which is given.

Source: American Iron & Steel Institute

STEEL USED IN A CONTAINER

Can Steel Contents Weights

Can Types	Gross Weight Used, oz
Paint (1 gal)	15.968
Fruit juice (No. 10)	11.080
Lard (3 lb)	8.288
Vegetable (No. 5)	5.920
Fruit (No. 3)	5.344
Olive oil (square 1 qt)	4.960
Soup (No. 2)	3.808
Grease (1 lb)	3.776
Fish (Tuna No. 1)	3.168
Meat (Square 12 oz)	2.848
Fish (Sardine No. 1 flat)	2.500
Condensed milk	2.480
Baby food	1.888

Note: Can weights are finished weights of the steel content.

Source: American Iron & Steel Institute

STEEL USED BY AUTO INDUSTRY

Production Level Estimates

Number of Cars and Trucks Produced	Estimated Total Steel and Strip Required (net tons)	Estimated Total Steel, All Types Required (net tons)
4,000,000	4,420,000	7,180,000
5,000,000	5,520,000	8,980,000
6,000,000	6,630,000	10,780,000

Source: THE IRON AGE

STEEL FOR AUTOMOBILE PARTS

Bar, Sheet and Strip Requirements

Estimates by THE IRON AGE, based on reports of steel sizes ordered from the mill. Passenger cars differ greatly in size, weight and design. It is not practical to compute averages on the basis of the data given below. The tables, do, however, give an indication of the specific steel requirements of auto plants for certain applications. The tables were compiled from data furnished by several auto producers and their steel suppliers. Some auto parts, oil pans and bumpers, for example, are made of more than one type of steel and the steel may be ordered double width.

	Typical Width, Inches	Gross Weight, lb
Cold-rolled sheet and strip—19 and 20 gage:		
Top	68–84	80–112
Hood top	43–72	60–80
Front fender	45–52	72–90[1]
Rear fender	42	80[1]
Quarter panel	45–59	72–90
Rear deck lid	39–47	44–62
Doors	35–50	36–54[2]
Bumpers	15–24	80 Max.
Oil pan	.....	.....
Hot-rolled sheet and strip—up to 18 gage:		
Floor pan, front	61–81	41–90
Floor pan, intermediate	55	37
Floor pan, rear	62–81	41–60
Oil pan	23–31	10–14
Frame	8–12¾	300–400
Wheel rims	7–9½	.....
Bumpers	6½–13	.....

	Typica Diam. Ordered, In.
Plain carbon hot-rolled bars	
Rear axle	1½
Spark plugs	⅞–$1\frac{5}{16}$
Camshafts	1⅞
Connecting rods	1¾
Motor support arm	1¼
Crankshaft sprocket	$2\frac{25}{32}$

Other auto parts for which carbon hot-rolled bars are usually specified include: Miscellaneous formed and forged parts, steering mechanism parts, engine and clutch parts, etc.

Plain carbon cold-finished bars:	
Transmission shafts	1⅝–$1\frac{43}{64}$
Transmission gear shift lever	1.0
Differential pinion shaft	0.766
Speedometer gear	2.0
Starter shaft	0.634
Spring shackle pins	0.489–½
Gear shifter shaft	¾
Piston pins	⅞

Other applications include: Heater parts, brake cylinder parts, front brake flange bolt, miscellaneous clutch parts, oil pump bracket bolt, door handle insert, door handle shaft, rear spring pin, reverse idler shaft, oil pump drive shaft, stud for rear shock absorber, distributor shaft, window regulator pin and cam thrust plunger.

	Typical Diam. Ordered, In.
Hot-rolled alloy bars	
Axle shafts	$1\frac{9}{16}$–1¾
Steering knuckles	1¼–2⅝
Steering arms	1¼–$1\frac{13}{16}$
Transmission gears	$1\frac{3}{16}$–1¾
Ring gears	3–4
Differential gears	1⅝–2
Springs, coil	0.592–0.750
Springs, leaf	0.231–0.313x1¾
Universal joint	1¾–1⅞
Propeller shafts	1⅞
King pins	1–$\frac{53}{64}$
Rear axle drive pinion	1⅝
Cold-finished alloy bars:	
Transmission shafts	1⅝
Piston pins	⅞
Oil pump drive shaft	½
Differential pinion	2⅜

1 Weight of 2 parts.
2 Total weight inner and outer panel.

STEEL IN A REFRIGERATOR
Use In Parts, Assembled Units, Pounds

Outer shell:	
Cold-rolled sheet	63.57
Cold-rolled strip	4.16
Liner:	
Enameling sheet	30.10
Compressor:	
Cold-rolled sheet	13.19
Electrical sheet	7.46
Provision compartment door:	
Cold-rolled strip	2.30
Cold-rolled sheet	15.75
Evaporator:	
Stainless sheet	10.03
Machine compartment door:	
Cold-rolled sheet	9.80
Condenser:	
Cold-rolled strip (fins)	7.26
Steel tubing	1.50
Condensing unit base assembly:	
Hot-rolled strip	3.91
Vegetable pan:	
Enameling sheet	1.23
Door trim:	
Stainless strip	1.11
Base trim:	
Stainless steel	0.29
Total	171.66

Source: American Iron and Steel Institute

IRON, STEEL IN A PIANO
Gray Iron Castings, Other Types, Pounds

Gray iron castings	194.00
Blued tuning pins:	
224 tuning pins	8.75
Machine screw stock:	
10 lag screws	1.07
76 action screws	0.98
3 Wood screws	6.80
Piano wire:	
224 strings	6.13
Cold-rolled bar stock:	
3 nose bolts	1.55
Steel stampings	1.02
Coppered pins:	
448 bridge pins	0.82
Nickel plated pins	0.55
Action springs	0.43
Total	222.10

Source: American Iron & Steel Institute

STEEL USED IN A TYPICAL AUTOMOBILE
Estimates From Various Sources of Sheet and Strip, and Total Steel Content

Source		Sheet and Strip	Total Steel
AMA	Materials used in a typical car 1942	....	3385 lb
AISI	Pounds of steel used in a typical car 1942	....	3544
THE IRON AGE	Steel required for a car in the lower price group	1740	2410
Confidential	Estimated steel consumption for a typical car, including scrap, 1941	....	2650
AISI	Steel delivered to the automobile industry 1946-47-48 per vehicle produced. (Inventory changes would affect this figure)	2454*	3992*
GM Research	Steel in typical car	2556	3320

* These figures undoubtedly include steel used for non-automotive applications.

WHAT MAKES AN AUTO
Materials in a 1950 4-Door Sedan

	Total (3824 lb car) (lb)	Approximate Requirements per 1000 lb* (lb)
Steel, Net	2556	669
Steel, Gross	3320[1]*	870
Gray Iron, Net	521	136
Gray Iron, Gross	641[2]*	168
Malleable Iron, Net	99.6	26.0
Malleable Iron, Gross	122.5[2]*	32.1
Aluminum and Alloys	11.4[3]	2.98[3]
Copper	26.0	6.8
Copper Alloys	15.6	4.08
Lead and Alloys	30.4	7.95
Zinc and Alloys	66.1	17.3
Antimony	1.1	.29
Manganese	18.8	4.9
Silicon	17.3	4.52
Chromium, Molybdenum and Nickel	7.2[3]	1.88[3]
Tin	1.37	.36
Fabric	92.3	24.2
Glass	76.3	20.0
Rubber Compounds	205.6	53.6
Plastics	5.2[3]	1.36[3]

[1] Based on an estimated 30 pct scrap loss, believed to be a conservative estimate. Scrap losses on bodies as high as 39 pct have been reported.
[2] Based on a 23 pct scrap loss.
[3] These figures vary over a wide range according to the manufacturer's specifications.
* Data not included in McCuen's paper.

Source: C. L. McCuen, General Motors Research Laboratories

STEEL IN PASSENGER CAR
Pounds of Steel by Type

	Lb.
Hot-rolled bars	532
Cold-rolled bars	81
Wire products	187
Pipe and tubes	10
Structural shapes	30
Hot-rolled sheets and strip	1,652
Cold-rolled sheets and strip	964
Plates	45
Terneplate	43
Total	3,544

Source: American Iron & Steel Institute

ALLOY STEELS IN AUTO
Typical Materials In Passenger Car

Part	SAE Steels Used
Axle Shafts	T 1330, 8630, 4063, 8640, 8653
Steering Knuckles and Arms	1340, 5130, 8640, 4053, 8830
Gears, Transmission	1340 Cyanided, 4032 Carb., 8620 Carb., 4820 Carb.
Gears, Differential	8620 Carb., 4620 Carb.
Springs, Coil and Leaf	4068, 9260, 5160
Bolts	1335, 4037, 4042, 3140, 8640

It is estimated that a typical passenger car uses from 260 to 280 lb of alloy steel.

MATERIALS USED IN TYPICAL 1950 FOUR-DOOR SEDAN

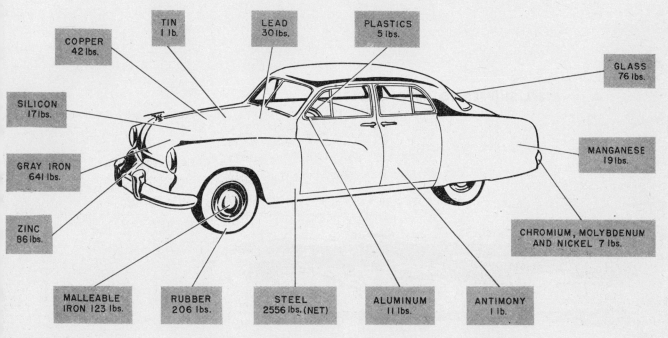

TIN
1 lb.

LEAD
30 lbs.

PLASTICS
5 lbs.

COPPER
42 lbs.

GLASS
76 lbs.

SILICON
17 lbs.

MANGANESE
19 lbs.

GRAY IRON
641 lbs.

ZINC
66 lbs.

CHROMIUM, MOLYBDENUM
AND NICKEL 7 lbs.

MALLEABLE
IRON 123 lbs.

RUBBER
206 lbs.

STEEL
2556 lbs. (NET)

ALUMINUM
11 lbs.

ANTIMONY
1 lb.

MOTOR VEHICLE PRODUCTION ESTIMATE

Estimated U. S. Output Listed By Companies

PASSENGER CARS	1946	1947	1948	1949	10 Months 1950*
Chevrolet	397,113	695,993	775,989	1,109,958	1,292,144
Pontiac	131,538	223,015	253,469	333,954	395,725
Oldsmobile	114,674	191,454	194,755	282,885	331,625
Buick	156,080	267,830	275,504	398,482	461,281
Cadillac	28,444	59,436	66,209	81,545	93,400
Total Gen. Motors	827,849	1,437,728	1,565,926	2,206,824	2,574,175
Plymouth	242,534	350,327	377,797	575,071	477,279
Dodge	156,070	231,804	239,164	298,399	278,078
DeSoto	62,860	81,552	92,920	108,440	101,974
Chrysler	76,693	108,103	119,061	141,825	137,757
Total Chrysler	538,157	771,786	828,942	1,123,735	995,088
Ford	372,917	601,665	549,077	841,170	1,066,845
Mercury	70,955	124,612	154,702	203,339	280,231
Lincoln	13,496	29,275	43,688	33,132	29,210
Total Ford	457,368	755,552	747,467	1,077,641	1,376,286
Total Big Three	1,823,374	2,965,066	3,142,335	4,408,200	4,945,549
Crosley	5,007	19,588	27,982	8,942	6,152
Graham					
Hudson	91,215*	100,862	143,697	142,462	114,467
Kaiser-Frazer	11,753	144,507	181,316	57,995	119,325
Nash	98,769	113,315	118,621	142,592	161,525
Packard	41,706	55,477	98,898	104,593	53,894
Studebaker	77,567	123,641	166,755	228,402	228,539
Willys	6,533	33,336	32,701	32,874	31,189
Total Independents	332,550	590,726	769,880	717,860	715,091
Total, Passenger Cars	2,155,924	3,555,792	3,912,215	5,126,060	5,660,640
MOTOR TRUCKS					
Chevrolet	270,151	335,346	389,690	383,543	419,063
GM Truck	33,850	61,918	92,677	83,840	90,944
Pontiac				2,490	1,798
Total Gen. Motors	304,001	397,264	482,367	469,873	511,805
Dodge	133,192	165,905	172,020	151,513	97,261
Ford	198,767	247,832	301,791	244,613	301,783
Total, Big Three	635,960	811,001	956,178	865,999	910,849
Crosley		3,055	2,673	375	439
Diamond T	8,889	16,205	12,684	5,545	5,891
Federal	6,026	10,114	3,898	1,649	1,524
Hudson	3,097	2,918			
International	113,546	153,009	166,784	110,572	83,355
Mack	4,855	17,072	11,570	9,025	9,258
Nash		129	1,051	676	468
Reo	16,743	20,349	11,452	3,600	6,689
Studebaker	43,196	67,810	67,983	63,473	41,886
White-Indiana	12,542	18,479	12,507	8,707	11,993
Willys	71,455	86,397	104,989	49,973	37,628
Miscellaneous	25,997	30,162	17,703	12,544	11,220
Total, Independents	306,346	425,699	413,294	266,139	210,351
Total, Trucks	942,306	1,236,700	1,369,492	1,132,138	1,121,200
Total, Cars and Trucks				6,258,198	6,781,840
Canadian, Cars and Trucks				290,981	325,879
Total Vehicles, U. S. and Canada				6,549,179	7,107,719

* Preliminary estimate.

Source: Ward's Automotive Reports

STEEL SHIPPED TO AUTO INDUSTRY

Net Ton Deliveries* for Cars, Trucks, Parts Makers

	Hot-Rolled Sheets	Cold-Rolled Sheets	Galvanized	All Other Coated Sheets	Elec. Sheets and Strips	Hot-Rolled Strip	Cold-Rolled Strip	Enameling Sheets	Total Steel Products
Pass. cars, trucks and other commercial vehicles	1,130,625	2,769,213	13,001	67,601	3,443	281,587	174,377	1,844	6,198,735
Parts, accessories and supplies	1,172,505	994,734	26,505	25,274	5,982	345,513	236,417	2,250	4,128,171
Automotive forgings									402,771
	2,303,130	3,763,947	39,506	92,893	9,425	627,100	410,794	4,094	10,729,677

* Nine Months 1950.

Source: American Iron & Steel Institute

AUTOMOBILE INDUSTRY WAGES

Employment and Average Earnings

	All Employees Number (thousands)	Production and Related Workers			
		Number (thousands)	Average Weekly Earnings	Average Weekly Hours	Average Hourly Earnings
1947	776.2	648.8	$57.45	39.0	$1.473
1948	792.8	657.6	61.86	38.4	1.611
1949	769.0	643.5	65.97	38.9	1.696
1950					
Jan.	797.4	675.4	70.14	40.9	1.715
Feb.	689.0	567.1	67.64	39.6	1.708
Mar.	698.9	575.6	69.08	40.4	1.710
Apr.	720.3	595.3	73.77	42.2	1.748
May	862.4	736.3	69.62	41.0	1.698
June	894.8	763.2	72.37	42.0	1.723
July	883.7	756.7	74.35	42.1	1.766
Aug.	901.8	774.1	75.12	42.3	1.776
Sept.	916.5	790.9	74.01	40.8	1.814

Source: Bureau of Labor Statistics

LOCOMOTIVES ORDERED IN U. S.

Steam, Diesel and Electric

	Steam	Diesel-Electric	Electric	Total
1929	1,055	80	95	1,230
1932	5	7	0	12
1935	30	60	7	97
1936	435	77	24	536
1937	173	145	36	354
1938	36	160	29	225
1939	119	249	32	400
1940	207	492	13	712
1941	302	1,104	38	1,444
1942	363	894	12	1,269
1943	413	635	0	1,048
1944	74	680	3	757
1945	148	691	6	845
1946	55	989	8	1,052
1947	79	2,149	1	2,229
1948	54	2,661*	2	2,717
1949	13	1,785	10	1,803
1950†	15	2,559	12	2,586

* 1948 Diesel orders shown as units. Previous orders shown as locomotives which may include one or more units.
† January through November.

Source: Railway Age

R. R. PASSENGER CARS

Steel Use In Tons Per Car

	Coach	Sleeper Roomette and Bedrooms	Baggage-Express
Billets	1.72	1.82	1.82
Shapes	4.84	4.84	4.77
Plates	5.79	5.79	6.11
Bars	2.84	2.84	2.88
Pipe—steel	.14	.19	.14
Sheets and strip	11.78	12.17	11.72
Wheels	3.80	3.80	3.80
Axles	1.70	2.05	2.05
Steel castings—body	.53	.53	.53
Steel castings—truck	4.89	5.17	5.17
Miscellaneous	.32	.32	.32
Totals	38.35	39.52	38.31

Note: Above covers cars with all-steel frame construction and aluminum and steel interior finish.

Source: American Railway Car Institute

R. R. EQUIPMENT EMPLOYMENT

Average Earnings by Week, Hour

	All Employees Number (thousands)	Production and Related Workers			
		Number (thousands)	Average Weekly Earnings	Average Weekly Hours	Average Hourly Earnings
1947	81.4	66.6	$57.06	40.5	$1.409
1948	84.8	69.6	62.24	40.0	1.556
1949					
Jan.	87.6	71.6	66.50	40.8	1.630
Feb.	88.2	72.1	65.53	40.7	1.610
Mar.	87.5	71.5	64.76	39.9	1.623
Apr.	84.6	68.8	62.42	38.6	1.617
May	83.0	67.4	63.39	39.2	1.617
June	81.3	65.6	62.63	38.9	1.610
July	73.5	58.4	61.16	37.8	1.618

Source: Bureau of Labor Statistics

Steel Requirements For Railroad Freight Cars,
Farm Machinery Made In U. S.

METAL FACTS SECTION 4

STEEL REQUIREMENTS FOR RAILROAD FREIGHT CARS
Steel Products Used in Principal Types of Cars, Net Tons

	Box 40'6" 50-T	Box 50'6" 50-T	Gon. H.S. 50-T	Gon. L.S. 70-T	Gon. 65' 70-T	Hopper 50-T	Hopper 70-T	Cov. Hopper 70-T	Ore	Flat 50-T	Flat 70-T	Refr. 40-T	Stock 40-T	Tank 10M-Gal ICC-103 50-T	Tank Hi-Press ICC-105 50-T	Average per Car Basis: Cars Delivered 1945-49
Billets and slabs	0.27	0.28	0.36	0.36	....	0.35	0.40	0.31	0.06	0.27	0.32	0.30	0.27	0.30	0.60	0.325
Shapes	4.15	5.14	3.52	5.35	5.40	3.89	4.81	4.96	2.67	5.27	7.32	4.15	4.15	2.50	3.20	4.201
Plates	2.85	2.92	8.71	8.07	12.60	5.87	7.86	6.06	6.66	7.39	8.76	2.85	2.85	10.70	16.60	5.575
Bars	0.63	1.33	0.58	0.78	1.00	0.75	0.75	0.94	1.11	0.87	1.86	0.63	0.63	0.10	0.12	0.698
Pipe	0.10	0.12	0.10	0.13	0.13	0.10	0.10	0.10	0.09	0.11	0.11	0.10	0.10	0.16	0.27	0.107
Sheets and strip	2.97	4.99	0.08	0.08	....	0.29	0.29	3.05	0.03	0.12	0.11	4.60	0.50	0.60	3.60	1.761
Wheels, rolled steel*	2.24	2.24	2.24	2.44	2.44	2.24	2.44	2.44	2.44	2.24	2.44	2.24	2.24	2.24	3.60	2.807
Axles	1.67	1.67	1.67	2.03	2.03	1.67	2.03	2.03	2.03	1.67	2.03	1.41	1.41	1.67	1.67	1.731
Other forgings	0.46	0.46	0.66	0.66	0.25	0.51	0.60	0.87	0.13	0.41	0.41	0.46	0.46	0.75	0.80	0.548
Steel castings	3.60	3.60	4.25	4.25	3.39	3.60	4.18	4.52	3.60	3.60	4.11	3.60	3.60	3.60	3.60	3.806
Miscellaneous	1.07	1.07	1.05	1.11	0.60	0.93	1.06	1.19	2.33	1.12	1.13	1.07	1.07	1.00	1.10	1.044
Totals	20.01	23.82	23.22	25.26	27.84	20.20	24.52	26.47	21.15	23.07	28.60	21.41	17.28	23.62	33.80	22.081

* If chilled iron wheels used, this amount eliminated.

Source: American Railway Car Institute

STEEL USED IN THE AVERAGE FREIGHT CAR

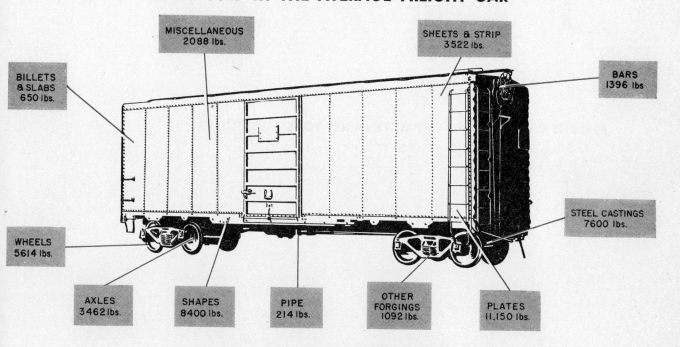

MISCELLANEOUS 2088 lbs.

SHEETS & STRIP 3522 lbs.

BILLETS & SLABS 650 lbs.

BARS 1396 lbs

WHEELS 5614 lbs.

STEEL CASTINGS 7600 lbs.

AXLES 3462 lbs.

SHAPES 8400 lbs.

PIPE 214 lbs.

OTHER FORGINGS 1092 lbs.

PLATES 11,150 lbs.

SELECTED FARM MACHINERY
Manufactured in the U. S. in Number of Units

	Tractor Mold Board Plows	Corn Binders	Corn (Field) Pickers	Silage Cutters	Grain Binders	Grain Threshers	Combines, Harv. and Thresh.	Manure Spreaders	Tractor Cultivators	One Way Disc Plows or Tillers	Hay Loaders	Pickup Hay Balers	Milking Machines	Power Sprayer and Dusters	Field Cultivators	Sweep Rakes
1929	122,897	15,246	8,620	8,065	65,069	13,818	36,957	61,000	34,634	No data	24,920	2,172	24,092	11,324	No data	18,273
1931	26,827	No data	3,243	3,156	15,356	3,954	5,907	19,707	15,631	7,085	10,042	1,311	14,896	5,915	No data	7,118
1935	57,862	19,290	1,845	7,294	47,680	4,619	3,872	31,462	54,519	6,980	8,813	No data	4,217	8,180	4,819	5,244
1936	116,213	19,364	4,052	12,850	66,970	8,622	16,983	53,361	115,957	9,651	9,841	No data	9,655	5,755		8,506
1937	149,006	16,694	13,586	10,197	32,295	4,996	29,403	60,057	127,188	15,027	27,256	No data	21,502	9,680	11,774	7,094
1938	117,960	12,765	16,722	11,743	47,619	8,649	48,046	27,344	90,760	13,245	17,481	No data	18,787	7,920	11,488	7,508
1939	98,672	5,535	16,044	9,125	15,242	2,781	41,537	33,363	65,547	9,408	15,350	454	22,798	9,904	6,004	4,783
1940	171,896	9,990	11,638	8,507	No data	2,054	46,552	46,075	104,345	14,148	20,226	1,464	44,374	6,845	8,138	6,497
1941	183,497	13,175	15,958	11,403	No data	2,459	54,296	69,618	175,285	17,074	29,930	8,200	55,711	9,915	13,115	9,397
1942	132,131	No data	13,640	8,332	5,171	2,146	41,722	56,881	141,704	11,274	19,426	8,801	37,287	10,363	11,313	9,812
1943	55,182	3,077	12,592	4,163	3,782	668	29,219	17,448	83,802	5,363	11,508	5,418	46,892	7,475	3,718	6,549
1944	121,689	9,709	25,371	8,757	11,317	1,858	44,704	49,522	181,554	12,945	21,065	12,126	78,421	13,875	17,618	14,599
1945	158,159	8,699	35,885	9,005	9,054	1,185	51,418	44,997	191,330	13,122	20,591	12,535	125,413	16,928	21,214	17,699
1946	162,113	7,218	34,554	9,294	No data	2,583	48,811	44,143	151,489	16,731	25,273	11,072	146,203	26,598	22,323	40,045
1947	244,115	No data	66,055	13,222	9,523	1,277	76,638	64,927	245,735	25,670	20,407	26,573	176,195	57,454	39,564	21,358
1948	308,805	No data	78,808	10,709	No data	2,161	90,668	118,206	359,057	35,429	28,472	48,469	128,599	119,952	74,892	14,901
1949	329,463	No data	90,410	7,752	No data	2,062	104,888	128,497	327,244	29,785	13,109	56,849	108,540	73,289	62,569	5,176

Source: U. S. Department of Commerce

4 METAL FACTS SECTION

Railroad Freight Data: Revenue Freight Loaded, Freight Car Carrying Capacity; Freight Cars Delivered; Passenger Cars Ordered

CARS OF REVENUE FREIGHT LOADED, BY PRODUCTS

Grain, Ore, Live Stock, Coal, Coke, Forest Products Shown

Period	Total Revenue Freight Loaded	Grain and Grain Products	Live Stock	Coal	Coke	Forest Products	Ore	Merchandise L.C.L.	Miscellaneous
1929	52,827,925	2,396,195	1,419,191	9,095,271	634,427	3,248,408	2,281,566	13,205,698	20,547,169
1932	28,179,952	1,653,381	949,287	5,338,938	223,766	899,198	210,367	9,069,736	9,835,279
1935	31,504,134	1,577,053	714,495	6,144,691	339,628	1,383,872	1,036,432	8,080,675	12,227,288
1936	36,109,112	1,804,767	759,092	6,937,416	480,043	1,682,582	1,623,008	8,275,977	14,546,227
1937	37,670,464	1,788,966	721,601	6,976,938	507,817	1,828,032	2,207,632	8,465,868	15,173,610
1938	30,457,078	1,967,318	702,920	5,540,739	274,639	1,417,869	845,965	7,681,847	12,025,781
1939	33,911,498	1,940,054	694,246	6,082,520	413,686	1,584,336	1,615,036	7,830,935	13,750,675
1940	36,357,854	1,834,593	685,282	6,819,614	548,686	1,799,650	2,148,428	7,679,389	14,842,212
1941	42,352,127	2,027,824	651,310	7,606,315	678,841	2,189,840	2,682,726	8,039,515	18,475,756
1942	42,771,102	2,185,022	745,180	8,356,430	731,777	2,445,231	3,015,745	5,536,792	19,754,925
1943	42,439,951	2,648,308	837,777	8,507,036	751,687	2,228,907	2,815,572	5,079,720	19,570,944
1944	43,408,295	2,520,733	892,145	8,889,518	750,685	2,271,450	2,648,589	5,427,928	20,007,247
1945	41,918,120	2,733,968	893,525	8,296,208	694,707	2,038,992	2,474,336	5,528,509	19,257,875
1946	41,341,278	2,497,043	924,919	8,004,021	586,890	2,263,246	1,995,721	6,325,295	18,744,143
1947	44,502,188	2,725,655	770,123	9,088,131	732,130	2,414,548	2,651,024	6,071,293	20,049,284
1948	42,833,902	2,467,286	630,873	8,729,745	735,801	2,359,193	2,780,635	5,457,824	19,672,545
1949	35,909,741	2,583,900	551,124	5,217,387	588,181	1,952,294	2,210,337	4,588,485	17,218,033
1950 to Nov. 25	35,270,376	2,209,593	442,246	6,499,434	652,005	2,004,800	2,432,772	3,888,718	17,140,808
1948: First quarter	9,856,383	510,690	124,469	2,155,710	187,379	562,616	182,100	1,394,022	4,749,497
Second quarter	10,910,817	552,185	154,344	2,195,189	170,088	585,696	931,153	1,399,437	4,922,725
Third quarter	11,246,528	740,063	144,110	2,227,097	183,791	653,999	1,021,096	1,327,183	4,949,189
Fourth quarter	10,820,174	664,348	207,950	2,151,749	194,543	566,982	646,286	1,337,182	5,051,134
1949: First quarter	8,987,425	562,133	119,723	1,757,363	196,483	458,307	222,606	1,208,392	4,462,418
Second quarter	9,753,724	622,159	112,749	821,236	169,795	499,311	950,859	1,197,220	4,380,395
Third quarter	9,070,307	762,897	143,368	1,248,681	120,231	493,018	886,050	1,110,096	4,305,966
Fourth quarter	8,098,285	636,711	175,284	1,390,107	101,672	501,658	150,822	1,072,777	4,069,254
1950: First quarter	8,127,115	525,216	103,957	1,480,017	147,090	456,864	147,072	1,041,296	4,225,603
Second quarter	9,760,148	552,226	103,628	1,891,185	185,982	557,694	693,573	1,065,858	4,701,002
Third quarter	10,611,999	683,245	118,840	1,872,773	192,140	617,211	1,062,017	1,095,869	4,969,904
Fourth quarter*	6,771,114	448,906	115,821	1,255,459	126,793	373,031	524,110	685,695	6,241,299

*Through Nov. 25

Source: Assn. of American Railroads

FREIGHT CAR CARRYING CAPACITY IN NET TONS

Data for Principal Types of Cars Used On Class 1 Railroads

	Box	Flat	Stock	Gondola and Hopper	Tank	Refrig.	Others	Average
1929	41.1	43.2	37.2	53.6	44.7	32.9	51.9	46.3
1932	42.	44.2	37.9	54.	45.	33.4	52.8	47.
1935	43.1	46.1	38.3	54.8	45.	35.2	53.4	48.3
1936	43.5	46.7	38.5	55.2	44.8	35.4	55.8	48.8
1937	43.9	46.9	38.9	55.4	45.	36.2	54.4	49.2
1938	44.2	47.1	39.1	55.6	45.	36.3	54.6	49.4
1939	44.5	47.3	39.3	55.7	45.	36.3	54.1	49.7
1940	44.8	47.7	39.5	56.	45.3	36.9	50.9	50.
1941	45.2	48.	39.5	56.2	45.3	37.	51.2	50.3
1942	45.5	48.6	39.6	56.3	46.1	36.8	51.4	50.5
1943	45.5	48.9	39.6	56.5	46.	36.8	50.8	50.7
1944	45.8	49.1	39.5	56.4	46.1	36.9	49.7	50.8
1945	46.2	49.2	39.5	56.6	46.1	36.9	50.2	51.1
1946	46.3	49.3	39.5	56.8	46.1	37.	49.4	51.2
1947	46.7	49.4	39.5	56.8	46.2	37.1	50.9	51.5
1948	47.1	49.6	39.6	57.2	46.3	37.1	51.4	51.9
1949	47.3	49.9	39.6	57.9	47.1	37.5	52.	52.4

Source: American Railway Car Institute

DOMESTIC RAILROAD PASSENGER CARS ORDERED

Coach, Dining and Combination Type Cars Shown In Data From 1929

	Coach	Coach and Comb.	Baggage and Express	Express Refr. and Milk	Sleeping and Comb.	Parlor, Club, etc.	Dining	Postal and Comb.	All Other	Total
1929	390	98	351	505	490	79	103	184	183	2383
1932	2	1	4	2	1	0	0	4	30	44
1935	14	16	7	55	18	6	10	7	0	133
1936	294	36	35	0	5	26	44	10	1	451
1937	136	23	58	110	171	18	37	8	6	567
1938	85	28	42	0	86	10	15	10	2	278
1939	97	20	9	0	125	18	38	12	2	321
1940	220	26	8	0	53	6	48	13	5	379
1941	164	13	69	0	197	16	36	46	8	549
1942	0	1	2	0	0	0	0	0	31	34
1943	14	2	3	0	0	0	4	12	1650	1685
1944	461	36	20	0	26	16	53	12	101	725
1945	296	17	134	25	570	84	98	54	1767	2993
1946	311	40	22	0	587	53	143	46	36	1238
1947	132	0	22	0	72	36	19	29	6	316
1948	143	0	51	0	156	20	25	10	101	506
1949*	46	0	6	0	30	6	14	6	1	109
1950*	16	0	38	0	1	0	0	10	32†	97

* January through November.
† Includes 31 self propelled units

Source: American Railway Car Institute

FREIGHT CARS DELIVERED

Data for Builders and Private Shops

Year	Car Builders' Shops	Railroad and Private Line Shops	Total
1913	172,729	3,320	176,049
1914	91,852	5,774	97,626
1915	46,704	11,522	58,226
1916	100,869	10,647	111,516
1917	99,500	16,205	115,705
1918	52,701	14,362	67,063
1919	82,845	12,136	94,981
1920	46,784	14,171	60,955
1921	39,259	1,033	40,292
1922	63,866	2,423	66,289
1923	146,247	29,501	175,748
1924	104,093	9,618	113,711
1925	94,707	11,028	105,735
1926	78,898	9,964	88,862
1927	54,830	8,540	63,370
1928	38,375	7,685	46,060
1929	68,712	12,878	81,590
1930	65,081	9,839	74,920
1931	7,497	5,706	13,203
1932	482	2,770	3,252
1933	863	1,300	2,163
1934	16,211	8,965	25,176
1935	5,965	1,550	7,515
1936	30,969	15,643	46,612
1937	61,929	15,569	77,498
1938	9,990	6,480	16,470
1939	19,491	5,641	25,132
1940	45,316	17,025	62,341
1941	63,396	17,227	80,623
1942	47,429	15,444	62,873
1943	24,616	7,220	31,836
1944	27,953	15,050	43,003
1945	31,011	12,853	43,864
1946	31,885	10,070	41,955
1947	52,990	15,532	68,522
1948	83,196	29,444	112,640
1949	62,955	29,607	92,562
1950:			
Jan.	1,006	1,389	2,395
Feb.	917	1,129	2,046
Mar.	830	882	1,712
April	223	748	971
May	1,211	982	2,193
June	3,165	709	3,874
July	2,138	1,326	3,464
Aug.	2,787	2,416	5,203
Sept.	2,395	2,736	5,131
Oct.	2,444	3,057	5,501
Total	17,116	15,374	32,490

Source: American Railway Car Institute

R. R. EMPLOYMENT, EARNINGS

Wages for Non-Supervisory Employees

	Non-Supervisory Employees			All Employees Number (thousands)
	Average Weekly Earnings	Average Weekly Hours	Average Hourly Earnings	
1947	$54.22	46.3	$1.171	1,352
1948	59.14	46.1	1.284	1,327
1949	60.53	43.1	1.414	1,191
1950				
Jan.	61.69	39.8	1.550	1,148
Feb.	62.37	39.8	1.567	1,123
Mar.	63.73	41.6	1.532	1,148
Apr.	61.69	39.9	1.546	1,188
May	61.75	40.2	1.536	1,135
June	64.19	41.9	1.532	1,240
July	61.19	39.4	1.553	1,246
Aug.	65.46	42.7	1.533	1,272
Sept.	N.D.	N.D.	N.D.	1,284

Source: Bureau of Labor Statistics

Index of Industrial Production; Earnings and
Wages in Shipbuilding and Aircraft; Truck-Trailer
Production; Hardware Sales

METAL FACTS SECTION 4

SHIPBUILDING EMPLOYMENT

Workers' Average Earnings

	Production and Related Workers				All Employees
	Average Weekly Earnings	Average Weekly Hours	Average Hourly Earnings	Number (thousands)	Number (thousands)
1947	$57.34	39.6	$1.448	140.6	159.4
1948	60.68	38.7	1.568	123.2	140.7
1949	61.67	37.0	1.623	85.0	100.3
1950					
Jan.	61.46	37.8	1.626	66.1	79.4
Feb.	61.16	37.5	1.631	67.6	81.2
Mar.	62.53	38.2	1.637	66.9	80.2
Apr.	62.08	37.9	1.638	66.6	79.9
May	63.21	38.4	1.640	67.2	80.0
June	62.54	38.3	1.633	68.6	81.1
July	64.20	38.1	1.685	67.9	81.2
Aug.	65.14	39.1	1.666	78.9	92.0
Sept.	63.63	38.4	1.657	76.3	89.2

Source: Bureau of Labor Statistics

AIRCRAFT AND PARTS WAGES

Employment and Average Earnings

	All Employees Number (thousands)	Production and Related Workers			
		Number (thousands)	Average Weekly Earnings	Average Weekly Hours	Average Hourly Earnings
1947	228.6	167.2	$54.98	39.9	$1.378
1948	228.1	166.6	61.21	41.0	1.493
1949	255.6	188.5	63.62	40.6	1.567
1950					
Jan.	251.9	184.3	65.20	40.7	1.602
Feb.	251.7	184.0	65.69	40.7	1.614
Mar.	252.4	184.0	65.29	40.5	1.612
Apr.	253.3	184.9	64.96	40.3	1.612
May	253.9	185.2	65.61	40.8	1.608
June	257.2	186.8	65.20	40.6	1.606
July	259.3	188.1	66.38	41.1	1.615
Aug.	274.0	200.3	68.74	42.2	1.629
Sept.	292.0	215.0	70.96	42.8	1.658

Source: Bureau of Labor Statistics

RETAIL HARDWARE SALES

Annual Listing From 1941

1941	$ 900,000,000
1942	984,000,000
1943	904,000,000
1944	1,025,000,000
1945	1,096,000,000
1946	1,700,000,000
1947	2,216,000,000
1948	2,410,000,000
1949	2,149,000,000
1950: January	127,000,000
February	125,000,000
March	152,000,000
April	171,000,000
May	201,000,000
June	205,000,000
July	205,000,000
August	214,000,000
September	205,000,000
Total—9 Months	1,605,000,000

Source: Dept. of Commerce

FEDERAL RESERVE INDEX OF INDUSTRIAL PRODUCTION

Durable and Nondurable Manufactures, Fuels, Metals

		Manufacturers			Minerals		
	Combined Index	Total	Durable Manufactures Total	Nondurable Manufactures Total	Total	Fuels	Metals
1935 monthly av.	87	87	83	90	86	89	73
1936 monthly av.	103	104	108	100	99	99	102
1937 monthly av.	113	113	122	106	112	109	127
1938 monthly av.	89	87	78	95	97	99	86
1939 monthly av.	109	109	109	109	106	105	113
1940 monthly av.	125	126	139	115	117	114	134
1941 monthly av.	162	168	201	142	125	122	149
1942 monthly av.	199	212	279	158	129	125	148
1943 monthly av.	239	258	360	176	132	132	126
1944 monthly av.	235	252	253	171	140	145	113
1945 monthly av.	203	214	274	166	137	143	101
1946 monthly av.	170	177	192	165	134	142	88
1947 monthly av.	187	194	220	172	149	155	118
1948 monthly av.	192	198	225	177	155	161	120
1949 monthly av.	191	115	218	183	145	149	119
1949: Jan.	187	195	225	170	143	156	68
Feb.	185	193	223	168	143	155	76
Mar.	181	190	221	164	131	137	93
Apr.	177	183	212	159	146	148	134
May	174	179	202	160	148	149	142
June	170	176	195	161	137	135	151
July	163	170	186	157	128	125	149
Aug.	173	180	194	169	134	134	135
Sept.	178	188	200	178	123	122	128
Oct.	169	179	176	181	112	120	63
Nov.	174	180	181	178	141	152	76
Dec.	178	186	201	175	128	136	81
1950 monthly av.	193	203	228	183	133	158	124
1950: Jan.	179	189	206	175	125	133	80
Feb.	177	188	204	176	113	118	81
Mar.	183	191	210	177	139	148	83
April	188	197	221	178	138	147	87
May	195	203	232	180	147	148	140
June	200	208	238	184	155	155	155
July	198	207	237	182	149	148	158
Aug.	212	221	249	198	163	162	169
Sept.	215	223	253	199	167	167	171

* IRON AGE estimate.

Source: Federal Reserve Board

TRUCK AND TRAILER PRODUCTION AND SHIPMENTS

Production of Principal Types of Trucking Equipment

	1949		1948		1947		1946	
	Production	Shipments	Production	Shipments	Production	Shipments	Production	Shipments
Total (Including Trailer Chassis)	33,097	34,273	44,478	46,960	53,096	55,372	76,234	73,001
Complete Trailers	31,571	32,747	42,395	44,877	49,795	52,071	70,619	67,386
Vans	18,317	18,999	23,199	23,715	23,254	24,833	34,651	31,577
Insulated and 'Refers'	2,642	2,756	2,279	2,724	1,852	2,474	3,384	3,202
Furniture	14,056*	14,623*	546	616	1,185	855	2,648	2,564
Other Closed Top	....	....	18,372	18,968	18,601	19,445	26,590	23,938
Open Top	1,619	1,620	2,002	2,023	1,616	1,759	2,029	1,873
Platforms	6,159	6,469	7,514	9,210	12,555	12,503	19,945	18,814
Cattle and Stake Racks	950	1,094	1,588	1,949	3,369	3,404	8,183	7,550
Grain Bodies	359	502	586	895	1,271	1,167		
All Other Platforms	4,850	4,873	5,340	6,366	7,915	7,932	11,762	11,264
Tanks	2,035	2,174	3,550	3,420	3,430	3,802	2,626	2,946
Petroleum	1,855	2,008	3,176	3,042	3,019	3,386	2,231	2,545
Other	180	166	374	378	411	416	395	401
Pole and Logging	1,260	1,309	3,671	3,902	5,356	5,320	7,568	7,565
Single Axle	642	681	2,064	2,184	3,815	3,696	5,970	6,042
Tandem Axle	6¹8	628	1,607	1,718	1,541	1,624	1,598	1,523
Low-Bed Heavy Haulers	1,426	1,433	1,821	1,834	2,405	2,417	1,976	1,987
Off-Highway**	....	....			808	795	619	631
Dump Trailers	470	522	504	654	622	797	697	977
All Other Trailers	1,904	1,841	2,136	2,142	1,365	1,604	2,537	2,889
Trailer Chassis	1,526	1,526	2,083	2,083	3,301	3,301	5,615	5,615
Total Dollar Value of Shipments	$119,098,000		$139,996,000		$138,383,093		$151,384,063	

* Combined with Other Closed Top.   ** Combined with "All Other Trailers" since August, 1948.

Source: Truck-Trailer Mfrs. Assn.

HOUSEHOLD APPLIANCES: SALES AND RETAIL VALUE
Cleaners, Ironers, Ranges, Irons, Refrigerators and Washing Machines

Product	1940		1941		1946		1947		1948		1949	
	Number Sold	Retail Value	Number Sold	Retail Value	Number Sold	Retail Value	Number Sold	Retail Value	Number Sold	Retail Value	Number Sold	Retail Value
Cleaners, vacuum:												
Floor type	1,340,590	$73,155,645	1,670,129	$93,600,906	2,289,500	$155,228,100	3,800,687	$285,368,000	3,500,000	$268,345,000	2,875,000	$219,937,500
Hand type	358,604	5,347,994	383,381	5,726,377	80,000	1,505,880			295,000	7,839,000	190,000	5,272,500
Ironing machines	175,466	10,219,140	259,668	14,489,056	175,000	13,146,000	599,250	75,821,800	470,000	65,221,900	300,000	42,000,000
Irons, total	5,171,000	18,853,500	5,585,000	21,099,750	9,600,000	82,959,000	9,400,000	100,046,000	6,500,000	80,925,000	6,310,000	81,639,500
Automatic	2,597,000	12,959,000	2,900,000	14,790,000	7,000,000	67,645,000	8,000,000	90,400,000	5,850,000	75,757,500	4,850,000	62,807,500
Non-automatic	2,574,000	5,894,500	2,685,000	6,309,750	2,600,000	15,314,000	1,400,000	9,646,000	650,000	5,167,500	495,000	3,440,250
Ranges	450,000	62,775,000	728,000	103,376,000	576,700	107,266,200	1,200,000	276,000,000	1,600,000	376,000,000	1,056,000	242,880,000
Refrigerators	2,600,000	395,200,000	3,500,000	542,500,000	2,100,000	434,700,000	3,400,000	867,000,000	4,530,000	1,177,800,000	4,450,000	1,134,750,000
Washing machines:												
Total	1,552,666	113,156,109	2,014,435	159,329,970	2,123,980	256,283,580	4,281,000	575,814,000	4,710,000	750,200,000	3,200,000	534,178,000
Electric (std. size)	1,454,831	104,485,962	1,892,435	148,556,150	2,047,380	247,303,000	3,657,000	541,236,000	4,285,600	722,123,600	3,065,000	525,188,000
Gas engine (std. size)	97,835	8,670,147	122,000	10,773,820	76,600	8,980,580	126,000	18,144,000	114,400	17,846,400	35,000	5,390,000
Small							498,000	16,434,000	310,000	10,230,000	100,000	3,600,000
Water heaters, storage	125,000	10,125,000	205,000	17,015,000	488,000	58,560,000	1,100,000	143,000,000	1,040,000	143,000,000	695,000	90,350,000

Source: Electrical Merchandising

DOMESTIC COOKING APPLIANCE SHIPMENTS
Electric, Gas, Coal, Oil, and Wood Ranges and Cook Stoves

	1939	1946	1947	1948	1949	1950 9 Mos.
Electric Ranges	296,846	576,723	1,043,711	1,363,742	903,806	1,218,186
Gas Ranges	1,502,301	1,691,526	2,268,526	2,579,265	1,954,910	2,123,742
Bungalow Ranges		70,355	70,179	61,428	38,013	29,662
Combination Ranges	100,167	115,642	171,517	128,585	87,022	71,777
Kerosene, Gasoline, Fuel Oil Ranges, Cook Stoves	470,000	516,308	559,579	466,777	185,939	1,012,002
Coal and Wood Ranges and Cook Stoves	633,151	405,107	449,356	295,527	170,741	114,972
Total Unit Shipments	3,002,465	3,375,916	4,562,868	4,895,324	3,340,431	4,570,341

Source: Institute of Cooking and Heating Appliance Manufacturers

ELECTRIC HOUSEHOLD REFRIGERATOR INDEX OF SALES
Index of Domestic Refrigerator Sales Billed; Average Month 1936 = 100

Year	Jan.	Feb.	Mar.	Apr.	May	June	July	Aug.	Sept.	Oct.	Nov.	Dec.	Avg.
1934	18.8	43.9	80.9	142.0	148.2	101.2	64.4	43.2	21.3	16.1	15.6	38.9	61.2
1935	56.2	70.8	124.5	155.7	142.8	93.5	89.8	64.1	31.2	25.3	27.3	44.0	77.1
1936	69.4	105.8	156.7	175.0	189.4	136.6	118.0	61.6	46.1	25.5	45.0	70.9	100.0
1937	100.8	144.5	207.4	197.2	196.1	157.6	113.5	70.9	48.7	39.9	52.8	64.5	116.2
1938	61.0	84.3	101.3	123.7	104.4	61.0	51.7	54.1	36.2	20.0	18.7	27.8	62.0
1939	87.9	117.4	142.8	147.7	155.5	152.6	93.2	53.8	41.5	35.2	31.4	52.6	92.6
1940	133.5	159.7	169.7	208.7	236.9	202.0	152.7	126.9	69.2	54.3	49.1	71.0	136.1
1941	231.7	220.8	260.5	297.3	267.3	233.1	211.4	168.5	102.4	82.8	57.3	62.6	183.0

Insufficient data available for computing indexes for the years 1942-1945 inclusive.

Year	Jan.	Feb.	Mar.	Apr.	May	June	July	Aug.	Sept.	Oct.	Nov.	Dec.	Avg.
1946	Average first 6 months—71.2						118.1	121.6	128.1	146.7	134.3	136.0	101.0
1947	131.7	113.4	154.3	167.6	176.4	183.0	173.3	133.1	179.7	197.1	181.9	211.2	166.9
1948	181.8	188.2	226.0	219.0	210.5	246.5	231.9	185.8	225.7	249.7	245.4	216.7	218.9
1949	253.1*	224.2	245.3	215.6	220.0	197.1*	209.9	204.6	205.9	168.0	137.4*	160.9	203.5
1950	226.0	280.0	356.0	330.0	328.0	332.0	304.0	293.0	302.0	236.0	n.a.	n.a.	298.7

* Revision. † 10 month average.
n.a.—Not available.

Source: National Electrical Manufacturers Assn.

DOMESTIC HEATING APPLIANCE SHIPMENTS
Gas, Wood, Coal, and Oil Heaters Shown

	1939	1946	1947	1948	1949	1950 9 Mos.
Gas	662,850	1,258,600	2,752,465	2,083,990	1,452,834	1,287,255
Wood (sheet metal airtight types)	474,450	866,360	636,209	511,647	519,305	360,566
Coal and Wood (other than sheet metal airtight types)	563,054	760,927	669,439	691,959	432,228	202,342
Kerosene, Gasoline and Fuel Oil:						
Vaporizing pot-type	294,634	1,006,174	1,953,807	1,185,607	713,720	659,833
Sleeve-type	63,481		50,442	49,258	27,692	
Unvented portable type	361,348	312,878	415,967	704,828	513,157	279,855
Total Unit Shipments	2,419,817	4,204,939	6,478,329	5,227,289	3,658,936	2,789,851

Source: Institute of Cooking and Heating Appliance Mfrs.; Dept. of Commerce

GAS RANGE SHIPMENTS
MILLIONS OF UNITS

1939
1946
1947
1948
1949
1950

REFRIGERATOR SALES INDEX

1939
1940
1941
1946
1947
1948
1949
1950

HOME HEATING UNIT SHIPMENTS
IN MILLIONS

1939
1946
1947
1948
1949
1950

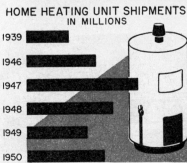

PRODUCTION OF ELECTRIC POWER IN MILLIONS OF KW-HR
Monthly Averages for Electric Utilities and Industrial Establishments

	Total	Electric Utilities	Industrial Establishments
1935 monthly average...	......	7,941	.....
1936 monthly average...	......	9,110	.....
1937 monthly average...	......	9,909	.....
1938 monthly average...	......	9,484	.....
1939 monthly average...	13,442	10,637	2,806
1940 monthly average...	14,992	11,820	3,172
1941 monthly average...	17,359	13,732	3,627
1942 monthly average...	19,429	15,493	3,931
1943 monthly average...	22,295	18,147	4,148
1944 monthly average...	23,294	19,016	4,278
1945 monthly average...	22,605	18,541	4,064
1946 monthly average...	22,467	18,598	3,869
1947 monthly average...	25,617	21,312	4,305
1948 monthly average...	28,067	23,558	4,509

1949:	Total	Electric Utilities	Industrial Establishments
January..........	30,374	25,550	4,804
February.........	27,463	22,996	4,467
March............	29,514	24,721	4,793
April............	27,745	23,215	4,530
May.............	27,875	23,348	4,526
June.............	28,025	23,617	4,407
July.............	27,946	23,684	4,262
August..........	29,492	25,021	4,471
September.......	28,358	23,922	4,436
October.........	28,110	24,288	3,876
November.......	28,539	24,328	4,268
December.......	31,096	26,321	4,814
1949 monthly average...	28,711	24,251	4,471

1950:	Total	Electric Utilities	Industrial Establishments
January..........	31,677	26,871	4,805
February.........	28,789	24,270	4,519
March............	31,864	26,997	4,867
April............	30,191	25,437	4,754
May.............	31,486	26,525	4,962
June.............	31,608	26,685	4,923
July.............	31,626	26,780	4,846
August..........	33,874	28,869	5,005
September.......	32,650	27,774	4,876
1950 monthly average...	31,529	26,690	4,839

Source: Federal Power Commission

APPLIANCE EMPLOYMENT
Hours and Average Earnings

	Production and Related Workers				All Employees
	Average Weekly Earnings	Average Weekly Hours	Average Hourly Earnings	Number (thousands)	Number (thousands)
1947	$51.68	40.6	$1.273	134.8	164.0
1948	56.08	40.2	1.395	125.5	154.8
1949	56.52	39.5	1.431	100.8	128.3
1950					
Jan.	59.09	40.5	1.459	100.6	126.0
Feb.	58.78	40.4	1.455	103.3	128.8
Mar.	58.68	40.3	1.456	104.8	130.5
Apr.	60.34	40.8	1.479	108.1	133.7
May	60.60	41.0	1.478	110.6	136.5
June	57.80	39.7	1.456	110.6	136.6
July	60.24	40.4	1.491	110.1	136.8

Source: Bureau of Labor Statistics

MOTORS AND GENERATORS
Index of Orders Integral HP Units

YEAR	1st Qtr.	2nd Qtr.	3rd Qtr.	4th Qtr.	Avg.
1934....	45.8	50.0	46.3	54.0	49.0
1935....	54.6	63.0	70.2	70.7	64.6
1936....	75.2	109.4	103.2	112.2	100.0
1937....	150.5	137.6	110.4	83.9	120.6
1938....	68.7	68.4	61.3	67.1	66.4
1939....	78.5	82.2	95.8	137.2	98.4
1940....	102.7	124.9	147.7	229.4	151.2
1941....	260.4	335.7	336.7	329.4	315.5
1942....	457.0	664.6	554.4	435.6	527.9
1943....	560.2	373.0	400.1	414.0	436.8
1944....	284.6	341.8	345.2	314.1	321.4
1945....	293.9	274.7	234.8	307.4	277.7
1946....	288.1	418.1	468.0	492.8	416.7
1947....	459.1	393.7	308.2	391.6	388.1
1948....	294.8	329.2	289.9	301.2	303.8
1949....	262.0	239.6	223.8	232.2	239.4
1950*....	338.0	337.0	551.0	.....	408.7†

* 9 month average
Source: National Electrical Manufacturers Assn.

VACUUM CLEANER SALES
Floor Uprite, Cylinder, Hand Units

Year	Floor Uprite & Cylinder, Units	Hand, Units
1929.............	1,253,112	142,543
1930.............	960,343	209,996
1931.............	687,250	191,047
1932.............	447,056	110,232
1933.............	580,644	191,818
1934.............	687,890	246,009
1935.............	850,109	294,441
1936.............	1,084,656	361,46L
1937.............	1,210,191	421,121
1938.............	967,002	295,610
1939.............	1,084,605	312,035
1940.............	1,340,590	358,604
1941.............	1,670,129	383,381
1942.............	579,567	85,167
War Years 1943–44–45		
1946.............	2,289,441	80,053
1947.............	3,800,687	186,457
1948.............	3,360,849	289,923
1949.............	2,889,518	191,110
1950: Jan.........	249,150	16,946
Feb..........	263,515	13,042
Mar.........	361,014	17,172
Apr.........	292,664	15,549
May.........	278,645	14,990
June........	250,190	13,479
July.........	279,967	22,490
Aug.........	341,232	28,536
Sept.........	327,524	20,186
(9 Mos.)...	2,643,901	162,390

Source: Vacuum Cleaner Manufacturers Assn.

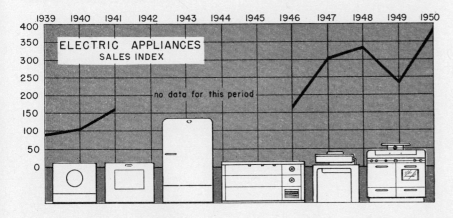

ELECTRIC APPLIANCES SALES INDEX

no data for this period

ELECTRIC APPLIANCES—MONTHLY SALES INDEX
Major Domestic Unit Sales Billed; Average Month 1936 = 100

Year	January	February	March	April	May	June	July	August	September	October	November	December	Average
1934...................	32.2	42.1	62.1	68.8	72.3	59.5	49.8	54.4	56.8	52.3	43.8	42.9	53.1
1935...................	43.3	58.8	82.4	93.4	100.1	77.3	70.7	72.8	75.7	83.4	69.0	66.6	74.5
1936...................	63.5	75.8	122.2	121.6	126.2	113.4	99.0	92.1	106.2	103.4	82.2	94.4	100.0
1937...................	95.2	104.4	170.4	163.0	148.3	144.4	117.1	102.9	109.1	90.9	62.5	58.1	113.9
1938...................	68.2	76.3	93.6	85.9	79.3	74.2	67.4	76.1	74.1	75.0	61.2	59.3	74.2
1939...................	87.5	90.9	111.2	93.9	102.7	95.7	73.1	86.8	92.2	93.3	78.6	65.2	89.2
1940...................	107.3	110.5	124.8	126.7	131.1	108.5	94.8	96.9	107.0	116.5	88.1	86.6	108.2
1941...................	133.5	146.1	154.8	191.2	188.1	186.4	185.5	148.0	179.2	145.8	110.1	131.5	160.4
			Insufficient data available for computing indexes for the years 1942-1945 inclusive										
1946...................	105.3	84.3	102.3	128.3	121.4	168.6	181.9	206.6	197.3	234.0	228.2	215.6	164.5
1947...................	223.0	247.3	301.3	306.2	310.1	329.8	280.7	265.8	343.8	377.8	333.1	352.2	305.9
1948...................	324.6	329.6	389.7*	341.1	318.3	358.5	275.8	334.0	387.7	363.8	341.8	279.3	337.0
1949...................	265.0	252.4	265.6*	203.4*	194.6*	226.0*	189.9*	239.8*	288.6*	266.5*	227.8*	237.7	238.1
1950...................	275.0	327.0	409.0	359.0	371.0	395.0	345.0	391.0	430.0	399.0	n.a.	n.a.	370.1†

* Revised.   † 10 month average.   n.a.—Not available.

Source: National Electrical Manufacturers Association

WHAT HOUSES ARE MADE OF

FHA Analysis of Components of Construction—a Partial List of Applications

For houses distributed according to design and relative use of materials on a national basis. The percentage of houses in 1000 using the material are listed under each component.

BASEMENT GIRDERS	Pct of Use Per 1000	Total Pct
Full basement		
Wood	36.2	
Steel	18.8	55.0
Partial and no basement		
Wood	45.0	45.0
		100.00

BASEMENT COLUMNS		
Full Basement		
Wood	19.9	
Steel	24.9	
Masonry	10.2	55.0
Partial basement		
Wood	5.1	
Steel	6.5	
Masonry	2.6	14.2
No basement		
Masonry piers	30.8	30.8
		100.00

BASEMENT WINDOWS		
Wood	24.2	
Steel	45.0	
No windows	30.8	100.00

WINDOWS ABOVE BASEMENT		
Wood	91.3	
Steel	8.7	
		100.00

GUTTERS & DOWNSPOUTS		
Galvanized steel	60.6	
Copper	6.7	
Wood with copper downspouts	5.7	
No gutters or downspouts	26.0	
		100.00

LATH & PLASTER		
Metal lath	1.3	
Wood lath	33.1	
Sheet lath	55.6	
Dry wall	9.8	
Dry wall and plaster	0.2	
		100.00

ELECTRIC WIRING	Pct of Use Per 1000	Total Pct
Knob & Tube	27.4	
BX cable	30.2	
Romex cable	24.4	
Flexible conduit	8.8	
Rigid conduit	8.8	
BX cable and flexible conduit	0.4	
		100.00

PLUMBING			
Fixture		Cast Iron	Steel
1 bathroom (4 fixtures)*		73.7	6.1
1½ bathroom (6 fixtures)		11.0	0.9
2 bathrooms (7 fixtures)		6.3	0.5
2½ bathrooms (9 fixtures)		1.4	0.1
		92.4	7.6
			100.00

* Each fixture count includes one kitchen sink.

STALL SHOWER		
Included	23.8	
No stall shower	76.2	
		100.00

TUB SHOWER		
Included	55.8	
No tub shower	44.2	
		100.00

LAUNDRY TRAYS		100.00

WATER PIPES		
Galvanized steel	70.0	
Wrough iron	0.6	
Copper	20.7	
Brass	8.7	
		100.00

SOIL PIPE UNDER BASEMENT		
Cast Iron	95.7	
Terra cotta	4.3	
		100.00

STORAGE TANKS		
Galvanized steel	82.2	
Copper	6.9	
Monel	2.8	
No tanks	8.1	
		100.00

HEATING	Pct of Use Per 1000	Total Pct
Warm air		
Gravity type furnace		
Steel	2.2	
Cast iron	21.3	23.5

FORCED AIR FURNACE		
Steel	19.0	19.0
Pipeless furnace	0.7	
Floor furnace	21.6	
Space heater	10.0	
Stoves	2.2	34.5

HOT WATER		
Gravity type		
Steel pipe	7.1	
Wrought iron pipe	0.3	7.4
Forced		
Steel pipe	3.0	
Wrought iron pipe	0.2	
Copper pipe	1.6	4.8

STEAM SYSTEM		
Steel pipe	8.3	
Wrought iron pipe	0.4	
No heating system	2.1	10.8
		100.0

BOILERS		
Steel	9.8	
Cast iron	11.1	
No boiler	79.1	100.00

STANDING RADIATION		
Hot Water		
Gravity		
Exposed cast iron	7.4	7.4
Forced		
Exposed cast iron	2.6	
Concealed cast iron	1.7	
Concealed copper	0.5	4.8

STEAM		
Exposed cast iron	4.7	
Concealed cast iron	3.0	
Concealed copper	1.0	8.7
No radiators	79.1	79.1
		100.00

NEW DWELLINGS BY TYPE AND NUMBER OF FAMILIES

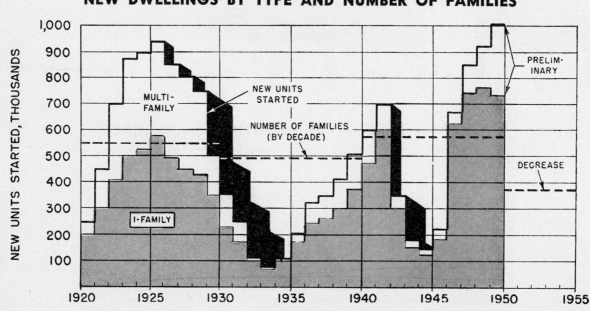

EXPENDITURES FOR NEW CONSTRUCTION BY TYPE

Spending for Private, Public, Utility, and Military Construction

Type of Construction	Expenditures (in millions of dollars)										
	1949	1950 (Nine Month Total)	1950								
			Jan.	Feb.	Mar.	April	May	June	July	Aug.	Sept.
Total new construction[2]	22,594	20,082	1,712	1,618	1,750	1,989	2,283	2,535	2,675	2,771	2,749
Private construction	16,204	15,039	1,298	1,262	1,313	1,483	1,690	1,883	1,997	2,050	2,059
Residential building (nonfarm)	8,290	9,121	742	717	741	882	1,035	1,171	1,253	1,286	1,294
Nonresidential building (nonfarm)	3,228	2,595	257	252	249	249	275	306	324	332	351
Industrial	972	703	69	70	69	70	73	78	83	90	101
Commercial	1,027	861	79	77	77	76	92	110	117	113	120
Warehouses, office and loft buildings	321	264	28	27	25	24	26	28	32	35	39
Stores, restaurants and garages	706	597	51	50	52	52	66	82	85	78	81
Religious	360	291	31	29	28	28	31	33	35	38	38
Educational	269	208	23	22	21	20	21	23	24	26	28
Social and recreational	262	182	20	18	17	17	19	21	23	24	23
Hospital and institutional	202	253	25	26	27	28	29	30	30	29	29
Hotel	136	97	10	10	10	10	10	11	12	12	12
Miscellaneous											
Farm construction	1,292	859	74	75	79	88	100	108	113	116	106
Public utilities	3,316	2,367	216	209	235	253	267	285	296	305	301
Railroad	352	229	22	16	21	26	27	28	29	30	30
Local transit											
Pipeline	2,431	1,782	164	161	176	187	199	215	222	230	228
Electric light and power											
Gas											
Telephone and telegraph	533	356	30	32	38	40	41	42	45	45	43
Public construction	6,390	5,092	414	356	437	506	593	652	678	721	735
Residential building	359	253	35	26	28	28	28	24	27	27	29
Nonresidential building	2,056	1,644	155	154	170	178	187	191	196	204	209
Industrial	177	128	7	7	11	13	17	16	18	19	20
Educational	934	819	80	79	84	87	90	94	98	102	105
Hospital and institutional	477	350	37	38	40	40	40	39	37	39	40
Miscellaneous	468	347	31	30	35	38	40	42	43	44	44
Military and naval facilities	137	86	9	9	8	9	8	10	10	11	12
Highway	2,129	1,740	90	55	100	145	210	250	275	305	310
Sewage disposal	619	479	49	46	49	52	54	55	56	58	60
Water supply											
Miscellaneous public service enterprises	203	131	12	10	11	13	15	17	18	18	17
Conservation and development	792	685	56	49	62	73	82	92	91	90	90
All other public	95	74	8	7	9	8	9	9	8	8	8

[1] Not shown separately.
[2] Less than $500,000.

Source: Dept. of Commerce, Dept. of Labor

TRANSPORTATION SPENDING

Plant, Equipment Expenditures

	Railroad	Other Transportation	Electric and Gas Utilities	Commercial and Miscellaneous
1935	$ 168	Included in Commercial and Miscellaneous		$1,784
1936	308			2,320
1937	524			2,876
1938	240			2,452
1939	280	$280	$480	1,850
1940	440	392	552	1,980
1941	560	340	710	2,490
1942	540	260	680	1,472
1943	460	192	540	732
1944	580	280	492	972
1945	550	320	630	1,480
1946	572	660	1,040	3,300
1947	1,010	800	1,900	4,430
1948	1,210	710	2,680	5,380
1949	1,350	520	3,140	5,120
1950	1,130	410	3,170	4,700

Source: Securities & Exchange Commission; U. S. Dept. of Commerce

NEW HOUSING STARTS

Monthly Starts of Non-Farm Units

Month	New Non-Farm Units Started			
	1947	1948	1949	1950
January	39,300	53,500	50,000	78,700
February	42,800	50,100	50,400	82,900
March	56,000	76,400	69,400	117,300
April	67,100	99,500	88,300	133,400
May	72,900	100,300	95,400	149,100
June	77,200	97,800	95,500	144,300
July	81,100	95,000	96,100	144,000
August	88,300	86,600	99,000	141,000
September	93,800	82,200	102,900	115,000
October	94,000	73,400	104,300	103,000
November	79,700	63,600	95,500	90,000*
December	58,800	52,900	78,300	71,000*
Total	849,000	931,300	1,027,100*	1,369,700*
Monthly av.	70,750	77,600	85,597*	114,142*

Source: U. S. Department of Labor
* IRON AGE estimate.

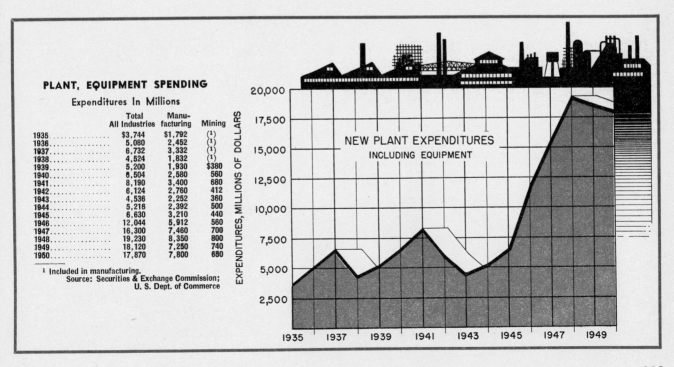

PLANT, EQUIPMENT SPENDING

Expenditures In Millions

	Total All Industries	Manufacturing	Mining
1935	$3,744	$1,792	(1)
1936	5,080	2,452	(1)
1937	6,732	3,332	(1)
1938	4,524	1,832	(1)
1939	5,200	1,930	$380
1940	6,504	2,580	560
1941	8,190	3,400	680
1942	6,124	2,760	412
1943	4,536	2,252	360
1944	5,216	2,392	500
1945	6,630	3,210	440
1946	12,044	5,912	560
1947	16,300	7,460	700
1948	19,230	8,350	800
1949	18,120	7,250	740
1950	17,870	7,800	650

[1] Included in manufacturing.
Source: Securities & Exchange Commission; U. S. Dept. of Commerce

NEW PLANT EXPENDITURES INCLUDING EQUIPMENT

CONSUMER EXPENDITURES, CLASSIFIED
Annual Rates in Billions of Dollars From 1935

| | Total | Durable Goods | | | Nondurable Goods | | | | | | Services | | | | | |
		Automobiles and Parts	Furniture and Household Equipment	Other Durable Goods	Clothing and Shoes	Food and Alcoholic Beverages	Gasoline and Oil	Semidurable Household furnishings	Tobacco	Other Nondurable Goods	Household Operation	Housing	Personal Service	Recreation	Transportation	Other Services
1935	56.2	1.9	2.5	0.8	5.9	16.3	1.7	0.5	1.4	3.5	3.0	7.6	1.2	1.3	1.5	7.1
1936	62.5	2.3	3.1	1.0	6.5	18.5	1.9	0.7	1.5	3.8	3.2	7.9	1.3	1.4	1.7	7.7
1937	67.1	2.4	3.4	1.2	6.7	20.0	2.1	0.7	1.7	4.0	3.5	8.4	1.5	1.6	1.8	8.2
1938	64.5	1.6	3.0	1.1	6.6	19.0	2.1	0.6	1.7	3.9	3.4	8.7	1.4	1.5	1.7	7.9
1939	67.5	2.1	3.4	1.2	7.0	19.3	2.2	0.8	1.8	4.2	3.6	8.9	1.4	1.6	1.9	8.1
1940	72.1	2.1	3.8	1.3	7.4	20.7	2.3	0.8	1.9	4.5	3.8	9.2	1.6	1.7	2.0	8.3
1941	82.3	3.3	4.8	1.6	8.8	24.4	2.6	1.0	2.1	5.1	4.0	9.9	1.8	1.8	2.2	8.9
1942	91.2	0.7	4.5	1.9	11.0	30.5	1.9	1.1	2.3	6.0	4.5	10.6	2.1	2.1	2.7	9.3
1943	102.2	0.8	3.8	2.2	13.7	35.3	1.2	1.3	2.6	6.9	5.0	11.1	2.5	2.3	3.5	10.1
1944	111.6	0.9	3.7	2.5	15.3	38.9	1.2	1.4	2.6	7.7	5.6	11.7	2.7	2.7	3.7	11.1
1945	123.1	1.1	4.4	3.0	17.1	43.0	1.6	1.4	2.9	8.8	6.1	12.2	2.9	3.0	3.9	11.6
1946	147.8	4.4	8.2	3.9	18.6	51.0	3.0	1.8	3.5	8.9	6.3	13.1	3.5	3.7	4.5	13.4
1947	166.9	7.2	10.8	4.0	19.1	57.8	3.5	1.9	3.9	10.0	7.0	14.5	3.7	3.9	4.8	14.9
1948	178.8	8.2	11.4	4.0	20.0	61.1	4.1	1.9	4.1	10.9	7.7	15.9	3.7	3.9	5.1	16.8
1948: First quarter†	175.2	7.5	11.2	3.9	19.3	61.0	3.9	1.9	4.1	11.1	7.6	15.4	3.7	3.9	5.0	15.8
Second quarter	178.7	8.0	11.9	4.0	20.2	61.2	4.2	1.9	4.1	10.9	7.6	15.8	3.7	3.9	4.9	16.6
Third quarter	180.3	8.7	12.1	4.0	19.9	60.5	4.2	2.0	4.3	10.9	7.7	16.0	3.7	4.0	5.2	17.2
Fourth quarter	180.9	8.5	10.4	3.9	20.5	61.7	4.3	1.9	4.1	10.8	7.9	16.3	3.7	4.1	5.3	17.6
1949	178.4	9.4	10.2	3.8	19.3	60.0	4.2	1.9	4.1	10.1	8.0	17.1	3.7	4.0	5.2	18.1
1949: First quarter	177.9	8.6	10.2	3.7	19.3	60.0	4.1	2.0	4.1	10.4	8.1	16.6	3.6	4.0	5.2	17.9
Second quarter	178.2	9.6	10.1	3.8	19.1	59.2	4.2	1.8	4.1	10.1	8.0	17.0	3.7	4.0	5.1	18.1
Third quarter	179.0	10.2	11.0	3.6	18.0	58.4	4.7	1.8	4.3	10.4	8.3	17.3	3.7	4.0	5.1	18.3
Fourth quarter	180.6	10.4	11.3	3.7	18.1	58.3	4.8	1.8	4.3	10.5	8.5	17.6	3.7	3.9	5.1	18.6
1950: First quarter	182.4	10.8	12.5	3.6	17.7	58.3	4.9	1.9	4.3	10.5	8.8	17.9	3.7	3.8	5.1	18.8
Second quarter	185.2	11.0	12.0	3.6	18.4	59.1	5.1	1.9	4.3	10.6	9.0	18.1	3.7	3.9	5.1	19.2
Third quarter	198.5	13.5	16.2	3.8	19.7	62.5	5.2	2.3	4.3	10.9	9.3	18.4	3.7	3.8	5.1	19.6

† Seasonally adjusted, quarterly totals, at annual rates.

Source: Dept. of Commerce

BUSINESS SALES AND INVENTORIES (Millions of Dollars)
Manufacturing, Wholesale and Retail Trade, Monthly Figures†

| | Business Sales | | | | Business Inventories, Book Value—End of Month | | | |
	Total Business Sales	Manufacturing (total)	Wholesale Trade (total)	Retail Trade (total)	Total Business Inventories	Manufacturing (total)	Wholesale Trade (total)	Retail Trade (total)
1935 monthly average			$1,965	$2,733				$4,364
1937 monthly average			2,649	3,512				5,339
1939 monthly average	$11,120	$5,112	2,505	3,503	$19,168	$10,782	$3,031	5,355
1940 monthly average	12,515	5,859	2,790	3,866	21,041	12,047	3,276	5,718
1941 monthly average	16,446	8,172	3,650	4,624	25,194	14,559	3,793	6,842
1942 monthly average	19,165	10,346	4,016	4,803	30,725	18,387	4,066	8,272
1943 monthly average	22,243	12,603	4,330	5,310	30,017	19,200	3,537	7,280
1944 monthly average	23,705	13,402	4,505	5,798	30,816	19,612	3,719	7,485
1945 monthly average	23,535	12,371	4,777	6,387	29,885	18,577	3,760	7,576
1946 monthly average	26,557	12,020	6,138	8,399	33,996	20,177	4,795	9,239
1947 monthly average	32,836	15,671	7,304	9,861	45,046	26,243	6,917	12,034
1948 monthly average	36,283	17,587	7,867	10,829	51,916	29,830	8,053	14,126
1949								
January	33,270	16,691	7,163	9,416	54,113	32,062	8,527	13,524
February	32,144	16,424	6,802	8,918	54,479	32,070	8,567	13,842
March	36,120	18,107	7,489	10,524	54,791	31,793	8,445	14,553
April	34,848	16,763	6,962	11,123	53,801	31,266	8,186	14,349
May	34,149	16,295	7,077	10,777	52,646	30,903	7,912	13,863
June	34,442	16,536	7,086	10,820	51,510	30,304	7,774	13,432
July	31,855	15,010	6,603	10,242	50,397	29,692	7,830	12,875
August	37,100	18,900	7,500	10,700	54,600	31,600	9,100	13,900
September	37,200	18,900	7,500	10,900	54,600	31,100	9,200	14,400
October	34,600	16,800	7,100	10,700	54,400	30,700	9,100	14,500
November	35,500	17,300	7,600	10,600	54,000	30,500	9,100	14,300
December	34,700	16,900	7,300	10,500	53,600	30,900	9,000	13,700
1949 monthly average	34,661	17,052	7,182	10,435	53,578	31,074	8,566	13,937
1950								
January	35,700	17,600	7,200	10,900	54,100	31,100	9,000	14,000
February	36,600	18,000	7,300	11,100	54,000	31,100	9,000	13,800
March	37,900	19,100	7,700	11,100	54,500	31,100	9,200	14,200
April	36,900	18,500	7,400	11,100	54,800	31,200	9,400	14,100
May	40,000	20,700	8,000	11,300	55,400	31,500	9,500	14,400
June	41,200	21,200	8,300	11,700	56,300	32,100	9,500	14,800

† Business sales and inventories are defined as the sum data for manufacturing and wholesale and retail trade.
Source: U. S. Dept. of Commerce

FARM TRACTOR PRODUCTION
Domestic Output; Nonfarm Excluded

| | Wheel Type | | Track Type | Total All Farm |
	Conventional	All Purpose		
1929	195,980		27,101	223,081
1931	36,109	25,831	7,089	69,029
1935	31,741	106,343	18,774	156,858
1936	39,068	154,879	27,299	221,246
1937	53,882	183,955	34,602	272,439
1938	41,377	131,060	16,837	189,274
1939	26,973	158,585	20,127	208,685
1940	25,163	224,271	24,762	274,196
1941	32,724	280,708	28,661	342,093
1942	21,135	150,988	29,578	201,701
1943	16,570	88,678	29,453	134,701
1944	43,228	205,903	44,860	293,991
1945	46,670	197,760	44,872	289,302
1946	37,393	220,881	25,902	284,176
1947	47,495	366,288	11,630	425,413
1948	25,617	394,120	12,780	591,382
1949	26,843	412,789	12,167	575,115

Source: Depts. of Commerce and Agriculture

TRACTOR SALES AND OUTPUT
Based On Belt Horsepower Range

	1948	1949
Production:		
Under 25 HP	321,824	316,924
25 to 35 HP	105,331	130,925
35 HP and over	18,670	27,920
Domestic Sales:		
Under 25 HP	288,025	271,413
25 to 35 HP	90,951	117,505
35 HP and over	16,266	24,803

Source: Farm Implement News

DISPOSITION OF INCOME

Totals By Billions of Dollars

	Total	Personal Tax and Nontax Payments	Disposable Personal Income	
			Total	Personal Saving
1935	59.9	1.9	58.0	1.8
1936	68.4	2.3	66.1	3.6
1937	74.0	2.9	71.1	3.9
1938	68.3	2.9	65.5	1.0
1939	72.6	2.4	70.2	2.7
1940	78.3	2.6	75.7	3.7
1941	95.3	3.3	92.0	9.8
1942	122.7	6.0	116.7	25.6
1943	150.3	17.8	132.4	30.2
1944	165.9	18.9	147.0	35.4
1945	171.9	20.9	151.1	28.0
1946	176.9	18.8	158.1	10.3
1947	193.5	21.5	172.0	5.1
1948	211.9	21.1	190.8	12.0
1948				
First quarter†	205.1	23.2	181.9	6.7
Second quarter	210.3	20.7	189.6	10.8
Third quarter	215.4	20.2	195.2	15.0
Fourth quarter	216.6	20.4	196.2	15.3
1949	213.5	19.0	195.0	15.0
1949				
First quarter	213.7	18.7	195.0	17.1
Second quarter	212.9	18.7	194.2	16.0
Third quarter	208.3	18.6	189.5	9.8
Fourth quarter	205.4	18.7	186.8	6.2
1950				
First quarter	216.4	18.7	197.7	15.3
Second quarter	215.1	19.5	195.6	10.4
Third Quarter	224.8	20.0	204.7	6.4

† Seasonally adjusted quarterly totals at annual rates
Source: U. S. Dept. of Commerce, Office of Business Economics

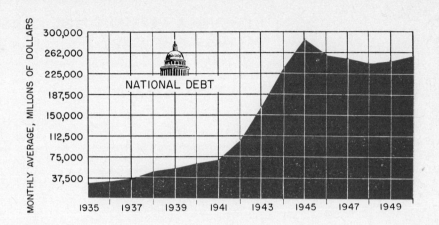

NATIONAL DEBT

GROSS NATIONAL DEBT OUTSTANDING

Interest-Bearing, Non-Interest Bearing (Millions of Dollars)

		Direct Debt				
		Interest-Bearing			Non-Interest Bearing	Obligations Guaranteed by U. S. Government
	Total	Total	Public Issues	Special Issues		
1935 monthly average	$30,557	$29,596	$28,868	$728	$961	$4,494
1936 monthly average	34,405	33,699	33,067	632	707	4,662
1937 monthly average	37,286	36,716	34,489	2,227	571	4,645
1938 monthly average	39,439	39,911	35,755	3,156	528	4,992
1939 monthly average	41,961	41,465	37,234	4,231	496	5,704
1940 monthly average	45,039	44,471	39,102	5,370	568	5,917
1941 monthly average	58,020	57,533	50,551	6,982	487	6,324
1942 monthly average	108,170	107,308	98,276	9,032	862	4,301
1943 monthly average	165,877	164,508	151,805	12,703	1,370	4,230
1944 monthly average	230,630	228,891	212,565	16,326	1,739	1,514
1945: June	258,682	256,357	237,545	18,812	2,326	433
1945: December	278,115	275,694	255,693	20,000	2,421	567
1946: June	269,422	268,111	245,779	22,332	1,311	476
1946: December	259,148	257,649	233,064	24,585	1,500	339
1947: June	258,286	255,113	227,747	27,366	3,173	90
1947: December	256,900	254,205	225,250	28,955	2,695	81
1948: June	252,292	250,063	219,852	30,211	2,229	73
1948: December	252,800	250,579	218,865	31,714	2,220	55
1949: June	252,770	250,762	217,986	32,776	2,009	27
1949: December	257,130	255,019	221,123	33,896	2,111	29
1950: January	256,865	254,869	221,367	33,502	1,997	27
February	256,368	254,406	221,535	32,871	1,962	27
March	255,724	253,506	221,408	32,098	2,218	24
April	255,718	253,516	221,714	31,802	2,202	22
May	256,350	254,183	222,315	31,868	2,167	20
June	257,357	255,209	222,853	32,356	2,148	20
July	257,541	255,403	222,884	32,518	2,138	16
August	257,874	255,764	223,059	32,705	2,110	18
September	257,216	254,968	221,572	33,396	2,247	20

Source: U. S. Treasury Dept.

FARM MACHINERY WAGES

Workers' Average Earnings

	Production and Related Workers				All Employees
	Average Weekly Earnings	Average Weekly Hours	Average Hourly Earnings	Number (thousands)	Number (thousands)
1947	$55.76	40.7	$1.370	140.3	178.9
1948	60.59	40.5	1.496	151.7	191.3
1949	61.11	39.3	1.555	142.4	181.3
1950					
Jan.	61.58	39.1	1.575	133.2	171.0
Feb.	63.24	40.0	1.581	137.4	175.2
Mar.	62.92	39.6	1.589	139.5	177.5
Apr.	62.96	39.7	1.586	142.4	180.5
May	63.88	40.1	1.593	141.5	180.7
June	63.88	40.2	1.589	141.1	180.4
July	63.88	40.1	1.593	140.5	180.1
Aug.	64.44	40.3	1.599	140.3	180.1
Sept.	63.90	40.6	1.574	107.4	146.0

Source: Bureau of Labor Statistics

FARM WHEEL TRACTORS BY AGE, DRAWBAR HP

Geographical Distribution; Garden and Homemade Tractors Excluded

Age and Drawbar HP Distribution by Age	Northeast Pct.	Corn Belt Pct.	Lake States Pct.	Plains Pct.	Southeast Pct.	Okla.-Texas Pct.	Mountain Pct.	Pacific States Pct.	United States Pct.
Under 5 years	36	30	32	27	40	28	48	39	32
5 to 9 years	37	44	40	38	44	42	36	34	41
10 to 14 years	12	16	13	14	10	18	7	9	14
15 to 19 years	9	7	11	19	4	10	7	9	10
20 years and over	6	3	4	2	2	2	2	9	3
Distribution by Drawbar HP									
Under 12 HP	31	18	24	15	19	27	13	32	21
12.0 to 18.4 HP	41	42	43	36	45	38	40	46	42
18.5 to 24.9 HP	23	33	28	36	28	24	31	15	29
25.0 HP and over	5	7	5	13	8	11	16	7	8

Source: Farm Implement News

4 METAL FACTS SECTION

Wholesale Trade: Sales and Number of Establishments—Electrical Goods, Appliances, Hardware, Plumbing, Machinery, Supplies, Metal Work, Iron and Steel Scrap

The information below is a condensation of statistics just released by the Bureau of the Census, U. S. Dept. of Commerce. It is contained in the Bureau's 1948 Census of Business, data for which was collected during 1949 and compiled and correlated during the past year. Additional data on these and other lines of business are now or will shortly be available for all states and for the nation as a whole as part of the Bureau's 1948 Census of Business.

DISTRIBUTOR AND JOBBER SALES
Not Including Branches Owned and Operated by Producers

	Electrical Goods—General Line, Apparatus Supplies		Electric Appliances, Specialties		Hardware		Plumbing, Heating Equipment, Supplies		Industrial Machinery Equipment, Supplies		Metal and Metal Work, except Scrap		Iron and Steel Scrap	
	No. of Establishments	1948 Sales (000 omitted)	No. of Establishments	1948 Sales (000 omitted)	No. of Establishments	1948 Sales (000 omitted)	No. of Establishments	1948 Sales (000 omitted)	No. of Establishments	1948 Sales (000 omitted)	No. of Establishments	1948 Sales (000 omitted)	No. of Establishments	1948 Sales (000 omitted)
CONTINENTAL U. S.	2,925	$2,386,546	2,518	$2,038,020	2,153	$2,013,997	3,748	$1,812,960	7,304	$2,999,989	1,803	$2,056,715	3,054	$1,699,428
NEW ENGLAND	202	109,525	147	134,887	138	74,074	341	139,666	409	130,286	108	X	201	72,765
Maine	10	9,867	17	8,259	12	13,730	17	11,462	18	5,560	5	1,154	13	2,008
New Hampshire	5	5,549	4	887	6	2,723	12	5,522	5	953	1	X	16	1,070
Vermont	4	2,287	3	57	5	5,831	6	4,442	8	2,153	3	544	11	936
Massachusetts	113	55,517	69	73,547	75	36,048	176	71,388	231	81,235	62	65,826	104	36,750
Rhode Island	20	10,037	14	14,030	14	6,523	32	10,994	54	11,237	10	5,236	10	5,799
Connecticut	50	26,268	40	38,107	26	9,219	98	35,858	93	29,148	27	17,983	47	26,202
Middle Atlantic	907	580,506	667	599,658	760	326,817	1,209	539,902	1,815	637,840	703	1,053,150	696	450,991
New York	569	359,531	462	354,062	535	202,930	686	292,345	1,171	395,096	532	885,475	292	1,629,985
New Jersey	120	60,461	60	72,959	93	21,795	241	91,343	231	52,758	63	59,044	107	47,923
Pennsylvania	218	160,514	145	172,637	132	102,092	282	156,214	413	189,986	108	108,631	297	240,083
EAST NORTH CENTRAL	566	515,235	536	397,144	344	354,700	688	295,574	1,511	544,331	401	456,461	894	706,045
Ohio	164	150,627	165	106,441	83	113,104	197	78,030	419	152,474	139	123,425	259	276,802
Indiana	57	49,406	59	43,758	31	39,655	71	30,418	137	59,494	23	43,198	125	36,497
Illinois	184	176,658	181	152,207	127	78,105	198	84,001	485	186,165	139	190,450	220	230,379
Michigan	107	95,861	86	62,857	75	76,144	149	70,270	323	103,235	85	88,693	183	125,950
Wisconsin	54	42,683	45	31,881	28	47,692	73	32,855	147	42,963	15	10,695	107	36,417
WEST NORTH CENTRAL	217	249,132	207	180,057	127	X	271	X	487	202,065	95	102,748	430	144,832
Minnesota	42	56,407	36	42,782	32	111,717	62	29,562	111	38,459	17	26,662	74	30,604
Iowa	43	45,881	32	22,486	19	27,096	41	25,847	47	22,381	7	4,080	84	18,791
Missouri	75	84,312	77	72,805	49	87,234	109	66,462	176	66,001	48	64,839	111	55,950
North Dakota	6	10,280	8	2,683	1	X	1	X	6	3,701	2	X	10	1,228
South Dakota	7	9,503	10	7,113	4	4,343	9	5,282	7	1,695	1	X	15	1,282
Nebraska	22	27,833	23	18,225	7	13,087	26	16,101	29	20,186	8	1,993	49	15,587
Kansas	22	14,916	21	13,963	15	19,437	23	14,194	111	49,642	12	4,641	87	21,390
SOUTH ATLANTIC	286	273,341	280	237,859	217	224,870	366	229,152	507	238,103	104	49,061	242	107,870
Delaware	9	8,132	3	325	3	2,268	12	6,010	4	X	2	X	5	1,721
Maryland	39	31,127	36	29,650	28	15,009	65	27,618	75	22,229	24	16,866	29	28,629
District of Columbia	17	20,760	27	29,526	11	11,293	27	31,688	21	X	7	2,358	5	1,406
Virginia	36	31,942	37	38,094	32	33,199	41	36,058	62	34,964	18	8,200	41	17,288
West Virginia	20	19,789	31	17,077	33	46,841	13	5,863	75	54,036	9	2,603	29	7,406
North Carolina	49	57,015	42	34,690	26	35,309	59	38,004	92	37,556	12	4,811	46	15,113
South Carolina	26	18,821	16	7,066	22	26,381	19	11,572	26	20,565	3	1,078	12	2,911
Georgia	38	41,526	39	47,564	36	32,814	50	28,542	77	35,049	11	4,347	51	23,895
Florida	58	44,229	49	33,867	26	21,756	80	43,797	75	27,910	18	8,712	24	9,501
EAST SOUTH CENTRAL	114	106,524	114	84,671	93	223,744	103	59,465	244	112,725	30	17,045	127	80,109
Kentucky	28	19,416	21	12,944	22	77,096	31	16,973	66	24,112	4	1,417	33	14,018
Tennessee	49	60,903	49	36,341	27	70,353	32	19,873	76	40,205	14	9,631	37	32,018
Alabama	25	16,420	38	29,431	25	63,259	21	13,449	60	32,389	7	2,772	39	31,256
Mississippi	12	9,785	6	5,955	19	13,036	19	9,170	42	16,019	5	3,225	18	2,817
WEST SOUTH CENTRAL	200	194,843	191	145,881	143	201,348	284	143,712	1,054	650,416	117	X	240	89,840
Arkansas	10	7,789	22	15,515	13	18,871	22	8,748	38	15,920	8	1,549	26	4,178
Louisiana	30	46,762	30	24,588	24	48,988	47	18,061	178	118,289	15	10,149	33	17,272
Oklahoma	29	27,985	28	19,849	11	9,887	44	21,790	218	129,901	16	X	61	10,195
Texas	131	112,307	111	85,929	95	123,602	171	95,111	620	386,306	78	60,956	120	58,195
MOUNTAIN	74	63,890	92	51,624	64	X	103	X	243	119,431	32	14,755	62	6,434
Montana	13	11,405	9	5,427	14	14,452	13	4,796	21	8,480	4	2,450	3	X
Idaho	6	X	3	X	6	9,876	6	2,031	21	4,128	2	X	4	604
Wyoming	3	X	5	X	2	X	3	X	25	24,395	1	X	7	368
Colorado	19	12,534	27	21,984	17	14,677	34	15,972	67	29,215	10	4,754	29	2,940
New Mexico	3	3,074	5	580	6	4,121	11	3,709	42	23,107	......	......	4	518
Arizona	16	12,632	15	4,470	9	10,077	12	4,996	22	10,322	6	5,044	7	382
Utah	15	14,920	24	16,721	7	21,674	21	11,184	34	17,708	9	2,084	6	1,086
Nevada	1	X	4	X	3	X	3	X	11	2,076	......	......	2	X
PACIFIC	359	293,550	284	266,239	267	266,790	383	202,741	1,034	364,792	213	187,399	162	40,542
Washington	61	56,652	48	30,858	53	55,798	50	26,277	150	45,039	31	23,484	26	8,021
Oregon	33	40,782	29	25,980	33	36,024	34	21,696	138	54,336	20	11,444	9	1,388
California	265	196,116	207	149,401	181	174,968	299	154,768	746	265,417	162	152,471	127	31,133

X = Suppressed to avoid disclosure.

Source: U. S. Dept. of Commerce, Bureau of the Census

IN THIS SECTION:

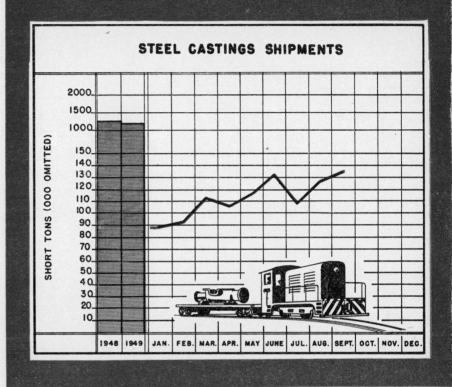

THE IRON AGE

SECTION 5

METAL INDUSTRY FACTS

Casting, Forging, Powder Metallurgy

STEEL CASTINGS SHIPMENTS

5 METAL FACTS SECTION

Steel Castings Production; Iron and Steel Foundry Employment; Earnings, Gray Iron and Semisteel Foundries; Earnings, Steel Casting Industry.

STEEL CASTINGS, PRODUCTION, SALES, ORDERS BY TYPE

Total Production and Sales Broken Into Railway Specialties and Miscellaneous Castings Over 20-Year Period.

Year	Production, Net Tons			Orders Booked, Less Cancellations, Net Tons		
	Total	Railway Specialties	Miscellaneous	Total	Railway Specialties	Miscellaneous
1930	991,872	368,690	623,182	884,433	333,199	551,234
1935	398,988	94,329	304,659	400,157	97,357	302,800
1940	797,947	290,255	507,692	816,919	266,418	550,501
1941	1,316,027	471,810	844,217	1,561,864	560,286	1,001,578
1942	1,679,178	309,352	1,369,826	2,187,347	219,145	1,968,202
1943	1,928,645	248,664	1,679,981	2,333,420	352,760	1,980,660
1944	1,843,386	338,007	1,505,379	1,914,294	322,630	1,591,664
1945	1,484,957[1]	311,833[1]	1,173,124[1]	1,529,912	352,382	1,177,530
1946	1,043,358[1]	286,131[1]	757,227[1]	1,069,842	283,511	786,331
1947	1,203,504[1]	341,987[1]	861,517[1]	1,330,081	449,432	880,649
1948	1,760,894[2]	442,258[2]	839,143[2]	5,514,224[3]	2,308,066[3]	3,206,158[3]
Jan.	141,068	35,129	73,153	491,745	209,398	282,347
Feb.	142,434	34,800	72,962	497,097	214,113	282,984
March	162,891	41,876	83,674	508,822	216,820	292,002
April	150,305	36,079	78,817	472,370	185,691	286,679
May	143,337	39,275	72,341	482,531	204,619	277,912
June	152,894	41,587	76,207	469,973	202,438	267,535
July	120,445	28,422	59,505	497,410	214,602	282,808
Aug.	140,223	35,056	72,482	472,481	201,347	271,134
Sept.	149,222	36,457	76,094	447,972	189,267	258,705
Oct.	153,845	38,833	76,092	424,352	169,707	254,645
Nov.	146,835	36,014	74,261	395,013	156,305	238,708
Dec.	157,395	38,730	77,555	354,458	143,759	210,699
	1,760,894	442,258	839,143	5,514,224	2,308,066	3,206,158
1949	1,243,502[2]	232,976[2]	623,321[2]	2,351,354[3]	809,888[3]	1,541,466[3]
Jan.	140,577	31,891	71,612	338,889	139,967	198,922
Feb.	135,042	32,545	66,880	320,202	130,460	189,742
Mar.	138,889	30,313	71,714	284,754	109,945	174,809
Apr.	119,953	23,834	59,443	250,506	99,240	151,266
May	106,178	22,165	53,372	191,473	85,851	105,622
June	116,052	26,940	57,172	173,237	58,215	115,022
July	78,710	14,625	35,499	155,494	48,236	107,258
Aug.	89,964	13,348	46,064	143,566	39,448	104,118
Sept.	86,502	11,823	44,030	127,664	28,526	99,138
Oct.	70,690	8,964	39,299	124,817	25,896	98,921
Nov.	76,437	7,270	43,415	117,865	23,114	94,751
Dec.	84,508	9,258	43,821	122,887	20,990	101,897
	1,243,502	232,976	623,321	2,351,354	809,888	1,541,466
1950						
Jan.	88,821	9,298	48,698	142,484	32,736	109,748
Feb.	91,827	10,920	51,125	165,186	51,208	113,978
Mar.	111,772	15,821	62,307	185,611	63,572	122,039
Apr.	106,964	17,406	57,727	201,643	71,080	130,563
May	117,944	20,552	63,293	198,078	65,669	132,409
June	131,097	27,065	67,572	206,799	71,806	134,993
July	98,269	15,734	53,140	255,418	94,835	160,583
Aug.	128,369	24,922	69,491	329,944	130,378	199,566
Sept.	134,574	96,738	71,443	427,969	203,899	224,070

[1] Shipments beginning with last quarter of 1945.
[2] Difference between total and classified use is the tonnage for own use and not for sale.
[3] Unfilled orders or backlog.
Note: Approximate coverage of industry is as follows: 1920-30, 80 pct; 1935, 90 pct; 1940-44, 96 pct; 1945-46, 100 pct; 1947, preliminary estimates of complete coverage, based on a sample of the foundries.

Source: Bureau of Census

IRON AND STEEL FOUNDRIES

Employment and Average Earnings

	All Employees Number (thousands)	Production and Related Workers		
		Number (thousands)	Average Weekly Earnings	Average Weekly Hours	Average Hourly Earnings
1947	256.8	229.4	$54.80	41.2	$1.330
1948	259.3	230.9	58.45	40.7	1.436
1949	217.0	188.9	55.09	37.2	1.481
1950:					
Jan.	198.3	172.0	58.17	38.7	1.503
Feb.	203.6	177.1	59.11	39.2	1.508
Mar.	208.6	182.1	60.33	39.9	1.512
Apr.	215.7	188.1	62.37	40.9	1.525
May	220.3	193.0	63.38	41.4	1.531
June	227.9	200.1	64.88	42.1	1.541
July	229.7	202.1	64.37	41.8	1.540

Source: Bureau of Labor Statistics

GRAY IRON, SEMISTEEL FOUNDRIES

Average Hours and Earnings of Workers

	Avg. Weekly Earnings, $	Avg. Weekly Hours	Avg. Hourly Earnings, $
1939	25.93	37.1	0.699
1943	47.39	47.3	1.003
1944	51.34	47.7	1.077
1945	50.86	46.2	1.101
1940	50.70	42.5	1.194
1947*	55.24	42.3	1.306
1948*	57.46	40.9	1.405
1949	54.38	37.5	1.450
1950: Jan.	57.74	39.2	1.473
Feb.	58.91	39.7	1.484
Mar.	59.81	40.3	1.484
Apr.	62.03	41.3	1.502
May	63.44	41.9	1.514
June	64.19	42.4	1.514
July	63.78	41.2	1.548

* All data for 1947, '48 and '49 calculated on revised BLS basis.

Source: Bureau of Labor Statistics

MALLEABLE CASTINGS, LABOR

Average Earnings and Hours for Industry

	Avg. Weekly Earnings, $	Avg. Weekly Hours	Avg. Hourly Earnings, $
1939	24.16	36.0	0.671
1940	25.43	37.5	0.678
1941	31.57	41.7	0.757
1942	37.15	42.5	0.874
1943	46.14	46.5	0.994
1944	50.98	47.9	1.064
1945	49.83	45.4	1.099
1946	49.51	40.9	1.211
1947*	54.39	40.2	1.353
1948*	59.19	40.4	1.465
1949	54.30	35.7	1.521
1950: Jan.	59.25	38.3	1.547
Feb.	59.25	38.6	1.535
Mar.	61.70	39.6	1.558
Apr.	63.25	40.6	1.558
May	63.32	40.8	1.552
June	65.75	41.8	1.573
July	64.80	41.3	1.569

* All data for 1947, '48 and '49 calculated on revised BLS basis.

Source: Bureau of Labor Statistics

STEEL CASTINGS EARNINGS

Average Hours and Earnings of Workers

	Avg. Weekly Earnings, $	Avg. Weekly Hours	Avg. Hourly Earnings, $
1939	27.97	36.9	0.759
1940	29.66	38.6	0.768
1941	37.00	43.7	0.844
1942	43.77	45.8	0.955
1943	48.79	46.4	1.052
1944	51.59	46.2	1.116
1945	49.98	43.9	1.138
1946	48.45	38.8	1.248
1947*	53.94	39.6	1.362
1948*	59.93	40.8	1.476
1949	56.73	37.3	1.521
1950: Jan.	57.75	37.6	1.536
Feb.	59.83	38.7	1.546
Mar.	60.61	39.1	1.550
Apr.	62.79	40.3	1.558
May	63.49	40.7	1.560
June	65.84	41.7	1.579
July	65.31	41.6	1.570

* All data for 1947, '48 and '49 calculated on revised BLS basis.

Source: Bureau of Labor Statistics

GRAY IRON SHIPMENTS

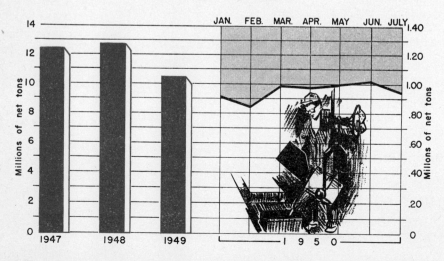

Steel Castings Shipments; Gray Iron Castings Shipments; Malleable Castings, Shipments and Orders and Earnings, Malleable Iron Casting.

METAL FACTS
SECTION 5

SHIPMENTS OF STEEL CASTINGS, ALLOY AND CARBON

By Types of Furnace and Grade of Steel, Net Tons

Type of Furnace and Grade of Steel	1946	1947	1948	1949	1950								
					January	February	March	April	May	June	July	August	September
Total	1,432,049	1,625,055	1,760,032	1,243,502	88,821	91,827	111,772	106,964	117,944	131,097	98,269	128,369	134,574
Electric	691,098	744,328	758,383	571,324	46,546	49,074	56,673	54,699	58,913	65,094	47,561	67,439	66,362
Carbon	489,466	487,486	511,183	386,803	31,636	33,696	39,102	37,407	41,261	40,695	28,007	40,447	41,793
Alloy (including stainless)	201,632	256,842	247,200	184,521	14,910	15,378	17,571	17,292	17,652	24,399	19,554	26,992	24,569
All Other	740,951	880,727	1,001,849	672,178	42,275	42,753	55,099	52,265	59,031	66,003	50,708	60,930	68,212
Carbon	622,777	753,519	856,525	557,429	32,980	33,147	43,356	42,505	46,941	55,670	42,115	51,750	56,730
Alloy (including stainless)	118,174	127,208	145,124	114,749	9,295	9,606	11,743	9,760	12,090	10,333	8,593	9,180	11,482

Source: Bureau of Census

SHIPMENTS OF GRAY IRON CASTINGS INCLUDING PIPE

Iron Castings Plus Soil and Pressure Pipe, Net Tons

	1947	1948	1949	1950								
				January	February	March	April	May	June	July	August	September
Total Gray Iron Castings, Shipments	12,540,960	12,785,909	10,549,284	913,321	864,189	995,782	981,126	1,095,111	1,136,129	961,450	1,201,569	1,159,240
For Sale	7,181,299	7,131,405	5,517,527	449,577	416,594	500,195	483,862	572,887	613,084	507,867	677,134	648,966
For Own Use	5,359,661	5,654,504	5,031,757	463,744	417,595	495,587	497,264	522,224	523,045	453,583	524,435	510,274
Unfilled Orders for Sale	33,512,992	31,179,282	....	914,185	873,455	921,575	922,255	977,833	1,039,619	1,286,579	1,670,380	1,794,118
Molds for Heavy Steel Ingots, Shipments	1,873,376	1,979,740	1,776,242	188,152	169,605	170,082	182,420	195,021	197,474	177,154	199,770	203,191
Chilled Iron R. R. Car Wheels, Shipments	752,976	719,784	555,569	34,254	33,417	44,898	42,768	46,219	45,672	35,066	52,508	44,707
Cast Iron Pressure Pipe and Fittings, Shipments	1,031,626	1,149,553	1,029,743	64,095	63,363	89,264	82,774	104,529	106,980	94,438	131,127	121,556
Cast Iron Soil Pipe and Fittings, Shipments	577,189	639,989	563,310	53,077	46,744	56,135	51,796	64,710	72,192	58,874	71,118	67,119
Misc. Gray Iron Castings, Shipments	8,305,793	8,296,843	6,624,420	573,743	551,060	635,403	621,368	684,632	713,811	595,918	747,046	722,667

Source: Bureau of Census

HEAT TREATING

"THE IRON AGE Mid-Century Reference of Heat Treating" begins on p. 267. For anyone in any way interested in heat treating it should prove invaluable. It is the most complete up-to-date index on time-temperature-transformation ever assembled. Both ferrous and nonferrous metals are covered in a guide which indexes and lists the most important papers and publications on this subject. Austenite transformations are affected by chemistry, grain size, segregation, cleanliness, etc., as well as by time and temperature. Many different references on these and on isothermal heat treating practices are covered with a modern reference index which also includes important foreign work in the field.

MALLEABLE IRON CASTINGS SHIPMENTS. ORDERS

Production, Shipments and New Orders, Net Tons

	Production, Net Tons	Shipments, Net Tons			New Orders, Less Cancellations, Net Tons			Shipments, Monthly Index*
		Total	For Sale	For Own Use	Total	For Sale	For Own Use	
1930	471,923	475,371	....	....	432,722	....	....	....
1935	466,395	455,208	....	....	452,611	....	....	96.1
1938	289,914	296,003	208,597	87,406	289,384	203,172	86,212	62.5
1939	480,578	466,068	331,421	134,647	489,482	354,249	135,233	98.4
1940	565,923	556,209	400,818	155,391	571,929	414,310	157,619	117.4
1941	843,038	832,173	619,365	212,808	884,881	663,688	221,193	175.7
1942	768,496	746,008	590,804	155,204	859,102	703,167	155,935	157.5
1943	849,764	844,639	653,884	190,755	1,054,224	826,422	227,802	178.3
1944	889,820	878,233	619,588	258,645	969,483	685,511	283,972	185.4
1945	....	790,731	520,887	269,844	766,711	426,159	340,552	166.9
1946	....	752,028	452,355	299,673	....	483,368	....	158.8
1947	....	895,054	513,228	381,826	....	447,975	....	188.9
1948	....	933,265	525,212	408,053	....	460,189	....	197.0
1949	....	713,330	371,214	34,416	430,530	226,483	204,047	155.8
1950: Jan.	....	62,874	32,918	29,956	....	34,390	....	159.3
Feb.	....	60,386	31,249	29,137	....	35,991	....	153.0
Mar.	....	66,259	38,639	27,620	....	41,456	....	167.8
April	....	69,822	36,279	33,543	....	42,663	....	176.9
May	....	76,161	42,432	33,729	....	43,256	....	192.9
June	....	82,345	46,613	35,732	....	56,322	....	208.6
July	....	67,514	37,198	30,316	....	55,715	....	171.0
Aug.	....	86,021	50,019	36,002	....	77,093	....	211.9
Sept.	....	82,479	46,927	35,552	....	67,136	....	208.9

Source: Bureau of Census

Note: Statistics represent coverage of approximately 90 pct for 1923-43; thereafter coverage is essentially complete
* Based on average monthly shipments for 5-year period 1935-39 (39,476 short tons).

5 METAL FACTS SECTION

Jet Engine Analysis; Cast Iron Radiation Shipments; Average Earnings In Forging Industry; Shipments of Forgings and Foundry Equipment Orders

HIGH-TEMPERATURE JET-ENGINE ALLOYS

Popular Grades Listed in Order of Their Decreasing Strategic Alloy Index, October

	C	Cr	Ni	Co	Mo	W	Cb	Ti	Fe	Other
S-816	0.4	20	20	44	4	4	4	...	3	...
MIT NT-2	1	20	30	20	3	2.2	...	...	21	Ta-2
S-590	0.4	20	20	20	4	4	4	...	25	...
61	0.4	28	1	67	...	5	...	...	...	...
NR 88 (Co-Cr(9W))	0.4	23	3	63	...	9	...	...	...	...
Vitallium	0.25	28	2.5	62	5.5	...	...	...	1	...
X-40	0.5	25	10	55	...	7	...	...	0.6	...
422-19	0.4	26	15	51	6	...	...	...	...	...
NR-90 (Co-Cr-Ni(5Mo.5W))	0.4	23	18	46	5	5	...	...	...	...
I-1360	0.10	10	70	...	5	...	2	...	4.5	Al-6 Be-0.5
N-155	0.3	20	20	20	3	2	1.0	...	0.32	N₂-0.11
6059	0.4	26	33	33	5	...	...	...	...	...
Inconel X	0.05	15	73	...	...	...	1	2.5	7	...
K-42-B	0.05	18	42	22	...	...	...	2.2	14	Al-0.2
EME	0.1	19	12	...	...	3.2	1.2	...	63	N₂-0.15
Refractalloy 26	0.05	18	37	20	3	...	...	2.8	18	Al-0.2
Nimonic 80	0.05	21	75	...	...	...	...	2.5	0.7	Al-0.6
19-9-DL	0.3	19	9	...	1.2	1.2	0.3	0.3	67	...
Inconel	0.05	14	78	...	...	...	...	...	7	Cu-0.2
Hastalloy B	0.1	...	64	...	28	...	...	...	6	...
Timken (16-25-6)	0.12	16	25	...	6	...	...	...	...	N₂-0.18
17W	0.5	13	19	...	1	2.5	...	...	60	...

CAST IRON RADIATION SHIPMENTS

By Type and Dollar Value

	Cast Iron Boilers 1000 lb	Value ($1000)	Cast Iron Radiators and Convectors 1000 sq ft	Value ($1000)
1948	263,303	......	60,333	......
1949	206,296	......	35,888	......
1950				
Jan.	10,595	$2,235	2,678	$1,428
Feb.	10,534	2,147	2,966	1,547
Mar.	11,144	2,273	3,015	1,571
Apr.	12,573	2,578	2,440	1,313
May	15,349	3,081	2,025	1,073
June	31,994	6,702	3,513	1,802
July	25,747	5,124	4,020	2,205
Aug.	40,329	8,175	6,449	3,506
Sept.	40,153	8,218	5,714	3,121

Source: Bureau of Census and Dept. of Commerce

SHIPMENTS OF COMMERCIAL STEEL FORGINGS

Alloy and Carbon in Drop and Upset and Press and Open Hammer Types—Net Tons

Date	Total	Drop and Upset Carbon Steel	Drop and Upset Alloy Steel	Press and Open Hammer Carbon Steel	Press and Open Hammer Alloy Steel
1946	1,164,041	564,491	228,743	224,962	145,845
1947	1,333,731	692,544	279,538	224,738	136,911
1948	1,413,266	693,874	344,928	227,662	146,802
1949	1,138,628	585,474	280,970	162,852	109,332
1950: January	92,994	49,192	24,266	10,053	9,483
February	92,547	50,880	22,560	10,224	8,883
March	108,677	60,781	26,964	11,508	9,424
April	99,193	55,661	25,289	9,756	8,487
May	113,657	64,334	29,125	9,719	10,479
June	117,333	67,747	28,314	10,804	10,468
July	94,929	55,596	23,485	7,047	8,801
August	123,608	67,670	31,935	12,301	11,702
September	122,408	64,456	33,297	13,652	11,003

Source: Bureau of Census

EARNINGS IN FORGING INDUSTRY

Average Earnings Per Worker

	Avg. Weekly Earnings, $	Avg. Weekly Hours	Avg. Hourly Earnings, $
1935	23.62	38.5	0.615
1936	26.11	41.7	0.627
1937	28.84	40.9	0.711
1938	23.97	32.3	0.744
1939	29.45	38.4	0.767
1940	32.56	41.2	0.791
1941	40.93	45.9	0.894
1942	49.93	47.9	1.047
1943	56.88	48.2	1.180
1944	59.62	47.7	1.251
1945	56.79	45.0	1.262
1946	52.77	39.9	1.324
1947*	59.79	40.7	1.469
1948*	65.16	40.8	1.597
1949	63.18	38.2	1.654
1950: Jan.	64 89	38.6	1.681
Feb.	66 94	39.4	1.699
Mar.	68.75	39.9	1.723
Apr.	68.80	40.0	1.720
May	72.89	41.7	1.748
June	72.51	41.6	1.743
July	73.08	41.5	1.761

* All data for 1947, '48 and '49 calculated on revised BLS basis.

Source: Bureau of Labor Statistics

FOUNDRY EQUIPMENT ORDER INDEX

FOUNDRY EQUIPMENT ORDERS AND SHIPMENTS

Index and Dollar Volume for New Orders and Repairs

	New Orders Closed New Equipment, $	Index	Shipments New Equipment, $	Repairs $	Total $
1949: January	693,747	149.9	1,213,737	816,018	1,029,755
February	668,095	144.4	1,387,142	823,916	2,211,058
March	882,645	190.8	955,240	767,386	1,722,626
April	797,085	172.0	998,808	716,807	1,715,615
May	564,814	121.9	950,194	578,681	1,528,875
June	763,920	164.9	1,136,552	578,198	1,714,650
July	679,432	146.6	1,027,326	419,055	1,446,381
August	588,975	127.1	1,057,651	509,963	1,567,614
September	771,864	166.6	770,285	574,653	1,344,938
October	618 489	133 5	979,891	567,492	1,547,383
November	1,250,059	270.4	814,423	534,669	1,349,092
December	929,343	201.0	782,906	514,488	1,297,394
1950: January	730,769	159.3	735,171	508,831	1,244,002
February	519,111	113.1	583,793	523,501	1,107,294
March	1,033,585	225.2	906,870	671,463	1,578,333
April	737,119	160.6	613,156	577,569	1,190,725
May	1,353,284	294.9	789,996	668,547	1,458,543
June	2,857,514	622.7	943,249	739,158	1,682,407
July	1,843,821	401.8	841,733	773,522	1,615,255
August	3,182,714	693.6	782,165	751,158	1,533,323
September	2,220,140	483.8	839,508	725,939	1,565,447

Source: Foundry Equipment Manufacturers Assn.

Shipments: Zinc, Aluminum, Lead, Copper and Magnesium Castings; Employment in Nonferrous Foundries; Sales of Industrial Furnaces.

METAL FACTS
SECTION 5

ALUMINUM CASTINGS, SHIPMENTS
By Type of Castings, 000 omitted

		Shipments			
	Total	Sand	Perm. Mold	Die	Unfilled Orders*
1947					
Total.....	441,996	155,112	174,515	110,538	......
1948					
Total.....	424,490	139,781	161,334	118,738	......
1949					
Jan.......	29,142	9,702	10.386	8,490	55,580
Feb.......	27,228	9,286	9.339	7,795	52,916
Mar.......	27,478	9,348	9,386	7,999	50.508
Apr.......	23.801	8,041	8,353	6,876	45.638
May.......	21.392	7,582	7,293	5,994	41,460
June.......	23,261	8,668	7.790	6,257	38.159
July.......	18,621	6,311	6,592	5,180	36.993
Aug.......	23,997	9 048	8.326	6,119	38.130
Sept.......	27,559	9,936	9,491	7,623	38.183
Oct.......	30,499	10.162	9.923	8,908	37.881
Nov.......	26.317	9,212	8.315	8,348	36.846
Dec.......	26,762	10.070	7,714	8,430	36,921
Total....	304,616	106,825	102,908	88,019	......
1950					
Jan.......	28,801	9,646	9,400	9,052	40.591
Feb.......	28,887	10,171	9 358	8,851	44.235
Mar.......	35 845	13 035	11,094	10,870	47.350
Apr.......	33 384	11,091	10 656	10.823	50.024
May.......	36,031	11,526	11.928	11,799	52.580
June.......	37,600	12,677	11,825	12,173	53.309
July.......	32,794	10 393	11,276	10.337	70.940
Aug.......	39 852	14,117	12,682	12,207	82,564
Sept.......	42,061	14,369	13,085	13,594	89,723

* For sale only.

Source: Bureau of Census

A listing of important trade associations and technical societies in the fields covered by this section begins on p. 150.... For a calendar of meetings in the metalworking field scheduled for 1951 see p. 114.... Don't miss "How to Sell to Uncle. Sam," a brief report on armed forces procurement, which begins on p. 269.... For major metal items bought by the government and where they are bought refer to p. 371.

NONFERROUS FOUNDRIES, LABOR
Employment, Hours and Earnings

	All Employees Number (thousands)	Production and Related Workers			
		Number (thousands)	Average Weekly Earnings	Average Weekly Hours	Average Hourly Earnings
1947	85.9	74.4	$54.92	40.0	$1.373
1948	85.2	73.2	59.96	40.0	1.499
1949	75.8	63.3	60.92	39.0	1.562
1950:					
Jan.	79.0	66.0	62.73	39.6	1.584
Feb.	80.8	67.8	62.29	39.5	1.577
Mar..	83.3	69.8	63.04	40.1	1.572
Apr...	84.3	70.7	64.03	40.5	1.581
May..	87.4	73.6	65.36	40.9	1.598
June.	91.8	77.7	66.64	41.6	1.602
July	92.1	78.0	64.27	40.5	1.587

Source: Bureau of Labor Statistics

COPPER CASTINGS SHIPMENTS
Copper and Copper-Base, 000 omitted

	Sand	Permanent Mold	Die	All Other	Total, All Types
1947.....	960,732	51,139	12,657	......	1,051,742
1948.....	930,790	59.009	12,672	......	1,030.825
1949.....	654,444	37,311	10,082	23,481	725.318
1950: Jan.	58,878	3,440	1,173	2,094	65,585
Feb.	60,257	3,626	1,100	2,046	67,029
Mar.	71,876	4,693	1,319	2,554	80,442
Apr.	64,773	3,848	1,128	2,731	72,478
May	71,605	3,751	1,076	2,676	79,108
June	74,990	3,896	1,165	2,972	83 023
July	62,414	3,789	941	1,889	69033
Aug.	85,948	4,258	1,159	2,648	94,013
Sept.	87,111	4,630	1,081	2,819	95,641

Source: Bureau of Census

ZINC CASTINGS SHIPMENTS
Zinc and Zinc-Base Alloys (1000 lb)

	Diecastings	All Other	Total
1947.............	429.535	6.873	436,408
1948.............	439,183	5,771	444,954
1949.............	....	....	374,865
1950: Jan.	36,908	269	37,177
Feb.	32,988	409	33,397
Mar.	42,658	436	43,094
Apr.	40,131	310	40,441
May.	47,029	425	47,454
June.	48,289	529	48,818
July.	41,924	264	42188,
Aug.	46,589	623	47,212
Sept.	48,712	367	49,079

Source: Bureau of Census

LEAD DIECASTINGS SHIPMENTS
Lead and Lead-Base (1000 lb)

	Total Shipments
1947..........................	14,137
1948..........................	14,877
1949..........................	9,101
1950:	
Jan..........................	659
Feb..........................	665
Mar..........................	847
Apr..........................	930
May..........................	982
June..........................	1,094
July..........................	1,045
Aug..........................	1,629
Sept..........................	1,479

Source: Bureau of Census

MAGNESIUM CASTINGS, ORDERS
Shipments, 000 omitted

	Shipments		Unfilled Orders*
	Total	For Sale	
1947			
Total............	7,693	7,050	.....
1948			
Total............	8,214	7,488	.....
1949			
Total............	9,364	8,781	.....
1950			
Jan............	814	762	2,237
Feb............	735	676	2,218
Mar............	903	849	2,322
Apr............	799	751	2,305
May............	810	762	2,282
June............	758	698	2,482
July............	763	713	3,587
Aug............	1,147	1,078	4,855
Sept............	1,231	1,154	4,952

* For sale only.

Source: Bureau of Census

PRESSED METAL EARNINGS
Average Hours and Earnings per Worker

Production and Related Workers

	Average Weekly Earnings	Average Weekly Hours	Average Hourly Earnings
1947.............	$53.71	40.6	$1.323
1948.............	58.39	40.3	1.449
1949.............	60.30	39.7	1.519
1950: Jan.......	63.37	40.7	1.557
Feb.......	62.35	40.7	1.532
Mar.......	62.59	40.8	1.534
Apr.......	62.92	41.1	1.531
May.......	63.47	41.0	1.548
June.......	66.22	42.1	1.573
July.......	65.46	41.3	1.585

Source: Bureau of Labor Statistics

INDUSTRIAL FURNACE SALES
Fuel Fired and Electric Types

Year	Fuel-Fired Industrial Furnaces, Including Hot Rolling Steel	Electric Resistance Furnaces	Total
1940........	$14,404,397	$ 8,238,613	$ 22,643,010
1941........	$34,124,751	$13,719,111	$ 47,843,862
1942........	$89,709,507	$39,052,122	$128,761,629
1943........	$16,951,800	$12,855,326	$ 29,807,126
1944........	$20,770,634	$10,233,549	$ 31,004,183
1945........	$22,102,225	$ 9,464,210	$ 31,566,435
1946........	$20,383,884	$ 8,429,840	$ 28,813,724
1947........	$22,569,770	$ 7,799,584	$ 30,369,354
1948........	$15,655,654	$ 5,836,410	$ 21,492,064
1949........	$ 9,982,440	$ 5,284,021	$ 15,266,461
1950 (9 Mos.)	$17,708,664	$ 8,616,188	$ 26,324,852

These figures constitute approximately 80% of the industry.   Source: Industrial Furnace Mfrs. Asso.

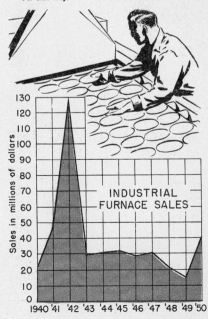

INDUSTRIAL FURNACE SALES

Sales in millions of dollars

1940 '41 '42 '43 '44 '45 '46 '47 '48 '49 '50

5 METAL FACTS SECTION

Prices: Copper, Lead, Zinc and Iron Powders; Shipments of Copper and Lead Powder; Imports of Iron Powders; Powder Part and Stamping Plants.

IRON POWDER, AVERAGE MONTHLY PRICES

Cents per pound, F.O.B. Mill Unless Otherwise Specified

1950	Swedish Sponge, c.i.f. N. Y., Ocean Bags, —100 Mesh	Domestic Sponge, 98+Pct Fe, Carload Lots, —100 Mesh	Electrolytic, Annealed, 99.5+Pct Fe, —100 Mesh	Electrolytic, Unannealed, —325 Mesh 99+Pct Fe	Hydrogen Reduced, —300 Mesh 98+Pct Fe	Carbonyl, 5-10 Microns, 98=99.8+ Pct Fe
Jan.	7.4 to 9.0	9.0 to 15.0	31.5 to 39.5	48.5	63.0 to 80.0	90.0 to $1.75
Feb.	7.4 to 9.0	9.0 to 15.0	31.5 to 39.5	48.5	63.0 to 80.0	90.0 to 1.75
March	7.4 to 9.0	9.0 to 15.0	31.5 to 39.5	48.5	63.0 to 80.0	90.0 to 1.75
April	7.4 to 9.0	9.0 to 15.0	31.5 to 39.5	48.5	63.0 to 80.0	70.0 to 1.75
May	7.4 to 9.0	9.0 to 15.0	31.5 to 39.5	48.5	63.0 to 80.0	70.0 to 1.35
June	7.4 to 9.0	9.0 to 15.0	31.5 to 39.5	48.5	63.0 to 80.0	70.0 to 1.35
July	7.4 to 9.0	9.0 to 15.0	36.0 to 39.5	48.5	63.0 to 80.0	70.0 to 1.35
Aug.	7.4 to 9.0	9.0 to 15.0	36.0 to 39.5	48.5	63.0 to 80.0	70.0 to 1.35
Sept.	7.4 to 9.0	9.0 to 15.0	36.0 to 39.5	48.5	63.0 to 80.0	70.0 to 1.35
Oct.	7.4 to 9.0	9.0 to 15.0	36.0 to 39.5	48.5	63.0 to 80.0	70.0 to 1.35
Nov.	7.4 to 9.0	9.0 to 15.0	36.0 to 39.5	48.5	63.0 to 80.0	70.0 to 1.35
Dec.	7.4 to 9.0	9.0 to 15.0	36.0 to 39.5	48.5	63.0 to 80.0	70.0 to 1.35
1950 Aver.	7.4 to 9.0	9.0 to 15.0	36.0 to 39.5	48.5	63.0 to 80.0	70.0 to 1.35
1949 Aver.	7.8 to 9.0	9.0 to 15.0	31.0 to 39.5	48.5	63.0 to 80.0	90.0 to 1.75

IMPORTS OF IRON POWDERS

Swedish Imports in Pounds per Month

1948	Total Weight, Lb
January	350,000
February	424,000
March	390,800
April	332,000
May	389,400
June	796,900
July	482,763
August	87,272
September	....
October	457,000
November	1,189,659
December	280,000
1948 Total	**5,179,794**
1949	
January	645,355
February	513,878
March	345,213
April	500,533
May	324,419
June	491,781
July	620,396
August	280,740
September	417,300
October	567,270
November	710,000
December	800,000
1949 Total	**6,216,883**
1950	
January	600,000
February	600,000
March	1,150,000
April	1,700,000
May	900,000
June	750,000
July	1,100,000
August	1,300,000
Estimated Total 1950	**12,000,000**

Source: Dept. of Commerce

SHIPMENTS OF LEAD POWDER

Net Tons

	Total	Bearings	Friction Materials	Protective Coatings	Miscl.
1943	731	...	...	...	...
1944	1441	...	...	...	...
1945	5195*	...	...	...	...
1946	905*	55	195	193	462
1947	785*	53	165	187	380
1948	1040*	74	319	141	506
1949	790	68	315	210	350
1950	918	112	230	132	444

Source: THE IRON AGE and *American Bureau of Metal Statistics.

COPPER POWDER SHIPMENTS

Net Tons

	Total	Bearings and Friction	Friction Materials	Graphite Metal Brushes	Misc.
1943	6,430	.....	......	.....	.....
1944	6,770	.....	......	.....	.....
1945	6,550	.....	......	.....	.....
1946	7,380	5,900	560	330	590
1947	8,700	7,170	615	385	600
1948	8,580	6,560	675	575	770
1949	7,014	4,374	1,158	450	1,032
1950	13,109	9,488	1,271	957	1,393

Source: THE IRON AGE, estimated

SHIPMENTS OF IRON POWDER

Total Net Tons, Four Major Classes

	Total	Bearings and Parts	Friction Materials	Magnetic Cores	Miscellaneous
1943	2,135	.....	.....	......	.....
1944	1,720	.....	.....	......	.....
1945	1,950	.....	.....	......	.....
1946	2,485	1,350	30	415	690
1947	3,115	1,560	30	600	845
1948	3,520	1,685	25	990	820
1949	3,235	1,746	14	935	540
1950	4,125	1,650	30	1,500	945

Source: THE IRON AGE

METAL POWDER PART PLANTS

Plants With 21 Workers or More

Alabama	..	Nevada	..
Arizona	..	New Hampshire	..
Arkansas	..	New Jersey	13
California	2	New Mexico	..
Colorado	..	New York	12
Connecticut	4	North Carolina	..
Delaware	..	North Dakota	..
District of Columbia	..	Ohio	9
Florida	..	Oklahoma	..
Georgia	..	Oregon	..
Idaho	..	Pennsylvania	13
Illinois	11	Rhode Island	1
Indiana	3	South Carolina	..
Iowa	1	South Dakota	..
Kansas	..	Tennessee	1
Kentucky	1	Texas	1
Louisiana	..	Utah	..
Maine	1	Vermont	..
Maryland	1	Virginia	..
Massachusetts	11	Washington	..
Michigan	14	West Virginia	..
Minnesota	1	Wisconsin	1
Mississippi	..	Wyoming	..
Missouri	..		
Montana	..	**Total**	**101**
Nebraska	1		

(Source: THE IRON AGE Basic Marketing Data)

AVERAGE COPPER POWDER PRICE

¢ per Pound, F.O.B. Mill—100 Mesh

1950	Electrolytic	Reduced
Jan.	28.625	28.50
Feb.	28.625	28.50
March	28.625	28.50
April	27.75	27.00
May	27.75	27.00
June	27.75	27.00
July	9.25*	9.75*
Aug.	9.25*	9.75*
Sept.	9.25*	9.75*
Oct.	10.25*	10.00*
Nov.	10.25*	10.00*
Dec.	10.25*	10.00*
1950 Average	9.75*	9.87*
1949 Average	29.82	30.06

* Change in method, above price, *plus metal value.*

Source: THE IRON AGE

AVERAGE ZINC POWDER PRICE

¢ per Pound, F.O.B. Mill—100 Mesh

1950	
Jan.	15.50 to 18.25
Feb.	15.50 to 18.25
March	15.50 to 18.25
April	15.75 to 18.50
May	15.75 to 18.50
June	18.14 to 21.17
July	20.50 to 23.85
Aug.	20.50 to 23.85
Sept.	20.50 to 23.85
Oct.	20.50 to 23.85
Nov.	20.50 to 23.85
Dec.	20.50 to 23.85
1950 Average	20.50 to 23.85
1948 Average	15.41 to 18.71

Source: THE IRON AGE

STAMPING PLANTS IN U. S.

Plants With 21 Workers or More

Alabama	44	Nevada	..
Arizona	2	New Hampshire	21
Arkansas	11	New Jersey	385
California	481	New Mexico	1
Colorado	28	New York	909
Connecticut	317	North Carolina	30
Delaware	9	North Dakota	1
District of Columbia	5	Ohio	885
Florida	36	Oklahoma	23
Georgia	54	Oregon	28
Idaho	3	Pennsylvania	549
Illinois	1092	Rhode Island	137
Indiana	310	South Carolina	5
Iowa	107	South Dakota	3
Kansas	39	Tennessee	53
Kentucky	60	Texas	92
Louisiana	18	Utah	8
Maine	13	Vermont	8
Maryland	78	Virginia	32
Massachusetts	397	Washington	34
Michigan	652	West Virginia	30
Minnesota	131	Wisconsin	271
Mississippi	7	Wyoming	3
Missouri	192		
Montana	..	**Total**	**7620**
Nebraska	30		

(Source: THE IRON AGE Basic Marketing Data)

Number of Foundries in Operation; Number of Diecasting Departments in U. S.; Number of Forge Shops and Heat Treating Plants.

METAL FACTS
SECTION 5

MALLEABLE IRON FOUNDRIES
Plants With 21 Workers or More

State	No.	State	No.
Alabama	1	Nevada	..
Arizona	..	New Hampshire	..
Arkansas	1	New Jersey	6
California	6	New Mexico	..
Colorado	..	New York	16
Connecticut	7	North Carolina	1
Delaware	1	North Dakota	..
District of Columbia	..	Ohio	24
Florida	..	Oklahoma	1
Georgia	1	Oregon	..
Idaho	1	Pennsylvania	15
Illinois	22	Rhode Island	1
Indiana	11	South Carolina	1
Iowa	1	South Dakota	..
Kansas	..	Tennessee	..
Kentucky	..	Texas	5
Louisiana	1	Utah	..
Maine	..	Vermont	..
Maryland	..	Virginia	..
Massachusetts	4	Washington	4
Michigan	13	West Virginia	2
Minnesota	2	Wisconsin	13
Mississippi	..	Wyoming	..
Missouri	3		
Montana	..	**Total**	**164**
Nebraska	..		

(Source: THE IRON AGE Basic Marketing Data)

NUMBER OF STEEL FOUNDRIES
Plants With 21 Workers or More

State	No.	State	No.
Alabama	6	Nevada	..
Arizona	1	New Hampshire	3
Arkansas	1	New Jersey	10
California	29	New Mexico	..
Colorado	4	New York	21
Connecticut	6	North Carolina	1
Delaware	3	North Dakota	..
District of Columbia	1	Ohio	32
Florida	1	Oklahoma	1
Georgia	4	Oregon	7
Idaho	..	Pennsylvania	68
Illinois	25	Rhode Island	2
Indiana	15	South Carolina	..
Iowa	4	South Dakota	..
Kansas	3	Tennessee	3
Kentucky	1	Texas	12
Louisiana	4	Utah	1
Maine	..	Vermont	..
Maryland	3	Virginia	3
Massachusetts	9	Washington	16
Michigan	19	West Virginia	4
Minnesota	5	Wisconsin	15
Mississippi	..	Wyoming	..
Missouri	8		
Montana	..	**Total**	**352**
Nebraska	1		

(Source: THE IRON AGE Basic Marketing Data)

DIECASTING SHOPS IN U. S.
Plants With 21 Workers or More

State	No.	State	No.
Alabama	1	Nevada	..
Arizona	..	New Hampshire	1
Arkansas	..	New Jersey	39
California	61	New Mexico	..
Colorado	7	New York	50
Connecticut	20	North Carolina	..
Delaware	..	North Dakota	..
District of Columbia	..	Ohio	67
Florida	3	Oklahoma	1
Georgia	5	Oregon	1
Idaho	1	Pennsylvania	38
Illinois	92	Rhode Island	8
Indiana	23	South Carolina	..
Iowa	5	South Dakota	..
Kansas	1	Tennessee	4
Kentucky	3	Texas	6
Louisiana	..	Utah	..
Maine	..	Vermont	..
Maryland	1	Virginia	3
Massachusetts	17	Washington	2
Michigan	52	West Virginia	1
Minnesota	13	Wisconsin	19
Mississippi	1	Wyoming	..
Missouri	17		
Montana	..	**Total**	**567**
Nebraska	4		

(Source: THE IRON AGE Basic Marketing Data)

NONFERROUS FOUNDRIES
Plants With 21 Workers or More

State	No.	State	No.
Alabama	16	Nevada	..
Arizona	1	New Hampshire	13
Arkansas	1	New Jersey	70
California	124	New Mexico	1
Colorado	11	New York	138
Connecticut	56	North Carolina	8
Delaware	2	North Dakota	..
District of Columbia	..	Ohio	166
Florida	13	Oklahoma	9
Georgia	16	Oregon	5
Idaho	..	Pennsylvania	140
Illinois	123	Rhode Island	8
Indiana	56	South Carolina	6
Iowa	22	South Dakota	..
Kansas	12	Tennessee	16
Kentucky	6	Texas	23
Louisiana	8	Utah	4
Maine	5	Vermont	2
Maryland	10	Virginia	10
Massachusetts	65	Washington	15
Michigan	115	West Virginia	9
Minnesota	23	Wisconsin	53
Mississippi	1	Wyoming	2
Missouri	33		
Montana	3	**Total**	**1429**
Nebraska	8		

(Source: THE IRON AGE Basic Marketing Data)

GRAY IRON FOUNDRIES
Plants With 21 Workers or More

State	No.	State	No.
Alabama	60	Nevada	..
Arizona	1	New Hampshire	17
Arkansas	2	New Jersey	71
California	87	New Mexico	1
Colorado	12	New York	140
Connecticut	44	North Carolina	30
Delaware	4	North Dakota	1
District of Columbia	1	Ohio	220
Florida	8	Oklahoma	13
Georgia	43	Oregon	15
Idaho	1	Pennsylvania	258
Illinois	161	Rhode Island	10
Indiana	97	South Carolina	9
Iowa	47	South Dakota	1
Kansas	24	Tennessee	45
Kentucky	16	Texas	36
Louisiana	10	Utah	7
Maine	8	Vermont	12
Maryland	18	Virginia	27
Massachusetts	76	Washington	22
Michigan	141	West Virginia	13
Minnesota	45	Wisconsin	86
Mississippi	6	Wyoming	1
Missouri	38		
Montana	3	**Total**	**1997**
Nebraska	9		

(Source: THE IRON AGE Basic Marketing Data)

FORGE SHOPS IN OPERATION
Plants With 21 Workers or More

State	No.	State	No.
Alabama	22	Nevada	1
Arizona	1	New Hampshire	10
Arkansas	3	New Jersey	87
California	89	New Mexico	..
Colorado	13	New York	147
Connecticut	61	North Carolina	8
Delaware	3	North Dakota	..
District of Columbia	5	Ohio	195
Florida	13	Oklahoma	9
Georgia	19	Oregon	15
Idaho	3	Pennsylvania	220
Illinois	148	Rhode Island	14
Indiana	66	South Carolina	1
Iowa	23	South Dakota	1
Kansas	14	Tennessee	22
Kentucky	18	Texas	43
Louisiana	10	Utah	5
Maine	9	Vermont	11
Maryland	17	Virginia	18
Massachusetts	106	Washington	25
Michigan	124	West Virginia	24
Minnesota	30	Wisconsin	51
Mississippi	6	Wyoming	1
Missouri	32		
Montana	4	**Total**	**1755**
Nebraska	8		

(Source: THE IRON AGE Basic Marketing Data)

SHEET METAL DEPARTMENTS
Plants With 21 Workers or More

State	No.	State	No.
Alabama	54	Nevada	2
Arizona	6	New Hampshire	12
Arkansas	8	New Jersey	280
California	405	New Mexico	3
Colorado	34	New York	612
Connecticut	116	North Carolina	42
Delaware	11	North Dakota	2
District of Columbia	7	Ohio	674
Florida	36	Oklahoma	35
Georgia	61	Oregon	39
Idaho	4	Pennsylvania	446
Illinois	708	Rhode Island	24
Indiana	216	South Carolina	5
Iowa	104	South Dakota	6
Kansas	55	Tennessee	64
Kentucky	58	Texas	127
Louisiana	25	Utah	9
Maine	12	Vermont	13
Maryland	76	Virginia	34
Massachusetts	237	Washington	59
Michigan	426	West Virginia	25
Minnesota	113	Wisconsin	223
Mississippi	7	Wyoming	3
Missouri	148		
Montana	3	**Total**	**5711**
Nebraska	42		

(Source: THE IRON AGE Basic Marketing Data)

HEAT TREATING SHOPS
Plants With 21 Workers or More

State	No.	State	No.
Alabama	30	Nevada	1
Arizona	2	New Hampshire	19
Arkansas	7	New Jersey	271
California	237	New Mexico	..
Colorado	21	New York	524
Connecticut	221	North Carolina	23
Delaware	9	North Dakota	..
District of Columbia	4	Ohio	623
Florida	15	Oklahoma	28
Georgia	26	Oregon	32
Idaho	2	Pennsylvania	496
Illinois	494	Rhode Island	76
Indiana	206	South Carolina	2
Iowa	64	South Dakota	3
Kansas	19	Tennessee	37
Kentucky	27	Texas	64
Louisiana	10	Utah	8
Maine	10	Vermont	16
Maryland	46	Virginia	21
Massachusetts	282	Washington	44
Michigan	440	West Virginia	23
Minnesota	59	Wisconsin	138
Mississippi	6	Wyoming	2
Missouri	117		
Montana	..	**Total**	**4819**
Nebraska	15		

(Source: THE IRON AGE Basic Marketing Data)

CHECK LIST OF AIR POLLUTION CONTROL ORDINANCES

City	Date	Air Contaminants Prohibited	Test Method	Dense Smoke Standard	Installation	Inspection	Sales Reports	Smokeless Fuel Control	Appeal	Advisory	Rule Making Authority
Akron	1949	DS FA (8) F	TM	R3					Yes 9	Yes 9	Yes
Atlanta	1941A	DS FA (2)		R3	Yes	Annual	Yes		Yes 3	Yes 13	
Baltimore	1939	DS FA (6)	TM	R2	Yes	Annual	Yes	User-Sales	Yes 5	Yes 5	Yes
Birmingham	1947	DS		R3	Yes			User	Yes 5		
Boston	1947	DS FA		R3							
Buffalo	1947	DS FA F		R3	Yes	Annual	Yes	User-Sales			
Camden	1948	DS FA F		R2	Yes	Annual	Yes	User	Yes		
Chattanooga	1946	DS FA F		R2	Yes	Annual			Yes 5		
Chicago	1947	DS FA F		R3	Yes	Annual	Yes	User-Sales	Yes 5		
Cincinnati	1947	DS FA (3-7) F		U2	Yes	Annual		User-Sales	Yes 7		Yes
Cleveland	1947	DS FA (5) F	TM	R2	Yes			User	Yes	Yes	Yes
Columbus	1949	DS FA (8) F	TM	R2	Yes	Annual		User-Sales	Yes 5	Yes 5	Yes
Denver	1948	DS FA F		R2	Yes			User	Yes		Yes
Des Moines	1947	DS		R3	Yes				Yes	Yes 9	Yes
Detroit	1947	DS FA (4) F	TM	R2	Yes	Annual	Yes	User-Sales	Yes 5		Yes
Duluth	1931	DS F		R3	Yes				Yes 7		
Erie	1948	DS FA F		R3	Yes	Annual			Yes 3	Yes 9	Yes
Evansville	1949A	DS		R2	Yes				Yes 12	Yes 12	Yes
Flint	1917	DS		None	Yes						
Fort Wayne	1949	DS FA F		R2	Yes				Yes	Yes 5	Yes
Gary	1917	DS FA		None							
Grand Rapids	1926	DS FA		R3	Yes				Yes 3		
Harrisburg	1920A	DS		R3	Yes	Periodic				Yes 1	
Hartford	1937	DS		R3**	Yes						
Houston	1942	DS		None				User			
Indianapolis	1948	DS FA (9) F	TM	R2	Yes	Annual	Yes	User-Sales	AB	Yes 7	Yes
Jacksonville	1945	DS FA		None							
Jefferson City	1945	DS FA F		R2	Yes	Annual			Yes 5	Yes 5	Yes
Kansas City	1948	DS FA F		R3	Yes	Annual		User	Yes 5	Yes 5	Yes
Knoxville	[3]	DS FA F		R2	Yes	Periodic		User	Yes 7	Yes 7	Yes
Lansing	1937	DS		U1						Yes 3	Yes
Long Beach	[1]	DS FA F		R2							
Los Angeles	1950	DS FA (1) F		R2	Yes	Periodic		User	Yes 3	Yes	Yes
Louisville	1949	DS FA F		R2	Yes	Annual		User-Sales	Yes 7	Yes 7	Yes
Memphis	[3]	DS FA F		R3	Yes			User			
Miami	1941	DS FA F		R3	Yes	Quarterly					
Milwaukee City	1948	DS FA (8) F	TM	R2	Yes	Annual	Yes	User-Sales	Yes 5	Yes 5	Yes
Minneapolis	1931	DS FA F		None	Yes			User			
Nashville	1947	DS FA (6) F	TM	R2	Yes	Annual	Yes	User-Sales	Yes 3		Yes
New Orleans	1934	DS		None	Yes						
New York	1950	DS FA F	TM	None	Yes	Periodic		User	Yes 5	Yes 3	Yes
Newark	1938	DS FA F		R2	Yes			User	Yes 3		Yes
Oakland	[1]	DS F		None							
Omaha	1947	DS FA (8) F		R2	Yes	Annual	Yes		Yes 5	Yes 5	Yes
Peoria	1947	DS FA* F		R3	Yes	Annual	Yes		Yes 5	Peoria	Yes
Philadelphia	1949	DS FA (8) F	TM	R2	Yes	Periodic			Yes 7	Yes 7	Yes
Pittsburgh	1946A	DS FA (6) F		R2	Yes	Annual	Yes	User-Sales	Yes 5		Yes
Portland	1943A	DS FA		R3**				User-Sales	Yes 5		
Providence	1947	DS FA* F		R2	Yes	Annual	Yes	Sales	Yes 5	Yes 5	Yes
Reading	1948[2]	DS FA IF		R2	Yes	Annual	Yes	Sales	Yes 5	Yes 5	Yes
Richmond	1947	DS FA (11)	TM	R3	Yes		Yes		Yes 5	Yes 7	Yes
Rochester	[1]	DS		Special							
Salt Lake City	1941	DS FA F		R2	Yes		Yes	User			
San Diego	1937	DS FA F		R3**							
San Francisco	[1]	DS FA		R3**							
Spokane	[3]	DS		None							
Springfield	[3]	DS		None							
St. Louis	1948	DS FA (10) F	TM	R2	Yes			User-Sales	Yes 5		Yes
St. Paul	1925	DS		R3						Yes 12	
Syracuse	1948	DS FA (3-8) F		R2	Yes		Yes	User-Sales			
Tacoma	1950	DS FA (7-3) F		R2	Yes				Yes 5		
Tampa	1943	None			Yes						
Toronto	1949	DS FA (3-8) F		R3	Yes	Periodic	Yes		Yes 7	Yes 7	Yes
Trenton	[1]	DS FA		None							
Utica	[3]	DS FA (6)		R3	Yes	Periodic					
Wilmington	1949	DS		R2							
Yonkers	1950	DS FA F		R2	Yes						
Youngstown	1950	DS FA (6) F	TM	R2	Yes	Annual	Yes	User-Sales	Yes 7	Yes 7	Yes

SYMBOL EXPLANATIONS

Date refers to the year of adoption of the basic code or its most recent revision.

"A" Ordinances now being amended.

[1] Smoke regulations incorporated in city health code, date of which was not furnished.

[2] Proposal ordinance, not yet formally approved.

[3] Smoke regulations incorporated in city fire code, undated.

"DS" in Table I refers to Dense Smoke as measured by the Ringlemann chart illustrated in Chart 1, or to the "Unbrascope" in which one thickness of 60% opacity glass equals No. 1 scale. 2 thicknesses equals No. 2 scale, 3 thicknesses No. 3 scale, and 4 thicknesses equals No. 4 scale.

FA (—) Limits of emission of solids vary as follows:

(1) .2% by volume SO_2
.4 gr./cu.ft. adjusted to 12% CO_2 at gas temperature except that dust or fumes may not exceed amounts shown in table of ordinance varying from 48/100% of the process weight at 50 lbs./hr. to 67/1000% of the process weight of 60,000 lbs./hr. Maximum permitted 40 lbs./hr.

(2) 90% collection entering collector, minimum.

(3) 85% collection entering collector, minimum.

(4) .3 gr./cu.ft. at 500° F. and 50% excess air.

(5) .425 gr./cu.ft. at 500° F. 50% excess air.
Must collect 75% in equipment installed before ordinance and 85% with new equipment.

(6) .75 gr./cu.ft. at 500° F. and 50% excess air which amount not more than .2 gr./cu.ft. shall be larger than 325 mesh, 44 microns.

(7) .85 lbs. per 1,000 lbs. of gas—50% excess air.

(8) .85 lbs. per 1,000 lbs. of gas adjusted to 12% CO_2.

(9) .75 gr./cu.ft. at 500° F. 50% excess air of which not more than .2 gr./cu.ft. at 850° F. shall be larger than 325 mesh.

(10) .85 lbs. per 1,000 lbs. of gas containing 50% excess air. Maximum .5 lbs. per 1,000 lbs. of gas shall be larger than 325 mesh.

(11) 2 lbs. per 1,000 lbs. of gases at 12% CO_2—must collect 75%.

(12) For steam: 2.2 lbs. of dust/1000 lbs. of steam at 100,000 lbs. steam/hr. to .8 lbs. of dust/1000 lbs. steam at 1 million lbs. steam/hr.

For other processes: .85 lbs./1000 lbs. gas adjusted to 50 pct. excess air. Not to exceed .40 lbs./1000 lbs. of gas shall be larger than 325 mesh.

Various city ordinances define particulate matter as follows:

Cinders: Particles not ordinarily considered fly ash or dust because of their greater size, entrained in the products of combustion and consisting essentially of fused ash and/or unburned combustibles.

Dust and Fly Ash: Gas-borne or air-borne particles larger than one micron (approximately 0.00004 inch); two cities specify above 10 microns.

"F"—Fumes: Gases, vapors, metallic oxides that are of such character as to create an unclean, destructive, offensive or unhealthful condition.

* These codes limit the emissions, amounts unknown to the author.

** Greater than.

"TM" in Table I refers to Test Method specified. All those so marked use the American Society of Mechanical Engineers test code. Those not marked will apparently accept any recognized or accurate method.

The A.S.M.E. test code for dust emission is now the most widely used test method; however, others are used and acceptable in some cities. There is a great need for a practical instrument that will traverse the stack, automatically adjust the velocity in the sampling tube to the stack gas velocity and at the same time secure an accurate dust sample and a volume record of the escaping gases at the same time the dust sample is taken. Instrument engineers are working on this problem and if it can be solved, the cost of testing various types of equipment will be greatly reduced.

A figure entered after "yes" in the Boards' column indicates the number of members. Where no figures are shown the governing ordinance does not fix a definite number of appeal or advisory board members. The omission of an entry for a particular city in one or more columns is to be interpreted as meaning that the ordinance contains no such provisions.

Courtesy of the WHITING CORP.

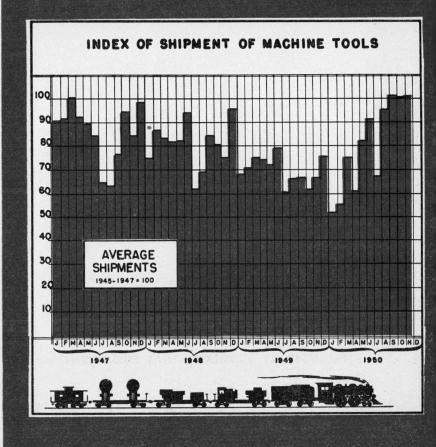

INDEX OF SHIPMENT OF MACHINE TOOLS

AVERAGE SHIPMENTS
1945-1947 = 100

INDEX OF MACHINE TOOL ORDERS AND SHIPMENTS

Average 1945 to 1947 = 100

	New Orders, Net	Foreign Orders, Net	Shipments 3 Month Average Centered		New Orders, Net	Foreign Orders, Net	Shipments 3 Month Average Centered		New Orders, Net	Foreign Orders, Net	Shipments*
1943: Jan......	162.7	.....	376.9	1946: Jan......	115.6	44.3	93.9	1948: Jan......	83.1	14.0	75.3
Feb......	215.8	.....	369.6	Feb......	79.8	24.0	98.4	Feb......	73.3	12.7	87.1
Mar......	289.8	.....	403.6	Mar......	100.6	26.8	96.1	Mar......	86.3	16.1	83.6
Apr......	193.4	.....	402.8	Apr......	123.4	25.3	96.1	Apr......	86.3	14.1	82.0
May......	164.4	.....	384.0	May......	107.9	24.1	97.7	May......	73.5	11.4	82.6
June......	137.0	.....	360.9	June......	109.1	35.7	90.8	June......	83.4	11.9	94.4
July......	91.6	.....	315.0	July......	99.0	29.3	90.2	July......	74.0	13.3	62.4
Aug......	111.6	.....	305.7	Aug......	99.9	22.4	86.1	Aug......	73.7	13.6	69.8
Sept......	104.8	.....	284.0	Sept......	86.4	18.3	93.3	Sept......	71.1	11.6	84.7
Oct......	104.5	.....	266.0	Oct......	85.3	22.1	92.6	Oct......	67.4	14.0	80.4
Nov......	107.5	.....	237.8	Nov......	73.2	24.5	95.2	Nov......	72.2	18.1	76.2
Dec......	94.0	.....	213.1	Dec......	72.7	21.8	92.4	Dec......	76.7	16.2	96.9
1944: Jan......	89.9	.....	188.6	1947: Jan......	71.1	21.0	93.1	1949: Jan......	87.0	21.9	68.8
Feb......	112.3	.....	178.6	Feb......	63.8	15.8	94.8	Feb......	80.9	26.5	70.3
Mar......	139.3	.....	161.7	Mar......	74.3	20.1	95.4	Mar......	93.5	22.3	75.8
Apr......	187.7	.....	152.3	Apr......	69.8	18.8	94.3	Apr......	70.1	23.1	74.7
May......	199.5	.....	140.5	May......	76.9	16.3	88.9	May......	63.7	15.8	72.8
June......	168.1	.....	130.8	June......	90.9	17.2	79.5	June......	53.6	15.7	79.0
July......	108.9	.....	123.3	July......	81.1	16.7	71.0	July......	48.0	14.0	60.7
Aug......	137.3	.....	117.1	Aug......	62.1	14.6	68.6	Aug......	51.5	18.8	67.3
Sept......	112.3	.....	124.4	Sept......	63.7	14.7	78.5	Sept......	57.7	13.7	67.6
Oct......	193.8	.....	123.7	Oct......	81.0	16.0	85.5	Oct......	56.8	13.7	62.3
Nov......	197.2	.....	126.1	Nov......	75.6	11.5	92.6	Nov......	84.3	17.0	67.6
Dec......	210.0	.....	127.2	Dec......	81.1	14.6	86.1	Dec......	82.5	22.4	75.7
1945: Jan......	197.7	.....	128.7					1950: Jan......	99.7	26.7	52.8
Feb......	191.6	.....	132.1					Feb......	89.2	18.8	56.1
Mar......	160.5	.....	136.3					Mar......	107.4	24.9	75.3
Apr......	94.9	.....	141.2					Apr......	98.9	17.4	61.6
May......	99.3	.....	143.0					May......	116.4	18.4	82.5
June......	72.5	.....	134.0					June......	124.1	23.0	91.9
July......	53.9	.....	124.8					July......	253.1	22.3	68.3
Aug......	11.5	.....	108.3					Aug......	305.1	34.2	95.7
Sept......	51.6	6.4	106.3					Sept......	280.6	27.2	101.6
Oct......	64.4	11.3	99.1					Oct......	290.5	48.8	101.1
Nov......	79.0	16.7	94.3								
Dec......	112.6	49.6	93.1								

* Beginning January 1948, net shipment index reported, instead of 3-month centered shipment average.

STEEL USED BY METALWORKING EQUIPMENT MAKERS

Net Tons

Type	1947	1948	1949	1950*
Semifinished..............................	4,541	5,680	2,737	2,702
Wire Rods..............................	9,754	7,923	8,029	13,904
Structural Shapes..............................	8,167	2,544	3,102	1,882
Plates..............................	65,825	58,012	59,760	76,323
Rails..............................	......	......	29	......
Bars				
Hot Rolled..............................	24,736	16,090	15,412	16,308
Cold Finished..............................	42,139	33,401	21,723	22,141
Tool Steel..............................	5,044	2,799	9,277	8,214
Pipe and Tubing..............................	4,911	7,822	2,827	1,523
Wire				
Drawn..............................	28,060	37,474	24,971	34,839
Nails and Staples..............................	1,670	2,293	2,180	13,153
Black Plate..............................	228	43	182	24
Tin and Terne Plate..............................	82	16	12	52
Sheets				
Hot Rolled..............................	38,591	18,375	10,718	8,212
Cold Rolled..............................	6,038	8,247	7,327	5,371
Coated..............................	814	......	554	5,166
Electrical Sheet and Strip..............................	4,220	3,584	993	1,078
Strip				
Hot Rolled..............................	9,911	7,047	4,364	4,688
Cold Rolled..............................	4,587	5,052	4,853	5,825
Total..............................	259,318	218,233	179,050	221,405

* Nine months.

Source: American Iron & Steel Institute
Compilation & Allocation by THE IRON AGE

ELECTRIC MOTOR EXPORTS

Value in Thousands of Dollars

	Fractional Hp 1/3 Hp and Under		Fractional Hp Over 1/3 and Under 1 Hp	
	No.	Value	No.	Value
1938............	103,980	$779	10,734	$273
1939............	135,544	849	17,285	345
1940............	154,395	1,005	15,225	350
1941............	198,735	1,250	28,863	603
1942............	132,523	735	16,532	462
1943............	69,974	569	8,991	261
1944............	65,300	738	15,463	408
1945............	75,212	878	24,384	621
1946............	156,222	1,306	37,200	1,050
1947............	275,255	3,002	80,303	3,079
1948............	248,717	3,353	80,739	2,895
1949............	204,663	2,372	40,810	1,536
1950 (7 Months)..	129,257	1,209	14,300	514

	Stationary, 1 to 200 Hp		Stationary, Over 200 Hp	
	No.	Value	No.	Value
1938............	9,875	$1,481	91	$499
1939............	12,654	1,480	100	472
1940............	16,664	2,485	131	585
1941............	28,626	2,855	167	1,001
1942............	25,712	3,114	73	265
1943............	37,136	5,064	235	1,203
1944............	40,540	7,514	577	3,636
1945............	54,434	9,061	338	1,968
1946............	64,871	9,374	439	2,263
1947............	108,747	13,479	538	2,848
1948............	93,183	15,627	432	3,064
1949............	48,041	14,008	511	7,743
1950 (7 Months)..	14,416	4,014	185	3,418

Source: Dept. of Commerce

ROLLER BEARING IMPORTS

Value in Thousands of Dollars

1938........	$334	1944........	$ 14
1939........	181	1945........	26
1940........	213	1946........	167
1941........	138	1947........	67
1942........	28	1948........	128
1943........	8	1949........	38
		1950 (7 months)..	7

Source: Bureau of Census

BALL BEARING IMPORTS

Value in Thousands of Dollars

1938........	$380	1944........	$481
1939........	267	1945........	85
1940........	145	1946........	107
1941........	676	1947........	39
1942........	54	1948........	55
1943........	20	1949........	49
		1950 (7 months)..	24

Source: Bureau of Census

PRODUCTION OF SELECTED TYPES OF MACHINE TOOLS
Thousands of Dollars

	1943 No.	1943 Value	1944 No.	1944 Value	1945 No.	1945 Value	1946 No.	1946 Value	1947 No.	1947 Value	1948 No.	1948 Value	1949 No.	1949 Value
Horizontal and Vertical Boring Machines	7,278	$103,144	3,070	$44,321	1,901	$29,415	1,888	$27,454	1,444	$25,825	1,268	$24,098	1,127	$29,430
Horizontal, Vertical and Radial Drills	41,581	94,747	21,994	46,623	11,731	22,784		33,970		33,517		32,816	6,305	25,271
Gear Cutting Machines	6,186	54,608	2,683	28,962	1,295	11,443	1,852	17,820	1,682	17,719	1,367	16,407	1,095	14,231
Grinding Machines	58,810	228,280	21,687	85,433	10,741	43,413	97,799	57,123		56,364	98,792	47,294	64,257	45,660
Honing and Lapping Machines													154	1,811
Lathes, Engine: Automatic and Hand Operated, Horizontal Turret	80,196	410,670	43,209	168,780	23,929	93,688	42,927	103,324		92,908	29,322	81,106	18,631	62,289
Milling Machines	30,819	192,695	10,975	71,015	5,799	35,407	9,929	41,155	7,504	35,278	6,064	34,914	4,397	31,400
Broaching Machines	802	7,507	416	3,151	281	2,222	573	4,657	532	4,956	343	3,779	290	3,411
Planers	618	20,852	344	10,962	226	7,344	206	4,853	152	4,018	157	4,828	99	3,699
Shapers and Slotters							2,110	7,159	1,787	6,880	1,369	5,826	666	2,831
Threading Machines							475	1,640	618	2,363	533	2,286	469	3,065

Source: Dept. of Commerce and War Production Board

INDEX OF GEAR ORDERS
Average Sales 1935 to 1939 = 100

	January	February	March	April	May	June	July	August	September	October	November	December
1936	89.1	90.2	91.7	104.6	105.9	102.9	111.6	113.5	118.2	115.8	115.8	134.6
1937	150.5	127.8	202.5	167.7	125.6	135.5	129.2	131.3	125.7	148.2	132.9	100.4
1938	96.7	78.9	93.5	72.1	68.3	59.9	68.3	75.3	84.8	72.2	68.8	77.3
1939	87.7	84.3	105.0	86.7	90.7	93.5	89.8	93.7	125.5	133.3	128.6	110.0
1940	126.5	113.4	114.4	128.5	130.9	126.9	132.9	184.4	177.3	198.0	170.1	202.1
1941	251.4	557.1	392.0	263.4	246.1	269.3	282.5	257.1	216.1	240.4	241.0	233.9
1942	298.9	323.4	455.3	376.1	430.4	362.7	345.7	395.8	354.9	228.4	329.9	302.2
1943	326.0	365.8	417.0	257.4	376.9	472.5	424.8	347.8	360.0	390.6	246.9	411.2
1944	252.5	203.3	418.8	247.4	323.4	274.5	221.4	220.6	285.5	279.0	220.3	226.9
1945	299.2	261.8	345.8	300.5	227.7	240.1	203.5	154.6	186.9	240.2	234.3	212.8
1946	265.8	225.4	265.9	290.9	258.8	279.0	362.2	330.9	292.9	245.4	280.9	386.1
1947	317.0	303.0	342.9	346.2	317.2	278.0	278.5	261.6	297.7	317.7	356.9	343.6
1948	346.8	324.4	389.8	320.9	283.6	324.1	348.4	335.6	320.4	333.3	309.0	325.9
1949	320.7	282.3	299.1	339.0	250.1	227.8	193.1	262.0	224.9	242.3	230.7	242.8
1950	289.2	272.9	358.4	328.6	363.1	401.0	410.7	617.4	.....	.....	.....	.....

Source: American Gear Manufacturers Assn.

MACHINERY MAKERS' SALES
Except Electrical—in Millions

	Sales	Profits,* After Taxes	Profits,* Pct of Sales
1930	3,498	149	4.3
1931	2,295	− 79	− 3.4
1932	1,342	−213	−15.9
1933	1,458	− 45	− 3.1
1934	1,898	85	4.5
1935	2,419	163	6.7
1936	3,358	284	8.5
1937	4,144	354	8.5
1938	3,006	154	5.1
1939	3,463	261	7.5
1940	4,568	448	9.8
1941	7,222	669	9.3
1942	9,437	574	6.1
1943	10,732	484	4.5
1944	11,012	555	5.0
1945	9,801	332	3.4
1946	9,117	378	4.2
1947	13,145	910	7.9
1948	14,721	1,029	7.0
1949	12,900	779	6.0

* Includes inventory profit adjustment in years prior to 1944.

Source: National Industrial Conference Board

FINANCIAL DATA ON MACHINERY MANUFACTURERS
Except Electrical—Millions of Dollars

	Total Income	Wages and Salaries	Interest	Taxes, Incl. Income and Excess Profit	Corporate Profits after Taxes — Total Profit	Dividends	Undistributed Profits	Income of Unincorporated Enterprises
1930	1,485	1,184	−22	36	271	214	57	16
1931	755	782	−23	13	−19	137	−156	2
1932	298	496	−21	5	−179	70	−249	−3
1933	476	500	−19	11	−67	47	−114	1
1934	735	685	−18	26	35	81	−46	7
1935	1,021	831	−18	38	158	105	53	12
1936	1,398	1,048	−18	73	275	182	93	20
1937	1,759	1,389	−12	101	258	220	38	23
1938	1,247	1,007	−16	46	196	140	56	14
1939	1,492	1,165	−16	66	258	154	104	19
1940	2,181	1,502	−19	240	426	200	226	32
1941	3,850	2,430	−22	774	611	238	373	57
1942	5,459	3,585	−27	1,076	561	211	363	145
1943	6,037	4,162	−24	1,017	498	188	310	231
1944	6,000	4,180	−17	818	555	189	366	300
1945	5,191	3,900	−14	563	332	182	150	287
1946	4,830	3,987	−23	358	378	230	148	195
1947	6,324	4,484	− 9	630	910	299	611	145
1948	6,999	5,359	− 6	527	1,029	380	399	125
1949	6,222	4,659	− 4	690	779	355	674	80

Source: National Industrial Conference Board

6 METAL FACTS SECTION

Sales of Welding Sets and Electrodes,
Welding and Brazing Departments in
Metalworking Plants

ARC WELDING MACHINE ORDERS
DC SETS, SINGLE OPERATOR, VARIABLE VOLTAGE

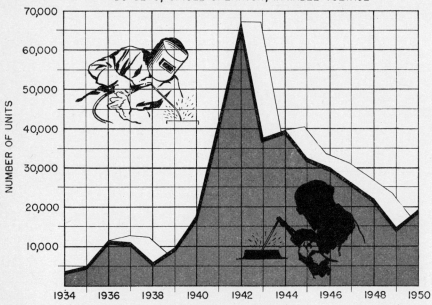

GAS OR ARC WELDING SHOPS
In Plants With Over 21 Workers

State	Count	State	Count
Alabama	72	Nebraska	50
Arizona	7	Nevada	2
Arkansas	10	New Hampshire	21
California	662	New Jersey	388
Colorado	50	New Mexico	4
Connecticut	167	New York	781
Delaware	18	North Carolina	52
District of Columbia	11	North Dakota	2
Florida	47	Ohio	1009
Georgia	87	Oklahoma	74
Idaho	5	Oregon	69
Illinois	908	Pennsylvania	758
Indiana	317	Rhode Island	56
Iowa	144	South Carolina	10
Kansas	79	South Dakota	6
Kentucky	68	Tennessee	90
Louisiana	46	Texas	192
Maine	23	Utah	21
Maryland	100	Vermont	21
Massachusetts	348	Virginia	56
Michigan	719	Washington	103
Minnesota	169	West Virginia	43
Mississippi	15	Wisconsin	332
Missouri	204	Wyoming	2
Montana	6	Total	8,424

(Source: THE IRON AGE Basic Marketing Data)

ARCWELDING SET ORDERS
Number of Units, Excluding Exports

Years	Single Operator, Variable Voltage, DC Sets			Transformer Welders	
	Motor Drive	Engine Drive	Generators Only	Industrial Type	Limited Input Type
1934	3,072	562	......	......	......
1935	4,307	860	......	......	......
1936	8,786	2,068	737	......	......
1937	8,182	1,738	1,069	......	......
1938	4,014	1,007	904	......	......
1939	7,242	1,525	995	......	......
1940	13,646	2,649	1,168		2,478
1941	35,856	4,412	1,415		4,217
1942	60,264	5,051	2,674		8,236
1943	30,437	4,747	2,068		4,439
1944	30,230	6,023	3,140		15,426
1945	20,716	8,776	2,795		21,448
1946	16,467	10,622	2,818	21,093	16,949
1947	13,677	10,822	1,169	9,719	13,034
1948	10,927	10,435	385	8,792	13,690
1949	7,393	6,193	256	7,295	12,647
1950: Jan.	543	412	13	617	1,026
Feb.	577	505	30	463	1,102
March	757	791	34	639	1,794
April	543	742	40	582	1,351
May	644	666	16	528	1,535
June	745	621	35	854	1,184
July	840	886	17	886	1,310
Aug.	994	754	20	1,225	1,780

Source: National Electrical Mfrs. Assn.

BRAZING DEPARTMENTS
In Plants With Over 21 Workers

State	Count	State	Count
Alabama	14	Nebraska	11
Arizona	1	Nevada	.
Arkansas	..	New Hampshire	3
California	191	New Jersey	173
Colorado	14	New Mexico	.
Connecticut	87	New York	295
Delaware	1	North Carolina	12
District of Columbia	3	North Dakota	.
Florida	18	Ohio	276
Georgia	16	Oklahoma	12
Idaho	..	Oregon	16
Illinois	288	Pennsylvania	207
Indiana	66	Rhode Island	27
Iowa	35	South Carolina	2
Kansas	20	South Dakota	2
Kentucky	21	Tennessee	19
Louisiana	9	Texas	44
Maine	6	Utah	3
Maryland	35	Vermont	4
Massachusetts	142	Virginia	10
Michigan	210	Washington	27
Minnesota	31	West Virginia	9
Mississippi	2	Wisconsin	83
Missouri	51	Wyoming	2
Montana	1	Total	2,499

(Source: THE IRON AGE Basic Marketing Data)

WELDING ELECTRODE SHIPMENTS
Cut Lengths and Coils—Pounds

Year	Total Electrodes	Mild Steel Electrodes	Alloy Steel Electrodes	Bronze and Copper Base	Aluminum and Aluminum Alloys	Hard-facing	Total Non-ferrous
1940	198,995,598	......	......	......	......	......	......
1941	377,564,483	......	......	......	......	......	......
1942	666,965,595	......	......	......	......	......	......
1943	971,929,787	......	......	......	......	......	......
1944	776,993,101	707,756,964	69,736,137	......	......	......	......
1945	494,819,155	435,789,217	59,029,938	......	......	......	......
1946	309,117,564	284,126,356	24,991,208	......	......	......	......
1947	335,078,645	307,756,469	25,172,362	809,668	285,036	50	2,149,768
1948	401,359,025	369,019,831	30,214,928	717,154	202,736	4,255	2,124,496
1949	299,932,909	273,463,740	24,753,807	572,601	139,804	13,185	1,715,362
1950*	193,146,193	197,097,222	23,678,279	260,649	117,759	3,960	1,211,992

* 8 months.

Source: National Electrical Mfrs. Assn.

RESISTANCE WELDING SHOPS
In Plants With Over 21 Workers

State	Count	State	Count
Alabama	49	Nebraska	41
Arizona	4	Nevada	1
Arkansas	8	New Hampshire	15
California	414	New Jersey	306
Colorado	22	New Mexico	...
Connecticut	174	New York	603
Delaware	9	North Carolina	26
District of Columbia	5	North Dakota	..
Florida	23	Ohio	707
Georgia	53	Oklahoma	31
Idaho	2	Oregon	34
Illinois	753	Pennsylvania	460
Indiana	269	Rhode Island	29
Iowa	97	South Carolina	6
Kansas	40	South Dakota	3
Kentucky	52	Tennessee	54
Louisiana	19	Texas	93
Maine	11	Utah	11
Maryland	66	Vermont	9
Massachusetts	266	Virginia	29
Michigan	505	Washington	48
Minnesota	116	West Virginia	26
Mississippi	2	Wisconsin	236
Missouri	172	Wyoming	..
Montana	2	Total	5,903

(Source: THE IRON AGE Basic Marketing Data)

Machine Tool Industry Labor, Electric
Industrial Truck and Conveying Equipment
Sales, Electric Machinery Makers' Steel Use

METAL FACTS SECTION 6

MACHINE TOOL LABOR

Workers in Machine Tool Industry

Year	Average Weekly Earnings	Average Weekly Hours	Average Hourly Earnings	Production Workers (thousands)
1947	$60.52	42.0	$1.441	74.5
1948	65.21	41.8	1.560	68.6
1949	64.16	39.7	1.616	57.3
1950: Jan.	63.64	39.6	1.607	36.0
Feb.	65.37	40.6	1.610	36.4
Mar.	66.95	41.1	1.629	36.6
Apr.	69.56	41.8	1.664	37.0
May	72.25	42.6	1.636	37.7
June	74.38	43.2	1.631	38.7
July	66.88	42.3	1.581	38.7
Aug.	71.81	44.6	1.610	41.4
Sept.	75.18	45.4	1.656	44.5

Source: Bureau of Labor Statistics

INDUSTRIAL TRUCK SHIPMENTS

Electric Powered—No. of Units

Year	Total	Domestic	Export
1935	925	850	75
1936	1,250	1,165	85
1937	1,850	1,740	110
1938	840	670	170
1939	1,080	910	170
1940	1,775	1,570	145
1941	3,095	2,830	250
1942	4,570	4,370	205
1943	4,490	4,285	215
1944	4,775	4,380	395
1945	3,850	3,625	225
1946	2,870	2,715	160
1947	4,130	3,565	570
1948	3,450	2,900	545
1949*	2,601	2,251	350
1950*	1,722	1,508	214

*Eight months.
Source: Electrical Industrial Truck Assn.

STEEL USED BY ELECTRICAL EQUIPMENT MAKERS

Mill Shipments—Net Tons

Item	1946	1947	1948	1949	1950 9 Months
Ingots, blooms, billets, slabs, sheet bars, and seamless tube rounds	13,928	38,423	11,451	3,537	2,110
Wire rods	17,317	27,086	15,784	7,040	8,549
Structural shapes	22,833	43,223	27,211	18,892	15,400
Plates (sheared and universal)	80,393	145,720	106,677	128,880	104,092
Track spikes			8		
Bars:					
Hot-rolled	94,717	103,346	109,706	74,741	83,096
Cold-finished	42,563	44,341	38,452	24,450	31,882
Concrete reinforcing					
Tool steel	380	342	257	128	90
Pipe and tubes:					
Butt weld	88,763	115,468			
Lap weld	6,837	13,132	138,827	127,995	127,627
Electric weld	1,181	2,103			
Seamless	3,823	1,393			
Conduit	28,190	34,367	48,949	32,887	
Mechanical and pressure tubing	2,676	5,577	8,373	7,329	8,084
Wire:					
Drawn	31,887	56,643	57,129	62,254	55,841
Nails and staples	659	429	847	538	432
Black plate, ordinary	1,345	1,781	4,277	2,984	5,732
Tin and terneplate:					
Hot dip	382	1,033	1,030	1,429	2,876
Electrolytic	330	1,544	1,017	303	449
Hot-rolled sheets	220,242	245,313	230,652	134,111	126,987
Cold-rolled sheets	85,653	122,030	139,197	90,536	114,936
Coated sheets	30,272	31,453	24,856	19,101	24,078
Electrical sheets and strip	270,568	436,614	450,893	342,528	419,230
Enameling sheets	1,978	2,744	3,606	1,342	4,254
Hot-rolled strip	61,096	78,885	81,159	54,235	57,606
Cold-rolled strip	46,481	42,530	94,118	69,085	83,505
Wheels	2		76	236	
Axles	10		8		
All other			140		
Total steel products	1,154,506	1,595,520	1,594,700	1,209,027	1,277,923

* IRON AGE estimate.
Source: American Iron & Steel Institute

A listing of important trade associations and technical societies
in metalworking and metal producing begins on p. 150. . . . For your
calendar of metalworking meetings scheduled for the coming year
turn to p. 114. . . . Don't miss "How to Sell to Uncle Sam," on p. 269.

CONVEYING EQUIPMENT INDEX

Average Sales 1935 to 1948 = 100

Year	Index	Year	Index
1929	191	1940	114
1930	154	1941	186
1931	84	1942	287
1932	47	1943	282
1933	44	1944	255
1934	64	1945	288
1935	77	1946	348
1936	104	1947	458
1937	133	1948	522
1938	86	1949	469
1939	96	1950	380*

* Nine months.
Source: Conveyer Equipment Mfrs. Assn.

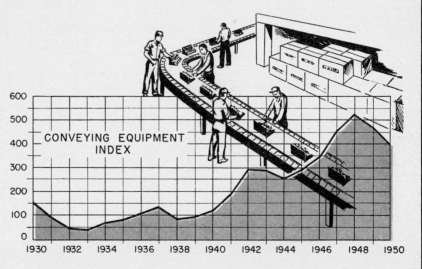

MACHINE TOOL EXPORTS

By Types—In Thousands of Dollars

	1934	1935	1936	1937	1938	1939	1940	1941	1942	1943	1944	1945	1946	1947	1948	1949	1950*
Engine Lathes Including Tool Room	939	1,369	2,825	3,649	6,644	6,534	16,025	13,094	12,939	23,056	19,377	7,918	8,872	7,707	6,335	6,603	2,493
Bench Lathes												764	1,423	2,332	1,269	1,119	479
Turret Lathes Including Vertical	568	881	1,847	3,839	5,986	7,486	17,844	18,162	21,824	33,997	10,829	2,576	2,793	2,824	811	1,977	1,631
Ram and Saddle Type Turret Lathes												1,893	4,070	3,888	2,299	1,879	1,665
Automatic Chucking and Between-Centers Lathes										10,407	5,821	2,112	5,377	6,798	1,745	3,760	4,031
Polishing and Buffing Machines								11,180	11,649	1,968	1,077	1,229	2,113	2,943	1,272	1,040	422
Other Lathes	610	945	1,337	1,420	2,166	3,399	14,138			6,910	9,469	3,062	6,171	5,661	2,612	1,241	808
Vertical Boring and Turning Mills								10,139	7,495	4,445	7,858	5,820	2,970	2,459	1,727	2,201	1,583
Other Boring Machines Including Precision	502	1,061	1,801	2,362	3,628	5,248	10,112			5,607	6,040	4,680	3,309	3,110	1,727	2,176	1,716
Tapping and Threading Machines										4,650	1,062	912	1,375	1,519	1,566	2,809	1,541
Automatic Screw Machines, Bar	1,017	1,391	2,236	3,759	4,392	5,605	20,036	17,657	16,137	17,579	15,706	763	2,258	3,288	2,905	5,372	3,211
Knee and Column Type Milling Machines	590	962	1,168	3,599	4,629	6,689	15,191	19,668	17,326	13,921	2,990	2,533	7,618	4,813	2,701	3,925	2,367
Other Milling Machines	1,281	2,005	2,458	3,639	9,955	12,563	23,831	27,865	18,751	24,499	14,547	5,376	10,868	8,569	5,487	4,175	3,729
Gear Cutting Machines	1,442	1,441	2,126	2,606	3,106	3,988	7,681	3,985	1,765	6,024	4,379	3,225	3,633	6,221	4,976	4,741	4,177
Sensitive Drilling Machines, Except Bench								3,690	2,824	1,911	677	1,129	1,065	1,539	1,098	1,010	502
Radial Drilling Machines	137	173	226	606	864	977	3,026	1,562	1,557	3,587	2,998	3,002	3,766	2,404	1,107	964	791
Other Drilling Machines	1,441	1,730	2,321	2,527	2,824	3,147	10,245	6,987	5,669	6,211	1,646	1,299	2,557	3,313	1,346	1,672	1,294
Planers	201	577	449	1,050	2,794	4,020	5,969	1,924	4,246	2,190	8,891	6,235	4,489	2,511	1,609	1,788	880
Shapers								2,469	3,298	3,243	1,731	1,713	3,162	2,109	1,183	934	459
Surface Grinders	356	934	1,081	1,746	2,769	2,559	5,600	5,450	5,587	5,429	4,218	1,869	3,468	3,482	2,003	2,543	1,618
External Grinders	772	890	1,039	1,568	4,082	3,963	7,136	5,824	3,660	9,214	5,682	2,810	3,412	3,183	1,217	3,590	2,781
Internal Grinders	974	1,088	1,259	2,451	3,990	4,218	8,294	3,294	3,000	5,614	2,934	1,554	1,972	2,673	1,195	2,360	1,671
Tool and Cutter, and Universal												2,409	3,281	3,865	2,069	2,295	1,439
Cylindrical Grinders	631	1,236	1,552	2,002	3,267	3,891	7,927	5,999	5,475	7,998	7,167	763	2,090	1,923	1,339	1,130	798
Gear Tooth Grinders										989	1,725	185	1,658	493	151	273	93
Honing and Lapping Machines										1,435	668	558	525	745	427	901	637
Thread Grinding Machines										3,528	3,631	331	462	346	137	335	234
Other Grinding Machines	607	688	1,088	1,623	3,417	5,478	12,494	7,586	14,332	15,251	6,969	4,095	3,870	4,655	3,338	2,247	1,018
Horizontal Boring Drilling and Milling Machines										6,602	10,970	4,105	7,010	2,875	2,426	3,689	2,823
Other Gear Honing and Finishing Machines												335	1,072	1,263	918	397	1,063
Broaching Machines										2,137	1,073	377	527	1,336	554	1,288	1,673
All Other Machine Tools										4,718	3,423	2,845	2,799	4,482	3,256	2,188	1,329
Total	12,047	17,352	24,854	38,445	64,516	79,767	185,554	166,533	157,534	237,122	163,599	78,487	110,036	105,328	62,806	72,621	49,957

* Nine months.

MACHINE TOOL EXPORTS

By Country of Destination—In Dollars

	1927	1928	1929	1930	1931	1932	1933	1934	1935	1936	1937	1938
France	1,217,500	2,886,662	3,592,614	1,992,599	759,537	526,257	405,427	1,975,837	1,451,995	1,400,987	3,466,243	4,287,101
Germany	2,310,028	1,715,764	1,362,332	587,683	793,569	72,836	221,762	398,234	272,731	85,174	167,425	901,531
Italy	440,196	669,615	1,141,937	590,466	356,591	252,761	282,415	496,933	3,165,623	1,165,769	1,244,058	748,165
Poland and Danzig	29,713	71,765	72,163		52,938	21,776	320,265	113,927	235,930	264,479	574,272	1,114,347
Russia	760,956	823,545	1,531,371	7,216,773	11,678,155	1,952,753	343,299	2,255,441	4,563,153	7,250,277	4,701,116	24,216,444
Sweden	288,787	427,075	897,584	376,004	165,646	23,883	52,570	325,710	526,722	593,672	1,008,294	672,932
United Kingdom	2,796,544	2,435,193	3,961,339	2,559,999	2,295,564	1,469,589	1,115,904	2,676,245	3,085,682	7,533,053	10,900,900	6,990,255
All Other Europe	828,508	2,038,274	1,779,379	1,183,099	289,675	187,220	149,008	338,399	537,530	1,111,733	2,049,471	2,529,292
Canada	1,691,225	2,780,950	2,358,537	1,442,128	680,868	699,615	197,290	483,045	518,641	1,254,268	2,951,367	1,472,015
All Other North and Central America	253,850	281,997	311,625	316,326	68,896	47,177	67,574	142,267	251,185	452,898	333,942	170,936
South America	870,367	751,245	608,346	720,826	80,060	43,988	86,087	197,945	351,886	352,199	612,980	743,017
Japan	421,036	496,368	570,295	554,805	159,614	801,893	1,025,236	2,188,601	1,635,837	2,604,994	8,976,817	18,501,722
All Other Asia	209,627	257,049	378,425	292,457	135,613	47,426	55,714	308,301	426,496	323,156	678,676	1,180,789
Oceania	365,313	186,609	195,240	123,676	26,332	24,967	35,175	155,486	179,819	230,699	485,955	606,130
Africa	85,018	125,329	100,373	86,379	27,949	18,104	30,971	90,654	149,158	230,725	293,347	380,880
Grand Total	12,568,722	15,957,440	18,861,560	18,043,220	17,571,067	6,190,269	4,407,410	12,078,037	17,389,095	24,912,911	38,537,642	64,628,143

	1939	1940	1941	1942	1943	1944	1945	1946	1947	1948	1949	1950*
France	15,769,287	26,076,868	180				2,370,233	26,393,443	11,620,848	6,449,691	9,061,505	9,020,265
Germany	469,497							544,661	746,808	35,673	2,423,223	1,464,512
Italy	513,992	608,847					258	35,184	456,147	2,570,124	13,010,953	13,144,821
Poland and Danzig	724,892							4,159,570	4,807,640	2,818,237	409,725	
Russia	14,327,013	12,332,013	3,679,052	35,577,260	119,586,711	122,228,745	54,165,818	33,437,984	15,442,605	1,804,652	110,000	
Sweden	851,859	413,495	7,316				384,781	4,668,897	7,730,980	2,147,573	2,485,968	1,388,618
United Kingdom	19,891,828	109,008,169	104,745,018	71,784,784	68,925,396	19,374,755	4,809,862	3,938,382	6,536,347	7,923,881	6,785,472	4,400,042
All Other Europe	2,315,372	1,663,162	58,593	36,378	140,060	64,397	482,400	11,740,467	17,739,793	13,120,488	15,056,817	6,914,047
Canada	2,548,717	12,673,371	43,433,161	29,805,367	15,770,581	3,994,192	4,706,734	6,052,670	8,218,856	6,743,314	8,013,379	6,118,303
All Other North and Central America	352,793	377,545	648,701	342,490	831,984	2,041,556	2,902,907	4,070,539	3,893,703	2,342,739	2,336,305	1,812,649
South America	478,071	1,027,104	1,690,849	658,992	4,424,132	3,681,161	4,313,313	8,951,945	13,784,469	8,967,120	5,367,279	1,963,948
Japan	18,063,085	14,798,533	162,174					137,010		72,207	43,956	178,018
All Other Asia	2,682,602	1,432,092	39,383,522	4,138,166	6,722,170	7,180,524	2,210,113	3,357,220	8,186,094	4,529,586	5,355,284	2,250,571
Oceania	538,140	4,055,689	5,907,428	12,634,105	17,704,485	1,472,925	536,400	385,842	3,395,267	1,121,707	1,102,687	757,921
Africa	239,369	1,077,542	2,262,611	2,556,816	3,016,273	3,560,855	1,704,048	2,198,031	2,631,610	1,939,677	1,138,020	396,496
Grand Total	79,818,943	185,717,037	166,533,438	157,534,358	237,121,792	163,599,140	78,486,867	110,035,671	105,328,177	62,806,037	72,620,513	49,957,177**

* Nine months. **Includes $146,966 destination not available

Source: National Machine Tool Builders Assn.

MECHANICAL RUBBER GOODS
Use By the Metalworking Industry in 1950*

Govt. Ind. Code	Description of Industry Groups	Total Mechanical Rubber Goods	Hose	Conveyer Belts	Flat Belts	Rubber V-Belts	Molded and Extruded Rubber	Sheet Rubber	Other Mechanical Rubber	Un-Itemized Purchases, not Expanded
25	METAL FURNITURE	$570,555	$103,968	$6,632	$4,236	$26,604	$408,109	$3,741	$12,315	$4,950
331	Steelworks and Rolling Mills	$2,709,021	$1,041,353	$738,024	$89,089	$421,016	$41,424	$136,901	$241,214	
332	Iron and Steel Foundries	$1,575,747	$357,145	$728,048	$67,354	$159,605	$37,472	$49,577	$18,496	$158,050
333-4	Nonferrous Smelting	$1,621,035	$236,793	$987,991	$41,290	$73,456	$28,287	$103,570	$149,648	
335	Nonferrous Rolling Mills	$242,091	$126,525	$4,981	$10,959	$29,888	$45,828	$11,955	$11,955	
336	Nonferrous Foundries	$453,799	$127,917	$278,433	$6,396	$21,319	$7,675	$3,837	$6,822	$1,400
339	Misc. Primary Metal	$498,809	$222,669	$11,494	$3,430	$110,480	$23,513	$25,313	$96,910	$5,000
	33—PRIMARY METALS	$7,100,502	$2,112,402	$2,748,971	$218,518	$815,764	$184,199	$331,153	$525,045	$164,450
341	Tin Cans and Tinware	$118,571	$13,270	$17,122	$5,565	$14,126	$42,377	$10,701	$15,410	
342	Cutlery, Hand Tools and Hardware	$542,676	$75,708	$41,283	$16,016	$62,954	$156,837	$15,506	$19,822	$154,550
343	Heating and Plumbing Equip.	$1,774,151	$238,992	$114,699	$10,569	$397,181	$639,575	$19,359	$352,076	$1,700
344	Fabricated Structural Products	$1,806,141	$773,220	$46,633	$7,094	$188,563	$173,161	$403,316	$198,529	$15,625
346	Metal Stamping	$1,400,222	$240,097	$49,295	$20,613	$91,150	$770,464	$123,861	$103,842	$900
347	Lighting Fixtures	$43,580	$8,269	$4,693		$8,269	$16,762	$5,587		
348	Fabricated Wire Products	$518,644	$103,541	$30,197	$139,720	$64,001	$180,284	$901		
349	Misc. Fabricated Metal Products	$350,857	$100,033	$9,127	$1,505	$44,617	$117,963	$3,232	$74,380	
	34—FABRICATED METAL PRODUCTS	$6,554,842	$1,553,130	$313,049	$201,082	$870,861	$2,097,423	$582,463	$764,059	$172,775
351	Engines and Turbines	$1,094,119	$222,091	$25,606	$465	$58,561	$312,093	$9,232	$466,071	
352	Agricultural Machy. and Tractors	$11,198,563	$2,005,257	$3,317,951	$209,505	$4,033,520	$1,084,694	$38,249	$374,348	$135,039
353	Construction and Mining Equipt.	$4,322,288	$1,264,958	$1,189,878	$169,133	$675,695	$473,511	$139,500	$196,613	$213,000
354	Metalworking Machinery	$1,711,119	$663,999	$78,339	$5,201	$423,082	$78,090	$38,643	$385,965	$37,800
355	Special Industry Machinery	$2,912,245	$393,067	$467,444	$212,172	$695,011	$852,881	$74,447	$203,723	$13,500
356	General Industrial Machinery	$6,777,610	$958,945	$2,538,854	$6,543	$1,189,986	$1,522,112	$143,101	$193,069	$225,000
357	Office and Store Machines	$5,537,719	$41,499	$24,089	$2,472	$34,742	$3,505,227	$1,835,829	$43,861	$50,000
358	Household Machines	$21,463,016	$5,516,601	$483,514	$81,430	$3,061,154	$11,762,692	$133,025	$294,600	$130,000
359	Misc. Machinery Parts	$2,597,363	$444,944	$78,121	$3,587	$221,759	$1,701,214	$78,291	$68,647	$800
	35—MACHINERY	$57,614,042	$11,511,361	$8,203,796	$690,508	$10,393,510	$21,292,514	$2,490,317	$2,226,897	$805,139
361	Elec. Wiring and Industrial Equip.	$3,664,072	$247,484	$92,815	$2,334	$116,564	$2,964,582	$120,511	$119,282	$500
362	Elec. Appliances, Not Elsewhere Classified	$255,295	$6,577		$41,852	$14,947	$172,189		$19,730	
364	Elec. Equipment For Transportation Equipment	$722,515	$87,802			$62,807	$448,623	$22,431	$100,852	
366	Communication Equipment	$2,081,371	$252,745	$6,901	$89,711	$93,516	$1,015,356	$477,012	$146,130	
369	Misc. Electrical Products	$71,598	$22,753			$9,809	$11,401	$13,902	$13,733	
	36—ELECTRICAL EQUIPMENT	$6,794,851	$617,361	$99,716	$133,897	$297,643	$4,612,151	$633,856	$399,727	$500
3714-16	Motor Vehicle Parts and Trailers	$4,573,628	$566,845	$320,960	$7,378	$446,547	$2,090,309	$97,147	$1,032,442	$12,000
372	Aircraft and Parts	$3,370,991	$608,025		$2,566	$110,671	$1,118,221	$616,290	$815,218	$100,000
373	Shipbuilding	$1,523,006	$570,300	$99,390		$59,938	$245,608	$316,705	$231,065	
374	Railroad Equipment	$2,229,018	$672,786	$15,162		$734,983	$464,826	$22,743	$318,518	
375	Motorcycles and Bicycles	$108,043	$3,230			$4,307	$100,506			
	37—TRANSPORTATION EQUIPMENT	$11,804,686	$2,421,186	$435,512	$9,944	$1,356,446	$4,019,470	$1,052,885	$2,397,243	$112,000
381-2	Mech. Control Instruments	$1,571,677	$105,658	$1,682		$9,250	$1,303,488	$44,991	$94,608	$12,000
383-7	Other Instruments	$370,555	$66,072	$605	$25,759	$86,668	$117,132	$31,602	$42,717	
	38—INSTRUMENTS	$1,942,232	$171,730	$2,287	$25,759	$95,918	$1,420,620	$76,593	$137,325	$12,000
391-6	Jewelry and Silverware	$119,080	$43,158	$4,149	$2,074	$62,261		$6,351		$1,087
3943	Children's Vehicles	$1,509,667	$3,203			$2,016	$1,504,448			
39 BAL.	Balance of 39 Group	$312,458	$36,244			$24,173	$183,846	$21,000	$46,945	$250
	39—MISC. MFG. (METAL)	$1,941,205	$82,605	$4,149	$2,074	$88,450	$1,688,294	$27,351	$46,945	$1,337
	Purchases of Metalworking Industry, Based on Expansion of the Sample	$94,322,915	$18,573,743	$11,814,112	$1,286,018	$13,945,196	$35,722,780	$5,198,359	$6,509,556	$1,273,151

*Exclusive of manufacturers of motor vehicles and bodies

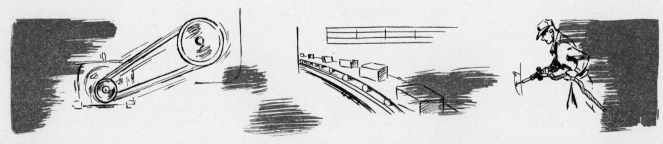

Present Trend and Future Use of Power
Transmission and Materials Handling
Equipment, Who Selects Equipment.

METAL FACTS
SECTION 7

POWER TRANSMISSION

Present Use and Future Trend*

Power Transmission Items	No, Now Using	Pct, Now Using	No, Answering Trend Question	Will Increase Use	Pct, Increasing	Will Decrease Use	Pct, Decreasing	Will Use Same Amt,	Pct, Will Use Same Amt,	Reason For Increasing Use		Reason For Decreasing Use	
										Change In Production	Change In Design	Change In Production	Change In Design
Ball Bearings	359	91.8	265	186	70.2	37	14.0	42	15.8	76	117	20	20
Roller Bearings	284	72.6	198	123	62.1	36	18.2	39	19.7	46	98	17	23
Needle Bearings	190	48.6	133	85	63.9	29	21.8	19	14.3	32	64	8	20
Flat Leather Belting	48	12.3	32	2	6.3	24	75.0	6	18.7	1	1	7	15
Flat Rubber Belting	61	15.6	43	19	44.2	16	37.2	8	18.6	12	10	6	9
V-Belts	322	82.4	221	139	62.9	37	16.7	45	20.4	75	84	14	22
Roller Chain Drives	223	57.0	149	82	55.0	33	22.1	34	22.9	42	47	9	25
Silent Chain Drives	84	21.5	51	19	37.3	21	41.2	11	21.5	7	14	6	16
Variable Speed Reducers	117	29.9	76	50	65.8	9	11.8	17	22.4	22	32	4	6
Hydraulic Transmissions	67	17.1	47	36	76.6	7	14.9	4	8.5	11	30	2	5
Gear Reducers	184	47.1	111	63	56.8	21	18.9	27	24.3	33	41	8	9
Shims	186	47.6	114	66	57.9	17	14.9	31	24.3	45	26	8	10
Electric Controls	264	67.5	174	118	67.8	13	7.5	43	24.7	63	64	11	5
Electronic Controls	84	21.5	56	47	83.9	2	3.6	7	12.5	16	41	0	2
Hydraulic Controls	159	40.7	100	75	75.0	10	10.0	15	15.0	32	58	4	3
Clutches	214	54.7	132	75	56.8	24	18.2	33	25.0	30	46	11	14
Flexible Couplings	241	61.6	152	84	55.3	26	17.1	42	27.6	46	54	12	14
Oil Seals	315	80.6	215	145	67.4	23	10.7	47	21.9	77	97	13	11

*Based on a questionnaire answered by 391 machinery manufacturers,

POWER TRANSMISSION

Who Selects Equipment*

Titles of Men Selecting the Types	No, Men Selecting Types
Chief Engineers	273
Design Engineers	212
Engineers (No prefix)	72
Various Other Engineers	48
Plant Superintendents	31
Works Managers	24
Production Managers	18
Foremen	4
Purchasing Executives	149
Top Administrative Executives	71
Sales Executives	12
Total in 370 Plants	914

* Based on survey of 370 plants,

MARKET RESEARCH SOURCES

The 1950 edition of "Market Research Sources," a reference guide for those engaged in marketing and market analysis, has just been published by the Office of Industry & Commerce, U. S. Dept. of Commerce. Designed as an aid to market research projects, the 264-p. book is also a national inventory of available market research material, the ninth in a series interrupted by World War II.

Since the last edition appeared in 1940, the present work attempts to bridge the entire 10-year period. However, since this period is so long, emphasis was placed mainly upon postwar materials. Information for the book was obtained through questionnaires sent to all organizations thought to be engaged in market research. Available from Superintendent of Documents, U. S. Government Printing Office, Washington 25, D. C., $2.25.

MATERIALS HANDLING

Present and Future Use of Equipment*

Type of Materials Handling Equipment	No, Plants Now Using	Pct, Of Plants Now Using	No, Plants Will Buy In Next 12 Months	Didn't Answer The Buy Question	No, Plants That Will Buy More Than in '49	No, Plants That Will Buy Less Than in '49	No, Plants Will Buy Same Amt, As '49
Electric Industrial Trucks	273	66	87	28	33	37	4
Straight Gas Ind, Trucks	274	66	80	25	39	26	2
Gravity Conveyors	246	59	99	28	41	41	1
Power Roller Conveyors	115	28	35	14	17	13	1
Overhead Conveyors	193	47	62	20	32	19	1
Portable Conveyors	162	39	43	21	21	16	2
Belt Conveyors	203	49	65	25	28	20	2
Chain Conveyors	137	33	35	18	14	15	2
Apron Conveyors	63	15	14	9	8	5	...
Electric Hoists	393	95	172	37	50	89	6
Air Hoists	204	49	62	31	15	34	2
Chain Hoists	344	83	84	51	13	46	6
Overhead Travel Cranes	312	75	55	37	30	15	1
Yard Crawler Cranes	72	17	7	2	3	1	...
Yard Tractor Cranes	81	20	8	9	2	2	1
Yard Truck-Mounted Cranes	48	12	3	3	1	1	...
Lifting Magnets	128	31	23	16	11	4	2
Pallets	282	68	157	26	71	57	5
Storage Batteries	247	60	141	20	38	77	7

*Based on a questionnaire answered by 415 plants,

MATERIALS HANDLING

Who Selects Equipment*

Titles of Men Selecting the Types	No, Men Selecting Types
Plant Engineers (& Maintenance)	171
Mfg, Engineering Including Master Mechanics. Methods & Planning Engineers. Equipment Engineers & Equipment Supervisors	123
Chief Engineers	46
Industrial & Mechanical Engineers	27
Other Engineers	22
Works Managers	122
Plant Superintendents	91
Production Managers	42
Dept, Supts,, & General Foremen	38
Purchasing Executives	131
Top Administrative Executives	105
Materials Handling Engineers. Traffic Mgrs / Transportation Supts	35
Total in 346 Plants	953

* Based on survey of 346 plants,

ABOUT THESE SURVEYS

The data in these market studies were compiled by THE IRON AGE from information received from representative metalworking companies — IRON AGE subscribers. In the surveys where quantities reported in the field sample were expanded to yield an industry estimate, expansion factors were used for the various industry groups. The factors were arrived at by dividing the number of production workers in the industry by the number of production workers in reporting plants.

7 METAL FACTS SECTION

Use of Plastics by the Metalworking Industry.
Future Trend in Plastics Use.
Scale Removal Survey.

PLASTICS
Use By Whole Metalworking Industry

Govt. Ind. Code	Description Of Industry Groups	Total Plastics Used in 1949	Molded Plastics Used	Extruded Plastics Used	Laminated Plastics Used
19	Ordnance....	$ 820,249	$ 816,876	$ 3,373	$ 2,542,900
25	Metal Furniture....	3,031,690	348,200	140,590	....
342	Cutlery. Hand Tools. Hardware....	4,679,802	4,366,129	261,557	52,116
343	Heating Equip., Plumbers Sup....	5,055,290	5,042,274	....	13,016
346	Stampings. (Commercial)....	2,057,325	1,977,650	....	79,675
347	Lighting Fixtures....	1,352,102	784,770	547,661	19,671
351	Engines & Turbines....	98,284	24,514	228	73,542
352	Agricultural Mchry., Tractors....	186,572	16,189	6,167	164,216
353	Construction & Mining Equip....	284,806	235,908	371	48,527
354	Metal-Working Machinery....	454,371	230,238	521	223,612
355	Special-Industry Machinery....	627,644	372,995	73,093	181,556
356	General Industrial Machinery....	409,545	282,408	8,578	118,559
357	Office & Store Machines....	7,423,117	6,739,570	478,772	204,775
358	Household Machines....	69,133,089	41,075,714	7,992,515	20,064,860
359	Valves. Ball Bearings....	259,510	186,112	5,557	67,841
361	Elec, Trans, & Indust'l, Equip,....	32,780,444	26,559,919	157,579	6,062,946
362	Elec, Appliances. Not Elsewhere Classified....	5,997,826	5,990,667	2,386	4,773
363	Insulated Wire & Cable....	3,596,320	....	3,596,320	....
364	Elec. Equip. for Transportation....	3,871,881	2,623,152	46,451	1,202,278
365	Electric Lamp Bulbs & Tubes....	440,000	440,000	....	....
366	Communication Equipment....	30,141,427	24,462,274	1,491,220	4,187,933
369	Batteries & X-Ray....	296,553	291,090	3,358	2,105
371	Motor Vehicles & Parts. Estimated....	27,700,000	18,900,000	5,022,000	3,078,000
372	Aircraft & Parts....	6,746,144	1,534,417	239,354	4,972,373
374	Railroad Cars....	298,470	100,000	....	198,470
38	Instruments. Photographic Equip,....	7,933,916	6,860,688	318,270	754,958
39	Misc, Toys. Pencils. Musical Instr,....	9,040,501	7,616,625	1,217,450	206,426
	Metalworking Industry....	224,016,878	157,878,379	21,613,371	44,525,128

Based on expansion of a sample survey covering 424 metalworking plants that use plastics.

PLASTICS
Use of Molded Types

Govt. Ind. Code	Description of Industry Groups	Buy 100 Pct. of Their Molded Plastics		Mold 100 Pct. of Their Molded Plastics		Buy and Mold Molded Plastics		
		No. Plants	Value Bought	No. Plants	Value Molded	No. Plants	Value Bought	Value Molded
19	Ordnance....	6	$ 788,481	..	....	..	....	....
25	Metal Furniture....	8	72,000	..	....	..	....	....
34	Fabricated Metal Prods....	67	2,190,214	6	$ 104,838	3	$ 58,903	$ 66,849
35	Machinery Mfrs,....	120	3,777,398	2	130,000	8	3,019,509	5,442,063
36	Electrical Equip....	64	6,785,650	13	1,408,100	20	1,336,725	4,357,875
37*	Transportation Equip,....	13	225,976	1	100,000	4	3,580	980
38	Instruments. Photographic Equip,..	11	1,041,500	1	350,000	5	32,800	148,200
39	Misc. Metal Products....	10	320,500	1	200,000	4	152,070	1,311,430
	Reporting Metalworking Plants....	299	15,201,719	24	2,292,938	44	4,603,587	11,327,397
	Pct. of Total Plants....	81	45	7	7	12	14	34

* Not including automotive Industry.

PLASTICS
Future Trend In Use

Govt. Ind. Code	Description of Industry Groups	Plastics Used In 1949 By 409 Plants	No. Plants That Will Use			Increase In Use Of Plastics	Decrease In Use Of Plastics	Net Increase In Use Of Plastics
			Same Amt.	More Plastics	Less Plastics			
19	Ordnance....	$ 790,395	6	....	....	....	....	....
25	Metal Furniture....	2,421,420	11	4	1	$ 303,250	$ 5,250	$ 298,000
34	Fabricated Metal Prods,....	2,483,283	43	27	4	194,080	3,813	190,267
35	Machinery Mfrs,....	19,281,049	104	54	....	1,878,259	....	1,878,259
36	Electrical Equip,....	20,034,555	48	54	3	1,321,388	62,300	1,259,088
37*	Transportation Equip,....	2,691,586	11	7	1	124,400	18,600	105,800
38	Instruments. Photographic Equipment....	1,913,050	8	6	3	129,810	93,750	36,060
39	Misc, Metal Products....	2,282,000	6	6	2	107,750	30,000	77,750
	Reporting Metalworking Plants....	51,897,338	237	158	14	4,058,937	213,713	3,845,224
	Pct. of Total Plants....	....	58	39	3	7.8	.4	7.4

*Not Including automotive industry.

SCALE REMOVAL

Question 1. *"Do you consider furnace scale detrimental to your dies and to the appearance of your product?"*

135 Forge shops (92 pct) consider furnace scale detrimental.
11 Forge shops (8 pct) do not consider it detrimental.

146 Total replies.

Seven of the 11 forge shops that do not consider furnace scale detrimental reported that none of their work could be classed as fairly long-run production jobs. One additional shop has only 10 pct of its work in the long-run production category.

Question 2. *"How do you remove scale from heated forging bars and billets?"*

Method of Scale Removal	Number of Plants Using. (Some Use Two Methods.)
Compressed Air	29
Wire Brushes	10
Breakdown Dies	8
High Pressure Water....	7
Water Spray	7
Hammer Blows	6
Steam Pressure	5
Edging or Fullering	5
Scraping Bars	4
Salt and Water	2
Roller Descalers	2
Chain Descaler	1
Mechanical Descaler ..	1
Number of shops reporting above	79
* Do Not Remove Scale..	23
Did Not Answer	12
**Answered Other Than Above	32
Total Replies	146

* Nine of the 23 shops that do not remove scale are users of induction heat. But as very few forge shops are 100 pct equipped with induction heat, it can be assumed that these 9 shops answered the question in the light of their more important jobs. Then there are the 11 shops that reported in Question 1, that furnace scale is not detrimental. Thus it would seem that some attempt at descaling is made in most forge shops that use closed dies, excepting that portion of the production which is induction heated.

** These 32 forge shops answered the scale removal question by mentioning operations such as sand and shot blasting, pickling, tumbling, grinding, etc., which indicates they were thinking of cleaning operations on the forgings rather than of the removal of furnace scale from the heated billets.

Use of Cutting Tools.
Present and Future Trends in Carbide Tool Use.

METAL FACTS
SECTION 7

FROM FORGING BARS AND BILLETS

To collect some information on how scale is removed from heated forging bars and billets prior to the actual forging operation, a questionnaire was sent to a cross-section of commercial forge shops and captive forging departments attached to manufacturing plants. The following report is based on 146 replies.

CUTTING TOOLS
Amount and Trend of Carbide Tool Use*

Type of Cutting Tool	No, Plants Using Each Type	No, Plants Using Carbide Tips	Pct, Using Carbide Tips	No, Plants Will Use More Carbide	No, Plants Will Use Less Carbide	No, Plants Will Use Same Amount
Milling Cutters. Solid........	217	97	44,7	71	4	22
Milling Cutters. Inserted Tooth..	201	168	83,6	143	4	21
End Mills.................	208	79	38,0	63	2	14
Hollow Mills...............	137	39	28,5	27	3	9
Counterbores..............	208	103	49,5	80	3	20
Spot Facers...............	202	98	48,5	79	5	14
Reamers.................	236	139	58,9	110	3	26
Twist Drills...............	227	50	22,0	38	3	9
Boring Tools. Multi-point......	170	138	81,2	107	1	30
Single Point Tools..........	248	226	91,1	187	5	34
Diamond Cutting Tools.......	47	....	....	....	....	....
Form Tools...............	196	109	55,6	88	2	19
Gear Cutters..............	114	5	4,4	4	0	1
Broaches................	149	10	6,7	7	1	2
Taps....................	212	5	2,4	3	0	2
Threading Chasers..........	177	3	1,7	2	0	1
Cold Saws................	149	7	4,7	5	0	2
Band Saws...............	165	....	....	....	....	....
Stamping Dies (Blanking)......	187	26	13,9	22	1	3

*Based on a questionnaire answered by 278 plants,

CUTTING TOOLS
Industry Groups Surveyed

Govt, Standard Industry Code	Industry Groups	No. Responses	No, Workers In Respondent Plants	Total Workers In Groups Surveyed	Pct, Coverage By Survey Sample
34	Fabricated Metal Products..............	29	16,731	264,400	6,3
35	Machinery Mfrs,....................	163	178,810	1,068,864	16,7
36	Electrical Equipment................	34	86,072	584,909	14,7
37	Transportation Equipment.............	52	144,410	818,083	17,6
	Totals.....................	278	426,023	2,736,256	15,6

Question 3. "Suppose that you could pass your heated forging stock through a water-tight chamber containing high pressure nozzles for descaling. Would such a hydraulic descaling chamber be a helpful device for forge shops?"

It would be helpful	59	.. 40.4 pct
It would not be helpful.	71	.. 48.6 pct
Don't know	16	.. 11.0 pct
No. plants reporting	146	.. 100.0 pct

Four of the 59 forge shops are now using such a high pressure hydraulic descaling chamber.

Question 4. "Do you use induction heat for heating forging stock?"

Now using induction heat.	19	.. 13 pct
Do not use induction heat.	127	.. 87 pct
No. plants reporting....	146	.. 100 pct

Question 5. "If you use induction heat, what percent of your output is induction heated?"

Pct of Output Induction Heated	No. Plants Using Induction Heat
1 to 10	5
11 to 25	4
26 to 50	3
51 to 75	1
76 to 100	3
Didn't state	3
Number using	19

Question 6. "Do you plan to increase your use of induction heat in the future? If so, to what percent of output?"

	Present pct of Output Induction Heated	Will Increase The Use of Induction Heat to pct Below
1 Shop	5	 100
1 Shop	10	 70
1 Shop	50	 75
1 Shop	70	 100
2 Shops	20	.... ?
2 Shops	?	.... ?

8 will increase their use of induction heat.

8 will not increase their use of induction heat.

2 already at 100 pct use of induction heat.

1 undecided.

19 Shops reporting use of induction heat.

Question 7. "If you are not using induction heat now, do you think you will use it later?"

Will use induction heat later for first time ..	30	.. 23.7 pct
Will not use induction heat in future	70	.. 55.1 pct
Didn't answer this question	27	.. 21.2 pct
No. reporting shops not using at present ...	127	.. 100.0 pct

Question 8. "What percent of your forging output can be classed as fairly long-run production jobs?"

Pct of Output classed as Long-run Production	No. Plants Reporting
1 to 10	19
11 to 25	15
26 to 50	29
51 to 75	19
76 to 100	30
None	34
No. Plants reporting..	146

Question 9. "Would you consider the installation of a completely engineered high pressure hydraulic descaling system?"

Yes	45
No	82
Didn't answer	15
Already use it	4
No. Plants reporting	146

In most forge shops where induction heat is used, it is used for a certain percentage of the forging output as shown in Question 5.

METAL CLEANING, FINISHING AND TESTING

Departments Operated by U. S. Metalworking Plants Employing 21 or More Plant Workers

WASHING OR DEGREASING

State	No.	State	No.
Alabama	25	Nebraska	24
Arizona	1	Nevada	..
Arkansas	5	New Hampshire	20
California	353	New Jersey	272
Colorado	19	New Mexico	..
Connecticut	253	New York	626
Delaware	6	North Carolina	18
District of Columbia	3	North Dakota	..
Florida	14	Ohio	653
Georgia	38	Oklahoma	20
Idaho	3	Oregon	19
Illinois	697	Pennsylvania	429
Indiana	230	Rhode Island	101
Iowa	77	South Carolina	4
Kansas	31	South Dakota	1
Kentucky	35	Tennessee	36
Louisiana	14	Texas	64
Maine	5	Utah	2
Maryland	58	Vermont	8
Massachusetts	288	Virginia	17
Michigan	528	Washington	19
Minnesota	91	West Virginia	18
Mississippi	6	Wisconsin	204
Missouri	127	Wyoming	1
Montana	1	**Total**	**5,464**

SAND BLASTING

State	No.	State	No.
Alabama	33	Nebraska	20
Arizona	3	Nevada	1
Arkansas	2	New Hampshire	17
California	208	New Jersey	154
Colorado	18	New Mexico	1
Connecticut	130	New York	98
Delaware	11	North Carolina	..
District of Columbia	1	North Dakota	..
Florida	13	Ohio	475
Georgia	25	Oklahoma	16
Idaho	2	Oregon	25
Illinois	350	Pennsylvania	419
Indiana	165	Rhode Island	30
Iowa	59	South Carolina	5
Kansas	22	South Dakota	1
Kentucky	22	Tennessee	40
Louisiana	16	Texas	72
Maine	13	Utah	10
Maryland	36	Vermont	10
Massachusetts	201	Virginia	20
Michigan	341	Washington	36
Minnesota	51	West Virginia	19
Mississippi	3	Wisconsin	146
Missouri	90	Wyoming	1
Montana	2	**Total**	**3648**

GALVANIZING OR TINNING

State	No.	State	No.
Alabama	12	Nebraska	6
Arizona	1	Nevada	..
Arkansas	..	New Hampshire	3
California	63	New Jersey	42
Colorado	3	New Mexico	..
Connecticut	36	New York	77
Delaware	1	North Carolina	4
District of Columbia	1	North Dakota	..
Florida	5	Ohio	115
Georgia	8	Oklahoma	3
Idaho	1	Oregon	1
Illinois	81	Pennsylvania	104
Indiana	38	Rhode Island	9
Iowa	17	South Carolina	..
Kansas	..	South Dakota	..
Kentucky	7	Tennessee	8
Louisiana	4	Texas	13
Maine	4	Utah	1
Maryland	20	Vermont	..
Massachusetts	63	Virginia	3
Michigan	58	Washington	6
Minnesota	18	West Virginia	7
Mississippi	3	Wisconsin	41
Missouri	30	Wyoming	1
Montana	..	**Total**	**918**

PICKLING

State	No.	State	No.
Alabama	16	Nebraska	7
Arizona	1	Nevada	..
Arkansas	2	New Hampshire	7
California	156	New Jersey	136
Colorado	8	New Mexico	..
Connecticut	157	New York	283
Delaware	3	North Carolina	7
District of Columbia	4	North Dakota	..
Florida	5	Ohio	296
Georgia	13	Oklahoma	6
Idaho	1	Oregon	7
Illinois	246	Pennsylvania	288
Indiana	105	Rhode Island	81
Iowa	24	South Carolina	1
Kansas	7	South Dakota	..
Kentucky	18	Tennessee	27
Louisiana	3	Texas	24
Maine	3	Utah	2
Maryland	25	Vermont	2
Massachusetts	177	Virginia	8
Michigan	201	Washington	16
Minnesota	25	West Virginia	14
Mississippi	1	Wisconsin	74
Missouri	61	Wyoming	2
Montana	..	**Total**	**2550**

PHYSICAL TESTING

State	No.	State	No.
Alabama	16	Nebraska	..
Arizona	..	Nevada	..
Arkansas	1	New Hampshire	9
California	138	New Jersey	137
Colorado	11	New Mexico	..
Connecticut	93	New York	242
Delaware	8	North Carolina	8
District of Columbia	2	North Dakota	..
Florida	4	Ohio	312
Georgia	11	Oklahoma	9
Idaho	..	Oregon	5
Illinois	280	Pennsylvania	257
Indiana	102	Rhode Island	16
Iowa	29	South Carolina	..
Kansas	14	South Dakota	2
Kentucky	17	Tennessee	20
Louisiana	5	Texas	26
Maine	5	Utah	4
Maryland	25	Vermont	2
Massachusetts	113	Virginia	9
Michigan	197	Washington	18
Minnesota	32	West Virginia	9
Mississippi	3	Wisconsin	91
Missouri	54	Wyoming	..
Montana	3	**Total**	**2348**

ELECTROPLATING

State	No.	State	No.
Alabama	6	Nebraska	9
Arizona	..	Nevada	1
Arkansas	3	New Hampshire	14
California	144	New Jersey	166
Colorado	10	New Mexico	..
Connecticut	187	New York	352
Delaware	2	North Carolina	6
District of Columbia	4	North Dakota	..
Florida	5	Ohio	292
Georgia	21	Oklahoma	8
Idaho	2	Oregon	2
Illinois	289	Pennsylvania	210
Indiana	114	Rhode Island	72
Iowa	30	South Carolina	1
Kansas	8	South Dakota	..
Kentucky	14	Tennessee	10
Louisiana	4	Texas	17
Maine	3	Utah	3
Maryland	22	Vermont	3
Massachusetts	175	Virginia	15
Michigan	221	Washington	9
Minnesota	36	West Virginia	11
Mississippi	..	Wisconsin	82
Missouri	56	Wyoming	2
Montana	..	**Total**	**2638**

PAINTING AND LACQUERING

State	No.	State	No.
Alabama	50	Nebraska	41
Arizona	3	Nevada	..
Arkansas	13	New Hampshire	28
California	551	New Jersey	391
Colorado	37	New Mexico	1
Connecticut	265	New York	860
Delaware	11	North Carolina	44
District of Columbia	8	North Dakota	1
Florida	38	Ohio	904
Georgia	68	Oklahoma	46
Idaho	4	Oregon	45
Illinois	960	Pennsylvania	661
Indiana	324	Rhode Island	101
Iowa	126	South Carolina	5
Kansas	62	South Dakota	5
Kentucky	56	Tennessee	66
Louisiana	21	Texas	126
Maine	19	Utah	13
Maryland	83	Vermont	14
Massachusetts	394	Virginia	43
Michigan	628	Washington	50
Minnesota	151	West Virginia	36
Mississippi	12	Wisconsin	319
Missouri	206	Wyoming	2
Montana	3	**Total**	**7895**

POLISHING OR BUFFING

State	No.	State	No.
Alabama	20	Nebraska	18
Arizona	1	Nevada	1
Arkansas	5	New Hampshire	26
California	285	New Jersey	292
Colorado	23	New Mexico	..
Connecticut	279	New York	659
Delaware	4	North Carolina	24
District of Columbia	6	North Dakota	1
Florida	15	Ohio	566
Georgia	39	Oklahoma	9
Idaho	..	Oregon	25
Illinois	545	Pennsylvania	03
Indiana	190	Rhode Island	107
Iowa	66	South Carolina	3
Kansas	25	South Dakota	1
Kentucky	42	Tennessee	31
Louisiana	7	Texas	53
Maine	12	Utah	4
Maryland	42	Vermont	11
Massachusetts	328	Virginia	22
Michigan	392	Washington	25
Minnesota	75	West Virginia	17
Mississippi	3	Wisconsin	183
Missouri	120	Wyoming	2
Montana	..	**Total**	**5,008**

All Data on This Page Were Obtained from THE IRON AGE Basic Marketing Data.

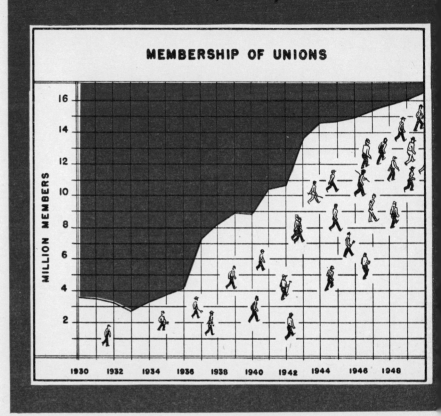

MEMBERSHIP OF UNIONS

IN THIS SECTION:

EMPLOYEES, MANUFACTURING BY STATES

Annual Averages for 1947 and 1949. Monthly Averages Thru August 1950 (In Thousands)

State	Annual Average 1947	Annual Average 1949	1950 Aug.	July	June	May	April	March	Feb.	Jan.
Alabama	224.1	205.4	223.3	212.0	208.8	206.2	205.0	205.0	204.3	207.2
Arizona	14.2	14.9	16.2	15.9	15.7	15.6	15.5	14.8	14.5	14.5
Arkansas	75.1	69.3	78.0	71.5	72.3	71.1	68.9	67.7	65.6	66.1
California	712.0	713.7	843.3	763.9	734.8	722.0	712.7	*697.4	684.0	683.0
Colorado	57.5	54.0	62.7	56.9	54.3	53.4	53.4	52.5	51.9	52.2
Connecticut	415.6		387.3	361.1	362.6	359.5	356.9	354.4	350.5	348.2
Delaware	45.9	44.3	50.7	47.0	46.5	44.8	45.0	*44.0	43.5	42.9
District of Columbia		17.1	15.7	15.7	16.4	16.3	16.1	16.1	16.0	16.1
Florida	92.7	88.4	N.A.	83.2	86.5	88.7	91.2	93.5	95.6	94.9
Georgia	273.7	262.3	291.0	270.3	265.3	266.0	267.1	266.1	264.0	263.8
Idaho	20.5	20.2	25.4	23.8	20.8	17.9	16.3	*16.2	16.2	17.2
Illinois	1,248.0	1,136.2	N.A.	N.A.						
Indiana	562.4	516.8	593.5	565.7	569.9	557.1	538.7	527.2	524.8	523.2
Iowa	149.6	144.6	145.9	149.8	148.9	147.7	147.5	147.1	147.0	146.1
Kansas	81.5	87.3	95.0	90.8	90.0	88.3	86.6	86.0	86.0	88.2
Kentucky		130.1	139.0	136.8	135.0	131.3	130.4	130.3	135.6	136.7
Louisiana	151.0	137.0	141.9	132.6	132.4	132.4	128.8	128.7	127.1	133.4
Maine	114.5	104.4	116.8	110.3	108.3	101.6	95.9	98.4	99.3	98.3
Maryland	230.3	210.4	227.8	212.2	213.5	209.3	207.7	*204.2	203.9	203.0
Massachusetts		651.2	680.6	645.0	644.5	632.8	636.2	642.4	639.8	639.2
Michigan	1,041.7	980.7	1,154.0	1,116.3	1,103.4	1,069.1	932.7	909.4	905.0	999.1
Minnesota	199.5	186.4	213.2	198.3	190.5	187.2	184.4	183.2	181.7	181.6
Mississippi	91.9	77.4	89.9	84.4	83.7	80.8	78.9	80.2	79.6	78.7
Missouri	348.8	334.1	355.5	343.2		334.6	330.8	333.0	330.5	328.1
Montana	18.4	17.9	20.1	19.6	18.7	18.5	17.1	*16.4	17.0	*17.3
Nebraska	49.3	48.2	50.4	49.6	48.3	46.6	46.1	45.4	45.6	45.9
Nevada	3.3	3.0	3.3	3.3	3.1	3.1	3.0	3.0	2.9	2.9
New Hampshire		74.5	80.2	76.1	75.7	74.5	74.9	76.8	76.9	75.3
New Jersey	775.3	702.9	756.6	704.4	709.3	696.6	696.6	*698.8	695.2	687.5
New Mexico	9.1	10.8	11.9	12.1	11.8	11.7	11.3	11.1	11.0	10.6
New York	1,903.7	1,764.5	1,905.6	1,755.7	1,744.3	1,739.0	1,742.1	1,775.0	1,773.6	1,753.8
North Carolina	412.1	384.3	432.4	388.5	392.0	391.2	393.1	395.5	398.2	400.6
North Dakota	6.1	5.8	6.0	6.1	5.8	5.5	5.4	*5.3	5.3	5.6
Ohio	1,245.1	1,098.3	1,236.0	1,178.2	1,150.6	1,131.2	1,120.1	1,104.6	*1,096.2	1,079.4
Oklahoma	62.4	64.4	N.A.	66.3	66.0	65.0	63.7	63.0	62.1	62.8
Oregon	132.8	127.2	147.4	140.1	137.6	129.0	120.9	*119.2	110.6	106.7
Pennsylvania	1,524.5	1,356.5	1,469.6	1,364.4	1,379.2	1,362.1	1,350.2	*1,340.3	1,343.8	1,333.1
Rhode Island	153.5	130.8	149.3	135.0	134.5	131.6	133.4	135.8	136.7	133.4
South Carolina	202.1	200.3	210.9	201.2	200.6	199.6	200.8	200.6	200.5	199.4
South Dakota	11.3	11.2	11.4	11.6	11.4	10.9	10.8	10.8	11.0	10.9
Tennessee	253.6	236.4	257.7	247.3	242.1	237.4	238.9	*239.7	236.7	235.8
Texas	*321.6	331.1	358.7	340.0	337.4	337.0	330.7	331.9	330.0	332.5
Utah	26.5	27.7	33.8	30.1	27.1	26.2	26.0	*25.1	*25.0	*25.3
Vermont	39.8	34.2	36.6	33.9	34.4	33.9	34.0	33.8	32.7	32.7
Virginia	234.5	217.4	237.2	215.2	213.3	211.4	211.4	*212.2	212.7	214.8
Washington	173.5	170.6	189.8	175.3	169.6	169.4	163.2	162.3	155.1	149.7
West Virginia	137.6	128.3	136.1	131.7	131.4	129.6	128.6	126.1	126.7	125.8
Wisconsin	*433.1	405.5	453.3	446.1	418.4	411.0	405.1	404.5	397.6	393.5
Wyoming	6.3	6.4	6.7	6.1	5.7	5.5	5.3	5.6	5.7	5.9

[1] Revised data in all except the first three columns will be identified by an asterisk for the first month's publication of such data.

[2] Average for 1943 may not be strictly comparable with current data for those States now based on Standard Industrial Classification.

[3] The manufacturing series for these States are based on the 1942 Social Security Board Classification (others are on the 1945 Standard Industrial Classification.)

Source: Bureau of Labor Statistics

TOTAL MEMBERS OF UNIONS

In Thousands

	AFL	CIO	Independent	Total All Unions
1897	265	.....	175	440
1898	278	.....	189	467
1899	349	.....	201	550
1900	548	.....	243	791
1901	788	.....	270	1,058
1902	1,024	.....	311	1,335
1903	1,466	.....	358	1,824
1904	1,676	.....	391	2,067
1905	1,494	.....	424	1,918
1906	1,454	.....	438	1,892
1907	1,539	.....	538	2,077
1908	1,587	.....	505	2,092
1909	1,483	.....	482	1,965
1910	1,562	.....	554	2,116
1911	1,762	.....	556	2,318
1912	1,770	.....	635	2,405
1913	1,996	.....	665	2,661
1914	2,021	.....	626	2,647
1915	1,946	.....	614	2,560
1916	2,073	.....	649	2,722
1917	2,371	.....	605	2,978
1918	2,726	.....	642	3,368
1919	3,260	.....	786	4,046
1920	4,079	.....	955	5,034
1921	3,907	.....	815	4,722
1922	3,196	.....	754	3,950
1923	2,926	.....	703	3,629
1924	2,866	.....	683	3,549
1925	2,877	.....	689	3,592
1926	2,804	.....	788	3,592
1927	2,813	.....	787	3,600
1928	2,896	.....	671	3,567
1929	2,934	.....	691	3,625
1930	2,961	.....	671	3,632
1931	2,890	.....	638	3,526
1932	2,532	.....	694	3,226
1933	2,127	.....	730	2,857
1934	2,608	.....	641	3,249
1935	3,045	.....	683	3,728
1936	3,422	.....	742	4,164
1937	2,861	3,718	639	7,218
1938	3,623	4,038	604	8,265
1939	4,006	4,000	974	8,980
1940	4,247	3,625	1,072	8,944
1941	4,569	5,000	920	10,489
1942	5,483	4,195	1,084	10,762
1943	6,564	5,285	1,793	13,642
1944	6,807	5,935	1,879	14,621
1945	6,931	6,000	1,865	14,796
1946	7,152	6,000	1,822	14,974
1947	7,578	6,000	1,836	15,414
1948	7,200	6,000	2,400*	15,600
1949	8,000	6,000	4,000*	16,000

* Estimate.   Source: Bureau of Labor Statistics

METAL PRODUCT EARNINGS

Average For Fabricated Products

	Production and Related Workers				All Employees
	Average Weekly Earnings	Average Weekly Hours	Average Hourly Earnings	Number (thousands)	Number (thousands)
1947	$52.06	40.8	$1.276	837	995
1948	56.68	40.6	1.396	812	976
1949	57.82	39.6	1.460	701	859
1950:					
Jan.	59.93	40.3	1.487	693	846
Feb.	59.68	40.3	1.481	698	851
Mar.	59.64	40.3	1.480	709	863
Apr.	60.56	40.7	1.488	722	876
May	60.89	40.7	1.496	742	894
June	62.68	41.4	1.514	769	921
July	62.71	41.2	1.522	770	925

Source: Bureau of Labor Statistics

ALL METAL MINING

Employment and Earnings Per Worker

	Production and Related Workers				All Employees
	Average Weekly Earnings	Average Weekly Hours	Average Hourly Earnings	Number (thousands)	Number (thousands)
1947	$54.63	41.8	$1.307	87.5	96.8
1948	60.80	42.4	1.434	94.7	105.1
1949	61.55	40.9	1.505	89.0	100.1
1950:					
Jan.	63.71	42.0	1.517	86.2	97.7
Feb.	62.81	41.9	1.499	86.9	97.9
Mar.	61.81	41.1	1.504	87.3	98.4
Apr.	62.90	41.6	1.512	87.2	98.5
May	63.11	41.6	1.517	88.5	99.9
June	63.40	41.6	1.524	90.1	101.9
July	63.17	41.1	1.537	91.4	103.2
Aug.	64.33	41.8	1.539	90.7	102.5
Sept.	63.97	40.8	1.568	91.3	102.9

Source: Bureau of Labor Statistics

DURABLE GOODS INDUSTRIES

Employment and Earnings Per Worker

	All Employees Number (thousands)	Production and Related Workers			
		Number (thousands)	Average Weekly Earnings	Average Weekly Hours	Average Hourly Earnings
1947	8,373	7,010	$52.46	40.6	$1.292
1948	8,315	6,909	57.11	40.5	1.410
1949	7,465	6,096	58.03	39.5	1.469
1950:					
Jan.	7,342	6,000	59.40	40.0	1.485
Feb.	7,324	5,982	59.47	40.1	1.483
Mar.	7,418	6,070	59.74	40.2	1.486
Apr.	7,548	6,195	61.01	40.7	1.499
May	7,813	6,452	61.72	40.9	1.509
June	7,971	6,598	62.94	41.3	1.524
July	7,978	6,597	63.01	41.1	1.533
Aug.	8,287	6,891	64.25	41.8	1.537
Sept.	8,435	7,024	65.09	41.7	1.561

Source: Bureau of Labor Statistics

TOTAL U. S. LABOR FORCES

Employment Status, Est. (000 omitted)

Average	Total Labor Force[1]	Civilian Labor Force	Employment	Unemployment
1929.......	49,440	49,180	47,630	1,550
1930.......	50,080	49,820	45,480	4,340
1931.......	50,680	50,420	42,400	8,020
1932.......	51,250	51,000	38,940	12,060
1933.......	51,840	51,590	38,760	12,830
1934.......	52,490	52,230	40,890	11,340
1935.......	53,140	52,870	42,260	10,610
1936.......	53,740	53,440	44,410	9,030
1937.......	54,320	54,000	46,300	7,700
1938.......	54,950	54,610	44,220	10,390
1939.......	55,600	55,230	45,750	9,480
1940.......	56,030	55,640	47,520	8,120
1941.......	57,380	55,910	50,350	5,560
1942.......	60,230	56,410	53,750	2,660
1943.......	64,410	55,540	54,470	1,070
1944.......	65,890	54,630	53,960	670
1945.......	65,140	53,860	52,820	1,040
1946.......	60,820	57,520	55,250	2,270
1947: Jan....	59,510	57,790	55,390	2,400
Feb....	59,630	58,010	55,520	2,490
Mar....	59,960	58,390	56,060	2,330
April...	60,650	59,120	56,700	2,420
May....	61,760	60,290	58,330	1,960
June[3]..	64,007	62,609	60,055	2,555
July....	64,035	62,664	60,079	2,584
Aug....	63,017	61,665	59,569	2,096
Sept...	62,130	60,784	58,872	1,912
Oct....	62,219	60,892	59,204	1,687
Nov...	61,501	60,216	58,595	1,621
Dec....	60,870	59,590	57,947	1,643
Aver...	61,607	60,168	58,027	2,142
1948: Jan....	60,455	59,214	57,149	2,065
Feb....	61,004	59,778	57,139	2,639
Mar....	61,005	59,769	57,329	2,440
April...	61,760	60,524	58,330	2,193
May....	61,660	60,422	58,660	1,761
June...	64,740	63,479	61,296	2,184
July...	65,135	63,842	61,615	2,227
Aug...	64,511	63,186	61,245	1,941
Sept...	63,578	62,212	60,312	1,899
Oct...	63,166	61,775	60,134	1,642
Nov...	63,138	61,724	59,893	1,831
Dec...	62,828	61,375	59,434	1,941
Aver...	62,748	61,442	59,378	2,064
1949: Jan...	61,546	60,078	57,414	2,664
Feb...	61,896	60,388	57,167	3,221
Mar...	62,305	60,814	57,647	3,167
April...	62,327	60,835	57,819	3,016
May...	63,452	61,983	58,694	3,289
June...	64,866	63,398	59,619	3,778
July...	65,278	63,815	59,720	4,095
Aug...	65,105	63,637	59,974	3,689
Sept...	64,222	62,763	59,411	3,351
Oct...	64,021	62,576	59,001	3,576
Nov...	64,363	62,927	59,518	3,409
Dec...	63,475	62,045	58,556	3,489
1950: Jan...	62,835	61,427	54,831	4,480
Feb...	63,003	61,637	54,694	4,684
Mar...	63,021	61,675	55,532	4,123
April...	63,513	62,183	56,822	3,515
May...	64,108	62,788	58,007	3,057
June...	66,177	64,866	59,072	3,384
July...	65,742	64,427	57,205	3,213
Aug...	66,204	64,867	57,901	2,500
Sept...	65,020	63,567	58,495	2,341

[1] Total labor force consists of the civilian labor force and the armed forces. However, about 150,000 persons in the armed forces in April 1940 who were stationed outside continental U. S. and who were not enumerated in the 1940 Census of Population are excluded from the total labor force. Figures since 1940 have correspondingly been reduced by 150,000 for purposes of comparability.

[2] Data for week ending March 30, 1940.

[3] Beginning in June 1947, the estimates are presented rounded to the nearest thousand. Because of rounding the individual figures do not necessarily add to the group totals.

Source: Bureau of Labor Statistics; Bureau of Census

EMPLOYEES IN SELECTED INDUSTRY GROUPS

Average Workers Incl. Production and Salaried Workers (000 Omitted)

Industry Group and Industry	1950							Annual Average		
	July	June	May	Apr.	Mar.	Feb.	Jan.	1949	1948	1947
Total Employees............	44,017	43,969	43,330	42,926	42,295	41,661	42,125	43,006	44,201	43,371
Mining †..........	922	944	939	939	938	595	861	932	981	943
Metal.................	103.3	101.8	100.4	98.5	98.4	97.9	97.7	100.1	105.1	96.8
Iron..............	36.6	36.0	35.9	33.8	33.9	33.6	34.0	33.7	36.6	33.1
Copper..........	28.4	28.1	27.9	28.0	27.8	27.7	27.6	27.3	27.8	22.5
Lead and zinc......	20.5	20.9	19.2	19.1	19.0	18.8	18.4	20.6	21.7	22.9
Anthracite.............		75.3	76.2	75.3	76.9	75.9	75.6	77.3	80.0	79.4
Bituminous-coal.........	382.1	411.2	412.6	419.0	422.9	82.6	347.7	399.0	438.2	431.8
Crude petroleum and natural gas production..	261.9	255.8	252.1	251.4	249.2	249.8	251.1	259.0	257.5	237.3
Nonmetallic mining and quarrying........	101.4	99.6	97.3	94.5	90.2	88.6	88.9	96.4	100.1	97.8
Contract construction.............	2,502	2,413	2,242	2,076	1,907	1,861	1,919	2,156	2,165	1,982
Manufacturing.............	14,777	14,681	14,421	14,162	14,103	13,997	13,980	14,146	15,286	15,247
Durable goods [2]	7,978	7,971	7,813	7,548	7,418	7,324	7,342	7,465	8,315	8,373
Nondurable goods [3]	6,799	6,710	6,608	6,614	6,685	6,673	6,638	6,681	6,970	6,874
Ordnance and accessories.............	23.5	23.5	23.2	22.8	22.4	21.8	21.3	24.8	28.1	26.9
Primary metal industries.............	1,222	1,217	1,190	1,171	1,144	1,137	1,121	1,101	1,247	1,231
Blast furnaces, steel works, and rolling mills..........	621.4	616.3	606.4	599.2	583.3	587.5	584.8	550.4	612.0	589.0
Iron and steel foundries.............	229.7	227.9	220.3	215.7	208.6	203.6	198.3	217.0	259.3	256.8
Primary smelting and refining of non-ferrous metals..............	54.3	55.2	54.6	54.2	54.4	54.1	51.1	52.3	55.6	55.1
Rolling, drawing, and alloying of non-ferrous metals............	96.0	96.0	94.9	93.2	92.4	90.6	89.0	87.0	103.8	111.5
Nonferrous foundries.............	92.1	91.8	87.4	84.3	83.3	80.8	79.0	75.8	85.2	85.9
Other primary metal industries.......	128.7	129.6	126.1	124.1	121.6	120.8	119.0	118.4	130.7	132.3
Fabricated metal products (except ordnance machinery and transportation equipment).	929	924	896	876	863	851	846	859	976	995
Tin cans and other tinware...........	51.3	48.6	45.6	44.6	43.5	41.8	41.2	45.8	43.7	47.7
Cutlery, hand tools, and hardware.....	153.0	156.4	154.4	152.5	151.2	147.3	145.2	142.3	154.4	156.6
Heating apparatus (except electric) and plumbers' supplies........	147.2	149.0	145.4	143.9	140.4	137.8	133.0	132.0	165.8	174.3
Fabricated structural metal products.....	201.3	198.4	192.4	190.3	187.6	185.1	186.2	198.5	215.9	206.7
Metal stamping, coating, and engraving....	172.7	170.5	162.2	156.3	152.9	152.1	151.2	147.9	172.2	180.4
Other fabricated metal products........	203.1	200.6	195.6	188.0	187.7	187.0	188.9	192.4	219.0	229.1
Machinery (except electrical).............	1,345	1,342	1,328	1,307	1,283	1,261	1,238	1,311	1,533	1,535
Engines and turbines.............	72.8	73.5	73.6	70.9	68.7	66.5	66.7	72.5	83.8	83.9
Agricultural machinery and tractors.....	180.1	180.3	180.6	180.5	177.5	175.2	171.0	181.3	191.3	178.9
Construction and mining machinery.....	99.1	97.8	95.9	95.4	95.2	93.4	91.3	101.3	122.6	120.2
Metalworking machinery...........	212.0	212.3	207.2	204.5	201.6	198.4	196.7	208.7	239.5	248.3
Special-industry machinery (except metal-working machinery).............	165.3	165.1	162.6	160.8	158.7	157.1	155.9	171.8	201.9	204.4
General industrial machinery........	185.0	183.7	181.3	178.8	175.7	174.0	172.8	186.4	209.8	208.6
Office and store machines and devices.....	89.5	89.4	88.4	88.0	87.0	85.4	84.7	90.6	109.1	108.2
Service-industry and household machines..	178.8	181.0	181.8	175.6	169.3	163.9	155.2	145.4	191.3	184.8
Miscellaneous machinery parts.........	160.5	158.8	156.6	152.6	149.3	147.0	143.9	153.2	183.4	197.3
Electrical machinery.............	817	809	800	791	779	772	762	759	869	918
Electrical generating, transmission, distri-bution, and industrial apparatus......	313.8	307.8	307.3	303.3	300.0	298.1	294.4	295.2	332.9	343.5
Electrical equipment for vehicles..........	70.0	69.6	67.8	66.6	65.1	65.5	65.1	64.5	69.0	74.3
Communication equipment..............	297.0	295.0	288.6	287.6	283.2	279.7	276.7	271.1	312.2	336.2
Electrical appliances, lamps, and miscel-laneous products.............	136.2	136.2	136.2	133.7	130.5	128.8	126.0	128.3	154.8	164.0
Transportation equipment.............	1,297	1,307	1,269	1,212	1,100	1,091	1,197	1,212	1,263	1,263
Automobiles.............	883.7	894.2	862.4	720.3	698.9	689.0	797.4	769.0	792.8	776.2
Aircraft and parts.............	259.3	257.2	254.4	253.3	252.4	251.7	251.9	255.6	228.1	228.6
Aircraft.............	172.8	170.7	169.3	167.9	166.5	166.1	166.8	169.7	151.7	151.4
Aircraft engines and parts........	52.8	52.1	50.8	50.7	50.6	50.2	50.1	51.8	46.7	47.8
Aircraft propellers and parts........	7.7	7.8	7.9	7.9	8.0	8.1	8.1	7.9	7.4	7.4
Other aircraft parts and equipment.....	26.0	26.6	26.4	26.8	27.3	27.3	26.9	26.2	22.4	22.0
Ship and boat building and repairing.....	81.2	81.0	80.1	79.9	80.2	81.2	79.4	100.3	140.7	159.4
Ship building and repairing[4].........	67.4	66.5	66.3	66.7	68.3	70.0	68.9	88.2	124.2	137.3
Railroad equipment.............	61.3	63.7	61.8	58.4	59.2	60.1	60.6	76.1	84.8	81.4
Other transportation equipment.......	11.6	11.1	10.7	10.1	9.6	9.1	7.7	10.9	16.6	17.0
Instruments and related products.............	242	243	239	236	234	232	233	238	260	265
Ophthalmic goods.............	24.8	24.9	25.0	25.0	25.1	25.1	25.1	26.8	28.2	30.1
Photographic apparatus.............	51.0	50.1	49.1	48.5	48.2	48.1	48.3	52.6	60.3	61.6
Watches and clocks.............	27.8	28.1	28.0	28.5	28.9	29.3	30.3	31.4	40.8	41.3
Professional and scientific instruments....	138.1	139.4	137.1	133.7	131.5	129.7	129.2	127.1	130.5	131.9
Miscellaneous manufacturing industries......	430	440	434	435	433	429	420	426	466	461
Jewelry, silverware, and plated ware....	51.1	52.5	52.7	53.2	53.2	54.4	54.2	55.4	60.3	53.1
Toys and sporting goods............	71.5	71.3	69.7	69.5	67.2	63.8	61.7	68.7	80.8	80.0
Costume jewelry, buttons, notions.....	52.1	52.8	51.5	53.1	56.5	59.4	56.7	57.7	62.3	61.0
Other miscellaneous manufacturing indus-tries............	254.8	263.1	259.8	259.8	256.5	251.3	246.9	243.8	262.8	......

Source: Bureau of Labor Statistics

EMPLOYMENT IN THE METALWORKING INDUSTRY

Plants With 21 Workers or More in 3-Digit Major Industry Groups by Government Codes

Titles of 3-Digit Groups	Number of Workers in Plants Employing Over 21 Plant Workers	Number of Plants Employing Over 21 Plant Workers	Number Plants by Size — With Over 100 Workers	With 51 to 100 Workers	With 21 to 50 Workers	3-Digit Govt. Code
33—Primary Metals						
Blast Furnaces, Steel Works and Rolling Mills.	541,536	219	209	5	5	331
Iron and Steel Foundries.	191,698	985	455	257	273	332
Smelting and Refining of Nonferrous Metals.	46,625	114	74	15	25	333-4
Rolling, Drawing and Alloying Nonferrous Metals.	100,826	149	92	27	30	335
Nonferrous Foundries.	50,119	368	100	81	187	336
Miscellaneous Primary Metal.	92,709	423	192	76	155	339
34—Fabricated Metal Products						
Tin Cans and Tinware.	43,806	143	95	23	25	341
Cutlery, Hand Tools and Hardware.	143,022	735	275	173	287	342
Heating Apparatus (Except Electrical) and Plumbers Supplies.	149,431	651	335	146	170	343
Fabricated Structural Products.	197,891	1,663	453	381	829	344
Metal Stamping and Coating.	180,704	1,050	318	236	496	346
Lighting Fixtures.	26,229	207	55	55	97	347
Fabricated Wire Products.	53,590	340	127	82	131	348
Miscellaneous Fabricated Metal Products...	101,401	644	222	163	259	349
35—Machinery (Except Electrical)						
Engines and Turbines.	72,717	102	66	22	14	351
Agricultural Machinery and Tractors.	162,532	418	166	98	154	352
Construction and Mining Equipment.	101,986	466	199	104	163	353
Metalworking Machinery.	207,448	1,222	380	258	584	354
Special Industry Machinery.	179,517	1,054	373	241	440	355
General Industrial Machinery and Equipment.	178,577	962	378	217	367	356
Office and Store Machines.	100,973	172	99	33	40	357
Service Industry and Household Machines..	194,578	412	210	100	102	358
Miscellaneous Machinery Parts.	137,514	655	184	133	338	359
36—Electrical Machinery and Equipment						
Electrical Generating Transmission and Industrial Equipment.	291,333	645	315	147	183	361
Electrical Appliances (Not elsewhere classified).	61,668	144	71	26	47	362
Insulated Wire and Cable.	21,844	48	38	8	2	363
Electrical Equipment for Transportation Equipment.	64,649	63	41	8	14	364
Electric Lamps (Bulbs, etc.).	23,251	31	22	2	7	365
Communication Equipment.	259,749	339	216	54	69	366
Miscellaneous Electrical Products.	25,591	105	46	23	36	369
37—Transportation Equipment						
Motor Vehicles and Equipment for.	751,427	817	472	139	206	371
Aircraft and Parts.	200,092	138	85	23	30	372
Ship and Boat Building.	162,344	147	113	15	19	373
Railroad Equipment.	98,236	77	54	13	10	374
Motorcycles, Bicycles and Parts.	12,405	35	16	8	11	375
Miscellaneous Transportation Equipment....	5,560	30	9	5	16	379
38—Instruments and Photographic Equipment						
Lab, Scientific and Engineering Instruments.	11,807	71	22	12	37	381
Mechanical Measuring and Control Instruments.	43,926	153	76	30	47	382
Optical Instruments.	13,091	15	8	5	2	383
Surgical and Dental Instruments.	12,461	79	23	25	31	384
Ophthalmic Goods.	6,024	15	9	4	2	385
Photographic Equipment.	39,009	56	27	9	20	386
Watches, Clocks, and Clock-operated Devices.	36,137	45	33	3	9	387
All Others, including Ordnance and Accessories, Furniture and Fixtures and Miscellaneous Manufacturing Industries (Metal).	295,643	1,371	537	335	499	...
Total for Metalworking Plants over 21 workers	5,691,658	17,578	7,290	3,820	6,468	...

Source: THE IRON AGE Basic Marketing Data

ELECTRICAL MACHINERY

Employment and Earnings Per Worker

	Production and Related Workers — Average Weekly Earnings	Average Weekly Hours	Average Hourly Earnings	Number (thousands)	All Employees Number (thousands)
1947	$51.26	40.3	$1.272	706	818
1948	55.66	40.1	1.388	656	869
1949	56.96	39.5	1.442	552	759
1950					
Jan.	58.44	40.5	1.443	561	762
Feb..	58.26	40.4	1.442	573	772
Mar.	58.44	40.5	1.443	580	779
Apr.	58.71	40.6	1.446	595	791
May	59.28	40.8	1.453	606	800
June	58.58	40.4	1.450	615	809
July	59.44	40.6	1.446	620	817
Aug.	60.21	41.1	1.465	655	854
Sept.	61.54	41.5	1.483	678	879

Source: Bureau of Labor Statistics

WORK STOPPAGES—1927-1950

Workers Involved and Man-days Idle

	Work Stoppages Beginning in Period — Number	Workers Involved Number (thousands)	Man-days Idle (all stoppages) — Number (thousands)	Per Worker Involved
1927	707	330	26,200	79.5
1928	604	314	12,600	40.2
1929	921	289	5,350	18.5
1930	637	183	3,320	18.1
1931	810	342	6,890	20.2
1932	841	324	10,500	32.4
1933	1,695	1,170	16,900	14.4
1934	1,856	1,470	19,600	13.4
1935	2,014	1,120	15,500	13.8
1936	2,172	789	13,900	17.6
1937	4,740	1,860	28,400	15.3
1938	2,772	688	9,150	13.3
1939	2,613	1,170	17,800	15.2
1940	2,508	577	6,700	11.6
1941	4,288	2,360	23,000	9.8
1942	2,968	840	4,180	5.0
1943	3,752	1,980	13,500	66.8
1944	4,956	2,120	8,720	4.1
1945	4,750	3,470	38,000	11.0
1946	4,985	4,600	116,000	25.2
1947	3,693	2,170	34,600	15.9
1948	3,419	1,960	34,100	.66
1949	3,606	3,030	50,500	.59
1950:				
Jan....	225	185	2,600	.38
Feb....	210	75	7,850	1.27
Mar....	260	80	3,750	.49
Apr....	400	160	3,150	.47
May...	450	325	3,000	.40
June...	425	260	2,750	.36
July...	425	225	2,900	.41
Aug....	560	350	2,900	.35
Sept...	525	275	3,500	.48

Source: Bureau of Labor Statistics.

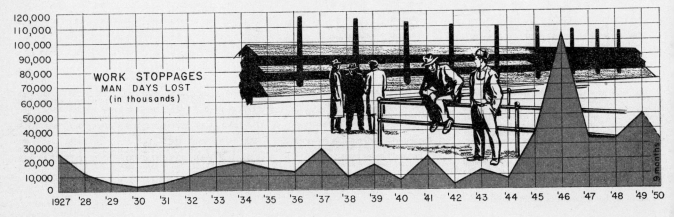

WORK STOPPAGES MAN DAYS LOST (in thousands)

120,000 110,000 100,000 90,000 80,000 70,000 60,000 50,000 40,000 30,000 20,000 10,000 0

1927 '28 '29 '30 '31 '32 '33 '34 '35 '36 '37 '38 '39 '40 '41 '42 '43 '44 '45 '46 '47 '48 '49 '50

9 months

CONSUMERS' PRICE INDEX IN LARGE CITIES

For Moderate-Income Families by Group of Selected Commodities, 1935-39 = 100

Period	All Items	Food	Apparel	Rent	Total	Gas and Electricity	House Furnishings	Miscel-laneous
1913	70.7	79.9	69.3	92.2	61.9	.....	59.1	50.9
1914	71.8	81.8	69.8	92.2	62.3	.....	60.7	51.9
1915	72.5	80.9	71.4	92.9	62.5	.....	63.6	53.6
1916	77.9	90.8	78.3	94.0	65.0	.....	70.9	56.3
1917	91.6	116.9	94.1	93.2	72.4	.....	82.8	65.1
1918	107.5	134.4	127.5	94.9	84.2	.....	106.4	77.8
1919	123.8	149.8	168.7	102.7	91.1	.....	134.1	87.6
1920	143.3	168.8	201.0	120.7	106.9	.....	164.6	100.5
1921	127.7	128.3	154.8	138.6	114.0	.....	138.5	104.3
1922	119.7	119.9	125.6	142.7	113.1	.....	117.5	101.2
1923	121.9	124.0	125.9	146.4	115.2	.....	126.1	100.8
1924	122.2	122.8	124.9	151.6	113.7	.....	124.0	101.4
1925	125.4	132.9	122.4	152.2	115.4	.....	121.5	102.2
1926	126.4	137.4	120.6	150.7	117.2	.....	118.8	102.6
1927	124.0	132.3	118.3	148.3	115.4	.....	115.9	103.2
1928	122.6	130.8	116.5	144.8	113.4	.....	113.1	103.8
1929	122.5	132.5	115.3	141.4	112.5	.....	111.7	104.6
1930	119.4	126.0	112.7	137.5	111.4	.....	108.9	105.1
1931	108.7	103.9	102.6	130.3	108.9	.....	98.0	104.1
1932	97.6	86.5	90.8	116.9	103.4	.....	85.4	101.7
1933	92.4	84.1	87.9	100.7	100.0	.....	84.2	98.4
1934	95.7	93.7	96.1	94.4	101.4	.....	92.8	97.9
1935	98.1	100.4	96.8	94.2	100.7	102.8	94.8	98.1
1936	99.1	101.3	97.6	96.4	100.2	100.8	96.3	98.7
1937	102.7	105.3	102.8	100.9	100.2	99.1	104.3	101.0
1938	100.8	97.8	102.2	104.1	99.9	99.0	103.3	101.5
1939	99.4	95.2	100.5	104.3	99.0	98.9	101.3	100.7
1940	100.2	96.6	101.7	104.6	99.7	98.0	100.5	101.1
1941	105.2	105.5	106.3	106.2	102.2	97.1	107.3	104.0
1942	116.5	123.9	124.2	108.5	105.4	96.7	122.2	110.9
1943	123.6	138.0	129.7	108.0	107.7	96.1	125.6	115.8
1944	125.5	136.1	138.8	108.2	109.8	95.8	136.4	121.3
1945	128.4	139.1	115.9	108.3	110.3	95.0	145.8	124.1
1946	139.3	159.6	160.2	108.6	112.4	92.4	159.2	128.8
1947	159.2	193.8	185.8	111.2	121.1	92.0	184.4	139.9
1948	171.2	210.2	198.0	117.4	133.9	94.3	195.8	149.9
1949	169.1	210.9	190.1	120.8	137.5	96.7	189.0	154.6
1950: Jan.	166.9	196.0	185.0	122.6	140.0	96.7	184.7	155.1
Feb.	166.5	194.8	184.8	122.8	140.3	97.1	185.3	155.1
Mar.	167.0	196.0	185.0	122.9	140.9	97.1	185.4	155.0
Apr.	167.3	196.6	185.1	123.1	141.4	97.2	185.6	154.8
May.	168.6	200.3	185.1	123.5	138.8	97.1	185.4	155.3
June.	170.2	204.6	185.0	123.9	139.9	97.0	185.2	155.3
July.	172.5	210.0	184.7	124.4	139.5	97.0	186.4	156.2
Aug.	173.0	209.0	185.9	124.8	140.9	97.0	189.3	158.1
Sept.	173.8	208.5	190.5	124.8	141.8	97.0	195.4	158.8

Source: Bureau of Labor Statistics

FEDERAL CIVILIAN WORKERS

Totals, Continental and All Areas

Year and Month	All Branches	Executive, Total	Legis-lative	Judicial
	Total (including areas outside continental United States)			
1947	2,153,170	2,142,825	7,127	3,218
1948	2,066,152	2,055,397	7,273	3,482
1949	2,100,407	2,089,151	7,661	3,595
1950: Jan.	1,976,093	1,964,246	8,062	3,784
Feb.	1,970 815	1,959,063	7,986	3,766
Mar.	1,970,603	1,958,806	8,048	3,749
Apr.	2,110,903	2,099,036	8,102	3,765
May.	2,061,939	2,050,132	8,048	3,759
June.	2,022,117	2,010,286	8,063	3,768
July.	1,986,705	1,974,902	8,031	3,772
	Continental United States			
1947	1,893,875	1,883,600	7,127	3,148
1948	1,846,840	1,836,158	7,273	3,409
1949	1,921,903	1,910,724	7,661	3,518
1950: Jan.	1,825,245	1,813,475	8,063	3,707
Feb.	1,820,625	1,808,950	7,986	3,689
Mar.	1,821,470	1,809,750	8,048	3,672
Apr.	1,959,746	1,947,956	8,102	3,688
May.	1,910,210	1,898,480	8,048	3,682
June.	1,871,293	1,859,539	8,063	3,691
July.	1,839,477	1,827,751	8,031	3,695

Source: Bureau of Labor Statistics

FEDERAL CIVILIAN PAYROLLS

For U. S. and All Areas (000 omitted)

Year and Month	All Areas All Branches
1947	$5,966,107
1948	6,223,486
1949	6,699,270
1950: January	553,090
February	521,041
March	583,186
April	539,430
May	577,915
June	573,659
July	558,231
August	618,049
September	585,147
	Continental United States
1947	$5,463,671
1948	5,731,115
1949	6,234,345
1950: January	516,707
February	488,138
March	546,866
April	506,707
May	541,195
June	536,052
July	522,981
August	580,732
September	550,704

Source: Bureau of Labor Statistics

ALL MANUFACTURING EMPLOYMENT AND WAGES

For Production and Related Workers, Average Employment, Hours and Earnings

	All Employees Number (thousands)	Production and Related Workers					
		Number (thousands)	Indexes (1939 Averages=100)		Average Weekly Earnings	Average Weekly Hours	Average Hourly Earnings
			Employment	Payroll			
1939	10,078	8,192	100.0	100.0	$23.86	37.7	$0.633
1940	10,780	8,811	107.5	113.6	25.20	38.1	.661
1941	12,974	10,877	132.8	164.9	29.58	40.6	.729
1942	15,051	12,854	156.9	241.5	36.65	42.9	.853
1943	17,381	15,014	183.3	331.1	43.14	44.9	.961
1944	17,111	14,607	178.3	343.7	46.08	45.2	1.019
1945	15,302	12,859	157.0	293.5	44.39	43.4	1.023
1946	14,461	12,105	147.8	271.1	43.74	40.4	1.084
1947	15,247	12,794	156.2	326.9	49.97	40.4	1.237
1948	15,286	12,717	155.2	351.4	54.14	40.1	1.350
1949	14,146	11,597	141.6	325.3	54.92	39.2	1.401
1950: Jan.	13,980	11,449	139.8	329.2	56.29	39.7	1.418
Feb.	13,997	11,460	139.9	330.0	56.37	39.7	1.420
Mar.	14,103	11,549	141.0	333.5	56.53	39.7	1.424
Apr.	14,162	11,597	141.6	337.2	56.93	39.7	1.434
May.	14,413	11,846	144.5	348.8	57.68	40.0	1.442
June.	14,666	12,072	147.4	362.2	58.74	40.4	1.454
July.	14,777	12,151	147.8	367.4	59.21	40.5	1.462
Aug.	15,442	12,794	156.1	394.0	60.28	41.2	1.463
Sept.	15,687	13,021	158.0	.....	60.68	41.0	1.480

Source: Bureau of Labor Statistics

INJURY RATES BY INDUSTRY—1949

Permanent and Temporary Disabilities by Frequency and Severity

Industry	Number of Units	Frequency Rates Fatal, Permanent Total	Permanent Partial Disability	Temporary Total Disability	All Disabilities	Rank (All Cases)	Severity Rates Rate	Rank
All Reporting Industries, 1948	6,707	.79	....	10.70	11.49	..	1.12	..
All Reporting Industries, 1949	7,185	.08	.64	9.42	10.14	..	1.02	..
Aircraft Manufacturing	17	.02	.61	3.62	4.25	2	.40	8
Air Transport	13	.03	.04	12.90	12.97	26	.38	6
Automobile	228	.02	.69	5.64	6.35	9	.57	13
Cement	139	.25	.80	4.13	5.18	6	2.21	34
Chemical	545	.09	.48	5.19	5.72	7	.60	14
Clay Products	120	.23	.86	21.24	22.33	35	2.33	35
Communications	59	.02	.01	2.11	2.14	1	.15	1
Construction	449	.24	.42	18.82	19.48	34	2.15	33
Electrical Equipment	190	.01	.64	4.18	4.83	3	.38	7
Electric Utilities	238	.31	.42	13.29	14.02	28	2.37	36
Food	571	.03	1.20	14.32	16.05	31	.90	21
Foundries	174	.11	1.02	12.74	13.87	27	1.43	28
Gas Utilities	425	.09	.43	17.40	17.92	33	.99	22
Glass	58	.01	.69	7.28	7.98	14	.46	9
Leather	74	....	.54	13.54	14.08	29	.46	10
Lumber	110	.44	1.82	45.46	47.72	40	4.67	39
Machinery	326	.03	1.36	9.40	10.79	21	.73	18
Marine Transport	51	.19	.78	23.48	24.45	37	2.09	32
Meat Packing	84	.11	.58	12.05	12.74	25	1.20	25
Mining, Coal	233	.68	1.58	39.22	41.48	39	6.84	40
Mining, other than Coal	234	.52	.98	32.13	33.63	38	4.63	38
Misc. Iron & Steel Products	346	.05	1.04	11.31	12.40	24	.89	20
Misc. Manufacturing	92	.04	.81	6.58	7.43	12	.63	15
Non-Ferrous Metals & Prods.	98	.10	1.28	10.53	11.91	23	1.54	30
Petroleum	239	.11	.36	10.07	10.54	20	1.03	24
Printing & Publishing	54	....	.37	6.40	6.77	11	.23	2
Pulp and Paper	419	.06	.86	10.70	11.62	22	1.03	23
Quarry	273	.49	1.07	15.87	17.43	32	4.02	37
Railroad Equipment	32	.09	2.46	5.80	8.35	15	1.62	31
Railroads††	..	....	....	....	14.05	..	..	..
Rubber	83	.02	.52	4.56	5.10	5	.51	11
Service	36	....	.13	6.24	6.37	10	.30	4
Sheet Metal	146	.01	.95	7.88	8.84	17	.69	17
Shipbuilding	42	.13	.32	8.41	8.86	18	1.28	26
Steel	142	.12	1.02	3.82	4.96	4	1.49	29
Storage & Warehousing	71	....	.36	9.78	10.14	19	.64	16
Textile	244	.02	.65	7.21	7.88	13	.57	12
Tobacco	41	....	.48	5.49	5.97	8	.23	3
Transit	202	.05	.21	15.30	15.56	30	.76	19
Wholesale and Retail Trade	40	.03	.04	8.62	8.69	16	.38	5
Wood Products	104	.03	1.67	21.55	23.25	36	1.32	27

Source: National Safety Council

INDEXES OF PLANT WORKERS

Manufacturing Employment, Payrolls
(1939 average = 100)

	Employment	Weekly Payroll
1939: Average	100.0	100.0
1940: Average	107.5	113.6
1941: Average	132.8	164.9
1942: Average	156.9	241.5
1943: Average	183.3	331.1
1944: Average	178.3	343.7
1945: Average	157.0	293.5
1946: Average	147.8	271.1
1947: Average	156.2	326.9
1948: Average	155.2	351.4
1949: Average	141.6	325.3
1950: Jan.	139.8	329.2
Feb.	139.9	330.0
March	141.0	333.5
Apr.	141.6	337.2
May	144.5	348.0
June	147.3	361.9
July	148.2	367.2
Aug.	156.1	394.0
Sept.	158.0	...

Source: Bureau of Labor Statistics

COKE, BYPRODUCTS INDUSTRY

Employment and Earnings Per Worker

	All Employees Number (thousands)	Production and Related Workers Number (thousands)	Average Weekly Earnings	Average Weekly Hours	Average Hourly Earnings
1947	18.6	15.9	$52.17	39.4	$1.324
1948	20.0	17.5	58.56	39.7	1.475
1949	19.5	16.9	61.07	39.3	1.554
1950: Jan.	20.2	17.4	61.93	39.8	1.556
Feb.	19.6	16.8	61.17	39.8	1.537
Mar.	19.7	17.0	58.90	38.1	1.546
Apr.	20.5	17.9	62.60	40.0	1.565
May	20.7	18.1	61.89	39.8	1.555
June	21.1	18.5	62.73	39.7	1.580
July	21.1	18.5	63.36	39.6	1.600
Aug.	21.4	18.6	63.76	40.2	1.586
Sept.	21.4	18.7	64.12	40.1	1.599

Source: Bureau of Labor Statistics

LABOR TURN-OVER RATES IN MANUFACTURING INDUSTRIES

Per 100 Employees, By Class of Turn-Over Per Month

Class of Turn-Over and Year	January	February	March	April	May	June	July	August	September	October	November	December
Total Accession:												
1950	3.6	3.2	3.6	3.5	4.4	4.8	4.7	[2]6.4				
1949	3.2	2.9	3.0	2.9	3.5	4.4	3.5	4.4	4.1	3.7	3.3	3.2
1948	4.6	3.9	4.0	4.0	4.1	5.7	4.7	5.0	5.1	4.5	3.9	2.7
1947	6.0	5.0	5.1	5.1	4.8	5.5	4.9	5.3	5.9	5.5	4.8	3.6
1946	8.5	6.8	7.1	6.7	6.1	6.7	7.4	7.0	7.1	6.8	5.7	4.3
1945	7.0	5.0	4.9	4.7	5.0	5.9	5.8	5.9	7.4	8.6	8.7	6.9
1939	4.1	3.1	3.3	2.9	3.3	3.9	4.2	5.1	6.2	5.9	4.1	2.8
Total Separation:												
1950	3.1	3.0	2.9	2.8	3.1	3.0	2.9	[2]4.3				
1949	4.6	4.1	4.8	4.8	5.2	4.3	3.8	4.0	4.2	4.1	4.0	3.2
1948	4.3	4.2	4.5	4.7	4.3	4.5	4.4	5.1	5.4	4.5	4.1	4.3
1947	4.9	4.5	4.9	5.2	5.4	4.7	4.6	5.3	5.9	5.0	4.0	3.7
1946	6.8	6.3	6.6	6.3	6.3	5.7	5.8	6.6	6.9	6.3	4.9	4.5
1945	6.2	6.0	6.8	6.6	7.0	7.9	7.7	17.9	12.0	8.6	7.1	5.9
1939	3.2	2.6	3.1	3.5	3.5	3.3	3.3	3.0	2.8	2.9	3.0	3.5
Quit:[4]												
1950	1.1	1.0	1.2	1.3	1.6	1.7	1.8	[2]3.0				
1949	1.7	1.4	1.6	1.7	1.6	1.5	1.4	1.8	2.1	1.5	1.2	.9
1948	2.6	2.5	2.8	3.0	2.8	2.9	2.9	3.4	3.9	2.8	2.2	1.7
1947	3.5	3.2	3.5	3.7	3.5	3.1	3.1	4.0	4.5	3.6	2.7	2.3
1946	4.3	3.9	4.2	4.3	4.2	4.0	4.6	5.3	5.3	4.7	3.7	
1945	4.6	4.3	5.0	4.8	4.8	5.1	5.2	6.2	6.7	5.6	4.7	4.0
1939[1]	.9	.6	.8	.8	.7	.7	.7	.8	1.1	.9	.8	.7
Discharge:												
1950	.2	.2	.2	.2	.3	.3	.3	[2].4				
1949	.3	.3	.3	.2	.2	.2	.2	.3	.2	.2	.2	.2
1948	.4	.4	.4	.4	.3	.4	.4	.4	.4	.4	.4	.3
1947	.4	.4	.4	.4	.4	.4	.4	.4	.4	.4	.4	.4
1946	.5	.5	.4	.4	.4	.3	.4	.4	.4	.4	.4	.4
1945	.7	.7	.7	.6	.6	.7	.6	.7	.6	.5	.5	.4
1939[3]	.1	.1	.1	.1	.1	.1	.1	.1	.2	.2	.2	.1
Lay-off:[4]												
1950	1.7	1.7	1.4	1.2	1.1	.9	.6	[2].6				
1949	2.5	2.3	2.8	2.8	3.3	2.5	2.1	1.8	1.8	2.3	2.5	2.0
1948	1.2	1.2	1.2	1.2	1.1	1.1	1.0	1.2	1.0	1.2	1.4	2.2
1947	.9	.8	.9	1.0	1.4	1.1	1.0	.8	.9	.9	.8	.9
1946	1.8	1.7	1.8	1.4	1.5	1.2	.6	.7	1.0	1.0	.7	1.0
1945	.6	.7	.7	.8	1.2	1.7	1.5	10.7	4.5	2.3	1.7	1.3
1939[1]	2.2	1.9	2.2	2.6	2.9	2.5	2.5	2.1	1.6	1.8	2.0	2.7

[1] Prior to 1943, rates relate to wage earners only.
[2] Preliminary figures.
[3] Prior to September 1940, miscellaneous separations were included with quits.
[4] Including temporary, indeterminate (of more than 7 days' duration) and permanent lay-offs.

Spendable Weekly Earnings; Transportation
Equipment; Death Rates by Industry; Accidents to
All Workers and Occupational Death Rates

METAL FACTS SECTION 8

TRANSPORTATION—EARNINGS

Employment and Hours Per Worker

| | Production and Related Workers | | | | All Employees |
	Average Weekly Earnings	Average Weekly Hours	Average Hourly Earnings	Number (thousands)	Number (thousands)
1947	$56.87	39.3	$1.447	1,038	1,263
1948	61.58	39.0	1.579	1,031	1,263
1949	64.95	39.2	1.657	987	1,212
1950					
Jan.	68.12	40.5	1.682	978	1,197
Feb.	66.58	39.7	1.677	872	1,091
Mar.	67.46	40.2	1.678	879	1,100
Apr.	70.46	41.3	1.706	899	1,122
May	69.62	41.0	1.698	1,045	1,269
June	72.37	42.0	1.723	1,077	1,308
July	71.71	41.5	1.728	1,070	1,297
Aug.	72.70	41.9	1.735	1,112	1,342
Sept.	72.41	41.0	1.766	1,143	1,374

Source: Bureau of Labor Statistics

NET SPENDABLE WEEKLY EARNINGS
FOR WORKER WITH 3 DEPENDENTS

CURRENT DOLLARS — 1939 DOLLARS

SPENDABLE WEEKLY EARNINGS OF WORKERS

Gross & Net Average Earnings of Production Workers in Manufacturing Industries[1]

| | Gross Average Weekly Earnings | | Net Spendable Average Weekly Earnings | | | |
| | | | Worker With No Dependents | | Worker With 3 Dependents | |
Period	Amount	Index (1939=100)	Current Dollars	1939 Dollars	Current Dollars	1939 Dollars
1941: Jan.	$26.64	111.7	$25.41	$25.06	$26.37	$26.00
1945: Jan.	47.50	199.1	39.40	30.81	45.17	35.33
July	45.45	190.5	37.80	29.04	43.57	33.47
1946: June	43.31	181.5	37.30	27.81	42.78	31.90
1939: Average	23.86	100.0	23.58	23.58	23.62	23.62
1940: Average	25.20	105.6	24.69	24.49	24.95	24.75
1941: Average	29.58	124.0	28.05	26.51	29.28	27.67
1942: Average	36.65	153.6	31.77	27.11	36.28	30.96
1943: Average	43.14	180.8	36.01	28.97	41.39	33.30
1944: Average	46.08	193.1	38.29	30.32	44.06	34.89
1945: Average	44.39	186.0	36.97	28.61	42.74	33.08
1946: Average	43.74	183.3	37.65	26.87	43.13	30.78
1947: Average	49.97	209.4	42.76	26.70	48.24	30.12
1948: Average	54.14	226.9	47.43	27.54	53.17	30.87
1949: Average	54.92	230.2	48.09	28.27	53.83	31.64
1950: Jan.	56.29	235.9	48.94	29.15	54.70	32.58
Feb.	56.37	236.3	49.00	29.25	54.76	32.69
March	56.53	236.9	49.13	29.24	54.90	32.68
April	56.93	238.6	49.46	29.39	55.23	32.81
May	57.54	241.2	49.95	29.45	55.74	32.86
June	58.70	246.0	50.90	29.73	56.73	33.13
July	59.21	248.2	51.32	29.57	57.13	32.94
Aug.	60.32	252.8	52.24	30.02	58.11	33.39

[1] Net spendable average weekly earnings are obtained by deducting from gross average weekly earnings, social security and income taxes for which the specified type of worker is liable. The amount of income tax liability depends on the number of dependents supported by the worker as well as on the level of his gross income. Net spendable earnings have, therefore, been computed for 2 types of income-receivers: (1) A worker with no dependents; (2) A worker with 3 dependents.

The computation of net spendable earnings for both the factory worker with no dependents and the factory worker with 3 dependents are based upon the gross average weekly earnings for all production workers in manufacturing industries without direct regard to marital status and family composition. The primary value of the spendable series is that of measuring relative changes in disposable earnings for 2 types of income-receivers. That series does not, therefore, reflect actual differences in levels of earnings for workers of varying age, occupation, skill, family composition, etc.

Source: Bureau of Labor Statistics

DEATH RATES BY INDUSTRY

Deaths of Workers, Major Industries

| Industry Group | Total Deaths 1949 | Deaths per 100,000 Workers | | |
		1949	1948	1947
Trade	1,500	14	14	15
Service	2,100	14	15	18
Manufacturing	2,300	15	16	17
Public utilities	400	28	29	31
Transportation	1,300	43	48	53
Agriculture	4,300	54	55	52
Construction	2,100	77	93	96
Mining, quarrying, oil and gas wells	1,000	116	154	167

Source: National Safety Council

ACCIDENTS TO ALL WORKERS

Death and Injury, Place of Accident

| | 1948 | | 1949 | |
Place of Accident	Deaths	Injuries	Deaths	Injuries
At work	16,500	1,950,000	15,000	1,850,000
Away from work	32,000	2,650,000	31,500	2,600,000
Motor vehicle	16,500	550,000	16,500	600,000
Public non-motor vehicle	8,000	1,000,000	7,800	950,000
Home	7,500	1,100,000	7,200	1,050,000

Source: National Safety Council

OCCUPATIONAL DEATH RATES

Deaths Per 10⁵ Workers, 1933-1948

Year	Deaths	No. of Workers (Millions)	Deaths per 100,000 Workers
1933	14,500	39	37
1934	16,000	42	38
1935	16,500	43	38
1936	18,500	45	41
1997	19,000	46	41
1938	16,000	44	36
1939	15,500	45	34
1940	17,000	46	37
1941	18,000	49	37
1942	18,500	52	36
1943	17,500	53	33
1944	16,000	52	31
1945	16,500	51	32
1946	16,500	53½	31
1947	17,000	56½	30
1948	16,500	57½	29
1949	15,000	57	26

Source: National Safety Council

REFINING OF ALUMINUM

Employment and Earnings Per Worker

| | Production and Related Workers | | | |
Year	Average Weekly Earnings	Average Weekly Hours	Average Hourly Earnings	Production Workers (thousands)
1947	$53.46	40.9	$1.307	7.3
1948	58.95	41.4	1.424	7.9
1949	61.95	41.3	1.500	7.8
1950: Jan.	61.16	40.8	1.499	8.0
Feb.	61.66	41.0	1.504	8.3
Mar.	62.03	40.7	1.524	8.4
Apr.	62.03	40.7	1.524	8.4
May	62.73	41.0	1.530	8.6
June	62.76	41.1	1.527	8.6
July	63.06	41.0	1.538	9.3
Aug.	62.99	40.9	1.540	9.3
Sept.	63.51	41.0	1.549	8.8

Source: Bureau of Labor Statistics

METALWORKING MACHINERY

Employment and Earnings Per Worker

| | Production and Related Workers | | | | All Employees |
Year	Average Weekly Earnings	Average Weekly Hours	Average Hourly Earnings	Number (thousands)	Number (thousands)
1947	$58.49	42.2	$1.386	196.1	248.3
1948	62.94	42.1	1.495	186.6	239.5
1949	61.11	39.5	1.547	157.9	208.7
1950					
Jan.	61.42	39.4	1.559	146.5	196.7
Feb.	63.86	40.6	1.573	149.2	198.4
Mar.	65.10	41.1	1.584	152.0	201.6
Apr.	67.21	41.8	1.608	155.4	204.5
May	68.57	42.3	1.621	158.3	207.2
June	69.93	42.9	1.630	162.9	212.6
July	71.16	43.1	1.649	161.5	212.0
Aug.	73.78	44.5	1.658	170.2	221.4
Sept.	74.38	44.3	1.679	181.3	233.1

Source: Bureau of Labor Statistics

CHANGES IN INJURY RATES, 1935-1939 TO 1949

Index Numbers Above 100 Indicate Percentage Increases From Base Period; Below 100, Decreases

Industry	Base Period	Frequency Rate Index Numbers						Frequency Change 1948–49	Severity Rate Index Numbers						Severity Change 1948–49
		1941	1943	1945	1947	1948	1949		1941	1943	1945	1947	1948	1949	
All Reporting Industries	1935–39	117	111	104	101	88	77	−12%	99	77	75	79	72	66	− 9%
Aircraft Manufacturing	1941	100	135	99	97	62	58	− 7%	100	157	193	137	147	133	− 9%
Air Transport	1942	...	169	131	126	116	100	−14%	...	180	114	141	125	25	−80%
Automobile	1935–39	72	98	98	96	81	61	−25%	79	78	77	81	80	70	−12%
Cement	1935–39	111	144	148	134	126	96	−24%	78	80	67	99	96	78	−19%
Chemical	1935–39	105	111	111	98	83	63	−24%	107	93	88	76	74	50	−33%
Clay Products	1935–39	168	184	105	131	106	121	+14%	129	174	83	180	153	226	+47%
Communications	1935–39	95	61	55	55	48	40	−18%	117	38	11	23	25	21	−17%
Construction	1935–39	105	60	77	94	64	76	0	74	76	69	81	77	66	−16%
Electrical Equipment	1935–39	101	125	111	105	97	84	−13%	86	83	76	78	78	66	−16%
Electric Utilities	1935–39	108	107	119	137	131	124	− 5%	76	94	78	100	88	99	+12%
Food	1935–39	99	133	140	126	111	99	−11%	114	102	110	102	96	79	−17%
Foundries	1935–39	89	112	92	105	88	58	−34%	91	108	130	92	119	98	−18%
Gas Utilities	1935–39	98	92	105	156	141	127	−10%	89	93	105	118	105	93	−11%
Glass	1935–39	84	128	108	125	109	91	−17%	68	111	112	90	66	63	− 4%
Leather	1935–39	115	124	98	121	112	102	− 9%	141	167	122	55	83	79	− 4%
Lumber	1935–39	96	97	119	110	90	88	− 3%	120	105	117	121	107	108	+ 1%
Machinery	1935–39	116	194	160	157	139	117	−16%	100	99	81	104	106	92	−13%
Marine Transportation	1935–39	161	205	238	118	104	96	− 7%	96	126	104	75	61	56	− 9%
Meat Packing	1935–39	61	99	115	86	69	49	−29%	118	89	75	62	53	100	+90%
Mining	1935–39	93	106	129	127	105	91	−13%	95	86	105	74	72	60	−17%
Misc. Iron and Steel Products	1935–39	127	120	116	100	107	95	−11%	129	97	113	80	101	88	−13%
Non-Ferrous Metals and Products	1935–39	128	190	166	136	118	116	− 2%	90	97	98	82	72	85	+18%
Petroleum	1935–39	86	94	105	96	90	77	−14%	88	79	81	81	71	63	−11%
Printing and Publishing	1935–39	105	149	133	117	105	72	−31%	70	152	82	128	86	46	−47%
Pulp and Paper	1935–39	104	129	123	110	91	67	−23%	99	102	85	83	68	61	−10%
Quarry	1935–39	143	137	79	137	153	140	− 9%	94	129	34	94	86	102	+19%
Railroad Equipment	1935–39	88	155	166	87	82	90	+10%	136	130	93	72	81	105	+29%
Rubber	1935–39	103	141	148	114	106	65	−39%	85	104	107	96	89	70	−22%
Service	1935–39	132	141	158	110	88	63	−29%	165	102	746	73	291	107	−63%
Sheet Metal Products	1935–39	109	79	126	98	74	69	− 9%	81	58	122	102	88	68	−23%
Shipbuilding	1935–39	185	226	148	145	96	84	−13%	94	101	83	157	80	92	+15%
Steel	1935–39	90	95	93	78	76	64	−15%	90	96	90	82	85	77	−10%
Textile	1935–39	134	177	158	116	116	104	−10%	91	131	117	93	100	98	− 2%
Transit	1935–39	95	129	170	168	114	99	−14%	75	87	97	88	63	49	−22%
Wood Products	1935–39	138	154	184	186	155	143	− 8%	99	125	170	189	145	126	−13%

Source: Individual company reports to the National Safety Council

UNSAFE ACTS AND CAUSES OF PERMANENT DISABILITIES

Deaths and Unsafe Acts (1937 to 1941 incl.) Broken Down For Ten Major Industries

Unsafe Act or Cause	All Industries*		Machinery	Steel	Sheet Metal	Metal Products	Non-Ferrous Metals	Chemical	Pulp and Paper	Food	Public Utility	Construction
	Number	Pct										
UNSAFE CONDITION												
Total Accidents	4,818	...	800	449	295	303	291	355	360	262	707	243
		100%	100%	100%	100%	100%	100%	100%	100%	100%	100%	100%
Hazardous arrangement or procedure	1,634	34	33	41	26	27	36	35	40	28	30	41
Improper guarding	1,214	25	22	22	36	24	21	22	28	26	30	18
Defective agencies	747	15	14	15	14	16	20	18	17	17	15	21
Unsafe dress or apparel	277	6	5	5	6	6	8	5	3	5	8	7
Improper Illumination, ventilation	32	1	1	**	**	**	**	1	**	2	1	2
No unsafe condition	914	19	25	16	18	27	15	19	13	22	16	11
UNSAFE ACT												
Total Accidents	3,112	...	564	244	200	187	202	214	208	182	453	187
		100%	100%	100%	100%	100%	100%	100%	100%	100%	100%	100%
Unnecessary exposure to danger	796	25	25	27	20	21	31	24	31	29	22	30
Unsafe, or improper use of equipment	467	15	19	15	21	13	13	11	17	7	12	12
Working on moving or dangerous equip.	428	14	13	15	13	12	9	18	14	19	9	9
Non-use personal protective equipment	275	9	7	9	6	7	9	7	6	4	20	9
Improper starting or stopping	284	9	12	8	3	12	10	9	8	7	9	13
Overloading, poor arranging	214	7	7	9	5	4	6	8	10	5	5	9
Making safety devices inoperative	157	5	5	1	9	8	4	4	2	4	8	2
Operating at unsafe speed	93	3	7	2	3	4	2	3	3	5	2	5
No unsafe act	398	13	9	14	20	19	16	16	9	20	10	11

* Includes information from industries other than the ten for which detailed information is shown.
** Less than half of one per cent.

Source: National Safety Council

In the preceding pages of statistics every effort has been made to include important data useful to the metalworking and metalproducing industry. A similar effort has been made to exclude data which might be considered of minor importance. However, the editors will appreciate comments on the scope of the material so that any important omissions can be corrected in future issues.—The Editors.

This is your handy synopsis of regulations and revisions under the Defense Production Act of 1950—the act which provides authority for the government controls now being used to gear the nation for defense.

YOU
YOU *and Government Controls*
YOU

AUTHORITY for the economic controls in this section is contained in The Defense Production Act of 1950. Full text of the Act appears in the Congressional Record of Aug. 31, 1950. The Act gives the President powers over the following:

(1) *Priorities and allocations*
(2) *Authority to requisition*
(3) *Expansion of productive capacity and supply*
(4) *Price and wage stabilization*
(5) *Settlement of labor disputes*
(6) *Control of consumer and real estate credit*

The broad aim of the Act is to provide the President with authority to accomplish economic adjustments necessary to back up our defense effort.

Charles E. Wilson, heading the Office of Defense Mobilization, answers only to the President. William Harrison is top man in National Production Authority which administers the controls.

Accelerated Plant Amortization

The National Security Resources Board was expected to lose its authority to grant certificates of necessity for fast tax write-offs to Wilson's ODM. Previously Congress had voted NSRB authority to stimulate industrial growth for indirect and direct defense output. It made possible 5-year accelerated amortization of defense plants and equipment.

Early in November, 1950, application form S and regulations for 60-month write-offs were distributed by NSRB for the first time since World War II. Business was thus able to apply for Certificates of Necessity—or permission to amortize facilities in the shortened span.

ODM will take NSRB's function of serving primary clearing house for applications, sorting them to governmental agencies for recommendations, and then making final decision. Certificates will not be issued for used or existing property unless a substantial increase in output for defense cannot be achieved in any other way.

Fast write-offs can be obtained on plants and facilities constructed or installed after Dec. 31, 1949. Applications for necessity certificates for facilities on which construction, reconstruction, or installation is begun or which are acquired after Sept. 23, 1950, must be filed within 6 months after construction begins or facilities are acquired. Mar. 23, 1951, is the filing deadline for facilities started or acquired on or before Sept. 23.

Applications are available at room 5803, Commerce Dept., Washington 25, D. C.; at 1725 F Street, N.W., Washington, D. C.; and at field offices of the Dept. of Commerce (see p. 374). Amortization deductions may be taken instead of depreciation and may be discortinued, with depreciation resumed, before the 5-year write-off period ends. Gains from the sale or exchange of property, to the extent that the adjusted basis is less than the adjusted basis determined without regard to accelerated depreciation shall be considered ordinary income.

Frank R. Creedon, ex-housing expediter, was named to pass on applications received by the NPA for fast tax write-offs. His Facilities Clearance Staff was assigned the processing of Certificates of Necessity handed to NPA.

Fast write-offs can be denied if it is felt that they will not foster competition or if it is believed a firm's management or financing is unsound.

Defense Loans

Government machinery to speed and aid defense production was set into action in December when NSRB untied the purse strings on a potential loan kitty of $2 billion. Passed by Congress in September, total amount borrowed at any one

January 4, 1951

365

time may not exceed $600 million. But Congress authorized appropriated funds of an additional $1.4 billion.

Loans will be granted when an applicant is unable to get funds from private or public sources. Field offices of certifying agencies—Depts. of Commerce, Agriculture, and Interior, and the Defense Transport Administration—will transmit applications to Washington. When dealing with non-certifying agencies, such as the Air Force, applicants may submit forms to them for transmittal to proper agencies in Washington.

Loans will be made *only* to further production on defense contracts. Application forms are available at field offices of certifying agencies. It is expected that ODM will also take over NSRB's administrative function here.

NPA Regulations

NPA Reg. 1, Inventory Control

Inventories of numerous steel and metal items must be held to a "practicable working minimum" under this order, effective Sept. 18. The order applies to all buyers and sellers for either production or resale for export. National stockpiling, purchasing for personal consumption are not involved.

Importing is unrestricted, but importers may not place domestic orders for the period such imports lift inventories above normal. Materials produced or marketed in minimum quantities may be ordered over permitted inventory levels temporarily. Orders should be regulated for a balance between production and inventory. Firms which historically pile up seasonal stocks must do so normally.

Suppliers may not ship to customers if the supplier knows that the customer is not entitled to deliveries. All stocks, even those held by others in account, must be figured in inventory. Excess inventories are subject to requisition under the Defense Production Act. Special items, those the supplier does not usually make, stock, sell, or which are difficult to dispose of, may be delivered in excess of inventory.

The initial list on which working inventory restrictions apply includes: *steel, iron, aluminum, copper, tin, nickel, zinc, tungsten, manganese, magnesium, columbium, cobalt, chemicals, rubber, and miscellaneous.* (For product breakdown, see THE IRON AGE, Sept. 21, p. 114.)

NPA Reg. 2, DO Priorities

Equal precedence to all defense orders, including atomic energy procurement, was made effec-

tive on Oct. 3 in NPA Reg. 2. Ore, scrap, foods, fuel, and electric power were omitted. A single rating with no degree of preference was authorized. Issuance of DO ratings will be through the procurement services of the Defense Dept. and Atomic Energy Commission.

Firms will give precedence to orders received first. If orders are received on the same date, precedence will be given to the order with the earliest delivery date. A rated order calling for earlier delivery than a rated order already accepted must not interfere with scheduled delivery of the accepted order. If both orders can be filled on schedule, it is not necessary to deliver the first order ahead of the second.

The date on which sufficient specifications have been furnished to the producer will usually be construed as the receiving date for the order. Cancellation of a rated order or a rating applicable to an order when the supplier has material in production to fill it, need not mean that he halt processing to go to other DO orders. He may continue processing material for the cancelled order to a "stage of completion that will avoid a substantial loss of total production."

But he may not incorporate materials needed for other rated orders and may not postpone other rated orders for more than 15 days. Rated orders for delivery of materials may be extended in most cases to obtain the material or items which will be physically incorporated in the material to be delivered. This includes containers and packaging items.

A person "losing" material which was delivered on a DO order may extend the rating for its replacement. To apply and extend ratings, the producer must label the order with a DO rating and with two digits supplied to him. He must put on it "certified under NPA Reg. 2" and the signature of the person placing the order.

Interpretation 1 to Reg. 2—The Dept. of Defense and the Atomic Energy Commission may assign suppliers of petroleum and food the right to apply DO ratings to secure drums, cans and other containers required for delivery, under an interpretation to NPA Reg. 2 (applying to steel). The ratings may be used only to secure minimum quantities of containers to fill specific defense orders.

NPA M-1, *Steel*

This order clarifies handling of steel orders under NPA Reg. 2. Steel producers need not accept orders received less than the specified number of days (lead time) before the first day of the month in which shipment is requested.

Unless ordered by NPA, producers need not accept DO orders for shipment in any one month in excess of certain specified percentages based on shipments for the 8-month period, January-August 1950.

Percentages of DO orders which producers must accept and lead time on the various products are subject to change. For latest revisions write to National Production Authority, Commerce Building, Washington 25, D. C.

Producers need not accept surplus orders in any month if the total exceeds specified percentages. In such case it is up to the government to find a producer to fill the order.

Supplement 1 to M-1—The first defense support program, issued as Supplement 1 to M-1, directs industry to provide 310,000 tons of steel a month during the first quarter of 1951 to support a 10,-000 per month freight car construction program. Repair and maintenance are included.

Steel obtained must be used only for repair and construction of freight cars. Steel shipped on these orders cannot be counted as produced under rated orders for determining percentages of defense production as set forth in Sec. 20.5 of M-1.

Supplement 2 to M-1—Allocation of 10,000 tons of steel monthly for the first quarter of 1951 for construction of nine Great Lakes ore carriers, two freight car ferriers and a limestone carrier is provided for in Supplement 2. Operating provisions are similar to the freight car program, including a required lead time of 45 days on orders.

Supplement 3 to M-1—Provides 8000 tons of steel monthly for Canadian freight car production.

NPA M-2, *Rubber*

This order restricts civilian consumption of natural rubber to a designated percentage of

---

Metalworking Form

Metalworking plants will soon have to file their first major form with National Production Authority. Similar to the old WPB "input-output" form, it is designed to give NPA complete data on materials input, man-hours worked, and output by product.

The form has already been discussed with industry representatives. Data on the fourth quarter of 1950 by Jan. 25, 1951 is the present target. Filing of the form will be on a regular quarterly basis after that.

Data compiled from this form will be used to check on inventory control and the use of critical materials.

---

consumption during the base period which is the year ended June 30, 1950. During November civilian users were allowed 75 pct of their consumption during the base period. During December the civilian allowance was cut to 63 pct.

NPA M-3, *Columbium Steels*

All columbium-bearing stainless steel must be set aside to meet DO-rated orders issued by the Defense Dept. and the Atomic Energy Commission. This order went into effect on Oct. 19, 1950, and also provides that no ferrocolumbium-bearing steel shall be used for any product if ferro-columbium-tantalaum bearing steel can be substituted.

Neither type of steel may be used if a substitute can be found for the latter.

NPA M-4, *Construction Ban*

Aim is to conserve materials by prohibiting construction which does not further the defense effort.

The order, effective Oct. 27, bans construction of buildings for amusement, recreational or entertainment purposes. It does not apply to construction already started at that time or to planned construction which will not cost more than $5,000. Also exempted are Defense Dept. and Atomic Energy Commission Projects.

This order should not be confused with Regulation X which increases down payments and shortens loan terms of Federal Housing Administration and Veteran's Administration loans for housing.

NPA M-5, *Aluminum Distribution*

This order established percentages and rules for handling DO orders on aluminum, and it applies to both primary and secondary production.

Primary producers must accept rated orders from independent fabricators up to 6½ pct of monthly scheduled production of primary pig and ingot. Ceilings were set for mandatory acceptance of rated orders.

Provision is also included for NPA to establish special programs (such as the steel freight car program) calling for rated orders. Producers and fabricators need not accept rated orders received less than 60 days before the first of the month in which shipment is asked.

NPA M-6, Warehouses

Primary purpose is to assure steel for small users. Steel producers must allot warehouse customers proportionate percentages of each steel product, based on average monthly shipments during the first 9 months of 1950.

Allotments will be made out of steel available after mills have met defense and other essential requirements. Producer does not have to take orders which are not for "substantially the same products," that is, which vary by other than minor differences in size and design.

Order also sets following ceilings on amounts of steel orders warehouses must accept from one customer at a time:

> Carbon steel . . . . 8000 lb
> Alloy (except stainless) . . . . 5000 lb
> Stainless bars, plates . . . . 1000 lb
> Stainless tubing, pipe . . . . 1000 lb

Distributor is not required to make deliveries totaling 40,000 lb or more at any one time, unless delivery includes 10 or more items, none of which exceed above limits.

Also, the order prohibits extension of a DO rating to obtain steel products for sale or resale in same form received except to replace items shipped from stock on DO orders.

The order was amended to cover Canadian warehouses.

NPA M-7, Aluminum Cutback

Use of aluminum for manufacture of non-defense goods is to be reduced in January to 80 pct of the average monthly consumption of the first half of 1950; February use will be cut to 75 pct of the same base; and, as of Mar. 1, non-essential consumption is limited to 65 pct of the base period. Use of aluminum for these purposes was restricted in December, 1950, to 100 pct.

Inventory restrictions are also imposed, limiting stocks to a 60-day supply or a practical working minimum, whichever is less.

Businesses using less than 1000 lb per year are exempt. Pending development of power require-

ments, the order does not apply to contracts placed prior to the order for delivery before April of aluminum conductor cable, wire or bus-bar for production or transmission of electricity.

It has been emphasized that the order applies to users of aluminum products and forms and does not limit production or conversion, or use in the production of other metals.

Direction 1 to NPA M-7 — This supplements order M-7 by providing for four types of adjustments which may be allowed for new businesses, changes in products, seasonal factors and, where the base period was affected by shutdowns of 15 days or more.

NPA M-8, Tin Inventories

Effective Nov. 13, 1950, possession of tin in any raw, semifinished or scrap form, or any alloy or compound in which tin is of chief value, is limited to a 60-day supply or a practical working minimum, whichever is less.

Use of tin for civilian goods is cut to 80 pct of the base period as of Feb. 1 and new tin is not to be used wherever secondary metal can be substituted. Tinplate manufacturers stocks of pig tin are limited to a 120 day supply.

The order applies to any product which contains 1.5 pct or more of tin.

NPA M-9, Zinc Distribution

This order is similar to M-5 in objective and scope.

The order took effect Nov. 16, 1950, and calls for a 30-day lead time. It goes on to state that no producer of zinc, zinc dust or zinc oxide will have to accept rated orders for shipment over 10 pct of his total scheduled production of these items during that month.

Fabricators do not have to ship anything on DO orders in excess of the following percentages: Zinc base alloys, 20 pct; zinc sheet, strip, wire, rod, shapes (rolled, drawn and extruded), and plates, 15 pct.

Without specific NPA direction, no dealer need accept rated orders in excess of 15 pct of the total zinc, zinc dust, zinc oxide and zinc products which are available to him during any one month.

NPA also provided for the setting up of production and delivery programs when needed. Provisions are also included for the assistance of those who have trouble in placing DO orders, for adjustments and exceptions, communications, reports and violations.

NPA M-10, Cobalt Stocks

Beginning Nov. 30, cobalt inventories were limited to a 30-day supply and the sole importer of the metal was directed how to allocate his December supply.

December non-defense use was limited to 60 pct, an increase from the 30 pct of the previous month. At this writing, the NPA was discussing

DEFENSE ORDER NUMBERS

Department of Defense:

DO-01 Aircraft
   02 Guided Missiles
   03 Ships
   04 Tanks, Automotive
   05 Weapons
   06 Ammunition
   07 Electronic and Communications Equipment
   08 Fuels and Lubricants
   09 Clothing and Equipage
   10 Transportation Equipment
   11 Building Materials and Equipment for Overseas (troop) Construction
   21 Miscellaneous
   22 Department of Defense Construction Contract
   98 Production, Equipment for Certain Contractors
   99 Miscellaneous—as referred to in Regulation 2 Sect. 11.9

Atomic Energy Commission:

DO-40 Operations
   41 Construction
   42 Construction Equipment

U. S. Coast Guard:

DO-60A Automotive
DO-60B Electronic and Communications Equipment
  60C Aids to Navigation
  60D Clothing, Small Stores
  60E Miscellaneous Stock
  61 Material for Aircraft
  62 Construction on Shore Projects
  63 Material for Ready-Built Ships

---

longer range plans for cobalt with cobalt consumers.

NPA M-11, Copper Distribution

NPA's purposes in this order were twofold: (1) to provide necessary supplies for defense needs and (2) to maintain equitable distribution among all users for that copper remaining after military requirements are met.

Percentage ceilings on the required acceptance of DO orders for copper, based on average monthly shipments during the first 6 months of 1950, are: Brass mill products, 20 pct; copper wire mill products including copper rods, cable and insulated wire, 5 pct; foundry and copper-base alloy products, 10 pct. Limits up to 25 pct are placed on certain products within these groups.

Distributors and jobbers have identical ceilings and base period except the distributors and wholesalers of wire mill products whose base is the preceding monthly inventory period.

A 45-day lead time is provided by this order, which is effective as of Jan. 1, 1951.

NPA M-12, Copper Cutback

Nonessential civilian use of copper is restricted by this order as follows: Production and use of wire mill products by total weight, 85 pct in January and February, 1951, and 80 pct in March; foundry products, 100 pct. The base period for these figures is January to June, 1950.

The order applies to all unalloyed copper and brass alloy, including scrap. It applies to all producers and users including copper or copper-base alloy (40 pct or more copper content) in production of other metals and alloys. Those who use less than 1000 lb of copper per calendar quarter are exempt. Use of copper for maintenance, repair and operating supplies is permitted up to 100 pct of the base period.

Producers' stocks are limited to a 45-day supply or a practical working minimum whichever is less, and users are restricted to 60-day inventories.

NPA M-13, Rayon

Producers of high tenacity rayon yarn need not accept priority orders received less than 30 days prior to first day of month in which shipment is requested. No producer need accept priority orders for any month in excess of 10 pct of his scheduled production.

NPA M-14, Nickel Cutback

Non-defense use of primary nickel for the first quarter of 1951 is cut back to 65 pct of the quarterly average of the first half of 1950. The order applies to electrolytic nickel, ingots, pigs, rolled and cast anodes, shot, oxides and residues derived directly from nickel. Those who consume less than 250 lb per quarter are exempt and use for maintenance, repair and operating supplies is allowed at 100 pct of the base period.

Inventories are restricted to a 30-day supply or a practical working minimum, whichever is less.

NPA M-15, Zinc Cutback

This order limits first quarter 1951 zinc consumption for non-defense purposes to 80 pct of the average use during the first 6 months of 1950. Inventories are set at 45 days or a practical working minimum, whichever is less.

Any zinc produced by electrolytic, electrothermic or fire refining processes, including scrap and other secondary metal, and any alloy containing 50 pct zinc by weight are included in this order. Zinc products specified include sheet, strip or ribbon, rod, wire, castings, plates, and shapes either drawn or extruded.

Two specific exemptions are provided: (1) Users of less than 3000 lb per quarter and (2) Highly specialized uses as well as zinc substituted for cadmium in electroplating. Maintenance and repair use are permitted at 100 pct of the base period.

NPA M-16, Copper Scrap Controls

Scrap dealer inventories are limited to one third (by weight) of total delivery in the first half of 1950 and mills are directed not to accumulate "excess" stocks of mill scrap.

Acceptance and delivery of copper scrap is confined to scrap dealers, refiners, brass mills, brass and bronze foundries, ingot makers and other producers who regularly use scrap copper in their normal operations.

Melting and other processing of mill scrap is limited to the mills themselves and sale of mill scrap is forbidden except through regular channels. Conversion or toll agreements are also made illegal in this order which covers all copper and copper-base alloy scrap containing 40 pct or more copper by weight.

Exceptions to any of the above regulations may be made only with specific NPA direction or approval.

NPA M-17, *Electrical Equipment*

Aim is to spread priority orders evenly among makers of certain kinds of electrical equipment. Order says makers of insulating washers, electronic tubes and fixed composition resistors must provide as much as 15 to 50 pct of their output for DO orders. They may refuse orders which would raise their total DO orders above these limits, though they aren't required to.

Personnel—Iron & Steel Division

NATIONAL PRODUCTION AUTHORITY, COMMERCE BUILDING, WASHINGTON 25
Phone Sterling 9200—Extension Indicated

		Room	Phone Ext.
Director	D. B. Carson Sharon Steel Corp.	3830A	4455 4456 4346 4347
Ass't. Director	F. T. McCue Chief, Iron & Steel Div., Dept. of Commerce	3323	3962 2369 2328
Staff Assistant	J. Levin	3323	2273
Staff Assistant	R. X. McGowan	3327	3349
Staff Assistant	E. S. Moorhead	3819	3483
International Economist	J. J. W. Palmer	3319	2263
Staff Economist	R. M. Weidenhammer	3323	2214
Legal Counsel	R. Bronson	5121	4621

Sections

		Room	Phone Ext.
Stainless Steel	C. B. Boyne, Chief Allegheny Ludlum Steel Corp.	3827	3323
Pig Iron	J. A. Claussen, Chief American Iron & Steel Inst.	3825	2343
Alloy & Cold drawn Bar	L. E. Creighton, Chief Rotary Electric Steel Co.	3827	3323
Rails & Accessories	J. J. Davis, Jr., Chief Inland Steel Co.	3819	3217
Program	C. Halcomb, Chief	3823	3152 3171
Pipe & Tube	A. P. Happer, Chief National Tube Co.	3316	2437 4437
Priorities & Statistical Control	K. H. Hunter, Chief	3329	3974
Plant Expansion	H. L. Leyda, Chief General Steel Co.	3309	3140
Tin Plate	A. M. Long, Chief Youngstown Sheet & Tube Co.	3825	3334

		Room	Phone Ext.
Structural Shapes	R. A. Marble, Chief Carnegie-Illinois Steel Corp.	3324	2767 2988
Wire	N. F. Melville, Chief Pittsburgh Steel Co.	3819	4656
Plate	W. E. Mullestein, Chief Lukens Steel Co.	3324	2767
	W. E. Bossert, Ass't. Chief Alan Wood Steel Co.		2988
Sheet & Strip	W. B. Quail, Chief Armco Steel Corp.	3320	2529 2700
Bars & Unfinished	J. W. Robinson, Chief Jones & Laughlin Steel Corp.	3326	3310 3151
Warehouse	A. Y. Sawyer, Chief Jos. T. Ryerson & Son, Inc.	3312	2050 2681
	Russell Link, Ass't. Chief Central Steel & Wire Co.	3312	2050
Forgings	H. F. Weaver, Chief Bethlehem Steel Corp.	3310	2004
	J. E. Sweeney, Ass't Chief Kropp Drop Forge Co.		2609
Castings	A. J. McDonald, Chief American Steel Foundries	3315	4520
Ferroalloys	James H. Critchett, Chief Electro Metallurgical Co.	3315	4455
Scrap	Marvin Plant, Chief H. Klaff Co.	3315	4520
Refractories	Marguerite Saurs, Chief General Refractories Co.		
Metallurgical & Technical	Col. Charles McKnight, Chief Aberdeen Proving Grounds		

GOVERNMENT PROCUREMENT

Major Metal Products Bought by the Armed Forces and Where They are Bought

These major products of the metalworking industry are bought by the military. Numbers at the right refer to the buying offices listed on the following pages. To sell any of these items write the appropriate office. If your product is not listed here write the Central Military Procurement Information Office, Munitions Board, Pentagon, Washington 25, D. C.

A

Aerial bombs, AP, depth....................13, 18
Aerial bombs, general, frag., etc. 13
Agricultural machinery and implements........ 2
Air conditioning and refrigeration equipment,
                        1, 2, 11, 15, 22, 30
Aircraft assemblies, components, propellers.15, 17, 20
Airplanes 15, 17
Ammunition, artillery, complete.............13, 18
Ammunition, artillery, components........4, 13, 18
Ammunition, small arms 4
Artillery, naval guns & mortars (cal. .60 and
    over) 5, 6, 7, 8, 18

B

Bituminous mixing, paving, and related equip-
    ment 2
Boats and accessories 2, 15, 19
Bomb fuzes 13, 18

C

Catapults, beaching gear 17
Cement handling and placing machinery and
    equipment 21
Communication and related equipment
                    12, 19, 20, 23, 26
Component parts and subassemblies, attachments
    and accessories for metalworking machinery.. 16
Compressors and pumps.............16, 19, 21, 28
Computing devices, sights (except bomb sights).4, 18
Concrete mixing, paving, placing, and related
    equipment 21
Containers and closures 20, 22, 24
Contractors' crawler carts, wagons, and trailers
    (full or half-track) 2
Contractors' jacks, supports for trench sidewalls,
    concrete forms, and related uses............. 21
Conveying, elevating and materials handling
    equipment 16, 21
Crushing, pulverizing, and screening machinery. 21
Cutlery, industrial 16
Cutting and forming tools for metal working
    machinery 16

D

Domestic water systems 21
Dredging machinery and components, except hulls 2

E

Electric distribution and control equipment
                    2, 16, 19, 20, 27, 28, 30
Electric generators and motors........2, 16, 19, 28
Explosives, HE 13, 18

F

Files, rasps and other hand tools.............. 16
Fire control equipment 4, 18
Fire fighting equipment 2, 15
Foundry equipment, except furnaces and ovens
                        16, 22
Fuel burning equipment 2, 3
Furniture and fixtures (incl. shelving and
    lockers) 16, 30

G

Gages, levels, micrometers, etc. 16
Graders and maintainers 21
Grenades and components.................... 13
Gun mounts, etc. (except aircraft)........5, 14, 18

H

Household electrical appliances 16

I

Industrial furnaces, kilns, lehrs, and ovens..... 30
Identification plates, badges, emblems, tags, and
    military insignia 10
Insulated wire and cable...........20, 23, 26, 27
Iron and steel products....................16, 20

J

Jigs, fixtures and metalworking accessories, ex-
    cept machine accessories 16

K

Kitchen utensils, tools and cutlery; and table-
    ware, except flatware and hollow ware.....11, 33

L

Landing vehicles (not tracked)................ 14
Landing vehicles, tracked 19
Lighting fixtures 16, 20 21, 27, 30, 31, 32
Lighting fixtures, automotive 14
Lighting fixtures, R. R. 3
Loaders, self-propelled, positive-feed........... 2
Locomotives, wheels and parts 3
Logging equipment 2

Armed Forces Buying Offices

Numbers at left refer to purchased products in list above.

1. Armed Services Medical Procurement Agency
   84 Sands Street
   Brooklyn 1, N. Y.

2. Chicago Procurement Office
   Corps of Engineers
   226 West Jackson Boulevard
   Chicago 6, Ill.

3. Commanding Officer
   Marietta Transportation Corps Depot
   Marietta, Pa.

4. Commanding Officer
   Frankford Arsenal
   Philadelphia, Pa.

5. Commanding Officer
   Rock Island Arsenal
   Rock Island, Ill.

6. Commanding Officer
   Springfield Armory
   Springfield, Mass.

7. Commanding Officer
   Watertown Arsenal
   Watertown, Mass.

8. Commanding Officer
   Watervliet Arsenal
   Watervliet, N. Y.

9. Commanding Officer
   Detroit Arsenal
   Center Line, Mich.

10. Commanding General
    New York Quartermaster Purchasing Office
    111 East 16th St.
    New York 3, N. Y.

11. Commanding Officer
    Chicago Quartermaster Purchasing Office
    1819 West Pershing Road
    Chicago 9, Ill.

12. Commanding Officer
    Signal Corps Procurement Agency
    2800 South 20th St.
    Philadelphia 45, Pa.

13. Ordnance Ammunition Center
    Joliet Arsenal
    Joliet, Ill.

14. Ordnance Tank & Automotive Center
    1501 Beard St.
    Detroit, Mich.

15. Procurement Division
    Air Materiel Command
    Wright-Patterson Air Force Base
    Dayton, Ohio

16. Officer in Charge
    Navy Purchasing Office
    Department of the Navy
    Washington 25, D. C.

17. Bureau of Aeronautics
    Department of the Navy
    Washington 25, D. C.

18. Bureau of Ordnance
    Department of the Navy
    Washington 25, D. C.

19. Bureau of Ships
    Department of the Navy
    Washington 25, D. C.

20. Aviation Supply Officer
    Aviation Supply Office
    400 Robbins Ave.
    Philadelphia 11, Pa.

21. Yards and Docks Supply Officer
    Yards and Docks Supply Office
    U. S. Naval Construction BN Center
    Port Hueneme, Calif.

22. Officer in Charge
    Navy Purchasing Office
    111 East 16th St.
    New York 3, N. Y.

23. Officer in Charge
    Navy Purchasing Office
    844 North Rush St.
    Chicago 11, Ill.

24. Officer in Charge
    Navy Purchasing Office
    180 Montgomery St.
    San Francisco, Calif.

25. Officer in Charge
    Navy Purchasing Office
    1206 South Santee St.
    Los Angeles, Calif.

26. Electronic Supply Officer
    Electronic Supply Office
    Great Lakes, Ill.

27. Commander
    U. S. Naval Shipyard
    Portsmouth, N. H.

28. Supply Officer in Command
    Naval Supply Depot
    Mechanicsburg, Pa.

29. Officer in Charge
    U. S. Navy Ship Store Office
    29th and 3rd Ave.
    Brooklyn 32, N. Y.

30. The Quartermaster General
    Headquarters USMC
    Washington, D. C.

31. Depot Quartermaster
    MC Depot of Supplies
    1100 South Broad St.
    Philadelphia, Pa.

32. Depot Quartermaster
    MC Depot of Supplies
    100 Harrison St.
    San Francisco, Calif.

33. Headquarters
    Army Quartermaster Market Center
    226 West Jackson Boulevard
    Chicago 6, Ill.

U. S. Dept. of Commerce Field Offices

Alabama
Atlanta 1, Ga., 30 Whitehall St., SW.
Mobile 10, 109 St. Joseph St.

Arizona
Phoenix 8, 234 N. Central Ave.

Arkansas
Memphis 3, Tenn., 229 Federal Bldg.

California
Los Angeles 12, 312 N. Spring St.
San Francisco 11, 555 Battery St.

Colorado
Denver 2, 828 17th St.

Connecticut
Hartford 1, 135 High St.

Delaware
Philadelphia 2, Pa., 42 S. 15th St.

Florida
Jacksonville 1, 311 W. Monroe St.
Miami 32, 36 NE 1st St.
Mobile 10, Ala., 109 St. Joseph St.

Georgia
Atlanta 1, 30 Whitehall St. SW.
Savannah, 125 Bull St.

Idaho
Portland 4, Oregon, 520 SW Morrison St.
Seattle 4, Wash., 909 1st Ave.

Illinois
Chicago 4, 332 S. Michigan Ave.
St. Louis 1, Mo., 1114 Market St.

Indiana
Chicago 4, Ill., 332 S. Michigan Ave.
Louisville 2, Ky., 631 Federal Bldg.

Iowa
Chicago 4, Ill., 332 S. Michigan Ave.

Kansas
Kansas City 6, Mo., 911 Walnut St.

Kentucky
Cincinnati 2, Ohio, 105 W. 4th St.
Louisville 2, 631 Federal Bldg.

Louisiana
New Orleans 12, 333 St. Charles Ave.

Maine
Boston 9, Mass., 2 India St.

Maryland
Baltimore 2, 103 S. Gay St.

Massachusetts
Boston 9, 2 India St.
Providence 3, R. I., 24 Weybossett St.

Michigan
Detroit 26, 230 W. Fort St.

Minnesota
Minneapolis 1, 401-2nd Ave. S.

Mississippi
Mobile 10, Ala., 109 St. Joseph St.

Missouri
Kansas City 6, 911 Walnut St.
Memphis 3, Tenn., 229 Federal Bldg.
St. Louis 1, 1114 Market St.

Montana
Butte, 14 W. Granite St.

Nebraska
Omaha 2, 1319 Farnam St.

Nevada
Reno, 111 W. 2nd St.

New Hampshire
Boston 9, Mass., 2 India St.

New Jersey
Newark, 325 Industrial Bldg., 1060 Broad St.
New York 4, N. Y., 42 Broadway.
Philadelphia 2, Pa., 42 S. 15th St.

New Mexico
Albuquerque, 203 W. Gold Ave.
El Paso 7, Tex., 310 San Francisco St.

New York
Buffalo 3, 117 Elicott St.
New York 4, 42 Broadway.

North Carolina
Atlanta 1, Ga., 50 Whitehall St., SW.
Charleston 3, S. C., 18 Broad St.

North Dakota
Minneapolis 1, Minn., 401-2nd Ave. S.

Ohio
Cincinnati 2, 105 W. 4th St.
Cleveland 14, 925 Euclid Ave.

Oklahoma
Oklahoma City 2, 102 NW 3rd St.

Oregon
Portland 4, 520 SW Morrison St.

Pennsylvania
Philadelphia 2, 42 S. 15th St.
Pittsburgh 19, 700 Grant St.

Rhode Island
Providence 3, 24 Weybossett St.

South Carolina
Charleston 3, 18 Broad St.

South Dakota
Minneapolis 1, 401-2nd Ave. S.

Tennessee
Atlanta 1, Ga., 50 Whitehall St., SW.
Memphis 3, 229 Federal Bldg.

Texas
Dallas 2, 1114 Commerce St.
El Paso 7, 310 San Francisco St.
Houson 14, 602 Federal Office Bldg.

Utah
Salt Lake City 1, 350 S. Main St.

Vermont
Boston 9, Mass., 2 India St.

Virginia
Richmond 19, 801 E. Broad St.

Washington
Portland 4, Ore., 520 SW Morrison St.
Seattle 4, 909-1st Ave.

West Virginia
Cleveland 14, Ohio, 925 Euclid Ave.
Pittsburgh 19, Pa., 700 Grant St.

Wisconsin
Milwaukee 1, 517 E. Wisconsin Ave.

Wyoming
Cheyenne, 304 Federal Office Bldg.

news of industry

Seek OK for New England Mill Fast Tax Writeoff

Project to cost $250 million . . . Door left open for major steel producer to back project . . . Expansion of metalworking capacity in New England forecast—*By George Baker.*

Washington — Rapid amortization plans for a 1,000,000-ton New England steel mill were ready for government approval this week.

The National Security Resources Board said it had been asked to expedite the application of the New England Development Corp. for fast tax writeoff of the proposed plant and equipment.

Officials of NEDC said financing of the $250 million project had not yet been settled. They hinted they were "holding the door open" for a "major steel producer" to join with them in backing the project, but indicated they would seek funds from the Reconstruction Finance Corp. if private capital were unavailable.

To Enlarge Port Facilities

Alfred C. Neal, vice-president of the Boston Federal Reserve Bank and a consultant for the New England Council, NEDC's parent organization, said the new integrated mill would be built on a 600-acre site between New London and Waterford, Conn. Plans are already underway for enlargement of port facilities south of Waterford, he said.

Clifford S. Strike, NEDC President, said in a letter to NSRB chief Stuart Symington accompanying the tax application that his company was "firmly committed" to the principles that (1.) The proposed mill should be pri-

vately operated, and that (2.) a "presently-operating" steel company should have preference as operator.

"Our purpose is still to join with a presently operating steel company in the design, construction, ownership and operation of the mill for which application is made, but if that course should fail, to proceed with the establishment of an independent company," Mr. Strike declared.

Advantages of Mill

Predicting a "substantial expansion" of new fabricating capacity in New England as a result of establishing the new mill, Mr. Strike said such expansion would occur at "minimum cost to the economy" because of the existing availability of labor, housing, and community facilities in the New London-Waterford area.

Sen. McMahon, D., Conn., predicted last week that the proposed mill would "not only command an adequate market for its products," but also enjoy a cost advantage of raw materials.

Coal, he said, would be shipped from West Virginia and would cost no more delivered at New London than to the steel mills of Chicago. The principal source of ore would be the Labrador deposits, from which ore would cost less delivered by water at New London than by rail-haul to Pittsburgh and Youngstown, he said.

Gray Market Control

Washington — NPA m o v e d last week to strengthen its control over supplies of critical materials and to put the finger on gray marketeers.

It issued a l o n g list of materials which may not be accumulated in excess of reasonable needs w h e t h e r for business, home, or personal consumption. It also forbids such accumulation for resale at more than the prevailing market price.

The list includes primary and semi-fabricated iron and steel, including pig iron, castings, forgings, and scrap, pressure and soil pipe, wire and rod, and primary and secondary aluminum.

Other materials in both basic and other forms, including alloys, are tin, c o p p e r , zinc, antimony, cadmium, cerium, chromium, cobalt, columbium, magnesium, manganese, mica, molybdenum, nickel, platinum, tantalum, tungsten, vanadium, industrial diamonds, and nonferrous scrap.

Swedish Steel Expands

Stockholm—A new mill producing hot-rolled strip up to 12 in. wide has been started at the Sandviken works in Sweden. It will have an annual capacity of about 20,000 tons. A tube mill with a capacity of 10,000 tons annually will be put into production soon. Cold-rolling mill capacity at Sandviken is being expanded.

INDUSTRIAL SHORTS

BRANCH STORE — A new factory branch store in Pittsburgh has been opened by the LINK-BELT CO. Otto W. Werner is district manager in the new store, which will stock all popular Link-Belt transmission and materials handling products.

ANOTHER PLANT — A $600,000 plant will be built on Egbert Road in Cleveland by the S. K. WELLMAN CO., manufacturers of Velvetouch friction linings. The plant will have its own railroad siding and will be completed next summer.

EXPANDING — A new plant is being constructed in Butler, Pa., by the AIR REDUCTION SALES CO. for the manufacture of oxygen and nitrogen. The plant is expected to be in operation the latter part of 1951.

TAKES OVER — The Anker-Holth Mfg. Co., Port Huron, Mich., manufacturers of hydraulic and air operated cylinders, chucks and collets, air valves and accessories, has been purchased by the WELLMAN ENGINEERING CO., Cleveland. J. C. Hodge, executive vice-president of Wellman, will supervise the operation of this new acquisition to be known as the Anker-Holth Div.

NEW MARKETS — Bethlehem Supply Co., Tulsa, and the Bethlehem Supply Co. of California, Los Angeles, have been appointed distributors by TUBE TURNS, INC., Louisville. They will handle Tube-Turn welding fittings and flanges.

CHAPTER LEADERS — Leo Chapin of Chapin & Fagin, Inc., Buffalo, was elected president of the Western New York chapter of the INSTITUTE OF SCRAP IRON & STEEL. J. L. Maher, Pennsylvania Wood & Iron Co., Inc., Buffalo, was named vice-president and Jack Reingold, Lake City Iron & Metal Co., Buffalo, re-elected secretary-treasurer.

SOUTHERN DEALER — Hyster Co., Portland, has appointed the AICHEL STEEL & SUPPLY CO., Jacksonville, Fla., as a dealer for their industrial materials handling equipment. They will handle the sales and service of Hyster equipment in eight Florida counties and twelve Georgia counties.

SALES OFFICES — New branch sales offices in Newark, N. J., and El Dorado, Ark., have been established by the RELIANCE ELECTRIC & ENGINEERING CO., Cleveland. The Syracuse district office directing the company's sales throughout northern and western New York State has been transferred to Buffalo.

WESTERN AGENT — The San Francisco and Los Angeles office of the ROUND CALIFORNIA CHAIN CO. are now acting as sales representatives for the Cleveland Cap Screw Co., producers of cap screws, socket screws, set screws and milled studs.

TUBE DIVISION — An Electronic Tube Division has been formed by the WESTINGHOUSE ELECTRIC CORP. and plans are in progress for three new plants to manufacture various types of tubes. E. W. Ritter has been appointed manager of this new division.

ACQUISITION — The entire tractor allied equipment business of Isaacson Iron Works has been acquired by the PULLMAN-STANDARD CAR MFG. CO., Chicago. Operation of the Isaacson plant at Rockford, Ill., will be continued by Pullman-Standard.

OPENING MINE — The VICTOR CHEMICAL WORKS, Chicago, is opening a mine on the Maiden Rock phosphate deposit and constructing a $5 million plant for processing the rock into elemental phosphorus in the vicinity of Butte, Mont.

GM to Build Thunderjets; Ominous Note for Auto Industry

Detroit — A news release by General Motors last week contained an ominous note Detroit has been fearing. Announcing that GM will build Republic F-84 Thunderjet fighter airplanes at its Buick-Olds-Pontiac plant at Kansas City, C. E. Wilson, president, said, "When tooling is completed the plant will be used exclusively for the manufacture of airplanes."

The question Detroit is now asking is just how many other plants built by the government and subsequently purchased and operated by the industry will be claimed for war production and how soon will recapture be ordered.

In addition to the Kansas City Plant, there are at least five major plants operated by the auto industry today that could be taken over by the government under the terms of similar purchase agreements.

Armco Rebuilds Hot Strip Mill

Middletown, Ohio — The $3 million modernization program for the hot strip mill at Armco Steel Corp.'s East Works will be completed during the third week of January.

An inventory of hot-rolled steel coils was built up in anticipation of the shutdown of this plant Jan. 2. This inventory will insure a steady supply of material during the shutdown to other departments. The openhearth department will continue to produce ingots.

Wartime Controls for England?

London — Some wartime controls may return to England with the government's decision to expand rearmament spending past present plans. Labor may again have to be directed into defense industries, prices and supplies may have to be controlled, and factories and buildings may have to be requisitioned.

U. S. Steel Speeds Fairless Works Plan

Motivated by defense needs . . . Plan early spring start, late 1952 finish . . . To have 1.8 million ton capacity . . . See output starting in year . . . National Tube to build pipe mill.

New York—U. S. Steel Corp. will build a new, wholly-integrated steel plant near Morrisville, Pa. It will be called the Fairless Works and is probably the biggest single expansion in steel's history, adding 1,800,000 annual ingot tons to the Corporation's capacity when completed by the end of 1952. Stress was laid on steel for defense in U. S. Steel's announcement for the project which will start early this spring.

Chairman of the Board Irving S. Olds said that within 6 to 12 months after construction opens, the first finished steel products are expected to be produced in the plant. The completed mill will produce a range of products, including bars, standard steel pipe, wire rods, hot and cold-rolled sheets and strip, and tinplate.

News of the mill is official confirmation of long-standing IRON AGE predictions that U. S. Steel would build an Eastern Mill in 1951. (THE IRON AGE, Feb. 2, 1950.) The Fairless Works will be the largest steelmaking aid to the defense effort authorized by U. S. Steel since the Korean war. Total of the firm's post-Korean expansion will add more than 4 million tons to its capacity.

Will Serve Two Areas

Mr. Olds stated that Fairless Works products will be distributed to Middle Atlantic and New England markets and mill location on the banks of the Delaware river, opposite Trenton, N. J., will expedite steel exports.

He said that the direness of the international situation and the need of American industry for defense program steel crystallized U. S. Steel's plans for an eastern seaboard mill. Plans were readied and put into effect when national focus was turned on the present crisis.

The Fairless Works will number among its products carbon high strength and alloy steel ingots, blooms, billets, slabs, bars, including bar-sized shapes, rounds, squares, concrete reinforcing bars, wire rods, light plates, standard steel pipe, hot and cold-rolled sheets and strip, vitrenamel sheets, blackplate, electrolytic and hot-dipped tinplate, and coal chemicals.

Breakdown by Products

The proposed plant will have an initial annual capacity to make 289,000 tons of cold-rolled sheets, 235,000 tons of hot-rolled sheets, 281,000 tons of standard pipe, 285,000 tons of bar products, and 170,000 tons of tin mill products.

Major construction at the Fairless plant will include: a coke and chemical plant, including two 85-oven byproduct coke batteries with a yearly potential of 916,000 tons of coke and more tonnages of coal chemical products; two blast furnaces with an annual capacity of 1,200,000 tons of pig iron; nine openhearths with an annual capacity of 1,800,000 tons of steel; an 80-in. hot strip mill and hot strip finishing facilities; finishing facilities for cold-rolled sheets and tinplate; a bloom-slab mill and auxiliary facilities, a billet mill and auxiliary facilities; and a bar mill with a size range from 3/8 in. to 2 in.

National Tube Facilities

U. S. Steel's subsidiary, National Tube Co., will build here facilities for making standard pipe, including a skelp mill, two Fretz Moon continuous butt weld pipe mills to produce annually 281,000 tons of 1/2-in. to 4-in. butt weld pipe; pipe galvanizing equipment, and a warehouse with a 30,000-ton capacity.

Ore docks to accommodate ocean-going ships—unloaders, ore

Turn to Page 382

October Finished Steel Shipments

As Reported to the American Iron & Steel Institute

STEEL PRODUCTS	Item	Current Month Carbon	Alloy	Stainless	Total	Pct cent of Total Shipments	To Date This Year Carbon	Alloy	Stainless	Total	Pct cent of Total Shipments
Ingots	1A	93,101	13,780	1,773	108,654	1.7	*580,631	101,554	14,031	*696,216	1.2
Blooms, slabs, billets, tube rounds, sheet bars, etc.	1B	154,321	42,854	1,001	198,176	3.0	1,419,917	354,320	8,203	1,782,440	3.0
Skelp	2	11,397	-	-	11,397	0.2	100,231	-	-	100,231	0.2
Wire rods	3	74,039	1,885	195	76,119	1.2	666,417	12,681	1,005	680,103	1.1
Structural shapes (heavy)	4	366,159	7,691	2	373,852	5.7	3,407,845	34,858	141	3,442,844	5.8
Steel piling	5	27,156	-	-	27,156	0.4	270,934	-	-	270,934	0.5
Plates	6	518,500	21,857	1,508	541,865	8.3	*4,420,991	147,570	9,576	4,578,137	7.7
Rails—Standard (over 60 lbs.)	7	137,607	27	-	137,634	2.1	1,454,256	311	-	1,454,567	2.4
Rails—All other	8	9,486	9	-	9,495	0.1	96,264	62	-	96,326	0.1
Joint bars	9	9,208	-	-	9,208	0.1	95,358	-	-	95,358	0.2
Tie plates	10	28,007	-.	-	28,007	0.4	352,642	-	-	352,642	0.6
Track spikes	11	12,710	-	-	12,710	0.2	117,867	-	-	117,867	0.2
Wheels (rolled & forged)	12	26,342	32	-	26,374	0.4	208,986	97	-	209,083	0.4
Axles	13	17,519	49	-	17,568	0.3	98,032	512	-	98,544	0.2
Bars—Hot rolled (incl. light shapes)	14	560,247	190,151	3,014	753,412	11.6	4,976,234	1,621,501	21,918	6,619,653	11.1
Bars—Reinforcing	15	159,332	-	-	159,332	2.5	1,369,533	260	-	1,369,793	2.3
Bars—Cold finished	16	130,584	24,464	3,662	158,710	2.4	1,115,143	205,978	24,247	1,345,368	2.3
Bars—Tool Steel	17	2,167	7,668	-	9,835	0.2	14,181	56,061	-	70,242	0.1
Standard pipe	18	238,147	89	3	238,239	3.7	2,152,618	339	14	2,152,971	3.6
Oil country goods	19	136,279	18,495	-	154,774	2.4	1,221,194	*186,759	-	*1,407,953	2.4
Line pipe	20	247,237	60	-	247,297	3.8	2,967,596	66	-	2,967,662	5.0
Mechanical tubing	21	54,373	21,101	503	75,977	1.2	430,888	171,865	2,929	605,682	1.0
Pressure tubing	22	20,277	2,293	806	23,376	0.4	175,953	20,253	6,345	202,551	0.3
Wire—Drawn	23	264,176	3,345	2,405	269,926	4.2	2,298,881	31,802	16,788	*2,347,471	3.9
Wire—Nails & staples	24	77,642	-	1	77,643	1.2	730,307	-	70	730,377	1.2
Wire—Barbed & twisted	25	20,521	-	-	20,521	0.3	195,570	-	-	195,570	0.3
Wire—Woven wire fence	26	42,368	-	-	42,368	0.7	406,361	-	-	406,361	0.7
Wire—Bale ties	27	8,463	-	-	8,463	0.1	67,927	-	-	67,927	0.1
Black plate	28	60,028	-	-	60,028	0.9	451,312	-	-	451,312	0.8
Tin & terne plate—hot dipped	29	154,727	-	-4	154,727	2.4	1,592,973	-	-	1,592,973	2.7
Tin plate—Electrolytic	30	232,782	-	-	232,782	3.6	2,382,456	-	-	2,382,456	4.0
Sheets—Hot rolled	31	675,905	27,080	1,902	704,887	10.8	*6,201,636	213,786	23,317	*6,438,739	10.8
Sheets—Cold rolled	32	805,214	12,617	11,365	829,196	12.8	*7,558,696	91,037	89,687	*7,739,420	13.0
Sheets—Galvanized	33	188,378	2,184	-	190,562	2.9	1,900,672	22,497	-	*1,923,169	3.2
Sheets—All other coated	34	20,937	-	-	20,937	0.3	193,547	-	-	193,547	0.3
Sheets—Enameling	35	25,530	-	-	25,530	0.4	216,569	-	-	216,569	0.4
Electrical sheets & strip	36	11,194	56,273	-	67,467	1.0	86,328	500,913	-	587,241	1.0
Strip—Hot rolled	37	221,294	5,742	594	227,630	3.5	1,879,128	37,204	6,361	1,922,693	3.2
Strip—Cold rolled	38	152,632	2,248	16,817	171,697	2.6	1,390,795	13,502	141,929	*1,546,226	2.6
TOTAL		5,995,986	461,994	45,551	6,503,531	100.0	*55,266,869	*3,825,788	366,561	59,459,218	100.0

During 1949 the companies included above represented 99.4% of the total output of finished rolled steel products as reported to the American Iron and Steel Institute.
*Revised.

DREVER

The hearth and side tile of this furnace, built by the Drever Company of Philadelphia, Pa., are made of CARBOFRAX silicon carbide tile. This is a single-end, under-fired furnace used for annealing, forming and general-purpose heat treating.

AMERICAN GAS

This gas-fired oven furnace is built by the American Gas Furnace Company of Elizabeth, N. J. It is designed to operate at temperatures up to 1800°F, for box carburizing, annealing large forgings, etc. The hearth, 42 inches wide by 85 inches long, is constructed of CARBOFRAX tile and is carried on CARBOFRAX supports.

In almost all heat-treating furnaces there are places where Super Refractories pay

IPSEN

This furnace contains a complete CARBOFRAX muffle. It is a gas-fired unit built by Ipsen Industries, Inc., of Rockford, Illinois, and is designed especially for bright annealing, hardening, carburizing and stress relieving.

For hearths and muffles where heat must travel *through* a refractory—for floors which must resist abrasion at high temperatures—for supports which must keep the floor flat and level under heavy loads—for burner ports and all other furnace parts subject to flame erosion, cracking or spalling — Super Refractories by CARBORUNDUM will pay their way, usually many times over.

A 40-page booklet, "Super Refractories for heat treatment furnaces," gives recommendations for many specific types of furnaces. A copy is yours for the asking.

THE CARBORUNDUM COMPANY

Dept. B-11, Refractories Div.   •   **Perth Amboy, New Jersey**

"Carbofrax" and "Carborundum" are registered trademarks which indicate manufacture by The Carborundum Company.

382

U. S. Steel's Fairless Works

(*Continued from page 380*)

bridges, and related equipment—will be built also. These will eventually receive ore cargoes from U. S. Steel's Cerro Bolivar ore mountain in Venezuela. Auxiliary equipment will include plant railways, roadways, utilities, etc.

Mr. Olds revealed that certificates of necessity had been issued by Washington to cover "a major part of the estimated cost of these facilities." Fairless Works will be operated by the newly-formed U. S. Steel Co., the result of a merger of four subsidiaries, and the pipe mill by National Tube. (See p. 388 for fast tax writeoff story.)

Swedish Steel Exports Rise; Pig Iron, Scrap Imports Also Up

London—During the first 9 months of 1950, Swedish exports of iron ore were 9,560,000 tons, compared with 10,340,000 tons for the same period in 1949.

Iron and steel exports increased from 114,600 tons to 130,600 tons, the rise being particularly marked in pig-iron, ferrous alloys and sponge iron.

Pig Iron Imports Up

The import of pig-iron increased from 67,500 tons to 73,-200 tons, while scrap imports remained at the 1949 level of about 120,000 tons. The import of rolled and forged iron and steel and cast-iron pipes, however, sank from 520,000 tons to 435,000 tons.

Pig-iron production totalled 585,700 tons; steel ingots and castings rose to 1,047,400 tons; rolled and forged iron and steel mounted to 671,600 tons.

To Build Swedish Limestone Works

Rattvik, Sweden—Claiming that Denmark and Finland have dominated the lime market in Scandinavia for too long, the Stora Kopparbergs A.B. will construct a limestone works near this city. Its products will feed, among other industries, the nearby Domnarvet Ironworks.

Use of Aluminum in Weapons Quickened by Start of Korean War

Pittsburgh — Aluminum use in weapons increased quickly after the start of Korean hostilities and will rise further as the defense program is spurred in 1951, said Roy A. Hunt, president of Aluminum Co. of America.

Although the aircraft industry will continue to be the major consumer, other defense applications will increase. Some aluminum uses are in the new 3.5-in. bore super bazooka, using about 13 lb; aircraft landing mats; tactical and floating bridges; radar towers and equipment; GI helmets; rockets and launching equipment; fire control towers, portable shelters; and mess kits.

Other Aluminum Uses

Other applications include: "invasion pipe" for fuel lines, containers for rocket fuel chemicals; ships and amphibious vehicles; aircraft armor; submarines and PT boats; unloading ramps and assault equipment; water and fuel tanks, field kitchen equipment, etc.

Mr. Hunt said that Alcoa had made progress in development of rolled aluminum "tapered sheet and plate" for plane wing skin panels and structures. Also developed was a new high-strength aluminum alloy rivet for bridges, railroad cars, and other structures.

New Dumas Steel Executive

Pittsburgh—David W. Thomas, formerly asst. general manager of sales, Jones & Laughlin Steel Corp., took over on Jan. 1 as executive vice-president and a director of Dumas Steel Corp. of Pennsylvania and its subsidiary companies, Dumas Steel Corp. of Illinois, New Jersey, Michigan.

Mr. Thomas also acquired a substantial interest in the company, which warehouses and distributes tin mill and sheet and strip products. He will also serve as general manager of M. G. Dumas & Sons, a partnership.

January 4, 1951

385

IT'S THE *Reliability* OF HEVI DUTY FURNACES

that assures
MORE PRODUCTION • LESS "DOWN-TIME" •
FEWER REJECTS • UNIFORM RESULTS

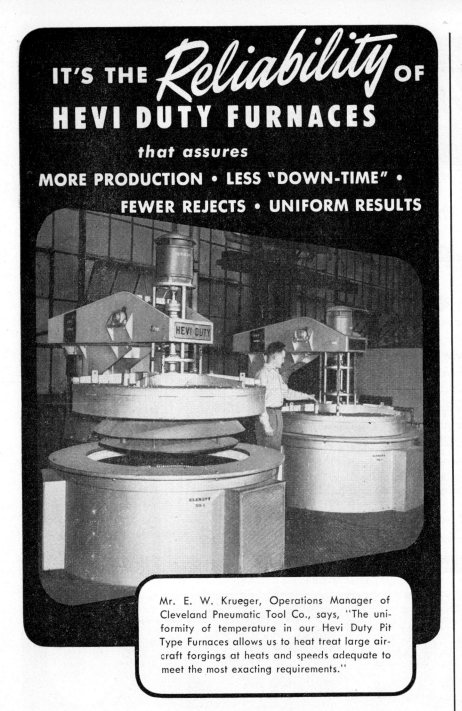

Mr. E. W. Krueger, Operations Manager of Cleveland Pneumatic Tool Co., says, "The uniformity of temperature in our Hevi Duty Pit Type Furnaces allows us to heat treat large aircraft forgings at heats and speeds adequate to meet the most exacting requirements."

These special pit type furnaces with a work space of 48" x 156" are typical of furnaces designed and built by Hevi Duty Electric Company to solve unusual heat treating problems.

The Hevi Duty return bend type heating elements are zoned to provide uniform temperatures in the entire depth of the work chamber.

For more information on how Hevi Duty Pit Type Furnaces can help you . . .

Write for Bulletin HD-1245

HEVI DUTY ELECTRIC COMPANY
HEAT TREATING FURNACES **HEVI·DUTY** ELECTRIC EXCLUSIVELY
DRY TYPE TRANSFORMERS — CONSTANT CURRENT REGULATORS
MILWAUKEE 1, WISCONSIN

• *News of Industry* •

Little Steel—No Profit

Grand Rapids, Mich.—Inability to obtain sheet steel supplies, and an 11-week strike of foundrymen were blamed for a loss during the fiscal year ended Sept. 30, 1950 by Hayes Mfg. Co. and its subsidiaries, American Engineering Co., Philadelphia, and Affiliated Engineering Co. Ltd., Montreal.

A net loss of $134,582 was sustained compared with net income of $1,111,706 in the previous year. The shortage in steel sheet necessitated use of certain types of steel which, because of high scrap loss, proved very costly, the company reported.

Pittsburgh Industry Level High

Pittsburgh — Business in the district showed a further increase last week, passing the previous all-time high of Dec. 11, 211.7, according to the University of Pittsburgh. Steel mills in the district operated at close to full capacity with 46 of the 47 available blast furnaces in operation.

Bituminous coal tonnage in Pennsylvania and electric power output reached new high records. Rail and river shipments reflected counter-seasonal increases, explained in part by movement of commodities accumulated during the period of heavy snow.

New motor car registrations last week were the lowest since early June; bank clearings showed a large counter-seasonal drop.

New Iridite Finish Saves Zinc

Baltimore — More plating production with less zinc is claimed for a new, low cost Iridite treatment for bright-type finishing of zinc plate in automatic machinery, according to Allied Research Products, Inc.

The protective chromate film can be produced on zinc plated coatings of less than .0001 in. thickness, the company claims. The coating, bluish bright or yellow iridescent, is flexible and can be applied in an immersion time of 20 seconds to a full minute. No bleaching operation is required.

January 4, 1951

387

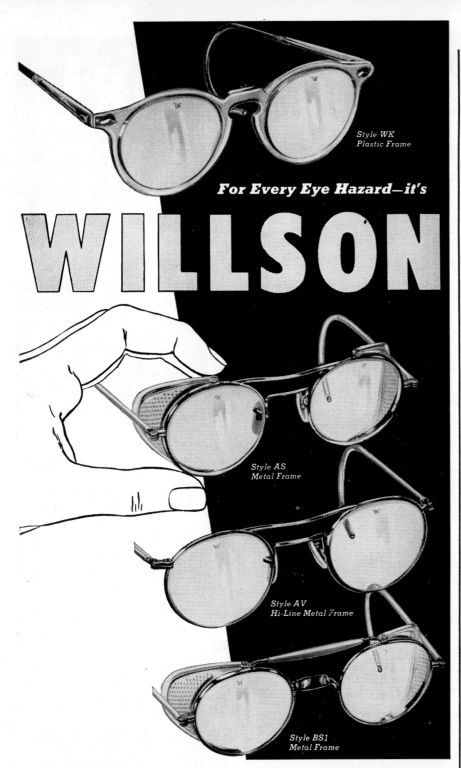

For Every Eye Hazard—it's

WILLSON

Style WK
Plastic Frame

Style AS
Metal Frame

Style AV
Hi-Line Metal Frame

Style BS1
Metal Frame

WILLSON*

Dependable Products Since 1870
*T.M. Reg. U.S. Pat. Off.

Protection • Comfort • Appearance

... only the most complete line of safety spectacles with Super-Tough* lenses gives you *all three* in metal or plastic frames. You'll find WILLSON safety spectacles an ideal combination of strength, comfort and good looks. And you need *all three* to get full cooperation from workers who must wear eye protection. See our new catalog for complete information. Get it from our nearest distributor, or write direct to WILLSON PRODUCTS, INC., 233 Washington St., Reading, Pennsylvania.

• News of Industry •

NSRB Grants 31 Plants Approval for Fast Tax Writeoffs

Washington—The National Security Resources Board announced approval of 31 other applications for fast writeoffs on expanded defense plant and equipment. The certificates apply to new production of malleable iron castings, barbed wire, precision steel castings, tungsten carbide, liquid oxygen, hydraulic pumps, tanks, fire brick, freight cars, ore-handling facilities, steel ingots, and other defense commodities.

Companies to which certificates have been issued, and amounts applied for, are as follows:

Albion Malleable Iron Co., Albion, Mich., $1,353,380; United Steel and Wire Co., Battle Creek, Mich., $30,600; Heintz Mfg. Co., Philadelphia, $204,000; Arwood Precision Casting Co., Brooklyn, N. Y., $94,-100; Capitol Foundry Co., Phoenix, Ariz., $1,452,500; Carboloy Co., Inc., Detroit, $2,-199,215 and $320,000; Blaw-Knox Co., Pittsburgh, $58,000; Thompson Products, Inc., Cleveland, $4,930,000; Air Reduction Co., Inc., New York, N. Y., $562,125; The New York Air Brake Co., Watertown, N. Y., $748,870; Dresser Industries, Inc., Bradford, Pa., $663,070; Merrill Brothers, Maspeth, N. Y., $141,934; Wheeling Steel Corp., Wheeling, W. Va., $8,750,000; Chrysler Corp., Detroit, Mich., $15,973,900.

Also: Harbison-Walker Refractories Co., Pittsburgh, $1,659,659 and $5,309,131; Thomas Steel Co., Warren, Ohio, $1,142,-417; Chesapeake and Ohio Railway Co., Cleveland, $9,941,184 and $31,587,000; Barden Corp., Danbury, Conn., $622,693; Lehigh and New England Railroad Co., Bethlehem, Pa., $2,275,000; National Tube Co., Pittsburgh, $46,631,420; Tennessee Coal, Iron and Railroad Co., Birmingham, Ala., $41,525,000; Geneva Steel Co., Salt Lake City, Utah, $4,263,000; Carnegie-Illinois Steel Corp., Pittsburgh, $351,414,-000; Roller Bearing Co. of America, Trenton, N. J., $1,453,961; Tennessee Products and Chemicals Corp., Nashville, Tenn., $805,961; Hofman Industries, Inc., Sinking Springs, Pa., $241,800; Jones and Laughlin Steel Corp., Pittsburgh, $2,000,-000; Washburn Wire Co., Phillipdale, R. I., $638,000; and Allegheny Ludlum Steel Corp., Brackenridge, Pa., $5,266,000.

Alcoa-CIO Agree on 2¢ Raise

Pittsburgh—An agreement within the range of the wage pattern recently established in the steel industry has been reached by Aluminum Co. of America and the United Steelworkers of America.

The agreement, affecting 17,000 Alcoa employees in 10 plants, includes (1) the addition of six paid holidays to the advance 10 pct wage increase which was effective the first payroll week in October, and (2) an additional 2¢ per hour at 4 southern plants at Alcoa, Tenn., Badin, N. C., Bauxite, Ark., and Mobile, Ala., and 3¢ per hour at Point Comfort, Tex., effective in the Dec. 11 payroll week.

January 4, 1951

Washington Asks Industry Advice on Price, Wage Controls

Washington — The government is asking officials of the steel, copper, and lead and zinc industries for advice on setting up price and wage controls.

The Economic Stabilization Agency invited leading producers to attend government-industry conferences on "stabilization problems" this week.

Economic Stabilization Administrator Alan Valentine and Price Stabilization Director Michael DiSalle said they would meet with representatives of the copper industry on January 3, the lead and zinc industry on January 4, and the steel industry on January 5.

Industrialists Invited

Steel products manufacturers invited to the price-wage conferences are: John A. Ingwersen, Armco Steel Corp.; H. B. Johnson, Atlantic Steel; Paul Mackall, Bethlehem Steel; F. S. Jones, Colorado Fuel & Iron Corp.; Walter Wiewel, Crucible Steel Co.; Joseph L. Block, Inland Steel; A. J. Hazlett, Jones & Laughlin Steel Corp.; James Hanks, Kaiser Co., Inc.; J. F. Wiese, Lukens Steel Co.; J. A. Henry, National Steel Corp.; A. C. Adams, Pittsburgh Steel Co.; J. M. Schlendorf, Republic Steel Corp.; David F. Austin, U. S. Steel Corp.; W. E. Watson, Youngstown Sheet & Tube; N. C. Reed, Wheeling Steel.

The copper manufacturers invited are: DeWitt Smith, Newmont Mining; James Douglas, Phelps Dodge Corp.; Simon Straus, American Smelting & Refining; Clarence Glass, Anaconda Copper Mining; C. R. Cox, president, Kennecott Copper Co.; and Morris Lacroix, Copper Range Co.

The lead and zinc manufacturers to which telegrams were sent are: Marshall Harvey, New Jersey Zinc Co.; Simon Straus, American Smelting & Refining Co.; Charles Ince, St. Joseph Lead Co.; Miles Zohler, Eagle Pitcher Lead Co.; Clarence Glass, Anaconda Copper Mining Co.

for Best Performance
KEOKUK ELECTRO-SILVERY

Pig for pig...car for car...the quality and uniformity
of Keokuk High Silicon Pig Iron never varies!

60 lb. pigs   **30 lb. pigs**   **12½ lb. piglets**

KEOKUK ELECTRO-METALS COMPANY
Keokuk, Iowa   •   *Wenatchee Division: Wenatchee, Washington*

SALES AGENTS: Miller and Company
332 S. Michigan Avenue, Chicago 4, Illinois • 3504 Carew Tower,
Cincinnati 2, Ohio • 407 North Eighth Street, St. Louis 1, Missouri

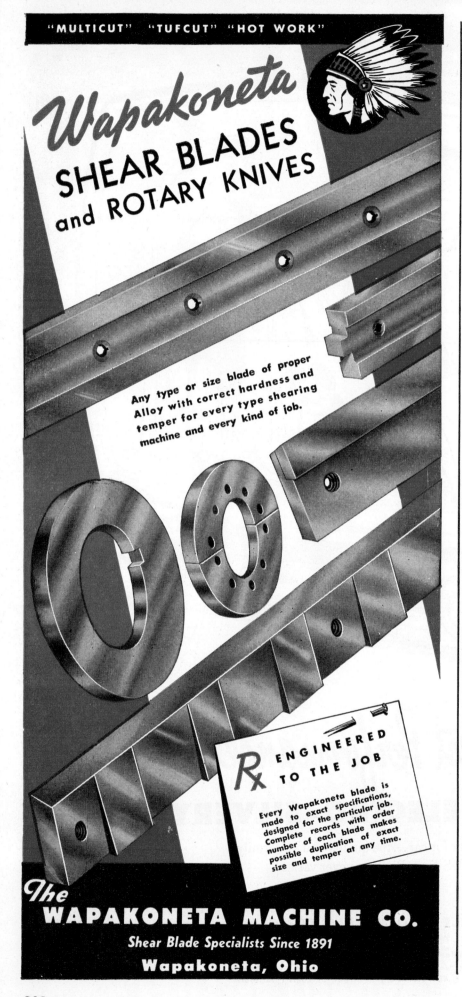

• *News of Industry* •

Steel Industry Will Meet The Acid Test in Defense Role

New York—The steel industry's 1950 record is significant and assuring, stated Walter S. Tower, president of the American Iron and Steel Institute, in his year-end statement.

U. S. producers made about 97 million tons of steel during the year, exceeding the previous record by about 7.5 million tons. This output was only 12 days short of 100 million tons and still it was below the abnormally high demand. By the end of 1952, planned expansions will bring steel capacity in this country to at least 110 million tons annually.

Payrolls Top 1949's

Since the end of World War II, steel companies have spent nearly $2.4 billion on their facilities. Steel payrolls exceeded $2.3 billion for the year, a rise of $300 million since 1949, reflecting increased wages and a zoom in employment from 602,000 to about 650,000 at the end of the year. Average hourly payments through most of the year were $1.72, which rose in December.

Most of the steel poured in 1950 went into consumer goods. Since 1946, steel companies have provided the steel for over 25 million new cars and trucks, 19 million new refrigerators, 4.5 million new homes, 54,000 miles of pipelines and numerous other items in record volume.

"The fact is that whether another world war at some early or later date decides the future fate of mankind, the United States can make all the steel needed for its military requirements and have a very generous amount left over for essential civilian uses," said Mr. Tower.

He pointed out, however, that other considerations might restrict civilian production.

Armament requirements for steel have been small and future requirements are not known, but the steel industry will meet the test, he said.

SWINDELL-DRESSLER

... constructs for **JONES & LAUGHLIN** the largest* coil sheet annealing furnace ever built.

Designed for high-speed production, the unit has every proved modern advantage—among them, high-capacity base fans plus high fuel input, contributing to outstandingly greater tonnage handled per shift. ● Let Swindell-Dressler consult with you on your own annealing-furnace requirements.

To the best of our knowledge, this 37'x19' furnace is the largest built to date in its field.

SWINDELL-DRESSLER Corporation

Designers and Builders of Modern Industrial Furnaces

Western Metal Congress Will Meet in California March 19-23

Cleveland — Papers by prominent metallurgical and mechanical engineers will highlight technical sessions of the American Society for Metals at the seventh Western Metal Congress and Exposition, March 19 to 23 in Oakland, Cal.

ASM, with 20 other national technical societies, will sponsor the 5-day educational meeting and display of new developments in producing, fabricating and applying metals.

Approximately 200 nationally known firms will display new developments. The ASM technical program, one of several sponsored by various societies, is under a committee headed by Earl R. Parker, University of California.

To Discuss Metals Problems

Sessions include papers by authorities, who will review frequent metallurgical problems.

More than 200 speakers are programmed for the Congress, with each ASM session devoted to an industry, such as aircraft, oil, large machinery, small equipment and shipbuilding. Other programs and exhibits will be devoted to mining, chemical and manufacturing industries.

Many officers and trustees of ASM will take part in the technical programs, including Walter E. Jominy, staff engineer, Chrysler Corp., and ASM president.

Seminar Subjects

Discussion subjects will include high temperature, low temperature, fatigue and weld failures. Speakers also will include: J. H. Hollomon, General Electric Co.; A. E. Focke, Diamond Chain Co.; D. S. Clark, California Institute of Technology; J. B. Dotson, Nordstrom Valve Co.

Another seminar will be devoted to failures resulting from general corrosion, stress-corrosion, corrosion-fatigue and corrosion problems in the aircraft and oil industries.

TRANTINYL

GUIDES
THE STEEL
INDUSTRY

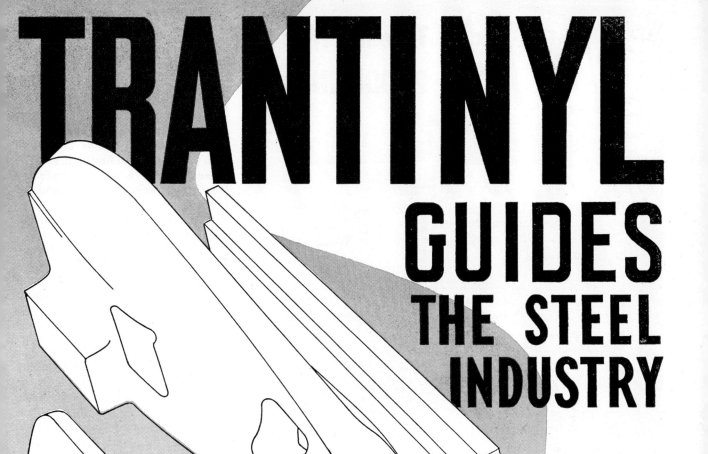

Straightening Machine Guides
for Rounds and Pipe

YOUNGSTOWN ALLOY CASTING CORP., YOUNGSTOWN, OHIO

Production · Quality · Yield

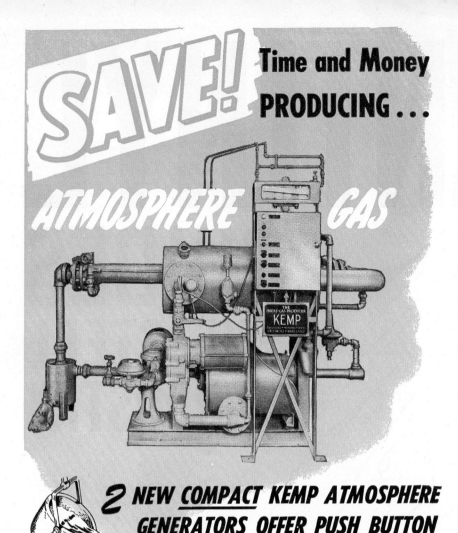

SAVE! Time and Money PRODUCING... ATMOSPHERE GAS

2 NEW COMPACT KEMP ATMOSPHERE GENERATORS OFFER PUSH BUTTON STARTING, FOOL-PROOF OPERATION

IF YOU need a compact source of atmosphere gas, *save time and money*, specify Kemp! Two new Kemp Atmosphere Generators (models MIHE-1 and 2) deliver 1000 and 2000 cfh respectively. Both offer all features of larger equipment: push button starting, automatic fire check, flow meter, etc. . . and assure that you get *same analysis* gas from 1% to 100% of capacity.

FOOL PROOF OPERATION

Kemp Generators burn ordinary gas just as it comes from the mains. A famous Kemp Carburetor, part of each installation, assures *complete combustion* without "tinkering" to produce

a clean, chemically inert gas containing 88% nitrogen, 12% CO_2 . . . a gas so pure it is used *without further processing* in copper annealing and in the manufacture of *aspirin* and *laboratory chemicals*, fine paints and a host of other products.

WRITE FOR DATA

Whether you need inerts for purging, fire protection, blanketing or any steel application . . . specify Kemp. For technical information write for Bulletin 1-11. *To find out how you can benefit:* tell us how you produce atmosphere gas now; we'll show you how Kemp can solve your problem. *Mail Coupon today!*

KEMP OF BALTIMORE

ATMOSPHERE GAS GENERATORS

CARBURETORS
BURNERS
FIRE CHECKS
ATMOSPHERE GENERATORS
ADSORPTIVE DRYERS
METAL MELTING UNITS
SINGEING EQUIPMENT
SPECIAL EQUIPMENT

THE C. M. KEMP MFG. CO., Dept. C-1
405 E. Oliver St., Baltimore 2, Md.

Gentlemen: Send me information on Kemp Generators. I am interested in Bulletin 1-11; data on larger equipment.

Name ....
Company ....
Address ....
City .... Zone ...... State ....

Defense, Consumer Spending Expected to Up Business Volume

New York—Stepped up defense ordering and larger consumer purchasing power are expected to boost business volume from 5 to 15 pct during the first half of 1951, according to a survey conducted by the Commerce and Industry Assn.

Of the 305 New York firms questioned, more than half expected a rise in volume of business. Of the others, 24 pct expect business volume to remain about the same, and only 18 pct anticipate a decline during the coming year.

Impact of Defense Spending

The impact of defense spending looms as the biggest factor in the business future of concerns questioned. The firms, employing about 235,000 persons, represent a cross-section of industry, and include machinery and metal products, paper, publishing, textiles, foods, chemicals, plastics, export, import, insurance, finance, real estate and transportation.

Barring a roll-back in prices, business almost unanimously looks for an increase in prices. More than 76 pct expect price rises of 5 to 25 pct. Business volume in 1950 equalled or was higher than 1949 volume more than 81 pct of the firms reported.

NE War Work to $138 Million

Boston—Defense contracts let in New England since beginning of the Korean conflict have climbed to $138 million, with the November total reaching a record $30 million, according to the New England Council.

Recent top-dollar contracts were the $2 million award to Bath Iron Works, Bath, Me., for conversion of two destroyers; an award of $1,635,250 to the Atlantic Parachute Co. of Lowell, Mass., and an award of $1,964,250 to the American Woolen Co.

An order for 43,137,000 plastic spoons was placed with the Van Brode Milling Co. of Clinton, Mass.

High-production set up to drill 19 holes in 5 sides of pump housing at the Heil Co, Milwaukee. 8 17" Drill Press heads (5 standard 2-spindle heads, and 2 with special 3- and 5-spindle heads) mounted on a special table with suitable controls make up this low-cost machine.

DELTA MILWAUKEE ®

Delta® Drilling from every Direction!

Build your own special equipment at low cost around Delta accuracy and flexibility!

Delta 17" Drill Press

Complete selection to meet every need — with the right chuck capacity, the right speed . . . in floor and bench types . . . single spindles, multi-spindle batteries, individual heads for special set-ups . . . power-feed — and a complete line of accessories for every model. The same selection in 14" drill presses. All told, 144 different models at prices from $77.50 to $2,892.50.

When you think of drilling think of Delta! Your own imagination plus the amazing adaptability of standard Delta drill presses or components can crack the toughest problem. Look what the Heil Co. did (above) with 8 Delta heads! One operator drills 19 holes in a casting—in a floor to floor time of 2.6 minutes! And at a fraction of the cost of a special-purpose machine, or a multi-station operation!

Do the same in your shop! The sealed, lubricated-for-life ball bearings in Delta drill heads let you drill from all directions — vertical, sideways, upside down, at all angles — without lubrication problems.

Send for complete details—and plan your jobs around the versatility of dependable Delta Tools — high in quality, low in cost! Delta's engineering service is always ready to help you.

Sold only through authorized dealers — available on easy time payments. . . . Look for the name of your Delta dealer under "Tools" in the classified section of your telephone directory.

DELTA POWER TOOL DIVISION

Rockwell
Manufacturing Company
MILWAUKEE 1, WISCONSIN

Delta • Multiplex • Crescent • Homecraft

From the world's most complete line

First in Selection!
First in Quality!
First in Value!

Free...

6 TIMES A YEAR

The Power Tool Journal—packed with detailed job data, fully illustrated — handbook of time- and money-saving shop ideas!

M-51

Tear out this coupon and mail today!

Delta Power Tool Division
ROCKWELL MANUFACTURING CO.
631A E. Vienna Ave., Milwaukee 1, Wisconsin

Send me free — ☐ The Power Tool Journal — 6 times a year.
☐ Catalogs and bulletins on complete Delta line.

Name..
Title..
Company..
Address..
City.. (......) State..............

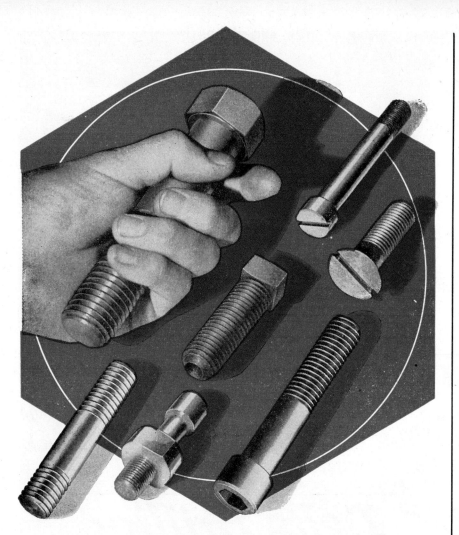

You profit by CLEVELAND'S policy of Specialization

Keeping "expert" in producing only Cap Screws, Set Screws and Milled Studs—plus "specials" made to customers' designs—is assurance that Cleveland's policy of Specialization brings you *Top Quality* Fasteners. We concentrate on making a *few* items *well*. . . . It's important, too, that by specializing we can make the much abused word "Service" really *mean* something. . . . It pays you to specify and buy Cleveland *Top Quality* Fasteners.

THE CLEVELAND CAP SCREW COMPANY
2917 East 79th Street, Cleveland 4, Ohio
Warehouses: Chicago, Philadelphia, New York, Providence

ORIGINATORS OF THE
KAUFMAN **DOUBLE EXTRUSION** PROCESS

Specialists for more than 30 years in

CAP SCREWS, SET SCREWS, MILLED STUDS

Ask your jobber for Cleveland Fasteners

Giant Motors, Air Compressor Ordered for New USAF Wind Tunnel

Pittsburgh—A U. S. Air Force order for $20 million worth of electrical equipment for the new jet engine and guided missile wind tunnel to be built at Tullahoma, Tenn., has been received by Westinghouse Electric Corp.

Two of the four motors will be the most powerful in the world, exceeding the 65,000 hp rating of motors in service at Grand Coulee Dam, Washington. The air compressor, to be built at Sunnyvale, Calif., will produce an air current faster than the speed of sound

Ask Stainless Pipe Standard

New York — Manufacturers of stainless steel pipe, meeting with representatives of the chemical industry at the American Standards Assn., have requested inclusion of Schedule 5S, for lightweight stainless steel pipe and fittings in an American Standard. Nominal wall thickness under schedule 5S are: ½ in. to 2 in. diameter tubing, 0.065 in.; 2½ in. to 4 in., 0.083 in.; 5 in. to 8 in., 0.109 in.; 10 in., 0.134 in.; 12 in. dia., 0.165 in.

Cook New President of EITA

Philadelphia — C. B. Cook of Cleveland has been elected president of the Electric Industrial Truck Assn. Elmer F. Twyman was elected vice-president; William Van C. Brandt was reelected secretary and treasurer.

Clark Equipment Co. of Battle Creek, Mich., was admitted to membership in the association, it was announced.

Katy Buys 11 Diesel-Electrics

St. Louis—Purchase of 11 diesel-electric locomotives by the Missouri Kansas Texas R.R. has been announced. Two 1600 hp units were purchased from American Locomotive Co., five 2200 hp units from Electro Motive Div. of General Motors Corp., and one 1600 hp unit from Fairbanks Morse Co.

---

15 blast furnaces in the U.S. have each produced over 1,000,000 tons of iron on a single "National" carbon lining ... and are still going strong!

BLAST FURNACE LININGS • BRICK • CINDER NOTCH LINERS • CINDER NOTCH PLUGS • SKIMMER BLOCKS • SPLASH PLATES • RUNOUT TROUGH LINERS • MOLD PLUGS • TANK HEATERS

U. S. Steel Limestone Units Merge; New Offices in Detroit

Pittsburgh—Merger of two subsidiaries of United States Steel Corp., Pittsburgh Limestone Corp. and Michigan Limestone & Chemical Co., as a single operating subsidiary has been announced by Benjamin F. Fairless, U. S. Steel president. The merger was effective Jan. 2, 1951.

New executive offices will be established in Detroit. District operating headquarters will continue at Rogers City, Mich., New Castle, Pa., and Buffalo, N. Y.

Irvin L. Clymer, head of both present subsidiaries, will become president of the new company. Other officers are: J. P. Kinville, assistant to president and treasurer; H. S. Lewis, vice-president, operations; C. F. Platz, vice-president, sales; H. R. Baltzersen, controller and assistant secretary; John G. Patterson II, secretary.

TTMA Annual Convention Jan. 21-23

Washington — Leland James, president of the American Trucking Assn. and head of Consolidated Freightways, Inc., of Portland, Oregon, will be the feature speaker at the annual convention of the Truck-Trailer Mfrs. Assn. in the Edgewater Gulf Hotel, Edgewater Park, Miss., January 21-23.

Federal officials handling transportation problems have been invited to attend the conference and give their views on over-the-road freight problems.

Willys Truck Sales Climb

Toledo—November sales of sedan delivery and half-ton trucks by Willys-Overland Motors, Inc., were 23 pct more than October and 20 pct over November of last year, according to Lyman W. Slack, vice-president of distribution.

Dealers' 10-day reports for the middle of the month indicated sales approximately two and a half times as great as those of the first 10 days of November. Sales continued to climb during the remainder of the month.

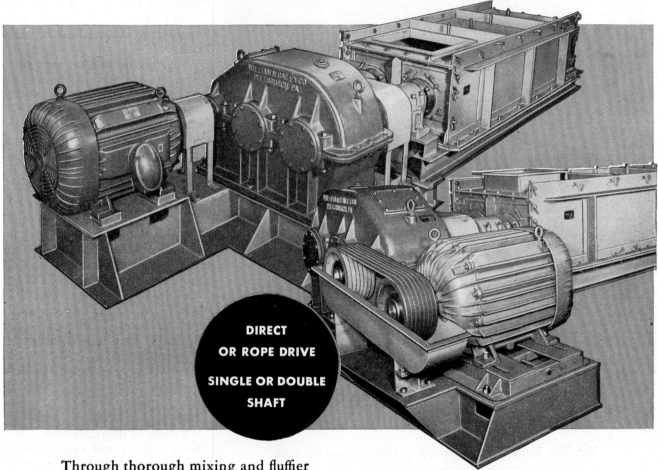

VAN DORN

Weldments Feature

★ Strength
★ Uniformity
★ Economy

Yes, Van Dorn Weldments are widely known for their outstanding quality—for they are backed by Van Dorn's complete fabricating facilities . . . experienced design engineers . . . specially trained workmen . . . 77 years' experience in metal working.

Consult us about your requirements—no obligation, of course. The Van Dorn Iron Works Co., 2685 East 79th Street, Cleveland 4, Ohio.

Send For
FREE WELDMENT BOOK
● *Profusely illustrated; describes the many advantages of weldments, and Van Dorn's extensive facilities.*

short 'n sweet...

SPERRY GYROSCOPE COMPANY ECONOMICALLY USES 150-TON H-P-M PRESS ON SHORT RUNS FOR MORE THAN A HUNDRED DIFFERENT DRAWING JOBS!

● Versatile and yet economical production is an accomplished fact in the pressed metal department of Sperry Gyroscope Company's Lake Success, N. Y., Plant.

With an H-P-M 150-ton FASTRA-VERSE Press, Sperry handles runs of 300 pieces per set-up on 101 different jobs—jobs that vary greatly in size, depth of draw, and gauge of metal (2SO, 3SO or 52SO aluminum sheet is used).

The big factor in this production picture can be found in the exclusive operational features of the H-P-M press itself. H-P-M's FASTRAVERSE hydraulic power system provides quick and easy adjustment of press speeds, strokes and pressures to suit each individual die set-up and part to be drawn . . . cutting set-up time to a minimum . . . protecting dies . . . and assuring parts production with negligible scrap loss.

Find out about versatile H-P-M FAST-RAVERSE Presses today—and how they can cut costs out of your present production methods— an H-P-M Engineer will gladly provide you with complete details.

Write today for your free copy of Bulletin 5005 which completely describes H-P-M FASTRAVERSE and other special purpose H-P-M Presses.

HPM
THE HYDRAULIC PRESS MFG. CO.

1006 MARION ROAD • MT. GILEAD, OHIO, U. S. A.

Makers of Presses for the Metal Working and Processing Industries - Plastic Molding Presses - Die Casting Machines - Hydraulic Pumps, Valves and Power Units

Wyandotte  for
heavy duty immersion cleaning

For heavy duty immersion cleaning you need Wyandotte W.L.G.* It conditions the water, removes fabricating compounds, rinses freely.

Try W.L.G. for still tank cleaning of any ferrous metal and some non-ferrous metals. (Such as copper and most copper alloys but NOT aluminum or its alloys.) Try W.L.G., too, for tumble barrel cleaning and in rotary type washing machines. It will do an excellent job for you prior to vitreous enameling, barrel plating of zinc or cadmium, dip type phosphate treatment before painting, or overhaul cleaning of engine parts, etc. Experienced Wyandotte Representatives are available. When you need technical assistance in your shop, call the nearest Wyandotte man.   *Reg. U. S. Pat. Off.

WYANDOTTE

Heavy duty immersion cleaner

- **Dissolves completely**
- **Conditions hard water**
- **Removes mineral and saponifiable fabricating compounds**
- **Cleans ferrous and non-ferrous metals**
- **Rinses freely**
- **Has long life in solution**

"Cleaning the World"

THE WYANDOTTE LINE—products for burnishing and burring, vat, electro, steam gun, washing machine, and emulsion cleaning, paint stripping, acid pickling, related surface treatments and spray booth compounds. *An all-purpose floor absorbent:* Zorball—**in fact, specialized products for every cleaning need.**

Wyandotte Chemicals Corporation
WYANDOTTE, MICHIGAN
Service Representatives in 88 Cities

Wyandotte
REG. U. S. PAT. OFF.

---

stops to provide pressure relief. A 220-440 v 5 hp motor has a magnetic brake. Water and electrical services are integral with the machine. *Grav-i-Flo Corp.*
For more data insert No. 37 on postcard, p. 37.

Ductility Tester
Detects surface and sub-surface imperfections in deep-drawing steel.

A new ductility testing machine provides a total capacity of 250,000-lb pressure and incorporates a 5-in. diam penetrator. Purpose of the unit is to detect surface and sub-surface imperfections in deep-

drawing steel over a comparatively large area. The machine is motorized, hydraulically operated and has separate controls for clamping the sample and for regulating the penetrating pressure. Equipped with a set of three dies for use with different gages of metal, the machine will test material up to $\frac{1}{4}$ in. thick. *Steel City Testing Machines, Inc.*
For more data insert No. 38 on postcard, p. 37.

Master Control System
Electronically operated, for combustion and process control.

A new electronic master control system, called Telemaster, provides such automatic control features as complete freedom of control centralization, simplified and smaller control panels, elimination of transmission lags and greater accuracy and speed of response. The use of an electronic link, connecting mas-

A Thrrrifty Thought

Have you considered using Boron as an alloying agent to help conserve the critical materials . . . Chrome, Manganese, Nickel and Molybdenum?

Borosil is a proven and economical alloy for making Boron additions. Borosil consists of 3 to 4% Boron, 40 to 45% Silicon and the remainder Iron. This diluted Boron alloy is ideally suited for ladle additions.

Borosil is immediately available in following sizes to meet your requirements . . . Standard lump, 2" x Down, ½" x Down, and 8 Mesh x Down.

THOMAS *Flexible* ALL METAL COUPLINGS
FOR POWER TRANSMISSION • REQUIRE NO MAINTENANCE

Patented Flexible Disc Rings of special steel transmit the power and provide for parallel and angular misalignment as well as free end float.

Thomas Couplings have a wide range of speeds, horsepower and shaft sizes: ½ to 40,000 HP — 1 to 30,000 RPM.

Specialists on Couplings for more than 30 years

PATENTED FLEXIBLE DISC RINGS

BACKLASH FRICTION WEAR and CROSS-PULL are eliminated *LUBRICATION IS NOT REQUIRED!*

THE THOMAS PRINCIPLE GUARANTEES PERFECT BALANCE UNDER ALL CONDITIONS OF MISALIGNMENT.

• • •

NO MAINTENANCE PROBLEMS.

• • •

ALL PARTS ARE SOLIDLY BOLTED TOGETHER.

Write for the latest reprint of our Engineering Catalog.

THOMAS FLEXIBLE COUPLING CO.
WARREN, PENNSYLVANIA

ter to actuator, eliminates the distance problem created by centralization. The Telemaster combines the null-balance principle of detection and the electronic transmission of control information, to form a

highly responsive control system that is said to be remarkably fast in completing adjustments, regardless of the distances involved. The benchboard control panel illustrated is evidence of the smaller and more compact panel units. This benchboard contains all the elements of the master control. *Republic Flow Meters Co.*
For more data insert No. 39 on postcard, p. 37.

Pyrometer Equipment
Temperature indication and control; protection for furnaces and ovens.

New pyrometer equipment offers accurate temperature indication, close temperature control of industrial processes and protection for furnaces, ovens and kilns. The

complete line consists of flush or surface-mounted indicators, controllers and protectors. The instrument is said to have a calibrated accuracy within ¾ of 1 pct of full scale. A 7-in. scale, fitted with an anti-glare cover, indicates any change in temperature equivalent to 1/10 of 1 pct of full scale.

HAVE YOU HEARD

how Farrel® can help solve your Rolling Mill problems?

For Example:

WITH FARREL ROLL GRINDERS—Reports from users indicate that the latest type Farrel machines regrind rolls in record time. In addition, they find that the rolls are accurately ground with a perfect surface free from marks of any kind. Faster grinding means increased productive capacity of the machine and lower labor cost per roll ground.

WITH FARREL ROLLING MILLS—For almost a century, Farrel mills have been helping to solve rolling mill production problems. Designed to meet specific requirements, they are built in a wide range of types and sizes for rolling nonferrous rods, strips or sheets, metal foils and cold strip steel. The company also designs and manufactures the reduction gear drives and pinion stands, coilers and special handling equipment required to make each installation a complete unit.

WITH SPEED REDUCERS FOR AUXILIARY DRIVES—Farrel speed reducers have been developed for continuous, trouble-free operation under difficult service conditions. Without sacrificing the advantages of general standards, the design of these units permits an engineering freedom in proportioning gears, shafts, bearings and even some housing dimensions to meet specific load, speed and service requirements. This flexibility has resulted in the solution of innumerable application problems.

INFORMATION and engineering consultation regarding any of the products mentioned on this page are available, without obligation.

FARREL-BIRMINGHAM COMPANY, INC., ANSONIA, CONN.
Plants: Ansonia and Derby, Conn., Buffalo, N. Y. *Sales Offices:* Ansonia, Buffalo, New York, Akron, Pittsburgh, Chicago, Los Angeles, Houston

━━━━━━━ FARREL® ROLLING MILL MACHINERY ━━━━━━━

Rolls • Rolling Mills • Rod Mill Tables and Manipulating Equipment • Universal Mill Spindles • Rod Coilers • Gears • Mill Pinions • Pinion Stands • Gear Drives of any Capacity • Flexible Couplings • Roll Grinding Machines • Roll Calipers • Lead Presses for Pipe or Rod

Farrel-Birmingham®

FB-645

Improve Quenching and You Get Better Heat Treating

Your Department can have a better arrangement with Niagara Equipment that saves much space and increases your production.

This quench bath cooler gives you control of temperature and pays for itself quickly with water savings

● The NIAGARA AERO HEAT EXCHANGER transfers the heat from the quench bath to atmospheric air by evaporative cooling. It never fails to remove the heat at the rate of input, giving you real control of the quench bath temperature. This prevents flashing of oil quenches. In all cases it improves physical properties, saves loss of your product from rejections and gives you faster production, increasing your heat treating capacity. You can put heat back into the quench bath to save the losses of a "warm-up" period.

Savings in piping, pumping and power as well as great savings in cooling water return the cost of the equipment to you in a short time. The Niagara Aero Heat Exchanger saves nearly all of the water consumed by conventional cooling methods.

For the complete story of other benefits and savings, write for Bulletin 96.

NIAGARA BLOWER COMPANY

Over 35 Years Service in Industrial Air Engineering

Dept. IA, 405 Lexington Ave.   **New York 17, N. Y.**

Experienced District Engineers in all Principal Cities

---

production ideas
Continued

Immediate control action follows. The indicating device is a milli-voltmeter, connected to a thermo-couple on the furnace. The controller provides on-off action of the final control element by a relay, mercury switch, or contactor through which electric power is supplied to the furnace or oven. The protector is used in conjunction with and to protect against the possible failure of a separate precision controller. *General Electric Co.*

For more data insert No. 40 on postcard, p. 37.

Ac Arc Welders
Designed for heavy duty, 'round-the-clock production welding.

The new industrial welders are available in sizes 200, 300 and 400 amp. capacities. One of the key construction features of the new 80

Series welders is the use of Hipersil steel transformer cores, which provide one-third greater flux-carrying capacity, said to reduce power consumption and operating costs. *Marquette Mfg. Co.*

For more data insert No. 41 on postcard, p. 37.

Steam Spray Gun
Dry, super-heated steam is used as an atomizing medium to heat paint.

A complete line of equipment for spraying paint with steam includes a new spray gun that uses super-heated steam instead of compressed air. The use of steam as an atomizing medium to heat finishing materials makes it possible to use materials of higher viscosity and allows the application of heavier coats without sagging or running. New insulation and radiation design features dissipate the heat caused by the steam in the gun, enabling the operator to use the gun continuously in comfort with bare hands. Hose supports for steam and mate-

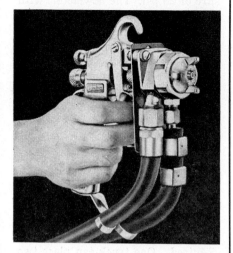

rials reduce the downward torque on the spray head, making it more easily balanced and less tiring for the operator. Other features include a built-in finger guard, an adjustable fluid needle and a spray head with one-piece, easy-to-clean steam cap and fluid nozzle. *American Brake Shoe Co., Kellog Div.*
For more data insert No. 42 on postcard, p. 37.

Regulator-Flowmeter

For the measurement of argon flow.

A new, direct-reading combination regulator and flowmeter, R-502, is designed for use with

Heliarc welding, argon metal arc welding, and other related processes. The instrument has a new three-stage regulator that maintains constant inlet pressure and

On cut-off jobs...
You benefit 4 ways with Wells Saws

1. Fast, continuous cutting action.
2. Greater accuracy on each job.
3. More pieces per length of stock.
4. Greater overall economy.

Illustrated is the popular Wells No. 8 with wet cutting system.

Our 25th year of service

HORIZONTAL band sawing is the modern, cost-cutting way to handle cut-off jobs . . . and Wells Saws are the leaders among horizontal metal cutting band saw machines. Simplicity of design means fewer moving parts and easy operation. Ruggedly built to increase productivity and reduce cutting costs, a Wells Saw pays for itself quickly and will give you years and years of dependable, satisfactory service.

BIG JOBS or LITTLE Jobs . . . There's a "WELLSAW" to meet your Metal Cutting Requirements. Check the table below and write for complete descriptive information or a job demonstration.

MODEL	49 A	No. 5	No. 8	No. 12
Capacity in inches: Rounds	3½	5	8	12¾
Rectangular	3½ x 6	5 x 10	8 x 16	12 x 16
Blade speeds, ft. per min.	54, 100, 190	60, 90, 130	60, 90, 130	50, 100, 150
Motor Size	1/6 H.P.	⅓ H.P.	½ H.P.	¾ H.P.
Floor Space, in inches	16½ x 38	21 x 50	24 x 72	32 x 78
Wet cutting system	No	Yes	Yes	Yes

Automatic stock projection available for Nos. 8 and 12.

Products by Wells are Practical

Wells METAL CUTTING BAND SAWS

WELLS MANUFACTURING CORPORATION
202 WASHINGTON AVE., THREE RIVERS, MICH.

414b

---

accurate flow. Factory presetting of the second stage of the regulator delivers argon at a constant pressure of 20 psi. The flowmeter, with a finger-tip control adjusting valve, permits accurate, steady flow rates up to 60 cu ft per hr. The same design features are incorporated in a second regulator-flowmeter, the R-503, for use with helium. *Linde Air Products Co.*
For more data insert No. 43 on postcard, p. 37.

Fingerlift Attachment
Eliminates pallets in handling crates; results in manpower saving.

A fingerlift-equipped electric truck handles crates without the use of pallets and no manpower other than the lift truck driver is required. One truck can place two or three crates at a time depending on size of crates. Design of

the attachment embodies a series of spring loaded fingers mounted on a horizontal shaft so that slight pressure on the tips of any of the finger causes them to retract by tilting backwards. A vertical apron below this shaft serves as a rest when the mast is tilted back. The whole assembly is mounted on a side shift mechanism. *A. O. Smith Corp.*
For more data insert No. 44 on postcard, p. 37.

Quench-Conveyer
For continuous heat treating of metal parts and forgings.

A quenching-and-conveying unit is designed for heat-treating individual pieces. The oil in the tank is recirculated and cooled. The belt, of metal, allows the quenched parts to drain as they move up the inclined conveyer, that is driven by a self-contained power unit. Cleats or flights can be attached. Overall di-

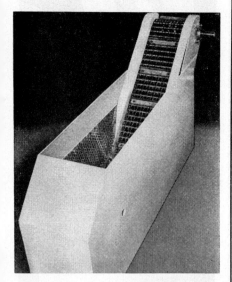

mensions are 8 ft long x 2 ft wide x 4 ft high. Larger quench-conveyers can be built for larger, heavier parts. *Klaas Machine & Mfg. Co.*
For more data insert No. 45 on postcard, p. 37.

Vertical Mill Attachment
Precision and ruggedness are the keynote of the unit's construction.

Retaining all the high performance features of the original design, a new improved streamlined, vertical mill attachment is versatile according to the manufacturer—taking the place and doing the work of

many specialized machines. Safety for the operator is provided by a protecting hood over power transmission parts. *Marvin Machine Products, Inc.*
For more data insert No. 46 on postcard, p. 37.
Resume Your Reading on Page 41

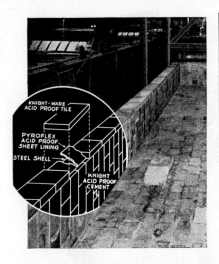

This Tank Will Live to a Ripe Old Age

It's PYROFLEX-Constructed

Pickling tanks lead a tough life. The Pyroflex - Constructed Pickling Tank above is in use in a continuous strip steel line in a large Ohio steel mill. It is subject to constant attack by acids, steam and other corrosive agents. To make this tank completely corrosion proof, Knight engineers installed Pyroflex sheet lining heat bonded to the steel shell, then covered with acid-proof brick set in Knight acid-proof cement. The result is a tank completely resistant to this highly corrosive type of service.

However, Pyroflex Construction is not always composed of these same materials. In designing various corrosion proof constructions such as tanks, chlorinating towers, floors, sewers, fume ducts, etc. Knight engineers may incorporate ceramics, carbon, glass, plastics or any other materials best suited to the individual situation. Consequently Pyroflex-Constructed units live to a ripe old age with less "down time" and lower maintenance costs.

When making inquiry regarding Pyroflex Constructions, please specify type of equipment in which interested, service conditions involved, etc.

MAURICE A. KNIGHT

301 Kelly Ave., Akron 9, Ohio

Acid and Alkali-proof Chemical Equipment

---

publications

Continued from Page 36

Major trends have been brought up to date. *United States Steel Supply Co.*

For free copy insert No. 9 on postcard, p. 37.

Rubber Testers

A summary of the activities of the V. L. Smithers Laboratories in testing rubber, rubber-like materials and compounding ingredients is presented in a new 16-p. brochure covering the scope of the laboratory. The booklet tells how this organization develops new compounds, tests suitability of raw materials for rubber compounds, performs physical and chemical testing to any specification, and can do limited manufacturing of small parts during development. *V. L. Smithers Laboratories.*

For free copy insert No. 10 on postcard, p. 37.

Cuts Waste Motion

How the Lull Hydraulic Traveloader eliminates a lot of the waste motions of backing, turning, stopping and starting in materials handling is described in a new 12-p. bulletin. The unit is shown to combine the features of a fork-lift truck, transporter, yard crane, spooled cable reeler and strip steel carrier into one unit. A few examples of the many jobs performed are shown. *Lull Mfg. Co.*

For free copy insert No. 11 on postcard, p. 37.

Versatile Lift Truck

Specifications for the new Model 230 Mercury Jeep, a tilting-tiering lift truck with 2000 lb capacity, are presented in a new 4-p. folder. The truck features exceptional maneuverability and unusual stability, as shown in the bulletin; dimensions and other details are also listed. *Mercury Mfg. Co.*

For free copy insert No. 12 on postcard, p. 37.

Welding Alloys, Fluxes

A new 32-p. pocket-size booklet serves as a buyers guide to the complete line of All-State alloys and fluxes for welding, brazing, soldering, cutting and tinning. It tells everything a buyer needs to know to select the particular alloys and fluxes that best meet his needs. All

(Turn to Page 416)

Greater Tonnage
Per Edge of Blade

A

AMERICAN
SHEAR KNIFE CO.
HOMESTEAD · PENNSYLVANIA

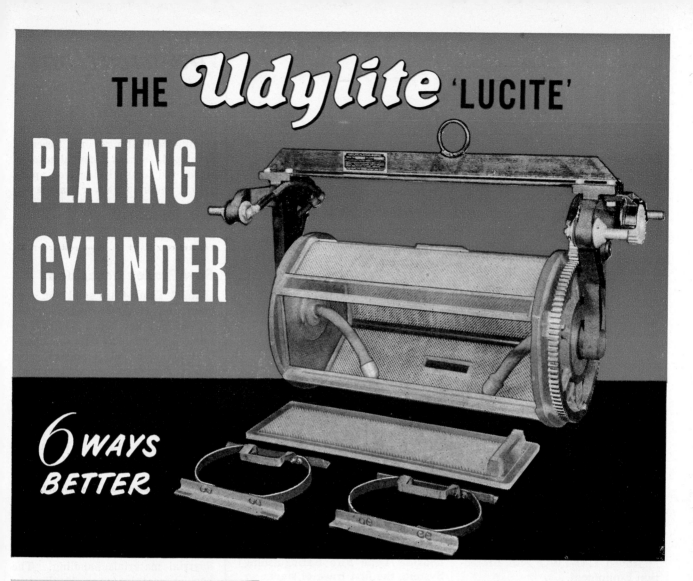

sleep's unaffected...
his factory's protected

Worry! Fret! Loss of sleep thinking about fire cutting into production time ... destroying valuable records ... costing lives of employees ... all are anxieties of the past when your factory's protected with modern, approved C-O-TWO Fire Protection Equipment.

For example, the new C-O-TWO Low Pressure Carbon Dioxide Type Fire Extinguishing Systems keynote flexibility to meet your particular fire protection needs. Flammable liquids, electrical equipment, storage and manufacturing processes can all be made firesafe from a single low pressure carbon dioxide storage tank . . . capacities range from one to fifty tons of fire killing carbon dioxide. If fire should strike the fast-acting, non-damaging, non-conducting carbon dioxide extin-

guishes the blaze in seconds . . . no water damage, no lingering odors.

Further, when a C-O-TWO Smoke or Heat Fire Detecting System is used in combination with a C-O-TWO Low Pressure Carbon Dioxide Type Fire Extinguishing System, the first trace of smoke or spark of fire in a protected area immediately sounds an alarm . . . then the fire quenching carbon dioxide is readily released into the threatened area.

So, whatever your fire protection problem, let an expert C-O-TWO Fire Protection Engineer help you in planning complete and up-to-date fire protection facilities now. Write us today . . . tell us about your particular fire hazards, our experience is at your disposal . . . no obligation of course.

C-O-TWO FIRE EQUIPMENT COMPANY
NEWARK 1 • NEW JERSEY
Sales and Service in the Principal Cities of United States and Canada
Affiliated with Pyrene Manufacturing Company
MANUFACTURERS OF APPROVED FIRE PROTECTION EQUIPMENT
Squeez-Grip Carbon Dioxide Type Fire Extinguishers • Dry Chemical Type Fire Extinguishers
Built-In High Pressure and Low Pressure Carbon Dioxide Type Fire Extinguishing Systems
Built-In Smoke and Heat Fire Detecting Systems

---

publications
Continued

current products are covered, including several new ones recently developed, such as a new aluminum solder rod for soldering iron application, a premium silver brazing rod and a silver brazing rod made especially for carbide tool tipping. *All-State Welding Alloys Co., Inc.*
For free copy insert No. 13 on postcard, p. 37.

Saw Blades Described

M&M Triple-Chip solid and segmental circular saw blades are described in a new 8-p. bulletin. Two tables give complete data and specifications for all standard size blades. Also described are two models of M&M automatic saw blade sharpeners, which impart the exclusive Triple-Chip tooth form. The details and advantages of this method of sawing are fully explained. *Motch & Merryweather Machinery Co.*
For free copy insert No. 14 on postcard, p. 37.

Crane Uses Shown

A new 20-p. bulletin covers the application of Lorain cranes to industrial materials handling. The booklet contains over 50 illustrations showing these versatile machines on the job in many types of industries, handling many types of material such as steel sheet, sand, scrap, pulpwood, sugar cane, paper, tires and airplanes. Rubber-tire Moto-Cranes and self-propelled Lorains and crawler mounted models are shown at work. Every page is filled with ideas on outdoor materials handling. *Thew Shovel Co.*
For free copy insert No. 15 on postcard, p. 37.

Induction Motor Bulletin

Features of A-C large two-pole squirrel cage induction motors are given in a new 6-p. bulletin. A cross-section view of a typical normal torque, low starting current motor shows the construction of stator winding, bearings, ventilation, squirrel cage winding, rotor, stator, and bearing brackets. Features described in the bulletin are available in A-C standard 40 C rise continuous rated, two-pole, 60-cycle, 3,600-rpm, bracket-bearing, squirrel cage

motors for direct-connected drives in all ratings 900 hp and larger, built for boiler feed pumps, oil pipeline pumps, centrifugal blowers, descaling pumps, and other high speed drives. *Allis-Chalmers Mfg. Co.*
For free copy insert No. 16 on postcard, p. 37.

Powered Hand Trucks

The new powered hand trucks recently announced by Clark are described in detail in a new 12-p. booklet. Separate sections of the book are devoted to each of the two power types: the Electro-Lift, battery-powered and motor-driven; and the Hydro-Lift, gas-powered and driven by hydraulic pump and hydraulic motor. The center-spread provides data concerning the mounting of the drive motors—both electric and hydraulic—inside the drive wheel; turning radius; the frame and other major units common to both power types and other important features. *Industrial Truck Div., Clark Equipment Co.*
For free copy insert No. 17 on postcard, p. 37.

Wire Rope Clamp

The streamlined neatness and holding power of the modern Safe-Line clamp for wire rope are pointed up by numerous illustrations of applications in a wide variety of industries, shown in a new 42-p. booklet. A questions-and-answers section provides general information about the clamps, showing how the inside of each half is made to fit the rope. *National Safe-Line Clamp Co.*
For free copy insert No. 18 on postcard, p. 37.

Heaters and Coolers

Brief descriptions and specifications of the complete line of Hunter gasoline-burning cab and cargo heaters and dry-ice cargo refrigeration systems are given in a new 4-p. folder. Illustrated with photographs and drawings of various models, the catalog also contains drawings of recommended installations. *Hunter Mfg. Co.*
For free copy insert No. 19 on postcard, p. 37.

Belting Info Bulletin

All types of conveyer and elevator belting are covered in a new 16-p. information bulletin. It contains a discussion of each of the various types of belting and suggestions for their application; and is complete with all the necessary tables, charts,

how to handle high assembly costs

KURZ-KASCH, Inc.
DAYTON, OHIO

• On an order for 120,000 plastic handles, to which metal sockets had to be attached, Kurz-Kasch, Inc., pioneer planners and moulders in plastics, found that manual assembly methods averaged only 125-150 units per hour per man . . . ran assembly costs dangerously high.

Converting to Buckeye air-powered screwdrivers, Kurz-Kasch stepped up productive output to 225-250 units per hour—a 66⅔ % increase that kept assembly costs in line, assured a profitable production operation.

In any business—including yours—there's a real need for efficient, modern Buckeye Air Tools. Screwdrivers, drills and nut runners . . . grinders, buffers, sanders . . . wrenches, shears and nibblers . . . there's a Buckeye Tool to do your work—faster, better, more economically. We'll prove that—in your plant, on your job—without obligation. May we call on you?

Buckeye Tools
CORPORATION
DIVISION 11 • DAYTON 1, OHIO

Portable Air and Electric Tools for Industry

and formulas for the selection of the right type of belt for the application. This new bulletin will be of particular interest to engineers and operating personnel interested in the selection of conveyer belts. *Thermoid Co.*
For free copy insert No. 20 on postcard, p. 37.

Brakes, Brake Motors

Features of C-W brakes and brake motors, incorporating brake linings of bonded metal, are described in a new 4-p. bulletin. The folder contains a checklist of advantages and a cutaway photo showing construction features of the compact unit. Dimensions of the various brake sizes available are provided; information on mounting, mechanical and electrical characteristics and other engineering data are presented. *Crocker-Wheeler Div. Elliott Co.*
For free copy insert No. 21 on postcard, p. 37.

For Induction Heating

Principles of Tocco induction heating are shown in a new 60-p. catalog describing equipment and advantages. Typical results of induction hardening and heat treating are presented, along with results of induction heating for forming, forging, annealing, brazing and soldering. The section on induction heating equipment lists numerous types and sizes of machines to meet specific requirements. Construction features are described, specifications are listed, and various typical installations are shown. *Tocco Div., Ohio Crankshaft Co.*
For free copy insert No. 22 on postcard, p. 37.

Wire Rope

A new 8-p. booklet on wire rope for excavating equipment incorporates a complete list of usage recommendations and the wire rope code. Drawings illustrate proper rigging on shovels, cranes, dragline excavators, trench hoes and skimmers. Hoist rope strand types are also detailed, showing both new and former constructions. *John A. Roebling's Sons Co.*
For free copy insert No. 23 on postcard, p. 37.

Resume Your Reading on Page 37

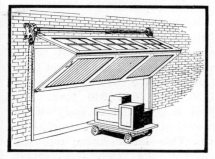
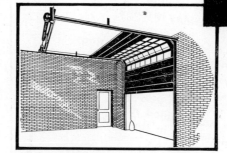

• News of Industry •

Attlee Hard of Hearing To Hands-Off Steel Industry Pleas

Sir Ellis Hunter says Cabinet had scrapped agreement reached in '47.

London — Renewed appeals to keep hands off the British steel industry might just as well have been directed to a deaf man with his hearing apparatus turned off.

Winston Churchill, in the House of Commons recently, appealed to Prime Minister Attlee to reconsider his decision to force steel nationalization on the country at a time of international turmoil. Mr. Attlee's silence did not mean consent.

Sir Ellis Hunter, president of the British Iron and Steel Federation, rallied after Mr. Churchill. He called attention to the dangers of altering the industry's structure in times like these.

Does He Mean Attlee?

"It would be a madman who would interfere at this stage with an industry that has served the country so well," said Sir Hunter sternly at a meeting of Dorman Long & Co. stockholders. He claimed that the industry and government had reached an "understanding" in 1947 to avoid nationalization. This agreement was later tossed aside by the Cabinet without explanation.

November steel production in Britain reached the highest rate ever achieved—equivalent to an annual rate of 19,568,640 net tons. Output in the first 11 months of 1950 was 16,919,840 tons. The year is expected to end with a record of 18,256,000 tons chalked up. This latter figure tops the government's "ambitious" target of 17,920,000 tons.

Domestic orders for steel fell in the first part of '50 but took a sharp upswing in recent months. Defense orders in England have still to play an important role in production. Action is being taken to limit steel exports. This with record steel production should help fill domestic demand.

To continue record steel output, high level users of steel are being requested to return their scrap as rapidly as possible.

K & R PRODUCTS

- ★ Straightening Rolls
- ★ Bending Rolls
- ★ Cold Roll Forming Machines
- ★ Gang Slitters
- ★ Flying Shears
- ★ Crimping Machines
- ★ Hydraulic Tube Benders
- ★ Hydraulic Bulldozers
- ★ Hydraulic Presses
- ★ Edging Machines
- ★ Special Metalworking Equipment

KANE & ROACH

INCORPORATED

 Syracuse, New York

Established 1887

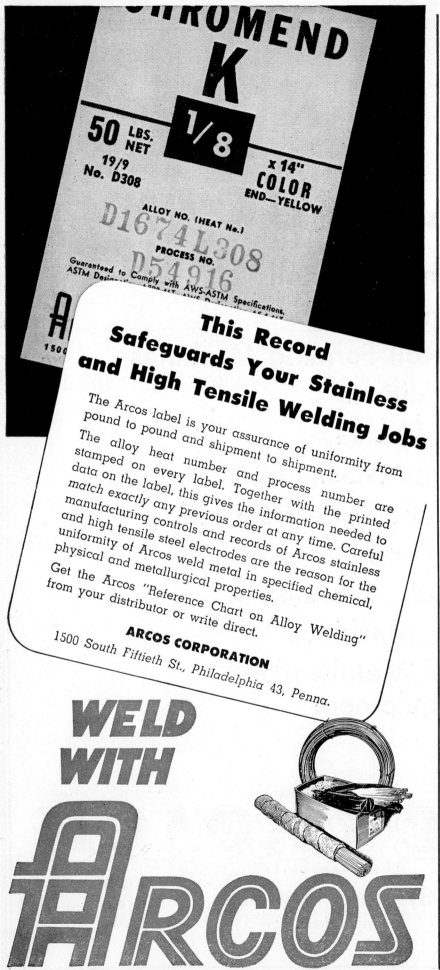
Materials Handling Society Plans Chicago Meeting April 30

Chicago—Sixteen chapters of the American Materials Handling Society will participate in the Materials Handling Conference to be held concurrently with the National Materials Handling Exposition at the International Amphitheatre, April 30 to May 4.

A. K. Strong Chairman

General chairman of the conference will be A. K. Strong, marine division, Columbian Rope Co., New York. Serving with him on the executive committee will be Donald W. Pennock, factory engineer, Carrier Corp., Syracuse, N. Y., and Irving M. Footlik, materials handling consultant, Chicago.

Participating chapters include Boston, Buffalo, Chicago, Cleveland, Detroit, Houston, Indianapolis, Los Angeles, Louisville, New York, North Texas, Pittsburgh, Syracuse, Toledo, Toronto, and Western Michigan.

Mechanization of Mulga Mine

Birmingham—The Mulga coal mine of the Woodward Iron Co. will be completely mechanized and production is expected to be increased about 25 pct. Production in 1949 was 462,392 tons and this year it is producing at a rate of more than 600,000 tons, the company announced.

Cost of mechanization is expected to be $1 million. A continuous belt to the mine mouth, "moles," mechanical coal diggers operated on the continuous belt principle, larger coal cars and automatic safety devices will be added.

Mechanization of the mine will not substantially decrease the underground force, but will result in larger output per miner.

Shows 43 Pct Profit Increase

Toledo — Bingham - Herbrand Corp., manufacturers of drop-forgings and metal stampings, reports its largest sales in history and a 43 pct increase in earnings for the fiscal year ending Sept. 30.

January 4, 1951

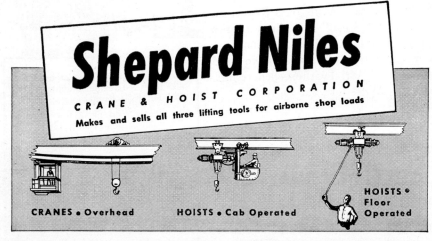
• News of Industry •

Southeast Iron and Steel Industry to Use More Rail Cars

Birmingham—The iron and steel
industry in the Southeast expects
to use 41,343 railroad cars to handle its shipments in the first quarter of 1951, reports R. M. Reid,
Tennessee Coal, Iron & Railroad
Company traffic manager and
chairman of the advisory committee of the Southeast Shippers Advisory Board. This is 12 pct more
than the same period in 1950.

"Business conditions within the
industry, both currently and pros-
pectively, are good," Mr. Reid said.
"Furnaces producing pig iron and
steel are expected to operate at
capacity.

"Expansion and modernization
programs now under way in the
industry contemplate considerable
increase in production capacity.

"The railroad car supply during the current quarter has been
extremely tight, with shortages reported by many members, particularly so in the case of boxcars
and pipe and pig iron gondolas.
But with car manufacturing plants
working at top speed, relief is in
sight."

Cladmetals Field to Expand

Carnegie, Pa.—Wide acceptance
among fabricators and the need to
conserve vital materials are forcing a period of expansion upon the
cladmetals industry, according to
Joseph Kinney, Jr., president,
American Cladmetals Co. Cladmetals, two metals bonded together
and providing the best characteristics of each, are being more
widely used in guided missiles, jet
power plants, communications
equipment and products of the
atomic energy laboratories.

Some ECA Steel Changes Made

Washington — Langdon S. Si-
mons, of the Economic Cooperation Administration, has gone to
Paris to head European headquarters' industry division iron and
steel branch. Charles G. McNaron
was elevated to the top post in the
Washington branch.

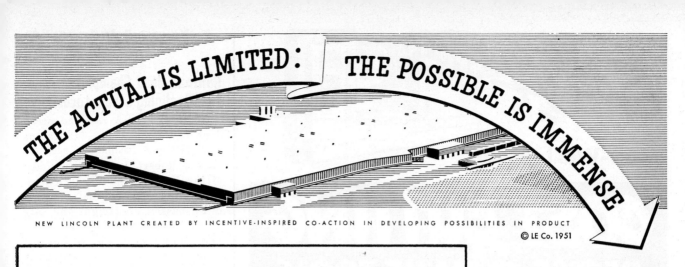

Specify

Max-WELL-Made

COST CUTTING
RECESS-O-MATIC TOOLS
Eliminate Secondary Operations

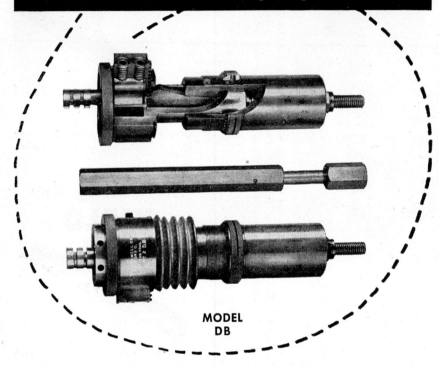

MODEL DB

● Universally adaptable RECESS-O-MATIC tools have been designed especially to perform recessing, back-chamfering, back counterboring and thread and grind reliefs, as well as other internal forming operations.

Because they can be used on your automatics, RECESS-O-MATIC tools completely eliminate secondary operations to perform these critical jobs. Large range and long stroke are features, and tools are easily and rapidly set-up or adjusted for diameters and locations to within 0.001-inch accuracy.

RECESS-O-MATIC tools can be piloted on the workpiece or operated by draw-bar. Circular form cutters with high-speed or Carbide tips assure immediate economy and dependable accuracy.

Write for catalog DB today, or send your drawings for recommendations.

THE MAXWELL COMPANY
386 BROADWAY • BEDFORD, OHIO

January 4, 1951

DRAVO *Counterflo* HEATERS

Apply Artificial Respiration.....

WHEN FOUNDRIES ARE OVERCOME BY FUMES

When you start to clear a foundry of smoke, noxious fumes and dust, it's not enough to push the foul air *OUT*. To complete the ventilating job, you must bring fresh air IN!

Natural air infiltration through doors and windows is usually not sufficient to replace exhausted foul air. Mechanical induction of sufficient make-up air takes care of this problem, but generally introduces another. During colder months, this replacement air must be heated, or working areas will be chilled far below comfort levels and production will suffer.

As many foundries have discovered, there's a sound, proven answer ready and waiting: just apply "artificial respiration" with Dravo *Counterflo* Heaters. When cold weather sets in, the heating function goes into instant action, tempering the make-up air to maintain comfortable working conditions throughout the building . . . and,

incidentally, overcoming negative pressure and thus increasing the efficiency of all combustion equipment. All through the warm months, the ventilating function provides a continuous supply of unwarmed fresh air to replace foul air.

There are many reasons why foundries make Dravo Heaters first-choice for this responsible job. The range of capacities—from 400,000 to 2,000,000 Btu per hour —provides the proper unit for every load and provides air handling capacity of 11,000 cfm per million Btu output. The heaters can be mounted in any position, and so accommodate themselves to space restrictions. Ready interchange between oil and gas is also a feature. The 80-85% efficiency spells operating economy, and the top-flight engineering, rugged mill-type construction incorporating a stainless steel combustion chamber, minimizes maintenance. Dependable automatic controls make a full-time attendant unnecessary.

Perhaps YOU have a foundry ventilating problem that is affecting worker morale and efficiency—or perhaps you are spending MORE than necessary for heating by old-fashioned methods. For a quick picture of what Dravo Heaters are doing in solving such problems, ask for Bulletin JK-520-1324.

DRAVO CORPORATION

DRAVO BLDG., PITTSBURGH 22, PA.

Manufactured and sold in Canada by
Marine Industries, Ltd. Sorel, Quebec

Export Associates:
Lynch, Wilde & Co. Washington 9, D. C.

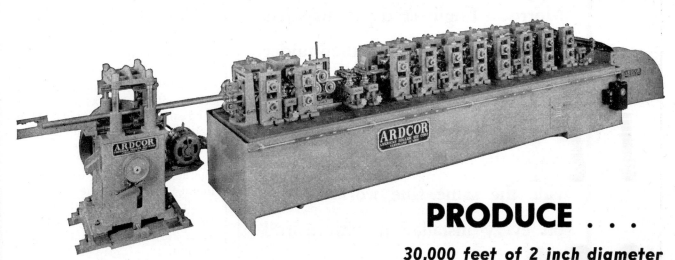

prefabricated parts with great resistance to the elements.

Other industries are also using more stainless steels, stemming from higher output or production innovations, said Dr. Thompson.

GE Labs Develop Liquid That May Serve Industry as Pipe Dope

Schenectady, N. Y.—"Anaerobic permafil," a material which remains liquid as long as a stream of air bubbles passes through it and then solidifies in a few minutes when removed from air, has been developed by the chemistry division of the General Electric Research Laboratory.

The material can penetrate fine cracks before hardening and a possible application is as a pipe dope for sealing threaded unions or as a tight seal for stopping leaks. Another use may be to do away with the lock nut needed to hold another nut onto a bolt. If the liquid is placed on the threads of a bolt just before the nut is screwed in, it hardens so tightly that great force is needed to remove the nut.

McLouth to Use Top Charging

Detroit — McLouth Steel Corp. has announced plans for converting its four electric furnaces to top charging. Together with extensions to buildings and the installation of two more soaking pits, the modernization program is expected to cost approximately $2 million. It will be completed by midsummer 1951.

Now, McLouth is producing 400,000 tons of steel annually. New equipment may permit production at a rate as high as ½ million tons a year a company spokesman indicated.

At the north end of the building an extension of 200 ft is being made. In addition 150 ft is being added to the south end of the McLouth mill to provide additional coil storage. A 200 ft addition to shipping facilities at the south end of the mill has just been completed.

"down time" costs more today!

that's why you'll save more

by using  APEX TOOLS

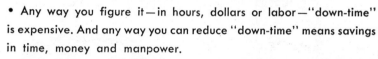

• Any way you figure it—in hours, dollars or labor—"down-time" is expensive. And any way you can reduce "down-time" means savings in time, money and manpower.

You'll have less "down-time" using Apex tools—impact sockets, universal sockets, extensions and adapters—because Apex tools are designed and built to stay on the job, to provide greater freedom from excessive tool breakage and quick wear-out.

Apex manufactures thousands of standard types and sizes, each precision-machined from high carbon electric furnace alloy steel, cold broached and heat-treated to withstand the severe strains and shocks of industrial service. If yours is a special application, just send sketch or blueprint for prompt quotation, without obligation.

Up to 5" hex opening

Up to 2½" size anvil

CATALOG 19 lists styles, dimensions, type and size of drives. Write, on your company letterhead please, for your copy.

sockets, extensions, adapters

THE APEX MACHINE & TOOL COMPANY
1029 S. Patterson Blvd., Dayton 2, Ohio

SAFETY FRICTION TAPPING CHUCKS • VERTICAL FLOAT TAPPING CHUCKS • SELF-RELEASING AND ADJUSTABLE STUD SETTERS • POWER BITS FOR PHILLIPS, FREARSON, SLOTTED HEAD, CLUTCH HEAD, HEX HEAD AND SOCKET SCREWS • HAND DRIVERS FOR PHILLIPS, FREARSON AND CLUTCH HEAD SCREWS • AIRCRAFT AND INDUSTRIAL UNIVERSAL JOINTS • SOCKETS AND UNIVERSAL JOINT SOCKET WRENCHES.

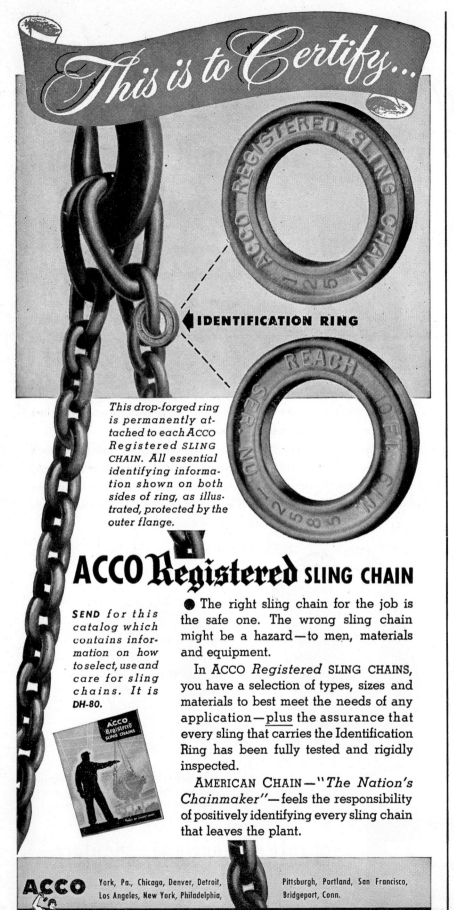

Titanium Will Take Place Among the World's Tonnage Metals

Chicago—The fourth most abundant structural metal in the earth, titanium, may find itself among tonnage metals within the next 5 years as research overcomes difficulty of producing it, said Dr. Julian Glasser, research metallurgist at Armour Research Foundation of Illinois Institute of Technology.

He said the element titanium was discovered 150 years ago but was not regarded as workable until about 1910. Its more attractive properties: lighter than iron, stronger than aluminum, and more corrosion-resistant than stainless steel, have only been discovered in the past few years.

Overcoming Difficulties

"Until recently metallurgists have been stumped in their efforts to find an economical method of extracting pure titanium from titanium ores," he said. "These smelting and refining difficulties are being rapidly overcome."

Commercial aircraft payloads could be increased with the use of titanium in frame and engine parts. The metal's resistance to salt water corrosion would make it practical for marine use, such as the manufacture of hulls, drive shafts, and propellors. With a melting point twice as high as aluminum, titanium could be used for exhaust manifolds and other "hot spots" that now require steel.

Dr. Glasser said that it is now known how to double the strength of the metal by proper alloying. He is working on a plan to make the Foundation a clearing house for all analytical methods on titanium and its alloys.

Aerojet to Build Calif. Plant

Azusa, Calif. — Aerojet Engineering Corp., General Tire & Rubber Co. subsidiary, has announced plans are virtually completed for acquisition of a 7200 acre site near Sacramento, for manufacture of rockets. Aerojet, is one of the world's largest manufacturers of rocket engines.

this Verson HYDRAULIC BULLDOZER forms heavy tractor parts

TRADE MARK

A leading manufacturer of crawler type tractors and road grading equipment uses the rugged Verson 500 ton Hydraulic Bulldozer illustrated above for heavy forming jobs. A typical one is the offset bending of 10 inch steel channels.

Whether your requirements are so specialized as to require a press such as the one illustrated above, or are run of the mine, Verson has the "know-how" and facilities to best fill your needs.

VERSON MECHANICAL PRESSES are the foremost in the mechanical field having compiled amazing records for accuracy, dependability and economy on all types of service.

VERSON HYDRAULIC PRESSES feature the revolutionary Hydrol Speed Circuit that minimizes high pressure piping and virtually eliminates the most common source of hydraulic press problems.

VERSON TRANSMAT PRESSES bring the advantages and economy of fully automatic metal forming to a wide range of mass produced products.

VERSON HIGH SPEED PRESSES offer phenomenal production rates for scores of products.

Before you buy another press be sure to find out what Verson can do for you. It will mean many dollars for the profit side of your ledger.

Behind your television screen...

Rubber Television Anode Shield Manufactured by Continental for the Ucinite Company

Continental Rubber gets into the act →

In the unseen act behind your television screen, a small cup-shaped rubber shield plays an important role. This shield fits over the anode on the side of the tube. Its function is to "seal in" high voltage current and thus prevent surface discharges that cause picture distortion.

Ordinary rubber compounds, of course, can't fill the bill. *This* rubber part must have exceptional dielectric properties and unusual stability under sustained heat. It must resist the deteriorating effects of ozone created by electrical discharges. In addition, the rubber shield must be precision molded to insure proper seating against the side of the television tube.

Continental engineers, working closely with Ucinite Company engineers, have met these exacting requirements. This technical cooperation typifies the service in rubber offered by Continental.

When *you* need better engineered rubber parts, why not enlist the service of specialists in molded and extruded rubber?

LET US SEND YOU THIS CATALOG

This new engineering catalog lists hundreds of standard grommets, bushings, rings and extruded shapes. It will be a valuable addition to your working file. Send for your copy today or . . .
See our Catalog in Sweet's File for Product Designers

MANUFACTURERS SINCE 1903

CONTINENTAL
RUBBER WORKS
1985 LIBERTY BOULEVARD • ERIE 6, PENNSYLVANIA

BRANCHES

Baltimore, Md.	Cleveland, Ohio	Kansas City, Mo.	Pittsburgh, Pa.
Boston, Mass.	Dayton, Ohio	Los Angeles, Calif.	Rochester, N. Y.
Buffalo, N. Y.	Detroit, Mich.	Memphis, Tenn.	St. Louis, Mo.
Chicago, Ill.	Hartford, Conn.	New York, N. Y.	San Francisco, Calif.
Cincinnati, Ohio	Indianapolis, Ind.	Philadelphia, Pa.	Syracuse, N. Y.

• News of Industry •

W. K. Skuce Named to Ready NPA's Controlled Materials Plan

Washington—Key appointments last week indicated the faster tempo of control activities. Perhaps the most important to the metals industry was appointment of Walter C. Skuce to the staff of NPA.

Mr. Skuce will direct planning for a controlled materials plan and presumably will operate the plan when it is ready for institution. He directed WPB's similar plan and also served as deputy vice-chairman of operations. Since 1945, Mr. Skuce has been with the Owens-Corning Fiberglas Corp.

General Clay to Serve

ODM Director Charles E. Wilson also appointed Gen. Lucius D. Clay and Sidney J. Weinberg as special assistants. General Clay, during World War II, was in direct charge of army procurement as deputy director of the services of supply.

His record in this job was considered outstanding. He later served as Deputy Director of the Office of War Mobilization and Reconversion. He is now chairman of the board of the Continental Can Co., from which firm he is on leave to take his new assignment.

Mr. Weinberg held several key jobs in WPB during his 4 years of service, including the post of vice-chairman.

Production Loss 45,000 Tons In Strike at Carnegie-Illinois

Youngstown—The 11 day strike of openhearth workers at the Ohio Works of Carnegie-Illinois Steel Corp., which ended Dec. 18, cost an estimated 45,000 ingot tons of production.

Members of Local 1330, United Steelworkers, voted to return to work when the company refused to discuss a grievance over new incentive pay rates in the openhearth department as long as the strike continued. The grievance will be processed through regular channels.

IN 1890

The largest forging machine weighed 40,000 pounds. With cast iron crankshaft and cast iron bed, the finest materials available, the 5″ Blakeslee Forging Machine was the quality machine of its day.

Mr. J. R. Blakeslee, founder of the Blakeslee Machine Co. (AJAX since 1894) stands beside the first 5″ Forging Machine. Patented in 1889.

FOR 60 YEARS

The urgent demands of industry in War and Peace, the supreme achievement of engineering skill, the use of the best materials have produced a superior product geared to the needs of the times. AJAX Forging Machines have excelled in performance throughout the years.

Today —

For excellence in design, performance and durability in Forging Machinery...CHOOSE

AJAX

Write for Bulletin 65-C

THE AJAX MANUFACTURING COMPANY
EUCLID BRANCH P.O. CLEVELAND 17, OHIO
110 S. DEARBORN ST.   DEWART BUILDING
CHICAGO 3, ILLINOIS   NEW LONDON, CONN.

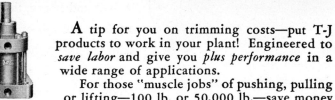

Nonferrous Metals Supply Worrying British Industry

London — Nonferrous metals shortages have become acute in the last few weeks. Restrictions of consumption are in force for zinc, aluminum, nickel, sheet steel, and tinplate.

New measures under consideration include restrictions on export of semi-manufactures, prohibition of use of these metals for non-essential articles, and institution of allocation systems.

Questioned regarding metal supply prospects Mr. George Strauss, Minister of Supply, told the House of Commons that zinc available to industry in 1951 is limited, further cuts in consumption are probable, and defense requirements would have to be met from the available supply.

During the first quarter of 1951 the shortage was likely to be more serious. Supply might be restricted to 50 pct. of the rate of consumption during the first 9 months of 1950.

Copper Shortage

A severe shortage of special shapes of copper will affect fabricators in 1951. The prospects for copper in early 1951 will not permit consumption at a higher rate than in the first half of 1950, a cut of about 10 pct. on the current rate of consumption.

Supplies of virgin aluminum will have to be restricted in 1951 to 15,000 tons a month. There is at present no real shortage of general steel, but steel production in 1951 may be affected by difficulties in supplies of steel-making raw materials, particularly imported scrap (mainly from Germany) and imported iron ore.

Truck Fleet Maintenance Clinic

New York—The first large-scale preventive maintenance clinic for operators of commercial vehicle fleets will be held at the meeting of the Technical Committee of the Transport Vehicle Show, Madison Square Garden Exhibition Hall, Feb. 1.

THE BEST LOCATION | IN THE NATION

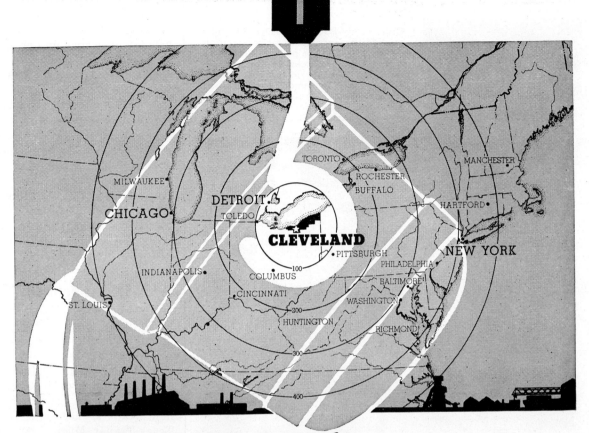

NORTHEAST OHIO chosen for

$150,000,000 STEEL EXPANSION

A MILLION MORE TONS of finished steel a year— that's the goal of a $150,000,000 steel industry expansion program now under way in the Cleveland-Northeast Ohio area!

THIS MAJOR DEVELOPMENT offers another exciting example of the extraordinary long-term advantages of the Best Location in the Nation.

This is the only industrial center in the world that offers ALL the advantages shown at right— *including a market of 81,000,000 people within overnight haul.*

IN PREPARING FOR YOUR NEXT EXPANSION use our free, confidential Location Engineering Service for information about this area's long-term advantages for your company. *In the long run, the short haul pays.*

Phone, wire or write, Development Department

Check these Advantages!

Only the Cleveland-Northeast Ohio area, *the best location in the nation,* offers industry this superior combination of long-term advantages:

- At the Market Center of America, with 81,000,000 people within 500 miles.
- Superlative transportation by land, water and air.
- Plenty of electric power at low rates.
- Highly skilled industrial workers.
- Many producers of parts, materials and supplies.
- Basic materials right at hand.
- Ample financial services.
- Complete business and industrial services.
- Favorable tax structure (no state income tax).
- Diversified industries to supply and be supplied.
- Unlimited fresh-water supply.
- Desirable plants and plant sites.
- Excellent living and cultural environment.

WRITE TODAY FOR FREE BOOKLET

Write today for free copy of new book about Northeast Ohio, entitled *"In the Long Run, The Short Haul Pays!"* Concise, authoritative, written for top management men.

THE CLEVELAND ELECTRIC ILLUMINATING COMPANY

75 PUBLIC SQUARE • CHerry 1-4200 • CLEVELAND 1, OHIO

January 4, 1951

441

ANY Electric Truck can be Equipped with READY-POWER

---

54 New Coke Ovens Installed At South African Iron and Steel

London—Fifty-four Becker coke ovens built by the Woodhall-Duckham Co. have gone into production as part of the Vanderbijl Park steelworks of the South African Iron and Steel Industrial Corp. They will carbonize 1,232 tons of coal a day. Total cost of the installation was $4,200,000.

Domestic sources now supply 60 pct. of South Africa's steel requirements, against 36 pct before the War. During 1951, the steel output of South African Iron and Steel Corp. is expected to expand to 1,230,000 ingot tons, rising to 1,344,000 tons in 1952.

89,979 Trailers Needed in '51

Washington — Total steel of 321,201 tons, plus 69,539,000 lbs of aluminum and 1,540,000 lbs of copper and copper base alloys will be needed by the trailer industry during 1951 to provide America's truckers with an estimated 89,979 new trailers, according to the Truck-Trailer Mfrs. Assn. Total axle demand will be 157,527, the TTMA explained.

Canadian Firm Plans Expansion

Montreal—Consolidated Mining & Smelting Co. of Canada Ltd., will proceed with new plant construction in British Columbia to cost about $15,000,000 according to R. E. Stavert, president. An addition to the electrolytic smelter will be constructed at a cost of about $3,200,000. The enlarged unit will increase capacity by about 70 tons daily.

Bussel Heads NJ Chapter ISIS

Newark — Irving Bussel of Plainfield Iron & Metal Co. was elected president of the New Jersey chapter of the Institute of Scrap Iron & Steel recently, and William Abramson was elected honorary president. Other officers include: Henry Fiestal, Herman Plavin, and Eric Lowenstein, vice-presidents; Murray Kunin, secretary; Eli Bussel, treasurer.

Automobile parts being protected for export shipment. (Left) Hoods and cowls pass through continuous criss-cross spray of NO-OX-ID before crating. (Right) Small parts are dipped in NO-OX-ID.

POSITIVE PROTECTION FOR YOUR PRODUCTS WITH DEARBORN NO-OX-ID

Whether you manufacture products for export or domestic markets—if they are made of metal, they need protection against the costly, constant threat of rust.

Whether your products require a coating that is transparent, heat resisting, cold resisting, lubricating or dry to the touch, there is a correct NO-OX-ID for your use. There is also a method of application suited to your operation. NO-OX-ID may be applied by hot or cold dip—either by hand or conveyor. It may be sprayed or brushed on—it may be protected in NO-OX-IDized wrappers.

NO-OX-ID will also play an important part in protecting the equipment in your plant, your out-buildings, storage tanks, and metal surfaces wherever corrosion threatens. Lower maintenance costs are made possible with NO-OX-ID.

Dearborn has been serving industry since 1887—put these years of experience to work for you, preventing corrosion on your products and in your plant. Consult with a Dearborn Engineer—he will advise you as to which NO-OX-IDs are best suited to your needs.

DEARBORN CHEMICAL COMPANY
General Offices: 310 S. Michigan Ave. • Chicago 4, Ill.

WRITE FOR THIS VALUABLE BOOKLET

A complete introduction to Dearborn NO-OX-IDs with valuable information to help you protect against rust in your plant and on your product. Mail the coupon.

DEARBORN CHEMICAL COMPANY
310 S. Michigan Ave., Dept. IA
Chicago 4, Ill.

Gentlemen: Please send me a copy of your booklet on NO-OX-ID Rust Preventives.

Name..................................

Company...............................

Title.................................

Address...............................

City.................State.............

Dearborn
Reg. U.S. Pat. Off.

THE ORIGINAL RUST PREVENTIVE

NO-OX-ID
IRON + OX = RUST

LEBANON ALLOY CASTINGS
Resist Sulphuric Acid Attack

Valve Bodies and Fittings cast at Lebanon in various special sulphuric acid resistant alloys.

FOR CHEMICAL AND
PROCESS INDUSTRY
APPLICATIONS . . .

LEBANON CIRCLE Ⓛ 34
NOMINAL ANALYSIS

Carbon Max.	0.07 Max.
Silicon	1.25
Manganese	0.75
Chromium	20.50
Nickel	28.50
Molybdenum.	2.50
Copper.	4.25

NOMINAL PHYSICAL PROPERTIES

Tensile Strength . . .	72,000
Yield Point	35,000
Elongation in 2''—%	45
Brinell Hardness . . .	150

Heat treatment: Water quenched.

*Circle L 34 (FA 20)
DuPont Specification 1364

DURING the period of development of special alloys to resist sulphuric acid and sulphuric and nitric acid combinations, Lebanon played an important part in proving their value as casting material. Lebanon Circle L 34 (Stainless Type FA 20*), analysis of which is given below, is an alloy created to meet this demand. Circle L 34, in addition to its resistance to sulphuric and nitric acid, offers good resistance to alkalis and alkali salts.

Our familiarity with the manufacture of castings of special alloy materials means that we can readily meet your requirements. Every Lebanon casting is made to exacting standards, inspected and thoroughly tested before shipping. A complete laboratory, including a million-volt X-Ray machine, is one of the facilities upon which our customers constantly rely.

Do you have copies of the Lebanon Data Sheets? If not, just let us know and we will send them along to you.

LEBANON STEEL FOUNDRY • LEBANON, PA.
"In the Lebanon Valley"

LEBANON Castings
ALLOY AND STEEL
CIRCLE L

SLAB ZINC

PRIME WESTERN, SELECT, BRASS SPECIAL, INTERMEDIATE, HIGH GRADE, SPECIAL HIGH GRADE

AMERICAN ZINC SALES COMPANY

Distributors for

AMERICAN ZINC, LEAD & SMELTING COMPANY

COLUMBUS, O.   CHICAGO   ST. LOUIS   NEW YORK

Unique Automatic Soldering Process Uses City Gas and Air

Newark, N. J.—Using air pressure mixed with city gas, Automatic Methods, Inc., makers of precision aircraft parts, have developed a new automatic soldering process.

From eight to 12 pieces of work on a circular table and one set of gas burners revolve simultaneously. Parts are thus preheated for the final fusion heat from another set of burners. With two operators for loading and unloading, this table has produced as many as 125 finished pieces per hour.

Ordinary city gas is mixed with air under 5 to 10 lb pressure. Work can be done at about 1/5 the cost of oxygen-acetylene soldering, the company said, while eliminating bottle storage. A single Leiman Air Pump provides adequate air pressure for several tables.

Profit Plan Quadruples Output

Denver—Under a profit sharing plan which averages nearly $700 a year to each eligible employee, the dollar volume of productive output has increased almost 400 pct in 5 years for the C. A. Norgren Co., manufacturer of pneumatic industrial equipment.

In the past 10 years, the company's wage rates have increased about 140 pct and materials now cost the company some 110 pct more but their prices have only been boosted 25 pct. This is attributed to the increased efficiency resulting from the incentive plan which pays about 21 pct of the worker's annual income.

To Relax Import Restrictions

Toronto — Restrictions against importation of capital goods from the United States into Canada will be relaxed by Hon. C. D. Howe, Minister of Trade and Commerce, effective Jan. 2, 1951. Included are heavy machinery, certain types of road equipment, automobiles, auto parts, chemicals, and electrical equipment.

Heat Treating

Continued from Page 268

formation of Steels," Industrial Heating, June 1944, p. 1110.

6. "Isothermal Annealing of Forgings," The Iron Age, Jan. 1, 1948, p. 164; Steel, Jan. 12, 1948, p. 51.

8. "Machinability—Cyclic Annealing," Metal Progress, 54, 1948, p. 509.

9. "Isothermal Treatment of Low Alloy Steels," Engineer, vol. 187, Mar. 25, 1949, p. 328.

10. "Report of the IRSID Committee on Boron Steels," Revue de Metallurgie Memoires, 1949, vol. 46, p. 859.

11. Handbook of Meehanite Metals Austempering, Martempering Cast Irons, Meehanite, 1948.

A

A-20. R. H. Aborn, "Metallurgical Changes at Welded Joints and the Weldability of Steel," Welding Journal, Jan. 9, 1940, p. 414-S.

A-21. R. H. Aborn, "Martempering," Metal Progress, January 1949, p. 65.

A-120. N. N. Alimov, "Isothermal Annealing Cycles, Temperatures, Times and Hardness," Lipchin & Sikov (Russian 1937) Iron and Steel Inst. (England) Translation No. 208, 1945.

A-125. A. H. Allen, "Isothermal Annealing Improves Forging Machinability," Steel, July 10, 1950, p. 84.

A-130. W. A. Anderson and R. F. Mehl, AIME, 161, 145, p. 140.

A-140. J. K. L. Anderson, "Determination of an Isothermal Transformation Diagram with an Optical Dialometer," Journal Iron and Steel Inst., vol. 162, 1949, p. 29.

A-145. J. H. Andrew, H. Lee, H. K. Lloyd and N. Stephenson, "Hydrogen and Transformation Characteristics of Steel," Journal Iron and Steel Inst., vol. 156, No. 2, 1947, p. 208.

A-180. R. S. Archer, J. Z. Briggs and C. M. Loeb, "Molybdenum, Steels, Irons, Alloys," Book, 1948.

A-200. R. Atkin, "The S Curve and Its Application to Industry," Australian Engineer; Australian Inst. of Metals, Mar. 7, 1947, p. 75.

A-210. C. R. Austin, "Interrupted Quench Treatment of Nodular Irons," The Iron Age, Dec. 1, 1949, p. 83.

A-211. C. R. Austin and J. R. Doig, "The Suppression of Pearlite in Manganese Molybdenum Steels," ASM Trans., vol. 36, 1946, p. 336.

A-214. J. B. Austin, "The Dependence of the Rate of Transformation of Austenite on Temperature," Trans. AIME, vol. 116, 1935, p. 309.

A-215. J. B. Austin and R. L. Rickett, "The Kinetics of the Decomposition of Austenite at Constant Temperature," Metals Tech. AIME T.P. 964, Trans. AIME, vol. 135, 1939, p. 964.

A-216. J. B. Austin, "Current Theories of the Hardening of Steel—50 Years Later," Metal Progress, August 1948, p. 201.

A-220. B. L. Averbach, "The Effect of Plastic Deformation on Solid Reactions: 1. Diffusion Reactions," "Cold Working of Metals," ASM book, 1950, p. 262.

A-221. B. L. Averbach, S. A. Kulin and Morris Cohen, "The Effect of Applied Stress and Strain on the Martensite Reaction," Part II, "Cold Working of Metals," ASM book, 1950, p. 290.

A-223. B. Averbach and M. Cohen, "X-Ray Determinations of Retained Austenite by Integrated Intensites," AIME T.P. 2342, Metal Tech., February 1948.

Continued

A-224. B. L. Averbach, L. S. Castleman and M. Cohen, "Measurement of Retained Austenite in Carbon Steel," ASM Trans., vol. 42, 1950, p. 112.

A-227. B. L. Averbach and M. Cohen, "The Isothermal Decomposition of Martensite and Retained Austenite," Trans. ASM, vol. 41, 1949, p. 1024.

B

B-1. H. J. Babcock, "Salt Bath Quenching Processes," Metals and Alloys, 20, October 1944, p. 964; "Commercial Practice," The Iron Age, Feb. 3, 1944, p. 44, Feb. 10, 1944, p. 62; also Industrial Heating, August 1946, p. 1288.

B-20. C. K. Baer and A. E. Nehrenberg, "Practical Aspects of Bainite Hardening of High-Speed Steel," The Iron Age, Sept. 4, 1947, p. 65.

B-21. C. K. Baer and P. Payson, "The Bainitic Hardening of High-Speed Steel," Trans. ASM, vol. 39, 1947, p. 488.

B-26. E. C. Bain, "Functions of the Alloying Elements in Steels," ASM book, 1939.

B-27. E. C. Bain and E. S. Davenport, "Transformations of Austenite at Constant Subcritical Temperatures," Trans. AIME, vol. 90, 1930, p. 117.

B-30. W. E. Bancroft, "Salt Baths for Hardening High-Speed Steel," Metal Progress, vol. 50, 1946, p. 941.

B-31. W. E. Bancroft and W. W. Wight, "The Practical Heat Treatment of High-Speed Steel Cutting Tools," Metal Progress, April 1948, p. 545.

B-40. J. B. Bassett and E. S. Rowland, "The Effect of Chromium on the Ms Point," Metals Technology, AIME, August 1948, Tech. Publ. No. 2417.

B-90. "The Pirotechnia of Vannoccio Biringuccio," Translated by C. S. Smith and M. T. Gnudi, AIME book, 1942, p. 371.

B-96. Wilhelm Bischof, "Untersuchungen uber die Zwischenstufenvergutung verschieden legierter Stahle (Research on Intermediate Stage Annealing of Different Alloy Steels), 29 Curves "S," Archiv fur das Eisenhuttenwesen, vol. 20, January-February 1949, p. 13.

B-120. J. R. Blanchard, R. M. Parks and A. J. Herzig, "The Effect of Molybdenum on the Isothermal Subcritical Transformation of Austenite in Low and Medium Carbon Steels," Trans. ASM, vol. 29, 1941, p. 317.

B-121. J. R. Blanchard, R. M. Park and A. J. Herzig, "The Effect of Mo on the Isothermal Subcritical Transformation of Austenite in Eutectoid and Hypereutectoid Steels," ASM Trans., vol. 31, 1943, p. 849.

B-150. A. L. Boegehold, "Hardenability Control for Alloy Steel Parts," Metal Progress, May 1948, p. 697.

B-151. B. N. Bose and M. F. Hawkes, "Eutectoid Transformation of Fe-N₂ Alloys," AIME Trans., vol. 188, February 1950, p. 307.

B-152. L. F. Bowne, "The Use of Direct Transformation Data in Determining Preheat and Postheat Requirements for Arcwelding Deep Hardening Steels and Weld Deposits," Welding Journal, vol. 25, 1946, p. 234.

B-153. H. E. Boyer, "Controlling Physical Properties by the Interrupted Quench," The Iron Age, July 3, 1947, p. 47.

B-154. H. E. Boyer, "The Interrupted Quench and Its Practical Aspect," ASM Trans. vol. 38, 1947, p. 209.

B-155. H. C. Boyer, "Problems in Heat Treating," Steel Processing, vol. 35, 1949, p. 203.

Turn to Page 450

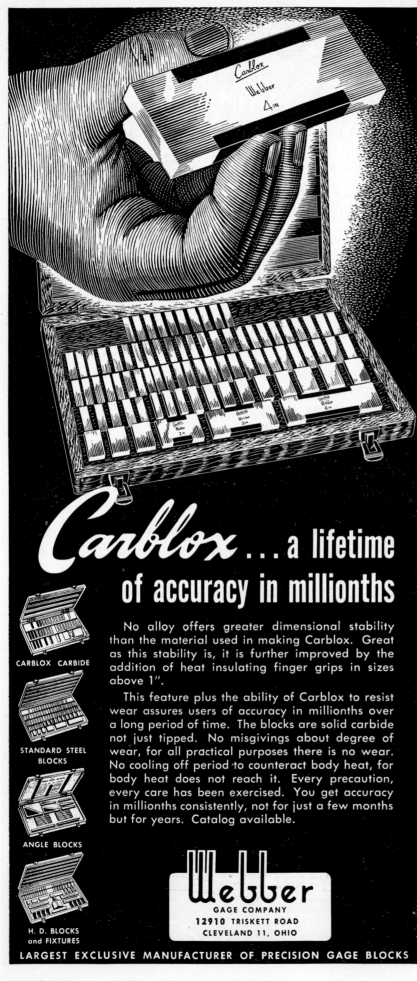
Heat Treating

B-156. H. E. Boyer, "Effect of Contamination on Quenching Media," The Iron Age, May 5, 1949, p. 88.

B-157. H. E. Boyer, "Quenching Media; Experimental Studies of Evaluation by the Jominy Test," Iron and Steel, May 1950, p. 177.

B-180. O. E. Brown, "Modified Isothermal Treatments Minimize Distortion on Carburized SAE 3312," The Iron Age, Apr. 17, 1947, p. 54.

B-181. W. H. Bruckner, "The Weldability of Steels," Welding Journal, vol. 21, 1942, p. 55-s.

B-182. W. H. Bruckner and J. Hino, "The Rate of Spheroidization and the Physical Properties of Pearlitic Malleable Iron After Isothermal Quenching," AFA Trans., 1944, p. 1189.

B-200. D. K. Bullens, "Steel and Its Heat Treatment," John Wiley & Sons, 1948, "Principles," vol. 1, p. 311; vol. 2, p. 274.

C

C-5. L. A. Carapella, "Computing A or Ms from Chemical Analysis," Metal Progress, June 1944, p. 108; ASM Trans., vol. 33, 1947, p. 277.

C-10. Carpenter Steel Co. Data Sheets—TTT, 1946-1947.

C-75. R. D. Chapman and W. E. Jominy, "Hardness Variations in C-Mo Steels After Tempering," Metal Progress, April 1950, p. 491.

C-80. A. L. Christenson, E. C. Nelson and C. E. Jackson, " 'S' Curves by Dilatometric Method," AIME Trans., vol. 162, 1945, p. 614.

C-100. D. S. Clark and D. S. Wood, "The Tensile Impact Properties of Some Metals and Alloys," ASM Trans., vol. 42, 1950, p. 45.

C-120. Climax Molybdenum Co., "Mo . . . Fundamental Effects in Steel," 1st and 2nd Editions, Pamphlet.

C-150. Morris Cohen, "Retained Austenite," Metal Progress, December 1948, p. 823.

C-151. Morris Cohen, "Retained Austenite," ASM Trans., vol. 41, 1949, p. 35.

C-153. Morris Cohen and P. Gordon, "Heat Treatment of High-Speed Steel," The Iron Age, Feb. 28, 1946, p. 42; Mar. 14, p. 68; Mar. 21, p. 61; Mar. 28, p. 55.

C-154. Morris Cohen, E. S. Machlin and V. G. Paranjpe, "Thermodynamics of the Martensitic Transformation," "Thermodynamics in Metallurgy," ASM book, 1950, p. 242.

C-155. Morris Cohen, "Tempering of Tool Steels," Metal Progress, May and June 1947, p. 781 and 962.

C-160. W. Connert and H. Kiessler, "Research on the Applicability of Intermediate Temperature Annealing," Stahl u Eisen, vol. 68, Apr. 22, 1948, p. 137.

C-170. A. Cottrell, "Tensile Properties of Unstable Austenite and Its Low Temperature Decomposition Products — Ni-Cr-Mo Steel," Journal Iron and Steel Inst., 1945, vol. 151, p. 93.

C-180. Crucible Steel Co. of America TTT Data Sheets, 1945-1949.

C-185. J. R. Cruciger and J. R. Vilella, "The Isothermal Transformation of Case Carburized SAE 4815," ASM Trans., vol. 32, 1944, p. 195.

C-190. C. Crussard, "Contribution to the Theory of the Martensitic Transformation," Conservatoire National des Arts et Metiers, Symposium on Metal Physics, Paris, 1948, p. 39.

C-210. P. A. Cushman, "Isothermal Heat Treatment Aids Bearing Production," The Iron Age, Nov. 27, 1947, p. 76.

Continued

D

D-0. H. L. Daasch, "Quenching Steel in Hot Baths," Metal Progress, November 1933, p. 27.

D-1. Yves Dardel, "Les Conceptions Americanines Relatives a la Trempabilite de L'acier," Publication du Centre de Documentation Siderurgique, 1948.

D-4. E. S. Davenport and E. C. Bain, "Transformation of Austenite at Constant Subcritical Temperatures," AIME Trans., vol. 90, 1930, p. 117.

D-5. E. S. Davenport, "Isothermal Transformation in Steels," ASM Trans., vol. 27, 1939, p. 837.

D-6. E. S. Davenport, "Austempering," Metal Progress, vol. 36, 1939.

D-7. E. S. Davenport, R. A. Grange and R. J. Hafsten, "Influence of Austenite Grain Size Upon Isothermal Behavior of SAE 4140 Steel," AIME Trans., vol. 145, 1941, p. 301.

D-8. E. S. Davenport, "Program in the Heat Treatment of Steel," Scientific American, April 1948, p. 149.

D-9. E. S. Davenport, "Isothermal Transformation Diagrams of Steel," ASM Handbook, 1948, p. 607.

D-50. G. Delbart, "Bulletin de la Societe Royale Belge des Ingenieurs et des Industriels," 1948, Series A. No. 3, p. 84.

D-52. G. Delbart and R. Potaszkin, "Properties of Cr-Mo Steel," Rev. de Metallurgie, vol. 43, 1945, p. 84.

D-53. G. Delbart and R. Potaszkin, "The Mechanical Properties of a Ni-Cr-Mo Steel Obtained by Stepped Quenching," Journal of the Iron and Steel Inst., vol. 157, 1947, p. 527.

D-54. G. Delbart and M. Ravery, "Research on Isothermal Quenching in France and in Foreign Countries," Revue de Metallurgie, vol. 46, June 1949, p. 399; July 1949, p. 475.

D-55. G. R. Delbart, "Recent French Studies on Hardening by Interrupted Quench," Instituto del Hierro y del Acero, 1, (2), October-December 1949, p. 76.

D-56. G. Delbart and M. Ravery, "Contribution to the Study of the Influence of Microstructure on Creep," Instituto del Hierro y del Acero, (1) January-March 1950, p. 2.

D-60. J. P. Deringer, "Bearing Races Improved by Isothermal Treatment," Metal Progress, July 1945, p. 80.

D-90. C. W. Dietz, "Short Anneal for Carburized SAE 3312," Metal Progress, December 1943, p. 1097.

D-140. J. R. Doig, "Crystal Structure and Phase Transformations," Metals Review, December 1949, p. 4.

D-150. T. J. Dolan and C. S. Yen, "Some Effects of the Metallurgical Structure on Fatigue Strength and Notch Sensitivity of Steel," ASTM Proc., vol. 48, 1948, p. 664.

D-160. C. K. Donoho, "The Temperature Range of Martensite Formation," Metal Progress Data Sheet, October 1946, p. 6766-B.

D-200. A. Dube and S. L. Gertsman, "Some Metallurgical Principles for the Efficient Heat Treatment of Steel," Canadian Inst. Mining and Met., Trans., 1945, p. 165.

D-210. Cenek Duchon, "Isothermal Quenching," Hutnicke-Listy, vol. 4, April 1949, p. 105, and May 1949, p. 142.

E

E-2. J. J. Ebner, "Carburizing-Martempering," Steel, Oct. 3, 1949, p. 72.

Turn to Page 452

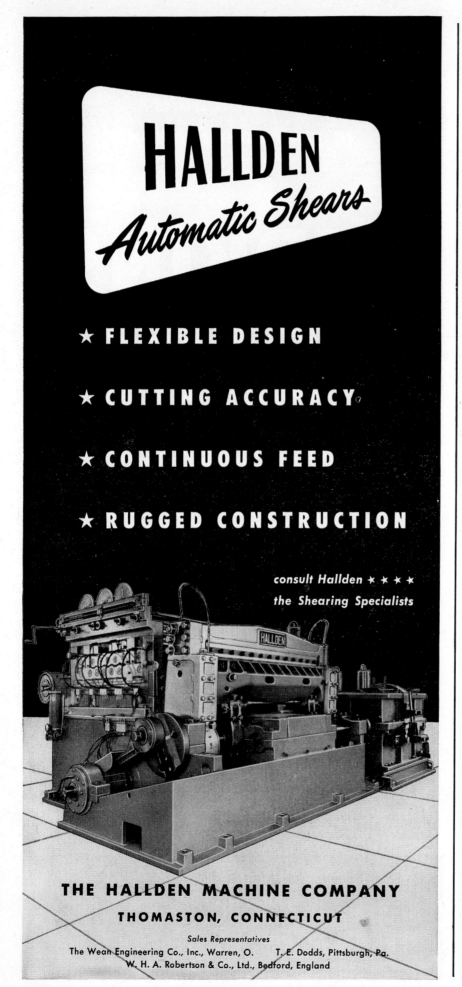
Heat Treating

E-40. C. T. Eddy, R. J. Marcotte and R. J. Smith, "Time - Temperature - Transformation Curves For Use in the Heat Treatment of Cast Steel," AIME Trans., vol. 162, 1945, p. 250.

E-120. R. M. Ellis, "Isothermal Treatment for Pistol Parts," The Iron Age, Feb. 8, 1945, p. 42.

E-123. H. J. Elmendorf, "The Effect of Varying Amounts of Martensite Upon the Isothermal Transformation of Austenite Remaining After Controlled Quenching," ASM Trans., vol. 33, 1944, p. 236.

E-125. A. R. Elsea, "Heat Treating During 1947," Metals Review, January 1948, p. 5.

E-140. G. M. Enos, G. J. Peer and J. C. Holwarth, "Dynamic Hot Hardness Testing—With Special Reference to Isothermal Transformations," Metal Progress, July 1948, P. 51.

E-200. G. V. Estulin, "The Study of Transformations in Austenitic Alloys by the Magnetic Method," Zavodskaya Laboratoriya, vol. 15, 1949, p. 1262. (Russian.)

F

F-1. V. Fabian, "Spannungsfreies, verzugsfreies, rissefreies Harten," Maschinenba, Der Betrieb, vol. 13, June 1934, p. 305.

F-51. I. Fesccenko-Czopiwski and J. Wilk, "Testing Quenching Media and Their Relation to Bain's S Curves," Prace Badawcze Huty Baildon, February 1939, p. 21.

F-90. J. C. Fisher, "Eutectoid Decompositions," "Thermodynamics in Physical Metallurgy," ASM book, 1950, p. 201.

F-91. J. C. Fisher, "The Free Energy Change Accompanying the Martensite Transformation in Steels," AIME Metals Trans., vol. 185, 1949, p. 688.

F-92. J. C. Fisher, J. H. Hollomon and D. Turnbull, "Kinetics of the Austenite-Martensite Transformation," AIME Metals Trans., vol. 185, 1949, p. 691.

F-120. S. G. Fletcher and Morris Cohen, "The Dimensional Stability of Steel," Part 1—"Subatmospheric Transformation of Retained Austenite," ASM Trans., vol. 34, 1945, p. 216.

F-121. S. G. Fletcher, B. L. Averbach and Morris Cohen, "The Dimensional Stability of Steel," ASM Trans., vol. 40, 1948, p. 703.

F-130. R. A. Flinn and J. Chipman, "The Acicular Structure in Nickel-Molybdenum Cast Irons," ASM Trans., vol. 30, 1942, p. 1255.

F-131. R. A. Flinn and J. A. Fellows, "A Quantitative Study of Austenite Transformation," ASM Trans., vol. 31, 1943, p. 41.

F-150. F. B. Foote, W. C. Truckmiller and W. P. Wood, "Electrical Resistance Method for Determination of Isothermal Austenite Transformations," ASM Trans., vol. 30, 1942, p. 1359.

F-155. A. C. Forsyth and R. P. Carreker, "Fatigue Limit of SAE 1095 After Various Heat Treatments," Metal Progress, November 1948, p. 683.

F-179. H. J. French and O. Z. Klopsch, "Quenching Diagrams for Carbon Steels," ASST Trans., vol. 6, 1924, p. 251.

F-180. H. J. French, "Fatigue and Hardening of Steels," ASM Trans., vol. 21, 1933, p. 899.

F-181. H. J. French, "Some Aspects of the Hardenability of Steels," Metal Progress, April 1949, p. 505.

F-190. M. L. Frey, "Timed Quenching," B. F. Shepherd, "Martempering," H. J. Elmen-

Continued

dorf, "Hot Quenching and Austempering—Incomplete Quenching A Discussion," Metal Progress, August 1944, p. 308.

G

G-50. S. L. Gertsman, "Delayed Quench for Steel Castings," Canadian Metals & Metallurgical Industries, vol. 11, September 1948, pp. 17, 32, 46.

G-150. P. Gordon, M. Cohen and R. S. Rose, "The Kinetics of Austenite Decomposition in High-Speed Steels," ASM Trans., vol. 31, 1943, p. 161.

G-151. Paul Gordon, M. Cohen and R. S. Rose, "The Effect of Quenching-Bath Temperature on the Tempering of High-Speed Steel," ASM Trans., 1944, p. 411.

G-155. J. Gorrissen, "Some Notes of Brittleness in Mild Steel," Journal of Iron and Steel Inst., vol. 162, (1), 1949, p. 17.

G-180. R. A. Grange and J. M. Kiefer, "Transformation of Austenite on Continuous Cooling and its Relation to Transformation at Constant Temperature," ASM Trans., vol. 29, 1941, p. 85.

G-181. R. A. Grange, W. S. Holt and E. T. Tkac, "Transformation of Austenite in an Aluminum - Chromium - Molybdenum Steel," AIME T.P. 2109, December 1946, Metals Technology.

G-182. R. A. Grange and H. M. Stewart, "The Temperature Range of Martensite Formation," AIME Trans., T.P. 1996, Metals Technology, June 1946; Steel, May 2, 1946, p. 126; Metal Progress, October 1946, p. 676-B; Materials & Methods, June 1946, p. 1621.

G-183. R. A. Grange, "Factors Influencing the Pearlitic Micro-Structure of Annealed Hypoeutectoid Steel," ASM Trans., 1947, p. 879.

G-184. R. A. Grange, J. F. Boyce and V. G. Peck, Transformation of 8630 Steel on Continuous Cooling and Isothermal Transformation Correlated with End Quench Hardenability Specimen," Metal Progress, Data Sheet, May 1950, p. 637 and 636B.

G-185. A. B. Greninger and A. R. Troiano, "Mechanism of Martensite Formation," AIME T.P. 1338, Metals Technology, June 1941; Trans., vol. 145, 1941, p. 289.

G-186. A. B. Greninger and A. R. Troiano, "The Kinetics of the Austenite-Martensite Reaction," ASM Trans., vol. 28, 1940, p. 537.

G-187. A. B. Greninger, "The Martensite Transformation in Beta Copper Aluminum Alloys," AIME Trans., vol. 133, 1939, p. 204.

G-188. A. B. Greninger and A. R. Troiano, "The Mechanism of Martensite Formation," AIME Trans., vol. 185, 1949, p. 590.

G-190. W. T. Griffith, L. B. Pfeil and N. P. Allen, "Special Report No. 24," Iron and Steel Inst., (England), vol. 24, 1939, p. 343.

G-191. W. T. Griffith, L. B. Pfeil and N. P. Allen, "Intermediate Transformation in Alloy Steels," Metal Progress, August 1939, p. 158.

G-200. M. Grossman, "Principle of Heat Treating," ASM book, 1941.

G-210. G. J. Guarneri and J. J. Kanter, "Some Characteristics of 4 to 6 Pct Cr and ½ Pct Mo Cast Steel," ASM Trans., vol. 40, 1948, p. 1147.

G-240. N. T. Gudtsov and T. N. Nazarova, "Influence of Boron on Kinetics of Austenite Transformation in Steel," Izvestiya Akademii Nauk SSSR, March 1950, p. 386.

Turn to Page 454

Heat Treating

H

H-1. R. J. Hafsten, "Metallurgy of SAE 52100 Ball Bearing Steel," The Iron Age, July 5, 1945, p. 54.

H-3. A. M. Hall, "Heat Treating—Theory and Practice," Metals Review, July 1949, p. 5.

H-8. H. Haneman and H. J. Wiester, On High Carbon Martensite, Archiv. fur das Eisenhuttenwesen, vol. 5, 1932, p. 377.

H-10. W. J. Harris and Morris Cohen, "Stabilization of the Austenite-Martensite Transformation," AIME Trans., vol. 180, 1949, p. 447.

H-11. W. J. Harris, "Comparison of Metallographic and X-Ray Measurements of Retained Austenite," Nature, London, Feb. 28, 1948, p. 315.

H-15. M. F. Hawkes and R. F. Mehl, "The Effect of Cobalt on the Rate of Nucleation and the Rate of Growth of Pearlite," AIME Metals Technology, August 1947, T.P. 2211.

H-50. W. F. Hess, "Effect of Cooling Rate on the Properties of Arcwelded Joints in C-Mo Steel," Welding Journal, vol. 21, 1942, p. 608-S.

H-51. W. F. Hess. L. L. Merrill, E. F. Nipper and A. P. Bunk, "The Measurement of Cooling Rates Associated with Arcwelding and Their Application to the Selection of Optimum Welding Conditions," Welding Journal, vol. 22, 1943, p. 377-s.

H-52. W. F. Hess, W. D. Doty and W. J. Childs, "The Heat Treatment of Spot Welds in Steel Plate," Welding Journal, vol. 26, 1947, p. 641-s.

H-85. W. C. Hiatt and W. B. Cheney, "Mass Marquenching," Automotive Industries, vol. 102, Apr. 15, 1950, p. 32, 114.

H-90. W. R. Hibard and G. E. Eichelman, "The Kappa Eutectoid Transformation in Copper Silicon Alloys," AIME Metals Technology, September 1948; Trans., vol. 180, 1949, p. 92.

H-95. W. Hiller, "The Heat Treatment of Steel," Osterreichescher Maschinenmarkt Und Elektrowirtschaft, vol. 4, Sept. 15, 1949, p. 314.

H-150. J. M. Hodge, "Principles and Applications of Isothermal Heat Treatment," Industrial Heating, August 1948, p. 1332.

H-151. J. M. Hodge, "Isothermal Heat Treatment," Steel, Oct. 11, 1948, vol. 123, p. 92; SAE Journal, vol. 56, September 1948, p. 18.

H-153. J. M. Hodge, J. L. Fiove and R. G. Storm, "The Hardenability Effect of Molybdenum," Journal of Metals, vol. 1, No. 3, 1949, p. 218.

H-160. J. H. Hollomon, L. D. Jaffe and M. R. Morton, "Anisothermal Decomposition of Austenite," AIME T.P. 2008, Metals Tech., August 1946.

H-161. J. H. Hollomon and L. D. Jaffe, "Ferrous Metallurgical Design," John Wiley & Sons, Inc., New York, 1947, p. 230, p. 270.

H-169. Houghton Line—Miscellaneous Articles, 1945 to date.

H-170. R. T. Howard and M. Cohen, "Austenite Transformations Above and Within the Martensite Ranges," AIME Trans., vol. 176, 1948, p. 384.

H-180. S. I. Hoyt, C. E. Sims and H. M. Banta, "Improving the Weldability of High Strength Low Alloy Steels," The Iron Age, May 31, 1945, p. 38; June 7, p. 70; June 14, p. 74.

H-200. F. C. Hull, R. A. Colton and R. F. Mehl, "Rate of Nucleation and Rate of Growth of Pearlite," AIME Trans., 1942, p. 185.

Continued

H-210. A. Hultgren, "Isothermal Transformation of Austenite," ASM Trans., vol. 39, 1947, p. 915.

I

I-10. International Nickel Co., "Isothermal Transformation Diagrams for Nickel Alloy Steels," Nickel Alloy Steels, Section 5, Data Sheet, A, 1947.

I-16. B. K. Ipatov, "Effect of Chemical Elements on the Isothermal Decomposition of Super-cooled Austenite (in cast iron) for Piston Rings," Chemical Abstract, vol. 40, 1946, p. 4997.

I-50. I. Isaitschew and V. Mirezkiy, "The Low Temperature Transformation of the Beta Phase in Copper-Zinc Alloys," J. Techn. Physics. (USSR) vol. 8, 1939, p. 1333.

J

J-1. L. D. Jaffe, "An Isothermal Formation of Bainite and Pro-Eutectoid Constituents in Steel," AIME Trans., T.P. 2290, Metals Technology, December 1945, p. 921.

J-10. Vojtecha Jarese, "The Martensite Transformation," Hutnicke Listy (Czech), vol. 4, October 1949, p. 309.

J-20. M. A. Jaswon and J. A. Wheeler, "Atomic Displacements in Martensite Transfromation," Acta Cryst. vol. 1, 1948, p. 216.

J-50. W. Jellinghaus, "The Influence of Mn on the Hardening of Carbon Steels," Mitt. Kaiser Wilhelmstr. F. Eisenforschung, vol. 15, 1933, p. 15.

J-51. W. Jellinghaus, "The Course of the Isothermal Austenite Transformation of a Chromium Magnet Steel and the Effect of Hardening Temperature and of Hardening Time," Archiv fur das Eisenhuttenwesen, vol. 20, July, August 1949, p. 243.

J-55. M. D. Jepson and F. G. Thompson, "The Acceleration of the Rate of Isothermal Transformation of Austenite" Journal Iron and Steel Inst., vol. 162, 1949, p. 49.

J-60. Jessop Steel Co., "Data Sheet on T-T-T Diagram for Steels."

J-150. H. Jolivet, "Transformation of Austenite on Cooling," Journal Iron and Steel Inst., vol. 140, 1939, p. 95.

J-151. H. Jolivet, "General Survey on the Decomposition of Austenite," Conservatoire National des Arts et Metiers Symposium on Metal Physics, Paris, 1948, p. 67.

K

K-1. J. F. Kahles, "Formation and Transformation Studies of Iron-Carbon Powder Alloys," ASM Trans., vol. 38, 1947, p. 618.

K-120. E. P. Klier and T. Lyman, "The Bainite Reaction in Hypoeutectoid Steels," AIME Trans., vol. 158, p. 394.

K-150. S. Koshiba, "Concerning the Study of Isothermal Transformations in High-Speed Steel," Part III (in Japanese), Nippon Kinzoku Gakkai-Si, vol. 13, May 1949, p. 40.

K-180. I. R. Kramer, S. L. Toleman and W. T. Haswell, "Iron Manganese Alloys," ASM Trans., vol. 42, p. 1260.

K-210. G. V. Kurdyumov, "On the Nature of Martensitic Transformations," Part III, "Diffusionless (Martensitic) Transformations in Alloys," Zhurnal Tekhnischeskoi Fiziki, vol. 18, 1948, No. 8, p. 1011.

Turn to Page 456

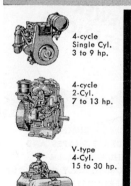

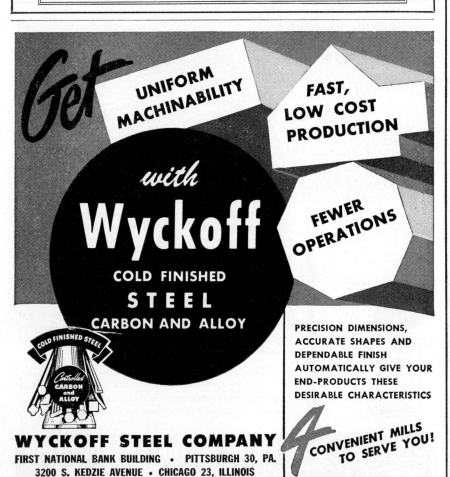
Heat Treating

K-211. G. V. Kurdyumov and L. G. Khandros, "On the Thermoelastic Equilibrium in Martensitic Transformations," Doklady Akadmii Nauk SSSR, vol. 66, 1949, No. 2, p. 211.

L

L-1. G. M. Lahr, "Conventional v. Salt Bath Hardening of Cast Iron Cylinder Liners," AFS Trans., vol. 56, 1948, p. 536.

L-10. H. Lange, "Kinetics of Austenite Transformation," Mitt. KW. Inst. 15, 1933, p. 263; Stahl und Eisen, vol. 54, 1934, p. 113.

L-15. P. Laurent, "The Nucleation in the Transformation of Steels," Conservaoire National des Arts et Metiers Symposium on Metal Physics, Paris, 1948, p. 5.

L-20. H. Lawrence, "Weldability in Steel,. Steel, Jan. 26, 1942, p. 90.

L-50. E. E. Legge, "The Industrial Application of Austempering," Metals & Alloys, August 1939, p. 228.

L-60. C. H. Lekberg, "Modern Methods for Interrupted Quenching," Industrial Heating, October 1946, p. 1591.

L-61. C. H. Lekberg, "Interrupted Quenching as a Metallurgical Tool," Steel, Oct. 27, 1947, p. 79.

L-70. B. S. Lement, B. L. Averbach and M. Cohen, "The Dimensional Stability of Steel," Part IV—"Tool Steels," ASM Trans., 1949, p. 1061.

L-90. C. A. Liedholm, "Transformation of SAE 4330 During Continuous Cooling," Metal Progress, vol. 45, 1944, p. 94.

L-91. C. A. Liedholm, S. E. Lopez and W. C. Coons, "Transformation of SAE X-4130 During Continuous Cooling," Metal Progress, vol. 46, 1946.

L-92. C. A. Liedholm, A. I. Rush and D. J. Blickwede, "Transformation of NE 8630 During Continuous Cooling," Metal Progress, vol. 46, 1946, p. 496-B.

L-93. C. A. Liedholm, S. E. Lopez and D. J. Blickwede, "Transformations of SAE 4315 During Continuous Cooling," Metal Progress, vol. 48, 1945, p. 696-B.

L-94. C. A. Liedholm and W. C. Coons, "Effect of Annealing Cycles on Cooling Transformations Upon Subsequent Isothermal Reactions," Metal Progress, January 1946, p. 104.

L-95. C. A. Liedholm, "Experimental Studies of Continuous Cooling Transformations," ASM Trans., vol. 38, 1947, p. 180.

L-96. C. A. Liedholm, A. I. Rush and W. C. Coons, "Transformation of SAE 6115 Steel—on Continuous Cooling," Metal Progress, March 1948, p. 392-B.

L-97. C. A. Liedholm. "Structural Changes During Continuous Cooling," Metal Progress, December 1948, p. 849.

L-100. J. F. Libsch, Wen-Pin Chuang, and W. J. Murphy, "The Effect of Alloying Elements on the Transformation Characteristics of Induction Heated Steels," ASM Trans., vol. 42, 1950, p. 121.

L-110. R. W. Linsay and J. E. Atherton, "Heat Treatment Study of Pearlite Malleable Cast Iron," American Foundryman, September 1945, p. 27.

L-120. I. P. Lipilin, "Heat Treatment of Uncooled Steel and Rationalization of the Annealing of Cooled Steel," (Russian), 1937 Iron and Steel Inst. Translation No. 230, July 1945.

Continued

L-121. I. P. Lipilin, "Isothermal Treatment of Hot Ingots and Forgings," Iron and Steel Inst. (England), Translation No. 216, 1945.

L-150. E. A. Loria and H. D. Shephard, "Acicular Transformations in Alloy Steels," ASM Trans., vol. 40, 1948, p. 758.

L-155. B. M. Loring, "The 'S' Curve of Chromium Nickel Steel," AIME Trans., vol. 150, 1942, p. 283.

L-200. W. Lueg and A. Pomp, "The Use of Salt Baths for Patenting Steel Wire," Stahl u Eisen, vol. 61, 1941, p. 266.

L-250. T. Lyman and A. R. Troiano, "Isothermal Transformation of Austenite in 1 Pct Carbon High Chromium Steels," AIME Trans., T.P. 1801, Metals Technology, September 1945; AIME Trans., Vol. 162, 1945, p. 196.

L-251. T. Lyman and A. R. Troiano, "Influence of Carbon Content Upon the Transformation in 3 Pct Chromium Steels," ASM Trans., vol. 37, 1946, p. 402.

M

M-1. D. J. Mack, "The Isothermal Transformation of an Eutectoid Aluminum Bronze," AIME Trans., T.P. No. 2242, 1947; "Discussion to T.P. 2398," p. 16, Metals Technology, June 1948.

M-5. G. K. Manning and C. H. Lorig, "The Relationship Between Transformation During Cooling," AIME T.P. 2014, Metals Technology, June 1946.

M-10. R. J. Marcotte and C. T. Eddy, "The Effect of Homogenization of Cast Steels," ASM Trans., vol. 40, 1948, p. 649.

M-14. D. L. Martin and W. G. Van Note, "Induction Hardening and Austenitizing Characteristics of Several Medium C Steels," ASM Trans., 1946.

M-15. J. Mazur, "Grain Size of Martensite After Treatment at Very Low Temperature" Nature, vol. 164, Aug. 27, 1949, p. 358.

M-16. Josef Mazur, "Structure of Tempered Martensite," Nature, vol. 164, Aug. 6, 1949, p. 230.

M-17. Josef Mazur and M. A. Jaswon, "X-Line Breaths of Martensite," Nature, vol. 164, 1949, p. 712.

M-18. C. E. McDermott, "Heat Treatment of Alloy Steels," Industrial Heating, vol. 17, June 1950, p. 980.

M-20. F. J. McMulkin, "Practical Tool Room Heat Treatment," The Iron Age, June 6, 1946, p. 60; June 13, p. 56; June 20, p. 64; June 27, p. 55.

M-30. A. W. McReynolds, "Electrical Observations of the Austenite-Martensite Transformation in Steel," Journal Applied Physics, vol. 17, 1946, p. 823.

M-50. W. L. Meinhart, "Low and Medium Alloy Cast Steels," The Valve World, vol. 44, February-March, 1947, p. 94.

M-55. Metallurgicus, "Cycle Annealing," Metal Progress, March 1944, p. 508.

M-60. B. Yu. Mett and R. I. Entin, "Causes of the Influence of Mo on the Kinetics of the Isothermal Decomposition of Austenite," Doklady Akad. SSSR 68, 1949, p. 681; C.A. 44, 1950, p. 4845 b.

M-80. Kenneth Midlam, "Annealing for Machinability," Metal Progress, October 1949, p. 504.

Turn to Page 458

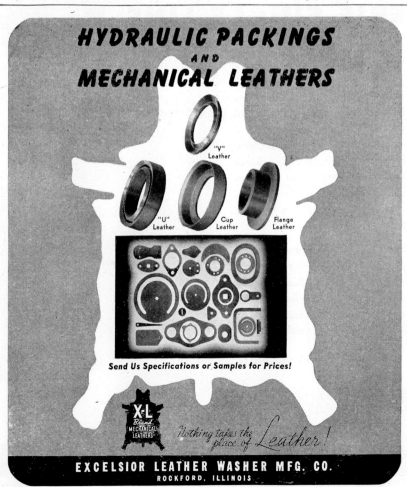
Heat Treating

Continued

M-90. A. Michel, "The Martensitic Quench and Tempering," Conservatoire National des Arts et Metiers, Symposium on Metal Physics, Paris, 1948, p. 55.

M-150. F. R. Morral, "Heat Treating Diagrams," Metal Progress, October 1945, p. 818.

M-151. F. R. Morral, "Modern Heat Treating—A Reference Index" The Iron Age, June 10, 1948, p. 83.

M-152. F. R. Morral, "Isothermal Heat Treating," Wire and Wire Products, January, February and March, 1949, p. 31, 152, 236.

M-153. F. R. Morral, "Quenching Steel in Molten Media," Steel, June 21, 1948, p. 92.

M-200. F. Munoz del Corral, "Thermodynamics of the Eutectoid Zone in Carbon and Low Alloy Steels," Inst. del Hierro y del Acero, vol. II (No. 4 and 6), 1949, pp. 27 and 52.

M-220. D. W. Murphy, W. P. Wood and C. D. D'Amico, "Austenite Transformation in Gray Iron," AFS Trans., vol. 46, 1939, p. 563.

N

N-1. C. Nagler and R. L. Dowdell, "Isothermal Transformation of Mo Cast Iron," AFS Prep. 47-17, 1947.

N-50. H. Neerfeld, "The Mechanism of the γ α Transformation in Iron," Stahl u Eisen, vol. 68, Mar. 25, 1948, p. 128.

N-51. H. Neerfeld, and K. Mathieu, "Mechanism of γ α Transformation," Metal Treatment, vol. 16, 1949, p. 77.

N-60. A. E. Nehrenberg, "Discussion to Paper by R. A. Grange and Stewart," AIME Trans., Vol. 167, 1946, p. 467.

N-100. Zenji Nishiyama and Michiyasu Doil, "Concerning the Mechanism of Formation of 'Lower Bainite' and Troostite in Steels," (In Japanese) Nippon Kinzoku Gakkai-Si (Journal of the Japan Inst. of Metals), vol. 13, June 1949, p. 3.

N-150. K. O. Nordin and E. Tholander, "Suitable Temperature and Time for Cycle Annealing," Jernkontorets Ann., vol. 131, 1947. p. 243.

O

O-1. D. B. Oakley and J. F. Oesterle, "Dliatometric Studies in the Transformation of Austenite in Molybdenum Cast Irons," ASM Trans., 1940, p. 832.

O-10. T. F. O'Brien, "Heat Treatment of Steel," Metals and Alloys, vol. 21, May 1945, p. 1335.

O-80. C. W. Ohly, "Austempering Cast Iron Serves as Cylinder Liners," Materials and Methods, May 1947, p. 89.

O-120. W. Olson and G. Nevins, "Use of Modified Martempering for Hardening Intricately Shaped Dies," Steel, Dec. 15, 1947, p. 88.

O-121. W. Olson and G. Nevins, "Modified Martempering," Industrial Gas, vol. 26, April 1948, pp. 10, 18.

O-250. S. Owaku, K. Iijima and N. Kashiwagi, "Concerning the Differences of Mechanical Properties Between Martempered and Austempered Carbon Steel," (In Japanese), Nippon Kinzoku Gakkai-Si (Journal of the Japanese Inst. of Metals), vol. 13, June 1949, p. 29.

Turn to Page 460

January 4, 1951

459

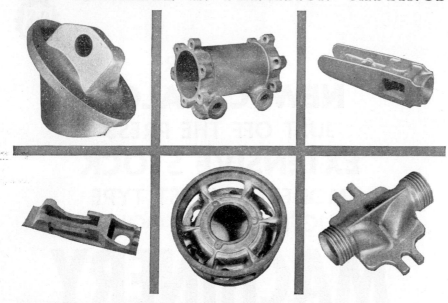

Heat Treating

P

P-1. P. Payson, W. L. Hodapp and J. Leeder, "The Spheroidizing of Steel," ASM Trans., 1939, p. 306.

P-2. P. Payson, "The Annealing of Steel," The Iron Age, June 24, 1943, p. 44; July 1, p. 48; July 8, p. 74; July 15, p. 70; July 22, p. 60.

P-3. P. Payson and J. L. Klein, "The Hardening of Tool Steels," ASM Trans., vol. 32, 1943, p. 218.

P-4. P. Payson and C. H. Savage, "Martensite Reactions in Alloy Steel," ASM Trans., vol. 33, 1944, p. 261.

P-5. P. Payson and A. E. Nehrenberg, "New Steel Features High Strength and High Toughness," The Iron Age, Oct. 21, 1948, p. 64; Oct. 28, p. 74.

P-6. P. Payson and R. A. Grange, "The Temperature Range of Martensite Formation in Steel," ASM Handbook, 1948, p. 611.

P-10. C. A. Payntor, "Scale Reduction in Controlled Atmosphere Cycle Annealing," The Iron Age, Dec. 15, 1949, p. 86.

P-50. B. M. Pearson, "Some Aspects of Salt Bath Furnaces Discussed in Their Application to the Wire Industry," Part III, Wire Industry, vol. 16, December 1949, p. 973.

P-55. W. S. Pellini and S. R. Queneau, "Development of Temper Brittleness in Alloy Steels," ASM Trans., vol. 39, 1947, p. 139.

P-60. Walter Peter, "Das Abkuhlungsvermogen flussiger Hartemittel," Archiv for das Eisenhuttenwesen, vol. 20, July-August 1949, p. 263.

P-61. P. Peter, "Cooling Power of Quenching Liquids and Influence on Hardening Processes," K. Wilhelm Inst. f. Eisenforschung, 1946. Manuscript No. 63.

P-100. J. Pomey, F. Goutel, R. Coudray and L. Abel, Societe Francaise de Metallurgie, Oct. 21, 1948, Revue de Metallurgie, Memoires, 1949, vol. 46, p. 825.

P-130. Anton Pomp and Gunter Gesche, "The Applicability of Isothermal Hardening in the Production of Unalloyed Steel Wires," (In German), Stahl und Eisen, vol. 70, Jan. 19, 1950, p. 52.

P-140. A. Portevin, "Incubation of Centers for Austenite Transformation," Metal Progress, May 1945, p. 932.

P-141. A. Portevin, "Morphology and Kinetics of the Constituents in Quenched Steels," Metal Progress, August 1946, p. 311.

P-142. A. Portevin and M. Garvin, "Fundamental Investigation of the Influence of the Rate of Cooling on the Hardening of Carbon Steels," Journal Iron and Steel Inst., vol. 99, 1919, p. 469.

P-150. C. B. Post and W. H. Fenstermacher, "Rates of Cooling in Blocks and Cylinders," ASM Trans., vol. 33, 1944, p. 19.

P-180. A. Preece, J. Nutting and A. Hartley, "The Overheating and Burning of Steel, Part III, The Influence of Excessive Reheating Temperatures on the Mechanical Properties and the Structure of Alby Steels," Journal Iron and Steel Inst., vol. 164, January 1950, p. 37.

P-210. M. A. Pugacz, G. J. Siegel and J. O. Steels," Metallic Creep, Book, 1949, p. 163.

Continued

Mack, "The Effect of Postheat in Welding Medium Alloy Steels," Welding Journal, vol. 23, 1944, p. 536-s.

P-220. W. I. Pumphrey, "Behavior of Chromium Steel in Jominy Hardenability Test," Journal Iron and Steel Inst., vol. 157, 1947, p. 27.

P-221. W. I. Pumphrey and F. W. Jones, "Austenite Breakdown," Iron and Steel (London), vol. 21, 1948, p. 561.

P-230. W. Pungel, "Compressed Air as a Coolant in the Patenting of Steel Wire," Stahl und Eisen, vol. 69, No. 8, 1949.

R

R-50. T. A. Read, A. Marcus and McCaughey, "Plastic Flow and Rupture of Steel at High Hardness Level," Fracture of Metals, ASM, 1948, p. 228.

R-55. Republic Steel Corp., "Alloy Steels," Book, 1949.

R-90. R. L. Rickett, "Planning Heat Treatment by S-curves," Metal Progress, vol. 43, 1943, p. 77.

R-91. R. J. Rickett, J. G. Cutton, C. B. Bernhart and J. R. Millikin, "Isothermal Transformation and End Quench Hardenability of Some NE Steels," ASM Trans., vol. 35, 1945, p. 22.

R-150. G. A. Roberts and R. F. Mehl, "The Mechanism and the Rate of Formation of Austenite from Ferrite Cementite Aggregates," ASM Trans., September 1943, p. 613.

R-151. G. A. Roberts and R. F. Mehl, "Effect of Inhomogeneity in Austenite on the Rate of the Austenite Pearlite Reaction in Plain Carbon Steels," AIME T.P. 1568, 1943; Trans., vol. 154, 1943, p. 318.

R-155. A. Rose and W. Fisher, "Influence of Cooling Velocities on the Transformation of Steels," Mitt. Kaiser Wilhelm Inst. f. Eisenforschung, 21, 1939, p. 133.

R-160. K. Rose, "Cyclic Annealing of Steel Forgings Saves Time, Better Quality," Materials and Methods, January 1948, p. 71.

R-170. D. Rosenblatt, "How to Predict Suitability and Determine Method of Martempering and Hypo-Eutectoid Steel," Steel, vol. 121, Oct. 20, 1947, p. 121.

R-171. D. Rosenblatt, "Isothemal Heat Treating of Large Steel Castings," The Iron Age, June 30, 1949, p. 42.

R-180. P. C. Rosenthal and C. K. Manning, "Heat Treatment of Heavy Cast Steel Sections," Steel, Nov. 18, 1946, p. 88.

R-185. E. S. Rowland and R. S. Lyle, "Measurement of Case Depths by Martensite Formation," Metal Progress, May 1945, p. 907.

R-210. D. W. Rudorff, "Abstracts of A. Gulyaev's Russian Article "On the Influence of Mo Content Upon the Properties of High-Speed W. Free Tool Steel," Metallurgia, July 1941, p. 88.

R-220. T. F. Russell and C. Mavrocordatos, "Experiences in the Study of Isothermal Transformations," Journal Iron and Steel Inst., vol. 162, 1949, p. 33.

R-221. J. V. Russell and F. T. McGuire, "A Metallographic Study of the Decomposition of Austenite in Mn Steels," ASM Trans., vol. 33, 1944, p. 103.

S

S-1. G. Sachs, "Comparison of Various Structural Alloy Steels by Means of the Static Notch-Bar Tensile Test," AIME, Metals Tech., December 1946, T.P. No. 2110, p. 6.

S-2. G. Sachs, L. J. Ebert and W. F. Brown, "Notch Tensile Characteristics of a Partially Austempered Low Alloy Steel," AIME Trans., vol. 176, 1948, p. 424.

S-10. J. Savage, "Mechanism of the Gamma-Alpha Transformation in Iron," Metal Treatment and Drop Forging, vol. 16, 1949, Summer Issue, p. 77.

S-30. F. M. Schmucker, "Discussion to Paper on the Hardenability Concept," AIME Trans., 1947, or Metals Tech., September 1946, p. 19.

S-35. H. Schneider, "Planning and Economy of Heat Treating Operation," Stahl und Eisen, vol. 68, 1948, p. 479.

S-40. D. A. Scott, W. M. Armstrong and F. A. Forward, "The Influence of Nickel and Molybdenum on the Isothermal Transformation of Austenite in Pure Iron-Nickel and Iron-Nickel-Molybdenum Alloys," ASM Trans., vol. 41, 1949, p. 1145.

S-50. A. P. Seasholtz, "Interrupted Quenching in Salt Baths," Metal Progress, October 1944, p. 730.

S-55. Richard P. Seelig, "Heat Treatment of Tool Steels by Martempering," The Iron Age, Sept. 1, 1949, p. 72.

S-60. Seidel and Tauscher, "Isothermal Hardening," Die Technik, vol. 4, 1949, p. 103.

S-70. J. Shaw, "Steel Treatments; Practical Aspects of Isothermal Annealing, Austempering, Martempering and Deep Freezing," Iron and Steel, vol. 21, September 1948, p. 391.

S-71. J. Shaw, "Practical Aspects of Isothermal Annealing," Steel Processing, vol. 34, November 1948, p. 600, 613.

S-80. L. J. Sheehan, "Salt Bath Hardening of NE Steels," Metals and Alloys, November 1943, p. 1087.

S-81. J. P. Sheehan, C. A. Julien and A. R. Troiano, "The Transformation Characteristics of Ten Selected Nickel Steels," ASM Trans., vol. 41, 1949, p. 1165.

S-86. B. F. Shepherd, "Martempering," The Iron Age, Jan. 28, 1943, p. 50; Feb. 4, 1943, p. 45.

S-87. B. F. Shepherd, "Mechanical and Metallurgical Advantages of Martempering Steel," Product Engineering, July 1945, p. 438.

S-87a. B. F. Shepherd, "Martempering Steel—Limitations of Hardness Penetration," Product Engineering, August 1945, p. 515.

S-88. B. F. Shepherd, "Some Observations on the Accuracy of Isothermal Diagrams," The Iron Age, Aug. 25, 1949, p. 61.

S-90. A. L. Simmons, "The 'S' Curve and Its Significance in the Practical Heat Treatment of Steel," The Australasian Eng. Science Sheet, June 7, 1944, p. 2.

S-110. P. Skulari, "Quenching of Steel from a Rontgenologists Point of View," Hutnicke Listy, vol. 3, 1948, p. 31.

S-130. C. S. Smith and W. E. Lindlief, "Micrographic Study of Cu-Al Alloys," AIME Trans., 104, 1933, p. 69.

S-131. E. W. P. Smith, "Effect of Residual Stresses on Fatigue of Compressor Valves," Metal Progress, April 1950, p. 480.

S-150. A. Sourdillon, "Theoretical and Practical Researches on Isothermal Quenching," Metallurgie, vol. 80, September 1948, pp. 11, 15, 17, 19.

S-151. A. Sourdillon, "The Decomposition of Austenite Under Isothermal Conditions and the Practical Application of this Reaction for the Treatment of Steels," Conservatoire National des Arts et Metiers, Symposium on Metal Physics, Paris, 1948, p. 19.

S-160. Paul Spencer and S. W. Poole, "Austenite Transformation in The Hardenable Chromium Stainless Steels," (In English), Metalen, vol. 4, September 1949, p. 1.

S-220. A. H. Sully, "Creep Properties of

Turn to Page 462

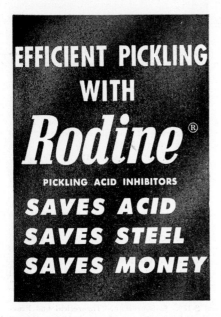

Heat Treating

Continued

S-250. W. P. Sykes, "The Ar¹ Reaction in Some Iron-Cobalt-Tungsten Alloys and the Same Modified With Chromium," ASM Trans., vol. 34, 1945, p. 415.

T

T-60. Eric Tholander, "Cycle Annealing in Quality Steel Production," Jernkontorets Ann., vol. 132, 1948, p. 367.

T-70. B. Thomas, "Salt Bath Quenching," Heat Treating and Forging, vol. 20, 1934, p. 285.

T-80. F. C. Thompson and L. R. Stanton, "Some Observation on the Austempering and Isothermal Transformation of Steels, With Special Ref. to the Production of Martensite," Iron and Steel Inst. Journal, vol. 151, 1945, p. 133.

T-81. F. C. Thompson and L. R. Stanton, "The Effect of Oxygen and the Isothermal Transformation of Steel and Suggested Test for Burning," Journal Iron and Steel Inst., vol. 153, 1946, p. 259.

T-82. F. C. Thompson and M. D. Jepson, "The Breakdown of Austenite Below the M Temperature," Journal Iron and Steel Inst., vol. 164, January 1950, p. 27.

T-85. J. M. Thompson, "Impact Resistance v. Hardness of Aircraft Low Alloy Steels," The Iron Age, Mar. 8, 1945, p. 72.

T-150. W. F. Toerge, "An Evaluation of Boron Treated Steels," The Iron Age, Dec. 8, 1947, p. 93.

T-180. A. R. Troiano, "An Investigation of the Metallographic and Physical Properties of New Types of Gun Steels," P.B. Report No. 15849, 1943.

T-181. A. R. Troiano and A. B. Greninger, "The Martensite Transformation," Metal Progress, August 1946, p. 303.

T-182. A. R. Troiano and J. E. de Moss, "Transformation in Krupp-Type Carburizing Steels," ASM Trans., vol. 39, 1947, p. 788.

T-183. A. R. Troiano, "Use of Hardness Data Restricted," Steel, Jan. 17, 1949, p. 66.

T-184. A. R. Troiano, "The Transformation and Retention of Austenite in SAE 2340, 5140 and T. 1350 Steels of Comparable Hardenability," ASM Trans., vol. 41, 1949, p. 1093.

T-210. K. I. Tulenkov, "Effect of Copper on Patenting Wire," Stal. vol. 7, 1947, p. 459.

U

U-1. U. S. Steel Corp., "Atlas of Isothermal Transformation Diagrams," 1943.

U-2. U. S. Steel Corp., "Suiting the Heat Treatment to the Job," booklet, 1946.

U-3. U. S. Steel Corp., "U.S.S. Carilloy Steels," booklet, 1948.

V

V-1. G. De Vries, "An End-Quenching Bar for Deep Hardening Steels," ASM Trans., vol. 41, 1949, p. 678.

W

W-50. F. Wever and H. Lange, "The Transformation Kinetics of Austenite," Mitt. Kaiser Wilhelmstr. Eisenforschung, vol. 14, 1932, p. 71.

W-51. F. Wever and H. Lange, "The Transformation Kinetics of Austenite," Mitt. Kaiser Wilhelminstitut fur Eisenforschung, vol. 15, 1933, p. 179.

W-52. F. Wever and K. Mathieu, "On Transformations in Mn Steels," Mitt. K. Wilhelm Inst. F. Eisenhuttenw., vol. 22, 1940, p. 9.

W-53. F. Wever and A. Rose, "The Influence of the Rate of Cooling on the Transformation and Properties of Vanadium Steels," Kaiser Wilhelminst. F. Eisenforschung, vol. 20, 1938, p. 213.

W-54. F. Wever, "The Problem of the Hardening of Steel and the Kinetics of Transformations," Stahl und Eisen, Sept. 15, 1949, p. 664.

W-80. A. M. White, "Variations in the Quenching Power of Salt Baths," Metal Progress, December 1949, p. 819.

W-81. J. H. Whitely, "The Extension of the Ar₁ Range with Carbide Formation in Mild Steel Due to High Temperature Treatment," Journal Iron and Steel Inst., vol. 164, 1950, p. 399.

W-85. S. L. Widrig and W. T. Groves, "Martempering of Automotive Gears and Shafts," Metal Progress, May 1950, p. 607.

W-90. H. T. Wieser, "The Bainite Structures in Steel and Their Origin," Arch. Eisenhuttenwesen, vol. 18, 1947, Nos. 5 and 6.

W-94. C. R. Wilks, E. Cook and H. S. Avery, "Further Development of the End Quench Hardenability Test," ASM Trans., vol. 35, 1945, p. 1.

W-95. C. T. Wilshaw, "Isothermal Heat Treatment for Precision Hardening," Metallurgia, vol. 39, November 1948, p. 3.

W-100. F. van Wijk, "Het TTT Diagrams," Metalen, vol. 2, August 1948, p. 253.

W-101. F. van Wijk, "Het TTT Diagrams," Centraal Instituut voor Material Onderzoek Afdeling Metalen, February 1949, p. 4.

W-110. K. Winterton, "The Effect of Overheating on the Transformation Characteristics of a Ni-Cr-Mo Steel," Journal Iron and Steel Inst., vol. 151, 1945, p. 79.

W-120. A. G. Witten, "Direct Quenching: Experimental Practice at Ruhrstahl," Iron and Steel, vol. 21, May 1948, p. 181.

W-180. W. J. Wrazej, "Lattic Spacing of Retained Austenite in Iron-Carbon Alloys," Nature, vol. 163, 1949, p. 212.

W-200. A. Wustefeld, "Equilibrium Disturbances in the γ-α Transformation of Iron Caused by Insufficient Diffusion," (in German), Archiv fur Metallkunde, vol. 3, December 1949, p. 436.

W-250. U. Wyss, "S-Curves and Nomenclature for Heat Treatment," Schweizer Archiv, vol. 14, April 1948, p. 127.

W-251. U. Wyss, "Effect of Bainite on Properties," Von Roll Mitteilungen, vol. 7, 1948, p. 51.

Z

Z-1. I. N. Zavarine, "Initial Stages of the Magnetic and Austenite Transformation in Carbon Steels," AIME Trans., T.P. No. 646, Metals Tech., October 1935.

Z-2. Karl Zankel, "Plant Experiences With Direct Resistance Heating for Patenting of Steel Wires," (in German), Stahl und Eisen, vol. 70, Jan. 19, 1950, p. 58.

Z-50. C. Zener, "Kinetics of the Decomposition of Austenite," AIME Trans., 1945, T.P. No. 1925.

Z-90. J. G. Zimmerman, R. H. Aborn, E. C. Bain, "Some Effects of Small Additions of Vanadium to Eutectoid Steels," ASM Trans., vol. 25, 1937, p. 755.

Z-250. V. Zyusin, V. Sadovski and S. Baranchuk, "Influence of Alloy Elements on the Position of the Martensite Point, Quantity of Retained Austenite and Stability of Austenite During Tempering," Metallurg, vol. 14, 1939, p. 75.

Resume Your Reading on Page 269

IRON AGE *markets and prices*

market briefs and bulletins

tinplate prices—Major producers of tinplate have announced changes in prices effective Jan. 1, with Carnegie-Illinois prices effective Jan. 16 (see THE IRON AGE, Nov. 2, 1950, p. 135). New prices for Wheeling, Weirton, and Inland Steel are: 1.50 lb base box, hot-dipped, $8.70; 1.25 lb hot-dipped, $8.45. Electrolytic prices: 0.25, $7.15; 0.50, $7.40; 0.75, $7.80; canmaking quality black plate, $6.25. Wheeling and Weirton's price for special coated manufacturing ternes is $7.50.

arsenal of democracy—Auto cutbacks are beginning to be offset by more defense orders. General Motors will make Republic F-84 Thunderjets at Kansas City. Willys-Overland has received four separate orders for jeeps, the latest one valued at $63 million. GM's Oldsmobile Div. will make 3½ in. rockets for the new super-bazooka. Ford will build aircraft engines in the old Tucker plant in Chicago. Cadillac is building tanks in Cleveland, and Continental is building tank engines.

tinplate—To date DO orders for tinplate have not been heavy. However, defense tonnage is expected to increase with application of tin consumption controls Feb. 1. Reason is that tin used for DO orders probably will be outside the quota, and canmakers are likely to slap on DO's whereas previously they were producing such items as ration cans from plate on hand.

refractories prices—General refractories prices are up. Standard chemically bonded chrome brick at Baltimore is up $5 to a new price of $82. Standard magnesite brick is $104 at Baltimore, and chemically bonded magnesite brick is now $93.

no reaction—Manufacturing companies in the midwest report little or no reaction on the part of suppliers to the government request for a voluntary rollback to Dec. 1 price levels. Suppliers' prices raised after Dec. 1 are reported to have gone up an average of 7 to 10 pct on a variety of products ranging from heavy chemicals to locomotive specialties. Suppliers are reported to feel they should not be required to roll back prices until there is a price adjustment on basic materials.

tube extrusion—National Tube Co. will build a large extrusion plant for manufacture of high alloy seamless specialty tubes, shapes, and bars at its Gary Works. The plant will utilize the recently developed French Ugine-Sejournet process of hot extrusion using glass as a lubricant. Included in facilities will be a 2500-ton hydraulic extrusion press. Capacity will be 3000 tons. Plant is expected to be in operation before the end of the year.

electronic parts makers hit—Material shortages and manpower dislocations will be major factors in 1951 to trouble makers of electronic parts and equipment. Manpower shortage will up demand for intercom systems.

stretching controls—NPA has directed General Services Administration to become exclusive buyer and seller of all natural rubber imported into the United States.

Steel Operations**

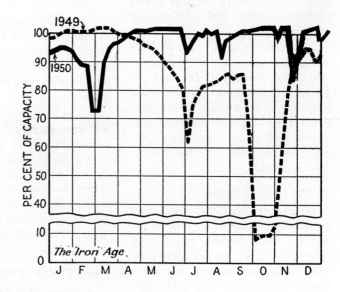

District Operating Rates—Per Cent of Capacity**

Week of	Pittsburgh	Chicago	Youngstown	Philadelphia	West	Buffalo	Cleveland	Detroit	Wheeling	South	Ohio River	St. Louis	East	Aggregate
Dec. 24	98.0*	104.0	86.0*	95.0*	100.0*	104.0*	96.5	99.0	103.0	106.0	90.6	85.0*	101.0*	99.0
Dec. 31	99.0	104.0	91.0	97.0	101.4	104.0	96.0	103.0	103.0	104.0	90.0	90.5	101.0	101.0

* Revised.
** Steel operations for the first half of 1950 are based on annual capacity of 99,392,800 net tons. Beginning July 1, 1950, operations are based on new annual capacity of 100,563,500 net tons.

January 4, 1951   463

nonferrous metals

outlook and market activities

NONFERROUS METALS PRICES

	Dec. 27	Dec. 28	Dec. 29	Dec. 30	Jan. 1	Jan. 2
Copper, electro, Conn. ...	24.50	24.50	24.50	24.50	....	24.50
Copper, Lake, delivered...	24.625	24.625	24.625	24.625	....	24.625
Tin, Straits, New York	$1.50	$1.51	$1.51*	....	....	$1.51*
Zinc, East St. Louis	17.50	17.50	17.50	17.50	....	17.50
Lead. St. Louis	16.80	16.80	16.80	16.80	....	16.80

Note: Quotations are going prices.

*Tentative.

by r. hatschek

New York—National Production Authority last week issued an order restricting the use of cadmium in 1951, modified order M-7 on aluminum, and told of plans to regulate aluminum scrap.

The cadmium order, M-19, specifically prohibits the use of the metal for any purpose not covered in the order. Those uses which are permitted are of very specific and vital nature to the war effort. Cadmium stocks are limited to a 30-day supply.

Direction No. 3 to order M-7 revises the quantity of aluminum which is permitted for use in strictly functional parts during March. The purpose is to give some relief to certain manufacturers and allow them more time to come up with suitable substitute materials.

75 Pct to Be Allowed

Instead of the 65 pct previously permitted, producers of component parts of non-defense goods may now use 75 pct of the aluminum they consumed during the base period provided that: (1) The aluminum components serve a functional purpose in the end product, (2) substitution of another material is impractical before March, and (3) the aluminum components do not exceed 1 pct of the total weight of the end product.

The component manufacturer must obtain certification from the manufacturer or assembler of the end product that these provisions are complied with.

Members of the aluminum foundry and castings industry met last week with officials of the NPA for the discussion of a proposed order to control the flow of aluminum scrap so that it will go through normal channels. General approval was given.

The order will be issued after further discussions with other industry groups and it is expected to be quite similar to NPA order M-16 which regulates copper scrap.

As this is being written, it is not yet clear just what effect this order will have on the price of scrap aluminum. People are just sitting back and waiting to see what the final form of the order will be and what the price control picture will look like in the New Year. The refiners would like to

MONTHLY AVERAGE PRICES

The average prices of the major non-ferrous metals in December based on quotations appearing in THE IRON AGE, were as follows:

	Cents Per Pound
Electrolytic copper, Conn. Valley..........	24.50
Lake copper, delivered	24.625
Straits tin, New York	$1.4483
Zinc, East St. Louis	17.50
Zinc, New York	18.22
Lead, St. Louis	16.80
Lead, New York	17.00

see lower prices because that would reduce the cost of lost metal and cut down on credit risks.

Certain brass and bronze ingot prices were reduced last week, reflecting lower raw material costs. The 88-10-2 group was lowered 1¢ to 1¼¢ per lb and manganese bronze came down 2¢ per lb. Other prices remained unchanged.

We have just concluded a year which saw almost unbelievable turmoil in the metal markets. Prices have climbed in an inflationary spiral of fantastic proportions; tin and mercury have just about doubled in price since the start of hostilities in Korea and many scrap metal prices have surpassed the price of new metal.

Industry Awaits New Controls

Supplies have become shorter and demand has risen for both civilian and military purposes. NPA was created and the consumption of many of the metals has been curtailed for non-essential use by this organization.

In the coming year we will see even more restrictions on metal uses as a controlled materials plan of some variety takes form in Washington. Price controls will be along as soon as the Economic Stabilization Agency can be organized to the point where its orders would be effective.

MILL PRODUCTS

(Cents per lb, unless otherwise noted)

Aluminum

(Base 30,000 lb, f.o.b. ship. pt. frt. allowed)

Flat Sheet: 0.188 in., 2S, 3S, 30.1¢; 4S, 61S-O, 32¢; 52S, 34.1¢; 24S-O, 24S-OAL, 32.9¢; 75S-O, 75S-OAL, 39.9¢; 0.081 in., 2S, 3S, 31.2¢; 4S, 61S-O, 33.5¢; 52S, 35.6¢; 24S-O, 24S-OAL, 34.1¢; 75S-O, 75S-OAL, 41.8¢; 0.32 in., 2S, 3S, 32.9¢; 4S, 61S-O, 37.1¢; 52S, 39.8¢; 24S-O, 24S-OAL, 41.7¢; 75S-O, 75S-OAL, 52.2¢.

Plate: ¼ in. and heavier: 2S, 3S-F, 28.3¢; 4S-F, 30.2¢; 52S-F, 31.8¢; 61S-O, 30.8¢; 24S-O, 24S-OAL, 32.4¢; 75S-O, 75S-OAL, 38.8¢.

Extruded Solid Shapes: Shape factors 1 to 5, 86.2¢ to 74.5¢; 12 to 14, 36.9¢ to 89¢; 24 to 26, 39.6¢ to $1.16; 36 to 38, 47.2¢ to $1.70.

Rod, Rolled: 1.5 to 4.5 in., 2S-F, 3S-F, 37.5¢ to 33.5¢; cold-finished, 0.375 to 3 in., 2S-F, 3S-F, 40.5¢ to 35¢.

Screw Machine Stock: Rounds, 11S-T3, ⅛ to 11/32 in., 53.5¢ to 42¢; ⅝ to 1½ in., 41.5¢ to 39¢; 1 9/16 to 3 in., 38.5¢ to 36¢; 17S-T4 lower by 1.5¢ per lb. Base 5000 lb.

Drawn Wire: Coiled, 0.051 to 0.374 in., 2S, 39.5¢ to 29¢; 52S, 48¢ to 35¢; 56S, 51¢ to 42¢; 17S-T4, 54¢ to 37.5¢; 61S-T4, 48.5¢ to 37¢; 75S-T6, 84¢ to 67.5¢.

Extruded Tubing, Rounds: 63S-T5, OD in in.: 1¼ to 2, 87¢ to 54¢; 2 to 4, 33.5¢ to 45.5¢; 4 to 6, 34¢ to 41.5¢; 6 to 9, 34.5¢ to 43.5¢.

Roofing Sheet, Flat: 0.019 in. x 28 in. per sheet, 72 in., $1.142; 96 in., $1.522; 120 in., $1.902; 144 in., $2.284. Gage 0.024 in. x 28 in., 72 in., $1.379; 96 in., $1.839; 120 in., $2.299; 144 in., $2.759. Coiled Sheet: 0.019 in. x 28 in., 28.2¢ per lb.; 0.024 in. x 28 in., 26.9¢ per lb.

Magnesium

(F.o.b. mill, freight allowed)

Sheet and Plate: FS1-O, ¼ in. 63¢; 3/16 in. 65¢; ⅛ in. 67¢; B & S Gage 10, 68¢; 12, 72¢; 14, 78¢; 16, 85¢; 18, 93¢; 20, $1.05; 22, $1.27; 24, $1.67. Specification grade higher. Base: 30,000 lb.

Extruded Round Rod: M, diam in., ¼ to 0.311 in., 74¢; ½ to ¾ in., 57.5¢; 1¼ to 1.749 in., 53¢; 2½ to 5 in., 48.5¢. Other alloys higher. Base: Up to ¾ in. diam, 10,000 lb; ¾ to 2 in., 20,000 lb; 2 in. and larger, 30,000 lb.

Extruded Solid Shapes, Rectangles: M. In weight per ft, for perimeters less than size indicated, 0.10 to 0.11 lb, 3.5 in., 62.3¢; 0.22 to 0.25 lb, 5.9 in., 59.3¢; 0.50 to 0.59 lb, 8.6 in., 56.7¢; 1.8 to 2.59 lb, 19.5 in., 53.8¢; 4 to 6 lb, 28 in., 49¢. Other alloys higher. Base, in weight per ft of shape: Up to ½ lb, 10,000 lb; ½ to 1.80 lb, 20,000 lb; 1.80 lb and heavier, 30,000 lb.

Extruded Round Tubing: M, wall thickness, outside diam, in., 0.049 to 0.057, ¼ in. to 5/16, $1.40; 5/16 to ⅜, $1.26; ½ to ⅝, 93¢; 1 to 2 in., 76¢; 0.165 to 0.219, ⅝ to ¾, 61¢; 1 to 2 in., 57¢; 3 to 4 in., 56¢. Other alloys higher. Base, OD in in.: Up to 1½ in., 10,000 lb; 1½ in. to 3 in., 20,000 lb; 8 in. and larger, 30,000 lb.

Titanium

(10,000 lb. base, f.o.b. mill)

Commercially pure and alloy grades: Sheet and strip, HR or CR, $15; Plate, HR, $12; Wire, rolled and/or drawn, $10; Bar, HR or forged, $6; Forgings, $6.

Nickel and Monel

(Base prices, f.o.b. mill)

	"A" Nickel	Monel
Sheets, cold-rolled	74	58
Strip, cold-rolled	80	62
Rods and bars	70	56
Angles, hot-rolled	70	56
Plates	72	57
Seamless tubes	103	93
Shot and blocks	..	51

Copper, Brass, Bronze

(Freight prepaid on 200 lb includes duty)

	Sheets	Rods	Extruded Shapes
Copper	41.03	....	40.63
Copper, h-r	....	36.88	....
Copper, drawn	....	38.18	....
Low brass	39.15	38.84	....
Yellow brass	38.28	37.97	....
Red brass	40.14	39.83	....
Naval brass	43.08	38.61	38.07
Leaded brass	....	32.63	36.70
Com'l bronze	41.13	40.82	....
Mang. bronze	45.96	40.65	41.41
Phos. bronze	60.20	60.45	....
Muntz metal	40.43	36.74	37.99
Ni silver, 10 pct	49.27	51.49	....
Arch. bronze	....	....	35:11

PRIMARY METALS

(Cents per lb, unless otherwise noted)

Aluminum ingot, 99+%, 10,000 lb, freight allowed	19.00
Aluminum pig	18.00
Antimony, American, Laredo, Tex.	32.00
Beryllium copper, 3.75-4.25% Be	$1.56
Beryllium aluminum 5% Be, Dollars per lb contained Be	$69.00
Bismuth, ton lots	$2.25
Cadmium, del'd	$2.55
Cobalt, 97-99% (per lb)	$2.10 to $2.17
Copper, electro, Conn. Valley	24.50
Copper, Lake, delivered	24.625
Gold, U. S. Treas., dollars per oz.	$35.00
Indium, 99.8%, dollars per troy oz.	$2.25
Iridium, dollars per troy oz.	$200
Lead, St. Louis	16.80
Lead, New York	17.00
Magnesium, 99.8+%, f.o.b. Freeport, Tex., 10,000 lb	24.50
Magnesium, sticks, 100 to 500 lb	42.00 to 44.00
Mercury, dollars per 76-lb flask f.o.b. New York	$137 to $142
Nickel, electro, f.o.b. New York	53.55
Nickel oxide sinter, f.o.b. Copper Cliff, Ont., contained nickel	46.75
Palladium, dollars per troy oz.	$24.00
Platinum, dollars per troy oz.	$90 to $93
Silver, New York, cents per oz.	80.00
Tin, New York	$1.51
Titanium, sponge	$5.00
Zinc, East St. Louis	17.50
Zinc, New York	18.22
Zirconium copper, 50 pct	$6.20

REMELTED METALS

Brass Ingot

(Cents per lb delivered, carloads)

85-5-5-5 ingot	
No. 115	29.00
No. 120	28.50
No. 123	28.00
80-10-10 ingot	
No. 305	35.00
No. 315	32.00
88-10-2 ingot	
No. 210	46.25
No. 215	43.25
No. 245	36.00
Yellow ingot	
No. 405	25.50
Manganese bronze	
No. 421	30.75

Aluminum Ingot

(Cents per lb, 30,000 lb lots)

95-5 aluminum-silicon alloys	
0.30 copper, max.	33.75-34.25
0.60 copper, max.	33.50-34.00
Piston alloys (No. 122 type)	31.50-32.00
No. 12 alum. (No. 2 grade)	30.75-31.25
108 alloy	31.25-31.75
195 alloy	32.75-33.25
13 alloy	34.00-34.50
ASX-679	31.25-31.75

Steel deoxidizing aluminum, notch-bar granulated or shot

Grade 1—95-97½%	32.50-33.00
Grade 2—92-95%	30.75-31.50
Grade 3—90-92%	30.00-30.50
Grade 4—85-90%	29.50-30.00

ELECTROPLATING SUPPLIES

Anodes

(Cents per lb, freight allowed, 500 lb lots)

Copper	
Cast, oval, 15 in. or longer	39½
Electrodeposited	33¾
Rolled, oval, straight, delivered	38⅞
Forged ball anodes	43
Brass, 80-20	
Cast, oval, 15 in. or longer	34¾
Zinc, oval	26½
Ball anodes	25½
Nickel 99 pct plus	
Cast	70.50
Rolled, depolarized	71.50
Cadmium	$2.80
Silver 999 fine, rolled, 100 oz lots, per troy oz., f.o.b. Bridgeport, Conn.	79½

Chemicals

(Cents per lb, f.o.b. shipping point)

Copper cyanide, 100 lb drum	52.15
Copper sulfate, 99.5 crystals, bbl.	12.85
Nickel salts, single or double, 4-100 lb bags, frt allowed	20½
Nickel chloride, 375 lb drum	27½
Silver cyanide, 100 oz lots, per oz.	67¼
Sodium cyanide, 96 pct domestic 200 lb drums	19.25
Zinc cyanide, 100 lb drums	45.85

SCRAP METALS

Brass Mill Scrap

(Cents per pound, add ½¢ per lb for shipments of 20,000 to 40,000 lb; add 1¢ for more than 40,000 lb)

	Heavy	Turnings
Copper	23	22¼
Yellow brass	20½	18¾
Red brass	21½	20¾
Comm. brass	21¾	21
Mang. bronze	19½	18⅝
Brass rod ends	19⅞	....

Custom Smelters' Scrap

(Cents per pound, carload lots, delivered to refinery)

No. 1 copper wire	21.00
No. 2 copper wire	20.00
Light copper	19.00
Refinery brass	18.50*
Radiators	15.00

*Dry copper content.

Ingot Makers' Scrap

(Cents per pound, carload lots, delivered to producer)

No. 1 copper wire	21.00
No. 2 copper wire	20.00
Light copper	19.00
No. 1 composition	20.00
No. 1 comp. turnings	19.75
Rolled brass	16.50
Brass pipe	18.50
Radiators	15.25
Heavy yellow brass	15.00
Aluminum	
Mixed old cast	20
Mixed old clips	21
Mixed turnings, dry	19¼
Pots and pans	20
Low copper	22¼

Dealers' Scrap

(Dealers' buying prices, f.o.b. New York in cents per pound)

Copper and Brass

No. 1 heavy copper and wire	19½—20
No. 2 heavy copper and wire	18—18¼
Light copper	17—17¼
New type shell cuttings	17—17¼
Auto radiators (unsweated)	14½—15
No. 1 composition	17—17½
No. 1 composition turnings	16½—17
Clean red car boxes	15½—16
Cocks and faucets	15½—16
Mixed heavy yellow brass	13—13½
Old rolled brass	14—14½
Brass pipe	17—17½
New soft brass clippings	17½—18
Brass rod ends	16½—17
No. 1 brass rod turnings	16—16½

Aluminum

Alum. pistons and struts	12½—13
Aluminum crankcases	15½—16
2S aluminum clippings	19—19¼
Old sheet and utensils	15½—16
Borings and turnings	13
Misc. cast aluminum	15½—16
Dural clips (24S)	15½—16

Zinc

New zinc clippings	14½—15
Old zinc	11—11¼
Zinc routings	8½— 9
Old die cast scrap	8— 8¼

Nickel and Monel

Pure nickel clippings	60—65
Clean nickel turnings	57—60
Nickel anodes	60—65
Nickel rod ends	60—65
New Monel Clippings	22—25
Clean Monel turnings	18—20
Old sheet Monel	20—22
Inconel clippings	26—28
Nickel silver clippings, mixed	13—14
Nickel silver turnings, mixed	12—13

Lead

Soft scrap, lead	15—15¼
Battery plates (dry)	8¾— 9

Magnesium

Segregated solids	9—10
Castings	5½— 6½

Miscellaneous

Block tin	85—90
No. 1 pewter	63—65
No. 1 auto babbitt	58—60
Mixed common babbitt	12¼—12½
Solder joints	18½—19
Siphon tops	58—60
Small foundry type	16¼—16½
Monotype	14¾—15
Lino. and stereotype	14½—14¾
Electrotype	12¾—13
Hand picked type shells	11½—11¾
Lino. and stereo. dross	8— 8¼
Electro. dross	6½— 6¾

SCRAP *iron and steel* | *markets prices trends*

Expect price freeze at formula . . . Railroad specialties, cast may be rolled back . . . New mill to put strain on eastern scrap market.

Scrap centers are shipping out old orders as fast as possible in anticipation of price controls from Washington. The prediction that steelmaking grades would be controlled at current formula levels still stands but some in the trade believe that railroad specialties and cast grades will be rolled back.

Whether to Dec. 1 levels is doubtful. A compromise level is far more likely. Last Tuesday Economic Stabilization Agency officials were to have met with three steel scrap and two foundry grades consumers, five scrap industry men, and five railroad representatives. With sentiment strong that voluntary controls will flop almost as soon as they are suggested, mandatory controls seem to be in the offing.

U. S. Steel Corp.'s announcement that it would build its Fairless Works by late 1952 will have a profound effect on the eastern scrap market. The mill will have a 1.8 million ton ingot capacity. That could mean annual scrap needs of almost 1 million tons of scrap steel—about half of that in purchased scrap.

Will U. S. Steel enter the Pittsburgh scrap area at all—taking from Peter to pay Paul? Or will it compete for scrap in New York and Philadelphia markets and then take the line of least resistance to start tapping the New England scrap market?

News also comes from Washington that the New England steel mill, whose advocates find the time ripe for building, is in the advanced stage of having approvals stamped on certificates of necessity for fast tax writeoff. When that mill is operating it will naturally draw heavily on New England scrap.

PITTSBURGH—With the exception of railroad specialties and cast, the trade expects prices to be controlled at present levels. Specialties and cast are likely to be rolled back. The meeting Jan. 2 with ESA officials will tell the story. Present at the meeting will be five consumers, including three from steel and two from foundries, five representatives of the scrap industry, and five from the railroads. It is conceded that mandatory controls will be applied, everybody agrees that voluntary controls won't work. Meanwhile, the flow of scrap has slowed somewhat but with few exceptions consumers are well situated.

PHILADELPHIA — The market here was quiet at press time waiting for new government regulations. The freight car shortage and bitter weather have cut into scrap shipments and yard activities. Some slight upgrading is again being reported but it is not prevalent. Yard cast is up $1 on the high side and chemical borings are stronger. The tone of the low phos market is softening.

NEW YORK—No price changes were reported in this market but old order shipments were moving fast and thick. Brokers were hoping that the ESA would control scrap prices at "realistic levels" to forestall drying up of scrap sources. News of U. S. Steel's Fairless Works started predictions on what that mill's demand would mean to the local market.

DETROIT—The Detroit scrap market is very quiet this week. Most market observers here feel controlled prices for scrap are just around the corner. Dealers are reported to be moving material out of their yards at a brisk pace, Apparently in anticipation of a price freeze or an actual rollback. Cast grades are quiet and there is considerable resistance to placing new orders.

CLEVELAND—Scrap is moving at the formula here and in the Valley this week as the trade awaits mandatory price controls. Brokers and dealers are trying to get the tonnage out and mills are buying unprepared material at good prices. Time and the cost of preparation are probably responsible for this. Some mills indicate that current shipments are less than consumption and in view of the weather, the inventory outlook is not reassuring. Best guess here is that No. 1 will be pegged at the present level, or possibly at a dollar or two under, but foundry material is due for a real slash.

CHICAGO—There was little activity in the Chicago scrap market this week. Openhearth grades of scrap are moving freely on old orders. One major consumer is reported to be out of the market for the next 45 days.

Several consumers are out of the market for short shoveling turnings and broker offerings are lower for all turnings grades. However, there is not sufficient consumer buying to arrive at a new firm price and quotations on these items reflect last consumer prices.

Low phos and cast grades dropped about $2 per gross ton as some foundries were resisting the higher prices. Consumer prices on railroad items, low phos and cast are expected to drop off sharply in the next few weeks.

BIRMINGHAM—The scrap metal market here is at a complete standstill. Neither users nor brokers are doing any buying and brokers who a week ago were frantically seeking scrap are turning down offers. Everyone who has made sales, however, is shipping as fast as possible as a result of a call for a price control meeting called in Washington for January 2.

CINCINNATI—Prices are unchanged in an anticipatory but active market here. Openhearth and blast furnace grades are moving freely at the formula and dealers are selling. Some tonnage is moving to other districts, including the Valley, which is an indicator of the terrific demand. Foundry grades are easing.

BUFFALO—With controls expected in the near future, the scrap market was content to mark time as dealers were shipping against substantial orders still outstanding. Snow and cold weather interfered with yard work.

BOSTON—A sudden lull in the market was felt here as controls were awaited. No. 1 heavy and other formula price items were selling over the top.

This Logemann scrap press is in operation in one of the larger industrial plants. It compresses scrap from three directions to produce high density, mill size bundles.

Self-Contained . . . .
Triple Compression . .
Automatically Controlled

LOGEMANN
SCRAP PRESSES

handle high tonnages with minimum labor . . . *at low cost*

LOGEMANN METAL BALERS

. . . are built in a large range of sizes to meet specific conditions. Let Logemann's engineering service help you arrive at the most efficient and economical way of handling your scrap.

The compact unit illustrated is completely self-contained with oil tank and pump located directly over the press . . . utilizing the advantages of short pipe lines. Automatic controls, mounted in front of pump, give the operator full visibility at all times. Controls operate rams successively within a single rigid box. There is no complex construction which means there is *no need for specially-trained maintenance crews.*

Both two-ram and three-ram models are available with automatic controls or for manual manipulation.

Logemann Bros. Co. have specialized in the production of scrap metal presses for sheet mills, stamping plants, scrap yards, and metal manufacturing plants of all types for nearly 75 years. Write for full information — please state the nature of your scrap and tonnage.

LOGEMANN BROTHERS COMPANY
3164 W. Burleigh Street • Milwaukee 10, Wisconsin

Iron and Steel
SCRAP PRICES

Going prices as obtained in the trade by THE IRON AGE based on representative tonnages. All prices are per gross ton delivered to consumer unless otherwise noted.

Pittsburgh

No. 1 hvy. melting	$45.75 to	$46.50
No. 2 hvy. melting	43.75 to	44.50
No. 1 bundles	45.75 to	46.50
No. 2 bundles	42.75 to	43.50
Machine shop turn.	37.75 to	38.50
Mixed bor. and ms. turns.	37.75 to	38.50
Shoveling turnings	39.75 to	40.50
Cast iron borings	39.75 to	40.50
Low phos. plate	56.00 to	56.50
Heavy turnings	46.50 to	47.00
No. 1 RR. hvy. melting	45.75 to	46.50
Scrap rails, random lgth.	64.50 to	65.00
Rails 2 ft and under	68.00 to	69.00
RR. steel wheels	63.00 to	64.00
RR. spring steel	63.00 to	64.00
RR. couplers and knuckles.	63.00 to	64.00
No. 1 machinery cast	67.50 to	68.00
Mixed yard cast.	57.50 to	58.00
Heavy breakable cast.	52.50 to	53.00
Malleable	71.00 to	72.00

Chicago

No. 1 hvy. melting	$44.25 to	$45.00
No. 2 hvy. melting	42.00 to	43.00
No. 1 factory bundles	44.00 to	45.00
No. 1 dealers' bundles	44.00 to	45.00
No. 2 dealers' bundles	41.00 to	42.00
Machine shop turn.	36.00 to	37.00
Mixed bor. and turn.	36.00 to	37.00
Shoveling turnings	38.00 to	39.00
Cast iron borings	38.00 to	39.00
Low phos. forge crops	55.00 to	56.00
Low phos. plate	52.00 to	53.00
No. 1 RR. hvy. melting	47.00 to	48.00
Scrap rails, random lgth.	62.00 to	63.00
Rerolling rails	65.50 to	66.50
Rails 2 ft and under	67.00 to	69.00
Locomotive tires, cut	58.00 to	59.00
Cut bolsters & side frames	54.00 to	55.00
Angles and splice bars	63.00 to	64.00
RR. steel car axles	100.00 to	105.00
RR. couplers and knuckles	58.00 to	59.00
No. 1 machinery cast.	62.00 to	64.00
No. 1 agricul. cast.	58.00 to	60.00
Heavy breakable cast.	53.00 to	55.00
RR. grate bars	48.00 to	49.00
Cast iron brake shoes	52.00 to	53.00
Cast iron car wheels	58.00 to	59.00
Malleable	78.00 to	82.00

Philadelphia

No. 1 hvy. melting	$44.00 to	$45.00
No. 2 hvy. melting	42.00 to	43.00
No. 1 bundles	44.00 to	45.00
No. 2 bundles	41.00 to	42.00
Machine shop turn.	36.00 to	37.00
Mixed bor. and turn.	35.00 to	36.00
Shoveling turnings	38.00 to	39.00
Low phos. punchings, plate	50.00 to	51.00
Low phos. 5 ft and under.	50.00 to	51.00
Low phos. bundles	48.00 to	49.00
Hvy. axle forge turn.	44.00 to	45.00
Clean cast chem. borings.	42.00 to	43.00
RR. steel wheels	53.00 to	54.00
RR. spring steel	53.00 to	54.00
Rails 18 in. and under	66.00 to	67.00
No. 1 machinery cast.	62.00 to	63.00
Mixed yard cast.	53.00 to	55.00
Heavy breakable cast.	53.00 to	54.00
Cast iron carwheels	67.00 to	68.00
Malleable	69.00 to	70.00

Cleveland

No. 1 hvy. melting	$45.25 to	$46.00
No. 2 hvy. melting	43.25 to	44.00
No. 1 busheling	45.25 to	46.00
No. 1 bundles	45.25 to	46.00
No. 2 bundles	42.25 to	43.00
Machine shop turn.	37.25 to	38.00
Mixed bor. and turn.	39.25 to	40.00
Shoveling turnings	39.25 to	40.00
Cast iron borings	39.25 to	40.00
Low phos. 2 ft and under.	47.75 to	48.50
Steel axle turn.	44.25 to	45.00
Drop forge flashings	45.25 to	46.00
No. 1 RR. hvy. melting	46.00 to	46.50
Rails 3 ft and under	70.00 to	71.00
Rails 18 in. and under	72.00 to	73.00
No. 1 machinery cast.	69.00 to	70.00
RR. cast.	71.00 to	72.00
RR. grate bars	50.00 to	51.00
Stove plate	55.00 to	56.00
Malleable	76.00 to	77.00

Youngstown

No. 1 hvy. melting	$45.75 to	$46.50
No. 2 hvy. melting	43.75 to	44.50
No. 1 bundles	45.75 to	46.50

Buffalo (center column top)

No. 2 bundles	$42.75 to	$43.00
Machine shop turn	37.75 to	38.50
Shoveling turnings	39.75 to	40.50
Cast iron borings	39.75 to	40.50
Low phos. plate	48.25 to	49.00

Buffalo

No. 1 hvy. melting	$44.50 to	$45.25
No. 2 hvy. melting	42.50 to	43.25
No. 1 busheling	42.50 to	43.25
No. 1 bundles	43.50 to	44.25
No. 2 bundles	41.50 to	42.25
Machine shop turn.	36.50 to	37.25
Mixed bor. and turn.	36.50 to	37.25
Shoveling turnings	38.50 to	39.25
Cast iron borings	36.50 to	37.25
Low phos. plate	48.25 to	49.00
Scrap rails, random lgth.	55.00 to	56.00
Rails 2 ft and under	60.00 to	61.00
RR. steel wheels	60.00 to	61.00
RR. spring steel	60.00 to	61.00
RR. couplers and knuckles	60.00 to	61.00
No. 1 machinery cast.	59.00 to	60.00
No. 1 cupola cast.	54.00 to	55.00
Small indus. malleable	60.00 to	61.00

Birmingham

No. 1 hvy. melting	$42.50 to	$43.50
No. 2 hvy. melting	38.50 to	39.50
No. 2 bundles	37.50 to	38.50
No. 1 busheling	38.00 to	39.00
Machine shop turn.	31.00 to	32.00
Shoveling turnings	32.00 to	33.00
Cast iron borings	27.00 to	28.00
Bar crops and plate	47.00 to	48.00
Structural and plate	46.00 to	47.00
No. 1 RR. hvy. melting	43.00 to	44.00
Scrap rails, random lgth.	58.00 to	59.00
Rerolling rails	61.00 to	62.00
Rails 2 ft and under	66.00 to	67.00
Angles & splice bars	59.00 to	60.00
Std. steel axles	61.00 to	62.00
No. 1 cupola cast.	59.00 to	60.00
Stove plate	54.00 to	55.00
Cast iron carwheels	46.00 to	47.00

St. Louis

No. 1 hvy. melting	$45.00 to	$47.00
No. 2 hvy. melting	41.00 to	42.00
No. 2 bundled sheets	40.00 to	41.00
Machine shop turn.	28.50 to	29.50
Shoveling turnings	35.00 to	36.00
Rails, random lengths	58.00 to	59.00
Rails 3 ft and under	66.00 to	68.00
Locomotive tires, uncut	57.00 to	58.00
Angles and splice bars	66.00 to	68.00
Std. steel car axles	100.00 to	105.00
RR. spring steel	57.00 to	58.00
No. 1 machinery cast.	65.00 to	66.00
Hvy. breakable cast.	56.00 to	58.00
Cast iron brake shoes	55.00 to	57.00
Stove plate	53.00 to	55.00
Cast iron car wheels	63.00 to	65.00
Malleable	55.00 to	57.00

New York

Brokers' Buying prices per gross ton, on cars:

No. 1 hvy. melting		$39.00
No. 2 hvy. melting		37.00
No. 2 bundles		36.00
Machine shop turn.		31.00
Mixed bor. and turn.		31.00
Shoveling turnings.		33.00
Clean cast chem. bor.	$38.00 to	39.00
No. 1 machinery cast.	52.00 to	53.00
Mixed yard cast.	47.00 to	48.00
Charging box cast.	47.00 to	48.00
Heavy breakable cast.	46.00 to	47.00
Unstrp. motor blocks	42.00 to	43.00

Boston

Brokers' Buying prices per gross ton, on cars:

No. 1 hvy. melting		$35.67
No. 2 hvy. melting		33.67
No. 1 bundles		38.00

Boston (continued, right column top)

No. 2 bundles		$32.67
Machine shop turn.		27.67
Mixed bor. and turn.	$26.67 to	27.67
Shoveling turnings		29.67
No. 1 busheling		35.67
Clean cast chem. borings.	33.00 to	34.00
No. 1 machinery cast.	48.00 to	49.00
Mixed cupola cast.	44.00 to	45.00
Heavy breakable cast.	42.00 to	43.00
Stove plate	42.00 to	43.00

Detroit

Brokers' Buying prices per gross ton, on cars:

No. 1 hvy. melting		$40.25
No. 2 hvy. melting		38.25
No. 1 bundles, openhearth		40.25
No. 1 bundles, electric furnace		42.75
New busheling		40.25
Flashings		40.25
Machine shop turn.		32.25
Mixed bor. and turn.		32.25
Shoveling turnings		34.25
Cast iron borings		34.25
Low phos. plate		42.75
No. 1 cupola cast.	$56.00 to	58.00
Heavy breakable cast.	47.00 to	49.00
Stove plate	46.00 to	48.00
Automotive cast.	60.00 to	62.00

Cincinnati

Per gross ton, f.o.b. cars:

No. 1 hvy. melting		$44.25
No. 2 hvy. melting		42.25
No. 1 bundles		44.25
No. 2 bundles, black		42.25
No. 2 bundles, mixed		41.25
Machine shop turn.		33.00
Mixed bor. and turn.		34.00
Shoveling turnings		34.00
Cast iron borings		34.00
Low phos.-steel		46.75
Low phos. 18 in. under		62.00
Rails, random lengths	$62.00 to	63.00
Rails, 18 in. and under	72.00 to	73.00
No. 1 cupola cast.	65.00 to	66.00
Hvy. breakable cast.	59.00 to	60.00
Drop broken cast.	71.00 to	72.00

San Francisco

No. 1 hvy. melting		$30.00
No. 2 hvy. melting		28.00
No. 1 bundles		30.00
No. 2 bundles		28.00
No. 3 bundles		25.00
Machine shop turn.		16.00
Elec. fur. 1 ft and under	$40.00 to	42.50
No. 1 RR. hvy. melting.		30.00
Scrap rails random lgth.		30.00
No. 1 cupola cast.	43.00 to	46.00

Los Angeles

No. 1 hvy. melting		$30.00
No. 2 hvy. melting		28.00
No. 1 bundles		30.00
No. 2 bundles		28.00
No. 3 bundles		25.00
Mach. shop turn.		16.00
Elec. fur. 1 ft and under.	$42.00 to	45.00
No. 1 RR. hvy. melting		30.00
Scrap rails, random lgth.		30.00
No. 1 cupola cast.		52.00

Seattle

No. 1 hvy. melting		$28.00
No. 2 hvy. melting		28.00
No. 1 bundles		22.00
No. 2 bundles		22.00
No. 3 bundles		18.00
Elec. fur. 1 ft and under.	$40.00 to	45.00
RR. hvy. melting		29.00
No. 1 cupola cast		45.00

Hamilton, Ont.

No. 1 hvy. melting		$30.00
No. 1 bundles		30.00
No. 2 bundles		29.50
Mechanical bundles		28.00
Mixed steel scrap		26.00
Mixed bor. and turn.		23.00
Rails, remelting		30.00
Rails, rerolling		33.00
Bushelings		24.50
Bush., new fact. prep'd.		29.00
Bush., new fact, unprep'd.		23.00
Short steel turnings		23.00
Cast scrap		45.00

Comparison of Prices

Steel prices in this page are the average of various f.o.b. quotations of major producing areas: Pittsburgh, Chicago, Gary, Cleveland, Youngstown.

Price advances over previous week are printed in Heavy Type; declines appear in *Italics*

Flat-Rolled Steel:	Jan. 2, 1951	Dec. 26, 1950	Dec. 5, 1950	Jan.3 1950
(cents per pound)				
Hot-rolled sheets	3.60	3.60	3.60	3.35
Cold-rolled sheets	4.35	4.35	4.35	4.10
Galvanized sheets (10 ga)	4.80	4.80	4.80	4.40
Hot-rolled strip	3.50	3.50	3.50	3.25
Cold-rolled strip	4.75	4.75	4.75	4.18
Plate	3.70	3.70	3.70	3.50
Plates wrought iron	7.85	7.85	7.85	7.85
Stains C-R-strip (No. 302)	36.50	36.50	36.50	33.00

Tin and Terneplate:
(dollars per base box)

Tinplate (1.50 lb) cokes.	$7.50	$7.50	$7.50	$7.50
Tinplate, electro (0.50 lb)	6.60	6.60	6.60	6.60
Special coated mfg. ternes	6.35	6.35	6.35	6.50

Bars and Shapes:
(cents per pound)

Merchant bars	3.70	3.70	3.70	3.45
Cold finished bars	4.55	4.55	4.55	3.995
Alloy bars	4.30	4.30	4.30	3.95
Structural shapes	3.65	3.65	3.65	3.40
Stainless bars (No. 302)	31.25	31.25	31.25	28.50
Wrought iron bars	9.50	9.50	9.50	9.50

Wire:
(cents per pound)

Bright wire	4.85	4.85	4.85	4.50

Rails:
(dollars per 100 lb)

Heavy rails	$3.60	$3.60	$3.60	$3.40
Light rails	4.00	4.00	4.00	3.75

Semifinished Steel:
(dollars per net ton)

Rerolling billets	$56.00	$56.00	$56.00	$54.00
Slabs, rerolling	56.00	56.00	56.00	54.00
Forging billets	66.00	66.00	66.00	63.00
Alloy blooms billets, slabs	70.00	70.00	70.00	66.00

Wire Rod and Skelp:
(cents per pound)

Wire rods	4.10	4.10	4.10	3.85
Skelp	3.35	3.35	3.35	3.15

Pig Iron:	Jan. 2, 1951	Dec. 26, 1950	Dec. 5, 1950	Jan.3 1950
(per gross ton)				
No. 2, foundry, del'd Phila.	$57.77	$57.77	$56.27	$50.42
No. 2, Valley furnace	52.50	52.50	51.00	46.50
No. 2, Southern Cin'ti	55.58	55.58	55.58	46.08
No. 2, Birmingham	48.88	48.88	48.85	39.38
No. 2, foundry, Chicago†	52.50	52.50	52.50	46.50
Basic del'd Philadelphia	56.92	56.92	55.42	49.92
Basic, Valley furnace	52.00	52.00	50.50	46.00
Malleable, Chicago†	52.50	52.50	52.50	46.50
Malleable, Valley	52.50	52.50	52.50	46.50
Charcoal, Chicago	70.56	70.56	70.56	68.56
Ferromanganese‡	181.20	181.20	181.20	173.40

†The switching charge for delivery to foundries in the Chicago district is $1 per ton.
‡Average of U. S. prices quoted on Ferroalloy page.

Scrap:
(per gross ton)

Heavy melt'g steel, P'gh	$46.13	$46.13	$43.75	$29.75
Heavy melt'g steel, Phila.	44.50	44.50	38.75	23.50
Heavy melt'g steel, Ch'go	*44.63*	44.75	39.75	25.50
No. 1 hy. com. sh't, Det..	40.25	40.25	41.25	24.50
Low phos. Young'n	48.63	48.63	46.25	31.75
No. 1 cast, Pittsburgh	67.75	67.75	62.75	37.50
No. 1 cast, Philadelphia	62.50	62.50	56.50	37.00
No. 1 cast, Chicago	*63.00*	65.00	63.00	38.50

Coke: Connellsville:
(per net ton at oven)

Furnace coke, prompt	$14.25	$14.25	$14.25	$14.00
Foundry coke, prompt	17.25	17.25	16.75	15.75

Nonferrous Metals:
(cents per pound to large buyers)

Copper, electro, Conn.	24.50	24.50	24.50	18.50
Copper, Lake, Conn.	24.625	24.625	24.625	18.625
Tin Straits, New York.	$1.51†	$1.50*	1.395	77.50
Zinc, East St. Louis	17.50	17.50	17.50	9.875
Lead, St. Louis	16.80	16.80	16.80	11.80
Aluminum, virgin	19.00	19.00	19.00	17.00
Nickel, electrolytic	53.55	53.55	51.22	42.97
Magnesium, ingot	24.50	24.50	24.50	20.50
Antimony, Laredo, Tex..	32.00	32.00	32.00	32.00

†Tentative. *Revised.

Composite Prices

Starting with the issue of May 12, 1949, the weighted finished steel composite was revised for the years 1941 to date. The weights used are based on the average product shipments for the 7 years 1937 to 1940 inclusive and 1946 to 1948 inclusive. The use of quarterly figures has been eliminated because it was too sensitive. (See p. 130 of May 12, 1949, issue.)

Finished Steel Base Price

Jan. 2, 1951	4.131¢ per lb
One week ago	4.131¢ per lb
One month ago	4.131¢ per lb
One year ago	3.837¢ per lb

Pig Iron

	$52.69 per gross ton
	52.69 per gross ton
	51.94 per gross ton
	45.88 per gross ton

Scrap Steel

	$45.09 per gross ton
	45.13 per gross ton
	40.75 per gross ton
	26.25 per gross ton

	High		Low		High		Low		High		Low	
1950	4.131¢	Dec. 1	3.837¢	Jan. 3	$52.69	Dec. 12	$45.88	Jan. 3	$45.13	Dec. 19	$26.25	Jan. 3
1949	3.837¢	Dec. 27	3.3705¢	May 3	46.87	Jan. 18	45.88	Sept. 6	43.00	Jan. 4	19.33	June 28
1948	3.721¢	July 27	3.193¢	Jan. 1	46.91	Oct. 12	39.58	Jan. 6	43.16	July 27	39.75	Mar. 9
1947	3.193¢	July 29	2.848¢	Jan. 1	37.98	Dec. 30	30.14	Jan. 7	42.58	Oct. 28	29.50	May 20
1946	2.848¢	Dec. 31	2.464¢	Jan. 1	30.14	Dec. 10	25.37	Jan. 1	31.17	Dec. 24	19.17	Jan. 1
1945	2.464¢	May 29	2.396¢	Jan. 1	25.37	Oct. 23	23.61	Jan. 2	19.17	Jan. 2	18.92	May 22
1944	2.396¢		2.396¢		$23.61		$23.61		19.17	Jan. 11	15.76	Oct. 24
1943	2.396¢		2.396¢		23.61		23.61		$19.17		$19.17	
1942	2.396¢		2.396¢		23.61		23.61		19.17		19.17	
1941	2.396¢		2.396¢		$23.61	Mar. 20	$23.45	Jan. 2	$22.00	Jan. 7	$19.17	Apr. 10
1940	2.30467¢	Jan. 2	2.24107¢	Apr. 16	23.45	Dec. 23	22.61	Jan. 2	21.83	Dec. 30	16.04	Apr. 9
1939	2.35367¢	Jan. 3	2.26689¢	May 16	22.61	Sept. 19	20.61	Sept. 12	22.50	Oct. 3	14.08	May 16
1938	2.58414¢	Jan. 4	2.27207¢	Oct. 18	23.25	June 21	19.61	July 6	15.00	Nov. 22	11.00	June 7
1937	2.58414¢	Mar. 9	2.32263¢	Jan. 4	32.25	Mar. 9	20.25	Feb. 16	21.92	Mar. 30	12.67	June 9
1936	2.32263¢	Dec. 28	2.05200¢	Mar. 10	19.74	Nov. 24	18.73	Aug. 11	17.75	Dec. 21	12.67	June 8
1935	2.07542¢	Oct. 1	2.06492¢	Jan. 8	18.84	Nov. 5	17.83	May 14	13.42	Dec. 10	10.33	Apr. 29
1932	1.89196¢	July 5	1.83910¢	Mar. 1	14.81	Jan. 5	13.56	Dec. 6	8.50	Jan. 12	6.43	July 5
1929	2.31773¢	May 28	2.26498¢	Oct. 29	18.71	May 14	18.21	Dec. 17	17.58	Jan. 29	14.08	Dec. 8

Weighted index based on steel bars, shapes, plates, wire, rails, black pipe, hot and cold-rolled sheets and strips, representing major portion of finished steel shipment. Index recapitulated in Aug. 28, 1941, issue and in May 12, 1949.

Based on averages for basic iron at Valley furnaces and foundry iron at Chicago, Philadelphia, Buffalo, Valley and Birmingham.

Average of No. 1 heavy melting steel scrap delivered to consumers at Pittsburgh, Philadelphia and Chicago.

IRON AGE
STEEL PRICES

Smaller numbers in price boxes indicate producing companies. For main office locations, see key on facing page.
Base prices at producing points apply only to sizes and grades produced in these areas. Prices are in cents per lb unless otherwise noted. Extras apply.

	Pittsburgh	Chicago	Gary	Cleveland	Canton Massillon	Middletown	Youngstown	Bethlehem	Buffalo	Conshohocken	Johnstown	Sparrows Point	Granite City	Detroit
INGOTS Carbon forging, net ton	$52.00[1]													
Alloy, net ton	$54.00[1,17]													$54.00[31]
BILLETS, BLOOMS, SLABS Carbon, rerolling, net ton	$56.00[1,5]	$56.00[1]	$56.00[1]						$56.00[3]		$56.00[3]			
Carbon forging billets, net ton	$66.00[1,5]	$66.00[1,4]	$66.00[1]	$66.00[4]	$66.00[4]				$66.00[3,4]	$73.00[26]	$66.00[3]			$69.00[31]
Alloy, net ton	$70.00[1,17]	$70.00[1,4]	$70.00[1]		$70.00[4]			$70.00[3]	$70.00[3,4]	$77.00[26]	$70.00[3]			$73.00[31]
PIPE SKELP	3.35[1] 3.45[5]						3.35[1,4]							
WIRE RODS	4.10[2] 4.30[18]	4.10[2,4,23]	4.10[6]	4.10[2]			4.10[6]				4.10[3]	4.20[3]		
SHEETS Hot-rolled (18 ga. & hvr.)	3.60[1,5,9,15] 3.75[28]	3.60[5,23]	3.60[1,6,8]	3.60[4]		3.60[7]	3.60[1,4,6] 4.00[13]		3.60[3]	4.00[26]		3.60[3]		3.80[12] 4.40[47]
Cold-rolled	4.35[1,5,9,15] 5.35[63]		4.35[1,6,8]	4.35[4]		4.35[7]	4.35[4,6]		4.35[3]			4.35[3]		4.55[12]
Galvanized (10 gage)	4.80[1,9,15]		4.80[1,8]		4.80[4]	4.80[7]	6.00[64]					4.80[3]		
Enameling (12 gage)	4.65[1]		4.65[1,8]			4.65[7]								
Long ternes (10 gage)	5.20[9,15]						6.00[64]							
Hi str. low alloy, h.r.	5.40[1,5] 5.75[9]	5.40[1]	5.40[1,8] 5.90[6]	5.40[4]			5.40[1,4,13]		5.40[3]	5.65[26]		5.40[3]		
Hi str. low alloy, c.r.	6.55[1,5] 6.90[9]		6.55[1,8] 7.05[6]	6.55[4]			6.55[4]		6.55[3]			6.55[3]		
Hi str. low alloy, galv.	7.20[1]													
STRIP Hot-rolled	3.60[9], 4.00[41] 58], 3.75[28] 3.50[5]	3.50[66]	3.50[1,6,8]			3.50[7]	3.50[1,4,6] 4.00[13]		3.50[3,4]	3.90[26]		3.50[3]		4.40[47]
Cold-rolled	4.65[5,9] 5.00[28] 5.35[63,40,58]	4.90[8,66]	4.90[8]	4.65[2]		4.65[7]	4.65[4,6] 5.35[13]		4.65[3]			4.65[3]		5.45[47] 5.60[68] 5.60[81]
Hi str. low alloy, h.r.	5.75[9]		5.50[1] 5.30[8] 5.80[6]				4.95[4], 5.50[1] 5.40[13]			5.55[26]				
Hi str. low alloy, c.r.	7.20[9]			6.70[5]			6.20[4], 6.55[13]							
TINPLATE† Cokes, 1.50-lb base box 1.25 lb, deduct 25¢	$7.50[1] $8.70[9,15]		$7.50[1] $8.70[6]				$8.70[4]					8.55[3]		
Electrolytic 0.25, 0.50, 0.75 lb box			Deduct $1.55, $1.30 and 90¢ respectively from 1.50-lb coke base box price											
BLACKPLATE, 29 gage Hollowware enameling	5.85[1] 6.15[15]		5.85[1]				5.30[4]							
BARS Carbon steel	3.70[1,5] 3.85[9]	3.70[1,4,23]	3.70[1,4,6,8]	3.70[4]	3.70[4]		3.70[1,4,6]		3.70[3,4]		3.70[3]			3.85[31]
Reinforcing‡	3.70[1,5]	3.70[4]	3.70[1,6,8]	3.70[4]			3.70[1,4]		3.70[3,4]		3.70[3]	3.70[3]		
Cold-finished	4.55[2,4,5, 52,71]	4.55[2,69,70, 23,73]	4.55[74,73]	4.55[2]	4.55[4,52]									4.70[84]
Alloy, hot-rolled	4.30[1,17]	4.30[1,4,23]	4.30[1,6,8]		4.30[4]		4.30[1,6]	4.30[3]	4.30[3,4]		4.30[3]			4.45[31]
Alloy, cold-drawn	5.40[17,52, 69,71]	5.40[4,23,69, 70,73]	5.40[4] 5.90[74]		5.40[4,52]			5.40[3]	5.40[3]					5.55[84]
Hi str. low alloy, h.r.	5.55[1,5]		5.55[1,8] 6.05[6]	5.55[4]			5.55[1]	5.55[3]	5.55[3]			5.55[3]		
PLATE Carbon steel	3.70[1,5,15]	3.70[1]	3.70[1,6,8]	3.70[4] 4.00[9]			3.70[1,4] 3.95[13]		3.70[3]	4.15[26]	3.70[3]	3.70[3]		
Floor plates			4.75[8]	4.75[5]						4.75[26]				
Alloy	4.75[1] 4.85	4.75[1]	4.75[1]				5.20[13]			5.05[26]	4.75[3]	4.75[3]		
Hi str. low alloy	5.65[1,5]	5.65[1]	5.65[1,8]	5.65[4,5]			5.65[4] 5.70[13]			5.90[26]	5.65[3]	5.65[3]		
SHAPES, Structural	3.65[1,5] 3.90[9]	3.65[1,23]	3.65[1,8]						3.70[3]	3.70[3]		3.70[3]		
Hi str. low alloy	5.50[1,5]	5.50[1]	5.50[1,8]					5.50[3]	5.50[3]		5.50[3]			
MANUFACTURERS' WIRE Bright	4.85[2,5] 5.10[18]	4.85[2] 4.[33]		4.85[2]					Kokomo=5.80[36]		4.85[3]	4.95[3]	Duluth=4.85[2]	
PILING, Steel Sheet	4.45[1]	4.45[1]	4.45[8]						4.45[3]					

Smaller numbers indicate producing companies. See key at right.
Prices are in cents per lb unless otherwise noted. Extras apply.

STEEL PRICES

Kansas City	Houston	Birm- ingham	WEST COAST Seattle, San Francisco, Los Angeles, Fontana		Product
			F = $79.00[19]		**INGOTS** carbon forging, net ton
	$62.00[83]		F = $80.00[19]		Alloy, net ton
		$56.00[11]	F = $75.00[19]		**BILLETS, BLOOMS, SLABS** Carbon, rerolling, net ton
	$74.00[83]	$66.00[11]	F = $85.00[19] SF, LA, S = $85.00[62]		Carbon forging billets, net ton
	$78.00[83]		F = $89.00[19,4] LA = $90.00[62]		Alloy net ton
					PIPE SKELP
	4.50[83]	4.10[4,11]	SF = 4.90[2] LA = 4.90[24,62]	Worcester = 4.40[2] Minnequa = 4.35[14]	**WIRE RODS**
		3.60[4,11]	SF, LA = 4.30[24] F = 4.55[19]	Niles = 5.25[64], Geneva = 3.70[16]	**SHEETS** Hot-rolled (18 ga. & hvr.)
		4.35[11]	SF = 5.30[24] F = 5.30[19]		Cold-rolled
		4.80[4,11]	SF, LA = 5.55[24]	Ashland = 4.80[7]	Galvanized (10 gage)
					Enameling (12 gage)
					Long ternes (10 gage)
		5.40[11]	F = 6.35[19]		Hi str. low alloy, h.r.
			F = 7.50[19]		Hi str. low alloy, c.r.
					Hi str. low alloy, galv.
4.10[83]	4.90[83]	3.50[4]	SF, LA = 4.25[24,62] F = 475[19], S = 4.50[62]	Atlanta = 4.05[65] Minnequa = 4.55[14]	**STRIP** Hot-rolled
			F = 6.30[19] LA = 6.40[27]	New Haven = 5.15[2], 5.85[68]	Cold-rolled
		5.30[11]	F = 6.70[19]		Hi str. low alloy, h.r.
					Hi str. low alloy, c.r.
					TINPLATE Cokes, 1.50-lb base box 1.25 lb. deduct 20¢
					Electrolytic 0.25, 0.50, 0.75 lb box

Deduct $1.55, $1.30 and 90¢ respectively from 1.50-lb coke base box price

Kansas City	Houston	Birm- ingham	WEST COAST	Eastern	Product
					BLACKPLATE, 29 gage Hollowware enameling
4.30[83]	4.10[83]	3.70[4,11]	SF, LA = 4.40[24]	Atlanta = 4.25[65] Minnequa = 4.15[14]	**BARS** Carbon steel
4.30[83]	4.10[83]	3.70[4,11]	SF, S = 4.45[62] F = 4.40[19] LA = 4.40[62]	Atlanta = 4.25[65] Minnequa = 4.50[14]	Reinforcing‡
				Newark = 5.00[69] Putnam = 5.10[69] Hartford = 5.10[4] Los Angeles = 6.00[4]	Cold-finished
4.90[83]	4.70[83]		LA = 5.35[62] F = 5.35[19]		Alloy, hot-rolled
				Newark = 5.75[69] Worcester = 2 Hartford = 5.85[4]	Alloy, cold-drawn
		5.55[11]	F = 6.60[19]		Hi str. low alloy, h.r.
	4.10[83]	3.70[4,11]	F = 4.30[19] S = 4.60[62] Geneva = 3.70[16]	Claymont = 4.15[29] Coatesville = 4.15[21] Minnequa = 4.50[14]	**PLATE** Carbon steel
				Harrisburg = 5.25[35]	Floor plates
			F = 5.70[19] Geneva = 5.65[16]	Coatesville = 5.25[21] Claymont = 4.85[29]	Alloy
		5.65[11]	F = 6.25[19]		Hi str. low alloy
4.25[83]	4.05[83]	3.65[4,11]	SF = 4.20[62] F = 4.25[16] LA = 4.25[24,62] S = 4.30[62]	Geneva 3.65[16] Minnequa 4.10[14]	**SHAPES, Structural**
		50[11]	F = 6.10[19]		Hi str. low-alloy
5.45[83]	5.25[83]	4.85[4,11]	SF, LA = 5.80[24]	Atlanta = 5.10[65] Worcester = 5.15[2] Minnequa = 5.10[14]	**MANUFACTURERS' WIRE** Bright

KEY TO STEEL PRODUCERS

With Principal Offices

1 Carnegie-Illinois Steel Corp., Pittsburgh
2 American Steel & Wire Co., Cleveland
3 Bethlehem Steel Co., Bethlehem
4 Republic Steel Corp., Cleveland
5 Jones & Laughlin Steel Corp., Pittsburgh
6 Youngstown Sheet & Tube Co., Youngstown
7 Armco Steel Corp., Middletown, Ohio
8 Inland Steel Co., Chicago
9 Weirton Steel Co., Weirton, W. Va.
10 National Tube Co., Pittsburgh
11 Tennessee Coal, Iron & R. R. Co., Birmingham
12 Great Lakes Steel Corp., Detroit
13 Sharon Steel Corp., Sharon, Pa.
14 Colorado Fuel & Iron Corp., Denver
15 Wheeling Steel Corp., Wheeling, W. Va.
16 Geneva Steel Co., Salt Lake City
17 Crucible Steel Co. of America, New York
18 Pittsburgh Steel Co., Pittsburgh
19 Kaiser Steel Corp., Oakland, Calif.
20 Portsmouth Div., Detroit Steel Corp., Detroit
21 Lukens Steel Co., Coatesville, Pa.
22 Granite City Steel Co., Granite City, Ill.
23 Wisconsin Steel Co., South Chicago, Ill.
24 Columbia Steel Co., San Francisco
25 Copperweld Steel Co., Glassport, Pa.
26 Alan Wood Steel Co., Conshohocken, Pa.
27 Calif. Cold Rolled Steel Corp., Los Angeles
28 Allegheny Ludlum Steel Corp., Pittsburgh
29 Worth Steel Co., Claymont, Del.
30 Continental Steel Corp., Kokomo, Ind.
31 Rotary Electric Steel Co., Detroit
32 Laclede Steel Co., St. Louis
33 Northwestern Steel & Wire Co., Sterling, Ill
34 Keystone Steel & Wire Co., Peoria, Ill.
35 Central Steel & Wire Co., Harrisburg, Pa.
36 Carpenter Steel Co., Reading, Pa.
37 Eastern Stainless Steel Corp., Baltimore
38 Washington Steel Corp., Washington, Pa.
39 Jessop Steel Co., Washington, Pa.
40 Blair Strip Steel Co., New Castle, Pa.
41 Superior Steel Corp., Carnegie, Pa.
42 Timken Steel & Tube Div., Canton, Ohio
43 Babcock & Wilcox Tube Co., Beaver Falls, Pa
44 Reeves Steel & Mfg. Co., Dover, Ohio
45 John A. Roebling's Sons Co., Trenton, N. J.
46 Simonds Saw & Steel Co., Fitchburg, Mass
47 McLouth Steel Corp., Detroit
48 Cold Metal Products Co., Youngstown
49 Thomas Steel Co., Warren, Ohio
50 Wilson Steel & Wire Co., Chicago
51 Sweet's Steel Co., Williamsport, Pa.
52 Superior Drawn Steel Co., Monaca, Pa.
53 Tremont Nail Co., Wareham, Mass.
54 Firth Sterling Steel & Carbide Corp., McKeesport, Pa.
55 Ingersoll Steel Div., Chicago
56 Phoenix Iron & Steel Co., Phoenixville, Pa.
57 Fitzsimmons Steel Co., Youngstown
58 Stanley Works, New Britain, Conn.
59 Universal-Cyclops Steel Corp., Bridgeville, Pa
60 American Cladmetals Co., Carnegie, Pa.
61 Cuyahoga Steel & Wire Co., Cleveland
62 Bethlehem Pacific Coast Steel Corp., San Francisco
63 Follansbee Steel Corp., Pittsburgh
64 Niles Rolling Mill Co., Niles, Ohio
65 Atlantic Steel Co., Atlanta
66 Acme Steel Co., Chicago
67 Joslyn Mfg. & Supply Co., Chicago
68 Detroit Steel Corp., Detroit
69 Wyckoff Steel Co., Pittsburgh
70 Bliss & Laughlin, Inc., Harvey, Ill.
71 Columbia Steel & Shafting Co., Pittsburgh
72 Cumberland Steel Co., Cumberland, Md.
73 La Salle Steel Co., Chicago
74 Monarch Steel Co., Inc., Hammond, Ind.
75 Empire Steel Co., Mansfield, Ohio
76 Mahoning Valley Steel Co., Niles, Ohio
77 Oliver Iron & Steel Co., Pittsburgh
78 Pittsburgh Screw & Bolt Co., Pittsburgh
79 Standard Forging Corp., Chicago
80 Driver Harris Co., Harrison, N. J.
81 Detroit Tube & Steel Div., Detroit
82 Reliance Div., Eaton Mfg. Co., Massillon, Ohio
83 Sheffield Steel Corp., Kansas City
84 Plymouth Steel Co., Detroit
85 Wickwire Spencer Steel, Buffalo
86 Angell Nail and Chaplet, Cleveland
87 Mid-States Steel & Wire, Crawfordsville, Ind.
88 National Supply, Pittsburgh, Pa.
89 Wheatland Tube Co., Wheatland, Pa.
90 Mercer Tube & Mfg. Co., Sharon, Pa.

STAINLESS STEELS

Base prices, in cents per pound, f.o.b. producing point

Product	301	302	303	304	316	321	347	410	416	430
Ingots, rerolling	14.25	15.00	16.50	16.00	24.25	19.75	21.50	12.75	14.75	13.00
Slabs, billets rerolling	18.50	19.75	21.75	20.75	31.75	26.00	28.25	16.50	20.00	16.75
Forg. discs, die blocks, rings	34.00	34.00	36.50	35.50	52.50	40.00	44.50	28.00	28.50	28.50
Billets, forging	26.25	26.25	28.25	27.50	41.00	31.00	34.75	21.50	22.00	22.00
Bars, wires, structurals	31.25	31.25	33.75	32.75	48.75	36.75	41.25	25.75	26.25	26.25
Plates	33.00	33.00	35.00	35.00	51.50	40.50	45.00	27.00	27.50	27.50
Sheets	41.00	41.00	43.00	43.00	56.50	49.00	53.50	36.50	37.00	39.00
Strip, hot-rolled	26.50	28.00	32.25	30.00	48.25	36.75	41.00	23.50	30.25	24.00
Strip, cold-rolled	34.00	36.50	40.00	38.50	58.50	48.00	52.00	30.50	37.00	31.00

STAINLESS STEEL PRODUCING POINTS—*Sheets:* Midland, Pa., 17; Brackenridge, Pa., 28; Butler, Pa., 7; McKeesport, Pa., 1; Washington, Pa., 38 (type 316 add 5¢), 39; Baltimore, 37; Middletown, Ohio, 7; Massillon, Ohio, 4; Gary, 1; Bridgeville, Pa., 59; New Castle, Ind., 55; Ft. Wayne, Ind., 67; Lockport, N. Y., 46.

Strip: Midland, Pa., 17; Cleveland, 2; Carnegie, Pa., 41; McKeesport, Pa., 54; Reading, Pa., 36; Washington, Pa., 38 (type 316 add 5¢); W. Leechburg, Pa., 28; Bridgeville, Pa., 59; Detroit, 47; Massillon, Canton, Ohio, 4; Middletown, Ohio, 7; Harrison, N. J., 80; Youngstown, 48; Lockport, N. Y., 46; New Britain, Conn., 58; Sharon, Pa., 13; Butler, Pa., 7.

Bars: Baltimore, 7; Duquesne, Pa. 1; Munhall, Pa., 1; Reading, Pa., 36; Titusville, Pa., 59; Washington, Pa., 39; McKeesport, Pa., 1, 54; Bridgeville, Pa., 59; Dunkirk, N. Y., 28; Massillon, Ohio, 4; Chicago, 1; Syracuse, N. Y., 17; Watervliet, N. Y., 28; Waukegan, Ill., 2; Lockport, N. Y., 46; Canton, Ohio, 42; Ft. Wayne, Ind., 67.

Wire: Waukegan, Ill., 2; Massillon, Ohio, 4; McKeesport, Pa., 54; Bridgeport, Conn., 44; Ft. Wayne, Ind., 67; Trenton, N. J., 45; Harrison, N. J., 80; Baltimore, 7; Dunkirk, 28.

Structurals: Baltimore, 7; Massillon, Ohio, 4; Chicago, 1, 67; Watervliet, N. Y., 28; Bridgeport, Conn., 44.

Plates: Brackenridge, Pa., 28 (type 416 add ½¢); Butler, Pa., 7; Chicago, 1; Munhall, Pa., 1; Midland, Pa., 17; New Castle, Ind., 55; Lockport, N. Y., 46; Middletown, 7; Washington, Pa., 39; Cleveland, Massillon, 4.

Forged discs, die blocks, rings: Pittsburgh, 1, 17; Syracuse, 17; Ferndale, Mich., 28.

Forging billets: Midland, Pa., 17; Baltimore, 7; Washington, Pa., 39; McKeesport, 54; Massillon, Canton, Ohio, 4; Watervliet, 28; Pittsburgh, Chicago, 1.

RAILS, TRACK SUPPLIES

F.o.b. Mill Cents Per Lb.	No. 1 Std. Rails	Light Rails	Joint Bars	Track Spikes	Axles	Screw Spikes	Tie Plates	Track Bolts Untreated
Bessemer-1	3.60	4.00	4.70	....	....	....	....	....
Chicago-4	....	....	....	6.15	....	....	....	....
Ensley-11	3.60	4.00	....	....	....	....	....	....
Fairfield-11	....	4.00	4.40	....	....	8.60	4.50	....
Gary-1	3.60	4.00	....	....	....	....	4.50	....
Ind. Harbor-8	3.60	....	4.70	6.15	5.25	8.60	4.50	....
Johnstown-3	....	4.00	....	....	5.60	8.60	....	....
Joliet-1	....	4.00	4.70	....	....	....	....	....
Kansas City-83	....	....	....	6.40	....	....	....	....
Lackawanna-3	3.60	4.00	4.70	....	....	8.60	4.50	....
Lebanon-3	....	....	....	6.15	....	....	....	9.60
Minnequa-14	3.60	4.50	4.70	6.15	....	8.60	4.50	9.60
Pittsburgh-77	....	....	....	....	....	9.35	....	9.60
Pittsburgh-78	....	....	....	....	....	....	....	9.60
Pittsburgh-5	....	....	....	6.15	....	....	....	....
Pittsburg-24	....	....	....	....	....	....	4.65	....
Seattle-62	....	....	....	6.10	....	....	4.35	....
Steelton-3	3.60	....	4.70	....	....	....	4.50	....
Struthers-6	....	....	....	5.60	....	....	....	....
Torrance-24	....	....	....	....	....	....	4.65	....
Youngstown-4	....	....	....	6.15	....	....	....	....

Track Bolts, heat treated, to railroads, 9.85¢ per lb.

BOILER TUBES

Seamless steel, electric welded commercial boiler tubes, locomotive tubes, minimum wall, per 100 ft at mill, c.l. lots, cut lengths 10 to 24 ft.

OD in in.	gage BWG	Seamless H.R.	Seamless C.D.	Electric Weld H.R.	Electric Weld C.D.
2	13	$22.67	$26.66	$21.99	$25.86
2½	12	30.48	35.84	29.57	34.76
3	12	33.90	39.90	32.89	34.80
3½	11	42.37	49.89	41.10	48.39
4	10	52.60	61.88	51.03	60.02

Pittsburgh Steel add, H-R: 2 in., 62¢; 2½ in., 84¢; 3 in., 92¢; 3½ in., $1.17; 4 in., $1.45. Add, C-R: 2 in., 74¢; 2½ in., 99¢; 3 in., $1.10; 3½ in., $1.37; 4 in., $1.70.

FLUORSPAR

Washed gravel fluorspar, f.o.b. cars, Rosiclare, Ill. Base price, per ton net: Effective CaF, content:

70% or more $41.00
60% or less 38.00

MERCHANT WIRE PRODUCTS

F.o.b. Mill	Standard & Coated Nails	Woven Wire Fence 9-15½ ga.	Fence Posts	Single Loop Bale Ties	Twisted Barbless Wire	Gal. Barbed Wire	Merch. Wire Ann'ld.	Merch. Wire Gal.
	Base Col.	Base Col.	Base Col.	Base Col.	Base Col.	Base Col.	¢/lb.	¢/lb.
Alabama City-4	118	126	....	123	....	136	5.70	5.95
Aliquippa, Pa.-5	118	132	....	....	136	140	5.70	6.15
Atlanta-65	113	133	....	126	126	143	5.95	6.40
Bartonville-34	118	130	140	123	143	143	5.95	6.15
Buffalo-85	....	....	....	....	....	....	....	....
Chicago-4	118	126	121	123	....	136	....	....
Cleveland-86	....	....	....	....	....	....	....	....
Cleveland-2	....	....	....	....	....	....	5.70	5.85
Crawfordsville-87	....	130	....	....	....	....	....	....
Donora, Pa.-2	118	130	....	123	....	140	5.70	5.85
Duluth-2	118	130	....	123	....	140	5.70	5.85
Fairfield, Ala.-11	118	126	....	123	....	136	5.70	5.95
Houston-83	126	138	....	....	....	148	6.10	6.55
Johnstown, Pa-3	118	130	....	....	140	....	5.70	6.15
Joliet, Ill.-2	118	130	....	123	....	140	5.70	5.85
Kokomo, Ind.-30	120	128	....	125	138	138	5.80	6.05
Los Angeles-62	....	....	....	....	....	....	....	....
Kansas City-83	130	130	142	135	....	152	6.30	6.75
Minnequa-14	123	138	130	128	146	146	5.95	6.45
Monessen-18	124	135	....	....	....	145	5.95	6.40
Moline, Ill.-4	....	....	121	....	....	....	....	....
Palmer-85	....	....	....	....	....	....	....	....
Pittsburg, Cal.-24	137	149	....	147	156	....	6.65	6.80
Portsmouth-20	124	137	....	....	147	147	6.10	6.60
Rankin, Pa.-2	118	130	....	....	....	140	5.70	5.85
San Francisco-14	....	....	....	....	....	....	....	....
So.Chicago, Ill.-4	118	126	116	123	....	136	5.70	5.95
So. San Francisco-14	....	....	....	147	....	160	6.65	7.10
Sparrows Pt.-3	120	....	....	125	142	132	5.80	6.25
Sterling, Ill.-33	118	130	140	123	140	140	....	....
Struthers, Ohio-6	....	....	....	....	....	....	....	....
Torrance, Cal.-24	138	....	....	....	....	....	6.65	....
Worcester-2	124	....	....	....	....	....	6.00	6.15
Williamsport, Pa.-51	....	....	....	....	....	....	....	....

Cut Nails, carloads, base, $6.75 per 100 lb. (less 20¢ to jobbers) at Conshohocken, Pa., (26), Wareham, lass. (53) Wheeling, W. Va., (15).

CAST IRON WATER PIPE

Per net ton

6 to 24-in., del'd Chicago . $105.30 to $108.80
6 to 24-in., del'd N. Y. ... 104.50 to 105.50
6 to 24-in., Birmingham . 91.50 to 96.00
6-in. and larger, f.o.b. cars, San Francisco, Los Angeles, for all rail shipment; rail and water shipment less .... $108.50 to $113.00
Class "A" and gas pipe, $5 extra; 4-in. pipe is $5 a ton above 6-in.

PIPE AND TUBING

Base discounts, f.o.b. mills. Base price about $200 per net ton.

	BUTTWELD														SEAMLESS					
	½ In.		¾ In.		1 In.		1¼ In.		1½ In.		2 In.		2½-3 In.		2 In.		2½-3 In.		3½-4 In.	
	Blk.	Gal.	Blk.	Gal.	Blk.	Gal.	Blk.	Gal.	Blk.	Gal.	Blk.	Gal.	Blk.	Gal.	Blk.	Gal.	Blk.	Gal.	Blk.	Gal.
STANDARD T. & C.																				
Bethlehem-3	34.0	12.0	37.0	16.0	39.5	19.5	40.0	20.0	40.5	21.0	41.0	21.5	41.5	22.0	....	....	....	....	....	....
Cleveland-4	36.0	14.0	39.0	18.0	41.5	21.5	42.0	22.0	42.5	23.0	43.0	23.5	43.5	24.0	....	....	....	....	....	....
Oakland-19	25.0	3.0	28.0	7.0	30.5	10.5	31.0	21.0	31.5	22.0	32.0	12.5	32.5	13.0	....	....	....	....	....	....
Pittsburgh-5	36.0	14.0	39.0	17.0	41.5	19.5	42.0	20.5	42.5	21.0	43.0	21.5	43.5	22.5	29.5	8.0	32.5	11.5	34.5	13.5
Pittsburgh-10	36.0	14.0	39.0	18.0	41.5	21.5	42.0	22.0	42.5	23.0	43.0	23.5	43.5	24.0	29.5	9.5	32.5	12.5	34.5	14.5
St. Louis-32	35.0	13.0	38.0	17.0	40.5	20.5	41.0	21.0	41.5	22.0	42.0	22.5	42.5	23.0	....	....	....	....	....	....
Sharon-90	36.0	13.0	39.0	17.0	41.5	20.0	42.0	20.5	42.5	21.0	43.0	21.5	43.5	22.0	....	....	....	....	....	....
Toledo-88	36.0	14.0	39.0	18.0	41.5	21.5	42.0	22.0	42.5	23.0	43.0	23.5	43.5	24.0	29.5	....	32.5	....	34.5	....
Wheeling-15	36.0	14.0	39.0	18.0	41.5	21.5	42.0	22.0	42.5	23.0	43.0	23.5	43.5	24.0	....	....	....	....	....	....
Wheatland-89	36.0	14.0	39.0	17.0	41.5	19.5	42.0	20.5	42.5	21.0	43.0	21.5	43.5	22.5	....	....	....	....	....	....
Youngstown-6	36.0	14.0	39.0	18.0	41.5	21.5	42.0	22.0	42.5	23.0	43.0	23.5	43.5	24.0	29.5	9.5	32.5	12.5	34.5	14.5
EXTRA STRONG, PLAIN ENDS																				
Bethlehem-3	33.5	13.0	37.5	17.0	39.5	20.5	40.0	21.0	40.5	22.0	41.0	22.5	41.5	23.0	....	....	....	....	....	....
Cleveland-4	35.5	15.0	39.5	19.0	41.5	22.5	42.0	23.0	42.5	24.0	43.0	24.5	43.5	25.0	....	....	....	....	....	....
Oakland-19	24.5	4.0	28.5	18.0	30.5	11.5	31.0	12.0	31.5	13.0	32.0	13.5	32.5	14.0	....	....	....	....	....	....
Pittsburgh	35.5	13.5	39.5	17.5	41.5	19.5	42.0	20.5	42.5	21.0	43.0	21.5	43.5	22.5	29.0	7.5	33.0	12.0	36.0	15.5
Pittsburgh-10	35.5	15.0	39.5	19.0	41.5	22.5	42.0	23.0	42.5	24.0	43.0	24.5	43.5	25.0	29.0	10.0	33.0	14.0	36.5	17.5
St. Louis-32	34.5	14.0	38.5	18.0	40.5	21.5	41.0	22.0	41.5	23.0	42.0	23.5	42.5	24.0	....	....	....	....	....	....
Sharon-90	35.5	14.0	39.5	18.0	41.5	21.0	42.0	21.5	42.5	22.0	43.0	22.5	43.5	23.0	....	....	....	....	....	....
Toledo-88	35.5	15.0	39.5	19.0	41.5	22.5	42.0	23.0	42.5	24.0	43.0	24.5	43.5	25.0	29.0	....	33.0	....	36.5	....
Wheeling-15	35.5	15.0	39.5	19.0	41.5	22.5	42.0	23.0	42.5	24.0	43.0	24.5	43.5	25.0	....	....	....	....	....	....
Wheatland-89	35.5	13.5	39.5	17.5	41.5	19.5	42.0	20.5	42.5	21.0	43.0	21.5	43.5	22.5	....	....	....	....	....	....
Youngstown-6	35.5	15.0	39.5	19.0	41.5	22.5	42.0	23.0	42.5	24.0	43.0	24.5	43.5	25.0	29.0	10.0	33.0	14.0	36.5	17.5

Galvanized discounts based on zinc at 17¢ per lb, East St. Louis. For each 1¢ change in zinc, discounts vary as follows: ½ in., ¾ in., and 1 in., 1 pt.; 1¼ in., 1½ in., 2 in., ¾ pt.; 2½ in., 3 in., ½ pt. Calculate discounts on even cents per lb of zinc, i.e., if zinc is 16.51¢ to 17.50¢ per lb, use 17¢. Jones & Laughlin discounts apply only when zinc price changes 1¢.

Threads only, buttweld and seamless, 1 pt. higher discount. Plain ends, buttweld and seamless, 3 in. and under, 3½ pts. higher discount. Buttweld jobbers' discount, 5 pct.

WAREHOUSE PRICES

Base prices, f.o.b. warehouse, dollars per 100 lb. (Metropolitan area delivery, add 20¢ to base price except Birmingham, San Francisco, Cincinnati, New Orleans, St. Paul (*), add 15¢; Philadelphia, add 25¢; Memphis, add 10¢; New York, add 30¢).

CITIES	SHEETS			STRIP		PLATES	SHAPES	BARS		ALLOY BARS			
	Hot-Rolled	Cold-Rolled (15 gage)	Galvanized (10 gage)	Hot-Rolled	Cold-Rolled		Standard Structural	Hot-Rolled	Cold-Finished	Hot-Rolled, A 4615 As-rolled	Hot-Rolled, A 4140 Ann.	Cold-Drawn, A 4615 As-rolled	Cold-Drawn, A 4140 Ann.
Baltimore	5.60	6.84	7.49²–8.07	6.04	....	5.80	6.14	6.04	6.84–6.89	10.24	10.54	11.89	12.19
Birmingham*	5.60	6.40	6.75	5.55	....	5.95	5.70	5.55	....	....	....	....	....
Boston	6.20	7.00–7.25	7.74–8.29	6.15	8.50¹⁶	6.48–6.78	6.20	6.05	6.79–6.84	10.25	10.55	11.90–12.00	12.20–12.30
Buffalo	5.60	6.40	7.74–8.09	5.86	....	6.05	5.80	5.60	6.40–6.45	10.15–10.85	10.45	11.80	11.95–12.10
Chicago	5.60	6.40	7.75	5.55	....	5.80	5.70	5.55	6.30	9.80	10.10	11.45	11.75
Cincinnati*	5.87	6.44	7.39	5.80	....	6.19	6.09	5.80	6.61	10.15	10.45	11.80	12.10
Cleveland	5.60	6.40	8.10	5.69	6.90	5.92	5.82	5.57	6.40	9.91	10.21	11.56	11.86
Detroit	5.78	6.53	7.89	5.94	....	5.99	6.09	5.84	6.56	10.11	10.41	11.76	12.06
Houston	7.00	8.25	....	....	....	6.85	6.50	6.65	9.35	10.35	11.25	....	12.75
Indianapolis, Del'd	6.00	6.80	8.15	5.95	....	6.20	6.10	5.95	6.80	....	....	....	....
Kansas City	6.00	6.80	7.45	6.15	7.50	6.40	6.30	6.15	7.00	10.40	10.70	12.05	12.35
Los Angeles	6.35	7.90	8.85	6.40	8.70¹⁶	6.40	6.35	6.35	7.55	11.30	11.30	13.20	13.50
Memphis*	6.33–6.38	7.08–7.18	....	6.33–6.38	....	6.43–8.02	6.33–6.48	6.08–6.33	7.16–7.32	....	....	....	....
Milwaukee	5.74	6.54	7.89	5.69–6.59	....	5.94	4.84	5.69	6.44–6.54	9.94	10.24	11.59	11.89
New Orleans*	5.70	6.95	....	5.75	7.25	5.95	5.75	5.75	7.30	....	....	....	....
New York*	5.67–5.97	7.19²²–7.24¹	8.14²	6.29–6.89	8.63¹⁶	6.28–6.58	6.10	6.12	6.99	10.05–10.15	10.35–10.45	11.70–11.80	12.10–12.20
Norfolk	6.50¹³	....	....	....	....	6.50¹³	6.60¹³	6.55¹³	....	....	....	....	....
Philadelphia*	5.90	6.55	8.00	6.10	....	6.05	5.90	6.05	6.61	9.90	10.20	....	....
Pittsburgh	5.60	6.40	7.75	5.65–5.95	....	5.75	5.70	5.55	6.15	9.80	10.10	11.45	11.75
Portland	6.60	....	8.50	7.30	....	6.80	6.95	6.90	....	....	....	....	....
Salt Lake City	7.95	....	9.70	8.70	....	8.05	8.30	8.65	9.00	....	....	....	....
San Francisco*	6.65	8.05²	8.55–8.90²	6.60	....	6.50	6.45	6.45	8.20	11.30	11.30	13.20	13.20–13.50
Seattle	7.05	8.60	9.20	9.05	....	6.75	6.65	6.75	9.05	....	....	....	....
St. Louis	5.80–5.85	6.65	8.00	5.80	8.00¹⁶–8.28	6.13	6.03	5.80	6.55–6.65	10.05	10.35	11.70	12.00
St. Paul*	6.16	6.96	8.31	6.11	....	6.36	6.26	6.11	6.96	10.36	10.66	12.01	12.31

BASE QUANTITIES (*Standard unless otherwise keyed on prices.*)

Hot-rolled sheets and strip, hot rolled bars and bar shapes, structural shapes, plate, galvanized sheets and cold-rolled sheets; 2000 to 9999 lb. Cold-finished bars; 2000 lb or over. Alloy bars; 1000 to 1999 lb. Cold-rolled strip; 2000 to 9999 lb.

All HR products may be combined to determine quantity bracket. All galvanized sheets may be combined to determine quantity bracket. CR sheets may not be combined with each other or with galv. sheets to determine quantity bracket.

Exceptions:
(1) 400 to 1499 lb; (2) 450 to 1499 lb; (3) 300 to 4999 lb; (4) 300 to 9999 lb; (5) 2000 to 5999 lb; (6) 1000 lb and over; (7) 500 to 1499 lb; (8) 400 lb and over; (9) 400 to 9999 lb; (10) 500 to 9999 lb; (11) 400 to 3999 lb; (12) 450 to 3749 lb; (13) 400 to 1999 lb; (14) 1500 lb and over; (15) 1000 to 9999 lb; (16) 6000 lb and over; (17) up to 1999 lb; (18) 1000 to 4999 lb; (19) 1500 to 3499 lb; (20) CR sheets may be combined for quantity; (21) 3 to 24 bundles; (22) 1500 to 9999 lb.

PIG IRON PRICES

Dollars per gross ton. Delivered prices do not include 3 pct tax on freight.

PRODUCING POINT PRICES

Producing Point	Basic	No. 2 Foundry	Malleable	Bessemer	Low. Phos.
Bethlehem	54.00	54.50	55.00	55.50	.....
Birmingham	48.38	48.88	.....	.....	.....
Buffalo	52.00	52.50	53.00	.....	.....
Chicago	52.00	52.50	52.50	53.00	.....
Cleveland	52.00	52.50	52.50	53.00	57.00
Daingerfield, Tex.	48.00	48.50	48.50	.....	.....
Duluth	52.00	52.50	52.50	53.00	.....
Erie	52.00	52.50	52.50	53.00	.....
Everett	.....	53.25	53.75	.....	.....
Fontana	58.00	58.50	.....	.....	.....
Granite City	53.90	54.40	54.90	.....	.....
Hubbard	52.00	52.50	52.50	.....	.....
Ironton, Utah	52.00	52.50	.....	.....	.....
Pittsburgh	52.00*	.....	.....	53.00	.....
Neville Island	52.00	52.50	52.50	53.00	.....
Geneva, Utah	52.00	52.50	.....	.....	.....
Sharpsville	52.00	52.50	52.50	53.00	.....
Steelton	54.00	54.50	55.00	55.50	60.00
Swedeland	56.00	56.50	57.00	57.50	.....
Toledo	52.00	52.50	52.50	53.00	.....
Troy, N. Y.	54.00	54.50	55.00	.....	60.00
Youngstown	52.00	52.50	52.50	53.00	.....

DELIVERED PRICES (BASE GRADES)

Consuming Point	Producing Point	Rail Freight Rate	Basic	No. 2 Foundry	Malleable	Bessemer	Low. Phos
Boston	Everett	$.60-.80	.....	53.85–54.05	54.55–54.75	.....	.....
Boston	Steelton	6.90	.....	.....	.....	.....	66.9?
Brooklyn	Bethlehem	4.29	.....	58.79	59.29	59.29	.....
Cincinnati	Birmingham	6.70	55.08	55.58	.....	.....	.....
Jersey City	Bethlehem	2.63	.....	57.13	57.63	58.13	.....
Los Angeles	Geneva-Ironton	7.70	.....	60.20	.....	.....	.....
Los Angeles	Fontana	.....	.....	59.70	60.20	.....	.....
Mansfield	Cleveland, Toledo	3.33	55.33	55.83	55.83	56.33	60.33
Philadelphia	Bethlehem	2.39	56.39	56.89	57.39	57.89	.....
Philadelphia	Swedeland	1.44	57.44	57.94	58.44	58.94	.....
Philadelphia	Steelton	3.09	57.09	57.59	58.09	58.59	63.09
Rochester	Buffalo	2.63	54.63	55.13	55.63	.....	.....
San Francisco	Geneva-Ironton	7.70	.....	60.20	.....	.....	.....
San Francisco	Fontana	.....	.....	59.70	60.20	.....	.....
Seattle	Geneva-Ironton	7.70	.....	60.20	.....	.....	.....
Seattle	Fontana	.....	.....	59.70	60.20	.....	.....
St. Louis	Granite City	0.75 Arb.	51.65	52.15	52.65	.....	.....
Syracuse	Buffalo	3.58	55.58	56.08	56.58	.....	.....

* Monessen, $54.00.

Producing points prices are subject to switching charges; silicon differential (not to exceed 50c per ton for each 0.25 pct silicon content in excess of base grade which is 1.75 to 2.25 pct for foundry iron); phosphorus differentials, a reduction of 28c per ton for phosphorus content of 0.70 pct and over; manganese differentials, a charge not to exceed 50c

per ton for each 0.50 pct manganese content in excess of 1.00 pct, $2 per ton extra may be charged for 0.5 to 0.75 pct nickel content and $1 per ton extra for each additional 0.25 pct nickel. Silvery iron (blast furnace) silicon 6.01 to 6.50 pct C/L per g.t.. f.o.b. Jackson, Ohio—$62.50; f.o.b. Buffalo, $63.75. Add $1.50 per ton for each additional 0.50 pct Si up to 17 pct.

Add 50c per ton for each 0.50 pct Mn over 1.00 pct. Add $1.00 per ton for 0.75 pct or more P. Bessemer ferro-silicon prices are $1.00 per ton above silvery iron prices of comparable analysis.

Charcoal pig iron base price for low phosphorus $62.00 per gross ton, f.o.b. Lyle, Tenn. Delivered Chicago, $70.56. High phosphorus charcoal pig iron is not being produced.

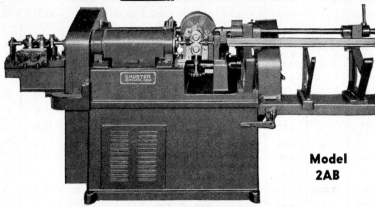
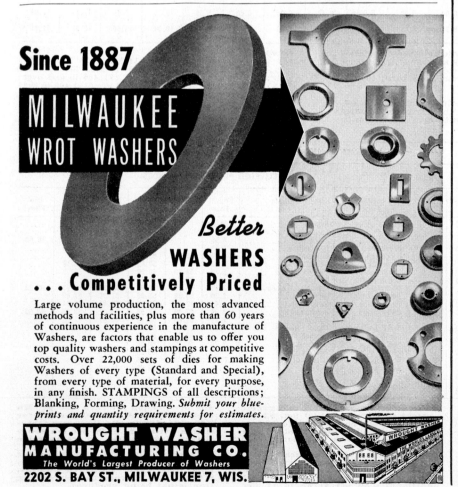
476

BOLTS, NUTS, RIVETS, SCREWS
Consumer Prices
(Base discount, f.o.b. mill, Pittsburgh, Cleveland, Birmingham or Chicago)

Machine and Carriage Bolts

	Pct Off list	
	Less Case	C.
½ in. & smaller x 6 in. & shorter	15	28½
9/16 in. & ⅝ in. x 6 in. & shorter	18½	30½
¾ in. & larger x 6 in. & shorter	17½	29½
All diam. longer than 6 in.	14	27½
Lag, all diam. x 6 in. & shorter	23	35
Lag, all diam. longer than 6 in.	21	33
Plow bolts	34	...

Nuts, Hot Pressed, Cold Punched—Sq

	Pct Off List			
	Less Keg (Reg.)	K.	Less Keg (Hvy.)	K.
½ in. & smaller	15	28½	15	28½
9/16 in. & ⅝ in.	12	25	6½	21
¾ in. to 1½ in. inclusive	9	23	1	16½
1⅝ in. & larger	7½	22	1	16½

Nuts, Hot Pressed—Hexagon

½ in. & smaller	26	37	22	34
9/16 in. & ⅝ in.	16½	29½	6½	21
¾ in. to 1½ in. inclusive	12	25	2	17½
1⅝ in. & larger	8½	23	2	17½

Nuts, Cold Punched—Hexagon

½ in. & smaller	26	37	22	34
9/16 in. & ⅝ in.	23	35	17½	30½
¾ in. to 1½ in. inclusive	19½	31½	12	25
1⅝ in. & larger	12	25	6½	21

Nuts, Semi-Finished—Hexagon

	Reg.		Hvy.	
½ in. & smaller	35	45	28½	39½
9/16 in. & ⅝ in.	29½	40½	22	34
¾ in. to 1½ in. inclusive	24	36	15	28½
1⅝ in. & larger	13	26	8½	23

	Light	
7/16 in. & smaller	35	45
½ in. thru ⅝ in.	28½	39½
¾ in. to 1½ in. inclusive	26	37

Stove Bolts

	Pct Off List
Packaged, steel, plain finished	56—10
Packaged, plated finish	41—10
Bulk, plain finish**	67*

*Discounts apply to bulk shipments in not less than 15,000 pieces of a size and kind where length is 3-in. and shorter; 5000 pieces for lengths longer than 3-in. For lesser quantities, packaged price applies.

**Zinc, Parkerized, cadmium or nickel plated finishes add 6¢ per lb net. For black oil finish, add 2¢ per lb net.

Rivets

	Base per 100 lb
½ in. & larger	$7.85
	Pct Off List
7/16 in. & smaller	36

F.o.b. Pittsburgh, Cleveland, Chicago, Birmingham, Lebanon, Pa.

Cap and Set Screws
(In bulk)

	Pct Off List
Hexagon head cap screws, coarse or fine thread, ¼ in. thru ⅝ in. x 6 in., SAE 1020, bright	54
¾ in. thru 1 in. up to & including 6 in.	48
¼ in. thru ⅝ in. x 6 in. & shorter high C double heat treat	46
¾ in. thru 1 in. up to & including 6 in.	41
Milled studs	35
Flat head cap screws, listed sizes	16
Fillister head cap, listed sizes	34
Set screws, sq head, cup point, 1 in. diam. and smaller x 6 in. & shorter	53

LAKE SUPERIOR ORES
(51.50% Fe; natural content, delivered lower lake ports)

	Per gross ton
Old range, bessemer	$8.70
Old range, nonbessemer	8.55
Mesabi, bessemer	8.45
Mesabi, nonbessemer	8.30
High phosphorus	8.30

After adjustments for analyses, prices will be increased or decreased as the case may be for increases or decreases after Dec. 2, 1950, in lake vessel rates, upper lake rail freights, dock handling charges and taxes thereon.

IRON AGE
FOUNDED 1855

MARKETS & PRICES

ELECTRODES

Cents per lb, f.o.b. plant, threaded electrodes with nipples, unboxed

Diam. in in.	Length in in.	Cents Per lb
GRAPHITE		
17, 18, 20	60, 72	17.00¢
8 to 16	48, 60, 72	17.00¢
7	48, 60	18.64¢
6	48, 60	19.95¢
4, 5	40	20.48¢
3	40	21.53¢
2½	24, 30	22.05¢
2	24, 30	24.15¢
CARBON		
40	100, 110	7.65¢
35	65, 110	7.65¢
30	65, 84, 110	7.65¢
24	72 to 104	7.65¢
20	84, 90	7.65¢
17	60, 72	7.65¢
14	60, 72	8.16¢
10, 12	60	8.42¢
8	60	8.67¢

CLAD STEEL

Base prices, cents per pound, f.o.b. mill

Stainless-carbon	Plate	Sheet
No. 304, 20 pct,		
Coatesville, Pa. (21)	*29.5	
Washgtn, Pa. (39)	*29.5	
Claymont, Del. (29)	*28.00	
Conshohocken, Pa. (26)		*24.00
New Castle, Ind. (55)	*26.50	*25.50
Nickel-carbon		
10 pct. Coatesville (21)	32.5	
Inconel-carbon		
10 pct Coatesville (21)	40.5	
Monel-carbon		
10 pct Coatesville (21)	33.5	
No. 302 Stainless - copper-stainless, Carnegie, Pa. (60)		77.00
Aluminized steel sheets, hot dip, Butler, Pa. (7)		7.75

*Includes annealing and pickling, or sandblasting.

TOOL STEEL

F.o.b. mill

W	Cr	V	Mo	Co	Base per lb
18	4	1	—	—	$1.10
18	4	1	—	5	$1.72
18	4	2	—	—	$1.245
1.5	4	1.5	8	—	78.5¢
6	4	2	6	—	84¢
High-carbon chromium					63.5¢
Oil hardened manganese					35¢
Special carbon					32.5¢
Extra carbon					27¢
Regular carbon					23¢

Warehouse prices on and east of Mississippi are 3¢ per lb higher. West of Mississippi, 5¢ higher.

ELECTRICAL SHEETS

22 gage, HR cut lengths, f.o.b. mill

	Cents per lb.
Armature	*6.75
Electrical	*7.25
Motor	*8.50
Dynamo	9.30
Transformer 72	9.85
Transformer 65	10.40
Transformer 58	11.10
Transformer 52	11.90

PRODUCING POINTS—Beech Bottom, W. Va., 15; Brackenridge, Pa., 28; Follansbee, W. Va., 63; Granite City, Ill., 22*, add 70¢; Indiana Harbor, Ind., 3; Mansfield, Ohio, 75; Niles, Ohio, 64, add 30¢; Vandergrift, Pa., 1; Warren, Ohio, 4; Zanesville, Ohio, 7.

COKE

	Net Ton
Furnace, beehive (f.o.b. oven)	
Connellsville, Pa.	$14.00 to $14.50
Foundry, beehive (f.o.b. oven)	
Connellsville, Pa.	$17.00 to $17.50
Foundry, oven coke	
Buffalo, del'd	$25.35
Chicago, f.o.b.	21.00
Detroit, f.o.b.	23.00
New England, del'd	24.80
Seaboard, N. J., f.o.b.	22.00
Philadelphia, f.o.b.	22.70
Swedeland, Pa., f.o.b.	22.60
Plainesville, Ohio, f.o.b.	24.00
Erie, Pa., f.o.b.	23.50
Cleveland, del'd	25.72
Cincinnati, del'd	25.06
St. Paul, f.o.b.	21.00
St. Louis, f.o.b.	24.90
Birmingham, del'd	20.79

IRON AGE
FOUNDED 1855

MARKETS & PRICES

Ferrochrome

Contract prices, cents per pound, contained Cr, lump size, bulk, in carloads, delivered. (65-72% Cr, 2% max. Si.)

0.06% C	.... 30.50	0.20% C	.... 29.50
0.10% C	.... 30.00	0.50% C	.... 29.25
0.15% C	.... 29.75	1.00% C	.... 29.00
2.00% C			28.75
65-69% Cr, 4-9% C			22.00
62-66% Cr, 4-6% C, 6-9% Si.			22.85

High-Nitrogen Ferrochrome

Low-carbon type: 67-72% Cr, 0.75% N. Add 5¢ per lb to regular low carbon ferrochrome price schedule. Add 5¢ for each additional 0.25% N.

S. M. Ferrochrome

Contract price, cents per pound, chromium contained, lump size, delivered.

High carbon type: 60-65% Cr, 4-6% Si, 4-6% Mn, 4-6% C.

Carloads	21.60
Ton lots	23.75
Less ton lots	25.25

Low carbon type: 62-66% Cr, 4-6% Si, 4-6% Mn, 1.25% max. C.

Carloads	27.75
Ton lots	30.05
Less ton lots	31.85

Chromium Metal

Contract prices, per lb chromium contained packed, delivered, ton lots. 97% min. Cr, 1% max. Fe.

0.20% Max. C.	$1.09
0.50% max. C.	1.05
.00 min. C	1.04

Low Carbon Ferrochrome Silicon

(Cr 34-41%, Si 42-49%, C 0.05% max.) Contract price, carloads, f.o.b. Niagara Falls, freight allowed; lump 4-in. x down, bulk 2-in. x down, 21.75¢ per lb of contained Cr plus 12.00¢ per lb of contained Si.

Bulk 1-in. x down, 21.90¢ per lb contained Cr plus 12.20¢ per lb contained Si.

Calcium-Silicon

Contract price per lb of alloy, dump, delivered.

30-33% Ca, 60-65% Si, 3.00% max. Fe

Carloads	19.00
Ton lots	22.10
Less ton lots	23.60

Calcium-Manganese—Silicon

Contract prices, cents per lb of alloy, lump, delivered.

16-20% Ca, 14-18% Mn, 53-59% Si.

Carloads	20.00
Ton lots	22.30
Less ton lots	23.30

CMSZ

Contract price, cents per pound of alloy, delivered.

Alloy 4: 45-49% Cr, 4-6% Mn, 18-21% Si, 1.25-1.75% Zr, 3.00-4.5% C.

Alloy 5: 50.56% Cr, 4-6% Mn, 13.50-16.00% Si, 0.75 to 1.25% Zr, 3.50-5.00% C

Ton lots	20.75
Less ton lots	22.00

V Foundry Alloy

Cents per pound of alloy, f.o.b. Suspension Bridge, N. Y., freight allowed, max St. Louis. V-5: 38-42% Cr, 17-19% Si, 8-11% Mn.

Ton lots	16.50¢
Less ton lots	17.75¢

Graphidox No. 4

Cents per pound of alloy, f.o.b. Suspension Bridge, N. Y., freight allowed, max. St. Louis. Si 48 to 52%, Ti 9 to 11%, Ca 5 to 7%.

Carload packed	18.00¢
Ton lots to carload packed	19.00¢
Less ton lots	20.50¢

SMZ

Contract price, cents per pound of alloy, delivered, 60-65% Si, 5-7% Mn, 5-7% Zr, 20% Fe, ½ in. x 12 mesh.

Ton lots	17.25
Less ton lots	18.50

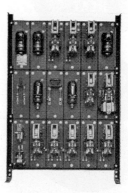

IRON AGE FOUNDED 1855 **MARKETS & PRICES**

FERROALLOYS

Ferromanganese
78-82% Mn. maximum contract base price, gross ton, lump size.

F.o.b. Birmingham	$174
F.o.b. Niagara Falls, Alloy, W. Va., Welland, Ont., Ashtabula, O.	$185
F.o.b. Johnstown, Pa.	$187
F.o.b. Sheridan, Pa.	$185
F.o.b. Etna, Clairton, Pa.	$175

$2.00 for each 1% above 82% Mn, penalty, $2.15 for each 1% below 78%.
Briquets—Cents per pound of briquet, delivered, 66% contained Mn.

Carload, bulk	10.45
Ton lots	12.05

Spiegeleisen
Contract prices gross ton, lump, f.o.b.

	16-19% Mn 3% max. Si	19-21% Mn 3% max. Si
Palmerton, Pa.	$74.00	$75.00
Pgh. or Chicago	75.00	76.00

Manganese Metal
Contract basis, 2 in. x down, cents per pound of metal, delivered.
96% min. Mn, 0.2% max. C, 1% max. Si, 2% max. Fe.

Carload, packed	29.75
Ton lots	31.25

Electrolytic Manganese
F.o.b. Knoxville, Tenn., freight allowed east of Mississippi, cents per pound.

Carloads	28
Ton lots	30
Less ton lots	32

Medium Carbon Ferromanganese
Mn 80% to 85%, C 1.25 to 1.50. Contract price, carloads, lump, bulk, delivered, per lb. of contained Mn ...... 19.15¢

Low-Carbon Ferromanganese
Contract price, cents per pound Mn contained, lump size, del'd., Mn. 85-90%.

	Carloads	Ton	Less
0.07% max. C, 0.06% P, 90% Mn	26.25	28.10	29.30
0.07% max. C	25.75	27.60	28.80
0.15% max. C	25.25	27.10	28.30
0.30% max. C	24.75	26.60	27.80
0.50% max. C	24.25	26.10	27.30
0.75% max. C, 7.00% max. Si	21.25	23.10	24.30

Silicomanganese
Contract basis, lump size, cents per pound of metal, delivered, 65-68% Mn, 18-20% Si, 1.5% max. C. For 2% max. C, deduct 0.2¢.

Carload bulk	9.90
Ton lots	11.55
Briquet, contract basis carlots, bulk delivered, per lb of briquet	11.15
Ton lots	11.75

Silvery Iron (electric furnace)
Si 14.01 to 14.50 pct, f.o.b. Keokuk, Iowa, or Wenatchee, Wash., $89.50 gross ton, freight allowed to normal trade area. Si 15.01 to 15.50 pct, f.o.b. Niagara Falls, N. Y., $83.00. Add $1.00 per ton for each additional 0.50% Si up to and including 18%. Add $1.00 for each 0.50% Mn over 1%.

Silicon Metal
Contract price, cents per pound contained Si, lump size, delivered, for ton lots packed.

96% Si, 2% Fe	21.70
97% Si, 1% Fe	22.10

Silicon Briquets
Contract price, cents per pound of briquet bulk, delivered, 40% Si, 1 lb Si briquets.

Carload, bulk	6.95
Ton lots	8.55

Electric Ferrosilicon
Contract price, cents per pound contained Si, lump, bulk, carloads, delivered.

25% Si	19.00	75% Si	14.30
50% Si	12.40	85% Si	15.55
90-95% Si			17.50

Calcium Metal
Eastern zone contract prices, cents per pound of metal, delivered.

	Cast	Turnings	Distilled
Ton lots	$2.05	$2.95	$3.75
Less ton lots	2.40	3.30	4.55

January 4, 1951

Other Ferroalloys

Alsifer, 20% Al, 40% Si, 40% Fe,
contract basis, f.o.b. Suspension
Bridge, N. Y.
    Carload .... 8.15¢
    Ton lots .... 9.55¢
Calcium molybdate, 45-40%, f.o.b.
Langeloth, Pa., per pound con-
tained Mo $1.15
Ferrocolumbium, 50-60%, 2 in x D,
contract basis, delivered, per
pound contained Cb.
    Ton lots $4.90
    Less ton lots 4.95
Ferro-Tantalum-columbium, 20%
Ta, 40% Cb, 0.30 C. Contract
basis, delivered, ton lots, 2 in. x
D, per lb of contained Cb plus Ta $3.75
Ferromolybdenum, 55-75%, f.o.b.
Langeloth, Pa., per pound con-
tained Mo $1.32
Ferrophosphorus, electrolytic, 23-
26%, car lots, f.o.b. Siglo, Mt.
Pleasant, Tenn., $3 unitage, per
gross ton $65.00
    10 tons to less carload 75.00
Ferrotitanium, 40%, regular grade,
0.10% C max., f.o.b. Niagara
Falls, N. Y., and Bridgeville, Pa.,
freight allowed, ton lots, per lb
contained Ti $1.38
Ferrotitanium, 25%, low carbon,
0.10% C max., f.o.b. Niagara
Falls, N. Y., and Bridgeville, Pa.,
freight allowed, ton lots, per lb
contained Ti $1.50
    Less ton lots $1.55
Ferrotitanium, 15 to 19%, high carbon, f.o.b. Niagara Falls, N. Y.,
freight allowed, carload per net
ton $177.00
Ferrotungsten, standard, lump or
¼ x down, packed, per pound
contained W, 5 ton lots, delivered $3.25
Ferrovanadium, 35-55%, contract
basis, delivered, per pound, contained V.
    Openhearth ....$3.00-$3.05
    Crucible 3.10- 3.15
    High speed steel (Primos)..... 3.25
Molybdic oxide, briquets or cans,
per lb contained Mo, f.o.b. Langeloth, Pa. $1.14
    bags, f.o.b. Washington, Pa.,
    Langeloth, Pa. $1.13
Simanal, 20% Si, 20% Mn, 20%
Al, contract basis, f.o.b. Philo,
Ohio, freight allowed, per pound
    Carload, bulk lump .... 14.50¢
    Ton lots, bulk lump .... 15.75¢
    Less ton lots, lump .... 16.25¢
Vanadium pentoxide, 88-92%,
V_2O_5 contract basis, per pound
contained V_2O_5 .... $1.2¢
Zirconium, 35-40%, contract basis,
f.o.b. plant, freight allowed, per
pound of alloy.
    Ton lots .... 21.00¢
Zirconium, 12-15%, contract basis,
lump, delivered, per lb of alloy.
    Carload, bulk .... 7.00¢

Boron Agents

Contract prices per lb of alloy, del.
Borosil, f.o.b. Philo, Ohio, freight
allowed, B 3-4%, Si 40-45%, per
lb contained B $5.25
Bortam, f.o.b. Niagara Falls
    Ton lots, per pound .... 45¢
    Less ton lots, per pound...... 50¢
Carbortam, Ti 15-21%, B 1-2%, Si
2-4%, Al 1-2%, C 4.5-7.5% f.o.b.
Suspension Bridge, N. Y., freight
allowed.
    Ton lots, per pound .... 10.00¢
Ferroboron, 17.50% min. B, 1.50% max
Si, 0.50% max. Al, 0.50% max. C, 1 in
x D. Ton lots $1.20
F.o.b. Wash., Pa.; 100 lb, up
    10 to 14% B .... .78
    14 to 19% B 1.20
    19% min. B 1.50
Grainal, f.o.b. Bridgeville, Pa.,
freight allowed, 100 lb and over.
    No. 1 .... $1.00
    No. 6 .... 68¢
    No. 79 .... 50¢
Manganese—Boron 75.00% Mn, 15-20%
B, 5% max. Fe, 1.50% max. Si, 3.00%
max. C, 2 in. x D, delivered.
    Ton lots $1.46
    Less ton lots 1.57
Nickel—Boron 15-18% B, 1.00% max. Al
1.50% max. Si, 0.50% max. C, 3.00%
max. Fe, balance Ni, delivered.
    Less ton lots $1.80
Silcaz, contract basis, delivered.
    Ton lots .... 45.00¢

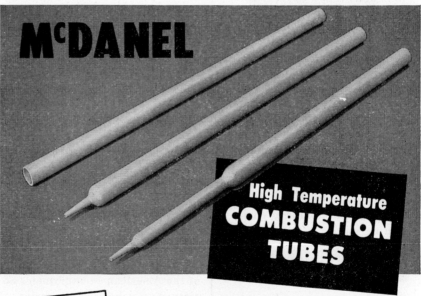

Trucks and Trailers

up to 50 ton capacity

Built with 80 years of skill by pioneers in the industry. Over a hundred standard two, four, and fifth wheel trucks and trailers. Special units designed and built to your specification. Complete engineering service.

WRITE FOR CATALOG

Name_____

Firm_____

Street_____

City & State_____

_____

THE KILBOURNE & JACOBS MFG. CO.
794 Congress St., Columbus 16, O.

• News of Industry •

NPA Seeks Plan to Curtail Use of Tungsten in Cutting Tools

Washington—The shortage of steel-hardening tungsten has forced NPA to seek measures for curtailment of the material's use in high-speed cutting tool steels. Reasons for the shortage, says NPA, is military stockpiling, jet engine production, and stoppage of Red Chinese exports. (THE IRON AGE, Nov. 30, 1950, p. 85).

NPA appointed an industry group to formulate a plan for tungsten cutbacks and substitution of more plentiful alloys. The NPA's directive will probably lower the content of tungsten in cutting tools from the current 18 pct. In World War II these steels had only a 6 pct tungsten content.

NPA was told by industry spokesmen that production of cutting tools will expand by 20 to 25 pct soon.

Try to Revive Scrap Exports

London—Aimed at boosting declining scrap steel exports to Britain, negotiations, which were held at Bonn and Dusseldorf, will be continued here this month. German scrap exports to Britain dropped from a monthly average of 130,000 tons during the first half of 1950 to 42,000 tons in October and scarcely 40,000 tons in November. At the same time, Britain's share in total German scrap exports dipped from 60 to 45 pct.

AFS Foundry Practice Lectures

Chicago—The Chicago chapter of the American Foundrymen's Society has scheduled a series of demonstrations on modern foundry practice during the coming year.

The first demonstration, at the People's Gas Auditorium Jan. 8, will illustrate better quality control through the laboratory. Later demonstrations will include modern molding, core-making and gating methods, improved foundry safety, defective castings and what to do about them.

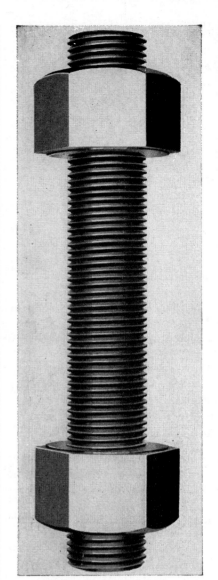

ERIE

Specialists for

36 YEARS... in PRECISION HIGH QUALITY ALLOY STUDS

Send your blueprints to

ERIE BOLT & NUT CO.
ERIE · PA.

A SUBSIDIARY OF

Barium STEEL CORPORATION
Steelwright to the Nation

STUDS · BOLTS · NUTS · ALLOYS
STAINLESS · CARBON · BRONZE

REPRESENTATION IN PRINCIPAL CITIES

J&L Has Sales Force Shakeup; Timberlake Named Sales Manager

Pittsburgh — A major shakeup in the sales force of Jones & Laughlin Steel Corp. was announced by A. J. Hazlett, vice-president in charge of sales, effective Jan. 1.

J. E. Timberlake, assistant general manager of sales, was named general manager of sales; H. E. Robinson, manager of strip and sheet sales, appointed assistant general manager of sales; C. M. Merritt, district sales manager, Detroit, appointed assistant general manager of sales; L. T. Willison, manager of cold-finished sales, appointed manager of strip and sheet sales; H. M. Knobloch, district sales manager, Indianapolis, appointed manager of cold-finished sales; L. C. Berkey, district sales manager, Chicago, appointed district sales manager, Detroit; I. A. Mlodoch, Chicago salesman, appointed district sales manager, Chicago; G. G. Marshall, assistant district sales manager, Buffalo, appointed district sales manager, Indianapolis; R. M. Laning, Detroit salesman, appointed assistant district sales manager, Detroit.

Hotpoint Sets Safety Record

Chicago—Hotpoint, Inc., manufacturers of kitchen and laundry appliances, finished the month of October, operating at full capacity without a single lost-time accident. The credit for this was attributed by William A. Kissock, vice-president in charge of industrial relations, to plant superintendent, foremen, supervisors, and the workers themselves.

B. & O. Uses Strata-Dome Cars

Baltimore — Three strata-dome sleeping cars built by Budd Co. were placed in service by the Baltimore & Ohio R. R. this week. The new cars, first to be used in the East, have glass domes and 24 upper level seats. On the lower level each car has five roomettes, one single bedroom, and three drawing rooms.

*Towmotor MH**

doubles storage capacity in your plant!

***MH IS MASS HANDLING—*the systematic movement of the most units, in the shortest time, at the lowest cost.

Valuable, costly storage space,

difficult or even impossible to reach by outmoded manual handling, becomes easily accessible with a Towmotor Fork Lift Truck. In lifting and stacking heavy loads right up under the rafters, Towmotor Mass Handling can *double* the amount of storage space *without* increasing the floor area!

HANDLES ANY TYPE MATERIAL

Improve your storage methods,
speed order filling, eliminate dangerous and costly "stock-falls." Select from 12 models plus standard and specially designed accessories for handling loads from 1500 to 15,000 lbs.—a Towmotor for *every* job. And learn how skilled Towmotor Preventive Maintenance keeps your equipment *on* the job—mail coupon below. Representatives in all Principal Cities in U. S. and Canada.

TOWMOTOR THE ONE-MAN-GANG **FORK LIFT TRUCKS and TRACTORS**

See how you can cut costs, increase profits—Mail Coupon Today!

See the
TOWMOTOR EXHIBIT
Booths 322-323
1951 Materials Handling Exposition, International Amphitheatre, Chicago
April 30—May 4

TOWMOTOR CORPORATION, DIV. 15
1226 E. 152nd Street, Cleveland 10, Ohio

Please send me current issue of "Handling Materials Illustrated" and information on Towmotor Preventive Maintenance.

Name_____Title_____

Company_____

Address_____

City_____State_____

RECEIVING • PROCESSING • STORAGE • DISTRIBUTION

CROSSING THE DELAWARE: Wire being spun into suspension cables for the $40 million Delaware Memorial Bridge by U. S. Steel's American Bridge Co. After completion in 1951, the 2-mile span will carry 4 million vehicles yearly, and will supplant ferry service between Pennsville, N. J., and New Castle, Del.

Uranium Out of Gold Mines

London—Uranium from South African gold mines will go to Britain and America. The problem has been to discover a sound method of extracting the material from the mines but the South African Dept. of Mines reported that the pilot plant stage has been reached.

Uranium is to be found in nearly all the gold mines of the Witwatersand and in the new gold field of the Orange Free State.

War and U.S. Utilities

New York—How will American utilities continue to function in the event of military attack, will be the subject of a panel discussion to be held at the winter meeting of the American Institute of Electrical Engineers, Jan. 22 to 26 at the Hotel Statler, here.

Britain Faces Zinc Shortage

London—Failure of a large zinc shipment to arrive from Belgium has forced the British to institute an allocation system for zinc on Jan. 1. The government is taking action to acquire zinc but a serious shortage is expected for at least the first half of the year.

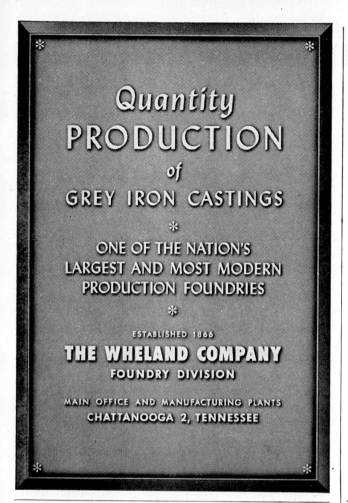

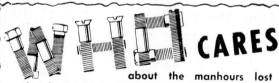

The Clearing House

NEWS OF USED, REBUILT AND SURPLUS MACHINERY

Strip Off the Cobwebs—Digging for used machines to take their production place in America's industrial fight for life against the Reds will be deeper and deeper into the barrel. Obsolescent machines will have their cobwebs stripped clean and be exhibited to buyers who will be suddenly enthusiastic. As the new year opens many of the good to excellent grades of used machinery have been snatched at remarkably high prices. The spotlight will be on used machines this year and they will play a strong role in the war effort.

More Machines Coming—It has been reported that some dealers have been holding back good machines—biding their time for the full force of defense orders to strike. They will not have long to wait.

Some manufacturers have been hanging on to used machines until they can unscramble what DO production will mean to them. They want to know whether their machines can be used for defense output. Many of these men will discover that they can release this machine and that machine.

Dealer Campaigns—Dealers themselves will try to stimulate the market. Their incentive will be orders they cannot fill. They will start canvassing. Some have started ringing doorbells already. A heavy turnout of used machines—of all vintages—is the result of crisis. But the market never sees all the machines that it could have. Some owners do not regard used machines as too valuable. Perhaps they don't have the time to scout the market. Consequently, machines stay in the plants and gather rust. Dealers are expected to plant both feet into this dormant market and bring out the machines for 1950.

The release of witheld machinery and dealer scouting will drag out more machinery for a demanding market. But no matter how many machines are mustered they will be insufficient to meet orders.

Market Softening?—Some feel that the market in certain types of used machinery may be softened by release of machines from the government's reserve pool. But it is debatable whether or not the government has stored enough to offset the pressing need. Builders of new machines will produce more this year—but not enough.

Delivery Dates Stretch—Delivery dates on new machines are stretching and stretching. The man who receives a defense order will try the used market for quick delivery. If he looked with disapproval before on a machine that had seen better days, the press of production schedules now will abolish that reluctance. Sales of the older machines will increase.

The reconditioning of used machines this year will see a lot of ingenuity and a struggle for scarce materials.

Ball Starts Rolling—The first trickle of DO orders started the ball rolling for new machinery ordering. Delivery dates were extended and those who normally would have disdained purchase of used machinery turned eagerly to that field. Those who normally used that market anyway found their needs increasing. Dealers' inventories in many cases were halved.

Manpower Woes—In 1950 subcontract work will be more widely distributed and the smaller shops, not reached previously, will be in the market with a roar. Used machine demand will be spurred.

The reconditioning industry will suffer from a manpower shortage. It started last year and will get fiercer this year. Last December the reconditioning program of at least one major machine tool builder was abolished by scarcity of skilled workers.

how ROTOBLAST* cleaning
SAVES $250⁰⁰ *a day*
for General Foundries
in MILWAUKEE

N<small>O COST-CONSCIOUS</small> executive can shrug off the kind of savings General Foundries in Milwaukee has racked up since the installation of Pangborn ROTOBLAST. Two hundred and fifty dollars daily savings amounts to more than $50,000 saved annually in regular foundry operations. Here's the story in a nutshell!

One ROTOBLAST Barrel with one operator working one nine-hour shift replaced 4 tumbling mills with two operators working two nine-hour shifts; and a ROTOBLAST Table Room took over the work of an air blast room, saving $100.80 every day on labor and compressed air costs alone.

WHAT ABOUT YOUR PLANT?

Chances are blast cleaning costs you $5000 to $10,000 *too much* each year. Investigate Pangborn ROTOBLAST as General Foundries did. Let a Pangborn engineer show you how ROTOBLAST can increase production and save you big money every year.

WRITE TODAY for Bulletin 214. It contains the complete story and shows typical installations. Included are specifications and a list of prominent users like General Electric, Westinghouse and others. Address your letter to PANGBORN CORPORATION, 1500 Pangborn Blvd., Hagerstown, Maryland.

* **ROTOBLAST TABLE-ROOM** (above) cleans the entire output of an air blast room in 40% less time and practically eliminates breakage of delicate castings.

● **ROTOBLAST BARREL** (above) at General Foundries does work of 4 tumbling mills in ¼ less time with a saving of 36 man-hours per day.

ROTOBLAST
saves you money these five ways:

SAVES LABOR: One ROTOBLAST machine and operator can do as much as a two-man crew and old-fashioned equipment.

SAVES SPACE: In many cases, one ROTOBLAST machine replaces five or more old-fashioned machines, requires less space.

SAVES TIME: Cases on record prove ROTOBLAST can cut cleaning time up to 95.8% compared with old-style methods.

SAVES POWER: Modern ROTOBLAST uses but 15-20 h.p. compared to old-fashioned equipment requiring 120 h.p. for same job.

SAVES TOOLS: On work cleaned with ROTOBLAST, cutting tools last up to 2/3 longer because no scale is left to dull edges.

All these savings mean INCREASED PROFITS for you!

No matter what you make

Tankers...

Back and forth, up and down, 'round and 'round, every motion of this giant shipyard crane must be under precise and dependable control. The safety and efficiency of many workers insist on Cutler-Hammer.

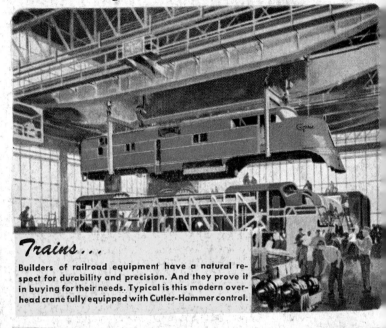

Trains...

Builders of railroad equipment have a natural respect for durability and precision. And they prove it in buying for their needs. Typical is this modern overhead crane fully equipped with Cutler-Hammer control.

Or Toys...

The investment many plants make in small motor-driven machines is amazing. So is the payroll of the people who run them. Where wasted time is so obviously costly, Cutler-Hammer control is top insurance.

Manufacturing *anything* today is a problem in teamwork ... teamwork between men, motors, and machines. Men are employed for their intelligence. Machines provide the facility for applying judgment and skill. Electric motors supply the brute force. And motor control is the connecting link that permits all these elements to work together as one.

Here is the reason experienced engineers and production men grant motor control an importance far greater than either its relative physical size or cost might suggest to the casual observer. It is not only a vital

Cutler-Hammer general purpose motor control is recommended by a majority of all electric motor manufacturers, is featured as standard equipment by machinery builders, is carried in stock by recognized electrical wholesalers everywhere.

factor in the efficient use of men, motors, and machines but the ever-watchful guardian of their safety. Its easily reached push buttons or automatic functions avoid both wasted steps and possible hazards. Its overload devices protect equipment from damage; production schedules from those intolerably costly interruptions.

No matter what *you* make, you too will find it pays to insist on Cutler-Hammer Motor Control for *dependable* performance. CUTLER-HAMMER, Inc., 1325 St. Paul Ave., Milwaukee 1, Wis. *Associate:* Canadian Cutler-Hammer, Ltd., Toronto.

The Iron Age

A CHILTON PUBLICATION

E NATIONAL METALWORKING WEEKLY

January 11, 1951

ENTS PAGE 2

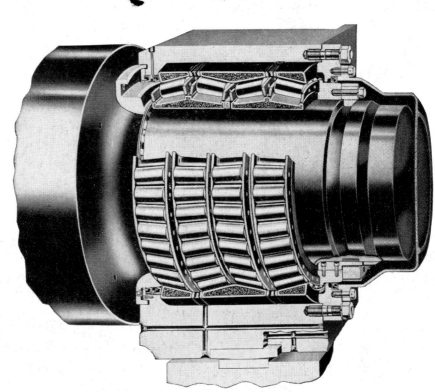
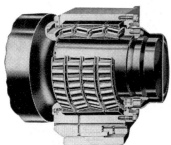

For worms and gears — in standard sets or to special requirements — or as worm-gear speed reducers, including the economical fan-cooled Speedaire unit — you can always depend on Cleveland.

High quality worms and gears to meet your needs

● You pay no more for Cleveland worms and gears — and yet, built into them are extra years of service and satisfaction.

Uniform, high quality has been an outstanding characteristic of Clevelands through 38 years — a generation devoted to the manufacture of fine worms and gears exclusively. Specifically, there are four ingredients of Cleveland quality:

1. Correctness of design — design proved best by years of performance.

2. The finest of materials, selected after years of experience and research.

3. Modern machine tool equipment, in a modern plant kept up-to-date by a policy of continuous replacement.

4. Machinists and other production workers who are craftsmen, trained in precision work.

So whatever your need, consult Cleveland. Sales representatives in all major industrial centers are at your service, to help you select correct types and sizes and discuss any phase of your power transmission problems.

Write for the latest Cleveland catalog, indicating your requirements. The Cleveland Worm & Gear Company, 3252 East 80th Street, Cleveland 4, Ohio.

Affiliate: The Farval Corporation, Centralized Systems of Lubrication. In Canada: Peacock Brothers Limited.

CLEVELAND
Worm Gear
Drives

COMPLETE STEEL SERVICE
for Industries of the West

3 STEELMAKING PLANTS

★ LOS ANGELES ★ SOUTH SAN FRANCISCO ★ SEATTLE

With its steelmaking plants located in Southern California, in the Bay Area, and in the Northwest, Bethlehem Pacific is equipped to provide Western industry with substantial tonnage of steel. Complete in every respect, these facilities include open-hearths, electric furnaces, various types of rolling mills, a wire mill, and metallurgical laboratories. Operations are all coordinated to produce the steel and to finish it into many products.

3 BOLT AND NUT PLANTS

★ LOS ANGELES ★ SOUTH SAN FRANCISCO ★ SEATTLE

Bethlehem Pacific operates bolt-and-nut manufacturing plants adjacent to its three steelmaking units. Each of these plants is equipped with automatic, high-speed machinery for producing a full line of bolts and nuts, as well as allied fasteners and specialties for different industries.

4 FABRICATING WORKS

★ LOS ANGELES ★ SOUTH SAN FRANCISCO
★ ALAMEDA ★ SEATTLE

Bethlehem Pacific's fabricating works are equipped to fabricate the steel for buildings, bridges, towers and miscellaneous structures of either small or large tonnage. Besides fabricating steel, this company also handles the erection of structural steel in any Western locality.

The plants mentioned here are some of the many specialized units within the Bethlehem Pacific organization. These facilities assure an economical, dependable source of materials for the builders, fabricators, manufacturers, railroads and miscellaneous steel-consuming industries in the eight Western states.

BETHLEHEM PACIFIC COAST STEEL CORPORATION
GENERAL OFFICES: SAN FRANCISCO

BETHLEHEM PACIFIC

BETHLEHEM STEEL

IRON AGE

CONTENTS

THE IRON AGE
Editorial, Advertising and Circulation
Offices, 100 E. 42nd St., New York 17,
N. Y.
GEORGE T. HOOK, Publisher
TOM C. CAMPBELL, Editor

EDITORIAL STAFF
Managing Editor   George F. Sullivan
Feature Editor   Darwyn I. Brown
News-Markets Editor   Wm. V. Packard
Machinery Editor   George Elwers
Associate Editors: William Czygan, H.
W. Van Camp, F. J. Winters; Assistant
Editors: R. L. Hatschek, J. Kolb, Ted
Metaxas, W. B. Olson; Regional Edi-
tors: E. C. Beaudet, Chicago; W. A.
Lloyd, Cleveland; W. G. Patton, De-
troit; John B. Delaney, Pittsburgh; Os-
good Murdock, R. T. Reinhardt, San
Francisco; Eugene J. Hardy, Karl Ran-
nells, George H. Baker, Washington;
Correspondents: Fred L. Allen, Birm-
ingham; N. Levenson, Boston; Fred Ed-
munds, Los Angeles; James Douglas,
Seattle; Roy Edmonds, St. Louis; F.
Sanderson, Toronto; F. H. Harley, London, England; Chilton Editorial Board:
Paul Wooton, Washington Representative.

BUSINESS STAFF
Production Manager   B. H. Hayes
Director of Research   Oliver Johnson
Mgr. Circul'n & Promotion   C. T. Post
Asst. Promotion Mgr.   James A. Crites
Asst. Dir. of Research   Wm. Laimbeer

REGIONAL BUSINESS MANAGERS
B. L. Herman, Philadelphia; Stanley J.
Smith, Chicago; Peirce Lewis, Detroit;
Paul Bachman, New England; Robert F.
Blair, Cleveland; R. Raymond Kay, Los
Angeles; C. H. Ober, New York; J. M.
Spackman, Pittsburgh; Harry Becker,
European Representative.

REGIONAL OFFICES
Chicago 3, 1134 Otis Bldg.; Cleveland
14, 1016 National City Bank Bldg.; Detroit 2, 103 Pallister Ave.; Los Angeles
28, 2420 Cheremoya Ave.; New England,
62 La Salle Rd., W. Hartford 7; New
York 17, 100 E. 42nd St.; Philadelphia
39, 56th & Chestnut Sts.; Pittsburgh 22,
814 Park Bldg.; Washington 4, National
Press Bldg.; European, 111 Thorley
Lane, Timperley, Cheshire England.

Circulation Representatives: Thomas
Scott, James Richardson.

One of the Publications Owned and
Published by Chilton Company, Inc.,
Chestnut and 56th Sts., Philadelphia 39,
Pa., U. S. A.

OFFICERS AND DIRECTORS
JOS. S. HILDRETH, President
Vice-Presidents: Everit B. Terhune, G.
C. Buzby, P. M. Fahrendorf, Harry V.
Duffy. William H. Vallar, Treasurer;
John Blair Moffett, Secretary; D. Allyn
Garber, Maurice E. Cox, Frank P.
Tighe, George T. Hook, Tom C. Camp-
bell, L. V. Rowlands, Directors. George
Maiswinkle, Asst. Treas.

Indexed in the Industrial Arts Index
and the Engineering Index. Published
every Thursday by the CHILTON CO.
(INC.), Chestnut and 56th Sts., Philadelphia 39, Pa. Entered as second class
matter Nov. 8, 1932, at the Post Office
at Philadelphia under the act of March
3, 1879. $8 yearly in United States, its
territories and Canada: other Western
Hemisphere Countries $15; other For-
eign Countries $25 per year. Single
Copies 35c. Annual Review and Metal
Industry Facts Issue, $2.00. Cable ad-
dress "Ironage" N. Y.

Member Audit Bureau of Circulations.
Member Society of Business Magazine
Editors.

Copyright, 1951, by Chilton Co. (Inc.)

DIGEST

ANUARY ELEVENTH · NINETEEN FIFTY-ONE · VOLUME 167 · NUMBER 2

ORTON

with GM *Dynaflow* Drive

NO SHOCK LOADING on gears, shafts and clutches! Smooth fluid application of power from the engine to load! Stresses cut in half, maintenance and time out for servicing cut to less than half!

CUSHIONED SHOCK MEANS A LOT — not only to machine but to operator! He has perfect control at all times—he can hover over a load, adjust a fraction of an inch without clutch or brake action! Cuts operator and equipment fatigue and wear!

THROTTLE CONTROL! POWER to start a heavy load without "slip-clutching" at high speed— POWER CONTROL to pick up heavy loads smoothly and quickly!

The GM *Dynaflow* Drive is a torque converter combined with a fluid clutch. The ORTON Crane with GM *Dynaflow* Drive AUTOMATICALLY PROVIDES THE CORRECT TORQUE in the exact amount needed to move the load!

ORTON
Crane and Shovel Co.
608 So. Dearborn Street
Chicago 5 • Illinois

IRON AGE

editorial

The Forgotten Man

IN a few years the steel industry will complete a 15 million ton expansion program. Ore boats are being built. Taconite plans are being rushed. Ore will be coming from Canada and Venezuela in great quantities in 3 to 4 years.

More coal and coke are in the cards for the new capacity. Freight cars are being built to take care of needed transportation. Men are being trained for new jobs. Machinery has been ordered, motors are being built and government priorities may soon give a green light to steel mill construction.

Everything looks jim dandy. All this augurs well for the country and for steel management. Defense needs will be met. Steel people will be in a position to make steel for war or defense and for essential civilian economy.

But next week there will be an annual convention at the Commodore Hotel in New York of some of the most individualistic people in the country. They are the ones on whose shoulders rests the responsibility for failure or success of the gigantic steel expansion program.

They are the scrap dealers and brokers who must each year gather at least 25 pct of the metallics that go into steelmaking. Someway, somehow they got together close to 25 million tons of market scrap from the factories, farms, byways and highways of the country in 1950.

This year their job will be harder. But their real job to come is a corker. They alone know what kind of a nightmare it will be. They must someway find an additional 3,500,000 tons of scrap a year when the current expansion in steel is completed.

They have no big units and properties to supply their product. They have to deal with thousands of sources and people all over the country to get what the mills need. They must cajole, curse, plead, beg, argue, bargain and turn somersaults to get a big part of the market scrap needed.

They know that if cream is ordered at skim milk prices you won't get cream. They know they will soon have ceilings, rules and red tape forced on them by people many of whom never had to get scrap from thousands of different sources.

They will be blamed when they don't get the scrap. They will be cussed out when the quality is not up to laboratory standards. Fortunately they can take this in their stride.

They produced the scrap before. They will do it again. They will need a lot of help with a minimum of red tape. They are the forgotten people in the defense program. They are free enterprise in its more robust form.

Tom Campbell

editor

G-E SYNCHRONOUS

SAVE MONEY

SAVE ON OPERATING COSTS . . . Municipal plant gets higher efficiency by continuous operation at constant speed of three 500 horsepower, 1.0 power factor, G-E synchronous motors, each coupled to a centrifugal storm-sewer pump.

SAVE ON INITIAL COST . . . Paper mill selected this 4000 hp, 200 rpm, G-E synchronous motor for driving the montague grinders at low speed. Maximum operating efficiency thus resulted.

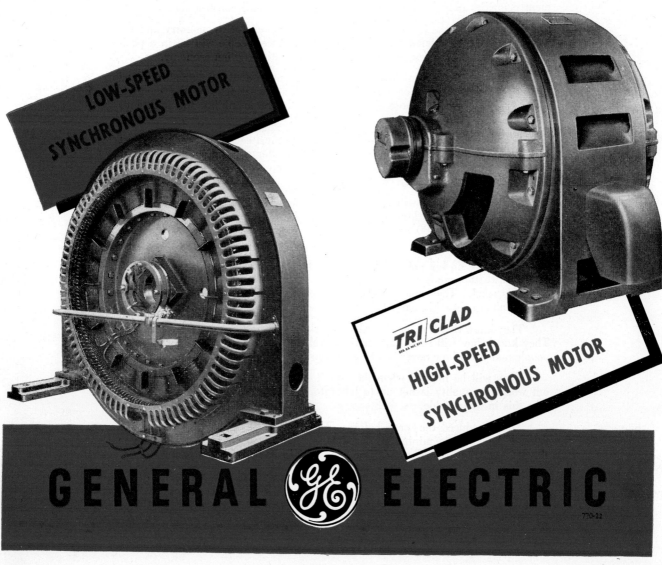

LOW-SPEED SYNCHRONOUS MOTOR

TRI CLAD
HIGH-SPEED SYNCHRONOUS MOTOR

GENERAL ⊕ ELECTRIC

770-22

IRON AGE *newsfront*

► Electroplated <u>plastic reflectors</u> are being replaced in some cases by steel stampings on which <u>aluminum is deposited by a vacuum process.</u> Thickness of the aluminum coat is about ½ to 1 micron. (One micron equals 0.00003937 in.)

► As the arms program gets up steam the <u>alloy requirements</u> per ton of steel will climb above their normal rate. During World War II alloy scrap did not come back to the mills in sizeable quantities until <u>some 7 months after the peak demand</u> for alloy steel occurred. The result was an intensified demand for <u>virgin alloying</u> elements in the early stages of the armament program.

► <u>Pilotless jet airplanes</u> are now being tested in Australia for use as <u>antiaircraft missiles.</u> Present test equipment carries a pilot to develop the radio control equipment. A simplified version of the Armstrong-Siddeley-Viper engine is being used. This is the turbo jet version of the Mamba, for which Curtiss-Wright has the American rights.

► Despite the 20 pct cutback in tin consumption ordered by NPA, U. S. tinplate producers will try <u>to hold output near current high levels</u> by persuading customers to use the lighter (electrolytic) coatings. They'll point out that it's either that or a <u>bad dislocation in supply.</u> In favor of speeding the change is the current <u>strong trend in favor of electrolytic</u> over hot-dipped tinplate.

► A <u>non-magnetic aluminum bronze alloy</u> has been developed for the Navy's Bureau of Ships. The iron content of the former alloys <u>has been replaced</u> with a non-magnetic element.

► Steel people would not be at all surprised to see the size of National Steel Corp.'s Eastern mill turn out to <u>be at least 50 pct larger</u> than most current guessing. In other words, it will probably have a capacity of at least <u>1,500,000 ingot tons a year.</u>

► Loans for defense plants tentatively approved under Stuart Symington's NSRB will be given a <u>careful review before getting an official OK</u> from William H. Harrison's DPA.

► This year the chances are better than they <u>have been in years</u> of coal labor negotiations coming to a <u>successful conclusion without the usual crippling strike.</u> It is not so much the size of present coal stocks as the change in character expected in the negotiations.

► The <u>first</u> binary phase diagrams for <u>titanium</u> sponsored by the Air Force have been completed. Among the compositions being studied are combinations of titanium with nickel, aluminum, carbon, oxygen, nitrogen and chromium. <u>The whole project should be completed by Spring.</u>

► The Naval Research Laboratory facilitates electron microscopy of metal samples by a technique of observing the same areas on a thin transparent film impression of a steel specimen in both the light and the electron microscope. Areas found with the light microscope <u>can be then observed with the higher magnification of the</u> electron microscope.

► An automotive main transmission shaft is being produced on <u>automatic screw machines</u> with <u>round</u> carbide insert tools. Seven pounds of metal are removed in <u>80 seconds.</u>

DRUG STERILIZER CONTROL · MUNITIONS FURNACE CONTROL · ARTWARE KILN CONTROL

AUTO PAINT OVEN CONTROL · SANITARY WARE KILN CONTROL

PLASTIC MOLDER CONTROL · ELECTRIC FURNACE CONTROL · WATER STILL CUTOFF

SPEEDOMAX (OR MICROMAX) STRIP-CHART ON-OFF CONTROLLER

SPEEDOMAX ROUND-CHART ON-OFF CONTROLLER

Dependable "ON-OFF" Controllers for Industry

THE kind of control instrument which industry calls on-off or 2-position is not only the oldest form of automatic regulator, but is one which many manufacturers still use, instead of more advanced types, for simple requirements. Usually, the instrument merely closes the valve when temperature reaches the control point, and opens valve again when temperature falls below point. The question of whether such on-off action is best for the given case can of course be settled by using the instrument with the best, most useful features. Here are some which L&N On-Off Controllers offer:

1. Instruments may be Recording Controllers with either strip-chart or round-chart, or Controllers with no charts at all.

2. Instruments can operate at high or moderate speed; can be located regardless of machine vibration, building tremors or distance from process.

3. Controls are outstandingly dependable because they "balance" temperature against a standard. Intermediate bearings and springs cannot increase, decrease or otherwise influence accuracy or sensitivity.

4. Low maintenance assured by machine-like design and construction.

5. More than 1000 standard ranges. Specials are available, but seldom needed.

Tell us your problem and we will send further information. Write either to our nearest office or to 4956 Stenton Avenue, Philadelphia 44, Pa.

MICROMAX MODEL C ON-OFF CONTROLLER

ELECTROMAX ON-OFF CONTROLLER

MEASURING INSTRUMENTS · TELEMETERS · AUTOMATIC CONTROLS · HEAT-TREATING FURNACES

LEEDS & NORTHRUP CO.

Jrl. Ad ND4-33(3)

THESE instruments are fully automatic; need no standardizing; are ideal even for hard-to-get-at or difficult locations.

IRON AGE *summary*

iron and steel industry trends

Military Slow to Decide on Needs
Money Ready But Procurement Lags
Most Steel People to Welcome CMP

THE real snag in the defense program is the slowness of the military to decide what it needs. Money which has been appropriated for defense is being spent at a snail's pace. It is now clear that much of it will not be converted into defense material during the present fiscal year—or soon after.

It is true that military orders are beginning to flow, but the contracts placed so far are puny compared with total defense needs, for which funds are available. If defense procurement is to be boosted sharply, the people in charge of defense planning will have to agree quickly on what is needed and how much.

The present system of DO orders will not assure an orderly flow of materials when military procurement reaches its peak. Before that happens—probably during the second quarter—a controlled materials plan will be in effect.

To Most—CMP is Welcome

Most steel producers will welcome a full CMP program for steel. For some it can't come soon enough. People administering the present DO system agree with them. Manpower to operate this and other programs is still Washington's big problem, but things are beginning to move on that score. In some instances defense officials are no longer directly contacting the men they want in Washington. Instead they are going to presidents of companies and saying in effect, "We need these men, you see that we get them."

Meanwhile, the steel market is becoming more confused. Some holders of DO orders are overstating the urgency of their needs, asking delivery of steel earlier than it is actually needed. Others are trying to protect their regular quotas by tapping new suppliers for their DO orders.

But some consumers with urgent needs covered by DO orders are not able to get steel when they need it. There are many such frustrated consumers running around the country wildly waving DO orders.

Bookings of defense orders are becoming more extended each day. DO orders for cold-rolled sheets are filled to April or May; hot-rolled sheets, June; plates, March; pipe, March or April. This is the average extent of DO bookings; it is not uniform among all producers.

Issue Steel Quotas for March

Some steel firms have done a good job of cleaning up order backlogs, and are now issuing quotas to regular customers for March on products such as bars, shapes and plates. Ordinarily these quotas would have been issued in January or February. The new quotas are slashed 40 to 50 pct from October allotments.

Those who thought that auto cutbacks would make steel easier are now beginning to find out how wrong they were. The same old fakers are still trying to peddle steel at 14 to 16 cents a pound (about 3 times regular mill price)—and they are finding takers when they can deliver.

Expensive multiple-pass conversion arrangements are continuing. For example, one deal calls for slabs from a Pennsylvania mill to be reduced in the East and Midwest and passed along finally to another mill in another city for finishing. Final cost of this steel is about $300 a ton, with freight charges, rolling fees, etc.

Claim Freight Car Building Mishandled

The freight car building program is not gathering steam as fast as had been expected. Some people in the industry claim the program is being mishandled, that materials are not flowing smoothly into car building plants. Some of them are clamoring for a redistribution of March steel allotments under the program. It is unlikely that production will reach the 10,000-car-per-month goal until June.

Steelmaking operations this week are scheduled at 102.5 pct of rated capacity, up 1½ points from last week.

(nonferrous summary, p 96)

Dear EDITOR

Letters From Readers

On The Right Track

Sir:

I have just read your editorial, "Hallelujah! We Are Started," in the Dec. 28, 1950, issue. I am in accord with your praise of Mr. Wilson. Certainly the President is to be complimented for his choice in this instance. Mr. Wilson warrants much more confidence than the usual set of political hacks appointed by this administration.

However, I could not help wondering just what you felt we were getting started on and where you thought we were going. Do you mean we are once again starting on the road to more Yaltas, Teherans and Potsdams? Are we once more to start on the road to world war, bleating the praises of Democracy and winding up with more people enslaved than before we started?

The shallowness of thinking in the past of our leaders can no better be shown than by recalling the criticism of "Balance of Power" politics in Europe. This was depicted as the ultimate in shameful policy. We have now awakened to find that we destroyed this balance of power all right, but hadn't the vision to see that in doing so we created a vacuum made to order for our then "ally" and our now very real enemy. We are now, just five years later, frantically trying to create a "Balance of Power" to meet this enemy. A complete reversal is a mild way of stating it.

How stupid can we really get? Is more of this what you are shouting "Hallelujah!" about?

L. L. JONES
Industrial Metal Products Co.
Ravenna, Ohio

Of course we are 5 years too late for a lot of things. Of course we are late because we have had no leadership—we have none yet with the possible exception of Mr. Wilson. We are at least getting started because we have a man in Wilson who knows what we are up against and what should be done.—Ed.

Aids Instructor

Sir:

I wish to express my appreciation for the charts, "Comparative Tool Steel Brands," sent to us. The chart will aid greatly in gathering generally used tool steels into groups so that the apprentice can see the choices available in each classification. Also, he can locate the types of steels that he uses in his work and compare its use with its proper classification. The chart will aid me as the instructor in having a ready-formed chart listing many of the common examples of tool steels, each under its proper classification.

C. A. CHRISTIAN
Metallurgy Instructor
School of Vocational & Adult Education
West Allis, Wis.

Long Fuel Hose, Maybe?

Sir:

Your "On The Assembly Line" column in the Dec. 7, 1950, issue headed "Natural Gas Engines" has come to our attention. We do appreciate your giving our story on these "Dual-fuel" engines this valuable attention, but the substitution of the the word "Trucks" for "units" in your magazine's write-up has caused some reverberations in this vicinity.

Dual-fuel units of the type described were designed for stationary or portable use on oil field drilling rigs, irrigation pumps, sawmills, etc., wherever natural gas is readily available. Of course, no means has been devised to carry natural gas as a fuel for any self-propelled vehicle.

Although the trucking field is only one of hundreds of applications of our engine, it seems the association of the word "Diesel" with trucks is almost automatic. Perhaps this is the reason the word "trucks" sneaked into your story. We have not found, and it is doubtful whether anyone ever will find a way to pipe natural gas as a fuel to trucks.

J. W. BROWN
Advertising Mgr.
Detroit Diesel Engine Div.,
General Motors Corp.

Praising Patton

Sir:

Just to let you know—your column, "On the Assembly Line," says more in a few lines than most of the so-called trade papers say in 10 pages. I never miss your swell "early" news. I congratulate you!

W. ALLEN
Bronx, New York

Maintains Story File

Sir:

Would it be possible for me to obtain two copies of the article, "Annealed Ductile Iron for Better Machinability," by J. F. Kales and R. Goldhoff, published in the Dec. 14, 1950 IRON AGE on p. 105?

These two copies will be for Prof. Boston and myself. I have recently been asked to act as secretary of the Metal Cutting Data Committee of the ASME and it is my responsibility to collect articles dealing with metal cutting. This article by Kales and Goldhoff is of excellent caliber and I am very glad to see THE IRON AGE publishing material of this nature.

W. W. GILBERT
Associate Professor
University of Michigan
Ann Arbor, Mich.

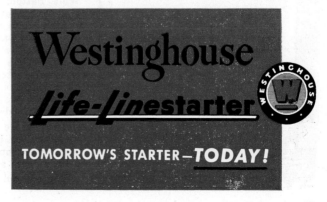
January 11, 1951

21

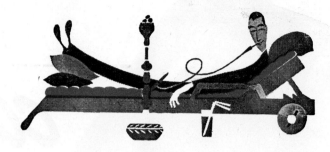

fatigue cracks

by Charles T. Post

stimulating

Not since the days when we pored over the late Don Marquis' *Archy and Mehetabel* have we experienced the same thrill as when we opened the fan mail on your favorite family journal's new format. Archy, you will recall, was a cockroach who jumped on the typewriter keys in order to write letters to Mehetabel, the cat. Since he couldn't jump on the letter key and shift key at the same time, there were no capitals. Republic Steel's Allan T. Frary created the same effect with his commentary, although we certainly don't mean to infer that Mr. Frary is a cockroach. Wrote Mr. Frary:

the adaptability of the iron age in refusing to follow slavishly such outmoded practices as capitalization and punctuation is most refreshing you are following such fearless leaders as helena rubenstein and surely modernity is to be admired above all things i think a logical next step would be a telegraphic style of wording the articles to match the telegraphic uncapitalization and unpunctuation in the headings see what you can do yours very truly allan t frary

After that, we picked up a crackling missive from R. J. Weber, assistant director of purchases, Great Lakes Steel, who started out, "I was a little late this week in reading my IRON AGE, for which I am now thankful." It developed that your f.f.j.'s Detroit editor, Walt Patton, had been needling Mr. Weber over the effervescent Detroit scrap market. "But now," Mr. Weber complained, "to further aggravate my ulcers, Walt had a picture taken with a halo around him and plastered it directly above his article *On the Assembly Line* . . . Mr. Post, how long should we remain friends?"

Then there was the scribbled blast written in violet ink " . . . smart alec. sophomoric . . . oh, for a little depth and dignity . . ."

The editors, swaying like reeds, are backing down. They have given up the idea of cutting a hole in the cover, like the late lamented Flair, and are even going to start the by-lines with capital letters.

Puzzlers

By J. A. Crites

Your new puzzle editor bows his head in shame for supplying the wrong answer to the smoke stack problem. When Charlie asked us to work it out we didn't realize he was tossing us an outside curve. Expect to hear from MIT any day now requesting that we send back our degree.

Our thanks to C. E. Norton, George Benoit and Carl Blass, Talon Inc., for setting us straight with the correct answer of 3.07 feet. We can't vouch for the answer to the Dec. 28 problem, as our chauffeur is on vacation, but Eugene Greth, Birdsboro Steel Fdry. & Mach. Co., Mrs. Hill, Lakeland, Fla., and Bob Huff, Canton, Ohio, claim that the man walked for 45 minutes.

We've had a week's rest from puzzles and our heads are clear once again, so let's start the New Year with a real toughie provided by the puzzle(d) brain of the editorial department, Bob Hatschek. The drawing shows a rectangle with one corner at the center and another on the circumference of a circle. Using the dimensions given, what is the diameter of the circle?

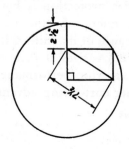

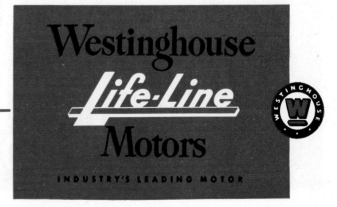

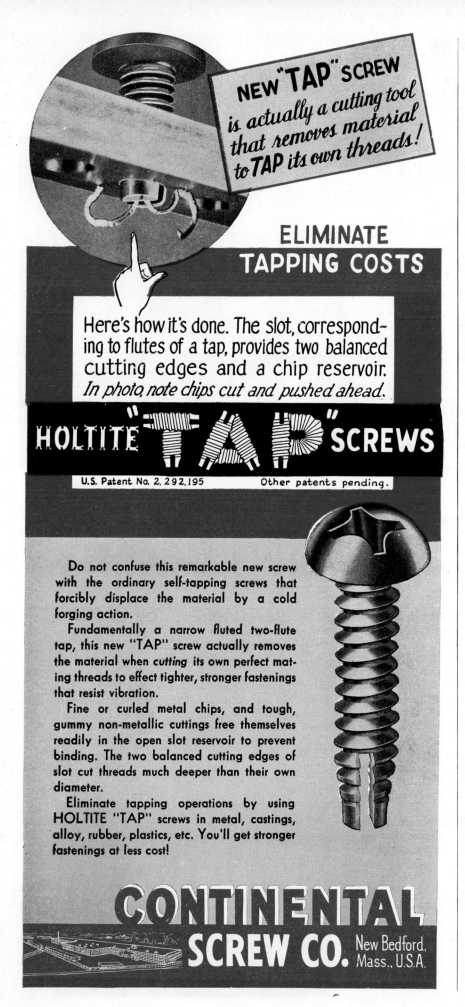
DATES
to
remember

Jan. 14-16—**Institute of Scrap Iron & Steel**, annual convention, Commodore Hotel, New York. Institute headquarters are at 1346 Connecticut Ave., N. W., Washington.

Jan. 15-16—**Industrial Furnace Manufacturers Assn.**, mid-winter meeting, Edgewater Beach Hotel, Chicago. Association headquarters are at 420 Lexington Ave., New York.

Jan. 15-18—**Plant Maintenance Show**, Public Auditorium, Cleveland. Exposition management Clapp & Poliak, Inc., 341 Madison Ave., New York.

Jan. 16—**American Boiler Manufacturers Assn. & Affiliated Industries**, mid-winter meeting, Cleveland. Association headquarters are at 264 Rockefeller Bldg., Cleveland.

Jan. 18-20—**Society of Plastics Engineers**, annual national technical conference, Statler Hotel, New York. Society president is J. H. DuBois, 160 Coit St., Irvington, N. J.

Jan. 19—**Malleable Founders Society**, semiannual meeting, Hotel Cleveland, Cleveland. Society headquarters are at 1800 Union Commerce Bldg., Cleveland.

Jan. 21-23—**Truck Trailer Manufacturers Assn.**, annual convention, Edgewater Gulf Hotel, Edgewater Park, Miss. Association headquarters are in the National Press Bldg., Washington.

Jan. 22-23—**Compressed Gas Assn.**, annual convention, Waldorf Astoria Hotel, New York. Association headquarters are at 11 W. 42nd St., New York.

Jan. 24-25—**Caster & Floor Truck Manufacturers Assn.**, winter meeting, Hotel New Yorker, New York. Association headquarters are at 7 W. Madison St., Chicago.

Jan. 28-Feb. 1 — **Associated Equipment Distributors**, annual meeting, Stevens Hotel, Chicago. Association headquarters are at 360 N. Michigan Ave., Chicago.

Feb. 19-22—**American Institute of Mining & Metallurgical Engineers**, annual meeting, Jefferson Hotel, St. Louis. Institute headquarters are at 29 W. 39th St., New York.

Mar. 5-7—**Hydraulic Institute**, quarterly meeting, Santa Barbara Biltmore Hotel, Santa Barbara, Calif. Institute headquarters are at 122 E. 42nd St., New York.

Mar. 5-7—**Manufacturers Standardization Society of the Valve and Fittings Industry**, annual meeting, Commodore Hotel, New York. Society headquarters are at 420 Lexington Ave., New York.

Mar. 5-7—**Pittsburgh Conference on Analytical Chemistry and Applied Spectroscopy**, William Penn Hotel, Pittsburgh. American Chemical Society national headquarters are at 1155 16th St., Washington.

Mar. 5-9—**American Society for Testing Materials**, spring meeting, Cincinnati. Society headquarters are at 1916 Race St., Philadelphia.

Mar. 6-8—**Society of Automotive Engineers**, passenger car, body and materials meetings, Hotel Book-Cadillac, Detroit. Society headquarters are at 29 W. 39th St., New York.

Mar. 12-15—**National Electrical Manufacturers Assn.**, spring meeting, Edgewater Beach Hotel, Chicago. Association headquarters are at 155 E. 44th St., New York.

machine tool high spots

by W. A. Lloyd

Bottleneck or Wonder?—Whether the machine tool industry will be branded a bottleneck by July 1, or generally regarded as a spectacular example of defense planning, will largely depend on a decision which will probably be made within the next 10 days in Washington.

Machine tool builders, at the request of NPA's machinery division, have submitted photostated copies of their order boards by January 8 for review. Rumor has it that this is the first step in the activation of the tentative production schedules (phantom orders) which carry a priority, and thus is the answer to the machine tool industry raw materials and components problem.

A Cautionary Note—While industry warns against undue optimism for immediate action, that it may be a long process complicated by secondary decision as to what agency will handle the project, money, and other factors, it appears that the industry's case is due for a realistic appraisal.

At the moment, the industry's backlog is 12.2 months at the present rate of shipments. The bulk of the defense business is still to be placed, according to industry sources, including some projects under consideration that are beyond anything yet seen. Potential volume of defense business is estimated at $1.5-billion.

Prepare for Avalanche—New order volume is $90-million a month, or more than $1-billion a year. Mutual Defense Assistance Program orders are coming in, and many companies have 30 pct rated business. Defense orders have increased materially during the past 30 days. The industry is swamped.

Some in the industry are moving swiftly to meet this avalanche. Under wraps are plans for several large plant expansions, at least two of which will be additions to present buildings. At least one of these projects will be announced next month.

More Sub-Contracting—Another expedient considered is sub-contracting capacity. It is likely that the industry will do much more sub-contracting than in World War II. One company is lining up five or six customer shops which have no defense business for sub-contract work. Another will sub-contract production of one complete line.

This will help solve the industry's manpower situation as well. In some areas, shops without defense business or even the promise have been reluctant to let their men go.

Finished by 1953?—In view of such preparations, the industry's tooling for defense would pyramid in 1951-1952 and by 1953 be pretty well completed. Then the civilian market might once again be a consideration.

A year ago, the industry was hungry for orders. Today, backlogs are higher in relation to current shipments than at any time in the industry's history. If the industry is given a priority as a result of the examination of the order boards, production will accelerate and 1950 shipments may be doubled, an achievement in any non-mass production industry.

November Shipments High—Some of the government's projects under construction or being tooled up are a clue to the urgency of this phase of national defense. On one project, if the machine tools are not received by May, the order is canceled.

In Cleveland, National Machine Tool Builders' Assn. reported that shipments of machine tools in November were the highest since August, 1945. NMTBA's preliminary index of November shipments was 110.9 compared with 100.9 in October and 67.6 in November, 1949. The November new order index was 292.7 compared with 289.6 in October and 84.3 in November, 1949.

FREE *publications*

New Stainless Bulletin

The analysis, corrosion resistance and working characteristics of Carpenter Stainless No. 20 steel are detailed in a new 20-p. bulletin. The booklet points out that one of the outstanding features of the material is its good corrosion resistance to hot sulphuric acid, which permits its use in 60° Be (78 pct) sulphuric acid solutions at temperatures of about 125°F. General corrosion resistance of the steel against more than 140 acids and corrodents is reported in a table. The booklet includes tables of physical constants and nominal mechanical properties. Heat treatment, workability, and recommended speeds for machining are also given. *Carpenter Steel Co.*

For free copy insert No. 1 on postcard.

Testing Machines

Features of the Universal medium capacity unit-type table model testing machine are presented in a new 4-p. brochure detailing characteristics of the unit for tension, compression, flexure, shear and transverse tests. Designed for volume production testing or laboratory research work, the machine is available in two capacities having three load scale ranges, as shown in the folder. *Testing Machine Div., National Forge & Ordnance Co.*

For free copy insert No. 2 on postcard.

Machine Tool Attachments

The Master portable motorized lathe converter, a metalworking machine with interchangeable heads or spindles to accomplish all types of machine shop operations, is described in a new 20-p. catalog telling how the unit will, in many cases, pay for itself in a short time. The latest models of the converter are shown, along with information on the various attachments and accessories for performing milling, boring, drilling, grinding and slotting operations in addition to the jobs normally performed on the lathe or turret. *Master Mfg. Co.*

For free copy insert No. 3 on postcard.

Car Shaker

Allis-Chalmers car shaker for unloading granular material from hopper-bottom gondola cars is described in a new 6-p. bulletin. Construction features of the shaker are given, along with specifications and a cross-section through the vibrating mechanism. The shaker, designed to save time and money and to eliminate danger to operating personnel, has application in power houses, steel mills, sand and gravel, chemical, coke and glass plants, coal mines and docks, sugar beet and paper mills, foundries, and building block and slag product manufacturing plants. *Allis-Chalmers Mfg. Co.*

For free copy insert No. 4 on postcard.

Aluminum Protection

The Pylumin process, providing a simple, inexpensive and rapid method of producing satisfactory paint base coatings on aluminum and aluminum alloys, is described in a new 10-p. booklet. This corrosion proof base for paint finishes acts quickly on aluminum, converting the surface into a nonmetallic film of complex basic oxides, forming a highly resistant coating and serving as a base for the finishes. Processing and instructions for operating are included. *Pyrene Mfg. Co.*

For free copy insert No. 5 on postcard.

Defense Welding Manual

The illustrated "Manual of Welding Engineering and Design" is the first in a series of free technical handbooks on the latest developments in welding materials and techniques. Details on the newest advances in Eutectic Low Temperature welding alloys with special reference to applications for defense production and maintenance are presented. In addition to technical data on characteristics, properties and applications and operational procedures for these alloys and fluxes, the manual contains handy information on the art of welding in all its phases. *Eutectic Welding Alloys Corp.*

For free copy insert No. 6 on postcard.

Chilling Equipment

Facts and information about Cascade Sub-Zero low temperature industrial chilling equipment are presented in a new 15-p. brochure listing specifications on various models for freezing to —120°F. Uses and general applications for the equipment are described, along with data on the procedure for treatment of steel by chilling. Technical data and tables for use with the equipment are also included. *Sub-Zero Products Div., Deepfreeze Distributing Corp.*

For free copy insert No. 7 on postcard.

Alloy Selection Guide

Two new cobalt-base alloys are described in a completely revised 96-p. edition of the booklet, "Haynes Alloys for High-Temperature Service." The new booklet contains technical data on 10 alloys that were specially developed for service at elevated operating temperatures. A section on each alloy gives a general description of the

Turn to Page 92

NEW *production ideas*

Quick-Release Pins

Used like a bolt; need no retaining cotter keys or nuts.

Used for shackle purposes or as tie-down fasteners, a Pip pin is a quick-release pin used like a bolt except that no separate retaining items such as cotter keys or nuts are needed. The pin is inserted into holes in the parts to be held. They cannot work loose, and must be deliberately removed to effect disassembly of any units they are holding. *Aviation Development, Inc.*

For more data insert No. 11 on postcard.

Wood Pattern Coating

Preserves patterns from dry rot, improves draws, lasts longer.

CK is a new type wood pattern coating for all types of foundry service. It is claimed to be so hard that it stands up exceptionally well under sand slingers and practically eliminates tiny holes in wood patterns resulting from the jabbing of vents in molds. It withstands heat up to 350° F, is impervious to moisture, and does not oxidize or weather. *Carboline Co.*

For more data insert No. 12 on postcard.

Cutting Oil Additive

Effective against development of rancidity and obnoxious odors.

A preservative for soluble-type cutting oils and coolants is a new odorless formulation that inhibits the growth of bacteria, stabilizes the emulsion and preserves the lubricating qualities of the oil for its full life. Normal use of coolants has been increased from 2 or 3 days to a period of 3 weeks when the additive has been used. The product is effective in a solution of 1 gal of additive to 1200 gal of prepared soluble cutting oil. *West Disinfecting Co.*

For more data insert No. 13 on postcard.

Barrel Filling Meter

Measures repeat quantities from 25 to 79 gal by 1-gal increments.

Production of a new 60 gpm 1½-in. pipe size barrel filling meter has been announced. Only a single gear change is necessary to obtain different quantity settings and changes may be made without use of tools. The meter is equipped with two counters: a totalizing counter registers the total meter through-put; a reset type counter indicates the number of containers filled. *Meter Div., A. O. Smith Corp.*

For more data insert No. 14 on postcard.

Radiation Detector

Permits direct radiation readings at a glance; weighs less than 1 lb.

Called a radiation monitor, a new atomic radiation detector is equipped with a self-contained power source, and has neither tubes nor batteries. It is the size of a quart oil can. Radiation measurements are read from the monitor simply by noting the position of a pointer as it moves across a graded scale. The speed at which the pointer moves across the scale is in proportion to the strength of radiation, and the distance it moves in a

use postcard below

production ideas

Continued

given time indicates the amount of radiation to which the instrument has been exposed during that time. *General Electric Co.*

For more data insert No. 15 on postcard.

Steam-Jet Cleaner

For locations where ample high pressure steam is available.

A new steam-jet cleaning unit known as Speedyjet makes available to companies which have ample high pressure steam supply the advantages of the Speedylectric system of steam-jet cleaning. The machine includes a high pressure detergent tank mounted on a lightweight all-metal dolly with rubber tired 10-in. wheels and handle bar grips for easy portability; 25 ft of high pressure steam hose; and 25 ft each of steam and detergent hose from the tank to the Speedylectric steam lance. The unit is equipped with pressure gage, 200 psi safety valve, and necessary control valves. It is built under the ASME code and carries National Board Stamping & Insurance Company certificate. In the Speedylectric system of steam-jet cleaning, solvent, detergent or paint stripper can be applied either alone or mixed with steam in any desired proportion. *Livingstone Engineering Co.*

For more data insert No. 16 on postcard.

Garage Door Operator

Opens or closes doors at touch of a push button on car dashboard.

The device said to fit any Kinnear Rol-Top door, is operated by a simple electric-magnetic control. Pressing a control button mounted on the dashboard of the car energizes a magnetic actuating unit placed in the driveway. A small electric motor raises and lowers the door from inside the garage by cable and pulley. The device also automatically turns on garage lights as the door is opened, and turns them off again when the door is closed. The magnetic assembly for the driveway can be placed at any point over which the car passes in entering and leaving the garage. *Kinnear Mfg. Co.*

For more data insert No. 17 on postcard.

Descaling Compound

Removes most scale in 15 to 30 min.

A compound used for descaling or derusting iron or steel parts in tumbling barrels is said to often save from 1 to 4 hr in finishing a load of parts. It can be used either where parts are self-tumbled or with abrasive mediums; is safe to handle; and does not throw off fumes. D-Scale-RW is an inhibited acid type powder with wetting agent added. Hot water speeds up descaling action. *Magnus Chemical Co., Inc.*

For more data insert No. 18 on postcard.

Tilt Dial for Scales

Allows greater legibility in reading scale above eye level.

Tilting dial faces downward 25° is an optional feature in the Hydroscale line of hydraulic crane scales with capacities up to 10,000 lb. It allows greater legibility in reading the scale above eye level and is helpful when readings must be made at substantial heights frequently encountered. Tilting does not consume headroom or interfere with swivel of either eye or hook. *Hydroway Scales, Inc.*

For more data insert No. 19 on postcard.

Plastic Finish

Dulls the reflecting surfaces of stainless steel in guided missiles.

A new plastic synthetic finish, VB 248, developed to cut glare from guided missiles, provides an effective coating that adheres to highly polished stainless steel used in various aircraft devices. Because of its good adhesion quality, it can be applied to other uses where glare is not the primary objective. VB 248 takes a baking temperature of 275°F for 1 hr. *United Lacquer Mfg. Corp.*

For more data insert No. 20 on postcard.

Horizontal Filter

Suited for cleaning foundry sand; filter areas are 10 to 165 sq ft.

The Oliver horizontal rotary filter, on which all operations are visible, is suited for filtering operations involving the washing and dewatering of coarse solids contami-

use postcard below

KAYDON 4-POINT CONTACT RADIAL BALL BEARING:
71.500" x 75.500" x 2.000"

Big **NON-ECCENTRIC** *Precision Bearings*
...that's what **KAYDON** *stands for!*

Eccentricity in the bearing shown above was held within **.0002″** ("practically unheard of" precision for bearings of this size).

Such accuracy doesn't just "happen". It's the result of KAYDON's development of all the required facilities, within this one organization, for producing all the types and sizes of bearings listed below. These unique facilities are fortified by engineering knowhow and broad experience in solving difficult bearing problems. KAYDON has its own modern atmospheric controlled heat treating, hardening with sub-zero conditioning, precision heat treating, metallurgical laboratory, microscopy and physical testing facilities.

Unbiased as to any one type of bearing design, KAYDON always is in position to recommend the one best suited to your specific use.

Counsel in confidence with KAYDON.

*Ground on Frauenthal Precision Grinder

KAYDON Types of Standard or Special Bearings: Spherical Roller • **Taper Roller** • Ball Radial • Ball Thrust • Roller Radial • Roller Thrust

THE **KAYDON** ENGINEERING CORP., MUSKEGON, MICH.

• ALL TYPES OF BALL AND ROLLER BEARINGS 4″ BORE TO 120″ OUTSIDE DIAMETER •

production ideas

Continued

nated with fine waste material, organic or inorganic. Foundry sands which must be free of organic material are washed with great efficiency, it is stated. Capacity and

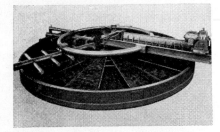

removal of water are high and the cake is discharged with moisture content ranging from 6 to 8 pct. Filters range from 4 to 15 ft diam, manufactured in steel, stainless steel and lead-protected. *Oliver United Filters, Inc.*

For more data insert No. 21 on postcard, p. 33.

Surface Grinder
Equipped with special fixture for grinding both ends of oil pump gear.

The No. 24-A rotary surface grinder with a special fixture for grinding both ends of oil pump gears has two sets of stations, one

for grinding one side and the other for the opposite side. After one side is ground, the operator turns the piece over for grinding the opposite side. The pieces are then automatically ejected. Work is constantly checked by automatic sizer which keeps all pieces within specified tolerances without attention of the operators. The surface grinder is a small edition of the No. 36-A model with the same design and construction features, but produced

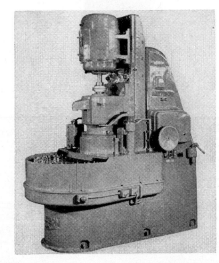

for use on smaller work pieces. Parts to be ground are placed directly on a rotary magnetic chuck,

or work table carrying work holding fixtures. They enter at one side of the automatically controlled cylinder or segmental wheel, pass under it, and come out finished to size at the opposite side. *Mattison Machine Works.*

For more data insert No. 22 on postcard, p. 33.

Powershear
Full capacity continuous shearing within its entire speed range.

Design and rugged construction of the Di-Acro Vari-O-Speed powershear provide full capacity continuous shearing within the machine's entire speed range of 30 to 200 rpm. The cutting cycle can be quickly adjusted to the fastest speed at which the operator can feed the material for any given shearing operation, providing maximum operator productivity as the necessity of engaging the clutch for each cutting stroke has been eliminated. Speed

of shearing stroke for both continuous and single cycle operation is controlled with a handle located at the operator's left. A non-repeating positive safety clutch allows single stroke operation with the shear blade moving at any desired speed within the unit's range. *O'Neil-Irwin Mfg. Co.*

For more data insert No. 23 on postcard, p. 33.

Engine Lathes
56 feeds and threads available without changing quadrant gearing.

Ranging in size from 40 to 80 in., a new line of heavy-duty engine lathes have an extra margin of power, strength, and rigidity, with heavier beds and more extensive automatic lubrication. The lathes, powered by ac or dc motors, feature a total of 56 feeds and threads, produced by the quick change feed box without changing gears in the enclosed quadrant. Quadrant gears are maintained on the end of the bed to produce special feeds and

threads. The 40-in. lathe is of high-grade semisteel and ribbed to resist strains and stresses developed during turning operations. The 6½-in. spindle mounted in the tailstock has a 12-in. travel. Lubrication is automatic. Drive for the 4-in. lathe is furnished by a 40 hp constant speed ac motor, or a 3:1 speed ratio dc motor. Controls on the carriage start and stop the main drive motor, set the directional rotation of the spindle and traversing the carriage. *Niles Tool Works Co. Div., Baldwin-Lima-Hamilton Corp.*

For more data insert No. 24 on postcard, p. 33.

Fire Extinguisher
Dry chemical extinguisher; 150-lb powder capacity; one-man mobility.

A wheeled dry chemical fire extinguisher uses two large upright steel cylinders mounted on two wheels, properly balanced to permit one-man mobility. The larger cylinder contains 150 lb of fire-smothering dry chemical, the smaller cylinder holds nitrogen under pressure of 2000 psi. Opening a valve on the nitrogen cylinder admits the nitro-

Turn to Page 89

36

THE IRON AGE

From East Texas to South Ohio

A current example of Stone & Webster Engineering Corporation's broad experience in design and construction for the natural gas industry is the six compressor stations on Texas Gas Transmission Corporation's recently completed 800-mile, high-pressure line.

The six stations along the line between Carthage Gas Field in East Texas and Middletown, Ohio, include gas engine driven compressors totalling 42,500 hp for boosting the gas pressure from 575 to 800 pounds for transmission.

STONE & WEBSTER ENGINEERING CORPORATION

A SUBSIDIARY OF STONE & WEBSTER, INC.

IRON AGE

introduces

Clark S. Judd has resigned as chairman of the board of the AMERICAN BRASS CO., New York, and will continue as a board member. William M. Moffatt, formerly vice-president in charge of manufacturing, becomes executive vice-president. Edward M. Bleser succeeds retiring secretary-treasurer Edwin J. Rockwell.

Everett D. Graff, formerly president, was elected chairman of the executive committee of JOSEPH T. RYERSON & SON, INC., Chicago. Thomas Z. Hayward was elected vice-president in charge of sales, and also a director and member of the executive committee.

Walter E. LaBelle, appointed assistant general manager of the fabricated steel construction division of BETHLEHEM STEEL CO., Bethlehem. Frank R. Barnako becomes manager of compensation and safety, succeeding Walter F. Ames, who has retired after 32 years with the company.

Dwight A. Bessmer, formerly director of purchases of the TIMKEN ROLLER BEARING CO., Canton, was appointed assistant to the president. R. J. Archibald was named assistant general purchasing agent.

John T. Kiley, executive vice-president of the JAMES FLETT ORGANIZATION, INC., Chicago, has been named president succeeding James Flett, who becomes chairman of the board.

Norman W. James, general purchasing agent of the PENNSYLVANIA SALT MFG. CO., Philadelphia, has withdrawn from active service with the company but will continue as a consultant and adviser on procurement problems.

E. R. Pettengill, appointed administrative assistant to the general manager of Pontiac Motor Div. of GENERAL MOTORS CORP., Pontiac, Mich. Buel E. Starr, named general manufacturing manager; A. F. Johnson, manufacturing manager; J. P. Charles, assistant chief engineer; Charles O. Johnson, general plant superintendent; and George Guinn, axle plant superintendent.

H. S. Geneen, assistant to the vice-president—general services of JONES & LAUGHLIN STEEL CORP., Pittsburgh, has been elected comptroller. W. H. Dupka, formerly vice-president and comptroller, will continue as vice-president and a director and will act as special consultant to the chairman of the board and president. Nils P. Johnson, appointed assistant to vice-president—general services.

Burton W. Lang, appointed vice-president of the AP PARTS CORP., Toledo. He will continue as director of purchasing and engineering; and also supervision, excluding sales, of the Miracle Power Div.

Ernest R. Schmidt, named vice-president in charge of manufacturing of the BUDD CO., Philadelphia. Raymond F. Littley becomes vice-president in charge of sales.

E. O. Clark, appointed industrial products sales manager for VICKERS INC., Detroit. J. C. Carpenter succeeds Mr. Clark as the Worcester district manager. M. J. Taup, formerly district manager of the Chicago office was appointed mobile products sales manager in Detroit.

Norman Chandler, president of the Times-Mirror Co. and publisher of the Los Angeles Times, was elected a director of KAISER STEEL CORP.

Turn to page 46

CHARLES L. HARDY, elected president of Joseph T. Ryerson & Son, Inc., Chicago.

JOHN A. COE, JR., becomes president of the American Brass Co., New York.

PAUL E. YOUNG, named director of purchases of the Timken Roller Bearing Co., Canton.

IRON AGE

salutes

Herbert W. Graham

WE hear a lot about far-seeing executives. When we are young we kind of doubt their existence. As we get older we know for sure there are a lot of them. We know also that they don't always shine brilliantly for everyone to see. Many times this is because they shun the limelight.

Such a man is Herbert W. Graham, vice-president-technology, Jones & Laughlin Steel Corp. You can't get it from him that he was co-founder and the first president of the Industrial Research Institute.

You would never know from talking to Herb Graham that years ago he was talking steel quality through better ores and better iron. In his job he was to look years ahead and see what the problems and their solutions will be.

No one can see the future. But those who are properly equipped can make a good guess as to what things will be. Herb Graham's predictions are so good they are almost uncanny.

His forward ideas are not restricted to ore, iron and steel. He was one of the first, years ago, to see the menace of Russian communism—at a time when a lot of people were calling it a noble experiment. In World War II you find that the U. S. Government picked him to head up the part of a little WPB sent to China to bolster their steel and iron production.

Mr. Graham has always had unlimited patience with young people. Many in the iron and steel industry today can trace their ability to get things straight to his personal and heart-to-heart talks. Others can trace their growth to his demand that they think, read and try things no matter how impossible they look.

Herb Graham went from Lehigh to J&L in 1914. What he doesn't know about steel would probably fill a very small pamphlet. But that is not the way he looks at it. He thinks the longer we live the more we find out how little we know. That's why he is recognized by those who know him as a valuable asset to his company, his industry, his friends and his country.

WILLIAM J. FLEMING, appointed vice-president in charge of engineering and manufacturing, General Electric X-Ray Corp., Milwaukee.

FRANK A. STROUCE, appointed general manager, fabricated steel construction, Bethlehem Steel Co., Bethlehem.

ARTHUR H. QUIGLEY, named chairman of the board of the American Brass Co., New York.

PAUL J. LARSEN, appointed assistant to the president of Borg-Warner Corp., Chicago.

IRON AGE *introduces*

Continued

Joseph H. Woodward II, elected a member of the board of directors of WHEELING STEEL CORP., Wheeling, W. Va.

Gunnar Palmgren, appointed assistant vice-president of SKF INDUSTRIES, INC., Philadelphia. **Arthur S. Roberts** was named general counsel and **Jack R. Bremer,** assistant purchasing agent.

F. L. Yetter, appointed senior vice-president of C. H. WHEELER MFG. CO., Philadelphia. He rejoins the company after a 20 month period of service as director of foreign affairs for the Kuljian Corp.

H. J. Henke, named superintendent of the East St. Louis, Ill., bitumastic protective coatings plant of KOPPERS CO., INC., Pittsburgh. **Edward Salner** was made manager of the precipitator department of the Metal Products Div.

Roland E. Govan, appointed sales promotion manager of the FALK CORP., Milwaukee.

Oliver W. Truax, Jr., appointed superintendent of industrial relations for the Donora Steel & Wire Works of AMERICAN STEEL & WIRE CO., Donora.

William S. Lowe, executive vice-president of the A. P. GREEN FIRE BRICK CO., Mexico, Mo., was elected president.

Freeman H. Dyke, appointed manager of U. S. METAL REFINING CO., Carteret, N. J., subsidiary of the American Metal Co., Ltd.

Emil R. Schaeffer, appointed manager of manufacturing, Switchgear Divs. of GENERAL ELECTRIC CO., Schenectady. **John W. Belanger** and **Nicholas M. DuChemin** were named general managers of the Large Apparatus Divs. and Small Apparatus Divs., respectively, of the Apparatus Dept.

Samuel A. Ott, appointed superintendent of melting of the MIDVALE CO., Philadelphia.

Charles S. Lang, appointed comptroller of the EDGEWATER STEEL CO., Pittsburgh.

L. A. Keeler, vice-president, director and comptroller of FAIRBANKS, MORSE & CO., Chicago, has retired after 39 years with the company.

Alphons J. John, named to head the employee-public relation's office at KEARNEY & TRECKER CORP., Milwaukee.

J. Carroll Bateman, appointed assistant director of public relations for the BALTIMORE & OHIO R. R., Baltimore.

Clyde B. Colwell, Jr., appointed assistant district manager for the Twin Cities district of U. S. STEEL SUPPLY CO., St. Paul, Minn.

Kenneth M. Allen, sales manager, was elected a director of the ROCKFORD MACHINE TOOL CO., Rockford, Ill.

William L. Hewes, assistant director of purchases of HERCULES POWDER CO., Wilmington, Del., has retired after 41 years of service with the company.

George E. Tate, formerly assistant treasurer of the FEDERAL FOUNDRY SUPPLY CO., Cleveland, was elected treasurer. He has been with the company for 25 years.

OBITUARIES

Harry Denby, 57, organizer of the Denby Wire & Iron Co., Cleveland, died recently.

John P. Hoelzel, 67, president of Pittsburgh Screw & Bolt Corp., Pittsburgh, died Dec. 26.

Ernest P. Waud, chairman of the executive committee of Griffin Wheel Co., Chicago, died recently.

G. Walter Sanborn, vice-president in charge of purchasing and traffic for United Engineering & Foundry Co., Pittsburgh, died recently.

Clermont C. Covert, 78, associated with W. & L. E. Gurley, Troy, N. Y., died recently.

Edwin J. Paulus, 62, general manager, fabricated steel construction, Bethlehem Steel Co., died recently.

Newton A. Woodworth, founder of the Ex-Cell-O Corp., Detroit, and N. A. Woodworth Co., Detroit, died Dec. 27.

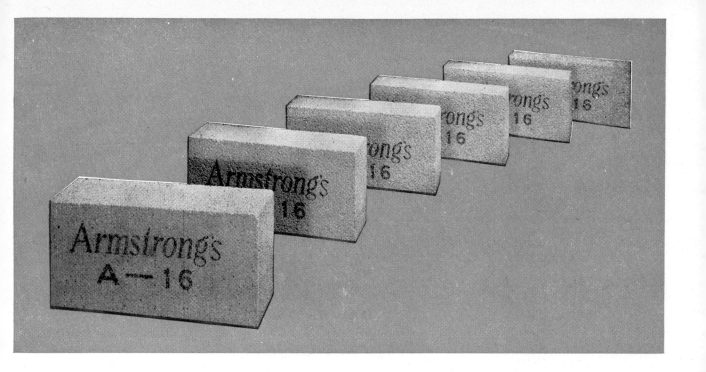

This improved insulating fire brick simplifies furnace design

To provide furnace builders with greater design flexibility, Armstrong has developed an improved A-16 insulating fire brick. An entirely new formulation gives this brick exceptionally high refractoriness when used directly exposed as furnace lining at temperatures to 1600° F. In addition, it will withstand temperatures to 2000° F. when used as back-up insulation behind insulating brick or fire brick furnace lining.

The improved properties of this better A-16 insulating fire brick offer furnace builders these important advantages.

1. At 1600° F., directly exposed, the A-16 will not shrink or soften under load. It provides a wide margin of safety in this application.

2. The ability of the improved A-16 to withstand 2000° F. temperatures behind the furnace lining allows simplification of furnace design by reducing the number of brick types required.

Perhaps the physical properties of this better A-16 Brick can help you improve furnace design and lower costs. Armstrong engineers will be glad to discuss your furnace constructions with you with these factors in mind. Just call the Armstrong office nearest you or write today to Armstrong Cork Company, 4901 Mulberry St., Lancaster, Penna.

Physical Properties of Armstrong's Improved A-16	
Temperature Limit—Direct Exposure.........	1600°
Temperature Limit—Back-Up Service.........	2000°
Crushing Strength—P.S.I.	175
P. C. E. Fusion......................	2984
Weight per Brick—pounds maximum........	1.80
Spalling Loss—average per cent...........	0.05
Shrinkage at 1600° F.—maximum per cent...	0.0
at 2000° F.—maximum per cent...	1.5
K-1200° Mean—Btu/sq. ft./hr./in.	1.36

ARMSTRONG'S INSULATING REFRACTORIES

on the assembly line

automotive news and opinions

Change rear springs on passenger cars . . . Shortages pose many problems . . . Chrysler building new V-8 powerplant.

by Walter G. Patton

Wider, Longer Leaves — Some interesting changes are being made in the rear springs of passenger cars. The latest spring leaves are wider and longer than those used in 1950 model cars. This improves the ride characteristics and also gives more resistance to sidesway.

In the past, most passenger car models have had 8 to 10 spring leaves in the rear. A 1951 Studebaker model has only three rear spring leaves. Most car producers will use not more than 5 spring leaves in the current models, thereby cutting almost in half the number of spring leaves previously specified.

Aluminum to Cast Iron — The government policy of encouraging the use of non-strategic materials is expected to result in many changes in automobile specifications. Many parts now made of aluminum are being changed over to cast iron. The adoption of cast iron for pistons and automatic transmission parts is already going forward. One manufacturer was surprised to learn he could save more than 80¢ per unit by using cast iron instead of aluminum for a certain transmission part.

Substitutions for Steel — If plastics are available, the industry may see substitutions of plastics (or even rubber) for steel. Scuff boards are an example. Extensive changes in plating are practically a certainty by next spring. Some important changes in the materials specified for bearings are under consideration. The substitution of cast iron for bronze, particularly in large non-automotive bearings, is already being made.

Almost without exception, the use of a substitute or alternate material increases the cost. This is another reason why auto manufacturers who were forbidden a price increase will find it difficult to hold their costs down under conditions of rising prices for materials and substantially reduced volume.

Shutdown of GM Plants — An omen to Detroit was the unanticipated temporary shutdown of five Buick-Oldsmobile-Pontiac assembly divisions because of a "sudden acute shortage of materials." A steel shortage was responsible. The GM BOP plants were closed down for 4 days, idling 13,000 employees. Studebaker Corp. and Chrysler have announced 20 pct cutbacks in production. Similarly, production of 1951 Buick models has been delayed by a shortage of materials at Fisher Body.

Single Leaf — Dead Duck — Considerable experimental work has been conducted to determine the practicability of a single leaf spring for rear suspensions of passenger cars. From an engineering standpoint, a single leaf spring is attractive. However, production costs of such a spring are far out of line. The amount of scrap steel produced is high. Many of the rolls employed today by steel mills to roll spring leaves to shape would have to be discarded.

Single leaf springs also require exceptionally high finish. Finally, the protection offered to car passengers by multi-leaf springs would have to be sacrificed. Detroit auto producers who have investigated the possibilities of single leaf rear springs say this idea is practically a dead duck.

Better Suggestion Pay — General Motors is liberalizing its employees' suggestion plan by increasing the maximum cash award from $1000 to $2500. The minimum award has been increased from $7.50 to $10.00.

Over a 9 year period GM has made awards totaling $5,740,000 for 145,000 suggestions adopted. Average payment is $40 per award. A total of 728 maximum awards have been paid out.

"Out of This World" — Chrysler Div. is getting limited production of its new high compression en-

46

THE IRON AGE

assembly line

Continued

gines at the Jefferson Ave. plant. While few details of the new powerplants have been disclosed, Chrysler engineers are telling their friends privately that the new engine is "out of this world."

When tooling for the new Chrysler engine was ordered, production estimates were set at 20 engines per hr. This was later increased to 40 per hr. Capacity was later doubled to 80 per hr. Current output is only a few units per day. Deliveries of equipment are still being made to raise the output to 80 engines per hr.

Oldsmobile Changeover — Oldsmobile is changing from coil springs in the rear of its 1951 models to leaf springs. This leaves Buick and Nash as the only cars with coil springs in the rear. Cost considerations as well as engineering advantages claimed for flat springs are believed to have influenced the change.

War Tells on Willys—Including a $63 million military order for Jeeps, Willys-Overland reports a bank of unfilled orders of $173 million. The backlog includes civilian Jeeps, trucks and station wagons, engines and miscellaneous parts.

Willys has received more government orders in the first 7 months of the Korean war than the total number of orders received during the first year of World War II. The new Jeeps are water-proofed to operate under several feet of water. In addition to Jeeps, Willys produced shells, steel and aluminum forgings, landing gears, fuel tanks, fuses and recoil cylinders during World War II.

GM Boosts Horsepower — General Motors Truck and Coach Div. has made several interesting improvements in its 1951 light model trucks. Horsepower of both engines used in the light line has been boosted 4 hp. All models have heavier axle ratings. The front axle of the GMC 1½ ton truck has

been increased from 3500 to 4500 lb capacity. A similar increase has been made in the rear axle.

Ventipanes have been added to give controlled cab ventilation. Seat cushions are adjustable. The cushion rests on roller balls that move easily to the desired position when the control rod is touched. Front brakes have been enlarged. Twin cylinders are used for rear brakes instead of single hydraulic mechanism. Some models have a new hand brake of the dual-shoe type.

A Lot of Language—Some idea of the extensive use of automatic teletype by the automobile industry is revealed by the fact that the Dearborn headquarters of Ford Motor Co. handles 12 million words of inter-plant communications per month.

Shortest Inventory Shutdown—The automobile industry has learned a great deal about taking inventory and changing models. An example of the latest technique is offered by Buick. This year Buick started its inventory in the forge shop and foundry and continued on a staggered basis in

each of the plants through the next several weeks.

Each plant was idle from only 2 to 4 days. This is the shortest inventory shutdown Buick has ever taken. About 25 pct of the 21,-000 hourly-rated Buick employees worked through the inventory. Average lost time per man was 2½ to 3 days.

Cars Cheaper by Pound—The automobile industry can make the point that its cars have improved both from the standpoint of passenger comfort and performance and that its price tags have gone up much less rapidly than food prices. For example, a Chrysler official has pointed out that in 1940 steak was 32¢ a lb and a Chrysler Crown Imperial sedan sold for 94¢ a lb. Today, he argues, steak costs $1.18 a lb and a Chrysler Imperial sells for 85¢ a lb.

Best Ford Year—Ford Motor Co. has just completed its best year in a quarter of a century. Total output of Ford-Lincoln and Mercury passenger cars, trucks and tractors during 1950 exceeded 2 million units. Payrolls aggregated $590 million.

THE BULL OF THE WOODS
By J. R. Williams

west coast progress report

by R. T. Reinhardt

Won't Take "No" for an Answer —Organized labor, business leaders and politicians in the West are united to bring to the Coast as much government shipbuilding as possible.

These forces insist the historical cost differential of shipbuilding in the West as opposed to that in the East and on the Gulf is more fictional than factual. The Kaiser interests produced approximately 35 pct of all vessels built during the past war with cost records equal to or superior to those of yards in any other part of the country.

Shipbuilders Ask Wage Increase —While the drive was being made to secure ship construction work for the West, the Pacific Coast District Metal Trades Council was asking for an 19¢ hourly wage increase. The existing contract expires June 30. Strikes in the Bay Area and Pacific Northwest have already interfered with ship repair and reconditioning.

It would require about a month to reactivate Richmond Yard No. 3 operated by Kaiser during the past war and those at Vancouver, Wash., Moore Drydock in Oakland, Bethlehem Pacific Coast Steel Co.'s yards and the Todd yards in the south.

Navy Yards Active — Terminal Island facilities in southern California are to be reopened on a full speed ahead basis and more than 6000 employees will be "found," according to a Navy spokesman. It is estimated 80 moth-balled vessels including merchantmen, destroyers, and small Navy ships will be put into shape.

The Navy is reportedly authorizing expenditures of more than $2 million for construction of dikes around the reactivated repair base to keep out sea water since the island has settled during recent years.

Navy reports indicate that orders for ships and equipment on the West Coast already include 30 mine sweepers. Of the 173 cargo barges recently put out to bid for the Army, 43 are scheduled on the West Coast.

Affect on Steel Demands—Reaction of steel users to the shipbuilding program are mixed. All point out that although steel production is several times as great as in 1940, it is still insufficient to meet normal demands and a shipbuilding program will seriously affect the overall economy.

The two principal plate producers in the West—Geneva in Utah and Kaiser in Fontana—have long range commitments for plate for pipe lines and are hard pressed to supply flat stock for hot and cold-rolled sheets.

Shortages Slow Auto Production —California automobile assembly plants are being hit by material shortages. Ford, General Motors and Chrysler have been least affected, but independents report assembly is down 20 to 25 pct.

Studebaker has backtracked to a 4-day week for assembly line personnel, and in Oakland, General Motors Fisher body plant was on a 3-day work basis during the first week of the new year.

The pinch for steel is pointed up by an arrangement completed by General Motors with Geneva Steel Co. and Columbia Steel Co. GM will ship 6000 tons of ingots monthly to Geneva for rolling into plates and hot-rolled strip, and Geneva will ship to points designated by GM. Geneva has rolling capacity in excess of its steel production, and General Motors can get ingots in Chicago.

Perambulating Furnace — In view of the West Coast's pig iron shortage, the rumor that Colorado Fuel & Iron Co. is looking over the idle blast furnace owned by Kaiser-Frazer Corp. at Ironton, Utah, for possible removal to Pueblo, Colo., is particularly interesting. This furnace of 600-ton capacity was originally erected at Duluth, Minn., moved to Joliet, Ill., and then during the past war to Ironton, Utah.

the federal view

by Eugene J. Hardy

this week in washington

Confusion Out of Chaos—Creation of the Defense Production Administration headed by former NPA Chief W. H. Harrison, as second in command to Mobilization Director C. E. Wilson, is another step to establishment of an all-powerful production agency similar to WPB. The executive order giving programming and policy authority to DPA and leaving actual issuance and enforcement of orders to NPA and other existing control agencies creates an administrative monstrosity.

DPA can be compared to the old Supply Priorities and Allocations Board, created in August, 1941, following the breakdown of the Office of Production Management. SPAB was replaced by WPB in January, 1942, and it can be expected that DPA as presently organized will not be long for this world.

Changes Coming—Defense Mobilizer Wilson in announcing the new set-up under the Presidential order admitted that further changes will be coming. DPA Boss Harrison went one step further in his closing staff meeting at NPA when he flatly stated that his new assignment was just another move toward centralized control.

Emphasis on Production — Despite its administrative shortcomings, the new set-up is expected to get production rolling and increased production is highest on Mr. Wilson's list.

Mr. Wilson is also known to be convinced that the DO priority system is unworkable and should be scrapped as soon as possible. This attitude on the part of the No. 1 man in the mobilization picture will hasten the advent of a Controlled Materials Plan.

NE Steels—In addition to increasing nickel production for both domestic and foreign sources, the Senate Armed Services Preparedness Subcommittee recommends that NPA urge the steel industry to produce NE steel wherever the saving in nickel will more than offset the increase in the use of other strategic materials.

The possibility of mandatory orders, if encouragement proves inadequate, is also suggested. The subcommittee also recommended that NPA call in major users of nickel-bearing materials and appoint an industry committee to formulate a workable program for segregation and speedy scrap recovery.

Manpower Problems Decentralized—Manpower problems are being parceled out to a country-wide system of regional and area Management-Labor Committees.

The Office of Defense Manpower is setting up 13 regional committees as well as area committees in all labor market areas in which significant manpower shortages exist or impend.

Regional committees will be set up in New York, Boston, Richmond, Philadelphia, Atlanta, Cleveland, Chicago, Minneapolis, Kansas City, Dallas, Denver, San Francisco, and Seattle. The regional committees will be composed of eight members, four from management, including one agriculture, and four from labor, with the Bureau of Employment Security regional director as head.

Work to the Worker—Make-up of the area committees will be similar. The committees will deal with manpower shortages and will also identify unused plant capacity and pools of surplus manpower and call them to the attention of the procurement agencies and prime contractors.

The Office of Defense Manpower, based on World War II experience, will attempt to bring the work to the worker to avoid needless migration and minimize strains on community facilities. Procurement agencies will, insofar as possible, consider the adequacy of labor supplies in specific localities in scheduling production, or building facilities.

One of the most important raw materials in steelmaking . . . one frequently underrated by the casual observer . . . is iron and steel scrap. With over 90% of all the steel in the U. S. being made by the open hearth process, the scrap used by steel producers totals approximately 50,000,000 tons each year.

The open hearth method of steel production is geared to a pig iron scrap consumption ratio of roughly 50-50. This is to the final advantage of the steel user, since a large scrap diet in steelmaking results in a number of benefits: (a) steel is made faster (since scrap has already been "refined" once before, the "melt" time in the open hearth is decreased); (b) vital raw materials are conserved (it takes almost 4 tons of iron ore, coal and limestone to make a ton of pig iron); (c) unless scrap prices are abnormally high, the price of steel is cheaper; (d) steel is of higher quality (since scrap has already undergone one refining process); (e) transportation facilities, instead of being used for the additional raw materials otherwise required, can be released for other uses; (f) steel mill capacities can be expanded more readily with less emphasis on the blast furnace and more on open hearths and rolling mills.

About two-thirds of the scrap consumed in making steel comes from the steel mills themselves. Crop ends and sheared edges move quickly back to the open hearth shop. The remaining third, flowing to the mills largely through the 6,500 scrap dealers in the U.S., comes from the wastage in metal working plants ("production" scrap), auto graveyards, old building, bridge and ship wrecking projects, railroads (worn rails, freight cars, etc.), neighborhood junk peddlers.

The scrap dealers must sort the scrap so that the undesirables are eliminated, the alloys segregated and the right kinds of scrap can be delivered in large tonnages to the mills for most efficient steelmaking practice.

Today, with steel production at record peaks and with capacity continually expanding, it is more important than ever to keep scrap flowing back to the steel mills from *every* source. Everyone waiting for steel can help himself by assisting the movement of his scrap through his regular channels.

THE SCRAP CYCLE

OPEN HEARTH BLOOMING MILLS FINISHING MILLS

STEEL MILL SCRAP YARD

HOME SCRAP

PURCHASE SCRAP

PRODUCTION SCRAP

MANUFACTURER

AUTO GRAVEYARD

SCRAP DEALER

JUNK

JUNK DEALER

CONSUMER

NEW PUNCH

does better job, slashes cost

A new type of punch, straight-ground and with a soft metal sleeve to absorb vibration, can produce holes with straight walls and no burr to replace drilled and reamed holes. It can make holes in stock thicker than hole diameter. Pieces per grind have been upped 700 pct in some cases, and die maintenance cut 80 pct.

By J. R. REINERTSON, *Midwest Engineer*
Pivot Punch and Die Corp., *Chicago*

PRODUCTION experience with a new type of punch perfected about 2 years ago is proving it a versatile and capable aid to tool engineers. The shock absorber punch has reduced punch breakage and increased the number of holes per grind in many varied applications. In addition it is used to perforate material where thickness equals, or is greater than, the hole diameter. And it has produced holes with 100 pct shear, or straight walls and no burr, enabling, in such cases, punched holes to replace drilled and reamed holes at a fraction of the former cost.

Increasing punch life is a question of primary importance to tool engineers. A broken punch means necessary but unprofitable labor. Scrapped parts, lost production, material handling, tool-room labor, and the minutes that an operator stands idle, represent the true cost of a broken punch. Maintenance costs on most production perforating dies are from 2 to 10 times the cost of tooling.

After an analysis of the various reasons for punch wear and punch breakage, the Pivot Punch and Die Corp. developed a method of straight grinding round punches. That is, punches are ground parallel to the punch axis. This increases the life of the cutting edge and eliminates the circumferential fracture lines set up by cylindrical grinding. In addition, the Whipsleeve, a vibration dampener or shock absorber, was developed to reduce punch breakage.

Vibration has proven to be one of the major conditions contributing to die maintenance costs.

Compression of the material in the product also compresses the steel in the punch. The impact as a punch hits the work and becomes subject to this compression, causes high-frequency vibration. The exact frequencies vary with speed of loading, punch size and the duration of compression. This action can be illustrated easily by experience in the toolroom. When a worker tries to chisel steel with a small diameter chisel, the vibration generated at the fulcrum point follows up the body of the chisel and stings his hand. As the result of pain and inability to get the job done with a small pencil type chisel, he therefore uses a heavy body chisel. The larger body chisel with a hard point and the top or head drawn back soft, absorbs the vibration before it reaches the hand. Vibrations in a chisel in the hand work the same way as those of a punch in a die.

Broken Down Edges Don't Shear Properly

At the left in Fig. 1 is the conventional heavy body punch that most toolmakers have standardized on where the center distance of the holes permits. The drawing exaggerates the surface resulting from the conventional cylindrical grind. This grinding leaves circumferential ridges not backed up by metal. The cutting edge is a ridge which rapidly breaks down as the punch enters the metal. With this edge broken down, a wedge, shown exaggerated in the drawing, remains. This changes the punch action from straight shear to a combination of shear and radial compression of material at the sides of the hole. Results are hole shrinkage, increased stripping pressure, and dimpling of stock when punching thin materials. When the microscopic edges of the punch break down direct shear results only from the smaller diameter of the wedge and the hole shrinks around the greater diameter of the punch. Shrinkage around any punch will speed up galling and will tear the hole.

It has been shown that the punch action sets up vibrations. It is a well-known principle of physics that the frequency of vibration of an object varies with the mass. The critical point of a punch, therefore, occurs where its diameter changes. At this point there is interference between the vibration frequency of the point and that of the heavier body of the punch, which produces a concentration of strain.

The different frequencies eventually cause fracture through fatigue. Initially, the incipient cracking progresses slowly and produces a fibrous fracture. When the cross-section area is reduced too far, the punch suddenly breaks because the sectional diameter will not support the strain imposed.

Tests have proven that a dull punch point will increase the die wear much more rapidly than if there is a sharp cutting edge on the punch. The small diameter of the taper or wedge end of the punch might only be a few tenths under the nominal diameter of the punch. But this can cause a side thrust which will exert extreme pressure and cause immediate failure on thin walled compound die sections, and cause trouble with any die set. Maintaining a sharp cutting or broaching edge will reduce the side pressure.

Straight Grind Backs Up Cutting Edge

On the right in Fig. 1 is the Pivot straight-ground punch, with grind lines parallel to the line of action and perpendicular to the probable line of fracture. In this sketch the surface produced by grinding has been exaggerated. The end view shows the effect produced by straight grinding. There is, in effect, a series of broaching teeth that are backed up along the length of the punch. These will not break down and alter the punch diameter, as do the ridges produced by cylindrical grinding.

There are other benefits from straight grinding. It is easier to prevent runout between the punch point and the body of the punch. And, the broaching teeth provide paths for the lubricants often used in punching operations.

The effect of cylindrical grinding is reduced in some shops by honing the point diameter of the punch. This, of course, adds to the cost of each punch, and by increasing the metal-to-metal contact surface, increases generated heat. It is not necessary to hone the straight-ground punch.

The second feature of the Pivot punch is a diecast sleeve of soft metal, which acts as a vibration dampener. This extends down about 1/16 in. below the critical point at which the punch changes diameter. As vibrations travel up the straight point section of the punch, they are absorbed by the soft Whipsleeve.

Fig. 2, illustrating the Whipsleeve, also shows how the sleeve can be used in guiding in a stationary or pressure type of stripper with a straight-through bushing. This permits guiding the punch right where the work is being done. It eliminates any possibility of the punch skidding.

Soft Sleeve Absorbs Vibration

The effect of this type of punch design, with its straight grind and the Whipsleeve, is illustrated in Fig. 3. On the left is the type of hole produced by the conventional punch. Hole diameter is almost never less than the thickness of the stock being punched. The punch shears a straight wall for about 1/3 of the hole. Two-thirds of the hole will break or tear out to a greater diameter than that of the punch, depending on the die clearance. This type of hole is, of course, not suitable for bearing or for subsequent tapping.

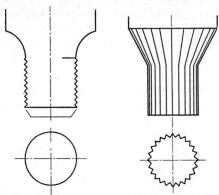

FIG. 1—The surface lines resulting from punch grinding are exaggerated in this drawing. Left, a conventional cylindrically-ground punch. The wedge-shaped tip left by the breakdown of the circumferential ridges left by grinding, shown exaggerated, is the cause of excessive galling. On the right is a straight-ground punch. The ridges left by grinding run parallel to the line of action of the punch and thus are backed up by metal and supported against breaking down.

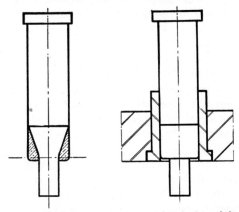

FIG. 2—The Whipsleeve, shown cross-hatched at left, is a diecast soft metal sleeve to absorb punch vibration, an important factor in punch life. The drawing on the right illustrates how the sleeve can be used in guiding the punch in a bushing in the stripper.

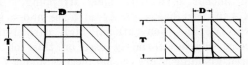

FIG. 3—Conventional punches produce holes like that shown on the left. Barely can T be greater than D. Punch shears for only about 1/3 of hole length. The rest of the hole tears or breaks out, to a diameter greater than that of the punch. A Pivot punch can produce a hole like that on the right, where the D is half of T, and the walls are straight for 2/3 of the hole length. When D is larger in relation to T, the punch can produce a 100 pct sheared hole with straight walls and no burr.

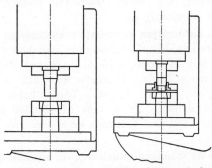

FIG. 4—Misalignment between the punch and the hole in the die block will result from a slight opening of the gap in the C-frame in the setup on the left. On the right, a Whipsleeve punch, guided in a bushing in the stripper, is not so easily thrown out of alignment.

The straight-ground punch, primarily because it retains a sharp edge without the minute reduction in diameter of the cylindrically-ground punch, is capable under proper conditions of producing a 100 pct sheared hole with straight walls and no burr. It can also be used for holes with a diameter less than the thickness of the stock being punched. As shown at the right in Fig. 3, in a hole with a diameter half the thickness of the stock, the punch shears straight for about 70 pct of the hole length.

The limitation of this type of punching is determined by comparing the shearing pressure required to punch the material against the compressive strength of the punch. The compressive strength for the Pivot punch is 405,250 psi. The compressive strength of a specific point diameter would thus be computed by multiplying the area of the punch, in square inches, by 405,250. For good engineering, Pivot recommends that the shearing pressure not exceed two-thirds of the compressive strength of the punch. However, a number of jobs are successfully operating where the shearing pressure exceeds this limitation.

Another important design point is the length of the straight, small-diameter point section of the punch. Keeping this short naturally increases the punch strength. Though punches can be supplied with greater point lengths, in use it is recommended that the length not exceed 1½ times the stock thickness. Also, for difficult work it is well to use as large as possible a ratio of body diameter to point diameter so that the punch will have a maximum mass in the cast sleeve to better absorb vibration.

Sleeve Aids Alignment

Fig. 4 illustrates the value of the use of the sleeve in guiding the punch. Should load cause a slight opening of the gap of the C-frame press, the punch at the left will not match with the hole in the die block. Die posts can be used for aligning, but no 2-in. die post is going to hold the ram straight on a 100-ton press. Such misalignment can greatly increase maintenance and punch replacement costs.

Fig. 4, on the right, shows the punch mounted in the punch pad in the same C-frame press as on the left. It shows how the Whipsleeve is guided in a stationary stripper through a drill bushing. There is no opportunity for the punch to skid and shear the button die. The sleeve is engaged in the guide bushing before the punch contacts the work.

A typical example of use of the Pivot punch is a production job at the P-K Tool & Manufacturing Co. of Chicago. Their blank measures roughly 2 x 2¾ in., of 1010 hot-rolled steel ⅛ in. thick, pickled and oiled. The piece contains six holes, four 0.139-in. diam holes to be tapped, and two holes of 0.174 in. diam. Production with conventional punches was about 8000 parts before the die had to be pulled out because a perforator was scored or broken. Vertical honing of the punches increased production to about 12,000 pieces per setup.

More than a million of these parts have now been run at P-K with Pivot Whipsleeve punches. Pieces per setup have averaged 50,000. Replacements for scoring or breakage are less than one

FIG. 5—Six holes are punched in this 1/8-in. thick AISI 1010 hot-rolled steel blank. Production per setup with conventional punches was about 8000 parts. Honing punches increased this to about 12,000. The Pivot punch gives 50,000 pieces per setup, and has cut die maintenance costs 80 pct.

FIG. 6—The three holes in this automotive hinge plate were formerly drilled and reamed for tapping. Pivot punches produce holes ready for tapping without further operations, at approximately the former cost of burring the reamed holes.

FIG. 7—The nine holes in this automotive transmission part are punched in one stroke, but in three 1/16-in. staggered steps to reduce press load. Hole diameter is 0.312 in., and stock thickness, 3/8 in. Runs of 100,000 pieces have been made without punch breakage or scoring.

punch per 100,000 pieces. Die maintenance costs are less than 20 pct of former costs, and press capacity, due to less downtime, has been increased 15 to 20 pct. This part is shown in Fig. 5.

At another plant, Pivot punches average 125,-000 pieces per grind, while conventional punches lasted only for 15,000 or 20,000 pieces before production was stopped for punch grinding or replacement of a broken punch. The job is punching of television chassis. The die has 300 punches. Punch pad and die block are jig bored. In one run of 300,000 chassis, only six punches had to be replaced, and then only when slugs piled up and caused punch breakage. On another job, production of over 100,000 pieces per grind is obtained in punching five 3/8-in. holes in T-angles of rerolled rails.

The backup hinge plate illustrated in Fig. 6 is a product of the Quality Hardware & Machine Co., Chicago. Four 0.270-in. diam holes are punched in 1/4-in. 1020 hot-rolled steel. In this case, 100 pct shear is obtained, and the punched holes are tapped for installation of the hinge on a leading make of automobile. The holes as punched have straight walls and no burr, and are the equal of holes formerly drilled, burred and reamed. The cost of punching these holes is approximately that of burring the drilled holes. The point length on the Pivot Whipsleeve punches used on this job is 3/8 in. It was found that punches with 1/2-in. point length broke too frequently.

Die Maintenance Cut 85 Pct

The Acme Steel Co., Chicago, produces a unit load anchor used with steel strapping. The 2 x 4-in. part has eight 1/4-in. holes and a slot 3/8 x 1 3/8 in. Conventional high carbon-high chrome punches formerly used on this job required grinding every 30,000 pieces—about 7 hr production. The average life of a punch was 350,000 parts. Pivot Whipsleeve punches average about 32 hr, or 200,000 parts, between grinds, and average life is 1,700,000 parts. Die maintenance cost is about 1/7 of former costs. The increase in press capacity, Acme figures, is about 1 hr a day. The Pivot punches Acme uses cost about 40¢ more than the conventional punches previously used.

In an automotive automatic transmission part, illustrated in Fig. 7, 9 holes are punched at one stroke, but in three 1/16-in.-staggered steps to reduce press loads. Diameter is 0.312 in. and stock thickness is 3/8 in. These holes were formerly drilled. Trial runs of 100,000 pieces were made without breakage or appreciable wear of the punch.

Since no standard punch will do all jobs, Pivot can supply over 69 million combinations of point diameter, point length, body diameter, overall length, and style. The proper combination is made to give maximum efficiency on each job.

Painting time on power transformer radiators was cut to less than an hour, as compared to from 6 to 24 hr by former methods. One coat of paint is eliminated, but the same film thickness is maintained. Handling is greatly reduced.

FLOW-COATING the primer coat on a radiator; a radiator with the finish coat applied is shown in the foreground.

Painting
Speeded

ON BULKY FABRICATIONS

IN the process of developing an improved method for flow-coating power transformer radiators, a number of finishing problems were solved. Some of the methods developed may be of use in handling and painting other long, narrow, complicated assemblies.

No other component of the modern power transformer has been so difficult to coat economically as the cooling radiator. Yet, it is extremely important to obtain good inhibitive and protective films on these radiator surfaces, since they have been the first to give trouble in field exposures over the years.

A large transformer may have as many as 20 or more cooling radiators. Such radiators are constructed with a horizontal, tubular header at each end between which are spaced the vertical cooling tubes; sometimes up to 30 in number. Most large transformers are constructed with

detachable radiators to comply with railroad clearance regulations.

If the radiator assembly is painted while detached, it means multiple handling of an awkward piece. If they are attached for coating with the tank, space problems are created within the fabricating shop, and portions of the tank itself are blanketed by the radiators. This makes painting of the tank very difficult.

The general practice had been to vertically flow-coat the tanks and radiators separately by pumping adequate quantities of paint through a hose to a nozzle in the hands of an operator. Complete immersion or dipping was discarded because of the large volume of paint required and the questionable tank stability, over long periods of time, of the available paints.

In contemplating a wholly new painting procedure, the following considerations were exam-

By M. P. GETTING, JR. (l.), *Asst. to Works Mgr.* and J. G. FINK (r.), *Chemist, Test Dept.*

Allis-Chalmers Mfg. Co., Pittsburgh

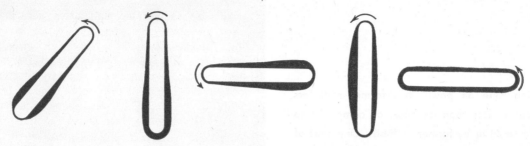

FIG. 1—Successive views of rotation, showing limits of the paint flow and how the paint flowed back and forth before setting up.

ined: (1) Increased production; (2) an improved uniformity of paint film thickness in place of the tapered thin top to thick bottom film, characteristic of the former method; and (3) improvement in handling procedures.

Assembly is Rotated

Past experience with flow coating radiators in a vertical position while hanging from conveyer rails 25 ft above the shop floor was a strong inducement to try other means. A fixture that would hold the radiator in a horizontal position and thus permit working from the floor level at all times was tried. This change in position would also provide the desired uniform film thickness and at the same time facilitate improvements in handling and overall production.

The practicality of flow-coating the assemblies in a horizontal position was examined. Experimentation showed that, with the radiator tube surfaces placed horizontal, after-drippage drain through the tubes would cause unsightly runs and tears.

The only solution was to take advantage of all the different positions the radiators might be placed in; that is, rotate it at slow speeds while the paint was being applied and during the initial setup period. It was felt that this might trap a certain amount of the excess liquid on the tube surface and reduce runs, while simultaneously creating a much thicker applied paint film. This was not only proved correct, but the number of paint coats was reduced from the usual three to two.

Flow-Out Problem Met

It was necessary to actually study liquid flow over the surfaces of the tubes. To this end, a small operating mechanism was constructed. The model was designed to hold short lengths of the tubes, simulating an actual radiator assembly. As nearly as possible, all conditions met in production were duplicated. A variable speed drive for the rotating mechanism was included so that the effect of speed changes could be studied. A blower with its intake over the enclosed drain pit and a paint pump in the circulating system were installed; these insured that no effects of aeration or agitation on the paint would be overlooked.

A number of paint manufacturers prepared samples of both primer and blue-gray finish

paint in adequate quantities to operate in the test machine. Some failures were experienced in applying the paint samples. Most of the problems were common to all paints in some degree, but a few seemed peculiar to only one or two formulations.

First and foremost was the matter of flow-out. Because of the two-coat system, heavier coats of paint were applied. This produced a condition similar to a brush-out application. Fig. 1 shows the limits of the paint flow and how the paint flowed back and forth over the surface before setting up.

The volume of paint in flow never completely circled the tube, but stopped short in each revolution. As the setting-up process advanced with thinner loss, the flow was reduced from an overall and unbroken flow front to many separate scalloped fronts. In an improperly formulated paint, these separate scalloped fronts failed to flow out laterally and were set up and baked as solid runs or ridges over the surface.

This failure was the one most commonly experienced with the different primers and the one most difficult to correct. Only one primer submitted worked perfectly at the first trial. It consists of zinc oxide, zinc chromate, and iron oxide pigments in a straight alkyd varnish, plus thinner and driers. This material has been in production for several months and to date has been completely trouble-free.

Bubbles Are Produced

When the stream of paint flowing at high velocity strikes the surface to be coated, numerous bubbles are produced. Many bubbles are also found in the circulating system if there is excessive turbulent flow. The same is true if the pump operates at insufficient static head in the drain pan, causing de-thinning of the paint as it passes through the pump. Improperly formulated paint forms bubbles which do not readily break on loss of solvent. These bubbles dry and bake as blisters in the film. Moreover, if the bubbles break late in the setting-up process, they will have a crater with a thin bottom.

Another difficulty encountered was in obtaining proper flow-out consistent with rapid setup. The frequent adjustment in obtaining smooth primer surface was to substitute higher and higher initial boiling point thinners; this increased setup time. In at least one case, setup time was over 45 min while the successful primer set up in 10 min. A 10-min performance was necessary for higher production.

Desired film thickness for the primer coat was 1.0 mil. Several of the primers submitted met this minimum, although in attempting to obtain a thick film it was necessary to use fairly high viscosities. In several instances, this resulted in an unsatisfactory flow-out condition.

The important problem, after the proper primer formulation had been made, was to correctly balance choice of the thinner initial boiling point range with viscosity. In several trials, corrections made in the formulation to eliminate one fault produced another, sometimes worse than the first, resulting in bubbles in the film.

Color Float Appeared

Trials with the finish coating disclosed not only the same problems encountered in the primers, but also the serious one of color float or pigment separation. This occurred particularly in paints containing more than one colored, opaque pigment and especially in dark gray coatings having a high percentage of black pigment. Only one finish paint consistently performed without apparent float. The most commonly observed float first appeared, depending on the thinner evaporation adjustment of the mix, from 30 sec to one min after application.

A dark wash developed at the flow front; as this progressed and setting-up advanced, the wash broke down into a number of dark and light streaks, which finally became fixed across the tubes normal to the long axis. This was observed in varying degrees in all of the finish coats except one. The desired film thickness for the finish was set at 2.0 mil to provide a total of 3.0 mil film thickness for two coats.

As with the primer, difficulties were encountered in obtaining smooth flow-out, adequate film thickness, rapid setup, high gloss, and absence of color float. One manufacturer was successful in completing satisfactory primer and top-coat trials, and was chosen to conduct further trials on the full-scale coating machines which had meanwhile been installed. The finish paint consists of titanium oxide, tinting color, inert and special-purpose pigments in a straight alkyd vehicle, plus thinners and driers.

The photo on p. 59 shows the coating machine from above, indicating the size of the unit and the radiators being coated. The full-size machine was built on the same principle as the test model, except for the radiator holding fixture. The fixture was originally conceived as a cage-like rack, extending the full length of the catch tank; this was supported by bearings at each end and chain driven at one end from an adjustable speed motor.

Holding Simplified

The radiators were lowered into the rack from above and clamped, according to their length, at two appropriate places. This rack was satisfactory, except that it was difficult to keep clean and furnished repositories for paint which later dripped down on to the radiator. The rack was completely eliminated and substituted by a holding fork at each end of the radiator. Each fork was mounted on a stub overhung shaft and supported by spaced ball bearings. The driving fork was fixed, but the idling fork was mounted in bearings supported by a carriage which ran on a rail at front and rear of the catch tank.

The carriage was equipped with drive chains between the axles so that ample traction was available to traverse with a hand crank. A hand

FIG. 2—The five-stage Bonderizing system used for hot-dip cleaning and phosphating of the transformer radiators. Assemblies up to 20 ft long are handled.

clamping wheel was furnished so that the adjustable fork could be locked, holding the radiator firmly for rotation. This reduced the amount of fixture requiring cleaning and practically eliminated damage to the paint film resulting from contact with the fixture. Only four small areas on each header need repainting by brush.

Not all the characteristics of the model were carried over to the production operation. A transverse surface, represented by the cylindrical headers, was introduced for the first time. In spite of this difficulty, perfectly smooth, rapid-setting prime coats of the proper thickness were obtained at the end of the first day by changing the viscosity.

Inconsistent Behavior

This success was not repeated, however, with the finish coat. Several weeks of intensive development and numerous adjustment trials on the machine were necessary. Color float was the serious obstacle. It was shown that a coating which would produce almost perfect results on a prototype might be subject to color separation on the full-scale radiators.

This inconsistency has been closely examined, but to date no set of conditions has been isolated to account for it. Through subsequent reformulation in the coating and final adjustments of the machine, it became possible to produce radiators, complete with headers, having extremely good appearance. A smooth surface and high gloss, including rapid setting-up time, and a total average film thickness of 3.0 mils resulted.

The new system makes possible straight line

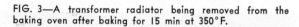

FIG. 3—A transformer radiator being removed from the baking oven after baking for 15 min at 350°F.

handling of a heavy, awkward fabricated shape in a relatively small floor space. The fabricated, tested radiators are delivered to the finishing department, laid down in the position they are handled throughout. The assemblies are first hand-wiped to remove soil and carbon smudge, which is difficult to clean off by an alkaline bath. They then move progressively through the five stages of a standard hot-dip cleaning and phosphating (Bonderizing) treatment, as shown in Fig. 2. Throughout the entire system, all handling is accomplished by two tractorized hoists running on separate monorails, supporting the ends of the radiators.

All dip tanks are 20 ft long to accommodate the largest piece manufactured. Short radiators are handled two at a time. The entire cleaning and phosphating processes consume about 22 min up to the time the pieces are delivered to another small lay-down space, ready to coat. They are then moved to the prime coating machine (p. 59) for coating, which takes approx 1 to 3 min. The machine revolves at 1 rpm during painting and while the primer sets up, consuming another 8 to 14 min, depending on the ambient temperature and humidity.

Coating Time Reduced

After set-up they are immediately moved over and past the finish-coat machine to the horizontal, top-opening oven, Fig. 3, and baked at 350°F for 15 min. Four electric timers furnish red light warnings at the completion of the set-up periods and at the termination of the baking cycle for both prime and finish coats. The radiator is laid down to cool and then placed in the finish coat machine. The coating time, setup time and baking time for this coat is approximately the same as for the primer. After baking, the radiator is moved to another small lay-down space and readied for the shipper. The whole operation, including cleaning and phosphating, is complete in 1 hr. The old method required from 6 to 24 hr for the three-coat paint film of equal thickness.

Several future refinements will further increase production and possibly reduce the number of working shifts. Preliminary experiments on applying the finish coat directly to the radiator, while still hot from the first bake, show considerable promise. This decreases the cooling time required between prime bake and finish application. It also makes possible a finish set-up time of approx 4 to 7 min. These trials were performed with properly adjusted paint on radiators at about 165°F.

This new procedure can prove advantageous to many manufacturers of bulky fabrications of irregular shape. It makes possible the application of a smooth, glossy, uniform film to irregularly-shaped objects with a minimum of turning, handling and coating, and does all this in a small, low space.

SWING GRINDING a huge Monel pickling hook, cast at Cooper Alloy Foundry Co.

USES BROADEN FOR Cast Monel

By N. S. MOTT
Chief Chemist and Metallurgist
The Cooper Alloy Foundry Co.
Hillside, N. J.

MONEL is the proprietary trade name (International Nickel Co., Inc.) given to a two-thirds nickel and one-third copper alloy; it was originally formed by the metallurgical reduction of a naturally-occurring mixture of copper and nickel ores. This reduction alloy was found to have valuable properties of corrosion resistance and mechanical strength. It was considered more advantageous to market it as such, rather than go through the exceedingly difficult and expensive separation of its components.

For many years, Monel has found widespread and diversified uses in chemical, pharmaceutical, food, textile, laundry, oil refinery, paper and pulp, architectural and household applications. It has also proved useful in many of the commonly encountered corrosives, such as sea water, dilute reducing acids, halogen gases, neutral and alkaline salts, non-oxidizing acid salts and strong caustic solutions.

The use of Monel in the cast form, in which the desirable corrosion resisting properties are maintained along with high strength and ductility, has become increasingly popular for shapes difficult or costly to fabricate. Castings can be made both in sand and permanent metal molds—according to standard static casting procedures as well as by recently perfected centrifugal methods. They are produced in three types of analyses, as shown in Table I, varying chiefly in silicon contents. The higher silicon alloys are used where greater hardness, strength and resistance to erosion or galling is desired, with some sacrifice as to ductility and shock resistance.

The use of cast Monel does not show a growth picture to equal what would be expected from an

Great care must be taken in melting Monel, or brittle metal may result. When handled properly, a wide range of desirable physical and mechanical properties can be had with good weldability and machinability.

examination of its properties, shown in Table II. The big reason for this lag is the fact that too many foundries have been careless of controls. Great care must be taken in melting Monel or brittle metal may result.

When Monel is heated to too high a temperature before pouring, oxidation or burning takes place despite the protective slag. An oxide film forms around the grains as they solidify, almost completely destroying the adhesion between them. This condition may also occur on the surface of the metal when it is heated in an oxidizing flame during welding or annealing operations.

Glass Slag Protects Melt

Monel metal burns so readily that crucible and induction melting are very difficult. Unless the metal is thoroughly protected from the air, brittle castings will result. Good practice is to melt in an acid arc furnace and protect the melt with a glass slag. When difficulty in melting scrap is experienced, calcium metal to the extent of 2 lb per 1500-lb heat is added to quiet the bath.

Pouring temperatures range from 2550° to 2600°F for large castings, and 2750° to 2800°F for small ones where running is difficult. No greater temperatures than 2800°F should be used if burning is to be avoided. To prevent embrittlement from the presence of sulfur, 1 oz of magnesium per 100 lb of metal is added to the ladle before pouring.

Sulfur, even in small amounts, may impair strength and lower ductility. It takes the form of a film or envelope of the eutectic of nickel and nickel sulfide or copper sulfide, around the grain boundaries. In casting, these sulfides are the last of the melt to solidify, distributing themselves between the primary grains with extremely damaging effects to strength and ductility.

Treating the molten metal with magnesium before casting causes the sulfur to combine forming a compound of high melting point. This replaces the eutectic envelope with granular particles of magnesium sulfide. In such form and random distribution, the sulfur will not interfere with strength and ductility.

Monel contains a small amount of carbon, which promotes fluidity and facilitates the production of sound castings. If it remains in solid solution, carbon does not have a serious effect on mechanical properties or corrosion resistance. If it is precipitated as graphite, however, serious reduction in strength and toughness may result. The presence of silicon reduces the solid solubility of carbon in Monel. The maximum amount of carbon to be tolerated is controlled by the silicon content. Standard recommendations show a maximum of 0.30 pct C for cast Monel; however, for "S" and "H" alloys, 0.15 pct C and even as low as 0.10 pct C may be preferable.

Forms Dendritic Structure

When a Monel casting solidifies, the crystals which first form are richer in nickel than the molten metal itself. The solidification proceeds too rapidly to permit smoothing out of this inequality; the cast metal, when entirely set, consists of tree-like skeletons of nickel-rich crystals within the arms or branches of which progressively more copper-rich metal has solidified. The metal thus has a cored or dendritic structure. Cast Monel metal is weakly magnetic, while the two silicon Monel alloys "S" and "H" are substantially non-magnetic.

Monel from its position in the electrochemical series is relatively noble; consequently, it does

Cast Monel containing 1.5 pct Si. 500X.

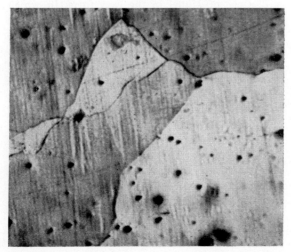

Monel "H" with 3.0 pct Si. 500X.

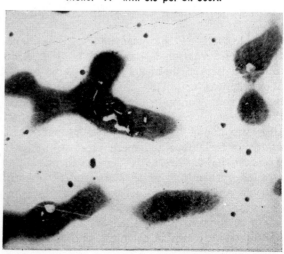

not readily evolve hydrogen from solutions in the absence of depolarizing agents. It is therefore most resistant to corrosion when conditions are reducing; the presence of oxygen or oxidizing agents, which facilitates the liberation of hydrogen, tend to promote attack. This resistance to corrosion under reducing conditions makes Monel very useful in some applications where stainless steels do not fare so well.

Being a non-ferrous alloy, Monel does not rust and discoloration and contamination from this source is obviated; however, Monel will tarnish in sulfur-bearing humid atmosphere. Monel does not suffer from the intergranular or pitting form of corrosion such as occurs in the austenitic chrome-nickel alloys; it also offers greater resistance to the effect of cavitation and impingement in salt water at high velocity.

Stress-corrosion cracking in hydrochloric acid or in chloride solutions and caustic embrittlement in strong caustic solutions are unknown. Monel is sensitive to increasing velocity of solution and this may be expected to somewhat increase the corrosion rate; also, its corrosion products are usually quite soluble and protective films from that source are not produced.

Used For Handling Acids

A most common use for Monel is in the handling of acids under reducing conditions. Sulfuric acid corrosion is resisted by Monel in concentrations of less than 80 pct at most temperatures, and hydrochloric acid may be handled by Monel in concentrations up to 20 pct at 160°F. The introduction of air or oxygen results in an accelerated rate of corrosion in these acids and is to be avoided. The presence in the acids of oxidizing salts, particularly those of iron or copper, may be expected to increase corrosion markedly.

In a variety of applications involving hydrofluoric acid, Monel has shown itself to be usefully resistant to all concentrations, including the anhydrous acid, over a considerable range of temperatures. In aqueous non-aerated solutions

TABLE I							
CAST MONEL ALLOYS Chemical Composition, Pct							
Type	Ni	Cu	Fe	Mn	Si	C	S
Monel............	63	32	1.5	0.75	1.5	0.15	0.015
Monel "H".......	63	31	2	0.75	3	0.10	0.015
Monel "S"........	63	30	2	0.75	4	0.10	0.015

of hydrofluoric acid, Monel has shown satisfactory resistance up to 250°F. Here again aeration appreciably increases corrosion rates and denickelization may occur in the acid when under pressure in the presence of air; however, aeration is not generally encountered in the closed vessels associated with operating equipment handling hydrofluoric acid.

Monel "S" and "H" show resistance equal to that of ordinary Monel in all acid media. In neutral and alkaline salts Monel shows good resistance, even in hot, aerated solutions. It is also quite resistant to acid salts if they are non-oxidizing and the solutions are free from air.

Monel is highly resistant to solutions of caustic alkalies at quite high concentrations and temperatures, being exceeded only by pure nickel. The corrosion rate of Monel in caustic solutions below 55 pct concentration is low at all temperatures, and aeration does not increase the rate. However, in the range of 55 to 75 pct of concentration, nickel is to be preferred, and above 75 pct, Monel corrodes too rapidly to be practical.

Resists Fluorine Action

At high temperatures, Monel is very useful in handling anhydrous halogens and halogen acids. It will resist the action of fluorine and hydrogen fluoride up to 1000°F, chlorine up to 800°F, and hydrogen chloride up to 450°F. In the absence of sulfur, Monel is resistant in an oxidizing atmosphere to 2000°F, and in a carbon monoxide reducing atmosphere to 1500°F. When sulfur is

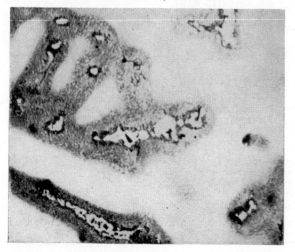

Monel "S" with 4.0 pct Si. 500X.

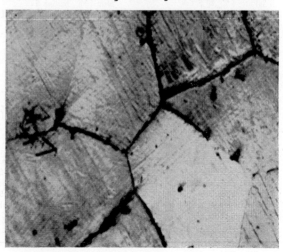

"Burnt" Monel showing oxidized grain boundaries. 500X.

TABLE II

CAST MONEL ALLOYS
Mechanical and Physical Properties

ALLOY	Monel	Monel "H"	Monel "S"		
HEAT TREATMENT	As Cast	As Cast	As Cast	Annealed	Hardened
Tensile Strength, 1000 psi	65 – 90	90 – 115	110 – 145	90	110 – 145
Yield Point, 1000 psi	32 – 40	60 – 80	80 – 115	65	80 – 115
Elongation in 2 in., pct	25 – 45	10 – 20	1 – 4	3	1 – 4
Hardness, Bhn	125 – 150	175 – 250	275 – 350	225 – 260	300 – 375
Charpy Impact, ft-lb	70	40	4		
Izod Impact, ft-lb	65 – 80	35 – 45	3 – 9		1 – 5
Modulus of Elasticity, 1 million psi	18.5	20	21	20.5	21.5
Specific Gravity	8.63	8.48	8.36		
Density, lb per cu in.	0.319	0.313	0.302		
Thermal Conductivity, Btu per sq ft/hr/°F/in.	180	180	180		
Specific Heat, Btu per lb per °F	0.127	0.129	0.130		
Melting Point, °F	2400 – 2450	2350 – 2400	2300 – 2350		
Resistivity, ohms per cir. mil ft	290	370	380		
Coefficient of Thermal Expansion, x 10⁻⁶					
70° to 212° F	7.8		6.8		
70° to 570°F	8.3		8.2		
70° to 1100°F	8.9		8.7		

TABLE III

CORROSION RESISTANCE OF CAST MONEL

ACIDS

Acetic 5%, 70 F * G
Acetic 5%, boiling E
Acetic 80%, 70 F * G
Acetic 80%, boiling E
Acetic Glacial, 70 F * E
Acetic Glacial boiling E
Benzoic 5%, 70 F E
Boric 5%, 176 F E
Chromic 10%, 70 F G
Chromic 10%, boiling N
Chromic 50%, boiling N
Citric 5%, 70 F E
Citric 25%, boiling G
Citric 50%, boiling G
Formic 5%, 70 F G
Hydrochloric 1%, 70 F * F
Hydrochloric 1%, boiling P
Hydrochloric 5%, 70 F * F
Hydrochloric 5%, boiling P
Hydrochloric 25%, 70 F P
Hydrochloric 25%, 176 F P
Hydrofluoric 48%, 70 F E
Hydrofluoric 48%, 176 F G
Lactic 5%, 70 F G
Malic, all temps. G
Nitric all concs., 70 F N
Nitric 65%, boiling N
Oleic all concs., all temps. E
Oxalic 5%, boiling G
Phosphoric 10%, 70 F * G
Phosphoric 85%, 70 F * E
Phosphoric 85%, boiling F
Stearic conc. to 200 F E
Sulfuric 2%, 70 F * G
Sulfuric 2%, 176 F * F
Sulfuric 2%, boiling F
Sulfuric 5%, 70 F * G
Sulfuric 5%, 176 F * F
Sulfuric 5%, boiling F
Sulfuric 10%, 70 F * G
Sulfuric 10%, 176 F * F
Sulfuric 10%, boiling F
Sulfuric 78% (60° Be), 176 F N
Sulfuric 93% (66° Be), 70 F F
Sulfuric 93%, 300 F N
Oleum, 70 F N

Mixed Acids 57% H₂SO₄, 28% HNO₃, 176 F N

ALKALIES

Ammonium Hydroxide, all concs. F
Calcium Hydroxide, 10%, boiling E
Calcium Hydroxide 50%, boiling E
Sodium Hydroxide or Potassium, all concs., 70 F E
Sodium Hydroxide <20%, boiling E
or Potassium 30%, boiling E
Potassium, Molten, 600 F G

NEUTRAL & ALKALINE SALTS

Barium Sulfide, 70 F E
Calcium Chloride 5%, 70 F E
Calcium Sulfate Sat., 70 F E
Magnesium Chloride 5%, 70 F E
Magnesium Sulfate 5%, 70 F E
Sodium Carbonate, all concs., 70 F E
Sodium Chloride 5%, 70 F E
Sodium Sulfate 5%, 70 F E
Sodium Sulfide 5%, 70 F E
Sodium Sulfite 5%, 70 F E

ACID SALTS

Alum 10%, boiling G
Aluminum Sulfate 10%, 70 F E
Ammonium Chloride 5%, 70 F G
Ammonium Sulfate 10%, 70 F E
Ammonium Sulfate 10%, boiling G
Ammonium Nitrate, all concs., 70 F E
Stannous Chloride 5%, 70 F G
Zinc Chloride, 5%, Boiling G

OXIDIZING ALKALINE SALTS

Calcium Hypochlorite 2%, 70 F P
Sodium Hypochlorite 5%, 70 F P
Sodium Peroxide G

OXIDIZING ACID SALTS

Ammonium Persulfate 5%, 70 F N
Cupric Chloride 1%, 70 F N
Cupric Sulfate 10%, 70 F F
Ferric Chloride 10%, 70 F N
Ferric Sulfate, boiling N
Mercuric Chloride 2%, 70 F N
Stannic Chloride 5%, 70 F N

WET AND DRY GASES

Chlorine Gas Dry, 70 F G
Chlorine Gas Wet, 212 F N
Sulfur Dioxide Dry, 575 F G
Sulfur Dioxide Wet, 70 F F
Sulfur Dioxide Solution, 70 F F
Sulfur Dioxide Spray, 70 F F
Hydrogen Sulfide Dry G
Hydrogen Sulfide Wet G

ORGANIC MATERIALS

Acetone, 70 F E
Acid Sludge (50% H₂SO₄), 200 F N
Alcohol—Methyl & Ethyl E
Analine Hydrochloride, 70 F G
Benzol, 176 P E
Carbon Tetrachloride E
Chloroform E
Ethyl Acetate, 70 F G
Formaldehyde, 70 F E
Phenol 5%, boiling G
Refinery Crudes G
Trichlorethylene, boiling E

PAPER MILL APPLICATIONS

Kraft Liquor G
Black Liquor G
Green Liquor G
White Liquor G
Sulfite Liquor, 176 F N
Chlorine Bleach P
Paper Makers Alum G

PHOTOGRAPHIC INDUSTRY

Humid Atmospheres E
Cellulose Acetate G
Acetic Anhydride E
Acetic Acid + .1% H₂SO₄ G
Developers G
Solutions Containing SO₂ E
Silver Nitrate, 70 F N

FERTILIZER MANUFACTURING

H₃PO₄ + H₂SO₄ + HF P

PICKLING OPERATIONS

H₂SO₄ + Dichromate, 176 F N
H₂SO₄ + Hcl, 176 F G

CORROSIVE WATERS

Acid Mine Water P
Abrasive Acid Mine Water N
Sea Water E
Brackish Water F

FOOD AND ASSOCIATED PRODUCTS

Brines E
Edible Oils E
Fats E
Fatty Acid Distillation G
Fruit Juices G
Ketchup G
Milk Pasteurizing G
Vinegar & Salt, 70 F F

RATINGS:
E—Excellent resistance. 0.004 max. in. per year of penetration. Corrosion so slight as to be harmless.
G—Good resistance. 0.004-0.042 in. per year of penetration. Satisfactory service expected; at most a slight etch.
F—Fair resistance. 0.042-0.120 in. of penetration per year. Satisfactory service under specific conditions. Light to moderate attack.
P—Poor resistance. 0.120-0.420 in. of penetration per year. Satisfactory for temporary service only.
N—No resistance. 0.420 min. in. of penetration per year. Rate of attack too great for any use.
*—Subject to pitting type corrosion.

Continued

present it is resistant under oxidizing conditions up to 600°F, and under reducing conditions to 500°F.

For non-galling, wear and erosion resisting castings with high hardness and strength as well as high corrosion resistance, it is most advantageous to use silicon as an alloying element to induce precipitation hardening. Two grades of castings of this type are regularly produced, Monel "S" with 4 pct Si and Monel "H" with 3 pct.

Because of its non-galling quality, it is possible to combine Monel "S" with regular Monel in moving assemblies, where scoring and seizing are encountered with other materials. The silicon addition forms a nickel silicide; this is precipitated as a dispersion of fine particles throughout the solid solution matrix. The quantity and form of this nickel silicide determines the hardness and mechanical properties of the alloy.

Although it takes about 3.5 to 4.5 pct Si to produce good hardening characteristics in the ordinary Monel composition, additions of from 2.5 to 3.5 pct produce some partial hardening; these are useful for obtaining intermediate hardness with better ductility. All silicon additions seem to work in the direction of better corrosion resistance, with the exception of alkaline attack.

Welds Readily

Monel metal may be readily welded by either the arc or oxyacetylene torch methods; in the case of the latter, however, a reducing flame is necessary to prevent the formation of copper oxide film around grains, which produces brittleness and loss of corrosion resistance. In the case of complicated castings, a preheat of 200° to 300°F is desirable. No intergranular corrosion is

CAST MONEL VALVES and fittings handle corrosive hydrochloric acid solutions for Ciba Pharmaceutical Products Co.

caused by the welding, and neither ductility or strength are altered noticeably. Post heat treatment is not necessary except for special reasons, such as stress relieving a fabricated structure. Passivation is not required to preserve corrosion resistance. Welding of Monel "S" and "H" is not recommended because of too great a tendency toward cracking. Only mechanical joints should be used with these alloys.

The machinability of regular Monel castings is good. That of Monel "H" is fair, and Monel "S" castings must be annealed by heating to 1650°F followed by air cooling to be made fairly machinable. After machining, Monel "S" must be re-hardened for use by heating at 1100°F for 4 hr followed by furnace cooling to 600°F, from which point it is air-cooled. In this state, it has a hardness of from 300 to 400 Bhn and is very erosion and galling resistant.

Large Meters Easily Read At A Distance

KING-SIZED electric meters, believed to be the largest ever built, will enable speeds and feeds to be read from a distance by the operators of Allis-Chalmers' new 27-ft boring mill. The size of this tool and the large workpieces it will machine mean a large operating area, and large meters were desirable so operators could read them easily and accurately from anywhere in this area.

Ordinarily when a large size indication of meter readings is desired, motion of the elements of a meter of conventional size is transmitted to an indicator on a large dial by means of a selsyn system or similar device. But this amounts

to magnification of the meter reading, so any meter error is also magnified. Also, response to changes in the value being measured is slowed. So for accuracy and response, it was preferable to build a direct-indicating meter on a scale to match the desired indicator dial size.

The largest meters known to have been built heretofore had dials 11 in. in diameter. But for A-C's new Lima-Hamilton boring mill, the Dittmore & Freimuth Electronics Engineering Co., Milwaukee, has built accurate meters 20 in. in diameter, with 8-in. indicator needles—believed to be the world's largest.

WELDED AND BRAZED

BRAKE BANDS USE

60 PCT LESS STEEL

By W. H. HAVILAND (l.)
Chief Process Engineer
and S. M. SPICE (r.)
Chief Welding Engineer
Buick Div., General Motors Corp.
Flint, Mich.

UNTIL recently brake bands for the Buick Dynaflow transmission were hogged out of rings. These rings were formed from stock 9/16 in. thick and submerged welded. The finished band was only ⅛ in. thick except where the integral lugs were left at each end. This method of production was used because the ears take a heavy thrust when the brake is applied. It was considered essential that the ears be made integrally until some method of attaching them with absolute security to a separately made band could be developed.

It was always recognized that cutting the band from such thick stock was expensive and wasteful of steel milled into chips. But this method was used pending development of one less costly and yet completely reliable. A new method has now been developed and is in use at the transmission plant of Buick.

Pieces Are Preformed

Production now starts with cold-rolled high-strength steel, 0.128 ± 0.002 in. thick and 1 25/32 in. wide. This stock is received in 8 to 12-ft lengths and is cold sawed into 19⅜-in. lengths. Stock is then production punched, one end at a time, to prepare each end for welding. Then each piece is preformed on each end in a press to give the ends proper curvature for rolling into circular bands.

A single lug to form ears on each end of the band is made from cold-drawn SAE 1030 steel 11/32 in. thick and 1 25/32 in. wide. This stock is cut into 2¾-in. lengths on a cut-off machine and each lug is then struck in a die to form it to the same radius as the OD of the band. Before assembly to the band, the inner face of the formed lug is painted with a thin film of brazing paste or flux.

Tacked With Projection Welds

A lug and a band are then clamped by shoes over a mandrel, forming part of a welding fixture on a projection welding machine, shown in Fig. 2. The lug is welded to the band with eight projection welds. In the fixture, the lug is centered over the gap in the rolled ring and remains as one piece until severed after all other operations on the band are completed. A copper alloy insert is used as a backing in the arbor below the welds and the shoes clamp the band so that its ends butt. The upper shoe fits the lug and has an alloy copper facing in contact with the lug.

Welding is so done that the gap around welds between the lug and band does not exceed 0.005 in. After this welding, a small stamped copper clip is placed at the joint, being clipped over the lug to make the assembly ready for brazing.

Fifteen assemblies are placed on each Nichrome tray that enters the brazing furnace. The furnace is a pusher type and is equipped with a generator that supplies an endothermic atmosphere containing approximately 40 pct

FIG. 1—Brake band blanks, with ends punched and preformed, are transformed into rings by this set of Tishken rolls.

Automatic transmission brake bands used to be machined from thick stock to leave lugs at each end. Now lugs are separate, attached by projection welding, then brazing. Steel required was formerly 5½ lb per brake; now it's 2½ lb.

H_2, 20 pct CO, with the remainder N_2. This atmosphere prevents scaling and minimizes decarburization of the steel.

In the furnace, the assemblies remain 15 min at a brazing temperature of 2030°F, then pass through a 30-ft cooling zone before emerging slightly above room temperature.

The brazed bands are belt sanded and machined to remove excess copper remaining outside the joints. Then the bands are run through a double-disk grinder that removes about 0.015 in. of metal from each edge of each band. Bands continue through a wire brush machine that removes burrs produced in the grinding.

Grit Blasting Causes Springiness

Next, bands go to a swaging press equipped with a segmental die having a tapered pin in the central hole. In this die, when the pin bottoms, the band is expanded 0.050 in. to give it a 6.094 in. OD. Then bands are transferred to a broach which produces radiused undercuts at the two ends of the lug. These cuts provide the seats for struts, applied at assembly of the transmission, for closing the band around the drum when braking is required.

After broaching and washing, the bands are passed through a Wheelabrator that grit-blasts the inner face. The blasting not only prepares the surface for cementing the lining, but puts the inner face under compression that tends to make the band expand. After the lug is cut apart, the compression causes the ends of the band to spread when the band is free. This keeps the band lining out of contact with the drum when assembled in the transmission except when the struts force the band to contract and act as a brake in service.

Band lining is produced in flat molded strips of band width, 0.045 in. thick. Strips are sprayed with phenolic cement on one face and the cement is dried before the lining is rolled into a ring and placed inside the band in a special fixture. The space between the ends of the lining is centered opposite the line where the ends of the band meet.

In the fixture, the lining is pressed against the inner face of the rings under a radial pressure of 225 psi. The faces of segments that apply this pressure are resistance heated to 400°F and each lining is clamped for 6 min. The heat fluxes and cures the phenolic resin cement, producing a permanent joint between the band and its lining.

When the assemblies are removed and cool, any protruding edges of the lining are sanded flush with the metal of the band. Then the lining is ready to be bored and circumferentially

FIG. 2—Setup in a Federal welder for projection welding a lug to the ends of the brake band ring. The lug is later severed to leave an ear on each end of the band ring.

grooved. This is done in setups in two-spindle boring machines.

After this boring, which holds an ID of 6.019-6.024 in., a set of carbide tools moves out radially to cut the circumferential oil grooves in the lining. Finally, the band is severed across the center of the lug, leaving an ear on each side. The cut is made on a milling machine, and burrs left in the cut are then removed by an abrasive belt and file. After passing inspection, bands are ready for assembly into the transmission.

It is expected that the new method will reduce the cost of bands to about one-third that involved in the prior method. A part of this saving is in steel required per band. This is reduced from over 5½ lb to less than 2 lb per

FIG. 3—The segmental die in this press is used to expand each brake band ring to bring the ID to final size.

band because loss in chips in the new method is much less than by previous methods.

NEW BOOKS

Current releases from the publishers that will be of interest to management, sales, engineering and production personnel in the metalworking industry.

"Engineering Economy," by H. G. Thuesen. Pointing out that engineering is essentially a means of obtaining desired results with economy, the book purposes to aid the engineering student to extend to economy the application of factual analyses in which he is proficient, and to develop an attitude that will cause him to approach engineering problems with regard for their economic as well as their physical implications. Prentice-Hall, Inc., 70 Fifth Ave., New York 11. $6.65. 502 p.

* * *

"Sales Engineering," by B. Lester. This second edition is concerned with the art of selling equipment and services that require engineering skill in their selection, application and use. The book describes the type of work this involves, the opportunities it offers for a career, and the skills and techniques that have been found successful in over 35 years of selling machinery and technical products to industry. John Wiley & Sons, Inc., 440 Fourth Ave., New York 16. $3.00. 226 p.

"The Growth and Development of Executives," by M. L. Mace. The author presents the results of his observations on the manner in which numerous industrial firms are undertaking to develop executive talent. The central theme of the book is the coaching concept, and his main conclusion is that the most effective way of providing for the growth and development of people is through the conscious coaching of subordinates by their immediate superiors. Harvard Business School, Div. of Research, Soldiers Field, Boston 63. $3.25. 200 p.

* * *

"Lower Prices Coming!" W. J. Baxter describes the shape of things to come, telling that present-day dollars will soon buy more of everything at lower prices. Containing explanatory cartoons by Rob't Day, the book predicts that one-third of the nation's four million business firms will either be eliminated or pass into stronger hands in the buyer's market that is ahead. International Economic Research Bureau, 76 William St., New York 5. $1.00. 92 p.

Germans Make Pig Iron Without Coking Coal

Using briquettes made of non-coking coal and ore fines, the low-shaft distillation furnace is in continuous production. The new furnace is only one third the size of conventional blast furnaces, yet tonnages of iron from both units are equal.

By B. M. PEARSON, *Saxonhurst, England*

WITH the Humboldt distillation process, pig iron is produced in a low-shaft blast furnace. Ore fines and a noncoking coal are used in the form of briquettes. Noncoking coals rich in gas and tar are most suitable.

The process was first developed during the war by L. Weber in conjunction with the Kloeckner-Humboldt-Deutz concern in Germany on the conception of using ore-coal briquettes in a low-shaft blast furnace. The briquettes were first given a low-temperature distillation in a Kloeckner-Humboldt-Deutz carbonization oven and then processed in the low-shaft blast furnace. However, after the preliminary development work, the Kloeckner-Humboldt-Deutz concern decided to combine coking with the reduction in the blast furnace. By doing the low-temperature carbonization part of the work in the upper part of the shaft and utilizing the heat of the throat gas, the process became simpler and more commercial.

The low-shaft blast furnace has a long, rectangular or round cross-section. The height of the shaft from the hearth amounts to about 13 to 17 ft. The low-temperature carbonization takes place more or less in the same manner as in the Germal Spuelgas low-temperature carbonization processes, while in the middle and lower part of the shaft, the reduction and melting takes place.

Ore and other constituents and the coal are combined in the briquette. Both—the ore constituents as well as the coal—are finely crushed. After the carbonization, when the charge has progressed down the shaft, a sufficiently mechanically strong ore-coke briquette is formed. Because of the highly favorable surface properties, the material is particularly favorable to the reduction reactions and by virtue of the good degree of distribution of the ore and coke, excellent heat transfer conditions are obtained in the shaft. A specific temperature drop is caused as a result of these factors, which makes possible conducting these two separate processes in the shaft without oxygen enrichment of the blast.

Coal Tar Recovered

Throat gases leave the furnace at temperatures which are only slightly higher than the normal blast furnace throat gas temperatures. The carbonization products from the coal are contained in the gas as low-temperature distillation vapors and gas. The calorific value of this low-temperature distillation throat gas at 1400 to 1450 kg-cal is considerably higher than with normal throat gas. After dust cleaning, the hydrocarbons are removed from the throat gas in a condenser plant. The thick tar which is recovered here is used as a binding agent in the briquetting process. It can, however, be partly or completely replaced by lime or the clay portion of the burden.

The charging of the burden into the blast furnace is not conducted batchwise as normally, but continuously. The regulation and control of the furnace and melting process takes place similarly as with the blast furnace, by variation in

Continued

the blast volume and in the blast temperature or by altering the burden or fuel charging. As the throughput time only amounts to 1½ to 2 hr, even after a very short period, a change in the burden is shown in the melting results. The small capacity of the low-shaft blast furnace makes possible a daily production per cubic meter of internal furnace volume of about 3.5 tons. This is 2½ times as much as the best Swedish output at Domnarfvet.

In 1949, on the basis of results obtained with a semi-large scale plant, the Kloeckner-Humboldt-Deutz concern proceeded with the construction of a further experimental low-shaft blast furnace. This furnace is provided with a complete condenser layout for recovery of the valuable distillates from the throat gas. A recuperator, which is operated with the furnace gas, serves for preheating the blast wind and the iron is run into a small casting bed.

The metallurgical and technical operational results have fulfilled expectations. Burnt pyrites residue and bauxite iron mud were smelted in the above manner in this furnace with an unwashed gas coal whose ash content amounted to 15 pct. The object of the test run was to smelt and produce a commercially usable pig iron.

Standard Burden Used

The charging of the furnace (ore and fuel) was not altered during the test run. In the second half of the test, because of the small manganese content of the burden, a manganese addition in the form of a high-content manganese slag was added. The lime-silica ratio amounted on the average to 1.5. Over 30 castings of this product were investigated. The pig iron produced had the following average composition: 3.3 pct C; 2.8 pct Si; 0.2 to 1.8 pct Mn and 0.03 pct S. The composition of the slag was 44.3 pct CaO; 29.3 pct SiO_2; 18.5 pct Al_2O_3; 2.4 pct MgO and 2.5 pct S. The furnace was run hot by means of a generously proportioned fuel addition. The iron was produced as a gray, fine grained iron.

In order to follow more closely the degree of reduction, the characteristics $K_{Si\,s}$ and $K_{Mn\,Si}$ were calculated for all the iron test pieces, in relation to the lime-silica ratio of the slag and developed into "standard" curves according to T. Kootz and W. Oelsen.

The carbon content varied between 3.1 and 3.5 pct. The reason that the carbon content was not higher in spite of the high fuel charge and the basic slag may well be ascribed to the very small furnace unit and to the low-blast preheating by means of the recuperator. In this connection, mention may be made of the method of operation of the small Siegerlaender "cold blast" blast furnace, in which the smaller furnace unit, with lower air-preheating, showed a corresponding smaller carbon content in the iron. More detailed and also broader conclusions from the test results of this very comprehensive development work are not yet available. Also, here, only broad reference can be made to the wide field on which research has been conducted of the ore-coal briquetting, the low-temperature carbonization and the condensation of the low-temperature distillates which are all closely associated in the low-temperature carbonization-smelting process.

New Process Much Cheaper

Comparisons made of the costs of iron production in a low-temperature carbonization blast furnace plant for producing pig iron with iron production costs in a normal blast furnace plant, which has to operate with a high proportion of sinter material in the burden, show the former method is cheaper. This is substantiated even if the iron production costs are calculated for the low-temperature carbonization blast furnace process and compared with the production cost of the iron from a normal blast furnace, if both were operating on the same burden.

The capital installation costs of a low-temperature carbonization blast furnace plant will obviously be lower than with a normal blast furnace plant, because of the considerably smaller furnace volume required per unit of production, by the smaller blast requirement and the abolition of a coking plant. Of this latter unit, only the by-product condenser unit is required for the low-shaft blast furnace. The ore-sinter unit is replaced by the briquetting layout.

A cost analysis in the normal sense, loses its significance, if a broader view is taken in those countries where coking coals are not available and where only fine ore deposits are available. Such countries could develop and build up an iron industry with this process in an economical manner.

But also even in those countries possessing reserves of coking coals, the use of commercial noncoking coals has special technical significance if it be considered that these coals, which are more easily mined, can now be used in conjunction with a by-product recovery process. The by-products in addition appear on the credit side of the production sheet balance.

Cheap Ore Fines Available

Finally, attention should be drawn to the large reserves of ore fines deposits existing in the world and to the extensive amounts of "artificial" iron ores available, such as scale, pickling waste, etc., which can be worked up cheaply and in a satisfactory manner by this new smelting process. The process is still of course in the development stage. Technicians and research workers of the German and foreign iron producing countries are extremely interested in the possibilities presented.

Scrap Men Watch and Wait for ESA Price Ceilings

Rumors are rampant . . . The industry airs its views in Washington, final meeting on Jan. 11 . . . New schedule of $1.50 deducted from formula is strong rumor—*By Bill Lloyd.*

Cleveland—Rumors were more numerous than No. 1 bundles in major scrap centers this week as the trade awaited an announcement by Economic Stabilization Agency of new ceiling prices and regulations on scrap.

Industry representatives attending conferences in Washington last week presented their views on the differentials the trade considers necessary for ceilings on steel and railroad scrap.

They are expected to complete their "suggestion" meeting Jan. 11, offering proposed differentials on cast and foundry grades of scrap on that date.

May Include Differentials

ESA officials take the view that the government alone will take the initiative in establishing maximum base prices—when the time comes—but industry proposals for establishing differentials as to base points and grades may well be incorporated in the forthcoming regulation as submitted.

About 15 representatives of the scrap, steel and railroad industries together with government officials attended last week's 2-day "suggestion meeting."

Basically, current government thinking is geared to the idea of bringing up to date the former OPA Reg. 4 applying to scrap prices at the close of World War II.

In the wake of the meeting, the scrap market is on edge, waiting. Mills and foundries need tonnage. Shipments generally are poor. Foundries report they can't buy tonnage at a lower price despite the fact that the trade seems reconciled to a big price cut in the cast grades.

Rule of Thumb

Out of the maze of conflicting reports and rumors it would appear that a rule of thumb for figuring out the new price schedule could be—deduct $1.50 from the formula prices on openhearth, low phos and blast furnace grades.

In any event, the new price schedule will probably look something like this. Readers are warned the following prices are not official.

In Pittsburgh, Sharon, Warren and Youngstown, No. 1 heavy melting steel will be pegged at $45 per gross ton delivered, including brokerage.

Expected Prices

Other primary grades are expected to fall in line about as follows:

No. 2 heavy melting steel, $43; No. 2 bundles, $42; low phos, 5 ft, $47.50; railroad heavy melting No. 1, $46; rails, random, $47; rails, 3 ft and under, $50; rails, 18 in. and under, $53; rerolling,

Turn Page

NPA Limits Scrap Stocks

Washington — To maintain movement of scrap steel to mills, NPA issued order M-20, limiting inventories of regular dealers, brokers, auto wreckers, and any scrap producer to a 60-day or working level, whichever is least. Exempt are shipbreakers, and similar long-term operators, as well as those in seasonal operations for later shipment by water.

Seeks New England Gas Line OK

Washington—Northeastern Gas Transmission Co. has asked permission from the Federal Power Commission to extend a proposed New England line by 441 miles through Massachusetts, New Hampshire and Maine. Estimated cost of the line is $14 million.

DO Powers Delegated to CAA

Washington—The National Production Authority has delegated defense rating authority to the Civil Aeronautics Administration in order to assure steel, aluminum and other materials and equipment for the Civil Air Transport and the Federal Airways System.

DO Authority for Overseas Work

Washington—Authority to issue DO ratings for construction equipment needed for overseas projects has been granted to the Defense Dept. by the National Production Authority through amendment to Delegation 1, effective Dec. 29.

INDUSTRIAL SHORTS

SMALL MOTORS PLANT—A new small motors plant will be built in Union City, Ind., by WESTINGHOUSE ELECTRIC CORP. Production is scheduled to start in late 1951 and the plant will employ about 500 people at full operation.

MORE RIVETS — The Cherry Rivet Co., Los Angeles, has merged with the TOWNSEND CO., New Brighton, Pa., manufacturers of rivets. The Cherry Rivet Co. will operate as the Cherry Div. of Townsend with William B. Hubbard, former president of Cherry, as managing director.

OPEN HOUSE—An open house held last week by DEARBORN MOTORS CORP., opened their new three-story office building, agricultural research center and warehouse at 2500 East Maple Road, Birmingham, Mich.

ADDS LINE—The Delta Star Electric Co., Chicago, manufacturers of high voltage electrical equipment, has been acquired by the H. K. PORTER CO., INC., Pittsburgh. No change in the operation or management of Delta is contemplated.

CANADIAN OUTLET — The RELIANCE ELECTRIC & ENGINEERING (CANADA) LTD., Welland, Ont. has been established as successor to the Commonwealth Electric Corp., Ltd., The Commonwealth company which manufactures alternating current motors and transformers was acquired by the Reliance Electric & Engineering Co., Cleveland, last year.

SOUTHERN REP—The American Flexible Coupling Co., Erie, Pa., manufacturers of American flexible couplings and Amerigear couplings for power transmission, has appointed the H. H. KUMLER CO. of Houston and Tulsa, as representative in Texas and Oklahoma.

TESTER AGENT—The Ernst portable hardness tester made by Snow, Deakin & Co., Ltd., England, has named FRANK W. FAERY CO., Detroit, as sole agent for this item in Michigan as well as Toledo.

AEC PROJECT — Donald W. Neville, vice-president of F. H. McGRAW & CO., New York, will head up the company's new $350 million construction project for the Atomic Energy Commission at Paducah, Ky. The company states that the project involves the largest single construction contract ever awarded to a construction company. It will require nearly 10,000 men and will take more than 2 years to complete.

SOUTH AFRICAN PLANT—A plant near Johannesburg, South Africa, has been purchased by LINK-BELT AFRICA, LTD., to manufacture conveyer machinery and other Link-Belt products. John E. Petersen, formerly divisional engineer at the Chicago plant of the Link-Belt Co., has been appointed managing director of the South African company.

EXPANDING—The CONSOLIDATED IRON-STEEL MFG. CO. has purchased the Chicago Pneumatic Tool Co.'s former plant in Cleveland. This acquisition was for the expansion of their Republic Structural Iron Works, for its steel warehouse and heavy steel fabrication business.

LARGER QUARTERS — FOLLANSBEE STEEL CORP. will quadruple its warehouse space in Pittsburgh with acquisition of a building occupied until recently by the Dilworth Porter Div. of Republic Steel Corp.

DISTRIBUTOR—Trabon Engineering Corp., Cleveland, has appointed the RITTER ENGINEERING CO., Pittsburgh, as exclusive distributor in the Pittsburgh district for their centralized lubrication systems.

$52; specialties, $50; No. 1 cast, $50; machine shop turnings, $35; shoveling turnings, $39; structurals, 3 ft, $48; structurals, 2 ft, $50; structurals, 1 ft, $51.

In Chicago, Philadelphia, Cincinnati and Buffalo the price of No. 1 heavy melting steel will probably be $1 or so under the $45 Pittsburgh price. Base price differentials, similar to those of the late formula, will apply. For example, price of No. 1 heavy in Cleveland will probably be $44.

If the foregoing prices prove to be official, it appears that an umbrella has been put over the crushers, in the form of a $4 premium for shovelings. Under the formula, this premium was $2.

It is believed the new price schedules will be announced about Jan. 15, or as soon after the Jan. 11 meeting as possible, and will become effective Feb. 1. This will give mills and shippers about 2 weeks to clean up hold orders.

Old orders still outstanding by Feb. 1 may be canceled, it is possible.

Expect Inventory Controls

It is expected inventory controls will be included in the new regulations. Also, it has been recommended (by foundries) that mills not be permitted to buy electric furnace tonnage unless they have electric furnace capacity, or in fact, any foundry grade of scrap.

Still in doubt is the brokers' commission. Brokers want a dollar, but it is believed that brokerage will be 75¢.

Points like Kansas City and Houston may be included in the new base schedule.

Allocation regulations are also expected to be a part of the new regulations. It is generally recognized that allocations are an essential part of scrap price control—that they will apply only when a consumer is in trouble.

Demand for scrap, with or without price control, will probably reach a new high this year. There is serious doubt that supply will be adequate.

Tin Restriction Hastens Hot Dip Method End

Was dying slow death anyway . . . February order limiting use of tin renews interest of canmakers in 1.00 lb unenameled electrolytic tinplate . . . May sacrifice speed for defense.

Pittsburgh—The need for conservation of tin will hasten the demise of the hot dip method of producing tinplate, which was dying a slow death anyway.

A government order restricting use of tin for civilian purposes beginning next month (THE IRON AGE, Dec. 28, '50, p. 81) renewed interest of can makers in a 1.00 lb unenameled electrolytic tinplate as a substitute for 1.25 and 1.50 lb hot dip.

Look for It in '51

On the basis of fairly large-scale tests, some of the major can companies are seriously interested.

However, on most electrolytic lines this heavier grade is produced only at considerable penalty in speed of the line. Nevertheless, it was believed that certain equipment may be available to produce the heavier coating weights, which could possibly include some intermediate coating weights between the present maximum of at least .75 and 1.00. Thus, mills, of course, will do everything within reason in the interest of national defense.

Production of hot dip tinplate in relation to electrolytic has been declining steadily in recent years. In the first 9 months of 1950 the product mix was 54.0 electrolytic, 36.1 hot dip, 9.9 black plate. This compares with 52.0 for hot dip and 24.0 for electrolytic in 1946. In 1949 the percentages were 48.0 electrolytic, 41.0 hot dip.

Tin Conservation Factor

This trend had been expected to continue at about the same pace, but the tin conservation program will speed it up. It would not be surprising if some present hot dip producers tried to abandon this product for all practical purposes.

On the basis of production in the first 9 months of 1950, shipments for the year were probably between 112 and 114 million base boxes. If tin is available, the industry probably will produce between 119 and 120 million base boxes this year. New electrolytic lines will be coming into production in the last half of '51.

East Germany Plans Steelworks

Berlin — Red-dominated East Germany will build a new State steel works at Leipzig, on the site of the former Hasag armament plant. Operation is scheduled for the third quarter this year. Also planned is a new steel foundry at Mettallgusswerk, in Leipzig, and expansion of Electrostahlgusswerk's cast steel production by 30 pct. The Brandenburg steel plant is operating a fourth new openhearth furnace.

Open New Scrap Metals Yard

New Haven, Conn. — Starting operations on Jan. 2, Eastcoast Scrap Iron and Steel Co., Inc., a subsidiary of Schiavone-Bonomo Corp., Jersey City, has been established at 299 Chapel St., here.

It is handling all grades of scrap iron, steel, and metals and has a large Galland-Henning hydraulic press for all grades of baling materials, shears, truck and travelling cranes. The yard is located on water for barge shipments and has a railroad siding.

Ask Data on Barium Products

Washington — The barium carbonate industry has been asked for data to assist in drawing up an allocation order which will assure an adequate supply for radar and other defense products and equalize the supply for nondefense. The proposed order will also affect distribution of barium chloride for steelmaking and manufacture of magnesium.

May Develop Iron Ore Land

Washington — Public domain lands in Minnesota may now be prospected and developed for mining of iron ore under new regulations approved by the Dept. of Interior. The regulations governing leases and permits from Interior's Bureau of Land Management are similar to those provided under general mining laws for leasing of minerals on acquired lands.

Defense Contracts to Metalworking Industry

Selected Contracts, Week of Jan. 8, 1951

Item	Quantity	Value	Company
Recorder-reproducer	300	$ 150,000	Sound, Inc., Chicago
Washing machines..	33	123,295	Chicago Dryer Co., Chicago
Test sets............	460	1,000,000	General Communications Co., Boston
Automatic pilot.....	27	273,000	Sperry Gyroscope Co., Great Neck, N. Y.
Tubes, electron.....	8000	270,400	Amperex Electronic Corp., Brooklyn, N. Y.
Tubes, electron.....	43,000	810,988	General Electric Co., Schenectady
Tubes, electron.....	50,000	862,500	General Electric Co., Schenectady
Drill, pneumatic....	.....	138,020	Aro Equipment Corp., Bryan, Ohio
Drill, pneumatic....	.....	90,000	Air Speed Tool Co., Los Angeles
Air welders.........	.....	91,000	General Electric Co., Dayton
Airplane kits.......	.....	100,000	North American Aviation, Los Angeles
Receiver-transmitter	.....	2,761,725	Hoffman Radio Corp., Los Angeles
Aircraft kits........	.....	100,000	Fairchild Aircraft & Engine Corp., Hagerstown, Md.
Kits	.....	264,105	Denison Engineering Co., Columbus
Block assy.	.....	224,787	New York Air Brake Co., New York
Aircraft heater assy.	.....	99,347	Surface Combustion Corp., Toledo
Valves, hydraulic...	.....	235,748	Saval Div. of Wm. R. Whittaker Co., Los Angeles
Parts, telescope.....	.....	1,140,000	Gilbert & Barker Mfg. Co., West Springfield, Mass.
Parts, telescope.....	.....	404,800	Universal Camera Corp., New York
Sight unit, M-34....	.....	550,165	The Auto-Soler Co., Atlanta
Fuel, water pump parts	.....	96,872	Borg-Warner Corp., Bedford, Ohio

National's Eastern Mill Rivals U. S. Steel's

Will have about 1¾ million ton capacity . . . About equal to U. S. Steel mill nearby . . . Both mills will probably expand later . . . Bethlehem advantage seen cut—*By John Delaney.*

Pittsburgh — National Steel Corp.'s new eastern mill near Camden, N. J., will have an initial annual ingot capacity of approximately 1¾ million tons. Thus it will compare in size with the mill U. S. Steel Corp. is building at Morrisville, Pa.

The new National plant will be situated on a rectangular 2000-acre plot on the Delaware River at Paulsboro, ten miles south of Camden and opposite the Philadelphia Southwest Airport. This is about 35 miles downriver from the site of the new U. S. Steel plant. It is considered likely that National will set up a new subsidiary to operate the eastern mill.

Expansion Likely Later

These two mills are likely to be expanded in size later. Initial capacity of the U. S. Steel plant will be 1,800,000 ingot tons, but eventually this may be lifted much higher—when ore is available—provided demand warrants it.

National Steel will invest approximately $400 million in its eastern operation. As a contribution to the defense effort, part or all of this cost will be covered by a Certificate of Necessity permitting amortization over 5 years.

The plant will include at least two blast furnaces, openhearths, slabbing-blooming mill, hot strip mill, sheet mill, an electrolytic tinplate line, an electro galvanizing line, by-product coke ovens, annealing equipment, and other integrated mill operations.

Ore for the blast furnaces will come by ocean-going carriers from the new Labrador-Quebec iron ore fields. This ore is perhaps 3 years away, but the mill will be turning out steel before that. The company will have finishing mills in operation meanwhile.

Ernest T. Weir, chairman of Na-

tional, said the new plant will provide "substantial" tonnages of steel for an expansion of domestic and foreign business. National's chief export trade product is tinplate.

The National and U. S. Steel mills will drastically alter the competitive picture in the East, where Bethlehem Steel heretofore has enjoyed an advantage. National also will be in a better position to market its products in the West.

No date has been set for start of construction of National's mill. U. S. Steel Corp. plans to break ground in about 2 months.

Present ingot capacity of National is 4,500,000 tons, but expansion plans exclusive of the new mill will boost this to 5,500,000 tons early next year. An additional 1,750,000 tons in the new plant would bring the total to 7,250,000 tons. This would make National the nation's fourth largest producer.

Few Midwest Suppliers Heed Rollback Order

Very few have rolled back prices to Dec. 1 levels . . . Determining validity of hikes would mean wide investigation . . . Suppliers seek raw material rollbacks—*By Gene Beaudet.*

Chicago—A check of manufacturers in the Chicago industrial area reveals that very few of their suppliers have rolled back their prices to Dec. 1 levels in response to the government's request to do so. Either their price increases were justified in accordance with the ESA's voluntary rollback order or they are just ignoring it.

To determine whether these increases are allowable under the present pricing standards would

"New machine—we're waiting for somebody to tell us how it works."

necessitate investigating a great number of companies supplying thousands of products to the metalworking industry. The rollback order will remain ineffective until some teeth are put into it.

Some Rescind Rises

Although some manufacturers of finished products in the area have rescinded price increases put into effect after Dec. 1, they did so without knowing definitely whether they were required to do so in the face of rising labor and material costs.

When the rollback order was announced on Dec. 19, a great many suppliers had already increased their prices during the first half of the month. Price boosts ranged from 5 to 10 pct on a variety of products from paper bags to heavy chemicals and from fasteners to forgings.

Some believe the order was issued not so much to effect a price rollback as to put a damper on future price increases. Suppliers who have increased prices after Dec. 1 claim they cannot restore former prices unless those of raw materials are also restored. When they can be assured a steady flow of materials at prices which will enable them to sell at Dec. 1 prices they will roll back their own, they say. Also, in this seller's paradise no one is going to lower his prices if his competitor isn't going to do the same.

Just Following Trend

Many of the suppliers hitched their price increase to the recent hike in steel prices and the rising cost of nonferrous metals. Unless these come down they will not budge. Since the government does not wish to jeopardize the wage gains which accompanied the steel price rise, steel prices probably won't be altered with the result that nothing will be done about other price increases that followed them. Furthermore, both suppliers and manufacturers of finished products claim their prices have not kept abreast of material and labor costs since the Korean War started and that any price increases since then only partly make up for them.

The following are a few of the products supplied manufacturers whose prices have jumped since Dec. 1 and have not yet been rescinded: foundry products, forgings, fasteners, electric motors and controls, ball bearings, gasoline engines, locomotive specialties, air brakes, coil springs, pipe fittings, hose, rubber tubing, soda ash, acetic acid, lubricating oils, paper bags, and insulation materials.

Buyers Are Hard-Pressed

Among the few items whose price increases were rescinded were air filters and small tools such as diamond and abrasive wheels.

Meanwhile, industrial buyers are harder pressed than ever to keep their plants adequately supplied with the many items going into their companies' finished products. Deliveries are becoming slower and more uncertain. Forward buying, which has become more and more extended since the

Korean War started, has gone out as far as practicable since the government is likely to step in at any time and restrict supplies.

At the beginning of December,

several large companies in the area which were buying 3 months in advance at the start of the Korean War, stepped up their forward buying from 5 to 6 months.

Local Market Mill to Be Built in Tennessee

Is new entry into future race for steel markets . . . Use local scrap, serve local market . . . Plan two electric furnaces . . . Mill will have freight umbrella protection—By Bill Packard.

Nashville, Tenn. — Tennessee Steel Corp. has just been incorporated in Nashville to build an electric furnace mill in the vicinity of Oneida, Scott County, Tenn. This marks a new entry in the fu-

Answer to High Rail Rates

New York—One answer to today's high freight rates is the erection of small steel plants in areas now remote from mills.

Under proper conditions electric furnaces, making carbon bar and flat-rolled products plus fast continuous mills permit steel costs as low as those of large integrated plants.

Under f.o.b. mill pricing such plants could sell their products in a market protected by a freight umbrella.

For a complete technical discussion of this type mill see THE IRON AGE, Apr. 6, 1950, p. 90.

ture race for steel markets. A small, low-cost mill, designed to serve a local market, will consume local scrap and sell its products in a protected market.

Heart of the new plant will be two 25-ton top-charge electric furnaces and one smaller unit. Finishing facilities will include a rod mill and strip mill. Annual capacity is rated at 100,000 tons, not counting a rail rerolling and slitting mill of 36,000 tons capacity.

Wire Mill Possibility

Finished products will include bar shapes and sections, household and agricultural pipe, hot-rolled strip, merchant and reinforcing bars, mine rails, cross ties,

mine and fence posts. A wire mill is among future possibilities.

Total cost of the mill is expected to be only about $5 million to $6 million, or about $50 per ton of capacity. Completely integrated new steel capacity has been estimated by various industry sources to cost as much as $200 to $300 a ton.

Financing is expected to be at least 80 pct private; there is a possibility that an RFC loan covering up to 20 pct of the cost will be sought. An application for a Certificate of Necessity is now being prepared. If approved, it will provide tax benefits in the form of 5-year amortization of the facilities.

Freight Umbrella Protection

The new mill will be designed to meet growing steel needs of industries in Tennessee, the Carolinas and adjoining states. Backers of the mill say they will aim at the local market by concentrating on prompt delivery, competitive prices, and production tailored to meet customers' special requirements.

Actually, the mill is being located in a market that will have the protection of a freight umbrella. The freight advantage results from the shift from basing point to f.o.b. method of selling steel. The competitive freight advantage will be equal to the difference in freight rates between this and other producing points to consumers in this area.

A leading figure in the new corporation is Dr. Huston St. Clair, of Tazewell, Va., an industrialist whose other interests include Jewell Ridge Coal Corp. and Virginia Smokeless Coal Co. Some years ago the St. Clair group acquired control of the Oneida & Western Railroad. Very low cost power is available from nearby Tennessee Valley Authority.

Piper Engineering Co. of Pittsburgh in association with Warren Worthington are preparing plant layouts and recommending equipment for the mill.

Harrison Heads DPA as Straw Boss to Wilson

Truman forms new Defense Production Administration to carry out policies of Wilson's ODM . . . Forms board to advise Wilson . . . Present agencies hold only administrative powers.

Washington—President Truman last week by executive order created a new agency, the Defense Production Administration, for the purpose of consolidating and speeding production and other mobilization efforts.

The new agency will be headed by William H. Harrison, erstwhile head of the National Production Authority. He thus becomes second in command to Mobilization Director Charles E. Wilson and the straw boss for carrying out policies and directives of Wilson's office.

Board to Advise Wilson

At the same time, the order also created a Defense Mobilization Board to assist and advise Wilson in all his major jobs—production, transportation, manpower, economic stabilization, and foreign aid. In addition to Wilson as chairman, the DMB will be comprised of the secretaries of Agriculture, Commerce, Defense, Interior, Labor, Treasury, and the chairmen of the Board of Governors of the Federal Reserve Board, Reconstruction Finance Corp., and National Security Resources Board.

"The Office of Defense Mobilization will determine general policies very much like the Office of War Mobilization did in World War II," Mr. Wilson said, "and the DPA will have about the same powers as the former WPB."

However, while WPB did both programming and operating in its own right, the new DPA will do the programming and leave the actual administration in the hands of the present operating agencies.

For instance, NPA currently remains as part of the Commerce Dept. but under a new chief, scheduled to be Manly Fleischman, erstwhile general counsel to the agency, but under the control of DPA, which assumes the authority for priorities, allocations and so on. The NPA will continue to issue orders but only after approval by Gen. Harrison as DPA head.

Likewise, most of the authority or power over production loans, procurement, certification of expansion plans for fast tax write-offs, etc.—previously held by other agencies—have also been moved over to the new DPA.

Insofar as military procurement is concerned, however, neither the

"Fix me up an ironclad contract I can wiggle out of if I want to."

ODM nor the DPA will have anything to do with the actual placing of orders. But both Wilson and Harrison can prod defense buying or report back to the White House if they think military purchasing is hitting the economy too hard.

With respect to food, the DPA can order diversion of agricultural products to industrial programs, such as grain for making industrial alcohol. But authority over all other food programs, including food for human and animal consumption, and domestic distribution of farm equipment and commercial fertilizer, remains within the control of the Agriculture Dept.

NSRB Stripped of Powers

The NSRB is stripped of much of its policy-making powers but it still will report directly to the White House on certain planning matters. As for operational matters, the chairman now merely becomes just a member of the advisory DMB.

The new DPA will also have overall direction and control over defense production and mobilization activities within other departments and agencies than those previously mentioned. These include:

Defense Transport Administration (domestic surface transport, storage, and port facilities); Commerce Dept. (air, coastwise, intercoastal, and overseas shipping) and the Interior Dept. (petroleum, solid fuels, minerals and metals, and power).

Cooperation with DPA

The Labor Dept. will work out labor and manpower problems and programs in cooperation with the DPA where defense and essential civilian production is concerned.

The Economic Stabilization Agency will work in cooperation with but independently of the DPA, going directly to Wilson, in working out its price-wage programs and controls.

DEFENSE MOBILIZATION ORGANIZATION

THE PRESIDENT

OFFICE OF DEFENSE MOBILIZATION
Director

EXECUTIVE OFFICE OF THE PRESIDENT

National Security Resources Board
National Security Council
Council of Economic Advisors
Bureau of the Budget

DEFENSE MOBILIZATION BOARD

Director of ODM, Chairman,
Secretaries of Treasury, Defense, Commerce,
Interior, Agriculture, and Labor, and Chairmen
of RFC, NSRB, and the Board of Governors of the
Federal Reserve System

ECONOMIC STABILIZATION AGENCY
Administrator

Prices	Wages

CREDIT CONTROLS

Federal Reserve Board | Housing and Home Finance Agency

Controls consumer credit and real estate construction credit

DEPARTMENT OF LABOR
Secretary

Formulates plans, programs, and policies, and utilize the public employment services system for meeting defense and essential civilian labor requirements

DEFENSE PRODUCTION ADMINISTRATION

Administrator
Production Executive Committee
Establishes overall production priorities
Determines program feasibility
Sets production program goals
Determine scope of production expansion
Estimates labor supply requirements for production programs
Represents U.S. on combined boards
Secures production plans from all agencies and develops methods and procedures for their execution

Requirements and Allocations Advisory Committee

FINANCIAL AGENTS UNDER EXECUTIVE ORDER NO.10161
Federal Reserve Board

Reconstruction Finance Corporation

General Services Administration

Make loans, act as fiscal agents, and make purchases on behalf of other agencies to promote measures for the expansion of productive capacity and supply

DEPARTMENT OF AGRICULTURE
Secretary

Food for human and animal consumption and domestic distribution of farm equipment and commercial fertilizer

Food for industrial use

DEPARTMENT OF INTERIOR
Secretary

Petroleum
Solid Fuels
Power
Minerals and Metals
Commercial Fisheries

DEPARTMENT OF COMMERCE
Secretary

Air transportation, Coastwise, Intercoastal, and Overseas Shipping

Production and distribution of industrial products (except as otherwise designated)

DEFENSE TRANSPORT ADMINISTRATION
Administrator

Domestic surface transportation, Storage, and Port Facilities

DEPARTMENT OF DEFENSE
Secretary

Develops requirements for military procurement and production programs; procures military equipment; develops stockpile programs

STATE
HOUSING AND HOME FINANCE AGENCY
FEDERAL SECURITY AGENCY
ATOMIC ENERGY COMMISSION
OTHERS

OTHER AGENCIES HAVING MOBILIZATION ACTIVITIES

PRIORITIES, ALLOCATIONS AND REQUISITIONING OPERATIONS

Harry S. Truman

Charles E. Wilson
ODM

W. H. Harrison
DPA

Alan Valentine
ESA

Stuart Symington
NSRB

Overall direction, control, and coordination of mobilization activities

Direction and control over defense production activities

The Iron Age

Handling Costs Cut, Pallets Eliminated by Fingerlift Truck

Milwaukee—Pallets have been outmoded and a marked reduction in material handling costs has been effected with introduction of a new crate handling method at A. O. Smith Water Heater Div., Kankakee, Ill.

Manpower savings of over 50 pct, elimination of pallets and pallet maintenance, lower lift truck maintenance, and less damage to crates and contents are claimed for the new "fingerlift" handling method developed at the Smith plant.

A 5-man team is doing the work formerly done by 22 operators, handlers and stockroom repairmen. Less waste space in warehouses with fewer aisles and additional stacking height is claimed.

Lift trucks fitted with a special fingerlift attachment eliminate the need for pallets and fork type lifting arm.

NO PALLETS: One man moves and stacks three crated water heaters in smooth operation. Formerly one man operated truck and two men stacked heaters on pallets.

FINGERS: Heart of the cost-cutting fingerlift crate handling device is row of spring actuated fingers in position to lift a crated water heater at the A. O. Smith Water Heater Div., Kankakee, Ill.

LINE TO CAR: One man driving fingerlift equipped truck moves crated heaters directly from assembly line and stacks them in boxcar.

Spring loaded fingers are mounted on a horizontal shaft. Pressure on the finger tips tilts them backwards. A vertical apron serves as a rest when the truck mast leans back. The whole assembly shifts right and left.

In operation the truck moves forward until the apron meets the crate. Some fingers protrude between the crate's vertical slats while others are pushed back. As the truck mast is raised, fingers between the slats engage a horizontal cleat or the crate top and raise the crate. The tilted fingers slide up the slats out of the way.

In a typical production line operation one man and truck place six crates on a dolly. With additional crates on the fingerlift, the truck and dolly move to the warehouse where the crates are stacked by the operator.

Formerly two men manhandled crates to dolly and truck, and two men stacked crates in the warehouse.

Two men operating fingerlift trucks between production line and boxcar can regularly load 1600 heaters into 10 cars in 7½ hours. This includes stacking in the car without use of pallets.

Arrangements for marketing the fingerlift have been made with Clark Equipment Co. of Battle Creek, Mich.

U.S. Has Copper Scrap Price Ceiling Order in Drafting Stage

Washington—Government is seriously considering price ceilings on copper scrap. Such an order is in the drafting stage, officials hinted.

No similar action is now being planned for primary copper, however. Officials of the Economic Stabilization Agency believe primary prices are stable enough.

ESA officials, following an industry-government meeting on copper here last week said they had received "assurances from members of the industry that they would not advance their prices without first notifying the ESA."

Industry representatives pointed out at the government meeting that wages comprise the largest single factor in determining current copper costs.

Pittsburgh Steel Expansion To Boost Ingot Capacity 46 Pct

Pittsburgh — Pittsburgh Steel Co. announced an expansion program that will increase ingot capacity by 488,000 tons to 1,560,000 tons—a rise of 46 pct.

The company also will build a new continuous hot and cold-rolled strip-sheet mill as well as the new high-lift blooming-slabbing mill ordered last August. This will put Pittsburgh Steel in the sheet and strip business for the first time.

Ingot capacity will be increased by enlarging the existing 12 open-hearth furnaces at Monessen, Pa., from the present 150-ton heat capacity to 250-ton capacity. Pig iron capacity will also go up.

A certificate of necessity covering $36,338,450 of the cost has been granted by NSRB.

toughen metal

improve surface

end stock waste

with

TORRINGTON SWAGERS

The Torrington Rotary Swaging Machine delivers 4000 hammer blows a minute...reduces, sizes, rounds, points and tapers rod, wire and tubing... work-hardens metal for toughness and resilience...produces a burnished surface...utilizes every bit of stock.

Torrington Swager performance is based on our 42 years of swaging experience. Send the coupon for your free copy of the booklet illustrating the machines and describing the art of rotary swaging.

THE TORRINGTON COMPANY
Swager Department
555 Field Street · Torrington, Conn.

For a free copy of this booklet, send the coupon today.

Please send a copy of "The Torrington Swaging Machine" to:

Name_____

Firm_____

Address_____5

November Iron & Steel Production by Districts
As Reported to American Iron & Steel Institute

BLAST FURNACE CAPACITY AND PRODUCTION —NET TONS	Number of Companies	Annual Blast Furnace Capacity July 1, 1950	PIG IRON		FERRO-MANGANESE AND SPIEGEL		TOTAL		Pct of Capacity	
			Nov.	Year to Date	Nov.	Year to Date	Nov.	Year to Date	Nov.	Year to Date
Distribution by Districts:										
Eastern.........	12	13,353,580	1,072,553	11,513,516	20,092	287,023	1,092,645	11,800,539	99.4	96.6
Pitts.-Youngstn..	16	26,735,520	1,844,894	21,896,633	26,609	230,634	1,871,503	22,127,267	85.1	90.4
Cleve.-Detroit....	6	7,044,600	539,431	6,220,587	....	....	539,431	6,220,587	93.1	96.5
Chicago........	7	15,897,190	1,206,572	12,530,250	....	....	1,206,572	12,530,250	92.2	86.1
Southern........	9	5,215,640	437,438	4,610,741	9,287	91,632	446,725	4,702,373	104.1	99.3
Western.........	4	3,375,200	229,962	2,410,119	....	....	229,962	2,410,119	82.2	78.6
Total.........	37	71,621,730	5,330,850	59,181,846	55,988	609,289	5,386,838	59,791,135	91.4	91.3

STEEL CAPACITY AND PRODUCTION —NET TONS	Number of Companies	Annual Steel Capacity July 1, 1950	TOTAL STEEL		Pct of Capacity		Alloy Steel* (Incl. under total steel)		Carbon Ingots-Hot Topped (Incl. under total steel)	
			Nov.	Year to Date	Nov.	Year to Date	Nov.	Year to Date	Nov.	Year to Date
Distribution by Districts:										
Eastern.........	24	20,387,460	1,589,865	17,103,875	94.8	92.9	123,324	1,181,705	304,056	3,133,642
Pitts.-Youngstn..	33	39,127,940	2,955,583	34,324,894	91.8	95.8	406,759	4,435,195	321,259	3,670,789
Cleve.-Detroit....	8	9,333,460	760,478	8,458,403	99.0	99.0	49,877	513,414	93,327	1,103,346
Chicago........	15	21,351,700	1,828,094	19,166,450	104.1	99.5	150,238	1,463,409	240,828	2,633,680
Southern........	8	4,588,320	396,548	4,385,107	105.0	104.8	2,461	48,803	7,707	57,703
Western.........	11	5,774,620	481,283	4,914,750	101.3	93.7	14,493	94,866	12,876	95,793
Total.........	78	100,563,500	8,011,851	88,353,479	96.8	96.6	747,152	7,737,392	980,053	10,694,953

* For the purpose of this report, alloy steel includes stainless and any other steel containing one or more of the following elements in the designated amounts: Manganese in excess of 1.65%, and Silicon in excess of 0.60%, and Copper in excess of 0.60%. It also includes steel containing the following elements in any amount specified or known to have been added to obtain a desired alloying effect: Aluminum, Chromium, Cobalt, Columbium, Molybdenum, Nickel, Titanium, Tungsten, Vanadium, Zirconium, and other alloying elements.

Republic, Hanna Seek Venezulean Ore

Have option on Maria Louisa (Sabeneta hill) claim . . . Exploration continuing . . . No deal yet on San Isidro . . . U. S. Steel to start construction on ore facilities this year.

Caracas, Venezuela — Tightening of the defense lines in the United States of America has placed the spotlight on iron ore discoveries in this country. It is to be expected that the close cooperation already given by the government to firms from North America will be continued.

Exploration is going forward by M. A. Hanna Co. and Republic Steel Corp. on their Maria Louisa concession at Sabeneta hill. That property is not far from the U. S. Steel's Cerro Bolivar concession. The two North American firms have an option on the Maria Louisa claim which was originally granted to Sr. Tabeo Schoen on a 50-year lease with right to renew for another 50 years.

The large San Isidro mountain, which is estimated to contain as much as 400 million or more tons of high-grade ore, is still the subject of interest to North American industry. So far no commitments have been made by the government but negotiations may be resumed in the near future.

Hauled by Rail to Port

If the Maria Louisa options turn out satisfactory to Republic and M. A. Hanna, it is likely that ore will eventually be moved to the contemplated U. S. Steel railroad and hauled over that line to seaport. Latest reports on U. S. Steel activities point to a readiness to start construction of needed facilities in 1951.

Main planning and design work on all parts of the giant undertaking at Cerro Bolivar are well along towards completion. Ore may be moving from there by mid 1954.

List U.S. Steel Co. Officers; Is Result of Subsidiaries Merger

Pittsburgh—Officers of United States Steel Co., resulting from the merger of Carnegie-Illinois Steel Corp., U. S. Steel Corp. of Delaware, H. C. Frick Coke Co., and U. S. Coal & Coke Co., follow:

B. F. Fairless, president; executive vice-presidents: C. F. Hood, operations; D. F. Austin, commercial; R. M. Blough, law and secretary; M. W. Reed, engineering and raw materials; G. W. Rooney, accounting.

Assistant executive vice-presidents: F. R. Burnette, engineering; B. S. Chapple, Jr., commercial; vice-presidents: R. C. Cooper, industrial engineering; J. D. Darby, sales; C. A. Ilgenfritz, purchases; R. W. Hyde, treasurer.

H. E. Isham, asst. executive vice-president, accounting; S. M. Jenks, vice-president, manufacturing; S. B. Kingham, asst. executive vice-president, accounting; K. L. Konnerth, vice-president, coal division; L. L. Lewis, associate general solicitor.

J. E. Lose, asst. executive vice-president, operations; vice-presidents: E. E. Moore, industrial relations administration; L. M. Parsons, Washington; E. G. Plowman, traffic; B. L. Rawlins, associate general solicitor and asst. secretary; R. F. Sentner, asst. executive vice-president, commercial; J. A. Stephens, vice-president, industrial relations.

Vice-presidents: G. M. Thursby, industrial relations administration, coal division; W. A. Walker, accounting; A. C. Wilby, Chicago; J. L. Young, chief engineer, R. Zimmerman, research.

Former chains on these mechanical picklers used to fail in 2½ months. Monel chains are giving 1½ years' service 24 hours a day in hot, 10% sulfuric acid. Average load is 5 tons. Reduced shut-downs have increased output substantially.

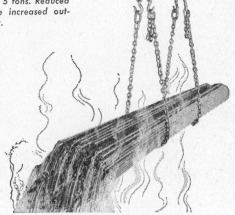

Monel sling chains handling 4 to 5 tons of steel tubing. 75 such chains are in this plant. Where 1¼" chains of another metal failed in 9 months, these Monel chains have already served 6 years.

The **Life is longer**
The **Weight is less**
The **Metal is Monel**

Monel® Pickling Chain — like *any* piece of Monel pickling equipment — pays for itself.

Any pickling-room foreman or superintendent who has used Monel will tell you that.

For he knows that Monel's superior resistance to corrosion by hot pickling acids and fumes means longer life and greater safety.

He knows, too, that the higher strength of Monel makes it possible to use *lighter* chain that saves up to 20% in dead weight.

Monel link chain is formed from hot-rolled rod, and welded. The welds retain all the strength and all the corrosion resistance of the parent metal.

Regular Monel chain ranges in size from ¼" to 1¼". In addition, special types of sprocket chain, as well as a complete line of accessories such as hooks, lifting links, U-bolts and open links are available.

Whether you are using chain as slings or in mechanical picklers, you'll get the maximum in safety, long life and light weight, if you make that chain *Monel!*

Mechanical pickler chains made of Monel for use in the pickling of steel pipe prior to galvanizing. Chains are so designed to permit quick and easy replacement of any individual part.

Although Nickel and Nickel Alloys are currently in short supply INCO advertisements will continue to bring you news of new products, applications, and technical developments.

THE INTERNATIONAL NICKEL COMPANY, INC.
67 Wall Street, New York 5, N. Y.

EMBLEM OF SERVICE

Monel
PICKLING
EQUIPMENT

extra life
extra capacity
extra safety

does sweat
make a product better?

Yesterday's blacksmith, for all his poetic sweat, couldn't begin to match, in quality or quantity, the output of a Clearing forging press.

Human labor is too costly to be wasted. Today's manufacturer must make machinery do more and more of his productive work. When he turns to Clearing presses for forging or other metal-shaping operations, he obtains maximum cost efficiency and usually an improved product as well.

That's because Clearing has carried press development far beyond the mere substitution of machines for muscle. There's a practical and economical answer to your particular metalworking problem.

Why don't you ask us?

CLEARING MACHINE CORPORATION
6499 WEST 65th STREET • CHICAGO 38, ILLINOIS

One man and this Clearing press can forge 450 connecting rods in 60 minutes.

CLEARING PRESSES
THE WAY TO EFFICIENT MASS PRODUCTION

STEEL

CONSTRUCTION NEWS

Recent fabricated steel awards included the following:

4730 Tons, East Boston, Mass., elevated structure and new highways from Porter and London Sts., East Boston, Bremen St., Neptune Road to McLellan Highway (extensions to the East Boston Expressway), Charles A. Fritz, district engineer. Completion date Oct. 15, 1952 through V. Barletta Co., Jamaica Plain, Mass., to Harris Structural Steel Co., New York.

1000 Tons, Jersey City, N. J., railroad bridge for Erie RR, to American Bridge Co., Pittsburgh.

606 Tons, Lehigh County, Pa., State Highway and Bridge Authority, bridges on Route LR 771 Sect. 2, to Bethlehem Steel Co., Bethlehem.

450 Tons, Philadelphia manufacturing buildings for Heintz Mfg. Co., to Bethlehem Fabricating Co., Bethlehem.

387 Tons, Berkshire, Vt., 3 span continuous W F Beam bridge, concrete floor beginning at routes 105 and 118 at East Berkshire. G. A. Pierce, St. Albans, Vt., district highway commissioner. Completion date Dec. 1, 1951. Oscar L. Olson, Montpelier, Vt., low bidder.

253 Tons, Darien, Conn., 3 span continuous rolled beam bridge. Paul Bacco and Son Inc., Stamford, Conn., low bidder.

253 Tons, Waukesha County, Wis., bridge project F 06-1/24/ to Milwaukee Bridge Co.

225 Tons, Scranton, Pa., store for Kresge Co., to Anthracite Bridge Co., Scranton.

140 Tons, Vineland, N. J., retail store for Sears Roebuck & Co., to Robinson Iron and Steel Co.

110 Tons, Marinette County, Wis., bridge project 5-0544/1/ to Milwaukee Bridge Co.

110 Tons, Philadelphia, State Police Barracks, to Max Corchin & Son, Philadelphia.

Recent fabricated steel inquiries included the following:

6000 Tons, Cromby, Pa., powerhouse for Philadelphia Electric Co., bids due Jan. 19.

1300 Tons, Newark, N. J., highway bridge for New Jersey State Highway Commission, Route 25, Sect. 1-G, bids due Jan. 23.

1000 Tons, Trenton, N. J., additional construction for U. S. Navy aeroturbine laboratory, bids due Jan. 25.

Recent reinforcing bar awards included the following:

699 Tons, East Boston, Mass., extensions to East Boston Expressway through V. Barletta Co., Jamaica Plain, to Bethlehem Steel Co., Bethlehem.

650 Tons, Milwaukee, Athletic Stadium, to Joseph T. Ryerson & Son, Chicago.

550 Tons, Newport, Ky., Atomic Energy Research Building, to H. J. Baker.

535 Tons, Crawford County, Pa., paving LR 82, to Bethlehem Steel Co.

525 Tons, Montgomery County, Pa., Pennsylvania Dept. of Highways, Route 769, Sect. 1D and 2A, F. A. Canuso & Son, Philadelphia, general contractor.

470 Tons, Louisville, Philip Morris and Co., to U. S. Steel Supply Co.

450 Tons, Rochester, Minn., service center building, to U. S. Steel Supply Co.

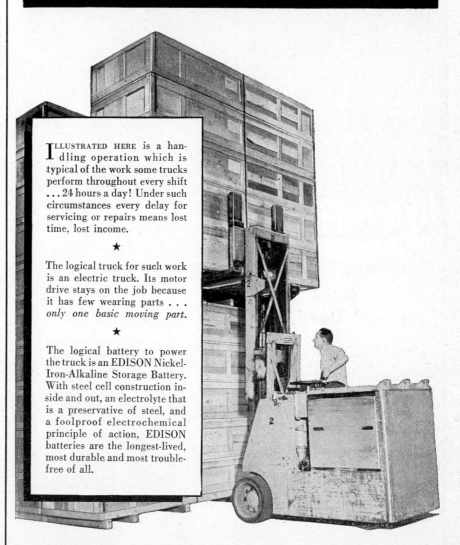

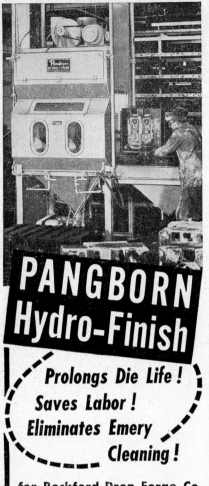
Steel Construction News

Continued

228 Tons, Lehigh County, Pa., Pennsylvania Dept. of Highways, Route 771, Sect. 2, C. W. Good, Lancaster, Pa., general contractor.

220 Tons, Newtown and Southbury, Conn., 4 span steel deck girder bridge, Mariani Construction Co., New Haven, Conn., low bidder.

210 Tons, Barrington, Ill., Jewel Tea Co. building to Truscon Steel Co.

190 Tons, Indiana County, Pa., paving LR-902, to Bethlehem Steel Co.

160 Tons, Auburn, Ala., men's dormitory, Alabama Polytechnic Institute, to Truscon Steel Co., Birmingham

160 Tons, McKeesport, Pa., hospital, to Lind Steel Co.

135 Tons, Whiting, Ind., Standard Oil Co., to U. S. Steel Supply Co.

130 Tons, DuPage County, Ill., Reactor Building, Argonne National Laboratory, to U. S. Steel Supply Co.

126 Tons, Berks County, Pa., Pennsylvania Dept. of Highways, Routes 06150 and 06038, Central Pennsylvania Quarry, Stripping & Construction Co., general contractor.

115 Tons, Pittsburgh, School of Industrial Administration, Carnegie Tech, to Dambach Co.

112 Tons, Darien, Conn., 3 span continuous rolled beam bridge, Paul Bacco and Son, Stamford, Conn.. low bidder.

100 Tons, Chicago, Central Steel & Wire Co. warehouse, to Ceco Steel Products Co., Chicago.

Recent reinforcing bar inquiries included the following:

2200 Tons, Louisville, housing project.

1450 Tons, Gary, Ind., water filtration plant.

970 Tons, Chicago, Wacker Drive from Madison to Washington St.

860 Tons, Allegheny County, Pa., road work LR 766.

800 Tons, Minneapolis, warehouse building.

625 Tons, Aurora, Minn., steam electric plant.

500 Tons, Louisville, high school.

500 Tons, Chicago, Auxiliary sewer contract 3A.

470 Tons, Rochester, Minn., Service center building.

400 Tons, Detroit, Great Lakes Steel Corp., blast furnace.

376 Tons, Westville, Ind., Dr. Norman Beatty Hospital.

235 Tons, Altoona, Blair County, Pa., Easterly Sewage Treatment Works.

215 Tons, Chicago, terminal building O'Hare Airport.

200 Tons, Iowa City, Iowa, children's hospital.

200 Tons, Cleveland, Shelby Mutual Insurance Bldg.

150 Tons, Orrville, Ohio, sewage treatment plant.

150 Tons, Akron, Ohio, Akron expressing system.

150 Tons, Milwaukee, Hall Chevrolet garage.

135 Tons, Albion, Mich., Albion College.

120 Tons, Moline, Ill., power station boiler room, Iowa-Illinois Gas and Electric Co.

115 Tons, Omaha, Missouri railroad bridge.

100 Tons, Detroit, annealing furnaces, Ford Motor Co.

Recent steel piling awards included the following:

196 Tons, Darien, Conn., 3 span continuous rolled beam bridge. Paul Bacco and Sons, Stamford, Conn., low bidder.

Tighten Cadmium Controls; Inventories Limited to 30 Days

Washington—Controls over both civilian and military use of cadmium were tightened last week in an NPA order specifying defense uses. The order, M-19, also limited inventories to a 30-day supply.

Among the cadmium-containing items which may be produced are: bearings for rolling mills and heavy duty diesels, resistance welding electrodes, shunt wire leads, silver brazing alloys containing not more than 19 pct cadmium, low melting point alloys for anchorage of punch press dies and drill jig bushings, copper base alloys containing no more than 1¼ pct (by weight) cadmium, zinc base alloys for specific purposes, and a long list of electrical items and parts.

Carnegie to Enlarge Blast Furnace; Add 112,000 Annual Tons

Youngstown, Ohio — Carnegie-Illinois Steel Corp. will increase blast furnace capacity at its Ohio Works by 112,000 tons a year with the rebuilding and enlarging of No. 5 blast furnace, which will be shut down soon. Daily rated capacity of the furnace will be increased by more than 300 tons.

At the same time two new turbo-blowers will be built to replace four obsolete, gas engine-driven blowers to provide additional wind pressure for the plant's blast furnaces, and two boilers supplying steam for the furnace steam blowing facilities will be equipped with new coal pulverizers.

Canada to Raise Cobalt Output

Ottawa—Exports of scarce cobalt to the United States will increase when Canada gets the ball rolling on its plan to expand production, government sources indicated. Increased output will help Canada meet her own and some U. S. needs. Canadian production in 1950 is estimated at 626,000 lb —a slight gain over 1949.

production ideas

Continued from Page 36

gen to the powder chamber through a normally-open valve, and pressurizes the dry chemical for discharge. A 50-ft hose has a dis-

charge nozzle with stirrup-type control lever, for off, fan and straight powder streams. The extinguisher is suitable for combating flammable liquid (Class B) and electrical (Class C) fires in industrial plants. *Walter Kidde & Co., Inc.*
For more data insert No. 25 on postcard, p. 33.

Hand Tachometer

Features extremely low torque; guaranteed accuracy of 0.5 of 1 pct.

Ranges of the new Smiths Model A.T.H. 10 dual-range hand tachometer are 0/1000 and 0/5000 rpm, each of which is printed on the dial in a contrasting color. Revolving

Alnico permanent magnet inside of the drag cup assures extreme sensitivity and accuracy over the entire scale range. The instrument is provided with a knurled knob for range selection and pushbutton for releasing or holding the pointer at the machine speed indication. The instrument is packed in a carrying case, complete with male and female

centers, 3½ in. extension and 6-in. circumference surface measuring disk. *Equipoise Controls, Inc.*
For more data insert No. 26 on postcard, p. 33.

Layout Kit

Scale models demonstrate the values obtained from 3-dimensional planning.

A 200-piece kit of ¼-in. scale models of machines, benches, trucks, conveyers, materials - handling equipment, office equipment, together with a 12 x 18-in. Lucite planning board, columns and layout tape enables the user to test the merit of three-dimensional planning before accepting or rejecting its values. *Visual Planning Equipment Co.*
For more data insert No. 27 on postcard, p. 33.

Coil and Sheet Marker

Automatically imprints trademarks, heat numbers, identification marks.

The printer was developed in cooperation with men in the strip steel mills, for the automatic imprinting of trademarks, heat numbers and inspector's identification

mark on each sheet or coil as it emerges from the temper mills or shear lines. The unit is fundamentally a revolving cylinder to which a rubber printing die is fastened. As the cylinder is revolved by the rubber drive tires in contact with the steel passing beneath, a clean, legible, inked impression is made. An internal feed inking unit insures control of ink distribution. The marker can be used for marking on a flat surface, or it can be mounted directly on top of the coil at the reel. *Jas. H. Matthews & Co.*
For more data insert No. 28 on postcard, p. 33.

Speed Reducers

Improved appearance, greater casting uniformity feature improved line.

Employing double-enveloping gearing, all operating parts in the improved standard line are directly

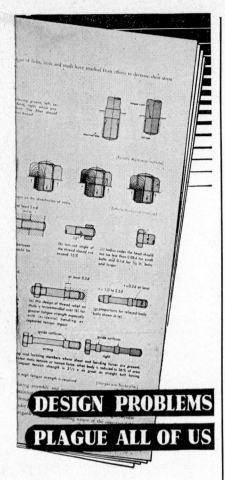

DESIGN PROBLEMS
PLAGUE ALL OF US

To serve well, a machine part—even when made of good steel, properly treated—must be properly designed.

A new 72 page booklet, sent free on request, discusses the vital relation between design, good steel and its satisfactory treatment.

---

production ideas
Continued

interchangeable with former models. Shown are reducers of 2, 2½ and 3 in. center distance. They are available in standard ratios of 5:1

to 50:1 (60:1 on the 3 in.). Horsepower ratings for these compact reducers range as high as 9.04 hp at 1750 rpm. *Cone-Drive Gear Div. Michigan Tool Co.*
For more data insert No. 29 on postcard, p. 33.

Hand Welding Equipment
Combines argon metal arc hand-welding torch and rod feed unit.

Fast welding is possible with a new argon metal arc hand-welding torch and automatic wire drive unit that uses consumable electrode as the filler metal. Welding rod is fed

from a coil into an argon-protected atmosphere at a steady predetermined rate. The equipment is particularly adaptable for welding aluminum in ranges of ⅛ to 1½ in. thick. Hand-welding can be applied on butt, lap, fillet, edge, and corner joints in the overhead and vertical, as well as in the horizontal and flat positions. *Linde Air Products Co.*
For more data insert No. 30 on postcard, p. 33.
Resume Your Reading on Page 37

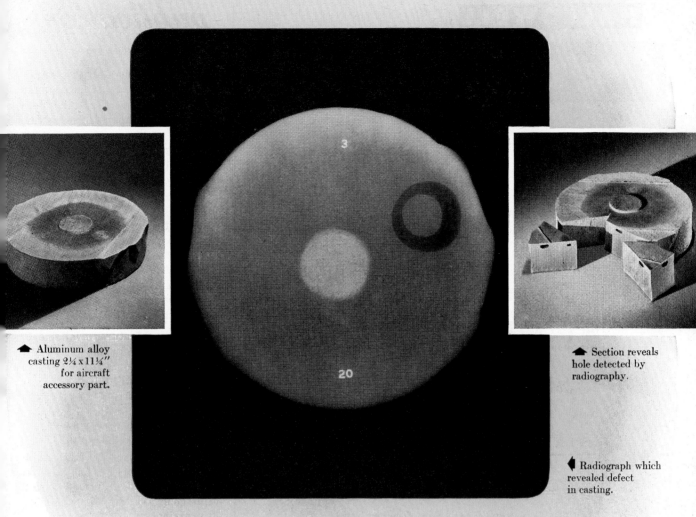

Aluminum alloy
casting 2¼ x 11¼"
for aircraft
accessory part.

Section reveals
hole detected by
radiography.

Radiograph which
revealed defect
in casting.

Minutes of Radiography
saved hours of machining

AFTER machining, this aluminum alloy casting was to be an important part in an aircraft accessory, vital to high-altitude flying. The finished part was needed quickly by the customer. Design specifications demanded high quality.

This was no time to wait for machining to disclose any defects. There was too much to lose —setup time, machining time, take-down time, as well as the reputation of the foundry.

Radiography saved all that. In a few minutes it revealed a defect that caused rejection of the rough casting at the foundry. Other castings, proved sound by radiography, were sent to the customer.

Cases like this show how more and more foundries are able to release only sound castings. Perhaps even more important, radiography is showing how to make consistently sound castings, by picturing the internal effects of changes in gating, venting, chilling, pouring temperature, and other variables.

Ask your x-ray dealer to explain how radiography can help you increase yield and cut costs.

EASTMAN KODAK COMPANY
X-Ray Division, Rochester 4, New York

Radiography . . .

another important function of photography

TRADE-MARK

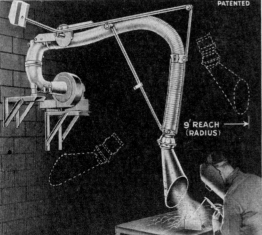
---

publications

Continued from Page 32

material, recommended uses, chemical composition, and physical and mechanical properties, in both tabular and graphic form. Nine pages of graphs compare the mechanical properties of the various Haynes alloys. Age-hardening data and fabrication procedures are also included. Engineers and metallurgists who design or specify equipment for high-temperature use will find the book an invaluable aid in the selection of alloys. *Haynes Stellite Div., Union Carbide & Carbon Corp.*

For free copy insert No. 8 on postcard, p. 33.

New Micrometers

Distinctive features available in the completely new Brown & Sharpe micrometers are shown in a new 12-p. catalog listing prices and specifications of the various models. Shown in detail are such items as carbide measuring faces; large diameter thimble, wide divisions, greater magnification; stainless steel construction and rust resistant finish; sliding taper thread adjustment and adjustable thimble, all contributing to easier precision measurement. *Brown & Sharpe Mfg. Co.*

For free copy insert No. 9 on postcard, p. 33.

Pit-Type Furnaces

Pit-type furnaces for controlled atmosphere heat treatment are discussed in a new 4-p. bulletin presenting a complete description of the application of these batch-type furnaces. Performance data, engineering construction features and applications of the furnaces to heat treatments such as gas case carburizing, homogeneous carburizing, dry cyaniding, clean hardening and bright annealing are presented. A practical formula for calculating size of load to be placed in a basket or fixture of given size is supplied, and the newest developments, such as the integrally built RX atmosphere gas generator, are presented in detail. Work handling methods with minimum labor costs and materials handling equipment investment are also described. *Surface Combustion Corp.*

For free copy insert No. 10 on postcard, p. 33.

Resume Your Reading on Page 33

IRON AGE *markets and prices*

market briefs and bulletins

supreme court rules on prices — The Supreme Court ruled this week that a firm can lower prices in "good faith" to meet competitors' prices even if competition among its customers is injured. In a case involving Standard Oil Co. of Indiana the Federal Trade Commission had ruled that "good faith" in cutting prices was not a binding factor since competition was injured. Justice Burton said, "Congress did not seek by the Robinson-Patman Act either to abolish competition or so radically curtail it that a seller would have no substantial right of self-defense against a price raid by a competitor."

continuous casting — Three American companies own a controlling interest in the newly formed Continuous Metalcast Corp., organized to take over U. S. and Canadian rights to the Junghans and Dunross patents and other related patents and facilities owned by Irving Rossi, new CMC president. Ownership is shared by: Allegheny Ludlum Steel Corp., 35 pct; Scovill Mfg. Co., 10 pct; and American Metal Co., Ltd., 10 pct; Mr. Rossi, 45 pct.

steel price stabilization — Steel industry and ESA officials have agreed a freeze on existing steel prices on a company-by-company basis is a sound and satisfactory approach to steel price stabilization. This is the first indication that ESA does not contemplate a rollback in steel prices. Earlier indications were prices might return to Dec. 1 levels.

tractor price rollback — Allis-Chalmers Mfg. Co. has rescinded tractor price increases of about 8 pct in compliance with ESA's order calling for a rollback to Dec. 1 price levels. Walter Geist, president, said the rollback will place the company in an "impossible" position unless its 8000 suppliers also roll back prices.

Chilean iron — Debevoise-Anderson Co. is now selling Chilean foundry grade pig iron for $64.55 in Philadelphia c.i.f. and duty paid. Other firms are reported to be importing both Chilean and Brazilian iron.

no end-use restrictions needed — Despite increasing defense requirements and supporting special programs, there is as yet no foreseeable need to restrict the end-use of steel, National Production Authority officials have told the Steel Products Advisory Committee. While additional steel allocations are in sight and some present regulations must be changed, such change would aim for as little disruption to steel distribution as possible, NPA said.

electrolytic zinc extras up — Weirton Steel Co. increased gage and width extras for 26 gage and heavier on electrolytic zinc coated sheets $3 to $7 per ton. Special killed quality is up $4, stretcher leveling extra $6, restricted thickness tolerance $5. Item quantity brackets under 2000 lb were eliminated and extras were advanced $4 to $6 per ton.

all-time record — Business activity in the Pittsburgh District apparently rose to an all-time record in the last week of 1950. The University of Pittsburgh bureau of business research reported the index of industrial production rose to 222.2 in that week, a new high record.

Steel Operations**

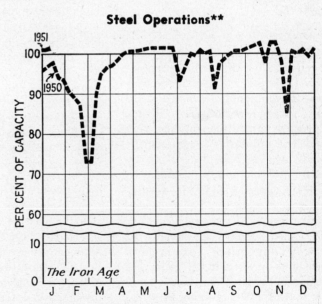

District Operating Rates—Per Cent of Capacity**

Week of	Pittsburgh	Chicago	Youngstown	Philadelphia	West	Buffalo	Cleveland	Detroit	Wheeling	South	Ohio River	St. Louis	East	Aggregate
Dec. 31	96.0*	104.0	92.5*	97.0	104.0*	104.0	97.0*	106.0*	103.0	104.0	90.0	90.5	101.0	101.0
Jan. 7	96.0	101.0	92.	98.0	104.0	104.0	97.0	106.0	97.0	106.0	90.0	90.5	98.0	102.5

* Revised.
** Steel operations for the first half of 1950 are based on annual capacity of 99,392,800 net tons. Beginning July 1, 1950, operations are based on new annual capacity of 100,563,500 net tons

January 11, 1951 95

nonferrous metals | outlook and market activities

NONFERROUS METALS PRICES

	Jan. 3	Jan. 4	Jan. 5	Jan. 6	Jan. 8	Jan. 9
Copper, electro, Conn. ...	24.50	24.50	24.50	24.50	24.50	24.50
Copper, Lake, delivered...	24.625	24.625	24.625	24.625	24.625	24.625
Tin, Straits, New York	$1.52	$1.57	$1.56	....	$1.59	$1.61*
Zinc, East St. Louis	17.50	17.50	17.50	17.50	17.50	17.50
Lead. St. Louis	16.80	16.80	16.80	16.80	16.80	16.80

Note: Quotations are going prices.

*Tentative.

by R. Hatschek

New York — Members of the zinc, lead and copper industries met in Washington last week with government officials on the subject of price controls and in view of the stability displayed by these metals, their prices will not be controlled for the present. Current prices for these metals were established as follows: Copper, Oct. 2; lead, Oct. 31; and zinc, Sept. 7.

Committee to Aid ESA

The Economic Stabilization Agency stated that it has been assured by industry members that prices would not be raised without advance notice. A full-time advisory committee for the zinc and lead industries is planned for assisting the ESA in setting up price stabilization programs.

It is reported that the government is soon to issue an order requiring all companies to notify the ESA 30 days in advance of raising any prices. Certain farm products are excluded from the proposed order. The effect would be that of a 30-day fixing of prices and is only intended to hold back inflationary trends until personnel for administering a full-scale price control program can be assembled.

Now that the new Congress has convened, the hue and cry for the retroactive suspension of the 2¢ copper import duty is once again heard in Washington. The new 1½¢ duty on lead is also the subject of Washington discussions. Under present-day conditions of supply and demand, and with prices under voluntary control and preparing to go under full control, these tariffs are doing little to help our defense production and are causing some difficulty by virtue of the split-price markets they cause.

At least in the case of the lead duty, one alternate to suspending the tariff has been suggested. This is to have some government agency, such as the Reconstruction Finance Corp., buy foreign lead and then resell it to consumers. This, however, would require more time than the needs of defense dictate.

Inco Lowers Price Hikes

In complying with the government request to hold prices back, International Nickel Co. last week reduced the amount of their recent price increases on nickel and Monel mill products. The rollbacks ranged from ½¢ to 5¢ per lb and are retroactive to Dec. 13, the date of the last increase. The new prices are 2½¢ higher than the nickel prices and 4¢ higher than the Monel prices prevailing before that time. Primary nickel prices were not affected by the reduction.

Ingot makers' buying prices for scrap aluminum dropped ½¢ to 1½¢ per lb with the result that secondary metal is selling at ¼¢ to ½¢ lower this week. Dealers' buying prices for aluminum scrap are about ½¢ lower on the bottom side of the price spread and the tone of the market is softer.

Copper Order in Drafting Stage

While primary copper is not due for immediate price control, copper scrap price regulations are said to be in the drafting stage in Washington. There is some strong feeling in the scrap metals trade that mandatory controls are the only ones that have any chance of working.

NPA proposals came out thick and fast last week. Another was for an order limiting the use of tin and aluminum in collapsible tubes for certain products. The purpose of this order is to enable the collapsible tube industry to produce at the current levels despite the reduced amount of metal available to these manufacturers during 1951.

The newly formed Defense Minerals Administration has indicated that it will approve a copper mine project in Michigan's upper peninsula. The project might involve a $100,000,000 loan from the government.

MILL PRODUCTS

(Cents per lb, unless otherwise noted)

Aluminum

(Base 30,000 lb, f.o.b. ship. pt. frt. allowed)

Flat Sheet: 0.188 in., 2S, 3S, 30.1¢; 4S, 61S-O, 32¢; 52S, 34.1¢; 24S-O, 24S-OAL, 32.9¢; 75S-O, 75S-OAL, 39.9¢; 0.081 in., 2S, 3S, 31.2¢; 4S, 61S-O, 33.5¢; 52S, 35.6¢; 24S-O, 24S-OAL, 34.1¢; 75S-O, 75S-OAL, 41.8¢; 0.032 in., 2S, 3S, 32.9¢; 4S, 61S-O, 37.1¢; 52S, 39.8¢; 24S-O, 24S-OAL, 41.7¢; 75S-O, 75S-OAL, 52.2¢.

Plate: ¼ in. and heavier: 2S, 3S-F, 28.3¢; 4S-F, 30.2¢; 52S-F, 31.8¢; 61S-O, 30.8¢; 24S-O, 24S-OAL, 32.4¢; 75S-O, 75S-OAL, 38.8¢.

Extruded Solid Shapes: Shape factors 1 to 5, 36.2¢ to 74.5¢; 12 to 14, 36.9¢ to 89¢; 24 to 26, 39.6¢ to $1.16; 36 to 38, 47.2¢ to $1.70.

Rod, Rolled: 1.5 to 4.5 in., 2S-F, 3S-F, 37.5¢ to 33.5¢; cold-finished, 0.375 to 3 in., 2S-F, 3S-F, 40.5¢ to 35¢.

Screw Machine Stock: Rounds, 11S-T3, ⅛ to 11/32 in., 53.5¢ to 42¢; ⅜ to 1½ in., 41.5¢ to 39¢; 1 9/16 to 3 in., 38.5¢ to 36¢; 17S-T4 lower by 1.5¢ per lb. Base 5000 lb.

Drawn Wire: Coiled, 0.051 to 0.374 in., 2S, 39.5¢ to 29¢; 52S, 48¢ to 35¢; 56S, 51¢ to 42¢; 17S-T4, 54¢ to 37.5¢; 61S-T4, 48.5¢ to 37¢; 75S-T6, 84¢ to 67.5¢.

Extruded Tubing, Rounds: 63S-T5, OD in in.: 1¼ to 2, 37¢ to 54¢; 2 to 4, 33.5¢ to 45.5¢; 4 to 6, 34¢ to 41.5¢; 6 to 9, 34.5¢ to 43.5¢.

Roofing Sheet, Flat: 0.019 in. x 28 in. per sheet, 72 in., $1.142; 96 in., $1.522; 120 in., $1.902; 144 in., $2.284. Gage 0.024 in. x 28 in., 72 in., $1.379; 96 in., $1.839; 120 in., $2.299; 144 in., $2.759. Coiled Sheet: 0.019 in. x 28 in., 28.2¢ per lb.; 0.024 in. x 28 in., 26.9¢ per lb.

Magnesium

(F.o.b. mill, freight allowed)

Sheet and Plate: FS1-O, ¼ in. 63¢; 3/16 in. 65¢; ⅛ in. 67¢; B & S Gage 10, 68¢; 12, 72¢; 14, 78¢; 16, 85¢; 18, 93¢; 20, $1.05; 22, $1.27; 24, $1.67. Specification grade higher. Base: 30,000 lb.

Extruded Round Rod: M, diam in., ¼ to 0.311 in., 74¢; ½ to ¾ in., 57.5¢; 1¼ to 1.749 in., 53¢; 2½ to 5 in., 48.5¢. Other alloys higher. Base: Up to ¾ in. diam, 10,000 lb; ¾ to 2 in., 20,000 lb; 2 in. and larger, 30,000 lb.

Extruded Solid Shapes, Rectangles: M. In weight per ft, for perimeters less than size indicated, 0.10 to 0.11 lb, 3.5 in., 62.3¢; 0.22 to 0.25 lb, 5.9 in., 59.3¢; 0.50 to 0.59 lb, 8.6 in., 56.7¢; 1.8 to 2.59 lb, 19.5 in., 53.8¢; 4 to 6 lb, 28 in., 49¢. Other alloys higher. Base, in weight per ft of shape: Up to ½ lb, 10,000 lb; ½ to 1.80 lb, 20,000 lb; 1.80 lb and heavier, 30,000 lb.

Extruded Round Tubing: M, wall thickness, outside diam, in., 0.049 to 0.057, ¼ in. to 5/16, $1.40; 5/16 to ⅜, $1.26; ½ to ⅝, 93¢; 1 to 2 in., 76¢; 0.165 to 0.219, ⅝ to ¾, 61¢; 1 to 2 in., 57¢; 3 to 4 in., 56¢. Other alloys higher. Base, OD in in.; Up to 1½ in., 10,000 lb; 1½ in. to 3 in., 20,000 lb; 3 in. and larger, 30,000 lb.

Titanium

(10,000 lb. base, f.o.b. mill)

Commercially pure and alloy grades: Sheet and strip, HR or CR, $15; Plate, HR, $12; Wire, rolled and/or drawn, $10; Bar, HR or forged, $6; Forgings, $6.

Nickel and Monel

(Base prices, f.o.b. mill)

	"A" Nickel	Monel
Sheets, cold-rolled	71½	57
Strip, cold-rolled	77½	60
Rods and bars	67½	55
Angles, hot-rolled	67½	55
Plates	69½	56
Seamless tubes	100½	90
Shot and blocks	....	50

Copper, Brass, Bronze

(Freight prepaid on 200 lb includes duty)

	Sheets	Rods	Extruded Shapes
Copper	41.03	....	40.63
Copper, h-r	....	36.88	....
Copper, drawn	....	38.18	....
Low brass	39.15	38.84	....
Yellow brass	38.28	37.97	....
Red brass	40.14	39.83	....
Naval brass	43.08	38.61	38.07
Leaded brass	....	32.63	36.70
Com'l bronze	41.13	40.82	....
Mang. bronze	45.96	40.65	41.41
Phos. bronze	60.20	60.45	....
Muntz metal	40.43	36.74	37.99
Ni silver, 10 pct	49.27	51.49	....
Arch. bronze	....	....	35.11

PRIMARY METALS

(Cents per lb, unless otherwise noted)

Aluminum ingot, 99+%, 10,000 lb, freight allowed	19.00
Aluminum pig	18.00
Antimony, American, Laredo, Tex.	32.00
Beryllium copper, 3.75-4.25% Be	$1.56
Beryllium aluminum 5% Be, Dollars per lb contained Be	$69.00
Bismuth, ton lots	$2.25
Cadmium, del'd	$2.55
Cobalt, 97-99% (per lb)	$2.10 to $2.17
Copper, electro, Conn. Valley	24.50
Copper, Lake, delivered	24.625
Gold, U. S. Treas., dollars per oz.	$35.00
Indium, 99.8%, dollars per troy oz.	$2.25
Iridium, dollars per troy oz.	$200
Lead, St. Louis	16.80
Lead, New York	17.00
Magnesium, 99.8+%, f.o.b. Freeport, Tex., 10,000 lb	24.50
Magnesium, sticks, 100 to 500 lb	42.00 to 44.00
Mercury, dollars per 76-lb flask f.o.b. New York	$182 to $185
Nickel, electro, f.o.b. New York	53.55
Nickel oxide sinter, f.o.b. Copper Cliff, Ont., contained nickel	46.75
Palladium, dollars per troy oz.	$24.00
Platinum, dollars per troy oz.	$90 to $93
Silver, New York, cents per oz.	90.16
Tin, New York	$1.61
Titanium, sponge	$5.00
Zinc, East St. Louis	17.50
Zinc, New York	18.22
Zirconium copper, 50 pct	$6.20

REMELTED METALS

Brass Ingot

(Cents per lb delivered, carloads)

85-5-5-5 ingot	
No. 115	29.00
No. 120	28.50
No. 123	28.00
80-10-10 ingot	
No. 305	35.00
No. 315	32.00
88-10-2 ingot	
No. 210	46.25
No. 215	43.25
No. 245	36.00
Yellow ingot	
No. 405	25.50
Manganese bronze	
No. 421	30.75

Aluminum Ingot

(Cents per lb, 30,000 lb lots)

95-5 aluminum-silicon alloys	
0.30 copper, max.	33.25-34.25
0.60 copper, max.	33.00-34.00
Piston alloys (No. 122 type)	31.00-31.50
No. 12 alum. (No. 2 grade)	30.50-31.00
108 alloy	30.75-31.25
195 alloy	32.25-32.75
13 alloy	33.50-34.00
ASX-679	30.75-31.25

Steel deoxidizing aluminum, notch-bar granulated or shot

Grade 1—95-97½%	32.00-32.50
Grade 2—92-95%	30.25-31.00
Grade 3—90-92%	29.50-30.00
Grade 4—85-90%	29.00-29.50

ELECTROPLATING SUPPLIES

Anodes

(Cents per lb, freight allowed, 500 lb lots)

Copper	
Cast, oval, 15 in. or longer	39⅛
Electrodeposited	33⅜
Rolled, oval, straight, delivered	38⅞
Forged ball anodes	43
Brass, 80-20	
Cast, oval, 15 in. or longer	34¾
Zinc, oval	26½
Ball anodes	25½
Nickel 99 pct plus	
Cast	70.50
Rolled, depolarized	71.50
Cadmium	$2.80
Silver 999 fine, rolled, 100 oz lots, per troy oz, f.o.b. Bridgeport, Conn.	79½

Chemicals

(Cents per lb, f.o.b. shipping point)

Copper cyanide, 100 lb drum	52.15
Copper sulfate, 99.5 crystals, bbl.	12.85
Nickel salts, single or double, 4-100 lb bags, frt allowed	20½
Nickel chloride, 375 lb drum	27½
Silver cyanide, 100 oz lots, per oz.	67¼
Sodium cyanide, 96 pct domestic 200 lb drums	19.25
Zinc cyanide, 100 lb drums	45.85

SCRAP METALS

Brass Mill Scrap

(Cents per pound, add ½¢ per lb for shipments of 20,000 to 40,000 lb; add 1¢ for more than 40,000 lb)

	Heavy	Turnings
Copper	23	22¼
Yellow brass	20⅛	18¾
Red brass	21½	20¾
Comm. bronze	21¾	21
Mang. bronze	19½	18⅝
Brass rod ends	19⅞	....

Custom Smelters' Scrap

(Cents per pound, carload lots, delivered to refinery)

No. 1 copper wire	21.00
No. 2 copper wire	20.00
Light copper	19.00
Refinery brass	18.50*
Radiators	15.00

*Dry copper content.

Ingot Makers' Scrap

(Cents per pound, carload lots, delivered to producer)

No. 1 copper wire	21.00
No. 2 copper wire	20.00
Light copper	19.00
No. 1 composition	20.00
No. 1 comp. turnings	19.75
Rolled brass	16.50
Brass pipe	18.50
Radiators	15.25
Heavy yellow brass	15.00
Aluminum	
Mixed old cast	18½
Mixed new clips	20½
Mixed turnings, dry	18½
Pots and pans	18½—18¾
Low copper	21½—21¾

Dealers' Scrap

(Dealers' buying prices, f.o.b. New York in cents per pound)

Copper and Brass

No. 1 heavy copper and wire	19½—20
No. 2 heavy copper and wire	18 —18½
Light copper	17 —17¼
New type shell cuttings	17 —17¼
Auto radiators (unsweated)	14½—15
No. 1 composition	17 —17½
No. 1 composition turnings	16½—17
Clean red car boxes	15½—16
Cocks and faucets	15½—16
Mixed heavy yellow brass	13 —13½
Old rolled brass	14 —14½
Brass pipe	17 —17½
New soft brass clippings	17½—18
Brass rod ends	16½—17
No. 1 brass rod turnings	16 —16½

Aluminum

Alum. pistons and struts	12 —13
Aluminum crankcases	15 —16
2S aluminum clippings	18½—19½
Old sheet and utensils	15 —16
Borings and turnings	12½—13
Misc. cast aluminum	15 —16
Dural clips (24S)	15 —16

Zinc

New zinc clippings	14½—15
Old zinc	11 —11¼
Zinc routings	8½— 9
Old die cast scrap	8 — 8¼

Nickel and Monel

Pure nickel clippings	60 —65
Clean nickel turnings	57 —60
Nickel anodes	60 —65
Nickel rod ends	60 —65
New Monel Clippings	22 —25
Clean Monel turnings	18 —20
Old sheet Monel	20 —22
Inconel clippings	26 —28
Nickel silver clippings, mixed	13 —14
Nickel silver turnings, mixed	12 —13

Lead

Soft scrap, lead	15 —15¼
Battery plates (dry)	8¾— 9

Magnesium

Segregated solids	9 —10
Castings	5½— 6½

Miscellaneous

Block tin	85 —90
No. 1 pewter	63 —65
No. 1 auto babbitt	58 —60
Mixed common babbitt	12¼—12½
Solder joints	18½—19
Siphon tops	58 —60
Small foundry type	16¼—16½
Monotype	14¾—15
Lino. and stereotype	14½—14¾
Electrotype	12¾—13
Hand picked type shells	11½—11¾
Lino. and stereo. dross	8 — 8¼
Electro. dross	6½— 6¾

SCRAP *iron and steel*

Trade sees ESA lopping off $1.50 from present formula prices . . . Hot demand forces mills into active buying in some markets.

In the fog of rumors and counter-rumors, a rule of the thumb for figuring out coming Economic Stabilization Agency scrap pricing schedules could be dimly seen. Still a rumor, with a little more weight than most, the rule is: deduct $1.50 from present formula prices on openhearths, low phos, and blast furnace grades. (See p. 75 for story on Washington scrap meetings and possible pricing results.)

Signs pointed to a violent demand that was forcing some mills into active buying despite signs that controls will sink prices below current formula levels. In Pittsburgh mills were "competing briskly" for scrap and upgrading continued. Some reported here that some users are paying more than the formula permits. At last week's Washington scrap meeting, the trade suggested a price of $44, plus $1 commission, for No. 1 heavy for the Pittsburgh area.

The watch and wait attitude was a damper to price rises and generally increases were negligible. The Detroit market edged toward price stability and the tonnage of free scrap moving over the formula was no longer significant.

PITTSBURGH — Despite indications that controlled prices will be below existing levels, mills are still competing briskly for available scrap. Upgrading continues commonplace and reports are that some consumers are paying more than the so-called formula. Final word on controlled prices is expected next week following Thursday's meeting of consumers and brokers with price control authorities in Washington. At last week's

session the industry recommended a price of $44, plus $1 commission, for No. 1 heavy melting at Pittsburgh. This would be exclusive of springboards a consumer might pay to bring in scrap long distances. Short turnings would be $38, plus $1 commission.

CHICAGO — Reports heard in the trade last week indicated that price controls on scrap would be imposed in the near future, possibly Jan. 15, with 2 weeks to clear up old orders. Ceiling prices on openhearth grades are expected to be $1.50 below the last formula prices. This would make No. 1 heavy melting steel and No. 1 bundles $43.50, No. 2 heavy melting $41.50 and No. 2 bundles $40.50. Short shoveling turnings are expected to be $6 per gross ton under No. 1 heavy melting and machine turnings $10 under No. 1.

PHILADELPHIA — Prices in this district remained stable with the exception of rail specialties which moved up $2 per ton to a range of $55 to $56. The freight car shortage continued to hamper scrap shipments and the strike of Philadelphia tugboat operators delayed unloading of several ships carrying scrap. Dealers in the area are selling all the material they can so that they will not be caught with a lot of high-priced inventory when scrap price controls are announced. Rollbacks are expected particularly in cast material and there is a possibility that cast grades will go to an f.o.b. shipping point pricing system.

NEW YORK—Movement of scrap and demand were lively in this market. The trade had its attention on the things to come from ESA and awaited a price control decision to stem from another scrap meeting in Washington this week. In this atmosphere of watchful waiting, the price line held on all items. It was reported some users were paying above the formula on some steelmaking grades.

DETROIT—In the face of threatened controls, the Detroit scrap market is edging cautiously toward price stability. While some dealers are apparently holding out, the tonnage of free scrap moving at higher than formula prices is no longer significant. Pressures to sell at formula have been increasing and most dealers have been responding by emptying their yards before the price drops. Cast grades have been somewhat weaker.

CLEVELAND — With buyers and brokers waiting for definite information from Washington, the market here and in the valley is in a state of suspended animation. Mills are buying practically anything that is offered and paying big springboards on remote tonnage. Shipments to some mills are not equal to consumption and tonnage is being taken from inventory to maintain operations.

ST. LOUIS—Major topic in the trade here is the new price schedule, which is expected to be announced Jan. 15, or thereabouts. Brokers are betting that No. 1 heavy melting steel will be pegged at $42 here and No. 2 at $39. Major consumers have placed their January orders and scrap is moving. Foundry grades are quiet, with buyers anticipating a break in prices.

BIRMINGHAM — All scrap steel in moving in the district at formula prices now. Cast iron is moving into the district in large quantities and the price, which has been out of line for some time is becoming normal and may drop a little more, brokers say.

CINCINNATI — Rumors of a rollback have the market here in high emotional gear, but steel mill grades are moving at quoted prices. Most persistent report has it that No. 1 heavy melting steel will be pegged at $42 here. Trading in the foundry grades is at low ebb, despite reports of a $5 to $7 price drop in the south. Mills want scrap and are showing no hesitancy in buying at the present level.

BOSTON — The market in scrap steel was active here this week, though prices remained unchanged. Brokers and dealers waited with crossed fingers for news from Washington on prices. Quite a demand for cast was noted.

BUFFALO — While the scrap trade awaits pending price controls, concern is in evidence over a shrinkage in supplies. A leading mill consumer was making sharp inroads on reserve stocks to maintain production. The thought prevails that available supplies are a more disturbing factor than prices. Speculations on possible controls seem to be that there would be no appreciable change in prices on steelmaking items. New business was deferred, but dealers still were shipping against old orders.

OUR FIRST HALF-CENTURY

50TH ANNIVERSARY

1901-1951

HARRY KLAFF
FOUNDER &
PRESIDENT

H. KLAFF & COMPANY, INC.

KLAFF

H. KLAFF & COMPANY, INC., Ostend & Paca Sts., Baltimore 30, Md.

Buyers of STAINLESS SCRAP, STRAIGHT CHROMES, NICHROME, PURE NICKEL, NICKEL ALLOYS & INCONEL

January 11, 1951

Iron and Steel
SCRAP PRICES

Going prices as obtained in the trade by THE IRON AGE based on representative tonnages. All prices are per gross ton delivered to consumer unless otherwise noted.

Pittsburgh

No. 1 hvy. melting	$45.75 to $46.50
No. 2 hvy. melting	43.75 to 44.50
No. 1 bundles	45.75 to 46.50
No. 2 bundles	42.75 to 43.50
Machine shop turn.	37.75 to 38.50
Mixed bor. and ms. turns.	37.75 to 38.50
Shoveling turnings	39.75 to 40.50
Cast iron borings	39.75 to 40.50
Low phos. plate	56.00 to 56.50
Heavy turnings	46.50 to 47.00
No. 1 RR. hvy. melting	45.75 to 46.50
Scrap rails, random lgth.	64.50 to 65.00
Rails 2 ft and under	68.00 to 69.00
RR. steel wheels	63.00 to 64.00
RR. spring steel	63.00 to 64.00
RR. couplers and knuckles	63.00 to 64.00
No. 1 machinery cast	67.50 to 68.00
Mixed yard cast.	57.50 to 58.00
Heavy breakable cast	52.50 to 53.00
Malleable	71.00 to 72.00

Chicago

No. 1 hvy. melting	$44.25 to $45.00
No. 2 hvy. melting	42.00 to 43.00
No. 1 factory bundles	44.00 to 45.00
No. 1 dealers' bundles	44.00 to 45.00
No. 2 dealers' bundles	41.00 to 42.00
Machine shop turn.	35.00 to 36.00
Mixed bor. and turn.	35.00 to 36.00
Shoveling turnings	37.00 to 38.00
Cast iron borings	37.00 to 38.00
Low phos. forge crops	54.00 to 55.00
Low phos. plate	52.00 to 53.00
No. 1 RR. hvy. melting	47.00 to 48.00
Scrap rails, random lgth.	62.00 to 63.00
Rerolling rails	65.50 to 66.50
Rails 2 ft and under	67.00 to 69.00
Locomotive tires, cut	58.00 to 59.00
Cut bolsters & side frames	54.00 to 55.00
Angles and splice bars	63.00 to 64.00
RR. steel car axles	95.00 to 100.00
RR. couplers and knuckles	58.00 to 59.00
No. 1 machinery cast.	62.00 to 64.00
No. 1 agricul. cast.	58.00 to 60.00
Heavy breakable cast.	53.00 to 55.00
RR. grate bars	48.00 to 49.00
Cast iron brake shoes	52.00 to 53.00
Cast iron car wheels	58.00 to 59.00
Malleable	78.00 to 82.00

Philadelphia

No. 1 hvy. melting	$44.00 to $45.00
No. 2 hvy. melting	42.00 to 43.00
No. 1 bundles	44.00 to 45.00
No. 2 bundles	41.00 to 42.00
Machine shop turn.	36.00 to 37.00
Mixed bor. and turn.	35.00 to 36.00
Shoveling turnings	38.00 to 39.00
Low phos. punchings, plate	50.00 to 51.00
Low phos. 5 ft and under.	50.00 to 51.00
Low phos. bundles	48.00 to 49.00
Hvy. axle forge turn.	44.00 to 45.00
Clean cast chem. borings..	42.00 to 43.00
RR. steel wheels	55.00 to 56.00
RR. spring steel	55.00 to 56.00
Rails 18 in. and under	66.00 to 67.00
No. 1 machinery cast.	62.00 to 63.00
Mixed yard cast.	53.00 to 55.00
Heavy breakable cast.	53.00 to 54.00
Cast iron carwheels	67.00 to 68.00
Malleable	69.00 to 70.00

Cleveland

No. 1 hvy. melting	$45.25 to $46.00
No. 2 hvy. melting	43.25 to 44.00
No. 1 busheling	45.25 to 46.00
No. 1 bundles	45.25 to 46.00
No. 2 bundles	42.25 to 43.00
Machine shop turn.	37.25 to 38.00
Mixed bor. and turn.	39.25 to 40.00
Shoveling turnings	39.25 to 40.00
Cast iron borings	39.25 to 40.00
Low phos. 2 ft and under.	47.75 to 48.50
Steel axle turn.	44.25 to 45.00
Drop forge flashings	45.25 to 46.00
No. 1 RR. hvy. melting.	46.00 to 46.50
Rails 3 ft and under	70.00 to 71.00
Rails 18 in. and under	72.00 to 73.00
No. 1 machinery cast.	69.00 to 70.00
RR. cast.	71.00 to 72.00
RR. grate bars	50.00 to 51.00
Stove plate	55.00 to 56.00
Malleable	76.00 to 77.00

Youngstown

No. 1 hvy. melting	$45.75 to $46.50
No. 2 hvy. melting	43.75 to 44.50
No. 1 bundles	45.75 to 46.50

No. 2 bundles	$42.75 to $43.00
Machine shop turn	37.75 to 38.50
Shoveling turnings	39.75 to 40.50
Cast iron borings	39.75 to 40.50
Low phos. plate	48.25 to 49.00

Buffalo

No. 1 hvy. melting	$44.50 to $45.25
No. 2 hvy. melting	42.50 to 43.25
No. 1 busheling	42.50 to 43.25
No. 1 bundles	43.50 to 44.25
No. 2 bundles	41.50 to 42.25
Machine shop turn.	36.50 to 37.25
Mixed bor. and turn.	36.50 to 37.25
Shoveling turnings	38.50 to 39.25
Cast iron borings	36.50 to 37.25
Low phos. plate	48.25 to 49.00
Scrap rails, random lgth...	55.00 to 56.00
Rails 2 ft and under	60.00 to 61.00
RR. steel wheels	60.00 to 61.00
RR. spring steel	60.00 to 61.00
RR. couplers and knuckles	60.00 to 61.00
No. 1 machinery cast.	59.00 to 60.00
No. 1 cupola cast.	54.00 to 55.00
Small indus. malleable	60.00 to 61.00

Birmingham

No. 1 hvy. melting	$42.50 to $43.50
No. 2 hvy. melting	40.50 to 41.50
No. 2 bundles	39.50 to 40.50
No. 1 busheling	38.00 to 39.00
Machine shop turn.	31.00 to 32.00
Shoveling turnings	32.00 to 33.00
Cast iron borings	27.00 to 28.00
Bar crops and plate	47.00 to 48.00
Structural and plate	46.00 to 47.00
No. 1 RR. hvy. melting.	43.00 to 44.00
Scrap rails, random lgth...	58.00 to 59.00
Rerolling rails	61.00 to 62.00
Rails 2 ft and under	66.00 to 67.00
Angles & splice bars	59.00 to 60.00
Std. steel axles	61.00 to 62.00
No. 1 cupola cast.	55.00 to 56.00
Stove plate	51.00 to 52.00
Cast iron carwheels	46.00 to 47.00

St. Louis

No. 1 hvy. melting	$43.75 to $44.50
No. 2 hvy. melting	41.75 to 42.50
No. 2 bundled sheets	40.75 to 41.50
Machine shop turn.	35.75 to 36.50
Shoveling turnings	37.75 to 38.50
Rails, random lengths	54.00 to 55.00
Rails 3 ft and under	62.00 to 63.00
Locomotive tires, uncut	52.00 to 53.00
Angles and splice bars	59.00 to 60.00
Std. steel car axles	94.00 to 95.00
RR. spring steel	57.00 to 58.00
No. 1 machinery cast.	55.00 to 56.00
Hvy. breakable cast.	48.00 to 49.00
Cast iron brake shoes	53.00 to 54.00
Stove plate	53.00 to 55.00
Cast iron car wheels	63.00 to 65.00
Malleable	55.00 to 57.00

New York

Brokers' Buying prices per gross ton, on cars:

No. 1 hvy. melting	$39.00
No. 2 hvy. melting	37.00
No. 2 bundles	36.00
Machine shop turn.	31.00
Mixed bor. and turn.	31.00
Shoveling turnings	33.00
Clean cast chem. bor.	$38.00 to 39.00
No. 1 machinery cast.	52.00 to 53.00
Mixed yard cast.	47.00 to 48.00
Charging box cast.	47.00 to 48.00
Heavy breakable cast.	46.00 to 47.00
Unstrp. motor blocks	42.00 to 43.00

Boston

Brokers' Buying prices per gross ton, on cars:

No. 1 hvy. melting	$35.67
No. 2 hvy. melting	33.67
No. 1 bundles	38.00

No. 2 bundles	$32.67
Machine shop turn.	27.67
Mixed bor. and turn.	$26.67 to 27.67
Shoveling turnings	29.67
No. 1 busheling	35.67
Clean cast chem. borings..	33.00 to 34.00
No. 1 machinery cast.	48.00 to 49.00
Mixed cupola cast.	44.00 to 45.00
Heavy breakable cast.	42.00 to 43.00
Stove plate	42.00 to 43.00

Detroit

Brokers' Buying prices per gross ton, on cars:

No. 1 hvy. melting	$40.25
No. 2 hvy. melting	38.25
No. 1 bundles, openhearth..	40.25
No. 1 bundles, electric furnace	42.75
New busheling	40.25
Flashings	40.25
Machine shop turn.	32.25
Mixed bor. and turn.	32.25
Shoveling turnings	34.25
Cast iron borings	34.25
Low phos. plate	42.75
No. 1 cupola cast.	$54.00 to 56.00
Heavy breakable cast.	45.00 to 47.00
Stove plate	44.00 to 46.00
Automotive cast.	58.00 to 60.00

Cincinnati

Per gross ton, f.o.b. cars:

No. 1 hvy. melting	$44.25
No. 2 hvy. melting	42.25
No. 1 bundles	44.25
No. 2 bundles, black	42.25
No. 2 bundles, mixed	41.25
Machine shop turn.	33.00
Mixed bor. and turn.	34.00
Shoveling turnings	34.00
Cast iron borings	34.00
Low phos.-steel	46.75
Low phos. 18 in. under	62.00
Rails, random lengths	$62.00 to 63.00
Rails, 18 in. and under	72.00 to 73.00
No. 1 cupola cast.	65.00 to 66.00
Hvy. breakable cast.	59.00 to 60.00
Drop broken cast.	71.00 to 72.00

San Francisco

No. 1 hvy. melting	$30.00
No. 2 hvy. melting	28.00
No. 1 bundles	30.00
No. 2 bundles	28.00
No. 3 bundles	25.00
Machine shop turn.	16.00
Elec. fur. 1 ft and under.	$40.00 to 42.50
No. 1 RR. hvy. melting.	30.00
Scrap rails random lgth...	30.00
No. 1 cupola cast.	43.00 to 46.00

Los Angeles

No. 1 hvy. melting	$30.00
No. 2 hvy. melting	28.00
No. 1 bundles	30.00
No. 2 bundles	28.00
No. 3 bundles	25.00
Mach. shop turn.	16.00
Elec. fur. 1 ft and under.	$42.00 to 45.00
No. 1 RR. hvy. melting	30.00
Scrap rails, random lgth.	30.00
No. 1 cupola cast.	52.00

Seattle

No. 1 hvy. melting	$28.00
No. 2 hvy. melting	28.00
No. 1 bundles	22.00
No. 2 bundles	22.00
No. 3 bundles	18.00
Elec. fur. 1 ft and under.	$40.00 to 45.00
RR. hvy. melting	29.00
No. 1 cupola cast	45.00

Hamilton, Ont.

No. 1 hvy. melting	$30.00
No. 1 bundles	30.00
No. 2 bundles	29.50
Mechanical bundles	28.00
Mixed steel scrap	26.00
Mixed bor. and turn.	23.00
Rails, remelting	30.00
Rails, rerolling	33.00
Bushelings	24.50
Bush., new fact. prep'd.	29.00
Bush., new fact. unprep'd.	23.00
Short steel turnings	23.00
Cast scrap	45.00

For the Purchase or Sale of
Iron and Steel Scrap...

CONSULT OUR NEAREST OFFICE

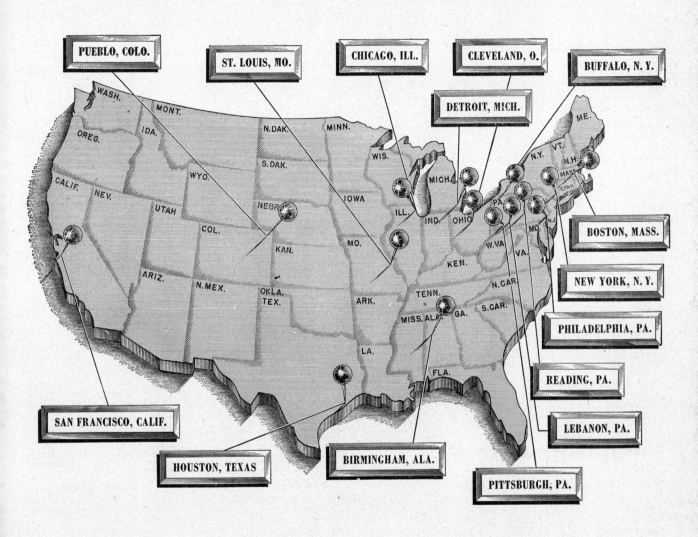

The energy and integrity of our organization is ready to serve your best interests ...
Since 1889, Luria Brothers & Company, Inc. have made fair dealings their constant aim.

CONSULT OUR NEAREST OFFICE FOR THE PURCHASE AND SALE OF SCRAP

LURIA BROTHERS AND COMPANY, INC.

LEADERS IN IRON AND STEEL SCRAP SINCE 1889

Comparison of Prices

Steel prices in this page are the average of various f.o.b. quotations of major producing areas: Pittsburgh, Chicago, Gary, Cleveland, Youngstown.

Price advances over previous week are printed in Heavy Type; declines appear in *Italics*

Flat-rolled Steel: (cents per pound)	Jan. 9, 1951	Jan. 2, 1951	Dec. 12, 1950	Jan. 10, 1950
Hot-rolled sheets	3.60	3.60	3.60	3.35
Cold-rolled sheets	4.35	4.35	4.35	4.10
Galvanized sheets (10 ga)	4.80	4.80	4.80	4.40
Hot-rolled strip	3.50	3.50	3.50	3.25
Cold-rolled strip	4.75	4.75	4.75	4.18
Plate	3.70	3.70	3.70	3.50
Plates wrought iron.....	7.85	7.85	7.85	7.85
Stains C-R-strip (No. 302)	36.50	36.50	36.50	33.00

Tin and Terneplate: (dollars per base box)				
Tinplate (1.50 lb) cokes.	$7.50	$7.50	$7.50	$7.50
Tinplate, electro (0.50 lb)	6.60	6.60	6.60	6.60
Special coated mfg. ternes	6.35	6.35	6.35	6.50

Bars and Shapes: (cents per pound)				
Merchant bars	3.70	3.70	3.70	3.45
Cold finished bars	4.55	4.55	4.55	3.995
Alloy bars	4.30	4.30	4.30	3.95
Structural shapes	3.65	3.65	3.65	3.40
Stainless bars (No. 302).	31.25	31.25	31.25	28.50
Wrought iron bars	9.50	9.50	9.50	9.50

Wire: (cents per pound)				
Bright wire	4.85	4.85	4.85	4.50

Rails: (dollars per 100 lb)				
Heavy rails	$3.60	$3.60	$3.60	$3.40
Light rails	4.00	4.00	4.00	3.75

Semifinished Steel: (dollars per net ton)				
Rerolling billets	$56.00	$56.00	$56.00	$54.00
Slabs, rerolling	56.00	56.00	56.00	54.00
Forging billets	66.00	66.00	66.00	63.00
Alloy blooms billets, slabs	70.00	70.00	70.00	66.00

Wire Rod and Skelp: (cents per pound)				
Wire rods	4.10	4.10	4.10	3.85
Skelp	3.35	3.35	3.35	3.15

Pig Iron: (per gross ton)	Jan. 9, 1951	Jan. 2, 1951	Dec. 12, 1950	Jan. 10, 1950
No. 2 foundry, del'd Phila.	$57.77	$57.77	$57.77	$50.42
No. 2, Valley furnace....	52.50	52.50	52.50	46.50
No. 2, Southern Cin'ti....	55.58	55.58	55.58	46.08
No. 2, Birmingham	48.88	48.88	48.88	39.38
No. 2, foundry, Chicago†.	52.50	52.50	52.50	46.50
Basic del'd Philadelphia..	56.92	56.92	56.92	49.92
Basic, Valley furnace....	52.00	52.00	52.00	46.00
Malleable, Chicago†	52.50	52.50	52.50	46.50
Malleable, Valley	52.50	52.50	52.50	46.50
Charcoal, Chicago	70.56	70.56	70.56	68.56
Ferromanganese‡	186.25	181.20	181.20	173.40

†The switching charge for delivery to foundries in the Chicago district is $1 per ton.
‡Average of U. S. prices quoted on Ferroalloy page.

Scrap: (per gross ton)				
Heavy melt'g steel, P'gh..	$46.13	$46.13	$46.25	$29.75
Heavy melt'g steel, Phila.	44.50	44.50	44.50	23.00
Heavy melt'g steel, Ch'go	44.63	44.63	44.50	26.50
No. 1 hy. com. sh't, Det..	40.25	40.25	43.13	23.50
Low phos. Young'n	48.63	48.63	48.63	31.75
No. 1 cast, Pittsburgh ...	67.75	67.75	66.75	37.50
No. 1 cast, Philadelphia..	62.50	62.50	59.50	37.00
No. 1 cast, Chicago	63.00	63.00	65.00	38.50

Coke: Connellsville: (per net ton at oven)				
Furnace coke, prompt...	$14.25	$14.25	$14.25	$14.00
Foundry coke, prompt...	17.25	17.25	17.25	15.75

Nonferrous Metals: (cents per pound to large buyers)				
Copper, electro, Conn....	24.50	24.50	24.50	18.50
Copper, Lake, Conn.....	24.625	24.625	24.625	18.625
Tin Straits, New York.	$1.61†	$1.50*	1.395	77.00
Zinc, East St. Louis.....	17.50	17.50	17.50	9.75
Lead, St. Louis	16.80	16.80	16.80	11.80
Aluminum, virgin	19.00	19.00	19.00	17.00
Nickel, electrolytic	53.55	53.55	51.22	42.97
Magnesium, ingot	24.50	24.50	24.50	20.50
Antimony, Laredo, Tex...	32.00	32.00	32.00	32.00

†Tentative. *Revised.

Composite Prices

Starting with the issue of May 12, 1949, the weighted finished steel composite was revised for the years 1941 to date. The weights used are based on the average product shipments for the 7 years 1937 to 1940 inclusive and 1946 to 1948 inclusive. The use of quarterly figures has been eliminated because it was too sensitive. (See p. 130 of May 12, 1949, issue.)

	Finished Steel Base Price	Pig Iron	Scrap Steel
Jan. 9, 1951	4.131¢ per lb.	$52.69 per gross ton....	$45.09 per gross ton.....
One week ago...........	4.131¢ per lb.	52.69 per gross ton....	45.09 per gross ton......
One month ago	4.131¢ per lb.	52.69 per gross ton....	45.08 per gross ton......
One year ago	3.837¢ per lb.	45.88 per gross ton....	26.25 per gross ton......

	High	Low	High	Low	High	Low
1951....	4.131¢ Jan. 2	4.131¢ Jan. 2	$52.69 Jan. 2	$52.69 Dec. 12	$45.09 Jan. 2	$45.09 Jan. 2
1950....	4.131¢ Dec. 1	3.837¢ Jan. 3	52.69 Dec. 12	45.88 Jan. 3	45.13 Dec. 19	26.25 Jan. 3
1949....	3.837¢ Dec. 27	3.3705¢ May 3	46.87 Jan. 18	45.88 Sept. 6	43.00 Jan. 4	19.33 June 28
1948....	3.721¢ July 27	3.193¢ Jan. 1	46.91 Oct. 12	39.58 Jan. 6	43.16 July 27	39.75 Mar. 9
1947....	3.193¢ July 29	2.848¢ Jan. 1	37.98 Dec. 30	30.14 Jan. 7	42.58 Oct. 28	29.50 May 20
1946....	2.848¢ Dec. 31	2.464¢ Jan. 1	30.14 Dec. 10	25.37 Jan. 1	31.17 Dec. 24	19.17 Jan. 1
1945....	2.464¢ May 29	2.396¢ Jan. 1	25.37 Oct. 23	23.61 Jan. 2	19.17 Jan. 2	18.92 May 22
1944....	2.396¢	2.396¢	$23.61	$23.61	19.17 Jan. 11	15.76 Oct. 24
1943....	2.396¢	2.396¢	23.61	23.61	$19.17	$19.17
1942....	2.396¢	2.396¢	23.61	23.61	19.17	19.17
1941....	2.396¢	2.396¢	$23.61 Mar. 20	$23.45 Jan. 2	$22.00 Jan. 7	$19.17 Apr. 10
1940....	2.30467¢ Jan. 2	2.24107¢ Apr. 16	23.45 Dec. 23	22.61 Jan. 2	21.83 Dec. 30	16.04 Apr. 9
1939....	2.35367¢ Jan. 3	2.26689¢ May 16	22.61 Sept. 19	20.61 Sept. 12	22.50 Oct. 3	14.08 May 16
1938....	2.58414¢ Jan. 4	2.27207¢ Oct. 18	23.25 June 21	19.61 July 6	15.00 Nov. 22	11.00 June 7
1937....	2.58414¢ Mar. 9	2.32263¢ Jan. 4	32.25 Mar. 9	20.25 Feb. 16	21.92 Mar. 30	12.67 June 9
1936....	2.32263¢ Dec. 28	2.05200¢ Mar. 10	19.74 Nov. 24	18.73 Aug. 11	17.75 Dec. 21	12.67 June 8
1932....	1.89196¢ July 5	1.83910¢ Mar. 1	14.81 Jan. 5	13.56 Dec. 6	8.50 Jan. 12	6.43 July 5
1929....	2.31773¢ May 28	2.26498¢ Oct. 29	18.71 May 14	18.21 Dec. 17	17.58 Jan. 29	14.08 Dec. 8

Weighted index based on steel bars, shapes, plates, wire, rails, black pipe, hot and cold-rolled sheets and strips, representing major portion of finished steel shipment. Index recapitulated in Aug. 28, 1941, issue and in May 12, 1949.

Based on averages for basic iron at Valley furnaces and foundry iron at Chicago, Philadelphia, Buffalo, Valley and Birmingham.

Average of No. 1 heavy melting steel scrap delivered to consumers at Pittsburgh, Philadelphia and Chicago.

this "pipe organ" plays a POWERFUL tune for you!

This picture shows the "works" of a modern boiler attached to a huge power generator that turns out electricity from coal to the tune of 150,000 kilowatts — enough to operate 800,000 washing machines simultaneously!

In these 12 miles of pipe, rising 10 stories above the ground, water is turned into super-heated steam by burning coal. The steam runs turbine-driven generators which produce electricity for home, farm and factory.

More than half of America's electricity is generated from coal. This past year more than *90 million tons* of coal went into making that electricity. That adds up to nearly one-fifth of the entire mine output of bituminous coal in 1950.

America is fortunate in having all the coal it *needs* to make all the electricity it *wants*. It is doubly fortunate in having an industry that can produce that coal in volume—efficiently and economically.

The American coal industry is made up of thousands of independent mine operators. In recent years, these progressive operators have invested hundreds of millions of dollars in new mine properties and mechanized equipment, in coal preparation plants and research—to bring all coal customers an increasingly *better* product for more *economical* utilization.

Today, no industry in America is better prepared than coal to meet the ever-increasing demands of both civilian and national defense production.

Granted a continuing supply of necessary equipment, transportation and trained man power, America's independently owned and operated coal mines will produce all the coal that's needed to continue to power the nation's progress, in peace or war.

IRON AGE
STEEL PRICES

Smaller numbers in price boxes indicate producing companies. For main office locations, see key on facing page.
Base prices at producing points apply only to sizes and grades produced in these areas. Prices are in cents per lb unless otherwise noted. Extras apply.

	Pittsburgh	Chicago	Gary	Cleveland	Canton Massillon	Middletown	Youngstown	Bethlehem	Buffalo	Conshohocken	Johnstown	Sparrows Point	Granite City	Detroit
INGOTS Carbon forging, net ton	$52.00[1]													
Alloy, net ton	$54.00[1,17]													$54.00[31]
BILLETS, BLOOMS, SLABS Carbon, rerolling, net ton	$56.00[1,5]	$56.00[1]	$56.00[1]						$56.00[3]		$56.00[3]			
Carbon forging billets, net ton	$66.00[1,5]	$66.00[1,4]	$66.00[1]	$66.00[4]	$66.00[4]				$66.00[3,4]	$73.00[26]	$66.00[3]			$69.00[31]
Alloy, net ton	$70.00[1,17]	$70.00[1,4]	$70.00[1]		$70.00[4]			$70.00[3]	$70.00[3,4]	$77.00[26]	$70.00[3]			$73.00[31]
PIPE SKELP	3.35[1] 3.45[5]						3.35[1,4]							
WIRE RODS	4.10[2] 4.30[18]	4.10[2,4,23]	4.10[6]	4.10[2]			4.10[6]				4.10[3]	4.20[3]		
SHEETS Hot-rolled (18 ga. & hvr.)	3.60[1,5,9,15] 3.75[23]	3.60[5,23]	3.60[1,6,8]	3.60[4]		3.60[7]	3.60[1,4,6] 4.00[13]		3.60[3]	4.00[26]		3.60[3]		3.80[12] 4.40[47]
Cold-rolled	4.35[1,5,9,15] 5.35[63]		4.35[1,6,8]	4.35[4]		4.35[7]	4.35[4,6]		4.35[3]			4.35[3]		4.55[12]
Galvanized (10 gage)	4.80[1,9,15]		4.80[1,8]		4.80[4]	4.80[7]	6.00[64]					4.80[3]		
Enameling (12 gage)	4.65[1]		4.65[1,8]			4.65[7]								
Long ternes (10 gage)	5.20[9,15]						6.00[64]							
Hi str. low alloy, h.r.	5.40[1,5] 5.75[9]	5.40[1]	5.40[1,8] 5.90[6]	5.40[4]			5.40[1,4,13]		5.40[3]	5.65[26]		5.40[3]		
Hi str. low alloy, c.r.	6.55[1,5] 6.90[9]		6.55[1,8] 7.05[6]	6.55[4]			6.55[4]		6.55[3]			6.55[3]		
Hi str. low alloy, galv.	7.20[1]													
STRIP Hot-rolled	3.60[9], 4.00[41,58] 3.75[23] 3.50[5]	3.50[66]	3.50[1,6,8]			3.50[7]	3.50[1,4,6] 4.00[13]		3.50[3,4]	3.90[26]		3.50[3]		4.40[47]
Cold-rolled	4.65[5,9] 5.00[23] 5.35[63,58]	4.90[8,66]	4.90[8]	4.65[2]		4.65[7]	4.65[4,6] 5.35[13,40]		4.65[3]			4.65[3]		5.45[47] 5.60[68] 5.60[81]
Hi str. low alloy, h.r.	5.75[9]		5.50[1] 5.30[8] 5.80[6]				4.95[4], 5.50[1] 5.40[13]			5.55[26]				
Hi str. low alloy, c.r.	7.20[9]			6.70[5]			6.20[4], 6.55[13]							
TINPLATE† Cokes, 1.50-lb base box 1.25 lb, deduct 25¢	$7.50[1] $8.70[9,15]		$7.50[1] $8.70[6]				$8.70[4]					8.80[3]		
Electrolytic 0.25, 0.50, 0.75 lb box	→ Deduct $1.55, $1.30 and 90¢ respectively from 1.50-lb coke base box price													
BLACKPLATE, 29 gage Holloware enameling	5.85[1] 6.15[15]		5.85[1]				5.30[4]							
BARS Carbon steel	3.70[1,5] 3.85[9]	3.70[1,4,23]	3.70[1,4,6,8]	3.70[4]	3.70[4]		3.70[1,4,6]		3.70[3,4]		3.70[3]			3.85[31]
Reinforcing‡	3.70[1,5]	3.70[4]	3.70[1,6,8]	3.70[4]			3.70[1,4]		3.70[3,4]		3.70[3]	3.70[3]		
Cold-finished	4.55[2,4,5,52,71]	4.55[2,69,70,23,73]	4.55[4,71,73]	4.55[2]	4.55[4,82]									4.70[84]
Alloy, hot-rolled	4.30[1,17]	4.30[1,4,23]	4.30[1,6,8]		4.30[4]		4.30[1,6]	4.30[3]	4.30[3,4]		4.30[3]			4.45[31]
Alloy, cold-drawn	5.40[17,52,69,71]	5.40[4,23,69,70,73]	5.40[4] 5.90[74]		5.40[4,82]			5.40[3]	5.40[3]					5.55[84]
Hi str. low alloy, h.r.	5.55[1,5]		5.55[1,8] 6.05[6]	5.55[4]			5.55[1]	5.55[3]	5.55[3]		5.55[3]			
PLATE Carbon steel	3.70[1,5,15]	3.70[1]	3.70[1,6,8]	3.70[4] 4.00[9]			3.70[1,4] 3.95[13]		3.70[3]	4.15[26]	3.70[3]	3.70[3]		
Floor plates			4.75[8]	4.75[5]						4.75[26]				
Alloy	4.75[1] 4.85	4.75[1]	4.75[1]				5.20[13]			5.05[26]	4.75[3]	4.75[3]		
Hi str. low alloy	5.65[1,5]	5.65[1]	5.65[1,8]	5.65[4,5]			5.65[4] 5.70[13]			5.90[26]	5.65[3]	5.65[3]		
SHAPES, Structural	3.65[1,5] 3.90[9]	3.65[1,23]	3.65[1,8]					3.70[3]	3.70[3]		3.70[3]			
Hi str. low alloy	5.50[1,5]	5.50[1]	5.50[1,8]					5.50[3]	5.50[3]		5.50[3]			
MANUFACTURERS' WIRE Bright	4.85[2,5] 5.10[18]	4.85[2] 4.33		4.85[2]				Kokomo=5.80[30]			4.85[3]	4.95[3]	Duluth=4.85[?]	
PILING, Steel Sheet	4.45[1]	4.45[1]	4.45[8]						4.45[3]					

Smaller numbers indicate producing companies. See key at right.
Prices are in cents per lb unless otherwise noted. Extras apply.

Kansas City	Houston	Birmingham	WEST COAST Seattle, San Francisco, Los Angeles, Fontana		STEEL PRICES
			F=$79.00[19]		INGOTS carbon forging, net ton
	$62.00[83]		F=$80.00[19]		Alloy, net ton
		$56.00[11]	F=$75.00[19]		BILLETS, BLOOMS, SLABS Carbon, rerolling, net ton
	$74.00[83]	$66.00[11]	F=$85.00[19] SF, LA, S=$85.00[62]		Carbon forging billets, net ton
	$78.00[83]		F=$89.00[19] LA=$90.00[62]		Alloy net ton
					PIPE SKELP
	4.50[83]	4.10[4,11]	SF=4.90[2] LA=4.90[24,62]	Worcester=4.40[2] Minnequa=4.35[14]	WIRE RODS
		3.60[4,11]	SF, LA=4.30[24] F=4.55[19]	Niles=5.25[64], Geneva=3.70[16]	SHEETS Hot-rolled (18 ga. & hvr.)
		4.35[11]	SF=5.30[24] F=5.30[19]		Cold-rolled
		4.80[4,11]	SF, LA=5.55[24]	Ashland=4.80[7]	Galvanized (10 gage)
					Enameling (12 gage)
					Long ternes (10 gage)
		5.40[11]	F=6.35[19]		Hi str. low alloy, h.r.
			F=7.50[19]		Hi str. low alloy, c.r.
					Hi str. low alloy, galv.
4.10[83]	4.90[83]	3.50[4]	SF, LA=4.25[24,62] F=4.75[19], S=4.50[62]	Atlanta=4.05[65] Minnequa=4.55[14]	STRIP Hot-rolled
			F=6.30[19] LA=6.40[27]	New Haven=5.15[2], 5.85[68]	Cold-rolled
		5.30[11]	F=6.20[19]		Hi str. low alloy, h.r.
					Hi str. low a'loy, c.r.
					TINPLATE Cokes, 1.50-lb base box 1.25 lb. deduct 20¢
			Deduct $1.55, $1.30 and 90¢ respectively from 1.50-lb coke base box price		Electrolytic 0.25, 0.50, 0.75 lb box
					BLACKPLATE, 29 gage Hollowware enameling
4.30[83]	4.10[83]	3.70[4,11]	SF, LA=4.40[24]	Atlanta=4.25[65] Minnequa=4.15[14]	BARS Carbon steel
4.30[83]	4.10[83]	3.70[4,11]	SF, S=4.45[62] F=4.40[19] LA=4.40[62]	Atlanta=4.25[65] Minnequa=4.50[14]	Reinforcing‡
				Newark=5.00[69] Putnam=5.10[69] Hartford=5.10[4] Los Angeles=6.00[4]	Cold-finished
4.90[83]	4.70[83]		LA=5.35[62] F=5.35[19]		Alloy, hot-rolled
				Newark=5.75[69] Worcester= [2] Hartford=5.85[4]	Alloy, cold-drawn
		5.55[11]	F=6.60[19]		Hi str. low alloy, h.r.
	4.10[83]	3.70[4,11]	F=4.30[19] S=4.60[62] Geneva=3.70[16]	Claymont=4.15[29] Coatesville=4.15[21] Minnequa=4.50[14]	PLATE Carbon steel
				Harrisburg=5.25[35]	Floor plates
			F=5.70[19] Geneva=5.65[16]	Coatesville=5.25[21] Claymont=4.85[29]	Alloy
		5.65[11]	F=6.25[19]		Hi str. low alloy
4.25[83]	4.05[83]	3.65[4,11]	SF=4.20[62] F=4.25[16] LA=4.25[24,62] S=4.30[62]	Geneva 3.65[16] Minnequa 4.10[14]	SHAPES, Structural
		50[11]	F=6.10[19]		Hi str. low-alloy
5.45[83]	5.25[83]	4.85[4,11]	SF, LA=5.80[24]	Atlanta=5.10[65] Worcester=5.15[2] Minnequa=5.10[14]	MANUFACTURERS' WIRE Bright

KEY TO STEEL PRODUCERS

With Principal Offices

1 U. S. Steel Co., Pittsburgh
2 American Steel & Wire Co., Cleveland
3 Bethlehem Steel Co., Bethlehem
4 Republic Steel Corp., Cleveland
5 Jones & Laughlin Steel Corp., Pittsburgh
6 Youngstown Sheet & Tube Co., Youngstown
7 Armco Steel Corp., Middletown, Ohio
8 Inland Steel Co., Chicago
9 Weirton Steel Co., Weirton, W. Va.
10 National Tube Co., Pittsburgh
11 Tennessee Coal, Iron & R. R. Co., Birmingham
12 Great Lakes Steel Corp., Detroit
13 Sharon Steel Corp., Sharon, Pa.
14 Colorado Fuel & Iron Corp., Denver
15 Wheeling Steel Corp., Wheeling, W. Va.
16 Geneva Steel Co., Salt Lake City
17 Crucible Steel Co. of America, New York
18 Pittsburgh Steel Co., Pittsburgh
19 Kaiser Steel Corp., Oakland, Calif.
20 Portsmouth Div., Detroit Steel Corp., Detroit
21 Lukens Steel Co., Coatesville, Pa.
22 Granite City Steel Co., Granite City, Ill.
23 Wisconsin Steel Co., South Chicago, Ill.
24 Columbia Steel Co., San Francisco
25 Copperweld Steel Corp., Glassport, Pa.
26 Alan Wood Steel Co., Conshohocken, Pa.
27 Calif. Cold Rolled Steel Corp., Los Angeles
28 Allegheny Ludlum Steel Corp., Pittsburgh
29 Worth Steel Co., Claymont, Del.
30 Continental Steel Corp., Kokomo, Ind.
31 Rotary Electric Steel Co., Detroit
32 Laclede Steel Co., St. Louis
33 Northwestern Steel & Wire Co., Sterling, Ill.
34 Keystone Steel & Wire Co., Peoria, Ill.
35 Central Steel & Wire Co., Harrisburg, Pa.
36 Carpenter Steel Co., Reading, Pa.
37 Eastern Stainless Steel Corp., Baltimore
38 Washington Steel Corp., Washington, Pa.
39 Jessop Steel Co., Washington, Pa.
40 Blair Strip Steel Co., New Castle, Pa.
41 Superior Steel Corp., Carnegie, Pa.
42 Timken Steel & Tube Div., Canton, Ohio
43 Babcock & Wilcox Tube Co., Beaver Falls, Pa
44 Reeves Steel & Mfg. Co., Dover, Ohio
45 John A. Roebling's Sons Co., Trenton, N. J.
46 Simonds Saw & Steel Co., Fitchburg, Mass.
47 McLouth Steel Corp., Detroit
48 Cold Metal Products Co., Youngstown
49 Thomas Steel Co., Warren, Ohio
50 Wilson Steel & Wire Co., Chicago
51 Sweet's Steel Co., Williamsport, Pa.
52 Superior Drawn Steel Co., Monaca, Pa.
53 Tremont Nail Co., Wareham, Mass.
54 Firth Sterling Steel & Carbide Corp., McKeesport, Pa.
55 Ingersoll Steel Div., Chicago
56 Phoenix Iron & Steel Co., Phoenixville, Pa.
57 Fitzsimmons Steel Co., Youngstown
58 Stanley Works, New Britain, Conn.
59 Universal-Cyclops Steel Corp., Bridgeville, Pa
60 American Cladmetals Co., Carnegie, Pa.
61 Cuyahoga Steel & Wire Co., Cleveland
62 Bethlehem Pacific Coast Steel Corp., San Francisco
63 Follansbee Steel Corp., Pittsburgh
64 Niles Rolling Mill Co., Niles, Ohio
65 Atlantic Steel Co., Atlanta
66 Acme Steel Co., Chicago
67 Joslyn Mfg. & Supply Co., Chicago
68 Detroit Steel Corp., Detroit
69 Wyckoff Steel Corp., Pittsburgh
70 Bliss & Laughlin, Inc., Harvey, Ill.
71 Columbia Steel & Shafting Co., Pittsburgh
72 Cumberland Steel Co., Cumberland, Md.
73 La Salle Steel Co., Chicago
74 Monarch Steel Co., Inc., Hammond, Ind.
75 Empire Steel Co., Mansfield, Ohio
76 Mahoning Valley Steel Co., Niles, Ohio
77 Oliver Iron & Steel Co., Pittsburgh
78 Pittsburgh Screw & Bolt Co., Pittsburgh
79 Standard Forging Corp., Chicago
80 Driver Harris Co., Harrison, N. J.
81 Detroit Tube & Steel Div., Detroit
82 Reliance Div., Eaton Mfg. Co., Massillon, Ohio
83 Sheffield Steel Corp., Kansas City
84 Plymouth Steel Co., Detroit
85 Wickwire Spencer Steel, Buffalo
86 Angell Nail and Chaplet, Cleveland
87 Mid-States Steel & Wire, Crawfordsville, Ind
88 National Supply, Pittsburgh, Pa.
89 Wheatland Tube Co., Wheatland, Pa.
90 Mercer Tube & Mfg. Co., Sharon, Pa.

STAINLESS STEELS

Base prices, in cents per pound, f.o.b. producing point

Product	301	302	303	304	316	321	347	410	416	430
Ingots, rerolling	14.25	15.00	16.50	16.00	24.25	19.75	21.50	12.75	14.75	13.00
Slabs, billets rerolling	18.50	19.75	21.75	20.75	31.75	26.00	28.25	16.50	20.00	16.75
Forg. discs, die blocks, rings	34.00	34.00	36.50	35.50	52.50	40.00	44.50	28.00	28.50	28.50
Billets, forging	26.25	26.25	28.25	27.50	41.00	31.00	34.75	21.50	22.00	22.00
Bars, wires, structurals	31.25	31.25	33.75	32.75	48.75	36.75	41.25	25.75	26.25	26.25
Plates	33.00	33.00	35.00	35.00	51.50	40.50	45.00	27.00	27.50	27.50
Sheets	41.00	41.00	43.00	43.00	56.50	49.00	53.50	36.50	37.00	39.00
Strip, hot-rolled	26.50	28.00	32.25	30.00	48.25	36.75	41.00	23.50	30.25	24.00
Strip, cold-rolled	34.00	36.50	40.00	38.50	58.50	48.00	52.00	30.50	37.00	31.00

STAINLESS STEEL PRODUCING POINTS—*Sheets:* Midland, Pa., 17; Brackenridge, Pa., 28; Butler, Pa., 7; McKeesport, Pa., 1; Washington, Pa., 38 (type 316 add 5¢), 39; Baltimore, 37; Middletown, Ohio, 7; Massillon, Ohio, 4; Gary, 1; Bridgeville, Pa., 59; New Castle, Ind., 55; Ft. Wayne, Ind., 67; Lockport, N. Y., 46.
Strip: Midland, Pa., 17; Cleveland, 2; Carnegie, Pa., 41; McKeesport, Pa., 54; Reading, Pa., 36; Washington, Pa., 38 (type 316 add 5¢); W. Leechburg, Pa., 28; Bridgeville, Pa., 59; Detroit, 47; Massillon, Canton, Ohio, 4; Middletown, Ohio, 7; Harrison, N. J., 80; Youngstown, 48; Lockport, N. Y., 46; New Britain, Conn., 58; Sharon, Pa., 13; Butler, Pa., 7.
Bars: Baltimore, 7; Duquesne, Pa. 1; Munhall, Pa., 1; Reading, Pa., 36; Titusville, Pa., 59; Washington, Pa., 39; McKeesport, Pa., 1, 54; Bridgeville, Pa., 59; Dunkirk, N. Y., 28; Massillon, Ohio, 4; Chicago, 1; Syracuse, N. Y., 17; Watervliet, N. Y., 28; Waukegan, Ill., 2; Lockport, N. Y., 46; Canton, Ohio, 42; Ft. Wayne, Ind., 67.
Wire: Waukegan, Ill., 2; Massillon, Ohio, 4; McKeesport, Pa., 54; Bridgeport, Conn., 44; Ft. Wayne, Ind., 67; Trenton, N. J., 45; Harrison, N. J., 80; Baltimore, 7; Dunkirk, 28.
Structurals: Baltimore, 7; Massillon, Ohio, 4; Chicago, 1, 67; Watervliet, N. Y., 28; Bridgeport, Conn., 44.
Plates: Brackenridge, Pa., 28 (type 416 add ½¢); Butler, Pa., 7; Chicago, 1; Munhall, Pa., 1; Midland, Pa., 17; New Castle, Ind., 55; Lockport, N. Y., 46; Middletown, 7; Washington, Pa., 39; Cleveland, Massillon, 4.
Forged discs, die blocks, rings: Pittsburgh, 1, 17; Syracuse, 17; Ferndale, Mich., 28; Baltimore, 7; Washington, Pa., 39; McKeesport, Pa., 54.
Forging billets: Midland, Pa., 17; Baltimore, 7; Washington, Pa., 39; McKeesport, 54; Massillon, Canton, Ohio, 4; Watervliet, 28; Pittsburgh, Chicago, 1.

RAILS, TRACK SUPPLIES

F.o.b. Mill Cents Per Lb.	No. 1 Std. Rails	Light Rails	Joint Bars	Track Spikes	Axles	Screw Spikes	Tie Plates	Track Bolts Untreated
Bessemer-1	3.60	4.00	4.70					
Chicago-4				6.15				
Ensley-11	3.60	4.00						
Fairfield-11	3.60	4.00	4.40			8.60	4.50	
Gary-1	3.60	4.00					4.50	
Ind. Harbor-8	3.60		4.70	6.15	5.60	8.60	4.50	
Johnstown-3					5.60	8.60		
Joliet-1	3.60			6.15				
Kansas City-83				6.40				
Lackawanna-3	3.60	4.00	4.70			8.60	4.50	
Lebanon-3				6.15				9.60
Minnequa-14	3.60	4.50	4.70	6.15		8.60	4.50	9.60
Pittsburgh-77						9.35		9.60
Pittsburgh-78								9.60
Pittsburgh-3				6.15				
Pittsburg-24							4.65	
Seattle-62				6.10			4.35	
Steelton-3	3.60		4.70				4.50	
Struthers-6					5.60			
Torrance-24							4.65	
Youngstown-4				6.15				

Track Bolts, heat treated, to railroads, 9.85¢ per lb.

BOILER TUBES

Seamless steel, electric welded commercial boiler tubes, locomotive tubes, minimum wall, per 100 ft at mill, c.l. lots, out lengths 10 to 24 ft.

OD in in.	gage BWG	Seamless H.R.	C.D.	Electric Weld H.R.	C.D.
2	13	$22.67	$26.66	$21.99	$25.86
2½	12	30.48	35.84	29.57	34.76
3	12	33.90	39.90	32.89	34.80
3½	11	42.37	49.89	41.10	48.39
4	10	52.60	61.88	51.03	60.02

Pittsburgh Steel add, H-R: 2 in., 62¢; 2½ in., 84¢; 3 in., 92¢; 3½ in., $1.17; 4 in., $1.45. Add, C-R: 2 in., 74¢; 2½ in., 99¢; 3 in., $1.10; 3½ in., $1.37; 4 in., $1.70.

MERCHANT WIRE PRODUCTS

CAST IRON WATER PIPE

Per net ton
6 to 24-in., del'd Chicago . $105.30 to $108.80
6 to 24-in., del'd N. Y. . . . 104.50 to 105.50
6 to 24-in., f.o.b. Birmingham . 91.50 to 96.00
6-in. and larger, f.o.b. cars, San Francisco, Los Angeles, for all rail shipment; rail and water shipment less . . . . . . $108.50 to $113.00
Class "A" and gas pipe, $5 extra; 4-in. pipe is $5 a ton above 6-in.

FLUORSPAR

Washed gravel fluorspar, f.o.b. cars, Rosiclare, Ill. Base price, per ton net: Effective CaF, content:
70% or more $41.00
60% or less 38.00

F.o.b. Mill	Standard & Coated Nails Base Col.	Woven Wire Fence 9-15½ ga. Base Col.	Fence Posts Base Col.	Single Loop Bale Ties Base Col.	Twisted Barbless Wire Base Col.	Gal. Barbed Wire Base Col.	Merch. Wire Ann'ld. ¢/lb.	Merch. Wire Gal. ¢/lb.
Alabama City-4	118	126		123		136	5.70	5.95
Aliquippa, Pa.-5	118	132			136	140	5.70	6.15
Atlanta-65	113	133		126	126	143	5.95	6.40
Bartonville-34	118	130	140	123	143	143	5.95	6.15
Buffalo-85								
Cleveland-86								
Cleveland-2							5.70	6.15
Crawfordsville-87		132			145		5.95	6.40
Donora, Pa.-2	118	130		123		140	5.70	6.15
Duluth-2	118	130		123		140	5.70	6.15
Fairfield, Ala.-11	118	130		123		136	5.70	6.15
Houston-83	126	138			148		6.10	6.55
Johnstown, Pa.-3	118	130			140		5.70	6.15
Joliet, Ill.-2	118	130		123		140	5.70	6.15
Kokomo, Ind.-30	120	132		125	138	138	5.80	6.05
Los Angeles-62							6.65	
Kansas City-83	130	130	142	135		152	6.30	6.75
Minnequa-14	123	133	130	128	146	146	5.95	6.40
Monessen-18	124	135			145		5.95	6.40
Moline, Ill.-4			136					
Palmer-85								
Pittsburg, Cal.-24	137	149		147	156	160	6.65	6.80
Portsmouth-20	124	137			147	147	6.10	6.60
Rankin, Pa.-2	118	130				140	5.70	6.15
So. Chicago, Ill.-4	118	126	140	123		136	5.70	5.95
S. San Fran.-14				147		160	6.65	7.10
Sparrows Pt.-3	120			125	142	142	5.80	6.25
Sterling, Ill.-33	118	130	140	123	140	140	5.70	6.15
Struthers, Ohio-6							5.70	6.15
Torrance, Cal.-24	138						6.65	
Worcester-2	124						6.00	6.45
Williamsport, Pa.-51			150					

F. Cut Nails, carloads, base, $6.75 per 100 lb. (less 20¢ to jobbers) at Conshohocken, Pa., (26), Wareham, Mass. (53) Wheeling, W. Va., (15).

PIPE AND TUBING

Base discounts, f.o.b. mills. Base price about $200 per net ton.

	BUTTWELD													SEAMLESS					
	½ In.		¾ In.		1 In.		1¼ In.		1½ In.		2 In.		2½-3 In.		2 In.		2½-3 In.		3½-4 In.
	Blk.	Gal.	Blk.	Gal.	Blk.	Gal.	Blk.	Gal.	Blk.	Gal.	Blk.	Gal.	Blk.	Gal.	Blk.	Gal.	Blk.	Gal.	Blk.	Gal.
STANDARD T. & C.																				
Sparrows Pt.-3	34.0	12.0	37.0	16.0	39.5	19.5	40.0	20.0	40.5	21.0	41.0	21.5	41.5	22.0						
Cleveland-4	36.0	14.0	39.0	18.0	41.5	21.5	42.0	22.0	42.5	23.0	43.0	23.5	43.5	24.0						
Oakland-19	25.0	3.0	28.0	7.0	30.5	10.5	31.0	21.0	31.5	12.0	32.0	12.5	32.5	13.0						
Pittsburgh-5	36.0	14.0	39.0	17.0	41.5	19.5	42.0	20.5	42.5	21.5	43.0	21.5	43.5	24.0	29.5		8.0	32.5	11.5	34.5 13.5
Pittsburgh-10	36.0	14.0	39.0	17.0	41.5	19.5	42.0	20.5	42.5	21.5	43.0	23.5	43.5	24.0	29.5		9.5	32.5	12.5	34.5 14.5
St. Louis-32	35.0	13.0	38.0	17.0	40.5	20.0	41.0	21.0	41.5	22.0	42.0	22.5	42.5	23.0						
Sharon-90	36.0	13.0	39.0	17.0	41.5	19.5	42.0	20.5	42.5	21.5	43.0	23.5	43.5	24.0						
Toledo-88	36.0	14.0	39.0	18.0	41.5	19.5	42.0	20.0	42.5	22.0	43.0	22.5	43.5	24.0	29.5			32.5		34.5
Wheeling-15	36.0	14.0	39.0	18.0	41.5	19.5	42.0	20.5	42.5	21.5	43.0	23.5	43.5	24.0						
Wheatland-89	36.0	14.0	39.0	17.0	41.5	19.5	42.0	20.0	42.5	22.5	43.0	22.5	43.5							
Youngstown-6	36.0	14.0	39.0	18.0	41.5	19.5	42.0	20.5	42.5	21.5	43.0	23.5	43.5	24.0	29.5		9.5	32.5	12.5	34.5 14.5
EXTRA STRONG, PLAIN ENDS																				
Sparrows Pt.-3	33.5	13.0	37.5	17.0	39.5	20.5	40.0	21.0	40.5	22.0	41.0	22.5	41.5	23.0						
Cleveland-4	35.5	15.0	39.5	19.0	41.5	22.5	42.0	23.0	42.5	24.0	43.0	24.5	43.5	25.0						
Oakland-19	24.5	4.0	28.5	8.0	30.5	11.5	31.0	12.0	31.5	13.0	32.0	13.5	32.5	14.0						
Pittsburgh-5	35.5	13.0	39.5	17.5	41.5	19.5	42.0	20.5	42.5	24.0	43.0	24.5	43.5	25.0	29.0		7.5	33.0	12.0	36.0 15.5
Pittsburgh-10	35.5	15.0	39.5	19.0	41.5	22.5	42.0	23.0	42.5	24.0	43.0	24.5	43.5	25.0	29.0		10.0	33.0	14.0	36.5 17.5
St. Louis-32	34.5	14.0	38.5	18.0	40.5	21.0	41.0	22.0	41.5	23.0	42.0	23.5	42.5	24.0						
Sharon-90	35.5	15.0	39.5	19.0	41.5	22.5	42.0	23.0	42.5	24.0	43.0	24.5	43.5	25.0						
Toledo-88	35.5	15.0	39.5	19.0	41.5	19.5	42.0	23.0	42.5	24.0	43.0	24.0	43.5	25.0			33.0			36.5
Wheeling-15	35.5	15.0	39.5	19.0	41.5	19.5	42.0	20.5	42.5	21.5	43.0	24.5	43.5	25.0						
Wheatland-89	35.5	15.0	39.5	17.5	41.5	19.5	42.0	20.5	42.5	22.5	43.0	22.5	43.5							
Youngstown-6	35.5	15.0	39.5	19.0	41.5	19.5	42.0	20.5	42.5	24.0	43.0	24.5	43.5	25.0	29.0		10.0	33.0	14.0	36.5 17.5

Galvanized discounts based on zinc at 17¢ per lb, East St. Louis. For each 1¢ change in zinc, discounts vary as follows: ½ in., ¾ in., and 1 in., 1 pt.; 1¼ in., 1½ in., 2 in., ¾ pt.; 2½ in., 3 in., ½ pt. Calculate discounts on even cents per lb of zinc, i.e., if zinc is 16.51¢ to 17.50¢ per lb, use 17¢. Jones & Laughlin discounts apply only when zinc price changes 1¢. Threads only, buttweld and seamless, 1 pt. higher discount. Plain ends, buttweld and seamless, 3 in. and under, 3½ pts. higher discount. Buttweld jobbers' discount, 5 pct.

WAREHOUSE PRICES

Base prices, f.o.b. warehouse, dollars per 100 lb. (Metropolitan area delivery, add 20¢ to base price except Birmingham, San Francisco, Cincinnati, New Orleans, St. Paul (*), add 15¢; Philadelphia, add 25¢; Memphis, add 10¢; New York, add 30¢).

CITIES	SHEETS			STRIP		PLATES	SHAPES	BARS		ALLOY BARS			
	Hot-Rolled	Cold-Rolled (15 gage)	Galvanized (10 gage)	Hot-Rolled	Cold-Rolled		Standard Structural	Hot-Rolled	Cold-Finished	Hot-Rolled, A 4615 As-rolled	Hot-Rolled, A 4140 Ann.	Cold-Drawn, A 4615 As-rolled	Cold-Drawn, A 4140 Ann.
Baltimore	5.60	6.84	7.49²–8.07	6.04	....	5.80	6.14	6.04	6.84–6.89	10.24	10.54	11.89	12.19
Birmingham*	5.60	6.40	6.75	5.55	....	5.95	5.70	5.55	....	....	....	....	....
Boston	6.20	7.00–7.25	7.74–8.29	6.15	8.50¹⁶	6.48–6.78	6.20	6.05	6.79–6.84	10.25	10.55	11.90–12.00	12.20–12.30
Buffalo	5.60	6.40	7.74 8.09	5.86	....	6.05	5.80	5.60	6.40 6.45	10.15 10.85	10.45	11.80	11.95–12.10
Chicago	5.60	6.40	7.75	5.55	....	5.80	5.70	5.55	6.30	9.80	10.10	11.45	11.75
Cincinnati*	5.87	6.44	7.39	5.80	....	6.19	6.09	5.80	6.61	10.15	10.45	11.80	12.10
Cleveland	5.60	6.40	8.10	5.69	6.90	5.92	5.82	5.57	6.40	9.91	10.21	11.56	11.86
Detroit	5.78	6.53	7.89	5.94	....	5.99	6.09	5.84	6.56	10.11	10.41	11.76	12.06
Houston	7.00	8.25	....			6.85	6.50	6.65	9.35	10.35	11.25		12.75
Indianapolis, Del'd	6.00	6.80	8.15	5.95	....	6.20	6.10	5.95	6.80	....	....	....	....
Kansas City	6.00	6.80	7.45	6.15	7.50	6.40	6.30	6.15	7.00	10.40	10.70	12.05	12.35
Los Angeles	6.35	7.90	8.85	6.40	8.70¹⁶	6.40	6.35	6.35	7.55	11.30	11.30	13.20	13.50
Memphis*	6.33–6.38	7.08–7.18	....	6.33–6.38	....	6.43–8.02	6.33–6.48	6.08–6.33	7.16–7.32	....	....	....	....
Milwaukee	5.74	6.54	7.89	5.69–6.59	....	5.94	4.84	5.69	6.44–6.54	9.94	10.24	11.59	11.89
New Orleans*	5.70	6.95	....	5.75	7.25	5.95	5.75	5.75	7.30	....	....	....	....
New York*	5.67–5.97	7.19²²7.24¹	8.14²	6.29–6.89	8.63¹⁶	6.28–6.58	6.10	6.12	6.99	10.05–10.15	10.35–10.45	11.70–11.80	12.10–12.20
Norfolk	6.50¹³	....	....			6.50¹³	6.60¹³	6.55¹³	....	....	....	....	....
Philadelphia*	5.90	6.55	8.00	6.10	....	6.05	5.90	6.05	6.61	9.90	10.20	....	....
Pittsburgh	5.60	6.40	7.75	5.65–5.95	....	5.75	5.70	5.55	6.15	9.80	10.10	11.45	11.75
Portland	6.60	....	8.50	7.30	....	6.80	6.95	6.90	....	....	....	....	....
Salt Lake City	7.95	....	9.70	8.70	....	8.05	8.30	8.65	9.00	....	....	....	....
San Francisco*	6.65	8.05²	8.55–8.90²	6.60	....	6.50	6.45	6.45	8.20	11.30	11.30	13.20	13.20–13.50
Seattle	7.05	8.60	9.20	9.05	....	6.75	6.65	6.75	9.05	....	....	....	....
St. Louis	5.80–5.85	6.65	8.00	5.80	8.00¹⁶–8.28	6.13	6.03	5.80	6.55–6.65	10.05	10.35	11.70	12.00
St. Paul*	6.16	6.96	8.31	6.11	....	6.36	6.26	6.11	6.96	10.36	10.66	12.01	12.31

BASE QUANTITIES *(Standard unless otherwise keyed on prices.)*

Hot-rolled sheets and strip, hot rolled bars and bar shapes, structural shapes, plate, galvanized sheets and cold-rolled sheets; 2000 to 9999 lb. Cold-finished bars; 2000 lb or over. Alloy bars; 1000 to 1999 lb. Cold-rolled strip; 2000 to 9999 lb.

All HR products may be combined to determine quantity bracket. All galvanized sheets may be combined to determine quantity bracket. CR sheets may not be combined with each other or with galv. sheets to determine quantity bracket.

Exceptions:

(1) 400 to 1499 lb; (2) 450 to 1499 lb; (3) 300 to 4999 lb; (4) 300 to 9999 lb; (5) 2000 to 5999 lb; (6) 1000 lb and over; (7) 500 to 1499 lb; (8) 400 lb and over; (9) 400 to 9999 lb; (10) 500 to 9999 lb; (11) 400 to 3999 lb; (12) 450 to 3749 lb; (13) 400 to 1999 lb; (14) 1500 lb and over; (15) 1000 to 9999 lb; (16) 6000 lb and over; (17) up to 1999 lb; (18) 1000 to 4999 lb; (19) 1500 to 3499 lb; (20) CR sheets may be combined for quantity; (21) 3 to 24 bundles; (22) 1500 to 9999 lb.

PIG IRON PRICES

Dollars per gross ton. Delivered prices do not include 3 pct tax on freight.

PRODUCING POINT PRICES

Producing Point	Basic	No. 2 Foundry	Malleable	Bessemer	Low Phos.
Bethlehem	54.00	54.50	55.00	55.50	.....
Birmingham	48.38	48.88	.....	.....	.....
Buffalo	52.00	52.50	53.00	.....	.....
Chicago	52.00	52.50	52.50	53.00	.....
Cleveland	52.00	52.50	52.50	53.00	57.00
Daingerfield, Tex.	48.00	48.50	48.50	.....	.....
Duluth	52.00	52.50	52.50	53.00	.....
Erie	52.00	52.50	52.50	53.00	.....
Everett	.....	53.25	53.75	.....	.....
Fontana	58.00	58.50	.....	.....	.....
Granite City	53.90	54.40	54.90	.....	.....
Hubbard	52.00	52.50	52.50	.....	.....
Ironton, Utah	52.00	52.50	.....	.....	.....
Pittsburgh	52.00*	.....	.....	53.00	.....
Neville Island	52.00	52.50	52.50	53.00	.....
Geneva, Utah	52.00	52.50	.....	.....	.....
Sharpsville	52.00	52.50	52.50	53.00	.....
Steelton	54.00	54.50	55.00	55.50	60.00
Swedeland	56.00	56.50	57.00	57.50	.....
Toledo	52.00	52.50	52.50	53.00	.....
Troy, N. Y.	54.00	54.50	55.00	.....	60.00
Youngstown	52.00	52.50	52.50	53.00	.....

DELIVERED PRICES (BASE GRADES)

Consuming Point	Producing Point	Rail Freight Rate	Basic	No. 2 Foundry	Malleable	Bessemer	Low. Phos
Boston	Everett	$.60–.80	.....	53.85–54.05	54.55–54.75	.....	.....
Boston	Steelton	6.90	.....	.....	.....	.....	66.90
Brooklyn	Bethlehem	4.29	.....	58.79	59.29	59.29	.....
Cincinnati	Birmingham	6.70	55.08	55.58	.....	.....	.....
Jersey City	Bethlehem	2.63	.....	57.13	57.63	58.13	.....
Los Angeles	Geneva-Ironton	7.70	.....	59.70	60.20	.....	.....
Los Angeles	Fontana	.....	.....	59.70	60.20	.....	.....
Mansfield	Cleveland, Toledo	3.33	55.33	55.83	55.83	56.33	60.33
Philadelphia	Bethlehem	2.39	56.39	56.89	57.39	57.89	.....
Philadelphia	Swedeland	1.44	57.44	57.94	58.44	58.94	.....
Philadelphia	Steelton	3.09	57.09	57.59	58.09	58.59	63.09
Rochester	Buffalo	2.63	54.63	55.13	55.63	.....	.....
San Francisco	Geneva-Ironton	7.70	.....	59.70	60.20	.....	.....
San Francisco	Fontana	.....	.....	59.70	60.20	.....	.....
Seattle	Geneva-Ironton	7.70	.....	59.70	60.20	.....	.....
Seattle	Fontana	.....	.....	59.70	60.20	.....	.....
St. Louis	Granite City	0.75 Arb.	51.65	52.15	52.65	.....	.....
Syracuse	Buffalo	3.58	55.58	56.08	56.58	.....	.....

* Monessen, $54.00.
Producing points prices are subject to switching charges; silicon differential (not to exceed 50c per ton for each 0.25 pct silicon content in excess of base grade which is 1.75 to 2.25 pct for foundry iron); phosphorus differentials, a reduction of 38c per ton for phosphorus content of 0.70 pct and over; manganese differentials, a charge not to exceed 50c

per ton for each 0.50 pct manganese content in excess of 1.00 pct, $2 per ton extra may be charged for 0.5 to 0.75 pct nickel content and $1 per ton extra for each additional 0.25 pct nickel.
Silvery iron (blast furnace) silicon 6.01 to 6.50 pct C/L per g.t., f.o.b. Jackson, Ohio—$62.50; f.o.b. Buffalo, $63.75. Add $1.50 per ton for each additional 0.50 pct Si up to 17 pct.

Add 50c per ton for each 0.50 pct Mn over 1.00 pct. Add $1.00 per ton for 0.75 pct or more P. Bessemer ferrosilicon prices are $1.00 per ton above silvery iron prices of comparable analysis.
Charcoal pig iron base price for low phosphorus $62.00 per gross ton, f.o.b. Lyle, Tenn. Delivered Chicago, $70.56. High phosphorus charcoal pig iron is not being produced.

BOLTS, NUTS, RIVETS, SCREWS
Consumer Prices
(Base discount, f.o.b. mill, Pittsburgh, Cleveland, Birmingham or Chicago)

Machine and Carriage Bolts

	Pct Off list	
	Less Case	C.
½ in. & smaller x 6 in. & shorter	15	28½
9/16 in. & ⅝ in. x 6 in. & shorter	18½	30½
¾ in. & larger x 6 in. & shorter	17½	29½
All diam. longer than 6 in.	14	27½
Lag, all diam. x 6 in. & shorter	23	35
Lag, all diam. longer than 6 in.	21	33
Plow bolts	34	....

Nuts, Hot Pressed, Cold Punched—Sq

	Pct Off List			
	Less Keg K. (Reg.)		Less Keg. K. (Hvy.)	
½ in. & smaller	15	28½	15	28½
9/16 in. & ⅝ in.	12	25	6½	21
¾ in. to 1½ in. inclusive	9	23	1	16½
1⅝ in. & larger	7½	22	1	16½

Nuts, Hot Pressed—Hexagon

½ in. & smaller	26	37	22	34
9/16 in. & ⅝ in.	16½	29½	6½	21
¾ in. to 1½ in. inclusive	12	25	2	17½
1⅝ in. & larger	8½	23	2	17½

Nuts, Cold Punched—Hexagon

½ in. & smaller	26	37	22	34
9/16 in. & ⅝ in.	23	35	17½	30½
¾ in. to 1½ in. inclusive	19½	31½	12	25
1⅝ in. & larger	12	25	6½	21

Nuts, Semi-Finished—Hexagon

	Reg.		Hvy.	
½ in. & smaller	35	45	28½	39½
9/16 in. & ⅝ in.	29½	40½	22	34
¾ in. to 1½ in. inclusive	24	36	15	28½
1⅝ in. & larger	13	26	8½	23

	Light	
7/16 in. & smaller	35	45
½ in. thru ⅝ in.	28½	39½
¾ in. to 1½ in. inclusive	26	37

Stove Bolts

	Pct Off List
Packaged, steel, plain finished	56—10
Packaged, plated finish	41—10
Bulk, plain finish**	67*

*Discounts apply to bulk shipments in not less than 15,000 pieces of a size and kind when length is 3-in. and shorter; 5000 pieces for lengths longer than 3-in. For lesser quantities, packaged price applies.

**Zinc, Parkerized, cadmium or nickel plated finishes add 6¢ per lb net. For black oil finish, add 2¢ per lb net.

Rivets

	Base per 100 lb
½ in. & larger	$7.85
	Pct Off List
7/16 in. & smaller	36

F.o.b. Pittsburgh, Cleveland, Chicago. Birmingham, Lebanon, Pa.

Cap and Set Screws
(In bulk)

	Pct Off List
Hexagon head cap screws, coarse or fine thread, ¼ in. thru ⅝ in. x 6 in., SAE 1020, bright	54
¾ in. thru 1 in. up to & including 6 in.	48
¼ in. thru ⅝ in. x 6 in. & shorter high C double heat treat	46
¾ in. thru 1 in. up to & including 6 in.	41
Milled studs	35
Flat head cap screws, listed sizes	16
Fillister head cap, listed sizes	34
Set screws, sq head, cup point, 1 in. diam. and smaller x 6 in. & shorter	53

LAKE SUPERIOR ORES
(51.50% Fe; natural content, delivered lower lake ports)

	Per gross ton
Old range, bessemer	$8.70
Old range, nonbessemer	8.55
Mesabi, bessemer	8.45
Mesabi, nonbessemer	8.30
High phosphorus	8.30

After adjustments for analyses, prices will be increased or decreased as the case may be for increases or decreases after Dec. 2, 1950, in lake vessel rates, upper lake rail freights, dock handling charges and taxes thereon.

ELECTRODES
Cents per lb, f.o.b. plant, threaded electrodes with nipples, unboxed

Diam. in in.	Length in in.	Cents Per lb
GRAPHITE		
17, 18, 20	60, 72	17.85
8 to 16	48, 60, 72	17.85
7	48, 60	19.57
6	48, 60	20.95
4, 5	40	21.50
3	40	22.61
2½	24, 30	23.15
2	24, 30	25.36
CARBON		
40	100, 110	8.03
35	65, 110	8.03
30	65, 84, 110	8.03
24	72 to 104	8.03
20	84, 90	8.03
17	60, 72	8.03
14	60, 72	8.57
10, 12	60	8.84
8	60	9.10

CLAD STEEL
Base prices, cents per pound, f.o.b. mill

Stainless-carbon	Plate	Sheet
No. 304, 20 pct,		
Coatesville, Pa. (21)	*29.5	
Washgtn. Pa. (39)	*29.5	
Claymont, Del. (29)	*28.00	
Conshohocken, Pa. (26)		*24.00
New Castle, Ind. (55)	*26.50	*25.50
Nickel-carbon		
10 pct. Coatesville (21)	32.5	
Inconel-carbon		
10 pct Coatesville (21)	40.5	
Monel-carbon		
10 pct Coatesville (21)	33.5	
No. 302 Stainless-copper-stainless, Carnegie, Pa. (60)		77.00
Aluminized steel sheets, hot dip, Butler, Pa. (7)		7.75

* Includes annealing and pickling, or sandblasting.

TOOL STEEL
F.o.b. mill

W	Cr	V	Mo	Co	Base per lb
18	4	1	—	—	$1.10
18	4	1	—	5	$1.72
18	4	2	—	—	$1.245
1.5	4	1.5	8	—	78.5¢
6	4	2	6	—	84¢
High-carbon chromium					63.5¢
Oil hardened manganese					35¢
Special carbon					32.5¢
Extra carbon					27¢
Regular carbon					23¢

Warehouse prices on and east of Mississippi are 3¢ per lb higher. West of Mississippi, 5¢ higher.

ELECTRICAL SHEETS
22 gage, HR cut lengths, f.o.b. mill

	Cents per lb.
Armature	*6.75
Electrical	*7.25
Motor	*8.50
Dynamo	9.30
Transformer 72	9.85
Transformer 65	10.40
Transformer 58	11.10
Transformer 52	11.90

PRODUCING POINTS—Beech Bottom, W. Va., 15; Brackenridge, Pa., 28; Follansbee, W. Va., 63; Granite City, Ill. 22*, add 70¢; Indiana Harbor, Ind., 3; Mansfield, Ohio, 75; Niles, Ohio, 64, add 30¢; Vandergrift, Pa., 1; Warren, Ohio, 4; Zanesville, Ohio, 7.

COKE

	Net Ton
Furnace, beehive (f.o.b. oven)	
Connellsville, Pa.	$14.00 to $14.50
Foundry, beehive (f.o.b. oven)	
Connellsville, Pa.	$17.00 to $17.50
Foundry, oven coke	
Buffalo, del'd	$25.35
Chicago, f.o.b.	21.00
Detroit, f.o.b.	23.00
New England, del'd	24.80
Seaboard, N. J., f.o.b.	22.00
Philadelphia, f.o.b.	22.70
Swedeland, Pa., f.o.b.	22.60
Plainesville, Ohio, f.o.b.	24.00
Erie, Pa., f.o.b.	23.50
Cleveland, del'd	25.72
Cincinnati, del'd	25.06
St. Paul, f.o.b.	21.00
St. Louis, f.o.b.	24.90
Birmingham, del'd	20.79

C-R SPRING STEEL
Base per pound f.o.b. mill

0.26 to 0.40 carbon	5.35¢
0.41 to 0.60 carbon	6.80¢
0.61 to 0.80 carbon	7.40¢
0.81 to 1.05 carbon	9.35¢
1.06 to 1.35 carbon	11.65¢

Worcester, add 0.30¢; Sharon, Carnegie, New Castle, add 0.35¢; Detroit, 0.26 to 0.40 carb., add 25¢; other grades add 15¢. New Haven, 0.26 to 0.40 carb., add 50¢; other grades add 5¢.

REFRACTORIES
(F.o.b. works)

Fire Clay Brick   Carloads, Per 1000

First quality, Ill., Ky., Md., Mo., Ohio, Pa. (except Salina, Pa., add $5)	$94.60
No. 1 Ohio	88.00
Sec. quality, Pa., Md., Ky., Mo., Ill.	88.00
No. 2 Ohio	79.20
Ground fire clay, net ton, bulk (except Salina, Pa., add $1.50)	13.70

Silica Brick

Mt. Union, Pa., Ensley, Ala.	$94.60
Childs, Pa.	99.00
Hays, Pa.	100.10
Chicago District	104.50
Western Utah and Calif.	111.10
Super Duty, Hays, Pa., Athens, Tex., Chicago	111.10
Silica cement, net ton, bulk, Eastern (except Hays, Pa.)	16.50
Silica cement, net ton, bulk, Hays, Pa.	18.70
Silica cement, net ton, bulk, Ensley, Ala.	17.60
Silica cement, net ton, bulk, Chicago District	17.60
Silica cement, net ton, bulk, Utah and Calif.	24.75

Chrome Brick   Per Net Ton

Standard chemically bonded, Balt., Chester	$82.00

Magnesite Brick

Standard, Baltimore	$104.00
Chemically bonded, Baltimore	93.00

Grain Magnesite   St. ⅜-in. grains

Domestic, f.o.b. Baltimore, in bulk fines removed	$62.70
Domestic, f.o.b. Chewelah, Wash., in bulk	36.30
in sacks	41.80

Dead Burned Dolomite

F.o.b. producing points in Pennsylvania, West Virginia and Ohio, per net ton, bulk Midwest. add 10¢; Missouri Valley, add 20¢ $13.00

METAL POWDERS
Per pound, f.o.b. shipping point, in ton lots, for minus 100 mesh.

Swedish sponge iron c.i.f. New York, ocean bags	7.4¢ to 9.0¢
Canadian sponge iron, del'd, in East	10.00¢
Domestic sponge iron, 98+% Fe, carload lots	9.0¢ to 15.0¢
Electrolytic iron, annealed, 99.5+% Fe	36.0¢ to 39.5¢
Electrolytic iron unannealed, minus 325 mesh, 99+% Fe	48.5¢
Hydrogen reduced iron, minus 300 mesh, 98+% Fe	63.0¢ to 80.0¢
Carbonyl iron, size 5 to 10 micron, 98%, 99.8+% Fe	70.0¢ to $1.35
Aluminum	29.00¢
Brass, 10 ton lots	30.00¢ to 33.25¢
Copper, electrolytic 10.25¢ plus metal value	
Copper, reduced 10.00¢ plus metal value	
Cadmium 100-199 lb. .95¢ plus metal value	
Chromium, electrolytic, 99% min., and quantity	$3.50
Lead 6.5¢ plus metal value	
Manganese	52.00¢
Molybdenum, 99%	$2.65
Nickel, unannealed	75.5¢
Nickel, annealed	81.5¢
Nickel, spherical, unannealed	78.5¢
Silicon	34.00¢
Solder powder . 6.5 to 8.5¢ plus met. value	
Stainless steel, 302	75.00¢
Tin 11.00¢ plus metal value	
Tungsten, 99%	$4.15
Zinc, 10 ton lots	20.50¢ to 23.85¢

FERROALLOYS

Ferrochrome

Contract prices, cents per pound, contained Cr, lump size, bulk, in carloads, delivered. (65-72% Cr, 2% max. Si.)

0.06% C	30.50	0.20% C	29.50
0.10% C	30.00	0.50% C	29.25
0.15% C	29.75	1.00% C	29.00
2.00% C	28.75		
65-69% Cr, 4-9% C	22.00		
62-66% Cr, 4-6% C, 6-9% Si	22.85		

High-Nitrogen Ferrochrome

Low-carbon type: 67-72% Cr, 0.75% N. Add 5¢ per lb to regular low carbon ferrochrome price schedule. Add 5¢ for each additional 0.25% N.

S. M. Ferrochrome

Contract price, cents per pound, chromium contained, lump size, delivered.
High carbon type: 60-65% Cr, 4-6% Si, 4-6% Mn, 4-6% C.

Carloads	21.60
Ton lots	23.75
Less ton lots	25.25

Low carbon type: 62-66% Cr, 4-6% Si, 4-6% Mn, 1.25% max. C.

Carloads	27.75
Ton lots	30.05
Less ton lots	31.85

Chromium Metal

Contract prices, per lb chromium contained packed, delivered, ton lots. 97% min. Cr, 1% max. Fe.

0.20% Max. C.	$1.09
0.50% max. C.	1.05
.00 min. C	1.04

Low Carbon Ferrochrome Silicon

(Cr 34-41%, Si 42-49%, C 0.05% max.) Contract price, carloads, f.o.b. Niagara Falls, freight allowed; lump 4-in. x down, bulk 2-in. x down, 21.75¢ per lb of contained Cr plus 12.00¢ per lb of contained Si. Bulk 1-in. x down, 21.90¢ per lb contained Cr plus 12.20¢ per lb of contained Si.

Calcium-Silicon

Contract price per lb of alloy, dump, delivered.
30-33% Ca, 60-65% Si, 3.00% max. Fe.

Carloads	19.00
Ton lots	22.10
Less ton lots	23.60

Calcium-Manganese—Silicon

Contract prices, cents per lb of alloy, lump, delivered.
16-20% Ca, 14-18% Mn, 53-59% Si.

Carloads	20.00
Ton lots	22.30
Less ton lots	23.30

CMSZ

Contract price, cents per pound of alloy, delivered.
Alloy 4: 45-49% Cr, 4-6% Mn, 18-21% Si, 1.25-1.75% Zr, 3.00-4.5% C.
Alloy 5: 50.56% Cr, 4-6% Mn, 13.50-16.00% Si, 0.75 to 1.25% Zr, 3.50-5.00% C.

Ton lots	20.75
Less ton lots	22.00

V Foundry Alloy

Cents per pound of alloy, f.o.b. Suspension Bridge, N. Y., freight allowed, max. St. Louis. V-5: 38-42% Cr, 17-19% Si, 8-11% Mn.

Ton lots	16.50¢
Less ton lots	17.75¢

Graphidox No. 4

Cents per pound of alloy, f.o.b. Suspension Bridge, N. Y., freight allowed, max. St. Louis. Si 48 to 52%, Ti 9 to 11%, Ca 5 to 7%.

Carload packed	18.00¢
Ton lots to carload packed	19.00¢
Less ton lots	20.50¢

SMZ

Contract price, cents per pound of alloy, delivered, 60-65% Si, 5-7% Mn, 5-7% Zr, 20% Fe, ½ in. x 12 mesh.

Ton lots	17.25
Less ton lots	18.50

Ferromanganese

78-82% Mn. maximum contract base price, gross ton, lump size.

F.o.b. Niagara Falls, Alloy, W. Va., Welland, Ont., Ashtabula, O.	$185
F.o.b. Johnstown, Pa.	$187
F.o.b. Sheridan, Pa.	$185
F.o.b. Etna, Clairton, Pa.	$188

$2.00 for each 1% above 82% Mn, penalty, $2.15 for each 1% below 78%. Briquets—Cents per pound of briquet, delivered, 66% contained Mn.

Carload, bulk	10.45
Ton lots	12.05

Spiegeleisen

Contract prices gross ton, lump, f.o.b.

	16-19% Mn 3% max. Si	19-21% Mn 3% max. Si
Palmerton, Pa.	$74.00	$75.00
Pgh. or Chicago	74.00	75.00

Manganese Metal

Contract basis, 2 in. x down, cents per pound of metal, delivered.
96% min. Mn, 0.2% max. C, 1% max. Si, 2% max. Fe.

Carload, packed	29.75
Ton lots	31.25

Electrolytic Manganese

F.o.b. Knoxville, Tenn., freight allowed east of Mississippi, cents per pound.

Carloads	28
Ton lots	30
Less ton lots	32

Medium Carbon Ferromanganese

Mn 80% to 85%, C 1.25 to 1.50. Contract price, carloads, lump, bulk, delivered, per lb. of contained Mn ... 19.15¢

Low-Carbon Ferromanganese

Contract price, cents per pound Mn contained, lump size, del'd, Mn. 85-90%.

	Carloads	Ton	Less
0.07% max. C, 0.06% P, 90% Mn	26.25	28.10	29.30
0.07% max. C	25.75	27.60	28.80
0.15% max. C	25.25	27.10	28.30
0.30% max. C	24.75	26.60	27.80
0.50% max. C	24.25	26.10	27.30
0.75% max. C, 7.00% max. Si	21.25	23.10	24.30

Silicomanganese

Contract basis, lump size, cents per pound of metal, delivered, 65-68% Mn, 18-20% Si, 1.5% max. C. For 2% max. C, deduct 0.2¢.

Carload bulk	9.90
Ton lots	11.55
Briquet, contract basis carlots, bulk delivered, per lb of briquet	11.15
Ton lots	11.75

Silvery Iron (electric furnace)

Si 14.01 to 14.50 pct, f.o.b. Keokuk, Iowa, or Wenatchee, Wash., $89.50 gross ton, freight allowed to normal trade area. Si 15.01 to 15.50 pct, f.o.b. Niagara Falls, N. Y., $83.00. Add $1.00 per ton for each additional 0.50% Si up to and including 18%. Add $1.00 for each 0.50% Mn over 1%.

Silicon Metal

Contract price, cents per pound contained Si, lump size, delivered, for ton lots packed.

96% Si, 2% Fe	21.70
97% Si, 1% Fe	22.10

Silicon Briquets

Contract price, cents per pound of briquet bulk, delivered, 40% Si, 1 lb Si briquets.

Carload, bulk	6.95
Ton lots	8.55

Electric Ferrosilicon

Contract price, cents per pound contained Si, lump, bulk, carloads, delivered.

25% Si	19.00	75% Si	14.30
50% Si	12.40	85% Si	15.55
90-95% Si			17.50

Calcium Metal

Eastern zone contract prices, cents per pound of metal, delivered.

	Cast	Turnings	Distilled
Ton lots	$2.05	$2.95	$3.75
Less ton lots	2.40	3.30	4.55

Other Ferroalloys

Alsifer, 20% Al, 40% Si, 40% Fe, contract basis, f.o.b. Suspension Bridge, N. Y.

Carload	8.15¢
Ton lots	9.55¢

Calcium molybdate, 45-40%, f.o.b. Langeloth, Pa., per pound contained Mo ... $1.15

Ferrocolumbium, 50-60%, 2 in x D, contract basis, delivered, per pound contained Cb.

Ton lots	$4.90
Less ton lots	4.95

Ferro-Tantalum-columbium, 20% Ta, 40% Cb, 0.30 C. Contract basis, delivered, ton lots, 2 in. x D, per lb of contained Cb plus Ta ... $3.75

Ferromolybdenum, 55-75%, f.o.b. Langeloth, Pa., per pound contained Mo ... $1.32

Ferrophosphorus, electrolytic, 23-26%, car lots, f.o.b. Siglo, Mt. Pleasant, Tenn., $3 unitage, per gross ton

gross ton	$66.00
10 tons to less carload	75.00

Ferrotitanium, 40%, regular grade, 0.10% C max., f.o.b. Niagara Falls, N. Y., and Bridgeville, Pa., freight allowed, ton lots, per lb contained Ti ... $1.38

Ferrotitanium, 25%, low carbon, 0.10% C max., f.o.b. Niagara Falls, N. Y., and Bridgeville, Pa., freight allowed, ton lots, per lb contained Ti ... $1.50

Less ton lots ... $1.55

Ferrotitanium, 15 to 19%, high carbon, f.o.b. Niagara Falls, N. Y., freight allowed, carload per net ton ... $177.00

Ferrotungsten, standard, lump or ¼ x down, packed, per pound contained W, 5 ton lots, delivered ... $3.25

Ferrovanadium, 35-55%, contract basis, delivered, per pound, contained V.

Openhearth	$3.00-$3.05
Crucible	3.10- 3.15
High speed steel (Primos)	3.25

Molybdic oxide, briquets or cans, per lb contained Mo, f.o.b. Langeloth, Pa. ... $1.14
bags, f.o.b. Washington, Pa., Langeloth, Pa. ... $1.13

Simanal, 20% Si, 20% Mn, 20% Al, contract basis, f.o.b. Philo, Ohio, freight allowed, per pound

Carload, bulk lump	14.50¢
Ton lots, bulk lump	15.75¢
Less ton lots, lump	16.25¢

Vanadium pentoxide, 88-92% V₂O₅, contract basis, per pound contained V₂O₅ ... $1.28

Zirconium, 35-40%, contract basis, f.o.b. plant, freight allowed, per pound of alloy.

Ton lots	21.00¢

Zirconium, 12-15%, contract basis, lump, delivered, per lb of alloy.

Carload, bulk	7.00¢

Boron Agents

Contract prices per lb of alloy, del.
Borosil, f.o.b. Philo, Ohio, freight allowed, B 3-4%, Si 40-45%, per lb contained B ... $5.25

Bortam, f.o.b. Niagara Falls

Ton lots, per pound	45¢
Less ton lots, per pound	50¢

Carbortam, Ti 15-21%, B 1-2%, Si 2-4%, Al 1-2%, C 4.5-7.5% f.o.b. Suspension Bridge, N. Y., freight allowed.

Ton lots, per pound	10.00¢

Ferroboron, 17.50% min. B, 1.50% max. Si, 0.50% max. Al, 0.50% max. C, 1 in. x D. Ton lots ... $1.20
F.o.b. Wash., Pa.; 100 lb, up

10 to 14% B	.78
14 to 19% B	1.20
19% min. B	1.50

Grainal, f.o.b. Bridgeville, Pa., freight allowed, 100 lb and over.

No. 1	$1.00
No. 6	68¢
No. 79	50¢

Manganese—Boron 75.00% Mn, 15-20% B, 5% max. Fe, 1.50% max. Si, 3.00% max. C, 2 in. x D, delivered.

Ton lots	$1.46
Less ton lots	1.57

Nickel—Boron 15-18% B, 1.00% max. Al, 1.50% max. Si, 0.50% max. C, 3.00% max. Fe, balance Ni, delivered.

Less ton lots	$1.80

Silcaz, contract basis, delivered.

Ton lots	45.00¢

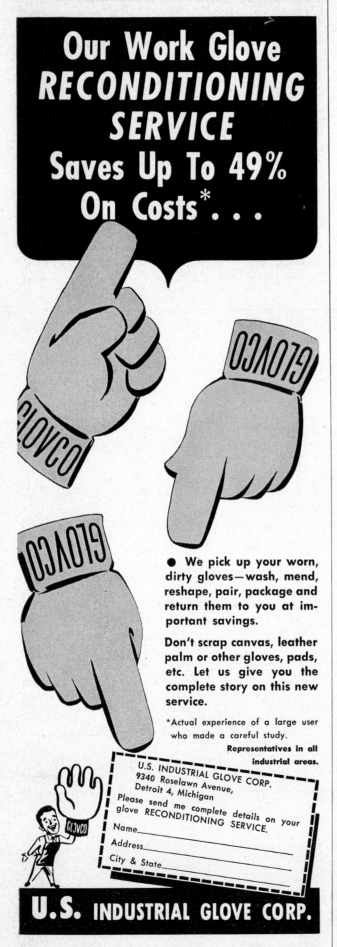
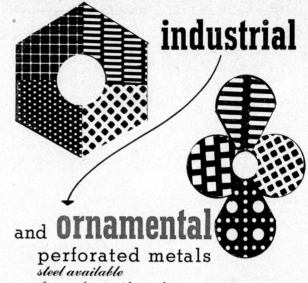

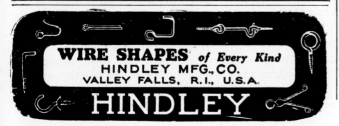

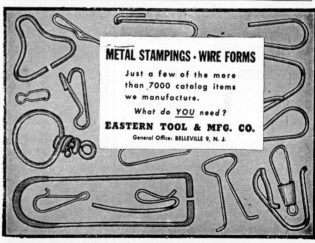

The Clearing House

NEWS OF USED, REBUILT AND SURPLUS MACHINERY

Up to '42 Mark—With the sifting down of increasing defense contracts to smaller plants and subcontractors, demand for used machines will reach high proportions this year, Cleveland used machinery dealers say. Although limited by the availability of machines, business should rival the 1942 peak, they think.

The market is expected to get brisker about Feb. 1 and dealers are trying to build up inventories in anticipation. They are not too successful.

On the Road—Dealers in their campaign to find used machines are sending men on the road with orders to find and buy almost any piece of equipment in working order. Others are paying bonuses in the form of "finders' fees" and some are cultivating relations with new machine tool salesmen for leads.

Particularly in short supply in the Cleveland district are turret lathes—and turning equipment of any kind, shears and tool room equipment. Tenor of the times is a statement from one dealer: "Anything that will work can be sold."

Rebuilding Boom—Dealers rebuilding used machines are trying to hire more men to meet schedules. They have more business than they can handle. Average rebuilding job, depending on the machine and its condition, runs about 3 months.

Starting to Move—The average large dealer is fairly well stocked with the big older machines. These items have not been too active. Now they are beginning to move slowly with faster movement predicted in the months ahead.

Private plants, where the dealer has a past relationship, continue to be the best source of used machines. Auctions are attracting plant buyers and dealers are buying for plants on commission.

Would Be Better—Used machinery business in the Chicago area would be tremendous if dealers had enough equipment to fill demand for late type equipment. Inquiries started upward again in December after a tapering off in November. Most buyers want machinery built in and after 1940. Turret lathes, screw machines, press brakes and large squaring shears are almost unobtainable.

Demand for older equipment is picking up and will continue to accelerate.

Near New Prices—Dealers are having a tough time replenishing stocks of late type equipment and prices are going up. Some auction machines bring within 5 pct of the new price and some dealers report that they are unable to buy at these high levels and still make a profit.

A few dealers, reasoning that they can get the full sale price from private sources, have discontinued the practice of giving discounts to fellow dealers.

Ear to the Ground—Dealers in the Chicago area have their ear to the ground, trying to follow the defense contract trend. A speedup was expected in January. With this the used machinery business will be stimulated.

Since it is not considered a risk for a firm to anticipate greater defense spending and consequently more war work, some companies are reportedly preparing for the near future by buying up used machinery. They will have the edge on the last-minute thinkers.

No Planned Schedules—NISA has written the National Production Authority a protest on the application of copper order M-12 to the trade. The order limits shops to the use of an amount of magnet wire (pounds) this month not greater than one-sixth of the average amount used in the first half of 1950.

KEEPS YOUR PRODUCTION LINES *MOVING*

Backed by 20 years of experience in engineering and installing lubricating equipment, Trabon can save you thousands of dollars. Write for this booklet which shows how it can be done.

Most of your machinery stoppages — due to bearing failures — could be avoided with Trabon. Shutdowns for lubrication can be eliminated, too. Trabon lubricates as your machines produce!

Trabon has a single indicator at the pump, giving proof when the lubricating cycle is complete. The progressive hydraulic operation makes it impossible to skip a bearing.

Trabon oil and grease systems are completely sealed, have no exposed moving parts . . . dirt, dust, water, grime, abrasive grit, are all barred from Trabon lubricating systems.

Trabon

OIL AND GREASE SYSTEMS

TRABON ENGINEERING CORPORATION
1814 East 40th Street • Cleveland 3, Ohio

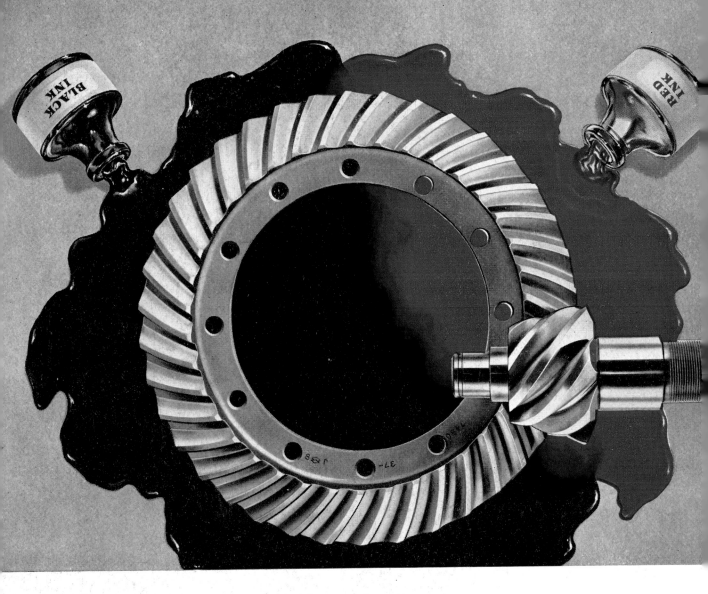

Where Does the Red Begin?

WHERE GEARS are concerned, that's a question you may want to ask yourself. Too often the red ink begins too soon. It may begin with gears not dependably up to your specifications. You may find it in production slow-downs due to gear installation difficulties. You may find that poor performance is building up your service costs.

You may discover that gear-troubles are causing your customers to think of competitors' products.

If the red ink begins at *any* of these points you'll be well rewarded by discussing gear problems with "Double Diamond" engineers. *"Double Diamonds" are produced to work in the black.* They provide low installed cost. They

serve economically and dependably on the job for which you buy them. They do credit to your product and your reputation.

We have thirty-six years of such gear-building behind us. We believe we know gears, and we believe we know the true facts about gear costs. We'd like to discuss these matters with you at your convenience.

DOUBLE DIAMOND
TRADE   MARK
GEARS

Automotive Gear Works, Inc.
RICHMOND, INDIANA

• • • • • FOR AUTOMOTIVE   FARM EQUIPMENT AND GENERAL INDUSTRIAL APPLICATIONS
☆Reg. U. S. Pat. Off.

HYPOID BEVEL

SPIRAL BEVEL

FLYWHEEL GEAR

ZEROL☆ BEVEL

STRAIGHT BEVEL

STRAIGHT SPUR

HELICAL SPUR

SPLINED STEM PINION

SPLINE SHAFT

The Iron Age

A CHILTON PUBLICATION

E NATIONAL METALWORKING WEEKLY

January 18, 195

ENTS PAGE 2

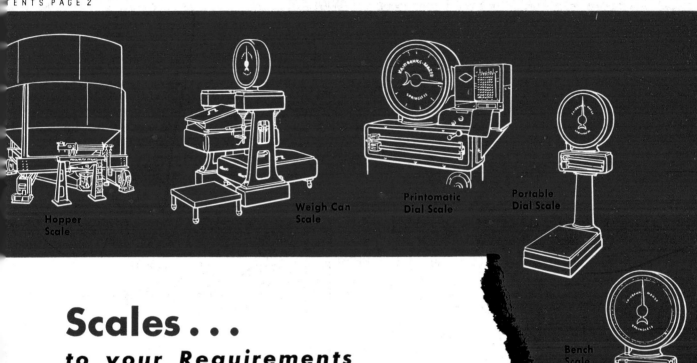

Hopper
Scale

Weigh Can
Scale

Printomatic
Dial Scale

Portable
Dial Scale

Bench
Scale

Counting
Scale

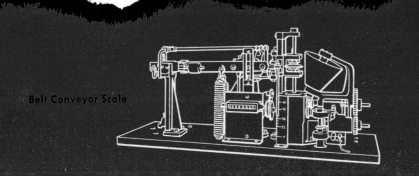

Belt Conveyor Scale

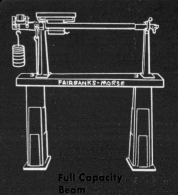

Full Capacity
Beam

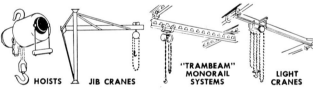

Tool Steel Topics

BETHLEHEM STEEL COMPANY, BETHLEHEM, PA.

the Pacific Coast Bethlehem products are sold by Bethlehem Pacific Coast Steel Corporation. *Export Distributor:* Bethlehem Steel Export Corporation

Made from BTR oil-hardening tool steel, this die recently produced 7,953,632 bottle caps before redressing was needed. Photo courtesy of R. M. Hollingshead Co., Camden, N. J.

BTR BLANKS AND FORMS 100,000 BOTTLE CAPS IN EIGHT HOURS

High-Production Die Still Going Strong After Four Years' Service

It takes a long time to wear out a die that's made from BTR. This popular, oil-hardening grade was selected by the R. M. Hollingshead Co., Camden, N. J., for this high-production die that blanks and forms 1-in. bottle caps from tin plate in almost fabulous quantities. Hardened to Rockwell C-61, the die is redressed about every three months. Records kept by William Schaefer, machine shop foreman, show that the die recently produced 7,953,632 caps between grinds. Such results indicate good tool design, correct heat-treatment and grinding . . . and quality tool steel to fit the job.

The performance record of this die over a four-year period is a good example of the long wear of which BTR is capable. Next to carbon tool steel, BTR is the most versatile of Bethlehem fine tool steels. It's safe-hardening in oil at 1475 F. It holds close dimensions during heat-treatment, has high resistance to wear and shock. BTR is an economical grade to buy, and it's easy to machine and heat-treat. There's not much more you could ask of a general-purpose tool steel!

Our Tool Steel Engineer Says:

Reduce tool failures by removing "feather" edges

A "feather" often remains on the working edges of tools after they are ground. Especially on cutting tools, it is best to remove these irregularities. Otherwise the cutting edge will get dull or fail prematurely. The experienced shop man carries a stone in his pocket for touching up such edges, for he knows that removing feather edges pays off in longer tool life.

This die of Lehigh S puts large dents in 3-in. steel tubing which is then fitted with baffles to make an efficient flue for space heaters.

Lehigh S Solves Problem for Space-Heater Manufacturer

In setting up the production of their patented "Heat Trap" flue for gas space heaters, the Day and Night Manufacturing Co., Monrovia, Calif., needed a tool steel with the absolute maximum of wear-resistance. The design called for a series of indents in a steel flue, staggered and baffled so as to retard rising hot gases in the flue and deflect them from side to side.

Lehigh S was the logical choice. This high-carbon, high-chromium grade (2.05 pct C; 12 pct Cr) has the highest hardness of all Bethlehem tool and die grades, ranging up to Rockwell C-66. And that's *hard!* Used for the form punches and inserts at wear points for the forming die illustrated, Lehigh S has given long service, requiring no maintenance after putting indents in more than 300,000 pieces of 3-in. steel tubing.

Heavy-Duty Shear Blades Made to Your Order

When you buy Bethlehem Shear Blades you get the benefit of our many years of experience in making all our own specialty shear blades for cutting sheets, strip, billets, bars, and plates in our own plants. Making our own shear blades involved many years of special development work in tool steels, and in blade design, heat-treatment, and grinding techniques. But we developed this product because we needed better blades than we were able to purchase, blades better able to stand up under heavy shock and high wear.

Bethlehem Shear Blades are usually made from Lehigh H, Lehigh L (for better shock resistance), or Lehigh S (for greatest wear-resistance where heavy shock is not a factor). Some are made from our hot-work and shock-resisting tool steels.

Among our specialty blades are: flying pinch knives for continuous sheet-strip mills, resquaring shear knives, heavy-duty knives for plates, rotary slitters, and many special-purpose blades.

Bethlehem blades have established fine performance records in the most severe types of shearing service. If you use blades requiring high-alloy tool steels let us tell you what we can do for you in supplying shear blades specially designed to your requirements.

Rotary slitters and shear blade made of Lehigh H, our most popular grade of high-carbon, high-chromium tool steel—for maximum production.

Bethlehem Tool Steel

IRON AGE

CONTENTS

THE IRON AGE
Editorial, Advertising and Circulation Offices, 100 E. 42nd St., New York 17, N. Y.
GEORGE T. HOOK, Publisher
TOM C. CAMPBELL, Editor

EDITORIAL STAFF
Managing Editor   George F. Sullivan
Feature Editor   Darwyn I. Brown
News-Markets Editor   Wm. V. Packard
Machinery Editor   George Elwers
Associate Editors: William Czygan, H. W. Van Camp, F. J. Winters; Assistant Editors: R. L. Hatschek, J. Kolb, Ted Metaxas, W. B. Olson, Regional Editors: E. C. Beaudet, Chicago; W. A. Lloyd, Cleveland; W. G. Patton, Detroit; John B. Delaney, Pittsburgh; Osgood Murdock, R. T. Reinhardt, San Francisco; Eugene J. Hardy, Karl Rannells, George H. Baker, Washington; Correspondents: Fred L. Allen, Birmingham; N. Levenson, Boston; Fred Edmunds, Los Angeles; James Douglas, Seattle; Roy Edmonds, St. Louis; F. Sanderson, Toronto; F. H. Harley, London, England; Chilton Editorial Board: Paul Wooton, Washington Representative.

BUSINESS STAFF
Production Manager   B. H. Hayes
Director of Research   Oliver Johnson
Mgr. Circul'n & Promotion   C. T. Post
Asst. Promotion Mgr.   James A. Crites
Asst. Dir. of Research   Wm. Laimbeer

REGIONAL BUSINESS MANAGERS
B. L. Herman, Philadelphia, Stanley J. Smith, Chicago; Peirce Lewis, Detroit; Paul Bachman, New England, Robert F. Blair, Cleveland; R. Raymond Kay, Los Angeles; C. H. Ober, New York; J. M. Spackman, Pittsburgh; Harry Becker, European Representative.

REGIONAL OFFICES
Chicago 3, 1134 Otis Bldg.; Cleveland 14, 1016 National City Bank Bldg.; Detroit 2, 103 Pallister Ave.; Los Angeles 28, 2420 Cheremoya Ave.; New England, 62 La Salle Rd., W. Hartford 7; New York 17, 100 E. 42nd St.; Philadelphia 39, 56th & Chestnut Sts.; Pittsburgh 22, 814 Park Bldg.; Washington 4, National Press Bldg.; European, 111 Thorley Lane, Timperley, Cheshire England.

Circulation Representatives: Thomas Scott, James Richardson.

One of the Publications Owned and Published by Chilton Company, Inc., Chestnut and 56th Sts., Philadelphia 39, Pa., U. S. A.

OFFICERS AND DIRECTORS
JOS. S. HILDRETH, President
Vice-Presidents: Everit B. Terhune, G. C. Buzby, P. M. Fahrendorf, Harry V. Duffy. William H. Vallar, Treasurer; John Blair Moffett, Secretary; D. Allyn Garber, Maurice E. Cox, Frank P. Tighe, George T. Hook, Tom C. Campbell, L. V. Rowlands, Directors. George Maiswinkle, Asst. Treas.

Indexed in the Industrial Arts Index and the Engineering Index. Published every Thursday by the CHILTON CO. (INC.), Chestnut and 56th Sts., Philadelphia 39, Pa. Entered as second class matter Nov. 8, 1932, at the Post Office at Philadelphia under the act of March 3, 1879. $8 yearly in United States, its territories and Canada: other Western Hemisphere Countries $15; other Foreign Countries $25 per year. Single Copies 35c. Annual Review and Metal Industry Facts Issue, $2.00. Cable address "Ironage" N. Y.
Member Audit Bureau of Circulations. Member Society of Business Magazine Editors.

Copyright, 1951, by Chilton Co. (Inc.)

DIGEST

ANUARY EIGHTEENTH • NINETEEN FIFTY-ONE • VOLUME 167 • NUMBER 3

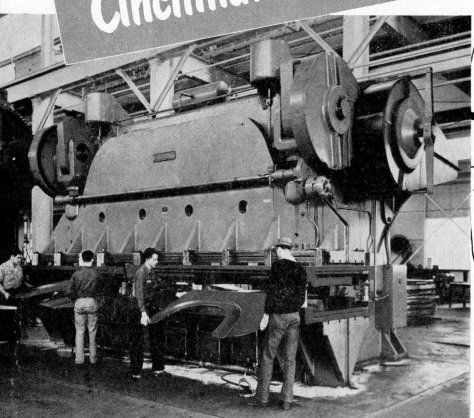
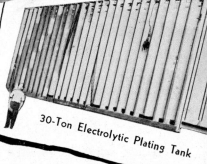

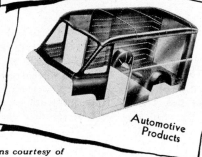

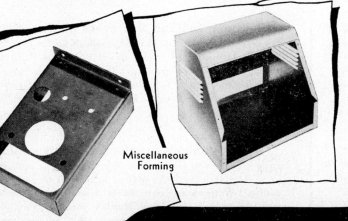

The Age of Folly

THE next few weeks should be an inventory period for those in charge of our government and our defense. What turns up might be of aid to the enemy. It might also be good for our souls. Anything good for our souls ought to be bad for our enemy.

We are in the midst of a defense program. The orders are coming in but they are coming in hit or miss. There is no overall comprehensive military plan to help business to give its best. Maybe it will come in time but will that be time enough?

Our No. 2 enemy is inflation. It can wreck us as surely as an all out war. It is getting away from those whose duty it is to keep it in check.

We hear talk of controls. We control the tail and let the dog go where he will. We clamp on ceilings—voluntary—knowing full well they won't work. We talk big stuff when the staff to run such a serious program as price and wage controls is hardly large enough to take a letter.

We put people in jobs of top responsibility whose sole qualification for the job is getting along with others. We have one excellent appointment at the top. He will need all the miracles in the Bible to get our defense and mobilization going in time to mean something.

We talk of a big army when our law and statistics show we can't even hit that goal anywhere near the time set—unless Congress changes the law. We don't have all the time in the world.

We have had more than 6 months—or 5 years—for the military to find out what kind of a war they should prepare for. If they don't know, who does? If they can't get on paper what we need, who can? If they lack leadership of the kind that moves forward with decision, what can we expect of the people who look to them and to others in Washington?

On the home front we hear about sacrifice. Aside from the real sacrifices of families and friends of casualties, where has there been any hardship in this country since the Civil War? Aside from these, what was really sacrificed in World War I or World War II? What will we give up this time? Ice cream, or shall we have it only on Sunday?

Let Washington not prate about sacrifice, or the home front take credit for walking instead of riding to the corner store. We are in for a Spartan existence unknown to us, before we can again earn the label of the best, the strongest and the freest people.

Tom Campbell

Editor

GET THESE TIME-PROVED

for the Tops in Threading Performance

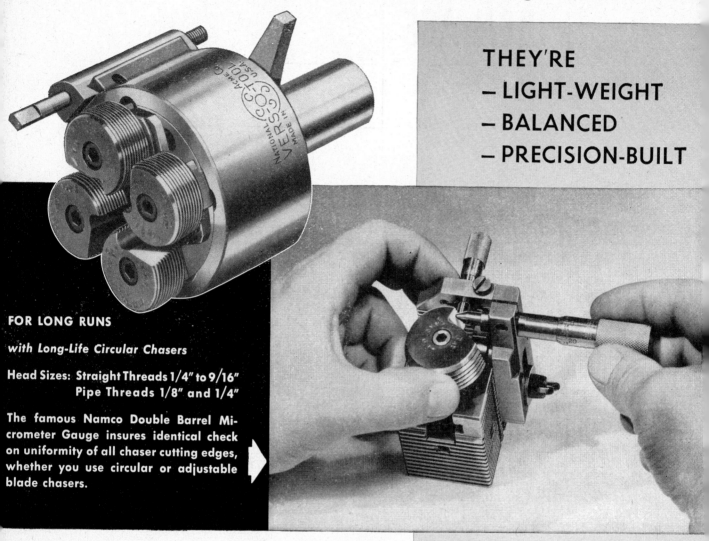

THEY'RE
- LIGHT-WEIGHT
- BALANCED
- PRECISION-BUILT

FOR LONG RUNS

with Long-Life Circular Chasers

Head Sizes: Straight Threads 1/4" to 9/16"
Pipe Threads 1/8" and 1/4"

The famous Namco Double Barrel Micrometer Gauge insures identical check on uniformity of all chaser cutting edges, whether you use circular or adjustable blade chasers.

BOTH USE GROUND-THREAD PRECISION CHASERS

● Namco Vers-O-Tool Circular Chasers are regrindable through a full 270°—and Vers-O-Tool Adjustable Blade Chasers are designed to give more regrinds than conventional types, with the blade adjustable to proper cutting position for any type of material.

● One micrometer gauge serves both circular and adjustable types. A minimum adjustment of .008" for economical regrinds insures a freshly ground chaser always at correct cutting position.

● Vers-O-Tool Heads, too, are hardened and ground throughout.

● Quick removal and replacement of chasers or blocks is made by loosening only two screws.

● Vers-O-Tool Heads are provided with radial adjustment for wear on all sizes. Diametric adjustment is made by one screw. Both adjustments take less than two minutes.

YOU CAN US

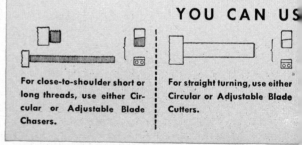

For close-to-shoulder short or long threads, use either Circular or Adjustable Blade Chasers.

For straight turning, use either Circular or Adjustable Blade Cutters.

Vers-O-Tools Give You More Threads per Dollar, with Closer Tolerances and Less Threading Down-Time.

Style DS Vers-O-Tool (Non-Revolving Type), 8 sizes, 3/16"-4 7/8" cutting range.

Style DR Vers-O-Tool (Revolving Type), 12 sizes, .056"-4 7/8" cutting range with circular chasers; 6 sizes, 3/16"-1 5/8" cutting range with adjustable blade chasers.

Style RST Collapsible Tap, equipped with blade chasers for thread sizes, 1 1/4"-4"; with circular chasers, from 3 1/2"-5".

IRON AGE *newsfront*

► A new punching compound does not carbonize until after a frictional heat of 450°F has been reached. Its high film strength is said to prevent metal-to-metal contact on heavy blanking dies.

► More than 2 million lb of aluminum were used in the superstructure of America's largest ocean liner, the S.S. United States. This is the largest application of aluminum ever made in this field. Unfortunately, the ship will probably have to be painted battleship gray.

► Output of nickel-bearing stainless steels has practically resolved itself into a case of nickel, nickel, who's got the nickel? After allowances for stockpiling and DO demands, the remaining free nickel is allocated among users on the basis of their previous consumption. As a result, producers of nickel-bearing stainless are most anxious for DO orders to maintain production on steels of this type.

► A specialized magnetic recorder uses variable speed electroplated disks as the recording medium. The apparatus is designed so that artificial delay times of variable duration can be obtained with recorded signals.

► Automobile and auto parts companies are passing along the hold-the-price-line story to their vendors by mail and word-of-mouth. Last month's changes in steel prices are not being questioned although some changes in extra charges have caused some eyebrow raising. One weakness in the auto industry position is this: Truck prices (which did not fall under the price freeze order) have been increased.

► Commercial availability of a new refractory has permitted construction of a new type of electric furnace in which the refractory material serves as a heating element. It can be built for either oxidizing or reducing atmospheres and for temperatures above 3600°F. Walls, bottoms, tops and insulation are of fused stabilized zirconia.

► Shortages of alloying elements have already caused substantial changes in the composition of large alloy dies for automobile stampings. The next step will be revival of the extended use of steel inserts to provide necessary strength and wear resistance.

► Steel sales people report that the number of government directives is increasing rapidly. Most are aimed at expediting orders not covered by DO priorities or too urgent to wait for steel under existing priority rules. They expect these directives to continue increasing until a controlled materials plan replaces the present faltering system.
   Meanwhile defense and essential civilian orders are raising hob with production schedules, including forcing switches into products that some mills don't normally make.

► The Naval Research Laboratory has developed two new insulating materials. One is a mica paper made from low grade ore and scrap to stand more heat and with greater capacitance than kraft paper. Electrical condensers should be the principal application. The other is an improved asbestos which forms readily into paper with high dielectric properties.

Good welder + good machine + GOOD PIPE = GOOD JOB!

7 POINTS OF UNIFORM GOODNESS IN YOUNGSTOWN STEEL PIPE

- uniform ductility
- uniform lengths
- uniform threading
- uniform weldability
- uniform wall thickness and size
- uniform strength and toughness
- uniform roundness and straightness

No matter how intricate the weld, you do it readily with Youngstown pipe. That's because Youngstown pipe is designed and made for easy welding--truly round, uniform in wall thickness, uniformly sized, and chemically and metallurgically right. The name "Youngstown" rolled into a length of pipe means it is GOOD PIPE.

Youngstown
STEEL PIPE

IRON AGE *summary*

iron and steel industry trends

Sweeping Changes in Steel Priorities
New Programs Coming, Others Reduced
Higher Limits on DO Quotas Expected

SWEEPING changes in steel priorities will result from new rules and regulations now being worked out by government and industry representatives. DO priority orders will be lifted out of the strict military category and given wider application. In addition, big increases in the tonnage allocated to DO and essential civilian programs will be felt soon.

Broadened DO applications will include such items as construction of new plants, steel mill expansion, construction of facilities to safeguard public health and safety, and other projects approved by NPA.

Additional allocation programs already in the cards call for 1.9 million tons of steel in the form of oil country goods for the petroleum industry. Other needs of the petroleum industry have not yet been settled. Another program will be needed to provide steel for up to 40 merchant ships.

Other Programs Due for Cutbacks

Two other programs will probably have their quotas shaved during the second quarter. Freight car builders are expected to be cutback from 308,000 to 288,000 tons per month. And allocations for a diesel locomotive program starting in April, will probably be somewhat lower than the original estimate of 70,000 tons per month.

Effective Mar. 1 (DO limits), on various steel products will be raised. Probable new percentages are: Stainless steels, semi - finished alloys, hot-rolled alloys, 35 pct; cold-finished alloy bars, 25 pct; carbon steel structurals, 20 pct; sheet piling, reinforcing bars, and cold-finished carbon bars, 15 pct; hot- and cold-rolled sheets, 12 pct; hot-rolled carbon bars, hot- and cold-rolled strip, wire rods, and rail steel bars, 10 pct; and tin mill products, 5 pct.

Although all steel items are in very tight supply, alloy steel demand is surging and boiling this week. A big chunk of alloy output is now going to the growing defense program. One stainless and alloy producer reports that 28½ pct of its orders are going for defense use. This percentage will increase in the next few months. The tank program alone is expected to take 100,000 tons of alloy steel within a 6 to 9 month period.

Bars Are Tighter Than Sheets

In the auto industry the tight market for flat-rolled steel has now been overmatched by the growing scarcity of carbon and alloy hot-rolled bars, ton for ton—despite the fact that bars cost less than sheets.

This week there is a marked increase in the number of government directives to steel producers. Most of these directives are spot requests for more DO tonnage. They are needed to expedite vital programs which cannot wait for steel through regular DO channels. Such directives are causing steel people to book DO tonnage beyond specified limits.

In order to meet quotas assigned to them, some mills have been forced to revise production schedules to the point where operations and profits have been affected. In some cases producers find that they must make products which they do not normally offer for sale.

Need Steel for Own Expansion

Steel producers are finding it hard to get steel for their own expansion programs. One company tried to work out a conversion deal with another producer for heavy structurals, but the plan was dropped because loss of the ingots involved would have hurt the mill's own rolling schedules.

Steelmaking operations this week are scheduled at 99.5 pct of rated capacity, up ½ point from last week's revised rate. This is based on new annual capacity of 104,229,650 net tons as of Jan. 1, 1951.

(nonferrous summary, p. 96)

"We have found GRAPH-MO an ideal steel for these cavity molds..."

REPORTS THE PARKER APPLIANCE CO.

SYNTHETIC rubber O-rings manufactured by The Parker Appliance Company, Cleveland, Ohio, are molded to extremely close tolerances and high finishes. To insure these qualities, the molds must be exact duplicates in dimension and finish. Parker formerly used various tool steels and boiler plate to make the molds, but found these steels hard to machine. And because they lacked stability after hardening, the molds did not always meet tolerance specifications.

Then they tried Graph-Mo—one of four Timken® graphitic tool steels. And Graph-Mo proved to be the answer. Parker Appliance reports, "We have found Graph-Mo an ideal steel for these cavity molds because it is free machining, holds a high polish and is dimensionally stable after hardening."

Graph-Mo is a special, oil-hardening graphitic tool steel. Because it contains free graphite, it can be machined faster and easier than other oil-hardening steels. Graph-Mo also offers unusual resistance to wear and abrasion, with less tendency to scuff or score.

Graph-Mo is one of four Timken graphitic tool steels. For further information, write for the new Timken Graphitic Steel Data Book. The Timken Roller Bearing Company, Steel and Tube Division, Canton 6, Ohio. Cable address: "TIMROSCO".

YEARS AHEAD—THROUGH EXPERIENCE AND RESEARCH

TIMKEN
TRADE-MARK REG. U.S. PAT. OFF.
Fine Alloy
STEEL
and Seamless Tubes

Specialists in alloy steel—including hot rolled and cold finished alloy steel bars—a complete range of stainless, graphitic and standard tool analyses—and alloy and stainless seamless steel tubing.

Wean-Hallden
LOW COST SYNCHRONIZED AUTOMATIC SHEAR LINES

THE installation of a Wean-Hallden Synchronized Automatic Shear Line assures you the most efficient shearing operation available today. The Wean-Hallden, while actually requiring *less floor space*, delivers up to *twice the production.*

Infinite variable lengths from 12-inches to 12-feet at speeds up to 200 FPM with accuracy better than commercial tolerances means faster production, reduced labor costs and minimum scrap loss for you. *Before You Buy—Investigate Wean-Hallden.*

Wean Equipment Corporation
CLEVELAND, OHIO

Dear EDITOR

Letters from Readers

Universal Question

Sir:

We would like some honest answers to the questions we are going to ask in this letter; we are sure your staff is in a position to help us get on the right road in these tangled times. Our facilities are above average for a small sheet metal plant. During the past war I was employed by the local division of Consolidated-Vultee Aircraft Corp., as General Foreman of the Sheet Metal Dept. That gives me some of the know-how regarding the volume production of sheet metal parts, as well as dealing with 800 people and their union representatives.

Our normal line of business has been the manufacture and erection of air conditioning duct work, also the manufacture to customer specifications of various job lot items such as lockers, cabinets, baskets and prefabricated duct work. Now for the questions, in case you have not guessed: "What, where and how in your opinion can we best serve in the defense effort?

W. ESSNER
Essner Metal Works
Fort Worth, Tex.

How to best serve the defense effort is a question being asked by companies all the way up the line to the biggest in the country, and as yet there doesn't seem to be any clear cut answer. Henry Ford II stated the other day that the Ford Motor Co. had not yet been given a clear picture as to what it was expected to do. The best guide we can give at the present time is to refer to the article "How To Sell To Uncle Sam" on p. 269 of the Jan. 4 Annual Review Issue of THE IRON AGE, and to p. 371 for the list of major metal products bought by the Armed Forces and where they are bought. —Ed.

Varied Reactions

Sir:

As a former assistant in a public library, and now the Librarian of an engineering research library in industry, I consider THE IRON AGE an old friend. I've been a reader of "Fatigue Cracks" from "Dix to Post," and quite naturally turned to that column for possible explanation of our f.f.j.'s "new look" in its Dec. 21, 1950, issue, learning that we are now to have IRON AGE with an aesthetic touch!

Lower-case type has had its day in pulps and slicks so it may as well have a try at the technical magazines, I suppose I can accept it, together with the dotted "i" and other artistic touches on the cover as long as it remains recognizable to our engineers and does not look like a changeling beside its sister issues on our library shelves. You see, magazines which change their size and shape, and even their lettering without due regard for uniformity of appearance when said magazine is shelved or bound, are the despair of librarians.

(Mrs.) O. K. NESBITT
Librarian
Lord Mfg. Co.
Erie, Pa.

Sir:

Some months ago, you changed the arrangement of THE IRON AGE, and I, personally, wish you had not. Having been a reader of your excellent magazine for many years, I feel entitled to at least express an opinion.

I do not like the new arrangement for the reason that I frequently refer to THE IRON AGE for price information and thoroughly dislike having to thumb over innumerable pages of advertising to find what I want. I do think the readers should be privileged to read the ads when desirous and pass them when not interested, and not, when trying to find information, have to thumb through a maze of advertising to obtain the information wanted.

T. O. HOLLAND
Mgr. of Purchases
Ames Baldwin Wyoming Co.
Parkersburg, W. Va.

We have had the same problem ourselves. If we want to refer quickly to specific price pages we first look them up on the contents page. It was to solve just such dilemma that we moved the contents to p. 2 for quick reference.—Ed.

Sir:

I appreciate reading THE IRON AGE. The readability is improving right along, and we find many facts we can use in our daily and weekly contacts with our supervisors.

The editorials by Tom C. Campbell on current topics are timely, and to the point. We enjoy and profit by reading them. I usually send them to our key men.

L. F. REINARTZ
Assistant Vice-President
Armco Steel Corp.
Middletown, Ohio

Sir:

Thought you'd like to know that quite a few here, many of whom know good typographical design and layout when they see it, were much impressed with your December 21st issue. In addition, they found chas. t. post's reference to it in "fatigue cracks" most interesting.

Of course we liked the new layout, also, but we haven't the background of these other people. We suspect that quite a number of your readers are going to say nice things about this new set-up.

H. J. MALLIA
Apparatus News Bureau
General Electric Co.
Schenectady

"no more GAMBLING on tool steel selection"

[⅓ actual size; Selector is in 3 colors]

Since the first announcement, hundreds of tool steel users have received their CRUCIBLE TOOL STEEL SELECTORS. The comments received indicate that this handy method of *picking the right tool steel right from the start* is going over big.

"Handiest selector I've ever seen"

"No more gambling on tool steel selection"

"You're right, the application should dictate the choice of the tool steel" . . . and many, many more favorable comments.

You'll want your CRUCIBLE TOOL STEEL SELECTOR. It uses the only logical method of tool steel selection — begin with the application to pick the right steel! And the answer you get with one turn of the Selector dial will prove satisfactory in every case, for the CRUCIBLE TOOL STEEL SELECTOR covers 22 tool steels which fit 98% of all Tool Steel applications. ALL the tool steels on the Selector are in Warehouse Stock . . . that means when you get the answer, you can get the steel . . . fast!

Write for your Selector today! We want you to have it, because we know you've never seen anything that approaches your tool steel problems so simply and logically. Just fill out the coupon and mail. Act now! CRUCIBLE STEEL COMPANY OF AMERICA, Chrysler Building, New York 17, N. Y.

Here's how it works:

To use the Selector, all you need know is the characteristics that come with the job: type and condition of material to be worked, the number of pieces to be produced, the method of working, and the condition of the equipment to be used.

FOUR STEPS—and you've got the right answer!

1. Move arrow to major class covering application
2. Select sub-group which best fits application
3. Note major tool characteristics (under arrow) and other characteristics in cut-outs for each grade in sub-group
4. Select tool steel indicated

That's all there is to it!

Here's an example:

Application—Deep drawing die for steel

Major Class—Metal Forming—Cold

Sub-Group — Special Purpose

Tool Characteristics — Wear Resistance

Tool Steel—Airdi 150

One turn of the dial does it!

And you're sure you're right!!

Crucible Steel Company of America
Dept. I, Chrysler Building
New York 17, N. Y.

Gentlemen:

Sure! I want my CRUCIBLE TOOL STEEL SELECTOR!

Name_____ Title_____

Company_____

Street_____

City_____ State_____

CRUCIBLE

first name in special purpose steels

TOOL STEELS

fifty years of Fine *steelmaking*

Branch Offices and Warehouses: ATLANTA • BALTIMORE • BOSTON • BUFFALO • CHARLOTTE • CHICAGO • CINCINNATI • CLEVELAND • DENVER • DETROIT HOUSTON, TEXAS • INDIANAPOLIS • LOS ANGELES • MILWAUKEE • NEWARK • NEW HAVEN • NEW YORK • PHILADELPHIA • PITTSBURGH • PROVIDENCE ROCKFORD • SAN FRANCISCO • SEATTLE • SPRINGFIELD, MASS. • ST. LOUIS • SYRACUSE • TORONTO, ONT. • WASHINGTON, D. C.

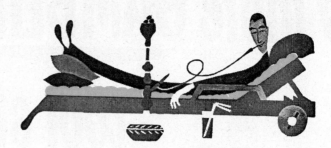

Fatigue Cracks

by Charles T. Post

Twenty Digits

Your f.f.j.'s Bill Czygan, who is responsible for the articles on minerals for Funk & Wagnall's *New International Year Book*, had quite a time rounding up last minute 1950 statistics for the new edition. He used the long distance telephone freely, but the telephone strike threw a partial crimp in the operation. The substitute operators were helpful, but as Bill listened for his connection with an official who could give him the statistics on antimony, he heard this dialogue between his man's secretary and the operator.

"Mr. ——— is not in his office, but possibly some one else can help Mr. Czygan. What information does he want?"

After a short consultation, the operator reported back. "I think he wants a doctor, dearie. He says it's about statistical anatomy."

Jet Saucepans

For a while it looked like the titanium situation was going to be tough, with the Cinderella metal being used only for the most vital military items, such as jet engines. But from a news item in *Advertising Age* magazine, it appears that titanium may take the place held by plastics in the last war when the steel and aluminum situation got real tough. Says *Advertising Age:*

"Federal Enameling and Stamping Co., McKees Rocks, Pa., has opened its most intensive advertising and promotion drive for its line of Vogue enameled kitchen utensils made with titanium."

When you walk into the kitchen, watch out for those flying saucepans!

New Scrap Source

According to U. S. Steel, "A century ago, workmen digging iron ore in a bog in central Virginia came across a deer's skeleton, still intact, that had turned to iron from long immersion in iron-bearing waters." That should give Armour and Swift the necessary know-how to go into the scrap business if they put a price ceiling on meat.

Puzzlers

By J. A. Crites

Many readers have been disturbed by the Dec. 28th puzzle. It seems that in walking for 45 min the man covers the same distance the car would have travelled in 15 min. Perhaps we should have pointed out that our commuter comes into Grand Central Station. It would then have been clear that the 12 mph averaged by the car was remarkable indeed. In spite of the confusion M. E. McKinney, International Harvester Co.; T. W. White and David Lieberman, Ther Electric & Machine Works, and Chas. G. Heilman, Commonwealth Industries Inc., all came through with the right answer.

After setting up several unsolvable equations, light finally dawned and we arrived at an answer of 15 in. for the diameter of the circle in last week's trick puzzle. Hope we are right for a change.

C. E. Norton, National Malleable & Steel Castings Co., poses this one: A boy tosses a ball straight up into the air and catches it when it returns. It goes up in 1 sec and returns in 1.2 sec. Taking g as 32.156 ft/sec^2, and assuming that the air resistance is directly proportional to the square of the velocity, find:

(1) The velocity of the ball when it leaves the boy's hand.

(2) The height to which it travels.

(3) The velocity of the ball when the boy catches it.

machine tool high spots

sales inquiries and production

by W. A. Lloyd

Priority Stage Set—Last week's meeting of machine tool industry representatives and the machinery division of NPA has seemingly set the stage for some concrete action by the government. As of now, there is no definite promise of a blanket priority for materials, but it appears that there is a program headed in that direction.

NPA has photostated copies of the order boards and a study is presumably being made to determine what will be involved in the granting of a blanket priority and a possible expansion of the industry.

Too Small for Volume—The armed services and their major contractors are aware that the industry is too small for the business volume reportedly on the way, a matter of $1 billion, or possibly more, in addition to what is already on the books. In short, the industry will probably get 3 years' business at the present rate of shipments within the near future.

This means drastic action, including sub-contracting, probably on broader scale than in World War II, more manpower, utilization of all plant capacity, including warehouse space in some cases, and some plant expansion. A month ago, there were seven ap-plications for certificates of necessity on file by machine tool builders.

Release Tentative Schedules—Under consideration, but considered likely by industry sources, is a release on part of the tentative production schedules, perhaps 40 pct of the present backlogs. It is believed that General Services Administration will handle the contracts with the industry, and the total is likely to be held to an aggregate of $750 million for metal cutting and forming machines.

The industry will do well to make shipments of $600 million this year, twice the 1950 volume. New order volume in December reportedly increased 15 to 20 pct over November, to a new postwar high and shipments increased about 20 pct over the preceding month. Based on the present index, December shipments were at the $40 million level.

Vanished Complacency—Despite the somewhat indefinite nature of the week's developments, it appears that complacency in Washington regarding the machine tool industry is practically over. It is believed that action will be taken on the blanket priority within a few weeks. Granting of such a priority plus certificates of necessity will put the contemplated ex-pansion plans in high gear.

Efforts are being made to get contracts to obtain ratings for some of the unrated orders they have placed. In addition, the conversion of plants to defense production will speed the rating process.

DO Ratings—NPA authorized use of DO ratings carried by defense orders to procure accessories for production equipment for companies working on rated orders. Ratings may be used for procuring jigs, dies, tools and fixtures where inability to obtain these production equipment accessories would result in failure to meet delivery dates.

Ratings may be used for accessories only if they are needed directly for the production of material for which a rating has been assigned. NPA said the action was taken as a means of granting some temporary assistance immediately, pending a long term program.

Abrasives Conference—In Washington, NPA officials and the abrasives industry advisory committee met to discuss the need for increased production of abrasives for the defense program. Industry spokesmen said they are now operating at nearly full capacity, turning out about as much abrasives as during the peak of World War II.

Large stage moves up and down for finer, faster focusing.

The PANPHOT combines permanently aligned microscope, camera and light source in one convenient unit.

The *Leitz* Panphot

Universal Camera Microscope

Only the Leitz PANPHOT enables you to switch from microscopic observation to photo-micrography *without moving from your chair,* for it's the only universal camera microscope with operating parts for both functions right at hand. Changeover from one to the other is fast, simple, dependable. Now available to industrial and technical laboratories, the PANPHOT is a perfect combination of research microscope and reflex camera.

The PANPHOT permits the use of transmitted light, reflected light, darkfield illumination and polarized light. The permanently aligned light source provides a filament lamp for observation and an arc light for photo-micrography.

Easy observation of the image to be photographed is provided by a large ground glass in the reflex mirror camera. The camera accommodates 3¼″ x 4¼″ plates or cut film for black and white or color work.

A full range of accessories is available to equip the PANPHOT for every phase of photo-micrography, photo-macrography and for drawing and projecting micro-images.

Write today for information to Dept. IA

E. LEITZ, Inc., 304 Hudson Street, New York 13, N. Y.

LEITZ MICROSCOPES • SCIENTIFIC INSTRUMENTS
LEICA CAMERAS AND ACCESSORIES

"K" 6 STATION 12-SPINDLE MULT-AU-MATIC

83%
INCREASE
In Production

Type "K" Mult-Au-Matic 550 Pcs
Type "D" Mult-Au-Matic 300 Pcs

A QUOTATION FROM THE FIELD:

We were especially impressed on this job with the ease in which the operator was able to load and unload this machine at the rate of 550 pcs. per hour compared with the operator on the 8 spindle double index Type "D" Mult-Au-Matic on the same operation, who was busy trying to produce 300 per hour."

Twin spindles and twin tooling at each station, and each station with its succeeding operations, provides a progressive, high efficient Production Method on Differential Side Gears.

Ask for information on Type "K" Mult-Au-Matic application to your work.

| STATION 2 | STATION 3 | STATION 4 | STATION 5 | STATION 6 |

efinement in design, higher spindle speeds, faster index and in many cases an improved method for 1st and d chucking on the same machine are only some of the factors that place the Type "K" Mult-AU-Matic in a ass by itself for Productive Economies.

HE BULLARD COMPANY BRIDGEPORT 2, CONNECTICUT

FREE *publications*

These publications describe money - saving equipment and services ... they are free with no obligation ... fill in and mail postcard.

Powdered Metal Parts

A revised catalog details powdered metal fabrication possibilities for various types of parts such as gears, bearings, filters, cams and electronic cores. Principle feature of the revised booklet is a supplement cataloging the company's new line of standard gears and self-lubricating bearings. *Powdered Metal Products Corp.*

For free copy insert No. 1 on postcard.

Surface Grinders

Mattison (Hanchett type) vertical spindle production surface grinders, for the accurate generation of flat surfaces, are described in a new 10-p. bulletin. Detailed descriptions of four models, differing chiefly in productive capacity, are presented, and the various features of the equipment are discussed. Photos show installations performing a variety of jobs, and complete specifications are listed. A section of the booklet deals with magnetic and special chucks, and laminated top plates. *Mattison Machine Works.*

For free copy insert No. 2 on postcard.

Lower Cleaning Costs

A new 8-p. bulletin entitled "Continuous Blast Cleaning Can Reduce Your Cleaning Costs" illustrates and explains the advantages offered by continuous airless abrasive blast cleaning and cites actual production figures for the five sizes of Wheelabrator Continuous Tumblasts. Operation of the units is shown, and examples of production records set are detailed. Models in a range of sizes to meet practically any cleaning problem are illustrated. *American Wheelabrator and Equipment Corp.*

For free copy insert No. 3 on postcard.

Electronics in Welding

How greater versatility, improved weld quality, balanced load, high power factor and 75 pct current reduction may be achieved in resistance welding is explained in a new 4-p. folder on Sciaky patented three-phase machines. The bulletin shows how the three-phase welding system embodying electronic principles operates; it lists representative examples of typical machine specifications and outlines the advantages of direct current at the welding electrodes. *Sciaky Bros., Inc.*

For free copy insert No. 4 on postcard.

Thermosetting Resins

Outstanding properties of Araldite triple-function resins for bonding, casting, and coating in product development are detailed in a new 6-p. folder. The bulletin contains a chart suggesting a wide range of applications for seven types of the material, and photos illustrate a few of the many varied uses of these ethoxyline resins. The material is shown to possess high resistance to corrosion and have adhesive properties toward metals, ceramics and other materials, in addition to high alkali and acid resistance. *Ciba Co., Inc.*

For free copy insert No. 5 on postcard.

Portable Electric Tools

A complete line of 360-cycle and 180-cycle portable electric tools is featured in a new catalog. Drills, screwdrivers, grinders, sanders and polishers are illustrated and described, and complete specifications on every tool are included. *Buckeye Tools Corp.*

For free copy insert No. 6 on postcard.

Maintenance Chart

Of interest to every plant and building maintenance superintendent is the brand new "Maintenance Checking Chart." This complete chart lists many common building maintenance problems and recommends a solution for each. The chart lists over 100 products and processes for maintenance of floors, roofs, interior and exterior walls, waterproofing, special paints and other items. *United Laboratories, Inc.*

For free copy insert No. 7 on postcard.

Heat Treat Bulletin

Designed to present current technical and operating information on heat treating metallurgy and practice, a new bulletin entitled the "Heat Treat Review" is for distribution to all persons concerned with heat treating operations. The magazine is intended to provide up-to-date information on heat treating processes as applied to all phases of the metal-working field. Metal melting and related metal processing activities are also covered. Industrial metallurgists and heat treaters are offered this magazine on a gratis basis by writing on their letterhead to this column. *Surface Combustion Corp.*

For free copy insert No. 8 on postcard.

Slide Chart on Stainless

Technical data and information on workability of stainless steels is presented on a new slide chart. The chart includes a standard analysis table of stainless steels and gives relative fabricating data for a variety of operations. These include soldering, welding, roll forming, hot and cold riveting, forging, buffing, deep drawing, *Turn to Page 90*

NEW *production ideas*

Taper Die Sinking Cutters

Have finish-ground ball nose, right-hand cut, straight shanks.

Taper die sinking cutters with full-cutting ball nose are supplied ready to use with ball nose finish-ground to cut to dead center; no preliminary hand grinding is necessary. Two styles of fluting are available: straight, for easy hand sharpening; and spiral for users who prefer helical cutting characteristics and have mechanical grinding equipment. Cutters have a 7° taper (14° included angle). *Pratt & Whitney, Div. Niles-Bement-Pond Co.*

For more data insert No. 18 on postcard.

Melting Furnace

Melts 25 lb lead in 4½ minutes, is adjustable to maintain temperatures.

A new L-P melting furnace, No. 500, constructed of steel and cast iron, burns 15 hr full blast or with intermittent melts; with a sustaining flame it burns up to 60 hr. It can be used with any standard liquid petroleum tank, no gas regulator required. A remote fuel service can be used; the L-P tank can be located any distance from the furnace. *Weldit, Inc.*

For more data insert No. 19 on postcard.

Magnetized Level

Combines level and angle indicator; sticks to round or flat surfaces.

The Magno-Level equipped with powerful Alnico permanent magnets sticks to round or flat surfaces at any angle, leaving hands free for line-up, straightening or fastening work in place. It has a clock-faced angle gage with balanced gravity needle, which determines any angle from 0 to 360°. The level comes in mechanics' pocket-size, 9x2 in., weighs 10 oz. *Buckeye Plastic Corp.*

For more data insert No. 20 on postcard.

Synchronous Generators

Available in four basic designs with ratings from 1.875 to 50 kva.

Designated as Types ATI, ASI, and ATB, new Tri-Clad high-speed synchronous generators have frequency ratings of 60 and 400 cycles. Three standard types of 60 cycle generators are offered, providing a range of characteristics for several different categories of voltage regulation and motor starting requirements. Variations of the basic machines are available with special characteristics for special applications. *General Electric Co.*

For more data insert No. 21 on postcard.

Diamond Abrasive Belts

Diamond impregnated solid nylon; for use on carbide dies, ¼ to 9 in. ID.

New diamond abrasive belts are made of solid nylon impregnated with diamond abrasive in grades of 1-5 microns to a sieve or mesh size of 100. The resilience of the nylon is said to provide a cushioning effect against shock and prevents the diamond chips from tearing out of their sockets. Belts are not affected by humidity and can be cleaned by washing in warm soap and water. They are impervious to oil, allowing the use of light oil

use postcard below

production ideas
Continued

as a coolant. Five different colors for coding indicate the abrasive size. *Hartford Special Machinery Co.*

For more data insert No. 22 on postcard.

Spacing Collars
Micrometer adjustable for accurate spacing of milling machine cutters.

Quick, accurate and definitely positive adjustment for spacing milling machine cutters is accomplished by improved micrometer adjustable spacing collars. They are made for standard milling machine arbors from 7/8 to 2 in., and have a maximum adjustment of 3/16 in. by thousandths. They are provided with new high speed keyways. Accurate spacing is made by loosening the cutter arbor nut and making the plus or minus adjustment with a special spanner wrench which is furnished. *Dayton Rogers Mfg. Co.*

For more data insert No. 23 on postcard.

Double Hook Hoist
Handles long items in quantity; lifts and dumps barrels, drums.

This hoist lifts 500 lb at 25 fpm or 250 lb at 50 fpm. Hooks are spaced 48 in. apart, but can be adjusted for lesser distance. It is a complete hoisting unit with reversing motor, trolley, cable and hooks. It is supplied with swivel and adjustable trolley wheels to fit any size or make of track and will travel any size curve. The unit is adaptable for reversible power drive, with speed changes from 54 to 500 rpm possible by changing pulley sizes. *Flinchbaugh Co.*

For more data insert No. 24 on postcard.

Portable Electric Oven
For baking and drying; low-priced; has uniform temperature throughout.

Fresh air is drawn into the oven and stale air driven out through specially located vents by a motor-driven fan. It is claimed that no stratification is possible. An adjustable damper gives wide range of constant temperature. Ovens can

use postcard below

be nested one on top of the other and used in groups, or operated as individual ovens. Selected ovens in the group can be cut-out or heated at different temperatures. They are made of heavy gage steel with asbestos air-cell insulation. *Grieve-Hendry Co., Inc.*

For more data insert No. 25 on postcard.

Electromagnet
Unit produces high flux density magnetic fields for laboratory use.

A new research tool now commercially available is the ADL electromagnet, a compact, versatile electromagnet for laboratory use. Its compact small cabinet requires only power and cooling connections. A minimum of operational supervision is required as it has built-in automatic controls and safety devices. The unit is said to produce the same magnetic fields as other electromagnets weighing many times as much. Other features include: variety of field patterns, accurately controlled air gap, simplicity of experimental setup, quiet operation and wide power range. *Arthur D. Little, Inc.*

For more data insert No. 26 on postcard.

Vacuum Furnace
Operated at high temperature, high vacuum or controlled atmospheres.

Engineered for versatility, operations such as heat treating, sintering, annealing, melting and pouring can be performed in this one packaged furnace. The power supply, vacuum pumping system, gages and controls are enclosed in a metal cabinet. The bell jar is hinged to a vertical base plate, with both sides accessible for servicing. The effective hot zone of the standard assembly is 5 in. high x 2½ in. diam. *National Research Corp.*

For more data insert No. 27 on postcard.

Centerless Grinder
For form grinding by in-feed method.

The new No. 4 centerless grinding machine announced by Scrivener operates upon the controlled-cycle principle. The grinding wheel measures 24 in. diam and up to 20 in. wide, the control wheel, 18 in. diam and up to 20 in. wide, with a maximum 9-in. opening between the wheels. Grinding wheel speed is 950 rpm. The control wheel has six speeds and an extra high speed for diamond truing the wheel. Power is

provided by a 35 bhp motor. This No. 4 centerless grinder is indicative of the field into which Scrivener centerless grinders are entering, namely, that of form ground work by the in-feed method. *Arthur Scrivener Ltd.*

For more data insert No. 28 on postcard.

Hydraulic Piston Grinder
Grinds cam shaped skirt portion of automotive pistons, 5 x 8 in.

The standard wheel of the 5x8 in. type H hydraulic piston grinding machine is 24 in. diam with a 3¼ in. face, driven by a 7½ hp

motor. This facilitates grinding pistons by the plunge grind method with wide wheel. When arranged for traverse grinding, there is an automatic feed at each reversal of the traverse until the piston is to finish size. With a plunge grinding cycle, feed is continuous until a predetermined size is reached, at which time the feed will stop. A reciprocating mechanism is used to re-

ciprocate the wheel for fine finishes. With an overhead wheel dressing mechanism the grinding wheel can be dressed without disturbing the grinding setup. A new live spindle type headstock has V-belt drive and the piston grinding unit has a rocking action to obtain the cam contour on the skirt of the piston. Arrangement for a semi-automatic cycle of operation is possible. *Landis Tool Co.*

For more data insert No. 29 on postcard.

Selectronic Gage
Classifies critical dimensions of parts for selective assembly.

The Pratt & Whitney Selectronic gage classifies critical tolerances of precision parts such as balls, rollers, pistons and piston pins. It

permits broader production tolerances in the manufacture of such parts because it provides a selective control for precision fitting at the time of assembly. Parts are loaded into a magazine-feeding mechanism from which they are automatically fed under an Electrolimit gaging head and subsequently routed into the proper classification bin. As each piece is gaged, an electric impulse passes through a commutator having size classification segments, and this actuates the chute-positioning mechanism. Only one set of masters, a minimum and maximum, is needed to adjust the gage. Selectronic gages are custom built. *Pratt & Whitney, Div. Niles-Bement-Pond Co.*

For more data insert No. 30 on postcard.

Mechanical Seals
Provide leakless operation of rotary shafts on pumps or other equipment.

No wear on the shaft is claimed for Garlock seals. Sealing is ef-

Turn to Page 91

Boring-Turning Mill
Pendant control electro-hydraulic shift simplifies overall operation.

Advanced design features of the new 12-ft Cincinnati Hypro vertical boring and turning mill are pendant control electro-hydraulic shift and individual traverse motors to rail and side heads. Control functions handled through the pendant station include remote shifting of the single shift for the two table

speed ranges that are obtained through a 50 hp adjustable voltage drive. The machine operator can observe cutting tool action and at the same time have finger tip control of the machine's feed and speeds. A metal cabinet encloses the motor-generator set and controls which operate the 50 hp motor. A new feed box provides 16 feeds between 0.004 and 0.750 in. Independent feed reverse for the saddle and ram means that either of these machine components can be moved up or down, in or out, individually. Control is by pushbutton. Three circular nonmetallic bed ways are used between the bed and table surfaces, offering improved contact and resulting in long, trouble-free service. Thread cutting, drum scoring, and taper turning are said to be greatly improved. *Giddings & Lewis Machine Tool Co.*

For more data insert No. 31 on postcard.

IRON AGE

introduces

Herbert Gordon, elected president of STERLING BOLT CO., Chicago. **Charles C. Gordon**, retired as president after more than 30 years with the company. Mr. Charles C. Gordon will become chairman of the board of directors. Other changes in personnel: **Harry Dorph**, associated with the company since its inception, has resigned, but will continue to serve on the board of directors. **P. T. Phillips**, elected vice-president and secretary.

Frank W. Jarvis, elected to the presidency of DIAMOND MAGNESIUM CO., Plainesville, Ohio.

William L. Hunger, formerly general manager, named vice-president and general manager of the Northern Equipment Div., CONTINENTAL FOUNDRY & MACHINE CO., Erie, Pa.

Paul M. Arnall, elected president of the LUKENHEIMER CO., Cincinnati. Mr. Arnall succeeds **Frank P. Rhame**, who resigned after 32 years with the company.

George H. Donaldson, named vice-president in charge of operations of both the CARBON LIMESTONE CO., and the CARBON CONCRETE BRICK CO., Lowellville, Ohio.

John P. MacLean, promoted to manager of the Buffalo district sales office of REPUBLIC STEEL CORP. Mr. MacLean succeeds **C. A. Cherry**, who resigned from the company.

John G. Munson, retired as vice-president—raw materials, UNITED STATES STEEL CORP. OF DELAWARE. Mr. Munson had a career of 30 years with U. S. Steel.

Charles W. Jinnette, retired recently, after 50 years of active service with the NORTON CO., Worcester.

Arnold Lenz, elected vice-president and member of the Administration Committee, GENERAL MOTORS CORP., New York. **Jack F. Wolfram**, recently appointed general manager of Oldsmobile; also elected vice-president and member of the administration committee.

Frederick W. von Raab, appointed manager of warehouse distribution for the CARPENTER STEEL CO., Reading, Pa.

Ray E. Kalmbach, named general manager of Wilson Foundry & Machine Co., Pontiac, Mich., a wholly-owned subsidiary of WILLYS-OVERLAND MOTORS, INC.

Ab Martin, appointed manager of the Fort Wayne, Ind., Works of GENERAL ELECTRIC CO., Apparatus Department. Mr. Martin succeeds **C. H. Matson**, who was named manufacturing consultant of the company's Small Apparatus Div. staff. **G. Stanley Berge**, appointed buyer for the Plastics Div., Pittsfield, Mass. **John L. Galt**, appointed manufacturing engineer, Chemicals Division Phenolic Products Plant; **Robert L. Gibson**, named general manager of the Chemical Department, also **Robert J. Baumann** was named marketing research section manager of the Chemical Department.

James J. Monaghan, appointed general sales manager of the Waterbury Factory division, of the PLUME & ATWOOD MFG. CO., Waterbury, Conn. **Walter L. French**, appointed to the position of acting sales manager for the Thomaston Brass Mill Div.; **Frederick D. Keeler**, resigned as sales manager recently.

Turn to Page 42

JOHN M. YAHRES, elected president of the Pittsburgh Screw & Bolt Corp., Pittsburgh.

DAVID W. THOMAS, appointed executive vice-president and director of Dumas Steel Corp., Pittsburgh.

CHARLES G. COOPER, elected a vice-president of the Cooper-Bessemer Corp., Mt. Vernon, Ohio.

IRON AGE

salutes

John I Snyder

H E'S young in years but old in experience. Forty-one year old John Snyder has the vigor to make his vision productive.

He's a bold thinker, not afraid to challenge the old, time-tested way of doing things—and change it if there is a better way.

He is the soul of brevity in word and act, can't tolerate waste motion in himself or others. He's really a plant efficiency expert, though he doesn't call himself that.

When he left Kuhn, Loeb & Co. in 1948 to become president of Pressed Steel Car Co., John Snyder found freight car building in the doldrums. Every sign indicated that this business was going to get a lot worse before it got better.

During this period when things could have gone to pot for his company, Mr. Snyder was working harder than ever before, finding new outlets and developing new products. He was also busy reorganizing the company, streamlining production, cutting costs, and getting his industrial house in order.

It was during this period, too, that John Snyder was directing a bold experiment in freight car building. This experiment resulted in the new Unicel freight car which was introduced last October (THE IRON AGE, Oct. 19, p. 89).

Although John Snyder is an industrialist, he might have done better than allright at several other jobs. He still likes to tinker with things electric, like radios and loudspeakers. But most of all he likes to make things grow. He is the proprietor of a nursery called Saltair at Shelter Island, New York.

RICHARD LESLIE MULLEN, elected vice-president of the Lehigh Structural Steel Co., Allentown, Pa.

GEORGE E. LOTT, elected vice-president in charge of purchasing, Automotive Div. of the Motor Products Corp., Detroit.

MARK M. BIDDISON, promoted to executive vice-president, General Chemical Div. of Allied Chemical & Dye Corp., New York.

JOHN E. TIMBERLAKE, appointed general manager of sales of Jones & Laughlin Steel Corp., Pittsburgh.

IRON AGE *introduces*

Continued

Thomas W. Russell, Jr., appointed assistant general purchasing agent of AMERICAN BRAKE SHOE CO., New York.

L. V. Johnson, appointed chief engineer of the NATIONAL TUBE CO., Pittsburgh.

R. K. Warren, appointed assistant manager of tool steel sales of CRUCIBLE STEEL CO. OF AMERICA, Syracuse, N. Y. Ira G. Sutton, appointed general superintendent of the Sanderson-Halcomb Works.

Robert W. Snowden, named as plant manager of the recently acquired New Brighton works of the HEPPENSTALL CO., Pittsburgh.

Albert Walton, named general manager of manufacturing by the BUDD CO., Philadelphia.

S. T. Mackenzie, appointed to the newly created post of sales manager of the BABCOCK & WILCOX CO., New York. R. W. Buntin succeeds Mr. Mackenzie as district sales manager of the Philadelphia office.

H. A. Forsberg, elected to the board of directors of CONTINENTAL FOUNDRY & MACHINE CO., Chicago. Mr. Forsberg has been associated with the company for more than 35 years.

J. C. Witherspoon, named assistant to general superintendent of the Donora Steel & Wire Works, of the AMERICAN STEEL & WIRE CO.; Kenneth C. Shearer succeeds Mr. Witherspoon as division superintendent, open hearth.

A. P. Hall, appointed a member of the board of directors of WALTER KIDDE & CO., INC., Belleville, N. J.

Frank Hallberg, named chief engineer of the ROSS OPERATING VALVE CO., Detroit.

Thomas C. Smith, named Milwaukee sales representative for ALLIS-CHALMERS MFG. CO. Others named: E. E. Strickland, Jr., New York, and Elwood C. Gerber, Pittsburgh. John F. Costigan, named assistant works manager, at the Norwood, Ohio, branch.

Leon S. Kuhn, newly appointed manager of sales, Portland district, for BETHLEHEM PACIFIC COAST STEEL CORP., San Francisco.

John C. Koch, appointed vice-president in charge of sales of the CONO-FLOW CORP., Philadelphia.

J. Richardson Dilworth, elected to the board of directors of ROCKWELL MFG. CO., Pittsburgh.

Robert J. Heggie, appointed general manager of sales of A. M. CASTLE & CO., Chicago, succeeding Earl E. Bates who retired recently.

Edgar L. McFerren, named chief engineer, succeeding K. F. Gallimore who will continue as a director, vice-president and consulting engineer of the GIDDINGS & LEWIS MACHINE TOOL CO., Fond du Lac, Wis. Fred C. Freund replaces Mr. McFerren as assistant to the executive vice-president and works manager; Ray G. Commo, promoted to supervisor of personnel and will head the industrial relations department.

William E. Close, appointed national account supervisor, eastern area, with headquarters in New York City, for the ACME STEEL CO. Vincent F. Murphy, replaces Mr. Close as New England district manager; Gardner W. MacDonald, Jr. and George R. Timm, assigned to the Boston sales territory; William G. Polley, sales engineer, assigned as area special representative in Atlanta. Clarence A. Carrell, appointed district manager of the southern division; G. R. "Red" Easley, appointed district manager, middle atlantic states; Judd B. Farr, assigned to the South Carolina territory; John J. Jorgensen, transferred to the Chattanooga, Tenn., sales territory.

John A. Petroskas, appointed chief metallurgist of the MIDVALE CO., Philadelphia.

OBITUARIES

Col. Eugene C. Peck, former general superintendent and a director of Cleveland Twist Drill Co., Cleveland, died recently at the age of 83.

Albert Browdy, scrap steel buyer for Republic Steel Co., Alabama, died recently after a short illness.

Carl E. Heussner, 51, chemist and engineer for Chrysler Corp., Detroit, died recently.

on the assembly line

automotive news and opinions

Auto producers resist vendor's price increases . . . Alloy shortages strike . . . Buick introduces 1951 models.

by Walter G. Patton

Dec. 1 Rollback — Automobile companies are passing along the hold-the-price line policy to their vendors. A letter from purchasing vice-president, Irving A. Duffy, told 6000 Ford suppliers last week to avoid price rises above Dec. 1 levels. There are also indications that some auto firms may ask their suppliers to certify that the price of their product qualifies under the government pricing formula. Several GM divisions have also notified vendors that their accounting department has been instructed not to accept any price increases above Dec. 1 levels.

Some exceptions have been made in the hold-the-line policy. Suppliers of rubber products, for example, have been permitted to make upward revisions in view of the steep climb in the price of both synthetic and natural rubber.

Truck Prices Up—There has been some opposition to the price position taken by the car manufacturers. Vendors are pointing out, for example, that auto firms are asking them to roll back prices voluntarily although some of these same companies have increased the price of their trucks.

Orders Up in Stars—When auto firms get a government contract nowadays, the orders sometimes reach astronomical proportions. Suppliers of trucks, for example, have reported substantial increases in government orders. An unconfirmed report indicates Ford may be asked to increase its output of aircraft engines at Chicago several times.

Cast Iron Pistons—The question of whether cast iron pistons will sweep the industry in 1951 is still undecided. Originally it was expected that Buick would start production on its 1951 Special Series with cast iron pistons. It is now definite that aluminum pistons will not be used during the first quarter at least. Both a downward revision in schedules and the slightly improved aluminum supply situation have contributed to the decisions to continue with aluminum pistons.

During the coming months in which automobile production schedules may be sharply reduced, it should be expected that many promised substitutions for critical aluminum and copper will not be necessary.

Auto Output Cut — Some informed observers now believe the cut in future automobile production schedules will not be proportional to changes in supplies of steel, aluminum, copper and other critical materials. Rather, it is reasonable to believe that as fast as government contracts are placed and auto workers can be transferred to war work, auto production schedules will be reduced. This is not an established policy but the trend seems to be running strongly in this direction.

Alloy Shortages — The shortage of alloying elements has already resulted in substantial changes in material specifications for the automobile industry. Nickel has practically disappeared from large forming dies. With chromium and molybdenum in shorter supply, Detroit foundries may find it necessary again to use steel inserts in the dies to prevent excessive wear of soft iron.

This practice was extensively used during World War II. One result of this practice is to increase substantially the cost of machining the die.

Big Chunk of Output — There are growing indications that the requirements of DO orders for hot-rolled bars may reach 50 pct of production even though steel producers are now required to take only 15 pct out of each month's output.

Some steel mills are booked as far ahead as June on DO orders for hot-rolled sheets. At the moment hot-rolled bars, both carbon

assembly line

Continued

and alloy, are as critical as hot and cold-rolled sheets. The possibility that this situation may be alleviated by conversion is very slim.

Old Order Confusion—Most Detroit observers are hoping that if a price freeze is ordered on steel scrap, it will be ordered as of a given date. Local observers have pointed out that where a price freeze is announced ahead of time, tremendous confusion in cleaning up old orders has invariably resulted.

Olds War Contract—A second defense contract has been announced by Oldsmobile which previously disclosed it will produce 3.5 in. rockets for the Army's new super bazooka. Olds will produce high velocity guns for the U. S. Army's medium tank. The 15-ft gun tubes will be machined in a new building now under construction at Lansing. The structure was originally intended for steel storage and plant engineering shops.

More than 200 machine tools will be needed, including turning and boring lathes, rifling and honing machines, milling, grinding and broaching machines. Some heat treat equipment will be needed. During World War II, Olds made 75 mm and 76 mm guns for medium tanks.

New Engine, Body—The 1951 Buick Special has a new Fisher body and a new engine. It also has a new chassis. Rear fenders are integral with the rear quarter panel, eliminating the use of fender welts.

Buick is continuing its unit bumper - and - grille construction. The wrap-around bumper is reinforced by two massive "bumper bombs" and two extra grille guards. The 25 grille guards are mounted on a frame which, with the "bombs," are bolted to the bumper bar. Grille bars are stampings rather than die castings.

Being attached to the bumper, the grille bar flexes with the bumper.

Tubular Axle Rods—Hub caps and wheel covers are a new design with the word Buick in script across the face. A one-piece bumper face plate wraps around the ends of the rear fenders. Buick is again using an X-member frame. Rear axle rods are tubular rather than channel type.

The F-263 valve-in-head straight eight engine has 7.2 to 1 compression ratio for Dynaflow transmissions. With Synchro-Mesh transmission, the compression ratio is 6.6 to 1. The new engine for the Special features lower height, shorter connecting rod and shorter pistons and uniform diameter crankshaft bearing journals. Hydraulic valve lifters will be used on all Series 50 and 70 models and on all Dynaflow-equipped Series 40 models.

Similar to Tanks—An important engineering change is the use of segmented brake linings, similar to brakes used on heavy tanks during the last wear. The segments are of unequal length and

are cemented to the brake shoes. Purpose of this design is to produce lower brake lining temperatures and provide additional cooling area. The brakes are also said to be self-cleaning.

Buick is offering E-X-Eye glass, developed jointly with Libbey-Owens-Ford, to reduce sun glare and heat. The windshield has a dark green glare-reducing band at the top, averaging 3¾ in. in width. The shaded top band then fades into a lighter shade designed to meet driving and styling requirements.

Vital Transportation—How necessary is an automobile? AMA has a ready answer: A survey made by Michigan State Highway Dept. showed that 75 pct of 434,-684 employees in 749 Michigan plants came to work in private autos. AMA says further that reports from 94 plants scattered throughout the country covering 140,000 war workers showed 73 pct rode in cars to their jobs. After the war, reports from 32 areas indicated that 52 pct of car trips are for the purpose of making a living, AMA contends.

THE BULL OF THE WOODS
By J. R. Williams

THE BAD MOVE

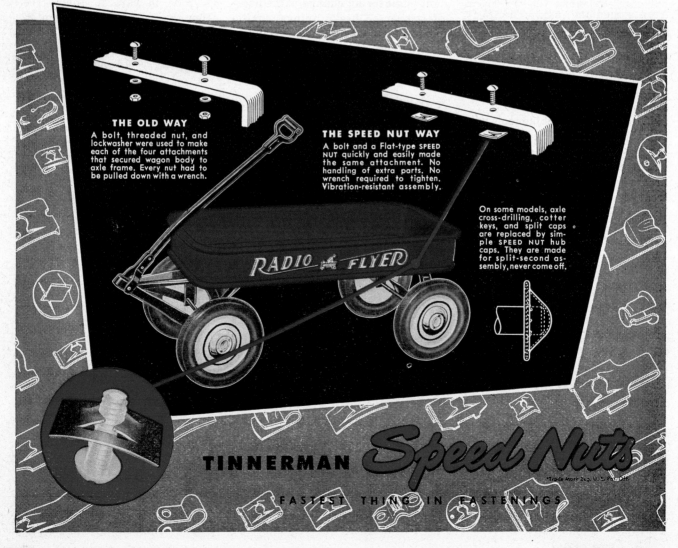

west coast progress report

digest of far west industrial activity

by R. T. Reinhardt

Big Things Brewing—Although plans and market studies can't fill cupolas and openhearths, a preview of things to come may afford hope for those who believe further steel expansion in the West is limited by availability of additional sources of metallics.

Still in the hush-hush stage are plans for limited production of pig iron in Canada and Mexico, and a third blast furnace at Fontana, Calif. These independent proposals seem to have a reasonable prospect of reaching the production stage.

It will be at least a year before any of these new producers can enter the market and in the meantime both foundries and steelmakers are digging deep for scrap.

As Was Expected—It was no surprise to western steel producers when they learned last week that representatives of at least one of the steel companies contemplating an eastern seaboard plant was making market studies of western consumption.

Deficiencies between production and consumption in the West have been estimated at from 1 million to 2 million tons but even the market analysts can't say with any degree of accuracy which finished products are in shortest supply.

Getting Tough—Foundries in Los Angeles County have been issued an ultimatum by the Los Angeles Air Pollution Control District to the effect that they must at least be able to produce purchase orders for smog control equipment.

Because of difficulty in obtaining suitable material the Control Board had issued and renewed variances from time to time to permit continued operation, but the latest order indicates a forthcoming clampdown.

Foundries which have made arrangements with manufacturers for installation will reportedly be granted a stay until equipment is delivered.

Los Angeles foundries recently raised wage scales approximately 6¢ an hour, which is approximately 1½ pct of a recent 5 pct increase in prices put into effect by the foundries. Increased costs of raw material—primarily pig iron and scrap—account for the other 3½ pct.

Hard on Tinplate — More tinplate will be used up by western canmakers this year than ever before.

American Can Co. is expected to have its new Los Angeles Harbor plant well under way by June with a capacity of 350 million units per year.

Pacific Can Co. is expanding its San Francisco plant by approximately 50 pct. Floor space has been increased by 85,000 sq ft and when the addition is completed the plant is expected to produce about 850 million units per year.

Plenty of Elbow Room—Development of a 5000 acre industrial community surrounding Kaiser Steel Corp. at Fontana, Calif., is under way.

Kaiser Steel, Southern California Edison Co., Southern Pacific, Santa Fe Railway, Southern California Instrument Co., the Metropolitan Water District and Union Pacific are all interested in the development, as is the Bank of America and other firms.

Rheem Expanding—Rheem Mfg. Co., Richmond, Calif., is expanding facilities by construction of a 200,000 sq ft building at a cost of approximately $1 million at San Pablo, Calif.

Rheem makes steel drums and household water and space heaters, and during the last war made depth charges and steel drums for the Armed Services.

From Alumina to Uranium—Built during World War II to produce alumina from alunite, the Kalunite plant in Salt Lake City will be used to convert various types of uranium ores to uranium oxide for the Atomic Energy Commission.

the federal view

this week in washington

by Eugene J. Hardy

Price Controls Orders — Temporary abandonment of plans for a general 30-day price freeze has given new impetus to the drafting of individual maximum price orders for basic products, including steel.

The fundamental problem that continues to plague the government's price stabilizers is simply this: Staff of fewer than 400 persons, many of them serving as per diem consultants, are swamped in a mass of pricing data on virtually every commodity and service the nation produces and sells. Unless the Economic Stabilization Agency decides to extend its present voluntary "hold - the - line" agreements with a number of basic industries, or re-examine the 30-day freeze proposal, the actual issuance of product-by-product price ceilings on a large scale would appear to be some weeks away.

On OPA Pattern—Preliminary drafts of ESA orders setting maximum prices on steel and numerous other metals are now being circulated among the price - control agency's limited staff. In some cases, the orders are in the completed stage, lacking only the actual price-ceiling figures and effective dates. Most of them parallel their counterparts which were in effect 5 years ago at the demise of OPA.

But with the exception of "a few cases," nobody in ESA is able to come up with the right formula for controlling prices in the great majority of the producing industries.

Small Business Agency — Don't be surprised if an agency similar to the controversial Smaller War Plants Corporation of World War II is a part of the Washington scene before 1951 rolls to a close. Small business proponents are rallying behind the Small Business Defense Plants Act, reintroduced by Sen. Sparkman, D., Ala., and Rep. Patman, D., Tex., chairmen of the Senate and House Small Business Committees, respectively.

The measure provides for loans to small business for plant expansion and construction; government aid in acquiring materials and machinery; and help in getting government contracts.

Production Men Wanted — Defense Mobilizer Charles E. Wilson wants production men from industry to fill top spots in the mobilization agency set-up. Mr. Wilson continues to emphasize the need for greater output from all industry rather than more controls designed to divide up the existing production pie. It is reported that he is none too happy about the type of individual now moving into key posts where contact with industry is the primary job.

Business and industry are going to have to come up with men to fill these spots unless they want to suffer with the misfits, has-beens, and hare-brained economists which characterized a number of the World War II agencies. This type of individual is control-minded and does not fit into Mr. Wilson's picture for expanding production.

Get the Monopolies—Congressman Celler, D., N. Y., said last week his campaign to "get the malefactors who want to monopolize steel and other industries has just begun."

As chairman of a now-defunct committee to investigate monopolistic practices during the recently-expired Congress, Mr. Celler went after "big steel" hammer-and-tongs in his preliminary efforts.

Celler Seen Stymied—The final report of Mr. Celler's committee did not back up his earlier charges, however. In a factual, but politically-inocuous 92-page report, the committee simply summarized testimony presented to it by various officials of the metalworking industries. Any conclusions or recommendations are conspicuous by their absence in the report.

The present general lack of enthusiasm for Fair Deal measures in the House would seem to indicate that Mr. Celler's campaign won't get very far in the new Congress.

NBS Meeting — The country's leading scientific societies will meet in Washington during 1951 in observance of the 50th anniversary of the National Bureau of Standards. NBS, created by Congress Mar. 3, 1901, is the principal agency of the Federal Government for scientific research.

ONE DRAW

reduces 40-in. diameter blank

66 PCT

By GEORGE ELWERS
Machinery Editor
THE IRON AGE

BLANKS nearly 40 in. in diam are being reduced approximately 66 pct to cups with a length-diameter ratio of nearly 1.7:1 in a single press stroke in drawing operations at Scaife Co., Pittsburgh. Beyond this, achieved in regular production, Scaife research has seen successful reductions as high as 78 pct in one stroke. The method used is reverse drawing, in which the press transforms a blank into a shallow cup, then literally turns the cup inside out as it continues the draw, all in one continuous stroke.

Scaife presently uses the process in manufacture of liquefied petroleum gas cylinders of 14½-in. diam. Dies are ready for production of a 20-in. size, and plans are being made to produce cylinders of other sizes from 6 to 36 in. in diam, as well as other Scaife products of various sizes. Scaife engineers haven't had much time yet to think of other potential applications, but don't doubt that there will be many. Along national defense lines, for example, reverse deep drawing might well be used for such products as shell bodies, shell casings, rocket and missile bodies, and rocket motor tubes.

Reverse deep drawing is not completely new. It has been used in Germany and at the time

Reverse drawing enables production of 14½-in. diam gas cylinder halves in a single press stroke. Diameter reduction of the 40-in., 12-gage, high-tensile steel blank is nearly 66 pct. Length to diameter ratio of the finished cup is almost 1.7:1. In this application of reverse drawing one press does the work of several, and handling and heat-treating between draws is eliminated.

Scaife became interested, Buhl Mfg. Co. and Wheeling Steel were making small parts of relatively light gage steel by this method. But nobody had ever successfully used steel of such thickness or made parts of such size, as Scaife contemplated. And, the press and dies developed by Schaife and the Hydraulic Press Mfg. Co., Mt. Gilead, Ohio, form the basis for the use of reverse deep drawing by the other companies now in the field.

Scaife hadn't done any drawing before adoption of reverse deep drawing. Its line of pressure vessels for air, gases and liquids was fabricated from sheet rolled into cylindrical shape. When Scaife decided to reduce manufacturing costs by going to the two-cup type of gas cylinder, it asked HPM to build a press and dies capable of making cups in a straight draw of approximately 50 pct reduction. The method then in use for producing the two-cup LP gas cylinder made each of the cups, which are later welded together to make the cylinder, in four drawing and ironing or sizing operations, with a stress-relieving heat treatment between each operation. But Scaife wanted to avoid the investment in equipment and floor space that this would entail.

Straight Draw Not Successful

The press and dies were built, and trial runs in HPM's plant proved that the 50 pct reduction could be accomplished in one draw—sometimes. Some heats of steel worked well, but others didn't, and it became apparent that the scrap rate would be prohibitively high. So it was decided to try reverse deep drawing, for which HPM designed a special press.

The 14½-in. diam cylinders currently being produced are formed from two cups, each identical as made on the press. They start with a blank about 38 in. in diam, of 0.10-in. nominal thickness. The finished cup is 14½ in. in diam, and about 24½ in. long, with a closed crowned top and a flange at the open bottom.

During the process, the steel work-hardens enough to make it a little too hard for the subsequent trimming operation. So when the cup is removed from the press, it is placed on its side on a roller conveyer which carries the flanged end under a row of gas burners which heat it to about 1400°F and draw back the hardness.

The handling of these cups after drawing has been thoroughly mechanized by Scaife through the use of roller conveyers. Once a man has lifted a cup from the press with tongs and placed it on the conveyer, further handling is almost entirely automatic, including travel along conveyers, turning the cup on end for washing and on its side for joining and welding, and delivery to and ejection from trimming and welding machines. From the press, the conveyer carries the cups past the burners and then through a washing machine to a Scaife-designed trimmer with two sets of tools which operate alternatively. A rotary knife on this machine simply trims the flange off of alternate cups. Every other cup is trimmed by the other set of tools, which not only cuts off the flange, but gives the cut edge a bead which will later be fitted inside the end of a plain trimmed cup to form a lap joint for welding.

Die Radii Are Critical Design Factors

The plain trimmed cups, which will become cylinder tops, are conveyed to an area where a boss hole is punched and a boss ring attached by submerged arcwelding. They then roll along the conveyer to meet the trimmed and beaded bottom cups at a hydraulic press, where the two are pressed together and roll down a conveyer to one of two welding machines. One of these machines is shown in Fig. 2, the second machine being out of sight at the left.

These Lincolnweld submerged arc machines weld the two cups together, and at the same time weld on a stand ring, a ring extending below the dished bottom of the cylinder to permit standing the cylinder upright. Scaife doesn't like to waste metal. These rings, now rolled

FIG. 1—Removing a finished cup from Scaife's 750-ton HPM press. Two of these cups, with their flanges trimmed, are welded together to make a gas cylinder. The roller conveyer at the left is the start of a system which carries the cups through washing, heat-treating, welding and other steps in manufacture, with almost no further manual handling.

from strip, will soon be made from metal trimmed from one of the cups. Both cups will be drawn to a little greater length to compensate for this. In another example of metal savings, the Info-Crown nameplate attached around the boss at the top of the cylinder is made from a corner left when the cylinder blank is cut from a square sheet.

Following welding, the cylinders undergo a preliminary air pressure test for leaks. Then they are heat-treated in a pusher-type controlled atmosphere furnace to restore tensile and ductility properties. Then come further tests, cleaning and painting.

At present, Scaife uses the HPM 750-ton press shown in Fig. 1. It has a 60x60-in. bed, 135-in. daylight and an 84-in. stroke. Full pressure is not required when working the steel being used for the 14½-in. cylinders. On current work, ram pressure is about 200 to 250 tons, blank holder pressure 125 to 150 tons, and cushion pressure about 75 to 100 tons. Drawing is done at the maximum press speed of 205 ipm. There is no indication that drawing could not be done faster were the press capable of it. HPM is now building for Scaife a 1500-ton press with an 84x84-in. bed, 108-in. stroke, 183-in. daylight, and a maximum speed of 260 ipm, which will be the largest press ever built for reverse deep drawing.

Proper die design is of great importance in success of reverse deep drawing. The operation is unusual in that no ironing is done. In fact, die clearances are very liberal. Except for a minimum which must be maintained, die clearance is not critical and is usually made quite large. Scaife has drawn material all the way from 0.050 to 0.110 in. thick with the same dies. Critical die design points are the radius on the draw ring, the radii on the hollow punch, and the angle on the hollow punch and the cushion. The approximate shapes at these points are illustrated in the accompanying box. Thickness can be very accurately held if these are correct, and if blank holder pressure and the pressure differential between the hollow punch and the cushion are correct.

Tool Steel Inserts Cut Die Wear

Inserts in the draw ring, and the heads of the hollow punch, solid punch, and cushion, are of high carbon-high chrome tool steel. In production of over 100,000 cylinders, these surfaces have shown no measureable wear. Lately, hardened Meehanite has been used instead of tool steel for some die parts, and while it does wear, indications are that it may be more economical in the long run than tool steel.

Scaife has experimented with various wet lubricants, but to date has found none that can stand up under the pressures and temperatures

FIG. 2—Automatic submerged arcwelding is used to join the cylinder halves. Simultaneously, a stand ring is welded on at the bottom of the cylinder.

of the process. It is now using a soap lubricant, applied wet in a thin film and dried, in a Scaife-designed machine.

The material used in production of the 14½-in. cylinders is an annealed high-strength low-alloy steel, used to keep weight as low as possible while still meeting the extremely rigid Interstate Commerce Commission physical specifications for LP gas containers. Scaife used to specify that the steel be pickled prior to annealing, but has discovered that the tight coat

FIG. 3—Wall thickness of cups is accurately held in reverse drawing. This is a typical thickness chart made from a cross-section of a cup for a 14½-in. cylinder half. Note that variation is less than ±0.005 in. except near the flange at the open end, which is trimmed off anyway.

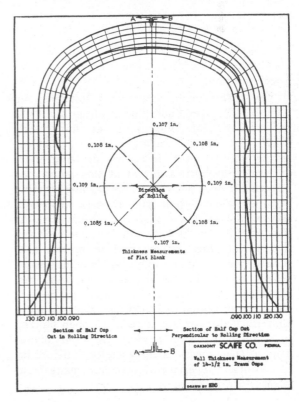

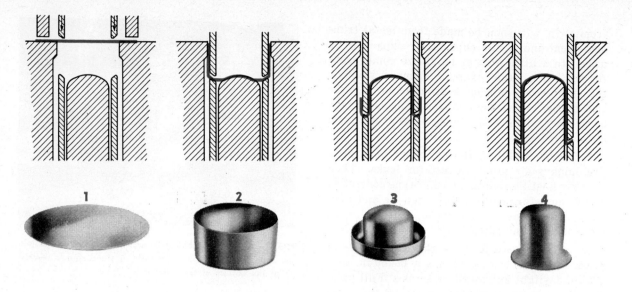

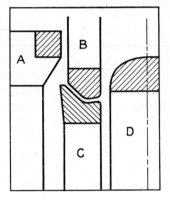

▶These simplified schematic drawings illustrate how reverse drawing works, using a Scaife LP gas cylinder half as an example.

(1) The process starts with a flat circular blank, held down by a blank holder against blank ring A. Downward motion of the ram causes formation of a shallow cup by the hollow punch, B.

(2) The blank holder pressure is removed at just the right time so that the cup is formed without a flange, and occupies the position shown, in the die. At this point the cup bottom is in contact with the stationary solid punch, D. And the descent of the hollow punch has pushed the cup against the ring, C, free to move down against oil pressure.

(3) Continued downward motion of the ram now literally turns the shallow cup inside out. Its bottom, which becomes the top of the final cup, is held and shaped by the solid punch. Its walls are drawn between the hollow punch and the cushion. Correct pressure for this operation is obtained by regulating the differential between the ram pressure forcing the hollow punch downward, and the resisting pressure of the cushion.

(4) The completed cup, with its flange trimmed off, forms half of a LP gas cylinder. All of this is accomplished in a single continuous stroke of the ram. Shaded areas in the sketch showing the approximate shape of the die parts, are tool steel inserts.

of reduced scale on steel annealed without prior pickling is, if uniform, beneficial to the drawing operation.

The ICC specifies that wall thickness on 14½-in. LP gas cylinders be not less than 0.083 in. The critical point occurs at the knuckle where the straight walls and the crowned end of the cylinder meet. In reverse drawing, there is less tendency to thin out at this point than in straight deep drawing. This permits starting with a slightly lighter gage of steel, while still easily holding better than the minimum thickness at this critical point. In fact, the uniformity of wall thickness obtained in reverse deep drawing is one of the important advantages of this process. Fig. 3 shows a graph of wall thickness of a section cut from a typical cup. It can be seen that wall thickness varies no more than ±0.005 in. except toward the open flanged end, which is cut off anyway. Another advantage of the process is the excellent uniformity of physical properties of cylinders made from reverse-drawn cups.

In its research, Scaife has successfully applied reverse drawing to many different materials, such as 302 stainless, aluminum, copper and Monel. It believes reverse drawing can be used for non-cylindrical shapes such as rectangular transformer cases, and for conical shapes. It sees no apparent limit to the thickness of metal that can be reverse drawn, and is, in fact, considering applying deep drawing to the manufacture of high-pressure vessels. Scaife also envisions the possibility of making an entire cylinder, closed at both ends, on the same press, thus eliminating the welded joint.

Scrap Rate Is Low

At the beginning of work with deep drawing, scrap loss at Scaife was, of course, quite high. But its overall average, now, including the high initial rate, is down to around 6.4 pct, and the current rate is comfortably below 4 pct, an excellent indication of the success attained with deep drawing on work which had once been considered impractical.

Cadmium-tin alloy plating stops corrosion

Extensive tests led to the development of a successful cadmium-tin alloy plating solution. The deposit is obtained from a fluoborate solution and contains approx 75 pct Cd and 25 pct Sn. Far greater corrosion resistance in low alloy steel is achieved than with cadmium or tin of comparable thicknesses.

CORROSION problems are serious ones in the manufacture and operation of aircraft engines, whether reciprocating, jet, or gas turbine. The reciprocating engine is particularly susceptible due to the low corrosion resistance of the steels normally employed. Jet and gas turbine engines have special problems of high temperature corrosive attack which will not be discussed here.

Previous methods of protecting steel parts in reciprocating aircraft engines have not been entirely satisfactory or desirable. Application of a thermosetting resin is being used extensively with some success. This method, however, has many limitations. It only offers physical protection; its thickness is 0.0005 in.; it is hard and brittle; and it chips easily.

Interest had been aroused[1] in the use of a thin tin deposit covered by an equally thin cadmium deposit which was subsequently heat treated to diffuse the two coatings. The total thickness of the finished coating was 0.0001 in. and was found to afford excellent protection to steel. An investigation was started to verify the corrosion resistance information that had been presented for the overlay cadmium-tin plate.

Test panels, measuring 2 x 4 x 1/16 in., were prepared from SAE 1020 steel and used for all tests. No variation of cleaning cycle was made throughout the investigation; a standard soak type alkaline cleaner followed by a rinse, neutralizing acid dip, and a final rinse was used for all panels. The primary interest was to produce an electro-deposit that would furnish high corrosion resistance for steel; the end results were successful (patent application filed for the plating bath developed).

Nearly every panel plated was subjected to the salt spray test so that a considerable amount of data were obtained. At first, the data were hard to believe but continued reproduction indicated good corrosion resistance. A deposit of 75 pct Cd and 25 pct Sn was chosen as the ideal, although some variation from this composition does not reduce corrosion resistance appreciably. Average values for the appearance of initial corrosion are listed in Table I.

Displays High Resistance

Many panels were left in the salt spray test after initial corrosion had occurred in order to determine the rate of advance. In all cases, the cadmium-tin alloy showed a very slow rate of advance. Numerous panels that exhibited initial corrosion at 600 to 700 hr were left for a total of 2000 hr at which time very little additional corrosion had taken place.

This characteristic of apparent anodic protection was highly desirable for the production of aircraft engine parts. During assembly, these parts often come in contact with each other. If this occurs, the effectiveness of the cadmium-tin coating is not destroyed. When chipping of a thermosetting resin takes place, its effectiveness

By B. E. SCOTT, *Senior Chemist,* and R. D. GRAY, Jr., *Former Senior Chemist*
Wright Aeronautical Corp., *Wood-Ridge, N. J.*

TABLE I

CORROSION IN SALT SPRAY

Cd-Sn Plate, Thickness, in.	Time,* hr
.00005	384
0.0001	1000
0.0003	3720
0.0004	none after 30 mo.
0.0005	none after 30 mo.
Cadmium	
0.0001	120
0.0003	360
Tin	
0.0001	48

* Time for initial corrosion to appear.

Cadmium-Tin Plating

Continued

is completely destroyed in the chipped area. Further evidence of anodic protection afforded by cadmium-tin was obtained by additional salt spray and humidity cabinet tests. Panels were cross-scratched through the deposit so that the base metal was exposed. Corrosion occurred in the scratch after 450 hr of salt spray test. No corrosion was evident after 1000 hr in the panels tested in the humidity cabinet.

Many aircraft engine parts have subsequently been plated with cadmium-tin and subjected to experimental operation. No detrimental effects of any nature have been found due to the deposit. On wearing surfaces, a burnishing effect appears to take place so that after considerable operating time, there is still evidence of a deposit. This may be due to a lower coefficient of friction than steel. Preliminary torquing tests with cadmium-tin and cadmium plated studs and bolts indicate more consistent values for the cadmium-tin.

Preliminary Tests Show Promise

Tin was first deposited from a regular sodium stannate bath to a thickness of 0.00005 in. followed by a similar amount of cadmium from a regular cyanide bath. The panels were then heated for 30 min in air at a temperature of $335° \pm 5°F$. For comparative purposes, panels were also plated 0.0001 in. thick with cadmium and to a similar thickness of tin. All of the panels were then subjected to salt spray[2] where they were examined every 24 hr. The first series of panels plated verified the previous information. The cadmium-tin overlay plate exhibited far better corrosion resistance than either of the regular plates. Microstructures are shown in Figs. 1 and 2.

Since the cadmium-tin deposits produced such promising results for resistance to salt spray corrosion, it was decided to investigate the possibilities of co-deposition of the two metals. A cadmium-tin plating solution[3] which could produce an alloy of cadmium containing up to 0.10 pct Sn was found. This tin content, however, was far below that deemed necessary for this program. Tin-zinc alloy plating,[4] as extensively used in Great Britain, was also examined.

Several plating baths were formulated using

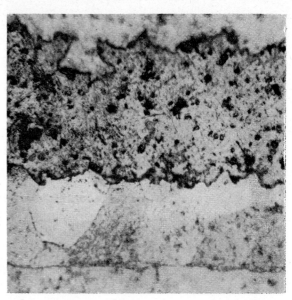

FIG. 1—Cadmium-tin overlay plate as deposited. Tin is in the large grains at the bottom, with the cadmium layer at the top. Etched 10 pct NaOH. 500X.

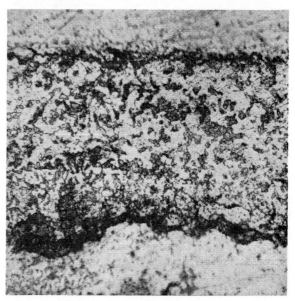

FIG. 2—Cadmium-tin overlay deposit after diffusing in air at 350° F for 30 min. Note diffusion of the tin through the cadmium matrix. Etched 10 pct NaOH. 500X.

FIG. 3—Co-deposited cadmium-tin from the new fluoborate bath. Etched 10 pct NaOH. 500X.

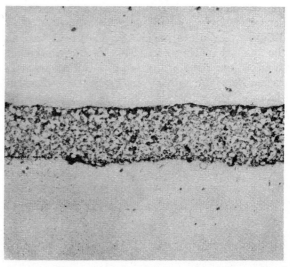

sodium stannate and cadmium oxide in a cyanide bath with little success. In all cases, practically pure cadmium resulted at the cathode. Inasmuch as tin is bivalent in an acid plating solution and tetravalent in an alkaline bath, the rate of deposition is double when operating below a pH of 7. This also results in a greater cathode efficiency and reduces hydrogen evolution at the cathode.

To study an acid plating bath, General Chemical Co. supplied solutions of cadmium fluoborate and tin fluoborate. It was hoped that a mixture of these solutions would produce an alloy plate sufficiently high in tin. Another advantage of such an acid solution over an alkaline bath is its higher electrical conductivity, which results in high anode and cathode current efficiency. Also, it was hoped that operation at room temperature would be feasible.

A number of fluoborate cadmium-tin baths were formulated and test specimens plated in them were submitted to salt spray tests. These baths produced deposits having tin contents ranging from 10 to 90 pct. After extensive testing it was determined that the optimum range of tin values was between 20 and 35 pct for maximum corrosion resistance. Microstructure of the cadmium-tin plate, co-deposited from the fluoborate bath, is shown in Fig. 3.

Operating pH Range is Narrow

Since the process produced an alloy plate, considerable time was spent in selecting the proper anodes. Anodes containing various percentages of tin and cadmium were cast and tried in the bath, as well as plain cadmium and tin anodes. The best anode corrosion and adequate maintenance of metal content in the bath were obtained from individual anodes of cadmium and tin with a surface area ratio of 1:3. It will be noted that this ratio is the opposite from the resultant deposit. A ratio of 1:1 for anode to cathode area was found to be satisfactory. No burning of the anodes occurred at this ratio. A smut formation on the anodes during operation of the bath made it necessary to bag them to prevent bath contamination.

The operating pH range was fairly narrow, best operation occurring between 2.5 and 3.0. If the pH drops appreciably below 2.5, the tin content of the deposit increases and corrosion resistance is lowered. The same is true if the bath is operated at a high current density.[5] The maximum operating range of current density was 10 to 80 amp per sq ft for a bright deposit of suitable tin content. The anode efficiency is high and, for all practical purposes, the cathode efficiency was 100 pct, which is typical of fluoborate plating solutions. Cathode efficiencies, calculate from Haring Cell data, are shown in Fig. 4.

Polarization effects at both the anode and the cathode were rather small. This was particularly

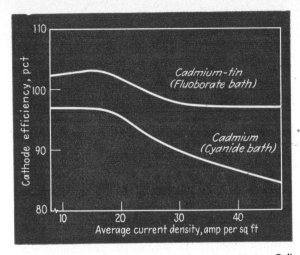

FIG. 4—Cathode efficiencies as obtained from Haring Cell data show the new fluoborate bath to average near 100 pct values.

true at the low current densities used to deposit 0.0001 in. of alloy. At high current densities, oxygen release at the anode changed the polarization picture somewhat. Measurements with a Haring Cell indicated that the bath has a resistivity or specific resistance of 2.4 ohm-cm. Since there is no pronounced cathode polarization effect, the throwing power of the bath is good.

Like many other plating baths, the use of agitation permits an increase in the limiting current density. Since the authors were not concerned with heavy deposits, the actual limiting current density for an agitated bath was not determined. The normal still plating time to deposit 0.0001 in. of the alloy is so small that increasing the plating rate by increasing the current density was not considered.

Plating Rate High

Due to the high cathode efficiency of the bath, the plating rate is quite high. Actual determinations of the plating rate were limited to short times and fairly low current densities as the primary interest was in deposits of about 0.0001 in. thick. It was found, however, that this data and a few determinations for longer plating periods correlated rather well with rate data calculated on the basis of 100 pct cathode efficiency shown in Fig. 5, and a deposit composition of 75 pct Cd and 25 pct Sn. The data will assume a slight curve toward lower thicknesses with a change in deposit composition, but not to any great extent. The change in rate is negligible in thicknesses of 0.0001 in. There will also be a slight departure from linearity as the current density increases due to its effect on deposit composition (increase in tin content).

No information was obtained on the effect of temperature on the operation of the bath. A primary object of the investigation was to develop a process that would operate satisfactorily at room temperature. As this object was fulfilled,

Continued

no work was done on the effect of temperature.

Without the addition agents specified in the accompanying box, the deposit is dull and rather coarse grained. A great many substances were tried as addition agents, most of which had no effect. Only a certain type of colloidal suspension supplied the necessary action, and only a few materials of this nature gave success. The most successful were Processed Protein, produced by Canada Packers, Inc., and Petone, produced by Cudahy. These materials gave a bright, fine-grained deposit; treeing, which had caused considerable trouble earlier, was completely absent.

Occasional Filtering Required

On long-time operation of the bath, it was found necessary to filter occasionally for clarification. The proteinaceous addition agents are not too stable, and the bath becomes cloudy with time.

It is well to add about ½ per liter of the Processed Protein or Peptone prior to the clarification. This restores the bath to its original brightness.

During the course of the investigation, it was necessary to develop analytical procedures for control purposes; deposits from all of the ex-

PLATING BATH COMPOSITION*

Cadmium Fluoborate (51.66 pct)	32 fl oz per gal
Stannous Fluoborate (43.50 pct)	9.3 fl oz per gal
Boric Acid	2.7 avdp oz per gal
Ammonium Fluoborate	6.7 avdp oz per gal
Fluoboric Acid (42 pct)	7.8 fl oz per gal
Phenol Sulfonic Acid (70 pct)	0.3 fl oz per gal
Processed Protein Powder	0.13 to 0.27 avdp oz per gal
Temperature	Room
Cathode Current Density	15 to 60 asf
Anodes	Individual tin and Cadmium (Ratio 3 Sn:1 Cd)
pH	2.5 to 3.0
Cathode and Anode Current Eff.	Approx 100 pct

*Cd-Sn fluoborate plating solution giving an average deposit of 75 pct Cd and 25 pct Sn.

perimental solutions were analyzed to determine their composition. These deposit analyses only involved the determination of tin. Cadmium was determined by difference. The deposit for analysis was usually plated upon stainless steel, from which the plate was easily lifted.

Bath Is Strongly Acid

Since this plating bath is rather strongly acid (ph 2.5 to 3.0) which is typical of the fluoborate baths in general, it is necessary to use either glass or rubber-lined equipment to prevent bath contamination and equipment damage. Acid resistant masking materials for parts and racks are also required.

The aircraft engine parts were plated in a 10-gal tank that has been in intermittent operation for 18 months. Some bath decomposition was noted over this period, necessitating occasional replenishment of cadmium and tin in the solution. Slightly over a gallon each of stannous fluoborate concentrate and cadmium fluoborate concentrate have been added over this period. Deposit compositions have remained fairly consistent with 25 to 30 pct Sn and the remainder cadmium. Parts were plated in the tank operated as a still tank, while small parts were plated in a portable barrel which was inserted in the still tank; both still tank and barrel operations are therefore feasible.

The authors wish to thank W. Paecht and J. Debiec for their assistance in plating details and analytical work, and C. Struyk, General Chemical Co., for advice on fluoborate plating solutions.

FIG. 5—Calculated plating rate data for the new method, based on 100 pct cathode efficiency and a deposit composition of 75 pct Cd and 25 pct Sn.

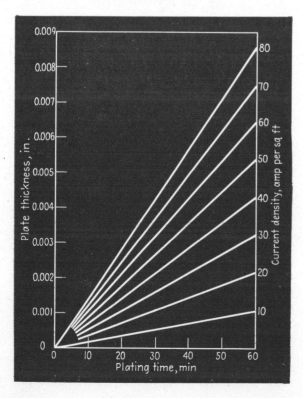

References

[1] Bureau of Aeronautics, Navy Dept.
[2] ASTM B-117-44T.
[3] U. S. Patent No. 2,093,031.
[4] R. M. Angles, "Electro-deposition of Tin-Zinc Alloys," Journal of the Electro-depositor's Tech. Soc., 21, p. 45 (1946).
[5] C. L. Faust, "Alloy Plating," Trans. of the Electrochemical Society, Vol. 80, 1941.

JOURNAL BEARINGS LUBRICATION TESTED

FRICTIONAL heat and the stability of protective oil films in plain journal bearings can be largely controlled by the arrangement of oil holes and grooves, according to tests conducted by S. A. McKee and H. S. White of the National Bureau of Standards. Their investigation is part of a continuing research program on plain journal bearing lubrication sponsored by the National Advisory Committee for Aeronautics.

The tests revealed that it is always desirable to avoid oil holes or grooves which interfere with the normal development of hydrostatic pressure in the oil film supporting the load in the bearing. However, in bearing installations where the direction or intensity of the load is not constant, it is not always possible to satisfy this requirement. Even though the data collected by McKee and White is based on test runs in which the direction of loads was constant, the values obtained should be useful in estimating the effect of more complex operating conditions.

The friction-testing machine used for the investigation consisted of four similar test bearings enclosed in a housing and mounted on a common shaft. Frictional torque was measured by a dynamometer scale acting through a torque arm fitted to the housing. Test shafts were carburized steel, heat treated to hardnesses ranging from 55 to 61 Rc and ground to a surface roughness ranging from 4 to 5 microinches. The bearings used in the tests were made up of solid steel sleeves with copper-lead linings. The diameter of each test bearing was measured at the axial center and near each end. All four journals in each shaft were checked. Nominal dimensions were a shaft diameter of 2 in. and a 1¼-in. bear-

RATINGS OF BEARINGS

Design of Oil Feed	Bearing set	Friction Ratings						Load-Carrying Capacity Ratings				
								First Run		Fourth Run		
		ZN/P=10 Δf	ZN/P=70 Δf	Average Δf for each set	Average Δf for each design	Rating		Critical ZN/P for each set	Average critical ZN/P for each design	Critical ZN/P for each set	Average critical ZN/P for each design	Rating
1 hole in bearing	31	0.00101	0.00149	0.00125	0.00130	A		3.2	3.2	1.7	1.6	A
	51	0.00106	0.00164	0.00135				3.1		1.5		
2 holes in bearing	32	0.00126	0.00187	0.00158	0.00147	B		3.5	3.5	2.6	2.7	B
	52	0.00113	0.00159	0.00136				3.8		2.8		
Axial groove in bearing	33	0.00101	0.00143	0.00122	0.00124	A		3.3	2.9	1.5	1.4	A
	53	0.00101	0.00149	0.00125				2.5		1.2		
4 holes in bearing	34	0.00125	0.00165	0.00145	0.00143	B		5.0	4.4	3.4	3.4	C
	54	0.00115	0.00166	0.00141				3.9		3.3		
Circum. groove in bearing	35	0.00186	0.00340	0.00263	0.00240	C		4.2	4.2	2.4	2.8	B
	55	0.00149	0.00284	0.00217				4.2		3.2		
1 hole in shaft	S31	0.00109	0.00166	0.00138	0.00136	A or B		2.2	2.6	1.8	1.8	A
	S51	0.00107	0.00162	0.00134				3.0		1.8		
2 holes in shaft	S32	0.00112	0.00169	0.00140	0.00143	B		2.7	2.8	2.0	1.9	A
	S52	0.00111	0.00181	0.00146				3.0		1.8		
1 hole with flat in shaft	S33	0.00137	0.00153	0.00145	0.00146	B		7.2	7.4	5.5	5.4	D
	S53	0.00126	0.00166	0.00146				7.7		5.2		

Values of the coefficient of friction, f, at ZN/P = 10 and ZN/P = 70 for each set of bearings tested are given in the friction ratings. The average value of f is given over this same range for each set and type of bearings. Critical values of ZN/P at which transition from stable to unstable lubrication occurred are given in the load-carrying capacity ratings.

ing length. With each oil feed arrangement, two sets of bearings of different clearances were used. These provided D/C ratios of 663 and 403, where D is the journal diameter and C is the diametral clearance. An SAE 20 motor oil was used in all tests at a constant oil inlet temperature of 200°F.

Constant Speed Held

The apparatus was warmed up before the start of each run and the data were obtained with the bearings at a steady rate of temperature distribution. With each set of bearings, tests were first made in the region of stable lubrication at the higher values of the generalized operating variable, ZN/P, where Z is the absolute viscosity of the lubricant, N is the speed of the shaft and P is the pressure on the projected area of the bearing. Each test run was made at a constant speed of 2030 rpm, with a number of constant loads which were successively increased at intervals during each run. Rate of oil flow was held at 15 cu in. per min, with the load on the shaft being increased until unstable lubrication

developed. Because these operating conditions tended to change the condition of bearing surfaces, four consecutive runs under each given set of conditions were made with each set of bearings tested.

As each set of bearings was operated at each given load for two minutes, observations of the frictional torque were made at one-minute intervals. When stable lubrication had developed in the test runs, the second torque reading was either equal to or lower than the first. For this reason, all friction data appearing in the accompanying table was obtained from the first and fourth test runs. The values obtained from the last runs were used for rating the load-carrying capacity of the oil films developed.

The temperature rise that developed in the bearings during the test runs was dependent on both the heat generated in shearing the oil in the bearings and the heat delivered by the oil entering the bearings. Data obtained from the tests as a whole indicate that, under the specific conditions involved, heat-dissipation characteristics displayed were dependent chiefly on the rate of oil flow through the bearings. Neither the clearance in the individual bearings nor the type of hole or groove arrangement used had any appreciable effect.

Indexing fixture aids drilling close holes

PLATEN end plugs are machined for IBM electric typewriters at the International Business Machine Corporation's Poughkeepsie, N. Y. plant. Such parts each require four step-drilled holes which are too closely spaced in one direction for all four to be readily drilled at the same time.

For this reason, and to attain a good produc-

tion rate, the illustrated indexing setup is employed. The indexing table carries three fixtures, each of which holds two workpieces. While each fixture is in the front position, two parts already drilled are removed and two undrilled parts are put in their place, after which the fixture is locked by a hand lever. This brings the combination clamp and bushing plate of the drill jig down against the top face of the two work pieces.

When this loaded fixture is indexed one station, it comes under four step drills that feed down and produce two holes in each piece. After the drills have retracted, the fixture indexes again and stops under a second set of four drills which are then in line with the remaining four holes in the jig. When these drills feed down, the four remaining holes, two in each piece, are produced. At the same time, a new pair of parts in the prior position are also drilled, hence eight holes are produced after each indexing.

With this setup, which works automatically except for loading and unloading; about 188 parts per hr are run. It is necessary to employ an 8-spindle drill press that can provide close center distances, or to use some equivalent setup that will operate two sets of four drills on the required centers.

Experiments on Forsterite Linings reported successful

According to this translation, the Germans have had good results with forsterite basic linings in induction furnaces. The raw material, Norwegian olivines, is plentiful and this practice may find wider use.

By B. M. PEARSON

Hassocks, Sussex, England

AS a result of experimentation and actual production experience in German steel plants, a new basic refractory material has been developed from the mineral forsterite. This refractory brick has substantially increased the number of melts that were obtained from high frequency induction furnace linings. Only highly refractory materials can be considered for this service, and the rarer and more expensive linings must also be excluded.

The research that resulted in the forsterite, or magnesium orthosilicate (Mg_2SiO_4) lining, was conducted by Stuetzel during 1942 and 1943 in the research department of Friedrich Krupp, Essen. The aim of the work was to find a refractory lining that could be used in induction furnaces of more than one ton capacity, melting those steels for which acid linings are too strongly reducing. A means of extending the working life of such linings and providing greater security against break-outs was desired. Along with the investigations of forsterite, tests were also made of magnesia linings, with different additions and various particle sizes.

Forsterite, containing 57 pct MgO and 43 pct SiO_2, is the only highly refractory compound in the system MgO-SiO_2 that is free of transformation changes. In contrast, there are the well-known technical difficulties caused by quartz, the silica stones and zirconium oxide. The melting point of forsterite is 3434°F. With excess magnesia, the melting curve rises after it has passed over at 3362°F, the forsterite-periclase eutectic. An excess of SiO_2 causes the melting temperature to fall to 2809°F, the melting point of the eutectic of clinoenstat (this is the metasilicate $MgSiO_3$, containing 40 pct MgO and cristobalite SiO_2). With 45 pct MgO, the melting point is about 3092°F. The spalling tendencies of forsterite are not as pronounced as periclase. In this respect, forsterite resembles quartz.

As a lining material, this refractory is gen-erally used in the massive form, and less often as a rammed mass. As far as is known, magnesium orthosilicate has never been used as a crucible lining for induction furnaces prior to the tests at Essen.[1] It was felt that it would be somewhat sensitive to slagging and iron oxides. Other quarters regarded the refractory as having satisfactory slag resistance. It does not appear, however, that forsterite can be considered as "the" basic lining. Such a basic lining—as satisfactory in every respect as the acid lining in its field—would not appear to be possible. Previous investigaions have shown that the reason for the basic behavior of forsterite is that its SiO_2 is firmly combined. Compared with the free silica of the quartzite linings, it is not reduced by the alloying metals of steels for which it is used. Accordingly, the steels themselves do not become contaminated with silicon and impoverished in manganese or chromium. In this respect, magnesium orthosilicate closely resembles magnesium oxide, and can replace this basic lining.

Other Basic Linings Limited

Other basic or basic to neutral linings offer great difficulties which can only be controlled by special measures or not at all. One of these refractories is magnesium oxide. While this material is completely basic, its tendency to crack when used in large crucible structures makes it one of the most undesirable types of linings. Other refractory compounds occupy an intermediate place in metallurgy and furnace operation.

Detailed information on the possibilities offered by these other materials and the difficulties involved in using them has been developed by W. Bottenberg and P. Bardenheuer[2] and by P. Bardenheuer and R. Bleckmann.[3] These investigations were confined to sinter magnesia and electro-magnesia. Spinel and forsterite were regarded as too little basic and too sensitive to temperature changes. Dolomite seemed too subject to weathering influences. Neither were alumina or corundum mentioned in this fundamental work, as they cannot be considered completely basic and possess insufficient resistance to temperature changes.

Special attention was paid to the slagging resistance of magnesite linings. After working with a reducing slag, it was established that destruction of the lining can only be prevented if penetrating slag can be removed immediately by some means. The particular disadvantages of magnesia linings, which are so favorable from the chemical-metallurgical aspects, are their sensitivity to temperature changes and thermal shock. Because of these characteristics there is always danger of break-throughs of molten steel to the water-cooled coils in induction furnaces.

One other material that is known to have particularly good resistance to thermal shock is the aluminum silicate mullite, $3Al_2O_3.2SiO_2$. As mullite is synthetically produced therefore it is not very economical. Like the silicate forsterite, $2MgO.SiO_2$, mullite can at least be characterized as having better resistance to thermal shock than many magnesite bricks.

Some Not Sufficiently Basic

If, as has been pointed out, corundum (Al_2O_3) and spinel ($MgO.Al_2O_3$) can be considered as not sufficiently basic, the same could also be said of silicate compounds containing 28 or even 40 pct of SiO_2. When used for melting chrome and manganese steels, these silicates might also react like acid linings.

Pure forsterite is seldom encountered as a natural mineral. However, there are the minerals called olivines, a close-mixed crystal series of forsterite and the corresponding iron orthosilicate known as fayalite (Fe_2SiO_4). These are not only encountered in nature as minerals, but even as massive rock formations, the peridotite, dunite or olivine rocks. Fortunately, these formations are usually rich in forsterite and are therefore refractory. Fayalite itself starts to melt at 2201°F, and a mixture of forsterite and about 15 pct fayalite commences to melt at 3092°F. For this reason, only those olivines with 10 pct or less of fayalite can be used for highly refractory linings. Olivine rocks always carry certain other additives which also reduce the melting point.

Rich amounts of olivine are often present in basic volcanic rocks such as the basalts, but they cannot be recovered. The earlier volcanic formations containing olivine are secondary in importance. Quantities are lower and are enclosed in lower melting basalt encrustations. Olivine rocks with the necessary low amounts of ad-

mixtures occur infrequently in Central Europe but are present in large amounts in South Norway. These deposits yield suitable forsterite. Formations have also been found in the Pyrenees, but they have yet to be evaluated.

How Forsterite Is Extracted

V. M. Goldschmidt[4], who worked on the Norwegian olivine rock and the Americans, R. E. Birch and F. A. Harvey[5], have described the method of extracting forsterite from this basic material. Magnesium oxide in the form of magnesia or sinter magnesite is added in such amounts to the crushed rock as to cause the decomposition of the fayalite content. The SiO_2 in this latter compound combines with MgO to form new forsterite, while the iron content forms a similarly refractory spinel magnesio-ferrite ($MgO.Fe_2O_3$), whose melting point is around 3272°F. The same reaction occurs with the chromite and magnetic iron ores, enstatite ($MgSiO_3$) and the magnesium hydrosilicates such as serpentine and talc, which are also present. Any excess of magnesium oxide remains as periclase.

It is also possible to process serpentine so as to form forsterite[6, 7]. Since it must first be kilned and undergoes considerable shrinkage during dehydration, it is preferable not to use this material.

Thermal shock tests of forsterite linings produced in this way have been performed. Bricks of the required shapes were prepared from a Norwegian olivine rock of the following composition: SiO_2, 40.7 pct; Al_2O_3, 0.7 pct; Fe_2O_3, 7.4 pct; CaO, 0.0 pct; MgO, 50.8 pct. The loss in weight on ignition was 0.36 pct.

The particle size was composed in agreement with recommendations by Goldschmitt[4]. These recommendations are for forsterite bricks having special resistance to thermal shock of 50 pct coarse olivine rock with a 3 to 1 mm particle size and 50 pct fine-grained material below 0.2 or 0.1 mm particle size, consisting half of olivine rock and half sinter-magnesite.

Handled Thirty-eight Melts

This lining was used in a one ton high frequency crucible, and thirty-eight melts, partly comprising hard manganese steels, were produced. This was the first of large scale tests conducted by M. Pohl. The crucible was very dense and tight, and was frequently allowed to cool during the tests. Unlike magnesite linings, it was noted that after melts were poured out there was no "after running" of the steel. The lining remained free of cracks and fissures.

Even in the hot condition the forsterite remained very elastic, because blows from pieces of scrap on charging did not damage it. A hole which developed during the thirty-sixth melt was successfully patched. In subsequent tests, patching had no apparent undue effects.

In general, the lining provided satisfactory

melting of steels which required a basic lining. A service life was established which could formerly only be achieved with a magnesia-zirconia composition. Accordingly, this expensive lining material may be replaced with forsterite. As for pure magnesite, the number of melts per lining was always considerably less.

Using laboratory samples of forsterite lining of the type just described, the following properties were established; density, 2.45; a slight after-expansion of about 0.1 pct, instead of the shrinkage that occurs with sinter magnesite; water absorption, 10 pct; apparent porosity, 25 pct. Thermal expansion was about 2.3 pct linear at 2822°F. This is similar to many magnesia samples, which generally show higher expansion rates. The heat conductivity of forsterite should be lower than with magnesite bricks.[5] In fact, forsterite appears to be less sintered though than is normal with magnesite linings. This has a lot to do with the greater sensitivity of magnesite to temperature changes.

It appears that the refractoriness of pure forsterite linings or those with a very small excess of magnesia is not always quite sufficient. At times, erosion occurs. This is due to certain constituents in the olivine rocks. The influence of these admixtures can be masked to a certain degree by a higher MgO addition, without endangering the inherent advantages of the forsterite lining.

Thermal Shock Tests Inconclusive

It must be emphasized that these thermal shock tests, like those made on standard-size, cylindrical test pieces, in no way give final evidence of the behavior of such linings in large-size crucibles such as high frequency induction furnaces. This is true both in the good and in the bad sense. As a matter of fact, the thermal shock test figures on individual test pieces were outstandingly bad. However, the differences between the demands made on samples in such limited tests and those made on complete linings in large crucibles are too great. Only extensive experience with crucibles of two tons capacity or more will permit sound estimates of a given type of basic lining. Forsterite has given good results when used to line a 2-ton crucible. The particle size was not entirely satisfactory, yet 14 melts were obtained with one lining and even with another. This second lining suffered premature destruction due to unfortunate circumstances. Sinter magnesite linings will not last through this many melts in the same type of furnace, even if special measures are taken. Usually, no more than 5 or 6 melts are obtained per lining.

Limited tests of forsterite in a 2.5 ton furnace by L. Luckemeyer-Hasse showed similar longevity. An average of twelve melts per lining was established, somewhat better than with magnesite linings under equivalent working conditions. In these tests, too, it was demonstrated again that forsterite linings do not crack or fissure, effectively minimizing the danger of breakouts.

This safety factor is the principal advantage of forsterite linings. It will continue to be so even when further experimentation and development provide greater durability.

It has also been shown that when certain percentages of the content of magnesite linings are forsterite they behave better than pure magnesite.[8] Therefore the excess olivine powder produced in crushing can be used as an up-grading constituent for magnesite. Similar mixtures in which ground scrap from forsterite crucible linings is present are significantly less inclined to cracking and fissuring, according to Luckemeyer-Hasse.

Quartz Can Be Substituted

Where olivine rock or fired serpentine is not available, magnesite linings can be given the advantage of forsteritic bonding by adding quartz, which opposes the spalling characteristics of the periclase grains. Preliminary investigations indicate that favorable results with such linings are completely possible. Such forsterite additions to magnesite have been studied by G. E. Seil[9]. Large-scale tests have not been undertaken.

Because of its dense structure, uncrushed olivine rock is quite resistant to slag attack, yet no precise information on rammed forsterite linings is available. There is one case where Stuetzel has reported that he observed a forsterite lining in prolonged contact with a lime-alumina slag. There was no ensuing damage.

Aside from the technical advantages afforded by forsterite, it is obvious that such linings will normally be somewhat cheaper than magnesite. One important economic advantage over sinter magnesite is that olivine rock, about two thirds of the lining mixture, requires no kilning.

REFERENCES

[1] German patent: Friedrich Krupp, Essen; No. K 164, 528, Gr. Yla, Kl. 31a, 1942.

[2] W. Bottenberg and P. Bardenheuer, Journal of Kaiser Wilhelm Iron and Steel Research Institute, p. 428, Vol. 24, Part 2, 1942.

[3] P. Bardenheurer and R. Bleckmann, Journal of Kaiser Wilhelm Iron and Steel Research Institute, p. 429, Vol. 24, Part 2, 1942.

[4] V. M. Goldschmidt, Industrial and Engineering Chemistry, p. 32, Vol. 30, 1938. Also numerous German patents.

[5] R. E. Birch and F. A. Harvey, Journal of American Ceramic Society, p. 175, Vol. 18, 1935.

[6] L. Litinski, Journal of German Ceramic Society, p. 565, Vol. 16, 1935.

[7] L. Pieper, Journal of German Ceramic Society, p. 41, Vol. 18, 1937.

[8] German patent: Friedrich Krupp, Essen; No. K 168, 373, Gr. Yla, Kl. 31a, 1943.

[9] G. E. Seil, Journal of American Ceramic Society, p. 1, Vol. 24, 1941.

CAST STEEL SAFE DOORS and frames delivered to Advance Foundry for backing up with gray iron and copper.

Foundry pours burglar-proof doors

DOOR SHELL PREHEATING is accomplished with an oil torch after lining with a layer of scrap copper rods and before pouring a 10¼-in. layer of gray iron.

IN order to make them impervious to drills and blowtorches, three sets of cast steel safe doors and frames were delivered to Advance Foundry Co., Dayton, for backing up with copper and cast iron. Door shells, empty, weighed 10,100 lb. Frame shells weighed 8170 lb, see A.

The first step in the backing operation was the placing of a layer of scrap copper rod in the shells of both the doors and frames. About 3500 lb of copper scrap was added to each door shell and about 875 lb to each frame shell. Next, both the shells and the scrap were preheated; the door shell with an oil torch, B, the frame shell by burning coke in the frame opening. Each unit was heated until the copper rods were glowing, C.

After heating, a 10¼-in. layer of gray iron, D, was poured over the copper rods. The cast gray iron layer in the door shell weighed 8800 lb; in the frame shell, 2200 lb.

Lastly, a 4-in. layer of cupola melted copper was poured over the layer of cast iron, E, into both the door and frame shells. Copper poured into the door weighed 5200 lb; into the frame, 2200 lb.

Final weights were: doors, 27,600 lb; frames. 13,445 lb. After proper finishing, these were sent to banks in California and Washington.

GLOWING COPPER RODS indicate that the door shell is ready to receive its layer of gray iron.

LIQUID GRAY IRON is poured into frame shell to a height of 10¼-in. Its weight is 2200 lb.

CUPOLA MELTED COPPER, poured over the gray iron layer in the door shell, finishes the job.

By L. SILVERMAN, *Chemist*
H. E. SCHWARTZ, *Chemist*
and B. CHALETT, *Metallurgist*

Eastern Smelting & Refining Co., *Los Angeles*

Rapid analysis

CUTS FURNACE HOLDING TIME

MANY smelters and foundries produce non-ferrous alloys "tailor-made," crucible style, in 1000-lb heats. In the work process, the furnace is charged with suitable materials, melted and sampled. At this point, the melt must be maintained at high temperature while a chemical analysis is made. Any saving in time is important. Since a control method is required primarily to indicate whether or not the heat is within specification limits, a rapid, not a precision method, is quite adequate.

It was suggested previously[1] that the base metal of a nonferrous alloy could be run colorimetrically. A new type procedure was then developed for colorimetric control of the base metal of an alloy and its important components.

An appropriate example is the group of manganese bronzes, such as ASTM B-30-48, 7A, 8A, 8B and 8C, which contain copper, zinc, iron, aluminum and manganese as major constituents. The 110,000-psi tensile manganese bronze alloy specifies 60 to 68 pct Cu, 2 to 4 pct Fe, 4 to 7 pct Al and 2.5 to 4 pct Mn. Thus, if a furnace is charged with raw materials of estimated content, a rapid chemical check of copper, iron and manganese, together with a visual inspection of the ingot, assures that a satisfactory product will result.

In brief, the alloy is dissolved in hydrochloric acid and water. The color intensity is then measured by the photometer and the apparent copper content estimated from the calibration curve. An aliquot is used to determine the iron as thiocyanate. Necessary correction is made on the copper curve only if iron, nickel and tin are present in sufficient amount. Manganese may be determined colorimetrically[2] or volumetrically[3] on an aliquot. Aluminum could also be determined colorimetrically with aluminon.[4, 5, 6]

For determination of copper, first weigh 0.500 g of drillings and transfer the sample directly to a dry 100-ml pyrex volumetric flask. Measure in 5 ml of HCl (sp gr 1.2) and place the flask in a bath of cold water. From a pipette, add 5 ml of 30 pct H_2O_2, at such a rate that the action will not be too rapid, while shaking the flask. About 3 ml of peroxide are needed for complete solution (slag will not be attacked).

Bubbles Show Decomposition

When solution is complete, set the flask on a steambath or warmplate (60° to 80°C) to decompose any residual peroxide and to volatilize most of the chlorine gas. A change in the type of bubbles that appear at the surface indicates the complete decomposition of the peroxide.

Remove the flask from the heat and allow it to cool on the bench. Fill the volumetric flask nearly to the mark with conc HCl (this is done in the hood). Set the flask in a bath of water at room temperature. When the liquid is at room temperature, adjust to exact volume by adding conc HCl from a dropping bottle. Stopper and mix well. This is flask "A."

By pipette, withdraw 25 ml of the green solution from flask "A" and transfer to a 50-ml flask, flask "B." Dilute the concentrated acid solution in flask "B" with water, just short of the 50-ml mark. Mix and then set the flask in a bath of water at room temperature. When cool, adjust the solution to the mark using a dropping bottle of distilled water. Flask "B" is the working flask.

Prepare the photometer with a 650-millimicron (red) filter and adjust to "0" density (100 pct transmittancy) using water. Pour a portion of the green solution from flask "B" into a cuvette and read the color density for copper using the 650-millimicron filter. From the copper calibration curve, obtain pct Cu in the manganese bronze.

By pipette, withdraw 1 ml of the solution from flask "B" and transfer it to a 50-ml flask, flask "C." By pipette, add 2 ml HCl, then half-fill the flask with water and mix. By pipette, add 5 ml of a 25 pct NaSCN solution, dilute to the mark with water and mix well. Do not change

Rapid control analysis of furnace heats with the photometer reduces the length of time the heat must be maintained at high temperature. A new procedure was developed for colorimetric control of the base metal and important constituents of manganese bronze.

TABLE II

SAMPLES FOR IRON CURVE

Flask No.	Cu, g	Zn, g	Fe, g	Fe, pct
0	0.320	0.18	0.0000	0.00
1	0.320	0.18	0.0025	0.50
2	0.320	0.18	0.0050	1.00
3	0.320	0.17	0.0100	2.00
4	0.320	0.17	0.0150	3.00
5	0.320	0.16	0.0200	4.00
6	0.320	0.16	0.0250	5.00

the order of additions. Let stand 2 min or more before reading.

Prepare the photometer with a 525-millimicron (green) filter and adjust to "0" density (100 pct transmittancy), using water. Pour a portion of the red solution from flask "C" into a cuvette and read the color density for iron, using the 525-millimicron filter. From the iron color calibration curve, obtain pct Fe in the manganese bronze.

Manganese Procedure

In the manganese procedure, a 0.1000-g sample should be used for 0 to 2.5 pct Mn, and 0.0500 g from 2.5 to 6.0 pct Mn. Weigh the sample and transfer it to a 250-ml volumetric flask. Add 20 ml of HNO_3 (1:1) and warm the flask until the sample decomposes. Remove the flask from the heat and allow to cool for several minutes on the bench. Add 10 ml of a 10 pct H_2NSO_3H solution. Mix (the brown fumes will disappear). Cool the flask to room temperature in a bath of running water.

Add 0.10 g of sodium bismuthate to the flask and mix again. Dilute the flask to the mark with cold water. Mix. Filter off about 25 ml through a dry filter paper into a dry beaker. Discard this portion. Filter a second portion and use this for the photometric determination of manganese as permanganate. A 525-millimicron filter may be used. Obtain pct Mn from the curve.

To prepare the standard manganese solution, weigh 0.288 g of $KMnO_4$ and transfer to a 400-ml beaker. Add 10 ml of water, 1 g of Na_2SO_3 and 5 ml of H_2SO_4. Boil for 5 min to expel excess SO_2. Cool the solution to room tempera-

ture and transfer to a 1-liter flask, dilute to the mark with water and mix well. 1 ml = 0.1 mg Mn. On a 0.1 gram sample, 1 ml is equivalent to 0.1 pct Mn, 5 ml are equivalent to 0.5 pct Mn, and so forth.

A set of 10 or more 100-ml volumetric flasks should be used in preparing the copper-color calibration curve. Each flask should be made up to contain 0.500 g of metal (copper plus zinc). Table I is an example.

Treat the flasks according to the procedure for copper. Plot the graph on regular coordinate paper using pct Cu as abscissa and color density as ordinate. The graph may be a straight line from 20 to 80 pct Cu, depending on the photometer.

Iron Determination

The iron color calibration curve is prepared with a set of seven or more 100-ml and 50-ml volumetric flasks. Each flask should be made up to contain 0.500 g of metal (copper plus zinc plus iron). Table II is an example. Treat the flasks according to the procedures for copper and iron, but read only the red thiocyanate solutions for the iron color calibration curve.

Plot the graph on regular coordinate paper using pct Fe as abscissa and color density as ordinate. The graph may be a straight line from 0.50 to 4.0 pct Fe. Prepare a set of seven 250-ml volumetric flasks for the manganese color calibration curves. Add 0.10 g of copper to each. Add to the seven respective flasks the following amounts of manganese solution: 0.0 ml (0.0 mg Mn); 1.0 ml (0.1 mg Mn); 5.0 ml (0.5 mg Mn); 10.0 ml (1.0 mg Mn); 15.0 ml (1.5 mg Mn); 20.0 ml (2.0 mg Mn); and 25.0 ml (2.5 mg Mn). This is for the 0 to 2.5 pct Mn series. A similar series for 2.5 to 6.0 pct Mn may be prepared by using just 0.050 g instead of 0.10 g of copper.

Treat the flasks as described in the procedure for manganese. From the data obtained plot color density as ordinate and plot mg Mn as abscissa; also, below mg Mn write in the equivalent pct Mn. Ordinary rectangular graph paper is used, since the color density values are logarithms of the pct transmittancy.

A copper sample of 0.500 g is convenient to weigh and the copper color will give a straight line graph for 20 to 80 pct Cu, which is well

TABLE I

SAMPLES FOR COPPER CURVE

Flask No.	Cu, g	Zn, g	Cu, pct
0	0.000	0.50	0.0
1	0.100	0.40	20.0
2	0.200	0.30	40.0
3	0.280	0.22	56.0
4	0.300	0.20	60.0
5	0.320	0.18	64.0
6	0.340	0.16	68.0
7	0.370	0.13	74.0
8	0.400	0.10	80.0
9	0.450	0.05	90.0

Continued

within the manganese bronze range. Larger samples would give too dark a color when filter photometers are used, but are satisfactory with a Backman spectrophotometer. Smaller samples may be used, but are less representative.

The sample is transferred directly to a 100-ml volumetric flask. This saves a re-transfer later from a beaker to the eventual 100-ml volumetric flask. The volumetric flask may be warmed in hot water or heated to 80°C on a hot plate without breakage.

The H_2O_2-HCl mix is especially useful for dissolving manganese bronze. This combination is rapid in action, the excess peroxide decomposes to water and chlorine gas is expelled by warming. If a HNO_3-HCl mix were used, some HNO_3 would remain unless the solution is evaporated: if an $HClO_4$ mix were used, fuming would be necessary to volatilize the other reagent, and there would be difficulty with high manganese alloys. An H_2SO_4 mix was not considered feasible.

Acid Content Varies Color

Preliminary experiments showed that the color density of a copper chloride solution varied with the excess amount of acid present. Data for a series of samples containing 64 pct Cu in mixes of 60 pct, 50 pct, etc., to 0 pct of water (by volume) and the balance of HCl were examined (Table III). Small changes in pct H_2O had direct influence on the color density, except in the range of 0 to 10 pct H_2O, meaning 100 to 90 pct HCl. In other words, small changes or errors in acid and water content in the range of 0 to 10 pct H_2O would not affect the results. Unfortunately, working with conc HCl solutions is not desirable because of the corrosive fumes.

A second choice is 50 pct H_2O. Nearly maximum absorption occurred at this point, and this concentration of water-acid was selected. In order to assure reproducible acid-water concentrations, a prescribed volume of liquid from the solvent (100 pct HCl) flask is pipetted into a second flask (flask B) and mixed with an equal volume of water.

As was expected, the color intensity of the solutions is increased with higher temperatures. It is therefore advisable to work at room temperature, which means a bath of water should be available at all times. Corrections for extreme hot and cold day variations may be noted by running a standard sample (Bureau of Standards No. 62b) at the same time.

The procedure described does not use "pct transmittancy" values, but employs instead the logarithms of these numbers, called "color densities." There is a twofold advantage in this system. First, the graphs may be plotted on ordinary coordinate paper; second, positive or negative corrections because of unusual concentration of elements or because of poor cuvettes may be algebraically added to the readings.

Ni, Cr, Can Cause Error

The only innovation in the manganese procedure is the use of H_2NSO_3H. The acidity is figured to be 3 pct HNO_3 by volume and the amount of bismuthate used will be more than 25 times the maximum manganese content. The blue color of copper nitrate will be about the same intensity in all the test samples of ordinary manganese bronzes.

This rapid method for the photometric determination of copper in manganese bronze should not be extended to other copper-base alloys without specific investigation. The presence of zinc (0 to 35 pct), aluminum (0 to 10 pct), manganese (0 to 5 pct), nickel (0 to 1 pct) or tin (0 to 1 pct) does not affect the copper or iron determination. These elements may be present within the stated ranges and do not, individually, affect the copper or iron readings.

On the other hand, a nickel content of 1.5 pct or more will give low readings for copper, as will tin content greater than 2 pct. If such alloys are frequently encountered, it would be advisable to prepare synthetic samples and apply proper corrections. For these reasons the field of application of this method should be limited to experimental coverage. Unexpected elements such as cadmium, antimony, arsenic, phosphorus, sulfur and titanium should cause no difficulty when present in amounts of less than 0.10 pct. Chromium might cause error.

The authors wish to thank Robert Bernstein for his assistance in developing this procedure.

TABLE III

EFFECT OF ACID—WATER CONTENT*

Water, Pct by Volume	Color Density Reading
65	60
55	62
45	63
35	62
25	61
15	60
10	60
5	60

* 64 pct Cu, 36 pct Zn.

References

[1] L. Silverman, THE IRON AGE, 163, No. 17, p. 88 (1948).

[2] W. W. Scott, "Standard Methods of Chemical Analysis," D. Van Nostrand Co., Inc., Fifth Edition, p. 562.

[3] L. Silverman, Ind. Eng. Chem., Anal. Ed., 14, p. 554 (1942).

[4] C. H. Craft and G. R. Makepeace, Ind. Eng. Chem., Anal. Ed., 17, p. 206 (1945).

[5] C. Goldberg, THE IRON AGE, 166, No. 3, p. 87 (1950).

[6] L. Silverman, Chemist-Analyst, 37, No. 3, p. 62 (1948).

New Giant Presses Will Speed Plane Production

U. S. Air Force orders huge forging and extrusion presses as part of $200 million program . . . Time, labor, and material savings possible with new methods—*By Bill Olson.*

New York — Long-range planning by the U. S. Air Force and hydraulic engineers in developing the world's biggest forging and extrusion presses has given the aircraft industry a 2-year head start in the race to build aircraft for defense.

The Air Force recently announced it had contracted with Hydropress, Inc., for a forging press of more than 50,000 tons capacity and an extrusion press of more than 15,000 tons capacity.

It is believed the presses ordered are those described last May in a Munitions Board booklet, "The Production of Large Forgings for Airplanes on Hydraulic Die Forging Presses."

For further details on the hydraulic press program see The Iron Age, Nov. 2, 1950, p. 72.

The presses are two of 25 to be ordered under a $200 million hydraulic press program, and will be ready for use in 1952. They will probably be installed at the Air Force pilot plant in Adrian, Mich., where much of the experimental work has been done. New production methods will be made available to the Army, Navy, and industry.

Biggest die forging press to date has been the 33,000-ton job taken by Russia from Germany as a part of war reparations. The Russians are believed building a 55,000-ton press from parts taken from the Krupp Works at Essen.

Wing sections, now made from many parts riveted together, will be produced at one stroke of the press. Much riveting will be eliminated, and tremendous savings in manpower, machine time, and materials will be effected.

Boost Plane Payload

Aircraft payload and effective range will be increased. Higher yield strengths possible from forged parts will permit marked reductions in weight. Even greater strength will be possible by using blanks from the extrusion press.

The enormous die working area, about 16 ft by 46 ft, will permit larger, stronger, lighter parts which can be assembled with a minimum of joints.

Germany's leadership in development of hydraulic presses was forced on her. Cut off from steel sources after World War I, the Germans developed their abundant supplies of aluminum and magnesium.

The need for tremendous pressures required to work the light metals, and the lack of abundant cheap power, turned the Germans to heavy hydraulic presses.

As the need for economy of materials and more efficient fabricating methods became apparent in the U. S., a few far-sighted Air

Turn Page

Steel Capacity Growth

New York—Steel industry expansion in 1950 added 4,800,000 tons of new capacity and total steel output potential, effective Jan. 1, 1951, was at the record high of 104,229,650 ingot tons, said the American Iron and Steel Institute. Blast furnace capacity, also on the expansion road, rose to a peak 72,471,780, as compared to 71,497,540 tons Jan. 1, 1950.

George S. Rose, Institute secretary, said steelmakers 3 or 4 months ago reported programs for expanding capacity by more than 9 million tons and that the figure would be raised by at least 50 pct to bring annual capacity to at least 115 million tons by the close of '52.

From Refrigerators to Jet Parts

Chicago—The new $20 million refrigerator plant recently completed by Hotpoint, Inc., will produce major components and assemblies for the J-48 jet engine. The war contract, said to be one of the largest received by a manufacturer of consumer goods in the area, was made with the Pratt & Whitney Div. of United Aircraft, E. Hartford, Conn.

Paris Tool Exhibit Planned

Paris—The first European Machine Tool Exhibition, sponsored by the European Committee of Cooperation of Machine Tool Industries, will meet in Paris, Sept. 1 to Sept. 10. Machine tool manufacturers of Europe, Canada and the United States are expected to take part.

Force leaders and hydraulic engineers centered their attention on the vast savings in materials and time possible with big presses.

Impressed with German techniques, the Air Force embarked on a long-range program for development of hydraulic forging and extrusion presses. Material problems and existing transportation facilities apparently kept the size of the forging press to 75,000 tons.

Only one producer had facilities to make the huge castings and forgings necessary for such a press. A potential bottleneck was eliminated by using laminated steel plate in place of heavy castings.

Tie Rods 250 Tons

By making all tie rods and other major parts of forged and rolled slabs, a tie rod that weighed 250 tons was designed. The heaviest member of that tie rod weighs 25 tons, which could be obtained from at least eight steel plants.

The press platen will be pulled down and pushed up. Drive of the press is by air hydraulic accumulators serviced by four pumps of 1000 hp each; if operated directly off the pumps, 28,000 hp would be required.

A survey of strategic bombing effects showed the heavy castings on German presses stood up remarkably well, but controls and hydraulic systems were usually wrecked.

Vital Parts Underground

The press described has about 60 pct of its 102 ft overall height below the floor. Many controls and most of the hydraulic system would be protected from all but heaviest bombing.

The 11,000 ton dead weight would have to float on a "concrete barge," located in a special building. Estimated cost of the press, installed with auxiliary equipment, would range from $12 to $15 million.

Die costs frequently estimated to be higher for a heavy press than for conventional tooling, may actually be lower.

An aircraft stabilizer, formerly built from 547 different parts riveted together, could be built from 8 parts made on three dies. Total tooling cost would be about a third the cost of all jigs, fixtures, and gadgets used under the old method.

HUGE PRESS: Model view of new 75,000 ton hydraulic press shows relative size of operator compared to press. Large part of press will be below the floor safe from air attack. Laminated plate structure replaces huge castings usually used.

Canadians Feel Steel Supply Pinch; Many Shops Cut Operations

Ottawa—Canada's steel supply, becoming more critical daily, has caused many industries to curtail operations and in some cases to close temporarily. No large defense contracts using steel have been let. Industry is worried what will happen when Canada swings into full defense production schedules.

Kenneth Harris, steel administrator, says steel controls may widen as Canada converts to defense work. Maximum production and maximum supplies of steel are of prime concern, he said.

Production Doubled Since '39

Canada entered the last war with steel capacity well ahead of ordinary requirements. Today, Canada's steel capacity is being used to the full, and many consumers are unable to obtain supplies for current needs, even though Canadian steel production has almost doubled since 1939.

Leading steel producers have announced expansion plans or are proceeding with work of this nature. Canada's total rated capacity for steel production may be boosted by about 25 pct in 1951.

John Munson, U.S. Steel Raw Materials Officer, Retires

Pittsburgh—John G. Munson, since 1939 vice-president of raw materials for the now-merged U. S. Steel Corp. of Delaware, has retired and will serve in an advisory capacity for a time. As raw materials officer, he was instrumental in the discovery of Cerro Bolivar iron ore deposits in Venezuela and development of beneficiation for Minnesota taconite ores.

A 1905 Yale graduate, Mr. Munson was born in Bellefonte, Pa. His first job after graduation was as a rodman on tunnel construction but in a short time, from 1906 to 1908, he was superintendent of projects in New Haven, Conn., and Baltimore, Md. In 1909 he joined the J. G. White Engineering Corp. as construction superintendent and later became operating manager of the Michigan Limestone and Chemical Co.

After the firm became a U. S. Steel subsidiary, he was made vice-president of Michigan Limestone and Bradley Transportation Co. in 1925. Mr. Munson was appointed president and director of both firms in 1928 and he became vice-president of U. S. Steel Corp. of Delaware in 1939.

Broader Steel Allocation, DO Extension Seen

Expect more allocations, DO extension late this month or early next . . . Petroleum industry first . . . To lift DO out of solely military . . . Rumor plans made—By Gene Beaudet.

Chicago—A government order calling for additional steel allocation programs and wider application of defense orders is expected at the end of this month or early February. Rumors resulting from a recent meeting of NPA's steel products advisory committee indicate plans for these programs and wider application of DO's have already been made. It is now up to the NPA steel task force committee to work out details of these projects when it meets later in January.

Out of Military Category

Present proposals are expected to lift DO's out of the strictly military category for the first time. They would be applied to construction of new plants, steel mill expansion and construction of facilities to safeguard public health, safety and other projects approved by the NPA.

Just how widely the DO's will be extended is not generally known, but if the plan is approved it will open the door to many more applications. It is said that these extended DO's may be applied against April steel production if the government can move quickly enough.

It is reported that an allocation program for the petroleum industry will soon be forthcoming. This is said to cover only oil country goods, with the tonnage set aside to be in the neighborhood of 1.9 million tons.

Steel requirements of the petroleum industry have been estimated at 12 million tons, so it is felt by steel and petroleum sources to be just a starter and that future allocations covering the rest of the industry will follow. Allocations for oil country goods were chosen first because they are hardest hit by the steel shortage.

Bite Into April Output

Another program of allocations expected to affect April steel production is one for the construction of 30 to 40 high speed merchant vessels which are needed quickly. Plate needed for construction of these ships is said to call for a wider and heavier plate around 1 in. thick. This will cause difficulty with those producers now rolling plate on strip mills.

Other reports state that some present programs will be cut down. Freight car allocations now running about 308,000 tons per month are expected to be reduced to 288,000 tons during the second quarter, according to informed sources. The diesel locomotive program planned to start in April will not get less than 70,000 tons per month during the second quarter as originally estimated.

Ford Orders 120 Gondola Cars

Greenville, Pa.—An order from the Ford Motor Co. for 120 special 70-ton all-steel mill type gondola cars, 40 ft in length, for handling hot billets was announced by the Greenville Steel Car Co.

Armor Plate Needed

Washington — The National Production Authority this week prepared to begin contacting steel firms which might be able to switch from some less essential types of production to output of armor plate. The action is held necessary, in addition to expanding present armor plate facilities, in view of the expected greatly stepped up need for defense.

Expansion of current capacity must begin immediately and NPA is taking steps which will assist in obtaining materials necessary for whatever conversion or construction is needed.

At the same time, a subcommittee of armor plate fabricators and finishers will begin setting up a program for obtaining and training manpower needed.

Contracts Top World War II Rate

Boston — New England's percentage of total national defense contract awards is topping the World War II rate for the first time since the Korean war opened and contract volume has doubled in the past month, reports the New England Council. A Council survey shows that during December contracts placed here were 10 pct over the national total.

NPA Order Cuts Firm's Output

Birmingham—Output of Stockham Valves and Fittings Co. will be slashed in half in the first quarter of 1951 because of government order NPA-M-12 which cuts brass use for non-defense purposes. Since the firm expects to be granted defense orders, no plans were made for cutting the work staff.

Gets Large Trailer Contract

Elba, Ala.—A $3 million U. S. contract for 747 heavy-duty flatbed trailers suitable for hauling heavy engineering equipment has gone to the Dorsey Trailer Co.

INDUSTRIAL SHORTS

INCREASING OUTPUT — The land, buildings and equipment of National Transit Pump & Machine Co., Oil City, Pa., has been acquired by the WORTHINGTON PUMP & MACHINERY CORP., Harrison, N. J. The plant will be utilized by Worthington to further its production of equipment related to the National Defense Program.

READY TO SERVE — The ALDEN EQUIPMENT CO., Los Angeles, has been formed and will represent the lines formerly handled by the Snyder Engineering Corp., including: Jeffrey Mfg. Co., Columbus, Ohio; Cleveland Worm & Gear Co., Cleveland; Farvel Corp., Cleveland; and Louden Machinery Co., Fairfield, Iowa. Snyder Engineering will continue with engineering, fabrication and construction activities.

NEW OPERATIONS — Plant No. 1 of the Pharis Tire & Rubber Co., Newark, Ohio, has been purchased by the WESTINGHOUSE ELECTRIC CORP. The plant will be converted and equipped to manufacture transmission units for Laundromat automatic washers.

CONSOLIDATES—A plant expansion and consolidation program of the ALFRED B. KING CO. with its subsidiaries, Churchward Welding Accessories and KIF Industrial Fabricators, was recently completed with the moving of these companies to their new 10,000 sq ft plant in North Haven, Conn.

BONDING PROCESS—A new method of bonding rubber to metal, called the Redux process, is described in the current issue of Rubber Developments issued by the NATURAL RUBBER BUREAU, Washington. The basic idea behind the procedure is to treat the rubber surface with concentrated sulfuric acid before bonding and then thoroughly washing in running water and drying.

BUILDING WAREHOUSE — Five acres of land in Baltimore has been purchased from the Baltimore & Ohio R. R. by the HILL-CHASE STEEL CO. OF MARYLAND for the erection of a new steel warehouse.

TAKES OVER — The JAMES CO., Seymour, Conn., manufacturers of chisels, bits and augers, has been purchased by John T. Doyle of Natick, Mass. The transfer includes the real estate, water rights on Little River and all the assets of the firm.

ACQUISITIONS — HAYES MFG. CORP., Grand Rapids, has acquired, for an undisclosed cash consideration, the substantial personal holdings of Allan P. Kirby, New York, in the Skyline Corp., Wichita, Kan., manufacturers of agricultural implements. Hayes has also purchased from Skyline, for cash, its 60 pct interest in Aircraft Armament, Inc., Baltimore, engineering firm specializing in aircraft armament and related equipment.

REORGANIZES—The Machinery Mfg. Co., Los Angeles, former builders of the Vernon line of jig borers, millers, shapers, and tool and cutter grinders, have reorganized under a new firm name, DIVERSIFIED METAL PRODUCTS CO. A development program is in process for precision machine tools.

MERGER — The Parker Plow Co., Richmond, Mich., has been merged with the DALZEN TOOL MFG. CO., Detroit. The former St. Clair Machine Products plant in St. Clair, Mich., will be reactivated into the Dalzen Mfg. Co. to make aircraft parts and heating equipment.

ADDS TWO BRANCHES — New branch offices at Denver and Houston have been opened by the HOWE SCALE CO., Rutland, Vt. Daniel O. Ferris and Henry K. Leonard are managers of the Denver and Houston offices respectively.

Truman's State of Economy Speech Puts the Stress on Output

Washington—While the President's annual economic message indicated an increasingly austere economy in 1951, Mr. Truman emphasized the need for greater production.

Expanded production will not only provide for national defense said Mr. Truman, but will also assure the maintenance of a strong economic base despite cutbacks in the output of civilian goods.

Emphasis on Output

A maximum production effort in 1951 should bring an "annual rate of output of about $310 billion at 1950 prices" by the end of 1951, said the President. National security costs were estimated at a rate of $45 to $55 billion by the end of 1951, although future committments will raise these costs to more than $140 billion for the fiscal years 1951 and 1953. These costs are now taking about 7 pct of national output and will increase to about 18 pct by next year, as compared with about 45 pct during the peak of World War II.

For the steel industry he called for an increase in capacity from the present 103 million tons to about 120 million tons within the next few years. The President warned that expansion of essential civilian production would mean a "much greater diversion from ordinary civilian uses." He also stressed the need for more Great Lakes ore boats and an expansion in iron ore supplies, including those in Venezuela and the Labrador-Quebec area, as well as a step-up in beneficiation of low-grade domestic ores.

Congress was also urged to authorize an immediate start on the St. Lawrence as an important artery for the transportation of iron ore and to increase the supply of power in the northeastern states. The nation's power facilities must be expanded by more than 20 million kw in the next 3 years, stated Mr. Truman.

New Zirconia Refractory Withstands 4600° F

Material has low rate of heat conductivity, high resistance to thermal shock . . . Finds wide use in chemical, petroleum and metalworking fields—*By Jack Kolb.*

Worcester, Mass.—A new refractory, fused stabilized zirconia, can withstand temperatures up to 4600°F as compared to super-duty fireclay, used up to 3100F°, and alumina brick, up to 3400°F. This zirconium dioxide product will be sold in bulk or molded shapes on a full commercial basis by Norton Co., here.

Large-Scale Uses

At present, few completely developed applications of the new refractory have been established, although a large number of experimental and pilot-plant test programs are under way in chemical, petroleum, metalworking and other industries.

Among present large-scale uses are setter plates for firing titanates in the electronic equipment field, furnace lining bricks for gas synthesis at high temperatures, and heating elements and insulation for large furnaces.

Demonstrations of this latter use at the Worcester, Mass., plant of the Norton Co. revealed some interesting possibilities. Laboratory-scale induction and resistance furnaces fitted with zirconia inner walls, bottoms and tops that also serve as the unit's heating elements, were operated at about 3600°F and 4000°F, respectively.

Low Rate of Heat

The induction furnace had an air atmosphere, while the resistance furnace was charged with hydrogen. Both must be preheated, as zirconia becomes a good conductor of electricity only at elevated temperatures.

Zirconia was used in brick, disc, tubular and granular form in these furnaces. Despite its high density, the new refractory material has a very low rate of heat conductivity and excellent resistance to thermal shock. It has exhibited low reactivity and is not subject to volatilization in either reducing or oxidizing atmospheres.

A large part of the reason for Norton's success in developing the new zirconium oxide refractory is the electric fusion process used to refine the ore. This is zircon sand, found in Australia and Florida, containing 33 pct silica. One furnace firing suffices to lower the silica content to ½ pct or lower. The principal stabilizing agent in the new refractory is lime.

Archibald H. Ballard, associate director of research and development at Norton, has stated that the basic problem still to be solved is improving manufacturing techniques for molding shapes and lowering the cost of manufacture.

A zirconia brick, 9½ x 4½ x 2½ in., weighs 16 pounds, almost twice as heavy as super-duty fireclay shapes of the same size. The zirconia brick costs 10 to 12 times more. Its insulating value, greater than all other commercial refractories, should offset this differential somewhat by making possible thinner wall construction. Expected improvements in service life should also improve the new refractory material's cost relationship.

New England Mill Start Seen in Six Months

Fast tax writeoff OK makes New England mill fairly certain . . . Will turn out about million tons of flat-rolled products . . . RFC loan will be made if it is needed—*By Bill Packard.*

New York—Government approval of the New England Steel Mill Development Corp.'s application for a certificate of necessity practically assures that a large integrated steel mill will be built near New London, Conn.

The mill will be able to turn out about a million tons of flat-rolled products annually. Construction, which will cost about $250 million, is expected to start in about 6 months.

Although details of financing, engineering and operation are not yet final, they should be completed within the next 30 days.

RFC Loan—If Needed

Backers of the project stressed that participation by an existing steel company was still open, but that the project would be pushed ahead regardless of the outcome of negotiations.

Approval of the certificate of necessity classifies the plant as necessary for defense and permits tax benefits in the form of 5-year amortization. It also clears the way for a loan from RFC.

New England insurance companies are ready to loan $120 million of the $250 million total cost. Another $40 million in equity capital is expected to be raised through New York bankers. This leaves $90 million to be raised by the participating steel company, or through a loan by a defense agency if a new corporation is formed to run the plant.

Most of the plant site is now owned by Connecticut, and the remaining land needed will be obtained through the state's power of eminent domain.

This is the third large new integrated steel mill to be approved for the East Coast area within recent weeks. The other two mills are to be built on the Delaware River below Philadelphia by U. S. Steel Co. and National Steel.

Anti-Inflation Camp—Allies in Discord

All factions plan strategy likely to hurt them least . . . ESA's Valentine reluctant to enter quickly into general price-wage controls . . . Auto rises probable—*By Ted Metaxas.*

New York—Washington, labor, and management are self-declared champions in the crusade against inflation—but they are allies in discord, divided even amongst themselves. All factions are advocating strategy that will injure them the least. It has developed into the campaign of the selfish motive.

When ESA clamped mandatory controls on auto prices, it was thought that it was unlimbering heavy guns. But Valentine feels that the time is not yet opportune for sweeping price and wage controls and last week auto men and John Hancock, assigned by DiSalle, discussed a formula for raising auto prices.

Lewis Stresses Output

Thus the call for a Dec. 1 roll-back of prices becomes a terribly confused affair with some manufacturers responding, others not. It is paring away the profits of some and permitting others the same gravy.

With a 3¢ to 5¢ cost-of-living wage adjustment due for Detroit auto workers by Mar. 1, ESA determination to control prices would justifiably have obviated all escalator clauses in union contracts. But now that probable quarterly auto price hikes would be permitted, escalator clauses seem to have a new lease on life.

UMW's John L. Lewis, one of the crusaders against inflation, at Washington Wage Stabilization Board meetings last week eloquently stated that the increased production of "free men" would offset the inflationary trend and thus direct controls of any kind would be unneeded.

Other unions are ostensibly bitter enemies of inflation—as long as it doesn't come out of their pocket. They point to "huge" cor-

poration profits and encourage the government to cut inflation at the expense of private enterprise. They urge retention of escalator clauses on the grounds that they will be meaningless anyway in a full price freeze that will not permit the cost-of-living index to advance.

The President's Council of Economic Advisers has declared against escalator clauses in a war-tempo economy. ESA is shying away from price controls on meat, food and other staples. Without these wage controls are difficult.

Former NAM president Ira Mosher told WSB last week that he was opposed to direct price-wage controls until all indirect steps prove fruitless. He said his group was divided on escalator clauses but that the clauses should be permitted unless they conflict with national wage policy. Also in Washington last week, officials of the dress industry uttered a unanimous, whole-hearted cry for a price chill.

Meanwhile ESA is trying to

"We got a defense order so we had to expand."

take the edge off inflation by controlling prices of raw materials. It is now working on scrap steel and iron with industry cooperation and some sort of mandatory controls may evolve, Under ESA discussion last week were price controls for the ferroalloy industry with tool steel men yelling for "immediate controls." Government officials said soothingly that the tool steel high price situation was "complicated chiefly by recent sharp rises in the price of imported tungsten."

Urges Holding Skilled Labor

Boston—Firms outside the New England industrial area are trying to lure away skilled workers and technicians with newspaper advertising and recruiting campaigns conducted by agents, said Walker Mason, newly-appointed chairman of the Industrial Committee of the New England Council.

He warned local industry to hold onto skilled help because defense contracts and subcontracting work would develop an urgent need for skilled labor.

Ford Postpones Construction

Detroit—Henry Ford II's decision to delay indefinitely construction of a Dearborn administrative wing is based on his belief that critical materials should not be used by the Ford Motor Co. for office buildings "when the nation needs weapons and materials to produce them." Ford had planned an 11-story structure for staff offices and a 6-story headquarters building for Lincoln-Mercury Div.

To Raise Electroshield Output

Carnegie, Pa.—Because of heavier demand for Electroshield metal sheets, a cladmetal of rolled copper bonded to a base sheet of magnetic low-carbon steel, American Cladmetals Co. is increasing production facilities. The company reports that Electroshield cuts copper use and is stronger than copper sheets.

More Scrap for More Steel for Defense

Scrap Institute holds 23rd annual convention in New York . . . Shop talk focus on defense and price controls . . . Many think best way to bring out scrap is unhindered market.

New York—Free enterprise in its healthiest form is still on the prowl. Anyone doubting this could have seen it for himself had he visited the 23rd annual convention of the Institute of Scrap Iron & Steel at the Commodore Hotel here the first 3 days of this week.

Corridor talk centered on price controls, inventory controls and other government regulations, as well as the defense effort and its effect on the already terrific demand for metal.

The usual buttonhole conferences on deals, grading, etc., came in for plenty of attention between sessions. But these were tempered a bit this year by the sure knowledge that the long hand of controls was reaching in the direction of their industry.

Privately, many scrap people are convinced that the best way to meet the unprecedented demand of hungry steel furnaces is by permitting free action of supply and demand through a free market. They believe that the best way to bring out the needed scrap metal is to pay the price. But they have also read the writing on the walls in Washington and it spells C O N- T R O L S.

Institute members came to the convention flushed from a record-breaking year in 1950. A total of 61 million gross tons of iron and steel scrap was consumed by steel mills and foundries in the U. S. last year, reported Ed Barringer, executive secretary. This was 20 pct greater than in 1949 and 5 pct above the previous peak year of 1948.

Consumption of close to 30 million tons of purchased scrap last year also topped the previous record of 29 million tons. Current rate of consumption is 32.5 million tons annually, and by the end of 1952 the annual requirement will

be at least 35 million tons of purchased scrap, Mr. Barringer declared.

The opening session Sunday morning was a workshop for officers of local and regional chapters. This was followed by a meeting of the national board of directors in the afternoon.

Stanley M. Kaplan, president, and Herman D. Moskowitz of the Institute's Defense Advisory Committee, spoke on the relation of

scrap iron and steel to the mobilization for national defense at the Monday morning session.

Major Alexander P. de Seversky, outstanding authority on aviation, was the principal speaker at the annual banquet Monday evening. He gave his views on how and where to apply our nation's strength so that we can maintain peace.

An unusual feature of the convention was an exhibit of machinery and equipment used in the scrap industry. This was of great interest to the many members who see increased mechanization as one of the best ways to help cut costs and meet the terrific demand for scrap.

DO's for Equipment Accessories

Washington — Under Amendment 3 to Reg. 2, DO ratings may be extended to obtain certain accessories for production equipment. However, ratings may be extended only for accessories needed for actual production of defense equipment. This does not include machine tools or other complete units of production equipment.

Specifically, ratings may be used for procurement of jigs, dies, tools and fixtures where inability to obtain these items would delay filling of defense orders. In the meantime, NPA is working out an assistance program for MOS (maintenance, repair and operations) needs.

Lewis Foundry to Expand

Pittsburgh—The Lewis Foundry & Machine Div. of Blaw-Knox Co. is moving ahead with a $1 million expansion and improvement program to help meet growing demand for rolling mill machinery.

The program will include plant changes and addition of new equipment to handle heavier types of rolling mill machinery, as well as increase overall capacity. Orders for machine tools have already been placed.

British Shipbuilding Stimulated

London — Britain's shipyards opened 1951 with nearly $850 million worth of orders, resulting from bookings during 1950 that were three times those of 1949.

Defense Contracts to Metalworking Industry
Selected Contracts, Week of Jan. 15, 1951

Item	Quan.	Value	Company
Drills	521	$ 214,652.00	Chicago Pneu. Tool, Chicago
Power unit	25	174,900.00	Pioneer Eng. Wk., Minneapolis
Radiosonde	75,000	3,041,250.00	Johnson Service Co., Milwaukee
Radio equipment	Various	11,485,239.00	Federal Tel. & Radio Corp., Clifton
Radio set	.....	1,732,291.00	The Lewyt Corp., Brooklyn
Dishwashing machine	365	717,033.25	Peters-Dalton Inc., Detroit
Teletype, model 14	144	100,000.00	Teletype Corp., Chicago
Radio set	591	600,000.00	Hoffman Radio Corp., Los Angeles
Vapor compressors	200	700,000.00	Cleveland Diesel Engine div. of GMC, Cleveland
Receiving set	381	405,600.00	Air Associates, Inc., Teterboro
Aircraft engine	178	398,250.00	Central Bank of Oakland, Oakland
Shock absorber	2,000	104,200.00	Delco Products Div.
Starter	5,245	209,312.70	Diamond T Motor Car Co., Chicago

U. N. Coal Committee Moves To Offset Coke, Coal Shortage

London—To offset serious coke and coal shortages in importing European countries, 18 nations in the coal committee of the United Nations Economic Commission for Europe have agreed on a pattern of trade.

The committee drew up a blueprint of supplies for importing countries covering 10.5 million tons of coal and 3 million tons of metallurgical and domestic coke for the coming 3 months of this year.

Total coal and coke import needs were estimated at nearly 19.5 million tons for the first quarter, while export possibilities revealed a deficit of almost 5 million tons of coal and about 1 million tons of coke.

The committee urged increased production and increased exports and economy of use. Britain's coal situation is grave. Coal production has not measured up to needs and inclement weather now is biting deep into below-average stocks.

Britain Starts Drive for Scrap

London—Some capacity in the iron and steel industry of Britain remains unused because raw materials supplies are tight. Greater scrap collections can solve part of this problem and thus the Iron and Steel Federation, the Joint Iron Council, and the National Federation of Scrap Iron, Steel, and Metal Merchants are pushing a drive for larger amounts of scrap. Letters have been sent to 15,000 iron and steel users in this country, pointing out that each extra ton of scrap means an extra ton of steel.

French Plate Mills to Expand Plate Output under Marshall Plan

Washington—Steel plate production, an essential part of France's rearmament, will be increased under two Marshall Plan projects.

The projects call for modernization and expansion of a plate and slab mill at Dillegen in the Saar, and a plate mill at Mont-Saint-Martin. Total cost is estimated at $14,640,000, one-third to be financed by the Marshall Plan.

Present French plate capacity is about 800,000 tons. This should rise to between 1,000,000 and 1,100,000 tons per year, it is reliably reported.

Completion of the two projects should take 2 years. Both plants were rehabilitated after World War II, but much essential equipment is obsolete.

STEEL PRODUCTION (Ingots and Steel for Castings)

As Reported to the American Iron & Steel Institute

Period	OPEN HEARTH Net Tons	Percent of Capacity	BESSEMER Net Tons	Percent of Capacity	ELECTRIC Net Tons	Percent of Capacity	TOTAL Net Tons	Percent of Capacity	Calculated Weekly Production (Net Tons)	Number of Weeks in Month
January, 1950	7,131,519	96.5	379,252	80.6	419,601	71.9	7,930,372	93.9	1,790,152	4.43
February	6,142,178	92.0	255,565	60.2	395,502	75.0	6,793,245	89.1	1,698,311	4.00
March	6,747,680	91.3	265,726	56.5	473,630	81.1	7,487,036	88.7	1,690,076	4.43
1st Quarter	20,021,377	93.3	900,543	65.9	1,288,733	76.0	22,210,653	90.6	1,727,111	12.86
April	7,314,733	102.2	407,909	89.5	490,030	86.7	8,212,672	100.4	1,914,376	4.29
May	7,597,837	102.8	437,006	92.9	517,044	88.6	8,551,887	101.3	1,930,449	4.43
June	7,218,570	100.9	406,944	89.3	506,001	89.5	8,131,515	99.4	1,895,458	4.29
2nd Quarter	22,131,140	102.0	1,251,859	90.6	1,513,075	88.2	24,896,074	100.4	1,913,611	13.01
1st 6 Months	42,152,517	97.7	2,152,402	78.3	2,801,808	82.2	47,106,727	95.5	1,820,902	25.87
July	7,220,214	96.9	380,317	79.8	470,763	78.4	8,071,294	94.7	1,826,085	4.42
August	7,315,215	98.0	405,118	84.8	509,984	84.7	8,230,317	96.3	1,857,859	4.43
September	7,258,961	100.7	409,216	88.7	525,017	90.3	8,193,194	99.3	1,914,298	4.28
3rd Quarter	21,794,390	98.5	1,194,651	84.4	1,505,764	84.4	24,494,805	96.7	1,865,560	13.13
9 months	63,946,907	98.0	3,347,053	80.4	4,307,572	82.9	71,601,532	95.9	1,835,937	39.00
October	7,731,280	103.6	436,835	91.5	571,980	95.0	8,740,095	102.3	1,972,933	4.43
*November	7,108,810	98.3	370,659	80.1	532,382	91.3	8,011,851	96.8	1,867,564	4.29
†December	7,438,703	99.9	380,011	79.8	541,084	90.1	8,359,798	98.1	1,891,357	4.42
†4th Quarter	22,278,793	100.6	1,187,505	83.8	1,645,446	92.2	25,111,744	99.1	1,911,092	13.14
†2nd 6 months	44,073,183	99.6	2,382,156	84.1	3,151,210	88.3	49,606,549	97.9	1,888,335	26.27
†Total	86,225,700	98.6	4,534,558	81.3	5,953,018	85.3	96,713,276	96.7	1,854,877	52.14

Note—The percentages of capacity operated in the first 6 months are calculated on weekly capacities of 1,668,287 net tons open hearth, 106,195 net tons Bessemer and 131,786 net tons electric ingots and steel for castings, total, 1,906,268 net tons; based on annual capacities as of January 1, 1950, as follows: Open hearth 86,984,490 net tons, Bessemer 5,537,000 net tons, Electric 6,871,310 net tons, total 99,392,800 net tons. Beginning July 1, 1950, the percentages of capacity operated are calculated on weekly capacities of 1,685,059 net tons open hearth, 107,806 net tons Bessemer and 135,856 net tons electric ingots and steel for castings, total, 1,928,721 net tons; based on annual capacities as of July 1, 1950, as follows: Open hearth 87,858,990 net tons, Bessemer 5,621,000 net tons, Electric 7,083,510 net tons, total 100,563,500 net tons.
* Revised.
† Preliminary figures, subject to revision.

Period	OPEN HEARTH Net Tons	Percent of Capacity	BESSEMER Net Tons	Percent of Capacity	ELECTRIC Net Tons	Percent of Capacity	TOTAL Net Tons	Percent of Capacity	Calculated Weekly Production (Net Tons)	Number of Weeks in Month
January, 1949	7,289,865	101.2	408,552	92.6	498,973	96.1	8,197,390	100.4	1,850,427	4.43
February	6,635,765	102.0	379,698	95.3	478,479	102.0	7,493,942	101.6	1,873,485	4.00
March	7,476,139	103.7	430,176	97.5	495,481	95.4	8,401,796	102.9	1,896,568	4.43
1st Quarter	21,401,769	102.3	1,218,426	95.2	1,472,933	97.7	24,093,128	101.6	1,873,494	12.86
April	7,017,712	100.6	404,095	94.6	374,358	74.4	7,796,165	98.6	1,817,288	4.29
May	6,891,293	95.6	400,741	90.9	306,956	59.1	7,598,990	93.0	1,715,348	4.43
June	5,956,402	85.4	349,196	81.8	199,058	39.6	6,504,656	82.2	1,516,237	4.29
2nd Quarter	19,865,407	93.9	1,154,032	89.1	880,372	57.7	21,899,811	91.3	1,683,306	13.01
1st 6 months	41,267,176	98.1	2,372,458	92.1	2,353,305	77.6	45,992,939	96.4	1,777,848	25.87
July	5,309,060	73.8	300,236	68.2	175,535	33.9	5,784,831	71.0	1,308,785	4.42
August	6,103,326	84.7	355,335	80.6	264,110	50.9	6,722,771	82.3	1,517,556	4.43
September	5,994,100	86.1	350,282	82.2	253,553	50.5	6,597,935	83.6	1,541,574	4.28
3rd Quarter	17,406,486	81.5	1,005,853	76.9	693,198	45.0	19,105,537	78.9	1,455,106	13.13
9 months	58,673,662	92.5	3,378,311	87.0	3,046,503	66.6	65,098,476	90.5	1,669,192	39.00
October	814,618	11.3			113,729	21.9	928,347	11.4	209,559	4.43
November	3,806,870	54.6	172,270	40.3	243,989	48.5	4,223,129	53.4	984,412	4.29
December	6,953,653	96.7	396,075	90.0	378,496	73.0	7,728,224	94.8	1,748,467	4.42
4th Quarter	11,575,141	54.2	568,345	43.4	736,214	47.8	12,879,700	53.2	980,190	13.14
2nd 6 months	28,981,627	67.8	1,574,198	60.2	1,429,412	46.4	31,985,237	66.0	1,217,558	26.27
Total	70,248,803	82.8	3,946,656	76.0	3,782,717	61.9	77,978,176	81.1	1,495,554	52.14

Note—The percentages of capacity operated are calculated on weekly capacities of 1,626,717 net tons open hearth, 99,559 net tons Bessemer and 117,240 net tons electric ingots and steel for castings, total 1,843,516 net tons; based on annual capacities as of January 1, 1949 as follows: Open hearth 84,817,040 net tons, Bessemer 5,191,000 net tons, Electric 6,112,890 net tons, total 96,120,930 net tons.

You Can't Buy

A BETTER BEARING

The know-how
of bearing making
can't be found
in books.
It's been accumulated
at New Departure
for generations
like folk lore.

Nothing Rolls Like a Ball...

NEW DEPARTURE
BALL BEARINGS

NEW DEPARTURE · DIVISION OF GENERAL MOTORS · BRISTOL, CONNECTICUT

122

• News of Industry •

ESA Hopes to Have Regional Field Offices Open This Month

Washington — The operational framework of the price control organization is slowly taking shape. The Economic Stabilization Agency has picked locations for its regional field offices. Administrative officials are to be dispatched to these cities at once and ESA hopes to have most of them open by the end of January.

Location of Headquarters

Regional headquarters will be established at Boston (for Me., N. H., Vt., Mass., Conn., and R. I.), New York City (N. Y. and N. J.) Philadelphia (Pa. and Del.), Richmond (Va., W. Va., Md., D. C., and N. C.), Atlanta (Ga., Tenn., S. C., Ala., Miss., and Fla.), Cleveland (Ohio, Mich., Ky.), Chicago (Ill., Wis., Ind.), Minneapolis (Minn., N. Dak., S. Dak., and Mont.), Kansas City (Mo., Ia., Neb., Kans.), Dallas (Tex., Okla., Ark., La.), Denver (Colo., Wyo., Utah, N. Mex.), San Francisco (Calif., Nev., Ariz.), and Seattle (Wash., Ore., Idaho).

In addition to these 13 regional offices, whose work will be largely administrative, the ESA plans to set up two branch headquarters, one each in Los Angeles and Detroit.

Regional offices will boss numerous district offices which will actually handle controls on the local levels. The total and locations for district offices are still on paper and cannot be set up until regional offices are established.

Expect Freight Car Increase

Washington—Deliveries of new domestic freight cars are expected to rise gradually in the first quarter of 1951 and possibly reach the 10,000 level goal by April or May, said the American Railway Car Institute and the Assn. of American Railroads. The largest number of new cars since 1922 was ordered last year. Total was 156,481 and deliveries were 43,991.

Chrysler Unveils 5 Major Developments

Engineering innovations include engine, brakes, steering, shock absorbers and torque converter . . . High compression engine uses standard gasoline—*By Walter G. Patton.*

Detroit — Chrysler engineering hit the jackpot in Detroit this week with the simultaneous announcement of five major engineering changes to be incorporated in its 1951 models. These advances include (1) a new 180 hp V-8 engine operating at 7.5 to 1 compression ratio on standard fuel, (2) power steering for passenger cars, (3) air-cooled brakes, (4) improved shock absorbers and (5) a new torque-converter type automatic transmission.

The new Chrysler engine is undoubtedly the most important contribution by Chrysler engineering in the postwar period. The new high compression type powerplant represents a somewhat different approach to the automotive engine problem although the principle of a hemisphere combustion chamber, spark plug located in the center and large valves has been utilized in aircraft engines and racing cars.

High Compression Engine

Design of the combustion chamber, coupled with a more adequate spark and larger valves permits the Chrysler engine to operate at 7.5 to 1 compression ratio on *standard fuel*. Chrysler design makes possible more efficient operation of a passenger car engine without requiring higher octane fuels. It is also believed that Chrysler can go to comparatively higher compression ratios with fewer engineering changes than will be required in the GM-type engines.

With only 2.3 pct more displacement, the new Chrysler engine achieves 33 pct greater hp. Maximum torque has been increased to 16 pct compared with the 1950 8-cylinder in-line engine. According to Chrysler engineers, the new design gives the highest output per cu in. of any engine in the industry today. The 180 hp rating is also the highest in the industry.

Power steering for passenger cars, developed by Gemmer Mfg. Co., Detroit, will be introduced first by Chrysler. Other auto makers are known to be interested in this development.

Hydraulic Power Steering

Power steering requires only about a tenth the physical effort previously necessary. The steering wheel can be guided using the pressure of only one finger and guidance with the thumb. This is made possible by the use of a hydraulic mechanism to do the work. Steering wheel travel has been reduced from five and a half to three and a half turns for complete travel of the wheel.

Chrysler's new Oriflow shock absorbers are also an advanced design. More precise control of the fluid flow in the shock absorber, it is claimed, makes possible a gradual change of resistance during jounce and rebound after severe spring deflection.

The new anti-shock devices have ten fewer parts than the previous designs. They are said to be less expensive than previous types to manufacture and are reported to give longer life than other designs.

Chrysler is introducing forced air cooling of its disc type brakes on all 1951 Imperial models. Forced air cooling is claimed to reduce (1) internal brake temperatures up to 35 pct and (2) brake lining wear up to **50 pct.** Because of a cooler brake, more braking effort can be used in making highspeed stops, it is contended. The new brakes have blades on the wheel discs which pull air over the housing while the wheels are turning.

Details of the new Chrysler automatic transmission are not yet available. Essentially, Chrysler is substituting a torque converter for the fluid coupling ahead of its automatic transmission.

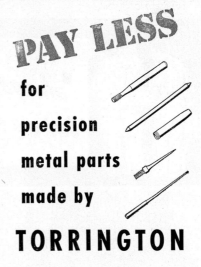
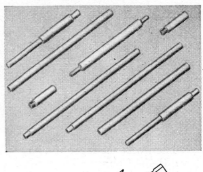

National Steel's Weir Asks Negotiation With Russia, China

Pittsburgh—E. T. Weir, chairman of National Steel Corp., favors direct negotiations between the United States and Russia and Red China in the interest of world peace. He said: "1. We are not prepared for war. What we need most is time to build up our military strength—not to prepare for war but to prevent war.

"2. Our European friends feel that our present tactics will lead to war with Communist China, which is one reason why we have been receiving only lukewarm support from them in Korea. War with China would also permit Russia to foment trouble in other parts of the world—trouble that we would be too busy to do anything about.

"3. While the decision of peace or war rests largely with us, we cannot make this decision without considering the views of the major European powers. These powers do not see eye-to-eye with us on our approach to settlement of the Asiatic problem.

"4. A demonstration of our willingness to negotiate on Korea and Formosa and the question of recognizing Red China will show the world once again our desire for peace. If negotiation fails, we still will have gained valuable time to strengthen our defenses."

Norton Opens Abrasive Plant

Worcester, Mass.—Norton Co. here has opened a new electric furnace plant to make silicon carbide abrasive at Cap-de-la-Madelaine, Quebec. The plant will make possible a 50 pct boost in the manufacture of Crystolon abrasive, Norton's trade name for silicon carbide.

Operates Smelter in New Plant

Anniston, Ala. — Lee Brothers Foundry, one of the largest brass foundries in the country, is operating a smelter in its new plant here. The furnace has a capacity of 10 tons.

Graphite Process Announced; May Spread Use of Home Product

Alabama flake graphite purified 98 pct . . . Vital to steelmaking.

Birmingham—A chemical process that will purify and concentrate flake graphite to 98 pct carbon has been announced by the University of Alabama and the U. S. Bureau of Mines.

Vital to Steels

The process, vital to defense, is expected to result in reactivation of three mills in Alabama used during World War II and possible building of others. The process was perfected by W. H. Weller, Jr., Birmingham coal and coke dealer.

Flake graphite is a vital ingredient in melting crucible steel and special alloys, and as a coating for black and smokeless powder. It is recognized as one of the ten top critical defense minerals.

Too Much Planning for A-bomb Can Hurt, Too Little Can be Fatal

New York—Too much planning against A-bomb attack can hurt by detracting from the defense effort and too little planning can be fatal, cautioned the Research Institute of America in a report, "Your Business and the A-Bomb."

Management can write to heads of their states for confidential information as to whether they are in probable target areas. Also available to industry is a handbook, "The Effects of Atomic Weapons," which is selling for $1.25 through the Superintendent of Documents, U. S. Government Printing Office, Wash. 25, D. C.

PA's Sponsor Chicago Show

Chicago—More than 100 leading manufacturers and industrial distributors will display their 1951 lines at the 17th Annual Products Show, sponsored by the Purchasing Agents Assn. of Chicago, at the Hotel Sherman on Feb. 20, 21, and 22. Total attendance is expected to exceed 15,000.

Behind your television screen...

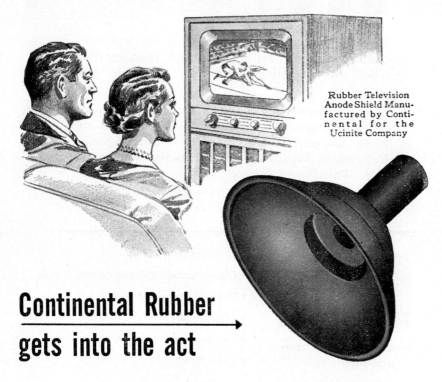

Rubber Television Anode Shield Manufactured by Continental for the Ucinite Company

Continental Rubber ➞
gets into the act

In the unseen act behind your television screen, a small cup-shaped rubber shield plays an important role. This shield fits over the anode on the side of the tube. Its function is to "seal in" high voltage current and thus prevent surface discharges that cause picture distortion.

Ordinary rubber compounds, of course, can't fill the bill. *This* rubber part must have exceptional dielectric properties and unusual stability under sustained heat. It must resist the deteriorating effects of ozone created by electrical discharges. In addition, the rubber shield must be precision molded to insure proper seating against the side of the television tube.

Continental engineers, working closely with Ucinite Company engineers, have met these exacting requirements. This technical cooperation typifies the service in rubber offered by Continental.

When *you* need better engineered rubber parts, why not enlist the service of specialists in molded and extruded rubber?

LET US SEND YOU THIS CATALOG

This new engineering catalog lists hundreds of standard grommets, bushings, rings and extruded shapes. It will be a valuable addition to your working file. Send for your copy today or . . .
See our Catalog in Sweet's File for Product Designers

MANUFACTURERS SINCE 1903

CONTINENTAL
RUBBER WORKS
1985 LIBERTY BOULEVARD • ERIE 6, PENNSYLVANIA

STEEL
CONSTRUCTION NEWS

Fabricated steel awards this week included the following:

600 Tons, Chicago, 23rd Street Viaduct, to American Bridge Co.

500 Tons, Repauno, N. J., building extensions for E. I. duPont de Nemours & Co., Inc., to Bethlehem Fabricating Co., Bethlehem.

400 Tons, Harvey, Ill., Y. M. C. A. Bldg., to Joseph T. Ryerson & Son, Inc.

275 Tons, Chicago, Racine Ave. pumping station for Sanitary District, to American Bridge Co.

135 Tons, Wabasha County, Minn., Bridge No. 6532, to American Bridge Co.

121 Tons, Cummington and Goshen, Mass., bituminous concrete and construction and widening of bridges over Crosby Brook, Swift River and Stony Brook. Thomas R. Rawson, North Woburn, Mass., low bidder.

115 Tons, Norman County, Minn., Bridge No. 6734 to Illinois Steel Bridge Co.

115 Tons, Brown County, Minn., Bridge No. 6756 to American Bridge Co.

100 Tons, Bethlehem, Pa., office building for United Steel Workers of America, to Bethlehem Steel Co., Bethlehem.

Fabricated steel inquiries this week included the following:

580 Tons, Redwing County, Minn., Bridge No. 6483.

420 Tons, Cook County, Ill., Bridge section 42SF for State of Illinois.

410 Tons, Redwing County, Minn., Bridge No. 6484.

300 Tons, St. Clair County, Ill., Bridge section 146F for State of Illinois.

250 Tons, Morrisville, Pa., new bids for administration building and toll collecting facilities, Delaware River Joint Toll Bridge Commission, bids due Jan. 30.

155 Tons, Darien, Conn., 70 foot square span composite steel girder bridge and 523 feet of widening and drainage. Bridge overpasses Route 1 and widening and damage is on Post Road. This project involves use of alpha composite construction of a patented design of spiral steel bars. E. T. Nettleton, New Haven, district engineer.

Reinforcing bar awards this week included the following:

390 Tons, Chicago, Housing Project Site No. 8, to Bethlehem Steel Corp.

130 Tons, DuPage County, Ill., building No. 208 for Argonne National Laboratory, to U. S. Steel Supply Corp.

115 Tons, Harvey, Ill., Y. M. C. A. Bldg., to Joseph T. Ryerson & Sons, Inc.

110 Tons, Oak Park, Ill., Oak Park Hospital addition, to Ceco Steel Products Co.

Reinforcing bar inquiries this week included the following:

157 Tons, Freeport, Maine, project on Route 1 extending around Freeport Village, concrete and bituminous concrete.

Plans Small Motors Plant

Union City, Ind.—To help satisfy increased demand for fractional horsepower motors, Westinghouse Electric Corp. will build a new small motors plant here, with production scheduled to start in late 1951. At full operation the plant will employ about 500.

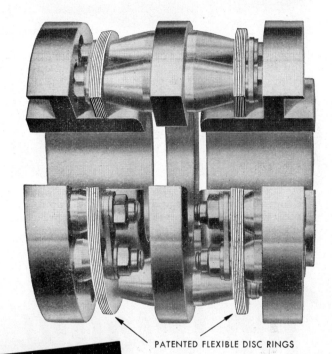

January 18, 1951

blanking, and perforating. Machinability, as measured by a range of low and high speeds of turning in surface feet per minute, is also given. The slide gives specifications for forging, annealing, hardening, and drawing Carpenter stainless steels, as well as information on corrosion resistance, Brinell and Rockwell hardness ranges after drawing, tensile strength, elongation, scaling temperatures safe for continuous service, and whether subject to intergranular corrosion. *Carpenter Steel Co.*
For free copy insert No. 9 on postcard, p. 37.

Corrugated Sheeting

How to use lightweight corrugated steel sheeting to effectively control movement of soil or water is described in a new, illustrated 10-p. booklet pointing out where Armco interlocking and flange type sheeting can be used to advantage. Photographic case-histories show that corrugated sheeting has ample strength, is fast driving and results in lower costs, and can be pulled and re-used many times. Also included in the booklet are data on driving and properties of both types of Armco sheeting as well as a method of figuring sizes and spacing of wales and struts. Contractors and engineers will find the booklet a handy reference. *Armco Drainage & Metal Products, Inc.*
For free copy insert No. 10 on postcard, p. 37.

Pre-Shaped Bar Stock

A new 4-p. bulletin describes a new steel bar stock, cold drawn in special sections to fit specific purposes. The bulletin points out that the pre-shaped feature eliminates many machining operations in the production of steel parts for machines and other products. In some cases, machining may be reduced to a simple cut off operation. Drawings of some typical pre-shaped steel sections are shown and an indication is given of the various analyses in which this specialty stock is available. *A. Milne & Co.*
For free copy insert No. 11 on postcard, p. 37.

Resume Your Reading on Page 37

production ideas

Continued from Page 39

fected by leakless and positive contact between carefully lapped metal-to-carbon or metal-to-metal mating surfaces. One of these elements rotates with the shaft and the other

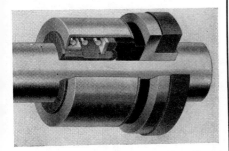

is stationary. The stationary element does not contact the shaft. Seals are made in several standard designs and in a wide range of highest grade materials. Design and material depend upon the service in which the seal is to be used. *Garlock Packing Co.*

For more data insert No. 32 on postcard, p. 37.

Material Handling Pump

Spray gun spurting eliminated by the new Mogul-Type Powerflo pump.

Mogul air-operated, high volume pumps, operating in 400 and 100-lb drums or in bucket-type containers, supply industrial material through

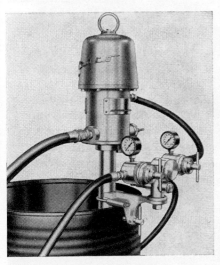

hoses for spray gun pole gun or extrusion gun application. No messy, time-wasting transfer operations are necessary. A device called the Evenflo prevents spurting. Rust and corrosion preventives, caulking compounds, adhesives, undercoaters, other industrial materials, even gummy mastics and non-self-level-

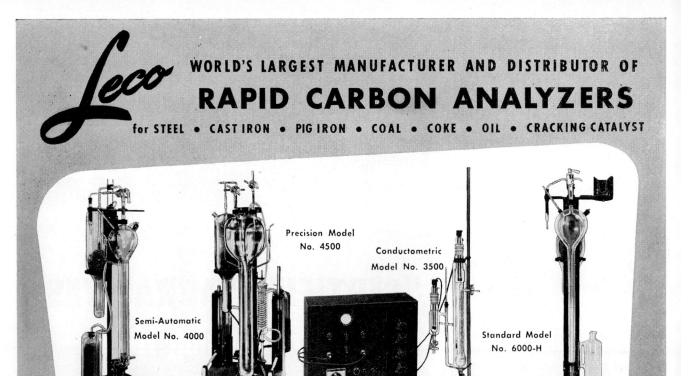
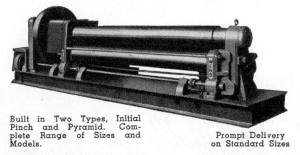

ing substances can be pumped with the new Graco Mogul. Power head of the 35-lb unit is cast aluminum. *Gray Co., Inc.*
For more data insert No. 33 on postcard, p. 37.

Wax Injection Press

For producing wax and plastic patterns for precision casting.

Pattern material is heated by oil circulating only through the revolving drum and crosshead, in the new Sherwood Model WP12 wax injection press. Thermostatically controlled temperatures to 400° F may be attained without overheating the

hydraulic ram mechanism. A separate heating unit for the crosshead and discharge nozzle facilitate free flow of pattern material. Ram pressures, varying with the power of the motor installed, may be developed to 1500 psi. The revolving drum holds four cylinders, each 3½ in. diam x 7 in. long, with 67 cu in. capacity. One section of the drum is cut out, providing ready access for servicing the hydraulic ram and crosshead. *Alexander Saunders & Co.*
For more data insert No. 34 on postcard, p. 37.

Automatic Drill

Speeds up drilling, countersinking cotter pin holes in clevis pins.

A new machine performs the operations of drilling cotter pin holes in clevis pins and screws and countersinking both sides at the rate of 1500 pieces per hr. The

production ideas

Continued

machine is fully automatic, employing 4 model-KH Govro-Nelson automatic drilling units which operate simultaneously in conjunction with and completely interlocked with a Geneva type, 8-station indexing dial and a hopper part-feeding mechanism. The ma-

chine stops automatically should a tool break or a malformed part jam in the mechanism. It slows down automatically when a tool becomes extremely dull. Indexing mechanism does not work unless tools are out of the work. *Govro-Nelson Co.*

For more data insert No. 35 on postcard, p. 37.

Motor Starter

Features protection of operating personnel and connected machine.

With ratings up to 600 v, 7½ hp polyphase, 5 hp single phase; or 220 v, 1½ hp dc, a new motor starter provides overload protection for single phase, polyphase and dc motors. The self-indicating handle, interlocked cover that prevents opening unless starter is off, and safety latch to lock starter off during servicing are personnel-protection features. Positive motor-protection is provided by the quick-make, quick-break, over-center toggle mechanism—De-ion arc-quenching—and the bimetallic disk-type thermal overload relay. Straight-through wiring facilitates installation and servicing. *Westinghouse Electric Co.*

For more data insert No. 36 on postcard, p. 37.

Resume Your Reading on Page 40

IRON AGE *markets and prices*

continuing conversion—Detroit auto producers are going ahead with conversion and apparently are having reasonable success with mill arrangements despite increasing tightness in the scrap and pig iron markets. For the first time in the past year or so, a tight ingot market was reported in Detroit. Washington action is having repercussions in Detroit. Unless use restrictions are balanced with quota cuts, artificial production dislocations are certain. For example, nickel is very scarce because it has been cut drastically while applications haven't been cut back nearly as much.

tinplate extras—U. S. Steel Co.'s tinplate prices, previously announced, were effective Jan 16. Extras apply on widths of 26 in. and under, with deductions for widths over 28 in. Length extras vary with base weight and length. Quantity extras apply under 7500 lbs. Resquaring extras are 40c for ends or sides, 60c for ends and sides. Hollowware enameling extras are 10c for 30 gage, 30c for 31 gage. Width extras and deductions apply as above. Length extras are 5c over 40 in. to 48 in.; 25c over 48 in. to 124 in.

steel capacity—Increased steelmaking capacity has made necessary a revision in operating rate. Revised rate for the week of Jan. 1, is 98.2, down 3.6 points from 101.8. Revised rate for the week of Jan. 8, is 99.1, down 3.6 points from 102.7. The revised figure is based on a rate of 104,229,650 tons.

shudder at the thought—Metallurgists shudder when they think what an all-out jet engine program could do to alloy steel distribution. In the postwar era, most firms shifted back to chrome, molybdenum, and nickel alloys. Now they are confronted with the necessity of shifting away again. The change may be coming fast.

cobalt bearing, electrical alloys—Allegheny Ludlum Steel Corp. has announced a 7½ pct increase in the price of cobalt-bearing high temperature and electrical alloys. The new prices were effective Jan. 12. Higher costs of alloys contributed to the price rise.

tool steel prices—Due to increases in the cost of tungsten since Jan. 1, increases of 2c to 13½c per lb in prices of high speed and tool steels have been announced by Allegheny Ludlum Steel Corp., Crucible Steel Co., Firth Sterling Steel & Carbide Corp., and Jessop Steel Co. Crucible's changes were effective Jan 13, the others Jan. 12.

Lone Star loan approved—Approval of a $73,425,201 loan to Lone Star Steel Co., Dallas, Tex., for construction of a tubular steel products mill to serve the oil industry has been announced by government agencies. The plant, to be built near Dainger Field, will be ready in about 18 months. RFC will loan $50 million of the sum, and the balance will be loaned under the Defense Production Act. Lone Star must provide $9 million outside the loan.

Wheeling adds coke capacity—Wheeling Steel Corp. will add 63 new coke ovens to its East Steubenville works at a cost of $8¾ million. The new battery, to be built by Koppers Co., will raise Wheeling's annual capacity to 145,000 tons.

Steel Operations**

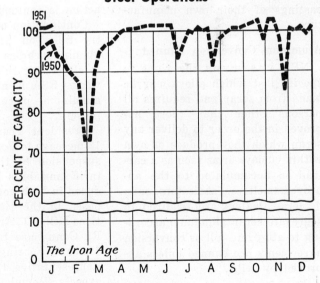

The Iron Age

District Operating Rates—Per Cent of Capacity**

Week of	Pittsburgh	Chicago	Youngstown	Philadelphia	West	Buffalo	Cleveland	Detroit	Wheeling	South	Ohio River	St. Louis	East	Aggregate
Jan. 7	96.0	101.0	93.5*	98.0	104.0	104.0	99.0*	107.0*	97.0	106.0	90.0	90.5	98.0	99.0*
Jan. 14	96.0	101.0	94.0	95.0	103.8	104.0	97.5	106.0	100.0	106.0	90.5	95.1	117.2	99.5

* Revised.
** Beginning Jan. 1, 1951, operations are based on an annual capacity of 104,229,650 net tons.

nonferrous metals

outlook and market activities

by R. Hatschek

New York — National Production Authority has issued an order closely controlling the movement of aluminum scrap. The order (M-22) is similar to the control order placed on copper scrap and provides that only certain approved smelters and fabricators may melt aluminum scrap. One exception is that foundries may, under certain conditions, remelt risers, sprues, gates and defective castings of their own manufacture.

Aluminum Conversion Banned

NPA reserves the right to specify just which alloys may be made from scrap and requires all persons other than those approved in the order to deliver any scrap which they produce or own within 60 days or as soon as a carload is accumulated to the approved smelters, fabricators, or to dealers. Dealers are required to segregate scrap aluminum according to alloy and toll or conversion agreements are banned unless approved by NPA.

At press time there were no changes in the prices of aluminum scrap or secondary ingots and it was still too early to tell what the general effects would be on the scrap and secondary metal industries.

Meanwhile, price control discus-

sions are continuing in Washington with the Economic Stabilization Agency using the old OPA price schedules as a guide. A brief summary of ESA thinking follows: Primary lead and zinc prices are stable enough and "immediate" controls are not planned; scrap, however, may be put under ceilings in the near future. Nickel scrap prices are in preliminary discussion stage and no immediate action is contemplated.

Continuation of the ESA-industry talks on price controls for aluminum, brass and copper scrap is slated for this week and next week. ESA is not expecting any aluminum price changes at present.

President Truman, in his Jan. 12 message to Congress, called for suspension of the copper import tariff and bills have been introduced in both houses for that purpose. In the House, Representatives Mills, D., Ark., and Patterson, R., Conn., are trying to arrange for early hearings on the subject. Representative Patterson says he expects "complete bipartisan cooperation" in enacting the suspension legislation.

Tin Market Surges, Dips

The tin market has started on another inflationary upswing with new alltime high prices being scored each day. Last week the

price was boosted several cents each day until on Friday it reached $1.75 per lb for prompt delivery. Early this week the price dipped on news of a possible international allocation program, then rose again.

The December report of statistics by the Copper Institute showed crude production, including both primary and secondary metal, at a total of 1,057,113 net tons for 1950, the highest total since 1944. Deliveries to fabricators during December added up to 121,954 tons and brought the year's total to 1,373,194, nearly as high as the postwar peak set in 1947.

Copper Production at Peak

Total domestic production in 1950 of refined copper totaled 1,270,768 net tons, topping all previous production records. Refined copper stocks, on the other hand, decreased another 2765 tons in December, leaving the stocks at a low of only 49,040 tons on hand.

The Handy and Harman summary of the silver market in 1950 indicates an increase in Western Hemisphere production of the metal amounting to about 6 pct to a total of 134,700,000 Troy ounces. Consumption by industry and the arts established a new postwar record, as did U. S. imports.

MILL PRODUCTS

(Cents per lb, unless otherwise noted)

Aluminum

(Base 30,000 lb, f.o.b. ship. pt. frt. allowed)

Flat Sheet: 0.188 in., 2S, 3S, 30.1¢; 4S, 61S-O, 32¢; 52S, 34.1¢; 24S-O, 24S-OAL, 32.9¢; 75S-O, 75S-OAL, 39.9¢; 0.081 in., 2S, 3S, 31.2¢; 4S, 61S-O, 33.5¢; 52S, 35.6¢; 24S-O, 24S-OAL, 34.1¢; 75S-O, 75S-OAL, 41.8¢; 0.032 in., 2S, 3S, 32.9¢; 4S, 61S-O, 37.1¢; 52S, 39.8¢; 24S-O, 24S-OAL, 41.7¢; 75S-O, 75S-OAL, 52.2¢.

Plate: ¼ in. and heavier: 2S, 3S-F, 28.3¢; 4S-F, 30.2¢; 52S-F, 31.8¢; 61S-O, 30.8¢; 24S-O, 24S-OAL, 32.4¢; 75S-O, 75S-OAL, 38.8¢.

Extruded Solid Shapes: Shape factors 1 to 5, 36.2¢ to 74.5¢; 12 to 14, 36.9¢ to 89¢; 24 to 26, 39.6¢ to $1.16; 36 to 38, 47.2¢ to $1.70.

Rod, Rolled: 1.5 to 4.5 in., 2S-F, 3S-F, 37.5¢ to 33.5¢; cold-finished, 0.375 to 3 in., 2S-F, 3S-F, 40.5¢ to 35¢.

Screw Machine Stock: Rounds, 11S-T3, ⅛ to 11/32 in., 53.5¢ to 42¢; ⅜ to 1½ in., 41.5¢ to 39¢; 1 9/16 to 3 in., 38.5¢ to 36¢; 17S-T4 lower by 1.5¢ per lb. Base 5000 lb.

Drawn Wire: Coiled, 0.051 to 0.374 in., 2S, 39.5¢ to 29¢; 52S, 48¢ to 35¢; 56S, 51¢ to 42¢; 17S-T4, 54¢ to 37.5¢; 61S-T4, 48.5¢ to 37¢; 75S-T6, 84¢ to 67.5¢.

Extruded Tubing, Rounds: 63S-T5, OD in in.: 1¼ to 2, 37¢ to 54¢; 2 to 4, 33.5¢ to 45.5¢; 4 to 6, 34¢ to 41.5¢; 6 to 9, 34.5¢ to 43.5¢.

Roofing Sheet, Flat: 0.019 in. x 28 in. per sheet, 72 in., $1.142; 96 in., $1.522; 120 in., $1.902; 144 in., $2.284. Gage 0.024 in. x 28 in., 72 in., $1.379; 96 in., $1.839; 120 in., $2.299; 144 in., $2.759. Coiled Sheet: 0.019 in. x 28 in., 28.2¢ per lb.; 0.024 in. x 28 in., 26.9¢ per lb.

Magnesium

(F.o.b. mill, freight allowed)

Sheet and Plate: FS1-O, ¼ in. 63¢; 3/16 in. 65¢; ⅛ in. 67¢; B & S Gage 10, 68¢; 12, 72¢; 14, 78¢; 16, 85¢; 18, 93¢; 20, $1.05; 22, $1.27; 24, $1.67. Specification grade higher. Base: 30,000 lb.

Extruded Round Rod: M, diam in., ¼ to 0.311 in., 74¢; ½ to ¾ in., 57.5¢; 1¼ to 1.749 in., 53¢; 2½ to 5 in., 48.5¢. Other alloys higher. Base: Up to ¾ in. diam, 10,000 lb; ¾ to 2 in., 20,000 lb; 2 in. and larger, 30,000 lb.

Extruded Solid Shapes, Rectangles: M. In weight per ft, for perimeters less than size indicated, 0.10 to 0.11 lb, 3.5 in., 62.3¢; 0.22 to 0.25 lb, 5.9 in., 59.3¢; 0.50 to 0.59 lb, 8.6 in., 56.7¢; 1.8 to 2.59 lb, 19.5 in., 53.8¢; 4 to 6 lb, 28 in., 49¢. Other alloys higher. Base, in weight per ft of shape: Up to ½ lb, 10,000 lb; ½ to 1.80 lb, 20,000 lb; 1.80 lb and heavier, 30,000 lb.

Extruded Round Tubing: M, wall thickness, outside diam, in., 0.049 to 0.057, ¼ in. to 5/16, $1.40; 5/16 to ⅜, $1.26; ½ to ⅝, 93¢; 1 to 2 in., 76¢; 0.165 to 0.219, ⅝ to ¾, 61¢; 1 to 2 in., 57¢; 3 to 4 in., 56¢. Other alloys higher. Base, OD in in.: Up to 1½ in., 10,000 lb; 1½ in. to 3 in., 20,000 lb; 3 in. and larger, 30,000 lb.

Titanium

(10,000 *lb. base, f.o.b. mill*)

Commercially pure and alloy grades: Sheet and strip, HR or CR, $15; Plate, HR, $12; Wire, rolled and/or drawn, $10; Bar, HR or forged, $6; Forgings, $6.

Nickel and Monel

(Base prices, f.o.b. mill)

	"A" Nickel	Monel
Sheets, cold-rolled	71½	57
Strip, cold-rolled	77½	60
Rods and bars	67½	55
Angles, hot-rolled	67½	55
Plates	69½	56
Seamless tubes	100½	90
Shot and blocks	....	50

Copper, Brass, Bronze

(Freight prepaid on 200 lb includes duty)

	Sheets	Rods	Extruded Shapes
Copper	41.03	..	40.63
Copper, h-r	....	36.88	....
Copper, drawn	....	38.18	....
Low brass	39.15	38.84	....
Yellow brass	38.28	37.97	....
Red brass	40.14	39.83	....
Naval brass	43.08	38.61	38.07
Leaded brass	..	32.63	36.70
Com'l bronze	41.13	40.82	....
Mang. bronze	45.96	40.65	41.41
Phos. bronze	60.20	60.45	....
Muntz metal	40.43	36.74	37.99
Ni silver, 10 pct	49.27	51.49	....
Arch. bronze	....	....	35.11

PRIMARY METALS

(Cents per lb, unless otherwise noted)

Aluminum ingot, 99+%, 10,000 lb, freight allowed	19.00
Aluminum pig	18.00
Antimony, American, Laredo, Tex.	32.00
Beryllium copper, 3.75-4.25% Be	$1.56
Beryllium aluminum 5% Be, Dollars per lb contained Be	$69.00
Bismuth, ton lots	$2.25
Cadmium, del'd	$2.55
Cobalt, 97-99% (per lb)	$2.10 to $2.17
Copper, electro, Conn. Valley	24.50
Copper, Lake, delivered	24.625
Gold, U. S. Treas., dollars per oz.	$35.00
Indium, 99.8%, dollars per troy oz.	$2.25
Iridium, dollars per troy oz.	$200
Lead, St. Louis	16.80
Lead, New York	17.00
Magnesium, 99.8+%, f.o.b. Freeport, Tex., 10,000 lb	24.50
Magnesium, sticks, 100 to 500 lb	42.00 to 44.00
Mercury, dollars per 76-lb flask f.o.b. New York	$187.50 to $198.00
Nickel, electro, f.o.b. New York	53.55
Nickel oxide sinter, f.o.b. Copper Cliff, Ont., contained nickel	46.75
Palladium, dollars per troy oz.	$24.00
Platinum, dollars per troy oz.	$90 to $93
Silver, New York, cents per oz.	90.16
Tin, New York	$1.74
Titanium, sponge	$5.00
Zinc, East St. Louis	17.50
Zinc, New York	18.22
Zirconium copper, 50 pct	$6.20

REMELTED METALS

Brass Ingot

(Cents per lb delivered, carloads)

85-5-5-5 ingot	
No. 115	29.00
No. 120	28.50
No. 123	28.00
80-10-10 ingot	
No. 305	35.00
No. 315	32.00
88-10-2 ingot	
No. 210	46.25
No. 215	43.25
No. 245	36.00
Yellow ingot	
No. 405	25.50
Manganese bronze	
No. 421	30.75

Aluminum Ingot

(Cents per lb, 30,000 lb lots)

95-5 aluminum-silicon alloys	
0.30 copper, max.	33.25-34.25
0.60 copper, max.	33.00-34.00
Piston alloys (No. 122 type)	31.00-31.50
No. 12 alum. (No. 2 grade)	30.50-31.00
108 alloy	30.75-31.25
195 alloy	32.25-32.75
13 alloy	33.50-34.00
ASX-679	30.75-31.25

Steel deoxidizing aluminum, notch-bar granulated or shot

Grade 1—95-97½%	32.00-32.50
Grade 2—92-95%	30.25-31.00
Grade 3—90-92%	29.50-30.00
Grade 4—85-90%	29.00-29.50

ELECTROPLATING SUPPLIES

Anodes

(Cents per lb, freight allowed, 500 lb lots)

Copper	
Cast, oval, 15 in. or longer	39⅛
Electrodeposited	33⅜
Rolled, oval, straight, delivered	38⅞
Forged ball anodes	43
Brass, 80-20	
Cast, oval, 15 in. or longer	34¾
Zinc, oval	26½
Ball anodes	25½
Nickel 99 pct plus	
Cast	70.50
Rolled, depolarized	71.50
Cadmium	$2.80
Silver 999 fine, rolled, 100 oz lots, per troy oz, f.o.b. Bridgeport, Conn.	79½

Chemicals

(Cents per lb, f.o.b. shipping point)

Copper cyanide, 100 lb drum	52.15
Copper sulfate, 99.5 crystals, bbl.	12.85
Nickel salts, single or double, 4-100 lb bags, frt allowed	20½
Nickel chloride, 375 lb drum	27½
Silver cyanide, 100 oz lots, per oz.	67¼
Sodium cyanide, 96 pct domestic 200 lb drums	19.25
Zinc cyanide, 100 lb drums	45.85

SCRAP METALS

Brass Mill Scrap

(Cents per pound, add ½¢ per lb for shipments of 20,000 to 40,000 lb; add 1¢ for more than 40,000 lb)

	Heavy	Turnings
Copper	23	22¼
Yellow brass	20⅛	18¾
Red brass	21½	20¾
Comm. bronze	21¾	21
Mang. bronze	19½	18⅝
Brass rod ends	19⅞	....

Custom Smelters' Scrap

(Cents per pound, carload lots, delivered to refinery)

No. 1 copper wire	21.00
No. 2 copper wire	20.00
Light copper	19.00
Refinery brass	18.50*
Radiators	15.00

*Dry copper content.

Ingot Makers' Scrap

(Cents per pound, carload lots, delivered to producer)

No. 1 copper wire	21.00
No. 2 copper wire	20.00
Light copper	19.00
No. 1 composition	20.00
No. 1 comp. turnings	19.75
Rolled brass	16.50
Brass pipe	18.50
Radiators	15.25
Heavy yellow brass	15.00
Aluminum	
Mixed old cast	18½
Mixed new clips	20½
Mixed turnings, dry	18½
Pots and pans	18½—18¾
Low copper	21½—21¾

Dealers' Scrap

(Dealers' buying prices, f.o.b. New York in cents per pound)

Copper and Brass

No. 1 heavy copper and wire	19½—20
No. 2 heavy copper and wire	18 —18½
Light copper	17 —17¼
New type shell cuttings	17 —17¼
Auto radiators (unsweated)	14½—15
No. 1 composition	17 —17½
No. 1 composition turnings	16½—17
Clean red car boxes	15½—16
Cocks and faucets	15½—16
Mixed heavy yellow brass	13 —13½
Old rolled brass	14 —14½
Brass pipe	17 —17½
New soft brass clippings	17½—18
Brass rod ends	16½—17
No. 1 brass rod turnings	16 —16½

Aluminum

Alum. pistons and struts	12 —13
Aluminum crankcases	15 —16
2S aluminum clippings	18½—19½
Old sheet and utensils	15 —16
Borings and turnings	12½—13
Misc. cast aluminum	15 —16
Dural clips (24S)	15 —16

Zinc

New zinc clippings	14½—15
Old zinc	11 —11¼
Zinc routings	8½— 9
Old die cast scrap	8 — 8¼

Nickel and Monel

Pure nickel clippings	60 —65
Clean nickel turnings	57 —60
Nickel anodes	60 —65
Nickel rod ends	60 —65
New Monel Clippings	22 —25
Clean Monel turnings	18 —20
Old sheet Monel	20 —22
Inconel clippings	26 —28
Nickel silver clippings, mixed	13 —14
Nickel silver turnings, mixed	12 —13

Lead

Soft scrap, lead	15 —15⅛
Battery plates (dry)	8¾— 9

Magnesium

Segregated solids	9 —10
Castings	5½— 6½

Miscellaneous

Block tin	85 —90
No. 1 pewter	63 —65
No. 1 auto babbitt	58 —60
Mixed common babbitt	12¼—12½
Solder joints	18½—19
Siphon tops	58 —60
Small foundry type	16¼—16½
Monotype	14¾—15
Lino. and stereotype	14½—14¾
Electrotype	12¾—13
Hand picked type shells	11½—11¾
Lino. and stereo. dross	8 — 8¼
Electro. dross	6½— 6¾

SCRAP *iron and steel*

markets prices trends

Prices surging upward as scrap field goes down last lap to controls ... Voluntary control rumor heard ... Price picture cloudy.

Markets in several important areas were boiling over with prices surging upward this week as scrap men went down the last lap to Economic Stabilization Agency controls—voluntary or mandatory.

Prices of steelmaking grades shot up $5.75 to $6.75 a ton in Buffalo when the principal local buyer came into the market to offset raiding by big out-of-district mills. Steelmaking grades in Philadelphia were up $5 a ton.

Some sources believe that the increases were caused by consumers who wanted to get orders placed ahead of any price controls that might be placed in effect.

In Pittsburgh it was rumored that controls would be on a voluntary basis with the big stick of threatened enforcement if they faltered. It is conceded that voluntary controls won't be too effective. They will merely be an extension of the formula, perhaps on a slightly lower price basis. Voluntary controls will not stop behind-the-contract deals and upgrading, some maintain.

ESA has indicated that it will control specific basic commodities first. Presumably it is simpler to control prices of items that wind up in the hands of relatively few producers than to regulate prices of products that reach millions.

PITTSBURGH — The trade is looking for an announcement within the next 10 days on price controls. Indications are that controls will be applied on a voluntary basis with the threat of enforced control if the voluntary system breaks down. It is generally agreed a voluntary system will not work. Meanwhile, demand continues strong with some mills experiencing difficulty obtaining material at present levels. Controlled prices are expected to be generally $1.50 lower than existing prices. Cast grades and railroad specialties are likely to be cut back more drastically.

CHICAGO — Activity in the scrap market was at a minimum this week as the trade awaited definite word on price controls. Brokers and dealers are lowering their offerings in expectation of lower controlled prices. Dealers are trying to cut down inventory. Few sales are being made to consumers. Cast grades and railroad items are expected to come down considerably when controls are put on.

PHILADELPHIA — Last-minute developments in the scrap trade here and in other centers have precipitated a wild market with prices for steelmaking grades substantially higher. No. 1 heavy melting and No. 1 bundles are **$5 per ton higher.** No. 2 is up $2, and No. 2 bundles are up $1. Low phos grades are up in sympathy. Earlier increases were scored by railroad specialties, chemical borings and malleable cast scrap. The reasons behind this renewed activity are (1) mills are in poor inventory situations, and (2) consumers expect shipments to drop off **severely in** the adjustment period when prices are fixed.

NEW YORK — The Scrap Institute convention held the spotlight in this section. Prices were stable and scrap shipments good. Washington developments and the possible pricing method were still a good topic for conversation. Scrap men think they are on the last lap to price controls with cast grades due for a rollback.

DETROIT—There is no change in the Detroit scrap market this week. Dealers and brokers are waiting for price controls and some orders have been accepted, "subject to subsequent government regulations. The amount of free scrap being sold is diminishing further. Cast grades are weaker in the face of uncertainty about price controls and the extent to which rearmament will replace industrial production.

CLEVELAND — A strong but subdued scrap market here and in the Valley is marking time this week in anticipation of mandatory price controls. Press time rumors had it that no announcement of new prices will be made this week and that industry and trade representatives may be called back for a final check after the regulations are written. Scrap is moving but the volume of shipments leaves much to be desired from a consumer's point of view. Foundry grades are strong but showing little activity.

ST. LOUIS — Further declines in the scrap iron list were reported during the week as a result of anticipation of price rollbacks by the ESA. This is especially true of railroad lists. There has been little buying by consumers because of the prospects of rollbacks.

BIRMINGHAM—The scrap steel market here is exceptionally strong. Northern buyers are taking everything they can get and local brokers and dealers are sending what they buy to that area after needs of local buyers are cared for. Republic Steel is paying $40.50 for No. 2 bundles and assuming freight charges from Atlanta, bringing the delivered price at Alabama City to $42.46. The North-South formula differential has been reduced to $3.00. The cast market continues weak and has dropped another dollar to $55.00. A sale of one carload of cast iron borings was reported at $34 a ton.

CINCINNATI—Prices are unchanged in a moderately active market here. Shipments are moving and brokers are trying to get some of their old paper cleaned up before announcement of price regulations. Foundry grades are very quiet and buyers are staying out of the market with lower prices seemingly on the way.

BOSTON—News of price controls from Washington was being awaited on all sides. Activity in the Boston area was generally good, with a few specialities reported selling at over the formula price. Mixed cupola cast moved up a $1 to a new price of $45 to $46.

BUFFALO—To offset raiding by out-of-district mills, the principal local buyer came into the market this week for a very substantial tonnage of steelmaking scrap at prices well above the preceding week. Steelmaking grades are up $5.75 to $6.75 per ton. Low phos increased in sympathy. At the same time it is understood that old orders were cancelled. These prices do not apply to allocated or earmarked material.

Iron and Steel

SCRAP PRICES

Going prices as obtained in the trade by THE IRON AGE based on representative tonnages. All prices are per gross ton delivered to consumer unless otherwise noted.

Pittsburgh

No. 1 hvy. melting	$45.75 to	$46.50
No. 2 hvy. melting	43.75 to	44.50
No. 1 bundles	45.75 to	46.50
No. 2 bundles	42.75 to	43.50
Machine shop turn.	37.75 to	38.50
Mixed bor. and ms. turns.	37.75 to	38.50
Shoveling turnings	39.75 to	40.50
Cast iron borings	39.75 to	40.50
Low phos. plate	56.00 to	56.50
Heavy turnings	46.50 to	47.00
No. 1 RR. hvy. melting	45.75 to	46.50
Scrap rails, random lgth.	64.50 to	65.00
Rails 2 ft and under	68.00 to	69.00
RR. steel wheels	63.00 to	64.00
RR. spring steel	63.00 to	64.00
RR. couplers and knuckles	63.00 to	64.00
No. 1 machinery cast.	67.50 to	68.00
Mixed yard cast.	57.50 to	58.00
Heavy breakable cast.	52.50 to	53.00
Malleable	71.00 to	72.00

Chicago

No. 1 hvy. melting	$44.25 to	$45.00
No. 2 hvy. melting	42.00 to	43.00
No. 1 factory bundles	44.00 to	45.00
No. 1 dealers' bundles	44.00 to	45.00
No. 2 dealers' bundles	41.00 to	42.00
Machine shop turn.	35.00 to	36.00
Mixed bor. and turn.	35.00 to	36.00
Shoveling turnings	37.00 to	38.00
Cast iron borings	37.00 to	38.00
Low phos. forge crops	54.00 to	55.00
Low phos. plate	52.00 to	53.00
No. 1 RR. hvy. melting	47.00 to	48.00
Scrap rails, random lgth.	62.00 to	63.00
Rerolling rails	65.50 to	66.50
Rails 2 ft and under	67.00 to	69.00
Locomotive tires, cut	58.00 to	59.00
Cut bolsters & side frames	54.00 to	55.00
Angles and splice bars	63.00 to	64.00
RR. steel car axles	95.00 to	100.00
RR. couplers and knuckles	58.00 to	59.00
No. 1 machinery cast.	62.00 to	64.00
No. 1 agricul. cast.	58.00 to	60.00
Heavy breakable cast.	53.00 to	55.00
RR. grate bars	48.00 to	49.00
Cast iron brake shoes	52.00 to	53.00
Cast iron car wheels	58.00 to	59.00
Malleable	78.00 to	82.00

Philadelphia

No. 1 hvy. melting	$49.00 to	$50.00
No. 2 hvy. melting	44.00 to	45.00
No. 1 bundles	49.00 to	50.00
No. 2 bundles	42.00 to	43.00
Machine shop turn.	36.00 to	37.00
Mixed bor. and turn.	35.00 to	36.00
Shoveling turnings	38.00 to	39.00
Low phos. punchings, plate	51.00 to	52.00
Low phos. 5 ft and under	51.00 to	52.00
Low phos. bundles	50.00 to	51.00
Hvy. axle forge turn.	44.00 to	45.00
Clean cast chem. borings.	44.00 to	45.00
RR. steel wheels	56.00 to	57.00
RR. spring steel	56.00 to	57.00
Rails 18 in. and under	66.00 to	67.00
No. 1 machinery cast.	62.00 to	63.00
Mixed yard cast.	53.00 to	55.00
Heavy breakable cast.	53.00 to	54.00
Cast iron carwheels	67.00 to	68.00
Malleable	70.00 to	72.00

Cleveland

No. 1 hvy. melting	$45.25 to	$46.00
No. 2 hvy. melting	43.25 to	44.00
No. 1 busheling	45.25 to	46.00
No. 1 bundles	45.25 to	46.00
No. 2 bundles	42.25 to	43.00
Machine shop turn.	37.25 to	38.00
Mixed bor. and turn.	39.25 to	40.00
Shoveling turnings	39.25 to	40.00
Cast iron borings	39.25 to	40.00
Low phos. 2 ft and under.	47.75 to	48.50
Steel axle turn.	44.25 to	45.00
Drop forge flashings	45.25 to	46.00
No. 1 RR. hvy. melting.	46.00 to	46.50
Rails 3 ft and under	70.00 to	71.00
Rails 18 in. and under	72.00 to	73.00
No. 1 machinery cast.	69.00 to	70.00
RR. cast.	71.00 to	72.00
RR. grate bars	50.00 to	51.00
Stove plate	55.00 to	56.00
Malleable	76.00 to	77.00

Youngstown

No. 1 hvy. melting	$45.75 to	$46.50
No. 2 hvy. melting	43.75 to	44.50
No. 1 bundles	45.75 to	46.50

(Center, under SCRAP PRICES)

No. 2 bundles	$42.75 to	$43.00
Machine shop turn	37.75 to	38.50
Shoveling turnings	39.75 to	40.50
Cast iron borings	39.75 to	40.50
Low phos. plate	48.25 to	49.00

Buffalo

No. 1 hvy. melting	$51.25 to	$52.00
No. 2 hvy. melting	49.25 to	50.00
No. 1 bushelings	49.25 to	50.00
No. 1 bundles	50.25 to	51.00
No. 2 bundles	47.25 to	48.00
Machine shop turn.	43.25 to	44.00
Mixed bor. and turn.	43.25 to	44.00
Shoveling turnings	45.25 to	46.00
Cast iron borings	43.25 to	44.00
Low phos. plate	51.25 to	52.00
Scrap rails, random lgth.	55.00 to	56.00
Rails 2 ft and under	60.00 to	61.00
RR. steel wheels	60.00 to	61.00
RR. spring steel	60.00 to	61.00
RR. couplers and knuckles	60.00 to	61.00
No. 1 machinery cast.	59.00 to	60.00
No. 1 cupola cast.	54.00 to	55.00
Small indus. malleable	60.00 to	61.00

Birmingham

No. 1 hvy. melting	$42.50 to	$43.50
No. 2 hvy. melting	40.50 to	41.50
No. 2 bundles	39.50 to	40.50
No. 1 busheling	40.50 to	41.50
Machine shop turn.	34.00 to	35.00
Shoveling turnings	32.00 to	33.00
Cast iron borings	33.00 to	34.00
Bar crops and plate	47.00 to	48.00
Structural and plate	46.00 to	47.00
No. 1 RR. hvy. melting.	43.00 to	44.00
Scrap rails, random lgth.	58.00 to	59.00
Rerolling rails	61.00 to	62.00
Rails 2 ft and under	66.00 to	67.00
Angles & splice bars	59.00 to	60.00
Std. steel axles	61.00 to	62.00
No. 1 cupola cast.	54.00 to	55.00
Stove plate	49.00 to	50.00
Cast iron carwheels	46.00 to	47.00

St. Louis

No. 1 hvy. melting	$43.75 to	$44.50
No. 2 hvy. melting	41.75 to	42.50
No. 2 bundled sheets	40.75 to	41.50
Machine shop turn.	33.75 to	34.75
Shoveling turnings	36.50 to	37.50
Rails, random lengths	49.00 to	50.00
Rails 3 ft and under	62.00 to	63.00
Locomotive tires, uncut	50.00 to	51.00
Angles and splice bars	59.00 to	60.00
Std. steel car axles	90.00 to	95.00
RR. spring steel	53.00 to	54.00
No. 1 machinery cast.	55.00 to	56.00
Hvy. breakable cast.	48.00 to	49.00
Cast iron brake shoes	53.00 to	54.00
Stove plate	45.00 to	47.00
Cast iron car wheels	60.00 to	62.00
Malleable	55.00 to	57.00

New York

Brokers' Buying prices per gross ton, on cars:

No. 1 hvy. melting		$39.00
No. 2 hvy. melting		37.00
No. 2 bundles		36.00
Machine shop turn.		31.00
Mixed bor. and turn.		31.00
Shoveling turnings.		33.00
Clean cast chem. bor.	$38.00 to	39.00
No. 1 machinery cast.	52.00 to	53.00
Mixed yard cast.	47.00 to	48.00
Charging box cast.	47.00 to	48.00
Heavy breakable cast.	47.00 to	48.00
Unstrp. motor blocks	42.00 to	43.00

Boston

Brokers' Buying prices per gross ton, on cars:

No. 1 hvy. melting		$35.67
No. 2 hvy. melting		33.67
No. 1 bundles		38.00

(Top right column)

No. 2 bundles		$32.67
Machine shop turn.		27.67
Mixed bor. and turn.	$26.67 to	27.67
Shoveling turnings		29.67
No. 1 busheling		35.67
Clean cast chem. borings	33.00 to	34.00
No. 1 machinery cast.	48.00 to	49.00
Mixed cupola cast.	45.00 to	46.00
Heavy breakable cast.	42.00 to	43.00
Stove plate	42.00 to	43.00

Detroit

Brokers' Buying prices per gross ton, on cars:

No. 1 hvy. melting		$40.25
No. 2 hvy. melting		38.25
No. 1 bundles, openhearth		40.25
No. 1 bundles, electric furnace		42.75
New busheling		40.25
Flashings		40.25
Machine shop turn.		32.25
Mixed bor. and turn.		32.25
Shoveling turnings		34.25
Cast iron borings		34.25
Low phos. plate		42.75
No. 1 cupola cast.	$54.00 to	56.00
Heavy breakable cast.	45.00 to	47.00
Stove plate	44.00 to	46.00
Automotive cast.	58.00 to	60.00

Cincinnati

Per gross ton, f.o.b. cars:

No. 1 hvy. melting		$44.25
No. 2 hvy. melting		42.25
No. 1 bundles		44.25
No. 2 bundles, black		42.25
No. 2 bundles, mixed		41.25
Machine shop turn.		33.00
Mixed bor. and turn.		34.00
Shoveling turnings		34.00
Cast iron borings		34.00
Low phos.-steel		46.75
Low phos. 18 in. under		62.00
Rails, random lengths	$62.00 to	63.00
Rails, 18 in. and under	72.00 to	73.00
No. 1 cupola cast.	65.00 to	66.00
Hvy. breakable cast.	59.00 to	60.00
Drop broken cast.	71.00 to	72.00

San Francisco

No. 1 hvy. melting		$30.00
No. 2 hvy. melting		28.00
No. 1 bundles		30.00
No. 2 bundles		28.00
No. 3 bundles		25.00
Machine shop turn.		16.00
Elec. fur. 1 ft and under	$40.00 to	42.50
No. 1 RR. hvy. melting.		30.00
Scrap rails random lgth.		30.00
No. 1 cupola cast.	43.00 to	46.00

Los Angeles

No. 1 hvy. melting		$30.00
No. 2 hvy. melting		28.00
No. 1 bundles		30.00
No. 2 bundles		28.00
No. 3 bundles		25.00
Mach. shop turn.		16.00
Elec. fur. 1 ft and under.	$42.00 to	45.00
No. 1 RR. hvy. melting		30.00
Scrap rails, random lgth.		30.00
No. 1 cupola cast.		52.00

Seattle

No. 1 hvy. melting		$28.00
No. 2 hvy. melting		28.00
No. 1 bundles		22.00
No. 2 bundles		22.00
No. 3 bundles		18.00
Elec. fur. 1 ft and under.	$40.00 to	45.00
RR. hvy. melting		29.00
No. 1 cupola cast		45.00

Hamilton, Ont.

No. 1 hvy. melting	$30.00
No. 1 bundles	30.00
No. 2 bundles	29.50
Mechanical bundles	28.00
Mixed steel scrap	26.00
Mixed bor. and turn.	23.00
Rails, remelting	30.00
Rails, rerolling	33.00
Bushelings	24.50
Bush., new fact. prep'd.	29.00
Bush., new fact, unprep'd.	23.00
Short steel turnings	23.00
Cast scrap	45.00

cast iron railroad car wheels

use:

Cast iron wheels are used by grey iron foundries in the making of new castings. They are particularly good scrap for the cupola because these wheels are heavy and are of uniform analysis forming a stable part of the cupola mixture. Though car wheels are broken up before being charged in the Cupola, they are accepted in the Open Hearth furnace without being broken. The veining on the inside rail of the wheel usually identifies cast iron from steel car wheels.

source:

Old Wheels from Railroad Cars.

This is one of a series illustrating the many and varied types of scrap required in the making of iron and steel for every use. Our national organization, manned by personnel who is steeped in every phase of scrap knowledge, is ready to meet your every scrap problem.

specifications:

Cast iron car and/or locomotive wheels

Comparison of Prices

Price advances over previous week are printed in Heavy Type; declines appear in *Italics*

Steel prices in this page are the average of various f.o.b. quotations of major producing areas: Pittsburgh, Chicago, Gary, Cleveland, Youngstown.

Flat-rolled Steel:

(cents per pound)	Jan. 16 1951	Jan. 9 1951	Dec. 19 1950	Jan. 17 1950
Hot-rolled sheets	3.60	3.60	3.60	3.35
Cold-rolled sheets.......	4.35	4.35	4.35	4.10
Galvanized sheets (10 ga)	4.80	4.80	4.80	4.40
Hot-rolled strip	3.50	3.50	3.50	3.25
Cold-rolled strip	4.75	4.75	4.75	4.21
Plate	3.70	3.70	3.70	3.50
Plates wrought iron.....	7.85	7.85	7.85	7.85
Stains C-R-strip (No. 302)	36.50	36.50	36.50	33.00

Tin and Terneplate:

(dollars per base box)				
Tinplate (1.50 lb) cokes.	$7.50	$7.50	$7.50	$7.50
Tinplate, electro (0.50 lb)	6.60	6.60	6.60	6.60
Special coated mfg. ternes	6.35	6.35	6.35	6.50

Bars and Shapes:

(cents per pound)				
Merchant bars	3.70	3.70	3.70	3.45
Cold finished bars	4.55	4.55	4.55	3.995
Alloy bars	4.30	4.30	4.30	3.95
Structural shapes	3.65	3.65	3.65	3.40
Stainless bars (No. 302).	31.25	31.25	31.25	28.50
Wrought iron bars	9.50	9.50	9.50	9.50

Wire:

(cents per pound)				
Bright wire	4.85	4.85	4.85	4.50

Rails:

(dollars per 100 lb)				
Heavy rails	$3.60	$3.60	$3.60	$3.40
Light rails	4.00	4.00	4.00	3.75

Semifinished Steel:

(dollars per net ton)				
Rerolling billets	$56.00	$56.00	$56.00	$54.00
Slabs, rerolling	56.00	56.00	56.00	54.00
Forging billets	66.00	66.00	66.00	63.00
Alloy blooms billets, slabs	70.00	70.00	70.00	66.00

Wire Rod and Skelp:

(cents per pound)				
Wire rods	4.10	4.10	4.10	3.85
Skelp	3.35	3.35	3.35	3.15

Pig Iron:

(per gross ton)	Jan. 16 1951	Jan. 9 1951	Dec. 19 1950	Jan. 17 1950
No. 2 foundry, del'd Phila..	$57.77	$57.77	$57.77	$50.42
No. 2, Valley furnace	52.50	52.50	52.50	46.50
No. 2, Southern Cin'ti....	55.58	55.58	55.58	47.08
No. 2, Birmingham	48.88	48.88	48.88	40.38
No. 2, foundry, Chicago†.	52.50	52.50	52.50	46.50
Basic del'd Philadelphia..	56.92	56.92	56.92	49.92
Basic, Valley furnace....	52.00	52.00	52.00	46.00
Malleable, Chicago†	52.50	52.50	52.50	46.50
Malleable, Valley	52.50	52.50	52.50	46.50
Charcoal, Chicago	70.56	70.56	70.56	68.56
Ferromanganese‡........	186.25	186.25	181.20	173.40

†The switching charge for delivery to foundries in the Chicago district is $1 per ton.
‡Average of U. S. prices quoted on Ferroalloy page.

Scrap:

(per gross ton)				
Heavy melt'g steel, P'gh.	$46.13	$46.13	$46.13	$29.75
Heavy melt'g steel, Phila.	49.50	44.50	44.50	23.00
Heavy melt'g steel, Ch'go	44.63	44.63	44.75	26.50
No. 1 hy. com. sh't, Det.	40.25	40.25	44.13	23.50
Low phos. Young'n	48.63	48.63	48.63	30.75
No. 1 cast, Pittsburgh ...	67.75	67.75	67.75	37.50
No. 1 cast, Philadelphia..	62.50	62.50	62.50	37.00
No. 1 cast, Chicago	63.00	63.00	65.00	38.50

Coke: Connellsville:

(per net ton at oven)				
Furnace coke, prompt...	$14.25	$14.25	$14.25	$14.00
Foundry coke, prompt...	17.25	17.25	17.25	15.75

Nonferrous Metals:

(cents per pound to large buyers)				
Copper, electro, Conn....	24.50	24.50	24.50	18.50
Copper, Lake, Conn.....	24.625	24.625	24.625	18.625
Tin Straits, New York..	$1.74†	$1.63*	1.55	76.25
Zinc, East St. Louis.....	17.50	17.50	17.50	9.75
Lead, St. Louis	16.80	16.80	16.80	11.80
Aluminum, virgin	19.00	19.00	19.00	17.00
Nickel, electrolytic	53.55	53.55	53.55	42.97
Magnesium, ingot	24.50	24.50	24.50	20.50
Antimony, Laredo, Tex...	32.00	32.00	32.00	28.75

†Tentative. *Revised.

Composite Prices

> Starting with the issue of May 12, 1949, the weighted finished steel composite was revised for the years 1941 to date. The weights used are based on the average product shipments for the 7 years 1937 to 1940 inclusive and 1946 to 1948 inclusive. The use of quarterly figures has been eliminated because it was too sensitive. (See p. 130 of May 12, 1949, issue.)

	Finished Steel Base Price	Pig Iron	Scrap Steel
Jan. 16, 1951	4.131¢ per lb	$52.69 per gross ton	$46.75 per gross ton
One week ago	4.131¢ per lb	52.69 per gross ton	45.09 per gross ton
One month ago	4.131¢ per lb	52.69 per gross ton	45.13 per gross ton
One year ago	3.837¢ per lb	46.05 per gross ton	26.42 per gross ton

	High		Low		High		Low		High		Low	
1951....	4.131¢	Jan. 2	4.131¢	Jan. 2	$52.69	Jan. 2	$52.69	Dec. 12	$46.75	Jan. 16	$45.09	Jan. 2
1950....	4.131¢	Dec. 1	3.837¢	Jan. 3	52.69	Dec. 12	45.88	Jan. 3	45.13	Dec. 19	26.25	Jan. 3
1949....	3.837¢	Dec. 27	3.3705¢	May 3	46.87	Jan. 18	45.88	Sept. 6	43.00	Jan. 4	19.33	June 28
1948....	3.721¢	July 27	3.193¢	Jan. 1	46.91	Oct. 12	39.58	Jan. 6	43.16	July 27	39.75	Mar. 9
1947....	3.193¢	July 29	2.848¢	Jan. 1	37.98	Dec. 30	30.14	Jan. 7	42.58	Oct. 28	29.50	May 20
1946....	2.848¢	Dec. 31	2.464¢	Jan. 1	30.14	Dec. 10	25.37	Jan. 1	31.17	Dec. 24	19.17	Jan. 1
1945....	2.464¢	May 29	2.396¢	Jan. 1	25.37	Oct. 23	23.61	Jan. 2	19.17	Jan. 2	18.92	May 22
1944....	2.396¢		2.396¢		$23.61		$23.61		19.17	Jan. 11	15.76	Oct. 24
1943....	2.396¢		2.396¢		23.61		23.61		$19.17		$19.17	
1942....	2.396¢		2.396¢		23.61		23.61		19.17		19.17	
1941....	2.396¢		2.396¢		$23.61	Mar. 20	$23.45	Jan. 2	$22.00	Jan. 7	$19.17	Apr. 10
1940....	2.30467¢	Jan. 2	2.24107¢	Apr. 16	23.45	Dec. 23	22.61	Jan. 2	21.83	Dec. 30	16.04	Apr. 9
1939....	2.35367¢	Jan. 3	2.26689¢	May 16	22.61	Sept. 19	20.61	Sept. 12	22.50	Oct. 3	14.08	May 16
1938....	2.58414¢	Jan. 4	2.27207¢	Oct. 18	23.25	June 21	19.61	July 6	15.00	Nov. 22	11.00	June 6
1937....	2.58414¢	Mar. 9	2.32263¢	Jan. 4	32.25	Mar. 9	20.25	Feb. 16	21.92	Mar. 30	12.67	June 9
1936....	2.32263¢	Dec. 28	2.05200¢	Mar. 10	19.74	Nov. 24	18.73	Aug. 11	17.75	Dec. 21	12.67	June 8
1932....	1.89196¢	July 5	1.83910¢	Mar. 1	14.81	Jan. 5	13.56	Dec. 6	8.50	Jan. 12	6.43	July 5
1929....	2.31773¢	May 28	2.26498¢	Oct. 29	18.71	May 14	18.21	Dec. 17	17.58	Jan. 29	14.08	Dec. 8

Weighted index based on steel bars, shapes, plates, wire, rails, black pipe, hot and cold-rolled sheets and strips, representing major portion of finished steel shipment. Index recapitulated in Aug. 28, 1941, issue and in May 12, 1949.

Based on averages for basic iron at Valley furnaces and foundry iron at Chicago, Philadelphia, Buffalo, Valley and Birmingham.

Average of No. 1 heavy melting steel scrap delivered to consumers at Pittsburgh, Philadelphia and Chicago.

January 18, 1951

Smaller numbers in price boxes indicate producing companies. For main office locations, see key on facing page.
Base prices at producing points apply only to sizes and grades produced in these areas. Prices are in cents per lb unless otherwise noted. Extras apply.

	Pittsburgh	Chicago	Gary	Cleveland	Canton Massillon	Middletown	Youngstown	Bethlehem	Buffalo	Conshohocken	Johnstown	Sparrows Point	Granite City	Detroit
INGOTS Carbon forging, net ton	$52.00[1]													
Alloy, net ton	$54.00[1,17]													$54.00[31]
BILLETS, BLOOMS, SLABS Carbon, rerolling, net ton	$56.00[1,5]	$56.00[1]	$56.00[1]						$56.00[3]		$56.00[3]			
Carbon forging billets, net ton	$66.00[1,5]	$66.00[1,4]	$66.00[1]	$66.00[4]	$66.00[4]				$66.00[3],[4]	$73.00[26]	$66.00[3]			$69.00[31]
Alloy, net ton	$70.00[1,17]	$70.00[1,4]	$70.00[1]		$70.00[4]			$70.00[3]	$70.00[3],[4]	$77.00[26]	$70.00[3]			$73.00[31]
PIPE SKELP	3.35[1] 3.45[5]						3.35[1,4]							
WIRE RODS	4.10[2] 4.30[18]	4.10[2,4,33]	4.10[6]	4.10[2]			4.10[6]				4.10[3]	4.20[3]		
SHEETS Hot-rolled (18 ga. & hvr.)	3.60[1,5,9,15] 3.75[28]	3.60[8,23]	3.60[1,6,8]	3.60[4]		3.60[7]	3.60[1,4,6] 4.00[13]		3.60[3]	4.00[26]		3.60[3]		3.80[12] 4.40[47]
Cold-rolled	4.35[1,5,9,15] 5.35[63]		4.35[1,6,8]	4.35[4]		4.35[7]	4.35[4,6]		4.35[3]			4.35[3]		4.55[12]
Galvanized (10 gage)	4.80[1,9,15]		4.80[1,8]		4.80[4]	4.80[7]	6.00[64]					4.80[3]		
Enameling (12 gage)	4.65[1]		4.65[1,8]			4.65[7]								
Long ternes (10 gage)	5.20[9,15]						6.00[64]							
HI str. low alloy, h.r.	5.40[1,5] 5.75[9]	5.40[1]	5.40[1,8] 5.90[6]	5.40[4]			5.40[1,4,13]		5.40[3]	5.65[26]		5.40[3]		
HI str. low alloy, c.r.	6.55[1,5] 6.90[9]		6.55[1,8] 7.05[6]	6.55[4]			6.55[4]		6.55[3]			6.55[3]		
HI str. low alloy, galv.	7.20[1]													
STRIP Hot-rolled	3.60[9], 4.00[41,58] 3.75[28] 3.50[5]	3.50[66]	3.50[1,6,8]			3.50[7]	3.50[1,4,6] 4.00[13]		3.50[3,4]	3.90[26]		3.50[3]		4.40[47]
Cold-rolled	4.65[5,9] 5.00[28] 5.35[63,58]	4.90[8,66]	4.90[8]	4.65[2]		4.65[7]	4.65[4,6] 5.35[13,40]		4.65[3]			4.65[3]		5.45[47] 5.60[68] 5.60[61]
HI str. low alloy, h.r.	5.75[9]		5.50[1] 5.30[8] 5.80[6]				4.95[4], 5.50[1] 5.40[13]			5.55[26]				
HI str. low alloy, c.r.	7.20[9]			6.70[5]			6.20[4], 6.55[13]							
TINPLATE† Cokes, 1.50-lb base box 1.25 lb, deduct 25¢	$8.70[1,9,15]		$8.70[1,6]				$8.70[4]					8.80[3]		
Electrolytic 0.25, 0.50, 0.75 lb box	Deduct $1.55, $1.30 and 90¢ respectively from 1.50-lb coke base box price													
BLACKPLATE, 29 gage Hollowware enameling	5.85[1] 6.15[15]		5.85[1]				5.30[4]							
BARS Carbon steel	3.70[1,5] 3.85[9]	3.70[1,4,23]	3.70[1,4,6,8]	3.70[4]	3.70[4]		3.70[1,4,6]		3.70[3,4]		3.70[3]			3.85[31]
Reinforcing‡	3.70[1,5]	3.70[4]	3.70[1,6,8]	3.70[4]			3.70[1,4]		3.70[3,4]		3.70[3]	3.70[3]		
Cold-finished	4.55[2,4,5, 52,71]	4.55[2,69,70, 23,73]	4.55[74,73]	4.55[2]	4.55[4,82]									4.70[84]
Alloy, hot-rolled	4.30[1,17]	4.30[1,4,23]	4.30[1,6,8]		4.30[4]		4.30[1,6]	4.30[3]	4.30[3,4]		4.30[3]			4.45[31]
Alloy, cold-drawn	5.40[17,52, 69,71]	5.40[4,23,69, 70,73]	5.40[4] 5.90[74]		5.40[4,82]			5.40[3]	5.40[3]					5.55[84]
HI str. low alloy, h.r.	5.55[1,5]		5.55[1,8] 6.05[6]	5.55[4]			5.55[1]	5.55[3]	5.55[3]		5.55[3]			
PLATE Carbon steel	3.70[1,5,15]	3.70[1]	3.70[1,6,8]	3.70[4] 4.00[9]			3.70[1,4] 3.95[13]		3.70[3]	4.15[26]	3.70[3]	3.70[3]		
Floor plates			4.75[8]	4.75[5]						4.75[26]				
Alloy	4.75[1] 4.85	4.75[1]	4.75[1]				5.20[13]			5.05[26]	4.75[3]	4.75[3]		
HI str. low alloy	5.65[1,5]	5.65[1]	5.65[1,8]	5.65[4,5]			5.65[4] 5.70[13]			5.90[26]	5.65[3]	5.65[3]		
SHAPES, Structural	3.65[1,5] 3.90[9]	3.65[1,23]	3.65[1,8]						3.70[3]	3.70[3]		3.70[3]		
HI str. low alloy	5.50[1,5]	5.50[1]	5.50[1,8]						5.50[3]	5.50[3]		5.50[3]		
MANUFACTURERS' WIRE Bright	4.85[2,5] 5.10[18]	4.85[2] 4.33		4.85[2]					Kokomo = 5.80[30]			4.85[3]	4.95[3]	Duluth = 4.85[2]
PILING, Steel Sheet	4.45[1]	4.45[1]	4.45[8]						4.45[3]					

STEEL PRICES

Smaller numbers indicate producing companies. See key at right.
Prices are in cents per lb unless otherwise noted. Extras apply.

Kansas City	Houston	Birmingham	WEST COAST Seattle, San Francisco, Los Angeles, Fontana	(other)	Category
			F=$79.00[19]		**INGOTS** carbon forging, net ton
	$62.00[83]		F=$80.00[19]		Alloy, net ton
		$56.00[11]	F=$75.00[19]		**BILLETS, BLOOMS, SLABS** Carbon, rerolling, net ton
	$74.00[83]	$66.00[11]	F=$85.00[19] SF, LA, S=$85.00[62]		Carbon forging billets, net ton
	$78.00[83]		F=$89.00[19] LA=$90.00[62]		Alloy net ton
					PIPE SKELP
4.50[83]		4.10[4,11]	SF=4.90[2] LA=4.90[24,62]	Worcester=4.40[2] Minnequa=4.35[14]	**WIRE RODS**
		3.60[4,11]	SF, LA=4.30[24] F=4.55[19]	Niles=5.25[54], Geneva=3.70[16]	**SHEETS** Hot-rolled (18 ga. & hvr.)
		4.35[11]	SF=5.30[24] F=5.30[19]		Cold-rolled
		4.80[4,11]	SF, LA=5.55[24]	Ashland=4.80[7]	Galvanized (10 gage)
					Enameling (12 gage)
					Long ternes (10 gage)
		5.40[11]	F=6.35[19]		Hi str. low alloy, h.r.
			F=7.50[19]		Hi str. low alloy, c.r.
					Hi str. low alloy, galv.
4.10[83]	4.90[83]	3.50[4]	SF, LA=4.25[24,62] F=4.75[19], S=4.50[62]	Atlanta=4.05[65] Minnequa=4.55[14]	**STRIP** Hot-rolled
			F=6.30[19] LA=6.40[27]	New Haven=5.15[2], 5.85[68]	Cold-rolled
		5.30[11]	F=6.20[19]		Hi str. low alloy, h.r.
					Hi str. low a'loy, c.r.
					TINPLATE Cokes, 1.50-lb base box 1.25 lb. deduct 20¢
					Electrolytic 0.25, 0.50, 0.75 lb box
					BLACKPLATE, 29 gage Hollowware enameling
4.30[83]	4.10[83]	3.70[4,11]	SF, LA=4.40[24]	Atlanta=4.25[65] Minnequa=4.15[14]	**BARS** Carbon steel
4.30[83]	4.10[83]	3.70[4,11]	SF, S=4.45[62] F=4.40[19] LA=4.40[62]	Atlanta=4.25[65] Minnequa=4.50[14]	Reinforcing‡
				Newark=5.00[69] Putnam=5.10[69] Hartford=5.10[4] Los Angeles=6.00[4]	Cold-finished
4.90[83]	4.70[83]		LA=5.35[62] F=5.35[19]		Alloy, hot-rolled
				Newark=5.75[69] Worcester=[2] Hartford=5.85[4]	Alloy, cold-drawn
		5.55[11]	F=6.60[19]		Hi str. low alloy, h.r.
	4.10[83]	3.70[4,11]	F=4.30[19] S=4.60[62] Geneva=3.70[16]	Claymont=4.15[29] Coatesville=4.15[21] Minnequa=4.50[14]	**PLATE** Carbon steel
				Harrisburg=5.25[35]	Floor plates
			F=5.70[19] Geneva=5.65[16]	Coatesville=5.25[21] Claymont=4.85[29]	Alloy
		5.65[11]	F=6.25[19]		Hi str. low alloy
4.25[83]	4.05[83]	3.65[4,11]	SF, LA=4.20[62] F=4.25[16] LA=4.25[24,62] S=4.30[62]	Geneva 3.65[16] Minnequa 4.10[14]	**SHAPES, Structural**
		50[11]	F=6.10[19]		Hi str. low-alloy
5.45[83]	5.25[83]	4.85[4,11]	SF, LA=5.80[24]	Atlanta=5.10[65] Worcester=5.15[2] Minnequa=5.10[14]	**MANUFACTURERS' WIRE** Bright

Deduct $1.55, $1.30 and 90¢ respectively from 1.50-lb coke base box price

KEY TO STEEL PRODUCERS

1 U. S. Steel Co., Pittsburgh
2 American Steel & Wire Co., Cleveland
3 Bethlehem Steel Co., Bethlehem
4 Republic Steel Corp., Cleveland
5 Jones & Laughlin Steel Corp., Pittsburgh
6 Youngstown Sheet & Tube Co., Youngstown
7 Armco Steel Corp., Middletown, Ohio
8 Inland Steel Co., Chicago
9 Weirton Steel Co., Weirton, W. Va.
10 National Tube Co., Pittsburgh
11 Tennessee Coal, Iron & R. R. Co., Birmingham
12 Great Lakes Steel Corp., Detroit
13 Sharon Steel Corp., Sharon, Pa.
14 Colorado Fuel & Iron Corp., Denver
15 Wheeling Steel Corp., Wheeling, W. Va.
16 Geneva Steel Co., Salt Lake City
17 Crucible Steel Co. of America, New York
18 Pittsburgh Steel Co., Pittsburgh
19 Kaiser Steel Corp., Oakland, Calif.
20 Portsmouth Div., Detroit Steel Corp., Detroit
21 Lukens Steel Co., Coatesville, Pa.
22 Granite City Steel Co., Granite City, Ill.
23 Wisconsin Steel Co., South Chicago, Ill.
24 Columbia Steel Co., San Francisco
25 Copperweld Steel Co., Glassport, Pa.
26 Alan Wood Steel Co., Conshohocken, Pa.
27 Calif. Cold Rolled Steel Corp., Los Angeles
28 Allegheny Ludlum Steel Corp., Pittsburgh
29 Worth Steel Co., Claymont, Del.
30 Continental Steel Corp., Kokomo, Ind.
31 Rotary Electric Steel Co., Detroit
32 Laclede Steel Co., St. Louis
33 Northwestern Steel & Wire Co., Sterling, Ill.
34 Keystone Steel & Wire Co., Peoria, Ill.
35 Central Steel & Wire Co., Harrisburg, Pa.
36 Carpenter Steel Co., Reading, Pa.
37 Eastern Stainless Steel Corp., Baltimore
38 Washington Steel Corp., Washington, Pa
39 Jessop Steel Co., Washington, Pa.
40 Blair Strip Steel Co., New Castle, Pa.
41 Superior Steel Corp., Carnegie, Pa.
42 Timken Steel & Tube Div., Canton, Ohio
43 Babcock & Wilcox Tube Co., Beaver Falls, Pa.
44 Reeves Steel & Mfg. Co., Dover, Ohio
45 John A. Roebling's Sons Co., Trenton, N. J.
46 Simonds Saw & Steel Co., Fitchburg, Mass.
47 McLouth Steel Corp., Detroit
48 Cold Metal Products Co., Youngstown
49 Thomas Steel Co., Warren, Ohio
50 Wilson Steel & Wire Co., Chicago
51 Sweet's Steel Co., Williamsport, Pa.
52 Superior Drawn Steel Co., Monaca, Pa.
53 Tremont Nail Co., Wareham, Mass.
54 Firth Sterling St. & Carbide Corp., McKeesport
55 Ingersoll Steel Div., Chicago
56 Phoenix Iron & Steel Co., Phoenixville, Pa
57 Fitzsimmons Steel Co., Youngstown
58 Stanley Works, New Britain, Conn.
59 Universal-Cyclops Steel Corp., Bridgeville, Pa
60 American Cladmetals Co., Carnegie, Pa.
61 Cuyahoga Steel & Wire Co., Cleveland
62 Bethlehem Pacific Coast Steel Corp., San Fran.
63 Follansbee Steel Corp., Pittsburgh
64 Niles Rolling Mill Co., Niles, Ohio
65 Atlantic Steel Co., Atlanta
66 Acme Steel Co., Chicago
67 Joslyn Mfg. & Supply Co., Chicago
68 Detroit Steel Corp., Detroit
69 Wyckoff Steel Co., Pittsburgh
70 Bliss & Laughlin, Inc., Harvey, Ill.
71 Columbia Steel & Shafting Co., Pittsburgh
72 Cumberland Steel Co., Cumberland, Md.
73 La Salle Steel Co., Chicago
74 Monarch Steel Co., Inc. Hammond, Ind.
75 Empire Steel Co., Mansfield, Ohio
76 Mahoning Valley Steel Co., Niles, Ohio
77 Oliver Iron & Steel Co., Pittsburgh
78 Pittsburgh Screw & Bolt Co., Pittsburgh
79 Standard Forging Corp., Chicago
80 Driver Harris Co., Harrison, N. J.
81 Detroit Tube & Steel Div., Detroit
82 Reliance Div., Eaton Mfg. Co., Massillon, Ohio
83 Sheffield Steel Corp., Kansas City
84 Plymouth Steel Co., Detroit
85 Wickwire Spencer Steel, Buffalo
86 Angell Nail and Chaplet, Cleveland
87 Mid-States Steel & Wire, Crawfordsville, Ind
88 National Supply, Pittsburgh, Pa.
89 Wheatland Tube Co., Wheatland, Pa.
90 Mercer Tube & Mfg. Co., Sharon, Pa.
91 Woodward Iron Co., Woodward, Ala.
92 Sloss-Sheffield Steel & Iron Co., Birmingham
93 Hanna Furnace Corp., Buffalo
94 Interlake Iron Corp., Cleveland
95 Lone Star Steel Co., Dallas
96 Mystic Iron Works, Everett, Mass.
97 Jackson Iron & Steel Co., Jackson, O.
98 Globe Iron Co., Jackson, O.
99 Pittsburgh Coke & Chemical Co., Pittsburgh
100 Shenango Furnace Co., Pittsburgh
101 Tennessee Products & Chemical Corp., Nashville
102 Koppers Co., Inc., Granite City, Ill.

STAINLESS STEELS

Base price, cents per lb, f.o.b. mill.

Product	301	302	303	304	316	321	347	410	416	430
Ingots, rerolling	14.25	15.00	16.50	16.00	24.25	19.75	21.50	12.75	14.75	13.00
Slabs, billets rerolling	18.50	19.75	21.75	20.75	31.75	26.00	28.25	16.50	20.00	16.75
Forg. discs, die blocks, rings.	34.00	34.00	36.50	35.50	52.50	40.00	44.50	28.00	28.50	28.50
Billets, forging	26.25	26.25	28.25	27.50	41.00	31.00	34.75	21.50	22.00	22.00
Bars, wires, structurals	31.25	31.25	33.75	32.75	48.75	36.75	41.25	25.75	26.25	26.25
Plates	33.00	33.00	35.00	35.00	51.50	40.50	45.00	27.00	27.50	27.50
Sheets	41.00	41.00	43.00	43.00	56.50	49.00	53.50	36.50	37.00	39.00
Strip, hot-rolled	26.50	28.00	32.25	30.00	48.25	36.75	41.00	23.50	30.25	24.00
Strip, cold-rolled	34.00	36.50	40.00	38.50	58.50	48.00	52.00	30.50	37.00	31.00

STAINLESS STEEL PRODUCING POINTS—*Sheets:* Midland, Pa., 17; Brackenridge, Pa., 28; Butler, Pa., 7; McKeesport, Pa., 1; Washington, Pa., 38 (type 316 add 5¢), 39; Baltimore, 37; Middletown, Ohio, 7; Massillon, Ohio, 4; Gary, 1; Bridgeville, Pa., 59; New Castle, Ind., 55; Ft. Wayne, Ind., 67; Lockport, N. Y., 46.

Strip: Midland, Pa., 17; Cleveland, 2; Carnegie, Pa., 41; McKeesport, Pa., 54; Reading, Pa., 36; Washington, Pa., 38 (type 316 add 5¢); W. Leechburg, Pa., 28; Bridgeville, Pa., 59; Detroit, 47; Massillon, Canton, Ohio, 4; Middletown, Ohio, 7; Harrison, N. J., 80; Youngstown, 48; Lockport, N. Y., 46; New Britain, Conn., 58; Sharon, Pa., 13; Butler, Pa., 7.

Bars: Baltimore, 7; Duquesne, Pa. 1; Munhall, Pa., 1; Reading, Pa., 36; Titusville, Pa., 59; Washington, Pa., 39; McKeesport, Pa., 1, 54; Bridgeville, Pa., 59; Dunkirk, N. Y., 28; Massillon, Ohio, 4; Chicago, 1; Syracuse, N. Y., 17; Watervliet, N. Y., 28; Waukegan, Ill., 2; Lockport, N. Y., 46; Canton, Ohio, 42; Ft. Wayne, Ind., 67.

Wire: Waukegan, Ill., 2; Massillon, Ohio, 4; McKeesport, Pa., 54; Bridgeport, Conn., 44; Ft. Wayne, Ind., 67; Trenton, N. J., 45; Harrison, N. J., 80; Baltimore, 7; Dunkirk, 28.

Structurals: Baltimore, 7; Massillon, Ohio, 4; Chicago, 1, 67; Watervliet, N. Y., 28; Bridgeport, Conn., 44.

Plates: Brackenridge, Pa., 28 (type 416 add ½¢); Butler, Pa., 7; Chicago, 1; Munhall, Pa., 1; Midland, Pa., 17; New Castle, Ind., 55; Lockport, N. Y., 46; Middletown, 7; Washington, Pa., 39; Cleveland, Massillon, 4.

Forged discs, die blocks, rings: Pittsburgh, 1, 17; Syracuse, 17; Ferndale, Mich., 28.

Forging billets: Midland, Pa., 17; Baltimore, 7; Washington, Pa., 39; McKeesport, 54; Massillon, Canton, Ohio, 4; Watervliet, 28; Pittsburgh, Chicago, 1.

RAILS, TRACK SUPPLIES

F.o.b. Mill Cents Per Lb	No. 1 Std. Rails	Light Rails	Joint Bars	Track Spikes	Axles	Screw Spikes	Tie Plates	Track Bolts Untreated
Bessemer-1	3.60	4.00	4.70	....	....	....	....	....
Chicago-4	....	....	....	6.15	....	....	....	....
Ensley-11	3.60	4.00	....	....	....	....	....	....
Fairfield-11	....	4.00	4.40	....	....	8.60	4.50	....
Gary-1	3.60	4.00	....	....	....	....	4.50	....
Ind. Harbor-8	3.60	....	4.70	6.15	5.25	8.60	4.50	....
Johnstown-3	....	4.00	....	....	5.60	8.60	....	....
Joliet-1	....	4.00	4.70	....	....	....	....	....
Kansas City-83	....	....	....	6.40	....	....	....	....
Lackawanna-3	3.60	4.00	4.70	....	....	8.60	4.50	....
Lebanon-3	....	....	....	6.15	....	....	....	9.60
Minnequa-14	3.60	4.50	4.70	6.15	....	8.60	4.50	9.60
Pittsburgh-77	....	....	....	....	....	9.35	....	9.60
Pittsburgh-78	....	....	....	....	....	....	....	9.60
Pittsburgh-5	....	....	....	6.15	....	....	....	....
Pittsburg-24	....	....	....	....	....	....	4.65	....
Seattle-62	....	....	....	6.10	....	....	4.35	....
Steelton-3	3.60	....	4.70	....	....	....	4.50	....
Struthers-6	....	....	....	6.15	....	....	....	....
Torrance-24	....	....	....	....	....	....	4.65	....
Youngstown-4	....	....	....	6.15	....	....	....	....

Track Bolts, heat treated, to railroads, 9.85¢ per lb.

BOILER TUBES

Seamless steel, electric welded commercial boiler tubes, locomotive tubes, minimum wall, per 100 *ft at mill, c.l. lots, cut lengths* 10 *to* 24 *ft.*

OD in in.	gage BWG	Seamless H.R.	Seamless C.D.	Electric Weld H.R.	Electric Weld C.D.
2	13	$22.67	$26.66	$21.99	$25.86
2½	12	30.48	35.84	29.57	34.76
3	12	33.90	39.90	32.89	34.80
3½	11	42.37	49.89	41.10	48.39
4	10	52.60	61.88	51.03	60.02

Pittsburgh Steel add, H-R: 2 in., 62¢; 2½ in., 84¢; 3 in., 92¢; 3½ in., $1.17; 4 in., $1.45. Add, C-R: 2 in., 74¢; 2½ in., 99¢; 3 in., $1.10; 3½ in., $1.37; 4 in., $1.70.

FLUORSPAR

Washed gravel fluorspar, f.o.b. cars, Rosiclare, Ill. Base price, per ton net: Effective CaF_2 content:

70% or more $41.00
60% or less 38.00

MERCHANT WIRE PRODUCTS

F.o.b. Mill	Standard & Coated Nails, Base Col.	Woven Wire Fence 9-15½ ga., Base Col.	Fence Posts, Base Col.	Single Loop Bale Ties, Base Col.	Twisted Barbless Wire, Base Col.	Gal. Barbed Wire, Base Col.	Merch. Wire Ann'ld., ¢/lb.	Merch. Wire Gal., ¢/lb.
Alabama City-4	118	126	....	123	....	136	5.70	5.95
Aliquippa, Pa.-5	118	132	....	....	136	140	5.70	6.15
Atlanta-65	113	133	....	126	126	143	5.95	6.40
Bartonville-34	118	130	140	123	143	143	5.95	6.15
Buffalo-85	....	....	....	....	....	....	....	....
Cleveland-86	....	....	....	....	....	....	....	....
Cleveland-2	....	....	....	....	....	....	5.70	6.15
Crawfordsville-87	....	132	....	....	....	145	5.95	6.40
Donora, Pa.-2	118	130	....	123	....	140	5.70	6.15
Duluth-2	118	130	....	123	....	140	5.70	6.15
Fairfield, Ala.-11	118	130	....	123	....	136	5.70	6.15
Houston-83	126	138	....	....	....	148	6.10	6.55
Johnstown, Pa.-3	118	130	....	....	140	....	5.70	6.15
Joliet, Ill.-2	118	130	....	123	....	140	5.70	6.15
Kokomo, Ind.-30	120	132	....	125	138	138	5.80	6.05
Los Angeles-62	....	....	....	....	....	....	6.65	....
Kansas City-83	130	130	142	135	....	152	6.30	6.75
Minnequa-14	123	138	130	128	146	146	5.95	6.45
Monessen-18	124	135	....	....	....	145	5.95	6.40
Moline, Ill.-4	....	....	136	....	....	....	....	....
Palmer-85	....	....	....	....	....	....	....	....
Pittsburg, Cal.-24	137	149	....	147	156	160	6.65	6.80
Portsmouth-20	124	137	....	....	147	147	6.10	6.60
Rankin, Pa.-2	118	130	....	....	....	140	5.70	6.15
So. Chicago, Ill.-4	118	126	140	123	....	136	5.70	5.95
S. San Fran.-14	....	....	....	147	....	160	6.65	7.10
Sparrows Pt.-3	120	....	....	125	142	142	5.80	6.25
Sterling, Ill.-33	118	130	140	123	140	140	5.70	6.15
Struthers, Ohio-6	....	....	....	....	....	....	5.70	6.15
Torrance, Cal.-24	138	....	....	....	....	....	6.65	....
Worcester-2	124	....	....	....	....	....	6.00	6.45
Williamsport, Pa.-51	....	....	150	....	....	....	....	....

Cut Nails, carloads, base, $6.75 per 100 lb. (less 20¢ to jobbers) at Conshohocken, Pa., (26), Wareham, Mass. (53) Wheeling, W. Va., (15).

CAST IRON WATER PIPE

Per net ton

6 to 24-in., del'd Chicago . $105.30 to $108.80
6 to 24-in., del'd N. Y. ... 104.50 to 105.50
6 to 24-in., Birmingham . 91.50 to 96.00
6-in. and larger, f.o.b. cars, San Francisco, Los Angeles, for all rail shipment; rail and water shipment less .... $108.50 to $113.00
Class "A" and gas pipe, $5 extra; 4-in. pipe is $5 a ton above 6-in.

PIPE AND TUBING

Base discounts, f.o.b. mills. Base price about $200 per net ton.

	Buttweld ½ In. Blk.	Buttweld ½ In. Gal.	Buttweld ¾ In. Blk.	Buttweld ¾ In. Gal.	Buttweld 1 In. Blk.	Buttweld 1 In. Gal.	Buttweld 1¼ In. Blk.	Buttweld 1¼ In. Gal.	Buttweld 1½ In. Blk.	Buttweld 1½ In. Gal.	Buttweld 2 In. Blk.	Buttweld 2 In. Gal.	Buttweld 2½-3 In. Blk.	Buttweld 2½-3 In. Gal.	Seamless 2 In. Blk.	Seamless 2 In. Gal.	Seamless 2½-3 In. Blk.	Seamless 2½-3 In. Gal.	Seamless 3½-4 In. Blk.	Seamless 3½-4 In. Gal.
STANDARD T. & C.																				
Sparrows Pt.-3	34.0	12.0	37.0	16.0	39.5	19.5	40.0	20.0	40.5	21.0	41.0	21.5	41.5	22.0	....	....	....	....	....	....
Cleveland-4	36.0	14.0	39.0	18.0	41.5	21.5	42.0	22.0	42.5	23.0	43.0	23.5	43.5	24.0	....	....	....	....	....	....
Oakland-19	25.0	3.0	28.0	7.0	30.5	10.5	31.0	21.0	31.5	22.0	32.0	12.5	32.5	13.0	....	....	....	....	....	....
Pittsburgh-5	36.0	14.0	39.0	17.0	41.5	19.5	42.0	20.5	42.5	21.0	43.0	21.5	43.5	22.5	29.5	8.0	32.5	11.5	34.5	13.5
Pittsburgh-10	36.0	14.0	39.0	18.0	41.5	21.5	42.0	22.0	42.5	23.0	43.0	23.5	43.5	24.0	29.5	9.5	32.5	12.5	34.5	14.5
St. Louis-32	35.0	13.0	38.0	17.0	40.5	20.5	41.0	21.0	41.5	22.0	42.0	22.5	42.5	23.0	....	....	....	....	....	....
Sharon-90	36.0	13.0	39.0	17.0	41.5	20.0	42.0	20.5	42.5	21.0	43.0	21.5	43.5	22.0	....	....	....	....	....	....
Toledo-88	36.0	14.0	39.0	18.0	41.5	21.5	42.0	22.0	42.5	23.0	43.0	23.5	43.5	24.0	29.5	....	32.5	....	34.5	....
Wheeling-15	36.0	14.0	39.0	18.0	41.5	21.5	42.0	22.0	42.5	23.0	43.0	23.5	43.5	24.0	....	....	....	....	....	....
Wheatland-89	36.0	14.0	39.0	17.0	41.5	19.5	42.0	20.5	42.5	21.0	43.0	21.5	43.5	22.5	....	....	....	....	....	....
Youngstown-6	36.0	14.0	39.0	18.0	41.5	21.5	42.0	22.0	42.5	23.0	43.0	23.5	43.5	24.0	29.5	9.5	32.5	12.5	34.5	14.5
EXTRA STRONG, PLAIN ENDS																				
Sparrows Pt.-3	33.5	13.0	37.5	17.0	39.5	20.5	40.0	21.0	40.5	22.0	41.0	22.5	41.5	23.0	....	....	....	....	....	....
Cleveland-4	35.5	15.0	39.5	19.0	41.5	22.5	42.0	23.0	42.5	24.0	43.0	24.5	43.5	25.0	....	....	....	....	....	....
Oakland-19	24.5	4.0	28.5	18.0	30.5	11.5	31.0	12.0	31.5	13.0	32.0	13.5	32.5	14.0	....	....	....	....	....	....
Pittsburgh-5	35.5	13.5	39.5	17.5	41.5	19.5	42.0	20.5	42.5	21.0	43.0	21.5	43.5	22.5	29.0	7.5	33.0	12.0	36.0	15.5
Pittsburgh-10	35.5	15.0	39.5	19.0	41.5	22.5	42.0	23.0	42.5	24.0	43.0	24.5	43.5	25.0	29.0	10.0	33.0	14.0	36.5	17.5
St. Louis-32	34.5	14.0	38.5	18.0	40.5	21.5	41.0	22.0	41.5	23.0	42.0	23.5	42.5	24.0	....	....	....	....	....	....
Sharon-90	35.5	14.0	39.5	18.0	41.5	21.0	42.0	21.5	42.5	22.0	43.0	22.5	43.5	23.0	....	....	....	....	....	....
Toledo-88	35.5	15.0	39.5	19.0	41.5	22.5	42.0	23.0	42.5	24.0	43.0	24.5	43.5	25.0	29.0	....	33.0	....	36.5	....
Wheeling-15	35.5	15.0	39.5	19.0	41.5	22.5	42.0	23.0	42.5	24.0	43.0	24.5	43.5	25.0	....	....	....	....	....	....
Wheatland-89	35.5	13.5	39.5	17.5	41.5	19.5	42.0	20.5	42.5	21.0	43.0	21.5	43.5	22.5	....	....	....	....	....	....
Youngstown-6	35.5	15.0	39.5	19.0	41.5	22.5	42.0	23.0	42.5	24.0	43.0	24.5	43.5	25.0	29.0	10.0	33.0	14.0	36.5	17.5

Galvanized discounts based on zinc at 17¢ per lb, East St. Louis. For each 1¢ change in zinc, discounts vary as follows: ½ in., ¾ in., and 1 in., 1 pt.; 1¼ in., 1½ in., 2 in., ¾ pt.; 2½ in., 3 in., ½ pt. Calculate discounts on even cents per lb of zinc, i.e., if zinc is 16.51¢ to 17.50¢ per lb, use 17¢. Jones & Laughlin discounts apply only when zinc price changes 1¢.

Threads only, buttweld and seamless, 1 pt. higher discount. Plain ends, buttweld and seamless, 3 in. and under, 3½ pts. higher discount. Buttweld jobbers' discount, 5 pct.

Base price, f.o.b., dollars per 100 lb. *(Metropolitan area delivery, add 20¢ except Birmingham, San Francisco, Cincinnati, New Orleans, St. Paul, add 15¢; Memphis, add 10¢; Philadelphia, add 25¢; New York, add 30¢).

Cities	Sheets Hot-Rolled	Sheets Cold-Rolled (15 gage)	Sheets Galvanized (10 gage)	Strip Hot-Rolled	Strip Cold-Rolled	Plates	Shapes Standard Structural	Bars Hot-Rolled	Bars Cold-Finished	Alloy Bars Hot-Rolled A 4615 As rolled	Alloy Bars Hot-Rolled A 4140 Annealed	Alloy Bars Cold-Drawn A 4615 As rolled	Alloy Bars Cold-Drawn A 4140 Annealed
Baltimore	5.60	6.84 / 8.07	7.49[2]	6.04		5.80	6.14	6.04	6.84 / 6.89	10.24	10.54	11.89	12.19
Birmingham*	5.60	6.40	6.75	5.55		5.95	5.70	5.55					
Boston	6.20	7.00 / 7.25	7.74 / 8.29	6.15	8.50[4]	6.48 / 6.78	6.20	6.05	6.79 / 6.84	10.25	10.55	11.90 / 12.00	12.20 / 12.30
Buffalo	5.60	6.40	7.74 / 8.09	5.86		6.05	5.80	5.60	6.40 / 6.45 / 6.85	10.15 / 10.85	10.45	11.80	11.95 / 12.10
Chicago	5.60	6.40	7.75	5.55		5.80	5.70	5.55	6.30	9.80	10.10	11.45	11.75
Cincinnati*	5.87	6.44	7.39	5.80		6.19	6.09	5.80	6.61	10.15	10.45	11.80	12.10
Cleveland	5.60	6.40	8.10	5.69	6.90	5.92	5.82	5.57	6.40	9.91	10.21	11.56	11.86
Detroit	5.78	6.53	7.89	5.94		5.99	6.09	5.84	6.56	10.11	10.41	11.76	12.06
Houston	7.00	8.25				6.85		6.65	9.35	10.35	11.25		12.75
Indianapolis, del'd	6.00	6.80	8.15	5.95		6.20	6.10	5.95	6.80				
Kansas City	6.00	6.80	7.45	6.15	7.50	6.40	6.30	6.15	7.00	10.40	10.70	12.05	12.35
Los Angeles	6.35	7.90	8.85	6.40	9.45[6]	6.40	6.35	6.35	8.20	11.30	11.30	13.20	13.50
Memphis*	6.33 / 6.38	7.08 / 7.18		6.33 / 6.38		6.43 / 8.02	6.33 / 6.48	6.08 / 6.33	7.16 / 7.32				
Milwaukee	5.74	6.54	7.89	5.69 / 6.59		5.94	5.84	5.69	6.44 / 6.54	9.94	10.24	11.59	11.89
New Orleans*	5.70	6.59		5.75	7.25	5.95	5.75	5.75	7.30				
New York*	5.67 / 5.97	7.19[5] / 7.24[1]	8.14[2]	6.29 / 6.89	8.63[4]	6.28 / 6.58	6.10	6.12	6.99	10.05 / 10.15	10.35 / 10.45	11.70 / 11.80	12.10 / 12.20
Norfolk	6.50[3]					6.50[3]	6.60[3]	6.55[3]					
Philadelphia*	5.90	6.55	8.00	6.10		6.05	5.90	6.05	6.61	9.90	10.20		
Pittsburgh	5.60	6.40	7.75	5.65 / 5.95		5.75	5.70	5.55	6.15	9.80	10.10	11.45	11.75
Portland	6.60 / 7.55	8.95	8.50 / 9.10	7.30		6.80	6.95	6.90		12.15			
Salt Lake City	7.95		9.70	8.70		8.05	8.30	8.65	9.00				
San Francisco*	6.65	8.05[2] / 8.90[2]	8.55	6.60	9.45[6]	6.50	6.45	6.45	8.20	11.30	11.30	13.20	13.20 / 13.50
Seattle	7.05	8.60	9.20	9.05		6.75	6.65	6.75	9.05				
St. Louis	5.80 / 5.85	6.65	8.00	5.80	8.00[4] / 8.28	6.13	6.03	5.80	6.55 / 6.65	10.05	10.35	11.70	12.00
St. Paul*	6.16	6.96	8.31	6.11		6.36	6.26	6.11	6.96	10.36	10.66	12.01	12.31

BASE QUANTITIES (Standard unless otherwise keyed): Cold finished bars; 2000 lb or over. Alloy bars; 1000 to 1999 lb. All others; 2000 to 9999 lb. All HR products may be combined for quantity. All galvanized sheets may be combined for quantity. CR sheets may not be combined with each other or with galvanized sheets for quantity.
EXCEPTIONS: (1) 400 to 1499 lb; (2) 450 to 1499 lb; (3) 400 to 1999 lb; (4) 6000 lb and over; (5) 1500 to 9999 lb.; (6) 2000 to 5999 lb.

PIG IRON

Dollars per gross ton, f.o.b., subject to switching charges.

Producing Point	Basic	No. 2 Foundry	Malleable	Bessemer	Low Phos.	Blast Furnace Silvery	Low Phos. Charcoal
Bethlehem-3	54.00	54.50	55.00	55.50			
Birmingham-4	48.38	48.88					
Birmingham-91	48.38	48.88					
Birmingham-92	48.38	48.88					
Buffalo-4	52.00	52.50	53.00				
Buffalo-93	52.00	52.50	53.00			63.75	
Chicago-94	52.00	52.50	52.50	53.00			
Cleveland-2	52.00	52.50	52.50	53.00	57.00		
Cleveland-4	52.00	52.50	52.50				
Daingerfield, Tex.-95	48.00	48.50	48.50				
Duluth-94	52.00	52.50	52.50	53.00			
Erie-94	52.00	52.50	52.50	53.00			
Everett, Mass.-96		53.25	53.75				
Fontana-19	58.00	58.50					
Geneva, Utah-16	52.00	52.50	52.50	53.00			
Granite City, Ill.-102	53.90	54.40	54.90				
Hubbard, O.-6	52.00	52.50	52.50				
Ironton, Utah-16	52.00	52.50					
Jackson, O.-97,98						62.50	
Lyle, Tenn.-101							66.00
Monessen-18	54.00						
Neville Island-99	52.00	52.50	52.50	53.00			
Pittsburgh-1	52.00			53.00			
Sharpsville-100	52.00	52.50	52.50	53.00			
Steelton-3	54.00	54.50	55.00	55.50	60.00		
Swedeland-26	56.00	56.50	57.00	57.50			
Toledo-94	52.00	52.50	52.50	53.00			
Troy, N. Y.-4	54.00	54.50	55.00		60.00		
Youngstown-6	52.00	52.50	52.50	53.00			

DIFFERENTIALS: Add 50¢ per ton for each 0.25 pct silicon over base (1.75 to 2.25 pct), 50¢ per ton for each 0.50 pct manganese over 1 pct, $2 per ton for 0.5 to 0.75 pct nickel, $1 for each additional 0.25 pct nickel. Subtract 38¢ per ton for phosphorus content over 0.70 pct. Silvery iron: Add $1.50 per ton for each 0.50 pct silicon over base (6.01 to 6.50 pct) up to 17 pct. $1 per ton for 0.75 pct or more phosphorus, manganese as above. Bessemer ferrosilicon prices are $1 over comparable silvery iron.

REFRACTORIES

Fire Clay Brick (F.o.b. works) Carloads, Per 1000
First quality, Ill., Ky., Md., Mo., Ohio, Pa. (except Salina, Pa., add $5).....$94.60
No. 1 Ohio 88.00
Sec. quality, Pa., Md., Ky., Mo., Ill. 88.00
No. 2 Ohio 79.20
Ground fire clay, net ton, bulk (except Salina, Pa., add $1.50)...... 13.70

Silica Brick
Mt. Union, Pa., Ensley, Ala. $94.60
Childs, Pa. 99.00
Hays, Pa. 100.10
Chicago District 104.50
Western Utah and Calif. 111.10
Super Duty, Hays, Pa., Athens, Tex., Chicago 111.10
Silica cement, net ton, bulk, Eastern (except Hays, Pa.) 16.50
Silica cement, net ton, bulk, Hays, Pa. 18.70
Silica cement, net ton, bulk, Ensley, Ala. 17.60
Silica cement, net ton, bulk, Chicago District 17.60
Silica cement, net ton, bulk, Utah and Calif. 24.70

Chrome Brick   Per Net Ton
Standard chemically bonded, Balt., Chester $82.00

Magnesite Brick
Standard, Baltimore $104.00
Chemically bonded, Baltimore 93.00

Grain Magnesite   St. ⅜-in. grains
Domestic, f.o.b. Baltimore, in bulk fines removed $62.70
Domestic, f.o.b. Chewelah, Wash., in bulk 36.30
in sacks 41.80

Dead Burned Dolomite
F.o.b. producing points in Pennsylvania, West Virginia and Ohio, per net ton, bulk Midwest, add 10¢; Missouri Valley, add 20¢....$13.00

COKE

Furnace, beehive (f.o.b. oven)   Net Ton
Connellsville, Pa. ......$14.00 to $14.50
Foundry, beehive (f.o.b. oven)
Connellsville, Pa. ....$17.00 to $17.50
Foundry, oven coke
Buffalo, del'd $25.35
Chicago, f.o.b. 21.00
Detroit, f.o.b. 23.00
New England, del'd 24.80
Seaboard, N. J., f.o.b. .. 22.00
Philadelphia, f.o.b. 22.70
Swedeland, Pa., f.o.b. ... 22.60
Plainesville, Ohio, f.o.b. 24.00
Erie, Pa., f.o.b. 23.50
Cleveland, del'd 25.72
Cincinnati, del'd 25.06
St. Paul, f.o.b. 21.00
St. Louis, f.o.b. 24.90
Birmingham, del'd 20.79

LAKE SUPERIOR ORES

(51.50% Fe; natural content, delivered lower lake ports)   Per gross ton
Old range, bessemer $8.70
Old range, nonbessemer 8.55
Mesabi, bessemer 8.45
Mesabi, nonbessemer 8.30
High phosphorus 8.30
After adjustments for analyses, prices will be increased or decreased as the case may be for increases or decreases after Dec. 2, 1950, in lake vessel rates, upper lake rail freights, dock handling charges and taxes thereon.

C-R SPRING STEEL

Base per pound f.o.b. mill
0.26 to 0.40 carbon .... 5.35¢
0.41 to 0.60 carbon .... 6.80¢
0.61 to 0.80 carbon .... 7.40¢
0.81 to 1.05 carbon .... 9.35¢
1.06 to 1.35 carbon ....11.65¢
Worcester, add 0.30¢; Sharon, Carnegie, New Castle, add 0.35¢; Detroit, 0.26 to 0.40 carb., add 25¢; other grades add 15¢; New Haven, 0.26 to 0.40 carb., add 50¢; other grades add 5¢.

BOLTS, NUTS, RIVETS, SCREWS

Consumer Prices
(Base discount, f.o.b. mill, Pittsburgh, Cleveland, Birmingham or Chicago)

Machine and Carriage Bolts

Pct Off list

	Less Case	C.
½ in. & smaller x 6 in. & shorter	15	28½
9/16 in. & ⅝ in. x 6 in. & shorter	18½	30½
¾ in. & larger x 6 in. & shorter	17½	29½
All diam. longer than 6 in.	14	27½
Lag, all diam. x 6 in. & shorter	23	35
Lag, all diam. longer than 6 in.	21	33
Plow bolts	34	...

Nuts, Hot Pressed, Cold Punched—Sq

Pct Off List

	Less Keg K. (Reg.)		Less Keg. K. (Hvy.)	
½ in. & smaller	15	28½	15	28½
9/16 in. & ⅝ in.	12	25	6½	21
¾ in. to 1½ in. inclusive	9	23	1	16½
1⅝ in. & larger	7½	22	1	16½

Nuts, Hot Pressed—Hexagon

½ in. & smaller	26	37	22	34
9/16 in. & ⅝ in.	16½	29½	6½	21
¾ in. to 1½ in. inclusive	12	25	2	17½
1⅝ in. & larger	8½	23	2	17½

Nuts, Cold Punched—Hexagon

½ in. & smaller	26	37	22	34
9/16 in. & ⅝ in.	23	35	17½	30½
¾ in. to 1½ in. inclusive	19½	31½	12	25
1⅝ in. & larger	12	25	6½	21

Nuts, Semi-Finished—Hexagon

	Reg.		Hvy.	
½ in. & smaller	35	45	28½	39½
9/16 in. & ⅝ in.	29½	40½	22	34
¾ in. to 1½ in. inclusive	24	36	15	28½
1⅝ in. & larger	13	26	8½	23

	Light	
7/16 in. & smaller	35	45
½ in. thru ⅝ in.	28½	39½
¾ in. to 1½ in. inclusive	26	37

Stove Bolts

Pct Off List

Packaged, steel, plain finished	56—10
Packaged, plated finish	41—10
Bulk, plain finish**	67*

*Discounts apply to bulk shipments in not less than 15,000 pieces of a size and kind where length is 3-in. and shorter; 5000 pieces for lengths longer than 3-in. For lesser quantities, packaged price applies.
**Zinc, Parkerized, cadmium or nickel plated finishes add 6¢ per lb net. For black oil finish, add 2¢ per lb net.

Rivets

½ in. & larger	Base per 100 lb $7.85
7/16 in. & smaller	Pct Off List 36

F.o.b. Pittsburgh, Cleveland, Chicago, Birmingham, Lebanon, Pa.

Cap and Set Screws
(In bulk)

Pct Off List

Hexagon head cap screws, coarse or fine thread, ¼ in. thru ⅝ in. x 6 in., SAE 1020, bright	54
¾ in. thru 1 in. up to & including 6 in.	48
¼ in. thru ⅝ in. x 6 in. & shorter high C double heat treat	46
¾ in. thru 1 in. up to & including 6 in.	41
Milled studs	35
Flat head cap screws, listed sizes	16
Fillister head cap, listed sizes	34
Set screws, sq head, cup point, 1 in. diam. and smaller x 6 in. & shorter	53

S. M. Ferrochrome
Contract price, cents per pound, chromium contained, lump size, delivered.
High carbon type: 60-65% Cr, 4-6% Si, 4-6% Mn, 4-6% C.

Carloads	21.60
Ton lots	23.75
Less ton lots	25.25

Low carbon type: 62-66% Cr, 4-6% Si, 4-6% Mn, 1.25% max. Si.

Carloads	27.75
Ton lots	30.05
Less ton lots	31.85

ELECTRODES

Cents per lb, f.o.b. plant, threaded electrodes with nipples, unboxed

Diam. in in.	Length in in.	Cents Per lb
	GRAPHITE	
17, 18, 20	60, 72	17.85
8 to 16	48, 60, 72	17.85
7	48, 60	19.57
6	48, 60	20.95
4, 5	40	21.50
3	40	22.61
2½	24, 30	23.15
2	24, 30	25.36
	CARBON	
40	100, 110	8.03
35	65, 110	8.03
30	65, 84, 110	8.03
24	72 to 104	8.03
20	84, 90	8.03
17	60, 72	8.03
14	60, 72	8.57
10, 12	60	8.84
8	60	9.10

CLAD STEEL

Base prices, cents per pound, f.o.b. mill

Stainless-carbon	Plate	Sheet
No. 304, 20 pct,		
Coatesville, Pa. (21)	*29.5	
Washgtn, Pa. (39)	*29.5	
Claymont, Del. (29)	*28.00	
Conshohocken, Pa. (26)		*24.00
New Castle, Ind. (55)	*26.50	*25.50
Nickel-carbon		
10 pct. Coatesville (21)	32.5	
Inconel-carbon		
10 pct Coatesville (21)	40.5	
Monel-carbon		
10 pct Coatesville (21)	33.5	
No. 302 Stainless-copper-stainless, Carnegie, Pa. (60)		77.00
Aluminized steel sheets, hot dip, Butler, Pa. (7)		7.75

*Includes annealing and pickling, or sandblasting.

TOOL STEEL

F.o.b. mill

W	Cr	V	Mo	Co	Base per lb
18	4	1	—	—	$1.235
18	4	1	—	5	$1.86
18	4	2	—	—	$1.38
1.5		1.5	8		78.5¢
6	4	2	6	—	.87¢
High-carbon chromium					63.5¢
Oil hardened manganese					35¢
Special carbon					32.5¢
Extra carbon					27¢
Regular carbon					23¢

Warehouse prices on and east of Mississippi are 3¢ per lb higher. West of Mississippi, 5¢ higher.

METAL POWDERS

Per pound, f.o.b. shipping point, in ton lots, for minus 100 mesh.

Swedish sponge iron c.i.f. New York, ocean bags	7.4¢ to 9.0¢
Canadian sponge iron, del'd, in East	10.00¢
Domestic sponge iron, 98+% Fe, carload lots	9.0¢ to 15.0¢
Electrolytic iron, annealed, 99.5+% Fe	36.0¢ to 39.5¢
Electrolytic iron unannealed, minus 325 mesh, 99+% Fe	48.5¢
Hydrogen reduced iron, minus 300 mesh, 98+% Fe	63.0¢ to 80.0¢
Carbonyl iron, size 5 to 10 micron, 98%, 99.8+% Fe	70.0¢ to $1.38
Aluminum	29.00¢
Brass, 10 ton lots	30.00¢ to 33.25¢
Copper, electrolytic	10.25¢ plus metal value
Copper, reduced	10.00¢ plus metal value
Cadmium 100-199 lb.	95¢ plus metal value
Chromium, electrolytic, 99% min., and quantity	$3.50
Lead	6.5¢ plus metal value
Manganese	52.00¢
Molybdenum, 99%	$2.65
Nickel	75.5¢
Nickel, annealed	81.5¢
Nickel, spherical, unannealed	78.5¢
Silicon	34.00¢
Solder powder	6.5¢ to 8.5¢ plus met. value
Stainless steel, 302	75.00¢
Tin	11.00¢ plus metal value
Tungsten, 99%	$4.15
Zinc, 10 ton lots	20.50¢ to 23.85¢

ELECTRICAL SHEETS

22 Ga. H-R cut lengths

F.o.b. Mill Cents Per Lb	Armature	Elec.	Motor	Dynamo	Transf. 72	Transf. 65	Transf. 58
Beech Botton-15		7.25	8.50	9.30	9.85	10.40	11.10
Brackenridge-28		7.25	8.50	9.30	9.85		
Follansbee-63	6.75	7.25	8.50	9.30	9.85	10.40	11.10
Granite City-22		7.95	9.20				
Ind. Harbor-9	6.75	7.25					
Mansfield-75	6.75	7.25	8.50	9.30			
Niles, O.-64	7.05	7.55					
Vandergrift-1	6.75	7.25	8.50	9.30	9.85	10.40	11.10
Warren, O.-4	6.75	7.25	8.50	9.30	9.85	10.40	11.10
Zanesville-7	6.75	7.25	8.50	9.30	9.85	10.40	11.10

Transformer 52, 80¢ above Transformer 58.

Ferrochrome
Contract prices, cents per pound, contained Cr, lump size, bulk, in carloads, delivered. (65-72% Cr, 2% max. Si.)

0.06% C	30.50	0.20% C	29.50
0.10% C	30.00	0.50% C	29.25
0.15% C	29.75	1.00% C	29.00
2.00% C			28.75
65-69% Cr, 4-9% C			22.00
62-66% Cr, 4-6% C, 6-9% Si.			22.85

High-Nitrogen Ferrochrome
Low-carbon type: 67-72% Cr, 0.75% N. Add 5¢ per lb to regular low carbon ferrochrome price schedule. Add 5¢ for each additional 0.25% N.

Chromium Metal
Contract prices, per lb chromium contained packed, delivered, ton lots. 97% min. Cr, 1% max. Fe.

0.20% Max. C.	$1.09
0.50% max. C.	1.05
.00 min. C	1.04

Low Carbon Ferrochrome Silicon
(Cr 34-41%, Si 42-49%, C 0.05% max.) Contract price, carloads, f.o.b. Niagara Falls, freight allowed; lump 4-in. x down, bulk 2-in. x down, 21.75¢ per lb of contained Cr plus 12.00¢ per lb of contained Si. Bulk 1-in. x down, 21.90¢ per lb of contained Cr plus 12.20¢ per lb of contained Si.

Calcium-Silicon
Contract price per lb of alloy, dump, delivered.
30-33% Ca, 60-65% Si, 3.00% max. Fe.

Carloads	19.00
Ton lots	22.10
Less ton lots	23.00

Calcium-Manganese—Silicon
Contract prices, cents per lb of alloy, lump, delivered.
16-20% Ca, 14-18% Mn, 53-59% Si.

Carloads	20.00
Ton lots	22.30
Less ton lots	23.30

CMSZ
Contract price, cents per lb of alloy, delivered.
Alloy 4: 45-49% Cr, 4-6% Mn, 18-21% Si, 1.25-1.75% Zr, 3.00-4.5% C.
Alloy 5: 50.56% Cr, 4-6% Mn, 13.50-16.00% Si, 0.75 to 1.25% Zr, 3.50-5.00% C.

Ton lots	20.75
Less ton lots	22.00

V Foundry Alloy
Cents per pound of alloy, f.o.b. Suspension Bridge, N. Y., freight allowed, max. St. Louis. V-5: 38-42% Cr, 17-19% Si, 8-11% Mn.

Ton lots	16.50¢
Less ton lots	17.75¢

Graphidox No. 4
Cents per pound of alloy, f.o.b. Suspension Bridge, N. Y., freight allowed, max. St. Louis. Si 48 to 52%, Ti 9 to 11%, Ca 5 to 7%.

Carload packed	18.00¢
Ton lots to carload packed	19.00¢
Less ton lots	20.50¢

SMZ
Contract price, cents per pound of alloy, delivered, 60-65% Si, 5-7% Mn, 5-7% Zr, 20% Fe, ½ in. x 12 mesh.

Ton lots	17.25
Less ton lots	18.50

FERROALLOYS

Ferromanganese

78-82% Mn. maximum contract base price, gross ton, lump size.

F.o.b. Niagara Falls, Alloy, W. Va., Welland, Ont., Ashtabula, O. $185
F.o.b. Johnstown, Pa. $187
F.o.b. Sheridan, Pa. $185
F.o.b. Etna, Clairton, Pa. $188

$2.00 for each 1% above 82% Mn, penalty, $2.15 for each 1% below 78%.
Briquets—Cents per pound of briquet, delivered, 66% contained Mn.

Carload, bulk 10.45
Ton lots 12.05

Spiegeleisen

Contract prices gross ton, lump, f.o.b.

	16-19% Mn 3% max. Si	19-21% Mn 3% max. Si
Palmerton, Pa.	$74.00	$75.00
Pgh. or Chicago	74.00	75.00

Manganese Metal

Contract basis, 2 in. x down, cents per pound of metal, delivered.
96% min. Mn, 0.2% max. C, 1% max. Si, 2% max. Fe.

Carload, packed 29.75
Ton lots 31.25

Electrolytic Manganese

F.o.b. Knoxville, Tenn., freight allowed east of Mississippi, cents per pound.

Carloads 28
Ton lots 30
Less ton lots 32

Medium Carbon Ferromanganese

Mn 80% to 85%, C 1.25 to 1.50. Contract price, carloads, lump, bulk, delivered, per lb. of contained Mn ..... 19.15¢

Low-Carbon Ferromanganese

Contract price, cents per pound Mn contained, lump size, del'd, Mn. 85-90%.

	Carloads	Ton	Less
0.07% max. C, 0.06% P, 90% Mn	26.25	28.10	29.30
0.07% max. C	25.75	27.60	28.80
0.15% max. C	25.25	27.10	28.30
0.30% max. C	24.75	26.60	27.80
0.50% max. C	24.25	26.10	27.30
0.75% max. C, 7.00% max. Si	21.25	23.10	24.30

Silicomanganese

Contract basis, lump size, cents per pound of metal, delivered, 65-68% Mn, 18-20% Si, 1.5% max. C. For 2% max. C, deduct 0.2¢.

Carload bulk 9.90
Ton lots 11.55
Briquet, contract basis carlots, bulk delivered, per lb of briquet 11.15
Ton lots 11.75

Silvery Iron (electric furnace)

Si 14.01 to 14.50 pct, f.o.b. Keokuk, Iowa, or Wenatchee, Wash., $89.50 gross ton, freight allowed to normal trade area. Si 15.01 to 15.50 pct, f.o.b. Niagara Falls, N. Y., $83.00. Add $1.00 per ton for each additional 0.50% Si up to and including 18%. Add $1.00 for each 0.50% Mn over 1%.

Silicon Metal

Contract price, cents per pound contained Si, lump size, delivered, for ton lots packed.

96% Si, 2% Fe 21.70
97% Si, 1% Fe 22.10

Silicon Briquets

Contract price, cents per pound of briquet bulk, delivered, 40% Si, 1 lb Si briquets.

Carload, bulk 6.95
Ton lots 8.55

Electric Ferrosilicon

Contract price, cents per pound contained Si, lump, bulk, carloads, delivered.

25% Si	19.00	75% Si	14.30
50% Si	12.40	85% Si	15.55
90-95% Si			17.50

Calcium Metal

Eastern zone contract prices, cents per pound of metal, delivered.

	Cast	Turnings	Distilled
Ton lots	$2.05	$2.95	$3.75
Less ton lots	2.40	3.30	4.55

Other Ferroalloys

Alsifer, 20% Al, 40% Si, 40% Fe, contract basis, f.o.b. Suspension Bridge, N. Y.
Carload ..... 8.15¢
Ton lots ..... 9.55¢

Calcium molybdate, 45-40%, f.o.b. Langeloth, Pa., per pound contained Mo $1.15

Ferrocolumbium, 50-60%, 2 in x D, contract basis, delivered, per pound contained Cb.
Ton lots $4.90
Less ton lots 4.95

Ferro-Tantalum-columbium, 20% Ta, 40% Cb, 0.30 C. Contract basis, delivered, ton lots, 2 in. x D, per lb of contained Cb plus Ta $3.75

Ferromolybdenum, 55-75%, f.o.b. Langeloth, Pa., per pound contained Mo $1.32

Ferrophosphorus, electrolytic, 23-26%, car lots, f.o.b. Siglo, Mt. Pleasant, Tenn., $3 unitage, per gross ton $65.00
10 tons to less carload 75.00

Ferrotitanium, 40%, regular grade, 0.10% C max., f.o.b. Niagara Falls, N. Y., and Bridgeville, Pa., freight allowed, ton lots, per lb contained Ti $1.38

Ferrotitanium, 25%, low carbon, 0.10% C max., f.o.b. Niagara Falls, N. Y., and Bridgeville, Pa., freight allowed, ton lots, per lb contained Ti $1.50
Less ton lots $1.55

Ferrotitanium, 15 to 19%, high carbon, f.o.b. Niagara Falls, N. Y., freight allowed, carload per net ton $177.00

Ferrotungsten, standard, lump or ¼ x down, packed, per pound contained W, 5 ton lots, delivered $3.25

Ferrovanadium, 35-55%, contract basis, delivered, per pound, contained V.
Openhearth ..... $3.00-$3.05
Crucible 3.10- 3.15
High speed steel (Primos) 3.25

Molybdic oxide, briquets or cans, per lb contained Mo, f.o.b. Langeloth, Pa. $1.14
bags, f.o.b. Washington, Pa., Langeloth, Pa. $1.13

Set Steel Output Records

Chicago—Record steel production was achieved during 1950 at the Gary and South Chicago works of the U. S. Steel Co. Production of openhearth ingots at the Gary works totaled 5,780,358 tons to top the previous record of 5,713,509 tons set in 1944, while at South Chicago, 3,898,145 tons were produced, bettering the 1942 record of 3,831,633 tons. At the company's Gary sheet and tin mill, total shipments from all departments came to 2,181,873 tons, well above the former record set in 1947.

Study OPA Scrap Ceilings

Washington—Government price stabilizers studied World War II price ceilings on iron and steel scrap this week as they moved toward imposition of new mandatory controls.

A 5-man industry subcommittee on specifications was scheduled to meet with Economic Stabilization Agency officials early this week

Simanal, 20% Si, 20% Mn, 20% Al, contract basis, f.o.b. Philo, Ohio, freight allowed, per pound
Carload, bulk lump ..... 14.50¢
Ton lots, bulk lump ..... 15.75¢
Less ton lots, lump ..... 16.25¢

Vanadium pentoxide, 88-92% V₂O₅ contract basis, per pound contained V₂O₅ $1.25

Zirconium, 35-40%, contract basis, f.o.b. plant, freight allowed per pound of alloy.
Ton lots ..... 21.00¢

Zirconium, 12-15%, contract basis, lump, delivered, per lb of alloy.
Carload, bulk ..... 7.00¢

Boron Agents

Contract prices per lb of alloy, del.

Borosil, f.o.b. Philo, Ohio, freight allowed, B 3-4%, Si 40-45%, per lb contained B $5.25

Bortam, f.o.b. Niagara Falls
Ton lots, per pound ..... 45¢
Less ton lots, per pound ..... 50¢

Carbortam, Ti 15-21%, B 1-2%, Si 2-4%, Al 1-2%, C 4.5-7.5% f.o.b. Suspension Bridge, N. Y., freight allowed.
Ton lots, per pound ..... 10.00¢

Ferroboron, 17.50% min. B, 1.50% max Si, 0.50% max. Al, 0.50% max. C, 1 in. x D. Ton lots $1.20
F.o.b. Wash., Pa.; 100 lb, up
10 to 14% B ..... .75
14 to 19% B 1.20
19% min. B 1.50

Grainal, f.o.b. Bridgeville, Pa., freight allowed, 100 lb and over.
No. 1 ..... $1.00
No. 6 ..... 68¢
No. 79 ..... 50¢

Manganese—Boron 75.00% Mn, 15-20% B, 5% max. Fe, 1.50% max. Si, 3.00% max. C, 2 in. x D, delivered.
Ton lots $1.46
Less ton lots 1.57

Nickel—Boron 15-18% B, 1.00% max. Al, 1.50% max. Si, 0.50% max. C, 3.00% max. Fe, balance Ni, delivered.
Less ton lots $1.80

Silcaz, contract basis, delivered.
Ton lots ..... 45.00¢

to discuss pricing recommendations submitted by the industry.

Approximately 50 industry officials met with ESA last week to discuss scrap differentials. The agency said pricing schedules that were applied to the industry by OPA were "used as guideposts."

Steel Doors Imprison Hot Atoms

Upton, N. Y.—Eleven-ton steel doors enclose three stainless steel cells backed by concrete walls 3-ft thick which seal off experiments with hot atoms at the new Hot Lab building here. The building is headquarters for processing "hot" materials, or radioisotopes, emerging from the Brookhaven reactor after neutron bombardment.

The steel doors are 1-ft thick, 3½-ft wide, and 11-ft high. They close in 5 seconds and stop automatically at the desired spot. These hot lab experiments are sealed off in the cells and operated by remote control. Researchers observe results through periscopes.

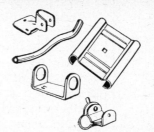

January 18, 1951

113

The Clearing House

NEWS OF USED, REBUILT AND SURPLUS MACHINERY

Temporary Slow-Down—Cuts in auto production in Detroit have temporarily slowed down spiraling demand for used and rebuilt machines in the Detroit area. While firms doing a large out-of-town business report no fluctuation in demand, some Detroit buyers are hesitant to buy because they believe that an appreciable production gap will ensue before major defense output starts.

Relinquish Reluctantly — Good used equipment is still as scarce as ever in Detroit. Faced with an indefinite war production role, owners of the good stuff are holding tight to what they have. Even some firms closed since World War II are sitting tight on machines that might fit into another defense role. When Washington finally sheds its befuddlement on its defense needs and starts war output rolling, owners will then shed surplus machines to a revived market.

A Crying Need—Some in Detroit feel that price ceilings on equipment would be a blessing at this time. Machine tool circles here are harping on the ceilings topic but Washington will yield no positive indication that controls are imminent. The need is shown by reports that a vertical mill, for example, which sold for $1385, was later resold for $2450 and then again changed hands at $3050.

Inflation has found green pastures in the used machinery field. Delivery dates on new machinery show no signs of shortening and, with no method of checking high-flying prices, premium prices for equipment may be expected for some time to come, is the consensus of the trade.

Anticipating Need — Detroit demand for tool room equipment has always been vital and this market has tightened up considerably in recent months. One popular theory is that tool and die shops reason that they will eventually need this equipment to build the jigs and fixtures for war work.

Duplicating Demand — Market analysts who have examined hot demand for machine tools here are convinced that much of the market's heat is based on duplication of inquiries by as many as ten firms which may be seeking the same scarce machine. Inquiries, they point out, do not for most items reflect the true condition of the market. What does reflect market demand more accurately is soaring prices, it is obvious.

Press Equipment—Also in the high demand brackets is press equipment. Inquiries for electrical and welding equipment, although continuing in good volume, have eased somewhat, says the trade.

Ringing Doorbells — Sales resistance to doorbell ringing in the hunt for surplus machines is rough. If the owner is willing to take the risk that his machine will not be important to his war output role and agrees to talk of selling—his price usually is too high.

Washington Session — Machinery Dealers' National Assn. reported that the industry will meet with U. S. officials on Feb. 8 and 9 to discuss prices, allocations, and priorities on used machine tools. Speakers from the Economic Stabilization Agency, National Production Authority, and the NSRB may address the meeting.

On the Block—Equipment of the Carey Machine Tool Co., Cleveland, was sold at public auction on Jan. 16. The heavy tool and die and manufacturing plant, which had purchased the majority of its machines new in the 1942-1945 period, put on the block lathes, shapers, milling machines, grinders, drills, honing machines, air compressors, planer and boring mills, and miscellaneous items.

NEW KING WITH CONTOURING ATTACHMENT
Speeds JET ENGINE Production

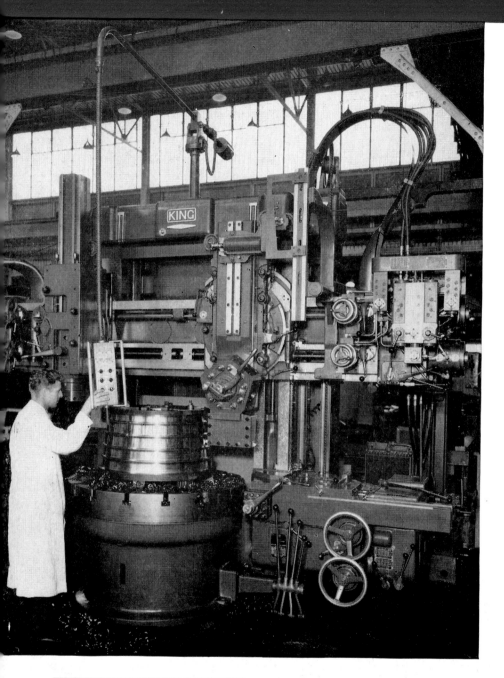

This 52" KING Boring & Turning Machine was specially built for large manufacturer of jet engines. Equipped with hydraulically controlled tracer attachment, swivel turret head, and special 4-way tool block on left-hand ram head, this versatile machine combines the following features:

1 — AUTOMATIC CONTOURING
2 — MANUAL ROUGHING WITH AUTOMATIC DEPTH CONTROL
3 — STANDARD BORING MILL FACILITIES

—ALL in ONE machine.

On any type of boring, facing, and turning—on work large or small —this machine sets a new standard in rapid production with dependable accuracy. The basic design and specifications are flexible, can readily be modified to meet individual requirements.

All KING machines, standard and special, are HEAVY, RUGGED, MASSIVE in construction. They have the extra weight and rigidity that assures maximum stock removal at the highest speeds within the range of modern cutting tools.

Tell us your requirements, and we'll tell you how a KING can meet them—with FASTER, MORE ACCURATE, MORE PROFITABLE PRODUCTION.

KING VERTICAL BORING & TURNING MACHINES
are made in
10 SIZES — 30" TO 144"

SEND FOR CATALOGS

Illustrated KING Catalogs, with full description and detailed specifications of machines, will be sent promptly on request. Catalog K-1 covers machines sizes 30", 36", and 42"; K-2, sizes 52", 62", and 72"; K-3, sizes 84" and 100"; K-4, sizes 120" and 144".

American Steel Foundries

KING MACHINE TOOL DIVISION
CINCINNATI 29, OHIO
Builders of King Vertical Boring & Turning Machines and Sebastian Lathes

The Iron Age

A CHILTON PUBLICATION

E NATIONAL METALWORKING WEEKLY

January 25, 195

ENTS PAGE 2

Farval lubricates press for "Big Inch" line pipe

● Since April, 1950, a new type of hydraulic press has been U-shaping forty-foot lengths of half-inch steel plate in the process of forming electric weld oil field pipe. Sizes produced range from 26 to 36 inches in diameter—for bigger "Big Inch" lines.

Lubrication is no problem on this press. It is served by three manually operated Farval systems —one of these lubricates 32 points on the gibs, while the other two lubricate 114 bearings on the dies.

With Farval on the job, there has been no need for extra men as oilers, no waste of lubricant, and even more important, no down time either to oil hard-to-get-at points or to replace worn-out bearings.

In this and in hundreds of other plants, on presses and other industrial machinery, Farval Centralized Lubrication has paid for itself in savings—savings in oiling labor, lubricants, bearing expense and production time.

Farval is the original Dualine system of centralized lubrication, proved practical in 20 years of service. The Farval valve has only two moving parts—is simple, sure and foolproof, without springs, ball-checks or pinhole ports to cause trouble. Through its full hydraulic operation, Farval unfailingly delivers grease or oil to each bearing—as much as you want, exactly measured —as often as desired. Indicators at every bearing show that each valve has functioned.

Write for Bulletin 25 for full details. The Farval Corporation, 3252 East 80th St., Cleveland 4, Ohio.

Affiliate of The Cleveland Worm & Gear Company, Industrial Worm Gearing. In Canada: Peacock Brothers Limited.

FARVAL— *Studies in Centralized Lubrication* No. 119

Three Farval centralized systems lubricate this 2000-ton hydraulic press. It forms steel plates, ¼" to ½" thick, into U-shape as a step in making electric-weld pipe.

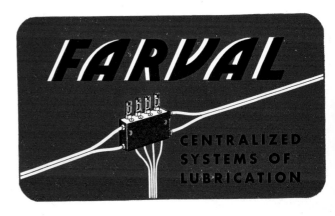

FARVAL

CENTRALIZED SYSTEMS OF LUBRICATION

5-6 yd truck mixer built by Challenge Manufacturing Company, Maywood, Calif. The use of Mayari R, the elimination of non-essential parts, and the use of fabricated parts in place of castings have reduced the overall deadweight of the unit by more than 1500 lbs.

They use Mayari R to double the life of truck mixers

When Challenge Manufacturing Company designed their modern concrete truck mixers they whipped the abrasion and corrosion problem by using low-alloy, high-strength Mayari R steel for blades and drums. Made from 3/16-in.-thick Mayari R, these parts have a service life estimated by the builders to be at least double that of similar blades and drums of carbon steel.

Its advantages over carbon steel have made Mayari R the choice of designers of a great variety of construction machinery and materials-handling equipment. Some of the more important advantages are:

1. Greater Strength—Its yield point of 50,000 psi is about twice that of plain carbon steel. You can use higher working stresses.

2. Higher Corrosion-Resistance—Mayari R has 5 to 6 times the atmospheric corrosion-resistance of carbon steel, and 2 to 4 times that of copper-bearing steel.

3. Better Abrasion-Resistance—This grade of steel has considerably better resistance to the abrasive action of many materials than does carbon steel.

4. Improved Resistance to Battering—Mayari R resists denting and battering as well as ordinary carbon steel 1.3 times as thick.

5. Longer Paint-Life—Depending on the type used, paint lasts 20 to 80 pct longer on Mayari R than on plain carbon steel.

Mayari R is used in the as-rolled condition and requires no special methods and no special equipment for fabricating or welding.

It is produced in sheets, plates, bars, structural shapes and cold-formed shapes. For further information write for Catalog 259.

Mayari R blades and drums being assembled and welded in the Challenge shops. The blades are designed so that end seals are not needed.

BETHLEHEM STEEL COMPANY
BETHLEHEM, PA.

On the Pacific Coast Bethlehem products are sold by Bethlehem Pacific Coast Steel Corporation. Export Distributor: Bethlehem Steel Export Corporation.

★ BETHLEHEM STEEL ★

Mayari R *makes it lighter...stronger...longer lasting*

IRON AGE

CONTENTS

THE IRON AGE
Editorial, Advertising and Circulation Offices, 100 E. 42nd St., New York 17, N. Y.

GEORGE T. HOOK, Publisher
TOM C. CAMPBELL, Editor

EDITORIAL STAFF

Managing Editor   George F. Sullivan
Feature Editor   Darwyn I. Brown
News-Markets Editor   Wm. V. Packard
Machinery Editor   George Elwers
Associate Editors: William Czygan, H. W. Van Camp, F. J. Winters; Assistant Editors: R. L. Hatschek, J. Kolb, Ted Metaxas, W. B. Olson; Regional Editors: E. C. Beaudet, Chicago; W. A. Lloyd, Cleveland; W. G. Patton, Detroit; John B. Delaney, Pittsburgh; Osgood Murdock, R. T. Reinhardt, San Francisco; Eugene J. Hardy, Karl Rannells, George H. Baker, Washington; Correspondents: Fred L. Allen, Birmingham; N. Levenson, Boston; Fred Edmunds, Los Angeles; James Douglas, Seattle; Roy Edmonds, St. Louis; F. Sanderson, Toronto; F. H. Harley, London, England; Chilton Editorial Board: Paul Wooton, Washington Representative.

BUSINESS STAFF

Production Manager   B. H. Hayes
Director of Research   Oliver Johnson
Mgr. Circul'n & Promotion   C. T. Post
Asst. Promotion Mgr.   James A. Crites
Asst. Dir. of Research   Wm. Laimbeer

REGIONAL BUSINESS MANAGERS

B. L. Herman, Philadelphia; Stanley J. Smith, Chicago; Peirce Lewis, Detroit; Paul Bachman, New England; Robert F. Blair, Cleveland; R. Raymond Kay, Los Angeles; C. H. Ober, New York; J. M. Spackman, Pittsburgh; Harry Becker, European Representative.

REGIONAL OFFICES

Chicago 3, 1134 Otis Bldg.; Cleveland 14, 1016 National City Bank Bldg., Detroit 2, 103 Pallister Ave.; Los Angeles 28, 2420 Cheremoya Ave.; New England, 62 La Salle Rd., W. Hartford 7; New York 17, 100 E. 42nd St.; Philadelphia 39, 56th & Chestnut Sts.; Pittsburgh 22, 814 Park Bldg.; Washington 4, National Press Bldg.; European, 111 Thorley Lane, Timperley, Cheshire, England.

Circulation Representatives: Thomas Scott, James Richardson.

One of the Publications Owned and Published by Chilton Company, Inc., Chestnut & 56th Sts., Philadelphia 39, Pa., U. S. A.

OFFICERS AND DIRECTORS

JOS. S. HILDRETH, President
Vice-Presidents: Everit B. Terhune, G. C. Buzby, P. M. Fahrendorf, Harry V. Duffy. William H. Vallar, Treasurer; John Blair Moffett, Secretary; D. Allyn Garber, Maurice E. Cox, Frank P. Tighe, George T. Hook, Tom C. Campbell, L. V. Rowlands, Directors. George Maiswinkle, Asst. Treas.

Indexed in the Industrial Arts Index and the Engineering Index. Published every Thursday by the CHILTON CO. (INC.), Chestnut and 56th Sts., Philadelphia 39, Pa. Entered as second class matter Nov. 8, 1932, at the Post Office at Philadelphia under the act of March 3, 1879. $8 yearly in United States, its territories and Canada; other Western Hemisphere Countries $15; other Foreign Countries $25 per year. Single Copies 35c. Annual Review and Metal Industry Facts issue, $2.00. Cable address "Ironage" N. Y.

Member Audit Bureau of Circulations. Member Society of Business Magazine Editors.

Copyright, 1951, by Chilton Co. (Inc.)

DIGEST

ANUARY TWENTY-FIFTH · NINETEEN FIFTY-ONE · VOLUME 167 · NUMBER 4

Where failures meant shutdowns they changed to grommet V belts

B. F. Goodrich grommet V belts cut costs 20 to 50%

THESE V belts operate in heavy-duty service 8 hours a day, 5 days a week. When the drive stops, the whole operation shuts down. It costs more to stop than keep going! Previous V belts suffered from shock loads, wore out fast. A BFG man recommended the grommet V belt to stand the jerks and hard pulls. The grommet V belts shown here have been in service 2 years, with no shut-offs or shut-downs for maintenance. Here's why the grommet V belt lasts 20 to 50% longer:

No cord ends—A grommet is endless, made by winding heavy cord on itself to form an endless loop. It has no overlapping ends. Because most of the failures in ordinary V belts occur in the region where cords overlap, the endless cord section in a grommet V belt eliminates such failures.

Concentrated cord strength—All of the cord material in a B. F. Goodrich grommet multiple-V belt is *concentrated* in twin grommets, positioned close to the driving faces of the pulley. No layers of cords to rub against one another and generate heat; cord and adhesion failures are reduced.

Better grip, less slip—Because a grommet is endless, a grommet V belt is more flexible, grips the pulleys better. Size for size, grommet multiple-V belts will give ⅓ more gripping power, pull heavier loads with a higher safety factor.

Only B. F. Goodrich has the grommet!—No other multiple-V belt is a grommet V belt (U. S. Patent No. 2,233,294). At present made in C, D and E sections only. See your local B. F. Goodrich distributor. Ask him to show you his "X-ray" belt that illustrates grommet construction clearly. *The B. F. Goodrich Company, Industrial and General Products Division, Akron, Ohio.*

Grommet V Belts BY

B.F. Goodrich
RUBBER FOR INDUSTRY

Guns, Butter and Pap

SINCE Charlie Wilson joined the defense effort things are moving a little faster. When he gets through shuffling people and things around they will move much faster. But there is only so much one can do. The rest is up to the people who have the responsibilities to see that things keep rolling.

It would be nice to sit back and say "Now things are going fine. Everything will be all right." But that just isn't so. Things are not fine nor are they going well. There will have to be a lot of heads bumped, personalities cut down and a stripped-for-action attitude taken before we get out of this snail's pace.

We seem to be fettered by too many words. We hear on every hand speeches about how we will keep our standard of living. Speakers high and mighty in the defense effort talk as if they would be robbing the people if we had a meatless day; or if we had less gas; or if we had to wear shiny pants; or if our wives had to turn our cuffs to get some extra wear; or if we had to read in a room that was a little below 72°.

Why all this fuss about standard of living? We are preparing for war or to prevent war so we can have a high standard of living and freedom. Is that term so sacred that we can't toss it in the ash can until we get strong and pay the bill as we go along?

We will still be living like kings compared to the rest of the world. We will live to see the day when we can prate about a television in every room, two dishwashers, hot and cold atmosphere, delicately perfumed house dust, 4-week vacations and hors d'oeuvres.

It is all right to prepare the people for things to come but we have had enough hot air on this subject from Washington to lift most of the rigid aircraft we have at present. What the people want is action. They have been ready for months. Let's tell them what they face in honest understandable terms and leave out the politicians' grandiose words that mean nothing.

Let's give the fellow, who knows the draft board will get him, some dope on how soon. Let's tell the industry that strives to keep its workers until defense orders come how long it will be. Let's tell what mistakes are being made and how they will be overcome. Let's get rid of the ones in high places who are not qualified to carry on such a big task.

In other words let's cut out some of the butter, all of the pap and concentrate on guns for a while at least.

Tom Campbell

Editor

The new **WATERBURY HI-PRO**

¼" Capacity . . . Speed, 150 to 200 Headed Blanks per minute . . .

ALL STEEL, SOLID DIE, DOUBLE STROKE—

Another High Speed Automatic COLD HEADER of Revolutionary Design . . . The culmination of nearly 100 years' experience and "know-how" in the design and manufacture of metal-working machinery, pioneering in the development of COLD HEADING EQUIPMENT.

For further information, address—PUBLICITY DEPT.

WATERBURY - FARREL
FOUNDRY AND MACHINE COMPANY
WATERBURY, CONNECTICUT • SALES OFFICES: CHICAGO, CLEVELAND, NEWARK, N.J.

IRON AGE *newsfront*

*news
methods
and product
forecast*

► A satisfactory side joint for containers made from electrolytically aluminized steel sheet has been developed in the laboratory. The method of joining the ends of cans made from this material will not be changed from the method now used on tinplate stock. The new process is not yet in commercial production.

► Tests indicate it may be practical to use porcelain, which has uniform physical properties and great gripping power, in place of mica in insulating electrical machinery commutators. Design of stronger commutators would ease a serious problem in design of high-speed motors and generators.

► Now in commercial use is a water conditioning process using a new synthetic resin. It can produce an effluent with zero hardness, low solids, alkalininity, silica and CO_2. Also, pH is high and only inexpensive salt and lime are needed for operation.

► Infra-red heating of test tubes has been developed in Switzerland as an improvement on the bunsen burner. Heating and cooling are a great deal faster.

► Some railroads are getting a little worried about the effect of new Eastern steel mills on their freight revenues. When these mills begin producing, the freight revenue pattern will be altered drastically. Shipments from Pittsburgh to the East, for example, are likely to fall off.

► To date, investigations (by at least one major firm) of ductile silicon and alloys of this metal have been negative. Alloys tested so far have proved too brittle. This characteristic appears to be due to the fact that silicon has a diamond crystal lattice structure.

► A new aluminum alloy, 78S, will soon be announced. This heat-treatable grade is 10 pct stronger than the old type 76S.

► People who study the long-range supply outlook for steelmaking scrap must consider a new and very important factor: Steel users are constantly finding new ways to reduce scrap loss in manufacturing. The tonnage of scrap in relation to new steel used by the auto industry, for instance, is constantly being lowered by more efficient manufacturing methods.

► The furore over lack of priorities for steel capacity expansion is still unheeded. But at least as serious and so far unnoticed is the lack of priorities on steel for maintenance and repair of existing steelmaking facilities.

► Hot-dipped aluminum coatings of steel fence have proved exceptionally satisfactory. Tests conducted so far by one aluminum manufacturer indicate that it will definitely be competitive with the galvanized product.

► Disliking the behavior of airplanes in atmospheric bumps, a French engineer designed an articulated wing plane which was flown this month. He uses the automotive shock absorber principle to control the "flexible" wings.

Silversmith's Way of Improving Tools Gives More Production Per Tool Dollar

Photos courtesy Towle Manufacturing Co., makers of sterling silver knives, forks, spoons and other tableware. Fork die shown is the King Richard Pattern.

VAPOCARB-HUMP CONTROL PANEL   VAPOCARB GAS GENERATOR   VAPOCARB-HUMP HARDENING FURNACE

Read About COST-CUTTING PROCESSES In These Catalogs

We supply complete Furnace Processes to regulate all action inside the heat-treating furnace, for hardening, tempering, normalizing, carburizing, nitriding, steam-treatment, dry cyaniding. See us if you want heavy production at low cost!

Address nearest office, or 4956 Stenton Ave., Phila. 44, Pa.

Jrl. Ad T-620(32)

TOWLE Manufacturing Company is one of the firms which successfully lengthens the production life of its forging dies. And Towle's method is basically "right" for other metal-working firms, whether they use expensive tools or simple ones, because Towle is interested in heavy production . . . the last possible piece from every die.

Towle's plan starts with the usual printed form for each die, on which are entered the heat-treating temperature, time, quench, hardness, etc., and the production from the tool, so that when it is retired the company can tell whether or not it produced well.

So far, of course, many plants use this routine; but Towle adds a "pay-off" step—they never throw a sheet away, regardless of the yield from its die. The sheet becomes a guide as to whether succeeding tools should be used

differently, or made of a different steel, or heat-treated differently.

As far as heat-treatment is concerned, the pay-off lies in Towle's facilities for either reproducing or changing the treatment, as they wish. Their Vapocarb-Hump Hardening and Homo Tempering equipments do exactly as the heat-treater says. With them, he can secure the desired structure, hardness and temper, just as a toolmaker can set the feed and speed of a filing machine. Guesswork is ended; the heat-treat becomes a place where specifications are followed to the letter.

Reasons for the dependability of these L&N Methods are given in the Catalogs at left; they explain why more and more plants are finding that it pays to Vapocarb-Hump Harden and Homo Temper all tools.

LEEDS NORTHRUP

IRON AGE *summary*

iron and steel industry trends

Price Controls and CMP Being Readied
Lack of Staff Seen Biggest Obstacle
Paper Work Snows Steel Sales Staffs

PRICE controls and a controlled materials plan are being readied in Washington this week. A general price freeze covering nearly all products and commodities will become effective about February 15. The CMP will be in effect by June, if not sooner.

Both of these anti-inflation weapons will be hampered in their early stages by a dire shortage of administrative people, but the cries for heavy artillery against inflation have become so frequent and so loud that the Government can no longer resist them.

Increasing labor and material costs are upsetting expansion and improvement plans of some manufacturing companies. They are finding money allotted to these projects in the planning stage is no longer sufficient to cover requirements when construction is ready to start. One company's estimate for custom made capital equipment was over 100 pct off.

Shifting DO Pattern Confuses Producers

Snowballing government orders, regulations, directives, revisions, and amendments have caused some people in industry who dislike government controls to call for a controlled materials plan. Steel producers are in a dither, trying to meet the constantly shifting needs of defense and essential civilian programs and still tell their regular customers what to expect. This everchanging pattern of DO and government-directed tonnage has upset their production schedules to the point where they are about ready to throw up their hands in disgust.

In addition, mills' clerical staffs are buried under mountains of paper work. For example, steel tonnage set aside for DO orders is based on shipments during a base period last year; government program tonnage is allocated directly; and warehouse allocations are based on another set of conditions. Just when clerical forces start to work their way clear, additional directives, new programs, or changed percentages, snow them under again.

While steel people feel that CMP is necessary to restore order to the confused market, they also fear it. Once the economy is controlled to this extent it will be hard to get the controls lifted. They fear that CMP will drag on like a millstone long after the emergency or war has passed.

Hard to Check Urgency of DO Orders

Meanwhile, military secrecy on the end use of alloy steel products is making it difficult for producers to check on the urgency of DO orders. They have no way of knowing whether a consumer is overstating the need for prompt delivery because ordnance applications are under wraps. They must take the word of the consumer.

Defense orders for stainless steel, particularly sheets, are growing by leaps and bounds. One producer who shipped 41 pct of his stainless sheets on DO orders in December has projected his February delivery to 55 pct and March delivery to 68 pct.

Defense tooling is now putting plenty of pressure on the machine tool market. It is becoming almost impossible to buy a standard machine today without a priority. Military people are insisting on standard machines wherever possible. In many cases they have the authority to buy standard equipment on the spot without consulting Washington. Also some new plants are expected to be kept in standby condition after the crisis. Standard machines are desirable from that standpoint too.

Steelmaking operations this week are scheduled at 101 pct of rated capacity, up 1½ points from last week. This will be another all-time record for steel produced in a single week.

(nonferrous summary, p 94)

January 25, 1951 15

SAVES $5,000 YEARLY ON STEEL COST

Unloading Time Cut 2 Hours Per Railroad Car

5-ton, 3-runway, 50-ft. span, completely motorized Cleveland Tramrail bridge operated by pushbuttons from floor. Bridge is shown interlocked with track extending out doorway over railroad. This Tramrail system has been in service since 1943.

A handsome dividend is being earned by the Kortick Manufacturing Co., San Francisco, Calif., on its Tramrail transfer bridge installation.

Because the bridge is of 5 tons capacity, the rods, bars and angle iron which Kortick uses for the manufacture of pole line hardware, can be bought and handled in 5-ton bundles. This eliminates a bundling charge made for smaller bundles. The savings is $2.00 per ton. As Kortick takes in an average of 200 tons per month, the monthly saving amounts to $400.

The bridge interlocks with an outside Tramrail track that extends over a railroad track. This enables the hoist carrier to deliver steel directly from railroad cars to any point inside the building served by the bridge. Because of this feature and the fact that heavier bundles are handled, a saving of about 2 hours unloading time is made per 50-ton car of steel, over their former method which employed a 3-ton hoist.

Obviously with total savings running in the neighborhood of $5,000 yearly, it did not take long for this Tramrail installation to pay for itself.

GET THIS BOOK!
BOOKLET No. 2008. Packed with valuable information. Profusely illustrated. Write for free copy

CLEVELAND TRAMRAIL DIVISION
THE CLEVELAND CRANE & ENGINEERING CO.
4861 EAST 284TH ST.   WICKLIFFE, OHIO.

CLEVELAND TRAMRAIL
OVERHEAD MATERIALS HANDLING EQUIPMENT

Better lubrication, lower maintenance costs for roll neck bearings —

Gulf xxx Lubricant

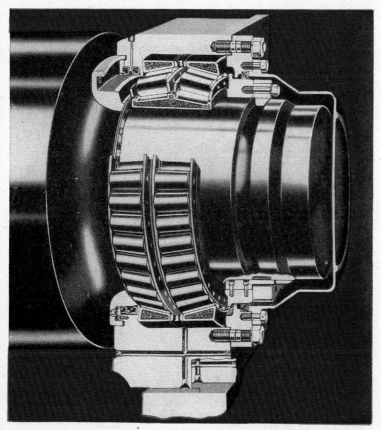

Photo courtesy The Timken Roller Bearing Company.

X **Exceptional extreme pressure characteristics**

X **High resistance to washout**

X **Effective protection against corrosion**

X **Good stability**

X **High pumpability**

Gulf XXX Lubricant provides the kind of lubrication that insures long life and low maintenance costs for roll neck roller bearings. Here's why! Gulf XXX Lubricant is a high quality grease that has exceptionally good extreme pressure characteristics—protects rollers and races subjected to shock loads or overloads. It provides that extra margin of protection so often required in rolling mill service.

Gulf XXX Lubricant stays put—is not washed out of the bearing, even when subjected to the washing action of large quantities of water. Thus bearings get continuous protection and grease consumption is kept to a minimum.

Another advantage of Gulf XXX Lubricant under wet conditions is its excellent rust-preventive characteristics — it covers every roller and raceway with a film that protects highly polished surfaces. You will eliminate bearing failures from

this cause when Gulf XXX Lubricant is in use.

Then, too, Gulf XXX Lubricant is a very stable grease—won't separate in storage or in service. It has excellent pumpability and is ideal for centralized lubricating systems.

For further information on Gulf XXX Lubricant and other Gulf quality lubricants for steel mills, call in a Gulf Lubrication Engineer today. Write, wire, or phone your nearest Gulf office. Gulf Oil Corporation · Gulf Refining Company, Gulf Building, Pittsburgh, Pennsylvania.

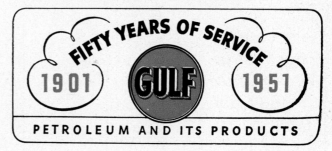

FIFTY YEARS OF SERVICE
1901 GULF 1951
PETROLEUM AND ITS PRODUCTS

Dear EDITOR

Letters From Readers

From Way Back When

Sir:

I am enclosing a very interesting document [shown below] which my father, Herbert L. Kelley, of Boston, found in the files of a Boston importing company (Silas Peirce & Co.), showing a receipted bill for a shipment of steel received from England just 100 years ago. It seems to me that prices were, surprisingly, not too far below our levels of the 30's.

R. C. KELLEY
Director of Purchases
Dresser Industries, Inc.
Cleveland

Big Investment

Sir:

Can you put us in touch with some concern which has solved a heating problem similar to ours? For the past 50 years we have heated our factory with individual stoves. It is now proposed to build a boiler room and heat the plant by steam. This will require an investment equivalent to about 40 pct of our present net worth. Will it pay?

Productive efficiency would undoubtedly be increased, but we are unable to form any definite estimate of the value of such an increase, or to determine how long it would take to recover the investment. Possibly other companies have installed similar heating plants and could give us the benefit of their experience, and help us form an estimate of the probable return from the investment.

C. H. WETZEL
President
Wayne Iron Works
Wayne, Pa.

How about it, readers; any information on a similar problem?—Ed.

Needs Tool Info

Sir:

As professor of industrial engineering at Illinois Institute of Technology, I am currently preparing and offering a course entitled Tool Engineering Economics. This course covers not only manufacturing processes in general but also, as the name implies, specific machines and the tooling of those machines.

In order to acquaint my students with the machines and tools that are available in the current market, I need specific information. You can be of great help to me in this matter by sending to me any of the following materials, or others that you might choose: Advertising brochures; catalogs; illustrative diagrams and photographs; orientation and training manuals; manuals of tooling and recommended tooling; and price lists and other related material. At the moment I am compiling a series of mimeographed notes for use in this course and eventually expect to develop a published textbook which will involve illustrations of appropriate machines and their tooling.

H. A. WILLIAMS
Illinois Institute of Technology
Chicago

Perhaps some of our readers can help Prof. Williams by supplying any of the information requested.—Ed.

where you can profit

from Union Drawn's Improved

MACHINABILITY

For years, *steel parts quality has been going up . . . unit costs coming down.*

That, in a few words, is what has resulted from *a continuous improvement* in Republic Union Cold Drawn Steel Bars. That is what you can learn for yourself by using these bars on production runs of duplicate steel parts on an automatic screw machine.

In every Union Drawn mill and laboratory, it's a 60-year-old tradition that MACHINABILITY comes first. As a result, many improvements have been and still are being made in Union Free Cut (B-1112), Union Supercut (B-1113) and their companion carbon, alloy and stainless steel grades.

Today, Union Drawn customers have learned to expect a high uniformity throughout bar after bar and shipment after shipment . . . and that one lot will machine just as readily as any other lot. They expect freedom from abrasive elements and long tool life. They expect smooth, bright machined surfaces. They expect high production efficiency and low unit costs for their steel parts.

They've learned to expect all these things, because they've been getting them for years.

The same experienced metallurgists and engineers who have been spending their time in customers' plants making certain that they get best possible results from Republic Union Cold Drawn Steel Bars are ready to help you, too. Call your nearest Republic District Sales Office or write us.

REPUBLIC STEEL CORPORATION
Union Drawn Steel Division • Massillon, Ohio
GENERAL OFFICES • CLEVELAND 1, OHIO
Export Department: Chrysler Building, New York 17, N. Y.

Republic
UNION COLD DRAWN
STEELS

REPUBLIC STEEL ®

Free - Machining Bessemer, Alloy and Enduro Stainless Steels
•
Union Cold Drawn Special Sections
•
Union Cold Drawn and Ground Rounds; Turned and Polished Rounds; and Turned, Ground and Polished Rounds (Union Precision Shafting.)

Fatigue Cracks

by Charles T. Post

Six Tricks to the Book

Just when we had become thoroughly discouraged about the possibility of reconciling widely divergent points of view in the world, we stumbled across a research project that lends new hope.

One of the country's best known research institutes is currently engrossed in a project for which the fee is being paid jointly by a Bible publisher and—of all things—a playing card manufacturer. In all the years Bibles have been printed, a certain process has been the same, untouched by the machine age. And highly mechanized as playing card manufacture is, a similar process has always been carried on by hand. Both sides finally recognized the joint nature of the problem, turned it over to the researchers under a flag of truce. Science, we are glad to report, is about to chalk up a complete triumph.

If parsons and poker players can be brought together under the aegis of science, perhaps there's a wee ray of hope for such minor matters as international differences.

Sell Research

From Armour Institute, we learn that science has taken still another step forward in its constant striving to create better things for better living.

Armour always has thrown itself wholeheartedly into everything it does and we can imagine that the entire staff and the formidable technical facilities of the Institute were engaged for months in giving birth to the latest boon to mankind—and we include advertisers under that heading.

Any day now you'll be encountering the new triumph—an electrical advertising sign that flashes on when a prospect approaches. Only thing that puzzles us is how the sign tells a prospect from a street cleaner. Possibly a built-in Dun's rating book.

Frustration

Clem Caditz wires from Snake Creek, Fla.:

BITTERLY DISAPPOINTED. CAUGHT A 63 POUND AMBERJACK BUT IT WASN'T EIGHTEEN OR TWENTY GAUGE. IT WAS ONLY FISH. LEAVING FOR HOME.

Puzzlers

The puzzler in the Jan. 11 issue has created quite a stir. Apparently everybody finally realized that the two diagonals of a rectangle are always equal. The obvious answer of 15 in. has been received from Jeanette Knapp, Chicago; Howard Fancher, Northville, N. Y.; B. L. Obear, Dexter, Maine; G. L. Griffith, Wright Aeronautical Corp.; Robert Huff, Canton, Ohio; and Nora LaDow, Birmingham.

A late comer on the smoke stack problem is Paul Bergevin, The Torrington Co., Ltd. His answer of 3.064 ft is good enough for us.

This week's puzzler sent in by Robert Huff, Canton, Ohio, is a good workout in plane geometry—with no tricks. A hole 4 in. in diameter is drilled through a metal block. Inserted in this hole are two roller bearings with the same length as the hole and radii of 1½ and ½ respectively. What is the radius of the largest ball bearing which can be thrust through the assembly?

machine tool high spots

by W.A.Lloyd

sales inquiries and production

Defense Inflates Demand—Demand for machine tools was threatening to reach sky-high proportions this week as some of the primary objectives of the defense program including the creation of facilities for the production of 50,000 planes, and a smaller, but imposing number of tanks and combat vehicles, began to unfold.

In Washington it was reported that the Air Forces plan to order $45 million in machine tools in the immediate future, as part of a preliminary commitment of $150 million, which in turn is part of a total program involving about $550 million in machine tools. These tools will be diverted to aircraft contractors, some of whom have not placed orders for machines as yet.

New Combat Vehicle—In Cleveland, an estimated $106 million increase in the Cleveland Tank Plant commitment, involving the development and building of a "new combat vehicle" was announced jointly by U. S. Army Ordnance and Cadillac officials. The increase raises total tank and combat vehicle commitments of the Cleveland plant to a current value of approximately half-billion dollars.

Question of Balance—Projects of this magnitude bring into critical focus the plans of the machine tool industry to double production this year, and the function of NPA. It seems that the fundamental problem facing NPA's machinery division is to match machine tool production, currently relatively low, with military requirements for machine tools, which are very high.

The question has been asked, "Why doesn't NPA do what WPB did in World War II?" The answer is that the circumstances are different, in both degree and timing.

Had Head Start—Last time, the machine tool industry tuned up on 2 years' of business for foreign customers, and with the advent of Pearl Harbor, was ready to go. The present defense program is set up for an eventuality which nobody can definitely predict.

Priorities for materials and pool orders appear to be the obvious answers to a rapid increase in machine tool production, an important objective not without official recognition in Washington.

Priority Step Coming? — But when the pool orders or Emergency Production Schedules, as they are formally designated, are activated, some distribution order, similar, but not identical to World War II's E-1-B will probably accompany the order.

A priority for materials is reportedly under consideration. When this step is taken, it will probably be done in a way least likely to be ill-received by other manufacturers, who feel that their products are also highly essential to the war effort. Just what this way will be poses a real public relations problem.

Defiance Line Sold—In Defiance, Ohio, the drill press line of Defiance Machine Co., an 80-year-old company which is going out of business, has been sold to Cleveland and Lima, Ohio, interests. Defiance Machine Co. sold its boring mill line to Kempsmith & Co., and its plastic machinery to the Baldwin Co. some months ago.

W. L. Thomas, president Thomas, Inc., machine tool distributors; A. E. Petrus, Petrus Industrial Machinery Sales Co., and George U. Crites, consulting engineer of Lima, purchased the drill press line from Defiance for an undisclosed sum, recently.

British DPC?—Britain, through the Ministry of Supply, will own all machine tools bought for the new armament program. Machines will be leased to manufacturers, but the government will retain the right to move them from one plant to another.

This will permit a flexibility in defense production and put to the best use a limited machine supply.

SIMPLIFY PNEUMATIC DESIGN

with this unique electrically - operated AIR CYLINDER with HYDRAULIC CONTROL

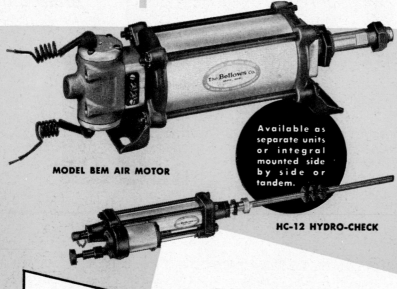

MODEL BEM AIR MOTOR

Available as separate units or integral mounted side by side or tandem.

HC-12 HYDRO-CHECK

Provides Absolute smoothness of piston movement — eliminates the natural "bounce" or "springiness" of air.

Permits Positive Control of Piston Speed in Either or both directions and at any point in piston travel.

WITH Bellows "Controlled-Air-Power" you can combine the speed, economy and flexibility of air-power, the smoothness of hydraulic operation, and inter-locked electrical control, all in a compact, space saving, easily installed assembly.

The Bellows Model BEM Air Motor (a double acting air cylinder) is a complete power unit in itself. Valve, electric valve operating controls, and speed controls are all built-in. The low-voltage built-in solenoid controls operate all day at high speed without hum, pounding, or excessive heat.

When used in the same assembly with the new Bellows Hydro-Check (an adjustable Hydraulic Resistance Unit) you obtain precision control and precision operation of pneumatic systems, easily adjusted to fit any operating requirement.

As a design engineer you'll be interested in knowing more about the Bellows system of pneumatic operation and controls. We'd like to send you two new bulletins showing how "Controlled-Air-Power" operates. No cost. No obligation. Just drop us a note and ask for your copies of Bulletins AV-300 and CL-30. Address The Bellows Co., Dept. IA-151, Akron 9, Ohio.

The Bellows Co.
Akron 9, Ohio
FIELD ENGINEER OFFICES IN ALL PRINCIPAL CITIES

PRESSES

FREE *publications*

These publications describe money - saving equipment and services ... they are free with no obligation ... just fill in and mail the postcard on the opposite page.

Universal Joints

Curtis standards of selection, heat treating, strength, accuracy, tolerance, concentricity and smoothness in the manufacture of universal joints are described in a new 6-p. folder. Information is presented on the extensive testing employed for improved quality, and a section of the bulletin presents information on correct universal joint selection. Construction features, as well as purchasing and engineering data, for both the ball type and standard block and pin type joints are detailed. *Curtis Universal Joint Co., Inc.*

For free copy insert No. 1 on postcard.

Broaches and Presses

The new 4-p. bulletin 10052 contains complete specifications and condensed information on a standard line of fluid power broaching machines and presses, illustrating and describing diversified special machines and listing the fluid power components manufactured for direct and resale purposes. *Oilgear Co.*

For free copy insert No. 2 on postcard.

Rust Prevention

Two new bulletins describe Derusto, a durable primer that prevents, absorbs and stops rust on all new and rusted metal. The bulletins show detailed results of a series of tests substantiating the claims made for this material, explaining what these tests mean to the customer in terms of greater efficiency, versatility and economy. Various examples of the wide field of application in industry, agriculture, state and civic facilities and around the home are also listed. *Master Bronze Powder Co.*

For free copy insert No. 3 on postcard.

British Machine Tools

One of Britain's largest machinery houses lists its complete stock of new and used machine tools, presses, sheet metal and woodworking machinery in a 202-p. catalog. Each item is illustrated, accompanied by detailed specifications and descriptive material. Services of a technical and advisory staff are offered purchasers. For overseas shipment, packing is done in the firm's own shops. *F. J. Edwards, Ltd.*

For free copy insert No. 4 on postcard.

Hard Surfacing Mn Steel

"Hard Surfacing Manganese Steel" is the title of a 4-p. bulletin outlining applications, precautions and suggestions on the proper procedures. The folder states that success in the facing of manganese is achieved by avoiding high temperatures throughout the body of the steel, a precaution which should be observed on pieces even as small as a shovel tooth. Where precautions as outlined have been observed, manganese has been successfully hard surfaced, saving users of manganese steel many thousands of dollars. *Rankin Mfg. Co.*

For free copy insert No. 5 on postcard.

Electrode Data

Contents of a 24-p. reference and instruction book, "Welding With Ampco Bronze Electrodes," include technical and pertinent information about every bronze electrode which Ampco manufactures, along with recommended welding techniques, welding procedures, and machining suggestions. Convenient charts covering the selection and preheating of bronze electrodes and the weldability of these electrodes are shown. *Ampco Metal, Inc.*

For free copy insert No. 6 on postcard.

Series-Arc Technique

The series-arc technique of submerged melt welding, a production welding method in which the depth of penetration of the weld metal into the base metal can be controlled, is explained in a new 28-p. illustrated booklet, "Welding with Multiple Electrodes in Series—A New Method of Unionmelt Welding." Use of this method in cladding operations with stainless steels, surface applications with some hard-facing rods, and in nonferrous cladding and surfacing applications are discussed. *Linde Air Products Co.*

For free copy insert No. 7 on postcard.

New Molding Brochure

A new 24-p. brochure covering fully automatic molding of thermosetting plastics describes the origins and growth of automatic molding, from the hand mold press to the fully automatic press. Cost savings by automatic molding are described, showing how it produces uniformity of parts, low mold and labor cost, less molding time, material savings, minimum investment, and controlled inventory. Typical applications for automatic molding are illustrated, together with its adaptability to a wide range of plastics products. Several case histories of successful users are presented. *F. J. Stokes Machine Co.*

For free copy insert No. 8 on postcard.

Radiation Protection

A selection of approved protective equipment of interest to industries directly concerned with the atomic energy field, as well as industrial plants using radioactive isotopes, is presented in a new 8-p.

Turn to Page 72

NEW *production ideas*

new and improved production ideas, equipment, services and methods described here offer production economies ... fill in and mail postcard.

Boring Tool Sets

Sixteen different combinations to meet varying requirements.

To facilitate the work of jig boring operators various groupings of boring tools are available in convenient, compact form with those shank diameters and lengths of tools required to carry on a particular type work. Hole diameters run as small as 1/16 in. Larger diameter tools have separate cutters, all interchangeable to fit the shanks supplied. Some sets contain ¾ and 1-in. adaptors to fit tools with ⅜-in. shank diam. *Bokum Tool Co.*

For more data insert No. 15 on postcard.

Fluid Transfer Pump

Transfers fluids at 22 gpm emptying 55 gal drum of SAE 30 oil in 2 min.

A new high speed, air-operated transfer pump can be used for transferring lubricants, thinners, coolants, naphthas, and non-corrosive chemicals without spillage, mess or waste. It fits all 2-in. opening drums; has a built-in, disk-type, precision-flo regulator to permit finger-tip regulation of the volume of output. The pump is steel construction, weighing 18 lb. *Lincoln Engineering Co.*

For more data insert No. 16 on postcard.

Aluminum Paint

Extra high heat resistant paint; withstands temperatures to 1700°F.

Known as Heat-Rem H-170, the new paint utilizes a silicone base and fuses with surface metal immediately upon application. It is said to form a bright, elastic finish resistant to moisture, corrosion, mild acids, alkalis and industrial fumes. It sets in 4 hr and dries completely overnight on hot surfaces. *Speco, Inc.*

For more data insert No. 17 on postcard.

Magnesium Anodes

Units contain anodes, backfill in cloth sack, copper wire attached.

The Anode-Pak units consist of a 17 or 32-lb anode packed with a chemically balanced backfill in a permeable cloth sack. A 10-ft insulated copper wire is attached and the complete unit shipped in a carton for instant installation and service. The use of the unit eliminates the need for mixing backfill at the site, and provides a backfill prepared under laboratory control to insure long installation life. *Apex Smelting Co.*

For more data insert No. 18 on postcard.

Induction Motors

Totally enclosed non-ventilated; indestructible Copperspun rotors.

The Fairbanks-Morse line of type QZE, totally enclosed, non-ventilated, squirrel cage, induction motors now includes continuous duty ratings built in NEMA standard frame 284: 7½ hp, 1800 rpm and 5 hp, 1200 rpm motors. Being completely sealed, there are no air passages to become clogged. Cooling is by radiation from the motor frames that are designed to maintain safe and uniform internal temperatures. Rotors are the in-

use postcard below

production ideas
Continued

destructible Copperspun. Cartridge type ball bearings with ample grease space permit sealing for the life of the bearing if desired, but with provisions for easy flushing and regreasing. *Fairbanks, Morse & Co.*

For more data insert No. 19 on postcard.

Sine Fixture Keys
Eliminate milling fixture key slots.

Sine fixture keys make it possible to establish the locating point, bore the fixture key holes and inspect the fixture all on one machine and in one setup. The flats of the sine fixture key base and the top of the shank are tapered to facilitate easy insertion. An additional feature is the locking device that enables the worker to rest the sine fixture key firmly in place by the slight turning of a set screw. *Jergens Tool Specialty Co.*

For more data insert No. 20 on postcard.

Unloading Valve
Features balance piston design for close accurate fit in valve bore.

Used in oil hydraulic circuits to unload one part of the circuit at no back pressure to the tank, a new hydraulic unloading valve is operated by pilot pressure from some other part of the circuit. Free flow to tank continues as long as the pilot pressure is higher than the setting of the valve. The Model 8826 unloading valve is available in sizes ¼ to 1½ in., in two pressure ranges of 50 to 150 psi and 500 to 1500 psi, adjustable from minimum to maximum in both ranges. *Rivett Lathe & Grinder, Inc.*

For more data insert No. 21 on postcard.

Pneumatic Hoist
Powered by rotary type air motor; lifting capacities, 250 to 2000 lb.

A new, lightweight, compact air hoist uses the worm-geared hoisting mechanism of the Detroit-Titan electric hoist, with an air-powered motor in place of an electric motor. The air motor is a sliding vane, rotary type; no pistons or reciprocating parts are involved. The hoist fitted with pendant operated, self-closing control, provides hoisting and lowering speeds that can be varied from a crawl, progressively, to full speed. *Detroit Hoist & Machine Co.*

For more data insert No. 22 on postcard.

Steam Turbine-Generators
High-speed, compact, streamlined; developed in 500 to 7500 kw ratings.

WA Series multi-stage, all-impulse steam turbine-generator units can operate with economical regenerative feedwater heating cycles and can be tied-in thermodynamically to provide a steam-power balance where low pressure process steam is utilized. Governor and regulating characteristics provide for paralleling with existing units and tie-lines. They incorporate the simplicity of three-bearing unit construction with quality multi-stage impulse turbine, housing type generator, and direct-connected exciter construction. *Allis-Chalmers Mfg. Co.*

For more data insert No. 23 on postcard.

Sealed-Hub Wheels
New Airlite Seal wheel offered at 50 pct below present price.

Of cast aluminum with solid rubber tread, the new sealed-hub industrial wheels feature a hub structure incorporating low-cost roller bearings and other economy features. The wheel is said to exclude virtually all foreign matter responsible for excessive bearing and axle wear and deterioration. Zerk fittings permit periodic lubrication of bearings and axle without tieup of handling equipment. Wheels range from 6 to 20 in. diam. *Aerol Co. Inc.*

For more data insert No. 24 on postcard.

Honing Machine
Small machine has working stroke of 15 in. and capacity from ¼ to 4 in.

The machine carries a 1¼-in. diam heat-treated alloy steel spindle, driven by a 3-hp motor through alloy steel reduction gears, with three spindle speeds available. Reciprocation is hydraulic with a 2-hp motor driving a Vickers pump with Vickers controls that permit reciprocating speeds from 1 to 70 fpm. Standard height under the

use postcard below

production ideas

Continued

spindle nose is 40 in. The machine is equipped with full pushbutton controls including pushbutton withdrawal at the end of the honing cycle. *C. Allen Fulmer Co.*

For more data insert No. 25 on postcard, p. 35.

Automatic Sorting Gage

Sorts bushings ½ in. diam x ¾ in. long at rate of 3600 per hr.

Bushings used in telephone lightning fuse units can be measured at the rate of 3600 per hr with an automatic sorting gage. The overall length is measured and each piece automatically delivered into two acceptable lengths and into over and under lengths. The machine is completely automatic; bushings are deposited in the hopper and the gage disposes them

into the proper tote boxes. Federal Electricators and power units are used to measure the bushings and control the segregating units. Signal lights show the operator what is going on at all times. *Federal Products Corp.*

For more data insert No. 26 on postcard, p. 35.

Transfer Press

Designed for the molding of small rubber parts around metal inserts.

Parts are produced on the new hydraulic transfer press at the rate of 20 units per 2-min cycle—10 units per min. The press is equipped with two transfer rams, each of 20 tons capacity. The moving-down die clamp has 60 tons capacity. Lower halves of the die are mounted on a rotating 3-station table providing nearly continuous processing of material, per-

mitting curing and unloading while material is being molded. The press has semi-automatic timed cycle controls, pushbutton operated, with inching features for all movements. The rotating table is mounted on a circular steam plate

to maintain die temperature when dies are out of pressing position. The clamp is provided with a smaller steam plate. Automatic controls maintain constant temperature. *Elmes Engineering Div., American Steel Foundries.*

For more data insert No. 27 on postcard, p. 35.

Hard Chrome Plater

Compact portable unit for hard chrome plating metal surfaces.

Parts up to 10 in. square can be hard chrome plated in the Model A-20 Chromaster. Powered by a dry disk, power pack, selenium rectifier, the unit is complete with plating bath tank, heavy duty rheostat, timer, ammeter and reversing switch for stripping action. The

hard chrome deposition can be controlled to tolerances of less than 0.0001 in. Operating at room temperature, Chromasol is a new, noncritical chrome plating solution available in a liquid concentrated form. It delivers a hard chrome plate that follows the exact charac-

teristics of the base metal to which it is applied. The rate of deposition remains constant at 0.002 iph. Using this process 1½ min is said to be the average time required to hard chrome cutting tools and wear parts. *Ward Leonard Electric Co.*

For more data insert No. 28 on postcard, p. 35.

Finishing Machine

Fluid-abrasive blast stops glare, reduces friction, holds lubricant.

In a new surface finishing machine work is placed in the sheet steel cabinet having an inverted pyramid hopper which contains 50 lb abrasive and 8 gal of water. Abrasive is kept in suspension by an agitator and propelled at an 85-oz impact against the work through a syphon-jet type gun attached to a flexible air hose. The operator directs the nozzle from outside the cabinet, working

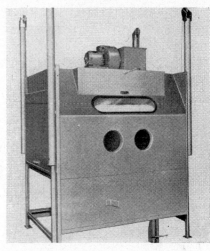

through arm holes, and observes work through an inspection window. Visibility is maintained by fluorescent lighting inside the cabinet and filtered exhaust system. Air is regulated by a foot throttle. The machine is available in seven standard sizes. *Jewett Mfg. Co.*

For more data insert No. 29 on postcard, p. 35.

Tensioning Setup

Removes foil processing problems.

Scrap losses and machine downtime due to foil breakage are said to be practically eliminated by a new precision tensioning means used on aluminum foil mills built by Lewis & Foundry & Machine Co. The tensioning control is based on use of a high capacity low pressure air brake. Tension produced by this brake can be precisely cali-

Turn to Page 73

View of Harbor Island Laboratory and Testing Station.

Lowering piling test specimens into place. Sea water is something more than a mixture of chemicals; its corrosive action over an extended period can be studied properly only by exposure of specimens to attack under natural conditions.

New testing station provides expanded facilities for corrosion studies

During the past 15 years, the Atlantic Ocean at Kure Beach served as a giant test tube for studying attacks of sea water and salt air upon more than 35,000 specimens, including virtually all types of metals and alloys.

Storm damage to the basin, in which the underwater tests were conducted, compelled establishment of a new and protected testing station. Accordingly, some 15 miles north, on Harbor Island, the new Inco Marine Laboratory was built to provide expanded facilities and an even better "Ocean Test Tube."

This new Harbor Island station, along with the atmospheric test racks retained on the shore of Kure Beach, now widen the scope of cooperative enterprise for fighting industry's common enemy — *corrosion*.

The vast amount of valuable data accumulated over the years will continue to be made available to all industry, as well as to government agencies for whom and with whose cooperation much of the research has been undertaken. You are invited to consult us on your corrosion problems.

Running water troughs. For studying the action of sea water flowing at moderate velocities, specimens are immersed in the troughs, shown above. The total length of trough used for this purpose now amounts to about 600 feet.

Atmospheric and spray test lot. Shown above is part of the atmospheric test lot at Kure Beach in which over 20,000 specimens have been exposed, some for over nine years. The racks face south, and the specimens, supported on porcelain insulators, are all set at a slope of 30 degrees.

EMBLEM OF **INCO** SERVICE
TRADE MARK

THE INTERNATIONAL NICKEL COMPANY, INC. 67 WALL STREET NEW YORK 5, N.Y.

IRON AGE

introduces,

William C. Oberg, appointed manufacturing consultant, U. S. STEEL CO., Pittsburgh. Mr. Oberg joined U. S. Steel in 1911 and prior to his present appointment, was general manager of operations, Pittsburgh district. **John H. Elliott,** appointed general manager—manufacturing.

Robert C. Tyson, elected vice-president of U. S. STEEL CORP., New York. Mr. Tyson will continue as comptroller in addition to his new post.

Kenneth F. Ames, promoted to sales manager, Plains division of the CATERPILLAR TRACTOR CO., Peoria, Ill. **Lee Morgan,** and **Gordon Fowler** will serve as assistant sales managers, Plains division. Other organizational changes: **E. A. Tiarks,** becomes assistant sales manager, Western division, **W. F. Jordan,** assistant sales manager, Eastern division.

Carl J. Meister, appointed vice-president and director of sales of the ATLAS CHAIN & MFG. CO., Philadelphia.

Maurice J. McCarthy, Jr., appointed manager of magnet wire sales of the ANACONDA WIRE & CABLE CO., Muskegon, Mich. **Richard B. Steinmetz,** appointed general manager of mills with headquarters at Hastings-on-Hudson, N. Y.

Milton E. Mengel, named Great Lakes regional manager of BURROUGHS ADDING MACHINE CO., Detroit. **J. Berryman** appointed superintendent of machine assembly and adjusting, and **K. Schwartz** as superintendent of production control, at the Plymouth, Mich. plant.

L. G. Porter, elected treasurer of BORG-WARNER CORP., Chicago.

Alan F. Dill, promoted to the newly-created post of defense regulations coordinator for the AMERICAN WIRE & STEEL CO., Cleveland.

Carl W. Hopp, named assistant manager of the Northwest Division of AMERICAN PIPE CONSTRUCTION CO., Portland, Ore. **Floyd E. Mulford,** advanced to position of assistant sales manager. **Don S. Browne** and **C. Herbert Johnson,** joined the sales staff. **Don S. Burnett,** named production manager.

Robert C. Ross, retired from active service with JOSEPH T. RYERSON & SON, INC., Chicago, after 47 years with the company.

James R. Hitt, appointed manager of the factory branch of the TRAILMOBILE CO., Newark, N. J.

Gordon F. Friauf, appointed general material supervisor at ALLIS-CHALMERS MFG. CO., Milwaukee. **Charles A. McCormack,** retired after 55 years with the company.

C. R. Carlin, elected vice-president in charge of production and **R. K. Lee,** elected vice-president in charge of research and engineering, for the ALLOY RODS CO., York, Pa. Other officers elected: **E. J. Brady,** president and chairman of the board; **M. G. Sedan,** executive vice-president; **W. D. Himes,** treasurer; and **H. L. Weaver,** secretary and assistant treasurer.

A. J. Morrison, elected chairman of the junior board of directors of DRAVO CORP., Pittsburgh. Three new members appointed to the board are **William D. Bickel,** manager of the power department; **Louis P. Struble,** manager of the Keystone Division, and **William H. Collins,** director of advertising.

H. THOMAS HALLOWELL, JR., elected president of the Standard Pressed Steel Co., Jenkintown, Pa.

C. S. BEATTIE, appointed executive vice-president and general manager of Delta-Star Electric Co., a division of H. K. Porter Co., Inc., Chicago.

ALBERT J. BERDIS, appointed general superintendent of U. S. Steel Company's Fairless Works, Morrisville, Pa.

IRON AGE

salutes

Erwin Loewy

HE is a man who has made American industrial strength mightier. His great hydraulic presses and mill machinery are revolutionizing design and production methods in aircraft and other industries. He is putting muscle in the industrial body.

Erwin Loewy, dynamic president of Hydropress, Inc., has built an international reputation for ability to accomplish the impossible. His latest giant is a forging press bigger than any ever built, limited only by manufacturing and transportation facilities.

After World War II the United States Air Force sought the why and how of German hydraulic press development. The Air Force turned to the one man who could best give the answers. Erwin Loewy went to Germany for a 30-day visit and stayed 10 months as an Air Force consultant.

Born in Czechoslovakia, Mr. Loewy studied engineering in Prague, France and Germany. He acquired a wide knowledge of the steel industry while working with a steel supply house in Duesseldorf. Later he became a guiding spirit in Schloemann Engineering Co. in Germany.

The coming of the Nazi forced Mr. Loewy and his associates to transfer headquarters to their British company, Loewy Engineering Co., Ltd. In 1940 he came to the United States and organized Hydropress, Inc.

Mr. Loewy first visited the U. S. in 1926 when he tried to sell heavy presses to American industry. In 1936 he supervised installation of the first Loewy press in this country at the Bridgeport Brass plant.

Prior to U. S. entry in World War II, Erwin Loewy warned OPM this country would need many extrusion presses. It took WPB a year-and-a-half to reach a decision. Then Hydropress built 80 heavy extrusion presses for American industry. He feels this country today stands in the same desperate need for heavy duty forging presses as it did in 1942 for extrusion presses.

SAM B. HEPPENSTALL, JR., elected vice-president in charge of sales of American Forge & Mfg. Co., Pittsburgh.

NORMAN F. SMITH, elected president of The Osborn Mfg. Co., Cleveland.

W. R. PERSONS, elected vice-president in charge of sales of The Lincoln Electric Co., Cleveland.

W. G. ANDREWS, appointed executive vice-president and general manager of Electrofilm Corp.

IRON AGE *introduces*

Continued

Edward O. Boshell, elected chairman of the board of directors and president of the WESTINGHOUSE AIR BRAKE CO., and its subsidiary, The Union Switch and Signal Co., Pittsburgh. **Herbert A. May**, elected senior vice-president of the parent company.

Alexander H. Gaal, appointed a vice-president of the EARLE M. JORGENSEN CO., Los Angeles. Mr. Gaal retains his position as merchandising manager.

Joseph G. Wortley, appointed manager of sales of the KENILWORTH STEEL CO., Kenilworth, N. J.

William K. Honan, appointed a regional manager of ALL-STATE WELDING ALLOYS CO., INC., White Plains, N. Y. Mr. Honan will direct sales and service for the company in all of New England, northern New York state, western Pennsylvania and Ohio.

Peter B. Kline, named manager of stainless sales for the EDGCOMB STEEL CO., Philadelphia.

J. Benjamin Cowan, promoted to the office of executive vice-president of PLASTEEL PRODUCTS CO., Washington, Pa.

Charles H. Disch, retired as vice-president and director of purchases of the WROUGHT WASHER MFG. CO., Milwaukee. Mr. Disch was with the company for 44 years.

A. M. Turner, elected assistant treasurer of the WILLIAMS & CO., INC., Pittsburgh. **W. A. Risher**, appointed manager of the nickel alloys department. **G. E. Pickett**, appointed manager of the stainless steel department.

C. B. House, Jr., and **Lee J. Mohler**, appointed sales managers of two newly established product line sections; the A-C Motor section and the D-C motor and generator section, respectively, of the GENERAL ELECTRIC CO., Lynn, Mass.

C. Russell Conklin, named manager of the Republic Rubber Div., of LEE RUBBER & TIRE CORP., Philadelphia. **Warren Ingersoll**, formerly in charge of the Philadelphia office, becomes assistant to the president.

H. T. Hallowell, Sr., becomes chairman of the board of STANDARD PRESSED STEEL CO., Jenkintown, Pa., the company that he founded in 1903. **Harold F. Gade**, appointed senior vice-president. Mr. Gade is a co-founder. **J. Whiting Friel**, named vice-president in charge of sales; **William I. Kryder**, elected secretary. Mr. Kryder succeeds **Ralph S. Mast**, who is retiring after 46 years of service with the company.

A. G. Hendrickson, joined A. O. SMITH CORP., Milwaukee, as welding equipment sales manager.

Robert C. Kuhn, appointed assistant district manager of the Cleveland sales office of the CRUCIBLE STEEL COMPANY OF AMERICA.

James S. McCullough, appointed sales promotion manager for LAMSON CORP., Syracuse, N. Y.

Edward J. Lilly, named sales engineer for the Butterfield Div., UNION TWIST DRILL CO. Mr. Lilly will be located in Philadelphia, representing the Butterfield Division in Philadelphia and Baltimore.

Howard H. Blouch, appointed sales manager of the Cleveland Plant of the CHROMIUM CORP. OF AMERICA, Cleveland.

John W. Codding, appointed manager of sales of the Boston district, BETHLEHEM STEEL CO., succeeding **Robert B. Wallace**, who has retired after 40 years of service.

OBITUARIES

Lionel M. Stern, 77, chairman of the board of The Colonial Iron Works Co., Cleveland, which he founded in 1916, died recently.

Robert N. Anderson, 52, district sales manager of Harnischfeger Corp., died recently.

John Avery, president of Roots-Connersville Blower Corp., since 1946, died recently.

George F. Meyer, 83, president of F. Meyer & Brother Co., and former president of The Meyer Furnace Co., both of Peoria, Ill., died recently.

"Good Enough" is NOT ENOUGH!

Revere Brass of carefully controlled grain sizes is used in the Andirons, the Fire Lighter, the Lighter Cover and the Torch Handle.

● Sometimes a routine laboratory procedure finds ways to make improvements even when everything already is "completely satisfactory". In fact, that is one of the main reasons for carrying out laboratory routines.

A case in point is the Decorative Polished Brass Fire Lighter produced by Peerless Manufacturing Corp., Louisville, Kentucky.

Here is a product that was rolling down the production line and on into homes all over the country. The consumers were satisfied and Peerless was pleased with the appearance of its product. There were no troubles. Nevertheless, the Revere Technical Advisory Service was asked to study the polishing methods and find out if even better procedures would be advantageous.

Just as a routine procedure our laboratory men cut up several of the partly drawn "Pots" and checked on the gauge diminution caused by drawing. The "Lab. Men" are continually doing things like that ;.. studying the successful products in order to pile up data which may be useful when they run into a "problem" product.

They found that with a different drawing sequence the draws, although still deep, could be made less severe. The new drawing sequence would permit the use of smaller grained metal. The smaller grain would make polishing easier, even though the product as it went out into the market could have *no* more than the same highly polished beauty it always had.

By testing to find if it could get one cost saving, this company got two.

Perhaps you also are thinking in terms of one slight improvement when two or more are readily available. The Revere Technical Advisory Service offers the laboratory routines which will find out. If you use copper, brass, bronze, aluminum, nickel silver—any alloy which Revere can make—just get in touch with the nearest Revere sales office.

REVERE
COPPER AND BRASS INCORPORATED
Founded by Paul Revere in 1801
230 Park Avenue, New York 17, New York

• • •

*Mills: Baltimore, Md.; Chicago and Clinton, Ill.;
Detroit, Mich.; Los Angeles and Riverside, Calif.;
New Bedford, Mass.; Rome, N. Y.
Sales Offices in Principal Cities, Distributors Everywhere:*

on the assembly line

automotive news and opinions

Chrysler show is tribute to engineers . . . V-8 engine features economy . . . Nash wins mechanical design citation.

by Walter G. Patton

Carmakers Have a Case—The opinion is growing in Detroit that automobile producers will be permitted to raise their prices based on a formula yet to be developed. The carmakers have a good case. One producer has estimated that between June and December the price of raw materials alone going into a car has increased more than $125 per car.

During the past 6 months, the price of crude rubber has jumped 130 pct. GRS rubber is up 6 pct. Synthetic rubber has advanced 12½ pct. Tin prices have increased 93 pct and lead is up 44 pct. The upward swing in zinc prices is 19 pct. Wool costs have gone up 59 pct.

Tribute to Engineers — The Chrysler engineering exhibit held last week at the Massachusetts Ave. plant in conjunction with the introduction of 1951 Chrysler models is undoubtedly the finest tribute yet paid to the automobile engineer. It was an engineer's show—a great personal triumph for the entire Chrysler engineering staff.

In addition to new Chrysler products—the 1951 line of cars, the new V-8 Fire Power engine, power steering, Oriflow shock absorbers, automatic transmission and air cooled brakes—Chrysler displayed impressive exhibits of the research tools used by the up-to-date engineer to develop these products.

Complex Rocker Arms—The new Chrysler V-8 engine is, of course, the No. 1 exhibit. Most ingenious feature of the new powerplant is the complex rocker arm assembly which requires two rocker arms, two hydraulic valve lifters and four push rods for each cylinder. This arrangement eliminates the necessity for an overhead cam, greatly simplifying the servicing problem.

Engine Breathes Better—Tests indicate the new engine will give an 11 pct improvement in economy. The valve position in the hemisphere head is such that the valves are approximately at right angles to each other. This permits improved "breathing" and is one of the reasons for the Chrysler claim of improved combustion efficiency, less build-up of carbon, varnish and other products of combustion. Incidentally, auto engineers agree that the build up of deposits in a dirty engine may reduce the effective octane rating of fuel from 11 to 15 points.

The new Chrysler engine will undoubtedly cost more to build than previous engines. Valves, for example, are equipped with two springs each.

Submarine Auto—Dodge is assembling four types of military vehicles on the same production lines used for civilian trucks. Last week the company began production on a $92 million order for military trucks, including cargo vehicles, telephone and maintenance trucks, utility trucks and wheel-drive field ambulances.

Incidentally, with a snorkel tube fitted on the engine and tail pipe, the new Dodge utility vehicles will operate in water which would normally be over the driver's head. After setting the throttle, the driver is able to sit on the roof and steer the vehicle with his toes. The ignition system is completely water-proofed. Breathing for the engine is provided through the front snorkel.

Squeak-Proof Brakes—Another Chrysler engineering first will undoubtedly be new molded brake lining used on trucks. The lining is said to be a design that eliminates squeaking of the brakes.

Some Overtime Scheduled — A substantial part of the decline in automobile output has been attributed to elimination of overtime work. Most Detroit sources believed that overtime in the auto plants would be largely eliminated during 1951. However, Buick has

assembly line

Continued

scheduled Saturday operations. There is a possibility that at least one other General Motors division will work Saturdays. This is another indication that car producers will continue to turn out as many cars as they possibly can in the face of growing government-imposed restrictions.

Chrysler Croning—In the Chrysler show a small pump casting was on exhibit made by the so-called Croning or shell mold precision casting method. Thus, Chrysler publicly joins Ford and General Motors in what promises to be the most important foundry development during the postwar period. (THE IRON AGE, Aug. 3, 1950.)

Rambler Gets Decorated—The 1951 Nash Rambler convertible has been awarded the "Modern Designs" citation for "general excellence in mechanical design." In bestowing the award on Meade F. Moore, Nash director of research, the new Nash front suspension that "reduces the unsprung weight and gives superior riding qualities in a shorter wheelbase automobile" was specifically cited.

Metal-Coated Plastic — Another interesting Chrysler exhibit was a plastic part plated with chromium. Just how the plating is accomplished was not disclosed but it is believed that electricity conductors are present in the plastic itself. No surface coating is necessary, according to Chrysler engineers.

Chrysler "Make Ready"—K. T. Keller, chairman of the board, indicated that Chrysler Corp. spent $50 million for "make ready" and tooling of its 1951 models. In addition to tooling the new engine and transmission for its 1951 models, Chrysler made many body changes requiring new dies for the fenders, top, grille and other formed parts. At the last minute, the die for the front corner post was scrapped to make possible the use of a narrower design.

One-Finger Steering—Hit of the Chrysler Show as far as the customers were concerned was power steering which reduces steering effort by nine-tenths. The pressure of one finger and the guidance of the thumb is all that is required to rotate the wheel. Hydraguide Power Steering will be available on all 1951 Chrysler Imperial and New Yorker models.

Price has not been announced but it is expected to be in the $125 to $150 range. Incidentally, most observers here predict power steering will be adopted by Cadillac and perhaps other GM divisions in 1952.

Available Immediately—The new Chrysler Fire Power V-8 engines will be available immediately in all Chrysler, New Yorker and Imperial models. Power steering will also be used on these models. No announcement was made last week about the Chrysler torque converter which, incidentally, requires a considerable amount of aluminum, a metal which will be taken heavily by defense.

Four Traveler Models — The Kaiser Traveler for 1951 will be available in four new models. With the rear panel open and the tail gate extended, the cargo capacity has been increased to 105½ cu ft. Floor area is 108 x 46 in. The spare tire is recessed into the floor. The Traveler, which doubles as a special purpose vehicle for ambulance, farm and sales work, is generally lower in price than station wagons which are often used for the same purpose.

Study Gear Failures—Gear design is an uncommon cause of failure in service, J. O. Almen, General Motors Research Laboratories consultant, told the Society of Automotive Engineers recently. Almen disclosed that in GM Research Laboratories more than 2 million gear histories were examined but only 100,000 failures could be attributed directly to design.

THE BULL OF THE WOODS

By J. R. Williams

THE CLASS DISTINCTION

1 1621—Glass was money! America's first glass factory was actually a mint —not for the manufacture of coins but to make glass beads for *use* as money when buying land, food and furs from the Indians.

2 1827—Blown glass was the rule until Enoch Robinson, a carpenter, figured glass could be *pressed* into shape . . . the glass pressing machine was born. Electricity to power new machines was still to come.

3 1899—Owens invented a machine to make bottles as the machine age arrived in glass. By 1915, Howell "Red Band" Motors were making important contributions to this and other industries.

ANOTHER HOWELL SUCCESS STORY

GLASS...from artisans to automatic machines

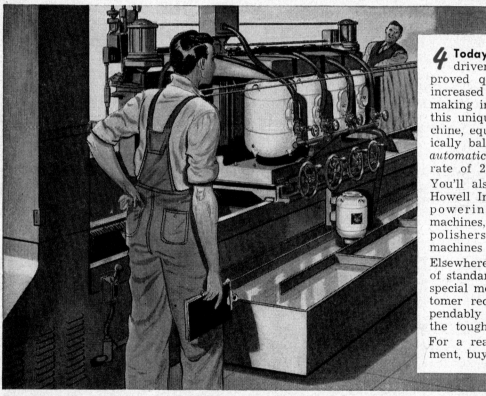

4 **Today**—Modern, electrically driven machines have improved quality, cut costs and increased output in the glass making industry. For example, this unique glass beveling machine, equipped with 7 dynamically balanced Howell Motors, *automatically* bevels glass at the rate of 2,000 inches per hour!

You'll also find precision-built Howell Industrial Type Motors powering bottle and bulb machines, conveyors, grinders, polishers, plate and window machines in the glass industry.

Elsewhere, Howell's wide range of standard NEMA motors, and special motors designed to customer requirements, serve dependably and efficiently under the toughest conditions.

For a really profitable investment, buy HOWELL!

Free enterprise encourages mass production, supplies more jobs — provides more goods for more people at less cost.

Howell totally enclosed, fan-cooled motor—windings completely sealed against dirt and weather.

HOWELL MOTORS

HOWELL ELECTRIC MOTORS CO., HOWELL, MICH.
Precision-built Industrial Motors Since 1915

west coast progress report

digest of far west industrial activity

by R.T. Reinhardt

Who Is Going to Do What?— Though the powers-that-be are loath to reveal who has applied for certificates of necessity to construct steel plants, it is known at least two applications are on file from western interests.

One unidentified group has applied for its certificate to construct a 1,200,000 ton capacity steel plant in central California claiming to have a deposit of 80 million tons of 64 pct iron ore in reserve.

Steel Plant in Nevada? — Another group claiming to control important iron ore deposits in Nevada is seeking to build an integrated steel plant in that state.

While conceded that western steel capacity is lagging behind even normal consumption, some steelmen argue that neither of these projects would be economically feasible. However, many steelmen held similar views in the early 1940's in regard to the Kaiser operation at Fontana.

Jittery Scrap—While western members of the scrap trade were attending the 23rd annual convention of the Institute of Scrap, Iron & Steel in New York last week, the California scrap market began to bubble and boil.

Although mills are still quoting an offering price of $30.00 per ton for No. 1 heavy melting in San Francisco and Los Angeles, considerable tonnages have moved at prices up to $34.00 per ton. Apparently the larger mills have been able to meet requirements at the lower figures but independents have had to go higher.

Particularly noteworthy has been an advance in the price of railroad scrap from transcontinental lines which has gone up to $46.00 per ton. Previously this grade was available at the current price of No. 1 heavy and is still available at that figure from railroads without transcontinental connections. Lines such as the Santa Fe and Southern Pacific can readily and economically haul their western scrap to Chicago where the current price is in the neighborhood of $45.00 per ton.

Awkward Spot—This puts western buyers in the awkward position of having to pay practically the Chicago price for railroad scrap or else see it leave this territory which is already pressed for metallics.

Western scrap dealers fully expect price freezes and hope they will be in the neighborhood of $35.00 per ton for No. 1 heavy, approximately twice the OPA figure during the last freeze. On the other hand, buyers are hoping for and anticipate a price in the neighborhood of $30.00 a ton.

In Los Angeles, scrap dealers are having a problem holding crane operators now being paid $1.50 per hour while contractors working for the government are paying as high as $2.35 per hour. This situation is cited as further justification for higher prices.

May Boost Aluminum Production—Aluminum producers in the Pacific Northwest may not much longer be faced with the need to curtail production because power supplied on an interruptible basis is periodically denied them.

If Congress approves the order of the Secretary of the Interior for the construction of a 140-mile high voltage transmission line connecting the Columbia Basin Power grid with that of the California Central Valley Project, 100,000 kilowatts of BPA power would be firmed up.

Bonneville now has an interruptible load of about 250,000 kilowatts, most of which is supplied to aluminum reduction plants in Washington and Oregon.

Kaiser Magnesium—Practically the same personnel will be in charge of production of magnesium at the Manteca, Calif., plant, to be reactivated in July by Kaiser Aluminum & Chemical Corp., that handled its operation during the past war. This unit has a rated capacity of 20 million lbs of magnesium metal per year.

CHASER LIFE *DOUBLED*

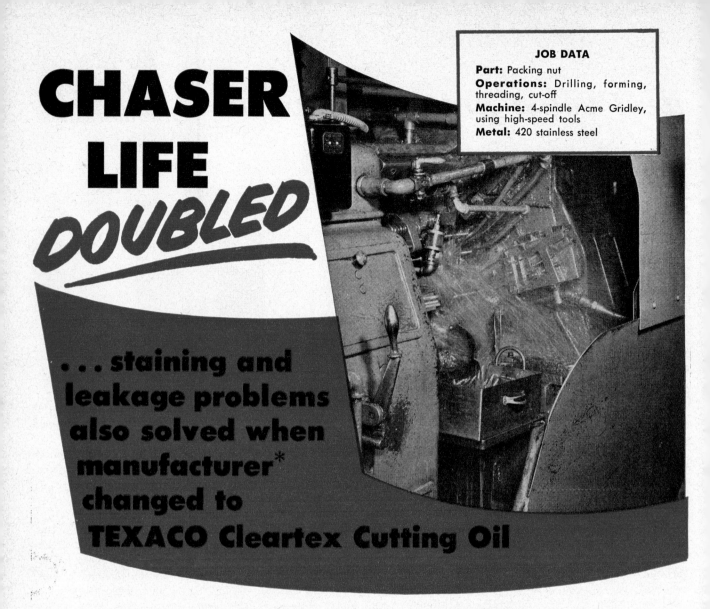

. . . staining and leakage problems also solved when manufacturer* changed to TEXACO Cleartex Cutting Oil

The stainless steel used on this job is one of the toughest metals to machine. Operators reported their greatest difficulty was frequent breakage of the threading chasers, none of which lasted more than three shifts (24 hours). In addition, leakage of machine lubricant into the cutting fluid caused contamination and high oil consumption.

At the suggestion of a Texaco Lubrication Engineer, the competitive cutting fluid and machine lubricant were both replaced by *Texaco Cleartex Cutting Oil.* Chasers now last six shifts (48 hours) —*double the life!* Because *Texaco Cleartex Cutting Oil* is dual-purpose—designed to serve as both cutting fluid and machine lubricant — contamination has been completely overcome and oil consumption

materially reduced.

Still another advantage gained from the change to *Texaco Cleartex Cutting Oil* is that either steel or brass can be worked without changing oils. *Texaco Cleartex Cutting Oil* does not stain.

Let a Texaco Lubrication Engineer—specializing in machining—help you gain similar cost-saving benefits in *your* plant. There is a complete line of Texaco Cutting, Grinding and Soluble Oils to assure better, faster, lower-cost machining, whatever the metal or the method of working it.

Just call the nearest of the more than 2,000 Texaco Distributing Plants in the 48 States, or write The Texas Company, 135 East 42nd Street, New York 17, New York.

*Name on request

the federal view

this week in washington

by Eugene J. Hardy

Trial CMP—A "trial run" for a Controlled Materials Plan is in the works at the Defense Dept. and NPA. The Munitions Board has reportedly asked the Army, Navy, and Air Force to have ready by Feb. 15, requirements for basic raw materials so that a start on CMP can be made. Extent of the "trial run" or the materials covered has not been revealed.

NPA says that a complete CMP for nonferrous metals is likely to come first. It is estimated that if complete allocation of steel under CMP were decided upon now, it would be fourth quarter 1951 before a staff could be ready to administer it.

Terminated Contracts — The World War II hassle over final review of terminated contracts is up again and this time Controller General Lindsay Warren who lost his earlier battle for review appears to have won the first round. The Defense Dept. has circulated to industry its proposed contract termination section of the Armed Services Procurement Regulations. The section does not contain a "finality" clause which means that a terminated contract agreed to by the firm involved and the contracting officer will not be final, but subject to further audit by Mr. Warren's General Accounting Office.

Mr. Warren has groused about losing his fight for review in the latter stages of World War II when he carried the fight before key Congressional Committees. Industry can be expected to go to Congress again, for GAO review of terminated contracts only means interminable delay.

Tax Battle Looms—Despite talk from the White House, generated by the Council of Economic Advisers, of a tax boost this year amounting to between $20 and $25 billion, Congress will not enact any such program, barring all-out war.

Top Treasury officials privately admit that there is little hope of gaining any more than $10 billion additional in taxes to ward off an estimated deficit of $16.5 billion. It is also likely that Congress will not enact a tax measure before mid-1951 at the earliest, despite White House screams for haste. Congress is none too happy about inclusion of the whole Fair Deal program in the Budget Message.

Government Plants — President Truman has followed up his recommendation for new legislation authorizing direct Government construction of industrial facilities with a budget estimate of $1.2 billion to cover this and other items. Even if Congress does not approve such Government construction a large portion of this amount will be used for loans, long-term purchase contracts, incentive payments, and government equipment for installation in defense plants.

Control Funds Up—Budget estimates of $330 million dollars for administration of economic controls indicate the extent to which controls will be imposed during the coming fiscal year. Currently, the control agencies are operating under a $30 million appropriation and there is a request before Congress for an additional $10 million.

While the amount requested for fiscal year 1952 is about ten times greater than existing appropriations, it is still well below World War II totals when the peak was greater than $2 billion. The $330 million is also about twice the amount granted OPA at its peak, although this sum is designed to cover all existing control agencies.

Point 4 Changes—The Administration's "Point 4" program of aid for underdeveloped areas of the world is changing direction as a result of the expanded mobilization effort. It is now being termed a security program for these areas which will be expected to speed up production of strategic materials in return for technical aid and dollars. Previously, the State Dept. regarded the program as an almost sacred universal "uplift" society and had rejected any idea of getting materials in return for this type of aid. The policy had been guided by the feeling that getting something in return would serve to "destroy the atmosphere."

INLAND DATA for STEEL USERS

INLAND STEEL CO.
38 S. Dearborn Street, Chicago 3, Illinois

The role of Scrap in Steel Making

One of the most important raw materials in steelmaking . . . one frequently underrated by the casual observer . . . is iron and steel scrap. With over 90% of all the steel in the U. S. being made by the open hearth process, the scrap used by steel producers totals approximately 50,000,000 tons each year.

The open hearth method of steel production is geared to a pig iron scrap consumption ratio of roughly 50-50. This is to the final advantage of the steel user, since a large scrap diet in steelmaking results in a number of benefits: (a) steel is made faster (since scrap has already been "refined" once before, the "melt" time in the open hearth is decreased); (b) vital raw materials are conserved (it takes almost 4 tons of iron ore, coal and limestone to make a ton of pig iron); (c) unless scrap prices are abnormally high, the price of steel is cheaper; (d) steel is of higher quality (since scrap has already undergone one refining process); (e) transportation facilities, instead of being used for the additional raw materials otherwise required, can be released for other uses; (f) steel mill capacities can be expanded more readily with less emphasis on the blast furnace and more on open hearths and rolling mills.

About two-thirds of the scrap consumed in making steel comes from the steel mills themselves. Crop ends and sheared edges move quickly back to the open hearth shop. The remaining third, flowing to the mills largely through the 6,500 scrap dealers in the U.S., comes from the wastage in metal working plants ("production" scrap), auto graveyards, old building, bridge and ship wrecking projects, railroads (worn rails, freight cars, etc.), neighborhood junk peddlers.

The scrap dealers must sort the scrap so that the undesirables are eliminated, the alloys segregated and the right kinds of scrap can be delivered in large tonnages to the mills for most efficient steelmaking practice.

Today, with steel production at record peaks and with capacity continually expanding, it is more important than ever to keep scrap flowing back to the steel mills from *every* source. Everyone waiting for steel can help himself by assisting the movement of his scrap through his regular channels.

THE SCRAP CYCLE

OPEN HEARTH   BLOOMING MILLS

FINISHING MILLS

STEEL MILL SCRAP YARD

HOME SCRAP

PURCHASE SCRAP

SCRAP DEALER

PRODUCTION SCRAP

AUTO GRAVEYARD

MANUFACTURER

JUNK

JUNK DEALER

CONSUMER

CONTINUOUS CASTING PROCESS

EMPLOYS A

moving mold

Each year sees more ideas and patents added to the files on continuous casting. Some are new approaches, but basically most are improvements or refinements of existing or expired patents. The Hazelett process is not new (THE IRON AGE, March 21, 1935, and April 11, 1940, p. 44). The former Hazelett machines are no longer in use.

A moving mold rather than a stationary or oscillating mold has been the aim of C. William Hazelett of Hazelett Strip Casting Process Co. for years. The latest design, which is 7 machines and 15 years later from the first unit Hazelett ever built, is shown in Fig. 1. The mold consists of two steel belts revolving over drum pulleys. The outside of the belt mold wall is shower-cooled with water. Molten metal is introduced into the cavity between the two belts and it solidifies and moves forward with the belts through the mill. The speed of the pilot plant mill in Fig. 1 varies from 27 to 35 fpm and a number of aluminum slabs 9 x ½ in., weighing 25 lb, have been cast. These slabs have an excellent surface as shown in Fig. 2. The edges of these slabs are also smooth with a slight convex contour.

The process appears to be well suited for continuous casting of flat shapes in aluminum.

By D. I. BROWN

Feature Editor

Water-cooled steel bands traveling over drum pulleys form the mold in the latest Hazelett machine. The mill requires very little space and power requirements are very small. Production machines for brass and aluminum are under consideration.

There is more work to be done on methods of introducing the metal into the mold. No attempt was made in trial runs to protect the aluminum from oxidation as the first aim was to establish that a sound section could be cast. Micros of one of the sections are shown in Fig. 3. The porosity and oxides, it is believed, can be eliminated by adding a suitable feeding device which will exclude air from the molten metal. A design for such a feeding method appears at the left of Fig. 4. The metal will thus be fed continuously into the concave mold section. The contours of the mold which hold the metal during solidification are of extreme importance. On p. 53 a scale model of the rolls and the metal band mold are shown. The convex rolls shape the metal band and this shape changes until a perfectly flat and rectangular section is produced prior to complete solidification of the metal throughout the section. These different mold contours are shown in the top righthand corner of Fig. 4.

Mill Occupies Small Space

The mill requires very little space. The pilot plant at Greenwich, Conn. occupies an area 15 x 15 ft square. This includes the controls, pumps, melting unit, etc. The control panel of the small unit is quite simple. Very little power is re-quired. The mill shown in Fig. 1 employs a 1-hp motor to drive the moving mold and a 5-hp motor for pumping water at a rate of 400 gpm.

The mill is only 6 deg off horizontal which is an added advantage. Cast slabs can be cut with a regular shear or the continuously cast slab could be fed into a 4-high single stand hot mill for reduction into strip. Very probably a re-heating furnace would be necessary so that the casting unit would not have to be confined and regulated to deliver a cast slab at precise rolling temperatures.

Satisfactory Edging A Problem

One of the big problems of the moving belt mold is satisfactory edging. The edge sides of the mold do not move in the present pilot model. The sides, called side dams, which appear in Fig. 4, are made of brass and are water-cooled. Although these dams have produced satisfactory edges, a movable side is being designed. Water which flows over both exterior sides of the metal belt is kept from overflowing the edge by a tight spring clip trough.

The tonnage which can be produced will not be known until a commercial installation is made. It is believed that a 28-in. wide mill could produce 40 to 100 tons of aluminum per hr, de-

FIG. 1—Pilot plant mill which has continuously cast aluminum and brass slabs.

FIG. 2—As-cast surface of aluminum slab, shown at the delivery end of the mill. The remarkably good surface finish is typical; the photograph has not been retouched in any way.

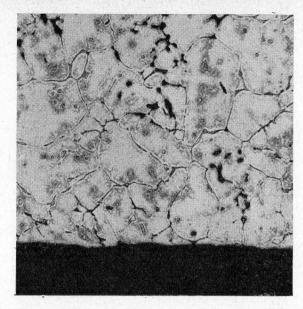

FIG. 3—Micro of cast aluminum shows porosity and oxide inclusions. These defects will be eliminated with proper protective feeding devices in production units. (120X.)

pendent on gage. Tonnage would vary inversely with the thickness and lineal production varies with the inverse square of the thickness of the slab. All parts of the Hazelett mill which control gage are water-cooled. Since no work (reduction) is done on the metal, very little power is needed to drive the mill.

The cast slab chills quickly and like other continuous casting methods, uniform analysis across the slab can be expected. It is now evident that the old troubles of segregation and folding which Hazelett encountered on previous designs have now been eliminated. Some thought has been given to casting of steel slabs with this machine but it is yet too early to tell if this can be done. There are problems of temperature and suitable refractories plus a lot of experimentation on speeds that must be made before the process can be evaluated for continuous casting steel sections. However, brass has been run through the machine and a production plant for 70-30 brass may be built this year. The process also has good possibilities for the casting of magnesium slabs.

FIG. 4—Schematic drawing of the Hazelett mill. A plug is inserted at X. This plug serves as a momentary dam to permit the metal to fill out the mold contour. The plug then passes through the mill ahead of the cast slab. A cross-section of the feeding spout (R) appears at upper right in position relative to the mold contour.

A Moving strip mold

B First pressure or flat roll

D Other flat work rolls

L Drum pulleys over which steel band mold revolves

M Molten aluminum in various stages of casting

N Water supply nozzles

P Concave pulleys which shape mold contour

R Spout which introduces the metal into the mold

T Water-cooled side dams which edge the cast slab

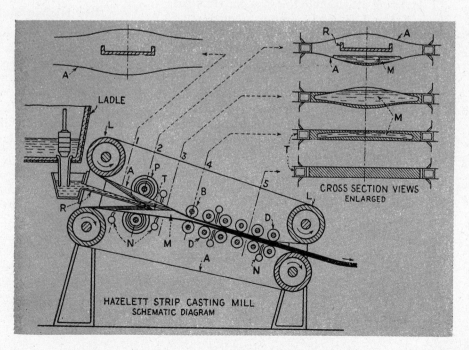

HAZELETT STRIP CASTING MILL
SCHEMATIC DIAGRAM

German and American
STAINLESS
compared

By C. A. ZAPFFE

Consulting Metallurgist

Baltimore

In April 1949, a Stahl-Eisen-Werkstoffblatt was published in Germany, standardizing the compositions of wrought stainless steels for the German industry. This listing is similar to the American Iron and Steel Institute classifications in this country, which provides American metallurgists with the familiar type numbers for stainless steels. Stainless steels were discovered and developed in Europe at the turn of this century,[1] spreading thereafter to America where they have attained world-wide records in production; a comparison of the current German and American standard listings is therefore both interesting and informative.[2]

Restricting attention to the wrought stainless steels, Tables I, II and III present a compilation of the standard analyses compiled in Germany and America in 1949. The tables are constructed with a view to matching similar grades. This is not always easy to do, and some of the groupings are entirely arbitrary. It is also important to note that a number of grades on the AISI list come under separate specifications in Germany on the basis of heat-resisting alloys, electrical resistors, and special steels.

Gaps in the tables therefore do not necessarily mean that a grade of a corresponding analysis is not made in Germany.

Because of shortages of nickel in Germany, particularly acute during World War II, manganese and nitrogen were substituted as austenitizing elements in the Class III (austenitic) grades. Some of the alloys are listed in Table IV. Results of the substitution were interesting; but these ersatz elements never did fully replace nickel, and they have been largely abandoned since the war. Table III lists the only standard German grade containing special additions of manganese; none contain nitrogen.

Use Higher Manganese Ranges

Nickel in German analyses still reflects a shortage. AISI Class III steels show a considerably greater liberality, particularly when stabilization of the austenite is desirable.

Minor manganese contents in general, and particularly in Class III, tend to be much higher in America, a maximum of 1.0 pct in Classes I and II (martensitic and ferritic, respectively) and 2.0 pct in Class III, comparing with the

Currently-used compositions of wrought stainless steels have recently been standardized in Germany in a manner similar to the AISI classifications in the United States. A comparison of the standard German and American listings is interesting in an historical sense and informative from a technical viewpoint.

German range of 0.2 to 0.4 pct for all classes. These maximum specifications permit, but do not require, high manganese contents; nevertheless, the statement as made is proper in its broad reference. This is primarily the result of an importance placed by American metallurgists on the improvement of hot workability afforded by manganese in carbon steel—also its slightly austenitizing effect. German metallurgists are not as strongly impressed with the effect of manganese on hot workability so far as stainless steels are concerned, and the point is worth considering.

Stabilizing Practice Differs

In stabilizing the Class III steels, German practice shows a number of distinctions: (a) tantalum is sometimes used, as well as titanium and columbium; (b) Class II steels are also often stabilized; (c) carbon contents of the stabilized grades tend to be higher than in American practice; (d) lower ratios of titanium and columbium to carbon are used, and (e) stabilization heat treatments are rarely administered to the stabilized grades.

The higher carbon content is attributable to the high cost of low-carbon ferrochromium, also to a scrap problem with regard to carbon pickup. Attention of German metallurgists, however, is on the recent procedure of decarburization by gaseous oxygen, which may allow a change in stabilization practice. As for the stabilization heat treatment, they do not regard its importance as having been demonstrated.

A proportion of ferrite is often preferred in German Class III steels as a guard against sensitization. They find that the presence of 10 to 20 pct of ferrite causes no appreciable change in mechanical properties, and in addition provides a surprisingly rapid recovery from sensitization. For example, a steel containing 22.6 pct Cr, 10.2 pct Ni, and 0.09 pct C —15 pct ferritic—developed sensitization in 1 hr at 600°C (1110°F); but after 50 hr at this temperature, sensitization had vanished.

This, they explain, is the result of diffusion of chromium from the ferrite, which by thermodynamic definition is chromium-rich with respect to accompanying austenite. American practice has hesitated to utilize a presence of ferrite, because ferrite (a) is subject to embrittlement in the range of 400° to 550°C (752° to 1022°F) (475° embrittlement), (b) is susceptible to embrittlement from sigma phase in the temperature range 600° to 950°C, (1112° to 1742°F) (c) is definitely disadvantageous to hot workability, (d) lowers creep resistance, and (e) probably favors stress-corrosion cracking.

Molybdenum More Widely Used

Molybdenum is much more widely used in Germany, being added to numerous alloys in all three classes, and particularly in Class III (see Table III). Molybdenum in stainless steel was an original German development, first patented in 1910 by the top discoverer of stainless steel—P. Monnartz[1]—and the use of that metal received a second impetus in its home country during the recent war. German practice rarely if ever uses the molybdenum grades for high-temperature service, whereupon embrittlement from sigma phase is not important. AISI Types 316 and 317 carry more molybdenum than the corresponding German grades; but for piercing operations German steels carry a

TABLE I

CLASS I—MARTENSITIC

| German Steel | | AISI No. | Analysis In Pct of Weight | | | | | | | |
No.	Name		C	Cr	Ni	Mo	Mn	Si	Other Elements
4001	X10 Cr 13........	403	<0.15	11.5–13.0	....	....	<1.00	<0.50	....
		410	<0.15	11.5–13.5	....	....	<1.00	<1.00	....
		(410-C)	<0.12 (∞0.20)	12.5–13.5	....	....	0.2–0.4	0.3–0.5	....
4021	X20 Cr 13........	....	0.17–0.22	12.5–13.5	....	....	0.2–0.4	0.3–0.5	....
*4120	X20 Cr Mo 13.....		0.17–0.22	12.5–13.5	....	1.0–1.3	0.2–0.4	0.3–0.5	....
		414	<0.15	11.5–13.5	1.25–2.5		<1.00	<1.00	....
		416	<0.15	12.0–14.0	....		<1.25	<1.00	P, S, Se >0.07; Zr, Mo 0.60
		420	<0.15	12.0–14.0	....		<1.00	<1.00	....
4034	X40 Cr 13........	....	0.38–0.43	12.5–13.5	....	....	0.2–0.4	0.3–0.5	....
*4122	X35 Cr Mo 17.....		0.30–0.40	16.0–17.0	....	1.0–1.3	0.2–0.4	0.3–0.5	....
		431	<0.20	15.0–17.0	1.25–2.5	....	<1.00	<1.00	....
4057	X22 Cr Ni 17.....	....	0.20–0.25	16.5–17.5	1.3 –1.8		0.2–0.4	0.3–0.5	....
		440-A	0.60–0.75	16.0–18.0		<0.75	<1.00	<1.00	....
		440-B	0.75–0.95	16.0–18.0		<0.75	<1.00	<1.00	....
		440-C	0.95–1.20	16.0–18.0		<0.75	<1.00	<1.00	....
*4112	X90 Cr Mo V.....	....	0.85–0.95	17.5–18.5	....	1.0–1.3	0.2–0.4	0.3–0.5	0.07–0.12 V

* Classified as special steels; the others are for general application.

higher molybdenum content than the American.

Free-machining modifications are much more widely explored and exploited in America. Germany seems still in the "sulfur stage," compared to our developments with selenium and the several combinations among sulfur, selenium, phosphorous, zirconium and molybdenum. Class III alloys containing silicon are more widely used in Germany, particularly for welding and for protection against pit corrosion.

Germans Lack Some U. S. 400 Grades

The following alloys, considered important in America, apparently remain more or less unused in Germany: (a) free-machining modifications of Types 410, 420, 440, 302, (b) free-spinning Type 305, (c) free-machining grades containing selenium, (d) Type 405, ferritized with an aluminum addition (3) 12-2 compositions, such as Type 414.

On the other hand, Germany utilizes: (a) partly ferritic Class III grades, besides that containing manganese, (b) austenites sometimes having additions of nitrogen, (c) a 12-12 analysis similar to that used in England, (d) a hardenable Class I analysis containing vanadium, (e) some special stabilized grades, particularly distinctive in Class II, (f) novel compositions employing molybdenum additions in all three classes.

In Class I compositions, manganese and silicon specifications are considerably lower for German alloys, the maximum of their specification being less than customary minimums for actual American analyses. The German Nos. 4021 and 4120 do not correspond to any standard American grade, but are similar to the nonstandard analysis sometimes referred to as Type 410-C. The Germans have therefore publicly recognized the necessity for an alloy intermediate between AISI Types 410 and 420

—a matter of some current concern in America. Their addition of more than 1 pct Mo to one of the twin listed alloys may deserve a continuation of our brief wartime notice given a similar steel.[3]

Germans Use No Free-Machining Class I's

No free-machining analyses are listed in the German standards for Class I. Their No. 4122 is unlike any American analysis, combining the carbon content of Type 420 with the chromium content of Type 440, and containing in addition more than 1 pct Mo.

The nickeliferous No. 4057 and Type 431 are virtually identical, but Germany lists no 12-2 analysis such as the American Type 414. The well-established series of three Type 440 steels in the American listing is represented by only one analysis in Germany, and that containing 1 pct Mo, also 0.1 pct V.

Regarding the Class II alloys, Germany apparently does not utilize an aluminum addition in the Type 410 analysis to prevent full hardening and thereby improve weldability in services where transformation stresses are advisably avoided—our Type 405. The grade containing several percent of aluminum, Type 406, would be listed in Germany under another classification.

U. S. and German 430 Types Vary

Type 430, one of the most prominent of all stainless steels in America, shows the following interesting contrasts with two corresponding German analyses: (a) titanium in proportions exceeding 7x pct C is added to both of the German steels; (b) one of these contains in addition nearly 2 pct Mo; (c) the chromium specifications of the German alloys allow no latitude at all in choosing ferrite-austenite proportions, while American practice allows freedom to choose a particular steel within this specification having strength at the cost of some corrosion resistance (low-chromium side),

TABLE II			CLASS II—FERRITIC					
German Steel		AISI No.	Analysis In Pct of Weight					
No.	Name		C	Cr	Mo	Mn	Si	Other Elements
4501	X8 Cr Ti 17	405	<0.08	11.5–13.5	....	<1.00	<1.00	0.10–0.30 Al
		406	<0.15	12.0–14.0	....	<1.00	<1.00	3.5–4.5 Al
		430	<0.12	14.0–18.0	....	<1.00	<1.00	
		....	<0.10	17.0–18.0	....	0.2–0.4	0.3–0.5	Ti >7 x Pct C
4523	X8 Cr Mo Ti 17	....	<0.10	16.5–17.5	1.6–1.9	0.2–0.4	0.3–0.5	Ti >7 x Pct C
		430–F	<0.12	14.0–18.0	....	<1.25	<1.00	P, S, Se >0.07; Zr, Mo <0.60
4104	X12 Cr Mo S 17		0.10–0.15	16.0–17.0	0.2–0.3	0.2–0.4	0.3–0.5	0.15–0.25 S
		446	<0.35	23.0–27.0	....	<1.50	<1.00	N <0.25
*4526	X12 Cr Mo Ti 25	....	<0.15	24.0–26.0	2.3–2.6	0.2–0.4	0.8–1.0	1.5–2.0 Ti

* Classified as special steels; the others are for general application.

TABLE III

CLASS III—AUSTENITIC

| German Steel | | AISI No. | Analysis In Pct of Weight | | | | | | |
No.	Name		C	Cr	Ni	Mo	Mn	Si	Other Elements
4300	X12 Cr Ni 18-8	301	0.08-0.20	16.0-18.0	6.0- 8.0	....	<2.00	<1.00	....
		302	0.08-0.20	17.0-19.0	8.0-10.0	....	<2.00	<1.00	....
			<0.15	17.5-18.5	8.0- 9.0	....	0.2-0.4	0.3-0.5	....
		302-B	0.08-0.20	17.0-19.0	8.0-10.0	....	<2.00	2.0-3.0	....
4330	X8 Cr Ni Si 18-8	....	<0.10	17.5-18.5	8.0- 9.0	....	0.2-0.4	1.5-2.5	....
		303	<0.15	17.0-19.0	8.0-10.0	....	<2.00	<1.00	P, S, Se >0.07; Zr, Mo <0.60
		304	<0.08	18.0-20.0	8.0-11.0	....	<2.00	<1.00	....
4301	X5 Cr Ni 18-9	....	<0.07	17.5-18.5	9.0-10.0	....	0.2-0.4	0.3-0.5	....
		305	<0.12	17.0-19.0	10.0-13.0	....	<2.00	<1.00	....
		308	<0.08	19.0-21.0	10.0-12.0	....	<2.00	<1.00	....
		309	<0.20	22.0-24.0	12.0-15.0	....	<2.00	<1.00	....
		310	<0.25	24.0-26.0	19.0-22.0	....	<2.00	<1.50	....
		314	<0.25	23.0-26.0	19.0-22.0	....	<2.00	1.5-3.0	....
		316	<0.10	16.0-18.0	10.0-14.0	2.0-3.0	<2.00	<1.00	....
4401	X5 Cr Ni Mo 18-10	....	<0.07	17.5-18.5	10.0-11.0	1.8-2.2	0.2-0.4	0.3-0.5	....
4571	X10 Cr Ni Mo Ti 18-10	....	<0.12	17.5-18.5	10.0-11.0	1.8-2.2	0.2-0.4	0.3-0.5	Ti >4 x Pct C
4580	X10 Cr Ni Mo Cb 18-10	....	<0.12	17.5-18.5	10.0-11.0	1.8-2.2	0.2-0.4	0.3-0.5	Cb >8 x Pct C
4413	X8 Cr Ni Mo Si 18-9	....	<0.10	17.5-18.5	9.0-10.0	1.8-2.2	0.2-0.4	2.0-2.5	....
		317	<0.10	18.0-20.0	11.0-14.0	3.0-4.0	<2.00	<1.00	....
*4449	X5 Cr Ni Mo 17-13	....	<0.07	16.5-17.5	12.5-13.5	4.5-5.0	0.2-0.4	0.3-0.5	....
		321	<0.08	17.0-19.0	8.0-11.0	....	<2.00	<1.00	Ti >5 x Pct C
4541	X10 Cr Ni Ti 18-9	....	<0.12	17.5-18.5	9.0-10.0	....	0.2-0.4	0.3-0.5	Ti >4 x Pct C
		347	<0.08	17.0-19.0	9.0-12.0	....	<2.00	<1.00	Cb >10 x Pct C
4550	X10 Cr Ni Cb 18-9	....	<0.12	17.5-18.5	9.0-10.0	....	0.2-0.4	0.3-0.5	Cb >8 x Pct C
*4307	X8 Cr Ni 12-12	....	<0.10	12.0-13.0	11.5-12.5	....	0.2-0.4	0.3-0.5	....
*4211	X12 Mn Cr 18-10	....	<0.15	9.5-10.5	0.7- 0.9	0.4-0.6	17.0-19.0	0.3-0.5	....
*4595	X5 Cr Ni Mo Cu 18-8	....	<0.07	17.0-18.0	17.0-18.0	1.8-2.2	0.2-0.4	0.3-0.5	1.8-2.2 Cu

* Classified as special steels; the others are for general application.

or corrosion resistance at the cost of some strength (high-chromium side); (d) carbon is kept a little lower in the German alloys because of the titanium addition; and (e) manganese and silicon contents are, as usual, lower in the German alloys.

The free-machining Type 430-F, produced in America with various free-machining additions as shown in Table II, is listed in Germany only for an addition of sulfur. Their carbon specification is also slightly different, setting a minimum at 0.10 pct and allowing additions somewhat higher than in American practice. Also, 0.25 pct Mo is added. Still further distinctions are essentially those given for the Type 430 analysis.

The high-chromium alloy, Type 446, commonly used in this country with no significant additions other than nitrogen for grain refining, is matched in Germany only by an alloy of considerably greater complexity. Their No. 4526: (a) has an addition of approximately 2 pct Ti, (b) contains 2.5 pct Mo, (c) has its silicon raised from the usual German 0.3 to 0.5 pct up towards 1 pct, (d) continues its low manganese level, in contrast to the augmented maximum of 1.5 pct in the American analysis, (e) restricts the carbon content to a maximum of 0.15 pct.

The table on Class III alloys is particularly interesting because of the important historical position of German metallurgists in the development of austenitic stainless steels.[1] The blanks in the German listing for our Types 308, 309, 310 and 314 should not be construed to mean an absence of similar compositions in Germany. Their comparable alloys would be listed elsewhere for heat-resisting applications.

U. S. Type 301 Not Used in Germany

The highly work-hardening Type 301 (17-7), having fairly wide usefulness in America, is not important in German practice. Their No. 4300, the analogue of our Type 302, is the popular 18-8 originally developed in Germany. Their current practice shows (a) a greater restriction in the respective ranges for carbon, chromium and nickel, (b) a generally lower silicon content, and (c) a considerably lower manganese content. This latter follows from their disregard for the effect of manganese on hot workability, also on austenite stability.

The German siliconized 18-8, No. 4330, is similar to AISI Type 302-B, differing in (a) the lower manganese content, (b) a lower carbon content, (c) a narrower specification for chromium, and (d) a lower limit on nickel. The German listing shows no analogue for America's popular free-machining grade, Type 303. Our 18-8 with specially low carbon—Type 304, also "ELC"—is closely matched by the German No. 4301, differing only in manganese and silicon contents, and in closer specifications on chromium and nickel.

A free-spinning analysis, similar to our Type 305, does not appear in the German listing. It is likely that the shortage of nickel in that country hinders the usefulness of an alloy whose low rate of work-hardening is largely the result of an aggravated nickel content.

Mo Abundant in German Class III's

Molybdenum, abundantly added to German stainless steels, appears in a particularly large number of their Class III modifications. The basic analysis of most of these rather closely approaches Type 316. The distinctions are: (a) closer specifications for all additions, (b) molybdenum on the low side near 2.0 pct (a practice also used by some in America), (c) a lower manganese content, (d) considerably lower nickel maximums, (e) lower silicon contents, except in No. 4413, which is a specially siliconized grade. The additions of titanium and columbium to Nos. 4571 and 4580 correspond to American practice for nonstandardized modifications of Type 316, except that the titanium and columbium to carbon ratio is greater in this country. The very low maximum of 0.07 pct C in No. 4401 warrants some attention.

Alloys of higher molybdenum content, such as our Type 317, are represented in Germany by No. 4449, which allows one of the highest nickel additions in any of their grades. Compared to Type 317, their steel has a higher molybdenum content, a lower carbon maximum, less chromium, and the usual lower manganese and silicon contents. Stabilized austenites containing titanium and columbium, analagous to our Types 321 and 347, show as their principal difference a slightly higher carbon maximum and a lower ratio of stabilizing element to total carbon content. Nickel contents are also lower, as well as manganese and silicon.

Two German Special Grades Popular

Among the special grades produced as standard stainless steels in Germany, two of them are virtually without analogue in this country. No. 4307 is the 12-12 analysis generally popular abroad, but receiving little attention over here. Their No. 4211 is the only high-manganese analysis on the postwar listing. Compare this with the listing in Table II. The chromium content of this alloy actually falls below the minimum required for "stainless" behavior in most service. Their No. 4595 is the elaborate molybdenum-copper Class III steel, comparable to some of the nonstandard grades studied in this country by Climax Molybdenum Co. This resembles Carpenter No. 20, except for the lower nickel analysis of the German steel.

In place of previous common chemical means, the Germans are now strongly leaning toward electrochemical methods for quantitative measurement of activation and passivation behavior. The process is essentially the one developed by Hittorf in that country half a century ago, involving measurement of anodic current density v. potential. The procedure, now adopted by Krupp, discloses three ranges of behavior; (1) normally active, (2) passivated, and (3) depassivated (breakdown of passivation). The data allow excellent systematization of both reagents and steels, with some particularly interesting results for H_2SO_4.

Study Stress-corrosion Cracking

During recent years, the phenomenon of stress-corrosion cracking has attracted attention in both countries.[4] German metallurgists relate stress-corrosion cracking to stability of austenite, more stable alloys being less sensitive. They find that coldworking decreases the corrosion-cracking resistance of stable austenite, but may actually increase that of unstable austenite—through electrochemical protection afforded by precipitated martensite. In their opinion, the intracrystalline phenomenon of stress-corrosion cracking has no relationship to sensitization. They find that Class II steels are also subject to the defect, but that the level of stress necessary for the phenomenon is too high to allow it to become important for most operating conditions.

Phosphorous has been found to counteract sensitization, probably because of its ferritizing tendency; but the observation has not resulted in any commercial application. Vanadium has been found to be ineffective as a carbide stabilizer, an addition as high as 25 pct still showing no inhibition of sensitization. Similar to opinions expressed in this country, particularly by Uhlig and Wulff, German metallurgists believe that pit corrosion does not necessarily relate to inclusions or visible inhomogeneities within the steel, but that it is a function of more subtle factors.

TABLE IV
NONSTANDARD GERMAN GRADES

C	Cr	Ni	Mo	Mn	N
0.07	20	5.0	.....	.....	0.25
0.07	20	5.5	1.2	.....	0.25
0.07	20	6.0	2.2	.....	0.25
0.10	15	1.5	.....	8	0.10
0.10	15	1.5	.....	14	0.10
0.10	19	1.5	.....	9	.....
0.10	20	1.5	.....	9	0.20

References

[1] C. A. Zapffe, "Who Discovered Stainless Steel?" THE IRON AGE, Oct. 14, 1948, p. 120.

[2] A. L. Field, "German Stainless Steel," THE IRON AGE, Dec. 20, 1945, p. 60.

[3] Metals and Alloys, July, 1943, p. 55.

[4] ASTM-AIME Symposium on Stress-Corrosion Cracking, 1944.

Three multiple-station automatic machines have increased output per manhour by more than 150 pct in machining Ford carburetor diecastings. On one casting, two machines do work which formerly required five machines and five operators. Savings in floor space, materials handling and labor costs result.

AUTOMATICS machine diecastings 150 pct faster

By HERBERT CHASE
Consultant, Forrest Hills

Complete revision of the machining lineup on the two major zinc alloy diecastings used in Ford carburetors has increased output per manhour by more than 150 pct at the Milford, Mich., plant of Ford Motor Co. These two castings are the main body and its mating air horn.

Formerly, the body machining required a row of five machines each having its own operator. Total output of the five machines was 1800 per 8-hr day. Now two machines, one 12-station and one 8-station, with one operator each, process 1600 carburetor bodies in 8 hr. A similar machine having 12 stations handles corresponding operations on the air horn. All three of the new machines are Morris vertical center column types in which most of the tools are supported from a common main head. These tools are lifted vertically before indexings occur and then are fed down simultaneously for the next set of operations. In some cases side or angle tools are also used.

Several Faces Can Be Machined

Each machine has one fixture per station. Each fixture is unloaded and reloaded and the workpiece is clamped by hand at the front station. It then progresses around horizontally, stopping at each successive station and finally returning to the front station with all machining except light burring completed. During some of the indexings, the fixtures are turned to bring a new portion of the casting in line with the tools. As a result, machining can be done on two sides, one end, and on top and bottom faces.

Where side heads are required, the tools in these are actuated by inter-connection with the main head of the machine, being fed inward as the latter feeds down and retracting when the main head retracts. Thus, all tools in effect are interlocked. Their motion depends upon that of the main head, which is raised between indexings and is lowered as the tools are fed into the workpieces at each machining station.

In indexing to the first working station in the first Morris machine, the fixture is turned 90°, as can be seen in Fig. 1. The table indexes automatically when the locking wrench is drawn back.

Some Heads Utilize High-Speed Motors

At station No. 2, the first working station on the 12-station machine, the pump chamber outlet hole is produced with a No. 40 drill. Four 8-32 and five 10-32 screw holes are also tapped using a multiple reversing tapping head. Another 10-32 holes is tapped at station No. 3, a No. 41 gun drill produces a pump outlet crosshole and a No. 28 drill, fed in by a high-speed angular head, drills an economizer hole to depth.

A pump rod hole is reamed and counterbored at station No. 4. Also at this station an econo-

FIG. 1—Locking a body casting in a fixture at the loading station of a 12-station Morris machine. In left background is first working station. During indexing fixture has rocked 90° to bring up proper face for machining at this station. Indexing occurs automatically when locking tool is retracted.

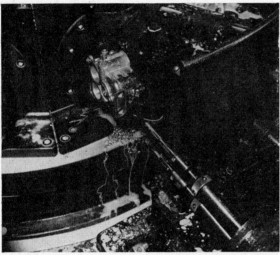

FIG. 2—Though most tools are mounted on the main vertical slide, these machines use some side heads. At this station, two stepped taps are driven by side heads.

FIG. 3—The final operation on the first machine handling body diecastings includes these tools: a step reamer, two inserted-blade reamers, and a rotary file or burring tool. The latter tool, given a compound motion by a cam, burrs an internal surface.

mizer body and two ejector pin marks are spot-faced and two No. 1 drills break out flash for throttle body screw holes. At station No. 5, cross drilling is done with one No. 41 drill fed to depth on a hole leading to the pump discharge and a step drill is applied to metering jet holes. A No. 59 drill, driven at 10,000 rpm by a high speed motor, produces an economizer metering hole.

Step drilling of a piston pump discharge hole and producing a pickup hole with a No. 90 drill is done at station No. 6. Then, at station No. 7, comes cross drilling with a No. 28 drill, to produce an economizer hole to depth, in an angular head. Spot-facing of two ejector pin marks, tapping of an economizer hole and a throttle body screw hole, are the operations at station No. 8.

Step Drills And Taps Used

At station No. 9 comes drilling of an economizer metering hole with a No. 59 drill in an angular head and drilling a No. 30 hole through the piston pump chamber. Then, at station No. 10, two No. 40 drills are used to clean out idler passage holes and two drills clean out the idler jet holes. Also used is a step drill for a pump chamber inlet hole, and a ball check seat is produced with a No. 50 drill.

At station No. 11 two step taps, Fig. 2, are used at main jet holes to produce threads for jet plugs. A No. 40 drill also makes a pickup hole.

Step reaming is done on pump chamber holes and two venturi holes are reamed at station No. 12, Fig. 3. Also used at this station is a rotary filer or burring tool. This tool is given a compound motion by a cam, first feeding down through a clearance hole, then radially part way into a side hole, and then vertically again to burr edges at the hole intersection. These motions are reversed in withdrawing the tool.

Machining Completed On Second Machine

After inspection, body castings go to the 8-station Morris machine to perform operations at points not accessible in the 12-station setup. After loading at station No. 1 of the second machine and indexing to station No. 2, a form or step drill is applied. At its end is a countersink. This tool is guided by a roller bearing bushing. Then, at station No. 3, a No. 42 drill starts a hole. At station No. 4 a drill in a horizontal head produces a hole and a vertical head using a step-drill produces another hole and counterbores it part way.

Station No. 5 includes burring from a horizontal head and use of a No. 42 gun drill in a

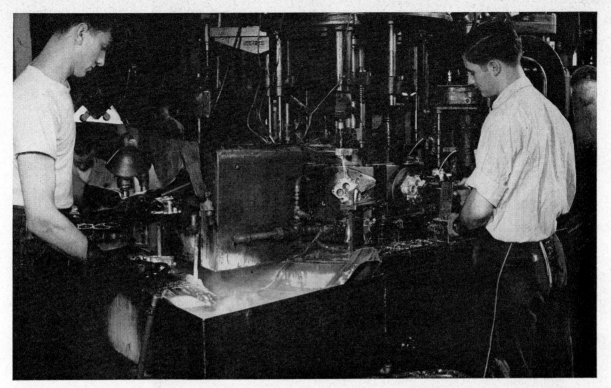

FIG. 4—At the loading station of the 8-station automatic, the operator on the right loads and unloads the fixtures. Finished castings go into the cleaning tank, from which the operator on the left removes them and blows them out with an air hose.

vertical head. Then, at station No. 6, a No. 42 drill is fed to depth to hold a 1.400-in. dimension. A No. 56 gun drill is used at station No. 7 to produce a hole for vacuum takeoff. At the final station in this machine, a ⅜-24 tap and a No. 42 drill in an angular head tap a hole and do burring operation respectively.

Castings Washed And Chromated

When the operator removes the casting, he places it in a chute and it slides into a hot washing solution from which it is taken by another operator, shown at the left in Fig. 4, who uses a jet of air to blow out the casting. All burring and inspection are done here. The casting is then ready for transfer to a tank in which the castings are given a chromate treatment designed to inhibit formation of white oxide, in case water in gasoline, used in service, is allowed to stand in contact with the casting.

Machining of the air horn is handled in the second 12-station Morris machine. Castings, loaded at station No. 1, are locked to the fixtures by a hand crank and after indexing to the second station come under a tool. Of the six blades in this cutter, three machine a 30° chamfer at the top of air horn, one spot-faces a 2.25-in. diam on the top, one faces a step outside the horn, and one makes an outside bevel.

One Station Not Used

Drilling the air vent tube is done at station No. 3. Station No. 4 is open. But at station No. 5, a form drill and spot-facer produce a 0.264 to 0.270-in. diam hole, a 36° included angle bevel of 0.452 to 0.458 in. diam. Also, a 90° countersink chamfers for a tap at the 0.452-in. diam. Five No. 9 drills at station No. 6 break away flash in five cored holes for the screws that fasten the horn to the body.

Tapping of one 5/16-24 thread for the fuel needle valve seat is done at station No. 7 and is followed at the next station by drilling a No. 41 hole in one ear for the float hinge pin. One 10-32 hole for a choke lever screw is tapped at this station. The hole for a float hinge pin is then drilled in the second ear at station No. 9, where also a reamer in a floating holder line reams the shaft hole.

Burring Is Only Other Machining Needed

A spot-facer at station No. 10 removes flash at a sector pin boss. Two ⅜-in. diam spot-facers clean off areas at the ejector at station No. 11. The final operation is the tapping of one inlet hole at the 12th station. Machined castings, as they are unloaded, are placed in a chute and fall into a hot wash from which they are removed, burred, inspected and placed on a conveyer. Degreasing is done before castings go to the chromic acid dip.

Machining of both castings, the body in two machines and the air horn in one, is thus virtually completed except for inspection. Both require some minor deburring which is done by hand, with high-speed tools.

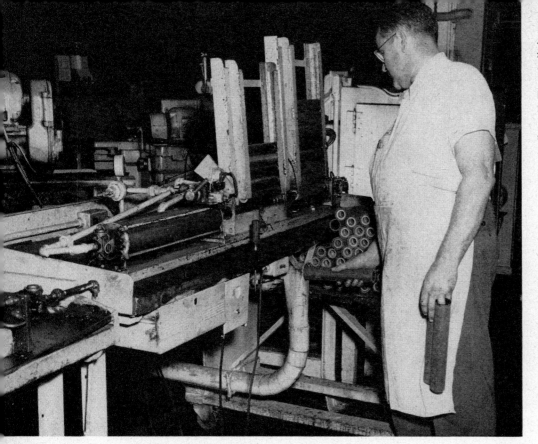

Assembles over 1000 typewriter units an hour

By replacing a hand-controlled press with semi-automatic, air-operated equipment of their own design, International Business Machines Corp., Poughkeepsie, N. Y., are now assembling power rolls for their electric typewriters at a rate of 1000 to 1200 an hour. This subassembly, similar to the platen in a regular typewriter, is made of thick-walled rubber with a tubular magnesium core. After being coated with rubber cement and allowed to dry, the core must be pressed into the thick-walled rubber tube. The latter then constitutes the friction driving surface of the roll.

When this job was done in a hand-controlled vertical press, it was a rather slow operation. Now the operator has only two duties to perform. One, he must keep the magazines feeding the new press filled. Two, the operator must chamfer the inner diameter of one end of each rubber tube before placing it in the press' magazine. For this purpose, the operator holds the tubing against a motor-driven grinding wheel installed just below bench level. A suction fan draws off the rubber particles.

As the magnesium tubes slide down the nearest of the two magazines in the illustration, the lowest one lines up with the ram of an air cylinder. At the same time, a rubber tube has also dropped into position, with its chamfered hole ready to receive the magnesium core. With both components lined up, the air ram advances and pushes the metal tube into the rubber one.

The second air ram, which is connected to the cradle holding the now-completed assembly, cannot be seen in the illustration. As soon as the metal tube's end is flush with that of its rubber container, a limit switch is tripped automatically. A solenoid then shifts the two air valves, causing air to return the longitudinal ram to its original position and advancing the transverse ram. This causes the cradle to upset and the sub-assembly rolls out into a holder. As soon as this second ram returns to position, the cradle rocks back and another rubber tube falls into it.

By R. B. SMITH

Assistant to the Director
Products and Applications Dept.
Reynolds Metals Co.
Louisville, Ky.

LIGHT METALS

and their alloys
CODIFIED

The confusion caused by varying designations for light metal alloys is on its way out. This new, uniform system is now officially adopted by ASTM. It will be combined with the temper designations in use since 1948.

The light metals industry has long sought an adequate system for codification of light metals and alloys, cast and wrought. Each producer has his own alloy nomenclature, resulting in use of many different designations for the same alloy. This makes it difficult to specify light metals and alloys without reference to the many commercial designations. It also presents a problem in the writing of specifications, for it is usually impractical to list all of the trade designations. The American Society for Testing Materials has been concerned with this difficulty for many years.

A system for codification of aluminum and aluminum-base alloys in ASTM specifications was adopted[1] in 1942 and modified[2] in 1945. For magnesium and magnesium-base alloys a somewhat different system was adopted[3] in 1944 and modified[4] in 1946. In both systems[5] letters designated alloying elements in the alloy. Numbers followed the letters to indicate the total number of alloying elements in aluminum alloys and the percentage of each designated alloying element in magnesium alloys. These codification systems were not considered entirely satisfactory, and several unsuccessful attempts[6] were made to change them. They were changed, however, in 1949 when a single system was adopted for light metals and alloys.

The new codification system is being used to designate aluminum and magnesium and their alloys in the latest issues of ASTM specifications. It is also used for the commercial designations of some new magnesium alloys which have not yet been incorporated into ASTM specs.

Coded By Alloying Element

Under this codification system, the designations for light metals and alloys are based on the chemical composition limits for the metal or alloy. In the system, an alloying element is defined as an element contained in the base metal within a specified range or in excess of a specified minimum percentage. The amount present is determined by the mean of the range (or minimum percentage) before rounding off. The designation for an alloy in ingot form for castings is the same as that assigned the same alloy in the form of castings, even though the composition may not be identical.

Designations for light alloys consist of not more than two letters representing the alloying elements specified in the greatest amount. These are arranged in order of decreasing percentages, or in alphabetical order if of equal percentages. They are followed by the respective percentages rounded off to whole numbers. A final letter is

TABLE I
ELEMENTS CODED

A — Aluminum	J — Phosphorus	R — Chromium
B — Bismuth	K — Zirconium	S — Silicon
C — Copper	L — Beryllium	T — Tin
D — Cadmium	M — Manganese	V — Arsenic
E — Cerium	N — Nickel	W — Sulfur
F — Iron	P — Lead	Y — Antimony
G — Magnesium	Q — Silver	Z — Zinc

TABLE II
MAGNESIUM ALLOY ANALYSIS

Aluminum	2.5 to 3.5
Manganese	0.20 min.
Zinc	0.6 to 1.4
Silicon	0.3 max.
Copper	0.05 max.
Nickel	0.005 max.
Iron	0.005 max.
Calcium	0.3 max.
Other impurities	0.3 max.

Aluminum and Aluminum-base Alloys

TABLE III

CHEMICAL COMPOSITION LIMITS—Pct

ASTM	Commercial	Si Min	Si Max	Fe Max	Cu Min	Cu Max	Mn Min	Mn Max	Mg Min	Mg Max	Cr Min	Cr Max	Ni Min	Ni Max	Zn Min	Zn Max	Sn Min	Sn Max	Pb Min	Pb Max	Bi Min	Bi Max	Ti Min	Ti Max	Others Each Max	Others Total Max	Al Min
850A		…	…	…	…	8.0	…	…	…	2.5	…	…	…	…	…	2.05									…	15.0[2]	85.0
900A		…	…	…	…	4.5	…	…	…	2.0	…	…	…	…	…	2.0									…	10.0[2]	90.0
920A		…	…	…	…	4.5	…	…	…	1.0	…	…	…	…	…	1.0									…	8.0[2]	92.0
950A		…	…	…	…	2.5	…	…	…	1.0	…	…	…	…	…	1.0									…	5.0[2]	95.0
980A		…	…	…	…	0.2	…	…	…	0.5	…	…	…	…	…	0.2									…	2.0[2]	98.
990A	2S	…	1.0 Si + Fe		…	0.20	…	0.10	…	…	…	…	…	…	…	0.10									0.05	0.15	99.0
9930A		…	0.30	0.50	…	0.10	…	…	…	0.05	…	…	…	…	…	…									0.05	0.70	99.3
996A	99.6	…	0.4 Si + Fe		…	0.05	…	…	…	…	…	…	…	…	…	…									0.05	0.15	99.6
9975A	99.75	…	0.10	0.20	…	0.05	…	…	…	0.03	…	…	…	…	…	…									0.03	0.25[2]	99.75
C4A	195	0.5	1.5	1.0	4.0	5.0	…	…	…	0.03	…	…	…	…	…	…							…	0.2	0.05	0.15	Remainder
CB60A[8]	11S	…	1.5	0.8	5.0	6.0	…	…	…	…	…	…	…	…	…	0.3			0.2	0.6	0.2	0.6	…	0.2	0.05	0.15	Remainder
CG42A	24S	…	0.50	0.50	3.8	4.9	0.30	0.90	1.2	1.8	…	0.10[3]	…	…	…	0.25									0.05	0.15	Remainder
Clad CG42A	Clad 24S (Core)	…	0.50	0.50	3.8	4.9	0.30	0.90	1.2	1.8	…	0.25	…	…	…	0.25									0.05	0.15	Remainder[2]
	(Clad)	…	0.70 Si + Fe		…	0.10	…	0.05	…	…	…	…	…	…	…	…									0.05	0.15	99.3
CG100A	122	…	2.0	1.5	9.2	10.8	…	0.5	0.15	0.35	…	…	…	0.3	…	0.5							…	0.2	…	0.3	Remainder
CM41A	17S	…	0.80	1.0	3.5	4.5	0.4	1.0	0.2	0.8	…	0.25	…	…	…	0.10							…	0.2	0.05	0.15	Remainder
CM41B	R317	…	1.0	1.0	3.5	4.5	0.4	1.0	0.2	0.8	…	0.25	…	…	…	0.10			0.3	0.7	0.3	0.7	…	…	0.05	0.15	Remainder
CN42A	142	…	0.7	1.0	3.5	4.5	…	0.3	1.2	1.8	…	0.2	1.7	2.3	…	0.3							…	0.2	0.05	0.15	Remainder
CN42C	18S	…	0.7	0.8	3.5	4.5	…	0.3	1.3	1.8	…	0.2	1.7	2.3	…	0.3							…	0.05	0.05	0.15	Remainder
CN42D	B18S	…	0.90	1.0	3.5	4.5	…	0.20	0.45	0.90	…	0.10	1.7	2.3	…	0.25							…	0.05	0.05	0.15	Remainder
CS41A	14S	0.5	0.90	1.0	3.9	5.0	0.4	1.2	0.20	0.8	…	0.10	…	…	…	0.25							…	[4]	0.05	0.15	Remainder
Clad CS41A	Clad 14S, Clad R301 (Core)	0.5	1.2	1.2	3.9	5.0	0.40	1.2	0.20	1.5	…	0.25	…	…	…	0.25							…	0.10	0.05	0.15	Remainder
	(Clad)	0.35	1.0	0.60	…	0.10	…	0.75	0.80	…	…	0.35	…	…	…	0.20							…	…	0.05	0.15	Remainder
CS41C	25S	0.50	1.2	1.0	3.9	5.0	…	1.2	…	0.05	…	0.10	…	…	…	0.25							…	0.15	0.05	0.15	Remainder
CS42A	B195	2.0	3.0	1.2	4.0	5.0	…	0.3	…	0.05	…	…	…	0.3	…	0.3							…	0.2	…	0.3	Remainder
CS43A	108	2.5	3.5	1.2	3.5	4.5	…	0.5	…	0.05	…	…	…	0.3	…	1.0							…	0.2	…	0.5	Remainder
CS66A	152 Type	5.0	6.0	1.2	5.5	7.5	…	0.8	0.2	0.4	…	…	…	…	…	0.8							…	0.2	…	0.8	Remainder

ASTM Specifications[1] (★ = applicable)

ASTM	B24	B26	B37	B85	B108	B178	B179	B209	B210	B211	B221	B234	B235	B241	B247
850A															★
900A			★												
920A			★												
950A			★												
980A			★												
990A								★							
9930A			★												
996A						★									
9975A						★									
C4A		★													
CB60A										★					
CG42A								★	★	★	★				
Clad CG42A								★							
CG100A							★								
CM41A										★	★				
CM41B							★								
CN42A															★
CN42C															★
CN42D															★
CS41A								★	★	★	★			★	★
Clad CS41A								★	★	★	★				
CS41C															★
CS42A					★										
CS43A							★								
CS66A							★								

Table continued on next page

Composition table (continued). Values are maximum (or min–max) percentages; "Remainder" denotes aluminum. Columns marked ★ in the original indicate applicable product forms.

Designation	Former Designation													Remainder			
CS72A	113	1.0	4.0	1.4	6.0	8.0	0.5	0.07		0.3		2.5		Remainder	0.5		0.2
CS104A	138 Type	1.0	4.0	1.2	6.0	8.0	0.5	0.07		0.3		2.5		Remainder	0.5		0.2
G1A	B50S, C50S, 150S	3.5	4.5	1.5	9.0	11.0	0.5	1.5		1.0		0.5		Remainder	0.5		0.2
G4A	214	3.5	4.5	1.2	9.0	11.0	0.5	1.5		1.0		0.5	0.10	Remainder	0.5	0.05	0.2
(G2)[6] G8A	218		0.50	0.80	0.25	0.16	0.3	3.5	4.5	0.3		0.3		Remainder		0.05	0.2
G10A	220		0.3	0.4	0.1	0.1	0.3	3.5	4.5	0.3		0.3	0.1	Remainder	0.2	0.05	
GR20A	52S	0.2	0.45 Si + Fe				0.1	7.5	8.5			0.1	0.1	Remainder	0.2		
GS10A	63S	0.2	0.6	0.50	0.2	0.10	0.10	9.5	10.6	0.10		0.20		Remainder	0.15	0.05	0.10
GS11A	61S	0.40	0.80	0.70	0.15	0.10	0.10	2.2	2.8	0.15	0.35	0.10		Remainder	0.15	0.05	0.15
GS11B	53S	45–65% of Mg	0.35		0.40		0.15	0.45	0.85		0.10			Remainder	0.15	0.05	0.15
GS42A	B214	1.4	2.2	0.6	0.3		0.2	0.80	1.2	0.20		0.3		Remainder	0.15	0.05	0.15
GZ42A	A214	1.4	2.2	0.5	0.3		0.2	1.1	1.4	0.10		0.3		Remainder	0.2	0.05	0.2
M1A	3S		0.3	0.6	0.1	0.3	0.8	3.5	4.5	0.2		1.4		Remainder	0.2	0.05	0.2
Clad M1A	Clad 3S (Core)	0.60	0.60	0.70	0.1	0.20	0.8	3.5	4.5	2.2		1.4		Remainder	0.15	0.05	0.2
	Clad 3S (Clad)	0.60 Si + Fe			0.20		0.3	3.5	4.5	2.2		0.10		Remainder	0.15	0.05	0.2
MG11A	4S	0.30	0.70	0.70	0.10		1.5		1.3		0.75	0.10		Remainder	0.15	0.05	0.15
S5A	43	4.5	6.0	0.8	0.1		0.3	0.05				0.3		Remainder	0.3	0.05	0.2
S5B	43 Type	4.5	6.0	0.6	0.1		0.3	0.05	0.2			0.3		Remainder	0.3	0.05	0.2
(S4)[6] S5C	43	4.5	6.0	0.8	0.37	2.0	0.3	0.05	0.2	0.5		0.3	0.1	Remainder	0.2		0.2
(S5)[6]	13	4.5	6.0	0.6	0.3	0.8	0.3	0.1		0.5		0.3	0.1	Remainder	0.2		0.2
(S9)[6]		11.0	13.0	0.8	0.6	2.0	0.3	0.1		0.5		0.3	0.1	Remainder	0.2		0.2
S12A	13	11.0	13.0	1.3	0.6		0.3	0.1		0.5		0.3	0.1	Remainder	0.2		0.2
SC51A	355	4.5	5.5	0.8	1.0	1.5	0.5	0.6	0.4			0.3		Remainder	0.15	0.05	0.2
(SC2)[6] SC54A	85	4.5	5.5	1.3	2.0	4.0	0.5	0.6		0.5		0.3	0.3	Remainder	0.15	0.05	
(SC5)[6] SC54B	85 Type	4.5	5.5	0.8	0.9	4.0	0.5	0.1		0.5		1.0	0.3	Remainder	0.5		
SC64A	A108	5.0	6.0	1.0	0.5	5.0	0.5	0.1		0.5		1.0	0.3	Remainder	0.5		0.2

TABLE III (Continued)

Aluminum and Aluminum-base Alloys

Alloy Designations			CHEMICAL COMPOSITION LIMITS—Pct																								ASTM Specifications[1]														
ASTM	Commercial		Silicon Min	Silicon Max	Iron Max	Copper Min	Copper Max	Manganese Min	Manganese Max	Magnesium Min	Magnesium Max	Chromium Min	Chromium Max	Nickel Min	Nickel Max	Zinc Min	Zinc Max	Tin Max	Lead Min	Lead Max	Bismuth Min	Bismuth Max	Titanium Min	Titanium Max	Others Each Max	Others Total Max	Aluminum Min	B24	B26	B37	B85	B108	B178	B179	B209	B210	B211	B221	B234	B235	B241	B247
SC64B	Allcast	....	5.5	7.0	1.0	3.3	4.3	...	0.5	...	0.1	...	...	...	0.3	...	1.0	...	...	...	...	...	...	0.2	....	0.5	Remainder		★			★										
		....	5.5	7.0	0.8	3.3	4.3	...	0.5	...	0.1	...	...	...	0.3	...	1.0	...	...	...	...	...	...	0.2	....	0.5	Remainder							★								
SC64C	319	....	5.5	7.0	1.2	3.0	4.5	...	0.8	...	0.5	...	...	...	0.5	...	1.0	...	...	...	...	...	...	0.2	....	0.5	Remainder		★			★										
		....	5.5	7.0	1.0	3.0	4.5	...	0.8	...	0.5	...	...	...	0.5	...	1.0	...	...	...	...	...	...	0.2	....	0.5	Remainder							★								
SC82A	Red X-8	....	7.0	8.6	1.0	1.0	2.0	0.2	0.6	0.2	0.6	...	0.3	...	0.2	...	1.0	...	...	...	...	...	...	0.3	....	0.5	Remainder		★													
		....	7.0	8.6	0.8	1.0	2.0	0.2	0.6	0.2	0.6	...	0.3	...	0.2	...	1.0	...	...	...	...	...	...	0.2	....	0.5	Remainder							★								
(SC6)[6] SC84A	A380	....	7.5	9.5	1.3	3.0	4.0	...	0.5	...	0.1	...	...	...	0.5	...	1.0	...	0.3	...	...	...	...	...	....	0.5	Remainder				★											
		....	7.5	9.5	0.8	3.0	4.0	...	0.5	...	0.1	...	...	...	0.5	...	0.5	...	0.3	...	...	...	...	...	....	0.5	Remainder							★								
(SC7)[6] SC84B	380	....	7.5	9.5	2.0	3.0	4.0	...	0.5	...	0.1	...	...	...	0.5	...	1.0	...	0.3	...	...	...	...	...	....	0.5	Remainder				★											
		....	7.5	9.5	0.8	3.0	4.0	...	0.5	...	0.1	...	...	...	0.5	...	0.9	...	0.3	...	...	...	...	...	....	0.5	Remainder							★								
SC122A	Red X-13	....	11.0	13.0	0.9	1.0	2.0	0.5	0.9	0.4	1.0	...	...	...	0.05	...	0.4	...	...	...	...	...	...	0.2	....	0.5	Remainder					★										
		....	11.0	13.0	0.7	1.0	2.0	0.5	0.9	0.4	1.0	...	...	...	0.05	...	0.4	...	...	...	...	...	...	0.2	....	0.5	Remainder							★								
SG11A	A51S	....	0.60	1.2	1.0	...	0.35	...	0.20	0.45	0.80	0.15	0.35	...	...	...	0.25	...	...	...	...	...	...	0.15	0.05	0.15	Remainder															★
SG70A	356	....	6.5	7.5	0.6	...	0.2	...	0.3	0.2	0.4	...	...	...	...	...	0.3	...	...	...	...	...	...	0.2	0.05	0.15	Remainder		★			★										
		....	6.5	7.5	0.5	...	0.2	...	0.3	0.2	0.4	...	...	...	...	...	0.3	...	...	...	...	...	...	0.2	0.05	0.15	Remainder							★								
(SG2)[6]	A360	....	9.0	10.0	1.3	...	0.6	...	0.3	0.4	0.6	...	...	...	0.5	...	0.5	0.1	...	...	...	...	...	...	....	0.2	Remainder				★											
(SG3)[6]	360	....	9.0	10.0	2.0	...	0.6	...	0.3	0.4	0.6	...	...	...	0.5	...	0.5	0.1	...	...	...	...	...	...	....	0.2	Remainder				★											
SG100A	360	....	9.0	10.0	0.8	...	0.6	...	0.3	0.4	0.6	...	...	...	0.5	...	0.5	0.1	...	...	...	...	...	...	....	0.2	Remainder							★								
SG121A	32S	....	11.5	13.5	1.0	0.50	1.3	...	...	0.80	1.3	...	0.10	0.50	1.3	...	0.25	...	...	...	...	...	...	0.05	0.05	0.15	Remainder															★
SN122A	A132	....	11.0	13.0	1.3	0.5	1.5	...	0.1	0.7	1.3	...	...	2.0	3.0	...	0.1	...	...	...	...	...	...	0.2	0.05	....	Remainder					★										
		....	11.0	13.0	1.0	0.5	1.5	...	0.1	0.9	1.3	...	...	2.0	3.0	...	0.1	...	...	...	...	...	...	0.2	0.05	....	Remainder							★								
ZC60A	C612	....	....	0.3	1.4	0.35	0.65	...	0.05	0.25	0.45	...	...	...	...	6.0	7.0	...	...	...	...	...	...	0.2	0.05	0.15	Remainder					★										
		....	....	0.3	1.3	0.35	0.65	...	0.05	0.25	0.45	...	...	...	...	6.0	7.0	...	...	...	...	...	...	0.2	0.05	0.15	Remainder							★								
ZC81A	Tenzaloy	....	....	0.3	1.0	0.4	1.0	...	0.6	0.2	0.5	...	0.3	...	0.1	7.0	8.0	...	...	...	...	...	...	0.2	0.1	0.2	Remainder		★													
ZC81B	Tenzaloy	....	....	0.3	1.3	0.4	1.0	...	0.6	0.2	0.5	...	0.3	...	0.1	7.0	8.0	...	...	...	...	...	...	0.2	0.1	0.2	Remainder					★										
ZC81A-B	Tenzaloy	....	....	0.25	0.9	0.4	1.0	...	0.6	0.2	0.5	...	0.3	...	0.1	7.0	8.0	...	...	...	...	...	...	0.2	0.05	0.2	Remainder							★								
ZG32A	Ternalloy 5	....	....	0.2	0.8	...	0.2	0.4	0.6	1.4	1.8	0.2	0.4	...	...	2.7	3.3	...	...	...	...	...	...	0.2	0.05	....	Remainder		★													
		....	....	0.2	0.8	...	0.2	0.4	0.6	1.4	1.8	0.2	0.4	...	...	2.7	3.3	...	...	...	...	...	...	0.2	0.05	....	Remainder					★										
		....	....	0.2	0.6	...	0.2	0.4	0.6	1.4	1.8	0.2	0.4	...	...	2.7	3.3	...	...	...	...	...	...	0.2	0.05	....	Remainder							★								

Composition limits, per cent (continued from preceding page; column headings not repeated on this portion)

Designation	Trade name	Si	Fe	Cu	Mn	Mg	Cr	Zn	Ti	Others, each	Others, total²	Al
ZG42A	Ternalloy 7	0.2	0.8	0.6	0.4	1.8–2.4	0.2	4.0–4.5	…	0.05	0.2	Remainder
ZG61A	40E	0.25	1.0	0.3	0.5	0.65	0.6	5.2–6.0	0.1	0.05	0.2	Remainder
ZG61B	A612	0.25	0.8	0.3	0.5	0.65	0.6	5.2–6.0	0.1	0.05	0.15	Remainder
ZG62A	75S	0.50	0.70	1.2–2.0	0.30	2.1–2.9	0.18–0.40	5.1–6.1	0.20	0.05	0.15	Remainder
Clad ZG62A (Core)	Clad 75S	0.50	0.70	1.2–2.0	0.30	2.1–2.9	0.18–0.40	5.1–6.1	0.20	0.05	0.15	Remainder
Clad ZG62A (Clad)		0.70 Si+Fe		0.10	0.10	0.10	…	1.25	…	…	0.10	Remainder

¹Specifications for:

B 24-46. Aluminum Ingots for Remelting.
B 26-50T. Aluminum-Base Alloy Sand Castings.
B 37-49. Aluminum for Use in Iron and Steel Manufacture.
B 85-49T. Aluminum-Base Alloy Die Castings.
B 108-50T. Aluminum-Base Alloy Permanent Mold Castings.
B 178-50T. Aluminum and Aluminum-Alloy Sheet and Plate for Use in Pressure Vessels.
B 179-50T. Aluminum-Base Alloys in Ingot Form for Sand Castings, Die Castings and Permanent Mold Castings.
B 209-50T. Aluminum and Aluminum-Alloy Sheet and Plate.
B 210-50T. Aluminum-Alloy Drawn Seamless Tubing.
B 211-49T. Aluminum and Aluminum-Alloy Bars, Rods and Wire.
B 221-49T. Aluminum and Aluminum-Alloy Extruded Bars, Rods and Shapes.
B 234-50T. Aluminum-Alloy Drawn Seamless Tubes for Condensers and Heat Exchangers.
B 235-50T. Aluminum-Alloy Extruded Tubes.
B 241-50T. Aluminum-Alloy Pipe.
B 247-50T. Aluminum-Alloy Die Forgings.

²Total of all impurities including those listed in composition limits.
³B209, B210, B211 and B221 permit 0.25 pct maximum chromium.
⁴B247 permits 0.15 pct maximum titanium.
⁵For cooking utensils, 0.6 pct maximum iron, 0.3 pct maximum copper, and 0.6 pct maximum manganese are permitted.
⁶The designation in parentheses, which does not conform to the designation system for light metals and alloys, is used in B85 to designate this alloy in the form of die castings.
⁷For general use, other than cooking utensils, 0.6 pct maximum copper is permitted.
⁸CB60A is erroneously designated as CP60A in B211.

arbitrarily assigned in alphabetical order to differentiate alloys which otherwise result in identical designations. The full name of the base metal precedes the designation, but it is omitted for brevity when the base metal being referred to is obvious. The letters used to represent alloying elements are shown in Table I.

When a range is specified for the alloying element, the rounded off mean is used in the designation. If only a minimum percentage is specified for the alloying element, the rounded off minimum percentage is used in the designation. When an alloying element is specified as the remainder, the percentage used in the designation is found by computing the possible range in accordance with the percentages specified for the other elements and rounding off the mean of the range. Elements specified as the remainder are ignored in the designation when only a minimum percentage is specified for the base metal.

Designations for unalloyed light metals consist of the specified minimum purity, all digits retained but dropping the decimal point. The digits are followed by a letter arbitrarily assigned in alphabetical order to differentiate metals of the same purity having different impurity requirements. The full name of the base metal precedes the designation, but it is omittd for brevity when the base metal being referred to is obvious.

Five Compositions Covered

ASTM specification B37-49, "Aluminum for Use in Iron and Steel Manufacture," covers five compositions of unalloyed aluminum varying in purity from 85.0 per cent minimum aluminum to 98.0 per cent minimum aluminum. In conformance with the codification system, they are designated 850A, 900A, 920A, 950A and 980A aluminum. The numbers in each designation indicate the specified minimum aluminum content with the decimal point dropped. The letter A in each designation serves to differentiate the metal from any other which might have the same minimum aluminum content but different impurity limits.

ASTM Specification B90-49T, "Magnesium-Base Alloy Sheet," covers two alloys, one of which is designated as magnesium alloy AZ31A. This alloy's composition limits are given in Table II. The designation AZ31A indicates that the alloy contains aluminum (code letter A) and zinc (code letter Z) as the two alloying elements specified in the greatest amount. Their specified percentages are rounded off to whole numbers, three and one respectively. The final letter A serves to differentiate this alloy from any other AZ31 alloy, such as magnesium alloy AZ31B in ASTM Specifications B91-49T, B107-

TABLE IV

Magnesium and Magnesium-base Alloys

Alloy Designations		Aluminum		Manganese	Zinc		Silicon	Copper	Tin		Nickel	Iron	Calcium	Total Others	Magnesium	B80	B90	B91	B92	B93	B94	B107	B199	B217
ASTM	Commercial	Min	Max	Min	Min	Max	Max	Max	Min	Max	Max	Max	Max	Max	Min									
9980A		...	...	...	...	...	...	0.02	...	...	0.001	...	...	0.20²	99.80				★					
AM80A	Dowmetal A	7.8	9.2	0.15		0.3	0.3	0.10			0.01			0.3	Remainder	★								
		8.0	9.0	0.18		0.20	0.2	0.08			0.01			0.3	Remainder					★				
AM100A	Mazlo AM240, Dowmetal G	9.3	10.7	0.10		0.3	0.3	0.10			0.01			0.3	Remainder	★						★		
		9.4	10.6	0.13			0.2	0.08			0.01			0.3	Remainder					★				
(AS100)³ AM100B		9.4	10.6	0.13			1.0	0.08			0.01			0.3	Remainder					★				
		9.0	11.0	0.10		0.3	1.0	0.05			0.03			0.3	Remainder						★			
AZ31A	Mazlo AM-C52S, Dowmetal FS-1	2.5	3.5	0.20	0.6	1.4	0.3	0.05			0.005	0.005	0.3	0.3	Remainder		★							
AZ31B	Mazlo AM-C52S, Dowmetal FS-1	2.5	3.5	0.20	0.6	1.4	0.3	0.05			0.005	0.005		0.3	Remainder		★					★		★
AZ61A	Mazlo AM-C57S, Dowmetal J-1	5.8	7.2	0.15	0.4	1.5	0.3	0.05			0.005	0.005		0.3	Remainder		★					★		★
AZ63A	Mazlo AM265, Dowmetal H	5.3	6.7	0.15	2.5	3.5	0.3	0.25			0.01			0.3	Remainder	★								
		5.5	6.5	0.18	2.7	3.3	0.2	0.20			0.01			0.3	Remainder					★				
AZ80A	Mazlo AM-C58S, Dowmetal O-1	7.8	9.2	0.12	0.2	0.8	0.3	0.05			0.005	0.005		0.3	Remainder			★						★
AZ91A	Mazlo AM263, Dowmetal R	8.5	9.5	0.15	0.5	0.9	0.2	0.08			0.01			0.3	Remainder						★			
		8.3	9.7	0.13	0.4	1.0	0.5	0.10			0.03			0.3	Remainder					★				
AZ91B	Dowmetal RC	8.5	9.5	0.15	0.5	0.9	0.2	0.25			0.01			0.3	Remainder						★			
		8.3	9.7	0.13	0.4	1.0	0.5	0.3			0.03			0.3	Remainder					★				
AZ91C⁴	Dowmetal R	8.3	9.7	0.13	0.4	1.0	0.3	0.10			0.01			0.3	Remainder	★								
		8.5	9.5	0.15	0.5	0.9	0.2	0.08			0.01			0.3	Remainder						★			
AZ92A	Mazlo AM260, Dowmetal C	8.3	9.7	0.10	1.6	2.4	0.3	0.25			0.01			0.3	Remainder	★							★	
		8.5	9.5	0.13	1.7	2.3	0.2	0.20			0.01			0.3	Remainder						★			
M1A	Mazlo AM3S, Dowmetal M	...	...	1.20			0.3	0.05			0.01		0.3	0.3	Remainder		★					★		★
M1B	Mazlo AM403, Dowmetal M	...	...	1.20			0.3	0.10			0.01			0.3	Remainder	★								
		...	...	1.30			0.1	0.08			0.01			0.2	Remainder						★			
TA54A	Mazlo AM65S, Dowmetal D	3.0	4.0	0.20		0.3	0.3	0.05	4.0	6.0	0.03			0.3	Remainder						★			

¹Specifications for:
B 80-49T. Magnesium-Base Alloy Sand Castings.
B 90-49T. Magnesium-Base Alloy Sheet.
B 91-49T. Magnesium-Base Alloy Forgings.
B 92-45, Magnesium Ingot and Stick for Remelting.
B 93-49T. Magnesium-Base Alloys in Ingot Form for Sand Castings, Die Castings, and Permanent Mold Castings.
B94-49T. Magnesium-Base Alloy Die Castings.

B107-49T. Magnesium-Base Alloy Bars, Rods, and Shapes.
B199-49T. Magnesium-Base Alloy Permanent Mold Castings.
B217-49T. Magnesium-Base Alloy Extruded Round Tubes.
²Total of aluminum, copper, iron, manganese, nickel, and silicon.
³The designation in parentheses, which does not conform to the designation system for light metals and alloys, is used in B93 and B94 to designate this alloy in the form of ingot and die castings.
⁴In ingot form for sand castings this alloy is designated as AZ91A in B93.

49T and B217-49T. This alloy differs from AZ31A in that it does not have a specified limit for calcium.

Table III covers aluminum and aluminum-base alloys, their ASTM and common commercial designations, ASTM chemical composition limits, and the ASTM specifications in which they appear. Table IV gives the same information for magnesium and magnesium-base alloys.

A new system for designating tempers was adopted[8] by the aluminum industry in 1948. It is also being used in the magnesium industry. Recent issues of many specifications designate tempers according to this system. The ASTM uses it in their specifications for aluminum and aluminum-base alloys. It will be used in their specifications for magnesium and magnesium-base alloys when they are next revised. It is

also planned to combine the codification system for light metals and alloys with the temper designation system for issuance by the ASTM as "Recommended Practices for Codification of Light Metals and Alloys, Cast and Wrought."

References

[1] Proceedings, ASTM, Vol. 42, 1942, p. 219.
[2] Proceedings, ASTM, Vol. 45, 1945, p. 139.
[3] Proceedings, ASTM, Vol. 44, 1944, p. 266.
[4] Proceedings, ASTM, Vol. 46, 1946, p. 259.
[5] R. B. Smith, "ASTM Code Systems for Aluminum Alloys and Magnesium Alloys," ASTM Bulletin, March 1948, p. 50.
[6] John C. Kiszka, "What's In An Alloy?" ASTM Bulletin, March 1948, p. 51.
[7] "Tentative Recommended Practices for Designating Significant Places in Specified Limiting Values," 1949 Book of ASTM Standards, Part 2, p. 1051.
[8] R. B. Smith, "New Temper Designations for Aluminum Alloys," THE IRON AGE, June 24, 1948, p. 72.

NEW TYPE QB CIRCUIT BREAKER
for NQB Lighting Panelboards

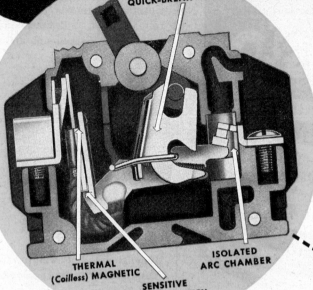

QUICK-MAKE,
QUICK-BREAK

THERMAL
(Coilless) MAGNETIC

SENSITIVE
MAGNETIC LATCH

ISOLATED
ARC CHAMBER

Completes the Line

TYPE **NMO**
MO Plug-In
Standard Duty breakers
for AC systems

TYPE **NQB**
QB heavy duty
breakers for
AC systems

TYPE **NAB**
ML heavy duty
breakers for
AC-DC systems

a **NEW** QB circuit breaker for NQB panelboards features an isolated arc chamber lined with arc resisting material which eliminates need for metal plates or other interrupting means. Operating mechanism is quick-make, quick-break. Stainless steel latch, independent of trip element, assures superior vibration characteristics. Thermal-(Coilless) Magnetic trip element is typical of other lighting panelboard types in Square D's broad line.

All Have 2-WAY PROTECTION

THERMAL element is a bi-metal providing positive and timed response to heating effects of both load current and surrounding atmosphere. The life of wire insulation is prolonged by limiting total temperature to a safe value.

MAGNETIC element responds instantaneously to the higher values of current characteristic of dangerous overloads and "shorts." Damage is minimized.

Both ARE NEEDED FOR **Complete** PROTECTION

Write for Bulletin 1640, Square D Company, 6060 Rivard Street, Detroit 11, Michigan
ASK YOUR ELECTRICAL WHOLESALER FOR SQUARE D PRODUCTS

SQUARE D COMPANY

DETROIT • MILWAUKEE • LOS ANGELES

SQUARE D COMPANY CANADA LTD., TORONTO • SQUARE D de MEXICO, S.A., MEXICO CITY, D. F.

publications

Continued from Page 34

booklet. Including photographs and details of 22 separate safety items, the booklet is concerned with problems of air and surface contamination involving radioactive or toxic contaminants. Described in the booklet are respiratory protective equipment, air sampling equipment, ventilation accessories, protective clothing, materials for contamination control, automatic artificial respiration instruments and oxygen therapy equipment. *Mine Safety Appliances Co.*
For free copy insert No. 9 on postcard, p. 35.

"Walkie" Battery Data

Nine new specification sheets covering "walkie" type batteries detail the battery to be used with a given make of truck. Each data sheet recommends battery types for light, normal, and heavy duty. A specification table on each sheet designates battery type, capacity, dimensions, and weight for each manufacturer's truck models. Layouts and tables indicate the type of terminals, plugs, or receptacles supplied to fit specific models. These specifications permit materials handling supervisors, battery room foremen, or purchasing agents quickly and easily to select the right battery for each truck and for the job it must do. *Gould-National Batteries, Inc.*
For free copy insert No. 10 on postcard, p. 35.

New Water Solvent

Immunol, the new 3-purpose solvent for use in metalworking plants, is described in a 12-p. booklet showing how to save money by eliminating additional cleaning operations. The solvent's chief use and purpose, as shown in the booklet, is to immunize any water against rust; this includes water in which soluble oils are used. Increased wetting-out properties of any solution are claimed and the solvent acts as a powerful detergent. Method of application for cleaning metals is given. *Haas Miller Corp.*
For free copy insert No. 11 on postcard, p. 35.
Resume Your Reading on Page 35

production ideas

Continued from Page 38

brated against air pressure and controlled by an air valve. Ordinary factory line compressed air is adequate. Changing tension requirements as the coil is dereeled

are made by adjusting the air pressure to the brake according to a calibration chart. *Linderman Devices.*

For more data insert No. 30 on postcard, p. 35.

Pillow Blocks

Self-aligning, precision ball bearing; shaft diam. ½ to 1¼ in.

A new line of pillow blocks and flanged cartridges feature a specially designed labyrinth seal, known as the Safety-Vent-Seal, that automatically provides the

correct amount of lubricant, excess grease being permitted to escape under pressure. The chrome alloy ball bearing used in these supports has a spherically ground OD to permit the bearing to align itself in the rigid, one-piece housing that is

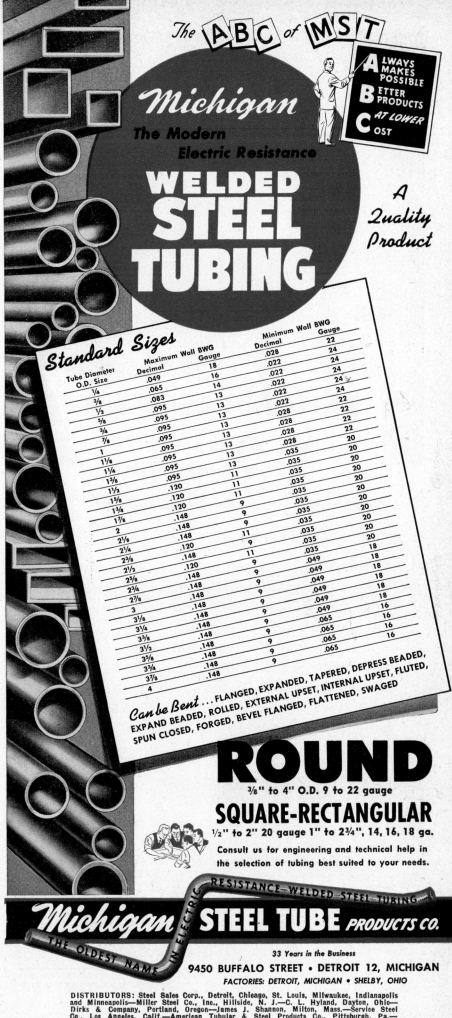

Battery of individually controlled Annealing Furnaces for heat treating Unitcastings.

UNITCAST Heat Treating Facilities MEET ALL PHYSICAL REQUIREMENTS

To meet Unitcast's standards, there is more than enough heat treating capacity to handle production. Because of Unitcast's and customer's requirements, these facilities are a necessity.

In heat treating, Unitcastings are grouped according to the grade of metal and thickness of cross section to assure meeting all physical requirements. And all Unit-castings are heat treated in this manner to insure better performance. Here's just one illustration of the many ways Unitcast's adequate plant facilities benefit you.

UNITCAST *Corporation*
QUALITY STEEL CASTINGS

Give us a chance to offer a "cast steel" answer for your parts problem. Our suggestions while your product is in the design stage will pay continuous dividends. Write or call today. Unitcast Corporation, Steel Casting Division, Toledo 9, Ohio. *In Canada:* Canadian-Unitcast Steel, Ltd., Sherbrooke, Quebec.

UNITCASTINGS ARE FOUNDRY ENGINEERED

---

production ideas
Continued

cast of Boston gear iron. This makes for accurate shaft alignment and quick mounting. *Boston Gear Works.*
For more data insert No. 31 on postcard, p. 35.

Strain Recorder
High-speed inkless, for static and dynamic load measurements.

A new recording SR-4 strain amplifier reproduces both static and rapidly changing SR-4 strain gage measurements of strains, forces, fluid pressures, displacements, vibrations, and acceleration, on a strip chart with rectangular coordinates. The instrument is a

direct-reading inkless, vacuum-tube voltmeter consisting of an ac powered strain gage amplifier of modulated carrier type in which the bridge is excited at 2500 cycles per sec by a built-in oscillator, a D'Arsonval moving coil recording galvanometer in which a current of 1-milliamp produces a writing arm torque of 200,000 dyne cms, and 1 cm deflection, and a paper drive mechanism. *Baldwin Locomotive Works.*
For more data insert No. 32 on postcard, p. 35.

Hand Serrating Tool
For use with Karbate graphite pipe.

The tool is simple, rugged, and easy to use, assuring a tight, workmanlike joint in minimum time. It facilitates quick assembly of Karbate impervious graphite pipe on the job site. Pipe sizes from 1 to 6 in. may be serrated. *National Carbon Div., Union Carbide & Carbon Corp.*
For more data insert No. 33 on postcard, p. 35.
Resume Your Reading on Page 39

news of industry

Price Freeze and CMP are Readied for Action

Prices expected to ice-up about Feb. 15 . . . Eric Johnston in, Valentine out as Wilson makes up mind . . . ESA battles over date to set prices . . . Controlled economy coming.

Washington—Two basic government anti-inflation weapons—price controls and a controlled-materials plan—are being readied for active service this week.

While no decision has been reached as to the effective date of each of these controlled-economy devices, top Administration advisors indicate a general price-freeze will be ordered by mid-February and a CMP by early June.

President Truman's decision to control prices via the general-freeze approach, rather than on a commodity-by-commodity basis (the "selective" approach) was revealed over the week-end in his appointment of Eric Johnston as Economic Stabilizer. Mr. Johnston's predecessor, Alan Valentine, had opposed the quick "freeze" approach to price stabilization.

Economic Stabilization Agency officials indicate they expect a price-freeze order to become effective about Feb. 15.

The level at which prices will be frozen is bitterly disputed within the agency, however, with some economists favoring a roll-back to Dec. 1 levels and others seeking to peg prices at Jan. 1 or Jan. 15 levels.

Decides Definitely on CMP

Charles E. Wilson, the government's top mobilization planner, disclosed his definite decision to adopt a Controlled Materials Plan at a Congressional hearing.

"We will ultimately come to it," he declared, indicating details of the plan were being worked out by William H. Harrison, head of the National Production Authority.

Equitable Distribution Sought

Mr. Harrison takes the view that a CMP is the only known method of bringing about "reasonably equitable and efficient distribution of scarce materials for civilian consumption."

But he also recognizes the administrative pitfalls inherent in any such system. Among these, he feels, are such drawbacks as the huge administrative staff required, the fact that such a plan must apply to every consumer without exception, and—most important—the military's current inability to make up its mind as to the extent of its materials needs.

NPA to Aid Farm Machine Makers

Washington—The National Production Authority is planning to work with industry and the Agriculture Dept. to keep steel and other materials flowing to agricultural equipment manufacturers. A special section will aid companies on an individual basis.

This decision was made after Farm Equipment Advisory committeemen reported farm machinery output might drop 25 pct under last year's rate by June.

Steel for Defense

Washington — From 12 to 14 pct of current steel production is channeled directly into defense production and large additional amounts go to supporting purposes, such as the freight car program, NPA's David B. Carson, of the Iron and Steel Div., told the Senate Small Business Committee last week.

He said present steel capacity of 104 million tons should be increased by over 10 million tons in 2 years but that problems of raw materials, transportation, ore boats, etc., would have to be overcome. NPA will continue a policy of seeing that military or defense orders get right of way at mills, Mr. Carson stated.

Bendix Buys Ford Plant

Detroit—Bendix Aviation Corp. has purchased the Hamilton, Ohio, plant of Ford Motor Co. for the production of aircraft parts and accessories. Ford used the Hamilton facilities until a few months ago for stamping operations. The new plant at Hamilton will be operated as a division of Bendix, according to Malcolm P. Ferguson, president of the company.

Ferguson Gets Arsenal Contract

New York—Contract for installation of process equipment at Picatinny Arsenal, Dover, N. J., has been awarded H. K. Ferguson Co. The $650,000 project will be completed within 6 months.

INDUSTRIAL SHORTS

EXPANSION PROGRAM — A $2.5 million expansion program is under way at the CLEVELAND PNEUMATIC TOOL CO., Cleveland. One million is being privately financed and covers plant expansion, re-arrangement and machine tools. The balance covers machine tools being acquired under a government facilities contract.

BRANCH PLANT — Approximately 180 acres at Hampstead, Md., have been purchased by BLACK & DECKER MFG. CO. for the erection of a branch plant to manufacture portable electric tools. Building is expected to start around April or May and about 300 to 400 people will be employed at the plant in a year's time.

CONSOLIDATION — Wood Works, the stainless steel processing plant of U. S. STEEL CO., is now the Wood Works plant of the company's Irvin Works, McKeesport, Pa. No changes are contemplated in the management personnel of Wood Works.

BUILDING NEW HOME — A new plant is being built in Englewood, a suburb of Denver, by C. A. NORGREN CO., manufacturers of pneumatic equipment. The company is also observing its 25th anniversary this year.

CHANGES NAME — Gordon & Kinney, Inc., Detroit, has adopted the new name of J. ALEX GORDON & CO. The company is sales representative for the Automatic Transportation Co., Chicago, covering the Detroit industrial area.

MORE SPACE — LATROBE ELECTRIC STEEL CO. has moved its Los Angeles office to larger quarters at 3537 E. Olympic Blvd. New location includes a 3500 sq ft warehouse for high speed tool and die steels, tool bits and drill rod.

WEST COAST AGENT—Eriez Mfg. Co. Erie, Pa., has appointed C. D. SUTTON, INC., as their representative in the Los Angeles area. Sutton will handle the complete Eriez line, which includes all permanent magnetic separation equipment of its own manufacture, Memco electromagnetic separation equipment and RCA electronic metal detectors.

BROADENS ACTIVITIES — West Coast regional headquarters have been established in Los Angeles by the BELLOWS CO., Akron, Ohio, manufacturers of Bellows "controlled-air-power" devices for industrial use. The company will also take over all distribution sales activities for Smith-Johnson Corp., Los Angeles, manufacturers of Senacon pneumatic equipment, formerly handled by Conapco, Inc.

WESTERN OUTLET — The WHITNEY CHAIN CO. of Hartford has established a new office and warehouse building in Los Angeles with A. J. Swisler as district manager. This branch will function as the engineering sales and service outlet for Whitney's complete line throughout southern California and Arizona.

NEW QUARTERS—The Baroid Sales Div. of the NATIONAL LEAD CO. has awarded a contract to the H. K. Ferguson Co. for construction of a new office building and research center in Houston.

GROUP OFFICIALS—Otto H. Fischer, president of Union Diesel Engine Co., Oakland, Calif., has been elected president of the DIESEL ENGINE MANUFACTURERS ASSN. William E. Butts, president of General Metals Corp., San Francisco, was elected to the board of directors.

Copper, Brass Price-Freeze Studied by Government, Industry

Bring OPA price lists up to date; . . . Some ingot cuts promised ESA

Washington — The government is studying price-freeze recommendations submitted by the copper and brass industries.

Industry representatives, including scrap dealers, refiners, and ingot makers have been bringing former OPA price lists up to date.

The Economic Stabilization Agency is studying the recommendations, but has not indicated when or how price ceilings will be imposed on the copper and brass industries.

Brass mill industry spokesmen told ESA they would agree to price stabilization if assured prices of raw materials, including scrap, were also stabilized.

Ingot makers indicated willingness to subscribe to a voluntary price stabilization agreement, ESA said. Under this proposal, companies would give ESA advance notice of any proposed price increase, provided there would be no increase in the primary metal market.

ESA said it had been assured by some ingot producers they were reducing their selling prices on certain grades of ingot, effective immediately, and accordingly will reduce their buying prices for the scrap they use.

NPA Amends Steel Order M-1

Washington—Certification that materials purchased for the freight car program will be used for no other purpose must be obtained under amendment to NPA M-1. Exact amounts of materials and required delivery dates must also be given.

Industrial alcohol, chlorine, natural and synthetic rubbers and other non-metallic materials have been added to the list of materials on NPA Notice 1 which may not be stocked in excess of reasonable needs or resold at higher than market prices.

MORE SCRAP FOR WAR: Scene is the exhibit room of the Institute of Scrap Iron and Steel Convention in New York's Commodore Hotel last week. The sign points out the importance of scrap in steelmaking and defense while men of the trade discuss expanded war volume that is needed and the coming clampdown of controls.

Steel Co. of Canada Plans 50 Pct Plant Capacity Expansion

Will boost potential to 1.9 million tons at cost of $40 million.

Toronto—The Steel Co. of Canada, Ltd., plans plant expansion to boost capacity by 50 pct at a cost of $40,000,000, H. G. Hilton, president, announced.

It will take about 18 months to complete the program. Principal features of the new undertaking are enlarged dock and storage facilities, additional coke ovens, a new blast furnace and a new open-hearth furnace shop in which will be installed four furnaces of 250 tons capacity each. On the completion of the new project the company will have four blast furnaces and capacity will be boosted 450,-000 tons to 1,207,000 tons annually. Steel ingot capacity will be increased by 650,000 tons to 1,900,-000 tons, enabling the company to produce over four times its average annual ingot rate during the years 1935 to 1939.

Increase in Flat-Rolled

While the additional steel will be rolled into the various products now being produced by the company, the major increase will be in hot and cold-rolled sheets, which have been scarce, the president stated. He emphasized that the expansion was a normally planned one and not caused by war conditions. Engineering work is well advanced and initial contracts have been placed.

Although the expansion program is the largest ever planned by the Hamilton industry in such a short time, the Steel Company has spent $65,000,000 on expansions to its Hamilton plant in the last 10 years.

Algoma Steel Corp., Ltd., is embarking upon a plant expansion program to cost about $10,000,000 which will involve installation of a strip and skelp mill. Morgan Construction Co., of Worcester, Mass., is reported to have the construction contract and Canadian General Electric Co., Ltd., a $1,600,000 contract to supply the main electrical drive. The new additions are expected to be in production in 1952.

Jones & Laughlin Splits Stock

Pittsburgh — Stockholders of Jones & Laughlin Steel Corp. have approved a proposal that common stock be split two-for-one, and have authorized an increase in indebtedness from $150 million to $180 million. They also approved a change from no par to $10 par.

NPA M-30 Limits Tungsten Use

Washington—The National Production Authority order M-30 sets up a tungsten allocation system and limits use of the metal for abrasives, high-speed steels, and pigments.

Effective Mar. 1, NPA authorizations based on end use must be obtained for tungsten for making high-speed steel. Effective at once, orders for class B high-speed steel must not exceed 20 pct of total monthly requirements.

Small users of 500 lb of high-speed steels per quarter are exempt. Inventories of 50 lb or more must report them and inventories are limited to a 60-day supply or working level, whichever is less.

Seeks Ways to Raise Benzene Production by 103 Million Gals

See 15 million gals extra from coke, 88 million gals from oil

Washington—A survey is being made by the Defense Solid Fuels Administration for the purpose of finding ways to increase benzene production from coke ovens. Output from this source is expected to be increased by 15 million gals over the next 2 years.

This announcement was made simultaneously with a meeting of benzene producers and users with National Production Authority officials, at which time a resolution was adopted asking the government to authorize construction of facilities to produce 88 million additional gals from petroleum.

Current needs are estimated at 252 million gals. Some 12 million gals are currently being produced from petroleum and 165 million gals are being recovered from coke ovens.

Petroleum Administration for Defense says enough applications for certificates of necessity have been received to result in production of more than the volume needed. Several have been granted and others are being studied.

TVA to Get 3 New Generators

Pittsburgh—Westinghouse Electric Corp. will build three vertical water-wheel generators of 31,250 kva capacity for the new Boone Dam of the Tennessee Valley Authority. The generators will cost approximately $2 million. All units are scheduled to operate by '53.

GSA Reopens Velasco, Tex., Manteca, Calif., Magnesium Plants

Washington—Arrangements for reopening two more reserve magnesium plants have been completed by the General Services Administration. Their total production over the next 2 years is estimated at about 200,000,000 lb.

Dow Chemical Co. has leased the plant it operated during the war at Velasco, Tex., for a 2-year period and will sell the entire output, estimated at 160,000,000 lb, to the government. Operations are scheduled to begin in May after $3 million worth of renovating and modernizing work.

Through another agreement, the Kaiser Magnesium Co. will operate the government plant at Manteca, Calif., which was operated by Permanente during the war. Some $700,000 will be spent in getting the plant ready for

A STEELY GRIP: Automatic tongs and an automatic locking device enables a craneman to singlehandedly load rolled steel rounds weighing up to 30,000 lb. Assisting in development of the tongs were mill designers, engineers, and operators at the Lorain, Ohio, plant of National Tube Co. Heppenstall Co., Pittsburgh, designed a unique automatic locking device.

operation by July. Output for the 2-year period is set at 40,000,000 lb.

The GSA has also contracted with Kaiser Aluminum & Chemical Corp. to supply Manteca with ferrosilicon and calcined dolomite. These magnesium components will come from a plant at Permanente,

Calif., and another at Natividad, Calif., both to be reactivated by Kaiser.

Dow is also completing installations at Madison, Ill., where the first continuous rolling mill for magnesium will produce for defense. The plant also will have extrusion equipment.

Confidence in Moses Pays Dividends in Peace

Coal grants voluntary wage hike, beating gun on wage-price controls . . . Lewis fire, brimstone tactics replaced by discreetness . . . Industry had built stocks,—*By John Delaney.*

Pittsburgh—The soft coal industry's confidence in Harry M. Moses is paying off.

For the first time, the industry has granted a wage increase to John L. Lewis and his United Mine Workers without a strike and without the customary namecalling.

The increase was granted voluntarily by the operators. Under their contract they didn't have to think about wages until next month. However, the imminence of price-wage controls was a factor in the early settlement.

Reduce February Stocks

Harry Moses and John Lewis did the job—so quietly and efficiently—that it left the industry and the rest of the country gasping. The negotiations included the usual give and take. But these two old friends, conscious of their responsibilities in the national emergency, came up with a nice, business-like settlement that nobody could get mad about. Both sides won concessions.

To say that a lot of people were surprised is an understatement. In anticipation of the usual crisis and possible strike, everybody was stocking up on coal. So much so that February probably will be one of the industry's poorest months as consumers reduce heavy inventories. Business will improve, though, as the defense program builds up steam and with

shipments of 5 million tons or more to Great Britain between now and June.

The Moses-Lewis meetings began last Dec. 27—less than 3 months after Moses resigned as president of H. C. Frick Coke Co., a U. S. Steel subsidiary, to represent the Northern Coal Operators and 200 million tons of capacity, little more than a third of which is so-called captive tonnage of steel producers. Moses is president of the Bituminous Coal Operators Assn.

The meetings continued, except for holiday recesses, until a tentative agreement was reached. The agreement called for a wage increase of $1.60 per day—20¢ an hour, increasing the basic daily pay of 370,000 coal miners to $16.35, effective Feb. 1. This represented, roughly, an average between what Moses offered and what Lewis demanded. Dismissed early was any consideration of a reduction in the work-day or an increase in the miners 30¢ per ton welfare fund royalty.

Join the Bandwagon

Moses took this agreement to the people he represented and asked their approval. He got it—unanimously.

The rest of the industry— Joseph E. Moody's Southern Coal Producers Assn., Harry Treadwell's Illinois group, and the western operators—almost trampled one another in their haste to say, "Me, too." Anthracite operators came along later.

The agreement assures peace in this vital industry until at least Mar. 31, 1952. It does not expire automatically, but only if notice of intent to cancel is given 60 days in advance. If such notice is not given, the contract continues in effect for 60 days after notice actually is served. This clause automatically eliminates danger of a no-contract, no-work strike without a full 60 days to reach settlement.

The Mar. 31 expiration date also is a concession to the operators. This gives them at least a full year before they start thinking about the possibility of new contract demands.

Coal operators will ask for a 5 or 6 pct price increase to cover cost of the pay hike.

Moses, Lewis Write the Peace

Reports of behind-the-scenes dictation by Benjamin F. Fairless, president of U. S. Steel Corp., or George Love, president of Consolidation Coal Co., are ridiculous. Moses saw neither of these men prior to the tentative agreement with Lewis.

An incident that occurred at the contract signing pointed up the harmony that now exists between Lewis and the industry in contrast to the bitterness of previous years. When someone handed Lewis a note advising that 11 miners had been killed in a West Virginia explosion, he didn't take it as a cue to tee off on the safety shortcomings of the industry. Instead, he looked up and said quietly:

"That, gentlemen, is what our men contribute to the country."

Two Furnaces Out of Blast

Pittsburgh—U. S. Steel Co. has blown out two blast furnaces this month. Its No. 5 furnace at the Ohio works was blown out Jan. 18 for relining and enlarging and its No. 2 furnace at Clairton went out on Jan. 7 for repairs.

AN INDUSTRIAL BEAUTY: In Ford's Dearborn, Mich., Rouge plant, toolmaker Paul F. Miller works on the surface of giant screw undergoing a thread-rolling operation that closes pores and gives the thread a high surface finish to cut frictional wear. He is taking more pains than a diamond cutter. The screw will control adjustments of rolls in Ford's steel rolling mill. Threads are 15 in. in diam and the screw is 13 ft long.

Steel Firms Negotiate For Steep Rock Iron Ore Land Rights

Cleveland—Pickands, Mather & Co., acting for a group of steel and iron ore producers, is negotiating with Steep Rock Iron Mines, Ltd., for an agreement to explore and an option to lease certain iron ore property in the Steep Rock Lake area in Western Ontario, said Elton Hoyt, 2nd, senior partner of Pickands, Mather & Co.

Others of the group are Bethlehem Steel Co., Youngstown Sheet & Tube Co., The Steel Co. of Canada, Ltd., and Interlake Iron Corp.

Mr. Hoyt said that, while details of the agreement are still to be worked out, exploratory work in the near future is planned. If sufficient ore should be proved, the company taking the lease will be managed by Pickands, Mather & Co., he said.

He declined to discuss tonnages but said it is hoped that the project will disclose deposits of some magnitude.

The property covers more than 1000 acres and is in the general vicinity of Inland Steel Co. land optioned from Steep Rock Iron Mines a year ago.

The area controlled by Steep Rock lies about 140 miles west of Port Arthur and Lake Superior, and is connected with Port Arthur by rail.

Carboloy Makes Heavier Metal

Detroit—Manufacture of a non-cutting metal heavier than cemented carbide and of 50 pct greater density than lead has been announced by Carboloy Co., Inc.

The new material, trade name Hevimet, will be widely used for static and dynamic balancing, since it provides maximum weight with minimum size. It will also serve as a screen for gamma rays in radiotherapy and other applications.

Alabama Plant to Make Munitions

Huntsville, Ala.—The former Dallas Mfg. Co. textile mill, sold and dismantled in 1949 and turned into a warehouse, will be converted into a munitions plant, according to Richard W. Wirt, Southern Railway official.

Roads Ask ICC for General 6 Pct Freight Rate Increase

Ask rise in handling charges at lower lake ports, boost for coal.

Washington—The railroads last week asked the Interstate Commerce Commission for authority to put into immediate effect a general 6 pct freight rate increase which they proposed 2 weeks ago. Refunds would be paid or allowed for any increases not finally approved by the ICC.

No increase has been asked for storing iron ore at lower Lake ports, nor in handling charges at upper Lake ports on shipments forwarded from there by water. But handling charges at the lower Lake ports would take the increase.

Coal Boost Sought

Instead of the general increase, a specific boost of 18¢ per net ton or 20¢ per gross ton is sought for coal. In the case of the Nickel Plate (New York, Chicago & St. Louis R.R.), the road would not increase bituminous rates for shipments picked up and delivered within the state of Ohio. This is to offset trucking competition.

Demurrage charges would not be increased, nor would allowances paid by the roads for drayage and similar services performed for the roads by shippers or receivers. But the proposed increase would apply to numerous other services, including protective service, switching, diversion, etc.

Also taking the general increase would be line haul rates on truck bodies, trailers or semi-trailers, as well as class rates along with joint water rates. Adjustments would be made later to restore normal differentials.

Alcan to Reopen Smelter

Montreal — Aluminum Co. of Canada, Ltd., proposes to reopen its smelter at Beauharnois, Que., next April and has arranged for a power supply of 100,000 hp to operate the plant. With this plant operating the company will add some 32,000 metric tons of primary aluminum ingots a year. The addition of the Beauharnois smelter to those already operating at Shawinigan Falls, Arvida and Isle Maligne, Que., will raise Aluminum Company's ingot capacity to well over 400,000 tons a year.

Steel Firms Give Workers Right Steer to Bond Savings Plan

Drive against inflation . . . Bulk of personnel sign up for savings.

New York—Broadsides against inflation are skillful appeal-to-reason campaigns through which many steel companies are signing thousands of their employees on the Payroll Savings Plan.

Metalworking plants were quick in the footsteps of National Tube Co., which evolved a successful technique in convincing workers that buying savings bonds on the payroll plan meant serving country and themselves. (THE IRON AGE, Oct. 26, 1950, p. 80.)

Carnegie-Illinois Steel Corp., now part of U. S. Steel Co., had only 18 pct of its staff on the plan before C. F. Hood, Carnegie president, opened a drive that saw

". . . But you *can't* quit. You've been in charge of misfiling for years!"

59,000 workers sign their names on the dotted line. The works now has 77 pct participation among 100,000 employees.

Crucible Starts from Scratch

Allegheny Ludlum's drive achieved 82.2 pct participation among 13,700 employees. Columbia Steel Co. recently completed its campaign, starting with less than 10 pct participation and finishing with 85.2 pct of 7500 workers. This was the record for all West Coast industry.

Incomplete results from Weirton Steel shows that the plant is at 53.6 participation. American Bridge Co. signed up 92.8 pct at its Ambridge plant and is working on other plants now. Starting from scratch and reinstating the plan, Crucible Steel Co. convinced 78 pct of its employees at the Syracuse plant to sign up.

Disregarding high-pressure sales tactics, Gerrard Steel Strapping Co. has 97 pct on the plan. Other firms now in the drive stage include Koppers Co., Inc.; Aluminum Co. of America, American Radiator and Standard Sanitary Corp.

Maintenance Show Speaker Asks Equipment Care for Defense Effort

Four-day show attracts 10,000 as 170 companies man exhibit booths.

Cleveland—Basic necessity for victory, even more than the number of men in the armed forces, is the productive capacity of a nation, Herman W. Steinkraus, president, Bridgeport Brass Co., Bridgeport, Conn., told engineers at the second annual Plant Maintenance Show banquet here.

Care for Defense Role

The former president of the U. S. Chamber of Commerce warned that "we will have to live for a good many years with a major defense program as a part of our annual effort."

This means that our equipment must be so geared that we do not break down under the load. If equipment and facilities are overloaded, the destruction is at a much faster rate than if loads are kept within the capacity of that equipment. In a defense program maintenance becomes important.

The banquet was sponsored by the Cleveland section and the management division of the American Society of Mechanical Engineers. Cooperating societies were the Cleveland Engineering Society and the Cleveland section of the Society for the Advancement of Management.

The 4-day Plant Maintenance show, which opened Jan. 15 at Public Auditorium here, attracted more than 10,000 visitors. More than 170 companies e x h i b i t e d

products and services. Theme was more efficient, cheaper plant upkeep.

Conference sessions, sponsored by the American Society of Mechaical Engineers and the Society for the Advancement of Management, featured talks by 44 experts on maintenance operations with emphasis centered on reducing maintenance costs.

At the sectional conference on maintenance in metalworking plants, F. A. French, chief plant engineer, John A. Roebling's Sons Co., Trenton, N. J., outlined a 13-point maintenance organization for larger plants.

No Chrome Stainless Cuts

Pittsburgh—There will be no immediate restrictions on the use of straight chrome grades of stainless steel for civilian purposes.

The government's order limiting civilian applications of stainless, expected shortly, will apply only to the nickel-chrome grades, or 300 series. There is nothing in the works at the p r e s e n t time pertaining to straight chrome types. NPA feels there is no need just now to restrict straight chrome applications for non-defense use.

PA's Pay More in Extras After Steel Rise

They feel cost pressure of higher extra charges on sheet and strip products after December base price rise . . . U. S. Steel Corp. is exception to trend of raising extra charges.

Pittsburgh — After steel base price increases last December, purchasing agents for steel consumers began to feel the cost pressure of higher extra charges on sheet and strip products, advanced by some producers, with the notable exception of U. S. Steel Corp.

Depending on their source of supply, some steel users are paying more in extras on hot and cold-rolled sheets, hot-rolled strip, galvanized sheets, and long ternes.

Increases in Extras

On the sheet and strip products they produce, extras were increased by Great Lakes Steel Corp., Weirton, Republic, Jones & Laughlin, A r m c o, Bethlehem, Youngstown Sheet & Tube, and others.

Hot-rolled sheet extra increases include: gage and width $2 per ton on all gages 48-in. and narrower, and $1 per ton over 48-in. up to 72-in.; side cutting, all gages and widths, generally up $1 per ton; cut lengths, up from $1 to $3 per ton; closer than standard side cutting, $1 to $2 per ton; restricted tolerances, for not more than 75 pct of standard tolerance, $5 per ton; for not more than 50 pct of standard tolerance, no change to $5 per ton.

Some mills now charge an item quantity extra of $3 to $4 for quantities under 20,000 lb. to 10,000 lb., whereas the former minimum quantity without extra was 10,000 lb. Extra for under 10,000 lb. to 6,000 lb. is up $4; under 6,000 lb. to 4,000 lb., up $6; under 4,000 lb. to 2,000 lb., up $5 to $10; under 2,000 lb., up $10.

Order quantity extra is up $5; item extra for exact quantity up $8; extra for circles up to $2 in some instances; sketches up $3 for regular, $5 for irregular; a new outside inspection extra of $3; resquaring extra up 5 pct; pickling extras up $2; corrugated extra up $3; oiling extra up $3; greased edges up $4; lined up $3; breaker passed or back coiled up $3; some heat treatment extras up $4 to $5; quality extras generally up $2; specific and restricted test requirements generally up $2; pack-

aging extras up $1.50 to $8 per ton on cut lengths; $2.50 to $5 per coil, and 50¢ to $16 per package.

Extra advances on cold-rolled sheets are generally the same as for hot-rolled. Cold-rolled gage and width extras are up $2 for widths of 48-in. and under, and $1 for widths over 48-in. to 72-in. Length extras are up from $1 to $6, although on the popular sizes the range of increase is $1 to $2. Cold-rolled primes only are up $5. Circles are up $2, sketch extras $3; a new inspection extra, $3.

On hot-rolled strip, gage and width extras for all thicknesses are up $1 on 2-in. wide, and $2 for over 2-in. to 12 in. Pickling extras are up $1 to $2; extras for cutting to length up $1 to $3; packaging extras up 50¢ to $3.

Coating Extras Up, Too

Galvanized sheet flattening extras are up $2 for 22 gage and heavier. Resquaring extra, not stretcher leveled, increased from 10 pct to 15 pct; if stretcher leveled, up from 12½ pct to 17½ pct. Packaging, quantity, and processing extras are revised.

All gage and width extras on long ternes are up $2. The length extra for 60-in. to 96-in. is now $4 for all gages instead of the former range of $1 to $4. An extra of $8 now exists for lengths of 96-in. to 144-in., where there was none before. Coating extra for heavier than commercial, up $3.

Bethlehem Unwraps Huge New Expansion Plan

Capacity to be expanded 1.6 million tons by end of next year ... Expanded 1 million tons last year ... Total cost is placed at about $300 million—*By Bob Hatschek.*

New York—Bethlehem Steel Co. is continuing the expansion which added 1,000,000 ingot tons of capacity in 1950 with an additional 1,600,000 tons which will bring Bethlehem's total capacity to 17,600,000 tons by the end of 1952. The total 2,600,000 ton program will cost about $300 million. It includes openhearths, blast furnaces, rolling mills, coke ovens, ore facilities, more power, transportation and other facilities.

This is Bethlehem's answer to other steel firms who, in planning to build new mills in the East, are invading Bethlehem's traditional territory. These eastern expansions point to a highly competitive steel market in this area when they are completed. The short-range defense program, however, is of prime importance.

The breakdown of new steel facilities is: Lackawanna, 1,080,000 tons; Sparrows Point, 740,000 tons; Steelton, 352,000 tons; Bethlehem, 188,000 tons; Johnstown, 180,000 tons; and Los Angeles, 60,000 tons.

Add Blast Furnace Capacity

A new blast furnace is to be built at Lackawanna and a sintering plant is going up at Sparrows Point along with other improvements to blast furnace equipment at these and other plants. A 76-oven battery and a 65-oven battery to be built at Lackawanna and Sparrows Point, respectively, will join the two 77-oven coke batteries already authorized last year for Johnstown in supplying blast furnaces with needed coke.

Necessary raw materials are included in the program with the acquisition and development of new ore, coke and limestone sources. Existing coal and limestone facilities have already been improved.

Besides planned improvements on its short line railroads, Bethlehem intends to build two new Great Lakes ore ships which will have enough capacity to haul a total of 1,400,000 tons of ore and limestone per year.

The first shipment of ore from the company's Venezuelan mines is expected to reach this country in a few weeks and it is expected that this source will supply about 1,000,000 tons of ore this year and the yield will increase annually thereafter. Other ore reserves are to be tapped and the output of mines already producing is to be increased.

Also reported is the acquisition by Bethlehem of land along the St. Lawrence River which is said by a Bethlehem spokesman to be for mining purposes.

Bethlehem reports encouraging progress in their work on the beneficiating of low-grade taconite ores. At the Cornwall, Pa., plant the company has recently added pelletizing to the concentrating and sintering operations that have been under way for years.

Tech Background Wanted

Together with Pickands, Mather & Co., and Youngstown Sheet & Tube Co., Bethlehem hopes to have a technical background that will make possible the erection of a plant at Aurora, Minn., for the production of usable ore from these deposits, which is expected to produce some 2,500,000 tons a year.

CONTROLS *digest*

For more details see "You and Government Controls," The Iron Age, Jan. 4, 1951, p. 365. For full text of NPA regulations write U. S. Dept. of Commerce, Div. of Printing Service, Room 6225, Washington 25, D. C.

Order	Subject	Effective Date
NPA Reg. 1	Inventory Control	Sept. 18
Interpretation 1, 2, 3		Nov. 10
NPA Reg. 2	Priorities System	Oct. 3
Amendment 1, 2	DO Ratings	Oct. 3, Dec. 29
Delegation 1, 2, 3, 4	DO Ratings	Nov. 1, Nov. 2, Nov. 8
NPA Reg. 3	Priorities with Canada	Nov. 8
NPA M 1	Steel	Oct. 12
Amendment 1	Special programs	Oct. 26
Amendment 2	DO Lead Time	Dec. 1
Supplement 1	Freight car program	Oct. 26
Supplement 2	Great Lakes Ship program	Nov. 15
Supplement 3	Canadian freight cars	Dec. 15
NPA M 2	Rubber	Nov. 1
Amendment 1		Dec. 11
NPA M 3	Columbian steels	Oct. 19
NPA M 4	Construction	Oct. 27
Amendment 1, 2.		Oct. 31, Nov. 15
NPA M 5	Aluminum	Oct. 27
NPA M 6	Steel warehouses	Nov. 8
Amendment 1, 2		Dec. 1, Dec. 15
NPA M 7	Aluminum use	Nov. 13
Amendment 1		Dec. 1
Direction 1, 2, 3.		Nov. 28, Dec. 16, Dec. 27
NPA M 8	Tin inventories	Nov. 13
Amendment 1		Dec. 18
NPA M 9	Zinc distribution	Nov. 16
NPA M 10	Cobalt stocks	Nov. 30
Amendment 1		Dec. 30
NPA M 11	Copper distribution	Nov. 29
NPA M 12	Copper use	Nov. 29
NPA M 13	Rayon	Dec. 1
NPA M 14	Nickel cutback	Dec. 1
NPA M 15	Zinc cutback	Dec. 1
NPA M 16	Copper scrap controls	Dec. 11
Amendment 1		Dec. 18
NPA M 17	Electrical components	Dec. 18
NPA M 18	Hog bristles	Dec. 21
NPA M 19	Cadmium	Jan. 1
NPA M 20	Scrap Inventory	Jan. 4
NPA M 21	Methylene Chloride	Jan. 11
NPA M 22	Aluminum Scrap	Jan. 12
ESA Reg. 1	Auto prices, wages	Dec. 18
NPA Notice 1	Hoarding	Dec. 27
NPA Delegation 5	Ores, Metals	Dec. 18

you supply the form...

BARBER COLMAN WILL DESIGN *form* **CUTTERS**

TO
- COMBINE CUTS
- PROLONG TOOL LIFE
- SPEED OPERATIONS
- DUPLICATE ACCURACY
- MAKE THE JOB EASIER

Complete Milling Cutter Service
Send BLUEPRINTS for QUOTATION

BARBER-COLMAN COMPANY
491 ROCK STREET
ROCKFORD, ILLINOIS

Some Warehouses Snub Small Firms on Steel, Claims NPA Man

Washington—More and more complaints are coming in from small manufacturers that some steel warehouses refuse to sell more critical steel items except on DO ratings, wrote D. B. Carson, director of the Iron and Steel Div. of NPA, to Walter S. Doxsey, president of American Steel Warehouse Assn.

Mr. Carson said that deliberate withdrawal of products from the market by warehouses to sell only on rated orders and thus secure more steel is a violation of order M-6 and may force a revision of the order unless "the few warehouses that seek advantage" cease the practice.

Mr. Carson continued that the order was issued to provide "a flow of steel products through warehouses" to small consumers normally dependent on them. He said that these users do not yet have DO's to a great degree.

ESA, Steel Industry Meetings Yield Voluntary Price Controls

Washington—In the first action of its kind, Economic Stabilization Agency has given the green light to voluntary price stabilization for the iron and steel industry.

Officially, the action is a formal request by ESA that the industry freeze prices of major iron and steel items at Jan. 15 levels and not to raise prices without first giving ESA a 20-day notice.

Such a program had been worked out at meetings between representatives of the industry and ESA. The industry agreed to go along with the government providing that the Federal Trade Commission and Justice Dept. did not object. Both approved.

The established price would be the highest price in the 30 days before Jan. 15. The mills would not change customary price practices, such as price differentials, allowances, etc., in such a way as to increase the net return under the frozen price.

The 3 R's of Reliance Service

Resourceful
Responsible
Responsive

RELIANCE *Job-Fitted* PRODUCTS AND SERVICES

COLD ROLLED STRIP STEEL

Coils . . . Cut Lengths . . . All Tempers

Slit, Sheared, Deburred

and Round Edge

From WAREHOUSE

or

DIRECT-FROM-MILL

SHEETS

Cold Rolled . . . Hot Rolled

Hot Rolled Pickled . . . Long Terne

Galvanized

Standard or production sizes

or cut to actual working

dimensions

from

WAREHOUSE STOCKS

Big plants . . . .extensive processing, handling and shipping facilities . . . a widespread organization — all these things help make Reliance Service *resourceful* and *responsible*.

But the things that make Reliance Service *responsive* are not measured by size or number. Over the years they reflect a concern's attitude toward its customers and their needs . . . a readiness to work closely with them . . . almost as an integral part of their business.

In our case they spell 28 years of day-in and day-out specialized experience, living with and licking sheet and strip steel problems . . . knowing the possibilities as well as the limitations of our products . . . knowing how they can best fit your jobs.

DEPENDABLE DAN OUR CUSTOMERS' MAN

Reliance Job Fitting Service is a way of doing business that <u>works</u> *for you . . . whether steel is plentiful or scarce, in peace time or in war (either cold or hot).*

STEEL—BACKBONE OF AMERICA'S ARMAMENT

For Immediate Action Call The Nearest Reliance Plant or Office:

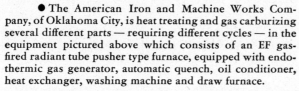
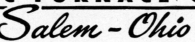
● *News of Industry* ●

Wheeling Builds Battery of 63 Coke Ovens at East Steubenville

Wheeling, W. Va. — Wheeling Steel Corp. is building a new battery of 63 coke ovens at its East Steubenville Works, an $8,750,000 project that will increase coke output from 120,000 tons to 145,000 tons per month.

The company also launched a new diesel-powered towboat, the *Capt. R. E. Reed*, at Decatur, Ala., where it was built by the Ingalls Ship Building Corp. The $96,000 boat replaces the *D. A. B.*, wrecked against a dam near Harmarville, Pa., last summer after the crew had rescued four persons from a yacht that had plunged over the dam. The boat will be used to push coal barges down the Allegheny and Ohio rivers to the plant.

Koppers Co. will build the coke ovens. Wheeling Steel now operates 251 units. To handle increased coal requirements, ten new coal barges will be added to the present fleet of 83.

U. S. Steel Ingot Capacity Up Sharply in Principal Areas

Pittsburgh—U. S. Steel Corp. ingot capacity in the Pittsburgh, Youngstown, and Chicago districts is up 1,661,600 tons over last year. Total capacity in these areas now tops 24,340,000 tons.

Pittsburgh area capacity is up 1,064,700 tons, Chicago 456,900 tons, and Youngstown 140,000.

This expansion was accomplished through enlargement of existing melting facilities, plus installation of modern, more efficient, and larger handling facilities and use of more iron ore sinter.

Belt Speeds Coal from Mine

Waltonville, Ill.—The world's highest lift conveyer belt has been installed here in a mine of the Chicago, Wilmington & Franklin Coal Corp. The belt, moving 7 miles per hour, can carry 1200 tons of coal an hour up a 3290 ft slope. A 1500 hp electric motor drives the head pulley.

Tempilstiks°

the amazing Crayons that tell temperatures

A simple method of controlling temperatures in:

- WELDING
- FLAME-CUTTING
- TEMPERING
- FORGING
- CASTING
- MOLDING
- DRAWING
- STRAIGHTENING
- HEAT-TREATING IN GENERAL

Also available in pellet and liquid form

It's this simple: Select the Tempilstik° for the working temperature you want. Mark your workpiece with it. When the Tempilstik° mark melts, the specified temperature has been reached.

$2 each

gives up to 2000 readings

Available in these temperatures (°F)

113	263	400	950	1500
125	275	450	1000	1550
138	288	500	1050	1600
150	300	550	1100	1650
163	313	600	1150	1700
175	325	650	1200	1750
188	338	700	1250	1800
200	350	750	1300	1850
213	363	800	1350	1900
225	375	850	1400	1950
238	388	900	1450	2000
250				

FREE —Tempil° "Basic Guide to Ferrous Metallurgy" — 16¼" by 21" plastic-laminated wall chart in color. Send for sample pellets, stating temperature of interest to you.

GORDON SERVICE

CLAUD S. GORDON CO.

Specialists for 36 Years in the Heat Treating and Temperature Control Field

Dept. 16 · 3000 South Wallace St., Chicago 16, Ill.
Dept. 16 · 2035 Hamilton Ave., Cleveland 14, Ohio

January 25, 1951

• News of Industry •

Pittsburgh Steel, Allegheny Ludlum Merger Decision Expected

Stockholders may vote in spring . . . Firms look each other over.

Pittsburgh — Merger of Allegheny Ludlum Steel Corp. and Pittsburgh Steel Co. is a distinct probability.

The two companies have inspected each other's facilities and have held formal discussions of terms. The decision, one way or another, will be made within a relatively short time. The question may be put to stockholders this spring.

Both companies are taking a good look at each other's financial structure and profit potential. Even advertising techniques of each company are being examined.

There would be no necessity to seek Dept. of Justice approval for the merger. The products produced by the companies conflict, so there would be no question of competition.

A Sensible Merger

The merger would be logical. Allegheny Ludlum is a leading producer of stainless and other alloy steels, plus a relatively small tonnage of carbon strip. It is semi-integrated and depends on others for its pig iron. Pittsburgh Steel is integrated, produces carbon seamless tubing and wire products, and will shortly enter the flat-rolled sheet and strip field for the first time.

Pittsburgh Steel has an excess of production, Allegheny Ludlum an excess of finishing facilities. At the present time, Pittsburgh Steel is selling part of the 950,-000 tons of pig iron it produces annually in the open market.. It is protected on iron ore.

Pittsburgh's present ingot capacity of 1,072,000 tons will shortly be increased to 1,560,000 tons. Allegheny Ludlum's ingot capacity is about 830,000 tons. Both companies have been expanding and modernizing their plants. Principal operations of both concerns are situated in western Pennsylvania.

DISCOBOLUS—By Myron

Precise Rhythm

so exact and explicit, faultless and flawlessly achieved in Myron's Discobolus, is the very goal of the entire personnel of this modern ball plant.

Every machine and every piece of equipment is of the latest design in this exclusive ball plant where balls only (not bearings) are made.

Interested ball users with proper credentials are invited to inspect these facilities.

Here you will see every contributing factor that assures you precision balls of absolute uniform quality.

Universal Balls have been used by the largest most meticulous bearing manufacturers in the U. S. A. and abroad since 1942.

The art of making balls to within ten millionths of an inch is the result of years of study and scientific research.

When you need precision balls of fine, very fine tolerance, perfect surface finish, sphericity and size accuracy that reduce friction, wear and maintenance costs to a minimum, balls that are guaranteed 100% inspected and individually gauged, specify Universal Precision Balls.

UNIVERSAL BALL CO.

PRECISION BALLS OF CHROME AND STAINLESS STEEL, BRONZE AND SPECIAL METALS.

WILLOW GROVE, Montgomery County, Pa.
Telephone, Willow Grove 1200

• News of Industry •

Scrap Committee, NPA Discuss Ways to Get More Scrap for War

Washington — Estimates that iron and steel scrap needs in 1951, year of expanded defense output, will surpass 1950 requirements of 29,700,000 tons by 3 million tons, prompted discussions between NPA and the Iron and Steel Scrap Industry Advisory Committee on methods to stimulate scrap.

Industry spokesman indicated that a concerted program will be needed to tap new scrap sources to meet the increased needs. The committee recommended securing more scrap from junked ships, release of obsolete machinery, recovery of street rails, recovery of metal from slag dumps, and a conservation program.

Ford to Build Rouge Coke Ovens

Detroit—Ford Motor Co. plans to open construction of 37 additional coke ovens at its Rouge plant. When the ovens are completed in late 1951, new capacity will be 1,430,000 tons annually. The ovens will furnish coke for new Ford foundry facilities being built at Cleveland and Rouge.

Ford also plans a coke screening plant and modernization of its coke byproducts plant.

Raise Steel Order Ceilings

Washington — Detailed changes were contained in an amendment to NPA M-1 issued this week, effective Jan. 22. Most percentage ceilings for acceptance of rated steel orders were raised, specific inventory controls at both production and consumption level were provided. Some ferrous products were added to the order and lead time of some items was changed.

A 45-day inventory is set for steel products and malleable and gray iron castings, while the maximum for pig iron is set at 30 days or a minimum working level. Percentage ceilings for acceptance of DO rated orders were also changed.

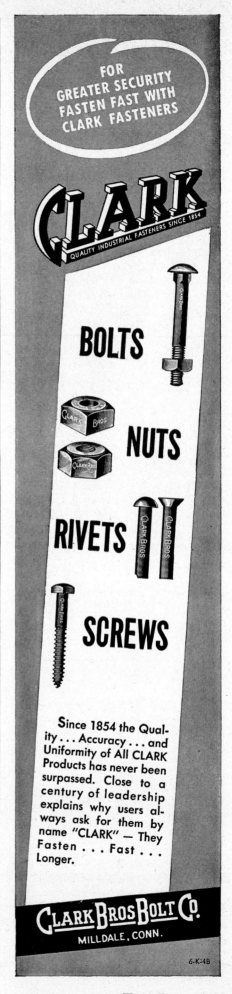

Seek NPA Aid in Chrome Shipping

Washington — NPA was asked last week to help break shipping bottlenecks in chrome ore imports.

Representatives of the ferro-chromium industry told NPA that expansion of their industry is well under way but production is hampered by difficulties in obtaining ore. Also, the industry is having difficulties in obtaining machinery and equipment.

In particular, the industry recommended that the ore pier at Beira, Africa, be set aside for handling chrome ore.

Expand Volta Redonda Capacity

Sao Paulo — Capacity of Volta Redonda, Brazil's pride and joy in steelmaking, will be expanded by 150,000 tons. Last year the mill produced 300,000 tons of steel, bettering 1949 output by about 75,000 tons.

Now under construction are a new blast furnace, two open-hearths, 21 coal chambers, and new rolling mill units. The mill now provides about 35 pct of Brazil's steel needs.

Alcoa Anti-Trust Suit Ended

New York — The 14-year-old anti-trust suit against Aluminum Co. of America was ended this week when Federal Judge John C. Knox accepted a stock disposal plan submitted by shareholders of Alcoa and Aluminum, Ltd., of Canada. Under the plan Alcoa shareholders will sell their holdings in the Canadian company over a 10-year period.

Mobile Plant Buys Local Foundry

Mobile, Ala. — The Pullman Stove & Pulley Mfg. Co. has purchased the foundry of Waterman Steamship Co. here.

The property consists of seven buildings on a 25-acre tract. It was used to supply Waterman Shipbuilding Corp., a subsidiary. The shipbuilding company will continue to obtain its requirements from the foundry.

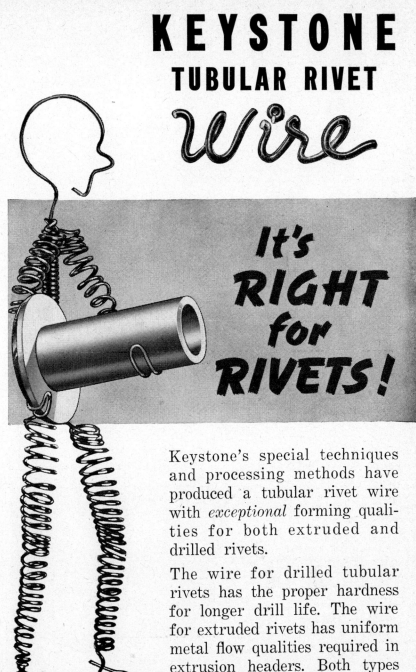

STEEL
CONSTRUCTION
NEWS

Fabricated steel awards this week included the following:

650 **Tons**, Philadelphia, warehouse for Frankford Grocery Co., to Bethlehem Steel Co., Bethlehem.

600 **Tons**, Salem, Mass., coal handling plant for New England Power Service Co. through William T. Donovan Co., Salem, to A. O. Wilson Structural Steel Co., Cambridge, Mass.

420 **Tons**, Dorchester, Mass., new Carney Hospital (now situated in South Boston, Mass), to A. O. Wilson Structural Steel Co., Cambridge, Mass.

210 **Tons**, Tolland, Conn., two span girder bridge, grading and drainage on Wilbur Cross Highway. Enfield Construction Co., Thompsonville, Conn., low bidder.

150 **Tons**, Philadelphia, Widener Memorial School, to Bethlehem Steel Co., Bethlehem.

Reinforcing bar awards this week included the following:

2000 **Tons**, Paducah, Ky., Powerhouse, to Concrete Steel Co.

1000 **Tons**, Evergreen Park, Ill., shopping center, to Ceco Steel Products Co., Chicago.

835 **Tons**, Milwaukee, Alverno College, to Ceco Steel Products Co., Chicago.

660 **Tons**, Eastlake, Ohio, Cleveland and Electric Illuminating Co., to U. S. Steel Supply Co.

650 **Tons**, Chicago, Harris Trust Bank vault, to Joseph T. Ryerson and Son, Chicago.

650 **Tons**, Chicago, Racine Avenue Pumping station sanitary district, to U. S. Steel Supply Co., Chicago.

500 **Tons**, Marietta, Ohio, Electro Metallurgical-Union Carbon and Carbide Co., to Bethlehem Steel Co.

375 **Tons**, Westville, Ind., hospital, to U. S. Steel Supply Co., Chicago.

315 **Tons**, Cincinnati, Beechmont Levy, to Pollak Steel Co., Cincinnati.

205 **Tons**, Gary, Ind., Municipal Court and Jail, to Olney J. Dean Co., Chicago.

200 **Tons**, Shelby, Ohio, Shelby Mutual Insurance building, to Pollak Steel Co., Cincinnati.

200 **Tons**, Wayne County, Ohio, project 540, to Pollak Steel Co., Cincinnati.

200 **Tons**, Meigs and Athens Counties, Ohio, project 519, to Truscon Steel Co.

175 **Tons**, Dayton, Oakview School, to Truscon Steel Co.

157 **Tons**, Freeport, Maine, project on Route 1, extending around Freeport Village. W. H. Hinman, Inc., North Anson, Maine, low bidder.

150 **Tons**, Tiffin, Ohio, American Radiator and Standard Sanitary Co., to U. S. Steel Supply Co.

140 **Tons**, Akron, Ohio, state highway project 492, to U. S. Steel Supply Co.

120 **Tons**, Chicago, International Harvester Co. vocational school, to Joseph T. Ryerson and Son, Chicago.

100 **Tons**, Detroit, annealing furnace, Ford Motor Co., to U. S. Steel Supply Co.

Reinforcing bar inquiries this week included the following:

1300 **Tons**, Chicago, Veterans Administration regional office and clinic building No. 11.

1200 **Tons**, Cincinnati, U. S. Engineers job.

600 **Tons**, Chicago, Twin Towers Apts.

335 **Tons**, Saginaw, Mich., sewage treatment plant.

290 **Tons**, Cleveland, St. Charles Hospital.

250 **Tons**, Detroit, U. S. Rubber Co. warehouse.

190 **Tons**, Blue Island, Ill., Illinois Bell Telephone Co.

170 **Tons**, Arlington Heights, Ill., Illinois Bell Telephone Co.

125 **Tons**, Chicago, administration building, Millers National Insurance Co.

100 **Tons**, Elmhurst, Ill., York community high school.

Cuba Nicaro Plant Reopening To Give U. S. 15 Pct More Nickel

Washington — Nickel supplies for the United States are seen as being increased by more than 15 pct by the end of the year when the Nicaro nickel plant in Cuba is reactivated.

The General Services Administration last week signed an agreement by which the Mining Equipment Corp. of New York will operate the plant after it is put in operating condition by the Frederick A. Snare Corp. at a cost of $5 million. The latter built the plant for the government in 1942. It has been inactive since 1947.

The rated capacity of the Nicaro works when constructed in 1942 was 43 million lb of high grade nickel oxide which would work out to about 32 million lb of nickel.

Transportation Facilities

The Nicaro plant includes rail and port terminals and more than 30 industrial type buildings including a reduction furnace building, wet ore building, and a large machine shop. The power plant has six 1500 kw and one 3000 kw generating units.

A pilot plant will also be built where research facilities will be turned toward development of a new process for producing cobalt as a by-product. The process is also expected to increase the nickel recovery rate.

Although the operating company is a subsidiary of the Dutch firm N. V. Billiton Maatschappij, all the output will be taken by the U. S. government. Operation will be on a fee basis which is expected to produce nickel oxide at about 40¢ a lb of contained nickel.

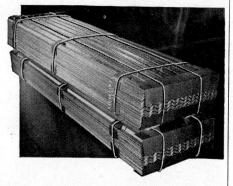

IRON AGE *markets and prices*

financing contracts—Methods of financing defense contracts and getting V-type loans were given by the Defense Dept. In order of military preference the financing procedures are: private lending, partial and progress payments, V-loans, and advance payment by the contracting agency. V-type loans will be authorized when defense contractors need financing in excess of what private lenders consider a normal risk. Branches of the armed services may guarantee the excess. Banks or financing agencies prepare the loan and send it to the interested military agency through the district Federal Reserve Bank.

farm priority—A program to take care of needs of farm equipment industry is being worked out. Members of the farm machinery industry have reported that they will be operating at a rate of 60 to 65 pct of that of last year by next June if they do not get help. The Agricultural Dept. is calling for a farm program equal to or greater than that of 1950.

Jorgensen invades midwest—Earl E. Jorgensen Co., steel distributors in Los Angeles and Oakland, Calif., and Dallas and Houston, Tex., will reverse the East to West trend by establishing facilities in Chicago. A site has been purchased and construction of a new warehouse will start soon.

steel for autos—Auto producers are aware they face a losing fight to keep production up. The industry will do well if it comes out of the first half of 1951 with 75 to 80 pct of its 1950 rate of output. For the second half of 1951, the guesses are now 50 to 60 pct of the 1950 rate, and the rate may go lower than this.

to handle products—Bethlehem Supply Co., Tulsa, Okla., has completed an agreement with Tube Turns, Inc., of Louisville, Ky., to distribute the latter's products to the petroleum industry in California.

expansion—Great Lakes Steel Corp. has opened construction on a fourth blast furnace on Zug Island and several of its openhearths are being rebuilt to raise capacity from 250 to 500 tons. The firm was granted a certificate of necessity for $42,833,800 recently. When the present program is finished in 1952, annual ingot capacity will be increased from the present 2.4 million tons to 3.6 million. Finishing capacity is also growing. Cold-rolled capacity is expected to reach 200,000 tons a month.

fluorspar—Oglebay Norton & Co. has announced increases in the price of metallurgical grade fluorspar effective Jan. 15, as follows: Less than 60 pct, $40; 70 pct or more, $43.

Kaiser at Permanente—Kaiser interests are investing approximately $1,700,000 to get its ferro-silicon plant at Permanente, Calif., in full production and to develop and enlarge its dolomite operations.

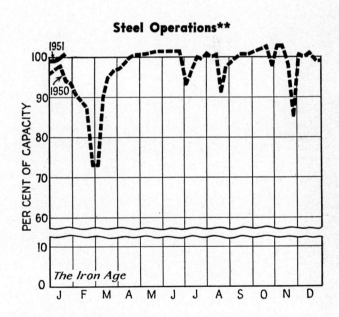

Steel Operations**

The Iron Age

PER CENT OF CAPACITY

J F M A M J J A S O N D

District Operating Rates—Per Cent of Capacity**

Week of	Pittsburgh	Chicago	Youngstown	Philadelphia	West	Buffalo	Cleveland	Detroit	Wheeling	South	Ohio River	St. Louis	East	Aggregate
Jan. 14	98.0*	101.0	96.0*	97.0*	103.8	104.0	97.0*	106.0	100.0	106.0	90.5	95.1	117.2	99.5
Jan. 21	96.0	100.5	95.5	99.0	106.7	104.0	98.0	106.0	101.0	106.0	91.0	95.1	111.3	101.0

* Revised.
** Beginning Jan. 1, 1951, operations are based on an annual capacity of 104,229,650 net tons.

nonferrous metals | *outlook and market activities*

NONFERROUS METALS PRICES

	Jan. 17	Jan. 18	Jan. 19	Jan. 20	Jan. 22	Jan. 23
Copper, electro, Conn. ...	24.50	24.50	24.50	24.50	24.50	24.50
Copper, Lake, delivered...	24.625	24.625	24.625	24.625	24.625	24.625
Tin, Straits, New York	$1.76	$1.7575	$1.755	....	$1.76	$1.77*
Zinc, East St. Louis	17.50	17.50	17.50	17.50	17.50	17.50
Lead. St. Louis	16.80	16.80	16.80	16.80	16.80	16.80

Note: Quotations are going prices.

*Tentative.

by R. Hatschek

New York — Prices dipped slightly on secondary aluminum ingots last week. The revision was from ¼¢ to ½¢ downward on most items. The reason behind this reduction is a slightly easier tone in the market for aluminum scrap.

Some of the secondary brass and bronze ingots also underwent a price revision last week. High tin alloys were boosted from ¼¢ to as much as 11¢ per lb because of the actions of the tin market. Other alloys were quoted fractionally lower because of increased availability of some scrap materials.

Still Wait Controls

Dealers' buying prices for scrap metals are generally unchanged, though the aluminum market is softer, as the trade awaits action from Washington on the price controls they know are coming. The replacement of Alan Valentine by Eric Johnston practically assures this in the near future.

The conscientious members of the scrap trade want controls. They point out that, while the majority would like to hold prices voluntarily, it is difficult to turn down higher offers when they see some of their competitors taking in higher prices.

The Spanish export price of mercury has been increased another $40 to $200 per flask, f.o.b. Spain. This latest increase brings the New York price up to $225 per 76-lb flask. The New York price at the start of hostilities in Korea was in a range of $70 to $71 per flask, at which price the Spaniards had undersold domestic producers and forced them out of the market. Then they started putting the price where they wanted it.

This new price, more than three times as high as it was only 7 months ago, is creating havoc in the U. S. market for mercury and little, if any, business had been transacted at the new record-high level as we went to press.

Mining Equipment Corp., of New York, is going to operate the Cuban Nicaro nickel plant. The plant, which has a capacity of about 30 million lb of nickel oxide per year, is expected to start producing within a year and all the output is slated for stockpiles.

News from Washington has it that the National Production Authority is planning to cut out all non-essential civilian uses of aluminum in an order similar to the one recently issued controlling the end-use of copper. This order is expected to be issued shortly and become effective on April 1.

Further NPA regulations governing inventories and end-uses of other ferrous and nonferrous metals are also in the works. Tin, antimony, nickel, tungsten, molybdenum and zinc are all slated for more stringent control.

To Add More Magnesium

General Services Administration has announced plans for the reactivation of the Velasco, Tex., and Manteca, Calif., government-owned magnesium plants. This is in addition to the previously announced reactivation of the plants at Wingdale, N. Y.; Canaan, Conn., and Painesville, Ohio, and will boost the nation's magnesium production some 200,000,000 lb over the next 2 years.

Dow Chemical Corp. will operate the Texas plant and Kaiser Aluminum & Chemical Co. will operate the one in California. Cost to the government will be $3,075,000 for the Velasco operations and $700,000 for the other.

Early this week National Lead Co. boosted the price of antimony 10¢ to 41 to 42¢ per lb, f.o.b. Laredo for R. M. M. brand. This was preceded by the announcement that the Bradley Mining Co. had resumed production and set up a price of 50¢ per lb, f.o.b. Cascade, Idaho. Bradley also set a price of 45¢ per lb for antimony oxide, also f.o.b. Cascade.

MILL PRODUCTS

(Cents per lb, unless otherwise noted)

Aluminum

(Base 30,000 lb, f.o.b. ship. pt. frt. allowed)

Flat Sheet: 0.188 in., 2S, 3S, 30.1¢; 4S, 61S-O, 32¢; 52S, 34.1¢; 24S-O, 24S-OAL, 32.9¢; 75S-O, 75S-OAL, 39.9¢; 0.081 in., 2S, 3S, 31.2¢; 4S, 61S-O, 33.5¢; 52S, 35.6¢; 24S-O, 24S-OAL, 34.1¢; 75S-O, 75S-OAL, 41.8¢; 0.032 in., 2S, 3S, 32.9¢; 4S, 61S-O, 37.1¢; 52S, 39.8¢; 24S-O, 24S-OAL, 41.7¢; 75S-O, 75S-OAL, 52.2¢.

Plate: ¼ in. and heavier: 2S, 3S-F, 28.3¢; 4S-F, 30.2¢; 52S-F, 31.8¢; 61S-O, 30.8¢; 24S-O, 24S-OAL, 32.4¢; 75S-O, 75S-OAL, 38.8¢.

Extruded Solid Shapes: Shape factors 1 to 5, 36.2¢ to 74.5¢; 12 to 14, 36.9¢ to 89¢; 24 to 26, 39.6¢ to $1.16; 36 to 38, 47.2¢ to $1.70.

Rod, Rolled: 1.5 to 4.5 in., 2S-F, 3S-F, 37.5¢ to 33.5¢; cold-finished, 0.375 to 3 in., 2S-F, 3S-F, 40.5¢ to 35¢.

Screw Machine Stock: Rounds, 11S-T3, ⅛ to 11/32 in., 53.5¢ to 42¢; ⅜ to 1½ in., 41.5¢ to 39¢; 1 9/16 to 3 in., 38.5¢ to 36¢; 17S-T4 lower by 1.5¢ per lb. Base 5000 lb.

Drawn Wire: Coiled, 0.051 to 0.374 in., 2S, 39.5¢ to 29¢; 52S, 48¢ to 35¢; 56S, 51¢ to 42¢; 17S-T4, 54¢ to 37.5¢; 61S-T4, 48.5¢ to 37¢; 75S-T6, 84¢ to 67.5¢.

Extruded Tubing, Rounds: 63S-T5, OD in in.: 1¼ to 2, 37¢ to 54¢; 2 to 4, 33.5¢ to 45.5¢; 4 to 6, 34¢ to 41.5¢; 6 to 9, 34.5¢ to 43.5¢.

Roofing Sheet, Flat: 0.019 in. x 28 in. per sheet, 72 in., $1.142; 96 in., $1.522; 120 in., $1.902; 144 in., $2.284. Gage 0.024 in. x 28 in., 72 in., $1.379; 96 in., $1.839; 120 in., $2.299; 144 in., $2.759. Coiled Sheet: 0.019 in. x 28 in., 28.2¢ per lb.; 0.024 in. x 28 in., 26.9¢ per lb.

Magnesium

(F.o.b. mill, freight allowed)

Sheet and Plate: FS1-O, ¼ in. 63¢; 3/16 in. 65¢; ⅛ in. 67¢; B & S Gage 10, 68¢; 12, 72¢; 14, 78¢; 16, 85¢; 18, 93¢; 20, $1.05; 22, $1.27; 24, $1.67. Specification grade higher. Base: 30,000 lb.

Extruded Round Rod: M, diam in., ¼ to 0.311 in., 74¢; ½ to ¾ in., 57.5¢; 1¼ to 1.749 in., 53¢; 2½ to 5 in., 48.5¢. Other alloys higher. Base: Up to ¾ in. diam, 10,000 lb; ¾ to 2 in., 20,000 lb; 2 in. and larger, 30,000 lb.

Extruded Solid Shapes, Rectangles: M. In weight per ft, for perimeters less than size indicated, 0.10 to 0.11 lb, 3.5 in., 62.3¢; 0.22 to 0.25 lb, 5.9 in., 59.3¢; 0.50 to 0.59 lb, 8.6 in., 56.7¢; 1.8 to 2.59 lb, 19.5 in., 53.8¢; 4 to 6 lb, 28 in., 49¢. Other alloys higher. Base, in weight per ft of shape: Up to ½ lb, 10,000 lb; ½ to 1.80 lb, 20,000 lb; 1.80 lb and heavier, 30,000 lb.

Extruded Round Tubing: M, wall thickness, outside diam, in., 0.049 to 0.057, ¼ in. to 5/16, $1.40; 5/16 to ⅜, $1.26; ½ to ⅝, 93¢; 1 to 2 in., 76¢; 0.165 to 0.219, ⅝ to ¾, 61¢; 1 to 2 in., 57¢; 3 to 4 in., 56¢. Other alloys higher. Base, OD in in.; Up to 1½ in., 10,000 lb; 1½ in. to 3 in., 20,000 lb; 3 in. and larger, 30,000 lb.

Titanium

(10,000 lb. base, f.o.b. mill)

Commercially pure and alloy grades: Sheet and strip, HR or CR, $15; Plate, HR, $12; Wire, rolled and/or drawn, $10; Bar, HR or forged, $6; Forgings, $6.

Nickel and Monel

(Base prices, f.o.b. mill)

	"A" Nickel	Monel
Sheets, cold-rolled	71½	57
Strip, cold-rolled	77½	60
Rods and bars	67½	55
Angles, hot-rolled	67½	55
Plates	69½	56
Seamless tubes	100½	90
Shot and blocks	....	50

Copper, Brass, Bronze

(Freight prepaid on 200 lb includes duty)

	Sheets	Rods	Extruded Shapes
Copper	41.03	....	40.63
Copper, h-r	....	36.88	....
Copper, drawn	....	38.18	....
Low brass	39.15	38.84	....
Yellow brass	38.28	37.97	....
Red brass	40.14	39.83	....
Naval brass	43.08	38.61	38.07
Leaded brass	....	32.63	36.70
Com'l bronze	41.13	40.82	....
Mang. bronze	45.96	40.65	41.41
Phos. bronze	60.20	60.45	....
Muntz metal	40.43	36.74	37.99
Ni silver, 10 pct	49.27	51.49	....
Arch. bronze	....	....	35.11

PRIMARY METALS

(Cents per lb, unless otherwise noted)

Aluminum ingot, 99+%, 10,000 lb, freight allowed	19.00
Aluminum pig	18.00
Antimony, American, Laredo, Tex.	42.00
Beryllium copper, 3.75-4.25% Be	$1.56
Beryllium aluminum 5% Be, Dollars per lb contained Be	$69.00
Bismuth, ton lots	$2.25
Cadmium, del'd	$2.55
Cobalt, 97-99% (per lb)	$2.10 to $2.17
Copper, electro, Conn. Valley	24.50
Copper, Lake, delivered	24.625
Gold, U. S. Treas., dollars per oz.	$35.00
Indium, 99.8%, dollars per troy oz.	$2.25
Iridium, dollars per troy oz.	$200
Lead, St. Louis	16.80
Lead, New York	17.00
Magnesium, 99.8+%, f.o.b. Freeport, Tex., 10,000 lb	24.50
Magnesium, sticks, 100 to 500 lb	42.00 to 44.00
Mercury, dollars per 76-lb flask f.o.b. New York	$225.00
Nickel, electro, f.o.b. New York	53.55
Nickel oxide sinter, f.o.b. Copper Cliff, Ont., contained nickel	46.75
Palladium, dollars per troy oz.	$24.00
Platinum, dollars per troy oz.	$90 to $93
Silver, New York, cents per oz.	90.16
Tin, New York	$1.77
Titanium, sponge	$5.00
Zinc, East St. Louis	17.50
Zinc, New York	18.22
Zirconium copper, 50 pct	$6.20

REMELTED METALS

Brass Ingot

(Cents per lb delivered, carloads)

85-5-5-5 ingot	
No. 115	29.00
No. 120	28.50
No. 123	28.00
80-10-10 ingot	
No. 305	35.00
No. 315	32.00
88-10-2 ingot	
No. 210	46.25
No. 215	43.25
No. 245	36.00
Yellow ingot	
No. 405	25.00
Manganese bronze	
No. 421	29.75

Aluminum Ingot

(Cents per lb, 30,000 lb lots)

95-5 aluminum-silicon alloys	
0.30 copper, max.	33.25-34.25
0.60 copper, max.	33.00-34.00
Piston alloys (No. 122 type)	30.50-31.00
No. 12 alum. (No. 2 grade)	30.00-30.50
108 alloy	30.25-30.75
195 alloy	31.25-31.75
13 alloy	33.50-34.00
ASX-679	30.50-31.00

Steel deoxidizing aluminum, notch-bar granulated or shot

Grade 1—95-97½%	32.00-32.50
Grade 2—92-95%	30.25-30.75
Grade 3—90-92%	29.25-29.75
Grade 4—85-90%	28.75-29.25

ELECTROPLATING SUPPLIES

Anodes

(Cents per lb, freight allowed, 500 lb lots)

Copper	
Cast, oval, 15 in. or longer	39⅛
Electrodeposited	33⅝
Rolled, oval, straight, delivered	38⅞
Forged ball anodes	43
Brass, 80-20	
Cast, oval, 15 in. or longer	34¾
Zinc, oval	26½
Ball anodes	25½
Nickel 99 pct plus	
Cast	70.50
Rolled, depolarized	71.50
Cadmium	$2.80
Silver 999 fine, rolled, 100 oz lots, per troy oz, f.o.b. Bridgeport, Conn.	79½

Chemicals

(Cents per lb, f.o.b. shipping point)

Copper cyanide, 100 lb drum	52.15
Copper sulfate, 99.5 crystals, bbl.	12.85
Nickel salts, single or double, 4-100 lb bags, frt allowed	20½
Nickel chloride, 375 lb drum	27½
Silver cyanide, 100 oz lots, per oz.	67¼
Sodium cyanide, 96 pct domestic 200 lb drums	19.25
Zinc cyanide, 100 lb drums	45.85

SCRAP METALS

Brass Mill Scrap

(Cents per pound, add ½¢ per lb for shipments of 20,000 to 40,000 lb; add 1¢ for more than 40,000 lb)

	Heavy	Turnings
Copper	23	22¼
Yellow brass	20⅛	18¾
Red brass	21½	20¾
Comm. bronze	21¾	21
Mang. bronze	19½	18⅝
Brass rod ends	19⅞	....

Custom Smelters' Scrap

(Cents per pound, carload lots, delivered to refinery)

No. 1 copper wire	21.50
No. 2 copper wire	20.00
Light copper	19.00
Refinery brass	19.50*
Radiators	15.00

*Dry copper content.

Ingot Makers' Scrap

(Cents per pound, carload lots, delivered to producer)

No. 1 copper wire	23.00
No. 2 copper wire	22.00
Light copper	21.00
No. 1 composition	22.00
No. 1 comp. turnings	21.50
Rolled brass	18.50
Brass pipe	20.50
Radiators	17.50
Heavy yellow brass	17.00
Aluminum	
Mixed old cast	18½—19
Mixed new clips	20½
Mixed turnings, dry	18½
Pots and pans	18½—19
Low copper	21½—22

Dealers' Scrap

(Dealers' buying prices, f.o.b. New York in cents per pound)

Copper and Brass

No. 1 heavy copper and wire	19½—20
No. 2 heavy copper and wire	18 —18½
Light copper	17 —17¼
New type shell cuttings	17 —17¼
Auto radiators (unsweated)	14½—15
No. 1 composition	17 —17½
No. 1 composition turnings	16½—17
Clean red car boxes	15½—16
Cocks and faucets	15½—16
Mixed heavy yellow brass	13 —13½
Old rolled brass	14 —14½
Brass pipe	17 —17½
New soft brass clippings	17½—18
Brass rod ends	16½—17
No. 1 brass rod turnings	16 —16½

Aluminum

Alum. pistons and struts	12 —13
Aluminum crankcases	15 —16
2S aluminum clippings	18½—19½
Old sheet and utensils	15 —16
Borings and turnings	12½—13
Misc. cast aluminum	15 —16
Dural clips (24S)	15 —16

Zinc

New zinc clippings	14½—15
Old zinc	11 —11¼
Zinc routings	8½— 9
Old die cast scrap	8 — 8¼

Nickel and Monel

Pure nickel clippings	60 —65
Clean nickel turnings	57 —60
Nickel anodes	60 —65
Nickel rod ends	60 —65
New Monel Clippings	22 —25
Clean Monel turnings	18 —20
Old sheet Monel	20 —22
Inconel clippings	26 —28
Nickel silver clippings, mixed	13 —14
Nickel silver turnings, mixed	12 —13

Lead

Soft scrap, lead	15 —15¼
Battery plates (dry)	8¾— 9

Magnesium

Segregated solids	9 —10
Castings	5½— 6½

Miscellaneous

Block tin	90 —100
No. 1 pewter	63 —65
No. 1 auto babbitt	58 —60
Mixed common babbitt	12¼—12½
Solder joints	18½—19
Siphon tops	58 —60
Small foundry type	16¼—16½
Monotype	14¾—15
Lino. and stereotype	14½—14¾
Electrotype	12¾—13
Hand picked type shells	11½—11¾
Lino. and stereo. dross	8 — 8¼
Electro. dross	6½— 6¾

SCRAP *iron and steel*

**Scrap men talk over ESA-bolstered rumor
of price controls on scrap this week . . .
Some areas report buying, others don't.**

Scrap men were trading rumors this week on the immediate imminence of a deep freeze on scrap prices. All the expectant buzzing in the field centered around a popular rumor that price controls were here, were coming tomorrow —or at any rate were due this week. The rumor was bolstered by an ESA statement that the order would go through this week after a few legal wrinkles had been ironed out. At press time the chill had not arrived but it was a short step to the brink.

Mills in some districts were buying right down to what seemed the controls deadline. Others, looking over their shoulders at higher scrap stocks, slowed up buying and waited for the price freeze and lower prices. In some markets, the price line was held. In others all sorts of upward surges were registered. So far, the formula was hurdled in Buffalo, Philadelphia, New York, Youngstown, and Boston. It proved that necessity could upset the best-laid plans and get ESA's dander up.

It was felt in Pittsburgh that, to be effective, the government would have to slap controls on the market immediately and that the order must specify that contracts in which the formula was scrapped be declared invalid.

PITTSBURGH—Mills here are holding out against higher prices in the hope of quick control action in Washington. To do any good, controls must be slapped on almost immediately, and any such order must specify that contracts in other areas where the so-called "formula" was tossed out not be completed. Otherwise consumers here would be starved while the higher priced orders were completed. To bring scrap in from the East, local mills would have to pay $56 to $57. Meanwhile, little if any business is being transacted. Machine shop turnings were up 50¢.

CHICAGO—The scrap market here was stronger last week although no new mill buying of openhearth grades was evident. Reaction to higher prices paid in the eastern districts, diminishing dealer inventories and the need for completing unfilled orders were factors adding strength to the market. Brokers are paying $45 and over to fill old orders for No. 1 heavy melting steel and reports have been heard of offerings over the formula for scrap to be shipped out of the area. Some foundries, unable to hold off any longer, are coming into the market and finding higher prices still prevailing.

PHILADELPHIA—Following last week's increases, blast furnace grades of scrap are $2 per ton higher this week. Broker buying on railroad lists is very careful and some brokers were surprised to get scrap on their conservative bids. No. 1 heavy melting and No. 1 bundles were incorrectly quoted last week although some small consumers are buying at those prices. Correct price for last week and this week is $47 to $48.

NEW YORK—The trade here felt the force of heavy buying. Need offset the desire to wait out imminent controls and lower prices. Last week the formula cracked down the middle and the price of No. 1 heavy jumped to as high as $44. All steelmaking grades hit the road up but there were some reports that the turnings group was softening.

DETROIT—With price controls just around the corner, no changes are being reported in Detroit scrap prices this week. However, the tone of the market continues strong. Reports of free scrap purchases in small tonnages as much as $7 over the No. 1 electric furnace bundle price continue to come in. The reason these sales are not reflected in the price spread is the small volume of scrap involved and belief that price controls are imminent. Despite occasional reports of a soft gray iron market, there have been actual sales of representative material here during the past week at the prices quoted.

CLEVELAND—The scrap market was running wild here and in the Valley at press time. Unofficially, the fireworks started last Thursday, when some Valley consumers began meeting competition from adjacent districts in the intermediate points. At least one major Valley consumer is paying $51.50 for No. 1 heavy melting steel locally, and $52.50 including springboards, for remote No. 1, in representative tonnages. Small remote tonnages of No. 1 have brought $55, including springboards.

ST. LOUIS—While there has been some buying of scrap iron in the St. Louis industrial district at prices higher than the formula, it has been mostly by smaller operators. The formula is being generally observed so that prices are unchanged. Steel mills inventories are said to be low.

BIRMINGHAM—Owners of scrap who have been holding for higher prices now are attempting to sell everything they have in anticipation of a price rollback. The result is that scrap outside the immediate Birmingham district is moving north, where mills are taking practically everything offered. Scrap in the Birmingham district is moving to Republic's plant at Alabama City. Atlantic Steel, with a large supply on hand, has stopped buying.

CINCINNATI—Despite an epidemic of high prices in other districts, the market here was unchanged from last week. A certain amount of raiding is going on, but local brokers have not yet been authorized by the mills to meet the competition.

BOSTON—Steelmaking grades in the local market moved up $4 per ton with some sales of No. 1 heavy melting reported as high as $42. The market was very active with buyers and sellers trying to protect their positions before controls.

BUFFALO—Dealers who sold steelmaking scrap at $5.75 to $6.75 a ton above formula report little material has moved against orders as supplies continue to shrink. Mills reserve stocks have been hit hard to maintain output. A definite shortage was reported in receipts.

WEST COAST—The California market broke loose this week with tonnages of No. 1 heavy melting moving at prices up to $34 a ton. Railroad scrap was outstanding with sales ranging to $46 for No. 1 railroad heavy melting. Roads with trans-continental connections have found they can haul their scrap in otherwise empty freight cars to Chicago and obtain the current higher price there.

Iron and Steel
SCRAP PRICES

Going prices as obtained in the trade by THE IRON AGE based on representative tonnages. All prices are per gross ton delivered to consumer unless otherwise noted.

Pittsburgh

No. 1 hvy. melting	$45.75 to $46.50
No. 2 hvy. melting	43.75 to 44.50
No. 1 bundles	45.75 to 46.50
No. 2 bundles	42.75 to 43.50
Machine shop turn.	38.25 to 39.00
Mixed bor. and ms. turns.	38.25 to 39.00
Shoveling turnings	39.75 to 40.50
Cast iron borings	39.75 to 40.50
Low phos. plate	56.00 to 56.50
Heavy turnings	46.50 to 47.00
No. 1 RR. hvy. melting	45.75 to 46.50
Scrap rails, random lgth.	64.50 to 65.00
Rails 2 ft and under	68.00 to 69.00
RR. steel wheels	63.00 to 64.00
RR. spring steel	63.00 to 64.00
RR. couplers and knuckles	63.00 to 64.00
No. 1 machinery cast.	67.50 to 68.00
Mixed yard cast.	57.50 to 58.00
Heavy breakable cast.	52.50 to 53.00
Malleable	71.00 to 72.00

Chicago

No. 1 hvy. melting	$44.25 to $45.00
No. 2 hvy. melting	42.00 to 43.00
No. 1 factory bundles	44.00 to 45.00
No. 1 dealers' bundles	44.00 to 45.00
No. 2 dealers' bundles	41.00 to 42.00
Machine shop turn.	36.00 to 37.00
Mixed bor. and turn.	36.00 to 37.00
Shoveling turnings	37.00 to 38.00
Cast iron borings	37.00 to 38.00
Low phos. forge crops	54.00 to 55.00
Low phos. plate	52.00 to 53.00
No. 1 RR. hvy. melting	47.00 to 48.00
Scrap rails, random lgth.	62.00 to 63.00
Rerolling rails	65.50 to 66.50
Rails 2 ft and under	67.00 to 69.00
Locomotive tires, cut	58.00 to 59.00
Cut bolsters & side frames	54.00 to 55.00
Angles and splice bars	63.00 to 64.00
RR. steel car axles	95.00 to 100.00
RR. couplers and knuckles	58.00 to 59.00
No. 1 machinery cast.	62.00 to 64.00
No. 1 agricul. cast.	58.00 to 60.00
Heavy breakable cast.	53.00 to 55.00
RR. grate bars	48.00 to 49.00
Cast iron brake shoes	52.00 to 53.00
Cast iron car wheels	58.00 to 59.00
Malleable	78.00 to 82.00

Philadelphia

No. 1 hvy. melting	$47.00 to $48.00
No. 2 hvy. melting	44.00 to 45.00
No. 1 bundles	47.00 to 48.00
No. 2 bundles	42.00 to 43.00
Machine shop turn.	38.00 to 39.00
Mixed bor. and turn.	37.00 to 38.00
Shoveling turnings	40.00 to 41.00
Low phos. punchings, plate	51.00 to 52.00
Low phos. 5 ft and under.	51.00 to 52.00
Low phos. bundles	50.00 to 51.00
Hvy. axle forge turn.	45.00 to 46.00
Clean cast chem. borings.	44.00 to 45.00
RR. steel wheels	56.00 to 57.00
RR. spring steel	56.00 to 57.00
Rails 18 in. and under	66.00 to 67.00
No. 1 machinery cast.	62.00 to 63.00
Mixed yard cast.	53.00 to 55.00
Heavy breakable cast.	53.00 to 54.00
Cast iron carwheels	67.00 to 68.00
Malleable	70.00 to 72.00

Cleveland

No. 1 hvy. melting	$51.00 to $52.00
No. 2 hvy. melting	49.00 to 50.00
No. 1 busheling	51.00 to 52.00
No. 1 bundles	51.00 to 52.00
No. 2 bundles	48.00 to 49.00
Machine shop turn.	43.00 to 44.00
Mixed bor. and turn.	45.00 to 46.00
Shoveling turnings	45.00 to 46.00
Cast iron borings	45.00 to 46.00
Low phos. 2 ft and under.	53.50 to 54.50
Steel axle turn.	50.00 to 51.00
Drop forge flashings	51.00 to 52.00
No. 1 RR. hvy. melting	51.50 to 52.00
Rails 3 ft and under	70.00 to 71.00
Rails 18 in. and under	72.00 to 73.00
No. 1 machinery cast.	69.00 to 70.00
RR. cast.	71.00 to 72.00
RR. grate bars	50.00 to 51.00
Stove plate	55.00 to 56.00
Malleable	76.00 to 77.00

Youngstown

No. 1 hvy. melting	$51.50 to $52.50
No. 2 hvy. melting	49.50 to 50.50
No. 1 bundles	51.50 to 52.50

Buffalo

No. 2 bundles	$48.50 to $49.50
Machine shop turn	43.50 to 44.50
Shoveling turnings	45.50 to 46.50
Cast iron borings	45.50 to 46.50
Low phos. plate	54.00 to 55.00

No. 1 hvy. melting	$51.25 to $52.00
No. 2 hvy. melting	49.25 to 50.00
No. 1 bushelings	49.25 to 50.00
No. 1 bundles	50.25 to 51.00
No. 2 bundles	47.25 to 48.00
Machine shop turn.	43.25 to 44.00
Mixed bor. and turn.	43.25 to 44.00
Shoveling turnings	45.25 to 46.00
Cast iron borings	43.25 to 44.00
Low phos. plate	51.25 to 52.00
Scrap rails, random lgth.	55.00 to 56.00
Rails 2 ft and under	60.00 to 61.00
RR. steel wheels	60.00 to 61.00
RR. spring steel	60.00 to 61.00
RR. couplers and knuckles	60.00 to 61.00
No. 1 machinery cast.	59.00 to 60.00
No. 1 cupola cast.	54.00 to 55.00
Small indus. malleable	60.00 to 61.00

Birmingham

No. 1 hvy. melting	$42.50 to $43.50
No. 2 hvy. melting	40.50 to 41.50
No. 2 bundles	39.50 to 40.50
No. 1 busheling	40.50 to 41.50
Machine shop turn.	34.00 to 35.00
Shoveling turnings	32.00 to 33.00
Cast iron borings	33.00 to 34.00
Bar crops and plate	47.00 to 48.00
Structural and plate	46.00 to 47.00
No. 1 RR. hvy. melting	43.00 to 44.00
Scrap rails, random lgth.	58.00 to 59.00
Rerolling rails	61.00 to 62.00
Rails 2 ft and under	66.00 to 67.00
Angles & splice bars	59.00 to 60.00
Std. steel axles	61.00 to 62.00
No. 1 cupola cast.	54.00 to 55.00
Stove plate	49.00 to 50.00
Cast iron carwheels	46.00 to 47.00

St. Louis

No. 1 hvy. melting	$43.75 to $44.50
No. 2 hvy. melting	41.75 to 42.50
No. 2 bundled sheets	40.75 to 41.50
Machine shop turn.	33.75 to 34.75
Shoveling turnings	36.50 to 37.50
Rails, random lengths	49.00 to 50.00
Rails 3 ft and under	62.00 to 63.00
Locomotive tires, uncut	50.00 to 51.00
Angles and splice bars	59.00 to 60.00
Std. steel car axles	90.00 to 95.00
RR. spring steel	53.00 to 54.00
No. 1 machinery cast.	55.00 to 56.00
Hvy. breakable cast.	48.00 to 49.00
Cast iron brake shoes	53.00 to 54.00
Stove plate	45.00 to 47.00
Cast iron car wheels	60.00 to 62.00
Malleable	55.00 to 57.00

New York

Brokers' Buying prices per gross ton, on cars:

No. 1 hvy. melting	$42.00 to $44.00
No. 2 hvy. melting	40.00
No. 2 bundles	39.00
Machine shop turn.	32.00 to 34.00
Mixed bor. and turn.	32.00 to 34.00
Shoveling turnings	34.00 to 36.00
Clean cast chem. bor.	40.00 to 41.00
No. 1 machinery cast.	52.00 to 53.00
Mixed yard cast.	47.00 to 48.00
Charging box cast.	47.00 to 48.00
Heavy breakable cast.	47.00 to 48.00
Unstrp. motor blocks	42.00 to 43.00

Boston

Brokers' Buying prices per gross ton, on cars:

No. 1 hvy. melting	$35.67 to $42.00
No. 2 hvy. melting	33.67 to 37.67
No. 1 bundles	38.00 to 42.00

(Boston cont.)

No. 2 bundles	$32.67 to $36.67
Machine shop turn.	27.67
Mixed bor. and turn.	$26.67 to 27.67
Shoveling turnings	29.67
No. 1 busheling	35.67
Clean cast chem. borings.	35.00 to 36.00
No. 1 machinery cast.	48.00 to 49.00
Mixed cupola cast.	45.00 to 46.00
Heavy breakable cast.	42.00 to 43.00
Stove plate	42.00 to 43.00

Detroit

Brokers' Buying prices per gross ton, on cars:

No. 1 hvy. melting	$40.25
No. 2 hvy. melting	38.25
No. 1 bundles, openhearth	40.25
No. 1 bundles, electric furnace	42.75
New busheling	40.25
Flashings	40.25
Machine shop turn.	32.25
Mixed bor. and turn.	32.25
Shoveling turnings	34.25
Cast iron borings	34.25
Low phos. plate	42.75
No. 1 cupola cast.	$54.00 to 56.00
Heavy breakable cast.	45.00 to 47.00
Stove plate	44.00 to 46.00
Automotive cast.	58.00 to 60.00

Cincinnati

Per gross ton, f.o.b. cars:

No. 1 hvy. melting	$44.25
No. 2 hvy. melting	42.25
No. 1 bundles	44.25
No. 2 bundles, black	42.25
No. 2 bundles, mixed	41.25
Machine shop turn.	33.00
Mixed bor. and turn.	34.00
Shoveling turnings	34.00
Cast iron borings	34.00
Low phos. melting	46.75
Low phos. 18 in. under	62.00
Rails, random lengths	$62.00 to 63.00
Rails, 18 in. and under.	72.00 to 73.00
No. 1 cupola cast.	65.00 to 66.00
Hvy. breakable cast.	59.00 to 60.00
Drop broken cast.	71.00 to 72.00

San Francisco

No. 1 hvy. melting	$30.00 to $34.00
No. 2 hvy. melting	28.00 to 32.00
No. 1 bundles	30.00 to 34.00
No. 2 bundles	28.00 to 32.00
No. 3 bundles	25.00
Machine shop turn.	16.00 to 18.00
Elec. fur. 1 ft and under.	40.00 to 42.50
No. 1 RR. hvy. melting	30.00 to 46.00
Scrap rails random lgth.	30.00 to 46.00
No. 1 cupola cast.	43.00 to 46.00

Los Angeles

No. 1 hvy. melting	$30.00 to $34.00
No. 2 hvy. melting	28.00 to 32.00
No. 1 bundles	30.00 to 34.00
No. 2 bundles	28.00 to 32.00
No. 3 bundles	25.00
Mach. shop turn.	16.00 to 18.00
Elec. fur. 1 ft and under.	40.00 to 42.50
No. 1 RR. hvy. melting	30.00 to 46.00
Scrap rails random lgth.	30.00 to 46.00
No. 1 cupola cast.	43.00 to 46.00

Seattle

No. 1 hvy. melting	$28.00
No. 2 hvy. melting	28.00
No. 1 bundles	22.00
No. 2 bundles	22.00
No. 3 bundles	18.00
Elec. fur. 1 ft and under.	$40.00 to 45.00
RR. hvy. melting	29.00
No. 1 cupola cast	45.00

Hamilton, Ont.

No. 1 hvy. melting	$30.00
No. 1 bundles	30.00
No. 2 bundles	29.50
Mechanical bundles	28.00
Mixed steel scrap	26.00
Mixed bor. and turn.	23.00
Rails, remelting	30.00
Rails, rerolling	33.00
Bushelings	24.50
Bush., new fact. prep'd.	29.00
Bush., new fact. unprep'd.	23.00
Short steel turnings	23.00
Cast scrap	45.00

Comparison of Prices

Price advances over previous week are printed in Heavy Type; declines appear in *Italics*

Steel prices in this page are the average of various t.o.b. quotations of major producing areas: Pittsburgh, Chicago, Gary, Cleveland, Youngstown.

Flat-Rolled Steel:	Jan. 23, 1951	Jan. 16, 1951	Dec. 26, 1950	Jan. 24, 1950
(cents per pound)				
Hot-rolled sheets	3.60	3.60	3.60	3.35
Cold-rolled sheets	4.35	4.35	4.35	4.10
Galvanized sheets (10 ga)	4.80	4.80	4.80	4.40
Hot-rolled strip	3.50	3.50	3.50	3.25
Cold-rolled strip	4.75	4.75	4.75	4.21
Plate	3.70	3.70	3.70	3.50
Plates wrought iron	7.85	7.85	7.85	7.85
Stains C-R-strip (No. 302)	36.50	36.50	36.50	33.00

Tin and Terneplate:				
(dollars per base box)				
Tinplate (1.50 lb) cokes.	$7.50	$7.50	$7.50	$7.50
Tinplate, electro (0.50 lb)	6.60	6.60	6.60	6.60
Special coated mfg. ternes	6.35	6.35	6.35	6.50

Bars and Shapes:				
(cents per pound)				
Merchant bars	3.70	3.70	3.70	3.45
Cold finished bars	4.55	4.55	4.55	3.995
Alloy bars	4.30	4.30	4.30	3.95
Structural shapes	3.65	3.65	3.65	3.40
Stainless bars (No. 302)	31.25	31.25	31.25	28.50
Wrought iron bars	9.50	9.50	9.50	9.50

Wire:				
(cents per pound)				
Bright wire	4.85	4.85	4.85	4.50

Rails:				
(dollars per 100 lb)				
Heavy rails	$3.60	$3.60	$3.60	$3.40
Light rails	4.00	4.00	4.00	3.75

Semifinished Steel:				
(dollars per net ton)				
Rerolling billets	$56.00	$56.00	$56.00	$54.00
Slabs, rerolling	56.00	56.00	56.00	54.00
Forging billets	66.00	66.00	66.00	63.00
Alloy blooms billets, slabs	70.00	70.00	70.00	66.00

Wire Rod and Skelp:				
(cents per pound)				
Wire rods	4.10	4.10	4.10	3.85
Skelp	3.35	3.35	3.35	3.15

Pig Iron:	Jan. 23, 1951	Jan. 16, 1951	Dec. 26, 1950	Jan. 24, 1950
(per gross ton)				
No. 2 foundry, del'd Phila.	$57.77	$57.77	$57.77	$50.42
No. 2, Valley furnace	52.50	52.50	52.50	46.50
No. 2, Southern Cin'ti	55.58	55.58	55.58	47.08
No. 2, Birmingham	48.88	48.88	48.88	40.38
No. 2, foundry, Chicago†	52.50	52.50	52.50	46.50
Basic del'd Philadelphia	56.92	56.92	56.92	49.92
Basic, Valley furnace	52.00	52.00	52.00	46.00
Malleable, Chicago†	52.50	52.50	52.50	46.50
Malleable, Valley	52.50	52.50	52.50	46.50
Charcoal, Chicago	70.56	70.56	70.56	68.56
Ferromanganese‡	186.25	186.25	181.20	173.40

†The switching charge for delivery to foundries in the Chicago district is $1 per ton.
‡Average of U. S. prices quoted on Ferroalloy page.

Scrap:				
(per gross ton)				
Heavy melt'g steel, P'gh	$46.13	$46.13	$46.13	$29.75
Heavy melt'g steel, Phila.	47.50	47.50*	44.50	23.00
Heavy melt'g steel, Ch'go	44.63	44.63	44.75	27.50
No. 1 hy. com. sh't, Det.	40.25	40.25	44.13	23.50
Low phos. Young'n	54.50	48.63	48.63	30.75
No. 1 cast, Pittsburgh	67.75	67.75	67.75	37.50
No. 1 cast, Philadelphia	62.50	62.50	62.50	37.00
No. 1 cast, Chicago	63.00	63.00	65.00	38.50

Coke: Connellsville:				
(per net ton at oven)				
Furnace coke, prompt	$14.25	$14.25	$14.25	$14.00
Foundry coke, prompt	17.25	17.25	17.25	15.75

Nonferrous Metals:				
(cents per pound to large buyers)				
Copper, electro, Conn.	24.50	24.50	24.50	18.50
Copper, Lake, Conn.	24.625	24.625	24.625	18.625
Tin Straits, New York	$1.77†	$1.75*	1.55	75.50
Zinc, East St. Louis	17.50	17.50	17.50	9.75
Lead, St. Louis	16.80	16.80	16.80	11.80
Aluminum, virgin	19.00	19.00	19.00	17.00
Nickel, electrolytic	53.55	53.55	53.55	42.97
Magnesium, ingot	24.50	24.50	24.50	20.50
Antimony, Laredo, Tex.	42.00	32.00	32.00	28.75

†Tentative. *Revised.

Composite Prices

Starting with the issue of May 12, 1949, the weighted finished steel composite was revised for the years 1941 to date. The weights used are based on the average product shipments for the 7 years 1937 to 1940 inclusive and 1946 to 1948 inclusive. The use of quarterly figures has been eliminated because it was too sensitive. (See p. 130 of May 12, 1949, issue.)

	Finished Steel Base Price	Pig Iron	Scrap Steel
Jan. 23, 1951	4.131¢ per lb	$52.69 per gross ton	$46.08 per gross ton
One week ago	4.131¢ per lb	52.69 per gross ton	46.08 per gross ton
One month ago	4.131¢ per lb	52.69 per gross ton	45.13 per gross ton
One year ago	3.837¢ per lb	46.05 per gross ton	26.75 per gross ton

	High	Low	High	Low	High	Low
1951	4.131¢ Jan. 2	4.131¢ Jan. 2	$52.69 Jan. 2	$52.69 Dec. 12	$46.08 Jan. 16	$45.09 Jan. 2
1950	4.131¢ Dec. 1	3.837¢ Jan. 3	52.69 Dec. 12	45.88 Jan. 3	45.13 Dec. 19	26.25 Jan. 3
1949	3.837¢ Dec. 27	3.3705¢ May 3	46.87 Jan. 18	45.88 Sept. 6	43.00 Jan. 4	19.33 June 28
1948	3.721¢ July 27	3.193¢ Jan. 1	46.91 Oct. 12	39.58 Jan. 6	43.16 July 27	39.75 Mar. 9
1947	3.193¢ July 29	2.848¢ Jan. 1	37.98 Dec. 30	30.14 Jan. 7	42.58 Oct. 28	29.50 May 20
1946	2.848¢ Dec. 31	2.464¢ Jan. 1	30.14 Dec. 10	25.37 Jan. 1	31.17 Dec. 24	19.17 Jan. 1
1945	2.464¢ May 29	2.396¢ Jan. 1	25.37 Oct. 23	23.61 Jan. 2	19.17 Jan. 2	18.92 May 22
1944	2.396¢	2.396¢	$23.61	$23.61	19.17 Jan. 11	15.76 Oct. 24
1943	2.396¢	2.396¢	23.61	23.61	$19.17	$19.17
1942	2.396¢	2.396¢	23.61	23.61	19.17	19.17
1941	2.396¢	2.396¢	$23.61 Mar. 20	$23.45 Jan. 2	$22.00 Jan. 7	$19.17 Apr. 10
1940	2.30467¢ Jan. 2	2.24107¢ Apr. 16	23.45 Dec. 23	22.61 Jan. 2	21.83 Dec. 30	16.04 Apr. 9
1939	2.35367¢ Jan. 3	2.26689¢ May 16	22.61 Sept. 19	20.61 Sept. 12	22.50 Oct. 3	14.08 May 16
1938	2.58414¢ Jan. 4	2.27207¢ Oct. 18	23.25 June 21	19.61 July 6	15.00 Nov. 22	11.00 June 7
1937	2.58414¢ Mar. 9	2.32263¢ Jan. 4	32.25 Mar. 9	20.25 Feb. 16	21.92 Mar. 30	12.67 June 9
1936	2.32263¢ Dec. 28	2.05200¢ Mar. 10	19.74 Nov. 24	18.73 Aug. 11	17.75 Dec. 21	12.67 June 8
1932	1.89196¢ July 5	1.83910¢ Mar. 1	14.81 Jan. 5	13.56 Dec. 6	8.50 Jan. 12	6.43 July 5
1929	2.31773¢ May 28	2.26498¢ Oct. 29	18.71 May 14	18.21 Dec. 17	17.58 Jan. 29	14.08 Dec. 8

Weighted index based on steel bars, shapes, plates, wire, rails, black pipe, hot and cold-rolled sheets and strips, representing major portion of finished steel shipment. Index recapitulated in Aug. 28, 1941, issue and in May 12, 1949.

Based on averages for basic iron at Valley furnaces and foundry iron at Chicago, Philadelphia, Buffalo, Valley and Birmingham.

Average of No. 1 heavy melting steel scrap delivered to consumers at Pittsburgh, Philadelphia and Chicago.

<u>I</u>f y<u>ou</u> use <u>Alloy</u> Steels...

...you should have this NEW helpful booklet!

HEAT TREATING
Republic Alloy Steels

TABLE OF CONTENTS

I Heat Treatment of Steels

II Transformation of Austenite Shown Graphically
(Isothermal Transformation Diagrams)

III Heat Treating Methods

Annealing	Nitriding
Hardening	Cyaniding
Martempering	Flame Hardening
Carburizing	Induction Hardening

IV Mechanical Properties of Alloy Steels

DATA & REFERENCE CHARTS

Critical Points	Carburizing Depths
Ms Calculation	Nitriding Depths
Mechanical Properties	

It's new . . . up-to-the-minute . . . 54 pages of valuable heat treating data that belongs on the desk of every alloy steel user.

Republic—world's largest producer of alloy and stainless steels—offers you this useful booklet without cost or obligation in any way.

Just fill in the coupon and mail *today*.

REPUBLIC
STEEL ®

REPUBLIC STEEL CORPORATION
Advertising Division
3104 East 45th Street, Cleveland 27, Ohio
Please send me a copy of your new booklet *Heat Treating Republic Alloy Steels.*

Name .... Title ....

Firm ....

Address ....

City .... State ....

STEEL PRICES

Smaller numbers in price boxes indicate producing companies. For main office locations, see key on facing page.
Base prices at producing points apply only to sizes and grades produced in these areas. Prices are in cents per lb unless otherwise noted. Extras apply.

	Pittsburgh	Chicago	Gary	Cleveland	Canton Massillon	Middletown	Youngstown	Bethlehem	Buffalo	Conshohocken	Johnstown	Sparrows Point	Granite City	Detroit
INGOTS Carbon forging, net ton	$52.00[1]													
Alloy, net ton	$54.00[1,17]													$54.00[31]
BILLETS, BLOOMS, SLABS Carbon, rerolling, net ton	$56.00[1,5]	$56.00[1]	$56.00[1]						$56.00[3]		$56.00[3]			
Carbon forging billets, net ton	$66.00[1,5]	$66.00[1,4]	$66.00[1]	$66.00[4]	$66.00[4]				$66.00[3,4]	$73.00[26]	$66.00[3]			$69.00[31]
Alloy, net ton	$70.00[1,17]	$70.00[1,4]	$70.00[1]		$70.00[4]			$70.00[3]	$70.00[3,4]	$77.00[26]	$70.00[3]			$73.00[31]
PIPE SKELP	3.35[1] 3.45[5]						3.35[1,4]							
WIRE RODS	4.10[2] 4.30[18]	4.10[2,4,23]	4.10[6]	4.10[2]			4.10[6]				4.10[3]	4.20[3]		
SHEETS Hot-rolled (18 ga. & hvr.)	3.60[1,5,9,15] 3.75[28]	3.60[8,23]	3.60[1,6,8]	3.60[4]		3.60[7]	3.60[1,4,6] 4.00[13]		3.60[3]	4.00[26]		3.60[3]		3.80[12] 4.40[47]
Cold-rolled	4.35[1,5,9,15] 5.35[63]		4.35[1,6,8]	4.35[4]		4.35[7]	4.35[4,6]		4.35[3]			4.35[3]		4.55[12]
Galvanized (10 gage)	4.80[1,9,15]		4.80[1,8]	4.80[4]	4.80[4]	4.80[7]	6.00[64]					4.80[3]		
Enameling (12 gage)	4.65[1]		4.65[1,8]			4.65[7]								
Long ternes (10 gage)	5.20[9,15]						6.00[64]							
HI str. low alloy, h.r.	5.40[1,5] 5.75[9]	5.40[1]	5.40[1,8] 5.90[6]	5.40[4]			5.40[1,4,13]		5.40[3]	5.65[26]		5.40[3]		
HI str. low alloy, c.r.	6.55[1,5] 6.90[9]		6.55[1,8] 7.05[6]	6.55[4]			6.55[4]		6.55[3]			6.55[3]		
HI str. low alloy, galv.	7.20[1]													
STRIP Hot-rolled	3.60[9] 4.00[1,58] 3.75[28] 3.50[5]	3.50[66]	3.50[1,6,8]			3.50[7]	3.50[1,4,6] 4.00[13]		3.50[3,4]	3.90[26]		3.50[3]		4.40[47]
Cold-rolled	4.65[1,9] 5.00[28] 5.35[63,58]	4.90[8,66]	4.90[8]	4.65[2]		4.65[7]	4.65[4,6] 5.35[13,40]		4.65[3]			4.65[3]		5.45[47] 5.60[68] 5.60[61]
HI str. low alloy, h.r.	5.75[9]		5.50[1] 5.30[8] 5.80[6]				4.95[4], 5.50[1] 5.40[13]			5.55[26]				
HI str. low alloy, c.r.	7.20[9]			6.70[5]			6.20[4], 6.55[13]							
TINPLATE† Cokes, 1.50-lb base box 1.25 lb, deduct 25¢	$8.70[1,9,15]		$8.70[1,6]				$8.70[4]					8.80[3]		
Electrolytic 0.25, 0.50, 0.75 lb box	Deduct $1.55, $1.30 and 90¢ respectively from 1.50-lb coke base box price													
BLACKPLATE, 29 gage Hollowware enameling	5.85[1] 6.15[15]		5.85[1]				5.30[4]							
BARS Carbon steel	3.70[1,5] 3.85[9]	3.70[1,4,23]	3.70[1,4,6,8]	3.70[4]	3.70[4]		3.70[1,4,6]		3.70[3,4]		3.70[3]			3.85[31]
Reinforcing‡	3.70[1,5]	3.70[4]	3.70[1,6,8]	3.70[4]			3.70[1,4]		3.70[3,4]		3.70[3]	3.70[3]		
Cold-finished	4.55[2,4,5,52,71]	4.55[2,69,70,23,73]	4.55[74,73]	4.55[2]	4.55[4,52]									4.70[84]
Alloy, hot-rolled	4.30[1,17]	4.30[1,4,23]	4.30[1,6,8]	4.30[4]			4.30[1,6]	4.30[3]	4.30[3,4]		4.30[3]			4.45[31]
Alloy, cold-drawn	5.40[17,52,69,71]	5.40[4,23,69,70,73]	5.40[4] 5.90[74]		5.40[4,52]			5.40[3]	5.40[3]					5.55[84]
HI str. low alloy, h.r.	5.55[1,5]		5.55[1,8] 6.05[6]	5.55[4]			5.55[1]	5.55[3]	5.55[3]		5.55[3]			
PLATE Carbon steel	3.70[1,5,15]	3.70[1]	3.70[1,6,8] 4.00[9]	3.70[4]			3.70[1,4] 3.95[13]		3.70[3]	4.15[26]	3.70[3]	3.70[3]		
Floor plates			4.75[8]	4.75[5]						4.75[26]				
Alloy	4.75[1] 4.85	4.75[1]	4.75[1]				5.20[13]			5.05[26]	4.75[3]	4.75[3]		
HI str. low alloy	5.65[1,5]	5.65[1]	5.65[1,8]	5.65[4,5]			5.65[4] 5.70[13]			5.90[26]	5.65[3]	5.65[3]		
SHAPES, Structural	3.65[1,5] 3.90[9]	3.65[1,23]	3.65[1,8]					3.70[3]	3.70[3]		3.70[3]			
HI str. low alloy	5.50[1,5]	5.50[1]	5.50[1,8]					5.50[3]	5.50[3]		5.50[3]			
MANUFACTURERS' WIRE Bright	4.85[2,5] 5.10[18]	4.85[2] 4.[33]		4.85[2]					Kokomo=5.80[39]		4.85[3]	4.95[3]	Duluth=4.85[2]	
PILING, Steel Sheet	4.45[1]	4.45[1]	4.45[8]						4.45[3]					

January 25, 1951

Smaller numbers indicate producing companies. See key at right.
Prices are in cents per lb unless otherwise noted. Extras apply.

IRON AGE
STEEL PRICES

Kansas City	Houston	Birmingham	WEST COAST Seattle, San Francisco, Los Angeles, Fontana		Product
			F=$79.00[19]		INGOTS carbon forging, net ton
	$62.00[83]		F=$80.00[19]		Alloy, net ton
		$56.00[11]	F=$75.00[19]		BILLETS, BLOOMS, SLABS Carbon, rerolling, net ton
	$74.00[83]	$66.00[11]	F=$85.00[19] SF, LA, S=$85.00[62]		Carbon forging billets, net ton
	$78.00[83]		F=$89.00[19] LA=$90.00[62]		Alloy net ton
					PIPE SKELP
4.50[83]		4.10[4,11]	SF=4.90[2] LA=4.90[24,62]	Worcester=4.40[2] Minnequa=4.35[14]	WIRE RODS
		3.60[4,11]	SF, LA=4.30[24] F=4.55[19]	Niles=5.25[64], Geneva=3.70[16]	SHEETS Hot-rolled (18 ga. & hvr.)
		4.35[11]	SF=5.30[24] F=5.30[19]		Cold-rolled
		4.80[4,11]	SF, LA=5.55[24]	Ashland=4.80[7]	Galvanized (10 gage)
					Enameling (12 gage)
					Long ternes (10 gage)
		5.40[11]	F=6.35[19]		HI str. low alloy, h.r.
			F=7.50[19]		HI str. low alloy, c.r.
					HI str. low alloy, galv.
4.10[83]	4.90[83]	3.50[4]	SF, LA=4.25[24,62] F=4.75[19], S=4.50[62]	Atlanta=4.05[65] Minnequa=4.55[14]	STRIP Hot-rolled
			F=6.30[19] LA=6.40[27]	New Haven=5.15[2], 5.85[68]	Cold-rolled
		5.30[11]	F=6.20[19]		HI str. low alloy, h.r.
					HI str. low alloy, c.r.
					TINPLATE Cokes, 1.50-lb base box 1.25 lb. deduct 20¢
					Electrolytic 0.25, 0.50, 0.75 lb box

Deduct $1.55, $1.30 and 90¢ respectively from 1.50-lb coke base box price

Kansas City	Houston	Birmingham	WEST COAST		Product
					BLACKPLATE, 29 gage Hollowware enameling
4.30[83]	4.10[83]	3.70[4,11]	SF, LA=4.40[24]	Atlanta=4.25[65] Minnequa=4.15[14]	BARS Carbon steel
4.30[83]	4.10[83]	3.70[4,11]	SF, S=4.45[62] F=4.40[19] LA=4.40[62]	Atlanta=4.25[65] Minnequa=4.50[14]	Reinforcing‡
				Newark=5.00[69] Putnam=5.10[69] Hartford=5.10[4] Los Angeles=6.00[4]	Cold-finished
4.90[83]	4.70[83]		LA=5.35[62] F=5.35[19]		Alloy, hot-rolled
				Newark=5.75[69] Worcester= [2] Hartford=5.85[4]	Alloy, cold-drawn
		5.55[11]	F=6.60[19]		HI str. low alloy, h.r.
	4.10[83]	3.70[4,11]	F=4.30[19] S=4.60[62] Geneva=3.70[16]	Claymont=4.15[29] Coatesville=4.15[21] Minnequa=4.50[14]	PLATE Carbon steel
				Harrisburg=5.25[35]	Floor plates
			F=5.70[19] Geneva=5.65[16]	Coatesville=5.25[21] Claymont=4.85[29]	Alloy
		5.65[11]	F=6.25[19]		HI str. low alloy
4.25[83]	4.05[83]	3.65[4,11]	SF, LA=4.20[62] F=4.25[16] LA=4.25[24,62] S=4.30[62]	Geneva 3.65[16] Minnequa 4.10[14]	SHAPES, Structural
		50[11]	F=6.10[19]		HI str. low-alloy
5.45[83]	5.25[83]	4.85[4,11]	SF, LA=5.80[24]	Atlanta=5.10[65] Worcester=5.15[2] Minnequa=5.10[14]	MANUFACTURERS' WIRE Bright

KEY TO STEEL PRODUCERS

1 U. S. Steel Co., Pittsburgh
2 American Steel & Wire Co., Cleveland
3 Bethlehem Steel Co., Bethlehem
4 Republic Steel Corp., Cleveland
5 Jones & Laughlin Steel Corp., Pittsburgh
6 Youngstown Sheet & Tube Co., Youngstown
7 Armco Steel Corp., Middletown, Ohio
8 Inland Steel Co., Chicago
9 Weirton Steel Co., Weirton, W. Va.
10 National Tube Co., Pittsburgh
11 Tennessee Coal, Iron & R. R. Co., Birmingham
12 Great Lakes Steel Corp., Detroit
13 Sharon Steel Corp., Sharon, Pa.
14 Colorado Fuel & Iron Corp., Denver
15 Wheeling Steel Corp., Wheeling, W. Va.
16 Geneva Steel Co., Salt Lake City
17 Crucible Steel Co. of America, New York
18 Pittsburgh Steel Co., Pittsburgh
19 Kaiser Steel Corp., Oakland, Calif.
20 Portsmouth Div., Detroit Steel Corp., Detroit
21 Lukens Steel Co., Coatesville, Pa.
22 Granite City Steel Co., Granite City, Ill
23 Wisconsin Steel Co., South Chicago, Ill
24 Columbia Steel Co., San Francisco
25 Copperweld Steel Co., Glassport, Pa.
26 Alan Wood Steel Co., Conshohocken, Pa.
27 Calif. Cold Rolled Steel Corp., Los Angeles
28 Allegheny Ludlum Steel Corp., Pittsburgh
29 Worth Steel Co., Claymont, Del.
30 Continental Steel Corp., Kokomo, Ind.
31 Rotary Electric Steel Co., Detroit
32 Laclede Steel Co., St. Louis
33 Northwestern Steel & Wire Co., Sterling, Ill.
34 Keystone Steel & Wire Co., Peoria, Ill.
35 Central Steel & Wire Co., Harrisburg, Pa
36 Carpenter Steel Co., Reading, Pa.
37 Eastern Stainless Steel Corp., Baltimore
38 Washington Steel Corp., Washington, Pa
39 Jessop Steel Co., Washington, Pa.
40 Blair Strip Steel Co., New Castle, Pa.
41 Superior Steel Co., Carnegie, Pa.
42 Timken Steel & Tube Div., Canton, Ohio
43 Babcock & Wilcox Tube Co., Beaver Falls, Pa
44 Reeves Steel & Mfg. Co., Dover, Ohio
45 John A. Roebling's Sons Co., Trenton, N. J
46 Simonds Saw & Steel Co., Fitchburg, Mass
47 McLouth Steel Co., Detroit
48 Cold Metal Products Co., Youngstown
49 Thomas Steel Co., Warren, Ohio
50 Wilson Steel & Wire Co., Chicago
51 Sweet's Steel Co., Williamsport, Pa.
52 Superior Drawn Steel Co., Monaca, Pa.
53 Tremont Nail Co., Wareham, Mass.
54 Firth Sterling St. & Carbide Corp., McKeesport
55 Ingersoll Steel Div., Chicago
56 Phoenix Iron & Steel Co., Phoenixville, Pa
57 Fitzsimmons Steel Co., Youngstown
58 Stanley Works, New Britain, Conn.
59 Universal-Cyclops Steel Corp., Bridgeville, Pa
60 American Cladmetals Co., Carnegie, Pa.
61 Cuyahoga Steel & Wire Co., Cleveland
62 Bethlehem Pacific Coast Steel Corp., San Fran.
63 Follansbee Steel Corp., Pittsburgh
64 Niles Rolling Mill Co., Niles, Ohio
65 Atlantic Steel Co., Atlanta
66 Acme Steel Co., Chicago
67 Joslyn Mfg. & Supply Co., Chicago
68 Detroit Steel Co., Detroit
69 Wyckoff Steel Co., Pittsburgh
70 Bliss & Laughlin, Inc., Harvey, Ill.
71 Columbia Steel & Shafting Co., Pittsburgh
72 Cumberland Steel Co., Cumberland, Md.
73 La Salle Steel Co., Chicago
74 Monarch Steel Co., Inc., Hammond, Ind.
75 Empire Steel Co., Mansfield, Ohio
76 Mahoning Valley Steel Co., Niles, Ohio
77 Oliver Iron & Steel Co., Pittsburgh
78 Pittsburgh Screw & Bolt Co., Pittsburgh
79 Standard Forging Corp., Chicago
80 Driver Harris Co., Harrison, N. J.
81 Detroit Tube & Steel Div., Detroit
82 Reliance Div., Eaton Mfg. Co., Massillon, Ohio
83 Sheffield Steel Corp., Kansas City
84 Plymouth Steel Co., Detroit
85 Wickwire Spencer Steel, Buffalo
86 Angell Nail and Chaplet, Cleveland
87 Mid-States Steel & Wire, Crawfordsville, Ind
88 National Supply, Pittsburgh, Pa.
89 Wheatland Tube Co., Wheatland, Pa.
90 Mercer Tube & Mfg. Co., Sharon, Pa.
91 Woodward Iron Co., Woodward, Ala.
92 Sloss-Sheffield Steel & Iron Co., Birmingham
93 Hanna Furnace Corp., Detroit
94 Interlake Iron Corp., Cleveland
95 Lone Star Steel Co., Dallas
96 Mystic Iron Works, Everett, Mass.
97 Jackson Iron & Steel Co., Jackson, O.
98 Globe Iron Co., Jackson, O.
99 Pittsburgh Coke & Chemical Co., Pittsburgh
100 Shenango Furnace Co., Pittsburgh
101 Tennessee Products & Chemical Corp., Nashville
102 Koppers Co., Inc., Granite City, Ill.

STAINLESS STEELS

Base price, cents per lb, f.o.b. mill.

Product	301	302	303	304	316	321	347	410	416	430
Ingots, rerolling	14.25	15.00	16.50	16.00	24.25	19.75	21.50	12.75	14.75	13.00
Slabs, billets rerolling	18.50	19.75	21.75	20.75	31.75	26.00	28.25	16.50	20.00	16.75
Forg. discs, die blocks, rings	34.00	34.00	36.50	35.50	52.50	40.00	44.50	28.00	28.50	28.50
Billets, forging	26.25	26.25	28.25	27.50	41.00	31.00	34.75	21.50	22.00	22.00
Bars, wires, structurals	31.25	31.25	33.75	32.75	48.75	36.75	41.25	25.75	26.25	26.25
Plates	33.00	33.00	35.00	35.00	51.50	40.50	45.00	27.00	27.50	27.50
Sheets	41.00	41.00	43.00	43.00	56.50	49.00	53.50	36.50	37.00	39.00
Strip, hot-rolled	26.50	28.00	32.25	30.00	48.25	36.75	41.00	23.50	30.25	24.00
Strip, cold-rolled	34.00	36.50	40.00	38.50	58.50	48.00	52.00	30.50	37.00	31.00

STAINLESS STEEL PRODUCING POINTS—*Sheets:* Midland, Pa., 17; Bracken-ridge, Pa., 28; Butler, Pa., 7; McKeesport, Pa., 1; Washington, Pa., 38 (type 316 add 5¢), 39; Baltimore, 37; Middletown, Ohio, 7; Massillon, Ohio, 4; Gary, 1; Bridgeville, Pa., 59; New Castle, Ind., 55; Ft. Wayne, Ind., 67; Lockport, N. Y., 46.
Strip: Midland, Pa., 17; Cleveland, 2; Carnegie, Pa., 41; McKeesport, Pa., 54; Reading, Pa., 36; Washington, Pa., 38 (type 316 add 5¢); W. Leechburg, Pa., 28; Bridgeville, Pa., 59; Detroit, 47; Massillon, Canton, Ohio, 4; Middletown, Ohio, 7; Harrison, N. J., 80; Youngstown, 48; Lockport, N. Y., 46; New Britain, Conn., 58; Sharon, Pa., 13; Butler, Pa., 7.
Bars: Baltimore, 7; Duquesne, Pa. 1; Munhall, Pa., 1; Reading, Pa., 36; Titusville, Pa., 59; Washington, Pa., 39; McKeesport, Pa., 1, 54; Bridgeville, Pa., 59; Dunkirk, N. Y., 28; Massillon, Ohio, 4; Chicago, 1; Syracuse, N. Y., 17; Watervliet, N. Y., 28; Waukegan, Ill., 2; Lockport, N. Y., 46; Canton, Ohio, 42; Ft. Wayne, Ind., 67.
Wire: Waukegan, Ill., 2; Massillon, Ohio, 4; McKeesport, Pa., 54; Bridgeport, Conn., 44; Ft. Wayne, Ind., 67; Trenton, N. J., 45; Harrison, N. J., 80; Baltimore, 7; Dunkirk, 28.
Structurals: Baltimore, 7; Massillon, Ohio, 4; Chicago, 1, 67; Watervliet, N. Y., 28; Bridgeport, Conn., 44.
Plates: Brackenridge, Pa., 28 (type 416 add ½¢); Butler, Pa., 7; Chicago, 1; Munhall, Pa., 1; Midland, Pa., 17; New Castle, Ind., 55; Lockport, N. Y., 46; Middletown, 7; Washington, Pa., 39; Cleveland, Massillon, 4.
Forged discs, die blocks, rings: Pittsburgh, 1, 17; Syracuse, 17; Ferndale, Mich., 28.
Forging billets: Midland, Pa., 17; Baltimore, 7; Washington, Pa., 39; McKeesport, 54; Massillon, Canton, Ohio, 4; Watervliet, 28; Pittsburgh, Chicago, 1.

RAILS, TRACK SUPPLIES

F.o.b. Mill Cents Per Lb	No. 1 Std. Rails	Light Rails	Joint Bars	Track Spikes	Axles	Screw Spikes	Tie Plates	Track Bolts Untreated
Bessemer-1	3.60	4.00	4.70					
Chicago-4				6.15				
Ensley-11	3.60	4.00						
Fairfield-11	3.60	4.00	4.40			8.60	4.50	
Gary-1	3.60	4.00					4.50	
Ind. Harbor-8	3.60	4.00	4.70	6.15	5.25	8.60	4.50	
Johnstown-3		4.00			5.60	8.60		
Joliet-1		4.00	4.70					
Kansas City-83				6.40				
Lackawanna-3	3.60	4.00	4.70			8.60	4.50	
Lebanon-3				6.15				9.60
Minnequa-14	3.60	4.50	4.70	6.15		8.60	4.50	9.60
Pittsburgh-77						9.35		9.60
Pittsburgh-78								9.60
Pittsburgh-5				6.15				
Pittsburgh-24								4.65
Seattle-62				6.10				4.35
Steelton-3	3.60		4.70					
Struthers-6								4.65
Torrance-24				6.15				
Youngstown-4				6.15				

Track Bolts, heat treated, to railroads, 9.85¢ per lb.

BOILER TUBES

Seamless steel, electric welded commercial boiler tubes, locomotive tubes, minimum wall, per 100 ft at mill, c.l. lots, cut lengths 10 to 24 ft.

OD in in.	gage BWG	Seamless H.R.	C.D.	Electric Weld H.R.	C.D.
2	13	$22.67	$26.66	$21.99	$25.86
2½	12	30.48	35.84	29.57	34.76
3	12	33.90	39.90	32.89	34.80
3½	11	42.37	49.89	41.10	48.39
4	10	52.60	61.88	51.03	60.02

Pittsburgh Steel add, H-R: 2 in., 62¢; 2½ in., 84¢; 3 in., 92¢; 3½ in., $1.17; 4 in., $1.45. Add, C-R: 2 in., 74¢; 2½ in., 99¢; 3 in., $1.10; 3½ in., $1.37; 4 in., $1.70.

FLUORSPAR

Washed gravel fluorspar, f.o.b. cars, Rosiclare, Ill. Base price, per ton net: Effective CaF, content:
70% or more $43.00
60% or less 40.00

MERCHANT WIRE PRODUCTS

F.o.b. Mill	Standard & Coated Nails Base Col.	Woven Wire Fence 9-15½ ga. Base Col.	Fence Posts Base Col.	Single Loop Bale Ties Base Col.	Twisted Barbless Wire Base Col.	Gal. Barbed Wire Base Col.	Merch. Wire Ann'l'd. ¢/lb.	Merch. Wire Gal. ¢/lb.
Alabama City-4	118	126		123		136	5.70	5.95
Aliquippa, Pa.-5	118	132			136	140	5.70	6.15
Atlanta-65	113	133		126	126	143	5.95	6.40
Bartonville-34	118	130	140	123	143	143	5.95	6.15
Buffalo-85								
Cleveland-86								
Cleveland-2							5.70	6.15
Crawfordsville-87		132			145		5.95	6.40
Donora, Pa.-2	118	130		123		140	5.70	6.15
Duluth-2	118	130		123		140	5.70	6.15
Fairfield, Ala.-11	118	130		123		136	5.70	6.15
Houston-83	126	138			148		6.10	6.55
Johnstown, Pa.-3	118	130		140			5.70	6.15
Joliet, Ill.-2	118	130		123		140	5.70	6.15
Kokomo, Ind.-30	120	132		125	138	138	5.80	6.05
Los Angeles-62							6.65	
Kansas City-83	130	130	142	135		152	6.30	6.75
Minnequa-14	123	138	130	128	146	146	5.95	6.45
Monessen-18	124	135				145	5.95	6.40
Moline, Ill.-4			136					
Palmer-85								
Pittsburg, Cal.-24	137	149		147	156	160	6.65	6.80
Portsmouth-20	124	137			147	147	6.10	6.60
Rankin, Pa.-24	118	130				140	5.70	6.15
So. Chicago, Ill.-4	118	126	140	123		136	5.70	5.95
S. San Fran.-14				147		160	6.65	7.10
Sparrows Pt.-3	120			125	142	142	5.80	6.25
Sterling, Ill.-33	118	130	140	123	140	140	5.70	6.15
Struthers, Ohio-6							5.70	6.15
Torrance, Cal.-24	138						6.65	
Worcester-2	124						6.00	6.45
Williamsport, Pa.-51			150					

Cut Nails, carloads, base, $6.75 per 100 lb. (less 20¢ to jobbers) at Conshohocken, Pa., (26), Wareham, Mass. (53) Wheeling, W. Va., (15).

CAST IRON WATER PIPE

Per net ton
6 to 24-in., del'd Chicago . $105.30 to $108.80
6 to 24-in., del'd N. Y. ... 104.50 to 105.50
6 to 24-in., Birmingham . 91.50 to 96.00
6-in. and larger, f.o.b. cars, San Francisco, Los Angeles, for all rail shipment; rail and water shipment less .... $108.50 to $113.00 Class "A" and gas pipe, $5 extra; 4-in. pipe is $5 a ton above 6-in.

PIPE AND TUBING

Base discounts, f.o.b. mills. Base price about $200 per net ton.

	BUTTWELD														SEAMLESS					
	½ In.		¾ In.		1 In.		1¼ In.		1½ In.		2 In.		2½-3 In.		2 In.		2½-3 In.		3½-4 In.	
	Blk.	Gal.	Blk.	Gal.	Blk.	Gal.	Blk.	Gal.	Blk.	Gal.	Blk.	Gal.	Blk.	Gal.	Blk.	Gal.	Blk.	Gal.	Blk.	Gal.
STANDARD T. & C.																				
Sparrows Pt.-3	34.0	12.0	37.0	16.0	39.5	19.5	40.0	20.0	40.5	21.0	41.0	21.5	41.5	22.0						
Cleveland-4	36.0	14.0	39.0	18.0	41.5	21.5	42.0	22.0	42.5	23.0	43.0	23.5	43.5	24.0						
Oakland-19	25.0	3.0	28.0	7.0	30.5	10.5	31.0	11.0	31.5	12.0	32.0	12.5	32.5	13.0						
Pittsburgh-5	36.0	14.0	39.0	17.0	41.5	19.5	42.0	20.5	42.5	21.0	43.0	23.5	43.5	22.5	29.5	8.0	32.5	11.5	34.5	13.5
Pittsburgh-10	36.0	14.0	39.0	18.0	41.5	21.5	42.0	22.0	42.5	23.0	43.0	24.0	43.5	24.0	29.5	9.5	32.5	12.5	34.5	14.5
St. Louis-32	35.0	13.0	38.0	17.0	40.5	20.5	41.0	21.0	41.5	22.0	42.0	22.5	42.5	23.0						
Sharon-90	36.0	13.0	39.0	17.0	41.5	20.0	42.0	20.5	42.5	21.0	43.0	23.5	43.5	24.0						
Toledo-88	36.0	14.0	39.0	18.0	41.5	21.5	42.0	22.0	42.5	23.0	43.0	23.5	43.5	24.0	29.5		32.5		34.5	
Wheeling-15	36.0	14.0	39.0	18.0	41.5	21.5	42.0	22.0	42.5	23.0	43.0	23.5	43.5	24.0						
Wheatland-89	36.0	13.0	39.0	17.0	41.5	19.5	42.0	20.5	42.5	21.0	43.0	23.5	43.5	22.5						
Youngstown-6	36.0	14.0	39.0	18.0	41.5	21.5	42.0	22.0	42.5	23.0	43.0	23.5	43.5	24.0	29.5	9.5	32.5	12.5	34.5	14.5
EXTRA STRONG, PLAIN ENDS																				
Sparrows Pt.-3	33.5	13.0	37.5	17.0	39.5	20.5	40.0	21.0	40.5	22.0	41.0	22.5	41.5	23.0						
Cleveland-4	35.5	15.0	39.5	19.0	41.5	22.5	42.0	23.0	42.5	24.0	43.0	24.5	43.5	25.0						
Oakland-19	24.5	4.0	28.5	8.0	30.5	11.5	31.0	12.0	31.5	13.0	32.0	13.5	32.5	14.0						
Pittsburgh-5	35.5	13.5	39.5	17.5	41.5	19.5	42.0	20.5	42.5	21.0	43.0	23.5	43.5	22.5	29.0	7.5	33.0	12.0	36.0	15.5
Pittsburgh-10	35.5	15.0	39.5	19.0	41.5	22.5	42.0	23.0	42.5	24.0	43.0	24.5	43.5	25.0	29.0	10.0	33.0	14.0	36.5	17.5
St. Louis-32	34.5	14.0	38.5	18.0	40.5	21.5	41.0	22.0	41.5	23.0	42.0	23.5	42.5	24.0						
Sharon-90	35.5	15.0	39.5	19.0	41.5	21.0	42.0	21.5	42.5	22.5	43.0	23.0	43.5	23.5						
Toledo-88	35.5	15.0	39.5	19.0	41.5	22.5	42.0	23.0	42.5	24.0	43.0	24.5	43.5	25.0	33.0				36.5	
Wheeling-15	35.5	15.0	39.5	19.0	41.5	22.5	42.0	23.0	42.5	24.0	43.0	24.5	43.5	25.0						
Wheatland-89	35.5	13.5	39.5	17.5	41.5	19.5	42.0	20.5	42.5	21.0	43.0	23.5	43.5	22.5						
Youngstown-6	35.5	15.0	39.5	19.0	41.5	22.5	42.0	23.0	42.5	24.0	43.0	24.5	43.5	25.0	29.0	10.0	33.0	14.0	36.5	17.5

Galvanized discounts based on zinc at 17¢ per lb, East St. Louis. For each 1¢ change in zinc, discounts vary as follows: ½ in., ¾ in., and 1 in. 1 pt; 1¼ in., 1½ in., 2 in., ¾ pt.; 2½ in., 3 in., ½ pt. Calculate discounts on even cents per lb of zinc, i.e., if zinc is 16.51¢ to 17.50¢ per lb, use 17¢. Jones & Laughlin discounts apply only when zinc price changes 1¢. Threads only, buttweld and seamless, 1 pt. higher discount. Plain ends, buttweld and seamless, 3 in. and under, 3½ pt. higher discount. Buttweld jobbers' discount, 5 pct.

January 25, 1951

WAREHOUSES

Base price, f.o.b., dollars per 100 lb. *(Metropolitan area delivery, add 20¢ except Birmingham, San Francisco, Cincinnati, New Orleans, St. Paul, add 15¢; Memphis, add 10¢; Philadelphia, add 25¢; New York, add 30¢).

Cities	Sheets Hot-Rolled	Sheets Cold-Rolled (15 gage)	Sheets Galvanized (10 gage)	Strip Hot-Rolled	Strip Cold-Rolled	Plates	Shapes Standard Structural	Bars Hot-Rolled	Bars Cold-Finished	Alloy Bars HR A 4615 As rolled	Alloy Bars HR A 4140 Annealed	Alloy Bars CD A 4615 As rolled	Alloy Bars CD A 4140 Annealed
Baltimore	5.60	6.84	7.49[2]/8.07	6.04		5.80	6.14	6.04	6.84/6.89	10.24	10.54	11.89	12.19
Birmingham*	5.60	6.40	6.75	5.55		5.95	5.70	5.55					
Boston	6.20	7.00/7.25	7.74/8.29	6.15	8.50[4]	6.48/6.78	6.20	6.05	6.79/6.84	10.25	10.55	11.90/12.00/12.10	12.20/12.30
Buffalo	5.60	6.40	7.74/8.09	5.86		6.05	5.80	5.60	6.40/6.45	10.15/10.85	10.45	11.80	11.95/12.10
Chicago	5.60	6.40	7.75	5.55		5.80	5.70	5.55	6.30	9.80	10.10	11.45	11.75
Cincinnati*	5.87	6.44	7.39	5.80		6.19	6.09	5.80	6.61	10.15	10.45	11.80	12.10
Cleveland	5.60	6.40	8.10	5.69	6.90	5.92	5.82	5.57	6.40	9.91	10.21	11.56	11.86
Detroit	5.78	6.53	7.89	5.94		5.99	6.09	5.84	6.56	10.11	10.41	11.76	12.06
Houston	7.00	8.25				6.85	6.50	6.65	9.35	10.35	11.25		12.75
Indianapolis, del'd	6.00	6.80	8.15	5.95		6.20	6.10	5.95	6.80				
Kansas City	6.00	6.80	7.45	6.15	7.50	6.40	6.30	6.15	7.00	10.40	10.70	12.05	12.35
Los Angeles	6.35	7.90	8.85	6.40	9.45[6]	6.40	6.35	6.35	8.20	11.30	11.30	13.20	13.50
Memphis*	6.33/6.38	7.08/7.18		6.33/6.38		6.43/8.02	6.33/6.48	6.08/6.33	7.16/7.32				
Milwaukee	5.74	6.54	7.89	5.69/6.59		5.94	5.84	5.69	6.44/6.54	9.94	10.24	11.59	11.89
New Orleans*	5.70	6.59			7.25	5.75	5.95	5.75	7.30				
New York*	5.67/5.97	7.19[5]/7.24[1]	8.14[2]	6.29/6.89	8.63[4]	6.28/6.58	6.10	6.12	6.99	10.05/10.15	10.35/10.45	11.70/11.80	12.10/12.20
Norfolk	6.50[3]					6.50[3]	6.60[3]	6.55[3]					
Philadelphia*	5.90	6.55	8.00	6.10		6.05	5.90	6.05	6.61	9.90	10.20		
Pittsburgh	5.60	6.40	7.75	5.65/5.95		5.75	5.70	5.55	6.15	9.80	10.10	11.45	11.75
Portland	6.60/7.55	8.95	8.50/9.10	7.30		6.80	6.95	6.90				12.15	
Salt Lake City	7.95		9.70	8.70		8.05	8.30	8.65	9.00				
San Francisco*	6.65	8.05[2]	8.55/8.90[2]	6.60	9.45[6]	6.50	6.45	6.45	8.20	11.30	11.30	13.20	13.20/13.50
Seattle	7.05	8.60	9.20	9.05		6.75	6.65	6.75	9.05				
St. Louis	5.80/5.85	6.65	8.00	5.80	8.00[4]/8.28	6.13	6.03	5.80	6.55/6.65	10.05	10.35	11.70	12.00
St. Paul*	6.16	6.96	8.31	6.11		6.36	6.26	6.11	6.96	10.36	10.66	12.01	12.31

BASE QUANTITIES (Standard unless otherwise keyed): Cold finished bars; 2000 lb or over. Alloy bars; 1000 to 1999 lb. All others; 2000 to 9999 lb. All HR products may be combined for quantity. All galvanized sheets may be combined for quantity. CR sheets may not be combined with each other or with galvanized sheets for quantity.

EXCEPTIONS: (1) 400 to 1499 lb; (2) 450 to 1499 lb; (3) 400 to 1999 lb; (4) 6000 lb and over; (5) 1500 to 9999 lb.; (6) 2000 to 5999 lb.

PIG IRON

Dollars per gross ton, f.o.b., subject to switching charges.

Producing Point	Basic	No. 2 Foundry	Malleable	Bessemer	Low Phos.	Blast Furnace Silvery	Low Phos. Charcoal
Bethlehem-3	54.00	54.50	55.00	55.50			
Birmingham-4	48.38	48.88					
Birmingham-91	48.38	48.88					
Birmingham-92	48.38	48.88					
Buffalo-4	52.00	52.50	53.00				
Buffalo-93	52.00	52.50	53.00			63.75	
Chicago-94	52.00	52.50	52.50	53.00			
Cleveland-2	52.00	52.50	52.50	53.00	57.00		
Cleveland-4	52.00	52.50	52.50				
Daingerfield, Tex.-95	48.00	48.50	48.50				
Duluth-94	52.00	52.50	52.50	53.00			
Erie-94	52.00	52.50	52.50	53.00			
Everett, Mass.-96			53.25	53.75			
Fontana-19	58.00	58.50					
Geneva, Utah-16	52.00	52.50	52.50	53.00			
Granite City, Ill.-102	53.90	54.40	54.90				
Hubbard, O.-6	52.00	52.50	52.50				
Ironton, Utah-16	52.00	52.50					
Jackson, O.-97,98						62.50	
Lyle, Tenn.-101							66.00
Monessen-18	54.00						
Neville Island-99	52.00	52.50	52.50	53.00			
Pittsburgh-1	52.00			53.00			
Sharpsville-100	52.00	52.50	52.50	53.00			
Steelton-3	54.00	54.50	55.00	55.50	60.00		
Swedeland-26	56.00	56.50	57.00	57.50			
Toledo-94	52.00	52.50	52.50	53.00			
Troy, N.Y.-4	54.00	54.50	55.00		60.00		
Youngstown-6	52.00	52.50	52.50	53.00			

DIFFERENTIALS: Add 50¢ per ton for each 0.25 pct silicon over base (1.75 to 2.25 pct), 50¢ per ton for each 0.50 pct manganese over 1 pct, $2 per ton for 0.5 to 0.75 pct nickel, $1 for each additional 0.25 pct nickel. Subtract 38¢ per ton for phosphorus content over 0.70 pct. Silvery iron: Add $1.50 per ton for each 0.50 pct silicon over base (6.01 to 6.50 pct) up to 17 pct. $1 per ton for 0.75 pct or more phosphorus, manganese as above. Bessemer ferrosilicon prices are $1 over comparable silvery iron.

January 25, 1951

REFRACTORIES

Fire Clay Brick *(F.o.b. works)* Carloads, Per 1000

First quality, Ill., Ky., Md., Mo., Ohio, Pa. (except Salina, Pa., add $5).....$94.60
No. 1 Ohio... 88.00
Sec. quality, Pa., Md., Ky., Mo., Ill... 88.00
No. 2 Ohio... 79.20
Ground fire clay, net ton, bulk (except Salina, Pa., add $1.50)...... 13.70

Silica Brick

Mt. Union, Pa., Ensley, Ala. $94.60
Childs, Pa. ... 99.00
Hays, Pa. ... 100.10
Chicago District ... 104.50
Western Utah and Calif. ... 111.10
Super Duty, Hays, Pa., Athens, Tex., Chicago ... 111.10
Silica cement, net ton, bulk, Eastern (except Hays, Pa.) ... 16.50
Silica cement, net ton, bulk, Hays, Pa. ... 18.70
Silica cement, net ton, bulk, Ensley, Ala. ... 17.60
Silica cement, net ton, bulk, Chicago District ... 17.60
Silica cement, net ton, bulk, Utah and Calif. ... 24.70

Chrome Brick Per Net Ton

Standard chemically bonded, Balt., Chester ... $82.00

Magnesite Brick

Standard, Baltimore ... $104.00
Chemically bonded, Baltimore ... 93.00

Grain Magnesite St. ⅜-in. grains

Domestic, f.o.b. Baltimore, in bulk fines removed ... $62.70
Domestic, f.o.b. Chewelah, Wash., in bulk ... 36.30
in sacks ... 41.80

Dead Burned Dolomite

F.o.b. producing points in Pennsylvania, West Virginia and Ohio, per net ton, bulk Midwest, add 10¢; Missouri Valley, add 20¢....$13.00

COKE

Furnace, beehive (f.o.b. oven) Net Ton
Connellsville, Pa. ... $14.00 to $14.50
Foundry, beehive (f.o.b. oven)
Connellsville, Pa. ... $17.00 to $17.50
Foundry, oven coke
Buffalo, del'd ... $25.35
Chicago, f.o.b. ... 21.00
Detroit, f.o.b. ... 23.00
New England, del'd ... 24.80
Seaboard, N. J., f.o.b. ... 22.00
Philadelphia, f.o.b. ... 22.70
Swedeland, Pa., f.o.b. ... 22.60
Plainesville, Ohio, f.o.b. ... 24.00
Erie, Pa., f.o.b. ... 23.50
Cleveland, del'd ... 25.72
Cincinnati, del'd ... 25.06
St. Paul, f.o.b. ... 21.00
St. Louis, f.o.b. ... 24.90
Birmingham, del'd ... 20.79
Neville Island, f.o.b. ... 23.00

LAKE SUPERIOR ORES

(51.50% Fe; natural content, delivered lower lake ports) Per gross ton

Old range, bessemer ... $8.70
Old range, nonbessemer ... 8.55
Mesabi, bessemer ... 8.45
Mesabi, nonbessemer ... 8.30
High phosphorus ... 8.30

After adjustments for analyses, prices will be increased or decreased as the case may be for increases or decreases after Dec. 2, 1950, in lake vessel rates, upper lake rail freights, dock handling charges and taxes thereon.

C-R SPRING STEEL

Base per pound f.o.b. mill

0.26 to 0.40 carbon ... 5.35¢
0.41 to 0.60 carbon ... 6.80¢
0.61 to 0.80 carbon ... 7.40¢
0.81 to 1.05 carbon ... 9.35¢
1.06 to 1.35 carbon ... 11.65¢

Worcester, add 0.30¢; Sharon, Carnegie, New Castle, add 0.35¢; Detroit, 0.26 to 0.40 carb., add 25¢; other grades add 15¢.
New Haven, 0.26 to 0.40 carb., add 50¢; other grades add 5¢.

BOLTS, NUTS, RIVETS, SCREWS
Consumer Prices
(*Base discount, f.o.b. mill, Pittsburgh, Cleveland, Birmingham or Chicago*)

Machine and Carriage Bolts

	Pct Off List Less Case	C.
½ in. & smaller x 6 in. & shorter	15	28½
9/16 in. & ⅝ in. x 6 in. & shorter	18½	30½
¾ in. & larger x 6 in. & shorter	17½	29½
All diam. longer than 6 in.	14	27½
Lag, all diam. x 6 in. & shorter	23	35
Lag, all diam. longer than 6 in.	21	33
Plow bolts	34	....

Nuts, Hot Pressed, Cold Punched—Sq
Pct Off List

	Less Keg K. (Reg.)		Less Keg K. (Hvy.)	
½ in. & smaller	15	28½	15	28½
9/16 in. & ⅝ in.	12	25	6½	21
¾ in. to 1½ in. inclusive	9	23	1	16½
1⅝ in. & larger	7½	22	1	16½

Nuts, Hot Pressed—Hexagon

½ in. & smaller	26	37	22	34
9/16 in. & ⅝ in.	16½	29½	6½	21
¾ in. to 1½ in. inclusive	12	25	2	17½
1⅝ in. & larger	8½	23	2	17½

Nuts, Cold Punched—Hexagon

½ in. & smaller	26	37	22	34
9/16 in. & ⅝ in.	23	35	17½	30½
¾ in. to 1½ in. inclusive	19½	31½	12	25
1⅝ in. & larger	12	25	6½	21

Nuts, Semi-Finished—Hexagon

	Reg.		Hvy.	
½ in. & smaller	35	45	28½	39½
9/16 in. & ⅝ in.	29½	40½	22	34
¾ in. to 1½ in. inclusive	24	36	15	28½
1⅝ in. & larger	13	26	8½	23
	Light			
7/16 in. & smaller	35	45		
½ in. thru ⅝ in.	28½	39½		
¾ in. to 1½ in. inclusive	26	37		

Stove Bolts
Pct Off List
- Packaged, steel, plain finished .... 56—10
- Packaged, plated finish ...... 41—10
- Bulk, plain finish** 67*

*Discounts apply to bulk shipments in not less than 15,000 pieces of a size and kind where length is 3-in. and shorter; 5000 pieces for lengths longer than 3-in. For lesser quantities, packaged price applies.

**Zinc, Parkerized, cadmium or nickel plated finishes add 6¢ per lb net. For black oil finish, add 2¢ per lb net.

Rivets

	Base per 100 lb
½ in. & larger	$7.85
	Pct Off List
7/16 in. & smaller	36

F.o.b. Pittsburgh, Cleveland, Chicago, Birmingham, Lebanon, Pa.

Cap and Set Screws
(*In bulk*)
Pct Off List
- Hexagon head cap screws, coarse or fine thread, ¼ in. thru ⅝ in. x 6 in., SAE 1020, bright 54
- ¾ in. thru 1 in. up to & including 6 in. 48
- ¼ in. thru ⅝ in. x 6 in. & shorter high C double heat treat 46
- ¾ in. thru 1 in. up to & including 6 in. 41
- Milled studs 35
- Flat head cap screws, listed sizes.... 16
- Fillister head cap, listed sizes 34
- Set screws, sq head, cup point, 1 in. diam. and smaller x 6 in. & shorter 53

S. M. Ferrochrome
Contract price, cents per pound, chromium contained, lump size, delivered.

High carbon type: 60-65% Cr, 4-6% Si, 4-6% Mn, 4-6% C.
- Carloads 21.60
- Ton lots 23.75
- Less ton lots 25.25

Low carbon type: 62-66% Cr, 4-6% Si, 4-6% Mn, 1.25% max. C.
- Carloads 27.75
- Ton lots 30.05
- Less ton lots 31.85

ELECTRODES
Cents per lb, f.o.b. plant, threaded electrodes with nipples, unboxed

Diam. in in.	Length in in.	Cents Per lb
	GRAPHITE	
17, 18, 20	60, 72	17.85
8 to 16	48, 60, 72	17.85
7	48, 60	19.57
6	48, 60	20.95
4, 5	40	21.50
3	40	22.61
2½	24, 30	23.15
2	24, 30	25.36
	CARBON	
40	100, 110	8.03
35	65, 110	8.03
30	65, 84, 110	8.03
24	72 to 104	8.03
20	84, 90	8.03
17	60, 72	8.03
14	60, 72	8.57
10, 12	60	8.84
8	60	9.10

CLAD STEEL
Base prices, cents per pound, f.o.b. mill

Stainless-carbon	Plate	Sheet
No. 304, 20 pct,		
Coatesville, Pa. (21)	*29.5	
Washgtn, Pa. (39)	*29.5	
Claymont, Del. (29)	*28.00	
Conshohocken, Pa. (26)	*24.00	
New Castle, Ind. (55)	*26.50	*25.50

Nickel-carbon
- 10 pct. Coatesville (21).. 32.5

Inconel-carbon
- 10 pct Coatesville (21).. 40.5

Monel-carbon
- 10 pct Coatesville (21).. 33.5

No. 302 Stainless - copper-stainless, Carnegie, Pa. (60) 77.00

Aluminized steel sheets, hot dip, Butler, Pa. (7)..... 7.75

*Includes annealing and pickling, or sandblasting.

TOOL STEEL
F.o.b. mill

W	Cr	V	Mo	Co	Base per lb
18	4	1	—	—	$1.235
18	4	1	—	5	$1.86
18	4	2	—	—	$1.38
1.5	4	1.5	8	—	78.5¢
6	4	2	6	—	.87¢

- High-carbon chromium .... 63.5¢
- Oil hardened manganese .... 35¢
- Special carbon .... 32.5¢
- Extra carbon .... 27¢
- Regular carbon .... 23¢

Warehouse prices on and east of Mississippi are 3¢ per lb higher. West of Mississippi, 5¢ higher.

METAL POWDERS
Per pound, f.o.b. shipping point, in ton lots, for minus 100 mesh.

Swedish sponge iron c.i.f. New York, ocean bags....	7.4¢ to 9.0¢
Canadian sponge iron, del'd, in East	10.00¢
Domestic sponge iron, 98+% Fe, carload lots	9.0¢ to 15.0¢
Electrolytic iron, annealed, 99.5+% Fe	36.0¢ to 39.5¢
Electrolytic iron unannealed, minus 325 mesh, 99+% Fe	48.5¢
Hydrogen reduced iron, minus 300 mesh, 98+% Fe	63.0¢ to 80.0¢
Carbonyl iron, size 5 to 10 micron, 98%, 99.8+% Fe	70.0¢ to $1.38
Aluminum	29.00¢
Brass, 10 ton lots ....30.00¢ to 33.25¢
Copper, electrolytic 10.25¢ plus metal value
Copper, reduced ...10.00¢ plus metal value
Cadmium 100-150 lb..95¢ plus metal value
Chromium, electrolytic, 99% min., and quantity	$3.50
Lead ....6.5¢ plus metal value
Manganese	52.00¢
Molybdenum, 99%	$2.65
Nickel, unannealed	75.5¢
Nickel, annealed	81.5¢
Nickel, spherical, unannealed .	78.5¢
Silicon	34.00¢
Solder powder..6.5¢ to 8.5¢ plus met. value
Stainless steel, 302	75.00¢
Tin ....11.00¢ plus metal value
Tungsten, 99%	$4.15
Zinc, 10 ton lots ....20.50¢ to 23.85¢

ELECTRICAL SHEETS
22 Ga. H-R cut lengths

F.o.b. Mill Cents Per Lb.	Armature	Elec.	Motor	Dynamo	Transf. 72	Transf. 65	Transf. 58
Beech Botton-15..		7.25	8.50	9.30	9.85	10.40	11.10
Brackenridge-28..		7.25	8.50	9.30	9.85		
Follansbee-63.	6.75	7.25	8.50	9.30	9.85	10.40	11.10
Granite City-22..		7.95	9.20				
Ind. Harbor-3.	6.75	7.25					
Mansfield-75.	6.75	7.25	8.50	9.30			
Niles, O.-64.	7.05	7.55					
Vandergrift-1.	6.75	7.25	8.50	9.30	9.85	10.40	11.10
Warren, O.-4.	6.75	7.25	8.50	9.30	9.85	10.40	11.10
Zanesville-7.	6.75	7.25	8.50	9.30	9.85	10.40	11.10

Transformer 52, 80¢ above Transformer 58.

Ferrochrome
Contract prices, cents per pound, contained Cr, lump size, bulk, in carloads, delivered. (65-72% Cr, 2% max. Si.)

0.06% C	30.50	0.20% C	29.50
0.10% C	30.00	0.50% C	29.25
0.15% C	29.75	1.00% C	29.00
2.00% C			28.75
65-69% Cr, 4-9% C			22.00
62-66% Cr, 4-6% C, 6-9% Si.			22.85

High-Nitrogen Ferrochrome
Low-carbon type: 67-72% Cr, 0.75% N. Add 5¢ per lb to regular low carbon ferrochrome price schedule. Add 5¢ for each additional 0.25% N.

Chromium Metal
Contract prices, per lb chromium contained packed, delivered, ton lots. 97% min. Cr, 1% max. Fe.
- 0.20% Max. C. $1.09
- 0.50% max. C. 1.05
- .00 min. C 1.04

Low Carbon Ferrochrome Silicon
(Cr 34-41%, Si 42-49%, C 0.05% max.) Contract price, carloads, f.o.b. Niagara Falls, freight allowed; lump 4-in. x down, bulk 2-in. x down, 21.75¢ per lb of contained Cr plus 12.00¢ per lb of contained Si.
Bulk 1-in. x down, 21.90¢ per lb contained Cr plus 12.20¢ per lb contained Si.

Calcium-Silicon
Contract price per lb of alloy, dump, delivered.
30-33% Ca, 60-65% Si, 3.00% max. Fe.
- Carloads 19.00
- Ton lots 22.10
- Less ton lots 23.00

Calcium-Manganese—Silicon
Contract prices, cents per lb of alloy, lump, delivered.
16-20% Ca, 14-18% Mn, 53-59% Si.
- Carloads 20.00
- Ton lots 22.30
- Less ton lots 23.30

CMSZ
Contract price, cents per lb of alloy, delivered.
Alloy 4: 45-49% Cr, 4-6% Mn, 18-21% Si, 1.25-1.75% Zr, 3.00-4.5% C.
Alloy 5: 50.56% Cr, 4-6% Mn, 13.50-16.00% Si, 0.75 to 1.25% Zr, 3.50-5.00% C.
- Ton lots 20.75
- Less ton lots 22.00

V Foundry Alloy
Cents per pound of alloy, f.o.b. Suspension Bridge, N. Y., freight allowed, max. St. Louis. V-5: 38-42% Cr, 17-19% Si, 8-11% Mn.
- Ton lots .... 16.50¢
- Less ton lots .... 17.75¢

Graphidox No. 4
Cents per pound of alloy, f.o.b. Suspension Bridge, N. Y., freight allowed, max. St. Louis. Si 48 to 52%, Ti 9 to 11%, Ca 5 to 7%.
- Carload packed .... 18.00¢
- Ton lots to carload packed . 19.00¢
- Less ton lots .... 20.50¢

SMZ
Contract price, cents per pound of alloy, delivered, 60-65% Si, 5-7% Mn, 5-7% Zr, 10% Fe, ½ in. x 12 mesh.
- Ton lots 17.25
- Less ton lots 18.50

FERROALLOYS

Ferromanganese
78-82% Mn. maximum contract base
price, gross ton, lump size.
F.o.b. Niagara Falls, Alloy, W. Va.,
Welland, Ont., Ashtabula, O. $185
F.o.b. Johnstown, Pa. $187
F.o.b. Sheridan, Pa. $185
F.o.b. Etna, Clairton, Pa. $188
$2.00 for each 1% above 82% Mn.
penalty, $2.15 for each 1% below 78%.
Briquets—Cents per pound of briquet,
delivered, 66% contained Mn.
Carload, bulk 10.45
Ton lots 12.05

Spiegeleisen
Contract prices gross ton, lump, f.o.b.

	16-19% Mn 3% max. Si	19-21% Mn 3% max. Si
Palmerton, Pa.	$74.00	$75.00
Pgh. or Chicago	74.00	75.00

Manganese Metal
Contract basis, 2 in. x down, cents per
pound of metal, delivered.
96% min. Mn, 0.2% max. C, 1% max.
Si, 2% max. Fe.
Carload, packed 29.75
Ton lots 31.25

Electrolytic Manganese
F.o.b. Knoxville, Tenn., freight allowed
east of Mississippi, cents per pound.
Carloads 28
Ton lots 30
Less ton lots 32

Medium Carbon Ferromanganese
Mn 80% to 85%, C 1.25 to 1.50. Contract
price, carloads, lump, bulk, delivered, per
lb. of contained Mn .... 19.15¢

Low-Carbon Ferromanganese
Contract price, cents per pound Mn contained, lump size, del'd., Mn. 85-90%.

	Carloads	Ton	Less
0.07% max. C, 0.06% P, 90% Mn	26.25	28.10	29.30
0.07% max. C	25.75	27.60	28.80
0.15% max. C	25.25	27.10	28.30
0.30% max. C	24.75	26.60	27.80
0.50% max. C	24.25	26.10	27.30
0.75% max. C, 7.00% max. Si	21.25	23.10	24.30

Silicomanganese
Contract basis, lump size, cents per
pound of metal, delivered, 65-68% Mn.
18-20% Si, 1.5% max. C. For 2% max. C,
deduct 0.2¢.
Carload bulk 9.90
Ton lots 11.55
Briquet, contract basis carlots, bulk
delivered, per lb of briquet 11.15
Ton lots 11.75

Silvery Iron (electric furnace)
Si 14.01 to 14.50 pct, f.o.b. Keokuk
Iowa, or Wenatchee, Wash., $89.50 gross
ton, freight allowed to normal trade area
Si 15.01 to 15.50 pct, f.o.b. Niagara Falls
N. Y., $83.00. Add $1.00 per ton for each
additional 0.50% Si up to and including
18%. Add $1.00 for each 0.50% Mn over
1%.

Silicon Metal
Contract price, cents per pound contained Si, lump size, delivered, for ton lots
packed.
96% Si, 2% Fe 21.70
97% Si, 1% Fe 22.10

Silicon Briquets
Contract price, cents per pound of
briquet bulk, delivered, 40% Si, 1 lb Si
briquets.
Carload, bulk 6.95
Ton lots 8.55

Electric Ferrosilicon
Contract price, cents per pound contained Si, lump, bulk, carloads, delivered.
25% Si..... 19.00   75% Si..... 14.30
50% Si..... 12.40   85% Si..... 15.55
90-95% Si 17.50

Calcium Metal
Eastern zone contract prices, cents per
pound of metal, delivered.

	Cast	Turnings	Distilled
Ton lots	$2.05	$2.95	$3.75
Less ton lots	2.40	3.30	4.55

Other Ferroalloys

Alsifer, 20% Al, 40% Si, 40% Fe,
contract basis, f.o.b. Suspension
Bridge, N. Y.
Carload .... 8.15¢
Ton lots .... 9.55¢

Calcium molybdate, 45-40%, f.o.b.
Langeloth, Pa., per pound contained Mo $1.15

Ferrocolumbium, 50-60%, 2 in x D,
contract basis, delivered, per
pound contained Cb.
Ton lots $4.90
Less ton lots 4.95

Ferro-Tantalum-columbium, 20%
Ta, 40% Cb, 0.30 C. Contract
basis, delivered, ton lots, 2 in. x
D, per lb of contained Cb plus Ta $3.75

Ferromolybdenum, 55-75%, f.o.b.
Langeloth, Pa., per pound contained Mo $1.32

Ferrophosphorus, electrolytic, 23-
26%, car lots, f.o.b. Siglo, Mt.
Pleasant, Tenn., $3 unitage, per
gross ton $65.00
10 tons to less carload 75.00

Ferrotitanium, 40%, regular grade,
0.10% C max., f.o.b. Niagara
Falls, N. Y., and Bridgeville, Pa.,
freight allowed, ton lots, per lb
contained Ti $1.31

Ferrotitanium, 25%, low carbon,
0.10% C max., f.o.b. Niagara
Falls, N. Y., and Bridgeville, Pa.,
freight allowed, ton lots, per lb
contained Ti $1.50
Less ton lots $1.55

Ferrotitanium, 15 to 19%, high carbon, f.o.b. Niagara Falls, N. Y.,
freight allowed, carload per net
ton $177.00

Ferrotungsten, standard, lump or
¼ x down, packed, per pound
contained W, 5 ton lots, delivered $3.25

Ferrovanadium, 35-55%, contract
basis, delivered, per pound, con-
tained V.
Openhearth .... $3.00-$3.05
Crucible 3.10- 3.15
High speed steel (Primos)..... 3.25

Molybdic oxide, briquets or cans,
per lb contained Mo, f.o.b. Langeloth, Pa. $1.14
bags, f.o.b. Washington, Pa.,
Langeloth, Pa. $1.13

Simanal, 20% Si, 20% Mn, 20%
Al, contract basis, f.o.b. Philo,
Ohio, freight allowed, per pound
Carload, bulk lump .... 14.50¢
Ton lots, bulk lump .... 15.75¢
Less ton lots, lump .... 16.25¢

Vanadium pentoxide, 88-92%
V₂O₅ contract basis, per pound
contained V₂O₅ $1.25

Zirconium, 35-40%, contract basis,
f.o.b. plant, freight allowed, per
pound of alloy.
Ton lots .... 21.00¢

Zirconium, 12-15%, contract basis,
lump, delivered, per lb of alloy.
Carload, bulk .... 7.00¢

Boron Agents
Contract prices per lb of alloy, del.
Borosil, f.o.b. Philo, Ohio, freight
allowed, B 3-4%, Si 40-45%, per
lb contained B $5.25

Bortam, f.o.b. Niagara Falls
Ton lots, per pound .... 45¢
Less ton lots, per pound..... 50¢

Carbortam, Ti 15-21%, B 1-2%, Si
2-4%, Al 1-2%, C 4.5-7.5%, f.o.b.
Suspension Bridge, N. Y., freight
allowed.
Ton lots, per pound .... 10.00¢

Ferroboron, 17.50% min. B, 1.50% max
Si, 0.50% max. Al, 0.50% max. C, 1 in
x D. Ton lots $1.30
F.o.b. Wash., Pa.; 100 lb, up
10 to 14% B .... .78
14 to 19% B 1.20
19% min. B 1.50

Grainal, f.o.b. Bridgeville, Pa.,
freight allowed, 100 lb and over.
No. 1 .... $1.00
No. 6 .... 68¢
No. 79 .... 50¢

Manganese—Boron 75.00% Mn, 15-20%
B, 5% max. Fe, 1.50% max. Si, 3.00%
max. C, 2 in. x D, delivered.
Ton lots $1.47
Less ton lots 1.57

Nickel—Boron 15-18% B, 1.00% max. Al
1.50% max. Si, 0.50% max. C, 3.00%
max. Fe, balance Ni, delivered.
Less ton lots $1.80

Silcaz, contract basis, delivered.
Ton lots .... 45.00¢

Defense Contracts to Metalworking Industry
Selected Contracts, Week of Jan. 22, 1951

Item	Quan.	Value	Company
Tanks	....	$99,000,000.00	Chrysler Corp., Detroit
Vehicles	....	76,000,000.00	Studebaker Corp., South Bend.
F-89 planes	......	....	Northrop Aircraft, Inc., Hawthorne
Ambulances	422	1,853,115.94	Watson Auto. Equip. Co., Wash., D. C.
Axles, gears	1,800	693,154.70	Federal Motor Trk. Co., Detroit
Retainer and axles	320	203,762.40	Ward LaFrance Trk. Co., Elmira
Engine	420	368,634.00	White Mtr. Co., Cleveland
Receiver-transmitter	....	621,741.00	Wilcox Electric Co., Inc., Kansas City
Airplanes	....	3,840,000.00	Douglas Aircraft Co., Inc., Santa Monica
Receiver-trans- mitter		1,559,237.00	Bendix Radio Div., Bendix Aviation Corp., Baltimore
Machmeters	......	338,164.00	Kollsman Instrument Div., Square D Co,. Elmhurst
Automatic pilots	....	2,000,000.00	Minneapolis-Honeywell Regulator Co., Minneapolis
Microwave systems	....	1,500,000.00	Philco Corp., Philadelphia
Trainers, simulators	....	2,000,000.00	Link Aviation, Inc., Binghamton
Flight computors	....	6,105,000.00	Sperry Gyroscope Co., Great Neck
Generators	......	1,163,808.00	Jack & Heintz Precision Ind., Inc., Cleveland
Amplifiers		315,997.00	Rauland Borg Corp., Chicago
Machinery		425,000.00	Eastman Kodak Co., Rochester
Oil filter assemblies	5,800	1,603,801.00	Purclator Products, Inc., Rahway
Helicopters	10	3,137,684.00	United Aircraft Corp., Bridgeport
Deck turrets	....	4,914,000.00	The Glenn L. Martin Co., Baltimore
Stowage cabinets	55,400	755,656.00	Sterod Mfg. Co., Newark, N. J.
Pumps	89	647,634.91	Blackmer Pump Co., Grand Rapids
Diesel engines	34	3,500,000.00	Packard Motor Car Co., Detroit
Power plants	25 ea.	130,000.00	O. E. Szekely, Philadelphia
Jet engine parts	....	5,150,000.00	Allison Div., General Motors Corp., Indianapolis
Power units	....	439,968.00	Sorensen & Co., Inc., Stamford

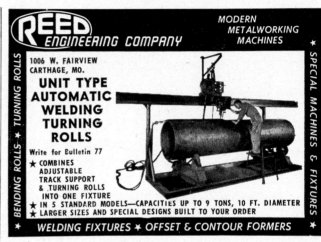

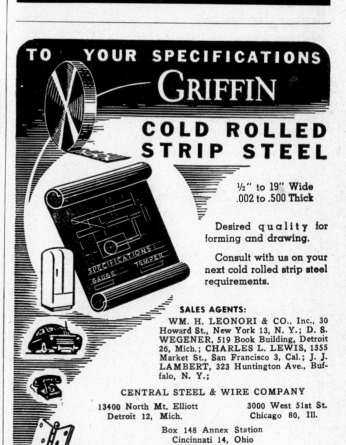

The Clearing House

NEWS OF USED, REBUILT AND SURPLUS MACHINERY

How to Plan—Dealers in rebuilt, reconditioned, and used machine tools will get hints on how to plan for their defense production roles at the Washington meeting to be held on Feb. 8 and 9 at the Wardman-Park Hotel. Members and non-members of the Machinery Dealers' National Assn. are urged to attend.

Speakers from the Defense Mobilization Board, the Defense Production Administration, Economic Stabilization Agency, National Production Authority, and NSRB will be on hand.

Things to Know—The trade may be able to get some inkling on Washington opinion on application of unbending NPA material restriction orders on an industry whose business volume fluctuates.

Rebuilders' rebuttal is that the industry has no planned schedules and that it was not on a regimented production line basis as are mass output industries. Problems of priorities, price controls, and probably production should also be of interest.

Reservations—J. M. P. Fox, MDNA executive director, announced that reservations have been made for 150 dealers at the Wardman-Park Hotel for Feb. 7, 8, and 9 and that rooms are mostly doubles. Dealers are asked to contact the hotel directly for an "MDNA Reservation" and send a copy of the request to the MDNA's national office, Chicago.

Duplicate Inquiries—Demand for used and rebuilt steel mill machinery in the Pittsburgh area has reached the point where anxious prospective buyers are resorting to a modification of the direct mail advertising technique.

A major dealer here reported that, while inquiries are heavy, he discovers that buyers are mailing the same inquiries to everyone in the business.

Cranes Scarce—Used cranes are still in scarcity. A few are circulating if buyers know where to look. Delivery dates on new equipment are so extended that used machinery dealers are swamped with inquiries. Generally, a new crane cannot be obtained for 9 months to a year.

With their own shortage difficulties, crane builders are being held back by slow deliveries of electrical equipment. One builder said that he must wait 40 weeks for delivery on motors.

Building Checkmate—Some crane users would like to build their own equipment. One interested party is checkmated by the lack of steel for end trucks and beams. According to one Pittsburgh dealer, one nice feature about the present market is that an inquiry usually leads to a sale —if the dealer can dig up the desired equipment.

Chief interest is in milling machines, lathes, radial drills and other standard equipment.

Defense Expectations—The high-pitched interest in automatics is due to a growing volume of defense business. Some are lining up equipment they think they will need. This tends to tighten the supply picture because some manufacturers who were ready to talk turkey on selling equipment as recently as a month ago have reconsidered.

Stock List—A 202-page stock list of both new and used machine tools, presses, sheet metal and woodworking machinery is offered by one of Britain's largest machinery houses. Equipment is illustrated, accompanied by detailed specifications and descriptive material. For overseas shipment, packing is done in the firm's own shops. F. J. Edwards, Ltd.

For free copy insert No. 20 on postcard on p. 35.

again and again

variable speed operation

makes a good job better

Better because variable speed operation pays off in higher rates of production, a more uniform better quality product and more efficient performance of your equipment and your operators.

Make the job better still by using Master Speedrangers because their all-metal construction makes them extremely compact and durable . . . more flexible and adaptable to a wide range of uses. They're available in sizes up to 5 horsepower with speed ranges up to 12 to 1 in most sizes.

Write for descriptive booklet Data 7525 and see how Master Speedrangers can help you get better results on material processing, handling and conveying equipment . . . mixers and agitators . . . machine tool drives . . . testing and calibrating equipment and many other applications.

THE MASTER ELECTRIC COMPANY • DAYTON 1, OHIO

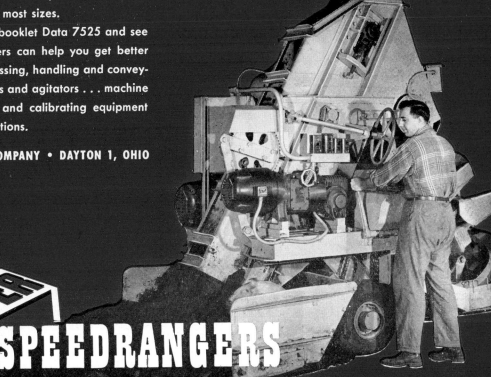

MASTER

SPEEDRANGERS

Ready for delivery now — from warehouse stock!

Two TIMKEN® wear-resistant steels that do 90% of your hollow parts jobs!

If you need steel tubing in a hurry for making hollow parts, let Timken® 52100 and "Nickel-moly" help you out. These two general purpose steels offer good hardenability and wear resistance. Between them, they can do nine out of ten of your hollow parts jobs. And they are available from Timken in warehouse quantities for immediate delivery.

Write for free stock list now. And remember, you're sure of uniformity in both these steels—from tube to tube and order to order—because of Timken's rigid quality controls. The Timken Roller Bearing Company, Steel and Tube Division, Canton 6, Ohio. Cable address: "TIMROSCO".

1. 52100 TUBING

A high carbon chrome steel. A direct quenching steel which gives through hardness in moderate sections. Can be heat treated to file hardness and tempered back to any desired point. Frequently may be used in place of more expensive steels. Typical uses include: aircraft parts, slitter knives, bearing races, collets, pump parts, bushings. Available in 101 sizes, ranging from 1″ to 10½″ O.D.

2. "NICKEL-MOLY" TUBING

A low carbon nickel-moly steel. A carburizing steel which gives high surface hardness with a tough core. Has exceptional stamina and shock absorbing qualities when heat treated. Used for: piston pins, bearings, sleeves, knitting machinery, farm equipment, pump parts, bushings, perforating guns. Available in 52 sizes, from 1.389″ to 10.223″ O.D.

YEARS AHEAD—THROUGH EXPERIENCE AND RESEARCH

TIMKEN
TRADE-MARK REG. U.S. PAT. OFF.
Fine Alloy
STEEL
and Seamless Tubes

Specialists in alloy steel—including hot rolled and cold finished alloy steel bars—a complete range of stainless, graphitic and standard tool analyses—and alloy and stainless seamless steel tubing

A CHILTON PUBLICATION

The Iron Age

E NATIONAL METALWORKING WEEKLY

February 1, 1951

ENTS PAGE 2

Nothing takes the place of

Chromel Alumel
thermocouples

When you're working with heat between 1000° and 2000° F. and accurate temperature measurement is essential to the results you want to produce, you'll find there is no suitable substitute for Hoskins CHROMEL-ALUMEL thermocouple alloys. They're unconditionally guaranteed to register true temperature— E.M.F. values within very close specified limits. Exceptionally durable . . . so resistant to oxidation that you need not pack the protection tube. Hence, highly responsive to temperature fluctuations. And, in spite of hard use, they maintain their fine degree of accuracy over far

longer periods of time than any other known base metal thermocouple materials.

So for positive long-life assurance of accurate temperature measurement, insist that your pyrometers be calibrated for CHROMEL-ALUMEL thermocouples. And important, too . . . be sure you use CHROMEL-ALUMEL *extension* leads instead of so-called "compensating" wires. For, when the couple and the lead are of identical alloy compositions there is no possibility of "cold-end" errors. Our Catalog 59-R contains a complete technical explanation . . . want a copy?

CHROMEL-ALUMEL couples and leads are available through your instrument manufacturer or pyrometer service company . . . ask for them by name!

HOSKINS MANUFACTURING COMPANY
4445 LAWTON AVE. • DETROIT 8, MICHIGAN
NEW YORK • CLEVELAND • CHICAGO
West Coast Representatives in Seattle, San Francisco, Los Angeles
In Canada: Walker Metal Products, Ltd., Walkerville, Ontario

Chromel ®

*the original nickel-chromium resistance alloy that first made electrical heating practical

MAY WE SPEAK OUR PIECE ABOUT
Gear Blanks?

These Bethlehem gear blanks are handsome to look at, and as good as they look. They're really something extra-special.

They're different from gear blanks made by conventional methods. In describing how they're made, we say that they're rolled and forged, or roll-forged. That is, the mill takes the hot blocks of steel, upsets them, and immediately rolls and forges in a single operation. Not just rolling, not just forging, but both . . . with the attendant *benefits* of both. Homogeneity, good grain structure, uniform density of metal.

The blanks are also rough-machined (something you don't have to worry about yourself!); then they're shipped to you ready for finish-machining. Sizes, approximately 10 in. to 42 in. OD; orders heat-treated or untreated, as you specify.

You'll like these blanks—their strength, their fine surface, their all-around goodness. Be sure you get them when planning your next output of spur, herringbone, bevel, or miter gears. And write for Booklet 216—it tells about gear blanks and the many other uses of Bethlehem circular steel forgings.

BETHLEHEM STEEL COMPANY, BETHLEHEM, PA.

On the Pacific Coast Bethlehem products are sold by Bethlehem Pacific Coast Steel Corporation. *Export Distributor:* Bethlehem Steel Export Corporation

BETHLEHEM
STEEL

BETHLEHEM ROLLED-AND-FORGED CIRCULAR PRODUCTS

IRON AGE

CONTENTS

THE IRON AGE

Editorial, Advertising and Circulation Offices, 100 E. 42nd St., New York 17, N. Y.

GEORGE T. HOOK, Publisher
TOM C. CAMPBELL, Editor

EDITORIAL STAFF

Managing Editor   George F. Sullivan
Feature Editor   Darwyn I. Brown
News-Markets Editor   Wm. V. Packard
Machinery Editor   George Elwers
Associate Editors: William Czygan, H. W. Van Camp, F. J. Winters; Assistant Editors: R. L. Hatschek, J. Kolb, Ted Metaxas, W. B. Olson; Regional Editors: E. C. Beaudet, Chicago; W. A. Lloyd, Cleveland; W. G. Patton, Detroit; John B. Delaney, Pittsburgh; Osgood Murdock, R. T. Reinhardt, San Francisco; Eugene J. Hardy, Karl Rannells, George H. Baker, Washington; Correspondents: Fred L. Allen, Birmingham; N. Levenson, Boston; Fred Edmunds, Los Angeles; James Douglas, Seattle; Roy Edmonds, St. Louis; F. Sanderson, Toronto; F. H. Harley, London, England; Chilton Editorial Board: Paul Wooton, Washington Representative.

BUSINESS STAFF

Production Manager   B. H. Hayes
Director of Research   Oliver Johnson
Mgr. Circul'n & Promotion   C. T. Post
Asst. Promotion Mgr.   James A. Crites
Asst. Dir. of Research   Wm. Laimbeer

REGIONAL BUSINESS MANAGERS

B. L. Herman, Philadelphia; Stanley J. Smith, Chicago; Peirce Lewis, Detroit; Paul Bachman, New England; Robert F. Blair, Cleveland; R. Raymond Kay, Los Angeles; C. H. Ober, New York; J. M. Spackman, Pittsburgh; Harry Becker, European Representative.

REGIONAL OFFICES

Chicago 3, 1134 Otis Bldg.; Cleveland 14, 1016 National City Bank Bldg., Detroit 2, 103 Pallister Ave.; Los Angeles 28, 2420 Cheremoya Ave.; New England, 62 La Salle Rd., W. Hartford 7; New York 17, 100 E. 42nd St.; Philadelphia 39, 56th & Chestnut Sts.; Pittsburgh 22, 814 Park Bldg.; Washington 4, National Press Bldg.; European, 111 Thorley Lane, Timperley, Cheshire, England.

Circulation Representatives: Thomas Scott, James Richardson.

One of the Publications Owned and Published by Chilton Company, Inc., Chestnut & 56th Sts., Philadelphia 39, Pa., U. S. A.

OFFICERS AND DIRECTORS

JOS. S. HILDRETH, President
Vice-Presidents: Everit B. Terhune, G. C. Buzby, P. M. Fahrendorf, Harry V. Duffy. William H. Vallar, Treasurer; John Blair Moffett, Secretary; D. Allyn Garber, Maurice E. Cox, Frank P. Tighe, George T. Hook, Tom C. Campbell, L. V. Rowlands, Directors. George Maiswinkle, Asst. Treas.

Indexed in the Industrial Arts Index and the Engineering Index. Published every Thursday by the CHILTON CO. (INC.), Chestnut and 56th Sts., Philadelphia 39, Pa. Entered as second class matter Nov. 8, 1932, at the Post Office at Philadelphia under the act of March 3, 1879. $8 yearly in United States, its territories and Canada; other Western Hemisphere Countries $15; other Foreign Countries $25 per year. Single Copies 35c. Annual Review and Metal Industry Facts issue, $2.00. Cable address "Ironage" N. Y.

Member Audit Bureau of Circulations. Member Society of Business Magazine Editors.

Copyright, 1951, by Chilton Co. (Inc.)

DIGEST

FEBRUARY FIRST · NINETEEN FIFTY-ONE · VOLUME 167 · NUMBER 5

contour the special job on a
Cincinnati Shaper...at low cost

The special job is often a time-eater — and a cost raiser.

This handy Cincinnati Shaper saves time — saves money — on many special jobs. Little time is lost on setups — costly fixtures and special equipment are not needed.

Contouring this 1200-pound tank stave die — roughed and finished in 4 hours — is done at low cost with simple tools and simple setup. It is an example of many jobs performed on versatile Cincinnati Shapers at lowered costs.

Write for Shaper Catalog N-5, where many uses of Cincinnati Shapers are illustrated, and the wide line described.

THE CINCINNATI SHAPER CO.
CINCINNATI 25, OHIO U.S.A.
SHAPERS · SHEARS · BRAKES

**Yes!
we build
Billet Mills**

JONES & LAUGHLINS, LTD.	Pittsburgh, Pa.	
CARNEGIE STEEL CO.	Duquesne, Pa.	189.
CARNEGIE STEEL CO.	Duquesne, Pa.	190
NATIONAL STEEL CO.	Youngstown, Ohio	1900
SHARON STEEL CO.	Sharon, Pa.	1901
GRAND CROSSING TACK CO.	Chicago, Ill.	1901
DOMINION IRON & STEEL CO.	Sydney, N. S.	1903
YOUNGSTOWN SHEET & TUBE CO.	Youngstown, Ohio	1905
LACKAWANNA STEEL CO.*	Buffalo, N. Y.	1906
INDIANA STEEL CO.	Gary, Ind.	1907
INDIANA STEEL CO.	Gary, Ind.	1907
PITTSBURGH STEEL CO.	Monessen, Pa.	1908
JONES & LAUGHLINS, LTD.	Aliquippa, Pa.	1909
JONES & LAUGHLIN STEEL CO.*	Aliquippa, Pa.	1909
CAMBRIA STEEL CO.*	Johnstown, Pa.	1909
REPUBLIC IRON & STEEL CO.	Youngstown, Ohio	1910
REPUBLIC IRON & STEEL CO.*	Youngstown, Ohio	1910
ATLANTA STEEL CO.	Atlanta, Ga.	1912
STEEL CO. OF CANADA*	Hamilton, Ont.	1912
BETHLEHEM STEEL COMPANY	Bethlehem, Pa.	1913
RIVER FURNACE COMPANY	Cleveland, Ohio	1913
RIVER FURNACE COMPANY*	Cleveland, Ohio	1913
UNITED STEEL CO.*	Canton, Ohio	1915
STEEL, PEECH & TOZER, LTD.	Rotherham, England	1916
DONNER STEEL COMPANY	Buffalo, N. Y.	1916
BETHLEHEM STEEL COMPANY	Sparrows Point, Md.	1917
BETHLEHEM STEEL COMPANY*	Sparrows Point, Md.	1917
TRUMBULL STEEL COMPANY	Warren, Ohio	1917
STEEL, PEECH & TOZER, LTD.	Sheffield, England	1917
TATA IRON & STEEL COMPANY	Sakchi, India	1917
TATA IRON & STEEL COMPANY*	Sakchi, India	1917
WICKWIRE STEEL COMPANY	Buffalo, N. Y.	1918
TRUMBULL STEEL COMPANY	Warren, Ohio	1919
WEIRTON STEEL COMPANY	Weirton, W. Va.	1919
WEIRTON STEEL COMPANY*	Weirton, W. Va.	1919
WHITAKER-GLESSNER COMPANY*	Portsmouth, Ohio	1919
ACIERIES DE LONGWY	Mont-St. Martin, France	1919
ACIERIES DE LONGWY*	Mont-St. Martin, France	1919
HOMECOURT, FORGES & ACIERIES	Homecourt, France	1919
HOMECOURT, FORGES & ACIERIES*	Homecourt, France	1919
DENAIN & ANZIN	Denain, France	1920
DENAIN & ANZIN*	Denain, France	1920
BROKEN HILL PROPRIETARY CO.*	Newcastle, Australia	1920
INLAND STEEL COMPANY***	Indiana Harbor, Ind.	1922
FORD MOTOR COMPANY	River Rouge, Mich.	1922
REPUBLIC IRON & STEEL CO.	Youngstown, Ohio	1923
REPUBLIC IRON & STEEL CO.**	Youngstown, Ohio	1923
YOUNGSTOWN SHEET & TUBE COMPANY	Youngstown, Ohio	1923
TENNESSEE COAL, IRON & R.R. CO.*	Birmingham, Ala.	1924
FORD MOTOR COMPANY*	River Rouge, Mich.	1925
INLAND STEEL COMPANY*	Indiana Harbor, Ind.	1925
AMERICAN STEEL & WIRE CO.	Worcester, Mass.	1926
INTERSTATE IRON & STEEL CO.	Chicago, Ill.	1927
JOHN A. ROEBLING'S SONS CO.	Trenton, N. J.	1927
SHEFFIELD STEEL CORPORATION	Kansas City, Mo.	1928
YOUNGSTOWN SHEET & TUBE CO.***	Indiana Harbor, Ind.	1929
FRIEDRICH KRUPP, A. G.***	Rheinhausen, Germany	1929
FRIEDRICH KRUPP, A. G.*	Rheinhausen, Germany	1929
BRITISH (G. K. B.) IRON & STEEL CO.*	Cardiff, Wales	1934
AUSTRALIAN IRON & STEEL, LTD.*	Port Kembla, Australia	1936
YOUNGSTOWN SHEET & TUBE CO.***	Youngstown, Ohio	1940
BETHLEHEM STEEL CO.	Lackawanna, N. Y.	1945
JOHN LYSAGHT, LTD.*	Scunthorpe, England	1947
OESTERREICHISCHE ALPINE MONTANGESELLSCHAFT	Leoben-Donawitz, Austria	1949
CONSETT IRON COMPANY, LTD.***	Consett, England	1950

*Mill also rolls sheet bar
**Mill also rolls sheet bar and skelp
***Mill also rolls slabs

RYERSON STEELGRAMS

Swift—changing conditions in today's steel market are so difficult to follow—perhaps these few paragraphs will prove helpful.

Warehouse steel stocks were again recognized as vital to defense by the Government's NPA order which allots a share of "free tonnage" production to steel distributors. The regulation is helpful. However, even at this early stage, Rated Orders and special government programs have substantially reduced total "free tonnage" — reducing the share going to distributors proportionately.

We are doing everything possible to maintain reasonable stocks for warehouse buyers. But, as we see it at the moment, we shall have less steel to distribute among our many customers in the coming months. It will be helpful if you order only for immediate needs and extend DO ratings whenever possible.

More steel will be available in some specialized cases. Example: Ryerson stocks of aircraft alloys. New program gives Ryerson plants a range of more than 400 sizes, finishes and conditions of aircraft alloy bars and strip. Included are alloys for aircraft parts manufacturers, airframe makers and engine builders conforming to new MIL-S and to AMS specifications. Aircraft quality stainless stocks have also been enlarged.

More on stainless and alloys — Some steel users may not know that the Government is issuing a single set of MIL (Military) specifications to replace the different U. S. Army, Navy, Air Force, Air Force—Navy, and Federal specifications previously in effect. The new specifications for a few products have yet to be published, but Ryerson alloy and stainless stocks assure a warehouse source for all the important MIL "specs" now in effect and, as additional products are covered, Ryerson stocks will be immediately brought into line.

Ryerson tubing stocks, not affected quite as much as some products by the tight steel market, are being enlarged to include Rockrite tubing (with close I. D. tolerance and better I. D. finish for hydraulic cylinder applications) and pressure tubing to JIC "specs". Fairly adequate stocks of both are in prospect. This is in addition to seamless and welded mechanical tubing, extra heavy wall hot rolled tubing, structural tubing.

Changes on the nation's railroads are not confined to rolling stock, in railway shops alloy chain is finding increased acceptance as a replacement for wrought iron slings. Reasons are easy to find. The alloy chain packs three times the tensile strength of wrought iron. Lasts 5 to 15 times longer. Taylor Made Alloy chain, available from Ryerson, costs little or no more than wrought iron. It is widely used for overhead lifting in most all industries. Other types of chain also available for prompt shipment.

Wire rope, especially desirable where chain may cause damage, is currently available in a wide range of types and sizes. Shipment from Ryerson is prompt.

Availability of high tin content babbitt metal is threatened by the short tin supply. Not affected — Ryerson production of Glyco babbitt metal. Made by a special process, it has physical properties equal to those of high—tin babbitt, costs considerably less, and remains in good supply.

Indications are that metal fabricators contemplating purchase of machinery and tools should make an early decision on placing orders. Ryerson can still make fairly prompt shipment on many types, but demand is strong and delivery schedules are lengthening. All but lighter tools are currently offered on the basis of 5 to 8 months.

JOSEPH T. RYERSON & SON, INC. STEEL-SERVICE PLANTS: NEW YORK • BOSTON • PHILADELPHIA • DETROIT • CINCINNATI
CLEVELAND • PITTSBURGH • BUFFALO • CHICAGO • MILWAUKEE • ST. LOUIS • LOS ANGELES • SAN FRANCISCO • 1-15-51

IRON AGE

editorial

We're Stuck With It

AT long last we have the price and wage freeze with us. The air will be rent with arguments from here on out. Cries from some will be high pitched; from others will come anguished yowls. It was that way last time; it will be that way this time.

Those who are opposed to controls will not change their minds. Those who wanted controls will find they are not the whole answer. Those who thought controls should have come long ago will say "I told you so." All will have a part of truth on their side. But none will be satisfied.

The months ahead will be tough on everyone. This country does not take to man-made controls. No man or group of men knows even a part of the answers. Revisions will come time and time again before we have anything approaching a fair setup. Those who brought on controls by their lack of restraint and greediness will be the same ones who will be responsible for the black markets to come.

Those who think that ceilings and controls are the answer to everything are in for trouble. Ceilings came simply because even in a war or defense period voluntary restraint means no more than lip service to many. Even though the majority would and could have gone along with a voluntary plan, there were enough others to wreck and make a mockery of such a setup.

Those who feel the Administration acted too late are right but neither the people nor Congress were ready 6 months ago to agree to controls. Those who want no controls at all have too much faith in formulas and paper economics. They have had little experience with human nature. Even the most conservative industrialists who wanted no controls 6 months ago, long ago privately said we should have them.

Controls will not stop inflation. The best they can do is to slow it up a little. There will be more price increases. There must be, if fair treatment is the standard. We have no Solomon to answer our complex 20th century problems. Wages and salaries will not really be frozen. They too will go up under the guise of correcting inequities and other high sounding phrases.

If we are to prevent an inflationary defeat for us and success for Stalin, we must do far more than put this dynamic economy under controls. We need higher taxes, far more stringent credit curbs, a much heavier savings program for all people, a paying off of private debts, a sharp reduction in non-defense spending and a brutal realization of how close we are coming to losing our liberty because of communism.

We are stuck with controls. Somehow they must be made to work. The stumbling around will be pitiful for a long time. Unless we attack inflation at its roots, reliance on controls alone will wreck us as surely as the commies will.

Tom Campbell

Editor

FROM LAMINATIONS TO REFRIGERATOR DOORS...
BLISS HAS THE RIGHT PRESS FOR THE JOB

A picture tour of Bliss Presses in action
at various General Electric Company plants

Whether your metal-stamping production is large or small, requiring automatic or hand-fed presses...mechanical and hydraulic...Bliss has the right press for your job.

Illustrated here are but a few examples of specially engineered Bliss equipment at work in various General Electric Company plants. Thousands of others are producing profits for leading manufacturers the world over.

For blanking, forming, drawing or squeezing operations, Bliss engineers are equipped to make unbiased analyses and recommendations for proper methods and equipment. Bliss is the only company that builds the complete range of press equipment required by industry.

Next time you need advice on metal-stamping production, call your Bliss representative. Show him your high-cost stampings. Selecting proper equipment and methods is "everyday" business with Bliss engineers, who are skilled in pressed-metal techniques and equipment. There's a good chance that they can give you the right answer.

E. W. BLISS COMPANY, TOLEDO 7, OHIO
Mechanical and Hydraulic Presses, Rolling Mills, Container Machinery

AT ERIE, PENNSYLVANIA: Doors for home refrigerators are drawn in this 350-ton Bliss "E" type straight side press equipped with Bliss-Marquette die cushions.

BLISS BUILT

FROM THE RIGHT PRESS FOR A GIVEN JOB...

IRON AGE *newsfront*

► Look for <u>pig iron to get tighter</u> as steelmaking capacity expands. Melting furnace construction takes <u>less time</u> than blast furnaces; the time lag will cut into merchant iron supplies from some plants.

► A laboratory process has been developed for making <u>hematite ore</u> (Fe_2O_3) <u>magnetic.</u> This will permit <u>magnetic separation</u> of low grade hematite. Until this development came along the magnetic separation of iron from its ore was only possible on magnetic ore (Fe_3O_4).

► <u>Aluminum cartridge cases</u> are being considered for small caliber ammunition. The <u>reduction in weight</u> would be particularly attractive in machine gun and small cannon ammunition for aircraft.

► Acute tinplate shortages are reported in South America, in England and on the Continent. Some foreign canneries have already <u>laid off help</u> because of the shortage but <u>U. S. exports are likely to go down</u> because of restrictions. Though thinner tin coatings will be more widely used, the outlook is for <u>more canning in glass</u> during the present emergency.

► By 1953, the <u>electric generating capacity reserve</u> over peak loads in the U. S. will increase from the current 11.8 pct to a more comfortable 19.9 pct, according to an industry observer known for his accurate estimates.
The only thing that <u>could upset this prediction</u> is a tremendous expansion in aluminum, magnesium and perhaps electric furnace steel. With government and industry pressure strong for boosting metal production, the <u>margin may turn out to be less comfortable</u> than is generally assumed.

► <u>German cars</u> will be assembled in <u>Brazil; Fiat</u> will assemble <u>in Mexico</u> and two English firms, <u>Austin</u> and the <u>Rootes group will build assembly plants in Mexico.</u> U. S. car manufacturers have had Mexican plants for some time but the European influx is significant.

► The British are trying to interest the U. S. in their <u>twin jet flying boat fighter</u> plane built by Saunders-Roe.

► A top-notch research institute is now studying <u>ways of improving the method of adding magnesium to nodular or ductile cast iron.</u> The aim is to overcome the difficulty of accurately controlling the percentage range of residual magnesium introduced into the bath and the efficiency of additions in terms of total recovery.
<u>Gaseous magnesium</u> and magnesium compounds of <u>low volatility</u> are being tried.

► Contrary to some generally held opinions, porcelain enamel <u>will not crack or chip from steel until the yield point</u> of the steel has been reached <u>or exceeded.</u> It fails only after a certain amount of <u>strain,</u> which has no relation to the strength of the metal.

► Tentative specifications for <u>iron powder rotating bands</u> on 90-mm and 105-mm shells have been developed. Efforts made during World War II to interest the Army in these bands were fruitless although the <u>Germans made wide use of them.</u> The principal gain would be to <u>take some pressure off critically short copper.</u>

"I wasn't asleep," said the Dormouse

EVERY boy and girl knows the drowsy Dormouse of Alice in Wonderland. He was elbowed and pinched by the Mad Hatter and the March Hare as he mumbled in his sleep at the tea party.

But our young people aren't so well versed in everyday economics. They have a sadly distorted picture of the profits of business. They don't realize why profits are necessary, how small they are, or how they are divided.

For instance, in a recent survey of high school seniors, it was discovered that they believe over 50% of the sales dollar is profit and they think stockholders receive 24% of it. Actually business profit averages less than 8%, with less than 3%

distributed as dividends. Business uses most of its profit, moderate as it is, for new plant and equipment, to improve products and to make more jobs.

Misconceptions among our youth bode ill for America's future. They open the door for too ready acceptance of dangerous isms and false foreign philosophies. Such misunderstanding of economics can be corrected only with facts supplied by business itself. You as a leader in your community must share this responsibility.

The American business man must not allow himself to be cast in the role of the Dormouse, pinched and pilloried by the March Hares of communism and the Mad Hatters of the "everything for nothing" state.

The Youngstown Sheet and Tube Company

General Offices -- Youngstown 1, Ohio

Export Offices -- 500 Fifth Avenue, New York

MANUFACTURERS OF CARBON, ALLOY AND YOLOY STEELS

ELECTROLYTIC TIN PLATE · COKE TIN PLATE · WIRE · COLD FINISHED CARBON AND ALLOY BARS · PIPE AND TUBULAR PRODUCTS · CONDUIT · RODS · SHEETS · PLATES · BARS · RAILROAD TRACK SPIKES.

IRON AGE *summary*

iron and steel industry trends

Capacity of 120 Million Tons Seen by '52
Eastern Capacity Second Only to Pittsburgh
Shell Steel Orders Lifted from DO List

THE greatest steel expansion in history will reach a climax about the end of 1952 when annual ingot capacity will exceed 120 million net tons. This new total results from a study of capacity expansion by companies and plants just completed by THE IRON AGE. Some programs listed are still under consideration; some that have been announced are likely to be on the conservative side.

When the last rivet is driven home the industry's competitive map will be largely redrawn. The Pittsburgh-Youngstown district will retain the No. 1 spot with capacity of more than 43.6 million ingot tons. The East will replace Chicago in the runner-up position with 28 million tons, compared with close to 24 million tons. Cleveland-Detroit capacity will be 13.3 million tons; the West 6.4 million, and the South 5.6 million. This totals 120.7 million tons, an increase of 21.4 million over capacity at Jan. 1, 1950.

Three Factors Promote Expansion

This tremendous expansion has been spurred by three factors: (1) Opportunity of amortizing part of the cost over 5 years for tax purposes; (2) the defense effort, and (3) encouraging results from market studies of the long range demand for steel.

Complaints about the wage-price freeze are frequent and loud. Early this week there were indications that some of the frozen area would be thawed. Price roll-backs were expected momentarily on some items. Indications were that in the future this order would act as a flexible restraint, rather than a deep-freeze.

Confusion still reigns in the steel market. Producers still lack any concrete knowledge of what is expected of them, except that it is plenty. As a result they are not able to give their customers any definite idea as to what they may expect. Pressure for more certain knowledge grows.

There are indications that the present priority system of placing defense orders in steel mills is starting to collapse under its own weight. Hot-rolled bars of projectile or shell quality steel have been lifted out of the DO category entirely. They are now subject to direct negotiation with NPA. This change also applies to shell quality billets, and rolled armor plate.

Government Directives Change Plans

Steel producers are finding it more and more difficult to maintain production schedules. The reason is that no production schedule is ever final. Just when they think they are all set a new government directive forces them to change their plans. The freight car program is interfering with the DO's, the oil country goods program is interfering with the freight car program, etc. Program requirements have reached the saturation point as far as some companies are concerned.

The steel picture would quickly become a lot clearer if the Military could make known its definite needs in terms of numbers of guns, tanks, ships, and planes. Until they do this the confusion will become worse. Such concrete clarification is believed to be at least 30 to 60 days away.

Some Progress to Clarification

However, some progress is finally being made towards this goal. The Military are now working out some arms requirements schedules. When this job is finished the needs can then be converted and scheduled by tons of steel required.

Steelmaking operations this week are scheduled at 101.5 pct of rated capacity, up half a point from the previous week. If equaled, this rate will yield another new all-time record for steel melted in a single week. The previous record was established last week.

(nonferrous summary, p. 170)

Nine welds for *14 cents!*

*(including loading
and unloading time)*

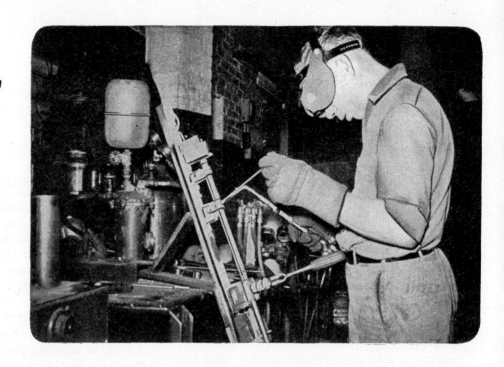

That's all it costs for labor to braze-weld the nine joints required for assembly of this smart tubular steel Collapsible Golf Bag Cart. It's a product of the Lake Manufacturing Co. of Lansing, Michigan and, to make the welds, they used ANACONDA "997" (Low Fuming) Welding Rod supplied by our distributor, Purity Cylinder Gases Inc., Grand Rapids.

Here again is striking evidence that ANACONDA Welding Rods are money-savers in modern production welding. In the list of ANACONDA Rods you are likely to find the welding rod that has exactly the right properties to serve you best and save you most in your manufacturing or repair-welding operations.

Anaconda specialists who know welding thoroughly will help you—arrange demonstrations of ANACONDA Welding Rods on your work any time you say. Let them show you. Just write The American Brass Company, Waterbury 20, Connecticut. In Canada: Anaconda American Brass Ltd., New Toronto, Ontario.

ANACONDA Welding Rods are sold by distributors throughout the United States.

51147

You can depend on
ANACONDA® *bronze welding rods*

DEPENDABLE CHEMICALS
for the Steel Industry

More than fifty years ago, General Chemical shipped the first of its quality chemicals to the steel industry. Today, as then, General Chemical continues to supply leaders in the industry with chemicals vital to efficient production. For your requirements, *be sure ... specify General Chemical ... first in "Basic Chemicals for American Industry."*

For Rimming Steel
SODIUM FLUORIDE

For Pickling, Descaling, Electroplating, Galvanizing, Tinning
SULFURIC ACID

HYDROCHLORIC ACID
  (Muriatic)

NITRIC ACID

HYDROFLUORIC ACID

FLUOBORIC ACID

BASIC CHEMICALS

FOR AMERICAN INDUSTRY

Other Products for the Steel Industry

COPPER FLUORIDE for gray steel; better fluidity and machinability, improved tensile and transverse strength.

BARIUM FLUORIDE for heat treating.

Oxalic Acid • Trisodium Phosphate • Sodium Metasilicate
Sodium Silicate • Sodium Bisulfite, Anhydrous • Sodium
Sulfite, Anhydrous • Phosphoric Acid • Perchloric Acid

For the Laboratory: Baker & Adamson Reagents.

GENERAL CHEMICAL DIVISION
ALLIED CHEMICAL & DYE CORPORATION
40 Rector Street, New York 6, N. Y.

Offices: Albany • Atlanta • Baltimore • Birmingham • Boston • Bridgeport • Buffalo • Charlotte
Chicago • Cleveland • Denver • Detroit • Houston • Los Angeles • Minneapolis • New York • Philadelphia
Pittsburgh • Providence • San Francisco • Seattle • St. Louis • Wenatchee and Yakima (Wash.)
In Wisconsin: General Chemical Company, Inc., Milwaukee, Wis.

In Canada: The Nichols Chemical Company, Limited • Montreal • Toronto • Vancouver

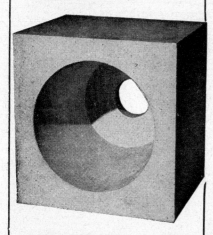

Dear EDITOR

Letters From Readers

Where To Spend It?

Sir:

I have not seen anything in your paper recently regarding Portsmouth Steel Co., Portsmouth, Ohio. They sold their plants about a year ago and have in their treasury about $12 million, which belongs to the stockholders.

Although they are still paying dividends, I have not heard of them doing any business since closing. The question is, what are they going to do with this money?

M. E. JOHNSON
West Long Branch, N. J.

This money has not been reinvested. As far as we are able to determine, it is still the intention of the controlling interests to reinvest their money at some later date, and they are still seeking a suitable investment.—Ed.

Readers' Opinions Solicited

Sir:

We have a client who is anxious to know if the sizing of black hot-rolled steel bars, some of which are up to 0.010 in. out of round, can be done economically in a draw bench in the as-rolled condition. It is desired to avoid the operation of pickling, as the product is not required to have bright finish. The presence of scale imbedded in the product is not objected to.

The amount of reduction would be about 0.010 to 0.015 in. on bars ⅜ to ¾ in. in diam. Material 28/32 and 25/40 tensile mild steel. Some of your readers may be able to give their experience on cold drawing under these conditions, indicating the life to be expected from tungsten carbide or other dies, speed of drawing, power required, lubricants, and so forth.

J. J. QUINN
Managing Director
Metal Products (Cork) Ltd.
Cork, Ireland

Unpickled bars are not customarily cold-drawn in this country. The scale would be too detrimental to the life of tungsten carbide dies. In fact, it would probably be cheaper to pickle than to redress or replace the dies.

With the small amount of reduction required, it might be possible to draw the material in the unpickled condition with cheaper dies. The best solution might be to run the bars through a roll straightening machine. These machines are capable of reducing the bars the specified amount and would also serve as a very fine scale breaker, except that the bars will show imperfections of scale marks. Perhaps our readers have some other ideas.—Ed.

Possible Solution

Sir:

Your article on extruding axle spindles, p. 108, June 15, 1950, was of great interest to us. Mr. Chase mentioned a swabbing compound of 60 pct machine oil, 25 pct Brooks compound and 15 pct Ceylon plumbago. Would you be good enough to give us further information as to this Brooks compound, as it may help us with some of our difficulties with dies.

W. R. McKAY
H. V. McKay Massey Harris Ltd.
Sunshine, Australia

The compound is made by the Brooks Oil Co., 934 Ridge Ave., Pittsburgh 12, Pa. More complete information may be obtained by writing directly to them.—Ed.

On Inspection Standards

Sir:

Your Dec. 14, 1950 issue carries an item pertaining to new uniform inspection standards. You state that Sec. XIV is a new regulation just issued by the Defense Dept. Since we now have several contracts and subcontracts we would like to know where and how this Sec. XIV can be obtained.

O. C. OLSEN
Mgr. Quality Control
Vendo Co.
Kansas City

Copies of Sec. XIV of the Armed Services Procurement Regulation may be obtained from the Munitions Board, Washington, D. C.—Ed.

Good Prediction

Sir:

I have not finished looking through your Jan. 4th issue but I have just re-read your editorial "What's Ahead" and I want to congratulate you on the cleancut, hardhitting presentation of the facts of life facing us this year. I particularly like your last sentence and I hope we do put up because if we don't I think we may *be* shut up. It's a good job, and it's an eye-opener, too.

G. VAN ALSTYNE
Advertising Mgr.
Air Reduction Sales Co.
New York

Capital "C" See?

Sir:

We have noted with interest the article "Lathe Tools Used in Milling Cutter" on p. 103 of your Dec. 14, 1950, issue, and appreciate your reference to our product. However, may we ask that in future references to the word "Carboloy" a capital "C" be used? "Carboloy" is our registered trademark and its use with a lower case "c" tends to jeopardize our trademark interests.

E. C. HOWELL
Merchandising Mgr.
Carboloy Co., Inc.
Detroit

Of course Carboloy is a well-known trademark, and we apologize for the typographical error.—Ed.

So you Want Accuracy Speed Durability... WELL HERE YOU ARE...

ON ERIE HAMMERS ALL STRESSED PARTS, UPPER WORKS, FRAME AND ANVIL ARE STEEL.

ERIE FOUNDRY COMPANY · ERIE, PA.

ERIE BUILDS *Dependable* **HAMMERS**

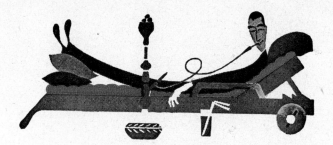

Fatigue Cracks

by Charles T. Post

Veto

Let this stand as a warning to guard carefully copies of your favorite family journal and report immediately to the F.B.I. if you see any suspicious characters snooping around them. At this moment you hold in your hand information which Soviet foreign agents undoubtedly have been instructed to get at all costs.

We weren't going to say much about it, but since the national news services, _Time,_ and a few assorted gossip columns have whispered across the country that your f.f.j. has stopped sending copies to Russia and friends at the request of the U. S. State Dept., you'll be relieved to know it's true. As a result, Fort Knox will receive nearly $10,000 less Russian gold this year, since the Soviets, like other eastern hemisphere subscribers, have been paying $25 per annual subscription . . . and cheerfully.

As recently as last fall, State's attitude, as we understood it, was that your f.f.j.'s depiction of the American industrial machine in action was effective propaganda behind the Iron Curtain. But times have changed, and apparently Moscow has become a little cozy with some of its technical magazines, so State asked if we would kindly cut off the Eastern European copies. It could be, too, that someone remembered your f.f.j.'s innocent little piece correctly appraising what was going on at Oak Ridge, Tenn., almost a year before that mushroom cloud rose over New Mexico. The censor caught that one, at the last minute and the same censor may not be working there any more.

So far as we know, no other publication has received a similar request from Dean Acheson's men, but then, there is no other publication like your f.f.j. None that carries such hush-hush data as Fatigue Cracks, anyhow.

Fishbowl

At the annual convention of the Institute of Scrap Iron & Steel, the promotion department filled a fishbowl with pieces of sheet scrap, offered a fancy wrist watch to the scrap man who could estimate most closely the number. The scrap experts stared, pondered, scratched their heads, then came up with estimates ranging from 200 to 90,000 instead of the actual 1653. The biggest sucker, of course, was your f.f.j., which paid $8.53 for about 15 lb of scrap, or about $1137 a ton.

Puzzlers

After the flood of letters on the trick circle problem we were a little disappointed to see so few answers to the ball problem in the Jan. 18 issue. Could it be that the rearmament program is taking up too much of our readers' time. War is hell! For those who tried it the answers are 47.618 fps, 19.357 ft and 27.481 fps.

H. M. Barnes, Chrysler Corp., is the latest to remind us that we were trying to make a mountain out of a mole hill with the circle problem in the Jan. 11 issue.

Here is a puzzler that is just a little different from the usual run of problems in this column. A. M. Woodall, The Ingalls Iron Works Co., poses this one. A 24 in. sphere consists of a spherical steel core with a specific gravity of 7.84 and a uniformly thick cork cover of 0.24 specific gravity. What is the thickness of the cork cover if the composite sphere has a specific gravity of unity?

60 million

just isn't enough

Sixty million is a lot of anything and that is the number of items Townsend can produce in one working day. Lately it just isn't enough to go around. We have strained every facility and every source of raw material to keep our production above average—but we still can't keep ahead of our orders.

So, if our delivery date for large and small cold-headed solid rivets and tubular rivets, special nails, fasteners, parts and other gadgets is longer than usual, please bear with us.

We believe our backlog of orders is in some measure caused by the savings we have created for our customers—so we intend to keep quality up to our rigid standards, no matter how busy we get.

Even if you must wait for delivery—you can count on Townsend quality control which has back of it 135 years of experience in wire drawing and cold-heading.

Townsend

COMPANY · ESTABLISHED 1816

Plants—New Brighton, Pa. · Chicago 38, Ill.

Division Sales Offices—Philadelphia, Detroit, Chicago

DATES
to remember

Feb. 19-22—American Institute of Mining & Metallurgical Engineers, annual meeting, Jefferson Hotel, St. Louis, Institute headquarters are at 29 W. 39th St., New York.

Mar. 5-7—Hydraulic Institute, quarterly meeting, Santa Barbara Biltmore Hotel, Santa Barbara, Calif. Institute headquarters are at 122 E. 42nd St., New York.

Mar. 5-7—Manufacturers Standardization Society of the Valve and Fittings Industry, annual meeting, Commodore Hotel, New York. Society headquarters are at 420 Lexington Ave., New York.

Mar. 5-7—Pittsburgh Conference on Analytical Chemistry and Applied Spectroscopy, William Penn Hotel, Pittsburgh. American Chemical Society national headquarters are at 1155 16th St., Washington.

Mar. 5-9—American Society for Testing Materials, spring meeting, Cincinnati. Society headquarters are at 1916 Race St., Philadelphia.

Mar. 6-8—Society of Automotive Engineers, passenger car, body and materials meetings, Hotel Book-Cadillac, Detroit. Society headquarters are at 29 W. 39th St., New York.

Mar. 12-15—National Electrical Manufacturers Assn., spring meeting, Edgewater Beach Hotel, Chicago. Association headquarters are at 155 E. 44th St., New York.

Mar. 13-15—Assn. of American Railroads, Engineering Div. and Construction & Maintenance Section, annual meeting, Palmer House, Chicago. Association headquarters are in the Transportation Bldg., Washington.

Mar. 13-16—National Assn. of Corrosion Engineers, conference and exhibition, Statler Hotel, New York. Association headquarters are in the Southern Standard Bldg., Houston.

Mar. 14-17—American Society of Tool Engineers, annual meeting, Hotel New Yorker, New York, Society headquarters are at 10700 Puritan Ave., Detroit.

Mar. 19-21—National Assn. of Waste Material Dealers, annual convention, Stevens Hotel, Chicago. Association headquarters are at 1109 Times Bldg., New York.

Mar. 19-21—Steel Founders Society of America, annual meeting, Edgewater Beach Hotel, Chicago. Society headquarters are at 920 Midland Bldg., Cleveland.

Mar. 19-23—Western Metal Congress and Exposition, Civic Auditorium and Exposition Hall, Oakland, Calif. American Society for Metals headquarters are at 7301 Euclid Ave., Cleveland.

Mar. 22-23—Pressed Metal Institute, annual technical meeting, Hotel Carter, Cleveland. Institute headquarters are at 13210 Shaker Square, Cleveland.

Apr. 2-3—Diamond Core Drill Manufacturers Assn., annual meeting, The Homestead, Hot Springs, Va. Association headquarters are at 122 E. 42nd St., New York.

Apr. 2-4—American Institute of Mining & Metallurgical Engineers, openhearth and blast furnace, coke oven and raw materials conference, Statler Hotel, Cleveland. Institute headquarters are at 29 W. 39th St., New York.

Apr. 2-5—American Society of Mechanical Engineers, spring meeting, Atlanta Biltmore Hotel, Atlanta. Society headquarters are at 29 W. 39th St., New York.

machine tool high spots

by W.A.Lloyd

April—Priority Date?—Despite a growing clamor for machine tools for the defense program, it appeared this week that April, or thereabouts, is a likely date for the release of the emergency production schedules and the priority for materials that is expected to accompany them.

It was reliably reported that NPA's machinery division has sent out tentative copies of the emergency production schedules to machine tool builders for verification—or a check on what types and sizes of machine tools are being ordered and what is in production.

Return by 60 Days—Informed observers assume that it will require about 60 days to get these reports back to Washington, make a breakdown on them, write the orders and get clearance for release. In all, a matter of probably 60 days.

Aircraft Shop Orders—Machine tool builders may receive purchase orders for machine tools for the maintenance shops of Boeing Aircraft Co. and Pratt & Whitney Div. of United Aircraft Corp., rated DO-97, it was reported this week.

Authority has been given by the Munitions Board to the Secretary of the Air Force for Boeing Aircraft Co. and to the secretary of the Navy for Pratt & Whitney Div. of United Aircraft Corp. to apply DO-97 on the purchase orders of these two companies for the purchase of maintenance, repair and operating equipment or supplies needed to repair breakdowns or prevent imminent stoppage or slowdown of production in these plants. It is not contemplated now that DO-97 will have wider application.

Warn NPA of Cutbacks—In Washington, spokesmen for the Electrical Motor Manufacturers and the Industrial Control Manufacturers Industry advisory committee warned of possible output cutbacks due to difficulties in obtaining copper and aluminum for defense orders at a joint meeting

ORDERS AND SHIPMENTS

1949	New Orders	Foreign	Shipments
Dec.	82.5	22.4	75.7
1950			
Jan.	99.7	26.7	52.8
Feb.	89.2	18.8	56.1
Mar.	107.4	24.9	75.3
Apr.	98.9	17.4	61.6
May	116.4	18.4	82.5
June	124.1	23.0	91.9
July	253.1	22.3	68.3
Aug.	305.1	34.2	95.7
Sept.	280.6	27.2	101.6
Oct.	289.6	49.5	100.9
Nov.	291.9	26.6	110.9
Dec.	410.1*	112.8*	135.7*

* Preliminary figures.
Average shipments 1945-47 = 100 pct.

with NPA officials. NPA said they would help on an individual company basis to fill DO orders and provide equipment to expand basic industries as a means of conserving copper and aluminum.

NPA Machinery Div.—Marshall M. Smith, former president of E. W. Bliss Co., was named director of NPA's machinery division. He has the responsibility of building up an organization to develop NPA programs for the machinery industry and evaluating defense needs for capital equipment, including industrial machinery of all types.

NPA also appointed two assistants in the machinery division, Herbert L. Tigges, Baker Brothers, Inc., Toledo, Ohio, as adviser and consultant on metalworking machinery problems, and P. L. Houser, International Harvester Co., Chicago, as acting chief of the machine tool section.

Reorganization — In Los Angeles, the Machinery Manufacturing Co., former builders of the Vernon line of jig borers, millers, shapers and tool and cutter grinders, announced a reorganization under a new name, Diversified Metal Products Co. A development program is in progress for precision machine tools which are in current demand.

FREE *publications*

Welding Accessories

The Weldit torch stand, safety check tank connection, and 2-way propane utility manifold are described in a new bulletin showing how these accessories provide more convenient and economical operation. The 2-way manifold makes a propane network more versatile, and can be attached to the safety check tank connection which automatically shuts off the flow of gas if the hose becomes ruptured or disconnected when the tank valve is open. The torch stand has a 360° radius so that the torch may be turned in any direction. The Weldit plumbers' melting furnace, for high efficiency at low cost, is also described. *Weldit, Inc.*

For free copy insert No. 1 on postcard.

Broach Care Chart

A timely and useful new 3-color poster chart for wall or bulletin board mounting is offered free to users of broaches and broaching machines. The chart is designed for in-plant use to increase broach life, improve their service performance and help lower the cost of maintaining broaches. Entitled "Broaches Help Pay Your Wages—Take Care of Them!" it lists the ten basic "Never and "Always" of broach care, intended to aid in realizing big dividends in broach savings. *Colonial Broach Co.*

For free copy insert No. 2 on postcard.

Serrated Blade Reamers

P & W Camlock serrated blade reamers, available in either high-speed steel or carbide tipped types, are described in a new 8-p. catalog telling how these adjustable blade reamers deliver high production and accurate finish in tough reaming operations. Sizes and prices for the full line of shell and chucking reamers are listed along with information on arbors, blade dimensions and data on component parts. *Pratt & Whitney Div., Niles-Bement-Pond Co.*

For free copy insert No. 3 on postcard.

Solving Pump Problems

Rotary pumps have been considered by many as too technical for the average industrial man to buy or sell without the aid of an extra pump technician. The cloak of mystery is pulled away in a new 32-p. booklet that explains in simple language the different steps to follow in selecting the proper pump. Data tables that will aid not only the beginner but also the experienced pump engineer are furnished. Other useful information on installing rotary pumps, locating trouble, pump care and how to order parts is also presented. *Geo. D. Roper Corp.*

For free copy insert No. 4 on postcard.

Motive Power Batteries

"Ironclad Batteries for Motive Power Service," is a new catalog describing the performance and utility of storage batteries for users of materials handling and haulage vehicles. The catalog consists of an information booklet and 5 data pages, the latter listing specifications of Exide Ironclad batteries, accessories and miscellaneous parts. This new catalog was designed for purchasing departments and for key personnel connected with the specification and purchase of motive power batteries. The information booklet lists user benefits for these batteries, illustrated by high power availability and uniform speed charts. *Electric Storage Battery Co.*

For free copy insert No. 5 on postcard.

Carbide Tools Booklet

All data in former Carboloy tool catalogs and supplements, in addition to information on many items not previously carried in stock, are presented in a new 60-p. catalog that not only lists tools and other items, but also tells how to select and apply them. Differences and limitations in the various grades of carbide are clarified, covering both the tool and wear-resistant grades. The catalog is divided into sections with a pictorial index, making it easy to use and a handy reference for the shop man, purchasing agent and design engineer. *Carboloy Co., Inc.*

For free copy insert No. 6 on postcard.

Reducing Valves

A new 6-p. bulletin containing complete technical information on Golden-Anderson's cushioned water pressure reducing valve also features the general arrangement of the G-A reducing pilot valve, with a detailed list of parts. Installation, operation, adjustment, servicing and specifications are fully described, along with tables showing general dimensions, approximate shipping weights and general list of materials. *Golden-Anderson Valve Specialty Co.*

For free copy insert No. 7 on postcard.

Motors and Generators

The new Life-Line type SK dc motors and generators are described in a new 19-p. booklet containing a transvision sequence showing construction details. It shows how the new design uses rolled steel frames, heavy steel brackets, steel angle feet and pre-lubricated double-sealed ball bearings to provide added strength and long life without outages. The *Turn to Page 154*

NEW *production ideas*

new and improved production ideas, equipment, services and methods described here offer production economies ... fill in and mail postcard.

Universal Joints

Ball type, designed for light duty applications, available in 4 sizes.

A new ball-type joint has steel forks bearing upon a bronze ball, with heat-treated centerless ground pivot bearing pins. The large pin is equipped with the Curtis patented oiler for proper lubrication of all bearing points. Ball surface offers minimum of friction loss, insuring long life for light load transmission or for hand operated controls. All sizes are furnished with riveted small pin. Sizes are ½, ¾, 1 and 1¼ in., single or double, solid or bored hubs. *Curtis Universal Joint Co., Inc.*

For more data insert No. 18 on postcard.

Improved Boring Tool

Provides accuracy to 0.0002-in. and speeds production operations.

Improvements in the E-Z set boring tools include increased tool rigidity through incorporation of larger dove-tail areas, ground fit male and female dove-tail, micrometer-like adjustment to facilitate accuracy, and elimination of distorting slots or gibs. The change from steep angle threads on the scroll mechanism to modified square type threads reduces back-lash to a minimum and augments tool rigidity and accuracy. E-Z Set boring tools cover boring range from ⅜ to 20 in. *Maxwell Co.*

For more data insert No. 19 on postcard.

Crucible Tongs

For safe handling of sample crucibles.

Jumbo crucible tongs are 21 in. long and made of 18-8 stainless steel. Positive control is assured by a patented handle that provides separate grips for the thumb and one finger. *Fisher Scientific Co.*

For more data insert No. 20 on postcard.

Table Way Lubricant

A slightly tacky, non-corrosive way lubricant for machine tools.

Febis K-53 has been developed as a special way lubricant for machine tools. It is slightly tacky, non-corrosive, mild EP lubricant that passes the Cincinnati Milling Machine Co.'s Stick-Slip Test of having a coefficient of static friction lower than its coefficient of kinetic friction. It also has high resistance to washing from metal surfaces and has mild rust preventive characteristics. *Esso Standard Oil Co.*

For more data insert No. 21 on postcard.

Hot-Topping Compound

Saves steel by cutting 2 in. from poured height of hot-tops.

Subjected to rigid tests before used in production, Mexatop, a new hot-topping compound has enabled one steel company to cut the poured height of hot-tops by 2 in. and reduce the metal in the hot-top by 1.5 pct on maximum weight ingots. Records are said to show a saving of 3000 to 4000 lb per heat. Mexatop gives a U-shaped cavity in the hot-top rather than the V-shape. The compound weighs 48 lb per cu ft and can be applied,

use postcard below

production ideas

Continued

it is said, for 3¢ per ingot ton. It is equally effective on casting risers. *U. S. Graphite Co.*

For more data insert No. 22 on postcard.

Fan Nozzles

Improved line produces more uniform coverage with less waste of spray.

Spray patterns have been made heavier in the center than at the edges of the new fan nozzles; side jets containing coarse droplets have been eliminated. There is less overspraying due to doubling up of the sprays from adjacent nozzles resulting in combined uniform covering. F Series nozzles include 13 disks made of stainless steel with flow rates of 1/10 to 10 gpm and spray angles of 50° to 90°. Disks are interchangeable in a brass base and cap assembly, having a $\frac{1}{4}$-in. male pipe connection. *Bete Fog Nozzles, Inc.*

For more data insert No. 23 on postcard.

Heat-Resistant Belt

Conveys hot materials to 600°F.

Called Super-Insulated Sahara, a new heat-resistant belting that conveys and elevates hot materials is made of heavy silver duck combined with asbestos and special insulating materials. It has proved successful in handling various hot materials, including red hot castings and foundry shake-out sand. *Imperial Belting Co.*

For more data insert No. 24 on postcard.

Air Vibrators

Long or standard stroke piston; operate on 80 psi line pressure.

Series 79 air vibrators are available in eight standard sizes for use on hoppers, tables, molding machines, chutes and other production equipment. For hopper installations, the vibrators can be used in conjunction with a Spo quick-acting hopper-gate-valve, that actuates the vibrator only when the hopper discharge gate is open. Vibrators are available in 2 and 2½-in. piston diam with long or standard stroke. Bodies are cast from semi-steel. Models are tapped for ¼-in. rigid or swivel type, straight or L connector for hose attachment. *Spo, Inc.*

For more data insert No. 25 on postcard.

Wire Drawing Compound

Magicoat is designed for drawing wire without any acid cleaning.

The new coating forms a dark, glossy oxide, with good lubricity. It is reported to have shown fine results on annealed stainless steel rod and wire, high carbon rod and wire, and low carbon wire and tests have proven that rod and wire coated with Magicoat are impervious to rust. The compound is used in hot solution, requiring only a coating tank as equipment. *Magnus Chemical Co.*

For more data insert No. 26 on postcard.

Milling Cutters

Feature truncated triangular blade.

Very close blade spacing is afforded in the new line of heavy duty milling cutters without loss of body or blade strength, it is claimed. A wedge type lock permits locking and unlocking the blade within a quarter to a half turn of an Allen wrench. The locking unit is self-contained and the wedge is actuated to and fro without the use of hammers or drifts. Each blade is backed up with a heavy, fine pitched screw that allows infinite adjustment throughout the life of the blade. Blades of Series 70 Tri-Bit face mills are high speed steel, super high speed steel, cast alloy, and carbide tipped. *Weddell Tools, Inc.*

For more data insert No. 27 on postcard.

Strain Analyzer

Electronic instrument for study of vibration, strain, dynamic stresses.

Known as the H-42A Strainalyzer, a self-contained electronic instrument records phenomena up to 50 kc and amplifies these weak signals up to 35,000 times. It makes possible the simultaneous observation and recording of four separate traces on a single 5-in. oscilloscope tube, each appearing in correct time relationship without the necessity of optical alignment. All four traces appear si-

use postcard below

RINGS THAT **GO** IN A STRAIGHT LINE

Since the inception of jet aircraft engines, American Welding has been closely associated with leading jet engine manufacturers*. Welded stainless steel rings that stand the gaff of supersonic speeds travel through our production lines — *fast!*

In addition to jet rings, we form, weld, heat-treat and machine a wide variety of rings, bands and assemblies to exact specifications, from both ferrous and non-ferrous metals.

Whatever your requirements, we can apply this same skill to your products. Send in your prints and quantities for prompt quotation, and be sure to ask for our illustrated booklet which will acquaint you with our company, our facilities and many of the products we furnish.

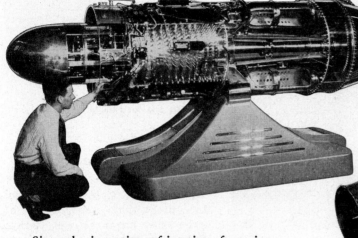

*1 — GENERAL ELECTRIC — J47
2 — PRATT & WHITNEY — J42
3 — ALLISON — J33
4 — WESTINGHOUSE — J34

THE **AW** **AMERICAN WELDING & MANUFACTURING CO.** • WARREN, OHIO

120 DIETZ ROAD • • WARREN, OHIO

production ideas
Continued

multaneously on a 5-in. screen for absolutely correct time and phase relationship. Recording is accomplished with a Fairchild Oscillo-Record camera. *Electronic Tube Corp.*

For more data insert No. 28 on postcard, p. 37.

Constant Tension Takeup
Dual-reel, continuous extrusion takeup has speed of 0 to 2600 fpm.

Built with integral capstan and tension stand, a new high-speed, constant-tension, dual-reel, continuous extrusion takeup for wire and cable features a speed range of 0 to 2600 fpm, with instantaneous acceleration of the empty reel to synchronous wire speed as soon as crossover is made. No interruption or slow down in the winding process is necessary to shift from

full to empty reel. Drives for reels, capstan and traverse are hydraulic and self-contained with fully enclosed, oil-immersed gears. Reel mounting features a demountable shaft and bearing housing assembly carried by a heavy bearing mounting on a lever-operated, tilting base, permitting loaded reels to be deposited gently on the floor upon the reel flanges. The unit is available complete, without the capstan, or with separate, floor mounted capstan and tension stand. *Industrial Ovens, Inc.*

For more data insert No. 29 on postcard, p. 37.

Mash Welder
Welds flat sheets of pickled mild steel to maximum 28 in. in width.

Mash welding is a resistance welding technique employing a seam or projection type welder to obtain a clean smooth end-to-end joint without metal overlap or protruding metal on the joined edges of the sheets. The joint is suitable for many purposes without further grinding or other finishing. The PMM2TL press type mash welding machine has been built for a specific application of joining a 28-in. wide mild steel sheet to form a continuous line for various mill operations. It incorporates the Sciaky three-phase system and is equipped with a locating and

clamping table to automatically locate the sheets to a proper overlap and hold them securely for the welding operation. Two steel idling wheels perform a rolling operation that reduces the overlap of the two sheets to a minimum thickness. Thickness can also be controlled by varying the amount of pressure provided by the upper head assembly. *Sciaky Bros. Inc.*

For more data, insert No. 30 on postcard, p. 37.

Planer-Miller
New Hypro machine performs multiple operations on huge parts.

With three planing heads and two milling heads, a new Hypro combination planer and miller will handle work up to 10½ ft wide, 9 ft high and 26 ft long. Right and left hand planer heads mounted on the rail may be operated individually or simultaneously. A right hand planer side head gives the machine conventional planer advantages. Rail heads may be traversed to clear the entire table for vertical milling head, also mounted on the rail. The head swivels to reach angular surfaces on the part being machined. A left hand milling side head augments the regular machine functions and swivels to reach the side of workpieces. Other

features include non-metallic table ways having forced lubrication; complete herringbone gear table

drive; dual rail control; and separate pendant control for planer and milling operations. *Giddings & Lewis Machine Tool Co.*

For more data insert No. 31 on postcard, p. 37.

Betatron
X-rays 20 in. of steel in 10 min.

The Allis-Chalmers 22 million volt Betatron is the newest tool for production radiography of large heavy metal castings. X-rays from the Betatron will penetrate 20 in. of steel in 10 min (4 in. of steel in a matter of seconds). Because of its wide latitude (up to 6 in.) fewer radiographs need to be taken and no time consuming

blocking materials are used. Detail is reportedly so excellent that a 1/32-in. crack is revealed in steel sections ranging from 2 to 12 in. in thickness. A 1/16-in. crack can easily be seen in steel sections 20 in. thick. *Picker X-Ray Corp.*

For more data insert No. 32 on postcard, p. 37.

Hot-Cold Test Stand
For testing small aircraft parts; temperatures —70° to +230°.

The test stand has a deep well that accommodates parts measuring up to 6x6x8 in. The item to be tested is placed in the well and

Turn to Page 157

Wire shapes shown
are greatly enlarged.

LOWER COST PARTS AND TRIM
"Shape-Engineered" from Wire

Your product, too, may have one or more parts which could be made better and more economically from Continental's shaped wire. Or, you may be able to add extra sales appeal with decorative Continental wire for smarter, lower-cost trim. Most manufacturers today are looking for ways to reduce product costs while improving the competitive appeal of things they make and sell. At Continental you will find engineers who are ready and eager to work with you to solve your "shape-engineering" problems. If you want service with the wire you buy, call on Continental. Wire or write us at Kokomo, Indiana.

Standard and Special Shaped—and Regular Round Wire in Many Alloys, Tempers and Finishes Continental wire is made in standard and special shapes in a great variety of sizes, tempers, alloys and finishes. Write today for your free copy of Continental's handy booklet of wire information for manufacturers.

*Tr. Mrk. Reg. U. S. Pat. Off.

CONTINENTAL
STEEL CORPORATION
GENERAL OFFICES • KOKOMO, INDIANA

PRODUCERS OF *Manufacturer's Wire* in many sizes, shapes, tempers and finishes, including Galvanized,   KOKOTE, Flame-Sealed, Coppered, Tinned, Annealed, Liquor Finished, Bright, Lead Coated, and special wire.   ALSO, Coated and Uncoated Steel Sheets, Nails, Continental Chain Link Fence, and other products.

IRON AGE

introduces

C. H. Wills, appointed director of sales for the MICHIGAN ABRASIVE CO., Detroit. **B. S. Meade** joined the firm in the capacity of general sales manager.

Edwin R. Bartlett, elected chairman of the board of directors of the HOOKER ELECTROCHEMICAL CO., Niagara Falls, N. Y. Also, **R. Lindley Murray** was promoted to the office of president of the company.

H. R. Cameron, appointed assistant chief engineer of the PITTSBURGH BRIDGE & IRON WORKS, Pittsburgh.

J. W. Bryant, named comptroller of RESERVE MINING CO., St. Louis County, Minn.

Thomas O. McMillan, appointed eastern district representative for the WARNER ELECTRIC BRAKE & CLUTCH CO., Lebanon, Pa.

W. P. L'Hommedieu, appointed assistant Pacific Coast district manager for the WESTINGHOUSE ELECTRIC CORP., San Francisco. **Bruce D. Henderson,** appointed general purchasing agent, with offices located in Pittsburgh. **Wesley H. Lees,** appointed general traffic manager for the company.

Domenic A. DiTirro, named to head up the sales and technical service engineering Divisions of the ROSS OPERATING VALVE CO., Detroit.

H. R. Shapaugh, appointed district manager of sales, southern branch, for the FRUEHAUF TRAILER CO., Dallas. Other district sales managers appointed: **V. H. Rossman,** Philadelphia; **F. L. Brower,** Birmingham; **M. J. MacQuarrie,** Buffalo; **C. L. Sargent,** Boston; **M. M. Williamson,** Oklahoma City, Okla.; **A. V. Howe,** So. Kearny, N. J.; **Glen W. Buse,** St. Paul, Minn.

Carl G. Holschuh, promoted to vice-president and assistant general manager for manufacture, of the SPERRY GYROSCOPE CO., Great Neck, N. Y. **Edward U. Da Parma,** becomes vice-president and works manager.

Richard E. Coe, elected assistant to the president of the ELECTRIC FURNACE CO., Salem, Ohio.

Charles H. Wagner, elected as a vice-president and director of the GEROTOR MAY CORP., Baltimore.

Ben Kaul, appointed to the new position of technical development engineer for the MULLINS MFG. CO., Salem and Warren, Ohio. Other promotions: **Michael Theil,** becomes superintendent of tools and dies. **Ralph Bradley** becomes general superintendent of engineering, tool design and estimating, and **Andrew W. Arnold,** promoted to superintendent of the Warren plant tool department.

Gilbert Soler, resigned as vice-president, manufacturing operations and director of ATLAS STEEL LTD., Welland, Ontario.

Carl J. Tsaloff, named manager of the Cadillac, Mich., plant of the B. F. GOODRICH CO. Mr. Tsaloff succeeds **Felix G. Tanner,** who has retired.

Steve Girard, appointed assistant general manager of KAISER-FRAZER CORP., Willow Run, Mich.

John J. Murphy, appointed in charge of the Washington, D. C., office, government contracts department, of the HUDSON MOTOR CAR CO.

Gerald J. Lynch, formerly assistant director of the office of defense products, has been named director of the Washington, D. C., office for the FORD MOTOR CO.

C. M. HOUCK, elected president of the Pittsburgh Testing Laboratory, Pittsburgh.

DAVID WHITE, appointed president of the Lester Engineering Co., Cleveland.

L. PIERCE RICHIE, elected vice-president in charge of purchases for the Oliver Corp., Chicago.

IRON AGE

salutes

John G. Munson

IN retiring as raw materials vice-president of U. S. Steel (he will continue to serve in an advisory capacity), John G. Munson must feel enormous satisfaction from a job well done. Few men of industry have ever faced sterner assignments; fewer still have achieved such shining success.

Mr. Munson became raw materials officer in 1939—just in time to tackle the tremendous job of supplying U. S. Steel and others with record quantities of materials needed to make steel for guns, tanks and ships of World War II. Production records tell how well he met the challenge.

But his toughest job was still to come. The war chewed up a lot of precious resources, including ore. The great Mesabi was being depleted at an alarming rate. And far-sighted steel people saw iron ore trouble ahead.

That was when Ben Fairless gave John Munson the unenviable assignment of solving the ore problem. He picked the right man. Mr. Munson knows how to make haste without fanfare or noise. Though retiring in nature, he is a brilliant raw materials man, as well as a keen judge of others.

These talents were to prove invaluable in organizing the most detailed search for ore ever conducted. He picked his men carefully, gave them wide latitude, then backed them to the hilt on every question that came up.

At the same time the great search for ore was going on in Venezuela, Mr. Munson was pressing development of methods for beneficiating Minnesota taconite ores. The rest of the story is well known. Fabulous Cerro Bolivar was discovered in Venezuela, and a million-ton capacity ore treating plant was built at Virginia, Minn., future site of large scale taconite beneficiation.

Because John Munson had faith, imagination and plenty of hard-won experience in the raw materials field, he finally won out—U. S. Steel has enough ore for 100 years, and it isn't all in one basket.

ROY F. HANCOCK, appointed assistant to the vice-president in charge of sales for the Vanadium Corp. of America, New York.

NEAL J. CRAIN, appointed director of purchases for the United Engineering & Foundry Co., Pittsburgh.

HAROLD G. INGERSOLL, elected as a vice-president of Borg-Warner Corp., Chicago.

FRANK J. THOMPSON, appointed director of purchases of the L. J. Mueller Furnace Co., Milwaukee.

IRON AGE *introduces*

Continued

P. F. Lindeman, promoted to vice-president in charge of operations and M. J. Russo, advanced to the position of vice-president in charge of purchasing of the PACIFIC CAN CO., San Francisco.

Carlton H. Rose, named manager of the Washington, D. C. office of NATIONAL LEAD CO.

C. B. Kershner, appointed purchasing agent for the BIRDSBORO STEEL FOUNDRY & MACHINE CO., Birdsboro, Pa.

Edwin E. McConnell and Lewis S. Greenleaf, Jr., elected members of the board of directors of the NORTON CO., Worcester. Thomas S. Green, retired from the board after a service of 13 years.

Robert Pollock, appointed district sales manager, New York, of the Wire Rope Divisions of AMERICAN CHAIN & CABLE CO., INC.

Arthur T. Baum, Jr., appointed director of personnel of the HYDRAULIC EQUIPMENT CO., Cleveland.

Edwin S. Ladley, named assistant director of purchases of HERCULES POWDER CO., Wilmington, Del.

Robert T. Haslam, elected to the board of directors of WORTHINGTON PUMP & MACHINERY CORP., Harrison, N. J.

Victor F. Stine, elected vice-president in charge of sales and engineering, and a director of the PANGBORN CORP., Hagerstown, Md. Lloyd L. Stouffer, becomes secretary and treasurer and a director of the company.

T. W. Krueger, appointed as assistant general sales manager of the DUFF-NORTON MFG. CO., Pittsburgh.

John V. Freeman, retired as director of the coal chemical sales division, commercial department, U. S. STEEL CO., Pittsburgh. Charles W. Baldwin, succeeds Mr. Freeman, and John W. Clinton becomes Mr. Baldwin's assistant. By retiring, Mr. Freeman ends 43 years of service with the company. Robert McC. Maxwell, appointed general product manager of the coal chemical sales division, commercial department.

Joseph J. Lusch, appointed manager of orders and schedules, a newly created department of BETHLEHEM PACIFIC COAST STEEL CORP., San Francisco.

W. E. Miles, elected vice-president in charge of crawler tractor and industrial sales for the OLIVER CORP., Chicago.

Delmar Woodhouse, elected secretary of KROPP FORGE CO., Chicago. Mr. Woodhouse will continue as comptroller of the company.

Robert J. Wagner, appointed industrial relations manager for the HARBISON-WALKER REFRACTORIES CO., Pittsburgh.

D. A. Coyle, named plant manager for the BUDD CO., Charlevoix plant, Detroit. W. H. Montee, succeeds Mr. Coyle as works manager of Charlevoix plant.

Robert E. Novy, elected a director of INLAND STEEL CONTAINER CO., Chicago. Edward E. Grosscup, promoted as manager of the Chicago plant; Thomas M. Dyer, transferred to New Orleans as manager, southern plant; Norman D. Rice, moved to Chicago as chief engineer in charge of engineering, research and development.

OBITUARIES

E. H. Weitzel, 82, retired vice-president and general manager of the Colorado Fuel & Iron Co., died in Los Angeles recently.

John F. Hennessy, manager of sales, Chicago district, Bethlehem Steel Co., for the past 22 years, died recently after a brief illness.

Albert A. Breault, Albany representative for Brace-Meuller-Huntly, Inc., for the past 17 years, died recently.

E. Arthur Kerschbaumer, 45, chairman of U. S. Ferro-Manganese Co., New Mexico, died suddenly on January 20, 1951.

Harry Hanson, vice-president and secretary of the Griffin Wheel Co., died suddenly in Chicago recently, after 48 years of service with the company.

Moses H. Moss, Cleveland district manager for Reliance Steel Div., Detroit Steel Corp., died recently.

Patterns in Pensions

Streamlining a Pension Pattern
TO FIT **YOUR** BUSINESS

THE success of your pension plan will depend upon a streamlining job which gears your pension system with *your* particular financial, personnel and industrial problems. And, if your pension plan is not streamlined to fit your company's circumstances, you may suffer serious loss in dollars and greatly reduce the effectiveness of your plan.

Our Pension Trust Division has helped develop hundreds of pension plans. This broad experience with all types of pension systems is yours for the asking. We shall be glad to estimate the cost of a pension plan for your company or discuss with you any pension problem you may have. No obligation, of course.

Write or call the
PENSION TRUST DIVISION
City Bank Farmers Trust Company
or
The National City Bank of New York
Ask for Booklet I. A. 2

We Act As Trustee Under Pension Plans and as Agent for Individual Trustees

CITY BANK FARMERS TRUST COMPANY
CHARTERED 1822
HEAD OFFICE: 22 WILLIAM STREET, NEW YORK

Affiliate of

THE NATIONAL CITY BANK OF NEW YORK
ESTABLISHED 1812

on the assembly line

automotive news and opinions

Plating is major auto problem . . . New cuts will hit hard soon . . . Reuther seeks UMW mutual insurance company.

by Walter G. Patton

Vanishing Bright Work—It now seems certain that the bright work on cars will begin to disappear rapidly after Mar. 1 if not before. A recent Washington order prohibits use of nickel for all decorative parts after that date. Nickel may be used for bumpers, bumper brackets and door handles — if you can get the nickel. However, auto firms have been getting not more than 65 pct maximum of their use during the first 6 months of 1950. Many firms have been getting only 45 pct of their base quota recently.

Painted Bumpers? — At least one car maker has been shipping service bumpers in the unplated condition. Several car producers are experimenting seriously with painted bumpers. Wide chrome trim strips along the side of the car are being painted. Painted bumpers seem to be the most practical solution found up to the present time. However, many engineers see plenty of service trouble ahead if painted bumpers are finally adopted.

Ships Less Copper—Part of the present confusion in the auto industry stems from an increasingly alarming copper situation. Deliveries of domestic copper are running as much as 2 months behind. Reports also indicate deliveries of copper from Chile have sagged bad-

ly. One explanation is that copper is being diverted in large quantities into so-called "deformed wire bars" that can be sold more profitably in other parts of the world than in U. S.

Standing Room Only—Cutbacks in automobile production will automatically lengthen the line of buyers which is forming. Cadillac reports 82,000 buyers standing in line. If Cadillac output is reduced 20 pct during the rest of '51, the resultant backlog represents about a year's output.

Lines of buyers for other cars are not as long as Cadillac, but the anticipated reduction of 20 to 30 pct in auto output in the first quarter will lengthen them appreciably.

Reuther's Insurance Plan — Walter Reuther, president of the UAW-CIO, will recommend to his members that the United Automobile Workers set up their own insurance company.

He says insurance companies are making sizable profits out of the worker's insurance dollars. He wants the group to handle its own insurance "on a mutual, non-profit basis." Reuther's program for 1951 for the U.A.W. is: (1) Increased pensions toward a goal of $200 a month minimum; (2) a guaranteed annual wage. Reuther also wants a labor-industry wage commission

to study ways and means of achieving a guaranteed annual wage.

New Pontiac Plant — A new sheet metal plant and a drive-out and shipping building have been announced by Pontiac. Construction is to be completed by midsummer. The drive-out and shipping building will handle 750 cars per day. Steel from the present drive-out building will be used in the new 303,000 sq ft structure.

The new sheet metal plant will extend 600 ft along Highwood Ave., adjacent to the present plating plant. This plant will be connected by an inclosed conveyer bridge which will carry fabricated sheet metal directly to the assembly lines, the plating plant, painting operations or storage.

Skirmishes with Unions — The aftermath of price freezing is always unpredictable. An example is the growing unrest in Detroit auto plants, traceable indirectly to the auto pricing order. Attempts by car manufacturers to hold down costs by boosting output in the face of regulated prices have resulted in considerable friction. Kaiser-Frazer, Briggs and others have had recent brushes with the union.

Not all of the labor strife here is directly attributable to the pricing situation. Detroit still has strikes resulting from attempts to

assembly line

Continued

discipline auto workers who are obviously guilty of breaking plant rules. Increased pressure to get out production plus the fear engendered by threatened layoffs have together created an uneasy labor situation.

New Vinyl Plastic—B. F. Goodrich Chemical Co. has introduced a new rigid, vinyl plastic said to be superior to available vinyls in the electrical insulation and structural fields. Indicated usage of "Geon 404" includes primary insulation on weatherproof line wire, military aircraft wire, military field wire, jackets on coaxial cable and similar applications.

Available in rigid sheets, rods and tubing, the material can be fabricated into such things as tanks for corrosives and acids, fume hoods and ducts and display paneling. The material is virtually unaffected by water, grease, air, salts, alkalies and acids and is non-inflammable.

Ford Hardtop Sedan — Ford is the latest car producer to introduce a hardtop sedan with the snappy styling of a convertible. The new Ford Victoria has a double drop frame with box-section side rails. Special flanges in the middle of the frame are built in to provide greater body strength. The new model was put in limited production this week.

Tanks' Steel Needs — If and when tank production reaches the 35,000 per year rate, a big tonnage of steel will be required. Estimated requirements for a medium tank is 41 tons. The new Chrysler heavy tank will require substantially more than this.

Modern Handling Pays — Basis for the current interest in materials handling in auto plants is this: A trailer handling loose material moved 20,000 lb of freight in a 48-hr period. In the same time, 93,320 lb of palletized freight were transported. To put it another way, revenue from the truck was rough-

ly four times as great where modern hauling methods are employed. One motor car manufacturer estimates a saving of $75 per car from improved materials handling methods adopted since World War II ended.

K-F in Plane Work — Early in April Kaiser-Frazer will start fabrication and assembly of components of the Lockheed P2V Navy Anti-Submarine Patrol Bomber. A building with 10 acres of floor space has been leased at Oakland, Calif. Equipment is already moving in. Other necessary facilities are on order.

This is the seventh large firm joining Lockheed's group of subcontractors who will build major sections of the F-94 Jet Fighter or the P2V Bomber. K-F will manufacture a portion of the fuselage after the trailing edge of the P2V's wing. The P2V will carry armament and electronic gear to detect submarines.

New Metal Container — Harnischfeger Corp. of Milwaukee is proposing a shipping container (made of steel or aluminum) which is 40 ft long, 8 ft wide and 8 ft high.

Containers are loaded on flat cars for long hauls. They can be transferred by crane to flat truck trailers for final delivery. A Chicago cotton goods concern is using two such steel containers carrying 20,000 lb of cotton each.

Chrysler Jet Plant — The new Chrysler jet engine plant will be located within 17 miles of the Detroit City Hall. Exact location has not been disclosed.

Pratt and Whitney Aircraft Div. of United Aircraft Corp. is negotiating a license with Chrysler for production of its J-48 Turbo-Wasp jet engine. The engine delivers 15,000 hp at maximum aircraft performance. It is now in production in Pratt and Whitney's plant at East Hartford, Conn. The Chrysler contract with the Navy Department involves an outlay of $50 million.

Bombers—Ford Motor Co. will add some 220,000 sq. ft. to its automatic transmission plant at Cincinnati to produce aircraft engine lubrication pumps for Pratt and Whitney B-36 bomber engines,

Estimates are Ford will be producing bomber engines in 15 months.

THE BULL OF THE WOODS

By J. R. Williams

THE BLUE FIELDS

COPR. 1951 BY NEA SERVICE, INC. T. M. REG. U. S. PAT. OFF.

M. & M. DUPLEX MILLING AND CENTERING MACHINE
Part — *automotive pinion*
Operation — *mill both ends and center drill*
Production — *220 pieces per hour at 100%*

FOR HIGHER PRODUCTION
Combine Operations
ON **MOTCH & MERRYWEATHER** SPECIAL MACHINES

The Motch & Merryweather milling head features rigidity at the tool point.

You can be sure of getting higher production with lower cost per piece by using Motch & Merryweather machines designed for multiple operations. The machine pictured here mills and center drills a vast range of parts, some of which are shown in white above. Our representative will help you obtain thorough-going accuracy, together with *production, PRODUCTION,* and *MORE PRODUCTION.* Contact us *now.*

Manufactured by
THE MOTCH & MERRYWEATHER MACHINERY COMPANY
715 PENTON BUILDING • CLEVELAND 13, OHIO
Builders of Circular Sawing Equipment, Production Milling, Automatic and Special Machines

PRODUCTION-WITH-ACCURACY MACHINES AND EQUIPMENT

west coast progress report

by R.T. Reinhardt

Good News—Best news foundries and primary steel producers heard last week was that Kaiser Steel Corp. had applied for a certificate of necessity involving approximately $55 million for the construction of a third blast furnace, coke ovens and blooming mill at Fontana, Calif. Foundries need the pig and many believe further expansion of primary steel production in the West is limited by availability of metallics.

Metalworking plants are complaining of a lack of government contracts or sub-contracts which would assure them of a steady supply of materials and are hard pressed to keep going with limited steel available.

This situation is believed especially acute in the West where many machine shops and other metalworking plants are small and not fully equipped to handle the few large sub-contracts offered.

Potential Nickel Source—Interest again is revived in the low grade nickel deposits in Douglas County, Ore.

According to S. W. Libbey, director of Oregon State Dept. of Geology and Metal Industries, the M. A. Hanna Co., Cleveland, Ohio, has an option on mineral rights of this deposit of some 20 million tons of ore. It is reported the deposit contains approximately 75 pct chromium oxide, 1.5 pct nickel, and some iron.

Two recovery methods may be used. One involves a wet process by which the nickel can be leached out, producing chromic oxide as a by-product. Mr. Libbey believes the ore contains enough iron and chromite to combine with the nickel into a stainless steel under proper smelting conditions.

Steel Essential in Tests—Boeing Airplane Co. of Seattle, Wash., reports that in tests conducted at its Wichita plant on the B-47 Stratojet approximately 700,000 lb of structural steel in fabricating jigs and scaffolding was used.

These tests subjected the wings to structural stresses greater than would normally be encountered in years of combat flying. In one phase, wing tips were bent through an arc of more than 20 ft—as much as 14 ft upward and 6 ft downward.

K-F to Make Aircraft Parts—Kaiser-Frazer Corp. has signed a contract with Lockheed Aircraft Corp. for fabrication and assembly of components for the Lockheed P2V Navy anti-submarine patrol bomber in San Leandro, Calif. K-F has leased the plant of Osborne Machinery Co.

William A. Cannon, formerly with Lockheed, will manage the K-F Oakland aircraft division and reports production work will start within 60 days. K-F is the seventh large firm to undertake subcontracts for Lockheed and will build fuselage waist sections and center section flaps.

Metals Big Business—During the past 5 years $130,700,000 new capital has been invested in Utah manufacturing plants, according to a survey by the University of Utah. The 5-year investment is more than the total value of the state's manufacturing plants in 1940.

Much of the investment is in primary metals and steel fabricating industries. The survey shows a total of $48 million for foundries in the Salt Lake and Ogden areas, facilities at Geneva steel plant and constructing a new copper refinery. An additional $14 million has been invested in steel fabricating plants in the area.

Chrysler Expansion—Chrysler Corp. is planning a $5 million plant at San Leandro, Calif., which company officials describe as a body-building unit for the Dodge division. However, there has been some conjecture that it may be utilized for production of war materials.

flamatic hardening gives a lift to piston rod performance

specified

Length: 14"
O.D.: 1¼"
Material: SAE 1050
Structure at surface: Rc 53-55

structure at transition zone: Rc 42

Close-up of hydraulic piston rod being Flamatic hardened, showing work centering device and special flame heads.

achieved

Flamatic selective surface hardening with electronic temperature control goes to great lengths to improve product performance, speed processing, and "shorten" costs as well. This slender 14" long hydraulic piston rod—formerly carburized—is now Flamatic hardened to Rc 53-55 in a matter of seconds . . . on a production line basis . . . and with distortion so slight that corrective operations are a thing of the past. Core and shaft ends are left soft.

A centering device and special flame head assembly readily adapts the standard Cincinnati No. 2 Flamatic to the job. Operation (automatic except for loading) is as straightforward and reliable as on gears, cams, etc., up to 18" OD and spindles up to 24" long.

Examine your present surface hardening processes in the light of a wide variety of Flamatic applications. Twelve interesting fully documented case histories are featured in the new 20-page Flamatic Catalog, Publication No. M-1724. Write for it, on your letterhead please.

the federal view

this week in washington

by Eugene J. Hardy

Move Toward CMP—Out of all the talk about a Controlled Materials Plan for basic metals finally comes the first concrete step in this direction. The NPA Program Bureau has developed basic instructions and forms for use by the various claimant agencies, including the military, so as to standardize the presentation of requirements for steel, copper, aluminum, etc.

Seemingly a minor step, it is the first move toward the development of a firm claimant program system. Obviously, CMP could not work unless all requirements are presented in the same form.

Spec Index Coming — For the first time in military procurement a standardized index of specifications and standards used by the armed services—Army, Navy, and Air Force—will soon be available. It's a five-volume job being prepared by the Munitions Board and will be available around Apr. 1.

It is designed for use by industry as well as government agencies. The index will not carry the complete standards and specifications, but will clearly identify them and provide information as to where copies may be obtained. Up to now, about 3600 uniform specs have been adopted and 2400 additional proposed uniform specs are in process.

NSRB Powers Gone — Defense Production Administration has taken over NSRB's job of issuing certificates of necessity for fast writeoff of plant expansion and also the issuing of certificates authorizing RFC loans. This was the first official action taken by newly-confirmed DPA Administrator W. H. Harrison.

Various agencies which previously issued certificates will continue to make recommendations on loans. Dept. of Commerce will make recommendations on loans for steel, chemical and other industrial expansion; and the Dept. of Interior will take similar action on loans for petroleum and mining activities. These agencies will make similar recommendations regarding certificates of necessity.

New Materials Study Group—NSRB's only remaining function is planning for mobilization that has already happened and is moving full steam ahead. Its long-range materials planning has been superseded by the President's appointment of a 5-man Materials Policy Commission, headed by William S. Paley, Columbia Broadcasting System.

The Commission will study the long-range requirements and supply outlook; the prospect and estimated extent of shortages; and the consistency and adequacy of the policies, plans and programs of both industry and Government. The Commission is expected to re-port on the prospect of balancing requirements and supply, including the outlook for allies of this country, within the next 6 to 9 months.

RFC Overhaul — Government loans for defense production will continue to grow in volume at the Reconstruction Finance Corp., despite congressional pressure for a top-to-bottom housecleaning of the giant lending agency.

In the Senate, the Banking and Currency Committee has thrown its weight behind two reorganization plans sponsored by Senator Fulbright, D., Ark. Mr. Fulbright proposes to substitute a single governor for the present 5-man board of directors, and to impose far-reaching limitations on the manner in which loans are granted and administered.

Name Douglas—Appointment of James Douglas as acting deputy administrator of the Defense Minerals Administration has been announced by Secretary of Interior Chapman. Mr. Douglas will assist DMA Administrator Boyd.

Amend Request—The railroads have amended their petition for an immediate 6 pct freight increase to include a similar increase in charges for handling iron ore at upper Lake Ports. The original petition had not included any increase in these charges.

February 1, 1951

97

INLAND DATA for STEEL USERS

INLAND STEEL CO.
38 S. Dearborn Street, Chicago 3, Illinois

Packaging your Steel sheets and strip

One way the steel user may be able to reduce the cost of steel delivered to his fabricating equipment, is by specifying the correct type of package the mill should provide. In the final analysis, his handling equipment, storage facilities, method of transportation from mill to plant and end-use of the steel will all have a bearing on the type and weight of package he needs. The following chart illustrates the most generally used types of packages for steel sheets and strip. We are always glad to recommend to the user, the most suitable type of package for the steels we ship.

Type of handling equipment in steel user's plant	The most generally used types of steel mill packages	
	for cut lengths	**for coils**
Overhead crane with SHEET LIFTER or COIL HOOK	sheets on lengthwise skids	cylinder method of loading coils / coil on skid, core horizontal
Overhead crane with CHAIN OR CABLE SLINGS	sheets on crosswise skids / sheets on lengthwise skids	cylinder method of loading coils / coil on skid, core horizontal
Overhead crane with ELECTRO-MAGNET	any type package as long as material is securely banded or tied	flat method of loading coils / coil on platform, core vertical
FORK TRUCK	sheets on crosswise skids	Ram truck or Fork truck used as ram — cylinder method of loading — coil on skid, core horizontal / Fork truck — coil on platform, core vertical

Sheet material with integral stiffening ribs and other structural details is under investigation by the aircraft industry, intent on lowering production costs. Among the methods of producing such structure, forging offers many advantages. Huge presses are on order, new forging techniques are being developed, to produce integrally-stiffened aircraft wing and fuselage structural panels.

INTEGRALLY-STIFFENED SKIN
REVOLUTIONIZES AIRCRAFT CONSTRUCTION

forged sections

FIRST OF A SERIES

The need for reduced production costs and increased structural efficiency in aircraft construction has led to investigation of a revolutionary new fabrication procedure. The industry is now investigating and developing the manufacture and use of large sections of integrally-stiffened surface structure. The idea is to make in one piece components which are now multipiece combinations in the conventional skin-and-stiffener structure.

Interest in this development is not limited to the aircraft industry. It is of great importance to those who supply the industry with tools and structural materials. And should, as seems possible, integrally-stiffened structure find application in other industries—such as automotive, containers, and building materials—the impact on industry in general will be substantial.

Much development is indicated to take full advantage of the potentialities of integrally-stiffened structure, in the production of aircraft structural materials, in metalworking machinery, and in production methods. Larger materials sizes are desirable. Larger presses and machine tools will be necessary to handle this material. Already the Air Force has ordered, for production development, presses for larger than any ever before built: a forging press with a capacity in excess of 50,000 tons, and an extrusion press with a capacity of over 15,000 tons.

Equipment will be needed to rapidly and economically do machining of great complexity.

By P. E. SANDORFF (l.), *Research Engineer*
and GEORGE W. PAPEN (r.), *Manager, Production Engineering Dept.*
Lockheed Aircraft Corp., *Burbank, Calif.*

Continued

Machines with elaborate automatic sequencing controls, and high-speed, multiple-spindles are being developed. A multihead slab milling machine with a 500-hp, 5000-rpm motor has been proposed.

To utilize the advantage of integrally-stiffened structure, bigger base stock is desirable—wider sheet and plate, and larger extrusion and forging billets. And, techniques and equipment for rolling tapered sheet, and sheet with rolled-in stiffening ribs, are being investigated.

These are examples of the type of development which will be stimulated by the use of integrally-stiffened structure. It is probable that such structure and the techniques of making and using it will be useful in other manufacturing operations. This would stimulate more extensive development. The total impact on industry promises to be substantial.

Several Manufacturing Methods Used

The name integrally-stiffened structure is applied to construction in which the skin and skin-stiffening elements are made of one part, instead of being built up of sheet material attached to many individual stiffeners. There are several methods of making such structure: It may be machined from heavy plate, or it may be forged from billet, or rolled similar to a sheet product, extruded or cast—or a combination of these processes may be used.

The immediate advantages of such a structure are the reduction in number of parts and attachments and the reduction in handling expenses and assembly tooling. Other advantages are also generally obtained, such as reduced weight, improved surface smoothness, and simplified sealing. Disadvantages are chiefly those associated

The development of integrally-stiffened structure represents a revolution in aircraft construction which is of vital importance to those who supply material and equipment to the aircraft industry. The machines, techniques, and materials developed may prove of importance in other industries as well.

This is the first of a series of four articles which will summarize development to date on the methods of producing integrally-stiffened structure: forging, casting, extruding, rolling, and machining. Advantages, limitations, and indicated applications of each will be discussed.

with fabrication of the integrally-stiffened sheet product.

Aircraft surface structure must conform to internal and external shape requirements while supporting specified loads. Generally these loads include normal pressure or air loads, wing and fuselage bending which causes axial stresses in the surface elements, and overall torsion which places shear in the skin.

Conventional skin-stressed structure has been developed to meet these requirements with high efficiency in terms of weight. Essentially such structure consists of: *(1) The external sheet or skin; (2) a system of stiffeners which rigidize the skin locally and, together with the skin, carry the major surface stresses; (3) a system of regularly spaced internal supports which establish the column length or the bending length of the skin-and-stiffener combination, and also transfer shear load; and (4) still another system of elements parallel to the skin-stiffeners, whose purpose is chiefly to preserve shape or carry beam shear.* Generally there is a taper in size and strength of all elements along the length of the

FIG. 1—An aircraft wing being assembled by conventional methods. In this single component, the dozens of individual stiffening elements visible demonstrate the magnitude of the fabrication and assembly job. Over a million rivets are required in assembling the skin-and-stiffener structure of one wing for a large plane.

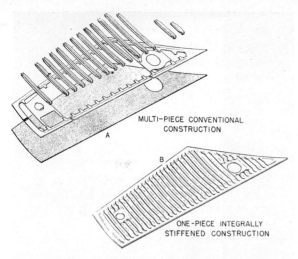

FIG. 2—A typical high-speed aircraft wing panel, as it would be made by conventional methods, and as it would look if made in one piece by integrally-stiffened construction. The conventional panel would have 19 components, requiring several hundred rivets for assembly.

assembly. A typical example of this construction is shown in Fig. 1.

This method of construction leaves much to be desired in obtaining a satisfactory compromise of the functional, structural and manufacturing requirements. It means the fabrication of many individual parts, few of them alike. Splices and joints are complex, and require much sealing in pressurized or tank structures. An incredible number of fasteners is required to assemble all the parts of an airplane.

Millions of Rivets Required

In larger sized aircraft, material stock sizes have begun to determine the number of parts and location of splices and joints. The number of attachments in the assembly under these conditions increases in a ratio approaching the cube of the linear dimension. For example, the wing surface of a Lockheed Constellation contains over 1 million rivets.

Structural weight suffers by compromise with what is practical from a manufacturing standpoint. Design at joints, splices and intersections of systems of elements is critical. Surface smoothness suffers from having many attachments through the skin, flush-milling often being required to smooth the surface. Compromise with production methods often leaves local areas unsatisfactory aerodynamically.

Design for trans-sonic and supersonic speeds has resulted in greatly accentuating these production difficulties. And the amount of equipment carried in modern aircraft makes space requirements more severe, as does the larger fuel volume necessary.

Among the developments aimed at reducing these problems are tapered sheet, tapered extrusions, and tailored sheet. Experimental quantities of sheet rolled with a taper are available,

and there are machine shops specializing in machining tapered sheet from plate. Tapered extrusions offer possibilities in material conservation, reduce machining time, and reduce the number of splices and parts required for section taper of stiffeners and beam caps. Some aircraft companies and private machine shops are setting up machines for producing tailored sheet, which is not only tapered but also includes such section changes as doublers and attachment pads.

Each of these, however, attacks only a small portion of the problem. Integrally-stiffened structure attacks all phases. It combines the advantages of tailored sheet with integral stiffeners, thus further reducing the number of parts, number of attachments and number of intersections. It makes possible the use of long-length stock incorporating taper and attachment pads, greatly reducing number and complexity of splices and effecting both weight and production savings.

The study reported in this article discusses and compares all the various methods of making integrally-stiffened structure. It is based on Lockheed research and experience, and on Air Force development work being carried on by Lockheed and other manufacturers.

Huge Forging Presses Used

One of the processes currently under investigation is press forging. Production of thin-skinned surface panels with deep-section integral stiffening by press forging has become more feasible with recent advancements in technique and press capacity. During the war Germany had a press of 30,000 tons capacity. Some large slab-shaped parts were made in quantity on this press, but none approached stiffened skin surface structure in minimum thickness or complexity of detail. The largest press in this country has a capacity of 18,000 tons and is operated by Wyman-Gordon

FIG. 3—An integrally-stiffened panel made by forging. This panel is 25 in. square, with 1-in. stiffeners spaced at 1½-in. intervals. Investigations to date have definitely established the practicability of making large surface panels by forging.

Co., Worcester, Mass. The Air Force has on order a forging press in excess of 50,000 tons capacity. (THE IRON AGE, Jan. 18, p. 75.)

Under a USAF contract Lockheed is now working with Wyman-Gordon to determine if integrally-stiffened structures can be profitably produced by press forging. Considerable progress has been made in development of dies and in forging technique. Results of an early phase of the program are illustrated in Fig. 3. This panel is 25 in. square with 1-in. stiffeners spaced at 1½-in. intervals. A few years ago the forging of such specimens was considered impossible; results to date definitely prove the feasibility and practicability of making large surface panels by this method, although more development work remains to be done.

The question of forging to finished contour or forging flat is still to be answered. Forging dies which will produce a part to finished contour may be more expensive than dies producing only a flat blank. However, if the dimensions can be held within required limits, it would eliminate forming. If dimensions cannot be held, or surface smoothness is insufficient, other additional machining or straightening operations are required. If the forging could be made to required contour dimensions, and surface smoothness was satisfactory, the problem of machining for desired accuracy at joints and other attachment

FIG. 5—The same removable panel shown in Fig. 4, as it would look if made as a one-piece integrally-stiffened structure by forging. This particular part was machined from plate, to simulate a forging. The joint on the right was necessitated by the limited size of plate available. If put into production as a forging, this part would be all one piece, with no joint.

FIG. 4—An exploded view showing the components in a conventional P-80 center wing lower removable panel. It has 49 separate parts, and requires 24 screws and nuts, and 1065 rivets in assembly.

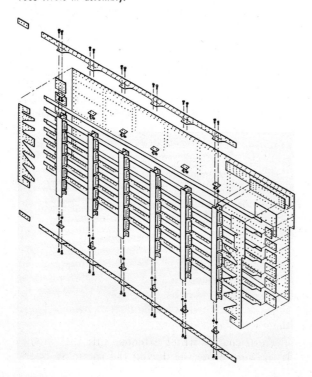

areas would be more difficult than if the part were flat.

Press forging would practically eliminate fabrication and subassembly operations in the aircraft plant. The high initial cost of dies and equipment, however, may offset the savings in other operations when total quantities are low or indefinite.

Forging Gives Weight Savings

In certain cases considerable weight advantage may be found by press forging. The wing panel illustrated in Fig. 2 weighs 76 lb in conventional construction; as an aluminum alloy forging, its weight is only 56 lb; if forged from magnesium alloy, 46 lb.

Fig. 5 illustrates the design of a wing surface panel for press forging. The panel must carry both end-compression and normal air pressure; in this case this is best accomplished with two sets of stiffening elements. In the forged design these are obtained by the waffle-grid arrangement. The weight is the same as that of the conventional design, but the part is one piece instead of being made from 49 components.

By DR. ROLAND B. SNOW
U. S. Steel Co. Research Laboratory
Kearny, N. J.

TEMPERATURES

of openhearth bottoms measured

Rammed bottoms of the same depth show similar thermal gradients providing equal insulation is used. Drill core data show all bottoms eroded to about the same depth after limited service regardless of composition or burning-in schedule.

PART I

The temperature attained at various levels in a pan-type openhearth bottom during the heating up, burning-in and operating periods are of practical importance to operators. Furnace time may be lost during burning-in by the injection of a series of steps which may have little actual value in the overall performance of a bottom. Temperature measurements in the brick work provide data for judging the expansion allowances for different hearth thicknesses and with different burning-in schedules. This is an important consideration if the brick work is to be tight during the normal operations. Temperature measurements in the rammed portion of a hearth not only show the possible depth of the ceramic set in the rammed layer but also provide information as to the strains which may be present in a bottom between tapping and charging. Tempera-

Part II will appear in The Iron Age *of February 8.*

tures in hearth sections of only slightly different construction may aid in designing a hearth having maximum protection against break-outs and a minimum heat loss.

The results reported here are based on measurements made with a total of 27 thermocouples distributed among six openhearth bottoms. With the exception of three chrome-alumel couples in one furnace, all couples were protected by at least one, and usually by two, closed end protection tubes of quartz glass or porcelain, depending upon their position in the bottom. In two of the hearths this outer protection tube extended from the tip

of the inner tube only as far as the upper course of the chrome brick and the inner protection tube, with only a 1/8-in. ID hole, extended through the remainder of the bottom.

Temperatures Automatically Recorded

The temperatures were recorded automatically. However, in some cases a complete record was not obtained for all the couples because of failure of the couple due to contamination by lead, tin or zinc, or because the recorder would not accommodate all of the couples. Only three of the platinum-platinum 10 pct rhodium couples were intact when removed from the furnaces but these were found to have retained their original calibration; the others all shorted out during service.

In each furnace the thermocouples were placed in the hearth just before the subhearth was rammed; the brickwork was removed from the area and a hole was burned through the pan. The brick were cut while replacing them so that they fit around the thermocouples protection tubes and the voids were filled with either fireclay or chrome-ore cold setting cement depending upon the brickwork. No breakout occurred as a result of the insertion of the couples in these bottoms. However, if a material other than a fine-grained, cold-setting cement is used around the protection tubes difficulty may be encountered in holding the tubes in place owing to the lack of bond between them and the brickwork.

Those couples which extended into the rammed layer were protected during the ramming opera-

Continued

tion by a 3-in. diam pipe held so as to prevent the rammer from damaging the couples and protection tubes. After the layer had been rammed the pipe was removed and the intervening space was rammed by packing loose material with blows of a mason's hammer on a 1-in. diam rod. Subse-

quent layers were rammed in a similar manner until the couple was covered; then normal ramming was carried out over the entire area.

Dr. R. B. Sosman reported temperature measurements in openhearth furnaces in his Howe Memorial Lecture entitled "Temperatures in the Openhearth Furnace."[1] Temperatures found in this furnace (A) and in the others of the same construction are indicated in Fig. 1; the tempera-

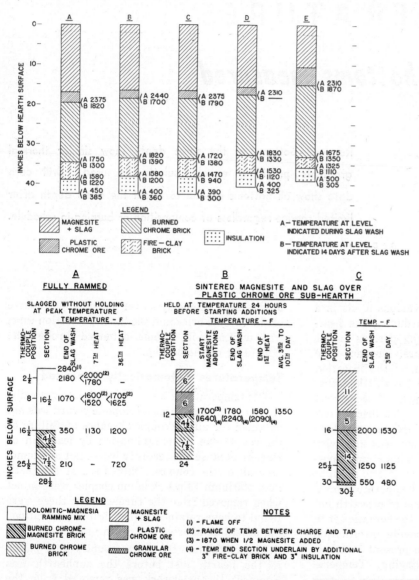

FIG. 1—Sketches of hearth sections with temperature data for grain magnesite—slag bottoms.

FIG. 2—Sketch of relatively thin hearth sections showing thermocouple positions and temperatures during burning-in and during steelmaking.

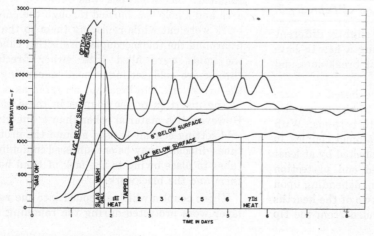

FIG. 3—Temperature record for thermocouples placed in hearth section A, Fig. 2.

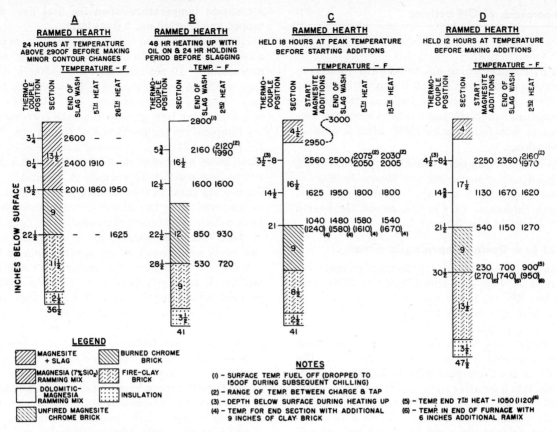

FIG. 4—Sketch of relatively thick hearth sections showing thermocouple position and temperatures at stages in burning-in and during steelmaking.

ture below the thin subhearth of plastic chrome was approximately 2400°F during slag washing and 1800°F during normal operation of the furnace. These furnaces, which are of approximately the same hearth construction, show nearly equivalent temperatures at corresponding levels.

The temperatures found in three relatively thin hearths of various construction are shown in Charts A, B and C in Fig. 2. In Chart A the hearth was slag washed without holding at peak temperature; normally such a hearth is held at 3000°F for 12 to 24 hr before making any addition. The continuous temperature record for this bottom is shown in Fig. 3. These data indicate a temperature of only 1040°F at a position 2½ in. below the hearth surface midway through the first heat. The simultaneous temperature 8 in. below the surface for the first seven heats is indicated. Peak temperatures usually occurred from 15 to 60 min after a heat was tapped. Minor fluctuations in temperatures which might be attributed to additions or to blocking of the heat did not show on the original chart. The cyclic nature of the curve for a position 8 in. below the surface is interesting but these peaks appeared from 3 to 5 hr after the peak occurred in the upper curve. The temperature at this position rose to 1500°, 1705°, and 1825°F during the 7th, 36th and 78th heats, respectively. The temperature 16½ in. below the surface was 1130°, 1200° and 1250°F during the 7th, 36th and 78th heats. The

couple 25½ in. below the surface, showed a temperature of 675°, 700° and 725°F during the 14th, 36th and 78th heats.

Center Insulation Cuts Heat Time

Chart B (Fig. 2) shows a slightly thinner hearth section where the brick work has the same construction as for the rammed hearth in Chart A. The temperature of the junction between the brick work and the plastic chrome ore subhearth at the time magnesite-slag additions were started was 1700°F and rose to 1870°F when half the magnesite-slag layer was added but was only 1780°F during the slag-washing period. During the 6th heat the temperature at this location was 1350°F, which is approximately 100°F below that of the corresponding extrapolated depth in the thicker hearth of Chart A. In the end of the furnace where the underlying brickwork includes 3 in. of fireclay brick and 3 in. of insulation, the temperature at the brick-plastic chrome ore interface was approximately 550° higher during slag washing and during the first heat than at a corresponding position in the uninsulated center portion of the hearth. The first helpers on these furnaces reported that lime and ore were usually up in the ends much before they were in the uninsulated center, indicating that insulation in the center might aid in reducing heat time on these furnaces.

Chart C in Fig. 2 is the hearth reported by Al-

February 1, 1951

105

win F. Frantz[2] which has almost the same construction as that of Chart B though it is slightly thicker. At the junction between the plastic chrome ore subhearth and the brickwork the temperature was found to be 1530° after 3 days of steelmaking.

Sketches of rammed hearths with, or without, magnesite-slag surfacing are shown in Fig. 4. These hearths are arranged according to total hearth thickness. Part of the record for hearth C is shown in Fig. 5.

Heat Loss During Charging Is Great

During the burning-in of the rammed material, furnace A, Fig. 4, a temperature of 2775° was reached 3¼ in. below the surface. The loss of heat from the hearth after chilling and charging is very marked. During the chilling and charging period the hearth lost 400° of temperature at a level 8¼ in. below the surface. The peaks on the temperature curve at this level occurred 2 to 5 hr after each heat was tapped. This couple failed during the 6th heat. The couple 13½ in. under the surface indicated a temperature of 1850°F after the first heat was tapped and remained nearly constant until the furnace was dampered 5 days later. The temperature rose during the subsequent 5-day period to 1950°F and remained nearly constant until the furnace was again taken off production 5 days later.

In Hearth B (Fig. 4) the temperature of the surface was apparently much lower. The couples 5¾ and 12½ in. under the surface barely reached a constant temperature when the first heat was tapped and shorted out 2 days later.

Hearth C received an 18-hr holding period above 2900°F prior to sintering of 4½ in. of a magnesite + 10 pct slag mixture. After a light slag wash the temperature 8½ in. below the surface dropped approximately 400° to 2100°F which is about 100° greater than the corresponding temperature for furnace A of this group. The temperature 14½ in. below the surface is of the same order of magnitude as was found at a corresponding position in furnace A (Fig. 4). An interesting point in this furnace is the difference in temperature at the Ramix-chrome brick interface, which is only approximately 150° greater in the end section, where 9 in. of additional fireclay brick are present in the hearth, than in the center of the hearth. Since fireclay brick will not hold steel, and since they show no great saving of heat where insulation is present, their use should be confined to locations at which it is necessary to fill space with a relatively low cost brick.

In Chart D the temperature 8¼ in. below the final surface reached the same order of magnitude as was observed in the other three furnaces by the time the second heat was tapped. The temperature at the 14⅝ and 21½-in. levels was considerably below a corresponding level in furnaces A and C of this group. An additional 6 in. in the thickness of the rammed layer increased the temperature of the chrome brick-fireclay brick interface by only 50°F.

References

[1] R. B. Sosman, "Temperatures in Openhearth Furnaces," T.P. 2435, AIME Metals Technology, 15, 1948.
[2] Alwin F. Frantz, "Furnace Bottom Temperature Gradients," AIME Openhearth Proc., 1938, p. 17.

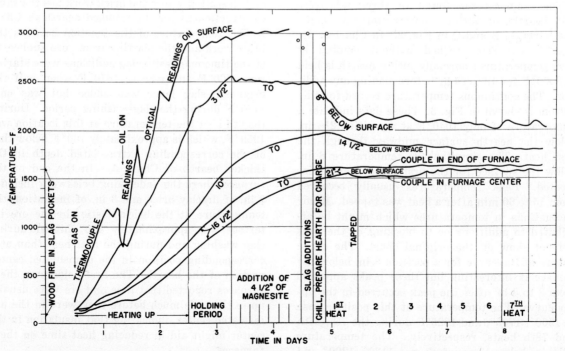

FIG. 5—Temperature record from thermocouples placed in hearth C, Fig. 4.

MAGNESIUM DOCKBOARD

employs extruded, cast, and wrought parts

By GENE BEAUDET
Chicago Editor

In an effort to stimulate industry-wide interest in magnesium applications, the Magnesium Co. of America, East Chicago, Ind., shortly after the war, started to look for a product they could manufacture that would be used by all industries. Their thinking was based on the belief that if they could manufacture such a basic item, it would result in a demand for other magnesium products from all types of industry.

After considering many possibilities, MAGCOA decided to build dockboards made from magnesium. Since every industrial plant has a loading dock on which material is transported from railroad cars and trucks, a dockboard made of magnesium would be the most likely means of acquainting industry in general with the qualities of magnesium products.

The development of heavy power loading equipment and its ability to handle increasingly greater loads had resulted in the need for an improved type of bridge ramp capable of supporting heavy loads more safely. In 5 years, magnesium dockboards have been placed in over 10,000 locations throughout the country. In addition, magnesium hand trucks, grain shovels, maritime gangplanks, can forks and many other items are now being manufactured.

Old Dockboards Inadequate

The growing acceptance of magnesium dockboards in materials handling is in great part due to the fact that the usual types of bridge ramps have proved inadequate in many cases. All too often a plain piece of heavy steel plate has been used. Heavy and cumbersome to handle, these plates present a definite safety hazard. In many cases accidents to personnel and damage to materials have resulted because the plates are incapable of withstanding heavy loads without buckling. They are also extremely difficult to secure properly and often shift out of position. Furthermore, their excessive weight makes them impossible to handle quickly and efficiently.

To overcome these difficulties, MAGCOA has developed a dockboard that is just as strong, considerably lighter and far safer than the conventional steel plate. Made entirely of magnesium, the dockboard weighs one-third to one-fourth as much

Just as strong but ¼ as heavy as steel plates, this all-welded magnesium dockboard is finding wide application. Each dockboard is individually designed. Some carry 30,000-lb axle loads, but typical designs carry around 1000-lb axle loads.

DOCKBOARDS about to enter stress relieving furnace where warping and internal stresses produced by welding are eliminated.

as steel plates of comparable strength. This factor speeds up operations, reduces handling accidents and cuts down on fatigue. In addition to the advantage of lighter weight, the dockboard has other features which add to its desirability. Reinforcing members on the underside of the dockboard increase its strength and prevent the dockboard from slipping out of position. The rounded slope of their special guard rails on the outer edges prevent runoffs of expensive loading equipment. These low guard rails or curbs also give maximum clearance for loading equipment and prevent damage to tires.

Mg Dockboards Custom-Built

Every dockboard is designed individually for each application because of the many variables at loading docks. Before a dockboard is manufactured, a company representative visits the site of the future installation and collects such data as the type of the materials handling equipment used and the maximum loads carried, the difference, if any, in height between the loading dock, the distance between the vehicle and the dock, the width of dockboard desired and any other information bearing on the proper design of the dockboard.

Each dockboard has three major components: the deckplate, the underframe and the guard rails. The deckplate, with a nonskid surface, is cut out of plate 36 by 48 in. wide by 60 to 144 in. long with thicknesses varying from $\frac{1}{4}$ to $\frac{5}{8}$ in. It is cut and beveled at each end by a carbide-tipped high-speed saw equipped with a trailing bevel cutter. On installations calling for a very wide dockboard, two plates are buttwelded together automatically by a mechanized Heliarc torch.

The underframe consists of standard structural magnesium shapes such as channels or I beams. These beams serve as reinforcing members to give added strength and are placed so that they prevent the dockboard from shifting out of position when in use. After the parts of the underframe are cut to specified lengths, they are tackwelded to the underside of the deckplate in the required positions.

The special guard rails are extruded. Together with the reinforcing members they have been designed to act as the principal longitudinal load carrying members and also act as side runoff preventatives.

After the guard rails are cut to size, they are tackwelded to the topside edges of the deckplate. However, they do not extend the full length of the edges. Nine inches from each of the four ends, tapered and rounded magnesium castings are welded to the extremities of the guard rails and to the deckplate. They contain hand holes on the outer side of the casting for safety and convenience in handling and allow a greater turning radius for loading vehicles. The plates and extrusions are made of F S alloy while the castings are made from H alloy.

When the components have been tackwelded into position, long filet welds are made which join the parts into one complete unit. Finished welds are smooth and uniform. The only finishing op-

SPECIALLY DESIGNED machine cuts and bevels magnesium tread plates. Machine bevels ⅝-in. plate in one operation.

INSPECTION prior to shipment. Finished dockboards are shown in background.

RAMP DOCKBOARD compensates for height differentials, provides smooth entry into truck and allows truck to park flush with loading dock.

eration that is necessary is quick wire brushing.

The welding process used in the entire operation is the Heliarc or inert gas shielding process developed by Linde Air Products Co. The use of this process makes the welding of magnesium an easy operation that can be done on a regular production basis. By this method an inert gas, usually argon, protects the arc from the air and eliminates the forming of oxides in the weld. Magnesium welding rods are used throughout the entire operation.

When all components have been joined by welding, the dockboard is passed into a stress relieving furnace where it is heated for periods of approximately 2 hr at temperatures ranging from 350° to 500°F to eliminate the small amount of warping and internal stresses resulting from the welding process. It is then removed and is ready for use.

In some cases a zinc chromate primer and corrosive resistant paint are applied to the finished dockboard. This is to protect the dockboard surface from corrosive atmospheres and conditions such as those encountered when they are used to unload refrigerator cars. Magnesium, however, has extremely good corrosion resistant properties under normal usage.

Mg Dockboards Easily Moved

Although some dockboards as much as 20 ft long and 6 ft wide, with the ability to support a 30,000 lb axle load, have been designed, a typical dockboard would be 60 in. wide and 48 in. long. Such a dockboard, capable of carrying an axle load of 1000 lb, weighs about 75 lb. A steel plate of equal strength would weigh four times that much and require the services of more than one worker to move it, whereas the magnesium dockboard can be easily moved and positioned by one man.

The load carrying capacity of a dockboard depends on its size and the thickness of plate used. A ¼-in. plate will carry up to 1000-lb axle loads, a ⅜-in. plate will carry up to 4000 lb, and ½-in. plate up to 12,000 lb, with suitable reinforcement.

FLARED dockboard increases maneuverability of heavy fork lift equipment where dock space is limited.

By B. M. PEARSON

Hassocks, Sussex, England

STEEL STRIP EXPERIMENTALLY

Continuous sheet and strip have been successfully made from iron powder in German laboratories and steel plants. Properties and characteristics of these experimental products are similar to those of normally rolled materials of the same chemical composition. The methods of fabricating powdered metals and alloys in continuous forms indicate practical solutions to the problems of rolling those alloys difficult to produce by ordinary openhearth-ingot-rolling processes. This is particularly true of those materials which, at present, are most easily readied for forming work by first producing them in the form of sponge and/or powder. For such materials, these new techniques offer a means of forming and shaping to specific sizes and thicknesses without any preliminary working.

Previously Believed Impossible

Previously, it has been thought impossible to produce forms from metal powder of any considerable length. The difficulty of avoiding variations in density inside pressed shapes has limited cross-sectional thicknesses as well. Prior to the recent developments in Germany, there was one method, proposed by G. Wasserman,[1] for producing sinter products of any desired length. This involves drawing down a tapered tube which has been filled with metal powder. A drawbench or enclosed grooved rolls are required.

Research was started on the continuous rolling of powdered metals when, in 1942, German metallurgists wanted some thin test pieces for special investigations[2] of RZ iron powders. It proved

surprisingly easy to produce strip by rolling.

Preliminary rolling tests based on this previous experience[3,4,5] showed that results depended largely on particle shape and sieve analysis, as with pressed and sintered products. Among the major factors affecting rolling of metal powders are the width of the opening between the rolls and their diameter, number and extent of the additional passes given the sintered strip, the turning speed of the rolls and the power loading reserve of the driving motor.

TABLE I

ANALYSIS OF RZ POWDER USED

	Particle Size in mm					
	<0.30	0.15 to 0.3	0.06 to 0.3	<0.15	0.06 to 0.15	<0.06
Composition, pct						
C	0.03	0.03	0.02	0.03	0.03	0.06
Mn	0.19	0.14	0.27	0.23	0.16	0.26
P	0.028	0.044	0.028	0.012	0.036	0.068
S	0.017	0.032	0.014	0.017	0.022	0.056
O_2	0.30	0.20	0.44	0.39	0.33	0.54
Sieving Analysis, pct						
>0.30	1.5	2.8	—	—	—	—
>0.15 ≤0.30	34.8	93.3	46.0	1.0	4.7	—
0.06 ≤0.15	49.0	3.0	51.3	78.9	93.6	—
<0.06	14.2	—	2.5	19.8	1.3	100
Pouring volumes cc 3/100 g	40.3	43.0	46.3	43.5	41.0	39.0
Rapping volumes cc 3/100 g	34.6	36.0	38.8	36.3	34.0	32.5
Filling density g/cc	2.48	2.33	2.16	2.30	2.44	2.56
Rapping density g/cc	2.89	2.78	2.58	2.78	2.94	3.08
Space Filling, pct	31.7	29.8	27.6	29.4	31.2	32.7

ROLLED FROM POWDER PART 1

Only an alloy's composition determines the properties obtainable by roll-forming, sintering and cold rolling it from the powder. This summary of the recent Report No. 6 from the German Iron & Steel and Engineering Societies tells how it has been done. For metals such as titanium, which are highly reactive with oxygen, this process may find application in producing certain shapes.

One of the first objects of the research was to investigate each of these influences and their effects on one another. At first, the work was confined to soft iron sheet and strip.

RZ iron powder with a normal sieve grading (particle size, 0.3 mm) was used almost exclusively for the tests. This is a melted-and-atomized powder with a spherical or spherical fragmented structure that provides a high grade, economical material. The chemical composition and the most important powder-metallurgy characteristics of this powder are given in Table I.

At first, attempts were made to feed the powder to the rolls by distributing it in a uniform thickness on sheet metal or paper. It was then introduced between the rolls, which were arranged vertically over one another as in normal practice. Undulations formed in the powder immediately before the rolls, particularly when compression was increased. These irregularities were drawn into the rolls and caused variations in thickness and compactness of the pressed strip. Cracks started at the edges as a result, and buckling or tearing of the under layer soon followed, with complete destruction of the strip.

Rolling Stand Turned On Side

Turning the rolling stand on its side was then tried and the powder fed from a box, arranged so that its slot-shaped opening was about the same length as the rolls and located some millimetres above the entry to them. It was soon established that below a definite roll clearance the rolls automatically took just the right quantity of powder.

Accordingly, the pressed strip showed a uniform thickness and density. The slot in the feed box need only be big enough to maintain a sufficient reserve of powder between the rolls above the entry. It was necessary to close off the rolls on the top side at the ends so that the powder would remain in the desired position.

By interrupting the rolling operation it was possible to follow in detail the formation of the

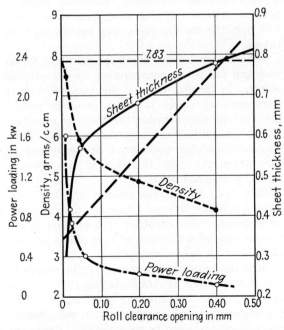

FIG. I—Influence of size of roll clearance opening on thickness, density and power consumption.

strip in the roll clearance. The powder is drawn down by the friction of the rolls. Increasing contact between the iron particles develops and a progressive interlocking of them takes place over the medial line of the roll opening. Finally, at least those particles on the surface remain permanently formed. Calculation of the strip thicknesses at the beginning and end of the forming demonstrated that an angle of nip of 8° accomplishes the pressing of the powder. The density of strip 0.45 mm thick under these conditions was 6.25 g per cc.

The factors governing the maximum and minimum sheet thicknesses obtainable with given equipment at different settings was determined. The maximum usable roll clearance is that which will provide a strip or sheet with sufficient strength to maintain structural soundness through the initial rolling and sintering steps. The lower limit is governed by the amount of deflection caused by the rolls impinging on one another—and thus, by the characteristics of the individual rolling mill itself. Yet a simple relationship between the roll clearances and sheet thicknesses is not obtained, at least in the middle range (see dotted straight line in Fig. 1). Instead, the curve representing sheet thickness rises steeply at first as the roll clearance increases and then continues in a relatively flat line.

Also Determined Densities

To aid in investigating the apparently complicated processes influencing sheet thickness, density was simultaneously ascertained. The curve representing density in Fig. 1 shows that this property increases in practically a linear manner as roll thickness decreases. However, below a definite, critical roll clearance, located at about 0.07 mm, the density rises very rapidly to high values.

Similar curves were developed for strip thickness and for power consumption by the driving motor. In the flat part of the curve for sheet thickness, the power is merely used to reduce the pore space by pressing the particles together. Below the critical roll clearance opening, however, considerable work must be performed to accomplish the cold forming of the already tightly compacted powder.

This steep rise in the amount of work indicated a relation between pressure and roll clearance opening. The densities of rolled test sheets were compared with those of thin pieces pressed in molds with known pressures.

Densities resulting from pressing pressures in Fig. 2 were used to etraploate the rolling pressures required for differing thicknesses. The rapid rise in pressure required to roll thinner sheet thicknesses can be seen clearly. Pressures up to about 6 tons per sq c could be applied

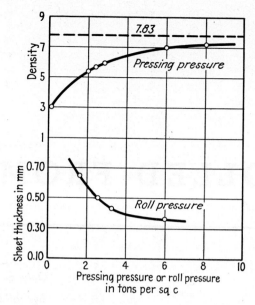

FIG. 2—Effect of pressing pressure on density and the influence of roll pressure on the thickness of rolled, non-sintered sheet. Test rolls, 70 mm diam.

with the small rolling stand used in these tests.

With the small, 70 mm diam rolls, pressed strip 0.35 to 0.75 mm thickness was prepared. Finished strip from this material ranged from 0.25 to 0.35 mm in thickness. Determining the most effective relationships between roll diameters and ranges of unsintered sheet thicknesses for commercial production would require rolling equipment at least approaching that used in normal practice, with rolls arranged side by side. However, to ascertain at least the approximate connections between these two factors, tests were conducted in rolling stands arranged normally, in vertical fashion. The diameters of the rolls involved were 200 mm in the smaller stand and 900 mm in the larger. Unsintered, pressed strips of about the same degree of compacting produced with varying thicknesses of powder feed were compared. Evaluation of these limited tests indicate clearly that the thicker the strip, the larger the roll diameter must be.

Influence of Roll Velocity

The influence of the linear velocity of the roll surfaces is apparently quite considerable, but since the turning speed of the experimental stands could not be controlled it could not be investigated. Rolling tests conducted in a plant having such equipment showed that thicker strip and sheet with a high degree of compacting could be produced, however.

Up to a certain limiting roll velocity, the tensile strength of unsintered strip became four or five times higher. But when the limit was exceeded. a coherent metal band was not formed. The amount of powder fed to the rolls was no longer sufficient. Roll diameter and the clearance between the rolls also influences this critical speed.

Particle size also helps to determine the thickness of sheets that can be produced, just as it is a deciding factor in finished surface quality. At related roll clearance openings, too fine a powder trickles through without being rolled and compacted. Within the range of those roll clearances that are usable with a given selection of particle sizes, the influence of powder gradings is not very great, Fig. 3. The thinnest sheet was obtained with a fine powder rolled through a small roll clearance. The thickest sheet was produced with powder of a normal grading and a larger opening. These powders generally approximated the complete particle size grading curve, with maximum space utilization effect.

Roll Clearance vs. Tensile Strength

Increasing the roll clearance opening decreases tensile strength of unsintered strip as well as density. Tensile strength falls from approximately 1.2 to 0.2 kg per sq mm when the roll clearance is increased from about 0.02 to 0.26 mm. With such low strength, the continuous strip cannot be drawn through the sintering furnace without damage. Because of its brittleness, unsintered strip cannot withstand any considerable bending or distortion.

The pressing phenomena involved in rolling metal powder leads to definite degrees of compactness or density. They also act markedly on tensile strength and the behavior and maintenance of sheet edges. For example, rolling various types of iron powder and also steel, bronze and aluminum powders under identical conditions caused large differences in the power consumption of the roll driving motor. This provided a means of evaluating the forming behavior of various powders. Knowledge of the tensile strengths of the test pieces obtained made it possible to determine the suitability of specific powders for sinter metallurgical purposes.

The properties of the roll surface are also important. If it is damp or moistened with a fine, adherent oil film, a thin, poorly compacted and brittle pressed strip results. It makes little differ-

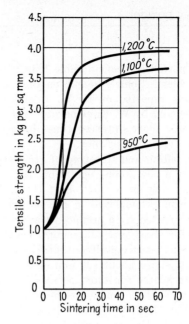

FIG. 4—Relationship of tensile strength to long sintering periods at various temperatures.

ence, at least where strip thickness is concerned, whether rolls are highly polished or are roughened.

Unlike a double-action press, where the direction of pressing lies in one plane, rolling proceeds along gliding planes. Beginning between the horizontal rolls, a continuing bonding and compacting of the powder particles take place. This proceeds up to the maximum strength obtainable with the given roll clearance and other factors present.

Effect of Pressing Pressure

The strength values obtained in rolled powders vary to about the same dimensional extent as with those powdered metal parts pressed in molds. From this it can be concluded that the forming phenomena in the roll clearance is governed by the pressing pressure. For this reason, the rolling of metal powder into strip or sheet may be considered as a continuing molding process performed by narrow, linear-type segmental regions along the surfaces of the rolls. This concept is of importance to powder metallurgy, because it indicates the possibility of commercially usable components and even continuous shapes being produced with roll stands and other specially developed equipment. An additional advantage is that rolling, compared with normal molding presses, require considerably lower-powered driving motors.

As the pressed strip issues from the rolls it is sintered, in a hydrogen atmosphere at a temperature of 1050 to 1100°C. The influence of temperature and time, which stand in inverse ratio to one another, have been a major consideration of this work. Because these investigations were primarily concerned with mold-pressed metal powders where greater wall thicknesses prevail,

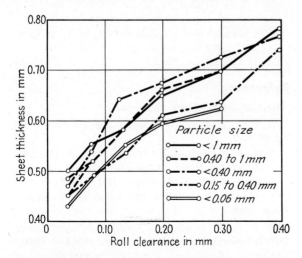

FIG. 3—How particle size affects sheet thickness, at varying roll clearances.

heating periods of considerable length were the main problem. Some research on short-time sintering was reported on by W. Eilender and R. Schwalbe[6] and by W. Englehardt.[7] However, up to now very short sintering times have not been measured with iron powder.

In the rolling and sintering of strip from iron powder as a continuous operation, the sintering period can only be a fraction of the time (1 to 3 hr) normally employed in powder metallurgy. The thin pressed strip produced was particularly suitable for short-time sintering, because of the rapid through-heating effect that was possible.

In tests, strips about 120 mm long and 20 mm wide were heated for short periods in a crucible containing a hydrogen atmosphere at 950, 1100 and 1200°C. Next, they were cooled in a second crucible in a nitrogen atmosphere. Periods of 5 to 60 sec were selected as the sintering times, as this represented the practical limits for this part of the projected continuous process.

Importance of Sintering Temperature

The curves in Fig. 4 shows clearly the great importance of temperature in short sintering periods. The first increase in strength occurs quickly and rises even more rapidly when higher temperatures are employed. Any further rise proceeds much more slowly. To reach a tensile strength of 2.5 kg per sq mm requires sintering for 100 sec at 950°C and only 10 sec at 1200°C.

The strength increase occurring in the first few seconds is caused by the test pieces requiring only a few seconds to reach the sintering temperature. The steep rise after this change point, especially at 1200°C and the flattening of the curve indicate that at least two phenomena are involved and super-imposed. The first of these obviously proceeds rapidly and the second requires a much longer time.

In an attempt to investigate the possibilities of even shorter sintering periods and higher temperatures, sample strips 10 mm wide were directly heated by direct current resistance heating. The test piece was placed in an insulated metal housing containing a protective atmosphere and was brought very rapidly to the required temperature. It was possible to control closely the rapidity of heating, its duration and the temperature. It was also possible to take measurements of the reaction of the specimens at selected points up to the maximum temperatures used in the tests, by means of cathode ray tube oscillograph.

High Temperatures Tested

The results of two series of tests at 1200 and 1400°C are given in Fig. 5. The time required for the heating up of the test pieces was ascertained to be about one second. Before the end of the first second of sintering at 1400 C following the preliminary heating up period, tensile strengths of more than 6 kg per sq mm are reached. In ordinary practice, such values could only be obtained after a prolonged sintering period. With this test equipment, the powder particles are sintered together almost instantaneously and as a result it is possible to perform this process much more rapidly than has been thought feasible. Such short sintering time also permit the use of short sintering furnaces in equipment setup for continuous operation.

Strip produced from RZ powder and sintered in this fashion showed no considerable reduction in volume, nor was this reduction greater than that occurring in sintered and pressed rings. Those metal powders produced by mechanical or chemical means did show more or less considerable sintering contraction, depending on the individual particle size and the pressing pressure applied.

_____

In Part II, to appear soon, cold-rolling and annealing experiments are described and the results of deep drawing tests are given. The making of steel strip is discussed, together with present and possible future costs of iron powder.—Ed.

_____

References

[1]*Metallforschung, p. 129, Vol. 2, 1947.*

[2]*G. Naeser, H. Steffe and W. Scholz, Stahl und Eisen, p. 346, Vol. 68, 1948.*

[3]*F. Skaupy, "Metallkeramik," Weiheim, 1950, fourth edition. R. Kieffer and W. Hotop, "Pulvermetallurgie und Sinterwerkstoffe," Berlin, Goettingen, Heidelberg, 1948, second edition.*

[4]*R. Kieffer and W. Hotop, "Sintereisen und Sinterstahl," Vienna, 1948.*

[5]*W. D. Jones, "Principles of Powder Metallurgy," London, 1937; P. Schwarzkopf, "Powder Metallurgy," New York, 1948.*

[6]*Archiv Eisenhuettenwesen, p. 267, Vol. 13, 1939-40.*

[7]*Zeitschrift Metallkunde, p. 12, Vol. 34, 1942.*

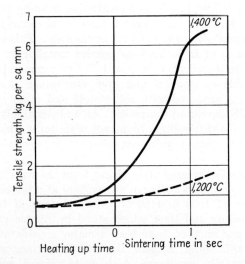

FIG. 5—Influence of short-time, high-temperature sintering on tensile strength.

SPECIAL SCALE
aids piston rod balancing

FIG. 2—Front of the Buick rod weighing machine with a rod in place and most of housing removed. Dial divisions are uniform. Sensitive dashpots in foreground make the scale dead beat.

To minimize engine vibration, G.M.'s Buick Motor Division exercises unusual care in weighing and balancing connecting rods employed in its Fireball engines. Each end of each rod has to come within ⅛ oz of standard weight. If weight at either end is excessive, metal has to be machined from bosses left at both ends to permit close balancing. Fig. 1 shows one of the new scales that Buick has developed to expedite weighing and insure holding the precise weights specified.

Each rod is set with its big end over two pins and its small end over a single pin of the weighing machine. Corresponding pointers move over two dials having 1/16-oz graduations and the pointers come to rest almost instantly because, although the scales are unusually sensitive, a suitable dashpot system makes the scales dead beat.

If readings do not come initially within the limits set, machining is done in the milling machine at left in Fig. 1. This machine has a fixture that holds the rod from the bores at each end. The amount of metal removed from each end depends upon the setting of two levers, each movable over a quadrant. Graduations on the quadrants correspond with those on the weighing scale and the levers are set to the reading that the respective scale pointers give. When this is done and the rod is in the fixture, the machine makes the corresponding cuts automatically. Then the rod is reweighed to be sure that cuts bring weights at both ends within the required limits.

In Fig. 2 the scale is shown with most of its housing removed to reveal the mechanism that Buick engineers developed to meet weighing needs. This development was undertaken because commercial scales previously employed had several drawbacks. These commercial scales

FIG. 1—New rod weighing scales developed by Buick, right. At left, the milling machine employed to remove excess metal when rods are found out of balance. Levers moving over quadrants in front of the machine are set, according to scale readings, to bring about correct balance.

lacked desired sensitivity and accuracy, did not have uniform graduations, and required overhaul and recalibration each one to three months. Moreover, if rods weighed were unduly heavy on one end, readings on the other end became inaccurate.

With the new scales, all these disadvantages are overcome. This is accomplished both through better design and through better construction. Indications involve only angular displacement of levers and counterweights and no steel tapes are required. The leverage system differs considerably from that of commercial scales. Knife edges are of hardened steel and the primary ones bear on tungsten carbide blocks while agate bearings are used with sector knife edges. If one end of the rod has excessive weight, weight indications on the other dial are not affected. Dials on which the graduations appear are adjustable and dial divisions are uniform. Preloading of dial hands is effected by counterweights but these weights, when properly adjusted, are so disposed that their deflection does not adversely affect the accuracy of readings.

Because of these features, the scales stay in adjustment. Some have been in use for more than a year without needing recalibration. This, of course, saves labor besides avoiding the uncertainties and need for frequent checking that were necessary with scales formerly used. When, to these advantages are added those of more rapid and precise weighing, the investment involved in designing and building the new scales is considered fully justified.

Checks hardness

'ON-THE-JOB'

Readings of metal hardness may now be taken any place in a plant or warehouse in a matter of seconds. It is done with a 30-oz, palm-sized hardness tester, made by Snow, Deakin and Co., Ltd., England, and distributed in this country by Newage International, Inc., New York. The device has been used to measure the hardness of flat, curved, round and other shapes. Sheet metal as thin as 0.020 in. has also been successfully tested.

The Ernst portable hardness tester is operated by pressing down the handgrips on the sides of the instrument. The unit's indentor is then actuated by a helical spring exerting a constant load of 15 lb. As the indentor or point penetrates the metal, it also compresses the base of a liquid-filled chamber, causing the liquid to move into a capillary tube. The tube extends up and around the tester's dial, and the point at which the liquid stops flowing represents the particular metal's hardness. Penetration of the metal is magnified 3000 times by the displacement of the liquid into the capillary tube.

Best results are obtained with the device by applying static pressure rather than by the sudden application of force. Only small indentations are made in metal surfaces, their maximum depth being 0.003 in. and maximum width 0.006 in. A hardened steel conical point is used with the Ernst tester for soft and medium hard metals and a diamond point for extremely hard alloys. The liquid in the capillary tube is colored green to facilitate reading and it contains antifreezing salts in solution.

The circular scales on which readings are made are interchangeable. Calibrated scales for Brinell, Rockwell, diamond pyramid or tons tensile are available.

THE ERNST PORTABLE hardness tester may be used to check the hardness of metals and alloys on the assembly line, in the warehouse and other such "on-the-job" points. Metals of a wide range of shapes and sizes may be tested with this device.

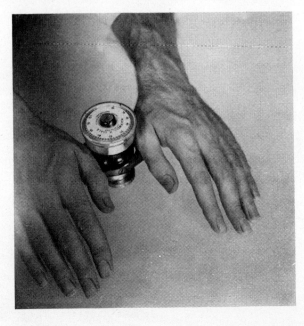

PARTS UNLIMITED

... in Jig Time

Cuts Irregular Shapes

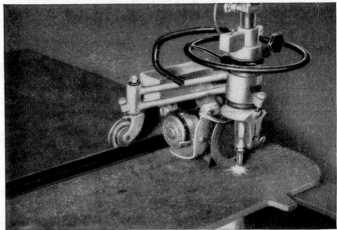
Cuts Straight Lines

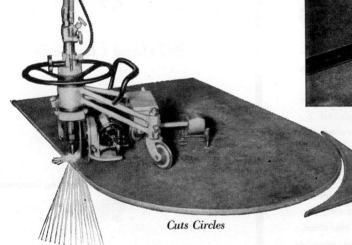
Cuts Circles

In large and small shops alike, the OXWELD CM-16 Portable Cutting Machine fills an unbelievably wide variety of oxygen cutting requirements. It cuts circles automatically. Hand-guided, it cuts irregular shapes. Operated on track, it cuts straight lines.

Indoors or out—wherever steel needs shaping—the CM-16 makes it easy to "tailor" parts as fast as the work can be laid out. *And its ready adaptability for special jobs is limited only by its operator's ingenuity!*

The CM-16 sets up as quickly as any manual outfit. It weighs only 45 lb., travels directly on the work, and is easy to carry from job to job. In normal use, it cuts up to 4 in. of steel; with standard accessories,

it cuts materials up to 18 in. thick and it cuts bevels.

Any LINDE representative will be glad to show you how the OXWELD CM-16 Portable Cutting Machine can boost production and cut fabricating costs in your shop. Write for catalog, Form 4487, or call the LINDE Office nearest you today for a free demonstration.

The terms "Linde" and "Oxweld" are registered trade-marks of Union Carbide and Carbon Corporation.

LINDE AIR PRODUCTS
A Division of Union Carbide and Carbon Corporation
30 East 42nd Street   **UCC**   New York 17, N. Y.
Offices in Other Principal Cities
In Canada: DOMINION OXYGEN COMPANY, LIMITED, Toronto

Oxweld
Trade-Mark

CM-16 PORTABLE CUTTING MACHINE

Now Available

NEW CLASS H*
MOTORS PROTECTED BY
DOW CORNING SILICONES

... the insulation that has already saved industry millions of maintenance dollars plus the hourly output of hundreds of thousands of men!

This most timely announcement caps the test program we started 8 years ago when silicone resins were introduced by Dow Corning Corporation. First we proved by accelerated life testing that silicone insulated motors had a good 10 to 1 advantage in life expectancy and wet insulation resistance. Then we sold silicone (Class H) insulation to the manufacturers of electrical equipment ranging from lift truck and traction motors to solenoid and brake coils. We also encouraged the better rewind shops to rebuild hard working industrial motors with Class H insulation.

Now we can proudly refer American industry to this goodly list of electrical manufacturers, all able and willing to supply electric machines protected by Class H insulation made with Dow Corning Silicones.

Take your special problems to the application engineer representing any of these companies or to our Product Development Engineers.

furnished by:

ALLIS-CHALMERS MANUFACTURING COMPANY

Continental Electric Co., Inc.

ELECTRO DYNAMIC

ELLIOTT COMPANY

KURZ & ROOT COMPANY
(INCORPORATED)

The Leland Electric Co.

THE LOUIS ALLIS CO.

The Reliance Electric & Engineering Company

THE B·A·WESCHE ELECTRIC COMPANY

**WESTINGHOUSE
ELECTRIC CORPORATION**

* "Class H" insulation is the kind of insulation that keeps motors running in spite of "Hell and High water." *(slanguage dictionary)*

DOW CORNING  CORPORATION
MIDLAND, MICHIGAN

news of industry

Steel Capacity in '52 Set at Over 120 Million Tons

Industry's greatest growth spree . . . Pittsburgh-Youngstown still on top . . . But East takes second place from Chicago . . . Estimate includes Barium's eastern mill—*By John Delaney.*

Stopgap Wage-Price Freeze

Washington—A stopgap wage-price order fell on industry, freezing nearly all commodities and services, except most farm products, at highest levels in a base period from Dec. 19, 1950, to Jan. 21, 1951. Wages were chilled at Jan. 25 levels. Lengthy adjustment on these hasty orders is coming. (See p. 128 for complete story.)

President Truman has signed an executive order calling on government agencies to lend personnel to the Office of Price Stabilization to aid in enforcing the price freeze.

Gary Coke Battery Enlarged

Gary—Reconstruction of the No. 13 coke oven battery of the United States Steel Co.'s Gary works was completed recently. The battery, enlarged from 69 to 77 ovens, will increase annual coke production from 340,000 to 380,000 tons. A similar project underway on the company's No. 15 coke oven battery is expected to be completed by July of this year.

Cole Named to NPA Steel Div.

Washington — Melvin W. Cole, Bethlehem Steel official, has been appointed deputy director of NPA Iron and Steel Div. Mr. Cole headed the Iron and Steel Div. of the Office of Industry Cooperation during the time of voluntary allocations in 1948. He also served with the WPB for 3 years during World War II.

Pittsburgh—The steel industry is on the greatest expansion spree in its history. Annual ingot capacity probably will exceed 120 million tons by the end of 1952, or shortly thereafter.

The expansion picture is changing so rapidly that steel marketing experts are at wit's end trying to put the pieces together. Some programs are still to be announced. Those that have been are likely to be on the conservative side.

When the last rivet is driven home, the industry's competitive map will be largely redrawn.

On the basis of announced programs and others known to be under consideration, the Pittsburgh-Youngstown district will retain the No. 1 spot with a probable capacity of more than 43.6 million ingot tons. However, the East will re-place Chicago in the runner-up position with 28 million tons as compared with close to 24 million tons. Cleveland-Detroit capacity will be 14 million; the West 6.4 million and the South 5.6 million. This totals about 121.5 million, an increase of 22.1 million tons over capacity at Jan. 1, 1950.

This estimate includes U. S. Steel Corp.'s new mill at Morrisville, Pa. (1.8 million tons); National Steel Corp.'s planned mill at Paulsboro, N. J. (estimated 1.5 million tons); Barium Steel Corp.'s mill now under consideration (1.3 million tons), and the New England mill (estimated 1.0 million tons). It also includes Gibraltar Steel Corp.'s mill (estimated 800,000 tons).

A survey by the American Iron & Steel Institute indicates that blast furnace capacity at Dec. 31,

New Steel Capacity Planned by Producing Districts

PITTSBURGH—A geographical breakdown of contemplated steel capacity increases by Dec. 31, 1952, including probable new capacities by producing districts:

District	Cap. at Jan. 1, 1950 (N.T.)	Probable Increase (N.T.)	Probable cap. at Dec. 31, 1952 (N.T.)
Pgh.-Youngstown	39,145,920	4,502,700	43,648,620
East	19,875,460	8,130,000	28,005,460
Chicago	20,777,520	2,994,900	23,772,420
Cleveland-Detroit	9,333,460	4,752,000	14,085,460
West	5,699,620	725,000	6,424,620
South	4,560,820	1,054,600	5,615,420
Totals	99,392,800	22,159,200	121,552,000

1952, will be close to 80 million tons, an increase of more than 7 million tons over Jan. 1, 1951 capacity.

This tremendous program has been spurred by three factors: (1) The opportunity of amortizing part of the cost over 5 years for tax purposes; (2) the defense effort, and (3) encouraging results of market studies on the long-range demand for steel.

In addition to materials and equipment for the expansion itself, the industry must provide for greatly expanded raw materials requirements, such as iron ore, coal, limestone, manganese, scrap, gas, fuel oil, and electrical power. More than 150 million tons of iron ore alone will be needed to support capacity operations—30 million tons more than the estimated consumption last year.

Steel Capacity Expansion Plans

(By Company and Location—Jan. 1, 1950 to Dec. 31, 1952)

Pittsburgh—Indications are that steel industry annual ingot capacity will exceed 120 million tons at Dec. 31, 1952. This is the expansion picture, based on latest information available at press time. Capacity increases are in relation to capacity at Jan. 1, 1950 of 99,392,800 tons.

Company	Planned Cap. Inc.* from Jan. 1, '50 to Dec. 31, '52 (Net Tons)	Location
U. S. Steel Corp.	1,064,700	Pittsburgh District
	456,900	Chicago District
	140,000	Youngstown District
	1,800,000	Morrisville, Pa.
	500,000	Fairfield, Ala.
	160,000	Geneva, Utah
Bethlehem Steel Corp.	1,080,000	Lackawanna, N. Y.
	740,000	Sparrows Point, Md.
	352,000	Steelton, Pa.
	188,000	Bethlehem, Pa.
	180,000	Johnstown, Pa.
	60,000	Los Angeles, Cal.
National Steel Corp.	1,200,000	Ecorse, Mich.
	300,000	Weirton, W. Va.
	1,500,000**	Paulsboro, N. J.
Armco Steel Corp.	580,000	Middletown, O.
	150,000	Houston, Tex.
	150,000	Kansas City
	137,000	Ashland, Ky.
	6,000	Butler, Pa.
Jones & Laughlin Steel Corp.	1,200,000	Pittsburgh
	350,000	Cleveland
Youngstown Sheet & Tube Co.	925,000	Indiana Harbor, Ind.
Republic Steel Corp.	852,000	Cleveland District
Inland Steel Co.	750,000	Indiana Harbor, Ind.
Detroit Steel Corp.	720,000	Detroit
Granite City Steel Co.	620,000	Granite City, Ill.
Sharon Steel Corp.	560,000	Farrell, Pa.
Pittsburgh Steel Co.	488,000	Monessen, Pa.
Colorado Fuel & Iron Corp.	325,000	Pueblo, Colo.
	40,000	Buffalo, N. Y.
Crucible Steel Co.	300,000	Midland, Pa.
Wheeling Steel Corp.	264,000	Wheeling, W. Va.
Kaiser Steel Corp.	180,000	Fontana, Calif.
McLouth Steel Corp.	100,000	Trenton, Mich.
Atlantic Steel Co.	100,000	Atlanta, Ga.
Allegheny-Ludlum Steel Corp.	80,000	Watervliet, N. Y.
Timken Roller Bearing Co.	75,000	Canton, O.
Alan Wood Steel Co.	50,000	Conshohocken, Pa.
Continental Steel Corp.	36,000	Kokomo, Ind.
Laclede Steel Co.	35,000	St. Louis, Mo.
Green River Steel Co.	30,000**	Owensboro, Ky.
Tennessee Steel Co.	100,000	Oneida, Tenn.
Connors Steel Div. of H. K. Porter Co.	37,600	Birmingham, Ala.
Empire Steel Corp.	75,000	Mansfield, O.
Keystone Steel & Wire Co.	22,000	Peoria, Ill.
New England Mill	1,000,000**	New London, Conn.
Barium Steel Corp.	1,300,000**	Phoenixville, Pa.
Gibraltar Steel Corp.	800,000	Detroit
Total	22,159,200	

*At least 4,836,850 net tons of this capacity is already in production. This includes 1.6 million tons of new capacity added by U. S. Steel last year and 1 million tons added by Bethlehem.
**Estimated

New Gibraltar Steel Corp. Plans Detroit Integrated Mill

Detroit—The newly-formed Gibraltar Steel Corp. is planning to build a new integrated steel mill of 800,000 tons annual capacity near Detroit. It will cost more than $100 million. Building of the plant is contingent on a large Reconstruction Finance Corp. loan. Detroit Steel Corp. also filed a certificate of necessity for steel expansion but details were not available at press time.

The plant would be located on a 900-acre tract on the Detroit River at Trenton, Mich., about 17 miles from Detroit. Backers of the project say it can be completed in 18 months if priorities are granted.

Steelmaking facilities would include a coke oven battery and blast furnace, four openhearth furnaces, blooming mill and hot and cold-rolled sheet mill. Finished steel capacity would be about 675,000 net tons of hot and cold-rolled sheet and strip.

Present plans call for an initial outlay of $10 million of private funds and a $90 million RFC loan. An additional $5 million of private funds would be raised when the plant is in operation. A certificate of necessity will be sought.

Cyrus Eaton, Cleveland financier head of Otis & Co., will be Gibraltar chairman of the board. Max Zivian, president of Detroit Steel Corp., will be president; and Carlton M. Higbie, president of Higbie Mfg. Co., will be vice-president and chairman of the executive committee.

Lone Star Steel's New Plant To Produce 350,000 Tons of Pipe

Dallas—Backed by a $73,425,201 loan from three government agencies (THE IRON AGE, Jan. 18, 1951, p. 95) construction of its integrated mill near existing facilities is being pushed by the Lone Star Steel Co. Ground breaking was to start "at once."

Planned are four openhearths with an average heat of 188 tons each. Rolling mills will be built with future expansion in mind. A two-high plate mill will produce plates measuring 44 in. by 110 in. A Steckel mill will further reduce plate thickness and roll the steel into coils. After feeding through

forming stands, the coils will be electrically welded into tube.

Estimated output of the proposed plant is 500,000 tons of steel ingots to make 350,000 tons of welded steel pipe in diameters from 2 in. to 16 in.

steels were run by Buick at Flint even prior to 1940.

Most automobile companies have made or are making studies to determine the extent to which boron-treated steels can be substituted for conventional SAE grades. In addition, committees of the Society of Automotive Engineers are studying both civilian and military alloy steel problems. A study of army jeep specifications has already been completed. Examination of the prospects for using boron-treated steels for army combat vehicles is in process.

Boron Steel Seen Substituting for Some Alloys

Changing alloy steel specs signal greater reliance on boron-containing steels . . . See autos, trucks, machinery, oil country goods hardest hit . . . Alloys short—*By Walter Patton.*

Detroit — Alloy steel specification changes already made and under consideration indicate that boron-containing steels will be used in large quantities by the end of this year. Although there may be important exceptions, through-hardened, boron-treated steels may replace many of the alloy steels containing chromium, nickel and molybdenum as alloying elements.

Products most likely to be affected, say metallurgists here, are automobiles and trucks, certain types of military combat vehicles, machinery, and oil country goods.

Aircraft alloy steels will be changed less rapidly than other required steels, but even these may have to give way if all-out war production is ordered by Washington.

Not Much Choice

"There is little choice left to us," a prominent Detroit steel buyer told The Iron Age this week. An all-out jet engine program would undoubtedly swallow up a very large percentage of all available chromium, molybdenum and nickel for steel alloying purposes."

The critical alloy shortage is developing for several reasons. Government stockpiling of nickel, molybdenum, tungsten and other alloying elements has been extensive. The stockpiling program is likely to continue and may even be enlarged, some believe.

In addition, military vehicles

need a much larger percentage of alloy steel. Sections involved are large, requiring high hardenability which usually means higher alloy content. In normal times, perhaps 7 pct of all constructional steel production is alloy. The percentage of total bar steel carrying alloy today is nearer 10 or 12 pct.

Used Widely During War

U. S. metallurgists have had wide experience with boron-treated steel. Such steels were used extensively during World War II. Most grades have been thoroughly tested in the laboratory and in service. Since World War II, some firms have continued to use boron-treated steels. Caterpillar Tractor Co. and Mack Truck Co. are examples. Many laboratory tests of boron-treated

---

Molybdenum Restrictions

Washington—NPA last Saturday ordered a temporary freeze on all non-rated orders for molybdenum except for making high-speed steels. At the same time, NPA issued an order (M-33) restricting molybdenum inventories to a 20-day supply.

Also, in another move, NPA issued directives by letter to producers, handlers, and marketers of molybdenum ordering that only 50 pct of the amount ordered on both rated and non-rated orders for high-speed steels be delivered.

Applied to Large Parts

Generally speaking, boron-treated steels have been most widely applied to large parts, requiring deep hardening. Although many tests have been made on carburizing grades having a hard, high carbon case and a soft core, service experience on these grades has been limited. The problem of possible distortion of boron-treated steels during heat treatment will require further study, say Detroit metallurgists.

Most Detroit engineers and metallurgists, remembering their successful experience during World War II, will approach the possibility of changing over to boron-treated steels with an open mind. Traditionally, the Air Corps has resisted such changes, insisting on steels with high chromium, nickel and molybdenum content.

Tungsten Cutting Tools

Another development in alloy steels is rapidly becoming a major headache for Detroit production experts. Drastic reduction in the use of tungsten cutting tools will result in widespread changes in tool specifications, it is believed. While many car companies have already changed over either to carbides or molybdenum-type steels, recent changes in the tungsten quota are expected to be felt in Detroit.

Restrictions on cobalt may result in further deviations in plant cutting tool practice.

INDUSTRIAL SHORTS

NCA OFFICERS—J. F. Pritchard, president of J. F. Pritchard & Co., Kansas City, has been elected president of the NATIONAL CONSTRUCTORS ASSN. J. J. O'Donnell, manager of personnel and labor relations of the Lummus Co., New York, was chosen vice-president.

PONTUSCO CORP. — Complete ownership of Pontusco Corp., has been acquired by the U. S. PIPE & FOUNDRY CO., Burlington. Pontusco formerly was jointly owned by U. S. Pipe & Foundry Co., and Compagnie de Pont-a-Mousson of Nancy, France.

GOLDEN JUBILEE — THE BUCKEYE BRASS & MFG. CO., Cleveland, manufacturer of bearing bronze, announces its fiftieth year of service to the industry.

COKE IS COOKING—ARMCO STEEL CORP. has awarded a contract to the Wilputte Coke Oven Div. of Allied Chemical & Dye Corp. for the erection of a coke oven plant at Middletown, Ohio. The new plant will have 76 coke ovens, and should have an annual capacity of 450,000 tons of blast furnace coke.

IN BUSINESS—G. G. GREULICH, formerly consulting engineer, Special Products Div., U. S. Steel Co., has opened an office at 610 Dupont Circle Bldg., Washington. He will represent Drilled-In Caisson Corp., W. E. O'Neil Construction Co., and Western Foundation Co.

NEW LOCATION—A new warehouse and general office building located in Cambridge, has been opened by WARD STEEL CO.

EXPANSION PROGRAM — A $500,000 expansion program including additional equipment and instruments to increase the availability of basic ingredients for company products was announced by KENNAMETAL, INC., Latrobe, Pa.

JOIN FORCES — The Baker-Raulang N. Y. Corp. and the Material Handling Equipment Co. have joined forces and will be known as MATERIAL HANDLING EQUIPMENT CO., located at 141 E. 44th St., New York.

MAKING COR-TEN — The ACME STEEL CO., Pittsburgh, has been licensed to manufacture Cor-Ten, corrosion resistant, high strength, low alloy steel developed by Carnegie-Illinois Steel Corp.

INCREASES OUTPUT—A new alumina plant will be built near Bauxite, Ark., by the ALUMINUM CO. OF AMERICA. The new plant will be operated by Aluminum Ore Co., wholly-owned subsidiary of Aluminum Co. of America, and will increase production 50 pct.

ACQUISITION—The Pittsburgh Valve & Fittings Div. of the Pitcairn Corp., Barbeton, Ohio, and the Pittsburgh Valve & Fittings Corp., a subsidiary of the Pitcairn Corp., has been acquired by ROCKWELL MFG. CO., Pittsburgh. Rockwell paid approximately $3 million for the purchase.

DISTRIBUTOR — Worthington Pump & Machinery Corp., Harrison, N. J., has named the HUTCHINSON FOUNDRY & STEEL CO., Hutchinson, Kan., a distributor for their construction equipment, including mixers, placers, air tools, centrifugal pumps and suction and discharge hoses.

MERGER—Crescent Truck Co., Lebanon, Pa., manufacturers of electric industrial trucks and tractors, has merged with BARRETT-CRAVENS CO., Chicago, and will operate as a division of the company. All sales will be conducted from the general office of Barrett-Cravens in Chicago, and manufacturing operations will continue at Lebanon.

NPA Nickel Order Amended To Ban Use in Non-Defense Items

Doesn't alter first quarter limits . . . More than 300 items in ban.

Washington—Nickel order (M-14) was amended last week to prohibit use of nickel bearing metals in a wide variety of non-defense products.

The order exempts purely functional uses if there is no suitable substitute. Some types of repair are permitted. The amendment does not change original first quarter limits of non-defense use of nickel to 65 pct of the base period average.

Ban Effective Apr. 1

Specifically, the order now provides that after Mar. 1 no nickel silver or nickel plate can be used in making the listed items. The effective date of the ban on high nickel alloys and nickel bearing stainless steel is Apr. 1.

A period of grace is allowed for items already in process before the effective dates of the order. Such work must be completed within 2 months after those dates.

More than 300 items under about 20 general classifications are prohibited under the amended order. Particularly affected are the automotive, construction, hardware and appliance industries.

Use of stainless steel in making most farm machinery, implements and tools is out, as well as for automobile bumpers, hubcaps and numerous other items. It is also banned for many uses in construction, appliance manufacture, general and miscellaneous purposes.

Essential Uses Only

Nickel alloy is banned for a variety of building materials, appliances, dry cleaning equipment, motor vehicle accessories, jewelry, and miscellaneous purposes. Use of nickel plate is prohibited for numerous hardware, appliance, furniture, auto accessories, and other categories.

Use of nickel silver is prohibited outright for all uses except dairy equipment, drafting and engineering instruments, hospital equipment and orthopedic appliances, slide fasteners, flat and hollow ware (not over 15 pct nickel), watch cases (not over 10 pct), and functional purposes for springs and communications and electrical equipment parts.

New Specs for Furnace Group Sought to Ease Nickel Shortage

Washington — Standardization of types and rewriting of heat treating furnace specifications are being urged by the industrial furnace and oven industry's advisory committee to NPA in an effort to help obtain scarce nickel and other materials.

The NPA has amended the nickel order (M-14) banning some end uses of nickel and is drafting an order controlling nickel scrap. The agency is also considering an MRO order for the furnace industry.

The industry is already using nickel substitutes wherever possible. But because of material shortages backlogs continue to grow. Orders have more than doubled the July level.

Canadian Iron Ore to England

Montreal—Dominion Steel & Coal Corp. has signed a 5-year contract to sell iron ore to Great Britain starting in 1952. The agreement covers annual shipments of 1 million gross tons, which will be supplied by the company's subsidiary, Dominion Wabana Ore, Ltd., Bell Island, Newfoundland. Additional mining, loading and shipping facilities at a cost of $6,000,000 will be built at Wabana.

GE Turbine Output Sets Record

Schenectady — Production of large turbine generators by the General Electric Co. during 1950 surpassed all company records. In the first full year of operation at the Schenectady plant combined capacity of units made totaled 2,866,000 kilowatts. Largest steam generator made had a rating of 165,000 kilowatts.

Shell Steel Mill Percentage Limits Abolished

NPA to quicken output of shell quality hot-rolled bars, billets, armor plate . . . Orders no longer DO's, subject to NPA negotiation . . . Bookings were extended—*By Gene Beaudet.*

Chicago — The recent government order revising certain provisions of NPA order M-1 indicates that the priority system of placing defense orders with steel mills is starting to collapse under its own weight.

With this revision hot-rolled bars of projectile or shell quality steel are lifted out of the DO category entirely and are subject to direct negotiation with NPA if necessary. It abolishes percentage limits over which mills are not required to book these items. It also applies to billets of projectile or shell quality and rolled armor plate.

Speculation on Reasons

Why such an order was issued is open to speculation. Some cold-drawn producers who are experiencing difficulty placing DO shell orders claim it is because DO bookings on these items are extended so far out that they cannot be filled in a reasonable length of time to satisfy contractors production schedules.

To fill these orders some cold drawers have been taking their consumer hot bar mill allotments in

---

Controls—Contracts

Two new regular weekly service features have been added by THE IRON AGE.

"Controls Digest" is a quick reference list of government orders and regulations relating to the metalworking industry and will be carried each week to help you keep abreast of latest government rulings. See page 126.

"Defense Contracts to Metalworking Industry" brings you selected major contracts awarded each week by government agencies. Potential sub-contractors will find the list on page 128 especially useful."

---

shell quality grades and getting them filled more quickly. They have then taken their DO tonnage in a common grade of hot-rolled bars and used them to replenish inventory or fill non-DO orders.

Some think mills have not put enough production into shell quality steels because they need a lot of conditioning, take away from other production, and are not as profitable as other grades. Others believe that they were not produced because there weren't enough shell orders out to justify increased production of these items until recently. Shell orders were scarce from August to November last year.

In December they picked up, continued to mount, and are expected to become even greater. As a result, mills were caught short. Some big bar mills in the area are presently booked into next December on defense orders, while others in the East are reported to be booked anywhere from September to January 1952.

Opening Up Bottleneck

To alleviate this bottleneck, NPA threw shell order bookings wide open. No DO limit was authorized because there was not enough shell steel being produced and therefore, no matter how high the percentage was raised there would not be enough. As shell orders increase they will be just absorbed by the mills. Procedure is not yet clear. Some mill sources believe they will receive NPA directives ordering them to produce certain tonnages of shell steels each month. Others think that holders of shell orders will place the orders with the mills. If they are unable to get them filled they will then apply to NPA which will direct certain mills to fill the order.

Expansion Rise to 6 Million Tons by '52 Listed by National

Pittsburgh — National Steel Corp.'s annual ingot capacity will rise to 6 million tons during 1952 —an increase of 500,000 tons over earlier announcements of expansion plans.

E. T. Weir, chairman, said that further developments in the company's flexible expansion program were responsible for the upward revision. The 1952 capacity will represent an increase of 1,500,000 tons over 1950 capacity. Present capacity is 4,750,000 tons.

This does not include the company's planned eastern mill at Paulsboro, N. J., which will have a capacity of approximately 1,500,000 tons.

When the program is completed, Great Lakes Steel Corp. capacity will be 3,600,000, an increase of 1,200,000 tons, and that of Weirton Steel Co. will be 2,400,000 tons, a boost of 300,000 tons.

Named to NPA Abrasive Group

Chicago—Arthur T. Dalton, secretary of Chicago Wheel & Mfg. Co., has been appointed to the advisory committee for the abrasive industry of the National Production Authority. During World War II Mr. Dalton was a representative on the abrasive advisory group of the War Production Board.

Amend Aluminum Scrap Order

Washington—The National Production Authority has postponed the effective date of the aluminum scrap order (M-22) until Mar. 1. The action was taken in order that additional firms could be included in the list of eligibles for processing scrap.

Zinc Industry Asks 60 Day Halt on Changes in NPA Order M15

Washington—Spokesmen for the zinc industry last week requested the National Production Authority to make no changes in the zinc order (M-15) over the next 30 to 60 days.

Both zinc producers and users believe the present unbalanced stocks and maldistribution has been caused primarily by attempts of users to bring inventories up to something near the permitted levels. Both groups think the situation will straighten itself out.

Zinc users told NPA they were opposed to any drastic limitation of end uses for fear of having to shut down. They said that many suppliers are filling rated orders out of regular stocks and are forced to hold nondefense allotments far below the 80 pct level imposed by M-15.

NPA Assigns Aluminum Authority

Washington — NPA authority has expanded its delegation of authority to the Secretary of Defense so as to permit rescheduling of deliveries of aluminum forms for the aircraft and guided-missiles program.

This will not affect production schedules. It merely permits an aluminum delivery to be shifted from one manufacturer to another when it is necessary to speed up either program.

NPA Readies Steel Strapping Order; Will Survey Metal Plants

Washington—The National Production Authority is preparing an order which will greatly restrict use of steel strapping in nonessential packaging. Industry spokesmen feel such an order is necessary.

Meanwhile, NPA has started a survey of metal consuming plants to get a better picture of how much material is going into various metal products.

Such information is needed to

CONTROLS *digest*

For more details see "You and Government Controls," The Iron Age, Jan. 4, 1951, p. 365. For full text of NPA regulations write U. S. Dept. of Commerce, Division of Printing Service, Room 6225 Commerce Bldg., Washington 25, D. C.

Subject	Order	Effective Date
General		
Inventory Control	NPA Reg. 1	Sept. 18
	Interpretation 1, 2, 3	Nov. 10
Priorities System	NPA Reg. 2	Oct. 3
DO Ratings	Amend. 1, 2	Oct. 3, Dec. 29
DO Ratings	Delegation 1, 2, 3, 4	Nov. 1, Nov. 2, Nov. 3
Priorities (Canada)	NPA Reg. 3	Nov. 8
Auto Prices, Wages	ESA Reg. 1	Dec. 18
Hoarding	NPA Notice 1	Dec. 27
Metals		
Aluminum distribution	NPA M 5	Oct. 27
Aluminum cutback	NPA M 7 (amended)	Dec. 1
	Direction 1	Nov. 28
	Direction 2	Dec. 16
	Direction 3	Dec. 27
Aluminum scrap	NPA M 22	Mar. 1
Cadmium	NPA M 19	Jan. 1
Cobalt stocks	NPA M 10 (amended)	Dec. 30
Collapsible tubes	NPA M 27	Jan. 27
Columbium steels	NPA M 3	Oct. 19
Copper distribution	NPA M 11	Nov. 29
Copper use	NPA M 12 (amended)	Dec. 30
Copper scrap	NPA M 16 (amended)	Jan. 1
Molybdenum cutback	NPA M 33	Jan. 27
Nickel cutback	NPA M 14 (amended)	Jan. 23
Ores, metals	NPA Del. 5	Dec. 18
Steel	NPA M 1 (amended)	Jan. 22
Freight car program	Supl. 1	Oct. 26
Great Lakes ships	Supl. 2	Nov. 15
Canadian freight cars	Supl. 3	Dec. 15
Steel warehouses	NPA M 6 (amended)	Nov. 15
Tin inventories	NPA M 8	Jan. 9
Tinplate, terneplate	NPA M 24	Jan. 27
Metal cans	NPA M 25	Jan. 27
Tinplate closures	NPA M 27	Jan. 27
Tungsten	NPA M 30	Jan. 22
Zinc distribution	NPA M 9	Nov. 16
Zinc cutback	NPA M 15	Jan. 15
Miscellaneous		
Chemicals	NPA M 32	Jan. 23
Construction	NPA M 4	Oct. 27
	Amendment 1, 2	Oct. 13, Nov. 15
Elec. components	NPA M 17	Dec. 18

set up a maintenance, repair, and operations program and orders, fast becoming necessary. Also the information provides more data for reviving the controlled materials plan now in the works.

Two industries—warm air heating and steel strapping—have already started task groups to provide data. The strapping industry expects to have first half requirements worked out when its advisory committee reconvenes with NPA on Feb. 12.

Bill Seeks U. S. Redress on Excessive Profits

Passed by House, now weighed by Senate, measure seeks recapture of excessive profits on war contracts . . . Would give 5-man board power to reopen, renegotiate contracts.

Washington—Senate tax-writers began this week to consider House-passed legislation permitting the government to recapture "excessive profits" on war contracts by renegotiation.

Rep. Doughton, D., N. C., who steered the renegotiation bill through the lower house to a 377-0 vote, said such a statute was necsary to protect the government against hasty cost estimates provided by contractors and subcontractors.

Board Can Reopen Contracts

The bill provides for a 5-man renegotiation board with authority to reopen contracts entered into by government agencies concerned with defense production. But a contractor or subcontractor must have received more than $100,000 in any one year before any of his contracts may be renegotiated.

The act is to become effective January 1, 1951, and affects all contracts entered into by the Depts. of Defense (including Army, Navy, and Air Force) and Commerce; the General Services Administration; Atomic Energy Commission, and any other agencies concerned with defense procurement.

Some Fields Exempt

Subcontractors whose income is derived from fees or commissions would be subject to the new act for any year in which they have receipts of $25,000 or more.

Exempt from renegotiation are

agricultural commodities, timber, and products of mines and oil and gas wells.

The bill provides for payment of 6 pct interest by the government in the case of recapture of funds, and 6 pct by the contractor or subcontractor from the date the government decides additional sums are payable by the contracting firm.

The act would replace any existing law passed in 1948 under which only military contracts are subject to renegotiation. The House Ways and Means Committee said this act was inadequate to safeguard the government in a time of huge defense expenditures.

"Now that I'm an executive, there are several young ladies at the office trying to take me away from you."

Plea for Higher Lead Import Levy Rejected by Tariff Group

Washington—An application filed by the Emergency Lead Committee and the New Mexico Miners & Prospectors Assn. requesting an investigation of, and increased levies on, imports of lead from Mexico has been dismissed by the Tariff Commission.

With termination of the Mexican Trade Agreement on Dec. 31, import rates which had been cut in half under the agreement have automatically returned to the 1930 rates. These duties are now 1½¢ a lb (lead content) for ores, flue dust and mattes; 2⅛¢ per lb on lead bullion, pigs, bars, scrap, and reclaimed lead.

Wright Calls for Subcontractors

Wood-Ridge, N. J. — Wright Aeronautical Corp. has sent out a call for subcontractors to make parts for America's warplanes. Most urgently wanted are firms with facilities to produce: hardened and ground parts (carburizing and nitriding facilities preferred); fabricated sheet metal—stainless steel (press and certified welding equipment required); gears; screw machine products; aluminum, magnesium, and steel castings, raw and finished; aluminum forgings, raw and finished; controls and accessories; and engine sub-assemblies.

Galvanized Ware Standards

Washington—Minimum grades for galvanized ware fabricated from pregalvanized sheets, as proposed by the Galvanized Ware Mfrs. Council have been published as Commercial Standard 169-50, according to the Dept. of Commerce. Copies are available from the Government Printing Office.

Scaife Gets Big Shell Contract

Pittsburgh — Scaife Co., Oakmont, Pa., has signed a $6 million Army contract for production of mortar shells. The job will not hinder the company's normal production of pressure vessels.

Stopgap Wage-Price Frost Falls on Industry

Steel prices stay under voluntary plan ... Nearly all products, services frozen at highest levels, Dec. 19 to Jan. 25 ... Rollbacks, flexible wage policy coming—By Gene Hardy.

Washington — The American businessman this week is confronted with two government orders that will have a profound effect on his method of operation for a long time to come. Putting into effect the first price and wage controls since the end of World War II, the Economic Stabilization Agency describes the new orders as stopgap measures.

The General Ceiling Price Regulation freezes prices for practically all commodities and services, except most raw farm products, at the highest levels prevailing during the base period Dec. 19, 1950, to Jan. 25, 1951. General Wage Stabilization Reg. 1 freezes all "wages, salaries and other compensation" at Jan. 25 levels, with new employees to be paid at the rates in effect Jan. 25.

Affecting all business, producing and distributing, the orders will be replaced as soon as possible with specific mark-up and dollars-and-cents ceilings and a flexible wage policy. Price Stabilizer M. V. DiSalle says that plans for a price rollback were dropped

since this would have delayed the freeze order for several weeks. Coming specific orders, however, will involve some rollbacks.

A more flexible wage policy is expected from Wage Stabilization Board Chairman Cyrus Ching sometime this week. It will probably sanction at least a 10 pct boost in wages above mid-1950 levels.

ESA officials are also working to close loopholes in the hastily drawn orders; provide relief in hardship cases; and provide for industries which voluntarily set price ceilings below those required by the freeze order.

Steel Under Voluntary Plan— Steel prices are not covered by the general freeze, but are still subject to the terms of the voluntary agreement (THE IRON AGE, Jan. 25, p. 86) under which the steel industry agreed to stabilize prices at the highest levels prevailing in the 30-day period preceding Jan. 15, 1951. Increases above the Jan. 15 level are not to be put into effect without giving ESA 20 days

notice. ESA spokesmen told THE IRON AGE that the voluntary agreement is still the controlling factor in steel pricing under the exemption provided in Sec. 14 (q) of GCPR.

General Price Formula—GCPR sets the ceiling prices for all commodities and services, with the exception of raw farm products and the exemptions noted below, at the highest price for which the commodity or service was delivered during the base period to a purchaser of the same class.

For all practical purposes, this means the price prevailing on Jan. 25. If the commodity or service was not delivered during the base period, the ceiling is the highest price at which it was offered. The offer must have been made in writing, but in the case of a retailer it may have been made by display.

Commodities Not Sold in Base Period — Commodities not delivered or offered for sale during the base period, but which fall within a category dealt with in the base period are priced in a different manner. Ceilings for such commodities are worked out by applying to current direct unit cost the percentage mark-up currently being received on a "comparison commodity," i.e., one in the same category as the item being priced.

Different Categories — In the case of manufacturers producing commodities in a different category from any dealt with or services that cannot be priced on the basis of being offered or delivered, still another formula is contained in GCPR. The ceiling price in such cases is the same as the ceiling of the most closely competitive seller of the same class selling the same commodity or service to the same class of purchaser.

Prices set in this manner are final and not subject to redetermination, but can be disapproved by the Office of Price Stabilization. Manufacturers must report to the Director of Price Stabilization on

---

Defense Contracts to Metalworking Industry
Selected Contracts, Week of Jan. 29, 1951

Item	Quan.	Value	Company
Governor parts	6,118 ea.	$398,869	Int'l Spare Parts Corp., Long Island, NY
Trailers, Trucks	35,883	34,786,484	Fruehauf Trailer Co., Detroit
Buses	....	6,913,228	A.C.F. Brill Mtrs. Co., Philadelphia
Trailers	....	1,167,684	Linn Coach & Trk. Div., Oneonta
Axles	....	193,200	Chrysler Corp., Detroit
Kits	300	210,773	Perfection Stove Co., Cleveland
Tank engines, parts	....	40,000,000	Ford Motor Co., Detroit
Tank transmissions	....	65,000,000	General Motors Corp., Detroit
Vehicle parts	....	475,665	Federal Motor Truck Co., Detroit
Buses	602	6,847,610	ACF-Brill Motors Co., Philadelphia
Engine and parts	....	17,374,896	Continental Motors, Detroit
Strip, studs, etc.	30,585	467,661	Allis-Chalmers, Milwaukee
Parts	446,137	896,708	GMC United Motor Serv. Co., Detroit
Generators	4,070	328,856	United Motors Ser. Div. GMC, Detroit
Engines	600	914,250	Biederman Motor Corp., Cincinnatti
Trucks	....	1,076,862	Willys Overland Motors, Inc., Toledo
Engines	700	803,669	International Harv. Co., Detroit
Trucks, Fork, Electric	46	193,200	The Baker Raulang Co., Cleveland
Trucks, Fork, Gas	80	303,600	The Yale & Towne Mfg. Co., Philadelphia
Facilities for manufacture of Electric vehicles		4,994,485	Electric Auto Lite Co., Toledo
Vehicles		90,000,000	Chrysler Corp., Detroit
Vehicles		50,000,000	Chrysler Corp., Detroit

---

such pricing and cannot sell the commodity until 10 days after mailing the report.

Wholesalers may follow the same formula, but cannot begin selling the commodity until 30 days after mailing the report.

The regulation requires the following report from all sellers pricing in this manner:

"Your report should state the name and address of your company; the new categories in which the commodities fall and the most comparable categories dealt in by you during the base period; the name, address and type of business of your most closely competitive seller of the same class; your reason for selecting him as your most closely competitive seller; a statement of your customary price differentials; and, if you are starting a new business, a statement whether you or the principal owner of your business are now or during the past 12 months have been engaged in any capacity in the same or a similar business at any other establishment, and if so, the trade name and address of each such establishment. Your report should also include the following:

(1) **"If you are a manufacturer:** Your proposed ceiling price and the specifications of the commodity you are pricing; the manufacturing processes involved; your unit direct costs; and the types of customers to whom you will be selling.

(2) **"If you are a wholesaler:** Your proposed ceiling price and your net invoice cost of the commodity being priced; the names and addresses of your sources of supply, the function performed by them (e.g. manufacturing, distributing, etc.), and the types of purchasers to whom they customarily sell; the types of customers to whom you plan to sell; and a statement showing that your proposed ceiling price will not exceed the ceiling price your customers paid to their customary sources of supply.

(3) **"If you are selling a service:** Your proposed ceiling price and a description of the most comparable service delivered by you during the base period showing your present direct labor and materials costs and ceiling price for it."

Still Another Method — If a seller cannot determine his ceiling prices under any of the foregoing provisions, which, in the opinion of Mr. Di Salle, provide adequate pricing instructions for virtually all transactions, he may apply in writing to the Director of Price Stabilization for a ceiling price.

This application must contain an explanation of why the seller is unable to determine a ceiling price under other provisions of GCPR; all pertinent information describing the commodity or service, and the nature of the business; proposed ceiling price and the method used to determine it; and the rea-

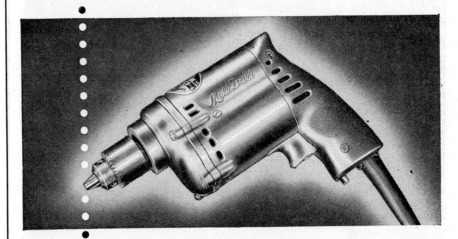
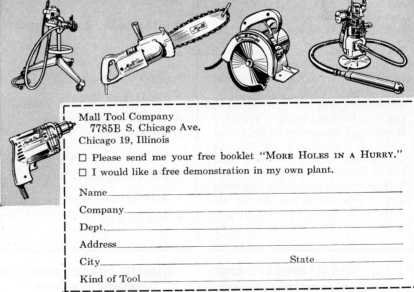

Zorball's Extra "Pick-up" Saves You Money 2 Ways!

SAVING NO. 1 — You save from $15 to $24 a ton on absorbent when you use Zorball. And we've got the test results — arrived at by *independent* laboratories — to prove it! You see, Zorball absorbs more oil per pound. So it takes less to do the job.

SAVING NO. 2 — You cut your man-hours of handling from 33% to 60% when you use Zorball. You see, your plant probably handles a floor absorbent five times. You unload it, put it on the floor, sweep it up, carry it out, load it on a truck. Because it takes less Zorball to do the job, you save plenty! Every time you use a ton of Zorball you save your maintenance crew from handling an extra 2½ to 7½ tons of less efficient absorbents. And your Wyandotte Representative or Supplier can *prove* it!

ZORBALL

—all-purpose floor absorbent

- *Picks up more*
- *Saves man-hours*
- *Tracks less*
- *Will not become muddy when wet*
- *Will not become dusty when dry*
- *Holds water and oil longer*
- *Anti-slip even when oil-soaked*
- *Will not burn*

THE WYANDOTTE LINE
—*all-purpose floor absorbent:* Zorball; *floor wax:* Anti-Slip Wax; *germicides:* Steri-Chlor, Spartec; *maintenance cleaners:* Detergent, F-100, El-Bee, Paydet; *detergent-sanitizers:* Tri-Bac, Kromet — **in fact, specialized products for *every* cleaning need.**

WYANDOTTE CHEMICALS CORPORATION
WYANDOTTE, MICHIGAN
Service Representatives in 88 Cities

Wyandotte
REG. U. S. PAT. OFF.

---

son it is believed the proposed price is in line with the level of ceiling prices otherwise established by GCPR. The commodity or service may not be sold until the seller is notified of the ceiling price.

Exports and Imports — Export and import sales are covered by the regulation. Importers handling commodities sold in substantially the same form, except for sorting, packaging, and simple processing, may adjust prices frozen at base period levels to offset an increase in landed costs since the base period, provided the commodities are covered by a contract date on or before Jan. 26, 1951.

Importers of crude and semi-finished steel, metal scrap, nonferrous metals, ferroalloys, minerals, and chemicals who reprice articles under this provision must file a report with the Director of Price Stabilization within 10 days after the first sale at the new price showing base period price, current foreign invoice price and total landed costs of commodities repriced.

Highest Price Line Limitation — Manufacturers of a selected list of consumer durables are also subject to a highest price line limitation. The list of items will be incorporated in a forthcoming supplementary order. This means that manufacturers of these commodities may not sell any of them at a price higher than the ceiling price for a commodity in that category.

For example: If the base period ceiling prices for a group of small "widgets" were $5.75, $6.75, and $8.75, firms will not be permitted to sell any "widgets" at a price in excess of $8.75.

Other Exemptions — Exempt from the order, in addition to the farm products affected by parity provisions, are most of the items which were exempt under OPA during World War II. These include: professional services, military and strategic commodities, advertising, books and magazines, insurance rates, utility and common carrier rates, sales of used household or personal effects at bonafide auctions, and handicraft made by Indians and Eskimos.

Records Which Must Be Kept Under GCPR

Base period records.

(1) You must preserve and keep available for examination those records in your possession showing the prices charged by you for the commodities or services which you delivered or offered to deliver during the base period, and also sufficient records to establish the latest net cost incurred by you prior to the end of the base period in purchasing the commodities (if you are a wholesaler or retailer).

(2) In addition, on or before Mar. 1, 1951, you must prepare and preserve a statement showing the categories in which you made deliveries and offers for delivery during the base period; or if you sold services you must prepare and preserve a statement listing the services which you delivered or offered to deliver during the base period.

(3) On or before Mar. 1, 1951, you must also prepare and preserve a ceiling price list, showing the commodities in each category (listing each model, type, style, and kind) delivered or offered for delivery by you during the base period together with a description or identification of each such commodity and a statement of the ceiling price. Your ceiling price list may refer to an attached price list or catalogue. If you are a retailer you may satisfy the requirement of this paragraph (3) by recording on your purchase invoices, covering the commodities (including every model, type, style, and kind) delivered or offered for delivery by you during the base period, the price at which you sold, or offered the commodities for delivery, during the base period.

(4) You must also prepare and preserve a statement of your customary price differentials for terms and conditions of sale and classes of purchasers, which you had in effect during the base period.

Current records.

If you sell commodities or services covered by the regulation you must prepare and keep available for examination by the Director of Price Stabilization for a period of 2 years, records of the kind which you customarily keep showing the prices which you charge for the commodities or services: In addition, you must prepare and preserve records indicating clearly the basis upon which you have determined the ceiling price for any commodities or services not delivered by you or offered for delivery during the base period.

Oppose Aluminum Scrap Order

New York—Opposition to the aluminum scrap order (NPA M-22) has been expressed by the Metal Dealers Div. of the National Assn. of Waste Material Dealers, Inc. The group claims smaller smelters and fabricators cannot maintain normal operations, and diversion of scrap from normal channels prevents "sweating" operations that would help ease freight car shortages.

fishin' is fun...
with care on the run

Here's a fellow that enjoys complete relaxation. He knows his plant is safeguarded from fire . . . a short circuit, a stray spark, a forgotten cigarette or spontaneous combustion can't cut into production time, destroy valuable records or endanger the lives of employees.

You too, can have this same peace of mind about fire by fully protecting your investment in materials, equipment and buildings with modern, approved C-O-TWO Fire Protection Equipment.

No matter what your property . . . factory, mill, warehouse, power station or research center . . . or a particular fire hazard such as spray booth, dip tank, pump room, electrical equipment enclosure or record vault . . . there is a type of C-O-TWO Fire Protection Equipment that gives you fast, positive action the instant fire strikes. Whether it's a C-O-TWO Squeez-Grip Carbon

Dioxide Type Fire Extinguisher for an incipient fire, or a C-O-TWO Built-In High Pressure or Low Pressure Carbon Dioxide Type Fire Extinguishing System for total flooding an entire fire hazardous area . . . C-O-TWO means experienced engineering that assures you of the best type equipment for the particular fire hazard concerned.

For example, at many locations a C-O-TWO Combination Smoke Detecting and Fire Extinguishing System is a "must". The first trace of smoke in a protected area sounds an alarm . . . then fast, clean, non-damaging, non-conducting carbon dioxide blankets the fire, putting it out in seconds, before it spreads and causes extensive damage.

So, let an expert C-O-TWO Fire Protection Engineer help you in planning complete and up-to-date fire protection facilities now. Write us today for complete free information . . . our experience is at your disposal.

TRADE MARK
REG. U.S. PAT. OFF.

C-O-TWO FIRE EQUIPMENT COMPANY
NEWARK 1 • NEW JERSEY
Sales and Service in the Principal Cities of United States and Canada
Affiliated with Pyrene Manufacturing Company
MANUFACTURERS OF APPROVED FIRE PROTECTION EQUIPMENT
Squeez-Grip Carbon Dioxide Type Fire Extinguishers • Dry Chemical Type Fire Extinguishers
Built-In High Pressure and Low Pressure Carbon Dioxide Type Fire Extinguishing Systems
Built-In Smoke and Heat Fire Detecting Systems

Rated Steel Order Limits Rise Under NPA M-1 Amendment

Provides specific inventory controls for producer and consumer.

Washington — Most percentage ceilings for acceptance of rated steel orders have been increased, specific inventory controls for producer and consumer have been provided, more ferrous products added, and some lead times changed under an amendment to NPA order M-1, effective immediately.

The order also designates producers who sell for further conversion as "producer suppliers" and those in conversion or fabrication as "converters." Previous allocation provisions now apply to them.

Make Monthly Allotment

A producer supplier must make a monthly allotment of his steel products remaining after filling rated and special program orders to each of his converter customers. It must equal the percentage of "his available production so remaining as the producer supplier's shipments to each converter customer bore to his total shipment during the base period from Jan. 1, 1950, through Sept. 30, 1950."

A producer supplier must accept orders from his converter customer up to the limit of his allotment—providing they agree with lead time provided by order. Products added to the original order include: steel castings and forgings, wire rope and strand, pig iron, and malleable gray iron castings.

The order was changed to provide minimum quantities below which producers are not obliged to accept order. They range from 500 lb to carloads, according to product, while in other cases the buyer and producer agree on quantity.

A 45-day inventory is set for steel products and malleable and gray iron castings, while the maximum for pig iron is set at 30 days or a minimum working level, whichever is less.

Some original lead times have

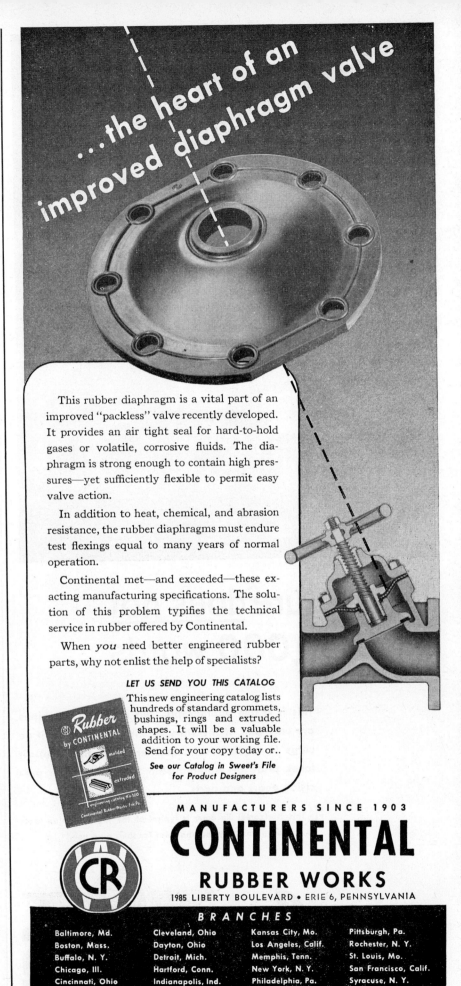

...the heart of an improved diaphragm valve

This rubber diaphragm is a vital part of an improved "packless" valve recently developed. It provides an air tight seal for hard-to-hold gases or volatile, corrosive fluids. The diaphragm is strong enough to contain high pressures—yet sufficiently flexible to permit easy valve action.

In addition to heat, chemical, and abrasion resistance, the rubber diaphragms must endure test flexings equal to many years of normal operation.

Continental met—and exceeded—these exacting manufacturing specifications. The solution of this problem typifies the technical service in rubber offered by Continental.

When *you* need better engineered rubber parts, why not enlist the help of specialists?

LET US SEND YOU THIS CATALOG

This new engineering catalog lists hundreds of standard grommets, bushings, rings and extruded shapes. It will be a valuable addition to your working file. Send for your copy today or..

See our Catalog in Sweet's File for Product Designers

MANUFACTURERS SINCE 1903

CONTINENTAL
RUBBER WORKS
1985 LIBERTY BOULEVARD • ERIE 6, PENNSYLVANIA

BRANCHES

Baltimore, Md.	Cleveland, Ohio	Kansas City, Mo.	Pittsburgh, Pa.
Boston, Mass.	Dayton, Ohio	Los Angeles, Calif.	Rochester, N. Y.
Buffalo, N. Y.	Detroit, Mich.	Memphis, Tenn.	St. Louis, Mo.
Chicago, Ill.	Hartford, Conn.	New York, N. Y.	San Francisco, Calif.
Cincinnati, Ohio	Indianapolis, Ind.	Philadelphia, Pa.	Syracuse, N. Y.

been changed, such as rolled armor plate and others requiring a longer production period because of manufacturing and special treating processes.

DO acceptance percentages for carbon steel products are now:

20 pct — structural shapes, rough castings (including high and low alloy and carbon), rough forgings, and both malleable and gray iron castings.

15 pct—piling, plates, reinforcing and cold-finished bars.

12 pct — hot and cold-rolled sheets.

10 pct—rails, wire rods, hot-rolled bars, mechanical and pressure tubing, hot and cold-rolled strip, and joint bars, tie plates, and track spikes.

7 pct — galvanized and other coated sheets, and electric sheets and strip.

5 pct — ingots, blooms, slabs, billets, skelp, line and standard pipe, barbed wire, bale ties, woven fence, drawn wire, nails and staples, tin mill blackplate, hot-dipped tin and terneplate, and electrolytic tinplate, and enameling.

Stainless Steel Ceiling

A ceiling of 25 pct is established for the following stainless steel items: ingots, blooms, slabs, billets, plate, hot-rolled bars, cold-finished bars, standard pipe, pressure and mechanical tubing, drawn wire, hot and cold-rolled sheets and strip. Stainless malleable and gray iron castings must be accepted up to 20 pct.

Acceptance ceilings for full alloy products are: 35 pct, blooms, billets, slabs, hot-rolled bars, mechanical tubing; 25 pct, ingots, wire ropes, cold-finished bars, pressure tubing, drawn wire; 15 pct, plates; 7 pct, electric sheet; and 5 pct, hot and cold-rolled strip and sheet.

Buffalo Firm 125 Years Old

Buffalo—Beals, McCarthy & Rogers, Inc., handlers of steel and industrial supplies, will observe their 125th anniversary with an open house and celebration Feb. 6 to 8.

STEEL CONSTRUCTION NEWS

New York—Total bookings of fabricated structural steel for 1950 are estimated at 2,529,832 tons and were the highest on record since 1930, according to reports received by the American Institute of Steel Construction, Inc. December bookings of 224,808 tons were 81% greater than for the corresponding month in the previous year, while the annual bookings exceeded 1949 by 77%.

1950 shipments amounted to 1,931,527 tons, an increase of 4% over the 1,853,536 tons shipped in 1949. The shipments for December were 175,575 tons, 30% over December of last year.

The backlog (tonnage available for future fabrication) for the next four months only stands at 736,340 tons, and for the period beyond these four months amounts to 1,177,695 tons, or a total potential for work ahead of 1,914,035 tons.

Following is the complete tabulation of bookings and shipments:

Estimated Total Tonnage for the Entire Industry

Contracts Closed	1950	1949	Avg. 1936/1940
January	119,317	130,418	107,578
February	117,664	108,764	96,280
March	189,420	149,079	124,558
April	155,011	98,802	110,783
May	192,319	116,975	126,237
June	266,612	96,952	125,835
July	272,745	126,255	152,481
August	259,212	98,953	113,135
September	251,054	120,373	137,982
October	236,170*	158,593	141,557
November	245,500*	103,557	129,757
December	224,808	124,251	143,313
Totals	2,529,832	1,432,972	1,509,496

Shipments	1950	1949	Avg. 1936/1940
January	135,253	152,746	92,578
February	129,628	145,879	88,626
March	156,781	185,885	115,031
April	164,440	179,206	123,650
May	168,113	171,101	123,225
June	172,096	172,260	129,969
July	141,576	147,960	127,422
August	180,688	183,868	136,389
September	157,000	162,139	137,255
October	183,318*	99,812	140,944
November	167,059*	117,180	127,873
December	175,575	135,500	121,664
Totals	1,931,527	1,853,536	1,464,626

*Revised

Tonnage Available for Fabrication Within the next four months (To April 30, 1951)

| 736,340 | 555,360 | 363,288 |

After the next four months (From May 1, 1951)

| 1,177,695 | 421,404 | 117,398 |

January 25, 1951

Fabricated steel awards this week included the following:

1250 **Tons,** Newark, N. J., highway bridge, Route 25A, Sect. 1G, El Dorer Construction Co., low bidder.

1080 **Tons,** Montgomery County, Pa., highway bridge, Pennsylvania Dept. of Highways, to American Bridge Co., Pittsburgh.

311 **Tons,** New Orleans, La., South Carrollton Avenue underpass for City of New Orleans, R. P. Farnsworth, contractor, to Virginia Bridge Company, Birmingham, Ala.

110 **Tons,** Seaford, Del., addition to plant of E. I. duPont de Nemours Co., to Bethlehem Fabricators, Inc., Bethlehem.

Fabricated steel inquiries this week included the following:

570 **Tons,** Newcastle, Del., highway bridge for Delaware Dept. of Highways, bids due Feb. 7.

500 **Tons,** Weston, N. J., bridge for the Reading Co., bids due Feb. 2.

350 **Tons,** State College, Pa., Burrowes Building, Pennsylvania State College, bids due Feb. 7.

February 1, 1951

for CONTINUOUS ELECTRIC POWER

• Diesel-Electric Locomotives

READY-POWER-equipped ELECTRIC-TRUCKS

Loading a Box-car with Ready-Power-Equipped Elwell-Parker Hi-Lift Platform Truck

Yale Crane Truck Equipped with Ready Power

Modern Diesel-electric locomotives and Ready-Power-equipped electric trucks operate alike. Both generate dependable electric power right on the vehicle; both operate economically; and both excel where long, continuous operation pays off. Your electric trucks will do more work at less cost when equipped with Ready-Power. There are models for every type, size and make of electric truck.'

Ready-Power-Equipped Automatic Fork Truck

THE READY-POWER CO.

3822 Grand River Ave., Detroit 8, Michigan

Contract Manufacture And Brandt—

B & O RR MAIN LINE (E & W)

MAIN PLANT

RR SIDING #1

BOILER & PLATE

RR SIDING #2

← U. S. ROUTE—BALTO. & WASH.
EXPRESS HIGHWAY ADJACENT

EXPANSION
AREA
423,000 SQ. FT.

SHOP STORAGE
AND PARKING
↓

STAMPING

PAINT &
BONDERIZING

(TRUCK SHIPPING AREA)

SHEET AND
LIGHT PLATE
FABRICA-
TION

ASSEMBLY
AND SPOT
WELDING

OFFICES

RIDGELY STREET

FOR RELIEF FROM PRODUCTION HEADACHES

in mass produced

STAMPINGS, SPOT WELDED ASSEMBLIES, WELDMENTS and PRESSED STEEL SHAPES

from all types of metal

Write for This Engineers' Fingertip File of Handy Working Information

● Brandt at your service means several hundred thousand square feet of facilities coordinated for your special production needs. Brandt—near steel mills, in the midst of major rail, water and highway transportation systems—offers assembly line scheduling, precision workmanship to exacting specifications and on-the-dot deliveries.

BRANDT
BALTIMORE

CHARLES T. BRANDT, INC.
1700 Ridgely Street, Baltimore 30, Md.

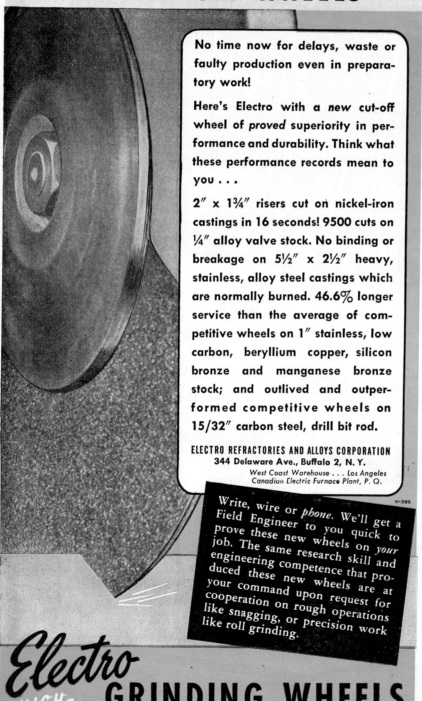
British Carmakers' Output May Fall with Sheet Steel Cut

London—Badgered by a grave nonferrous metals shortage, car makers in England thought they at least had one cloud with a silver lining. Steel mills were setting output records and the auto industry reasoned that they would be cut only 5 pct. With this steel present production could be maintained.

But this month car makers were told to expect a cut in sheet steel that may reduce output by 15 to 20 pct. Many companies will be forced on a 4-day week. Some relief in the sheet supply picture may come with the opening of new mills at Margam, South Wales, this summer.

Blame for the cut is put on slumping sheet imports and the defense program. Output was estimated at 140,000 passenger cars and 65,000 commercial vehicles in the last quarter of 1950.

Signode Plans Weirton Growth

Pittsburgh — Signode Steel Strapping Co. will expand its Weirton, W. Va., operations with construction of a new plant 420 ft long and 150 ft wide. Employment, now totaling 25, will increase to 250. The original plant, a quonset-type building, will be used as a storehouse.

Won't Build Giant Airliners

London—Britain will postpone building any more Bristol Brabazon airliners beyond the first two it now has. The project will remain a research experiment. Work on the giant airliner project opened in 1945 and $32 million was spent so far.

Blaw-Knox to Build Gun Mounts

Pittsburgh—Lewis Foundry & Machine Div. of Blaw-Knox Co. will produce anti-aircraft gun mounts for the U. S. Navy. During World War II, the company produced Bofors naval anti-aircraft gun mounts.

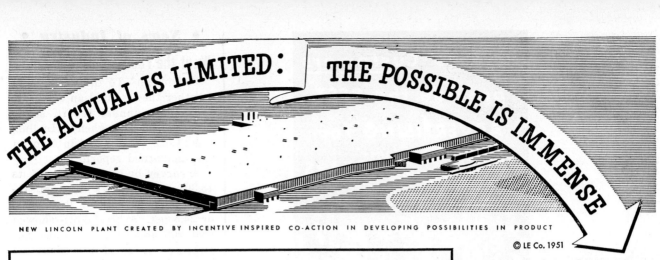

• *News of Industry* •

Want the Facts—Hard and Cold

Pittsburgh—To the question of whether they wanted an elaborate or a plain annual report, stockholders of Allegheny Ludlum Steel Corp. voted 2-to-1 in favor of the unadorned report.

A survey by the company of its 13,304 stockholders brought replies from 3266 as of last week, or 24.5 pct. A breakdown showed that 966 or 29.6 pct of those answering preferred the fancy report; 1787 or 54.7 pct the plain, factual report; and 436 or 13.3 pct simply financial statistics and auditors' letter. A combination of the latter two totaled 2223, or 68 pct.

The results were contrary to the popular belief that stockholders like multi-color reports with plenty of charts and pictures.

Westinghouse Plans Expansion

Pittsburgh—Westinghouse Electric Corp. announced an expansion program that will increase generator production capacity at its East Pittsburgh plant by 65 pct.

The program calls for construction of two buildings to provide more than 300,000 additional sq ft for large generator production, making possible the building of larger than 150,000 kw high-speed 3600 rpm generators.

Three old buildings will be razed to make room for the new structures.

Steel Forgings Down in Nov.

Washington — November shipments of commercial steel forgings totaled 130,000 tons, compared with 137,000 tons in October and 73,000 tons in November of 1949. Unfilled orders at the end of November totaled 657,000 tons.

Armco's Sebald Starts Trust Fund

Middletown, Ohio — A trust fund of $50,000 to aid sick and needy children in the community has been established by W. W. Sebald, president of Armco Steel Corp., in "appreciation for good neighborliness of the people of Middletown."

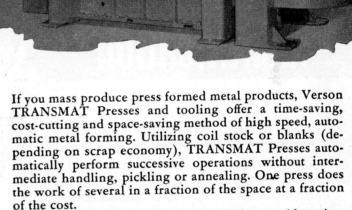

February 1, 1951

141

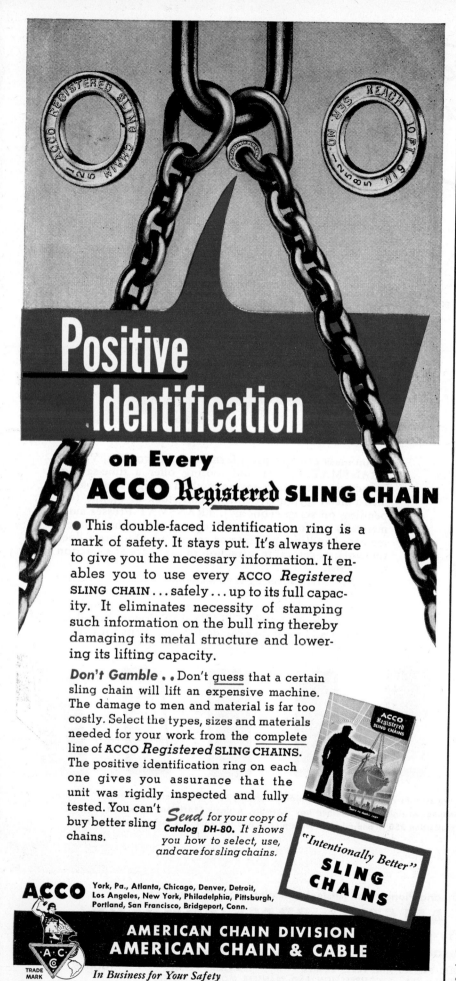

Positive Identification

on Every ACCO Registered SLING CHAIN

● This double-faced identification ring is a mark of safety. It stays put. It's always there to give you the necessary information. It enables you to use every ACCO *Registered* SLING CHAIN . . . safely . . . up to its full capacity. It eliminates necessity of stamping such information on the bull ring thereby damaging its metal structure and lowering its lifting capacity.

Don't Gamble . . Don't guess that a certain sling chain will lift an expensive machine. The damage to men and material is far too costly. Select the types, sizes and materials needed for your work from the complete line of ACCO *Registered* SLING CHAINS. The positive identification ring on each one gives you assurance that the unit was rigidly inspected and fully tested. You can't buy better sling chains.

Send for your copy of **Catalog DH-80.** *It shows you how to select, use, and care for sling chains.*

"Intentionally Better" **SLING CHAINS**

ACCO York, Pa., Atlanta, Chicago, Denver, Detroit, Los Angeles, New York, Philadelphia, Pittsburgh, Portland, San Francisco, Bridgeport, Conn.

AMERICAN CHAIN DIVISION
AMERICAN CHAIN & CABLE
In Business for Your Safety

Raw Material Shortages May Lower British Steelmaking in '51

London—British steel output in 1950 reached a new high of 18,247,824 tons—or 328,000 tons over the Government mark and 828,000 tons above production in 1949. But now that the industry is on the doorstep to initiative-deadening nationalization, steel men will not make any optimistic predictions. This despite the 500,000 tons of new capacity to come in this year.

Raw material shortages are likely to cut steel production in the early months of 1950. Coke deliveries are currently below consumption and stockpiles are low. A major coal producer, England was forced to divert shipping from iron ore to import coal. Stocks of imported ore, at a good level last year, have been severely cut.

Imports of German scrap have been dwindling and are expected to dip to 1,125,000 tons in '51 as compared with 2,250,000 tons last year. A scrap drive has started in England but steelmakers doubt whether this will offset the deficit.

In addition to nationalization woes, melting shop workers will ask a 40-hr week at negotiations this month.

ACF Smooths Way for P.A.'s

New York—An attempt to lighten the load of its purchasing agents, and of salesmen calling at American Car & Foundry Co., has been made by ACF with its new "welcome" booklet.

The booklet lists purchasing personnel for the various ACF divisions. Engineers, inspectors and others who have contact with suppliers are also listed. Salesmen are advised what the company makes and the best hours to call.

Construction Boomed in '50

New York—Construction in 37 eastern states during 1950 showed a 40 pct increase over 1949 figures, for a total of some $14½ billion, according to the F. W. Dodge Corp. Residential construction was up 59 pct for a total of $6,741,028,000.

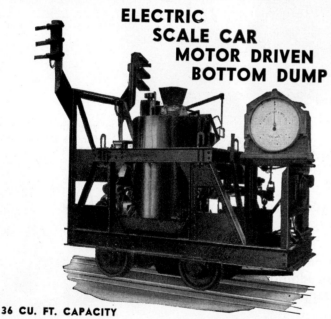

New Hot Strip Mill to Alter France's Role as Sheet Importer

Paris—France will drop her role as an importer of steel sheets now that USINOR's 66-in. continuous hot strip mill at Denain, North France, was put into operation late last month. First of its type in Europe, with an approximate output of 700,000 tons annually, the mill will in few months be able to fully supply the Montatair cold reduction mill. Montatair has been importing coils from America.

The Denain mill has a slabbing mill able to roll 15 ton ingots straight from steelmaking furnaces; four roughing stands and six finishing stands; a coiler with flying shears. With capacity set at 800,000 tons annually and production expected to reach 700,000 tons, Denain will ship about 360,000 tons per year to Montatair—which will cold-roll sheets primarily for the car industry in Paris.

To meet the steel needs of Denain, Usinor has enlarged two blast furnaces at Trith-Saint-Leger and is building a blast furnace and openhearth at Denain. SOLLAC's hot strip mill in Lorraine, with an 830,000 ton capacity, will be in production sometime in 1952.

BCR to Meet in Columbus Feb. 7

Columbus, Ohio—"Research to Meet Competition" will be the theme of the annual meeting of Bituminous Coal Research, Inc., at the Deshler-Wallick Hotel Feb. 7. Improved methods of handling and using coal and development of new coal products will be discussed. Locomotive and mining development programs will be featured at an exhibit.

Dr. Mehl Takes U. S. Post

Pittsburgh—Dr. Robert F. Mehl, director of the Metals Research Laboratory and head of the Dept. of Metallurgical Engineering at Carnegie Institute of Technology, has been appointed chairman of the Metallurgical Advisory Board of the government's National Research Council.

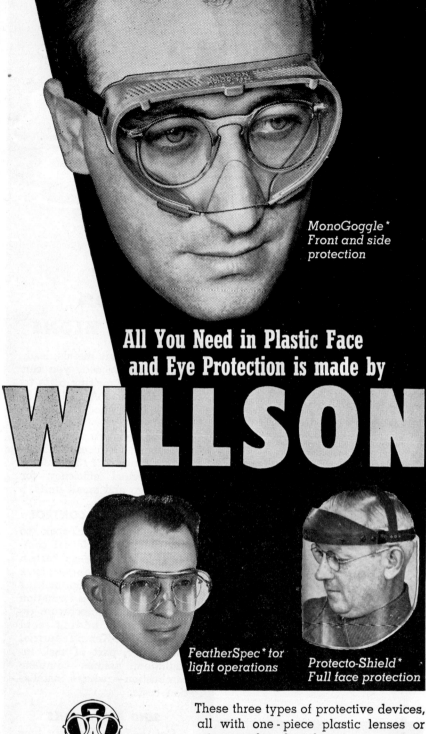

MonoGoggle*
Front and side
protection

All You Need in Plastic Face and Eye Protection is made by

WILLSON

FeatherSpec* for
light operations

Protecto-Shield*
Full face protection

WILLSON*

Dependable Products Since 1870

These three types of protective devices, all with one-piece plastic lenses or visors and each with many variations, give you a wide selection to meet specific requirements of work hazards. Their light weight and comfortable fit insure workers' willingness to wear them for long hours on the job. Complete information on plastic protection and other eye and respiratory safety equipment is available in the new WILLSON catalog. Get your copy from our nearest distributor or write direct to WILLSON PRODUCTS, INC., 231 Washington Street, Reading, Pa.

*T.M. Reg. U.S. Pat. Off.

Weirton Names Ross Manager Of Labor Relations Department

Weirton, W. Va.—Edward A. Ross, former president of the defunct Weirton Independent Union, Inc., which represented Weirton Steel Co. employees in labor negotiations, has been appointed manager of labor relations of the company.

Ross, an employee in Weirton's strip steel department for 18 years, was president of the WIU from 1946 until 1950, when the union was disbanded by federal court order. This union was succeeded by the Independent Steelworkers Union, which won collective bargaining rights over the United Steelworkers of America, CIO.

NE Industry Advised to Expand

Hartford—A vigorous program of industrial plant and equipment "face-lifting" for New England manufacturers is advocated by Walter H. Wheeler, Jr., president of the New England Council.

Mr. Wheeler, president of Pitney-Bowes, Inc., believes New England is not planning enough plant expansion to maintain its competitive position.

ASLE Convention April 16-18

Philadelphia—Internal combustion engineers from some of the country's leading automotive and petroleum producing companies will take part in a panel on Diesel power at the convention of the American Society of Lubrication Engineers here Apr. 16 to 18. The meeting will be at the Bellevue-Stratford Hotel.

Union Pacific Orders 1000 Cars

Omaha, Neb.—Plans to build 1000 new freight cars during 1951 at a cost of $6½ million, have been announced by A. E. Stoddard, president of Union Pacific R.R. Freight car orders during the past year total 8500. Union Pacific's freight car program to date, including cars on order, now totals more than $50 million.

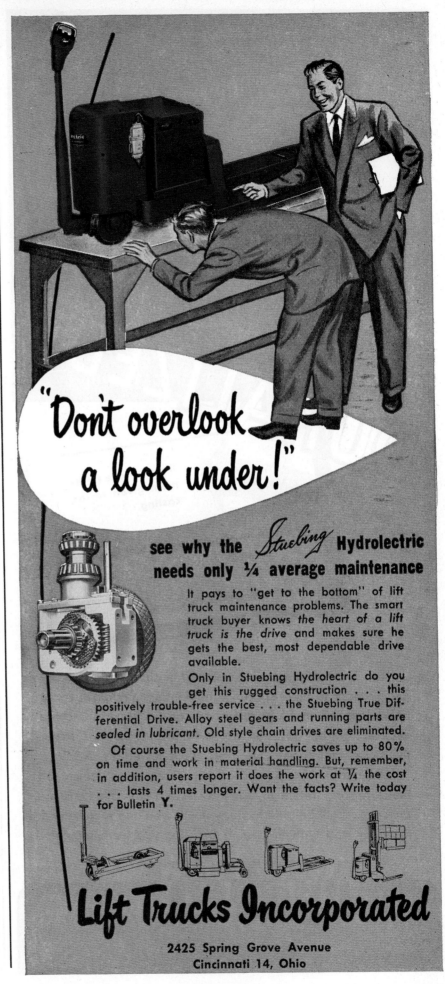

• *News of Industry* •

Plan New West Texas Oil Line

Pittsburgh — A 440-mile 26-in. diam. crude oil pipe line will be built by Gulf Oil Corp. and four other oil companies to make more West Texas oil available to refineries on the Gulf Coast, the Ohio Valley and Great Lakes region.

Gulf Oil has filed plans with the Petroleum Defense Authority for the line, which will have an estimated daily capacity of 300,-000 bbls. Associated with Gulf are Cities Service, Pure Oil, Sun Oil and Standard of Ohio.

Work will get underway in late summer or early fall with completion early in 1952. The line will have a connection in Eastern Texas to north-bound crude lines serving the Ohio and Great Lakes areas.

Form ASTE Book Committee

Detroit—The American Society of Tool Engineers has formed a new "A.S.T.E. Book Committee" to replace its former ASTE Handbook Committee. The new committee will determine fields of industrial production in which specialized tooling information is required and develop books and manuals under its supervision.

Chicago Firm Wins ISIS Award

New York—Iron & Steel Products, Inc., Chicago, won first place in the 1950 safety contest of the Institute of Scrap Iron & Steel. The Chicago firm was credited with 44,690 accident-free man-hours. Second place went to Abrams Metal Co., Philadelphia, and third place to Mervis Iron & Metal Co., of Danville, Ill.

Unions Sign Longer Contracts

New York—Unions are signing more long-term labor pacts with provisions for some method of altering wages, according to a survey of 229 contracts completed by the National Industrial Conference Board. A "decided shift" to contracts longer than a year took place after outbreak of the Korean war but was evident previously.

• *News of Industry* •

Shortage, Higher British Defense Needs to Force Zinc Cuts

London—Further cuts in British zinc consumption were promised by the Minister of Supply who announced in Parliament that the shortage was not easing and that the supply of zinc, ordinary grade, may have to be restricted to about 50 pct of the rate of use during the first 9 months of 1950.

The effective date of the Statutory Order prohibiting the use of zinc and copper for certain manufactures has been put forward to March 1. A further concession is that users will have until July 1 to use up stocks.

Credit Curbs Hit Auto Sales

Detroit—Government credit restrictions have taken their toll as shown by November new car registrations which declined 130,000 units while trucks fell off 13,000 units from October, reports R. L. Polk & Co., statisticians. Polk estimates new car registrations in '50 as over 5 million and truck sales near 1.1 million units.

Soil Pipe Makers Agree on Sizes

Birmingham — Industry - w i d e standardization of cast iron soil pipe sizes is expected to follow a meeting here of the technical committee of the Cast Iron Soil Pipe Institute and the standardization committee of the National Assn. of Master Plumbers.

Institute Elects Wernisch

Chicago—George R. Wernisch of Ceco Steel Products Corp., has been elected chairman of the Metal Roof Deck Technical Institute. Other officers are: E. Klein, U. S. Gypsum Co., vice-chairman; E. A. Miller, Detroit Steel Products Co., secretary-treasurer.

Steel Casting Shipments Off

Washington—Shipments of steel castings in November were 146,000 tons, down slightly from the October figure of 150,000 tons. Unfilled orders at the end of November reached a total of 538,000 tons.

Now available for oil hardening in entire range of thicknesses...

Brown & Sharpe Ground Flat Stock

For templates, cutting tools, gages, machine parts and many similar pieces, there's a type of Brown & Sharpe Stock exactly suited to your specific requirements.

To give you even greater benefits from the money-saving, time-saving advantages of accurately pre-ground stock, Brown & Sharpe offers a choice of oil or water hardening steel in 16 different thicknesses from 1/64" to 1".

In eight thicknesses up to and including 3/16", a single type of ground flat stock now serves for hardening in either oil or water . . . a distinct Brown & Sharpe feature.

With this complete range of 145 stock sizes, you can meet a wide variety of requirements. Stock for oil hardening is for parts with intricate sections, sharp corners or abrupt changes in form . . . for water hardening, where slightly higher hardness is needed.

Continuous, repeat markings of type on each piece of Brown & Sharpe Ground Flat Stock make identification easy. Protective envelopes in different colors simplify handling.

Write for new descriptive folder. Brown & Sharpe Mfg. Co., Providence 1, R. I., U. S. A.

We urge buying through the Distributor

Brown & Sharpe   B·S

• *News of Industry* •

Heppenstall to Boost Steel Forging Output with Other Plant

Pittsburgh — To speed production of steel forgings for defense, The Heppenstall Co. has taken over a plant at New Brighton, Pa., and will coordinate facilities there with production in its Pittsburgh works.

Heppenstall purchased the William Leard Corp. plant from the Harkit Corp. of Pittsburgh.

Plant Sets Safety Record

LaGrange, Ill.—A new national record for heavy industry operation without a lost time accident has been set by Plant No. 3 of Electro-Motive Div. of General Motors at Cleveland. Employees at the plant worked 5,294,960 hr without a lost time accident. The record was set between May 9, 1949, and Dec. 11, 1950, covering a calendar period of 588 days. The previous record, set in 1941 by the Wilmington, Del., plant of the Pullman Co., was 4,265,572. The new record was recognized by the National Safety Council on Jan. 3.

ADCI Plans For Doehler Award

New York—Nominations for the annual Doehler Award of the American Die Casting Institute are being received between now and April 30, the Institute has announced. The award, a plaque and $500, will be made at the annual meeting in September.

Any individual, group, or technical society is eligible, whether or not engaged in the die casting business.

Cobalt Production Swings Up

New York—United States and Canadian production of cobalt, stringently rationed component of magnet metal, will total $4\frac{1}{4}$ million lbs by the end of 1952, according to the American Institute of Mining and Metallurgical Engineers. U. S. cobalt use prior to June, 1950, was 8 million lbs annually, 90 pct imported from Belgian Congo.

Design, Fabricating Firms Merge Into Salem-Brosius, Inc.

Pittsburgh—The Edgar E. Brosius Co., of Pittsburgh and the Salem Engineering Co., Salem, Ohio, have merged and will be known as Salem-Brosius, Inc. But individual company identifications will be retained for business purposes.

The merger was announced in a joint statement by Ward A. Wickwire, Sr., president of Brosius, and Sam Keener, president of Salem Engineering.

Government Information Offices

Washington — Three new field offices of the Commerce Dept. have been opened in the United States and another in Puerto Rico to handle priority matters, allocations, small business programs, to guide business in interpreting NPA orders, and provide U. S. procurement information.

Locations of the new offices are: 507 Strauss Bldg., 809 South Calhoun St., Fort Wayne, Ind.; 251 Sonna Bldg., Main St., Boise, Ida.; Davenport Institute, 4 Fulton St. East, Grand Rapids, Mich.; and 2 Puerto Reconstruction Administration Ground, Bldg. N, San Juan, Puerto Rico.

Modification Center to Reopen

Birmingham — The Bechtel-McCone aircraft modification plant here, built by the government during World War II at a cost of $13 million, will be re-opened soon.

The announcement by Under-Secretary for Air John A. McCone apparently means Chase Aircraft Company of West Trenton,, N. J., which had leased part of the plant for manufacture of cargo aircraft, may lose its lease.

Electric Maintenance Meeting

Milwaukee — The Electrical Maintenance Engineers of Milwaukee will hold their 12th annual Industrial Electrical Equipment Exposition here on Feb. 1 and 2. On display will be equipment from 65 manufacturers.

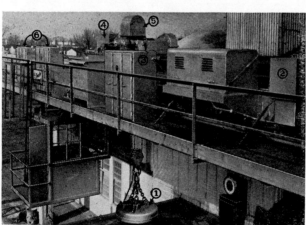
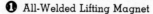
booklet discusses the use of cast brass brush-holders, stainless steel springs and the unique construction of the end turns. Types, enclosures and mountings for many different applications are shown. *Westinghouse Electric Corp.*
For free copy insert No. 8 on postcard, p. 37.

Bending Manual

"It's Easy to Bend" is the title of a new 32-p. bending manual. Numerous illustrations show Di-Acro benders; the ideas contained in the booklet apply to any rotary type bending machine and should be of value to anyone interested in the bending of metals. Standard radius and tube forming accessories are described, with information on rod parters, Ejectomatic gage, and units for notching, bending, punching and shearing. Detailed descriptions of numerous standard bending procedures are presented. *O'Neil-Irwin Mfg. Co.*
For free copy insert No. 9 on postcard, p. 37.

Data on Lubricants

Combining both technical data and historical information about the company, a new 24-p. brochure traces Brooks' history from its beginning as a lamp oil producer to its position today as one of the largest compounders of industrial lubricants. Included in the technical section are details on Leadolene, Klingfast and Roll Oil F. Case histories are cited which indicate how these lead-base lubricants have compared with other products on such applications as open and enclosed gears, corrosion protection, rolling mills, circulating systems, bearings, leaking gear cases, railroad switchplates and track curves, gear reductions and wire drawing machines. *Brooks Oil Co.*
For free copy insert No. 10 on postcard, p. 37.

School Lab Machines

Four new bulletins describing G-E ac and dc rotating machines for school laboratories group 19 motor generator sets for instructional purposes into four broad classifications. Quick evaluation of the suitability of these sets for each school's particular needs can be

made more easily and more accurately. The bulletins cover motor generator sets for the study of dc machines, synchronous machines, ac motors and dc exploring coil sets for oscillograph studies in dc armatures. *General Electric Co.*
For free copy insert No. 11 on postcard, p. 37.

Metallic Bellows Info

How many common types of bellows and methods of attaching end fittings are available? Is stainless steel, nickel or brass the material most frequently used? What affects the choice of material? How can you double the flexibility and halve the spring rate of a bellows? How can you limit the total pressure generated by a bellows at a specified temperature? These and many other questions are answered in an 8-p. bulletin entitled "What to Consider When Selecting A Metallic Bellows." The bulletin contains charts, diagrams, applications, and a detailed analysis of bellows construction, materials and flexibility. *Clifford Mfg. Co.*
For free copy insert No. 12 on postcard, p. 37.

Testing Machines

A new 30-p. catalog on Riehle screw power universal testing machines and accessories includes illustrations, details of construction, specifications and dimensions of testing machines up through 400,-000 lb capacity. Information is also given on special tools, instruments and accessories for special tests. *Riehle Testing Machines Div., American Machine & Metals, Inc.*
For free copy insert No. 13 on postcard, p. 37.

For Steel Handling

Featured in a new straddle truck catalog is the Hyster Model MHS, especially designed for handling steel. A variation of the standard 30,000 lb capacity Model MH straddle truck, the new model is intended for extreme service encountered in materials handling in the metal working industry. Principal among the number of improvements for extended utility shown in the booklet are double-row roller chains in the hoist mechanism; solid bar rather than channel sections in the lifting links; additional carrying capacity of the suspension springs; heavier frame in the cross members

February 1, 1951

publications
Continued

and corner sections; and the suspension springs having added carrying capacity to accommodate consistent handling of capacity loads. *Hyster Co.*
For free copy insert No. 14 on postcard, p. 37.

Production Tools

Standard Scully-Jones production tools are described and illustrated in 11 new catalog bulletins. These new bulletins replace the company's Tool Engineering Manual 500 and any other literature previously published. The catalogs and price lists cover: Drill and tap chucks; arbors and adapters; quick change chucks; tap holders and drivers; counterbores, countersinks and core drills; adjustable adapters; sleeves and sockets; floating holders; centers; recessing tools; and work rest blades. *Scully-Jones & Co.*
For free copy insert No. 15 on postcard, p. 37.

Lab Safety Manual

The newly revised edition of a 40-p. booklet entitled "Manual of Laboratory Safety" brings the original material up to date by the inclusion of recently developed data, techniques and equipment. The new manual will prove to be useful in the implementation of complete laboratory safety programs. The original edition of this manual has been translated into many foreign languages and is widely used throughout the world. Ten commandments for laboratory safety are listed, along with information on accident prevention, first aid, fire-fighting and safety equipment. *Fisher Scientific Co.*
For free copy insert No. 16 on postcard, p. 37.

Hand and Foot Valves

A new 4-p. technical bulletin describes the Ross ¼ and ⅜ in. 880 Series hand and foot valves. Installation data, engineering drawings and explanations of interchangeability of parts and ease of modification are included. The 880 Series was developed for quick control of small cylinders and for pilot operation of master valves. *Ross Operating Valve Co.*
For free copy insert No. 17 on postcard, p. 37.
Resume Your Reading on Page 37

production ideas

Continued from Page 40

a thermal selector set at the desired temperature to which the deep well is then chilled or heated. The part under test assumes the temperature of the deep well and can then be withdrawn and checked for operation. To test small parts mounted on larger assemblies, that

cannot be placed in the deep well, the thermal fluid can be circulated in a closed system a short distance from the test stand in insulated lines. This mobile hot-cold test stand measures 30 x 40 x 54 in. *Electro Mechanical Devices Div., George L. Nankervis Co.*
For more data insert No. 33 on postcard, p. 37.

Tube Seal

Insures foolproof seal against leakage in tube sheet closures.

A new packing and packing installation tool are special equipment for a new method of sealing tube sheet closures on heat transfer equipment for use with cor-

rosive fluid. Sealing involves no bolting or threading. The packing itself is molded composition to match the service. Thrust of the tool's cylindrical blade into the packing's annular space and against the filler ring results

production ideas

Continued

in distention of the packing, enabling it to pass over the end of the exchanger tube and be inserted in the tube sheet opening. With removal of the blade, the packing recovers its shape, thereby exerting its sealing pressure radial to the axis of the tube along the length of the filler ring. *Greene, Tweed & Co.*

For more data insert No. 34 on postcard, p. 37.

Multi-Drive Power Table

For rotary sheet metal work.

Hand operated bench machines are instantly converted to power machines with the multi-drive table. The portable welded steel table has positions for four machines. An electric foot treadle controls

the driving motor, leaving the operator's cranking arm free so that both hands can be used to guide the work in the rolls. The power unit is a Niagara worm reduction unit mounted on anti-friction bearings and operating in a bath of oil. The table comes complete with eight steel universal joints, four coupling shafts and all eletrical equipment. *Niagara Machine & Tool Works.*

For more data insert No. 35 on postcard, p. 37.

Hydraulic Eye Bender

Largest OD of eye which can be bent —with stationary mandrel—is 6½ in.

The spindle of the new hydraulic eye bender is actuated by a hydraulic cylinder with rack and pinion. Reversal is accomplished by a solenoid-operated valve which is

controlled by a limit switch adjustable to vary the degree of rotation of the bending spindle. The hold down clamp is hydraulically actuated and arranged so that the clamping of the stock is completed before the bending spindle is ro-

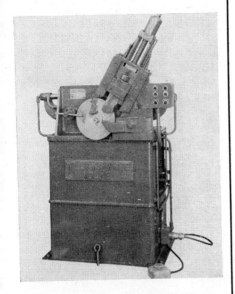

tated. Control for single cycle or continuous operation is by a foot-button mounted on a flexible cable. The machine has a recommended capacity of bending 1 in. diam round stock, hot, around a 1½ in. mandrel. *Williams-White & Co.*
For more data insert No. 36 on postcard, p. 37.

Powered Wheelbarrow

Compact, maneuverable, with rugged chassis and increased capacity.

Capacity has been increased to 1500 lb, bucket or platform load, in the improved Model 15 Prime-Mover powered wheelbarrow. Other new features include forward di-

rect drive with half speed reverse under power; dependable 5 hp Wisconsin engine; constant mesh transmission; and conveniently placed operator's controls. The engine and gasoline tank are located in an enclosed panel on top and at rear of the chassis. Two sizes of plat-

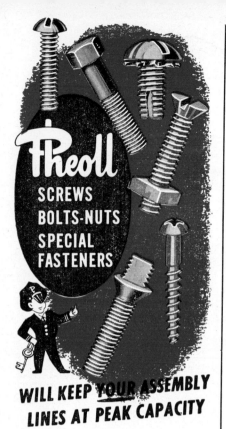

production ideas
Continued

forms with stakes are quickly interchangeable with the bucket. Turning radius is 33 in. The unit is 31½ in. wide permitting easy access through doorways and on elevators. *Prime-Mover Co.*
For more data insert No. 37 on postcard, p. 37.

Redesigned Pul-Pac
Handles unit fork-truck loads without use of conventional pallets.

Principal design change from the early Pul-Pac is the adoption of a pantograph-type linkage to actuate the gripper-jaw and pusher rack. The new construction allows a shorter hydraulic stroke, eliminating bending stresses to which the long pistons were subjected. The pantograph absorbs strong side forces formerly exerted on the long pistons. Pul-Pac structure back of the uprights is eliminated, contributing to maximum visibility and safety for the driver. *Clark Equipment Co.*
For more data insert No. 38 on postcard, p. 37.

Crankshaft Grinder
Refinishes shafts up to 18 ft long.

The principle of the moving grinding wheel is incorporated in a 20-ton grinder for regrinding diesel crankshafts. The supersize machine reportedly can chuck up and grind an 18-ft diesel shaft with ease and precision. The 4½-ft diam grinding wheel, on the largest model, is moved hydraulically on precision ways from journal to journal at selected speeds from 1 to 35 ipm. Hydraulic controls are also used to give rapid, smooth approach and retraction to the grinding wheel. Adjustment for various lengths of crankshafts is made through movement of the headstock, with the final setting made at the tailstock

through an adjustable quill. Head and tailstock spindles are mounted in 12½ in. Timken OD bearings. Shaft is held by 24-in. pot chucks and main bearings are ground between centers. The overall height is 7 ft; work is placed at eye-level. Electrical controls are at the operator's finger tips. Three models are available accommodating crankshaft swings varying from 32 to 50 in. and lengths from 108 to 216 in. Grinding wheel diameters range from 36 to 54 in. with widths from 1 to 5 in. *Lemco Products, Inc.*
For more data insert No. 39 on postcard, p. 37.

Measuring System
For precision location of table and work on P & W jig borer.

Accurately locating large work under the machine spindle on the P & W No. 4E jig borer is facilitated by a measuring system based

on the P&W Electrolimit gaging principle. Basic 1-in. spacing is obtained from a master measuring bar by electrical means, without making physical contact with the bar. Two master bars are built into the machine at right angles with one another, one for positioning longitudinally and one for positioning transversely. Cylindrical reference scales are used to locate the table to approximate settings. To locate a hole, the micrometer is set at the inch frac-

tion and the power rapid traverse operated until the reference scale reads the approximate setting. Final adjustment is made by hand-wheel. All scales read from zero in either direction and are adjustable to set zero for a starting position. Locating can start from either end or from the center of the work. *Pratt & Whitney, Div. Niles-Bement-Pond Co.*
For more data insert No. 40 on postcard, p. 37.

Electric Pallet Truck
Compact, powerful; handles pallet loads weighing 4000 lb maximum.

Among the advanced features of the Model W pallet truck are a new contactor panel, a positive-action brake with foolproof dead-man control, improved differential action, and all-rubber, dual trailer

wheels for smoother operation. Operator controls are located for finger-tip operation with right or left hand. A key switch provides positive turn off of power to the dual control buttons. Other features include smooth hydraulic lift, the rapid raising of heavy loads, powerful electric drive, and fast, agile maneuverability. *Towmotor Corp.*
For more data insert No. 41 on postcard, p. 37.

Goggle Padding Mask
Assures extra tight fit for better protection of worker.

A new molded rubber detachable padding mask for heavy duty coverall safety cup goggles is attached by a beaded molding that slips over the rims of the eye cups, providing a firm, light-tight joint. It is replaceable and can be changed without use of any tools. The mask may be purchased as an accessory with Willson cup goggles, or bought separately for application to goggles already in use. *Willson Products, Inc.*
For more data insert No. 42 on postcard, p. 37.
Resume Your Reading on Page 41

YOU LEARN A LOT IN A CENTURY

WIREBOUND BOXES and CRATES

WOODEN BOXES and CRATES

CORRUGATED FIBRE BOXES

BEVERAGE CASES

STARCH TRAYS

PALLETS

We have . . . especially about boxes and crates, because we have been designing and manufacturing them for nearly a century.

Today we are proud to offer you SUPERSTRONG . . . the crowning product of our long experience. Here you have a complete line of tough sturdy shipping containers - custom built to your product to give maximum protection at lowest possible cost.

Send out a call for a SUPERSTRONG man - it will pay you to get the full SUPERSTRONG story.

RATHBORNE, HAIR AND RIDGWAY BOX CO.
1440 WEST 21st PLACE · CHICAGO 8, ILLINOIS

PEDRICK BENDERS

Do not use Mandrels!

The illustration shows a Pedrick Machine bending a 4″ Extra Heavy Pipe Cold and without a Mandrel. The radius is about three times the nominal diameter of the pipe and the flattening effect is almost unnoticeable. This machine is in the service of the Hajoca Corporation, manufacturers of plumbing supplies at their new plant in Philadelphia. The bending time is computed in seconds and the relay control duplicates the work where same is desired without manual attention. If you are interested in saving money in your pipe fabricating department, write for our illustrated folder.

PEDRICK TOOL AND MACHINE COMPANY
3640 N. Lawrence Street, Philadelphia 40, Pa.

IRON AGE *markets and prices*

steel bookings—Mill bookings are running fairly current on DO's since the limits were revised upwards recently. However some products are still out of kilter. One mill has openings in July for hot-rolled sheets, June for hot-rolled strip and rail steel bars. Cold-rolled sheets, tinplate and plain carbon plate are open for May. Carbon bars and reinforcing bars are open for May-June rolling. A check of other companies shows about the same. The exception is big bar mills which are booked from Sept., 1951 to Jan., 1952.

takes up option—National Steel Corp. has exercised an option to buy a 15 pct interest in Reserve Mining Co., organized to develop an industrial process for extracting iron ore from taconite. Armco Steel Corp. and Republic Steel Corp. hold the remaining interest. Reserve Mining controls deposits at the eastern end of the Mesabi Range estimated to hold 1.5 billion tons of taconite, which should yield 500 million tons of 60 pct iron ore. Present plans call for production of 300,000 tons of ore per year in the form of pellets.

adjustments in copper use—Adjustments to permit builders to use inventory stock of hardware, piping and brass mill products covered in NPA order M-12 may soon be made. This would ease the situation for home builders who under M-12 amendment 1 "may not accept for delivery of or use such product for this purpose after Apr. 30, 1951."

conversion—It appears that legitimate steel conversion has at least the temporary blessing of Washington. The reason is simple: Conversion represents 10 to 20 pct of total steel output today. Rather than lose this large amount of steel output Washington gave conversion the nod—for the present at least.

how urgent—If a controlled materials plan is impossible at this time, steel people would like to be advised at least of the urgency of one order as related to another. They feel that it should not be their responsibility to make the decision. On some products in certain companies the present system shows signs of bogging down.

warehouse quotas—Some warehousemen claim their allotments have been cut 25 pct overall so far this year, while on some individual products it runs as high as 50 pct. They say their biggest cuts are coming from nonintegrated steel producers. But the nonintegrated producers get their allotments from integrated mills after DO's and allocation programs are taken out. Thus what the warehouses get from the nonintegrated producers is a percentage of a percentage. Toughest items are bars and tubing.

price confusion—Dealings in tin, lead, zinc and copper futures on the New York commodity exchange were halted Monday as trading officials met in emergency sessions in an effort to clarify the murky price control situation. Traders and exchange operators were in the dark over application of the price freeze. Confusion resulted from uncertainty as to how prices would be applied, and the fact that the freeze did not consider futures orders separately.

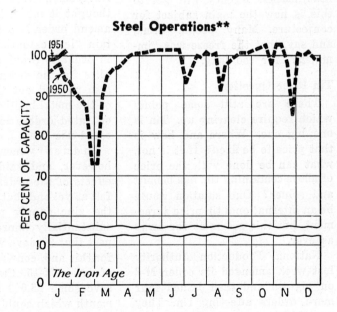

Steel Operations**

The Iron Age

District Operating Rates—Per Cent of Capacity**

Week of	Pittsburgh	Chicago	Youngstown	Philadelphia	West	Buffalo	Cleveland	Detroit	Wheeling	South	Ohio River	St. Louis	East	Aggregate
Jan. 21.......	97.0*	100.5	96.0*	99.0	106.7	104.0	99.0*	108.0*	101.0	106.0	91.0	95.1	111.3	101.0
Jan. 28.......	97.0	101.5	96.5	99.0	103.8	104.0	97.0	108.0	100.0	106.0	90.5	95.1	98.0	101.5

* Revised.
** Beginning Jan. 1, 1951, operations are based on an annual capacity of 104,229,650 net tons.

nonferrous metals | *outlook and market activities*

NONFERROUS METALS PRICES

	Jan. 24	Jan. 25	Jan. 26	Jan. 27	Jan. 29	Jan. 30
Copper, electro, Conn. ...	24.50	24.50	24.50	24.50	24.50	24.50
Copper, Lake, delivered...	24.625	24.625	24.625	24.625	24.625	24.625
Tin, Straits, New York	$1.80	$1.83	$1.82	....	$1.83	$1.83*
Zinc, East St. Louis	17.50	17.50	17.50	17.50	17.50	17.50
Lead, St. Louis	16.80	16.80	16.80	16.80	16.80	16.80

Note: Quotations are going prices.

*Tentative.

by R. Hatschek

New York — The long-awaited price freeze is finally upon us but setting prices at record-high levels is looked upon as ridiculous by many. What is expected next is a definite price list, at least for scrap metals, in which the price for new metal will be the guide.

Just how soon the Economic Stabilization Agency will get to this is now the main subject for conjecture. Many people think, and say, that the freeze was "imminent" for too long.

Tin Price Question

There are still some points which require clearing up. Tin is one big one. Where and how is that price to be fixed? If it is not, what can be done with the price of alloys containing tin, like babbitt and solder? One solution would be an international tin price agreement, but this seems as far away as ever.

National Production Authority last week amended its order M-8 on pig tin and then issued four more orders affecting tin. They are: M-24 on tinplate and terneplate, M-25 on metal cans, M-26 on tinplate closures, and M-27 on collapsible tubes.

Other orders affecting nonferrous metals were an amendment to M-14, prohibiting the use of nickel for non-essential purposes; M-30 on tungsten; and M-33 on molybdenum. More complete details on these orders can be found in the section of this issue devoted to news.

Industry Disagrees

Following the meeting with members of the zinc industry, NPA officials indicated that they thought it might be necessary to amend order M-8 to prohibit certain "less essential" uses of zinc in order to provide sufficient supplies for the defense effort. NPA also pointed out that some users of the metal had been getting zinc on rated orders long before they could use it.

Industry members protested, however, and said that the full effects of the order have not been felt as yet and that, when they are, the zinc supply picture will be substantially improved. They expect that 90 days will be required for this and, considering all facets of order M-15, they expect it to save some 25,000 tons of zinc a month which could be used for essential production and stockpile purposes.

Nonferrous metal shortages are helping to create a very uncertain future for the auto industry. Copper, nickel, zinc and alumium restrictions are all hampering the car manufacturers, it is reported.

Detroit interests attribute the worsening copper situation to three factors—(1) A slowdown in domestic shipments, (2) the government stockpile program, and (3) late developments in Chile. Chilean producers are reported to be selling more copper to countries other than the United States. Copper is being made into deformed wire bars which can be sold more profitably in the world markets than ingots to this country.

Copper Stockpiling Needs

The Munitions Board stockpiling is taking some 15,000 to 20,000 tons of copper per month and the amount already on hand is reported to be a little more than a quarter of the minimum requirement.

William H. Harrison, Defense Production Administrator, does not paint an optimistic picture of the future of the copper industry. He mentioned the expansion taking place in the steel and aluminum industries and indicated that this would not happen with copper. Mr. Harrison stated that a controlled materials plan would be in effect by summer and said that this would be a great aid in supplying the nation's needs of this metal.

MILL PRODUCTS

(Cents per lb, unless otherwise noted)

Aluminum

(Base 30,000 lb, f.o.b. ship. pt. frt. allowed)

Flat Sheet: 0.188 in., 2S, 3S, 30.1¢; 4S, 61S-O, 32¢; 52S, 34.1¢; 24S-O, 24S-OAL, 32.9¢; 75S-O, 75S-OAL, 39.9¢; 0.081 in., 2S, 3S, 31.2¢; 4S, 61S-O, 33.5¢; 52S, 35.6¢; 24S-O, 24S-OAL, 34.1¢; 75S-O, 75S-OAL, 41.8¢; 0.032 in., 2S, 3S, 32.9¢; 4S, 61S-O, 37.1¢; 52S, 39.8¢; 24S-O, 24S-OAL, 41.7¢; 75S-O, 75S-OAL, 52.2¢.

Plate: ¼ in. and heavier: 2S, 3S-F, 28.3¢; 4S-F, 30.2¢; 52S-F, 31.8¢; 61S-O, 30.8¢; 24S-O, 24S-OAL, 32.4¢; 75S-O, 75S-OAL, 38.8¢.

Extruded Solid Shapes: Shape factors 1 to 5, 36.2¢ to 74.5¢; 12 to 14, 36.9¢ to 89¢; 24 to 26, 39.6¢ to $1.16; 36 to 38, 47.2¢ to $1.70.

Rod, Rolled: 1.5 to 4.5 in., 2S-F, 3S-F, 37.5¢ to 33.5¢; cold-finished, 0.375 to 3 in., 2S-F, 3S-F, 40.5¢ to 35¢.

Screw Machine Stock: Rounds, 11S-T3, ⅛ to 11/32 in., 53.5¢ to 42¢; ⅜ to 1½ in., 41.5¢ to 39¢; 1 9/16 to 3 in., 38.5¢ to 36¢; 17S-T4 lower by 1.5¢ per lb. Base 5000 lb.

Drawn Wire: Coiled, 0.051 to 0.374 in., 2S, 39.5¢ to 29¢; 52S, 48¢ to 35¢; 56S, 51¢ to 42¢; 17S-T4, 54¢ to 37.5¢; 61S-T4, 48.5¢ to 37¢; 75S-T6, 84¢ to 67.5¢.

Extruded Tubing, Rounds: 63S-T5, OD in in.: 1¼ to 2, 37¢ to 54¢; 2 to 4, 33.5¢ to 45.5¢; 4 to 6, 34¢ to 41.5¢; 6 to 9, 34.5¢ to 43.5¢.

Roofing Sheet, Flat: 0.019 in. x 28 in. per sheet, 72 in., $1.142; 96 in., $1.522; 120 in., $1.902; 144 in., $2.284. Gage 0.024 in. x 28 in., 72 in., $1.379; 96 in., $1.839; 120 in., $2.299; 144 in., $2.759. Coiled Sheet: 0.019 in. x 28 in., 28.2¢ per lb.; 0.024 in. x 28 in., 26.9¢ per lb.

Magnesium

(F.o.b. mill, freight allowed)

Sheet and Plate: FS1-O, ¼ in. 63¢; 3/16 in. 65¢; ⅛ in. 67¢; B & S Gage 10, 68¢; 12, 72¢; 14, 78¢; 16, 85¢; 18, 93¢; 20, $1.05; 22, $1.27; 24, $1.67. Specification grade higher. Base: 30,000 lb.

Extruded Round Rod: M, diam in., ¼ to 0.311 in., 74¢; ½ to ¾ in., 57.5¢; 1¼ to 1.749 in., 53¢; 2½ to 5 in., 48.5¢. Other alloys higher. Base: Up to ¾ in. diam, 10,000 lb; ¾ to 2 in., 20,000 lb; 2 in. and larger, 30,000 lb.

Extruded Solid Shapes, Rectangles: M. In weight per ft, for perimeters less than size indicated, 0.10 to 0.11 lb, 3.5 in., 62.3¢; 0.22 to 0.25 lb, 5.9 in., 59.3¢; 0.50 to 0.59 lb, 8.6 in., 56.7¢; 1.8 to 2.59 lb, 19.5 in., 53.8¢; 4 to 6 lb, 28 in., 49¢. Other alloys higher. Base, in weight per ft of shape: Up to ½ lb, 10,000 lb; ½ to 1.80 lb, 20,000 lb; 1.80 lb and heavier, 30,000 lb.

Extruded Round Tubing: M, wall thickness, outside diam, in., 0.049 to 0.057, ¼ in. to 5/16, $1.40; 5/16 to ⅜, $1.26; ½ to ⅝, 93¢; 1 to 2 in., 76¢; 0.165 to 0.219, ⅝ to ¾, 61¢; 1 to 2 in., 57¢; 3 to 4 in., 56¢. Other alloys higher. Base, OD in in.; Up to 1½ in., 10,000 lb; 1½ in. to 3 in., 20,000 lb; 3 in. and larger, 30,000 lb.

Titanium

(10,000 lb. base, f.o.b. mill)

Commercially pure and alloy grades: Sheet and strip, HR or CR, $15; Plate, HR, $12; Wire, rolled and/or drawn, $10; Bar, HR or forged, $6; Forgings, $6.

Nickel and Monel

(Base prices, f.o.b. mill)

	"A" Nickel	Monel
Sheets, cold-rolled	71½	57
Strip, cold-rolled	77½	60
Rods and bars	67½	55
Angles, hot-rolled	67½	55
Plates	69½	56
Seamless tubes	100½	90
Shot and blocks	....	50

Copper, Brass, Bronze

(Freight prepaid on 200 lb includes duty)

	Sheets	Rods	Extruded Shapes
Copper	41.03	....	40.63
Copper, h-r	....	36.88	....
Copper, drawn	....	38.18	....
Low brass	39.15	38.84	....
Yellow brass	38.28	37.97	....
Red brass	40.14	39.83	....
Naval brass	43.08	38.61	38.07
Leaded brass	....	32.63	36.70
Com'l bronze	41.13	40.82	....
Mang. bronze	45.96	40.65	41.41
Phos. bronze	60.20	60.45	....
Muntz metal	40.43	36.74	37.99
Ni silver, 10 pct	49.27	51.49	....
Arch. bronze	....	....	35.11

PRIMARY METALS

(Cents per lb, unless otherwise noted)

Aluminum ingot, 99+%, 10,000 lb, freight allowed	19.00
Aluminum pig	18.00
Antimony, American, Laredo, Tex.	42.00
Beryllium copper, 3.75-4.25% Be	$1.56
Beryllium aluminum 5% Be, Dollars per lb contained Be	$69.00
Bismuth, ton lots	$2.25
Cadmium, del'd	$2.55
Cobalt, 97-99% (per lb)	$2.10 to $2.17
Copper, electro, Conn. Valley	24.50
Copper, Lake, delivered	24.625
Gold, U. S. Treas., dollars per oz.	$35.00
Indium, 99.8%, dollars per troy oz.	$2.25
Iridium, dollars per troy oz.	$200
Lead, St. Louis	16.80
Lead, New York	17.00
Magnesium, 99.8+%, f.o.b. Freeport, Tex., 10,000 lb	24.50
Magnesium, sticks, 100 to 500 lb	42.00 to 44.00
Mercury, dollars per 76-lb flask f.o.b. New York	$225.00
Nickel, electro, f.o.b. New York	53.55
Nickel oxide sinter, f.o.b. Copper Cliff, Ont., contained nickel	46.75
Palladium, dollars per troy oz.	$24.00
Platinum, dollars per troy oz.	$90 to $93
Silver, New York, cents per oz.	90.16
Tin, New York	$1.83
Titanium, sponge	$5.00
Zinc, East St. Louis	17.50
Zinc, New York	18.22
Zirconium copper, 50 pct	$6.20

REMELTED METALS

Brass Ingot

(Cents per lb delivered, carloads)

85-5-5-5 ingot	
No. 115	29.00
No. 120	28.50
No. 123	28.00
80-10-10 ingot	
No. 305	35.00
No. 315	32.00
88-10-2 ingot	
No. 210	46.25
No. 215	43.25
No. 245	36.00
Yellow ingot	
No. 405	25.00
Manganese bronze	
No. 421	29.75

Aluminum Ingot

(Cents per lb, 30,000 lb lots)

95-5 aluminum-silicon alloys	
0.30 copper, max.	33.25-34.25
0.60 copper, max.	33.00-34.00
Piston alloys (No. 122 type)	30.50-31.00
No. 12 alum. (No. 2 grade)	30.00-30.50
108 alloy	30.25-30.75
195 alloy	31.25-31.75
13 alloy	33.50-34.00
ASX-679	30.50-31.00

Steel deoxidizing aluminum, notch-bar granulated or shot

Grade 1—95-97½%	32.00-32.50
Grade 2—92-95%	30.25-30.75
Grade 3—90-92%	29.25-29.75
Grade 4—85-90%	28.75-29.25

ELECTROPLATING SUPPLIES

Anodes

(Cents per lb, freight allowed, 500 lb lots)

Copper	
Cast, oval, 15 in. or longer	39¼
Electrodeposited	33⅜
Rolled, oval, straight, delivered	38⅞
Forged ball anodes	43
Brass, 80-20	
Cast, oval, 15 in. or longer	34¾
Zinc, oval	26½
Ball anodes	25½
Nickel 99 pct plus	
Cast	70.50
Rolled, depolarized	71.50
Cadmium	$2.80
Silver 999 fine, rolled, 100 oz lots, per troy oz, f.o.b. Bridgeport, Conn.	79½

Chemicals

(Cents per lb, f.o.b. shipping point)

Copper cyanide, 100 lb drum	52.15
Copper sulfate, 99.5 crystals, bbl.	12.85
Nickel salts, single or double, 4-100 lb bags, frt allowed	20½
Nickel chloride, 375 lb drum	27½
Silver cyanide, 100 oz lots, per oz.	67¼
Sodium cyanide, 96 pct domestic 200 lb drums	19.25
Zinc cyanide, 100 lb drums	45.85

SCRAP METALS

Brass Mill Scrap

(Cents per pound, add ½¢ per lb for shipments of 20,000 to 40,000 lb; add 1¢ for more than 40,000 lb)

	Heavy	Turnings
Copper	23	22¼
Yellow brass	20½	18¾
Red brass	21½	20¾
Comm. bronze	21¾	21
Mang. bronze	19½	18⅝
Brass rod ends	19⅝	....

Custom Smelters' Scrap

(Cents per pound, carload lots, delivered to refinery)

No. 1 copper wire	21.50
No. 2 copper wire	20.00
Light copper	19.00
Refinery brass	19.50*
Radiators	15.00

*Dry copper content.

Ingot Makers' Scrap

(Cents per pound, carload lots, delivered to producer)

No. 1 copper wire	23.00
No. 2 copper wire	22.00
Light copper	21.00
No. 1 composition	22.00
No. 1 comp. turnings	21.50
Rolled brass	18.50
Brass pipe	20.50
Radiators	17.50
Heavy yellow brass	17.00
Aluminum	
Mixed old cast	18½—19
Mixed new clips	20½
Mixed turnings, dry	18½
Pots and pans	18½—19
Low copper	21½—22

Dealers' Scrap

(Dealers' buying prices, f.o.b. New York in cents per pound)

Copper and Brass

No. 1 heavy copper and wire	19½—20
No. 2 heavy copper and wire	18 —18½
Light copper	17 —17¼
New type shell cuttings	17 —17¼
Auto radiators (unsweated)	14½—15
No. 1 composition	17 —17½
No. 1 composition turnings	16½—17
Clean red car boxes	15½—16
Cocks and faucets	15½—16
Mixed heavy yellow brass	13 —13½
Old rolled brass	14 —14½
Brass pipe	17 —17½
New soft brass clippings	17½—18
Brass rod ends	16½—17
No. 1 brass rod turnings	16 —16½

Aluminum

Alum. pistons and struts	12 —13
Aluminum crankcases	15 —16
2S aluminum clippings	18½—19½
Old sheet and utensils	15 —16
Borings and turnings	12½—13
Misc. cast aluminum	15 —16
Dural clips (24S)	15 —16

Zinc

New zinc clippings	14½—15
Old zinc	11 —11¼
Zinc routings	8½— 9
Old die cast scrap	8 — 8½

Nickel and Monel

Pure nickel clippings	60 —65
Clean nickel turnings	57 —60
Nickel anodes	60 —65
Nickel rod ends	60 —65
New Monel Clippings	22 —25
Clean Monel turnings	18 —20
Old sheet Monel	20 —22
Inconel clippings	26 —28
Nickel silver clippings, mixed	13 —14
Nickel silver turnings, mixed	12 —13

Lead

Soft scrap, lead	15 —15¼
Battery plates (dry)	8¾— 9

Magnesium

Segregated solids	9 —10
Castings	5½— 6½

Miscellaneous

Block tin	90 —100
No. 1 pewter	63 —65
No. 1 auto babbitt	58 —60
Mixed common babbitt	12¼—12½
Solder joints	20 —21
Siphon tops	58 —60
Small foundry type	18¼—18½
Monotype	16¾—17
Lino. and stereotype	16¼—16¾
Electrotype	14¾—15
Hand picked type shells	11½—11¾
Lino. and stereo. dross	8 — 8¼
Electro. dross	6½— 6¾

SCRAP *iron and steel*

Markets dull on eve of price rollbacks . . . NPA issues scrap inventory control order . . . Cleveland, Cincinnati markets lively.

It was the eve of price rollbacks on scrap as this issue hit the presses and everything was mostly quiet throughout the markets—except blood pressure of men in the trade. They had played guessing games with Washington before and had discovered that the capitol was unpredictable. But this time it looked like "it."

Before the rollback broke, it was impossible to divine the backward trend. Astounding was the lack of rumors on the scope of the rollback. It seemed that everyone in Washington was this time keeping mum.

With the exception of Cleveland and Cincinnati, which played it wild and wooly on trading till what seemed the final minute, the markets reported low and spotty activity. Most were content to see what the rollbacks would be.

NPA has amended order M-20 so that it can order increases or decreases in consumer steel scrap inventories and allocate scrap and specifically direct the manner and quantities of delivery. The order doesn't change the 60-day limit on dealer and broker inventories nor mills' practical working minimum.

The guessing contest held by THE IRON AGE at the scrap convention in New York was won by Herman Caplan, of M. W. Singer & Co., Pittsburgh, with a shrewd guess of 1680 pieces of scrap in the fish bowl. Actual count: 1653.

PITTSBURGH—As a protective measure to halt the flow of scrap to other districts, the largest consumer here has agreed to pay a competitive price pending imposition of controls. This has had the effect of tentatively advancing prices on melting grades $5 per ton, at the least.

Turnings were up similarly on the basis of purchases by another mill. Under this arrangement, the consumer will take in scrap without immediate billing, with the price dependent on the nature of the control order.

If the order is effective after Jan. 24, when the arrangement was made, the competitive price as of that time will be paid on scrap already shipped. If the order is retroactive to an earlier date, however, the mill will pay only the control price. Chances are that the order will not be retroactive, although it is expected to specify that uncompleted orders not be filled if the price is higher than the control figure.

CHICAGO—Prior to the announcement of a price freeze last week some dealers were being offered as high as $47 per gross ton for a few carloads of No. 1 heavy melting steel for shipment to the East. Local mills, however, were still getting scrap at formula prices. Some dealers were reluctant to ship to the East because of fear of rejections. It was also reported that some foundries were offering $48 per gross ton for immediate shipment of small tonnages of No. 1 steel to get scrap in under the deadline. Otherwise there was not much activity as the trade was waiting the arrival of rollbacks.

PHILADELPHIA—There were few price changes prior to the government's price freeze order, although the market was suffering from general confusion. Some of the local consumers stayed out of the market waiting for it but quick shipments of insignificant tonnages could demand their own prices from others. The $5 increase in Pittsburgh caused some steel scrap to drift out of this district.

NEW YORK—On the eve of price controls the scrap market here was confused. Brokers were waiting for the price rollback, but last week the melting grades got a shot in the arm and advanced $1 on No. 1 to a ceiling of $45.

DETROIT—The Detroit scrap market is standing virtually still in the face of reports that price rollbacks are imminent. While most scrap sources anticipate a rollback in prices will be imposed simultaneously with controls, there is a wide variation of opinion as to the price level that will be set by Washington. Meanwhile, the present situation is badly confused. Even further confusion is anticipated when controls are finally announced. In the meantime, demand for

mill grades is holding although interest in cast grades appears to be noticeably softer than it was a few weeks ago.

CLEVELAND—Scrap is moving freely and in large tonnages here and in the Valley on what is thought to be the eve of price controls. Deals are numerous and the price of No. 1, for spot tonnages on the ground, is practically anybody's guess. Dealers and brokers are moving every pound they can. The market for blast furnace grades is confused, but major consumers were able to buy tonnage this week at $40, a substantial drop from last week's level. Foundry grades are strong but not moving.

ST. LOUIS—Pending issuance of expected price controls buying of scrap iron in the St. Louis market has been confined to small lots needed by consumers to tide them over an emergency. In such cases prices paid have been higher than the formula now in effect. Receipts have been cut down as a result of bad weather conditions which also have halted processing operations. Prices are unchanged.

BIRMINGHAM—The scrap market is quiet here, with most buyers apparently waiting for the government to decide if there will be a price rollback. There have been no price changes. A prominent consumer, which last week announced it was out of the market, came back in this week when it was learned dealers were buying in Georgia and selling to Northern mills.

CINCINNATI—A strong but confused scrap market here was ready to greet controls with fixed emotions. Brokers raised their buying prices for No. 1 heavy melting steel and blast furnace grades over the week end to meet competition from other districts. Anybody with an order is shipping everything he can get his hands on. Foundry grades are strong but inactive. Demand is there, but foundries waited for lower control prices.

BOSTON—Prices inched further and further from the formula price of 8 weeks ago, $35.67 for No. 1 heavy melting, as scrap moved freely in a lively market. Prices on most items were up, with No. 1 heavy melting and No. 1 bundles at $42 to $43.

BUFFALO—As the trade here awaited rollbacks, dealers rushed scrap to a top consumer at recently-set higher prices. It was generally conceded that the spurt in prices would be a temporary situation. While the price rise brought out more scrap, supply is uncertain.

This Logemann scrap press is in operation in one of the larger industrial plants. It compresses scrap from three directions to produce high density, mill size bundles.

Self-Contained . . . . .
Triple Compression . . .⎫
Automatically Controlled⎭

LOGEMANN
SCRAP PRESSES

handle high tonnages with minimum labor . . . *at low cost*

LOGEMANN METAL BALERS

. . . are built in a large range of sizes to meet specific conditions. Let Logemann's engineering service help you arrive at the most efficient and economical way of handling your scrap.

The compact unit illustrated is completely self-contained with oil tank and pump located directly over the press . . . utilizing the advantages of short pipe lines. Automatic controls, mounted in front of pump, give the operator full visibility at all times. Controls operate rams successively within a single rigid box. There is no complex construction which means there is *no need for specially-trained maintenance crews.*

Both two-ram and three-ram models are available with automatic controls or for manual manipulation.

Logemann Bros. Co. have specialized in the production of scrap metal presses for sheet mills, stamping plants, scrap yards, and metal manufacturing plants of all types for nearly 75 years. Write for full information — please state the nature of your scrap and tonnage.

LOGEMANN BROTHERS COMPANY
3164 W. Burleigh Street   •   Milwaukee 10, Wisconsin

Iron and Steel

SCRAP PRICES

Going prices as obtained in the trade by THE IRON AGE based on representative tonnages. All prices are per gross ton delivered to consumer unless otherwise noted.

Pittsburgh

No. 1 hvy. melting	$50.75 to $51.50
No. 2 hvy. melting	48.75 to 49.50
No. 1 bundles	50.75 to 51.50
No. 2 bundles	47.75 to 48.50
Machine shop turn.	43.25 to 44.00
Mixed bor. and ms. turns.	43.25 to 44.00
Shoveling turnings	44.75 to 45.50
Cast iron borings	44.75 to 45.50
Low phos. plate	56.00 to 56.50
Heavy turnings	51.50 to 52.00
No. 1 RR. hvy. melting	50.75 to 51.50
Scrap rails, random lgth.	64.50 to 65.00
Rails 2 ft and under	68.00 to 69.00
RR. steel wheels	63.00 to 64.00
RR. spring steel	63.00 to 64.00
RR. couplers and knuckles	63.00 to 64.00
No. 1 machinery cast	67.50 to 68.00
Mixed yard cast	57.50 to 58.00
Heavy breakable cast	53.00 to 53.50
Malleable	71.00 to 72.00

Chicago

No. 1 hvy. melting	$44.25 to $45.00
No. 2 hvy. melting	42.00 to 43.00
No. 1 factory bundles	44.00 to 45.00
No. 1 dealers' bundles	44.00 to 45.00
No. 2 dealers' bundles	41.00 to 42.00
Machine shop turn.	36.00 to 37.00
Mixed bor. and turn.	36.00 to 37.00
Shoveling turnings	37.00 to 38.00
Cast iron borings	37.00 to 38.00
Low phos. forge crops	54.00 to 55.00
Low phos. plate	52.00 to 53.00
No. 1 RR. hvy. melting	47.00 to 48.00
Scrap rails, random lgth	62.00 to 63.00
Rerolling rails	65.50 to 66.50
Rails 2 ft and under	67.00 to 69.00
Locomotive tires, cut	58.00 to 59.00
Cut bolsters & side frames	54.00 to 55.00
Angles and splice bars	63.00 to 64.00
RR. steel car axles	95.00 to 100.00
RR. couplers and knuckles	58.00 to 59.00
No. 1 machinery cast	62.00 to 64.00
No. 1 agricul. cast	58.00 to 60.00
Heavy breakable cast	54.00 to 55.00
RR. grate bars	48.00 to 49.00
Cast iron brake shoes	52.00 to 53.00
Cast iron car wheels	58.00 to 59.00
Malleable	78.00 to 82.00

Philadelphia

No. 1 hvy. melting	$47.00 to $48.00
No. 2 hvy. melting	44.00 to 45.00
No. 1 bundles	47.00 to 48.00
No. 2 bundles	42.00 to 43.00
Machine shop turn.	38.00 to 39.00
Shoveling turnings	40.00 to 41.00
Low phos. punchings, plate	52.00 to 53.00
Low phos. 5 ft and under	52.00 to 53.00
Low phos. bundles	50.00 to 51.00
Hvy. axle forge turn.	46.00 to 47.00
Clean cast chem. borings	44.00 to 45.00
RR. steel wheels	56.00 to 57.00
RR. spring steel	56.00 to 57.00
Rails 18 in. and under	66.00 to 67.00
No. 1 machinery cast	62.00 to 63.00
Mixed yard cast	53.00 to 55.00
Heavy breakable cast	53.00 to 54.00
Cast iron carwheels	67.00 to 68.00
Malleable	70.00 to 72.00

Cleveland

No. 1 hvy. melting	$51.00 to $52.00
No. 2 hvy. melting	49.00 to 50.00
No. 1 busheling	51.00 to 52.00
No. 1 bundles	51.00 to 52.00
No. 2 bundles	48.00 to 49.00
Machine shop turn.	37.00 to 38.00
Mixed bor. and turn.	39.00 to 40.00
Shoveling turnings	39.00 to 40.00
Cast iron borings	39.00 to 40.00
Low phos. 2 ft and under	53.50 to 54.50
Steel axle turn.	50.00 to 51.00
Drop forge flashings	51.00 to 52.00
No. 1 RR. hvy. melting	51.50 to 52.00
Rails 3 ft and under	70.00 to 71.00
Rails 18 in. and under	72.00 to 73.00
No. 1 machinery cast	69.00 to 70.00
RR. cast	71.00 to 72.00
RR. grate bars	50.00 to 51.00
Stove plate	55.00 to 56.00
Malleable	76.00 to 77.00

Youngstown

No. 1 hvy. melting	$51.50 to $52.50
No. 2 hvy. melting	49.50 to 50.50
No. 1 bundles	51.50 to 52.50

Buffalo

No. 1 hvy. melting	$51.25 to $52.00
No. 2 hvy. melting	49.25 to 50.00
No. 1 bushelings	49.25 to 50.00
No. 1 bundles	50.25 to 51.00
No. 2 bundles	47.25 to 48.00
Machine shop turn.	43.25 to 44.00
Mixed bor. and turn.	43.25 to 44.00
Shoveling turnings	45.25 to 46.00
Cast iron borings	43.25 to 44.00
Low phos. plate	51.25 to 52.00
Scrap rails, random lgth.	55.00 to 56.00
Rails 2 ft and under	60.00 to 61.00
RR. steel wheels	60.00 to 61.00
RR. spring steel	60.00 to 61.00
RR. couplers and knuckles	60.00 to 61.00
No. 1 machinery cast	59.00 to 60.00
No. 1 cupola cast	54.00 to 55.00
Small indus. malleable	60.00 to 61.00

Birmingham

No. 1 hvy. melting	$42.50 to $43.50
No. 2 hvy. melting	40.50 to 41.50
No 2 bundles	39.50 to 40.50
No. 1 busheling	40.50 to 41.50
Machine shop turn.	34.00 to 35.00
Shoveling turnings	32.00 to 33.00
Cast iron borings	33.00 to 34.00
Bar crops and plate	47.00 to 48.00
Structural and plate	46.00 to 47.00
No. 1 RR. hvy. melting	43.00 to 44.00
Scrap rails, random lgth.	58.00 to 59.00
Rerolling rails	61.00 to 62.00
Rails 2 ft and under	66.00 to 67.00
Angles & splice bars	59.00 to 60.00
Std. steel axles	61.00 to 62.00
No. 1 cupola cast	54.00 to 55.00
Stove plate	49.00 to 50.00
Cast iron carwheels	46.00 to 47.00

St. Louis

No. 1 hvy. melting	$43.75 to $44.50
No. 2 hvy. melting	41.75 to 42.50
No. 2 bundled sheets	40.75 to 41.50
Machine shop turn.	33.75 to 34.75
Shoveling turnings	36.50 to 37.50
Rails, random lengths	49.00 to 50.00
Rails 3 ft and under	62.00 to 63.00
Locomotive tires, uncut	50.00 to 51.00
Angles and spice bars	59.00 to 60.00
Std. steel car axles	90.00 to 95.00
RR. spring steel	53.00 to 54.00
No. 1 machinery cast	55.00 to 56.00
Hvy. breakable cast	48.00 to 49.00
Cast iron brake shoes	53.00 to 54.00
Stove plate	45.00 to 47.00
Cast iron car wheels	60.00 to 62.00
Malleable	55.00 to 57.00

New York

Brokers' Buying prices per gross ton, on cars:

No. 1 hvy. melting	$44.00 to $45.00
No. 2 hvy. melting	41.00 to 42.00
No. 2 bundles	40.00 to 41.00
Machine shop turn.	32.00 to 34.00
Mixed bor. and turn.	32.00 to 34.00
Shoveling turnings	34.00 to 36.00
Clean cast chem. bor.	40.00 to 41.00
No. 1 machinery cast	52.00 to 53.00
Mixed yard cast	47.00 to 48.00
Charging box cast	47.00 to 48.00
Heavy breakable cast	47.00 to 48.00
Unstrp. motor blocks	42.00 to 43.00

Boston

Brokers' Buying prices per gross ton, on cars:

No. 1 hvy. melting	$42.00 to $43.00
No. 2 hvy. melting	37.50 to 38.50
No. 1 bundles	42.00 to 43.00

(Detroit top column)

No. 2 bundles	$40.00 to $41.00
Machine shop turn	30.00 to 31.00
Mixed bor. and turn.	30.00 to 31.00
Shoveling turnings	32.00 to 33.00
No. 1 busheling	41.00 to 42.00
Clean cast chem. borings	35.00 to 36.00
No. 1 machinery cast	48.00 to 49.00
Mixed cupola cast	44.00 to 45.00
Heavy breakable cast	42.00 to 43.00
Stove plate	42.00 to 43.00

Detroit

Brokers' Buying prices per gross ton, on cars:

No. 1 hvy. melting	$40.25
No. 2 hvy. melting	38.25
No. 1 bundles, openhearth	40.25
No. 1 bundles, electric furnace	42.75
New busheling	40.25
Flashings	40.25
Machine shop turn.	32.25
Mixed bor. and turn.	32.25
Shoveling turnings	34.25
Cast iron borings	34.25
Low phos. plate	42.75
No. 1 cupola cast	$54.00 to 56.00
Heavy breakable cast	45.00 to 47.00
Stove plate	44.00 to 46.00
Automotive cast	58.00 to 60.00

Cincinnati

Per gross ton, f.o.b. cars:

No. 1 hvy. melting	$45.00
No. 2 hvy. melting	43.25
No. 1 bundles	45.50
No. 2 bundles, black	42.25
No. 2 bundles, mixed	41.25
Machine shop turn.	35.00
Mixed bor. and turn.	35.00
Shoveling turnings	36.00
Cast iron borings	36.00
Low phos.-steel	46.75
Low phos. 18 in. under	62.00
Rails, random lengths	$62.00 to 63.00
Rails, 18 in. and under	72.00 to 73.00
No. 1 cupola cast	45.00 to 47.00
Hvy. breakable cast	59.00 to 60.00
Drop broken cast	71.00 to 72.00

San Francisco

No. 1 hvy. melting	$30.00 to $34.00
No. 2 hvy. melting	28.00 to 32.00
No. 1 bundles	30.00 to 34.00
No. 2 bundles	28.00 to 32.00
No. 3 bundles	25.00
Machine shop turn.	16.00 to 18.00
Elec. fur. 1 ft and under	40.00 to 42.50
No. 1 RR. hvy. melting	30.00 to 46.00
Scrap rails random lgth.	30.00 to 46.00
No. 1 cupola cast	45.00 to 47.00

Los Angeles

No. 1 hvy. melting	$30.00 to $34.00
No. 2 hvy. melting	28.00 to 32.00
No. 1 bundles	30.00 to 34.00
No. 2 bundles	28.00 to 32.00
No. 3 bundles	25.00
Mach. shop turn.	16.00 to 18.00
Elec. fur. 1 ft and under	40.00 to 42.50
No. 1 RR. hvy. melting	30.00 to 46.00
Scrap rails random lgth.	30.00 to 46.00
No. 1 cupola cast	52.00 to 54.00

Seattle

No. 1 hvy. melting	$28.00
No. 2 hvy. melting	28.00
No. 1 bundles	22.00
No. 2 bundles	22.00
No. 3 bundles	18.00
Elec. fur. 1 ft and under	$40.00 to 45.00
RR. hvy. melting	29.00
No. 1 cupola cast	45.00

Hamilton, Ont.

No. 1 hvy. melting	$30.00
No. 1 bundles	30.00
No. 2 bundles	29.50
Mechanical bundles	28.00
Mixed steel scrap	26.00
Mixed bor. and turn.	23.00
Rails, remelting	30.00
Rails, rerolling	33.00
Bushelings	24.50
Bush., new fact. prep'd.	29.00
Bush., new fact. unprep'd.	23.00
Short steel turnings	23.00
Cast scrap	45.00

Comparison of Prices

Price advances over previous week are printed in Heavy Type; declines appear in *Italics*

Steel prices in this page are the average of various f.o.b. quotations of major producing areas: Pittsburgh, Chicago, Gary, Cleveland, Youngstown.

Flat-Rolled Steel:

(cents per pound)	Jan. 30 1951	Jan. 23 1951	Jan. 2 1951	Jan. 31 1950
Hot-rolled sheets	3.60	3.60	3.60	3.35
Cold-rolled sheets	4.35	4.35	4.35	4.10
Galvanized sheets (10 ga)	4.80	4.80	4.80	4.40
Hot-rolled strip	3.50	3.50	3.50	3.25
Cold-rolled strip	4.75	4.75	4.75	4.21
Plate	3.70	3.70	3.70	3.50
Plates wrought iron	7.85	7.85	7.85	7.85
Stains C-R-strip (No. 302)	36.50	36.50	36.50	33.00

Tin and Terneplate:

(dollars per base box)				
Tinplate (1.50 lb) cokes	$7.50	$7.50	$7.50	$7.50
Tinplate, electro (0.50 lb)	6.60	6.60	6.60	6.60
Special coated mfg. ternes	6.35	6.35	6.35	6.50

Bars and Shapes:

(cents per pound)				
Merchant bars	3.70	3.70	3.70	3.45
Cold finished bars	4.55	4.55	4.55	*4.145
Alloy bars	4.30	4.30	4.30	3.95
Structural shapes	3.65	3.65	3.65	3.40
Stainless bars (No. 302)	31.25	31.25	31.25	28.50
Wrought iron bars	9.50	9.50	9.50	9.50

Wire:

(cents per pound)				
Bright wire	4.85	4.85	4.85	4.50

Rails:

(dollars per 100 lb)				
Heavy rails	$3.60	$3.60	$3.60	$3.40
Light rails	4.00	4.00	4.00	3.75

Semifinished Steel:

(dollars per net ton)				
Rerolling billets	$56.00	$56.00	$56.00	$54.00
Slabs, rerolling	56.00	56.00	56.00	54.00
Forging billets	66.00	66.00	66.00	63.00
Alloy blooms billets, slabs	70.00	70.00	70.00	66.00

Wire Rod and Skelp:

(cents per pound)				
Wire rods	4.10	4.10	4.10	3.85
Skelp	3.35	3.35	3.35	3.15

Pig Iron:

(per gross ton)	Jan. 30 1951	Jan. 23 1951	Jan. 2 1951	Jan. 31 1950
No. 2 foundry, del'd Phila.	$57.77	$57.77	$57.77	$50.42
No. 2, Valley furnace	52.50	52.50	52.50	46.50
No. 2, Southern Cin'ti	55.58	55.58	55.58	47.08
No. 2, Birmingham	48.88	48.88	48.88	40.38
No. 2, foundry, Chicago†	52.50	52.50	52.50	46.50
Basic del'd Philadelphia	56.92	56.92	56.92	49.92
Basic, Valley furnace	52.00	52.00	52.00	46.00
Malleable, Chicago†	52.50	52.50	52.50	46.50
Malleable, Valley	52.50	52.50	52.50	46.50
Charcoal, Chicago	70.56	70.56	70.56	68.56
Ferromanganese‡	186.25	186.25	181.20	173.40

†The switching charge for delivery to foundries in the Chicago district is $1 per ton.
‡Average of U. S. prices quoted on Ferroalloy page.

Scrap:

(per gross ton)				
Heavy melt'g steel, P'gh	$51.13	$46.13	$46.13	$30.75
Heavy melt'g steel, Phila.	47.50	47.50	44.50	23.00
Heavy melt'g steel, Ch'go	44.63	44.63	44.63	27.50
No. 1 hy. com. sh't, Det.	40.25	40.25	40.25	23.50
Low phos. Young'n	54.50	54.50	48.63	31.75
No. 1 cast, Pittsburgh	67.75	67.75	67.75	37.50
No. 1 cast, Philadelphia	62.50	62.50	62.50	37.00
No. 1 cast, Chicago	63.00	63.00	63.00	38.50

Coke: Connellsville

(per net ton at oven)				
Furnace coke, prompt	$14.25	$14.25	$14.25	$14.00
Foundry coke, prompt	17.25	17.25	17.25	15.75

Nonferrous Metals:

(cents per pound to large buyers)				
Copper, electro, Conn.	24.50	24.50	24.50	18.50
Copper, Lake, Conn.	24.625	24.625	24.625	18.625
Tin, Straits, New York	$1.83†	$1.78*	$1.50	74.50
Zinc, East St. Louis	17.50	17.50	17.50	9.75
Lead, St. Louis	16.80	16.80	16.80	11.80
Aluminum, virgin	19.00	19.00	19.00	17.00
Nickel, electrolytic	53.55	53.55	53.55	42.97
Magnesium, ingot	24.50	24.50	24.50	20.50
Antimony, Laredo, Tex.	42.00	42.00	32.00	28.75

†Tentative. *Revised.

Composite Prices

[Starting with the issue of May 12, 1949, the weighted finished steel composite was revised for the years 1941 to date. The weights used are based on the average product shipments for the 7 years 1937 to 1940 inclusive and 1946 to 1948 inclusive. The use of quarterly figures has been eliminated because it was too sensitive. (See p. 130 of May 12, 1949, issue.)]

Finished Steel Base Price

Jan. 30, 1951	4.131¢ per lb.
One week ago	4.131¢ per lb.
One month ago	4.131¢ per lb.
One year ago	3.837¢ per lb.

Pig Iron

	$52.69 per gross ton
	52.69 per gross ton
	52.69 per gross ton
	46.05 per gross ton

Scrap Steel

	$47.75 per gross ton
	46.08 per gross ton
	45.09 per gross ton
	27.08 per gross ton

	High		Low		High		Low		High		Low	
1951	4.131¢	Jan. 2	4.131¢	Jan. 2	$52.69	Jan. 2	$52.69	Jan. 2	$47.75	Jan. 30	$45.09	Jan. 2
1950	4.131¢	Dec. 1	3.837¢	Jan. 3	52.69	Dec. 12	45.88	Jan. 3	45.13	Dec. 19	26.25	Jan. 3
1949	3.837¢	Dec. 27	3.3705¢	May 3	46.87	Jan. 18	45.88	Sept. 6	43.00	Jan. 4	19.33	June 28
1948	3.721¢	July 27	3.193¢	Jan. 1	46.91	Oct. 12	39.58	Jan. 6	43.16	July 27	39.75	Mar. 9
1947	3.193¢	July 29	2.848¢	Jan. 1	37.98	Dec. 30	30.14	Jan. 7	42.58	Oct. 28	29.50	May 20
1946	2.848¢	Dec. 31	2.464¢	Jan. 1	30.14	Dec. 10	25.37	Jan. 1	31.17	Dec. 24	19.17	Jan. 1
1945	2.464¢	May 29	2.396¢	Jan. 1	25.37	Oct. 23	23.61	Jan. 2	19.17	Jan. 2	18.92	May 22
1944	2.396¢		2.396¢		$23.61		$23.61		19.17	Jan. 11	15.76	Oct. 24
1943	2.396¢		2.396¢		23.61		23.61		$19.17		$19.17	
1942	2.396¢		2.396¢		23.61		23.61		19.17		19.17	
1941	2.396¢		2.396¢		$23.61	Mar. 20	$23.45	Jan. 2	$22.00	Jan. 7	$19.17	Apr. 10
1940	2.30467¢	Jan. 2	2.24107¢	Apr. 16	23.45	Dec. 23	22.61	Jan. 2	21.83	Dec. 30	16.04	Apr. 9
1939	2.35367¢	Jan. 3	2.26689¢	May 16	22.61	Sept. 19	20.61	Sept. 12	22.50	Oct. 3	14.08	May 16
1938	2.58414¢	Jan. 4	2.27207¢	Oct. 18	23.25	June 21	19.61	July 6	15.00	Nov. 22	11.00	June 7
1937	2.58414¢	Mar. 9	2.32263¢	Jan. 4	32.25	Mar. 9	20.25	Feb. 16	21.92	Mar. 30	12.67	June 8
1936	2.32263¢	Dec. 28	2.05200¢	Mar. 10	19.74	Nov. 24	18.73	Aug. 11	17.75	Dec. 21	12.67	June 8
1932	1.89196¢	July 5	1.83910¢	Mar. 1	14.81	Jan. 5	13.56	Dec. 6	8.50	Jan. 12	6.43	July 5
1929	2.31773¢	May 28	2.26498¢	Oct. 29	18.71	May 14	18.21	Dec. 17	17.58	Jan. 29	14.08	Dec. 8

Weighted index based on steel bars, shapes, plates, wire, rails, black pipe, hot and cold-rolled sheets and strips, representing major portion of finished steel shipment. Index recapitulated in Aug. 28, 1941, issue and in May 12, 1949.

Based on averages for basic iron at Valley furnaces and foundry iron at Chicago, Philadelphia, Buffalo, Valley and Birmingham.

Average of No. 1 heavy melting steel scrap delivered to consumers at Pittsburgh, Philadelphia and Chicago.

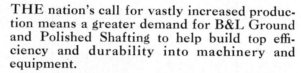

IRON AGE
STEEL PRICES

Smaller numbers in price boxes indicate producing companies. For main office locations, see key on facing page.
Base prices at producing points apply only to sizes and grades produced in these **areas.** Prices are in cents per lb unless otherwise noted. Extras apply.

	Pittsburgh	Chicago	Gary	Cleveland	Canton Massillon	Middletown	Youngstown	Bethlehem	Buffalo	Conshohocken	Johnstown	Sparrows Point	Granite City	Detroit
INGOTS Carbon forging, net ton	$52.00[1]													
Alloy, net ton	$54.00[1,17]													$54.00[31]
BILLETS, BLOOMS, SLABS Carbon, rerolling, net ton	$56.00[1,5]	$56.00[1]	$56.00[1]						$56.00[3]		$56.00[3]			
Carbon forging billets, net ton	$66.00[1,5]	$66.00[1,4]	$66.00[1]	$66.00[4]	$66.00[4]				$66.00[3,4]	$73.00[26]	$66.00[3]			$69.00[31]
Alloy, net ton	$70.00[1,17]	$70.00[1,4]	$70.00[1]		$70.00[4]			$70.00[3]	$70.00[3,4]	$77.00[26]	$70.00[3]			$73.00[31]
PIPE SKELP	3.35[1] 3.45[5]						3.35[1,4]							
WIRE RODS	4.10[2] 4.30[18]	4.10[2,4,33]	4.10[6]	4.10[2]			4.10[6]				4.10[3]	4.20[3]		
SHEETS Hot-rolled (18 ga. & hvr.)	3.60[1,5,9,15] 3.75[28]	3.60[8,23]	3.60[1,6,8]	3.60[4]		3.60[7]	3.60[1,4,6] 4.00[13]		3.60[3]	4.00[26]		3.60[3]		3.80[12] 4.40[47]
Cold-rolled	4.35[1,5,9,15] 5.35[63]		4.35[1,6,8]	4.35[4]		4.35[7]	4.35[4,6]		4.35[3]			4.35[3]		4.55[12]
Galvanized (10 gage)	4.80[1,9,15]		4.80[1,8]		4.80[4]	4.80[7]	6.00[64]					4.80[3]		
Enameling (12 gage)	4.65[1]		4.65[1,8]			4.65[7]								
Long terne (10 gage)	5.20[9,15]						6.00[64]							
Hi str. low alloy, h.r.	5.40[1,5] 5.75[9]	5.40[1]	5.40[1,8] 5.90[6]	5.40[4]			5.40[1,4,13]		5.40[3]	5.65[26]		5.40[3]		
Hi str. low alloy, c.r.	6.55[1,5] 6.90[9]		6.55[1,8] 7.05[6]	6.55[4]			6.55[4]		6.55[2]			6.55[2]		
Hi str. low alloy, galv.	7.20[1]													
STRIP Hot-rolled	3.60[9], 4.00[41,58], 3.75[28] 3.50[5]	3.50[66]	3.50[1,6,8]			3.50[7]	3.50[1,4,6] 4.00[13]		3.50[3,4]	3.90[26]		3.50[3]		4.40[47]
Cold-rolled	4.65[5,9] 5.00[28] 5.35[63,58]	4.90[8,66]	4.90[8]	4.65[2]		4.65[7]	4.65[4,6] 5.35[13,40]		4.65[3]			4.65[3]		5.45[47] 5.60[68] 5.60[81]
Hi str. low alloy, h.r.	5.75[9]		5.50[1] 5.30[8], 5.80[6]				4.95[4], 5.50[1] 5.40[13]			5.55[26]				
Hi str. low alloy, c.r.	7.20[9]			6.70[5]			6.20[4], 6.55[13]							
TINPLATE† Cokes, 1.50-lb base box 1.25 lb, deduct 25¢	$8.70[1,9,15]		$8.70[1,6]				$8.70[4]					8.80[3]		
Electrolytic 0.25, 0.50, 0.75 lb box	Deduct $1.55, $1.30 and 90¢ respectively from 1.50-lb coke base box price													
BLACKPLATE, 29 gage Holloware enameling	5.85[1] 6.15[15]		5.85[1]				5.30[4]							
BARS Carbon steel	3.70[1,5] 3.85[9]	3.70[1,4,23]	3.70[1,4,6,8]	3.70[4]	3.70[4]		3.70[1,4,6]		3.70[3,4]		3.70[3]			3.85[21]
Reinforcing‡	3.70[1,5]	3.70[4]	3.70[1,6,8]	3.70[4]			3.70[1,4]		3.70[3,4]		3.70[3]	3.70[3]		
Cold-finished	4.55[2,4,5,52,71]	4.55[2,69,70,23,73]	4.55[74,73]	4.55[2]	4.55[4,82]									4.70[84]
Alloy, hot-rolled	4.30[1,17]	4.30[1,4,23]	4.30[1,6,8]		4.30[4]		4.30[1,6]	4.30[6]	4.30[3,4]		4.30[3]			4.45[31]
Alloy, cold-drawn	5.40[17,52,69,71]	5.40[4,23,69,70,73]	5.40[4] 5.90[74]		5.40[4,32]				5.40[3]	5.40[3]				5.55[84]
Hi str. low alloy, h.r.	5.55[1,5]		5.55[1,8] 6.05[6]	5.55[4]			5.55[1]	5.55[3]	5.55[3]		5.55[3]			
PLATE Carbon steel	3.70[1,5,15]	3.70[1]	3.70[1,6,8]	3.70[4] 4.00[9]			3.70[1,4] 3.95[13]		3.70[3]	4.15[26]	3.70[3]	3.70[3]		
Floor plates			4.75[8]	4.75[5]						4.75[26]				
Alloy	4.75[1] 4.85	4.75[1]	4.75[1]				5.20[13]			5.05[26]	4.75[3]	4.75[3]		
Hi str. low alloy	5.65[1,5]	5.65[1]	5.65[1,8]	5.65[4,5]			5.65[4] 5.70[13]			5.90[26]	5.65[3]	5.65[3]		
SHAPES, Structural	3.65[1,5] 3.90[9]	3.65[1,23]	3.65[1,8]						3.70[3]	3.70[3]	3.70[3]			
Hi str. low alloy	5.50[1,5]	5.50[1]	5.50[1,8]						5.50[3]	5.50[3]	5.50[3]			
MANUFACTURERS' WIRE Bright	4.85[2,5] 5.10[18]	4.85[2] 4.33		4.85[2]					Kokomo = 5.80[30]		4.85[3]	4.95[3]	Duluth = 4.85[2]	
PILING, Steel Sheet	4.45[1]	4.45[1]	4.45[8]						4.45[3]					

STEEL PRICES

Smaller numbers indicate producing companies. See key at right.
Prices are in cents per lb unless otherwise noted. Extras apply.

Kansas City	Houston	Birmingham	WEST COAST Seattle, San Francisco, Los Angeles, Fontana		
			F=$79.00[19]		**INGOTS** Carbon forging, net ton
	$62.00[83]		F=$80.00[19]		**Alloy, net ton**
		$56.00[11]	F=$75.00[19]		**BILLETS, BLOOMS, SLABS** Carbon, rerolling, net ton
$74.00[83]		$66.00[11]	F=$85.00[19] SF, LA, S=$85.00[62]		Carbon forging billets, net ton
$78.00[83]			F=$89.00[19] LA=$90.00[62]		Alloy net ton
					PIPE SKELP
	4.50[83]	4.10[4,11]	SF=4.90[2] LA=4.90[24,62]	Worcester=4.40[2] Minnequa=4.35[14]	**WIRE RODS**
		3.60[4,11]	SF, LA=4.30[24] F=4.55[19]	Niles=5.25[64], Geneva=3.70[16]	**SHEETS** Hot-rolled (18 ga. & hvr.)
		4.35[11]	SF=5.30[24] F=5.30[19]		Cold-rolled
		4.80[4,11]	SF, LA=5.55[24]	Ashland=4.80[7]	Galvanized (10 gage)
					Enameling (12 gage)
					Long ternes (10 gage)
		5.40[11]	F=6.35[19]		Hi str. low alloy, h.r.
			F=7.50[19]		Hi str. low alloy, c.r.
					Hi str. low alloy, galv.
4.10[83]	4.90[83]	3.50[4]	SF, LA=4.25[24,62] F=4.75[19], S=4.50[62]	Atlanta=4.05[65] Minnequa=4.55[14]	**STRIP** Hot-rolled
			F=6.30[19] LA=6.40[27]	New Haven=5.15[2], 5.85[68]	Cold-rolled
		5.30[11]	F=6.20[19]		Hi str. low alloy, h.r.
					Hi str. low alloy, c.r.
					TINPLATE Cokes, 1.50-lb base box 1.25 lb, deduct 20¢
					Electrolytic 0.25, 0.50, 0.75 lb box
Deduct $1.55, $1.30 and 90¢ respectively from 1.50-lb coke base box price					
					BLACKPLATE, 29 gage Hollowware enameling
4.30[83]	4.10[83]	3.70[4,11]	SF, LA=4.40[24]	Atlanta=4.25[65] Minnequa=4.15[14]	**BARS** Carbon steel
4.38[83]	4.10[83]	3.70[4,11]	SF, S=4.45[62] F=4.40[19], LA=4.40[62]	Atlanta=4.25[65] Minnequa=4.50[14]	Reinforcing‡
				Newark=5.00[69] Putnam=5.10[69] Hartford=5.10[4] Los Angeles=6.00[4]	Cold-finished
4.90[83]	4.70[83]		LA=5.35[62] F=5.35[19]		Alloy, hot-rolled
				Newark=5.75[69] Worcester= [2] Hartford=5.85[4]	Alloy, cold-drawn
		5.55[11]	F=6.60[19]		Hi str. low alloy, h.r.
	4.10[83]	3.70[4,11]	F=4.30[19] S=4.60[62] Geneva=3.70[16]	Claymont=4.15[29] Coatesville=4.15[21] Minnequa=4.50[14]	**PLATE** Carbon steel
				Harrisburg=5.25[35]	Floor plates
			F=5.70[19] Geneva=5.65[16]	Coatesville=5.25[21] Claymont=4.85[29]	Alloy
		5.65[11]	F=6.25[19]		Hi str. low alloy
4.25[83]	4.05[83]	3.65[4,11]	SF, LA=4.20[62] F=4.25[16] LA=4.25[24,62], S=4.30[62]	Geneva 3.65[16] Minnequa 4.10[14]	**SHAPES, Structural**
		50[11]	F=6.10[19]		Hi str. low alloy
5.45[83]	5.25[83]	4.85[4,11]	SF, LA=5.80[24]	Atlanta=5.10[65] Worcester=5.15[2] Minnequa=5.10[14]	**MANUFACTURERS' WIRE** Bright

KEY TO STEEL PRODUCERS

1 U. S. Steel Co., Pittsburgh
2 American Steel & Wire Co., Cleveland
3 Bethlehem Steel Co., Bethlehem
4 Republic Steel Corp., Cleveland
5 Jones & Laughlin Steel Corp., Pittsburgh
6 Youngstown Sheet & Tube Co., Youngstown
7 Arco Steel Corp., Middletown, Ohio
8 Inland Steel Co., Chicago
9 Weirton Steel Co., Weirton, W. Va.
10 National Tube Co., Pittsburgh
11 Tennessee Coal, Iron & R. R. Co., Birmingham
12 Great Lakes Steel Corp., Detroit
13 Sharon Steel Corp., Sharon, Pa.
14 Colorado Fuel & Iron Corp., Denver
15 Wheeling Steel Corp., Wheeling, W. Va.
16 Geneva Steel Co., Salt Lake City
17 Crucible Steel Co. of America, New York
18 Pittsburgh Steel Corp., Pittsburgh
19 Kaiser Steel Corp., Oakland, Calif.
20 Portsmouth Div., Detroit Steel Corp., Detroit
21 Lukens Steel Co., Coatesville, Pa.
22 Granite City Steel Co., Granite City, Ill.
23 Wisconsin Steel Co., South Chicago, Ill.
24 Columbia Steel Co., San Francisco
25 Copperweld Steel Co., Glassport, Pa.
26 Alan Wood Steel Co., Conshohocken, Pa.
27 Calif. Cold Rolled Steel Corp., Los Angeles
28 Allegheny Ludlum Steel Corp., Pittsburgh
29 Worth Steel Co., Claymont, Del.
30 Continental Steel Corp., Kokomo, Ind.
31 Rotary Electric Steel Co., Detroit
32 Laclede Steel Co., St. Louis
33 Northwestern Steel & Wire Co., Sterling, Ill.
34 Keystone Steel & Wire Co., Peoria, Ill.
35 Central Steel & Wire Co., Harrisburg, Pa.
36 Carpenter Steel Co., Reading, Pa.
37 Eastern Stainless Steel Corp., Baltimore
38 Washington Steel Corp., Washington, Pa.
39 Jessop Steel Co., Washington, Pa.
40 Blair Strip Steel Co., New Castle, Pa.
41 Superior Steel Corp., Carnegie, Pa.
42 Timken Steel & Tube Div., Canton, Ohio
43 Babcock & Wilcox Tube Co., Beaver Falls, Pa.
44 Reeves Steel & Mfg. Co., Dover, Ohio
45 John A. Roebling's Sons Co., Trenton, N. J.
46 Simonds Saw & Steel Co., Fitchburg, Mass.
47 McLouth Steel Corp., Detroit
48 Cold Metal Products Co., Youngstown
49 Thomas Steel Co., Warren, Ohio
50 Wilson Steel & Wire Co., Chicago
51 Sweet's Steel Co., Williamsport, Pa.
52 Superior Drawn Steel Co., Monaca, Pa.
53 Tremont Nail Co., Wareham, Mass.
54 Firth Sterling St. & Carbide Corp., McKeesport
55 Ingersoll Steel Div., Chicago
56 Phoenix Iron & Steel Co., Phoenixville, Pa.
57 Fitzsimmons Steel Co., Youngstown
58 Stanley Works, New Britain, Conn.
59 Universal-Cyclops Steel Corp., Bridgeville, Pa.
60 American Cladmetals Co., Carnegie, Pa.
61 Cuyahoga Steel & Wire Co., Cleveland
62 Bethlehem Pacific Coast Steel Corp., San Fran.
63 Follansbee Steel Corp., Pittsburgh
64 Niles Rolling Mill Co., Niles, Ohio
65 Atlantic Steel Co., Atlanta
66 Acme Steel Co., Chicago
67 Joslyn Mfg. & Supply Co., Chicago
68 Detroit Steel Corp., Detroit
69 Wycoff Steel Co., Pittsburgh
70 Bliss & Laughlin, Inc., Harvey, Ill.
71 Columbia Steel & Shafting Co., Pittsburgh
72 Cumberland Steel Co., Cumberland, Md.
73 La Salle Steel Co., Chicago
74 Monarch Steel Co., Inc., Hammond, Ind.
75 Empire Steel Co., Mansfield, Ohio
76 Mahoning Valley Steel Co., Niles, Ohio
77 Oliver Iron & Steel Co., Pittsburgh
78 Pittsburgh Screw & Bolt Co., Pittsburgh
79 Standard Forging Corp., Chicago
80 Driver Harris Co., Harrison, N. J.
81 Detroit Tube & Steel Div., Detroit
82 Reliance Div., Eaton Mfg. Co., Massillon, Ohio
83 Sheffield Steel Corp., Kansas City
84 Plymouth Steel Co., Detroit
85 Wickwire Spencer Steel, Buffalo
86 Angell Nail and Chaplet, Cleveland
87 Mid-States Steel & Wire, Crawfordsville, Ind.
88 National Supply, Pittsburgh
89 Wheatland Tube Co., Wheatland, Pa.
90 Mercer Tube & Mfg. Co., Sharon, Pa.
91 Woodward Iron Co., Woodward, Ala.
92 Sloss-Sheffield Steel & Iron Co., Birmingham
93 Hanna Furance Corp., Detroit
94 Interlake Iron Corp., Cleveland
95 Lone Star Steel Co., Dallas
96 Mystic Iron Works, Everett, Mass.
97 Jackson Iron & Steel Co., Jackson, O.
98 Globe Iron Co., Jackson, O.
99 Pittsburgh Coke & Chemical Co., Pittsburgh
100 Shenango Furnace Co., Pittsburgh
101 Tennessee Products & Chemical Corp., Nashville
102 Koppers Co., Inc., Granite City, Ill.

STAINLESS STEELS

Base price, cents per lb, f.o.b. mill.

Product	301	302	303	304	316	321	347	410	416	430
Ingots, rerolling	14.25	15.00	16.50	16.00	24.25	19.75	21.50	12.75	14.75	13.00
Slabs, billets rerolling	18.50	19.75	21.75	20.75	31.75	26.00	28.25	16.50	20.00	16.75
Forg. discs, die blocks, rings	34.00	34.00	36.50	35.50	52.50	40.00	44.50	28.00	28.50	28.50
Billets, forging	26.25	26.25	28.25	27.50	41.00	31.00	34.75	21.50	22.00	22.00
Bars, wires, structurals	31.25	31.25	33.75	32.75	48.75	36.75	41.25	25.75	26.25	26.25
Plates	33.00	33.00	35.00	35.00	51.50	40.50	45.00	27.00	27.50	27.50
Sheets	41.00	41.00	43.00	43.00	56.50	49.00	53.50	36.50	37.00	39.00
Strip, hot-rolled	26.50	28.00	32.25	30.00	48.25	36.75	41.00	23.50	27.00	24.00
Strip, cold-rolled	34.00	36.50	40.00	38.50	58.50	48.00	52.00	30.50	37.00	31.00

STAINLESS STEEL PRODUCING POINTS—*Sheets:* Midland, Pa., 17; Brackenridge, Pa., 28; Butler, Pa., 7; McKeesport, Pa., 1; Washington, Pa., 38 (type 316 add 5¢), 39; Baltimore, 37; Middletown, Ohio, 7; Massillon, Ohio, 4; Gary, 1; Bridgeville, Pa., 59; New Castle, Ind., 55; Ft. Wayne, Ind., 67; Lockport, N. Y., 46.
Strip: Midland, Pa., 17; Cleveland, 2; Carnegie, Pa., 41; McKeesport, Pa., 54; Reading, Pa., 36; Washington, Pa., 38 (type 316 add 5¢) ; W. Leechburg, Pa., 28; Bridgeville, Pa., 59; Detroit, 47; Massillon, Canton, Ohio, 4; Middletown, Ohio, 7; Harrison, N. J., 80; Youngstown, 48; Lockport, N. Y., 46; New Britain, Conn., 58; Sharon, Pa., 13; Butler, Pa., 7.
Bars: Baltimore, 7; Duquesne, Pa. 1; Munhall, Pa., 1; Reading, Pa., 36; Titusville, Pa., 59; Washington, Pa., 39; McKeesport, Pa., 54; Bridgeville, Pa., 59; Dunkirk, N. Y., 28; Massillon, Ohio, 4; Chicago, 1; Syracuse, N. Y., 17; Watervliet, N. Y., 28; Waukegan, Ill., 2; Lockport, N. Y., 46; Canton, Ohio, 42; Ft. Wayne, Ind., 67.
Wire: Waukegan, Ill., 2; Massillon, Ohio, 4; McKeesport, Pa., 54; Bridgeport, Conn., 44; Ft. Wayne, Ind., 67; Trenton, N. J., 45; Harrison, N. J., 80; Baltimore, 7; Dunkirk, 28.
Structurals: Baltimore, 7; Massillon, Ohio, 4; Chicago, 1, 67; Watervliet, N. Y., 28; Bridgeport, Conn., 44.
Plates: Brackenridge, Pa., 28 (type 416 add ½¢) ; Butler, Pa., 7; Chicago, 1; Munhall, Pa., 1; Midland, Pa., 17; New Castle, Ind., 55; Lockport, N. Y., 46; Middletown, Washington, Pa., 39; Cleveland, Massillon, 4.
Forged discs, die blocks, rings: Pittsburgh, 1, 17; Syracuse, 17; Ferndale, Mich., 28.
Forging billets: Midland, Pa., 17; Baltimore, 7; Washington, Pa., 39; McKeesport, 54; Massillon, Canton, Ohio, 4; Watervliet, 28; Pittsburgh, Chicago, 1.

RAILS, TRACK SUPPLIES

F.o.b. Mill Cents Per Lb	No. 1 Std. Rails	Light Rails	Joint Bars	Track Spikes	Axles	Screw Spikes	Tie Plates	Track Bolts Untreated
Bessemer-1	3.60	4.00	4.70					
Chicago-4				6.15				
Ensley-11	3.60	4.00						
Fairfield-11		4.00	4.40			8.60	4.50	
Gary-1	3.60	4.00					4.50	
Ind. Harbor-8	3.60			6.15	5.25	8.60	4.50	
Johnstown-3						5.60	8.60	
Joliet-1		4.00	4.70					
Kansas City-83				6.40				
Lackawanna-3	3.60	4.00	4.70			8.60	4.50	
Lebanon-3				6.15				9.60
Minnequa-14	3.60	4.50	4.70	6.15		8.60	4.50	9.60
Pittsburgh-77						9.35		9.60
Pittsburgh-78								9.60
Pittsburgh-5				6.15				
Pittsburg-24							4.65	
Seattle-62				6.10			4.35	
Steelton-3	3.60		4.70				4.50	
Struthers-6				6.15				
Torrance-24							4.65	
Youngstown-4				6.15				

Track Bolts, heat treated, to railroads, 9.85¢ per lb.

BOILER TUBES

Seamless steel, electric welded commercial boiler tubes, locomotive tubes, minimum wall, per 100 ft at mill, c.l. lots, cut lengths 10 to 24 ft.

OD in in.	gage BWG	Seamless H-R.	C.D.	Electric Weld H.R.	C.D.
2	13	$22.67	$26.66	$21.99	$25.86
2½	12	30.48	35.84	29.57	34.76
3	12	33.90	39.90	32.89	34.80
3½	11	42.37	49.89	41.10	48.39
4	10	52.60	61.88	51.03	60.02

Pittsburgh Steel add, H-R: 2 in., 62¢; 2½ in., 84¢; 3 in., 92¢; 3½ in., $1.17; 4 in., $1.45. Add, C-R: 2 in., 74¢; 2½ in., 99¢; 3 in., $1.10; 3½ in., $1.37; 4 in., $1.70.

FLUORSPAR

Washed gravel fluorspar, f.o.b. cars, Rosiclare, Ill. Base price, per ton net: Effective CaF, content:

70% or more	$43.00
60% or less	40.00

MERCHANT WIRE PRODUCTS

F.o.b. Mill	Standard & Coated Nails Base Col.	Woven Wire Fence 9-15½ ga. Base Col.	Fence Posts Base Col.	Single Loop Bale Ties Base Col.	Twisted Barbless Wire Base Col.	Gal. Barbed Wire Base Col.	Merch. Wire Ann'l'd. ¢/lb.	Merch. Wire Gal. ¢/lb.
Alabama City-4	118	126		123		136	5.70	5.95
Aliquippa, Pa.-5	118	132			136	140	5.70	6.15
Atlanta-65	113	133		126	126	143	5.95	6.40
Bartonville-34	118	130	140	123	143	143	5.95	6.15
Buffalo-85							4.85	
Cleveland-86	125							
Cleveland-2							5.70	6.15
Crawfordsville-87		132				145	5.95	6.40
Donora, Pa.-2	118			123		140	5.70	6.15
Duluth-2	118	130		123		140	5.70	6.15
Fairfield, Ala.-11	118	130		123		136	5.70	6.15
Houston-83	126	138				148	6.10	6.55
Johnstown, Pa.-3	118	130			140		5.70	6.15
Joliet, Ill.-2	118	130		123		140	5.70	6.15
Kokomo,Ind.-30	120	132		125	138	138	5.80	6.05
Los Angeles-62						6.65		
Kansas City-83	130	130	142	135		152	6.30	6.75
Minnequa-14	123	138	130	128	146	146	5.95	6.45
Monessen-18	124	135				145	5.95	6.40
Moline, Ill.-4			136					
Palmer-85								
Pittsburg, Cal.-24	137	149		147	156	160	6.65	6.80
Portsmouth-20	124	137			147	147	6.10	6.60
Rankin, Pa.-2	118					140	5.70	6.15
So.Chicago,Ill.-4	118	126	140	123		136	5.70	5.95
S. San Fran.-14				147		160	6.65	7.10
Sparrows Pt.-3	120			125	142	142	5.80	6.25
Sterling, Ill.-33	118	130	140	123	140	140	5.70	6.15
Struthers, Ohio-6							5.70	6.15
Torrance,Cal.-24	138						6.65	
Worcester-1	124						6.00	6.45
Williamsport, Pa.-51			150					

Cut Nails, carloads, base, $6.75 per 100 lb. (less 20¢ to jobbers) at Conshohocken, Pa. (26), Wareham, Mass. (53) Wheeling, W. Va., (15).

CAST IRON WATER PIPE

Per net ton

6 to 24-in., del'd Chicago $105.30 to $108.80
6 to 24-in., del'd N. Y. 108.50 to 109.50
6 to 24-in., Birmingham 91.50 to 96.00
6-in. and larger, f.o.b. cars, San Francisco, Los Angeles, for all rail shipment; rail and water shipment less $108.50 to $113.00
Class "A" and gas pipe, $5 extra; 4-in. pipe is $5 a ton above 6-in.

PIPE AND TUBING

Base discounts, f.o.b. mills. Base price about $200 per net ton.

	BUTTWELD														SEAMLESS					
	½ In.		¾ In.		1 In.		1¼ In.		1½ In.		2 In.		2½-3 In.		2 In.		2½-3 In.		3½-4 In.	
	Blk.	Gal.	Blk.	Gal.	Blk.	Gal.	Blk.	Gal.	Blk.	Gal.	Blk.	Gal.	Blk.	Gal.	Blk.	Gal.	Blk.	Gal.	Blk.	Gal.
STANDARD T. & C.																				
Sparrows Pt.-3	34.0	12.0	37.0	16.0	39.5	19.5	40.0	20.0	40.5	21.0	41.0	21.5	41.5	22.0						
Cleveland-4	36.0	14.0	39.0	18.0	41.5	21.5	42.0	22.0	42.5	23.0	43.0	23.5	43.5	24.0						
Oakland-19	25.0	3.0	28.0	7.0	30.5	10.5	31.0	11.0	31.5	12.0	32.0	12.5	32.5	13.0						
Pittsburgh-5	36.0	14.0	39.0	17.0	41.5	19.5	42.0	20.5	42.5	21.5	43.0	22.5	43.5	22.5	29.5		8.0	32.5	11.5	34.5	13.5
Pittsburgh-10	36.0	14.0	39.0	17.0	41.5	19.5	42.0	20.5	42.5	21.5	43.0	23.5	43.5	22.5	29.5		9.5	32.5	12.5	34.5	14.5
St. Louis-32	36.0	13.0	38.0	17.0	40.5	20.5	41.0	21.0	41.5	22.0	42.0	22.5	42.5	23.0						
Sharon-90	36.0	13.0	39.0	18.0	41.5	21.5	42.0	22.0	42.5	23.0	43.0	23.5	43.5	24.0						
Toledo-88	36.0	14.0	39.0	18.0	41.5	21.5	42.0	22.0	42.5	23.0	43.0	23.5	43.5	24.0						
Wheeling-15	36.0	14.0	39.0	18.0	41.5	21.5	42.0	22.0	42.5	23.0	43.0	23.5	43.5	24.0	29.5			32.5		34.5	
Wheatland-89	36.0	14.0	39.0	17.0	41.5	20.5	42.0	20.5	42.5	21.5	43.0	22.5	43.5	22.5						
Youngstown-6	36.0	14.0	39.0	18.0	41.5	21.5	42.0	22.0	42.5	23.0	43.0	23.5	43.5	24.0	29.5		9.5	32.5	12.5	34.5	14.5
EXTRA STRONG, PLAIN ENDS																				
Sparrows Pt.-3	33.5	13.0	37.5	17.0	39.5	20.5	40.0	21.0	40.5	22.0	41.0	22.5	41.5	23.0						
Cleveland-4	35.5	14.0	39.5	19.0	41.5	22.5	42.0	23.0	42.5	24.0	43.0	24.5	43.5	25.0						
Oakland-19	24.5	4.0	28.5	8.0	30.5	11.5	31.0	12.0	31.5	13.0	32.0	13.5	32.5	14.0						
Pittsburgh-5	35.5	13.5	39.5	17.5	41.5	19.5	42.0	20.5	42.5	21.5	43.0	22.5	43.5	25.0	29.0		7.5	33.0	12.0	36.5	15.5
Pittsburgh-10	35.5	13.5	39.5	17.5	41.5	19.5	42.0	20.5	42.5	21.5	43.0	24.5	43.5	25.0	29.0		10.0	33.0	14.0	36.5	17.5
St. Louis-32	34.5	14.0	38.5	18.0	40.5	21.5	41.0	22.0	41.5	23.0	42.0	23.5	42.5	24.0						
Sharon-90	35.5	14.0	39.5	19.0	41.5	22.5	42.0	23.0	42.5	24.0	43.0	24.5	43.5	25.0						
Toledo-88	35.5	14.0	39.5	19.0	41.5	22.5	42.0	23.0	42.5	24.0	43.0	24.5	43.5	25.0	29.0			33.0		36.5	
Wheeling-15	35.5	15.0	39.5	19.0	41.5	22.5	42.0	23.0	42.5	24.0	43.0	24.5	43.5	25.0	29.0			33.0		36.5	
Wheatland-89	35.5	13.5	39.5	17.5	41.5	20.5	42.0	20.5	42.5	21.5	43.0	22.5	43.5	25.0						
Youngstown-6	35.5	15.0	39.5	19.0	41.5	22.5	42.0	23.0	42.5	24.0	43.0	24.5	43.5	25.0	29.0		10.0	33.0	14.0	36.5	17.5

Galvanized discounts based on zinc at 17¢ per lb, East St. Louis. For each 1¢ change in zinc, discounts vary as follows: ½ in., ¾ in., and 1 in., 1 pt.; 1¼ in., 1½ in., 2 in., ¾ pt.; 2½ in., 3 in., ½ pt. Calculate discounts on even cents per lb of zinc, i.e., if zinc is 16.51¢ to 17.50¢ per lb, use 17¢. Jones & Laughlin discounts apply only when zinc price changes 1¢. Threads only, buttweld and seamless, 1 pt. higher discount. Plain ends, buttweld and seamless, 3 in. and under, 3½ pts. higher discount. Buttweld jobbers' discount. 5 pct.

Base price, f.o.b., dollars per 100 lb. *(Metropolitan area delivery, add 20¢ except Birmingham, San Francisco, Cincinnati, New Orleans, St. Paul, add 15¢; Memphis, add 10¢; Philadelphia, add 25¢; New York, add 30¢).

WAREHOUSES

Cities	Sheets Hot-Rolled	Sheets Cold-Rolled (15 gage)	Sheets Galvanized (10 gage)	Strip Hot-Rolled	Strip Cold-Rolled	Plates Standard Structural	Shapes	Bars Hot-Rolled	Bars Cold-Finished	Alloy Bars Hot-Rolled A 4615 As rolled	Alloy Bars Hot-Rolled A 4140 Annealed	Alloy Bars Cold-Drawn A 4615 As rolled	Alloy Bars Cold-Drawn A 4140 Annealed
Baltimore	5.60	6.84	7.49²–8.07	6.04		5.80	6.14	6.04	6.84–6.89	10.24	10.54	11.89	12.19
Birmingham*	5.60	6.40	6.75	5.55		5.95	5.70	5.55					
Boston	6.20	7.00–7.25	7.74–8.29	6.15	8.50⁴	6.48–6.78	6.20	6.05	6.79–6.84	10.25	10.55	11.90–12.00	12.20–12.30
Buffalo	5.60	6.40	7.74–8.09	5.86		6.05	5.80	5.60	6.40–6.45	10.15–10.85	10.45	11.80	11.95–12.16
Chicago	5.60	6.40	7.75	5.55		5.80	5.70	5.55	6.30	9.80	10.10	11.45	11.75
Cincinnati*	5.87	6.44	7.39	5.80		6.19	6.09	5.80	6.61	10.15	10.45	11.80	12.10
Cleveland	5.60	6.40	8.10	5.69	6.90	5.92	5.82	5.57	6.40	9.91	10.21	11.56	11.86
Detroit	5.78	6.53	7.89	5.94		5.99	6.09	5.84	6.	10.11	10.41	11.76	12.06
Houston	7.00	8.25				6.85	6.50	6.65	9.35	10.35	11.25		12.75
Indianapolis, del'd	6.00	6.80	8.15	5.95		6.20	6.10	5.95	6.80				
Kansas City	6.00	6.80	7.45	6.15	7.50	6.30	6.15	7.00	10.40	10.70	12.05	12.35
Los Angeles	6.35	7.90	8.85	6.40	9.45⁶	6.40	6.35	6.35	8.20	11.30	11.30	13.20	13.50
Memphis*	6.33–6.38	7.08–7.18		6.33–6.38		6.43–8.02	6.33–6.48	6.08–6.23	7.16–7.32				
Milwaukee	5.74	6.54	7.89	5.69–6.59		5.94	5.84	5.69	6.44–6.54	9.94	10.24	11.59	11.89
New Orleans*	5.70	6.59		5.75	7.25	5.95	5.75	5.75	7.30				
New York*	5.67–5.97	7.19⁵–7.24¹	8.14²	6.29–6.89	8.63⁴	6.28–6.58	6.10	6.12	6.99	10.05–10.15	10.35–10.45	11.70–11.80	12.10–12.20
Norfolk	6.50²					6.50³	6.60³	6.55³					
Philadelphia*	5.90	6.80	8.00	6.10		6.05	5.90	6.05	6.86	9.90	10.20		
Pittsburgh	5.60	6.40	7.75	5.65–5.95		5.75	5.70	5.55	6.15	9.80	10.10	11.45	11.75
Portland	6.60–7.55	8.95	8.50–9.10	7.30		6.80	6.95	6.90			12.15		
Salt Lake City	7.95		9.70–10.50²	8.70–8.75		8.05	6.75–8.30	7.95–8.65	9.00				
San Francisco*	6.65	8.05²	8.55–8.90²	6.60	9.45⁶	6.50	6.45	6.45	8.20	11.30	11.30	13.20	13.20–13.50
Seattle	7.05	8.60	9.20	9.05		6.75	6.65	6.75	9.05				
St. Louis	5.80–5.85	6.65	8.00	5.80	8.00⁴–8.28	6.13	6.03	5.80	6.55–6.65	10.05	10.35	11.70	12.00
St. Paul*	6.16	6.96	8.31	6.11		6.36	6.26	6.11	6.96	10.36	10.66	12.01	12.31

BASE QUANTITIES (Standard unless otherwise keyed): Cold finished bars; 2000 lb or over. Alloy bars; 1000 to 1999 lb. All others; 2000 to 9999 lb. All HR products may be combined for quantity. All galvanized sheets may be combined for quantity. CR sheets may not be combined with each other or with galvanized sheets for quantity.
EXCEPTIONS: (1) 400 to 1499 lb; (2) 450 to 1499 lb; (3) 400 to 1999 lb; (4) 6000 lb and over; (5) 1500 to 9999 lb.; (6) 2000 to 5999 lb.

PIG IRON

Dollars per gross ton, f.o.b., subject to switching charges.

Producing Point	Basic	No. 2 Foundry	Malleable	Bessemer	Low Phos.	Blast Furnace Silvery	Low Phos. Charcoal
Bethlehem-3	54.00	54.50	55.00	55.50			
Birmingham-4	48.38	48.88					
Birmingham-91	48.38	48.88					
Birmingham-92	48.38	48.88					
Buffalo-4	52.00	52.50	53.00				
Buffalo-93	52.00	52.50	53.00			63.75	
Chicago-94	52.00	52.50	52.50	53.00			
Cleveland-2	52.00	52.50	52.50	53.00	57.00		
Cleveland-4	52.00	52.50	52.50				
Daingerfield, Tex.-95	48.00	48.50	48.50				
Duluth-94	52.00	52.50	52.50	53.00			
Erie-94	52.00	52.50	52.50	53.00			
Everett, Mass.-96		53.25	53.75				
Fontana-19	58.00	58.50					
Geneva, Utah-16	52.00	52.50	52.50	53.00			
Granite City, Ill.-102	53.90	54.40	54.90				
Hubbard, O.-6	52.00	52.50	52.50				
Ironton, Utah-16	52.00	52.50				62.50	
Jackson, O.-97,98							66.00
Lyle, Tenn.-101	54.00						
Monessen-18	54.00				53.00		
Neville Island-99	52.00	52.50	52.50	53.00			
Pittsburgh-1	52.00				53.00		
Sharpsville-100	52.00	52.50	52.50	53.00			
Steelton-3	54.00	54.50	55.00	55.50	60.00		
Swedeland-26	56.00	56.50	57.00	57.50			
Toledo-94	52.00	52.50	52.50	53.00			
Troy, N.Y.-4	54.00	54.50	55.00		60.00		
Youngstown-6	52.00	52.50	52.50	53.00			

DIFFERENTIALS: Add 50¢ per ton for each 0.25 pct silicon over base (1.75 to 2.25 pct), 50¢ per ton for each 0.50 pct manganese over 1 pct, $2 per ton for 0.5 to 0.75 pct nickel, $1 for each additional 0.25 pct nickel. Subtract 38¢ per ton for phosphorus content over 0.70 pct. Silvery iron: Add $1.50 per ton for each 0.50 pct silicon over base (6.01 to 6.50 pct) up to 17 pct. $1 per ton for 0.75 pct or more phosphorus, manganese as above. Bessemer ferrosilicon prices are $1 over comparable silvery iron.

REFRACTORIES

Fire Clay Brick
(F.o.b. works) Carloads, Per 1000
First quality, Ill., Ky., Md., Mo., Ohio, Pa (except Salina, Pa., add $5) $94.60
No. 1 Ohio 88.00
Sec. quality, Pa., Md., Ky., Mo., Ill. 88.00
No. 2 Ohio 79.20
Ground fire clay, net ton, bulk (except Salina, Pa., add $1.50) 13.70

Silica Brick
Mt. Union, Pa., Ensley, Ala. $94.60
Childs, Pa. 99.00
Hays, Pa. 100.10
Chicago District 104.50
Western Utah and Calif. 111.10
Super Duty, Hays, Pa., Athens, Tex., Chicago 111.10
Silica cement, net ton, bulk, Eastern (except Hays, Pa.) 16.50
Silica cement, net ton, bulk, Hays, Pa. 18.70
Silica cement, net ton, bulk, Ensley, Ala. 17.60
Silica cement, net ton, bulk, Chicago District 17.60
Silica cement, net ton, bulk, Utah and Calif. 24.70

Chrome Brick
Per Net Ton
Standard chemically bonded, Balt., Chester $82.00

Magnesite Brick
Standard, Baltimore $104.00
Chemically bonded, Baltimore 93.00

Grain Magnesite
St. ⅜-in. grains
Domestic, f.o.b. Baltimore, in bulk fines removed $62.70
Domestic, f.o.b. Chewelah, Wash., in bulk 36.80
in sacks 41.80

Dead Burned Dolomite
F.o.b. producing points in Pennsylvania, West Virginia and Ohio, per net ton, bulk Midwest, add 10¢; Missouri Valley, add 20¢ $13.00

COKE

Furnace, beehive (f.o.b. oven) Net Ton
Connellsville, Pa. ..... $14.00 to $14.50
Foundry, beehive (f.o.b. oven)
Connellsville, Pa. ..... $17.00 to $17.50
Foundry, oven coke
Buffalo, del'd $25.35
Chicago, f.o.b. 21.00
Detroit, f.o.b. 23.00
New England, del'd 24.80
Seaboard, N. J., f.o.b. 22.00
Philadelphia, f.o.b. 22.70
Swedeland, Pa., f.o.b. 22.60
Plainesville, Ohio, f.o.b. 24.00
Erie, Pa., f.o.b. 23.50
Cleveland, del'd 25.72
Cincinnati, del'd 25.06
St. Paul, f.o.b. 21.00
St. Louis, f.o.b. 24.90
Birmingham, del'd 20.79
Neville Island, f.o.b. 23.00

LAKE SUPERIOR ORES

(51.50% Fe; natural content, delivered lower lake ports)
Per gross ton
Old range, bessemer $8.70
Old range, nonbessemer 8.55
Mesabi, bessemer 8.45
Mesabi, nonbessemer 8.30
High phosphorus 8.30
After adjustments for analyses, prices will be increased or decreased as the case may be for increases or decreases after Dec. 2, 1950, in lake vessel rates, upper lake rail freights, dock handling charges and taxes thereon.

C-R SPRING STEEL

Base per pound f.o.b. mill
0.26 to 0.40 carbon ..... 5.35¢
0.41 to 0.60 carbon ..... 6.80¢
0.61 to 0.80 carbon ..... 7.40¢
0.81 to 1.05 carbon ..... 9.35¢
1.06 to 1.35 carbon ..... 11.65¢
Worcester, add 0.30¢; Sharon, Carnegie, New Castle, add 0.35¢; Detroit, 0.26 to 0.40 carb., add 25¢; other grades add 15¢; New Haven, 0.26 to 0.40 carb., add 50¢; other grades add 5¢.

IRON AGE FOUNDED 1855 MARKETS & PRICES

ELECTRODES

Cents per lb, f.o.b. plant, threaded electrodes with nipples, unboxed

Diam. in in.	Length in in.	Cents Per lb
GRAPHITE		
17, 18, 20	60, 72	17.85
8 to 16	48, 60, 72	17.85
7	48, 60	19.57
6	48, 60	20.95
4, 5	40	21.50
3	40	22.61
2½	24, 30	23.15
2	24, 30	25.36
CARBON		
40	100, 110	8.03
35	65, 110	8.03
30	65, 84, 110	8.03
24	72 to 104	8.03
20	84, 90	8.03
17	60, 72	8.03
14	60, 72	8.57
10, 12	60	8.84
8	60	9.10

CLAD STEEL

Base prices, cents per pound, f.o.b. mill

Stainless-carbon	Plate	Sheet
No. 304, 20 pct,		
Coatesville, Pa. (21)	*29.5	
Washgtn, Pa. (39)	*29.5	
Claymont, Del. (29)	*25.00	
Conshohocken, Pa. (26)		*24.00
New Castle, Ind. (55)	*26.50	*25.50
Nickel-carbon		
10 pct. Coatesville (21)	32.5	
Inconel-carbon		
10 pct Coatesville (21)	40.5	
Monel-carbon		
10 pct Coatesville (21)	33.5	
No. 302 Stainless - copper-stainless, Carnegie, Pa. (60)	77.00	
Aluminized steel sheets, hot dip, Butler, Pa. (7)	7.75	

* Includes annealing and pickling, or sandblasting.

TOOL STEEL

F.o.b. mill

W	Cr	V	Mo	Co	Base per lb
18	4	1	—	—	$1.235
18	4	1	—	5	$1.86
18	4	2	—	—	$1.38
1.5	4	1.5	8	—	78.5¢
6	4	2	6	—	.87¢
High-carbon chromium					63.5¢
Oil hardened manganese					35¢
Special carbon					32.5¢
Extra carbon					27¢
Regular carbon					23¢

Warehouse prices on and east of Mississippi are 3¢ per lb higher. West of Mississippi, 5¢ higher.

METAL POWDERS

Per pound, f.o.b. shipping point, in ton lots, for minus 100 mesh.

Swedish sponge iron c.i.f. New York, ocean bags	7.4¢ to 9.0¢
Canadian sponge iron, del'd, in East	10.00¢
Domestic sponge iron, 98+% Fe, carload lots	9.0¢ to 15.0¢
Electrolytic iron, annealed, 99.5+% Fe	36.0¢ to 39.5¢
Electrolytic iron unannealed, minus 325 mesh, 99+% Fe	48.5¢
Hydrogen reduced iron, minus 300 mesh, 98+% Fe	63.0¢ to 80.0¢
Carbonyl iron, size 5 to 10 micron, 98%, 99.8+% Fe	70.0¢ to $1.3t
Aluminum	29.00¢
Brass, 10 ton lots	30.00¢ to 33.25¢
Copper, electrolytic	10.25¢ plus metal value
Copper, reduced	10.00¢ plus metal value
Cadmium 100-199 lb.	95¢ plus metal value
Chromium, electrolytic, 99% min., and quantity	$3.50
Lead	6.5¢ plus metal value
Manganese	52.00¢
Molybdenum, 99%	$2.65
Nickel, unannealed	75.5¢
Nickel, annealed	81.5¢
Nickel, spherical, unannealed	78.5¢
Silicon	34.00¢
Solder powder	6.5¢ to 8.5¢ plus met. value
Stainless steel, 302	75.00¢
Tin	11.00¢ plus metal value
Tungsten, 99%	$4.1t
Zinc, 10 ton lots	20.50¢ to 23.85¢

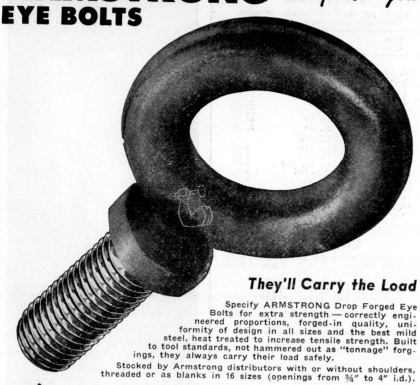
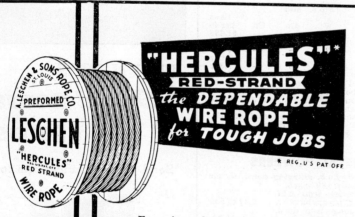
IRON AGE MARKETS & PRICES
FOUNDED 1855

ELECTRICAL SHEETS
22 Ga. H-R cut lengths

F.o.b. Mill Cents Per Lb.	Armature	Elec.	Motor	Dynamo	Transf. 72	Transf. 65	Transf. 58
Beech Botton-15		7.25	8.50	9.30	9.85	10.40	11.10
Brackenridge-28		7.25	8.50	9.30	9.85		
Follansbee-63	6.75	7.25	8.50	9.30	9.85	10.40	11.10
Granite City-22			7.95	9.20			
Ind. Harbor-3	6.75	7.25					
Mansfield-75		7.25	8.50	9.30			
Niles, O.-64	7.05	7.55					
Vandergrift-1	6.75	7.25	8.50	9.30	9.85	10.40	11.10
Warren, O.-4	6.75	7.25	8.50	9.30	9.85	10.40	11.10
Zanesville-7	6.75	7.25	8.50	9.30	9.85	10.40	11.10

Transformer 52, 80¢ above Transformer 58.

Ferrochrome

Contract prices, cents per pound, contained Cr, lump size, bulk, in carloads, delivered. (65-72% Cr, 2% max. Si.)

0.06% C	30.50	0.20% C	29.50
0.10% C	30.00	0.50% C	29.25
0.15% C	29.75	1.00% C	29.00
2.00% C			28.75
65-69% Cr, 4-9% C			22.00
62-66% Cr, 4-6% C, 6-9% Si			22.85

High-Nitrogen Ferrochrome

Low-carbon type: 67-72% Cr, 0.75% N. Add 5¢ per lb to regular low carbon ferrochrome price schedule. Add 5¢ for each additional 0.25% N.

Chromium Metal

Contract prices, per lb chromium contained packed, delivered, ton lots. 97% min. Cr, 1% max. Fe.

0.20% Max. C	$1.09
0.50% max. C	1.06
.00 min. C	1.04

Low Carbon Ferrochrome Silicon

(Cr 34-41%, Si 42-49%, C 0.05% max.) Contract price, carloads, f.o.b. Niagara Falls, freight allowed; lump 4-in. x down, bulk 2-in. x down, 21.75¢ per lb of contained Cr plus 12.00¢ per lb of contained Si.

Bulk 1-in. x down, 21.90¢ per lb contained Cr plus 12.20¢ per lb contained Si.

Calcium-Silicon

Contract price per lb of alloy, dump delivered.
30-33% Ca, 60-65% Si, 3.00% max. F.

Carloads	19.00
Ton lots	22.10
Less ton lots	23.10

Calcium-Manganese—Silicon

Contract prices, cents per lb of alloy, lump, delivered.
16-20% Ca, 14-18% Mn, 53-59% Si.

Carloads	20.00
Ton lots	22.30
Less ton lots	23.30

CMSZ

Contract price, cents per lb of alloy, delivered.
Alloy 4: 45-49% Cr, 4-6% Mn, 18-21% Si, 1.25-1.75% Zr, 3.00-4.5% C.
Alloy 5: 50.56% Cr, 4-6% Mn, 13.50-16.00% Si, 0.75 to 1.25% Zr, 3.50-5.00% C

Ton lots	20.75
Less ton lots	22.00

V Foundry Alloy

Cents per pound of alloy, f.o.b. Suspension Bridge, N. Y., freight allowed, max. St. Louis. V-5: 38-42% Cr, 17-19% Si, 8-11% Mn.

Ton lots	16.50¢
Less ton lots	17.75¢

Graphidox No. 4

Cents per pound of alloy, f.o.b. Suspension Bridge, N. Y., freight allowed, max. St. Louis. Si 48 to 52%, Ti 9 to 11%, Ca 5 to 7%.

Carload packed	18.00
Ton lots to carload packed	19.00
Less ton lots	20.50¢

SMZ

Contract price, cents per pound of alloy, delivered, 60-65% Si, 5-7% Mn, 5-7% Zr, 20% Fe, ½ in. x 12 mesh.

Ton lots	17.25
Less ton lots	18.50

FERROALLOYS

Ferromanganese
78-82% Mn. maximum contract base price, gross ton, lump size.
F.o.b. Niagara Falls, Alloy, W. Va.,
Welland, Ont., Ashtabula, O...... $185
F.o.b. Johnstown, Pa............... $187
F.o.b. Sheridan, Pa............... $185
F.o.b. Etna, Clairton, Pa......... $188
$2.00 for each 1% above 82% Mn, penalty, $2.15 for each 1% below 78%.
Briquets—Cents per pound of briquet, delivered, 66% contained Mn.
Carload, bulk 10.45
Ton lots 12.05

Spiegeleisen
Contract prices gross ton, lump, f.o.b.

	16-19% Mn 3% max. Si	19-21% Mn 3% max. Si
Palmerton, Pa.	$74.00	$75.00
Pgh. or Chicago	74.00	75.00

Manganese Metal
Contract basis, 2 in. x down, cents per pound of metal, delivered.
96% min. Mn, 0.2% max. C, 1% max. Si, 2% max. Fe.
Carload, packed 29.75
Ton lots 31.25

Electrolytic Manganese
F.o.b. Knoxville, Tenn., freight allowed east of Mississippi, cents per pound.
Carloads 28
Ton lots 30
Less ton lots..................... 32

Medium Carbon Ferromanganese
Mn 80% to 85%, C 1.25 to 1.50. Contract price, carloads, lump, bulk, delivered, per lb. of contained Mn............19.15¢

Low-Carbon Ferromanganese
Contract price, cents per pound Mn contained, lump size, del'd, Mn 85-90%.

	Carloads	Ton	Less
0.7% max. C, 0.06% P, 90% Mn......	26.25	28.10	29.30
0.07% max. C......	25.75	27.60	28.80
0.15% max. C......	25.25	27.10	28.30
0.30% max. C......	24.75	26.60	27.80
0.50% max. C......	24.25	26.10	27.30
0.75% max. C, 7.00% max. Si.....	21.25	23.10	24.30

Silicomanganese
Contract basis, lump size, cents per pound of metal, delivered, 65-68% Mn, 18-20% Si, 1.5% max. C. For 2% max. C, deduct 0.2¢.
Carload bulk 9.90
Ton lots 11.55
Briquet, contract basis carlots, bulk delivered, per lb of briquet....... 11.15
Ton lots 11.75

Silvery Iron (electric furnace)
Si 14.01 to 14.50 pct, f.o.b. Keokuk, Iowa, or Wenatchee, Wash., $89.50 gross ton, freight allowed to normal trade area. Si 15.01 to 15.50 pct, f.o.b. Niagara Falls, N. Y., $83.00. Add $1.00 per ton for each additional 0.50% Si up to and including 18%. Add $1.00 for each 0.50% Mn over 1%.

Silicon Metal
Contract price, cents per pound contained Si, lump size, delivered, for ton lots packed.
96% Si, 2% Fe.............. 21.70
97% Si, 1% Fe.............. 22.10

Silicon Briquets
Contract price, cents per pound of briquet bulk, delivered, 40% Si, 1 lb Si briquets.
Carload, bulk 6.95
Ton lots 8.55

Electric Ferrosilicon
Contract price, cents per pound contained Si, lump, bulk, carloads, delivered.

25% Si.....	19.00	75% Si.....	14.30
50% Si.....	12.40	85% Si.....	15.55
		90-95% Si	17.50

Calcium Metal
Eastern zone contract prices, cents per pound of metal, delivered.

	Cast	Turnings	Distilled
Ton lots	$2.05	$2.95	$3.75
Less ton lots..	2.40	3.30	4.55

February 1, 1951

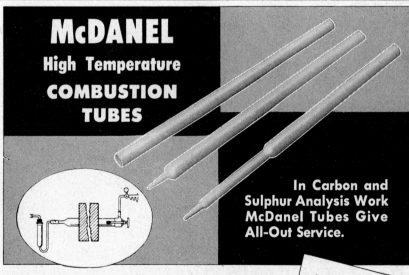

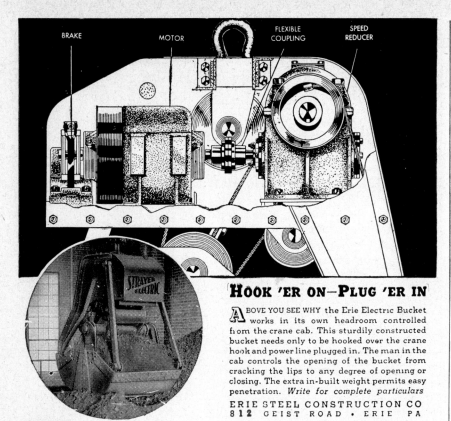

BRAKE · MOTOR · FLEXIBLE COUPLING · SPEED REDUCER

HOOK 'ER ON—PLUG 'ER IN

ABOVE YOU SEE WHY the Erie Electric Bucket works in its own headroom controlled from the crane cab. This sturdily constructed bucket needs only to be hooked over the crane hook and power line plugged in. The man in the cab controls the opening of the bucket from cracking the lips to any degree of opening or closing. The extra in-built weight permits easy penetration. *Write for complete particulars*

ERIE STEEL CONSTRUCTION CO
812 GEIST ROAD · ERIE PA

BUCKETS · BINS · AGGREMETERS
ELECTRIC OVERHEAD TRAVELING CRANES
PORTABLE CONCRETE PLANTS

ERIE STEEL CONSTRUCTION CO., ERIE, PA.

Since 1887

MILWAUKEE WROT WASHERS

Better WASHERS

...Competitively Priced

Large volume production, the most advanced methods and facilities, plus more than 60 years of continuous experience in the manufacture of Washers, are factors that enable us to offer you top quality washers and stampings at competitive costs. Over 22,000 sets of dies for making Washers of every type (Standard and Special), from every type of material, for every purpose, in any finish. STAMPINGS of all descriptions; Blanking, Forming, Drawing. *Submit your blueprints and quantity requirements for estimates.*

WROUGHT WASHER MANUFACTURING CO.
The World's Largest Producer of Washers
2202 S. BAY ST., MILWAUKEE 7, WIS.

Other Ferroalloys

Alsifer, 20% Al, 40% Si, 40% Fe, contract basis, f.o.b. Suspension Bridge, N. Y.
  Carload .... 8.15¢
  Ton lots .... 9.55¢
Calcium molybdate, 45-40%, f.o.b. Langeloth, Pa., per pound contained Mo. $1.15
Ferrocolumbium, 50-60%, 2 in x D, contract basis, delivered, per pound contained Cb.
  Ton lots $4.90
  Less ton lots 4.95
Ferro - Tantalum - columbium, 20% Ta, 40% Cb, 0.30 C. Contract basis, delivered, ton lots, 2 in. x D, per lb of contained Cb plus Ta $3.75
Ferromolybdenum, 55-75%, f.o.b. Langeloth, Pa., per pound contained Mo $1.32
Ferrophosphorus, electrolytic, 23-26%, car lots, f.o.b. Siglo, Mt. Pleasant, Tenn., $3 unitage, per gross ton $65.00
  10 tons to less carload 75.00
Ferrotitanium, 40%, regular grade, 0.10% C max., f.o.b. Niagara Falls, N. Y., and Bridgeville, Pa., freight allowed, ton lots, per lb contained Ti $1.35
Ferrotitanium, 25%, low carbon, 0.10% C max., f.o.b. Niagara Falls, N. Y., and Bridgeville, Pa., freight allowed, ton lots, per lb contained Ti $1.50
  Less ton lots $1.55
Ferrotitanium, 15 to 19%, high carbon, f.o.b. Niagara Falls, N. Y., freight allowed, carload per net ton $177.00
Ferrotungsten, standard, lump or ¼ x down, packed, per pound contained W, 5 ton lots, delivered $3.25
Ferrovanadium, 35-55%, contract basis, delivered, per pound, contained V.
  Openhearth .... $3.0-$3.05
  Crucible 3.10- 3.15
  High speed steel (Primos) 3.25
Molybdic oxide, briquets or cans, per lb contained Mo, f.o.b. Langeloth, Pa. $1.14
  bags, f.o.b. Washington, Pa., Langeloth, Pa. $1.13
Simanal, 20% Si, 20% Mn, 20% Al, contract basis, f.o.b. Philo, Ohio, freight allowed, per pound
  Carload, bulk lump .... 14.50¢
  Ton lots, bulk lump .... 15.75¢
  Less ton lots, lump .... 16.25¢
Vanadium pentoxide, 88-92% V_2O_5 contract basis, per pound contained V_2O_5 .... $1.28
Zirconium, 35-40%, contract basis, f.o.b. plant, freight allowed, per pound of alloy.
  ton lots .... 21.00¢
Zirconium, 12-15%, contract basis, lump, delivered, per lb of alloy.
  carload, bulk .... 7.00¢

Boron Agents

Contract prices per lb of alloy, del.
Borosil, f.o.b. Philo, Ohio, freight allowed, B 3-4%, Si 40-45%, per lb contained B $5.25
Bortam, f.o.b. Niagara Falls
  Ton lots, per pound .... 45¢
  Less ton lots, per pound ...... 50¢
Carbortam, Ti 15-21%, B 1-2%, Si 2-4%, Al 1-2%, C 4.5-7.5%, f.o.b. Suspension Bridge, N. Y., freight allowed.
  Ton lots, per pound .... 10.00¢
Ferroboron, 17.50% min. B, 1.50% max. Si, 0.50% max. Al, 0.50% max. C, 1 in. x D. Ton lots $1.20
  F.o.b. Wash., Pa.; 100 lb, up
  10 to 14% B................ .75
  14 to 19% B................ 1.20
  19% min. B................ 1.50
Grainal, f.o.b. Bridgeville, Pa., freight allowed, 100 lb and over.
  No. 1 .... $1.00
  No. 6 .... 68¢
  No. 79 .... 50¢
Manganese—Boron 75.00% Mn, 15-20% B, 5% max. Fe, 1.50% max. Si, 3.00% max. C, 2 in. x D, delivered.
  Ton lots $1.46
  Less ton lots 1.57
Nickel—Boron 15-18% B, 1.00% max. Si, 0.50% max. C, 3.00% max. Fe, balance Ni, delivered.
  Less ton lots $1.80
Silcaz, contract basis, delivered.
  Ton lots .... 45.00¢

The Clearing House

NEWS OF USED, REBUILT AND SURPLUS MACHINERY

Price Controls — New machine tools of equal quality are more amenable to price controls than their used fellows. The government's price chill applied to used machinery of varying quality may result in a jungle of red tape. It will have, whatever its shortcomings in a difficult field, one overall result—sapping a lusty market whose prices had more spring than a jack-in-the-box.

Evaluation of condition, working order, quality of rebuilt and reconditioned machines will again have to be considered. The groundwork was laid by the old OPA.

Ripe for Controls—The nature of the used machinery market, the scramble for equipment and resultant high prices made the field ripe for price controls. Some dealers have been complaining that it was difficult to buy and sell because of market uncertainties. Some dealers feared that they were selling themselves out of business by not being able to replace many machines they were selling at prices buyers were willing to pay.

Cry in the Wilderness—As in every other industry, there have been many who oppose price control on the grounds that it interferes with basic capitalistic laws of supply, demand, and resultant prices. Their argument was weakened because too many buyers have despaired on hearing prices of used machines that rivalled those of new ones and too many dealers sold a machine for a certain sum one day and had to pay much more later to replace it. The stand of the rugged individualists is a cry in the wilderness.

The used market has exhibited unruliness and no signs of toning down. It was asking for controls.

Out of This World—In Cleveland recently used machine tool prices marched to a new high as demand for good equipment turned the market into a brawl for available machines. Particularly in demand were turret lathes, radial drills, production milling machines, and tool room and metal forming equipment of any type.

Dealers moaned that prices were "out of this world." Cited was the case of a production milling machine which sold for $2450 2 months ago and some weeks later sold for $3850. A No. 5 Warner & Swasey turret lathe in good condition brought $12,500, the price of a new machine, at a recent auction. Only 6 months ago a comparable machine sold for $6500.

Drag Out the Ancients—Cleveland demand is growing for older machines, 20 years and older, many of which reposed in the retirement of inventory for a few years. A definite market is shaping up, although buyers refused to pay inflated prices.

Now that defense production is taking form and with the Air Force planning to order a fabulous number of machine tools, more buyers will be forced to dig into this obsolete reserve. It was reported in Cleveland that two 1921 Cone machines brought an offer of $2100 each. As new machine tool buyers fall into the used machinery field under the stimulus of defense orders and extended delivery dates on new machines, they, too, may look over the venerable items.

Not at Peak Yet—Demand has not yet reached the 1942 peak when dealers sacrificed dignity and went as far as dragging machines out of scrap yards. Prices being paid at auctions were getting so high in the Chicago area that some dealers could not attend. Users were bidding them out of the market. Dealers who did attend usually were bidding for clients.

how ROTOBLAST* saves $62,500 annually for General Foundries in MILWAUKEE

No COST-CONSCIOUS executive can shrug off the kind of savings General Foundries in Milwaukee has racked up since the installation of Pangborn ROTOBLAST. Two hundred and fifty dollars daily savings amounts to more than $50,000 saved annually in regular foundry operations. Here's the story in a nutshell!

One ROTOBLAST Barrel with one operator working one nine-hour shift replaced 4 tumbling mills with two operators working two nine-hour shifts; and a ROTO- BLAST Table Room took over the work of an air blast room, saving $100.80 every day on labor and com- pressed air costs alone.

WHAT ABOUT YOUR PLANT?

Chances are blast cleaning costs you $5000 to $10,000 *too much* each year. Investigate Pangborn ROTO- BLAST as General Foundries did. Let a Pangborn engineer show you how ROTOBLAST can increase pro- duction and save you big money every year.

WRITE TODAY for Bulletin 214. It contains the com- plete story and shows typical installations. Included are specifications and a list of prominent users like General Electric, Westinghouse and others. Address your letter to PANGBORN CORPORATION, 1500 Pang- born Blvd., Hagerstown, Maryland.

• *ROTOBLAST TABLE- ROOM (above) cleans the entire output of an air blast room in 40% less time and practi- cally eliminates break- age of delicate castings.*

●*ROTOBLAST BARREL (above) at General Foundries does work of 4 tumbling mills in ¼ less time with a saving of 36 man-hours per day.*

ROTOBLAST
saves you money these five ways:

$ **SAVES LABOR:** One ROTOBLAST ma- chine and operator can do as much as a two-man crew and old-fashioned equipment.

$ **SAVES SPACE:** In many cases, one ROTOBLAST machine replaces five or more old-fashioned machines, requires less space.

$ **SAVES TIME:** Cases on record prove ROTOBLAST can cut cleaning time up to 95.8% compared with old-style methods.

$ **SAVES POWER:** Modern ROTOBLAST uses but 15-20 h.p. compared to old-fashioned equipment requiring 120 h.p. for same job.

$ **SAVES TOOLS:** On work cleaned with ROTOBLAST, cutting tools last up to 2/3 longer because no scale is left to dull edges.

All these savings mean INCREASED PROFITS for you!

Accurate Records Prove ROTOBLAST Makes Important Savings on:

LABOR: With ROTOBLAST, General Foundries cut cleaning time daily from 54 to 14 man-hours—$100.80 saved per day.

BREAKAGE: On extremely fragile castings General Foundries reduced breakage 83%, saving $150 a day.

FINISH: Thorough removal of all burnt-in sand makes machining easier. Saves customers money.

Look to Pangborn for the Latest Developments in Blast Cleaning and Dust Control Equipment

MORE THAN 25,000 PANGBORN MACHINES SERVING INDUSTRY

Pangborn

FEMA

'Trademark of Pangborn Corporation

BLAST CLEANS CHEAPER with the right equipment for every job

WARNER & SWASEY TUR-
RET LATHE EQUIPPED WITH
CUTLER-HAMMER BUL.
9739 MOTOR CONTROL.

CHOICE OF THE LEADERS

CUTLER·HAMMER

MOTOR CONTROL

C·H

THE MARK OF BETTER MACHINES

AMERICAN WHEELABRATOR 27" x 36" W/A
TUMBLAST EQUIPPED WITH C-H CONTROL.

CUTLER·HAMMER
MOTOR CONTROL
C·H

HIGH-SPEED GRAY OPENSIDE PLANER
"CUB" EQUIPPED WITH CUTLER-HAMMER
BUL. 6250 MOTOR CONTROL.

CUTLER·HAMMER
MOTOR CONTROL
C·H

ALL-ELECTRIC AUTOMATIC STEAM GEN-
ERATOR MADE BY THE CUSTOM ENGI-
NEERING COMPANY, CUTLER-HAMMER
CONTROL AND CUTLER-HAMMER TUBU-
LAR HEATING UNITS ARE STANDARD
EQUIPMENT.

Command Performance

Among the numerous manufacturers of every type of machine
made are always a certain few
recognized leaders who have
won success by the excellence
of their product. Basic to such
excellence, of course, is good
engineering. And good engineering invariably means the
utmost discrimination in the
selection of any purchased components. There in one, two,
three order is the reason why
Cutler-Hammer Motor Control
is so frequently the repeated selection of outstanding machine
builders. Able engineers respect
able engineering. And that is
why Cutler-Hammer Motor
Control is so widely accepted
as the mark of better machines.
CUTLER-HAMMER, Inc.,
1325 St. Paul Avenue, Milwaukee 1, Wisconsin. *Associate:*
Canadian Cutler-Hammer,
Ltd., Toronto.

A CHILTON PUBLICATION

The Iron Age

E NATIONAL METALWORKING WEEKLY

February 8, 1951

TENTS PAGE 2

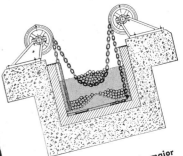

Weldco Mechanical Pickler in major Ohio steel plant, operated with two 600 AT and one 300 AT Cleveland Speed Reducers. Photo by courtesy of Youngstown Welding & Engineering Company.

Unique mechanical bar pickler driven by three CLEVELANDS

THIS pickler descales steel bars prior to cold drawing. The excellence of its work depends on its drive. An unusual arrangement of three Cleveland Worm Gear Speed Reducers lowers and raises the bars in and out of the tank at a prescribed rate, resulting in thoroughly uniform, complete descaling at low cost. No overpickling and no underpickling!

For any job where a powerful, trouble-free, right-angle drive is desired, Cleveland is first choice. Wherever they serve, engineers know from experience that they can depend on Clevelands. They give satisfactory service, no matter how severe the conditions.

Cleveland sales representatives are ready to discuss your power transmission needs with you—help you select correct types and sizes.

For specifications and other details, write for our current catalog. The Cleveland Worm & Gear Company, 3252 East 80th St., Cleveland 4, Ohio.

Affiliate: The Farval Corporation, Centralized Systems of Lubrication. In Canada: Peacock Brothers Limited.

CLEVELAND
Worm Gear
Speed Reducers

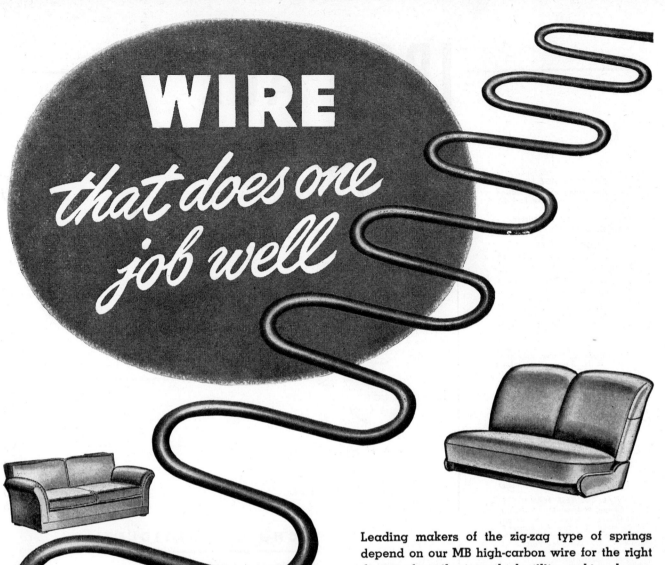

WIRE
that does one job well

Rows of these elements, stretched and anchored within the frames of automobile seats and furniture, provide a foundation of resilient steel for comfortable seating.

Leading makers of the zig-zag type of springs depend on our MB high-carbon wire for the right degree of tensile strength, ductility, and toughness. The proper temper of MB wire is governed by the type of upholstery construction in each case. This application is but one of countless examples of Bethlehem's ability to produce steel wire in special grades — each of which does one job well.

Bethlehem has pioneered in many kinds of wire for specific uses. Each grade has certain characteristics which lead to good performance and low costs.

Right now is a good time to bring your wire problems to us. Whether you're trying to trim down costs or improve the quality of your products, you can depend on Bethlehem wire.

BETHLEHEM STEEL COMPANY, BETHLEHEM, PA.

On the Pacific Coast Bethlehem products are sold by
Bethlehem Pacific Coast Steel Corporation
Export Distributor: Bethlehem Steel Export Corporation

BETHLEHEM WIRE

IRON AGE

CONTENTS

THE IRON AGE
Editorial, Advertising and Circulation Offices, 100 E. 42nd St., New York 17, N. Y.
GEORGE T. HOOK, Publisher
TOM C. CAMPBELL, Editor

EDITORIAL STAFF

Managing Editor   George F. Sullivan
Feature Editor   Darwin I. Brown
News-Markets Editor   Wm. V. Packard
Machinery Editor   George Elwers
Associate Editors: William Czygan, H. W. Van Camp, F. J. Winters; Assistant Editors: R. L. Hatschek, J. Kolb, Ted Metaxas, W. B. Olson; Regional Editors: E. C. Beaudet, Chicago; W. A. Lloyd, Cleveland; W. G. Patton, Detroit; John B. Delaney, Pittsburgh, Osgood Murdock, R. T. Reinhardt, San Francisco; Eugene J. Hardy, Karl Rannells, George H. Baker, Washington; Correspondents: Fred L. Allen, Birmingham; N. Levenson, Boston; Fred Edmunds, Los Angeles; James Douglas, Seattle; Roy Edmonds, St. Louis; F. Sanderson, Toronto; F. H. Harley, London, England; Chilton Editorial Board: Paul Wooton, Washington Representative.

BUSINESS STAFF

Production Manager   B. H. Hayes
Director of Research   Oliver Johnson
Mgr. Circul'n & Promotion   C. T. Post
Asst. Promotion Mgr.   James A. Crites
Asst. Dir. of Research   Wm. Laimbeer

REGIONAL BUSINESS MANAGERS

B. L. Herman, Philadelphia; Stanley J. Smith, Chicago; Peirce Lewis, Detroit; Paul Bachman, New England; Robert F. Blair, Cleveland; R. Raymond Kay, Los Angeles; C. H. Ober, New York; J. M. Spackman, Pittsburgh; Harry Becker, European Representative.

REGIONAL OFFICES

Chicago 3, 1134 Otis Bldg.; Cleveland 14, 1016 National City Bank Bldg., Detroit 2, 103 Pallister Ave.; Los Angeles 28, 2420 Cheremoya Ave.; New England, 62 La Salle Rd., W. Hartford 7; New York 17, 100 E. 42nd St.; Philadelphia 39, 56th & Chestnut Sts.; Pittsburgh 22, 814 Park Bldg.; Washington 4, National Press Bldg.; European, 111 Thorley Lane, Timperley, Cheshire England.

Circulation Representatives: Thomas Scott, James Richardson.

One of the Publications Owned and Published by Chilton Company, Inc., Chestnut & 56th Sts., Philadelphia 39, Pa., U. S. A.

OFFICERS AND DIRECTORS

JOS. S. HILDRETH, President
Vice-Presidents: Everit B. Terhune, G. C. Buzby, P. M. Fahrendorf, Harry V. Duffy, William H. Vallar, Treasurer; John Blair Moffet, Secretary; D. Allyn Garber, Maurice E. Cox, Frank P. Tighe, George T. Hook, Tom C. Campbell, L. V. Rowlands, Directors. George Maiswinkle, Asst. Treas.

Indexed in the Industrial Arts Index and the Engineering Index. Published every Thursday by the CHILTON CO. (INC.), Chestnut and 56th Sts., Philadelphia 39, Pa. Entered as second class matter Nov. 8, 1932, at the Post Office at Philadelphia under the act of March 3, 1879. $8 yearly in United States, its territories and Canada; other Western Hemisphere Countries $15; other Foreign Countries $25 per year. Single Copies 35c. Annual Review and Metal Industry Facts issue, $2.00. Cable address "Ironage" N. Y.

Member Audit Bureau of Circulations. Member Society of Business Magazine Editors.

Copyright, 1951, by Chilton Co. (Inc.)

DIGEST

FEBRUARY EIGHTH · NINETEEN FIFTY-ONE · VOLUME 167 · NUMBER 6

HARDEN MOLYBDENUM HIGH SPEED STEEL TOOLS WITHOUT DECARB

Typical installation for hardening high-speed tools. Preheat, high heat and quench furnaces. The center unit operating at 2200°F. is equipped with submerged electrodes which have an average life of one year.

Tungsten is scarce—and, just as happened during World War II, may become much scarcer. This means wider use of high-speed molybdenum steel tools with their critical hardening problems for which the Ajax Electric Salt Bath supplies far and away the most logical, efficient and economical answer. Actually, it was the inherent characteristics of the salt bath that, to a large extent, made feasible the adoption of molybdenum high-speed steels in place of the tungsten types.

Scaling, decarb, oxidation, pitting and other surface defects are *automatically* avoided. Distortion is reduced to a negligible minimum. Immersion in the bath seals the work from all atmosphere. A protective film of salt protects the tools fully, right up to the instant of quenching.

Heating is amazingly rapid and uniform. Thanks to the exclusive Ajax electrodynamic stirring action, the temperature will not vary more than 5°F. *in any part of the bath*. Because of its faster heating cycles, productive capacity of an Ajax salt bath is two or three times that of other heat treating methods.

In short, the Ajax furnace makes it just as easy and practical to harden molybdenum steels as any other kind—and the equipment works equally well in heat-treating tungsten steels, high carbon—high chromium and all other tool steels.

Be prepared! Ajax Bulletin 123 tells the complete story. Write for your copy today.

More molybdenum high-speed tools are hardened in Ajax Salt Bath furnaces than in any other equipment!

Following are but a few leading users of Ajax furnaces:

AC Spark Plug Div.
American Twist Drill Co.
Brown & Sharpe Mfg. Co.
Buick Motor Div.
Chevrolet Motor Div.
Cleveland Twist Drill Co.
Commercial Steel Treating Co.
Henry Disston & Sons Co.
Ford Motor Co.
Frigidaire Div.
General Electric Co.
Gorham Tool Co.
Greenfield Tap & Die Co.
Landis Machine Co.
McCroskey Tool Corp.

Midvale Co.
Morse Twist Drill Co.
Mueller Brass Co.
National Cash Register Co.
National Screw Co.
National Tool Co.
Oliver Iron & Steel Co.
Pipe Machinery Co.
Pratt & Whitney Div.
Republic Steel Co.
Stanley Works
Thompson Products Co.
Threadwell Tap & Die Co.
Union Twist Drill Co.
Wesley Steel Treating Co.
Westinghouse Electric Co.

AJAX ELECTRIC COMPANY, INC.

904 Frankford Ave.   Philadelphia 23, Pa.

World's largest manufacturer of electric heat treating furnaces exclusively

AJAX HULTGREN ELECTRIC SALT BATH FURNACES

IRON AGE

editorial

Russia Is Winning—So Far

WITHOUT hurting herself one iota, Russia has put the greatest nation in the world in a whirling state of confusion. Without apparently losing a single Russian, Stalin has forced a country that loves liberty and happiness to take on some of the trappings of a controlled state.

Of course there is a good reason for all this: We must be ready to defend the right to live and work and worship and think as free men. It is clear to even the most rugged isolationist that Russia is not out for fun. It is crystal clear to those who have followed her moves closely that she hopes to rule the world—by war if need be.

What has she done to us and to our allies? How much of the war—we are at war whether we want to say so or not—has she won? The answer is painfully clear. She has won so much that there are millions in this country who privately think we are doomed as a free nation.

We were sucked into Korea because our foreign policy was atrocious. Once we were in we had to support the United Nations: We sponsored U. N. as a possible hope for peace.

We are restricting, taxing and spending for war materiel. We must do this if we are to match Russia, lest she take everything for nothing. This will put us into a strait-jacket before we are through. It may give some of the fellow travelers a chance to keep us there for years to come.

Russia tries to drive a wedge between us and our allies by diabolical maneuvering. If we swallow this kind of stuff we are stupid. She has forced her satellite Red China to do her bidding and at the same time estranged us from people who should be our friends.

Her propaganda for communism has been so far superior to ours for democracy that some people think we really *are* aggressive-minded. Russia is a past master at deceit, lies and intrigue. Our sense of decency is an asset to her at every turn.

Russia still has a full bag of tricks—at the United Nations, in Asia, in Europe, in the United States. She will use them all to defeat us if she can.

We must control inflation. We must cut non-defense spending. We must not criticize our allies until we have all the facts. We must not let our defense effort lag nor let it wreck our economy. We must get rid of controls as soon as we can. We must have infinite faith in ourselves and we must elect leaders in whom we can have faith.

Tom Campbell

Editor

Basic Parts of America's Industrial Power...

The Production-Tested Legion of
MONARCH PRECISION LATHES

Here's visible evidence that, whatever your turning problems, there's a specific Monarch Lathe to do the job. And, being a Monarch Lathe built to Monarch standards, you can count on peak production at minimum cost.

You won't see every Monarch Lathe on these pages —we couldn't get them all in. But note the variety. Note the *3* types of tracer controls—a choice that only Monarch offers. And please note this: regularly, since 1909, Monarch lathes have been first to feature almost every major lathe improvement later considered as standard for the industry. You're ahead of the field with Monarch—in longer life, in improved accuracy, in lowered costs.

For complete information—with performance data, photos and case histories—we have prepared specialized Bulletins. Just indicate your interest, and we'll send the ones you want. *The Monarch Machine Tool Company, Sidney, Ohio.*

10" MACHINES

10" x 20" Model EE Toolmaker's Lathe

10" Precision Manufacturing Lathe

10" Precision Manufacturing Lathe with Turret

The Speedi-Matic

ROLL TURNING LATHES

Monarch Heavy Duty Roll Turner

Model N Roll Turning machine

SERIES 60 LINE

12" Series 60 Toolmaker's Lathe

16" Series 60 Engine Lathe

20" Series 60 Toolmaker's Lathe

20" Series 60 Engine Lathe

IRON AGE *newsfront*

► A great many large aircraft parts will <u>eventually</u> be made from huge forgings and extrusions but mass production along these lines is <u>at least 2 years away.</u> <u>Thick skin magnesium</u> construction may be an interim or supplementary step. The number of webs, stiffeners, rivets, etc., can be enormously reduced and production stepped up sharply if this technique proves itself—as tests made so far indicate it will.

► Another, and perhaps equally important aircraft development, is a <u>cast magnesium wing section</u> which has been produced for test purposes. Studies are now going on to work out a way to cast entire wings.

► A new nickel mine is now being developed in Canada. Prospects look good but nickel users should not get their hopes up too soon. It is not expected to be in production until 1954.

► Incandescent lamps with <u>aluminum bases are being tested for consumer reaction.</u> Mass production has been made possible by development of a suitable <u>high-temperature aluminum sheet</u> as well as the <u>solder and flux</u> to permit <u>high speed automatic soldering.</u>

► Steel castings can be made radiographically sound, the Naval Research Laboratory reports, <u>without padding or chills,</u> provided the <u>distance from the perimeter of the riser to the edge of the plate is</u> <u>$4\frac{1}{2}$ times the casting thickness.</u>

► An <u>artificial fog strip</u> along a section of the Autobahn near Frankfurt, Germany, guides drivers in bad weather. Laid along both edges of the concrete, the device throws up a wall of white fog about a foot thick, which headlights easily pick out. <u>Operating costs are reported to be low</u> though the installation is <u>still too expensive</u> to permit its use except at dangerous spots.

► The cost of crushing taconite to extremely fine powder can apparently be cut to <u>about a third that of present methods,</u> according to laboratory tests. The improved process also gives <u>greater recovery of iron</u> from the ore. A process for reducing these ores to metallic iron <u>without prior sintering or pelletizing</u> is now being evaluated.

► Some steel executives are beginning to wonder just <u>what this country will do with all the steel</u> once the current international situation clears up—one way or the other. But <u>some</u> long range guessers are <u>optimistic</u>—fearing to make the same mistake they made 10 years ago. They predict a <u>boom period.</u>

► Army Engineers have developed a 10,000-gal storage tank that can be set up in <u>10 minutes.</u> It is made of a sandwich of Buna N synthetic rubber and nylon cloth with a nylon film lining. Though primarily intended for combat engineer work it might be used as a <u>temporary fuel storage tank.</u>

► Commercial production of <u>columbium-bearing stainless steel</u> from an <u>all-scrap charge</u> is growing in importance because of the columbium scarcity. The technique has already been referred to for foundry work; it is <u>now being used in a steel mill.</u>

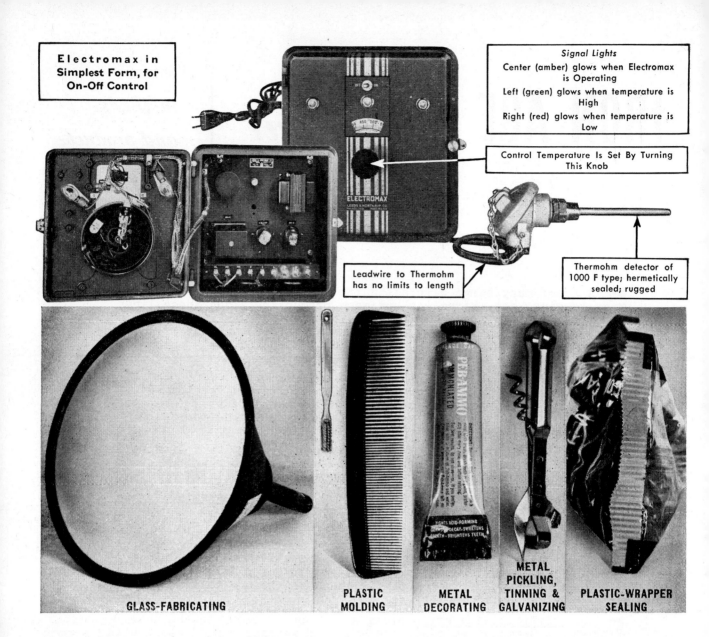

PROTECT PRODUCTION WITH ELECTROMAX CONTROL

ELECTROMAX CONTROLLERS give modern *electronic* regulation to thousands of important manufacturing processes. They exactly fill the bill for non-recording controllers of outstanding dependability.

Electromax has the sensitivity, accuracy and dependability of its big brother Speedomax Recording Controller. Likewise, it is not affected by vibration or building tremors—can even be mounted on the frame of a molding press. The instrument needs almost no attention, because it has only one moving part —a covered, plug-in type relay. There's usually no need to open its door for months at a time.

You can specify any one of 3 types of control action:

1. On-Off or 2-position Control

2. Proportioning, automatic reset and rate (D.A.T.) Control

3. Proportioning and manual reset (P.A.T.) Control

For further information, write our nearest office, or 4956 Stenton Ave., Philadelphia 44, Pa.

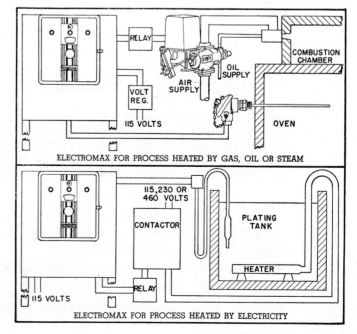

ELECTROMAX FOR PROCESS HEATED BY GAS, OIL OR STEAM

RELAY
COMBUSTION CHAMBER
OIL SUPPLY
AIR SUPPLY
VOLT REG.
115 VOLTS
OVEN

ELECTROMAX FOR PROCESS HEATED BY ELECTRICITY

115, 230 OR 460 VOLTS
CONTACTOR
PLATING TANK
HEATER
115 VOLTS
RELAY

IRON AGE *summary*

*iron and steel
industry trends*

Rail Strike Costs 100,000 Tons Steel
Cripples Shipments of Finished Steel
Regular Customers Face Quota Slashes

STEEL people will be struggling for many weeks to unsnarl the production and shipping mess caused by the rail tie up. Production schedules have been shattered; movement of vital raw materials has been blocked; and finished steel urgently needed by manufacturers has been frozen in the shipping yards.

So far more than 100,000 net tons of steel have been lost because of the wildcat strike. This production is lost forever. It can not be made up at a later date because the industry is straining its productive equipment almost to the breaking point to meet the double-barreled demand of military and civilian users.

Production Pulled Down from Behind

Steel production men who had been breaking output records week after week saw their operating rates pulled down from behind. This week the industry has tentatively scheduled steelmaking operations at 96.5 pct of rated capacity, down 4½ points from last week's revised rate.

Consumers hit quickest and hardest by the rail strike were those depending on current steel shipments to keep their operations going. Although every possible priority was given to shipments of defense (DO) orders, some of these were delayed too. Meanwhile, steel people engaged every available truck in an effort to deliver the growing stack of finished steel.

Lost production which had been slated for DO or essential civilian orders will have to be rescheduled at a later date. This means that other orders which had been already scheduled will have to be pushed aside. For the moment they will be deferred, but they may never be produced if programmed tonnage grows too big. At best the already critical production scheduling headache has been amplified and extended. It will take many weeks to work off—if possible.

King winter also blew freezing breath on output during the past week. In the Pittsburgh area the cold forced gas companies to curtail deliveries to numerous industrial plants. As a result at least three steel companies lost production.

Steel for Defense Snowballs

Meanwhile, the amount of steel going into defense and essential civilian programs is snowballing. Percentage of total output going into these directed uses varies among products and companies. There is widespread feeling among steel producers that they have almost reached the saturation point on plates, carbon bars, structurals and sheets. Some steel companies report as much as 50 to 70 pct of these products are currently being booked for directed programs.

One large company has already cut overall quotas of free steel to regular civilian customers 50 pct for March and April. Even this quota is tentative; it will be even more drastically slashed if more government orders or directives force them to again revise production schedules.

Government Smiles on Conversion

Steel conversion arrangements face no peril from government curtailment—at least for the present. Government officials obviously are influenced by the fact that total steel output now getting a healthy boost through the activity of resourceful converters. In one instance a government agency actually urged a steel consumer now getting steel as an essential user to augment its supply through conversion. The consumer shied away because of cost.

The long awaited rollback of scrap prices was expected to slow activity in the once explosive scrap market to a snail's pace. Buyers were ready to accept tonnage, but dealers and brokers wanted to feel their way along for at least a week or two until the new order could be fully digested.

(nonferrous summary, p. 134)

February 8, 1951

15

50% Increase in Production to Meet Demands for Brad Foote Gears

1951 may be rugged for all industrialists—including users of BRAD FOOTE gears —and the BRAD FOOTE GEAR WORKS. Already we're receiving from our friends heavy and urgent demands for early delivery.

Whether the coming months bring us immediate war—preparation for future war —or, as we hope, the assurance of long years of uninterrupted peace, the BRAD FOOTE GEAR WORKS will be ready to meet any contingency.

We have made material additions to our plant equipment—consisting of important, modern, improved, high-speed mechanisms.

We have mapped out and installed new, streamlined production systems.

With these developments, we have obtained approximately 50% greater output without one minute of the long, tedious delays which are virtually unavoidable when new plants are constructed and equipped.

Brad Foote Gear Works is set to go.

We thank our old friends. We welcome new ones. We are far better prepared than ever before with thoroughgoing engineering cooperation—with the finest gears we have ever built—with prompt delivery.

When may we go to work for you?

Gunnar L. Gunderson
President
BRAD FOOTE GEAR WORKS

BRAD FOOTE GEAR WORKS, Inc.

BISHOP 2-1070 • OLYMPIC 2-7700 • 1309 SOUTH CICERO AVENUE
CICERO 50, ILLINOIS

Free your hands with a *ZIP!*

P&H Zip-LIFT

P&H. ZIP-LIFT

HARNISCHFEGER CORP · MILWAUKEE WIS

HANDLE IT "THRU-THE-AIR"—FASTER—FOR LESS

Skilled hands shouldn't be load-lifters. There's more important work for them to do — more profitably!

Take the hands out of handling — make your man-hours more productive by using Zip-Lifts wherever loads must be handled frequently — along assembly lines, beside machine tools, etc. Make it a push button job.

There's nothing like the Zip-Lift for all-round service and quality — America's favorite wire rope electric hoist.

You pay so little more for ADDED VALUES like these—

SAFER — Full magnetic control with current reduced to 110 volts at push button. Plugging crane type limit switch. Large double brakes. P&H has never stretched a motor rating. That's *your* protection.

LIFETIME CONSTRUCTION — Precision built — shaved gears run in oil — grease-sealed bearings — fully enclosed.

SEE YOUR ZIP-LIFT DEALER, or write us for Bulletin H-20 — it's filled with time-saving ideas for you.

P&H ELECTRIC HOISTS
4401 W. National Avenue
Milwaukee 14, Wisconsin

HARNISCHFEGER
CORPORATION
P&H

EXCAVATORS · OVERHEAD CRANES · HOISTS · ARC WELDERS & ELECTRODES · SOIL STABILIZERS · CRAWLER & TRUCK CRANES · DIESEL ENGINES · CANE LOADERS · PRE-ASSEMBLED HOMES

Dear EDITOR

Letters from Readers

Trend to Local Mills?

Sir:

We are developing plans for the erection of a small steel mill here in Kansas City and were somewhat surprised to find that this subject had been covered in your Apr. 6, 1950 issue, of which we do not seem to have a copy. Would it be possible to obtain this issue or a reprint of the article relating to the small steel mill?

We are also interested in any information you may have relating to the approximate cost of setting up such a mill. We are primarily interested in equipment cost, since we plan to erect the equipment with our own organization.

R. V. SCHROEDER
Schroeder Steel Engineering Co.
Kansas City, Kan.

For the past two years we have been banging away on the possibility of such mills and trying to convince the industry of their practicability by publishing documented stories. The story on p. 79 of the Jan. 11 issue is again on a small steel mill for a local market and carries cost figures.—Ed.

Staunch Backer

Sir:

Thought you might be interested in a letter I sent to the Atomic Energy Commission regarding the DO-Priority symbols used by them:

I note with interest your letter to the Editor of THE IRON AGE, reproduced in the Dec. 28, 1950, issue, wherein you mention that the magazine was in error regarding certain DO symbols. You indicate that the Atomic Energy Commission uses DO Symbols 40-41-42-43-44, and are used to secure materials under contract for or by the A.E.C.

May I point out that THE IRON AGE was quoting from Dept. of Defense releases, particularly the release entitled: "DO Rating of Orders for Production Equipment." If the AEC is also issuing DO-ratings—and your letter states that this is so—then more than one firm must have just read about it in this excellent magazine. Our firm receives copies of regulations, directives, press releases, and other public information items, but nowhere has any of these AEC symbols appeared. . . .

It's hard to keep ahead of all the government BULL-etins. I try to do so—your staff does a much better job than I do—yet apparently we all ran out of official "dope." Just keep up the good job you are doing.

W. H. EVANS
Special Assistant
Hofmann Industries, Inc.
Sinking Spring, Pa.

Finally Remembered

Sir:

We have your issue of Jan. 11 and upon reading it, came across the editorial entitled "The Forgotten Man," written by your editor, Tom C. Campbell. We thoroughly agree with his sentiments and have had numerous copies printed and are sending them to our customers.

M. WILKOF
Morris Steel, Inc.
Canton, Ohio

Sir:

If there are any reprints to be had of your fine editorial in THE IRON AGE of Jan. 11, will appreciate 25 of same and being billed for them.

M. NEWBERGER
Summer & Co.
Buffalo

Classification Complexities

Sir:

Having been a reader of your publication for many years via the "route slip" system, I have found much useful information in its pages. One of the features frequently consulted is the table of finished steel shipments that appears monthly, and on this I would like some further information.

During 1950 the finished steel shipments of electrical sheet and strip have been reported in two classifications: "carbon" and "alloy." Does this reflect the AISI classification of alloy, and, if so, does the carbon classification cover the field and armature grades only? A further question concerns electrical grade. Presupposing this grade is not included in the carbon classification, is there any data available on shipments of the electrical grade?

F. J. MOYLAN
Product Representative
Inland Steel Co.
East Chicago, Ind.

The table is AISI 10, and all descriptive terms and definitions are those of the American Iron & Steel Institute. We are told by them that the field and armature grades are alloy, and that the carbon classification is used for intermittent pole lines. The Institute does not furnish us shipment data on the electrical grade.—Ed.

Seeks Directory

Sir:

Will you please inform me where I might obtain a directory of structural fabricators, shipyards, and used machinery dealers, particularly those handling heavier plate working machinery?

J. L. HOLT
Consultant
Butler, Pa.

The directory most closely fitting this description is the "Directory of Iron & Steel Plants" published by Steel Publications, Inc., 4 Smithfield St., Pittsburgh 30. We do not know of any directory of used machinery dealers, although a membership list might be available from the Machinery Dealers National Assn., 20 N. Wacker Drive, Chicago. The Clearing House Section of THE IRON AGE sometimes carries offerings of machinery of this type.—Ed.

install for these 6 reasons

ABOUT THESE IMPORTANT FEATURES WITH THE "SCREWDRIVER TEST"

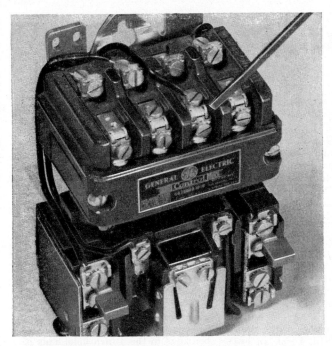

3   Mr. Perito: "*Are all the terminals easy to get at?*"
Every one of them is *up front* where it's easy
to get at, and wire. And they're *big* terminals with
panhead screws and saddle-type connectors that
ride up with the screw head. The stripped wire
simply slides into place and is easily secured with a
turn of your screwdriver.

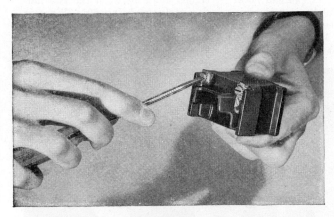

4   Mr. Perito: "*Tough-looking coil! Is it new?*"
Right! It's called the "Strongbox Magnet Coil"
and it's an exclusive with the new G-E starter
line. Feel how solid it is! If your electrician's
screwdriver slips, it can't hurt the windings—
they're safely locked in a block of molded plastic. And
oil, dust or water can't get at them, either!

5   Mr. Perito: "*How do I set the overloads?*"
Easy—and you don't have to take the starter
apart to do it. Flip that little lever and it's on
"Automatic." Flip it back and it's on "Manual."
Heaters are in the front, can be changed without
disturbing any wiring.

6   Mr. Perito: "*What about maintenance?*"
Once this new G-E starter is installed, it *stays*
installed. There's no need to remove the case for
ordinary maintenance or even to replace or
reverse contacts. Just remove the arc chute and
there are your terminals.

WHY DON'T *YOU*

"BUY ONE AND COMPARE?"

See for yourself why this
new line of G-E motor starters lasts longer, costs less to
install than almost any other
starter you can buy. Your G-E
representative or authorized
G-E agent or distributor can
supply you from stock in
NEMA sizes 0, 1, 2 and 3 for
a-c motors up to 50 hp. For
a complete description, write
for Bulletin GEA-5153. Section 730-18, Apparatus Dept.,
General Electric Company,
Schenectady 5, New York.

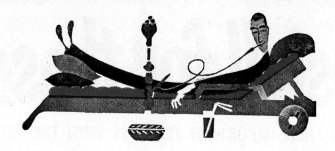

Fatigue Cracks

by Charles T. Post

Aptronyms

For a Friday dish, you can have Ruth R. Haddock, who writes publicity for the Xman Trout Ranch, fresh frozen trout packers in Nevada, or Paul R. Fish, recently named advertising director of *Hunting & Fishing* magazine.

Margaret's Friend

H. S. T. dropped over to the Washington Statler the other night to present his old friend Paul Wooten with the Silver Quill Award of the National Business Publications for outstanding service in behalf of business papers. Paul, as Washington member of the Chilton Editorial Board, keeps an eye on the cross-currents of government for your favorite family journal and its sister publications.

In presenting the trophy, the President said: "You never forget kind treatment when you move into a strange place. Just to show you the difference in the attitudes of people when a strange man comes to town, my daughter at that time was about ten years old—I hope you won't spread that around—and Paul Wooten lived in the apartment below us. And he was as kind to Margaret as anybody could be. And when anybody is kind to Margaret, I never forget it. And neither do I forget it when they are not."

Puzzlers

Still no answers to the ball problem in the January 28 issue. Our timing must have been off. Maybe we will repeat it in the spring when a young man's fancy turns to—among other things—baseball.

The great American mind once again conquers all obstacles. E. J. Sampson, Brockton, Mass., just happened to find on his bench a ball bearing with a radius of 0.46636 inches which he claims fits nicely between the 3 inch and 1 inch roller bearings in the 4 inch hole. This is close enough to the right answer of 0.461538461538 inches so we will add his name to the honor roll.

Here we go with another ladder problem from A. M. Woodall, The Ingalls Iron Works Co. A ladder is so placed in a street that the top of the ladder will just reach the top of a 40 foot high building on one side of the street or a 30 foot building on the other side, the included angle between the two ladder positions being 60°. What is the length of the ladder, street width and the location of the foot of the ladder?

machine tool high spots

sales inquiries and production

by W.A.Lloyd

Pool Orders in 10 Days—Big news for the machine tool industry is in the making this week, according to Washington sources.

First, release of the emergency production schedules (pool orders) is expected to start within 10 days. These orders will not be released on a mass basis, but probably in dribbles. It is understood that the orders will be released as soon as verification copies come back corrected from machine tool companies.

Thinking Reversed—Industry spokesmen predicted last week that pool orders would not be released until Apr. 1, or thereabouts. Apparently the thinking at that time was that a mass release would be made after verification had been received from all companies.

The change will accelerate the program considerably. However, some companies as of Feb. 1 had not received the copies for verification, which could easily push the release of their schedules back to Apr. 1.

General Purpose Order—Also in the wind is a general purpose order, which reportedly has been approved. It is believed similar but not identical to World War II's E-1-B, covering distribution of machine tools. Company order boards will probably be divided into two parts, 75 pct for the armed forces and 25 pct for foreign and essential civilian use. Mutual Defense Assistance Program orders will probably be consigned to this category, as was lend-lease in World War II.

Finally, priorities are expected to follow pool orders within days. The priority will not be of the blanket type but will enable machine tool companies to proceed with sub-contracting plans and materially increase their production.

Insurance for Industry — One function of the emergency production schedules will be as a sort of insurance policy for machine tool companies, in that they give a company authority to get a priority on material for increasing production and also, protect machine tool companies against the possibility of the bottom dropping out of the defense program if the Reds should suddenly extend an olive branch.

Demand Peak On Way—Coming up is a violent peak in machine tool demand which is expected to reach an estimated $1.3 billion in new orders this year and then begin tapering off gradually.

All defense orders will be rated. A general purpose order will, however, leave some big users of machine tools, including the automobile industry, dangling on some equipment, like special purpose machines which have not been started through the shops, etc. MDAP business will be assigned a new rating, DO-35.

Bands of Priorities—Also, it is understood that the Air Force is placing about $100 million of their projected $550 million program. These developments suggest that bands of priorities will probably be necessary to put first things first.

Recently the U. S. Navy placed orders for about $6 million worth of machine tools for its various bureaus. Still to come is an estimated $30 million under MDAP which will be split among France, Belgium and Holland. In addition, the present $125 million British program may be doubled.

Release Pool Machines—In Dayton, Ohio, Wright-Patterson Air Force Base, headquarters of the Air Materiel Command, announced that machine tools are being released from a 40,000-unit pool, collected after World War II, from private contractors and stored since 1946 in two depots, Bell Bomber plant, Marietta, Ga., and the former Martin Bomber plant in Omaha, Neb.

This Firefighter can be two places at once!

You can protect several danger spots at one time with a Kidde built-in carbon dioxide fire extinguishing system. ¶ Widely separated fire hazards...even on different floors can be protected by a single Kidde system. If fire strikes a protected space, directional valves rush fire-smothering carbon dioxide gas to the stricken area. The same CO_2 can set off mechanisms to shut doors and windows . . . turn off fans and machinery. After doing its job, the clean, dry CO_2 evaporates completely. ¶ Whatever your fire detection and protection problem may be, a Kidde expert will be glad to help. When you think of CO_2 call Kidde.

Walter Kidde & Company, Inc., 250 Main Street, Belleville 9, N. J.
In Canada: Walter Kidde & Company of Canada, Ltd., Montreal, P.Q.

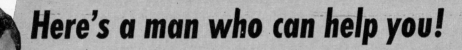
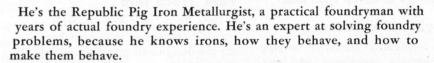

FREE *publications*

Al Finishing Manual

The 1950 edition of the 124-p. process manual, "Finishes For Aluminum," is a revision supplying basic information on the various processes for applying surface finishes to aluminum; it also details the characteristics of the finishes produced. Information is given on 10 cleaning treatments, 15 mechanical finishes, 16 chemically produced finishes, 11 electrolytic oxide finishes, organic finishes, and specialized finishes such as luminous paints and vitreous enamels. A section is also included on controls and tests. A guide for approximating typical costs of applying 20 different treatments to aluminum is shown. Another new table gives typical finishing practices for a wide variety of aluminum products to serve as a suggestion when selecting a finish. *Reynolds Metals Co. Address requests to this column on company letterhead.*

Bearing Maintenance

A continuing study of bearing maintenance techniques and successful maintenance, installation and removal procedures is being published, in pamphlet form, on every type of bearing. A file folder type of binder is being sent to each bearing user who requests it in which succeeding issues can be compiled. At the present time too many bearings are being replaced for reasons other than normal fatigue, which in most cases is due to faulty maintenance practice. Proper distribution and use of the material to be published is intended to reduce this loss to a reasonable minimum. *Anti-Friction Bearing Distributors Assn. Address requests on company letterhead to this column.*

Contour Projector Booklet

What the Kodak Contour Projector Model 2 is—and how it can be used to magnify dimensions, shapes, and surfaces in production or tool making—is the subject of a new 8-p. descriptive booklet. Pointing out that the projector is a potent weapon against rising inspection costs, the booklet describes both the features and application of the machine. Some of the special jobs that the projector can do include, as shown in the booklet, looking into deep recesses, exploring and measuring sizable concavities in one continuous operation at high magnification, and checking intricate dimensional relationships. Specifications, optics, and accessories are described in detail. *Industrial Optical Sales Div., Eastman Kodak Co.*

For free copy insert No. 1 on postcard.

Fork Truck Info

Data in a new 8-p. descriptive bulletin translates into user benefits the design and construction features of the new Baker FT fork trucks in 3000 and 4000 lb capacity. The bulletin contains pictures and descriptions of major components of the trucks, dimension drawings showing maneuverability and detailed specifications. Features that assure ease of handling and maintenance are described, and pictures showing the trucks working in various industries and 16 different applications are included. The bulletin contains illustrations of 14 of the many attachments which can be applied to the trucks for the handling of material in sizes, shapes and forms not practical with standard forks. *Baker Industrial Truck Div., Baker-Raulang Co.*

For free copy insert No. 2 on postcard.

Core Binder

The use of Totanin in all branches of the foundry industry as a core binder, a binder for dry sand mixtures, and for mold washes is described in a new 8-p. booklet discussing the many advantages of this water soluble powder. Several typical mixtures for both general and special purposes are shown, and this British company offers free technical advice on any specific problems not covered in the booklet. *Lambeth & Co. (Liverpool) Ltd.*

For free copy insert No. 3 on postcard.

Book on Refractories

"Modern Refractory Practice" is a practical 440-p. engineering handbook, a comprehensive technical treatise, and a catalog of Harbison-Walker products, combined in a single volume. The new edition has been completely rewritten and increased in size. Scale drawings of 20 types of furnaces, illustrating up-to-date industrial practice, constitute one of the most important features. The drawings show in detail not only the design of the furnaces, but also the types of refractories generally used, and alternate types for special conditions of operation. The discussion of service conditions and requirements for refractories in furnaces of a wide variety should prove helpful to furnace operators. A chapter is devoted to suggestions of a practical nature regarding the selection, care and use of refractories, including handling, installation and service factors which affect the life of refractories. Properties of refractories are fully covered, and another chapter contains a discussion

Turn to Page 122

NEW *production ideas*

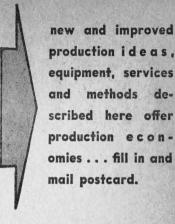

new and improved production ideas, equipment, services and methods described here offer production economies . . . fill in and mail postcard.

Coating Service

For protecting metal or wood parts against corrosion or abrasion.

Application of natural or synthetic coatings for metal or wood equipment and products to provide protection against corrosion or abrasion is offered as a new service. Equipment so bonded is said to last longer, reduces plant shut-down and decreases maintenance costs. Coatings, either dipped or sprayed, may be applied to any type equipment, inside or out, regardless of size, shape, use or quantity. All work is done at the plant of the *American Rubberizing Co.*

For more data insert No. 13 on postcard.

Micrometer

Interchangeable anvils give one micrometer a range of 6 to 12 in.

Six anvils are furnished with the micrometer, all readily interchangeable and providing the full range in steps of 1 in. Each anvil is marked to show capacity and is fitted with an adjusting collar that compensates for wear and acts as a seat when clamped in position by a locking collar. Suitable wrenches are furnished to make necessary adjustments. The complete set is packed in a durable wood case. *L. S. Starrett Co.*

For more data insert No. 14 on postcard.

Carbide Boring Tools

Standard type to fit each of the more popular boring machines.

A new solid carbide boring tool is available from stock in all the carbide grades listed in Super's new Catalog 50 and can be produced in other suitable grades upon request. The company now offers a total of nine types of standard carbide boring tools. *Super Tool Co.*

For more data insert No. 15 on postcard.

Improved 4-Ton Punch Press

8-in. open height permits the use of higher dies and special tooling.

The improved 4-ton deep throat press punches to the center of an 18-in. circle. Frame construction has been strengthened at all stress points and a knock-out has been added. With the exception of the frame, trip link and legs, all parts have been standardized and are interchangeable with the regular 4-ton model, expediting shipment of replacements. *Benchmaster Mfg. Co.*

For more data insert No. 16 on postcard.

Low Cost Iridites

Two chromate finishes for bright finishing of zinc plated surfaces.

Iridite No. 8P is sold in powder form, providing the advantages of lower freight rates, easier handling and elimination of the use of carboys. It is extremely flexible and economical in use. Cost per gallon of working solution ranges from $8\frac{1}{4}$¢, when operating in the yellow color ranges, to 35¢ per gal when operating in the blue-bright ranges. Iridite No. 12 is a chromate treatment for bright zinc plate that both passivates and imparts a chrome-

use postcard below

production ideas

Continued

like appearance to the slated surface. Since it provides relatively little chemical polishing action for the zinc, it should be applied only to bright zinc deposits. It is shipped in carboys in concentrated form. Both products are applied by chemical dip method using standard finishing shop equipment. *Allied Research Products, Inc.*

For more data insert No. 17 on postcard.

Spot Welding Control Units

For low-capacity, spot-type resistance welding machines.

New synchronous and nonsynchronous control equipment uses air-cooled thyratron tubes to make and break the welding current. There are no moving parts. All components are mounted on a side-swinging panel, enclosed in a NEMA type I enclosure for ease of inspection and maintenance. Units can be mounted on or near the weld-

ing machine. Rms current ratings range up to 50 amp at a 10 pct duty cycle for synchronous units; up to 100 amp at 10 pct duty cycle for the nonsynchronous. *Westinghouse Electric Corp.*

For more data insert No. 18 on postcard.

Inductrol Power Packs

A convenient unit for low-voltage, regulated ac lighting, power supply.

Called an Inductrol Power Pack, a new midget load center unit substation incorporates in one steel housing an air circuit breaker, a dry-type transformer and an air-cooled induction regulator. Available in single or three-phase ratings, it has a capacity range of 15 to 100 kva, with incoming circuit rated 480 or 600 v, 60 cycles and a regulated output at 120/240 or 208Y/120 v. Units can be used also to regulate power supplied to resistance heating and infrared heating equipment, electronic apparatus, precision instruments and control circuits. *General Electric Co.*

For more data insert No. 19 on postcard.

use postcard below

Plate-Edge Preparation

Device cuts single or double bevel accurately, with or without a land.

Employing a spring-balanced, free floating carriage and caster-wheel assembly to permit bevel cutting over plate undulations while maintaining a constant tip-to-work distance, a new plate edge preparation device may be mounted on any gas cutting machine equipped with a 3-in. square torch bar. Torches may be individually positioned vertically or laterally without changing the bevel angle. Ability of the device to cut a single or double bevel accurately, with or without a land, recommends it especially for use in shops or factories that do steel fabrication work. *Air Reduction Sales Co.*

For more data insert No. 20 on postcard.

Fire Detection System

Sees fire, does not depend on heat, smoke or other indications of fire.

Fireye fire detector provides instantaneous detection of fire. Based on the photo-electric principle, it is capable of detecting a very small fire, yet ignores extraneous light of any intensity. The protection block consisting of six detectors and one control panel provides coverage up to 120 by 80 ft. Each detector monitors any area within a radius of 20 ft. Connections can be made to a wide variety of existing alarm and automatic extinguishing systems. *Fireye Corp.*

For more data insert No. 21 on postcard.

Scrap Separator

Processes nonferrous chips and fine borings with less than 10 pct iron.

For the automatic separation of magnetic and non-magnetic products, a non-electric permanent Alnico double drum magnetic separator has been developed. The separator incorporates two magnetic Perma-Drums, one mounted directly above the other, enclosed in a dust-tight housing. Non-magnetic material flows over the drum shell in a normal trajectory. Magnetics are held fast to the surface of the shell for one half revolution until they are carried to a point beyond the magnetic field, to be separately discharged. As the material is spouted from the first to the second drum, it is turned over, so that a more effective secondary separation

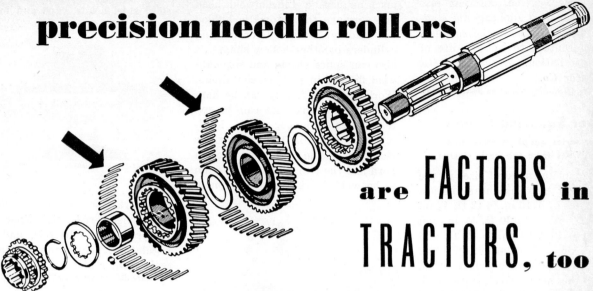

production ideas

Continued

takes place. Nine different size units cover most applications. Magnetic permanence of the magnets are guaranteed to last the life of the installation. *Dings Magnetic Separator Co.*

For more data insert No. 22 on postcard, p. 35.

Power Squaring Shears

New series adopts construction variations from the basic design.

A complete range of sizes in the new power squaring shear line has capacities of 3/16 in. to 12 ft, ¼ in. to 14 ft, ⅜ in. to 20 ft, ½ in. and ¾ in. to 14 ft, 1 in. to 12 ft, and 1¼ in. x 6 ft. The smaller units are all-welded rolled steel construction, using the heavy steel plate work chute as a structural member. Models ¼ in. x 14 ft and larger are assembled rolled steel construction with structural members dovetailed into each other and bolted. All members have been designed to give the assembly a safe measure of strength and rigidity without excess weight. An air-operated disk

clutch has been installed in the flywheel, controlled by a solenoid through a jog or foot switch. Full cutting capacity is obtained with 80 lb air pressure. A spring-operated disk brake automatically stops the shear in event of air or power failure. Positive, automatic hydraulic hold-downs are standard on all except 3/16-in. units. All models can be equipped with 10-ft range squaring arm with steel scale and hinged gage and stop, 50-in. range front gage, light-gage for scribe line shearing and motorized front-operated micrometer back gage. *Columbia Machinery & Engineering Corp.*

For more data insert No. 23 on postcard, p. 35.

Hidden Arc Seam Welder

Seam welder automatically welds seams in 14 gage to ¼ in. metal.

This universal horn type welding machine uses a Lincolnweld head and carriage for automatic hidden arc welding. Designed for welding cylinders or other hollow shapes, it also can splice sheets and through-weld flanges in making containers. Work up to 18 ft long can be handled and the machine can be extended to take longer pieces. Minimum diameter is 12 in. Work is placed over the rigid box section horn and the two edges of the seam to be welded are gripped by pneu-

matically operated heavy copper fingers. Back-up for the weld is provided by a patented back-up device. Automatic brazing or inert-gas-shielded arc welding on stainless steel and nonferrous metals also can be done on the machine. *Lincoln Electric Co.*

For more data insert No. 24 on postcard, p. 35.

Space-Saving Cylinders

Compactness of 30-station welding machine due to square cylinders.

Designed by Hautau Engineering Co. of Detroit, for volume production of automotive transmission brake bands, a new special 30-station Cyclewelding machine is said to owe its economical compactness of design largely to the use of space-saving square-design cylinders. The machine makes maximum use of standard parts for easy replacement. Each of the 30 stations is an independent press with its own, replaceable standard thermostatic controls, electrical connections and square-design cylinders. The 30 stations are built into a compact 9½-ft diam circular table, allowing convenient accessibility to

center slip rings and air headers from a standing position. It is stated the use of circular cylinders of the same bore would require an 18-ft diam table. Cylinders have solid steel heads, caps and mount-

SPACE SAVING "SQUARE DESIGN" CYLINDERS

ings, scratch-resistant, hard chrome plated piston rods, dirt wiper seals, rustproof brass barrels, and self-regulating, wear-compensating seals. *Miller Motor Co.*

For more data insert No. 25 on postcard, p. 35.

Punch Press

Changes from single to continuous ramming without stopping the press.

A new 4-in-1 four-ton punch press has a deep, 12¾-in. throat, a 400-lb cast frame and patented clutch drive dog built into the clutch collar instead of a slot in the crankshaft.

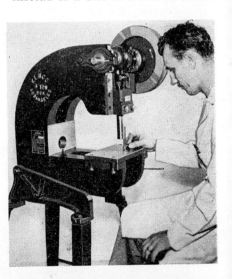

This was engineered to eliminate weakening the one-piece shaft by deep milling. A special trip mechanism permits the operator to change from single to continuous ramming without stopping the press. An adjustable bed permits quick conversion from the standard press to long punch, half or horn press. Connecting rod bearings are of steel encircled bronze-lead alloy,

Turn to Page 127

IRON AGE

introduces

E. M. Heinmiller, elected president to succeed A. J. McAllister, who has retired from the FAIRFIELD MFG. CO., Lafayette, Ind.

Robert F. Rentschler, named vice-president assigned to special duties; James M. Heppenstall, appointed treasurer and Lester E. Leinbach appointed secretary of the BIRDSBORO STEEL FOUNDRY & MACHINE CO., Birdsboro, Pa.

Paul A. Duke, named product engineer for ATLANTIC STEEL CO., Atlanta.

Oscar L. Olson, appointed president and general manager of SWEDISH CRUCIBLE STEEL CO., Detroit.

Arthur Peacock, named assistant secretary-treasurer and comptroller of BORG-WARNER INTERNATIONAL CORP., Chicago.

J. L. Hiers, named assistant general manager, Woodhouse Chain Works, ROUND ASSOCIATE CHAIN CO., Trenton, N. J.

Robert Krogh, named in charge of sales in the Cincinnati area, for the ISPEN INDUSTRIES, INC.

Paul Abel, elected vice-president in charge of engineering for the YODER CO., Cleveland.

Philip D. Moore, appointed manager of employee and community relations of CARBOLOY CO., INC., Detroit.

L. G. Graper, named technical advisor for the LONE STAR STEEL CO., Dallas.

Douglas E. Thompson, appointed manager of by-products sales of the BUDD CO., Philadelphia.

William G. Gerstacker, named chief engineer of the COLONIAL IRON WORKS CO., Cleveland.

Herbert L. Mausk, elected vice-president sales, railway division, and Ellsworth H. Sherwood, elected assistant vice-president sales, railway division of the NATIONAL MALLEABLE & STEEL CASTINGS CO., New York.

Eric Springer, named general manager El Segundo division; Fred Herman, named general manager Long Beach division and Leo Carter for the Santa Monica division of DOUGLAS AIRCRAFT CO. Harry Woodhead, named general manager of the Tulsa, Okla., division.

Walter L. Davidson, named sales manager, heating department of DRAVO CORP., Pittsburgh.

John A. McKinley, promoted to the position of pigment sales supervisor for METALS DISINTEGRATING CO., INC., Elizabeth, N. J. John P. Halloran, appointed manager of the company's Chicago office.

E. B. Forslund, appointed manager of the New York Sales office of the MERCURY MFG. CO., replacing Conrad Hibbeler, who has retired.

Peyton S. Hopkins, named to manage the Washington, D. C., office of the RUST ENGINEERING CO., succeeding Richard E. Butler, who is retiring after 20 years with the company.

J. M. East, appointed vice-president and general manager of the KING & KRINGEL MACHINERY CORP., Denver.

E. C. Iverson, appointed chief engineer of the TOWMOTOR CORP., Cleveland.

Turn to page 70

ALEX G. McKENNA, named executive vice-president of Kennametal Inc., Latrobe, Pa.

ROBERT H. OWENS, named president and general manager of Roots-Connersville Blower Corp., Connersville, Ind.

H. W. FAGERT, elected president, general manager and board member of the R. D. Fageol Co., Detroit.

IRON AGE

salutes

John L. Neudoerfer

JOHN L. NEUDOERFER, new president of Wheeling Steel Corp., is impressive without seeming or wanting to be. A visit with Mr. Neudoerfer is like sitting down for a chat with an old family friend. He wears the presidency of Wheeling like a comfortable old felt hat.

He's an old-timer in the steel business, one who came up through the ranks. But he is not inclined to belabor this point, however proud he must be of it. He rarely becomes sufficiently disturbed to raise his voice above a normal conversational level. People who work for him love him for it.

When John Neudoerfer was a boy in Portsmouth, O., his father wanted him to become an electrical engineer. Had it been any other town, maybe that is the way it would have been. But in Portsmouth the steel industry made too great an impression on the youngster. So at 20 he took a job as clerk in the order entry department of a company that later became part of Wheeling Steel. That was it.

Later, Mr. Neudoerfer took to the road as a steel peddler. He knows what it's like to sell steel when the going is tough, too. In fact, he was elected vice-president in charge of sales in 1931—a year that a lot of people would like to forget—and is still waiting for the "normal" year that is always just around the corner.

John Neudoerfer has a large capacity for hard work, but quietly. This side of his personality is wearing off on his associates, with the result that steel is made and sold at Wheeling without abnormal rises in blood pressures.

Somehow you get the impression that the Wheeling ship is in good hands—that a good, safe course is being charted for the years ahead.

W. W. WARNER, elected vice-president in charge of engineering of the Davey Compressor Co., Kent, Ohio.

K. C. GARDNER, JR., vice-president in charge of operations for United Engineering & Foundry Co., Pittsburgh, was elected a member of the board of directors and executive committee.

CYRIL J. BINNE, appointed to the position of works manager of the Morris Machine Tool Co., Cincinnati.

R. SMITH SCHENK, appointed executive vice-president of Sun Tube Corp., Hillside, N. J.

IRON AGE *introduces*

Continued

Harold R. Foss, named assistant director of the office of defense products, FORD MOTOR CO., Dearborn, Mich. Other appointees: **Donald C. Pippel, John S. French, Kenneth D. Holloway** and **W. E. Simms** were appointed as contract administrators.

Dean, Hammond, appointed vice-president in charge of engineering of KAISER-FRAZER CORP., Willow Run, Mich. **S. W. Taylor,** appointed to the newly created post of executive engineer.

Robert M. Critchfield, named assistant general manager, Allison Div., in Indianapolis for GENERAL MOTORS CORP.

John P. McLaney, Webster C. English, named to general machinery division offices in the south by ALLIS-CHALMERS MFG. CO., Charlotte, N. C., and **Andrew J. Beall, Jr.,** named to the New Orleans office.

Charles W. Pinkerton, named office supervisor of the Coatesville District sales office of LUKENS STEEL CO. Mr. Pinkerton replaces **John W. Martin** who has been recalled to active duty with the Air Force.

Robert L. Pettibone, appointed chief metallurgical engineer of the SINTERCAST CORP. OF AMERICA, Yonkers, N. Y.

Arthur T. Baum, Jr., elected personnel director HYDRAULIC EQUIPMENT CO., Cleveland.

Charles H. Merbitz, appointed sales representative of the type metal department of Federated Metals Div., AMERICAN SMELTER & REFINING CO., Philadelphia.

Edwin H. Howell, appointed special representative for the GENERAL ELECTRIC CO., in Washington, D. C. **Donald E. Craig,** named to succeed Mr. Howell as manager of sales of the meter and instrument divisions, with headquarters in Lynn, Mass.

Frederic W. Thomas, appointed director of purchases, and **George R. Fox** becomes assistant to the executive vice-president in charge of the plant expansion program, of the JOY MFG. CO., Pittsburgh.

R. Bruce Vasey, joined DAVID ROUND & SON, Cleveland, in the capacity of sales promotion manager.

A. L. Geisinger, appointed a vice-president by DIAMOND ALKALI CO., Cleveland. Mr. Geisinger will have charge of the company's activity in the organic chemistry field.

Kline A. Ables, succeeds C. C. Wolf as assistant general purchasing agent of PHELPS DODGE CORP., Douglas, Ariz. Mr. Wolf will continue with the company however, having special duties in connection with the Bisbee East Ore Body program.

Tom B. Nantz, named plant manager for the B. F. GOODRICH CHEMICAL CO., Cleveland.

Russell W. Knode, formerly assistant export manager, named manager of the export department of the JEFFREY MFG. CO., Columbus, Ohio. **L. E. Bixby,** named manager of the contract division.

Henry E. Warren, Jr., appointed assistant general superintendent, and **Forest J. Smith,** appointed assistant to general superintendent of the Fairless Works, of U. S. STEEL CO., Morrisville, Pa.

OBITUARIES

Walter Geist, 56, president of the Allis-Chalmers Mfg. Co., died January 29, 1951, in Milwaukee.

Ralph A. Shaffer, 76, associated with Simonds Saw and Steel Co. for nearly 50 years died recently at his home in West Newton, Mass.

Paul William Lawrence, 60, founder and president of the Lawrence Steel Co., at Los Angeles died recently.

Arthur D. Saul, 72, president of Avery and Saul Co., Cambridge, Mass., died recently at Arlington, Mass.

Frank M. Nyiro, 37, a salesman for Republic Steel Corp., Chicago, was killed in a traffic accident recently.

Preston L. Kelsey, 47, sales executive of the Norge Division, Borge-Warner Corp., Chicago, died recently.

Hubert C. Reynolds, engineer attached to the executive staff of Chrysler Corp., died recently in Detroit.

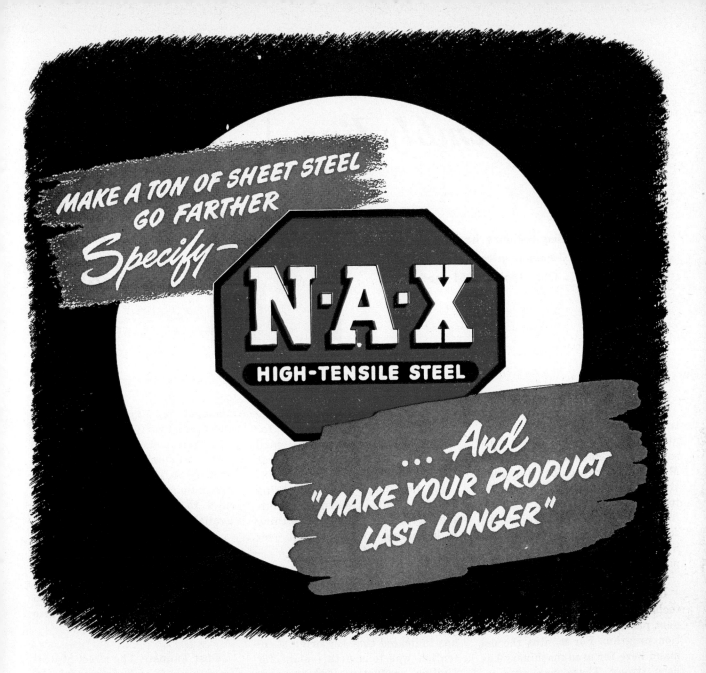

MAKE A TON OF SHEET STEEL GO FARTHER Specify—

N·A·X HIGH-TENSILE STEEL

...And "MAKE YOUR PRODUCT LAST LONGER"

Now, more than ever before, America must make full use of its steel-making capacity and conserve its natural resources. Now, more than ever, there is national significance in the phrases, *"Make a ton of sheet steel go farther"* and *"Make your product last longer."*

These low-alloy, high-tensile steels do "make a ton of sheet steel go farther"—for their inherently higher strength is 50% greater than mild carbon steel. That means, in turn, that 25% less section can be used with safety, and where rigidity is important, this can usually be compensated for through slight design change.

"Make your product last longer" is no idle claim. The much greater resistance of N·A·X HIGH-TENSILE to corrosion, abrasion, and fatigue assures longer lasting products even at reduced thickness.

Explore the potential economies to be derived from the use of low-alloy, high-strength steels— and then specify them. Their use can add materially to our national conservation program.

GREAT LAKES STEEL CORPORATION
N-A-X Alloy Division, Ecorse, Detroit 29, Michigan

NATIONAL STEEL CORPORATION

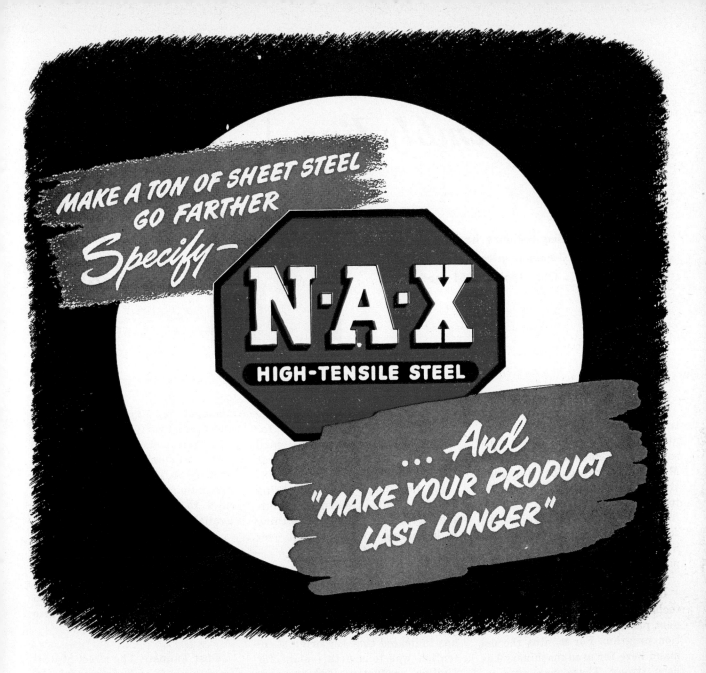

on the assembly line

Special machine builders barraged by orders . . . Gemmer introduces power steering . . . Olds shows 1951 models.

by Walter G. Patton

Million Dollar Backlogs — Detroit's already crowded special machine builders are being barraged with new defense orders. Million dollar backlogs for relatively small builders of special tools are common. One firm has indicated the percentage of defense orders on its order board has jumped from 1 to 30 pct in the past few weeks.

Burden on Used—Used machine tools are expected to play a prominent part in Detroit's war production program. For months the demand here for used machinery has been strong. There was some tapering off locally—but not nationally—during the final 2 months of 1950. Since the turn of the year, business has been brisk.

Many used machines are bringing prices higher than the original selling price. There are also reports that several used machinery dealers are trying to lease their equipment rather than sell the machine outright. There was some leasing of equipment here during World War II.

Skilled Help Scarce — Despite threatened layoffs in auto plants, highly skilled help is very difficult to find in Detroit. Skilled tool makers are in great demand. There have been recent reports of raid-

ing of high grade engineering talent. Some of the demands for engineers originate with small concerns setting up to take on war business. Detroit's population of small tool shops and engineering firms multiplied tremendously during World War II. The same thing is beginning to happen all over again.

Speculation on Chrysler—There is still considerable speculation about the new Chrysler engine plant at Trenton, Mich. Chrysler has indicated that the original intention was to use this plant for civilian production. Latest guess is that the company had in mind a new plant to build marine, truck and industrial engines.

The Little Luxuries—Radios and heaters are among the list of auto accessories that are expected to become short. Most car accessories are expected eventually to be listed as non-essential. Meanwhile, car dealers are expected to husband carefully their supplies of rear seat radio speakers, antennas, spot lights, fog lights, rear view mirrors, electric clocks, windshield visors and other accessories.

Types of War Work—As pointed out by Arnold Lenz, new general

manager of Pontiac, recently, there are two types of war work. The first consists of items like small ammunition, all kinds of shells, small rockets and cartridge cases. Such items can be tooled up in 4 to 8 months, depending on availability of machines.

The second class of items includes guns, tanks, planes, engines of both reciprocating and jet types. These latter items may require from 8 months to more than a year for tooling and they also take up a lot of floor space.

Dust Tunnel—The effect of dust on engine life and engine performance is being studied at Dexter, Mich., in a new dust tunnel and air laboratory built by Fram Corp., Providence, R. I.

This is the first tunnel designed and equipped especially to determine the effect of dust on motor vehicles. Dust conditions of a city street or the Sahara Desert can be duplicated in a matter of minutes. Effect of dust on engine wear and the effectiveness of filtering devices can be accurately judged.

Constant Analysis—In a separate building Fram engineers have established an air cleaner laboratory. Here, carburetors, air filters and oil filters are tested.

During the tests, air is injected

assembly line

Continued

into the tunnel's air stream which is constantly checked and analyzed for dust content. Weather and temperature conditions can be varied at will. Length of the test depends on the test car and the degree of protection provided for the engine. Tests are terminated when high blow-by, low oil pressure, audible knocks or loss of power indicate mechanical failure.

The new Fram facilities at Dexter are available for use by engineers and research men throughout the industry.

Power Steering—Many automotive executives regard power steering as the next major engineering advance. This week Gemmer Mfg. Co., Detroit, introduced the first power steering for passenger cars. (Power steering has been used for heavy duty and "off-the-road" vehicles for several years in its development phases.)

The new device will be available on 1951 Chrysler models. Other passenger car makers are also expected to offer power steering as soon as the new devices are available in quantity. In addition to Chrysler, Gemmer supplies Ford, Hudson, Kaiser-Frazer, Lincoln, Packard and Nash.

Increase Gear Ratios—With the advent of low-pressure tires gear ratios had to be increased. Responsiveness to steering was reduced correspondingly. Power steering makes possible the use of a 16 to 1 ratio. Most cars have about 26 to 1 ratio.

Gemmer's new "Hydraguide" quickens the response of the wheel in the driver's hands. Approximately 40 pct less steering wheel movement is needed. About 75 to 80 pct less physical effort is required to turn the wheel. Power control is instantaneous. The wheel straightens automatically after making a turn. When the engine is not running, the car steers like a conventional car al-

though with greater physical effort.

Power Through Pistons—In the Gemmer design, power is applied through two pistons, operating in hydraulic cylinders placed on either side of an auxiliary power arm. This power arm is attached to the shaft between the roller gear and Pitman arm. The piston heads are connected by a yoke. A hardened roller on needle bearings permits accurate movement of the power arm. Steering action occurs only when pressure is applied to this roller *and only on one side at a time.*

Oldsmobile Features—Improved engine efficiency, new springing that eliminates the dip on fast starts, new decorative treatment, a redesigned frame and an improved "hot operating" type of muffler have been incorporated in the new 1951 Oldsmobile.

Compression ratio of the Series 88 and 98 models has been raised

to 7½ to 1. The increase has been made possible by redesigning the combustion chamber. A new carburetor, distributor, air cleaner and water-proof sleeves on the spark plugs result in improved engine performance.

More Leg Room—The new Olds leaf-type rear springs are 58 in. long and 2½ in. wide. Leg room has been increased in the rear seat by 2½ in. The cross-member of the frame is I-beam type instead of channel steel construction. The new Olds Hydra-Matic transmission permits rocking of the car out of ice, snow or mud, thus eliminating one advantage often claimed for a torque converter type transmission.

The use of standard gasoline at 7½ to 1 compression ratio has been made possible by redesigning the combustion chamber. Flame travel is shorter. A more effective "quench area" above the pistons is provided. Better gasoline and air mixtures are available.

THE BULL OF THE WOODS   By J. R. Williams

THE LOOKOUTER

15 blast furnaces in the U.S. have each produced over 1,000,000 tons of iron on a single "National" carbon lining ... and are still going strong!

NUTS TO THIS 'NATIONAL' CARBON... NOTHING I DO SEEMS TO HURT IT!

HY HEET

BLAST FURNACE LININGS • BRICK • CINDER NOTCH LINERS • CINDER NOTCH PLUGS • SKIMMER BLOCKS • SPLASH PLATES • RUNOUT TROUGH LINERS • MOLD PLUGS • TANK HEATERS

west coast progress report

digest of far west industrial activity

by R.T.Reinhardt

Utah Steel Production Up—Steel production in Utah during 1950 was far ahead of 1949, according to the University of Utah.

Ingot production was 1,400,000 tons, up 42 pct from 1949. Pig iron production was 1,215,000 tons, an increase of 32 pct; and coke production was 1,206,700 tons, an increase of 20 pct. Coal production was 6,300,000 tons, an increase of 7.4 pct.

Copper and gold production showed a large increase over 1949 but lead, zinc and silver were down.

Strip Mill Announced—Seidelhuber Iron and Bronze Works of Seattle, Wash., plans an electric furnace and small strip mill, possibly with a maximum width of 12-in.

A $1 million corporation has been formed by Frank Seidelhuber, Jr., vice-president of the parent company.

Good 6-Months Report—Kaiser Steel Corp.'s first earning report since it sold $125 million worth of securities and paid off its RFC loan indicates that for the 6 months ended Dec. 31, 1950, net income after Federal taxes was $4,322,792.00, equivalent to $1.23 per common share, after payment of preferred dividends for November and December.

Net sales were $47,177,365.00 and miscellaneous income was $1,-642,710.00. Profit for the 6 month period before taxes amounted to $7,879,854.00 and income taxes totaled $3,557,062.00.

Kaiser Aluminum & Chemical Corp. is negotiating for private financing involving $115 million to pay off indebtedness to the government and expand production facilities, probably in Texas.

More Gas for Utah—Salt Lake City industrialists hope a new natural gas field, on which Utah Natural Gas Co. has applied for a $32 million loan to build a pipe line in Salt Lake City, will solve their fuel problems.

The field is located in southeastern Utah where the first well is producing 1,500,000 cu ft daily.

Another potential source of gas is New Mexico provided the Utah Pipe Line Co. is granted permission by the Federal Power Commission to build a 392 mile long pipe line.

Power Hungry Northwest — A $26 million hydro-electric dam on the Lewis River in southwestern Washington is planned by the Pacific Power & Light Co. which would add 100,000 kw to the system by the end of 1952.

Columbia Shows Signs of Life—Rumors grew that Columbia Steel's President Alden G. Roach would, before long have an important an-

nouncement regarding the partially-occupied Los Angeles works of Columbia. The plant was operated during World War II by Alcoa.

Rheem Into Aircraft — Rheem Mfg. Co. has formed an aircraft division headed by Laurence H. Cooper, formerly with Pacific Airmotive Corp. and has contracted for a building with 200,000 sq ft on 50 acres of land at Southgate, near Los Angeles. During the last war Rheem did considerable contract work for many southern California air frame manufacturers.

Hand Tool Pinch—Users of hand tools in the metalworking industries in the West are finding that their suppliers of eastern made tools are quoting as much as 5 months on deliveries.

Principal bind seems to be on those tools utilizing both iron and steel castings, few of which are made on the West Coast. Western hand tool producers are making prompt deliveries as in the past and apparently have been unaffected thus far by material shortages.

Wrenches and other tools in which a number of alloys are used are particularly tight. Even DO orders issued by the Armed Services here in the West on eastern manufacturers are being filled 4 months after placement and another 30 days in transit.

Cut Production Costs

LATROBE
DESEGATIZED BRAND
HIGH SPEED STEELS
HI CARBON – HI CHROME DIE STEELS

* FULL UNIFORMITY

* QUALITY CONTROL

CAREFUL SELECTION OF RAW MATERIALS

CONSISTENT MELTING PROCESSES

ACCURATE FINISHING STANDARDS

RIGID INSPECTION PRACTICES

Latrobe's Desegatized Brand high speed steels and hi carbon - hi chrome die steels will help you cut production costs. Rigorous quality control - from material selection through product inspection - plus the full uniformity found in all Desegatized Brand steels assures better tool and die performance and longer production life.

In Desegatized Brand steels, the all-important carbide particles are evenly distributed throughout the entire cross section - NO HARMFUL CARBIDE SEGREGATES ARE PRESENT! This results in extra toughness and strength . . . cracks, checks and warpage in heat treatment are radically minimized . . . superior machining and grinding abilities result.

Specify Latrobe's Desegatized Brand tool and die steels for better performance and resulting lower production costs.

Send for booklet "WHY DESE-GATIZED" showing superiority of Desegatized Brand steels over average standard process steels.

WHY ? DESEGATIZED

LATROBE ELECTRIC STEEL COMPANY
LATROBE, PENNSYLVANIA

Branch Offices and Warehouses located in: DETROIT, TOLEDO, DAYTON, PITTSBURGH, LOS ANGELES, PHILA-DELPHIA, CHICAGO, CLEVELAND, NEW YORK, BOSTON, SEATTLE, MILWAUKEE, HARTFORD, ST. LOUIS, BUFFALO.

Sales Agents: DALLAS, HOUSTON, WICHITA, DENVER, BIRMINGHAM.

the federal view

this week in washington

by Eugene J. Hardy

Steel Balks at CMP — For the first time since the government began carving up the steel pie, the National Production Authority and the steel industry have differed widely. Here's the story: NPA, as is well known, hopes to institute a Controlled Materials Plan by mid-year. In addition, an order limiting the amount of steel that can be used by major civilian consumers, notably the auto industry, is in the works.

Last week, the Steel Products Advisory Committee went on record as opposing both CMP and cutbacks in specific uses of steel. It said, in formal resolutions, that no cutbacks should be made without prior consultation with the committee as to the uses of the steel that would be freed under such orders. Generally, the committee felt that existing procedures DO orders and allocation programs will provide adequate steel for defense and essential civilian needs.

Harrison's Decision — The decision to invoke CMP and percentage cutbacks was made by Defense Production Administrator W. H. Harrison. Chances are that he will go right ahead with these plans. In any case, there is no thought of imposing anything like WPB Order M-216 which prohibited the use of iron and steel in about 1200 items.

Wage Disputes Agency — A behind-the-scenes yak session concerns the advisability of making the Wage Stabilization Board the disputes-settling body for defense industries. Labor would welcome such a set-up and industry doesn't like it. Industry wants WSB to continue as a policy-setting body, for if it gets into disputes it is felt that every wage controversy will go immediately to WSB as the agency that can change policy.

Mark-Up Formula — Planning at the Office of Price Stabilization indicates that eventually practically all price control will be based on a mark-up formula permitting cost increases to be passed on to the consumer. The only exceptions would be basic raw materials which would be covered by specific dollar-and-cents ceilings. OPA got around to a similar method of control toward the end of World War II, but in a very limited way.

Basing Points Again — Interested Congressmen are still pulling for legislation denied to end the basing point controversy and affirm the legality of freight absorption and delivered prices.

A bi-partisan group of six Senators led by Sen. McCarran, D., Nev., has introduced S. 719 which would rivet into law the Supreme Court decision in the Standard Oil of Indiana case involving good faith price discrimination (THE IRON AGE, Jan. 11, p. 95). The measure would amend the Clayton Act so that it will be "a complete defense to a charge of price discrimination for the seller to show that its price differential has been made in good faith to meet the equally lower price of a competitor."

"Complete Solution" — Enactment of S. 719, says Sen. McCarran, "will end the so-called basing-point controversy." Sen. Johnson, D., Colo., another sponsor of the bill and Chairman of a committee which has blasted the Federal Trade Commission for its inaction since the President vetoed S. 1008, calls the measure a "complete solution to the freight absorption problems, for freight absorption is merely one means by which a seller reduces his price to meet price competition."

Contracts — President Truman has authorized the Defense and Commerce Depts. to negotiate contracts without asking for competitive bids. The action, taken under a recent act of Congress, authorizes the ignoring of "advertising, competitive biddings, and bid payment, performance, or other bonds or other forms of security." Cost-plus-a-percentage-of-cost contracts are not permitted.

BLUEPRINT FOR HARD WORK: This is Moisie River Canyon near Seven Islands. The point from where this picture was taken is the end of a tunnel now being bored. The railroad will follow the Moisie River up the terrain on the right side.

Personal initiative builds 360-mi railroad to Quebec-Labrador iron ore field

Seven Islands, Quebec—Personal initiative is at work with a bang here—even though the temperatures range from 5° above to 15° or 20° below zero. This will be the railroad terminal and the location of mammoth ore docks and storage for the Quebec-Labrador iron ore development (see IRON AGE, Nov. 4, 1948, p. 155).

What many called publicity just 3 years ago is

RETURN VISIT: On the left is Norman Delmage, winter boss at Burnt Creek, 320 air miles north of Seven Islands, Quebec (roughly 1100 air miles north of New York City). On the right is Tom Campbell, IRON AGE editor—writer and photographer on this story who was also there in 1948.

today a live, surging race to get ore out of upper Quebec and Labrador by spring 1954. Preliminary construction of the railroad has started; full scale work will begin this spring.

The ore is needed. The five American steel companies (see IRON AGE, Oct. 19, 1950, p. 93) which are part of the Iron Ore Co. of Canada are banking on getting the material as soon as possible.

Newcomers wag their heads over the difficulties to be faced in building the 360 mile railroad from here to Knob Lake. But those who have been here a couple of months say "Sure it's tough, but we will do it, and ahead of time."

Excuses don't count up here. Nobody wastes time telling why things can't be done; they use that time to find ways of doing things. There is a minimum of fanfare and a maximum of self reliance. Rules there are, but they aren't needed too much—there is not much else to do in waking hours except work.

On the following pages is a pictorial report made by the writer at Seven Islands and at Knob Lake and Burnt Creek 320 miles to the north on Jan. 9, 10, 11 and 12.

Fast Work: This temporary dock at Seven Islands was built in record time. Between early October and early December last year the dock had been completed and about $8 million worth of equipment and material unloaded before the freeze-up. Track was laid from yards to dock so equipment could be unloaded onto flat cars from small boats on the side runways to the dock and from big boats at the end of the dock.

Waiting for Work: Dump trucks, regular trucks, big trucks, little trucks and snowmobiles have all been moved in for one of the biggest railroad construction jobs in recent history. Here are a few pieces of the equipment. The weird-looking cars in the middle are snowmobiles with treads in the back and skiis in the front for steering. They make about 25 to 30 miles an hour over the snow no matter what the depth. They can haul about 12 people.

Sleeping Giants: These shovels, Caterpillars and other machines were shipped in before the freeze-up on the St. Lawrence River. Canadian and American firms did a wonderful job in getting equipment together in a couple of months time. Many of these shovels will be knocked down and flown 85 miles north from Seven Islands to Waguna, a base construction camp. About 100 miles of the road will be completed this year.

On Top of the Job: That fellow on top is both happy and anxious. He is Fred Bolton of Armco Drainage & Metal Products of Canada. He is happy about the stockpile of culvert pipe for the big railroad job and anxious to get more that will be needed. Since Fred is an ingenious, friendly and hardworking guy the project will get what it needs. Fred is taking a picture of an Armco steel building being erected a few feet away. This job is his pet.

Genial Brass: Here are the two big fellows on the 360 mile railroad project. Do they look worried? To the left is Hector MacNeil, chief engineer, Quebec North Shore & Labrador R.R. Formerly a Canadian National R.R. chief he knows his stuff. To the right is Karl Collet, supreme representative of contractors, Cartier, Mannix and Morris-Knudson. He knows his way around. These men will take the raps and the praise. There will be lots of both.

Give and Take: There have been and will be many of these chatty and informal meetings before the railroad is finished. To extreme left is Karl Collett, contractor boss, and to extreme right is Jack Little, field boss on the ore project. They are knee deep in a serious discussion—lumber to build camp after camp for engineers and workmen. Meetings like these between ore company men and contractors' people are setting records in fellowship.

A Big Morale Builder: In bush, mining, railroad, construction and lumber camps food has to be good. But the cook is the one who has to be almost perfect. Food—lots of it and properly prepared—is put down as 50 pct of the morale building in any camp. On the right with the dough on his hands is Joe Davis, cook at Seven Islands airport-base for field and engineer corps. Those things in the pan on the stove are light fluffy donuts.

Blast Away: The rock floor where these men are standing has been partly drilled and dynamite placed in holes. About 8 ft will be blasted off the hillside. A tunnel will be driven through the mountain in the background. The foreground will be approach to 700 ft bridge across the Moisie River shown on the first page of this story. This bridge—150 ft above the river—will eliminate five tunnels in original plans. It's cold, but work goes on.

Pile Driving at 16 Below: On Jan. 10 these fellows were hard at work repairing the end of the temporary dock at Seven Islands. It took a lot of beating from boats, ice and waves. Permanent ore docks will be farther up the St. Lawrence River. Shipping will be open for ore boats 9½ to 10 months a year. In emergencies the season could be 12 months but ice breakers might be needed at times. By 1954 heat may be used to thaw ore.

Winter Scene: Here is the base camp for the iron ore project. Burnt Creek is the name. The Knob Lake airport is about 12 miles from the camp. About all that is being done now at Burnt Creek is repairing and maintenance of equipment. Only access is by plane. Buildings are log cabins and quonset huts. When mining starts in 1954 the season will be at least 5½ months a year. Some feel a longer mining season is possible, if necessary.

No Shutdown: This is part of the maintenance and repair shop at Burnt Creek. Drills, trucks, jeeps, snowmobiles and everything else is worked on here. When this picture was taken on Jan. 10 the temperature was about 26° below zero outside. A maintenance force of about 20 men is here throughout the winter. The lowest temperature in December was 42° below zero, the highest 39° above and the mean 0°. It will be colder this month and next.

Hut Flies Everything: Hollinger Ungava Transport (HUT) planes number eight. Three are Douglas C-47's, others are Norseman and Stinson. This Doug has landed at Knob Lake air field—and Canadian weather station. To left on plane is pilot Wes MacIntosh; to right is copilot Hank Gates. These fellows have hauled everything from 75-ton shovels to big churn drills—knocked down of course. They and their buddies have a lot of work ahead of them.

Integrally-stiffened sheet can be made by rolling-in stiffening ridges as the sheet stock is processed at the mill. Such material will find many aircraft structural uses, and has potential uses in other industries. Castings, because of low strength and high weight, will find only limited use in replacing fabricated aircraft assemblies.

INTEGRALLY-STIFFENED SKIN REVOLUTIONIZES AIRCRAFT CONSTRUCTION

rolled and cast sections

SECOND OF A SERIES

One of the most promising methods of making integrally-stiffened sheet is by rolling stiffened ridges into the sheet stock as it is processed at the mill. The problem to date has been the determination of sizes, proportions, and materials which would be most satisfactory for structural applications and still be reasonable to produce by rolling. Sections suitable for rolling are illustrated in Fig. 6.

Rolled-ribbed sheet is far superior in rigidity to unstiffened sheet of the same total weight. Because of limitations of the rolling operation, however, it cannot be made to compare in efficiency with a built-up skin-and-stiffener structure. Its advantages therefore lie only in applications where adequate skin-stiffening by ordinary methods is impossible or impractical. A large portion of the exposed surface of every airplane falls in this category.

Good For Lightly Loaded Surfaces

In such places as trailing edge surfaces and control surfaces, applied loads are so light that skin gages are the minimum as determined by handling requirements, stiffeners are as close as production expense will allow, and surface roughness and "oilcanning" still remain a prob-

lem. For this purpose, the light gage section shown in Fig. 7 has been proposed.

One factor in use of this material is the expense of getting started. The procurement of rolled-ribbed sheet in a structural alloy will involve considerable initial expenditure for rolling equipment. Ribbed sheet was once rolled in production by the Aluminum Co. of America for the refrigerator trade. In this instance a soft alloy was used. The section produced is the lowermost one shown in Fig. 6.

Developmental work on the equipment and techniques of rolling ribbed-sheet stock is currently in progress at Reynolds Metals Co. under Air Force contract. Results to date have indicated that the desired shapes can be produced in any alloy, but that very heavy rolling equipment will be required to make light gage sections such as that of Fig. 7. There have been experiments with reducing the gage of rolled sections by etching.

Application of rolled-ribbed sheet to aircraft structures has been under continued investigation at Lockheed and several experimental designs have been constructed using ribbed sheet made by machining from plate.

As a result of these studies the section shown

By P. E. SANDORFF, *Research Engineer*
and GEORGE W. PAPEN, *Manager, Production Engineering Dept.*
Lockheed Aircraft Corp., *Burbank, Calif.*

FIG. 6—Samples of some integrally-stiffened sheet sections which can be produced on a rolling mill. Three of these were simulated by machining from plate. The bottom section was actually rolled. It was produced, a few years ago, for the refrigerator trade.

Integrally-stiffened skin

continued

in Fig. 7 has become standardized. The total weight of this product is the same as that of plain 0.020-in. sheet, but its rigidity is more than 20 times as great. This one section, it has been found, can be applied much like ordinary sheet stock in place of 0.016-in., 0.020-in., and 0.025-in. skin used in conventional designs, with reduction in parts, increase in rigidity, and possible weight saving.

An experimental aileron tab structure was

FIG. 7—A proposed rolled-ribbed sheet section developed by Lockheed. Its weight would be equivalent to standard sheet 0.020-in. thick, but rigidity in the direction of stiffeners would be 20 times greater.

constructed identical in function and strength to the aileron tab of the Constellation airplane. The surfaces and beam of this tab were formed in one piece from simulated rolled-ribbed sheet stock. This skin section replaced the 0.016-in. outer skin, 0.016-in. beaded inner skins, and the 0.032-in. beam web in the conventional design. Enough weight was saved here with rolled-ribbed sheet to permit use of a casting for the central actuator fitting. Thus considerable simplification was achieved, and it was estimated that even if the rolled-ribbed sheet were to be machined for production, a net saving could be achieved. Parts and cost comparison are indicated in Table I, and the structure is shown in Fig. 8.

Used For Wing Trailing Edge Structure

The trailing edge surfaces of the Constellation wing carry no wing bending loads, but only the direct air loads of low magnitude which are transferred forward immediately to the main wing structure. Consequently the aft surfaces are made as light as possible, the skin gages and stiffening being determined chiefly by handling requirements, manufacturing problems, and oilcanning tendencies.

An equivalent structure made with rolled-ribbed sheet is illustrated in Fig. 9. The excellent smoothness is evident from the photograph. Only half as many ribs were required, and the necessity for contour-formed chords was eliminated. Comparative data and cost estimates for the 60-in. section in conventional structure and as designed with rolled-ribbed skin are presented in Table I.

On lightly loaded trailing edge structure, the use of rolled-ribbed sheet with stiffening elements oriented chordwise often provides sufficient rigidity and strength so that all internal framework can be eliminated. For example, the aileron trailing edge of the Constellation airplane is constructed of 0.020-in. skin supported by many light ribs spaced 4 in. apart. An alternate design using rolled-ribbed sheet gives a

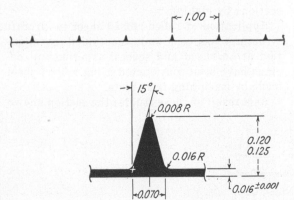

FIG. 8—The 11 parts of an aileron tab structure using ribbed sheet. Its estimated production cost, with the sheet produced by machining from heavy plate, would be $129. The same structure produced by conventional means would have 33 parts, not counting rivets, and would cost $202. If sheet with rolled-in ribs were used, the cost saving would be considerably more.

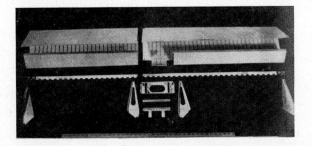

TABLE I
ROLLED-RIBBED STRUCTURES COST LESS

	Aileron Tab		Wing Aft Structure	
	Integrally Stiffened Construction	Conventional Construction	Integrally Stiffened Construction	Conventional Construction
Total weight per unit...	4.65 lb	4.80 lb	28.00 lb	28.00 lb
Total number detail Parts per airplane..	22	66	116	152
Total number different parts per airplane.........	15	48	47	61
Rivets per assembly..	220	490	1310	1380
Spotwelds per assembly.........	......	560	......	2260
Cost (based on production of 50 airplanes)				
Material.............	$25.02*	$ 4.57	$102.30*	$ 17.63
Labor..............	46.16	84.57	102.40	227.90
Tooling.............	58.05	112.85	79.60	123.10
Total Cost........	$129.23	$202.09	$284.30	$368.63

* Includes total cost machining the integrally stiffened sheet from 0.125 in. plate stock.

structure in which all ribs were eliminated and a slight weight advantage was also indicated.

Several other advantageous applications for rolled-ribbed sheet have been suggested. Some of these are: Ducts, tanks, shell structures, leading edge skins, rib webs, fairing, equipment and furnishings, instrument cases, cabinets, junction boxes, cabin partitions and doors. Many suggested uses are outside the aircraft field; for example, roofing and siding, household furnishings, containers, etc.

Conventional Sheet Metal Tools Used

No new tools or special techniques are required to use rolled-ribbed sheet. It may be treated very much like ordinary sheet stock. However, sufficient bend radius must be allowed for bends across the stiffener sections, or ribs removed in the bend area.

Rolled-ribbed stock may be cut and trimmed with conventional power shears, if the stiffeners are protected from the clamping rams by a piece of heavy sheet used as a buffer plate. The portion to be trimmed away is placed under the blade, as this becomes irregularly bent. Gentle curvatures may be handled on ordinary rolls and sharp bends may be made with the power brake using conventional punch and dies. Excellent joggles have been formed on the power brake using shims and plates.

In some cases it is desirable to remove the stiffener elements over a portion of the rolled-ribbed sheet, to permit sharp bends, such as for a tab trailing edge, or to allow attachment to a plain flange. This has been accomplished satisfactorily as a routing operation, using a flat-bottomed cutter turning at high speed, and clamping plates adjacent to the area to be worked.

Casting, both sand and permanent mold, as a production method has inherent advantages because it eliminates many operations in preparation of the material as well as in fabrication and assembly of the part. It also permits the complexity of detail which is usually necessary for high structural efficiency. That it is not used more widely is due to several disadvantages.

One big disadvantage is that strength of cast material is generally only about half as much as that for the wrought alloy. Then there are technological limitations. As the size of castings is increased, the problems of warpage, shrinkage, homogeneity and porosity become more severe. If minimum thicknesses are too large, cast structure will not be able to compete on a weight basis. It should be noted, though, that casting methods are under constant development. Recent advancements in technique make possible designs of unusual size and thickness. New alloys also may provide several advantages. There is the magnesium-cerium alloy which has exceptional properties at elevated temperatures. There is also a magnesium-zirconium alloy which needs only aging to obtain good physicals. Heat treat, with attendant warpage, is not needed.

Intake Duct Cost

Some cast surface panels have been designed in which some saving in weight and considerable saving in cost are indicated. However, attempts have been made to apply casting design in similar fashion to other surface panels in both the F-90 as well as the F-80 airplanes, but weight penalties were too great. An example of another possible type of application for casting in the intake duct shown in Fig. 10. In this instance, a weight penalty is involved but possible cost savings are so great as to make it

FIG. 9—A wing aft structure fabricated with simulated rolled-ribbed skin. A large number of complex fabricated parts can be eliminated through use of rolled-ribbed skin in this part. And cost is considerably less.

merit consideration. Casting is particularly adaptable to this structure because it permits great irregularity in the shape and location of various elements, and eliminates forming and assembly operations which in this case are unusually difficult and costly.

Stiffening By Formed Beads Has Been Used

In several airplanes, notably the Republic Seabee, the Thorpe Sky-Skooter and, to a lesser extent, the Ford Trimotor, another method of obtaining integral stiffening was used. Integral stiffening was accomplished by rows of formed beads in the external skin surfaces.

This proven method has great advantage in simplification, reduction in parts, and reduction in cost. The Seabee airframe weighed 120 lb less, used 350 less parts, and required 2300 less manhours to assemble, when simplified by use of beaded structure. And the airframe tooling cost, based on 5000 planes a year, was only $400,000 as against $1,750,000 for the conventional prototype of the plane.

Rolled-Ribbed Better than Beaded Sheet

Despite this striking comparison, there is considerable objection to the use of formed-stiffened sheet in higher speed aircraft. It is aerodynamically undesirable because the formed stiffening elements cause irregularity in the airfoil surface. Forming properties limit the depth and shape of the integral stiffening element or bead to a small value. Thus generally this type of formed-stiffened sheet does not have the rigidity that would be available in the same weight of rolled-ribbed sheet. And, the beaded sheet is inadequate for loads of any magnitude acting in the plane of the sheet transversely to the direction of the beads.

It is probable that rolled-ribbed sheet will eventually be available as a purchasable mate-

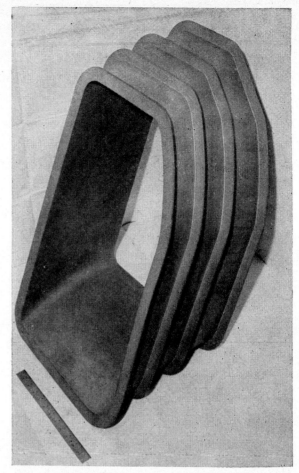

FIG. 10—A cast magnesium air intake scoop, equivalent to a multipiece assembly now in use. This casting has a wall thickness of 0.100 in. For complex structures like this, casting offers an advantage, despite the fact that cast parts will usually weigh more than their fabricated counterparts.

rial. This product will furnish all the functional advantages of formed-stiffened sheet, with few of its objectionable qualities.

This is the second in a series of four articles covering the manufacture and application of cast, extruded, forged, rolled, and machined integrally-stiffened structure.

NEW BOOKS

Inspection Organization and Methods, by J. E. Thompson, provides industrial executives and supervisors with tested methods for improving efficiency, simplifying procedures, and reducing costs in inspection departments. The procedures given may be applied regardless of the product being made or the quality level being maintained. Complete data necessary for the orderly planning, accomplishment and recording of inspection examination and testing are supplied. All modern equipment is discussed. McGraw-Hill Book Co., 330 W. 42nd St., New York 18. $5.00. 370 p.

Executive Action, by E. P. Learned, D. N. Ulrich and D. R. Booz, is addressed to business executives and to others who are interested in the practical aspects of business administration. It is a study of the problems which executives face in trying to get effective coordination at the top level as well as among the various parts of an industrial enterprise. It undertakes to state and deal with the problem of coordination in human terms, emphasizing the human factors in the background of executive action. Harvard Business School, Div. of Research, Soldiers Field, Boston 63. $3.25. 218 p.

MOLYBDENUM LUBRICANT

proves itself in tough tests

By ALFRED SONNTAG, *President*
The Alpha Corp., Greenwich, Conn.

During the past 2 years a large number of tests and practical applications have indicated that molybdenum disulfide is an exceptionally valuable addition to the small family of base lubricants. Some of its lubricity and antiseizing properties at extreme bearing pressures and at very high or very low temperatures surpass any other commercially available lubricant.

Molybdenum disulfide is a chemical combination of molybdenum and sulfur, chemically noted as MoS_2. It appears in nature as a mineral. It greatly resembles graphite in appearance and feel, but it is more than twice as heavy, having a specific gravity of approximately 5.

The chart gives typical results of a large number of press fit tests. Hardened, ground, and polished dowel pins 1.001 in. in diam were pressed into bushings hardened, ground and polished to a diameter of 1.000 in. The press fit interference of 0.001 resulted in a calculated bearing pressure of 10,000 psi. The parts were assembled in a Baldwin precision hydraulic testing machine at a uniform speed of 0.6 ipm. The chart shows the maximum force required to fully insert the pin for a variety of lubricants used on pin and bushing.

The solid black portion of the load scale in the chart represents the chatter range which may interpret the severity of localized seizure. The strange and exceptional fact that no load fluctuation was observed with silicone oil where friction reached the highest value remains to be more fully investigated. It may be assumed, however, that in this case seizure was not localized but was uniform over the entire surface, and was continuous. For white lead in oil the chatter range is indicated in dotted lines, because it was not observed on every specimen.

Chatter Distorts Parts

The worst effects of chatter during press fitting, besides the damage to surface finishes, are the dimensional distortions of the parts. Thin-walled sleeve bearings 4 in. in diam, with 3/16-in. walls, 2¾ in. long, manufactured with a required accuracy of 0.0001 in., distorted 0.0005 in. at calculated press fit pressures of only 1575 psi when chatter occurred.

On the basis of such results, a lubricating grade of molybdenum disulfide is finding in-

Molybdenum disulfide has long been known to have lubricating properties. But only during the last 2 years has it been available, free of abrasive impurities, for commercial use. Test and application data now accumulating show this lubricant has great value for high-temperature, high-pressure use, for breaking in machine bearings, and other rough duty.

creasing commercial applications for the press fitting of sleeve and antifriction bearings and many other parts. Corrosion problems make colloidal graphite in water, and lard, which were next in line of performance in the above tests, less desirable.

MoS_2 mixed into a paste consistency with solvents or with lubricating oils having a viscosity of SAE 10 or lighter compare favorably with the dry powder application in the press fit test. However, a large number of test mixtures with heavier oils and greases were tested with less satisfactory results. This can be seen in the values for MoS_2—grease SG, in the chart.

According to a widely accepted theory, the molecular structure of MoS_2 is of the laminar or sandwich type, composed of a layer of molybdenum atoms with a layer of sulfur atoms on each side. The sulfur atom layer has an affinity for metal surfaces and adheres strongly to them upon contact. The bond between two adjacent sulfur atom layers is weak and they slip easily upon one another. This theory accounts for the tenacity of adherence as well as the lubricity

SUPERIOR LUBRICITY of molybdenum disulfide is demonstrated by this table of test results. Data were obtained by measuring load required to force a 1.001-in. pin into a 1.000-in. bushing, making a 10,000 psi bearing pressure, as shown in cross-section at top right. Black areas represent load range in which chatter was observed. The area shaded for white lead in oil represents range in which chatter was observed in some, but not all, tests. Inset shows, exaggerated, how MoS_2 particles are scraped off pin when mixing with grease destroys adherence by coating particles.

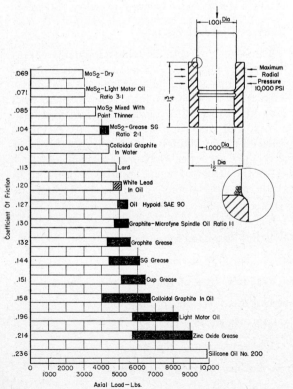

of MoS_2. With reference to adherence, it should be noted that repeated and severe scrubbing with solvents will not remove all of the MoS_2. How much is removed in this manner has not been determined, but friction tests show that a sufficient deposit remains to lubricate, and a mild abrasive operation is required to remove all traces. Because the sulfur in MoS_2 is chemically combined, it does not exhibit the chemical reaction with metals that free sulfur does.

Ordinary mixtures of the heavier oils and greases seem to coat the MoS_2 particles, thereby destroying their affinity for attachment. In the inset in the chart, an enlarged cross-section of the bushing corner is shown. The elastic deformation of the pin and the sizes of coated MoS_2 particles are highly exaggerated. Oil or grease film coated MoS_2 particles are mostly retained at the entrance.

For Lifetime Lubrication

For a variety of other applications, however, mixtures of MoS_2, even with heavy oils and greases, have been highly successful. In one particular problem of gear lubrication a single coating of a mixture consisting by weight of one part of MoS_2 and 1½ parts of a medium heavy oil served as a long-sought-for lifetime lubricant. In such cases, mechanical action crushes through the oil or grease film, and the affinity of the MoS_2 for attachment is restored.

There will be uses in the low and high temperature field. MoS_2 appears to be unaffected by low temperatures, and while it oxidizes at elevated temperatures, the rate of oxidation in air doesn't assume practical proportions below 750°F. And in the absence of air it is usable to at least 1000°F. Other types of lubricants now available for low or high temperatures are limited to relatively low bearing pressures.

When a lubricating grade of MoS_2 was first made available to industry, a large number of different applications now being made were never suspected. This was mainly because it was thought that aside from the metal forming field, bearing pressures as extreme as those in heavy press fits were rare. But experience has shown that actual bearing pressures in moving parts are nearly always underestimated and the need for extreme bearing pressure lubricants exist where often not suspected.

By way of example, a check was made on wear test specimens which had been ground with more than usual commercial care and accuracy. One is shown in the accompanying photograph. It was found that less than 10 pct of the total area made metal-to-metal contact in the beginning of a run. Another investigator, using electrical methods for measuring actual metal contact areas of commercially ground surfaces, found only about 5 pct.

MoS_2 is being used now successfully in the machine tool industry for breaking-in. In some

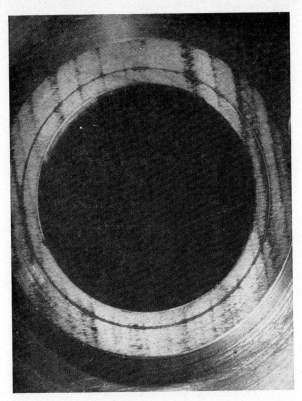

CALCULATIONS of bearing area usually assume that the entire area shares the load. But this is not true during breaking-in, as this wear test ring shows. Dark areas, only about 10 pct of total area, show where wear occurred. Thus during breaking-in, lubricant was subjected to much higher than calculated bearing pressures.

cases the powder is rubbed into the bearing surfaces, serving as an undercoat for conventional lubrication, and thereby protecting high spots against galling and seizing. In other uses it is applied in paste form, mixed in varying percentages with oils and greases. For breaking-in heavy pinion assemblies, mixtures of 2 pct MoS_2 with grease have proved successful with gears reported running cool for the entire break-in period of 9 hr, whereas without the addition of MoS_2, excessive heat required disassembly and scraping every 2 hr.

Cuts Torque on Threads

The use of MoS_2 on threads for low, room and elevated temperatures is increasing. To reach a tension of 4000 lb, which amounts to 13,000 psi in a ¾-10 threaded assembly, 70 pct less torque was required, when a mixture of MoS_2 and light oil was used on threads and under the washer of the nut, compared with zinc oxide, white lead and graphite grease.

A series of tests on threaded connections lubricated with MoS_2 and exposed to temperatures of 800°F for prolonged periods showed that the break-away torque was 10 pct less than the makeup torque, leaving clean and undamaged threads. Reports that MoS_2 prevents the freezing of threaded connections after being subjected to temperatures up to 1100°F, are quite frequent.

In the field of stainless steel lubrication, the reception of MoS_2 has been good, especially for thread lubrication and in general for mating stainless steel parts. It has been used with good results for very severe stainless steel drawing and cold forming operations.

Others report that if occasionally applied to precision drawing dies, MoS_2 preserves the finish and reduces the frequency of expensive polishing with diamond compounds. In other cases expensive hand finishing of dies was dispensed with because the picking-up of metal at high spots in the dies was eliminated by occasional applications of MoS_2.

A method of applying a bonded coating of MoS_2 was developed some years ago by T. E. Norman. It consists of mixing equal parts by weight of MoS_2 with corn syrup, the latter serving as an organic binder, and painting this mixture on a metal surface which must be heated to at least 650°F. This forms a thin and tenacious coating approximately 0.0002 in. thick, bonded to the metal.

The Cleveland Laboratories of the NACA have reported on experiments with such coatings and found them to be very effective in reducing friction at high sliding velocities and very extreme contact pressures, and for reducing fretting corrosion. While MoS_2 by itself appears to have no anti-corrosion properties, Norman-processed samples have shown considerable corrosion resistance in salt spray tests.

Grease Film Type Developed

The advantages of such coatings for practical applications, less severe than the ones on which the NACA tests were based, remains to be investigated. The NACA bonded coatings were limited to steel surfaces, but the same method has been used experimentally on stainless steel, aluminum, brass, and copper, and by appearance an equally good coating was obtained.

In another series of NACA tests at extreme bearing pressures and sliding velocities, comparatively low friction coefficients and wear rates were obtained with hot pressed bearing material compositions of silver, copper and MoS_2, the best being 85 pct silver, 5 pct copper and 10 pct MoS_2.

While there are a large number of applications where the dry film application is preferable, grease film stores more MoS_2, adds protection against corrosion, serves better to transfer or spread frictional heat, and is easier to apply.

After several years of development work with hundreds of compounds, a mixture of grease consistency was finally developed and will soon be available for extreme bearing pressures.

Plating
improved WITH

Greater plating speed and brighter deposits can be attained through use of a recently-introduced electroplating innovation. Although the principles of periodic reverse current plating, as the process is called, have been known for almost 40 years, it was only in recent times that the technique has gained commercial acceptance. Several patents have been issued on the process, the most recent of which are the Jernstedt patents No. 2,451,340 and 2,451,341, issued Oct. 12, 1948.

Briefly stated, the process combines plating and electrolytic polishing in the same operation; it permits the use of much higher current densities than can possibly be used with ordinary direct current plating. When the current is reversed, some of the deposit is redissolved. If the conditions of chemical balance, current density, and timing are correct, the reverse current acts as a smoothing agent by removing many surface imperfections. Pits are bridged over, burrs are rounded, and scratches are smoothed. In addition, edges do not build up as badly with periodic reverse as they do when ordinary plating methods are employed. Among the many advantages of periodic reverse plating is the fact that it permits the use of higher currents, thereby increasing the rate of deposi-

tion. Brightness is improved, and the method produces smooth deposits of close-grain structure up to a thickness of 3/16 in. Porosity is reduced, and the deposit is distributed with greater uniformity.

Plating and reversal currents with a plating time of 7.5 sec. and reversal time of 2.5 sec. are shown in Fig. 1. The curve is theoretical and does not show the loss of time required to accomplish switching by various contacting or generator field switching devices. This time loss, however, is very slight and for all practical purposes, negligible.

Improves Corrosion Resistance

The immediate question which arises is the apparent loss of plating efficiency: the plating cycle is not only interrupted during the reversal of current, but a substantial quantity of deposit is also redissolved, by deplating. The deposition therefore cannot possibly follow Faraday's Law, which states that 1 g equivalent of metal is deposited when 96,500 Coulombs of electricity is passed through a solution—assuming a current efficiency of 100 pct. Nevertheless, the loss of current efficiency due to the current reversal is more than compensated for by the reductions in time and in polishing costs. Also,

By G. W. SLOMIN
Technical Director
Hollywood Bronze Supply
Hollywood, Calif.

REVERSE CURRENT TECHNIQUES

Periodic reverse current plating makes possible greater plating speed and smoother, finer-grained deposits. The process combines plating and electrolytic polishing in one operation, the current reversal reducing surface imperfections and holding edge buildup to a minimum. Brightness is also improved.

since pin holes and porosity are reduced to a minimum, greater corrosion resistance is possible.

A number of devices are available for producing periodic reverse current; these are generally divided into three classes. The first class embraces chronometrically-driven devices such as is shown in Fig. 2, which energize relays or other contacting devices to accomplish reversal. The total cycle is fixed from 10 to 15 sec, and only the reverse cycle is adjustable.

The second class is the electronic timing devices. These units employ two separate electron tube timing circuits so that both the plating and reverse cycles can be adjusted. The tubes are usually of the thyratron gas-filled type having very sharp cut-off current characteristics. Timing is accomplished by having a predetermined grid bias and then charging a condenser through a variable resistance. When the condenser is fully charged, it causes the tube to fire (conduct), acting as a short circuit across the condenser. The discharged condenser then starts recharging, and the cycle is thereby repeated. In order to vary the timing cycle, it is only necessary to vary the resistance; this increases or decreases the charging rate on the condenser. The two thyratron circuits are connected to small relays; these operate the master relay, which performs the actual reversing operation.

Timing devices which reverse the polarity in generator fields comprise the third class, and may be of the chronometric or electronic type. However, the relay need not be as large as those used for direct high current reversal, where the current source is a rectifier. This latter type should therefore be much more economical, since high amperage relays and magnetic contactors are rather expensive.

Has Broad Range of Uses

Cyanide-type plating solutions have been found the most suitable for periodic reverse plating. The method is used extensively for silver, copper, gold, brass, cadmium, zinc and tin plating. It can be used for any type of plating where the conditions of the solution and metal being plated permit a complete electrochemical reaction reversal. Such solutions as chromium and rhodium, which are plated from insoluble anodes, naturally are not suitable for periodic reverse plating. There is no reason, however, why the use of periodic reverse plating should be restricted to the cyanide group, since excellent results have been ob-

FIG. 1—Schematic diagram showing plating and reversal currents, with a plating time of 7.5 sec and reversal time of 2.5 sec. The curve is theoretical.

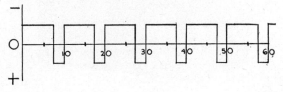

tained with copper fluoborate, copper sulfate, and many other types of acid solutions.

No positive statement can be made about timing. Cycles which are suitable for one type of solution and article are not suitable for others. A total cycle of from 10 to 15 sec and a reverse cycle of from ½ sec to as much as 5 sec can be used. Some timers are made with two cycle adjustments from 0 to 20 sec each, giving the user a wide choice of ranges.

The demand for electroplating on aluminum has been increasing, especially since it is now possible to plate the difficult No. 13 high-silicon diecasting alloy. A patent recently applied for by the author describes a process for preparing this material for plating—U. S. Patent Application No. 166,839, Docket No. 9222. In addition to being somewhat porous, this alloy is also very susceptible to corrosion. The periodic reverse current method is recommended for the purpose of sealing the pores and making the copper and nickel deposits impervious. Since the difference in potential between the base metal (aluminum) and the plated coating in the presence of moisture is tremendous, even the tiniest pin hole will cause a rapid breakdown. For this reason, any plated coating intended to protect aluminum must be substantially free from pin holes.

Smoother, More Uniform Plate

One of the most recent applications of periodic reverse current technique is for silver and copper plating on printed electronic circuits. These circuits are used in hearing aids, front-end tuners on television sets, and in radar and radio circuits in guided missiles for military use.

The plating in these circuits must be of very uniform cross section and of considerable thickness. If plastic material is used as a base or chassis, an electrically conductive coating is

FIG. 2—Chronometric type laboratory model Ramyr periodic reverse current unit on which only the reverse cycle is adjustable.

printed directly on the plastic which binds itself firmly to the base material. Resistors, condensers, and inductances are then ingeniously printed (plated) into the circuit in steps. If glass is used, a silver mirror is deposited directly on the glass by chemical reduction. To plate these circuits by conventional methods would require from 2 to 2.5 times the time required with periodic reverse plating. Also, the quality of the periodic reverse plated surface is superior both in smoothness and in uniformity.

Plates Radar Wave Guides

Another application used by a large aircraft manufacturer doing considerable electronic research work, is periodic reverse plating of wave guides for radar. These wave guides are made of aluminum and are first given a pretreatment. This makes it possible to plate on a thin film of copper, over which silver is plated to a thickness of about 0.001 to 0.0012 in. This is done in a special bath containing brighteners and considerably more silver than standard formulas call for.

After the silver is deposited, it emerges from the bath with a bright satin finish unlike the dull gray or yellowish nonmetallic-appearing finish produced by ordinary dc plating methods. However, silver tarnishes rapidly, so a flash or light plate of indium is applied. The indium may be diffused into the surface of silver by heating, thus protecting the silver from tarnishing. Other aluminum parts so plated and intended for electrical work may be stored for considerable lengths of time. They can be easily soldered, without the use of acid fluxes which, because of their corrosive effect, cannot be used in electronic work.

Permits High Current Density

Many other useful applications will no doubt be found for periodic reverse plating. Much research work remains to be done in developing suitable brighteners, surface tension depressants and plating solution formulas which will lend themselves readily to the alternate oxidation and reduction reactions which take place. In connection with alkaline solutions, much progress has already been made, as for example the remarkable success obtained with modified bright high-speed copper solutions.

Considerable improvement is still desirable for using this type of plating in acid solutions, especially the acid fluoborates. Copper fluoborate shows considerable promise in this respect, since it is a high-speed process even without periodic reverse, capable of plating 1.5 to 2.0 times faster than copper sulfate—sulfuric acid solutions. When periodic reverse is applied to a copper fluoborate solution, extremely high current densities can be used with no apparent effect on the smoothness or other qualities of the deposit.

40-ton ram truck

INCREASES YIELD AND PRODUCTION

THIS IS the world's largest ram truck, which has made it possible to increase the weight of strip coils produced by Bethlehem Steel Corp., at Lackawanna, N. Y.

THE TAPERED, cast steel ram may be used for one big coil or split to handle several smaller ones. Dual controls permit the truck to be operated from either side of the cab.

A 165-HP diesel-electric unit powers the articulated wheels and driving mechanism of this new Yale & Towne ram truck.

With a capacity only two tons less than its 42-ton weight, the new, and world's largest, ram truck is already at work in the Lackawanna, N. Y., plant of Bethlehem Steel Corp. The truck is one of a new series being designed and manufactured by Yale and Towne Mfg. Co., Philadelphia, to meet the steel industry's need for equipment able to match the mile-a-minute pace of modern continuous strip mills.

The 15-ft high monster has made it possible to increase the size of coils produced in the Lackawanna mill from 40,000 to 60,000 lb, and this figure could be upped to 80,000 lb if necessary. The two new ram trucks now in service at the Bethlehem plant are handling strip 72 in. wide by 65 in. OD, 24 in. ID.

The new equipment's greater capacity is important, because until now it has been possible to roll strip faster than the mill could be fed or its products carried away. As much as 17 pct of the rolling time of a typical fast strip mill has been consumed by handling. Doubling the size of the coils produced increases yield as well as overall output. Ends of coils rolled while the mill is accelerating and decelerating are off-gage and must be rejected.

Trucks Will Work On Rough Floors

Plants having uneven floor surfaces will find the new truck able to retain equal wheel loading despite bumps and depressions. Both its front drive wheels and trailing wheels, which do the steering, are fully articulated. Safe, low-pressure hydraulic systems power both the fingertip-controlled steering mechanism and lifting equipment. The truck can be turned around in a 14-ft aisle.

Yale and Towne's new ram truck obtains its power supply from a 165-hp diesel-electric unit, of the same size used in a 25-ton locomotive. Dual controls make it possible to operate the unit from either side of the cab.

One big strip coil can be handled by the new ram truck's tapered cast steel ram or it can be split in two to take several smaller ones. Each half of the ram can be operated independently.

By DR. ROLAND B. SNOW

U. S. Steel Co. Research Laboratory

Kearny, N. J.

TEMPERATURES

of openhearth bottoms measured

Part II: As a result of precise temperature measurements and core drilling of openhearth bottoms, better design, materials and methods are now possible. A type of hearth construction as a result of this project is suggested.

Temperature measurements in rammed portions of openhearth bottoms show not only the depth of ceramic set and possible strain present, but they also clearly depict the thermal gradients present. Some of these data were presented in Part I of this article. Other information contained here will help in designing better bottom construction.

Thermal gradients, mostly near tap time, in two hearths are given in Fig. 6. They show that after steelmaking has started, the subsurface layers are relatively cool; the gradient is extremely steep adjacent to the surface in Hearth A, Fig. 2, but the gradient in the remainder of this hearth is nearly parallel to the gradient found in Hearth C. Fig. 4. These gradients are not for steady-state heat flow, but for the high points in a cyclic variation in the inner layers. The displacement of the curves undoubtedly results from the hearth thickness and thickness of the insulation used. Thus the relief of the strain set up in the surface layer due to thermal contraction between the tapping of a heat and the charging of the next is confined to the hearth

layer immediately below the surface. Since the temperature change may be as much as 2000°F, cracks may be present in each hearth after charging and in some cases a slab may split off parallel to the surface.

The displacement of the temperature peaks at a level some 8 in. below the surface by some 3 to 5 hr after a heat was tapped illustrates the slow passage of heat through a hearth. If a surface layer has shelled off because of the thermal contraction during charging, this defect may not heal until after liquid metal is present on the surface. If the defect is beneath a large mass of lime, then, owing to the violent agitation, the entire surface layer may come loose and expose a cold surface to the action of steel, though the boiling action usually continues and it is difficult to determine whether boiling is from charged lime or action on the hearth. This type of bottom defect may be caused in part by strains set up during charging combined with the relatively low temperature which is present in the subsurface layers. This steep temperature gradient near the surface permits heats to be successfully worked on an essentially steel bottom covered by a few inches of dolomite providing they are kept on the cold side until near the end of the processing cycle.

Thermal Expansion Allowed For

A temperature of approximately 1800°F is reached at a level of 15 in. below the surface after steelmaking starts in relatively thick hearths, regardless of the hearth composition. In thinner, uninsulated hearths the temperature may be of the same order of magnitude only 8 in. below the surface while the temperature 12 in. below the surface may be of the order of 1300°F.

An expansion allowance for 3000°F must be provided for brickwork which is to serve as the base for a magnesite-slag surface but after steel

FIG. 6—Temperature gradients through rammed openhearth bottoms.

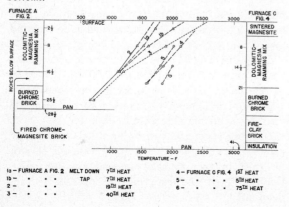

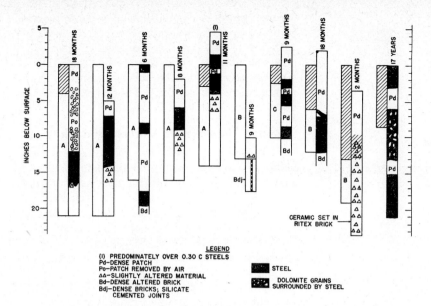

FIG. 7—Sketches showing original composition of different openhearth furnace bottoms and corresponding drill cores after limited service.

LEGEND

(I) PREDOMINATELY OVER 0.30 C STEELS
Pd—DENSE PATCH
Po—PATCH REMOVED BY AIR
△△—SLIGHTLY ALTERED MATERIAL
Bd—DENSE ALTERED BRICK
Bdj—DENSE BRICKS; SILICATE CEMENTED JOINTS

■ STEEL

▨ DOLOMITE GRAINS SURROUNDED BY STEEL

production is started the normal temperature is only 1300°F (15 in. below the surface). Since the expansion allowance has been made only to provide for thermal expansion, then upon cooling 1200°F the brick work will contract and voids will be present between the brick. This is especially true when magnesite brick, which have a high coefficient of expansion, are used.

One of the advantages of a rammed hearth would seem to lie in the fact that allowances for expansion in the brickwork need be made for only 2000°F and a tight brick subhearth should result during normal operations. If deep holes occur in in the hearth they will be of local nature and the compression of the brick owing to thermal expansion should aid in preventing steel from penetrating the joints. The weight of the metal bath has always been assumed to be sufficient to prevent the heaving of brickwork in the bottom.

Working Surface 10 in. Below Blueprint Level

No advantage has been shown by any one type of construction over the others as judged from drill core data as shown in Figs. 7 and 8. These data suggest that the working surface may often be as low as 10 in. below blueprint level when a hearth has been used chiefly to make steels under 0.20 pct C. The record lost time obtained on a new hearth is achieved by not replacing the original hearth material which is worn away through the action of the steel and slag. After the hearth becomes so low that maintenance material is added to the flat, the delay time increases and usually approaches the shop average three to six months after it has been installed. All types of bottom material have been eroded to about the same extent and for this reason we are skeptical of new products offered for use in our furnaces.

In Fig. 9 a suggested construction for a 41-in. deep hearth, based on these temperature measurements, as well as drill core data, is given. This hearth should be brought up to temperature in a manner governed only by the requirements for proper heating of a new silica roof and after reaching temperature, 5 in. of double-burned dolomite is to be burned on within 10 hr. The furnace should be held at temperature for only 1 hr or so and then slagged to seal the pores. The hearth should be given a 30-min chill to harden the hearth before the first heat is charged.

Fast Burning-in Recommended

This rapid burning-in schedule is suggested because no unfavorable results were noted after using this type of schedule, however, the type of bonds in one of the nearly pure magnesia ramming mixes may not be adaptable to this type of schedule. Drill cores failed to show any undue erosion in this type of hearth as compared to other furnaces which had been given much more extended heating and holding periods.

Drill cores have shown repeatedly that double-burned dolomite has sintered to a porous mass and during the succeeding heats owing to insufficient initial slagging, the voids between the grains were filled with steel. A good slag wash should aid in eliminating the pores near the surface of such a sintered mass. Another advantage of this sintered dolomite surface is its apparent ability to resist cracking during chilling. Cracks usually develop on all other preparations almost immediately after the flame has been shut off, but a sintered dolomite layer does not usually show cracks until a temperature of 2000°F is reached.

The rammed layer will prevent the brickwork from becoming too hot during the burning-in period when an expansion allowance for 2000°F is used. However, the 10-in. rammed layer and

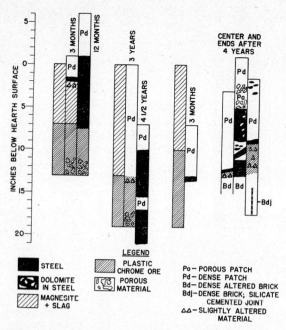

FIG. 8—Sketches showing original composition of open-hearth furnace bottoms with plastic chrome ore subhearths and corresponding drill cores.

Legend

- **STEEL**
- **DOLOMITE IN STEEL**
- **MAGNESITE + SLAG**
- **PLASTIC CHROME ORE**
- **POROUS MATERIAL**
- Po — POROUS PATCH
- Pd — DENSE PATCH
- Bd — DENSE ALTERED BRICK
- Bdj — DENSE BRICK; SILICATE CEMENTED JOINT
- △△ — SLIGHTLY ALTERED MATERIAL

the 9-in. underlying brick layer make potentially a 19-in. monolithic subhearth. The liquids from a rammed layer of magnesia base mix with high silicate content will drain downward to cement the rammed layer to the magnesite brick as well as seal the brick joints and the pores in the brick. Drill cores from one hearth of this type showed a segment where the rammed layer was ceramically bonded to the underlying unfired magnesia-chrome brick, Fig. 7. This ceramic bond extended throughout the upper 4½ in. thickness of the brick as well as between the brick.

Dense Brick Prevents Penetration

Dense magnesite brick should be used because one hearth was observed where steel had penetrated to the magnesite brick and a ⅛-in. thick fin of steel had penetrated 3 in. of the 9 in. soldier course. The brick adjacent to the metal was dense while that portion below the metal had the porosity of the normal magnesite brick. The use of a more dense brick should have minimized possible shrinkage of the brick while proper expansion allowances would also have been an aid in preventing steel from entering the brick work. The use of two 4½-in. rowlock courses would not seem to provide as great a protection against floating out of brick as does the 9-in. soldier course.

Chrome brick is suggested below the magnesite brick because of the tendency for magnesite brick to slate after standing for long periods of time. Several instances occurred in which silicate liquids coming from the overlying magnesite base materials had filled the voids as well as the brick joints to produce a monolithic mass of well sintered dense chrome particles during service.

The banks should be covered by a 1 to 2-in.

layer of sintered dolomite prior to charging and in order to save furnace time the banks must be installed so that they have an angle of about 45° with the flat. If banks are steeper than this, a sintered layer cannot be burned-in with a minimum of time nor can the banks be dressed before or after the first heat is tapped.

Cheaper Than Plastic Chrome Hearth

This hearth should be less costly from several points of view than one prepared using a plastic chrome ore subhearth, although the core drilling (Fig. 8) shows this latter type of construction to have an excellent record in thinner hearths and it has stood up as well as other materials in thicker furnace bottoms. Drill cores taken 3 months after start of steelmaking showed that the upper 4 in. of a 6-in. thick layer was dense and that the entire layer was chemically intact. In addition, 4 in. of the original magnesite was still in place and chemically unaltered. After an additional 9 months of operation, this furnace was found to be giving considerable delays but upon core drilling a thick steel layer was found to overlie the subhearth material which was intact and chemically unaltered.

In a thicker type of hearth after 3 years of service, the upper 1 in. of the original material was slightly altered but only 4 in. of the 6-in. layer had been matured during the burning-in process. However, upon redrilling the hearth 1½ years later, this entire layer was missing although the underlying chrome brick had become ceramically bonded to form a dense mass.

Acknowledgment

The author wishes to thank J. W. Bain, Dr. R. B. Sosman and John Topping for their work and help on this project.

References

1 R. B. Sosman, "Temperatures in Openhearth Furnaces," T.P. 2435. AIME Metals Technology, 15, 1948.

2 Alwin F. Frantz, "Furnace Bottom Temperature Gradients," AIME Openhearth Proceedings, 1938, p. 17.

FIG. 9—Recommended construction for openhearth bottoms.

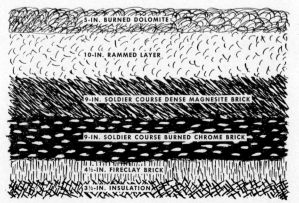

5-IN. BURNED DOLOMITE

10-IN. RAMMED LAYER

9-IN. SOLDIER COURSE DENSE MAGNESITE BRICK

9-IN. SOLDIER COURSE BURNED CHROME BRICK

4½-IN. FIRECLAY BRICK

3½-IN. INSULATION

news of industry

Taconite is Steel Industry's Ace-in-the-Hole

Once a stepchild, abundant low-grade taconite is subject of serious study . . . Two major projects under way on Mesabi . . . Beneficiation success means steel security—By Bill Lloyd.

Steel Scrap Rollback

New York—Based on a delivered Pittsburgh key price of $44 a ton for No. 1 heavy melting steel, new ceilings were placed on iron and steel scrap by the Office of Price Stabilization effective Feb. 7.

In commenting on the order, OPS Director Michael V. DiSalle said that although the regulation fixes prices at generally prevailing December levels, the month "is not being used as a base period necessarily reflecting general stability" and prices will be re-examined later. (For complete order and reaction of trade story see p. 136.)

Ceilings of the order are in force regardless "of any contract or other obligation" existing on the effective date of the regulation.

Electromet Buys Tungsten Ores

Pine Creek, Calif.—Purchase of low grade tungsten ores and concentrates will be made by Electro Metallurgical Div. of Union Carbide & Carbon Corp., according to H. L. McKinley, general superintendent, Pine Creek mine and mill.

Navy Planes Planned at Lustron

Washington — Government-owned facilities at Columbus, Ohio, scene of the ill-fated Lustron housing activities, will be turned over to the Navy Dept. on orders from the Defense Production Administration.

The plant will be used for manufacture of aircraft as soon as facilities can be installed, probably by mid-summer.

Cleveland — Steel industry expansion to over 120 million annual tons by the end of 1952 (THE IRON AGE, Feb. 1, 1951, p. 121) can put a crippling strain on once-vast Lake Superior iron ore deposits and make American steelmaking vulnerable to war-cut supply routes and international misunderstandings that may result from heavy dependence on foreign iron ore.

Major Mesabi Projects

This underlines the importance of beneficiation of low-grade taconite ores as a means of preserving Lake Superior fields and providing a security supplement for foreign ore. The holdback now is perfection of methods to make beneficiation more feasible.

Two major projects for beneficiation of magnetic taconite are now under way on the Mesabi Range: Erie Mining Co., managed by Pickands, Mather & Co. for Bethlehem Steel and Youngstown Sheet & Tube; and the Reserve Mining Co., managed by Oglebay, Norton & Co. for Republic Steel, Armco Steel, and National Steel Corp.

Eugene Grace, Bethlehem president, said that Erie Mining may build a beneficiation plant at Aurora, Minn., to produce 2.5 million annual tons of usable ores. Hopes for this plant are based on encouraging progress with ores in the Northwest and Bethlehem experience in Cornwall, Pa., mines, where ores have been concentrated and pelletizing and sinter-

ing operations held. Erie Mining has for 2 years operated a pilot plant at Aurora.

National Steel recently acquired a 15 pct interest in Reserve Mining which controls iron ore deposits containing 1.5 billion tons of taconite at the eastern end of the Mesabi Range in Minnesota. A yield of 500 million tons of 60 pct iron ore pellets is expected. Reserve plans to install equipment to produce 300,000 tons of pellets a year.

After completion of the smaller plant, Reserve intends to build a one-unit plant to produce 2.5 million tons of pellets a year, docks and harbor at Beaver Bay, Lake Superior, two mining towns, and a 47-mile railroad, to cost about $60 million. Eventual construction of a plant with a 10 million ton capacity and a total investment of about $160 million is also planned.

Site of Future Facilities

U. S. Steel Corp. now has a washing and sintering plant at Virginia, Minn., using sub-marginal ore, 40 to 45 pct Fe, for a 60 pct Fe product. This plant may be the core of future taconite beneficiation.

Taconite experts hope some day to be able to beneficiate both magnetic and non-magnetic taconite. Magnetic taconite, which has the greater part of its iron oxide as magnetite, is so called because magnetic separation can be used on it. This method cannot be used yet with hematite or other types

INDUSTRIAL SHORTS

DOUBLES CAPACITY — Plans for a 100 pct expansion of facilities of the Aeroproducts Div. of GENERAL MOTORS CORP., Dayton, Ohio, are completed. The construction of a new building at the rear of the present structure, will double the present manufacturing area, affording a total of over 500,000 sq ft of manufacturing, laboratory testing and office area.

CHAIRMAN SEATED—A. vanderZee, vice-president, Chrysler Corp., has been elected chairman of the sales managers committee of the AUTOMOBILE MANUFACTURERS ASSN., Detroit. Mr. vanderZee succeeds Wiliam F. Hufstader, vice-president in charge of distribution, General Motors Corp.

ELECTIONS — Eight warehouses joined the AMERICAN STEEL WAREHOUSE ASSN.: Bushnell Steel Products, Inc., Hialeah, Fla.; Cold Metal Products Co. of California, Los Angeles; W. L. Coston & Sons, Birmingham; August Feine & Sons Co., Inc., Buffalo; General Steel Co., Fort Worth, Tex.; Great Western Steel Co., Chicago; Murray-Baker-Frederick, Inc., New Orleans, and Precision Steel Warehouse, Inc., Chicago.

SIGNED AND SEALED — The Titanium Alloy Mfg. Div. of NATIONAL LEAD CO. has contracted for the purchase of the assets of the Hi-Alloy Castings and Tri-State Foundry Co. of Elwood City, Pa. The additional electric furnace capacity and ample power facilities of this plant is expected to augment present production of the Niagara Works of the division in Niagara Falls.

NEW SALES REP.—Rigidized Metals Corp. have acquired three new sales representatives; RUBERT J. WAGNER, Los Angeles; the DISQUE STEEL PRODUCTS CO., Indianapolis, and the ALDER STEEL PRODUCTS CO., Minneapolis.

BUSINESS IS GOOD — The H. K. FERGUSON CO., New York, industrial engineers and builders, entered 1951 with a backlog more than 50 pct greater than the previous year. The management disclosed that 1950 was the third best year in the company's 32-year history from a sales standpoint and that new business in 1950 tripled the volume of 1949.

DIVIDE DIVISION — The expansion of the Ingersoll Steel Div. has prompted BORG-WARNER CORP. to divide the division. The New Castle plant continues the name of Ingersoll Steel Div., while the Chicago and Kalamazoo plants are now known as the Ingersoll Products Div.

SELLS OUT—Purchase by the OHIO ELECTRIC MFG. CO., Cleveland, of all tools, patents and rights to manufacture the Taylor & Fenn line of drilling machines has been completed. The Taylor & Fenn Co. was established in 1846 and is one of the country's pioneer machine tool builders.

MORE POWER — The BALDWIN - LIMA - HAMILTON CORP., Philadelphia, has completed arrangements with the Electric Light & Power Plant of Weatherly, Pa., for the delivery of a 1000 kw diesel engine generating unit to supplement the present steam power because of increasing industrial needs.

SIX NEW GENERATORS — STONE & WEBSTER ENGINEERING CO., Boston, has been contracted by the Chelan County Public Utility, Washington district, to construct a $26,000,000 power facilities plant at Rock Island Dam on the Columbia river. An agreement between the Puget Sound Power & Light Co. and the Public Utility district was reached to add 135,000 kw with six new generators.

of taconite because the iron minerals are non-magnetic.

The big problem in beneficiation is agglomeration. Taconite can be broken down with crushers and ball mills, and the iron taken out with separators. But pelletizing is harder than was supposed.

Flotation Method

Experts believe that with low-cost natural gas for heat, non-magnetic taconite can be made susceptible to magnetic treatment by conversion of its oxides to magnetite. The cost factor is big.

Several companies have been using flotation which would have priority over roasting because of lower cost. Some figure that six or seven times as many workers will be needed to produce one carload of taconite concentrate to a carload of open pit free shipping ore. Offsetting factors are taconite's abundance and low tax rate.

Plant capacity costs have been estimated at from $15 to $20 an annual ton, depending on what dock and rail facilities are required. Costs would decline later. It is believed that foreign ores can compete with taconite as far West as Pittsburgh. By a rough rule, taconite concentrate costs about three times as much as open pit ore and one-third more than underground. The only fair comparison, though, is by an iron unit basis.

Backed By Cash

Recently, E. W. Davis, director of the Mines Experiment Station, University of Minnesota, published a figure of $9.24 as a total cost of a ton of taconite pellets delivered to lower lake ports. Lake Erie price 64 pct Fe dry, 62.5 pct Fe natural x $0.15243 (the unit price) yields $9.53, indicating a profit of .29 cents per gross ton.

The steel industry's conviction that taconite beneficiation must work is being backed with cash.

Start Joint Aircraft Agency

Washington — The Munitions Board has established an Aircraft Production Resources Agency at Wright-Patterson Air Forces

Base, Dayton, Ohio. The new agency will act as a joint Army-Navy-Air Force organization for the military services and the aircraft industry.

Acting in the place of the former Aircraft Scheduling Unit of the Munitions Board, the agency will expand former duties and consolidate requirements for materials and other resources needed in the combined military aircraft and associated programs.

NPA May Allocate Moly Soon To Fight Cutting Tool Pile-Up

Washington—An allocation system for molybdenum, similar to that for tungsten, was a definite probability this week.

Major reason is order backlogs for tool and other high-speed steels are piling up and manufacturers are in the middle. Tungsten suppliers have been ordered to cut deliveries to 20 pct of requirements (M-33) while molybdenum inventories have been cut to 20 days and shipments to 50 pct of requirements.

Manufacturers of cutting tools tell NPA orders for both defense and supporting programs have jumped. For instance, tool steel requirements for hack saw blades and metal cutting band saws have increased by a third, largely in sizes not normally required.

Representatives of these industries have requested NPA to permit them to increase inventories from the 45-day to a 90-day limit. They estimate requirements for 1951 will be about 8000 tons.

Forge-Tapered Wing Spars

Pittsburgh—Successful experimental fabrication of forge-tapered aluminum wing spars was announced by the McDonnel Aircraft Corp. and Aluminum Co. of America. The new method provides a bulb of aluminum in the web of what otherwise is an I-beam type of extrusion. The extrusion is then forged so that the bulb is progressively flattened and the web tapers from 10 in. at one end to about 15½ in. at the other.

Powder Metallurgy May Offset Metals Cuts

Auto appliance cutbacks may make available powder metallurgy capacity . . . Powder metal parts eliminates much-machining, can free machines for defense work—By Walter Patton.

Detroit — Many metalworking firms caught by recent restrictions placed on copper, tin, aluminum and other strategic materials may find powdered metal parts an answer to their production problems.

For the next few months, cutbacks in auto and appliance production are expected to make available a substantial amount of capacity in the fast-growing powder metallurgy industry.

Product Range Broadens

Industry sources report that for the present at least the supply of iron powder will meet anticipated demands of industry. However, if present experimental work results in adoption of iron powder rotating bands for shells capacity will have to be greatly expanded.

Since the end of World War II, the powder metal industry has made tremendous forward strides, and the number of products produced from metal powders has broadened. Whereas most products made with this method 5 years ago weighed only a few ounces, parts weighing 5 lb or more are now being made. Dimensional obstacles have also been removed. Parts 18 in. in diameter have been formed successfully.

Another advantage of specifying powder metal is the elimination of a large volume of machining. Redesigning of intricate machine parts for powdered metal production often eliminates broaching, milling, drilling, facing or other operations, thereby freeing a considerable amount of machine capacity for defense purposes.

Big backlogs reported by machine tool producers may also turn many production engineers

Steel Company Earnings—1950 and 1949

Company	Fourth Quarter '50	Fourth Quarter '49	1950 12 Months	1949 12 Months
U. S. Steel	$36,516,115	$32,735,397	$215,337,655	$165,908,829
Bethlehem Steel Corp.	32,171,657	16,385,137	122,976,071	99,283,539
Republic Steel Corp.	7,410,093	10,794,449	63,794,711	46,142,323
Jones & Laughlin Steel Corp.	13,263,000	922,000	39,744,000[2]	22,248,000
Youngstown Sheet & Tube Co.	11,394,492	3,219,020	40,616,403	31,777,010
Armco Steel Corp.	8,256,886	7,325,371	46,000,000	30,018,415
Inland Steel Corp.	5,930,414	1,171,070	38,015,676	25,013,707
Sharon Steel Corp.	....	....	9,284,643	3,325,964
Wheeling Steel Corp.	4,646,050	371,968[5]	18,314,517	7,896,265
Colorado Fuel & Iron Corp.	2,032,721	823,004[5]	4,578,332[1]	[1]591,828
Alan Wood Steel Co.	928,362	420,668	2,546,902	2,255,840
Thomas Steel Co.	....	....	929,945[4]	1,135,070
Kaiser Steel Corp.	....	....	4,322,792[3]	
Keystone Steel & Wire Co.	2,300,123	2,141,051	3,138,188[1]	[1]3,557,248
Granite City Steel Co.	5,727,405	....	5,727,405	2,958,108
Pittsburgh Steel Co.	....	....	7,000,000[6]	844,810

(1) 6 months
(2) Preliminary
(3) Includes $852,000 non-recurring net profit
(4) 9 months
(5) net loss
(6) Tentative

in the direction of powder metallurgy, the trade believes.

Other Advantages Seen

For example: A product badly needed for defense was recently placed in production in 6 weeks using powder metal. Estimates placed the waiting period for new broaching equipment at 18 months.

Metallurgists point out the advantages of using powder metals are not confined to greater freedom of design, a wider choice of materials and elimination of machining operations. Other potential advantages include: (1) Quieter operation in service, particularly in the case of gears, pump parts and business machines; (2) Savings in assembly cost; (3) Reduced overall cost and (4) Greater production per sq ft of floor space.

Steel Importers Seek Price Freeze Relief

Try to drive out foreign steel hustlers . . . Meet in Washington this week . . . New Institute claims established importers were frozen at low voluntary price control period.

New York—Established steel importers are trying to drive out the hustlers who smelled a gold rush in foreign steel and jumped into the business with little knowledge but with an ambition to profit. They met in Washington this week with Economic Stabilization Agency officials to convince them to work some relief into the price freeze law so that the importers can stay in business.

The importers claimed that they were playing it above the table and in complying with a voluntary price freeze request 2 months ago held back markups. Thus the freeze caught them with their prices at a patriotic minimum while the speculators were playing the sky's the limit and can now continue operations with nearly the same profit margin.

Backs Against the Wall

Under the newly-formed American Institute of Imported Steel, 115 Broadway, New York City, steel importers charged that they faced ruin because the steel they could order now would have to be delivered months later at prices much above those of their low base period. Meanwhile, the hustlers could afford to pay high prices and could throw out a dragnet for nearly all foreign steel business.

The established firms, who claim that they do 95 pct of the importing in normal times, will then sit impotently on the sidelines—unable to buy because their dollars are tied by the freeze. Inflation would also be furthered because while most of the steel was being sold by established importers before, it may now get into less scrupulous hands. Result would be a great deal more foreign steel going at higher prices.

The steel import hustlers are a product of the steel shortage and high civilian demand. Smaller manufacturers had a willing ear for the traveling salesman of some line unrelated to steel who happened to discover a steel mill in Belgium or some other place that could ship so many tons of cold-rolled sheets. The prices of course were "understandably" terrific but the manufacturer was faced with balking on contracts and cutting down production.

With Little Knowledge

Some of these speculators knew absolutely nothing about steel and when they caught something they thought good, they started quick research to find out just what kind of steel it was. Others acted as contact men, investing little or no money. They merely found a firm that needed steel and guaranteed purchase, risking nothing except their consciences.

President of the new Institute is Nicholas Schilling, Amerlux Steel Products Corp. Vice-presidents are: L. J. Falling, Ovington Steel, Inc., and Henry Hack, Industrial Sales Corp.

Seek Pool Orders for Tools

Washington—The National Production Authority is stepping up its preparations for issuing pool orders for machine tools.

Probably the first segment of the industry to be affected will be the makers of vertical and hori-

COLD WEATHER INSURANCE: When cold winds blew and the supply of natural gas was curtailed, U. S. Steel Corp. switched its openhearth furnaces to fuel oil with the aid of this 4 million gal storage tank recently completed at the Duquesne Works. Furnaces are equipped for emergency conversion to oil.

zontal boring machines as well as the planer type milling machines. This was evident last week after a meeting of officials of the boring machine industry with NPA officials.

Industry representatives said that they are now already booked far ahead for some types of boring machines. In addition, they are having trouble getting materials such as castings of machine tool grade and manpower problems are beginning to be felt.

In view of increased demands expected as industry expands to meet defense production needs, pool orders are seen as helping the machine tool industry make advance scheduling. Spokesmen also indicated that they may ask for certificates of necessity (for fast tax write-offs) for their own expansion plans.

Tinless Cans Stitch in Time for NPA Cuts

Canco discloses tin-saving methods with tinless cans and new soldering methods . . . May take the edge off 20 pct tin cut . . . Tin free solders and plastic cement used.

New York—American Can Co.'s "Operation Survival" has unearthed means to slash tin use in metal containers with development of tinless cans and new seam-soldering methods. The news comes as a stitch in time following NPA's recent 20 pct cut in civilian tin use.

W. C. Stolk, executive vice-president, said that Canco's project, seeking American independence from foreign sources of can making materials, will soften the impact of tin restrictions on can making, customer industries, and consumers. The effects of the cuts will be as serious as the in-industry's capacity to produce tin-less cans, he continued.

Breakdown of Methods

Progress of "Operation Survival" was listed as follows:

(1) Cans have been made of tinmill blackplate and low tin-bearing solder at speeds comparable to tinplate can output.

(2) Cans have also been made with tin-free solders which may be turned to universal use.

(3) Tinless cans have been made with a special plastic cement for side seams instead of solder. These cans are now being tested by several packers of oil and anti-freeze.

The NPA tin order assured adequate supplies for perishable foods containers but put many commercial products on the tinless black iron can basis. Canco's **new processes** will have the most immediate application to these. A stumbling step before had been in soldering side seams on tinless cans but now Canco seems to have overcome the obstacle.

Organic Coatings Goal

"Operation Survival" has another goal, that of discovering organic plate coatings from materials available on this continent. Canco has put a corps of scientists

"It's right there in the bottom bin, Al."

on the project to work full time in conjunction with over 20 firms who are possible suppliers of substitute numerous can making materials.

"An Irreducible Minimum"

Mr. Stolk also said that the can industry has under its own "austerity" program cut tin usage down to the bone. In 1941, it used 41,000 gross tons of tin to make 25 billion cans and in 1950 used only 31,000 tons to make 33 billion cans. Thus the industry is faced with paring away 20 pct of tin supplies from "an irreducible minimum." Without the advent of tinless can on a commercial basis this feat would probably be impossible.

Revise Building Estimate for '51

New York—F. W. Dodge Corp. has revised upward previous estimates of 1951 construction volume and nature. Dodge now expects a total decline of 18 pct rather than 19 pct from 1950 volume and anticipates that limitations on commercial building will be offset by increases in manufacturing plant, power plant, direct military and civil defense construction projects.

Build Big Ford Ore Carrier

Detroit — A 647-ft ore carrier, the William C. Ford, will be built by Great Lakes Engineering Works for Ford Motor Co. The 19,000 ton vessel will be powered by a 7000 hp oil-fired turbine. Construction of three other ore carriers and a large ice-breaker for use in Mackinac Straits has also been announced.

Men for Fairless Works

Pittsburgh—U. S. Steel's Fairless Works now has top bracket operating personnel. They are Albert J. Berdis, general superintendent of the proposed plant; Henry E. Warren, Jr., assistant general superintendent; and Forest J. Smith, assistant to the general superintendent.

CONTROLS *digest*

For more details see "You and Government Controls," The Iron Age, Jan. 4, 1951, p. 365. For full text of NPA regulations write U. S. Dept. of Commerce, Division of Printing Service, Room 6225 Commerce Bldg., Washington 25, D. C.

Subject	Order	Effective Date
General		
Inventory Control	NPA Reg. 1	Sept. 18
	Interpretation 1, 2, 3,	Nov. 10
Priorities System	NPA Reg. 2	Oct. 3
DO Rating	Amend. 1	Oct. 3
DO Rating	Amend. 2	Dec. 29
DO Ratings	Delegation 1, 2, 3, 4	Nov. 1, 2, 3
Priorities (Canada)	NPA Reg. 3	Nov. 8
Hoarding	NPA Notice 1	Dec. 27
Auto Prices, Wages	ESA Reg. 1	Dec. 18
Ceiling Price Regulation	CPR 1	Jan. 26
Military supplies	Supplement 1	Feb. 1
Wage Increases	CPR 2	Feb. 9
Coal Prices	CPR 3	
Metals		
Aluminum distribution	NPA M 5	Oct. 27
Aluminum cutback	NPA M 7 (amended)	Feb. 1
	Direction 1	Nov. 28
	Direction 2	Dec. 16
	Direction 3	Dec. 27
Aluminum scrap	NPA M 22	Mar. 1
Cadmium	NPA M 19	Jan. 1
Cobalt stocks	NPA M 10 (amended)	Dec. 30
Collapsible tubes	NPA M 27	Jan. 27
Columbium steels	NPA M 3	Oct. 19
Copper distribution	NPA M 11	Nov. 29
Copper use	NPA M 12 (amended)	Dec. 30
Copper readjustment	M-12 Direction 1	Feb. 1
Copper scrap	NPA M 16 (amended)	Jan. 1
Molybdenum cutback	NPA M 33 (amended)	Feb. 2
Nickel cutback	NPA M 14 (amended)	Jan. 23
Ores, metals	NPA Del. 5	Dec. 18
Steel	NPA M 1 (amended)	Jan. 22
Freight car program	Supl. 1	Oct. 26
Great Lakes ships	Supl. 2	Nov. 15
Canadian freight cars	Supl. 3	Dec. 15
Steel scrap	NPA M 20 (amended)	Jan. 29
Steel warehouses	NPA M 6 (amended)	Nov. 15
Tin inventories	NPA M 8	Jan. 9
Tinplate, terneplate	NPA M 24	Jan. 27
Metal cans	NPA M 25	Jan. 27
Tinplate closures	NPA M 27	Jan. 27
Tungsten	NPA M 30	Jan. 22
Zinc distribution	NPA M 9	Nov. 16
Zinc cutback	NPA M 15	Jan. 15
Miscellaneous		
Chemicals	NPA M 32	Jan. 23
Construction	NPA M 4	Oct. 27
	Amend. 1	Oct. 13
	Amend. 2	Nov. 15
Elec. components	NPA M 17	Oct. 18
Iron, Steel Scrap Prices	OPS	Feb. 7

Controls This Week

NPA Orders

M-5, Aluminum distribution Amendment—Establishes new limits on DO orders for producers and fabricators based on average monthly shipments during first 8 months of 1950. Effective Feb. 1.

M-7, Aluminum cutback, as amended—Further curtails the use of aluminum in consumer goods. Effective Feb. 1.

M-12, Copper use, Direction 1—Permits readjustment of base period where operations were shut down 15 days or more during first half of 1950.

M-16, Copper scrap, as amended—Foundries and other producers are permitted to melt and process copper scrap generated in their own plants. Effective Jan. 31.

Wage and Price Orders

CPR-1—General price freeze. Effective Jan. 26.

CPR-1, Supplement 1—Exempts certain strategic supplies and services from the general price freeze. Effective Feb. 1.

CPR-2, Wages—Permits 15-day catch period for wage increases agreed upon before Jan. 25.

CPR-3, Coal prices—Permits adjustments in coal prices to coal wage increases.

CPR-... Iron and steel scrap price schedule, effective Feb. 7. Puts ceilings on scrap prices.

English Tractor Output Up

London—Farm tractor production last year was 53,000 units, of which 20,000 went to domestic users. Home buying rose during 1950 after a slow start.

Exempt Many Military Items From Price Freeze Restrictions

Much materiel and services are included . . . In effect until Apr. 1.

Washington — Supplementary CPR 1, exempting all commodities and services peculiar to military needs from the general freeze imposed by CPR 1, was signed late last week by Price Director DiSalle. It remains in effect until Apr. 1 to provide time to study whether the items exempted should be more limited in scope.

In effect, it exempts most commodities (and their components, but not the raw materials therefore) sold to a defense agency or defense contractor for strictly military use.

The list includes: aircraft, ammunition, artillery, weapons, gas masks, mines and mine sweeping equipment, rockets, small arms, ships, torpedoes, grenades, parachutes and similar items.

Services Included

Nor do the ceiling prices apply to a broad list of services. These include repairs and maintenance of vessels, stevedoring, servicing and maintenance of aircraft, construction services, and research.

It exempts emergency sales and services to defense agencies provided a report of such sale is filed with the director of price stabilization giving details of the transaction.

Reason for the exemptions is that specifications and production plans for such goods are subject to frequent change. Since most of them are peculiar to the military, defense agencies are seen as best controlling prices, in addition, most contracts are subject to renegotiation to eliminate excess profits.

J&L's Dupka Named ESA Consultant

Washington—Walter H. Dupka, vice-president and a director of the Jones & Laughlin Steel Corp., has been named an iron and steel consultant to the Economic Stabilization Agency.

Aluminum Cutback Extended; Defense Orders Get Bigger Share

Take 45 pct of primary production . . . Cut use in 200 consumer items.

Washington — Amendments to NPA orders M-5 and M-7, issued last week, require producers and fabricators of aluminum to take larger percentages of rated orders and prohibits use of aluminum for manufacture of more than 200 end items.

Establish Limit

Effective immediately, under the amended M-5, the ceilings on DO orders for producers and fabricators are now as follows, based on average monthly shipments during the first 8 months of 1950:

Sheet (coiled and flat), plate, circle and blanks, 40 pct; extrusions and tubing, 45 pct; rolled shapes, 30 pct; rod, bar, wire and cable, 35 pct; forgings and pressings, 60 pct; secondary ingots, 45 pct, and all other mill products, each 40 pct.

However, producers of primary and secondary aluminum are not required to take rated orders in any one month totaling more than 45 pct of scheduled primary production for that month. Nor must fabricators take more rated orders than 45 pct of their average shipments for the first 8 months of 1950.

The 60-day lead time remains unchanged, and there has been no increase in the 25 pct ceiling on rated orders for jobbers and distributors.

Effective Apr. 1, Amend 2 to M-7 prohibits the use of aluminum in the manufacture of more than 200 end items specified in List A. Items started before Mar. 31 must be completed before May 31. Effective June 1, use of aluminum for decorative or ornamental purpose is banned.

Included in List A are the following items which may not be made after Apr. 1:

Residential type roofing and siding, automobile hardware, wire fencing, metal lath, store fronts, domestic laundry accessories, fur-

PIDGEON HOLE PARKING: A new parking system developed by Pidgeon-Hole Parking, Inc., and installed at Spokane, Wash., will use large tonnages of structural steel. A mobile hydraulic elevator picks up the car, travels along a 19½ ft corridor, deposits the car in the right place, and returns. Operation takes from 45 to 60 seconds. Fifty-five units with capacity of more than 80,000 cars are scheduled for installation in Los Angeles County.

niture and furniture hardware, varied types of foil, storm windows and venetian blinds, wheelbarrows, flag and tent poles, screening (except insect), garden tools, and many other items.

Granite Steel Buys Koppers Plant

Granite City, Ill. — The Missouri-Illinois pig iron and coke plant of Koppers Co., Inc., has been purchased by Granite City Steel Co. Adjacent to the Granite Steel works, the property includes: one 600-ton and one 500-ton blast furnace, a 49-oven coke battery, and related equipment for pig iron production.

John N. Marshall, Granite president, assured St. Louis area foundries and fabricators that the sale of pig iron will continue.

Copper Scrap Order M-16 Eased

Washington — Under an amendment to the copper alloy order (M-16), miscellaneous producers such as foundries are now permitted to melt and process copper scrap generated in their own plants.

The amended NPA order also permits them to accept from dealers the types of scrap named in the order for melting and processing, provided the materials are needed for their own production.

Inland Steel Opens Ore Mine

Chicago — A new iron ore mine will be opened by Inland Steel Co. It lies 2 miles east of Crystal Falls, Mich., and will be called the Cayia Mine for A. J. Cayia, Inland's manager of ore mines and quarries and head of the Inland Lime and Stone Co. Development of the mine will start immediately. Production is expected late in 1952. Eventual production of 200,000 annual tons is hoped for.

Ore will be shipped from Chicago and North Western docks at Escanaba, Mich.

Inco Makes Peak Nickel Shipments

Copper Cliff, Ont. — International Nickel Co., Inc., delivered 256 million lb of nickel in all forms last year. Deliveries in 1949 totaled 209,292,257 lb. Sales of all Inco products in 1950 amounted to $228 million as compared to $182,806,452 for 1949.

The firm reported current nickel output as being at maximum capacity and is expected to increase this year. Inco expects to complete by 1953 its project of fully converting from surface to underground mining. This has taken the bulk of Inco's $100 million in capital expenditures over the past decade and was motivated by diminishing open pit ores.

Coal Price Ceilings Permit Adjustment for Mine Pay Increase

Special anthracite regulation gives 90¢ a ton increase over Jan. 2 level.

Washington—Immediately after authorizing a catch-up period for wage increases agreed upon before the Jan. 25 wage freeze, the Office of Price Stabilization began work on an order allowing adjustment in coal prices to meet the $1.60 a day wage increase granted the miners.

As issued last week, CPR (ceiling price regulation) 3 set ceiling prices on bituminous, lignite and Virginia anthracite for mines east of the Mississippi at the highest price received between July 1, 1948 and June 30, 1949 or in the period Jan. 1-15, 1951. Ceilings for mines west of the Mississippi would be the highest prices charged between Mar. 1, 1950 to Jan. 15, 1951.

CPR-3 also provides these ceilings may be increased by the amount of additional cost resulting from the recent wage agreement. This was estimated as averaging about 25¢ per ton, varying from mine to mine.

A special regulation was issued covering Pennsylvania anthracite. Its effect is to remove anthracite from the general freeze order and establish specific prices, permitting a 90¢ a ton increase over Jan. 2 price levels.

Industry Objects

Industry members of the Wage Stabilization Board were united in opposition to a grace period.

Regulation 2 permits wage increases agreed upon prior to Jan. 25 to be granted provided such increases were scheduled to take effect by Feb. 9. The grace period also allowed arbitrated wage hikes and intraplant pay "adjustments."

Federal, state and municipal pay increases, fixed by statute, as well as increases necessary to bring pay up to establish minimum wage standards are exempt from the order.

The coal price order was seen as setting a pattern for other adjustments in prices. Officials of the OPS said the grace period would probably affect as many as 500 labor contracts.

Building Booms Despite Curbs

Washington — Despite governmental ban on some types of construction, dollar volume of building activity for January boomed to a fifth more than for last year, Commerce Dept. figures show. A total of $2.1 billion went into place.

Industrial construction amounted to $125 million, compared with $69 million last year—an 80 pct increase.

Despite credit curbs, residential construction continued at a record level of $900 million for the month, a fifth higher than last year. Military construction was up to $25 million, three times the amount for January 1950.

White Starts ESC Program

Cleveland — Formation of an Emergency Service Corps program by the White Motor Co. to keep White trucks and buses rolling during the national emergency has been announced by J. N. Bauman, vice-president.

First phase of the program calls for registration of all White equipment in the United States. The program will aim to keep available White parts on hand in localities where needed.

Twin Coach Gets Bus Order

Kent, Ohio—One of the largest single bus orders ever awarded has been received by the Twin Coach Co. from the Army for production of 1650 transport buses. Total cost is $21,450,000.

Design is similar to a basic combination coach and cargo carrier developed by L. J. Fageol, president of Twin Coach.

Appliance Sales Volume Leaps

Chicago — Factory sales of standard size household washers totaled 4,289,931 during 1950, reports American Home Laundry Mfrs. Assn. This is an increase of 41.4 pct over 1949 sales. Sales of dryers during 1950 jumped 201.2 pct over '49 and ironer sales gained 33.1 pct.

November Finished Steel Shipments

As Reported to the American Iron & Steel Institute

STEEL PRODUCTS	Item	Current Month					To Date This Year				
		Carbon	Alloy	Stainless	Total	Per cent of Total Shipments	Carbon	Alloy	Stainless	Total	Per cent of Total Shipments
Ingots	1A	69,132	12,611	1,294	83,037	1.4	649,763	114,165	15,325	779,253	1.2
Blooms, slabs, billets, tube rounds, sheet bars, etc.	1B	151,662	43,925	944	196,531	3.2	1,577,893	398,245	9,147	1,985,285	3.0
Skelp	2	11,858	-	-	11,858	0.2	112,089	-	-	112,089	0.2
Wire rods	3	70,807	1,473	390	72,670	1.2	737,224	14,154	1,395	752,773	1.1
Structural shapes (heavy)	4	382,673	6,596	6	389,275	6.4	3,790,518	41,454	147	3,832,119	5.8
Steel piling	5	37,416	-	-	37,416	0.6	308,350	-	-	308,350	0.5
Plates	6	510,809	28,334	967	540,110	8.9	4,937,750	175,904	10,543	5,124,197	7.8
Rails—Standard (over 60 lbs.)	7	118,576	18	-	118,594	2.0	1,572,832	329	-	1,573,161	2.4
Rails—All other	8	11,995	118	-	12,113	0.2	108,259	180	-	108,439	0.2
Joint bars	9	9,677	-	-	9,677	0.2	105,035	-	-	105,035	0.2
Tie plates	10	33,243	-	-	33,243	0.5	385,885	-	-	385,885	0.6
Track spikes	11	10,094	-	-	10,094	0.2	127,961	-	-	127,961	0.2
Wheels (rolled & forged)	12	28,704	26	-	28,730	0.5	237,690	123	-	237,813	0.4
Axles	13	14,198	53	-	14,251	0.2	112,230	565	-	112,795	0.2
Bars—Hot rolled (incl. light shapes)	14	502,146	165,900	2,730	670,776	11.1	5,472,066	1,787,401	24,749	7,284,216	11.1
Bars—Reinforcing	15	152,405	-	-	152,405	2.5	1,521,938	260	-	1,522,198	2.3
Bars—Cold finished	16	105,820	24,130	2,900	132,850	2.2	1,220,963	230,108	27,147	1,478,218	2.3
Bars—Tool Steel	17	1,931	7,421	-	9,352	0.2	16,112	63,482	-	79,594	0.1
Standard pipe	18	214,140	113	2	214,255	3.5	2,366,758	452	16	2,367,226	3.6
Oil country goods	19	111,449	16,224	-	127,673	2.1	1,332,643	202,983	-	1,535,626	2.3
Line pipe	20	217,881	131	-	218,012	3.6	3,185,477	197	-	3,185,674	4.9
Mechanical tubing	21	46,921	19,173	353	66,447	1.2	477,809	191,038	3,282	672,129	1.0
Pressure tubing	22	19,432	1,456	422	21,310	0.4	195,385	21,709	6,767	223,861	0.3
Wire—Drawn	23	263,459	3,482	1,992	268,933	4.4	2,562,360	35,284	18,679	2,616,303	4.0
Wire—Nails & staples	24	74,658	-	2	74,660	1.2	804,965	-	72	805,037	1.2
Wire—Barbed & twisted	25	19,898	-	-	19,898	0.3	215,468	-	-	215,468	0.3
Wire—Woven wire fence	26	39,631	-	-	39,631	0.7	445,992	-	-	445,992	0.7
Wire—Bale ties	27	8,113	-	-	8,113	0.1	76,040	-	-	76,040	0.1
Black plate	28	53,240	-	-	53,240	0.9	504,552	-	-	504,552	0.8
Tin & terne plate—hot dipped	29	154,595	-	-	154,595	2.6	1,747,568	-	-	1,747,568	2.7
Tin plate—Electrolytic	30	221,407	-	-	221,407	3.7	2,603,863	-	-	2,603,863	4.0
Sheets—Hot rolled	31	627,883	27,606	1,654	657,143	10.9	6,829,519	241,392	24,971	7,095,882	10.8
Sheets—Cold rolled	32	733,266	11,639	8,318	753,223	12.4	8,291,962	102,676	98,005	8,492,643	13.0
Sheets—Galvanized	33	163,633	1,350	-	164,983	2.7	2,064,305	23,847	-	2,088,152	3.2
Sheets—All other coated	34	19,136	-	-	19,136	0.3	212,683	-	-	212,683	0.3
Sheets—Enameling	35	18,570	-	-	18,570	0.3	235,139	-	-	235,139	0.4
Electrical sheets & strip	36	11,188	48,922	-	60,110	1.0	97,516	549,835	-	647,351	1.0
Strip—Hot rolled	37	191,517	4,412	420	196,349	3.2	2,070,645	41,616	6,781	2,119,042	3.2
Strip—Cold rolled	38	154,547	2,275	13,653	170,475	2.8	1,545,342	15,777	155,582	1,716,701	2.6
TOTAL		5,587,710	427,388	36,047	6,051,145	100.0	60,860,529	4,253,176	402,608	65,516,313	100.0

During 1949 the companies included above represented 99.4% of the total output of finished rolled steel products as reported to the American Iron and Steel Institute.

* Revised.

Better Inspection Methods Urged by Industry and Military

New York—Less lost time between factory and front line will result if recommendations of industry and the armed services on inspection methods are applied in defense plants, according to the National Industrial Conference Board.

The recommendations, contained in a survey of 300 companies, are based on World War II experience. Industry recommended the military eliminate duplication among the services, give personnel more training, ease impractical or too-rigid specifications.

Military inspection personnel recommended industry study contract specifications more thoroughly, keep better records, and develop better inspection systems, particularly among smaller and medium-sized companies.

Gray Iron Coatings Manual

Cleveland — Product economies and conservation of vital alloys now under rigid government control are described in "Metallic and Non-Metallic Coatings for Gray Iron," a manual released by the Gray Iron Founders' Society.

Scotland Host to 18 New U.S. Industrial Plants Since Last War

Firms find power rates, rentals, and labor supply are favorable.

Glasgow — Eighteen American manufacturers, making products known to almost every home or farm, have set up shop in Scotland since World War II and are employing more than 12,000 men.

Chief of these is International Business Machines.

Low power rates, factory rentals of 12¢ to 17¢ a sq ft per year, and a supply of capable labor have appealed to American industrialists with foreign markets.

Two of the oldest American plants in Scotland are that of the Singer Co., started about the time of the Civil War, and that of Babcock & Wilcox, opened in the 1890's.

Other manufacturers who have opened Scottish plants are: National Cash Register Co., Remington Rand, Burroughs Adding Machine, Honeywell Regulator Co., Rance, Joy Sullivan, Thos. A. Edison, Mine Safety Appliances, Massey Harris, Euclid, UK Time, Westclox, Pal Personna Blades Co., and Northern Beverage Drinking Straws.

The shape's the thing . . .

The selection of a suitable steel and its subsequent satisfactory performance can be made easy by good design.

How and in what shape a part is made is, we hold, of fundamentally greater importance than of what it is made.

In designing a piece of machinery it is necessary to consider Design, the choice of steel, and its Heat Treatment. All three are highly significant factors, but of them we believe Design to be vital because even the best in steel and treatment will not save a poorly designed part.

To evaluate the importance of good design and its vital relationship to the selection of steel and its heat treatment, we have prepared a book— "Three Keys to Satisfaction". This starts by discussing mainly design factors involved in stress concentrations, and includes useful sketches comparing poor and good features of design from the aspect of subsequent metallurgy. It is available on request to all engineers and designers.

Defense Contracts to Metalworking Industry
Selected Contracts, Week of Feb. 5, 1951

Item	Quan.	Value	Company
Buses	1650	$21,450,000	Twin Coach Co., Kent, Ohio
Dishwashing machine	177	288,612	Insinger Machine Co., Philadelphia
Oscilloscope	600	432,523	Waterman Prod.'s Co., Philadelphia
Signal generator	750	412,687	Measurements Corp., Boonton, N. J.
Radar sets	500	129,210	Telephonics Corp., Huntington, N. Y.
Radar beacons	...	493,806	Motorola, Inc., Chicago
Transmissions	269	119,436	American Auto Parts Co., Kansas City, Mo.
Ammeters	30,795	104,130	Neff Equipment Co., Toledo
Track	15,240	748,498	Allis Chalmers, Milwaukee
Tank	1381	25,000,000	Cadillac Mtr. Car Corp., Detroit
Trailer	104	197,091	Miller Trailer, Bradenton, Fla.
Machine tools	...	328,000	Amgears, Inc., Chicago
Truck, set	688	1,076,862	Willys Overland Mtrs., Toledo
Parts	4910	703,566	Willys Overland Mtrs., Toledo
Gearings	372,517	757,881	United Motors Service, Detroit
Shafts	...	280,710	Gear Grinding Machine, Detroit
Truck	181	1,010,710	International Harvester, Detroit
Engines	700	803,669	International Harvester, Detroit
Generator	4070	328,856	United Mtrs. Service, Detroit
Engine	600	914,250	Beiderman Mtrs. Corp., Cincinnati
Truck	1288	1,723,700	Chevrolet Mtr. Div., Detroit
Engine	400	938,236	International Spare Parts, New York
Engine	368	659,025	Ward LaFrance Trk. Corp., Elmira, N.Y.
Aircraft parts	...	6,500,000	Consolidated-Vultee, San Diego
Azel indicator	...	4,259,818	Gilfillan Bros., Inc., Los Angeles
Facilities for manufacture of			
Airplanes		10,000,000	Kaiser-Frazer Corp., Willow Run, Mich.
Engines		14,700,000	Ford Mtr. Co., Detroit
....		30,000,000	Chrysler Corp., Detroit
Tanks		140,000,000	Chrysler Corp., Detroit

Sees Worldwide Copper Shortage

Riverside, N. J. — An all-time high production rate of copper with no substantial increase in supplies of raw copper ore is breeding a worldwide crisis in copper supply, said James T. Duffy, Jr., Riverside Metal Co. president. He advocated opening up of greater supplies of raw copper from South America by repealing the 2¢ per lb copper tariff and slowing down copper stockpiling.

Launch U.S. Built Cargo Ship

Birmingham—The S. S. Schuyler Otis Bland, first cargo vessel built under the government's new shipbuilding program, was launched at Pascagoula, Miss., last week. The ship, built by Ingalls Shipbuilding Corp., cost about $5 million.

Foresee 40 Million TV Sets

Chicago—A potential television market of 8 million sets a year with a $3 billion volume is forecast by John S. Meck, president of John Meck Industries and Scott Radio Laboratories. Total receiver use will be about 40 million sets, with replacements estimated at once in 5 years. Set production in 1950 was above 7,400,000.

Canadian Plants to Make Jeeps

Ottawa—Orders for production of jeeps and other motor vehicles have been placed by the Department of Defense with Canadian Commercial Corp., a government owned purchasing agency.

Canadian Commercial will negotiate with automotive companies for tooling. The vehicles will probably be made in plants located at Oshawa and Windsor.

December Iron & Steel Production by Districts

As Reported to American Iron & Steel Institute

BLAST FURNACE CAPACITY AND PRODUCTION—NET TONS	Number of Companies	Annual Blast Furnace Capacity July 1, 1950	PIG IRON Dec.	PIG IRON Year to Date	FERRO-MANGANESE AND SPIEGEL Dec.	FERRO-MANGANESE AND SPIEGEL Year to Date	TOTAL Dec.	TOTAL Year to Date	Pct of Capacity Dec.	Pct of Capacity Year to Date
Distribution by Districts										
Eastern	12	13,353,580	1,133,083	12,646,599	23,291	310,314	1,156,374	12,956,913	102.2	97.0
Pitts.-Youngstn.	16	26,735,520	2,094,359	23,990,992	29,516	260,150	2,123,875	24,251,142	93.7	90.7
Cleve.-Detroit.	6	7,044,600	560,978	6,781,565	...	...	560,978	6,781,565	93.9	96.3
Chicago	7	15,897,190	1,152,086	13,682,336	...	...	1,152,086	13,682,336	85.5	86.1
Southern	9	5,215,640	441,696	5,052,437	11,800	103,432	453,496	5,155,869	102.6	99.6
Western	4	3,375,200	246,224	2,656,343	...	...	246,224	2,656,343	86.1	79.3
Total	37	71,621,730	5,628,426	64,810,272	64,607	673,896	5,693,033	65,484,168	93.8	91.5

STEEL CAPACITY AND PRODUCTION—NET TONS	Number of Companies	Annual Steel Capacity July 1, 1950	TOTAL STEEL Dec.	TOTAL STEEL Year to Date	Pct of Capacity Dec.	Pct of Capacity Year to Date	Alloy Steel* (Incl. under total steel) Dec.	Alloy Steel* Year to Date	Carbon Ingots-Hot Topped (Incl. under total steel) Dec.	Carbon Ingots-Hot Topped Year to Date
Distribution by Districts:										
Eastern	24	20,387,460	1,669,102	18,772,977	96.6	93.2	132,407	1,31.,112	293,720	3,427,362
Pitts.-Youngstn.	33	39,127,940	3,207,119	37,532,013	96.7	95.9	458,015	4,893,210	335,212	4,006,001
Cleve.-Detroit.	8	9,333,460	786,147	9,244,550	99.4	99.0	48,013	561,427	91,906	1,195,252
Chicago	15	21,351,700	1,755,398	20,921,848	97.0	99.3	150,588	1,613,997	242,570	2,876,250
Southern	8	4,588,320	434,186	4,819,293	111.6	105.3	5,775	54,578	7,926	65,629
Western	11	5,774,620	491,338	5,406,088	100.4	94.2	8,466	103,332	13,119	108,912
Total	78	100,563,500	8,343,290	96,696,769	97.9	96.7	803,264	8,540,656	984,453	11,679,406

* For the purpose of this report, alloy steel includes stainless and any other steel containing one or more of the following elements in the designated amounts: Manganese in excess of 1.65%, and Silicon in excess of 0.60%, and Copper in excess of 0.60%. It also includes steel containing the following elements in any amount specified or known to have been added to obtain a desired alloying effect: Aluminum, Chromium, Cobalt, Columbium, Molybdenum, Nickel, Titanium, Tungsten, Vanadium, Zirconium, and other alloying elements.

Steel Products Committee Recommends Warehouse Changes

Washington — The Steel Products Advisory Committee recommended to the National Production Authority last week the following regulation changes for warehouses: (1.) Amendment of order M-6, change of allotments to provide fixed percentages of average monthly tonnages delivered by producers; (2.) to require warehouses to accept rated orders for sale from inventory on the same basis of producers under M-1, but that there be no extension of such DO orders to producers, and that M-1 be amended to change allotment to further converters to the same formula as for warehouses.

The committee also advised that steel output is adequate to supply both defense and essential civilian needs under present NPA controls without specific cutbacks. It recommended that no end use controls should be imposed without prior consultation with the industry.

Sees Welding Flash on Upswing

New York — More arc welders in more crowded plants as the defense program takes a production upswing will make the incapacitating "welding flash" an increasingly active pest and rob industry of skilled manhours.

Dr. Walter E. Fleischer, medical director of Armco Steel's Rustless Div. and member of the National Society for the Prevention of Blindness, said that the term "welding flash" is a misnomer since the temporary blindness and inability to focus eyes is caused by a more constant exposure to ultra-violet radiations of the welding arc rather than to a sudden flash.

At the onset of shipbuilding increase in 1942 at least 40 pct of all new injuries in shipyards were to the eyes and a large part of these were from "welding flash," said Dr. Fleischer. He estimated that there were over 100,000 eye injuries from flash in U. S. shipyards in 1944.

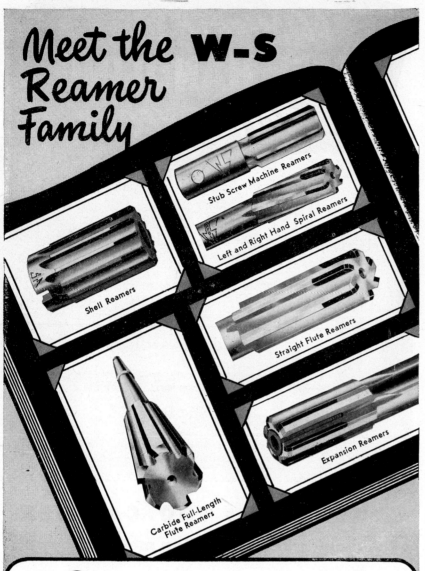
Colorado Fuel and Iron To Buy Worth Steel Capital Stock

Pueblo, Colo.—The Worth Steel Co. plant on the Delaware River, at Claymont, will be sold to Colorado Fuel and Iron Corp. in a stock sale transaction scheduled for Mar. 5 completion, reported Charles Allen, Jr., Colorado chairman, and Edward W. Worth, chairman of Worth Steel.

The plant will operate as a subsidiary, Claymont Steel Corp. Colorado Fuel and Iron is studying expansion possibilities to use the eastern plant's tidewater location. Besides extending its product range to the Worth line of steel plate and oil and gas transmission pipe, Colorado will add 468,000 tons to its present capacity of 1,560,000 tons. Its expansion program includes another 350,000 tons.

Involved in the stock transaction are 60,000 shares of capital stock, $100 par value, owned by the Worth family. Principal products of Colorado Fuel's two integrated plants at Buffalo and Pueblo and subsidiaries are wire, rails, and structural steel.

Detroit Steel's $50 Million Expansion Plan to Double Capacity

Detroit—The $50 million expansion program at the Portsmouth, Ohio, works announced last week by Detroit Steel Corp. will double the company's ingot capacity to 1,290,000 tons per year. Detroit Steel Corp. also plans to increase its finishing capacity from 180,000 tons to more than a million tons.

Present plans call for completion of the project by 1952. The new facilities include a second blast furnace rated at 1400 tons, four additional openhearth furnaces of 250 tons each, a new blooming mill, a new 54-in. hot strip mill and a new 54-in. cold-rolled sheet mill.

Detroit Steel Corp. operates cold-rolled strip mills in Detroit and New Haven, Conn. The steel melting capacity is concentrated at Portsmouth.

Ore Consumption Rises

Cleveland—Consumption of Lake Superior district iron ore by U. S. and Canadian blast furnaces rose to 7,289,138 gross tons in December, as compared with 6,860,823 gross tons in November and 6,788,405 gross tons in December, 1949, reported the Lake Superior Iron Ore Assn.

Total 1950 consumption of Lake Superior district iron ore rose to 83,536,678 gross tons, from 70,998,420 gross tons in 1949.

Iron ore stocks on hand at furnaces and Lake Erie docks totaled 37,168,873 gross tons Jan. 1, compared with 41,542,602 gross tons on Dec. 1 and 38,628,510 gross tons on Jan. 1, 1950.

Furnaces depending principally on Lake Superior district iron ore in blast Jan. 1 totaled 175 in the U. S. and nine in Canada.

Steel Nationalization on Feb. 15

London—Unheralded by British steel men, nationalization of the iron and steel industry will be enforced on Feb. 15. Laying the red tape groundwork, the Ministry of Supply announced recently that after May 15 licenses will be needed to produce more than 5000 tons of iron ore per year, 5000 tons of blast furnace pig iron or steel ingots, and 5000 tons of hot-rolled steels.

After that date such output, apart from licensees, will be limited to the Iron and Steel Corp. and nationalized companies.

Centrifugal Pump Line to Grow

Pittsburgh — Wilson - Snyder Manufacturing Div. of Oil Well Supply Co., U. S. Steel subsidiary, will expand its line of centrifugal pumps to include 19 general purpose pumps ranging from 5 to 250 hp of a type formerly made by National Transit Pump and Machine Co., Oil City, Pa.

Wilson-Snyder has acquired the patterns, drawings, tools, testing equipment and inventory for the centrifugal pumps formerly manufactured by National Transit.

ECA Finances Metals Exploration

Washington — A new exploration program in French Equatorial Africa to be financed by the Marshall Plan may uncover copper, lead and zinc for United States stockpiles, it is reported by sources here.

ECA has advanced $1,855,000 and the equivalent of $2,385,000 in French counterpart francs to the Mid-African Exploration Co., a subsidiary of Newmont Mining Co., of New York City and to its associated French companies, Explorations Minieres au Congo and Society Miniere du Niari. Repayment of Marshall Plan funds will come in the form of metals to the U. S. stockpile.

GE X-Ray Speeds Increased

Milwaukee — High-speed automatic inspection of thousands of industrial products at low cost will be possible with use of a new crystal detection method, according to General Electric X-Ray Corp.

GE will raise by 100 pct the number of engineers studying X-ray inspection under a special program during 1951. The GE course includes a 3-month period in Milwaukee, plus training in the field.

To Make Tank Transports

Birmingham — The Huntington Processing and Packaging Co. of Huntington, W. Va., has leased Bay No. 2 at the World War II Bechtel-McCone plane modification plant. It will make and assemble Army tank transports weighing 64,000 lb each and replacement parts. The firm, already recipient of a $1 million contract, is negotiating for another $1 million order.

Cleveland Designers Meet Feb. 5

Cleveland—The eighth annual Machine Design Conference, sponsored by the Machine Design Div. of the Cleveland Engineering Society, was to be held Feb. 5 in the society's headquarters.

Canadian Pig Iron Record

Toronto — Canadian pig iron production set a new record for the first 11 months of 1950 with 2,111,563 net tons poured compared with 1,982,350 tons in 1949. November production totaled 208,301 net tons compared with 205,811 tons in October and 157,327 tons for November 1949. Operations were 92.3 pct of capacity.

Production of ferroalloys in November totaled 16,920 net tons compared with 16,959 tons during October and 14,758 tons in November 1949.

Australia Gets Diesel Cars

Philadelphia—The first foreign shipment of the Budd Co.'s self-propelled rail diesel cars left Port Richmond this week destined for Commonwealth Railways of Australia. The shipment consisted of three rail diesel cars and four standard coaches purchased from a United States RR.

Aluminum Output Up 19 Pct

New York—Primary aluminum production during 1950 totaled 1,437,255,518 lbs, an increase of 19 pct over 1949 production, according to the Aluminum Assn. Sheet and plate shipments accounted for 1,155,318,982 lbs. Production will be expanded 20 pct during 1950, it was reported.

Swedish Steel Shortage Acute

London — The Swedish steel shortage is becoming so acute that some of the smaller industries are faced with suspended production. Appeals have been made to the Board of Trade for equitable distribution.

Iron Castings Shipments Off

Washington — November, 1950, shipments of malleable iron castings totaled 85,163 net tons, down slightly from the October figure of 89,968 tons, but 64 pct above the November, 1949, figure of 49,439 tons.

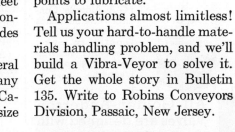

STEEL CONSTRUCTION NEWS

Fabricated steel awards this week included the following:

7000 Tons, E. Pikeland Township, Pa., Cromby Station (powerhouse) for Philadelphia Electric Co., to Bethlehem Steel Co., Bethlehem.

5500 Tons, Oak Creek, Wis., Wisconsolidated Electric Power Co. Plant units No. 1 and 2 to Milwaukee Bridge and Iron Co., Worden Allen Co., and Wisconsin Bridge Co.

590 Tons, Redwing County, Minn., bridge 6483 to American Bridge Co.

415 Tons, Redwing County, Minn., bridge 6484 to American Bridge Co.

320 Tons, St. Paul, beam spans for Great Northern RR Co., to American Bridge Co.

211 Tons, Potawattamie County, Iowa, bridge project F-554, to Pittsburgh Des Moines Steel Co.

190 Tons, Cass County, Iowa, bridge project SW-1853, to Pittsburgh Des Moines Steel Co.

Reinforcing bar awards this week included the following:

1200 Tons, Louisville, housing project to Jones and Laughlin Steel Co.

1200 Tons, Cincinnati, U. S. Health Center, to Pollak Steel Co.

1000 Tons, Louisville, housing project, to Laclede Steel Co.

950 Tons, Allegheny County, Pa., LR 765, to U. S. Steel Supply Co.

800 Tons, Minneapolis, warehouse for L. F. Donaldson Co., to U. S. Steel Supply Co.

525 Tons, Montgomery County, Pa., Pennsylvania Dept. of Highways Route 769 Sect. 1D, 2A, F. A. Canuso & Sons, general contractors.

435 Tons, Philadelphia, Southwest Sewage Treatment Plant, Progressive Builders, Pennsauken, N. J., general contractors, to Bethlehem Steel Co., Bethlehem.

375 Tons, Pottstown, Pa., new plant building for Doehler-Jarvis Corp., H. E. Baton Construction Co., Philadelphia, general contractors.

315 Tons, Rock Island, Ill., Central Junior High School, to Laclede Steel Co. through C. H. Langman and Son, Rock Island, Ill.

310 Tons, Philadelphia, elementary school at Longshore and Algon Ave., McCloskey & Co., general contractors, to Bethlehem Steel Co., Bethlehem.

Reinforcing bar inquiries this week included the following:

1000 Tons, Newport, Ind., Wabash ordnance plant.

900 Tons, Chicago, Lake Shore Briar Apts., 329 W. Briar Place, bids taken Feb. 5.

600 Tons, Detroit, caisson job.

355 Tons, Chicago, Congress Street superhighway.

300 Tons, Peoria, Ill., apartment building.

250 Tons, Clearfield, Pa., Harbinson Walker Refractories.

200 Tons, Ankeny, Iowa, Carney School.

180 Tons, Milwaukee, St. Charles Boys Home.

100 Tons, Racine, Massey Harris Mfg. Co.

100 Tons, Chicago, Club Aluminum Co.

100 Tons, Chicago, National Video Corp.

Tool and Die Makers Assn. Asks NPA for Labor Safeguards

New York—Officials of the National Tool and Die Manufacturers' Assn. were to meet this week with NPA officials in Washington to discuss safeguards for their numerically small but valuable work force against draft board depletion.

At a meeting here last week, Herbert F. Jahn, Assn. president, and Centre W. Holmberg, past president, pointed out that the tool and die making industry was unique in importance because it provided the tooling to set off the spark making vast defense output possible.

They said that surplus labor in their field was at best scanty and that loss of even the young experienced workers was a blow. Almost entirely new tooling was needed to push off production in the current crisis because most World War II tooling had been destroyed, it was indicated.

Under Selective Service, a 2A occupational deferment classification is open to industrial workers. Material on importance of industries and critical jobs has been published by the Depts. of Commerce and Labor but the local draft board remains the sole judge.

Copper Use Base Adjustment

Washington — Direction 1 to M-12 was issued last week by National Production Authority permitting a readjustment of the base period use averages for copper and copper base alloys if operations were shut down for 15 days or more during first half of 1950.

It provides that the month or months of the shutdown may be omitted in figuring the monthly average.

Ford Ups Prices in England

London — Ford Motor Co. in England has increased auto prices from 2½ pct to 10 pct. Still the cheapest British car, the 8 hp Ford Anglia now costs $1005 as compared to $921 previously. Other car makers are expected to follow suit.

SPEED CLIPS* help ROPER
"boil down" assembly costs

● "Until recently each vent grill cowl on our ranges was attached with a five-piece fastener," reports the Geo. D. Roper Corporation, Rockford, Illinois.

"Now we are making the same attachment with a *single* SPEED CLIP! As with all 65 of the Tinnerman fasteners used on each of our ranges, the assembly savings on this new application are substantial."

Everywhere you look today you find new proof of SPEED NUT savings power. If you haven't made a recent check of your products, we will be glad to conduct a thorough Fastening Analysis. Ask your Tinnerman representative for details on this service, and write for your copy of SPEED NUT Savings Stories. TINNERMAN PRODUCTS, INC., Box 6688, Department 12, Cleveland 1, Ohio. In Canada: Dominion Fasteners Limited, Hamilton. In Great Britain: Simmonds Aerocessories, Limited, Treforest, Wales.

SPEED CLIP replaces five-piece fastener. Provides secure attachment of cowl —yet permits easy removal for cleaning.

New 1951 Roper "Town and Country" Gas Range

TINNERMAN *Speed Nuts*

FASTEST THING IN FASTENINGS

They have FAR-REACHING qualities . . .

BATTERY trucks such as this one offer far-reaching advantages in warehouse duty. Fast and versatile, they save much time, space and hand labor. Smooth-running and fume-free, they cut product damage. Using dependable, low-maintenance electric drives, they run with a minimum of down-time.

Couple battery trucks with EDISON batteries and you'll have the most reliable handling team going! EDISON cells are built of rugged steel inside and out, and their electrolyte preserves steel. They are electrochemically foolproof and are not injured even by accidental short-circuiting or reverse charging. They take jars, jolts and accidents as part of the day's routine. That's why they're an outstanding investment.

Write today for free booklet SB 2039 and a current price quotation. You'll find EDISON batteries cost little more than other makes...and they pay this back over and over in terms of low upkeep and long, long life.—

Edison Storage Battery Division of Thomas A. Edison, Incorporated, West Orange, New Jersey. In Canada, International Equipment Company, Ltd., Montreal and Toronto.

EDISON
Nickel · Iron · Alkaline
STORAGE BATTERIES

Typical Truck Battery

publications

Continued from Page 34

on arch construction and design. "Modern Refractory Practice" is offered without charge to users of refractories, to libraries, and to heads of departments in universities and technical schools. For general distribution or for student use, a charge is made which is much lower than the cost of preparation. *Harbison-Walker Refractories Co. Address requests for the book to this column on company letterhead.*

Lifting Magnets

The line of Rapid heavy-duty lifting magnets, in round, rectangular and bi-polar types, are described in a new 8-p. British bulletin listing complete specifications. Tables showing dimensions, lifting capacities and other technical data are included. *The Rapid Magnetting Machine Co., Ltd.*

For free copy insert No. 4 on postcard, p. 35.

Safety Switch

The Autocon, an auxiliary high-level safety switch designed to operate either audible or visual alarms, is described in a new bulletin showing typical applications in water tanks, rivers and sumps. The unit needs only a ½-in. rise in water level above normal to operate, is not affected by temperature and operates independently of all other controls, as shown on the data sheet. *Automatic Control Co.*

For free copy insert No. 5 on postcard, p. 35.

Dust Collectors

A new 38-p. catalog contains illustrations and specifications of the complete line of Dustkop dust collectors available in standard, pretested units. Illustrations are included of almost every typical dry grinding dust control problem; considerable space is also devoted to buffing and polishing dusts as well as to the control of chips and shavings from both wood and metal-working machines. A cross index permits locating the recommended unit, either by known cfm capacity requirement or by the general classification of the dust involved.

publications
Continued

Control of vapor and mist from various wet grinding and machining operations is also dealt with. *Aget-Detroit Co.*
For free copy insert No. 6 on postcard, p. 35.

Lift Truck Accessories

A new standard accessories folder pictures the various standard accessories provided for fast, cost-cutting mass handling of unusual materials and special types of loads. As pointed out in the folder, many difficult handling problems can be solved easily by combining a Towmotor lift truck with the correct accessory to pick up, deposit, upend, or revolve the load. The folder shows such accessories as the crane arm, extension back rest, unloader, scoop, side shifter, cotton truck, hydraulic scoop, bale clamp, and many others. It also covers such special attachments as a multiple drum carrier designed to pick up and carry one to four heavy drums at a time. *Towmotor Corp.*
For free copy insert No. 7 on postcard, p. 35.

Crane Scale Brochure

A new 6-p. brochure completely describes the operation and applications of the Hydroscale hydraulic crane scale. Pertinent dimensions of all 34 standard models are tabulated. The new tilt-face-dial model is illustrated and described, as is the Hydro-Stand, a portable frame for supporting the scale when not in use. A partial list of users including the names of 100 nationally known firms is given. *Hydroway Scales, Inc.*
For free copy insert No. 8 on postcard, p. 35.

Weight, Length Calculator

A handy weight and length calculator for all strip metals is designed to compute at a glance the weight and length of strip metals in coils or straight lengths. Although designed so that basic calculations are for cold rolled strip steel, a factor table is included which enables the user to find the answer for aluminum, brass, copper, magnesium, Monel, zinc, and many other metals. It can save time and money by lopping hours

Weirton chose Monel...

Scrubber tanks of Monel help keep maintenance costs low in Weirton Steel Company's new electrolytic tin-plating line

Capable of a continuous coating speed of 2500 feet per minute, the Weirton Steel Company's new No. 4 Electrolytic Tin-Plating Line is said to be the largest and fastest in industry.

The rated capacity of the new line is 5,000,000 base boxes per year, raising the Weirton Tin Mill production potential to 15,000,000 base boxes annually.

Pickling tanks in the line are 100 feet long...oversize because of the high speed of the strip passing through. The scrubber section, where the steel sheet is washed with hot water to remove carried-over pickling acid, is made of Monel®. Monel was chosen for this application because of its excellent resistance to hot pickling acids...an essential quality for low maintenance costs.

Equipment for the new line was manufactured by the Wean Engineering Company of Warren, Ohio, and the Westinghouse Electric Corporation of Pittsburgh, Pennsylvania. The line was designed by the Weirton Steel Company's own engineering department.

If you — like the Weirton Steel Company — have metal problems involving corrosion or high temperatures, remember that INCO's Technical Service Department is always ready to help you solve them.

THE INTERNATIONAL NICKEL COMPANY, INC.
67 Wall Street, New York 5, N. Y.

End of Weirton high-speed electrolytic tin-plating line, showing finished tin plate being coiled. The line is the largest and fastest of its kind, making the Weirton, West Virginia, plant the world's largest tin mill.

*   *   *

Although Nickel and Nickel Alloys are currently in short supply, INCO advertisements will continue to bring you news of products, applications, and technical developments.

*   *   *

MONEL

EMBLEM OF SERVICE — INCO — TRADE MARK

...FOR MINIMUM MAINTENANCE

"Mopping up"
a production problem
with CLEARING presses

O-Cedar Corp'n, Chicago, recently introduced a new type of floor mop which has made a big hit with American housewives. A quartet of Clearing presses is turning out the several stamped parts required in an uninterrupted production stream. Two of the presses are fed automatically from coiled strip stock and progressive dies result in a finished stamping at every stroke.

To produce their modern mops, O-Cedar chose modern Clearing presses for their precision and dependability. If you have, or are expecting, a mass production requirement of large or small parts, it will pay you to consult Clearing.

CLEARING MACHINE CORPORATION
6499 WEST 65TH STREET ★ CHICAGO 38, ILLINOIS

CLEARING PRESSES
THE WAY TO EFFICIENT MASS PRODUCTION

publications

Continued

from jobs where conventional computing methods are used. It can be used by engineers, estimators, purchasing agents, press room foremen, and slitter operators. *Precision Steel Warehouse, Inc.*
For free copy insert No. 9 on postcard, p. 35.

Turbine-Generators

Nearly 50 turbine-generator installations, both utility and industrial, are pictured and described in a new 40-p. bulletin covering turbine-generators (500 kw and above). Brief discussions of generator and exciter cooling methods are included. A reference section offers a detailed drawing showing a typical turbine-condenser installation arrangement. Dimensions and weights of standard Elliott units are tabulated for easy reference. *Elliott Co.*
For free copy insert No. 10 on postcard, p. 35.

Squaring Shear Bulletin

The new series Columbia steel squaring shear line, recently improved and enlarged to include models for shearing mild steel plate from 3/16 to 1¼ in. thick, is described in an 8-p. bulletin. The booklet illustrates and details the 3 variations from basic design developed to meet various service requirements, and new features such as the air-operated clutch installed in the flywheel. Other mechanical presses and power press brakes offering efficient, economical operation for metal fabrication are also shown. *Columbia Machinery & Engineering Corp.*
For free copy insert No. 11 on postcard, p. 35.

Air Power Control

The Bellows system of using an opposed hydraulic force to smooth out the natural bounce and springiness of air is described in a new 8-p. bulletin giving details of the Hydro-Check. This unit sets up an opposed, steadying resistance to the thrust of air cylinder pistons, providing a smoother piston rod movement, as shown in the booklet. *Bellows Co.*
For free copy insert No. 12 on postcard, p. 35.
Resume Your Reading on Page 35

production ideas

Continued from Page 38

insuring long life and maximum efficiency of lubrication. *Kenco Mfg. Co.*

For more data insert No. 26 on postcard, p. 35.

Electric Hammer

Has one working part; special power unit; 3600 blows per min.

The power unit of the new Model 437 portable electric hammer consists of two alternately energized

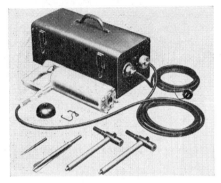

magnetic coils, eliminating gears, cranks and connecting rods. A patented contour grip handle makes the tool easy to hold and operate during long use. The 1⅛-in. hammer has an operating range of ¾ to 1⅛-in. diam star drills and extreme operating limits of ⅜ to 1½ in. diam star drills. It is 16¼ in. long and weighs 20 lb. *Skilsaw, Inc.*

For more data insert No. 27 on postcard, p. 35.

Parts Feeder

Multiple discharge tracks increase capacity; handles rivets to blades.

The feeding capacity of Syntron vibratory parts feeders can be

doubled or tripled by equipping them with two or three feeding tracks instead of one as originally furnished. Movement of parts is in the same direction on all tracks,

production ideas

Continued

and the discharges may be located all at one point or at various points around the circumference of the bowl, convenient to processing stations. *Syntron Co.*

For more data insert No. 28 on postcard, p. 35.

Angle Computer

Simplifies lay-out of dies, tools; inspects machined parts, castings.

Studler angle computers have three individual directions of rotation assembled into one unit—the radial, vertical and the horizontal.

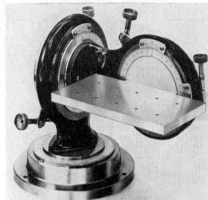

The 4½ x 9 in. surface plate can be revolved 360° in each plane. It is moved to the approximate required position and then by operating an actuating screw the exact position is found to 0.001 in. or to a minute of a degree. The surface plate is cast iron with eighteen ¼-20 tapped holes for clamping the casting or part to the plate. *Angle Computer Co.*

For more data insert No. 29 on postcard, p. 35.

Micro Circle Cutter

Cuts bolts in metals, plastics, wood.

The micro circle cutter is adjustable in an infinite number of hole diameters within its range, with a micrometer type adjusting screw to assure precise settings. Locking the beam is an easy, quick operation. Two type cutters are available: round shank for drill presses or hand drills; square tapered shank for hand braces. Maximum hole diameters are 4 and 6 in. All are equipped with a ¼ in. high speed steel cutting bit. *Precise Measurements Co.*

For more data insert No. 30 on postcard, p. 35.

Contour Grinder

Improved to increase rigidity and to obtain greater precision.

Improvements in the Visual-Grind contour grinding machine includes a heavy casting of aluminum alloy for the support for the entire optical projection section. Fins in the lamp housing increase radiation and dispersion of heat to prolong lamp life; lamp housing adjustment is by hand wheel, worm gear and screw, rising and falling on dovetail ways; pre-set lens tube insures positive focus. The longitudinal and cross traverse movement of the optical section is on hardened steel ways and rollers for easy adjustment and complete counterbalancing. Bijur one-shot lubrication is standard on all Visual-Grind units. *Cleveland Grinding Machine Co.*

For more data insert No. 31 on postcard, p. 35.

Grease Rig

Two-wheeled service cart dispenses lubricants to industrial bearings.

Compact and highly maneuverable, this grease rig moves rapidly along plant aisles and between closely placed production machines. Since all grease and oil equipment on the rig is removable even re-

motely located machines that are inaccessible to the cart can be greased with the cart's equipment. All equipment is hand-operated. An oil pump dispenses oil either in single shots or in a steady stream. Two models are available: one with bucket-type unit of 30-lb capacity; the other pumps from a 25 to 40 lb refinery filled pail. *Gray Co., Inc.*

For more data insert No. 32 on postcard, p. 35.

Foundry Laboratory Oven

Bakes test cores uniformly; maximum temperature of 550°F.

Of rugged construction, the core-baking oven has a heavily insulated chamber 10 in. wide x 12 in. high x 18 in. deep, designed for maximum temperature of 550°F with sensitive, automatic, thermostatic control. A special double type air-diffusing system insures a large volume of air entering the oven with an equal amount of air intake

at both the front and back of the chamber. In this way with a minimum of three to four air changes per min, convected heat is used to best advantage for drying and baking, rapidly eliminating the gases and moisture. *Claud S. Gordon Co.* For more data insert No. 33 on postcard, p. 35.

Weight Indicator

16-in. diam dial for closer readings; and compensation for tare loads.

The new Dillon weight indicator will weigh such materials as steel, wire, aluminum foil, scrap, etc., and is especially advantageous where long or bulky objects cannot be easily moved to a central weighing point. Pivots and bearings of the industrial scale are highly polished, hardened tool steel and a 360° swivel hook is standard. Accuracy is to within one division of the indicated reading at any point on the dial. *W. C. Dillon & Co., Inc.* For more data insert No. 34 on postcard, p. 35.

Drum Clamp

Handles cylindrical objects either individually or as pallet loads.

The device picks up individual drums or barrels, and loads a pallet which is then handled after two

production ideas
Continued

curved rubber-faced grab plates are removed from the forks. Adjustable from 32 in. inside spacing to 19 in., the two forks move simultaneously in or out by separate hydraulic cylinders. A pressure reducer valve controls gripping pressure and an accumulator keeps the pressure constant for safety in moving drums. *Baker Raulang Co.*
For more data insert No. 35 on postcard, p. 35.

Dimensional Air Gage
Measures the dimension variation directly on its graduated scale.

Called the Dimensionair, this gage is reported to have exceptional measuring range and clearance combined with almost absolute stability. The 0.003 in. range of the

gage enables the user to determine the size of a hole before he reaches the ultimate size required. Irregular and tapered holes are easily gaged. Setting the gage is simple, quick and positive. The master jet is fixed; no complicated adjustments are required. The instrument operates on air pressure between 40 and 100 lb. Tolerances are read directly on the scale just as on a dial indicator. Variations in millionths are easily determined. *Federal Products Corp.*
For more data insert No. 36 on postcard, p. 35.

Bench Blast Cabinet
Uses soft abrasives, sand or metal, for cleaning small metal parts.

Two light fixtures for illuminating the interior, an exhaust fan and a dust bag for making the operation dustless are equipment on a new handy sandblast cabinet for clean-

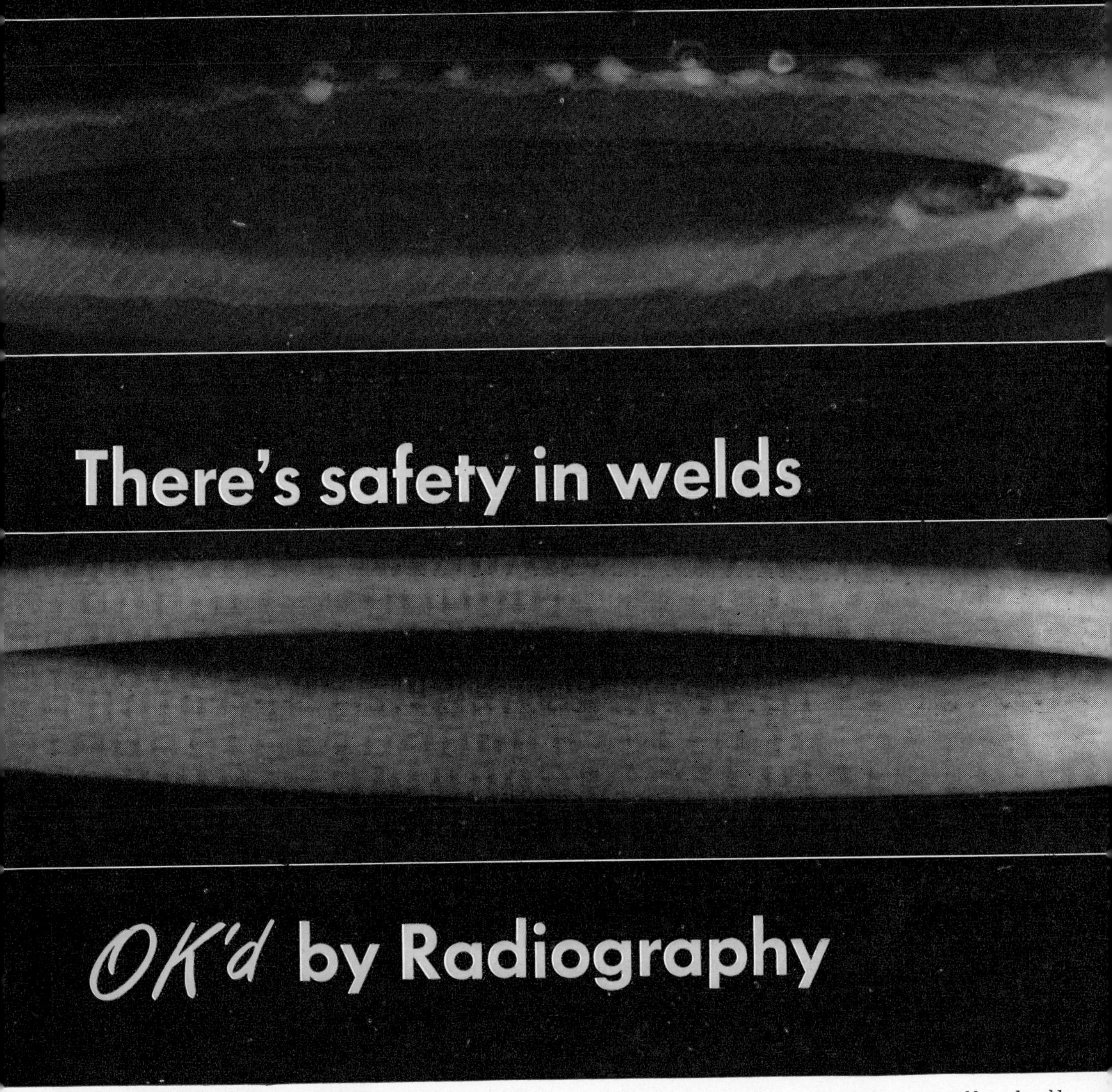

There's safety in welds

OK'd by Radiography

Radiographs showing welds in gas tanks. Lower radiograph shows acceptable tank weld.

These radiographs show the welds in propane gas tanks. The upper discloses a lack of fusion and heavy gas porosities. Out of a lot of several hundred tanks, Radiography showed a dozen to be hazardous—twelve potential accidents that were prevented.

Because Radiography can prove the soundness of welds it is opening new fields to welders in manufacturing pressure vessels and in other applications where welding was once barred, it is now an accepted procedure.

This is why Radiography can help you build your business as well as earn a reputation for highly satisfactory work.

If you would like to know more about what it can do for you in your own work, discuss it fully with your x-ray dealer.

EASTMAN KODAK COMPANY
X-ray Division
Rochester 4, New York

Radiography...
another important function of photography

Kodak
TRADE-MARK

Bearing balls are loaded into this specially-built Holcroft furnace; they move over a shaker hearth, down a chute, into a quench tank, and are then removed by a conveyor.

this custom-built Holcroft furnace

HARDENS BEARING BALLS TO EXACT SPECIFICATIONS

This continuous shaker-hearth furnace is typical of the many kinds of heat-treat furnaces built by Holcroft.

Designed to meet exact hardness specifications, this furnace heat treats 150 pounds of bearing balls per hour. The operating cycle totals less than 30 minutes.

The adjustable shaker hearth maintains even heating of the work and uniform load distribution. Low-cost heat is provided by Holcroft removable electric heating elements with three-zone automatic control. If desired, Holcroft gas-fired radiant tube burners can be used. Because the furnace is above floor level and has no permanent connections, it can be moved quickly and easily to any part of the production line.

No matter what your heat treat problem may be, Holcroft can provide a furnace that will do the job quickly, efficiently and at a low unit cost. Write today for further information.

BLAZING THE HEAT-TREAT TRAIL

---

production ideas
Continued

ing dies, tools, pistons, piston rings, valves and other small parts. It uses ground corn cobs or ground nut shells to remove surface impurities without scoring the metal.

Two rubber sleeves for both arms of the operator have rubber gloves attached. *W. W. Sly Mfg. Co.*
For more data insert No. 37 on postcard, p. 35.

Permeability Meter
Familiar orifice method has been added for rapid control testing.

The latest developments in permeability testing are embodied in the new Dietert No. 335 Perm-

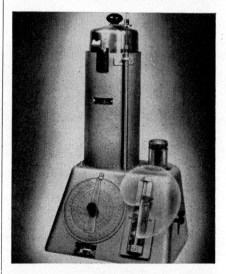

meter. The construction complies with the requirements for standard A.F.S. stopwatch permeabilities, independent of operator attention. A clear plastic permeability scale marks an improvement in ac-
For more data insert No. 38 on postcard, p. 35.
curacy for this method. *Harry W. Dietert Co.*

Resume Your Reading on Page 39

IRON AGE *markets and prices*

coke prices—While increases in coke prices had not been announced at press time, price of coke is expected to go up. Ceiling Price Regulation 3 passed last week permitted increases in coal prices to accommodate increases to miners allowed under CPR 2. Ceilings for mines west of the Mississippi would be the highest prices charged between Mar. 1, 1950 and Jan. 15, 1951. Average increase in coal would be about 25¢ per ton. A special anthracite regulation gives a 90¢ a ton increase over the Jan. 2 level.

product mix—Plates are being shipped to defense and essential civilian consumers in ever increasing quantities. One large producer is currently scheduling more than 60 pct of its plate output for these programs. Another is turning out plate on its strip facilities. Still another producer who doesn't normally sell plate is now turning it out for the freight car program. Plate requirements are expected to continue growing.

faster procurement—The Secretary of Defense and the Munitions Board have issued directives to military departments emphasizing the need for speed in placing contracts for major military items. They also urge development of adequate production bases for later increases. It will probably take 60 days to translate major defense programs into numbers of items.

stainless—You might get some stainless steel without a DO order, but it won't be easy, and it's getting harder. One stainless producer is virtually booking nothing but DO's. If a customer tries to place an order without a DO they check to see if he can get one. If not, the order goes in the hold file to be filled whenever possible.

army construction—The Philadelphia District of the Army Corps of Engineers plans $100 million worth of building in Pennsylvania, New Jersey and Delaware. Design is in progress in some cases. Architects and design engineers are being approached in others. Total value of the steel for these jobs is not yet known.

foreign pig—Increased steelmaking at home may give added importance to foreign pig iron. The demand for pig to feed expanding steel furnaces is growing steadily. Some producers whose product went to foundries are finding more profit in making pig for steelmaking operations. This leaves foundries high and dry. With large export of finished military goods ahead, and a tighter scrap market at home, foreign pig for foundries could become increasingly important during the next 2 years.

revolution—Weirton Steel Co. has developed a revolutionary electro-tinplating process that will mean savings of 25 to 50 pct in consumption of strategic tin and at the same time increase production of tinplate. With the new process the electrolytic tinplate is coated on one side with sufficient tin to protect contents of the can and on the other side with just enough tin to prevent corrosion. The usual practice is to apply the same weight coating on both sides. This new tinplate is now being marketed by Weirton.

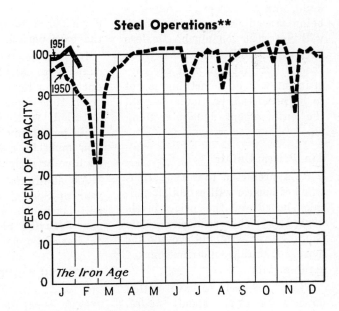

Steel Operations**

The Iron Age

District Operating Rates—Per Cent of Capacity**

Week of	Pittsburgh	Chicago	Youngstown	Philadelphia	West	Buffalo	Cleveland	Detroit	Wheeling	South	Ohio River	St. Louis	East	Aggregate
Jan. 28	97.0	100.0*	94.0*	99.0	103.8	104.0	97.0	108.0	100.0	106.0	90.5	95.1	98.0	101.0*
Feb. 4	96.0	99.5	91.0	96.0	105.8	104.0	51.5	109.0	100.0	106.0	88.2	95.1	105.0	96.5†

* Revised.
** Beginning Jan. 1, 1951, operations are based on an annual capacity of 104,229,650 net tons.
† Tentative.

nonferrous metals | *outlook and market activities*

NONFERROUS METALS PRICES

	Jan. 31	Feb. 1	Feb. 2	Feb. 3	Feb. 5	Feb. 6
Copper, electro, Conn. ...	24.50	24.50	24.50	24.50	24.50	24.50
Copper, Lake delivered...	24.625	24.625	24.625	24.625	24.625	24.625
Tin, Straits, New York	$1.825	$1.825	$1.825	....	$1.825	$1.825*
Zinc, East St. Louis	17.50	17.50	17.50	17.50	17.50	17.50
Lead. St. Louis	16.80	16.80	16.80	16.80	16.80	16.80

Note: Quotations are going prices.

*Tentative.

by R.Hatschek

New York — The nonferrous scrap trade is in a state of loaded quiet. The quiet was brought about by the iron and steel scrap price rollback order of the Economic Stabilization Agency which finally went into effect on Wednesday.

Nobody has much material on hand, and whatever is around is being moved fast so the rollback will not cost too much. Dealers here expect rollbacks in this trade "soon" but just how fast the government will do something is not to be predicted, particularly with the enforcement squabble going on.

Tin Prices Unfair

It is predicted that the order, when it comes, will establish ceilings based on the price levels quoted by the refineries. This would be realistic and provide for more equitable distribution of scrap metals.

Tin prices seem to have settled down to a fairly steady figure. This, however, is only outward, as many of the sellers have been frozen out of the high prices quoted. Each company has its own ceiling at present; that is, the highest it was able to sell at before the price fix. A standard must be established for this com-

modity soon in the interest of eliminating these inequities.

National Production Authority, because of numerous requests for adjustment under order M-12, have added Direction 1 to the copper order. The new addition permits the user to make his own adjustment without specific appeal to NPA if his business was shut down for a 15-day period during the base period.

If such is the case, the consumer is to calculate his base production after eliminating the down time from his base period. Detailed, written records of all facts pertaining to the recalculation must be made out and kept on file for at least 2 years.

An additional 70,000 tons per year of Special High Grade zinc will become available when the new Peruvian plant of the Cerro de Pasco Copper Corp. gets into

MONTHLY AVERAGE PRICES

The average prices of the major non-ferrous metals in January based on quotations appearing in THE IRON AGE, were as follows:

	Cents Per Pound
Electrolytic copper, Conn. Valley	24.50
Lake copper, delivered	24.625
Straits tin, New York	$1.7172
Zinc, East St. Louis	17.50
Zinc, New York	18.22
Lead, St. Louis	16.80
Lead, New York	17.00

production. An Export - Import Bank loan, up to a maximum of $20,-800,000, will finance the construction of these facilities. When operations are scheduled to proceed is not known.

Aluminum Output Up

The Aluminum Association reports fourth quarter 1950 production of 382,176,940 lb of aluminum, bringing the total for the year up to 1,437,255,518 lb. This exceeds 1949 production by 19 pct, and the outlook for 1951 is an increase to about 1.7 billion lb or more, with further increases in 1952.

Aluminum sheet and plate shipments totaled 1,155,318,982 lb in 1950, an increase of 48 pct above the previous year. Shipments of permanent-mold rough castings (not including pistons) totaled 34,336,366 lb and foil shipments added up to 90,679,719 lb.

It is reported that a representative of Chilean industry and the Chilean government will soon come to this country in order to appeal for an increase in the price of copper. The higher price, it is claimed, would not be artificial and would lead to higher production of the metal.

At press time, unauthorized strike of rail switchmen was still tying up shipments of badly needed copper and other supplies.

MILL PRODUCTS

(Cents per lb, unless otherwise noted)

Aluminum

(Base 30,000 lb, f.o.b. ship. pt. frt. allowed)

Flat Sheet: 0.188 in., 2S, 3S, 30.1¢; 4S, 61S-O, 32¢; 52S, 34.1¢; 24S-O, 24S-OAL, 32.9¢; 75S-O, 75S-OAL, 39.9¢; 0.081 in., 2S, 3S, 31.2¢; 4S, 61S-O, 33.5¢; 52S, 35.6¢; 24S-O, 24S-OAL, 34.1¢; 75S-O, 75S-OAL, 41.8¢; 0.032 in., 2S, 3S, 32.9¢; 4S, 61S-O, 37.1¢; 52S, 39.8¢; 24S-O, 24S-OAL, 41.7¢; 75S-O, 75S-OAL, 52.2¢.

Plate: ¼ in. and heavier: 2S, 3S-F, 28.3¢ 4S-F, 30.2¢; 52S-F, 31.8¢; 61S-O, 30.8¢; 24S-O, 24S-OAL, 32.4¢; 75S-O, 75S-OAL, 38.8¢.

Extruded Solid Shapes: Shape factors 1 to 5, 36.2¢ to 74.5¢; 12 to 14, 36.9¢ to 89¢; 24 to 26, 39.6¢ to $1.16; 36 to 38, 47.2¢ to $1.70.

Rod, Rolled: 1.5 to 4.5 in., 2S-F, 3S-F, 37.5¢ to 33.5¢; cold-finished, 0.375 to 3 in., 2S-F, 3S-F, 40.5¢ to 35¢.

Screw Machine Stock: Rounds, 11S-T3, ⅛ to 11/32 in., 53.5¢ to 42¢; ⅜ to 1½ in., 41.5¢ to 39¢; 1 9/16 to 3 in., 38.5¢ to 36¢; 17S-T4 lower by 1.5¢ per lb. Base 5000 lb.

Drawn Wire: Coiled, 0.051 to 0.374 in., 2S, 39.5¢ to 29¢; 52S, 48¢ to 35¢; 56S, 51¢ to 42¢; 17S-T4, 54¢ to 37.5¢; 61S-T4, 48.5¢ to 37¢; 75S-T6, 84¢ to 67.5¢.

Extruded Tubing, Rounds: 63S-T5, OD in in.: 1¼ to 2, 37¢ to 54¢; 2 to 4, 33.5¢ to 45.5¢; 4 to 6, 34¢ to 41.5¢; 6 to 9, 34.5¢ to 43.5¢.

Roofing Sheet, Flat: 0.019 in. x 28 in. per sheet, 72 in., $1.142; 96 in., $1.522; 120 in., $1.902; 144 in., $2.284. Gage 0.024 in. x 28 in., 72 in., $1.379; 96 in., $1.839; 120 in., $2.299; 144 in., $2.759. Coiled Sheet: 0.019 in. x 28 in., 28.2¢ per lb.; 0.024 in. x 28 in., 26.9¢ per lb.

Magnesium

(F.o.b. mill, freight allowed)

Sheet and Plate: FS1-O, ¼ in. 63¢; 3/16 in. 65¢; ⅛ in. 67¢; B & S Gage 10, 68¢; 12, 72¢; 14, 78¢; 16, 85¢; 18, 93¢; 20, $1.05; 22, $1.27; 24, $1.67. Specification grade higher. Base: 30,000 lb.

Extruded Round Rod: M, diam in., ¼ to 0.311 in., 74¢; ½ to ¾ in., 57.5¢; 1¼ to 1.749 in., 53¢; 2½ to 5 in., 48.5¢. Other alloys higher. Base: Up to ¾ in. diam, 10,000 lb; ¾ to 2 in., 20,000 lb; 2 in. and larger, 30,000 lb.

Extruded Solid Shapes, Rectangles: M. In weight per ft, for perimeters less than size indicated, 0.10 to 0.11 lb, 3.5 in., 62.3¢; 0.22 to 0.25 lb, 5.9 in., 59.3¢; 0.50 to 0.59 lb, 8.6 in., 56.7¢; 1.8 to 2.59 lb, 19.5 in., 53.8¢; 4 to 6 lb, 28 in., 49¢. Other alloys higher. Base, in weight per ft of shape: Up to ½ lb, 10,000 lb; ½ to 1.80 lb, 20,000 lb; 1.80 lb and heavier, 30,000 lb.

Extruded Round Tubing: M, wall thickness, outside diam, in., 0.049 to 0.057, ¼ in. to 5/16, $1.40; 5/16 to ⅜, $1.26; ½ to ⅝, 93¢; 1 to 2 in., 76¢; 0.165 to 0.219, ⅝ to ¾, 61¢; 1 to 2 in., 57¢; 3 to 4 in., 56¢. Other alloys higher. Base, OD in in.; Up to 1½ in., 10,000 lb; 1½ in. to 3 in., 20,000 lb; 3 in. and larger, 30,000 lb.

Titanium

(10,000 lb base, f.o.b. mill)

Commercially pure and alloy grades: Sheet and strip, HR or CR, $15; Plate, HR, $12; Wire, rolled and/or drawn, $10; Bar, HR or forged, $6; Forgings, $6.

Nickel and Monel

(Base prices, f.o.b. mill)

	"A" Nickel	Monel
Sheets, cold-rolled	71½	57
Strip, cold-rolled	77½	60
Rods and bars	67½	55
Angles, hot-rolled	67½	55
Plates	69½	56
Seamless tubes	100½	90
Shot and blocks	....	50

Copper, Brass, Bronze

(Freight prepaid on 200 lb includes duty)

	Sheets	Rods	Extruded Shapes
Copper	41.03	....	40.63
Copper, h-r	....	36.88	....
Copper, drawn	....	38.18	....
Low brass	39.15	38.84	....
Yellow brass	38.28	37.97	....
Red brass	40.14	39.83	....
Naval brass	43.08	38.61	38.07
Leaded brass	....	32.63	36.70
Com'l bronze	41.13	40.82	....
Mang. bronze	45.96	40.65	41.41
Phos. bronze	60.20	60.45	....
Muntz metal	40.43	36.74	37.99
Ni silver, 10 pct	49.27	51.49	....
Arch. bronze	....	....	35.11

PRIMARY METALS

(Cents per lb, unless otherwise noted)

Aluminum ingot, 99+%, 10,000 lb, freight allowed	19.00
Aluminum pig	18.00
Antimony, American, Laredo, Tex.	42.00
Beryllium copper, 3.75-4.25% Be	$1.56
Beryllium aluminum 5% Be, Dollars per lb contained Be	$69.00
Bismuth, ton lots	$2.25
Cadmium, del'd	$2.55
Cobalt, 97-99% (per lb)	$2.10 to $2.17
Copper, electro, Conn. Valley	24.50
Copper, Lake, delivered	24.625
Gold, U. S. Treas., dollars per oz.	$35.00
Indium, 99.8%, dollars per troy oz.	$2.25
Iridium, dollars per troy oz.	$200
Lead, St. Louis	16.80
Lead, New York	17.00
Magnesium, 99.8+%, f.o.b. Freeport, Tex., 10,000 lb	24.50
Magnesium, sticks, 100 to 500 lb	42.00 to 44.00
Mercury, dollars per 76-lb flask, f.o.b. New York	$225.00
Nickel, electro, f.o.b. New York	53.55
Nickel oxide sinter, f.o.b. Copper Cliff, Ont., contained nickel	46.75
Palladium, dollars per troy oz.	$24.00
Platinum, dollars per troy oz.	$90 to $93
Silver, New York, cents per oz.	90.16
Tin, New York	$1.825
Titanium, sponge	$5.00
Zinc, East St. Louis	17.50
Zinc, New York	18.22
Zirconium copper, 50 pct	$6.20

REMELTED METALS

Brass Ingot

(Cents per lb delivered, carloads)

85-5-5-5 ingot	
No. 115	29.00
No. 120	28.50
No. 123	28.00
80-10-10 ingot	
No. 305	35.00
No. 315	32.00
88-10-2 ingot	
No. 210	46.25
No. 215	43.25
No. 245	36.00
Yellow ingot	
No. 405	25.00
Manganese bronze	
No. 421	29.75

Aluminum Ingot

(Cents per lb, 30,000 lb lots)

95-5 aluminum-silicon alloys	
0.30 copper, max.	33.25-34.25
0.60 copper, max.	33.00-34.00
Piston alloys (No. 122 type)	30.50-31.00
No. 12 alum. (No. 2 grade)	30.00-30.50
108 alloy	30.25-30.75
195 alloy	31.25-31.75
13 alloy	33.50-34.00
ASX-679	30.50-31.00

Steel deoxidizing aluminum, notch-bar granulated or shot

Grade 1—95-97½%	32.00-32.50
Grade 2—92-95%	30.25-30.75
Grade 3—90-92%	29.25-29.75
Grade 4—85-90%	28.75-29.25

ELECTROPLATING SUPPLIES

Anodes

(Cents per lb, freight allowed, 500 lb lots)

Copper	
Cast, oval, 15 in. or longer	39⅛
Electrodeposited	33⅜
Rolled, oval, straight, delivered	38⅞
Forged ball anodes	43
Brass, 80-20	
Cast, oval, 15 in. or longer	34¾
Zinc, oval	26½
Ball anodes	25½
Nickel 99 pct plus	
Cast	70.50
Rolled, depolarized	71.50
Cadmium	$2.80
Silver 999 fine, rolled, 100 oz lots, per troy oz, f.o.b. Bridgeport, Conn.	79½

Chemicals

(Cents per lb, f.o.b. shipping points)

Copper cyanide, 100 lb drum	52.15
Copper sulfate, 99.5 crystals, bbl.	12.85
Nickel salts, single or double, 4-100 lb bags, frt. allowed	20½
Nickel chloride, 375 lb drum	27½
Silver syanide, 100 oz lots, per oz.	67¼
Sodium cyanide, 96 pct domestic 200 lb drums	19.25
Zinc cyanide, 100 lb drums	45.85

SCRAP METALS

Brass Mill Scrap

(Cents per pound, add ½¢ per lb for shipments of 20,000 to 40,000 lb; add 1¢ for more than 40,000 lb)

	Heavy	Turnings
Copper	23	22¼
Yellow Brass	20½	18¾
Red brass	21½	20¾
Comm. bronze	21¾	21
Mang. bronze	19½	18⅝
Brass rod ends	19⅞	....

Custom Smelters' Scrap

(Cents per pound, carload lots, delivered to refinery)

No. 1 copper wire	21.50
No. 2 copper wire	20.00
Light copper	19.00
Refinery brass	19.50*
Radiators	15.00

*Dry copper content.

Ingot Makers' Scrap

(Cents per pound, carload lots, delivered to producer)

No. 1 copper wire	23.00
No. 2 copper wire	22.00
Light copper	21.00
No. 1 composition	22.00
No. 1 comp. turnings	21.50
Rolled brass	18.50
Brass pipe	20.50
Radiators	17.50
Heavy yellow brass	17.00

Aluminum

Mixed old cast	18½—19
Mixed new clips	20½
Mixed turnings, dry	18½
Pots and pans	18½—19
Low copper	21½—22

Dealers' Scrap

(Dealers' buying prices, f.o.b. New York in cents per pound)

Copper and Brass

No. 1 heavy copper and wire	19½—20
No. 2 heavy copper and wire	18 —18½
Light copper	17 —17¼
New type shell cuttings	17 —17¼
Auto radiators (unsweated)	14½—15
No. 1 composition	17 —17½
No. 1 compositon turnings	16½—17
Clean red car boxes	15½—16
Cocks and faucets	15½—16
Mixed heavy yellow brass	13 —13½
Old rolled brass	14 —14½
Brass pipe	17 —17½
New soft brass clippings	17½—18
Brass rod ends	16½—17
No. 1 brass rod turnings	16 —16½

Aluminum

Alum. pistons and struts	12 —13
Aluminum crankcases	15 —16
2S aluminum clippings	18½—19½
Old sheet and utensils	15 —16
Borings and turnings	12½—13
Misc. cast aluminum	15 —16
Dural clips (24S)	15 —16

Zinc

New zinc clippings	14½—15
Old zinc	11 —11¼
Zinc routings	8½— 9
Old die cast scrap	8 — 8¼

Nickel and Monel

Pure nickel clippings	60 —65
Clean nickel turnings	57 —60
Nickel anodes	60 —65
Nickel rod ends	60 —65
New Monel clippings	22 —25
Clean Monel turnings	18 —20
Old sheet Monel	20 —22
Inconel clippings	26 —28
Nickel silver clippings, mixed	13 —14
Nickel silver turnings, mixed	12 —13

Lead

Soft scrap, lead	15 —15¼
Battery plates (dry)	8¾— 9

Magnesium

Segregated solids	9 —10
Castings	5½— 6½

Miscellaneous

Block tin	90 —100
No. 1 pewter	63 —65
No. 1 auto babbitt	58 —60
Mixed common babbitt	12¼—12½
Solder joints	20 —21
Siphon tops	58 —60
Small foundry type	18¼—18½
Monotype	16¾—17
Lino. and stereotype	16½—16¾
Electrotype	14¾—15
Hand picked type shells	11½—11¾
Lino. and stereo. dross	8 — 8¼
Electro. dross	6½— 6¾

SCRAP *iron and steel*

OPS finally issues long-expected iron and steel scrap price schedule . . . Rollback to December levels . . . Trading comes to halt.

Cleveland—Buyers were breathing easier this week following Office of Price Stabilization announcement of the long-expected scrap price schedule which at press time had brought trading to an abrupt halt in major scrap markets and generally deadened the market. Effective date of the order is Feb. 7.

Secondary effects of the OPS order will be numerous and varied. Most immediate will be a 30 to 60-day slowup in the movement of tonnage, which will be enough to push some major consumers to the brink of allocations.

Earmarked Tonnage

Also to be expected are more consumer demands on customers for earmarked tonnage, in what will probably be a general effort to screw the lid down on captive scrap and bring it back home.

Consumers like the new prices, a statement which will surprise nobody, but the realists among the buyers are warning that scrap procurement may well become the steel industry's biggest headache.

Most brokers were accepting the OPS order philosophically, but their pleasure at the $1 brokerage was dampened somewhat by the "lack of protection" afforded them by the order. One broker put it this way, "every mill in the country will be doing business with 200 brokers in the next 6 months. Every guy and his brother will become a scrap broker."

Most dealers were satisfied with the order, although some difference of opinion exists as to the fair allowance for the preparation of low phos at $2.50 as compared with $6 for preparing a hydraulic bundle.

With scrap in its present short supply, the effect of the $2 differential between No. 1 and No. 2 heavy melting steel is problematical. If a dealer should, for example ship a car of No. 2 for No. 1 and the mill rejects it, some other mill will probably be glad to take it. This may lead to only one grade, No 1, regardless of what it is.

Prices on the foundry grades represent substantial reductions from recent prices, but according to dealers, the new schedule is much better than the one OPA handed them and the $4 a ton trucking charge will help. Immediate allocation for foundries will probably be necessary.

What apparent inequities presently exist in the order will probably be ironed out leaving only the vital question of supply still to be answered.

In Pittsburgh, both consumers and scrappies are happy that OPS not only listened to but adopted the recommendations they made in pre-control discussions. Some dealers are unhappy over the amount of the rollback.

Some dealers are going to eliminate their most unprofitable items. Most people feel that consumers will not be able to go right out and pick up tonnage. Some claim that the spread between such items as cut and uncut bolsters and side frames and cut and uncut locomotive tires are not sufficient. The trade thinks many will stop preparing these items if they prove unprofitable and that consumers will have to petition Washington to get some adjustment made.

Iron and Steel Scrap Price Schedule

IRON AND STEEL SCRAP

Pursuant to the Defense Production Act of 1950 (Pub. Law 774, 81st Cong.) and Executive Order 10161 (15 F. R. 6105), and in accordance with Economic Stabilization Agency General Order No. 2 (16 F. R. 738), it is hereby ordered that price ceilings on the sale of iron and steel scrap shall be effective as provided in this Ceiling Price Regulation No. .... A statement of the considerations involved in the issuance of this regulation is incorporated hereinafter as Appendix A.

SCOPE OF THE REGULATION

- 1   Prohibitions against dealing in iron and steel scrap at prices above the ceiling.
- 2   Geographical application.

CEILING PRICES

- 3   Basing point prices for steel scrap of dealer and industrial origin.
- 4   Ceiling shipping point prices for steel scrap of dealer and industrial origin.
- 5   Switching charge deductions.
- 6   Ceiling delivered prices for shipment by rail, vessel, or combination thereof, for steel scrap of dealer and industrial origin.
- 7   Basing point prices for steel scrap of railroad origin.
- 8   Ceiling on-line prices for steel scrap of railroad origin.
- 9   Ceiling delivered prices for shipment by rail, vessel, or combination thereof, for steel scrap of railroad origin.

• 10 Ceiling prices for railroad steel scrap sold by sellers other than railroads.
• 11 Ceiling shipping point and on-line prices for all cast iron scrap.
• 12 Ceiling delivered prices for shipment by rail, vessel, or combination thereof, for all cast iron scrap.
• 13 Ceiling prices for shipment by truck for all steel or cast iron scrap.

GENERAL PROVISIONS

• 14 Unlisted grades.
• 15 In transit preparation.
• 16 Ceiling preparation charges.
• 17 Premiums for alloy content.
• 18 Mixed shipments.
• 19 Commissions.
• 20 Unprepared scrap.
• 21 Transportation.
• 22 Weights to govern.

SPECIFICATIONS

• 23 Steel grades of dealer and industrial origin.
• 24 Steel grades of railroad origin.
• 25 All cast iron grades.

MISCELLANEOUS PROVISIONS

• 26 Imported scrap.
• 27 Exported scrap.
• 28 Definitions.
• 29 Records and reports.
• 30 Less than maximum prices.
• 31 Evasion.
• 32 Enforcement.
• 33 Petitions for amendment.
Appendix A Statement of Consideration.
Authority: §§ 312.1 to 312.33 issued under sec. 704, Pub. Law 774, 81st Cong. Interpret or apply Title IV, Pub. Law 774, 81st Cong., E.O. 10161, Sept. 9, 1950, 15 F. R. 6105.

SCOPE OF THE REGULATION

• 1 **Prohibitions against dealing in iron and steel scrap at prices above the ceiling.**
On and after the 7th day of February 1951, regardless of any contract or other obligation:

(a) No person shall sell or deliver iron or steel scrap to a consumer of scrap or his broker at prices higher than the ceiling prices established by this regulation;

(b) No person shall sell, deliver, buy or receive prepared iron or steel scrap at prices higher than the applicable ceiling prices established by this regulation;

(c) No industrial producer or railroad or governmental agency (whether federal, state or local) shall sell or deliver unprepared iron or steel scrap to any person at prices higher than the applicable ceiling prices established by this regulation. No person shall buy or receive unprepared iron or steel scrap from such industrial producer or railroad or governmental agency at prices higher than the applicable ceiling prices established by this regulation;

(d) No consumer of scrap or his broker shall buy or receive iron or steel scrap at prices higher than the ceiling prices established by this regulation;

(e) No person shall export or sell iron or steel scrap to an exporter at prices higher than the ceiling prices established by this regulation;

(f) No person shall charge or pay a fee for the service of preparing iron or scrap in excess of the ceiling preparation charges established by this regulation;

(g) No person shall sell or deliver iron or steel scrap upon condition that the buyer shall sell or deliver to any person any other commodity. No person shall buy or receive iron or steel scrap upon the condition that he shall sell or deliver to any person any other commodity;

(h) No person shall act as both broker and dealer in the purchase of any single lot or item of iron or steel scrap, where the price paid for such lot or item of iron or steel scrap would exceed the applicable ceiling prices established by this regulation;

(i) No person shall agree, offer, solicit or attempt to do any of the foregoing.

• 2 **Geographical application.** This regulation shall apply to sales, deliveries, and preparation of iron or steel scrap in the forty-eight states of the United States and the District of Columbia.

CEILING PRICES

312.3 **Basing point prices for steel scrap of dealer and industrial origin.**

(a) **Basing point prices from which maximum shipping prices are computed.**

(1) Basing point prices for the base grade, No. 1 heavy melting steel, Grade 1:

Basing Point:	Price per Gross Ton
Alabama City, Ala.	$ 39.00
Ashland, Ky.	42.00
Atlanta, Ga.	39.00
Bethlehem, Pa.	42.00
Birmingham, Ala.	39.00
Brackenridge, Pa.	44.00
Buffalo, N. Y.	43.00
Butler, Pa.	44.00
Canton, Ohio	44.00
Chicago, Ill.	42.50
Cincinnati, Ohio	43.00
Claymont, Del.	42.50
Cleveland, Ohio	43.00
Coatesville, Pa.	42.50
Conshohocken, Pa.	42.50
Detroit, Mich.	40.00
Duluth, Minn.	40.00
Harrisburg, Pa.	42.50
Houston, Tex.	37.00
Johnstown, Pa.	44.00
Kansas City, Mo.	39.50
Kokomo, Ind.	42.00
Los Angeles, Cal.	35.00
Middletown, Ohio	43.00
Midland, Pa.	44.00
Minnequa, Colo.	38.00
Monessen, Pa.	44.00
Phoenixville, Pa.	42.50
Pittsburg, Calif.	35.00
Pittsburgh, Pa.	44.00
Portland, Ore.	35.00
Portsmouth, Ohio	42.00
St. Louis, Mo.	41.00
San Francisco, Calif.	35.00
Seattle, Wash.	35.00
Sharon, Pa.	44.00
Sparrows Point, Md.	42.00
Steubenville, Ohio	44.00
Warren, Ohio	44.00
Weirton, W. Va.	44.00
Youngstown, Ohio	44.00

(2) **Differentials per gross ton above or below the price of Grade 1 (No. 1 heavy melting steel) for other grades of steel scrap.**

OPEN HEARTH AND BLAST FURNACE GRADES

Grades	Differentials
2. No. 2 Heavy Melting Steel	— $ 2.00
3. No. 1 Busheling	Base
4. No. 1 Bundles	Base
5. No. 2 Bundles	— 3.00
6. Machine Shop Turnings	— 10.00
7. Mixed Borings and Short Turnings	— 6.00
8. Shoveling Turnings	— 6.00
9. No. 2 Bushelings	— 4.00
10. Cast Iron Borings	— 6.00

ELECTRIC FURNACE AND FOUNDRY GRADES

Grades	Differentials
11. Billet, Bloom and Forge Crops	+ 7.50
12. Bar Crops and Plate Scrap	+ 5.00
13. Cast Steel	+ 5.00
14. Punchings and Plate Scrap	+ 2.50
15. Electric Furnace Bundles	+ 2.00
16. Cut Structural and Plate Scrap 3 ft. and under	+ 3.00
17. Cut Structural and Plate Scrap 2 ft. and under	+ 5.00
18. Cut Structural and Plate Scrap 1 ft. and under	+ 6.00
19. Briquetted Cast Iron Borings	Base
20. Foundry steel, 2 feet and under	+ 2.00
21. Foundry steel, 1 foot and under	+ 4.00
22. Springs and Crankshafts	+ 1.00
23. Alloy Free Turnings	— 3.00
24. Heavy Turnings	— 1.00

SPECIAL GRADES

Grades	Differentials
25. Briquetted Turnings	Base
26. No. 1 Chemical Borings	— 3.00
27. No. 2 Chemical Borings	— 4.00
28. Wrought Iron	+ 10.00
29. Shafting	+ 10.00

(b) **Restrictions on use.**
(1) The prices established for Grade 11 (billet, bloom and forge crops), Grade 23 (alloy free turnings) and Grade 24 (heavy turnings) may be charged only when shipped to a consumer directly from an industrial producer of such grades; otherwise the ceiling prices for such grades shall not exceed the prices established for the corresponding grades of basic open hearth and blast furnace scrap.

(2) The prices established for Grade 26 (No. 1 chemical borings) and Grade 27 (No. 2 chemical borings) may be charged only when such grades are sold for use for chemical or annealing purposes; otherwise the ceiling prices for such grades shall not exceed the price established for Grade 10 (cast iron borings).

(3) The price established for Grade 28 (wrought iron) may be charged only when sold to a producer of wrought iron; otherwise the ceiling price for such grade shall not exceed the ceiling price established for the corresponding grade of basic open hearth.

(c) **Special pricing provisions.** (1) Sellers of Grade 26 (No. 1 chemical borings) and Grade 27 (No. 2 chemical borings) may make an extra charge of $1.50 per gross ton for loading in box cars or 75 cents per gross ton for covering gondola cars with a weather-resistant covering.

(2) The ceiling price of pit scrap, ladle scrap, salamander scrap, skulls, skimmings or scrap recovered from slag dumps and prepared to charging box size, shall be computed by deducting from the price of No. 1 heavy melting steel of dealer and industrial origin, the following amounts:

Where the iron content is 85% and over .... — $ 4.00
Where the iron content is 75% and over .... — 6.00
Where the iron content is less than 75% .... — 10.00

(3) The ceiling price for any inferior grade of iron or steel scrap not listed in section • 3 (a) (2) hereof, shall not exceed the price of No. 1 heavy melting steel less $15.00.

• 4 **Ceiling shipping point prices for steel scrap of dealer and industrial origin.** (a) For shipping points located within a basing point named in section • 3 hereof, the ceiling shipping point price for any grade of steel scrap shall be the price established at such basing point, minus the applicable switching charge deduction set forth in section • 5 hereof.

(b) For shipping points located outside the basing points named in section •3 hereof, the ceiling shipping point price of any grade of iron or steel scrap shall be the price established for the scrap at the most favorable basing point, minus the lowest established charge for transporting scrap from the shipping point to such basing point by rail or water carrier, or combination thereof. (The most favorable basing point is the basing point named in section •3 hereof which will yield the highest shipping point price.)

(c) Where water rates are involved in the computations under subsection (b) the following additional deductions must be made. A flat charge of $1.25 per gross ton for dock charges, except, however, that at Memphis, Tennessee, the deduction shall be 95 cents per gross ton; at Great Lakes ports, $1.50 per gross ton; and at New England ports, $1.75 per gross ton.

Where the shipping point is located outside of the switching district of the city from which the water rate is applicable, the lowest established charge for transporting scrap by rail from the shipping point to the f.a.s. vessel point must be deducted. No deduction for switching charges need be made where the shipping point is located within the switching district of the city from which the water rate is applicable. If there is no established charge for transporting scrap by rail from the shipping point to the f.a.s. vessel point, water rates may not be used in computing shipping point prices.

(d) The ceiling shipping point price for No. 1 heavy melting steel (with differentials established in section •3 hereof for all other grades) at all shipping points in New York City (or Brooklyn, New York) shall be $36.99 per gross ton.

(e) Ceiling shipping point prices at all shipping points in Hudson and Bergen Counties, New Jersey, shall be computed from the Bethlehem, Pa., basing point.

(f) Ceiling shipping point prices at all shipping points in the State of New Jersey shall be computed by the use of all rail transportation charges.

(g) The ceiling shipping point price for No. 1 heavy melting steel (with differentials established in section •3 hereof for all other grades) need not fall below $32.00 per gross ton.

•5 **Switching charge deductions.** The switching charges to be deducted from the basing point price of dealer and industrial scrap as set forth in section •3 hereof, or the basing point price of non-operating railroad scrap, as set forth in section •7 hereof, in order to determine the ceiling shipping point prices for such scrap originating in basing points, are as follows:

(a) Basing point:	Dollars per Gross Ton
Alabama City, Ala.	$ .43
Ashland, Ky.	.47
Bethlehem, Pa.	.52
Birmingham, Ala.	.50
Brackenridge, Pa.	.53
Buffalo, N. Y.	.83
Butler, Pa.	.65
Atlanta, Ga.	.51
Canton, Ohio	.51
Chicago, Ill.	1.34
Cincinnati, Ohio	.65
Claymont, Del.	.79
Cleveland, Ohio	.76
Coatesville, Pa.	.50
Conshohocken, Pa.	.20
Detroit, Mich.	.95
Duluth, Minn.	.50
Harrisburg, Pa.	.51
Houston, Tex.	.57
Johnstown, Pa.	.75

Bills of Lading

Pittsburgh — The Economic Stabilization Agency stated that ceiling prices on scrap will apply on bills of lading dated subsequent to effective date of the order which is 12.01 A. M., Wednesday, Feb. 7. Date of actual delivery to the consumer's mill or foundry is not a factor.

Kansas City, Mo.	.78
Kokomo, Ind.	.51
Los Angeles, Cal.	.66
Middletown, Ohio	.26
Midland, Pa.	.75
Minnequa, Colo.	.33
Monessen, Pa.	.51
Phoenixville, Pa.	.51
Pittsburg, Calif.	.65
Pittsburgh, Pa.	.99
Portland, Ore.	.52
Portsmouth, Ohio	.51
St. Louis, Mo.	.51
San Francisco, Cal.	.66
Seattle, Wash.	.59
Sharon, Pa.	.75
Sparrows Point, Md.	.20
Steubenville, Ohio	.51
Warren, Pa.	.75
Weirton, W. Va.	.70
Youngstown, Ohio	.75

(b) The Pittsburgh, Pa., basing point includes the switching districts of Bessemer, Homestead, Duquesne and Munhall, Pa.

(c) The Cincinnati, Ohio, basing point includes the switching district of Newport, Ky.

(d) The St. Louis, Mo., basing point includes the switching districts of Granite City, East St. Louis and Madison, Ill.

(e) The San Francisco, Cal., basing point includes the switching districts of South San Francisco, Niles and Oakland, Cal.

(f) The Claymont, Delaware, basing point includes the switching districts of Chester, Pa.

(g) The Chicago, Ill., basing point includes the switching district of Gary, Ind.

(h) The Los Angeles, Cal., basing point includes the Firestone switching district.

•6 **Ceiling delivered prices for shipment by rail, vessel, or combination thereof, for steel scrap of dealer and industrial origin.** (a) The ceiling delivered price of any grade of steel scrap delivered by rail, vessel, or combination thereof, shall be the shipping point price as determined in section •4 hereof, plus the actual charge for transporting the scrap from the shipping point to the point of delivery by the means of transportation employed.

(b) If delivery to the consumer involves vessel movement, the actual charges incurred at a public dock may be added to the actual transportation charges. Where the dock facilities are owned or controlled by the shipper of the scrap, a maximum charge of $1.25 per gross ton may be added to the actual transportation charges; except that the maximum charge shall be 95 cents per gross ton at Memphis, Tenn., $1.50 per gross ton at any Great Lakes port, or $1.75 per gross ton at any New England port.

(c) In the case of water movement by deck scow or railroad lighter, no established charges at the dock or any charge or cost customarily incurred at the dock may be included in the delivered price. In lieu thereof a maximum charge of $1.25 per gross ton may be included in the delivered price.

•7 **Basing point prices for steel scrap of**

---

railroad origin. (a) **Basing point prices from which ceiling on-line and ceiling delivered prices are computed.**

(1) Basing point prices for the base grade. No. 1 railroad heavy melting steel. Grade 1:

	Price per Gross Ton
Alabama City, Ala.	$ 41.00
Ashland, Ky.	44.00
Atlanta, Ga.	41.00
Bethlehem, Pa.	44.00
Birmingham, Ala.	41.00
Brackenridge, Pa.	46.00
Buffalo, N. Y.	45.00
Butler, Pa.	46.00
Canton, Ohio	46.00
Chicago, Ill.	44.50
Cincinnati, Ohio	45.00
Claymont, Del.	44.50
Cleveland, Ohio	45.00
Coatesville, Pa.	44.50
Conshohocken, Pa.	44.50
Detroit, Mich.	42.00
Duluth, Minn.	42.00
Harrisburg, Pa.	44.50
Houston, Tex.	39.00
Johnstown, Pa.	46.00
Kansas City, Mo.	41.50
Kokomo, Ind.	44.00
Los Angeles, Cal.	37.00
Middletown, Ohio.	45.00
Midland, Pa.	46.00
Minnequa, Colo.	40.00
Monesen, Pa.	46.00
Phoenixville, Pa.	44.50
Pittsburg, Cal.	37.00
Pittsburgh, Pa.	46.00
Portland, Ore.	37.00
Portsmouth, Ohio	44.00
St. Louis, Mo.	43.00
San Francisco, Cal.	37.00
Seattle, Wash.	37.00
Sharon, Pa.	46.00
Sparrows Point, Md.	44.00
Steubenville, Ohio	46.00
Warren, Ohio	46.00
Weirton, W. Va.	46.00
Youngstown, Ohio	46.00

(2) **Differentials per gross ton above or below the price of Grade 1 (No. 1 railroad heavy melting steel) for other grades of railroad steel scrap:**

Grades	Differentials
2. No. 2 Heavy Melting Steel	— $ 2.00
3. No. 2 Steel Wheels	Base
4. Hollow Bored Axles	Base
5. No. 1 Busheling	— 3.50
6. No. 1 Turnings	— 3.00
7. No. 2 Turnings, Drillings and Borings	— 12.00
8. No. 2 Cast Steel	— 6.00
9. Uncut Frogs and Switches	Base
10. Flues, Tubes and Pipes	— 8.00
11. Structural, Wrought Iron and/or Steel, Uncut	— 6.00
12. Destroyed Steel Cars	— 8.00
13. No. 1 Sheet Scrap	— 9.50
14. Scrap Rails, Random Lengths	+ 2.00
15. Rerolling Rails	+ 7.00
16. Cut Rails, 3 feet and under	+ 5.00
17. Cut Rails, 2 feet and under	+ 6.00
18. Cut Rails, 18 inches and under	+ 8.00
19. Cast Steel No. 1	+ 3.00
20. Uncut Tires	+ 2.00
21. Cut Tires	+ 5.00
22. Uncut Bolsters and Side Frames	Base
23. Cut Bolsters and Side Frames	+ 3.00
24. Angle and Splice Bars	+ 5.00
25. Solid Steel Axles	+ 12.00
26. Steel Wheels, No. 3 Oversize	Base
27. Steel Wheels, No. 3	+ 5.00
28. Spring Steel	+ 5.00
29. Couplers and Knuckles	+ 5.00
30. Wrought Iron	+ 8.00

(b) **Restrictions on use.** (1) The price established for grade 15 (rerolling rails) may be charged only when purchased and sold for rerolling use; otherwise, the ceiling price for such grade shall not exceed the ceiling price established for grade 14 (scrap rails in random lengths). (The term "rerolling rails" includes any rails which are sold to be used for rerolling, irrespective of whether or not such rails are usable for relaying.)

(2) The price established for grade 30 (Wrought Iron) may be charged only when sold to a producer of Wrought Iron; otherwise, the ceiling price for such grade shall not exceed the ceiling price established for the base grade, No. 1 railroad heavy melting steel.

• **8. Ceiling on-line prices for steel scrap of railroad origin.** The term "on-line prices" means the ceiling prices that the originating railroad may charge for scrap delivered to a consumer located on the line of the railroad.

(a) **On-line prices for operating railroads operating in a basing point.** The ceiling on-line price of any grade of steel scrap originating from an operating railroad operating in a basing point name in section • 7 hereof shall be the price established in that section for the scrap at the highest priced basing point in which the railroad operates.

(b) **On-line prices for operating railroads not operating in a basing point.** The ceiling on-line price of any grade of steel scrap originating from an operating railroad not operating in a basing point named in section • 7 hereof shall be the price established for the scrap at the most favorable basing point named in that section minus the foreign line proportion of the lowest established charge for transporting scrap by rail from the scrap accumulation point of the railroad to such basing point. (The "scrap accumulation point" shall be that point from which the greatest tonnage of scrap was shipped in the calendar year, 1950). The ceiling on-line price of No. 1 railroad heavy melting steel need not fall below $34.00 per gross ton (with differentials established in section • 7 hereof for all other grades).

The "most favorable basing point" is the basing point named in section • 7 hereof which will yield the highest ceiling on-line price.

On and after the effective date of this regulation, no operating railroad not operating in a basing point named in section • 7 hereof may sell or offer to sell iron and steel scrap to a consumer or his broker (without obtaining prior written approval from the Office of Price Stabilization) unless it has filed with the Office of Price Stabilization, Washington 25, D. C., a statement in writing setting forth its ceiling on-line price for No. 1 railroad heavy melting steel and describing the method by which the said ceiling on-line price was calculated and such statement has been approved in writing by the Office of Price Stabilization, Washington, D. C. The statement shall include: the most favorable basing point selected, the price at such basing point, the location of the scrap accumulation point, the lowest established charge for transporting scrap by rail from such accumulation point to the named basing point, and the foreign line proportion of such lowest established charge.

(c) **Non-operating railroad.** (1) The ceiling on-line (or shipping point) price of any grade of steel scrap originating from a non-operating railroad shall be the price established for the scrap at the most favorable basing point named in section • 7 hereof minus the lowest established charge for transporting scrap by rail from the scrap accumulation point of the railroad to such basing point. (The "scrap accumulation point" shall be that point from which the greatest tonnage of scrap was shipped in the calendar year 1950; except, that the non-operating railroad may be permitted to

use more than one accumulation point upon filing with the Office of Price Stabilization notice thereof showing the tonnage shipped from such additional point during 1950). The ceiling on-line price of No. 1 railroad heavy melting steel need not fall below $34.00 per gross ton (with differentials established in section • 7 hereof for all other grades). The "most favorable basing point" is the basing point named in section • 7 hereof which will yield the highest ceiling on-line or shipping point price.

(2) Where the non-operating railroad is located within a basing point set forth in section • 7 hereof, the switching charge deductions established in section • 5 hereof shall be applicable.

312.9 **Ceiling delivered prices for shipment by rail, vessel, or combination thereof, for steel scrap of railroad origin.** (a) **When delivered to a consumer located on the line of a railroad.** The ceiling delivered price of any grade of steel scrap originating from an operating railroad and delivered to a consumer's plant located on the line of that railroad shall be the ceiling on-line price established in section • 8 hereof.

(b) **When delivered to a consumer located off the line of the originating railroad.** The ceiling delivered price of any grade of steel scrap originating from an operating railroad and delivered to a consumer located off the line of that railroad, by rail, vessel or combination thereof, shall be the ceiling on-line price established in section • 8 hereof, plus the foreign line proportion of the through rate from the point of shipment to the consumer's plant via the junction nearest such plant in terms of transportation charges, or the commercial rate from such nearest junction to the consumer's plant (unless off-line routing at another point is directed by order of a government agency). In no case may a railroad seller participate in the transportation charges incurred in off-line delivery of steel scrap unless the ceiling on-line price for the scrap is reduced by the amount of the participation in the off-line charges.

(c) **When delivered to a consumer from a non-operating railroad.** The ceiling delivered price of any grade of steel scrap originating from a non-operating railroad shall be the ceiling price established in section • 8 (c) hereof, plus transportation charges to the point of delivery. Such transportation charges shall be computed in the same manner as charges allowable under section • 6 or • 15 hereof for dealer of industrial scrap.

• **10 Ceiling prices for railroad steel scrap sold by sellers other than railroads.** (a) Railroad steel scrap prepared by a dealer or moving through a dealer's yard (except for unprepared scrap prepared in-transit pursuant to section • 15 hereof or sold by any other person than a railroad as defined in this regulation, shall be classified and priced under sections • 3 and • 4 hereof except that for Grades Nos. 3, 4, 8, 14, 15, 16, 17, 18, 19, 20, 21, 22, 23, 24, 25, 26 and 27 of steel scrap set forth in section • 7(a)(2) hereof the ceiling shipping point prices shall be the same as those established for non-operating railroads in section • 8(c) hereof, and the ceiling delivered prices shall be the same as those established for non-operating railroads in section • 9(c) hereof.

(b) Where a dealer or contractor demolishes railroad equipment on the property of, or in a yard provided exclusively for that purpose by the railroad awarding the contract, the resultant railroad scrap may be sold at prices not in excess of the ceiling prices established in section • 8(c) hereof for non-operating railroads; **Provided,** That in each case the dealer or contractor awarded such contract by a railroad reports to the Office of Price Stabilization, Washington 25, D. C., within 7 days after the

award of the contract the name of the selling railroad, the type of equipment involved, the location at which demolition will take place, and the estimated tonnage of each grade of scrap resulting; also such other relevant information as he considers necessary or advisable to explain the transaction.

• **11 Ceiling shipping point and ceiling on-line prices for all cast iron scrap.** (a) The ceiling price per gross ton for any of the following grades of cast iron scrap shall be the price shown in the following table, f.o.b. the shipping point:

Grades	Price per Gross Ton
1. Cast iron No. 1 (cupola cast)	$ 49.00
2. Cast iron No. 2 (charging box cast)	47.00
3. Cast iron No. 3 (heavy breakable cast)	45.00
4. Cast iron No. 4 (burnt cast)	41.00
5. Cast iron brake shoes	41.00
6. Stove plate	46.00
7. Clean auto cast	52.00
8. Unstripped motor blocks	48.00
9. Wheels No. 1	47.00
10. Malleable	55.00
11. Drop broken machinery casts	52.00

(b) **Restrictions on use.** (1) The ceiling shipping point or on-line price which a basic open hearth consumer may pay for cast iron No. 1 (cupola cast), wheels No. 1, clean auto cast or malleable shall be the ceiling price established for cast iron No. 3 (heavy breakable cast).

(2) The ceiling shipping point or on-line price which any foundry consumer other than a malleable iron producer may pay for Grade 10 (malleable) shall be the ceiling price established for cast iron No. 1 (cupola cast).

• **12 Ceiling delivered prices for shipment by rail, vessel, or combination thereof, for all cast-iron scrap.** (a) The ceiling delivered price for shipment by rail, vessel, or combination thereof of any grade of cast iron scrap of dealer or industrial origin shall be the shipping point price as determined in section • 11 hereof plus the actual charge for transporting the scrap from the shipping point to the point of delivery by the means of transportation employed. If delivery to the consumer involves water movement the actual charges incurred at a public dock may be added to the actual transportation charges. Where the dock facilities are owned or controlled by the shipper of the cast iron scrap, the following maximum dock charges may be added to the actual transportation charges: At Memphis, Tenn., 95 cents per gross ton; at any Great Lakes port, $1.50 per gross ton; at all New England ports, $1.75 per gross ton; and at all other ports, $1.25 per gross ton.

• **13 Ceiling delivered prices for shipment by truck for all steel or cast iron scrap.** (a) Where delivery of any grade of iron or steel scrap is made by public carrier truck, the ceiling delivered price shall be the ceiling shipping point price, or in the case of railroad scrap, the ceiling on-line price, as established in section • 4, • 8, • 10 or • 11 hereof, whichever is applicable, plus the actual public carrier charge.

(b) Where delivery of any grade of iron or steel scrap is made in a truck owned or controlled by the shipper or broker of the scrap, the ceiling delivered price shall be the ceiling shipping point price, or in the case of railroad scrap, the ceiling on-line price, as established in section • 4, • 8, • 10 or • 11 hereof, whichever is applicable, plus the established rail carload freight rate for shipping scrap from the rail siding nearest the point of delivery, except that, the transportation charge for delivering any grade of iron or steel scrap in a truck owned or controlled by the shipper shall not be in excess of $4.00 and need not fall below $2.50 per gross ton.

General Provisions

•14 **Unlisted grades.** If the seller is unable to determine a ceiling price for any grade of iron or steel scrap under the applicable provisions hereof (which, in the opinion of the Director of Price Stabilization, provided adequate pricing instructions for all recognized grades), he shall file an application for approval of a ceiling price with the Office of Price Stabilization, Washington 25, D. C. The application shall set forth: (1) a complete description of the material, and (2) the ceiling price being requested.

The seller may not deliver or sell at his requested price until he has received written approval of the price from the Office of Price Stabilization.

•15. **Intransit preparation.** (a) A consumer may designate a dealer or dealers to prepare steel scrap of dealer and industrial origin intransit on a preparation fee basis under one of the following circumstances:

(1) Where unprepared steel scrap of dealer and industrial origin is allocated for preparation intransit by the National Production Authority.

(2) Where a consumer purchases unprepared scrap of dealer and industrial origin in rail carload lots.

(3) Where Grade 6 (machine shop turnings) or other grades of long or bushy turnings are allocated by the National Production Authority in rail carload lots to a consumer, or where a consumer purchases such turnings in rail carload lots for crushing.

(4) Where Grade 10 (cast iron borings) is allocated by the National Production Authority to a consumer for briquetting.

(b) A consumer may designate a dealer or dealers to prepare steel scrap of railroad origin intranst on a preparation fee basis only where a consumer without adequate preparation facilities purchases unprepared steel scrap from an originating railroad.

(c) A consumer may designate a dealer or dealers to prepare cast iron scrap intransit on a preparation fee basis where such consumer is without adequate preparation facilities.

(d) No fee may be paid to the person preparing scrap intransit pursuant to the provisions of this section if the scrap originates in the preparer's yard or if title to the scrap resides in the preparer at any time after the scrap leaves its shipping point, unless such scrap is allocated by the National Production Authority.

(e) The maximum preparation fee for preparing any grade of iron or steel scrap intransit shall be the applicable fee established in section •16 hereof.

(f) Whenever intransit preparation of iron or steel scrap is permissible pursuant to the provisions of this section, the ceiling delivered price shall be the ceiling shipping point price or ceiling on-line price for unprepared scrap plus the rail transportation charges incurred in moving the scrap to the point of preparation, plus the applicable ceiling preparation fee as established in section •16 hereof, plus the transportation charges from the preparation yard to the point of delivery as established and restricted in section •6, •9, •12 or •13 hereof, whichever is applicable.

•16 **Ceiling preparation charges.** (a) The ceiling fees which may be charged for intransit preparation of any grade of steel scrap of dealer or industrial origin which is allocated by the National Production Authority to a consumer, shall be as follows:

(1) For preparing into Grade No. 1 (No. 1 heavy melting steel), Grade No. 2 (No. 2 heavy melting steel) or Grade No. 3 (No. 1 busheling), $8.00 per gross ton.

(2) For hydraulically compressing Grade No. 4 (No. 1 bundles), $6.00 per gross ton or Grade No. 5 (No. 2 bundles), $8.00 per gross ton.

(3) For crushing Grade No. 6 (machine shop turnings), $3.00 per gross ton.

(4) For preparing into Grade No. 25 (briquetted turnings), $6.00 per gross ton.

(5) For preparing into Grade No. 19 (briquetted cast iron borings), $6.00 per gross ton.

(6) For preparing into Grade No. 12 (bar crops and plate scrap), Grade No. 13 (cast steel), Grade No. 14 (punchings and plate scrap), or Grade No. 18 (cut structural and plate scrap, 1 foot and under), $10.00 per gross ton.

(7) For preparing into Grade No. 17 (cut structural and plate scrap, 2 feet and under) or Grade No. 21 (foundry steel, 1 foot and under), $10.00 per gross ton.

(8) For preparing into Grade No. 16 (cut structural and plate scrap, 3 feet and under), or Grade No. 20 (foundry steel, 2 feet and under), $10.00 per gross ton.

(9) For hydraulically compressing Grade No. 15 (electric furnace bundles), $8.00 per gross ton.

(10) For preparing into Grade No. 28 (wrought iron), $10.00 per gross ton.

(b) The ceiling fees which may be charged for intransit preparation of any grade of steel scrap of railroad origin shall be as follows:

(1) For preparing into Grade No. 1 (No. 1 railroad heavy melting steel) and Grade No. 2 (No. 2 railroad heavy melting steel), $8.00 per gross ton.

(2) For hydraulically compressing Grade No. 13 (No. 1 sheet scrap), $6.00 per gross ton.

(3) For preparing into Grade No. 16 (Cut Rails, 3 feet and under), $4.00 per gross ton.

(4) For preparing into Grade No. 17 (Cut Rails, 2 feet and under), $5.00 per gross ton.

(5) For preparing into Grade No. 18 (Cut Rails, 18 inches and under), $7.00 per gross ton.

(6) For preparing into Grade No. 21 (cut tires), $4.00 per gross ton.

(7) For preparing into Grade No. 23 (cut Bolsters and side Frames), $4.00 per gross ton.

(c) The ceiling fees which may be charged for intransit preparation of cast iron shall be limited to the following:

For preparing Grade No. 8 (unstripped motor blocks) into Grade No. 7 (clean auto cast), $9.00 per gross ton, and Grade No. 3 (heavy breakable cast) into Grade No. 1 (cast iron No. 1), $4.00 per gross ton.

(d) Whenever scrap has arrived at its point of delivery and the consumer engages a dealer to prepare such scrap, no fee may be charged or paid for such service unless the consumer obtains prior written approval from the Office of Price Stabilization, Washington 25, D. C.

(e) No preparation charge other than the charges set forth in this section may be made for the preparation of any grade of iron or steel scrap unless the consumer has secured prior written approval of such charge from the Office of Price Stabilization, Washington 25, D. C.

•17 **Premiums for alloy content.** With the exception of the premium specifically authorized in this section no premium may be charged for alloys contained in iron or steel scrap. Except as outlined below the premiums are not confined to a particular use.

(a) **Nickel.** A premium of $1.25 per gross ton for each ¼ of 1 pct may be charged in addition to the applicable ceiling price for No. 1 heavy melting steel where the scrap contains not less than 1 pct and not over 5.25 pct nickel.

(b) **Molybdenum.** A premium of $2.00 per gross ton may be charged in addition to the applicable ceiling price for No. 1 heavy melting steel for scrap containing not less than .15 pct molybdenum. A premium of $3.00 per gross ton may be charged in addition to the applicable ceiling price for No. 1 heavy melting steel for scrap containing not less than .65 pct molybdenum.

(c) **Manganese.** A premium of $4.00 per gross ton over the applicable basing point price for No. 1 heavy melting steel or No. 1 railroad heavy melting steel may be charged where scrap contains not less than 10 pct manganese and is in sizes larger than 12 x 24 x 8 inches. A premium of $14.00 per gross ton over the applicable basing point price for No. 1 heavy melting steel or No. 1 railroad heavy melting steel may be charged where scrap contains not less than 10 pct manganese and is cut to sizes of 12 x 24 x 8 inches or smaller. The manganese premiums provided in this paragraph (c) are only applicable if the scrap is sold for electric furnace use except on allocation by the National Production Authority.

(d) **Silicon.** The adjustments established under section •4 hereof for electric furnace, and foundry grades shall not be applicable if the scrap contains silicon between .5 pct and 1.75 pct.

(e) **Chromium.** Steel scrap conforming to SAE 52100 may command a premium of $1.00 per gross ton in addition to the applicable ceiling price for the corresponding grade when sold for electric furnace use only, but in no event shall the ceiling price plus the premium provided herein exceed the ceiling price for No. 1 heavy melting steel plus $1.00.

(f) **Multiple alloys.** Where any grade of scrap contains two alloy elements for which premiums have been established in this section, the total premiums may not exceed the ceiling premium for any one contained alloy.

•18 **Mixed shipments.** When grades of scrap commanding different ceiling prices under the provisions of this regulation are included in one vehicle, the ceiling price shall be the applicable ceiling price in section •4, •8, •10 or •11 hereof for the lowest grade contained in the vehicle, except when the grades are invoiced as separate grades and the grades are so loaded in the vehicle that they can readily be distinguished and separately weighed.

•19 **Commissions.** (a) No commission shall be payable on sales made under this regulation except by a consumer to a broker for brokerage services rendered to the consumer. Where scrap is allocated by the National Production Authority other than from a government agency, the seller may designate a broker. Where scrap is allocated by the National Production Authority from a governmental agency, the consumer may designate a broker. In the event that a broker purchases iron or steel scrap for sale to a consumer, such consumer may pay such broker a commission not exceeding $1.00 per gross ton. No commission shall be payable unless:

(1) The broker is regularly and primarily engaged in the business of buying and selling iron and steel scrap;

(2) The broker guarantees the quality and delivery of an agreed tonnage of scrap;

(3) The scrap is purchased by the consumer at a price no higher than the ceiling prices established in this regulation;

(4) The broker sells the scrap to the consumer at the same price, with the same

discounts and allowances, at which he purchased it, and does not include in the shipping point price any cost, fee, or charge incurred in placing the scrap at its shipping point;

(5) The broker does not split or divide the commission in whole or in part, with the seller or sellers of the scrap, or with another broker, or sub-broker, or with the consumer;

(6) The commission is shown as a separate item on the invoice.

(b) No commission shall be payable to a person for scrap which he prepares.

(c) No commission shall be payable to a person controlling, or holding directly or indirectly a substantial financial interest in the person preparing the scrap, or to a person employed or controlled by the person preparing the scrap, or to a person in whom the person preparing the scrap holds directly or indirectly a substantial financial interest or control.

• 20 **Unprepared scrap.** (a) The term "unprepared scrap" shall have its customary trade meaning and shall not include such demolition projects as bridges, box cars or automobiles, which must be so priced that the prepared scrap will be delivered to the consumer within the ceiling delivered prices established by this regulation.

(b) For unprepared steel scrap other than materials suitable for hydraulic compression, the ceiling basing point prices shall be $8.00 per gross ton beneath the price of the prepared base grades, No. 1 heavy melting steel or No. 1 railroad heavy melting steel, as established in section • 3 or • 7.

(c) For unprepared material which when compressed constitutes No. 1 bundles the ceiling basing point price shall be $6.00 per gross ton beneath the ceiling basing point price for No. 1 bundles or when compressed constitutes No. 2 bundles the ceiling basing point price shall be $8.00 per gross ton beneath the ceiling basing point price for No. 2 bundles, as established in section • 3 hereof.

(d) Any iron casting which cannot be broken with an ordinary drop into Grade No. 2 (cast iron No. 2) or Grade No. 1 (cast iron No. 1) as established in section • 11 hereof may not be classified as Grade No. 3 (cast iron No. 3). Where such iron casting requiring blasting or other special preparation is sold to a consumer other than the shipping point price for Grade No. 3 (cast iron No. 3) as established in section • 11 hereof must be reduced by the amount of the additional charges required for preparation.

• 21 **Transportation charges.** (a) The rail or vessel charges, or combination rail-vessel charges, used in computing ceiling shipping point or ceiling on-line prices in section • 4 or • 8 hereof need not reflect any increase in rates which became effective after January 1, 1951, nor need such charges reflect any transportation tax.

(b) Any tax imposed upon the transportation charges from the shipping point to the point of delivery, may be included in the ceiling delivery price.

(c) No vessel charge shall be deemed an established charge within the provisions of this regulation unless regular vessel movement of scrap, except for seasonal restrictions, is being made to the most favorable basing point as of the effective date of this regulation, as a customary business practice.

(d) Where rail or vessel charges vary because of seasonal factors, the lowest established charge shall be the lowest charge in effect at any time during the year.

• 22 **Weights to govern.** (a) Except as

Scrap Prices Hold

New York—Restrained by the general price freeze order and the pending price rollback regulation, scrap prices in all markets were unchanged from last week to Tuesday, Feb. 6, with the exception of two minor price dips in Birmingham and some upward price revisions for Seattle.

In Birmingham, No. 1 RR. heavy melting dropped from last week's $43 to $44 down to $42.50 to $43.50 and No. 1 cupola cast lost $1, becoming $53 to $54. The Seattle price of No. 1 heavy rose to $35; No. 2 heavy, $35; electric furnace 1 ft and under, $50; and No. 1 cupola cast, $45 to $50.

---

otherwise provided in this section, settlement for all scrap shall be made on the basis of weights at the point of delivery.

(b) **Rail shipments.** If the consumer is a member of a weighing association, settlement shall be on the basis of mill weights. If the consumer does not have weighing facilities, settlement shall be made on the basis of railroad weights at the point of delivery.

No adjustment need be made for shortages of 500 pounds or less per car between shipping point weights and weights at the point of delivery. If the shortage exceeds 500 pounds per car, adjustment must be made for the full shortage.

(c) **Vessel shipment.** When shipment is wholly or partially by vessel, weights at the dock prior to vessel movement shall govern. If the scrap moves from the shipping point to the dock by rail and weights at the shipping point have been determined, no adjustment need be made for differences of 500 pounds or less per car between shipping point weights and weights at the dock. If the difference exceeds 500 pounds per car, adjustment must be made for the full shortage in the car.

(Provisions 23 through 25 give specifications of all grades of scrap.)

Miscellaneous Provisions

• 26 **Imported scrap.** (a) This Ceiling Price Regulation No. is not applicable to imported scrap as defined in section • 28(f) hereof.

• 27 **Exported scrap.** The ceiling price for any grade of iron or steel scrap sold for export or to an exporter shall be the ceiling shipping point or on-line price as established in section • 4, • 8, • 10 or • 11 hereof, whichever is applicable, plus all transportation charges allowable under the appropriate section, to the place of export. For scrap exported by vessel, this ceiling export price shall be f.a.s. vessel at the place of export, and the actual cost incidental to shipment and export from that point may be added, if shown as separate charge on the invoice.

• 28 **Definitions.** (a) "Person" includes an individual, corporation, partnership, association, or any other organized group of persons or legal successor or representative of any of

---

the foregoing, and includes the United States or any agency thereof, or any other government, or any of its political subdivisions, or any agency of any of the foregoing.

(b) "Iron and steel scrap" means all ferrous materials, either alloyed or unalloyed, of which iron or steel is a principal component, which are the waste of industrial fabrication, or objects that have been discarded on account of obsolescence, failure or any other reason, when sold to a consumer as defined in paragraph (c) of this section, or his broker.

(c) "Consumer" means a purchaser of iron or steel scrap for use in the production of iron or steel products by melting or rerolling; or any person purchasing iron or steel scrap for use as a reduction agent in the production of chemicals or pigments, for use in the production of non-ferrous materials, for use as ballast or counterweights, or for annealing; and includes any governmental agency or subdivision.

(d) "Operating railroad" means a railroad, terminal association, or switching company which operates a railway line and derives at least a portion of its revenue from the carrying of freight.

(e) "Non-operating railroad" means all railroads other that operating railroads, as defined in paragraph (d) of this section, and includes suburban and interurban electric railroads, street railways, refrigerator car, stock car, sleeping car and tank car companies engaged primarily in the transportation business, but does not include mine or logging roads.

(f) "Imported scrap" means all iron and steel scrap having a point of origin outside the 48 states of the United States and the District of Columbia.

(g) "Free of alloys" means that any alloys contained in the steel are residual and have not been added for the purpose of making an alloy steel. Steel scrap will be considered free of alloys where the residual alloying elements do not exceed the following amounts:

Nickel	0.45
Chromium	.20
Molybdenum	.10
Manganese	1.65

and where the combined residuals other than the manganese do not exceed a total of .60 pct.

(h) "Lowest established charge." The term shall mean the rail or vessel freight rate for transporting material generally classified as iron or steel scrap and shall not refer to freight charges for transporting any special grade thereof even though the latter grade is actually being shipped.

(i) "Shipping point." Scrap is at its shipping point in the case of all rail, rail-vessel, rail-truck or truck-rail movement when it has been placed f.o.b. railroad cars for shipment to the consumer; in the case of all-vessel, vessel-rail or vessel-truck movement, when it has been placed f.a.s. vessel for shipment to the consumer; and, in the case of all-truck movement, when it has been placed f.o.b. truck for shipment to the consumer.

(j) "Point of delivery" shall mean that point at which scrap has arrived for unloading at the plant of the consumer.

(k) "Dealer and industrial origin" shall mean all sources of scrap other than railroads as defined in this regulation.

(l) "Scrap accumulation point" shall be that point from which the greatest tonnage of scrap was shipped in the calendar year 1950.

(Provisions 29 through 33 deal with records and reports, below ceiling prices, evasion and enforcement of the order, and petitions for amendment.)

*F*or the Purchase or Sale of
Iron and Steel Scrap...
CONSULT OUR NEAREST OFFICE

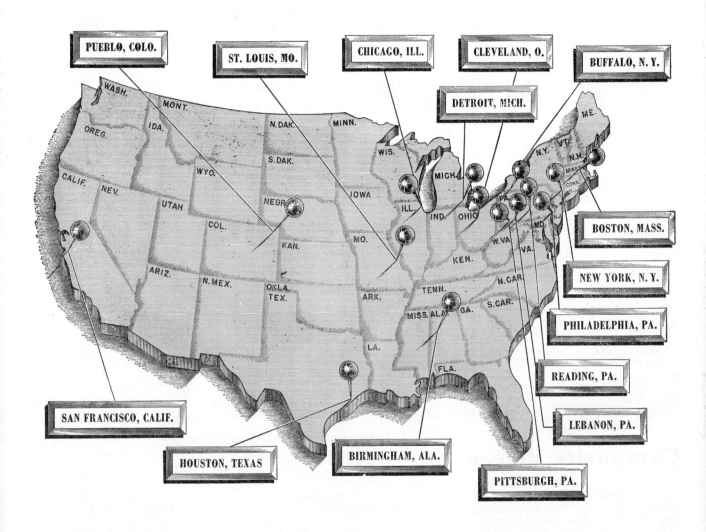

The energy and integrity of our organization is ready to serve your best interests ...
Since 1889, Luria Brothers & Company, Inc. have made fair dealings their constant aim.

CONSULT OUR NEAREST OFFICE FOR THE PURCHASE AND SALE OF SCRAP

LURIA BROTHERS AND COMPANY, INC.

Main Office
LINCOLN-LIBERTY BLDG.
Philadelphia 7, Pennsylvania

Yards
LEBANON, PA. • READING, PA.
DETROIT (ECORSE), MICH.
MODENA, PA. • PITTSBURGH, PA.

Branch Offices

BIRMINGHAM, ALA.	CHICAGO, ILL.	HOUSTON, TEXAS	PITTSBURGH, PA.
Empire Bldg.	100 W. Monroe St.	1114 Texas Av. Bldg.	Oliver Bldg.
BOSTON, MASS.	CLEVELAND, O.	LEBANON, PA.	PUEBLO, COLO.
Statler Bldg.	1022 Midland Bldg.	Luria Bldg.	334 Colorado Bldg.
BUFFALO, N.Y.	DETROIT, MICH.	NEW YORK, N.Y.	READING, PA.
Genesee Bldg.	2011 Book Bldg.	100 Park Avenue	Luria Bldg.
	ST. LOUIS, MO.	SAN FRANCISCO, CAL.	
	2110 Railway Exchange Bldg.	Pacific Gas & Elec. Co. Bldg.	

LEADERS IN IRON AND STEEL SCRAP SINCE 1889

Comparison of Prices

Steel prices in this page are the average of various f.o.b. quotations of major producing areas: **Pittsburgh, Chicago, Gary, Cleveland, Youngstown.**

Flat-Rolled Steel:

(cents per pound)	Feb. 6, 1951	Jan. 30, 1951	Jan. 9, 1951	Feb. 7, 1950
Hot-rolled sheets	3.60	3.60	3.60	3.35
Cold-rolled sheets	4.35	4.35	4.35	4.10
Galvanized sheets (10 ga)	4.80	4.80	4.80	4.40
Hot-rolled strip	3.50	3.50	3.50	3.25
Cold-rolled strip	4.75	4.75	4.75	4.21
Plate	3.70	3.70	3.70	3.50
Plates wrought iron.....	7.85	7.85	7.85	7.85
Stains C-R-strip (No. 302)	36.50	36.50	36.50	33.00

Tin and Terneplate:

(dollars per base box)				
Tinplate (1.50 lb) cokes.	$7.50	$7.50	$7.50	$7.50
Tinplate, electro (0.50 lb)	6.60	6.60	6.60	6.60
Special coated mfg. ternes	6.35	6.35	6.35	6.50

Bars and Shapes:

(cents per pound)				
Merchant bars	3.70	3.70	3.70	3.45
Cold finished bars.......	4.55	4.55	4.55	*4.145
Alloy bars	4.30	4.30	4.30	3.95
Structural shapes	3.65	3.65	3.65	3.40
Stainless bars (No. 302).	31.25	31.25	31.25	28.50
Wrought iron bars......	9.50	9.50	9.50	9.50

Wire:

(cents per pound)				
Bright wire	4.85	4.85	4.85	4.50

Rails:

(dollars per 100 lb)				
Heavy rails	$3.60	$3.60	$3.60	$3.40
Light rails	4.00	4.00	4.00	3.75

Semifinished Steel:

(dollars per net ton)				
Rerolling billets	$56.00	$56.00	$56.00	$54.00
Slabs, rerolling	56.00	56.00	56.00	54.00
Forging billets	66.00	66.00	66.00	63.00
Alloy blooms billets, slabs	70.00	70.00	70.00	66.00

Wire Rod and Skelp:

(cents per pound)				
Wire rods	4.10	4.10	4.10	3.85
Skelp	3.35	3.35	3.35	3.15

Pig Iron:

(per gross ton)	Feb. 6, 1951	Jan. 30, 1951	Jan. 9, 1951	Feb. 7, 1950
No. 2 foundry, del'd Phila.	$57.77	$57.77	$57.77	$50.42
No. 2, Valley furnace....	52.50	52.50	52.50	46.50
No. 2, Southern Cin'ti....	55.58	55.58	55.58	49.08
No. 2, Birmingham......	48.88	48.88	48.88	42.38
No. 2, foundry, Chicago†	52.50	52.50	52.50	46.50
Basic del'd Philadelphia..	56.92	56.92	56.92	49.92
Basic, Valley furnace....	52.00	52.00	52.00	46.00
Malleable, Chicago†	52.50	52.50	52.50	46.50
Malleable, Valley	52.50	52.50	52.50	46.50
Charcoal, Chicago	70.56	70.56	70.56	68.56
Ferromanganese‡	186.25	186.25	181.20	173.40

†The switching charge for delivery to foundries in the Chicago district is $1 per ton.
‡Average of U. S. prices quoted on Ferroalloy page.

Scrap:

(per gross ton)				
Heavy melt'g steel, P'gh..	$51.13	$51.13	$46.13	$31.25
Heavy melt'g steel, Phila.	47.50	47.50	44.50	23.00
Heavy melt'g steel, Ch'go	44.63	44.63	44.63	27.50
No. 1 hy. com. sh't, Det.	40.25	40.25	40.25	23.50
Low phos. Young'n......	54.50	54.50	48.63	31.75
No. 1 cast, Pittsburgh...	67.75	67.75	67.75	37.50
No. 1 cast, Philadelphia..	62.50	62.50	62.50	37.00
No. 1 cast, Chicago......	63.00	63.00	63.00	38.50

Coke: Connellsville:

(per net ton at oven)				
Furnace coke, prompt...	$14.25	$14.25	$14.25	$14.00
Foundry coke, prompt...	17.25	17.25	17.25	15.75

Nonferrous Metals:

(cents per pound to large buyers)				
Copper, electro, Conn....	24.50	24.50	24.50	18.50
Copper, Lake, Conn.....	24.625	24.625	24.625	18.625
Tin Straits, New York...	*$1.825*†	*$1.83**	$1.63	74.50
Zinc, East St. Louis.....	17.50	17.50	17.50	9.75
Lead, St. Louis..........	16.80	16.80	16.80	11.80
Aluminum, virgin	19.00	19.00	19.00	17.00
Nickel, electrolytic	53.55	53.55	53.55	42.97
Magnesium, ingot	24.50	24.50	24.50	20.50
Antimony, Laredo, Tex...	42.00	42.00	32.00	27.25

†Tentative. *Revised.

Composite Prices

Starting with the issue of May 12, 1949, the weighted finished steel composite was revised for the years 1941 to date. The weights used are based on the average product shipments for the 7 years 1937 to 1940 inclusive and 1946 to 1948 inclusive. The use of quarterly figures has been eliminated because it was too sensitive. (See p. 130 of May 12, 1949, issue.)

	Finished Steel Base Price	Pig Iron	Scrap Steel
Feb. 6, 1951............	4.131¢ per lb...........	....$52.69 per gross ton....	......$47.75 per gross ton......
One week ago.........	4.131¢ per lb...........	.... 52.69 per gross ton....	...... 47.75 per gross ton......
One month ago........	4.131¢ per lb...........	.... 52.69 per gross ton....	...... 45.09 per gross ton......
One year ago	3.837¢ per lb...........	... 46.38 per gross ton....	...... 27.25 per gross ton......

	High	Low	High	Low	High	Low
1951....	4.131¢ Jan. 2	4.131¢ Jan. 2	$52.69 Jan. 2	$52.69 Jan. 2	$47.75 Jan. 30	$45.09 Jan. 2
1950....	4.131¢ Dec. 1	3.837¢ Jan. 3	52.69 Dec. 12	45.88 Jan. 3	45.13 Dec. 19	26.25 Jan. 3
1949....	3.837¢ Dec. 27	3.3705¢ May 3	46.87 Jan. 18	45.88 Sept. 6	43.00 Jan. 4	19.33 June 28
1948....	3.721¢ July 27	3.193¢ Jan. 1	46.91 Oct. 12	39.58 Jan. 6	43.16 July 27	39.75 Mar. 9
1947....	3.193¢ July 29	2.848¢ Jan. 1	37.98 Dec. 30	30.14 Jan. 7	42.58 Oct. 28	29.50 May 20
1946....	2.848¢ Dec. 31	2.464¢ Jan. 1	30.14 Dec. 10	25.37 Jan. 1	31.17 Dec. 24	19.17 Jan. 1
1945....	2.464¢ May 29	2.396¢ Jan. 1	25.37 Oct. 23	23.61 Jan. 2	19.17 Jan. 2	18.92 May 22
1944....	2.396¢	2.396¢	$23.61	$23.61	19.17 Jan. 11	15.76 Oct. 24
1943....	2.396¢	2.396¢	23.61	23.61	$19.17	$19.17
1942....	2.396¢	2.396¢	23.61	23.61	19.17	19.17
1941....	2.396¢	2.396¢	$23.61 Mar. 20	$23.45 Jan. 2	$22.00 Jan. 7	$19.17 Apr. 10
1940....	2.30467¢ Jan. 2	2.24107¢ Apr. 16	23.45 Dec. 23	22.61 Jan. 2	21.83 Dec. 30	16.04 Apr. 9
1939....	2.35367¢ Jan. 3	2.26689¢ May 16	22.61 Sept. 19	20.61 Sept. 12	22.50 Oct. 3	14.08 May 16
1838....	2.58414¢ Jan. 4	2.27207¢ Oct. 18	23.25 June 21	19.61 July 6	15.00 Nov. 22	11.00 June 7
1937....	2.58414¢ Mar. 9	2.32263¢ Jan. 4	32.25 Mar. 9	20.25 Feb. 16	21.92 Mar. 30	12.67 June 9
1936....	2.32263¢ Dec. 28	2.05200¢ Mar. 10	19.74 Nov. 24	18.73 Aug. 11	17.75 Dec. 21	12.67 June 8
1932....	1.89196¢ July 5	1.83910¢ Mar. 1	14.81 Jan. 5	13.56 Dec. 6	8.50 Jan. 12	6.43 July 5
1929....	2.31773¢ May 28	2.26498¢ Oct. 29	18.71 May 14	18.21 Dec. 17	17.58 Jan. 29	14.08 Dec. 8

Weighted index based on steel bars, shapes, plates, wire, rails, black pipe, hot and cold-rolled sheets and strips, representing major portion of finished steel shipment. Index recapitulated in Aug. 28, 1941, issue and in May 12, 1949.

Based on averages for basic iron at Valley furnaces and foundry iron at Chicago, Philadelphia, Buffalo, Valley and Birmingham.

Average of No. 1 heavy melting steel scrap delivered to consumers at Pittsburgh, Philadelphia and Chicago.

At Cummins Engine Company

Cummins Diesel Engine — Model NHRBS — 600 — 300 HP

MAGNAFLUX* INSPECTION
SAVES $600 — $800 a Week

and INSURES dependable engine quality!

Magnaflux inspection of injector bodies at CUMMINS ENGINE COMPANY, INC., Columbus, Indiana

Inspecting rough forged connecting rods for Magnaglo fluorescent indications under black light.

Cummins Engine Company Diesels are recognized for dependable service in the field. This they insure in manufacture by fully effective Magnaflux-Magnaglo* inspection of critical parts.

By using Magnaglo to detect defective forgings and castings *in the rough*, Cummins Engine Company eliminates useless finishing operations. Direct savings in machining time, equipment and labor are currently averaging $600 to $800 a week—with production capacity increased in similar ratio.

Forgings and castings to be inspected are hand-loaded onto the Magnaflux unit's endless conveyor and automatically processed with Magnaglo. At the inspection station pertinent defects are indicated under the black light by glowing fluorescent lines. Depending upon the kind of parts in process, up to 1200 pieces per hour can be inspected.

Cummins' operation may not be typical of your problem but Magnaflux has solutions for most industries. Invite an experienced Magnaflux engineer to discuss them with you.

Magnaflux and Magnaglo are U. S. registered trademarks of Magnaflux Corporation

Reg. U. S. Pat. Off.

MAGNAFLUX CORPORATION
5902 Northwest Highway, Chicago 31, Illinois
NEW YORK • CLEVELAND • DETROIT • DALLAS • LOS ANGELES
Export Distributor: Curtis Wright Corp.   *In Canada:* Williams & Wilson, Ltd.

IRON AGE

STEEL PRICES

Smaller numbers in price boxes indicate producing companies. For main office locations, see key on facing page. Base prices at producing points apply only to sizes and grades produced in these areas. Prices are in cents per lb unless otherwise noted. Extras apply.

	Pittsburgh	Chicago	Gary	Cleveland	Canton Massillon	Middletown	Youngstown	Bethlehem	Buffalo	Conshohocken	Johnstown	Sparrows Point	Granite City	Detroit
INGOTS Carbon forging, net ton	$52.00[1]													
Alloy, net ton	$54.00[1,17]													$54.00[31]
BILLETS, BLOOMS, SLABS Carbon, rerolling, net ton	$56.00[1,5]	$56.00[1]	$56.00[1]						$56.00[3]		$56.00[3]			
Carbon forging billets, net ton	$66.00[1,5]	$66.00[1,4]	$66.00[1]	$66.00[4]	$66.00[4]				$66.00[3,4]	$73.00[26]	$66.00[3]			$69.00[31]
Alloy, net ton	$70.00[1,17]	$70.00[1,4]	$70.00[1]		$70.00[4]			$70.00[3]	$70.00[3,4]	$77.00[26]	$70.00[3]			$73.00[31]
PIPE SKELP	3.35[1] 3.45[5]						3.35[1,4]							
WIRE RODS	4.10[2] 4.30[18]	4.10[2,4,33]	4.10[6]	4.10[2]			4.10[6]				4.10[3]	4.20[3]		
SHEETS Hot-rolled (18 ga. & hvr.)	3.60[1,5,9,15] 3.75[28]	3.60[8,23]	3.60[1,6,8]	3.60[4]		3.60[7]	3.60[1,4,6] 4.00[13]		3.60[3]	4.00[26]		3.60[3]		3.80[12] 4.40[47]
Cold-rolled	4.35[1,5,9,15] 5.35[63]		4.35[1,6,8]	4.35[4]		4.35[7]	4.35[4,6]		4.35[3]			4.35[3]		4.55[12]
Galvanized (10 gage)	4.80[1,9,15]		4.80[1,8]		4.80[4]	4.80[7]	6.00[64]					4.80[3]		
Enameling (12 gage)	4.65[1]		4.65[1,8]			4.65[7]								
Long terne (10 gage)	5.20[9,15]						6.00[64]							
Hi str. low alloy, h.r.	5.40[1,5] 5.75[9]	5.40[1]	5.40[1,8] 5.90[6]	5.40[4]			5.40[1,4,13]		5.40[3]	5.65[26]		5.40[3]		
Hi str. low alloy, c.r.	6.55[1,5] 6.90[9]		6.55[1,8] 7.05[6]	6.55[4]			6.55[4]		6.55[2]			6.55[2]		
Hi str. low alloy, galv.	7.20[1]													
STRIP Hot-rolled	3.60[9], 4.00[41] 5[8], 3.75[28] 3.50[5]	3.50[66]	3.50[1,6,8]			3.50[7]	3.50[1,4,6] 4.00[13]		3.50[3,4]	3.90[26]		3.50[3]		4.40[47]
Cold-rolled	4.65[5,9] 5.00[28] 5.35[63,58]	4.90[8,66]	4.90[8]	4.65[2]		4.65[7]	4.65[4,6] 5.35[13,40]		4.65[8]			4.65[3]		5.45[47] 5.60[68] 5.60[81]
Hi str. low alloy, h.r.	5.75[9]		5.50[1] 5.30[8], 5.80[6]				4.95[4], 5.50[1] 5.40[13]			5.55[26]				
Hi str. low alloy, c.r.	7.20[9]			6.70[5]			6.20[4], 6.55[13]							
TINPLATE† Cokes, 1.25-lb base box 1.50 lb, add 25¢	$8.70[1,5,9,15]		$8.70[1,6,8]				$8.70[4]					$8.80[3]		
Electrolytic 0.25, 0.50, 0.75 lb box	0.25 lb. base box, $7.15[1,4,5,8,9]; $7.25[3,11]; $7.35[22] 0.50 lb., add 25¢; 0.75 lb. add 65¢													
BLACKPLATE, 29 gage Hollowware enameling	5.85[1] 6.15[15]		5.85[1]				5.30[4]							
BARS Carbon steel	3.70[1,5] 3.85[9]	3.70[1,4,23]	3.70[1,4,6,8]	3.70[4]	3.70[4]		3.70[1,4,6]		3.70[3,4]		3.70[3]			3.85[21]
Reinforcing‡	3.70[1,5]	3.70[4]	3.70[1,6,8]	3.70[4]			3.70[1,4]		3.70[3,4]		3.70[3]	3.70[3]		
Cold-finished	4.55[2,4,5,52,71]	4.55[2,69,70,23,73]	4.55[74,73]	4.55[2]	4.55[4,82]									4.70[84]
Alloy, hot-rolled	4.30[1,17]	4.30[1,4,23]	4.30[1,6,8]	4.30[4]			4.30[1,6]	4.30[8]	4.30[3,4]		4.30[3]			4.45[31]
Alloy, cold-drawn	5.40[17,52,69,71]	5.40[4,23,69,70,73]	5.40[4] 5.90[74]		5.40[4,32]				5.40[3]	5.40[3]				5.55[84]
Hi str. low alloy, h.r.	5.55[1,5]		5.55[1,8] 6.05[6]	5.55[4]			5.55[1]	5.55[3]	5.55[3]		5.55[3]			
PLATE Carbon steel	3.70[1,5,15]	3.70[1]	3.70[1,6,8]	3.70[4] 4.00[9]			3.70[1,4] 3.95[13]		3.70[3]	4.15[26]	3.70[3]	3.70[3]		
Floor plates			4.75[8]	4.75[5]						4.75[26]				
Alloy	4.75[1]	4.75[1]	4.75[1]				5.20[13]			5.05[26]	4.75[3]	4.75[3]		
Hi str. low alloy	5.65[1,5]	5.65[1]	5.65[1,8]	5.65[4,5]			5.65[4] 5.70[13]			5.90[26]	5.65[3]	5.65[3]		
SHAPES, Structural	3.65[1,5] 3.90[9]	3.65[1,23]	3.65[1,8]					3.70[3]	3.70[3]		3.70[3]			
Hi str. low alloy	5.50[1,5]	5.50[1]	5.50[1,8]					5.50[3]	5.50[3]		5.50[3]			
MANUFACTURERS' WIRE Bright	4.85[2,5] 5.10[18]	4.85[2] 4.33		4.85[2]				Kokomo = 5.80[30]			4.85[3]	4.95[3]	Duluth = 4.85[2]	
PILING, Steel Sheet	4.45[1]	4.45[1]	4.45[8]						4.45[3]					

STEEL PRICES

Smaller numbers indicate producing companies. See key at right.
Prices are in cents per lb unless otherwise noted. Extras apply.

Kansas City	Houston	Birmingham	WEST COAST Seattle, San Francisco, Los Angeles, Fontana		Product
			F=$79.00[19]		**INGOTS** Carbon forging, net ton
	$62.00[83]		F=$80.00[19]		Alloy, net ton
		$56.00[11]	F=$75.00[19]		**BILLETS, BLOOMS, SLABS** Carbon, rerolling, net ton
	$74.00[83]	$66.00[11]	F=$85.00[19] SF, LA, S=$85.00[62]		Carbon forging billets, net ton
	$78.00[83]		F=$89.00[19] LA=$90.00[62]		Alloy net ton
					PIPE SKELP
	4.50[83]	4.10[4,11]	SF=4.90[2] LA=4.90[24,62]	Worcester=4.40[2] Minnequa=4.35[14]	**WIRE RODS**
		3.60[4,11]	SF, LA=4.30[24] F=4.55[19]	Niles=5.25[64], Geneva=3.70[16]	**SHEETS** Hot-rolled (18 ga. & hvr.)
		4.35[11]	SF=5.30[24] F=5.30[19]		Cold-rolled
		4.80[4,11]	SF, LA=5.55[24]	Ashland=4.80[7]	Galvanized (10 gage)
					Enameling (12 gage)
					Long ternes (10 gage)
		5.40[11]	F=6.35[19]		Hi str. low alloy, h.r.
			F=7.50[19]		Hi str. low alloy, c.r.
					Hi str. low alloy, galv.
4.10[83]	4.90[83]	3.50[4]	SF, LA=4.25[24,62] F=4.75[19], S=4.50[62]	Atlanta=4.05[65] Minnequa=4.55[14]	**STRIP** Hot-rolled
			F=6.30[19] LA=6.40[27]	New Haven=5.15[2], 5.85[68]	Cold-rolled
		5.30[11]	F=6.20[19]		Hi str. low alloy, h.r.
					Hi str. low alloy, c.r.
		$8.55	SF = $9.20		**TINPLATE** Cokes, 1.25-lb base box 1.50 lb, add 25¢
					Electrolytic 0.25, 0.50, 0.75 lb box
					BLACKPLATE, 29 gage Hollowware enameling
4.30[83]	4.10[83]	3.70[4,11]	SF, LA=4.40[24]	Atlanta=4.25[65] Minnequa=4.15[14]	**BARS** Carbon steel
4.38[83]	4.10[83]	3.70[4,11]	SF, S=4.45[62] F=4.40[19], LA=4.40[62]	Atlanta=4.25[65] Minnequa=4.50[14]	Reinforcing‡
				Newark=5.00[69] Putnam=5.10[69] Hartford=5.10[4] Los Angeles=6.00[4]	Cold-finished
4.90[83]	4.70[83]		LA=5.35[62] F=5.35[19]		Alloy, hot-rolled
				Newark=5.75[69] Worcester= [2] Hartford=5.85[4]	Alloy, cold-drawn
		5.55[11]	F=6.60[19]		Hi str. low alloy, h.r.
	4.10[83]	3.70[4,11]	F=4.30[19] S=4.60[62] Geneva=3.70[16]	Claymont=4.15[29] Coatesville=4.15[21] Minnequa=4.50[14]	**PLATE** Carbon steel
				Harrisburg=5.25[35]	Floor plates
			F=5.70[19] Geneva=5.65[16]	Coatesville=5.25[21] Claymont=4.85[29]	Alloy
		5.65[11]	F=6.25[19]		Hi str. low alloy
4.25[83]	4.05[83]	3.65[4,11]	SF, LA=4.20[62] F=4.25[16] LA=4.25[24,62] S=4.30[62]	Geneva 3.65[16] Minnequa 4.10[14]	**SHAPES, Structural**
		50[11]	F=6.10[19]		Hi str. low alloy
5.45[83]	5.25[83]	4.85[4,11]	SF, LA=5.80[24]	Atlanta=5.10[65] Worcester=5.15[2] Minnequa=5.10[14]	**MANUFACTURERS' WIRE** Bright

KEY TO STEEL PRODUCERS

1 U. S. Steel Co., Pittsburgh
2 American Steel & Wire Co., Cleveland
3 Bethlehem Steel Co., Bethlehem
4 Republic Steel Corp., Cleveland
5 Jones & Laughlin Steel Corp., Pittsburgh
6 Youngstown Sheet & Tube Co., Youngstown
7 Arco Steel Corp., Middletown, Ohio
8 Inland Steel Co., Chicago
9 Weirton Steel Co., Weirton, W. Va.
10 National Tube Co., Pittsburgh
11 Tennessee Coal, Iron & R. R. Co., Birmingham
12 Great Lakes Steel Corp., Detroit
13 Sharon Steel Corp., Sharon, Pa.
14 Colorado Fuel & Iron Corp., Denver
15 Wheeling Steel Corp., Wheeling, W. Va.
16 Geneva Steel Co., Salt Lake City
17 Crucible Steel Co. of America, New York
18 Pittsburgh Steel Co., Pittsburgh
19 Kaiser Steel Corp., Oakland, Calif.
20 Portsmouth Div., Detroit Steel Corp., Detroit
21 Lukens Steel Co., Coatesville, Pa.
22 Granite City Steel Co., Granite City, Ill.
23 Wisconsin Steel Co., South Chicago, Ill.
24 Columbia Steel Co., San Francisco
25 Copperweld Steel Co., Glassport, Pa.
26 Alan Wood Steel Co., Conshohocken, Pa.
27 Calif. Cold Rolled Steel Corp., Los Angeles
28 Allegheny Ludlum Steel Corp., Pittsburgh
29 Worth Steel Co., Claymont, Del.
30 Continental Steel Corp., Kokomo, Ind.
31 Rotary Electric Steel Co., Detroit
32 Laclede Steel Co., St. Louis
33 Northwestern Steel & Wire Co., Sterling, Ill.
34 Keystone Steel & Wire Co., Peoria, Ill.
35 Central Steel & Wire Co., Harrisburg, Pa.
36 Carpenter Steel Co., Reading, Pa.
37 Eastern Stainless Steel Corp., Baltimore
38 Washington Steel Corp., Washington, Pa.
39 Jessop Steel Co., Washington, Pa.
40 Blair Strip Steel Co., New Castle, Pa.
41 Superior Steel Corp., Carnegie, Pa.
42 Timken Steel & Tube Div., Canton, Ohio
43 Babcock & Wilcox Tube Co., Beaver Falls, Pa.
44 Reeves Steel & Mfg. Co., Dover, Ohio
45 John A. Roebling's Sons Co., Trenton, N. J.
46 Simonds Saw & Steel Co., Fitchburg, Mass.
47 McLouth Steel Corp., Detroit
48 Cold Metal Products Co., Youngstown
49 Thomas Steel Co., Warren, Ohio
50 Wilson Steel & Wire Co., Chicago
51 Sweet's Steel Co., Williamsport, Pa.
52 Superior Drawn Steel Co., Monaca, Pa.
53 Tremont Nail Co., Wareham, Mass.
54 Firth Sterling St. & Carbide Corp., McKeesport
55 Ingersoll Steel Div., Chicago
56 Phoenix Iron & Steel Co., Phoenixville, Pa.
57 Fitzsimmons Steel Co., Youngstown
58 Stanley Works, New Britain, Conn.
59 Universal-Cyclops Steel Corp., Bridgeville, Pa.
60 American Cladmetals Co., Carnegie, Pa.
61 Cuyahoga Steel & Wire Co., Cleveland
62 Bethlehem Pacific Coast Steel Corp., San Fran.
63 Follansbee Steel Corp., Pittsburgh
64 Niles Rolling Mill Co., Niles, Ohio
65 Atlantic Steel Co., Atlanta
66 Acme Steel Co., Chicago
67 Joslyn Mfg. & Supply Co., Chicago
68 Detroit Steel Corp., Detroit
69 Wycoff Steel Co., Pittsburgh
70 Bliss & Laughlin, Inc., Harvey, Ill.
71 Columbia Steel & Shafting Co., Pittsburgh
72 Cumberland Steel Co., Cumberland, Md.
73 La Salle Steel Co., Chicago
74 Monarch Steel Co., Inc., Hammond, Ind.
75 Empire Steel Co., Mansfield, Ohio
76 Mahoning Valley Steel Co., Niles, Ohio
77 Oliver Iron & Steel Co., Pittsburgh
78 Pittsburgh Screw & Bolt Co., Pittsburgh
79 Standard Forging Corp., Chicago
80 Driver Harris Co., Harrison, N. J.
81 Detroit Tube & Steel Div., Detroit
82 Reliance Div., Eaton Mfg. Co., Massillon, Ohio
83 Sheffield Steel Corp., Kansas City
84 Plymouth Steel Co., Detroit
85 Wickwire Spencer Steel, Buffalo
86 Angell Nail and Chaplet, Cleveland
87 Mid-States Steel & Wire, Crawfordsville, Ind.
88 National Supply, Pittsburgh, Pa.
89 Wheatland Tube Co., Wheatland, Pa.
90 Mercer Tube & Mfg. Co., Sharon, Pa.
91 Woodward Iron Co., Woodward, Ala.
92 Sloss-Sheffield Steel & Iron Co., Birmingham
93 Hanna Furance Corp., Detroit
94 Interlake Iron Corp., Cleveland
95 Lone Star Steel Co., Dallas
96 Mystic Iron Works, Everett, Mass.
97 Jackson Iron & Steel Co., Jackson, O.
98 Globe Iron Co., Jackson, O.
99 Pittsburgh Coke & Chemical Co., Pittsburgh
100 Shenango Furnace Co., Pittsburgh
101 Tennessee Products & Chemical Corp., Nashville
102 Koppers Co., Inc., Granite City, Ill.
103 Page Steel & Wire Div., American Chain & Cable., Monessen, Pa.

STAINLESS STEELS

Base price, cents per lb, f.o.b. mill.

Product	301	302	303	304	316	321	347	410	416	430
Ingots, rerolling	14.25	15.00	16.50	16.00	24.25	19.75	21.50	12.75	14.75	13.00
Slabs, billets rerolling	18.50	19.75	21.75	20.75	31.75	26.00	28.25	16.50	20.00	16.75
Forg. discs, die blocks, rings	34.00	34.00	36.50	35.50	52.50	40.00	44.50	28.00	28.50	28.50
Billets, forging	26.25	26.25	28.25	27.50	41.00	31.00	34.75	21.50	22.00	22.00
Bars, wires, structurals	31.25	31.25	33.75	32.75	48.75	36.75	41.25	25.75	26.25	26.25
Plates	33.00	33.00	35.00	35.00	51.50	40.50	45.00	27.00	27.50	27.50
Sheets	41.00	41.00	43.00	43.00	56.50	49.00	53.50	36.50	37.00	39.00
Strip, hot-rolled	26.50	28.00	32.25	30.00	48.25	36.75	41.00	23.50	30.25	24.00
Strip, cold-rolled	34.00	36.50	40.00	38.50	58.50	48.00	52.00	30.50	37.00	31.00

STAINLESS STEEL PRODUCING POINTS—*Sheets:* Midland, Pa., 17; Bracken-ridge, Pa., 28; Butler, Pa., 7; McKeesport, Pa., 1; Washington, Pa., 38 (type 316 add 5¢), 39; Baltimore, 37; Middletown, Ohio, 7; Massillon, Ohio, 4; Gary, 1; Bridgeville, Pa., 59; New Castle, Ind., 55; Ft. Wayne, Ind., 67; Lockport, N. Y., 46.
Strip: Midland, Pa., 17; Cleveland, 2; Carnegie, Pa., 41; McKeesport, Pa., 54; Reading, Pa., 36; Washington, Pa., 38 (type 316 add 5¢); W. Leechburg, Pa., 28; Bridgeville, Pa., 59; Detroit, Mich.; Massillon, Canton, Ohio, 4; Middletown, Ohio, 7; Harrison, N. J., 80; Youngstown, 48; Lockport N. Y., 46; New Britain, Conn., 58; Sharon, Pa., 13; Butler, Pa., 7.
Bars: Baltimore, 7; Duquesne, Pa., 1; Munhall, Pa., 1; Reading, Pa., 36; Titusville, Pa., 59; Washington, Pa., 39; McKeesport, Pa., 1, 54; Bridgeville, Pa., 59; Dunkirk, N. Y., 28; Massillon, Ohio, 4; Chicago, 1; Syracuse, N. Y., 17; Watervliet, N. Y., 28; Waukegan, Ill., 2; Lockport, N. Y. 46; Canton, Ohio, 42; Ft. Wayne, Ind., 67.
Wire: Waukegan, Ill., 2; Massillon, Ohio, 4; McKeesport, Pa., 54; Bridgeport, Conn., 44; Ft. Wayne, Ind., 67; Trenton, N. J., 45; Harrison, N. J., 80; Baltimore, 7; Dunkirk, 28; Monessen, 103.
Structurals: Baltimore, 7; Massillon, Ohio, 4; Chicago, 1, 67; Watervliet, N. Y., 28; Bridgeport, Conn., 44.
Plates: Brackenridge, Pa., 28 (type 416 add ½¢); Butler, Pa., 7; Chicago, 1; Munhall, Pa., 1; Midland, Pa., 17; New Castle, Ind., 55; Lockport, N. Y., 46; Middletown, 7; Washington, Pa., 39; Cleveland, Massillon, 4.
Forged discs, die blocks, rings: Pittsburgh, 1, 17; Syracuse, 17; Ferndale, Mich., 28.
Forging billets: Midland, Pa., 17; Baltimore, 7; Washington, Pa., 39; McKeesport, 54; Massillon, Canton, Ohio, 4; Watervliet, 28; Pittsburgh, Chicago, 1.

RAILS, TRACK SUPPLIES

F.o.b. Mill Cents Per Lb	No. 1 Std. Rails	Light Rails	Joint Bars	Track Spikes	Axles	Screw Spikes	Tie Plates	Track Bolts Untreated
Bessemer-1	3.60	4.00	4.70					
Chicago-4				6.15				
Ensley-11	3.60	4.00						
Fairfield-11		4.00	4.40		8.60		4.50	
Gary-1	3.60	4.00					4.50	
Ind. Harbor-8	3.60		4.70	6.15	5.25	8.60	4.50	
Johnstown-3		4.00			5.60	8.60		
Joliet-1		4.00	4.70					
Kansas City-83				6.40				
Lackawanna-3		4.00	4.70	6.15		8.60	4.50	
Lebanon-3				6.15				9.60
Minnequa-14	3.60	4.50	4.70	6.15		8.60	4.50	9.60
Pittsburgh-77						9.35		9.60
Pittsburgh-78								9.60
Pittsburgh-5				6.15				
Pittsburg-24							4.65	
Seattle-62				6.10			4.35	
Steelton-3	3.60		4.70				4.50	
Struthers-6				6.15				
Torrance-24							4.65	
Youngstown-4				6.15				

Track Bolts, heat treated, to railroads, 9.85¢ per lb.

BOILER TUBES

Seamless steel, electric welded commercial boiler tubes, locomotive tubes, minimum wall, per 100 ft at mill, c.l. lots, cut lengths 10 to 24 ft.

OD gage in in.	BWG	Seamless H.R.	C.D.	Electric Weld H.R.	C.D.
2	13	$22.67	$26.66	$21.99	$25.86
2½	12	30.48	35.84	29.57	34.76
3	12	33.90	39.90	32.89	34.80
3½	11	42.37	49.89	41.10	48.39
4	10	52.60	61.88	51.03	60.02

Pittsburgh Steel add, H-R: 2 in., 62¢; 2½ in., 84¢; 3 in., 92¢; 3½ in., $1.17; 4 in., $1.45. Add, C-R: 2 in., 74¢; 2½ in., 99¢; 3 in., $1.10; 3½ in., $1.37; 4 in., $1.70.

FLUORSPAR

Washed gravel fluorspar, f.o.b. cars, Rosiclare, Ill. Base price, per ton net: Effective CaF, content:

70% or more	$43.00
60% or less	40.00

MERCHANT WIRE PRODUCTS

F.o.b. Mill	Standard & Coated Nails — Base Col.	Woven Wire Fence 9-15½ ga. — Base Col.	Fence Posts — Base Col.	Single Loop Bale Ties — Base Col.	Twisted Barbless Wire — Base Col.	Gal. Barbed Wire — Base Col.	Merch. Wire Ann'ld. ¢/lb.	Merch. Wire Gal. (1) ¢/lb.
Alabama City-4	118	126		123		136	5.70	5.95
Aliquippa, Pa.-5	118	132			136	140	5.70	6.15
Atlanta-65	121	133		126	126	143	5.95	6.40
Bartonville-34	118	130	140	123	143	143	5.95	6.15
Buffalo-85								4.85
Cleveland-86	125							
Cleveland-2							5.70	6.15
Crawfordsville-87		132				145	5.95	6.40
Donora, Pa.-2	118	130		123		140	5.70	6.15
Duluth-2	118	130		123		140	5.70	6.15
Fairfield, Ala.-11	118	130		123		136	5.70	6.15
Houston-83	126	138				148	6.10	6.55
Johnstown, Pa.-3	118	130			140		5.70	6.15
Joliet, Ill.-2	118	130		123		140	5.70	6.15
Kokomo, Ind.-30	120	132		125	138	138	5.80	6.05
Los Angeles-62							6.65	
Kansas City-83	130	130	142	135		152	6.30	6.75
Minnequa-14	123	128	130	128	146	146	5.95	6.40
Monessen-18	124	135				145	5.95	6.40
Moline, Ill.-4			136					
Palmer-85								
Pittsburg, Cal.-24	137	149		147	156	160	6.65	6.80
Portsmouth-20	124	137			147	147	6.10	6.60
Rankin, Pa.-2	118	130				140	5.70	6.15
So. Chicago, Ill.-4	118	126	140	123		136	5.70	5.95
S. San Fran.-14				147		160	6.65	7.10
Sparrows Pt.-3	120				125	142	5.80	6.25
Sterling, Ill.-33	118	130	140	123	140	140	5.70	6.15
Struthers, Ohio-6							5.70	6.15
Torrance, Cal.-24	138						6.65	
Worcester-2	124						6.00	6.45
Williamsport, Pa.-51			150					

Cut Nails, carloads, base, $6.75 per 100 lb. (less 20¢ to jobbers) at Conshohocken, Pa., (26), Wareham, Mass. (53), Wheeling, W. Va. (15).
(1) Alabama City and So. Chicago do not include zinc extra.

CAST IRON WATER PIPE

Per Net Ton

6 to 24-in., del'd Chicago. $105.30 to $108.80
6 to 24-in., del'd N. Y. . . . 108.50 to 109.50
6 to 24-in., Birmingham. 91.50 to 96.00
6-in. and larger, f.o.b. cars, San Francisco, Los Angeles, for all rail shipment; rail and water shipment less . . . . $108.50 to $113.00
Class "A" and gas pipe, $5 extra; 4-in. pipe is $5 a ton above 6-in.

PIPE AND TUBING

Base discounts, f.o.b. mills. Base price about $200 per net ton.

	BUTTWELD														SEAMLESS					
	½ In.		¾ In.		1 In.		1¼ In.		1½ In.		2 In.		2½-3 In.		2 In.		2½-3 In.		3½-4 In.	
	Blk.	Gal.	Blk.	Gal.	Blk.	Gal.	Blk.	Gal.	Blk.	Gal.	Blk.	Gal.	Blk.	Gal.	Blk.	Gal.	Blk.	Gal.	Blk.	Gal.
STANDARD T. & C.																				
Sparrows Pt.-3	34.0	12.0	37.0	16.0	39.5	19.5	40.0	20.0	40.5	21.0	41.0	21.5	41.5	22.0						
Cleveland-4	36.0	14.0	39.0	18.0	41.5	21.5	42.0	22.0	42.5	23.0	43.0	23.5	43.5	24.0						
Oakland-19	25.0	3.0	28.0	7.0	30.5	10.5	31.0	11.0	31.5	12.0	32.0	12.5	32.5	13.0						
Pittsburgh-5	36.0	14.0	39.0	18.0	41.5	19.5	42.0	20.5	42.5	21.0	43.0	21.5	43.5	22.5	29.5	8.0	32.5	11.5	34.5	13.5
Pittsburgh-10	36.0	14.0	39.0	18.0	41.5	21.5	42.0	22.0	42.5	23.0	43.0	23.5	43.5	24.0	29.5	9.5	32.5	12.5	34.5	14.5
St. Louis-32	35.0	13.0	38.0	17.0	40.5	19.5	41.0	20.5	41.5	21.0	42.0	21.5	43.0	23.0						
Sharon-90	36.0	13.0	39.0	17.0	41.5	20.0	42.0	20.5	42.5	21.0	43.0	21.5	43.5	24.0						
Toledo-88	36.0	14.0	39.0	18.0	41.5	21.5	42.0	22.0	42.5	23.0	43.0	23.5	43.5	24.0	32.5		34.5			
Wheeling-15	36.0	14.0	39.0	18.0	41.5	21.5	42.0	22.0	42.5	23.0	43.0	23.5	43.5	24.0						
Wheatland-89	36.0	14.0	39.0	18.0	41.5	19.5	42.0	20.0	42.5	21.0	43.0	21.5	43.5	22.5						
Youngstown-6	36.0	14.0	39.0	18.0	41.5	21.5	42.0	22.0	42.5	23.0	43.0	23.5	43.5	24.0	29.5	9.5	32.5	12.5	34.5	14.5
EXTRA STRONG, PLAIN ENDS																				
Sparrows Pt.-3	33.5	13.0	37.5	17.0	39.5	20.5	40.0	21.0	40.5	22.0	41.0	22.5	41.5	23.0						
Cleveland-4	35.5	15.0	39.5	19.0	41.5	22.5	42.0	23.0	42.5	24.0	43.0	24.5	43.5	25.0						
Oakland-19	24.5	4.0	28.5	8.0	30.5	11.5	31.0	12.0	31.5	13.0	32.0	13.5	32.5	14.0						
Pittsburgh-5	35.5	13.5	39.5	17.5	41.5	20.5	42.0	21.5	42.5	22.0	43.0	22.5	43.5	23.0	29.0	7.5	33.0	12.0	36.0	15.5
Pittsburgh-10	35.5	15.0	39.5	19.0	41.5	22.5	42.0	23.0	42.5	24.0	43.0	24.5	43.5	25.0	29.0	10.0	33.0	14.0	36.5	17.5
St. Louis-32	34.5	14.0	38.5	18.0	40.5	21.5	41.0	22.0	41.5	23.0	42.0	23.5	43.0	24.5						
Sharon-90	35.5	14.0	39.5	18.0	41.5	21.0	42.0	21.5	42.5	22.0	43.0	22.5	43.5	24.5						
Toledo-88	35.5	15.0	39.5	19.0	41.5	22.5	42.0	23.0	42.5	24.0	43.0	24.5	43.5	25.0	33.0		36.5			
Wheeling-15	35.5	15.0	39.5	19.0	41.5	22.5	42.0	23.0	42.5	24.0	43.0	24.5	43.5	25.0						
Wheatland-89	35.5	13.5	39.5	17.5	41.5	20.5	42.0	21.5	42.5	22.0	43.0	22.5	43.5	23.0						
Youngstown-6	35.5	15.0	39.5	19.0	41.5	22.5	42.0	23.0	42.5	24.0	43.0	24.5	43.5	25.0	29.0	10.0	33.0	14.0	36.5	17.5

Galvanized discounts based on zinc at 17¢ per lb, East St. Louis. For each 1¢ change in zinc, discounts vary as follows: ½ in., ¾ in., and 1 in., 1 pt.; 1¼ in., 1½ in., 2 in., ¾ pt.; 2½ in., 3 in., ½ pt. Calculate discounts on even cents per lb of zinc, i.e., if zinc is 16.51¢ to 17.50¢ per lb, use 17¢. Jones & Laughlin discounts apply only when zinc price changes 1¢. Threads only, buttweld and seamless, 1 pt. higher discount. Plain ends, buttweld and seamless, 3 in. and under, 3½ pts. higher discount. Buttweld jobbers' discount, 5 pct.

Base price, f.o.b., dollars per 100 lb. *(Metropolitan area delivery, add 20¢ except Birmingham, San Francisco, Cincinnati, New Orleans, St. Paul, add 15¢; Memphis, add 10¢; Philadelphia, add 25¢; New York, add 30¢).

WAREHOUSES

Cities	Sheets Hot-Rolled	Sheets Cold-Rolled (15 gage)	Sheets Galvanized (10 gage)	Strip Hot-Rolled	Strip Cold-Rolled	Plates	Shapes Standard Structural	Bars Hot-Rolled	Bars Cold-Finished	Alloy Bars Hot-Rolled A 4615 As rolled	Alloy Bars Hot-Rolled A 4140 Annealed	Alloy Bars Cold-Drawn A 4615 As rolled	Alloy Bars Cold-Drawn A 4140 Annealed
Baltimore	5.60	6.84	7.49[2]–8.07	6.04		5.80	6.14	6.04	6.84–6.89	10.24	10.54	11.89	12.19
Birmingham*	5.60	6.40	6.75	5.55		5.95	5.70	5.55					
Boston	6.20	7.00–7.25	7.74–8.29	6.15	8.50[4]	6.48–6.78	6.20	6.05	6.79–6.84	10.25	10.55	11.90–12.00	12.20–12.30
Buffalo	5.60	6.40	7.74–8.09	5.86		6.05	5.80	5.60	6.40–6.45	10.15–10.85	10.45	11.20	11.95–12.19
Chicago	5.60	6.40	7.75	5.55		5.80	5.70	5.55	6.30	9.80	10.10	11.45	11.75
Cincinnati*	5.87	6.44	7.39	5.80		6.19	6.09	5.80	6.61	10.15	10.45	11.80	12.10
Cleveland	5.60	6.40	8.10	5.69	6.90	5.92	5.82	5.57	6.40	9.91	10.21	11.56	11.86
Detroit	5.78	6.53	7.89	5.94		5.99	6.09	5.84	6.	10.11	10.41	11.76	12.06
Houston	7.00	8.25				6.85	6.50	6.65	9.35	10.35	11.25		12.75
Indianapolis, del'd	6.00	6.80	8.15	5.95		6.20	6.10	5.95	6.80				
Kansas City	6.00	6.80	7.45	6.15	7.50	6.40	6.30	6.15	7.00	10.40	10.70	12.05	12.35
Los Angeles	6.35	7.90	8.85	6.40	9.45[6]	6.40	6.35	6.35	8.20	11.30	11.30	13.20	13.50
Memphis*	6.33–6.38	7.08–7.18		6.33–6.38		6.43–8.02	6.33–6.48	6.08–6.33	7.16–7.32				
Milwaukee	5.74	6.54	7.89	5.69–6.59		5.94	5.84	5.69	6.44–6.54	9.94	10.24	11.59	11.89
New Orleans*	5.70	6.59		5.75	7.25	5.95	5.75	5.75	7.30				
New York*	5.67–5.97	7.19[5]–7.24[1]	8.14[2]	6.29–6.89	8.63[4]	6.28–6.58	6.10	6.12	6.99	10.05–10.15	10.35–10.45	11.70–11.80	12.10–12.20
Norfolk	6.50[3]					6.50[3]	6.60[3]	6.55[3]					
Philadelphia*	5.90	6.80	8.00	6.10		6.05	5.90	6.05	6.86	9.90	10.20		
Pittsburgh	5.60	6.40	7.75	5.65–5.95		5.75	5.70	5.55	6.15	9.80	10.10	11.45	11.75
Portland	6.60–7.55	8.95	8.50–9.10	7.30		6.80	6.95	6.90			12.15		
Salt Lake City	7.95		9.70–10.50[2]	8.70–8.75		8.05	6.75–8.30	7.95–8.65	9.00				
San Francisco*	6.65	8.05[2]	8.55–8.90[2]	6.60	9.45[6]	6.50	6.45	6.45	8.20	11.30	11.30	13.20	13.20–13.50
Seattle	7.05	8.60	9.20	9.05		6.75	6.65	6.75	9.05				
St. Louis	5.80–5.85	6.65	8.00	5.80	8.00[4]–8.28	6.13	6.03	5.80	6.55–6.65	10.05	10.35	11.70	12.00
St. Paul*	6.16	6.96	8.31	6.11		6.36	6.26	6.11	6.96	10.36	10.66	12.01	12.31

BASE QUANTITIES (Standard unless otherwise keyed): Cold finished bars; 2000 lb or over. Alloy bars; 1000 to 1999 lb. All others; 2000 to 9999 lb. All HR products may be combined for quantity. All galvanized sheets may be combined for quantity. CR sheets may not be combined with each other or with galvanized sheets for quantity.
EXCEPTIONS: ([1]) 400 to 1499 lb; ([2]) 450 to 1499 lb; ([3]) 400 to 1999 lb; ([4]) 6000 lb and over; ([5]) 1500 to 9999 lb.; ([6]) 2000 to 5999 lb.

PIG IRON

Dollars per gross ton, f.o.b., subject to switching charges.

Producing Point	Basic	No. 2 Foundry	Malleable	Bessemer	Low Phos.	Blast Furnace Silvery	Low Phos. Charcoal
Bethlehem-3	54.00	54.50	55.00	55.50			
Birmingham-4	48.38	48.88					
Birmingham-91	48.38	48.88					
Birmingham-92	48.38	48.88					
Buffalo-4	52.00	52.50	53.00				
Buffalo-93	52.00	52.50	53.00			63.75	
Chicago-94	52.00	52.50	52.50	53.00			
Cleveland-2	52.00	52.50	52.50	53.00	57.00		
Cleveland-4	52.00	52.50	52.50				
Daingerfield, Tex.-95	48.00	48.50	48.50				
Duluth-94	52.00	52.50	52.50	53.00			
Erie-94	52.00	52.50	52.50	53.00			
Everett, Mass.-96		53.25	53.75				
Fontana-19	58.00	58.50					
Geneva, Utah-19	52.00	52.50	52.50	53.00			
Granite City, Ill.-102	53.90	54.40	54.90				
Hubbard, O.-6	52.00	52.50	52.50				
Ironton, Utah-16	52.00	52.50					
Jackson, O.-97,98						62.50	
Lyle, Tenn.-101							66.00
Monessen-18	54.00						
Neville Island-99	52.00	52.50	52.50	53.00			
Pittsburgh-1	52.00			53.00			
Sharpsville-100	52.00	52.50	52.50	53.00			
Steelton-3	54.00	54.50	55.00	55.50	60.00		
Swedeland-26	56.00	56.50	57.00	57.50			
Toledo-94	52.00	52.50	52.50	53.00			
Troy, N. Y.-4	54.00	54.50	55.00		60.00		
Youngstown-6	52.00	52.50	52.50	53.00			

DIFFERENTIALS: Add 50¢ per ton for each 0.25 pct silicon over base (1.75 to 2.25 pct), 50¢ per ton for each 0.50 pct manganese over 1 pct, $2 per ton for 0.5 to 0.75 pct nickel, $1 for each additional 0.25 pct nickel. Subtract 38¢ per ton for phosphorus content over 0.70 pct. Silvery iron: Add $1.50 per ton for each 0.50 pct silicon over base (6.01 to 6.50 pct) up to 17 pct. $1 per ton for 0.75 pct or more phosphorus, manganese as above. Bessemer ferrosilicon prices are $1 over comparable silvery iron.

REFRACTORIES
(F.o.b. works)

Fire Clay Brick — *Carloads, Per 1000*
First quality, Ill., Ky., Md., Mo., Ohio, Pa. (except Salina, Pa., add $5) $94.60
No. 1 Ohio 88.00
Sec. quality, Pa., Md., Ky., Mo., Ill. 88.00
No. 2 Ohio 79.20
Ground fire clay, net ton, bulk (except Salina, Pa., add $1.50) 13.75

Silica Brick
Mt. Union, Pa., Ensley, Ala. $94.60
Childs, Pa. 99.00
Hays, Pa. 100.10
Chicago District 104.50
Western Utah and Calif. 111.10
Super Duty, Hays, Pa., Athens, Tex., Chicago 111.10
Silica cement, net ton, bulk, Eastern (except Hays, Pa.) 16.50
Silica cement, net ton, bulk, Hays, Pa. 18.70
Silica cement, net ton, bulk, Ensley, Ala. 17.60
Silica cement, net ton, bulk, Chicago District 17.60
Silica cement, net ton, bulk, Utah and Calif. 24.70

Chrome Brick — *Per Net Ton*
Standard chemically bonded, Balt., Chester $82.00

Magnesite Brick
Standard, Baltimore $104.00
Chemically bonded, Baltimore 93.00

Grain Magnesite — *St. ⅜-in. grains*
Domestic, f.o.b. Baltimore, in bulk fines removed $62.70
Domestic, f.o.b. Chewelah, Wash., in bulk 36.30
in sacks 41.80

Dead Burned Dolomite
F.o.b. producing points in Pennsylvania, West Virginia and Ohio, per net ton, bulk Midwest, add 10¢; Missouri Valley, add 20¢ $13.00

COKE
Furnace, beehive (f.o.b. oven) — *Net Ton*
Connellsville, Pa. .... $14.00 to $14.50
Foundry, beehive (f.o.b. oven)
Connellsville, Pa. .... $17.00 to $17.50
Foundry, oven coke
Buffalo, del'd $25.35
Chicago, f.o.b. 21.00
Detroit, f.o.b. 23.00
New England, del'd 24.80
Seaboard, N. J., f.o.b. 22.00
Philadelphia, f.o.b. 22.70
Swedeland, Pa., f.o.b. 22.60
Plainesville, Ohio, f.o.b. 24.00
Erie, Pa., f.o.b. 23.50
Cleveland, del'd 25.72
Cincinnati, del'd 25.06
St. Paul, f.o.b. 21.00
St. Louis, f.o.b. 24.90
Birmingham, del'd 20.79
Neville Island 23.00

LAKE SUPERIOR ORES
(51.50% Fe; natural content, delivered lower lake ports)

Per gross ton
Old range, bessemer $8.70
Old range, nonbessemer 8.55
Mesabi, bessemer 8.45
Mesabi, nonbessemer 8.30
High phosphorus 8.30

After adjustments for analyses, prices will be increased or decreased as the case may be for increases or decreases after Dec. 2, 1950, in lake vessel rates, upper lake rail freights, dock handling charges and taxes thereon.

C-R SPRING STEEL
Base per pound f.o.b. mill
0.26 to 0.40 carbon .... 5.35¢
0.41 to 0.60 carbon .... 6.80¢
0.61 to 0.80 carbon .... 7.40¢
0.81 to 1.05 carbon .... 9.35¢
1.06 to 1.35 carbon .... 11.65¢

Worcester, add 0.30¢; Sharon, Carnegie, New Castle, add 0.35¢; Detroit, 0.26 to 0.40 carb., add 25¢; other grades add 15¢. New Haven, 0.26 to 0.40 carb., add 50¢; other grades add 5¢.

IRON AGE FOUNDED 1855 — MARKETS & PRICES

BOLTS, NUTS, RIVETS, SCREWS
Consumer Prices
(Base discount, f.o.b. mill, Pittsburgh, Cleveland, Birmingham or Chicago)

Machine and Carriage Bolts

	Pct Off List	
	Less Case	C.
½ in. & smaller x 6 in. & shorter	15	28½
9/16 in. & ⅝ in. x 6 in. & shorter	18½	30½
¾ in. & larger x 6 in. & shorter	17½	29½
All diam. longer than 6 in.	14	27½
Lag, all diam. x 6 in. & shorter	23	35
Lag, all diam. longer than 6 in.	21	33
Plow bolts	34	....

Nuts, Hot Pressed, Cold Punched—Sq
Pct Off List

	Less Keg (Reg.)	K.	Less Keg (Hvy.)	K.
½ in. & smaller.	15	28½	15	28½
9/16 in. & ⅝ in.	12	25	6½	21
¾ in. to 1½ in. inclusive	9	23	1	16½
1⅝ in. & larger.	7½	22	1	16½

Nuts, Hot Pressed—Hexagon

½ in. & smaller.	26	37	22	34
9/16 in. & ⅝ in.	16½	29½	6½	21
¾ in. to 1½ in. inclusive	12	25	2	17½
1⅝ in. & larger.	8½	23	2	17½

Nuts, Cold Punched—Hexagon

½ in. & smaller.	26	37	22	34
9/16 in. & ⅝ in.	23	35	17½	30½
¾ in. to 1½ in. inclusive	19½	31½	12	25
1⅝ in. & larger.	12	25	6½	21

Nuts, Semi-Finished—Hexagon

	Reg.		Hvy.	
½ in. & smaller.	35	45	28½	39½
9/16 in. & ⅝ in.	29½	40½	22	34
¾ in. to 1½ in. inclusive	24	36	15	28½
1⅝ in. & larger.	13	26	8½	23

Light		
7/16 in. & smaller	35	45
½ in. thru ⅝ in.	28½	39½
¾ in. to 1½ in. inclusive	26	37

Stove Bolts
Pct Off List

Packaged, steel, plain finished	56—10
Packaged, plated finish.......	41—10
Bulk, plain finish**..........	67*

*Discounts apply to bulk shipments in not less than 15,000 pieces of a size and kind where length is 3-in. and shorter; 5000 pieces for lengths longer than 3-in. For lesser quantities, packaged price applies.
**Zinc, Parkerized, cadmium or nickel plated finishes add 6¢ per lb net. For black oil finish, add 2¢ per lb net.

Rivets

	Base per 100 lb.
½ in. & larger...................	$7.85
	Pct Off List
7/16 in. & smaller................	36

F.o.b. Pittsburgh, Cleveland, Chicago, Birmingham, Lebanon, Pa.

Cap and Set Screws
(In bulk) — Pct Off List

Hexagon head cap screws, coarse or fine thread, ¼ in. thru ⅝ in. x 6 in., SAE 1020, bright..........	54
¾ in. thru 1 in. up to & including 6 in.	48
¼ in. thru ⅝ in. x 6 in. & shorter high C double heat treat.........	46
¾ in. thru 1 in. up to & including 6 in.	41
Milled studs	35
Flat head cap screws, listed sizes....	16
Fillister head cap, listed sizes.......	34
Set screws, sq head, cup point, 1 in. diam. and smaller x 6 in. & shorter	53

S. M. Ferrochrome
Contract price, cents per pound, chromium contained, lump size, delivered.

High carbon type: 60-65% Cr, 4-6% Si, 4-6% Mn, 4-6% C.

Carloads	21.60
Ton lots	23.75
Less ton lots.....................	25.25

Low carbon type: 62-66% Cr, 4-6% Si, 4-6% Mn, 1.25% max. C.

Carloads	27.75
Ton lots	30.05
Less ton lots.....................	31.85

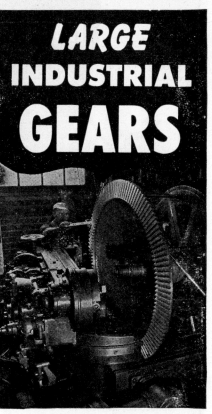

IRON AGE MARKETS & PRICES
FOUNDED 1855

ELECTRICAL SHEETS
22 Ga. H-R cut lengths

F.o.b. Mill Cents Per Lb.	Armature	Elec.	Motor	Dynamo	Transf. 72	Transf. 65	Transf. 58
Beech Botton-15		7.25	8.50	9.30	9.85	10.40	11.10
Brackenridge-28		7.25	8.50	9.30	9.85		
Follansbee-63	6.75	7.25	8.50	9.30	9.85	10.40	11.10
Granite City-22		7.95	9.20				
Ind. Harbor-3	6.75	7.25					
Mansfield-75	6.75	7.25	8.50	9.30			
Niles, O.-64	7.05	7.55					
Vandergrift-1	6.75	7.25	8.50	9.30	9.85	10.40	11.10
Warren, O.-4	6.75	7.25	8.50	9.30	9.85	10.40	11.10
Zanesville-7	8.75	7.25	8.50	9.30	9.85	10.40	11.10

Transformer 52, 80¢ above Transformer 58.

Ferrochrome
Contract prices, cents per pound, contained Cr, lump size, bulk, in carloads, delivered. (65-72% Cr, 2% max. Si.)

0.06% C ... 30.50		0.20% C ... 29.50
0.10% C ... 30.00		0.50% C ... 29.25
0.15% C ... 29.75		1.00% C ... 29.00
2.00% C 28.75
65-69% Cr, 4-9% C 22.00
62-66% Cr, 4-6% C, 6-9% Si. 22.85

High-Nitrogen Ferrochrome
Low-carbon type: 67-72% Cr, 0.75% N. Add 5¢ per lb to regular low carbon ferrochrome price schedule. Add 5¢ for each additional 0.25% N.

Chromium Metal
Contract prices, per lb chromium contained, packed, delivered, ton lots. 97% min. Cr, 1% max. Fe.

0.20% Max. C.	$1.09
0.50% Max. C.	1.05
.00 min. C.	1.04

Low Carbon Ferrochrome Silicon
(Cr 34-41%, Si 42-49%, C 0.05% max.) Contract price, carloads, f.o.b. Niagara Falls, freight allowed; lump 4-in. x down, bulk 2-in. x down, 21.75¢ per lb of contained Cr plus 12.00¢ per lb of contained Si.
Bulk 1-in. x down, 21.90¢ per lb contained Cr plus 12.20¢ per lb contained Si.

Calcium-Silicon
Contract price per lb of alloy, dump, delivered.
30-33% Ca, 60-65% Si, 3.00% max. Fe.

Carloads	19.00
Ton lots	22.10
Less ton lots	23.00

Calcium-Manganese—Silicon
Contract prices, cents per lb of alloy, lump, delivered.
16-20% Ca, 14-18% Mn, 53-59% Si.

Carloads	20.00
Ton lots	22.30
Less ton lots	23.30

CMSZ
Contract price, cents per lb of alloy, delivered.
Alloy 4: 45-49% Cr, 4-6% Mn, 18-21% Si, 1.25-1.75% Zr, 3.00-4.5% C.
Alloy 5: 50.56% Cr, 4-6% Mn, 13.50-16.00% Si, 0.75 to 1.25% Zr, 3.50-5.00% C.

Ton lots	20.75
Less ton lots	22.00

V Foundry Alloy
Cents per pound of alloy, f.o.b. Suspension Bridge, N. Y., freight allowed, max. St. Louis. V-5: 38-42% Cr, 17-19% Si, 8-11% Mn.

Ton lots	16.50¢
Less ton lots	17.75¢

Graphidox No. 4
Cents per pound of alloy, f.o.b. Suspension Bridge, N. Y., freight allowed, max. St. Louis. Si 48 to 52%, Ti 9 to 11%, Ca 5 to 7%.

Carload packed	18.00¢
Ton lots to carload packed	19.00¢
Less ton lots	20.50¢

SMZ
Contract price, cents per pound of alloy, delivered, 60-65% Si, 5-7% Mn, 5-7% Zr, 20% Fe, ½ in. x 12 mesh.

Ton lots	17.25
Less ton lots	18.50

February 8, 1951

Straightening Time Cut 66%

in Steel Fabricating Plant by Using a Standard Model Dake Press

When a steel fabricating company recently sought a faster method for straightening I-beams and channels after welding, first reports indicated that a high-priced bulldozer would be required or that special equipment would have to be built for the job.

Dake engineers advised otherwise: "If you will equip our regular 50PA Air-Operated Press with a special table and screw nose," they said, "you should be able to materially reduce your straightening costs on all of your structural work." They bought the press and adapted the press to the job. (See illustration above.) The result . . . straightening time was sliced 66%; and they tell us the press paid for itself in the first two months of use.

If you have any kind of straightening, bending or pressing jobs where pressure is to be applied to metals, plastics, wood, etc., consider a regular Dake press first. If a regular model will not work satisfactorily, we will tell you so and will be glad to quote on custom-built equipment.

The complete line of regular-model Dake presses is illustrated and described in the folder which we invite you to send for . . . now.

Write for this Folder

Dake Engine Company, 602 Seventh St., Grand Haven, Michigan

- -

DAKE arbor and hydraulic **PRESSES**

     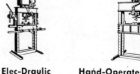

Single Leverage   Ratchet Type   Combination   Elec-Draulic   Hand-Operated Hydraulic

FERROALLOYS

Ferromanganese

78-82% Mn. maximum contract base price, gross ton, lump size.

F.o.b. Niagara Falls, Alloy, W. Va., Welland, Ont., Ashtabula, O.	$185
F.o.b. Johnstown, Pa.	$187
F.o.b. Sheridan, Pa.	$185
F.o.b. Etna, Clairton, Pa.	$188

$2.00 for each 1% above 82% Mn, penalty, $2.15 for each 1% below 78%.

Briquets—Cents per pound of briquet, delivered, 66% contained Mn.

Carload, bulk	10.95
Ton lots	12.55

Spiegeleisen

Contract prices gross ton, lump, f.o.b.

	16-19% Mn 3% max. Si	19-21% Mn 3% max. Si
Palmerton, Pa.	$74.00	$75.00
Pgh. or Chicago	74.00	75.00

Manganese Metal

Contract basis, 2 in. x down, cents per pound of metal, delivered. 96% min. Mn, 0.2% max. C, 1% max. Si, 2% max. Fe.

Carload, packed	29.75
Ton lots	31.25

Electrolytic Manganese

F.o.b. Knoxville, Tenn., freight allowed east of Mississippi, cents per pound.

Carloads	28
Ton lots	30
Less ton lots	32

Medium Carbon Ferromanganese

Mn 80% to 85%, C 1.25 to 1.50. Contract price, carloads, lump, bulk, delivered, per lb. of contained Mn. . . . 19.15¢

Low-Carbon Ferromanganese

Contract price, cents per pound Mn contained, lump size, del'd, Mn 85-90%.

	Carloads	Ton	Less
0.7% max. C, 0.06% P, 90% Mn	26.25	28.10	29.30
0.07% max. C	25.75	27.60	28.80
0.15% max. C	25.25	27.10	28.30
0.30% max. C	24.75	26.60	27.80
0.50% max. C	24.25	26.10	27.30
0.75% max. C, 7.00% max. Si	21.25	23.10	24.30

Silicomanganese

Contract basis, lump size, cents per pound of metal, delivered, 65-68% Mn, 18-20% Si, 1.5% max. C. For 2% max. C, deduct 0.2¢.

Carload bulk	9.90
Ton lots	11.55
Briquet, contract basis carlots, bulk delivered, per lb of briquet	11.15
Ton lots	11.75

Silvery Iron (electric furnace)

Si 14.01 to 14.50 pct, f.o.b. Keokuk, Iowa, or Wenatchee, Wash., $89.50 gross ton, freight allowed to normal trade area. Si 15.01 to 15.50 pct, f.o.b. Niagara Falls, N. Y., $83.00. Add $1.00 per ton for each additional 0.50% Si up to and including 18%. Add $1.00 for each 0.50% Mn over 1%.

Silicon Metal

Contract price, cents per pound contained Si, lump size, delivered, for ton lots packed.

96% Si, 2% Fe	21.70
97% Si, 1% Fe	22.10

Silicon Briquets

Contract price, cents per pound of briquet bulk, delivered, 40% Si, 1 lb Si briquets.

Carload, bulk	6.95
Ton lots	8.55

Electric Ferrosilicon

Contract price, cents per pound contained Si, lump, bulk, carloads, delivered.

25% Si	19.00	75% Si	14.30
50% Si	12.40	85% Si	15.55
90-95% Si			17.50

Calcium Metal

Eastern zone contract prices, cents per pound of metal, delivered.

	Cast	Turnings	Distilled
Ton lots	$2.05	$2.95	$3.75
Less ton lots	2.40	3.30	4.55

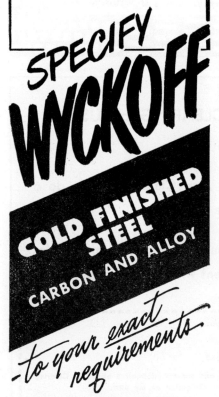
IRON AGE MARKETS & PRICES
FOUNDED 1855

Other Ferroalloys

Alsifer, 20% Al, 40% Si, 40% Fe, contract basis, f.o.b. Suspension Bridge, N. Y.
- Carload .... 9.90¢
- Ton lots .... 11.30¢

Calcium molybdate, 45-40%, f.o.b. Langeloth, Pa., per pound contained Mo. $1.15

Ferrocolumbium, 50-60%, 2 in x D, contract basis, delivered, per pound contained Cb.
- Ton lots $4.90
- Less ton lots 4.95

Ferro - Tantalum - columbium, 20% Ta, 40% Cb, 0.30 C. Contract basis, delivered, ton lots, 2 in. x D, per lb of contained Cb plus Ta $3.75

Ferromolybdenum, 55-75%, f.o.b. Langeloth, Pa., per pound contained Mo $1.32

Ferrophosphorus, electrolytic, 23-26%, car lots, f.o.b. Siglo, Mt. Pleasant, Tenn., $3 unitage, per gross ton $65.00
- 10 tons to less carload 75.00

Ferrotitanium, 40%, regular grade, 0.10% C max., f.o.b. Niagara Falls, N. Y., and Bridgeville, Pa., freight allowed, ton lots, per lb contained Ti $1.35

Ferrotitanium, 25%, low carbon, 0.10% C max., f.o.b. Niagara Falls, N. Y., and Bridgeville, Pa., freight allowed, ton lots, per lb contained Ti $1.50
- Less ton lots $1.55

Ferrotitanium, 15 to 19%, high carbon, f.o.b. Niagara Falls, N. Y., freight allowed, carload per net ton $177.00

Ferrotungsten, standard, lump or ¼ x down, packed, per pound contained W, 5 ton lots, delivered $3.25

Ferrovanadium, 35-55%, contract basis, delivered, per pound, contained V.
- Openhearth .... $3.0-$3.05
- Crucible 3.10- 3.15
- High speed steel (Primos) 3.25

Molybdic oxide, briquets or cans, per lb contained Mo, f.o.b. Langeloth, Pa. $1.14
- bags, f.o.b. Washington, Pa., Langeloth, Pa. $1.13

Simanal, 20% Si, 20% Mn, 20% Al, contract basis, f.o.b. Philo, Ohio, freight allowed, per pound
- Carload, bulk lump .... 14.50¢
- Ton lots, bulk lump .... 15.75¢
- Less ton lots, lump .... 16.25¢

Vanadium pentoxide, 88-92% V₂O₅ contract basis, per pound contained V₂O₅ $1.28

Zirconium, 35-40%, contract basis, f.o.b. plant, freight allowed, per pound of alloy.
- ton lots .... 21.00¢

Zirconium, 12-15%, contract basis, lump, delivered, per lb of alloy.
- carload, bulk .... 7.00¢

Boron Agents

Contract prices per lb of alloy, del.

Borosil, f.o.b. Philo, Ohio, freight allowed, B 3-4%, Si 40-45%, per lb contained B $5.25

Bortam, f.o.b. Niagara Falls
- Ton lots, per pound .... 45¢
- Less ton lots, per pound .... 50¢

Carbortam, Ti 15-21%, B 1-2%, Si 2-4%, Al 1-2%, C 4.5-7.5%, f.o.b. Suspension Bridge, N. Y., freight allowed.
- Ton lots, per pound .... 10.00¢

Ferroboron, 17.50% min. B, 1.50% max. Si, 0.50% max. Al, 0.50% max. C, 1 in. x D. Ton lots $1.20

F.o.b. Wash., Pa.; 100 lb, up
- 10 to 14% B .... .75
- 14 to 19% B 1.20
- 19% min. B 1.50

Grainal, f.o.b. Bridgeville, Pa., freight allowed, 100 lb and over.
- No. 1 .... $1.00
- No. 6 .... 68¢
- No. 79 .... 50¢

Manganese—Boron 75.00% Mn, 15-20% B, 5% max. Fe, 1.50% max. Si, 3.00% max. C, 2 in. x D, delivered.
- Ton lots $1.46
- Less ton lots 1.57

Nickel—Boron 15-18% B, 1.00% max. Al, 1.50% max. Si, 0.50% max. C, 3.00% max. Fe, balance Ni, delivered.
- Less ton lots $1.80

Silcaz, contract basis, delivered.
- Ton lots .... 45.00¢

THE CLEARING HOUSE

The Clearing House

NEWS OF USED, REBUILT AND SURPLUS MACHINERY

An Increasing Burden — Washington is shuffling around the machine tool question indecisively. It has held back priorities and information from the new machine tool industry and although it is now fumbling around with plans and schedules, the damage of delay has been done.

As order books fattened unhealthily and delivery dates stretched to the horizon, the burden of feeding machines to industry so that it could maintain vigorous civilian production and prepare for war work has fallen increasingly on the used machinery field.

Collection Campaign—The trade has responded. It has been moving desirable equipment as quickly as inventory and collection permitted. But there is a limit to the late model machines available and it is anticipated that before the yoked new machine tool industry can get going, buyers will be scraping the bottom of the barrel.

To make up the lag between now and the time machine tool production can be quickened, dealers will have to "encourage" firms to strip off the cobwebs on some machines and put them into circulation. It should be pointed out to manufacturers that to hold back equipment when America is rearming for what could be a desperate battle is selfish and unpatriotic.

The Human Touch — Digging out this idle equipment should become a campaign with dealers. They must jog the memory of manufacturers. They must point out the need of the times and the selfishness of not searching plants. Finally, they should appeal to profit-consciousness. But no matter how they do it, they should get out the machines.

Chicago Demand — In the Chicago area, used machinery demand stayed high-pitched. Some government subcontracts have been let in the area. They have not made themselves felt too keenly but they should be regarded as only the beginning. Demand was principally for machines to maintain high civilian output.

Some observers point out that contrary to the pre-World War II situation, some machine tool users are reasonably assured of continuing non-defense business and filling in with defense work. Since manufacturers before realized that a greater portion of their capacity would go to war, they were more uncertain of what demands on them would be. Consequently they weren't as deeply into the market as now.

Some Items Tighter — Demand for late type equipment in Chicago is still at a peak. Turret lathes, vertical and horizontal boring mills, and automatic screw machines are difficult and almost impossible to pick up. Large press brakes and squaring shears have been tight for some time. Prices had been running at 75 to 80 pct of new machine prices.

Buyers were still scratching around for late model machines and although a shift to older machines was evident, it was minor.

Rebuilding Questionnaire—Rebuilding of machine tools from their reserves is now an irksome problem to the Air Force which has drained off nearly all machine tools in usable condition.

To find out what the rebuilding potential is, MDNA has mailed to its members a questionnaire on ability and desire to rebuild machines. MDNA asks its members to understand that volunteering this information will aid not only the Air Force but Navy and Ordnance procurement offices. It is hoped that the questionnaire will unearth more skilled rebuilding facilities than have been evident.

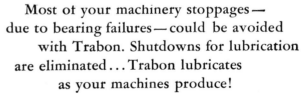

Where Does the Red Begin?

WHERE GEARS are concerned, that's a question you may want to ask yourself. Too often the red ink begins too soon. It may begin with gears not dependably up to your specifications. You may find it in production slow-downs due to gear installation difficulties. You may find that poor performance is building up your service costs.

You may discover that gear-troubles are causing your customers to think of competitors' products.

If the red ink begins at *any* of these points you'll be well rewarded by discussing gear problems with "Double Diamond" engineers. *"Double Diamonds" are produced to work in the black.* They provide low installed cost. They

serve economically and dependably on the job for which you buy them. They do credit to your product and your reputation.

We have thirty-six years of such gear-building behind us. We believe we know gears, and we believe we know the true facts about gear costs. We'd like to discuss these matters with you at your convenience.

TRADE MARK

Automotive Gear Works, Inc.
RICHMOND, INDIANA

•••• **FOR AUTOMOTIVE**

FARM EQUIPMENT AND GENERAL INDUSTRIAL APPLICATIONS ••

☆Reg. U. S. Pat. Off.

HYPOID BEVEL

SPIRAL BEVEL

FLYWHEEL GEAR

ZEROL☆ BEVEL

STRAIGHT BEVEL

STRAIGHT SPUR

HELICAL SPUR

SPLINED STEM PINION

SPLINE SHAFT

The Iron Age

A CHILTON PUBLICATION

THE NATIONAL METALWORKING WEEKLY

February 15, 1951

CONTENTS PAGE 2

Duplexing installation in which hot metal is carried to the Hydro-Arc Furnace with a ladle.

Cupola-to-Electric DUPLEXING

— a solution to low-quality coke problems

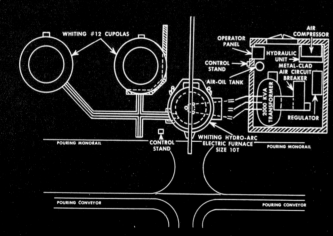

Typical cupola-to-electric duplexing layout complete with pouring system

By using a Hydro-Arc Furnace that matches total cupola capacity, melters are increasing production, getting proper pouring temperatures at all times, and reducing machine shop rejections.

Other savings (such as continuity in pouring, increased yield from alloys, and finer grain castings of higher strength) help to make cupola-to-electric duplexing repay its entire cost in a comparatively short time.

The versatility of Hydro-Arc Electric Furnaces, combined with the ingenuity of Whiting engineers, make this equipment adaptable to almost any foundry requirements. A Whiting representative will gladly call to discuss it with you.

WHITING
CORPORATION

15601 Lathrop Ave.   Harvey, Illinois

Offices in Chicago, Cincinnati, Detroit, Houston, Los Angeles, New York, Philadelphia, Pittsburgh, and St. Louis. Representatives in other principal cities. Canadian Subsidiary: Whiting Corporation (Canada) Ltd., Toronto, Ontario. Export Department: 30 Church St., New York 7, N. Y.

Cylinder Door Shell and Head Assembly, made principally from Bethlehem Weldments. Shell,
7 ft, 9 in. o.d., and 4 in. thick; head thickness, 1¼ in.; height, 75 in.; weight, 17,789 lb.

Welding Plays Big Part in 17,789-lb Assembly

This huge assembly, recently completed by Bethlehem, is a cylinder door shell and head assembly for an autoclave used in creosoting. It is 75 in. high, and weighs 17,789 lb. The shell is 7 ft, 9 in. o.d., and 4 in. thick, and its head is 1¼ in. thick. For strength and durability, as well as for the economies afforded by a substantial saving in weight, the assembly was made principally by welding.

Bethlehem Weldments offer the combination of strength, durability, and weight-saving to manufacturers because they are made of rolled steel plates, structural shapes and other sections of the exact thicknesses required, and with the necessary rigidity to do the job. They are accurately flame-cut to customer specifications, then welded into simple parts or intricate assemblies.

Bethlehem Weldments can be made in varied sizes. They permit freedom of design, for the formed and flame-cut rolled steel may be bent, pressed, or otherwise formed prior to welding, without damage to the physical structure of the steel.

They can also be used economically in combination with steel castings or forgings. If you would like to know more about Bethlehem Weldments, just give us a call or drop a line to us at Bethlehem, Pa.

BETHLEHEM STEEL COMPANY
BETHLEHEM, PA.

On the Pacific Coast Bethlehem products are sold by Bethlehem Pacific Coast Steel Corporation. *Export Distributor:* Bethlehem Steel Export Corporation

BETHLEHEM WELDMENTS

IRON AGE

CONTENTS

THE IRON AGE
Editorial, Advertising and Circulation Offices, 100 E. 42nd St., New York 17, N.Y.
GEORGE T. HOOK, Publisher
TOM C. CAMPBELL, Editor

EDITORIAL STAFF
Managing Editor   George F. Sullivan
Feature Editor   Darwyn I. Brown
News-Markets Editor   Wm. V. Packard
Machinery Editor   George Elwers
Associate Editors: William Czygan, H. W. Van Camp, F. J. Winters; Assistant Editors: R. L. Hatschek, John Kolb, Ted Metaxas, W. B. Olson; Regional Editors: E. C. Beaudet, Chicago; W. A. Lloyd, Cleveland; W. G. Patton, Detroit; John B. Delaney, Pittsburgh, Osgood Murdock, R. T. Reinhardt, San Francisco; Eugene J. Haray, Karl Rannells, George H. Baker, Washington; Correspondents: Fred L. Allen, Birmingham; N. Levenson, Boston; Fred Edmunds, Los Angeles; James Douglas, Seattle; Roy Edmonds, St. Louis; F. Sanderson, Toronto; F. H. Harley, London, England; Chilton Editorial Board: Paul Wooton, Washington Representative.

BUSINESS STAFF
Production Manager   B. H. Hayes
Director of Research   Oliver Johnson
Mgr. Circul'n & Promotion   C. T. Post
Asst. Promotion Mgr.   James A. Crites
Asst. Dir. of Research   Wm. Laimbeer

REGIONAL BUSINESS MANAGERS
B. L. Herman, Philadelphia; Stanley J. Smith, Chicago; Peirce Lewis, Detroit; Paul Bachman, New England; Robert F. Blair, Cleveland; R. Raymond Kay, Los Angeles; C. H. Ober, New York; J. M. Spackman, Pittsburgh; Harry Becker, European Representative.

REGIONAL OFFICES
Chicago 3, 1134 Otis Bldg.; Cleveland 14, 1016 National City Bank Bldg., Detroit 2, 103 Pallister Ave., Los Angeles 28, 2420 Cheremoya Ave.; New England, 62 La Salle Rd., W. Hartford 7; New York 17, 100 E. 42nd St.; Philadelphia 39, 56th & Chestnut Sts.; Pittsburgh 22, 814 Park Bldg.; San Francisco 3, 1355 Market St.; Washington 4, National Press Bldg.; European, 111 Thorley Lane, Timperley, Cheshire England.

Circulation Representatives: Thomas Scott, James Richardson.

One of the Publications Owned and Published by Chilton Company, Inc., Chestnut & 56th Sts., Philadelphia 39, Pa., U. S. A.

OFFICERS AND DIRECTORS
JOS. S. HILDRETH, President
Vice-Presidents: Everit B. Terhune, G. C. Buzby, P. M. Fahrendorf, Harry V. Duffy, William H. Vallar, Treasurer; John Blair Moffet, Secretary; D. Allyn Garber, Maurice E. Cox, Frank P. Tighe, George T. Hook, Tom C. Campbell, L. V. Rowlands, Directors. George Malswinkle, Asst. Treas.

Indexed in the Industrial Arts Index and the Engineering Index. Published every Thursday by the CHILTON CO. (INC.), Chestnut and 56th Sts., Philadelphia 39, Pa. Entered as second class matter Nov. 8, 1932, at the Post Office at Philadelphia under the act of March 3, 1879. $8 yearly in United States, its territories and Canada; other Western Hemisphere Countries $15; other Foreign Countries $25 per year. Single Copies 35c. Annual Review and Metal Industry Facts Issue, $2.00. Cable address "Ironage" N. Y.
Member Audit Bureau of Circulations. Member Society of Business Magazine Editors.

Copyright, 1951, by Chilton Co. (Inc.)

DIGEST

EBRUARY FIFTEENTH • NINETEEN FIFTY-ONE • VOLUME 167 • NUMBER 7

ACCURATE

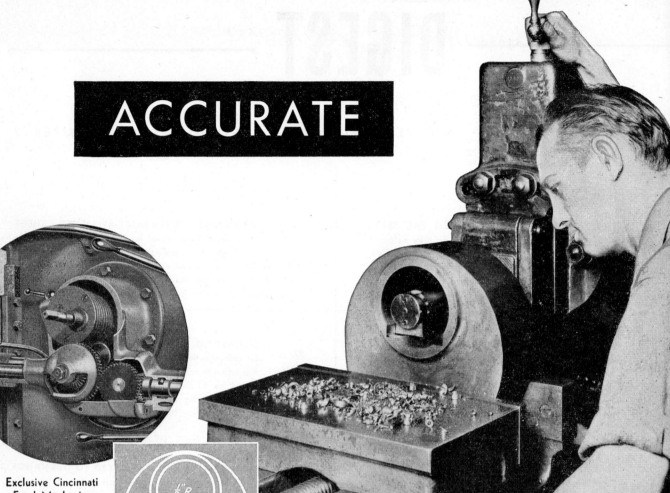

Exclusive Cincinnati
Feed Mechanism

Shaping internal keyways to close limits.

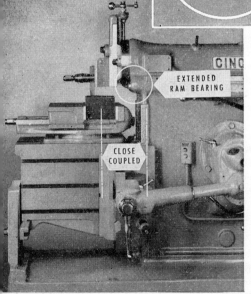

Tool has cut seven inches, and ram has
not moved beyond bearing support.

ACCURATE FEEDING

No bumps, no gaps in the feed on a Cincinnati Shaper. The unique
feed mechanism, with a cam for each feed always in contact with the
follower, maintains both accuracy and a superior finish to the work.

ACCURATE CUTTING

To further increase accuracy, a Cincinnati Shaper literally hugs the
work. Extended ram bearings and full table clearance keep the work
close to the column, reduce vibration and
deflection, and consequent inaccuracies. A
Cincinnati Shaper is the closest coupled
shaper in the field.

For dependable, day in, day out accuracy,
investigate a Cincinnati.

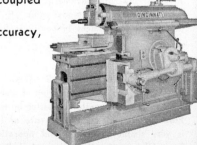

*Write for complete
Shaper Catalog N-5.*

editorial

Whose Money Is It?

THE President has asked for unprecedented taxes for defense purposes. No one would want to shirk on the cost of making this country strong. No one has raised his voice on this score. From the farm to the city, from the home to the office, all have applauded the desire to make this country so strong we can't suffer defeat. We believe in pay-as-we-go.

So far so good. But just raising taxes and spending money is not the whole answer. The way the budget has been presented and the lack of a real honest effort to cut down non-defense spending has jolted many people. It would jolt many more to action—if they realized who pays the bill.

There has been some effort by our government to cut down on its spending —but it has been small potatoes (not the expensive kind the government buys). There is evidence that no attempt has been made by the Administration—nor will one be made—to realistically cut down regular government spending. We still have federal aid to education in tremendous sums. Maybe we do need aid for education, but we need an impartial committee study to see where some of this money goes and what good it does.

We have new-fangled ideas on socialized medicine despite the experience in England. If they are pushed through they will cost billions. Now is the time to keep them from mushrooming. Sooner or later the farm support program may drive housewives to revolt. A subsidy for farm prices, supported by a tax on the people who must pay higher prices because of this rigmarole is something close to insanity.

We have the government going further and further into the public power business when private power concerns can do a much better job. Some of these things may be only a drop in the bucket. But there are so many drops that they add up to gallons.

Some Congressmen log roll and will vote for anything if they can get something for their own community. That something can wait. Some businesses put pressure on for this or that when it can wait or be eliminated. Government is pressured for all sorts of things by many of us but no one wants to restrain himself.

When we finally realize that "The Government" is only a collection of all of us and that our own money is going down the drain maybe things will be different.

When we see what the taxes do to our bankroll—if any—and to incentive— if any remains—maybe each of us will demand a cut-to-the-bone in government services which have no bearing on defense, which are socialistic in nature and which in themselves are a danger to the very freedom we are fighting to protect.

Tom Campbell

Editor

Fifteen seconds is the machining time for this exacting interrupted cut, made on an Acme-Gridley 6" RPA-8 Spindle Chucking Automatic, using carbide tooling.

HOLD HIGH CONCENTRICITY on high-speed interrupted cuts
...put the job on an Acme-Gridley Automatic

Here's more proof that an Acme-Gridley's basic design advantages pay off in the ability to take it—on the toughest kind of tricky jobs—up to the limitations of modern carbide tooling speeds.

To take interrupted cuts at high speed and still maintain concentricity, an automatic must have rigid, rugged strength in the frame; *an Acme-Gridley's got it.* And direct, positive camming keeps accuracy always up to snuff.

Adaptability is another important advantage of Acme-Gridleys; they'll handle a wide variety of tooling (including independent power-driven auxiliaries where needed). That way, better distribution of cuts or the combining of operations can cut machining and handling times.

All these features add up to give you "more good

pieces in the pan," more tough production problems licked. Get the full story on these time-saving, money-saving Acme-Gridley 4, 6 and 8 spindle Chucking Automatics—ask for Bulletin CM 51.

JOB FACTS

PART—Hydraulic Lift Box
MATERIAL—1035 Steel Casting
MACHINE—Acme-Gridley 6" RPA-8 Spindle Chucking Automatic
TOOLING—Carbide
TOLERANCES—.003" on Large Hole; .001" on Small Hole
MACHINING TIME—15 Seconds (240/hr.)

Machine Obsolescence is the Creeping Paralysis That Strangles Profit.

IRON AGE *newsfront*

► A great many of the machines which are now coming out of government reserves require <u>extensive</u> rebuilding to put them in like-new condition. Cost is often as high as <u>60 pct of current new machine cost</u>—which is often <u>higher than the original cost</u> of the machine being rebuilt.

► Nickel is now selling in the black market for <u>$3.00 a pound,</u> up a dollar from the last reported quotation. Even at this price it is <u>very hard to find.</u> One of the ways nickel gets into the black market involves <u>no cash:</u> A legitimate user turns over his regular approved shipment to a dealer who pays for it with twice as much <u>equally usable scrap.</u>

► Because of the <u>FTC ban on basing point selling</u> of steel the government is paying various prices for its steel, depending on the producing point. This should please the <u>theoretical economists.</u> <u>What they may not realize</u> is that the basing point ban is <u>costing the government</u> (like other consumers) <u>more money</u> because most producers follow their usual practice of selling f.o.b. mill with no freight absorption.

► As much as <u>50 pct of the pig iron</u> being bought by some midwestern foundries is <u>imported.</u>

► The automobile industry can't move far these days without running into a material restriction. A GM Saginaw steering gear uses <u>15 different materials.</u> In it there are <u>18 different kinds of steel.</u> The Delco-Remy Div. has a slightly different problem: Last year it used <u>42,000 baby nipples</u> to mask the terminals of automobile starting motors during painting.

► Use of <u>approved packaging</u> entitles shippers to <u>rate reductions</u> on the French railways. One test in which packages are rotated in a spiked barrel is called "the brutal manipulation."

► If present experimental applications of <u>iron powder in projectiles</u> are adopted, the domestic iron powder capacity would have to be expended <u>tremendously</u>—some conservative estimates say by at least 10 times if foreign sources are ruled out of strategic planning.
  This would put the U. S. about where Germany was in 1944, when the Nazi's iron powder output topped <u>32,000 tons</u> to meet demands of their <u>shell rotating band</u> production.

► Inspection of <u>internal tolerances</u> of assembled parts can now be done with a betatron <u>without having to tear down the assembly</u> for measurements. Entire engines for military vehicles have been inspected in this way.

► One of the new uses for metal powders is for <u>turbine buckets</u> for the <u>hot end</u> of a jet engine. Pressed iron powder blades have been used in the compressor section. But now one of the <u>new metal alloys</u> is being tested for the <u>high temperature</u> application.

► <u>Radially fed gear shaving,</u> long thought impractical, is being successfully used in Detroit on internal gears. The cutter <u>does not reciprocate;</u> the <u>gear feeds radially</u> into it. Production is <u>twice</u> that of an ordinary gear shaver.

► A Chicago steel warehouse is planning to install a <u>rolling mill.</u> They expect to have it finished by the middle of this year.

Christendom was saved by steel

ALL day long, waves of Arab horsemen beat upon the ranks of Charles Martel's veteran militia. But time after time, the enemy cavalry recoiled before storms of iron-tipped javelins, their shining scimitars unsuccessful. On the second morning, the Saracen leader, Abderrahman, was slain, pierced with many spears. The Moslem horde fled back across the Pyrenees, never again to menace the Western world.

Time after time, as at Tours in 732 A.D., Christian civilization has been threatened by seemingly invincible enemies. Yet history proves that victory invariably has gone to the nation or alliance which excelled in the production and use of iron and steel.

In the present era of alarms and crises, it is reassuring to realize that America has greater capacity for making steel than all the rest of the world combined. Furthermore, the American steel industry is expanding at a rate far faster than that of all the dictator-directed economies behind the Iron Curtain. Our free and independent steel making and metal working industries can and will forge sinews for the peace we want or for the war we may be forced to fight.

So remember this: It is not only the threat of Muscovy to fear—America has itself to fear also—its misguided sentimentalists, its sheltered saboteurs—who seem to play communism's game by frittering away our strength and our resources.

IRON AGE *summary*

iron and steel industry trends

Steel expansion requires 10 million tons steel... Detroit angry over expected steel slash ... CMP means seat for every ticket

STEEL capacity expansion during the next 2 years will require about 10 million tons of steel. But so far the government has not recognized that it takes steel to make steel by setting up priorities for steel expansion.

In order to keep their expansion programs on schedule steel companies have resorted to the ancient system of barter. Reason for the trading is that few steel companies can produce all the numerous items required in a construction program. Wide flange beams for example are made by only two companies and their order books are extended far into the future.

Thus, if an expanding steel company wants to keep its program moving it has to trade some of its products with another company that makes what it needs. Tonnages involved in this method of "horse trading" are considerable.

By Government Command—Only

Obviously new steel mills proposed by people not now in the steel business cannot be built unless steel is provided under a government-directed program. They have no steel to trade and present producers cannot be expected to supply them during a period of extreme shortage —unless the government directs them to do so.

This week an irate and perplexed auto industry is pondering over reports from Washington that steel use in autos may be slashed as much as 40 pct during the second quarter. Such a cutback could mean unemployment of nearly half a million men—unless placing of defense orders is miraculously speeded.

There is increasing evidence that government programs are beginning to compete with each other for steel. For example, plates are needed in tanks, ships, freight cars, and a number of other essential products. The problem of juggling production schedules to meet requirements of each program is being intensified by government directives for additional tonnages of steel.

Many in industry fear that too many tickets are being printed for steel's big production performance. Demand for tickets from military and civilian customers is terrific. Someone ought to count the seats and make sure that only one ticket is issued for each seat (each ton of steel). Matching of available production against requirements is the way the controlled materials plan will function when it is put into effect later this year.

Expand Iron Powder for Defense

Domestic iron powder capacity will have to be expanded many times its present size if the Ordnance Corps adopts iron powder rotating bands for shells. A long development program is believed nearing the decision stage now. Depending on whether the war is hot or cold, and also on the outcome of iron powder bullet development work, the required expansion might be more than ten times present capacity.

Pressure is growing for closer scrutiny of strategic metals being shipped to Europe. Criticism is being leveled at continued Marshall Plan buying of these metals from American stocks and sources—especially when domestic controls are being drawn steadily tighter.

Sick Switchmen Hit Where It Hurts

Steelmaking operations this week are scheduled at 98.5 pct of rated capacity, up 5½ points from last week's revised rate. When the final figures are toted up it will be found that the striking railroad switchmen took a toll of more than 200,000 tons of lost steel production. Although the transportation tangle is being quickly unraveled, steel producers' production schedules will feel the effects of the strike for several weeks.

(nonferrous summary, p. 142)

drop forgers

come to us for BIG forged hammer parts

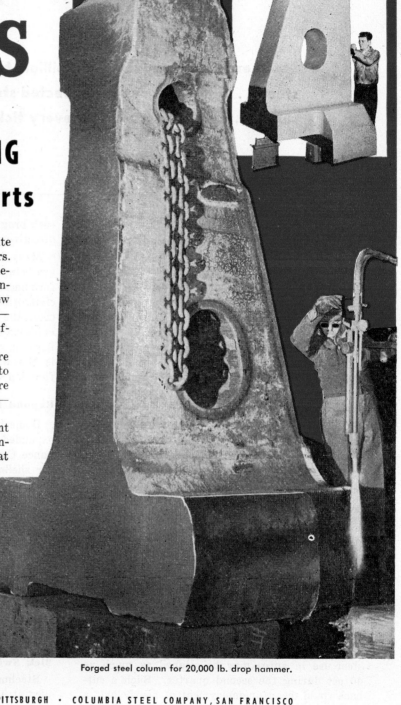

THE drop forging industry has licked quite a few problems in the last few years. Every day, more intricate shapes are demanded. And, particularly since 1940, this industry has done a fine job of forging the new high alloys, stainless steels and light metals—materials that were considered extremely difficult to forge a few years back.

But the new metals and involved shapes are tough on forging equipment. That's why, to cut maintenance costs, many drop forgers are using hammer parts made *from* forgings—the form of steel they *know* will stand up.

Forged anvil bases and columns represent an obvious advancement in drop hammer construction. They stand up under the great impact loads encountered when forging difficult metals, guaranteeing longer life, lower operating costs and reduced "lost time."

If you want the best in heavy forgings, get them from the Homestead District Works of United States Steel Company. That's where we make the steel, forge it, heat-treat it, and rough or finish machine it to your specifications. All work is done by highly experienced men, using the finest equipment.

Forged steel column for 20,000 lb. drop hammer.

UNITED STATES STEEL COMPANY, PITTSBURGH • COLUMBIA STEEL COMPANY, SAN FRANCISCO
TENNESSEE COAL, IRON & RAILROAD COMPANY, BIRMINGHAM • UNITED STATES STEEL EXPORT COMPANY, NEW YORK

Commercial Forgings

0-1671

UNITED STATES STEEL

Dear EDITOR

letters from readers

Shares Views

Sir:

I read your editorial in the Jan. 25 issue and I agree that all of us can very well make some sacrifices in our standard of living in view of the world situation. Everybody would agree to this—BUT people would tell you that they don't believe in making sacrifices in their standard of living when the Government in Washington believes in raising its standard of living day by day. Why should people out in the country believe they should get leaner and leaner when the Government at Washington believes in getting fatter and fatter? Has the Government made one single gesture of economy as an example?

E. M. KEAYS
Robert W. Baird & Co.
Milwaukee

Typical Reaction

Sir:

Enclosed is two bucks for another copy of your annual. Your annual issue is one which everyone interested in the steel industry will want to keep for its source material. That statistical section was a marvelous job, and everybody connected with the magazine is entitled to congrats.

W. K. GUTMAN
Goodbody & Co.
New York

Plenty of Interest Now

Sir:

I will greatly appreciate your sending me tearsheets for the articles on p. 66 in THE IRON AGE of Dec. 28, 1950 on continuous casting, and the issue of Dec. 22, 1949, p. 59. I have been informed that THE IRON AGE also published a very excellent article on the subject in the Feb. 24, 1944 issue. I believe that it would be a real contribution to the national emergency, if the articles were reprinted, what with the coming steel shortages. Interest in continuous casting will be stimulated as a result of plant expansion and the scramble for metals in the future.

J. R. HYNES
White Plains, N. Y.

We don't have to stimulate interest in continuous casting, as there has been a very active program by many companies during the past year. The Jan. 25 issue covers the latest Hazelett continuous casting mill, and the first disclosure of an aluminum bar casting machine appears on p. 87 of this issue.—Ed.

The Changing Times

Sir:

In the past, we were very much under the impression that practically all warehouses had established the same quantity extras. Also, the mills all had about the same quantity extras. Any difference in price usually was reflected in the warehouse base price and the mill base price.

Today, according to prices we have received, it seems that the various warehouses have different quantity extras as well as different base prices, the same thing holding true for the mills. Would you be so good as to check us on this and let us know whether we are or are not correct.

H. B. STAMM
Purchasing Agent
Columbia Mills, Inc.
Syracuse, N. Y.

About 10 years ago, the warehouses in each region of the country generally had similar base quantities and extras. It has been common to find regional similarities in pricing practices since. These are reflected in the footnote to the warehouse prices published weekly in THE IRON AGE. However, the pressure of the current situation has resulted in variations in mill extras, with variations from mill to mill. Quite probably, these are reflected in the actions of individual warehouses, depending upon the mill from which each receives the bulk of his stock.—Ed.

Credit Original Author

Sir:

I was amazed in reading the article "Germans Make Pig Iron without Coking Coal" by a B. M. Pearson, on p. 71 of the Jan. 11 number of THE IRON AGE, to find that it contained no reference whatsoever to the original article by Dr. Fritz Jaeger of which Pearson's article is but a somewhat condensed translation. This article appeared in "Stahl und Eisen," Aug. 3, 1950 . . .

G. LETENDRE
Director
Dept. of Mines & Metallurgy
Universite Laval
Quebec, Canada

THE IRON AGE regrets exceedingly the oversight which permitted this condensed translation to appear without credit to the author and to "Stahl und Eisen." The same apology is due on the forsterite lining article (Jan. 18, p. 65) which was also translated and abstracted by Mr. Pearson. On the latter, Mr. Pearson indicated "Stahl und Eisen" as his reference; we failed to realize it was a translation from that magazine.—Ed.

Kudos

Sir:

This is just a short note to express our very sincere appreciation of the fine treatment you gave R. B. Smith's article on codification of light metals in your Jan. 25 issue. Everyone here is very pleased with your handling of this material—especially the large 3½-p. chart, which is really a "dilly."

G. W. BIRDSALL
Mgr., Editorial Dept.
Reynolds Metals Co.
Richmond, Va.

IS MR. O. V. IN YOUR STOCK?

Perhaps you feel that any kind of cold rolled strip steel in your inventory is better than none. We agree that in times of critical shortages this may sometimes be true. But OVERSIZE VARIATION in strip thickness, a not uncommon characteristic in some strip and/or slit-sheet products can materially reduce your productive yield per ton—is a hidden cost that increases your steel bill. Best way to control Mr. O. V., locked in a stock permanently, is to specify, when deliveries are possible, Thinsteel precision cold rolled strip in low carbon, high carbon (annealed or tempered) and stainless grades. Thinsteel assures you extreme accuracy to gauge and uniformity of all characteristics in coil after coil - - means more feet per pound, more finished parts per ton.

CMP's expansion program, which includes new rolling facilities and auxiliary equipment, is under way and will help to provide, during 1951, additional capacity to meet increasing demand for Thinsteel products.

CMP
THINSTEEL
TRADE MARK

PRECISION COLD ROLLED
CMP
STRIP STEEL

the Cold Metal Products co.
YOUNGSTOWN I, OHIO

NEW YORK • CHICAGO • INDIANAPOLIS • DETROIT • ST. LOUIS • LOS ANGELES

WAREHOUSE STOCKS OF CMP THINSTEEL ARE AVAILABLE FROM:

THE COLD METAL PRODUCTS CO. of CALIFORNIA, 6600 McKinley Avenue, Los Angeles
Phone: PLeasant 3-1291
THE KENILWORTH STEEL CO., 750 Boulevard, Kenilworth, New Jersey
Phones: N. Y., COurtlandt 7-2427; N. J., UNionville 2-6900
PRECISION STEEL WAREHOUSE, INC.. 4425 W. Kinzie, Chicago • Phone: COlumbus 1-2700

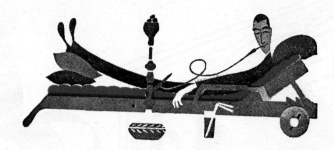

Fatigue Cracks

by Charles T. Post

Welcome Price Control

It's nice to be able to report that at least *somebody* likes the new scrap price ceilings. From early reports, it appears that the nation's police held a celebration the likes of which has not been seen since VJ-day.

Soaring scrap prices had created too much temptation for certain gentry possessed with trucks, hoists, and not too many scruples. Take the case of the Portland, Ore., heating equipment dealer who woke up one night to see a 600-lb boiler being hoisted onto a truck from his equipment lot across the street. Before he could get his trousers on, the thieves had taken off. Then there was the logging operator who towed his rig into the deep woods and left it preparatory to beginning operations the next day. The minute he left, someone popped out from behind the nearest fir tree and towed it into the still deeper woods for cutting up into No. 1 Machinery Cast.

With agricultural scrap at $60, the farmer who reported that someone had sawed the wooden handles off his plow and stolen the blade should not have been too surprised. Fifty years ago, the plow would have been ignored and the horse taken.

Now, with ceiling prices, the incentive will be to turn scrap into finished products again. If you have an open hearth furnace in the back lot, you had better keep your eye on it.

Or, as the sign in the clip joint said, "Keep your eye on your wife; to heck with your coat."

Back Copies Wanted

Ziegler Sargent, v.p. of Sargent & Co., the builders' hardware firm, dropped in the other day to find out if we had the back issues of your f.f.j. he wanted. In 1864, his firm supplemented its product advertising with "Help Wanted" ads designed to attract immigrant labor to its new plant in New Haven. Until Sept. 22 of that year, your f.f.j. was known as the *Hardware Reporter & Iron and Steel Mfrs. Circular*; then, as *The Iron Age and Hardware, Iron & Industry Reporter*. If you happen to have any of these issues containing the "Help Wanted" ads, please let us know.

Puzzlers

Apparently some of your f.f.j.'s readers are just getting caught up on their reading. L. F. Scana, North American Aviation has just come through with the right answer to the "walking man" puzzle and C. M. Williamson, Sears, Roebuck & Co., recognized that the diameter of the circle was 15 in.

T. W. White and D. A. Lieberman, Ther Electric & Machine Works find that they can just squeeze a well-oiled ball bearing of 0.4615-in. radius through the hole in the Jan. 25 puzzle. First one in with the correct answer of 6.43008 in. to the steel and cork sphere problem is C. E. Norton, Chicago.

For this week's puzzle, H. K. Moore, Boston, wants us to find the correct numerical values for the various letters in the denominator and quotient below. Note: "O" refers to the letter "O" and not zero.

```
                   S T U F F
         HOT ) 1 F 8 T H 9 F U
               1 S U 8
               U O 9 H
               U S 9 9
                 9 S 9
                 T 1 S
                 W H O F
                 U 1 S U
                   U 1 S U
                   U 1 S U
```

DATES
to remember

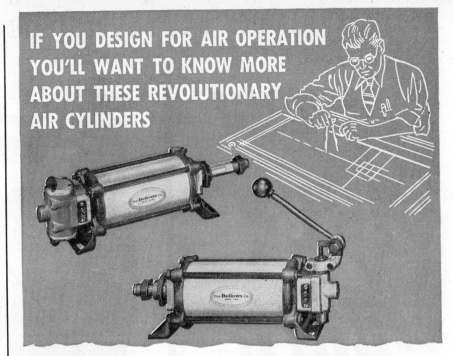
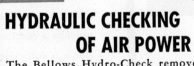

machine tool high spots

by W.A.Lloyd

Capitol Skull Session — First pool orders will probably go to builders of vertical and horizontal boring mills and planer-type milling machines, it was indicated this week.

Representatives of the boring machine industry met with NPA officials in Washington to review immediate and future needs for vertical and horizontal boring mills and the planer-type milling machines and the ability of the industry to meet those needs.

Forceful Pressure—NPA officials said that as the mobilization program gains momentum there will be increasingly heavy demands on the industry to provide boring machines of all types needed before manufacturers can tool up for military production.

NPA officials are now considering issuing "pool" orders to help speed the building of these machine tools. They emphasized that the primary purpose of pool orders is to enable the machine tool manufacturers to make orderly advance scheduling of their full production for defense, and to assure them that they will get the materials they need, when they need them. Such a program was put into effect during World War II.

Expansion Help — Industry spokesmen said they are now

booked far ahead for some types of boring machines. In order to facilitate expansion of present facilities in certain parts of the industry, certificates of necessity may be requested to help firms charge off depreciation at an accelerated rate. In some cases, direct government loans may be required, they said.

Staffing Extra Shifts—Industry representatives said they are having trouble getting the manpower for extra shifts and in getting castings for boring machines, particularly castings of the machine tool grade.

NPA officials said they would aid wherever possible in placing defense orders for castings, and urged the industry to assist in locating idle boring mills in plants in their localities.

Press Output Increase—Lake Erie Engineering Corp., a major producer of presses, is spending $1 million for new machine tools to increase capacity of its Kenmore, N. Y. (near Buffalo) plant 30 pct. Robert E. Dillon, president, said his company "probably" would increase the physical size of the plant.

Meanwhile, builders of all types of machine tools are bending their effort to step up production. In the East, a major manu-

facturer of elevators will reportedly produce certain assemblies and possibly complete machines for one company. In the Midwest, a manufacturer of printing machinery, will produce lathes.

Bottleneck Stigma—The industry is battling to forestall a bottleneck brand, which would be as ridiculous factually as it would be unfortunate public relations-wise.

Facts are that the industry is swamped with orders. Best estimates of machine tool demand indicate that it will reach a peak, possibly $1.3 billion this year, and taper off gradually. But with some companies already quoting deliveries on some machines for first quarter of 1953, the situation is obviously something less than fluid.

Automatic Handling—In Cleveland, the automatic handling, feeding and unloading of materials between machining processes, is a must in industry today, W. R. Slattery, of the manufacturing engineering staff of Ford Motor Co. told 300 engineers at the eighth annual machine design conference, at Cleveland Engineering Society here.

He described the function of automation, a mass production method soon to be in operation at Ford's engine plant and foundry here.

FREE *publications*

These publications describe money-saving equipment and services ... they are free with no obligation ... just fill in and mail the postcard on the opposite page.

Cold Sawing Machines

Heavy duty models of the Ohler hydraulic high-speed cold sawing machines are described in a new 4-p. bulletin listing complete specifications. Features of the equipment that result in greater efficiency at lower cost are detailed, along with information on cooling, ease of operation, the hydraulic system, and cutting speeds. The model 1500 automatic saw sharpening machine, providing accurate grinding and equal height to each tooth, is also described. *Klingelhofer Machine Tool Co.*

For free copy insert No. 1 on postcard.

Plant Safety Kit

The Towmotor plant safety kit contains 4 big plant markers measuring 14 x 22 in. for marking off lift truck routes, and 4 safety posters for display on bulletin boards. The latter are humorously illustrated with attention-getting cartoons emphasizing 4 major causes of accidents, and the heavy cardboard markers have bold black lettering on a yellow background. Also included are 2 operator guides showing how to get maximum service from efficient Towmotor operation, and how to lift, transport and stack all types of products. This practical kit should aid materially in reducing plant accidents and promoting safer materials handling. *Towmotor Corp.*

For free copy insert No. 2 on postcard.

Metal Turnings Crusher

Reasons for crushed turnings are listed in a new 8-p. booklet describing American ring turnings crushers, designed especially for shredding long curly turnings of low or high carbon steel, alloy steel, aluminum, brass or bronze as produced by automatic screw machines, lathes and planers. Design and construction features are detailed and information is given on approximate capacities, speeds and power. A clearance and foundation plan is shown, along with photos and descriptions of various installations. *American Pulverizer Co.*

For free copy insert No. 3 on postcard.

Exhaust and Dust Collector

Advantages of employing the unit system of dust collection are discussed in a new 14-p. bulletin describing dust exhauster and collector units. Some of the outstanding features of 1100-cfm units are covered, and complete specifications are listed. Performance curves are shown, along with typical arrangements of unit systems and information on suggested volumes and pipe sizes. Essential information for ordering units from this British company is explained. The booklet also lists prices for the various 3-phase, single-phase and dc models. *Keith Blackman Ltd.*

For free copy insert No. 4 on postcard.

Metal Protectives

A new 4-p. bulletin on Protect-O-Metal weld spatter preventives and metal protection compounds supplies full details on composition, application, and potential savings provided by the three grades. In addition to describing spatter-proofing properties, the folder tells how compound No. 8 provides corrosion protection for long periods—of special value to manufacturers and fabricators who may store metal stock, semi-finished materials and dies out-of-doors prior to welding operations. *G. W. Smith & Sons, Inc.*

For free copy insert No. 5 on postcard.

Aluminum-Coated Steel

Aluminized steel — steel with a special coating of aluminum—is discussed in a new 24-p. booklet describing the steel's aluminum surface, its heat and corrosion resistance and outstanding heat reflectivity—80 pct up to 900°F. Photographs and a listing of applications show where manufacturers have used Aluminized in a wide variety of products. Also included are data on mechanical and forming properties, available sizes and gages, as well as detailed recommendations for welding by various methods, brazing and finishing. *Armco Steel Corp.*

For free copy insert No. 6 on postcard.

For Resurfacing Floors

Plastic Rock, a floor resurfacing material composed of siloxide rock, asphaltic paste and setting powder, is described in a new 4-p. bulletin telling how this material, when combined with water, forms a mortar-like mixture which is troweled the same as concrete. The bulletin illustrates typical applications and gives information on physical characteristics and uses. The folder explains how more than 53 million sq ft presently in use have stood the test of time. *United Laboratories, Inc.*

For free copy insert No. 7 on postcard.

Mill Motors and Controls

Westinghouse 600-Series mill motors and Class 9500 dc magnetic mill auxiliary controllers are described in a new 20-p. booklet. Design features and construction details of the mill motors are discussed. The booklet points out that the motors are built to meet the AISE specifications. The new mag-

Turn to page 126

NEW *production ideas*

new and improved production ideas, equipment, services and methods described here offer production economies ... fill in and mail postcard.

Spiral Milling Attachment

Designed for larger machines—No. 3 dial to No. 6 dual power dial types.

The new Cincinnati heavy duty universal spiral milling attachment is driven from the machine spindle. It has 360° swivel range in two planes, offering the versatility of smaller attachments. To obtain utmost rigidity, the primary bracket is clamped to the face of the column and also to the front end of the Dynapoise overarm. Outboard supports for extra heavy milling operations may be obtained as an extra. Spindle and all shafts are mounted on anti-friction bearings; the spindle nose conforms to No. 50 standard. *Cincinnati Milling & Grinding Machines, Inc.*
For more data insert No. 14 on postcard.

Chromated Anti-Rust Paint

Can be applied right over rust without wire brushing or scraping.

Known as Rustrem Chromate Special, the new paint is available in clear, black and aluminum. It possesses all the penetrating and sealing qualities of standard Rustrem and stands up under extreme conditions of temperature and moisture. It is suitable for interior and exterior use. *Speco, Inc.*
For more data insert No. 15 on postcard.

Large Diameter Cylinders

For heavy production machinery; 15, 30 and 195 tons lifting power.

A 20-in. diam model air cylinder produces over 30 tons of lifting power at rated operating pressure of 200 psi. Cylinders are the counterbalance type, adaptable for use on presses and other heavy production machinery, and available also in 18, 16, 14, 12, 10 and 8-in. bores. At its rated 2500 psi operation under shock load conditions, the 12-in. bore model high pressure hydraulic cylinder produces 140 tons of thrust, and in non-shock load conditions, produces over 195 tons of thrust at 3500 psi operation. Cylinders have non-breakable solid steel heads, caps, and mountings, scratch-resistant, hard chrome plated piston rods, piston rod dirt wipers, precision-honed barrels of 15 microinch finish, and self-regulating, wear compensating, leakproof and tamper-proof seals. Non-corrosive brass barrels eliminate rust from air moisture. *Miller Motor Co.*
For more data insert No. 16 on postcard.

Industrial Trailers

Of welded, heavy gage steel; for heavy hauling; singly or in tandem.

Three models are available with a fifth wheel at both ends or at one end only. All wheels are Timken roller bearing equipped. A 5-ton capacity trailer with 16-in. diam pneumatic-tired wheels for floor and load protection has a clearance of 40½ in. and stake pockets for use when side or end stakes are required. Model TF-100 has solid rubber tires, stands less than 23 in. high, and has four stake holes on each side. A 15-ton capacity for

use postcard below

production ideas

Continued

heaviest industrial hauling has an overall height of less than 24 in. It has dual solid rubber-tired wheels and a removable stake near each corner. *Phillips Mine & Mill Supply Co.*

For more data insert No. 17 on postcard.

Rust Resisting Finish

Atomite provides deep black finish for carbon and low chrome steels.

Atomite processing, an immersion treatment using no current, gives a gloss black on smooth surfaces or a non-reflecting dull mat finish on etched or sand-blasted surfaces. Atomite will not affect heat treated parts and reportedly remains deep black at 1000°F. It is oil absorptive; aids lubrication. The process requires no expensive equipment. It is recommended for use in place of zinc or cadmium on steel. *Atomite Black Co.*

For more data insert No. 18 on postcard.

Fusible Panelboard

With toggle switches for lighting-appliance branch circuit control.

The new NTPR panelboards are available with 4 to 40 circuits for use on ac or dc applications. They carry the approval and label of the Underwriters' Laboratories, Inc. Construction features embody a 17 in. wide x 4¼ in. deep box with 4-in. wide wiring gutters. *Square D Co.*

For more data insert No. 19 on postcard.

DC Power Supplies

Metal-enclosed; utilize selenium rectifier stacks; reliable control.

Applicable wherever dc power is required, the new conversion equipment may be used for excitation of synchronous motors; operation of dc elevators, cranes and machine tools; and for conversion of ac feeders to dc. The rectifier units are mounted in a metal casing consisting of one to four separate sections, mounted vertically, one on top of the other, and bolted together. The units supply either 125 or 250

v dc from a 208, 230 or 460 v, three phase, 60 cycle ac supply. Convection-cooled and fan-cooled units are available. Under proper operating conditions, the efficiency is said to run as high as 81 to 84 pct, with power factor of 95. *General Electric Co.*

For more data insert No. 20 on postcard.

Air Compressor

400 cycle ac, designed for positive operation at 50,000 ft altitudes.

The pump is equipped with an ac motor of 1/5 hp, 115 v, 400 cycle, single phase, 4 amp, 7200 rpm. The minimum capacity at 50,000 ft is 80 cu in. per min while maintaining 32 in. Hg absolute pressure. Sea level capacity is 1750 cu in. free air per min. Principal use is the pressurizing of radar installations in aircraft, maintaining atmosphere of dry, oil-free air. Unit has a service life of 1000 hr. *Lear, Inc., Romec Div.*

For more data insert No. 21 on postcard.

Adjustable Micrometer

One does work of 12 or 24.

A V-notch adjustable micrometer that can be set and read with speed and accuracy, has a series of 12 or 24 V-shaped notches spaced 1-in. apart in a tool steel blade. A carrier, sliding on the blade and holding a standard 1-in. micrometer head, is positioned in the desired notch and locked in place by a spring clamp. The 1-in. distance between notches is divided into 0.001 in. by the micrometer head. Adding the micrometer head reading to the V-notch number is all the reading required. Available in 12 and 24-in. length ranges, with a 12-24-in. micrometer. *Lester Micrometer Co.*

For more data insert No. 22 on postcard.

Plating Brighteners

Exceptional brilliance, uniformity and high covering power claimed.

Manufacturers who must change plating specifications from critical chromium, nickel and copper can attain exceptional brilliance with new cadmium and zinc brighteners, it is reported. Cadmium brightener is available as a liquid or powder additive. Because barrel solutions may be operated at high temperatures (up to 105°F) maximum production is maintained. Wide latitude of operable concentration range

use postcard below

Let's face it . . . every day the tempo of American industrial production accelerates to keep pace with a program of increasing national preparedness. Here at Monarch we are ready to serve industry and government requirements with a background of over 37 years of casting experience.

HERE'S WHAT MONARCH OFFERS

. . . 300,000 square feet of manufacturing area devoted entirely to the production of ★ **Aluminum Permanent Mold Castings** ★ **Aluminum Die Castings** ★ **Zinc Die Castings.**

. . . Monarch pioneered in the development of aluminum permanent mold castings and today offers the most modern permanent mold production methods.

. . . Monarch also offers a modern die casting division devoted exclusively to precision casting of aluminum and zinc.

. . . Monarch coordinates the production of both permanent mold and die castings under the supervision of two completely staffed engineering departments to assure sound, economical casting design.

. . . Monarch uses complete physical and metallurgical laboratory facilities to maintain highest quality control methods and inspection standards.

. . . Monarch services include finishing and assembly operations for individual permanent mold and die castings or complete product assembly.

. . . Monarch offers modern, company-owned toolroom, maintenance and warehousing facilities within a plant that is strategically located for rail, air or truck shipment.

Here at Monarch we welcome the opportunity to work with you in giving the widest possible casting service, utilizing the full scope of our unique casting facilities.

NOTE: This advertisement forms the nucleus of an interesting folder giving the complete story of Monarch's facilities. We will forward this folder upon request.

MONARCH ALUMINUM MFG. COMPANY • *Detroit Avenue at W. 93rd Street* • *Cleveland 2, Ohio*

publications

Continued

provides ease of control. Barrel and still zinc brighteners, available as liquid additives, are readily controlled by visual inspection of deposits. All give deposits of exceptional brilliance, uniformity and high covering power. *R. O. Hull & Co., Inc.*
For more data insert No. 23 on postcard, p. 37.

Radial Relief Grinder
Stepless speed control from 0 to 80 rpm by turning a dial knob.

Outstanding feature of the new model is stepless speed control, achieved with a selenium rectifier. The motor is a dc, 110 v, gear reduction type offering 40:1 ratio

and giving 44 in. rounds torque. The fixture which can be used with a number of standard tool grinders is offered with or without the stand and grinder. *Royal Oak Tool & Machine Co.*
For more data insert No. 24 on postcard, p. 37.

Heat Treating Unit
Controlled atmosphere; maximum operating temperature of 2100° F.

A semi-automatic controlled atmosphere unit for bright heat treating is rated at 100 lb per hr. The hearth is 12 in. wide x 18 in. long x 10 in. high. The unit consists of a furnace sealed to a combination cooling chamber and quenching tanks. The work is manually loaded into the furnace and the transfer from the furnace to the cooling or quenching section is done without breaking the atmosphere seal. The furnace is electrically heated, using eight bars for 16 kw input. The cooling chamber is water jacketed with automatic temperature control. The

quench tank has built-in oil heating and cooling coil also with automatic temperature control. A pneumatic operated elevator is used in quench-

ing and the oil has two speed propulsion. All doors are pneumatically operated. *Ipsen Industries, Inc.*
For more data insert No. 25 on postcard, p. 37.

Zinc Diecasting Machine
Air-operated, capable of a free cycling speed of 1000 shots per hr.

Completely automatic cycling and adjustable timing dwell on the opening and closing of the toggle and injection of the molten metal are features of a new zinc diecasting machine. The machine will produce castings up to 1 lb capacity utilizing die blocks from 1½ in. thick x 8 x 9

in. with an allowable increase in die thickness to 3 in. for each half. The machine is ruggedly constructed with a 200-lb pot and powerful toggle arrangement to insure relatively flash free castings. *A B C Die Casting Co.*
For more data insert No. 26 on postcard, p. 37.

Carbide Diemakers Tools
Rotary finishing tools in a set for finishing soft or hardened dies.

A set of eight ¼-in. shank carbide rotary finishing tools designed for the tool and diemaker, have

cuts, tooth patterns, and shapes selected to cover the greatest possible range of usefulness. Made of a selected grade of carbide resistant to flaking and chipping, they finish hardened or unhardened dies smoothly and accurately. Di-Car Set No. 40 is furnished in a convenient flat wooden case. *Severance Tool Industries, Inc.*
For more data insert No. 27 on postcard, p. 37.

Double Disk Grinder
Grinds two parallel flat surfaces on small workpieces in 1 operation.

Two 18-in. diam solid center abrasive disks are each driven by a 3 or 5 hp motor. Disks are each 2-in. thick. The 32-in. diam rotary

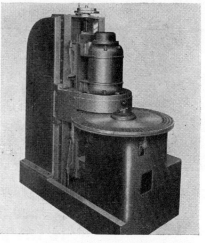

work carrier is made to suit the types and sizes of the workpieces to be ground. Finger tip speed control is provided for an infinite range of work carrier speeds between ⅛ and 1 rpm. A bayonet lock for the rotary work carrier permits rapid change of the carrier plate when changing work setup or dressing the disks. Both grinding heads may be independently adjusted by means of graduated hand wheels, and tilted for jobs requiring progressive grinding of the workpiece. The path of the workpieces is directly across the center of the abrasive disks. *Gardner Machine Co.*
For more data insert No. 28 on postcard, p. 37.

Positioner for Welding
Allows instant start and stop to synchronize with welding machine.

The positioner designed for automatic welding has a solenoid actuated clutch that allows instant
Turn to Page 130

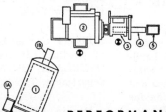

IRON AGE

introduces

M. D. Conroy, appointed vice-president in charge of industrial relations; **J. W. Hargate,** vice-president in charge of purchasing, and **W. F. Hoelscher,** secretary of the GRANITE CITY STEEL CO., St. Louis. The two vice-presidential posts are new positions created by the board of directors.

John W. Ochler, named sales manager of the enginering works division of DRAVO CORP., Pittsburgh.

N. H. Balaam, transferred from northern California district sales office of KAISER STEEL CORP., to Washington, D. C., to manage the recently-opened offices there.

W. C. Thompson, appointed district sales manager, Cleveland district for the COLD METAL PRODUCTS CO.

Worthington J. Gross, appointed manager governmental division, Washington, D. C., and **Bert C. Landstrom,** appointed district representative for the seven Eastern states and the Northeastern part of Canada for the ATHEY PRODUCTS CORP.

Edwin J. Heimer, appointed sales manager of hand lift and motorized hand trucks of the Philadelphia division of the YALE & TOWNE MFG. CO. **W. Glen Tipton** is retiring after 23 years of service with the company.

Walter Zimmermann, named district manager for the COLUMBIA TOOL STEEL CO., Cincinnati. Mr. Zimmermann replaces **James Terry** who has resigned.

F. O. Dutton, joined the staff of BENDIX HOME APPLIANCES — Division Avco Mfg. Corp., South Bend, Ind. Mr. Dutton devotes the major portion of his time to special procurement assignments.

Chester F. Delbridge, appointed general sales manager of the K-G EQUIPMENT CO., INC., New York.

C. Fred Watkins, appointed general sales manager for the AMERICAN SWISS FILE & TOOL CO., Newark, N. J.

Thomas A. Claiborne, transferred from the Houston office to the Cleveland district office of the VANADIUM CORP. OF AMERICA, as service engineer.

Frank L. Hooper, appointed general sales manager of KALEX CORP., New York.

Kenneth C. Specht, named manager of trade sales for NATIONAL LEAD CO., New York.

Robert C. Smith, named manager of product education for WILLYS-OVERLAND MOTORS, farm sales department, Toledo.

Marvin Friedman, appointed production manager and secretary of the ANDREL PRODUCTS CORP., New York.

J. J. Llanso, appointed general export manager of WORTHINGTON PUMP & MACHINERY CORP., Harrison, N. J.

Harold G. Lolley, joined the ROSEDALE FOUNDRY & MACHINE CO., Pittsburgh, as foundry superintendent.

Benjamin E. Feeley, appointed production control manager for HUNT-SPILLER MFG. CORP., Boston. Mr. Feeley succeeds **R. G. Fredette,** who resigned.

Turn to page 76

WALLACE B. PHILLIPS, elected president of Pyrene Mfg. Co., Newark, N. J.

ALBERT J. BOLD, elected executive vice-president of the Superior Metal Fabricating Co., Niles, Ohio.

L. W. EVANS, named vice-president of Rheem Mfg. Co., South Gate, Calif.

IRON AGE

salutes

Frank R. Milliken

NEXT week the American Institute of Mining & Metallurgical Engineers will honor Frank R. Milliken, assistant manager, Titanium Div. of National Lead Co., for "advancing the technique of the metallurgy and beneficiation of titanium-bearing ores."

Frank Milliken belongs to the corps of young engineers who are helping build a more powerful America. For 10 years Mr. Milliken has sparked National Lead's drive for ore to meet industry's needs for titanium products. Jet engines, paint, paper and shoe paste depend on a steady flow of titanium ores.

In 1941, National Lead, looking for the man to head up production at its MacIntyre Development at Tawahus, N. Y., 50 miles south of Lake Placid, called Frank Milliken from Utah where he was chief metallurgist for a group of consulting engineers.

The Tawahus mine and mill were carved from wilderness. Putting wide experience in mineral dressing and development of ore flow sheets to work, Frank Milliken had a large part in design and development of the Tawahus plant.

With ingenuity, drive and persuasiveness, Mr. Milliken had the Tawahus plant, first in the country, in full operation 19 months after designs were started. He solved the problem of ilmenite recovery by flotation from slime ores. The plant is now producing well in excess of its 4000 tons a day rated capacity.

Friendly, quiet, even-tempered Frank Milliken lives at Darien, Conn., has two sons. He plays golf and is an enthusiastic fisherman and hunter.

CLEM W. GOTTSCHALK, appointed assistant vice-president—Traffic of the Jones & Laughlin Steel Corp., Pittsburgh.

JAMES W. KINNEAR, JR., appointed assistant to vice-president —Manufacturing of U. S. Steel Co., Pittsburgh.

C. L. FIX, named works manager of Mullins Mfg. Corp.; Liberty plant at Warren, Ohio.

GEORGE EBERT, appointed comptroller of the Riverside Metal Co., Riverside, N. J.

IRON AGE *introduces*

Continued

Edmund Fitzgerald, elected a member of the board of directors of ALLIS-CHALMERS MFG. CO., Milwaukee.

Deane R. Ebey, named co-ordinator of defense activities for plastics at the DOW CHEMICAL CO., Midland, Mich. **Robert L. Curtis,** succeeds Mr. Ebey in the Los Angeles office, as supervisor of plastic sales.

John P. Mansfield, elected vice-president and director of the PLYMOUTH MOTOR CORP., Detroit. Mr. Mansfield is one of the veterans of the Chrysler organization, which is the parent company.

Harry C. O'Brien, retired as head of the container bureau, sheet and strip division, U. S. STEEL CO., Pittsburgh, after 47 years in the steel industry.

David A. Challis, Jr., appointed assistant general manager of sales, U. S. STEEL CO., Pittsburgh. **Walther H. Haggard,** named sales representative in New York for the coal chemical sales division.

R. K. Laurin, appointed assistant advertising manager of the meter & valve div., of ROCKWELL MFG. CO., Pittsburgh.

E. R. Walsh, III, appointed general sales manager of ALLOY RODS CO., York, Pa.

Joseph W. S. Davis, named assistant to the vice-president, eastern regional sales, by the AMERICAN LOCOMOTIVE CO., New York.

Seton Porter and **John E. Bierwirth,** elected to the board of directors of DOREMUS & CO., New York.

Fielder Israel, named assistant to the president of GENERAL DRY BATTERIES, INC., Cleveland.

Orvin K. Gaskins, appointed manager of aircraft and assigned sales, Ewart plant of the LINK-BELT CO., Indianapolis.

Thur Schmidt, appointed assistant to the president, Ingersoll Products Div., BORG-WARNER CORP., Chicago.

James B. Fenner, named vice-president and comptroller of the ELECTRIC AUTOLITE CO., Toledo. Other vice-presidents elected: **H. E. Hasemeyer, R. M. Lake, C. L. Lancaster** and **Lyman A. Wine.**

John W. Willard, assumes new responsibilities as sales training manager and director of personnel for LAMSON CORP., Syracuse, N. Y.

Arthur I. Schell, appointed superintendent, No. 7 machine shops of the MIDVALE CO., Philadelphia.

George L. Marchant, named manager of the Boston district of the replacement tire sales division of the B. F. GOODRICH CO. Mr. Marchant succeeds L. L. Black who is retiring. Mr. Black had been with the company since 1916 and held a number of executive sales posts.

Charles Bangert, Jr., appointed manager of engineering for the TRUMBULL ELECTRIC MFG. CO., Plainville, Conn. **J. J. Pascher,** appointed district sales manager, New York district, for the company.

Ralph R. Newquist, named executive vice-president of the ROOTS-CONNERSVILLE BLOWER CORP., Connersville, Ind.

L. D. Rigdon, named assistant to vice-president in charge of manufacturing, and **C. G. Wallis,** named manager of the headquarters manufacturing department, of WESTINGHOUSE ELECTRIC CORP., Pittsburgh.

George P. Extrom, elected treasurer of the GISHOLT MACHINE CO., Madison, Wis. Mr. Extrom has been with the company for nearly 35 years and has been acting as assistant secretary for the past 10 years.

OBITUARIES

Willard N. Lynch, president of Keystone Drawn Steel Co., Spring City, Pa., died recently.

Leslie R. Taylor, 60, president of International Heater Co., died recently in New York.

H. W. Porter, president of H. K. Porter, Inc., Sommerville, Mass., died recently.

Yellott F. Hardcastle, 67, director of the Pennsylvania Salt Mfg. Co., Philadelphia, died recently.

on the assembly line

automotive news and opinions

by Walter G. Patton

Carmakers weigh big output slash . . . Dodge peps up its new truck engines . . . Rail walkout affects industry.

NPA Brews Storm—A puzzled and perplexed automobile industry was trying this week to digest the true significance of reports from Washington that auto output may be slashed as much as 40 pct during April, May and June. If this promise holds it will mean (1) widespread unemployment in the industry, (2) wholesale cancellations of steel conversion contracts, (3) compounding of the confusion that already exists about future steel supplies.

Layoffs have already stung the industry which now claims as many as half a million workers could be idled by NPA material cutbacks. The industry's position is that NPA has failed to show either that the steel and other metal reductions are necessary or are likely to become necessary.

Rail Walkout Effects — If the NPA cutbacks were not enough, the railroad strike also took its toll. Last week Ford Motor Co. sent half the force at its huge Rouge plant home for an indefinite period. Approximately 30,000 men were affected. Ford is also laying off at its assembly plants scattered throughout the country.

GM was similarly hit, reporting 70,200 idle at 26 plants. Nash has reported 14,000 idle, Studebaker has laid off 12,750. Chrysler was also affected. While railroad switchmen came straggling back to work, the auto workers faced a bleak future. Once again the adage was proved: the duration is always longer than the strike.

Wayne University Exhibit—Detroit's fast-growing group of stress engineers had an opportunity last week to see a display at Wayne University of the latest equipment for measuring stress—strain gages, amplifiers, oscilloscopes, transducers, stress-coating, photo elasticity and high-speed photography.

Approximately 300 members and guests of the Society for Experimental Stress Analysis saw a demonstration of high-speed motion pictures taken of a beam breaking under the impact of a falling weight. Pictures were taken at a rate of 7500 frames per second.

Lecture Session—Dr. J. H. Meier, of Bucyrus-Erie Co., Milwaukee, president of S.E.S.A., described the latest methods and equipment used for measuring loads and performance characteristics of power shovels and earth-moving machinery. Another speaker was Richard Kemp, National Advisory Committee for Aeronautics, who reported the results of studies of turbine blade vibration and strain in high temperature operations of aircraft turbines.

Using German Thunder—Cold extrusion, a metallurgical development used extensively in Germany during World War II to conserve steel, is expected to be extended substantially by the auto industry in the years ahead. Both Chrysler and Ford are cold extruding several parts.

The process is also being used by several auto parts plants for the production of shells. Advantages of cold extruded parts include high strength resulting from work hardening, elimination of machining and substantial savings in material.

Dodge Truck Changes—Dodge engineers have extended twin carburetion and twin exhaust as a means of giving truck buyers in the 2¾ to 3½ ton class more power and greater economy. Engine output on these models has been increased 18 to 20 pct, resulting in higher average gross speed, faster hill climbing, greater economy and less driver fatigue.

Other new features in Dodge trucks include higher governor settings, redesigned fuel pumps, "hotter" spark plugs with improved moisture-proofing, larger generators and more efficient cooling systems.

Oriflow Shocks for Trucks—Light, ½ to 1 ton models are

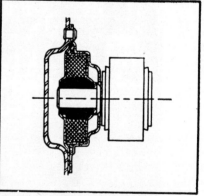

assembly line

Continued

equipped with the new Oriflow shock absorbers. Brake cylinders are now anodized for positive protection against rust and corrosion. A new cycle-bond molded tapered brake lining has been developed to give more positive action and reduce any tendency to grab or squeal.

Four piston rings are used. The top ring is chrome-plated. Chrysler is also offering fluid drive on light models up to 1 ton, including the Route-Van.

Steel Quota Reductions—Steel delivery promises are being cut still further, indicating a continued drop in automobile output. Some mills report consumers' quotas will be reduced as much as 50 pct during March and April. Steel sources report that DOs are taking as much as 50 pct on sheets and almost 70 pct of output on carbon bars.

The freight car program, increased production of military vehicles and the demands for steel mill expansions have all contributed to the increased defense requirements. Another factor is increased tonnage for shell production.

Here to Stay—More than 3.5 million GM cars have already been equipped with automatic transmissions.

The first Hydramatic, introduced in 1939 by Oldsmobile, was sold to 10 pct of the new Olds car buyers. Demand increased to 74 pct in 1946. Last year 94 pct of Olds buyers ordered Hydramatics.

In 1940 only 2 pct of new Cadillac owners wanted automatic transmissions. The 1946 percentage reached 86. Last year the total was more than 97 pct.

Pontiac has a record of 65 pct for Hydramatic since its introduction 2 years ago. Last year 77 pct of all Buicks were Dynaflow-equipped. Production of the Chevrolet Powerglide has now reached 2000 units a day.

Ready for Trouble—Defense work in the automobile industry has not been confined to engineering and tooling. Ford, for exaxmple, has formed a Security Committee to formulate a company-wide disaster preparedness program. Top Ford executives headed by John S. Bugas, vice-president industrial relations, sit on the committee.

Detailed plans to protect the company against sabotage or internal attacks are being developed. Plans to protect all confidential reports against espionage are being worked out. These efforts have been carefully integrated with Federal, state and local defense planning.

Code of Ethics—Packard sales executives have drawn up a new code for Packard dealers, reaffirming a position taken 5 years ago. Here are some of the fair trade practices advocated by Packard sales executives:

(1) Fair trade-in allowance and acceptance of the customer's order *without* a trade-in.

(2) Make new car deliveries in the same sequence in which the orders are placed.

(3) Buy and sell new and used cars at prices established by regulation.

(4) No "loading" of accessories on new cars.

(5) Bill customers of service department for parts and labor at established prices and provide estimates of costs in advance.

Arsenal to Warehouse—For the past 5 years Buick Motor Div. has been using the government-owned Grand Blanc tank arsenal for a parts warehouse. Last week Buick bought this 500,000 sq ft plant which was operated by Fisher Body during World War II. Buick will continue to use the building as a parts warehouse.

Small Arms Order—This week Saginaw Steering Gear Div. announced the contract for the manufacture of parts for small arms. The parts will be produced in Steering Gear Plant No. 2. Tooling is being placed in anticipation of production within the next several months. During World War II Saginaw Steering Gear made machine guns and other war materials.

THE BULL OF THE WOODS
By J. R. Williams

MULTIPRESS® SWAGES 'EM 800% FASTER

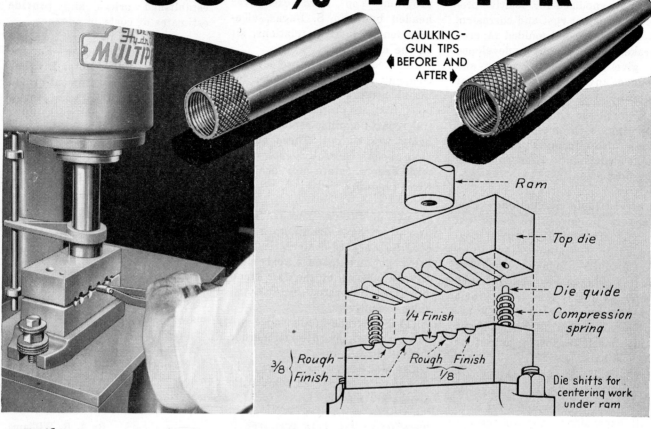

CAULKING-GUN TIPS ◀ BEFORE AND AFTER ▶

Ram

Top die

Die guide

Compression spring

1/4 Finish

3/8 } Rough Finish

Rough Finish 1/8

Die shifts for centering work under ram

Vibratory Control Feature Plays Big Part in Record Production at Crew Manufacturing Co.

A swaging operation that used to take 3⅓ minutes is now done in *24 seconds* at the Crew Manufacturing Co., Cleveland, Ohio. An 8-ton Multipress makes the big difference.

The job is to taper half-inch tube steel to form caulking gun tips with apertures of ⅛″, ¼″ and ⅜″. Multipress does it faster, gets

> A typical 4-ton Multipress equipped with a 6-station index table. Capacities to 50 tons available.

more uniform results, and has eliminated scrap losses.

Vibratory Ram Action—an accessory available only on Multipress—is a big factor in this amazing speed-up. It delivers short, rapidly repeated strokes of uniform, pre-set pressure, forming the parts in a quick series of easy stages. The operator holds the tubes with inside pliers, and rotates them as he feeds them to the desired depth. Top and bottom halves of the die, separated by compression springs, open slightly between each vibratory ram effort, making it easy to feed the parts.

The die contains both roughing and finishing cavities for all three sizes of parts. It is simply moved to right or left to bring the de-

sired cavities directly under the press ram—no die changes are required.

Worker fatigue has also been sharply reduced by the quieter, easier, oil-smooth operation of the Multipress.

Gains like these are an old story with Multipress, on an extremely wide variety of production jobs. Multipress — an oil-hydraulic tool featuring advanced engineering design—can readily be tailored to your specific needs, in eight different frame sizes, with capacities ranging up to 50 tons. Available accessories include indexing tables, dial feed tables, harmonic stock feeds, straightening accessories, and foil marking attachments. Write today for full details!

west coast progress report

by R.T. Reinhardt

digest of far west industrial activity

Poor Metallics Prospect—Western steel producers and foundries are faced with the same problem as many of their customers—where to get the raw materials with which to operate at capacity levels?

Western steel producers and foundries face a deficit of approximately one-half million net tons of metallics annually if they anticipate operating at capacity levels with existing facilities. By 1952, on completion of new steel ingot and cast iron pipe producing facilities, this deficit will reach an estimated 1 million net tons.

Changing Situations — At the outbreak of World War II the seven western states formed a surplus scrap area with No. 1 heavy melting selling at $13 per gross ton in mid-1940 and with 1,300,000 net tons of scrap and pig iron required for capacity operations of ingot and casting furnaces. In 1940, 437,000 net tons of scrap were exported from the Pacific Coast.

How rapidly the picture has changed is indicated by the sharp increase in the scrap price at Los Angeles and San Francisco which last year rose from $20 per gross ton for No. 1 heavy melting in May to $30 per gross ton in November. Current frozen price is $35 per gross ton.

Future Metallics Supply—It is estimated the future Far Western supply of metallics will not exceed 4 million net tons, and pig iron production from present blast furnaces probably will not exceed rated capacity of 2,189 thousand net tons. This would be an increase of 310,000 tons over 1950 actual production.

Ability to maintain capacity operations at the Kaiser furnaces at Fontana depends on continued receipt of 72,000 net tons of Colorado coke annually; if cut off, pig iron output would drop 93,000 net tons a year.

Scrap Imported — Kaiser and Geneva in Utah, including the Ironton furnace, have a combined capacity of 2,189,000 net tons per year. In assaying the metallics available for production of steel ingots and steel and iron for castings, B. E. Etcheverry, Kaiser cost director, reports local production of purchased scrap cannot be counted on to exceed the 1950 figure of 1,800,000 net tons and points out the balance of 2 million net tons of pig iron consumed in 1950 reflected imports of 50,000 tons and a reduction in consumers' inventory of 150,000 tons.

Prompt scrap is less of a factor in the West than nationally because of local processing operations. The high percentage of steel products are not processed after leaving the mill.

Present Metallic Demand—Western producers of ingots and iron and steel castings used 2 million net tons of purchased scrap and 2 million tons of pig iron in 1950. With capacity on Jan. 1, 1951, of 4,640,000 net tons, 549,000 tons over 1950 output, 440,000 additional tons of purchased scrap and pig will be required.

Pacific States Cast Iron Pipe Co. at Ironton, Utah, needs 100,000 tons of pig iron to operate at capacity, 40,000 tons over their receipts in 1950. Operation of West Coast steel producers at their January 1951 capacity and operation of other consumers at 1950 rate would require 4,480,000 tons of purchased scrap and pig iron.

Another Record—New production records were set at Kaiser Steel Corp., Fontana, in January: 78,466 tons of steel products for shipment compared to 77,754 tons in August 1950, previous high; 76,274 tons of pig iron against 69,960, the previous record; and the openhearth poured 110,789 tons of ingots, almost 3000 tons above the best previous month. Iron ore shipped from Eagle Mountain totaled 100,562 tons, a new high.

Heppenstall KNIVES

...give you an "EDGE" on competition!

In metal cutting, shearing, or trimming operations you can keep costs 'way down . . . and production up . . . by standardizing on Heppenstall Knives!

If you're not using them, don't be satisfied with the "average service" you think you're getting with your present knives. Specify Heppenstall Knives . . . and honestly, you'll be surprised at the difference!

Long-time users know that Heppenstall Knives, made from our own electric induction steels, are the finest knives obtainable. They consistently deliver greater tonnage per edge . . . more and cleaner cuts per grind . . . per knife . . . and per dollar of original cost. Why not order a set today?

Heppenstall Company, Pittsburgh 1, Pa. Sales Offices in Principal Cities.

BAR KNIFE

SHEET BAR KNIFE

HALF SLITTER

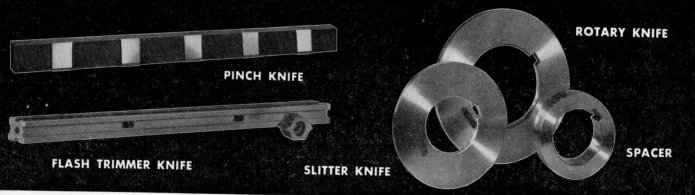

PINCH KNIFE

FLASH TRIMMER KNIFE

SLITTER KNIFE

ROTARY KNIFE

SPACER

◇H◇ **Heppenstall**

-The most dependable name in forgings...

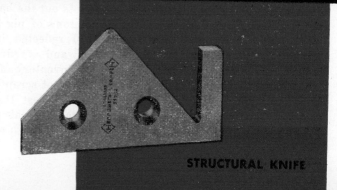

STRUCTURAL KNIFE

the federal view

this week in washington

by Eugene J. Hardy

Payments for Tool Wear — The Munitions Board and the military services are consulting with industry on permitting accelerated depreciation for abnormally intensive use of machinery and equipment in defense plants.

The military knows two or three shift operation can break down machinery in perhaps 5 years, when the normal depreciation period might be 20 years.

What is likely to result is not accelerated tax depreciation but additional compensation in contracts to take care of such abnormal wear and tear. In addition, the military will provide tools from the National Industrial Reserve to replace worn-out equipment or to meet initial needs.

Seaway Chances Brighter—New support in Congress for the St. Lawrence seaway may provide the momentum necessary to get the controversial project started after many years of delay.

The need for an efficient and cheap means of moving Labrador iron ore to the Great Lakes and midwestern steelmaking centers has caused a number of congressmen to alter earlier positions. The opposition camp has dwindled. Only eastern seaport and pro-railroad members are now hold-outs.

In Time for Need? — Seaway proponents are citing the vital need for ore and other steelmaking materials in the rearmament program, but their critics point out that at least 5 years would pass before even a single boatload of ore could navigate the proposed waterway.

One of the influences affecting the fate of the proposal is what attitude the Senate and House will take toward President Truman's budget. There is considerable pressure on the lawmakers to trim non-defense expenditures, and a snowballing movement to cut all "nonessential" appropriations might result in another year's postponement of the project.

Cut Investigation Time — Military security clearance regulations are being revised to prevent unnecessary production delays while plants are being investigated. Security investigations of plant employees might take as much as 120 days while the contract involved might have a 45-day delivery date.

Under the new program, the military departments will eliminate investigations when only "Restricted" contracts are involved, and on "Confidential" contracts an interim clearance will be used pending completion of a full security investigation. Contracts bearing a higher security classification will still require full investigation.

Also in preparation are a manual standardizing investigative procedures and a uniform security agreement for the three services.

Uniform Inspection — General Services Administration, cooperating with the Munitions Board and the military services, has issued a Government-wide regulation in inspection services and testing.

Generally, inspection will be at the supply source if the items are in continuous volume production, or if quality control and inspection are related to a plant's production methods, or if inspection at any other point would cause delay or expense. Inspection will be at destination for off-the-shelf items, brand name or simple commercial items, and on products from plants where the volume of buying is not enough to justify a full-time inspector.

Ore Shipping to be Approved— Canadian ore boats are going to get a piece of the Great Lakes ore-shipping business again this year.

By law, iron ore and other products moving between U. S. ports must be shipped in U. S. vessels, but Congress has suspended this statute each year since the start of World War II because of the need for ships.

Last year, U. S. shippers and vessel owners thought they were about ready to dispense with Canadian shipping companies, but today's tremendous demand makes it likely that Canadian vessels will again be permitted to move iron ore until Dec. 31, 1951.

Approval of legislation to further suspend the ban on shipping via vessels of Canadian registry will probably get Congressional approval.

Help Yourself to Better Bearing Performance

Here are two famous bearing materials that give you superior bearing performance at nominal initial cost. Both are readily available at Ryerson.

Glyco babbitt metal is a lead base alloy with physical properties equal to those of high tin babbitt. Introduced in this country by Ryerson almost 50 years ago, Glyco babbitt is made by an exclusive process which gives the greatest possible homogeniety of texture and unvarying uniformity. It is available in five grades covering all bearing applications—light or heavy shock loads, low or high shaft speeds.

Ryertex is a phenolic laminated-textile composition developed under Ryerson sponsorship. Possessing an extremely low coefficient of friction, it may be used with practically any lubricant—water, oil or grease, alone or in combination. Adaptable to almost any size or shape, Ryertex bearings are out-lasting and out-performing other types of bearings in many steel and paper mill applications, in the marine field and in other industries.

Write for full details on these money-saving bearing materials.

RYERTEX and GLYCO BABBITT

JOSEPH T. RYERSON & SON, INC.— PLANTS AT: NEW YORK • BOSTON • PHILADELPHIA • CINCINNATI • CLEVELAND
PITTSBURGH • DETROIT • BUFFALO • CHICAGO • MILWAUKEE • ST. LOUIS • LOS ANGELES • SAN FRANCISCO

THE IRON AGE
FOUNDED 1855
FEATURE ARTICLES

CONTINUOUS CAST aluminum bars produced by the Properzi process

By D. I. BROWN
Feature Editor

Nichols Wire & Aluminum Co., Davenport, Ia., has been continuously casting high purity aluminum bars since July 1950. The casting machine was designed and built by Mr. Ilario Properzi of S.p.A. Continuus, Milan, Italy.

The machine casts an equilateral triangular section 7/8 in. on a side. The headpiece above is a photomacrograph of the cast section. The cast section is then fed into a 15-stand continuous rod mill also of Italian design. The rolled rod in coil form is later cold drawn into various wire sizes. The two most popular sizes of rod rolled at Nichols are 9/32-in. and 3/8-in. diam. The end product of this material has been mostly consumer wire products.

The machine is an extremely simple device which casts at a speed of 10 to 30 fpm. The average weight of aluminum cast per hour is 1000 lb. Three 100-kw Ajax induction furnaces melt the pig and feed the casting machine. Scrap loss from pig to rod is extremely low averaging less than 1 pct and all scrap is remelted.

High purity aluminum 99.5 pct or better has

PART I The continuous casting of aluminum bars has proved eminently successful in this country. The Properzi, Italian-made machine casts at a rate of 10 to 30 fpm. The casting machine is very simple in design and operation. Three men easily run the entire operation including the 15-stand continuous rolling mill which converts the cast section into coiled rod.

CONTINUOUS CAST ALUMINUM rod, arrow, emerging from the Properzi machine. The small control wheel, center, adjusts turning speed of the wheel mold. The two larger control wheels control the tilt of the ladle and the machine itself.

been the chief metal processed. The Nichols Co. plans to cast and roll alloy grades of aluminum in the near future. Mechanical properties of the rods and wire made by this process are higher than those of the same metal processed by conventional methods. The Properzi casting machine and rolling mill require little floor space and a minimum number of men. Power requirements are also quite low.

THE HOLDING LADLE feeds through the spout A, into the mold cavity. The metal enters the cavity just above the brush marked B. The brush distributes the oil on the outside of the steel band C. In the background is the holding induction furnace which feeds hot metal into the ladle.

The three Ajax furnaces melt continuously. Two of these tilting furnaces feed the third unit. Molten aluminum is run out through refractory-lined cast iron troughs into the third furnace which serves as a holding unit. The third furnace then pours into the main trough which feeds the hot metal reservoir or ladle mounted on the casting machine. Three furnaces are used to permit melting flexibility so that small runs of alloy can be made if desired.

A schematic drawing of the casting machine, Fig. 1, consists of two revolving drum wheels and a steel band. The band passes over the drum wheels; tension on the top wheel keeps the band tight. This band serves as one side of the mold cavity which is cut in the copper portion of the bottom wheel. A cross-section of the

ONE OPERATOR controls feeding of the molten metal from three furnaces and the casting process. Pushbutton controls for pouring the three furnaces appear in the lower center portion of the photo. Below and to the left is the control button for stopping and starting the casting machine. The gas burner which heats the ladle can be seen just below the main feeding trough at the upper right.

copper mold with the band in place is shown in Fig. 1 also. The rim of the lower wheel is a copper casting which is bolted to the inner steel drum or hub. Circulating water is contained inside the hollow hub section of the lower two-piece wheel. The bottom portion of the casting wheel is immersed in a tank of water also.

The lower or casting wheel is $36\frac{1}{4}$ in. in diam. It revolves at a rate of $1\frac{1}{4}$ to $2\frac{1}{2}$ rpm when casting. Speed of casting is essentially governed by the 3/16-in. round orifice of the spout which leads from the holding ladle to the

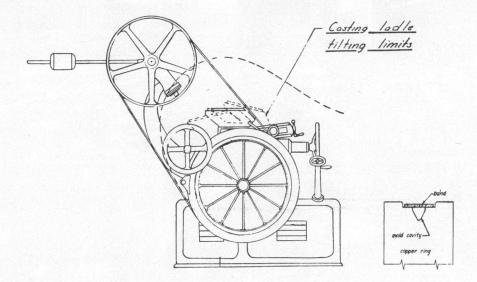

FIG. 1—Schematic view of the Properzi continuous casting machine. The extent to which the ladle can be tilted is indicated. A cross-section of the mold cavity cut in the copper ring appears at the right. The steel band is tightly stretched around the casting wheel to form the third side of the mold.

steel band—copper mold junction. The molten stream is fed into the mold cavity tangentially and in a down direction.

The ladle feeding the spout is 22x8x4 in. deep and holds about 20 lb of metal. This refractory-lined container is under-fired with a gas flame from one side. The hot gases sweep under the length of the ladle and are exhausted along the spout, so that the spout is heated at all times to prevent metal solidification or temperature loss.

Pouring Temperature Controlled

The pouring temperature at the melting furnaces is 1275° to 1285°F. Immersion thermocouples connected to automatic recording pyrometers control tapping temperature. The runout troughs from the melting furnaces are not heated. The holding furnace pours at 1220° to 1240°F and this temperature is maintained in the ladle and through the spout and is the temperature at which the metal is fed into the wheel mold cavity.

The melting furnaces are not fully emptied. They tap only enough metal to maintain a suitable charge in the holding furnace. There is considerable flexibility in furnace operation as the only *must* in the entire metal feeding procedure is that the ladle on top of the casting machine be kept reasonably full.

Solidification is fast in this process. Two sides of the mold are formed by the copper cavity and the third side is the steel band. The water inside the wheel plus the water circulating in the outside tank extract the heat from the mold.

The operator adjusts the casting speed and

the tilt of the machine and/or the spout to produce optimum casting rates and control of section. An oil film is run onto the outside of the steel band opposite the point at which the metal is fed into the wheel mold. White lead is mixed with the oil and speed of casting is regulated by the oil evaporation pattern formed on the outside of the steel band.

The cast section travels with the wheel to a point part way up the side opposite the operator. A stripping device then ejects the section to one side and the section loops back over the operator's position into the first pass of the mill. Cotton waste wipers clean and dry both the band and the mold cavity before again receiving a molten charge.

The 7/8-in. triangular section was chosen because it is the simplest shape to extract from a wheel mold. Also this shape is the best section for the subsequent 3-roll rolling pass de-

THE THREE FURNACES and the casting machines require very little space. The cast bar feeds back over the operator's head into a 15-stand continuous rolling mill which produces coiled rod.

sign of the continuous mill. It was thought by the designers that alternate triangular and circular passes have advantages over the traditional square-oval methods. The performance of the product and the mill operation itself appear to fully confirm this belief. Other reasons for the cast shape and odd roll pass design will be discussed later.

Casting Is Self Stripping

Two corners of the triangular cast section were modified to facilitate positive stripping from the wheel mold. The straight-line contour is short and does not interfere with filling out the first roughing pass of the mill. Once the cast section is started, the operation is continuous. The section is not broken and the section automatically strips itself from the wheel and feeds directly into the rolling mill.

The only scrap regularly encountered is at the beginning or end of a production run. At

times improper control of metal feed on the machine may cause a break in the cast section, but usually the unit works continuously. At present the process only runs for 8 hr a day but it could run around the clock if so desired.

No artificial shielding from air of the molten stream from melting to holding furnace or holding to spout is needed. The aluminum forms its own protective envelope or sock and the metal fed into the mold runs through this natural sock at all times and is fully protected from oxidation.

Part II of the article will appear in next week's issue of The Iron Age. The second article will include the 15-stand continuous rolling mill plus a macro etch study of the rolled rod and mechanical properties of wire drawn from the rod made by this continuous process.

Machining integrally-stiffened sheet from plate will have extensive application, despite high loss in chips. Elaborate equipment is not essential, though machines with special features will be needed to bring cost and machining time down. Machining is now in use to make production and experimental structure, and to simulate structure which will eventually be produced by other means.

INTEGRALLY-STIFFENED SKIN

REVOLUTIONIZES AIRCRAFT CONSTRUCTION

machined

sections

THIRD OF A SERIES

Machining from thick plate provides a ready means of making integrally-stiffened structure. It is highly flexible, permitting variations in section to incorporate taper, local reinforcements, integral doublers, and heavy attachment panels. The simple rectangular stiffener shape available by machining is generally considered poor from a structural standpoint. But this disadvantage is offset by freedom to reduce stiffener spacing and thus make the skin more effective under compression. Applications to date have shown substantial weight savings.

The size of machined parts is limited only by size of machining equipment and material. Large size parts with any desired taper eliminate the need for splices and so save both their cost and weight.

The one great disadvantage of machining is that 75 to 95 pct of the original material is cut away in chips. Cost of raw material is therefore high. Machining time is also high, with present equipment.

In spite of this, machining from plate will,

in certain applications, show cost advantage as well as simplification and weight savings, over conventional structure.

High-speed equipment and methods now used extensively in milling aircraft parts have greatly increased the practicability and potentialities of machining as a primary method of fabrication. Machining may be used to duplicate any other type of integral stiffening for experimental study or for prototype construction. When extruded and forged integrally-stiffened designs become available, it may be desirable to apply the same machining methods to reduce skin thicknesses and incorporate taper, local trim and reinforcement pads.

End Milling Is Practical

The most readily applied method of machining integrally-stiffened sheet is that of end-milling—milling with the axis of the cutting tool perpendicular to the machined surface.

Elaborate equipment is not essential. Fig. 11 shows the manufacture of a bulkhead rib for an integral fuel tank. This operation was done

By P. E. SANDORFF, *Research Engineer*

and GEORGE W. PAPEN, *Mgr., Production Engineering Dept.*

Lockheed Aircraft Corp., Burbank, Calif.

Continued

FIG. 11—Setup for machining an experimental bulkhead rib for an integral wing tank. Material is thick aluminum plate.

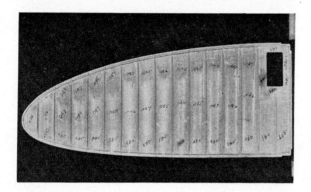

FIG. 12—Experimental integral tank bulkhead rib machined from plate on setup shown in Fig. 11. Web, stiffeners, flanges and doubler pad are all one piece. Machining permits convenient tapering of web thickness as desired.

FIG. 13—Machining integrally-stiffened sheet on a modified planer. Vacuum bed holds down workpiece.

on a small Milwaukee milling machine with standard cutters and accepted methods. The finished part, shown in Fig. 12, is equivalent to a 13-piece assembly in conventional construction. For production, a Cincinnati Hydrotel or other high-speed duplicating machine would be more practical than the method illustrated.

By using high-speed cutting heads and special beds the machining time can be considerably reduced. Fig. 13 shows a modified 16-ft planer which is used at Lockheed for experimental manufacture of integrally-stiffened sheet. A high-cycle motor is mounted on one of the planer heads driving a fly-cutter or end mill at a speed of about 10,000 rpm.

Fig. 14 illustrates machining of an experimental leading edge structure, equivalent to that used on the Constellation outer wing, which was machined from ¼-in. plate. The skin is of 0.040 in. nominal thickness, and a doubler pad 0.072-in. thick is left on all edges to simplify attachment. Forming of this part to curvature is accomplished after machining by repeated bumping on a power brake. Rolling has also been used for similar sections.

Slab Milling Has Advantages

For rapid removal of a large mass of metal, slab milling is much better suited than flycutting or end milling. The advantages are apparent chiefly for quantity production because heavier equipment and higher horsepower are available. The process is generally less flexible in application.

For the machining of integrally-stiffened surfaces Onsrud spar-milling equipment has been applied with excellent results. Fig. 15 shows a 75-ft spar mill in operation machining a spanlength wing panel from ⅞-in. plate. The skin thickness of the finished part tapers from 0.091 to 0.045 in. The depth of cut is cam guided and is accurate to within a few thousandths of an

FIG. 14—Setup for machining an experimental leading edge panel from ¼-in. aluminum plate. After machining, sheet with integral stiffeners is trimmed and formed to contour.

inch. Taper in skin thickness as well as local reinforcements and integral pads for end-attachments are readily obtained. Details of the machine setup are shown in Fig. 16.

Contour Machining Studied

Discussion thus far has been limited to the production of flat integrally-stiffened panels. However, most applications will undoubtedly require contoured surfaces. The forming of flat integrally-stiffened panels to required contour will be discussed in another part of this article. Machining to required contour has also been investigated. It has been suggested that plate of the required cross-section thickness be formed to contour and then machined to final shape. This naturally would require less machining time and conserve material over machining from a solid billet large enough to encompass the curvature. The type of equipment required to machine to the contoured shape must of necessity be a high-speed duplicating type machine based on the Keller or Hydrotel principle. The best that is expected of this type equipment is only a slight improvement on the end-mill type operation. Consequently the machining operation would be slow and costly.

Whether or not machining from billet or rolled flat stock to the finished shape proves feasible and economical, it will probably be desirable to do some trimming and finish-machining on parts conforming to contour. Forging integral panels to finished contour with subsequent machining for joints and other areas requiring closer tolerances than can be maintained by forging appears feasible. It is believed that high production equipment capable of machining a finished formed integrally-stiffened part should be developed.

A most useful piece of special equipment in machining thin-skinned sections to close toler-ances is the vacuum-clutch bed plate. The vacuum plates designed and constructed at Lockheed may be seen in Figs. 13 and 16. They consist of a network of narrow surface grooves fed internally to a vacuum system. The sheet to be machined is fixed to the bed plates with a few mechanical hold-down clamps and sealed around all edges with zinc chromate filleting putty. With this arrangement, skin as thin as 0.016 in., accurate to ±0.002 in., is obtained.

Use Stretcher-Leveled Stock

The use of a roller hold-down to apply a concentrated hold-down force adjacent to the cutter was investigated and found to be of questionable value. To make thick plate lie flat, the loads which the roller hold-down must apply are so large as to introduce severe machine design problems. For thin plate the vacuum plate appears more satisfactory.

An important practice introduced by Lockheed which greatly reduces the problems of warpage is the use of stretcher-levelled plate stock. If the finished, machined part before removal from the flat bed of the machine contains unbalanced internal stresses it will warp when the hold-down clamps are removed. Such unbalanced stresses may arise from two sources: The plate before machining may contain locked-up residual stresses and the machining operation may introduce a stress condition. Early experiments at Lockheed indicated that when proper cutters were used, virtually all of the warping was caused by the residual stress which existed in the plate before machining. A study was made to determine the exact residual stress distribution in as-rolled and in stretcher-levelled plate and the results proved the value of the stretcher-levelling operation. All plate up to 0.375 in. are now stretcher-leveled. Thicker plates are roller leveled.

Unfortunately plate no thicker than ⅞ in. can

FIG. 15—A 75-ft spar mill being used to machine integrally-stiffened sheet from ⅞-in. plate. Taper in skin thickness, and local reinforcements and attachment pads are readily obtained with this setup.

FIG. 16—Details of the spar mill setup for machining integrally-stiffened structure. Depth of cut, cam-guided, is accurate to within a few thousandths. Though mechanical clamps are used, workpiece is mainly held by vacuum bed.

be obtained in the stretcher-levelled condition at present, and such plate is limited to about 3 ft in width and 24 ft in length.

An experimental wing structure has been constructed of machined surface panels. This assembly was made interchangeable with the long-range Constellation outer wing which also serves as an integral tank for carrying fuel. Using data obtained in the construction of this wing, a complete study was made of the value of the machining process in its present stage of development, as compared with conventional methods, for producing this type of structure. The following conclusions were reached.

Conclusions Are Significant

The external surfaces of the machined structure are exceptionally smooth and free of rivets. No skin buckling occurs under any design load condition. All splices and bulkhead flange attachments are made with a single row of rivets through thick skin pads which are integral with the panels. On removable doors a ⅛-in. thick flange is provided. There are no chordwise splices over the entire 20-ft span. The machined taper in skin thickness and stiffener height provides optimum structural properties at all stations.

With the machined integrally-stiffened structure, a weight saving of 230 lb per airplane was realized. This amounted to 25 pct of the weight of the structure subject to redesign. Half of this was due to structural weight saved by elimina-

What kind of machines?

Lockheed engineers list the following as features they would like to see in a machine tool designed especially for machining integrally-stiffened structure:

Vacuum bed 72 in. or more in width, 40 ft long.

Power feed for machining across either dimension of the bed.

Accuracy of indexing cutter head to 0.010 in. in any horizontal direction, and 0.005 vertically.

Fifty horsepower, 20,000 rpm, end milling head.

Five-hundred horsepower, 5000 rpm, drive for slab milling plate stock with gang cutters.

Completely automatic system for sequencing, actuating and controlling depth and location of all cutting operations.

TABLE II

MACHINED STRUCTURE V. CONVENTIONAL CONSTRUCTION

Outer Wing Structure
Pct of Total Cost of Conventional Design

	Conventional Structure	Machined Integrally-Stiffened Structure
Fabrication	7	17
Assembly	38	20
Tooling	21	29
Raw Material	16	25
Sealing	18	14
Total	100	105

tion of splices and by more efficient use of material; half was due to weight of fuel tank sealing compound saved at stiffener-skin attachments.

On the basis of production of 50 items, the comparison of costs was estimated as shown in Table II. Assembly cost—the major cost item in conventional airplane construction—is greatly reduced by integrally-stiffened design. But current methods of machining, it is seen, involve increased fabrication, tooling and material costs which at present over-balance the saving in assembly.

Further Study Indicated

The cost data obtained in this case clearly show that further development should be directed at reducing raw material cost and speeding up the machining process. Tooling costs may also be worthy of attention. In quantity production, however, more elaborate tooling would be justified.

In machining surface panels from thick aluminum alloy plate, 80 to 95 pct of the original stock is cut away in chips and trim. Chips have low salvage value. There is therefore an advantage in machining from an outline section which might be prepared, for example, by forging or extrusion.

It is probable that more economical methods for reclaiming chips will be developed if machining practices are adopted extensively. But even when machining from plate shows considerable dollar advantage to the airframe manufacturer, consideration should be given to material transportation and mill processing problems which might occur in case of national emergency.

Machining time and cost of machining would be considerably less if equipment more suited to fabrication of surface panels were available. Automatic control would also be an advantage. A machine of this type is being built by Giddings & Lewis Machine Tool Co., Fond-du-Lac, Wis.

CONTINUOUS STRIP EXPERIMENTALLY ROLLED FROM POWDER PART II

Sheet made of rolled and sintered iron powder requires cold rolling and annealing, and it can be made into steel by carburizing and other methods. While present powder costs are high, there has been no incentive to develop large-scale production methods. This is a translation of a German paper written by Dr. Franz Zirm, which appeared in Stahl und Eisen, vol. 70, 1950.

Metal powder parts that are produced by pressing in molds are generally not given further processing after sintering. Some porosity is often desirable. When higher tensile and rupturing strength is required, a post-pressing at high temperatures and a subsequent sintering is necessary. This method is customary when producing parts from sinter steel. In the case of strip and sheet, such post-compacting is absolutely necessary unless a porous structure is required.

Several of these subsequent rolling passes are required. The percentage of reduction in the first rolling pass given strip and sheet after

---

In Part I, which appeared in the issue of Feb. 1, 1951, the relationships between various rolling factors, particle size, density and non-sintered properties were discussed. The quick sintering method developed during these investigations was described.—Ed.

---

sintering should not exceed a certain amount. Otherwise, transverse cracks occur. This limit would seem to be about 30 pct, for strips of the thickness of those on which tests were conducted. Subsequent passes, after intermediate heat treatment, are limited to 10 to 20 pct reductions. After

the fourth pass, the strip can be handled like regularly produced sheet and can even be given a heavy cold reduction.

The progressive changes in density and thickness occurring in pressed and sintered strip of varying initial density and thickness (0.45 to 0.55 mm) with increasing reduction is shown in Fig. 6. The degree of reduction for each pass is also indicated. The greater reduction that took place in the first pass is due to the reduction of the considerable pore space remaining after the original forming and sintering of the strip. With the fourth pass, the density of soft iron is almost attained.

Annealed Between Rolling Passes

In between the cold rolling passes, the test strips, which were about 400-mm long and 100-mm wide, were annealed for a short time in a muffle-type furnace through which hydrogen gas was passing. This furnace ended in a water-cooled cooling zone. A final annealing for stress relief was given after the last pass. This experimental arrangement resembled what might be a suitable organization of rolling stands, sintering and annealing furnaces and other equipment in a full-scale continuous process.

The increases in tensile strength and elongation caused by successive rolling passes are shown

TRANSLATED BY B. M. PEARSON, Hassocks, Sussex, England, from Stahl und Eisen, vol. 70, No. 22, dated Oct. 26, 1950. Part I of this story in The Iron Age, Feb. 1, was also translated from this paper written by Dr. Franz Zirm.

Continued

in Fig. 7. The curves representing these properties show a similarity in their nature and resemble those determined by W. Eilender and R. Schwalbe[6], describing the influence of sintering time on tensile strength and elongation. As can be seen from the curves in Fig. 7, the tensile strength rises rapidly up to the fourth reduction pass and increases only slightly thereafter, tending to reach a permanent maximum value. This value roughly corresponds to the tensile strength calculated from the chemical composition of the test strips. The reason for this is probably the changed density of the materials, which generally characterizes the number of pores present.

Higher Elongation Requires More Passes

From the curve in Fig. 6, it can be seen that density rises more after the first pass than with any of those following. The increase is greater than that which occurs in tensile strength. As the structure of the material becomes pore-free it not only becomes greatly strengthened but, also, the notch effect recedes into the background. The strengthening effect may be ascribed to crystallization phenomena.

As for elongation values, these still change considerably even with the fifth pass, but after that point they also remain relatively the same. While a good tensile strength begins to be obtained with the third rolling pass, higher elongation requires at least five passes.

The strength increase in the test pieces after each of the cold passes was measured before annealing, Fig. 8. Although the first cold pass does improve strength, as compared with the sintered condition, an additional increase is effected by the annealing following it (from 8 to 20 kg per sq mm). This first annealing is the only one that

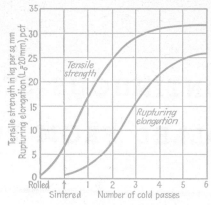

FIG. 7—Influence of increasing deformation on tensile strength and elongation.

causes such an increase, and is due to a continuation of the sintering process, particularly of the secondary particles which are brought closer together by the initial cold-rolling.

With the second cold pass, a work hardening can already be discerned, for the tensile strength rises from 20 to about 44 kg per sq mm. A relaxing effect takes place after the subsequent annealing to about 27 kg per sq mm. With additional cold-rolling and annealing, the tensile strength gradually rises to the maximum permitted by the composition.

Lower Annealing Temperature Used

Determining the temperature at which the final heat treatment of the cold-rolled strip should be performed requires consideration of a characteristic property of synthetic bodies. This is the increased grain growth at certain sintering temperatures[6, 8], the opposite of the case with normally produced metals. Strength and other properties are strongly influenced by this annealing for stress relief. To prevent the coarsening of grain size which starts at temperatures of 850 to 900°C, lower temperatures are used (about 650°C). In this way, stresses introduced by the cold rolling are removed and the structure of the strip is recrystallized without any coarsening of the grain.

The grain size and the distribution of that grain size also greatly influences processing behavior and mechanical properties. The finer powders with uniform particle size distribution gave the best results. Coarse grained sieved fractions, whose fine fraction was not lower than 0.06 mm, gave the lowest values. According to the results in Table II, with increasing deformation the differences in tensile strength balance out up to a certain degree. However, from the standpoint of processing behavior, normal powder with a particle size of 0.30 mm was the best. This is in conformity with results of previous work.

Tests of the deep drawing and bending properties of the specimen strips were made according to German standards for similar materials. The results, Table III, indicate that the speci-

FIG. 6—Change effected in density, thickness and percentage of reduction with each cold-rolling pass. Annealed after each pass.

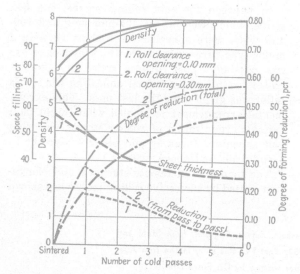

men strips satisfied this requirement.

Backward and forward bend cycle tests of the strip revealed outstanding results. Bend cycle figures of 50 to 200 were recorded, and the best values were obtained with strips prepared from powder of normal sieve classification.

According to F. Sauerwald and J. Hunczek[9] and F. Sauerwald and S. Kubik[10], if the initial forming of the strip and sheet could be a hot operation or if a hot pass could be given the pressed strip immediately before sintering, a very high degree of compacting would be reached. A more extensive removal of porosity and the consequent improved density would increase tensile strength and elongation. Unfortunately, such experiments could not be conducted, as the thin test strips produced cooled off too quickly in the cooled rolls. These rolls were running fairly slowly.

However, a single test was made on a reversing two-roll stand (roll diameter, 900 mm) which clearly indicated the value of such hot compacting. A press strip about 9 mm thick, with a density of 5.55 g per cc, was subjected to a hot rolling, producing a 43 pct reduction. The density increased to 7.45 g per cc and the elongation value was found to be 14 pct. Another sample of the same material that was given a cold pass showed only 2 pct elongation.

Equipment Layout Described

How equipment for the continuous production of sheet and strip from iron powder might be laid out is shown in Fig. 9. Horizontally arranged, parallel forming rolls receive the metal powder from a hopper, forming it into a pressed strip which is sintered in a protective atmosphere. The sintered material then passes through any desired sequence of cold passes and annealings, with a final relaxing heat treatment.

Various possibilities exist for the direct rolling of metal powders of these materials which either wholly or in part cannot be produced by normal ingot-and-rolling-mill methods. For example, there are three possible ways in which steel sheet can be produced: from steel powder, from mixtures of soft iron powder and carbon carriers such as graphite, or from carburized soft

FIG. 8—Change in tensile strength caused by each cold-rolling pass and its subsequent annealing pass.

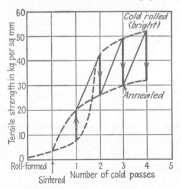

TABLE II
TENSILE STRENGTHS AND PARTICLE SIZES

| | Particle Size in mm | | | | | |
	<0.30	0.15 to 0.30	0.06 to 0.30	<0.15	0.06 to 0.15	<0.06
	Tensile Strength in kg/sq mm					
Sintered...........	8.2	4.2	4.3	6.8	6.6	n. o.
1st Pass...........	20.5	19.7	14.4	22.4	n. o.	18.1
2nd Pass...........	30.0	27.3	23.2	29.9	25.2	n. o.
3rd Pass...........	30.6	29.7	27.9	31.8	26.6	31.0

n. o.—Not observed.

TABLE III
RESULTS OF DEEP DRAWING TESTS

Particle Size, mm	Sheet Thickness, mm	Depth, mm
<0.30	0.25	6.9
<0.30	0.24	7.1
<0.15	0.29	8.1

iron press strips. As experience in the production of sinter steel parts by powder metallurgy[4, 11] indicates, carburization of the press-strip is most suitable. The thin cross-section of the strip and sheet produced from metal powder makes this particularly desirable.

Carburization was effected with coke-oven gas and tests were conducted at various temperatures, with and without the addition of the benzene vapor used as the protective atmosphere. Carbon was absorbed in a very short time, Fig. 10. After one minute at 1100°C, carbon content rose from 0.02 to 0.8 pct, and at 1200°C to 1.3 pct. This produced rollable strip with high tensile strength. Microscopic examination of a test piece, treated at 1200°C in coke-oven gas with benzene vapor added and containing 1.33 pct carbon, showed a good carburized structure. Pores were completely absent and the grain boundaries were sharply defined and completely individual, indicating a normal structure. Needles inside the grains were apparently caused by the high carbon content and rapid cooling. RZ powder provided the best results in these tests, as against electrolytic and carbonyl powders, which behave anomalously in this respect[12].

Made Iron Into Steel by Carburizing

The tests indicated that obtaining a required degree of carburization by conducting the sintering and reheating of soft iron strip in a carbon-containing atmosphere is technically possible. Detailed research is still needed to determine the best possible composition of the gaseous carburizing atmosphere for optimum results in the short heating time that would have to be used.

A special arrangement of the feeding hopper in front of the forming rolls was used to produce a compound, multi-layered sheet from powders of different chemical compositions. A 2 pct C steel powder was given outer layers of soft iron, the resulting sandwich being rolled into a homogeneous sheet. Diffusion and increasing deformation tended to make the carbon migrate to the outer layers low in carbon. To prevent decarburization, nitrogen was used as a protective atmosphere.

The chromium and aluminum oxides, which cannot be reduced by hydrogen and are stable when formed, create difficulties in the sintering stage. For this reason, when using such materials to produce high-alloy sheet from metal powders it is necessary and relatively easy to bring the strip to very high temperatures with an electrical current. A hot pass under hydrogen is also likely to be required and would not be difficult to apply.

Since iron powder can be decarburized to a very considerable extent by treatment with hydrogen, this sinter-metallurgical process also offers special advantages in the manufacturing of magnetically soft iron. The good magnetic properties of electrolytic iron powder can be improved by the addition of proper elements and should prove outstandingly suitable.

Bronze Powder Also Made Into Sheet

As to other metals, up to now only bronze powder has been investigated and it has been successfully made into sheet by the methods already described.

Various German technicians have given their opinions on this application of continuous processes to powder metallurgy. They consider that the work represents a decisive step forward because many of those sizes of sintered products that could not be made up to the present can now be produced by the new method. In addition, other workers have performed experiments which confirm the present findings.

It has also been demonstrated that for every

TABLE IV
PRODUCTION COSTS VS. MONTHLY OUTPUT

Production of Iron Powder tons/month	Method of Production	Production Costs per Ton Iron Powder	
		German Marks	U. S. Dollars
5	Hematite crude iron—electric furnace........	1,200 to 1,300	285.60 to 304.40
50	Hematite crude iron—electric furnace........	600 to 650	142.80 to 154.70
500	Basic Bessemer Steel and Carburization..........	275 to 300	65.45 to 71.40
5,000	Basic Bessemer Steel and Carburization..........	170 to 190	40.46 to 45.22

sheet thickness there is an applicable roll diameter, powder size and degree of compacting. With RZ powders, it has been found that the most suitable ratio between sheet thickness and roll diameter is 1 to 100.

It was felt that special emphasis must be placed on the characteristics of the powders used. Good flow properties are especially important. RZ powder is more suitable than powder consisting of scale or plate-shaped particles. With these latter types, there is always a danger that if the powder feed should slacken, non-uniform thickness and irregularities will occur in the sheet. The angle of rest of such powders varies according to the geometrical arrangement of their particles. If attempts are made to achieve uniform thickness in faulty sheet made of these powders by further passes, even with inter-annealing, a tendency to cracking will be encountered.

Heating by Electrical Resistance Questioned

One technician has disagreed with the suggestion that direct electrical resistance heating through the press strip could be used to provide the required sintering heat. As is well known, the specific resistance of sinter metal bodies decreases with progressive sintering effect. Insufficient resistance to develop the necessary heating effect would occur precisely at that point where a high power loading would be needed.

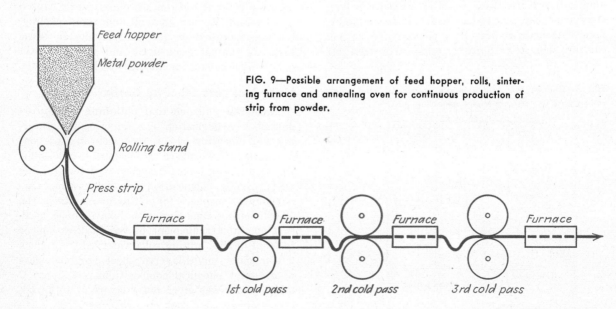

FIG. 9—Possible arrangement of feed hopper, rolls, sintering furnace and annealing oven for continuous production of strip from powder.

Another approach to the sintering operation suggests performing this step as the powder is pressed between the rolls. Such a process has been developed in Germany under the name of the "Goldesel" process, embodying graphitic rolls. This equipment was originally designed for conducting reactions between oxides and carbon. Bars have been produced from iron powder about 10 mm in thickness.

The graphitic rolls were placed in circuit with a high voltage transformer, and the greatest heating effect extended over about half of the narrowest part of the roll clearance. Care must be taken so that the temperature does not rise too high an amount. Otherwise, a reaction can occur between the iron powder and the graphite rolls to produce cast iron.

"Goldesel" Process Criticized

Another technician who stated that he is well acquainted with the Goldesel process has pointed out that if this type of equipment is used to process an iron powder having a considerably lower specific resistance than the graphite rolls it will be difficult to exercise control over the flow of current between the rolls. An impractically low voltage would be required with a correspondingly high current. This would not be feasible because the rolls would not be able to conduct that amount of current.

Some experiments based on the present findings were conducted at the Voeklingen steelworks and experimental iron powder strip was rolled. The results were in agreement with the work reported here. One fact was determined

which amplifies the information developed to date. By sintering the press-strip in a hydrogen atmosphere, the carbon and sulfur contents dropped to less than 0.03 and 0.003 pct, respectively.

The reason for tests being conducted in the Voeklingen works was less to develop a cheaper method of producing strip than to develop a bigger market for iron powder. Powder metallurgy suffers today from the too-high production costs involved in producing its raw materials. The consumption of iron powder by powder metallurgy parts manufacturers is so small at present than an iron or steelworks has little interest in producing this material.

Requires Large-Scale Powder Production

The development of full-scale production of sheet and strip from powder would change this present situation. Such a change would require an iron and steel works producing thousands of tons of iron powder a month. Production costs per ton, based on different monthly outputs have been estimated and are shown in Table IV.

Large scale production of iron powder from basic Bessemer steel could be achieved by carburizing the steel. The object would be to obtain a synthetic hematite crude iron that would then be atomized and heat treated. Should good ore factors be available that would permit the making of a hematite pig iron low in phosphorus, then under certain circumstances the cost figures given in Table IV could be still further reduced.

H. Hofmeister[13] has intimated that in certain cases strip for food containers could become a commercial proposition. He gives as an example those sulfur-containing ores and fuel which are unsuitable for processing in a blast furnace but which can be handled in a Stuerzelberg plant. The iron produced is then powdered and processed to strip, by-passing the steel-making and much of the rolling mill work.

Possible to Produce High Alloy Sheet

Special attention should also be given to high-alloy sheet. For example, Permalloy sheet can easily be made from powder. At the moment, unfortunately, technical difficulties are encountered in the production of electrical resistance heating strip, but these may be overcome. A favorable feature here is the fact that direct electrical heating will permit very high sintering temperatures to be used.

FIG. 10—Carburization of pressed, non-sintered iron strip to produce steel at varying temperatures and in different atmospheres.

	Coke oven gas plus
Coke oven gas	Benzene vapor
A—1200°C	E—1200°C
B—1100°C	F—1100°C
C—1000°C	G—1000°C
D— 900°C	H— 900°C

References

[8] F. Sauerwald, Zeitschrift Elektrochemisch, p. 79, Vol. 29, 1923
F. Sauerwald and L. Holub, Zeitschrift Elektrochemisch, p. 750, Vol. 39, 1933
[9] Zeitschrift Metallkunde, p. 22, Vol. 21, 1929
[10] Zeitschrift Elektrochemisch, p. 33, Vol. 38, 1932
[11] H. Bernstorff and H. Silbereisen, Archiv Metallkunde, p. 295, Vol. 2, 1948
[12] D. Duftschmid and E. Houdremont, Stahl und Eisen, p. 1613, Vol. 51, 1931
[13] Leistung und Fortschritt, p. 4, 1948

DIECASTING MACHINES FED
AUTOMATICALLY

Electromagnetic molten metal pumps feed metal directly into diecasting machines, eliminating the hand ladling formerly used. Two pumps act as holding furnaces, receiving metal from one melting unit and insuring a uniform supply of molten metal at constant temperature to two cold chamber machines.

By HERBERT CHASE
Consultant, Forest Hills, N. Y.

Within recent months, the production of electrical connectors has become a major activity at the Scintilla Magneto Div., Bendix Aviation Corp., Sidney, N. Y. Such connectors, made in many sizes and patterns, each involve two or more die cast aluminum shell-like components surrounding and supporting one or more dielectric insulators; the insulators are molded from a flexible plastic called Scinflex. Holes cored in the plastic inserts position the current-carrying contacts and hold the latter in correct relative position.

As the connectors are employed primarily in aircraft where lives depend upon correct functioning of electrical equipment, exacting specifications have to be met and products of highest quality are essential. To attain this and at the same time realize economy in manufacture while still holding high production schedules, Scintilla has recently installed one of the latest and most advanced setups for die casting the shell-like components. Typical examples of these castings appear in Fig. 1; at the center is shown a gate of four castings attached to the runners and "biscuit," as the casting comes from the die.

Most of the castings have sections ranging from 1/16 to $\frac{1}{4}$ in. in thickness and are cored out to receive the plastic insulators. Some types include elbows that are cored from both ends. All castings have to be sound and high pressure is required to fill out the one to four impressions in a given die or set of die blocks. Many dies are of the unit type and are inter-

FIG. 1—Typical diecast aluminum connector components and a gate of castings as it comes from the die. Flash is not removed from some of the castings shown.

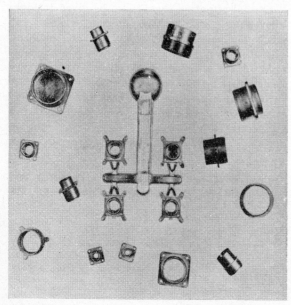

FIG. 2—Layout of melting, pumping and casting units: (1, 2) diecasting machines; (3) melting furnace; (4) heated runway; (5, 7) electromagnetic pumps; and (6, 8) pump nozzles.

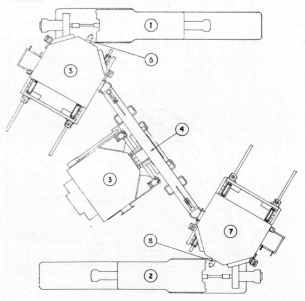

changeable in common holders which accommodate either one, two or four blocks.

To insure castings of uniform quality and at the same time to attain a high production rate, it is essential to supply the metal at a uniform temperature. It is also desirable to eliminate the human variables involved in hand ladling metal into the cold chamber of the casting machine and to make the casting cycle fully automatic. By these means, even the minor variations in timing and in volume of metal fed can be virtually eliminated.

Gives Close Control

To attain these conditions, two of the latest type Lester-Phoenix casting machines were installed, along with a set of three Ajax low frequency induction furnaces. The furnaces are also of the latest design, capable of supplying molten aluminum within exceptionally close temperature limits. One of these furnaces melts the aluminum and feeds it as required to the two electromagnetic pumps one of which is adjacent to each casting machine, as shown in Fig. 2. The melting furnace is located between the two electromagnetic pumps, the latter serving also as holding furnaces. An electrically heated runway of refractory material is used to transfer molten metal from the melter to the two pumps. The nozzles of the pumps discharge into the cold chambers of the two die casting machines.

Each electromagnetic pump is electrically interconnected with a precise timer and with the controls of the casting machine served, so that the pump discharges a predetermined weight of metal into the cold chamber at the precise and unvarying time in each cycle for which the automatic controls are set. There is, thus, close control of the weight and volume of metal injected as well as of its temperature. Moreover, injection is always at the same time in the cycle, which is set initially for optimum casting production.

No hand ladling is needed. Human variations in measuring the metal and in timing its application in the cycle are avoided. When the die has been spray lubricated, the operator merely presses a button that starts the cycle. This first causes the casting machine to close and lock the dies. Immediately thereafter, the timer operating the electromagnetic pump causes the latter to discharge the set weight of metal into the cold chamber. Then the ram advances and injects the metal into the die.

Of special interest is the construction and operation of the electromagnetic pump, because no mechanical pump is suited for handling molten aluminum at the temperature required. Moreover, if one was available, it would be most difficult to operate it intermittently and to vary the delivery to supply molten metal in precisely correct amount, especially during the short interval allowable in an efficient casting cycle.

Molten Metal Forms Secondary

Construction of the Ajax electromagnetic pump is illustrated in Fig. 3. The level of the molten metal in the hearth is at or near that shown, but varies somewhat as metal is pumped out and as a new supply is fed into the furnace. The level of the molten metal in the pumping nozzle (G) is higher and very near the tip, so that metal travels only a short distance every time a shot is made. Two primary coils (A) surround the laminated core (B) fed from an ac 60-cycle power source. The secondary consists of two loops of molten aluminum that fill the channels (C) and (E), as well as the hearth above them, the channels being inside the refractory (D) in the shaded area. High current on the order of 30,000 amp is induced in the secondary loops (E).

As there is a strong magnetic field with flux lines approximately circular around channel (E), the current in the fluid conductor causes it to move in the direction of the arrows. Elec-

FIG. 3—Sectional views, at right angles to each other, through the Ajax electromagnetic pump, which lifts molten metal and discharges it through a nozzle to the diecasting machine.

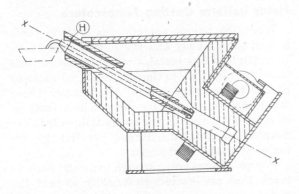
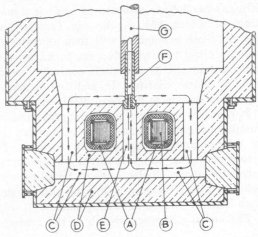

tromagnetic pressure is at a maximum in the channel at the top of which an orifice (F) is placed.

The rate of metal flow through this orifice depends upon the diameter of the orifice and the pressure inducing the flow. Actually, the orifice remains fixed; the pressure is varied by changing the voltage applied to the primary coils. Thus, the weight of metal poured can be varied by controlling the duration of current flow in the primary circuit. Connected to the orifice is a tube (G) made from silicon carbide refractory and surrounded, in its upper portion, by a resistance heating unit (H). The heating unit keeps the tube, where it is above the level of molten metal in the furnace, at the proper temperature up to the spout where the metal is discharged.

Depending on the size of the orifice, a metal flow ranging from ½ to 5 lb per sec can be attained. Consequently, timers are set to discharge a given weight of metal which the casting machine plunger immediately forces into the dies.

After a preset interval for the castings to solidify, the dies open automatically and the casting is pushed free. The operator merely lifts out the gate of castings and lays it in a tote box to cool. When this is done, the die is visually checked (and lubricated, if necessary) and the button starting the next cycle is pressed.

Output Increased 25 Pct

Metal injected always comes from the lower part of the hearth and is free of any dross or oxide such as may be introduced in hand ladling. Temperature is held within ± 5°F and is set at 1200°F for the SAE 306 aluminum alloy employed. Metal and casting conditions are so nearly perfect that the output of acceptable castings is upped about 25 pct over that for hand ladling. About 150 shots (die fillings) per hr are attained as against a maximum of about 120 per hr for fastest hand ladling. Such economies will soon amortize the higher initial cost of induction furnaces, electromagnetic pumps and their controls, besides yielding better castings. In addition, a marked reduction in rejects has been attained.

It requires only two men to operate the two casting machines and part of a third man's time to charge and tilt the melting furnace. The electromagnetic pump requires no production labor. Usually each electromagnetic pump needs refilling about once in 2 hr and this is done with little or no loss in casting time.

The melting furnace, shown at the center of

FIG. 4—Ajax melting furnace, center, and two electromagnetic pumps to which molten metal is fed through the electrically heated launder. Trough tilts either way and serves both pumps.

Fig. 4, is at a higher level than the two pumps and is set on trunnions for nose tilting. Directly below the spout is a covered refractory-lined trough or launder into which the metal is discharged when the furnace is tilted. This launder is electrically heated and is arranged so that it can be tilted one way to fill one pump and the opposite way to fill the other.

Each holding and pumping furnace is set on rails, positioned so that the pump nozzle is slightly above and to one side of the cold chamber filling opening. Metal discharges from the pump nozzle and flows down a trough, a distance of a few inches, directly into the cold chamber. This close coupling is important, and was attained by close cooperation between the designers of the die casting machines and of the electromagnetic pumps. A close-up of one electromagnetic pump appears in Fig. 5. As the case is well insulated and all heat is applied by the induction coil inside the base, very little heat is radiated and comfortable working conditions for the machine operator are assured.

Holds Uniform Casting Temperature

When the pumps operate, the level in their hearth falls slowly and the pumps tend to deliver slightly less metal. Compensation for this is made from time to time by slight adjustment of the timers that control the pumps. These timers are set to operate the pumps a fraction of a second longer as the levels fall, so that the quantity of metal discharged per impulse remains virtually unchanged.

Pumps discharge through silicon carbide tubes that are heated electrically so that the metal always issues at the casting temperature set. The electromagnetic pumps remain in fixed

FIG. 5—Close-up of one electromagnetic pump, center, serving the diecasting machine at the left.

FIG. 6—Diecasting machine being charged with a measured quantity of molten metal from the pump. Automatic charging is followed by closing and locking of the dies.

position and need not be tilted. They also remain covered except when being filled. The pumps hold about 900 lb of aluminum alloy and the melting furnace about 1200 lb.

Some forty different dies are needed to produce the different castings required in the Scintilla line of electrical connectors. Most of these dies are small and are made to fit unit holders. In general, the dies have four cavities, all of which are filled at each shot of the machine. When both machines use four-cavity dies at a time, about 16,000 castings are produced in two 8-hr shifts.

Casting Cycle Is Automatic

Each of the new die casting machines, Fig. 6, are designated model HHP-1CC Lester and have automatic controls so that they run through the cycle automatically, unless stopped by the operator. In some cases, the operator uses a hand-operated ejector but in most cases knockouts operate automatically and the operator need only remove the gates of castings by hand. When side cores are needed, they can be arranged for either angle pin or hydraulic pulling, as desired. The machines are self-contained units equipped with hydraulic pumps that operate at 2000 psi. Rams in cold chambers are of 2-in. diam, hence, the pressure applied to the metal is about 11,000 psi. Total locking pressure applied to the dies is 150 tons.

This plant continues to operate two older and larger Lester-Phoenix machines, known as type HHP 3XS. These have 600-ton locking pressures and are employed for making castings of larger size than the connectors. With these machines, hand ladling is done from gas fired holding furnaces of 200-lb capacity, filled by hand from a 400-lb gas fired melting furnace.

With the large machines and hand-ladling, the number of die fillings ranges from 40 to 100 per hr, depending upon the size and type of casting produced. In many cases, inserts must be placed in the die by hand; this slows the cycle, but provides castings in which the inserts are held together in correct relative position in a manner attainable only by die casting.

Among the castings produced in this manner are magneto rotors, such as in Fig. 7, having a steel shaft and laminations as inserts. These inserts are clamped hydraulically or by air pressure in the die and are held securely while the aluminum alloy is cast around them. Thus, the casting operation effects an assembly and yields a product that would cost more if it had to be produced and assembled by other means.

Several of the castings made in the larger machines require side cores that are operated by the hydraulic system of the machine. The larger machines are equipped with prefilling arrangements. They also have nitrogen accumulators that step up the speed and pressure of the injection ram near the end of its stroke.

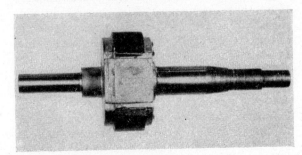

FIG. 7—Magneto rotor has a steel shaft and a set of steel laminations. These are applied as inserts in the die, bound together by diecasting aluminum around the inserts.

Operator installing Heli-Coil insert in retapped hole with a high-speed inserting tool.

The installed thread insert can be seen in place in the motor frame casting, left, half a turn below the surface.

Helical inserts speed thread repair in castings

The maintenance department serving one of New York City's subway lines has the frequent problem of replacing worn and stripped threads in the axle-cap bolt holes of its subway car motor-frame castings. Repair of these holes is expedited by the use of stainless steel helical-wire thread inserts.

These inserts permit the use of the same size cap screws in the repaired holes as were used in the original holes. This eliminates the matching operations that would be necessary if oversize threads and cap screws were used to solve the damaged thread problem. Use of these inserts also eliminates the need for drilling out larger clearance holes in mating parts. In addition, these preformed wire inserts provide threads that are stronger, more wear-resistant, and more corrosion-resistant than the original threads.

Thread repair is accomplished in the following manner: The damaged thread is cleaned out with a drill slightly larger in outside diameter than the major diameter of the original thread. The hole is then retapped using an oversize, special-threaded tap, and the helical thread insert is installed.

Threads in a motor frame were repaired in this manner. This casting had a badly worn

thread, a completely stripped thread, and a broken 2¼-in. cap screw. Original holes had 1 9/32-7 tapped threads.

After removal of the broken stud, these three holes were repaired by drilling out with a 1 21/64-in. drill, tapping with a special oversize Heli-Coil tap identified with a 1 9/32-7 marking, and installing a stainless steel Heli-Coil thread insert to bring the hole back to size. This insert, having a diamond-shaped cross-section, has threads on its outside diameter conforming to the special tap and internal threads conforming to the original 1 9/32-7 thread.

The entire operation was completed in approximately 55 min. The formed wire inserts provided smooth threads to permit frequent assembly and disassembly operations with a minimum of thread wear. Also, corrosion caused by infiltration of water or other reactive liquids and gases will not cause deterioration of these threads.

The strength of the 18-8 stainless steel more than compensates for the loss of material in the bolt-hole boss. Also, increased loading strength is achieved because the helical insert automatically adjusts itself to mating threads on both the casting and the stud, thereby distributing the load properly over each thread.

news of industry

Ordnance Holds Key to Vast Iron Powder Growth

Shell rotating band and bullet projects would require vast quantities of iron powder . . . If adopted, program would mean multi-expansion of capacity—*By Bill Packard.*

New York—Iron powder may go to war in a big way. Domestic iron powder capacity will have to be expanded many times its present size if the Ordnance Corps adopts iron powder rotating bands for shells. A long development program is believed nearing the decision stage now. Depending on whether the war is hot or cold, and also on the outcome of iron powder bullet development work, the required expansion might be over ten times capacity now.

The idea of making rotating bands by powder metalluragy is not new. Neither are iron powder rotating bands. We made some copper bands by powder metallurgy during the last war. But the Germans went us one better. Spurred by a terrific copper shortage, they used iron powder.

German Output Zoomed

The German rotating band program was reflected in their iron powder production statistics. In 1938 they produced no more than 300 tons of iron powder. But in 1944 they hit a peak of almost 33,000 tons. They produced more than a billion rotating bands in addition to vast numbers of bullets and parts—all from iron powder. Their rotating bands ranged from 20 mm to 88 mm. Their manufacturing methods have been exploited in our own development work.

Intensive study of iron powder rotating bands has been underway at Watertown Arsenal, Stephens Institute and Purdue University during the past 2 years. A Shell Committee was formed last August to study materials, engineering and manufacture of shells. A Powder Metallurgy Committee from industry was formed to advise the Shell Committee on metallurgical problems. A total of 27 men from industry, serving on five subcommittees, are working on powder metallurgy.

Ordered for Test Firing

Specifications for revolving bands made of iron powder have been set up based on work done at Watertown Arsenal. A moderate quantity of these bands has been ordered from industry for test firing. A decision on their future should not be long in coming.

Rotating bands made by powder metallurgy are precision jobs. Both inside and outside diameters are circular and concentric. Surfaces are precisely flat and parallel. Cost is competitive with metal tubing. No machining is required.

Although there are only three domestic producers currently making iron powder, there are more than 100 plants making metal powder parts. There is no shortage of presses needed to convert the powder into parts. Also, many presses now making cores

Turn Page

Firms Gets U.S. Steel Contracts

Pittsburgh — Morrisville Contractors, a combination of four construction firms, has been given the contract for foundations, floors, roads, tracks, and sewers for the Morrisville, Pa., plant of U. S. Steel Corp. The contractors include Walsh Construction Co., Davenport; S. J. Groves & Sons, Inc., Minneapolis; Perini & Sons, Inc., Framingham, Mass., and Slattery Construction Co., Inc., New York.

Morrisville Plant Openhearths

Pittsburgh — Koppers Co. Inc. will engineer and construct the nine 275-ton openhearth furnaces to be built at the new Morrisville, Pa., plant of U. S. Steel Co. The Wilputt Coke Oven Div. of Allied Chemical and Dye Corp. will design and erect two coke oven batteries of 87 ovens each at the mill.

INDUSTRIAL BRIEFS

CENTURY MARK — The E. HORTON & SON CO., Windsor Locks, Conn., in the lathe chuck industry, is now in its 100th year of operation.

"NOT LEGAL" — The pending merger of the PERFECT CIRCLE CORP. and THOMPSON PRODUCTS, INC., Hagerstown, Ind., will not be completed. The Department of Justice advised that the merger would be in violation of the anti-trust law and it would institute litigation if merger were put through.

SOLE U. S. REP.—KALEX CORP., N. Y., are the exclusive distributors in the U. S. for Cary of Switzerland, makers of high precision gages.

NEW LOCATION — The plant of EMPIRE SOLVENTS, INC., has moved to Clifton, N. J. Their general offices and laboratory are located in N. Y.

UNDER CONSTRUCTION — Construction has begun on the new office and warehouse building being erected for PETER A. FRASSE & CO., INC., Syracuse, N. Y. The building will permit the consolidation of the entire Frasse Syracuse operation under one roof.

OPEN HOUSE—BEALS, McCARTHY & ROGERS, INC., marked their 125th anniversary with a 3-day open house celebration at their new office-warehouse in Buffalo. During the 125 years of existence the firm outgrew its quarters eight times.

PATENT RIGHTS—Patent and manufacturing rights for the Tromp Heavy Density Coal Cleaning System have been acquired for the Western Hemisphere by McNALLY PITTSBURGH MFG. CORP., Pittsburgh. The Tromp system is widely used in England, France and Holland for the cleaning of the low-gravity and high-gravity coals.

NEW HIGH—The net earnings of the PENNSYLVANIA SALT MFG. CO., Philadelphia, after taxes, for 1950, were the highest in the company's 100 years. These earnings were 49 pct higher than profits earned in 1949 and 118 pct more than the average annual profit for the preceding decade.

ASSN. SECRETARY — Robert T. Griebling will serve as executive secretary of the AIR POLLUTION & SMOKE PREVENTION ASSN. OF AMERICA, INC. The headquarters of the association will move from Chicago to Pittsburgh and will be housed in Mellon Institute.

SIGNAL EQUIPMENT — LEWYT CORP., Brooklyn, has been awarded a $4,500,000 contract by the U. S. Army Signal Corps., to manufacture communication equipment.

AMERICAN AGENT — Exclusive representation for the Pouplier Steel Mills, Hagen-Kabel, Germany, has been given the NEW AMSTERDAM IMPORT CO., New York. The Pouplier Mills have increased their capacity.

TENTATIVE CONTRACT — BROWN & ROOT, INC., Houston engineering and construction firm is the lowest bidder on the general contract covering erection of Lone Star Steel company's $73.5 million integrated steel mill to be built at the E. Texas works. A formal contract is awaiting approval by directors and RFC officials.

ACROSS THE RIVER—Transfer of the sales and manufacturing facilities of the S. G. FRANTZ CO., INC., from New York to Trenton, N. J., has been completed. The new plant provides ample space for sales and administrative offices, as well as a large area for manufacturing operations.

or parts could be quickly converted to revolving bands if the word is given. Production rates for these presses are very high.

But the most compelling reason for switching from copper to iron powder is the availability of material. The outlook for substantially increasing supplies of copper is bleak. But raw materials for iron powder are abundant.

Plenty of Raw Materials

While most domestic iron powder is made from mill scale, it can also be made from high grade iron ore or steel scrap. During the last war the Germans made it from chopped wire and scrap, as well as sponge iron.

Last year domestic iron powder producers shipped 4125 net tons of powder. During the same period we imported 6000 tons from Sweden. Domestic capacity is being expanded, but not by the leaps and bounds that will be necessary if Ordnance adopts iron powder widely in revolving bands and bullets. The switch is not expected to be made overnight.

NPA to Aid Diesel Engine Industry

Washington—A plan by which the National Production Authority will help the diesel engine industry obtain material for production is being worked out. However, the industry has been told to expect production in the near future to be limited to highly essential uses.

Inco of Canada Chairman Dies

New York—Robert Crooks Stanley, 74, chairman of the board and former president of International Nickel Co. of Canada, Ltd., died here this week. Mr. Stanley was noted for discovering Monel metal and held several patents on processing and refining of metals. He studied engineering at Stevens Institute of Technology and Columbia School of Mines and was a metallurgist since 1901, when he joined Oxford Copper Co. After being made a director of International in 1917, he was named president in 1922.

U.S. Shipbuilding Program Starts With Awards to 5 Yards

First of 25 ships to be delivered in 480 days . . . Cost $8 million each.

Washington — The first large scale government shipbuilding program since World War II has been set in motion with award of 25 Mariner ship contracts to five shipyards at a cost of approximately $8 million per ship.

Congress appropriated $350 million for the new ships last month and bids invited from shipyards on Jan. 10 were opened Jan. 31. Of 11 yards responding, the following were accepted: Newport News Shipbuilding & Dry Dock Co., Newport News, Va.; Ingalls Shipbuilding Corp., Pascagoula, Miss.; Bethlehem Steel Co., Sparrows Point, Md.; Bethlehem Steel Co., Quincy, Mass.; Sun Shipbuilding & Dry Dock Corp., Chester, Pa.

At prices awarded, higher cost yards will probably receive less profit per ship than lower cost yards, the Maritime Administration reported. Contracts call for delivery of the first ship from Newport News and Bethlehem-Quincy in 480 days, with other deliveries up to 730 days.

R-108 Prolongs Life of Steel

Pittsfield — Development of R-108, an ingredient to give improved alkali and acid resistance to paints, has been announced by the Chemicals Div. of General Elec. Used on steel, the coating conserves expensive and hard-to-get alloys, GE claims. Steel drum life can be extended, and experiments are being made with R-108 to replace tin used in food containers.

B & O Ore Pier Ready in April

Baltimore—Foreign ore shipments from Liberia and Venezuela can be handled here soon after completion in April of the Baltimore & Ohio Railroad's new $5 million ore pier at Curtis Bay.

Two Dravo ore unloading machines will be able to unload a ship in 24 hours, handling from 1000 to 1500 tons an hour. First of its kind on the Eastern seaboard, the pier will be expanded to accommodate two ships simultaneously as soon as the flow of ore justifies it.

OPS Studies Formula Prices For Nonferrous Foundry Industry

Washington — Formula price-control for the nonferrous foundry industries is being studied by the Office of Price Stabilization.

Nonferrous foundry representatives last week urged OPS to permit the industry to continue using individual company formulas under any price regulation the government may issue.

OPS was told the multiplicity of foundries and wide diversity of production make formula pricing "inescapable" in the affected industries.

Foundry representatives requested the order be issued as soon as possible to remove the industry from provisions of the current general price regulation.

NMTA Urges Industry Restudy Employment Practices for Women

Job breakdown, control redesign suggested . . . Training needed.

Chicago—With the number of women in industry showing a sharp upward turn, and still the nation's biggest reservoir of untapped labor, the National Metal Trades Assn. urges manufacturers to review employment and shop practices in light of World War II experience.

Job breakdowns, redesign of operating controls and safety devices to accommodate women's smaller stature, and revision of material handling facilities will enable women to attain greater production levels.

Recruiting in the 25 to 35 year age group may be complicated by lack of child care facilities since there are relatively more women with young children than before the last war.

While many states relaxed laws governing employment of women during World War II, NMTA recommends review of state and federal laws on lifting loads, hours,

Defense Contracts to Metalworking Industry

Selected Contracts, Week of Feb. 12, 1951

Item	Quan.	Value	Company
Aircraft engines	136	$1,224,000	Capitol Airlines Nat'l Airport, Washington, D. C.
Automatic pilot comp's.	...	1,969,611	Sperry Gyroscope Co., Great Neck, N. Y.
Propeller assemblies	...	984,872	Curtis-Wright Corp., Caldwell, N. J.
Carburetor parts	...	875,378	Bendix Products Div., South Bend
Aircraft parts	...	4,271,273	North American Aviation, Los Angeles
Aircraft generators	...	1,146,014	General Electric Co., Dayton
Wheel & brake assemblies	...	1,279,000	Bendix Products Div., South Bend
Radios	2266	2,000,000	Radio Corp. of America, Camden, N. J.
Aircraft Comp's	...	14,000,000	Lockheed Aircraft Corp., Burbank, Calif.
Trucks	483	892,659	General Motors Corp., Detroit
Trucks	4500	12,380,000	Studebaker Corp., South Bend
Trucks	320	379,046	Chevrolet Motor Corp., Detroit
Carburetors	90,000	602,500	Lally's Des Moines, Iowa
Trucks	3050	8,000,000	International Harvester Co., Chicago
Trucks, gas tanks	4173	11,557,528	Reo Motors Inc., Lansing, Mich.
Trucks	595	3,090,446	Federal Motor Truck Co., Detroit
Motors	489	35,000,000	Cadillac Mtr. Car Div., Detroit
Buses	1772	7,255,954	Ford Motor Co., Washington, D. C.
Automobiles	164	229,591	Buick Motor Div., Detroit
Trucks	10,298	18,515,441	Ford Motor Co., Washington, D. C.
Trucks	5030	5,734,738	Ford Motor Co., Washington, D. C.
Trucks	536	834,713	Chevrolet Motor Div., Detroit
Mobile bakery	58	560,277	American Machine & Foundry Co.
Direction finder	46	800,000	Stewart Warner Corp., Chicago
Prototype Diesels	6	1,000,000	Continental Aviation & Eng., Detroit
Energizers	200	520,000	General Electric Co., Washington
Motor parts	29,188	478,768	ACF Brill Mtrs. Co., Philadelphia
Crane shovels	30	1,000,000	Bay City Shovel, Inc., Bay City, Mich.
Road rollers	150	600,000	Calion Iron Wks., Calion, Ohio
Parts	...	600,000	Thew Shovel, Lorain, Ohio
Construction equip	11	450,304	Pioneer Eng. Works, Inc., Minneapolis
Bomb components	20,000	4,690,410	Griffin Mfg. Co., Dallas
Sights	...	500,000	Argus, Inc., Ann Arbor, Mich.
Air compressors	125	800,000	Joy Mfg. Co., Chicago
Air compressors	175	1,000,000	Davey Compressor, Kent, Ohio

pay, machinery and safety measures.

NMTA recommends simple attire and proper hair control to prevent accidents. Since women usually lack the mechanical background of men, NMTA suggests special training, and urges that supervisers be briefed to cope with different emotional reactions.

U. S. Scrambles for Metals ECA Gives Europe

Congressional ire grows as copper, lead, zinc, aluminum shipments under Marshall Plan reach $605 million in past 9 months . . . Favor joint defense approvals—*By Karl Rannells.*

Washington—Increasing criticism is being leveled at continued Marshall Plan buying of strategic materials from American stocks and sources, especially when domestic controls are being drawn steadily tighter.

Total purchase authorizations for four of the more critical metals is given in the Economic Cooperation Administration's year-end report as $605 million. This is for the period from April 1948 through December 1950.

While a majority in Congress view the Marshall Plan as an economic necessity, there is a growing feeling that there should be a closer screening of Marshall Plan demands. And there is increasing support for the belief held by Sen. McCarran, Sen. Wherry, R., Nebr.; Rep. Reed, R., N. Y.; Rep. Rees, R., Kans., and others, that shipments of strategic materials from this country should be approved only when necessary for joint defense.

U. S. Supplies Third of Total

But best available figures indicate that to date the totals within ECA's stated period approach nearer $625 million. Roughly broken down, this amounts to about $350 million worth of copper and copper products; $130 million worth of aluminum; $85 million in zinc and its products; and about $60 million worth of lead and its products.

Actual deliveries, of course, lag somewhat behind the purchase approvals. Nevertheless, ECA reports through November showed that paid shipments of these metals were running at about 80 pct of total authorizations. Roughly a third was being shipped from the United States.

A substantial portion of these total authorizations was approved prior to the setting up of the National Production Authority—and thus is water over the dam. However, great concern is being created because purchase approvals have slowed down but little since NPA began slapping controls and restrictions on domestic supplies, use and distribution.

As an illustration, in addition to $8 million worth of aluminum some $17 million worth of copper and its products were authorized by the ECA during the first 2 months of control—November and December. A third of the copper was to be bought in the United States and the total just about equals the current stockpiling buying rate.

"That isn't all scrap—my machine is under there somewhere."

Moreover, ECA announced in mid-January that it had authorized Germany to buy some $2 million worth of copper and copper products from the United States. A few days later it authorized a similar purchase by the Dutch which amounted to roughly $367,000.

These approvals were announced 2 and 3 weeks after NPA had issued its amendment to the original copper cutback order (M-12) which barred use of copper in manufacture of more than 300 end items. Similar restrictions have been placed on aluminum, nickel and tin.

Restrictions Run Wide Range

What is making it bad from all viewpoints is that the prohibited lists are not confined to strictly non-essential articles. They also apply to various types of tools, building materials, hardware and so on.

"It is manifestly unjust to allow the export of such materials if they are to be used in Europe for purposes which are prohibited here at home," Sen. McCarran, D., Neb., declared on the Senate floor recently.

Neither business nor labor understand why the government continues to follow two apparently conflicting policies—strict domestic conservation with one hand and distribution abroad with the other. They say it will bring production cutbacks and unemployment.

Japanese Copper to Europe

Nor do they understand why between 15,000 and 20,000 tons of Japanese copper was permitted to be sent to Europe and the Far East over a 21-month period while copper was short here.

The ECA takes the position that Marshall Plan nations need such raw materials in order to keep factories going and to keep from being a greater burden to this country.

It explains the Japanese shipments by saying this "enables the United States to use more of its own production for defense mobilization."

Woodward Expansion Adds To Coking, By-products Facilities

Raises to 154 number of new ovens announced in area in past 5 months.

Birmingham—A new $4 million expansion program has been announced by Bradford G. Colcord, president of Woodward Iron Co. Construction will start at once.

Major item is 30 additional coke ovens with a capacity of 115,000 net tons annually. It will bring to 154 the total of new coke ovens announced for the Birmingham area in the past 5 months and will increase annual coke production approximately 600,000 tons.

Others that have announced plans for new coke ovens and on which work actually has started are: Republic Steel Corp., 65 new ovens; Sloss-Sheffield Steel & Iron Co., 30, and Alabama By-Products Co., 29.

At present Woodward has 226 coke ovens producing some 850,000 tons annually.

Includes By-Products Facilities

The Woodward program also calls for additional coal and coke handling facilities for increased production of coal chemical by-products, including ammonium sulphate, coal tar, benzene, xylene, toluene, napthalene and pyridine.

The company is constructing a new $4½ million blast furnace to produce about 237,250 gross tons of pig iron a year. Later it plans to add steam and power equipment and transportation facilities.

Income More Than Doubled

Chicago—A. M. Castle & Co., Chicago steel distributors, report a net 1950 income of $1,319,789 as compared with $539,775 for 1949. Net sales of the company for 1950 came to $18,709,876.

ASIE Honors Westinghouse

New York—Westinghouse Electric Corp. has been given the Merit Award of the American Society of Industrial Engineers for leadership in research, engineering, design and manufacture in the home laundry field.

ANTI-SMOG EQUIPMENT: General Metals Corp. iron plant at Vernon, Calif., has a new weapon against smog in Los Angeles area. It is a Whiting Corp. five section Bag Type Dust Suppressor serving two No. 4 cupolas. Shown at upper right are cupolas with conditioning chambers attached to upper stacks. All gases and remaining dust, fumes, and smoke are channelled to the dust suppressor (left) for final cleaning. The tough Los Angeles County Air Pollution Control District has approved the installation.

Pittsburgh Coal Builds Coal Pipeline for Surface Mining Site

Pittsburgh — Transportation of coal by pipeline is here.

Pittsburgh Consolidated Coal Co. is building a 3-mile coal pipeline system near Cadiz, Ohio, at the Georgetown surface mining operation of the Hanna Coal Co. Div. The project is expected to be in operation this summer.

Experiments by Pitt-Consol at a small pilot operation at Library, Pa., apparently convinced the company that pipeline movement of coal is feasible. The $550,000 demonstration-size line is expected to show up any bugs that still must be worked out.

Coal will be pumped through the 12-in. pipeline in the form of a coal-water "slurry." At the other end of the line the coal will be drained and dried. It was believed that fine coal for power plant use and perhaps stoker size coal could be transported in this manner.

After crushing, the coal will be washed and mixed with water to form a slurry. Special pumps have been designed to push this mixture through the line under pressure. The company expects to pump several thousand tons of coal per day through the line.

U.S. Okays Green River Steel Loan; Considers North American

Washington—Green River Steel Corp. last week received a government loan for $8,356,000 for construction of an electric furnace at Owensboro, Ky., and government officials this week met to consider application by North American Steel Co., of Clinton, Iowa, on request for a $100 million steel mill loan.

The two loans covering construction of the Owensboro plant will bring an additional 189,000 tons of ingot capacity annually. The plant will employ from 800 to 1000. Operations are expected to begin within a year. The corporation has an option on a 127-acre site in a coal reserve.

North American Steel Co. plans to make 1 million tons of finished steel annually, plus 400,000 tons of pig iron. To be built on the Mississippi River, south of Clinton, at Comanche, Ia., the new plant will produce sheet, bar, and slat steel.

Robinson Gets Ordnance Post

Cincinnati—Harry S. Robinson, retired general manager and treasurer of the Cincinnati Shaper Co., has been named chief of the Cincinnati Ordnance District.

High Price of Mechanization

Milwaukee, Wis.—Allis-Chalmers Mfg. Co. has paid a high price for mechanization. This is not as dire as it sounds. The firm has bought its most expensive single machine tool for the West Allis Works—a 30 ft heavy boring and turning mill, its second largest machine tool.

A Lima-Hamilton Corp. product, the new mill can machine single pieces up to 30 ft, 5 in. diam and 17 ft high. Supplementing production of a 40-ft boring mill, largest in the shops, the 30-in. mill increases capacity for manufacture of large generators, condensers, steam and hydraulic turbines.

It weighs about 500 tons and is 48 ft tall, 37 ft of which is over the floor line, and is 59 ft wide, with a depth of 29 ft. The mill has an elevating type crossrail on which are mounted two swivelling rail heads with 14-in. octagonal boring bars about 18 ft in length.

Push button control from four stations operate 36 motors. Shown in the photograph on the mill's table is a bottom guide vane for a hydraulic turbine.

Koppers Co. Reports Earnings

Pittsburgh—Koppers Co., Inc., reports net income of $11,615,498 during 1950 compared with $7,111,997 in 1949. Sales and receipts in 1950 were $213,791,687 compared with $192,314,685 in 1949.

Study U.S. Coal Mining Methods

London — A 16-man English team will study the American coal mining industry from top to bottom in a program sponsored by the ECA. The group, which sailed for the U. S. last week, will visit a dozen bituminous coal fields.

More Non-Defense Steel Cuts To Hit Industry Apr. 1, NPA Says

Further cuts in aluminum and copper planned . . . Blow to auto production.

Washington — Further limitations on non-defense use of steel were in the final draft stage this week. The new order will cut back steel use for durable goods on an industry-by-industry basis.

It is scheduled to become effective Apr. 1. A National Production Authority official said the method was selected as a preferable alternative to imposing end-use restricting as in the case of aluminum and copper. NPA feels manufacturing industries are in best position to determine where steel allotments can be used to best advantage.

No Cut for Auto Parts

Further limitations on aluminum and copper uses were also being completed. The three orders will hit the automotive industry hard. Some estimates are production will have to be cut back 50 pct instead of the expected 25-30 pct.

However, officials said it is not planned at present to apply the steel cut-back to the automotive parts industry. They indicated production would probably be allowed at 100 pct of the average rate during first half 1950.

Steel Firms Move Mountains And Reroute Rivers for Expansion

New York—Steel companies will move mountains of ore, reroute rivers, move cemeteries in their concerted push for vast steel expansion.

A river will be set on another course so that one steel firm can get room for a new mill building. Another company will gingerly move the contents of two cemeteries for expansion land. This involves shifting 250 graves and headstones, reported the American Iron and Steel Institute.

One firm plans to insert a large section in the middle of one of its ore vessels so the ship can haul more ore. Houses were moved wholesale by two firms. One of them moved 100.

Now under construction is a 360-mile railroad to connect Labrador-Quebec ore fields. Other big construction projects are going on in foreign lands to provide ore for steel capacity that will be over 120 million tons by the end of 1952.

Dual Tin Coat May Alter Production, Pricing

Right now it means tin savings . . . May cause revision of tin cut order . . . Weirton offers tinplate now . . . Its Halogen process readily adaptible to dual coatings—*By John Delaney.*

Pittsburgh—The dual coatings electrolytic tinplate process developed by Weirton Steel Co. could have important effects on the producing methods and pricing policies of the industry.

Of more immediate importance, the process will help conserve tin. Weirton estimates that tin metal savings will be between 25 and 30 pct. The company's announcement stated also that the process may enable the government to revise recently-announced restrictions on tin consumption and end uses of tin mill products. Weirton already is offering the new tinplate to its customers.

Unequal Tin Coatings

The dual coatings process means that a coating of sufficient weight to protect the contents of a can may be deposited on one side of the plate, with just enough for appearance and protection against corrosion on the other. Before the Weirton development, the industry-wide practice was to apply the same coating weight on both sides.

The Halogen process, used by Weirton, electrolytically coats each side of the plate individually, and is readily adaptable to dual coating. This same type line is operated by Republic Steel Corp. and is being currently installed by Jones & Laughlin Steel Corp. at its Aliquippa plant. However, all other lines in the industry coat both sides simultaneously. Whether they can be adapted economically to dual coating is a problem now under study.

Since the new process requires less tin, electrolytic tinplate prices could eventually be revised to reflect this saving, although this is not an immediate probability in view of recent advances in the price of pig tin.

Revise Basis Box Weights

One immediate effect was the revision by Weirton of six standard basis box weights of tinplate, revealing that the company now is producing 1.00 lb electrolytic as a substitute for 1.25 lb hot dip, in itself a tin conservation measure which most consumers of 1.25 and 1.50 lb hot dip had anticipated. (THE IRON AGE, Jan. 11, '51, p. 77.)

For example, the former 1.25 lb basis weight hot dip is now produced by Weirton with 1.00 lb for the interior of the can and 0.25 lb for the exterior—a saving of 50 pct in tin. It also means an increase of 100 pct in surface coverage with the same quantity of tin.

In the former 0.50 lb basis

"Yoo Hoo, Boss—I'm back from the lavatory—."

weight the saving on tin is 25 pct and the increase in area covered is 33.3 pct. The former 0.75 lb basis weight shows a saving of 33.3 pct with an increase in area of 50 pct.

Exports Mean Hardship

Some mills believe that Government restrictions on end use are not sufficient to balance the reduction in the amount of tin they are permitted to consume. Any export allocation orders that may be given the industry could impose a real hardship on both producers and consumers.

Worrying some producers is the effect government restrictions will have on electrolytic operations. Their problem revolves around the necessity of satisfying hot dip requirements for perishable packs at home and abroad. Electrolytic operations will suffer in proportion to the amount of hot dip required. This would penalize electrolytic operations, and make it more difficult to hold trained electrolytic line workers.

Production of black plate is expected to be increased at the expense of electrolytic because coffee, oil and shortening have already been put on black plate.

The industry also expects that some producers will be asked to make chemically or electro-chemically treated black plate for ends of processed food cans. This will mean either the installation of new equipment or the conversion of some electrolytic lines.

USAF Div. to Open Bottlenecks

Dayton, Ohio—To open the bottlenecks for firms working on Air Force Contracts, USAF will expand its Industrial Planning Div. and give it the new name of Production Resources Div., more in keeping with its added duties. Industrial planning work will continue by a separate group under the new division.

The new agency will attempt to aid manufacturers fill manpower needs and locate scarce metals and materials to complete Air Force contracts. Headquarters will be at the Wright-Patterson Air Force Base here.

CONTROLS *digest*

For more details see "You and Government Controls," The Iron Age, Jan. 4, 1951, p. 365. For full text of NPA regulations write U. S. Dept. of Commerce, Division of Printing Service, Room 6225 Commerce Bldg., Washington 25, D. C.

Subject	Order	Effective Date
General		
Inventory Control	NPA Reg. 1	Sept. 18
	Interpretation 1, 2, 3	Nov. 10
Priorities System	NPA Reg. 2	Oct. 3
DO Rating	Amend. 1	Oct. 3
DO Rating	Amend. 2	Dec. 29
DO Ratings	Delegation 1, 2, 3, 4	Nov. 1, 2, 3
Priorities (Canada)	NPA Reg. 3	Nov. 8
Hoarding	NPA Notice 1	Dec. 27
Auto Prices, Wages	ESA Reg. 1	Dec. 18
Ceiling Price Regulation	CPR 1	Jan. 26
Military supplies	Supplement 1	Feb. 1
Wage Increases	CPR 2	Feb. 9
Coal Prices	CPR 3	Feb. 1
Metals		
Aluminum distribution	NPA M 5	Oct. 27
Aluminum cutback	NPA M 7 (amended)	Feb 1
	Direction 1	Nov. 28
	Direction 2	Dec. 16
	Direction 3	Dec. 27
Aluminum scrap	NPA M 22	Mar. 1
Cadmium	NPA M 19	Jan. 1
Cobalt stocks	NPA M 10 (amended)	Dec. 30
Collapsible tubes	NPA M 27	Jan. 27
Columbium steels	NPA M 3	Oct. 19
Copper distribution	NPA M 11	Nov. 29
Copper use	NPA M 12 (amended)	Dec. 30
Copper readjustment	M-12 Direction 1	Feb. 1
Copper scrap	NPA M 16 (amended)	Jan. 1
Molybdenum cutback	NPA M 33 (amended)	Feb. 2
Nickel cutback	NPA M 14 (amended)	Feb. 1
Ores, metals	NPA Del. 5	Dec. 18
Steel	NPA M 1 (amended)	Jan. 22
Freight car program	Supl. 1	Oct. 26
Great Lakes ships	Supl. 2	Nov. 15
Canadian freight cars	Supl. 3	Dec. 15
Steel scrap	NPA M 20 (amended)	Jan. 29
Steel warehouses	NPA M 6 (amended)	Nov. 15
Tin inventories	NPA M 8	Jan. 9
Tinplate, terneplate	NPA M 24	Jan. 27
Metal cans	NPA M 25	Jan. 27
Tinplate closures	NPA M 27	Jan. 27
Tungsten	NPA M 30	Jan. 22
Zinc distribution	NPA M 9	Nov. 16
Zinc cutback	NPA M 15	Jan. 15
Miscellaneous		
Chemicals	NPA M 32	Jan. 23
Construction	NPA M 4	Oct. 27
	Amend. 1	Oct. 13
	Amend. 2	Nov. 15
Elec. components	NPA M 17	Oct. 18
Iron, Steel Scrap Prices	OPS	Feb. 7

Industry Controls This Week:

NPA Orders

M-14, Nickel use, as amended—Makers of Nickel alloy may not extend priority ratings to replace nickel used before Jan 1 stainless steel and high nickel content materials. Effective Feb. 1.

Seek Electronics Priorities

Washington—The Assn. of Electronic Parts and Equipment Mfrs. will present to NPA a resolution to obtain critical materials for fabrication of maintenance, repair and operating supplies for their industry, reports Kenneth C. Prince, mobilization committee. The plan will suggest a priority system.

Add 2396 Locomotives in 1950

Washington—Class I railroads put 2396 new locomotives in service during 1950, more than in any other year in the past 27 years, according to the Assn. of American Railroads. Of these, 2372 were diesel, 12 steam and 12 electric. New locomotives in 1949 totaled 1865, of which 1808 were diesels.

L&N Orders 5200 Freight Cars

Birmingham—The largest single order ever given the Pullman-Standard Car Mfg. Co. here, 5200 freight cars, was placed by Louisville & Nashville Railroad. The order is worth $27.5 million.

Ben Fairless Wants Termite Control Against Red Saboteurs

New York—Benjamin Fairless, president of U. S. Steel Corp., warned against the invisible Red army of trained termites who could bore from within to undermine American productive capacity—most feared by Moscow. He spoke at rites awarding him the Sales Executives Club Applause Award for outstanding salesmanship and public service at the Roosevelt Hotel here last week.

Armco's Hook Also Speaks

Also on the speaker's rostrum, Charles R. Hook, Armco Steel Corp. president, spoke against government financing of mills proposed by "certain groups who wanted to get into the steel business on a shoestring." He said that he was not eager to "run a race with a competitor who has little to lose because he is being financed by the American taxpayer."

Tactics of the trained termites, said Mr. Fairless, will be to attack management through the labor press and create strikes. They will also strive to play economic group against economic group and plot against public confidence in big business, he continued. Mr. Fairless advocated "Termite Control" by teamwork, knowledge of each other's problems by industry and government, and passing information to the public.

Plan Steel Mill in Virginia

Washington — Present fast tax writeoff provisions may give a real push to the regional steel mill for a local market. Another plan that may fit the pattern was disclosed here with Tidewater Industries, Inc., application for a certificate of necessity. The mill would be located in the James River basin, east of Richmond, Va.

Tidewater obtained a charter from the Virginia State Corp. Commission and it is said that the mill would use ore from South America and southwest Virginia coal and limestone.

Republic Metallurgical Service

helps leading bearing producer *save 30%*
IN HEAT TREATMENT COSTS

When you can take a top-quality precision bearing, improve the quality still further — *and cut production costs in the process* — there's sure to be an interesting story involved.

In this case, it's the story of many months of close cooperation between the metallurgical staffs of a leading roller-bearing producer and Republic Steel. It's a story that may be summarized like this:

Having determined that no appreciable advantages could be obtained from a change in alloy steel analyses, Republic's Field Metallurgist recommended a change in heat treatment cycle. The change was made. After a thorough testing period, the following benefits were noted:

1. **Furnace time required for carburizing — substantially reduced.**
2. **Re-heat treat — almost completely eliminated.**
3. **Parts distortion resulting from heat treat — also reduced.**

As a result, overall heat treatment costs were reduced by approximately 30% ... grinding time of carburized parts was effectively lessened ... bearing quality was further improved.

Perhaps you, too, are using the *right* analysis of alloy steel, but could profit through more efficient processing of that steel.

Republic — world's largest producer of alloy and stainless steels — offers you the *confidential* services of its 3-Dimensional Metallurgical Service without cost or obligation. Write, wire or phone.

REPUBLIC STEEL CORPORATION
Alloy Steel Division • Massillon, Ohio
GENERAL OFFICES • CLEVELAND 1, OHIO
Export Dept.: Chrysler Bldg., New York 17, N.Y.

"HOW ABOUT SECURITY?"
Labor has security. The farmer has security. But what about business, the third partner in today's economy? Shouldn't it have security, too? Read what Peter R. Levin has to say on this subject in "What Kind of Security for Business?" We'll send you reprints — if you'll write us.

Republic
ALLOY STEELS

REPUBLIC STEEL ®

Other Republic Products include Carbon and Stainless Steels—Sheets, Strip, Plates, Pipe, Bars, Wire, Pig Iron, Bolts and Nuts, Tubing

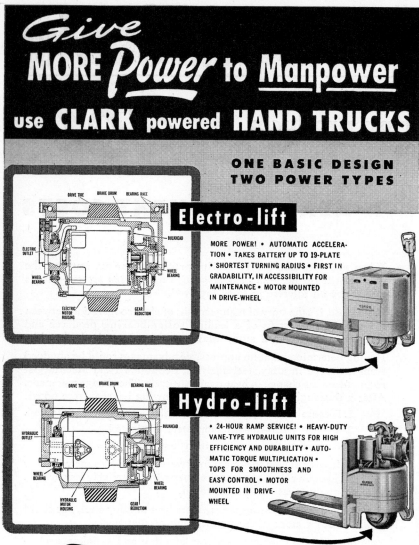

PA's Report Delivery Slowup, Price Hikes on Supplies Received

Chicago—The January report of the business survey committee of the Purchasing Agents Assn. of Chicago reveals that 70 pct of members reported suppliers' deliveries are slowing down and 76 pct reported paying higher prices for the suppies received.

Order backlogs continued for 60 pct reporting while buying policies of over 75 pct have extended beyond 90 days.

A large majority of those queried believe a realistic priorities allocation of materials should be instituted immediately. Three out of four of the reporting members feel present voluntary steel allocation allotments are not equitable.

Aluminum Assn. Elects Officers

New York—A. P. Cochran, of Cochran Foil Co., Inc., Louisville, Ky., has been elected president of the Aluminum Assn. A. V. Davis, of Alcoa, was re-elected chairman, and Donald M. White was reappointed secretary and treasurer. Vice-presidents are: I. T. Bennett, Revere Copper & Brass, Inc.; L. M. Brile, Fairmont Aluminum Co.; E. G. Fahlman, Permold Co.

Firm to Build at Olean, N. Y.

Milwaukee—Plans for erection of a plant at Olean, N. Y., to make protective power line equipment have been announced by Line Material Co. The 70,000 sq ft plant, on a 24 acre tract east of Olean, is expected to be in production by next fall. The local plant will be given over to munitions production.

NE Contracts Over $222 Million

Boston — Defense contract awards amounting to more than $222 million have been awarded in the New England area, according to the New England Council. The 6-state region is contributing 6 pct of national defense production compared with 9 pct during the peak of World War II.

OPS Steel Warehouse Order In Works; Would Affect Importers

Washington—Price adjustments for steel warehousers and importers are being considered by government price stabilizers.

The Office of Price Stabilization is drafting a new pricing regulation for the steel warehouse business that would put prices on a formula basis.

W. F. Sterling, metals price consultant, is studying means of affording relief to steel importers. The trade complains prices have been frozen at lower levels than those of competitors who recently entered the importing business. This makes it increasingly difficult for old firms to obtain foreign steel.

Information Service Set Up

Washington—The Office of Publication Information of the Defense Dept. has established an Industrial Services Branch for spreading information of interest to industry. The branch will combine functions of the Industrial Services Div. of the War Dept. and the Industrial Incentive Div. of Navy Dept. of World War II.

Introduce New Tungsten Electrode

Fitchburg, Mass. — New Hi-Thoria tungsten electrodes, producing a stable arc over a wider range of currents and resisting contamination by weld metal, have been announced by General Electric's Welding Divs. here The firm claims major applications will be for inert arc welding with direct current, straight polarity with either argon or helium gas. The electrodes reportedly reduce costs.

Solar Aids Sub-Contractors

New York—Solar Steel Corp. has opened a Washington information office to help small business get information on sub-contracts, contract specifications, and government procurement procedures. The free service is directed by Nathan Siegal, 219 Woodward Bldg.

• News of Industry •

Armour Foundation Scientists Can Now X-Ray Steel 8 in. Thick

Chicago—Scientists at Armour Research Foundation of Illinois Institute of Technology can now take X-ray pictures through solid steel 8 in. thick

A radioactive source shielded by 16 to 30 in. of concrete emits 65 billion gamma rays per second and has a penetration power similar to 1.8 grams of radium. With this source, hidden flaws in metal castings, welds, and soldered joints can be detected and crystals sensitive to radiation can be studied, according to Dr. Richard C. Humphreys, assistant chairman of the Foundation's physics department.

Technically termed cobalt 60, the radiation source enables physicists to make shadowgrams of subject material on photograph film placed between two sheets of lead. The exposures frequently require up to 48 hr.

English Boost Coal 58¢ a Ton

London—The National Coal Board has approved a boost in coal prices, as of Feb. 5, to compensate for government pay raises to miners aimed at increasing production.

The increase, 58¢ a long ton at the mine, will add $19,600,000 to the steel industry's annual fuel bill, or more than $1 a ton on finished steel. Whether or not the industry will absorb the increase has not been decided. Present fuel supplies are low and a long winter would result in large-scale shutdowns.

Ships Package Power Plant

Sunnyvale, Calif.—The largest and heaviest assembly of electrical apparatus, a 157,000-lb power plant, was shipped from Westinghouse Electric Corp.'s plant, here to Thomasville, Ga. To add 5000 kw to that city's power supply, the unit was delivered as a packaged unit on a special low-bed railroad car. It included a steam condenser, steam turbine, and electric generator.

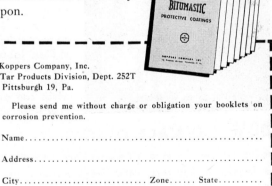

• News of Industry •

Joint Oil Products Terminal In Birmingham to Cover 61 Acres

Birmingham—Construction has begun on a million-dollar oil products terminal to be jointly owned and operated by Pan American, Pure Oil and Gulf Refining Companies.

The terminal, with storage tanks, pipelines, pumping stations and railroad sidings, will cover more than 61 acres.

Rives Construction Company, Birmingham, has the general contract. The storage tanks will be built by the Chicago Bridge & Iron Company and the railroad sidings by the Louisville & Nashville R.R.

Osborn to Modernize Plants

Cleveland—A program to cut smoke output at the Osborn Mfg. Co.'s plant in Cleveland and modernize its Henderson, Ky., plant has been announced. New equipment at Cleveland will include a coal and ash handling system, storage silo, and railroad coal unloading equipment.

A new 200 hp boiler will be installed at the Kentucky plant. Osborn, makers of industrial brushes and foundry molding machines, will spend $500,000.

Austria Blooming Mill Order

Pittsburgh—Lewis Foundry & Machine Div. of Blaw-Knox Co. has received an Austrian order for a two-high reversing blooming mill for installation at the Donawitz Steel Works of the Alpine Montan Co., largest steel producer in that country. The order amounts to more than $1 million and is the second received by Lewis from Austria for rolling mills and machinery through ECA.

U.S. Pays English Mill Fees

London—American engineering firms building a billet mill, slabbing mill, and blast furnace at Consett Iron Co., Ltd., County Durham, will be paid $583,000 from Marshall Plan funds, the Economic Cooperation Administration has announced.

**38 factory-trained fieldmen
in constant circulation**

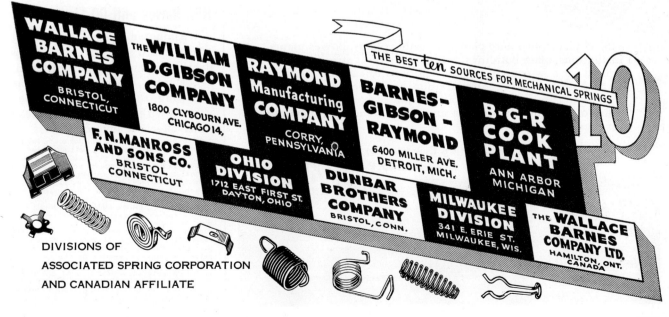

Practical Experience
PLUS
Unexcelled Facilities
in the FABRICATION
and
ERECTION
of
STRUCTURAL STEEL
in every industry

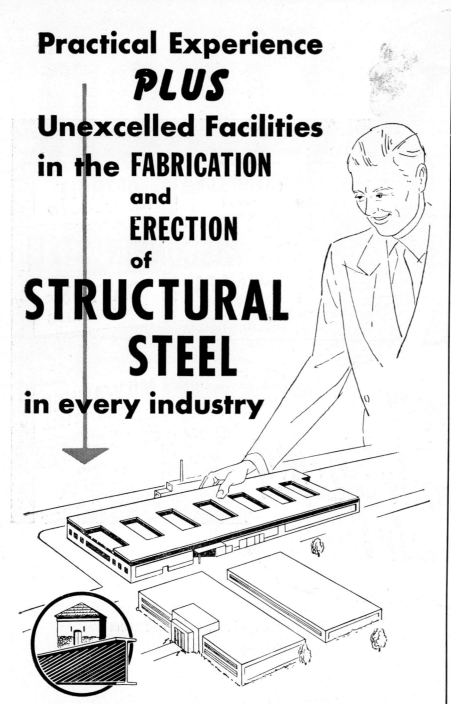

Steel plants, furniture plants, assembly plants, power plants, institutions, office buildings, bridges, wherever structural steel is used for new construction or additions to existing facilities —the Fort Pitt Bridge organization stands ready to assume the responsibility for fabrication and erection—backed by years of skill and experience and an outstanding reputation for dependability.

"Steel Permits Streamlining Construction with Safety, Endurance and Economy."

STEEL CONSTRUCTION NEWS

Fabricated steel awards this week included the following:

132 Tons, Rapides Parish, Louisiana, highway bridge for Louisiana Highway Department, Forcum & James Company, contractors, to Virginia Bridge Company, Birmingham.

100 Tons, Coffee County, Alabama, highway bridge, for Alabama Highway Department, E. W. Norrell, contractor, to Virginia Bridge Co., Birmingham.

Reinforcing bar awards this week included the following:

1300 Tons, Chicago, Veterans Administration office and clinic building 11., to Joseph T. Ryerson and Son.

1000 Tons, Duluth, Oliver Iron Mining Co., to U. S. Steel Supply Co.

970 Tons, Chicago, Wacker Drive, Madison to Washington Sts., to Joseph T. Ryerson and Son.

900 Tons, Mobile, Ala., grain elevator, Jacks Construction Co., to Ceco Steel Products Co., Birmingham.

600 Tons, Columbus, Ga., housing project, Columbus Housing Authority, to Ceco Steel Products Co., Birmingham.

500 Tons, Chicago, Kostner Ave. sewer contract 3A, to U. S. Steel Supply Co.

500 Tons, Louisville, school, to Truscon Steel Co.

310 Tons, Chicago, Catholic Order of Foresters building, to Joseph T. Ryerson and Son.

300 Tons, Peoria, Ill., apartment building, to Olney J. Dean Co.

250 Tons, Milwaukee, Cutler Hammer Co., to Joseph T. Ryerson and Son.

238 Tons, Huntsville, Ala., Redstone Arsenal buildings, Butler & Cobbs Co., contractors, to Truscon Steel Co., Birmingham.

190 Tons, Blue Island, Ill., Illinois Bell Telephone Co., to U. S. Steel Supply Co.

Reinforcing bar inquiries this week included the following:

7700 Tons, Chicago, 87th and Dorchester Sts. housing project.

1400 Tons, Peoria, Ill., U. S. Engineers.

1000 Tons, Lakewood, Ohio, Edgewater Drive apts.

405 Tons, Brockenridge, Pa., Allegheny Ludlum Steel Corp.

250 Tons, Keokuk, Iowa, senior high school.

165 Tons, Franklin, Wis., administration and dormitory building.

135 Tons, Milwaukee, Chain Belt Co.

125 Tons, Akron, Ohio, Goodyear Rubber Co., Plant 2.

NPA Raises Mill DO Limits

Washington — Steel mills got official word from National Production Authority's general counsel, Manley Fleischman, that the following DO limits are revised upward within the prescribed lead time, effective immediately:

Mechanical tubing, 15 pct; alloy mech. tubing, 60 pct; sheet bar carbon, 5 pct; sheet bar alloy, 5 pct; wire rods, 15 pct; cold-finished bars, carbon, 25 pct; alloy bars, 40 pct; drawn wire, 10 pct; rough forgings, carbon, 30 pct; rough forgings, alloy, 30 pct; blooms, billets, slabs, carbon, 10 pct total. (Was 5 pct on each and is a reduction.)

Alloy blooms, billets, slabs, 45 pct total; tube rounds, carbon, 15 pct; alloy tube rounds, 60 pct; hot-rolled bars, 15 pct; hot-rolled bars, projectile and shell quality, 35 pct of tonnage represented by above, 15 pct; alloy bars, 45 pct; projectile and shell quality alloy bars, 35 pct of tonnage represented by the above, 45 pct; reinforcing bars, 20 pct; hot-rolled sheets, 17 pct; cold-rolled sheets, 15 pct; galvanized sheets, 10 pct; hot-rolled strip, 12 pct; cold-rolled strip, 12 pct; sheets, all other coated, 10 pct; and effective with May, carbon and alloy plates, 20 pct.

The "Heat" is on

AT WISCONSIN STEEL

A hundred tons of molten steel...yet it's only part of the day's work at our mill as we tap heat after heat of quality steel.

We are straining our plant capacity to the utmost. The "heat" is on us and the entire industry to provide enough steel to meet the increasing demands of our changing economy.

At Wisconsin, we are not compromising rigid standards of quality. We are not making delivery promises we are unable to keep. Our policy is, and always has been, to produce and deliver as we promise. We are putting the "heat" on production to the limit of our ability. We feel sure that our customers will understand when we cannot supply their full requirements.

INTERNATIONAL HARVESTER

WISCONSIN STEEL COMPANY, affiliate of INTERNATIONAL HARVESTER COMPANY
180 North Michigan Avenue, Chicago 1, Illinois

WISCONSIN STEEL

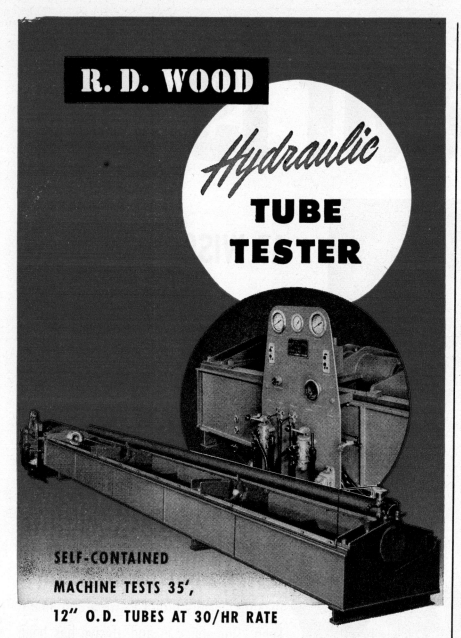

R.D. WOOD

Hydraulic TUBE TESTER

SELF-CONTAINED

MACHINE TESTS 35',

12" O.D. TUBES AT 30/HR RATE

HYDROSTATIC testing of tubes is fast and easy on this completely self-contained machine. It handles tubes 4½" to 12" of maximum 35' length at preset test pressures of 700 to 1500 pounds, sealed on the ends, outside or inside diameters as desired. Maximum diameter and length tubes are tested at an average rate of one every 2 minutes, but smaller size or shorter length tubes give proportionately larger production.

The entire cycle of automatic tube admission, centering, clamping, testing, draining and ejection is single-operator worked from one control panel. Write today for complete information.

HYDRAULIC PRESSES AND VALVES FOR EVERY PURPOSE · ACCUMULATORS · ALLEVIATORS · INTENSIFIERS

R.D. Wood Company

EST. 1803   PUBLIC LEDGER BUILDING, PHILADELPHIA 5, PA.

publications
Continued from Page 36

netic controllers for mill auxiliaries are discussed in the second section. These controllers use the newly-developed type M contactor, which is available in NEMA ratings from 25 to 2500 amp. The different controllers in the line are listed, with a typical circuit diagram presented and explained. Operation of the type AP plugging relays is detailed. Standard accessories for the controllers are also described. *Westinghouse Electric Corp.*
For free copy insert No. 8 on postcard, p. 37.

For Separating, Lifting

The line of Rapid magnetic separating and lifting equipment, claiming high functional efficiency and long life with negligible maintenance, is described in a new 8-p. bulletin. Various sizes and models of laboratory and production units are shown, along with several types of lifting magnets and electromagnetic chute separators made by this British company. A representative list of materials which have been treated by the magnetic equipment described is included. *Rapid Magnetic Machines Ltd.*
For free copy insert No. 9 on postcard, p. 37.

Fine Small Tubing

Information on the analyses available, production limits, commercial tolerances, temper designations and product descriptions of seamless and Weldrawn tubing, available in sizes from 0.010 to 1⅜ in. OD, is presented in a new 4-p. bulletin. Items described in the folder include mechanical tubing, shaped tubing, aircraft tubing, instrument tubing, and tubing for electronic products. Information on ordering and a list of distributors are shown. *Superior Tube Co.*
For free copy insert No. 10 on postcard, p. 37.

Instrument Uses Reviewed

The acceleration of research through the use of industrial and related instruments and apparatus is the subject of a new 84-p. book describing many types of equipment, which, alone or in combination with other apparatus, are being used in research and analytical studies. The book details the

CrysCoat
is in Good Company!

*Prepares Metal Surfaces for Painting

Patented Material and Process

"MEALMASTER", (Knox Stove Co.) the new, revolutionary combination Coal-Electric, Oil-Electric range that cooks, bakes and heats with either fuel is one of Americas' finest ranges. Beautifully designed, sturdily constructed ... "Mealmaster" is built to give dependable long-life service. And quality manufacture is carried on through to the durable finish. Here all painted surfaces are first CrysCoated for long-lasting paint adherence and protection against the spread of rust in case of accidental damage to the finish.

The Oakite *CrysCoat* Process may be just what you're looking for. With minimum equipment ... in minimum time ... at minimum cost you can (1) clean metal surfaces and condition them for painting; (2) improve the adhesion of paint to metal; (3) prevent corrosion before metal is painted; (4) localize corrosion under paint if finish is broken.

The Oakite *CrysCoat* Process Offers These Extras:

1. Eliminates operations ... uses less equipment
2. Cuts operating time
3. Uses less chemicals for cleaning and conditioning
4. Reduces heating costs
5. Saves cost of expensive acid-proof tanks and equipment
6. Saves cost of frequent descaling and desludging
7. Drag-out costs are less because of low original cost of solution
8. Saves paint
9. Cuts cost of rejects caused by rusting before painting

FREE ... illustrated folder describes the Oakite *CrysCoat* Process for use in before-paint-treatment of steel, aluminum sheet and castings, zinc die castings and galvanized surfaces. If you are engaged in the fabrication of civilian goods or the speedy production of defense orders—send for Folder F7642.

OAKITE PRODUCTS, INC., 30H Thames St., NEW YORK 6, N.Y.
Technical Service Representatives in Principal Cities of U. S. & Canada

SPECIALIZED INDUSTRIAL CLEANING
OAKITE
TRADE MARK REG. U. S. PAT. OFF.
MATERIALS · METHODS · SERVICE

February 15, 1951

For low-cost electrocleaning
use Wyandotte

publications
Continued

robotized polarograph, titrator and still applications, and describes various types of spectrometers and continuous gas analyzers. The section on precision laboratory measuring instruments includes mention of electronic indicators, the Electrometer, pyrometers for measuring low temperatures and radiation pyrometers for measuring temperatures up to 7000°F. This section also includes information on high vacuum gages, and pressure and force transducers. A third section reviews research apparatus components such as converters, balancing motors and servo amplifiers which constitute integral operating parts of research and analytical apparatus. *Brown Instruments Div., Minneapolis-Honeywell Regulator Co.*
For free copy insert No. 11 on postcard, p. 37.

Stud Driver Bulletin

A new 4-p. bulletin on Aero-Thread stud drivers covers the uses and operation of both hand and power models. Driving and removing studs of any standard or special thread form is illustrated, showing how the tool will drive and extract any stud without marring the stud's threads or mushrooming its end. Detailed instructions explain how to regulate the stud driver, how to drive and extract studs, and how to remove them from the driver. *Heli-Coil Corp.*
For free copy insert No. 12 on postcard, p. 37.

Die Casting Data

A new booklet on die castings—their advantages, how they are made, how they should be designed—provides basic information and help to anyone who has anything to do with die castings; it also contains essential technical information for designers and engineers. Steps in the manufacture of die castings are pictured, and the booklet includes information on draft, tolerance, wall thickness and core size requirements, tables of chemical and physical specifications for alloys, and a production timetable. *Die Castings Div., Hoover Co.*
For free copy insert No. 13 on postcard, p. 37.
Resume Your Reading on Page 37

What SUN has done for others...

STRATEGIC MULTI-MILLION-DOLLAR WIND TUNNEL DEPENDS ON **SUNVIS** TO OIL-CUSHION THE SENSITIVE BALANCE SYSTEM FOR MEASURING STRESSES

MANUFACTURER OF BUSINESS MACHINES COATS FACTORY AIR SUPPLY FILTERS WITH **SUNTAC** - IMPROVES PURIFICATION BY 50%

SUNISO IN THE COMPRESSOR ASSURES ICE FOR MAJOR SPORTS ARENA (ONE REFRIGERATION FAILURE COULD COST THE RINK $25,000)

SUN CUP **LC GREASE** PROVES EFFECTIVE IN MAST AND HOUSING OF TV AERIALS UNDER ALL WEATHER CONDITIONS-AND UNDER TEMPERATURES FROM -20° TO +150°

RIVER TOWBOAT SWITCHES FROM OIL TO **SUN ADHESIVE PRESSURE GREASE** FOR STERN-TUBE BEARINGS. RESULTS: COMPLETE SUCCESS, LONGER LIFE, BIG CUTS IN COSTS

...SUN can do for you!

Hydraulic Eye-Bender...

for production shaping of small stock and forming round or oval eyes, hooks, etc.

Above
Starting bend

Below
Finished eye

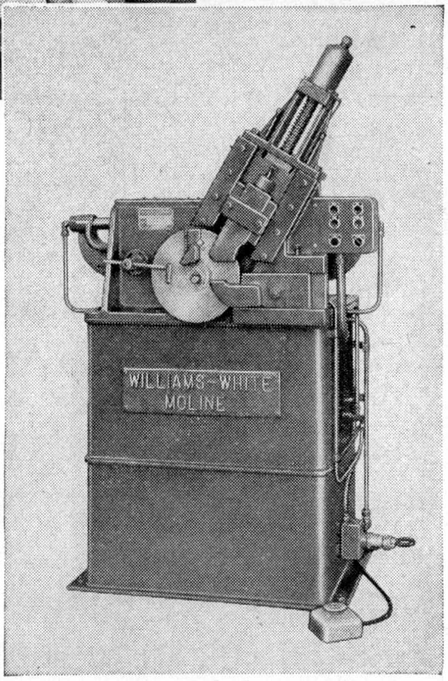

- Completely new, self-contained, hydraulically operated bender
- Welded steel construction
- Hydraulic pump with direct drive, 5HP electric motor
- Footbutton control; "inching" button provided for setting dies.
- Capacity: 1" diam. stock (hot) around a 1½" mandrel
- Strokes per minute, 20

The machine described above is typical of the up-to-date, efficient machines by WILLIAMS-WHITE & CO.

Write for free information regarding this and other WILLIAMS-WHITE machines, including presses, bulldozers, punches, shears, rolls and hammers for every type of heavy production.

MAKERS OF QUALITY PRODUCTION TOOLS FOR NEARLY 100 YEARS

WILLIAMS-WHITE & CO.
703 THIRD AVE., MOLINE, ILLINOIS

production ideas
Continued from Page 40
Continued from Page 40

start and stop of the work table with the advantage that the welding machine and the work table can be synchronized to start at the same time, by pushbutton control. The work table which tilts at any position about 360° rotates at infinitely variable speeds from zero

to 5 rpm with back-lash reduced to a minimum, allowing smooth, jerk-free rotation on Timken taper roller bearings. The work arm can be any length up to 16 in. An air cylinder attached to the table spindle provides that a pull-bar attached to the cylinder through the hollow spindle will clamp the workpiece to the table with advantageous speed. *Aronson Machine Co.*

For more data insert No. 29 on postcard, p. 37.

Heat Treating Furnace

The small production type furnace with the big furnace features.

Lite-Cast refractories are used in the heat treating chamber, insuring a quick heat up for efficiency

and long life. Specifications: chamber size, 7 x 7 x 12 in.; maximum temperature, 2000°F; heat up time, 3 speeds, slow, medium and fast. Controls: indicating type of thermocouple thermometer; electronic,

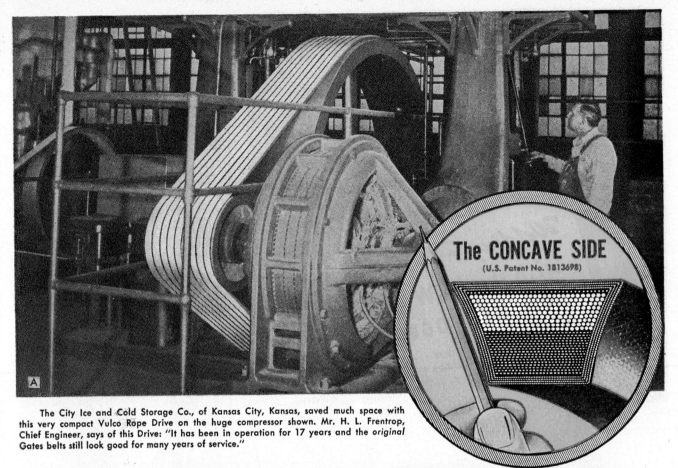

The CONCAVE SIDE
(U.S. Patent No. 1813698)

The City Ice and Cold Storage Co., of Kansas City, Kansas, saved much space with this very compact Vulco Rope Drive on the huge compressor shown. Mr. H. L. Frentrop, Chief Engineer, says of this Drive: "It has been in operation for 17 years and the original Gates belts still look good for many years of service."

This Simple Test Tells WHY the Concave Sides of Gates Vulco Ropes Mean *Longer Belt Life!*

Prove this *yourself*—in two minutes' time.

Take any V-belt that has *straight* sides. *Bend* that V-belt while you grip its sides between your fingers and your thumb. You will *feel* the sides of the belt *bulge out*—as shown in figure 1-A, below.

Clearly, that outbulge forces the sides of the belt to press *unevenly* against the V-pulley —and this concentrates the *wear* where the bulge is greatest.

Now, make the same test with the belt that is built with the Concave Sides—the Gates Vulco Rope.

Figures 2 and 2-A show clearly what happens when you bend a Vulco Rope. Instead of *bulging,* the precisely engineered Concave Sides merely *fill out* and become perfectly straight. There is no side-bulge. This belt, when bent, precisely fits its sheave groove.

Because there is *no bulging,* the sides of the Gates Vulco Rope always grip the *full* face of the V-pulley *evenly* and therefore wear uni-

formly—resulting in *longer belt life* and *lower belt costs for you.*

Only V-belts made by Gates are built with concave sides. Whenever you buy V-belts, be sure that you get the V-belt with the Concave Sides—The Gates Vulco Rope!

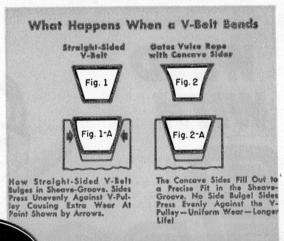

What Happens When a V-Belt Bends

Straight-Sided V-Belt | Gates Vulco Rope with Concave Sides

Fig. 1 | Fig. 2

Fig. 1-A | Fig. 2-A

How Straight-Sided V-Belt Bulges in Sheave-Groove. Sides Press Unevenly Against V-Pulley Causing Extra Wear At Point Shown by Arrows.

The Concave Sides Fill Out to a Precise Fit in the Sheave-Groove. No Side Bulge! Sides Press Evenly Against the V-Pulley—Uniform Wear—Longer Life!

CS-511

THE GATES RUBBER COMPANY
DENVER, U. S. A.
The World's Largest Makers of V-Belts

Gates VULCO ROPE **DRIVES**
Engineering Offices and Jobber Stocks **IN ALL INDUSTRIAL CENTERS** of the U. S. and 71 Foreign Countries

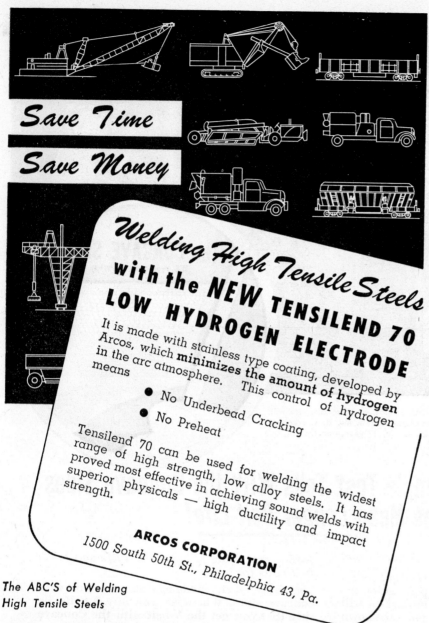

production ideas
Continued

pyrometric types; gold fuse overheating control. The furnaces are made in sizes and types to specifications up to 12 x 12 x 24 in. chamber. *Monogram Products Co., Inc.*
For more data insert No. 30 on postcard, p. 37.

Camera Microscope

For metallurgical work; built-in camera; magnification 4,5 to 2200X.

Among the outstanding features of this Reichert universal camera microscope MeF are the instant changeover from bright to dark ground illumination, the instantaneous transition from visual ob-

servation to photography and from ordinary to polarized light. Methods of illumination include vertical and oblique internal having bright grounds; flat oblique multilateral and unilateral external with dark grounds. The instrument is convenient for micrography. Drawing and projection micro hardness tester accessories are available. *William J. Hacker & Co.*
For more data insert No. 31 on postcard, p. 37.

Integral HP Gear-Motors

Maximum flexibility of mounting, easy to assemble on any apparatus.

With the addition of ventilated integral hp gear-motors, the Janette line includes ventilated, enclosed, and totally enclosed fan-cooled types of gear motors. The single phase type motors are available in 1 hp and smaller ratings; polyphase and dc motors are available through 7½ hp. Integral hp, class 2 gear-

Rubber Parts...

NEW CATALOG CONTAINS DATA ON COMPOUNDS, APPLICATIONS AND FABRICATION METHODS

This 16-page, illustrated, multi-colored catalog now is available to design, production, purchasing and management personnel. This publication has been compiled to familiarize readers with Stalwart-developed rubber compounds which feature resistance to (1) abrasion, (2) chemicals, (3) high and low temperatures, (4) petroleum products and derivatives, and (5) weathering. Sections of the catalog are devoted to the new and outstanding Silicone Rubber compounds, the major methods of fabrication, and Stalwart production facilities.

More than 60 Stalwart-developed compounds are listed by code number. Charted individually in conjunction with these compounds are their physical properties and general characteristics, as well as suggested applications.

Catalog 51SR-1 will be sent upon receipt of coupon or on letterhead request.

THE STALWART RUBBER COMPANY

Please send (without obligation) **your new 16-page, illustrated, multi-colored Catalog 51SR-1.**

NAME _____ TITLE _____

COMPANY _____

ADDRESS _____

CITY _____ ZONE _____ STATE _____

$\mathcal{S}$TALWART RUBBER COMPANY

2164 NORTHFIELD ROAD • BEDFORD, OHIO

to answer the HOT question...
specify LEBANON HEAT-RESISTANT Centrifugal Castings

CYLINDRICAL shapes cast in permanent molds by the exclusive Lebanon CENTRI-DIE process, are succeeding where other castings have failed. There are important reasons why Lebanon is able to produce these tough, service-proved castings with such outstanding qualities. First . . . *Lebanon experience*, covering some 39 years, has taught us how to work with difficult-to-cast heat and corrosion alloys. Second . . . *Lebanon testing* involves every proved

method (including the use of a million-volt X-Ray machine) to insure absolute structural integrity. Third . . . *Lebanon exclusive processes*, like our CENTRI-DIE method of casting, were developed to give castings superior physical properties, more uniformity and to retain high resistance to many types of destructive agents. For example, today's jet engines which are subject to extremely high temperatures, depend upon Lebanon CENTRI-DIE castings. Lebanon Castings can be made to meet A.I.S.I., A.S.T.M., A.M.S., Army and Navy specifications.

Write for your copy of the Lebanon CENTRI-DIE Bulletin so that you may have, at first hand, all the facts on this important process.

LEBANON STEEL FOUNDRY • LEBANON, PA.

"In the Lebanon Valley"

Other Lebanon quality products include centrifugal castings produced in refractory molds—illustration shows a typical casting made by this process.

LEBANON Castings
ALLOY AND STEEL

CIRCLE
L

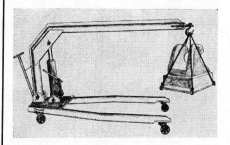

WE INCREASED PRODUCTION
71% WITH J&L "E" STEEL

J&L STEEL

(a story* about how to win customers and influence prospects)

"Got a minute? Well, let me tell you about what happened at our machine shop a couple of months ago when we first tried that new J&L "E" Steel. You wouldn't believe it was possible! (Confidentially, neither did we until we proved it to ourselves.) Here's what happened.

"We got an order to produce a big lot of plunger stops for solenoid starter switches. They're tricky to run, and you've got to be pretty careful every second. We'd read about "E" Steel in some of J&L's ads, and decided we might try some on this job.

"So we ordered some 17/32" E-33 "E" Steel stock, set up our B&S #2 and B&S #0 Automatics and began to turn out parts. We had used B-1113 for this job before and had been getting 350 pieces per hour. But we soon realized we could machine much faster with "E" Steel, and **we kept increasing speed until we were getting an average of 600 parts per hour. That's a 71%**

production increase!

"Next thing we discovered was that our tools were lasting twice as long and the chips were coming off better with "E" Steel than they did with B-1113. We also found that the finish on the parts had improved from 20% to 25%.

"That's why we've been using "E" Steel. We turn out work much faster and can take on more jobs. Our men like the way "E" Steel machines and our customers get better parts and better service. Everybody benefits!"

Get your copy of the booklet titled "A Progress Report on 'E' Steel." It outlines a series of 11 case histories from machine shops that have used "E" Steel with excellent results. Write for your copy.

―――――――

* *Based on an actual case history.*

Jones & Laughlin Steel Corporation
403 Jones & Laughlin Building
Pittsburgh 30, Penna.

Please send me a free copy of "A Progress Report on 'E' Steel."

Name_____

Title_____

Company_____

Address_____

_____

"E" Steel (U.S. Pat. No. 2,484,231) is easily identified by the distinctive blue color on the end of every bar.

JONES & LAUGHLIN STEEL CORPORATION

From its own raw materials, J&L manufactures a full line of carbon steel products, as well as certain products in OTISCOLOY and JALLOY (hi-tensile steels).

PRINCIPAL PRODUCTS: HOT ROLLED AND COLD FINISHED BARS AND SHAPES • STRUCTURAL SHAPES • HOT AND COLD ROLLED STRIP AND SHEETS • TUBULAR, WIRE AND TIN MILL PRODUCTS • "PRECISIONBILT" WIRE ROPE • COAL CHEMICALS

TIPS
by the dozen on a sure thing!

WEIGER-WEED

WW

TRADE MARK

SPOT WELDING TIPS

Resistance Welding knows this symbol. In shops small and large, it means *dependability* in Tips for sound, clean welds—efficient cooling—speedy welding—long tip life—less down time—welding at a saving! WW Tips are made of alloys of correct physical and electrical properties, precision-machined, water-tight and electrically tight fitting.

Replaceable tips, both straight and offset, WW leak-proof holders, seam welding wheels, electrodes and dies and special alloys for making your own dies are available in numerous standard sizes which you will find in the WW Catalog entitled "Standard Replaceable Welding Tips—Standard Water-Cooled Holders." Weiger Weed & Company, Division of Fansteel Metallurgical Corporation, 11644 Cloverdale Avenue, Detroit 4, Michigan.

Send for this free booklet of latest information on Resistance Welding.

WEIGER-WEED

WW

TRADE MARK

12801-A

Resistance Welding ELECTRODES
DIES · TIPS · WHEELS · HOLDERS

---

production ideas
Continued

through the extruder, assuring that the proper amount of insulating material is deposited to cover Underwriters' requirements. It saves material by preventing ex-

cessive amounts being deposited. The Federal Electricator is used in transferring the measurements to the speed control. The second indicator is used in setting the gage. Signal lights indicate what is going on at all times. *Federal Products Corp.*

For more data insert No. 34 on postcard, p. 37.

8000-Lb Line Pull Hoist

Safe and positive load control; economy in power consumption.

Clyde's band friction clutches enable the operator of the new hoist to handle full capacity loads with exceptional ease. Equalized linkage gives smooth and even friction

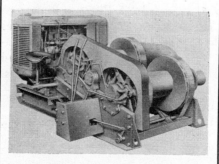

engagement and release. Outside friction surface affords better heat dissipation. Large diameter brakes permit safe and accurate load control by merely "toeing" the brake lever. Shafts rotate on ball bear-

---

Top-Flight Business Leaders
SHIP TODAY
VIA *TWA*

TWA's new, fast, all-cargo "Sky Merchant" Fleet speeds your shipments to important markets in U. S. and overseas.

Experienced shippers know the smartest way to ship is via dependable TWA *All-cargo* "Sky Merchants."

Direct routes and connections serve more than 60 important market centers in the U. S. *All-cargo* flights overseas every week end, as well as frequent flights direct to London, Frankfurt, Paris, Zurich, Geneva, Milan, Rome.

Check these outstanding advantages:

1. Save shipping time.
2. Obtain faster, wider distribution.
3. Replenish stocks practically overnight.
4. Reduce risk of pilferage, damage, loss.
5. Save costs on crating and insurance.
6. Receive careful, dependable handling of all shipments by TWA cargo specialists.
7. And remember, TWA service meets the urgency of every emergency.

Make a memo—NOW—to phone TWA (Trans World Airlines) for information, rates, schedules, quick pick-up service. Request interesting folder from Cargo Sales Manager, TWA, 60 East 42nd Street, New York 17, N. Y.

All TWA flights carry Air Mail and Air Cargo.

TWA
TRANS WORLD AIRLINES
U.S.A. · EUROPE · AFRICA · ASIA

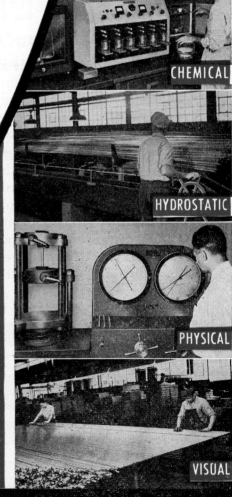

FROM NINE CORES
..TO ONE!

UNITCAST ENGINEERING
SAVES ON PRODUCTION COSTS ..
IMPROVES QUALITY!

The illustrated steel casting was formerly made from nine hand made cores, resulting not only in slow production but loss of accuracy. So Unitcast Engineering went to work. By replacing the nine hand made cores with one unit blown core, increased production was balanced, quality improved, and all core holes on every casting were in perfect alignment. Here's just one of the many ways Unitcast facilities provide better customer service, improve the product and keep production costs competitive.

UNITCAST
Corporation
QUALITY STEEL CASTINGS

Give us a chance to offer a "cast steel" answer for your parts problem. Our suggestions while your product is in the design stage will pay continuous dividends. Write or call today. Unitcast Corporation, Steel Casting Division, Toledo 9, Ohio. *In Canada:* Canadian-Unitcast Steel, Ltd., Sherbrooke, Quebec.

UNITCASTINGS ARE FOUNDRY ENGINEERED

---

production ideas
Continued

ings to provide a higher degree of hoist efficiency and economy with longer, trouble free service. These Frame-5 hoists are available with gasoline, diesel or electric power. *Clyde Iron Works, Inc.*
For more data insert No. 35 on postcard, p. 37.

Side-Dump Trucks
For use in machine shops; handle dry material—waste, parts, bulk.

The side-dump feature makes disposal of machine chips and scrap easy, eliminating shoveling and other time-consuming operations. The trucks can be drawn by hand

or powered, singly or in trains. They can also be used for temporary storage of materials. The hod is made of sheet metal, welded at the joints, and counterbalanced to render the dumping easy. Frame is structural steel; wheels, iron or rubber. Capacity is approximately 1 cu yd. *Klaas Machine & Mfg. Co.*
For more data insert No. 36 on postcard, p. 37.

Pressure Valve
Incorporates Shear-Seal principle that gives extreme pressure control.

The Shear-Seal principle points up the fact that to shear off the fluid flow requires the least amount of effort. A pressure balanced, self-aligning, tubular valve seat keeps perfect intimate contact with the mating surface of an optically flat porting disk. Rotary movement of the disk opens and closes the flow passages. Fluid flow is always through the hole in the center of the Shear-Seal, never across sealing surfaces. The wiping and lapping action between sealing members during each operation is said to improve the sealing properties of the valve with use. Bodies are high tensile hydraulic bronze

THOMAS *Flexible* ALL METAL COUPLINGS

FOR POWER TRANSMISSION • REQUIRE NO MAINTENANCE

Patented Flexible Disc Rings of special steel transmit the power and provide for parallel and angular misalignment as well as free end float.

Thomas Couplings have a wide range of speeds, horsepower and shaft sizes: ½ to 40,000 HP — 1 to 30,000 RPM.

Specialists on Couplings for more than 30 years

PATENTED FLEXIBLE DISC RINGS

BACKLASH FRICTION WEAR and CROSS-PULL are eliminated LUBRICATION IS NOT REQUIRED!

THE THOMAS PRINCIPLE GUARANTEES PERFECT BALANCE UNDER ALL CONDITIONS OF MISALIGNMENT.

• • •

NO MAINTENANCE PROBLEMS.

• • •

ALL PARTS ARE SOLIDLY BOLTED TOGETHER.

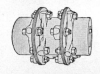

Write for the latest reprint of our Engineering Catalog.

THOMAS FLEXIBLE COUPLING CO.
WARREN, PENNSYLVANIA

---

production ideas
Continued

and available with regular in-line porting, straight, or manifold porting. Production models cover a complete range of types and pressures and their service ratings include all common industrial media. *Barksdale Valves.*

For more data insert No. 37 on postcard, p. 37.

Double-Step Ladders

Steps on both ends; two or more people can use ladder at one time.

When no one is on the ladder it rolls easily on swivel casters. The weight of a person, however, causes the spring mounted casters to deflect so that rubber-tipped legs en-

gage the floor and the ladder will not roll. Frame of the ladder is welded tubular steel; steps are expanded steel. The ladder is 30 in. high x 17½ in. wide x 48 in. deep. Top step has a 20-in. tread, others have a 7-in. tread. *Ballymore Co.*

For more data insert No. 38 on postcard, p. 37.

Sealing Washers

Of fabricated compound, seals out air, dust, water and water vapor.

The washer was developed for the automobile and other industries confronted with the problem of sealing bolts, screws and other similar parts. It has strong adherence to faying surfaces, and has proved effective, it is stated, in eliminating squeaks and rattles. The washer is made in standard sizes. Inner dimensions permit it to be slipped freely over the shaft, bolt or screw. As the bolt or screw is tightened, the sealer is forced into the annular space between the bolt and the rim of the hole, effecting a water-tight seal. *Presstite Engineering Co.*

For more data insert No. 39 on postcard, p. 37.

Resume Your Reading on Page 41

IRON AGE *markets and prices*

higher limits on DO orders—Steel mill officials in the Midwest do not believe increases in DO limits (see story, p. 124) will change their position noticeably on extended DO orders. One mill official states that some consumers were aware of the revisions before the mill and were holding their DO's ready to put them on as soon as the order came out. In fact some consumers holding DO's called up 2 days previous to the order's issuance to place their tonnage. Mills are holding back April quotas until they can be revised. Some mills expect an additional cutback in quotas of 10 pct for April.

stainless steel—The small amount of stainless steel left over for non-rated customers is leading those in the industry to believe the mills are booking way over their DO percentages on stainless. One producer is taking on no more non-rated consumer business, except one product (hot-rolled annealed bars) until the end of the second quarter. It is not likely the mills will open their books on stainless sheet during the third quarter because of the great influx of rated orders and a considerable carry-over expected from the second quarter. This comes after the mills didn't open for stainless sheet at all in the second.

super NE steels—Alloy steels containing only half as much strategic alloys as the famous NE steels have been perfected and are being produced to conserve supplies of scarce nickel, molybdenum and chrome, the American Iron & Steel Institute reported early this week. The new alloys contain an average of 0.30 pct nickel, 0.12 moly and one series contains 0.25 chrome and the other series 0.43 chrome. They also make use of boron treatment, which increases strength without reducing toughness. AISI's technical committee on alloy steel has been working on these new steels for several months because of the shortage of alloys caused by the jet program.

auto cutback—NPA is getting ready to restrict the amount of steel going into the auto industry. They have hinted at a cutback of as much as 40 pct. Last year the industry consumed over 15.5 million tons of finished steel, almost 22 pct of the national total. A 40 pct restriction would channel 6.2 million tons of steel to other uses. Much of the steel consumed in Detroit is cold-rolled sheet, production of which in some cases can be shifted to plate. Because of the danger of large-scale unemployment the initial restriction on auto steel will probably be considerably less than 40 pct.

back to normal—Fully recovered from the recent rail strike, U. S. Steel Co. has all 11 blast furnaces operating in South Chicago, and 11 of 12 operating at Gary. The one furnace at Gary is down for relining. Lack of cars caused by the rail strike is still being felt, but it is expected the pile-up of material at the finishing mills will be eliminated within the next several days.

substitute—Indications are that auto makers are planning to substitute paint for plating. Either aluminum or matching car paint will probably be tried. The paint may be used either with or without an overall plastic coating.

westward ho—Commercial Shearing and Stamp Co. of Chicago and Youngstown, O., will construct a $750,000 plant in Salt Lake City, on a 20-acre site in Industrial Center which it expects to have in operation by August.

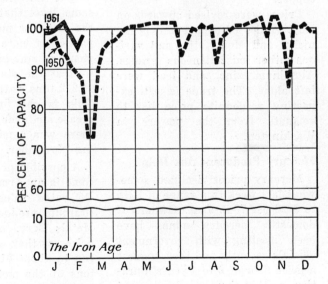

Steel Operations**

District Operating Rates—Per Cent of Capacity**

Week of	Pittsburgh	Chicago	Youngstown	Philadelphia	West	Buffalo	Cleveland	Detroit	Wheeling	South	Ohio River	St. Louis	East	Aggregate
Feb. 4	94.0*	94.2*	91.0	96.0	95.0*	104.0	22.0*	108.0*	100.0	106.0	88.2	95.1	105.0	93.0*
Feb. 11	96.0	100.5	90.0	98.0	101.7	104.0	86.5	109.0	100.0	104.0	88.0	95.1	112.6	98.5

* Revised.
** Beginning Jan. 1, 1951, operations are based on an annual capacity of 104,229,650 net tons.

nonferrous metals | *outlook and market activities*

NONFERROUS METALS PRICES

	Feb. 7	Feb. 8	Feb. 9	Feb. 10	Feb. 12	Feb. 13
Copper, electro, Conn....	24.50	24.50	24.50	24.50	....	24.50
Copper, Lake delivered...	24.625	24.625	24.625	24.625	....	24.625
Tin, Straits, New York....	$1.825	$1.825	$1.825	....	....	$1,825*
Zinc, East St. Louis	17.50	17.50	17.50	17.50	....	17.50
Lead, St. Louis	16.80	16.80	16.80	16.80	....	16.80

Note: Quotations are going prices.

*Tentative.

by R.Hatschek

New York—Following the general price freeze order, nonferrous scrap dealers boosted their buying prices on many items to a level equal to or near the highest they paid during last December. Conversion deals, authorized by the National Production Authority, have warranted a price of 21½¢ per lb for No. 1 heavy copper.

Prices were revised upwards on most grades of copper and brass, nickel and Monel, tin, and various other miscellaneous grades. Aluminum, zinc, and lead were left alone. The trade is still expecting a definite price list to emanate from the powers in Washington.

Mercury Producers Ask Help

Mercury prices declined somewhat last week to a range of $216 to $220 per 76-lb flask. Owners of domestic mercury mines have been meeting with government officials recently and they suggest a price floor of 2 to 4 years' duration, so that they may be assured of adequate returns for reopening their mines.

At present, U. S. mercury production is at an extremely low ebb, reported to be the lowest level in 100 years, and the price of this commodity has been set wherever the European producers want it. The present high level was reached only after practically all domestic producers were forced out of the market by the underselling of Spanish and Italian interests.

January Output Stable

Production figures of the American Zinc Institute show January output continuing at about the same level that prevailed during the last few months of 1950. Of particular note is the fact that stocks of zinc increased from 8884 tons at the start of the year to 10,212 tons at the end of January. This is the first significant increase in over a year, although there was a minor increase during November.

A possible preview of things to come is an Army Ordnance Dept. DO rated order for 75,000 lb of titanium products from Titanium Metals Corp. of America. With prices as they are today, this will run to about $1 million. Some 60 tons of the metal were produced in 1950, but increased production will no doubt have the effect of reducing the current high costs.

Titanium Boom Coming?

It is already economically practical to use titanium in aircraft for the weight saving and the cost of a more efficient ground force will be more than paid for by the saving of lives in the field. The use and production of titanium can be expected to mushroom in these critical times.

As we go to press, the Singapore tin market is at approximately $1.91 to $1.92 per lb for April delivery. With a domestic ceiling of $1.825 (actually varying according to the individual sellers) an impossible situation has arisen and there has been no trading up to noon Tuesday. It is expected that the tin trade will appeal to the government for a solution to this problem. We continue to tentatively quote the most common ceiling price.

Wilson Asks Tariff Repeal

While brass mills are laying off workers and going to a 4-day work week and users of copper and brass mill products are yelling for relief in the copper shortage, Defense Mobilizer Charles E. Wilson got on record as being against the 2¢ tariff. It is reported that he asked the Senate Banking Committee to use its influence to have the duty repealed. Mr. Wilson contends that the copper shortage is not as acute as some people claim and that the elimination of the tax would permit the import of sufficient supplies of the vital metal.

MILL PRODUCTS

(Cents per lb, unless otherwise noted)

Aluminum

(Base 30,000 lb, f.o.b. ship. pt. frt. allowed)

Flat Sheet: 0.188 in., 2S, 3S, 30.1¢; 4S, 61S-O, 32¢; 52S, 34.1¢; 24S-O, 24S-OAL, 32.9¢; 75S-O, 75S-OAL, 39.9¢; 0.081 in., 2S, 3S, 31.2¢; 4S, 61S-O, 33.5¢; 52S, 35.6¢; 24S-O, 24S-OAL, 34.1¢; 75S-O, 75S-OAL, 41.8¢; 0.032 in., 2S, 3S, 32.9¢; 4S, 61S-O, 37.1¢; 52S, 39.8¢; 24S-O, 24S-OAL, 41.7¢; 75S-O, 75S-OAL, 52.2¢.

Plate: ¼ in. and heavier: 2S, 3S, 28.3¢; 4S-F, 30.2¢; 52S-F, 31.8¢; 61S-O, 30.8¢; 24S-O, 24S-OAL, 32.4¢; 75S-O, 75S-OAL, **38.8¢.**

Extruded Solid Shapes: Shape factors 1 to 5, 36.2¢ to 74.5¢; 12 to 14, 36.9¢ to 89¢; 24 to 26, 39.6¢ to \$1.16; 36 to 38, 47.2¢ to \$1.70.

Rod, Rolled: 1.5 to 4.5 in., 2S-F, 3S-F, 37.5¢ to 33.5¢; cold-finished, 0.375 to 3 in., 2S-F, 3S-F, 40.5¢ to 35¢.

Screw Machine Stock: Rounds, 11S-T3, ⅛ to 11/32 in., 53.5¢ to 42¢; ⅜ to 1½ in., 41.5¢ to 39¢; 1 9/16 to 3 in., 38.5¢ to 36¢; 17S-T4 lower by 1.5¢ per lb. Base 5000 lb.

Drawn Wire: Coiled, 0.051 to 0.374 in., 2S, 39.5¢ to 29¢; 52S, 48¢ to 35¢; 56S, 51¢ to 42¢; 17S-T4, 54¢ to 37.5¢; 61S-T4, 48.5¢ to 37¢; 75S-T6, 84¢ to 67.5¢.

Extruded Tubing, Rounds: 63S-T5, OD in in.: 1¼ to 2, 37¢ to 54¢; 2 to 4, 33.5¢ to 45.5¢; 4 to 6, 34¢ to 41.5¢; 6 to 9, 34.5¢ to 43.5¢.

Roofing Sheet, Flat: 0.019 in. x 28 in. per sheet, 72 in., \$1.142; 96 in., \$1.522; 120 in., \$1.902; 144 in., \$2.284. Gage 0.024 in. x 28 in., 72 in., \$1.379; 96 in., \$1.839; 120 in., \$2.299; 144 in., \$2.759. Coiled Sheet: 0.019 in. x 28 in., 28.2¢ per lb.; 0.024 in. x 28 in., 26.9¢ per lb.

Magnesium

(F.o.b. mill, freight allowed)

Sheet and Plate: FS1-O, ¼ in. 63¢; 3/16 in. 65¢; ⅛ in. 67¢; B & S Gage 10, 68¢; 12, 72¢; 14, 78¢; 16, 85¢; 18, 93¢; 20, \$1.05; 22, \$1.27; 24, \$1.67. Specification grade higher. Base: 30,000 lb.

Extruded Round Rod: M, diam in., ¼ to 0.311 in., 74¢; ½ to ¾ in., 57.5¢; 1¼ to 1.749 in., 53¢; 2½ to 5 in., 48.5¢. Other alloys higher. Base: Up to ¾ in. diam, 10,000 lb; ¾ to 2 in., 20,000 lb; 2 in. and larger, 30,000 lb.

Extruded Solid Shapes, Rectangles: M. In weight per ft, for perimeters less than **size** indicated, 0.10 to 0.11 lb, 3.5 in., 62.3¢; 0.22 to 0.25 lb, 5.9 in., 59.3¢; 0.50 to 0.59 lb, 8.6 in., 56.7¢; 1.8 to 2.59 lb, 19.5 in., 53.8¢; 4 to 6 lb, 28 in., 49¢. Other alloys higher. Base, in weight per ft of shape: Up to ½ lb, 10,000 lb; ½ to 1.80 lb, 20,000 lb; 1.80 lb and heavier, 30,000 lb.

Extruded Round Tubing: M, wall thickness, outside diam, in., 0.049 to 0.057, ¼ in. to 5/16, \$1.40; 5/16 to ⅜, \$1.26; ½ to ⅝, 93¢; 1 to 2 in., 76¢; 0.165 to 0.219, ⅝ to ¾, 61¢; 1 to 2 in., 57¢; 3 to 4 in., 56¢. Other alloys higher. Base, OD in in.; Up to 1½ in., 10,000 lb; 1½ in. to 3 in., 20,000 lb; 3 in. and larger, 30,000 lb.

Titanium

(10,000 lb base, f.o.b. mill)

Commercially pure and alloy grades: Sheet and strip, HR or CR, \$15; Plate, HR, \$12; Wire, rolled and/or drawn, \$10; Bar, HR or forged, \$6; Forgings, \$6.

Nickel and Monel

(Base prices, f.o.b. mill)

	"A" Nickel	Monel
Sheets, cold-rolled	71½	57
Strip, cold-rolled	77½	60
Rods and bars	67½	55
Angles, hot-rolled	67½	55
Plates	69½	56
Seamless tubes	100½	90
Shot and blocks	....	50

Copper, Brass, Bronze

(Freight prepaid on 200 lb includes duty)

	Sheets	Rods	Extruded Shapes
Copper	41.03	....	40.63
Copper, h-r	....	36.88	....
Copper, drawn.	....	38.18	....
Low brass	39.15	38.84	....
Yellow brass	38.28	37.97	....
Red brass	40.14	39.83	....
Naval brass	43.08	38.61	38.07
Leaded brass.	....	32.63	36.70
Com'l bronze.	41.13	40.82	....
Mang. bronze.	45.96	40.65	41.41
Phos. bronze..	60.20	60.45	....
Muntz metal ..	40.43	36.74	37.99
Ni silver, 10 pct	49.27	51.49	....
Arch. bronze ..	....	....	35.11

PRIMARY METALS

(Cents per lb, unless otherwise noted)

Aluminum ingot, 99+%, 10,000 lb, freight allowed	19.00
Aluminum pig	18.00
Antimony, American, Laredo, Tex.	42.00
Beryllium copper, 3.75-4.25% Be...	\$1.56
Beryllium aluminum 5% Be, Dollars per lb contained Be	\$69.00
Bismuth, ton lots	\$2.25
Cadmium, del'd	\$2.55
Cobalt, 97-99% (per lb)	\$2.10 to \$2.17
Copper, electro, Conn. Valley	24.50
Copper, Lake, delivered	24.625
Gold, U. S. Treas., dollars per oz.	\$35.00
Indium, 99.8%, dollars per troy oz.	\$2.25
Iridium, dollars per troy oz.	\$200
Lead, St. Louis	16.80
Lead, New York	17.00
Magnesium, 99.8+%, f.o.b. Freeport, Tex., 10,000 lb	24.50
Magnesium, sticks, 100 to 500 lb	42.00 to 44.00
Mercury, dollars per 76-lb flask, f.o.b. New York	\$216-\$220
Nickel, electro, f.o.b. New York	53.55
Nickel oxide sinter, f.o.b. Copper Cliff, Ont., contained nickel	46.75
Palladium, dollars per oz.	\$24.00
Platinum, dollars per troy oz.	\$90 to \$93
Silver, New York, cents per oz.	90.16
Tin, New York	\$1.825
Titanium, sponge	\$5.00
Zinc, East St. Louis	17.50
Zinc, New York	18.22
Zirconium copper, 50 pct	\$6.20

REMELTED METALS

Brass Ingot

(Cents per lb delivered, carloads)

85-5-5-5 ingot	
No. 115	29.00
No. 120	28.50
No. 123	28.00
80-10-10 ingot	
No. 305	35.00
No. 315	32.00
88-10-2 ingot	
No. 210	46.25
No. 215	43.25
No. 245	36.00
Yellow ingot	
No. 405	25.00
Manganese bronze	
No. 421	29.75

Aluminum Ingot

(Cents per lb, 30,000 lb lots)

95-5 aluminum-silicon alloys	
0.30 copper, max.	33.25-34.25
0.60 copper, max.	33.00-34.00
Piston alloys (No. 122 type)	30.50-31.00
No. 12 alum. (No. 2 grade)	30.00-30.50
108 alloy	30.25-30.75
195 alloy	31.25-31.75
13 alloy	33.50-34.00
ASX-679	30.50-31.00

Steel deoxidizing aluminum, notch-bar granulated or shot

Grade 1—95-97½%	32.00-32.50
Grade 2—92-95%	30.25-30.75
Grade 3—90-92%	29.25-29.75
Grade 4—85-90%	28.75-29.25

ELECTROPLATING SUPPLIES

Anodes

(Cents per lb, freight allowed, 500 lb lots)

Copper

Cast, oval, 15 in. or longer	39⅛
Electrodeposited	33⅜
Rolled, oval, straight, delivered.	38⅞
Forged ball anodes	43
Brass, 80-20	
Cast, oval, 15 in. or longer	34¾
Zinc, oval	26½
Ball anodes	25½
Nickel 99 pct plus	
Cast	70.50
Rolled, depolarized	71.50
Cadmium	\$2.80
Silver 999 fine, rolled, 100 oz lots, per troy oz., f.o.b. Bridgeport, Conn.	79½

Chemicals

(Cents per lb, f.o.b. shipping points)

Copper cyanide, 100 lb drum	52.15
Copper sulfate, 99.5% crystals, bbl.	12.85
Nickel salts, single or double, 4-100 lb bags, frt. allowed	20½
Nickel chloride, 375 lb drum	27½
Silver syanide, 100 oz lots, per oz.	67¼
Sodium cyanide, 96 pct domestic 200 lb drums	19.25
Zinc cyanide, 100 lb drums	45.85

SCRAP METALS

Brass Mill Scrap

(Cents per pound, add ½¢ per lb for shipments of 20,000 to 40,000 lb; add 1¢ for more than 40,000 lb)

	Heavy	Turnings
Copper	23	22¼
Yellow Brass	20½	18¾
Red brass	21½	20¾
Comm. bronze	21¾	21
Mang. bronze	19½	18⅝
Brass rod ends	19⅞	....

Custom Smelters' Scrap

(Cents per pound, carload lots, delivered to refinery)

No. 1 copper wire	21.50
No. 2 copper wire	20.00
Light copper	19.00
Refinery brass	19.50*
Radiators	15.00

*Dry copper content.

Ingot Makers' Scrap

(Cents per pound, carload lots, delivered to producer)

No. 1 copper wire	23.00
No. 2 copper wire	22.00
Light copper	21.00
No. 1 composition	22.00
No. 1 comp. turnings	21.50
Rolled brass	18.50
Brass pipe	20.50
Radiators	17.50
Heavy yellow brass	17.00
Aluminum	
Mixed old cast	18½—19
Mixed new clips	20½
Mixed turnings, dry	18½
Pots and pans	18½—19
Low copper	21½—22

Dealers' Scrap

(Dealers' buying prices, f.o.b. New York in cents per pound)

Copper and Brass

No. 1 heavy copper and wire.	21½
No. 2 heavy copper and wire.	20
Light copper	19
New type shell cuttings	19
Auto radiators (unsweated)..	15½—16
No. 1 composition	19—19½
No. 1 composition turnings	18½—19
Clean red car boxes	17½—18
Cocks and faucets	17½—18
Mixed heavy yellow brass..	14½—15
Old rolled brass	15½—16
Brass pipe	18½—19
New soft brass clippings	17½—18
Brass rod ends	16½—17
No. 1 brass rod turnings	16—16½

Aluminum

Alum. pistons and struts	12—13
Aluminum crankcases	15—16
2S aluminum clippings	18½—19½
Old sheet and utensils	15—16
Borings and turnings	12½—13
Misc. cast aluminum	15—16
Dural clips (24S)	15—16

Zinc

New zinc clippings	14½—15
Old zinc	11—11¼
Zinc routings	8½—9
Old die cast scrap	8—8¼

Nickel and Monel

Pure nickel clippings	90—100
Clean nickel turnings	80—90
Nickel anodes	90—100
Nickel rod ends	90—100
New Monel clippings	30—35
Clean Monel turnings	20—25
Old sheet Monel	25—30
Inconel clippings	30—35
Nickel silver clippings, mixed.	16—18
Nickel silver turnings, mixed	15—16

Lead

Soft scrap, lead	15—15¼
Battery plates (dry)	8¾—9

Magnesium

Segregated solids	9—10
Castings	5½—6½

Miscellaneous

Block tin	120—125
No. 1 pewter	80—85
No. 1 auto babbitt	75—80
Mixed common babbitt	12¼—12½
Solder joints	23—24
Siphon tops	75—80
Small foundry type	18¼—18½
Monotype	16¾—17
Lino. and stereotype	16½—16¾
Electrotype	15—15½
Hand picked type shells	11½—11¾
Lino. and stereo. dross	8¾—9
Electro. dross	6¾—7

SCRAP *iron and steel*

markets
prices
trends

**Scrap men seek clarification on pricing order
... Light needed on some vague clauses and
inequities ... Market activity sags.**

What the scrap trade needs is a little light on the subject of iron and steel scrap pricing. When, bit by bit, official interpretations and rulings are extracted from Washington the dead market of last week may quicken. Clarification must come quickly for capacity steel output is at stake.

The trade last week spent most of its time in interpreting the order and trying to arrive at something favorable for them. But there was too much room for doubt, and scrappies then wondered if OPS would later swat their ideas aside. Others saw only painful tidings in small print clauses and sent up a howl.

Reports of order inequities and fuzzy wording came from all scrap centers. The chief complaint in Pittsburgh was against the ban on broker-to-broker commissions and split commissions.

PITTSBURGH—The need for clarification and amendment of the scrap price control order is apparent. A rereading of the schedule has brought to light some apparent inequities and loose wording that ESA will be asked to rectify. Number one on the list is the prohibition against broker-to-broker commissions and split commissions. Some brokers say they will be seriously handicapped if the restriction is allowed to stand. The trade would also like more specific definitions on grading. Another question to be answered is whether preparation fees may be split. The preparation allowance of $2.50 for low phos is considered by many to be too low. Very little trading has been done under the new schedule. Yards were virtually swept clean in last week's rush to ship before the controlled prices became effective.

CHICAGO—Some quarters in the trade expect scrap movement during February to be slow until various points in the recent price control order are clarified. Shipments held up because of the recent rail strike started to pick up early in the

week although the situation was far from normal. The bulk of material moving was that loaded before the recent control order. The problem facing members of the trade is the determination of what grades consumers will accept under the price control order and from what shipping points they will accept them.

PHILADELPHIA—Trade reaction to last week's price rollback order was generally favorable. The prices are pretty close to what was anticipated in this area. There is one question: Will openhearths be permitted to buy electric furnace scrap? It is felt that the intention was that the openhearths would not be allowed to do this but the order is not clear. A combination of the scrap order, extremely cold weather, the car shortage and the switchmen's strike contributed to a very slow week in this area. Mills are poorly supplied.

NEW YORK—Brokers here are waiting for Washington to give official interpretation to ambiguous clauses of the scrap pricing order. Meanwhile the market is sluggish after last week's bolt to ship everything but the kitchen sink before deadline time. On the limited sales going on now, some complain they don't know if prices will stand up under OPS interpretation of the order. The market will remain dull until the smoke has been cleared through OPS rulings.

DETROIT—Two situations have developed here on which interpretations are expected momentarily. By using a Cleveland base and shipping by water to Cleveland, mills in Pittsburgh and Cleveland, it appears, might pay $40.20 for scrap as compared with a $39.05, Detroit ceiling. Another issue concerns the $2 differential for electric furnace bundles. Since few local scrap sources prepare bundles 14 x 14 x 20, most of the Detroit bundles are openhearth size. However, some electric furnace buyers here have argued their bundles should be regarded as electric furnace material. The market is quiet. Weather has hindered scrap movements. Lists are expected to go under allocation late this month at ceiling prices.

CLEVELAND—One major consumer in this district was getting allocations and the market generally was breaking all records in reverse. Yards are pretty well cleaned out as a result of the feverish activity of the past month and at the moment, the market is practically inert. Foundries need tonnage and some may

have to be allocated within 30 days, according to trade sources. The market seems to be in an interim period which may last anywhere from 2 weeks to a month, during which little tonnage will move. Biggest problem will be making supply adequate to the demand.

ST. LOUIS—Most railroads in the St. Louis industrial district are revising their prices on lists for which bids were submitted by brokers in accordance with ceilings. One road has torn up all bids and is starting all over again, and consumers are ready to take on the scrap most of them delayed buying because of the imminence of ceilings. The movement from the country has been sharply curtailed for lack of cars since the strike embargo was lifted, and cold weather has halted collections and processing.

BIRMINGHAM—The scrap market here has been fairly active since the price rollback, users who had been holding off buying in anticipation of such action going back into the market to replenish stockpiles, many of which were badly depleted. Dealers are finding offerings in the Southeast plentiful and, in addition to supplying customers in the area, are shipping to northern mills.

CINCINNATI—Trading is at low ebb here in the wake of the new scrap price schedule. Little tonnage is moving other than plant scrap which is going into dealers' yards. Foundries need tonnage but yard inventories of cast grades are reported low. The lack of activity here is not a matter of price but a hopeful expectancy that some amendments will be made to the order, particularly in preparation charges. Little trading is expected here for a month.

BOSTON—Activity in the local market was good and dealers generally expressed satisfaction with operation during the first week of controlled prices. It is generally felt ceilings are fair, and all items moved at ceiling price except unstripped motor blocks which sold at $38 to $39.

BUFFALO—Interest in the scrap market here shifted from government controls to a drastic shrinkage in supplies. The rail strike and sub-zero temperatures added to processing problems. Collections were off as some cars were weeks overdue at dealers' yards. Mills continue to draw on reserve stocks to maintain operations. Orders placed at the higher precontrolled levels were carried over at the reduced prices.

144

THE IRON AGE

Highest Quality Steels
MADE WITH
VANCORAM
FERRO VANADIUM

	Typical Composition
IRON FOUNDRY GRADE	Vanadium . . .38-42% Silicon . . . . .7-11% Carbon . . . .about 1%
GRADE "A" *(Open Hearth)*	Vanadium . . .35-45% 50-55% Silicon . . .max. 7.50% Carbon . .max. 3.00%
GRADE "B" *(Crucible)*	Vanadium . . .35-45% 50-55% Silicon . . .max. 3.50% Carbon . .max. 0.50%
GRADE "C" *(Primos)*	Vanadium . . .35-45% 50-55% 70-80% Silicon . . .max. 1.25% Carbon . .max. 0.20%

VANADIUM CORPORATION OF AMERICA
420 LEXINGTON AVENUE, NEW YORK 17, N. Y. • DETROIT • CHICAGO • CLEVELAND • PITTSBURGH

MAKERS OF FERRO-ALLOYS

CHEMICALS AND METALS

Iron and Steel SCRAP PRICES

(Maximum basing point prices, per gross ton, as set by OPS, effective Feb. 7, 1951. Shipping point and delivered prices calculated as shown below.)

Switching Charge (Dollars per gross ton) / **Basing Points:**

- Pittsburgh $0.99, Johnstown .75, Brackenridge .53, Butler .75, Midland .75, Monessen .51, Sharon .75
- Youngstown .75, Canton .51, Steubenville .51, Warren .75, Weirton .70
- Cleveland .76, Buffalo .83, Cincinnati .65, Middletown .26
- Chicago 1.34, Claymont .79, Coatesville .50, Conshohocken .51, Harrisburg .51, Phoenixville .51
- Sparrows Pt. .20, Bethlehem .52, Ashland, Ky. .47, Kokomo, Ind. .51, Portsmouth, O. .51
- St. Louis .51
- Detroit .95, Duluth .50
- Kansas City .78
- Birmingham .50, Alabama City .43, Atlanta .51
- Minnequa .33
- Houston .57
- Los Angeles .66, Pittsburg, Cal. .65, Portland, Ore. .52, San Francisco .66, Seattle .53

GRADES

Grade	Pittsburgh grp.	Youngstown grp.	Cleveland grp.	Chicago grp.	Sparrows Pt. grp.	St. Louis	Detroit/Duluth	Kansas City	Birmingham grp.	Minnequa	Houston	Los Angeles grp.
No. 1 heavy melting	$44.00	$44.00	$43.00	$42.50	$42.00	$41.00	$40.00	$39.50	$39.00	$38.00	$37.00	$35.00
No. 2 heavy melting	42.00	42.00	41.00	40.50	40.00	39.00	38.00	37.50	37.00	36.00	35.00	33.00
No. 1 busheling	44.00	44.00	43.00	42.50	42.00	41.00	40.00	39.50	39.00	38.00	37.00	35.00
No. 1 bundles	44.00	44.00	43.00	42.50	42.00	41.00	40.00	39.50	39.00	38.00	37.00	35.00
No. 2 bundles	41.00	41.00	40.00	39.50	39.00	38.00	37.00	36.50	36.00	35.00	34.00	32.00
Machine shop turnings	34.00	34.00	33.00	32.50	32.00	31.00	30.00	29.50	29.00	28.00	27.00	25.00
Mixed borings and turnings	38.00	38.00	37.00	36.50	36.00	35.00	34.00	33.50	33.00	32.00	31.00	29.00
Shoveling turnings	38.00	38.00	37.00	36.50	36.00	35.00	34.00	33.50	33.00	32.00	31.00	29.00
Cast iron borings	38.00	38.00	37.00	36.50	36.00	35.00	34.00	33.50	33.00	32.00	31.00	29.00
No. 1 chemical borings	41.00	41.00	40.00	39.50	39.00	38.00	37.00	36.50	36.00	35.00	34.00	32.00
Forge crops	51.50	51.50	50.50	50.00	49.50	48.50	47.50	47.00	46.50	45.50	44.50	42.50
Bar crops and plate	49.00	49.00	48.00	47.50	47.00	46.00	45.00	44.50	44.00	43.00	42.00	40.00
Punchings and plate	46.50	46.50	45.50	45.00	44.50	43.50	42.50	42.00	41.50	40.50	39.50	37.50
Electric furnace bundles	46.00	46.00	45.00	44.50	44.00	43.00	42.00	41.50	41.00	40.00	39.00	37.00
Cut struct., plate, 3 ft and less	47.00	47.00	46.00	45.50	45.00	44.00	43.00	42.50	42.00	41.00	40.00	38.00
Cut struct., plate, 2 ft and less	49.00	49.00	48.00	47.50	47.00	46.00	45.00	44.50	44.00	43.00	42.00	40.00
Cut struct., plate, 1 ft and less	50.00	50.00	49.00	48.50	48.00	47.00	46.00	45.50	45.00	44.00	43.00	41.00
Heavy turnings	43.00	43.00	42.00	41.50	41.00	40.00	39.00	38.50	38.00	37.00	36.00	34.00
No. 1 RR heavy melting	46.00	46.00	45.00	44.50	44.00	43.00	42.00	41.50	41.00	40.00	39.00	37.00
Scrap rails, random lengths	48.00	48.00	47.00	46.50	46.00	45.00	44.00	43.50	43.00	42.00	41.00	39.00
Scrap rails, 3 ft and less	51.00	51.00	50.00	49.50	49.00	48.00	47.00	46.50	46.00	45.00	44.00	42.00
Scrap rails, 2 ft and less	52.00	52.00	51.00	50.50	50.00	49.00	48.00	47.50	47.00	46.00	45.00	43.00
Scrap rails, 18 in. and less	54.00	54.00	53.00	52.50	52.00	51.00	50.00	49.50	49.00	48.00	47.00	45.00
Rerolling rails	53.00	53.00	52.00	51.50	51.00	50.00	49.00	48.50	48.00	47.00	46.00	44.00
Uncut tires	48.00	48.00	47.00	46.50	46.00	45.00	44.00	43.50	43.00	42.00	41.00	39.00
Cut tires	51.00	51.00	50.00	49.50	49.00	48.00	47.00	46.50	46.00	45.00	44.00	42.00
Cut bolsters and side frames	49.00	49.00	48.00	47.50	47.00	46.00	45.00	44.50	44.00	43.00	42.00	40.00
RR specialties	51.00	51.00	50.00	49.50	49.00	48.00	47.00	46.50	46.00	45.00	44.00	42.00
Solid steel axles	58.00	58.00	57.00	56.50	56.00	55.00	54.00	53.50	53.00	52.00	51.00	49.00
No. 3 steel wheels	51.00	51.00	50.00	49.50	49.00	48.00	47.00	46.50	46.00	45.00	44.00	42.00

SWITCHING DISTRICTS—These basing points include the indicated switching districts: Pittsburgh; Bessemer, Homestead, Duquesne, Munhall. Cincinnati; Newport. St. Louis; Granite City, East St. Louis, Madison. San Francisco; South San Francisco, Niles, Oakland. Claymont; Chester. Chicago; Gary. Los Angeles; Firestone.

SHIPPING POINT PRICES (Except RR scrap)—For shipping points within basing points, the ceiling shipping point price is the basing point price, less switching charge. The ceiling for shipping points outside basing points is the basing point price yielding the highest shipping point price, less the lowest established freight charge. Dock charge, where applicable, is $1.25 per gross ton except: Memphis, 95¢; Great Lakes ports, $1.50, and New England ports, $1.75. Maximum shipping point price on No. 1 heavy melting steel in New York City is $36.99 per gross ton with set differentials for other grades. Hudson and Bergen County, N. J., shipping point prices are computed from Bethlehem basing point. All New Jersey computations use all-rail transport. Ceiling need not fall below $32 per gross ton for No. 1 heavy melting steel, with set differentials for other grades. Cast scrap shipping point prices are given in table.

DELIVERED PRICES (Except RR scrap)—Ceiling is the shipping point price plus actual freight charge, tax included. Dock charges, where applicable, are as above.

DELIVERED PRICES (RR scrap)—Ceiling on-line price of a RR operating in a basing point is the top in the highest priced basing point in which the RR operates. For off-line prices, RR's not operating in basing point, non-operating RR's, and RR scrap sold by someone other than a RR see text of order, THE IRON AGE, Feb. 8, 1951, p. 137-C.

UNPREPARED SCRAP—Maximum is $8 per gross ton less than prepared base grades (No. 1 heavy & No. 1 RR heavy). Scrap suitable for compressing into No. 1 bundles is $6 less than No. 1 bundles; suitable for compressing into No. 2 bundles, $8 less than No. 2 bundles. For cast material requiring special preparation, price is breakable cast less preparation costs.

COMMISSIONS—Brokers are permitted a maximum of $1 per gross ton commission which must be separate on the bill.

ALLOY PREMIUMS—Alloy extras are permitted on: nickel, molybdenum, manganese, silicon, and chromium. Quantities and charges may be found in the order, THE IRON AGE, Feb. 8, 1951, p. 137-D.

RESTRICTIONS ON USE—Ceiling prices on some scrap items may fluctuate with use by consumers. If some scrap is purchased for its established specialized use, the ceiling price set in the order stands. But if some special grades are purchased for other uses, the ceiling price charge shall be the price of the scrap grade being substituted. For example, the price established for Grade 28 (wrought iron) may be charged only when sold to a producer of wrought iron. Otherwise the ceiling price shall not exceed the ceiling price for the corresponding grade of basic openhearth. Restrictions on use are placed on the following grades: Chemical borings, wrought iron, rerolling rails, cupola cast, clean auto cast, and malleable. Ceiling prices on billet bloom and forge crops, alloy-free turnings, and heavy turnings may be charged only when shipped directly from industrial producer.

CEILING DELIVERED PRICES FOR TRUCK SHIPMENT OF ALL STEEL OR CAST IRON SCRAP—If delivery is made by truck public carrier, ceiling delivered price shall be the ceiling shipping point price (or in the case of railroad scrap, the pertinent ceiling on-line price) plus the actual public carrier charge. Scrap delivered by shipper or broker trucks shall have a ceiling delivered price consisting of the ceiling shipping point price (or railroad ceiling on-line price) plus the established rail carload freight rate for shipping scrap from the rail siding nearest the point of delivery. Transportation charges for delivery in a shipper or broker truck shall not exceed $4 and need not fall below $2.50.

OPS Correction on CPR 5

In F. R. Doc. 51-1937 (16 F. R. 1061), the fourth sentence of Section 23 (a) (5) reading: "May not include galvanized, vitreous enameled stock tin plate, terne plate, or other metal coated material" is corrected to read as follows: "May include galvanized, but not vitreous enameled stock tin plate, terne plate, or other metal coated material."

(s) Michael V. DiSalle
Director of
Price Stabilization

Cast Scrap

(F.o.b. all shipping points)

Cupola cast	$49.00
Charging box cast	47.00
Heavy breakable cast	45.00
Cast iron brake shoes	41.00
Stove plate	46.00
Clean auto cast	52.00
Unstripped motor blocks	43.00
Cast iron carwheels	47.00
Malleable	55.00
Drop broken machinery cast	52.00

Boston, unstripped motor blocks....$38 to $39

CEILING SHIPPING POINT, CEILING ON-LINE PRICES FOR ALL CAST IRON SCRAP—The above table shows blanket ceiling prices per gross ton for all cast iron scrap, f.o.b. shipping points.

CEILING DELIVERED PRICES—The ceiling delivered price for shipment by rail, vessel, or both of dealer and industrial cast iron scrap shall be the shipping point price plus the actual transportation charges to the point of delivery. Public dock charges may be added to actual transportation charges. Where dock facilities are owned or controlled by the shipper, certain fixed charges apply. (See steel scrap footnote).

CEILING DELIVERED PRICES FOR TRUCK SHIPMENT OF ALL STEEL OR CAST IRON SCRAP—(See steel scrap footnote).

RESTRICTIONS ON USE—(See steel scrap footnote).

CEILING INTRANSIT PREPARATION CHARGES (Dollars per gross ton)

No. 1 heavy; No. 2 heavy; No. 1 RR heavy; No. 2 RR heavy; No. 1 busheling; No. 2 bundles; electric furnace bundles..$ 8.00
No. 1 bundles; briquetted turnings or cast iron borings; No. 1 RR sheet scrap..... 6.00
Crushing machine shop turnings........ 3.00
Bar crops and plate; punchings and plate; structural and plate, 1 ft & less, and 3 ft and less; foundry steel, 1 ft & less and 2 ft & less; wrought iron.... 10.00
Rails, 3 ft & less; cut tires; cut bolsters & side frames 4.00
Rails, 2 ft & less 5.00
Rails, 18 in. & less 7.00

February 15, 1951

malleable scrap

use:

Malleable iron scrap is the principal ingredient used in the making of new malleable castings. These castings are very ductile and can absorb tremendous pressures or heavy hammering without fracturing.

Malleable castings have a varied range of applications and are widely used in the railroad, agricultural and automotive industries.

source:

Scrap malleable parts of automobiles, railroad cars, pipe fittings, etc.

This is one of a series illustrating the many and varied types of scrap required in the making of iron and steel for every use. Our national organization, manned by competent personnel, is ready to meet your every scrap problem.

specifications:

The scrap must be prepared to meet the physical requirements of the cupola and air furnaces, being no longer than 1/3 the diameter of the cupola. Air furnaces can use slightly larger pieces.

Malleable scrap must be free of metallic alloys, chrome and sulphur because these chemicals produce "hard spots" in the castings.

Rust is very undesirable because of its hydrogen and oxygen properties, upsetting the calculations of the metallurgist.

Comparison of Prices

Steel prices in this page are the average of various f.o.b. quotations of major producing areas: Pittsburgh, Chicago, Gary, Cleveland, Youngstown.

Price advances over previous week are printed in Heavy Type; declines appear in *Italics*

Flat-Rolled Steel:

(cents per pound)	Feb. 13, 1951	Feb. 6, 1951	Jan. 16, 1951	Feb. 14, 1950
Hot-rolled sheets	3.60	3.60	3.60	3.35
Cold-rolled sheets	4.35	4.35	4.35	4.10
Galvanized sheets (10 ga)	4.80	4.80	4.80	4.40
Hot-rolled strip	3.50	3.50	3.50	3.25
Cold-rolled strip	4.75	4.75	4.75	4.21
Plate	3.70	3.70	3.70	3.50
Plates wrought iron.....	7.85	7.85	7.85	7.85
Stains C-R-strip (No. 302)	36.50	36.50	36.50	33.00

Tin and Terneplate:

(dollars per base box)				
Tinplate (1.50 lb) cokes.	$7.50	$7.50	$7.50	$7.50
Tinplate, electro (0.50 lb)	6.60	6.60	6.60	6.60
Special coated mfg. ternes	6.35	6.35	6.35	6.50

Bars and Shapes:

(cents per pound)				
Merchant bars	3.70	3.70	3.70	3.45
Cold finished bars.......	4.55	4.55	4.55	*4.145
Alloy bars	4.30	4.30	4.30	3.95
Structural shapes	3.65	3.65	3.65	3.40
Stainless bars (No. 302).	31.25	31.25	31.25	28.50
Wrought iron bars......	9.50	9.50	9.50	9.50

Wire:

(cents per pound)				
Bright wire	4.85	4.85	4.85	4.50

Rails:

(dollars per 100 lb)				
Heavy rails	$3.60	$3.60	$3.60	$3.40
Light rails	4.00	4.00	4.00	3.75

Semifinished Steel:

(dollars per net ton)				
Rerolling billets	$56.00	$56.00	$56.00	$54.00
Slabs, rerolling	56.00	56.00	56.00	54.00
Forging billets	66.00	66.00	66.00	63.00
Alloy blooms billets, slabs	70.00	70.00	70.00	66.00

Wire Rod and Skelp:

(cents per pound)				
Wire rods	4.10	4.10	4.10	3.85
Skelp	3.35	3.35	3.35	3.15

Pig Iron:

(per gross ton)	Feb. 13, 1951	Feb. 6, 1951	Jan. 16, 1951	Feb. 14, 1950
No. 2 foundry, del'd Phila.	$57.77	$57.77	$57.77	$50.42
No. 2, Valley furnace....	52.50	52.50	52.50	46.50
No. 2, Southern Cin'ti...	55.58	55.58	55.58	49.08
No. 2, Birmingham....	48.88	48.88	48.88	42.38
No. 2, foundry, Chicago†	52.50	52.50	52.50	46.50
Basic del'd Philadelphia..	56.92	56.92	56.92	49.92
Basic, Valley furnace....	52.00	52.00	52.00	46.00
Malleable, Chicago†	52.50	52.50	52.50	46.50
Malleable, Valley	52.50	52.50	52.50	46.50
Charcoal, Chicago	70.56	70.56	70.56	68.56
Ferromanganese‡	186.25	186.25	186.25	173.40

†The switching charge for delivery to foundries in the Chicago district is $1 per ton.
‡Average of U. S. prices quoted on Ferroalloy page.

Scrap:

(per gross ton)				
Heavy melt'g steel, P'gh..	$44.00*	$51.13	$46.13	$31.25
Heavy melt'g steel, Phila.	42.50*	47.50	49.50	23.00
Heavy melt'g steel, Ch'go	42.50*	44.63	44.63	27.50
No. 1 hy. com. sh't, Det.	40.00*	40.25	40.25	23.50
Low phos. Young'n....	46.50*	54.50	48.63	31.75
No. 1 cast, Pittsburgh...	49.00†	67.75	67.75	37.50
No. 1 cast, Philadelphia..	49.00†	62.50	62.50	35.50
No. 1 cast, Chicago......	49.00†	63.00	63.00	38.50

*Basing Pt. †Shipping Pt.
Not including broker's fee after Feb. 7, 1951.

Coke: Connellsville:

(per net ton at oven)				
Furnace coke, prompt...	$14.25	$14.25	$14.25	$14.00
Foundry coke, prompt...	17.25	17.25	17.25	15.75

Nonferrous Metals:

(cents per pound to large buyers)				
Copper, electro, Conn...	24.50	24.50	24.50	18.50
Copper, Lake, Conn.....	24.625	24.625	24.625	18.625
Tin Straits, New York...	$1.825†	$1.825*	$1.75	74.50
Zinc, East St. Louis.....	17.50	17.50	17.50	9.75
Lead, St. Louis..........	16.80	16.80	16.80	11.80
Aluminum, virgin	19.00	19.00	19.00	17.00
Nickel, electrolytic	53.55	53.55	53.55	42.97
Magnesium, ingot	24.50	24.50	24.50	20.50
Antimony, Laredo, Tex..	42.00	42.00	32.00	27.25

†Tentative. *Revised.

Composite Prices

[Starting with the issue of May 12, 1949, the weighted finished steel composite was revised for the years 1941 to date. The weights used are based on the average product shipments for the 7 years 1937 to 1940 inclusive and 1946 to 1948 inclusive. The use of quarterly figures has been eliminated because it was too sensitive. (See p. 130 of May 12, 1949, issue.)]

Finished Steel Base Price	Pig Iron	Scrap Steel
Feb. 13, 1951...........4.131¢ per lb.........	....$52.69 per gross ton....	......$43.00 per gross ton......
One week ago.........4.131¢ per lb.........	.... 52.69 per gross ton....	...... 47.75 per gross ton......
One month ago........4.131¢ per lb.........	.... 52.69 per gross ton....	...... 46.75 per gross ton......
One year ago ....3.837¢ per lb.........	.... 46.38 per gross ton....	...... 27.25 per gross ton......

	High	Low	High	Low	High	Low
1951....	4.131¢ Jan. 2	4.131¢ Jan. 2	$52.69 Jan. 2	$52.69 Jan. 2	$47.75 Jan. 30	$43.00 Feb. 7
1950....	4.131¢ Dec. 1	3.837¢ Jan. 3	52.69 Dec. 12	45.88 Jan. 3	45.13 Dec. 19	26.25 Jan. 3
1949....	3.837¢ Dec. 27	3.3705¢ May 3	46.87 Jan. 18	45.88 Sept. 6	48.00 Jan. 4	19.33 June 28
1948....	3.721¢ July 27	3.193¢ Jan. 1	46.91 Oct. 12	39.58 Jan. 6	43.16 July 27	39.75 Mar. 9
1947....	3.193¢ July 29	2.848¢ Jan. 1	37.98 Dec. 30	30.14 Jan. 7	42.58 Oct. 28	29.50 May 20
1946....	2.848¢ Dec. 31	2.464¢ Jan. 1	30.14 Dec. 10	25.37 Jan. 1	31.17 Dec. 24	19.17 Jan. 1
1945....	2.464¢ May 29	2.396¢ Jan. 1	25.37 Oct. 23	23.61 Jan. 2	19.17 Jan. 2	18.92 May 22
1944....	2.396¢	2.396¢	$23.61	$23.61	19.17 Jan. 11	15.76 Oct. 24
1943....	2.396¢	2.396¢	23.61	23.61	$19.17	$19.17
1942....	2.396¢	2.396¢	23.61	23.61	19.17	19.17
1941....	2.396¢	2.396¢	$23.61 Mar. 20	$23.45 Jan. 2	$22.00 Jan. 7	$19.17 Apr. 10
1940....	2.30467¢ Jan. 2	2.24107¢ Apr. 16	23.45 Dec. 23	22.61 Jan. 2	21.83 Dec. 30	16.04 Apr. 9
1939....	2.35367¢ Jan. 3	2.26689¢ May 16	22.61 Sept. 19	20.61 Sept. 12	22.50 Oct. 3	14.08 May 16
1838....	2.58414¢ Jan. 4	2.27207¢ Oct. 18	23.25 June 21	19.61 July 6	15.00 Nov. 22	11.00 June 7
1937....	2.58414¢ Mar. 9	2.32263¢ Jan. 4	32.25 Mar. 9	20.25 Feb. 16	21.92 Mar. 30	12.67 June 9
1936....	2.32263¢ Dec. 28	2.05200¢ Mar. 10	19.74 Nov. 24	18.73 Aug. 11	17.75 Dec. 21	12.67 June 8
1932....	1.89196¢ July 5	1.83910¢ Mar. 1	14.81 Jan. 5	13.56 Dec. 6	8.50 Jan. 12	6.43 July 5
1929....	2.31773¢ May 28	2.26498¢ Oct. 29	18.71 May 14	18.21 Dec. 17	17.58 Jan. 29	14.08 Dec. 8

Weighted index based on steel bars, shapes, plates, wire, rails, black pipe, hot and cold-rolled sheets and strips, representing major portion of finished steel shipment. Index recapitulated in Aug. 28, 1941, issue and in May 12, 1949.

Based on averages for basic iron at Valley furnaces and foundry iron at Chicago, Philadelphia, Buffalo, Valley and Birmingham.

Average of No. 1 heavy melting steel scrap delivered to consumers at Pittsburgh, Philadelphia and Chicago.

February 15, 1951

February 15, 1951

IRON AGE

STEEL PRICES

Smaller numbers in price boxes indicate producing companies. For main office locations, see key on facing page.
Base prices at producing points apply only to sizes and grades produced in these areas. Prices are in cents per lb unless otherwise noted. Extras apply.

	Pittsburgh	Chicago	Gary	Cleveland	Canton Massillon	Middletown	Youngstown	Bethlehem	Buffalo	Conshohocken	Johnstown	Sparrows Point	Granite City	Detroit
INGOTS Carbon forging, net ton	$52.00[1]													
Alloy, net ton	$54.00[1,17]													$54.00[31]
BILLETS, BLOOMS, SLABS Carbon, rerolling, net ton	$56.00[1,5]	$56.00[1]	$56.00[1]						$56.00[3]		$56.00[3]			
Carbon forging billets, net ton	$66.00[1,5]	$66.00[1,4]	$66.00[1]	$66.00[4]	$66.00[4]				$66.00[3,4]	$73.00[26]	$66.00[3]			$69.00[31]
Alloy, net ton	$70.00[1,17]	$70.00[1,4]	$70.00[1]		$70.00[4]			$70.00[3]	$70.00[2,4]	$77.00[26]	$70.00[3]			$73.00[31]
PIPE SKELP	3.35[1] 3.45[5]						3.35[1,4]							
WIRE RODS	4.10[2] 4.30[18]	4.10[2,4,33]	4.10[6]	4.10[2]			4.10[6]				4.10[3]	4.20[3]		
SHEETS Hot-rolled (18 ga. & hvr.)	3.60[1,5,9,15] 3.75[28]	3.60[6,23]	3.60[1,6,8]	3.60[4]		3.60[7]	3.60[1,4,6] 4.00[13]		3.60[3]	4.00[26]		3.60[3]		3.80[13] 4.40[47]
Cold-rolled	4.35[1,5,9,15] 5.35[63]		4.35[1,6,8]	4.35[4]		4.35[7]	4.35[4,6]		4.35[3]			4.35[3]		4.55[13]
Galvanized (10 gage)	4.80[1,9,15]		4.80[1,8]		4.80[4]	4.80[7]	6.00[64]					4.80[3]		
Enameling (12 gage)	4.65[1]		4.65[1,8]			4.65[7]								
Long terne (10 gage)	5.20[9,15]						6.00[64]							
Hi str. low alloy, h.r.	5.40[1,5] 5.75[9]	5.40[1]	5.40[1,8] 5.90[6]	5.40[4]			5.40[1,4,13]		5.40[3]	5.65[26]		5.40[3]		5.95[12]
Hi str. low alloy, c.r.	6.55[1,5] 6.90[9]		6.55[1,8] 7.05[6]	6.55[4]			6.55[4]		6.55[2]			6.55[2]		7.10[12]
Hi str. low alloy, galv.	7.20[1]													
STRIP Hot-rolled	3.60[9], 4.00[41] 5[8], 3.75[28] 3.50[5]	3.50[66]	3.50[1,6,8]			3.50[7]	3.50[1,4,6] 4.00[13]		3.50[3,4]	3.90[26]		3.50[3]		4.40[47] 3.80[12]
Cold-rolled	4.65[5,9] 5.00[28] 5.35[63,58]	4.90[8,66]	4.90[8]	4.65[2]		4.65[7]	4.65[4,6] 5.35[13,40]		4.65[3]			4.65[3]		4.85[12] 5.45[47] 5.60[68,81]
Hi str. low alloy, h.r.	5.75[9]		5.50[1] 5.30[8], 5.80[6]				4.95[4], 5.50[1] 5.40[13]			5.55[26]				5.95[12]
Hi str. low alloy, c.r.	7.20[9]			6.70[5]			6.20[4], 6.55[13]							
TINPLATE† Cokes, 1.25-lb base box (1.50 lb. add 25¢)	$8.45[1,5,9,15]		$8.45[1,6,8]				$8.45[4]					$8.55[3]		
Electrolytic 0.25, 0.50, 0.75 lb box	0.25 lb. base box, $7.15[1,4,5,8,9]; $7.25[3,11]; $7.35[22] 0.50 lb., add 25¢: 0.75 lb. add 65¢													
BLACKPLATE, 29 gage Holloware enameling	5.85[1] 6.15[15]		5.85[1]				5.30[4]							
BARS Carbon steel	3.70[1,5] 3.85[9]	3.70[1,4,23]	3.70[1,4,6,8]	3.70[4]	3.70[4]		3.70[1,4,6]		3.70[3,4]		3.70[3]			3.85[21]
Reinforcing‡	3.70[1,5]	3.70[4]	3.70[1,6,8]	3.70[4]			3.70[1,4]		3.70[3,4]		3.70[3]	3.70[3]		
Cold-finished	4.55[2,4,5,] 52,71	4.55[2,69,70,] 23,73	4.55[74,73]	4.55[2]	4.55[4,82]									4.70[84]
Alloy, hot-rolled	4.30[1,17]	4.30[1,4,23]	4.30[1,6,8]		4.30[4]		4.30[1,6]	4.30[8]	4.30[3,4]		4.30[3]			4.45[31] 4.65[12]
Alloy, cold-drawn	5.40[17,52,] 69,71	5.40[4,23,69,] 70,73	5.40[4] 5.90[74]		5.40[4,32]				5.40[3]	5.40[3]				5.55[84]
Hi str. low alloy, h.r.	5.55[1,5]		5.55[1,8] 6.05[6]	5.55[4]			5.55[1]	5.55[3]	5.55[3]		5.55[3]			
PLATE Carbon steel	3.70[1,5,15]	3.70[1]	3.70[1,6,8]	3.70[4] 4.00[9]			3.70[1,4] 3.95[13]		3.70[3]	4.15[26]	3.70[3]	3.70[3]		
Floor plates			4.75[8]	4.75[5]						4.75[26]				
Alloy	4.75[1]	4.75[1]	4.75[1]				5.20[13]			5.05[26]	4.75[3]	4.75[3]		
Hi str. low alloy	5.65[1,5]	5.65[1]	5.65[1,8]	5.65[4,5]			5.65[4] 5.70[13]			5.90[26]	5.65[3]	5.65[3]		
SHAPES, Structural	3.65[1,5] 3.90[9]	3.65[1,23]	3.65[1,8]					3.70[3]	3.70[3]		3.70[3]			
Hi str. low alloy	5.50[1,5]	5.50[1]	5.50[1,8]					5.50[3]	5.50[3]		5.50[3]			
MANUFACTURERS' WIRE Bright	4.85[2,5] 5.10[18]	4.85[2] 4,33		4.85[2]					Kokomo = 5.80[30]		4.85[3]	4.95[3]	Duluth = 4.85[2]	
PILING, Steel Sheet	4.45[1]	4.45[1]	4.45[8]						4.45[3]					

Smaller numbers indicate producing companies. See key at right.
Prices are in cents per lb unless otherwise noted. Extras apply.

STEEL PRICES

Kansas City	Houston	Birmingham	WEST COAST Seattle, San Francisco, Los Angeles, Fontana		Product
			F = $79.00[19]		**INGOTS** Carbon forging, net ton
	$62.00[83]		F = $80.00[19]		Alloy, net ton
		$56.00[11]	F = $75.00[19]		**BILLETS, BLOOMS, SLABS** Carbon, rerolling, net ton
	$74.00[83]	$66.00[11]	F = $85.00[19] SF, LA, S = $85.00[62]		Carbon forging billets, net ton
	$78.00[83]		F = $89.00[19] LA = $90.00[62]		Alloy net ton
					PIPE SKELP
	4.50[83]	4.10[4,11]	SF = 4.90[2] LA = 4.90[24,62]	Worcester = 4.40[2] Minnequa = 4.35[14]	**WIRE RODS**
		3.60[4,11]	SF, LA = 4.30[24] F = 4.55[19]	Niles = 5.25[64], Geneva = 3.70[16]	**SHEETS** Hot-rolled (18 ga. & hvr.)
		4.35[11]	SF = 5.30[24] F = 5.30[19]		Cold-rolled
		4.80[4,11]	SF, LA = 5.55[24]	Ashland = 4.80[7]	Galvanized (10 gage)
					Enameling (12 gage)
					Long ternes (10 gage)
		5.40[11]	F = 6.35[19]		Hi str. low alloy, h.r.
			F = 7.50[19]		Hi str. low alloy, c.r.
					Hi str. low alloy, galv.
4.10[83]	4.90[83]	3.50[4]	SF, LA = 4.25[24,62] F = 4.75[19], S = 4.50[62]	Atlanta = 4.05[65] Minnequa = 4.55[14]	**STRIP** Hot-rolled
			F = 6.30[19] LA = 6.40[27]	New Haven = 5.15[2], 5.85[68]	Cold-rolled
		5.30[11]	F = 6.20[19]		Hi str. low alloy, h.r.
					Hi str. low alloy, c.r.
		$8.55	SF = $9.20		**TINPLATE** Cokes, 1.25-lb base box (1.50 lb, add 25¢)
					Electrolytic 0.25, 0.50, 0.75 lb box
					BLACKPLATE, 29 gage Hollowware enameling
4.30[83]	4.10[83]	3.70[4,11]	SF, LA = 4.40[24]	Atlanta = 4.25[65] Minnequa = 4.15[14]	**BARS** Carbon steel
4.38[83]	4.10[83]	3.70[4,11]	SF, S = 4.45[62] F = 4.40[19], LA = 4.40[62]	Atlanta = 4.25[65] Minnequa = 4.50[14]	Reinforcing‡
				Newark = 5.00[69] Putnam = 5.10[69] Hartford = 5.10[4] Los Angeles = 6.00[4]	Cold-finished
4.90[83]	4.70[83]		LA = 5.35[62] F = 5.35[19]		Alloy, hot-rolled
				Newark = 5.75[69] Worcester = [2] Hartford = 5.85[4]	Alloy, cold-drawn
		5.55[11]	F = 6.60[19]		Hi str. low alloy, h.r.
	4.10[83]	3.70[4,11]	F = 4.30[19] S = 4.60[62] Geneva = 3.70[16]	Claymont = 4.15[29] Coatesville = 4.15[21] Minnequa = 4.50[14]	**PLATE** Carbon steel
				Harrisburg = 5.25[35]	Floor plates
			F = 5.70[19] Geneva = 5.65[16]	Coatesville = 5.25[21] Claymont = 4.85[29]	Alloy
		5.65[11]	F = 6.25[19]		Hi str. low alloy
4.25[83]	4.05[83]	3.65[4,11]	SF = 4.20[62] F = 4.25[16] LA = 4.25[24,62] S = 4.30[62]	Geneva 3.65[16] Minnequa 4.10[14]	**SHAPES, Structural**
		50[11]	F = 6.10[19]		Hi str. low alloy
5.45[83]	5.25[83]	4.85[4,11]	SF, LA = 5.80[24]	Atlanta = 5.10[65] Worcester = 5.15[2] Minnequa = 5.10[14]	**MANUFACTURERS' WIRE** Bright

KEY TO STEEL PRODUCERS

1 U. S. Steel Co., Pittsburgh
2 American Steel & Wire Co., Cleveland
3 Bethlehem Steel Co., Bethlehem
4 Republic Steel Corp., Cleveland
5 Jones & Laughlin Steel Corp., Pittsburgh
6 Youngstown Sheet & Tube Co., Youngstown
7 Arco Steel Corp., Middletown, Ohio
8 Inland Steel Co., Chicago
9 Weirton Steel Co., Weirton, W. Va.
10 National Tube Co., Pittsburgh
11 Tennessee Coal, Iron & R. R. Co., Birmingham
12 Great Lakes Steel Corp., Detroit
13 Sharon Steel Corp., Sharon, Pa.
14 Colorado Fuel & Iron Corp., Denver
15 Wheeling Steel Corp., Wheeling, W. Va.
16 Geneva Steel Co., Salt Lake City
17 Crucible Steel Co. of America, New York
18 Pittsburgh Steel Co., Pittsburgh
19 Kaiser Steel Corp., Oakland, Calif.
20 Portsmouth Div., Detroit Steel Corp., Detroit
21 Lukens Steel Co., Coatesville, Pa.
22 Granite City Steel Co., Granite City, Ill.
23 Wisconsin Steel Co., South Chicago, Ill.
24 Columbia Steel Co., San Francisco
25 Copperweld Steel Co., Glassport, Pa.
26 Alan Wood Steel Co., Conshohocken, Pa.
27 Calif. Cold Rolled Steel Corp., Los Angeles
28 Allegheny Ludlum Steel Corp., Pittsburgh
29 Worth Steel Co., Claymont, Del.
30 Continental Steel Corp., Kokomo, Ind.
31 Rotary Electric Steel Co., Detroit
32 Laclede Steel Co., St. Louis
33 Northwestern Steel & Wire Co., Sterling, Ill.
34 Keystone Steel & Wire Co., Peoria, Ill.
35 Central Steel & Wire Co., Harrisburg, Pa.
36 Carpenter Steel Co., Reading, Pa.
37 Eastern Stainless Steel Corp., Baltimore
38 Washington Steel Corp., Washington, Pa.
39 Jessop Steel Co., Washington, Pa.
40 Blair Strip Steel Co., New Castle, Pa.
41 Superior Steel Corp., Carnegie, Pa.
42 Timken Steel & Tube Div., Canton, Ohio
43 Babcock & Wilcox Tube Co., Beaver Falls, Pa.
44 Reeves Steel & Mfg. Co., Dover, Ohio
45 John A. Roebling's Sons Co., Trenton, N. J.
46 Simonds Saw & Steel Co., Fitchburg, Mass.
47 McLouth Steel Corp., Detroit
48 Cold Metal Products Co., Youngstown
49 Thomas Steel Co., Warren, Ohio
50 Wilson Tube & Wire Co., Chicago
51 Sweet's Steel Co., Williamsport, Pa.
52 Superior Drawn Steel Co., Monaca, Pa.
53 Tremont Nail Co., Wareham, Mass.
54 Firth Sterling St. & Carbide Corp., McKeesport
55 Ingersoll Steel Div., Chicago
56 Phoenix Iron & Steel Co., Phoenixville, Pa.
57 Fitzsimmons Steel Co., Youngstown
58 Stanley Works, New Britain, Conn.
59 Universal-Cyclops Steel Corp., Bridgeville, Pa.
60 American Cladmetals Co., Carnegie, Pa.
61 Cuyahoga Steel & Wire Co., Cleveland
62 Bethlehem Pacific Coast Steel Corp., San Fran.
63 Follansbee Steel Corp., Pittsburgh
64 Niles Rolling Mill Co., Niles, Ohio
65 Atlantic Steel Co., Atlanta
66 Acme Steel Co., Chicago
67 Joslyn Mfg. & Supply Co., Chicago
68 Detroit Steel Corp., Detroit
69 Wycoff Steel Co., Pittsburgh
70 Bliss & Laughlin, Inc., Harvey, Ill.
71 Columbia Steel & Shafting Co., Pittsburgh
72 Cumberland Steel Co., Cumberland, Md.
73 La Salle Steel Co., Chicago
74 Monarch Steel Co., Inc., Hammond, Ind.
75 Empire Steel Co., Mansfield, Ohio
76 Mahoning Valley Steel Co., Niles, Ohio
77 Oliver Iron & Steel Co., Pittsburgh
78 Pittsburgh Screw & Bolt Co., Pittsburgh
79 Standard Forging Corp., Chicago
80 Driver Harris Co., Harrison, N. J.
81 Detroit Tube & Steel Div., Detroit
82 Reliance Div., Eaton Mfg. Co., Massillon, Ohio
83 Sheffield Steel Corp., Kansas City
84 Plymouth Steel Co., Detroit
85 Wickwire Spencer Steel, Buffalo
86 Angell Nail and Chaplet, Cleveland
87 Mid-States Steel & Wire, Crawfordsville, Ind.
88 National Supply, Pittsburgh, Pa.
89 Wheatland Tube Co., Wheatland, Pa.
90 Mercer Tube & Mfg. Co., Sharon, Pa.
91 Woodward Iron Co., Woodward, Ala.
92 Sloss-Sheffield Steel & Iron Co., Birmingham
93 Hanna Furance Corp., Detroit
94 Interlake Iron Corp., Cleveland
95 Lone Star Steel Co., Dallas
96 Mystic Iron Works, Everett, Mass.
97 Jackson Iron & Steel Co., Jackson, O.
98 Globe Iron Co., Jackson, O.
99 Pittsburgh Coke & Chemical Co., Pittsburgh
100 Shenango Furnace Co., Pittsburgh
101 Tennessee Products & Chemical Corp., Nashville
102 Koppers Co., Inc., Granite City, Ill.
103 Page Steel & Wire Div., American Chain & Cable., Monessen, Pa.

STAINLESS STEELS

Base price, cents per lb, f.o.b. mill.

Product	301	302	303	304	316	321	347	410	416	430
Ingots, rerolling	14.25	15.00	16.50	16.00	24.25	19.75	21.50	12.75	14.75	13.00
Slabs, billets rerolling	18.50	19.75	21.75	20.75	31.75	26.00	28.25	16.50	20.00	16.75
Forg. discs, die blocks, rings	34.00	34.00	36.50	35.50	52.50	40.00	44.50	28.00	28.50	28.50
Billets, forging	26.25	26.25	28.25	27.50	41.00	31.00	34.75	21.50	22.00	22.00
Bars, wires, structurals	31.25	31.25	33.75	32.75	48.75	36.75	41.25	25.75	26.25	26.25
Plates	33.00	33.00	35.00	35.00	51.50	40.50	45.00	27.00	27.50	27.50
Sheets	41.00	41.00	43.00	43.00	56.50	49.00	53.50	36.50	37.00	39.00
Strip, hot-rolled	26.50	28.00	32.25	30.00	48.25	36.75	41.00	23.50	30.25	24.00
Strip, cold-rolled	34.00	36.50	40.00	38.50	58.50	48.00	52.00	30.50	37.00	31.00

STAINLESS STEEL PRODUCING POINTS—*Sheets:* Midland, Pa., 17; Brackenridge, Pa., 28; Butler, Pa., 7; McKeesport, Pa., 1; Washington, Pa., 38 (type 316 add 5¢), 39; Baltimore, 37; Middletown, Ohio, 7; Massillon, Ohio, 4; Gary, 1; Bridgeville, Pa., 59; New Castle, Ind., 55; Ft. Wayne, Ind., 67; Lockport, N. Y., 46.
Strip: Midland, Pa., 17; Cleveland, 2; Carnegie, Pa., 41; McKeesport, Pa., 54; Reading, Pa., 36; Washington, Pa., 38 (type 316 add 5¢); W. Leechburg, Pa., 28; Bridgeville, Pa., 59; Detroit, 47; Massillon, Canton, Ohio, 4; Middletown, Ohio, 7; Harrison, N. J., 80; Youngstown, 48; Lockport N. Y., 46; New Britain, Conn., 58; Sharon, Pa., 13; Butler, Pa., 7.
Bars: Baltimore, 7; Duquesne, Pa., 1; Munhall, Pa., 1; Reading, Pa., 36; Titusville, Pa., 59; Washington, Pa., 39; McKeesport, Pa., 1, 54; Bridgeville, Pa., 59; Dunkirk, N. Y., 28; Massillon, Ohio, 4; Chicago, 1; Syracuse, N. Y., 17; Watervliet, N. Y., 28; Waukegan, Ill., 2; Lockport, N. Y. 46; Canton, Ohio, 42; Ft. Wayne, Ind., 67.
Wire: Waukegan, Ill., 2; Massillon, Ohio, 4; McKeesport, Pa., 54; Bridgeport, Conn., 44; Ft. Wayne, Ind., 67; Trenton, N. J., 45; Harrison, N. J., 80; Baltimore, 7; Dunkirk, 28; Monessen, 103.
Structurals: Baltimore, 7; Massillon, Ohio, 4; Chicago, 1, 67; Watervliet, N. Y., 28; Bridgeport, Conn., 44.
Plates: Brackenridge, Pa., 28 (type 416 add ½¢); Butler, Pa., 7; Chicago, 1; Munhall, Pa., 1; Midland, Pa., 17; New Castle, Ind., 55; Lockport, N. Y., 46; Middletown, 7; Washington, Pa., 39; Cleveland, Massillon, 4.
Forged discs, die blocks, rings: Pittsburgh, 1, 17; Syracuse, 17; Ferndale, Mich., 28.
Forging billets: Midland, Pa., 17; Baltimore, 7; Washington, Pa., 39; McKeesport, 54; Massillon, Canton, Ohio, 4; Watervliet, 28; Pittsburgh, Chicago, 1.

RAILS, TRACK SUPPLIES

F.o.b. Mill Cents Per Lb	No. 1 Std. Rails	Light Rails	Joint Bars	Track Spikes	Axles	Screw Spikes	Tie Plates	Track Bolts Untreated
Bessemer-1	3.60	4.00	4.70					
Chicago-4				6.15				
Ensley-11	3.60	4.00						
Fairfield-11		4.00	4.40			8.60	4.50	
Gary-1	3.60	4.00		6.15	6.15	5.20	4.50	
Ind. Harbor-8	3.60			6.15		8.60	4.50	
Johnstown-3		4.00			5.60	8.60		
Joliet-1		4.00	4.70					
Kansas City-83				6.40				
Lackawanna-3	3.60	4.00	4.70			8.60	4.50	
Lebanon-1				6.15				9.60
Minnequa-14	3.60	4.50	4.70	6.15		8.60	4.50	9.60
Pittsburgh-77						9.35		9.60
Pittsburgh-78								9.60
Pittsburgh-5				6.15				
Pittsburg-24							4.65	
Seattle-62				6.10			4.35	
Steelton-3	3.60	4.70					4.50	
Struthers-6				6.15				
Torrance-24							4.65	
Youngstown-4				6.15				

Track Bolts, heat treated, to railroads, 9.85¢ per lb.

BOILER TUBES

Seamless steel, electric welded commercial boiler tubes, locomotive tubes, minimum wall, per 100 ft at mill, c.l. lots, cut lengths 10 to 24 ft.

OD in in.	gage BWG	Seamless H.R.	C.D.	Electric H.R.	Weld C.D.
2	13	$22.67	$26.66	$21.99	$25.86
2½	12	30.48	35.84	29.57	34.76
3	12	33.90	39.90	32.89	34.80
3½	11	42.37	49.89	41.10	48.39
4	10	52.60	61.88	51.03	60.02

Pittsburgh Steel add, H-R: 2 in., 62¢; 2½ in., 84¢; 3 in., 92¢; 3½ in., $1.17; 4 in., $1.45. Add, C-R: 2 in., 74¢; 2½ in., 99¢; 3 in., $1.10; 3½ in., $1.37; 4 in., $1.70.

FLUORSPAR

Washed gravel fluorspar, f.o.b. cars, Rosiclare, Ill. Base price, per ton net:
Effective CaF, content:
70% or more $43.00
60% or less 40.00

MERCHANT WIRE PRODUCTS

F.o.b. Mill	Standard & Coated Nails Base Col.	Woven Wire Fence 9-15½ ga. Base Col.	Fence Posts Base Col.	Single Loop Bale Ties Base Col.	Twisted Barbless Wire Base Col.	Gal. Barbed Wire Base Col.	Merch. Wire Ann'ld. ¢/lb.	Merch. Wire Gal. (1) ¢/lb.
Alabama City-4	118	126		123		136	5.70	5.95
Aliquippa, Pa.-5	118	132			136	140	5.70	6.15
Atlanta-65	121	133		126	126	143	5.95	6.40
Bartonville-34	118	130	140	123	143	143	5.95	6.15
Buffalo-85							4.85	
Cleveland-86	125							
Cleveland-2							5.70	6.15
Crawfordsville-87		132				145	5.95	6.40
Donora, Pa.-2	118	130		123		140	5.70	6.15
Duluth-2	118	130		123		140	5.70	6.15
Fairfield, Ala.-11	118	130		123		136	5.70	6.15
Houston-83	126	138			148		6.10	6.55
Johnstown, Pa.-3	118	130			140		5.70	6.15
Joliet, Ill.-2	118	130		123		140	5.70	6.15
Kokomo, Ind.-30	120	132		125	138	138	5.80	6.05
Los Angeles-62							6.65	
Kansas City-83	130	130	142	135		152	6.30	6.75
Minnequa-14	123	138	130	128	146	146	5.95	6.45
Monessen-18	124	135				145	5.95	6.40
Moline, Ill.-4			136					
Palmer-85								
Pittsburg, Cal.-24	137	149		147	156	160	6.65	6.80
Portsmouth-20	124	137			147	147	6.10	6.60
Rankin, Pa.-2	118	130				140	5.70	6.15
So. Chicago, Ill.-4	118	126	140	123		136	5.70	5.95
S. San Fran.-14					147		6.65	7.10
Sparrows Pt.-3	120			125	142	142	5.80	6.25
Sterling, Ill.-33	118	130	140	123	140	140	5.70	6.15
Struthers, Ohio-6							5.70	6.15
Torrance, Cal.-24	138						6.65	
Worcester-2	124						6.00	6.45
Williamsport, Pa.-51			150					

Cut Nails, carloads, base, $6.75 per 100 lb. (less 20¢ to Jobbers) at Conshohocken, Pa., (26), Wareham, Mass. (53), Wheeling, W. Va., (15).
(1) Alabama City and So. Chicago do not include zinc extra.

CAST IRON WATER PIPE

Per Net Ton
6 to 24-in. del'd Chicago.$105.30 to $108.80
6 to 24-in. del'd N. Y.... 108.50 to 109.50
6 to 24-in., Birmingham. 91.50 to 96.00
6-in. and larger, f.o.b. cars, San Francisco, Los Angeles, for all rail shipment; rail and water shipment less ...$108.50 to $113.00
Class "A" and gas pipe, $5 extra; 4-in. pipe is $5 a ton above 6-in.

PIPE AND TUBING

Base discounts, f.o.b. mills. Base price about $200 per net ton.

	BUTTWELD														SEAMLESS					
	½ In.		¾ In.		1 In.		1¼ In.		1½ In.		2 In.		2½-3 In.		2 In.		2½-3 In.		3½-4 In.	
	Blk.	Gal.	Blk.	Gal.	Blk.	Gal.	Blk.	Gal.	Blk.	Gal.	Blk.	Gal.	Blk.	Gal.	Blk.	Gal.	Blk.	Gal.	Blk.	Gal.
STANDARD T. & C.																				
Sparrows Pt.-3	34.0	12.0	37.0	16.0	39.5	19.5	40.0	20.0	40.5	21.0	41.0	21.5	41.5	22.0						
Cleveland-4	36.0	14.0	39.0	18.0	41.5	21.5	42.0	22.0	42.5	23.0	43.0	23.5	43.5	24.0						
Oakland-19	25.0	3.0	28.0	7.0	30.5	10.5	31.0	11.0	31.5	12.0	32.0	12.5	32.5	13.0						
Pittsburgh-5	36.0	14.0	39.0	17.0	41.5	19.5	42.0	20.5	42.5	21.0	43.0	23.5	43.5	22.5	29.5	9.5	32.5	11.5	34.5	14.5
Pittsburgh-10	36.0	14.0	39.0	18.0	41.5	21.5	42.0	22.0	42.5	23.0	43.0	23.5	43.5	22.5	29.5	9.5	32.5	12.5	34.5	14.5
St. Louis-32	35.0	13.0	38.0	17.0	40.5	20.5	41.0	21.0	41.5	22.0	42.0	22.5	42.5	23.0						
Sharon-90	36.0	14.0	39.0	18.0	41.5	21.5	42.0	22.0	42.5	23.0	43.0	23.5	43.5	24.0						
Toledo-88	36.0	14.0	39.0	18.0	41.5	21.5	42.0	22.0	42.5	23.0	43.0	23.5	43.5	24.0	29.5		32.5		34.5	
Wheeling-15	36.0	14.0	39.0	18.0	41.5	21.5	42.0	22.0	42.5	23.0	43.0	23.5	43.5	24.0						
Wheatland-89	36.0	14.0	39.0	18.0	41.5	21.5	42.0	22.0	42.5	23.0	43.0	23.5	43.5	24.0						
Youngstown-6	36.0	14.0	39.0	18.0	41.5	21.5	42.0	22.0	42.5	23.0	43.0	23.5	43.5	24.0	29.5	9.5	32.5	12.5	34.5	14.5
EXTRA STRONG, PLAIN ENDS																				
Sparrows Pt.-3	33.5	13.0	37.5	17.0	39.5	20.5	40.0	21.0	40.5	22.0	41.0	22.5	41.5	23.0						
Cleveland-4	35.5	15.0	39.5	19.0	41.5	22.5	42.0	23.0	42.5	24.0	43.0	24.5	43.5	24.5						
Oakland-19	24.5	4.0	28.5	8.0	30.5	11.5	31.0	12.0	31.5	13.0	32.0	13.5	32.5	14.0						
Pittsburgh-5	35.5	15.0	39.5	17.5	41.5	19.5	42.0	20.5	42.5	22.0	43.0	22.5	43.5	22.5	29.0		7.5	33.0	12.0	36.0	15.5
Pittsburgh-10	35.5	15.0	39.5	19.0	41.5	22.5	42.0	23.0	42.5	24.0	43.0	24.5	43.5	24.5	29.0	10.0	33.0	14.0	36.5	17.5
St. Louis-32	34.5	14.0	38.5	18.0	40.5	21.5	41.0	22.0	41.5	23.0	42.0	23.5	42.5	24.0						
Sharon-90	35.5	15.0	39.5	19.0	41.5	21.5	42.0	22.0	42.5	23.0	43.0	23.5	43.5	24.0						
Toledo-88	35.5	15.0	39.5	19.0	41.5	22.5	42.0	23.0	42.5	24.0	43.0	24.5	43.5	24.0	29.0		33.0		36.5	
Wheeling-15	35.5	15.0	39.5	19.0	41.5	22.5	42.0	23.0	42.5	24.0	43.0	24.5	43.5	24.5						
Wheatland-89	35.5	15.0	39.5	19.0	41.5	22.5	42.0	23.0	42.5	24.0	43.0	24.5	43.5	24.5						
Youngstown-6	35.5	15.0	39.5	19.0	41.5	22.5	42.0	23.0	42.5	24.0	43.0	24.5	43.5	24.0	29.0	10.0	33.0	14.0	36.5	17.5

Galvanized discounts based on zinc at 17¢ per lb, East St. Louis. For each 1¢ change in zinc, discounts vary as follows: ½ in., ¾ in., and 1 in., 1 pt.; 1¼ in., 1½ in., 2 in. ¾ pt.; 2½ in., 3 in., ½ pt. Calculate discounts on even cents per lb of zinc, i.e., if zinc is 16.51¢ to 17.50¢ per lb, use 17¢. Jones & Laughlin discounts apply only when zinc price changes 1¢.
Threads only, buttweld and seamless, 1 pt. higher discount. Plain ends, buttweld and seamless, 3 in. and under, 3½ pts. higher discount. Buttweld jobbers' discount, 5 pct.

WAREHOUSES

Base price, f.o.b., dollars per 100 lb. *(Metropolitan area delivery, add 20¢ except Birmingham, San Francisco, Cincinnati, New Orleans, St. Paul, add 15¢; Memphis, add 10¢; Philadelphia, add 25¢; New York, add 30¢).

Cities	Sheets Hot-Rolled	Sheets Cold-Rolled (15 gage)	Sheets Galvanized (10 gage)	Strip Hot-Rolled	Strip Cold-Rolled	Plates	Shapes Standard Structural	Bars Hot-Rolled	Bars Cold-Finished	Alloy Bars Hot-Rolled A 4615 As rolled	Alloy Bars Hot-Rolled A 4140 Annealed	Alloy Bars Cold-Drawn A 4615 As rolled	Alloy Bars Cold-Drawn A 4140 Annealed
Baltimore.........	5.60	6.84	7.49²–8.07	6.04	.....	5.80	6.14	6.04	6.84–6.89	10.24	10.54	11.89	12.19
Birmingham*......	5.60	6.40	6.75	5.55	.....	5.95	5.70	5.55	.....	.....	.....	.....	.....
Boston...........	6.20	7.00–7.25	7.74–8.29	6.15	8.50⁴	6.48–6.78	6.20	6.05	6.79–6.84	10.25	10.55	11.90–12.00	12.20–12.30
Buffalo..........	5.60	6.40	7.74–8.09	5.86	.....	6.05	5.80	5.60	6.40–6.45	10.15–10.85	10.45	11.80	11.95–12.10
Chicago..........	5.60	6.40	7.75	5.55	.....	5.80	5.70	5.55	6.30	9.80	10.10	11.45	11.75
Cincinnati*.......	5.87	6.44	7.39	5.80	.....	6.19	6.09	5.80	6.61	10.15	10.45	11.80	12.10
Cleveland........	5.60	6.40	8.10	5.69	6.90	5.92	5.82	5.57	6.40	9.91	10.21	11.56	11.86
Detroit..........	5.78	6.53	7.89	5.94	.....	5.99	6.09	5.84	6.	10.11	10.41	11.76	12.06
Houston..........	7.00	8.25	.....	.....	.....	6.85	6.50	6.65	9.35	10.35	10.35	.....	12.75
Indianapolis, del'd.	6.00	6.80	8.15	5.95	.....	6.20	6.10	5.95	6.80	.....	.....	.....	.....
Kansas City.......	6.00	6.80	7.45	6.15	7.50	6.40	6.30	6.15	7.00	10.40	10.70	12.05	12.35
Los Angeles.......	6.35	7.90	8.85	6.40	9.45⁶	6.40	6.35	6.35	8.20	11.30	11.30	13.20	13.50
Memphis*.........	6.33–6.38	7.08–7.18	.....	6.33–6.38	.....	6.43–8.02	6.33–6.48	6.08–6.33	7.16–7.32	.....	.....	.....	.....
Milwaukee........	5.74	6.54	7.89	5.69–6.59	.....	5.94	5.84	5.69	6.44–6.54	9.94	10.24	11.59	11.89
New Orleans*......	5.70	6.59	.....	5.75	7.25	5.95	5.75	5.75	7.30	.....	.....	.....	.....
New York*........	5.67–5.97	7.19⁵–7.24¹	8.14²	6.29–6.89	8.63⁴	6.28–6.58	6.10	6.12	6.99	10.05–10.15	10.35–10.45	11.70–11.80	12.10–12.20
Norfolk..........	6.50³	.....	.....	.....	.....	6.50³	6.60³	6.55³	.....	.....	.....	.....	.....
Philadelphia*.....	5.90	6.80	8.00	6.10	.....	6.05	5.90	6.05	6.86	9.90	10.20	.....	.....
Pittsburgh........	5.60	6.40	7.75	5.65–5.95	.....	5.75	5.70	5.55	6.15	9.80	10.10	11.45	11.75
Portland..........	6.60–7.55	8.95	8.50–9.10	7.30	.....	6.80	6.95	6.90	.....	12.15	.....	.....	.....
Salt Lake City.....	7.95	.....	9.70–10.50²	8.70–8.75	.....	8.05	6.75–8.30	7.95–8.65	9.00	.....	.....	.....	.....
San Francisco*.....	6.65	8.05²	8.55–8.90²	6.60	9.45⁶	6.50	6.45	6.45	8.20	11.30	11.30	13.20	13.20–13.50
Seattle...........	7.05	8.60	9.20	9.05	.....	6.75	6.65	6.75	9.05	.....	.....	.....	.....
St. Louis.........	5.80–5.85	6.65	8.00	5.80	8.00⁴–8.28	6.13	6.03	5.80	6.55–6.65	10.05	10.35	11.70	12.00
St. Paul*.........	6.16	6.96	8.31	6.11	.....	6.36	6.26	6.11	6.96	10.36	10.66	12.01	12.31

BASE QUANTITIES (Standard unless otherwise keyed): Cold finished bars; 2000 lb or over. Alloy bars; 1000 to 1999 lb. All others; 2000 to 9999 lb. All HR products may be combined for quantity. All galvanized sheets may be combined for quantity. CR sheets may not be combined with each other or with galvanized sheets for quantity.
EXCEPTIONS: (1) 400 to 1499 lb; (2) 450 to 1499 lb; (3) 400 to 1999 lb; (4) 6000 lb and over; (5) 1500 to 9999 lb.; (6) 2000 to 5999 lb.

PIG IRON

Dollars per gross ton, f.o.b., subject to switching charges.

Producing Point	Basic	No. 2 Foundry	Malleable	Bessemer	Low Phos.	Blast Furnace Silvery	Low Phos. Charcoal
Bethlehem-3........	54.00	54.50	55.00	55.50	.....	.....	.....
Birmingham-4.......	48.38	48.88	.....	.....	.....	.....	.....
Birmingham-91......	48.38	48.88	.....	.....	.....	.....	.....
Birmingham-92......	48.38	48.88	.....	.....	.....	.....	.....
Buffalo-4..........	52.00	52.50	53.00	.....	.....	.....	.....
Buffalo-93.........	52.00	52.50	53.00	.....	.....	63.75	.....
Chicago-94.........	52.00	52.50	52.50	53.00	.....	.....	.....
Cleveland-2........	52.00	52.50	52.50	53.00	57.00	.....	.....
Cleveland-4........	52.00	52.50	52.50	.....	.....	.....	.....
Daingerfield, Tex.-95.	48.00	48.50	48.50	.....	.....	.....	.....
Duluth-94..........	52.00	52.50	52.50	53.00	.....	.....	.....
Erie-94...........	52.00	52.50	52.50	53.00	.....	.....	.....
Everett, Mass.-96...	.....	53.25	53.75	.....	.....	.....	.....
Fontana-19.........	58.00	58.50	.....	.....	.....	.....	.....
Geneva, Utah-16.....	52.00	52.50	52.50	53.00	.....	.....	.....
Granite City, Ill.-102.	53.90	54.40	54.90	.....	.....	.....	.....
Hubbard, O.-6.......	52.00	52.50	52.50	.....	.....	.....	.....
Ironton, Utah-16....	52.00	52.50	.....	.....	.....	.....	.....
Jackson, O.-97,98....	.....	.....	.....	.....	.....	62.50	66.00
Lyle, Tenn.-101.....	.....	.....	.....	.....	.....	.....	.....
Monessen-18........	54.00	.....	.....	.....	.....	.....	.....
Neville Island-99....	52.00	52.50	52.50	53.00	.....	.....	.....
Pittsburgh-1........	52.00	.....	.....	53.00	.....	.....	.....
Sharpsville-100.....	52.00	52.50	52.50	53.00	.....	.....	.....
Steelton-3.........	54.00	54.50	55.00	55.50	60.00	.....	.....
Swedeland-26.......	56.00	56.50	57.00	57.50	.....	.....	.....
Toledo-94..........	52.00	52.50	52.50	53.00	.....	.....	.....
Troy, N. Y.-4.......	54.00	54.50	55.00	.....	60.00	.....	.....
Youngstown-6.......	52.00	52.50	52.50	53.00	.....	.....	.....

DIFFERENTIALS: Add 50¢ per ton for each 0.25 pct silicon over base (1.75 to 2.25 pct), 50¢ per ton for each 0.25 pct manganese over 1 pct, $2 per ton for 0.5 to 0.75 pct nickel, $1 for each additional 0.25 pct nickel. Subtract 38¢ per ton for phosphorus content over 0.70 pct. Silvery iron: Add $1.50 per ton for each 0.50 pct silicon over base (6.01 to 6.50 pct) up to 17 pct. $1 per ton for 0.75 pct or more phosphorus, manganese as above. Bessemer ferrosilicon prices are $1 over comparable silvery iron.

REFRACTORIES

(F.o.b. works)

Fire Clay Brick — Carloads, Per 1000

First quality, Ill., Ky., Md., Mo., Ohio, Pa. (except Salina, Pa., add $5)....	$94.60
No. 1 Ohio	88.00
Sec. quality, Pa., Md., Ky., Mo., Ill..	88.00
No. 2 Ohio	79.20
Ground fire clay, net ton, bulk (except Salina, Pa., add $1.50)	13.75

Silica Brick

Mt. Union, Pa., Ensley, Ala.	$94.60
Childs, Pa.	99.00
Hays, Pa.	100.10
Chicago District	104.50
Western Utah and Calif.	111.10
Super Duty, Hays, Pa., Athens, Tex., Chicago	111.10
Silica cement, net ton, bulk, Eastern (except Hays, Pa.)	16.50
Silica cement, net ton, bulk, Hays, Pa.	18.70
Silica cement, net ton, bulk, Ensley, Ala.	17.60
Silica cement, net ton, bulk, Chicago District	17.60
Silica cement, net ton, bulk, Utah and Calif.	24.70

Chrome Brick — Per Net Ton

Standard chemically bonded, Balt., Chester	$82.00

Magnesite Brick

Standard, Baltimore	$104.00
Chemically bonded, Baltimore	93.00

Grain Magnesite — St. ⅜-in. grains

Domestic, f.o.b. Baltimore, in bulk fines removed	$62.70
Domestic, f.o.b. Chewelah, Wash., in bulk	36.30
in sacks	41.80

Dead Burned Dolomite

F.o.b. producing points in Pennsylvania, West Virginia and Ohio, per net ton, bulk Midwest, add 10¢; Missouri Valley, add 20¢....	$13.00

COKE

	Net Ton
Furnace, beehive (f.o.b. oven) Connellsville, Pa.	$14.00 to $14.50
Foundry, beehive (f.o.b. oven) Connellsville, Pa.	$17.00 to $17.50
Foundry, oven coke	
Buffalo, del'd	$25.35
Chicago, f.o.b.	23.00
Detroit, f.o.b.	24.00
New England, del'd	24.80
Seaboard, N. J., f.o.b.	22.00
Philadelphia, f.o.b.	22.70
Swedeland, Pa., f.o.b.	22.60
Plainesville, Ohio, f.o.b.	24.00
Erie, Pa., f.o.b.	23.50
Cleveland, del'd	25.72
Cincinnati, del'd	25.06
St. Paul, f.o.b.	22.50
St. Louis	25.40
Birmingham, del'd	21.69
Neville Island	23.00

LAKE SUPERIOR ORES

(51.50% Fe; natural content, delivered lower lake ports)

	Per gross ton
Old range, bessemer	$8.70
Old range, nonbessemer	8.55
Mesabi, bessemer	8.45
Mesabi, nonbessemer	8.30
High phosphorus	8.30

After adjustments for analyses, prices will be increased or decreased as the case may be for increases or decreases after Dec. 2, 1950, in lake vessel rates, upper lake rail freights, dock handling charges and taxes thereon.

C-R SPRING STEEL

Base per pound f.o.b. mill

0.26 to 0.40 carbon	5.35¢
0.41 to 0.60 carbon	6.80¢
0.61 to 0.80 carbon	7.40¢
0.81 to 1.05 carbon	9.35¢
1.06 to 1.35 carbon	11.65¢

Worcester, add 0.30¢; Sharon, Carnegie, New Castle, add 0.35¢; Detroit, 0.26 to 0.40 carb., add 25¢; other grades add 15¢. New Haven, 0.26 to 0.40 carb., add 50¢; other grades 5¢.

IRON AGE MARKETS & PRICES
FOUNDED 1855

BOLTS, NUTS, RIVETS, SCREWS
Consumer Prices
(Base discount, f.o.b. mill, Pittsburgh, Cleveland, Birmingham or Chicago)

Machine and Carriage Bolts

	Pct Off List Less Case	C.
½ in. & smaller x 6 in. & shorter	15	28½
9/16 in. & ⅝ in. x 6 in. & shorter	18½	30½
¾ in. & larger x 6 in. & shorter	17½	29½
All diam. longer than 6 in.	14	27½
Lag, all diam. x 6 in. & shorter	23	35
Lag, all diam. longer than 6 in.	21	33
Plow bolts	34	....

Nuts, Hot Pressed, Cold Punched—Sq
Pct Off List

	Less Keg (Reg.)	K.	Less Keg (Hvy.)	K.
½ in. & smaller	15	28½	15	28½
9/16 in. & ⅝ in.	12	25	6½	21
¾ in. to 1½ in. inclusive	9	23	1	16½
1⅝ in. & larger	7½	22	1	16½

Nuts, Hot Pressed—Hexagon

½ in. & smaller	26	37	22	34
9/16 in. & ⅝ in.	16½	29½	6½	21
¾ in. to 1½ in. inclusive	12	25	2	17½
1⅝ in. & larger	8½	23	2	17½

Nuts, Cold Punched—Hexagon

½ in. & smaller	26	37	22	34
9/16 in. & ⅝ in.	23	35	17½	30½
¾ in. to 1½ in. inclusive	19½	31½	12	25
1⅝ in. & larger	12	25	6½	21

Nuts, Semi-Finished—Hexagon

	Reg.		Hvy.	
½ in. & smaller	35	45	28½	39½
9/16 in. & ⅝ in.	29½	40½	22	34
¾ in. to 1½ in. inclusive	24	36	15	28½
1⅝ in. & larger	13	26	8½	23
	Light			
7/16 in. & smaller	35	45		
½ in. thru ⅝ in.	28½	39½		
¾ in. to 1½ in. inclusive	26	37		

Stove Bolts
Pct Off List

Packaged, steel, plain finished	56—10
Packaged, plated finish	41—10
Bulk, plain finish**	67*

*Discounts apply to bulk shipments in not less than 15,000 pieces of a size and kind where length is 3-in. and shorter; 5000 pieces for lengths longer than 3-in. For lesser quantities, packaged price applies.
**Zinc, Parkerized, cadmium or nickel plated finishes add 6¢ per lb net. For black oil finish, add 2¢ per lb net.

Rivets
Base per 100 lb.

½ in. & larger	$7.85
	Pct Off List
7/16 in. & smaller	36

F.o.b. Pittsburgh, Cleveland, Chicago, Birmingham, Lebanon, Pa.

Cap and Set Screws
(In bulk)   *Pct Off List*

Hexagon head cap screws, coarse or fine thread, ¼ in. thru ⅝ in. x 6 in., SAE 1020, bright	54
¾ in. thru 1 in. up to & including 6 in.	48
¼ in. thru ⅝ in. x 6 in. & shorter high C double heat treat	46
¾ in. thru 1 in. up to & including 6 in.	41
Milled studs	35
Flat head cap screws, listed sizes	16
Fillister head cap, listed sizes	34
Set screws, sq head, cup point, 1 in. diam. and smaller x 6 in. & shorter	53

S. M. Ferrochrome

Contract price, cents per pound, chromium contained, lump size, delivered.
High carbon type: 60-65% Cr, 4-6% Si, 4-6% Mn, 4-6% C.

Carloads	21.60
Ton lots	23.75
Less ton lots	25.25

Low carbon type: 62-66% Cr, 4-6% Si, 4-6% Mn, 1.25% max. C.

Carloads	27.75
Ton lots	30.05
Less ton lots	31.85

February 15, 1951

IRON AGE
FOUNDED 1855   MARKETS & PRICES

ELECTRODES

Cents per lb., f.o.b. plant, threaded electrodes with nipples, unboxed

Diam. in in.	Length in in.	Cents Per lb.
	GRAPHITE	
17, 18, 20	60, 72	17.85
8 to 16	48, 60, 72	17.85
7	48, 60	19.57
6	48, 60	20.95
4, 5	40	21.50
3	40	22.61
2½	24, 30	23.15
2	24, 30	25.36
	CARBON	
40	100, 110	8.03
35	65, 110	8.03
30	65, 84, 110	8.03
24	72 to 104	8.03
20	84, 90	8.03
17	60, 72	8.03
14	60, 72	8.57
10, 12	60	8.84
8	60	9.10

CLAD STEEL

Base prices, cents per pound, f.o.b. mill

Stainless-carbon	Plate	Sheet
No. 304, 20 pct,		
Coatesville, Pa. (21)	*29.5	
Washgtn. Pa. (39)	*29.5	
Claymont, Del. (29)	*28.00	
Conshohocken, Pa. (26)		*24.00
New Castle, Ind. (55)	*26.50	*25.50
Nickel-carbon		
10 pct Coatesville (21)	32.5	
Inconel-carbon		
10 pct Coatesville (21)	40.5	
Monel-carbon		
10 pct Coatesville (21)	33.5	
No. 302 Stainless-copper-stainless, Carnegie, Pa. (60)	77.00	
Aluminized steel sheets, hot dip, Butler, Pa. (7)	7.75	

*Includes annealing and pickling, or sandblasting.

TOOL STEEL

F.o.b. mill

W	Cr	V	Mo	Co	Base per lb
18	4	1	—	—	$1.235
18	4	1	—	5	$1.86
18	4	2	—	—	$1.38
1.5	4	1.5	8	—	78.5¢
6	4	2	6	—	.87¢
High-carbon chromium					63.5¢
Oil hardened manganese					35¢
Special carbon					32.5¢
Extra carbon					27¢
Regular carbon					23¢

Warehouse prices on and east of Mississippi are 3¢ per lb higher. West of Mississippi, 5¢ higher.

METAL POWDERS

Per pound, f.o.b. shipping point, in ton lots, for minus 100 mesh.

Swedish sponge iron c.i.f. New York, ocean bags	7.4¢ to 9.0¢
Canadian sponge iron, del'd, in East	10.00¢
Domestic sponge iron, 98+% Fe, carload lots	9.0¢ to 15.0¢
Electrolytic iron, annealed, 99.5+% Fe	36.0¢ to 39.5¢
Electrolytic iron unannealed, minus 325 mesh, 99+% Fe	48.5¢
Hydrogen reduced iron, minus 300 mesh, 98+% Fe.	63.0¢ to 80.0¢
Carbonyl iron, size 5 to 10 micron, 98%, 99.8+% Fe	70.0¢ to $1.35
Aluminum	29.00¢
Brass, 10 ton lots	30.00¢ to 33.25¢
Copper, electrolytic	10.25¢ plus metal value
Copper, reduced	10.00¢ plus metal value
Cadmium, 100-199 lb.	95¢ plus metal value
Chromium, electrolytic, 99% min., and quantity	$3.50
Lead	6.5¢ plus metal value
Manganese	52.00¢
Molybdenum, 99%	$2.65
Nickel, unannealed	75.5¢
Nickel, annealed	81.5¢
Nickel, spherical, unannealed	78.5¢
Silicon	34.00¢
Solder powder	6.5¢ to 8.5¢ plus met. value
Stainless steel, 302	75.00¢
Tin	11.00¢ plus metal value
Tungsten, 99%	$4.15
Zinc, 10 ton lots	20.50¢ to 23.85¢

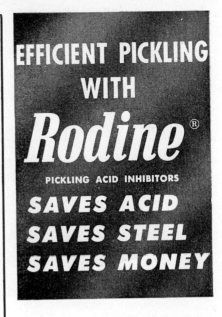

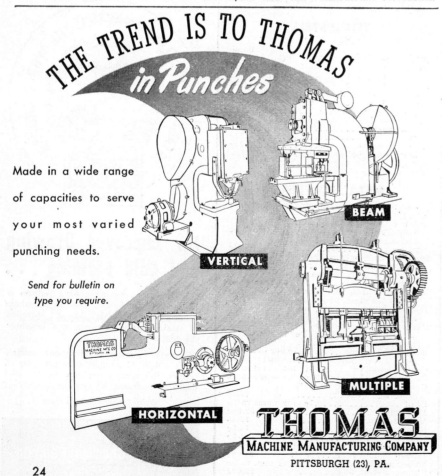
IRON AGE MARKETS & PRICES
FOUNDED 1855

ELECTRICAL SHEETS

F.o.b. Mill Cents Per Lb.	Armature	Elec.	Motor	Dynamo	Transf. 72	Transf. 65	Transf. 58
Beech Botton-15...		7.25	8.50	9.30	9.85	10.40	11.10
Brackenridge-28...		7.25	8.50	9.30	9.85		
Follansbee-63...	6.75	7.25	8.50	9.30	9.85	10.40	11.10
Granite City-22...		7.95	9.20				
Ind. Harbor-3...	6.75	7.25					
Mansfield-75...	6.75	7.25	8.50	9.30			
Niles, O.-64...	7.05	7.55					
Vandergrift-1...	6.75	7.25	8.50	9.30	9.85	10.40	11.10
Warren, O.-4...	6.75	7.25	8.50	9.30	9.85	10.40	11.10
Zanesville-7...	8.75	7.25	8.50	9.30	9.85	10.40	11.10

22 Ga. H-R cut lengths

Transformer 52, 80¢ above Transformer 58.

Ferrochrome
Contract prices, cents per pound, contained Cr, lump size, bulk, in carloads, delivered. (65-72% Cr, 2% max. Si.)

0.06% C ... 30.50		0.20% C ... 29.50
0.10% C ... 30.00		0.50% C ... 29.25
0.15% C ... 29.75		1.00% C ... 29.00
2.00% C			28.75
65-69% Cr, 4-9% C			22.00
62-66% Cr, 4-6% C, 6-9% Si.			22.85

High-Nitrogen Ferrochrome
Low-carbon type: 67-72% Cr, 0.75% N. Add 5¢ per lb to regular low carbon ferrochrome price schedule. Add 5¢ for each additional 0.25% N.

Chromium Metal
Contract prices, per lb chromium contained, packed, delivered, ton lots. 97% min. Cr, 1% max. Fe.

0.20% Max. C	$1.09
0.50% max. C	1.05
.00 min. C	1.04

Low Carbon Ferrochrome Silicon
(Cr 34-41%, Si 42-49%, C 0.05% max.) Contract price, carloads, f.o.b. Niagara Falls, freight allowed; lump 4-in. x down, bulk 2-in. x down, 21.75¢ per lb of contained Cr plus 12.00¢ per lb of contained Si.
Bulk 1-in. x down, 21.90¢ per lb contained Cr plus 12.20¢ per lb contained Si.

Calcium-Silicon
Contract price per lb of alloy, dump, delivered.
30-33% Ca, 60-65% Si, 3.00% max. Fe.

Carloads	19.00
Ton lots	22.10
Less ton lots	23.00

Calcium-Manganese—Silicon
Contract prices, cents per lb of alloy, lump, delivered.
16-20% Ca, 14-18% Mn, 53-59% Si.

Carloads	20.00
Ton lots	22.30
Less ton lots	23.30

CMSZ
Contract price, cents per lb of alloy, delivered.
Alloy 4: 45-49% Cr, 4-6% Mn, 18-21% Si, 1.25-1.75% Zr, 3.00-4.5% C.
Alloy 5: 50.56% Cr, 4-6% Mn, 13.50-16.00% Si, 0.75 to 1.25% Zr, 3.50-5.00% C.

Ton lots	20.75
Less ton lots	22.00

V Foundry Alloy
Cents per pound of alloy, f.o.b. Suspension Bridge, N. Y., freight allowed, max. St. Louis. V-5: 38-42% Cr, 17-19% Si, 8-11% Mn.

Ton lots	16.50¢
Less ton lots	17.75¢

Graphidox No. 4
Cents per pound of alloy, f.o.b. Suspension Bridge, N. Y., freight allowed, max. St. Louis. Si 48 to 52%, Ti 9 to 11%, Ca 5 to 7%.

Carload packed	18.00¢
Ton lots to carload packed	19.00¢
Less ton lots	20.50¢

SMZ
Contract price, cents per pound of alloy, delivered, 60-65% Si, 5-7% Mn, 5-7% Zr, 20% Fe, ½ in. x 12 mesh.

Ton lots	17.25
Less ton lots	18.50

Simply clean surface

STEP 1

Simply apply **dy√chek** Dye Penetrant *(by brush, spray, or dip)*

STEP 2

Simplified Non-Destructive Testing

Simply remove excess dye with **dy√chek** Dye Remover

STEP 3

Simply apply **dy√chek** Developer

STEP 4

New Way to INSPECT METALS

Save dollars... save time... and be sure!

HERE ARE FACTS ON

dy√chek TRADE-MARK

the dye penetrant inspection method
PATENT PENDING

AND... FLAWS ARE REVEALED

CRACK, COLD SHUT, OR SIMILAR OPENING

PITS OR POROSITY

TIGHT CRACK OR COLD SHUT, OR PARTIALLY WELDED LAP

QUESTIONS AND ANSWERS

Q. What is Dy-Chek?

A. Dy-Chek is the revolutionary new dye penetrant method of inspection developed by *Northrop Aircraft Research*. It consists of three special liquid compounds easily applied by brush, spray, or dip.

Q. What does it do?

A. Dy-Chek reveals the location, extent, and nature of any flaw having a surface opening or discontinuity in any metal.

Q. What kind of metal surface can Dy-Chek inspect?

A. Any kind, magnetic or non-magnetic, including castings, forgings, machined parts, plate, sheet, tubing, pipe, and weldments.

Q. Are special lights required?

A. No lights, booths, electricity, or special installations are necessary.

Q. Is Dy-Chek inspection expensive?

A. Not at all. No fees or licensing is required — only the moderate cost of the special liquids. Dy-Chek materials cover large areas per gallon. Dye Remover is water-soluble, therefore water can be used freely in Step 3.

Q. Can Dy-Chek be used in the field, for preventive maintenance, as well as in a plant for manufacturing and receiving inspection?

A. Yes, the complete portability of Dy-Chek is one of its great advantages.

LEARN HOW the Dy-Chek method of non-destructive testing can save you time and money in your business. Ask for complete details today.

dy√chek COMPANY
TRADE MARK

division of Northrop Aircraft, Inc.

1505 EAST BROADWAY HAWTHORNE, CALIFORNIA

dy√chek —*the dye penetrant inspection method*

Dy√Chek Company
1505 East Broadway, Hawthorne, California
Send by return mail complete details on Dy-Chek, the Dye Penetrant Method of inspection for any metal.

Name_____ Title_____

Company_____

Address_____

City_____ Zone____ State____

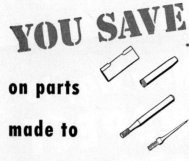

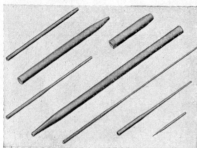
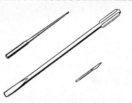
IRON AGE FOUNDED 1855 — MARKETS & PRICES

FERROALLOYS

Ferromanganese

78-82% Mn. maximum contract base price, gross ton, lump size.

F.o.b. Niagara Falls, Alloy, W. Va., Welland, Ont., Ashtabula, O.	$185
F.o.b. Johnstown, Pa.	$187
F.o.b. Sheridan, Pa.	$185
F.o.b. Etna, Clairton, Pa.	$188

$2.00 for each 1% above 82% Mn, penalty, $2.15 for each 1% below 78%.

Briquets—Cents per pound of briquet, delivered, 66% contained Mn.

Carload, bulk	10.95
Ton lots	12.55

Spiegeleisen

Contract prices gross ton, lump, f.o.b.

	16-19% Mn 3% max. Si	19-21% Mn 3% max. Si
Palmerton, Pa.	$74.00	$75.00
Pgh. or Chicago	74.00	75.00

Manganese Metal

Contract basis, 2 in. x down, cents per pound of metal, delivered. 96% min. Mn, 0.2% max. C, 1% max. Si, 2% max. Fe.

Carload, packed	29.75
Ton lots	31.25

Electrolytic Manganese

F.o.b. Knoxville, Tenn., freight allowed east of Mississippi, cents per pound.

Carloads	28
Ton lots	30
Less ton lots	32

Medium Carbon Ferromanganese

Mn 80% to 85%, C 1.25 to 1.50. Contract price, carloads, lump, bulk, delivered, per lb. of contained Mn............19.15¢

Calcium Metal

Eastern zone contract prices, cents per pound of metal, delivered.

	Cast	Turnings	Distilled
Ton lots	$2.05	$2.95	$3.75
Less ton lots	2.40	3.30	4.55

Silicomanganese

Contract basis, lump size, cents per pound of metal, delivered, 65-68% Mn, 18-20% Si, 1.5% max. C. For 2% max. C, deduct 0.2¢.

Carload bulk	9.90
Ton lots	11.55

Briquet, contract basis carlots, bulk

delivered, per lb of briquet	11.15
Ton lots	11.75

Silvery Iron (electric furnace)

Si 14.01 to 14.50 pct, f.o.b. Keokuk, Iowa, or Wenatchee, Wash., $89.50 gross ton, freight allowed to normal trade area. Si 15.01 to 15.50 pct, f.o.b. Niagara Falls, N. Y., $83.00. Add $1.00 per ton for each additional 0.50% Si up to and including 18%. Add $1.00 for each 0.50% Mn over 1%.

Silicon Metal

Contract price, cents per pound contained Si, lump size, delivered, for ton lots packed.

96% Si, 2% Fe	21.70
97% Si, 1% Fe	22.10

Silicon Briquets

Contract price, cents per pound of briquet bulk, delivered, 40% Si, 1 lb Si briquets.

Carload, bulk	6.95
Ton lots	8.55

Electric Ferrosilicon

Contract price, cents per pound contained Si, lump, bulk, carloads, delivered.

25% Si	19.00	75% Si	14.30
50% Si	12.40	85% Si	15.55
90-95% Si			17.50

Low-Carbon Ferromanganese

Contract price, cents per pound Mn contained, lump size, del'd, Mn 85-90%.

	Carloads	Ton	Less
0.7% max. C, 0.06% P, 90% Mn	26.25	28.10	29.30
0.07% max. C	25.75	27.60	28.80
0.15% max. C	25.25	27.10	28.30
0.30% max. C	24.75	26.60	27.80
0.50% max. C	24.25	26.10	27.30
0.75% max. C, 7.00% max. Si	21.25	23.10	24.30

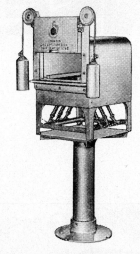

IRON AGE FOUNDED 1855 **MARKETS & PRICES**

Other Ferroalloys

Alsifer, 20% Al, 40% Si, 40% Fe, contract basis, f.o.b. Suspension Bridge, N. Y.	
Carload	9.90¢
Ton lots	11.30¢
Calcium molybdate, 45-40%, f.o.b. Langeloth, Pa., per pound contained Mo	$1.15
Ferrocolumbium, 50-60%, 2 in x D, contract basis, delivered, per pound contained Cb.	
Ton lots	$4.90
Less ton lots	4.95
Ferro - Tantalum - columbium, 20% Ta, 40% Cb, 0.30 C. Contract basis, delivered, ton lots, 2 in. x D, per lb of contained Cb plus Ta	$3.75
Ferromolybdenum, 55-75%, f.o.b. Langeloth, Pa., per pound contained Mo	$1.32
Ferrophosphorus, electrolytic, 23-26%, car lots, f.o.b. Siglo, Mt. Pleasant, Tenn., $3 unitage, per gross ton	$65.00
10 tons to less carload	75.00
Ferrotitanium, 40%, regular grade, 0.10% C max., f.o.b. Niagara Falls, N. Y., and Bridgeville, Pa., freight allowed, ton lots, per lb contained Ti	$1.35
Ferrotitanium, 25%, low carbon, 0.10% C max., f.o.b. Niagara Falls, N. Y., and Bridgeville, Pa., freight allowed, ton lots, per lb contained Ti	$1.50
Less ton lots	$1.55
Ferrotitanium, 15 to 19%, high carbon, f.o.b. Niagara Falls, N. Y., freight allowed, carload per net ton	$177.00
Ferrotungsten, standard, lump or ¼ x down, packed, per pound contained W, 5 ton lots, delivered	$3.25
Ferrovanadium, 35-55%, contract basis, delivered, per pound, contained V.	
Openhearth	$3.00-$3.05
Crucible	3.10- 3.15
High speed steel (Primos)	3.25
Molybdic oxide, briquets or cans, per lb contained Mo, f.o.b. Langeloth, Pa.	$1.14
bags, f.o.b. Washington, Pa., Langeloth, Pa.	$1.13
Simanal, 20% Si, 20% Mn, 20% Al, contract basis, f.o.b. Philo, Ohio, freight allowed, per pound	
Carload, bulk lump	14.50¢
Ton lots, bulk lump	15.75¢
Less ton lots, lump	16.25¢
Vanadium pentoxide, 88-92% V_2O_5 contract basis, per pound contained V_2O_5	$1.28
Zirconium, 35-40%, contract basis, f.o.b. plant, freight allowed, per pound of alloy.	
ton lots	21.00¢
Zirconium, 12-15%, contract basis, lump, delivered, per lb of alloy.	
carload, bulk	7.00¢

Boron Agents

Contract prices per lb of alloy, del.	
Borosil, f.o.b. Philo, Ohio, freight allowed, B 3-4%, Si 40-45%, per lb contained B	$5.25
Bortam, f.o.b. Niagara Falls	
Ton lots, per pound	45¢
Less ton lots, per pound	50¢
Carbortam, Ti 15-21%, B 1-2%, Si 2-4%, Al 1-2%, C 4.5-7.5%, f.o.b. Suspension Bridge, N. Y., freight allowed.	
Ton lots, per pound	10.00¢
Ferroboron, 17.50% min. B, 1.50% max. Si, 0.50% max. Al, 0.50% max. C, 1 in. x D. Ton lots	$1.20
F.o.b. Wash., Pa.; 100 lb, up	
10 to 14% B	.75
14 to 19% B	1.20
19% min. B	1.50
Grainal, f.o.b. Bridgeville, Pa., freight allowed, 100 lb and over.	
No. 1	$1.00
No. 6	68¢
No. 79	50¢
Manganese—Boron 75.00% Mn, 15-20% B, 5% max. Fe, 1.50% max. Si, 3.00% max. C, 2 in. x D, delivered.	
Ton lots	$1.46
Less ton lots	1.57
Nickel—Boron 15-18% B, 1.00% max. Al, 1.50% max. Si, 0.50% max. C, 3.00% max. Fe, balance Ni, delivered.	
Less ton lots	$1.80
Silcaz, contract basis, delivered.	
Ton lots	45.00¢

MONARCH CURED-ON TIRES

Soft Touch for Floors

Easy-going Monarch Tires on your hand trucks will make your floors last longer, reduce your floor repair bills—Monarch Tires never groove or chip floors. Monarch-equipped caster wheels are instantly responsive to changes in direction. Make sure the hand trucks you buy are equipped with Monarch Tires. Available in oil-resistant synthetics.

The leading manufacturers of industrial trucks, both hand and powered, use Monarch Tires as original equipment.

THE
MONARCH
RUBBER COMPANY

301 LINCOLN PARK • HARTVILLE, OHIO

SPECIALISTS IN INDUSTRIAL SOLID TIRES AND MOLDED MECHANICAL RUBBER GOODS

Sweden to Make More Sponge Iron to Recapture Lost Markets

Stockholm—Sweden is planning greater production and building new sponge iron plants to fend off harmful effects of high prices of charcoal pig iron and unwanted alloys of poorer scrap metal in making its high-grade steels.

With fuel costs of charcoal iron almost double those of coke pig iron and scrap in shortage and of poorer quality, Swedish steelmakers want to recapture lost special steel markets and jack up backsliding exports of quality steels to a pre-war point of 200,000 tons per year. Now, exports are 120,000 tons a year.

Planning New Plants

New sponge iron plants are being built at Sandviken and Hellefors, while Bofors, Gagersta, and Uddeholm companies are considering joint production of the material from Toulluvaara ore. Others are also planning furnaces.

The Sandviken works brings up the problem of unwanted alloying elements in scrap by saying that they cannot use outside scrap for their special steels. For many years the firm has been charging 15 to 20 pct sponge iron instead of scrap in its acid openhearth furnaces. Soderfors and Bofors also use heavy charges of sponge and domestic scrap.

The generally-used Wiberg-Soderfors process on a run with Grangesberg concentrate will make sponge with 94.5 pct reduction. If high enough in Fe content lump ore can be used. Soderfors is now testing Venezuelan ore to determine if it is suitable for a home industry in Venezuela.

A complementary method of making sponge, the Hoganas process uses a 71.2 pct concentrate from Malmbergot and has been supplying approximately half of America's needs. Sponge iron as a substitute for a scrap and to water down alloys has been considered in the United States where the Bureau of Mines conducted tests during World War II. The report was favorable.

February 15, 1951

The Clearing House

NEWS OF USED, REBUILT AND SURPLUS MACHINERY

Cause for Mystification—Washington conferences among Economic Stabilization Agency, National Production Authority, and members of the used machinery field were expected to clarify confusion as to the scope of price controls on used machines and equipment.

A survey of used machinery firms in New York last week disclosed almost complete mystification in regard to price controls. Some admitted that used machinery may be covered by the general control order while others stated confidently that the field was still free. Another check with the local ESA office yielded information that used machinery was covered.

Someone Who Should Know—The machine tool rebuilding field, which was lagging not too long ago, is booming to near-capacity operations, Charles A. Simmons, Sr., dean of the industry and president of the Simmons Machine Tool Corp., Albany, N. Y., told THE IRON AGE.

"The huge stocks available 90 days ago, including many held for 3 years, are gone, leaving mostly large special purpose tools on hand," said Mr. Simmons. "Six to 10 weeks is the average delivery time on rebuilding orders."

Still Some Capacity—Despite the sharp upswing caused by intense demand for equipment, machine tool rebuilders still have substantial capacity to take on new business, stated Mr. Simmons.

He continued that industry would have unlimited capacity at its disposal if the hundreds of used machinery builders who now merely paint and polish would devote their facilities to rebuilding and "thus serve industry's requirements."

Again on Prices—Mr. Simmons, who was World War II chief of the used tool division of the office of Production Management, contends that realistic price ceilings are needed immediately. He favors reemployment of the system used in World War II, with modifications to compensate fairly for rebuilt products.

Heard around the country is a rising complaint that rebuilding capacity is inadequate. Assurance of fair compensation for rebuilt products would be vital to nurturing a capable and sufficient machine rebuilding industry.

Advantages of Organization—Overall industry stands at the doorstep of fast-stepping crisis production.

There is an advantage to organization of used machinery dealers. National organizations can immediately classify them and supply important information to the government in filling defense requirements. It means that a dealer can put himself in the position of serving his country—and make certain that he will not miss any business.

Demand Spurred—Detroit demand for used machinery has picked up during recent weeks. Demand for tool room equipment is particularly potent.

In the production fever of World War II, many sellers of used machinery set up shops "in back of the warehouse" to take on war contracts. This trend is not yet evident in Detroit but the war work rush may soon revive it.

Machine Rebuilding—This area has also seen machine rebuilding on the upswing but it is retarded by shortage of skilled manpower. Some believed that extensive layoffs from auto plants because of cutbacks would release enough men into the labor pool so that the rebuilders could grab off their share.

But makers of new tools have such large backlogs that their plants are reportedly absorbing skilled workers as soon as they leave the auto industry's door.

WHEN A STANDARD PRESS WON'T DO...

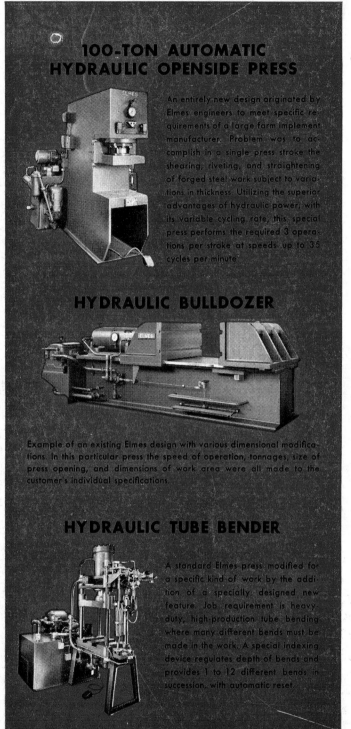

100-TON AUTOMATIC HYDRAULIC OPENSIDE PRESS

An entirely new design originated by Elmes engineers to meet specific requirements of a large farm implement manufacturer. Problem was to accomplish in a single press stroke the shearing, riveting, and straightening of forged steel work subject to variations in thickness. Utilizing the superior advantages of hydraulic power, with its variable cycling rate, this special press performs the required 3 operations per stroke at speeds up to 35 cycles per minute.

HYDRAULIC BULLDOZER

Example of an existing Elmes design with various dimensional modifications. In this particular press the speed of operation, tonnages, size of press opening, and dimensions of work area were all made to the customer's individual specifications.

HYDRAULIC TUBE BENDER

A standard Elmes press modified for a specific kind of work by the addition of a specially designed new feature. Job requirement is heavy duty, high-production tube bending where many different bends must be made in the work. A special indexing device regulates depth of bends and provides 1 to 12 different bends in succession, with automatic reset.

Call in ELMES *for a* Special Press

custom-engineered to meet your job requirements

Designing special hydraulic presses to meet unusual job requirements has always been a major function of Elmes engineers. Whether you need a press newly designed throughout, or one embodying changes from existing designs, Elmes century-long background plus advanced engineering skill and the most modern production facilities are your best assurance of satisfaction.

In standard presses, Elmes service is equally complete. The Elmes standard line includes a full range of hydraulic metal-working presses, hobbing presses, forcing presses, laboratory presses, and compression and transfer molding presses.

All Elmes equipment, standard or special, provides the superior advantages of hydraulic power . . . full power exerted at any point in the stroke . . . length of stroke and pressing force variable to suit work.

The Elmes engineering staff is always available for counsel, recommendations, and cost estimates. When *you* have a "pressing problem," it will pay you to *call in Elmes*.

ELMES
100th
Anniversary
1851-1951
HYDRAULIC EQUIPMENT

Send for Bulletin . . . "Metal-Working Presses"
Covers single-action, double-action, and triple-action presses . . . standard designs . . . special applications . . . automatic feeds. Ask your Elmes distributor or write direct for Bulletin 1010-B.

AMERICAN STEEL FOUNDRIES • ELMES ENGINEERING DIVISION

Distributors in Principal Industrial Centers   Also Manufactured in Canada

------ PLANT ADDRESS ------ 1161 Tennessee Avenue CINCINNATI 29, OHIO

METAL-WORKING PRESSES · PLASTIC MOLDING PRESSES · EXTRUSION PRESSES · PUMPS · ACCUMULATORS · VALVES · ACCESSORIES

The **Iron Age**

A CHILTON PUBLICATION

THE NATIONAL METALWORKING WEEKLY

February 22, 195

CONTENTS PAGE 2

Greater Productivity

...More Horsepower...Less Man Power

TODAY American Industry is under pressure to meet fantastic demands. Only yesterday, intense competition was the problem. Manufacturers have found the answer to both situations in more productive machine tools. The New Britain-Gridley Division, The New Britain Machine Company, New Britain, Conn., U.S.A.

AUTOMATIC BAR AND CHUCKING MACHINES • PRECISION BORING MACHINES
LUCAS HORIZONTAL BORING, DRILLING AND MILLING MACHINES

NEW BRITAIN

NEW BRITAIN *Automatics*

Farval pays for itself quickly, many times over

...saving oiling labor
...saving lubricant
...saving bearing expense
...saving production time

WITH Farval you lubricate your machinery or equipment mechanically. Farval does the job quickly and dependably.

Any type of bearing surface, enclosed or open, can be Farval-lubricated with grease or oil. Measured charges of lubricant are metered to each bearing through the unique Dualine Valve, delivered under pressure from a central reservoir, either by a manually operated pump or one actuated by an automatic time-clock mechanism.

Farval is not a new idea. It has proved its value in service over a 23-year period, protecting millions of bearings in every phase of industry—in manufacturing plants, mining and quarrying operations, transportation —wherever there are bearings that have to be lubricated. Thousands of installations on mills, presses, conveyors, cranes, engines and other industrial equipment provide records of money saved. Savings take four forms:

1. Labor saving—Farval eliminates hand oilers. Minimum attention only is required—to inspect system, refill lubricant reservoirs, etc.

2. Lubricant saving—Correct amounts are used without waste, frequently reducing oil or grease consumption as much as 75%.

3. Bearing expense saving—No more burned out or damaged bearings with Farval protection. Expense of replacement eliminated.

4. Production time saving—Farval lubricates while equipment is running. No shutting down to oil. No taking a machine out of production to repair or replace bearings.

In short, savings are so positive that you soon recover the entire cost of a Farval system—and savings continue as extra dividends.

If you want figures on savings possible with Farval on the types of machines you operate, just write us. Tell us what equipment you have and ask for Bulletin 25. The Farval Corporation, 3252 East 80th Street, Cleveland 4, Ohio.

Affiliate of The Cleveland Worm & Gear Company, Industrial Worm Gearing. In Canada: Peacock Brothers Limited.

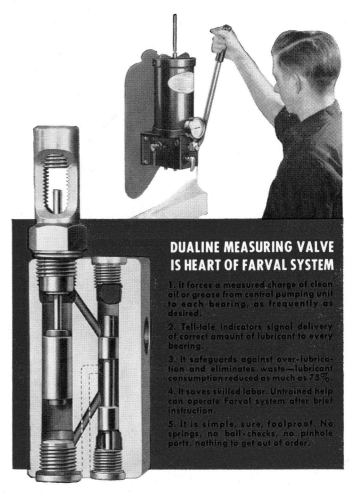

DUALINE MEASURING VALVE IS HEART OF FARVAL SYSTEM

1. It forces a measured charge of clean oil or grease from central pumping unit to each bearing, as frequently as desired.

2. Tell-tale indicators signal delivery of correct amount of lubricant to every bearing.

3. It safeguards against over-lubrication and eliminates waste—lubricant consumption reduced as much as 75%.

4. It saves skilled labor. Untrained help can operate Farval system after brief instruction.

5. It is simple, sure, foolproof. No springs; no ball-checks, no pinhole ports, nothing to get out of order.

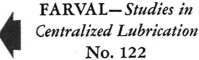

FARVAL—*Studies in Centralized Lubrication* No. 122

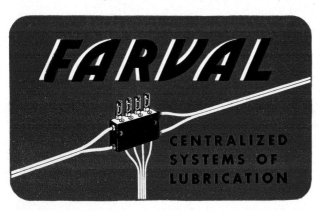

FARVAL

CENTRALIZED SYSTEMS OF LUBRICATION

Press Forgings by Bethlehem

SMALL

Carbon-steel hoist shaft, finish-machined. Length, 14 ft; wt, 4478 lb. Maximum diameter, 12 ¾ in.

Here are three widely-different types of steel shafts recently produced in our forge and machine shops. They range in weight from approximately 2¼ to 53 tons.

Shafts are but one of the many classes of products forged by Bethlehem each year. The three pieces shown, however, do illustrate two important points: our ability to handle press forgings in a wide range of sizes, and our ability to machine them exactly as specified by the customer.

No matter what you need in forgings . . . little fellows, heavyweights, or any sizes in between . . . check first with Bethlehem. We are equipped to do the job you want—the way you want it.

MEDIUM

Multiflanged mill shaft, rough-machined. Length, 23 ft 1¼ in.; wt, 28,640 lb. Diameters of end flanges, 38⅞ in. and 42⅜ in.; center flanges, 49¾ in.

LARGE

Vertical shafting for hydroelectric unit. Rough-turned, smooth-bored. Length, 21 ft 5¾ in.; wt, 106,880 lb. Diameters of center flanges, 82½ in., 78 in., and 73½ in.

IRON AGE

CONTENTS

THE IRON AGE
Editorial, Advertising and Circulation Offices, 100 E. 42nd St., New York 17, N. Y.
GEORGE T. HOOK, Publisher
TOM C. CAMPBELL, Editor

EDITORIAL STAFF
Managing Editor George F. Sullivan
Feature Editor Darwyn I. Brown
News-Markets Editor Wm. V. Packard
Machinery Editor George Elwers
Associate Editors: William Czygan, H. W. Van Camp, F. J. Winters; Assistant Editors: R. L. Hatschek, John Kolb, Ted Metaxas, W. B. Olson; Regional Editors: E. C. Beaudet, Chicago; W. A. Lloyd, Cleveland; W. G. Patton, Detroit; John B. Delaney, Pittsburgh; Osgood Murdock, R. T. Reinhardt, San Francisco; Eugene J. Hardy, Karl Rannells, George H. Baker, Washington; Correspondents: Fred L. Allen, Birmingham; N. Levenson, Boston; Fred Edmunds, Los Angeles; James Douglas, Seattle; Roy Edmonds, St. Louis; F. Sanderson, Toronto; F. H. Harley, London, England; Chilton Editorial Board: Paul Wooton, Washington Representative.

BUSINESS STAFF
Production Manager B. H. Hayes
Director of Research Oliver Johnson
Mgr. Circul'n. & Promotion C. T. Post
Asst. Promotion Mgr. James A. Crites
Asst. Dir. of Research Wm. Laimbeer

REGIONAL BUSINESS MANAGERS
B. L. Herman, Philadelphia; Stanley J. Smith, Chicago; Peirce Lewis, Detroit; Paul Bachman, New England; Robert F. Blair, Cleveland; R. Raymond Kay, Los Angeles; C. H. Ober, New York; J. M. Spackman, Pittsburgh; Harry Becker, European Representative.

REGIONAL OFFICES
Chicago 3, 1134 Otis Bldg.; Cleveland 14, 1016 National City Bank Bldg., Detroit 2, 103 Pallister Ave. Los Angeles 28, 2420 Cheremoya Ave.; New England, 62 La Salle Rd., W. Hartford 7; New York 17, 100 E 42nd St.; Philadelphia 39, 56th & Chestnut Sts.; Pittsburgh 22, 814 Park Bldg.; San Francisco 3, 1355 Market St.; Washington 4, National Press Bldg.; European, 111 Thorley Lane, Timperley, Cheshire, England.

Circulation Representatives: Thomas Scott, James Richardson.

One of the Publications Owned and Published by Chilton Company, Inc., Chestnut & 56th Sts., Philadelphia 39, Pa., U. S. A.

OFFICERS AND DIRECTORS
JOS. S. HILDRETH, President
Vice-Presidents: Everit B. Terhune, G. C. Buzby, P. M. Fahrendort, Harry V. Duffy, William H. Vallar, Treasurer; John Blair Moffet, Secretary; D. Allyn Garber, Maurice E. Cox, Frank P. Tighe, George T. Hook, Tom C. Campbell, L. V. Rowlands, Directors. George Maiswinkle, Asst. Treas.

Indexed in the Industrial Arts Index and the Engineering Index. Published every Thursday by the CHILTON CO. (INC.), Chestnut and 56th Sts., Philadelphia 39, Pa. Entered as second class matter Nov. 8, 1932, at the Post Office at Philadelphia under the act of March 3, 1879. $8 yearly in United States, its territories and Canada; other Western Hemisphere Countries $15; other Foreign Countries $25 per year. Single Copies 35c. Annual Review and Metal Industry Facts Issue, $2.00. Cable address "Ironage" N. Y.

Member Audit Bureau of Circulations. Member Society of Business Magazine Editors.

Copyright, 1951, by Chilton Co. (Inc.)

DIGEST

FEBRUARY TWENTY-SECOND • NINETEEN FIFTY-ONE • VOLUME 167 • NUMBER 8

IRON AGE

editorial

First Things Come First

NO one in his right mind would deny that defense orders should come first, should be produced quickly and that sacrifices should be made. Industry is not only ready to do what the armed forces and the government want but it is putting the needle in for speed.

There is alarming talk coming from Washington about drastically cutting back this or that. We hear that the auto industry will be cut off from so much steel as they have been denied non-ferrous metals. That is well and good—*if* the government has the orders that will immediately use up the material that has been cut back.

Appliances, toys and what not may soon be restricted by the National Production Authority. That is all right too if the material saved by the cutback can be used for defense purposes. But the story up to this time does not speak too well for some of Mr. Wilson's departments.

The Defense Act specifically says that defense and indirect defense items should have the right of way. That goes without saying. The American people are not only in favor of that but they think the government is moving at a snail's pace.

There are no cases where the armed services are not getting complete cooperation from steel and other basic industries. But there are cases where industry is not getting cooperation from government.

Some companies are rushing production of material—on orders from Washington—when the plants to make the end product haven't even tooled up. There are cases where there has been no integration of the program as a whole. Scarce material is being taken from the civilian economy before defense programs can take it.

You expect a certain amount of this looseness in tooling up for defense. We had it before and we will have it again. But this time we are not in an all-out war. The economy has to be strong to take care of huge expenditures and taxes for defense. If we waste by making haste before a program is ready we hit that economy where it hurts—in unemployment and loss of production.

The law also says that after the defense program has been adequately taken care of the rest of the material being made by industry should be equitably distributed throughout the civilian economy. That is not the trend today. The NPA seems interested in cutting back specific industries like autos and appliances. The Defense Act doesn't read that way.

Industry should be cut back on non-defense activity when and as the armed services get their orders in. To cut back on any civilian activity before defense orders are ready to absorb the cutback is not only foolish, it is dangerous.

Tom Campbell

Editor

FIRST PRESS DESIGNED AND MANUFACTURED IN THE UNITED STATES FOR THE COLD EXTRUSION OF STEEL

● **Developed by Lake Erie Engineering Corporation in collaboration with Mullins Manufacturing Corporation of Salem, Ohio.**

Press has a bed area 72″ x 60″, 108″ daylight opening and 60″ stroke. It stands 35′ 39″ above the floor and extends 21′ below the floor, where a 250 ton hydraulic ejector is located in the bed of the press. The press weighs over 700,000 pounds and is complete with a high-speed self-contained pumping unit, powered by 900 HP motors. Many of these specifications are in excess of those required for production equipment and are incorporated in the press to provide flexibility for experimental and research work.

IRON AGE *newsfront*

► A new <u>storage battery</u> using plates made of nickel powder is reported to <u>have better life</u> than standard batteries and to operate well at <u>temperatures down to –40°F.</u> Its <u>size</u>--for the same capacity--is <u>considerably less</u> than standard units.

► Inquiries are out from an aircraft company for a <u>revolutionary new type contour milling machine.</u> It is to be designed with table travel, ram travel and head tilt about two different axes automatically controlled from three different templates.

► A large farm implement manufacturer plans to swing over to a <u>boron steel</u> on a <u>big chunk of its alloy parts production</u> within a month. The grade is not an AISI standard steel. It will use Grainal No. 1 with a 0.30 to 0.60 Cr content in both low and medium carbon ranges.

► Iron castings have been made experimentally as <u>substitutes for diecast zinc door handles and trim</u> on some appliances. Made by the shell mold--or Croning--process, these castings have a <u>finish that does not require further machining.</u>

► Ferrite cores used as deflection yokes and horizontal output transformers in television are now being made with <u>lithium replacing the nickel</u> formerly used. Theory is that the switch proved practical because lithium atoms are about the same size as nickel atoms.

Another growing use of <u>lithium</u> is in ceramics. A big manufacturer of lithium compounds estimates that lithium compounds displaced some <u>10,000 tons of lead in ceramics last year</u>--including porcelain enamel, television tube glass, etc.

► The Government's new <u>Metallurgical Advisory Committee</u> is now being formed under the chairmanship of Dr. Robert Mehl. The group will concentrate its activities on <u>metals research.</u> Contrary to some surmises, its powers--at least as they are now set up--<u>will not be as broad</u> as the War Metallurgy Board of World War II.

► An order for 1.5 million 105-mm shells will be produced by <u>hot extrusion.</u> The shell body will be made in <u>3</u> steps in 300-ton mechanical presses. This represents a <u>simplification of some World War II</u> hot extrusion practice.

► Both the Army and the Air Force have pooled funds to develop a plane which will combine the vertical qualities of a <u>helicopter</u> with the faster <u>straight flight</u> characteristics of a conventional plane. Some <u>17 companies</u> have submitted plans for such a plane to the Air Materiel Command.

► A <u>porcelain enamel finish for aluminum</u> has been developed but is not expected to be offered for commercial use at present. Main application difference between enamel on steel and on aluminum is that the latter <u>must of course be applied at much lower temperatures.</u> The laboratory product has been made in <u>several colors.</u>

► <u>Workable or not,</u> the NPA seems determined to clap steel under a controlled materials plan by July 1. Writing the rules for steel will be easier than for any other major industry because NPA's steel section is <u>best organized and staffed.</u> But tying steel into other and completely disorganized sections of the economy <u>will be another matter.</u> Manufacturers will be driven into a frenzy before it is over but NPA officials face <u>actual physical and mental exhaustion.</u>

► Bad news for steel sheet users: Every <u>ton of tank plate</u> produced on a <u>sheet mill</u> means a loss of about <u>4 tons</u> of sheets.

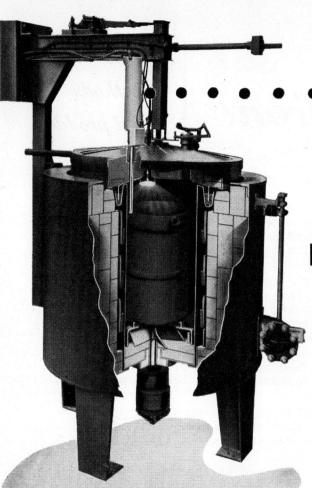

Now!

Homocarb Furnaces Feature Microcarb AUTOMATIC Atmosphere Control

Microcarb Control is part of the Series H Homocarb furnace. This new furnace with its many important features . . . solid bottom retort, convection cooler, new fan housing and work support, aerodynamically designed vanes and discharge jets . . . is a superior heat treating tool.

*N*OW heat treaters can do what formerly has been impossible . . . that is, continuously measure and control the carbon potential of a furnace atmosphere directly in terms of per cent carbon.

A new development by Leeds & Northrup Company, called "Microcarb" Control, makes this possible. It regulates atmospheric carbon content during heat treating as accurately as temperature is regulated. Atmosphere can be adjusted to increase or decrease the carbon potential automatically, as required for the job . . . whether it's surface carburizing, homogeneous carburizing, carbon restoration, hardening or annealing.

Principal feature of the Microcarb carbon control system is its Carbohm detecting element. This device projects into the furnace work chamber like a thermocouple; electrically senses the carbon potential of the furnace atmosphere. Connected to the element is a Microcarb Controller, which automatically adjusts the flow of Homocarb fluid to hold carbon potential of furnace gas at any selected value between 0.15 and 1.15 per cent carbon. For the heat treater's guidance, a Micromax recorder draws a continuous record of per cent of carbon as detected by the Carbohm element.

Microcarb Control is supplied for use with Leeds & Northrup Homocarb furnaces. It can be ordered as an integral part of new Homocarb equipments, or can be added to certain furnaces now in service.

For further information write to our nearest office or to Leeds & Northrup Company, 4956 Stenton Avenue, Philadelphia 44, Pennsylvania.

IRON AGE *summary*

Small firms hit by cutbacks . . . But defense orders aren't taking up the slack . . . Big tooling lag a factor . . . NPA readies CMP.

NEVER was the pain of an economy shifting from peace to war goods more evident than it is this week. Dr. NPA is finding that Mr. Economy is a very sensitive patient, who requires extremely accurate medication. Too much stimulant here or too little sedative there might prove fatal.

This week injured members are sending cries of protest through the patient's nervous system. Hardest hit, as usual, are the small metal fabricators. They are being starved by material cutbacks. Juicy defense contracts, which could nourish them are not being received in quantity. Many of these small fabricators will eventually get defense contracts or subcontracts—if they can hold out that long. Meanwhile, they are in a tough spot and making themselves heard.

Dislocation from War Work Shift

This economic dislocation largely results from the time lag in shifting production from peace to war goods. Some of the major contracts that already have been placed will require as much as 18 months for tooling up before assembly line production can begin. This explains why the machine tool industry is staggering under an ever increasing backlog of orders, while many small manufacturers face production curtailment. Many of them cannot weather such a long storm.

The small manufacturer's salvation is to land a defense contract or a subcontract. To do this he must sell the one product he has left—productive capacity.

Increasing the limits of defense (DO) orders which steel mills must accept is also hitting the small manufacturer—especially if his steel has been coming from mills now forced to roll plate on sheet or strip mills. For example, the increase to 20 pct on carbon plates and 17 pct on hot-rolled sheets means that the hot-rolled sheet producer using his mill for rolling plates is diverting at least 37 pct of his sheet capacity to DO orders. This does not include tonnage he must provide for essential civilian programs, warehouses, and non-integrated mills. During the second quarter some mills will be channeling more than 50 pct of their hot-rolled sheet into essential programs.

Means Greater Loss of Sheets

Any increases in orders for tank plate will multiply the effect on sheet production. One producer estimates that every ton of tank plate produced on a sheet mill means a loss of 4 tons of sheet. This is due to the rigid specifications for this type of plate and the extreme care required in processing it.

In addition to existing allocation programs, the following are slated to start in May: Merchant vessels, barges, locomotives for the U. S. and Canada, oil country goods and wheel head equipment for the petroleum industry, maritime ship program, ocean-going ship repair, drums and pails. Still under consideration are heavy power equipment, power plants and highways. It is estimated that these programs will take about a million tons of steel during May.

The National Production Authority seems determined to install its new controlled materials plan on steel, copper and aluminum on July 1— ready or not. Unless a lot of detail work is done between now and then, they will not be ready. CMP in name only, or prematurely installed, could do more harm than good.

CMP Needs a Lot of Spadework

Just putting the CMP label on a plan will neither guarantee priorities nor guide production. To be effective CMP will have to be preceded by long and careful planning, detailed screening of material, requests from all types of consumers, and a selective buildup of administrative people.

Steelmaking operations this week are scheduled at 99.5 pct of rated capacity, up 1 point from the previous week.

(nonferrous summary, p. 120)

The 3 R's of Reliance Service

Resourceful
Responsible
Responsive

WEAN

SHEET AND TIN PLATE SHEARING *Lines*

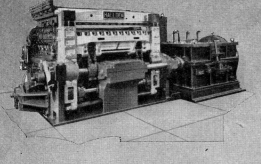

SPECIALISTS IN SHEET, TIN *and* **STRIP MILL EQUIPMENT**

HIGH-SPEED, high-tonnage production ... unsurpassed accuracy . . . rugged construction that minimizes operating and maintenance costs.

Modern Wean sheet and tin plate shearing lines for converting strip in coil form to flat sheets provide all these advantages.

THE WEAN ENGINEERING CO., INC.
WARREN, OHIO

Dear EDITOR

letters from readers

Which Is Legal?

Sir:

In the Jan. 4 issue under the heading of "How To Sell To Uncle Sam," on p. 270, you state that:

"An important point concerns obtaining of contracts with the aid of an agent (a full-time employee is not considered an agent) or what is sometimes known as a "five percenter" because he works on a commission basis. There is no law against employing an agent to look after a supplier's interests or even to obtain government contracts. But, and this is a big if, if such is done it must be reported on the contracts together with the amount of the fee paid. Failure to do so is cause for cancellation. And payment on a contingency or commission basis is definitely forbidden—only specific salaries or fees are permitted."

Frankly, I am not able to make head or tail out of this statement; in one section you interpret this to say that so long as the contractor states that he is paying a fee, together with the amount he is paying to a bonafide agent, that such a fee is permitted. On the other hand you state that a contingency or commission basis is definitely forbidden.

J. W. MOORE
John Moore Specialty Co.
Chicago

The situation is this: It is legal for a contractor to include in his cost a salary or flat fee paid to an agent, but it is illegal to include a percentage brokerage or commission fee for individual contracts.—Ed.

Wants Steel Piles

Sir:

I am trying to find out whether or not there is on the market, a steel post which could be driven into the ground to support a frame garage, as a substitute for laying a cement foundation. Could you refer me to a company which might be most apt to have such a product in its line?

P. G. PRESCOTT
Chicago

Although heavy structural steel bearing piles are frequently used to support large buildings, we don't know whether anything is made which would be feasible or within reason from a cost standpoint for a frame garage. A call to a local office of Joseph T. Ryerson & Sons, Inc.; Ceco Steel Products Co.; Bethlehem Steel Co.; or U. S. Steel Supply Co. there in Chicago should serve to settle the possibility one way or the other.—Ed.

Needs Prompt Delivery

Sir:

I am trying to contact those concerns who are in position to build a large 400-ton high speed self-contained joggling and forming press, all steel "C" frame type. I have already been in contact with a number of the larger machinery manufacturers, but none of them are able to take on additional business for prompt delivery.

L. S. PECK
Portland, Ore.

The possibility of securing prompt delivery on a 400-ton hydraulic joggling and forming press is rather remote; it may be necessary to go a little farther afield than normally in the hope that some other press firms may have patterns and be able to take on the work. Perhaps some of our readers can offer suggestions??—Ed.

Special Tubing Required

Sir:

We have a recollection of seeing recently advertisements or notices of a company who constructs a multi-walled pipe by rolling a sheet and welding the outside. The process would seem to solve a problem we now have and we would like to get in touch with the manufacturer of such pipe. Can you supply the name?

G. C. WHEELER
Engineering Dept.
North American Philips Co., Inc.
Lewiston, Me.

Bundy Tubing Co., Detroit 14, Mich., manufactures a double-walled tube made from a single strip which is rolled and then welded.—Ed.

Prompt Service

Sir:

We wish to thank you for the very prompt attention given our wire request for copies of the article by D. I. Brown entitled "Cold Extrusion of Shells Saves Steel," in the Oct. 19, 1950 issue. The copies were received this morning. It is a very interesting article and several of our prospective customers requested copies of us.

G. D. MILLER
George D. Miller Co.
Cleveland

Timely Titanium Topic

Sir:

With the potentialities of titanium looming rather large on the metallurgical horizon, we wonder whether you would be good enough to inform us which domestic companies seem to hold the largest reserves of this material.

R. A. BING
Head of Research Dept.
Sutro & Co.
San Francisco

From recent reports, the Quebec Iron & Titanium Corp., 120 Broadway, New York, probably has access to the largest reserves of titanium ore in this hemisphere. There are no actual reserves of the metal and most production is currently going into research and development projects.—Ed.

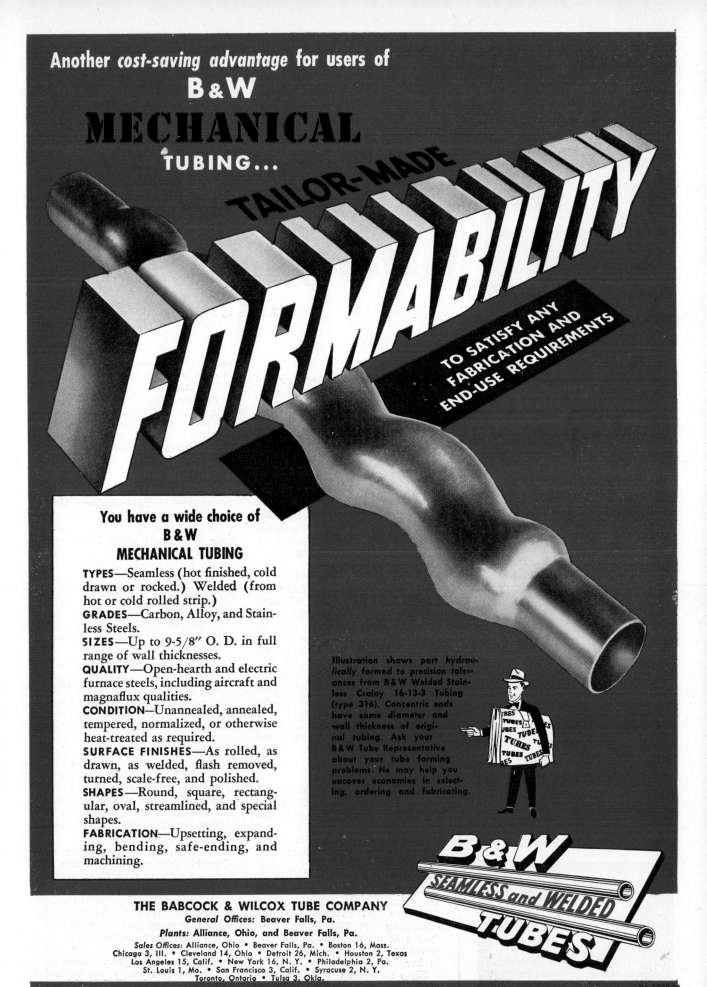

for top precision

Production to close tolerances mostly applies to metal working. But the technique of Western Felt production and processing has built an enviable reputation for engineering precision.

Chemical specifications must be perfectly met—parts from wool softness to rock hardness are cut to close tolerances. As an extremely versatile material Western Felts are resilient, flexible, compressible. They resist oil, water, heat, age—do not ravel, fray or lose shape. New uses found daily. It pays to depend on Western Felt.

Check Possible Uses for Your Product
• Excluding dirt, grit, dust • Retaining lubricants • Thermostatic insulation • Isolating vibration • Cushioning shock • Padding, packing, seals • Air and liquid filters • Gaskets, channels, etc. • Grinding, polishing, etc. • Weight reduction • Instrument mounts

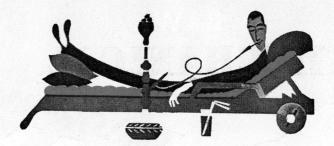

Fatigue Cracks

by *Charles T. Post*

Brass Tacks

This matter of getting down to brass tacks seems a lot easier since reading our erudite British contemporary, "*The Metal Bulletin.*" Probably no one but an upholsterer has very much direct contact with brass tacks, as such. Brass tacks have always been something you got down to. Having a certain amount of pride, a growing paunch, and a lazy disposition, we've never cottoned up to the idea of getting down to anything, let alone brass tacks. Much nicer to recline on a couch with water pipe and glass nearby, as seen above.

The *Metal Bulletin*, however, recently came across a volume entitled "*A Dictionary of Rhyming Slang.*" "Brass tacks," it turns out, is merely rhyming slang for "the facts." You can get down to them without stooping, use the terms interchangeably.

Oh, yes. It seems that rhyming slang for pipe is "cherry-ripe." If you happen to have a few thousand feet of cherry-ripe in your warehouse, your f.f.j.'s editors assure us it would be a pipe to sell it profitably.

Shortages

After learning last week that the scrap shortage was resulting in a wave of thefts of unguarded machinery and equipment, we were astounded to learn that impending shortages were having their effect on other fields.

The police of Perth Amboy, N. J., have picked up a woman worker at the plant of the Maiden-Form Brassiere Co., charged her with smuggling out 8000 brassieres—"parts at a time," whatever that would be—and stashing them away in her basement.

Since no woman we know needs 8000 brassieres, we can only assume that the thief saw a chance to cash in on an impending shortage, with possibly a sideline selling to owners of 1951 Fords with sagging radiator grilles. It all goes to show you can't check your plant security too closely these days, no matter what you make.

Puzzlers

Not all the nation's mathematical brains are in its factories. Had there been a prize for the first answer to come in to last week's code problem, it would have gone to Jim Carlin, head proof reader at the printing plant. Before the page on which Fatigue Cracks appears, was even printed on both sides, he figured out that HOT has a numerical value of 357 and that STUFF can be expressed as 47266. We'd say that Jim is pretty 357 47266, himself.

E. J. Sampson, Robert W. Huff, and Howard Fancher correctly deduced that the ladder in the February 8 problem is 41.633 ft long, the street 40.414 ft wide, and the base of the ladder placed 11.547 ft from the base of the taller building. Reader Sampson, Robert A. Wallace, McDowell Manufacturing Co., and S. A. Kenorf of Crucible Steel's Park Works correctly probed the cork cover on the steel ball. John W. Higby, Madrid, Iowa, finally drilled through the 2-in. cube mentioned last November.

T. H. Rattray, purchasing agent, Engelke Engineering, Inc., has a circular military type wrist watch. The second hand measures exactly ½ in. from the pivot to the outside end of the hand. He wants to know how many land miles the outside end of the hand travels, in its normal circular motion, for the period of a normal year. Actually, he knows, and wants you to find out.

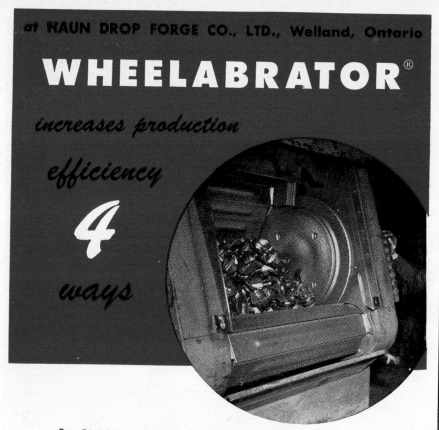

DATES *to remember*

Mar. 5-7—Hydraulic Institute, quarterly meeting, Santa Barbara Biltmore Hotel, Santa Barbara, Calif. Institute headquarters are at 122 E. 42nd St., New York.

Mar. 5-7—Manufacturers Standardization Society of the Valve and Fittings Industry, annual meeting, Commodore Hotel, New York. Society headquarters are at 420 Lexington Ave., New York.

Mar. 5-7—Pittsburgh Conference on Analytical Chemistry and Applied Spectroscopy, William Penn Hotel, Pittsburgh. American Chemical Society national headquarters are at 1155 16th St., Washington.

Mar. 5-9—American Society for Testing Materials, spring meeting, Cincinnati. Society headquarters are at 1916 Race St., Philadelphia.

Mar. 6-8—Society of Automotive Engineers, passenger car, body and materials meetings, Hotel Book-Cadillac, Detroit. Society headquarters are at 29 W. 39th St., New York.

Mar. 7—Bituminous Coal Research, Inc., annual meeting, Deshler-Wallick Hotel, Columbus, Ohio. Organization headquarters are at 2609 First National Bank, Pittsburgh.

Mar. 12-15—National Electrical Manufacturers Assn., spring meeting, Edgewater Beach Hotel, Chicago. Association headquarters are at 155 E. 44th St., New York.

Mar. 13-15—Assn. of American Railroads, Engineering Div. and Construction & Maintenance Section, annual meeting, Palmer House, Chicago. Association headquarters are in the Transportation Bldg., Washington.

Mar. 13-16—National Assn. of Corrosion Engineers, conference and exhibition, Statler Hotel, New York. Association headquarters are in the Southern Standard Bldg., Houston.

Mar. 14-17—American Society of Tool Engineers, annual meeting, Hotel New Yorker, New York, Society headquarters are at 10700 Puritan Ave., Detroit.

Mar. 19-21—National Assn. of Waste Material Dealers, annual convention, Stevens Hotel, Chicago. Association headquarters are at 1109 Times Bldg., New York.

Mar. 19-21—Steel Founders Society of America, annual meeting, Edgewater Beach Hotel, Chicago. Society headquarters are at 920 Midland Bldg., Cleveland.

Mar. 19-23—Western Metal Congress and Exposition, Civic Auditorium and Exposition Hall, Oakland, Calif. American Society for Metals headquarters are at 7301 Euclid Ave., Cleveland.

Mar. 22-23—Pressed Metal Institute, annual technical meeting, Hotel Carter, Cleveland. Institute headquarters are at 13210 Shaker Square, Cleveland.

Apr. 2-3—Diamond Core Drill Manufacturers Assn., annual meeting, The Homestead, Hot Springs, Va. Association headquarters are at 122 E. 42nd St., New York.

Apr. 2-4—American Institute of Mining & Metallurgical Engineers, openhearth and blast furnace, coke oven and raw materials conference, Statler Hotel, Cleveland. Institute headquarters are at 29 W. 39th St., New York.

Apr. 2-5—American Society of Mechanical Engineers, spring meeting, Atlanta Biltmore Hotel, Atlanta. Society headquarters are at 29 W. 39th St., New York.

machine tool high spots

sales inquiries and production

by W.A.Lloyd

January Shipments Dip—The peak which some experts predicted the machine tool business would reach this year appears to be virtually at hand. According to informed sources, January order volume may have been the highest since July, 1942, indicating a preliminary order index of possibly 450, compared with an index of 410 in December.

It is believed shipments dipped in January, due chiefly to shortages of materials, indicating a preliminary index of 115, compared with an index of 135 in December. As a result, backlog or the ratio of unfilled orders to shipments has increased, possibly to 13 or 14 to 1.

Exports Taper Off — Big increase in new order volume is the result of domestic placements. Foreign demand, says the trade, is tapering off.

The estimated decrease in shipments is serious in view of the machine tool requirements of the defense program and the growing shortage of machine tools which now exists. Companies are enlarging their subcontract work, and one company indicated that within a few weeks an estimated 60,000 hours of subcontract work will be coming into the shop for assembly.

Plug and Ring Gages—In Washington, standardizing and cataloging of commercial type plug and ring gages has been announced by the Munitions Board, Dept. of Defense. The development of military standards and cataloging will reduce to about 187,000 catalog items the more than 1 million descriptions of plug and ring gages previously used.

First series of military standards covering plain plug and ring gages constituting one-half of the total items under development have been approved for publication.

Buys British Firm—In Chicago, Independent Pneumatic Tool Co. has acquired all the stock of Armstrong Whitworth Machine Tools, Ltd., Newcastle, one of Great Britain's biggest pneumatic tool builders. Neil C. Hurley, Jr., Pneumatic president, said the purchase will permit increasing standardization of British and American tools for arms production. One reason for the move was to enable his firm to acquire a stronger foothold in world markets, he said.

Problems Before NPA—One of the machine tool industry's key suppliers, the anti-friction bearing industry, placed its problems in expanding facilities and obtaining alloy steel before NPA officials this week. The Anti-Friction Bearing Manufacturers Advisory Committee outlined the industry's requirements for alloy steel, machine tools, machinery, plant floor space and related facilities.

NPA officials told the committee that as orders for bearings to meet the growing needs of the defense program continue to increase during the next 2 years, it will become necessary to make some adjustment with respect to civilian use unrelated to the rearmament program.

Tool and Die Barriers—Shortages of special types of steel and manpower are hampering the tool and die industry, the Tool and Die Manufacturers Advisory Committee told NPA officials in discussing problems confronting the industry in preparing plants for war work.

NPA officials advised the committee to submit specific information on cases in which undue difficulty is encountered in obtaining supplies, so that steps can be taken to correct the situation.

Shortages of journeymen tool and die makers is causing the industry plenty of concern and government assistance was requested to help find a solution.

FREE *publications*

These publications describe money-saving equipment and services . . . they are free with no obligation . . . just fill in and mail the postcard on the opposite page.

Current-Metering Manual

A new 40-p. manual of watthour meters comprehensively covers the fundamentals of alternating-current metering. Containing charts, diagrams and photos, the brochure shows how electricity is measured; describes operating principles of alternating-current watthour meters; and explains techniques involved in the use, testing and maintenance of meters. The brochure can be used as a reference in the meter schools of companies to show proper application and maintenance. *General Electric Co.*

For free copy insert No. 1 on postcard.

Fabrication Facts

"Beyond Your Blueprints" is the title of a new 16-p. illustrated catalog providing many useful facts regarding steel and alloy plate fabrication. It explains the many specialized techniques and services of this company in the fabrication of tanks and vessels for the petroleum and chemical processing industries. Another useful feature of the catalog is the extensive section devoted to corrosion data charts— which lists the resistance values of commonly used metals with reference to hundreds of chemicals. *Nooter Corp. Address requests to this column on company letterhead.*

Steam Capacity Chart

The new Mipco steam capacity chart provides means for determining steam capacity required from safety valves to give 100 pct protection in case of pressure-reducing valve failure. A typical example of a problem is given, with an explanation of how the chart is used for solution. *Marine & Industrial Products Co.*

For free copy insert No. 2 on postcard.

Two-Cycle Diesel Engines

The complete line of Series 71 2-cycle GM Diesel engines for application in the industrial, petroleum and marine fields is described in a new catalog. The book covers single and multiple engine units from 2 to 24 cylinders with power ranging from 32 continuous to 780 intermittent hp. It contains data on design and interchangeability of parts; a "Select Your Power" chart covering 57 standard power take-off and 7 torque converter models; engine illustrations and an outline of service facilities. *Detroit Diesel Engine Div., General Motors Corp. Address requests to this column on company letterhead.*

Self-Locking Nuts

Advantages of Greer self-locking nuts are presented in a new 8-p. stock and price list. Information on types, materials, dimensions and finishes for coarse and fine machine screw hex nuts, light and heavy weight nuts, and clinch nuts, is shown. Complete prices and discounts are listed. *Greer Stop Nut Co.*

For free copy insert No. 3 on postcard.

Rubber Compounds, Parts

A new 16-p. illustrated catalog lists by code number approx 30 compounds which are representative of more than 500 rubber stocks developed to meet special requirements. Full information is presented on compounds which feature resistance to abrasion, chemicals, high and low temperatures, petroleum products and their derivatives, and weathering. A special section deals with the recently-developed Silicone rubber compounds. *Stalwart Rubber Co.*

For free copy insert No. 4 on postcard.

Conveyer Chain Folder

A new 4-p. folder gives dimensions and pertinent data on S-815 flat-top conveyer chain and its cut tooth sprocket wheels — for the transportation of small containers, bottles, packages or parts through various operations. The bulletin shows how each pitch of chain consists of only a hinge type beveled-edged flat-top link, and a pin to hinge adjacent links to each other with an overlap, assuring a continuous, smooth carrying surface and smooth transfers. *Link-Belt Co.*

For free copy insert No. 5 on postcard.

For Drainage Problems

"An Economical Answer to Limited Headroom—Fast Runoff," is the title of a new, illustrated folder describing Armco Pipe-Arch and Multi-Plate Pipe-Arch, and shows why they carry more water than round pipe. Test data and case histories also show that they have more than sufficient strength to withstand both live and dead loads. The folder discusses erosion and corrosion problems and tells how to solve them. Tables give recommended sizes and gages to meet various loading conditions. *Armco Drainage & Metal Products, Inc.*

For free copy insert No. 6 on postcard.

Metal Corrosion-Proofing

Prufcoat metal reactive primer P-10, providing a simple 2-step system for corrosion-proofing old or moist metal surfaces, is described in a new technical bulletin detailing method of application and advantages. A question-and-answers section provides most of the necessary information about this new metal-treating formulation, *Turn to Page 103*

NEW *production ideas*

Roll Temperature Unit

Measures temperature of moving roll surface without touching the roll.

Temperature detected by the unit is recorded automatically by either a Micromax or Speedomax instrument supplied as an integral part of the complete equipment. The recorder can be equipped to operate signals or controls. Applicable to roll diameters down to 9 in. and to flat surfaces, the new detecting unit operates independent of surface speed, emission characteristics, and finish. It can be mounted at the center of the roll or at any other location, wherever actual temperature measurement is desired. *Leeds & Northrup Co.*

For more data insert No. 20 on postcard.

Pivot Polishing Machine

Machine uses carbide or ceramic wheels for wet polishing pivots.

The Hauser Type 241 polishing machine will replace in many instances centerless grinding, it is claimed, and can be operated by unskilled labor. It polishes pivots straight, taper or radius and will polish shoulder at the same time as the cylinder at right angle or bevel. Mild steel, hardened steel, stainless steel, brass, nickel, bronze can be burnished. The machine takes work in collet or on centers. It is rated at 600 or more pivots per hr. *Hauser Machine Tool Corp.*

For more data insert No. 21 on postcard.

Tube, Pipe Fittings

Simplify installation and reduce pipe line costs.

Three principal fittings in corrosion-resistant alloys are an insert flange, an aligning connector and a tube and pipe union. The insert flange consists of a corrosion-resistant serrated insert in a carbon steel flange, requiring only an expanding tool and a plain wrench for working with it. It is made for standard tubing ODs and gages, and nominal pipe sizes from ½ to 6 in. The aligning connector is used in connecting standard heavy-wall pipe to light-wall pipe. Tubing OD and pipe sizes are ½ to 4 in. The tube and pipe union combines the best features of the screwed pipe union and the sanitary tube union, and is said to remove leakage problems often encountered with corrosion - resistant ground joints. *Horace T. Potts Co.*

For more data insert No. 22 on postcard.

Rubber-Fabric Belt

Will not slip, permits split-second timing, has up to 16,000 fpm speeds.

Known as the Gilmer Timing Belt, a rubber and fabric belt with teeth fulfills the need for a power drive that will not slip and permits split-second precision timing. It attains speeds up to 16,000 fpm and is said to operate more quietly than precision gears running in an oil bath. The new belt does not stretch and operates on fixed centers without takeup adjustments. Since it needs no initial tension it has high efficiency with low bearing pres-

use postcard below

---

production ideas

Continued

sure. The belt requires no lubrication, but oil will not harm it. It is compact and speed ratios up to 30:1 are possible with it. The belt's flexibility permits pulley diameters as small as ½ in. at 10,000 rpm even with a heavy load. *U. S. Rubber Co.*

For more data insert No. 23 on postcard.

Tungsten Electrode
Reduces inert-arc welding cost.

The new Hi-Thoria tungsten electrodes produce a stable arc over a wider range of currents and will resist contamination by weld metal. Hi-Thoria tungsten is said to have strength comparable to standard pure tungsten. It runs cooler than standard tungsten and does not become molten. The end of the electrode remains square and intact and consumption is reduced. The new electrode is manufactured in 3 to 24 in. lengths and from 0.040 to ¼ in. diam. Major applications of the new tungsten will be for inert-arc welding with dc, straight polarity using either argon or helium gas. This type is used to weld mild steel, stainless steel, copper and alloys. *General Electric Co.*

For more data insert No. 24 on postcard.

No-Rust Compound
Protects metal surfaces against corrosion, indoors or outdoors.

Gulf No-Rust No. 6 is a rust preventive of the thin film type and will provide approximate surface coverage of 390 sq ft per gal. It has no tendency to settle or separate in storage, and due to excellent adhesion the coating when once applied and dried will not crack, chip, scale or distintegrate at temperatures down to 0°F, nor will it flow at temperatures as high as 190°F. The rust preventive is said to deposit a coating not exceeding 0.008 in. thick by dipping at a temperature of 70°F and will dry sufficiently within 4 hr to permit handling without removal of the coating. No-Rust No. 6 is suitable for application by brushing, spraying, or dipping, and is removed with stoddard solvent, kerosene, or similar petroleum solvents. *Gulf Oil Co.*

For more data insert No. 25 on postcard.

Bundling Chain
Bundles materials for storage.

The Acco bundling chain with automatic lock permits bundles to be stored indefinitely and held securely eliminating the use of pins, pear shaped links, and wires. The drop forged automatic bundle lock is available as a separate unit or as part of a chain assembly. The lock is manufactured for 17/32, 9/16, ⅝ and 21/32-in. chain. Assemblies can be furnished with wrought iron, low carbon, high test or alloy chain. *American Chain Div., American Chain & Cable Co., Inc.*

For more data insert No. 26 on postcard.

Emergency Light
For Civilian Defense emergencies, provides 80 hr continuous light.

For use in defense plants and in emergencies, a portable light is powered by a heavy duty rechargeable long life battery. A special 2-filament bulb furnishes work or rescue light for 80 continuous hours on one filament—or a higher power flood-light for 20 consecutive hours on the second filament. A thumb-operated 3-way toggle switch controls both filaments. Beam can be tilted instantly by fingertip pressure. *Carpenter Mfg. Co.*

For more data insert No. 27 on postcard.

Heavy Duty Casters
Said to move maximum loads with a minimum of vibration and shock.

To meet explosives plant safety requirements, new heavy duty casters for pneumatic industrial wheels are spark-proof and generate minimum friction heat due to rollability guaranteed to be 20 pct greater than that of ordinary industrial casters. Cased bearings eliminate the race wear common with ordinary ball bearings. As a mounting for 10-in. diam pneumatic wheels, the caster has designed load rating of 1200 lb. *Aerol Co., Inc.*

For more data insert No. 28 on postcard.

Control Valves
Manufactured to operate 1 to 4 single or double-acting cylinders.

Hydreco V16 Series control valves conserve mounting space by incorporating check valves within

use postcard below

WESTINGHOUSE
RECTIFIER WELDERS
Save ON ANY JOB

Westinghouse D-C Rectifier Welders handle applications of *all* sizes better, faster and cheaper than m. g. sets. Field reports prove the unit is ready for tomorrow's even bigger welding jobs.

Take the 2,000,000-gallon water tank created by Pittsburgh-Des Moines Steel for the city of Niagara Falls, New York. Welding of the monster prefabricated sections was done by a unique battery of d-c rectifier units supplied by one large diesel-driven generator. This arrangement replaced separate engine-driven welding generators formerly used.

With the rectifier welders, as compared to those formerly used, fuel costs alone were slashed 70% ... maintenance was reduced 85% ... equipment weight was cut 15,000 pounds. Initial cost of these rectifier welders and power supply generator was 50% less than that of rotating d-c welders of equivalent capacity.

You may never have to weld a 2,000,000-gallon tank, but you can always save with Westinghouse D-C Rectifier Welders on all your applications— large or small. Call your nearest Westinghouse distributor or write Westinghouse Electric Corporation, Dept. DC-32, Welding Division, Buffalo, N. Y.

J-21609

YOU CAN BE **SURE**.. IF IT'S

Westinghouse

Rectifier Welders

production ideas

Continued

their respective control plungers and using the hollow plunger center for oil passage. Relief valves designed into the valve body further reduce space requirements for this type of equipment. These valves can be used in the limited space for mounting hydraulic controls found on many types of materials handling equipment. *Hydraulic Equipment Co.*

For more data insert No. 29 on postcard, p. 37.

Cold Sawing Machine

Full automatic, hydraulic high speed; capacity to 5-in. rounds.

This cold saw has the features of the Models 660 and 1000 (see IRON AGE, Aug. 17, 1950, p. 40) plus the new control for full automatic operation. Hydraulic feed

mechanism feeds the material accurately in lengths of 0 to 16 in. for continuous production cutting. The machine can be converted for semi-automatic operation with a single hand lever control. All controls are interlocked to avoid operational errors. A hydraulic vise clamps the material on both sides of the saw blade and centers the stock directly under the center of the blade, providing a short, efficient and burr-free cut. *Klingelhofer Machine Tool Co.*

For more data insert No. 30 on postcard, p. 37.

Spring Grinder

Double vertical spindle disk grinder has semi-automatic cycling.

Grinding coil springs more quickly and economically, with a corresponding increase in accuracy and all-round quality is

claimed for a new disk grinder. Advantages listed are extra flexibility, time saving, increased wheel life, conservation of floor space, and overhead economies. The machine grinds springs from ½ to 6 in. long, from ¼ to 4 in. diam. and from 0.0625 to 0.500 in. wire diam. The abrasives are especially constructed to grind a variety of

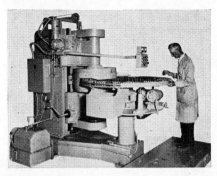

spring types as well as materials such as oil tempered steel, music wire, bronze wire, etc. This eliminates downtime for wheel changeover. The springs pass across the center of 30-in. diam abrasives with no center holes, and are finished during each cycle. The new method tends, also, to obviate the need for secondary operations such as reaming or chamfering, squaring and scale testing. *Charles H. Besly & Co.*

For more data insert No. 31 on postcard, p. 37.

Power Squaring Shears

12 gage shears in 52 in., 6, 8 and 10 ft cutting lengths.

To insure top performance at the 12 gage rating, Wysong tests each shear on 10 gage sheets. In the test, cutting is full length at 60 strokes per min. Bed, end-frames, holddown and knife-bar are one-piece, Hi-tensile castings, contain-

ing 30 pct steel. Standard equipment includes motor with controls and electrical equipment; ball-bearing, precision back-gage adjustable to 1/128th in.; 2 front gage brackets and front gage; side and bevel gages; stainless steel scale

embedded in table to aid in positioning sheets; slatted metal finger guard; non-repeat unit and 4-edge blades. The 52-in. shear has front operation for the precision back gage, and an automatic stroke counter. *Wysong & Miles Co.*

For more data insert No. 32 on postcard, p. 37.

Roll Handling Truck

Built-in signal system indicates truck position in narrow aisles.

This truck is required to handle 1500 lb rolls, 32 in. diam x 42 in. long in and out of five high storage racks along both sides of 54-in. wide aisles. A signal system built into the truck lets the operator know the aisle and his position in the aisle as the truck moves along. While traveling in aisles, the truck is steered by guide rollers running

against the side of the aisle tracks. In other places the truck is steered manually. Electric storage battery power moves the truck and runs the hydraulic pump. Once the truck reaches its position in the aisle a few controls are set and the carriage automatically starts to raise to the proper level, move sideways, pick up or deposit a roll, return to the center position where the carriage lowers to a normal position. *Lewis-Shepard Products, Inc.*

For more data insert No. 33 on postcard, p. 37.

Cutter Vise

Holds cutter firmly—indexes quickly.

A new cutter vise holds inserted-blade milling cutters firmly in a convenient position while blades are being reset. With the cutter rigidly clamped, wedges can be driven and screws tightened more rapidly. Power-operated jaws of the vise are

Turn to Page 108

NEW Airco Oxygen Process reclaims nickel...chromium from stainless and high-alloy scrap

DURIRON COMPANY, of Dayton, Ohio, a well-known, mid-western foundry, wanted a method for reclaiming highly-critical nickel—and chromium—from their stainless and other high-alloy scrap. They wanted to re-use this tightly-allocated metal for making castings in their own shop.

W. T. Bryan, Duriron Co., and **H. C. Linde,** Airco Technical Sales Representative, working together, used oxygen refining as a means of removing carbon from the alloy steel bath. On the basis of experience, it was found that the carbon removal was accomplished without excessive oxidation of chromium from the high alloy scrap charge. Equally important, all of the nickel charged was recovered. This permitted the foundry to reclaim all scrap.

The Duriron Company was highly pleased with these results, and have adapted this process as standard practice ...and, now produce low-carbon, high-alloy castings from material that otherwise would be useless to them.

For further information about this modern method for reclaiming high-priority nickel — and chromium — from your scrap, call or write your nearby Airco office for Technical Sales assistance.

AIR REDUCTION

AIR REDUCTION SALES COMPANY • AIR REDUCTION MAGNOLIA COMPANY
AIR REDUCTION PACIFIC COMPANY
REPRESENTED INTERNATIONALLY BY AIRCO COMPANY INTERNATIONAL
Divisions of Air Reduction Company, Incorporated
Offices in Principal Cities

IRON AGE

introduces

W. A. Roberts, elected president of ALLIS-CHALMERS MFG. CO., New York. W. C. Johnson, elected executive vice-president; Fred Mackey, vice-president in charge of manufacturing, general machinery division.

L. A. Dixon, elected a director of the ROCKWELL MFG. CO., Pittsburgh.

Ernest S. Theiss, appointed chief engineer of the DAVEY COMPRESSOR CO., Kent, Ohio.

Victor P. Johnson, joined the sales staff of BIGELOW-LIPTAK CORP., New York.

Herbert B. Nechemias, appointed manager of the industrial sales department at WAGNER ELECTRIC CORP., St. Louis, succeeding J. S. Smith who was appointed director of purchasing.

Barry Herbert Fisher, appointed sales representative, Baltimore, for the U. S. GRAPHITE CO., of Saginaw, Mich.

Earl M. Landis, appointed to the newly created post of training director for HARRIS-SEYBOLD CO., Cleveland.

Tomlinson Fort, elected a vice-president of WESTINGHOUSE ELECTRIC CORP., Pittsburgh. Others elected: L. W. McLeod and L. E. Lynde.

Robert G. Boulter, appointed manager of sales planning and analysis for the Laminated & Insulating Products Div., Coshocton, Ohio, of the GENERAL ELECTRIC CO.

Walter G. Mason, appointed as director of personnel for the ARTHUR G. McKEE & CO., Cleveland.

E. H. Nichols, appointed district sales manager for TRUSCON STEEL CO., Birmingham.

Charles E. Leasure, named works accountant of the Butler Div., of ARMCO STEEL CORP., Middletown, Ohio.

Earl Erich, promoted to product director for linings and coatings and George Kanelis recently joined the engineering department of ATLAS MINERAL PRODUCTS CO., Mertztown, Pa.

W. A. Edwards, appointed district manager of the TRUMBULL ELECTRIC MFG. CO. With headquarters at Norwood, Ohio, Mr. Edwards will be in charge of the East Central district.

A. R. Wise, appointed assistant general manager of the CLEVELAND TAPPING MACHINE CO., Cleveland. Mr. Wise continues as vice-president and sales manager of the company.

Maurice J. Erisman, named assistant chief engineer, Pershing Road Chicago plant of LINK-BELT CO. Homer J. Foye replaces Mr. Erisman at the Los Angeles plant as chief engineer.

Meritt Myers, named to the newly created post, director of production planning of the AMERICAN STOVE CO., St. Louis.

H. F. Detrick, appointed general manager of the A. O. SMITH CORP., with offices in San Francisco.

C. F. Cooper, appointed acting district sales manager for northern California for the KAISER STEEL CORP., with headquarters in Oakland.

Turn to page 56

C. A. KRAL, appointed a vice-president in the engineering and construction division at Concepcion, Chile, for Koppers Co., Inc.

R. W. WALKER, named executive vice-president and a director of Brunswick Ordnance Corp., New Brunswick, N. J., a wholly owned Mack Trucks, Inc., subsidiary.

DAVID S. GIBSON, appointed assistant to the vice-president, purchases and traffic, of Worthington Pump and Machinery Corp., Harrison, N. J.

IRON AGE

salutes

Clifford F. Hood

BEING executive vice-president-operations of U. S. Steel Co. is a challenge that Cliff Hood is meeting in customary fashion—head on.

What's more he likes it. He doesn't even have to say it. The zestful way he works at squeezing one more ingot from the production pot is enough.

Thirty-two years in the steel business, virtually all of it in a supervisory or executive capacity, has taught him the importance of getting along with other people. He not only believes that a man should be praised for a job well done—he does it. And he's not shy about spreading the word around either. That's another reason why people like to work for him.

He puts all he has into whatever he does. His excellent bond drive at Carnegie-Illinois is being used by the Treasury Dept. as a model in other plants.

Mr. Hood, born on a farm near Monmouth, Ill., Feb. 8, 1894, might have been a farmer except for happenstance. When he was a youth, an electrical engineer moved into town and aroused his interest in this field. As a result, he graduated from the University of Illinois with a degree in electrical engineering.

He served as assistant cable sales manager for Packard Electric Co. before joining the electric cable department of American Steel & Wire Co. in 1917. After service in World War I he moved up the ladder steadily, becoming president in 1938. He was made president of Carnegie-Illinois in 1950.

When he can find the time, which is not often enough to suit him, he likes to play a strictly sociable round of golf. If he manages to hold his score to the low 90s he goes home happy.

WALTER J. DAILY, appointed vice-president of the vacuum cleaner division of Lewyt Corp., Brooklyn, N. Y.

HOWARD G. GOLEM, appointed as director of procurement for Consolidated Vultee Aircraft Corp., San Diego, Calif.

A. H. LEWIS, JR., appointed manager of the Syracuse, N. Y., branch of Crucible Steel Company of America.

ORREN S. LESLIE, assumed the managership of the Beloit, Wis., works of Fairbanks, Morse & Co.

IRON AGE *introduces*

Continued

H. N. May, appointed chief of material for the San Diego division of CONSOLIDATED VULTEE AIRCRAFT CORP.

Jerome L. Strauss, appointed as vice-president of the contract manufacturing division and **Irving J. Bottner** as treasurer of LEWYT CORP., Brooklyn, N. Y.

John H. Clough, elected a director of the GRISCOM-RUSSELL CO., New York.

Harry G. Call, named a vice-president; **I. O. Goodnight,** treasurer and **G. A. Kessel,** assistant comptroller of the ELECTRIC AUTO-LITE CO., Toledo.

Robert I. Baxter, appointed manager of sales for the PENN STEEL CASTINGS CO., New York.

S. W. Hickey, appointed assistant manager of the railroad products department of FAIRBANKS, MORSE & CO., Chicago.

Sheldon Dale, promoted to the newly created position of director of research and development for CORY CORP., Chicago.

Herbert L. Schultz, appointed plant manager of MID-WEST ABRASIVE CO., Owosso, Mich.

Robert W. Lea, joined OLIN INDUSTRIES, INC., East Alton, Ill. Mr. Lea was formerly the president of the Johns-Manville Corp.

H. B. West, appointed sales engineer, Syracuse district, for CRUCIBLE STEEL COMPANY OF AMERICA.

William M. O'Donnell, appointed to the executive staff of AMERICAN METALLURGICAL PRODUCTS CO., Pittsburgh. Mr. O'Donnell will be engaged in sales and metallurgical development.

W. F. Hurlburt, Sr., elected chairman of the board of directors of AUTOMATIC SWITCH CO., Orange, N. J. Other officers elected: **W. F. Hurlburt, Jr.,** president; **H. V. Darrin,** vice-president and secretary; **David M. Darrin,** vice-president and treasurer.

Patrick J. Patton, appointed Milwaukee manager for the commercial sales division of the DE LAVAL STEAM TURBINE CO.

Harry Brandvik, appointed representative for KENNAMETAL, INC., at their new district office in Minneapolis. **William J. Collins,** appointed as representative in the New England district, and **Frank Price** as service engineer in the Middle Atlantic district.

T. W. Haines, named district manager for Philadelphia and eastern Pennsylvania of the MORSE TWIST DRILL & MACHINE CO. Mr. Haines has been replaced in New York by **R. W. Kuhn** and **R. E. Bennett.**

E. A. Williams, Jr., joined the operating department of the NORTH AMERICAN REFRACTORIES CO., Philadelphia. Mr. Williams was formerly vice-president in charge of production of the Climax Fire Brick Co.

Clyde E. Albro, appointed sales development supervisor for mica products for GENERAL ELECTRIC CO., Schenectady.

OBITUARIES

Paul Pauren Ildings, 50, director of General Motors Corp. for Portugal, died February 13, 1951.

John Hughes, 85, formerly assistant to the president of U. S. Steel Corp., New York, died recently.

Paul Prescott, 33, structural engineer with Truscon Steel Co., Boston, died recently.

W. L. Iliff, 60, manager of Eastern sales, Hyatt Bearings Div., General Motors Corp., Harrison, N. J., died recently. Mr. Iliff started with the company in 1914.

Francis A. Troendle, 61, treasurer and assistant secretary of The Midvale Co., Philadelphia, died suddenly.

Henry Plackett, 63, superintendent of the sheet rolling mill, Park Works of Crucible Steel Co., since 1931, died at Pittsburgh recently.

Fred H. Loftus, 56, president of Loftus Engineering Corp., Pittsburgh, died recently.

Sherwood A. Moore, president of Sherwood Moore Iron Works, Birmingham, died recently at St. Petersburg, Fla.

NUTONE and REVERE "RING the BELL"!

NuTone "SYMPHONIC" EIGHT-NOTE WESTMINSTER DOOR CHIME WALNUT FINISH COVER AND BRASS CHIME TUBES.

NUTONE'S Symphonic Door Chime, made by NuTone Incorporated, Cincinnati 27, Ohio. The company has recently added to its line Westminster Chime and Strike Clocks.

EASY polishing on centerless polishing machines is an important feature of Revere Brass Tubes.

POLISHED tubes are dipped in clear synthetic finish and up-ended to drain before baking.

● In the early days of NuTone, when the company was laying the foundation for a business that became the world's largest producer of door chimes, an important decision had to be made. A metal had to be selected for the chimes, one that would produce a soft, pleasant, resonant tone; a metal that was hard and durable; that would polish easily and retain a gleaming, luxurious surface for many years.

NuTone experimented with different metals, tested various products. Finally a Revere Brass Tube was selected, which was not surprising, because Revere itself had conducted extensive laboratory investigations into the factors responsible for pleasing tone. For the past 14 years, throughout NuTone's history, Revere Brass Tube has been used in increasing quantities. Revere has also collaborated in economy as well as quality, assisting on production problems, in the specification of multiple

lengths to lessen scrap, and so on. This is a story of cooperation between two industries, and between a large company and one that used to be small, but is now the largest in its field . . . Revere is proud of the results of this long and happy association.

February 22, 1951

on the assembly line

automotive news and opinions

Race develops between civilian and defense tooling . . . Civilian programs hang on . . . See auto taxes too high.

by Walter G. Patton

No Engine Cancellations—Closest heat in the race between civilian and defense production is in special machine tools. Motor car producers are still going ahead with their plans for new V-8 high compression engines. There have been no cancellations and will be no breaks in the projected engine programs unless defense takes over. There is real danger this may happen but it hasn't happened yet.

Men and Materials—Right now Detroit machine tool builders face two very tough shortages: materials and manpower. Steel is very tight—and getting tighter. A shortage of steel bars is slowing down machine tool production. Some machine tool builders believe pooled orders for steel, giving preference to machine tool builders, will be absolutely essential if civilian machine tool decks are to be cleared for defense work.

High Auto Taxes—Tax target for today is certainly the automobile. Industry statisticians estimate that a $2000 car delivered at Detroit during 1949 carried a measurable tax burden of $475.75. About 24¢ out of every automotive dollar goes for taxes. During 1949, special motor vehicle taxes collected from the public are estimated at $3845 million.

It is not to be wondered that the industry last week protested the government's plan for a 20 pct excise tax on new automobiles. As AMA figures it, the current 7 pct excise tax is too high and many other commodities are tax free. The industry is also protesting that the rate of increase on automobiles proposed by the Treasury is higher than the tax burden suggested for any other commodity, accounting for 40 pct of the new program.

Wanted—Clear Picture—Here is a fact not generally considered: If war work takes over suddenly, cancellations of civilian machine tool orders will make World War II cancellations look like peanuts. The present emergency has found machine tool builders loaded. Eight major car engine and body tooling jobs are now in process—more than at any time in the industry's history.

This work is going ahead—for the present. Some observers feel the critical materials situation plus the growing defense requirements will eventually upset existing plans. This question is being asked: Is it fair to ask auto makers to give up tooling in which they have already invested millions until a clearer picture comes out of Washington?

Reckoning the Chances—As matters now stand, the prospects for new engine programs look like this: The Ford 6 and Lincoln seem to have a good chance to reach completion. The Ford 8 and Mercury may get squeezed. DeSoto seems to have a good chance but there is some doubt about Dodge. The new Buick engine is doubtful —but work is proceeding.

Beating the Deadline?—While there has been much conjecture about 1952 car models, these facts should be kept in mind: (1) Each car manufacturer is going ahead with his plans. There have been no major cancellations of die work. (2) The changes involved in 1952 models are the most extensive in the history of the industry with the exception of the original postwar models.

The outlook is for increased activity to complete present die work. This work should be out of the foundries next month or April at the latest. The dies then go on to tool and die shops. This work will undoubtedly go forward unless it is stopped by defense. Whether the finished dies will be used or mothballed for the duration is anybody's guess.

Foundries Tighten Belts — Detroit foundries have been hard hit

assembly line

by the critical alloy situation. Automobile dies have always contained substantial amounts of nickel, chromium, molybdenum and other alloys. These alloy additions assure adequate hardness and other desirable properties in large sections. Some dies are now being made without the usual alloy content.

Foundries are also having pig iron supply difficulties. Others report silicon is very tight. One result: New automotive dies may be on the soft side. Foundry sources hasten to add, however, they will work quite satisfactorily.

Ford Steelmaking — Progress made in the Ford steel operation at the Rouge has been tremendous. From 1940 to 1945, Ford blast furnaces averaged 41,000 tons annually. Output in 1950 was more than a million tons, a gain of 127 pct. Ford openhearth ingot production averaged about 710,000 during 1940-45. In 1950, output reached 1,200,000 tons, a gain of more than 73 pct.

Guesswork in Capacity—There is always a certain amount of guesswork in capacity figures. Rated production capacity of the Ford Motor Co. is about 6300 cars a day. Still, Ford was able to boost its peak output to nearly 9000 units a day during 1950.

Testing for Leaks — The day may come when water tests are extensively used on the assembly line. De Soto uses such a test and reports excellent results. The water is forced on the car under high pressure. The test not only discloses leaks but quickly indicates variations in dies and assemblies.

Fisher Body has announced a 4 minute sealing test is being employed. The test is intended to duplicate road conditions encountered at high speed. In the test, 30 high pressure jets dash 500 gal of water at the body from all directions. Fisher uses a comparable water test at its assembly plants to check the sealing of each body coming off the assembly line.

Checking for Roadability—Other tests used currently by Fisher Body include: (1) a "shake rig" test in which the front end of the car is held rigid while the rear end is oscillated to simulate the twisting motion encountered on the road, (2) measuring maximum deflection over the length of the car with maximum passenger loads in the front and rear seats, (3) a "dust test" in which body sealing is checked by blowing powdered chalk dust into a specially constructed chamber, (4) checking road noise by placing front or rear wheels between revolving rollers that are interchangeable to simulate different road surfaces. Offset cams are used to reproduce surfaces ranging from rough cobblestones to superhighways.

A Lot of Sand—Materials requirements for production foundries are staggering. To produce the various types of molds for aluminum castings at Fabricast Div. of General Motors a total of 40,000 tons of sand are used per year. This includes 12,000 tons of bank sand, 10,000 tons of silica sand, and 18,000 tons of lake sand.

Detroit's War Work—Four more major defense contracts have recently been announced by the automobile industry. (1) Hudson will build Wright R3350 reciprocating aircraft engines. (2) K-F has been awarded its third aircraft order—to build Wright R-1300 aircraft engines. (These will be built at the K-F engine division in Detroit.) (3) Buick has been announced as a prime contractor to produce British-designed J-65 Sapphire jet engines for American fighter planes. Amount of the contract is $25 million. (During World War II Buick built Pratt and Whitney bomber engines.) (4) Chrysler Div. of Chrysler Corp. will build V-12 air-cooled tank engines of Continental design at New Orleans.

Must Be Easy Reading—General Motors is continuing the successful operation of its Information Rack Service. During the past 25 months, GM has distributed 21 million copies of 148 booklets to employees. Social and economic material accounted for 36 pct of the total; home and family, 18 pct; safety and health, 16 pct; inspirational, 13 pct.

THE BULL OF THE WOODS
By J. R. Williams

THE INDIRECT ROUTE

Double Output...

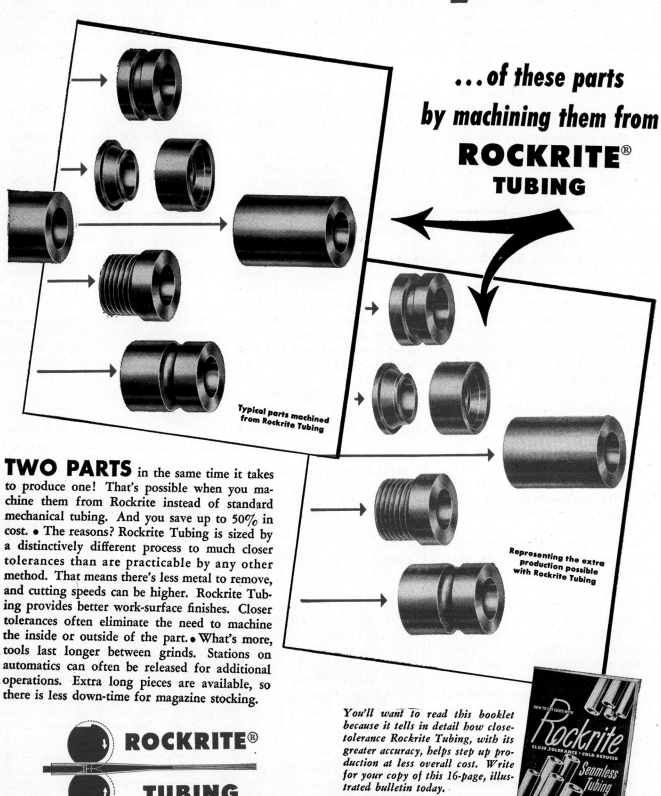

...of these parts
by machining them from

ROCKRITE®
TUBING

Typical parts machined
from Rockrite Tubing

Representing the extra
production possible
with Rockrite Tubing

TWO PARTS in the same time it takes to produce one! That's possible when you machine them from Rockrite instead of standard mechanical tubing. And you save up to 50% in cost. • The reasons? Rockrite Tubing is sized by a distinctively different process to much closer tolerances than are practicable by any other method. That means there's less metal to remove, and cutting speeds can be higher. Rockrite Tubing provides better work-surface finishes. Closer tolerances often eliminate the need to machine the inside or outside of the part. • What's more, tools last longer between grinds. Stations on automatics can often be released for additional operations. Extra long pieces are available, so there is less down-time for magazine stocking.

ROCKRITE®
TUBING

You'll want to read this booklet because it tells in detail how close-tolerance Rockrite Tubing, with its greater accuracy, helps step up production at less overall cost. Write for your copy of this 16-page, illustrated bulletin today.

HOW TO CUT COSTS WITH
Rockrite
CLOSE TOLERANCE • COLD REDUCED
Seamless
Tubing

TUBE REDUCING CORPORATION · WALLINGTON, NEW JERSEY

west coast progress report

by R.T. Reinhardt

New Steel Plants—Latest development in the proposed steel plant for "someplace in central California" is the filing of a certificate of necessity for $24 million by the Yolo Steel & Metal Co.

The backers claim to have a large deposit of magnetite ore running more than 50 pct Fe in central California. The entire proposal involves a blast furnace, openhearth with 1 million ton per year capacity and rolling mills, to cost approximately $264 million.

Seattle Mill — In the Pacific Northwest the Seidelhuber Steel Rolling Mill Corp. has been formed with Frank Seidelhuber, Jr., president; Frank Seidelhuber, Sr., and William S. Leckendy, vice-presidents; Wayne Booth, secretary; Roy C. Erickson, treasurer, and Henry R. Seidelhuber and Frank L. Cassidy, directors.

Company officials say ground will be broken within 4 months and the mill will employ about 150 men on a three shift basis within 18 months. The mill will produce strip.

Cost Advantage—President Seidelhuber states, "There is no other mill within 1000 miles, which gives us a $30 a ton advantage on freight alone, and then too, our scrap price is lower than back East." He adds that "with a little expansion we could use 1000 tons of sheet a month and the mill will produce

3000 tons which means we will have 2000 tons to sell to small manufacturers who are already expressing interest."

At present he buys ingots locally for $106 a ton and then pays to have the ingots rolled into sheets at a total cost of approximately 10¢ a pound.

The parent company, Seidelhuber Iron & Bronze Co., last week reported that it has a 3-year contract with the Army Ordnance Dept. for steel landing mats, 5-gallon gas cans and practice bombs.

K-F Closes at Long Beach—Production of automobiles for the Kaiser-Frazer Corp. at Long Beach was discontinued last Saturday at midnight. The company had been assembling 25 cars a day for approximately 2 years in the former Douglas Aircraft Corp. plant, and the facilities will be reconverted to aircraft production.

This assembly unit was one of several planned by the K-F Corp. where output would be somewhere between 25 and 100 units per day. A similar plant has been in operation in Portland for the past 6 months.

Few Tears Shed — Announcement by Kaiser Aluminum & Chemical Corp. that New Orleans, La., has been selected as the site for construction of its new 100,000 ton per year aluminum reduction plant

came as no surprise to westerners. As reluctant as they were to see this industry and heavy payrolls go to another area, power conscious industrialists of the Northwest privately are relieved.

There has long been opposition to further expansion of aluminum reduction facilities in the Pacific Northwest because of the high rate of electrical consumption per manhour.

Low Cost Power—Low rate for electrical power, the magnet drawing aluminum reduction facilities to the Pacific Northwest, may be equalled in the New Orleans project. Kaiser Aluminum & Chemical Corp. expects the cost of electricity generated with natural gas from the Gulf areas to compete favorably with the low rates in existence from the Bonneville Power Administration.

Scrap Headaches — Although western scrap dealers are almost completely satisfied with recent price regulations there are some objections to limits on preparation costs, and some off-grading has been reported.

Although there has been no real evidence of hoarding by dealers, scrap is tight particularly in the Northwest. Pacific Car & Foundry at Renton which has a large defense order is asking for more scrap than it is getting.

REDUCE ROLL NECK MAINTENANCE COSTS

Lubricate with TEXACO REGAL OILS

To OBTAIN economical and trouble-free performance of oil film roll neck bearings, use *Texaco Regal Oils*. These heavy-duty turbine-quality oils keep circulating systems clean, thus assuring a constant flow of cool, clean lubricant to the bearings. Bearings last longer . . . efficiency and production go up . . . maintenance costs go down.

Texaco Regal Oils are especially resistant to oxidation, emulsification and sludging, and are designed to carry heavy loads—even under high operating temperatures. You'll agree with operators everywhere that *Texaco Regal Oils* assure better performance . . . better results.

For efficiency and economy in pinion stands and reduction drives, protect heavy-duty enclosed gears with *Texaco Meropa Lubricants*. Gear and bearing life is greatly prolonged with these "extreme pressure" and foam-resistant lubricants.

Let Texaco's cost-saving lubricants work for you. A Texaco Lubrication Engineer will gladly help you select the proper ones for your operation. Just call the nearest of the more than 2,000 Texaco Distributing Plants in the 48 States, or write The Texas Company, 135 East 42nd Street, New York 17, N. Y.

TEXACO Regal Oils
(HEAVY CIRCULATING OILS)

the federal view

this week in washington

by Eugene J. Hardy

More Cutbacks Coming—Relaxation of metal orders here and there actually represents efforts to equalize the impact of limitations, thus affording a little relief to industry. Present tight supply situation is due to grow worse before getting better. Steel is due to be brought under cutback restrictions.

NPA opinion is divided as to whether the proposed industry-by-industry cutback is the right approach. But there is agreement that the use of steel for the civilian economy must be reduced by at least 20 pct during the second quarter. The relaxing of some restrictions on copper, scheduled for this week, will bring only spotty relief. Another 5 pct copper cutback to the present 20 pct is seen as certain for the second quarter. No changes in aluminum limitations are currently planned for the second quarter although the supply is growing tighter.

Stockpile Storage—Distribution and storage of materials in the strategic stockpile is now being made on the basis of relative industry consumption — pin-pointed by cities, instead of broad areas. In other words, manganese and tin will be stored near steel-producing centers, rubber close by the major tire-producing plants, etc.

The new plan is based on a Munitions Board review of industrial consumption of stockpile materials, which has been substantially completed. As a result, the Board points out millions of ton miles of wartime transportation requirements, will, in effect, be "stockpiled." Materials will be stored closer to possible claimants minimizing cross-hauls and back-hauls.

Metal Buying Centers—The Defense Minerals Administration is studying the feasibility of reviving the metals procurement depot system set up by the Metals Reserve Corp. during World War II. Reason is that increased domestic metal production is foreseen in the flood of applications being received by DMA for government aid in expanding and enlarging mining operations.

Applications under process run the gamut from opening new mines to expansion of existing facilities and reopening of marginal mines. Metal received through government contracts would be channeled mostly back to industry (defense projects). Production under DMA help will not be felt for at least 18 months.

Tighter A-T Penalties?—In the coming months the Federal Trade Commission will press its annual fight for more teeth in existing anti-trust laws. The House Inter-state and Foreign Commerce Committee has already been told penalties are too light and that the commission leans more toward the $50,000 maximum (per count) proposed under a bill which died in the last Congress.

The FTC is also drafting a proposal which would amend the Clayton Act to provide the same type of enforcement provisions contained in the Wheeler-Lea Act —civil penalties up to $5,000 for violation of cease and desist orders after they become final.

On Deaf Ears—President Truman's demand for $16 billion in new taxes is falling upon deaf ears on Capitol Hill.

Current congressional sentiment indicates that the most the Treasury can expect to receive in the way of new revenue next year is about half this amount.

A Flat Refusal—Senate and House tax-writers first exercised their constitutional prerogatives on revenue matters last week when they flatly refused to go along with White House demands for "immediate" enactment of a $10 billion tax bill as a "first installment."

Committee thinking is that Mr. Truman will be lucky to get one bill providing for about $8 billion in new revenue instead of what are seen as bloated demands.

REDESIGNED FREEZER DOOR

USES LESS STEEL

By J. V. KIELB
Director of Development,
Seeger Refrigerator Co.,
St. Paul

A unique new home freezer door design cuts materials cost by permitting use of lighter gage steel. But it introduced knotty problems in drawing and porcelain enameling. These were solved by refinements in design and processing methods.

Several interesting problems were overcome in the design and manufacture of a new freezer door, resulting in lower cost. This lowering of product cost was not easy. The manufacturing methods of a good organization are such that the possible reduction in direct labor is often small. Therefore, in order to reduce product cost, sometimes the only outlet is to reduce the purchase part cost, such as by the elimination of parts or through reducing gage thickness of materials.

Such a problem was involved in the design of a new door for home freezers. Before the decision was made on this door, many questions were asked, reviewed, and investigated, ranging between the most suitable door from a manufacturing standpoint to consumer preferences. Considered were a stainless steel door, a fabric surface with stainless steel trim, a painted steel door, and a white porcelain door. The stainless, although acceptable to the sales department, was too expensive. The fabric top surface was rejected because it would necessitate keeping a large inventory of different colors and patterns to meet the needs of all types of homes. The plain painted door did not test satisfactorily, showing a tendency to rust.

After much investigation, it was found that the porcelain finished surface, acid resistant, would be the most widely acceptable. Field reports have shown that this type of finished surface is one of the most practicable in home usage today. With this in mind, work was started to develop a complete new door design which would be completely different and also low in cost.

The result is an exterior door which is new in design and appearance. It is unique because it

FIG. 1—The first drawing operation forms a splash guard on the door blank.

has no lock handle mechanism for lifting or closing, or sealing the door. This door is also reduced in thickness from 2¼ to 1¼ in., giving a better appearance while still maintaining low heat loss. The lifting action of the door was accomplished by placing an offset in the front flanges. Sealing was obtained through a reverse action in the hinge mechanism. This not only holds the door open, but as it closes, the spring mechanism reverses itself and keeps the door closed.

Since this was to be a white porcelain door finish, there arose countless problems due to the fancy design. It was found that cold-working stresses built up due to limited radii on the top and bottom corners of the splash board and the front offset handle embossment, which had to be eliminated before porcelain could be applied. This door developed into a rigid section particularly at the outside corners of the splash board, the height of the splash board, and the front offset handle embossment. If any cracking or rupture of the metal appeared in these radii, it generally resulted in hair lining, chippage or cracking of the porcelain.

Radii At Critical Points Increased

In the first draw operation, illustrated in Fig. 1, fracture of the metal appeared on the top left and right curve sections of the splash board, while the second draw operation generally resulted in a tearing out of these weak sections at the radii. At the start of the model, the openings at these points were welded before applying porcelain. During trial runs, the radii at these critical points were increased and blended together with other radii at these curve surfaces, so that maximum drawn qualities were obtained.

Fig. 1 shows the first draw operation, which is

done from a developed size of enameled steel. In the design of this door, it was first thought that it would be necessary to use 18-gage steel in order to have a heavier door for sealing and preventing the door from warping. Also from the porcelain standpoint there would be less rejects on first coat operation against crackling, chippage or hair lining. From a punch press room standpoint, the heavier gage would have less rejects, and better drawing characteristics. However, it was found that the embossments resulting from the splash board, the offset handle, and the radii on the sides and front and back flanges added greatly to the

FIG. 2—Two operations are performed simultaneously on this press. The second draw is done in the background, and formation of the door offset flange in the foreground.

rigidity of the door. Therefore, it was possible to consider 20 and 22-gage materials, in high tensile steel. This design change resulted in a good cost reduction of raw material.

The material is roller leveled after the sheet is cut to size. In this operation, the splash board section is drawn on a 200-ton cushioned press. After this operation, the part is taken to a 350-ton Clearing press where the second operation is performed. In the background of Fig. 2 is the exterior door drawn to about 4 in. from the developed sheet. This developed sheet covers the side, the inside flanges, and trim of edges. On the right, in the foreground, the operation which forms the bumped flange is illustrated. This bump is such that it gives a gripping action for handling and lifting the door. Both of these operations are handled in this press by three operators, and the hit is simultaneous on both operations.

The part then moves to another press where the corners are folded over as illustrated in Fig. 3. This handling requires four hits of the press. Then the door is passed to the next press where the hinge holes are punched in the back flange. The door is then placed on another press where all flanges are trimmed and formed. The side flanges are handled first, and then the front flange and finally the hinge back flange. The back is again bumped to make sure it is flat for the hinge assembly.

As production on this freezer model is limited, simple dies are used to keep down the overall die cost. During operation sequence, the part is inspected periodically. In the final operations, presses are grouped together, thus eliminating double handling and trucking. If the model had warranted greater production, then many of the operations could be combined to reduce direct labor, though original tool cost would be increased.

After the door is completed in the press room, it goes to the metal door assembly room where strap braces are spotwelded to the front and rear flanges. The corner flanges are kept to a minimum to reduce warping and buckling of the metal at these points, which reduces metal finishing and maintains a good door seal. Many

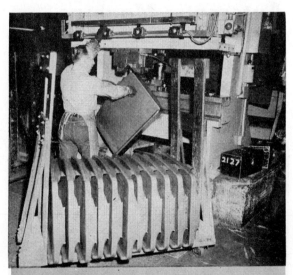

FIG. 3—Corner forming of the freezer door on a single strike die.

tests were conducted to determine whether corner gussets were necessary for having a flat door, and it was found that good results could be obtained without them. This eliminated four extra pieces of metal and also the spotwelding of these parts.

Porcelain Coats Dipped and Sprayed

After assembly, the door is placed on a chain conveyor, inspected and sent to the cleaning-pickling room. In process through the porcelain shop, the door is thoroughly cleaned and dried. The ground coat is put on by dipping and baked at 1450°F in a continuous furnace. The door is then inspected and placed on the finish coat conveyor, sprayed and baked. The only wiping is a 1¼-in. edge wipe on the inside flanges and corners, and the hinge holes on the back flange.

The white finish coat rejections were high at

the start, but now have been reduced to a minimum. The defects causing most of these rejects were hair lining on the outside rear radii of the splash board due to drawing stresses, and chipping on the under side of flanges, particularly the side flanges. This chippage was caused by many things such as radii of edge flanges, flanges not broken 90°, spraying too much finish coat on the door edge flanges, and improper hanging of door through baking.

Door Flanges Broken 90 Degrees

Upon investigation of these items, it was finally decided to see that the flanges on the door were broken 90° or slightly more, to see that the radii of the corners were not fractured and that good flow of metal appeared, to see that the door was hung properly through the drying and baking furnace, and finally to see that the holes in the flanges were reamed after porcelain. All this was accomplished by closer inspection of the metal part after leaving the metal shop and final inspection of the door in porcelain shop. Proper handling of the door throughout the plant was also stressed.

Fig. 4 shows a finished freezer door from the porcelain shop, illustrating its flatness and overall exterior appearance. At the start of this program, quite a few warped doors came from the porcelain shop, making it difficult to get a door seal. By changing the technique of hanging the door through the porcelain furnace and reducing the amount of deposit of finish coat on the door, the warping was reduced to a minimum. At the start, the door was hung in the porcelain shop by the corner strap braces, which caused distortion of the door and chippage of the under side flange and radii. Hanging the door by the holes in the flanges in the porcelain shop caused warp-

FIG. 4—A completed door, as it comes from the porcelain shop. The difficult contours, flatness, and good finish show clearly.

ing and chipping. This was changed to hanging the doors by special wire hangers which were placed on the inside radii of the side flanges, thus placing the door load on the radii which were more rigid than the flanges.

Each door is sent to the door assembly line

before finally being placed on a freezer. Before starting assembly, the door is inspected and the inner door pan holes are reamed because of porcelain buildup. The insulation is placed in the door and the inner door pan and gasket are placed over the insulation. Then clips are driven into the door.

In order to have a floating door with good sealing properties, clips were used to give flexibility of door assembly. It has been found on this horizontal door that a flexible or floating inner door pan gives better sealing than would the rigid type of construction. This floating action is accomplished by making the hole in the inner door pan larger than the hole in the exterior door. Fastening of the inner door is done by a clip which is the same size as the exterior door hole, but overlaps the inner door pan. This assembly is placed on a freezer and the hinges are attached to the exterior shell and door. The freezer then passes through final inspection, on to the warehouse for run-in tests and crating.

This door construction is similar to that used on new ranges, but the splash board on the freezer door is a drawn section, while on the kitchen ranges it is a formed open-back section. It was once thought that this type of construction was impractical if not impossible, but by coordinating good design and good tooling, the door design became a reality.

Small Parts Coated in Automatic Machine

Efficiency in the painting or waxing of small steel parts is increased 200 to 300 pct in an automatically-operated spinning cabinet at Tinnerman Products, Inc., Cleveland.

The cabinet, designed and installed by Tinnerman engineers, also eliminates the necessity of workmen lifting and lowering baskets of fasteners weighing approximately 90 lb from floor level to and from a height of approximately 4 ft.

The basket to be filled with unpainted fasteners is placed on a lift, operated on a track in the front of the cabinet. Approximately 50 lb of fasteners is dumped from a can into the basket. The operator presses a button on the front of the cabinet, and the lift is raised by an electrically-operated hoist to the level of the front opening of the cabinet.

The operator then slides the basket into the cabinet and onto a metal disk. A drum, operated by two air cylinders beneath it, and filled to a depth of 7 in. with paint or liquid wax, is then raised to permit the liquid to cover the metal parts.

After the fasteners have been submerged the drum is lowered until the bottom of the basket is above the surface of the paint but still inside the drum. The basket is spun on the disk at 450 rpm for approximately 45 sec. At the end of this interval a dog contacts the basket and stops its motion.

The drum is lowered further to clear the bottom of the basket. Another basket is slid into the cabinet, pushing the first one out onto a conveyer track. This has been raised, by a series of pulleys and a compensating weight, to the level of the opening on the side of the cabinet corresponding to the opening on the front.

The basket of finished parts then rides down the conveyer into a pivoted rack, where the parts are placed in a tray ready for baking.

AUTOMATICALLY-OPERATED spinning cabinet developed by engineers at Tinnerman Products, Inc., for painting or waxing Speed Nuts and other small metal parts.

CONTINUOUS CAST aluminum bars produced by the Properzi process

By D. I. BROWN
Feature Editor

PART II

A novel 3-roll cluster pass 15-stand type of continuous mill reduces the continuous cast aluminum bar to coiled rod. Finished product shows better than standard mechanical properties. Major end use is for nails and manufactured wire products.

The rolling mill which converts the continuous cast aluminum bar into rod at Nichols Wire & Aluminum Co. is also of Italian design. The mill is driven by a 50-hp motor. Power is transmitted to a 26-in. diam V-belt pulley and this directly turns the drive shaft which runs the length of the mill.

The top roll of each roll cluster at each stand is connected to the drive shaft by a sprocket and chain drive. Each stand has a simple gear reducer which controls roll speed and the

speeds at each stand cannot be individually varied. Speed of the mill can only be changed by varying the speed of the motor.

There are three rolls in each pass of the 15-stand mill. Usually only 13 stands are employed to roll the rod sizes used at Nichols. The even numbered passes roll a triangular section and the odd numbered passes produce a round. The bar does not turn or twist through the mill.

The crystalline structure of the cast section,

Diam. In Inches	Lot	Pct Elong. In 10 in.	Ultimate Tensile PSI	Conductivity Measurement
TESTS ON AS-DRAWN WIRE				
0.0765	Standard specification for electrical conductor cable..........	1.4	28,000	60.97
0.0765	Average values on 11 tests............................ #1, Coil #2	1.8	34,170	59.6
0.0825	Standard specification............................	1.5	27,500	60.97
0.0825	Average values on 12 tests............................ #1, Coil #2	1.9	34,179	59.85
0.1050	Standard specification............................	1.5	26,000	60.97
0.1050	Average values on 12 tests............................ #1, Coil #15	2.3	30,552	60.44
0.1320	Standard specification............................	1.7	25,000	60.97
0.1320	Average values on 12 tests............................ #1, Coil #3	2.4	29,788	60.05
0.1480	Standard specification............................	1.8	24,500	60.97
0.1480	Average values on 12 tests............................ #1, Coil #1	2.9	28,408	60.27
0.1480	Annealed (rod)............................ #1, Coil #1	2.7	26,150	60.99
0.1660	Standard specification............................	2.0	24,000	60.97
0.1660	Average values on 12 tests............................ #1, Coil #2	2.9	26,890	60.15
0.1865	Standard specification............................	2.0	24,000	60.97
0.1865	Average values on 12 tests............................ #1, Coil #1	3.2	25,267	60.71

see headpiece, presents three 120° angles of preferential working. The mill rolls set at 120° alternately work the corners. A square section having four preferential angles of crystallinity, the designers believe, would require a much more complex mill.

The geometrical shape progression of rolling was chosen so that all main shafts of the rolling stands could be horizontal. Any other

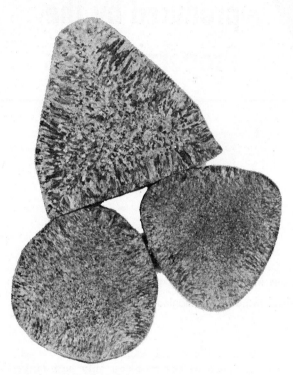

FIG. 2—Cross-sections of the as-cast bar and after first and second pass on the mill. At the top is the as-cast bar; left, first breakdown and right, the section after the second reduction. Etched with Turners reagent, 2X.

arrangement would require both horizontal and vertical shafts to avoid angular torsions or twists to the bar.

Screwdown pressure at each stand can be adjusted but only by moving the roll housings in or out on the main frame to which they are bolted. Roll diameters are about 8 in. The rod is coiled at the end of the mill. Coil weights average 225 lb although a wide range of coil weights can be made. Just after the rod leaves the finishing pass an air blast cleans the oil lubricant from the surface of the rod.

The macrograph of the as-cast section, see headpiece, shows a relatively fine crystalline structure. From the few cross-sectional samples examined, it appears that an occasional small center cavity is formed in the cast section. These cavities are not continuous, but appear at random. This flaw is not due to piping as

solidification is too fast. It is believed they form from a combination of factors which can be eliminated.

First the metal from which the samples were cast was not fluxed and second a turbulence at the discharge end of the spout is sometimes experienced. Further control of pouring and better direction of metal flow into the mold cavity will soon be made and it is believed that these refinements will preclude the occasional porosity in the as-cast section which eventually is completely eliminated in rolling to final size.

In Fig. 2 the initial section plus the rod through the first and second pass are shown. The contour of the round to triangular roll pass can be seen and the refinement of the as-cast structure is plainly evident.

The as-cast structure disappears after the reduction taken by pass No. 7 as shown in Fig. 3. The finish size has a bearing on where as-cast structure disappears. The rod shown in Fig. 3 is rolled to a finish diam of 9/32 in. Other finish sizes, because of different mill draft on each stand, may shift the position at which the cast structure is worked out of the original bar.

The finished rod is exceptionally sound, fine-grained and the surface of the coiled rod has

FIG. 3—A magnification, 7X, of the cross-section after seventh pass, shown above. The large grains at the perimeter are due to recrystallization because of rolling temperature at this pass. After the last reduction, the cross-section shows an equiaxed fine grain structure of very sound metal.

a much better than the average finish on rod made by conventional methods.

Mechanical and electrical properties of continuously cast and rolled Nichols aluminum are shown in the Table. The strength specifications for conductor cable are easily satisfied. To meet the rigid conductivity test, the rod can be finished at higher temperatures or the

THE CAST BAR at the right enters the continuous rolling mill. Each stand is separately chain-driven of the main drive shaft. The mill is 28 ft 8 in. long and the pass level of the mill is 46½ in. above the floor. Mill adjustments are easy and fast to make although few adjustments while rolling have been found necessary.

wire can be annealed by conventional methods.

Tests on a sample drawn from an as-rolled unannealed rod which fell just below the minimum conductivity are also shown in the Table. From annealed rod the samples from the same coil fully met the conductivity requirements. The test samples not marked annealed in wire size 0.1480 in. diam were taken from a coil finished at low temperatures so that some cold work was induced in the finished rod.

The success of the Properzi continuous casting machine in this country merits attention. It would be possible for small plants to gear their production of finished product very close to actual day-by-day consumption of semi-finished stock. The process also offers a means of dispersing some types of aluminum-producing mills to sections in which industry is not highly concentrated. Aluminum rivet wire makers can now get out of the big target areas much easier than heretofore. The process has good possibilities to makers of small diameter aluminum screw stock in sizes of ½-in. diam or less.

Nichols Wire & Aluminum Co. has on order a new mill designed to improve the operating characteristics of the experimental rolling mill. The casting machine needs no drastic modifications and when the control refinements are added, this machine will be capable of even better than present performance.

Part I of this two-part story covering the melting and continuous casting machine was published in last week's Iron Age.—Ed.

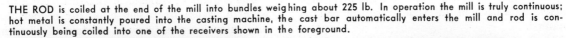

THE ROD is coiled at the end of the mill into bundles weighing about 225 lb. In operation the mill is truly continuous; hot metal is constantly poured into the casting machine, the cast bar automatically enters the mill and rod is continuously being coiled into one of the receivers shown in the foreground.

Skin with integral T-shaped stiffeners can be extruded. It will find wide application where loads are high and there are few irregularities in contour. Physical properties are high. Forming of integrally-stiffened parts produced by any of the methods can be done on standard sheet-metal equipment, using only slightly different techniques.

INTEGRALLY-STIFFENED SKIN

REVOLUTIONIZES AIRCRAFT CONSTRUCTION

extruded sections and forming methods

FOURTH OF A SERIES

For surface structure such as wing panels, fuselage and empennage surfaces, where loads are high and there are few irregularities in contour or structural continuity, integrally-stiffened extrusion shows exceptional possibilities. Extruded sections have high physical properties and because of the excellent detail configuration they will generally carry unusually high compressive stresses even with widely spaced supports. Thus both weight advantage and simplification of internal structure can be obtained.

The T-stiffener configuration makes for simplicity and efficiency where attachments, splices and joints are required. Because extrusion is obtainable in long lengths, reduction in the number of chordwise splices is generally possible. For some applications it may be worthwhile to machine the extruded section to obtain taper in skin thickness and section depth and to make integral reinforcements and attachment pads. It seems possible that future development will see production at tapered extruded sections.

Several shapes of practicable dimensions for integrally-stiffened aircraft surfaces have been extruded. Lockheed is using such shapes for tank panels on the F-94C.

The maximum size of the extruded section is determined primarily by the dimensions of the extrusion press and length is limited by billet size. The available extrusion pressure limits the complexity of the section shape and determines minimum thicknesses and fillets for successful extrusion of a particular shape.

The new extrusion press which the Air Force has ordered from Hydropress, presumably for its pilot plant at Adrian, Mich., will have a pressure in excess of 15,000 tons, far higher than any extrusion press now in existance. The limitations are interrelated and differ with various materials; the larger size extrusions in the harder alloys must have correspondingly thicker webs.

To take maximum advantage of press capacities Dow Chemical Co. developed the "octopus" type section shown in Fig. 17b. After extrusion the section was split and flattened to form a 17-in. wide stiffened sheet. A rail-shaped section was produced experimentally, about 1942, in 0-1HTA magnesium alloy. Considerable difficulty was experienced in obtaining satisfactory flatness in the surface after heat treatment. The more efficient T-stiffened section shown in Fig. 17c was extruded in the flat by Dow in 1946 of

By P. E. SANDORFF, *Research Engineer*
and GEORGE W. PAPEN, *Mgr., Production Engineering Dept.*
Lockheed Aircraft Corp., Burbank, Calif.

ZK-60 magnesium alloy, under an NACA contract.

To facilitate extrusion the section itself must contain no hollow elements. A logical configuration is provided by regularly spaced T-stiffeners, the spacing being determined by skin buckling requirements and the stiffener flanges providing high crippling strength and high section moment of inertia. An unsymmetrical flange may be advantageous for attachment but is not quite as efficient in bending or column action, particularly if the web and skin are thin.

Could Be Used In Wing Structures

The sections of Fig. 17 might be used in the upper surface structure of the wing of a large transport airplane. This section is naturally limited in width by the extrusion press die diameter if it is desired to extrude it flat.

Under a contract with the Air Force, Reynolds Metals Co. has completed the development of tools and processes to extrude the section shown in Fig. 17b, and split, straighten and heat-treat the product. Successful results have been obtained in extruding the hollow shape in 61S, 24S and 75S alloys.

It is believed parts of widths and thicknesses comparable to standard rolled sheet sizes can be produced on present equipment. Considerable variation in section details will also be permissible. Development of the processes necessary for obtaining satisfactory flatness in the finished heat-treated section has also progressed with considerable success.

To obtain sections of width larger than available die diameters, and yet avoid some of the extrusion and straightening problems, the semicircular sections shown in Fig. 17a have been proposed by Alcoa. The thickness limitations in this case are approximately the same as for flat extrusions.

To use many extruded and forged shapes to best advantage, some machining may be necessary. Skin thickness will be reduced, stiffener sections sized, and tapers in thickness and depth incorporated, leaving doubler pads for end attachments and local reinforcements. These machining operations are similar to those used in machining plate stock and essentially the same type of equipment is required.

Preshaping Cuts Costs

In savings in raw material alone, as compared with machining from plate stock, the use of rough outline sections shaped by extrusion or progressive forging show advantage. Though the extruded or forged shape costs more per pound, enough raw material is saved as compared with plate stock to show substantial reductions in total material cost.

In applying extrusion and machining together the advantages of better section inherent in extrusion can often be used to improve structural efficiency and simplify internal structure. Thus,

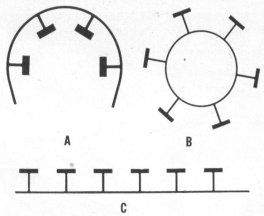

FIG. 17—How integrally-stiffened structure would be made by extrusion. The section shown in C, extruded flat, would be the most desirable. But to get larger sections from a press of given size, section B has been proposed. This hollow extruded cylinder would be slit and flattened to the shape shown in C. Certain problems in flattening would be avoided through use, instead of B, of the semicircular section shown in A.

an extruded section can later be machined to incorporate the desired degree of taper.

The application of integrally-stiffened construction to contoured surfaces such as wings and fuselages introduces the question of obtaining the proper curvature or contour.

Integrally-stiffened panels can be produced to the final shape, if desired, by forging or machining. Sections produced by rolling or extruding will have to be formed to contour subsequent to the basic operation. It may be that the warping due to heat treating, machining, stretching or the normal forging tolerances will require some degree of straightening operation on the panel regardless of original method of obtaining contour.

In view of the above it has been considered imperative to develop the forming techniques along with the basic operation of obtaining the desired cross-section. The Air Force has sponsored an extensive investigation into the forming problem through a research program now completed at the Lockheed plant.

It was assumed at the start that the section to be formed would be neither consistent nor constant in cross-section shape and in plan form.

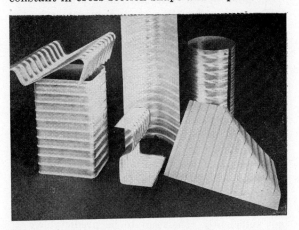

FIG. 18—Sample forming in integrally-stiffened sheet. All of these shapes were formed with conventional sheet metal equipment.

FIG. 19—One of the integrally - stiffened cylinders extruded by Reynolds Metals Co. in an Air Force research Program.

Integrally Stiffened Skin

Continued

Springback, therefore, would be difficult to determine. The skin between the stiffening elements would tend to buckle during the forming operation, leaving a wavy surface, and in extreme cases, the stiffener elements might actually punch through the skin. The stiffening elements would tend to buckle during forming and would have to be supported. Preliminary tests have proved that most of these fears are justified.

All of the common methods of forming sheet material are being investigated. For example: Bumping, a means of obtaining a contour or large radius by forming an infinite number of bends which blend into the desired curvature; rolling, using a Farnum contour roll or some similar type rolling equipment; die forming, use of hard-faced dies in a mechanical or hydraulic press; stretching, use of various type stretch presses or stretch dies in a large press. Each of the above methods depends to a large extent on specific type of equipment and has certain advantages and disadvantages.

Low Melting Point Being Studied

Support of the stiffeners and prevention of inter-stiffener buckling of skin appear to be the paramount difficulties. An attempt is being made to solve these problems by the use of dies, rollers and mandrels cut to fit over the stiffener. Also, investigations are being conducted relative to the use of a low melting point matrix which would encase the part and have the effect of making it act like a plate. Should this prove successful, it would eliminate much expensive punch, roll or die development.

The major fault found with this procedure on previous work is that the part after removal of the matrix materials tends to assume a still different contour. This relaxation or springback is not sufficiently consistent to be predictable.

As forming either completely from the flat or straightening after machining or forging will be

necessary, considerable work remains to be done to arrive at a satisfactory production method.

Conclusions of Lockheeds study of development to date are herewith presented.

The cost of airframe construction can be reduced by the judicious use of integrally-stiffened structure. The major cost item at present is in assembly and assembly tooling. By combining skin and stiffeners into one unit, assembly costs may be reduced considerably.

Size of Machine Parts Not Limited

Additional advantages of integrally-stiffened structure may be found in its greater rigidity, surface smoothness, and its structural efficiency, which often results in weight saving.

Machining from thick plate provides a ready means of making integrally-stiffened structure. It is highly flexible in design, permitting variations in section to incorporate taper, local reinforcements, integral doublers and heavy attachment panels. The simple rectangular stiffener shape available by machining is generally considered poor from a structural standpoint; this disadvantage is offset by freedom to reduce stiffener spacing and thus make the skin more effective under compression, and applications to design have shown substantial weight savings.

The size of machined parts is limited only by size of machining equipment and material availability; large size parts with any desired taper eliminate the need for splices and so save both their cost and weight. The one great disadvantage of machining is that of the original material, 75 to 95 pct is cut away in chips. Cost of raw material is therefore high. Machining time is also a large item with present-day equipment.

In spite of this, machining from plate will in certain applications show cost advantage as well as simplification and weight savings over conventional structure. It appears most valuable as an interim method or for prototype construction until it becomes possible to obtain blank stock of the outsize dimension, made by some other process.

FIG. 20—The integrally - stiffened sheet made by slitting the cylinder of Fig. 19, and flattening and stretching it.

Manufacture of integrally-stiffened surface by extrusion promises many advantages: Low cost, high material strength, and wide latitude in detail section design. Because of recent advances in technique, very thin as well as very heavy sections can be made available in flat sheets of relatively large width.

Section Taper Desirable

In general, taper in stiffener and skin section as well as local variations in thickness of reinforcement and attachment purposes will often be necessary to preserve the weight advantage of using extrusion; these irregularities can be obtained by machining but this represents an increase in cost.

No difficulty is anticipated with moderate forming to single curvatures, but any considerable forming will introduce new production problems. Therefore, while extrusion basically appears exceptionally attractive for weight saving and simplification of structure, its application will probably be limited to long-length, essentially flat panels unbroken in structure and requiring a minimum of tailoring and tapering. Advancement of machining technique will broaden the field of application.

Press forging shows great possibilities for cost savings where high quantity production is expected. While the basic section obtainable by forging is not as efficient as that which can be extruded, forgings in general will still be structurally equivalent for many applications, because of the additional detail which may be incorporated in the forged part, such as taper of any kind, irregular spacing and angularities, local variations and reinforcements, and edge doublers.

A minimum of machining and forming, perhaps none at all, will be required to finish the press forged parts. At present it appears that the application of press forging will be limited to small or moderately sized parts, and that, because of minimum thickness limitations, the lightly loaded applications will probably show weight penalties.

Rolled-ribbed sheet of very light gage offers special advantages in application to lightly loaded structure, where rigidity, shape, and surface smoothness are desirable but loads are so low that skin thickness is taken at the practical minimum for handling or fabrication purposes. In such cases, the much more rigid rolled-ribbed sheet may be had for the same weight, permitting a reduction and simplification of internal structure and consequent saving in cost. At the same time surface smoothness and rigidity would in general be improved.

Other Means Give More Strength

Where design is determined by strength requirements rather than rigidity, however, rolled ribbed sections are much inferior structurally to those obtainable by extrusion or other methods.

Each of the various manufacturing methods has both limitations and advantages making it particularly well suited for some applications yet unsatisfactory for others. When properly applied, each method—machining, extrusion, forging and rolling—affords considerable benefit in its own field of application.

New Process Enables Hidden Arc Welding on Vertical Surfaces

Automatic hidden arc welding is no longer limited to jobs where the joint is in a position for downhand welding. A new process developed by the Lincoln Electric Co., Cleveland, makes possible hidden arc welding of horizontal joints on surfaces positioned anywhere from flat to vertical. The new process consists of new welding methods, procedures and equipment which overcome previous difficulties of directing the electrode and retaining flux and molten metal in a joint not lying flat.

Referred to as 3 o'clock welding, the process offers advantages such as the saving in handling and setup time required when each weld must be positioned for downhand welding, and permitting welds from both sides of a joint simultaneously. In addition, smaller sizes of electrode wire are used, tendency for burn through is reduced, and back-up strips can be eliminated where two arcs on opposite sides of the work are used.

The accompanying drawing shows a horizontal seam in vertical plate being welded from both sides simultaneously. The joint is stationary as two electrodes are moved along opposite sides of the work. Flux is carried on a moving belt so that it is stationary in relation to the work.

METAL
FINISHING *forges ahead*

By ADOLPH BREGMAN
*Consulting Engineer,
New York*

The metal finishing industry has made more progress in the past 5 years than in any like period in its history. Many new processes have been produced, and marked improvements in old techniques are evident. Shortages of some materials are getting more critical, and emphasis is on developing substitutes.

Metal finishing as an industry has experienced an unparalleled growth and advancement during the postwar years. Without attempting to evaluate this progress by a mathematical formula, it is no exaggeration to state that its rate of progression is nearer to geometric than arithmetic. In brief—it is a healthy, progressive and productive industry.

Metal finishing broadly may be divided into the following categories: Mechanical (polishing, buffing, tumbling); chemical (cleaning, dips, contact or immersion plates, etches, etc.); electrolytic (electroplates and anodizing of aluminum and magnesium); and non-metallic (lacquers, enamels, synthetics applied by spray, dip, brush, roller-coating, etc.).

Belt polishing is an old operation which has lately come back into popularity. The equipment consists essentially of idler pulleys and back stands which eliminate the specialized work of heading up abrasive wheels. The abrasive belt presents a large surface to the work and attains much longer life than the abrasive wheel without its successive headings. An important factor in belt polishing is the use of contoured contact wheels on which the belt follows the contours of irregular or complicated shapes.

By the development of more flexible equipment, proper contact wheels with the correct face width and diameter, density, speeds, etc., possible uses for abrasive belt finishing have been greatly extended. Equipment is now available for a wide range of work in various shapes and sizes, providing suitable belt tension controls. The belts may be made of canvas, leather, rubber, cloth, and similar materials. The contact wheels may be serrated or con-

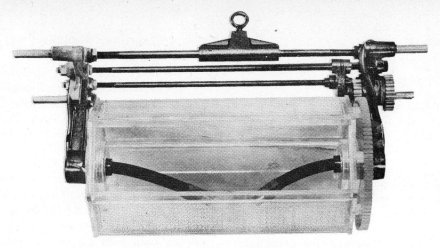

MERCIL TYPE PLEXIGLAS cylinder with hanger equipment and flexible dangler contacts.

toured, resilient or hard, as required for the job.[1]

Liquid abrasives are a comparatively young development. The old type of bar polishing compounds have always produced excessive waste through stubs, melting and throwing off of the polishing compound and the formation of heavy beads. During recent years, polishing compounds have been applied to the cotton in a liquid medium, aqueous or nonaqueous (the former being preferable), by spray through a gun which may be operated with a foot valve. This permits the polisher to devote his hands exclusively to work. Liquid abrasives also provide more uniform application to the wheel, giving longer wheel life as well as saving a substantial portion of the operator's time and material used.[2]

Tumbling for low-cost finishing is one of the most promising of the processes now in use. The art is old, but general realization is growing that there are many applications for tumbling which have not yet been explored. Costs are low and finishes are obtainable comparable to cutting down and greaseless polishing on the wheel. By ball burnishing, lustres are achieved which come very close to the mirror finish on the buffing wheel.[3]

Removes Stubborn Soils

One of the most interesting newcomers to cleaning is the di-phase cleaner. It consists of an aqueous alkaline solution and a hydro-carbon solvent which, in the bath, separate into two phases or layers. This type of cleaner is particularly advantageous in the removal of buffing compounds and similar stubborn soils. In many instances, it has eliminated the necessity for solvent degreasing. In the bath, each phase removes the soil which it preferentially wets or dissolves. This action may be augmented by surface active agents. Because of the diverse soils removable, freedom from hazards and the variable schedules possible, di-phase cleaning practice is very flexible.

Another newcomer is the liquid abrasive blast, in which the abrasive is propelled by water instead of air. The use of a wide range of abrasives is possible and a fine finish is produced, finer than with sand or steel and with no distortion of the work or embedding of abrasive. If dry steel shot is used and embedding occurs, rust will follow. The use of water as a propelling medium eliminates the embedding and such attendant evils as silicosis hazard.

Another important advance in metal cleaning is the sodium hydride pickle for removing scale from stainless steel. This process has found

ADDING ZINC to the zinc pot. Structure at the left is the exit end of the cooling furnace. Photo courtesy of Armco Steel Corp.

wide application, especially in plants large enough to warrant the installation of a substantial set up of fused caustic soda and hydrogen.[4]

Chemical polishing has only lately come to the fore, using phosphoric, nitric and acetic acids in various combinations. Applied to copper and copper alloys, the results have so far not been substantially better than the nitric-sulphuric dip. However for aluminum and its alloys, the results seem to be far superior.

Simplifies Plating On Aluminum

Electrolytic polishing of silver and stainless steel has made long strides.[5] Electropolishing is more easily applicable to flatware than to hollow ware. Although the process has not proved to be a full replacement for the wheel in all cases, it has reduced buffing to such an extent as to make it a notable cost-saver. The combination of electropolishing and chemical polishing has provided a finish on aluminum which is said to be the equal of anodizing in reflectivity.

The zincate bath has greatly forwarded the electroplating of aluminum. In this process, a sodium zincate solution is used to deposit a film of zinc on the cleaned aluminum surface, by contact. The work with the zinc deposit may then be removed, rinsed and plated with copper, nickel and other materials, as desired. Similar methods have been worked out for plating on magnesium, using zinc pyrophosphate instead of sodium zincate. The solution operates satisfactorily but there are reports of porous deposits which later flake off. The electrodeposits on magnesium have not yet been found wholly satisfactory for outdoor exposure.

PRP Is Outstanding Advance

In electroplating equipment, there is a trend away from rectifiers and back to generators because of the greater reliability of the latter, especially under overload and other critical conditions. The rectifier has suffered in many instances from the impure air in plating plants which, since the rectifiers were air-cooled, found its way into the stacks and corroded them into a breakdown. A new type of rectifier with oil-cooled stacks may remedy this condition.

Another innovation in low-voltage current-supplying equipment is the homopolar or ascyclic generator,[6] which is said to produce current more economically by (a) reduction of mounting area; (b) increased generator efficiency; (c) lower installation and operating cost; (d) greater flexibility; (e) greater dependability.

Periodic reverse plating is without doubt one of the outstanding accomplishments of recent years. It consists of plating with direct current for a few seconds, then reversing for a much shorter period; and repeating these periodic reversals to obtain smoother, more dense and brighter deposits. PRP has also made it possible to plate large irregular rack loads without burning the outside pieces or skimping the pieces on the inside of the rack.[7]

Another new development is the tin-zinc plating bath with deposits varying from 50 to 80 pct Sn. The corrosion resistance of this deposit is similar to zinc, and cadmium and can be readily soldered and welded.[8]

Speculum plating has received more attention in England, than in the United States, producing a deposit of approximately 55 pct Cu and 45 pct Sn. The control of this bath poses a problem, using copper and tin anodes in alkaline solutions and controlling the rates of deposit from these anodes, in some instances by separate current sources to each type of anode. Recently, attempts have been made to operate this solution with insoluble anodes, replenishing the solution with copper and tin salts.

Leveling Solutions Gain Interest

In the graphic arts, a large user of electroplating, important advances have been made in nickel plating of stereotypes in the nickel chloride-acetate bath; the use of the cobalt-nickel solution in plating electrotypes; tin plating of electrotype shells; the use of the copper fluoborate bath for plating electrotypes and rotogravure-cylinders; iron deposits on electrotypes and in the manufacture of engraving plates; and zinc plating of deep-etch offset lithographic plates.[9]

A recent move in chromium plating has been the use of the fluosilicate solution. This bath is said to possess the ability to plate bright even with current interruption, a wider bright range and better throwing power. Barrel plating of chromium should be a much easier operation with this type of solution since the make-and-break of the current through the work in the barrel will not adversely affect the deposit.[10]

Leveling solutions have attracted a great deal of interest. Such solutions deposit a plate heavier in the recesses and lighter on the high spots of irregular surfaces; it eliminates much of the grinding and polishing before plating. In this type of solution, the important factors are the organic addition agents and metallic constituents of the baths. However, a "level" deposit is not necessarily a bright deposit. A deposit may be irregular in surface contour and still be bright. Still, wheel finishing a

SPEEDYELECTRIC STEAM-JET cleaner in use at Norton Co., Worcester, Mass., cleaning machines preparatory to repainting.

level deposit is an easier operation than on an irregular deposit.[11]

The acid copper bath is enjoying a revival because of the greater ease of buffing and polishing the deposit, and the higher speeds obtainable with improved solutions. Nickel plating with fluoborate solutions is receiving close attention.[12]

Metal coating by high vacuum evaporation has taken a firm foothold in the application of metals to glass, plastics, paper, fabrics and thin metal sheet. Beginning as a laboratory technique, it is now also in expanding commercial use for optical mirrors, glass light bulbs, quartz crystals, mica sheets for condensers, molded plastic toys, Christmas tree decorations, automobile horn buttons, plaques, costume jewelry, sequins, ribbons, wrappings, and other products.[13]

In anodizing aluminum, preference is shown for the sulphuric acid solution in general commercial work because of the ease of coloring or dyeing the oxide coat to any desired color, including pastels. Recently, however, a multi-color printing process has been developed in which the dyes are applied by roller coating, silk screen and other methods, and then sealed. This process is said to be equally applicable to the chromic or sulfuric acid anodized surface of aluminum.[14]

A new scratch and wear resistant hard coating for aluminum which makes it usable in many applications formerly restricted to steel alloys has been developed by Glenn L. Martin Co. "MHC" finish, as it is called, gives aluminum a scratch and wear resistant coating which is file hard, smooth and heat resistant. Wear resistance is superior to that of hard chrome plating or cyanide case-hardened steel. Cost may be less than chrome plating or heat treating steel.

Magnesium has been anodized by the use of sodium hydrate-phenol solutions. The process has been marketed under the trade name

GRAVURE ROLLS are among the articles that can be plated with a minimum of rejects through use of SRHS solution. Such self-regulating baths are always in good plating balance. Photo courtesy of United Chromium, Inc.

"Manodizing" by Hanson-Van Winkle-Munning Co., Matawan, N. J.

Electroforming has broadened into a primary process of manufacture, and now widely used for molds for casting plastics, rubber, etc. It is also used in a variety of applications for final manufactured products such as pen and pencil tips and similar objects. One of the most striking uses of electroforming has been in the manufacture of band instruments.[15]

The present shortages of plating materials has forced a turn to the use of iron instead of copper or nickel. Electroforming and the graphic arts have found electrodeposited iron suitable in a number of instances, using the sulfate-chloride and the all-chloride solutions. Iron can be employed to build up worn parts and to salvage worn or mismachined pieces. Some of the products of electroformed iron include printing plates, computing cams, radar, plumbing, letter embossing dies and record stampers.

One matter which has claimed increasing attention among electroplaters is the disposal of waste to prevent the pollution of streams. Methods of waste disposal in use are: (a) electrolytic decomposition of cyanide; (b) chlorination to form the cyanate and then nitrogen; and (c) ion exchange, which was originally applied in electroplating installations to purify the water supply and is now in use for the recovery of metals and chromic acid.[16]

In the field of nonmetallic finishing, a recent innovation consists of hot lacquers (about 150°F) which permit substantial increases in the solids content of the material used, often making possible the application of the finish with one coat instead of two, without sagging; also, very important, eliminating blushing.

Shortages Are More Acute

Organic coatings are now being applied under even higher temperatures by flame spraying.[17] The technique is analogous to the metallizing process of atomizing and applying molten metals and alloys. Polythene or polymerized ethylene can be used as a coating without preliminary dispersion in solvents and without a later baking. This method is suggested for coating metal products and for building up strip coatings on lubricated patterns or mold cavities to produce plastic products in small quantities at low cost. Styrene is used in copolymers with butadiene, drying oils, and alkyd resins to obtain faster drying, harder films and better water and chemical resistance.

A major advance in coatings has been made by silicone resins, which are exceptionally resistant to chemical fumes, dilute and concentrated acids, alkalies, salts and oils. Silicone-based finishes have great heat stability, weather resistance and durability.

The electrostatic spray has made an important contribution to the metal finishing industry, making it possible to coat objects of complex shape on all sides with a minimum of labor and lost or wasted material. This process is also useful for detearing of the work.

Rack coatings have been improved by the use of plastisol, applying heavy coats with one dip over a prime coating. One procedure which has spread rapidly is the use of chromate coatings as protectors of zinc and also cadmium. These chromates range in appearance from clear to a variety of colors and have been found excellent preventives of corrosion under adverse atmospheric conditions. Clear chromate is also applicable to other metals such as copper and brass for tarnish prevention.

The most pressing problem of the metal finishing industry at this time is the shortage of materials, such as cadmium, nickel, copper and zinc. Chemicals in a wide variety are available only in limited quantities. Unfortunately, as fast as a substitute is found, it is either another of the scarce materials, or it rapidly becomes scarce.

References

[1]E. E. Oathout, "Abrasive Belt Polishing," AES Proceedings, 1950.

[2]E. T. Candee and S. L. Doughty, Jr., "Water Base Buffing Liquid," AES Proceedings, 1950.

[3]A. Bregman, "Tumbling for Low Cost Finishing," Metal Progress, May 1950.

[4]A. Bregman, "Metal Cleaning Progress and Tests for Cleaners," Metal Progress, March 1950, p. 394.

[5]C. L. Faust and E. E. Graves, "Industrial Electropolishing," AES Proceedings, 1948.

[6]G. J. Berry, "The Acyclic Generator for Electrolytic Processing," 98th meeting of the Electrochemical Society, Oct. 12, 1950, Buffalo.

[7]A. Bregman, "Periodic Reverse-Current Electroplating," Metal Progress, Aug. 1950, p. 199.

[8]E. E. Halls, "Electroplated Tin-Zinc Alloy Coatings on Iron and Steel," Metallurgia, Dec. 1949; Metal Finishing, Apr. 1950.

[9]E. I. Peters, "Advances in Electrodeposition in the Graphic Arts," AES Proceedings, 1950. K. L. Koersler and R. R. Sloan, "High-Speed Nickel Plating of Curved Stereotypes," AES Proceedings, 1950.

[10]J. E. Starek, H. Mallstedt and F. Parsal, "A Self-Regulating High Speed Chromium Plating Bath," AES Proceedings, 1950. W. Czygan, "Self Regulating Solution Speeds Chromium Plating," THE IRON AGE, Feb. 16, 1950.

[11]C. L. Faust, "Leveling and Smoothing by Electropolishing and Chemical Polishing;" G. W. Jernstedt, "Leveling With P. R. Current Plating;" L Weisberg, "Leveling in Cobalt-Nickel Solutions;" A. H. DuRose, W. P. Karash and K. S. Willson, "Surface Contour and Leveling," all in AES Proceedings, 1950.

[12]R. J. O'Connor, "Production Barrel Plating," Plating, 1950.

[13]P. Godley, "Metals Coated by High Vacuum Evaporation," THE IRON AGE, Apr. 1, 1948, p. 90.

[14]Process developed by Sinclair & Valentine, 611 W. 129th St., New York.

[15]F. K. Savage, et al, "Electroforming Techniques," AES Proceedings, 1944, p. 173.

[16]Information on this AES Research Project and a full list of other projects can be obtained from American Electroplaters' Society, P.O. Box 168, Jenkintown, Pa.

[17]T. A. Dickenson, "Flame-Spraying Plastic Coating," Organic Finishing, October, 1950.

COLLOIDAL GRAPHITE

By W. E. LANG
Service Engineer,
Acheson Colloids Corp.,
Port Huron, Mich.

Lubricates Diecasting Machines

Colloidal graphite lubricates various working parts of the diecasting machine, in addition to acting as the die lubricant. It offers stability at high temperatures, prevents adhesion, and resists the scrubbing effect of the hot metal.

DIECASTING of zinc and aluminum alloys, because of the high temperatures involved, poses problems in lubricating the machines and die cavities. These difficulties cannot usually be solved with conventional petroleum lubricants, which either decompose rapidly at temperatures above 300°F or do not possess the required "lubricity." Colloidal graphite, because of its stability at high temperatures, excellent lubricating qualities, ability to prevent adhesion and lack of tendencies to build-up, finds many applications in the lubrication of both the dies themselves and the working parts of the machines,

Lubrication Increases Die Life

Lubrication of the faces of the die cavity is required to insure proper metal flow. It also increases the life of the dies by providing a lubricating film on the die face. This film resists the scrubbing effect of the hot metal and inhibits its tendency to combine with the iron in the die surfaces.

Colloidal graphite is especially well suited for this purpose since it will not volatilize when in contact with the hot metal and cause pock marks due to gas formation. It will perform these functions when present in extremely thin films which will not affect dimensions or cause undue discoloration of the parts being cast. As it is not volatilized or otherwise destroyed in the casting process, it need not be applied as often as other lubricants. This fact alone often results in an increase of as much as 25 pct in production.

Either water or oily materials can be used as carriers to apply the colloidal graphite. The choice depends on the metal being cast, subsequent finishing operations, the configuration of the cavity and the design of the die. Water is a very desirable carrier because it completely dries before the die is closed. This eliminates gummy deposits on the dies and adjacent parts of the machine and does not constitute a source of fumes, nor is it a fire hazard.

However, the use of water requires greater care in application because it will deposit the colloidal graphite only where it is applied. It will not spread to adjacent parts of the die face or creep into ejection pin bearings. As a result, it will not lubricate these parts where no other provisions exist. These objections are often easily remedied.

Proper spray equipment and care in application will assure complete coverage of the die face in most cases. Ejection pin lubrication, where these pins protrude a sufficient distance, will be taken care of by the die lubricant itself which plates the surface of the pins, just as it does the die face. A graphoid surface of microscopic thickness is formed which provides good lubrication and protection against the tendency of metal to adhere to the surface.

Where ejection pins do not protrude sufficiently to receive a coating in the normal cavity spraying process, a solution was worked out which has given very good results over a period of years. This consists of merely providing oil passages which lead from oil holes at the top of the ejector pin mounting plate to points about midway from each end of the pins. The lubricant, being applied at the center of the pin travel, works out at the ends rather than accumulating sticky deposits at the center.

Oil Residue Flushed Out

The gummy carbonaceous material resulting from the oil breaking down is repeatedly flushed out at the ends; there is no accumulation of residue to bind the pins or cause scuffing and rapid wear. A few drops of a lubricant consisting of about 6 oz of colloidal graphite in oil (Oildag) to 1 gal of SAE No 30 oil should be applied twice per shift. This permits the dies to be operated with no ejection pin service for as long as 1000 working hr or 100,000 shots.

If it is not possible to provide positive means of lubrication in this way, coating the pins when they are installed with a concentrated dispersion of semi-colloidal graphite in oil (Dag Dispersion No. 170) will often provide satisfactory lubrication for a considerable length of time. After the oil evaporates or works out, enough graphite will remain to provide adequate lubrication.

To insure proper adhesion of the colloidal graphite to the die face when using it in the

SPRAYING a Dag colloidal graphite dispersion in the cavity of a permanent mold. Courtesy of Cox-Ware Corp., Kirkwood, Mo.

water dispersed form, all oily materials must be removed with a suitable solvent. The die temperature should also be raised to at least 250°F before being sprayed.

Special spray guns have been devised that overcome the inadequacies of conventional paint spray guns or blow guns having a tube attached. These special guns will spray either at right angles or 180° angles at the same time. This permits spraying two surfaces simultaneously.

Very thin films of graphite are adequate for coating die faces. A mixture of one part of colloidal graphite in water (Aquadag) to 100 parts of water is normal. Greater dilutions are entirely feasible if the dies are shallow and have sufficient draft. At a dilution of 1:100 the lubricant cost is approx 30¢ per gal. As the film of graphite is not destroyed each time a shot is made, the frequency of spraying is often reduced considerably. In many cases one application in 10 or more cycles is adequate. This appreciably increases production rates.

One of the greatest advantages of using colloidal graphite in water exists in the casting of aluminum and its alloys, because of higher prevailing temperatures. Superior results have

also been observed in many cases with zinc. The small amount of graphite left on the surface of the castings is seldom objectionable as it apparently has no effect on subsequent plating or painting operations.

In case of barrel polishing, a mottled effect is often observed. This is apparently caused by the lubricating effect of the thin films of graphite protecting the underlying surface against the polishing action of the tumbling process. This may be objectionable when the castings are not subjected to further surface treatment.

Graphite Used With Oil and Water

To overcome this objection as well as those involving coating problems due to the difficulty in reaching all parts of a deep cavity with a water dispersion, colloidal graphite in oil (Oildag) has often been used in small amounts in conventional oily die lubricants. About 2 pct of Oildag in the normally-used lubricant, or even kerosene, frequently yields improved results with greater intervals between spraying.

Colloidal graphite in both water and oil carriers is used succesfully in diecasting the conductors and cooling-fan blades of electric motor rotors. The type of carrier chosen depends on the particular demands of the individual process. In general, the inside of the cap which forms the fan blading and consists of one end of the fixture in which the laminations are clamped, the side walls of the die or mold in which it is placed and any other faces subjected to contact with the molten aluminum are coated with a water dispersion.

The bottom face of the mold and the ejector pin which passes through it are swabbed with a mixture of 3 pct Oildag in an SAE No. 30 oil. As graphite is inert in the presence of Freon, there is no objection to its use in making rotors for hermetically sealed units, which account for a major percentage of the production of these rotors.

Colloidal Graphite Stays Put

On the diecasting machine itself there are several points where the ability of colloidal graphite to stay put has been found to result in better lubrication. The tip of the ram has been very successfully lubricated by brushing on a heavy concentration of semi-colloidal graphite in oil (Dag Dispersion No. 170) applied without dilution. This product, consisting of 50 pct graphite in oil, contains no soaps to form objectionable residues as is the case with greases.

Any other sliding or rotating parts of the machine that are exposed to elevated temperatures will be provided with better lubrication if about 2 pct of Oildag is mixed with the lubricant currently being used.

news of industry

NPA Set on CMP—Ready or Not, Here it Comes

A practical controlled materials plan means a lot of spade-work . . . You can't rub it like Aladdin's lamp and wish . . . Last CMP was child of painful mutation—*By Bill Packard.*

New York—You are going to get a controlled materials plan by July 1, but it won't work like Aladdin's lamp. Just putting the CMP label on a plan will neither guarantee your priorities nor guide your production.

To be effective CMP will have to be preceded by long and careful planning, detailed screening of material requests from all types of consumers, and a selective buildup of administrative people. Above all, it cannot possibly be more efficient than the people administering it.

CMP wasn't perfect during the last war, though it did work better than any other system tried. It grew out of a long, painful period of trial and error. When it was finally installed, most of the people needed for planning, screening requirements and administration had already been on the job for many months. It was a child of painful mutation, not divine creation.

CMP—Ready or Not

Its chief advantage was that it brought the maze of conflicting and confusing priorities into a single program under a single authority. It made it impossible to issue more tickets than there were seats for any given production because it matched the tickets against the seats; requirements against production. It slashed red tape.

The National Production Authority seems determined to in-

stall its new CMP on steel, aluminum and copper July 1, ready or not. Unless a lot of detail work is done between now and then, they will not be ready. A CMP in name only, or prematurely installed, could do more harm than good.

Job's Harder This Time

Under CMP the entire economy must be organized. This includes both producers and consumers. That is the only way to work out who can give what to whom and when. Right now the iron and steel section of NPA is believed to be the only one that is thoroughly organized. Aluminum and copper are still limping along with skeleton staffs.

In some ways making CMP work this time will be harder than it was before. During the last war all steel produced went to only two classes of users—direct war and essential civilian. During 1943, a typical war year, 38 pct of total steel output went to direct war uses and 62 pct went to other essential uses.

But during the present emergency no one has suggested that defense and essential civilian uses will take all of our expanded steel output. In fact there is general agreement that there will be large quantities of steel left over to be divided among regular consumers. Not all they want, not by a long sight. But still a lot.

One of NPA's toughest prob-

Turn Page

Turn Page

Founders' Price Formula

Washington — Formula-type price ceilings for the gray iron foundry and malleable iron castings industries are being drafted by the Office of Price Stabilization.

Representatives of the two industries pointed out in OPS meetings last week that the existing price freeze does not provide for the formula-type pricing used in their industries. They asked for a separate and flexible type of price regulation.

OPS said it hopes to come up with a regulation that would preclude the necessity for relief appeals except in extraordinary cases.

Reactivate All Magnesium Plants

Washington—With reactivation of the government's sixth and final reserve magnesium plant at Spokane, Wash., all six of the Munition Board's plants will be back into production by the middle of this year. Entire output of the Spokane plant will go to the stockpile or for allocation among key industries. The Spokane plant will be operated by the Pacific Northwest Alloys, Inc.

Quickie Strikes Are Settled

Birmingham — Two short-lived strikes in Alabama have been settled and the men will return to work immediately. One was at the Gadsden plant of Allis-Chalmers Co. and the other at the North Birmingham plant of the U. S. Pipe and Foundry Co.

INDUSTRIAL BRIEFS

PLANT CONVERSION — REPUBLIC PLATING & PROCESSING CO., Chicago, will soon complete conversion of its plant facilities to process aluminum through sulphuric and chromic acid anodizing. The anodizing process will be available exclusively to firms engaged in defense production.

EXPANDS DIVISION—The engineering, personnel and departmental facilities of the valve division of the MINNEAPOLIS-HONEYWELL REGULATOR CO., at Philadelphia has expanded by 400 pct. The expansion program includes research, developing applications for new and existing products and for speeding production and deliveries.

ASSN. PRESIDENT — Harold W. Delzell, will serve as president of the TIRE & RIM ASSN., INC., for the next 2 years. The organization founded by tire and rim manufacturers in 1903 is the technical standardizing body of the tire and rim industries. Mr. Delzell is section manager, field engineering department of The B. F. Goodrich Co.

APPOINTS DISTRIBUTOR — The Ready Tool Co., Bridgeport, Conn., appointed the DAVID E. GROSSMAN CO., New York, as their metropolitan New York and worldwide export distributor for RED-E machine tools.

NEW LINE—TINIUS OLSEN TESTING MACHINE CO., Willow Grove, Pa., is manufacturing a new line of low cost hydraulic testing machines for simplified, accurate tension, compression, transverse and flexure testing.

NEW SITE FOR SALES — A new district sales office in Denver for servicing of chemical processing industries in Colorado, Utah, New Mexico, and Wyoming, has been opened by the PATTERSON FOUNDRY & MACHINE CO.

SUBSIDIARY FORMED— Sealol Corp., of Providence, manufacturers of "Sealol" mechanical seals for rotating shafts, has formed a subsidiary company, SEALOL MFG. CO., to be located in Keene, N. H. Research engineering and sales will continue to be handled by the organization at Providence.

ASST. DIRECTOR—Creation of a new assistant directorship at BATTELLE INSTITUTE, Columbus, Ohio, with Dr. Bruce W. Gonser named to the post, is the result of the company's enlarged program in up-to-now unexplored aspects of metallurgy and chemistry of metals.

LEASES PLANT—The government-owned Valley Stream plant has been leased by the FAIRCHILD ENGINE DIV. of Fairchild Engine & Airplane Corp. It will be used for the manufacture of jet engine components and for the production of parts and assemblies for an auxiliary power plant used in aircraft.

WINS DESIGN AWARD— Ralph A. Ostbert, president, Edward Ermold Co., New York, received a special certificate of award from DESIGN NEWS for excellence in general mechanical design of the Ermold Automatic Unpacker. Function of the machine is to automatically unpack containers from cases and cartons and deposit the containers on a conveyor line.

NEW IDEA—A plan to bring appliance distributors directly into the defense production effort, was advanced by THOR CORP., Chicago. The firm submitted to the government a proposal to convert into packaging centers for the armed forces more than 3,500,000 sq ft of warehouse facilities operated by its 77 distributors.

NEW PLANT—Ground will be broken soon for the new Mississippi plant of ROCKWELL MFG. CO. This makes a total of 15 plants across the country for this organization.

lems will be deciding who gets how much of the material that is left over after defense and essential civilian needs are allotted. One way to do it would be to allot consumers their proportionate percentage of the remaining "free" material, based on consumption during a previous period.

Apparently they do not plan to do that. Advance information that they plan to cut back steel use by auto makers, perhaps as much as 40 pct, has the makings of a real Donnybrook. Why single out autos? What about stoves and refrigerators? Or baby carriages, bobby pins or curling irons? That's what Detroit (including the United Auto Workers) is asking.

NPA Caught in Middle

There is plenty to be said on the other side. Many small manufacturers have been complaining that material restrictions are forcing them to their knees while auto production stays high.

NPA is caught in the middle. If they follow their projected course on steel cutbacks for autos (provided it is legal), they will gain about 6 million tons of finished steel per year to divide among other users. But they will have also set a precedent for bickering and high pressure from all consumers or groups who think they should get a bigger share. Not to mention the wrath of UAW.

Running CMP will be hard enough without that. Providing material for defense and essential civilian uses will be a tough job. But if NPA doesn't come up with an acceptable plan for dividing the remainder among regular customers, they might as well throw in the towel.

Urges Students Find New Alloys

State College, Pa.—Engineering students at Pennsylvania State College have been urged by John J. B. Rutherford, metallurgist of Babcock & Wilcox Tube Co., to seek new alloying elements to replace columbium, aluminum, nickel and molybdenum, now in short supply. Citing the threat of continuing armament for years to come, Mr. Rutherford urged the students to pioneer in finding substitute alloys.

January Steel Output Sets Monthly Record at 8,830,000 Tons

New York—January steel production was a record 8,830,000 tons, at an annual output rate of 104 million tons of ingots and steel for castings, reports the American Iron & Steel Institute. The yearly rate would top actual 1950 production by 7 million tons.

The October 1950 record was surpassed by 90,000 tons and January 1950 output by 900,000 tons. Revised December output brought total 1950 production to 96,696,769 tons, a 24 pct increase over 1949.

Study Corrosion as It Happens

Chicago — Armour Research Foundation scientists can now measure corrosion of any metal as it takes place with a new method similar to television scanning. A metal cylinder is dipped into a corrosive solution such as sea water, rotated several hundred times a minute, and scanned with a stationary probe electrode which is a plastic arm containing 11 silver wires.

Placed about .02 in. from the cylinder, the electrode detects minute electrical currents caused by corrosion. Researchers are thus able to measure and study the process as it happens. Armour has undertaken the project under the sponsorship of the National Advisory Committee for Aeronautics.

Bethlehem Plans Blast Furnace

Buffalo — Bethlehem Steel Co. will build a new blast furnace, reportedly one of the world's largest, at its Lackawanna plant. The new furnace will raise output by 500,000 tons per year, Bethlehem Steel announced.

Mining manganese the easy way: Pick it up and chuck it into a wheelbarrow.

MANGANESE—Tough Nut to Expanding Steel

DMA puts manganese ore under allocation . . . Russian exports fade to a trickle . . . India has tripled shipments . . . Vast ore find in Brazil may prove the answer—*By Bob Hatschek.*

New York—With steel capacity growing at a phenomenal rate, many raw material supply difficulties must be surmounted. One of the toughest is manganese, vital to steelmaking. Steelmen are frankly worried about it because they must import about 90 pct of their manganese needs.

Manganese Allocated

To further illustrate our manganese-short* position, Defense Minerals Administration has placed strategic manganese ore under an allocation program. After Mar. 31 all ore of 35 pct or more manganese content may be delivered only in accordance with authority issued for the month by DMA. Applications for allocation authority must be filed by the fifteenth of the month preceding the month in which delivery is required.

Ore for government stockpiling or for resale is not covered but all other purchasers must use the ore as specified by DMA. They must also report inventories on hand.

The five main sources of our manganese have been Brazil, Gold Coast, India, Union of South Africa, and Russia. These countries have combined to supply the U. S. with 90 pct of imported manganese ore, or 80 pct of what industry uses.

In 1948 Russia shipped 34 pct of U. S. imports. By 1950 this dropped to a trickle, only 3.6 pct of total manganese imports.

To make up for this fading

Imports on Manganese Ore

	1948 Tonnage	1948 Pct of Total	1949 Tonnage	1949 Pct of Total	1950* Tonnage	1950* Pct of Total
Brazil	143,917	11.4	151,560	10.2	129,721	7.1
Gold Coast	132,681	10.5	371,314	23.9	328,099	17.9
India	213,445	17.0	429,203	27.6	633,170	34.5
Union of So. Africa	216,575	17.1	354,265	22.8	475,316	25.6
U.S.S.R.	427,229	34.0	201,409	13.0	65,563	3.6
TOTAL	1,256,597		1,544,526		1,837,950	

*Preliminary.
Total includes imports from all countries.
Source: Bureau of Mines.

source, U. S. steelmakers turned elsewhere. India has almost tripled her manganese exports to this country since 1948. Gold Coast and Union of South Africa shipments have more than doubled in the same period, while receipts from Brazil have remained about the same.

Fields in Amapa, Brazil

What seems the most optimistic note in the whole manganese supply picture is the vast ore reserve that is now being developed in the Territory of Amapa, Brazil (THE IRON AGE, Aug. 17, 1950, p. 101). Some geologists have estimated that there may be as much as 50 million tons of high-grade ore along the Amapari River. It is reported some of the ore assays as high as 68 pct manganese.

Ore can be picked up on the surface and thrown up onto trucks. A road from Macapa, at the mouth of the Amapari, up the river to the ore deposits is already under construction and a 140-mile railroad is to be built along the same route. Dredging operations are also under way in the harbor. A series of falls prevents practical river transport.

A firm, jointly owned by Bethlehem Steel Co. (49 pct.) and Industria e Comercio de Minerios, S. A. (51 pct), is doing the development work and is expected to be financed by a $35 million loan from the International Bank for Reconstruction and Development. Thus far the loan has not been officially applied for and has only been informally discussed by the World Bank.

Ore Export Deadline

Under the terms of the 50-year concession granted by the Territorial Government, export of ore must begin by Dec. 31, 1953, but, with world conditions as they are and with Bethlehem's currently accelerated expansion program, it is likely that this deadline will be more than complied with. In fact, if transportation needs are met, a possible 300,000 tons of ore can be exported by January 1953.

Need Rebuilding for Reserve Machine Tools

Used, rebuilt machinery field may get price controls and priorities . . . Washington asks cooperation . . . Dealers suggest return to OPA system of pricing—*By Ted Metaxas.*

New York—Hard and fast price controls and materials priorities will be granted to the used and rebuilt machinery field. The government will try to further vitalize an industry that has taken an increasing burden of supplying tools for civilian output and defense work while new machine tool makers were rooted by Washington inertia of plans and priorities too late.

Last week dealers and rebuilders went to a command conference in Washington under the auspices of the Machinery Dealers National Assn. Expecting to be told crisis plans for their industry, they got instead an appeal for cooperation and an opportunity to suggest acceptable price controls and priorities.

Paint, Polish Tactics

Washington stressed rebuilding capacity. In effect, rebuilders were asked to pull government chestnuts out of the fire by whipping into shape some machines that had complacently been buried in reserve pools as operable and later proved lemons.

Not many dealers are willing to

"I'd like to report a leak!"

enter rebuilding wholeheartedly. It is not as profitable as paint, polish, and salesmanship. And with the rush for used equipment, many dealers can empty their warehouses while even the paintbrushes get stiff.

Larger Capacity Possible

Recently Charles A. Simmons, head of the Simmons Machine Tool Corp., Albany, N. Y., told THE IRON AGE that the rebuilding industry, lagging not too long ago, has reached near-capacity operations but that it could have almost unlimited capacity if paint and polish tactics were supplanted by the brass tacks of rebuilding.

At Washington, dealers suggested that government financing be used to amplify rebuilding facilities. Some of this spending may be beneficial. But arrangements of coming OPA-style price controls to yield a larger profit for rebuilt machines may furnish the needed profit lure to activate "hidden" rebuilding capacity.

The pledge of priorities indicates the sudden esteem in which Washington holds the rebuilding industry. Rebuilders have been hit not only by labor shortages but by unbending NPA restrictions on such important items as copper. The industry noted that it did not have regimented production line schedules, fluctuated widely, and because of the crisis boom had no realistic base periods for controls.

The used machinery field has been on the spiral staircase of inflation with prices of the used rivalling the new — when they were available. Delivery dates on new machines stretched out of sight and both traditional customers and need-converted buyers competed for limited stocks of late used equipment.

Currently the market is in the loose grip of the general price freeze. It means that Dealer A who sold a 1940 machine for $3000 as his highest base period price is stuck with that figure. Dealer B who sold the same machine for $4000 is frozen more comfortably. Dealer A is getting double punishment, stung the first time and not able to compete favorably now.

So MDNA men recommended a

return to the World War II OPA system. It would once again classify machines in year ranges, establish grades of "as is" and "rebuilt," and allow percentages of new equipment prices.

Dealers must fill the gap before new machine makers can get rolling. They will have to sharpen up their collection campaigns. But many remember that in the past war they were furtively visiting scrap metal yards to retrieve venerable machines. Things shouldn't be that tough this time.

First step in getting subcontract work is to locate prime contractors. These are listed weekly by the Dept. of Commerce in its "Consolidated Synopsis of Award Contracts," available at field headquarters and more than 5000 cooperating outlets. The bigger contracts are listed in THE IRON AGE each week.

Hire a Good Salesman

Trade groups advise the small businessman to hire a good salesman—to sell productive capacity instead of products.

Small producers of hard-goods items are hardest hit. Mobilization has aimed at extending basic industrial capacity.

Surveys show 67 pct of World War II prime contracts went to 100 companies who farmed out about a third of their contracts. Responsibility for maximum volume of subcontracting will probably be left to the prime contractors.

Wider use of competitive bidding on standard items to give small companies a bigger share is being considered by DPA—a reversal of the recent policy of switching most procurement to a negotiated basis for speed.

Consider Legislation

The government, in answer to criticism, may name a special assistant in charge of small business. Legislation to create a Small Business Defense Plants Corp. is being considered by the Banking Committee of the House and Senate.

Steps are being taken to help small manufacturers and prime contractors get together. One is a clinic session sponsored by the Air Force Procurement Office and the Commerce & Industry Assn. this week in New York. Prime contractors from five states will explain their needs.

Another assist is by the Chicago Assn. of Commerce & Industry and the Commerce & Industry Assn. of New York. They try to help members and non-members locate prospects, and they work with prime contractors and pro-

Small Business Must Sell Productive Capacity

Material restrictions cut small businessman's profits . . . Subcontracts will save his business if he gets out and sells his productive capacity to prime contractors.—*By Bill Olson*

New York—Everyone agrees the material-short, order-hedged small businessman is in a tough spot. His howls are sending shivers up Congressional spines and his problems are political dynamite. But when the chips are down, the small businessman will get out and do his own selling job, just as he has before.

Valuable help in this selling job will come from trade associations, the Dept. of Commerce and procurement offices.

End-use restriction dates are coming up fast and material shortages are cutting profit margins. Workers are listening to the siren call of higher wages prime contractors can offer, and if lost now are irreplaceable.

Sell Productive Capacity

The small businessman's salvation is to land a subcontract from a prime contractor by peddling the one product small business has left—productive capacity.

Biggest help from Washington so far is Secretary of Defense Marshall's order to distribute contracts "as widely as possible" and his recommendation that subcontracting by prime contractors be encouraged.

Some big trade organizations

are not directly trying to help small companies get subcontracts. They feel the job of getting subcontracts is the same as staying in business generally, and that they help most by supplying prompt, accurate information on government rulings, and by trying to influence top level government.

Subcontracting is widely used by the automobile and aircraft industries. During emergencies, prime contractors often desperately need the productive capacity of many small, capable plants.

Where to Get Leads

Prime contractors, as listed by the Dept. of Commerce in "Consolidated Synopsis of Contract Award Information."

Products the government wants, as listed by the Dept. of Commerce in "Consolidated Synopsis of U. S. Government Procurement Information."

Procurement Offices and Dept. of Commerce Field Headquarters, as Listed in THE IRON AGE, Jan. 4, 1951, p. 371-374.

Trade associations.

Local Chamber of Commerce.

Local military posts and bases.

Prime Contractor Must Know

A prime contractor wants the following information about a prospective subcontractor:

Description of plant, facilities and location;

Items made and processes used;

Previous subcontracting experience, items produced, and contracting companies;

Estimate of available machine capacity;

Listing of type, size, age, and condition of machines;

Tolerances normally used, and closest tolerance to which you can work;

Materials used in plant;

Number and kind of employees, and qualifications of key personnel;

Current financial condition;

Nature of cost records and time used;

Shipping facilities available.

curement officers to find open machine time.

It works like this: A small firm, in a machine report, describes the capacity it has to offer. The report is cross-indexed by machine type. A prime contractor

seeking open boring mill time calls the association. Firms who have reported boring mill capacity are recommended.

The New York association estimates this service in World War II helped 1500 small businesses get

$82 million in original subcontract orders.

If the prime contractor is interested, he may send a field engineer to inspect the plant, methods, and cost and wage rates.

Lack of working capital does not rule out the possibility of handling subcontracts. A prime contractor may be willing to make partial payments as work progresses. A subcontractor may be able to obtain a loan under Regulation V of the Federal Reserve Board. The loan cannot be used to expand or build plants.

Industry Controls This Week:

NPA Orders:

M-1, Steel supplement 4—Sets aside 9000 tons of steel for ship repair and conversion during April, May and June.

M-4, amended—Permits some additions to commercial buildings without NPA approval.

M-12, Copper amendment — Adds additional end uses and relaxes some former restrictions. Effective Mar. 1 for List A, Apr. 1 for List B. Amendment effective Feb. 19.

M-37, Bans zinc conversion—Toll agreements on zinc scrap conversion must have NPA permission. Dealers' scrap stocks are limited, and galvanizers' dross may be used only for production of zinc dust. Effective Feb. 14.

M-38, Lead inventories—Stocks of lead and materials containing lead are limited to a 60-day supply or practical working minimum, whichever is lower. Effective Feb. 16.

M-39, Antimony — Stocks of antimony and materials containing antimony are limited to a 60-day supply or practical working minimum, whichever is lower. Effective Feb. 16.

DMA Orders:

MO-2, Manganese inventory—Provides temporary allocation program and inventory control for manganese ore of 35 pct or more metal content. Effective Mar. 31.

MO-4, Tungsten inventory—Temporarily controls delivery of all tungsten concentrates containing 40 pct or more tungsten tri-oxide. Effective Feb. 15.

Set Aside Ship Repair Steel

Washington—Supplement 4 to M-1 has been issued by National Production Authority providing for issuance of NPA directives

CONTROLS *digest*

For more details see "You and Government Controls," The Iron Age, Jan. 4, 1951, p. 365. For full text of NPA regulations write U. S. Dept. of Commerce, Division of Printing Service, Room 6225 Commerce Bldg., Washington 25, D. C.

Subject	Order	Effective Date
General		
Inventory Control	NPA Reg. 1	Sept. 18
	Interpretation 1, 2, 3	Nov. 10
Priorities System	NPA Reg. 2	Oct. 3
DO Rating	Amend. 1	Oct. 3
DO Rating	Amend. 2	Dec. 29
DO Ratings	Delegation 1, 2, 3, 4	Nov. 1, 2, 3
Priorities (Canada)	NPA Reg. 3	Nov. 8
Hoarding	NPA Notice 1	Dec. 27
Auto Prices, Wages	ESA Reg. 1	Dec. 18
Ceiling Price Regulation	CPR 1	Jan. 26
Military supplies	Supplement 1	Feb. 1
Wage Increases	CPR 2	Feb. 9
Coal Prices	CPR 3	Feb. 1
Metals		
Aluminum distribution	NPA M 5	Oct. 27
Aluminum cutback	NPA M 7 (amended)	Feb 1
	Direction 1	Nov. 28
	Direction 2	Dec. 16
	Direction 3	Dec. 27
Aluminum scrap	NPA M 22	Mar. 1
Antimony	NPA M-39	Feb. 16
Cadmium	NPA M 19	Jan. 1
Cobalt stocks	NPA M 10 (amended)	Dec. 30
Collapsible tubes	NPA M 27	Jan. 27
Columbium steels	NPA M 3	Oct. 19
Copper distribution	NPA M 11	Nov. 29
Copper use	NPA M 12 (amended)	Dec. 30
	Amend.	Feb. 19
Copper readjustment	M-12 Direction 1	Feb. 1
Copper scrap	NPA M 16 (amended)	Jan. 1
Manganese ore inventory	DMA MO-2	Mar. 31
Lead	NPA M 38	Feb. 16
Molybdenum cutback	NPA M 33 (amended)	Feb. 2
Nickel cutback	NPA M 14 (amended)	Feb. 1
Ores, metals	NPA Del. 5	Dec. 18
Steel	NPA M 1 (amended)	Feb. 15
Freight car program	Supl. 1	Oct. 26
Great Lakes ships	Supl. 2	Nov. 15
Canadian freight cars	Supl. 3	Dec. 15
Ship repair, conversion	Supl. 4	Feb. 16
Steel scrap	NPA M 20 (amended)	Jan. 29
Steel warehouses	NPA M 6 (amended)	Nov. 15
Tin inventories	NPA M 8	Jan. 15
Tinplate, terneplate	NPA M 24	Jan. 27
Metal cans	NPA M 25	Jan. 27
Tinplate closures	NPA M 27	Jan. 27
Tungsten	NPA M 30	Jan. 22
Tungsten concentrates	DMA MO-4	Feb. 15
Zinc distribution	NPA M 9	Nov. 16
Zinc cutback	NPA M 15	Jan. 15
Zinc scrap	NPA M 37	Feb. 14
Miscellaneous		
Chemicals	NPA M 32	Jan. 23
Construction	NPA M 4	Oct. 27
	Amend. 1	Oct. 13
	Amend. 2	Nov. 15
Elec. components	NPA M 17	Oct. 18
Iron, Steel Scrap Prices	OPS	Feb. 7

requiring delivery of 9000 tons of steel products for ship repair and conversion during April, May and June.

This set-aside is based on recommendations of the Maritime Commission which says shipyard inventories of plates, shapes, bars, sheet and pipe have now reached the depletion stage.

The directives will be issued by NPA calling for acceptance of certified orders from specified shipyards which are in need of the materials for repair and conversion work.

Direct Reduction Won't Arrive Overnight

Process has been worked out in pilot stage . . . But engineers believe it won't make blast furnaces obsolete . . . Freezing of ore bed overcome . . . Better blast furnaces seen.

New York—The steel industry is moving closer in its pursuit of a practical method of direct reduction of iron ore. Long the dream of steelmakers, direct reduction is now an accomplished fact in the pilot stage.

But engineers believe the days of the blast furnace are far from numbered—that it will still be a very useful and profitable melting agent even if direct reduction eventually becomes common commercial practice. They believe this will take years.

Direct reduction is merely extraction of oxygen from iron ore, relatively simple under the right conditions. To do this reducing gases must be brought into intimate contact with every grain of the ore.

Stalemate at 70 Pct

In early attempts at direct reduction atomized gas was blown in fine dispersion through the powdered ore bed making contact with all the ore and rendering it fluid. This worked fine until reduction was 70 pct completed. Then the ore bed froze and uniform contact between the gas and ore was no longer possible. Neither was the continued removal of reduced ore from the apparatus. This dead end street has delayed industry's search for a practical method of direct reduction.

In a pilot operation, H. A. Brassert & Co., New York, has overcome this problem by converting the fine ore into baked pellets. These pellets can be made from ore fines or flue dust which cannot be used in the blast furnace without sintering or pelletizing.

Since the pellets are round and porous the reducing gas can percolate through them freely. Reduction of a descending column of these pellets in a vertical shaft is done under atmospheric pressure at 850°-900°C in about 60 min. Under 42-lb pressure, reduction has been completed in as low as 8 min.

The reduced pellets, now metallic, can be used immediately as charge stock in the electric or openhearth furnace. If used as feed stock they must be briquetted

"I hate to disillusion the boss. He goes for this honor system in a big way—"

to make a heavy, solid melting stock which will readily go through the slag. Briquetting of the pellets right after reduction has been technically worked out.

Summarizing the steps the process shapes up like this: (1) Baked pellets are made in the top of the reducing furnace. (2) Pellets are reduced in bottom of furnace by reducing gas such as reformed natural gas. (3) Reduced pellets are discharged and used directly as charge stock or briquetted for feed stock.

While none of these operations are new to industry, their practical combination on a commercial scale is not so simple. There are many problems still to be worked out for different ores and different uses of reduced iron. If gangue content is high, refining is complicated by excessive slag, longer melting time, higher fuel consumption. In such case it is better to remove the gangue from the ore by beneficiation before it is reduced.

Blast Furnace Improvement

There are some ores in which the silica is chemically combined with the iron oxide. Such ores are not suitable for direct reduction since the only known way to separate the gangue from the metal is by melting it in the blast furnace.

Mr. Brassert believes there is still plenty of room for improved efficiency and lower cost through improvement of the blast furnace. For example, part of the coke used in the furnace may be replaced by oil or gas, if properly applied and certain alterations in design and operating practice are made.

Such improvements may result in a 2000-ton furnace which will be smaller and cheaper than the present 1500-ton furnaces. This would mean lower pig iron costs, since natural gas and oil are cheaper fuels than coke is today.

Meanwhile, experimental work is continuing in both directions. The furnace of the future will probably result from mutation, not revolution.

Crucible Introduces Two New Alloys, Light on Critical Items

Pittsburgh—Skimping on use of critical alloying materials and containing no cobalt or columbium, two new stainless and heat-resisting alloys, CSA 39 and Crucible 422, have been introduced by Crucible Steel Co. for applications requiring high strength at hot temperatures.

Possible applications include aircraft jet engine parts and high temperature industrial equipment. CSA 39 is an iron base alloy with about 27 pct nickel, 18 pct chromium, 9 pct molybdenum, and 3 pct tungsten. Fitted for use at temperatures between 1300 and 1600°F, it does not need special hot-cold working practices for high-strength required. It can be hardened by heat treatment.

Also an iron base alloy, Crucible 422 contains 13 pct chromium, 1 pct tungsten, 1 pct molybdenum, less than 1 pct nickel, and less than ½ pct vanadium. Designed for 1000 to 1100°F temperature use, it can be hardened by normal heat treating.

NPA Amends Copper Order M-12

Washington—The National Production Authority has amended copper order M-12 to include additional prohibited end uses (List B) but temporarily relax inventory restrictions to permit more gradual adjustment to the cut-off order.

Effective date for List A remains Mar. 1 but List B is not effective until Apr. 1. Manufacturers may use up copper remaining in inventory on the cut-off dates for A and B items, provided the metal or forms are "wholly unsuitable" for items not on the lists.

This provision also applies to copper scheduled for February (List A) and March (List B) but delivered before Apr. 1 and May 1.

Because there is not enough galvanized water pipe, the order relaxes restrictions on copper tubing for home plumbing. List B adds more than 50 end items to the prohibited copper use list. Major goods banned include refrigerators, air conditioners and outboard motors.

Foote Mineral Co. Describes New, Enlarged Uses of Lithium

Exton, Pa.—Several new and enlarged uses of lithium and other minerals were described here last week at the stockholders' meeting of Foote Mineral Co. H. Conrad Meyer, president, also reported record sales of $5,447,000 for 1950, a 51 pct gain over 1949.

Zirconium, which Foote is making in ductile form, was also shown. Its uses are growing, though Foote now sells a good part of its zirconium for igniting flashlight bulbs.

New uses for lithium include an improved low temperature dry cell, in greases and in ceramics. Based on past performance, company engineers expect lithium to eventually displace as much as 32,000 tons of lead a year in the ceramics industry. One big use now is in glass television tubes, in which Corning Glass uses a lithium compound in place of lead oxide. Lithium also replaces nickel in some TV tube ferrite cores.

Alcoa Votes Debt Limit Rise

Pittsburgh—Aluminum Co. of America has been authorized by its stockholders to increase its indebtedness to as much as $500 million, an increase of $300 million over the previous limit, to permit financing of the company's defense expansion program.

Roy A. Hunt, president, said net income for 1950 will be approximately $45 million, after "ample" provision for renegotiation of contracts.

Chevrolet to Make Jet Engines

Detroit—Additional jet engine facilities will be established as result of a contract between the Air Force and Chevrolet Motor Div. of General Motors. The engines will be built at a government plant at Tonawanda, N. Y., used by Chevrolet during World War II for production of Pratt & Whitney radial type engines. Production is scheduled to begin in 1952.

Defense Contracts to Metalworking Industry

Selected Contracts, Week of Feb. 19, 1951

Items	Quan.	Value	Company
Generator sets	10 ea.	$ 400,000	Westinghouse Electric Corp., Washington, D. C.
Rocket assemblies 4,670,000	4,580,000	General Motors Corp., Lansing, Mich.
Compressors parts ...	7084	63,320	Hardie-Tynes Mfg. Co., Birmingham
Pump parts	14,176	605,068	Dravo Corp., Philadelphia
Turbine parts	5852	319,428	Dravo Corp., Philadelphia
Diesel parts	48,930	413,905	The Buda Co., Harvey, Ill.
Diesel parts	20,000	140,700	General Motors Corp., Detroit
Bullgraders	41	97,170	Bucyrus-Erie Co., Milwaukee
Spare parts	...	100,827	International Spare Parts Corp., Long Island, N. Y.
Shovel equipment ...	...	325,000	Thew Shovel Co., Elyria, Ohia
Automobiles	35	150,000	Ford Motor Truck Co., Dearborn
Road rollers	90	90,000	American Steel Wks., Kansas City
Scrapers	100	600,000	R. G. LeTourneau, Peoria, Ill.
Scrapers	50	300,000	Southwest Welding, Alhambra, Calif.
Trailers	50	425,000	Steel Products, Savannah
Trailers	50	425,000	Rogers Bros. Corp., Albion, Pa.
Trailers	30	900,000	Thew Shovel Co., Lorain, Ohio
Tractors	175	3,600,000	R. G. LeTourneau, Peoria, Ill.
Generators	200	1,000,000	The Buda Co., Harvey, Ill.
Generators	150	700,000	Hill Diesel Eng. Co., Lansing
Generators	325	1,600,000	Ready-Power Co., Detroit
Generators	200	740,000	Consolidated Diesel Electric Corp., Stamford, Conn.
Generators	50	300,000	Stewart & Stevenson Services, Dallas
Mortar parts	1 lot	244,879	Muncie Gear Works, Inc., Muncie, Ind.
Tooling	1 lot	212,269	La Pointe Machine Tool Co., Hudson, Mass.
Fork trucks	624	2,215,546	Clark Equipment Co., Buchanan, Mich.
Construction facilities Steel forgings	...	2,038,445	Kropp Forge Ordnance, Melvindale, Mich.

British Steel Industry Is Taken Over by Labor Government

Conciliatory approach aims to keep trained steelmen in the industry.

London — The government-appointed Iron & Steel Corp. of Great Britain on Feb. 15 took over 91.8 pct of England's basic iron and steel production, including all companies producing more than 5000 tons of pig-iron or steel a year.

Cost to the government so far has been $500 million for 87 companies. The value of 59 others is being argued. Sore point with the steel companies is the fact that compensation for 24 companies is reported to represent only 75 pct of the book value of assets.

Biggest problem the government faces is how to keep the men who know steel in the steel industry. Government intention is to establish a team representing the Iron & Steel Corp. and the Iron & Steel Federation representing the original owners.

By a conciliatory approach the government hopes to entice steelmen into its new corporation—now lacking in trained steelmen.

Bethlehem Grants Pay Boost

New York—An 18½¢ to 23¢ per hour wage increase granted to workers in Bethlehem Steel Co. shipyards in the East prevented a 17,000-man strike set for Feb. 28. The increase won by the Industrial Union of Marine and Shipbuilding Workers of America, C. I. O., will be retroactive to Jan. 1 if it is approved by the Wage Stabilization Board.

Pittsburgh Industry Slowed

Pittsburgh—Industrial production during January fell due to lower steel operations. Because of temporary gas shortages during the cold wave, some mills were forced to reduce working schedules. Bituminous coal production and electric output rose slightly. Retail sales were at record levels.

Steel Ingot, Casting Output At All-Time Canadian High in '50

Toronto — Canadian production of steel ingots and castings in 1950 was at the all-time record total of 3,384,131 net tons, 85.1 pct of capacity, and compares with 3,186,930 tons in 1949.

Output for 1950 included 3,298,-068 tons of steel ingots and 86,063 tons of steel castings. Steel ingots and castings produced in December, 1950, amounted to 291,-242 tons, a daily average of 86.2 pct of capacity, and compares with 289,488 tons or 88.5 pct for November and 263,949 tons or 78.1 pct for December, 1949.

Sheffield Steel Plans Expansion

Houston—Sheffield Steel Corp. is waiting for government approval of financing arrangements to push through its plan for a 50 pct capacity expansion of its plant here. Construction cost is set as $71,518,981. Two certificates of necessity, one for $59,-275,000 for expansion of coke, pig iron, and steel products, and another, $12,243,981 for greater output of steel ingots and plates, have already been approved.

Construction plans include a new blast furnace, another open-hearth, a seamless tubing mill to make oil industry products, and blooming mill expansion. Sheffield is a subsidiary of Armco Steel.

Kaiser Aluminum Expansion

New York—Kaiser Aluminum & Chemical Corp. has announced plans for $115 million of private financing to increase productive capacity of its aluminum plants.

Of this, $79 million will be spent for construction of an aluminum reduction plant in the New Orleans area. Estimated annual capacity will be 200,000 lbs. Also included are a power project using natural gas as fuel to generate low-cost electricity, and development of bauxite deposits in Jamaica. An existing bauxite plant at Baton Rouge, La., will be expanded to increase production of alumina to 540,000 tons a year.

How to starve wood's worst enemy

An important coke oven by-product of Kaiser Steel's Fontana plant is creosote oil—an antiseptic chemical that protects wood throughout its lifetime against the ravenous appetite of the termite.

Creosote oil is just one of a dozen by-products, produced by Kaiser Steel, which are important to a wide variety of western industries.

Another is benzol, a basic ingredient of synthetic rubber, which is in critical demand today. Others, like toluol, phenol, xylol, are essential ingredients in such diverse products as explosives, paint, dyes, fabrics, enriched gasoline ... many of them vital to our military needs.

More evidence that the West Coast's only integrated *independent* steel plant is bringing more industry, more jobs, more wealth to the West!

It's good business to do business with

Kaiser Steel

built to serve the West

PROMPT, DEPENDABLE DELIVERY AT COMPETITIVE PRICES • plates • continuous weld pipe • electric weld pipe • hot rolled strip • hot rolled sheet • alloy bars carbon bars • structural shapes • cold rolled strip • cold rolled sheet • special bar sections • semi-finished steels • pig iron • coke oven by-products
For details and specifications, write: **KAISER STEEL CORPORATION, LOS ANGELES, OAKLAND, SEATTLE, PORTLAND, HOUSTON, TULSA, NEW YORK**

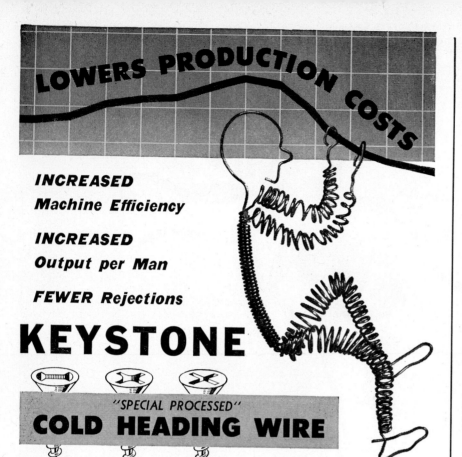

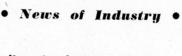
Radioactive Isotopes Used To Study Steelmaking Chemistry

New York—Radioactive isotopes, which emit rays or particles, are being used to study the physical chemistry of steelmaking, distribution of carbon in steel, friction, diffusion of elements, and studies of some types of gages and measuring instruments, reports the American Iron & Steel Institute.

Radiocarbon 14 is being used by scientists in steel research to determine segregation habits and mechanisms by which carbon hardens steel. Other experiments are on the method of changes in metal during heat treatment, diffusion of solid iron during annealing, hardening, and recrystallization, effects on metal in high speed ball bearings.

Steelworkers Less Migratory

New York—Steelworkers are proving less migratory and are holding on to their jobs. Turnover of steel industry workers in 1950 dropped more rapidly than in overall manufacturing, said the American Iron & Steel Institute on the basis of Bureau of Labor Statistics.

In the first 8 months of 1950, blast furnace, steel works, and rolling mill workers had a separation rate of only 1.6 for each 100 employees as against 3.1 for each 100 in all manufacturing. Among 92 industries surveyed, 64 rated higher in separation than iron and steel in August 1950 while 21 had lower rates.

Claim Waxes Boost Tool-Life

Racine, Wis.—Drawing of stainless steel beyond theoretical capacity, and extended life for drawing dies is possible with special blends of waxes in conventional lubricants, according to S. C. Johnson & Son, Inc. Company tests indicate waxes may serve as a replacement for copper flashing on stainless steel wire used for cold heading. Upsetting operations are also improved, the company claims.

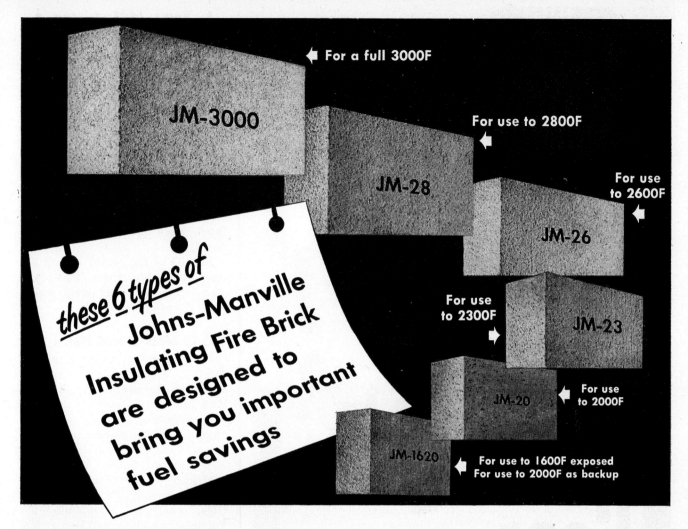

For a full 3000F

JM-3000

For use to 2800F

JM-28

For use to 2600F

JM-26

For use to 2300F

JM-23

For use to 2000F

JM-20

For use to 1600F exposed
For use to 2000F as backup

JM-1620

these 6 types of Johns-Manville Insulating Fire Brick are designed to bring you important fuel savings

You can make important savings in fuel by taking advantage of the quick heating characteristics of J-M Insulating Fire Brick. These light-weight brick permit a quicker rise to proper operating temperature in the furnace because of their low heat storage capacity, and low thermal conductivity. Where furnaces are being intermittently operated these are two especially important characteristics.

These same insulating materials can also be obtained in large size units called Johns-Manville Insulating *Fireblok*. This product has many advantages over the smaller size fire brick for certain types of jobs . . . from both a construction and stability standpoint. The Fireblok units can be quickly applied because they are easy to cut and fit. Fireblok insulations provide additional heat savings be-

cause they reduce the number of joints, and require less mortar for bonding.

It will pay you to let a Johns-Manville insulation engineer explain the many ways in which you can save by using these insulations in your furnaces. Just write for further information to Johns-Manville, Box 290, New York 16, N.Y.

	JM-1620	JM-20	JM-23	JM-26	JM-28	JM-3000
Densities, lb per cu ft.................	29	35	42	48	58	63-67
Transverse Strengths, psi.............	60	80	120	125	120	200
Cold Crushing Strengths, psi..........	70	115	170	190	150	400
Linear Shrinkage†, percent...........	0.0 at 2000 F	0.0 at 2000 F	0.3 at 2300 F	1.0 at 2600 F	4.0 at 2800 F	0.8 at 3000 F
Reversible Thermal Expansion, percent.	0.5—0.6 at 2000 F †	0.5—0.6 at 2000 F	0.5—0.6 at 2,000 F	0.5—0.6 at 2000 F	0.5—0.6 at 2000 F	0.5—0.6 at 2000 F
Conductivity* at Mean Temperatures						
500 F.........................	0.77	0 97	1.51	1.92	2.00	3.10
1000 F.........................	1.02	1.22	1.91	2.22	2.50	3.20
1500 F.........................	1.27	1.47	2.31	2.52	3.00	3.35
2000 F.........................	—	1.72	2.70	2.82	3.50	3.60
Recommended Service						
Back up........................	2000 F	2000 F	2300 F	2600 F	2800 F	3000 F
Exposed........................	1600 F	2000 F	2300 F	2600 F	2800 F	3000 F

†24-hr. simulative service panel test for JM-3000; 24-hr. soaking period for other brick.

*Conductivity is expressed in Btu in. per sq ft per F per hour of the designated mean temperatures.

Note: Above tests are in accordance with A.S.T.M. tentative standards.

Johns-Manville *first in* INSULATIONS

BLS Plans Steel Wage Survey

Washington—A survey on the wage structure of the basic iron and steel industry has been started this month by the Bureau of Labor Statistics. A representative slice of the industry will be asked to provide detailed information on selected occupations, average hourly earnings for all workers, and some information on related wage practices and their cost.

Results of the survey should be made available about mid-1951. The latest iron and steel wage survey was made in 1938.

USS to Break Ground Mar. 1

Pittsburgh — Ground-breaking for U. S. Steel Co.'s new Fairless Works at Morrisville, Pa., will be held Mar. 1.

Participating officials will include Gov. John S. Fine, of Pennsylvania; Gov. Alfred Driscoll, of New Jersey; Calvin W. Moyer, chairman of the Bucks County, Pa., commissioners; Irving S. Olds, chairman; Benjamin F. Fairless, president, and Enders M. Voorhees, chairman of the finance committee, U. S. Steel Corp., and C. F. Hood, executive vice-president, operations, U. S. Steel Co.

Discuss Changed Market Picture

New York—Market organization changes by major firms to meet new selling conditions resulting from allocations and shortages will be discussed at the 2-day national marketing conference to be held by the American Management Assn. on Mar. 12 to 13 at the Waldorf-Astoria Hotel, here.

Chesapeake Orders 2500 Cars

New York—An order for 2500 hopper cars has been received by the American Car & Foundry Co. from the Chesapeake & Ohio Railway. To have a capacity of 70 tons each, the cars will be built at American Car's Huntington, W. Va., plant. This order supplements another from Chesapeake for 3000 hopper cars.

TRAMRAIL CRANES
Indispensable for Efficient Production

Plenty of cranes in this Diesel motor plant ease the work and boost production.

Even though most parts could be moved by hand in this electrical factory, production is speeded and safety improved by employing inexpensive cranes with electric hoists

Three things which are held extremely important to modern industrial plants are achieved by the use of simple Cleveland Tramrail overhead cranes:

(1) Production is speeded
(2) Costs are cut
(3) Safety is improved

Cranes save many costly man-hours of skilled mechanics by enabling one man, in most cases, to pick up and move heavy or awkward parts that ordinarily require hard and dangerous work by several men when lifting and tugging by hand.

Even where light loads are lifted only a few times a week, it has come to be realized that the cost of Cleveland Tramrail cranes is well justified because they are a tremendous factor in the elimination of hernias, smashed hands and feet, wrenched backs and other unnecessary injuries.

Progressive plants regard overhead materials handling equipment as indispensable.

GET THIS BOOK!
BOOKLET No. 2008. Packed with valuable information. Profusely illustrated. Write for free copy

CLEVELAND TRAMRAIL DIVISION
THE CLEVELAND CRANE & ENGINEERING CO.
4804 EAST 284TH ST., WICKLIFFE, OHIO

CLEVELAND TRAMRAIL
OVERHEAD MATERIALS HANDLING EQUIPMENT

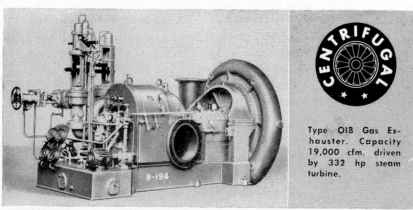

STEEL CONSTRUCTION NEWS

Fabricated steel inquiries this week included the following:

275 Tons, Chicago, procurement office U. S. Engineers I-beam railway bridges.

Reinforcing bar awards this week included the following:

800 Tons, Denver, Rocky Mountain Arsenal to Utah Construction Co., San Francisco.

600 Tons, Chicago, Continental Grain Co. concrete tanks to Ryan Construction Co., Omaha.

405 Tons, Brackenridge, Pa., Allegheny Ludlum Steel Corp. to U. S. Steel Supply Co.

290 Tons, Waterloo, Iowa, junior high school to Laclede Steel Co.

235 Tons, Altoona, Pa., Easterly Sewage Treatment Works to U. S. Steel Supply Co.

200 Tons, Iowa City, Iowa, children's hospital to Laclede Steel Co.

170 Tons, Arlington Heights, Ill., dial office Illinois Bell Telephone Co. to Jos. T. Ryerson and Son.

Reinforcing bar inquiries this week included the following:

900 Tons, Sterling, Ill., Northwestern Steel and Wire Co.

700 Tons, Lexington, Ky., hotel

150 Tons, Des Moines, Iowa, Solar Aircraft Co.

116 Tons, Madison, Wis., International Resident Dormitory, U. of Wisconsin.

Federated Metals, Philco, RCA Join Conservation Campaign

New York—Industry is seeking new ways to conserve critical materials. Federated Metals Div. of American Smelting & Refining Co., Philco Corp., and Radio Corp. of America joined the conservation drive last week.

Federated Metals, said to be the second largest user of tin, announced that immediate saving of 50 pct and more of tin in solder was possible. Leaner in tin content, the new products will be priced lower than the products they will replace.

Federated proposes use of silver, most available metal that can be used as a substitute, as part of the solder content, replacing tin. No working efficiency loss and lower costs are claimed. The firm also announced formation of the Metals Conservation Committee to plot out conservation methods.

Both Philco and R. C. A. announced television sets which make drastic savings in critical alloys and metals.

American Can Co. and Weirton Steel Co. had previously reported new methods to save tin on cans and solder material.

publications

Continued from Page 36

pointing out that complete surface cleaning is not usually required. *Prufcoat Laboratories, Inc.*
For free copy insert No. 7 on postcard, p. 37.

Hoisting Equipment Data

The new 92-p. general catalog No. 81 contains product illustrations, complete engineering specifications and list prices currently effective on the entire line of David Round hoisting equipment. Products shown include chain hoists, trolleys, cranes, sheaves, hoist chain, electric hoist, winches and crabs. Full data on repair parts for each of the various types of equipment is also given, along with other data and technical information of value to engineers. *David Round & Son.*
For free copy insert No. 8 on postcard, p. 37.

Fan Catalog

Design and construction specifications with complete performance data on various types of desk and stand fans, air circulators, ceiling fans, kitchen ventilators, exhaust, attic and window fans are presented in a new 32-p. illustrated catalog. Included is detailed dimensional information. *Emerson Electric Mfg. Co. Address requests to this column on company letterhead.*

Alignment Instrument

An illustrated circular describing the "Tumico King Way" alignment instrument tells how it is used for levelling and aligning new machine tools, particularly lathes, grinders, planers, etc., and is especially useful for rebuilding and rescraping used machines to perfect alignment. Pictures show six successive steps in realigning and rescraping a lathe bed. *George Scherr Co.*
For free copy insert No. 9 on postcard, p. 37.

Scaffolding Practice

The convenience, economy and other advantages of Trouble Saver sectional tubular steel scaffolding for maintenance work in industrial buildings are shown in a new 11-p. bulletin. This reference source on modern scaffolding practice in maintenance jobs gives detailed information on erection and dis-

mantling of basic units, building up complete assemblies, available frames and components and a variety of actual applications of a special nature. Illustrations cover many on-the-job applications ranging from small assemblies to elaborate erections covering entire buildings. *Patent Scaffolding Co., Inc.*

For free copy insert No. 10 on postcard, p. 37.

Plastic Coatings

Use of vinyl plastic coatings for the control of corrosion on exteriors of steel, concrete, brick, formed block and plywood structures, and as a tank lining, is detailed in a new illustrated bulletin. Specific properties are given and a chemical resistance chart is included, as well as information concerning application. Coatings described are of thermoplastic resin base and inert, noncontaminating enough for food processing, yet tough enough for use on railroad tank cars or sea-going barges. *Casey & Case Coating Co. Address requests to this column on company letterhead.*

Packaged Air Control

The Bellows Electroaire valve—a complete packaged air control unit, is described in a new 6-p. bulletin. Consisting of four-way directional valve, and independent speed regulators for control of piston rod speed of air cylinders in either or both directions, the unit is shown to embody unique low voltage solenoid controls guaranteed against burnout. Detailed technical data and wiring diagrams are also shown. *Bellows Co.*

For free copy insert No. 11 on postcard, p. 37.

Graphite for Parting

How colloidal graphite dispersions are used profitably in the metalworking and other industries is shown in a new 6-p. bulletin. Details given are of such specific applications as the parting of sintered metal clutch plates from each other, the separation of ingots from molds, and the removal of

FARQUHAR HYDRAULIC PRESS

turns out better forgings *faster*

for Cameron Iron Works

This Giant 5000-ton Farquhar Hydraulic Press has a big job to do at the Cameron Iron Works, of Houston, Texas—and it's doing it!

Cameron needed faster and better production of tubing head spools which are used in the oil industry for capping wells. These parts had formerly been produced from steel castings. By using the built-to-specification Farquhar Press to turn out 800-lb. forgings of the spools instead, Cameron speeded up production, saved time and labor.

Advantages of forgings by the Farquhar Press over the castings are: Cheaper to produce . . . Free from porosity . . . Uniform in physical properties . . . Controlled in grain structure. Cameron gets higher quality at lower costs for this operation—still can convert the press for other production jobs in the future.

Farquhar Presses Cut Your Costs

Just one more example of cost-cutting Farquhar performance in heavy production. Farquhar Presses are built for the job . . . presses that assure faster production due to rapid advance and return of the ram . . . greater accuracy because of the extra guides on moving platen . . . easy, smooth operation with finger-tip controls . . . longer die life due to positive control of speed and pressure on the die . . . long, dependable service with minimum maintenance cost!

Farquhar engineers are ready to help solve whatever production problem you may have. Give them a call.

Send for Free Catalog showing Farquhar Hydraulic Presses in all sizes and capacities for all types of industry. Write to: A. B. Farquhar Co., *Hydraulic Press Division*, 1503 Duke St., York, Pa.

GET THE DETAILS on how our Deferred Payment Plan helps you pay for your Farquhar Hydraulic Press out of the savings it produces!

Farquhar HYDRAULIC PRESSES

for Bending · Forming · Forcing · Straightening · Assembling · Drawing
Extruding · Joggling · Forging · and other Metal-working Operations

glass forms from molding machines. The folder explains that this lubricant is unaffected by heat up to 3500°F in inert atmospheres, and is widely used to prevent sticking, corrosion, galling, and freezing of parts. *Acheson Colloids Corp.*

For free copy insert No. 12 on postcard, p. 37.

Charts to Aid Production

Isometrics at work in the plant today is the subject of a new 10-p. explanatory booklet showing how the individual plant can make maximum production per worker a reality. It tells how Isometrics show the untrained worker, by means of illustrated charts, the correct rotation of assembled parts, eliminating special training and supervisory assistance. The method is adaptable to all types of industry, particularly the radio, aircraft and automotive fields. *Isometric Co.*

For free copy insert No. 13 on postcard, p. 37.

Die Cushion Catalog

Die cushions for mechanical presses are described in a new 20-p. booklet cataloging the entire Danly die cushion line with complete size, capacity and dimensional data. A valuable feature of the booklet is a series of cushion selection charts covering a wide range of sizes and types of die cushions. All are shown in photos and engineering drawings. *Danly Machine Specialties, Inc.*

For free copy insert No. 14 on postcard, p. 37.

Tiny Tantalum Capacitors

A series of sub-miniature tantalum capacitors, notable for stability over wide ranges of time and temperature, is announced in a new bulletin telling how, for its capacity ratings, this is the smallest electrolytic capacitor ever known—excluding connection leads, it occupies less than 1/10 cu in. Nine standard capacitors are listed, ranging from 30 mfd at 6 v dc to 3.5 mfd at 75 v dc. *Fansteel Metallurgical Corp.*

For free copy insert No. 15 on postcard, p. 37.

Resume Your Reading on Page 37

Conserve that Stainless!

IF you possess any stainless steel of doubtful parentage, now is the time to identify it. Most stainless alloying elements are scarce—some have reached the critical stage.

Any mixed supplies of stainless steels you have in stock have become precious, and well worth sorting out.

To help you, Frasse engineering service has recently revised and reissued our Data Chart, Sec. A No. 3—which describes 10 simple methods for separating stainless from carbon and alloy steels, nickel stainless from moly grades, straight chrome from chrome nickel grades, etc. A detailed expla-

nation of each testing method is also included.

The chart is printed on durable cardboard stock, regular file card size, and can be filed, tacked on a wall, or slipped under glass for speedy reference.

A copy of this useful chart may be obtained by using the coupon below. Mail it today! *Peter A. FRASSE and Co., Inc., 17 Grand St., New York 13, N. Y. (Walker 5-2200) • 3911 Wissahickon Ave., Philadelphia 29, Pa. (Baldwin 9-9900) • 50 Exchange St., Buffalo 3, N. Y. (Washington 2000) • 157 Richmond Ave., Syracuse 4, N. Y. (Syracuse 3-4123) • Jersey City • Hartford • Rochester • Baltimore*

FRASSE for Stainless Steels

- Bars
- Sheets
- Strip
- Plates
- Angles
- Wire
- Tubing
- Pipe
- Fittings

Peter A. FRASSE and Co., Inc.   1-IA
17 Grand Street
New York 13, N. Y.

Gentlemen: Please send me, without obligation, a copy of your new data chart, Sec. A No. 3—listing methods for identifying Stainless Steels.

Name_____ Title_____

Firm_____

Address_____

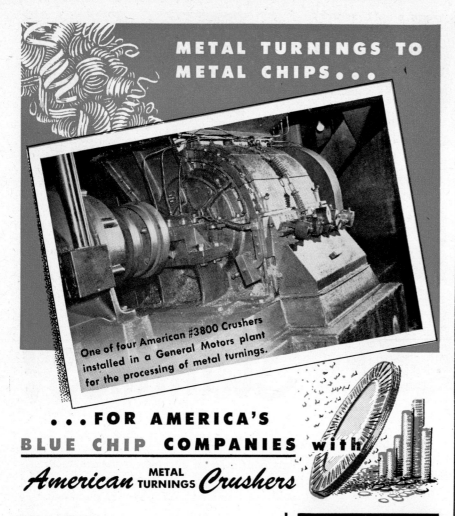

production ideas
Continued from Page 40

opened and closed by an air-pressure valve as operator indexes the cutter. Pointer mounted on vise is used in setting blades to the same height. Arbors for cutters with

1½ and 2½ in. diam bores are standard equipment. Arbors for other bore diameters are available as special equipment. *Ingersoll Milling Machine Co.*
For more data insert No. 34 on postcard, p. 37.

Tilting Motor Base
Accommodates all sizes and types of fractional motors up to 1 hp.

Adjustable in width and length to accommodate fractional hp motors, a lightweight tilting motor

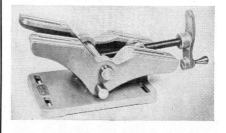

base also acts as a belt tightener when used with variable speed drives and for easy belt changing on cone step pulleys. A handle screw adjustment provides exact speed control and changes while the machine is in use. The base is 5½ x 7 in., shipping weight 10 lb. *Lovejoy Flexible Coupling Co.*
For more data insert No. 35 on postcard, p. 37.

Dispatch Carrier
Gear head motor can turn the bucket one complete revolution.

The carrier illustrated was originally designed for delivery of core

INCREASE PRODUCTION NOW...

WITH Present Plant Manpower Present Plant Space

The next time you walk through your plant, cast your eyes toward the ceiling and you'll realize that there is mighty valuable space that can be put to work—without increasing your plant capacities and without increasing plant manpower.

An American MonoRail engineer will show you how you can use your "air rights". With thousands of overhead handling installations from which to draw, each with many money and time saving advantages, it will pay you to investigate American MonoRail Overhead Handling Systems. Send for bulletin C-1.

THE AMERICAN MONORAIL COMPANY

13103 ATHENS AVENUE   **CLEVELAND 7, OHIO**

February 22, 1951

For Automatic Feeding to Punch Presses—Press Brakes

A press brake equipped with Wittek No. 6-L Automatic Roll Feed

You Can't Beat WITTEK

Wittek Roll Feeds are made in standard models to meet every requirement in the automatic feeding of strip stock to punch presses or press brakes. The distinguishing feature is their simple and economical method of operation which does away with complicated parts thereby assuring *speed* and *accuracy* in the feeding of various kinds and thicknesses of material.

Wittek Adjustable Reel Stands are designed as companion units to Wittek Automatic Roll Feeds and are available in seven different models to handle *ALL* types of coiled strip stock and wire being fed to punch presses or similar production machinery.

Special units of Wittek Automatic Roll Feeds and Adjustable Reel Stands are engineered to meet unusual requirements.

Write for complete descriptive literature

WITTEK Manufacturing Co.
4329 W. 24th Place
Chicago 23, Ill.

Automatic **ROLL FEEDS AND REEL STANDS** (WMco)

EF

Easier HEAT TREATMENT of LARGE, HEAVY CASTINGS

● The gantry crane shown with this battery of EF batch type furnaces picks up castings from a receiving platform — loads them into the furnaces — removes them after heating — lowers them into the quench — removes them after quenching and places them on an unloading platform.

Our wide experience in all phases of heat treating and related material handling problems, puts us in a preferred position to solve most any ferrous or non-ferrous annealing or heat treating problem. We solicit your inquiries.

THE ELECTRIC FURNACE CO.
Salem - Ohio
GAS FIRED, OIL FIRED AND ELECTRIC FURNACES
FOR ANY PROCESS, PRODUCT OR PRODUCTION

---

production ideas
Continued

sand to storage hoppers at core makers benches and core blowing machines. It consists of a standard MonoTractor for horizontal propulsion on the MonoRail tracks, a

twin hook Electro Lift hoist and a special bucket mounted so that the gear head motor can turn it one complete revolution. Control devices can perform selective stopping and starting at stations. *American MonoRail Co.*

For more data insert No. 36 on postcard, p. 37.

Channel Marking Machine
Stamps identification on aluminum or other metal channel sections.

A channel section is marked by pulling the handle of the marker from left to right. This action rolls a deep, clear-cut mark in the channel without distorting the metal. A spring returns the mandrel to

MARKED CHANNEL

position for the next marking. The roll die can be made with lettering engraved on the solid roll. For part numbers or other changing identification marks, interchangeable type setups can be provided. The base or mandrel section is machined to suit individual channel shapes. *M. E. Cunningham Co.*

For more data insert No. 37 on postcard, p. 37.

Adjustable Shelving

Steel-wood shelving features sturdiness, strength, safety.

No bolts are used to attach the hard wood shelving to the steel uprights. A pressed steel clip attaches each shelf to the steel upright giving maximum in adjustability and strength to each wood shelf. Steel-wood shelving is available 3 ft wide x 1 or 1½ ft deep x 7 ft high. *Lyons Metal Products, Inc.*

For more data insert No. 38 on postcard, p. 37.

Stroboscopic Tachometer

Measures speeds without physical connection with rotating equipment.

The fundamental range of flashing speed of the Strobotac is 600 to

14,400 per min. These speeds can be read directly from a dial calibrated in rpm. By using multiples of the flashing speed, the range of measurement can be extended to about 100,000 rpm. By multiple images, speeds below 600 rpm can be measured. The Strobotac operates on 105 to 125 v, 50/60 cycles, consumes approximately 35 w. It measures 7½ x 8¾ x 9⅞ in. overall. *Electronic Measurements Co.*

For more data insert No. 39 on postcard, p. 37.

Multi-Use Primer

Rust inhibiting, for use on ferrous or aluminum surfaces.

A new rust inhibiting primer is basically a rust inhibiting synthetic primer that reduces with

production ideas
Continued

Toluol or Xylol for spraying or dipping. The product is said to bake or air-dry with equal facility and can be cured simultaneously with its top coat in a one-bake operation. A 15-min. baking operation at 300°F is sufficient to thoroughly dry Multi-Primer. Ten minutes of air-drying is adequate to allow handling. Available in gray, red, yellow and black. *James B. Sipe & Co.*

For more data insert No. 40 on postcard, p. 37.

Crank Pin Grinder

For production grinding crank pins of 4, 6, or 8 cylinder crankshafts.

Refinements to speed production and insure dependable operation built into this improved model include lubrication to the carriage and wheelbase ways from a separate reservoir with pump and filter; a safety pressure switch to prevent operation of the machine unless pressure exists in the system. A

new handfeed for the carriage positions the crankshaft laterally as the grinding wheel moves toward the work, permitting even grinding on each side of the crankshaft sidewall. Speeds of the hydraulic traverse are adjustable at the front of the machine. There are separate

controls for positioning speed of the carriage and for right hand and left hand cushioning speeds. Microsphere spindle bearings are lubricated by pressure. An overhead wheel dresser obtainable to speed the operating cycle is hydraulically operated and permits dressing the wheel without changing the work setup. A variable

Turn to Page 115

production ideas

Continued from Page 112

speed motor maintains correct surface speed of the wheel regardless of wheel diameter. *Landis Tool Co.*
For more data insert No. 41 on postcard, p. 37.

Metal Separator

Reclaims valuable metal from skimmings, slags and dross.

This dry process separator recovers waste metal at once and makes it available for immediate resmelting; eliminates the accumulations of skimming over a

period of time; and produces a high percentage of metal recoveries. The operating features are: No heat—no water; automatic operation; low maintenance cost; and no skilled operator needed. The metal separator is available in two sizes. *Peerless Metal Separator Co.*
For more data insert No. 42 on postcard, p. 37.

Fork Lift Truck

Will tier three pallets high; lifts 117 in. from floor-to-forks.

A Tier-Master fork lift truck with telescoping uprights is 72 in. high with the mast lowered; overall height of the mast extended is 142 in. The truck is designed to tier three pallets high and still easily move in and out of trucks, through low doors and other restricted clearance areas without transferring loads from one fork truck to another. Roller chain lift mechanism allows unobstructed view between the uprights and lifts at a speed of more than 45 fpm. Lev-R-Matic drive controls allow forward or back operation at the
Turn to Page 117

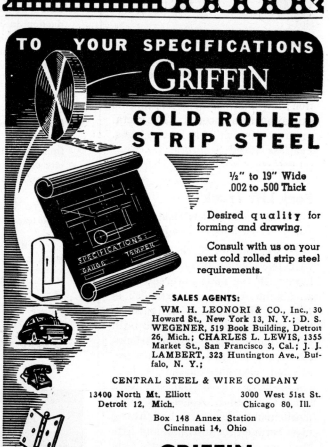

push or pull of a single lever without shifting gears. The Tier-Master is a stand-up type, 2000-lb capacity fork lift truck powered by a three-cylinder air-cooled, gas operated Mobilift engine. *Mobilift Corp.*

For more data insert No. 43 on postcard, p. 37.

Boring Heads

Safety smooth, round contour and micrometer offset adjustment.

Five new offset boring heads are of lightweight design. The smallest has a 2¾ in. diam, ½ in. bar capacity and weighs 3 lb. The largest has 6½ in. diam, 1½ in. bar capacity and weighs 24 lb. Bar off-

set of the new series ranges from ⅝ to 1½ in. All heads are machined from solid stock and ground after hardening. The tool blocks have the extension nose, but the nose on the new model is round. Boring tools may be inserted in the head either vertically or horizontally. *Flynn Mfg. Co.*

For more data insert No. 44 on postcard, p. 37.

Demineralizer

Features new direct reading meter.

With the direct reading meter, anyone can tell the purity of the water at any time and maintain a constant purity check on the flow of demineralized water. For convenience, the instrument is calibrated in parts per million and also in ohms electrical resistance. The demineralizer is complete with a needle type regulating valve, a drain valve and a base for bench mounting. *Barnstead Still & Sterilizer Co.*

For more data insert No. 45 on postcard, p. 37.

Resume Your Reading on Page 41

IRON AGE *markets and prices*

steel cutback—NPA, within the next 10 days, will cut back steel for consumer durable goods to 80 pct of the average quarterly use of the first half of 1950. Copper and aluminum will be cut to 75 and 65 pct, respectively. Manufacturers will be required to use the same proportion of conversion steel. They can look forward to a third quarter cut of 70 pct in steel. NPA chief, Manly Fleischman, does not anticipate a sizable cut in auto production, since there are no unit limits. The second quarter cut is expected to save about 1 million tons of steel, mostly sheet.

a slight thaw—Beginning Feb. 15, NPA will take applications at field offices for construction of retail stores, warehouses, and other commercial buildings frozen as of Jan. 15. Approvals hinge on proof that buildings are necessary for defense, public health or safety, or to prevent hardship. With an NPA okay, the Federal Reserve Board amended Reg. X, effective Feb. 15, to require 50 pct of cost on commercial construction.

steel plate set-asides—An indication of the gathering speed of the defense effort is the increase in set-asides of carbon and alloy plates scheduled for May 1. The present 15 pct set-aside called for by the amended steel order (M-1) will be raised to 20 pct. Changes in military requirements, however, cut the percentage reserve for alloy sheet bars from 35 to 5 pct in the recent amendment, effective Feb. 15.

British steel hike—Rising coal and coke prices to the tune of up to $30 million increased costs to the British steel industry will definitely necessitate higher steel prices in England, according to the Minister of Supply. The new schedule is now being worked out on the higher basis but the new prices are still expected to be well below those prevalent on the Continent.

defense orders—Some of the biggest defense orders so far placed require a long period of tooling up before the goods start to roll. This partly explains why machine tool backlogs are growing while manufacturers are being pinched by material cutbacks and lack of defense contracts.

so you have trouble—A manufacturer of kitchen equipment placed an order for stainless sheet last year and was promised delivery in February. Later they were told they would have to be pushed back into the fourth quarter of 1951. Then came the M-14 order and they had to be taken off the books. They use almost all stainless steel and so far have no defense orders.

tungsten from down under—The U. S. and U. K. governments have placed long-term contracts with King Island Scheelite, Ltd., an Australian producer, for $15,680,000 worth of strategic tungsten. The American contract will run for 7 years, the British for 5.

steel for expansion—One mill reports that steel expansion is taking as much structural shapes as they are contributing to the freight car program. While this is not believed general for the industry, it does point up the fact that it takes steel to make steel.

Steel Operations**

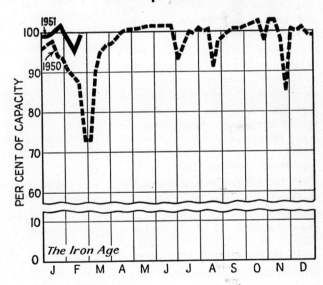

District Operating Rates—Per Cent of Capacity**

Week of	Pittsburgh	Chicago	Youngstown	Philadelphia	West	Buffalo	Cleveland	Detroit	Wheeling	South	Ohio River	St. Louis	East	Aggregate
Feb. 11........	98.0*	100.5	92.0*	98.0	101.7	104.0	82.5*	108.0*	100.0	104.0	88.0	95.1	112.6	98.5
Feb. 18........	97.0	101.5	88.0	99.0	103.5	104.0	96.0	109.0	99.0	104.0	86.0	87.2	112.6	99.5

* Revised.
** Beginning Jan. 1, 1951, operations are based on an annual capacity of 104,229,650 net tons.

nonferrous metals | *outlook and market activities*

NONFERROUS METALS PRICES

	Feb. 14	Feb. 15	Feb. 16	Feb. 17	Feb. 19	Feb. 20
Copper, electro, Conn...	24.50	24.50	24.50	24.50	24.50	24.50
Copper, Lake delivered..	24.625	24.625	24.625	24.625	24.625	24.625
Tin, Straits, New York...	$1.83	$1.83	$1.83	....	$1.83	$1.83*
Zinc, East St. Louis	17.50	17.50	17.50	17.50	17.50	17.50
Lead, St. Louis	16.80	16.80	16.80	16.80	16.80	16.80

Note: Quotations are going prices.

*Tentative.

by R. Hatschek

New York—Scrap metals prices are ranging all over the lot. In anticipation of the freeze some people in the trade ran up their prices so that they might charge higher prices legally and, because of the highly competitive nature of the business, the freeze is not working well. Dealers and consumers are expecting Washington to set ceiling prices at any time.

Demand for secondary brass and bronze is only fair because of the lack of DO rated orders in the brass industry. Brass mills have been forced to severely curtail their operations because of this lack of defense work and the fact that they are not permitted to use enough of their metal for other than war work.

Aluminum Demand High

On the other hand, demand for secondary aluminum ingot is good following a slightly depressed period. It is felt that the drop in demand was the result of consumers trimming down their inventories in compliance with government regulations. DO orders on aluminum are more frequent than on brass and bronze.

National Production Authority has amended order M-12 on copper. The amendment added about 50 more items on the end-use list for which copper is prohibited and it also eased the inventory provisions of the original order. NPA has also placed lead and antimony under control in orders M-38 and M-39. More complete details will be found in the *News of Industry* section.

Boost Alumina Output

It is reported that the Shullsburg, Wis., zinc-lead mine of Calumet and Hecla Consolidated Copper Co. is now producing about 650 tons of ore a day. About 1200-ton-per-day production is expected from the mine by the middle of the year. The added metal from this mine will be welcome to a zinc-starved industry.

Also increasing production is the East St. Louis works of the Aluminum Ore Co., an Aluminum Co. of America subsidiary. At present the plant has increased production by about 50 pct and the goal set for Mar. 15 is a 100 pct boost in output. The cost of expanding this plant, which makes alumina from bauxite, is set at over $500,000.

The Emergency Lead Committee has filed a petition to the U. S. Tariff Commission for investigation and revision of the lead import duty, now 2⅛¢ per lb. The committee's recommendation is a tariff which slides inversely with the domestic price of lead, that is the lower the price, the higher the tariff.

They specifically suggest these rates: When lead is 17¢ per lb and over, the duty would be 1 1/16¢ on metal and ¾¢ on lead in ore; when lead is 12¢ to 17¢, duty would be 2⅛¢ on metal and 1½¢ on lead in ore; when lead is less than 12¢, duty would be 3 3/16¢ on metal and 2¼¢ on lead in ore. This, it is claimed, would give the domestic producers of lead a more favorable position in time of slack demand and would permit greater imports in times of excessive demand as at present.

Imports Top Home Output

The combination of high demand and devaluated currency in Mexico and the sterling countries contributed to imports in 1950 that were greater than domestic production. It was pointed out that this was the first time in history that this has happened. The ratio was 550,000 tons imported to 425,000 tons produced by domestic lead mines.

The Singapore tin market was still above New York levels last week but was coming down gradually. It is expected that the current lack of orders from the U. S. will soon bring Far East prices down to a point where imports will again be possible.

MILL PRODUCTS

(Cents per lb, unless otherwise noted)

Aluminum

(Base 30,000 lb, f.o.b. ship. pt. frt. allowed)

Flat Sheet: 0.188 in., 2S, 3S, 30.1¢; 4S, 61S-O, 32¢; 52S, 34.1¢; 24S-O, 24S-OAL, 32.9¢; 75S-O, 75S-OAL, 39.9¢; 0.081 in., 2S, 3S, 31.2¢; 4S, 61S-O, 33.5¢; 52S, 35.6¢; 24S-O, 24S-OAL, 34.1¢; 75S-O, 75S-OAL, 41.8¢; 0.032 in., 2S, 3S, 32.9¢; 4S, 61S-O, 37.1¢; 52S, 39.8¢; 24S-O, 24S-OAL, 41.7¢; 75S-O, 75S-OAL, 52.2¢.

Plate: ¼ in. and heavier: 2S, 3S-F, 28.3¢ 4S-F, 30.2¢; 52S-F, 31.8¢; 61S-O, 30.8¢; 24S-O, 24S-OAL, 32.4¢; 75S-O, 75S-OAL, 38.8¢.

Extruded Solid Shapes: Shape factors 1 to 5, 36.2¢ to 74.5¢; 12 to 14, 36.9¢ to 89¢; 24 to 26, 39.6¢ to $1.16; 36 to 38, 47.2¢ to $1.70.

Rod, Rolled: 1.5 to 4.5 in., 2S-F, 3S-F, 37.5¢ to 33.5¢; cold-finished, 0.375 to 3 in., 2S-F, 3S-F, 40.5¢ to 35¢.

Screw Machine Stock: Rounds, 11S-T3, ⅛ to 11/32 in., 53.5¢ to 42¢; ⅜ to 1½ in., 41.5¢ to 39¢; 1 9/16 to 3 in., 38.5¢ to 36¢; 17S-T4 lower by 1.5¢ per lb. Base 5000 lb.

Drawn Wire: Coiled, 0.051 to 0.374 in., 2S, 39.5¢ to 29¢; 52S, 48¢ to 35¢; 56S, 51¢ to 42¢; 17S-T4, 54¢ to 37.5¢; 61S-T4, 48.5¢ to 37¢; 75S-T6, 84¢ to 67.5¢.

Extruded Tubing, Rounds: 63S-T5, OD in in.: 1¼ to 2, 37¢ to 54¢; 2 to 4, 33.5¢ to 45.5¢; 4 to 6, 34¢ to 41.5¢; 6 to 9, 34.5¢ to 43.5¢.

Roofing Sheet, Flat: 0.019 in. x 28 in. per sheet, 72 in., $1.142; 96 in., $1.522; 120 in., $1.902; 144 in., $2.284. Gage 0.024 in. x 28 in., 72 in., $1.379; 96 in., $1.839; 120 in., $2.299; 144 in., $2.759. Coiled Sheet: 0.019 in. x 28 in., 28.2¢ per lb.; 0.024 in. x 28 in., 26.9¢ per lb.

Magnesium

(F.o.b. mill, freight allowed)

Sheet and Plate: FS1-O, ¼ in. 63¢; 3/16 in. 65¢; ⅛ in. 67¢; B & S Gage 10, 68¢; 12, 72¢; 14, 78¢; 16, 85¢; 18, 93¢; 20, $1.05; 22, $1.27; 24, $1.67. Specification grade higher. Base: 30,000 lb.

Extruded Round Rod: M, diam in., ¼ to 0.311 in., 74¢; ½ to ¾ in., 57.5¢; 1¼ to 1.749 in., 53¢; 2½ to 5 in., 48.5¢. Other alloys higher. Base: Up to ¾ in. diam, 10,000 lb; ¾ to 2 in., 20,000 lb; 2 in. and larger, 30,000 lb.

Extruded Solid Shapes, Rectangles: M. In weight per ft, for perimeters less than size indicated, 0.10 to 0.11 lb, 3.5 in., 62.3¢; 0.22 to 0.25 lb, 5.9 in., 59.3¢; 0.50 to 0.59 lb, 8.6 in., 56.7¢; 1.8 to 2.59 lb, 19.5 in., 53.8¢; 4 to 6 lb, 28 in., 49¢. Other alloys higher. Base, in weight per ft of shape: Up to ½ lb, 10,000 lb; ½ to 1.80 lb, 20,000 lb; 1.80 lb and heavier, 30,000 lb.

Extruded Round Tubing: M, wall thickness, outside diam, in., 0.049 to 0.057, ¼ in. to 5/16, $1.40; 5/16 to ⅜, $1.26; ½ to ⅝, 93¢; 1 to 2 in., 76¢; 0.165 to 0.219, ⅝ to ¾, 61¢; 1 to 2 in., 57¢; 3 to 4 in., 56¢. Other alloys higher. Base, OD in in.; Up to 1½ in., 10,000 lb; 1½ in. to 3 in., 20,000 lb; 3 in. and larger, 30,000 lb.

Titanium

(10,000 lb base, f.o.b. mill)

Commercially pure and alloy grades: Sheet and strip, HR or CR, $15; Plate, HR, $12; Wire, rolled and/or drawn, $10; Bar, HR or forged, $6; Forgings, $6.

Nickel and Monel

(Base prices, f.o.b. mill)

	"A" Nickel	Monel
Sheets, cold-rolled	71½	57
Strip, cold-rolled	77½	60
Rods and bars	67½	55
Angles, hot-rolled	67½	55
Plates	69½	56
Seamless tubes	100½	90
Shot and blocks	....	50

Copper, Brass, Bronze

(Freight prepaid on 200 lb includes duty)

	Sheets	Rods	Extruded Shapes
Copper	41.03	....	40.63
Copper, h-r	....	36.88	....
Copper, drawn	....	38.18	....
Low brass	39.15	38.84	....
Yellow brass	38.28	37.97	....
Red brass	40.14	39.83	....
Naval brass	43.08	38.61	38.07
Leaded brass	....	32.63	36.70
Com'l bronze	41.13	40.82	....
Mang. bronze	45.96	40.65	41.41
Phos. bronze	60.20	60.45	....
Muntz metal	40.43	36.74	37.99
Ni silver, 10 pct	49.27	51.49	....
Arch. bronze	....	....	35.11

PRIMARY METALS

(Cents per lb, unless otherwise noted)

Aluminum ingot, 99+%, 10,000 lb, freight allowed	19.00
Aluminum pig	18.00
Antimony, American, Laredo, Tex.	42.00
Beryllium copper, 3.75-4.25% Be	$1.56
Beryllium aluminum 5% Be, Dollars per lb contained Be	$69.00
Bismuth, ton lots	$2.25
Cadmium, del'd	$2.55
Cobalt, 97-99% (per lb)	$2.10 to $2.17
Copper, electro, Conn. Valley	24.50
Copper, Lake, delivered	24.625
Gold, U. S. Treas., dollars per oz.	$35.00
Indium, 99.8%, dollars per troy oz.	$2.25
Iridium, dollars per troy oz.	$200
Lead, St. Louis	16.80
Lead, New York	17.00
Magnesium, 99.8+%, f.o.b. Freeport, Tex., 10,000 lb	24.50
Magnesium, sticks, 100 to 500 lb	42.00 to 44.00
Mercury, dollars per 76-lb flask, f.o.b. New York	$216-$220
Nickel, electro, f.o.b. New York	53.55
Nickel oxide sinter, f.o.b. Copper Cliff, Ont., contained nickel	46.75
Palladium, dollars per troy oz.	$24.00
Platinum, dollars per troy oz.	$90 to $93
Silver, New York, cents per oz.	90.16
Tin, New York	$1.83
Titanium, sponge	$5.00
Zinc, East St. Louis	17.50
Zinc, New York	18.22
Zirconium copper, 50 pct	$6.20

REMELTED METALS

Brass Ingot

(Cents per lb delivered, carloads)

85-5-5-5 ingot	
No. 115	29.00
No. 120	28.50
No. 123	28.00
80-10-10 ingot	
No. 305	35.00
No. 315	32.00
88-10-2 ingot	
No. 210	46.25
No. 215	43.25
No. 245	36.00
Yellow ingot	
No. 405	25.00
Manganese bronze	
No. 421	29.75

Aluminum Ingot

(Cents per lb, 30,000 lb lots)

95-5 aluminum-silicon alloys	
0.30 copper, max.	33.25-34.25
0.60 copper, max.	33.00-34.00
Piston alloys (No. 122 type)	30.50-31.00
No. 12 alum. (No. 2 grade)	30.00-30.50
108 alloy	30.25-30.75
195 alloy	31.25-31.75
13 alloy	33.50-34.00
ASX-679	30.50-31.00

Steel deoxidizing aluminum, notch-bar granulated or shot

Grade 1—95-97½%	32.00-32.50
Grade 2—92-95%	30.25-30.75
Grade 3—90-92%	29.25-29.75
Grade 4—85-90%	28.75-29.25

ELECTROPLATING SUPPLIES

Anodes

(Cents per lb, freight allowed, 500 lb lots)

Copper	
Cast, oval, 15 in. or longer	39⅛
Electrodeposited	33⅜
Rolled, oval, straight, delivered	38⅞
Forged ball anodes	43
Brass, 80-20	
Cast, oval, 15 in. or longer	34¾
Zinc, oval	26½
Ball anodes	25½
Nickel 99 pct plus	
Cast	70.50
Rolled, depolarized	71.50
Cadmium	$2.80
Silver 999 fine, rolled, 100 oz lots, per troy oz, f.o.b. Bridgeport, Conn.	79½

Chemicals

(Cents per lb, f.o.b. shipping points)

Copper cyanide, 100 lb drum	52.15
Copper sulfate, 99.5 crystals, bbl.	12.85
Nickel salts, single or double, 4-100 lb bags, frt. allowed	20½
Nickel chloride, 375 lb drum	27½
Silver syanide, 100 oz lots, per oz.	67¼
Sodium cyanide, 96 pct domestic 200 lb drums	19.25
Zinc cyanide, 100 lb drums	45.85

SCRAP METALS

Brass Mill Scrap

(Cents per pound, add ½¢ per lb for shipments of 20,000 to 40,000 lb; add 1¢ for more than 40,000 lb)

	Heavy	Turnings
Copper	23	22¼
Yellow Brass	20½	18¾
Red brass	21½	20¾
Comm. bronze	21¾	21
Mang. bronze	19½	18⅝
Brass rod ends	19⅞	....

Custom Smelters' Scrap

(Cents per pound, carload lots, delivered to refinery)

No. 1 copper wire	21.50
No. 2 copper wire	20.00
Light copper	19.00
Refinery brass	19.50*
Radiators	15.00

*Dry copper content.

Ingot Makers' Scrap

(Cents per pound, carload lots, delivered to producer)

No. 1 copper wire	23.00
No. 2 copper wire	22.00
Light copper	21.00
No. 1 composition	22.00
No. 1 comp. turnings	21.50
Rolled brass	18.50
Brass pipe	20.50
Radiators	17.50
Heavy yellow brass	17.00

Aluminum

Mixed old cast	18½—19
Mixed new clips	20½
Mixed turnings, dry	18½
Pots and pans	18½—19
Low copper	21½—22

Dealers' Scrap

(Dealers' buying prices, f.o.b. New York in cents per pound)

Copper and Brass

No. 1 heavy copper and wire	21½
No. 2 heavy copper and wire	20
Light copper	19
New type shell cuttings	19
Auto radiators (unsweated)	15½—16
No. 1 composition	19 —19½
No. 1 composition turnings	18½—19
Clean red car boxes	17½—18
Cocks and faucets	17½—18
Mixed heavy yellow brass	14½—15
Old rolled brass	15½—16
Brass pipe	18½—19
New soft brass clippings	17½—18
Brass rod ends	16½—17
No. 1 brass rod turnings	16 —16½

Aluminum

Alum. pistons and struts	12 —13
Aluminum crankcases	15 —16
2S aluminum clippings	18½—19½
Old sheet and utensils	15 —16
Borings and turnings	12½—13
Misc. cast aluminum	15 —16
Dural clips (24S)	15 —16

Zinc

New zinc clippings	14½—15
Old zinc	11 —11¼
Zinc routings	8½— 9
Old die cast scrap	8 — 8¼

Nickel and Monel

Pure nickel clippings	90 —100
Clean nickel turnings	80 —90
Nickel anodes	90 —100
Nickel rod ends	90 —100
New Monel clippings	30 —35
Clean Monel turnings	20 —25
Old sheet Monel	25 —30
Inconel clippings	30 —35
Nickel silver clippings, mixed	16 —18
Nickel silver turnings, mixed	15 —16

Lead

Soft scrap, lead	15 —15¼
Battery plates (dry)	8¾— 9

Magnesium

Segregated solids	9 —10
Castings	5½— 6½

Miscellaneous

Block tin	120 —125
No. 1 pewter	80 —85
No. 1 auto babbitt	75 —80
Mixed common babbitt	12¼—12½
Solder joints	23 —24
Siphon tops	75 —80
Small foundry type	18¼—18½
Monotype	16¾—17
Lino. and stereotype	16½—16¾
Electrotype	15 —15½
Hand picked type shells	11½—11¾
Lino. and stereo. dross	8¾— 9
Electro. dross	6¾— 7

SCRAP *iron and steel*

Dealers slow in collections . . . Mills buy foundry grades for openhearths . . . Trade generally approves order, asks revisions.

Some scrap consumers are saying that dealers are in semi-retirement and can be seen walking around with vacation folders in their pockets. The dealers have been given a quadruple dose of take-it-easy pills: (1) That heavy strength-sapping shipping before the order deadline, (2) removal of the gamble for higher prices next week that spurred collection, (3) bad weather in some districts, (4) confusion over facets of the order.

In other districts the scrap movement started to gain momentum.

Mills are not pleased at their disinterest. They need s c r a p. Local eastern and out-of-district mills were buying foundry grades Nos. 20 and 21 for openhearth use—and were paying the premium price.

NPA last week ordered electric furnace grades Nos. 11 through 18 out of the reach of openhearth users and a similar order was expected for foundry grades Nos. 20, 21. In Washington, scrap men told the Office of Price Stabilization that the trade was "generally satisfied" with the order but asked for revisions and definitions. Some scrap men feel that these interpretations and amendments are too slow in coming.

PITTSBURGH—Controls have slowed activity to a walk in this area. The prohibition against use of electric furnace grades in openhearths has calmed worried electric furnace producers. A similar prohibition against openhearth consumption of foundry scrap is expected. Specialty steel producers look for establishment of a controlled price of about $150 for stainless scrap this week. This scrap is now bringing as much as $200 per ton, a price most mills refuse to pay. Allo-

cated scrap was not a factor here early in the week, although it was reported that some eastern and midwestern mills were receiving allocated tonnages. It is understood NPA has compiled a list of generators of 100 tons or more of scrap per month, for allocation.

CHICAGO—Bad weather is hindering dealers' collection of scrap here so that they have little inventory not already committed. Industrial scrap flowing into yards is going out as fast as it comes in. Close inspection of incoming scrap for grading purposes will cause slight delays in shipment. New orders are easy to come by but difficult to fill. Foundries who held off buying previous to price controls are desperately trying to pick up tonnage. Most railroad scrap is going by allocation. Greater market activity is expected as old orders become filled and the severe weather lets up.

PHILADELPHIA—Western mills came into this market and started buying foundry grades of scrap (grades 20 and 21) and soon the local mills followed along. The idea was to replace the electric furnace material (grades 11 to 18) which they had been buying but which the government has ordered them not to buy as of last week. Mill inventories are low but the trade is now getting used to the controls and scrap is moving along a bit better.

NEW YORK—The market here is stubbornly dull. Dealers have no immediate incentive to start speculative collections and the scrap order itself is confusing some. The incentive to stay in business will later perk up scrap collection. But right now the mills need scrap and they aren't getting it. Some openhearth users are buying foundry grades and paying the price. No. 2 bundles are doing a fast exit out of the market.

DETROIT—The scrap situation here was badly confused. Because of clauses in the scrap order permitting use of combined rail and water rates, Detroit brokers report they had orders on their books for the same grades at $39.05, $40.10 and $40.20. There were reports that the Detroit base might have to be knocked out temporarily.

Further confusion centered around the question of openhearth and electric furnace bundles. Since few Detroit bundles meet the size qualifications set forth in the scrap order, dealers are claiming the **right to sell to electric melters at electric** furnace prices even though size qualifica-

tions are not fully met. Also, some confusion exists over flashings, not officially graded.

CLEVELAND—Movement of tonnage is down to a trickle in a subdued and uncertain market here and in the Valley. Two major consumers and a few foundries in this district are on allocations. Some openhearths are buying cast grades, indicative of rapidly diappearing inventories. Some report the new regulations confusing, particularly on premium grades. Further clarification is awaited.

ST. LOUIS—The scrap market has settled down with a feeling the base ceiling prices fixed by OPS are fair to all interests. It is believed there are some differentials yet to be worked out. Railroads feel their prices should be at shipping points. Mills are buying as they need the material. The movement has been slow because of the ice weather in the producing territories.

BIRMINGHAM — The scrap situation in this area is still unsettled. With prices stabilized everyone seems anxious to sell and dealers are buying freely. The largest buyer in the area has been out of the market for the past 3 weeks, but some foundries are buying. One large eastern mill is reported supplementing its heavy melting purchases with foundry grades.

CINCINNATI—Scrap is beginning to move here. Mills are hungry and need tonnage and two are receiving some allocated material, industrial and railroad. This may well be the last month there will be any railroad or industrial tonnage that is not allocated. Foundries appear to be in fairly good shape, but the demand for cast material is terrific.

BOSTON—Scrap moved steadily in a fairly good local market. Unstripped motor blocks again sold at $38 to $39 with the ceiling price $43. The feeling here is that the government in setting ceiling prices was off-base on this item. Mills in the Midwest can now buy the same grade closer to home at a lower price when freight is added.

BUFFALO—Scrap shipments improved but mills were still short. Better weather aided dealers' yard activities. New business was reported in cast at ceiling levels. Dealers were mostly satisfied with fixed prices but complained against the 83¢ switching charge here.

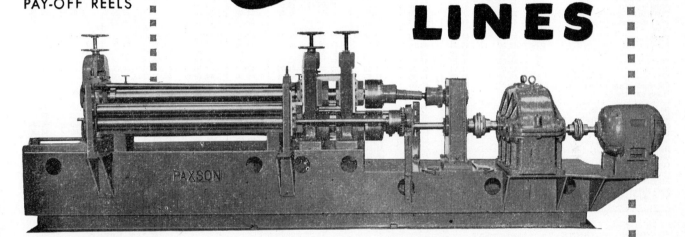

Iron and Steel SCRAP PRICES

(Maximum basing point prices, per gross ton, as set by OPS, effective Feb. 7, 1951. Shipping point and delivered prices calculated as shown below.)

Switching Charge (Dollars per gross ton) → Basing Points →	Pittsburgh $0.99 / Johnstown .75 / Brackenridge .53 / Butler .65 / Midland .75 / Monessen .51 / Sharon .75	Youngstown .75 / Canton .51 / Steubenville .51 / Warren .75 / Weirton .70	Cleveland .76 / Buffalo .83 / Cincinnati .65 / Middletown .26	Chicago 1.34 / Claymont .79 / Coatesville .50 / Conshohocken .20 / Harrisburg .51 / Phoenixville .51	Sparrows Pt. .20 / Bethlehem .52 / Ashland, Ky. .47 / Kokomo, Ind. .51 / Portsmouth, O. .51	St. Louis .51	Detroit .95 / Duluth .50	Kansas City .78	Birmingham .50 / Alabama City .43 / Atlanta .51	Minnequa .33	Houston .57	Los Angeles .66 / Pittsburg, Cal. .65 / Portland, Ore. .52 / San Francisco .66 / Seattle .59
GRADES												
No. 1 heavy melting	$44.00	$44.00	$43.00	$42.50	$42.00	$41.00	$40.00	$39.50	$39.00	$38.00	$37.00	$35.00
No. 2 heavy melting	42.00	42.00	41.00	40.50	40.00	39.00	38.00	37.50	37.00	36.00	35.00	33.00
No. 1 busheling	44.00	44.00	43.00	42.50	42.00	41.00	40.00	39.50	39.00	38.00	37.00	35.00
No. 1 bundles	44.00	44.00	43.00	42.50	42.00	41.00	40.00	39.50	39.00	38.00	37.00	35.00
No. 2 bundles	41.00	41.00	40.00	39.50	39.00	38.00	37.00	36.50	36.00	35.00	34.00	32.00
Machine shop turnings	34.00	34.00	33.00	32.50	32.00	31.00	30.00	29.50	29.00	28.00	27.00	25.00
Mixed borings and turnings	38.00	38.00	37.00	36.50	36.00	35.00	34.00	33.50	33.00	32.00	31.00	29.00
Shoveling turnings	38.00	38.00	37.00	36.50	36.00	35.00	34.00	33.50	33.00	32.00	31.00	29.00
Cast iron borings	38.00	38.00	37.00	36.50	36.00	35.00	34.00	33.50	33.00	32.00	31.00	29.00
No. 1 chemical borings	41.00	41.00	40.00	39.50	39.00	38.00	37.00	36.50	36.00	35.00	34.00	32.00
Forge crops	51.50	51.50	50.50	50.00	49.50	48.50	47.50	47.00	46.50	45.50	44.50	42.50
Bar crops and plate	49.00	49.00	48.00	47.50	47.00	46.00	45.00	44.50	44.00	43.00	42.00	40.00
Punchings and plate	46.50	46.50	45.50	45.00	44.50	43.50	42.50	42.00	41.50	40.50	39.50	37.50
Electric furnace bundles	46.00	46.00	45.00	44.50	44.00	43.00	42.00	41.50	41.00	40.00	39.00	37.00
Cut struct., plate, 3 ft and less	47.00	47.00	46.00	45.50	45.00	44.00	43.00	42.50	42.00	41.00	40.00	38.00
Cut struct., plate, 2 ft and less	49.00	49.00	48.00	47.50	47.00	46.00	45.00	44.50	44.00	43.00	42.00	40.00
Cut struct., plate, 1 ft and less	50.00	50.00	49.00	48.50	48.00	47.00	46.00	45.50	45.00	44.00	43.00	41.00
Heavy turnings	43.00	43.00	42.00	41.50	41.00	40.00	39.00	38.50	38.00	37.00	36.00	34.00
No. 1 RR heavy melting	46.00	46.00	45.00	44.50	44.00	43.00	42.00	41.50	41.00	40.00	39.00	37.00
Scrap rails, random lengths	48.00	48.00	47.00	46.50	46.00	45.00	44.00	43.50	43.00	42.00	41.00	39.00
Scrap rails, 3 ft and less	51.00	51.00	50.00	49.50	49.00	48.00	47.00	46.50	46.00	45.00	44.00	42.00
Scrap rails, 2 ft and less	52.00	52.00	51.00	50.50	50.00	49.00	48.00	47.50	47.00	46.00	45.00	43.00
Scrap rails, 18 in. and less	54.00	54.00	53.00	52.50	52.00	51.00	50.00	49.50	49.00	48.00	47.00	45.00
Rerolling rails	53.00	53.00	52.00	51.50	51.00	50.00	49.00	48.50	48.00	47.00	46.00	44.00
Uncut tires	48.00	48.00	47.00	46.50	46.00	45.00	44.00	43.50	43.00	42.00	41.00	39.00
Cut tires	51.00	51.00	50.00	49.50	49.00	48.00	47.00	46.50	46.00	45.00	44.00	40.00
Cut bolsters and side frames	49.00	49.00	48.00	47.50	47.00	46.00	45.00	44.50	44.00	43.00	42.00	40.00
RR specialties	51.00	51.00	50.00	49.50	49.00	48.00	47.00	46.50	46.00	45.00	44.00	42.00
Solid steel axles	58.00	58.00	57.00	56.50	56.00	55.00	54.00	53.50	53.00	52.00	51.00	49.00
No. 3 steel wheels	51.00	51.00	50.00	49.50	49.00	48.00	47.00	46.50	46.00	45.00	44.00	42.00

SWITCHING DISTRICTS—These basing points include the indicated switching districts: Pittsburgh; Bessemer, Homestead, Duquesne, Munhall. Cincinnati; Newport. St. Louis; Granite City, East St. Louis, Madison. San Francisco; South San Francisco, Niles, Oakland. Claymont; Chester. Chicago; Gary. Los Angeles; Firestone.

SHIPPING POINT PRICES (Except RR scrap) —For shipping points within basing points, the ceiling shipping point price is the basing point price, less switching charge. The ceiling for shipping points outside basing points is the basing point price yielding the highest shipping point price, less the lowest established freight charge. Dock charge, where applicable, is $1.25 per gross ton except: Memphis, 95¢; Great Lakes ports, $1.50, and New England ports, $1.75. Maximum shipping point price on No. 1 heavy melting steel in New York City is $36.99 per gross ton with set differentials for other grades. Hudson and Bergen County, N. J., shipping point prices are computed from Bethlehem basing point. All New Jersey computations use all-rail transport. Ceiling need not fall below $32 per gross ton for No. 1 heavy melting steel, with set differentials for other grades. Cast scrap shipping point prices are given in table.

DELIVERED PRICES (Except RR scrap)—Ceiling is the shipping point price plus actual freight charge, tax included. Dock charges, where applicable, are as above.

DELIVERED PRICES (RR scrap) — Ceiling on-line price of a RR operating in a basing point is the top in the highest priced basing point in which the RR operates. For off-line prices, RR's not operating in basing point, non-operating RR's, and RR scrap sold by someone other than a RR see text of order, THE IRON AGE, Feb. 8, 1951, p. 137-C.

UNPREPARED SCRAP—Ceiling price is $8 a ton less than prepared base grades (No. 1 heavy & No. 1 RR heavy). Scrap suitable for compressing into No. 1 bundles is $6 less than No. 1 bundles; suitable for compressing into

No. 2 bundles, $8 less than No. 2 bundles. For cast material requiring special preparation, price is breakable cast less preparation costs.

COMMISSIONS—Brokers are permitted a maximum of $1 per gross ton commission which must be separate on the bill.

ALLOY PREMIUMS—Alloy extras are permitted on: nickel, molybdenum, manganese, silicon, and chromium. Quantities and charges may be found in the order, THE IRON AGE, Feb. 8, 1951, p. 137-D.

RESTRICTIONS ON USE—Ceiling prices on some scrap items may fluctuate with use by consumers. If some scrap is purchased for its established specialized use, the ceiling price set in the order stands. But if some special grades are purchased for other uses, the ceiling price charge shall be the price of the scrap grade being substituted. For example, the price established for Grade 28 (wrought iron) may be charged only when sold to a producer of wrought iron. Otherwise the ceiling price shall not exceed the ceiling price for the corresponding grade of basic openhearth. Restrictions on use are placed on the following grades: Chemical borings, wrought iron, rerolling rails, cupola cast, clean auto cast, and malleable. Ceiling prices on billet bloom and forge crops, alloy-free turnings, and heavy turnings may be charged only when shipped directly from industrial producer. NPA prohibits openhearth users from buying electric furnace grades, Nos. 11 through 18.

CEILING DELIVERED PRICES FOR TRUCK SHIPMENT OF ALL STEEL OR CAST IRON SCRAP—If delivery is made by truck public carrier, ceiling delivered price shall be the ceiling shipping point price (or in the case of railroad scrap, the pertinent ceiling on-line price) plus the actual public carrier charge. Scrap delivered by shipper or broker trucks shall have a ceiling delivered price consisting of the ceiling shipping point price (or railroad ceiling on-line price) plus the established rail carload freight rate for shipping scrap from the rail siding nearest the point of delivery. Transportation charges for delivery in a shipper or broker truck shall not exceed $4 and need not fall below $2.50.

Cast Scrap

(F.o.b. all shipping points)

Cupola cast	$49.00
Charging box cast	47.00
Heavy breakable cast	45.00
Cast iron brake shoes	41.00
Stove plate	46.00
Clean auto cast	52.00
Unstripped motor blocks	43.00
Cast iron carwheels	47.00
Malleable	55.00
Drop broken machinery cast	52.00

Boston, unstripped motor blocks....$38 to $39

CEILING SHIPPING POINT, CEILING ON-LINE PRICES FOR ALL CAST IRON SCRAP—The above table shows blanket ceiling prices per gross ton for all cast iron scrap, f.o.b. shipping points.

CEILING DELIVERED PRICES—The ceiling delivered price for shipment by rail, vessel, or both of dealer and industrial cast iron scrap shall be the shipping point price plus the actual transportation charges to the point of delivery. Public dock charges may be added to actual transportation charges. Where dock facilities are owned or controlled by the shipper, certain fixed charges apply. (See steel scrap footnote.)

CEILING DELIVERED PRICES FOR TRUCK SHIPMENT OF ALL STEEL OR CAST IRON SCRAP—(See steel scrap footnote).

RESTRICTIONS ON USE—(See steel scrap footnote).

CEILING INTRANSIT PREPARATION CHARGES (Dollars per gross ton)

No. 1 heavy; No. 2 heavy; No. 1 RR heavy; No. 2 RR heavy; No. 1 busheling; No. 2 bundles; electric furnace bundles ..$ 8.00
No. 1 bundles; briquetted turnings or cast iron borings; No. 1 RR sheet scrap...... 6.00
Crushing machine shop turnings........ 3.00
Bar crops and plate; punchings and plate; structural and plate, 1 ft & less, and 3 ft and less; foundry steel, 1 ft & less and 2 ft & less; wrought iron...... 10.00
Rails, 3 ft & less; cut tires; cut bolsters & side frames 4.00
Rails, 2 ft & less 5.00
Rails, 18 in. & less 7.00

SCRAP *at your Service!*

The facilities and experienced personnel in each of our offices, stand ready to supply your every scrap requirement whenever and wherever needed.

LURIA BROTHERS AND COMPANY, INC.

CONSULT OUR NEAREST OFFICE FOR THE PURCHASE AND SALE OF SCRAP

PLANTS	MAIN OFFICE		OFFICES		
LEBANON, PENNA.	LINCOLN-LIBERTY BLDG.	BIRMINGHAM, ALA.	CHICAGO, ILLINOIS	HOUSTON, TEXAS	PITTSBURGH, PA.
READING, PENNA.	Philadelphia 7, Penna.	Empire Building	100 W. Monroe St.	1114 Texas Av. Bldg.	Oliver Building
DETROIT (ECORSE), MICHIGAN		BOSTON, MASS.	CLEVELAND, OHIO	LEBANON, PENNA.	PUEBLO, COLORADO
MODENA, PENNA.		Statler Building	1022 Midland Bldg.	Luria Building	334 Colorado Bldg.
PITTSBURGH, PENNA.		BUFFALO, N. Y.	DETROIT, MICHIGAN	NEW YORK, N. Y.	READING, PENNA.
ERIE, PENNA.		Genesee Building	2011 Book Building	100 Park Avenue	Luria Building
		ST. LOUIS, MISSOURI		SAN FRANCISCO, CALIFORNIA	
		2110 Railway Exchange Bldg.		Pacific Gas & Elec. Co., Bldg.	

LEADERS IN IRON AND STEEL SCRAP SINCE 1889

Comparison of Prices

Steel prices in this page are the average of various f.o.b. quotations of major producing areas: Pittsburgh, Chicago, Gary, Cleveland, Youngstown.

Price advances over previous week are printed in Heavy Type; declines appear in *Italics*

Flat-Rolled Steel:

(cents per pound)	Feb. 20 1951	Feb. 13 1951	Jan. 23 1951	Feb. 21 1950
Hot-rolled sheets	3.60	3.60	3.60	3.35
Cold-rolled sheets	4.35	4.35	4.35	4.10
Galvanized sheets (10 ga)	4.80	4.80	4.80	4.40
Hot-rolled strip	3.50	3.50	3.50	3.25
Cold-rolled strip	4.75	4.75	4.75	4.21
Plate	3.70	3.70	3.70	3.50
Plates wrought iron.....	7.85	7.85	7.85	7.85
Stains C-R-strip (No. 302)	36.50	36.50	36.50	33.00

Tin and Terneplate:

(dollars per base box)				
Tinplate (1.50 lb) cokes.	$7.50	$7.50	$7.50	$7.50
Tinplate, electro (0.50 lb)	6.60	6.60	6.60	6.60
Special coated mfg. ternes	6.35	6.35	6.35	6.50

Bars and Shapes:

(cents per pound)				
Merchant bars	3.70	3.70	3.70	3.45
Cold finished bars.......	4.55	4.55	4.55	*4.145
Alloy bars	4.30	4.30	4.30	3.95
Structural shapes	3.65	3.65	3.65	3.40
Stainless bars (No. 302).	31.25	31.25	31.25	28.50
Wrought iron bars......	9.50	9.50	9.50	9.50

Wire:

(cents per pound)				
Bright wire	4.85	4.85	4.85	4.50

Rails:

(dollars per 100 lb)				
Heavy rails	$3.60	$3.60	$3.60	$3.40
Light rails	4.00	4.00	4.00	3.75

Semifinished Steel:

(dollars per net ton)				
Rerolling billets	$56.00	$56.00	$56.00	$54.00
Slabs, rerolling	56.00	56.00	56.00	54.00
Forging billets	66.00	66.00	66.00	63.00
Alloy blooms billets, slabs	70.00	70.00	70.00	66.00

Wire Rod and Skelp:

(cents per pound)				
Wire rods	4.10	4.10	4.10	3.85
Skelp	3.35	3.35	3.35	3.15

Pig Iron:

(per gross ton)	Feb. 20 1951	Feb. 13 1951	Jan. 23 1951	Feb. 21 1950
No. 2 foundry, del'd Phila.	$57.77	$57.77	$57.77	$50.42
No. 2, Valley furnace....	52.50	52.50	52.50	46.50
No. 2, Southern Cin'ti....	55.58	55.58	55.58	49.08
No. 2, Birmingham......	48.88	48.88	48.88	42.38
No. 2, foundry, Chicago†	52.50	52.50	52.50	46.50
Basic del'd Philadelphia..	56.92	56.92	56.92	49.92
Basic, Valley furnace....	52.00	52.00	52.00	46.00
Malleable, Chicago†	52.50	52.50	52.50	46.50
Malleable, Valley	52.50	52.50	52.50	46.50
Charcoal, Chicago	70.56	70.56	70.56	68.56
Ferromanganese‡	186.25	186.25	186.25	173.40

†The switching charge for delivery to foundries in the Chicago district is $1 per ton.
‡Average of U. S. prices quoted on Ferroalloy page.

Scrap:

(per gross ton)				
Heavy melt'g steel, P'gh..	$44.00*	$44.00*	$46.13	$31.75
Heavy melt'g steel, Phila.	42.50*	42.50*	47.50	23.00
Heavy melt'g steel, Ch'go	42.50*	42.50*	44.63	27.50
No. 1 hy. com. sh't, Det.	40.00*	40.00*	40.25	22.50
Low phos. Young'n	46.50*	46.50*	54.50	32.75
No. 1 cast, Pittsburgh...	49.00†	49.00†	67.75	37.50
No. 1 cast, Philadelphia..	49.00†	49.00†	62.50	35.50
No. 1 cast, Chicago......	49.00†	49.00†	63.00	39.50

*Basing Pt. †Shipping Pt.
Not including broker's fee after Feb. 7, 1951.

Coke: Connellsville:

(per net ton at oven)				
Furnace coke, prompt...	$14.25	$14.25	$14.25	$14.00
Foundry coke, prompt...	17.25	17.25	17.25	15.75

Nonferrous Metals:

(cents per pound to large buyers)				
Copper, electro, Conn....	24.50	24.50	24.50	18.50
Copper, Lake, Conn.....	24.625	24.625	24.625	18.625
Tin, Straits, New York..	$1.83†	$1.83*	$1.78	74.50
Zinc, East St. Louis.....	17.50	17.50	17.50	9.75
Lead, St. Louis..........	16.80	16.80	16.80	11.80
Aluminum, virgin	19.00	19.00	19.00	17.00
Nickel, electrolytic	53.55	53.55	53.55	42.97
Magnesium, ingot	24.50	24.50	24.50	20.50
Antimony, Laredo, Tex...	42.00	42.00	42.00	27.25

†Tentative. *Revised.

Composite Prices

Starting with the issue of May 12, 1949, the weighted finished steel composite was revised for the years 1941 to date. The weights used are based on the average product shipments for the 7 years 1937 to 1940 inclusive and 1946 to 1948 inclusive. The use of quarterly figures has been eliminated because it was too sensitive. (See p. 130 of May 12, 1949, issue.)

	Finished Steel Base Price	Pig Iron	Scrap Steel
Feb. 20, 1951	4.131¢ per lb	$52.69 per gross ton	$43.00 per gross ton
One week ago	4.131¢ per lb	52.69 per gross ton	43.00 per gross ton
One month ago	4.131¢ per lb	52.69 per gross ton	46.08 per gross ton
One year ago	3.837¢ per lb	46.38 per gross ton	27.42 per gross ton

	High		Low		High		Low		High		Low	
1951....	4.131¢	Jan. 2	4.131¢	Jan. 2	$52.69	Jan. 2	$52.69	Jan. 2	$47.75	Jan. 30	$43.00	Feb. 7
1950....	4.131¢	Dec. 1	3.837¢	Jan. 3	52.69	Dec. 12	45.88	Jan. 3	45.13	Dec. 19	26.25	Jan. 3
1949....	3.837¢	Dec. 27	3.3705¢	May 3	46.87	Jan. 18	45.88	Sept. 6	43.00	Jan. 4	19.33	June 28
1948....	3.721¢	July 27	3.193¢	Jan. 1	46.91	Oct. 12	39.58	Jan. 6	43.16	July 27	39.75	Mar. 9
1947....	3.193¢	July 29	2.848¢	Jan. 1	37.98	Dec. 30	30.14	Jan. 7	42.58	Oct. 28	29.50	May 20
1946....	2.848¢	Dec. 31	2.464¢	Jan. 1	30.14	Dec. 10	25.37	Jan. 1	31.17	Dec. 24	19.17	Jan. 1
1945....	2.464¢	May 29	2.396¢	Jan. 1	25.37	Oct. 23	23.61	Jan. 2	19.17	Jan. 2	18.92	May 22
1944....		2.396¢		2.396¢		$23.61		$23.61		$19.17	Jan. 11	15.76	Oct. 24
1943....		2.396¢		2.396¢		23.61		23.61		$19.17		$19.17	
1942....		2.396¢		2.396¢		23.61		23.61		19.17		19.17	
1941....		2.396¢		2.396¢	$23.61	Mar. 20	$23.45	Jan. 2	$22.00	Jan. 7	$19.17	Apr. 10
1940....	2.30467¢	Jan. 2	2.24107¢	Apr. 16	23.45	Dec. 23	22.61	Jan. 2	21.83	Dec. 30	16.04	Apr. 9
1939....	2.35367¢	Jan. 3	2.26689¢	May 16	22.61	Sept. 19	20.61	Sept. 12	22.50	Oct. 3	14.08	May 16
1838....	2.58414¢	Jan. 4	2.27207¢	Oct. 18	23.25	June 21	19.61	July 6	15.00	Nov. 22	11.00	June 7
1937....	2.58414¢	Mar. 9	2.32263¢	Jan. 4	32.25	Mar. 9	20.25	Feb. 16	21.92	Mar. 30	12.67	June 9
1936....	2.32263¢	Dec. 28	2.05200¢	Mar. 10	19.74	Nov. 24	18.73	Aug. 11	17.75	Dec. 21	12.67	June 8
1932....	1.89196¢	July 5	1.83910¢	Mar. 1	14.81	Jan. 5	13.56	Dec. 6	8.50	Jan. 12	6.43	July 5
1929....	2.31773¢	May 28	2.26498¢	Oct. 29	18.71	May 14	18.21	Dec. 17	17.58	Jan. 29	14.08	Dec. 8

Weighted index based on steel bars, shapes, plates, wire, rails, black pipe, hot and cold-rolled sheets and strips, representing major portion of finished steel shipment. Index recapitulated in Aug. 28, 1941, issue and in May 12, 1949.

Based on averages for basic iron at Valley furnaces and foundry iron at Chicago, Philadelphia, Buffalo, Valley and Birmingham.

Average of No. 1 heavy melting steel scrap delivered to consumers at Pittsburgh, Philadelphia and Chicago.

IRON AGE
STEEL PRICES

Smaller numbers in price boxes indicate producing companies. For main office locations, see key on facing page.
Base prices at producing points apply only to sizes and grades produced in these areas. Prices are in cents per lb unless otherwise noted. Extras apply.

	Pittsburgh	Chicago	Gary	Cleveland	Canton Massillon	Middletown	Youngstown	Bethlehem	Buffalo	Conshohocken	Johnstown	Sparrows Point	Granite City	Detroit
INGOTS Carbon forging, net ton	$52.00[1]													
Alloy, net ton	$54.00[1,17]													$54.00[31]
BILLETS, BLOOMS, SLABS Carbon, rerolling, net ton	$56.00[1,5]	$56.00[1]	$56.00[1]						$56.00[3]		$56.00[3]			
Carbon forging billets, net ton	$66.00[1,5]	$66.00[1,4]	$66.00[1]	$66.00[4]	$66.00[4]				$66.00[3,4]	$73.00[26]	$66.00[3]			$69.00[31]
Alloy, net ton	$70.00[1,17,6]	$70.00[1,4,6]	$70.00[1]		$70.00[4]			$70.00[3]	$70.00[3,4]	$77.00[26]	$70.00[3]			$73.00[31]
PIPE SKELP	3.35[1] 3.45[5]						3.35[1,4]							
WIRE RODS	4.10[2] 4.30[18]	4.10[2,4,33]	4.10[6]	4.10[2]			4.10[6]		4.10[85]		4.10[3]	4.20[3]		
SHEETS Hot-rolled (18 ga. & hvr.)	3.60[1,5,9,15] 3.75[28]	3.60[8,23]	3.60[1,6,8]	3.60[4,5]		3.60[7]	3.60[1,4,6] 4.00[13]		3.60[3]	4.00[26]		3.60[3]	4.30[22]	3.80[12] 4.40[47]
Cold-rolled	4.35[1,5,9,15] 5.35[63,7]		4.35[1,6,8]	4.35[4,5]		4.35[7]	4.35[4,6]		4.35[3]			4.35[3]	5.05[22]	4.55[12]
Galvanized (10 gage)	4.80[1,9,15]		4.80[1,8]		4.80[4]	4.80[7]	5.50[44] 6.00[64]					4.80[3]	5.50[22]	
Enameling (12 gage)	4.65[1]		4.65[1,8]	4.65[4]		4.65[7]	4.65[6]						5.35[22]	
Long terne (10 gage)	5.20[9,15]		5.20[1]			5.20[7]	6.00[64]							
Hi str. low alloy, h.r.	5.40[1,5] 5.75[9]	5.40[1]	5.40[1,8] 5.90[6]	5.40[4,5]			5.40[1,4,13] 5.90[6]		5.40[3]	5.65[26]		5.40[3]		5.95[12]
Hi str. low alloy, c.r.	6.55[1,5] 6.90[9]		6.55[1,8] 7.05[6]	6.55[4,5]			6.55[4] 7.05[6]		6.55[3]			6.55[3]		7.10[12]
Hi str. low alloy, galv.	7.20[1]											6.75[3]		
STRIP Hot-rolled	3.60[9], 4.00[41], 58, 3.75[28] 3.50[5,7]	3.50[66]	3.50[1,6,8]			3.50[7]	3.50[1,4,6] 4.00[13]		3.50[3,4]	3.90[26]	3.50[3]	3.50[3]		4.40[47] 3.80[12]
Cold-rolled	4.65[5,7,9] 5.00[28] 5.35[40,63,58]	4.90[8,66]	4.90[8]	4.65[2,5]		4.65[7]	4.65[4,6] 5.25[48,49] 5.35[13,40]		4.65[3]			4.65[3]		4.85[12] 5.45[47] 5.60[68,81]
Hi str. low alloy, h.r.	5.75[9]		5.50[1] 5.30[8], 5.80[6]				4.95[4], 5.50[1] 5.40[13] 5.80[6]		4.95[3]	5.55[26]		4.95[3]		5.95[12]
Hi str. low alloy, c.r.	7.20[9]		{6.55[2] {6.70[5]				{6.20[4], 6.55[13] {7.05[6]		6.40[3]			6.40[3]		
TINPLATE† Cokes, 1.25-lb base box (1.50 lb, add 25¢)	$8.45[1,5,9,15]		$8.45[1,6,8]				$8.45[4]					$8.55[3]		
Electrolytic 0.25, 0.50, 0.75 lb box	0.25 lb. base box, $7.15[1,4,5,8,9]; $7.25[3,11]; $7.35[22] 0.50 lb., add 25¢; 0.75 lb. add 65¢													
BLACKPLATE, 29 gage Holloware enameling	5.85[1] 6.15[15] 6.25[5]		5.85[1]				5.30[4]							
BARS Carbon steel	3.70[1,5] 3.85[9]	3.70[1,4,23]	3.70[1,4,6,8]	3.70[4]	3.70[4]		3.70[1,4,6]		3.70[3,4]		3.70[3]			3.85[31]
Reinforcing‡	3.70[1,5]	3.70[4]	3.70[1,6,8]	3.70[4]			3.70[1,4,6]		3.70[3,4]		3.70[3]	3.70[3]		
Cold-finished	4.55[2,4,5] 52,69,71	4.55[2,69,70] 23,73	4.55[4,74] 73	4.55[2]	4.55[4,82]		4.55[6,57]		4.60[70]					4.70[84]
Alloy, hot-rolled	4.30[1,17]	4.30[1,4,23]	4.30[1,6,8]		4.30[4]		4.30[1,6]	4.30[8]	4.30[3,4]		4.30[3]			4.45[31] 4.65[12]
Alloy, cold-drawn	5.40[17,52] 69,71,2	5.40[4,23,69] 70,73 5.45[2]	5.40[4,73] 74		5.40[4,82] 32		5.40[6,25,57]	5.40[8]	5.40[3]					5.55[84]
Hi str. low alloy, h.r.	5.55[1,5]		5.55[1,8] 6.05[6]	5.55[4]			5.55[1]	5.55[3]	5.55[3]			5.55[3]		
PLATE Carbon steel	3.70[1,5,15]	3.70[1]	3.70[1,6,8]	3.70[4] 4.00[9]			3.70[1,4] 3.95[13]		3.70[3]	4.15[26]	3.70[3]	3.70[3]		
Floor plates	[1]		4.75[8]	4.75[5]						4.75[26]				
Alloy	4.75[1]	4.75[1]	4.75[1]				5.20[13]			5.05[26]	4.75[3]	4.75[3]		
Hi str. low alloy	5.65[1,5]	5.65[1]	5.65[1,8]	5.65[4,5]			5.65[4] 5.70[13]			5.90[26]	5.65[3]	5.65[3]		
SHAPES, Structural	3.65[1,5] 3.90[9]	3.65[1,23]	3.65[1,8]					3.70[3]	3.70[3]		3.70[3]			
Hi str. low alloy	5.50[1,5]	5.50[1]	5.50[1,8]					5.50[3]	5.50[3]		5.50[3]			
MANUFACTURERS' WIRE Bright	4.85[2,5] 5.10[18]	4.85[2] 4,23,33		4.85[2]				Kokomo=5.80[30]			4.85[3]	4.95[3]	Duluth=4.85[2]	
PILING, Steel Sheet	4.45[1]	4.45[1]	4.45[8]						4.45[3]					

Smaller numbers indicate producing companies. See key at right.
Prices are in cents per lb unless otherwise noted.   Extras apply.

IRON AGE
STEEL PRICES

Kansas City	Houston	Birmingham	WEST COAST Seattle, San Francisco, Los Angeles, Fontana		STEEL PRICES
			F=$79.00[19]		**INGOTS** Carbon forging, net ton
	$62.00[83]		F=$80.00[19]		Alloy, net ton
		$56.00[11]	F=$75.00[19]		**BILLETS, BLOOMS, SLABS** Carbon, rerolling, net ton
	$74.00[83]	$66.00[11]	F=$85.00[19] SF, LA, S=$85.00[62]	Geneva=$66.00[16]	Carbon forging billets, net ton
	$78.00[83]		F=$89.00[19] LA=$90.00[62]		Alloy net ton
					PIPE SKELP
	4.50[83]	4.10[4,11]	SF=4.90[2], F=4.90[19] LA=4.90[24,62]	Worcester=4.40[2] Minnequa=4.35[14] Portsmouth=4.30[20]	**WIRE RODS**
		3.60[4,11]	SF, LA=4.30[24] F=4.55[19]	Niles=5.25[64], Geneva=3.70[16] Ashland=3.60[7]	**SHEETS** Hot-rolled (18 ga. & hvr.)
		4.35[11]	SF=5.30[24] F=5.30[19]		Cold-rolled
		4.80[4,11]	SF, LA=5.55[24]	Ashland=4.80[7] Kokomo=5.20[30]	Galvanized (10 gage)
				Ashland=4.65[7]	Enameling (12 gage)
					Long ternes (10 gage)
		5.40[11]	F=6.35[19]		Hi str. low alloy, h.r.
			F=7.50[19]		Hi str. low alloy, c.r.
					Hi str. low alloy, galv.
4.10[83]	4.90[83]	3.50[4,11]	SF, LA=4.25[24,62] F=4.75[19], S=4.50[62]	Atlanta=4.05[65] Minnequa=4.55[14] Ashland=3.50[7]	**STRIP** Hot-rolled
			F=6.30[19] LA=6.40[27]	New Haven=5.15[2], 5.85[68] Trenton=6.00[45]	Cold-rolled
		5.30[11]	F=6.20[19] SF, LA=6.05[62] S=6.30[62]		Hi str. low alloy, h.r.
			F=6.95[19]		Hi str. low alloy, c.r.
		$8.55[11]	SF=9.20[24]		**TINPLATE** Cokes, 1.25-lb base box (1.50 lb, add 25¢)
					Electrolytic 0.25, 0.50, 0.75 lb box
		6.35[11]			**BLACKPLATE, 29 gage** Hollowware enameling
4.30[83]	4.10[83]	3.70[4,11]	SF, LA=4.40[24]	Atlanta=4.25[65] Minnequa=4.15[14]	**BARS** Carbon steel
4.38[83]	4.10[83]	3.70[4,11]	SF, S=4.45[62] F=4.40[19], LA=4.40[62]	Atlanta=4.25[65] Minnequa=4.50[14]	Reinforcing‡
				Newark=5.00[69] Putnam=5.10[69] Hartford=5.10[4] Los Angeles=6.00[4]	Cold-finished
4.90[83]	4.70[83]		LA=5.35[62] F=5.35[19]		Alloy, hot-rolled
				Newark=5.75[69] Worcester=5.75[2] Hartford=5.85[4]	Alloy, cold-drawn
		5.55[11]	F=6.60[19]		Hi str. low alloy, h.r.
	4.10[83]	3.70[4,11]	F=4.30[19] S=4.60[62] Geneva=3.70[16]	Claymont=4.15[29] Coatesville=4.15[21] Minnequa=4.50[14]	**PLATE** Carbon steel
				Harrisburg=5.25[35]	Floor plates
			F=5.70[19] Geneva=5.65[16]	Coatesville=5.25[21] Claymont=4.85[29]	Alloy
		5.65[11]	F=6.25[19]		Hi str. low alloy
4.25[83]	4.05[83]	3.65[4,11]	SF=4.20[62] F=4.25[16] LA=4.25[24,62] S=4.30[62]	Geneva 3.65[16] Minnequa 4.10[14]	**SHAPES, Structural**
		50[11]	F=6.10[19]		Hi str. low alloy
5.45[83]	5.25[83]	4.85[4,11]	SF, LA=5.80[24]	Atlanta=5.10[65] Worcester=5.15[2] Minnequa=5.10[14] Portsmouth=5.25[20]	**MANUFACTURERS' WIRE** Bright

KEY TO STEEL PRODUCERS

1 U. S. Steel Co., Pittsburgh
2 American Steel & Wire Co., Cleveland
3 Bethlehem Steel Co., Bethlehem
4 Republic Steel Corp., Cleveland
5 Jones & Laughlin Steel Corp., Pittsburgh
6 Youngstown Sheet & Tube Co., Youngstown
7 Armco Steel Corp., Middletown, Ohio
8 Inland Steel Co., Chicago
9 Weirton Steel Co., Weirton, W. Va.
10 National Tube Co., Pittsburgh
11 Tennessee Coal, Iron & R. R. Co., Birmingham
12 Great Lakes Steel Corp., Detroit
13 Sharon Steel Corp., Sharon, Pa.
14 Colorado Fuel & Iron Corp., Denver
15 Wheeling Steel Corp., Wheeling, W. Va.
16 Geneva Steel Co., Salt Lake City
17 Crucible Steel Co. of America, New York
18 Pittsburgh Steel Co., Pittsburgh
19 Kaiser Steel Corp., Oakland, Calif.
20 Portsmouth Div., Detroit Steel Corp., Detroit
21 Lukens Steel Co., Coatesville, Pa.
22 Granite City Steel Co., Granite City, Ill.
23 Wisconsin Steel Co., South Chicago, Ill.
24 Columbia Steel Co., San Francisco
25 Copperweld Steel Co., Glassport, Pa.
26 Alan Wood Steel Co., Conshohocken, Pa.
27 Calif. Cold Rolled Steel Corp., Los Angeles
28 Allegheny Ludlum Steel Corp., Pittsburgh
29 Worth Steel Co., Claymont, Del.
30 Continental Steel Corp., Kokomo, Ind.
31 Rotary Electric Steel Co., Detroit
32 Laclede Steel Co., St. Louis
33 Northwestern Steel & Wire Co., Sterling, Ill.
34 Keystone Steel & Wire Co., Peoria, Ill.
35 Central Steel & Wire Co., Harrisburg, Pa.
36 Carpenter Steel Co., Reading, Pa.
37 Eastern Stainless Steel Corp., Baltimore
38 Washington Steel Corp., Washington, Pa.
39 Jessop Steel Co., Washington, Pa.
40 Blair Strip Steel Co., New Castle, Pa.
41 Superior Steel Corp., Carnegie, Pa.
42 Timken Steel & Tube Div., Canton, Ohio
43 Babcock & Wilcox Tube Co., Beaver Falls, Pa.
44 Reeves Steel & Mfg. Co., Dover, Ohio
45 John A. Roebling's Sons Co., Trenton, N. J.
46 Simonds Saw & Steel Co., Fitchburg, Mass.
47 McLouth Steel Corp., Detroit
48 Cold Metal Products Co., Youngstown
49 Thomas Steel Co., Warren, Ohio
50 Wilson Steel & Wire Co., Chicago
51 Sweet's Steel Co., Williamsport, Pa.
52 Superior Drawn Steel Co., Monaca, Pa.
53 Tremont Nail Co., Wareham, Mass.
54 Firth Sterling St. & Carbide Corp., McKeesport
55 Ingersoll Steel Div., Chicago
56 Phoenix Iron & Steel Co., Phoenixville, Pa.
57 Fitzsimons Steel Co., Youngstown
58 Stanley Works, New Britain, Conn.
59 Universal-Cyclops Steel Corp., Bridgeville, Pa.
60 American Cladmetals Co., Carnegie, Pa.
61 Cuyahoga Steel & Wire Co., Cleveland
62 Bethlehem Pacific Coast Steel Corp., San Fran.
63 Follansbee Steel Corp., Pittsburgh
64 Niles Rolling Mill Co., Niles, Ohio
65 Atlantic Steel Co., Atlanta
66 Acme Steel Co., Chicago
67 Joslyn Mfg. & Supply Co., Chicago
68 Detroit Steel Corp., Detroit
69 Wycoff Steel Co., Pittsburgh
70 Bliss & Laughlin, Inc., Harvey, Ill.
71 Columbia Steel & Shafting Co., Pittsburgh
72 Cumberland Steel Co., Cumberland, Md.
73 La Salle Steel Co., Chicago
74 Monarch Steel Co., Inc., Hammond, Ind.
75 Empire Steel Co., Mansfield, Ohio
76 Mahoning Valley Steel Co., Niles, Ohio
77 Oliver Iron & Steel Co., Pittsburgh
78 Pittsburgh Screw & Bolt Co., Pittsburgh
79 Standard Forging Corp., Chicago
80 Driver Harris Co., Harrison, N. J.
81 Detroit Tube & Steel Div., Detroit
82 Reliance Div., Eaton Mfg. Co., Massillon, Ohio
83 Sheffield Steel Corp., Kansas City
84 Plymouth Steel Co., Detroit
85 Wickwire Spencer Steel, Buffalo
86 Angell Nail and Chaplet, Cleveland
87 Mid-States Steel & Wire, Crawfordsville, Ind.
88 National Supply, Pittsburgh, Pa.
89 Wheatland Tube Co., Wheatland, Pa.
90 Mercer Tube & Mfg. Co., Sharon, Pa.
91 Woodward Iron Co., Woodward, Ala.
92 Sloss-Sheffield Steel & Iron Co., Birmingham
93 Hanna Furance Corp., Detroit
94 Interlake Iron Corp., Cleveland
95 Lone Star Steel Co., Dallas
96 Mystic Iron Works, Everett, Mass.
97 Jackson Iron & Steel Co., Jackson, O.
98 Globe Iron Co., Jackson, O.
99 Pittsburgh Coke & Chemical Co., Pittsburgh
100 Shenango Furnace Co., Pittsburgh
101 Tennessee Products & Chemical Corp., Nashville
102 Koppers Co., Inc., Granite City, Ill.
103 Page Steel & Wire Div., American Chain & Cable., Monessen, Pa.

STAINLESS STEELS

Base price, cents per lb, f.o.b. mill.

Product	301	302	303	304	316	321	347	410	416	430
Ingots, rerolling	14.25	15.00	16.50	16.00	24.25	19.75	21.50	12.75	14.75	13.00
Slabs, billets rerolling	18.50	19.75	21.75	20.75	31.75	26.00	28.25	16.50	20.00	16.75
Forg. discs, die blocks, rings	34.00	34.00	36.50	35.50	52.50	40.00	44.50	28.00	28.50	28.50
Billets, forging	26.25	26.25	28.25	27.50	41.00	31.00	34.75	21.50	22.00	22.00
Bars, wires, structurals	31.25	31.25	33.75	32.75	48.75	36.75	41.25	25.75	26.25	26.25
Plates	33.00	33.00	35.00	35.00	51.50	40.50	45.00	27.00	27.50	27.50
Sheets	41.00	41.00	43.00	43.00	56.50	49.00	53.50	36.50	37.00	39.00
Strip, hot-rolled	26.50	28.00	32.25	30.00	48.25	36.75	41.00	23.50	30.25	24.00
Strip, cold-rolled	34.00	36.50	40.00	38.50	58.50	48.00	52.00	30.50	37.00	31.00

STAINLESS STEEL PRODUCING POINTS—*Sheets:* Midland, Pa., 17; Bracken-ridge, Pa., 28; Butler, Pa., 7; McKeesport, Pa., 1; Washington, Pa., 38 (type 316 add 5¢), 39; Baltimore, 37; Middletown, Ohio, 7; Massillon, Ohio, 4; Gary, 1; Bridgeville, Pa., 59; New Castle, Ind., 55; Ft. Wayne, Ind., 67; Lockport, N. Y., 46.
Strip: Midland, Pa., 17; Cleveland, 2; Carnegie, Pa., 41; McKeesport, Pa., 54; Reading, Pa., 36; Washington, Pa., 38 (type 316 add 5¢); W. Leechburg, Pa., 28; Bridgeville, Pa., 59; Detroit, 47; Massillon, Canton, Ohio, 4; Middletown, Ohio, 7; Harrison, N. J., 80; Youngstown, 48; Lockport N. Y., 46; New Britain, Conn., 58; Sharon, Pa., 13; Butler, Pa., 1.
Bars: Baltimore, 7; Duquesne, Pa., 1; Munhall, Pa., 1; Reading, Pa., 36; Titusville, Pa., 59; Washington, Pa., 39; McKeesport, Pa., 54; Bridgeville, Pa., 59; Dunkirk, N. Y., 28; Massillon, Ohio, 4; Chicago, 1; Syracuse, N. Y., 17; Watervliet, N. Y., 28; Waukegan, Ill., 2; Lockport, N. Y., 46; Canton, Ohio, 42; Ft. Wayne, Ind., 67.
Wire: Waukegan, Ill., 2; Massillon, Ohio, 4; McKeesport, Pa., 54; Bridgeport, Conn., 44; Ft. Wayne, Ind., 67; Trenton, N. J., 45; Harrison, N. J., 80; Baltimore, 7; Dunkirk, 28; Monessen, 103.
Structurals: Baltimore, 7; Massillon, Ohio, 4; Chicago, 1, 67; Watervliet, N. Y., 28; Bridgeport, Conn., 44.
Plates: Brackenridge, Pa., 28 (type 416 add ½¢); Butler, Pa., 7; Chicago, 1; Mun-hall, Pa., 1; Midland, Pa., 17; New Castle, Ind., 55; Lockport, N. Y., 46; Middletown, 7; Washington, Pa., 39; Cleveland, Massillon, 4.
Forged discs, die blocks, rings: Pittsburgh, 1, 17; Syracuse, 17; Ferndale, Mich., 28.
Forging billets: Midland, Pa., 17; Baltimore, 7; Washington, Pa., 39; McKeesport, 54; Massillon, Canton, Ohio, 4; Watervliet, 28; Pittsburgh, Chicago, 1.

RAILS, TRACK SUPPLIES

F.o.b. Mill Cents Per Lb	No. 1 Std. Rails	Light Rails	Joint Bars	Track Spikes	Axles	Screw Spikes	Tie Plates	Track Bolts Untreated
Bessemer-1	3.60	4.00	4.70					
Chicago-4				6.15				
Ensley-11	3.60	4.00						
Fairfield-11		4.00	4.40			8.60	4.50	
Gary-1	3.60	4.00					4.50	
Ind. Harbor-8	3.60		4.70	6.15	5.25	8.60	4 50	
Johnstown-3		4.00			5.60	8.60		
Joliet-1		4.00	4.70					
Kansas City-83				6.40				
Lackawanna-3	3.60	4.00	4.70			8.60	4.50	
Lebanon-3				6.15				9.60
Minnequa-14	3.60	4.00	4.70	6.15		8.60	4.50	9.60
Pittsburgh-77						9.35		9.60
Pittsburgh-78								9.60
Pittsburgh-5				6.15				
Pittsburg-24								4.65
Seattle-62				6.10				4.35
Steelton-3	3.60		4.70				4.50	
Struthers-6				6.15				
Torrance-24								4.65
Youngstown-4				6.15				

Track Bolts, heat treated, to railroads, 9.85¢ per lb.

BOILER TUBES

Seamless steel, electric welded commer-cial boiler tubes, locomotive tubes, mini-mum wall, per 100 ft at mill, c.l. lots, cut lengths 10 to 24 ft.

OD in in.	gage BWG	Seamless H.R.	C.D.	Electric Weld H.R.	C.D.
2	13	$22.67	$26.66	$21.99	$25.86
2½	12	30.48	35.84	29.57	34.76
3	12	33.90	39.90	32.89	34.80
3½	11	42.37	49.89	41.10	48.39
4	10	52.60	61.88	51.03	60.02

Pittsburgh Steel add, H-R: 2 in., 62¢; 2½ in., 84¢; 3 in., 92¢; 3½ in., $1.17; 4 in., $1.45. Add, C-R: 2 in., 74¢; 2½ in., 99¢; 3 in., $1.10; 3½ in., $1.37; 4 in., $1.70.

FLUORSPAR

Washed gravel fluorspar, f.o.b. cars, Rosiclare, Ill. Base price, per ton net: Effective CaF₂ content:
70% or more $43.00
60% or less 40.00

MERCHANT WIRE PRODUCTS

F.o.b. Mill	Standard & Coated Nails Base Col.	Woven Wire Fence 9-15½ ga. Base Col.	Fence Posts Base Col.	Single Loop Bale Ties Base Col.	Twisted Barbless Wire Base Col.	Gal. Barbed Wire Base Col.	Merch. Wire Ann'l'd. ¢/lb.	Merch. Wire Gal. (1) ¢/lb.
Alabama City-4	118	126		123		136	5.70	5.95
Aliquippa, Pa.-5	118	132			136	140	5.70	6.15
Atlanta-65	121	133		126	126	143	5.95	6.40
Bartonville-34	118	130	140	123	143	143	5.95	6.15
Buffalo-85							4.85	
Cleveland-86	125							
Cleveland-2							5.70	6.15
Crawfordsville-87		132			145	145	5.95	6.40
Donora, Pa.-2	118	130		123		140	5.70	6.15
Duluth-12	118	130		123		140	5.70	6.15
Fairfield, Ala.-11	118	130		123		136	5.70	6.15
Houston-83	126	138				148	6.10	6.55
Johnstown, Pa.-3	118	130			140		5.70	6.15
Joliet, Ill.-2	118	130		123		140	5.70	6.15
Kokomo, Ind.-30	120	132		125	138	138	5.80	6.05
Los Angeles-62							6.65	
Kansas City-83	130	130	142	125		152	6.30	6.75
Minnequa-14	123	138	130	128	146	146	5.95	6.45
Monessen-18	124	135				145	5.95	6.40
Moline, Ill.-4			136					
Palmer-85								
Pittsburgh, Cal.-24		137	149		147	156	160 6.65	6.80
Portsmouth-20	124	137			147	147	6.10	6.60
Rankin, Pa.-2	118	130				140	5.70	6.15
So.Chicago,Ill.-4	118	126	140	123		136	5.70	5.95
S. San Fran.-14				147		160	6.65	7.10
Sparrows Pt.-3	120			125	142	142	5.80	6.25
Sterling, Ill.-33	118	130	140	123	140	140	5.70	6.15
Struthers, Ohio-6							5.70	6.15
Torrance,Cal.-24	138						6.65	
Worcester-2	124						6.00	6.45
Williamsport, Pa.-51		150						

Cut Nails, carloads, base, $6.75 per 100 lb. (less 20¢ to Jobbers) at Conshohocken, Pa., (26), Ware-ham, Mass. (53), Wheeling, W. Va., (15).
(1) Alabama City and So. Chicago do not include zinc extra.

CAST IRON WATER PIPE

Per Net Ton
6 to 24-in., del'd Chicago . $105.30 to $108.80
6 to 24-in., del'd N. Y. ... 108.50 to 109.50
6 to 24-in., Birmingham . 91.50 to 96.00
6-in. and larger, f.o.b. cars, San Francisco, Los Angeles, for all rail shipment; rail and water shipment less ....$102.50 to $113.00 Class "A" and gas pipe, $5 extra; 4-in. pipe is $5 a ton above 6-in.

PIPE AND TUBING

Base discounts, f.o.b. mills. Base price about $200 per net ton.

	BUTTWELD													SEAMLESS					
	½ In.		¾ In.		1 In.		1¼ In.		1½ In.		2 In.		2½-3 In.		2 In.		2½-3 In.		3½-4 In.
	Blk.	Gal.	Blk.	Gal.	Blk.	Gal.	Blk.	Gal.	Blk.	Gal.	Blk.	Gal.	Blk.	Gal.	Blk.	Gal.	Blk.	Gal.	Blk.	Gal.
STANDARD T. & C.																				
Sparrows Pt.-3	34.0	12.0	37.0	16.0	39.5	19.5	40.0	20.0	40.5	21.0	41.0	21.5	41.5	22.0						
Cleveland-4	36.0	14.0	39.0	18.0	41.5	21.5	42.0	22.0	42.5	23.0	43.0	23.5	43.5	24.0						
Oakland-19	25.0	3.0	28.0	7.0	30.5	10.5	31.0	11.0	31.5	12.0	32.0	12.5	32.5	13.0						
Pittsburgh-5	36.0	14.0	39.0	17.6	41.5	19.5	42.0	20.5	42.5	21.0	43.0	21.5	43.5	22.5	29.5	8.0	32.5	11.5	34.5	13.5
Pittsburgh-10	36.0	14.0	39.0	17.6	41.5	19.5	42.0	20.5	42.5	21.0	43.0	21.5	43.5	22.5	29.5	9.5	32.5	14.5	34.5	14.5
St. Louis-32	35.0	13.0	38.0	17.0	40.5	20.5	41.0	21.0	41.5	22.0	42.0	22.5	42.5	23.0						
Sharon-90	36.0	13.0	39.0	17.0	41.5	20.0	42.0	20.5	42.5	21.5	43.0	23.0	43.5	24.0						
Pittsburgh-88	36.0	14.0	39.0	18.0	41.5	21.5	42.0	22.0	42.5	23.0	43.0	23.5			32.5		34.5			
Wheeling-15	36.0	14.0	39.0	17.6	41.5	19.5	42.0	20.5	42.5	21.0	43.0	21.5	43.5	22.5						
Wheatland-89	36.0	14.0	39.0	17.6	41.5	19.5	42.0	20.5	42.5	21.0	43.0	21.5	43.5	22.5						
Youngstown-6	36.0	14.0	39.0	18.0	41.5	21.5	42.0	22.0	42.5	24.0	43.0	24.5	43.5	25.0	29.5	9.5	32.5	14.5	34.5	14.5
EXTRA STRONG, PLAIN ENDS																				
Sparrows Pt.-3	33.5	13.0	37.5	17.0	39.5	20.5	40.0	21.0	40.5	22.0	41.0	22.5	41.5	23.0						
Cleveland-4	35.5	15.0	39.5	19.0	41.5	22.5	42.0	23.0	42.5	24.0	43.0	24.5	43.5	25.0						
Oakland-19	24.5	4.0	28.5	8.0	30.5	11.5	31.0	12.0	31.5	13.0	32.0	13.5	32.5	14.0						
Pittsburgh-5	35.5	13.5	39.5	17.5	41.5	19.5	42.0	20.5	42.5	21.0	43.0	21.5	43.5	22.5	29.0	7.5	33.0	12.0	36.0	15.5
Pittsburgh-10	35.5	15.0	39.5	19.0	41.5	22.5	42.0	23.0	42.5	24.0	43.0	24.5	43.5	25.0	29.0	10.0	33.0	14.0	36.5	17.5
St. Louis-32	34.5	14.0	38.0	18.0	40.5	21.5	41.0	22.0	41.5	23.0	42.0	23.5	42.5	24.0						
Sharon-90	35.5	14.0	39.5	18.0	41.5	21.0	42.0	21.5	42.5	22.5	43.0	23.0	43.5	24.0						
Pittsburgh-88	35.5	15.0	39.5	19.0	41.5	22.5	42.0	23.0	42.5	24.0	43.0	24.5			33.0		36.5			
Wheeling-15	35.5	15.0	39.5	19.0	41.5	22.5	42.0	23.0	42.5	24.0	43.0	24.5	43.5	25.0						
Wheatland-89	35.5	13.5	39.5	17.5	41.5	21.5	42.0	22.5	42.5	24.0	43.0	24.5	43.5	25.0						
Youngstown-6	35.5	15.0	39.5	19.0	41.5	22.5	42.0	23.0	42.5	24.0	43.0	24.5	43.5	25.0	29.0	10.0	33.0	14.0	36.5	17.5

Galvanized discounts based on zinc at 17¢ per lb, East St. Louis. For each 1¢ change in zinc, discounts vary as follows: ½ in., ¾ in., and 1 in., 1 pt.; 1¼ in., 1½ in., 2 in., ¾ pt.; 2½ in., 3 in., ½ pt. Calculate discounts on even cents per lb of zinc, i.e., if zinc is 16.51¢ to 17.50¢ per lb, use 17¢. Jones & Laughlin discounts apply only when zinc price changes 1¢. Threads only, buttweld and seamless, 1 pt. higher discount. Plain ends, buttweld and seamless, 3 in. and under, 3½ pts. higher discount. Buttweld jobbers' discount, 5 pct.

WAREHOUSES

Base price, f.o.b., dollars per 100 lb. *(Metropolitan area delivery, add 20¢ except Birmingham, San Francisco, Cincinnati, New Orleans, St. Paul, add 15¢; Memphis, add 10¢; Philadelphia, add 25¢; New York, add 30¢).

Cities	Sheets Hot-Rolled	Sheets Cold-Rolled (15 gage)	Sheets Galvanized (10 gage)	Strip Hot-Rolled	Strip Cold-Rolled	Plates Standard	Shapes Structural	Bars Hot-Rolled	Bars Cold-Finished	Alloy Bars Hot-Rolled A 4615 As rolled	Alloy Bars Hot-Rolled A 4140 Annealed	Alloy Bars Cold-Drawn A 4615 As rolled	Alloy Bars Cold-Drawn A 4140 Annealed
Baltimore	5.60	6.84	7.49²–8.07	6.04		5.80	6.14	6.04	6.84–6.89	10.24	10.54	11.89	12.19
Birmingham*	5.60	6.40	6.75	5.55		5.95	5.70	5.55					
Boston	6.20	7.00–7.25	7.74–8.29	6.15	8.50⁴	6.48–6.78	6.20	6.05	6.79–6.84	10.25	10.55	11.90–12.00	12.20–12.30
Buffalo	5.60	6.40	7.74–8.09	5.86		6.05	5.80	5.60	6.40–6.45	10.15–10.85	10.45	11.80	11.95–12.10
Chicago	5.60	6.40	7.75	5.55		5.80	5.70	5.55	6.30	9.80	10.10	11.45	11.75
Cincinnati*	5.87	6.44	7.39	5.80		6.19	6.09	5.80	6.61	10.15	10.45	11.80	12.10
Cleveland	5.60	6.40	8.10	5.69	6.90	5.92	5.82	5.57	6.40	9.91	10.21	11.56	11.86
Detroit	5.78	6.53	7.89	5.94		5.99	6.09	5.84	6.56	10.11	10.41	11.76	12.06
Houston	7.00	8.25				6.85	6.50	6.65	9.35	10.35	11.25		12.75
Indianapolis, del'd	6.00	6.80	8.15	5.95		6.20	6.10	5.95	6.80				
Kansas City	6.00	6.80	7.45	6.15	7.50	6.40	6.30	6.15	7.00	10.40	10.70	12.05	12.35
Los Angeles	6.35	7.90	8.85	6.40	9.45⁶	6.40	6.35	6.35	8.20	11.30	11.30	13.20	13.50
Memphis*	6.33–6.38	7.08–7.18		6.33–6.38		6.43–8.02	6.33–6.33	6.08–6.33	7.16–7.32				
Milwaukee	5.74	6.54	7.89	5.69–6.59		5.94	5.84	5.69	6.44–6.54	9.94	10.24	11.59	11.89
New Orleans*	5.70	6.59		5.75	7.25	5.95	5.75	5.75	7.30				
New York*	5.67–5.97	7.19⁵–7.24¹	8.14²	6.29–6.89	8.63⁴	6.28–6.58	6.10	6.12	6.99	10.05–10.15	10.35–10.45	11.70–11.80	12.10–12.20
Norfolk	6.50³					6.50³	6.60³	6.55³					
Philadelphia*	5.90	6.80	8.00	6.10		6.05	5.90	6.05	6.86	9.90	10.20		
Pittsburgh	5.60	6.40	7.75	5.65–5.95		5.75	5.70	5.55	6.15	9.80	10.10	11.45	11.75
Portland	6.60–7.55	8.95	8.50–9.10	7.30		6.80	6.95	6.90			12.15		
Salt Lake City	7.95		9.70–10.50²	8.70–8.75		8.05	6.75–8.30	7.95–8.65	9.00				
San Francisco*	6.65	8.05²	8.55–8.90²	6.60	9.45⁶	6.50	6.45	6.45	8.20	11.30	11.30	13.20	13.20–13.50
Seattle	7.05	8.60	9.20	9.05		6.75	6.65	6.75	9.05				
St. Louis	5.80–5.85	6.65	8.00	5.80	8.00⁴–8.28	6.13	6.03	5.80	6.55–6.65	10.05	10.35	11.70	12.00
St. Paul*	6.16	6.96	8.31	6.11		6.36	6.26	6.11	6.96	10.36	10.66	12.01	12.31

BASE QUANTITIES (Standard unless otherwise keyed): Cold finished bars; 2000 lb or over. Alloy bars; 1000 to 1999 lb. All others; 2000 to 9999 lb. All HR products may be combined for quantity. All galvanized sheets may be combined for quantity. CR sheets may not be combined with each other or with galvanized sheets for quantity.
EXCEPTIONS: (¹) 400 to 1499 lb; (²) 450 to 1499 lb; (³) 400 to 1999 lb; (⁴) 6000 lb and over; (⁵) 1500 to 9999 lb.; (⁶) 2000 to 5999 lb.

PIG IRON

Dollars per gross ton, f.o.b., subject to switching charges.

Producing Point	Basic	No. 2 Foundry	Malleable	Bessemer	Low Phos.	Blast Furnace Silvery	Low Phos. Charcoal
Bethlehem-3	54.00	54.50	55.00	55.50			
Birmingham-4	48.38	48.88	48.88				
Birmingham-91	48.38	48.88	48.88				
Birmingham-92	48.38	48.88	48.88				
Buffalo-4	52.00	52.50	53.00				
Buffalo-93	52.00	52.50	53.00			63.75	
Chicago-94	52.00	52.50	52.50	53.00			
Cleveland-2	52.00	52.50	52.50	53.00	57.00		
Cleveland-4	52.00	52.50	52.50				
Daingerfield, Tex.-95	48.00	48.50	48.50				
Duluth-94	52.00	52.50	52.50	53.00			
Erie-94	52.00	52.50	52.50	53.00			
Everett, Mass.-96		53.25	53.75				
Fontana-19	58.00	58.50					
Geneva, Utah-16	52.00	52.50	52.50	53.00			
Granite City, Ill.-102	53.90	54.40	54.90				
Hubbard, O.-6	52.00	52.50	52.50				
Ironton, Utah-16	52.00	52.50					
Jackson, O.-97,98						62.50	
Lyle, Tenn.-101							66.00
Monessen-18	54.00						
Neville Island-99	52.00	52.50	52.50	53.00			
Pittsburgh-1	52.00			53.00			
Sharpsville-100	52.00	52.50	52.50	53.00			
Steelton-3	54.00	54.50	55.00	55.50	60.00		
Swedeland-26	56.00	56.50	57.00	57.50			
Toledo-94	52.00	52.50	52.50	53.00			
Troy, N. Y.-4	54.00	54.50	55.00		60.00		
Youngstown-6	52.00	52.50	52.50	53.00			

DIFFERENTIALS: Add 50¢ per ton for each 0.25 pct silicon over base (1.75 to 2.25 pct), 50¢ per ton for each 0.50 pct manganese over 1 pct, $2 per ton for 0.5 to 0.75 pct nickel, $1 for each additional 0.25 pct nickel. Subtract 38¢ per ton for phosphorus content over 0.70 pct. Silvery iron: Add $1.50 per ton for each 0.50 pct silicon over base (6.01 to 6.50 pct) up to 17 pct. $1 per ton for 0.75 pct or more phosphorus, manganese as above. Bessemer ferrosilicon prices are $1 over comparable silvery iron.

REFRACTORIES

Fire Clay Brick *(F.o.b. works)* Carloads, Per 1000
First quality, Ill., Ky., Md., Mo., Ohio, Pa. (except Salina, Pa., add $5) $94.60
No. 1 Ohio **88.00**
Sec. quality, Pa., Md., Ky., Mo., Ill. .. 88.00
No. 2 Ohio 79.20
Ground fire clay, net ton, bulk (except Salina, Pa., add $1.50) **13.75**

Silica Brick
Mt. Union, Pa., Ensley, Ala. $94.60
Childs, Pa. **99.00**
Hays, Pa. **100.10**
Chicago District **104.50**
Western Utah and Calif. **111.10**
Super Duty, Hays, Pa., Athens, Tex., Chicago **111.10**
Silica cement, net ton, bulk, Eastern (except Hays, Pa.) **16.50**
Silica cement, net ton, bulk, Hays, Pa. 18.70
Silica cement, net ton, bulk, Ensley, Ala. 17.60
Silica cement, net ton, bulk, Chicago District 17.60
Silica cement, net ton, bulk, Utah and Calif. 24.70

Chrome Brick Per Net Ton
Standard chemically bonded, Balt., Chester **$82.00**

Magnesite Brick
Standard, Baltimore **$104.00**
Chemically bonded, Baltimore ... **93.00**

Grain Magnesite St. ⅜-in. grains
Domestic, f.o.b. Baltimore, in bulk fines removed $62.70
Domestic, f.o.b. Chewelah, Wash., in bulk 36.30
in sacks 41.80

Dead Burned Dolomite
F.o.b. producing points in Pennsylvania, West Virginia and Ohio, per net ton, bulk Midwest, add 10¢; Missouri Valley, add 20¢....**$13.00**

COKE

Furnace, beehive (f.o.b. oven) Net Ton
Connellsville, Pa. .....$14.00 to $14.50
Foundry, beehive (f.o.b. oven) Connellsville, Pa. .....$17.00 to $17.50
Foundry, oven coke
Buffalo, del'd $26.69
Chicago, f.o.b. 23.00
Detroit, f.o.b. 24.00
New England, del'd 24.80
Seaboard, N. J., f.o.b. 22.00
Philadelphia, f.o.b. **22.70**
Swedeland, Pa., f.o.b. 22.60
Painesville, Ohio, f.o.b. .. 24.00
Erie, Pa., f.o.b. 23.50
Cleveland, del'd 25.72
Cincinnati, del'd **25.06**
St. Paul, f.o.b. 22.50
St. Louis 25.40
Birmingham, del'd 21.69
Neville Island 23.00

LAKE SUPERIOR ORES

(51.50% Fe; natural content, delivered lower lake ports)

Per gross ton
Old range, bessemer **$8.70**
Old range, nonbessemer **8.55**
Mesabi, bessemer 8.45
Mesabi, nonbessemer 8.30
High phosphorus 8.30

After adjustments for analyses, prices will be increased or decreased as the case may be for increases or decreases after Dec. 2, 1950, in lake vessel rates, upper lake rail freights, dock handling charges and taxes thereon.

C-R SPRING STEEL

Base per pound f.o.b. mill
0.26 to 0.40 carbon .... **5.35¢**
0.41 to 0.60 carbon .... **6.80¢**
0.61 to 0.80 carbon .... **7.40¢**
0.81 to 1.05 carbon .... **9.35¢**
1.06 to 1.35 carbon .... **11.65¢**
Worcester, add 0.30¢; Sharon, Carnegie, New Castle, add 0.35¢; Detroit, 0.26 to 0.40 carb., add 25¢; other grades add 15¢. New Haven, 0.26 to 0.40 carb., add 50¢; other grades add 5¢.

BOLTS, NUTS, RIVETS, SCREWS
Consumer Prices
(Base discount, f.o.b. mill, Pittsburgh, Cleveland, Birmingham or Chicago)

Machine and Carriage Bolts

	Pct Off List Less Case	C.
½ in. & smaller x 6 in. & shorter	15	28½
9/16 in. & ⅝ in. x 6 in. & shorter	18½	30½
¾ in. & larger x 6 in. & shorter	17½	29½
All diam. longer than 6 in.	14	27½
Lag, all diam. x 6 in. & shorter	23	35
Lag, all diam. longer than 6 in.	21	33
Plow bolts	34	....

Nuts, Hot Pressed, Cold Punched—Sq

	Pct Off List Less Keg (Reg.)	K.	Less Keg (Hvy.)	K.
½ in. & smaller	15	28½	1	28½
9/16 in. & ⅝ in.	12	25	6½	21
¾ in. to 1½ in. inclusive	9	23	1	16½
1⅝ in. & larger	7½	22	1	16½

Nuts, Hot Pressed—Hexagon

½ in. & smaller	26	37	22	34
9/16 in. & ⅝ in.	16½	29½	6½	21
¾ in. to 1½ in. inclusive	12	25	2	17½
1⅝ in. & larger	8½	23	2	17½

Nuts, Cold Punched—Hexagon

½ in. & smaller	26	37	22	34
9/16 in. & ⅝ in.	23	35	17½	30½
¾ in. to 1½ in. inclusive	19½	31½	12	25
1⅝ in. & larger	12	25	6½	21

Nuts, Semi-Finished—Hexagon

	Reg.		Hvy.	
½ in. & smaller	35	45	28½	39½
9/16 in. & ⅝ in.	29½	40½	22	34
¾ in. to 1½ in. inclusive	24	36	15	28½
1⅝ in. & larger	13	26	8½	23

Light

7/16 in. & smaller	35	45
½ in. thru ⅝ in.	28½	39½
¾ in. to 1½ in. inclusive	26	37

Stove Bolts
Pct Off List
Packaged, steel, plain finished 56—10
Packaged, plated finish...... 41—10
Bulk, plain finish**.......... 67*

*Discounts apply to bulk shipments in not less than 15,000 pieces of a size and kind where length is 3-in. and shorter; 5000 pieces for lengths longer than 3-in. For lesser quantities, packaged price applies.
**Zinc, Parkerized, cadmium or nickel plated finishes add 6¢ per lb net. For black oil finish, add 2¢ per lb net.

Rivets
Base per 100 lb.
½ in. & larger.................. $7.85
Pct Off List
7/16 in. & smaller................ 36
F.o.b. Pittsburgh, Cleveland, Chicago, Birmingham, Lebanon, Pa.

Cap and Set Screws
(In bulk)
Pct Off List
Hexagon head cap screws, coarse or fine thread, ¼ in. thru ⅝ in. x 6 in., SAE 1020, bright.......... 54
¾ in. thru 1 in. up to & including 6 in. 48
¼ in. thru ⅝ in. x 6 in. & shorter high C double heat treat.......... 46
¾ in. thru 1 in. up to & including 6 in. 41
Milled studs 35
Flat head cap screws, listed sizes.... 16
Fillister head cap, listed sizes...... 34
Set screws, sq head, cup point, 1 in. diam. and smaller x 6 in. & shorter 53

S. M. Ferrochrome
Contract price, cents per pound, chromium contained, lump size, delivered.
High carbon type: 60-65% Cr, 4-6% Si, 4-6% Mn, 4-6% C.
Carloads 21.60
Ton lots 23.75
Less ton lots 25.25
Low carbon type: 62-66% Cr, 4-6% Si, 4-6% Mn, 1.25% max. C.
Carloads 27.75
Ton lots 30.05
Less ton lots.................. 31.85

ELECTRODES
Cents per lb., f.o.b. plant, threaded electrodes with nipples, unboxed

Diam. in in.	Length in in.	Cents Per lb.
	GRAPHITE	
17, 18, 20	60, 72	17.85
8 to 16	48, 60, 72	17.85
7	48, 60	19.57
6	48, 60	20.95
4, 5	40	21.50
3	40	22.61
2½	24, 30	23.15
2	24, 30	25.36
	CARBON	
40	100, 110	8.03
35	65, 110	8.03
30	65, 84, 110	8.03
24	72 to 104	8.03
20	84, 90	8.03
17	60, 72	8.03
14	60, 72	8.57
10, 12	60	8.84
8	60	9.10

CLAD STEEL

Base prices, cents per pound, f.o.b. mill

	Plate	Sheet
Stainless-carbon No. 304, 20 pct,		
Coatesville, Pa. (21)..	*29.5	
Washg'tn. (39)..	*29.5	
Claymont, Del. (29)...	*28.00	
Conshohocken, Pa. (26)		*24.00
New Castle, Ind. (55).	*26.50	*25.50
Nickel-carbon 10 pct Coatesville (21)..	32.5	
Inconel-carbon 10 pct Coatesville (21)..	40.5	
Monel-carbon 10 pct Coatesville (21)..	33.5	
No. 302 Stainless-copper-stainless, Carnegie, Pa. (60)		77.00
Aluminized steel sheets, hot dip, Butler, Pa. (7).....		7.75

*Includes annealing and pickling, or sandblasting.

TOOL STEEL
F.o.b. mill

W	Cr	V	Mo	Co	Base per lb
18	4	1	—	—	$1.235
18	4	1	—	5	$1.86
18	4	2	—	—	$1.38
1.5	4	1.5	8	—	78.5¢
6	4	2	6	—	.87¢

High-carbon chromium .... 63.5¢
Oil hardened manganese........... 35¢
Special carbon .... 32.5¢
Extra carbon .... 27¢
Regular carbon .... 23¢

Warehouse prices on and east of Mississippi are 3¢ per lb higher. West of Mississippi, 5¢ higher.

METAL POWDERS

Per pound, f.o.b. shipping point, in ton lots, for minus 100 mesh.

Swedish sponge iron c.i.f. New York, ocean bags... 7.4¢ to 9.0¢
Canadian sponge iron, del'd, in East .... 10.00¢
Domestic sponge iron, 98+% Fe, carload lots .... 9.0¢ to 15.0¢
Electrolytic iron, annealed, 99.5+% Fe .... 36.0¢ to 39.5¢
Electrolytic iron unannealed, minus 325 mesh, 99+% Fe 48.5¢
Hydrogen reduced iron, minus 300 mesh, 98+% Fe.. 63.0¢ to 80.0¢
Carbonyl iron, size 5 to 10 micron, 98%, 99.8+% Fe 70.0¢ to $1.35
Aluminum .... 29.00¢
Brass, 10 ton lots ....30.00¢ to 33.25¢
Copper, electrolytic.10.25¢ plus metal value
Copper, reduced ...10.00¢ plus metal value
Cadmium, 100-199 lb..95¢ plus metal value
Chromium, electrolytic, 99% min., and quantity $3.50
Lead ....6.5¢ plus metal value
Manganese .... 52.00¢
Molybdenum, 99% 2.65
Nickel, unannealed .... 75.5¢
Nickel, annealed .... 81.5¢
Nickel, spherical, unannealed 78.5¢
Silicon .... 34.00¢
Solder powder..6.5¢ to 8.5¢ plus met. value
Stainless steel, 302 ... 75.00¢
Tin ....11.00¢ plus metal value
Tungsten, 99% $4.15
Zinc, 10 ton lots ......20.50¢ to 23.85¢

ELECTRICAL SHEETS
22 Ga. H-R cut lengths

F.o.b. Mill Cents Per Lb.	Armature	Elec.	Motor	Dynamo	Transf. 72	Transf. 65	Transf. 58
Beech Botton-15...		7.25	8.50	9.30	9.85	10.40	11.10
Brackenridge-28...		7.25	8.50	9.30	9.85		
Follansbee-63...	6.75	7.25	8.50	9.30	9.85	10.40	11.10
Granite City-22...		7.95	9.20				
Ind. Harbor-3...	6.75	7.25					
Mansfield-75...	7.25	7.75	9.00	9.80			
Niles, O.-64...	7.05	7.55					
Vandergrift-1...	6.75	7.25	8.50	9.30	9.85	10.40	11.10
Warren, O.-4...	6.75	7.25	8.50	9.30	9.85	10.40	11.10
Zanesville-7...	8.75	7.25	8.50	9.30	9.85	10.40	11.10

Transformer 52, 80¢ above Transformer 58.

Ferrochrome
Contract prices, cents per pound, contained Cr, lump size, bulk, in carloads, delivered. (65-72% Cr, 2% max. Si.)
0.06% C ... 30.50   0.20% C ... 29.50
0.10% C ... 30.00   0.50% C ... 29.25
0.15% C ... 29.75   1.00% C ... 29.00
2.00% C 28.75
65-69% Cr, 4-9% C 22.00
62-66% Cr, 4-6% C, 6-9% Si. 22.85

High-Nitrogen Ferrochrome
Low-carbon type: 67-72% Cr, 0.75% N. Add 6¢ per lb to regular low carbon ferrochrome price schedule. Add 5¢ for each additional 0.25% N.

Chromium Metal
Contract prices, per lb chromium contained, packed, delivered, ton lots. 97% min. Cr, 1% max. Fe.
0.20% Max. C. $1.09
0.50% max. C. 1.05
.00 min. C. 1.04

Low Carbon Ferrochrome Silicon
(Cr 34-41%, Si 42-49%, C 0.05% max.)
Contract price, carloads, f.o.b. Niagara Falls, freight allowed; lump 4-in. x down, bulk 2-in. x down, 21.75¢ per lb of contained Cr plus 12.00¢ per lb of contained Si.
Bulk 1-in. x down, 21.90¢ per lb contained Cr plus 12.20¢ per lb of contained Si.

Calcium-Silicon
Contract price per lb of alloy, dump, delivered.
30-33% Ca, 60-65% Si, 3.00% max. Fe.
Carloads 19.00
Ton lots 22.10
Less ton lots 23.00

Calcium-Manganese—Silicon
Contract prices, cents per lb of alloy, lump, delivered.
16-20% Ca, 14-18% Mn, 53-59% Si.
Carloads 20.00
Ton lots 22.30
Less ton lots 23.30

CMSZ
Contract price, cents per lb of alloy, delivered.
Alloy 4: 45-49% Cr, 4-6% Mn, 18-21% Si, 1.25-1.75% Zr, 3.00-4.5% C.
Alloy 5: 50.56% Cr, 4-6% Mn, 13.50-16.00% Si, 0.75 to 1.25% Zr, 3.50-5.00% C.
Ton lots 20.75
Less ton lots 22.00

V Foundry Alloy
Cents per pound of alloy, f.o.b. Suspension Bridge, N. Y., freight allowed, max. St. Louis. V-5: 38-42% Cr, 17-19% Si, 8-11% Mn.
Ton lots .... 16.50¢
Less ton lots .... 17.75¢

Graphidox No. 4
Cents per pound of alloy, f.o.b. Suspension Bridge, N. Y., freight allowed, max. St. Louis. Si 48 to 52%, Ti 9 to 11%, Ca 5 to 7%.
Carload packed .... 18.00¢
Ton lots to carload packed .... 19.00¢
Less ton lots .... 20.50¢

SMZ
Contract price, cents per pound of alloy, delivered, 60-65% Si, 5-7% Mn, 5-7% Zr, 20% Fe, ½ in. x 12 mesh.
Ton lots 17.25
Less ton lots 18.50

FERROALLOYS

Ferromanganese

78-82% Mn. maximum contract base price, gross ton, lump size.

F.o.b. Niagara Falls, Alloy, W. Va., Welland, Ont., Ashtabula, O.	$185
F.o.b. Johnstown, Pa.	$187
F.o.b. Sheridan, Pa.	$185
F.o.b. Etna, Clairton, Pa.	$188

$2.00 for each 1% above 82% Mn, penalty, $2.15 for each 1% below 78%.

Briquets—Cents per pound of briquet, delivered, 66% contained Mn.

Carload, bulk	10.95
Ton lots	12.55

Spiegeleisen

Contract prices gross ton, lump, f.o.b.

	16-19% Mn 3% max. Si	19-21% Mn 3% max. Si
Palmerton, Pa.	$74.00	$75.00
Pgh. or Chicago	74.00	75.00

Manganese Metal

Contract basis, 2 in. x down, cents per pound of metal, delivered.
96% min. Mn, 0.2% max. C, 1% max. Si, 2% max. Fe.

Carload, packed	29.75
Ton lots	31.25

Electrolytic Manganese

F.o.b. Knoxville, Tenn., freight allowed east of Mississippi, cents per pound.

Carloads	28
Ton lots	30
Less ton lots	32

Medium Carbon Ferromanganese

Mn 80% to 85%, C 1.25 to 1.50. Contract price, carloads, lump, bulk, delivered, per lb. of contained Mn ... 19.15¢

Calcium Metal

Eastern zone contract prices, cents per pound of metal, delivered.

	Cast	Turnings	Distilled
Ton lots	$2.05	$2.95	$3.75
Less ton lots	2.40	3.30	4.55

Silicomanganese

Contract basis, lump size, cents per pound of metal, delivered, 65-68% Mn, 18-20% Si, 1.5% max. C. For 2% max. C, deduct 0.2¢.

Carload bulk	9.90
Ton lots	11.55
Briquet, contract basis carlots, bulk delivered, per lb of briquet	11.15
Ton lots	11.75

Silvery Iron (electric furnace)

Si 14.01 to 14.50 pct, f.o.b. Keokuk, Iowa, or Wenatchee, Wash., $92.50 gross ton, freight allowed to normal trade area. Si 15.01 to 15.50 pct, f.o.b. Niagara Falls, N. Y., $83.00. Add $1.00 per ton for each additional 0.50% Si up to and including 18%. Add $1.00 for each 0.50% Mn over 1%.

Silicon Metal

Contract price, cents per pound contained Si, lump size, delivered, for ton lots packed.

96% Si, 2% Fe	21.70
97% Si, 1% Fe	22.10

Silicon Briquets

Contract price, cents per pound of briquet bulk, delivered, 40% Si, 1 lb Si briquets.

Carload, bulk	6.95
Ton lots	8.55

Electric Ferrosilicon

Contract price, cents per pound contained Si, lump, bulk, carloads, delivered.

25% Si	19.00	75% Si	14.30
50% Si	12.40	85% Si	15.55
90-95% Si	17.50		

Low-Carbon Ferromanganese

Contract price, cents per pound Mn contained, lump size, del'd, Mn 85-90%.

	Carloads	Ton	Less
0.7% max. C, 0.06% P, 90% Mn	26.25	28.10	29.30
0.07% max. C	25.75	27.60	28.80
0.15% max. C	25.25	27.10	28.30
0.30% max. C	24.75	26.60	27.80
0.50% max. C	24.25	26.10	27.30
0.75% max. C, 7.00% max. Si	21.25	23.10	24.30

IRON AGE FOUNDED 1855 — MARKETS & PRICES

Other Ferroalloys

Alsifer, 20% Al, 40% Si, 40% Fe, contract basis, f.o.b. Suspension Bridge, N. Y.
Carload .... 9.90¢
Ton lots .... 11.30¢
Calcium molybdate, 45-40%, f.o.b. Langeloth, Pa., per pound contained Mo. $1.15
Ferrocolumbium, 50-60%, 2 in x D, contract basis, delivered, per pound contained Cb.
Ton lots $4.90
Less ton lots 4.95
Ferro - Tantalum - columbium, 20% Ta, 40% Cb, 0.30 C. Contract basis, delivered, ton lots, 2 in. x D, per lb of contained Cb plus Ta $3.75
Ferromolybdenum, 55-75%, f.o.b. Langeloth, Pa., per pound contained Mo $1.32
Ferrophosphorus, electrolytic, 23-26%, car lots, f.o.b. Siglo, Mt. Pleasant, Tenn., $3 unitage, per gross ton $65.00
10 tons to less carload 75.00
Ferrotitanium, 40%, regular grade, 0.10% C max., f.o.b. Niagara Falls, N. Y., and Bridgeville, Pa., freight allowed, ton lots, per lb contained Ti $1.35
Ferrotitanium, 25%, low carbon, 0.10% C max., f.o.b. Niagara Falls, N. Y., and Bridgeville, Pa., freight allowed, ton lots, per lb contained Ti $1.50
Less ton lots $1.55
Ferrotitanium, 15 to 19%, high carbon, f.o.b. Niagara Falls, N. Y., freight allowed, carload per net ton $177.00
Ferrotungsten, standard, lump or ¼ x down, packed, per pound contained W, 5 ton lots, delivered $3.25
Ferrovanadium, 35-55%, contract basis, delivered, per pound, contained V.
Openhearth ....$3.00-$3.05
Crucible 3.10- 3.15
High speed steel (Primos) 3.25
Molybdic oxide, briquets or cans, per lb contained Mo, f.o.b. Langeloth, Pa. $1.14
bags, f.o.b. Washington, Pa., Langeloth, Pa. $1.13
Simanal, 20% Si, 20% Mn, 20% Al, contract basis, f.o.b. Philo, Ohio, freight allowed, per pound
Carload, bulk lump .... 14.50¢
Ton lots, bulk lump .... 15.75¢
Less ton lots, lump .... 16.25¢
Vanadium pentoxide, 88-92% V₂O₅ contract basis, per pound contained V₂O₅ $1.28
Zirconium, 35-40%, contract basis, f.o.b. plant, freight allowed, per pound of alloy.
ton lots .... 21.00¢
Zirconium, 12-15%, contract basis, lump, delivered, per lb of alloy.
carload, bulk .... 7.00¢

Boron Agents

Contract prices per lb of alloy, del.
Borosil, f.o.b. Philo, Ohio, freight allowed, B 3-4%, Si 40-45%, per lb contained B $5.25
Bortam, f.o.b. Niagara Falls
Ton lots, per pound .... 45¢
Less ton lots, per pound ...... 50¢
Carbortam, Ti 15-21%, B 1-2%, Si 2-4%, Al 1-2%, C 4.5-7.5%, f.o.b. Suspension Bridge, N. Y., freight allowed.
Ton lots, per pound ...... 10.00¢
Ferroboron, 17.50% min. B, 1.50% max. Si, 0.50% max. Al, 0.50% max. C, 1 in. x D. Ton lots $1.20
F.o.b. Wash., Pa.; 100 lb, up
10 to 14% B.................... .75
14 to 19% B.................... 1.20
19% min. B.................... 1.50
Grainal, f.o.b. Bridgeville, Pa., freight allowed, 100 lb and over.
No. 1 .... $1.00
No. 6 .... 68¢
No. 79 .... 50¢
Manganese—Boron 75.00% Mn, 15-20% B, 5% max. Fe, 1.50% max. Si, 3.00% max. C, 2 in. x D, delivered.
Ton lots $1.46
Less ton lots 1.57
Nickel—Boron 15-18% B, 1.00% max. Al, 1.50% max. Si, 0.50% max. C, 3.00% max. Fe, balance Ni, delivered.
Less ton lots $1.80
Silcaz, contract basis, delivered.
Ton lots .... 45.00¢

131

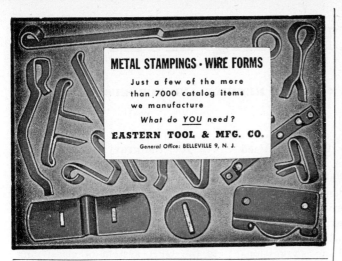

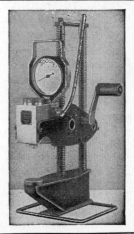

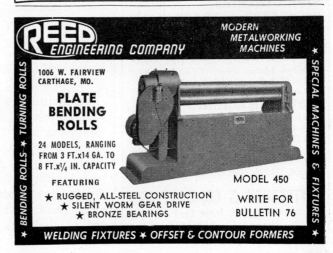

The Clearing House

NEWS OF USED, REBUILT AND SURPLUS MACHINERY

Road Back to Controls—Used machinery dealers are back from their junket to Washington where they put government men straight on the state of the industry and its problems. They heard a plea for cooperation loaded with emphasis on rebuilding and made suggestions that will certainly yield a return to the World War II system of price controls and adoption of material priorities for rebuilding and maintenance of DO related equipment.

Expand Rebuilding—The exclamation point was put on rebuilding by government men because many stockpile reserve tools may stay stockpiled unless some rebuilding capacity can be opened to make them operable. While rebuilding capacity is considered by most unequal to the present task, many will admit that it can be greatly expanded if a greater profit lure is dangled.

Another incentive that machinery men suggested to Washington was financial assistance in expansion of rebuilding facilities. This might entail certificates of necessity for fast tax writeoffs and direct loans.

Priorities Will Help—Used machinery men were told that a priority system is in the planning process. It is needed to direct strategic materials, such as copper products, to the trade. Lack of these items under NPA restrictions has been turning shortage screws on the industry. Now relief is seen as near. Naturally priorities will be granted for DO orders only.

Impractical Price Freeze—The used machinery field is currently struggling with the general price freeze order. It chilled prices at the highest point in the given base period. But in the used field each dealer was frozen at differing prices—and as those on the short end of the stick can vehemently

tell you, the gravy is being ladled unequally.

Return to OPA System—Thus the 65 to 75 dealers at the Washington session under the auspices of MDNA recommended a return to the OPA system of classifying machinery by year ranges, "as is" and "rebuilt grades," with the controlled price being determined by set percentages by year range and grade.

Government men also wanted the industry's help in locating needed tools as quickly as possible. Membership in a national organization would serve to consolidate information and accomplish this function.

Busy but Worried—In Pittsburgh, some dealers had their best business since the war but were worrying about their inability to replace what they sell—with inventories ebbing. One dealer has sold almost all his milling machines and geared head lathes. Some of the milling machines were about 30 years old.

Transition from civilian to defense work has forced some buyers to postpone closing of machinery deals. This will hold true in other markets also. One Pittsburgh dealer said that deals agreed to almost 2 weeks ago have not yet been closed because buyers must take heed of revised shop layouts before bringing in new equipment.

Crane Demand—More used cranes could be sold in Pittsburgh than are available. Prospective buyers must hunt about more than usual because the few cranes that can be had don't fill the bill.

This reflects strong demand for new cranes. New crane makers are quoting 15 to 18 months delivery even for defense orders. Add to this the fact that buyers cannot get new cranes unless they first get the steel to build them. That's facing two shortages for one product.

$ 20067

When ITE Circuit Breaker Co. found it necessary to build their own rolling mill to get relatively small quantities of extremely accurate strip, they were confronted with the problem of securing compact drive units for the rolls, each pair of which must operate at different speeds. They found as many others have, that from Master's broad line of Gearmotors they could select standard units which would give them the RIGHT horsepower, the RIGHT shaft speed in one compact unit that they could use RIGHT where they wanted it.

Probably you will never design a rolling mill. But the next time you need motor drives for your plant or product, remember that Master Motors, available

tough problem . . . easy solution

in thousands and thousands of types and ratings, give you a selection you can get nowhere else.

Open, enclosed, splash proof, fan-cooled, explosion proof . . . horizontal or vertical . . . for all phases, voltages and frequencies . . . in single speed, multi-speed and variable speed types . . . with or without flanges or other special features . . . with 5 types of gear reduction up to 432 to 1 ratio . . . with electric brakes . . . with mechanical variable speed units . . . and for every type of mounting . . . Master has them all and so can be completely impartial in helping you select the one best motor drive for YOU.

Select the RIGHT power drive from Master's broad line and you can increase the saleability of your motor driven products . . . improve the economy and productivity of your plant equipment.

THE MASTER ELECTRIC COMPANY • DAYTON 1, OHIO

MASTER GEARMOTORS

You get UNIFORMITY every time with TIMKEN® forging steels

When you're set up for production with a given analysis of Timken® forging steel, you don't have to alter your shop practices with every new shipment of stock. Timken forging bars give you uniform forgeability, uniform machinability, and uniform response to heat treatment. As a result, you have fewer delays, fewer rejects, lower production costs. And the quality of your finished product is uniformly high.

The uniformity of Timken forging steel is maintained by close quality control at every step in manufacture . . . from melting through final inspection. For example, the Timken Company uses a Direct Reading Spectrometer—first in the industry—to make possible instantaneous checking and analysis control of every heat. And Timken employs many other special techniques—many of them practical only in a large, flexible specialty mill—which insure the high surface and internal quality of Timken steel.

For help with your forging bar problems, get an on-the-job analysis by our Technical Staff. And write on your letterhead for your copy of the complete catalogue of our steels, "Timken Steel Products". The Timken Roller Bearing Company, Steel and Tube Division, Canton 6, Ohio. Cable address: "TIMROSCO".

YEARS AHEAD—THROUGH EXPERIENCE AND RESEARCH

TIMKEN

TRADE-MARK REG. U.S. PAT. OFF.

Fine Alloy

STEEL

and Seamless Tubes

Specialists in alloy steel—including hot rolled and cold finished alloy steel bars—a complete range of stainless, graphitic and standard tool analyses—and alloy and stainless seamless steel tubing.

$ 20067